Feedback Loops Figures

At the end of the "Understanding" and the "Treating" sections for each major disorder in the edition, you will usually find a Feedback Loops capstone section—e.g., *Feedback Loops in Action: Understanding Schizophrenia* and *Feedback Loops in Treatment: Schizophrenia*—which include figures that illustrate how feedback loops work and the interactions among the various factors.

Feedback Loops in Action Figures

- Summarize the neurological, psychological, and social factors that are associated with a given disorder
- Illustrate the dynamic interactive nature of the factors
- Provide a recurring illustrative format, which allows students to compare and contrast the specific factors of the feedback loops across disorders

Feedback Loops in Treatment Figures

- Summarize the neurological, psychological, and social treatments for a given disorder
- Illustrate the interactive nature of successful treatment
- Provide a recurring illustrative format, which allows students to compare and contrast the specific factors involved in treatment feedback loops across disorders

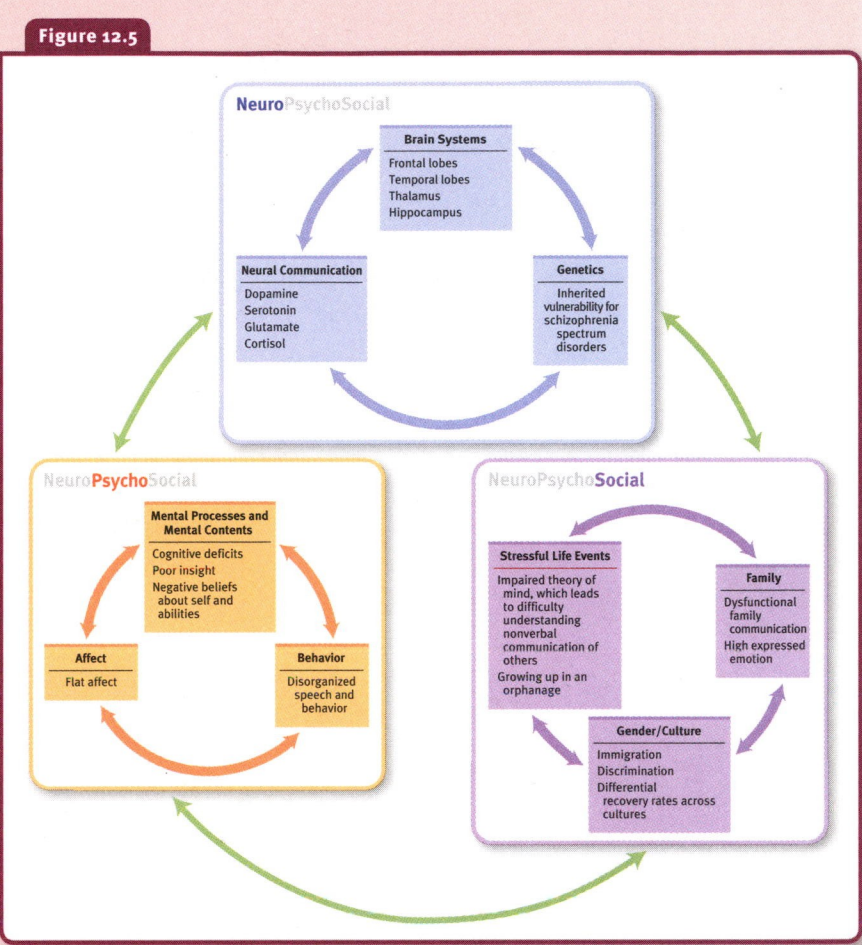

Figure 12.5

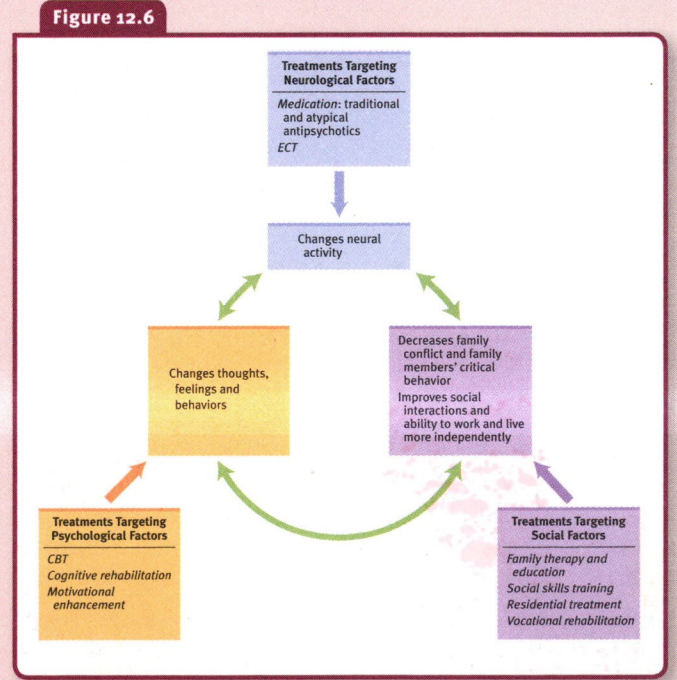

Figure 12.6

ABNORMAL
PSYCHOLOGY

ROBIN S. ROSENBERG
STEPHEN M. KOSSLYN
Harvard University

Worth Publishers

Grateful acknowledgment is given for permission to reprint the following art: p. 1: Nicolas Wilton; p. 32: Leigh Wells; p. 70: Michael Gillette/Heart Agency; p. 108: Diane Fenster; p. 152: Bruno Mallart/Images.com; p. 190: Alan Witschonke; p. 246: Don Kilpatrick/Morgan Gaynin; p. 330: Noma Bliss; p. 380: Richard Tuschman/Stock Illustration Source; p. 434: Katherine Streeter/Frank Sturges Reps; p. 472: Stephen Tunney; p. 518: Craig LaRotonda/Revelation Art; p. 564: Illustration by Sean Rodway/ Photography by Paul Hampartsoumian/Advocate Art; p. 624: Alan Baker/Heart Agency; p. 680: Dave Cutler; p. 716: Clifford Alejandro.

The Permissions and Attributions section (page P-1 at the back of this book) constitutes an extension of this copyright page. Grateful acknowledgment is given for the use of all quotations and previously published material.

Senior Publisher: Catherine Woods
Acquisitions Editor: Erik Gilg
Executive Marketing Manager: Katherine Nurre
Associate Director of Market Development: Carlise Stembridge
Development Editor: Jim Strandberg
Media and Supplements Editor: Sharon Prevost
Photo Editor: Christine Buese
Photo Researcher: Patricia Cateura
Art Director, Cover Designer: Babs Reingold
Interior Designers: Babs Reingold and Charles Yuen
Layout Designer: Paul Lacy
Associate Managing Editor: Tracey Kuehn
Project Editors: Dana Kasowitz
              Jenna Gray, Pre-PressPMG
Illustration Coordinators: Bill Page, Eleanor Jaekel
Illustrations: Pre-PressPMG, Keith Kasnot, Chris Notarile, Matt Holt
Production Manager: Barbara Anne Seixas
Composition: Pre-PressPMG
Printing and Binding: Worldcolor Versailles
Cover Art: *Let me show you the world in my eyes*. Eric Ceccarini

Library of Congress Control Number: 2009921876

ISBN-13: 978-0-7167-1728-7
ISBN-10: 0-7167-1728-X

Printed in the United States of America

First printing 2010

Worth Publishers
41 Madison Avenue
New York, NY 10010
www.worthpublishers.com

To our mothers, Bunny and Rhoda,
and our sons, David, Neil, and Justin

Robin S. Rosenberg is a clinical psychologist in private practice and has taught psychology courses at Lesley University and Harvard University. In addition, she is coauthor (with Stephen Kosslyn) of *Psychology in Context* and *Fundamentals of Psychology in Context*. She is the editor of *Psychology of Superheroes* and a contributor to *The Psychology of Harry Potter* and *Batman Unauthorized*. She is board certified in clinical psychology by the American Board of Professional Psychology, and has been certified in clinical hypnosis; she is a fellow of the American Academy of Clinical Psychology and a member of the Academy for Eating Disorders. She received her B.A. in psychology from New York University and her M.A. and Ph.D. in clinical psychology from the University of Maryland, College Park. Dr. Rosenberg completed her clinical internship at Massachusetts Mental Health Center and had a postdoctoral fellowship at Harvard Community Health Plan before joining the staff at Newton-Wellesley Hospital's Outpatient Services, where she worked before leaving to expand her private practice. Dr. Rosenberg specializes in treating people with depression, anxiety, and eating disorders, and she is interested in the integration of different therapy approaches. She was the founder and coordinator of the New England Society for Psychotherapy Integration. Dr. Rosenberg enjoys using superhero stories to illustrate psychological principles and can sometimes be found at comic book conventions.

Stephen M. Kosslyn is the John Lindsley Professor of Psychology and former chair of the Department of Psychology at Harvard University, as well as former Head Tutor (directing the undergraduate program in Psychology). He currently is Dean of Social Science at Harvard as well as Associate Psychologist in the Department of Neurology at the Massachusetts General Hospital. He received a B.A. from UCLA and a Ph.D. from Stanford University, both in psychology. His research has focused primarily on the nature of visual mental imagery, visual perception, and visual communication; he has authored or coauthored 9 books and over 300 papers on these topics. Kosslyn has received the APA's Boyd R. McCandless Young Scientist Award, the National Academy of Sciences Initiatives in Research Award, the Cattell Award, a Guggenheim Fellowship, the J-L. Signoret Prize (France), and an honorary Doctorate of Science from the University of Caen (France), and he has been elected to Academia Rodinensis pro Remediatione (Switzerland), the Society of Experimental Psychologists, and the American Academy of Arts and Sciences. Kosslyn works hard, but not every waking moment; his hobbies are bass guitar (he has played rock-and-roll and blues with the same group for many years) and French (he has struggled with the language ever since living in France for a year in 1996).

BRIEF CONTENTS

CONTENTS

CHAPTER 3

Clinical Diagnosis and Assessment 70

CHAPTER 4

Foundations Of Treatment 108

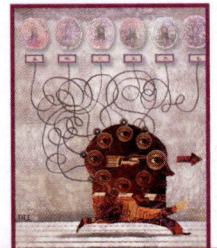

CHAPTER 5

CHAPTER 6

Mood Disorders and Suicide 190

CHAPTER 7

CHAPTER 8

Dissociative and Somatoform Disorders 330

CHAPTER 9

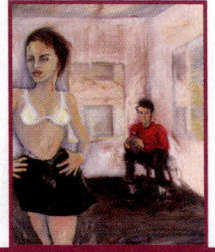

CHAPTER 11

Gender and Sexual Disorders.................**472**

CHAPTER 14

Childhood Disorders............624

CHAPTER 15

Cognitive Disorders............................ 680

CHAPTER 16

Ethical and Legal Issues 716

This is an exciting time to study psychopathology. Research on the entire range of psychological disorders has blossomed during the last decade, yielding new insights about psychological disorders and their treatments. However, the research results are outpacing the popular media's ability to explain them. We've noticed that when study results are explained in a television news report or a mainstream magazine article, "causes" of mental illness are often reduced to a single factor, such as genes, brain chemistry, irrational thoughts, or social rejection. But that is not an accurate picture. Research increasingly reveals that psychopathology arises from a confluence of three types of factors: *neurological* (brain and body, including genes), *psychological* (thoughts, feelings, and behaviors), and *social* (relationships and communities). Moreover, these three sorts of factors do not exist in isolation, but rather mutually influence each other.

We are a clinical psychologist (Rosenberg) and a cognitive neuroscientist (Kosslyn) who have been writing collaboratively for many years. Our observations about the state of the field of psychopathology—and the problems with how it is sometimes portrayed—led us to envision an abnormal psychology textbook that is guided by a central idea, which we call the *neuropsychosocial approach*. This approach allows us to conceptualize the ways in which neurological, psychological, and social factors interact to give rise to mental disorders. These interactions take the form of feedback loops in which every type of factor affects every other type. Take depression, for instance, which we discuss in Chapter 6: Someone who attributes the cause of a negative event to himself or herself (such attributions are a psychological factor) is more likely to become depressed. But this tendency to attribute the cause of negative events to oneself is influenced by social experiences, such as being criticized or abused. In turn, such social factors can alter brain functioning (particularly if one has certain genes), and abnormalities in brain functioning affect social interactions, and so on—round and round.

The neuropsychosocial approach grew out of the venerable biopsychosocial approach; instead of focusing broadly on biology, however, we take advantage of the bountiful harvest of findings about the brain that have filled the scientific journals over the past two decades. Specifically, the name change signals a focus on the brain itself; we derive much insight from the findings of neuroimaging studies, which reveal how brain systems function normally and how they have gone awry with mental disorders, and we also learn an enormous amount from findings regarding neurotransmitters and genetics.

Although mental disorders cannot be fully understood without reference to the brain, neurological factors alone cannot explain these disorders; rather, mental disorders develop through the complex interaction of neurological factors with psychological and social factors. We argue strongly that psychopathology cannot be reduced to "brain disease," akin to a problem someone might have with his or her liver or lungs. Instead, we show that the effects of neurological factors can only be understood in the context of the other two types of factors addressed within the neuropsychosocial approach. Thus, we not only present cutting-edge neuroscience research results but also put them in their proper context. (In fact, an understanding of a psychological disorder cannot be reduced to *any* single type of factor, whether genetics, irrational thoughts, or family interaction patterns.)

Our emphasis on feedback loops among neurological, psychological, and social factors led us to reconceptualize and incorporate the classic diathesis-stress model. In the classic view, the diathesis was almost always treated as a biological state, and the stress was viewed as a result of environmental events. In contrast, after describing the conventional diathesis-stress model in Chapter 1, we explain how the neuropsychosocial approach provides a new way to think about the relationship between diathesis and stress. Specifically, we show how one can view any of the three sorts of factors as a potential source of either a diathesis (a precondition that makes a person vulnerable) or a stress (a triggering event). For example, living in a dangerous neighborhood, which is a social factor, creates a diathesis for which psychological events can serve as the stress, triggering an episode of depression. Alternatively, being born with a very sensitive amygdala may act as a diathesis for which social events—such as observing someone else being mugged—can serve as a stressor that triggers an anxiety disorder.

Thus, the neuropsychosocial approach is not simply a change in terminology ("bio" to "neuro"), but rather a change in basic orientation: We do not view any one sort of factor as "privileged" over the others, but regard the interactions among the factors—the feedback loops—as paramount. In our view, this approach incorporates what was best about the biopsychosocial approach and the diathesis-stress model. The resulting new approach led naturally to a set of unique features, as we outline next.

Unique Coverage

Through its integration of cutting-edge neuroscience research and more traditional psychosocial research on psychopathology and its treatment, this textbook provides students with a sense of the field as a coherent whole, in which different research methods illuminate different aspects of abnormal psychology. Our integrated neuropsychosocial approach allows students to learn not only how neurological factors affect mental processes (such as memory) and mental contents (such as distorted beliefs), but also how neurological factors affect emotions, behavior, social interactions, and responses to environmental events. And further, the approach allows students to learn how neurological, psychological, and social factors affect each other.

The 16 chapters included in this book span the traditional topics covered in an abnormal psychology course. The neuropsychosocial theme is reflected in both the overall organization of the text and the organization of its individual chapters. We present the material in a decidedly contemporary context that infuses both the foundational chapters (Chapters 1–5) as well as the chapters that address specific disorders (Chapters 6–15).

In the chapter that provides an overview of explanations of abnormality (Chapter 2), neurological, psychological, and social factors are discussed as etiological factors. Our coverage is not limited merely to categorizing causes as examples of a given type of factor; rather, we explain how events pertaining to a given type of factor influence and create feedback loops with other factors. Consider depression again: The loss of a relationship (social factor) can affect thoughts and feelings (psychological factors), which—given a certain genetic predisposition (neurological factor)—can trigger depression. Using the neuropsychosocial approach, we show how disparate fields of psychology and psychiatry (such as neuroscience and clinical practice) are providing a unified and overarching understanding of abnormal psychology.

Our chapter on diagnosis and assessment (Chapter 3) uses the neuropsychosocial framework to organize methods of assessing abnormality. We discuss how abnormality may be assessed through measures that address the different types of factors: neurological (e.g., neuroimaging data or lab tests, and we note that even measures taken from the blood ultimately reflect brain events), psychological (e.g., clinical interviews, questionnaires, or inventories), and social (e.g., family interviews or a history of legal problems).

Similarly, in the treatment chapter (Chapter 4), we describe treatment from the neuropsychosocial perspective, explaining how each type of treatment is designed to target and change specific factors (e.g., medications aimed at neurotransmitter levels, cognitive-behavior therapy that focuses on thoughts and behaviors, or family therapy that addresses family interactions). We also explain how successful treatment—of any type—affects *all* factors, positively influencing neurological functioning, thoughts, feelings, behaviors, and social interactions.

The research methods chapter (Chapter 5) also provides unique coverage. We explain the general scientific method, but we do so within the neuropsychosocial framework. Specifically, we consider methods used to study neurological and other biological factors (e.g., neuroimaging), psychological factors (e.g., self-reports of thoughts and moods), and social factors (e.g., observational studies of dyads or groups or of cultural values and expectations). We show how the various measures themselves reflect the interactions among the different types of factors. For instance, when researchers ask participants to *report* family dynamics, they are relying on psychological factors—participants' memories and impressions—to provide measures of social factors. Similarly, when the number of items checked off on a stressful life events scale is used to infer the actual stress experienced by individual participants, social and environmental factors are providing a proxy measure of the psychological and neurological consequences of stress. The chapter also discusses research on treatment from the neuropsychosocial framework.

The clinical chapters (Chapters 6–15), which address specific disorders, also rely on the neuropsychosocial approach to organize the discussions of both etiology and treatment of the disorders. Moreover, when we discuss a particular disorder, we address the three basic questions of psychopathology: What exactly constitutes this psychological disorder? How does it arise? How can it be treated?

Pedagogy

All abnormal psychology textbooks cover a lot of ground: Students must learn new concepts, facts, and theories. We want to make that task easier, to help students consolidate the material they learn and to come to a deeper understanding of the material. The textbook uses a number of pedagogical tools to achieve this goal.

Feedback Loops Within the Neuropsychosocial Approach

This textbook highlights and reinforces the theme of feedback loops among neurological, psychological, and social factors in several ways:

- In the "Understanding" sections of each chapter (for instance, "Understanding Panic Disorder"), when two or more types of factors are part of a feedback loop, we explicitly call out these relationships by highlighting the margin in beige where we mention such feedback loops, and include an icon in the margin that notes the specific factors involved. The icon specifies which types of factors and feedback loops are directly implicated by a particular study, set of findings, or theory ("N" for neurological, "P" for psychological, and "S" for social). For instance, in the margin here is the icon we use to note specific evidence or theory that implicates psychological and social factors—and the feedback loop between them—as contributing to a particular psychological disorder.

Social Factors: Modeling

Sometimes, simply seeing other people exhibit fear of a particular stimulus is enough to make the observer become afraid of that stimulus (Mineka, Cook, & Miller, 1984). For example, if as a young child, you saw your older cousin become agitated and anxious when a dog approached, you might well learn to do the same. Similarly, repeated warnings about the dangers of a stimulus can increase the risk of de-
_____ ____ __ _____ __ _____ __ _____ ___y & Barlow, 2002). After __

- Similarly, in the "Treating" sections of each chapter (for instance, "Treating Panic Disorder"), highlighting and icons in the margin mark the relevant feedback loops. In addition, an arrow points to the type of factor that is the direct target of relevant treatment. (However, we stress that even though one sort of factor is the direct target, it rarely—if ever—is the only one affected by the therapy.) For instance, below is the icon we use to note when treatment that directly targets a psychological factor in turn can affect neurological factors and create feedback loops between the two kinds of factors.

were afraid of touching dirt, she would touch dirt but would not then wash her hands. Through exposure and response prevention, patients learn that nothing bad happens if they don't perform their compulsive behavior; the anxiety is lessened without resorting to the compulsion, their fear and arousal subside, and they experience mastery. They survived the anxiety and exerted control over the compulsion. When patients success-

- At the end of the "Understanding" and the "Treating" sections, we typically have concluding sections that explicitly call attention to interactions among the three factors and that walk students through a description of how the three types of factors affect one another via feedback loops. Examples of these sections are *Feedback Loops in Action: Understanding Panic Disorder* and *Feedback Loops in Treatment: Panic Disorder*.

FEEDBACK LOOPS IN ACTION: Understanding Panic Disorder

Cognitive explanations of panic disorder can help show how a few panic attacks can progress to panic disorder, but not everyone who has panic attacks develops panic disorder. It is only when neurological, biological, and psychological factors interact that panic disorder develops (Bouton, Mineka, & Barlow, 2001). Cognitive processes such as catastrophic thinking and anxiety sensitivity (psychological factors) are triggered, in part, by environmental and social stressors (social factors). Indeed, such stressors may lead an individual to be aroused (neurological factor), but he or she then misinterprets the cause of this arousal (psychological factor). This misinterpretation may increase the arousal (Wilkinson et al., 1998), making it more likely that symptoms of panic—rapid heartbeat or shallow breathing—will follow.

For example, a man's argument with his wife might arouse his anger and

FEEDBACK LOOPS IN TREATMENT: Panic Disorder

Invariably, medication—which changes neurological functioning—stops exerting its beneficial effect when the patient stops taking it. The positive changes in neural communication and brain activity, and the associated changes in thoughts, feelings, and behaviors do not endure. Eventually, the symptoms of panic disorder return. For some patients, though, medication is a valuable first step, providing enough relief from symptoms that they are motivated to obtain CBT, which can change their reactions (psychological factor) to perceived bodily sensations (neurological factor). When a patient receives both medication and CBT, however, the medication should be at a low enough dose that the patient can still feel the sensations that led to panic in the past (Taylor, 2000). In fact, the dose should be gradually decreased so that the patient can experience enough anxiety to be increasingly able to make use of cognitive-behavioral methods. It is the CBT that leads to enduring changes: Researchers have found that adding medication to CBT doesn't provide an advantage over CBT alone (de Beurs et al., 1999). This finding has led to CBT's being recommended even for those who prefer medication (Ellison & McCarter, 2002).

- At the end of most *Feedback Loops in Action* and *Feedback Loops in Treatment* sections, we include a neuropsychosocial "Feedback Loops" figure; this figure illustrates the feedback loops among the neurological, psychological, and social factors.

- The *Feedback Loops in Action* figures serve several purposes: (1) They provide a visual summary of the most important neuropsychosocial factors that contribute to the various disorders; (2) they illustrate the interactive nature of the factors; (3) their overall structure is the same for each disorder, which allows students to compare and contrast the specifics of the feedback loops across disorders.

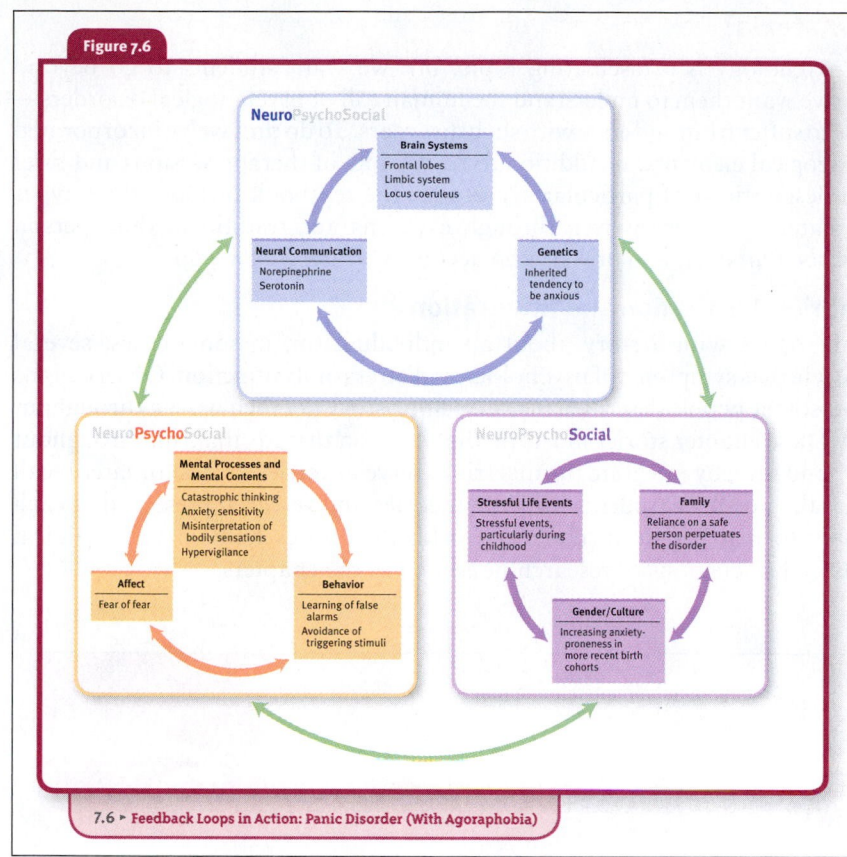

Figure 7.6

7.6 ▸ Feedback Loops in Action: Panic Disorder (With Agoraphobia)

- Like the *Feedback Loops in Action* figures, the *Feedback Loops in Treating a Disorder* figures serve several purposes: (1) The figures provide a visual summary of the treatments for the various disorders; (2) they illustrate the interactive nature of successful treatment, the fact that a treatment may directly target one type of factor but change in that factor in turn affects other factors; (3) their overall structure is the same for each disorder, which allows students to compare and contrast the specifics of the feedback loops across disorders.

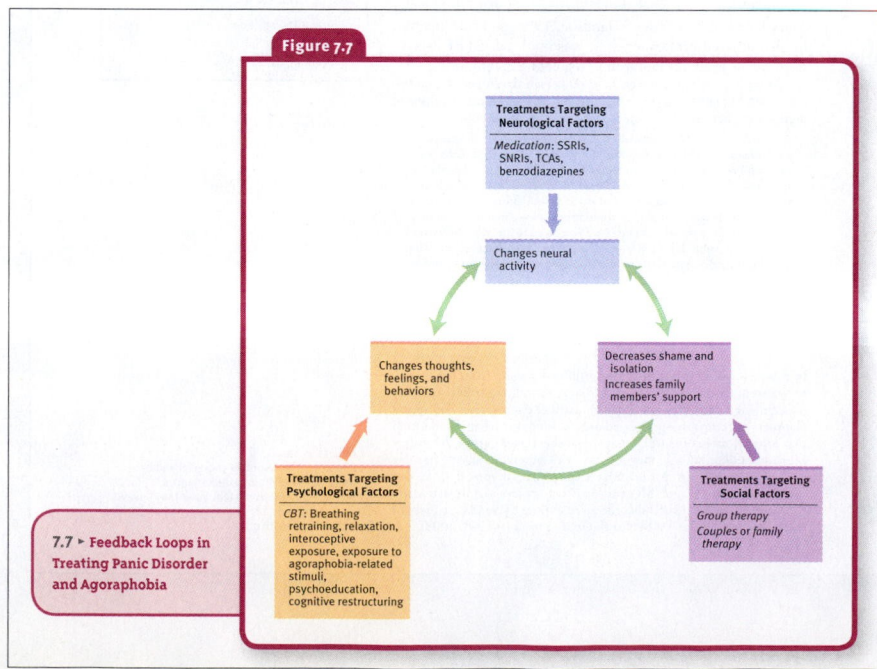

Figure 7.7

7.7 ▸ Feedback Loops in Treating Panic Disorder and Agoraphobia

Clinical Material

Abnormal psychology is a fascinating topic, but we want students to go beyond fascination; we want them to understand the human toll of psychological disorders—what it's like to suffer from and cope with such disorders. To do this, we've incorporated several pedagogical elements. In addition to transcripts of therapy sessions and brief first-person descriptions of particular symptoms, the textbook includes three types of clinical material: a story woven through each chapter, traditional third-person cases (*From the Outside*), and first-person accounts (*From the Inside*).

Chapter Stories: Illustration and Integration

Each chapter opens with a story about an individual (or, in some cases, several individuals) who has symptoms of psychological distress or dysfunction. Observations about the person or people described in the opening story are then woven throughout the chapter. These chapter stories illustrate the common threads that run throughout the chapter (and thereby integrate the material), serve as retrieval cues for later recall of the material, and show students how the theories and research presented in each chapter apply to real people in the real world; the stories humanize the clinical descriptions and discussions of research presented in the chapters.

CHAPTER

6

Mood Disorders and Suicide

Chapter Outline

Depressive Disorders
The Building Block of Depressive Disorders: Major Depressive Episode
Major Depressive Disorder
Dysthymic Disorder
Understanding Depressive Disorders
Treating Depressive Disorders

Bipolar Disorders
Building Blocks for Bipolar Disorders
The Two Types of Bipolar Disorder
Cyclothymic Disorder
Understanding Bipolar Disorders
Treating Bipolar Disorders

Suicide
Suicidal Thoughts and Suicide Risks
Understanding Suicide
Preventing Suicide

Kay Redfield Jamison, a psychologist who studies mood disorders, is uniquely qualified to report and reflect on such disorders. Not only has she made mood disorders her area of professional expertise, but she has also lived with such a disorder. In her memoir, *An Unquiet Mind* (1995), Jamison recounts her experiences. The youngest of three children in a military family, she and her siblings attended four different elementary schools—some in foreign countries—by the time she was in 5th grade. She describes her father, a meteorologist and Air Force officer, as expansive, with infectious good moods, and impulsive, often giving the children gifts. It was "like having Mary Poppins for a father" (Jamison, 1995, p. 17). However, he also suffered periods when he was immobilized by depression, and he generally had trouble regulating his emotions.

As we'll see in this chapter, Jamison herself developed difficulties regulating her emotions. She recounts that when she was a senior in high school, her mood became so dark that her thinking

> . . . was torturous. I would read the same passage over and over again only to realize that I had no memory at all for what I had just read. Each book or poem I picked up was the same way. Incomprehensible . . . I could not begin to follow the material presented in my classes. . . . It was very frightening . . . [my mind] no longer found anything interesting or enjoyable or worthwhile. It was incapable of concentrated thought and turned time and time again to the subject of death: I was going to die, what difference did anything make? Life's run was only a short and meaningless one, why live? I was totally exhausted and could scarcely pull myself out of bed in the mornings. . . . I wore the same clothes over and over again, as it was otherwise too much of an effort to make a decision about what to put on. I dreaded having to talk with people, avoided my friends whenever possible, and sat in the school library in the early mornings and late afternoons, virtually inert, with a dead heart and a brain as cold as clay.
> (Jamison, 1995, pp. 37–38)

In this passage, Jamison describes problems arising from her *mood*, a persistent emotion lurking in the background, regardless of what is occurring. The category of psychological disorders called **mood disorders** encompasses prolonged and marked disturbances in mood that affect how people feel, what they believe and expect, how they think and talk, and how they interact with others. In any particular year, about 8% of Americans experience a mood disorder (Substance Abuse and Mental Health Services Administration [SAMHSA], 2008). Mood disorders are among the leading causes of disability worldwide (World Health Organization [WHO], 2008).

Mood disorders
Psychological disorders characterized by prolonged and marked disturbances in mood that affect how people feel, what they believe and expect, how they think and talk, and how they interact with others.

The chapter stories present individuals as clinicians and researchers often find them—with sets of symptoms: It is up to the clinician or researcher to make sense of the symptoms, determining which of them may meet the criteria for a particular disorder, which may indicate an atypical presentation, and which may arise from a comorbid disorder. Thus, we ask the student to see situations from the point of view of clinicians and researchers, who must sift through the available information to develop hypotheses about possible diagnoses and then obtain more information to confirm or disconfirm these hypotheses.

In the first two chapters, the opening story is about a mother and daughter—Big Edie and Little Edie Beale—who were the subject of a famous documentary in the 1970s and whose lives have been portrayed more recently in the play and HBO film *Grey Gardens*. In these initial chapters, we offer a description of the Beales' lives and examples of their *very* eccentric behavior to address two questions central to psychopathology: How is abnormality defined? Why do psychological disorders arise?

The chapter stories in subsequent chapters focus on different examples of symptoms of psychological disorders, drawn from the lives of other people. For example, in Chapter 7, we discuss the reclusive billionaire Howard Hughes and the football star Earl Campbell, both of whom suffered from symptoms of anxiety; in Chapter 12, we discuss the Genain quadruplets—all four of whom were diagnosed with schizophrenia. To provide a flavor of how we use such stories, here's an example from the beginning of Chapter 13 on personality disorders. The chapter begins like this:

> Rachel Reiland wrote a memoir called *Get Me Out of Here,* about living with a personality disorder. In the opening of the book, Reiland remembers Cindy, the golden-haired grade-school classmate who was their teacher's favorite. At the end of a painting class, Cindy's painting was beautiful, with distinctive trees. Unfortunately, Rachel's painting looked like a "putrid blob." Rachel then recounts:
>
>> "I seethed with jealousy as Mrs. Schwarzheuser showered Cindy with compliments. Suddenly, rage overwhelmed me. I seized a cup of brown paint and dumped half of it over my picture. Glaring at Cindy, I leaned across the table and dumped the other half over her drawing. I felt a surge of relief. Now Cindy's picture looked as awful as mine.
>>
>> "'Rachel!' Mrs. Schwarzheuser yelled. 'You've completely destroyed Cindy's beautiful trees. Shame on you. You are a *horrible* little girl. The paint is everywhere—look at your jeans.'
>>
>> "My blue jeans were soaked with brown paint. They looked ugly. I looked ugly. Mrs. Schwarzheuser frantically wiped up paint to keep it from dripping onto the floor. Everyone was watching.
>>
>> "I felt my body go numb. My legs, arms, and head were weightless. Floating. It was the same way I felt when Daddy pulled off his belt and snapped it. Anticipation of worse things to come—things I had brought on myself because I was different.
>>
>> " 'In all my years, I've never seen a child like you. You are the *worst* little girl I've ever taught. Go sit in the corner, immediately.'
>>
>> "Shame on Rachel. That language I understood. And deserved....
>>
>> "Mrs. Schwarzheuser was right. I was horrible." (Reiland, 2004, pp. 1–2)

We return to Reiland's story throughout Chapter 13, noting when her symptoms resemble those of one personality disorder or another, as well as the ways in which her symptoms may not meet the diagnostic criteria for various personality disorders. The stories in other chapters are handled similarly.

From the Outside

The feature called *From the Outside* provides third-person accounts (typically case presentations by mental health clinicians) of disorders or particular symptoms of disorders. These accounts provide an additional opportunity for memory consolidation of the material, an additional set of retrieval cues, a further sense of how symptoms and disorders affect real people; these cases also serve to expose students to professional case material. The *From the Outside* feature covers an array of disorders, including cyclothymic disorder (Case 6.5) in Chapter 6, panic disorder (Case 7.2) in Chapter 7, transvestic fetishism in Chapter 11 (Case 11.6), and separation anxiety disorder (Case 14.8) in Chapter 14. Often several *From the Outside* cases are included in a chapter; for instance, in Chapter 8 , we include *From the Outside* cases on dissociative amnesia (Case 8.1), dissociative fugue (Case 8.2), depersonalization disorder (Case 8.3), somatization disorder (Case 8.5), and body dysmorphic disorder (Case 8.8).

CASE 12.1 • FROM THE OUTSIDE: Disorganized Schizophrenia

Emilio is a 40-year-old man who looks 10 years younger. He is brought to the hospital, his twelfth hospitalization, by his mother because she is afraid of him. He is dressed in a ragged overcoat, bedroom slippers, and a baseball cap and wears several medals around his neck. His affect ranges from anger at his mother ("She feeds me shit . . . what comes out of other people's rectums") to a giggling, obsequious seductiveness toward the interviewer. His speech and manner have a childlike quality, and he walks with a mincing step and exaggerated hip movements. His mother reports that he stopped taking his medication about a month ago and has since begun to hear voices and to look and act more bizarrely. When asked what he has been doing, he says, "eating wires and lighting fires." His spontaneous speech is often incoherent and marked by frequent rhyming and clang associations (speech in which sounds, rather than meaningful relationships, govern word choice).

Emilio's first hospitalization occurred after he dropped out of school at age 16, and six

---

From the Inside

In every chapter in which we address a disorder in depth, we present at least one first-person account of what it is like to live with that disorder or particular symptoms of it. In addition to providing high-interest personal narratives, these *From the Inside* cases help students to consolidate memory of the material (because they mention the symptoms the individual experienced), provide additional retrieval cues, and are another way to link the descriptions of disorders and research findings with real people's experiences.

CASE 6.1 ▸ FROM THE INSIDE: Major Depressive Episode

Another experience of depression was captured by the writer William Styron in his memoir, *Darkness Visible*.

In depression this faith in deliverance, in ultimate restoration, is absent. The pain is unrelenting, and what makes the condition intolerable is the foreknowledge that no remedy will come—not in a day, an hour, a month, or a minute. If there is mild relief, one knows that it is only temporary; more pain will follow. It is hopelessness even more than pain that crushes the soul. So the decision-making of daily life involves not, as in normal affairs, shifting from one annoying situation to another less annoying—or from discomfort to relative comfort, or from boredom to activity—but moving from pain to pain. One does not abandon, even briefly, one's bed of nails, but is attached to it wherever one goes.

(Styron, 1990, p. 62)

The *From the Inside* cases illuminate what it is like to live with disorders such as agoraphobia (Case 7.3), obsessive-compulsive disorder (Case 7.6), hypochondriasis (Case 8.7), alcohol dependence (Case 9.5), gender identity disorder (Case 11.1), schizophrenia (Case 12.2), attention-deficit/hyperactivity disorder (Case 14.7), and dementia (Case 15.4), among others.

Learning About Disorders: Consolidated Tables to Consolidate Learning

In addition to explaining each disorder in the text, we provide two types of tables to help students organize and consolidate information related to diagnosis: DSM-IV-TR diagnostic criteria tables, and *Facts at a Glance* tables.

DSM-IV-TR Diagnostic Criteria Tables

The American Psychiatric Association's manual of psychiatric disorders—the *Diagnostic and Statistical Manual of Mental Disorders,* 4th edition, text revision (DSM-IV-TR)—provides tables of the diagnostic criteria for each of the listed disorders. For each disorder that we discuss at length, we present its full DSM-IV-TR diagnostic criteria table so that students become familiar with how the diagnostic criteria are presented in the manual; the criteria—and criticisms of them—are also explained in the text itself.

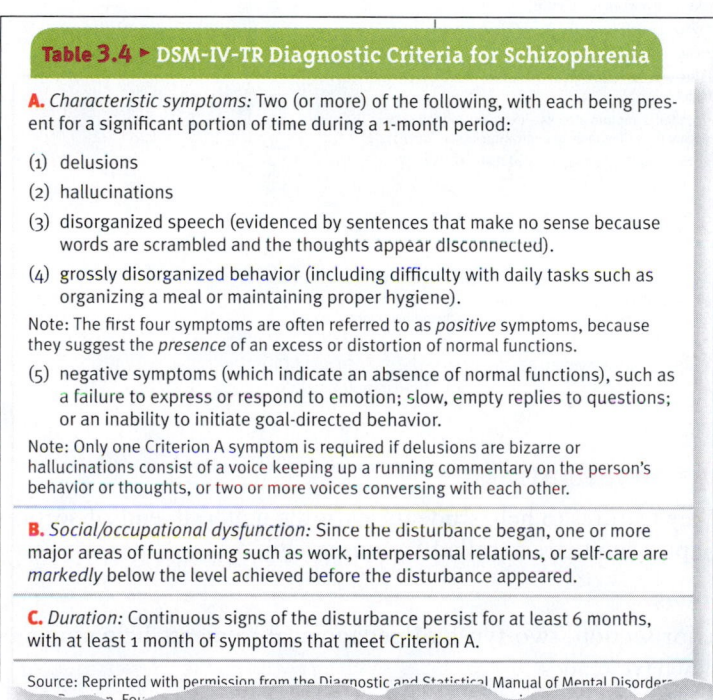

Table 3.4 ► DSM-IV-TR Diagnostic Criteria for Schizophrenia

A. *Characteristic symptoms:* Two (or more) of the following, with each being present for a significant portion of time during a 1-month period:

(1) delusions

(2) hallucinations

(3) disorganized speech (evidenced by sentences that make no sense because words are scrambled and the thoughts appear disconnected).

(4) grossly disorganized behavior (including difficulty with daily tasks such as organizing a meal or maintaining proper hygiene).

Note: The first four symptoms are often referred to as *positive* symptoms, because they suggest the *presence* of an excess or distortion of normal functions.

(5) negative symptoms (which indicate an absence of normal functions), such as a failure to express or respond to emotion; slow, empty replies to questions; or an inability to initiate goal-directed behavior.

Note: Only one Criterion A symptom is required if delusions are bizarre or hallucinations consist of a voice keeping up a running commentary on the person's behavior or thoughts, or two or more voices conversing with each other.

B. *Social/occupational dysfunction:* Since the disturbance began, one or more major areas of functioning such as work, interpersonal relations, or self-care are *markedly* below the level achieved before the disturbance appeared.

C. *Duration:* Continuous signs of the disturbance persist for at least 6 months, with at least 1 month of symptoms that meet Criterion A.

Source: Reprinted with permission from the Diagnostic and Statistical Manual of Mental Disorders

In Chapter 7, for example, full DSM-IV-TR diagnostic criteria tables are included for generalized anxiety disorder, panic attack, panic disorder (with or without agoraphobia), agoraphobia, social phobia, specific phobia, obsessive-compulsive disorder, and posttraumatic stress disorder.

Facts at a Glance Tables for Disorders

An important innovation is summary tables that provide key facts about prevalence, comorbidity, onset, course, and gender and cultural factors for each disorder. These facts are presented in easy-to-read tables, which are titled with the name of the disorder, followed by the term *Facts at a Glance* (for instance, *Obsessive-Compulsive Disorder Facts at a Glance*). These tables give students the opportunity to access this relevant information in one place and to compare and contrast the facts for various disorders.

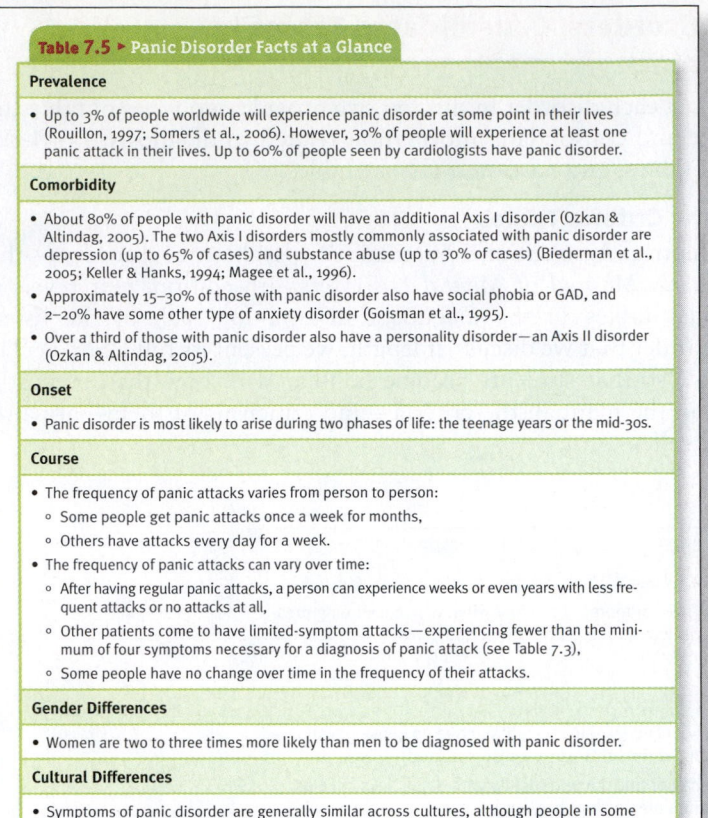

Table 7.5 ▸ Panic Disorder Facts at a Glance

Prevalence

- Up to 3% of people worldwide will experience panic disorder at some point in their lives (Rouillon, 1997; Somers et al., 2006). However, 30% of people will experience at least one panic attack in their lives. Up to 60% of people seen by cardiologists have panic disorder.

Comorbidity

- About 80% of people with panic disorder will have an additional Axis I disorder (Ozkan & Altindag, 2005). The two Axis I disorders mostly commonly associated with panic disorder are depression (up to 65% of cases) and substance abuse (up to 30% of cases) (Biederman et al., 2005; Keller & Hanks, 1994; Magee et al., 1996).
- Approximately 15–30% of those with panic disorder also have social phobia or GAD, and 2–20% have some other type of anxiety disorder (Goisman et al., 1995).
- Over a third of those with panic disorder also have a personality disorder—an Axis II disorder (Ozkan & Altindag, 2005).

Onset

- Panic disorder is most likely to arise during two phases of life: the teenage years or the mid-30s.

Course

- The frequency of panic attacks varies from person to person:
  - Some people get panic attacks once a week for months,
  - Others have attacks every day for a week.
- The frequency of panic attacks can vary over time:
  - After having regular panic attacks, a person can experience weeks or even years with less frequent attacks or no attacks at all,
  - Other patients come to have limited-symptom attacks—experiencing fewer than the minimum of four symptoms necessary for a diagnosis of panic attack (see Table 7.3),
  - Some people have no change over time in the frequency of their attacks.

Gender Differences

- Women are two to three times more likely than men to be diagnosed with panic disorder.

Cultural Differences

- Symptoms of panic disorder are generally similar across cultures, although people in some cultures may experience or explain the symptoms differently, such as "wind overload" among the Khmer (Hinton et al., 2002, 2003).

Summarizing and Consolidating

We include two more key features to help students learn the material: end-of-section reviews and end-of-chapter summaries (called *Summing Up*).

End-of-Section Reviews

At the end of each major section, two types of pedagogical elements help students review the material they have read:

- *Key Concepts and Facts Summary.* This feature uses bulleted lists to summarize the fundamental concepts and facts discussed in the section.

Key Concepts and Facts About Understanding Schizophrenia

- A variety of neurological factors are associated with schizophrenia:
  - Abnormalities in brain structure and function have been found in the frontal and temporal lobes, the thalamus, and the hippocampus. Moreover, certain brain areas do not appear to interact with each other properly. People with schizophrenia are more likely to have enlarged ventricles than are other people. The brain abnormalities give rise to biological markers in some individuals.
  - These brain abnormalities appear to be a result of, at least in some cases, maternal malnourishment or illness during pregnancy or to fetal ...

- alone, though, cannot explain why a given individual develops the disorder.
- Psychological factors that are associated with schizophrenia and shape the symptoms of the disorder include:
  - cognitive deficits in attention, memory, and executive functioning;
  - dysfunctional beliefs and attributions; and
  - difficulty recognizing and conveying emotions.
- Various social factors are also associated with schizophrenia:
  - an impaired theory of mind, which makes it difficult to under ...

- *Making a Diagnosis.* This feature is designed to help students consolidate the information about diagnostic criteria by applying the criteria to symptoms *as they are expressed in real people*. For each disorder, we ask students to diagnose the

individual in a case that was presented in a *From the Inside* or *From the Outside* section. Students are asked to reread the case carefully and determine which DSM-IV-TR criteria are met and are not met and whether there is enough information to warrant a diagnosis. If the students would like more information in order to make a diagnosis (or to decide whether a diagnosis is not appropriate), we ask them to describe what information—specifically—they want and to explain how it would inform their diagnosis. The *Making a Diagnosis* feature can be used as homework or as a springboard for small-group or class discussions.

Making a Diagnosis

- Reread Case 12.1 about Emilio, and then determine whether or not his symptoms met the minimum criteria for a diagnosis of schizophrenia. Specifically, list which criteria apply and which ones do not. If you would like more information to determine his diagnosis, what information—specifically—would you want, and in what ways would the information influence your decision? If you decide that a diagnosis of schizophrenia is appropriate for Emilio, do you think he has the deficit or nondeficit subtype, and why?

End-Of-Chapter Review: Summing Up

The end-of-chapter review, called *Summing Up*, has three elements, each of which is designed to help students further consolidate the material in memory and to foster their critical thinking about the material (which itself furthers learning):

- *Section summaries.* These summaries repeat the important information in the end-of-section summaries, allowing students to review what they have learned in the broader context of the entire chapter's material.

SUMMING UP

Summary of Depressive Disorders

A major depressive episode (MDE) is the building block for a diagnosis of major depressive disorder (MDD); when a person has an MDE, he or she is diagnosed with MDD. Symptoms of an MDE can arise in three areas: affect, behavior, and cognition.

Depression is becoming increasingly prevalent in younger cohorts. Depression and anxiety disorders have a high comorbidity—around 50%. MDD may arise with melancholic features, catatonic features, or psychotic features. Symptoms may also fall into less common patterns, as in atypical depression and chronic depression.

A diagnosis of dysthymic disorder requires fewer symptoms than does a diagnosis of MDD; however, the symptoms of dysthymic disorder must persist for a longer time than do symptoms of MDD. People who have both dysthymic disorder and MDD are said to have double depression.

Neurological factors related to depression include low activity in the frontal lobes, and abnormal functioning of dopamine, serotonin, and norepinephrine. The stress–diathesis model of depression highlights th[...]

Thinking like a clinician

Suppose that a friend began to sleep through morning classes, seemed uninterested in going out and doing things together, and became quiet and withdrawn. What could you conclude or not conclude based on these observations? If you were concerned that these were symptoms of depression, what other symptoms would you look for? What if your friend's symptoms did not appear to meet the criteria for an MDE—what could you conclude or not conclude? If your friend was, in fact, suffering from depression, how might the three types of factors explain the depressive episode? What treatments might be appropriate?

Summary of Bipolar Disorders

The four building blocks for diagnosing bipolar disorders are major depressive episode (MDE), manic episode, mixed episode, and hypomanic episode. Symptoms of a manic episode include grandiosity, pressured speech, flight of ideas, distractibility, poor judgment, decreased need for sleep, and psychomotor agitation. A mixed episode is characterized by symptoms of both an MDE and a manic episode and may include [...] suici[...]

Social factors that are associated with bipolar disorders include disruptive life changes and social and environmental stressors. The different factors create feedback loops that can lead to a bipolar disorder or make the patient more likely to relapse.

Mood stabilizers are one treatment that targets neurological factors; when manic, patients may receive an antipsychotic medication or a benzodiazepine.

Treatment that targets psychological factors—particularly CBT—helps patients recognize warning signs of mood episodes, develop better sleeping strategies, and, when appropriate, stay on medication.

Treatments that target social factors include interpersonal and social rhythm therapy (IPSRT), which can increase the regularity of daily events and decrease social stressors; family therapy and education; and group therapy or a self-help group, which is intended to decrease shame and isolation.

Thinking like a clinician

You get in touch with a friend from high school who tells you that she recently had a hypomanic episode. What are two possible DSM-IV-TR diagnoses that she might have had (be specific)? What will determine which dia[...]

- *Thinking Like a Clinician* questions. These questions ask students to apply what they have learned to other people and situations. These questions allow students to test their knowledge of the chapter's material; they may be assigned as homework or used to foster small-group or class discussion.

> **Thinking like a clinician**
> Suppose you are a mental health clinician working in a hospital emergency room in the summer; a woman is brought in for you to evaluate. She's wearing a winter coat, and in the waiting room, she talks—or shouts—to herself or an imaginary person. You think that she may be suffering from schizophrenia. What information would you need in order to make that diagnosis? What other psychological disorders could, with only brief observation, appear similar to schizophrenia?

- *Key Terms*. The final element of *Summing Up* is a list of the key terms used in that chapter—the terms that are presented in boldface in the text and are defined in the marginal glossary—with the pages on which the definitions can be found.
- At the very end of *Summing Up*, students are directed to the book-specific website, **www.worthpublishers.com/rosenberg**, for more study aids and resources pertinent to the chapter.

Integrated Gender and Cultural Coverage

The textbook has extensive culture and gender coverage integrated throughout the entire textbook. The list of coverage and corresponding page numbers are too numerous to list here, but you can find this coverage—in two different indexes—one for Culture and one for Gender—on Worth's free book companion site, which can be reached by going to www.worthpublishers.com/rosenberg. These indexes will help you locate the many different places where we offer this coverage in order to better facilitate learning in your classroom.

Media and Supplements

Online Video Tool Kit for Abnormal Psychology

The Online Video Tool Kit for Abnormal Psychology spans the full range of standard topics for a course in abnormal psychology, combining both research and news footage from the BBC Motion Gallery and CBS News, as well as other great sources. With its superb collection of brief (1 to 5 minutes) clips and emphasis on the neuropsychosocial bases of behavior, the Online Video Tool Kit for Abnormal Psychology gives students a fresh new way to experience the realities of living with psychological disorders from a patient's and a clinician's perspective.

Within the Online Video Tool Kit for Abnormal Psychology, Worth Publishers brings together some of the most famous and important psychology research and news footage ever filmed—and matches it with specific areas of coverage in this textbook. No other abnormal psychology video product available for student purchase offers such a high-quality collection of clips.

Instructors can create assignments and customize their students' experience by annotating the descriptions that accompany each video clip. Or instructors can choose to assign the Online Video Tool Kit for Abnormal Psychology to their students without customizing any of the material. Video clips are keyed to the textbook and

are accompanied by multiple-choice questions so that students can assess their understanding of what they've seen. Student responses are submitted to an online gradebook, making the Online Video Tool Kit for Abnormal Psychology a seamless part of the abnormal psychology course.

Also Available for Instructors: The Video Tool Kit for Abnormal Psychology on CD and close-captioned DVD

The CD and DVD includes the same video clips as the online version. Instructors can play clips to introduce key topics, to illustrate and reinforce specific core concepts, or to stimulate small-group or full classroom discussions. Clips may also be used to challenge students' critical thinking skills—either in class or via independent, out-of-class assignments.

Free Book Companion Site at www.worthpublishers.com/rosenberg

The companion website serves students as a *free*, continuously available online study guide, while providing instructors with a variety of presentation, assessment, and course management resources. Among its many features are Web quizzes by J. D. Rodgers, Hawkeye Community College, and Kanoa Meriwether, University of Hawaii–West Oahu.

CourseSmart eBook at www.coursesmart.com

CourseSmart is a new way for instructors and students to access textbooks online anytime and from anywhere. With thousands of titles related to hundreds of courses, CourseSmart helps instructors choose the best textbook for their class and give their students the option of buying the assigned textbook as a lower cost eTextbook.

Instructor's Resource Manual, by Meera Rastogi, University of Cincinnati (1-4292-3472-5)

The resource manual offers chapter-by-chapter support for instructors using the text, as well as tips for communicating the neuropsychosocial approach to abnormal psychology to students. For each chapter, the manual offers the following:

- A brief outline
- Learning objectives
- List of key terms
- A chapter guide, including an extended chapter outline, point-of-use references to art in the text, and listings of class discussions/activities, assignments, and extra credit projects for each section

The manual recommends additional media for enhancing lectures and assignments, including films, books, magazine and journal articles, and web sites.

Test Bank, by Joy Crawford, University of Washington, and Judith Levine, Farmingdale State College (Printed: 1-4292-3468-7; CD [Mac and Windows on one disc], 1-4292-3473-3)

The test bank offers over 1700 questions, including multiple-choice, true/false, fill-in, and essay questions. The CD version makes it easy for instructors to add, edit, and change the order of questions.

Student Study Guide, by Joe Etherton, Texas State University (1-4292-3470-9)

This helpful student resource offers chapter-by-chapter help for studying and exam preparation.

Acknowledgments

We want to thank the following people, who generously gave of their time to review one or more—in some cases all—of the chapters in this book. Their feedback has helped make this a better book.

Eileen Achorn, University of Texas at San Antonio
Tsippa Ackerman, Queens College
Paula Alderette, University of Hartford
Richard Alexander, Muskegon Community College
Leatrice Allen, Prairie State College
Liana Apostolova, University of California, Los Angeles
Hal Arkowitz, University of Arizona
Randolph Arnau, University of Southern Mississippi
Tim Atchison, West Texas A&M University
Linda Bacheller, Barry University
Yvonne Barry, John Tyler Community College
David J. Baxter, University of Ottawa
Bethann Bierer, Metropolitan State College of Denver
Dawn Bishop Mclin, Jackson State University
Nancy Blum, California State University, Northridge
Robert Boland, Brown University
Kathryn Bottonari, University at Buffalo/SUNY
Joan Brandt Jensen, Central Piedmont Community College
Franklin Brown, Eastern Connecticut State University
Eric Bruns, Campbellsville University
Gregory Buchanan, Beloit College
Jeffrey Buchanan, Minnesota State University–Mankato
NiCole Buchanan, Michigan State University
Danielle Burchett, Kent State University
Glenn M. Callaghan, San Jose State University
Christine Calmes, University at Buffalo/SUNY
Rebecca Cameron, California State University, Sacramento
Alastair Cardno, University of Leeds
Kan Chandras, Fort Valley State University
Jennifer Cina, University of St. Thomas
Carolyn Cohen, Northern Essex Community College
Sharon Cool, University of Sioux Falls
Craig Cowden, Northern Virginia Community College
Judy Cusumano, Jefferson College of Health Sciences
Daneen Deptula, Fitchburg State College
Dallas Dolan, The Community College of Baltimore County
Mitchell Earleywine, University at Albany/SUNY
Christopher I. Eckhardt, Purdue University
Diane Edmond, Harrisburg Area Community College
James Eisenberg, Lake Erie College
Frederick Ernst, University of Texas–Pan American
John P. Garofalo, Washington State University–Vancouver
Franklin Foote, University of Miami
Sandra Jean Foster, Clark Atlantic University
Richard Fry, Youngstown State
Murray Fullman, Nassau Community College
Irit Gat, Antelope Valley College
Marjorie Getz, Bradley University
Andrea Goldstein, South University
Steven Gomez, Harper College
Carol Globiana, Fitchburg State University

Cathy Hall, East Carolina University
Debbie Hanke, Roanoke Chowan Community College
Sheryl Hartman, Miami Dade College
Wanda Haynie, Greenville Technical College
Brian Higley, University of North Florida
Debra Hollister, Valencia Community College
Kris Homan, Grove City College
Farrah Hughes, Francis Marion University
Kristin M. Jacquin, Mississippi State University
Annette Jankiewicz, Iowa Western Community College
Paul Jenkins, National University
Cynthia Kalodner, Towson University
Richard Kandus, Mt. San Jacinto College
Jason Kaufman, Inver Hills Community College
Jonathan Keigher, Brooklyn College
Mark Kirschner, Quinnipiac University
Cynthia Kreutzer, Georgia Perimeter College, Clarkston
Thomas Kwapil, University of North Carolina at Greensboro
Kristin Larson, Monmouth College
Dean Lauterbach, Eastern Michigan University
Robert Lichtman, John Jay College of Criminal Justice
Michael Loftin, Belmont University
Jacquelyn Loupis, Rowan-Cabarrus Community College
Donald Lucas, Northwest Vista College
Mikhail Lyubansky, University of Illinois, Urbana-Champaign
Eric J. Mash, University of Calgary
Janet Matthews, Loyola University
Dena Matzenbacher, McNeese State University
Timothy May, Eastern Kentucky University
Paul Mazeroff, McDaniel University
Dorothy Mercer, Eastern Kentucky University
Paulina Multhaupt, Macomb Community College
Mark Nafziger, Utah State University
Craig Neumann, University of North Texas
Christina Newhill, University of Pittsburgh
Bonnie Nichols, Arkansas NorthEastern College
Rani Nijjar, Chabot College
Janine Ogden, Marist College
Randall Osborne, Texas State University—San Marcos
Patricia Owen, St. Mary's University
Crystal Park, University of Connecticut
Karen Pfost, Illinois State University
Daniel Philip, University of North Florida
Skip Pollack, Mesa Community College
William Price, North Country Community College
Linda Raasch, Normandale Community College
Christopher Ralston, Grinnell College
Lillian Range, Our Lady of Holy Cross College
Judith Rauenzahn, Kutztown University
Jacqueline Reihman, State University of New York at Oswego
Sean Reilley, Morehead State University
David Richard, Rollins College
Harvey Richman, Columbus State University
J.D. Rodgers, Hawkeye Community College
David Romano, Barry University

Sandra Rouce, Texas Southern University
David Rowland, Valparaiso University
Lawrence Rubin, St. Thomas University
Stephen Rudin, Nova Southeastern University
Michael Rutter, Canisius College
Thomas Schoeneman, Lewis and Clark College
Stefan E. Schulenberg, University of Mississippi
Christopher Scribner, Lindenwood University
Russell Searight, Lake Superior State University
Daniel Segal, University of Colorado at Colorado Springs
Frances Sessa, The Pennsylvania State University, Abington
Fredric Shaffer, Truman State University
Eric Shiraev, George Mason University
Susan J. Simonian, College of Charleston
Melissa Snarski, University of Alabama
Jason Spiegelman, Community College of Beaver County
Michael Spiegler, Providence College
Barry Stennett, Gainesville State College
Carla Strassle, York College of Pennsylvania
Nicole Taylor, Drake University
Paige Telan, Florida International University
Carolyn Turner, Texas Lutheran University
MaryEllen Vandenberg, Potomac State College of West Virginia
Elaine Walker, Emory University
David Watson, MacEwan University
Karen Wolford, State University of New York at Oswego
Shirley Yen, Brown University
Valerie Zurawski, St. John's University
Barry Zwibelman, University of Miami

We would also like to thank the thoughtful group of instructors who generously attended our 2009 APA focus group in Toronto and who also offered many excellent suggestions, some of which—even in the book's eleventh hour—found their way into the book. They are:

Gina M. Brelsford, Penn State University, Harrisburg
NiCole T. Buchanan, Michigan State University
Farah Ibrahim, University of Colorado Denver
Marva Lewis, Tulane University
John McIlvried, University of Indianapolis
Ilyse O'Desky, Kean University
Crystal Park, University of Connecticut, Storrs
Jeanne M. Slattery, Clarion University

Although our names are on the title page, this book has been a group effort. Special thanks to a handful of people who did armfuls of work in the early stages of the book's life: Nancy Snidman, Children's Hospital Boston, for help with the chapter on developmental disorders; Shelley Greenfield, McLean Hospital, for advice about the etiology and treatment of substance abuse; Adam Kissel, for help in preparing the first draft of some of the manuscript; Lisa McLellan, senior development editor, for conceiving the idea of "Facts at a Glance" tables; Susan Clancy for help in gathering relevant literature; and Lori Gara-Matthews and Anne Perry for sharing a typical workday of a pediatrician and a school psychologist, respectively.

To the people at Worth Publishers who have helped us bring this book from conception through gestation and birth, many thanks for your wise counsel, creativity, and patience. Specifically, thanks to: Erik Gilg, our acquisitions editor, for his continual assistance and good humor; Jim Strandberg, a freelancer, our final development editor who kept us on track and focused on the end goal and made us laugh along the way; Michael Kimball, our development editor for most of the first and second drafts and from whom we learned so much about writing; Catherine Woods, senior publisher, for having faith in our vision for this book, providing support at every step along the way, and for putting us in Erik's capable hands; Jane Hoover of Lifland et al., Bookmakers, copyeditor extraordinaire, for reading every word so carefully and catching errors and ambiguities; Babs Reingold, art director, for creating our wonderful design; Jaclyn Castaldo, assistant editor, for her good humor and diligence in handling the endless pages of manuscript and helping us with the reviews; Jenna Gray, project editor at PrePress, Dana Kasowitz, project editor at Worth, and Tracey Kuehn, associate managing editor at Worth, for keeping the final phases of the book on track; Patricia Cateura, photo researcher, and Christine Buese, photo editor, for helping us add photographs to the pages; Diane Kraut, permissions freelancer, for the thankless task of tracking down and obtaining permissions to use quotes, tables, and figures; Nancy Brooks, freelance editor, for carefully matching our words to photos and figures; to the team at Worth who help us introduce ourselves and our book to psychologists who teach abnormal psychology classes: Carlise Stembridge, associate marketing director; Kate Nurre, Executive Marketing Manager; and, Tom Kling, Worth's National Psychology Consultant. We also thank our fantastic supplements team: Sharon Prevost, media and supplements editor, for recruiting a talented team of academic authors and helping them bring the supplements to life: Joe Etherton, Texas State University and Judy Levine, Farmingdale State College (we give both of them an extra special shout out of thanks); Meera Rastogi, University of Cincinnati; Joy Crawford, University of Washington; J. D. Rodgers, Hawkeye Community College; Kanoa Meriwether, University of Hawaii–West Oahu; and the media team of Ramón Rivera Moret, video researcher and producer, Andrea Musick, Senior Media and Supplements Editor, and Alex Levering, freelance editor.

On the personal side, we'd like to thank our children—Neil, David, and Justin—for their unflagging love and support during this project and for their patience with our foibles and passions. We also want to thank: our mothers—Bunny and Rhoda—for allowing us to know what it means to grow up with supportive and loving parents; Steven Rosenberg, for numerous chapter story suggestions; Merrill Mead-Fox, Melissa Robbins, Jeanne Serafin, Amy Mayer, Kim Rawlins, and Susan Pollak, for sharing their clinical and personal wisdom over the last two and a half decades; Michael Friedman and Steven Hyman, for answering our esoteric pharmacology questions; and Jennifer Shephard and Bill Thompson, who helped track down facts and findings related to the neurological side of the project.

ABNORMAL
PSYCHOLOGY

The History of Abnormal Psychology

"Big Edie" (Edith Bouvier Beale, 1894–1977) and her daughter, "Little Edie" (Edith Beale, 1917–2002), lived together as adults for 29 years. Their home was a 28-room mansion, called Grey Gardens, in the chic town of East Hampton, New York. But the Beales were not rich society women, entertaining in grand style. They had few visitors, other than people who delivered food to them daily, and they lived in impoverished circumstances. For the most part, they inhabited only two of the second-floor rooms and an upstairs porch. The house, a wood-shingled seaside home, was falling apart, the paint on the shingles long since having been worn away by the elements. These intelligent women were not simply poor recluses, though. They were unconventional, eccentric women who flaunted the rules of their time and social class.

Let's consider Big Edie first. In her later years, Big Edie had difficulty walking, and her bedroom was the hub of the Beale women's lives. It contained a small refrigerator, a hot plate, and up to 52 cats. The room had two twin beds, one for Little Edie to use when in the room, the other for Big Edie. Big Edie made her bed into an unusual nest of blankets (no sheets), and the mattress was so soiled that the grime and the cat droppings were indistinguishable. Cats constantly walked across the bed or rested on it (or on Big Edie), but there was no litter box for them. Consider this exchange between mother and daughter:

> Big Edie: This cat's going to the bathroom right in back of my portrait. [A painting of Big Edie is resting on the floor, against the wall.]
>
> Little Edie: Oh; isn't that awful?
>
> Big Edie: No. I'm glad he is. I'm glad somebody's doing something they want to do.
>
> (Maysles & Maysles, 1976)

The room was mopped once a week (Wright, 2007).

Amid the squalor, food was heated or cooked on a hot plate next to Big Edie's bed. Big Edie hadn't left the house in decades (except for one occasion; Sheehy, 1972) and would let Little Edie out of her sight for only a few minutes before yelling for her to return to the bedroom. When Big Edie fell off a chair and broke her leg at the age of 80, she refused to leave the house to see a doctor, and refused to allow a doctor to come to the house to examine her leg. As a result, she developed bedsores that became infected and she died at Grey Gardens 7 months later (Wright, 2007).

Nicolas Wilton

Abnormal psychology
The subfield of psychology that addresses the causes and progression of psychological disorders; also referred to as *psychopathology*.

Psychological disorder
A pattern of thoughts, feelings, or behaviors that causes significant personal *distress*, significant *impairment* in daily life, and/or significant *risk of harm*, any of which is unusual for the context and culture in which it arises.

Little Edie was also unusual, most obviously in her style of dress. Little Edie always covered her head, usually with a sweater that she kept in place with a piece of jewelry. She professed not to like women in skirts, but invariably wore skirts herself, typically wearing them upside down so that the waistband was around her knees or calves and the skirt hem bunched around her waist. She advocated wearing stockings *over* pants, and she suggested that women "take off the skirt, and use it as a cape" (Maysles & Maysles, 1976).

Big Edie and Little Edie had limited financial means, but this wasn't the only reason for their plight. As Little Edie said, "We didn't live conventionally" (Graham, 1976). Although they were odd, could their behavior be chalked up to eccentricity, or did one or both of them have a psychological disorder? It depends on how "psychological disorder" is defined.

The sort of psychologist who would evaluate Big Edie and Little Edie would specialize in **abnormal psychology** (or *psychopathology*), the subfield of psychology that addresses the causes and progression of psychological disorders (also referred to as *psychiatric disorders, mental disorders,* or *mental illness*). How would a mental health clinician—a mental health professional who evaluates or treats people with psychological disorders—determine whether Big Edie or Little Edie (or both of them) had a psychological disorder? The clinician would need to evaluate whether the women's behavior and experience met three general criteria for psychological disorders.

The Three Criteria for Determining Psychological Disorders

Big Edie and Little Edie came to public attention in 1971 when their unusual living situation was described in the national press. Health Department inspectors had raided their house and found the structure to be in violation of virtually every regulation. "In the dining room, they found a 5-foot mountain of empty cans; in the upstairs bedrooms, they saw human waste. The story became a national scandal. Health Department officials said they would evict the women unless the house was cleaned" (Martin, 2002). The Beales were able to remain in their house after Big Edie's niece (Jacqueline Kennedy Onassis, the former first lady) paid to have the dwelling brought up to the Health Department's standards. Several years after this incident, Little Edie is reported to have said, "Do you know, they can get you in East Hampton for wearing red shoes on a Thursday?" (Maysles & Maysles, 1976), attributing the threatened eviction not to the state of their living environment, but to the color of the shoes she wore on a particular day.

In 1976, the Beales were again brought before the public eye with the release of the documentary film *Grey Gardens*, of which they were the "stars." During the filming, there were so many fleas in the house that the filmmakers strapped flea collars on their ankles before entering (Martin, 2002). At the time of the filming, Big Edie was 79 and her daughter 57, and the film captures their unusual lifestyle.

To determine whether Big Edie or Little Edie had a psychological disorder we must first define a **psychological disorder**: A pattern of thoughts, feelings, or behaviors that causes significant personal *distress*, significant *impairment* in daily life, and/or significant *risk of harm*, any of which is unusual for the context and culture in which it arises (American Psychiatric Association, 2000). Notice the word "significant" in the definition, which indicates that the diagnosis of psychological disorder is applied only when the symptoms have a substantial effect on a person's life. As we shall see shortly,

Big Edie and Little Edie Beale were clearly unconventional and eccentric. But did either of them have a psychological disorder? Psychological disorders involve significant distress, impairment in daily life, and/or risk of harm.

Archive Photos/Getty Images

all three elements (distress, impairment, and risk of harm) do not need to be present; if two (or even one) of the elements are present to a severe enough degree, then the person's condition may merit the diagnosis of a psychological disorder (see Figure 1.1). Let's consider these three elements in more detail.

Distress

Distress can be defined as anguish or suffering and all of us experience distress at different times in our lives. However, when a person with a psychological disorder experiences distress, it is often *out of proportion* to a situation. The state of being distressed, in and of itself, is not abnormal—it is the degree of distress or the circumstances in which the distress arises that mark a psychological disorder. Some people with psychological disorders exhibit their distress: They may cry in front of others, share their anxieties, or vent their anger on those around them. But other people with psychological disorders contain their distress, leaving family and friends unaware of their emotional suffering. For example, a person may worry excessively but not talk about the worries, or a depressed person may cry only when alone, putting on a mask to convince others that everything is all right.

Please note that severe distress, by itself, doesn't necessarily indicate a psychological disorder. The converse is also true: The absence of distress doesn't necessarily indicate the absence of a psychological disorder. A person can have a psychological disorder without experiencing distress, although it is uncommon. For instance, someone who chronically abuses stimulant medication, such as amphetamines, may not feel distress about misusing the drug but that person nonetheless has a psychological disorder (specifically, a type of *substance use disorder*).

Did either Big Edie or Little Edie exhibit distress? People who knew them describe the Beale women as free spirits, making the best of life. Like many people, they were distressed about their financial circumstances; but, of course, they had real financial difficulties, so these worries were not unfounded. Little Edie did show significant distress in other ways, though. She was angry and resentful about having to be a full-time caretaker for her mother, and the film *Grey Gardens* clearly portrays this: When Big Edie yells for Little Edie to return to her side, Little Edie says in front of the camera, "I've been a subterranean prisoner here for 20 years" (Maysles & Maysles, 1976).

Although Little Edie appears to be significantly distressed, her distress is reasonable *given the situation*. Being the full-time caretaker to an eccentric and demanding mother for decades would undoubtedly distress most people. Because her distress makes sense in its context, it is not an element of a psychological disorder. Big Edie, in contrast, appears to become significantly distressed when she is alone for more than a few minutes, and this response is unusual for the context. We can consider Big Edie's distress as meeting this criterion for a psychological disorder.

Impairment in Daily Life

Impairment is a significant reduction of an individual's ability to function in some area of life. A person with a psychological disorder may be impaired in functioning at school, at work, or in relationships. For example, a woman's drinking problem—and the morning hangovers—may interfere with her ability to do her job. Similarly, a middle-aged man who constantly—20 times a day or more—pesters his wife about whether he has adequately combed his remaining hair over his bald spot may find that his behavior has created considerable marital problems.

But where do mental health clinicians draw the line between normal functioning and impaired functioning? It is the *degree* of impairment that indicates a psychological disorder. When feeling "down" or nervous, we are all likely to function less well—for example, we may feel irritable or have difficulty concentrating.

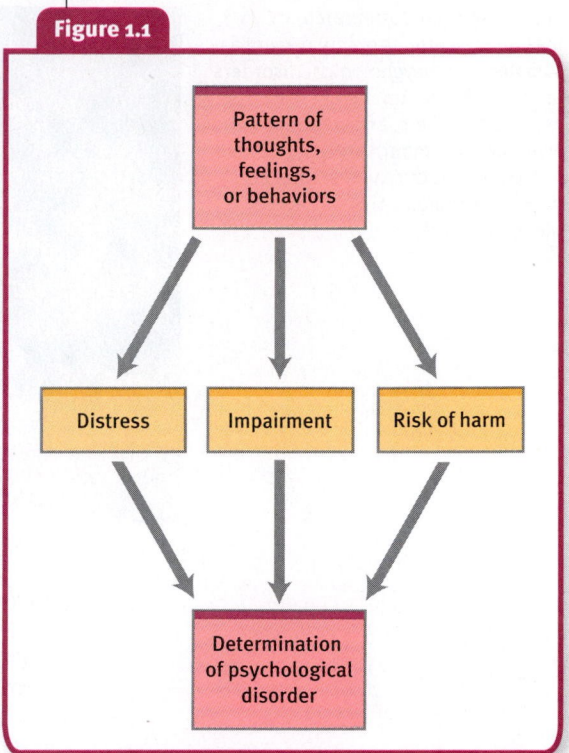

Figure 1.1

1.1 ▶ Determining a Psychological Disorder: Three Criteria The severity of an individual's distress, impairment in daily life, and/or risk of harm determine whether he or she is said to have a psychological disorder. All three elements don't need to be present at a significant level: When one or two elements are present to a significant degree, this may indicate a psychological disorder, provided that the person's behavior and experience are not normal for the context and culture in which they arise.

Researchers have attempted to measure the effects of impairment associated with psychological disorders on the ability to function at work: For every 100 workers, an average of 37 work days per month are lost because of reduced productivity or absences due to psychological disorders (Kessler & Frank, 1997).

Alex Maloney/zefa/Corbis

With a psychological disorder, though, the degree of impairment is atypical for the context—the person is impaired to a greater degree than most people in a similar situation. For instance, after a relationship breakup, most people go through a difficult week or two, though they still go to school or to work. They may not accomplish much, but they soon begin to bounce back. Some people, however, are more impaired after a breakup—they may not make it out of the house or even out of bed; they may not bounce back after a few weeks. These people are significantly impaired.

One type of impairment directly reflects a particular pattern of thoughts: a **psychosis** is an impaired ability to perceive reality to the extent that normal functioning is not possible. There are two forms of psychotic symptoms: hallucinations and delusions. **Hallucinations** are sensations that are so vivid that the perceived objects or events seem real, although they are not. Hallucinations can occur in any of the five senses, but the most common type is auditory hallucinations, in particular, hearing voices. However, a hallucination—in and of itself—does not indicate psychosis or a psychological disorder. Rather, this form of psychotic symptom must arise in a context that renders it unusual and indicates impaired functioning.

The other psychotic symptom is **delusions**—persistent false beliefs that are held despite evidence that the beliefs are incorrect or exaggerate reality. The content of delusions can vary across psychological disorders. Common themes include an individual's belief that:

- other people—the FBI, aliens, the neighbor across the street—are after the individual (*paranoid* or *persecutory delusions*);

- his or her intimate partner is dating or interested in another person (*delusional jealousy*);

- he or she is more powerful, knowledgeable, or influential than is true in reality and/or that he or she is a different person, such as the president or Jesus (*delusions of grandeur*);

- his or her body—or a part of it—is defective or functioning abnormally (*somatic delusion*).

Were the Beale women impaired? The fact that they lived in such squalor implies an inability to function normally in daily life. They knew about hygienic standards but didn't live up to them. Whether the Beales were impaired is complicated, however, by the fact that they viewed themselves as bohemians, set their own standards, and did not want to conform to mainstream values (Sheehy, personal communication, December 29, 2006). Their withdrawal from the world can be seen as clear evidence that they were impaired, though. Perhaps they couldn't function in the world, and so retreated to Grey Gardens.

The women also appear to have been somewhat paranoid: In the heat of summer, they left the windows nailed shut (even on the second floor) for fear of possible intruders. And Little Edie seems to have bizarre beliefs—for example, that wearing red shoes on a Thursday led to the threatened eviction—which may suggest that she had problems in understanding cause-and-effect in social interactions. The women's social functioning was impaired to the extent that their paranoid beliefs led to strange behaviors that isolated them. In addition, their beliefs led them to behave in ways that made the house so uncomfortable—extreme temperatures and fleas—that relatives wouldn't visit. And Big Edie's distress at being alone for even a few minutes indicates that her ability to function independently was impaired. It seems, then, that a case could be made that both of them—Big Edie more so than Little Edie—were impaired and unable to function normally.

Psychosis
An impaired ability to perceive reality to the extent that normal functioning is not possible. The two types of psychotic symptoms are hallucinations and delusions.

Hallucinations
Sensations that are so vivid that the perceived objects or events seem real, although they are not. Hallucinations can occur in any of the five senses.

Delusions
Persistent false beliefs that are held despite evidence that the beliefs are incorrect or exaggerate reality.

Risk of Harm

Some people take more risks than others. They may drive too fast or drink too much. They may diet too strenuously, exercise to an extreme, gamble away too much money, or have unprotected sex with multiple partners. For such behavior to indicate a psychological disorder, it must be outside the normal range. The criterion of danger, then, refers to symptoms of a psychological disorder that lead to life or property being put at risk, either accidentally or intentionally. For example, a person with a psychological disorder may be in danger when:

• depression and hopelessness lead him or her to attempt suicide;

• auditory hallucinations interfere with normal safety precautions, such as checking for cars before crossing the street;

• body image and other psychological disturbances lead the person to refuse to eat enough food to maintain a healthy weight, which in turn leads to malnutrition and medical problems.

Psychological disorders can also lead individuals to put other people's lives at risk. Examples of this type of danger include:

• auditory hallucinations that command the individual to harm another person;

• suicide attempts that put the lives of other people at risk, such as driving a car into oncoming traffic;

• paranoia so extreme that a parent kills his or her children in order to "save" them from a greater evil.

The house in which Little Edie and Big Edie lived had clearly become dangerous. Wild animals—raccoons and rats—roamed the house, and the ceiling was falling down. But having too little money to make home repairs doesn't mean that someone has a psychological disorder. Some might argue that perhaps the Beale women simply weren't aware of the danger. They were, however, aware of *some* dangers: When their heat stopped working, they called a heating company to repair it, and ditto for the electricity. They had a handyman come in regularly to repair fallen ceilings and walls and to fill holes that rats might use to enter (Wright, 2007). It's hard to say, however, whether they realized the extent to which their house itself had become dangerous.

On at least one occasion in her early 30s, Little Edie appears to have been a danger to herself. Her cousin John told someone about "a summer afternoon when he watched Little Edie climb a catalpa tree outside Grey Gardens. She took out a lighter. He begged her not to do it. She set her hair ablaze" (Sheehy, 2006). From then on, her head was at least partially bald, explaining her ever-present head covering.

Aside from Little Edie's single episode with the lighter, it's not clear how much the Beale women's behavior led to a significant risk of harm. Big Edie recognized most imminent dangers and took steps to ensure her and her daughter's safety. The women were not overtly suicidal nor were they interested in harming others. The only aspect of their lives that suggests a risk of harm was the poor hygienic standards they maintained.

Using this book's definition of a psychological disorder, did either of the Beales have a disorder? Big Edie exhibited *distress* that was inappropriate to her situation; both women appeared to have an *impaired* ability to function. The *risk of harm* to the women, however, is less clear-cut.

Everett Collection

Context and Culture

As we noted earlier, what counts as a significant level of distress, impairment, or risk of harm depends on the context in which it arises. That human waste was found in an empty room at Grey Gardens might indicate abnormal behavior, but the fact that the plumbing was out of order for a period of time might provide a reasonable explanation. Of course, knowing that the human waste was allowed to remain in place after the plumbing was fixed would probably decide the question of whether the behavior was abnormal.

In addition, the Beales appeared to have delusions—that people wanted to break into the house or kidnap them, and that then-President Nixon might have been responsible for the 1971 "raid" on their house by the town health inspectors (Wright, 2007). But these delusions aren't necessarily as farfetched as they might sound. Their house *was* broken into in 1968, and, as relatives of Jackie Kennedy, they had cars with Secret Service agents posted outside their house while John F. Kennedy was president.

Behavior that seems inappropriate in one context may make sense from another point of view. Having a psychological disorder isn't merely being different—we wouldn't say that someone was abnormal simply because he or she was avant-garde or eccentric or acted on unusual social, sexual, political, religious, or other beliefs. And as we've seen with the Beales, the effects of context can blur the line between being different and having a disorder. Table 1.1 provides additional information about psychological disorders.

Culture, too, can play a crucial role in how mental illness is diagnosed. To psychologists, **culture** is the shared norms and values of a society; these norms and values are explicitly and implicitly conveyed to members of the society by example and through the use of reward and punishment. Different societies and countries have their own cultures, each with its own view of what constitutes mental health and mental illness, and even what constitutes distress. For example, in some cultures, distress may be conveyed by complaints of fatigue or tiredness rather than by sadness or depressed mood. Some sets of symptoms that are recognized as disorders in other parts of the world are not familiar to most Westerners. One example, described in Case 1.1, is *koro*, a disorder that arises in some people from countries in southeast Asia. Someone with *koro* rapidly develops an intense fear that his penis—or her nipples and vulva—will retract into the body and cause death (American Psychiatric Association, 2000). This disorder may break out in clusters of people, like an epidemic (Bartholomew, 1998; Sachdev, 1985). Similar genital-shrinking fears have been reported in India and in West African countries (Dzokoto & Adams, 2005; Mather, 2005).

Table 1.1 ▶ Psychological Disorders: Facts at a Glance

- Psychological disorders are a leading cause of disability and death, ranked second, after heart disease (Murray & Lopez, 1996).
- About half of all Americans will likely develop at least one of 30 common psychological disorders, such as depression, anxiety, or substance abuse, over the course of their lives; in half of the cases, symptoms will begin by age 14 (Kessler, Berglund, et al., 2005).
- Those born more recently have a higher likelihood of developing a psychological disorder than those born earlier (Kessler, Berglund, et al., 2005).
- Within a given year, about 25% of Americans experience a diagnosable or diagnosed mental disorder; of these cases, almost a quarter are severe (Kessler, Chiu, et al., 2005).
- Disadvantaged ethnic groups—Hispanics and Blacks—do not have a higher risk for psychological disorders overall (Breslau et al., 2005).

CASE 1.1 ▶ FROM THE OUTSIDE: Cultural Influence on Symptoms

Although most cases of *koro* appear to resolve quickly, in a minority of cases, symptoms may persist.

A 41-year-old unmarried, unemployed male from a business family, presented with the complaints of gradual retraction of penis and scrotum into the abdomen. He had frequent panic attacks, feeling that the end had come. The symptoms had persisted more than 15 years with a waxing and waning course. During exacerbations he spent most of his time measuring the penis by a scale and pulling it in order to bring it out of [his] abdomen. He tied a string around it and attached it to a hook above to prevent its shrinkage during [the] night. . . . He did not have regular work and was mostly dependent on the family.

(Kar, 2005, p. 34)

Another example of a set of symptoms not familiar in Western cultures is *possession trance*, which occurs when spirits (perhaps of a loved one who has died or an ancestor) purportedly take over an individual's body (often a woman's) and cause it to participate in a ritual. Possession trance occurs in many cultures and, in context, does not indicate psychosis; it can be a way for people who traditionally have less power to speak their minds in a culturally sanctioned way (Bourguignon, 2004).

Culture
The shared norms and values of a society that are explicitly and implicitly conveyed to its members by example and through the use of reward and punishment.

Constellations of symptoms, such as *koro* and possession trance, that are generally observed only in certain countries or cultures are said to be *culture-bound*.

Even within a country or culture, there are different segments—*subcultures*—that have their own norms and values, and these subcultures may support divergent views about mental health and mental illness. For instance, families who immigrated to the United States from Southeast Asia tend to value self-control and are more likely to interpret a child's pattern of physically active or aggressive behavior as a problem than are most Americans, who view such behavior in children as normal and healthy.

In addition, culture can shape the form taken by psychological distress and any ensuing problematic behaviors. As we shall see in the rest of this chapter, culture—and its evolution over time—affects the way individuals with mental illness see themselves and how other people respond to them. However, cultural norms about psychopathology are not set in stone but can shift. Consider that, in 1851, Dr. Samuel Cartwright of Louisiana wrote an essay in which he declared that slaves' running away was evidence of a serious mental disorder, which he called "drapetomania" (Eakin, 2000). More recently, homosexuality was officially considered a psychological disorder in the United States until 1973, when it was removed from the *Diagnostic and Statistical Manual of Mental Disorders*, the manual used by mental health clinicians to classify psychological disorders.

Cultural norms also affect how mental health professionals view mental illness. In fact, in the 1960s and 1970s, some researchers and psychiatrists believed that culture and context were so important that behavior that was merely unusual or undesirable had come to be labeled as mental illness. Thomas Szasz (1960) argued that because all people engage in "us-versus-them" thinking, it is easy for a society to stigmatize people who are noticeably different. That is, culturally undesirable behaviors, emotional difficulties, and coping problems may be inaccurately called mental illness. In fact, Szasz proposed that mental illness is actually a myth.

Although culture is undeniably important, it does not entirely define mental illness. As we shall show in this book, many studies have documented both commonalties across a wide range of culture and the contribution of neurological factors to the development and expression of mental illness. The assertion that mental illness is a myth is therefore not true and has been relegated to history. However, it is always important for mental health professionals to ensure that the diagnosis of mental illness is not used simply to label people who are different or, as in the former Soviet Union, who question the policies of the government or those in authority. Diagnosing someone with a mental illness assigns a label that may influence how the diagnosed person feels about himself or herself and how that person is seen and treated by others (Eriksen & Kress, 2005).

Let's examine the behavior of the Beales within their context and culture. Big Edie's father claimed that his ancestors were prominent French Catholics; she and her siblings grew up financially well off. She was a singer and a performer, but, as a product of her time, she was expected to marry well (McKenna, 2004). Her father arranged for her to wed New York lawyer Phelan Beale, from a socially prominent Southern family (Rakoff, 2002). Little Edie was born about a year later, followed by two brothers. Big Edie was very close to her daughter, even keeping her out of school when Little Edie was 11 and 12, ostensibly for "health reasons." However, Little Edie was well enough to go to the movies with her mother every day and on a shopping trip to Paris (Sheehy, 2006).

Charles & Josette Lenars/Corbis

Although you may view the intentional facial scarring of this man from a tribe in West Africa as unusual, you probably do not view it as an indicator of a psychological disorder. But what if your neighbor or classmate had similar scarring—might you view it as a sign of a psychological disorder? Notice that the context of the behavior and the culture of the person influence your assessment.

After she was married, Big Edie continued to sing, to write songs with her accompanist, and even to record some of those songs. At that time, however, cultural conventions required a woman of Big Edie's social standing to stop performing after marrying, even if such performances generally were limited to social functions. Big Edie's need to perform was almost a compulsion, though, and she would head straight to the piano at family gatherings. Her nieces and nephews were eager to hear her sing, but the adults in her extended family, and her own children, were not. Her parents and siblings barely tolerated her at family gatherings (Davis, 1969). Clearly, even as a young woman, Big Edie was already behaving in ways that were at odds with cultural norms.

In 1934, when Little Edie was 16, Big Edie and her husband divorced; at that time, divorce was much less common and much less socially acceptable than it is today. This event marked the start of Big Edie's life as a recluse (Davis, 1969). By 1936, the house and grounds began to suffer from neglect (Davis, 1996). In 1942, Big Edie's husband stopped supporting her financially after she showed up late for their son's wedding, dressed inappropriately—another time when Big Edie's behavior was unusual for the context and culture. Big Edie's father was also angry with her for her inappropriate behavior, but he didn't want her to starve. He set up a trust fund for her, which provided a small monthly allowance, barely enough to pay for food and other necessities.

Like her mother, Little Edie was artistically inclined. She aspired to be an actress, dancer, and poet, and she claimed that wealthy men such as Howard Hughes and Joe Kennedy, Jr. (John F. Kennedy's older brother, who died in World War II) proposed marriage, which she refused. Little Edie's cousin said of her, "She had a very, very fertile imagination" (Martin, 2002). In 1946, she left home to live in New York City and work as a model, but her father disapproved of this as he had disapproved of his wife's musical performances (Sheehy, 2006).

In 1952, after 6 years of being separated from her daughter, Big Edie became seriously depressed (Sheehy, 2006), although there is no information about her specific symptoms. She spent 3 months calling Little Edie daily, begging her to return to Grey Gardens. Eventually, Little Edie moved back to take care of Big Edie. When she did, her artistic aspirations became only dreams and fantasies. The documentary film *Grey Gardens* vividly captures Little Edie's palpable disappointment at the path her life took—becoming a round-the-clock caretaker to her mother, a disappointed woman herself.

So far, we've seen that psychological disorders lead to significant distress, impairment in daily life, and/or risk of harm. We've also seen that the determination of a disorder depends on the culture and context in which these elements occur. A case could be made that the Beale women did have psychological disorders; let's consider each one in turn. Big Edie exhibited significant distress when alone for more than a few minutes; her reclusiveness and general lifestyle suggest an impaired ability to function independently in the world—perhaps to the point where there might be a risk of harm to herself or her daughter. Her behavior and experience appear to satisfy the first two criteria, which is enough to indicate that she had a psychological disorder. Moreover, Big Edie suffered from depression at some point after Little Edie moved to New York, and she experienced enough distress that she begged her daughter to return to Grey Gardens.

As for Little Edie, her distress was appropriate for the context, and thus would not meet the first criterion. Her ability to function independently, though, appears to have been significantly impaired, which also increased the risk of harm to herself and her mother. It appears that she too suffered from a psychological disorder. However, these conclusions must be tentative—they are based solely on films of the women and other people's descriptions and memories of them.

Now that we know what is required to determine whether someone has a psychological disorder, we'll spend the rest of this chapter looking at how psychopathology has been explained through the ages, up to the present.

Key Concepts and Facts About The Three Criteria for Determining Psychological Disorders ▪

- A psychological disorder is a pattern of thoughts, feelings, or behaviors that causes significant distress, impaired functioning in daily life, and/or risk of harm.

- The distress involved in a psychological disorder is usually out of proportion to the situation.

- Impairment in daily life may affect functioning at school, at work, at home, or in relationships. Moreover, people with a disorder are impaired to a greater degree than most people in a similar situation. A psychosis is a relatively easily identifiable type of impairment that includes hallucinations or delusions.

- A psychological disorder may lead to behaviors that create a significant risk of harm to the person or to others.

- Mental health clinicians and researchers recognize that context and culture in part determine whether a person's state involves significant distress, impairment, or risk of harm. In particular, people from different cultures may express distress differently, and some sets of symptoms, such as possession trance, may, in fact, not be a disorder in certain cultures.

Views of Psychological Disorders Before Science

Psychological disorders have probably been around as long as there have been humans. In every age, people have tried to answer the fundamental questions of why mental illness occurs and how to treat it. In this section, we begin at the beginning, by considering the earliest known explanations of psychological disorders.

Ancient Views of Psychopathology

Symptoms of psychopathology can take a toll both on the people suffering from a disorder and on others affected by their symptoms. Throughout history, humans have tried to understand the causes of mental illness in an effort to counter its detrimental effects. The earliest accounts of abnormal thoughts, feelings, and behaviors focused on two possible causes: (1) supernatural forces and (2) an imbalance of substances within the body.

Supernatural Forces

Societies dating as far back as the Stone Age appear to have explained psychological disorders in terms of supernatural forces (Porter, 2002)—magical or spiritual in nature. Both healers and common folk believed that the mentally ill were possessed by spirits or demons, and possession was often seen as punishment for some religious, moral, or other transgression.

    In the ancient societies that understood psychological disorders in this way, treatment often consisted of *exorcism*—a ritual or ceremony intended to force the demons to leave the individual's body and restore the person to a normal state. The healer led the exorcism, which in some cultures consisted of reciting incantations, speaking with the spirit, and inflicting physical pain to induce the spirit to leave the individual's body (Goodwin, Hill, & Attias, 1990). This belief in supernatural forces was common in ancient Egypt and Mesopotamia (and, as we shall see shortly, arose again in the Middle Ages in Europe and persists today in some cultures). Although it is tempting to regard such a view of psychopathology—and its treatment—as barbaric or uncivilized, the healers were simply doing the best they could in trying to understand and treat devastating impairments.

Chinese *Qi*

Healers in China in the 7th century B.C.E. viewed psychological disorders as a form of physical illness, reflecting imbalances in the body and spirit. This view, which continues to be common in China to this day, rests on the belief that all living things

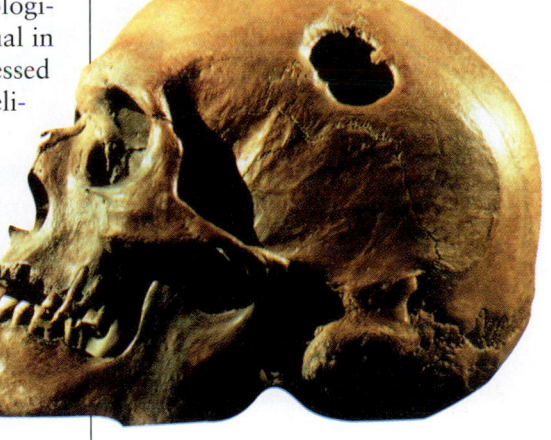

Archaeologists have found evidence of *trephination*, the boring of a hole in the skull, dating as far back as 7,000 years ago. In some ancient cultures, insanity was thought to arise from supernatural forces; one explanation for trephination is that the hole allowed these supernatural forces to escape. Treatment for mental illness is usually related to the prevailing explanation of the cause of the mental illness.

Eurelios/Photo Researchers

have a life force, called *qi* (pronounced "chee" as in *cheetah*), which flows through the body along 12 channels to the organs. Illness results when *qi* is blocked or seriously imbalanced. This is one of the oldest biological explanations of psychological disorders. Even today, Chinese treatment for various problems, including some psychological disorders, aims to restore the proper balance of *qi*. Practitioners use a number of techniques, including acupuncture and herbal medicine.

Ancient Greeks and Romans

Like the ancient Chinese, the ancient Greeks viewed mental illness as a form of bodily illness (U.S. National Library of Medicine, 2005). According to their theory, mental illness arose through an imbalance of four *humors* (that is, bodily fluids): black bile, blood, yellow bile and phlegm. Each humor corresponded to one of four basic elements: earth, air, fire, water. The ancient Greeks believed that differences in character reflected the relative balance of these humors, and an extreme imbalance of the humors resulted in illness—including mental illness (see Table 1.2). Most prominent among the resulting mental disorders were *mania* (marked by excess uncontrollability, arising from too much of the humors blood and yellow bile) and *melancholy* (marked by anguish and dejection, and perhaps hallucinations, arising from too much black bile). The goal of treatment was to restore the balance of humors through diet, medicine, or surgery (such as bleeding, or letting some blood drain out of the body if the person had too much of the humor blood).

Table 1.2 ▸ The Four Humors

Element	Humor	Material and Function	Character
Earth	Black Bile	A dark liquid that causes other fluids and parts of the body to darken (such as stool, hair, skin)	Gloomy or sullen
Air	Blood	A red liquid that promotes vitality	Lively and energetic, but easily angered
Fire	Yellow Bile	A gastric fluid that promotes digestion	Irritable and biting
Water	Phlegm	A lubricant and coolant that is most evident in excess (as in tears or sweat)	Indifferent and apathetic

Beginning with the physician Hippocrates (460–377 B.C.E.), the ancient Greeks emphasized reasoning and rationality in their explanations of natural phenomena, rejecting supernatural explanations. In many ways, Hippocrates was a visionary: He suggested that the brain, rather than any other bodily organ, is responsible for mental activity, and that mental illness arises from abnormalities in the brain (Shaffer & Lazarus, 1952). Today, the term *medical model* is used to refer to Hippocrates' view that all illness, including mental illness, has its basis in biological disturbance. Nevertheless, regardless of how insightful the Greeks' basic theory of disorders may have been, their treatments were not sophisticated by today's standards. Such treatments included music, bathing, diets, and bleeding.

Galen (131–201 C.E.), a Roman doctor, extended the ideas of the Greeks. Galen proposed that imbalances in humors produced emotional imbalances—and such emotional problems in turn could lead to psychological disorders. His view of the importance of emotions extended to treatment: Just as the humors must be balanced for physical health, so too must the emotions (U.S. National Library of Medicine, 2005). However, the fall of the Roman Empire and the spread of Christianity throughout Europe affected the view of psychopathology: The views that biological or emotional forces contributed to psychopathology waned, as did scientific investigations into its causes.

Forces of Evil in the Middle Ages and the Renaissance

With the rise of Christianity in Europe, psychopathology came to be attributed to forces of evil; this view persisted from the Middle Ages until the early Renaissance.

The Middle Ages

During the Middle Ages (approximately 500–1400 C.E.), the Greek emphasis on reason and science lost influence, and madness was once again thought to result from supernatural forces, now being conceived as a consequence of a battle between good and evil for the possession of an individual's soul. Prophets and visionaries were believed to be possessed or inspired by the will of God. For example, French heroine Joan of Arc reported that she heard the voice of God command her to lead a French army to drive the British out of France. The French hailed her as a visionary. In contrast, other men and women who reported such experiences usually were believed to be possessed by the devil or were viewed as being punished for their sins. Treatment consisted of attempts to end the possession: exorcism, torture (with the idea that physical pain would drive out the evil forces), starvation, and other forms of punishment to the body. Such inhumane treatment was not undertaken everywhere, though. As early as the 10th century, Islamic institutions were caring humanely for those with mental illness (Sarró, 1956).

The Renaissance

During the Renaissance (15th through 17th centuries), mental illness continued to be viewed as a result of demonic possession, and witches (who were possessed by, or in league with, the devil) were held responsible for a wide variety of ills. Indeed, witches were blamed for other people's physical problems and even for societal problems, such as droughts or crop failures. As before, treatment was primarily focused on ridding the individual of demonic forces, in one way or another.

During the Renaissance, people believed that witches put the whole community in jeopardy through their evil acts and through their association with the devil (White, 1948). The era is notable for its witch hunts, which were organized efforts to track down individuals who were believed to be in league with the devil and to have inflicted possession on other people (Kemp, 2000). Once found, these "witches" were often burned alive. The practice of witch burning spread throughout Europe and the American colonies:

> Judges were called upon to pass sentence on witches in great numbers. A French judge boasted that he had burned 800 women in 16 years on the bench; 600 were burned during the administration of a bishop in Bamberg. The Inquisition, originally started by the Church of Rome, was carried along by Protestant Churches in Great Britain and Germany. In Protestant Geneva 500 persons were burned in the year 1515. Other countries, where there were Catholic jurists, boasted of as many burnings. In Treves, 7,000 were reported burned during a period of several years.
>
> (Bromberg, 1937, p. 61, quoted in White, 1948, p. 8)

Rationality and Reason in the 18th and 19th Centuries

At the end of the Renaissance, rational thought and reason gained acceptance again. French philosopher René Descartes proposed that mind and body are distinct, and that bodily illness arises from abnormalities in the body, whereas mental illness arises from abnormalities in the mind. Similarly, according to the 17th-century British philosopher John Locke, insanity is caused by irrational thinking, and so could be treated by helping people regain their rational and logical thought process.

Bettmann/Corbis

Joan of Arc (1412–1430) was a young Frenchwoman who led a French army and successfully drove the English out of France. She said that God spoke to her and told her to help her people. The French viewed her as a visionary, but the English believed her to be possessed by the devil.

Asylums

Institutions to house and care for people who are afflicted with mental illness.

Asylums were initially meant to be humane settings for those with mental illness. A victim of their success, asylums became overcrowded as a result of an influx of delinquents and people with certain medical illnesses. With overcrowding, the primary purpose of asylums became incarceration rather than treatment, as was true of the Hospital of St. Mary of Bethlehem ("Bedlem") in the early 18th century.

Burstein Collection/Corbis

Franz Mesmer believed that hysteria arises from blocked electromagnetic forces. He stated that his technique used the magnetic forces in his own hand to unblock electromagnetic forces in the patient when he moved his hand over—but not touching—her body. In fact, this treatment probably induced either a placebo effect or a hypnotic trance.

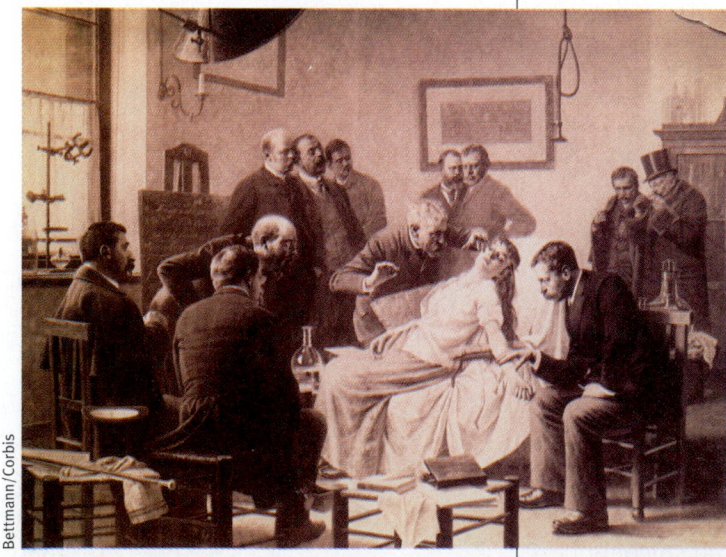

Bettmann/Corbis

However, deficits in rationality and reason turned out to be insufficient as an explanation for psychological disorders or as a foundation for treatment. In the Western world, the mentally ill were treated differently from country to country and decade to decade. As we see in the following sections, various approaches were tried in an effort to cope with the mentally ill and with mental illness itself.

Asylums

The Renaissance was a time of widespread innovation and enlightened thinking. For some people, this enlightenment extended to their view of how to treat those with mental illness—humanely. Some groups founded **asylums**, institutions to house and care for individuals who were afflicted with mental illness. Such institutions coped with the mentally ill as people. In general, asylums were founded by religious orders; the first of this type was opened in Valencia, Spain, in 1409 (Sarró, 1956). In subsequent decades, asylums for the mentally ill were built throughout Europe.

Initially, asylums were places of refuge for the mentally ill. But before long, delinquents and others were sent to asylums, and the facilities became overcrowded. Their residents were then more like inmates than patients. At least in some cases, people were sent to asylums simply to keep them off the street, without any effort to treat them.

Perhaps the most famous asylum from this era was the Hospital of St. Mary of Bethlehem in London (commonly referred to as "Bedlem" or later as "Bedlam," which became a word meaning "confusion and uproar"). In 1547, that institution shifted from being a general hospital to an asylum used to incarcerate the mad, particularly those who were poor. Residents were chained to the walls or floor or put in cages and displayed to a paying public much like animals in a zoo (Sarró, 1956). Officials promoted such displays as educational, allowing the public to observe what was believed to be the excesses of sin and passion. The idea was that such exhibitions would deter people from indulging in behaviors believed to lead to mental illness.

Novel Humane Treatments

At the same time that asylums were incarcerating many of the mentally ill, some people were trying to treat psychological disorders. For example, in Europe during the 18th and 19th centuries, a common psychological disorder, particularly among women, was *hysteria*—a disorder marked by physical symptoms such as paralysis, blindness, and bodily tics for which doctors could find no specific medical cause. Franz Mesmer (1734–1815) caused a stir among the French by proposing a new theory to explain hysteria. His view was that all living things possessed *animal magnetism*—a fluid of electromagnetism that flowed in the body through fine channels—and that hysteria was caused by blocked electromagnetic forces. Treatment, according to Mesmer, should unblock the flow. The technique he used to do so came to be called *mesmerism*. It consisted of the healer's passing his hands (which contained his own magnetism) very close to the patient's body to unblock the patient's flow of electromagnetism; Mesmer called these hand motions "magnetic passes" (Crabtree, 2000).

Although Mesmer's treatment was sometimes successful, this didn't necessarily indicate that his theory was correct. For example, the successes might have occurred simply because of a placebo effect (such as occurs when a sugar pill helps patients recover, as we will discuss in Chapter 5), or possibly because the treatment induced a hypnotic trance, which is used even today to alleviate pain and other medical symptoms. A scientific commission, headed by Benjamin Franklin, investigated mesmerism and discredited the theory of electromagnetism and the treatment based on that theory (Chaves, 2000). Nonetheless, Mesmer's treatment was more humane than many that had come before it.

The humane treatment of people with psychological disorders found a great supporter in French physician Phillipe Pinel (1745–1826). He and others transformed the lives of asylum patients at the Salpêtrière and Bicêtre Hospitals (for women and men, respectively) in Paris: In 1793, Pinel removed their chains and stopped "treatments" that involved bleeding, starvation, and physical punishment (Porter, 2002). Pinel and his colleagues believed that "madness" is a disease; they carefully observed patients and distinguished between different types of "madness." Pinel also identified *partial insanity*, where the individual was irrational with regard to one topic but was otherwise rational. He believed that such a person could be treated through psychological means, such as reasoning with him or her, which was one of the first *mental* treatments for *mental* disorders.

During the same period in England, King George III (1738–1820) displayed psychotic symptoms during his reign. In 1788, Francis Willis, who ran a private asylum, treated King George by creating blisters on his skin to draw out the "evil humors." When the king exhibited "mad" behaviors, Willis punished him, for example, by restraining him in a type of straightjacket, in an effort to bring him to his senses (Fraser, 2000). Willis used restraint when he felt it was necessary but also tried to talk people out of their delusions, which is another *mental* treatment for mental disorders. More recently, scientists have proposed that King George probably suffered from *porphyria*, a rare genetic disorder of metabolism that can cause delusions and confusion; in the king's case, it was likely triggered by exposure to arsenic (Cox et al., 2005). When the king recovered from his bout of porphyria, the methods that Willis had used to treat his "madness" were, for a short time, hailed as cures for insanity.

Moral Treatment

During King George III's reign, a group of Quakers in York, England, developed a treatment that was based on their personal and religious belief systems. Mental illness was seen as a temporary state during which the individual was deprived of his or her reason. **Moral treatment** consisted of providing an environment in which people with mental illness were treated with kindness and respect. The "mad" residents lived out in the country, worked, prayed, rested, and functioned as a community. Over 90% of the residents treated this way for a year recovered (Whitaker, 2002), at least temporarily.

Moral treatment also began to be used in the United States. Around the time that Pinel was unchaining the mentally ill in France, Doctor Benjamin Rush (1745–1813), a physician at the Pennsylvania Hospital in Philadelphia, moved the mentally ill from filthy basement cells to rooms above ground level, provided them with mattresses and meals, and treated them with respect.

In Massachusetts and other states, however, the mentally ill were still frequently incarcerated with felons under deplorable conditions. This began to change in the 1840s after Dorothea Dix (1802–1887), a schoolteacher, witnessed the terrible conditions that mental patients were forced to endure in asylums. She was inspired to engage in lifelong humanitarian efforts to ensure that the mentally ill were housed separately from criminals and treated humanely, in both public and private asylums (Viney, 2000). Dix also helped to raise millions of dollars for building new mental health facilities throughout the United States. Her work is all the more remarkable because she undertook it at a time when women did not typically participate in such political endeavors.

Moral treatment proved popular, and its success had an unintended consequence: Unlike private asylums, public asylums couldn't turn away patients, and thus their population increased tenfold as the mentally ill were joined by people with epilepsy and others with neurological disorders, as well as many who might otherwise have gone to jail. As a result, public institutions housing the mentally ill

King George III of England exhibited signs of psychosis—hallucinations and delusions. Among the treatments the king received were various forms of punishment, which the man in charge of his care, Francis Willis, believed would induce the king to "come to his senses." The king's madness was probably a result of a medical condition, porphyria, unidentified at that time, and Willis's treatment probably delayed his recovery.

Humanitarian Dorothea Dix worked tirelessly for humane treatment of the mentally ill in the United States (Viney, 2000).

Moral treatment
The treatment of the mentally ill that provided an environment in which people with mental illness were treated with kindness and respect and functioned as part of a community.

again became overcrowded and underfunded, and moral treatment—or treatments of any kind—were no longer provided (Porter, 2002). Sedation and management became the new goals.

Neurasthenia

By the end of the 19th century in Europe and North America, "madness" was generally seen as caused by a medical abnormality. The specific type of medical abnormality varied, however, from country to country and from decade to decade. In the United States, the pace of life increased with the advent of the telegraph and the railroad. More and more men and women were diagnosed with *neurasthenia*—literally, nerve weakness—which was accompanied by the symptoms of low mood and mental and physical fatigue. Treatment, administered by a physician, included rest, sedatives, and induced vomiting or bleeding.

Key Concepts and Facts About Views of Psychological Disorders Before Science

- The oldest known view of psychopathology is that it arose fro supernatural forces, either magical or spiritual in nature. Treatment included exorcism. Ancient and modern Chinese views of psychopathology consider its cause to be blocked or significantly imbalanced *qi*. The ancient Greeks attributed mental illness to an imbalance of bodily humors. The term *medical model* refers to Hippocrates' view that illness (including psychological disorders) is due to a biological disturbance.

- The Middle Ages saw a resurgence of the view that supernatural forces cause psychopathology; prophets and visionaries were believed to be possessed or inspired by the will of God. This view persisted into the Renaissance, when mental illness was viewed as the result of demonic possession, and witches were thought to be possessed by, or in league with, the devil. Treatment of the mentally ill consisted of exorcism; those believed to be witches were burned alive. By the end of the Renaissance, however, the mentally ill began to be treated more humanely, and asylums were built throughout Europe; over time, however, these asylums became a place to keep the mentally ill poor off the street, which led to overcrowded facilities.

- In the years immediately following the Renaissance, mental illnesses were thought to arise from irrational thinking, but this ap-

proach did not lead to consistent cures. Mesmer proposed that hysteria was caused by blocked electromagnetic forces in the body, and he developed a humane technique—mesmerism—to unblock the flow. His treatment was sometimes successful, possibly because it induced a hypnotic trance.

- Beginning in the 1790s, Pinel championed humane treatment for those in asylums in France. Based on careful observation, he proposed that there were different types of madness, and he used a mental treatment—reasoning with patients—to treat mental disorders. In other European settings, patients were given moral treatment, which centered on having them live and work within a community in the countryside.

- In the United States, Benjamin Rush initiated the effort to treat the mentally ill more humanely; similarly, Dorothea Dix strove to ensure that the mentally ill were housed separately from criminals and treated humanely. However, public institutions for the mentally ill became overcrowded and underfunded, which reduced the amount and quality of the treatment that was provided. By the end of the 19th century in Europe and North America, "madness" was generally viewed as caused by a medical abnormality. The characterization of the specific type of medical abnormality varied, however, from country to country and from decade to decade.

The Transition to Scientific Accounts of Psychological Disorders

Each of the prescientific explanations of psychological disorders proved inadequate. However, those who cared for and had responsibility for the mentally ill were making their best guesses about the cause of such illness and how best to cope with those who were afflicted. They were trying to help the individuals who experienced incredible distress and inability to function. But because the explanations proved inadequate over the course of time—and the responses to the mentally ill derived from them were not satisfactory—pressure built for more effective and enduring treatments.

There is one positive legacy from the prescientific era: The mentally ill came to be regarded as ill, and so were treated humanely, at least in some places and some eras. If the Beales had lived in the 18th century or earlier, they might have ended up as exhibits in an English asylum. If they had lived at the end of the 19th century, they would probably have been treated much better—although their chances of receiving effective treatment would still have been hit-or-miss. Fortunately, the situation improved dramatically during the 20th century. If the Beales were diagnosed today, they would almost certainly receive treatments that would enable them to function more effectively in the world. Let's now consider the crucial transition from prescientific times to today, the period when investigators worked to develop genuinely scientific theories about mental illness.

Freud and the Importance of Unconscious Forces

Sigmund Freud (1856–1939), a Viennese neurologist, played a major role in making the study of psychological disorders a science. He not only developed new methods, for both diagnosis and treatment (many of which are still in use today), but also proposed a rich and intricate theory, which continues to have massive influence on many clinicians. The beginnings of Freud's contributions to the study of psychopathology can be traced to 4 months he spent studying with the French neurologist Jean-Martin Charcot (1825–1893). Charcot, a professor at the Salpêtrière hospital in Paris, treated women with hysteria, which he believed arose from abnormal neurological functioning. Charcot proposed that people with hysteria have susceptible nerves, and that their hysterical symptoms could be cured by *hypnosis*, a trancelike state of consciousness in which a person is susceptible to suggestions about his or her thoughts, feelings, and behaviors. Charcot would induce a hypnotic trance in hysterical patients and suggest that their symptoms would go away, which they often did.

Initially, Freud used hypnosis with his patients in Vienna, though he found that not everyone was equally hypnotizable and that patients' symptoms often returned. This led Freud to develop another method to help patients with hysteria: *free association*, a technique in which patients are encouraged to say whatever thoughts occur to them. Free association was part of Freud's treatment that involved talking—often referred to as the "talking cure"—which rested on his idea that hysteria (and mental disorders in general) arises in part because of unconscious conflicts. His idea was that talking freely would help a person to reduce his or her unconscious conflicts and so provide some relief from the psychological disorder.

Psychoanalytic Theory

Freud developed a far-reaching theory of the origins, nature, and treatment of psychopathology based on both his work with patients (who were mostly middle-class and upper-middle-class women with hysteria) and his observations about himself. His theory, **psychoanalytic theory** (the Greek word *psyche* means "mind"), proposes that thoughts, feelings, and behaviors are a result of conscious and unconscious forces continually interacting in the mind. Freud often discussed *motivations*, which are thoughts (such as goals), feelings (such as guilt), or a mixture of thoughts and feelings that impel one to behave in a specific way. Psychoanalytic theory also suggests that the mind is organized so as to function across three levels of consciousness:

- The *conscious* consists of thoughts and feelings that are in awareness; this is normal awareness.

- The *preconscious* consists of thoughts and feelings that a person does not perceive, but that might enter conscious awareness in the future.

- The *unconscious* includes thoughts and feelings that cannot be perceived or called into awareness on command, but which have power to influence a person.

Psychoanalytic theory
The theory that thoughts, feelings, and behaviors are a result of conscious and unconscious forces continually interacting in the mind.

Id
According to Freud, the seat of sexual and aggressive drives, as well as of the desire for immediate gratification of physical and psychological needs.

Superego
According to Freud, the seat of the conscience, which works to impose morality.

Ego
According to Freud, the psychic structure that is charged with mediating between the id's demands for immediate gratification and the superego's high standards of morality, as well as the constraints of external reality.

Psychosexual stages
According to Freud, the sequence of five distinct stages of development (oral, anal, phallic, latency, and genital) through which children proceed from infancy to adulthood; each stage has a key task that must be completed successfully for healthy psychological development.

Figure 1.2

1.2 ▸ The Iceberg Metaphor of the Organization of the Mind According to Freud Freud proposed that the mind is made up of three structures: id, ego, and superego. Each individual is aware (conscious) of some of what is in his or her ego and superego; some of the preconscious contents of the ego and the superego can be brought into awareness, and some of those contents—along with all of the id—remain unconscious.

According to Freud, people have sexual and aggressive urges from birth onward. Freud argued that when we find such urges unacceptable, they are banished to our unconscious, where they inevitably gain strength and eventually demand release. Unconscious urges can be released as conscious feelings or thoughts, or as behaviors. Freud believed that abnormal experiences and behaviors arise from this process. For example, according to psychoanalytic theory, one woman's extreme fear of eating dust—which drove her to cover cooked food on the stove, not to serve food until she had brushed off her clothes and the tablecloth, and to wash her plate repeatedly to remove any speck of dust—arose from unconscious sexual impulses related to "taking in" semen (the dust symbolically represented semen; Frink, 1921).

Freud (1923/1961) also distinguished three psychological structures of the mind—the id, the ego, and the superego:

- The **id** is the seat of sexual and aggressive drives, as well as of the desire for immediate gratification of physical and psychological needs. These physical needs (such as for food and water) and psychological drives (sexual and aggressive) constantly require satisfaction. The id follows the *pleasure principle*, seeking gratification of needs without regard for the consequences.

- The **superego**, the seat of an individual's conscience, works to impose morality. According to Freud, the superego is responsible for feelings of guilt, which motivate the individual to constrain his or her sexual and aggressive urges that demand immediate gratification. People with an inflexible morality—an overly rigid sense of right and wrong—are thought to have too strong a superego.

- Meanwhile, the **ego** tries to mediate the id's demands for immediate gratification and the superego's high standards of morality, as well as the constraints of external reality. Normally, the ego handles the competing demands well. However, when the ego is relatively weak, it is less able to manage the conflicts among the id, superego, and reality, which then cause anxiety and other symptoms.

Figure 1.2 shows how the three mental structures are related to the three kinds of consciousness. As is evident, both the ego and the superego are privy to conscious thoughts, but also have access to preconscious ones (which can be called to mind voluntarily). Similarly, some aspects of both of these structures lie beneath consciousness, in the unconscious. The id is entirely in the realm of the unconscious. Thus, according to Freud, you cannot be directly aware of the basic urges that drive your thoughts, feelings, and behaviors. You only find out about these urges by observing their effects on the ego and the superego—usually in the form of conflicts. One of Freud's lasting contributions to the field of psychopathology—and all of psychology, in fact—is the notion of the unconscious, the mental processes that occur outside of our awareness and influence our motivations, thoughts, feelings, and behaviors.

Psychosexual Stages

Freud also identified five distinct stages of development (the oral, anal, phallic, latency, and genital stages) through which children proceed from infancy into adulthood. Four of these stages involve particular *erogenous zones*, which are areas of the body (the mouth, genitals, and anus) that can satisfy the id's urges and drives. Freud called these five stages **psychosexual stages** because he believed that each erogenous zone demands some form of gratification and that each stage requires a person successfully to complete a key task for healthy psychological development. All of these stages arise during infancy or childhood, although they may not be resolved until adulthood, if ever.

According to Freud, a child who fails to satisfy the needs of a psychosexual stage will develop a *fixation*, a tendency for thoughts, feelings, and behaviors to relate to that particular stage of psychosexual development, even as the child passes to the next stage. Under stress, a person with a fixation might regress to the thoughts, feelings, and behaviors of the earlier stage. For example, according to Freud (1905/1955), people with a fixation at the oral stage use food or alcohol to alleviate anxiety.

Mental Illness, According to Freud

Freud proposed two general categories of mental illness: *neuroses* and *psychoses*. A **neurosis** is a pattern of thoughts, feelings, or behaviors that expresses an unresolved conflict between the ego and the id or between the ego and the superego. One type of neurosis—what Freud called an *anxiety neurosis*—involves extreme "free-floating fear" that latches onto different objects or possibilities; people with anxiety neuroses may "interpret every coincidence as an evil omen, and ascribe a dreadful meaning to all uncertainty" (Freud, 1920, p. 344).

Freud (1938) defined *psychosis* as a break from reality characterized by conflict between the ego's view of reality and reality itself. (Note that this is *not* the definition of *psychosis* provided earlier in this chapter; that will be the one employed throughout the rest of this book.) According to the psychoanalytic view, then, schizophrenia involves a psychosis because it is an escape from reality into one's own internal world (Dorcus & Shaffer, 1945).

Freud was also revolutionary in proposing that parents' interactions with their child are central in the formation of personality. For instance, parents who are too strict about toilet training their toddler may inadvertently cause their child to become fixated at the anal stage. A person who has such a fixation may develop obsessional thoughts and compulsions about being clean and orderly, as in *obsessive-compulsive disorder*, which is marked by persistent and repetitive thoughts and behaviors (American Psychiatric Association, 2000).

In Freud's view, mental illness is caused by unconscious conflicts that express themselves as psychological symptoms. He revolutionized treatment of psychological disorders by listening to what patients had to say.

Bettmann/Corbis

Defense Mechanisms

In addition to proposing an explanation for how internal psychological conflict arises, Freud, along with his daughter, the noted psychoanalyst Anna Freud (1895–1982), suggested how such conflicts are resolved: The ego frequently employs unconscious **defense mechanisms**, which work to transform the conflicts in a way that prevents unacceptable thoughts and feelings from reaching consciousness. If successful, defense mechanisms can decrease anxiety (see Table 1.3). Freud proposed several defense mechanisms, and Anna Freud extended this work. Conflicts and threats do not necessarily cause psychological disorders, but they may do so when a particular defense mechanism is relied on too heavily.

Psychoanalytic Theory Beyond Freud

Psychoanalytic theory has been modified by Freud's followers; these variations fall under the term *psychodynamic theory* and have attracted many adherents. Psychodynamic theorists have focused on areas that Freud did not develop fully:

- normal versus abnormal development of the self (Kohut, 1971);

- the contribution of additional sources of motivation, such as feelings of inferiority (Ansbacher & Ansbacher, 1956);

- the development and work of the ego (Hartmann, 1939);

Neurosis
According to psychoanalytic theory, a pattern of thoughts, feelings, or behaviors that expresses an unresolved conflict between the ego and the id or between the ego and the superego.

Defense mechanisms
Unconscious processes that work to transform psychological conflict so as to prevent unacceptable thoughts and feelings from reaching consciousness.

Table 1.3 ▸ Common Defense Mechanisms

Defense Mechanism	How the Defense Mechanism Transforms the Conflict	Example
Repression (considered to be the most important defense mechanism)	Unintentionally keeping conflict-inducing thoughts or feelings out of conscious awareness	You "forget" about the time you saw someone getting mugged across the street.
Denial	Not acknowledging the conflict-inducing thoughts or feelings to oneself (and others)	You are addicted to painkillers, but won't admit it even though the addiction has caused you to miss work.
Rationalization	Justifying the conflict-inducing thoughts, feelings, or behaviors with explanations	After a father hits his daughter, he justifies his behavior to himself by saying she deserved it.
Projection	Ascribing (projecting) the conflict-inducing thoughts or feelings onto others	Instead of admitting that you don't like a classmate, you say the person doesn't like you.
Reaction Formation	Transforming the conflict-inducing thoughts or feelings into their opposite	Your feelings of attraction to your colleague at work are transformed into distaste and disgust, and you begin to feel repulsed by the colleague.
Sublimation	Channeling the conflict-inducing thoughts or feelings into less threatening behaviors	When a father's frustration and anger at his teenage daughter mount, he channels his feelings by going for a 20-minute run.

- the possibility that our species has certain inborn and unconscious archetypes (an *archetype* is an abstract, ideal characterization of a person, object, or concept) that channel some aspects of motivation (Jung, 1983).

In addition, Karen Horney (1885–1952) and other psychologists conducted research on the ways that moment-to-moment interactions between child and parent can contribute to psychological disorders (Horney, 1937; Kernberg, 1986; Sullivan, 1953). This emphasis on the contribution that an infant's social world can make to psychopathology is one of the lasting contributions of psychodynamic theory. Treatment based on psychodynamic theory is generally referred to as *psychodynamic therapy* and will be discussed in Chapter 4. Various modifications of psychodynamic therapy have been developed, based on specific alterations of Freud's theory.

Evaluating Freud's Contributions

One challenge to psychodynamic theory is that its guiding principles, and those of its corresponding treatments, rest primarily on subjective interpretations of what patients say and do. Another challenge is that the theory is not generally amenable to scientific testing. For instance, a fear of eating dust could be due to a sublimation of sexual impulses (a fixation at the oral stage) or a reaction formation to an unconscious desire to play with fecal matter (a fixation at the anal stage). The problem is not that there can be more than one hypothesis based on psychodynamic theory, but rather that there is no evidence and no clear means for obtaining evidence that either hypothesis (or both) is correct.

The Humanist Response

Some psychologists, such as Abraham Maslow (1908–1970), reacted adversely to Freud's ideas, especially two notions: (1) that mental processes are mechanistic (with the same sort of cause-and-effect relations that govern all machines), driven by sexual and aggressive impulses, and (2) that humans don't really have free will because our behavior is in response to unconscious processes. These psychologists proposed a different view of human nature and mental illness that came to be called *humanistic psychology*, which focuses on free will, innate goodness, creativity, and the self (Maslow, 1968). Mental health clinicians with this outlook, such as Carl Rogers (1902–1987), are often called *humanists*. Rogers (1942) proposed that symptoms of distress and mental illness arise when a potential route to personal growth is blocked, as can occur when a person lacks a coherent and unified sense of self or when there is a mismatch—or *incongruence*—between the ideal self (the qualities a person wants to have) and the real self (the qualities the person actually has). For example, suppose a woman believes she should *always* be energetic (ideal self), but her real self is someone who is often energetic, but not always. The incongruence between the two selves can lead her to feel bad about herself, which in turn creates feelings of apathy and guilt.

Rogers developed *client-centered therapy* to help people reduce such incongruence and to help them create solutions to their problems by releasing their "real selves." In accordance with this approach of self-empowerment, Rogers (1942) stressed that his *clients* were not *patients*, who are seen to be "sick" and lacking in power. Referring to people as "clients" indicated that they had control over their own lives and were interested in self-improvement through engagement with mental health services (Kahn, 1998).

However, although the emphasis on self-empowerment has proven useful, the humanist approach falls shorts as a general method for conceptualizing and treating mental illness. As we shall see, other factors (e.g., biological and social) must be considered.

Building on the humanist nomenclature, other clinicians have recognized that clients are consumers of mental health services who often choose from a variety of possible treatments. Nevertheless, it is also acceptable to use the term *patient*, and in this book we use the term *patient* and *patients* to emphasize the suffering and distress experienced by people with psychological disorders.

Lasting Contributions of Psychodynamic and Humanist Approaches

As the humanist response made clear, psychodynamic theory was not solidly rooted in science. Nevertheless, despite its limitations, psychodynamic theory rested on a fundamental insight that was crucial for the development of later theories and treatments: **Mental processes** are the internal operations that underlie cognitive and emotional functions (such as perception, memory, and guilt feelings) and most human behavior. In addition, psychodynamic theory's focus on **mental contents**—the specific memories, knowledge, goals, and other material that are stored and processed in the mind—has led to much fruitful research. Furthermore, the notion that some mental processes and mental contents are hidden away from consciousness has proven invaluable to understanding psychopathology. Psychodynamic theory is still used by some mental health clinicians to help them understand aspects of mental illness. Moreover, psychodynamic approaches cleared the way for more scientific approaches to understand psychological disorders, which we consider next.

Mental processes
The internal operations that underlie cognitive and emotional functions (such as perception, memory, and guilt feelings) and most human behavior.

Mental contents
The specific material that is stored in the mind and operated on by mental processes.

Key Concepts and Facts About The Transition to Scientific Accounts of Psychological Disorders

- Freud played a major role in making the study of psychological disorders a science, largely by developing new methods for diagnosis and treatment; he also proposed an extensive theory of psychopathology. Freud's methods included hypnosis (which he later abandoned) and free association.

- According to Freud's psychoanalytic theory, thoughts, feelings, and behaviors are a result of conscious and unconscious forces—such as sexual and aggressive urges—continually interacting in the mind. Moreover, he proposed that the mind is structured so as to function across three levels of consciousness: the conscious, the preconscious, and the unconscious. Freud stressed that many mental processes occur outside our awareness but nonetheless influence thoughts, feelings, and behaviors. Unacceptable urges are banished to the unconscious, where they inevitably gain strength and eventually demand release.

- Freud proposed three psychic structures in the mind—id, ego, and superego—which are continually interacting and negotiating. The ego frequently employs defense mechanisms to transform conflict in a way that prevents unacceptable thoughts and feelings from reaching consciousness.

- According to Freud, each individual passes through five psychosexual stages from infancy to adulthood, of which four involve particular erogenous zones. For healthy psychological development, each stage requires the successful completion of a key task; otherwise, the person will develop a fixation. Mental illness can take the form of neurosis or psychosis. Freud also proposed that parents' interactions with their child are central in forming the child's personality.

- Freud's followers focused on a variety of issues related to the development of the self and of the ego, the role of motivation, the possibility of unconscious archetypes, and the ways moment-to-moment interactions between child and parent can contribute to psychological disorders. Various forms of psychodynamic therapy have been proposed, each drawing primarily on a different aspect of psychodynamic theory. A drawback of psychodynamic theory is that it has proven difficult to test scientifically.

- Humanistic psychologists such as Carl Rogers viewed psychodynamic theory as too mechanistic and opposed to free will. Rogers proposed that symptoms of distress and mental illness arise when a potential route to personal growth is blocked, as can occur when there is incongruence between the ideal and real selves. Rogers developed client-centered therapy to decrease incongruence in clients.

- Lasting contributions of psychodynamic theory include the focus on mental processes and mental contents and the concept that such processes and contents can be hidden from awareness.

Scientific Accounts of Psychological Disorders

In the early 20th century, advances in science led to an interest in theories of psychological disorders that could be tested rigorously. Several different scientific approaches (and accompanying theories) that emerged at that time are still with us today; they focus on different aspects of psychopathology, including behavior, cognition, social forces, and biology. These scientific accounts and theories have thrived because studies have shown that they explain some aspects of mental illness. Let's examine these modern approaches to psychopathology and how they could explain Big Edie and Little Edie's lifestyle.

Behaviorism

All of the views discussed so far focus on forces that affect mental processes and mental contents. However, some psychologists in the early 20th century took a radically different perspective and focused on directly observable behaviors. Spearheaded by American psychologists Edward Lee Thorndike (1874–1949), John B. Watson (1878–1958), and Clark L. Hull (1884–1952), and, most famously, B. F. Skinner (1904–1990), **behaviorism** focuses on understanding directly observable behaviors rather than unobservable mental processes and mental contents (Watson, 1931). The behaviorists' major contribution to understanding psychopathology was to propose scientifically testable mechanisms that may explain how maladaptive behavior arises (Skinner,

Behaviorism
The approach to psychology that focuses on understanding directly observable behaviors in order to understand mental illness and other psychological phenomena.

1986, 1987). These psychologists focused their research on the association between a behavior and its consequences—factors that influence whether a behavior is likely to recur. For instance, to the extent that using a drug has pleasurable consequences, an individual is more likely to use the drug again.

At about the same time in Russia, Nobel-Prize–winning physiologist Ivan Pavlov (1849–1936) accidentally discovered an association between a reflexive behavior and its antecedents, an association created by a process sometimes referred to as *Pavlovian conditioning* (Pavlov, 1936). He studied salivation in dogs, and he noticed that dogs increased their salivation both while they were eating (which he predicted—the increased salivation when eating is a reflexive behavior) and *right before* they were fed (which he did not predict). After investigating why this latter salivation might occur, he determined that the dogs began salivating when they heard the approaching footsteps of the person feeding them. The feeder's footsteps (a neutral stimulus) became associated with the stimulus of food in the mouth, thus leading the dogs to salivate when hearing the sound of footsteps; the dogs' past association between the feeder's footsteps and subsequent food led to a behavior change.

Pavlov investigated the reflexive behavior of salivation, but other researchers have found that reflexive fear-related behaviors (such as a startle response) can be conditioned in the same fashion. These findings contributed to the understanding of how the severe fears and anxieties that are part of many psychological disorders can arise—how neutral stimuli that have in the past been paired with fear-inducing objects or events can, by themselves, come to induce fear or anxiety. We will consider such conditioning in more detail in Chapter 2.

Among the most important insights of behaviorism, then, is that a person's behavior, including maladaptive behavior, can result from learning—from a previous association with an object, situation, or event. Big Edie appears to have developed maladaptive behaviors related to a fear of being alone. This may have been a result of past negative experiences with (and the resulting associations to) being alone. The behaviorist approach has also accounted for some aspects of substance abuse, including alcoholism, which can arise because of the association between drinking and feeling more relaxed soon after drinking: Based on past experiences with alcohol, someone who wants to become less tense may reach for a bottle. Behaviorists have discovered different ways that associations can be learned, and each sort of learning can affect psychological disorders (we will discuss forms of learning in Chapter 2 and treatments based on these forms of learning in Chapter 4).

Behaviorism ushered in new explanations of—and treatments for—some psychological disorders, but researchers soon learned that not all psychological problems could readily be explained as a result of maladaptive learning. Rather, mental processes and mental contents are clearly involved in the development and maintenance of many psychological disorders. The behaviorists' emphasis on controlled, objective observation and on the importance of the situation, however, had a deep and lasting impact on the field of psychopathology.

Behaviorism focuses on observable behaviors and their consequences. According to behaviorists, maladaptive behaviors that are related to psychological disorders, such as drinking too much alcohol, can arise because the pleasurable consequences of the behavior lead people to want to engage in it again.

The Cognitive Contribution

Psychodynamic and behaviorist explanations of psychological disorders seemed incompatible. Psychodynamic theory emphasized private mental processes and mental contents; behaviorist theories emphasized directly observable behavior. Then, the late 1950s and early 1960s saw the rise of *cognitive psychology*, the area of psychology that studies mental processes starting from the analogy of information processing by a computer. Researchers developed new, behaviorally based methods to track the course of hidden mental processes, and these mental processes began to be demystified. If a mental process is like a computer program, direct connections can be made between observable events (such as changes in the time it takes to respond to different stimuli) and mental processes.

Cognitive psychology has contributed to the understanding of psychological disorders by focusing on specific changes in mental processes. For instance, people with *anxiety disorders*—a category of disorders that involves extreme fear, panic, and/or avoidance of a feared stimulus—tend to focus their attention in particular ways, creating a bias in what they expect and remember. In turn, these biased memories appear to support the "truth" of their inaccurate view about the danger of the stimulus that elicits their fear. For instance, a man who is very anxious in social situations may pay excessive attention to whether other people seem to be looking at him; when people glance in his general direction, he will then notice the direction of their gaze and infer that they are looking at him. Later, he will remember that "everyone" was watching him.

Other cognitive explanations of psychological disorders focused on the content of people's thoughts. Psychiatrist Aaron Beck (b. 1921) and psychologist Albert Ellis (1913–2007) each focused on how people's irrational and inaccurate thoughts about themselves and the world can contribute to psychological disorders (Beck, 1967; Ellis & Maclaren, 1998). For example, people who are depressed often think very negatively and inaccurately about themselves, the future, and the world. They think that they are inept, ugly, or unlovable or they have other equally unhappy thoughts. They often believe that they will *always* be so, and that no one will care about them; or, if someone does care, this person will leave as soon as he or she sees how really inept, ugly, or unlovable the depressed person is. Such thoughts could make anyone depressed! For cognitive therapists, treatment involves shifting, or *restructuring*, people's faulty beliefs and irrational thoughts that led to psychological disorders. Such cognitive techniques will be discussed in more detail in Chapter 4.

Cognitive therapy might have been appropriate for the Beale women, who had unusual beliefs. Consider the fact that Little Edie worried about leaving her mother alone in her room for more than a few minutes because she might come back and find her mother dead, or that a stranger might break in, despite the fact that the windows were nailed shut (Graham, 1976). Big Edie also had unusual beliefs. One time, a big kite was hovering over Grey Gardens and she called the police, concerned that the kite was a listening device or a bomb (Wright, 2007).

The focus on particular mental processes and mental contents illuminates some aspects of psychological disorders. But just as behaviorist theories do not fully address why individuals develop the *particular* beliefs and attitudes they have, cognitive theories do not fully explain why an individual's mental processes and contents are biased in a *particular* way. For instance, Little Edie's brothers, who grew up in the same household, were not eccentric, nor did they appear to harbor unusual beliefs or behave in bizarre ways. Knowledge about social and neurological factors (i.e., those that affect the brain and its functioning) helps to complete the picture.

Social Forces

We can view behavioral and cognitive explanations as psychological: Both refer to thoughts, feelings, or behaviors of individuals. In addition to these sorts of factors, we must also consider social factors, or factors that involve more than a single person. There is no unified social explanation for psychological disorders, but various researchers and theorists in the last half of the 20th century recognized that social forces affect the emergence and maintenance of mental illness. Many of these social forces, such as the loss of a relationship, abuse, trauma, neglect, poverty, and discrimination, produce high levels of stress.

Looking at the earliest years of life, Freud had a valuable insight when he recognized that the way parents treat their children can make them more vulnerable to mental illness. Two researchers who focused on the interactions between the infant and the primary caretaker were John Bowlby (1969) and Mary Ainsworth (1989; Ainsworth & Bell, 1970). They examined *attachment style*, which characterizes the particular way a person relates to intimate others. Specifically, they observed young American children with their mothers and characterized each child's attachment style by noting his or her behavior when the mother briefly left the room. Researchers have delineated four types of attachment styles:

1. *Secure attachment.* These children became upset when their mother left, but quickly calmed down upon her return (Ainsworth & Bell, 1970).

2. *Resistant/anxious attachment.* These children became angry when their mother left and remained angry upon her return, sometimes even hitting her (Ainsworth & Bell, 1970).

3. *Avoidant attachment.* These children had no change in their emotions based on mother's presence or absence (Ainsworth & Bell, 1970).

4. *Disorganized attachment.* These children exhibited a combination of resistant and avoidant styles, and also appeared confused or fearful with their mother (Main & Solomon, 1986).

Children who did not have a secure attachment style (those with a resistant/anxious, avoidant, or disorganized style) were more likely to develop symptoms of psychological disorders (Main & Solomon, 1986; Minde, 2003). However, attachment styles can be different in different cultures; these four attachment styles and their association with psychological disorders are not necessarily accurate descriptions of attachment styles for all cultures or countries (Rothbaum et al., 2000).

Research on social factors also points to the ways that relationships—and the social support they provide—can buffer the effects of negative life events (Hyman, Gold, & Cott, 2003; Swift & Wright, 2000). For example, researchers have found that healthy relationships can mitigate the effects of a variety of negative events, such as abuse (during childhood or adulthood), trauma, discrimination, and financial hardship. The converse is also true: The absence of protective relationships increases an individual's risk for developing a psychological disorder in the face of a significant stressor (Dikel, Engdahl, & Eberly, 2005). (Note that *stressor* is the technical term used to refer to any stimulus that induces stress.)

The Beale women experienced many stressors: financial problems, the dissolution of Phelan and Big Edie's marriage, and, in later years, social isolation. Their extended family and their community ostracized them, at least in part because they were independent-minded and artistic women. In addition, Little Edie endured her own unique social stresses: Both her parents were excessively controlling, though in different ways. Her father restricted her artistic pursuits. And Little Edie could scarcely leave her mother's room before her mother was calling urgently for her to return; this intense attachment and close physical proximity echo their relationship when Little Edie was a child.

Like the other factors, social factors do not fully account for how and why psychological disorders arise. For instance, social explanations cannot tell us why, of people who experience the same circumstances, some will go on to develop a psychological disorder and others won't.

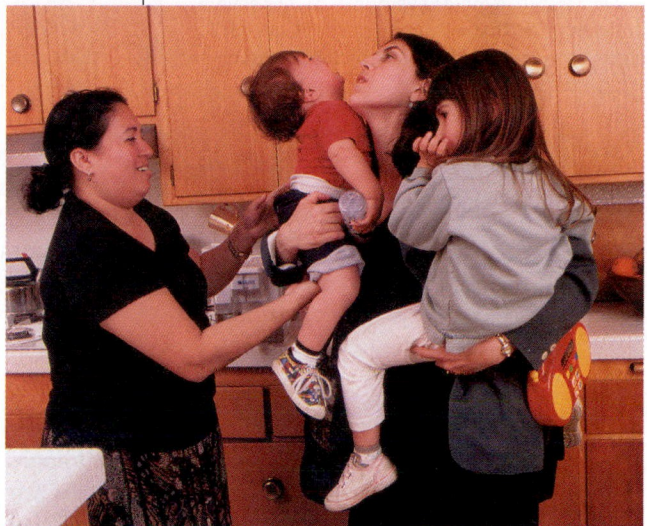

Children who do not have a secure attachment style have a higher likelihood of subsequently developing symptoms of psychological disorders (Main & Solomon, 1986; Minde, 2003).

Michael Newman/Photo Edit

Biological Explanations

As some researchers explored the behavioral, cognitive, and social factors that contribute to psychological disorders and their treatment, other researchers continued to focus on biological causes of psychological disorders and their medical treatments. Many biological researchers were impressed by the discovery in 1913 that one type of mental illness—which was then called *general paresis*, or *paralytic dementia*—was caused by a sexually transmitted disease, syphilis. The final stage of this disease damages the brain and leads to abrupt changes in mental processes, including psychotic symptoms (Hayden, 2003). The discovery of a causal link between syphilis and general paresis heralded a resurgence of the medical model, the view that psychological disorders have underlying biological causes. According to the

The bacterium *Treponema pallidum* is responsible for the sexually transmitted disease syphilis. Left untreated, syphilis eventually causes severe brain damage that in turn gives rise to abrupt changes in mental processes, including psychotic symptoms.

medical model, once the biological causes are identified, appropriate medical treatments can be developed, such as medications. In fact, antibiotics that treat syphilis also prevent the related mental illness, which was dramatic support for applying the medical model to at least some psychological disorders.

Since that discovery, scientists have examined genes, neurotransmitters (chemicals that allow brain cells to communicate with each other), and abnormalities in brain structure and function associated with mental illness. However, explaining psychological disorders simply on the basis of biological factors ultimately strips mental disorders of the context in which they occur—in thinking people who live in families and societies—and provides a false impression that mental disorders arise from biological factors alone. As we shall see throughout this book, multiple factors usually contribute to a psychological disorder, and treatments targeting only biological factors are not necessarily the most effective.

What biological factors might have contributed to the Beales' unusual lifestyle and beliefs? Unfortunately, the documentaries and biographies about the two women have not addressed this issue, so there is no way to know. All we know is that one of Big Edie's brothers was a serious gambler, another died as a result of a drinking problem, and one of her nieces also battled problems with alcohol; taken together, these observations might suggest a family history of impulse control problems. We might be tempted to infer that such tendencies in this family reflect an underlying genetic predisposition, but we must be careful: Families share more than their genes, and common components of the environment can also contribute to psychological disorders.

The Modern Synthesis of Explanations of Psychopathology

In the last several decades, researchers and clinicians increasingly recognize that psychological disorders cannot be fully explained by any single type of factor or theory. Two approaches to psychopathology integrate multiple factors: the *diathesis–stress model* and the *biopsychosocial approach*.

The Diathesis–Stress Model

The diathesis–stress model is one way to bring together the various explanations of how psychological disorders arise. The **diathesis–stress model** rests on the claim that a psychological disorder is triggered when a person with a predisposition—a *diathesis*—for the particular disorder experiences an environmental event that causes significant stress (Meehl, 1962; Monroe & Simons, 1991; Rende & Plomin, 1992). Essentially, the idea is that if a person has a predisposition to a psychological disorder, stress may trigger its occurrence. But the same stress would not have that effect for a person who did not have the predisposition; also, a person who did have a diathesis for a psychological disorder would be fine if he or she could avoid high-stress situations. Both factors are required. For example, the diathesis–stress model explains why, if one identical twin develops depression, the co-twin (the other twin of the pair) also develops depression in less than a quarter of the cases (Lyons et al., 1998). Because identical twins share 100% of their genes, a co-twin should be virtually guaranteed to develop the disorder if genes alone cause it to develop. But even identical twins experience different types and levels of stress. Their genes are identical, but their environments are not; thus, both twins do not necessarily develop the psychological disorder over time. The diathesis–stress model is illustrated in Figure 1.3.

A diathesis may be a biological factor, such as a genetic vulnerability to a disorder, or it may be a psychological factor, such as a cognitive vulnerability to disorder, such as can occur when irrational or inaccurate negative thoughts about oneself contribute to depression. The *stress* is often a social factor, which can be acute, such as being the victim of a crime, or less intense but chronic, such as recurring spousal abuse, poverty, or overwork. It is important to note that not

Figure 1.3

1.3 ▶ The Diathesis–Stress Model
According to the diathesis–stress model of depression, people who are more vulnerable to depression (high diathesis) will become depressed after experiencing less stress than people who are less vulnerable to depression (low or absent diathesis). Put another way, given the same level of stress, those who are more vulnerable to depression will develop more symptoms of depression than those who are less vulnerable.

everybody experiences the same social factor in the same way. And what's important is not simply the objective circumstance; it's how a person perceives it. For example, think about roller coasters: For one person, they are great fun; for another, they are terrifying. Similarly, Big Edie and Little Edie didn't appear to mind their isolation and strange lifestyle and may even have enjoyed it; other people, however, might find living in such circumstances extremely stressful and depressing. Whether because of learning, biology, or an interaction between them, some people are more likely to perceive particular events and stimuli as stressors (and therefore to experience more stress) than others. The diathesis–stress model was the first approach that integrated existing, but separate, explanations for psychological disorders.

The Biopsychosocial and Neuropsychosocial Approaches

To understand the bases of both diatheses and stress, we need to look more carefully at the factors that underlie psychological disorders.

Three Types of Factors

Historically, researchers and clinicians grouped the factors that give rise to psychological disorders into three general types: *biological* (including genetics, the structure and function of the brain, and the function of other bodily systems); *psychological* (thoughts, feelings, and behaviors); and, *social* (social interactions and the environment in which they occur). The **biopsychosocial approach** to understanding psychological disorders rests on identifying these three types of factors and documenting the ways in which each of them contributes to a disorder.

That is, the biopsychosocial approach leads researchers and clinicians to look for ways in which the three types of factors contribute to both the diathesis (the predisposition) and the stress. For instance, having certain genes (a biological factor), having biases to perceive certain situations as stressful (a psychological factor), and living in poverty (a social factor) all can contribute to a diathesis; similarly, chronic lack of sleep (a biological factor), feeling that one's job is overwhelming (a psychological factor), or having a spouse who is abusive (a social factor) can contribute to stress.

However, two problems with the traditional biopsychosocial approach have become clear. First, the approach does not specifically focus on the organ that is responsible for cognition and affect, that allows us to learn, that guides behavior, and that underlies all conscious experience—namely, the brain. The brain not only gives rise to thoughts, feelings, and behaviors, but also mediates all other biological factors; it both registers events in the body and affects bodily events.

Second, sometimes the biopsychosocial approach was used to identify a set of factors that together caused a disorder. However, the factors were often considered in isolation, as if they were items on a list. Considering the factors in isolation is reminiscent of the classic South Asian tale about a group of blind men feeling different parts of an elephant, each trying to determine what the animal is. One person feels the trunk, another the legs, another the tusks, and so on, and each reaches a different conclusion. Even if you combined all the people's separate reports, you might miss the big picture of what an elephant is: That is, an elephant is more than a sum of its body parts; the parts come together to make a dynamic and wondrous creature.

We are beginning to understand how the three types of factors combine and affect each other. That is, factors that researchers previously considered to be independent are now known to influence each other. For example, the way that parents treat their infant was historically considered to be exclusively a social factor—the infant was a receptacle for the caregiver's style of parenting. However, more recent research has revealed that parenting style is in fact a complex set of interactions between

It's a snake!

It's a spear!

It's a fan!

It's a wall!

It's a rope!

It's a tree!

The whole elephant cannot be described by a group of blind men if each of them is feeling only a small part of the animal's body. In the same way, past explanations of psychological disorders that focused on only one or two factors created an incomplete understanding of such disorders.

Diathesis–stress model
The model that proposes that a psychological disorder is triggered when a person with a predisposition—a diathesis—for the particular disorder experiences an environmental event that causes significant stress.

Biopsychosocial approach
The view that a psychological disorder arises from the combined influences of three types of factors—biological, psychological, and social.

caregiver and infant. Consider that if the infant frequently fusses, this will elicit a different pattern of responses from the caregiver than if the infant frequently smiles; if the infant is fussy and "difficult," the caregiver might handle him or her with less patience and warmth than if the infant seems happy and easy-going. And the way the caregiver handles the infant in turn affects how the infant responds to the caregiver. In turn, these early interactions between child and caregiver (a social factor) contribute to a particular attachment style, which is associated with particular biases in paying attention to and perceiving emotional expressions in faces (psychological factors; Fraley & Shaver, 1997; Maier et al., 2005).

In fact, some researchers who championed the biopsychosocial approach acknowledged that explanations of psychological disorders depend on the interactions of biological, psychological, and social factors (Engel, 1977, 1980). But these researchers did not have the benefit of the recent advances in understanding the brain, and hence were not able to specify the nature of such interactions in much detail.

These two problems led to a revision of the traditional biopsychosocial approach, to align it better with recent discoveries about the brain and how psychological and social factors affect brain function. We call this updated version of the classic approach the *neuropsychosocial approach*, which is explained in the following section.

The Neuropsychosocial Approach: Refining the Biopsychosocial Approach

The neuropsychosocial approach has two defining features: the way it characterizes the factors and the way it characterizes their interactions. As we discuss below, this approach emphasizes the brain rather than the body (hence the *neuro-* in its name) and maintains that no factor can be considered in isolation.

Emphasis on the Brain. As psychologists and other scientists have learned more about the biological factors that contribute to psychological disorders, the primacy of the role of the brain—and even particular brain structures and functions—in contributing to psychological disorders has become evident. Ultimately, even such disparate biological factors as genes and bodily responses (e.g., the increased heart rate associated with anxiety) are best understood in terms of their relationship with the brain.

Because of the importance of the brain's influence on all biological functioning involved in psychological disorders, this book generally uses the term *neurological* rather than *biological* and the term *neuropsychosocial* rather than *biopsychosocial* to refer to the three types of factors that contribute to psychological disorders.

Emphasis on Feedback Loops. In addition, neurological, psychological, and social factors are usually involved simultaneously and are constantly interacting (see Figure 1.4). These interactions occur through feedback loops: Each factor is affected by the others, and *also* feeds back to affect the other factors. Hence, no one factor can be understood in isolation, without considering the other factors. For example, problems in relationships (social factor) can lead people to experience stress (psychological factor); in turn, when people feel stressed, their brains cause their bodies to respond with a cascade of events.

As you will see throughout this book, interactions among neurological, psychological, and social factors are common. Icons that look like this will highlight parts of the text that illustrate specific ways that these factors interact with one another:

- indicates feedback between neurological and psychological factors:
- indicates feedback between neurological and social factors:
- indicates feedback between psychological and social factors: and
- indicates feedback among all three pairs of factors:

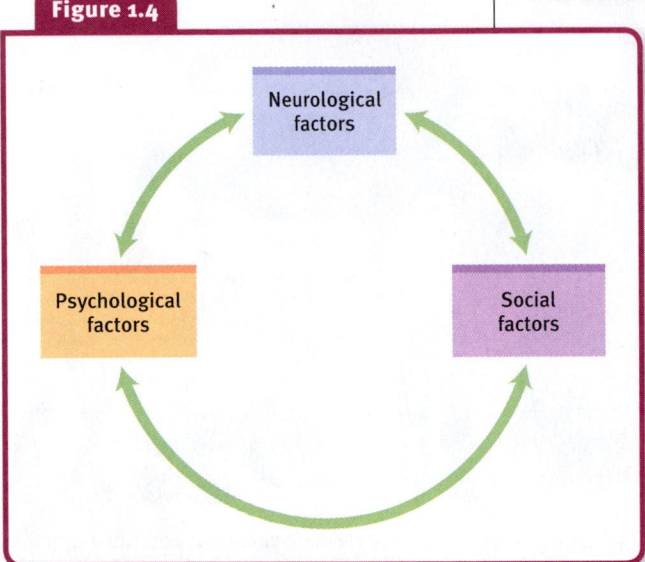

Figure 1.4

1.4 ▸ The Neuropsychosocial Approach According to the neuropsychosocial approach, neurological, psychological, and social factors *interact with one another* via feedback loops to contribute to the development of psychopathology.

Such icons will be in the margin of the page; the relevant portion of text will also be highlighted in the margin. Any of the types of factors can spark us to behave in a certain way or can help us control ourselves so that we do *not* behave in a certain way.

In short, the **neuropsychosocial approach** can allow us to understand how neurological, psychological, and social factors—which affect and are affected by one another through feedback loops—underlie psychological disorders.

In the next chapter, we will discuss the neuropsychosocial approach to psychological disorders in more detail, examining neurological, psychological, and social factors as well as the feedback loops among them. In that chapter, we will also continue our evaluation of the Beales and the specific factors that might contribute to their unusual behavior. In subsequent chapters, we will consider the stories of various other people.

Chapters 2 though 5 will provide you with knowledge to understand psychopathology in general: neurological, psychological, and social factors that contribute to psychological disorders (Chapter 2); issues related to diagnosing and assessing psychopathology (Chapter 3); treating psychological disorders (Chapter 4); and researching psychological disorders (Chapter 5). Chapters 6 through 15 address specific categories of psychological disorders (such as anxiety disorders). The final chapter (Chapter 16) discusses ethical and legal issues related to psychological disorders.

As you will see in these subsequent chapters, the definition of a psychological disorder provided earlier in this chapter—a pattern of thoughts, feelings, or behaviors that causes significant distress, impaired functioning in daily life, and/or risk of harm—forms the basis for the definitions of specific disorders. However, we note in Chapter 3 and other chapters that the extent of distress, impaired functioning, and/or risk of harm that is required for a diagnosis of a psychological disorder is not always clear. Rather, each of these three elements exists on a continuum. Two individuals with psychological disorders are likely to have symptoms that reflect different locations on each continuum.

Neuropsychosocial approach
The view that a psychological disorder arises from the combined influences of neurological, psychological, and social factors—which affect and are affected by one another through feedback loops.

Key Concepts and Facts About Scientific Accounts of Psychological Disorders

- Psychologists Edward Thorndike, John Watson, Clark Hull, and B. F. Skinner spearheaded behaviorism, focusing on directly observable behaviors rather than unobservable mental processes and mental contents. They investigated the association between a behavior and its consequence, and proposed scientifically testable mechanisms to explain how maladaptive behavior arises. Behaviorism helps explain how maladaptive behavior can arise from previous associations with an object, situation, or event. Behaviorism led to innovative treatments.

- Ivan Pavlov discovered and investigated what is sometimes referred to as Pavlovian conditioning—the process whereby a reflexive behavior comes to be associated with a stimulus that precedes it. Pavlovian conditioning helps explain the severe fears and anxieties that are part of some psychological disorders: Neutral stimuli that have in the past been paired with fear-inducing objects or events can subsequently, by themselves, induce fear or anxiety.

- Cognitive psychology has led to the scientific investigation of mental processes that affect how people pay attention to stimuli and develop biases in what they expect and remember. Such biases in turn can confirm the inaccurate views that perpetuate a psychological disorder. Aaron Beck and Albert Ellis each focused on how people's irrational and inaccurate thoughts about themselves and the world can contribute to psychological disorders, and each developed a type of treatment to address the irrational and inaccurate thoughts.

- Social forces that help explain psychological disorders include difficulties with attachment and the role of relationships in buffering negative life events.

- The discovery of the biological cause of one type of mental illness—general paresis—led to investigations into possible biological causes of other types of mental illness. Although researchers investigate various biological and neurological abnormalities to understand psychopathology, exclusively biological explanations ultimately strip mental disorders of the context in which they occur and provide a false impression that mental disorders arise from biological (primarily neurological) factors alone.

- Psychological disorders cannot be fully explained by any single type of factor or theory. One approach to integrating different factors is the diathesis–stress model, which proposes that if a person has a predisposition to a psychological disorder, stressors may trigger its occurrence.

- The biopsychosocial approach rests on the idea that both diathesis and stress can be grouped into three types of factors: biological, psychological, and social. As research on biological factors associated with psychological disorders has advanced, the important effects of the brain on other biological functions have become clear. In addition, recent research allows investigators to begin to understand the feedback loops among the three types of factors. For these reasons, this book uses the term *neuropsychosocial* rather than *biopsychosocial*.

SUMMING UP

Summary of The Three Criteria for Defining Psychological Disorders

A psychological disorder is a pattern of thoughts, feelings, or behaviors that causes significant distress, impaired functioning in daily life, and/or risk of harm. The distress involved in a psychological disorder is out of proportion to the situation.

Impairment in daily life may be evident in functioning at school, at work, at home, or in relationships. Moreover, people with a psychological disorder are impaired to a greater degree than most people in a similar situation. A psychosis is a relatively easily identifiable type of impairment that includes hallucinations or delusions. A psychological disorder may lead to behaviors that create a significant risk of harm to the person or to others.

Mental health clinicians and researchers recognize that context and culture in part determine whether a person's state involves significant distress, impairment, or risk of harm. In particular, people from different cultures may express distress differently, and some sets of symptoms, such as those of possession trance, may, in fact, not be a disorder in certain cultures.

Thinking like a clinician

Suppose Pietro was hearing the voice of a deceased relative, and he was from a culture where such experiences were considered normal—or at least not abnormal. But he was distressed about hearing the voice, to the point where he was having a hard time doing his job. Should Pietro be considered to have a psychological disorder? If so, why? If not, why not? What additional information would you want to help you decide, if you weren't sure?

Summary of Views of Psychological Disorders Before Science

The oldest known view of psychopathology is that it arose from supernatural (magical or spiritual) forces. Treatment included exorcism. The ancient Greeks attributed mental illness to an imbalance of bodily humors. The term *medical model* refers to Hippocrates' view that illness (including psychological disorders) arises from a biological disturbance.

The Middle Ages saw a resurgence of the view that supernatural forces cause psychopathology. This view persisted into the Renaissance, when mental illness was viewed as the result of demonic possession, and witches were thought to be possessed by, or in league with, the devil. Treatment of the mentally ill consisted of exorcism. By the end of the Renaissance, however, the mentally ill began to be treated more humanely, and asylums were built throughout Europe; over time, however, these asylums became a place to keep the mentally ill poor off the street, which led to overcrowded facilities.

In the years immediately following the Renaissance, mental illnesses were thought to arise from irrational thinking, but this approach did not lead to consistent cures.

Beginning in the 1790s, Pinel championed humane treatment for those in asylums in France. Based on careful observation, he proposed that there were different types of madness. In other European settings, patients were given moral treatment, which centered on having them live and work within a community in the countryside.

In the United States, Benjamin Rush initiated the effort to treat the mentally ill more humanely; similarly, Dorothea Dix strove to ensure that the mentally ill were housed separately from criminals and treated humanely. However, public institutions for the mentally ill became overcrowded and underfunded. By the end of the 19th century in Europe and North America, "madness" was generally viewed as caused by a medical abnormality.

Thinking like a clinician

Why might explanations of mental illness as arising from supernatural forces have been popular for so long? How does prevailing treatment of abnormality follow from beliefs about the cause of mental illness? Use specific examples.

Summary of The Transition to Scientific Accounts of Psychological Disorders

Freud played a major role in making the study of psychological disorders a science, largely by developing new methods for diagnosis and treatment; he also proposed an extensive theory of psychopathology. According to Freud's psychoanalytic theory, thoughts, feelings, and behaviors are a result of conscious and unconscious forces—such as sexual and aggressive urges—continually interacting in the mind. Moreover, he proposed that the mind is structured so as to function across three levels of consciousness: the conscious, the preconscious, and the unconscious. Freud stressed that many mental processes occur outside our awareness but nonetheless influence thoughts, feelings, and behaviors. Unacceptable urges are banished to the unconscious, where they inevitably gain strength and eventually demand release.

Freud proposed three psychic structures in the mind—id, ego, and superego—which are continually interacting and negotiating. According to Freud, each individual passes through five psychosexual stages from infancy to adulthood, of which four involve particular erogenous zones. For healthy psychological development, each stage requires the successful completion of a key task. Freud also proposed that parents' interactions with their child are central in forming the child's personality.

Freud's followers focused on a variety of issues related to the development of the self and of the ego, the role of motivation, the possibility of unconscious archetypes, and the ways moment-to-moment interactions between child and parent can contribute to psychological disorders. A drawback of psychodynamic theory is that it has proven difficult to test scientifically.

Humanistic psychologists such as Carl Rogers viewed psychodynamic theory as too mechanistic and opposed to free will. Rogers proposed that symptoms of distress and mental illness arise when a potential route to personal growth is blocked, as can occur when the ideal and real selves are incongruent. Rogers developed client-centered therapy to decrease incongruence in clients.

Lasting contributions of psychodynamic theory include the focus on mental processes and mental contents and the concept that such processes and contents can be hidden from awareness.

Thinking like a clinician

Based on what you have read, why do you think Freud's theory has diminished in influence? Why have certain aspects of psychodynamic theory continued to influence modern perspectives?

Summary of Scientific Accounts of Psychological Disorders

Psychologists Edward Thorndike, John Watson, Clark Hull, and B. F. Skinner spearheaded behaviorism, which focused on directly observable behaviors rather than unobservable mental processes and mental contents. They investigated the association between a behaviors and its consequence, and proposed scientifically testable mechanisms to explain how maladaptive behavior arises. Behaviorism helps explain how maladaptive behavior can arise from previous associations with an object, situation, or event. Behaviorism led to innovative treatments.

Ivan Pavlov discovered and investigated what is sometimes referred to as Pavlovian conditioning—the process whereby a reflexive behavior comes to be associated with a stimulus that precedes it. Pavlovian conditioning helps explain the severe fears and anxieties that are part of some psychological disorders.

Cognitive psychology has led to the scientific investigation of mental processes that affect how people pay attention to stimuli and develop biases in what they expect and remember. Such biases in turn can confirm the inaccurate views that perpetuate a psychological disorder. Aaron Beck and Albert Ellis each focused on how people's irrational and inaccurate thoughts about themselves and the world can contribute to psychological disorders, and each developed a type of treatment to address the irrational and inaccurate thoughts.

Social forces that help explain psychological disorders include difficulties with attachment and the role of relationships in buffering negative life events.

The discovery of the biological cause of one type of mental illness—general paresis—led to investigations into possible biological causes of other types of mental illness.

However, psychological disorders cannot be fully explained by any single type of factor or theory. One approach to integrating different factors is the diathesis–stress model, which proposes that if a person has a predisposition to a psychological disorder, stressors may trigger its occurrence.

The biopsychosocial approach proposes that both diathesis and stress can be grouped into three types of factors: biological, psychological, and social. As research on biological factors associated with psychological disorders has advanced, the important effects of the brain on other biological functions have become clear. In addition, recent research allows investigators to begin to understand the feedback loops among the three types of factors. For these reasons, this book uses the term *neuropsychosocial* rather than *biopsychosocial*.

Thinking like a clinician

Natasha's uncle Alex was severely depressed about 5 years ago—to the point where he went into the hospital for a week. Natasha's parents had talked about Uncle Alex having a "chemical imbalance." Based on what you have read, which of the various modern perspectives were her parents adopting? If her parents had used other modern perspectives to explain Alex's depression, to what would they have attributed his depression? Be specific.

How would the two integrationist approaches (diathesis–stress and biopsychosocial) explain Alex's depression? (*Hint*: Use Figures 1.3 and 1.4 to guide your answers.) What do the two approaches have in common, and in what ways do they differ from each other?

Key Terms

Abnormal psychology (p. 4)

Psychological disorder (p. 4)

Psychosis (p. 6)

Hallucinations (p. 6)

Delusions (p. 6)

Culture (p. 8)

Asylums (p. 14)

Moral treatment (p. 15)

Psychoanalytic theory (p. 17)

Id (p. 18)

Superego (p. 18)

Ego (p. 18)

Psychosexual stages (p. 18)

Neurosis (p. 19)

Defense mechanisms (p. 19)

Mental processes (p. 21)

Mental contents (p. 21)

Behaviorism (p. 22)

Diathesis–stress model (p. 27)

Biopsychosocial approach (p. 27)

Neuropsychosocial approach (p. 29)

More Study Aids

For additional study aids related to this chapter, go to:

www.worthpublishers.com/rosenberg

Understanding Psychological Disorders:
The Neuropsychosocial Approach

During the last year of Big Edie's life, the Beale women had a guest, Lois Wright, stay with them. Lois slept in a spare bedroom, on a canvas cot that she had brought with her. However, the floor of her room was so thoroughly layered with years of cat droppings and fleas that she put newspaper down on the floor every night before she went to bed.

Sometimes, when Lois wanted to leave the house and go into town for her own food or supplies, the Beales wouldn't let her out. They were afraid that if they unlocked the door for Lois, a "spy might try to gain entrance" (Wright, 2007, p. 35) or Lois might be kidnapped while in town, by people wanting information about Grey Gardens.

As we saw in Chapter 1, clearly the Beale women had odd thoughts and feelings and engaged in unusual behaviors. As we asked in Chapter 1, were they merely eccentric? Did Big Edie or Little Edie (or both of them) have a psychological disorder? Could either of them have had more than one psychological disorder? If one or both had a disorder, how could we understand why? The neuropsychosocial approach allows us to consider the factors that lead someone to develop a psychological disorder, which is known as its **etiology**.

Let's consider the Beale women in terms of the neuropsychosocial approach. First, we can ask about *neurological* factors: Was something abnormal about their genes or brains? Perhaps their neurons or neurotransmitters functioned abnormally, and that led to their odd behavior. Second, we can ask about *psychological* factors: How might their thoughts and feelings have motivated them, and what role might their mental processes have played? For instance, might Pavlovian conditioning have been involved in Big Edie's apparent fear of being alone? And third, we can ask about *social* factors, such as their financial circumstances, their family relationships, the straight-laced society they were members of, and other cultural forces affecting them. To what extent might the disdain shown to Big Edie and Little Edie by their extended family have influenced their unusual behavior?

At any moment in a day of the Beales' lives (or anyone's life, for that matter), all three types of factors are operating: neurological, psychological, and social. Depending on the state of a person's brain (which is affected, for example, by various chemicals produced by the body), social factors (such as an angry friend or a stressful job interview) have a greater or lesser impact. This impact in turn affects psychological factors (the person's thoughts, feelings, and behaviors) in different ways. And then the psychological factors can affect both

Etiology
The factors that lead a person to develop a psychological disorder.

Leigh Wells

neurological factors and social factors, continuing the interaction among these different influences. Thus, considering only one type of factor would lead to an incomplete understanding of psychological disorders. That is why we consider each type of factor—neurological, psychological, and social—in detail in this chapter, to provide information that we will use in later chapters as we probe the etiology of specific psychological disorders. It is important to note, however, that the neuropsychosocial approach does not focus on each type of factor individually; rather, we must always consider how the three factors interact and affect one another via feedback loops.

Neurological Factors in Psychological Disorders

Big Edie had always been unconventional. She didn't seem to care what other people thought of her behavior. And although she loved performing—seemingly to the point of compulsion—she was a recluse for most of her adult life, seeing almost no one but her children. How did such a lifestyle arise? And what about Little Edie's paranoid beliefs? Could neurological factors account for the odd beliefs and behaviors of this mother and daughter? In fact, accumulating research indicates that genes can contribute to the development of disorders by affecting both the structure and function of the brain (Hasler et al., 2004; Gottesman, 1991; Greenwood & Kelsoe, 2003).

Neurological factors that contribute to psychological disorders include abnormalities in the structure of the brain, in the operations of specific chemicals (such as those that affect transmission of information among brain cells), and in specific genes. Researchers and clinicians sometimes focus on neurological factors when they explain psychopathology—noting, for example, that depression is correlated with abnormal levels of a particular chemical (serotonin) in the brain, or that an irrational fear of spiders develops partly from an overly reactive brain structure involved in fear (the amygdala; Larson et al., 2006). However, as you know, the neuropsychosocial approach maintains that explanations based on neurological factors alone rarely provide the whole story. For instance, one person's serotonin levels might become abnormal because of his social position (Raleigh et al., 1984), and another person's amygdala might be overly reactive because of her experiences with threatening people (Phelps et al., 2000). Each thought, feeling, and behavior, as well as each social experience and the environment in which we live and work, affects our neurological functioning. In other words, as noted above, the three types of factors typically interact with one another through *feedback loops*. Neurological factors contribute to psychopathology, but they must be considered in the context of the other factors.

To understand the role of neurological factors in explanations of psychopathology, we next consider brain structure and function, neurons and neurotransmitters, and genetics and the ways that genes interact with the environment.

Brain Structure and Brain Function

Have you ever been high in the mountains and looked up at a crystal clear night sky? The number of stars is staggering. In fact, there are about 100 billion stars in our galaxy—which nicely approximates the number of brain cells in each of our brains. Think of packing all those points of light into a single skull! And just as the stars in a galaxy are organized into clusters and arms, and the entire ensemble turns majestically around the galactic core, our billions of brains cells are organized into brain structures that work together in specific ways. In fact, the number of possible connections among the brain's cells is truly astronomical—by some estimates, there are more possible connections among brain cells than there are atoms in the universe (Thompson, 1993)!

Not surprisingly, such complexity leads to many opportunities for the functioning of the brain to go awry. The brain is the organ of thinking, feeling, and behavior, and thus it must play a key role in psychopathology. In the following sections, we discuss the brain so that you can begin to understand the neurological aspects of specific psychological disorders that we consider later in the book. We start with the big picture by considering the overall structure of the brain and its organization into large systems. Then we turn to increasingly more detailed components, considering how individual brain cells interact within these systems.

A Quick Tour of the Nervous System

Psychopathology involves deficits in how a person thinks, feels, and behaves. The brain, of course, is ultimately responsible for all of these functions. Let's briefly consider how different parts of the brain contribute to cognitive and emotional capacities when the brain is structured and functions normally. In later chapters, when we need to know more to understand a specific psychological disorder, we'll look more closely at specific parts of the brain and how they can malfunction.

The Central Nervous System and the Peripheral Nervous System

The central nervous system (CNS) has two parts: the brain and the spinal cord. The CNS is the seat of memory and consciousness, as well as perception and voluntary action (Smith & Kosslyn, 2006). However, the CNS is not the only neurological foundation of our internal lives. The peripheral nervous system (PNS) also plays an important role and is of particular interest in the study of psychopathology.

The Autonomic Nervous System

Like the CNS, the PNS is divided into two parts, in this case the sensory-somatic nervous system and the autonomic nervous system (see Figure 2.1). The *sensory-somatic nervous system* is involved in connecting the brain to the world, via both the senses (inputs) and the muscles (outputs). The *autonomic nervous system (ANS)* is probably of greater relevance to psychopathology, in part because it plays a key role in how we respond to stress (as we'll discuss shortly). The ANS controls many involuntary functions, such as those of the heart, digestive tract, and blood vessels (Goldstein, 2000; Hugdahl, 2001). The ANS itself has two major components: the sympathetic nervous system and the parasympathetic nervous system. The *sympathetic nervous system* revs you up so that you can respond to an emergency: It speeds up the heart (providing more blood and oxygen to the limbs) and dilates the pupils of the eyes (making you more sensitive to light). The sympathetic system also slows down functions that are not essential in an emergency, such as those involved in digestion. The sum result of the sympathetic nervous system's being activated is called the *fight-or-flight response,* (or the *stress response,* because it occurs when people experience stress).

As part of the fight-or-flight response, the *hypothalamic-pituitary-adrenal axis (HPA axis)* manages the production of the hormone cortisol, which readies the muscles for physical exertion by helping the body release fuel more effectively. Under chronic stress, a person's level of cortisol often doesn't

Figure 2.1

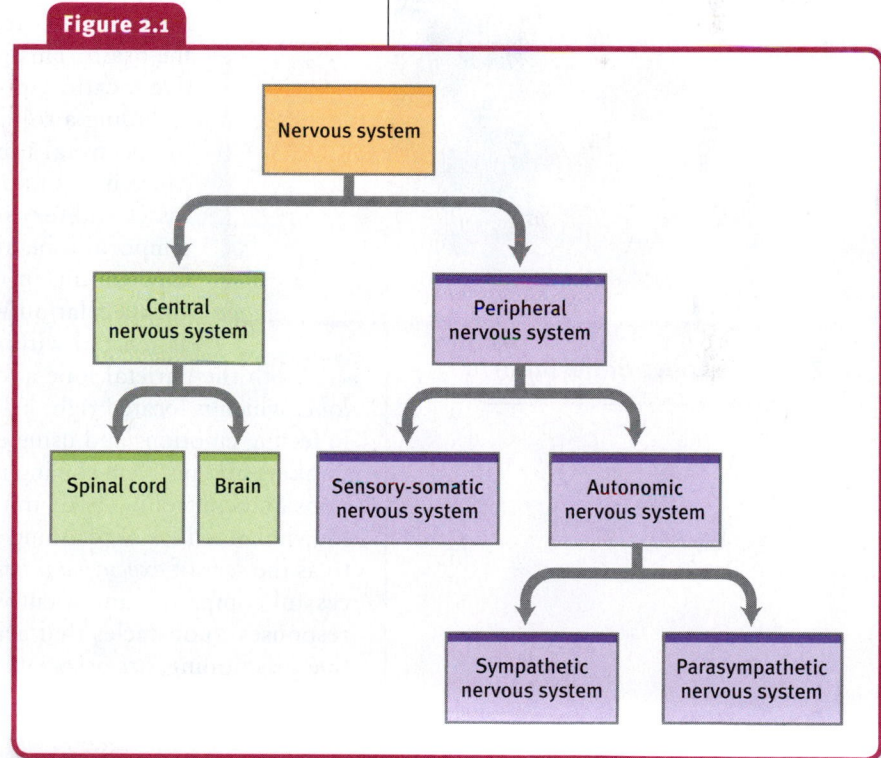

2.1 ▶ The Nervous System The autonomic nervous system (ANS) is part of the peripheral nervous system (PNS), and malfunctioning of the ANS can produce abnormal responses to stress.

return to baseline. The HPA axis and cortisol levels are involved in depression and stress-related psychological disorders such as *posttraumatic stress disorder (PTSD),* an anxiety disorder that can arise after a person experiences a traumatic event.

The other part of the ANS is the *parasympathetic nervous system,* which settles you down after a crisis is over: The parasympathetic nervous system slows the heart, contracts the pupils, and also increases the activity of the digestive tract. The parasympathetic system typically counteracts the effects of the sympathetic nervous system, and psychopathology may arise if it fails to do so effectively. In fact, dysfunctional activity in the parasympathetic nervous system has been associated with various psychological problems, such as anxiety disorders, disruptive behavior, and hostility (Pine et al., 1998).

The Four Brain Lobes

Let's now focus on one part of the CNS, the brain. As shown in Figure 2.2, the brain has four major lobes: occipital lobe, parietal lobe, temporal lobe, and frontal lobe. The brain is divided into two hemispheres (or half-spheres), left and right, and each hemisphere has all four lobes (although they do not have identical functions in the two hemispheres). Let's start with the back of the brain. When the eyes are stimulated by light, they send neural impulses into the brain; the first area to process this information in detail is the *occipital lobe,* which is at the very back of the brain. This lobe is entirely dedicated to the function of vision.

Two major neural pathways lead forward from the occipital lobes. One extends up into the *parietal lobe,* at the top, back of the brain. This lobe processes spatial information, such as the relative location of objects. The parietal lobe also has other functions, including a role in self-awareness. The second neural pathway from the occipital lobe leads down to the *temporal lobe* (so named because it lies under the temple), which stores visual memories, processes auditory information, and decodes the meaning of speech; the temporal lobe also contributes to conscious experience. Abnormal functioning in the temporal lobe can produce intense emotions, such as elation when a person is manic (Gyulai et al., 1997), and is associated with auditory hallucinations (Plaze et al., 2006).

Both the parietal lobe and the temporal lobe send information to the *frontal lobe,* which is located right behind the forehead. The frontal lobe plays crucial roles in feeling emotions and using emotional responses in decision making, as well as in thinking and problem solving more generally; it is also involved in programming actions and controlling body movements. Because these functions are so important to the vital activities of planning and reasoning, the frontal lobe is sometimes referred to as the seat of *executive functioning;* its role is much like that of the head of a successful company—an executive—who plans the company's future and formulates responses to obstacles that arise. Abnormalities in the frontal lobe, and in executive functioning, are associated with *schizophrenia,* a psychological disorder characterized by profoundly unusual and impaired behavior, expression of emotion, and mental processing (Bellgrove et al., 2006; Morey et al., 2005).

The Cortex and Beneath the Cortex

The **cerebral cortex** is the outer layer of cells on the surface of the brain; it contains the majority of the brain's **neurons,** the cells that process information related to our physical, mental, and emotional functioning. Most of the brain functions just described are carried out primarily in the cortex of the corresponding lobes. But many important brain functions are carried out in *subcortical areas,* beneath the cortex, as shown in Figure 2.3.

Figure 2.2

Frontal lobe
Parietal lobe
Temporal lobe
Occipital lobe

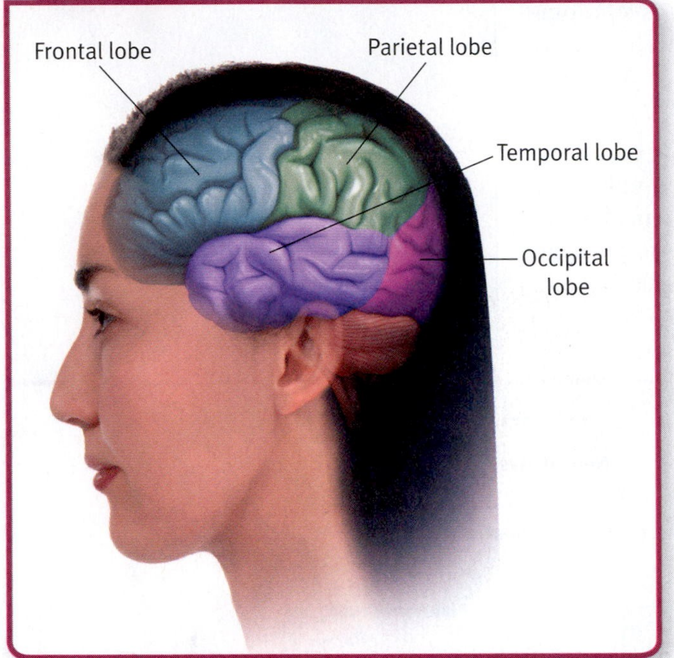

2.2 ▶ **The Lobes of the Brain**

Cerebral cortex
The outer layer of cells on the surface of the brain.

Neurons
Brain cells that process information related to physical, mental, and emotional functioning.

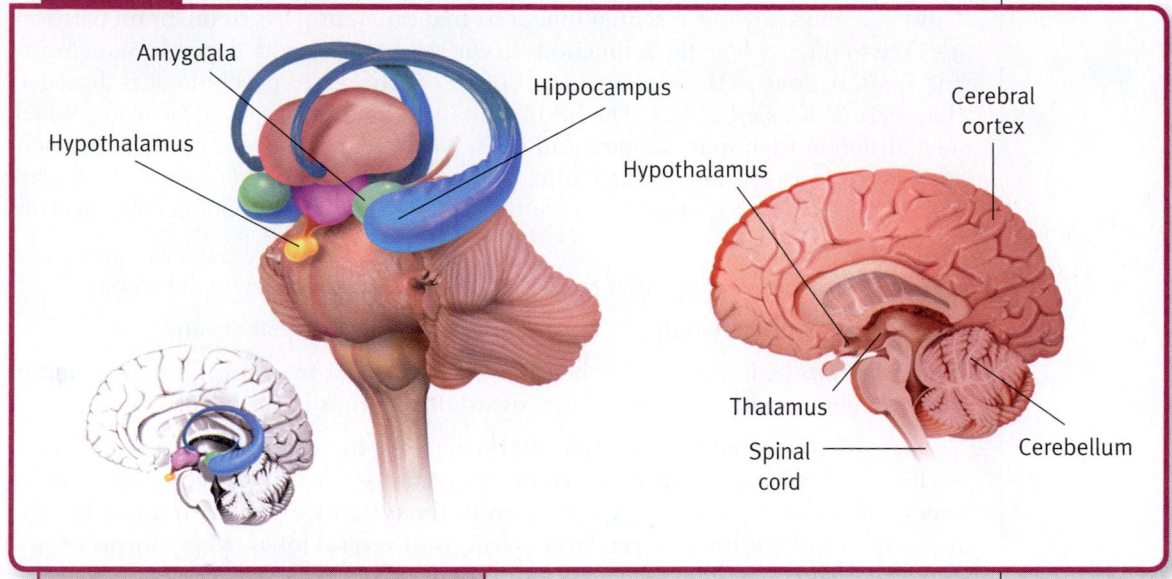

2.3 ▸ **Key Subcortical Brain Areas**

The *limbic system* plays a key role in emotions; among its most important components are the hypothalamus, the hippocampus, and the amygdala:

- The *hypothalamus* governs bodily functions associated with eating, drinking, and controlling temperature, and it plays a key role in many aspects of our emotions and in our experience of pleasure (Swaab, 2003).

- The *amygdala* is central to producing and perceiving strong emotions, especially fear (LeDoux, 2000).

- The *hippocampus* works to store new information in memory of the sort that later can be voluntarily recalled; (Squire, 2002).

In addition to components of the limbic system, other important subcortical areas are the thalamus, the nucleus accumbens, the basal ganglia, and the cerebellum:

- The *thalamus* is critical for controlling sleep and maintaining attention (and parts of it are closely involved with the limbic system; Lambert & Kinsley, 2005). Some people with schizophrenia have abnormalities in the structure and function of the thalamus, a finding that is consistent with their difficulties in focusing attention (Andreasen et al., 1994; Andrews et al., 2006).

- The *nucleus accumbens* plays a major role in registering reward and learning from experience (Breiter & Rosen, 1999). The functioning of the nucleus accumbens is involved in substance abuse (Leone, Pocock, & Wise, 1991).

- The *basal ganglia* are involved in automatic responses. Some psychological disorders disrupt the basal ganglia and can cause repetitive thoughts or behavior. For example, the basal ganglia operate abnormally in people who have *obsessive-compulsive disorder*, which is characterized by preoccupying thoughts and repetitive behaviors that the person feels compelled to do (Rauch et al., 2006).

- The *cerebellum* helps to manage physical coordination, attention, and many automatic motions (Ivry et al., 2002).

Both physical abnormalities and abnormal levels of activity in these subcortical brain areas can contribute to psychological disorders.

Neurons

Now that you know the essential functions that different parts of the brain perform, it's time to discuss *how* these functions occur. All brain activity depends on neurons, and malfunctions at the neuronal level often contribute to psychological disorders (Lambert & Kinsley, 2005). The brain contains numerous types of neurons, which have different functions, shapes, and sizes. Most neurons interact with other neurons. In some cases, neurons *activate*, or act to "turn on," other neurons; in other cases, neurons *inhibit*, or act to "turn off," other neurons. We can classify neurons into three main types:

- *sensory neurons* receive input from the sense organs (eyes, ears, and so on);

- *motor neurons* carry output that stimulates muscles and glands; and

- *interneurons* lie between other neurons—sensory neurons, motor neurons, and/or other interneurons—and make up most of the neurons in the brain.

Sets of connected neurons that work together to accomplish a basic process, such as making you recoil when you touch a hot stove, are called **brain circuits**; sets of brain circuits are organized into **brain systems**, which often can involve most of an entire lobe—or even large portions of several lobes. Many forms of psychopathology arise because specific brain circuits are not working properly, either alone or as part of a larger brain system. To understand brain circuits, consider an analogy to a row of dominoes: When one domino falls, it causes the next in line to fall, and so on, down the line. Similarly, when a neuron within a brain circuit is activated, it in turn activates sequences of other neurons. However, unlike a domino in a row, the average neuron is connected to about 10,000 other neurons—and thus a complex pattern of spreading activity occurs when a brain circuit is activated. For each input, a brain system produces a specific output—for instance, an interpretation of the input, an association to it, or a response based on it. Ultimately, it is the pattern of activated neurons that is triggered—by a sight, smell, thought, memory, or other event—that gives rise to our cognitive and emotional lives. A pattern of neurons firing makes us desire that third piece of chocolate cake or causes us to recoil when a spider saunters out from behind it. Brain systems allow us to think, feel, and behave.

Psychopathology can arise when neurons fail to communicate appropriately, leading brain circuits to produce incorrect outputs. For example, people with schizophrenia appear to have abnormal circuitry in key parts of their frontal lobes (Pantelis et al., 2003; Vidal et al., 2006). To understand such problems—and possible treatments for them—you need to know something about the structure and function of the neuron and its methods of communication.

The Cell Body

To see how neurons can fail to communicate appropriately, we must take a closer look at their anatomy. Figure 2.4 shows that a neuron has three parts: a receiving end, a sending end, and a middle part, called the *cell body*. Neurons, like all human cells, have a *nucleus*, which regulates all of the functions of the neuron, and a *cell membrane*, which forms an outer covering. When a neuron receives a sufficient amount of excitatory input, very small holes in the cell membrane—called *channels*—open, and the neuron's internal balance of chemicals will change to the point where the neuron fires. It is this firing that sends information to other neurons (Lambert & Kinsley, 2005).

Each neuron registers the sum total of inputs, both those that try to stimulate it to fire and those that try to inhibit it from firing. The neuron, then, balances the two sorts of inputs against each other and only fires if the stimulating influences substantially outweigh the inhibiting ones (Kandel, Schwartz, & Jessell, 2007). To understand how firing occurs, we need to look at the two other major parts of the neuron: the axon and the dendrites.

Brain circuits
Sets of connected neurons that work together to accomplish a basic process.

Brain systems
Sets of brain circuits that work together to accomplish a complex function.

The Axon

The *axon* is the part of the neuron that sends signals when a neuron fires. The axon is a long, threadlike structure covered by a layer of fatty material, known as the myelin sheath, that insulates it electrically. Though a neuron has only a single axon, it often branches extensively, allowing signals to be sent simultaneously to many other neurons (Shepherd, 1999). When a neuron has been stimulated to the point that it fires, a wave of chemical activity moves from the cell body down the axon very quickly. This wave is called an **action potential**. When the action potential reaches the end of the axon, it typically causes chemicals to be released. These chemicals are stored in structures called *terminal buttons*, and they affect other neurons, muscles, or glands.

Figure 2.4

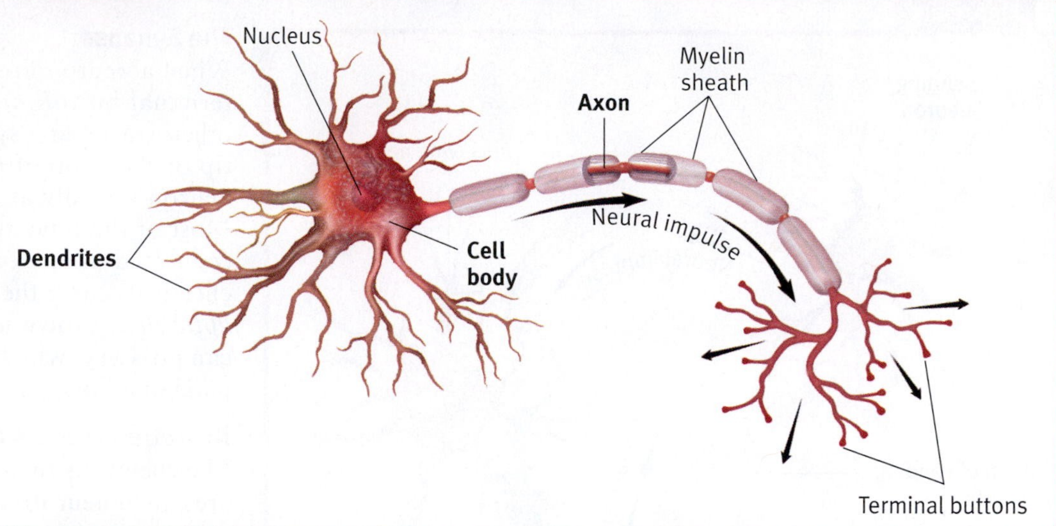

2.4 ▸ **The Neuron**

If stimulation does not cause a neuron to fire when it should, the circuit of which it is a part will not function correctly—and psychopathology may result. Let's consider why a neuron might not fire when stimulated appropriately.

The Dendrites

Neurons fire when they are appropriately stimulated. But how are they stimulated? Two ways: First, through *dendrites*, which receive signals from other neurons. These dendrites are highly branched, so a single neuron can receive many different signals at the same time. Received signals move along the dendrites to the cell body (Kandel, Schwartz, & Jessell, 2007). Second, in some cases, neurons receive inputs directly on their cell bodies. Such inputs are produced not only by other neurons, but also by *glial cells*. Glial cells are involved in the "care and feeding" of neurons, and act as a kind of support system (in fact, *glial* means "glue" in Greek; Lambert & Kinsley, 2005). The brain has about ten times as many glial cells as neurons, which implies that glial cells are important. In fact, researchers have learned that glial cells do much more than provide support services; they can directly stimulate neurons, and play a role in modulating input from other neurons (Parpura & Haydon, 2000).

Given the roles of neurons and glial cells in brain function, it is not surprising that researchers have found that at least some patients with psychological disorders (specifically, the sorts of mood disorders we consider in Chapter 6) have lost both types of cells. One possible reason for such deficits may be that stress early in childhood (and even to the mother, prior to a child's birth) can disrupt the development of both neurons and glial cells (Zorumski, 2005).

Chemical Signals

The way neurons communicate is crucial for understanding psychopathology. In many cases, psychological disorders involve faulty signaling among neurons, and effective medications operate by altering the ways in which signals are produced or processed (Kelsey, Newport, & Nemeroff, 2006). Subsequent chapters of this book will describe how particular signaling problems contribute to some psychological disorders and how certain medications compensate for such problems. To understand these problems with chemical signaling, we now need to consider the following: what

Action potential
The wave of chemical activity that moves from the cell body down the axon when a neuron fires.

happens at the synapse, what neurotransmitters and neuromodulators do, the nature of receptors, and what can go wrong with chemical communication among neurons.

The Synapse

When a neuron fires and chemicals are released at the terminal button, those chemicals usually contact another neuron at a **synapse**, which is the place where the tip of the axon of one neuron nestles against another neuron (usually at a dendrite) and sends signals to it. Most of the time, the sending neuron is not physically connected to the receiving neuron, though. Instead, the chemicals carry the signal across a gap, called the *synaptic cleft*, shown in Figure 2.5. Events at the synapses can go awry, which can underlie a variety of types of psychopathology.

Neurotransmitters and Neuromodulators

The chemicals that are released at the terminal buttons are called **neurotransmitters**. Neurotransmitters can be distinguished from **neuromodulators**, which are chemicals that modulate (alter) the way neurotransmitters affect the receiving neuron. Some neuromodulators affect the function of neurotransmitters by altering events at the synapse, for instance, by slowing down the rate at which molecules of a neurotransmitter are removed from the synaptic cleft after having been released. However, researchers have discovered that some chemicals that act as neurotransmitters can also act as neuromodulators in certain circumstances, and vice versa (Dowling, 1992). Thus, what originally seemed to be a sharp distinction, between neurotransmitters and neuromodulators, has become blurred. Researchers now often use the term *neurotransmitter* broadly, to include both sorts of substances, or they refer to both sorts as *neurotransmitter substances*.

It is worth looking briefly at the major neurotransmitter substances that play roles in psychological disorders. However, keep in mind that no neurotransmitter substance works in isolation and that no psychological disorder can be traced solely to the function of a single neurotransmitter substance. Nevertheless, imbalances in some of these substances have been linked, to some extent, with certain psychological disorders.

Dopamine is involved in reward and motivation, and it also plays roles in executive functions in the frontal lobe, including those that orchestrate body movements. Too little dopamine is thought to play a role in attention-deficit/hyperactivity disorder and depression (Bressan & Crippa, 2005). Too much dopamine is thought to play a role in inappropriate aggression and schizophrenia (Buchsbaum et al., 2006).

Serotonin is largely an inhibitory neurotransmitter involved in mood and sleep, as well as motivation. Too little serotonin may play a role in depression and obsessive-compulsive disorder (Mundo et al., 2000); too much of it may reduce a person's motivation.

Acetylcholine plays a particularly important role in the hippocampus, where it is involved in the processes that store new information in memory. It is also found in the ANS and is involved in the fight-or-flight response (which plays a role in panic responses, as we discuss in Chapter 7). Too little acetylcholine is apparently involved in the production of delusions (Rao & Lyketsos, 1998), and too much can contribute to spasms, tremors, and convulsions (Eger et al., 2002).

Figure 2.5

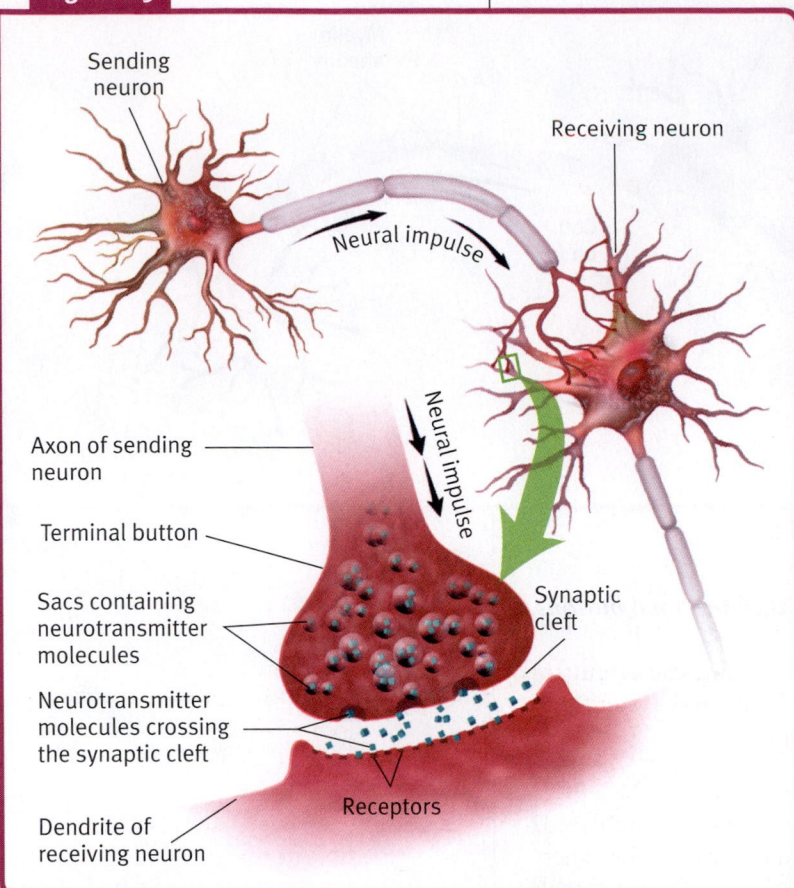

Sending neuron

Receiving neuron

Neural impulse

Axon of sending neuron

Neural impulse

Terminal button

Sacs containing neurotransmitter molecules

Synaptic cleft

Neurotransmitter molecules crossing the synaptic cleft

Receptors

Dendrite of receiving neuron

2.5 ▸ The Synapse

Synapse
The place where the tip of the axon of one neuron sends signals to another neuron.

Neurotransmitters
Chemicals that are released at the terminal buttons and cross the synaptic cleft.

Neuromodulators
Chemicals that modulate (alter) the way neurotransmitters affect the receiving neuron. Some chemicals that act as neurotransmitters can also act as neuromodulators in certain circumstances, and vice versa.

Adrenaline (also called *epinephrine*) plays a role in attention and in the fight-or-flight response (Nemeroff, 1998). Too little of this substance in the brain contributes to depression, and too much can lead to over-arousal and feelings of apprehension or dread.

Noradrenaline (also called *norepinephrine*) also plays a role in attention and the fight-or-flight response. Too little contributes to distractibility, fatigue, and depression (Meana et al., 1992); too much has been implicated in schizophrenia and anxiety disorders (Nutt & Lawson, 1992).

Glutamate is a fast-acting excitatory neurotransmitter found throughout the brain. It plays a role in registering pain and in the formation of new memories. Too much glutamate is involved in various disorders, including substance abuse (Kalivas & Volkow, 2005), and too little is associated with other disorders, notably schizophrenia (Muller & Schwarz, 2006).

Gamma-amino butyric acid (GABA) is a common inhibitory substance. Too little of it is associated with anxiety and (possibly) panic disorder (Goddard et al., 2001); too much appears to undermine motivation.

Endogenous cannabinoids are involved in emotion, attention, memory, appetite, and the control of movements (Wilson & Nicoll, 2001). Too little of these substances is associated with chronic pain; an excess is associated with eating disorders, memory impairment, attention difficulties, and possibly schizophrenia (Giuffrida et al., 2004).

You may have noticed that these descriptions of what the chemical substances do are fairly general. There's a reason for that: The effects of these substances depend only in part on their nature; the effects also depend on the nature of the receiving neurons. Thus, we must next look more closely at what's on the receiving end of these chemical substances.

Chemical Receptors

A neuron receives chemical signals at its **receptors**, specialized sites that respond only to specific molecules (see Figure 2.5). Located on the dendrites or on the cell body, receptors work like locks into which only certain kinds of keys will fit (Kelsey, Newport, & Nemeroff, 2006; Lambert & Kinsley, 2005). However, instead of literally locking or unlocking the corresponding receptors, the neurotransmitter molecules *bind* to the receptors and affect them either by exciting them (making the receiving neuron more likely to fire) or by inhibiting them (making the receiving neuron less likely to fire). We noted earlier that a sending neuron can make a receiving neuron more or less likely to fire, and now we see how these effects occur: The sending neuron releases specific neurotransmitters.

Although each neuron produces only a small number of neurotransmitters, those chemicals often bind to many different types of receptors (Kelsey, Newport, & Nemeroff, 2006). When a neuron fires, the effect of this event depends on how its neurotransmitters bind to receptors on the receiving neuron. The same chemical can have different effects on a neuron depending on which kind of receptor it binds to. For example, dopamine acts as a neurotransmitter in the subcortical reward circuits of the nucleus accumbens. In fact, most abused substances directly or indirectly affect dopamine activity, which in turn activates those reward circuits; this pleasurable experience leads many individuals to want to use the abused substance again to reexperience that state (Tomkins & Sellers, 2001). However, dopamine also acts as a neuromodulator in the frontal lobes (Robbins, 2000), and disruption of its role in executive functions may be critical in schizophrenia.

Abnormal Communications Among Neurons

How can communications among neurons at the synaptic cleft go awry, and thereby lead to psychological disorders? Scientists point to at least three ways in which such communications can be disrupted: First, neurons might have too many or too few dendrites or receptors, making the neurons more or less sensitive, respectively, to even normal amounts of neurotransmitter substances in the synaptic

Receptors
Specialized sites on dendrites and cell bodies that respond only to specific molecules.

cleft (Meana, Barturen, & Garcia-Sevilla, 1992). If the neurons in an inhibitory circuit are abnormal in this way, the brain may have difficulty dampening down repetitive thoughts or behaviors—as occurs in certain disorders we will discuss later in this book.

Second, the sending neurons might produce too much or too little of a neurotransmitter substance. Third, the events after a neuron fires may go awry (Kelsey, Newport, & Nemeroff, 2006). In particular, when a neuron fires and sends neurotransmitter chemicals to another neuron, not all of these molecules bind to receptors. Rather, some of the molecules linger in the synaptic cleft and need to be removed. Special chemical processes operate to **reuptake** these leftover neurotransmitters, moving them back into the sending neuron. Sometimes reuptake does not operate correctly, which may contribute to a psychological disorder. For example, neurons might not reabsorb enough of the molecules from the synaptic cleft, which results in chronically high levels of neurotransmitter (Kandel, Schwartz, & Jessell, 2007; Kelsey, Newport, & Nemeroff, 2006). You might think that this would mean that the receiving neuron is habitually stimulated too much, but in fact the neuron alters its sensitivity to the neurotransmitter so that abnormally high amounts must be produced by the sending neuron to be registered. And if abnormally high amounts are not in fact produced, the functional results are the same as if not enough neurotransmitter were being produced. As we saw earlier, many psychological disorders are associated with too little of a specific neurotransmitter substance.

Hormones and the Endocrine System

Not all neurotransmitter substances are released across synapses. **Hormones** are neurotransmitter substances that are released directly into the bloodstream and often function primarily as neuromodulators; their effect is more general and more widespread than that of neurotransmitters released into synapses (Kelsey, Newport, & Nemeroff, 2006). Like other neurotransmitter substances, hormones can activate or modulate the activity of neurons. For example, some hormones play a key role in helping animals respond to stressful situations by altering the functioning of the ANS (Kandel, Schwartz, & Jessell, 2007). However, traumatic events can disrupt this often–helpful mechanism and contribute to psychological disorders such as depression (Claes, 2004).

Hormones are produced by glands in the *endocrine system*, which secretes substances into the bloodstream. Hormones affect various organs throughout the body. As we noted when we discussed the HPA axis, *cortisol* is a particularly important hormone, which helps the body to cope with challenges by making more resources available (by breaking down fats and proteins and converting them to sugar); cortisol is produced by the adrenal glands (which are located right above the kidneys), and abnormal amounts of cortisol have been linked to anxiety and depression. Some substances, such as adrenaline, function as neurotransmitters in the brain and also as hormones in the body (Lambert & Kinsley, 2005). As noted earlier, we cannot link a psychological disorder solely to the relative amounts of a given transmitter substance: We must also take into account the nature of the neurons (and the circuits in which they participate) that have receptors for that substance.

The Genetics of Psychopathology

Researchers knew about the inheritance of traits long before the discovery of DNA (deoxyribonucleic acid, the long molecule that contains many thousands of genes). Everyone knows that people "take after" their parents in some ways, and genes are responsible for this phenomenon. Genes affect not only physical traits but also the brain and, through the brain, thinking, feeling, and behavior; moreover, genes affect how vulnerable people are to particular psychological disorders (Plomin et al., 1997, 2003).

The study of genetics dates back to Gregor Mendel, an Augustinian monk who lived and worked in what is now the Czech Republic. In 1866, he published a paper

Reuptake
The process of moving leftover neurotransmitter molecules in the synapse back into the sending neuron.

Hormones
Neurotransmitter substances that are released directly into the bloodstream and often function primarily as neuromodulators.

that formulated the core ideas of **Mendelian inheritance**, or the transmission of traits by separate elements (which turned out to be genes). The two most important aspects of Mendelian inheritance are that:

1. Each parent transmits a distinct "element" to its offspring, which specifies each trait.

2. One element may dominate the other in the expression (or nonexpression) of the trait in the offspring. The element that is not *dominant* is called *recessive*. The offspring will show the effect of the recessive element only if neither parent transmits the dominant element, leaving the offspring with two copies of the recessive element, one from each parent.

In the middle of the 20th century, James Watson and Francis Crick famously identified the "elements" that Mendel hypothesized as **genes**, which correspond to segments of DNA that control the production of particular proteins and other substances (see Figure 2.6). For many traits, gene variants—referred to as *alleles*—determine how the trait is manifested. The sum of an organism's genes is called its **genotype**. In contrast, the sum of its observable traits is called its **phenotype**, and many aspects of the phenotype are determined by how the genotype is expressed in a particular environment.

At one time differences in eye color were used as an example of the effects of having different alleles, with brown being dominant and blue recessive. This example has mostly been dropped from textbooks for a simple reason: Eyes come in a huge range of colors, not just two (if you need to be convinced of this, check out the eye colors of your friends). Thus, Mendelian inheritance doesn't really explain differences in eye color. In fact, most traits do not arise from simple combinations of dominant and recessive genes. Rather, for most traits, many genes work together to cause particular effects. Such sets of genes give rise to traits, such as height, that are expressed along a continuum, and the joint actions of these genes produce **complex inheritance** (Plomin et al., 1997). Traits that arise from complex inheritance cannot be linked to a few distinct genes, but rather emerge from the interactions among the effects of numerous genes. Almost all psychological disorders that have a genetic component, such as schizophrenia and depression, arise in part through complex inheritance (Faraone, Tsuang, & Tsuang, 2001; Plomin et al., 2003).

Behavioral Genetics

Studies that investigate the contributions of genes to mental illness rely on the methods of **behavioral genetics**, which is the field that investigates the degree to which the variability of characteristics in a population arises from genetic versus environmental factors (Plomin et al., 2003). With regard to psychopathology, behavioral geneticists consider these questions: What is the role of genetics in causing a particular mental disorder? What is the role of the environment? And what is the role of interactions between genes and the environment?

Throughout this book, we discuss the relative contributions of genes and the environment to the development of specific mental disorders. We must always keep in mind, however, that any conclusions about the relative contributions of the two influences are always tied to the specific environment in which the contributions are measured. To see why, consider the following example (based on Lewontin, 1976). Imagine three situations in which we plant two apple trees of the same variety, one of which has genes for large apples and one of which has genes for small apples.

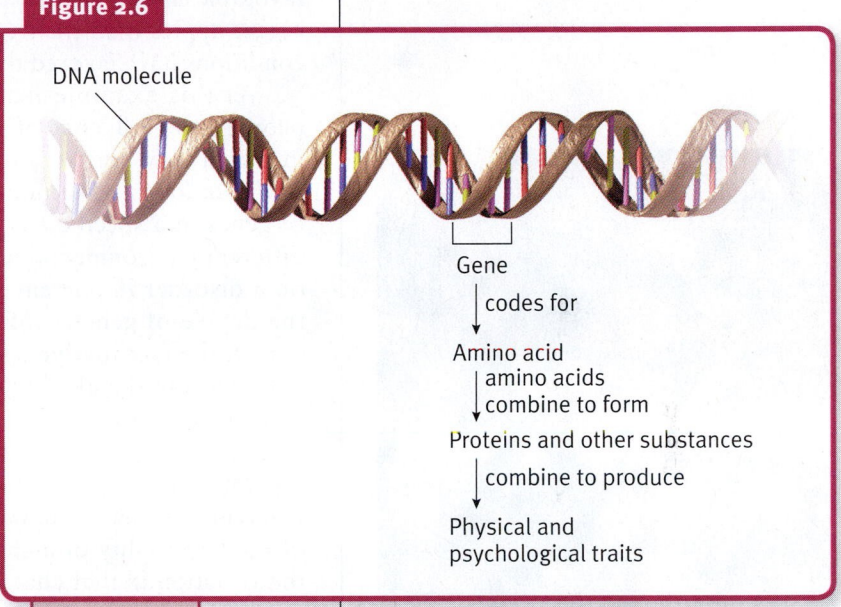

Figure 2.6

DNA molecule

Gene

codes for

Amino acid

amino acids combine to form

Proteins and other substances

combine to produce

Physical and psychological traits

2.6 ▸ DNA

Mendelian inheritance
The transmission of traits by separate elements (genes).

Genes
Segments of DNA that control the production of particular proteins and other substances.

Genotype
The sum of an organism's genes.

Phenotype
The sum of an organism's observable traits.

Complex inheritance
The transmission of traits that are expressed along a continuum by the interaction of sets of genes.

Behavioral genetics
The field that investigates the degree to which the variability of characteristics in a population arises from genetic versus environmental factors.

In the first case, we keep the environment the same for the two trees. Unfortunately for them, however, it is not a very friendly environment: The soil is bad, the trees are in the shade, and there isn't much water. Both trees produce small apples. In this case, the environment overshadows the genetic influence for large apples.

In the second case, the trees are luckier. We keep the environment the same for the two trees, but the soil is rich, the trees are in the sun, and they receive plenty of water. What happens? The tree with genes for large apples produces larger apples than the tree with genes for small apples.

In the third case, the tree with genes for large apples is planted in the impoverished environment, and the tree with genes for small apples is planted in the favorable environment. Now, the tree that has genes for small apples might produce bigger apples than the tree with genes for large apples because the environmental conditions have favored the former and acted against the latter.

As this example makes clear, for trees and other organisms—including people—the influence of genes must be described in relation to the environment in which they function. In other words, genes and environment interact through *feedback loops*—and in fact, that's why the phenotype is described as the product of genes in a specific environment. The same genes can have different effects in different environments. A research finding of a certain degree of genetic influence on a disorder in one environment does not necessarily have any relationship to the degree of genetic influence on the disorder in other environments. For example, the fact that genes can predispose an individual to alcoholism has different effects in the alcohol-embracing culture of France and the alcohol-shunning culture of Pakistan.

Heritability

Behavioral genetics characterizes the relative influence of genetic factors in terms of the heritability of a characteristic. **Heritability** is an estimate of how much of the variation in that characteristic within a population (in a specific environment) can be attributed to genetics. For example, the heritability of *generalized anxiety disorder* (which is characterized by anxiety that is not associated with a particular situation or object, as we will discuss in detail in Chapter 7) is about .32 in citizens of Western countries (Hetteman, Neale, & Kendler, 2001). This means that about a third of the variation in generalized anxiety disorder in this population is genetically determined. Note that this estimate of .32 does *not* mean that any particular person's likelihood of developing the disorder is determined 32% by genes and 68% by environment.

How do researchers estimate the heritability of a given psychological disorder? There is no sure-fire research method, because many variables can affect the results. For example, if researchers find a similar prevalence of a mental disorder in children and their parents, can they assume genetic inheritance? Not necessarily; they would have to rule out any effects of the environment that might be operating. As an extreme example, suppose that for generations, the members of a given family always prepare their meals in lead pots, and hence each generation of children *becomes* mentally retarded because of lead poisoning. This mental retardation is not a result of genetics. Furthermore, it is difficult to assess "the environment" for a given person. The environment must be understood not in objective terms, but rather in terms of how situations and events are perceived and understood. For instance, for siblings in a given family, does having divorced parents constitute the same environment? Not exactly: A child's age at the time of parents' divorce can influence how the child experiences the divorce. A preschooler might believe he or she somehow caused the divorce, whereas an older child—who is more mature cognitively, emotionally, and socially—is less likely to make that inference (Allison & Furstenberg, 1989; Hoffman, 1991). Researchers can entirely avoid such age effects between siblings by studying twins.

David Young-Wolff/PhotoEdit

In Western countries, genes account for about .32 of the variation in generalized anxiety disorder; in other words, in this context, this disorder is about 32% heritable. This does not mean that the likelihood that a given person living in a Western country will develop generalized anxiety disorder is determined 32% by the genes and 68% by the environment; it means that about a third of the variation across the whole population of that environment (Western countries) is determined by genetics.

Heritability
An estimate of how much of the variation in a characteristic within a population (in a specific environment) can be attributed to genetics.

Twin and Adoption Studies

Twin studies compare some characteristic, or set of characteristics, in two groups of twins, identical and fraternal. Identical twins have basically the same genetic makeup, because they began life as a single fertilized egg (or *zygote*) that then divided to become two embryos. Such twins are **monozygotic** (*mono-* means "one"). However, even identical twins do not have absolutely identical sets of genes: They may differ in how often particular genes are repeated, which in turn has effects on how the genes operate (Bruder et al., 2008). Fraternal twins begin life as different fertilized eggs, and so are **dizygotic** (*di-* means "two"). Fraternal twins are like any other nonidentical siblings in terms of their genetic similarity: They have about 50% overlap in the genes that vary among humans. When researchers compare the characteristics of monozygotic twins and dizygotic twins, controlling as much as possible for the environment, they can attempt to draw conclusions about the relative contribution of genes to those characteristics in that environment. For instance, such studies have suggested that schizophrenia is about 50% heritable (Gottesman, 1991). However, we must be cautious about such estimates: Not only can identical twins have slightly different sets of genes, but they begin to have different experiences before birth—in fact, one twin is usually heavier and larger at birth, because of differences in the amounts of nutrients the two fetuses receive in the womb (Cheung, Bocking, & Dasilva, 1995; Hollier, McIntire, & Leveno, 1999).

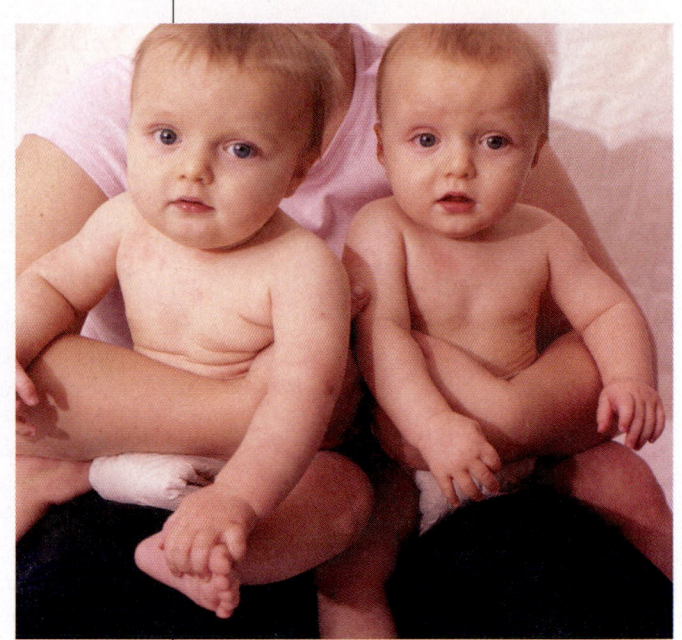

It is not easy to sort out the effects of genetics from those of the environment by studying identical twins. Each twin has unique experiences even before he or she is born: One twin may get less nutrients or be exposed to more toxins while in the mother's womb; that is, there can be different environments for the twins even before birth.

Sometimes researchers try to discover the roles of genes and the environment in mental disorders by conducting *adoption studies*: They study twins who were separated at birth and raised in different homes, then compare them to twins who were raised in the same home. In addition, researchers also study unrelated children who were adopted and raised together, then compare them to unrelated children who were reared in different homes. But even in adoption studies, it's not easy to disentangle the effects of genes and the environment. The reason is that genetic differences influence the environment—a relationship that is characterized by the *reciprocal gene–environment model*. For instance, suppose that a pair of twins has genes that lead them to be high-strung and very active. Even if these twins are raised apart in different environments, their parents may react similarly to them—trying to keep them calm and out of trouble, which might mean that they wouldn't be taken on family outings as often as children who were less of a handful. Or perhaps their genes lead the twins to be bright and ask a lot of questions. In this case, both sets of adoptive parents might take them to museums and talk to them a lot. The point is that even in different adopted households, genes can influence how twins are treated and what they experience. Thus, although twin and adoption studies can be fascinating, their findings must be interpreted cautiously.

The problems with twin and adoption studies have led many researchers to take advantage of recent technological advances in genetics: It is now possible to assess, inexpensively and quickly (for many genes), whether a particular person has a specific allele of a gene (Schena et al., 1995). Researchers have used such techniques to attempt to find associations between the presence or absence of specific alleles and psychological disorders. For example, Rasmussen and colleagues (2006) found that people who develop schizophrenia relatively late in life tend to have one particular allele of a certain gene, which may act either to make them susceptible to late-developing schizophrenia or to delay the onset of the disease in them until later in life. However, such research has proven difficult because many genes contribute to most disorders, and they interact in complex ways. Thus, any one gene is likely to have a relatively small role in most psychological disorders.

Monozygotic twins
Twins who have basically the same genetic makeup (although it may differ in how often specific genes are repeated) because they began life as a single fertilized egg (zygote), which then divided into two embryos; also referred to as *identical twins*.

Dizygotic twins
Twins who developed from two fertilized eggs and so have the same overlap in genes (50%) as do siblings not conceived at the same time; also referred to as *fraternal twins*.

Paul Whitehill/Photo Edit

FEEDBACK LOOPS IN ACTION: **The Genes and the Environment**

We've seen how genes can affect the environment, but—to the surprise of many—the genes themselves are also affected by the environment, including psychological and social factors. We consider the feedback loop between the environment and the genes in the following two sections.

The Environment Affects the Genes

Many people seem to think of genes as instructions for building the brain and the body, guiding the construction process and then ceasing to function. For most genes, this is not so. Even in adulthood, a person's genes are being regulated by the environment (Hyman & Nestler, 1993). Consider a simple example: Did you ever try to learn to play piano? If you did, your fingers were probably sore after even a half-hour of practice. But if you stuck with it, you could play for longer and longer periods with no discomfort. What happened? Your muscles got stronger—but how? When you first began, the stress of using your fingers in new ways actually damaged the muscles (which is why they felt sore). Then, a series of chemical events inside the muscle cells of your fingers *turned on* genes in the nuclei of these cells. These genes directed the cells to produce more proteins, to build up the muscles, which made them stronger. If you stopped playing for a period of time, those genes would turn off, and the muscles would become weaker. Which is why your fingers might be sore when you first resumed playing after having taken a long break.

The point is that some genes are activated, or turned on, as a result of experience, of interacting with the world (Kandel, Schwartz, & Jessell, 2007). This is true of genes in the brain that produce neurotransmitters and that cause new synapses to form. In fact, when you learn, genes in your brain are turned on, which causes new connections among neurons to be formed. This is true even when you learn maladaptive behaviors, which can produce, among other problems, a *phobia*—an intense, irrational fear of an object or situation.

Moreover, genetic factors can contribute to a neurological vulnerability for a psychological disorder. For example, genetic factors can lead a person to be prone to learning maladaptive behaviors.

However, genes are not destiny. More often than not, having specific genes does not determine behavior, but rather predisposes one to be affected by the environment in certain ways. That is, genes can predispose a person for a specific disorder, but those genes may have that effect only when triggered by psychological or social factors.

The Genes Affect the Environment

We've just seen how the environment affects the genes, and we've already noted that the reverse also occurs. Let's now look in more detail at ways in which the genes affect the environment. Many researchers (Plomin et al., 1997; Scarr & McCartney, 1983) distinguish three ways in which genes affect the environment—passive interaction, evocative interaction, and active interaction:

1. *Passive interaction.* The parents' genes affect the child's environment—and the child passively receives these influences. For instance, some parents avoid large social groups because they are shy, which is in part a result of their genes; this means that their child does not have many social experiences. The child may not have inherited the parents' shy temperament, but the parents' genes nonetheless act through the environment to affect the child.

2. *Evocative interaction* (also called *reactive interaction*). A person's inherited traits encourage other people to behave in particular ways, and hence the person's social environment will be affected by his or her genes. For example, if you are very tall and heavy-set, others may respond to you somewhat cautiously—in a way they would not if you were short and frail. Similarly, others may approach or avoid you (fairly or not!) in response to your temperament (e.g., shy, calm, high-strung); any specific temperament will appeal to some and not to others. Thus, even your circle

of friends will be somewhat determined by your genes, and those friends will then affect you in certain ways depending on their own characteristics.

3. *Active interaction.* Each of us actively seeks out some environments and avoids others, and our genes influence which environments feel most comfortable to us. For example, a person who is sensitive to environmental stimulation might prefer spending a quiet evening at home curled up with a good book instead of going to a loud, crowded party at a friend's house.

The interactions between genes and the environment involve all of the factors considered by the neuropsychosocial approach, and hence create complex feedback loops. Once the environment (including social factors, such as one's choice of friends) has been influenced by genes, the environment affects the genes (as well as one's knowledge, beliefs, attitudes, and so on).

Again, the import of these observations for psychological disorders is clear. Genes can make a person at risk for a particular psychological disorder, but other factors—psychological and social—can influence the expression of the genes. And the specific psychological and social factors that affect a person arise, in part, from that person's genes (which affect, for example, aspects of his or her appearance). Thus, even though genes may make some people vulnerable to specific kinds of mental illness, the path from genes to illness is neither straight nor inevitable.

Key Concepts and Facts About Neurological Factors in Psychological Disorders

- The nervous system has two major parts: the central nervous system (CNS), which is composed of the brain and spinal cord, and the peripheral nervous system (PNS), which is composed of the sensory-somatic nervous system and the autonomic nervous system (ANS).

- The ANS controls many involuntary functions, such as those of the heart, blood vessels, and digestive tract. The ANS has two major components:

  - The sympathetic nervous system, which produces more adaptive bodily functioning in an emergency with the fight-or-flight response. As part of this response, the hypothalamic-pituitary-adrenal axis (HPA axis) manages the production of cortisol, which helps the muscles prepare for physical exertion. The HPA axis and high levels of cortisol are involved in depression and stress-related psychological disorders.

  - The parasympathetic nervous system, which typically brings the body back to its normal state after a fight-or-flight response. The parasympathetic system typically counteracts the effects of the sympathetic nervous system, and psychopathology may arise if it fails to do so effectively.

- The brain is divided into two hemispheres; the lobes of which (along with their key functions) are: occipital lobe (involved in vision), parietal lobe (involved in processing spatial information and self-awareness), temporal lobe (involved in processing auditory information, including speech, and memory), and frontal lobe (site of executive functioning).

- Subcortical (beneath the cortex) areas of importance (along with their key functions) are as follows:

  - The limbic system, which plays a key role in emotions and includes the hypothalamus (involved in controlling eating,

drinking, temperature, and emotions), the amygdala (central to producing and perceiving strong emotions), and the hippocampus (involved in storing new information in memory);

  - The thalamus (involved in controlling sleep and maintaining attention);

  - The nucleus accumbens (involved in registering reward and learning from experience);

  - The basal ganglia (involved in automatic responses); and

  - The cerebellum (involved in physical coordination and automatic motions).

- There are three types of neurons: sensory neurons, motor neurons, and interneurons (most neurons are interneurons). Neurons communicate with each other to create patterns of activation in brain circuits, which in turn are organized into large brain systems; these systems may be disrupted in cases of psychopathology.

  - A neuron has a cell body, an axon that ends in terminal buttons, and dendrites that receive signals from other neurons. The neuron is covered by a cell membrane that has channels that open when the neuron fires.

  - When a neuron fires, neurotransmitters released from the terminal buttons travel across the synaptic cleft to receptors on the dendrite or cell body of another neuron. Neuromodulators may affect the functioning of neurotransmitters by altering events at the synapse.

- Neurotransmitter substances include dopamine (involved in reward, motivation, and executive functioning), serotonin (involved in mood, sleep, and motivation), acetylcholine (involved in memory and the fight-or-flight response), adrenaline and noradrenaline

continued on next page

(involved in attention and the fight-or-flight response), glutamate (involved in registering pain and the formation of new memories), GABA (involved in anxiety and motivation), and endogenous cannabinoids (involved in emotion, attention, memory, appetite, and the control of movements).

- Neurotransmitters can bind to different types of receptors; the type of receptor a neurotransmitter binds to determines its effect.

- Neuronal communication can go awry when (1) neurons have an abnormal number of dendrites or receptors, affecting sensitivity to neurotransmitters in the synaptic cleft; (2) sending neurons release abnormal amounts of neurotransmitter into the synapse; (3) reuptake of neurotransmitter molecules does not operate correctly.

- Hormones, produced by glands in the endocrine system, often function as neuromodulators; an important hormone related to some psychological disorders is cortisol.

- Genes can influence the development of psychopathology. Complex inheritance best explains the influence of genes on psychological disorders. Scientists who study behavioral genetics seek to determine the roles of genes, the environment, and their interactions in both normal and abnormal thoughts, feelings, and behaviors. Heritability is an estimate of how much of the variation of a characteristic across a population, *in a specific environment*, is determined by genes.

- Behavioral geneticists may use twin and adoption studies to determine the relative influences of genes and environment. Twins are either monozygotic or dizygotic. The environment can affect genes by influencing when—and which—genes are turned off and on. Genes can affect the environment in three ways: (1) passive interaction, (2) evocative interaction, and (3) active interaction.

Psychological Factors in Psychological Disorders

Both of the Beale women had idiosyncratic ideas and inclinations. For instance, Little Edie, in talking about World War II, expressed an unusual view about who should be soldiers and sent off to fight a war—people who are not physically healthy and hardy. With such people as soldiers, she claimed, the war would be over sooner (Maysles, 2006). In addition, Big Edie was known to command Little Edie to change her attire, repeatedly, up to 10 times each day (Maysles, 2006). Psychological factors, such as learning, can help to account for people's beliefs and behavior. Could aspects of Big Edie and Little Edie's views and lifestyle have been learned? And how might their emotions—such as Big Edie's fear of being alone or Little Edie's resentment of her mother's control—influence their thoughts and behavior? Let's examine the role that previous learning, mental processes and contents, and emotions can play in psychological disorders.

Behavior and Learning

As we saw in Chapter 1, psychological disorders involve distress, impaired functioning, and/or risk of harm. These three elements can be expressed in behaviors, such as occurs when people disrupt their daily lives in order to avoid feared stimuli or when they drink too much alcohol to cope with life's ups and downs. Many behaviors related to psychological disorders can be learned. As we shall see, some psychological disorders can be explained, at least partly, as a consequence of one of three types of learning: classical conditioning, operant conditioning, and observational learning.

Classical Conditioning

Classical conditioning
A type of learning that occurs when two stimuli are paired so that a neutral stimulus becomes associated with another stimulus that elicits a reflexive behavior; also referred to as *Pavlovian conditioning*.

In a landmark study of an 11-month-old infant, known as "Little Albert," behaviorists John B. Watson and Rosalie Rayner (1920) demonstrated how to produce a phobia. The researchers conditioned Little Albert to be afraid of white rats, using the basic procedure of Pavlovian conditioning (see Chapter 1), except in this case the reflexive behavior was related to fear rather than salivation. To do this, they made a very loud sound immediately after a white rat (which was used as the neutral stimulus) moved into the child's view; they repeated this procedure several times. Whenever Little Albert subsequently saw a white rat, he would cry or exhibit other signs of fear. The process that generated Little Albert's fear of white rats is called **classical conditioning**—a type of learning that occurs when two stimuli are paired so that a neutral stimulus becomes associated with another stimulus that elicits a reflexive behavior; classical conditioning is also referred to (less commonly) as Pavlovian conditioning. By experiencing pairings of the two stimuli (the white rat and the loud noise in the case of Little Albert), the person comes to respond to the neutral stimulus alone (the white rat) in the same way that he or she had responded to the stimulus that elicited the reflexive behavior (the loud noise).

How, specifically, does classical conditioning occur? Using the lingo of psychologists, the stimulus that reflexively elicits a behavior is called the **unconditioned stimulus (UCS)**, because it elicits the behavior without prior conditioning. In the case of Little Albert, the loud noise was the UCS, and the behavior it reflexively elicited was a startle response associated with fear. Such a reflexive behavior is called an **unconditioned response (UCR)**. The neutral stimulus that, when paired with the UCS, comes to elicit the reflexive behavior is called the **conditioned stimulus (CS)**. It is called the conditioned stimulus because its ability to elicit the response is *conditional* on its being paired with a UCS. In Little Albert's case, the CS was the white rat. The **conditioned response (CR)** is the response that comes to be elicited by the previously neutral stimulus (the CR is basically the same behavior as the UCR, but the behavior is elicited by the CS). In Little Albert's case, the CR was the startle response to the rat alone (and ensuing fear-related behaviors, such as crying and trying to avoid the rat). The process of classical conditioning is illustrated in Figure 2.7.

Although various reflexive behaviors, such as salivation, can be classically conditioned (Pavlov, 1927), the ones most important for understanding psychopathology are those related to emotional responses such as fear and arousal (Davey, 1987; Schafe & LeDoux, 2004). When emotions and emotion-related behaviors are classically conditioned, they are referred to as **conditioned emotional responses**. People who have the personality characteristic of being generally emotionally reactive—referred to as being high in *neuroticism*—are more likely to develop conditioned emotional responses than are people who do not have this personality characteristic (Bienvenu et al., 2001).

Conditioned responses can also *generalize,* so that they are elicited by stimuli that are similar to the conditioned stimulus, a process called **stimulus generalization**. For instance, Little Albert became afraid not only of white rats, but also of other white furry things. He even became afraid of a piece of white cotton! His fear of rats had generalized to similar stimuli.

As we shall see in detail in later chapters, classical conditioning is of interest to those studying psychological disorders because it helps to explain:

- various types of anxiety disorders, particularly phobias, like Little Albert's phobia;
- mechanisms related to substance abuse and dependence (Hyman, 2005);
- the development of specific types of sexual disorders (Domjan, Cusato, & Krause, 2004).

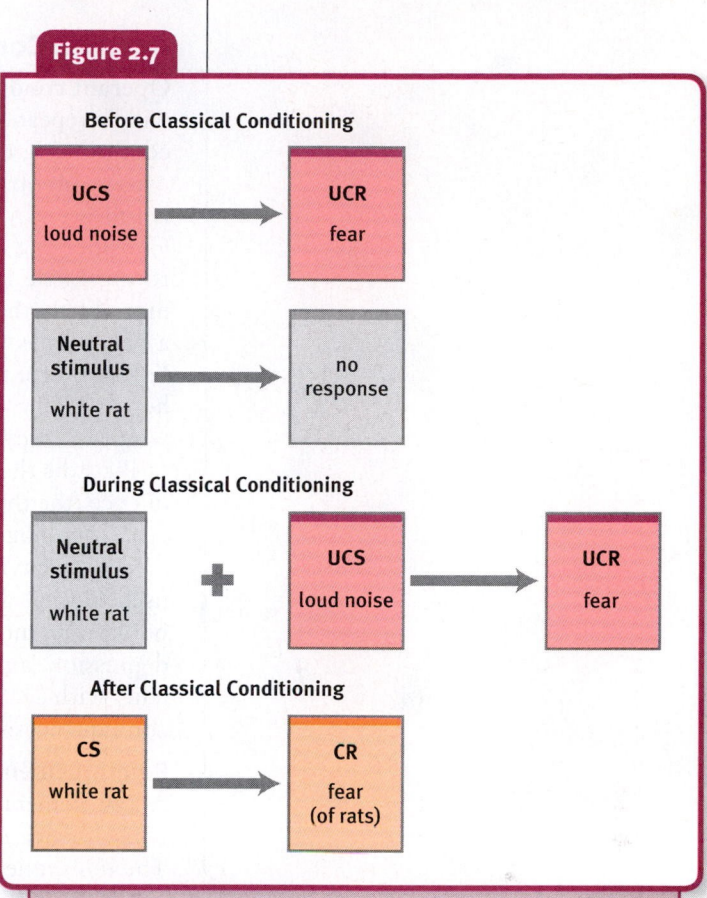

Figure 2.7

2.7 ▸ Classical Conditioning of a Fear: Little Albert

Unconditioned stimulus (UCS)
A stimulus that reflexively elicits a behavior.

Unconditioned response (UCR)
A behavior that is reflexively elicited by a stimulus.

Conditioned stimulus (CS)
A neutral stimulus that, when paired with an unconditioned stimulus, comes to elicit the reflexive behavior.

Conditioned response (CR)
A response that comes to be elicited by the previously neutral stimulus that has become a conditioned stimulus.

Conditioned emotional responses
Emotions and emotion-related behaviors that are classically conditioned.

Stimulus generalization
The process whereby responses come to be elicited by stimuli that are similar to the conditioned stimulus.

Operant Conditioning

Operant conditioning is a type of learning in which the likelihood that a behavior will be repeated depends on the consequences associated with the behavior. Operant conditioning usually involves voluntary behaviors, whereas classical conditioning usually involves reflexive behaviors. With operant conditioning, when a behavior is followed by a positive consequence, the behavior is more likely to be repeated. Consider Big Edie's behavior of crying out for Little Edie to come back into the room. Little Edie then returns to the room (a positive consequence), making it more likely that Big Edie will cry out for Little Edie to return in the future. When a behavior is followed by a negative consequence, it is less likely to be repeated. For instance, the last time Big Edie left Grey Gardens was in 1968, when she and her daughter went to a party at a friend's house; upon returning home, the Beale women discovered that thieves had taken $15,000 worth of heirlooms. It seemed to Big Edie that her behavior (leaving the house) was followed by a negative consequence (the theft), and so she never left again.

Psychologist B. F. Skinner showed that operant conditioning can explain a great deal of behavior, including abnormal behavior, and operant conditioning can be used to treat abnormal behaviors (Skinner, 1965). As we shall see throughout this book, operant conditioning contributes to various psychological disorders, such as depression, anxiety disorders, substance abuse disorder, eating disorders, and problems with self-regulation in general. Operant conditioning relies on two types of consequences: reinforcement and punishment.

Reinforcement

A key element in operant conditioning is **reinforcement**, the process by which the consequence of a behavior *increases* the likelihood of the behavior's recurrence. The consequence—an object or event—that makes a behavior more likely in the future is called a *reinforcer*. In the case of Big Edie's fear of being alone, the behavior was Big Edie's calling out to her daughter to return to her room, and it was followed by a reinforcer: Little Edie's return to her mother's side. The consequences do not need to be explicit in order for reinforcement to occur. That is, subsequent behavior change in response to reinforcement is likely to occur even when the individual is not *told* what behavior is being reinforced.

We need to consider two types of reinforcement: positive reinforcement and negative reinforcement. **Positive reinforcement** occurs when a desired reinforcer is received after the behavior, which makes the behavior more likely to occur again in the future. For instance, when someone takes a drug, the chemical properties of the drug may lead the person to experience a temporarily pleasant state (the reinforcer), which he or she may want to experience again, thus making the person more likely to take the drug again.

In contrast, **negative reinforcement** occurs when an aversive or uncomfortable stimulus is *removed* after a behavior, which makes that behavior more likely to be repeated in the future. For example, suppose that a man has a strong fear—a phobia—of dirt. If his hands get even slightly dirty, he will have the urge to wash them and will be uncomfortable until he does so. The act of washing his hands is negatively reinforced by the consequence of removing his discomfort about the dirt, which makes him more likely to wash his hands again the next time they get a bit dirty. Similarly, someone who feels sad and then eats some ice cream may briefly feel better; the act of eating the ice cream is negatively reinforced by the consequence of feeling less sad, which in turn increases the likelihood that the person will reach for ice cream the next time he or she feels sad. Negative reinforcement is often confused with punishment; as we see next, however, the two are very different.

Punishment

Positive reinforcement and negative reinforcement both *increase* the probability of a behavior's recurring. In contrast, **punishment** is a process by which an event or object that is the consequence of a behavior *decreases* the likelihood that the behavior will occur again. Just as there are two types of reinforcement, there are two types

---

Operant conditioning
A type of learning in which the likelihood that a behavior will be repeated depends on the consequences associated with the behavior.

Reinforcement
The process by which the consequence of a behavior *increases* the likelihood of the behavior's recurrence.

Positive reinforcement
The type of reinforcement that occurs when a desired reinforcer is received after a behavior, which makes the behavior more likely to occur again in the future.

Negative reinforcement
The type of reinforcement that occurs when an aversive or uncomfortable stimulus is *removed* after a behavior, which makes that behavior more likely to be produced again in the future.

Punishment
The process by which an event or object that is the consequence of a behavior *decreases* the likelihood that the behavior will occur again.

of punishment: positive punishment and negative punishment. **Positive punishment** takes place when a behavior is followed by an undesirable consequence, which makes the behavior less likely to recur. In other words, an undesired stimulus is added in response to a behavior. For example, imagine that every time a young boy sings along with a song playing on the radio, his older sister makes fun of him (an undesirable consequence): In the future, he won't sing as often when she's around. That boy has experienced positive punishment.

Some parents use corporal punishment—spanking or slapping a child after a misbehavior—as positive punishment, believing that hitting a child after a misbehavior will decrease the likelihood of that behavior's recurring. Although a specific misbehavior may—or may not—become less likely if it is followed by corporal punishment, nonphysical forms of punishment can work just as well; examples of nonphysical punishments include time out and being grounded (Larzelere & Kuhn, 2005). (As we shall discuss shortly, though, these nonphysical punishments are *negative* rather than positive punishments.) Moreover, one reason to avoid using corporal punishment is that being physically punished in childhood may, for some children, lead to an increased risk of depression and substance abuse in adulthood (Afifi et al., 2006).

Negative punishment occurs when a behavior is followed by the removal of a pleasant or desired event or circumstance, which decreases the probability of that behavior's recurrence. Negative punishment occurs, for example, when a teenager stays out too late with friends and then her parents take away her access to television (or cell phone, email, use of the car, or something else she likes) for a week. Big Edie's father tried to use negative punishment to modify her behavior: He decreased her monthly allowance, repeatedly reduced her inheritance, and even told her that he was doing this because of her eccentric behavior. His attempts at negative punishment did not work, however, which indicates that the consequence he picked—taking away some money—was not meaningful enough to Big Edie.

The four types of operant conditioning are compared in Table 2.1.

School detention is an attempt at positive punishment: Imposing the consequence of detention on students who exhibit troublesome behaviors should decrease the likelihood of those behaviors in the future.

Table 2.1 ▶ Four Types of Operant Conditioning

Type of Conditioning	How It Occurs	Result	Example
Positive Reinforcement	Desired consequence is produced by behavior.	Increased likelihood of the behavior	A pleasant effect from drug use makes drug use *more likely* to recur.
Negative Reinforcement	Undesired event or circumstance is removed after behavior.	Increased likelihood of the behavior	The uncomfortable feeling of having dirty hands is relieved by washing them (which makes such washing *more likely* to recur).
Positive Punishment	Undesired consequence is produced by behavior.	Decreased likelihood of the behavior	A sister's humiliating comment about her brother's singing along with the radio makes future singing in her presence *less likely* to recur.
Negative Punishment	Pleasant event or circumstance is removed after behavior.	Decreased likelihood of the behavior	Removing a television from a teenager's room after he stays out too late makes staying out too late *less likely* to recur.

Positive punishment
The type of punishment that takes place when a behavior is followed by an undesirable consequence, which makes the behavior less likely to recur.

Negative punishment
The type of punishment that takes place when a behavior is followed by the removal of a pleasant or desired event or circumstance, which decreases the probability of that behavior's recurrence.

Learned helplessness
The state of "giving up" that arises when an animal is in an aversive situation where it seems that no action can be effective.

Observational learning
The process of learning through watching what happens to others; also referred to as *modeling*.

Receiving frequent punishments or negative criticisms is associated with depression in some people: Over time, some individuals who experience such aversive events eventually give up trying to avoid or escape them and become depressed. Martin Seligman and his colleagues suggested that this giving up is learned through operant conditioning (Miller & Seligman, 1973, 1975). The process appears analogous to what happens to animals in similar circumstances. Consider a classic study by Overmier and Seligman (1967): When caged dogs were electrically shocked, at first they would respond to the shocks, trying to escape in order to avoid them. But when they could not escape the continued shocks, they eventually stopped responding and simply endured, huddling on the floor. Even after they were put in a new cage in which they could easily avoid the shocks, they remained on the floor. This phenomenon is called **learned helplessness**: In an aversive situation where it seems that no action can be effective, the animal stops trying to escape (Mikulincer, 1994). Learned helplessness may also occur in humans, and is considered to underlie certain types of depression. For example, sometimes people are emotionally abused—continually criticized, humiliated, and belittled—and no matter how hard they try to be "better" (and so prevent the abuse), the emotional abuse continues. When people in such a situation give up trying, they may become depressed and become vulnerable to a variety of stress-related problems.

FEEDBACK LOOPS IN ACTION: Classical Conditioning and Operant Conditioning Revisited

Classical conditioning and operant conditioning involve neurological factors: the underlying brain mechanisms that pair stimuli in the case of classical conditioning, and the underlying brain mechanisms for reward and punishment in the case of operant conditioning. And based on temperament (another neurological factor, which we'll discuss shortly), people who are more emotionally reactive are more likely to develop conditioned emotional responses than are others (Bienvenu et al., 2001). Social factors can also contribute to maladaptive learning: The presence of others or emotional responses from others can serve as reinforcement or punishment (Kringelbach, Aranjo, & Rolls, 2001), leading people to behave in maladaptive ways. For example, if a parent punishes a child in some way (even through facial expressions) for playing with another child, that punished child may grow up to feel that it is somehow "wrong" to enjoy others' company and come to avoid others when possible. Similarly, a specific individual, such as a punitive relative, can become a conditioned stimulus, eliciting fear.

Let's suppose that a student gave a presentation that didn't go well and some classmates snickered during one part (social factor). Let's also suppose that this student had an inherited vulnerability (a neurological factor; Biederman et al., 2001; Kagan, 1989) that increased his or her risk of developing a conditioned emotional response—in this case, to making presentations (Mineka & Zinbarg, 1995). And let's further suppose that the student developed negative, irrational thoughts about public speaking (psychological factor; Abbott & Rapee, 2004; Antony & Barlow, 2002). The neurological factors and social factors may increase the likelihood that the student will develop a *social phobia*—an intense fear of public humiliation or embarrassment, accompanied by an avoidance of social situations likely to elicit this fear.

People who are uncomfortable in particular social situations may leave such situations as early as possible; this early departure is negatively reinforced because, once they leave, they no longer feel uncomfortable. Such negative reinforcement of social anxiety can contribute to a psychological disorder called *social phobia*—unreasonable anxiety or fear in social situations (American Psychiatric Association, 2000).

Observational Learning

Not all learning involves directly experiencing the associations that underlie classical and operant conditioning. **Observational learning** (also referred to as *modeling*) results from watching what happens to others (social factor; Bandura, Ross, & Ross, 1961); from our observations, we develop a guide for our own behavior as well as expectations about what is likely to occur when we behave the same way (psychological factor). Observational learning is primarily a *psychological* factor: Mental processes (who and what behaviors are paid attention to, how the information is perceived and interpreted, how motivated the individual is to imitate the behavior) are a primary force. However, social factors are also involved, which include who the model is, his or her status, and his or her relationship to the observer. For instance, people who have high status or are attractive are more likely to hold our attention—so we are more likely to model their behavior (Brewer & Wann, 1998).

Through observational learning, children can figure out the types of behavior that are acceptable in their family (Thorn & Gilbert, 1998), even if the observed behaviors are maladaptive. For example, when children observe parents managing conflict through violence or by drinking alcohol, they may learn to use such coping strategies themselves. From a young age, Little Edie spent much of her time with her mother, and during the 2 years she was kept out of school, she was with her mother practically day and night. Thus, in her formative years, Little Edie had ample opportunity to watch her mother's eccentric behavior and may have modeled her own eccentric behavior on that of her mother. Further, observational learning and operant conditioning can work together: When Little Edie modeled her behavior after her mother's, she was no doubt reinforced by her mother.

Mental Processes and Mental Contents

As Freud emphasized (see Chapter 1), both mental processes and mental contents play important roles in the etiology of psychological disorders. Let's take a closer look at these two types of contributing factors.

Mental Processes

We all have biases in our mental processes; hearing the same conversation, we can differ in what we pay attention to, how we interpret what we hear, and what we remember. Suppose a group of friends is sitting around chatting after dinner. One of them says, "I feel really bad." Each friend may understand and respond to this sentence in a different way: One friend may pay a lot of attention to it, understand it to mean, "You've made me feel very bad by what you said earlier" (and then spend the rest of the night feeling guilty for inflicting emotional pain on someone else). Another friend may "tune out" the complaint and not even remember it later. A third friend may pay attention to it, but infer that the person is physically unwell and wonder whether to recommend seeing a doctor.

With some psychological disorders, mental processes involved in attention, perception, and memory may be biased in particular ways:

- *Attention* results in selecting or enhancing certain stimuli, including those that may be related to a disorder (van den Heuvel et al., 2005). Women with an eating disorder, for instance, are more likely than women without such a disorder to focus their attention on the parts of their bodies they consider "ugly" (Jansen, Nederkoorn, & Mulkens, 2005).

- *Perception* results in registering and identifying specific stimuli, such as spiders or particular facial expressions of emotion (Buhlmann, Etcoff, & Wilhelm, 2006). As one example of bias in perception, depressed people are less likely than nondepressed people to rate neutral or mildly happy faces as "happy" (Surguladze et al., 2004).

- *Memory* involves storing, retaining, and accessing stored information, including that which is emotionally relevant to a particular disorder (Foa et al., 2000).

Consider the disorder *hypochondriasis,* which is marked by a preoccupation with bodily sensations, combined with a belief of having a serious illness despite a lack of medical evidence. People suffering from hypochondriasis have a memory bias: They are better able to remember health-related words than non–health-related words (Brown et al., 1999), which is not surprising considering that the disorder involves a preoccupation with illness.

Thus, various mental processes can contribute to psychopathology by influencing what people pay attention to, how they perceive various stimuli, and what they remember. In turn, these alterations in mental processes influence the content of people's thoughts by shifting their awareness of various situations, objects, and stimuli.

Mental Contents

The contents of people's thoughts can play a role in the development of psychological disorders, as noted in Chapter 1. Psychiatrist Aaron Beck (1967) proposed that dysfunctional, maladaptive thoughts are the root cause of psychological problems. These dysfunctional thoughts are **cognitive distortions** of reality. An example of a dysfunctional belief is a woman's conviction that she is unlovable—that if her boyfriend *really* knew her, he couldn't love her. Cognitive distortions can make a person vulnerable to psychological disorders and are sometimes referred to as *cognitive vulnerabilities* (Riskind & Alloy, 2006). Beck (1967) also argued that recognizing these false and dysfunctional thoughts, and adopting realistic and adaptive thoughts, can reduce psychological problems. Cognitive distortions can arise as a result of maladaptive learning from previous experiences. A man with a classically conditioned fear of rodents, for instance, may come to believe that rodents are *dangerous* because of the fear and anxiety he experiences when he's with them. Operant conditioning can also give rise to cognitive distortions. For instance, a child who is repeatedly rejected by her father can grow up to believe that nobody could love her. In this case, the conditioning could have occurred every time she tried to hug her father, if he removed her arms from his body and turned away. Several common cognitive distortions are presented in Table 2.2.

Table 2.2 ▸ Cognitive Distortions

Cognitive Distortion	Definition	Example
All-or-Nothing Thinking	Seeing things in black and white	You think that if you are not perfect, you are a failure.
Overgeneralization	Seeing a single negative event as part of a never-ending pattern of such events	While having a bad day, you predict that subsequent days will also be bad.
Mental Filter	Focusing too strongly on negative qualities or events to the exclusion of the other qualities or events	Although your overall appearance is fine, you focus persistently on the bad haircut you recently had.
Disqualifying the Positive	Not recognizing or accepting positive experiences or events, thus emphasizing the negative	After giving a good presentation, you discount the positive feedback you received and focus only on what you didn't like about your performance.
Jumping to Conclusions	Making an unsubstantiated negative interpretation of events	Although there is no evidence for your inference, you assume that your boss didn't like your presentation.
Personalization	Seeing yourself as the cause of a negative event when in fact you were not actually responsible	When your parents fight about finances, you think their problems are somehow your fault, despite the fact that their financial troubles weren't caused by you.

Source: Copyright © 1980 by David D. Burns, M.D. Reprinted by permission of HarperCollins Publishers, William Morrow. For more information see the Permissions section.

Mental health professionals need to keep in mind, however, cultural factors that may contribute to what appear to be maladaptive cognitive distortions, but in fact reflect appropriate social behavior in a patient's culture. For instance, some cultures, such as that of Japan, have a social norm of responding to a compliment with a self-deprecating statement. It is only through careful evaluation that a clinician can discern whether such self-deprecating behavior reflects a patient's attempt to show good manners or his or her core maladaptive dysfunctional beliefs about self.

Biases in mental processes and distortions in mental contents affect each other (see Figure 2.8), and their interactions can make people more vulnerable to psychopathology. Unfortunately, once someone has a psychological disorder, these biases and distortions can become self-perpetuating: People see what they believe they will see. Someone who feels unlovable, for instance, becomes alert for—and will remember—any hint of rejection, which then confirms the belief of being unlovable.

Emotion

Part of being human is to know the ups and downs of emotions—such as joy, elation, happiness, love, pride, sadness, fear, anger, guilt, relief. When our emotions are negative—that is, when they make us feel uncomfortable—we often try to make ourselves feel better. When we are afraid, we try to avoid what's making us afraid or calm ourselves down; when we feel guilty, we seek to relieve the guilt. Yet not everyone experiences the normal range of emotions or is equally effective in regulating emotions. Many psychological disorders include problems that involve emotions: not feeling or expressing enough emotions (such as showing no response to a situation where others would be joyous or sad), having emotions that are inappropriate or inappropriately excessive for the situation (such as feeling sad to the point of crying for no apparent reason), or having emotions that are difficult to regulate (such as not being able to overcome a fear of flying, even though you know that such fear is irrational) (American Psychiatric Association, 2000).

But what, specifically, are emotions? To psychologists, an **emotion** is a short-lived experience evoked by a stimulus that produces a mental response, a typical behavior, and a positive or negative subjective feeling. The stimulus that initiates an emotion could be physical: It can be a kiss, the letter *F* on an essay you get back from a professor, or the sounds of a tune you listen to on your computer. Alternatively, the stimulus can occur only in the mind, such as *remembering* a sad occasion or tune or *imagining* your perfect mate.

Mental health clinicians and researchers sometimes use the word **affect** to refer to an emotion that is associated with a particular idea or behavior, similar to an *attitude*. *Affect* is also used to describe how emotion is expressed, as when noting that a patient has **inappropriate affect**—the patient's expression of emotion is not appropriate to what he or she is saying or not appropriate to the situation. An example is a person laughing at a funeral or talking about something very sad or traumatic while smiling, or, conversely, talking about a happy event while looking sad or angry. **Flat affect** is a lack of, or considerably diminished, emotional expression, such as occurs when someone speaks robotically and shows little facial expression. People with some psychological disorders, such as schizophrenia, frequently display inappropriate or flat affect. Affect that changes very rapidly—too rapidly—is said to be *labile*, and it may indicate a psychological disorder; for instance, some people with depression may quickly shift emotions from sad to angry or irritable.

In the film *Grey Gardens*, Little Edie and her mother often displayed inappropriate affect, and Little Edie's emotions were sometimes labile, rapidly changing from anger to happy excitement to relative calm. For instance, at one point, Big Edie recounts that when Little Edie had moved to New York City, Big Edie wanted Mr. Beale to return to Grey Gardens. Little Edie immediately started yelling, "You're making

Figure 2.8

Biased mental processes		Distorted mental contents
Attention Perception Memory	⟷	Cognitive distortions

2.8 ▶ Biased Mental Processes and Distorted Mental Contents Biases in mental processes can influence the contents of people's thoughts by making certain stimuli more prominent and easier to call to mind, which can lead to cognitive distortions. The reverse is also true: Cognitive distortions can create a bias in what people pay attention to, perceive, and remember.

Girl Ray/Getty Images

Some disorders are characterized by inappropriate affect—expressions of emotion that are inappropriate to the situation. This young man appears to have inappropriate affect.

Emotion
A short-lived experience evoked by a stimulus that produces a mental response, a typical behavior, and a positive or negative subjective feeling.

Affect
An emotion that is associated with a particular idea or behavior, similar to an attitude.

Inappropriate affect
An expression of emotion that is not appropriate to what a person is saying or not appropriate to the situation.

Flat affect
A lack of, or considerably diminished, emotional expression, such as occurs when someone speaks robotically and shows little facial expression.

me very angry!" (Maysles & Maysles, 1976), even though one moment before she had been relatively calm, and they were talking about events that had transpired over 20 years earlier.

A **mood** is a persistent emotion that is not attached to a stimulus. A mood lurks in the background and influences mental processes, mental contents, and behavior. For example, when you wake up "on the wrong side of the bed" for no apparent reason and feel grumpy all day, you are experiencing a type of bad mood. Some psychological disorders, such as depression, involve disturbances in mood.

Emotions and Behavior

Emotions and behavior can be closely linked in various ways (see Figure 2.9). People are more likely to participate in activities and behave in ways that are consistent with their emotions (Bower & Forgas, 2000). When people are sad, they tend to hunch their shoulders and listen to slow music rather than upbeat music. When people are afraid, they tend to freeze, like a deer caught in the headlights. And when people are depressed, they often don't have the inclination or energy to see friends, which can lead to social isolation.

Fortunately, the relationship between emotions and behavior also works in the other direction: A change in behavior can lead to a change in emotion. When depressed people make an effort to see friends or engage in other activities that they used to enjoy, they often become less depressed (Jacobson, Martell, & Dimidjian, 2001). The fact that changing behaviors can alter emotions is the basis of a number of psychological treatments (to be discussed in Chapter 4). The point is that emotions can kindle—and be kindled by—behavior; emotions and behavior dynamically interact.

Emotions, Mental Processes, and Mental Contents

Emotions not only affect behavior, but also affect mental processes and mental contents (see Figure 2.10). In fact, emotions and moods contribute to biases in attention, perception, and memory (Blaney, 1986; Eich, Macauley, & Ryan, 1994; Forgas, 1995; MacKay & Ahmetzanov, 2005; Mogg & Bradley, 2005; Yovel & Mineka, 2005). When anxious, people are more likely to judge a neutral stimulus as anxiety-related (Mogg & Bradley, 2005). Similarly, when feeling down, people are more likely to see the world through "depressed" lenses, to have a negative or pessimistic slant in general—not only will they find it easier to remember past periods of sadness, but they will also tend to view the future as hopeless; they will see more reasons to be sad than will people who aren't down (Lewis & Critchley, 2003).

In addition, the causality also works in the other direction: Mental processes can affect emotions. For example, emotions are affected by attributions. That is, we all regularly try to understand why events in our lives occur, and thus make *attributions*, assigning causes for particular occurrences. A person's mood can be affected by the attributions he or she makes. For instance, college students who tend to attribute negative events to general, enduring negative qualities about themselves ("I am stupid") are more likely to become depressed after a negative event (such as getting a bad grade) (Metalsky et al., 1993).

One particular type of attribution can actually protect against depression: The *self-serving attributional bias* occurs when people typically attribute positive events—but not negative events—to their own personality traits. For example, suppose you receive a pay raise or a good grade. If you are prone to the self-serving bias, you will attribute this positive event to some enduring quality that you believe you possess: intelligence, perseverance, ability, or some similarly positive trait. This bias serves to increase or preserve a positive view of yourself. People who are depressed rarely display the self-serving attributional bias, which is con-

Figure 2.9

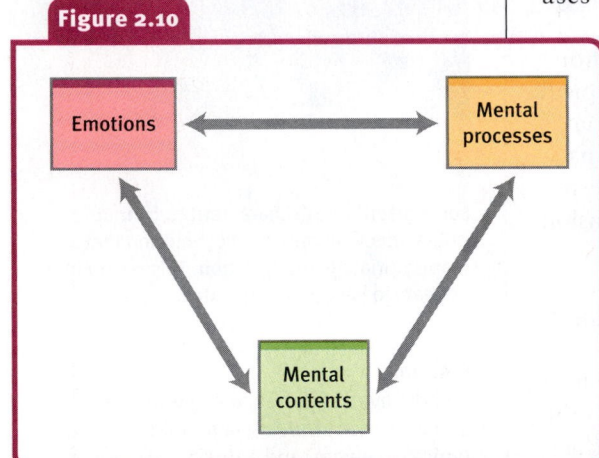

Emotions ⟷ Behavior

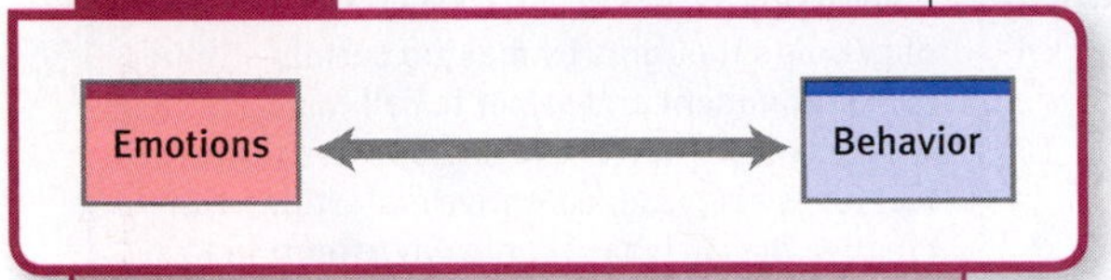

2.9 ▶ Emotions and Behavior An emotion often leads a person to behave in a particular way that matches the emotional state. By the same token, behavior that is not consistent with an emotional state can lead to a change in the emotion, bringing it more into line with the behavior.

Figure 2.10

Emotions ⟷ Mental processes

Mental contents

2.10 ▶ Emotions, Mental Processes, and Mental Contents Emotions can influence what people pay attention to, perceive, and remember, and they can color the contents of people's thoughts. The influence also operates in the other directions: Mental processes and mental contents can alter people's emotions.

Mood
A persistent emotion that is not attached to a stimulus; it exists in the background and influences mental processes, mental contents, and behavior.

sistent with their negative view of themselves, their past, and their future (Mezulis et al., 2004). This bias, although present in all cultures, is less evident among members of Asian cultures than among members of Western cultures (Mezulis et al., 2004), perhaps because members of Asian cultures often tend to attribute positive events to the efforts of groups of people, not a single individual.

And, of course, emotion can affect the sorts of attributions we make. For instance, Walter Scott and colleagues (2003) found that, among depressed individuals, those who were irritable and hostile were more likely to blame their negative life events on others, whereas those who were predominantly sad were more likely to blame themselves for such negative events.

Emotions, Moods, and Psychological Disorders

Many psychological disorders are marked by impaired or inappropriate emotions, emotional experiences, or emotional expression. For example, excesses of mood, as occur in depression (prolonged and profound sadness) and mania (prolonged and inappropriate elation or euphoria), are part of mood disorders. And schizophrenia can involve flat affect—deficits in emotion expression. Furthermore, some *dissociative disorders*, which involve a separation of normally integrated mental processes, include the absence of the normal emotional experiences (Hunter et al., 2003).

Some psychological disorders, such as those that involve high levels of fear or anxiety, often are accompanied by emotions or moods that don't fit the context in which they arise (Davidson, Jackson, & Klein, 2000). We are all likely to feel anxious and afraid if faced with a car that seems to be out of control and barreling toward us, but most of us will not experience that same level of anxiety or fear when simply driving across a bridge, giving a presentation, seeing a spider, or getting a tetanus shot. As we shall see in Chapter 7, some people do experience such misplaced emotions.

In addition, psychological disorders may arise from or produce difficulty in *regulating* emotions—such as an inability to dampen down anxiety when its intensity is inappropriate. Difficulty in regulating emotions and related thoughts and behaviors can lead to three types of problems (Cicchetti & Toth, 1991; Weisz et al., 1997): (1) *Externalizing problems* are characterized by too little control of emotion and related behaviors, such as aggression, and by disruptive behavior. They are called externalizing problems because their primary effects are on others and/or their environment; these problems are usually observable to others. (2) *Internalizing problems* are characterized by negative internal experiences, such as anxiety, social withdrawal, and depression. Internalizing problems are so named because their primary effect is on the troubled individual rather than on others; such problems are generally less observable to others. (3) *Other problems* include emotional or behavioral problems that do not fit into these categories. This "other" category includes eating disorders and learning disorders (Achenbach et al., 1987; Kazdin & Weisz, 1998).

Significant difficulty in regulating emotions can begin in childhood and last through adulthood, forming the basis for some disorders. For example, *personality disorders* are inflexible and maladaptive stable personality traits that lead to distress or dysfunction (Gratz et al., 2006). As we discuss in Chapter 13, several personality disorders are characterized by difficulties in emotional regulation, marked by impulsive behavior or rapid changes in emotion. Problems in regulating emotion can also occur in some forms of eating disorders and substance-related disorders (Sim & Zeman, 2005; Thorberg & Lyvers, 2006).

Brain Bases of Emotion

Emotion is a psychological response, but it is also a neurological response. We can learn much about the psychological aspects of emotion by considering how it arises from brain function. For example, research by Richard Davidson and colleagues,

Fear involves a reflexive activation of the amygdala, not necessarily accompanied by any cognitive interpretation of the stimulus. Other emotions, such as guilt, depend on such interpretation. The ease of treating an emotional problem may be related to the nature of the underlying mechanism that gives rise to the experience of that emotion.

Temperament
The various aspects of personality that reflect a person's typical emotional state and emotional reactivity (including the speed and strength of reactions to stimuli).

conducted largely by measuring the brain's electrical activity, has demonstrated that there are two general types of human emotions, approach emotions and withdrawal emotions, each relying on its own system in the brain. *Approach emotions* are positive emotions, such as love and happiness, and tend to activate the left frontal lobe more than the right. *Withdrawal emotions* are negative emotions, such as fear and sadness, and tend to activate the right frontal lobe more than the left (Davidson, 1992a, 1992b, 1993, 1998, 2002; Davidson et al., 2000; Lang, 1995). Researchers have also found that people who generally have more activation in the left frontal lobe tend to be more optimistic than people who generally have more activation in the right. This is important because depression has been associated with relatively less activity in the left frontal lobe (Davidson, 1993, 1994a, 1998; Davidson et al., 1999). As a result of genetics, learning, or (most likely) some combination of the two, some people are temperamentally more likely to experience positive (approach) emotions, whereas others are more likely to experience negative (withdrawal) emotions (Fox et al., 2005; Rettew & McKee, 2005).

Joseph LeDoux (1996) has further suggested that different brain systems contribute to different emotions. This is important for psychopathology and its treatment because some of these systems lie outside of awareness and are not easy to control voluntarily. In contrast, other brain systems rely on conscious interpretation of stimuli or events, and hence might be more easily targeted during psychotherapy. In particular, LeDoux argues that some of the brain systems that underlie emotions work like reflexes, *independent* of conscious thought or interpretation. For example, fear involves activation of the amygdala, but not necessarily any cognitive interpretation of the stimulus (you become afraid before you've thought through the situation). Other emotions, such as guilt, *depend* on such cognitive processes. Why the difference? In our evolutionary past, fear may have been particularly important to survival, signaling the presence of an immediate danger—and hence it was advantageous to have a very rapidly acting brain system for identifying to-be-feared objects. Guilt is different; not only may the consequences often be less severe that those of fear-inducing events, but also the consequences of guilt-inducing events may not be as immediate as the threats that evoke fear—you can take your time responding to what made you feel guilty, wallowing in your guilt at your leisure.

Temperament

Temperament is closely related to emotion: **Temperament** refers to the various aspects of personality that reflect a person's typical emotional state and emotional reactivity (including the speed and strength of reactions to stimuli). Temperament is in large part innate, and it influences behavior in early childhood and even in infancy. Temperament is of interest in the study of psychological disorders for two reasons (Nigg, 2006): First, it may be part of the neurological vulnerability for certain disorders; having a particular temperament may make a person especially vulnerable to certain psychological disorders, even at an early age. For instance, people who are temperamentally more emotionally reactive are more likely to develop psychological disorders related to high levels of anxiety. Second, it is possible that in some cases a psychological disorder is simply an extreme form of a normal variation in temperament. For instance, some researchers argue that social phobia is on a continuum with shyness but is an extreme form of it; shyness involves withdrawal emotions and lack of sociability, and is viewed as a temperament (Schneider et al., 2002).

The Beale women had unusually reactive temperaments—reacting strongly to stimuli. One or the other of them would respond to a neutral or offhand remark with emotion that was out of proportion: hot anger, bubbling joy, or snapping irritability. It's not a coincidence that mother and daughter seemed similar in this respect. Much evidence indicates that genes contribute strongly to temperament (Gillespie et al., 2003); in fact, some researchers report that genes account for about half of the variability in temperament (Oniszcenko et al., 2003). Researchers have associated some aspects of temperament to specific genes, such as genes that affect receptors for the neurotransmitter dopamine and a gene involved in serotonin production, and have shown that these genes can influence depression and problems controlling impulses (Nomura et al., 2006; Propper & Moore, 2006). Genes that affect dopamine receptors have also been shown to influence emotional reactivity (Oniszczenko & Dragan, 2005). However, these genes have stronger effects on children raised in harsh family environments, and, as we stressed earlier, the effects of genes need to be considered within the context of specific environments (Roisman & Fraley, 2006; Saudino, 2005).

Researchers and scholars going back at least as far as Plato in ancient Greece have proposed many ways to conceive of variations in temperament (Buss, 1995; J. A. Gray, 1991; Eysenck, 1990). C. Robert Cloninger and his colleagues have proposed one particularly influential contemporary theory of temperament, which describes temperament in terms of four dimensions—novelty seeking, harm avoidance, reward dependence, and persistence—each of which is associated with a brain system that relies predominantly on a particular neurotransmitter (Cloninger, 1987; Cloninger, Svrakic, & Przybeck, 1993).

Novelty seeking consists of searching out novel stimuli and reacting to them positively; this dimension of temperament also involves being impulsive, avoiding frustration, and losing one's temper easily. Novelty seeking is thought to be associated with the actions of dopamine (which is known to play a central role in the effects of reward on behavior). A high level of novelty seeking is associated with a variety of disorders that involve impulsive or aggressive behaviors (Yoo et al., 2006).

Harm avoidance consists of reacting very negatively to harm and, whenever possible, avoiding it. This dimension of temperament may be associated with the actions of serotonin (which, as noted earlier, is involved in mood and motivation). For instance, people with anxiety disorders tend to have higher levels of harm avoidance than do people without anxiety disorders (Ball, Smolin, & Shekhar, 2002; Rettew et al., 2006; Wiborg et al., 2005).

Reward dependence involves the degree to which behaviors that have led to desired outcomes in the past are repeated; for example, a person may continually seek out social approval because he or she has received approval in the past. This dimension of temperament is associated with the actions of norepinephrine (which plays a role in attention and the stress response). A low level of reward dependence, in combination with a high level of impulsivity, is found in people who have substance use disorders (Tcheremissine et al., 2003).

The fourth dimension of temperament is *persistence*, which consists of making continued efforts in the face of frustration when attempting to accomplish something. Originally, this dimension was viewed as an aspect of reward dependence (and hence affected by norepinephrine), but subsequent research has suggested that certain genes that lead to low levels of dopamine may be associated with it (Czermak et al., 2004). A low level of persistence is found in attention-deficit/hyperactivity disorder (Yoo et al., 2006).

In fact, researchers have found associations between specific genes and these dimensions of temperament (Gillespie et al., 2003; Keltikangas-Järvinen et al., 2006; Rybakowski et al., 2006). The specific results suggest that complex inheritance, not Mendelian inheritance, is at work. Temperament apparently arises from the joint activity of many different factors. However, not surprisingly, the underlying neurological bases for the four dimensions of temperament are more complex than originally conceived. For example, researchers have linked novelty and reward dependence with certain genes and with levels in the blood of a specific variant of *monoamine oxidase (MAO)*, an enzyme (Shiraishi et al., 2006); people who have low levels of MAO tend to seek out sensations by engaging in high-stimulation activities, such as sky diving (Zuckerman, 1994).

Skip Nall/Getty Images

Because of temperament, some people will avoid situations that have a risk of harm. Such people are more likely to have high levels of anxiety and to develop anxiety disorders.

Key Concepts and Facts About Psychological Factors in Psychological Disorders

- Three types of learning can contribute to psychological disorders:

  - Classical conditioning of emotional responses such as fear and anxiety. Conditioned emotional responses can generalize from the original conditioned stimulus to other, similar stimuli.

  - Operant conditioning of voluntary behaviors through positive and negative reinforcement and punishment. Certain types of depression in humans can be thought of as similar to learned helplessness in animals.

  - Observational learning, which can guide the observer's behaviors and expectations, leading to maladaptive behaviors.

- Mental processes and mental contents play important roles in the etiology and maintenance of psychological disorders.

  - Mental processes influence what people pay attention to, how they perceive and interpret various situations and events, and what they remember.

  - Mental contents can be associated with various psychological disorders in the form of irrational thoughts that are cognitive distortions of reality, creating cognitive vulnerabilities. Once someone has a psychological disorder, these biases and distortions can become self-perpetuating.

- Emotional disturbances contribute to some psychological disorders. Such disturbances include:

  - not feeling or expressing emotions to a normal degree;

  - expressing emotions that are inappropriate or inappropriately excessive for the situation; and

  - having difficulty regulating emotions.

- Emotions, behaviors, mental contents, and mental processes are often intertwined, and so disturbances in one will affect the others. For instance, emotional and mood disturbances can lead to biases in mental processes, and mental processes can affect emotions. Moreover, a person's attributions and mood can affect each other.

- Emotions involve both a psychological and a neurological response to a stimulus. Researchers distinguish between two basic types of emotions—approach (positive) and withdrawal (negative)—each of which relies on different brain systems. Some people are temperamentally more likely to experience approach emotions, whereas others are more likely to experience withdrawal emotions.

- Having a particular temperament may make a person especially vulnerable to certain psychological disorders, even at an early age. In some cases, a psychological disorder may be an extreme form of a normal variation in temperament. Evidence indicates that genes contribute strongly to temperament; however, the effects of genes need to be considered within the context of specific environments.

- Temperament is conceived of as having four dimensions: novelty seeking, harm avoidance, reward dependence, and persistence. Cloninger proposed that each of these dimensions is associated with the action of a particular neurotransmitter and is influenced by complex inheritance and other factors.

Social Factors in Psychological Disorders

We exist in a world filled with social forces: our relationships with family, friends, colleagues, and neighbors; the messages we receive through the media; the norms of our culture. These social forces help to shape who we become; they can help to protect us from developing psychological disorders, or they can make us more vulnerable to or exacerbate psychological disorders. Social forces begin to exert their influence before adulthood, and they can affect each generation differently, as a culture changes over time: For instance, the more recently an American is born, the more likely he or she is to develop a psychological disorder (Kessler et al., 2005), perhaps because of social trends such as the increased divorce rate, an increased sense of danger, and a diminished sense of local community (Twenge, 2000).

Consider Big Edie and Little Edie. The social factors that influenced them include their relationships with other members of their family, their financial circumstances, the prevailing community and cultural standards of appropriate behavior for women—and the discrimination they encountered. Let's examine each type of social factor—family, community, and culture—as well as the stress they can create, in more detail.

Family Matters

Certain aspects of family life form the basis for the type of attachment a child has to the primary caregiver, which influences how a child comes to view himself or herself and learns what to expect from other people. Other family-related social factors include the style of interaction among family members, child maltreatment, and parental psychological disorders. All of these factors can contribute to the emergence or persistence of psychological disorders.

Family Interaction Style and Relapse

If family members exhibit hostility, voice unnecessary criticism, or are emotionally overinvolved, then the family environment is characterized by **high expressed emotion**. Based on what we know of the Beale women, their family environment would likely be classified as high expressed emotion. Consider these typical comments by Big Edie to her daughter: "Well, you made a rotten breakfast," followed moments later by, "Everything is perfectly disgusting on account of you" (Maysles & Maysles, 1976). Big Edie and Little Edie were also clearly overinvolved with each other: They spent virtually all their waking hours together, participated in all aspects of each others' lives, and responded to each other in exaggerated ways.

British researchers found that among people with schizophrenia, those whose families showed high expressed emotion were more likely to have the disorder recur; the same association between high expressed emotion and relapse has been found in other studies in the United States and China (Butzlaff & Hooley, 1998; Yang et al., 2004). This may be because high expressed emotion is associated with family members' belief that the patient has the ability to control his or her symptomatic behaviors, which sometimes leads the family members to push the patient to change (Miura et al., 2004). Unfortunately, these exhortations may well backfire—instead of encouraging the patient to change, they may produce the sort of stress that makes the disorder worse! When family members are educated about the patient's disorder and taught more productive ways of communicating with the patient, relapse rates generally decline (Miklowitz, 2004).

High expressed emotion is not associated with relapse in all cultural or ethnic groups; members of different groups interpret such emotional expression differently. Among Mexican American families, for instance, the family member with schizophrenia is more likely to have a recurrence if the family style is the less common one of being distant and aloof; high expressed emotion is not related to recurrence (Lopez et al., 1998). And among African American families, high expressed emotion is actually associated with a better outcome (Rosenfarb, Bellack, & Aziz, 2006). One possible explanation is that in African American families, confrontations are interpreted as signs of honesty (Rogan & Hammer, 1998) and may signal love and caring.

Child Maltreatment

Child maltreatment comes in various forms—neglect, verbal abuse, physical abuse, and sexual abuse—and is associated with a higher risk for a variety of psychological disorders (Cicchetti & Toth, 2005), including personality disorders (Battle et al., 2004; Bierer et al., 2003). Child maltreatment exerts its influence indirectly, through the following:

- *An altered bodily and neurological response to stress.* For instance, children who have been maltreated have higher baseline levels of cortisol than do children who have not been maltreated. Such alteration of the stress response in those who have been maltreated continues into adulthood (Tarullo & Gunnar, 2006; Watts-English et al., 2006).

- *Behaviors that are learned as a consequence of the maltreatment.* For instance, maltreatment may result in a type of learned helplessness, so the children are more likely to be victimized as adults (Renner & Slack, 2006).

High expressed emotion
A family interaction style characterized by hostility, unnecessary criticism, or emotional overinvolvement.

Although high expressed emotion is associated with relapse in a European-American family member with schizophrenia, this is not true among Mexican Americans; the likelihood of relapse of a patient with schizophrenia in a Mexican American family is higher when family members are emotionally distant. The family shown here does not appear to be emotionally distant.

- *Biases in discriminating and responding to facial expressions.* For instance, children who have been physically abused are more likely to perceive photographs of faces as conveying anger than are children who have not been physically abused (Pollak et al., 2000).

- *Difficulties in attachment.* Children who have been maltreated are less likely to develop a secure type of attachment than are children who have not been maltreated (Baer & Martinez, 2006).

- *Increased social isolation.* For instance, children who have been physically abused report feeling more socially isolated than children who have not been physically abused (Elliot et al., 2005).

However, not everyone who experienced maltreatment as a child develops a psychological disorder (Haskett et al., 2006; Katerndahl, Burge, & Kellogg, 2005).

Parental Psychological Disorders

Another family-related factor that may contribute to psychological disorders is the presence of a psychological disorder in one or both parents (Pilowsky et al., 2006). It is difficult to pinpoint the specific mechanism responsible for this association, however, because it could be due to any number—or combination—of factors. For instance, a parent may transmit a genetic vulnerability for a psychological disorder to a child. Alternatively, the specific patterns of interaction between an affected parent and a child may lead to particular vulnerabilities in learning, mental processes, cognitive distortions, emotional regulation, or social interactions—any or all of which can increase the risk of a psychological disorder as the child grows older (Finzi-Dottan & Karu, 2006).

What is clear is that the association between a parent's having a psychological disorder and the increased risk of the child's later developing a psychological disorder isn't due solely to genetic vulnerability. One study found that when depressed mothers received treatment, their symptoms improved and so did their children's symptoms of anxiety, depression, and disruptive behaviors. Prior to their mother's successful treatment, a third of the children had symptoms severe enough to be classified as psychological disorders. The more positively a mother responded to her treatment, the less likely her children were to continue to have symptoms (Weissman et al., 2006).

Community Support

Social support—the comfort and assistance that an individual receives through interactions with others—can buffer the stressful events that occur throughout life (Silver & Teasdale, 2005). Conversely, a lack of social support can make people more vulnerable to various psychological disorders (Scarpa, Haden, & Hurley, 2006). College students who experience high levels of stress, for instance, are less likely to be depressed if they have relatively high levels of social support (Pengilly & Dowd, 2000). Here's another example of the buffering effects of social support: When people are exposed to trauma during military service, they are less likely to develop posttraumatic stress disorder—anxiety and other symptoms that arise as a result of experiencing a trauma—if they have strong social support when they return home (Dikel, Engdahl, & Eberly, 2005; King et al., 1998).

The Beale women did not have much social support in their extended family or community, but they had each other, which clearly played a role in limiting whatever distress they may have felt about their lifestyle and circumstances. Little Edie noted, "My mother really was the most extraordinary member of the family. She was always singing. . . . I was happy to be alone with mother because we created the sort of life we liked, and it was very private and beautiful" (Wright, 2006, p. 17). On another occasion, Little Edie said of their singing, "That's really the only thing that we live for really. That we love and enjoy"

Social support can lessen the detrimental after-effects of a stressful event such as an untimely death. People who do not have such support have a higher risk of developing a psychological disorder.

Mike Theiler/Getty Images

Social support
The comfort and assistance that an individual receives through interactions with others.

(Graham, 1976). Had the Beale women not supported each other and shared good times, the symptoms of psychological disorders that they displayed might have been worse.

Social Stressors

Living in poverty is associated with a higher rate of psychological disorders. Another social factor associated with psychological disorders is discrimination. Let's examine these two factors—financial hardship and discrimination—in more detail.

Socioeconomic Status

Socioeconomic groups are defined in terms of education, income, and occupational level; these indicators are sometimes referred to collectively as *socioeconomic status (SES)*. People from low SES backgrounds have a higher rate of psychological disorders than people from higher SES backgrounds (Costello et al., 1996, 2003; Kessler et al., 1995; Mittendorfer-Rutz et al., 2004; Robins & Regier, 1991). Socioeconomic factors may contribute to the development of psychological disorders in several ways. One theorized mechanism is through **social causation**: socioeconomic disadvantages and stress *cause* psychological disorders (Freeman, 1994). Specifically, the daily stressors of urban life, especially as experienced by people in a lower socioeconomic level, trigger mental illness in those who are vulnerable. For instance, living with inadequate housing, very limited financial means, and few job opportunities corresponds to the stress component of the diathesis–stress model discussed in Chapter 1 (Costello et al., 2003). Case 2.1 describes Anna, whose depression was precipitated by financial stressors.

CASE 2.1 ▸ FROM THE OUTSIDE: Depression and Social Selection

Anna was a single mother in her 30s when she sought treatment for her depression. At the time, she was having difficulty getting out of bed and was struggling to maintain order and basic routines at home for herself and her children. She had separated from her husband and lost her job 5 years prior to her first visit to the clinic. Since that time she had been struggling financially. She had a number of part-time jobs to try to make enough money to keep her family fed and clothed. However, she was often short of funds and felt very worried and stressed by their straitened [sic] financial situation. She noted she often felt worse after the summer as she became overwhelmed by the demands of a new school year and the thought of Christmas. As a result of encountering difficulty finding a permanent full-time position, her confidence waned, and she feared that she had lost her job skills. She had recently returned to school to take some business courses to update and extend her qualifications. . . .

Anna expressed regrets about her divorce. She had not realized at the time what a massive and difficult journey it would prove to be. She regretted uprooting her children and found her worries about money very stressful and disconcerting because she had never had to worry about finances before. Anna was a committed and dedicated mother who, even as she struggled to feed her children, put on a happy face to hide her stress because she did not want to worry them.

(Watson, Goldman, & Greenberg, 2007, pp. 83–84)

Another mechanism that may be responsible for the connection between psychological disorders and low SES is **social selection**: The hypothesis that those who are mentally ill "drift" to a lower socioeconomic level because of their impairments (Mulvany et al., 2001; Wender et al., 1973); social selection is sometimes referred to as *social drift*. In fact, research suggests that the relationship between psychological disorders and SES cuts both ways: low SES both contributes to disorders and is a consequence of having a disorder (Conger & Donnellan, 2007; Fan & Eaton, 2001; Johnson et al., 1999; Shaw et al., 1998).

Social causation
The hypothesis that the daily stressors of urban life, especially as experienced by people in a lower socioeconomic level, trigger mental illness in those who are vulnerable.

Social selection
The hypothesis that those who are mentally ill "drift" to a lower socioeconomic level because of their impairments; also referred to as *social drift*.

A study by Jane Costello and colleagues (2003) tested the influence of social selection and social causation on psychopathology in children. These researchers tracked over 300 Native American children between the ages of 9 and 13 for 8 years; the children were seen annually. At the start of the study, over half of the children were living in poverty. Halfway through the study, a casino opened on the reservation, raising the income of all the Native American families and pulling a quarter of them above the poverty line. Before the casino opened, children whose families were below the poverty line had more psychiatric symptoms than children whose families were above it. After the casino opened, the number of psychiatric symptoms among children who were no longer living in poverty was the same as among those who had never lived in poverty. Once the socioeconomic disadvantages and accompanying family stress were removed, children functioned better and their symptoms improved, an outcome that supports the role of social causation in this setting (Rutter, 2003).

Discrimination

Being the object of discrimination is associated with an increased risk of distress and psychological disorders (Bhui et al., 2005; Chakraborty & McKenzie, 2002; Kessler, Mickelson, & Williams, 1999; Mays & Cochran, 2001; Simons et al., 2002; United States Public Health Service, 2001). Women, for example, may experience sexual harassment and assault, limitations on their freedom (such as a prohibition against working outside the home), or glass ceilings (unstated limits on social or occupational possibilities). Such experiences may lead to increased stress and vulnerability to psychological disorders. For instance, sexual harassment of women in the workplace is associated with subsequent increased alcohol use by those women (Freels et al., 2005; Rospenda, 2002). Similarly, members of ethnic, racial, or sexual minority groups may experience harassment at—or discrimination in—school, housing, or jobs, which can create a sense of powerlessness and lead to chronically higher levels of stress (Bhugra & Ayonrinde, 2001; Burke, 1984; Mills et al., 2004; Williams & Williams-Morris, 2000), which in turn increases the risk for developing psychological disorders.

Despite the increased risk for disorders that is associated with discrimination, American Blacks and Hispanics are no more likely to experience psychological disorders than are Whites (Kessler et al., 1994; Breslau et al., 2005, 2006). How can we understand this paradoxical finding? People from nonmajority ethnic groups may also experience more protective factors—factors that buffer the effects of discrimination (Breslau et al., 2006; Lee & Newberg, 2005). Protective factors include social support, a sense of ethnic identity, spirituality, and religious participation. When non-Whites do have a disorder, however, their symptoms are more persistent than are those of Whites with the same disorder (Bresalu et al., 2005). Moreover, non-Whites are less likely to receive treatment for their psychological disorders (United States Public Health Service, 2001).

Bullying

Whereas discrimination involves untoward behavior toward someone because of his or her status as a member of a particular group (based on ethnicity, race, religion, sexual orientation, or another characteristic), *bullying* involves untoward behavior that may be unrelated to the victim's membership in an ethnic, racial, or other

The stigma and discrimination encountered by some gays and lesbians can make them—and others experiencing discrimination—more vulnerable to psychological disorders (Herek & Garnets, 2007; Mays & Cochran, 2001).

Max Whittaker/Getty Images

group. Research indicates that being a victim of childhood bullying can contribute to psychological problems in childhood and adulthood (Arseneault et al., 2008; Fosse & Holen, 2004; Kumpulainen et al., 1998), and it is particularly likely to lead to internalizing problems. (Bullying itself is one type of externalizing problem; Kaltiala-Heino et al., 2000; Kumpulainen et al., 1998.)

War

War often inflicts extreme and prolonged stress on soldiers and civilian victims. How an individual responds to the effects of war is determined by a variety of factors (discussed at length in Chapter 7), such as proximity to the fighting and the duration of combat. Since the mandated extended tours of duty for American soldiers in Iraq and Afghanistan, approximately 20% of returning troops have symptoms of posttraumatic stress disorder or depression (Tanielian & Jaycox, 2008).

Culture

Every culture promotes an ideal of healthy functioning—of a "normal" personality—and a notion of unhealthy functioning. These ideals differ somewhat from culture to culture and can shift over time (Doerfel-Baasen & Rauh, 2001). Some cultures, such as those of many Asian, Latin American, and Middle Eastern countries, are *collectivist*, placing a high value on getting along with others; in such cultures, the goals of the group (family or community) traditionally take precedence over those of the individual. In contrast, other cultures, such as those of Australia, Canada, the United Kingdom, and the United States, are *individualist*, valuing independence and autonomy; the goals of the individual take precedence over the goals of the group (Hui & Triandis, 1986). In either case, if an individual has personality traits that are different from those valued by the culture, other people's responses to the person may lead him or her to feel humiliated and to develop poor self-esteem, which increases the risk of developing psychological disorders.

Collectivist cultures tend to emphasize getting along with others and rank the community's well-being over the individual's; these values are reversed in individualist cultures. Individuals whose personalities differ from their culture's ideal may face humiliation and even discrimination and may come to see themselves in a negative light—all of which can make them more vulnerable to psychological disorders.

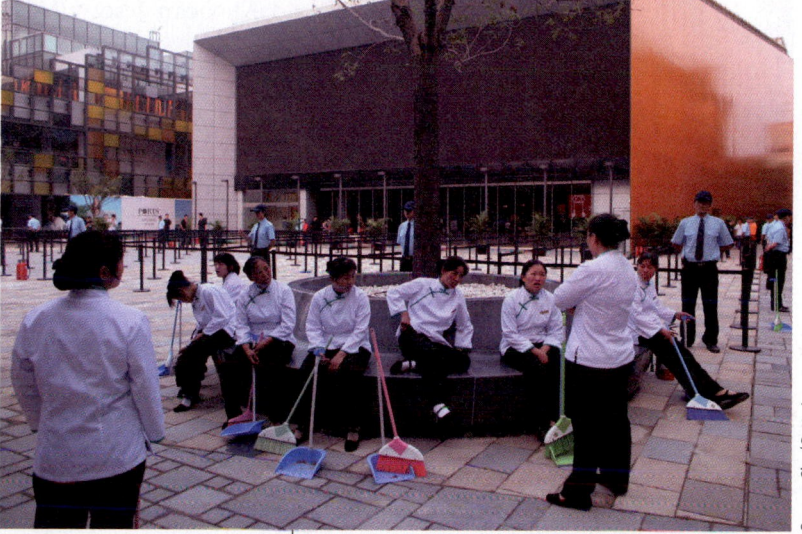

Cancan Chu/Getty Images

Culture Can Suppress or Facilitate Behaviors

The *problem suppression-facilitation model* (Weisz et al., 1987) addresses how culture can influence mental health and mental illness. According to the model, cultural factors—such as values, social norms, and accepted child-rearing practices—can affect a child's behavior by minimizing or amplifying the child's natural behavioral tendencies. Consider a child who has a tendency to be very energetic and active. Cultures such as that of China, which value the ability to sit still for long periods of time, seek to minimize such a behavioral tendency. Hong Kong schools require children to sit and focus on schoolwork for long periods of time, and the children are not allowed to leave their seats. From an early age, then, energetic and active children must learn how to control their behavioral tendencies. This contrasts with American culture, where the school day is organized to allow children in primary grades to move around the classroom frequently (Sandberg, 2002).

Acculturation

Moving from one culture to another often leads people to adopt the values and behaviors of the new culture, a process that is termed *acculturation*. This can be very stressful and can create tension between parents—who moved to the new culture as adults—and their children, whose formative years were spent in the new culture. As these children grow up, they may be forced to choose between the values and views of their parents' culture and those of the new culture, which can be stressful and can make them more likely to develop psychological disorders (Escobar, Nervi, & Gara,

2000). However, the degree to which acculturation is stressful and increases the risk for psychological disorders depends on other factors, such as the degree of difference in values between the native and new cultures, the reasons for leaving the native country (traumatic causes for leaving such as war and famine can have strong effects), the change in SES status that results from immigration, and the degree of discrimination encountered in the new culture. In the absence of these other factors, moving to a new culture is not necessarily associated with later psychological disorders (Kohn, 2002).

Paradoxically, individuals who have immigrated to the United States tend to have lower rates of psychological disorders than their American-born counterparts of similar age (Alegría et al., 2008; Nguyen, 2006). One possible explanation for this counterintuitive finding is that people who voluntarily leave their native countries to live elsewhere may be particularly psychologically hardy and better able to weather the stresses of immigration. Moreover, not all groups of immigrants are equally psychologically robust: Puerto Rican immigrants are afflicted with psychological disorders at the same rates as their American-born counterparts whose families immigrated earlier from Puerto Rico. Immigrants from Mexico, in contrast, are less likely to suffer from psychological disorders than are American-born people of Mexican descent (Alegría et al., 2008).

Key Concepts and Facts About Social Factors in Psychological Disorders ■

- Social factors can help to protect us from developing psychological disorders, or they can make us more vulnerable to or exacerbate psychological disorders. Such factors begin to exert their influence before adulthood and can affect each generation differently, as a culture changes over time.

- A family's style of interacting that involves high expressed emotion can contribute to relapse in patients with schizophrenia from particular ethnic or cultural groups.

- Being maltreated as a child indirectly contributes to the development of psychological disorders by:
  - increasing stress,
  - teaching maladaptive behaviors,
  - promoting biases in discriminating among and responding to facial expressions,
  - creating difficulties in attachment, and
  - increasing social isolation.

- Psychological disorders in parents can contribute to psychological disorders in their children, although it is difficult to pinpoint the specific mechanism through which this influence occurs.

- Social support can buffer against stress, and a lack of social support can make people more vulnerable to psychological disorders.

- Low SES is associated with a higher rate of psychological disorders; both social causation and social selection contribute to this relationship.

- Being the object of discrimination is associated with an increased risk of distress and psychological disorders.

- Different personality traits and behaviors are valued in different cultures; thus, acculturation can lead to conflict among family members, creating stress and a risk of psychological disorders.

Feedback Loops in Action: Learned Helplessness

We have stressed that neurological, psychological, and social factors do not occur in isolation, but rather affect each other. Let's examine the phenomenon of *learned helplessness* in more detail to understand the feedback loops between the three sorts of factors (Zhukov & Vinogradova, 1998). Consider that when rats receive uncontrollable shock (as compared to controllable shock), neurological events in the brain change (Amat et al., 2001); for example, serotonin levels decrease (Amat et al., 1998; Edwards et al., 1992; Petty, Kramer, & Wilson, 1992), and the density of receptors for the neurotransmitter GABA increases in particular brain regions (Kram et al., 2000). Furthermore, rats can be bred to be more inclined or more resistant to developing learned helplessness, which suggests that genetic factors may contribute to whether a rat is vulnerable to this outcome (Kohen et al., 2003).

Moreover, studies of rats have also demonstrated the influence of social factors. For example, in one study, rats received inescapable shocks either alone or in pairs. The pairs of rats fought when shocked. But these rats, when tested individually 2 days later, were less likely to show learned helplessness than the rats that were originally shocked alone (Zhukov & Vinogradova, 1998). Perhaps the fighting helped to distract the paired rats from the shocks, or perhaps the neural events that provoked the rats to fight also protected them from subsequent learned helplessness.

What does this have to do with humans? Consider the fact that social factors can create an aversive situation from which an individual cannot escape, such as abuse (physical, sexual, or emotional), social discrimination, or poverty (for Anna, in Case 2.1). Characteristics of the environment, such as uncontrollable noise and crowding, are associated with a learned helplessness response (Evans & Stecker, 2004). These events lead to changes in psychological factors, such as the individual's beliefs ("I can't escape, so I might as well give up"), goals ("No matter what I do it doesn't help, so I must simply endure it"), and behavior (staying put). In turn, these events lead to neurological changes, such as a reduced serotonin level in the brain, which is associated with depression. And we've already seen how learned helplessness may contribute to some cases of depression.

Let's conclude this chapter by briefly examining how neurological, psychological, and social factors might have affected each other via feedback loops in the case of Big Edie and Little Edie. Both women were artistic, unconventional, and independent (psychological factor), but their social class and the time in which they lived made their behavior "inappropriate," leading them to be discriminated against within their extended family and community (social factor). In turn, the social constraints of their day prevented them from having jobs or careers, and so they were unable to support themselves; they were financially dependent on others (social), which created its own stress (neurological and psychological). These external realities, in turn, may have heightened their feeling that people were out to get them (psychological factor). Moreover, it is possible that they had neurological characteristics—such as emotional reactivity—that predisposed them to behave in certain ways, which in turn evoked certain responses from others.

We will draw on the neuropsychosocial approach—considering all three types of factors *and their feedback loops*—to understand the various psychological disorders discussed in this book. Neurological factors (genetics, brain structure and function, and bodily responses), psychological factors (learning and behavior, mental processes and mental contents, and emotions), social factors (social stressors, relationships, family, culture, and socioeconomic status), and the interactions among these factors all play a role in explaining psychological disorders.

SUMMING UP

Summary of Neurological Factors

The nervous system has two major parts: the central nervous system (CNS), which is composed of the brain and spinal cord, and the peripheral nervous system (PNS), which is composed of the sensory-somatic nervous system and the autonomic nervous system (ANS). The ANS controls many involuntary functions, such as those of the heart, blood vessels, and digestive tract. The ANS has two major components: (1) The sympathetic nervous system produces more adaptive bodily functioning in an emergency with the fight-or-flight response. As part of this response, the hypothalamic-pituitary-adrenal axis (HPA axis) manages the production of cortisol, which helps the muscles prepare for physical exertion. The HPA axis and high levels of cortisol are involved in depression and stress-related psychological disorders. (2) The parasympathetic nervous system typically brings the body back to its normal state after a fight-or-flight response.

The brain is divided into two hemispheres, which each have four major lobes: occipital lobe, parietal lobe, temporal lobe, and frontal lobe. Subcortical (beneath the cortex) areas of importance are as follows: (1) the limbic system, which includes the hypothalamus, the amygdala, and the hippocampus; (2) the thalamus; (3) the nucleus accumbens; (4) the basal ganglia; and (5) the cerebellum.

There are three types of neurons: sensory neurons, motor neurons, and interneurons (most neurons are interneurons). Neurons communicate with each other to create patterns of activation—brain circuits—which are organized into large brain systems; these systems may be disrupted in cases of psychopathology. A neuron has a cell body, an axon that ends in terminal buttons, and dendrites that receive signals from other neurons. The neuron is covered by a cell membrane that has channels that open when the neuron fires. When a neuron fires, neurotransmitters released from the terminal button travel across the synaptic cleft to receptors on the dendrite or cell body of another neuron. Neuromodulators may affect the functioning of neurotransmitters by altering events at the synapse.

Neurotransmitter substances include dopamine, serotonin, acetylcholine, adrenaline and noradrenaline, gluatamate, GABA, and endogenous cannabinoids.

Neurotransmitters can bind to different types of receptors; the type of receptor a neurotransmitter binds to determines its effect. Neuronal communication can go awry when (1) neurons have an abnormal number of dendrites or receptors, affecting sensitivity to neurotransmitters in the synapse; (2) sending neurons release abnormal amounts of neurotransmitter into the synapse; (3) reuptake of neurotransmitter molecules does not operate correctly. Hormones, produced by glands in the endocrine system, often function as neuromodulators; an important hormone related to some psychological disorders is cortisol.

Genes can influence the development of psychopathology. Complex inheritance best explains the influence of genes on psychological disorders. Scientists who study behavioral genetics seek to determine the roles of genes, the environment, and their interactions in both normal and abnormal thoughts, feelings, and behaviors. Heritability is an estimate of how much of the variation of a characteristic across a population, *in a specific environment*, is determined by genes.

Behavioral geneticists may use twin and adoption studies to determine the relative influences of genes and environment. Twins may be monozygotic or dizygotic. Genes can affect the environment in three ways: (1) passive interaction, (2) evocative interaction, and (3) active interaction.

Thinking like a clinician

Dominic is adopted, and his biological father was an alcoholic; alcoholism has a genetic component. Dominic's adoptive parents are very religious and don't drink alcohol. What factors in Dominic's environment might affect the expression of any genes that he might have that can contribute to alcoholism? Suppose scientists determine that, among alcoholics, a particular brain area has an abnormally high level of activity of the neurotransmitter dopamine. Further suppose that Dominic has too much activation of dopamine neurons in this area. Does this mean that his brain is wired wrong, and he should just resign himself to eventually becoming an

alcoholic? How might psychological and social factors affect dopamine levels?

Summary of Psychological Factors

Three types of learning can contribute to psychological disorders: (1) Classical conditioning of emotional responses, such as fear and anxiety, produces conditioned emotional responses that can generalize from the original conditioned stimulus to other, similar stimuli. (2) Operant conditioning of voluntary behaviors occurs through positive and negative reinforcement and positive and negative punishment. (3) Observational learning can guide the observer's behavior and expectations, leading to maladaptive behaviors.

Mental processes and mental contents play important roles in the etiology and maintenance of psychological disorders. Mental processes influence what people pay attention to, how they perceive and interpret various situations and events, and what they remember. Mental contents can be associated with various psychological disorders in the form of irrational thoughts that are cognitive distortions of reality, creating cognitive vulnerabilities.

Emotional disturbances such as the following contribute to some psychological disorders: not feeling or expressing emotions to a sufficient degree, expressing emotions that are inappropriate or inappropriately excessive for the situation, and having difficulty regulating emotions. Emotions, behaviors, mental contents, and mental processes are often intertwined, and so disturbances in one will affect the others. Moreover, a person's attributions and mood can affect each other.

Researchers distinguish between two basic types of emotions—approach (positive) and withdrawal (negative)—each of which relies on different brain systems. Some people are temperamentally more likely to experience approach emotions, whereas others are more likely to experience withdrawal emotions.

Having a particular temperament may make a person especially vulnerable to certain psychological disorders, even at an early age. In some cases, a psychological disorder may be an extreme form of a normal variation in temperament. Evidence indicates that genes contribute strongly to temperament; however, the effects of genes need to be considered within the context of specific environments.

Temperament is conceived of as having four dimensions: novelty seeking, harm avoidance, reward dependence, and persistence.

Thinking like a clinician

Maya is depressed; she's often tearful and feels hopeless about the future and helpless

to change the negative things in her life. Give specific examples of the ways that types of learning might have influenced her negative expectations of life and led to her current depression. (It's okay to speculate here, but be specific.) Based on what you have read, how can Maya's thought patterns and emotions lead to her feeling depressed (or make the depression worse)?

Summary of Social Factors

Social factors can help to protect us from developing psychological disorders, or they can make us more vulnerable to or exacerbate psychological disorders. Such factors begin to exert their influence during childhood and can affect each generation differently, as a culture changes over time.

A family's style of interacting that involves high expressed emotion can contribute to relapse in patients with schizophrenia from particular ethnic or cultural groups. Being maltreated as a child indirectly contributes to psychological disorders by increasing stress, teaching maladaptive behaviors, promoting biases in discriminating among and responding to facial expressions, creating difficulties in attachment, and increasing social isolation. Psychological disorders in parents can contribute to psychological disorders in their children, although it is difficult to pinpoint the specific mechanism through which this influence occurs.

Social support can buffer against stress, and a lack of social support can make people more vulnerable to psychological disorders. Low SES is associated with a higher rate of psychological disorders; both social causation and social selection contribute to this relationship. Being the object of discrimination is associated with an increased risk of distress and psychological disorders. Different personality traits and behaviors are valued in different cultures; thus, acculturation can lead to conflict among family members, creating stress and a risk of psychological disorders.

Thinking like a clinician

Gonsalvo and Bill, roommates, are both first-year college students. Gonsalvo has left his family and country and moved to another continent to study in the United States; Bill's family lives a few hours' drive away. What social factors may influence whether either young man develops a psychological disorder during the time at college? Be specific about possible factors that might lead *each man* to be vulnerable. What social factors may protect them from developing a disorder? What additional information would you want to help you answer these questions, and how might such information affect your predictions?

Summary of Feedback Loops in Action

Research has demonstrated that rats that receive uncontrollable shocks undergo different brain changes (neurological factor) than do rats that receive controllable shocks. When a second rat is present during the shocks (social factor), subsequent behavior indicates that learned helplessness is less severe than occurs when rats are shocked alone. Similar mechanisms may contribute to depression in humans, which is associated with behavior that resembles learned helplessness. In humans, social factors such as abuse, discrimination, and poverty can lead to changes in beliefs (psychological factor), as well as changes in the brain (neurological factor) that are associated with depression.

Thinking like a clinician

Always a shy child, Lara vividly remembered the time in high school when it had been her turn to read aloud from a short story she'd written: She began blushing as soon as she got up in front of the class, she stumbled over her words, and the class roared with laughter at a part that wasn't meant to be funny. She felt humiliated and had nightmares about it for weeks. In college she tried to avoid classes that required class presentations.

Using the neuropsychosocial approach, point out the various factors likely to have contributed to Lara's fear of public speaking, and how those factors may have interacted with one another. In order to answer this question fully, what other information might you want to know about Lara's life, and why?

Key Terms

Etiology (p. 33)
Cerebral cortex (p. 36)
Neurons (p. 36)
Brain circuits (p. 38)
Brain systems (p. 38)
Action potential (p. 39)
Synapse (p. 40)
Neurotransmitters (p. 40)
Neuromodulators (p. 40)
Receptors (p. 41)
Reuptake (p. 42)
Hormones (p. 42)
Mendelian inheritance (p. 43)
Genes (p. 43)
Genotype (p. 43)
Phenotype (p. 43)
Complex inheritance (p. 43)
Behavioral genetics (p. 43)
Heritability (p. 44)
Monozygotic twins (p. 45)
Dizygotic twins (p. 45)
Classical conditioning (p. 48)
Unconditioned stimulus (UCS) (p. 49)
Unconditioned response (UCR) (p. 49)
Conditioned stimulus (CS) (p. 49)
Conditioned response (CR) (p. 49)
Conditioned emotional responses (p. 49)

Stimulus generalization (p. 49)
Operant conditioning (p. 50)
Reinforcement (p. 50)
Positive reinforcement (p. 50)
Negative reinforcement (p. 50)
Punishment (p. 50)
Positive punishment (p. 51)
Negative punishment (p. 51)
Learned helplessness (p. 52)
Observational learning (p. 52)
Cognitive distortions (p. 54)
Emotion (p. 55)
Affect (p. 55)
Inappropriate affect (p. 55)
Flat affect (p. 55)
Mood (p. 56)
Temperament (p. 58)
High expressed emotion (p. 61)
Social support (p. 62)
Social causation (p. 63)
Social selection (p. 63)

More Study Aids

For additional study aids related to this chapter, go to:

www.worthpublishers.com/rosenberg

Clinical Diagnosis and Assessment

Jeannette Walls had an unusual childhood. She and her three siblings—Lori, Brian, and Maureen—had smart, engaging parents who taught them each to read by the time they were 3, explained and demonstrated to them scientific principles, instilled a love of reading and appreciation for the arts, and made their children each feel that they were special. As Jeannette Walls recounts in her memoir, *The Glass Castle* (2005), her father, Rex, was an intelligent man who was a skilled electrical engineer. Her mother, Rose Mary, was an artist and had been trained to be a teacher. Yet Rex had difficulty holding onto jobs, and most of the time Rose Mary didn't have a paying job. However, she wasn't as busy raising her children as you might think: Both parents gave their children enormous freedom to explore and experiment; they also often left the children to fend for themselves.

Rex and Rose Mary would uproot and move the family in the middle of the night, sometimes giving the kids 15 minutes to pack their things and pile into the car. They'd leave town in order to avoid bill collectors or child welfare officials, moving to whatever small town caught Rose Mary's and Rex's fancy. Neither parent spent much time fulfilling the many daily responsibilities of parenting, such as preparing meals. For instance, even at the age of 3, if Jeannette was hungry, she knew not to ask her parents for something to eat, but to make it herself. She figured out how to make hot dogs: put water in a pot and boil the dogs, standing on a chair by the gas stove in order to do it. During one stint of hot dog making when she was 3, her dress caught on fire. She was so severely burned that she was hospitalized for 6 weeks and had skin grafts. Her hospital stay ended when her father had a fight with her doctor about whether her bandages should remain on; her father carried Jeannette from her hospital room in the middle of the night and out to the car, where her family was waiting for her. They headed out of town to wherever the road took them; Jeannette's scars never properly healed.

The family referred to this and other late night moves from one dusty town to another as doing "the skedaddle." A few months after taking Jeannette out of the hospital, the family did the skedaddle again. During Jeannette's early childhood, Rex would get a job as an electrician or an engineer (often making up stories about previous jobs he'd had or degrees he'd earned). When they left a town, Rex would explain to the family that they were running from federal investigators, who were chasing him for some unnamed episode in the past; Rose Mary admitted to the children that frequently they were running from bill collectors. Sometimes they moved simply because Rex was bored.

Rex and Rose Mary tried to make their tumbleweed life into an adventure for their children, and they succeeded to some extent when the children were young. However, the parents' own problems got in the way of their responsibilities. When Rex would lose his job, sometimes he'd stay home. He drew up blueprints for a solar-powered "glass castle" or worked on his design for a tool that would find gold in rocks. And increasingly during Jeannette's childhood, he'd gamble and drink (where he found the money for liquor wasn't always clear, but sometimes he took the family's food money or his children's earnings from their part-time jobs). In what Jeannette describes as his "beer phase," Rex would drive fast and sing loudly. When he began to drink the "hard stuff," Rose Mary would get frantic because Rex would become angry: He'd beat his wife, throw furniture around, and yell. Then, he'd collapse.

When Jeannette was in elementary school and high school, her family was so poor that the children ended up eating only one meal a day—the lunch leftovers at school that they were able to scavenge from the trash. Under duress from her children and the threat of visits from child welfare officials, Rose Mary tried two different stints of working as a teacher, but she hated it so much that she had a hard time getting out of bed to get ready for work, and she had difficulty doing the paperwork required by the job. After a year, Rose Mary refused to work anymore; she claimed that she needed to put herself first—to paint, sculpt, and write novels and short stories—even though Rex still was not working and there was no other regular income.

Did Rex and Rose Mary have psychological disorders? To answer that question, we must return to the criteria for a psychological disorder that we discussed in Chapter 1: a pattern of thoughts, feelings, or behavior that lead to distress, impairment in daily life, and risk of harm, in the context of the culture. Did Rose Mary or Rex experience significant distress? Remarkably, Jeannette's account of her family conveys little sense that her parents were distressed by their situation. What about impaired functioning? The fact that neither parent was able to hold a job consistently certainly indicates impairment in daily life.

With regard to risk of harm, Rose Mary and Rex put themselves and their children at risk countless times in various ways: They—and their children—regularly went without food (and neither parent was sufficiently motivated to earn money in order to buy food). Rex repeatedly drove while intoxicated, sometimes at 90 miles an hour or more. The family members' physical safety was put at risk in other ways. Jeannette recalls how her parents insisted that the doors and windows of the house be left open at night for better air circulation, but vagrants would come in. One night when Jeannette was 10 years old, she woke up to find a vagrant sexually groping her. When the children asked their parents to close the doors at night, their parents refused: "They wouldn't consider it. We needed the fresh air, they said, and it was essential that we refuse to surrender to fear" (Walls, 2005, p. 103). The parents put themselves at risk of harm in other ways, including intense fighting. For example, during one fight, Rex and Rose Mary went at each other with knives—and then their fighting suddenly switched off, and the couple ended up laughing and hugging. Rose Mary admitted to her children that she was an "excitement addict," and her quest for excitement and Rex's drinking and related behavior often led the family into dangerous situations.

According to Jeannette's descriptions, then, both Rex and Rose Mary Walls would seem to have had some type of psychopathology. On what basis should you evaluate and classify their behavior? How would a mental health professional go about identifying their psychological problems? How should you go about determining whether a specific diagnosis is warranted? For mental health professionals, a **diagnosis** is the identification of the nature of a disorder (American Psychiatric Association, 2000). A diagnosis is made by assigning a patient's symptoms to a specific classification. Classifying a set of symptoms as a disorder allows you to know more than was initially apparent. By analogy, once you've categorized an object as an "apple," you know that it has seeds inside, can be squeezed to produce juice or cider, and may have a relationship with the absence of doctors. Depending on how much is known about a given disorder, a diagnosis may suggest the disorder's possible causes, its course over time, and its possible treatments. In Rex's case, for example, a diagnosis for his pattern of drinking and related behavior would be what mental health clinicians call *alcohol dependence* (which we discuss in more detail in Chapter 9). Having a diagnosis might indicate why he—and other people with the same set of symptoms—may have developed the disorder and whether the symptoms would be likely to shift in frequency or intensity over time. Moreover, the diagnosis might indicate that certain types of treatment, such as those based on behavioral principles (see Chapter 2), might be more effective than other types of treatment (we will discuss different types of treatment in detail in Chapter 4).

A diagnosis is based on information about the patient obtained through interviews, observations, and tests. Such information is part of a **clinical assessment**—the process of obtaining relevant information and making a judgment about mental illness based on the information. Clinical assessments often go further than providing information needed to make a diagnosis. They also can provide information about the specific ways in which and the degree to which an individual is impaired, as well as about areas of functioning that are not impaired. When we discuss the mental health—or mental illness—of Rex and Rose Mary Walls, we are trying to approximate a clinical assessment based on the words—and judgments—of their daughter, Jeannette—someone who knew them intimately. Rex died at the age of 59. Were he alive today and it were possible to make a clinical assessment of him and Rose Mary, we would be in a position to determine with greater confidence whether either of them could be diagnosed with a psychological disorder.

Diagnosing Psychological Disorders

Rose Mary and Rex Walls created an endurance contest for their growing children. A typical example was when Lori was diagnosed by the school nurse as severely near–sighted and in need of glasses. Rose Mary didn't approve of eyeglasses, commenting, "If you had weak eyes . . . they needed exercise to get strong" (Walls, 2005, p. 96). Rose Mary thought that glasses were like crutches. She herself had refused to wear glasses for years, and initially refused to get glasses for Lori; she relented when school officials required the glasses for Lori to attend school.

Rose Mary also had entrenched illogical and dysfunctional beliefs about the importance of keeping land in the family and not selling it under any circumstance. After Rose Mary's mother died (when Jeannette was 9 years old), Rose Mary inherited property in Texas. That property was worth a lot of money (nearly $1 million), yet she refused to sell it, despite the fact that she and her children lived in poverty, with no electricity, no indoor plumbing, no heat, and not enough food.

Rose Mary wasn't the only parent with unusual beliefs. Rex recounted to his family that the reason he hadn't found a job after months of unemployment in a coal mining town was because the mines were controlled by the unions, which were controlled by the mob, and he was nationally blackballed after he was kicked out of the electrician's union in Arizona (where he had previously worked). In order to get a job in the mines, he explained, he must help reform the United Mine Workers of America. And so he claimed that he spent his days investigating that union.

Diagnosis
The identification of the nature of a disorder.

Clinical assessment
The process of obtaining relevant information and making a judgment about mental illness based on the information.

Unusual beliefs may not have been the only factor that motivated Rose Mary and Rex's behavior; they also seemed to have a kind of tunnel vision that led them to see their own needs and desires while being indifferent to those of their children. When Jeanette was 5 and the family was again moving, her parents rented a U–Haul truck and placed all four children (including the youngest, Maureen, who was then an infant) and some of the family's furniture in the dark, airless, windowless back of the truck for the 14 hours it would take to get to their next "home." Rex and Rose Mary instructed the children to remain quiet in this crypt—which was also without food, water, or toilet facilities—for the entire journey. The parents also expected the children to keep baby Maureen silent so that police wouldn't discover the children in the back: It was illegal to transport people in the trailer. What explanation did the parents give their children for locking them up this way? They said that only two people could fit in the front of the truck.

In order to determine whether Rex and Rose Mary Walls had psychological disorders, we would have to compare their behavior and psychological functioning to some standard of normalcy. A diagnostic *classification system* provides a means of making such comparisons. We saw in Chapter 1 that various classification systems were used over the centuries; these systems categorized different types of disorders according to different principles. The ancient Greeks, for instance, classified mental disorders based on behavior that was attributed to either too much or too little of bodily humors.

The first modern classification system for characterizing mental disorders was developed by Emil Kraepelin (1856–1926), a distinguished German psychiatrist (Boyle, 2000). Kraepelin focused on both the symptoms themselves and their *course*—how they progressed over time. Through systematic and lengthy observations of patients, he outlined some of the hallmarks of what would later be called *schizophrenia*. Today's modern diagnostic system is based, in part, on Kraepelin's system.

Let's first examine general issues about classification systems and diagnosis and then consider the system that is now most commonly used—the system described in the most recent edition of the *Diagnostic and Statistical Manual of Mental Disorders*.

Why Diagnose?

You've probably heard that categorizing people is bad: It pigeonholes them and strips them of their individuality—right? Not necessarily. Imagine that classification systems for psychological disorders did not exist—that different sorts of unusual behavior could be described, but there were no labels for them. For instance, suppose that the diagnosis "depression" didn't exist. How, then, could clinicians and patients distinguish between a common response to a negative event (such as having a relationship break up)—feeling sad, rejected, and unlovable—and an episode of depressed mood that might lead to a suicide attempt or to chronic alcohol abuse? Moreover, without a classification system and the consequent ability to label disorders, such as depression, there would not be a word or a phrase to describe people's experiences. Said another way, there would be no yardstick of normality against which to measure people's experiences—their thoughts, feelings, and behaviors. It would therefore be difficult for clinicians and researchers to learn from one case to the next or to decide how best to help each person with unusual symptoms or combinations of symptoms.

By categorizing psychological disorders, clinicians and researchers can know more about a patient's symptoms and about how to treat the patient. To be specific, classification systems of mental disorders provide the following benefits:

- *They provide a type of shorthand, which enables clinicians and researchers to use a small number of words instead of lengthy descriptions.* For instance, Kitty Dukakis, wife of 1988 Democratic presidential candidate Michael Dukakis, suffered from depression (Dukakis & Scovell, 1991). By using the term *depression*,

AP Photo/Evan Agostini

Simone Lins/AFP/Getty Images/Newscom

Jason Moore/ZUMA Press/Newscom

Without a classification system for psychological disorders, the problems that Pete Wentz, Carolina Reston, and Keith Urban appear to have suffered from—bipolar disorder, anorexia nervosa, and substance abuse, respectively—would be nameless. Among other purposes, a classification system allows clinicians to diagnose and treat symptoms more effectively, allows patients to know that they are not alone in their experiences, and helps researchers to investigate the factors that contribute to psychological disorders and to evaluate treatments.

clinicians don't need to spell out the various elements that constitute her disorder: for example, that she had depressed mood and a significant lack of energy and enthusiasm (Dukakis & Tye, 2006).

• *They allow clinicians and researchers to group certain abnormal thoughts, feelings, and behaviors into unique constellations.* To say that someone has a diagnosis of depression effectively communicates to a mental health professional that the patient has a particular constellation of symptoms. When a clinician hears that Kitty Dukakis suffered from depression, for instance, the clinician can infer that she has some or all of the following symptoms: depressed mood, reduced pleasure in activities, fatigue or tiredness, a sense of worthlessness, difficulty concentrating, recurrent thoughts about death, and significant changes in appetite, sleep, and energy level (American Psychiatric Association, 2000). Notice how long this list of symptoms is—the term *depression* conveys much of the needed information more succinctly.

• *A particular diagnosis may also convey information about the etiology (causes) of the disorder, its course, and indications for its treatment.* Depression, for instance, can further be specified as either a single—that is, first—episode or as a recurrence. A diagnosis of recurrent depression implies a heightened neurological and/or cognitive vulnerability to depression and a longer and more variable course, and it indicates that the disorder may require multiple types of treatments in order to reduce symptoms (Peterson et al., 2007). Despite treatment, Kitty Dukakis suffered numerous bouts of depression, which suggests that many types of factors contributed to her disorder and that she was at significant risk for additional episodes.

Steve Liss/Time Life Pictures/Getty Images

Kitty Dukakis became intimately familiar with her symptoms of depression: "It is June 20, 2001, Michael's and my 38th wedding anniversary. It also is the end of my fourth month of depression, my crisis period. I'm normally a person with enormous enthusiasm for and interest in the world. All that is just missing now. Fun or enjoyment are things I cannot even imagine. I don't speak to my kids on the phone, or to my sister" (Dukakis & Tye, 2006).

• *Classification systems also enable researchers to study the causes, the course, and the effects of treatments for various disorders.* If there were no diagnoses, then how would researchers be able to study mental illness and its treatment? They wouldn't be able to group together individuals with similar problems systematically and reliably. Not only did Kitty Dukakis suffer from depression, but she was also dependent on amphetamine pills—"uppers"—and alcohol (Dukakis & Tye, 2006). Some researchers investigate differences between people who suffer from both depression and substance abuse (as Dukakis did) and those who suffer only depression. Researchers have also examined the effect of substance abuse on the course of depression (Agosti & Levin, 2006).

Other researchers have examined how best to treat people with both substance abuse and depression, compared to those with only substance abuse (Dodge, Sindelar, & Sinha, 2005; Torrens et al., 2005). Such comparisons are possible only because the diagnoses are part of a classification system.

• *A diagnosis can indicate that an individual is in need of attention (including treatment), support, or benefits.* For example, children diagnosed with a learning disorder may receive special accommodations or services at school. For some adults, a diagnosis may allow them to have special accommodations at home or work or to receive certain services paid for by their health insurance plan or by government programs. For some people involved in criminal justice proceedings, a diagnosis of a psychological disorder, such as schizophrenia, may make the difference between being sent to a mental health facility and going to prison or jail.

• *Some people find great relief in learning that they are not alone in having particular problems* (see Case 3.1). People may derive a measure of comfort from merely being given a label for their problems—knowing not only that there is a term for their disturbing thoughts, feelings, and behaviors, but also that they are not the only one with the specific difficulties. Moreover, once they have a name for the symptoms they are experiencing, they can learn more about the disorder and treatments for it.

CASE 3.1 ▶ FROM THE OUTSIDE: On Being Diagnosed with a Disorder

Sally, an articulate and dynamic 46-year-old woman, came to share her experiences with our psychiatry class. For much of her adult life, she had suffered from insomnia, panic attacks, and intense fear. Then, six years ago, a nightmare triggered memories of childhood sexual abuse and she was finally diagnosed with posttraumatic stress disorder.

Being diagnosed, she told us, was an intense relief.

"All those years, I thought I was just crazy," she said. "My whole family used to call me the crazy one. Once, my brother called my mom and asked, 'So, how's my crazy sister?' But all of a sudden I wasn't crazy any more. It had a name. It had a real reason. I could finally understand why I felt the way I did,' she said."

(Rothman, 1995)

A Cautionary Note About Diagnosis

Having a classification system for mental illness has many advantages, but assigning the appropriate diagnosis can be a challenge. For example, clinicians may be biased to make—or not make—particular diagnoses for certain groups of people. Patients, once diagnosed with a disorder, may be stigmatized because of it. Relatives and friends, as well as patients, often struggle to answer this question: Does having a psychological disorder exempt patients from being responsible for their behavior? Let's examine the possibilities of bias and stigma in more detail.

Diagnostic Bias

A **diagnostic bias** is a systematic error in diagnosis (Meehl, 1960). Such a bias can cause groups of people to receive a particular diagnosis disproportionately, on the basis of an unrelated factor such as sex, race, or age (Kunen et al., 2005). Studies of diagnostic bias show, for example, that in the United States, black patients are more likely than white patients to be diagnosed with schizophrenia instead of a mood disorder (Abreu, 1999; Garb, 1997; Neighbors et al., 2003; Trierweiler et al., 2005). Black patients are also prescribed higher doses of medication than are white patients (Strakowski, Shelton, & Kolbrener, 1993).

When the mental health clinician is not familiar with the social norms of the patient's cultural background, the clinician may misinterpret certain behaviors as

Diagnostic bias
A systematic error in diagnosis.

pathological, and thus be more likely to diagnose a psychological disorder. So, for instance, the clinician might view a Caribbean immigrant family's closeness as "overinvolvment" rather than as normal for that culture.

Other groups, such as low-income Mexican Americans, may have their mental illnesses under–diagnosed (only a percentage of cases are diagnosed) (Schmaling & Hernandez, 2005). Part of the explanation for the under-diagnosis may be that the constellation of symptoms experienced by some Mexican Americans does not fit within the classification system currently used in North America; another part of the explanation may be language differences between patient and clinician that make accurate assessment difficult (Kaplan, 2007; Villaseñor & Waitzkin, 1999).

Diagnosis as a Stigmatizing Label

When someone has a psychological disorder, the diagnosis may be seen as a stigmatizing label that influences how other people—including the mental health clinician—view and treat the person. It may even change how a diagnosed person behaves and feels about himself or herself (Eriksen & Kress, 2005). Such labels can lead some people with a psychological disorder to blame themselves and try to hide their problems (Corrigan & Watson, 2001; Wahl, 1999). Feelings of shame may even lead them to refrain from obtaining treatment (U.S. Department of Health and Human Services, 1999).

Great strides have been made toward destigmatizing mental illness, although there is still a way to go. In 2006, actor Tom Cruise said about actor Brooke Shield's postpartum depression, "When you talk about postpartum, you can take people today, women, and what you do is you use vitamins. There is a hormonal thing that is going on, scientifically, you can prove that. But when you talk about emotional, chemical imbalances in people, there is no science behind that" (Grove, 2005). However, to the contrary, clinicians and researchers do in fact have scientific evidence that chemical imbalances can be involved in a psychological disorder. And, fortunately, many people challenged Cruise's statements by providing facts, leading to greater awareness of postpartum depression. One organization devoted to confronting the stigma of mental illness is the National Alliance for the Mentally Ill (nami.org), which has a network of advocates—called StigmaBusters—who combat incorrect and insensitive portrayals of mental illness in the media.

The National Alliance for the Mentally Ill protested the airing of a television show, *Crumbs*, and its portrayal of the lead character, Mother Crumb, who was hospitalized with a "nervous breakdown." When her mental illness led to violent behavior, audience laughter followed. The show both trivialized mental illness and reinforced stereotypes of the mentally ill.

Gale Adler/© ABC/Courtesy: Everett Collection

Reliability and Validity in Classification Systems

Classification systems are most useful when they are reliable and valid. If a classification system yields consistent results over time, it is **reliable**. To understand what constitutes a reliable classification system, imagine the following scenario about Rose Mary Walls: Suppose she decided to see a mental health clinician because she was sleeping a lot, crying every day, and losing weight. Further, she consented to have her interview with the clinician filmed for other clinicians to watch. Would every clinician who watched the videoclip hear Rose Mary's words and see her behavior in the same way? Would every clinician diagnose her as having the same disorder? If so, then the classification system they used would be deemed reliable. But suppose that various clinicians came up with different diagnoses or were divided about whether Rose Mary even had a disorder. They might make different judgments about how her behaviors or symptoms fit into the classification system. That is, they might interpret the same behaviors and characteristics differently. For instance, some clinicians might interpret Rose Mary's experiences and behaviors as appropriate to the situation—as understandable given the regular disruptions to her social and family life. If there were significant differences of opinion about her diagnosis among the clinicians, the classification system they used probably is not reliable.

Reliable
Classification systems (or measures) that consistently produce the same results.

Problems concerning reliability in diagnosis can occur when:

• *the criteria for disorders are unclear*, and thus require the clinician to use considerable judgment about whether symptoms meet the criteria; or

• *there is significant overlap among disorders*, which can then make it difficult to distinguish among them.

However, just because clinicians agree on a diagnosis doesn't mean that the diagnosis is correct! For example, in the past, there was considerable agreement about the role of the devil in producing mental disorders, but we now know that this isn't a valid explanation. Science is not a popularity contest; what the majority of observers believe at any particular point in time is not necessarily correct. Thus, another requirement for any classification system is that it needs to be **valid**—the categories must characterize what they are supposed to be classifying. Each disorder should have a unique set of criteria that are necessary for the diagnosis to be made.

The reliability and validity of classification systems are important in part because such systems are often used to study the etiology of a psychological disorder, its **prognosis** (the likely course and outcome of the disorder), and whether particular treatments will be effective. In order to use a classification system in this way, however, the **prevalence** of each disorder—the number of people who have the disorder in a given period of time—must be large enough that researchers are likely to encounter people with the disorder. (A related term is *incidence*, which refers to the total number of new cases of a disorder that are identified in a given time period.)

In addition, to be valid, the criteria must not be too restrictive or too broad. If the criteria for diagnosing a particular disorder are so restrictive that the disorder's prevalence is very low, not much will be discovered about its course or the most effective treatments. On the other hand, if the criteria for a disorder are so broad that the disorder is very common, the criteria may reflect a set of different (but perhaps related) problems or even include aspects of normal—not abnormal—psychological functioning; in either case, the classification is not of much use (Kutchins & Kirk, 1997).

In sum, a classification system should be as reliable and valid as possible in order to be useful for patients, clinicians, and researchers. Next, we'll examine the most commonly used classification system for psychological disorders—the system in the *Diagnostic and Statistical Manual of Mental Disorders (DSM)*.

The Diagnostic and Statistical Manual of Mental Disorders

Suppose that child welfare officials had spoken with Rex and Rose Mary Walls and required that the parents be evaluated by mental health professionals. How would a mental health clinician go about determining whether or not either of them had a disorder? What classification system would the clinician probably use? The classification system that most clinicians use in the United States is found in the *Diagnostic and Statistical Manual of Mental Disorders*, which is currently in its fourth edition. This guide, published by the American Psychiatric Association (2000), describes the characteristics of many psychological disorders and identifies *criteria*—the kinds, number, and duration of relevant symptoms—for diagnosing each disorder. This classification system is *categorical*—someone either has a disorder or does not.

A different classification system, described in the *International Classification of Diseases* (ICD), is used in some other parts of the world. The World Health Organization (WHO) develops the ICD, which is currently in its tenth edition. The primary purpose of the ICD is to provide a framework for collecting health statistics worldwide. Unlike the DSM, however, the ICD includes many diseases and

Valid
Classification systems (or measures) that actually characterize what they are supposed to characterize.

Prognosis
The likely course and outcome of a disorder.

Prevalence
The number of people who have a disorder in a given period of time.

disorders, not just psychological disorders. In fact, until the sixth edition, the ICD only classified causes of death. With the sixth edition, the editors added diseases, of which mental disorders were one type. Current versions of the mental disorders sections of the ICD and the DSM have been revised to overlap substantially. Research on prevalence that uses one classification system is now applicable to the other system.

The Evolution of DSM

When the original version of the DSM was published in 1952, it was the first manual to address the needs of clinicians rather than researchers (Beutler & Malik, 2002). At that time, psychodynamic theory was popular, and the DSM strongly favored the psychodynamic approach in its classifications. For example, it organized mental illness according to different types of conflicts among the id, ego, superego, and reality, as well as different patterns of defense mechanisms employed (American Psychiatric Association, 1952). The second edition of the DSM, published in 1968, had only minor modifications. The first two editions were criticized for problems with reliability and validity, which arose in part because their classifications relied on psychodynamic theory. Clinicians had to draw many inferences about the specific nature of patients' problems, including the specific unconscious conflicts that motivated patients' behavior.

The authors of the third edition (DSM-III), published in 1980, set out to create a classification system that had better reliability and validity. Unlike the previous editions, DSM-III:

1. did not rest on the psychodynamic theory of psychopathology (or on any other theory);

2. focused more on what can be observed than on what can be inferred;

3. listed explicit criteria for each disorder and began to use available research results to develop those criteria; and

4. included a system for clinicians and researchers to record diagnoses as well as additional information—such as related medical history—that may affect diagnosis, prognosis, and treatment.

Some of the criteria in DSM-III were not clear, however, and various inconsistencies were identified. So, in 1987, a revised version was published. DSM-III-R (R for "Revised") provided more explicit criteria than did previous editions, which meant that it had greater reliability (Malik & Beutler, 2002). Researchers in different hospitals could collect information about prevalence, etiological factors, course, or treatment from patients with a particular disorder and be reasonably certain that they all were studying the same disorder. However, this research revealed certain limitations of DSM-III-R, including continuing problems with validity (Malik & Beutler, 2002). For instance, criteria were too restrictive for some disorders; thus, even though some individuals, such as those with preoccupations of physical illness, were clearly distressed or impaired, their symptoms did not meet enough of the criteria for a diagnosis (Rief et al., 1996; Wise & Birket-Smith, 2002).

The Multiaxial System of DSM-IV-TR

The weaknesses of DSM-III-R led to DSM-IV, published in 1994, which specified new disorders and revised the criteria for some of the disorders included in DSM-III-R. In 2000, the American Psychiatric Association published an expanded version of DSM-IV that included more current information about each disorder, such as new information about prevalence, course, issues related to gender and cultural factors, and **comorbidity**—the presence of more than one disorder at the same time in a given patient. This revised edition is called DSM-IV-TR, where *TR* stands for "Text Revision." The list of disorders and almost all of

Comorbidity
The presence of more than one disorder at the same time in a given patient.

Table 3.1 ▶ The 17 Categories of Psychological Disorders in DSM-IV-TR

Adjustment Disorders
Anxiety Disorders
Delirium, Dementia, and Amnestic and Other Cognitive Disorders
Disorders Usually First Diagnosed in Infancy, Childhood, or Adolescence
Dissociative Disorders
Eating Disorders
Factitious Disorders
Impulse-Control Disorders
Mental Disorders Due to a General Medical Condition
Mood Disorders
Other Conditions That May Be a Focus of Clinical Attention
Personality Disorders
Schizophrenia and Other Psychotic Disorders
Sexual and Gender Identity Disorders
Sleep Disorders
Somatoform Disorders
Substance-Related Disorders

Source: Reprinted with permission from the Diagnostic and Statistical Manual of Mental Disorders, Text Revision, Fourth Edition, (Copyright 2000) American Psychiatric Association.

Table 3.2 ▶ The Fives Axes of DSM-IV-TR

Axis I: Clinical Disorders
Axis II: Personality Disorders and Mental Retardation
Axis III: General Medical Conditions
Axis IV: Psychosocial and Environmental Problems
Axis V: Global Assessment of Functioning

Source: Reprinted with permission from the Diagnostic and Statistical Manual of Mental Disorders, Text Revision, Fourth Edition, (Copyright 2000) American Psychiatric Association.

the criteria were not changed, but the text discussion of the disorders was revised. DSM-IV and DSM-IV-TR define 17 major categories of psychological problems, listed in Table 3.1, and nearly 300 specific mental disorders—almost triple the number in DSM-III. As work progresses on the fifth edition of DSM, some researchers and clinicians support the inclusion of additional disorders, such as "Internet addiction" (Block, 2008) and "night eating syndrome" (Stunkard, Allison, & Lundgren, 2008).

DSM-III introduced five *axes* (which is why it is called *multiaxial*), each of which delineates specific kinds of information to be noted about a patient. These axes are still included in DSM-IV-TR (see Table 3.2), and they may be used for diagnosing a patient, for planning treatment, for prognosis, or for research purposes. In addition to these axes, an appendix in DSM-IV-TR outlines aspects of the cultural context that clinicians should consider when making a diagnosis for a particular patient.

The first two axes specify the diagnosed disorders. Disorders listed on *Axis I* include most of the disorders in DSM-IV-TR and in this book, such as social phobia and bulimia nervosa. If an individual has comorbid Axis I disorders, all of the disorders are listed. For instance, if an individual has both social phobia and bulimia nervosa, both disorders would be listed on Axis I.

Disorders listed on Axis II include mental retardation and *personality disorders*—personality traits that are so inflexible and self-defeating that they impair functioning (discussed in detail in Chapter 13). The authors of DSM-III's multiaxial system believed that the presence of mental retardation or a personality disorder in a patient could significantly affect the expression of symptoms of other disorders—those on Axis I. Having a separate axis—Axis II—to specify such disorders ensures that these types of symptoms receive special attention. For example, suppose that a man who has moderate mental retardation lately seems to be "not himself"—he's been crying often, but when asked why, he says he doesn't know. His mental retardation makes it difficult for him to express himself well. The clinician diagnosing the man would need to determine how his mental retardation affects the way he expresses symptoms of a comorbid psychological disorder, such as depression or anxiety. Moreover, the presence of mental retardation may indicate that certain treatments would be more appropriate than others.

On *Axis III*, mental health clinicians or researchers list any physical disorders or disabilities that might be relevant to the disorders on Axis I or II. For instance, an elderly woman with poor eyesight who recently suffered a hip fracture after a fall may now feel so anxious about leaving home that she has *panic attacks*—episodes of extreme fear, terror, or dread. In order to diagnose and treat this woman's problems appropriately, a clinician would need to know about both her visual problems and her recent hip fracture; both medical problems would be noted on Axis III.

The first three axes focus on current psychological and medical disorders. *Axis IV* focuses on the wider context of the disorder: social and environmental problems that could affect the diagnosis, treatment, and prognosis of a disorder. Knowing that a depressed patient's mother recently died, for instance, may influence both the diagnosis and recommended treatment, if any. Social problems that affect a person's psychological state are often called *psychosocial* problems. Such psychosocial and environmental problems include (American Psychiatric Association, 2000, pp. 31–32):

1. problems with the person's primary support group (e.g., marital conflict or divorce, or some type of maltreatment);

2. problems with the social environment (e.g., the death of a friend or discrimination);

3. educational problems (e.g., academic problems or difficulties with a teacher);

4. occupational problems (e.g., unemployment or stressful working conditions);

5. housing problems (e.g., homelessness or an unsafe neighborhood);

6. economic problems (e.g., extreme poverty);

7. problems with access to health care (e.g., inadequate health insurance or lack of transportation to health care facilities); and

8. legal difficulties (e.g., being arrested or being a victim of a crime).

Axis V requires the clinician or researcher to provide a numerical estimate (between 1 and 100) of the patient's global functioning within the past year. As shown in Table 3.3, the number indicates the highest level of functioning the patient has achieved in his or her work, relationships, and leisure time or the patient's current level of functioning. This information can be used to plan treatment and estimate the level of functioning likely to be attained after treatment.

Consider a 25-year-old woman, Lia, who has suffered from delusions and hallucinations from time to time over the last 5 years and has been diagnosed with schizophrenia. Lia was briefly hospitalized because her hallucinations had gotten much worse, but she's now out of the hospital and stable. A clinician would want to know how well Lia had been doing during the past year as a guide to what level of functioning might be possible for her. If her symptoms had been relatively under control and she had been attending college part-time, the prognosis would probably be better than if she had been living at home, not doing anything during the day, and not always able to care for herself. Similarly, if Lia had been able to attend college, treatment might focus, in part, on identifying factors associated with the onset of more severe symptoms and on developing coping strategies and social support to help her resume her higher level of functioning. Had she previously been unable to care for herself, treatment would focus on helping Lia develop basic self-care abilities—maintaining hygiene, preparing meals—and creating some type of daily structure to organize her time.

Table 3.3 ▸ Axis V: Global Assessment of Functioning Scale

91–100	Superior functioning in a wide range of activities, life's problems never seem to get out of hand, is sought out by others because of his or her many positive qualities. No symptoms.
81–90	Absent or minimal symptoms (e.g., mild anxiety before an exam), good functioning in all areas, interested and involved in a wide range of activities, socially effective, generally satisfied with life, no more than everyday problems or concerns (e.g., an occasional argument with family members).
71–80	If symptoms are present, they are transient and expectable reactions to psychosocial stressors (e.g., difficulty concentrating after family argument); no more than slight impairment in social, occupational, or school functioning (e.g., temporarily falling behind in schoolwork).
61–70	Some mild symptoms (e.g., depressed mood and mild insomnia) OR some difficulty in social, occupational, or school functioning (e.g., occasional truancy or theft within the household), but generally functioning pretty well, has some meaningful interpersonal relationships.
51–60	Moderate symptoms (e.g., flat affect and circumstantial speech, occasional panic attacks) OR moderate difficulty in social, occupational, or school functioning (e.g., few friends, conflicts with peers or coworkers).
41–50	Severe symptoms (e.g., suicidal ideation, severe obsessional rituals, frequent shoplifting) OR any serious impairment in social, occupational, or school functioning (e.g., no friends, unable to keep a job).
31–40	Some impairment in reality testing or communication (e.g., speech is at times illogical, obscure, or irrelevant) OR major impairment in several areas, such as work or school, family relations, judgment, thinking, or mood (e.g., depressed man avoids friends, neglects family, and is unable to work; child frequently beats up younger children, is defiant at home, and is failing at school).
21–30	Behavior is considerably influenced by delusions or hallucinations OR serious impairment in communication or judgment (e.g., sometimes incoherent, acts grossly inappropriately, suicidal preoccupation) OR inability to function in almost all areas (e.g., stays in bed all day; no job, home, or friends).
11–20	Some danger of hurting self or others (e.g., suicide attempts without clear expectation of death, frequently violent, manic excitement) OR occasionally fails to maintain minimal personal hygiene (e.g., smears feces) OR gross impairment in communication (e.g., largely incoherent or mute).
1–10	Persistent danger of severely hurting self or others (e.g., recurrent violence) OR persistent inability to maintain minimal personal hygiene OR serious suicidal act with clear expectation of death.
0	Inadequate information.

Source: Reprinted with permission from the DSM-IV-TR Casebook: A Learning Companion to the Diagnostic and Statistical Manual of Mental Disorders, Fourth Edition, Text Revision, (Copyright 2002) American Psychiatric Association.

The Global Assessment of Functioning Scale asks the clinician to "consider psychological, social, and occupational functioning on a hypothetical continuum of mental health—illness. Do not include impairment in functioning due to physical or environmental limitations" (American Psychiatric Association, 2000, p. 34).

Criticisms of DSM-IV-TR

Most mental health professionals agree that DSM-IV-TR is an improvement over previous editions, but its classification system has been criticized on a number of grounds. To understand the criticisms, we will focus on the DSM-IV-TR criteria

Table 3.4 ► DSM-IV-TR Diagnostic Criteria for Schizophrenia

A. *Characteristic symptoms:* Two (or more) of the following, with each being present for a significant portion of time during a 1-month period:

(1) delusions

(2) hallucinations

(3) disorganized speech (evidenced by sentences that make no sense because words are scrambled and the thoughts appear disconnected).

(4) grossly disorganized behavior (including difficulty with daily tasks such as organizing a meal or maintaining proper hygiene).

Note: The first four symptoms are often referred to as *positive* symptoms, because they suggest the *presence* of an excess or distortion of normal functions.

(5) negative symptoms (which indicate an absence of normal functions), such as a failure to express or respond to emotion; slow, empty replies to questions; or an inability to initiate goal-directed behavior.

Note: Only one Criterion A symptom is required if delusions are bizarre or hallucinations consist of a voice keeping up a running commentary on the person's behavior or thoughts, or two or more voices conversing with each other.

B. *Social/occupational dysfunction:* Since the disturbance began, one or more major areas of functioning such as work, interpersonal relations, or self-care are *markedly* below the level achieved before the disturbance appeared.

C. *Duration:* Continuous signs of the disturbance persist for at least 6 months, with at least 1 month of symptoms that meet Criterion A.

Source: Reprinted with permission from the Diagnostic and Statistical Manual of Mental Disorders, Text Revision, Fourth Edition, (Copyright 2000) American Psychiatric Association.

for a diagnosis of schizophrenia as an example (see Table 3.4); this disorder is discussed in more detail in Chapter 12. The criticisms raised in this discussion apply to most DSM-IV-TR disorders. Let's examine those criticisms in detail.

Determining Clinical Significance

Consider symptoms A3 and A4 in Table 3.4: disorganized speech and grossly disorganized behavior. DSM-IV-TR instructs the clinician to determine what constitutes *clinically significant* disorganized speech or behavior. Part of the problem is that this decision, to a certain extent, is subjective. Similarly, in Criterion B, dysfunction must be *markedly* below the person's previous level of functioning. But DSM-IV-TR does not specify what, exactly, *markedly* means (Caplan, 1995; Frances, First, & Pincus, 1995). Not all professionals would consider the same patient's dysfunction marked *enough* to qualify as a symptom of schizophrenia. These problems are complicated further if the clinician relies on the patient's description of his or her previous level of functioning; the patient's view of the past may be clouded by the present symptoms.

In a similar vein, consider the category of disorders known as *adjustment disorders* (see Table 3.1): These disorders are characterized by a response to an identifiable stressor that is *in excess of what would normally be expected*. The clinician must determine whether an individual's response is excessive. However, different people have different coping styles, and what seems to one clinician like an excessive response may be deemed normal by another clinician.

Disorders as Categories, Not Continua

DSM-IV-TR is structured so that someone either has or does not have a given disorder. It's analogous to the old adage about pregnancy: A woman can't be a little bit pregnant—she either is or isn't pregnant. But critics argue that many disorders may exist along continua (continuous gradations), meaning that patients can have different degrees of a disorder (Kendell & Jablensky, 2003).

Some psychologists propose that when the fifth edition of DSM is developed, each disorder should be classified on a continuum, where the number or severity of symptoms indicates the degree of severity of the disorder (Malik & Beutler, 2002; Westen et al., 2002). Subsequent editions of DSM may include a way to diagnose disorders along a continuum in addition to a version of the current categorical system (First, 2006). If disorders were specified along a continuum, planning appropriate goals and treatments would be easier, and prognoses might be more accurate.

Consider, for example, two young men who have had the diagnosis of schizophrenia for 5 years. Aaron has been living with roommates and attending college part-time; Max is living at home, continues to hallucinate and have delusions, and cannot hold down a volunteer job. Over the holidays, both men's symptoms got worse and both were hospitalized briefly. Since being discharged from the hospital, Aaron has only mild symptoms, but Max still can't function independently even though he no longer needs to be in the hospital. The categorical diagnosis of schizophrenia lumps both of these patients together, but the intensity of their symptoms suggests that clinicians should have different expectations, goals, treatments, and prognoses for them. As shown in Figure 3.1, on a dimensional scale, one of them is likely to be diagnosed with mild schizophrenia, whereas the other is likely to be diagnosed with severe schizophrenia.

Similarly, consider Allie and Lupe, both of whom are afraid of bugs and spiders. Lupe mildly dislikes insects and avoids them whenever possible, but she doesn't freak out when she sees a spider; Lupe's fear of bugs doesn't reach the cutoff for a disorder (it doesn't significantly impair her functioning or cause her excessive distress). Allie, in contrast, lives in fear of spiders and refuses to open her windows because she worries that spiders might invade her apartment. As a result, the air is stifling hot in her apartment during the summer. Allie's fear and avoidance of spiders are probably severe enough to be considered a disorder.

Heterogeneous Groups Have the Same Disorder

For many DSM-IV-TR disorders, including schizophrenia, a person needs to have only some of the symptoms in order to be diagnosed with the disorder. For example, under Criterion A in Table 3.4, a person needs to have only two out of the five symptoms. This means that some people with schizophrenia may have delusions and hallucinations, whereas others may have disorganized speech and disorganized behavior, but *no* delusions or hallucinations. Moreover, still other people classified as having schizophrenia may have negative symptoms and delusions, but not exhibit disorganized behavior or experience hallucinations. Taken together, these three groups of people with schizophrenia are *heterogeneous*—they are different from each other.

If the different combinations of symptoms do in fact reflect a single underlying disorder (in other words, if the category is valid), this is not a problem. But it is possible—and many researchers believe it is likely (Messias & Kirkpatrick, 2001; Tek et al., 2001)—that people who have different combinations of symptoms have distinct types of schizophrenia, perhaps with different causes and prognoses. If so, then it is an error to group them together. And this may be true for most disorders in DSM-IV-TR. People with different combinations of symptoms may have developed the disorder in different ways, and different treatments might be effective. Thus, the DSM-IV-TR diagnostic system may obscure important differences among types of a given mental disorder (Malik & Beutler, 2002).

Symptoms Are Weighted Equally

In the DSM-IV-TR system, the diagnostic criteria for a given disorder, in essence, produce a checklist; each criterion (and the symptoms reflected in it, such as the five symptoms in Criterion A in Table 3.4) is generally weighted equally (Malik & Beutler, 2002). But each symptom in the list of criteria for a given disorder may not be equally important for diagnosis. For instance, patients with schizophrenia who primarily have delusions or hallucinations are generally less impaired and have a better prognosis than those who primarily have negative symptoms such as flat affect (diminished emotional expression) or difficulty initiating goal-directed behavior (McGlashan & Fenton, 1993).

Duration Criteria Are Arbitrary

Each set of criteria for a disorder specifies a minimum amount of time that symptoms must be present for a patient to qualify for that diagnosis (see Criterion C in Table 3.4). However, the specification of a particular duration, such as that noted for bulimia nervosa (which requires that the symptoms be present for at least 3 months), is often arbitrary and not supported by research (Sullivan, Bulik, & Kendler, 1998).

The requirement for a specific duration also means that someone's diagnostic status can change literally overnight. For instance, for the diagnosis of social phobia, symptoms of significant fear in social situations must have persisted for at

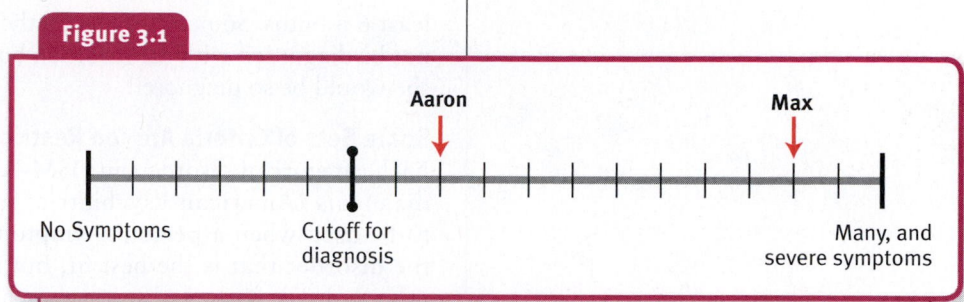

Figure 3.1

Aaron   Max

No Symptoms   Cutoff for   Many, and
                     diagnosis   severe symptoms

3.1 ▸ A Disorder as on a Continuum If a disorder such as schizophrenia is best characterized along a continuum, then two people, Aaron and Max, diagnosed with schizophrenia but with different severity or numbers of symptoms, would fall at different points on the continuum. Aaron has fewer symptoms and is able to function better than Max. According to DSM-IV-TR, they both have the same disorder. However, their illnesses have different courses and prognoses and will likely require different types of treatment. None of this information is captured by the categorical diagnostic system of DSM-IV-TR.

least 6 months. Someone who had these symptoms for 5 months and 29 days would not be diagnosed with the disorder, but if the symptoms persisted another day, he or she would be so diagnosed.

Some Sets of Criteria Are Too Restrictive

Each category of disorders in DSM-IV-TR includes a *not otherwise specified (NOS)* diagnosis (American Psychiatric Association, 2000)—a nonspecific diagnosis to be used when a person's symptoms do not meet all the necessary criteria for the disorder that is the best fit, but the individual is significantly distressed and impaired. For instance, someone who had some—but not enough—of the symptoms to meet the criteria for schizophrenia or another psychotic disorder would be diagnosed as having *psychotic disorder NOS*; this would be the case, for example, for someone with only negative symptoms of schizophrenia (Criterion A5 in Table 3.4).

With some disorders, though, the criteria are so restrictive that *most* of the distressed and impaired patients with appropriate symptoms don't meet all the relevant criteria to be diagnosed with that disorder; this is true for people with eating disorders (Sloan, Mizes, & Epstein, 2005): Most people with an eating disorder are diagnosed with the more general (and less reliable) *eating disorder NOS*, rather than with *bulimia nervosa* or *anorexia nervosa*, the two diagnoses in the eating disorders category. The criteria for bulimia and anorexia are sufficiently restrictive that most people with eating-related problems who have significant distress, dysfunction, or risk of harm have symptoms that fall short of the criteria. Those diagnosed with *eating disorder NOS* are a very heterogeneous group of people, who have varying problems associated with food and eating.

When NOS diagnoses occur frequently for a particular category of disorders, as is the case with eating disorders, the criteria for the disorders may not meaningfully capture the important elements needed for diagnosis—and hence the set of criteria should be reevaluated.

Psychological Disorders are Created to Ensure Payment

With each edition of DSM, the number of disorders has increased, reaching almost 300 with DSM-IV. Does this mean that more types of mental disorders have been discovered and classified? Not necessarily. This increase may, in part, reflect economic pressures in the mental health care industry (Eriksen & Kress, 2005). Today, in order for a mental health facility or provider to be paid or a patient to be reimbursed by health insurance companies, the patient must have symptoms that meet a DSM-IV-TR diagnosis. Prior to DSM-III-R, this requirement for payment did not generally exist. The more disorders that are included in a new edition of DSM, then, the more likely it is that a patient's treatment will be paid for or reimbursed by health insurance companies. But this does not imply that all of the disorders are valid from a scientific perspective.

Medical Illnesses are Made into Psychological Disorders

The DSM is beginning to include medical disorders, which are not clearly *psychological* disorders (Eriksen & Kress, 2005). For example, *breathing-related sleep disorder*, which is included in DSM-IV-TR, is caused in part by an obstruction of the breathing passage, a medical condition. No research evidence or medical discoveries warranted the addition of this sleep disorders to Axis I of the DSM. Rather, the decision was made by a small number of psychiatrists on the DSM committee in order to ensure that treatment of this sleep disorder by mental health clinicians would be paid for by health insurance companies; treatment by mental health clinicians for disorders that are not included in the DSM is less likely be paid for by most health insurance plans (Houts, 2002).

However, the push to include medical conditions in DSM is not entirely based on financial considerations: Clinicians have found that treatments developed for some psychological disorders can also be used to treat some medical disorders successfully (Deckersbach et al., 2006). For example, a number of psychological treatments can help reduce symptoms of irritable bowel syndrome, a medical disorder marked by intestinal cramping, bloating, and diarrhea (Blanchard et al., 2006; Whitehead, 2006). Even so, this does not justify including a medical disorder in the DSM.

Social Factors are Deemphasized

Perhaps because DSM-IV-TR does not generally address etiological factors (the causes of a disorder), it does not explicitly recognize social factors that *contribute* to disorders (as opposed to the listing of current psychosocial problems on Axis IV). DSM-IV-TR states that its diagnoses are not supposed to apply to conflicts between an individual and society, but rather to conflicts within an individual. However, this distinction is often difficult to make (Caplan, 1995). For instance, people can become depressed in response to a variety of social stressors: after losing their jobs, after they are exposed to systematic discrimination, after emigrating from their native country, or after experiencing other social and societal conflicts.

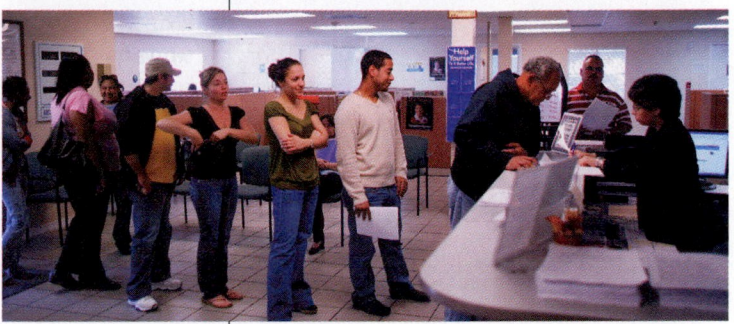

One criticism of DSM-IV-TR is that social factors that contribute to psychological disorders—such as being laid off from work—are not incorporated into the diagnosis (Caplan, 1995).

Comorbidity is Common

About half of the people who are diagnosed with a DSM-IV-TR disorder have at least one additional disorder; that is, they exhibit comorbidity (Kessler et al., 2005). This raises the question of whether the disorders in DSM-IV-TR describe unique clusters of symptoms. For instance, half of the people who are clinically depressed—that is, whose depression meets the criteria for the DSM-IV-TR disorder *major depressive disorder*—also have an anxiety disorder (Kessler et al., 2003). Such a high rate of comorbidity suggests that, for a significant number of people, the two DSM-IV-TR disorders may represent different facets of the same underlying problem. This possibility raises questions about validity and makes DSM-IV-TR diagnoses less useful to clinicians and researchers.

Overlooks Commonalities Across Diagnostic Categories

The structure of DSM-IV-TR makes it difficult for researchers to identify commonalities that underlie disorders across the 17 categories. Such commonalities arise either when particular disorders are frequently comorbid—as is common with depression and anxiety—or when various disorders have some symptoms in common. In either case, commonly comorbid disorders may be better classified as different expressions of the same core problem, rather than the way DSM-IV-TR does—as completely separate disorders.

For example, many emotional and behavioral problems can be categorized as hinging on either overcontrol or undercontrol; such problems often begin in childhood and persist into adulthood. Problems that involve overcontrol are referred to as *internalizing* problems because they are largely characterized by the internal experiences associated with them; examples include depression and various types of anxiety. Problems that involve undercontrol are referred to as *externalizing* problems because they are largely characterized by their effects on others and on the environment; examples include aggression and disruptive behaviors, such as occur in attention-deficit/hyperactivity disorder and delinquency. Not all emotional or behavioral problems fit into these categories, however, and an "other" category was created to include eating disorders and learning disorders (Achenbach, McConaughy, & Howell, 1987; Kazdin & Weisz, 1998). But DSM-IV-TR doesn't provide any way to classify or group disorders that involve internalizing or externalizing problems, making it more challenging for researchers to identify commonalities.

Although the criticisms of DSM-IV-TR have merit, the clinical chapters of this book (Chapters 6–15) are generally organized according to DSM-IV-TR categories and criteria. DSM-IV-TR is by far the most widely used classification system for diagnosing psychological disorders, and it will no doubt provide the foundation for a revised edition in the future.

The People Who Diagnose Psychological Disorders

Who, exactly, are the mental health professionals who might diagnose Rex or Rose Mary Walls, or anyone else who might be suffering from a psychological disorder? As you will see, there are different types of mental health professionals, each with a different type of training. The type of training can influence the kinds of information that clinicians pay particular attention to, what they perceive, and how they interpret the information. However, regardless of the type of training and educational degrees they receive, all mental health professionals must be licensed in the state in which they practice (or board-certified in the case of psychiatrists); licensure indicates that they have been appropriately trained to diagnose and treat mental disorders. However, there are no laws that prevent people who have not been trained in approved ways—and therefore are not licensed by the state—from calling themselves psychotherapists.

Clinical Psychologists and Counseling Psychologists

A **clinical psychologist** generally has a doctoral degree, either a Ph.D. (doctor of philosophy) or a Psy.D. (doctor of psychology), that is awarded only after several years of coursework (on mental processes, learning theory, psychological testing, the assessment of psychological disorders, psychological treatments, and ethics) and several years of treating patients while receiving supervision from experienced clinicians. People training to be clinical psychologists also take other courses that may include neuropsychology and psychopharmacology. In addition, clinical psychologists with a Ph.D. will have completed a *dissertation*—a major, independent research project. Programs that award a Psy.D. in clinical psychology place less emphasis on research.

Clinical neuropsychologists are a particular type of clinical psychologist. Clinical neuropsychologists concentrate on characterizing the effects of brain damage and neurological diseases (such as Alzheimer's disease) on thoughts (that is, mental processes and mental contents), feelings (affect), and behavior. Sometimes, they help design and conduct rehabilitation programs for patients with brain damage or neurological disease.

Counseling psychologists might have a Ph.D. from a psychology program that focuses on counseling or might have an Ed.D. (doctor of education) degree from a school of education. Their training is similar to that of clinical psychologists except that counseling psychologists tend to have more training in vocational testing, career guidance, and multicultural issues, and they generally don't receive training in neuropsychology. Counseling psychologists also tend to work with healthier people, whereas clinical psychologists tend to have more training in psychopathology and often work with people who have more severe problems (Cobb et al., 2004; Norcross et al., 1998). The distinction between the two types of psychologists, however, is less clear-cut than in the past, and both types may perform similar work in similar settings.

Clinical psychologists and counseling psychologists are trained to perform research on the nature, diagnosis, and treatment of mental illness. They also both provide *psychotherapy*, which involves helping patients better cope with difficult experiences, thoughts, feelings, and behavior. Both types of psychologists also learn how to administer and interpret psychological tests in order to diagnose and treat psychological problems and disorders more effectively.

Psychiatrists, Psychiatric Nurses, and General Practitioners

Someone with an M.D. (doctor of medicine) degree can choose to receive further training in a residency that focuses on mental disorders, becoming a **psychiatrist**. A psychiatrist is qualified to prescribe medications; psychologists in the United States, except for appropriately trained psychologists in New Mexico and Louisiana, currently may not prescribe medications (other states are considering allowing appropriately trained psychologists to prescribe). But psychiatrists usually have not been taught how to interpret and understand psychological tests and have not

Clinical psychologist
A mental health professional who has a doctoral degree that requires several years of related coursework and several years of treating patients while receiving supervision from experienced clinicians.

Counseling psychologist
A mental health professional who has either a Ph.D. degree from a psychology program that focuses on counseling or an Ed.D. degree from a school of education.

Psychiatrist
A mental health professional who has an M.D. degree and has completed a residency that focuses on mental disorders.

been required to acquire detailed knowledge of research methods used in the field of psychopathology.

Psychiatric nurses have an M.S.N. (master of science in nursing) degree, plus a C.S. (clinical specialization) certificate in psychiatric nursing; a psychiatric nurse may also be certified as a psychiatric nurse practitioner (N.P.). Psychiatric nurses normally work in a hospital or clinic to provide psychotherapy; in these settings, they work closely with physicians to administer and monitor patient medications. Psychiatric nurses are also qualified to provide psychotherapy in private practice and are permitted in some states to monitor and prescribe medications independently (Haber et al., 2003).

Although not considered a mental health professional, a *general practitioner* (GP), or family doctor—the doctor you may see once a year for a checkup—may inquire about psychological symptoms, may diagnose a psychological disorder, and may recommend to patients that they see a mental health professional. Responding to pressure to reduce insurance companies' medical costs, general practitioners frequently prescribe medication for some psychological disorders. However, studies have found that treatment with medication is less effective when prescribed by a family doctor than when prescribed by psychiatrists, who are specialists in mental disorders and more familiar with the nuances of such treatment (Lin et al., 2000; Wang et al., 2005; Wilson, Duszynski, & Mant, 2003). Responding to general practitioners, medical staff in hospitals' emergency departments must also determine whether some individuals who arrive there have a psychological disorder and, if so, what immediate treatment to recommend.

Mental Health Professionals with Master's Degrees

In addition to psychiatric nurses, some other mental health professionals have master's degrees. Most **social workers** have an M.S.W. (master of social work) degree and may have had training to provide psychotherapy to help individuals and families. Social workers also teach clients how to find and benefit from the appropriate social services offered in their community. For example, they may help clients to apply for Medicare or may facilitate home visits from health care professionals. Most states also license *marriage and family therapists* (M.F.T.s), who have at least a master's degree and are trained to provide psychotherapy to couples and families. Other therapists may have a master's degree (M.A.) in some area of counseling or clinical psychology, which indicates that their training consisted of fewer courses and research experience, and less supervised clinical training than that of their doctoral-level counterparts. Some counselors may have had particular training in *pastoral counseling*, which provides counseling from a spiritual or faith-based perspective.

Table 3.5 reviews the different types of mental health clinicians.

Table 3.5 ▸ Clinicians Who Diagnose Mental Disorders

Type of Clinician	Specific Title and Credentials
Doctoral-Level Psychologists	Clinical psychologists (including clinical neuropsychologists) and counseling psychologists have a Ph.D., Psy.D., or Ed.D. degree and have advanced training in the treatment of mental illness.
Medical Personnel	Psychiatrists and general practitioners have a M.D. degree; psychiatrists have had advanced training in the treatment of mental illness. Psychiatric nurses have a M.S.N. degree and have advanced training in the treatment of mental illness.
Master's-Level Mental Health Professionals	Social workers with a master's degree (M.S.W.), marriage and family therapists (M.F.T.), and master's level counselors (M.A.) are mental health clinicians who have received specific training in helping people with problems in daily living or with mental illness. Psychiatric nurses have master's level training.

Psychiatric nurse
A mental health professional who has an M.S.N. degree, plus a C.S. certificate in psychiatric nursing.

Social worker
A mental health professional who has an M.S.W. degree and may have had training to provide psychotherapy to help individuals and families.

Key Concepts and Facts About Diagnosing Psychological Disorders

- Among other purposes, classification systems for diagnosis allow: (1) patients to be able to put a name to their experiences and to learn that they are not alone; (2) clinicians to distinguish "normal" from "abnormal" psychological functioning and to group together similar types of problems; and (3) researchers to discover the etiology, course, and effectiveness of treatments for abnormal psychological functioning.

- Classification systems also have drawbacks. They can be subject to diagnostic bias—perhaps on the basis of the patient's sex, race, or ethnicity. For some people, being diagnosed with a psychological disorder is experienced as stigmatizing, which changes how the person feels about himself or herself or is seen by others.

- Classification systems should be both reliable and valid. Reliability is less likely when the criteria for disorders are not clear and when the criteria for different disorders significantly overlap.

- The most commonly used classification system in the United States is the *Diagnostic and Statistical Manual of Mental Disorders*, presently in its fourth edition, text revision (DSM-IV-TR). The DSM-IV-TR:

  - generally does not focus on etiology (the causes of disorders), but instead focuses on what can be observed rather than inferred;

  - lists explicit criteria for each disorder and includes a multiaxial system for clinicians and researchers to record diagnoses as well as additional information (medical status, comorbid psychological disorders, psychosocial and environmental problems, assessments of current and past functioning) that may affect diagnosis, prognosis, and treatment.

- DSM-IV-TR has been criticized on numerous grounds:

  - What constitutes clinically significant distress or impaired functioning is subjective and can vary widely from one clinician to another.

  - Disorders are classified as categorical rather than as on continua.

  - The way the criteria are structured leads to heterogeneous groups being diagnosed with the same disorder.

  - Every criterion for a given disorder is generally weighted equally to the others.

  - The duration criteria can be arbitrary and not necessarily supported by research.

  - Some sets of criteria are too restrictive.

  - With each edition of the DSM, the number of psychological disorders grows (DSM-IV-TR identifies almost 300 disorders). Many diagnoses have been created in order to ensure payment from health insurance providers.

  - Diagnoses have been added for disorders that clearly are medical problems.

  - Social factors that lead or contribute to psychological disorders are deemphasized.

  - There is a high comorbidity rate: Half the people diagnosed with one disorder have at least one other disorder.

  - Commonalities that underlie disorders across the categories are difficult to identify.

- Psychological disorders are generally diagnosed by clinical and counseling psychologists, psychiatrists, psychiatric nurses, and social workers. Other clinicians in a position to diagnose psychological disorders include general practitioners, pastoral counselors, and marriage and family therapists. Each type of clinician has received somewhat different training and therefore may gather different types of information and use that information in different ways.

Assessing Psychological Disorders

People came to know about Rose Mary and Rex Walls through the eyes of their daughter, Jeannette. In her memoir, Jeannette reports incidents that seem to be clear cases of neglect and irresponsible behavior. How might a mental health clinician or researcher have gone about assessing Rose Mary's or Rex's mental health? Although mental health clinicians might read Jeannette Walls's memoir, hear her speak about her parents, or even see brief video clips of Rose Mary Walls, the information conveyed by those accounts isn't adequate to make a clinical assessment: Jeannette's memoir—and Rose Mary's brief statements on videotape—portray what Jeannette and the video directors chose to include; we don't know about events that were not discussed or portrayed, and we don't know how accurate Jeannette's childhood memories are. Other people's accounts of an individual's mental health generally provide only narrow slices of information—brief glimpses *as seen from their own points of view*, none of which is that of a mental health clinician. Without use of the formal tools and techniques of clinical assessment, any conclusions are likely to be speculative.

Were it possible to obtain information about Rose Mary and Rex Walls directly, what specific information would a clinician want to know in order to make a diagnosis and recommendations for treatment? More generally, what types of information are included in a clinical assessment? The answer depends, in part, on several factors related to the assessment:

- *The reason for the assessment* determines the questions that are to be asked and answered by the assessment; possible reasons for making an assessment include:
  - *To obtain additional information in order to make a diagnosis;*
  - *To monitor the course of the symptoms;*
  - *To determine what type of treatment might be most beneficial;* or
  - *To monitor the progress of treatment.*
- *The type of clinician making the assessment* determines, by virtue of his or her training, the types of information to be obtained.
- *The setting in which the clinician works* determines how much information is gathered; if the assessment is part of a research project, it may be more comprehensive than an assessment that is not part of a research project.
- *Financial issues related to the assessment* determine what specific methods of obtaining information will—and will not—be paid for. Health insurance companies, for instance, may be reluctant to pay for assessment methods that are not crucial in determining diagnosis or appropriate treatment.

Just like classification systems, assessment tools and techniques must be *reliable*. Other clinicians or researchers who make a clinical assessment of the same patient using the same method should obtain the same information. Similarly, assessment tools and techniques should be *valid*—they should assess the problem or aspect of functioning that they are intended to assess. And just because an assessment tool or technique is reliable, that doesn't necessarily mean it is valid. For instance, a questionnaire designed to assess the extent of an individual's preoccupying worries might be very reliable, but the questions might ask about preoccupying thoughts generally. If so, then people newly in love (and preoccupied with thoughts of their new partner) would achieve high scores; in that case, the test might measure *preoccupation* reliably, but not be a valid measure of preoccupation with worries per se.

In addition, clinicians should take into account an individual's cultural background when determining which assessment tools to use and how to interpret the resulting information. Not all assessment tools have comparison data for people from various ethnic backgrounds; comparing an individual's data or scores against those of a culturally dissimilar group will provide information that is not necessarily valid (Poortinga, 1995).

A complete clinical assessment can include various types of information about three main categories of factors: neurological and other biological factors (the structure and functioning of brain and body), psychological factors (behavior, emotion and mood, mental processes and contents, past and current ability to function), and social factors (the social context of the patient's problems, the living environment and community, family history and family functioning, history of the person's relationships, and level of financial resources and social support available). Most types of assessment focus primarily on one type of factor. We'll consider assessments of each of these main types of factors in the following sections.

Assessing Neurological and Other Biological Factors

In some cases, clinicians assess neurological (and other biological) functioning in order to determine whether abnormal mental processes and mental contents, affect, or behaviors arise from a medical problem, such as a brain tumor or abnormal hormone levels. In other cases, researchers seek to understand neurological and other biological factors that may be related to a particular disorder, because this

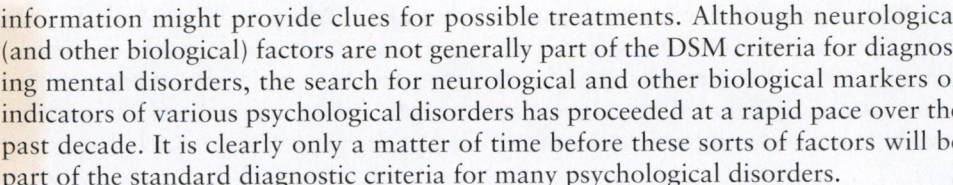

information might provide clues for possible treatments. Although neurological (and other biological) factors are not generally part of the DSM criteria for diagnosing mental disorders, the search for neurological and other biological markers or indicators of various psychological disorders has proceeded at a rapid pace over the past decade. It is clearly only a matter of time before these sorts of factors will be part of the standard diagnostic criteria for many psychological disorders.

Assessing Abnormal Brain Structures with X-Rays, CT Scans, and MRIs

Some psychological disorders, such as schizophrenia, appear to involve structural abnormalities of the brain. This is why clinical assessments sometimes make use of scans of a patient's brain. *Neuroimaging techniques* provide images of the brain. The oldest neuroimaging technique involves taking pictures of a person's brain using *X-rays*. A computer can then analyze these X-ray images and reconstruct a three-dimensional image of the brain. **Computerized axial tomography (CT)** (*tomography* is from a Greek word for "section") builds an image of a person's brain, slice by slice, creating a CT scan (sometimes called a CAT scan).

A more recent technology, **magnetic resonance imaging (MRI)**, makes especially sharp images of the brain, which allows more precise diagnoses when brain abnormalities are subtle. MRI makes use of the magnetic properties of different atoms, which resonate at different frequencies. Here's the basic idea: First, a large magnet is turned on, which causes atoms in the brain to line up with its magnetic field. Each atom has a north and south pole. Because opposite magnetic poles attract and like poles repel, the atoms become aligned with the magnetic field. Second, another magnetic field, presented from a different angle, is activated. This field will turn some of the atoms away from their alignment with the first field. Which atoms are affected by this second field? This depends on the rate at which this second field is pulsing: Different kinds of atoms resonate with different frequencies of pulses and align with this second magnetic field. The crucial part of an MRI is that when the second field is turned off completely, the atoms that had lined up with it will now reorient themselves with the first field. When the atoms that oriented with the second field move back to be aligned with the first one, they create a signal that can be recorded. This signal is translated into an image that shows where the atoms were located. By detecting different atoms and combining the signals into images, MRI can indicate the location of damaged tissue and can reveal particular parts of the brain that are larger or smaller than normal. For instance, an MRI can reveal the shrinkage of brain tissue that typically arises with chronic alcoholism (Rosenbloom, Sullivan, & Pfefferbaum, 2003); had Rex Walls had an MRI, it might well have shown that his brain had such shrinkage.

CT scans and MRIs can provide amazing images of the structure of the living brain. For example, some people with schizophrenia have larger ventricles (interior, fluid-filled spaces in the brain) than do people who do not have the disorder (Schneider-Axmann et al., 2006). These larger ventricles may occur, at least in part, because some of the surrounding brain tissue is smaller than normal, particularly in the thalamus (Gaser et al., 2004).

Assessing Brain Function With PET Scans and fMRI

Some mental disorders are associated not with abnormal brain structures (physical makeup), but rather with abnormal brain functioning (how the brain operates). By analogy, a laptop computer can fail to read CDs because the drawer for the CD won't open or the disk won't fit in the slot (a structural problem) or because the program that reads the disks gets corrupted (a functional problem). In a similar way, the brain can produce abnormal thoughts, feelings, and behaviors because either its structure or its functioning is awry. Researchers use different types of brain scans to assess brain functioning.

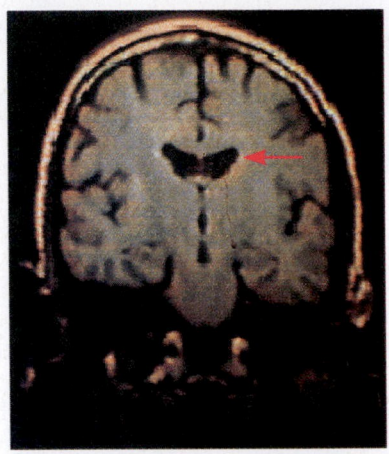

Schizophrenia

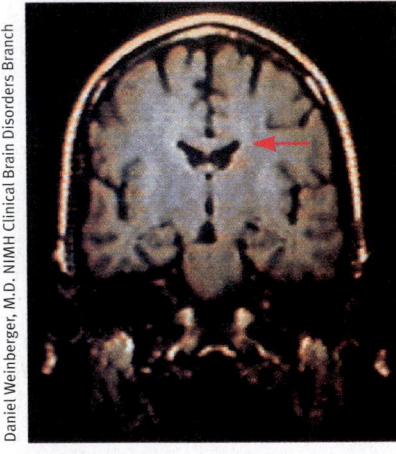

No schizophrenia

People with schizophrenia tend to have abnormally large ventricles (fluid-filled spaces in the brain). Compare these two images: The ventricles are indicated by the red arrows.

Daniel Weinberger, M.D. NIMH Clinical Brain Disorders Branch

We've just talked about how certain neuroimaging techniques can reveal brain structure, but how can researchers observe brain functioning? A key fact is that when a part of the brain is active, more blood (which transports oxygen and nutrients) flows to it, a little like the way that more electricity flows into a house when more appliances are turned on. The neurons draw more blood while they are sending and receiving signals than they do when they are not activated, because the activity increases their need for oxygen and nutrients. Because neurons in the same area of the brain tend to work together, specific areas of the brain will have greater blood flow while a person performs particular tasks.

In the field of psychopathology, researchers use functional neuroimaging to identify brain areas related to specific aspects of a disorder. For example, in one study, researchers asked participants with social phobia, who were afraid of speaking in public, to speak to a group and also to speak in private while their brains were scanned. As shown in Figure 3.2, speaking in public activated key parts of the limbic system, particularly the amygdala, more than did speaking in private (Tillfors et al., 2001). As noted in Chapter 2, the amygdala is involved in strong emotion, particularly fear. This part of the brain was not activated when people without a social phobia were tested. Other researchers have reported similar results for other sorts of phobias (Pissiota et al., 2003; Rauch et al., 1995).

The functional neuroimaging technique used in the study of social phobia just described was **positron emission tomography (PET)**, one of the most important methods for measuring blood flow (or energy consumption) in the brain. PET requires introducing a very small amount of a radioactive substance into the bloodstream. While a person performs a task, active regions of the brain take up more blood (and thus more of the radioactive substance) than less active regions. The relative amounts of radiation from different areas of the brain are measured and sent to a computer, which constructs a three-dimensional image of the brain that shows the levels of activity in the different areas. In PET images, higher radiation (greater activity) typically is indicated with brighter colors. PET scanning has drawbacks, such as the need to introduce radioactive substances and the need to have the person perform the same task for at least 40 seconds; in addition, a single test can cost $2,000.

Figure 3.2

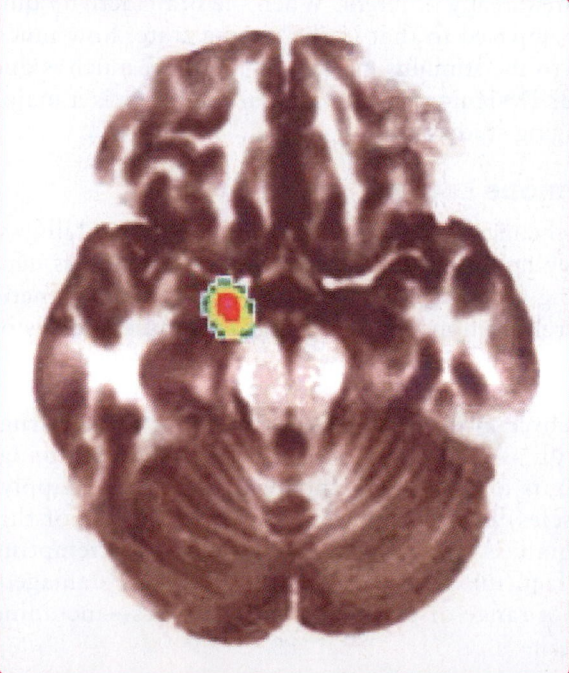

3.2 ▸ Social Phobia and the Amygdala Results from PET scans showing increased activation in the region of the amygdala when people with social phobia spoke to an audience compared to when they spoke in private; brighter colors indicate greater activation. The PET results are superimposed on an MRI scan to show the location of activated areas (Tillfors et al., 2001).

Computerized axial tomography (CT)
A neuroimaging technique that uses X-rays to build a three-dimensional image (CT or CAT scan) of the brain.

Magnetic resonance imaging (MRI)
A neuroimaging technique that creates especially sharp images of the brain by measuring the magnetic properties of atoms in the brain; MRI allows more precise diagnoses when brain abnormalities are subtle.

Positron emission tomography (PET)
A neuroimaging technique that measures blood flow (or energy consumption) in the brain and requires introducing a very small amount of a radioactive substance into the bloodstream.

Functional magnetic resonance imaging (fMRI) is currently the most widely used method for measuring human brain function. Neuroimaging with fMRI typically relies on three facts: (1) Iron affects the way that the hydrogen atoms in water molecules respond to the magnetic fields used in fMRI. (2) The presence of oxygen diminishes this effect of iron. (3) Hemoglobin, the crucial component of red blood cells that allows them to carry oxygen throughout the body and brain, has iron atoms in its structure. The key here is that the effects of the iron are different when the hemoglobin carries oxygen than when it has been stripped of its oxygen (because the oxygen was used for cell metabolism). When a region of the brain is activated, it draws blood more quickly than the oxygen carried by the hemoglobin in the blood can be used. This means that red blood cells with oxygenated hemoglobin accumulate in the activated region—and this increase is what is measured in an fMRI scan. Brain regions that are not activated (or are activated less strongly) when a person is performing a particular task (such as speaking in public or looking at pictures) draw less blood, and the oxygen carried by the blood gets used up. The difference in oxygen levels due to brain activity is reflected in the fMRI images.

The advantages of fMRI over PET include the absence of radiation and the ability to construct brain images showing activation that occurs in just a few seconds. Disadvantages include the requirement that a participant must lie very still in the narrow tube of a noisy machine (which some people find uncomfortable); in addition, any metal object containing iron cannot be brought into the machine.

Neither PET nor fMRI simply detects which parts of the brain are "on" or "off" at a particular time. Even at rest, the brain is never completely "off," so activity in the brain during a particular task is always measured *relative* to activity during another condition. In many neuroimaging studies, researchers compare activity when the participants are performing a given task with activity when they are "resting." However, researchers cannot know what is happening in the brain while a particular participant is at rest. For instance, even if two participants are both daydreaming while supposedly at rest, they may be thinking about different things, which would produce different resting states in their brains. A person with depression might be thinking about how hopeless everything seems, whereas someone with schizophrenia may be thinking about a particular delusion. The same stimulus in the task itself might affect the two participants' brains differently, but the two resting states are already different. When the brain activity during performance of the task is compared to that in the resting state, how much of the observed difference is due to the stimulus in the task and how much is due to differences in the resting state? Designing proper comparison tasks is a major challenge in functional neuroimaging studies.

Neurotransmitter and Hormone Levels

Many researchers study how biochemical imbalances contribute to mental illness. However, researchers are just beginning to develop reliable ways to assess neurotransmitter levels in functioning human brains (Gujar et al., 2005). **Magnetic resonance spectroscopy (MRS)** relies on magnetic resonance to assess levels of neurotransmitter substances in the brain. For example, Smith and her colleagues (2001) used MRS to scan the brains of children whose mothers used cocaine while they were pregnant, thereby exposing their unborn infants to this drug. Even though the children were, on average, 8 years old at the time of scanning, they had abnormally high amounts of creatine (a chemical involved in supplying energy to neurons and muscles) in their frontal lobes. High levels of this substance indicate increased numbers of glial cells, which may be attempting to repair damaged tissue. If, in fact, the children's frontal lobes were damaged, the damage could contribute to a range of psychological disorders—including problems inhibiting aggression.

Functional magnetic resonance imaging (fMRI)
A neuroimaging technique that uses MRI to obtain images of brain functioning, which reveal the extent to which different brain areas are activated during particular tasks.

Magnetic resonance spectroscopy (MRS)
A neuroimaging technique that uses magnetic resonance to assess levels of neurotransmitter substances in the brain.

In addition to using MRS, researchers measure the levels of chemical by-products of neurotransmitters in blood, urine, or cerebrospinal fluid (the fluid that surrounds the brain and spinal cord) in order to get a sense of the role of neurotransmitters in psychological disorders. For example, Geracioti and colleagues (2006) studied the cerebrospinal fluid of patients who had major depression or posttraumatic stress disorder (PTSD) and found in both groups higher than normal levels of a by-product of *substance P* (a neurotransmitter substance known to be involved in registering pain). The researchers also found that more of this by-product was present when the patients with PTSD viewed aversive videos (which triggered their symptoms) than when they viewed neutral videos. Such studies can not only provide information about neurological and other biological differences that characterize people who have different disorders, but also help reveal why specific stimuli can exacerbate the symptoms of a disorder.

Furthermore, PET techniques that use *ligands*, radioactive molecules that mimic neurotransmitters, can reveal where receptors for given neurotransmitters are located in the brain. As noted in Chapter 2, some aspects of mental illness may be related to dysfunctional receptor systems. For example, Tauscher and colleagues (2001) injected a ligand that mimics serotonin into the blood of healthy volunteers and observed how much of that ligand bound to one type of serotonin receptor. They also found that people who had higher levels of anxiety showed less binding of this ligand.

Researchers and clinicians also want to assess the levels of specific hormones to determine whether they may contribute to mental illness. For instance, symptoms of depression are sometimes caused by low levels of the hormone *thyroxin*, which is measured by a blood test (Pfennig et al., 2004). Depressed individuals who have low levels of thyroxin might be prescribed thyroid supplements as part of their treatment (Altshuler et al., 2001).

Neuropsychological Assessment

An assessment of neurological factors may include **neuropsychological testing**, which uses behavioral responses to test items in order to draw inferences about brain functioning. Assessing neuropsychological functioning allows clinicians and researchers to distinguish the effects of brain damage from the effects of psychological problems (for example, disrupted speech can be caused by either of these). Neuropsychological assessment is also used to determine whether brain damage is contributing to psychological problems (for example, frontal lobe damage can disrupt the ability to inhibit aggressive behavior). Unlike functional neuroimaging, which identifies brain areas activated during a given task (relative to another task), neuropsychological testing gives a broad picture of the brain's functioning. A neuropsychological assessment determines the sorts of basic functions that the brain can do effectively, can do with effort, or cannot perform. Moreover, the results can suggest that specific parts of the brain may be damaged. Although much less precise, such testing is significantly less expensive and easier to administer than neuroimaging, and it can be given in any quiet room.

Neuropsychological tests range from those that assess complex abilities (such as judgment or planning) to those that assess a relatively specific ability, such as the ability to recognize faces (measured by the Facial Recognition Test; Benton et al., 1983). For example, in one version of the Facial Recognition Test, a patient is shown a photo of a "target" face, then a set of six photos of faces from which the patient must pick out the target. In another version of the Facial Recognition Test, the six photos differ in lighting or orientation, and the patient must pick out the three that show the target face. Other neuropsychological tests, such as the Bender Visual-Motor Gestalt Test-II (2nd edition) (Bender, 1963; Brannigan & Decker, 2003), assess more

Neuropsychological testing
The employment of assessment techniques that use behavioral responses to test items in order to draw inferences about brain functioning.

The Rey Osterrieth Test requires the test-taker to copy a complex figure, and then draw it from memory; the test assesses visual perception, organizational ability, and memory.

Photo Edit

complex functions. In the Bender Visual-Motor Gestalt Test, patients are shown a series of drawings that range from simple to complex and are asked to reproduce them. This test assesses the integration of visual and motor functioning, which involves many distinct parts of the brain. The test may be used to help diagnose various problems, including learning disorders and memory problems (Brannigan & Decker, 2006).

There are also sets of neuropsychological tests, such as the Luria-Nebraska Neuropsychological Battery (Golden, Hammeke, & Purisch, 1980), which consists of 14 tests that measure different abilities, or the Halstead-Reitan Neuropsychological Battery (Reitan & Davison, 1974), which consists of 10 tests that measure different abilities. When specific neuropsychological tests suggest possible brain areas that may be affected, the status of those areas can be verified by neuroimaging. A neuropsychologist may administer a whole battery of tests or only specific tests, depending on the reason for the assessment and what information is already known about the patient's brain damage and ability to function.

Assessing Psychological Factors

If Rose Mary and Rex Walls had been willing to see a mental health clinician, how would the clinician have gone about assessing psychological factors relating to their unusual behavior and beliefs? What would such an assessment entail? During an assessment, clinicians and researchers often seek to identify the ways in which psychological functioning is disordered and the ways in which it is not. For instance, a clinical assessment would shed light on the extent to which Rex Walls's problems were primarily a result of his drinking or arose from underlying impairments that may have been masked by his pronounced drinking. According to Jeannette's memoir, during the two stretches when Rex was sober, his functioning significantly improved.

Certain areas of psychological functioning—mental processes and mental contents, affect, and behavior—are often directly related to DSM-IV-TR criteria for specific disorders. Further, these areas are frequently the most relevant for determining a person's current and future ability to function in daily activities.

Mental health researchers and clinicians employ a variety of assessment techniques and tools to ascertain psychological functioning, including interviews and tests of cognitive and personality functioning. Which tools and techniques are used depends on the purpose of the assessment. In the case of Rex and Rose Mary Walls, the purpose of the assessment could be to determine whether either one or both of them: (1) was so impaired that he or she posed a potential imminent danger to self or others, and thus might best be admitted to a psychiatric unit of a hospital to be observed around the clock; (2) was impaired enough to qualify for disability payments; (3) had a psychological disorder, and if so, what specific disorder it was and what type of treatment might be appropriate. If an assessment had been made while Rex and Rose Mary's children were still living with them, it could have helped the clinician determine whether either or both parents were competent to be responsible for their underage children.

Clinical Interview

An important tool used to assess psychological functioning is the **clinical interview**, a meeting between clinician and patient during which the clinician asks questions related to the patient's symptoms and functioning. A clinical interview provides two types of information: the content of the answers to the interview questions, and the manner in which the person answered them (Westen & Weinberger, 2004). Questions may focus on symptoms, general functioning, degree and type of impairment, and the patient's relevant history.

In an *unstructured interview*, the clinician asks whatever questions he or she deems appropriate, depending on the patient's responses. In contrast, in a *structured interview*, the clinician uses a fixed set of questions to guide the interview. The advantage of an unstructured interview is that it allows the clinician to pursue

Clinical interview
A meeting between clinician and patient during which the clinician asks questions related to the patient's symptoms and functioning.

topics and issues specific to the patient. However, different clinicians who use this approach to interview the same patient may arrive at different diagnoses, because each clinician's interview may cover different topics and therefore gather different information. Another problem with unstructured interviews is that the interviewer may neglect to gather important information about the context of the problem and the individual's cultural background. In contrast, a structured interview is likely to yield a more reliable diagnosis because each clinician asks the same set of questions. However, such a diagnosis may be less valid, because the questions asked may not be relevant to the patient's particular symptoms, issues, or concerns (Meyer, 2002). That is, different clinicians using a structured interview may agree on the diagnosis, but all of them may be missing the boat about the nature of the problem and may diagnose the wrong disorder. A *semistructured interview* combines elements of both of the other types: Specific questions guide the interview, but the clinician also has the freedom to pose additional questions that may be relevant, depending on the patient's answers to the standard questions.

Observation

All types of interviews provide an opportunity for the clinician or researcher to observe and make inferences about different aspects of a patient:

- *Appearance.* Has he or she bathed recently? Is he or she dressed appropriately? In addition to these obvious aspects of appearance, signs of disorders can sometimes be noted by carefully observing subtle aspects of a person's appearance. For example, patients with the eating disorder bulimia nervosa (to be discussed in Chapter 10) may regularly induce vomiting; as a result of repeated vomiting, their parotid glands, located in the cheeks, may swell and create a somewhat puffy look to the cheeks (similar to a chipmunk's cheeks). Such patients may also have scars on their hands where repeated exposure to stomach acid has damaged the skin (which occurs when they put their hands down their throats to induce vomiting).

- *Behavior.* The patient's body language, facial expression, movements, and speech can provide insights into different aspects of psychological functioning:

  - *Emotions.* What emotions does the patient convey? The clinician can observe the patient's expression of distress (or lack thereof) and emotional state (upbeat, "low," intense, uncontrollable, inappropriate to the situation, or at odds with the content of what the patient says).

  - *Movement.* The patient's general level of movement—physical restlessness or a complete lack of movement—may indicate abnormal functioning.

  - *Speech.* Clinicians observe the rate and contents of the patient's speech: Speaking very quickly may suggest anxiety, mania, or certain kinds of substance abuse; speaking very slowly may suggest depression or other kinds of substance abuse.

  - *Mental processes.* Do the patient's mental processes appear to be unusual or abnormal? Does the patient appear to be talking to someone who is not in the room, which would suggest that he or she is having hallucinations? Can the patient remember what the clinician just asked? Does the patient flit from topic to topic, unable to stay focused on answering a single question?

Another aspect of the patient's speech that clinicians may note is whether it follows grammatical rules and a logical pattern. Here's a clear example of an abnormal speech pattern that indicates impaired mental processes: "If we need soap when you can jump into a pool of water, and then when you go to buy your gasoline, my folks always thought they should get pop, but the best thing is to get motor oil . . ." (Andreasen, 1979, p. 41).

Behaviors observed during a clinical interview can, in some cases, provide more information than the patient's report about the nature of the problem. In other cases, such observations round out an assessment; it is the patient's own report of the problem—its history and related matters—that provides the foundation of the interview. In any case, the clinician must keep in mind that "unusual" behavior should perhaps be interpreted differently for patients from different cultural backgrounds. For instance, Japanese people, as a rule, express less emotion in their faces (Ekman, 1984). A clinician should not necessarily interpret a Japanese immigrant's reduced emotional expression as indicating flat affect. Conversely, should a Japanese immigrant display anger that would seem "normal" for an American, the clinician might inquire further about the patient's anger and ability to control his or her emotions. Moreover, the same principle applies to different age groups; for example, what is usual for a middle-aged adult might not be usual for an older adult (Baden & Wong, 2008).

Patient's Self-Report

Some symptoms cannot be observed directly, such as the hallucinations that characterize schizophrenia, or the worries and fears that characterize some anxiety disorders. Thus, the patient's own report of his or her experiences becomes a crucial part of the clinical assessment.

At some point in the interview process, the clinician will ask about the patient's history—past factors or events that may illuminate the current difficulties. For example, the clinician will ask about current and past psychiatric or medical problems and about how the patient understands these problems and possible solutions to them. The clinician will inquire about substance use, sexual or physical abuse or other traumatic experiences, economic hardships, and relationships with family members and others. This information helps the clinician put the patient's current difficulties in context and determine whether his or her psychological functioning is maladaptive or adaptive, given the environmental circumstances (Kirk & Hsieh, 2004).

Some patients, however, intentionally report having symptoms that they don't actually have or exaggerate symptoms they do have, either for material gain or to avoid unwanted events (such as criminal prosecution)—such behavior is the hallmark of **malingering**. For instance, a malingering soldier may exaggerate his or her anxiety symptoms and claim to have posttraumatic stress disorder in order to avoid further combat. Malingering contrasts with **factitious disorder**, which occurs when someone intentionally pretends to have symptoms or even induces symptoms so that he or she can assume a "sick" role and receive attention. A soldier with factitious disorder might exaggerate or invent anxiety symptoms *not* to avoid combat, but for the attention he or she might receive from other soldiers or from clinicians. Whereas both malingering and factitious disorder involve deception—inventing or exaggerating symptoms—the motivations are different. Unlike those with malingering, people with factitious disorder do not deceive others about their symptoms for material gain or to avoid negative events.

Most patients intend to report their current problems and history as accurately as possible. Nevertheless, even honest self-reports are subject to various biases. Most fundamentally, patients may accurately report what they remember, but their memory of the frequency, intensity, or duration of their symptoms may not be entirely accurate. As we noted in Chapter 2, emotion can bias what we notice, perceive, and remember.

Another bias that can affect what patients say about their symptoms is *reporting bias*—inaccuracies or distortions in a patient's report because of a desire to appear in a particular way (Meyer, 2002). In some cases, patients may not really know the answer to a question asked in a clinical interview. For instance, when asked, "Why did you do that?" they may not have thought about their motivation before and may not *really* be aware of what it was, but instead create an answer on the spot (Westen & Weinberger, 2004).

In other cases, people's psychological functioning is sufficiently impaired that they confuse their internal world—their memories, fears, beliefs, fantasies, or dreams—with reality, which leads to inaccuracies in self-reports; delusions are such an impairment. For instance, Rex Walls frequently told stories about his past, including his

Malingering
Intentional false reporting of symptoms or exaggeration of existing symptoms, either for material gain or to avoid unwanted events.

Factitious disorder
A psychological disorder marked by the false reporting or inducing of medical or psychological symptoms in order to assume a "sick" role and receive attention.

years with the Air Force; his stories often involved his heroic actions that saved others (such as fixing a broken sluicegate at Hoover Dam or safely landing a plane after an engine failed). According to Jeannette, "Dad always fought harder, flew faster, and gambled smarter than everyone else in his stories. Along the way, he rescued women and children and even men who weren't as strong and clever" (Walls, 2005, p. 24). A clinical assessment could help determine the extent to which Rex's stories were merely embellishments to make him look good or were delusions. It can be useful to obtain information from family, friends, or other people who are in a position to confirm or modify a patient's report in order to distinguish delusions from embellishments.

Here's an example of how simply asking patients about themselves during clinical interviews may not always lead to an accurate picture of their psychological functioning, despite their honesty. One of the authors of this book (Rosenberg) once worked in a hospital emergency room, evaluating people who came to the emergency room for psychiatric reasons. One day, she was asked to interview a man in his 30s who was dressed appropriately and spoke somewhat slowly. He had a history of schizophrenia and depression, and his psychiatrist was affiliated with the hospital. The patient reported that he came to the hospital because his mother wanted him to come (in fact, she drove him there), but he wasn't exactly sure why. He said that he wasn't hearing voices, and he didn't feel sad, depressed, or suicidal. In response to questions, his mental processes and mental contents seemed normal. Rosenberg telephoned his psychiatrist, who was puzzled about why the patient had come to the emergency room. The psychiatrist could shed no light on the matter; he had an appointment scheduled with the patient the following week, but he did not know why the patient's mother brought him to the hospital.

Rosenberg asked the patient's permission to speak with his mother; he consented. The mother, a woman in her 60s, reported that she thought her son had been more depressed lately. She went on to explain that for the last month he hadn't gotten out of bed unless he had a doctor's appointment. On those days, she harangued him until he bathed, groomed himself, and put on appropriate clothes (as she had also done the day he came to the emergency room). The other days he stayed in bed in his pajamas. When Rosenberg spoke to the psychiatrist, he had not known that his patient was depressed, or that the only reason the patient was appropriately dressed and groomed for appointments was because of his mother's insistence. When Rosenberg then spoke with the patient again, explaining what the mother had said, he admitted that he had a hard time getting out of bed, and didn't have much energy or interest in things, although he didn't *feel* depressed. He agreed that it made sense for him (and his mother) to be interviewed by staff in the inpatient psychiatric unit to determine whether he should be hospitalized; Rosenberg did not see him again, but later found out that he in fact had been hospitalized for depression.

This experience brings home the limitations of relying solely on people's self-reports of their emotional states (Achenbach et al., 2005; Meyer, 2002). This patient said that he didn't feel depressed, but key aspects of his behavior at home, in particular, his difficulty getting out of bed and his lack of energy or interest in previously interesting activities, were clear symptoms of depression. But because the patient didn't realize that these behaviors were a problem, he didn't report that he was having those symptoms. Thus, although a patient's self-report is important, it has limitations. Similarly, when interviewing children, the clinician must be sensitive to the fact that they may lack adequate insight and/or the verbal ability to be reliable reporters of their mental health status.

Semistructured Interviews

Because clinicians sometimes want to be sure to cover specific ground with their questions, they may use a semistructured interview format, asking a list of standard questions but formulating their own follow-up questions. The follow-up questions are based on patients' responses to the standard questions. One set of questions that assesses a patient's mental state at the time of the interview is the *mental status exam*. In a mental status exam, the clinician asks the patient to

Creatas/Punchstock

Some problematic behaviors may be obvious to a mental health professional while interacting with a patient. Other behaviors, which occur infrequently or only in specific types of environments, such as avoiding stepping on cracks (which some people with obsessive compulsive disorder do) are less likely to be observed. If the patient doesn't view these behaviors as a problem, he or she may not report them.

Photo Edit

As part of the mental status exam, patients are asked whether they know their own name, the date and year, and who is currently president. Patients who do not know these facts may have some type of memory impairment. Further tests will be done to determine the specific memory problems, their cause, and possible treatments.

describe the problem, its history, and the patient's functioning in different areas of life. Other standard questions in the mental status exam probe the patient's ability to reason, to perform simple mathematical computations, and to assess possible problems in memory and judgment. The clinician uses the patient's answers to the standard questions to develop hypotheses about possible diagnoses and difficulties with functioning, and then asks other questions to obtain additional information. For instance, as part of the mental status exam, patients are routinely asked whether they remember their own name, the date and year, and who is president. If the patient doesn't remember correctly who the current president is, the clinician might ask other, more detailed questions involving different aspects of memory—such as memories of other languages spoken, of more distant events or important personal events in the recent past—which may reflect an underlying neurological problem. People from other cultures may answer some of the questions in a mental status exam in unconventional ways, and clinicians must take care not to infer that "different" is "abnormal."

The mental status exam assesses cognitive, emotional, and behavioral functioning broadly, and the standard questions are not designed to obtain specific information that corresponds to the categories in DSM-IV-TR. The interviewer can arrive at a diagnosis based on answers to both standard and follow-up questions, but the goal of the mental status exam is more than diagnosis: It seeks to create a portrait of the individual's general psychological functioning.

The mental status exam contrasts with another semistructured interview format—the *Structured Clinical Interview for DSM-IV, Axes I and II* (SCID-I and SCID-II; First et al., 1997, 2002), which is generally used when the interview is part of a research project and is designed to assist the researcher in diagnosing patients according to the DSM-IV-TR. The SCID provides modules that correspond to different categories of disorders. Each module starts off with a question to assess whether the individual has symptoms related to that category of disorders. If the patient does not have such symptoms, the rest of the questions in the module are skipped. If symptoms are present, the SCID lists the questions the interviewer should ask. The questions correspond to DSM-IV-TR criteria lists, such as that in Table 3.4. Based on the patient's responses, the interviewer can readily determine which disorder (if any) is the most appropriate diagnosis. Such DSM-related tools generally do not require the interviewer to interpret patients' answers.

Clinical interviews provide a wealth of information, about the patient's symptoms and the patient's general functioning, as well as about the context in which the symptoms arose and continue. However, a thorough clinical interview can be time-consuming and may not be as reliable and valid as assessment techniques that utilize tests.

Tests of Psychological Functioning

Many different tests are available to assess different areas of psychological functioning. Some tests assess a relatively wide range of abilities and areas of functioning (such as intelligence or general personality characteristics). Other tests assess a narrow range of abilities, particular areas of functioning, or specific symptoms (such as the ability to remember new information or the tendency to avoid social gatherings).

Cognitive Assessment

One tool to assess cognitive functioning is an intelligence test. Clinicians typically use the *Wechsler Adult Intelligence Scale*, 4th edition (WAIS-IV, revised in 2008) or the *Wechsler Intelligence Scale for Children*, 4th edition (WISC-IV, revised in 2003), depending on the age of the patient. Numerical results of these tests yield an *intelligence quotient* (IQ); the average intelligence in a population is set at a score of 100, with normal intelligence ranging from 85 to 115. IQ scores of 70 to 85 are considered to be in the *borderline* range, and scores of 70 and below signify mental impairment. However, the single intelligence score is not the only important information that the WAIS-IV and WISC-IV provide. Both of these tests include subtests that assess four types of abilities:

- *verbal comprehension* (i.e., the ability to understand verbal information);
- *perceptual reasoning* (i.e., the ability to reason with nonverbal information);
- *working memory* (i.e., the ability to maintain and mentally manipulate new information); and
- *processing speed* (i.e., the ability to focus attention and quickly utilize information).

In addition, the WAIS-IV and WISC-IV are devised so that the examiner can compare an individual's responses on each of the subtests to the responses of other people of the same age and sex. Information about specific subtests helps the examiner determine the individual's pattern of relative strengths and weaknesses in intellectual functioning.

Current versions of intelligence tests have been designed to minimize the influence of cultural factors, in part by excluding test items that might require cultural knowledge that is unique to one group (and would thus put members of other groups at a disadvantage) (Kaufman et al., 1995; Poortinga, 1995). Moreover, newer tests and revisions of older tests include specific norms for different ethnic groups.

Neuropsychological testing, described earlier, can also be used for cognitive assessment. Many of the tests in a typical neuropsychological battery assess basic cognitive functions, such as perception, memory, and language comprehension. Other cognitive testing focuses purely on cognitive functions, without any regard to which parts of the brain give rise to these functions. For example, memory tests can discover whether a person has significantly greater difficulty recalling events from the relatively distant past than recalling recent events.

Personality Assessment

Various psychological tests assess different aspects of personality functioning.

Inventories In order to assess general personality functioning, a clinician may use an *inventory*—a questionnaire with items pertaining to many different problems and aspects of personality. An inventory can indicate to a clinician what problems and disorders might be most likely for a given person. Inventories usually contain test questions that are sorted into different *scales*, with each scale assessing a different facet of personality. The most commonly used inventory is the *Minnesota Multiphasic Personality Inventory,* 2nd edition (MMPI-2; Butcher & Rouse, 1996). Originally developed in the 1930s to identify people with mental illness, it was revised in 1989 to include norms of people from a wider range of racial, ethnic, and other groups and to update specific items. The MMPI-2 consists of 567 questions about the respondent's behavior, emotions, mental processes, mental contents, and other matters. The respondent rates each question as being true or false about himself or herself. The inventory generally takes between 60 and 90 minutes to complete. (There is also a short form, with 370 items.) The inventory is available in three formats: paper and pencil, an audiocassette recording, and a computer version. The MMPI-2 has been translated into many languages and is used in many different countries.

Responses on the MMPI-2 are sorted into two types of scales: validity scales and clinical scales. *Validity scales* assess whether the individual's responses are likely to be valid—that is, whether they represent an accurate self-report. The validity scales assess the degree to which the respondent answers in order to appear psychologically healthier or more impaired than he or she actually is (as occurs with malingering or factitious disorder). If the score on any of the validity scales is extremely high, an individual's responses are thought to be invalid. *Clinical scales* assess symptoms of various disorders and problems (see Table 3.6). The pattern of scores on the various scales creates a profile, as illustrated in Figure 3.3. Different profiles are associated with different patterns of personality functioning and impairment.

Table 3.6 ▸ MMPI-2 Scales

Scale	Sample Item	What Is Assessed
? (Cannot Say)	The score is the number of items that were unanswered or answered as both true and false.	An inability or unwillingness to complete the test appropriately, which could indicate the presence of symptoms that interfere with concentration.
L (Lie)	Sometimes want to swear (F).	Attempts to present himself or herself in a positive way, not admitting even minor shortcomings.
F (Infrequency)	Something wrong with mind (T).	Low scores suggest attempts to try to fake appearing to have "good" mental health or psychopathology; high scores suggest some type of psychopathology.
K (Correction)	Often feel useless (F).	More subtle attempts to exaggerate "good" mental health or psychopathology. This scale is also associated with education level—more educated people score higher than those with less education.
1. Hs (Hypochondriasis)	Body tingles (F).	An abnormal concern over bodily functioning and imagined illness.
2. D (Depression)	Usually happy (F).	Symptoms of sadness, poor morale, and hopelessness.
3. Hy (Hysteria)	Often feel very weak (T).	A propensity to develop physical symptoms under stress, along with a lack of awareness and insight about one's behavior.
4. Pd (Psychopathic Deviate)	Am misunderstood (T).	General social maladjustment, irresponsibility, or lack of conscience.
5. Mf (Masculinity-Femininity)	Like mechanics magazines (T for women).	The extent to which the individual has interests, preferences, and personal sensitivities more similar to those of the opposite sex.
6. Pa (Paranoia)	No enemies who wish me harm (F).	Sensitivity to others, suspiciousness, jealousy, and moral self-righteousness.
7. Pt (Psychasthenia)	Almost always anxious (T).	Obsessive and compulsive symptoms, poor concentration, and self-criticism.
8. Sc (Schizophrenia)	Hear strange things when alone (T).	Delusions, hallucinations, bizarre sensory experiences, and poor social relationships.
9. Ma (Hypomania)	When bored, stir things up (T).	Symptoms of hypomania—elated or irritable mood, "fast" thoughts, impulsiveness, and physical restlessness.
10. Si (Social Introversion)	Try to avoid crowds (T).	Discomfort in social situations and preference for being alone.

Note: (T) indicates that when the item is marked as true, it contributes toward a high score on the scale; (F) indicates that when the item is marked as false, it contributes toward a high score on the scale. The dark green rows above refer to the validity scales, and the light green rows refer to the clinical scales.

Source: Excerpted from the MMPI-2 Booklet of Abbreviated Items. Copyright © 2005 by the Regents of the University of Minnesota. All rights reserved. Used by permission of the University of Minnesota Press. "MMPI-2" and "Minnesota Multiphasic Personality Inventory 2" are trademarks owned by the Regents of the University of Minnesota.

Although the MMPI-2 does help a clinician or researcher to understand the nature of various clinical disorders, the results do not yield a specific DSM-IV-TR diagnosis (because this test was not designed to do so).

Projective Tests Psychologists may also wish to assess facets of patients' personalities that are less likely to emerge in a self-report, such as systematic biases in mental processes. In a **projective test**, the patient is presented with an ambiguous stimulus (such as an inkblot or a group of stick figures) and is asked to make sense of and explain the stimulus. For example, what does the inkblot look like, or what are the stick figures doing? The idea behind such a test is that the particular structure a patient imposes on the ambiguous stimulus reveals something about the patient's mental processes or mental contents. This is the theory behind the well-known *Rorschach test*, which was developed by

Projective test
A tool for personality assessment in which the patient is presented with ambiguous stimuli (such as inkblots or stick figures) and is asked to make sense of and explain them.

Figure 3.3

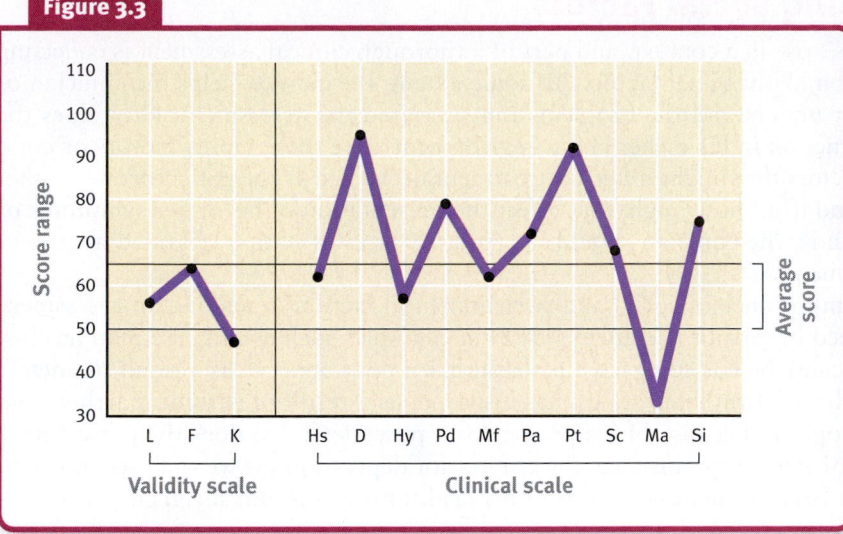

3.3 ▶ An MMPI-2 Profile for Validity and Clinical Scales This is the MMPI-2 profile of a depressed 47-year-old man. His highest clinical scores are on the D and Pt scales, followed by Pd and Si. People with this profile typically are significantly depressed, agitated, and anxious. They may brood about their own deficiencies and have concentration problems (Greene, 2000).

Herman Rorschach (1884–1922). This test includes ten inkblots, one on each of ten cards. The ambiguity of the shapes permits a patient to imagine freely what the shapes resemble.

Rorschach tests and projective tests in general have been criticized for two related reasons (Anastasi, 1988; Entwisle, 1972): (1) They do not appear to be valid (that is, to assess what they are said to measure); and, (2) they are not necessarily reliable (the assessment of a patient on one day is not necessarily the same as an assessment made on another day). John Exner (1974) addressed these criticisms by developing a systematic, comprehensive scoring system for the Rorschach test. This system has been tested extensively with a variety of populations, and it has been shown to be reasonably reliable (Sultan et al., 2006). Research shows that Exner's system also assesses psychosis reasonably well (Dao & Prevatt, 2006; Garb et al., 2005; Meyer & Archer, 2001). However, it is not as effective in assessing psychological disorders in general (Lilienfeld et al., 2000; Wood, Lilienfeld, et al., 2001). Furthermore, the norms of Exner's scoring system might lead to misdiagnosing people as having a disorder they do not, in fact, have (Wood, Nezworski, et al., 2001). Thus, although the Rorschach test may provide information regarding aspects of a patient's personality and mental functioning, it is not the only tool available to do so, and it has clear drawbacks.

Another projective test, the *Thematic Apperception Test (TAT)*, uses detailed black-and-white drawings that often include people. The TAT was developed by Christiana Morgan and Henry Murray (1935) and is used to discern motivations, thoughts, and feelings without having to ask a person directly. The patient is asked to explain the drawings in various ways: The clinician may ask the patient what is happening in the picture, what has just happened, what will happen next, or what the people in the picture might be thinking and feeling. Like the Rorschach test, the TAT elicits responses that presumably reflect unconscious beliefs, desires, fears, or issues (Murray, 1943).

Responses on the TAT may be interpreted freely by the clinician or scored according to a scoring system. However, only 3% of clinicians who use the TAT rely on a scoring system (Pinkerman, Haynes, & Keiser, 1993). Furthermore, the TAT has been criticized because responses to the drawings can be ambiguous. In particular, a clinician cannot distinguish between a patient's thoughts, feelings, or usual behavior and how the person *wants* to think, feel, or behave (Lilienfeld, Wood, & Garb, 2000). This fundamental ambiguity calls into question the rationale for using the test, which is to understand the patient's mental processes and contents without having to ask about them directly.

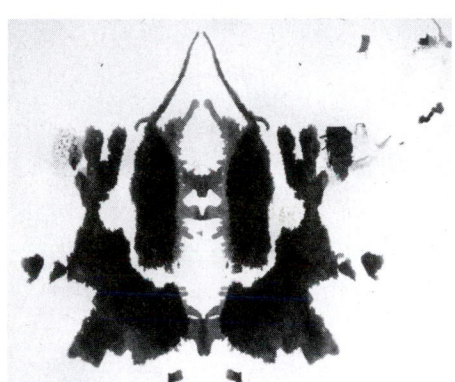

The Rorschach test is a projective test that consists of inkblots. Patients are asked what each inkblot—like the one here—looks like. The Rorschach test is based on the idea that the test-taker imposes a structure onto the ambiguous inkblot; the patient's responses are thought to reveal something about himself or herself.

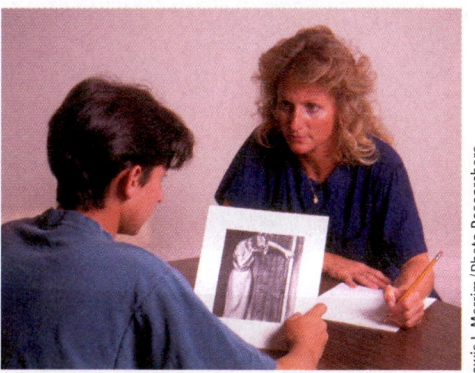

As part of the Thematic Apperception Test, patients are asked to describe the motivations, thoughts, and feelings of people portrayed in various drawings. Some clinicians consider a patient's answers to reflect unconscious beliefs, feelings, and desires.

Assessing Social Factors

Symptoms arise in a context, and part of a thorough clinical assessment is collecting information about social factors. To some extent, the context helps the clinician or researcher understand the problems that initiated the assessment: How does the patient function in his or her home environment? Are there family factors or community factors that might influence treatment decisions? Is the patient from another culture, and if so, how might that affect the presentation of his or her symptoms or influence how the clinician should interpret other information obtained as part of the assessment?

The importance of social and environmental factors in making an assessment is illustrated by Arthur Kleinman (1988) in examples such as this: If a man has lost energy because he has contracted malaria, has a poor appetite as a result of anemia (due to a hookworm infestation), has insomnia as a result of chronic diarrhea, and he feels hopeless because of his poverty and powerlessness, does the person have depression? His symptoms meet the criteria for depression (as we shall see in Chapter 6), but isn't his distress a result of his health problems and social circumstances and their consequences? Summing up his experiences as depression might limit our understanding of his situation and the best course of treatment.

Family Functioning

As noted in Chapter 2, various aspects of family functioning can affect a person's mental health. This was certainly true of the Walls family, where Rex's drinking and irresponsibility led Rose Mary to become overwhelmed and to "shut down"—staying in bed for days and crying. Similarly, their marriage appeared to have a role in Rex's drinking problem: While living on the streets of New York, Rex developed tuberculosis and was hospitalized for 6 weeks, during which time he became sober. A hospital administrator helped him obtain a job as a maintenance man in a resort in upstate New York; Rose Mary didn't want to leave the city, so he went without her. He worked and lived at the resort for almost three seasons and continued to stay sober while he was there—his longest stretch of time without a drink. As winter came, Rose Mary called him and persuaded him to come back to the city to be with her; he resumed drinking as soon as he returned (Walls, 2005).

In order to assess family functioning, clinicians may interview all or some family members or ask patients about how the family functions. Some clinicians and researchers try to assess family functioning more systematically than through interviews or observations. One tool for doing so is the *Family Environment Scale* (Moos & Moos, 1986), which requires family members to answer a set of questions. Their answers are integrated to create a profile of the family environment—how the family is organized, different types of control and conflict, family values, and emotional expressiveness. Such information helps the clinician or researcher to understand the patient within the context of his or her family and identifies possible areas of family functioning that could be improved (Ross & Hill, 2004). Another family assessment tool that focuses on family functioning is the *Family Adaptability and Cohesion Scales, Version 3* (Olson et al., 1985), which consists of 20 questions about family adaptability and cohesion that are answered by one or more family members.

Researchers have studied families in which one member has a particular type of disorder and compared these findings to those from families without such a member (Cook-Darzens et al., 2005). For example, in one Chinese study, researchers gave versions of both the Family Environment Scale and the Family Adaptability and Cohesion Scales to families that had a member with schizophrenia and families that had no member with schizophrenia. Families with a member with schizophrenia had more conflict and were less cohesive (Phillips et al., 1998). As with other assessment tools, however, an individual's or a family's data should be compared to norms of people from similar cultural backgrounds.

Note that the presence of certain distinctive characteristics in families with a member who has a psychological disorder does not necessarily indicate that these characteristics *caused* the disorder; it is possible that something about the affected family member (such as particularly intense symptoms of his or her disorder or some other characteristic) elicits certain types of behavior from other members of the family. So, for instance, families with a member who has schizophrenia may be less cohesive because the ill family member's symptoms and ensuing family stress lead other members to seek support from friendships. That is, the ill member's symptoms may decrease family cohesion, not the other way around. Thus, the assessed family environment may contribute toward, or be a product of, the family member's illness—or the family environment and the member's illness may both reflect other factors, such as living in extreme poverty.

Community

When making a clinical assessment, the clinician should try to learn about the patient's community in order to understand what normal functioning is in that environment. As we saw in Chapter 2, people who have low socioeconomic status (SES) are more likely to have psychological disorders. Those people live in poorer communities, which tend to have relatively high crime rates—and so they are more likely to witness a crime, be a victim of crime, or to live in fear. What, then, is "normal" functioning in this context?

In an effort to understand a patient within his or her social environment, "community" may be defined loosely—it can refer not only to where the patient lives, but also to where he or she spends a lot of time, such as school or the workplace. Some jobs and work settings can be particularly stressful or challenging, and a comprehensive assessment should take such information about a patient into account. Consider that some work settings place very high demands on employees—high enough that some may become "burned out" (Aziz, 2004; Lindblom et al., 2006). Symptoms of burnout (a psychological condition, though not a psychological disorder in DSM-IV-TR) include feeling chronically mentally and physically tired, dissatisfied, and performing inefficiently—which resemble symptoms of depression (Maslach, 2003; Mausner-Dorsch & Eaton, 2000).

In some cases, such as when determining whether an elderly patient whose memory is deteriorating is able to continue living at home alone, a thorough assessment may require the participation of a wide range of people in the patient's community (Gilmour, Gibson, & Campbell, 2003). The patient's medical doctor, neighbors, relatives, and community-based elder services coordinator may each contribute vital information to the assessment.

The clinician should also assess the patient's capacity to manage daily life in his or her community, considering factors such as whether the patient's psychological problems interfere with the sources for social support and ability to communicate his or her needs and interact with others in a relatively normal way. Similarly, the clinician may be asked to determine whether the patient would benefit from training to enhance his or her social skills (Combs et al., 2008).

Culture

To assess someone's reports of distress or impairment, a clinician must understand the person's culture. Different cultures have different views about complaining or describing symptoms, which influence the amount and type of symptoms people will report to a mental health clinician—which, in turn, can affect the diagnosis a clinician makes. For instance, compared to white British teenagers with anorexia nervosa, who say they are afraid of becoming fat and report being preoccupied with their weight (both symptoms are part of the criteria set for anorexia), British teenagers of South Asian background do not report these symptoms, but are more likely to report a loss of appetite (Tareen,

Getty Images

Clinicians should inquire about the problems and strengths of a patient's community, such as the presence of violence and the sources for support. Such information helps us understand the wider context of the patient's symptoms, as well as interventions that might be helpful.

Hodes, & Rangel, 2005). Thus, the reported symptoms of the British teenagers of South Asian background may not meet enough of the criteria for a diagnosis of anorexia (although they may still have significant distress, impairment, or risk of harm).

Such cultural differences may underlie, at least in part, the dramatic differences in the apparent rates of serious mental illness across countries, shown in Figure 3.4 (WHO World Mental Health Survey Consortium, 2004). (A mental illness was considered *serious* if the individual was unable to carry out his or her normal activities for at least 30 days in the past year.) These rates were based on data gathered in face-to-face interviews. Notice how much higher the rates are in the United States compared to other developed and developing countries. One explanation for this discrepancy is that Americans are less inhibited about telling strangers about their psychological problems. People in other countries might have minimized the frequency or severity of their symptoms.

Figure 3.4

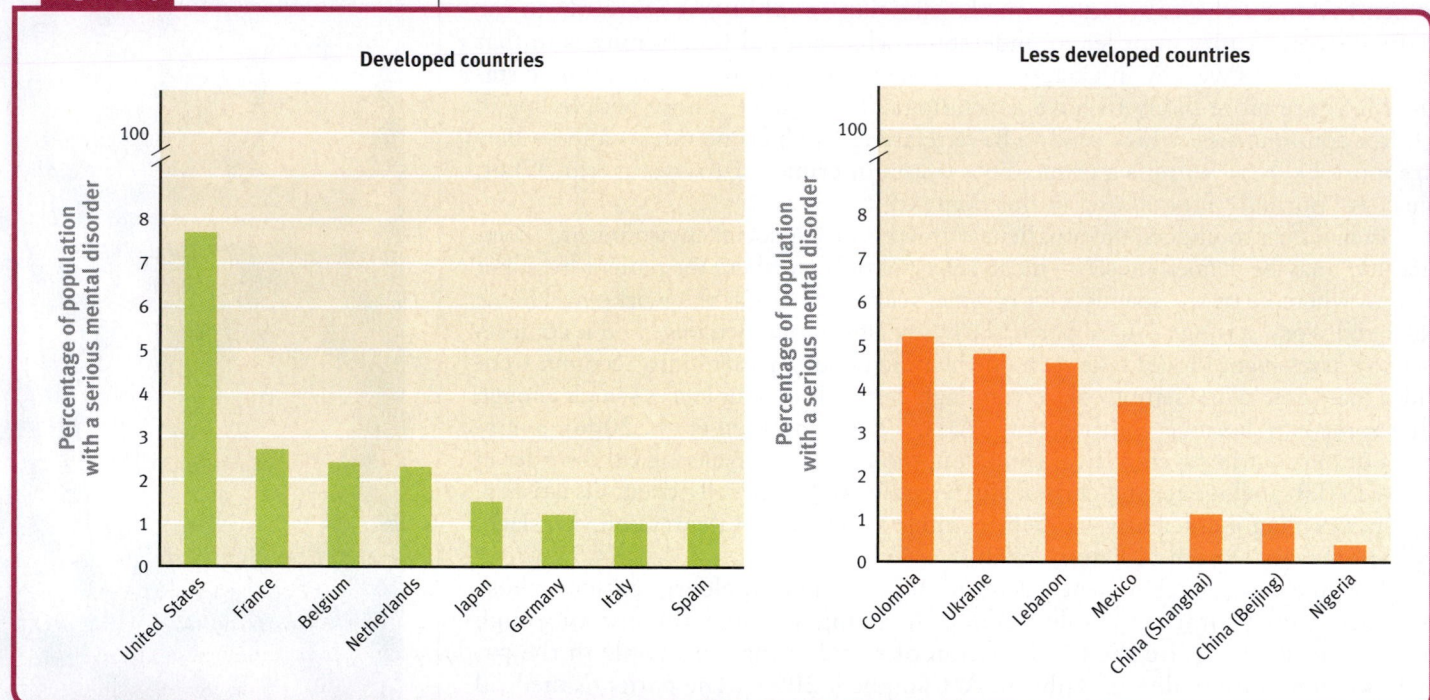

3.4 ▸ Rates of Serious Mental Illness Across Countries From 2001 to 2003, the World Health Organization conducted surveys to measure the prevalence of serious mental disorders in the populations of various countries. The results revealed significant differences among countries (WHO World Mental Health Survey Consortium, 2004).

Source: Copyright 2004 by the American Medical Association. For more information see the Permissions section.

Assessment as an Interactive Process

Mental health researchers and clinicians learn about patients from assessing psychological and social factors and, to a lesser extent, neurological and other biological factors. Information about each type of factor should not be considered in isolation, but rather should influence how the clinician understands the other types of information.

Knowledge of psychological factors must be developed in the context of the patient's culture. Psychiatrist Paul Linde (2002) recounts his experiences working in a psychiatric unit in Zimbabwe: The residents of that country generally understand that bacteria can cause an illness such as pneumonia, but they nonetheless wonder why the bacteria struck a particular individual at a specific point in time (a question that contemporary science is just beginning to try to answer). They look to ancestral spirits for an answer to such a question, even when a particular person is beset with mental rather than physical symptoms. A first experience of hallucinations and delusions may signal the beginning of a long and chronic course of schizophrenia, or it may be a one-time occurrence brought on in part by extreme stress or severe substance intoxication. In the latter case in Zimbabwe, the hallucinations and delusions are viewed as signs that the individual is being called to become a healer, a *n'anga*, and not as indicators of mental illness.

Thus, knowledge of the patient's culture influences how an outside researcher such as Linde understands the symptoms. When a patient in Zimbabwe claims to be hearing voices of dead ancestors, Linde undoubtedly interprets this symptom somewhat differently than he would if a white, American-born patient made the same claim. At the same time, knowledge of a patient's family history of chronic schizophrenia (which may indicate a neurological factor—genetic, in this case) will also influence the interpretation of the patient's symptoms. Thus, assessment of each type of factor can influence the assessment of the other types.

However, comprehensive assessment of all three factors in the same patient is extremely costly and rarely undertaken. Formal testing beyond a brief questionnaire that the patient completes independently can be relatively expensive, and often health insurance companies will not pay for routine assessments; they will pay only for specific assessment procedures or tests that they have authorized in advance, based on indications of clear need (Eisman et al., 2000). Beyond an interview, other forms of assessment are most likely to occur as part of a legal proceeding (e.g., custody hearing or sentencing determination) or as part of a research project related to psychological disorders and their treatment.

Key Concepts and Facts About Assessing Psychological Disorders

- An assessment may be performed in order to obtain additional information for a diagnosis, monitor the course of symptoms, determine what type of treatment might be most beneficial, or monitor the progress of treatment.

- Assessment tools and techniques must be reliable and valid, and clinicians should take care to compare a patient's assessment data to an appropriate norm for the patient's background.

- Neurological and other biological factors may be assessed with various methods. Neuroimaging techniques can assess brain structure (X-rays, computerized axial tomography, and magnetic resonance imaging) and brain function (positron emission tomography and functional magnetic resonance imaging). Neurotransmitter levels can be assessed through magnetic resonance spectroscopy, and neurotransmitter and hormone by-products can be measured in blood, urine, and cerebrospinal fluid. Neuropsychological testing can assess brain functioning.

- Various methods are used to assess psychological factors. These include the clinical interview (unstructured, structured, or semistructured), observing the patient (e.g., appearance and behavior), the patient's self-report, and the reports of others involved in the patient's life. Each method has advantages and limitations. Specific aspects of psychological functioning can be assessed through tests of cognitive abilities and personality functioning can be assessed with inventories, questionnaires, and projective tests.

- Some techniques used to assess psychological factors (such as interviews and questionnaires) also can be used to assess social factors—such as family functioning—as well as to provide a more detailed portrait of the patient's community and culture. These social factors affect, and are affected by, neurological and psychological factors.

Diagnosing and Assessing Rose Mary and Rex Walls

Now that you know something about diagnosis and assessment, let's review what we know—and what we don't know—about the Rose Mary and Rex Walls, starting with Rex. We know that he drank alcohol—regularly and to excess. In fact, he drank so much and so chronically that when he stopped drinking he developed *delirium tremens* (also known as the DTs)—withdrawal symptoms marked by hallucinations and shaking. He clearly would have been diagnosed as having *alcohol dependence* (disorders related to the abuse of and dependence on alcohol and other substances are discussed in Chapter 9).

We don't know whether the tall tales he told about himself were delusions or merely attempts to make himself look good in his own eyes and those of other people. Based on Jeannette's descriptions of her father, it appears that Rex also strove to be the center of attention. This pattern of self-centered behavior suggests that he may have had a personality disorder (specifically, what is known as *narcissistic personality disorder*, discussed in Chapter 13). Several other personality disorders might also be appropriate diagnoses, including *paranoid personality disorder*, given his frequent statements about the FBI and unions being after him or against him, and *antisocial personality disorder*, given his frequent disregard for the rights and safety of others—including his wife and children—and his clear violation of the law (at one time he created and carried out a scheme to defraud banks). Given his long history of drinking, though, it is hard to sort out how much of his behavior arose from the effects of alcohol dependence and how much might have been caused by an underlying personality disorder. However, the vast majority of people who abuse or are dependent on alcohol do not develop Rex's other problems—and thus it's not likely that his alcoholism can account for these other problems.

What about Rose Mary? Based on Jeannette's descriptions of her mother's difficulties with work—her lack of motivation to work despite the family's dire circumstances, her difficulty getting out of bed in the morning in order to get to work, and her inability to complete her school-related paperwork without assistance—Rose Mary may have suffered from depression. It is possible, though, that these behaviors instead may have been expressions of anger and resentment about feeling forced to work when her husband was so irresponsible. She was bitter that she hadn't become a famous artist and blamed her lack of success on her children. In addition, given her own preoccupations with her worth as an artist, even as her children were starving, she may well have had *narcissistic personality disorder*.

However, again we need to be cautious: No mental health clinician can know with certainty what, if any, specific disorder Rose Mary or Rex Walls may have had. We cannot make a direct clinical assessment of neurological, psychological, or social factors; we can only infer such factors from their daughter's account, which does not provide the kind of information needed to make an accurate clinical assessment.

Clinicians and researchers diagnosing and assessing patients should keep in mind the possibility that symptoms of a psychological disorder can arise from medical problems. These medical problems can range from a brain tumor, stroke, or hormone imbalance to a condition like anemia, the symptoms of which may overlap with those of depression. For Rose Mary and Rex Walls, it's possible that malnutrition (and for Rex, the effects of chronic heavy drinking) adversely affected their psychological functioning. Therefore, patients should obtain appropriate medical evaluations to ensure that their psychological symptoms are not caused by a medical problem. Only after ruling out medical illnesses can the mental health clinician or researcher have confidence in a diagnosis of a psychological disorder.

SUMMING UP

Summary of Diagnosing Psychological Disorders

Among other purposes, classification systems for diagnosis allow: (1) patients to be able to put a name to their experiences and to learn that they are not alone; (2) clinicians to distinguish "normal" from "abnormal" psychological functioning and to group together similar types of problems; and (3) researchers to discover the etiology, course, and success of treatments for abnormal psychological functioning.

Classification systems also have drawbacks. They can be subject to diagnostic bias—perhaps on the basis of the patient's sex, race, or ethnicity. Classification systems should be both reliable and valid. Reliability is less likely when the criteria for disorders are not clear and when the criteria for different disorders significantly overlap.

The most commonly used classification system in the United States is the *Diagnostic and Statistical Manual of Mental Disorders*, presently in its 4th edition, text revision (DSM-IV-TR). The DSM-IV-TR: (1) generally does not focus on etiology (the causes of disorders), but focuses instead on what can be observed rather than inferred; and (2) lists explicit criteria for each disorder and includes a system for clinicians and researchers to record diagnoses as well as additional information that may affect diagnosis, prognosis, and treatment.

DSM-IV-TR has been criticized on numerous grounds, including the subjectivity of some of the criteria of some disorders, the categorical nature of the classification system, and the large number of disorders contained in it.

Psychological disorders are primarily diagnosed by clinical and counseling psychologists, psychiatrists, psychiatric nurses, and social workers. Each type of clinician has received somewhat different training and therefore may gather different types of information and use that information in different ways.

Thinking like a clinician

Your abnormal psychology class watches a videotape of a clinical interview with Peter, a man who has been diagnosed with schizophrenia. Your professor has been researching new criteria for diagnosing schizophrenia and has asked you and your classmates to determine whether Peter does, in fact, have schizophrenia according to the new criteria. If you and your classmates disagree with each other about his diagnosis, what might that indicate about the criteria's reliability and validity, and what might it indicate about the interview itself?

The professor then asks you to decide whether Peter has schizophrenia as defined by the DSM-IV-TR criteria. What are some of the advantages and disadvantages of using DSM-IV-TR? Based on what you have read, what factors, other than the specifics of Peter's symptoms, might influence your assessment? (*Hint*: Think of biases.) Should Peter be diagnosed with schizophrenia, might there be any benefits to him that come with the diagnosis, based on what you have read? What might be the possible disadvantages for Peter of being diagnosed with schizophrenia? Be specific in your answers.

Summary of Assessing Psychological Disorders

An assessment may be performed in order to: (1) obtain additional information for a diagnosis, (2) monitor the course of symptoms, (3) determine what type of treatment might be most beneficial, or (4) monitor the progress of treatment. Assessment tools and techniques must be reliable and valid, and clinicians should take care to compare a patient's assessment data to an appropriate norm for the patient's background.

Neurological (and other biological) factors may be assessed with various methods. Neuroimaging techniques can assess brain structure (X-rays, computerized axial tomography, and magnetic resonance imaging) and brain function (positron emission tomography and functional magnetic resonance imaging). Neurotransmitter levels can be assessed through magnetic resonance spectroscopy, and neurotransmitter and hormone by-products can be measured in blood, urine, and cerebrospinal fluid. Neuropsychological testing can assess brain functioning.

Various methods are used to assess psychological factors. These include the clinical interview, observing the patient, the patient's self-report, and the reports of others involved in the patient's life. Each method has advantages and limitations. Specific aspects of psychological functioning can be assessed through tests of cognitive abilities and personality functioning can be assessed with inventories, questionnaires, and projective tests.

Some techniques used to assess psychological factors can also be used to assess social factors—such as family functioning—as well as to provide a more detailed portrait of the patient's community and culture. These social factors affect, and are affected by, neurological and psychological factors.

Thinking like a clinician

Suppose that you have decided to become a mental health professional. What type of training (and what type of degree) would you obtain and why?

Now suppose that you are working in an emergency room, assessing possible mental illness in patients. You have been asked to determine whether a 55-year-old woman, who was brought in by her son, has a psychological disorder severe enough for her to be hospitalized. Based on what you have read, if you could use only one assessment method of each type (neurological, psychological, and social), what methods would you pick and why?

Key Terms

Diagnosis (p. 73)

Clinical assessment (p. 73)

Diagnostic bias (p. 76)

Reliable (p. 77)

Valid (p. 78)

Prognosis (p. 78)

Prevalence (p. 78)

Comorbidity (p. 79)

Clinical psychologist (p. 86)

Counseling psychologist (p. 86)

Psychiatrist (p. 86)

Psychiatric nurse (p. 87)

Social worker (p. 87)

Computerized axial tomography (CT) (p. 91)

Magnetic resonance imaging (MRI) (p. 91)

Positron emission tomography (PET) (p. 91)

Functional magnetic resonance imaging (fMRI) (p. 92)

Magnetic resonance spectroscopy (MRS) (p. 92)

Neuropsychological testing (p. 93)

Clinical interview (p. 94)

Malingering (p. 96)

Factitious disorder (p. 96)

Projective test (p. 100)

More Study Aids

For additional study aids related to this chapter, go to:

www.worthpublishers.com/rosenberg

Diagram of a
simple flower

Foundations of Treatment

"Leon is a 45-year-old postal employee who was evaluated at a clinic. He claims to have felt constantly depressed since the first grade, without a period of 'normal' mood for more than a few days at a time. His depression has been accompanied by lethargy, little or no interest or pleasure in anything, trouble concentrating, and feelings of inadequacy, pessimism, and resentfulness. His only periods of normal mood occur when he is home alone, listening to music or watching TV.

"On further questioning, Leon reveals that he cannot ever remember feeling comfortable socially. Even before kindergarten, if he was asked to speak in front of a group of his parents' friends, his mind would 'go blank.' He felt overwhelming anxiety at children's social functions, such as birthday parties, which he either avoided or, if he went, attended in total silence. He could answer questions in class only if he wrote down the answers in advance; even then, he frequently mumbled and couldn't get the answer out. He met new children with his eyes lowered, fearing their scrutiny, expecting to feel humiliated and embarrassed. He was convinced that everyone around him thought he was 'dumb' or 'a jerk.'

"As he grew up, Leon had a couple of neighborhood playmates, but he never had a 'best friend.' His school grades were good, but suffered when oral classroom participation was expected. As a teenager, he was terrified of girls, and to this day he has never gone on a date or even asked a girl for a date. This bothers him, although he is so often depressed that he feels he has little energy or interest in dating.

"Leon attended college and did well for a while, then dropped out as his grades slipped. He remained very self-conscious and 'terrified' of meeting strangers. He had trouble finding a job because he was unable to answer questions in interviews. He worked at a few jobs for which only a written test was required. He passed a civil service exam at age 24 and was offered a job in the post office on the evening shift. He enjoyed this job as it involved little contact with others. He was offered several promotions but refused them because he feared the social pressures. Although by now he supervises a number of employees, he still finds it difficult to give instructions, even to people he has known for years. He has no friends and avoids all invitations to socialize with co-workers. . . . Leon has never experienced sudden anxiety or a panic attack in social situations or at other times. Rather, his anxiety gradually builds to a constant high level in anticipation of social situations." (Spitzer et al., 2002, pp. 124–125)

Diane Fenster

Treatment (for psychological disorders)
The use of a procedure or substance to reduce or eliminate psychological problems or symptoms of psychological disorders and/or improve quality of life.

Biomedical treatments
Treatments that are designed to reduce target symptoms and/or improve quality of life by changing brain functioning, hormonal activity, or another aspect of bodily functioning.

Psychopharmacology
The use of medication to reduce or eradicate symptoms of psychological disorders; also the study of such treatment.

Agonists
Medications that mimic the effects of a neurotransmitter or neuromodulator and activate a particular type of receptor.

A clinician might consider many different types of treatment for Leon's depression and anxiety, depending both on Leon's specific symptoms and on the type of treatment the clinician is trained to provide. **Treatment** for psychological disorders is the use of a procedure or substance to reduce or eliminate psychological problems or symptoms and/or improve quality of life.

Notice that the definition of *treatment* does not explicitly mention abnormality. In fact, many people who seek treatment do not have symptoms that warrant a DSM-IV-TR diagnosis. They have problems in their relationships or work or are struggling with a personal issue; they simply want to talk things through and receive guidance and support. Because these sorts of problems are not "abnormal," such people, and their treatment, are not specifically discussed in this book.

As our definition implies, treatment has two possible goals: (1) to reduce or eliminate specific symptoms, and/or (2) to improve the general quality of life. With regard to the first goal, successful treatment may reduce or eliminate *some* symptoms, but not necessarily all of them. A given treatment focuses on diminishing particular symptoms, referred to as the *target symptoms*. For instance, in treating Leon's social anxiety, medications may target the physical symptoms of anxiety (such as an increased heart rate when he thinks he must talk to others). Cognitive techniques may target unrealistic and maladaptive thoughts about social interactions ("I will be totally humiliated if I try to talk to someone at work"). Behavioral techniques may target the physical symptoms as well as the avoidant behavior. Each type of treatment targets specific symptoms, either by addressing the symptoms directly (for example, by using behavioral techniques) or by altering the factors that give rise to the symptoms (for example, changing the levels of neurotransmitter substances). A given type of treatment may improve certain symptoms but not others.

What about the second goal of treatment? Treatment may also seek to improve the *quality of life*—patients' psychological, social, and material well-being (Gladis et al., 1999). Researchers and clinicians recognize that health is not simply the absence of disease, but is a state of having mental and social well-being (World Health Organization, 1948). Research examining how treatment improves patients' quality of life asks whether their relationships with friends, relatives, and coworkers have improved, whether the patients can take better care of themselves, and whether they can function more fully in society (Abraham et al., 2006; Beasley et al., 2006; Keyes, 2007).

Generally, clinicians who are trained to diagnose psychological disorders (see Chapter 3) are also trained to treat such disorders. Mental health treatment may take place in hospitals, psychiatric institutions, clinics, private offices, religious institutions, or, less frequently, in patients' homes or workplaces. Who provides a particular patient's treatment and where it is provided depend on that patient's health insurance coverage and finances, the availability of appropriate treatment within the patient's community, and possibly the patient's ability to travel in order to obtain specialized treatment.

One way to categorize the treatments themselves is according to the type of factor they target: neurological, psychological, or social (see Table 4.1). But ultimately, all treatments have the same broad goal—to decrease symptoms and/or improve quality of life. The goal of treatment can be likened to an X on a map—the place toward which the treatment nudges the patient; each type of treatment provides a different path toward that destination. Different treatments, when successful, bring the patient to the same general place, but follow different paths.

Table 4.1 ▶ Aspects of Neurological, Psychological, and Social Factors That May Change as a Result of Successful Treatment

Neurological Factors	Psychological Factors	Social Factors
• Neuronal activity • Levels of transmitter substances • Level of stress hormones • Amount of substance used (for those with substance abuse) • Bodily symptoms of arousal (as in anxiety disorders or sexual disorders) • Appetite • Sleep	• Mental processes • Mental contents • Specific behaviors, including those associated with caring for oneself • The experience and regulation of emotions	• Relationships (social support, pattern of family and work interactions) • Social isolation • Socioeconomic status

Although a given treatment targets a particular factor or set of factors, the treatment also creates feedback loops among factors: As some symptoms are reduced or quality of life improves, these changes in turn affect additional factors, other than those directly targeted. A rising tide raises all boats. Throughout this book, we highlight sections that discuss these treatment-initiated feedback loops by placing in the margin our feedback loop icon, along with an arrow pointing to the type of factor that is being directly targeted by the treatment. For instance, suppose that medication (which directly targets a neurological factor) successfully treated Leon's social phobia so that he was able to interact with people more freely (social factor) and not be anxious beforehand or ruminate about it afterward (psychological factor). Because social situations would no longer fill him with dread, he would in turn be less aroused in such situations (neurological factor).

Let's review the most common methods of treatment, considering them in terms of the type of factor that is each treatment's primary target.

Treatments That Target Neurological Factors

One way to treat Leon's depression and anxiety would be to make neurological factors the direct target of treatment. **Biomedical treatments** reduce target symptoms and/or improve quality of life by changing brain functioning, hormonal activity (which is regulated by the brain), or another aspect of bodily functioning (which typically is also regulated by the brain; see Table 4.1). Thus, the general goal of these treatments is to change neurological functioning directly in some way; as we shall discuss, several different methods can achieve this goal.

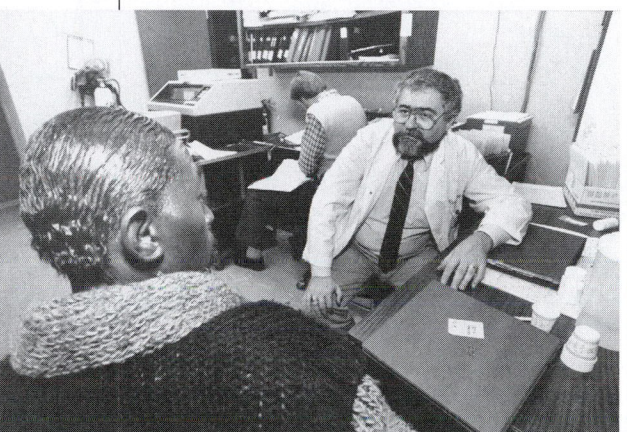

Medications that Change Brain Functioning

Throughout the ages and across cultures, healers have treated abnormal thoughts (mental processes and mental contents), feelings (affect), and behaviors by dispensing medicines to sufferers. Using medication to reduce or eradicate symptoms of psychological disorders, and the study of such treatment, is termed **psychopharmacology**. Medications that affect mental process or mental contents, affect, or behavior are called *psychotropic* medications. Psychotropic medication is most frequently administered as pills, but can also be administered via skin patches (which allow it to be absorbed through the skin), or by injection.

By definition, biomedical treatments target neurological factors, but such treatments also affect other sorts of factors. In particular, the relationship between the patient and the person providing the treatment is itself an intervention that addresses social factors: The patient receives support, advice, and, at least some of the time, the feeling that someone cares. Biomedical treatments—like any type of treatment—also address psychological factors by giving the patient hope and a framework for understanding his or her symptoms and problems.

Goals of Medication

Medications generally are intended to affect neurological factors (such as over-arousal in anxiety disorders) or psychological factors (such as thoughts, feelings, and behaviors related to depression) by increasing or decreasing specific types of brain activity; that is, medications cause particular sets of neurons to fire more or less than they otherwise would.

The key point about successful treatment with medication is that the beneficial effects go beyond altering brain activity—the changes in brain activity, in turn, influence psychological factors (mental processes, mental contents, affect, and behavior) and social factors (interactions with family members, friends, and coworkers). These positive psychosocial changes in turn influence neurological and other biological processes.

Methods of Medication

Medication can alter neural activity in several ways. Figure 4.1 on the next page shows a *synapse*—the space between the sending neuron's terminal button and the receiving neuron's dendrite—and the various methods by which medications can alter neuronal activity. Medications can alter activity in the synapse by:

- mimicking the effects of a neurotransmitter or a neuromodulator, thereby activating a particular type of receptor; such medications are called **agonists**.

Keith Philpott/Time Life Pictures/Getty Images

4.1 ▸ Using Medication to Change Brain Functioning Medications can alter events at the synapse, and thereby change brain functioning. A medication can (a) mimic the effects of a neurotransmitter substance (that is, act as an agonist); (b) bind to receptors and thereby prevent neurotransmitter molecules from binding (that is, act as an antagonist); (c) cause extra amounts of a neurotransmitter to be released from the terminal button into the synapse; or (d) partially block reuptake of leftover neurotransmitter molecules in the synaptic cleft (that is, act as a reuptake inhibitor). Drugs can also alter the level or activity of other substances that are produced in glial cells that surround a synapse, which in turn influence the amount of neurotransmitter in the synaptic cleft.

Figure 4.1

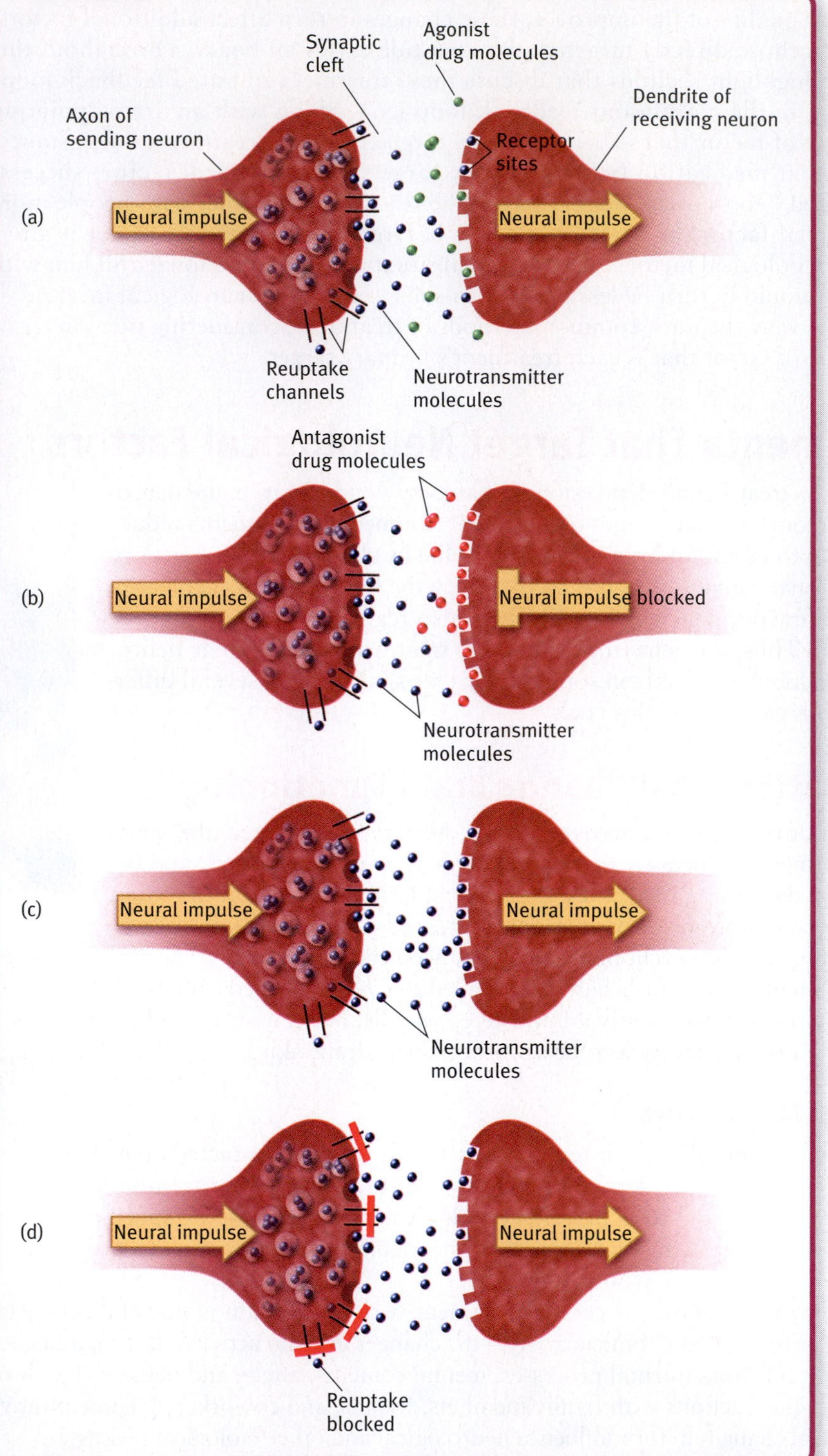

Antagonists
Medications that bind to a receptor site on a dendrite (or cell body) and prevent the neurotransmitter in the synapse from binding to that receptor or cause less of it to bind.

- binding to a receptor site, which prevents the neurotransmitter in the synapse from binding to the receptor (or causes less of it to bind); such medications are called **antagonists**.
- causing the release of extra amounts of a neurotransmitter from the terminal button into the synapse.
- increasing or decreasing the level or activity of other substances that activate or inactivate a neurotransmitter.

- partially blocking *reuptake* (the process by which neurotransmitter molecules left in the synapse are reabsorbed into the terminal button to be recycled for later use), thereby increasing the amount of neurotransmitter in the synaptic cleft. Such medications are referred to as **reuptake inhibitors**.

Just as imbalances of different neurotransmitters are associated with different symptoms (see Chapter 2), different medications affect the various neurotransmitters differently, which changes synaptic activity among only some sets of neurons. That is, medications are *selective* in their effects. For instance, *selective serotonin-reuptake inhibitors* (SSRIs, such as Prozac, Zoloft, and Celexa, taken for depression or anxiety) affect serotonin activity. Similarly, *noradrenaline reuptake inhibitors* (such as Strattera, taken for attention-deficit/hyperactivity disorder) affect noradrenaline (also called norepinephrine) activity.

As more is learned about brain systems and neurotransmitters, researchers are able to develop new medications to target symptoms more effectively and with fewer side effects. Thus, for any given disorder, the number of medication options is likely to increase over time. Next, we'll take a brief look at the medications used to treat key disorders. When we discuss specific disorders in later chapters, we will address medications for treating them in more detail.

Schizophrenia

Mental health clinicians most commonly treat schizophrenia and other psychotic disorders with a class of medications referred to as **antipsychotic medications** (or *neuroleptic medications*); these medications reduce certain psychotic symptoms, such as hallucinations. However, they do not cure the disorder. The original, or traditional, antipsychotics include Haldol and Thorazine. A newer group of antipsychotics, called *second-generation antipsychotics* or *atypical antipsychotics*, may reduce additional symptoms such as withdrawal, apathy, and lack of interest and improve cognitive functioning (Keefe et al., 1999). However, as we will discuss in Chapter 12, research has shown that atypical antipsychotics are not necessarily superior to traditional antipsychotics (Green, 2007; Kahn et al., 2008; Keefe et al., 2006). Both traditional and a typical antipsychotics affect the neurotransmitter dopamine, along with other neurotransmitters, and can have considerable side effects (such as significant weight gain).

Depression

Depression is often treated with SSRIs, SNRIs, *tricyclic antidepressants* (TCAs), or *monoamine oxidase inhibitors* (MAOIs). TCAs have been used since the 1950s, and until SSRIs were available, were the most commonly used type of medication to treat depression. MAOIs have the drawback of possibly causing potentially fatal changes in blood pressure if the person taking them eats food that contains tyramine (a substance found in cheese and wine). These medications may also be prescribed for other types of disorders, such as various anxiety disorders or eating disorders (Rosenbaum et al., 2005).

Anxiety Disorders

For the long-term treatment of anxiety disorders, antidepressants such as tricyclics, SSRIs, or SNRIs can be effective (Rosenbaum et al., 2005). The optimal dosage for treating anxiety symptoms generally differs from the optimal dosage for treating depression (Gorman & Kent, 1999; Kasper & Resinger, 2001; Rivas-Vazques,

Reuptake inhibitors
Medications that partially block the process by which a neurotransmitter is reabsorbed into the terminal button, thus increasing the amount of the neurotransmitter in the synaptic cleft.

Antipsychotic medications
Medications that reduce certain psychotic symptoms; also called *neuroleptic medications*.

Medications, particularly antidepressants, are prescribed for an ever widening range of conditions. By 2008, 11% of female Americans and 5% of male Americans were taking antidepressants (Barber, 2008). Medications have helped many people, but should personality traits (such as shyness or grouchiness) long considered to be in the normal range be treated with medication?

BananaStock/Jupiterimages

Benzodiazepines
A class of medications commonly known as tranquilizers.

Electroconvulsive therapy (ECT)
A procedure that causes a controlled brain seizure in an effort to reduce or eliminate the symptoms of certain psychological disorders.

Transcranial magnetic stimulation (TMS)
A procedure that sends sequences of short, strong magnetic pulses into the cerebral cortex via a coil placed on the scalp.

2001). For short-term treatment of anxiety symptoms, psychiatrists may prescribe **benzodiazepines** (commonly referred to as *tranquilizers*) such as Valium or Xanax.

Changing Brain Function Through Brain Stimulation

Medication changes brain functioning through a circuitous route: The medication is generally swallowed, then absorbed into the bloodstream, and ultimately transported to the particular synapses. Two other biomedical techniques can change patients' brain functioning more directly: electroconvulsive therapy and transcranial magnetic stimulation. The former has been in use for many years, and thus much is known about who might or might not benefit from it; the latter is relatively new, and so guidelines about its use are only beginning to be formulated.

Electroconvulsive Therapy

Electroconvulsive therapy (ECT) is a procedure that causes a controlled brain seizure in an effort to reduce or eliminate the symptoms of certain psychological disorders. An electric current is passed through the head via electrodes that are placed on the scalp. The current causes a seizure. Just before ECT treatment, the patient receives a muscle relaxant, and the treatment occurs while the patient is under anesthesia. Because of the risks associated with anesthesia, ECT is performed in a hospital and may require a hospital stay. A typical course of ECT can involve six to twelve sessions over several weeks, with about three sessions per week. Some patients report memory loss for events that transpired before the ECT treatments (Kho, Van Vreeswijk, & Murre, 2006).

Researchers do not yet understand why ECT is effective in treating depression. In the 1940s and 1950s, ECT was a major neurological treatment, but was used less often after effective medications were developed. ECT became politically unpopular when the public discovered that the procedure was sometimes used to make troublesome patients docile. Moreover, some patients reported cognitive difficulties as a result of ECT. Today, the cognitive impairments and other side effects of ECT have been significantly reduced, and laws prevent ECT from being used simply to calm unruly patients. Given these improvements, the use of ECT to alleviate severe and treatment-resistant depression—the disorder for which this procedure is most effective—has increased since the 1980s (Glass, 2001), and now is administered to about 12.5 per 100,000 people in the general U.S. population. ECT is more commonly used for older adults than younger adults (Rapoport, Mamdani, & Herrmann, 2006). It is also used more frequently for wealthy patients than for those in publicly funded hospitals, perhaps in reaction to the fact that ECT was previously overused in such hospitals (Sackeim, Devanand, & Nobler, 1995).

Transcranial Magnetic Stimulation

In contrast to ECT, which transmits electrical impulses, **transcranial magnetic stimulation (TMS)** sends sequences of short, strong magnetic pulses into the cerebral cortex via a coil placed on the scalp. Each pulse lasts only 100–200 microseconds. TMS has varying effects on the brain, depending on the exact location of the coil and the frequency of the pulses, and researchers are still working to understand how the magnetic field affects brain chemistry and brain activity (George, Lisanby, & Sackheim, 1999).

Studies indicate that TMS can be used effectively to treat depressed people for whom medication has not helped (Bretlau et al., 2008), and it may work as well as ECT (Avery et al., 2006; Dannon et al., 2002; Rosa et al., 2006). In 2008, the U.S. Food and Drug Administration approved TMS as a treatment for depression that should be used after traditional treatments have failed.

Other studies have suggested that TMS may reduce symptoms that arise in a variety of disorders, not only in depression (Alonso et al., 2001; Grisaru et al.,

Transcranial magnetic stimulation is a new technique that might treat some kinds of depression more effectively than ECT.

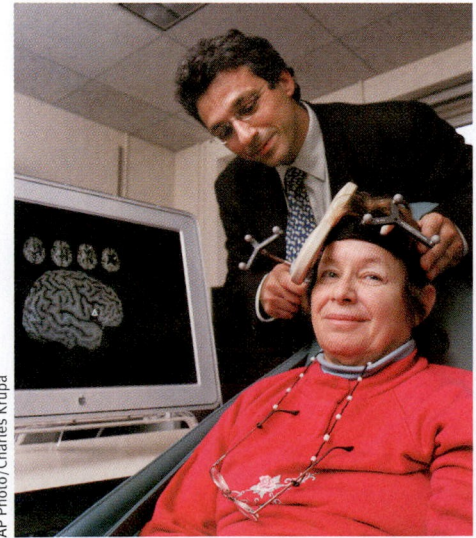

AP Photo/Charles Krupa

1998; Hoffman et al., 2005). Additional studies are needed to confirm these experimental results and determine the optimal location of the coil, as well as the frequency and strength of the pulses, for treating each disorder.

TMS offers several advantages over ECT: It produces minimal side effects and is easier to administer (no anesthesia or hospitalization is needed). In fact, the most commonly reported short-term side effect, a slight headache, affects only about 5–20% of those receiving TMS.

Although ECT and TMS can provide relief for some disorders, these direct methods of brain stimulation are generally used only when other types of treatment have been unsuccessful.

Biofeedback

Biofeedback is a technique by which a person is trained to bring normally involuntary or unconscious bodily activity, such as heart rate or muscle tension, under voluntary control. It works as follows: Electrical leads are placed on the body in the appropriate locations to measure the targeted biological activity (such as pulse rate or muscle tension level), and the patient can see the activity (displayed on a graph or as a sequence of flashing lights) or hear it (in the form of musical tones or beeps transmitted through headphones or a speaker). At first, patients can only slightly affect the biological activity, but over time—largely by a process of trial-and-error—each patient discovers his or her own way to induce the desired change. When the person does something that produces a desired change, this feedback serves as a positive reinforcer—which makes it more likely that the person will repeat that behavior to produce that change in the future. With training, a patient eventually can learn to keep the

Will & Deni McIntyre/Photo Researchers

Biofeedback is designed to allow patients to control biological activity that is normally involuntary. Successful use of biofeedback draws on learning principles. This woman is learning to identify and decrease muscle tension.

targeted biological activity within the desired range (Blanchard, 2000). Biofeedback is used to treat involuntary muscle tension associated with some anxiety disorders and some sexual disorders (Chapters 7 and 11; Reiner, 2008).

Changing Brain Structure Through Neurosurgery

Neurosurgery—brain surgery—is used only rarely to treat people with symptoms of psychological disorders. It is a treatment of last resort, used when all other treatments have failed and the disorder is sufficiently severe that it prevents even a semblance of normal life (Davidovsky, Fleta, & Moreno, 2007; Morgan & Crisp, 2000; Price et al., 2001). During neurosurgery, either specific brain structures are destroyed or their connections with other parts of the brains are severed, thereby changing brain functioning; these changes in brain functioning in turn reduce the intensity or frequency of the symptoms. For example, neurosurgery can be a last resort treatment for obsessive-compulsive disorder (OCD), a disorder in which individuals are extremely preoccupied with performing mental rituals, such as counting to 100 after having a self-defined "bad thought," or physical rituals, such as repeatedly going back to check that the door is locked after leaving home. Such rituals can be repeated for hours at a time. For patients with extremely severe symptoms of OCD, when all else has failed, neurosurgery may be used to destroy a small part of the anterior cingulate cortex. This procedure can disrupt the brain circuit that keeps patients engaged in their mental or physical ritual (Jenike, Baer, & Minichiello, 1998).

Biofeedback
A technique by which a person is trained to bring normally involuntary or unconscious bodily activity, such as heart rate or muscle tension, under voluntary control.

Targeting Neurological Factors in Younger and Older Populations

Patients at two ends of the developmental continuum—children (including adolescents) and the elderly—may respond somewhat differently than do young and middle-aged adults to the same biomedical treatments. Let's explore how biomedical treatments may be modified for these special populations.

Targeting Neurological Factors in Younger Patients

The Food and Drug Administration is the federal agency in the United States charged with determining whether a medication is safe for use and, if so, for what disorders and at what dosages. However, most medications are tested on and approved for use with adults. (One exception is the skin patch containing a daily dose of *methylphenidate* for the treatment of attention-deficit/hyperactivity disorder.) However, some medications that are effective for adults may not alleviate symptoms in children; for example, tricyclic antidepressants are not an effective treatment for depression in children (Stein, Weizman, & Bloch, 2006). Other medications are prescribed for patients *off-label*, meaning that the medication has not been approved for treating the given disorder or for treating children and/or adolescents. For younger patients, the dosage and frequency of medications that are prescribed off-label may need to be adjusted, and these patients may need to be monitored for adverse side effects more frequently than are adults.

Electroconvulsive therapy has rarely been used to treat children and adolescents, and so there isn't much research to guide clinicians about what kind of disorders and symptoms are appropriate to treat with ECT in younger patients and what level of electric current is best (Sporn & Lisanby, 2006). Interest in using brain stimulation techniques to treat children and adolescents is increasing because side effects of various antidepressant medications, such as increased risk for suicide, have been noted in young patients (Stein et al., 2006).

Targeting Neurological Factors in Older Patients

As adults become older, their bodies, and certain cognitive functions, change—although in most cases these changes do not significantly interfere with normal functioning. For instance, older adults tend to process information more slowly (Salthouse, 2005) and may have difficulty remembering names of objects or people (Nicholas et al., 1985). In addition to these cognitive changes among the elderly, their symptoms of some disorders may be different; for example, depressed elders tend to have more agitation and more memory problems than do depressed younger adults (Segal, Pearson, & Thase, 2003).

Mental health clinicians who treat older adults should be prepared to modify biomedical treatments for this population. Consider that older adults are typically more sensitive to medications and so need lower dosages than do younger adults (Fick et al., 2003). In fact, if older adults are given a dose that is standard for younger adults, they may experience symptoms that mimic psychological disorders—such as being sedated (which can cause them to be slower, both physically and cognitively) and confused.

In addition, many elderly people take medications to treat physical problems, and these medications can adversely affect their mood, cognitive functioning, or behavior. Indeed, one study found that elders who do not live in institutional care (such as nursing homes) take an average of five prescription medications each day (Rajska-Neumann & Wieczorowska-Tobis, 2007). Such medications, or their interactions, can cause symptoms that appear to be related to depression, such as difficulty concentrating, sedation, and confusion. Thus, an elderly patient may *appear* to be depressed, but not actually be.

When older people actually are depressed, electroconvulsive therapy is often markedly more effective than it is for younger people. In addition, older depressed patients may be more likely to receive ECT because they may experience more side effects of antidepressant medication and so not be able to stay on the medication long enough—and at a high enough dosage—for their depression to lift (Rabheru, 2001).

Of all the biomedical treatments presented in this section, the most appropriate treatment for Leon's depression and anxiety would be medication. ECT or TMS would not be considered appropriate because Leon's depressive symptoms don't seem severe enough. Biofeedback is not a treatment for depression. Surgery is much too drastic for Leon's problems, even if it were certain that surgery could cure depression or anxiety (which it cannot, at least not at present). However, some of the treatments that target psychological and social factors (discussed in subsequent sections) are likely to be as effective as medication for treating depression and anxiety—if not more so. Further, the positive effects of treatments that target psychological and social factors often continue after the treatment ends. In contrast, even if medication were effective for Leon's depression and anxiety, his symptoms would probably return after he stopped taking the medication.

Key Concepts and Facts About Treatments That Target Neurological Factors

- The goal of treatment is to reduce or eliminate problems or symptoms and/or to improve quality of life. Various procedures and substances are used to treat psychological disorders.

- Treatments that target neurological factors, sometimes referred to as biomedical treatments, include medications, brain stimulation (electroconvulsive therapy and transcranial magnetic stimulation), biofeedback, and, in rare cases, neurosurgery.

- Medications can alter synaptic activity by:
  - mimicking the effects of a neurotransmitter or a neuromodulator (agonists);
  - binding to a receptor site, which prevents the neurotransmitter in the synapse from binding to the receptor or causes less of it to bind (antagonists);
  - causing the release of extra amounts of a neurotransmitter from the terminal button into the synapse;
  - increasing or decreasing the level or activity of other substances that activate or inactivate a neurotransmitter; or
  - partially blocking reuptake of a neurotransmitter from the synapse.

- Electroconvulsive therapy (ECT) induces a controlled brain seizure by passing current through electrodes on the scalp; this treatment is performed in a hospital, under anesthesia, and usually involves up to a dozen sessions over several weeks. ECT is most effective for treating severe depression.

- Transcranial magnetic stimulation (TMS) delivers very brief magnetic pulses into the cerebral cortex. TMS is approved as a treatment for depression when other treatments have failed. Unlike ECT, TMS does not require anesthesia (and so need not be administered in a hospital), and it has fewer side effects.

- Biofeedback is a technique by which patients can bring involuntary bodily activity, such as heart rate or muscle tension, under voluntary control. Biofeedback training sessions require the patient to monitor the targeted bodily activity and, through trial and error, discover how to modify this activity.

- Neurosurgery, usually considered a treatment of last resort, is sometimes used to modify brain structures that contribute to severe disorders in cases where other treatments have not been effective.

- Biomedical treatments used with adults may need to be modified for use with children or elderly patients.

Treatments That Target Psychological Factors

Many of the types of treatments that might be most appropriate for Leon's depression and anxiety are *psychosocial* therapies or treatments—treatments that target psychological factors or social factors. Treatments that target psychological factors specifically focus on mental processes, mental contents, affect, and behaviors (see Table 4.1). A variety of treatments directly target psychological factors; we'll consider psychodynamic therapy, client-centered therapy, and cognitive-behavior therapy. These treatments differ in the specific psychological factors that they target, their goals, and the methods used. However, when successful, all of these treatments affect mental processes, mental contents, affect, and behaviors.

Psychodynamic Therapy

Sigmund Freud's psychoanalytic theory (see Chapter 1) radically changed conceptions of how psychological problems arise and how best to treat those problems. Freud promoted *psychic determinism*, the theory that all behavior, no matter how minor (except for biological functions), has underlying psychological causes. In particular, he believed that the unconscious contains drives and urges concerning sex and aggression, and the individual's behaviors are responses to those unconscious drives or urges. Such drives arise from the id, one of three psychic structures of the mind. The drives are restrained and regulated by the superego, which houses the internalized morals of society and the family. And the ego mediates among the id, the superego, and the constraints of reality.

Freud held that psychological problems arise in large part from conflicts among the urges of the id and from the regulatory actions of the superego and ego. Rather than treating such problems medically—with medications or medical procedures, as was done in Europe at the end of the 19th century—Freud treated patients by having them talk about their problems and trying to discern the unconscious causes of the problems.

The Goals of Psychoanalysis and Psychodynamic Therapy

Psychoanalysis refers to the intensive psychotherapy based on Freud's view that psychopathology arises from unconscious conflict. The ultimate goal of psychoanalysis is to help patients manage impulses and urges more adaptively. To attain this end, the patient tries to: (1) understand the events in his or her past (especially interactions with his or her parents), and (2) understand how those events and his or her unconscious urges influence current difficulties. The theory holds that once patients become aware of the unconscious urges that are creating problems, they will be capable of more adaptively handling impulses arising from those urges. That is, when patients have attained sufficient *insight* into their problems, they can make more satisfying and productive choices; insight, according to proponents of psychodynamic therapy, is the main catalyst of change.

Psychoanalysis is time-consuming and expensive (and rarely covered by health insurance plans). Patients meet with their *psychoanalyst* (a therapist who provides psychoanalysis) four or five times per week, and the average patient participates in 835 sessions over at least 4 years (Voth & Orth, 1973). Psychoanalysis is difficult to study scientifically because each patient receives a unique course of treatment (tailored to his or her own personal issues) over a long period of time. Nevertheless, the available studies have not usually found this treatment to be effective for many disorders. Psychoanalysis is less common today than in previous decades because of the time and cost involved and its uncertain benefits.

The more common treatment that is based on psychoanalysis is **psychodynamic therapy**, which involves less frequent sessions, less emphasis on aggressive and sexual drives, and more attention to present experiences (in contrast to psychoanalysis's focus on past experiences). Very brief forms of this less intensive treatment can consist of as few as 12 to 20 sessions (Bloom, 1997; Malan, 1976; Sifneos, 1992). Table 4.2 outlines the major differences between psychoanalysis and psychodynamic therapy.

Both psychoanalysis and psychodynamic therapy are designed to help patients understand that their unconscious motivations influence their behavior in specific ways and to help them make better choices. According to Freud, however, such treatment is not a cure, but a method for transforming deep misery into mundane unhappiness.

Psychoanalysis
The intensive psychotherapy based on Freud's view that psychopathology arises from unconscious conflict.

Psychodynamic therapy
A form of psychotherapy based on psychoanalysis but that involves less frequent sessions, less emphasis on aggressive and sexual drives, and more attention to present experiences.

Table 4.2 ▸ Differences Between Psychoanalysis and Psychodynamic Therapy

	Psychoanalysis	Psychodynamic Therapy
Frequency	Four or five times a week	Usually not more than twice a week
Duration	Years, or indefinitely	A few years or less
Seating Arrangements	Patient lies on a couch; the analyst sits behind the patient, off to the side, out of the patient's view.	Patient and therapist both sit on chairs, facing each other.
Emphasis	More emphasis on sexual and aggressive urges and childhood experiences	Less emphasis on sexual and aggressive urges; more emphasis on current—rather than past—experiences

David Young-Wolff/Photo Edit

Methods of Psychodynamic Therapy

Freud and his followers developed a variety of techniques to allow the analyst and patient to glimpse the workings of the patient's unconscious and to promote insight.

The Therapeutic Alliance

Both psychoanalysis and psychodynamic therapy emphasize the importance of a **therapeutic alliance,** the positive relationship between the therapist and the patient (Greenberg & Mitchell, 1983; Klein, 1932; Kohut, 1977; Sullivan, 1953; Winnicott, 1958). This patient-therapist collaboration, a social factor, provides the trust and good will needed to undertake the challenging work of the therapy. The therapeutic alliance also can supply patients with a *corrective emotional experience*, an opportunity to work through past unresolved experiences in a safe environment with the therapist (Alexander & French, 1946). This experience can lead to improvements in symptoms, personality, and behavior.

Free Association

One method that Freud developed in order to determine patients' unconscious conflicts is **free association,** in which patients report aloud their train of thought, uncensored. Psychodynamic therapists believe that the content and pattern of patients' unedited thoughts reveal unconscious urges and responses to those urges.

Interpretation

Free association is usually used in conjunction with **interpretation,** in which the therapist infers the unconscious meaning or motivation behind a patient's words and behaviors and shares this inference with the patient. Thus, the therapist might first note a patient's thought pattern during free association and then point out possible unconscious meaning in the patient's associations. The therapist also uses interpretation when a patient makes a speech error, such as saying "father" instead of "bother"; such errors are thought to be laden with meaning and are often called *Freudian slips*. According to Freud, interpretation should help the patient become aware of his or her unconscious conflicts. The patient's own interpretations are not generally considered as accurate as the therapist's because the patient's unconscious urges and conflicts are presumed to make him or her less objective.

Dream Analysis

Another method that Freud developed to plumb a patient's unconscious is **dream analysis,** in which the therapist interprets the content of a patient's dreams. Freud

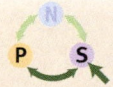

Therapeutic alliance
The positive relationship between the therapist and the patient.

Free association
The psychodynamic technique in which patients report aloud their train of thought, uncensored.

Interpretation
The psychodynamic technique in which the therapist infers the unconscious meaning or motivation behind a patient's words and behaviors and shares these inferences with the patient.

Dream analysis
The psychodynamic technique in which the therapist interprets the content of a patient's dreams.

Psychoanalysts and psychodynamic therapists interpret unconscious meaning from patients' slips of the tongue, referred to as *Freudian slips*.

called dreams the "royal road to the unconscious" (1900/1958) and proposed that dreams have both:

- a *manifest content*, which is the content of the dream itself, as recounted by the patient (such as a nightmare that Leon might have about standing in front of a group of people who are laughing at him); and

- a *latent content*, which is the hidden, true meaning expressed by the unconscious.

In dream analysis, the therapist carefully examines the dream's manifest content in order to infer its latent content. A psychodynamic therapist might infer that Leon's nightmare expressed a reaction to his own aggressive urges. In other words, in his nightmare, Leon's wish to hurt others was transformed (via the process of reaction formation—see Chapter 1) into his being hurt by their laughter.

Using Resistance

At some point during psychodynamic therapy, patients are likely—overtly or covertly, consciously or unconsciously—to hinder treatment; such behavior is referred to as *resistance*. Patients may come late to therapy sessions (or forget to come at all) or refuse to free associate, to discuss a dream, or to answer the therapist's questions. Resistance is most likely to arise when disturbing or painful memories or thoughts come into consciousness. Rather than viewing resistance as a problem, the psychodynamic therapist views it as a natural part of treatment and uses it as an opportunity to increase awareness and insight. The therapist interprets the resistance as indicating the patient's wish to avoid certain feelings or thoughts.

Using Transference

Another inevitable part of psychodynamic therapy and psychoanalysis is **transference**, which occurs when patients interact with the therapist in the same manner that they did with their parents or other important figures in their lives. In fact, transference is an integral part of psychodynamic therapy, and the therapist encourages it by nonjudgmentally asking the patient about his or her feelings toward the therapist and encouraging the patient to explore and accept such feelings. As part of a corrective emotional experience, patient and therapist talk about the patient's feelings toward the therapist, which serves to help the patient better understand his or her transferred feelings and how they influence his or her behavior. According to psychodynamic theory, as the patient becomes aware of such feelings, he or she is able to accept them and have more choice about how—and whether—to express them.

CASE **4.1** ▸ FROM THE OUTSIDE: **A Patient's Transference**

A psychoanalyst describes a patient, Ms. B, and her transference:

Ms. B began her multiyear psychoanalysis when she was 29 years old, and felt she was "stagnating in my own anger." Ms. B was passed over for advancement and thought that she might have to leave the [law] firm [where she'd worked for a number of years].

The eldest of five sisters and two brothers, Ms. B came from a middle-class neighborhood in New York City where her parents owned a "mom and pop candy store that everyone called 'Pop's' because my mother was always pregnant." She describes her mother as

Transference
The psychodynamic process by which patients interact with the therapist in the same manner that they did with their parents or other important figures in their lives.

depressed, living in fantasies, and preoccupied with having children. Ms. B's first sister (C) was born when Ms. B was 2 years old. She recalls the years following C's birth as being filled with a constant need to be with her mother and a sense of panic and rage at her mother's "unavailability." She longed for her mother's exclusive attention and would have temper tantrums when her mother could not be with her. Separation, even for a short time, was experienced as traumatic. . . .

Ms. B felt that I was an empathic and reliable person who was available to her in a special way. She also felt that I did not like her and was bored by her. When I was quiet during a session she felt I was punishing her. "Sometimes you're like my mother and sometimes my father."

As our work continued, the transference oscillated between Ms. B's view of me as being "indifferent" toward her and more interested in other female patients (particularly her "arch rival"—a patient she would see in the waiting room) and her view of me as not comforting her, not telling her that everything will be all right: "I want you to get rid of that woman . . . you're indifferent to me. Make me feel better. . . . it feels just like mother."

(Frosch, 2002, pp. 612–614)

In sum, psychoanalysis and psychodynamic therapy rely on six methods to help a patient understand his or her unconscious urges and conflicts and to promote insight and change: the therapeutic alliance, free association, interpretation, dream analysis, and the use of resistance and transference.

Client-Centered Therapy

As discussed in Chapter 1, therapists who provide treatment within the framework of humanistic psychology view psychopathology as arising from blocked personal growth. **Client-centered therapy**, a humanistic therapy developed by psychologist Carl Rogers, is intended to promote personal growth so that a client can reach his or her full potential.

The Goal of Client-Centered Therapy

Rogers believed that a client's symptoms arise from an incongruence between the *real self* (that is, the person the client knows himself or herself to be) and the *ideal self* (that is, the person he or she would like to be). This incongruence leads to a fragmented sense of self and blocks the potential for personal growth. The goal of treatment, according to Rogers, should be to decrease the incongruence, either by modifying the ideal self or by realizing that the real self is closer to the ideal self than previously thought, which in turn leads to a more integrated sense of self, and an enhanced ability for the client to reach his or her full potential. According to the theory, the client's emotional pain should diminish as the real self and the ideal self become more congruent.

Methods of Client-Centered Therapy

The two basic tenets of client-centered therapy are that the therapist should express *genuine empathy* and *unconditional positive regard* toward clients.

Genuine Empathy

The therapist does not interpret the client's words, but rather accurately reflects back the key parts of what the client said, which allows the client to experience the therapist's *genuine empathy* (Kirschenbaum & Jourdan, 2005). Were Leon in client-centered therapy, for instance, the therapist would try to convey his or her empathy for Leon's situation by paraphrasing his descriptions of his feelings and reactions to situations. According to Rogers (1951), if the therapist simply repeats the same words, reflects the client's words inaccurately, or seems to express false empathy, the therapy tends to fail.

Client-centered therapy
A humanistic therapy developed by Carl Rogers that is intended to promote personal growth so that a client can reach his or her full potential.

Unconditional Positive Regard

The therapist also conveys unconditional positive regard for the client, expressing positive feelings for the client, regardless of the client's expressed thoughts, emotions, and behaviors. The therapist can honestly do so by continually showing that the client is inherently worthy as a human being, distinguishing between the client as a person and the particular thoughts, feelings, and actions of the client (about which the therapist may not necessarily have a positive opinion).

According to proponents of client-centered therapy, when clients experience genuine empathy and unconditional positive regard from the therapist, they come to accept themselves *as they are*, which decreases the incongruence between real and ideal selves.

Cognitive-Behavior Therapy

Behaviorism and cognitive psychology each led to explanations for how psychopathology can arise (see Chapter 2); in turn, each of these approaches gave rise to its own form of therapy. **Behavior therapy** rests on two ideas: (1) Maladaptive behaviors, cognitions, and emotions stem from previous learning, and (2) new learning can allow patients to develop more adaptive behaviors, cognitions, and emotions. In contrast, **cognitive therapy** rests on these ideas: (1) Mental contents—in particular, conscious thoughts—influence a person's feelings and behavior; (2) irrational thoughts and incorrect beliefs contribute to mood and behavior problems; and, (3) correcting such thoughts and beliefs leads to more rational thoughts and accurate beliefs and therefore will lead to better mood and more adaptive behavior.

Although these two forms of therapy began separately, their approaches are complementary and are frequently combined; when methods from cognitive and behavior therapy are implemented in the same treatment, it is called **cognitive-behavior therapy (CBT)**. Let's look first at the unique elements of each type of therapy and then consider cognitive-behavior therapy.

The Goals of Behavior Therapy

Founded by Joseph Wolpe (1915–1997) behavior therapy is based on well-researched principles of learning (see Chapter 2). Behavior therapy stresses changing behavior rather than identifying unconscious motivations or root causes of problems (Wolpe, 1997). Behavior therapy has appealed to psychologists in part because of the ease in determining whether the treatment is effective: The patient's maladaptive behavior either changes or it doesn't.

In some cases, a behavior itself may not be immediately maladaptive, but it may be followed by unwanted consequences at a later point in time. For instance, Leon may not necessarily view avoiding social interactions as a problem, but he may worry about losing his job—a consequence—if he doesn't adequately supervise his employees because of his social anxiety. The ultimate goal is for the patient to replace problematic behaviors with more adaptive ones; the patient acquires new behaviors through classical and operant conditioning (and, to a lesser extent, modeling).

Methods of Behavior Therapy

The therapist, consulting with the patient, directs new learning; together they may focus on the *ABCs* of an unwanted behavior pattern:

- the *antecedents* of the behavior (the stimuli that trigger the behavior),
- the *behavior* itself, and
- the *consequences* of the behavior (which may reinforce the behavior).

In Leon's case, a behavioral therapist might focus on the ABCs of his social phobia: The behavior is Leon's avoidance of social interactions. The antecedents might include his (irrational) thoughts about what will happen if he goes into a social situation ("They will laugh at me, and I will feel humiliated"), which in turn

Behavior therapy
The form of treatment that rests on the ideas that (1) maladaptive behaviors, cognitions, and emotions stem from previous learning and (2) new learning can allow patients to develop more adaptive behaviors, cognitions, and emotions.

Cognitive therapy
The form of treatment that rests on the ideas that (1) mental contents influence feelings and behavior; (2) irrational thoughts and incorrect beliefs lead to psychological problems; and, (3) correcting such thoughts and beliefs will therefore lead to better mood and more adaptive behavior.

Cognitive-behavior therapy
The form of treatment that combines methods from cognitive and behavior therapies.

lead him to feel anxious. The consequences of his avoidant behavior include relief from the anticipatory anxiety.

The therapist assigns *homework*, important tasks that the patient completes between therapy sessions. Homework for Leon, for instance, might consist of his making eye contact with a coworker during the week, or even striking up a brief conversation about the weather. To prepare for this task, Leon might spend part of a therapy session practicing making eye contact or making small talk with his therapist. The success of behavior therapy is measured in terms of the change in frequency and intensity of the maladaptive behavior and the increase in adaptive behaviors.

The Role of Classical Conditioning in Behavior Therapy

As we saw with Little Albert in Chapter 2, classical conditioning can give rise to fears and phobias and, more generally, conditioned emotional responses. To treat the conditioned emotional responses that are associated with a variety of symptoms and disorders and to create new, more adaptive learning, behavioral therapists may employ classical conditioning principles.

Treating Anxiety and Avoidance A common treatment for anxiety disorders, particularly phobias, is based on the principle of **habituation**: The emotional response to a stimulus that elicits fear or anxiety is reduced by exposing the patient to the stimulus repeatedly. The technique of **exposure** involves such repeated contact with the (feared or arousing) stimulus in a controlled setting, and usually in a gradual way. The patient first creates a hierarchy of feared events, arranging them from least to most feared (see Table 4.3), and then begins the exposure process by having contact with the least-feared item on the hierarchy. With sustained exposure, the symptoms diminish within 20–30 minutes or less; that is, habituation to the fear- or anxiety-inducing stimuli occurs. Over multiple sessions, this process is repeated with items higher in the hierarchy until all items no longer elicit significant symptoms.

Exposure—and therefore habituation—to fear- or anxiety-related stimuli does not normally occur outside of therapy because people avoid the object or situation,

---

Table 4.3 ▸ Sample Hierarchy of Fear and Avoidance for Social Situations

If Leon constructed a hierarchy of his fears and avoidance of social situations, it might look something like this completed form. The "Fear" column contains the rating (from 0 to 100, with 100 = very intense fear) that indicates how the patient would feel if he or she were in the given situation. The "Avoidance" column contains the rating (from 0 to 100, with 100 = always avoids the situation) that indicates the degree to which the person avoids the situation. Although Leon avoids almost all the situations on the completed form, some situations arouse more fear than others.

Situation	Fear	Avoidance
Give a 1-hour formal lecture to 30 coworkers	100	100
Go out on a date	98	100
Ask a colleague to go out on a date	97	100
Attend a retirement party for a coworker who is retiring	85	100
Have a conversation with the person sitting next to me on the bus	70	100
Ask someone for directions or the time	60	99
Walk around at a crowded mall	50	98
Answer the telephone without checking caller ID	30	85

Source: Adapted from Antony & Swinson, 2000, p. 171.

Habituation
The process by which the emotional response to a stimulus that elicits fear or anxiety is reduced by exposing the patient to the stimulus repeatedly.

Exposure
The behavioral technique that involves repeated contact with a feared or arousing stimulus in a controlled setting.

thereby making exposure (and habituation) unlikely. Patients in therapy can experience exposure in three ways:

- *imaginal exposure*, which relies on forming mental images of the stimulus;

- *virtual reality exposure*, which consists of exposure to a computer-generated (often very realistic) representation of the stimulus; and

- *in vivo exposure*, which is exposure to the actual stimulus.

Leon's social phobia could be treated in any or all of these ways: He could vividly imagine interacting with others, he could use virtual reality software to have the experience of interacting with others without actually doing so, or he could interact with others in the flesh.

Exposure—imaginal, in vivo, or virtual reality— can be used successfully to treat people with a variety of anxiety disorders, including a fear of heights and posttraumatic stress disorder (Krijn et al., 2004; Reger & Gahm, 2008).

Virtual reality exposure combines aspects of the other two types of exposure: As with imaginal exposure, the patient isn't actually exposed to the fear- or anxiety-producing stimulus, and, as with in vivo exposure, the patient experiences a vivid situation that isn't totally under his or her control—similar to a real situation. Virtual reality exposure has been used to treat a variety of psychological disorders, including posttraumatic stress disorder (Ready et al., 2006), even among active duty soldiers (Reger & Gahm, 2008); fear of flying (Rothbaum et al., 2006); social phobia (specifically, fear of public speaking, with a virtual audience; Anderson et al., 2005); and fear of heights (Krijn et al., 2004). Patients are less likely to refuse treatment with virtual reality exposure than with in vivo exposure (Garcia-Palacios et al., 2007). Moreover, virtual reality exposure may be more effective than in vivo exposure for some people and some disorders (Powers & Emmelkamp, 2008).

Another technique for treating fear, anxiety and avoidance is **systematic desensitization**, which is learning to become relaxed in the presence of a feared stimulus. Whereas exposure relies on habituation, systematic desensitization relies on the fact that a person cannot be relaxed and anxious at the same time. Systematic desensitization is used less frequently than exposure because it is usually not as efficient or effective; however, it may be used to treat a fear or phobia when a patient chooses not to try exposure or has tried it but was disappointed by the results.

The first step of systematic desensitization is learning to become physically relaxed through *progressive muscle relaxation*, relaxing the muscles of the body in sequence from feet to head. Once the patient has mastered this ability, the therapist helps the patient construct a hierarchy of possible experiences relating to the feared stimulus, ordering them from least to most feared, just as is done for exposure (see Figure 4.1). Over multiple therapy sessions, the patient practices becoming relaxed and then continuing to remain relaxed while imagining increasingly feared experiences.

Although systematic desensitization and biofeedback both involve relaxation, systematic desensitization uses relaxation as the first step in reducing anxiety in response to feared stimuli and does not utilize any equipment. In contrast, the goal of biofeedback is learning to control what are generally involuntary responses.

Treating Compulsive Behaviors In some cases, avoidance or fear of a specific stimulus is not the primary maladaptive behavior. For people with OCD, the maladaptive behavior is a compulsive, ritualistic action that patients feel they *must* perform in response to some stimulus. After grocery shopping, for example, a person may feel compelled to reorganize all the canned goods in the cupboard so that the contents remain in alphabetical order. Similarly, some people with bulimia nervosa feel compelled to make themselves throw up after eating even a bite of a dessert. These compulsive behaviors temporarily serve to decrease anxiety that has become part of a conditioned emotional response to a particular stimulus (e.g., randomly arranged canned goods or the sensation of dessert in the mouth).

Systematic desensitization
The behavioral technique of learning to relax in the presence of a feared stimulus.

AP Photo/Ted S. Warren

To treat compulsive behaviors, behavior therapists may use a variant of exposure called **exposure with response prevention**, whereby the patient is carefully prevented from engaging in the usual maladaptive response after being exposed to the stimulus (Foa & Goldstein, 1978). Using this technique with someone who compulsively alphabetizes his or her canned goods, for instance, involves exposing the person to a cupboard full of canned goods arranged randomly and then, as agreed, preventing the typical maladaptive response of alphabetizing the cans. The person then habituates to the ensuing anxiety. Similarly, someone with bulimia might eat a bite or two of a dessert and, as planned, not throw up. This technique will be described more fully when we discuss treatments for OCD (Chapter 7) and bulimia nervosa (Chapter 10).

Treating Habitual Maladaptive Behaviors Some disorders—substance-related disorders, eating disorders, and sexual disorders—involve habitual maladaptive behaviors that are elicited by certain stimuli. For instance, some people drink alcohol to excess (habitual maladaptive behavior) only when they are in bars or clubs (the stimulus). Others may binge (habitual maladaptive behavior) when they eat dessert (the stimulus). Still others may become inappropriately sexually aroused (habitual maladaptive behavior) in response to touching women's shoes (the stimulus).

To treat such disorders, the behavior therapist may seek to limit the patient's contact with the stimulus. This technique, called **stimulus control**, involves changing the frequency of a maladaptive conditioned response by controlling the frequency or intensity of exposure to the stimulus that elicits the response. For example, the person who drinks too much in bars would refrain from going to bars; the person who binges after eating even a bit of dessert might avoid buying desserts or going into bakeries. Stimulus control will be described more fully when we discuss treatment for substance abuse (Chapter 9).

The Role of Operant Conditioning in Behavior Therapy

Whereas classical conditioning methods can be used to decrease maladaptive behaviors related to conditioned emotional responses, operant conditioning techniques can be used to modify maladaptive behaviors more generally. When operant conditioning principles such as reinforcement and punishment are used to change maladaptive behaviors, the process is called **behavior modification**.

Making Use of Reinforcement and Punishment The key to successful behavior modification is setting appropriate *response contingencies*, which are the specific consequences that follow maladaptive or desired behaviors. It is these specific consequences (namely, reinforcement or punishment) that modify an undesired behavior. The goal of behavior modification is to have someone perform a desired behavior more often or perform an undesired behavior less often (or not at all) by shifting the consequences of the behavior through reinforcement, removing reinforcement, or—less frequently—through punishment.

Some behaviors are too complex to learn or perform immediately and must be developed gradually. Let's consider a woman who has had the eating disorder anorexia nervosa for a number of years. As we discuss in detail in Chapter 10, this eating disorder involves an inadequate intake of calories, which is a consequence of the individual's irrational belief about being "fat." (People with anorexia are at least 15% under their ideal weight.) When people with anorexia are in the early stages of recovery, eating a normal quantity of food can seem impossible. They may not be able to go from their daily intake of perhaps a serving of yogurt, a glass of milk, an egg white and a piece of fruit to three square meals a day along with a snack or two between meals. Sometimes the desired behavior change (in this case, resuming normal eating) can only occur gradually, and reinforcement follows small and then increasingly larger components of the desired new complex behavior. Thus, a woman recovering from anorexia nervosa might be reinforced for increasing her dinner from only a glass of milk and an apple to also include a small helping of fish. On subsequent meals, she might be expected to eat the fish (without reinforcement) and be reinforced for adding a piece of bread. This process would continue until she ate normal meals.

As part of behavioral treatment, someone with bulimia may use stimulus control initially to limit her intake of foods that she is likely to purge. If she habitually purges after eating cookies, for instance, she may want to avoid eating—or buying—cookies. Once she is out of the habit of purging, she may use exposure with response prevention to learn to eat cookies without purging.

FoodPix/Jupiterimages

Exposure with response prevention
The behavioral technique in which a patient is carefully prevented from engaging in his or her usual maladaptive response after being exposed to a stimulus that usually elicits the response.

Stimulus control
The behavioral technique for changing the frequency of a maladaptive conditioned response by controlling the frequency or intensity of exposure to the stimulus that elicits the response.

Behavior modification
The use of operant conditioning principles to change maladaptive behavior.

The procedure of reinforcing a small component of behavior at a time, and then progressively adding components of changed behavior until the desired complex behavior is exhibited is called **shaping**. The process of adding components is called *successive approximation*.

Making Use of Extinction In addition to using reinforcement and punishment, therapists also rely on the principle of **extinction**, which is the process of eliminating a behavior by not reinforcing it. To see how extinction can work to change behavior, let's consider someone who has a mild version of Leon's problem of social phobia. This man only gets anxious in certain types of social situations, such as going to a party where there will be unfamiliar people. Working with a therapist, the man might realize that in the past, when his wife has suggested they go to a party, he puts up such a fuss that she doesn't push him to go—it's not worth the effort to drag him to the party and have him complain before, during, and after it. Therapist and patient might decide that the maladaptive behavior to change is his *complaining*, because it leads his wife to decline the invitation (or to leave him at home). Patient and therapist agree to have the wife come to a therapy session and propose to her that she *extinguish* her husband's complaining. That is, when he complains about parties, she should ignore these comments, and they both then go to the party. In contrast, when he talks about other things, she can respond with interest.

Keeping Track of the ABCs Through Self-Monitoring In order to determine the antecedents and consequences of maladaptive behaviors, patients often use *self-monitoring* tools, such as keeping a daily log of activities, feelings, and thoughts. By completing self-monitoring logs like the one in Figure 4.2, a patient can become aware of possible *triggers*, or antecedents to a problematic behavior. The date, day of the week, and time of day can help the patient to identify triggers related to time. Information about the context can help the patient to identify whether particular situations or environments have become conditioned stimuli. Identifying thoughts, feelings, interactions with others, or other stimuli that triggered the problematic behavior (right-hand column in Figure 4.2) can help the patient and the therapist to plan the direction the therapy should take. Daily self-monitoring logs are used in treatments for anxiety, poor mood, smoking, compulsive gambling, overeating, and sleep problems, among others.

Behavioral techniques that rely on operant conditioning principles are often used in inpatient psychiatric units, where clinicians can intensively monitor and treat patients 24 hours a day, 7 days a week. Under these conditions, caregivers can change the response contingencies for desired and undesired behavior. In order to change behavior, treatment programs for psychiatric patients, mentally retarded children and adults, and prison inmates often employ **secondary reinforcers**, objects and events that do not directly satisfy a biological need but are desirable nonetheless. Examples of secondary reinforcers are praise or the opportunity to enjoy a favorite activity, such as watching television or using a computer. In addition, a common form of secondary reinforcement relies on a system in which participants can earn a "token" or chit by engaging in desired behaviors. The tokens or chits can be exchanged at a "store" for small items such as candy or for privileges such as permission to go out for a walk. A treatment program that uses such secondary reinforcers to change behavior is called a **token economy**.

The Goals of Cognitive Therapy

Unlike behavior therapy, cognitive therapy focuses not on what can be directly observed (stimuli, responses, and consequences of responses), but rather on internal states and events—namely, on the way people perceive and interpret objects and events can influence their mental health. In particular, many individuals with psychological disorders have automatic but irrational thoughts or incorrect beliefs that were formed as a result of past experiences. Such dysfunctional thoughts and beliefs, in turn, contribute to maladaptive behaviors and poor mood. Cognitive therapy is designed to modify the automatic thoughts and beliefs that contribute to psychological disorders.

Shaping
The process of reinforcing a small component of behavior at a time and then progressively adding components until the desired complex behavior occurs.

Extinction
The process of eliminating a behavior by not reinforcing it.

Secondary reinforcers
Objects and events that do not directly satisfy a biological need but are desirable nonetheless.

Token economy
A treatment program that uses "tokens" or chits as secondary reinforcers to change behavior.

Figure 4.2

Time of day	Problematic behavior	Context: Where the behavior occurred	What event triggered the behavior (thoughts, feelings, interactions with others)?
Name: *Leon*	Day: *Monday*		Date: *Oct 10*
9 am	Avoidance: Even though I want some, I don't get coffee from cafeteria.	Sitting at desk at work, hard to fully wake up.	Wanted coffee, but worried that someone else will be in the food area and I'll feel uncomfortable around them. Then started to feel depressed and hopeless about my situation and my life.
10:15 am	Avoidance: Problem arises at work and I should talk to a colleague about it but I don't – I avoid it. I send an email instead even though that will take longer to resolve problem.	Checking over some documents at work.	Realized that a coworker made a mistake, but the thought of talking to her made me anxious. Sad and angry that I can't make this phone call.
noon	Avoidance and social isolation.	Eat my lunch at my desk rather than eat with others.	Thought about eating with others, but became anxious about their looking at me or talking to me. Then felt very sad about my life.

4.2 ▸ A Daily Self-Monitoring Log Leon's self-monitoring log (from a time when he worked the day shift) suggests that his depressed and hopeless feelings follow the anxiety he experiences after simply thinking about possible social interactions, which he then avoids. Treatment might focus on his social anxiety and avoidance at the outset; as those lessen, so should his depression.

Leon, for example, has irrational, dysfunctional thoughts about being evaluated, and he expects to feel embarrassed and humiliated. Thus, he avoids interacting with others. His thoughts and beliefs lead to his avoidant behaviors—and his thoughts, beliefs, and behaviors, in turn, lead to his depression. With cognitive therapy, Leon would have an opportunity to reassess whether his automatic thoughts and beliefs are realistic and, if not, learn to substitute more realistic ones that will make social interactions less anxiety-provoking. Leon should then be more likely to participate in social situations, which in turn may reduce his depression. In general, then, cognitive therapy promotes more rational and realistic thoughts and beliefs, which in turn alter the patient's behavior, which should then lead the symptoms to subside.

Rational-emotive behavior therapy (REBT)
The form of treatment in which a patient's irrational thoughts are transformed into rational ones, which in turn leads to more positive emotions and adaptive behaviors.

Methods of Cognitive Therapy

The two pioneers in the field of cognitive therapy are Albert Ellis and Aaron Beck (see Chapters 1 and 2). Although there are some differences between the specific methods these men proposed, they both placed importance on working with patients to identify and challenge irrational and illogical thoughts and on giving patients between-session homework.

Ellis's Rational Emotive Behavior Therapy

To help people counter their irrational, destructive thoughts with rational ones, Ellis developed *rational-emotive therapy*, in which the therapist challenges the patient's irrational thoughts in detail and then encourages the patient to cultivate more realistic thoughts (Hollon & Beck, 1994, 2004). Over the years, however, Ellis incorporated behavioral techniques into his therapy. His treatment is now referred to as **rational-emotive behavior therapy (REBT)**, in which a patient's irrational thoughts are transformed into rational ones, which in turn leads to more positive emotions and adaptive behaviors. At the same time, the REBT therapist tries to promote self-acceptance, so the patient comes to learn that shortcomings, errors, and failures are simply part of life rather than crimes or evidence of moral weakness. Thus, this therapy also is designed to reduce self-blame (based on faulty beliefs), which is viewed as getting in the way of rational thinking.

The REBT therapist accomplishes these goals by systematically proceeding through a sequence of observational and interventional steps that can be labeled A, B, C, D, E, and F. As shown in Figure 4.3, the series is as follows: (A) An *activating event* triggers (B) the patient's *belief*, which leads to (C) a highly charged emotional *consequence*. (Note that the event itself does not lead to the consequence; the process

Figure 4.3

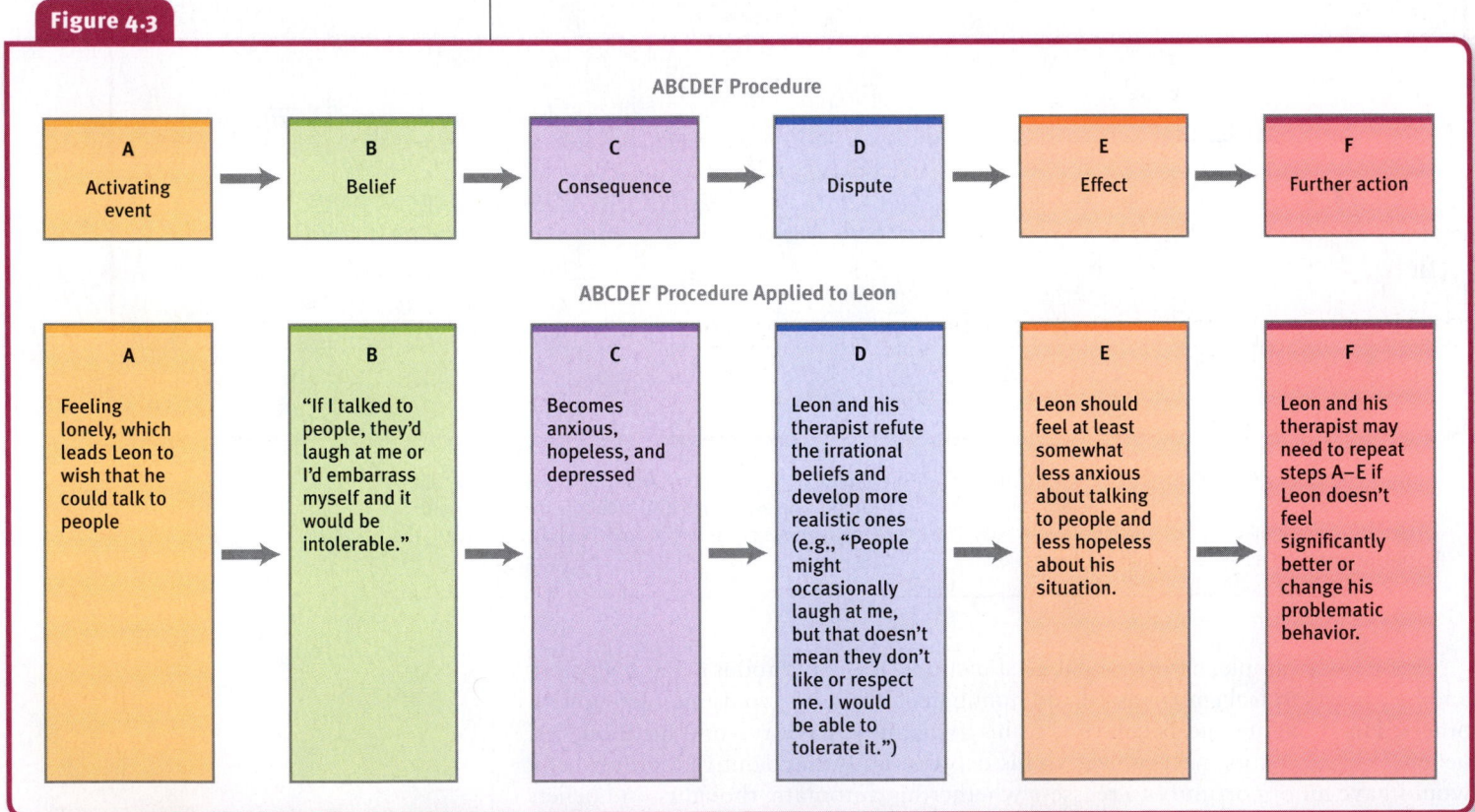

ABCDEF Procedure

A	B	C	D	E	F
Activating event	Belief	Consequence	Dispute	Effect	Further action

ABCDEF Procedure Applied to Leon

A	B	C	D	E	F
Feeling lonely, which leads Leon to wish that he could talk to people	"If I talked to people, they'd laugh at me or I'd embarrass myself and it would be intolerable."	Becomes anxious, hopeless, and depressed	Leon and his therapist refute the irrational beliefs and develop more realistic ones (e.g., "People might occasionally laugh at me, but that doesn't mean they don't like or respect me. I would be able to tolerate it.")	Leon should feel at least somewhat less anxious about talking to people and less hopeless about his situation.	Leon and his therapist may need to repeat steps A–E if Leon doesn't feel significantly better or change his problematic behavior.

4.3 ▸ The ABCDEF Procedure of Rational Emotive Behavior Therapy Rational emotive behavior therapy helps patients systematically become aware of and challenge their irrational thoughts. As patients dispute such thoughts, develop more realistic ones, and come to accept themselves more, their symptoms—such as feeling depressed—should lessen.

requires mediation through the patient's belief.) The therapist helps the patient (D) *dispute* any irrational beliefs by highlighting their destructive or illogical quality. A successful dispute leads to (E) an *effect* or an *effective new philosophy*, a new idea or a new pattern of emotion or behavior. Finally, the patient can fortify the effect through (F) *further action*.

Each REBT session is devoted to one aspect of the patient's overall problem. The patient and therapist often start a session by agreeing on the desired effect of the session's intervention. In Leon's case, the desired effect for a session might be to modify enough of his beliefs about being laughed at that he feels able to say hello to a coworker the next day. A main intervention during the dispute step involves helping the patient distinguish between a belief that something is necessary (a "must," such as "When I talk to someone, I must be suave and brilliant") and a belief that something is simply preferred ("When I talk to someone, I'd like them to think of me as suave and brilliant"). Sometimes the therapist argues with the patient as part of the dispute process. The therapist might also use role-playing to help patients develop new patterns of thinking and acting (Ellis & MacLaren, 1998).

Beck's Cognitive Restructuring

Beck's approach to cognitive therapy, like Ellis's, builds on the premise that psychological problems result from faulty automatic thoughts. Such thoughts are negative and pop into awareness without effort. For example, consider the situation of a young man, Yoshi, who, as a child, was accused by his parents of being selfish in relation to his younger brother; he grew up believing that he is a selfish person. Whenever he expresses a preference ("I'd like to see *this* movie tonight, not that one"), Yoshi feels that he is being selfish and feels bad about himself. Yoshi may live his life trying to avoid seeming selfish, and so strive to be totally flexible, never expressing preferences or desires that might conflict with those of others. His automatic thought, then, is that he is selfish; it pops into his awareness without effort.

Beck proposed that such negative thoughts arise from systematic *cognitive distortions*, which create a cognitive vulnerability—a diathesis, to use the term introduced in Chapter 1—for particular disorders (Beck, 2005). Table 4.4 shows several common cognitive distortions that lead to negative automatic thoughts.

Beck proposes that the problems created by negative automatic thoughts can diminish as the patient tests these thoughts (and discovers they are faulty) and adopts more rational and realistic thoughts. Beck developed methods to identify and reduce cognitive distortions and thereby modify automatic negative thoughts. Whereas REBT depends on the therapist's efforts to persuade patients that their beliefs are irrational, Beck's approach to cognitive therapy encourages patients to see their beliefs and automatic negative thoughts as testable hypotheses, about which they collect data. Both patient and therapist then examine the data to determine whether the patient's hypotheses are supported (or, as more often occurs, refuted). From this point of view, interactions in the world are opportunities for real-life "experiments" that can confirm, modify, or challenge the patient's beliefs (Hollon & Beck, 1994, 2004). Beck and his colleagues have developed this treatment scientifically, assessing depression, anxiety, and other problems before and after treatment; they have obtained this information in order to evaluate the degree to which the treatment works for each kind of problem, and to determine which elements cause the most positive change (Beck, 2005; Beck, Emery, & Greenberg, 2005; Beck, Freeman, & Davis, 2004; Newman et al., 2002).

This kind of cognitive therapy often relies on a patient's written self-report of each day's dysfunctional thoughts (see Figure 4.4, which shows a completed log for Leon). Patients are instructed to identify the context in which each automatic thought occurred, rate their emotional state at the time, and record the thought itself. Then they are asked to record their *rational* response to the automatic thought (which is like the dispute step in REBT) and a new rating of

Table 4.4 ▶ Five Common Cognitive Distortions

Cognitive Distortion	Definition	Example
Dichotomous Thinking (also called black-and-white thinking)	Maintaining only extremes of an idea, as in thinking that if you are not perfect, you are worthless	*"I'm trying to stop drinking and I had a beer; I blew it, so I might as well have five or six more."*
Mental Filtering	Directing attention to the negative qualities of something while overlooking—or filtering out—its positive qualities	*Noticing only what you weren't able to accomplish on a given day, not what you did accomplish*
Mind Reading	Believing that you can tell what other people are thinking, particularly what they think about you	*Thinking that other people are aware of what a failure you are and that they can tell that you are incompetent and detestable*
Catastrophic Exaggeration	Thinking that the worst possible circumstance will come to pass and that you won't be able to handle it	*Fearing that people will see who you "really" are (unworthy, incompetent, unlovable) and you'll never be able to show your face again*
Control Beliefs	Believing that unless you keep your life tightly under control, things will spin totally out of control and you will be permanently helpless	*Feeling certain that if you lose something, bad things will happen, which you won't be able to prevent or repair*

their emotional state, the outcome. For example, a rational response to Yoshi's automatic thought about being selfish might be that it is acceptable to express a strong preference sometimes, that it doesn't necessarily indicate selfishness, and that he is often very flexible.

As shown in Figure 4.4, when a patient challenges the logic and truth of an automatic thought and then develops a rational response, it is likely that the new emotional state will be rated as less distressing. Sometimes, however, it is difficult to challenge automatic thoughts; a patient may be so accustomed to the "truth" of the automatic thought that he or she cannot perceive the thought as irrational or distorted. This would be the case if Leon were unable to see why his belief that other people will laugh at him is irrational.

The process of reorganizing how a person interprets situations and events, which relies on dysfunctional or irrational automatic thoughts with more rational ones, is called **cognitive restructuring**. The therapist helps the patient to consider the accuracy of automatic thoughts or habitual ways of interpreting himself or herself and the world and then to develop more realistic thoughts or interpretations.

Methods of Cognitive-Behavior Therapy

CBT relies in part on the methods developed by Ellis and Beck but also uses a variety of additional ones. For example, CBT therapists may also employ **psychoeducation**, which is the process of educating patients about research findings and therapy procedures relevant to their situation. The therapist may provide such information during a therapy session, may suggest a book or Web site that has relevant information, or may give the patient reading materials to take home. This new knowledge helps patients to develop a less distorted, more realistic understanding of their problems and to formulate more appropriate treatment goals (Cuijpers, 1998; Miklowitz et al., 2003; Rice & Moller, 2006).

Cognitive restructuring
The process of reorganizing how a person interprets situations and events, which relies on replacing dysfunctional or irrational automatic thoughts with more rational ones.

Psychoeducation
The process of educating patients about research findings and therapy procedures relevant to their situation.

Figure 4.4

Name: _Leon_		Day: _Monday_	Date: _Oct 10_	
Situation	Emotion(s)	Automatic thought(s) (ATs)	Rational response	Outcome
Actual event or stream of thoughts	Rate (1–100%)	ATs that preceded emotion. Rate of belief in ATs (1–100%)	Write rational response to ATs. Rate belief in rational response (1–100%)	Rerate at (1–100%)
I needed to talk to a colleague about a work problem.	_Anxiety (85%)_	_If I talk with her, I will somehow be humiliated—either I will humiliate myself or she will laugh at me for reasons I won't understand. (90%)_	_It is possible I may be humiliated, but it is unlikely. Even if I do or say something inappropriate, she may not even notice or think it's stupid. (60%)_	_Anxiety (60%)_
Same situation	_Sadness and hopelessness (70%)_	_I am so pathetic. I'm afraid to do something as trivial as talk to a colleague._	_I may be afraid to talk to her, but I am working on my anxiety so that the next time I'll be able to do it._	_Sadness and hopelessness (50%)_

4.4 ▶ A Daily Record of Dysfunctional Thoughts Leon's daily record can identify his train of irrational automatic thoughts and the types of events that trigger those thoughts. By countering such thoughts with rational responses, the thoughts seem less believable and the intensity of the emotions should decrease. (Format adapted from Beck et al., 1979.)

In the decades since behavior therapy and cognitive therapy emerged, clinicians and researchers have found that attempting to change both cognitions and behaviors can, for some disorders, reduce symptoms and improve quality of life more than addressing either cognitions or behaviors alone. Behavioral and cognitive approaches work together: When cognitive techniques change thoughts, changes in emotions and behaviors often follow, and when behavioral techniques change behaviors, changes in emotions, social interactions, and thoughts about oneself and the world often follow. Consider exposure therapy: The behavioral technique also challenges the cognitive distortion of catastrophic exaggeration. When patients see that horrible things do not occur upon exposure to a feared stimulus, their cognitive distortions are modified (Emmelkamp, 2004). Moreover, new cognitions may be maintained through principles of reinforcement or punishment (Roth & Fonagy, 2005).

Dialectical Behavior Therapy—CBT Plus More

CBT forms the nucleus of a relatively new type of therapy called **dialectical behavior therapy (DBT)**, which was originally developed specifically for treating people with *borderline personality disorder*, an Axis II disorder (to be discussed in detail in Chapter 13). *Dialectical* refers to the aim of helping patients to tolerate and integrate contradictory feelings, beliefs, and desires. DBT, like CBT, employs particular tools and methods to change specific thoughts, feelings, and behaviors. DBT was

Dialectical behavior therapy (DBT)
The form of treatment that includes elements of CBT as well as an emphasis on validating the patient's experience, a Zen Buddhist approach, and a dialectics component.

developed to treat people, generally women, who regularly hurt themselves physically (such as by cutting or burning themselves) or who make suicidal gestures or attempts (Linehan, 1993), and for whom other forms of therapy—including CBT—had not been successful. DBT has also been used with patients who have significant difficulty regulating their emotions and containing their impulses, such as some people with drug dependence (van den Bosch et al., 2005) and some people with bulimia nervosa (Safer, Telch, & Agras, 2001).

DBT, which generally involves individual and group therapy, includes elements of CBT, such as skills building, cognitive restructuring, and a warm and strong collaborative bond between patient and therapist. DBT adds three other components:

- *An emphasis on validating the patient's experience.* It is assumed that the patient's thoughts, feelings and behaviors in a given situation make sense in the context of his or her life, past experiences, and strengths and weaknesses. The therapist helps the patient recognize the context of the patient's experience.

- *A Zen Buddhist approach.* Patients are helped to identify and then, without judgment, accept any painful realities of their lives. Patients are encouraged to "let go" of emotional attachments that cause them suffering. Mindfulness—nonjudgmental awareness—is the goal. Patients entering DBT are often full of self-loathing and judge themselves harshly, which only serves to make them feel worse and resort to impulsive behaviors to soothe themselves; treatment is intended to reduce such unproductive judgments.

- *A dialectics component.* This therapy is a process of acknowledging and coming to terms with opposing elements—feelings, beliefs, desires. The therapist helps the patient to change what can be changed but also to accept what cannot be changed (Robins, Ivanoff, & Linehan, 2001). Patients entering DBT tend to see themselves and others in rigid all-or-nothing terms. The dialectics component helps them become less rigid in how they see themselves and others. For instance, they learn to see that most people—including themselves—can be generally good people, who sometimes make mistakes; mistakes don't necessarily indicate that people are bad or evil.

Incorporating Technology Into Treatment

In their efforts to make treatment more effective and efficient, researchers and clinicians have been inspired to incorporate technologies into treatment—usually as part of between-session work—and to broaden the ways that treatment can occur so that it need not always involve having the patient and therapist in the same room (Gega, Marks, & Mataix-Cols, 2004).

Using Technology for Between-Session Work

Patients in CBT often perform significant between-session work, such as completing self-monitoring logs, challenging their irrational or automatic thoughts, constructing hierarchies of fear and avoidance, and trying out new behaviors. Several kinds of technology can help make these between-session tasks easier to remember and to perform and can make it easier to collect and analyze the data obtained from the tasks:

- Self-monitoring is made easier with hand-held devices—such as PDAs and smartphones—or computer software. An alarm can be set to go off at programmed or random times, reminding patients to:

  o assess their thoughts, mood, and symptom level (such as anxiety);

  o perform certain mental tasks (such as coming up with a rational response to an automatic thought); or

  o perform certain physical behaviors (such as trying a relaxation technique).

- Computer software or Web sites can be used to facilitate cognitive restructuring or provide educational information or blank forms that can be completed online (Carroll et al., 2008; Eisen et al., 2008; Kurtz et al., 2007; Litz et al., 2007).

- Computer software can provide virtual reality exposure treatment, which can be particularly helpful when it would be difficult to have a therapist along for an in vivo exposure (such as on an airplane, for those with a fear of flying).

Researchers have found that 4 weeks of computer-assisted CBT treatment for anxiety plus 8 weeks of self-monitoring with a hand-held device was as effective as 12 weeks of the usual CBT (Newman et al., 1997; Przeworski & Newman, 2004).

Cybertherapy

Therapy most frequently occurs when therapist and patient are together in the same room, but technology has offered an alternative possibility—therapy at a distance. One well-established use of technology (at the low-tech end of the spectrum) is phone calls between therapists and patients for emergencies. For patients who are not able to get to a therapist's office, because they live in a rural area, are housebound with a medical illness, or because their phobias prevent a face-to-face meeting with a therapist, therapy conducted over the telephone may be better than no treatment (Ludman et al., 2007; Mohr, Hart, et al., 2005; Tate & Zabinski, 2004).

Newer technology has made possible another form of treatment that allows patient and therapist to be in different locations: **cybertherapy**, or Internet-based therapy. In such therapy, the patient and the therapist interact online. Clinicians have developed a number of different cybertherapeutic techniques (Santhiveeran & Grant, 2005):

- *E-therapy, or e-mail exchanges between patient and therapist.* Patient and therapist do not meet face to face. E mail exchanges can be valuable to both patient and therapist in providing a real-time written record of the conversation (Murphy & Mitchell, 1998), and the task of organizing a thoughtful written communication itself can be therapeutic (Pennebaker, 1999);

- *E-mail exchanges between patient and therapist who also meet face-to-face.* Such e-mails may include updates on between-session homework assignments and questions or comments raised by a prior session (Barnett & Scheetz, 2003; Ruwaard et al., 2007).

- *Real-time chat room involving a patient and a therapist.*

- *Real-time face-to face video chats* (using webcams) between a patient and a therapist (Jerome & Zaylor, 2000).

Cybertherapy can be particularly helpful for rural or housebound patients, enabling them to meet with a therapist.

Leon, because of his anxiety about meeting new people, might find cybertherapy initially more comfortable than face-to-face therapy. However, most therapists have reservations about using the Internet as a vehicle for therapy. Concerns about various forms of cybertherapy include (Heinlen et al., 2003):

- *Imposters.* The individual posing as a therapist may be neither professionally trained nor licensed.

- *Privacy.* With Internet or e-mail communications, confidentiality and privacy cannot be guaranteed (Young, 2005).

- *Incomplete communication.* E-mail communications lack important nonverbal cues (such as body language, facial expressions, and tone of voice); a therapist in face-to-face therapy sessions uses such information to assess a patient's problems and responses to treatment suggestions (Bloom, 1998). However, the use of webcams may reduce this concern.

Some studies have shown that treatment via cybertherapy is more effective than none at all (Lange et al., 2001; Ritterband et al., 2003), but little research so far has compared cybertherapy to in-person therapy (either in general or for specific disorders). For instance, although e-mail has been used in family therapy

Cybertherapy
Internet-based therapy.

when a member of the family was too far away to attend sessions and with people who have severe medical problems that make it difficult to come to a therapist's office (King, Engi, & Poulos, 1998), its effectiveness in such situations has not yet been tested rigorously.

Targeting Psychological Factors in Younger and Older Populations

As when biomedical treatments are given to children and older adults, treatments that target psychological factors in these special populations may need to be modified.

Targeting Psychological Factors in Younger Patients

Many of the treatments that target psychological factors can be used with children and adolescents, although a mental health clinician may need to modify a particular method so that it is appropriate for the cognitive and emotional level of the younger patient. In addition, the clinician may ask parents to assist with between-session homework assignments. A therapist employing CBT with a child, for instance, may ask the parents to become directly involved by helping the child complete daily self-monitoring logs or by providing reinforcement in response to the child's desired behavior change.

In addition, special therapeutic methods have been developed for younger children, who may not be able to discuss their problems in detail or may have poor insight into their problems. One such method is *play therapy*, which uses toys, games, and play-based activities to elicit therapeutic change. Play therapy is used in varying ways by clinicians with different therapeutic approaches. For instance, a psychodynamic child therapist may view a child's play during a therapy session as a communication of unconscious feelings, much like free association is viewed for adults in psychodynamic therapy; the role of the clinician is then to interpret the child's play. In contrast, a cognitive-behavior therapist is likely to use play therapy to enhance a child's social and problem-solving skills; in that case, play therapy might be the medium through which modeling or role-playing occurs, where new behaviors are practiced and reinforced (Waas & Kleckler, 2000). Unfortunately, researchers have yet to evaluate whether specific uses of play therapy are effective.

Targeting Psychological Factors in Older Patients

To the extent that elderly patients have significant cognitive slowing or memory problems (or other types of impaired cognition), psychosocial treatments may need to be modified. For instance, with CBT, elderly patients may need the therapist to explain information more frequently, or they may require more opportunities to practice changing their behaviors.

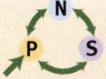

In sum, we've seen that various approaches to therapy directly target psychological factors: thoughts, feelings, and behaviors. The methods of psychodynamic therapies, client-centered therapy, CBT, and DBT—and the technological innovations that can supplement such treatments—all address the psychological factors that contribute to psychological disorders.

Although in this section we have focused on psychological factors, note that the relationship between the therapist and patient is a social event: A patient's interaction with a therapist can provide support, advice, a framework for understanding symptoms and problems and the sense that someone cares. Moreover, as with all successful treatments, changing a psychological factor affects neurological factors as well as social factors: As patients more successfully regulate their emotions, think about themselves more realistically, and behave differently, their neurological functioning also changes.

Key Concepts and Facts About Treatments That Target Psychological Factors

- Psychodynamic therapy and psychoanalysis are intended to help patients more adaptively manage unconscious conflicts that arise in large part from id-driven impulses and urges. They do so by helping a patient develop insight into events in his or her past (especially interactions with parents) and how these events and unconscious forces influence current difficulties. Psychoanalysis is more time-consuming than is psychodynamic therapy.

- Psychodynamic therapy and psychoanalytic methods focus on the therapeutic alliance, and use free association, interpretation, dream analysis, resistance, and transference.

- Client-centered therapy is designed to integrate the sense of self by decreasing the incongruence between a patient's real and ideal selves. According to the theory of client-centered therapy, with an integrated sense of self comes reduced emotional pain. To accomplish these aims, therapists show the patient genuine empathy and unconditional positive regard.

- Behavioral methods often focus attention on the antecedents and consequences of a maladaptive behavior, as well as on the behavior itself. Specific methods based on classical conditioning include exposure (sometimes with response prevention), systematic desensitization, and stimulus control. Methods based on operant conditioning make use of reinforcement and punishment and may involve shaping, extinction, and self-monitoring.

- Cognitive methods based on Ellis's rational emotive behavior therapy (REBT) may follow steps (A through F) that are designed to dispute beliefs that lead to maladaptive consequences. Methods based on Beck's cognitive restructuring challenge patients' maladaptive automatic negative thoughts and encourage patients to test the accuracy of their beliefs through real-life

experiments. This hypothesis testing leads patients to develop more rational responses to the automatic thoughts.

- The behavioral aspects of cognitive-behavior therapy (CBT) are intended to transform maladaptive behaviors that stem from previous learning, whereas the cognitive aspects of CBT are intended to modify irrational thoughts and incorrect beliefs that influence feelings and behavior maladaptively. Changing behaviors and thoughts in turn alters feelings as well. CBT often includes psychoeducation.

- Dialectical behavior therapy (DBT) relies on CBT methods and also has the therapist validate the patient's experience, help the patient accept and integrate contradictory feelings and thoughts, and teach the patient a Zen Buddhist approach of being nonjudgmental.

- Technology is being incorporated into treatment through the use of electronic methods for self-monitoring and cognitive restructuring. Virtual reality exposure is also sometimes used in therapy. Moreover, cybertherapy brings treatment to patients who are unable or unwilling to go to the office of a mental health clinician, and it can be a means through which patient and therapist can maintain contact between visits. However, cybertherapy has drawbacks: The therapist could be an imposter, confidential information may not remain private, and the lack of nonverbal cues for the therapist may skew the treatment in a less helpful direction.

- Treatments for children and older patients that target psychological factors may need to be modified for those populations. For instance, children may engage in play therapy (however, clinicians who have different theoretical orientations will use this method differently).

Treatments That Target Social Factors

Treatments that target social factors aim to reduce symptoms or improve quality of life by changing a person's relationships for the better and by creating, expanding, or improving a person's sense of community. Such treatments may directly or indirectly address the patient's problems. For example, when treatment that directly targets improving a family's communication leads to better family functioning, the positive change can lead to the patient's feeling more supported, which in turn can reduce symptoms. As we shall see, some treatments that target social factors would be appropriate for Leon's problems of depression and social anxiety, whereas other treatments that target social factors would be less appropriate. All these treatments have in common their focus on the patient *in the context* of other people: family members, group therapy members, coworkers, community members.

Interpersonal Therapy

Interpersonal therapy focuses on the patient's relationships and is loosely based on psychodynamic theory.

Interpersonal therapy (IPT)
The form of treatment that is intended to improve the patient's skills in relationships so that they become more satisfying.

The Goal of Interpersonal Therapy

Originally developed to treat depression, the theory underlying **interpersonal therapy (IPT)** is that symptoms of psychological disorders such as depression and bulimia nervosa become exacerbated when a patient's relationships aren't functioning well. The goal of IPT is thus to improve the patient's skills in relationships so that they become more satisfying; as relationships improve, so do the patient's thoughts and feelings, and the symptoms of psychological disorders lessen. The therapist who provides IPT tries to link specific aspects of the patient's current relationships with one of four kinds of problems in relationships (see Table 4.5; Klerman et al., 1984); each type of problem suggests a distinct goal for treatment. For example, with depressed patients, the task is to identify ways that current relationships are not satisfying and then to set about enhancing those aspects of the relationships. Perhaps a patient feels that a boyfriend does not communicate enough, and hence the patient feels a lack of intimacy; a goal in this case would be to work on ways to improve communication, which should in turn increase feelings of intimacy.

Table 4.5 ▸ Four Themes of Relationship Problems in Interpersonal Therapy

Theme	Example	Goal
Unresolved Grief	A relationship lost through death	Facilitate mourning of the lost relationship and help the patient develop other interests and activities
Role Transition	Difficulty coping with changes in life (e.g., getting a new job, having a baby, retiring) that lead to a new role for a patient or family member	Help patient develop appropriate expectations about what is needed for the new role, as well as whatever skills and social support are needed
Role Dispute	Differing expectations about an enduring relationship (such as that between coworkers, family members, or neighbors), which lead to chronic significant conflict	Help identify the particular dispute and develop ways to move forward; encourage patient to try to change patterns in the relationship or assess whether expectations are realistic
Interpersonal Deficits	Exhibiting behaviors that lead to social isolation and poor communication, such as staying in bed all day or not answering the phone	Decrease social isolation by focusing on present relationship with a therapist and forming additional relationships

Methods Used in Interpersonal Therapy

IPT was conceived of as a short-term therapy, usually lasting 16 sessions. Moreover, the therapist uses a treatment manual to guide the goals, techniques, and topics for each session to ensure that all methods of the treatment are implemented.

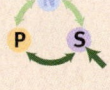

To achieve the goals summarized in Table 4.5, the therapist providing IPT uses a variety of methods, some borrowed from psychodynamic and cognitive behavioral therapy; these methods helps patients to:

• consider the consequences of their actions in a relationship,

• role-play their interactions with significant others,

• become more aware of feelings that they have tried to ignore or push aside,

• improve their communication skills, and

• tell others how they feel in an appropriate manner (Elkin, 1994; Shea et al., 1992; Weissman, Markowitz, & Klerman, 2000).

Family and Systems Therapy

Some therapies target family functioning in order to change maladaptive patterns of interaction and to increase the support family members provide to each other.

Family Therapy

Family therapy is a treatment that involves either an entire family or some portion of a family. What constitutes a "family"? For our purposes, a *family* is any group of people that functions as a family: an extended family that includes several generations, a blended family of children and parents originally from different households, any other nontraditional family, as well as a traditional nuclear family that consists of mother, father, and their children (Carter & McGoldrick, 1999). Family therapy can be performed using any theoretical approach; the main focus is on the family, rather than an individual patient.

Systems Therapy: A Different Way of Thinking About the Family

The most prevalent theoretical orientation in family therapy is **systems therapy** (sometimes referred to as *family systems therapy*), which is designed to change the communication or behavior patterns of one or more family members. According to this approach, the family is a system that strives to maintain *homeostasis*, a state of equilibrium, so that change in one member affects other family members. Systems therapy is guided by the view that when one member changes (perhaps through therapy), change is forced on the rest of the system (Bowen, 1978; Minuchin, 1974).

To a systems therapist, the "patient" is the family, and the individual member with a psychological disorder is referred to as the *identified patient*. Systems therapy focuses on communication and power within the family. The symptoms of the identified patient are understood to be a result of that individual's intentional or unintentional attempts to maintain or change a pattern within the family or to convey a message to family members.

The Goals of Systems Therapy

The goals of systems therapy are to identify and then change maladaptive patterns of interaction and communication among family members (Gurman, 2000). For instance, had Leon and his parents participated in systems therapy when he was younger, perhaps the therapist might have found that Leon's parents didn't mind the fact that Leon didn't socialize with others; he was a good companion and having him around more meant that the parents spent less time alone as a couple. The therapist might have reframed the problem as one in which Leon needed to spend more time with others so that his parents could have more opportunities to practice spending time alone as a couple before Leon went off to college and they were alone all the time.

Methods of Systems Therapy

A systems therapist normally begins by interviewing family members about the history of the family. This interview establishes which family members are close to and distant from each other and determines how feelings, issues, and conflicts tend to be handled within the family. The systems therapist might discover, for example, that one parent is underinvolved (doesn't interact much with his or her child, for instance), and the other is overinvolved (spending inordinate amounts of time with the child, perhaps finishing his or her sentences). In addition, the parents may have a conflicted relationship. Treatment might then focus on rectifying such imbalances in the family system. The patterns and conflicts are often illustrated graphically; Figure 4.5 illustrates an angry, antagonistic relationship between parents, which influences the child's behavior (Kitzmann, 2000).

Family therapy
The form of treatment that involves either the family as a whole or some portion of it.

Systems therapy
The form of treatment that is designed to change the communication or behavior patterns of one or more family members in the context of the family as a whole; also known as *family systems therapy*.

Figure 4.5

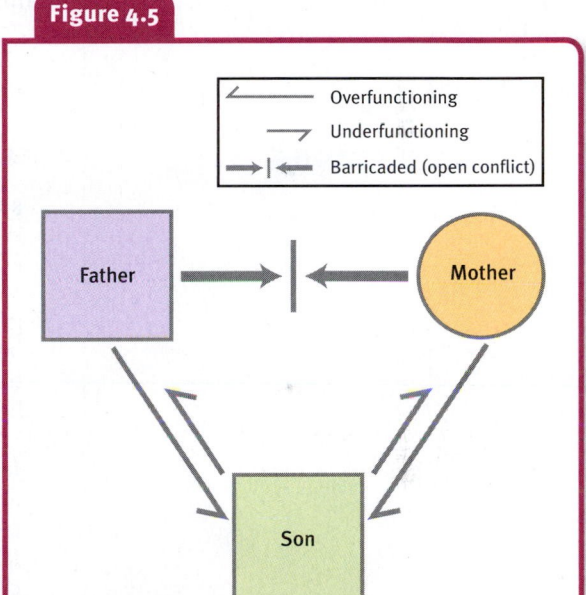

4.5 ▸ Graphing the Family System Systems therapists may graphically illustrate the predominant family dynamic. This figure shows conflict in the parents' relationship with each other. It also shows that each parent tries to be involved with and control the son (overfunctioning, represented by the long arrows), who has withdrawn from both parents (underfunctioning, represented by the short arrows). Part of the problem in this family system may be that the parents are constantly vying for attention from the son as an extension of their conflict with each other.

Source: Adapted from Ackerman, 1980, pp. 152, 154.

Consider an example of the methods of systems therapy in action: A mother and stepfather and the mother's two daughters from a previous marriage, Maria, age 17, and Lena, age 14, come to family therapy. Lena has taken to wearing all black and, despite her mother's clear admonition against it, has gotten tattoos and nose rings. Although she's doing okay in school, she frequently fights with her mother and her stepfather about her dress and her attitude. Lena likes her stepfather, but he and Lena's mother have been squabbling a lot for the last couple of years, and there's been a lot of tension between them, which makes Lena uncomfortable. Maria is a high school senior and is planning to go to college next year; she's just biding her time until she leaves home. During a therapy session, a systems therapist might rephrase what each family member has said in order to **validate** their experiences—demonstrate that the therapist understands each one's feelings and desires. The therapist may also try to ensure that each family member understands every other member's experience. In addition, the therapist might **reframe**—offer new ways to conceive of, or frame, the problem—in this case, Lena's behavior. Instead of viewing her behavior as a bad thing, the therapist might point out that what Lena is doing is trying to bring her mother and stepfather together by having them focus on her. If she is the focus of their negative attention, then they'll get along better with each other. The therapist might then suggest that perhaps Lena fears that if her behavior and attitude improve, the anger and tension between the mother and stepfather will increase. The therapist might praise Lena's willingness to be a lightning rod for the family tension.

Case 4.2 illustrates family systems therapy for a marital conflict.

CASE 4.2 ▶ FROM THE OUTSIDE: Family Systems Therapy for Depression

Ruben, a Cheyenne Native American, and his wife, Angie, a Hungarian, were at an impasse. Living on the East Coast and childless, with financial problems, they came to therapy when Ruben was offered an apprentice job with a large manufacturer, a position arranged by a member of Angie's family. Angie worked as a secretary, while Ruben held a series of temporary jobs. Instead of being happy about the new position, Ruben had become depressed and even was thinking of turning it down. Furious, Angie was threatening to leave him. . . . Angie came from a family in which women typically made decisions about work and finances, and thus helped direct the family's mobility. For her, financial stability was critical.

Ruben became depressed because he faced a major conflict. On the one hand, in his family, asking for guidance and direction through healing rituals was a way to begin to find answers to problems. Before he and Angie married, Ruben made a commitment to participate in a year-long purification ritual, both for the blessings he hoped it would bestow on his family, and to maintain his traditional ways while living as a part of the dominant American culture. Ruben felt strongly about his prior commitment to perform the ritual, and he realized that if he takes the job, he might not be able to perform the ritual as he originally intended (and thus be unable to fulfill part of his commitment to his heritage); on the other hand, his wife desired that he take the job, and he felt that the future of his marriage might be at stake if he did not take it. The goal of systems therapy was not to reduce Ruben's guilt should he not perform the Cheyenne ritual; rather, it was to help Ruben more clearly identify the conflict and his feelings, and explore acceptable ways that he could resolve the situation. This may involve helping Angie to understand the ritual and its significance to Ruben.

(Adapted from Sutton & Broken Nose, 1996, pp. 38–39)

In certain cases, a systems therapist might employ **paradoxical intention**—by suggesting that the problem behavior be allowed to continue, or even increase in intensity or frequency. This technique is paradoxical because it seems at odds with the general goal of treatment; it is also called *prescribing the symptom* (Stanton, 1981). With Lena's family, the systems therapist might use paradoxical intention by suggesting that Lena continue to behave in ways that make her mother and

Validate
A systems therapy technique by which the therapist demonstrates an understanding of each family member's feelings and desires.

Reframe
A systems therapy technique in which the therapist offers new ways to conceive of, or frame, the family's or identified patient's problem.

Paradoxical intention
A systems therapy technique in which the therapist suggests that the problem behavior be allowed to continue or even increase in intensity or frequency.

stepfather angry, at least until the adults have more practice working out their difficulties. Paradoxical intention is generally only used with families who have not otherwise made changes suggested by the therapist.

Note that systems therapy originated with therapists who worked almost exclusively with families. This history has caused systems therapy to be confused with *family therapy*. The two are not the same: Some systems therapists use a systems approach to treat only one individual, whereas some family therapists use a psychodynamic or behavioral approach rather than a systems approach.

Group Therapy

In **group therapy**, a number of patients (typically 6–8) with similar needs meet together with one or two therapists. This form of therapy can occur in a single session, in sessions that continue over years, or within some specified time limit (such as 12 weeks). Like family therapy, group therapy can be rooted in any of a variety of theoretical orientations, such as psychodynamic or cognitive-behavioral. If the therapist has a cognitive-behavioral orientation, participants in the group are likely to be assigned homework between sessions and will then discuss their homework in the group. Some therapy groups are restricted to people who have a specific problem or disorder (such as people with depression), and the group offers members psychoeducation, emotional support, or training in CBT techniques. Other therapy groups (which may be psychodynamic in approach) are open to people who are united simply by their desire to understand their relationships and to develop better ways to interact with others—romantic partners, colleagues, or other people in their lives. A psychodynamic therapist might use transference, resistance, and interpretation to help members learn about themselves and change the ways that they relate to others. In groups in which the goal is to improve interpersonal interactions, the group itself can be a forum for experimenting with new ways of interacting.

The most appropriate type of group therapy for Leon might well be one that targeted his social phobia. Just being in a group with strangers would, in and of itself, be exposure treatment for him; moreover, he might feel less alone and ashamed when hearing about other group members' similar problems and struggles.

Beyond information and support, group therapy provides interaction with others who share similar problems and goals. Hearing members talk about experiences that are similar to their own can help patients understand their own experiences more clearly and think about them in a different way. For instance, if Leon were in group therapy, after hearing about other members' experiences, he might feel less anxious being around them and realize that, just as he wasn't judging the other group members, they probably were not judging him. In turn, he might then feel more willing to be with other people. Whether group therapy helps people explore their relationships or develop skills for cognitive restructuring of automatic negative thoughts, being with other members who are struggling with the same issues decreases the sense of hopelessness, isolation, and shame that some patients feel about their problem or disorder.

Community-Based Treatment

Treatment most often occurs within a patient's community—his or her neighborhood, town, or city. Most people seeking mental health care receive **outpatient treatment**—treatment that does not involve an overnight stay in a hospital. Outpatient treatment may occur in a therapist's private office, a community mental health center or mental health clinic, an outpatient unit of a hospital, or, for those seeking pastoral counseling, within their church, synagogue, or mosque. For some people with severe symptoms, outpatient treatment consisting of weekly sessions of up to 1 hour may not be adequate, and more intensive treatment may be needed or desired. Intensive treatment may take place in a hospital, clinic, or mental health facility and may last for several hours each day or evening to 24 hours a day.

Group therapy
The form of treatment in which several patients with similar needs meet together with one or two therapists.

Outpatient treatment
Treatment that does not involve an overnight stay in a hospital.

Inpatient Treatment

Inpatient treatment is the term for treatment that occurs while a patient is in a psychiatric hospital or in a psychiatric unit of a general hospital. This is the most intensive level of treatment and is provided in two main circumstances: (1) when individuals, because of a psychological disorder, are believed to be at risk of harming themselves or another person (or have already done so); and (2) when individuals do not appear able to take adequate care of themselves. The initial goals of hospitalization are to ensure the patients' safety, the safety of others, and reduce the intensity or frequency of the patients' symptoms.

Partial Hospitalization

Partial hospitalization consists of treatment provided at a hospital or other facility, but the patient does not sleep there; such treatment is more intensive than what is available through once-a-week outpatient visits, but is less intensive than the treatment received through hospitalization. Partial hospitalization is appropriate for people who are not actively dangerous to themselves or others, and such programs may last from 2 to 12 hours daily. *Day treatment programs* and *evening programs* are examples of partial hospitalization. Such programs often provide many different kinds of group therapy and teach skills for coping with symptoms such as delusions, feelings of hopelessness, or continued bingeing and vomiting. These programs also provide an opportunity for patients to discuss problems and concerns they have with specific medications, such as how to minimize side effects.

Residential Treatment

Residential treatment consists of staying in a staffed facility where patients sleep, eat breakfast and dinner, and perhaps take part in evening groups. Typically patients must go elsewhere during the day, such as to a partial hospitalization program, school, or work. Residential treatment is for people who do not need the intensity of inpatient care, but nonetheless need supervised care during the evening and night.

Self-Help

Some people choose to attend self-help groups, either as a supplement to their therapy or instead of therapy. Like group therapy, self-help groups (sometimes referred to as *support groups*) tend to focus on a particular problem or disorder. Self-help groups generally do not have a leader who is clinically trained, although a mental health professional may sometimes advise the group (Shepherd et al., 1999).

The first popular self-help program was Alcoholics Anonymous (AA), which is still widely used. AA is designed around a 12-step process of recovery from alcoholism and a belief in a "higher power" (for most participants, God), which, according to AA, is crucial to the recovery process. Most other 12-step programs, such as Narcotics Anonymous, follow this model.

There are other self-help programs that use a different approach, however, such as that of the Depression and Bipolar Support Alliance, which serves people suffering from depression or bipolar disorder and their friends and families. This program provides education about the disorders and holds groups for patients where they can learn from and support one another. Like the Depression and Bipolar Support Alliance, self-help organizations may also offer information and support groups for friends and family members (Citron, Solomon, & Draine, 1999). If a member wants the services of a mental health clinician, a self-help organization often can provide the names of therapists in the community who are experienced in treating people with a given disorder.

Like group therapy, self-help groups can diminish feelings of shame and isolation, as well as provide support and valuable information. However, sometimes the lack of a trained leader may lead to negative group interactions that go unchecked.

Inpatient treatment
Treatment that occurs while a patient is in a psychiatric hospital or in a psychiatric unit of a general hospital.

Partial hospitalization
Treatment is provided at a hospital or other facility, but the patient does not sleep there.

Residential treatment
Treatment in which patients stay in a staffed facility where they sleep, eat breakfast and dinner, and perhaps take part in evening groups.

Much self-help does not take place in groups, but instead often relies on an individual's reading a book, listening to audio materials, or visiting Web sites. The number and variety of self-help books and materials have vastly expanded in recent years. These publications provide help for a wide variety of problems—such as depression, panic disorder, attention-deficit/hyperactivity disorder, and eating disorders—and many of the publications incorporate the theories and techniques described in this chapter. Research reveals that self-help materials are most likely to help people with depression and anxiety (Cuijpers, 1997), headache, sleep disturbances, and fears (Gould & Clum, 1993), and anxiety (Finch, Lambert, & Brown, 2000; Hirai & Clum, 2006; Scogin et al., 1990). In contrast, self-help materials have not been as successful in helping people change habits such as smoking, drinking, or overeating (Cuijpers, 1997). As you might expect, self-help materials are more likely to be helpful when people closely follow the recommended techniques (Gould & Clum, 1983).

Using self-help materials as part of therapy is sometimes called **bibliotherapy**, and therapists often advise patients to read relevant books (Campbell & Smith, 2003, Starker, 1988) in order to understand better the possible causes of their symptoms and ways to treat the disorder.

The Internet also provides a variety of self-help opportunities, including educational materials, chat rooms that serve as support groups (which may or may not be led by someone claiming to be a therapist), and interactive self-help treatments (Andersson et al., 2006; Carlbring et al., 2006). However, information can be posted online by anyone for any purpose, so online resources may not be accurate. Like some "therapists" who engage in cybertherapy, people in an online support group may be lying about their identity, may not provide accurate diagnoses, and may recommend inappropriate courses of treatment (Finn & Banach, 2000; Waldron, Lavitt, & Kelley, 2000).

Using the Internet or computer software, people can also benefit from interactive self-help programs that automatically adapt to the user's responses. These interactive programs may be more complex than a self-help book or video, but they are unlikely to surpass live therapy in terms of patient satisfaction and quality of treatment (Jacobs et al., 2001). As with cybertherapy, some online interactive self-help programs that use a cognitive-behavioral approach result in a better outcome than engaging in no treatment at all (Carlbring et al., 2006). Further research is needed, however, to assess the efficacy of these programs in comparison with live treatment.

Prevention Programs

Prevention programs are designed to prevent or inhibit the development or progression of psychological problems or disorders (Mrazek & Haggerty, 1994). The specific techniques in a prevention program might target any or all neuropsychosocial factors, but the creation of such programs relies crucially on social factors. One such program is the Big Brother/Big Sister program, which targets both psychological and social factors in children deemed at risk of developing problems because they don't have regular positive contact with an adult family member; the Big Brother or Big Sister provides such contact with an adult who serves as a mentor. Prevention programs have also been created to address suicide and drug abuse, to provide counseling for rape victims, and to provide early intervention for people who have been identified as having an elevated risk of a particular psychological disorder. This last group includes:

- those with a family history of a particular disorder,
- those who have experienced a traumatic event, and
- children whose parents have divorced.

Any treatment technique and theoretical orientation may be employed in a prevention program.

For many people, self-administered treatment programs available through books and other media appear to be more effective than no treatment at all (Bilch et al., 2008; Hirai & Clum, 2006, 2008).

Bibliotherapy
The use of self-help materials as part of therapy.

Prevention programs
Programs that are designed to prevent or inhibit the development or progression of psychological problems or disorders.

Some prevention programs, such as some stress management programs, are funded privately by health insurance companies for people they insure or by corporations for their employees. Other prevention programs, such as rape crisis centers, are publicly funded and available to the public.

Many prevention programs focus on children, parents, or families with children. Although most children whose parents are divorced do not develop a mental disorder, children with divorced parents are more likely to develop a disorder than are children whose parents are not divorced. To minimize the incidence of psychological disorders in this population, some prevention programs help parents interact more effectively with their children (Pruett, Insabella, & Gustafson, 2005). These programs, at least in the short run, can diminish children's mental health problems. Such interventions target social factors (parent-child interactions) with the goal of improving or preserving the child's mental health.

For instance, consider a study by Sharlene Wolchik and colleagues (2002), which was designed to discover whether the positive effects of a prevention program for children of divorced parents continue over time (specifically, 6 years after the program) and whether having both mothers and their children involved in the program is better than having only the mothers involved. Participants were 218 families; at the time of the prevention program, the children were 9–12 years old, and the families were randomly assigned to one of three groups:

1. an 11-session "mother-only" group that received CBT. The intervention was designed to improve the mothers' relationships with their children, teach effective disciplinary methods, and reduce conflict between mothers and fathers;

2. an 11-session "mother program/child program" group that received CBT; the intervention for the mothers was the same as described above, and the intervention for the children was designed to improve their coping skills and their relationships with their mothers and to decrease their negative thoughts about the divorce and its aftereffects;

3. a control group of mothers and children who received books on adjusting to divorce.

Six years after the program, the researchers assessed psychological disorders in the children with a comprehensive computerized questionnaire, completed by the children and their parents. Results indicated that both the mother-only and the mother/child interventions helped prevent psychological disorders in those children who had more psychological problems before the intervention (more than 6 years previously); however, the fewer problems that children had at the start of the program, the less of an impact the intervention made. This makes sense because for these less symptomatic children, there was a smaller range within which the intervention could have an effect. When the two types of interventions were compared, they were found to be equally effective.

In conclusion, treatment can occur with varying intensity or frequency, depending, in part, on a patient's needs. Options include inpatient and partial hospitalization, residential treatment, outpatient treatment, or prevention programs. All of these community-based treatments target social factors—the patient in *context*. Such treatments may also target neurological and/or psychological factors. However, for a given patient, his or her health insurance company may not pay for or reimburse all types of treatment, or may limit the duration of treatment. Later, we'll examine the financial side of treatment in a bit more detail.

Targeting Social Factors in Younger and Older Populations

Treatments for children and older adults that target social factors may need to be modified for these special populations.

Targeting Social Factors in Younger Patients

As discussed in Chapter 2, all of us are influenced by factors in our social environment—and in some ways, this is particularly true of children, who are not yet able to function independently in the world and must rely heavily on the people around them. In targeting social factors, family therapy is a frequent form of treatment for children with psychological disorders. In some cases, family therapy may focus on parental guidance, instructing parents how to interact more effectively with their children; the children may not necessarily be present for all—or even any—of these discussions (Dishion & Stormshak, 2007).

Social factors may also be targeted in group therapy for children and adolescents, for instance, to help them develop appropriate social skills with peers. Other groups are for parents, to help them further develop parenting skills and make them feel less isolated. Mental health clinicians may also advise school personnel or specific teachers, to help them better understand a given child or to develop more effective ways of interacting with the child or resolving peer conflicts (Dishion & Stormshak, 2007).

Targeting Social Factors in Older Patients

Elderly patients can have psychological disorders that leave them unable to care for themselves, such as the cognitive disorder *dementia*, which involves significant memory problems (to be discussed in more detail in Chapter 15). In such cases, treatment may involve family therapy to help the patient and family members plan long-term care. The family may decide to have the elderly patient move in with a family member or into an assisted living facility. Given the medical problems that often develop or become worse with age, family therapy sessions may include members of an elder's healthcare team (Tisher & Dean, 2000).

Treating a Multicultural Population

One social factor that may not be targeted directly by a treatment may nevertheless serve as a potential backdrop to treatment, namely the demographic characteristics of the patient—ethnic background, race, or sexual orientation. The United States has an increasingly multicultural population, as shown in Figure 4.6. By the year 2025, approximately 40% of adults and almost half of all children in the United States will be from a racial or ethnic minority group (U.S. Census Bureau, 2000). Individual members of each ethnic or racial group, however, may have many different reasons for having immigrated to the United States, may have different values and traditions, and may vary in other ways that can influence treatment.

How Ethnicity Can Influence Treatment

Information about a patient's ethnic background, race, or sexual orientation can influence the type of treatment used or lead a clinician to modify the treatment. Moreover, if patient and therapist have different backgrounds, this may lead to misunderstandings about treatment goals, methods, and expectations. For instance, experiences with discrimination and prejudice can lead someone to have negative automatic thoughts about the futility of continuing to look for a better job ("What's the point, they won't hire me anyway"); the patient sees the problem (depression about feeling stuck in a dead-end, low-paying job) as having an external

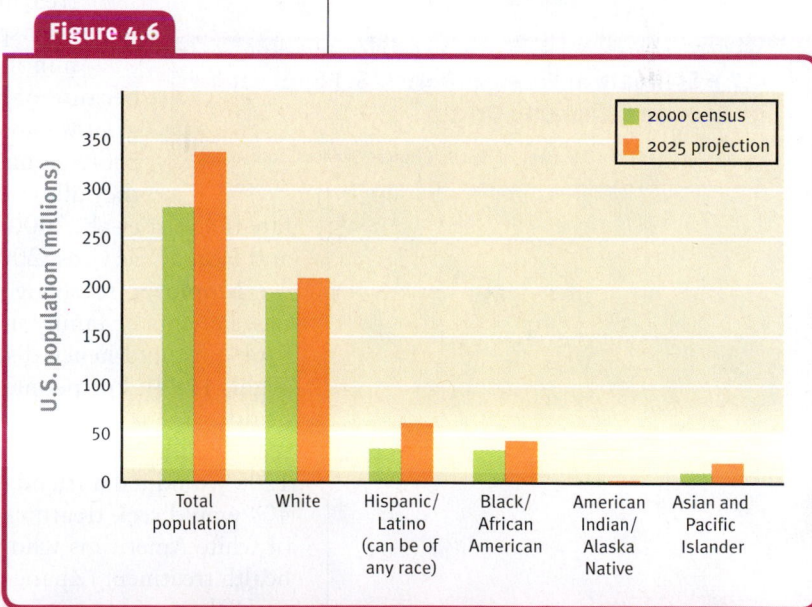

Figure 4.6

4.6 ▶ The Multicultural Population of the United States

Source: Adpated from U.S. Dept. of Health & Human Services, 2001, p. 6.

cause—discriminatory hiring practices. In contrast, the therapist may see the problem as internal, in that the patient's pessimistic thinking leads the patient to behave in ways that create a self-fulfilling prophecy. In this case, patient and therapist would be working toward very different points in addressing what each perceives as the root cause of the patient's depression about finding a better job. The patient's thoughts, however, are not necessarily irrational, and if the therapist is not sensitive to that possibility and aware of how past discrimination has affected the patient's sense of self and the world, then the two of them will continue to have different goals for and expectations of treatment, possibly leading the treatment to be ineffective or the patient to drop out of treatment.

Using Mental Health Services

Although members of minority groups and Whites have similar lifetime prevalences of psychological disorders in the United States, minorities generally do not use mental health services as often as do Whites (U.S. Department of Health and Human Services, 2001). Several factors, some pragmatic, may contribute to this difference. First, members of minority groups are less likely to have health insurance coverage, which creates a financial burden on them and their families (who must pay for treatment). In addition, immigrants may not speak English well enough to communicate effectively about their psychological problems; if bilingual clinicians or translators are not available, then patients must rely on family or friends to translate for them—which can create a disincentive to seek treatment (U.S. Department of Health and Human Services, 2001). Figure 4.7 compares the proportion within each ethnic group living in the United States that is native-born versus foreign-born; the foreign-born may not be able to communicate well in English. Asian Americans and Hispanics are the ethnic groups most likely to have been born elsewhere.

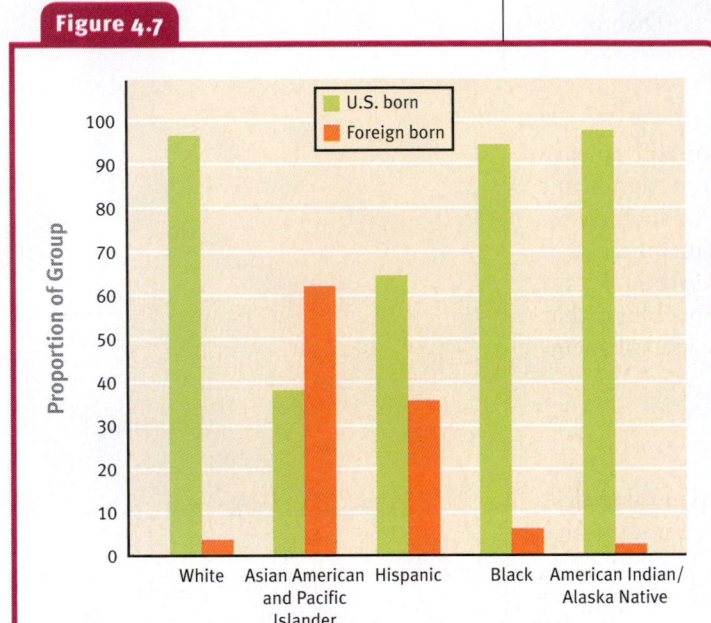

Figure 4.7

4.7 ▶ Estimate of Foreign-Born U.S. Population by Race and Hispanic Origin

Source: Adapted from U.S. Dept. of Health & Human Services, 2001, p. 109.

Beyond these practical barriers to treatment, two additional factors may explain why minorities use mental health treatments less often than do Whites: a basic mistrust of such treatments, and the stigma of receiving treatment. Mistrust may spring in part from past experiences, in which members of minority groups may have felt disrespected or judged unfairly because of their ethnicity or race. In addition, members of minority groups may be aware of past abuses by mental health institutions and professionals—and some fear that they will be "experimented on" if they allow such institutions or professionals to have control over their fate (LaVeist et al., 2000; Neal-Barnett & Smith, 1997; U.S. Department of Health and Human Services, 2001).

Moreover, receiving mental health care may carry a stigma in some communities. Patients or family members may feel ashamed or embarrassed by the patient's problems, and hence discourage the patient from receiving treatment (Ng, 1997; Wahl, 1999). For people already experiencing discrimination, becoming a mental health patient can add another source of discrimination, making them reluctant to seek treatment. For instance, one study found that among Asian Americans, only 12% would tell a friend or family member about psychological problems, and only 4% would seek treatment from a mental health clinician; this contrasts with 25% of white Americans who would both tell friends and family and would seek mental health treatment (Zhang et al., 1998).

When minority patients do seek treatment, their symptoms tend to be more severe at the time of assessment than is typical for Whites (Snowden & Cheung 1990; Sue et al., 1991). One explanation for this finding is that some people may hope that the symptoms will disappear on their own and will consult a mental health clinician only after the symptoms continue for a long period or become so bad as to be intolerable. In addition, some patients (and their family members) seek alternative services—for example, from a minister or traditional healer from their community—before they turn to standard mental health services; they might consult mental health clinicians only when other types of treatments have failed (Chung, 2002; Nebelkopf & Phillips, 2004).

Furthermore, minority patients are less likely to come to mental health clinicians directly; instead, they often seek treatment from their primary care physician (Snowden & Pingitore, 2002; U.S. Department of Health and Human Services, 2001). (As mentioned in Chapter 3, though, primary care physicians generally treat mental health problems less effectively than do mental health clinicians.) Compared to white patients, members of minority groups (Blacks, Latinos, and Asian Americans) prefer counseling over medication (Givens et al., 2007).

Bridging a Cultural Gap Between Patient and Clinician

Let's examine in more detail factors that mental health professionals must take into account when providing treatment and discuss ways that mental health professionals address the unique needs of different populations. (Of course, even when clinician and patient have similar backgrounds, the clinician should always try to understand the patient's unique experiences that influence the disorder and that may influence treatment and recovery.)

Research has shown that when mental health services are tailored to the needs of a specific cultural group, members of that group are more likely to make use of, and benefit from, the treatments. The term *cultural competence* refers to the ability of the mental health system and individual clinicians to provide treatment in a way that is sensitive to people from different backgrounds.

A clinician's cultural competence rests on an awareness of the biases and assumptions he or she has about mental health, mental illness, and treatment in general and in reference to particular ethnic groups; cultural competence also reflects an understanding of the different biases and assumptions held by people from other ethnic groups. The clinician and patient together develop treatment goals that respect the context in which the patient lives—family, cultural, and spiritual values, the patient's identity, cultural explanations of the psychological problems the patient is experiencing, and issues related to the relationship with the mental health clinician (Malik & Velazquez, 2002).

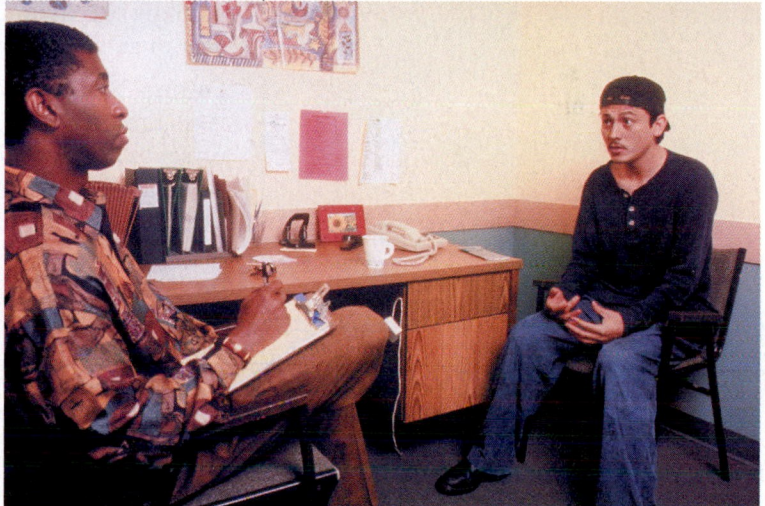

Therapists should be aware of cultural differences that may exist between themselves and their patients, and they should try to learn how patients' experiences of their culture influence their understanding of their problems and their goals for treatment.

For instance, a Latina woman may attribute her depression to *nervios*, or nerves, whereas a clinician, hearing about a history of depression in her family, might partly attribute her depression to family-related factors (U.S. Department of Health and Human Services, 2001). Or a patient of Asian descent may frame his or her problem with depression in bodily terms rather than psychological ones. In both cases, the clinician should not dismiss the patient's views but rather should incorporate them into the treatment goals and plans that are developed with the patient.

Cultural Competence and Medication

Clinicians who prescribe medication should be aware that people from different ethnic groups may respond to medication differently than do Whites. In fact, members of different ethnic groups may metabolize drugs differently. Asian Americans and African Americans, for instance, may be more sensitive to the effects of psychotropic medications than are Whites; a standard dose for a white patient might be too high a dose for an African American or Asian American patient and would lead to more and greater side effects—which in turn might lead the patients to stop taking the medication (Lin et al., 1997; Lin & Cheung, 1999; U.S. Department of Health and Human Services, 2001). As noted earlier, Blacks generally prefer counseling to medication for psychological problems, at least in part because of concerns about side effects and how effective the medication will be (Cooper-Patrick et al., 1997). Such concerns can arise because of metabolic differences (Dwight-Johnson et al., 2000). (Note that although these findings about medication apply to groups of people, they may not necessarily apply to a given individual who is of African or Asian descent.)

Culturally Specific Treatment

Clinicians may address a patient's culture in a variety of ways, depending on the patient's facility with English and the community in which the patient lives. When immigrant patients do not speak English well, treatment should be provided by a clinician who speaks the patient's language, or who makes use of a translator. Community health centers in ethnic neighborhoods are most likely to have such resources available. In fact, such health centers may have specific programs to reach out to community members about mental health treatment and may use approaches that are consistent with the particular ethnic group's view of mental health and mental illness. Such culturally sensitive approaches result in increased use of mental health services and decreased rates of dropping out of treatment (Lau & Zane, 2000; U.S. Department of Health and Human Services, 2001), particularly among patients who are less assimilated and who do not speak English well (U.S. Department of Health and Human Services, 2001).

Cultural Sensitivity in Treatment

A therapist should not assume that a patient's different ethnic or racial background or sexual orientation will necessarily lead to misunderstandings. As long as the therapist is sensitive to *possible* differences and asks the patient about ways that his or her culture or sexual orientation may influence symptoms or treatment, the difference in backgrounds need not be a stumbling block. In fact, ethnic similarity of patient and therapist alone does not reduce the likelihood of dropping out of treatment or produce better outcomes (Ito & Maramba, 2002; Karlsson, 2005). This finding suggests that therapists can bridge most gaps that arise from different backgrounds as long as there is no significant language barrier. Case 4.3 illustrates why therapists shouldn't make assumptions about how cultural differences *must* influence treatment.

CASE 4.3 ▸ FROM THE OUTSIDE: Emotional or Physical Problem?

Mrs. Corrales, a 70-year-old Puerto Rican, was referred to a mental health clinic by her local priest. Mrs. Corrales had no friends within [her neighborhood]. She had migrated from Puerto Rico eight years earlier to live with her two sons and her 45-year-old single and mildly developmentally impaired daughter. Two years before she came to the clinic, her sons had moved to a nearby city in search of better jobs. Mrs. Corrales remained behind with her daughter, who spoke no English and did not work. Among other questions, the Latin American therapist asked her if she was losing weight because she had lost her appetite, to which she quipped: "No, I've lost my teeth, not my appetite! That's what irks me!" Indeed, Mrs. Corrales had almost no teeth left in her mouth. Apparently, her conversations with the priest (an American who had learned to speak Spanish during a Latin American mission and was sensitive to the losses [that people endure as the result] of migration) had centered on the emotional losses she had suffered with her sons' departure. The priest thought this was the cause of her "anxious depression." Though well meaning, he had failed to consider practical issues. Mrs. Corrales had no dental insurance, did not know any dentists, and had no financial resources.

(Falicov, 1998, p. 255)

The therapist should check with each patient to determine whether demographic differences of many kinds—in age, weight, ethnic background, country of origin, or religion, as well as race, gender, or sexual orientation—might influence treatment (Davison, 2005; Eubanks-Carter, Burckell, & Goldfried, 2005; Helms & Cook, 1999; Higgenbotham, West, & Forsyth, 1988; McGoldrick, Jordano, & Pearce, 1996; Ramirez, 1999). If such differences are salient for the patient, the therapist should inquire about the patient's relevant experiences and concerns and discuss how to shift the plans for and goals of treatment (Zane et al., 2004). For instance, Joe, a devout Catholic seeking treatment for depression related to his unhappy marriage, might explain to his Protestant therapist that, because of his religion, divorce was out of the question. Joe and his therapist could then together devise possible goals and strategies for treatment that did not conflict with Joe's religious beliefs.

Finances and Managed Care

Perhaps unfortunately, finances are another social factor that must be taken into account when treating mental illness. Mental health services make up just a small part of overall health care costs in the United States and Canada, but as the cost of providing medical care has risen significantly, external pressure to limit mental health care spending has increased. To contain costs, health insurance companies have developed a system of **managed care**, a plan that restricts access to specialized medical care by limiting benefits or reimbursement. A managed care organization tries to minimize the expense of providing health care without restricting services that it deems medically necessary. So, for instance, to keep mental health care costs down, a managed care organization might:

- restrict the number of days that a patient can remain in an inpatient unit, and will no longer pay for such treatment after that time has passed;
- restrict the mental health facilities where a patient may receive care (to those that have agreed to be paid a previously negotiated rate);
- pay for partial hospitalization rather than inpatient care;
- restrict the number of days a patient can remain in partial hospitalization; and
- limit the number of outpatient sessions or restrict the mental health clinicians whose services will be covered.

These limitations can harm patients, their families, and even society at large. In an effort to minimize the adverse effects of such restrictions, the U.S. Congress in 2008 passed the Wellstone-Domenici Mental Health Parity Act. This act requires most insurance plans to provide comparable levels of treatment benefits for mental health and physical health (as well as for substance abuse). For example, if an insurance plan does not restrict the total number of days a patient can remain in a hospital for a medical problem, it cannot restrict the total number of days a patient can remain in a hospital for a psychological disorder. Health insurers may still limit benefits—but the limitations must be equivalent for physical and mental health.

The majority of Americans who have health insurance have their mental health coverage handled through a managed care system (Open Minds, 1999). In response to managed care, therapists of every theoretical orientation have worked to maintain the same effectiveness in fewer sessions or in less intensive forms of treatment.

Some research suggests that having a time limit on psychotherapy may accelerate the rate of change for some—but not all—patients (Reynolds et al., 1996). However, patients who have complex or multiple problems are less likely to benefit from a limit on the number of sessions (Lambert & Ogles, 2004). Further research is needed to determine whether, for each psychological disorder short-term therapy can provide long-term positive change without increased rates of relapse.

Managed care
A type of health insurance plan that restricts access to specialized medical care by limiting benefits or reimbursement.

Key Concepts and Facts About Treatments That Target Social Factors

- Treatments that target social factors are designed to reduce symptoms and/or improve quality of life by changing a person's relationships for the better and by creating, expanding, or improving a person's sense of community.

- Interpersonal therapy (IPT) is intended to address a patient's problematic relationships and improve his or her interpersonal skills so that relationships become more satisfying; the theory is that as relationships improve, the symptoms of psychological disorders will lessen. IPT focuses on four themes in problems with relationships: unresolved grief, role transition, role dispute, and interpersonal deficits. The methods of IPT include focusing on the consequences of patients' actions, role-playing interactions with significant others, encouraging patients to heighten their awareness of feelings they have minimized, and helping patients to improve their communication skills.

- Family therapy can be conducted using most theoretical approaches; depending on the specific approach, the focus of family therapy may be an individual patient in the context of his or her family, or the family itself. In contrast, systems therapy views the entire family as the unit of change and is designed to improve communication or behavior patterns among family members—who may not be the identified patient—and in doing so change the system. Methods of systems therapy include validating each family member's experience, reframing the problem, and using paradoxical intention.

- Group therapy, in which several patients with similar needs meet together with one or two therapists, can be based on various theoretical approaches, such as psychodynamic therapy or CBT; the theoretical approach determines the specific methods employed.

- Treatment can occur in different settings and with differing levels of intensity, ranging from once-a-week outpatient treatment to partial hospitalization, residential treatment, and inpatient treatment. People can also receive help for psychological disorders in self-help groups and through bibliotherapy.

- Prevention programs target those at risk for a variety of psychological disorders; these interventions may focus on neurological, psychological, or social factors.

- Treatments for children and elderly patients that target social factors may need to be modified for those specific populations.

- Therapists should try to be aware of—and discuss with patients—any cultural, demographic, or other significant difference between themselves and their patients that could affect the goals and expectations of treatment or create miscommunication and misunderstanding.

- Culturally competent mental health clinicians provide treatment that is sensitive to people from different backgrounds. Mental health services that are tailored to the needs of a specific cultural or ethnic group are more likely to be used by members of that group.

- The bulk of the costs for mental health treatments are borne by health insurance programs; managed care organizations in particular may restrict treatment in an effort to minimize costs.

Creating a Treatment Plan

We've considered many different types of treatment. How does a patient and his or her mental health clinician decide on a particular course of treatment? Let's review the process of choosing one or more types of treatment for a given problem, using Leon's depression and social phobia as an example.

Choosing a Specific Treatment

How would a clinician decide what type of treatment to offer to Leon, or any other patient? The answer depends, in part, on the types of treatment the clinician has been trained to provide. For instance, in general, psychologists may be more likely to target psychological or social factors, whereas psychiatrists may be more likely to target neurological factors.

The specific treatment or treatments provided to a patient also depend on what types of treatment he or she is willing to try. Ideally, a patient has looked at reputable Web sites to learn more about his or her symptoms and the types of treatments that have been found to be effective. Leon might have developed a sense of what type of treatment he wanted to try and might have sought out a clinician who was qualified to provide that treatment.

Which types of treatment might be most appropriate for Leon's particular problems—depression and social phobia? Given that his problems did not incapacitate him or lead him to be likely to hurt himself or others, outpatient treatment would be the most appropriate. Among the biomedical treatments, medication (most likely an SSRI) for Leon's anxiety and depression would be a reasonable place to start. Among the treatments targeting psychological factors, CBT is the one for which there is the most research support for both social phobia and depression; as we'll see in Chapter 6, though, a variety of other treatments can help alleviate depression. Among treatments targeting social factors, group therapy could be particularly helpful for Leon's social phobia—simply being in a group, whatever its theoretical orientation, would be an exposure treatment for him. The social support might also lessen his depression.

Choosing One or More Treatments

Some patients receive only one type of treatment, whereas other patients may receive more than one type—why? A given patient may receive more than one form of treatment, depending on the nature of the problem, the patient's preferences, and whether a single treatment sufficiently alleviates symptoms or improves quality of life. Moreover, constraints arising from health insurance coverage or finances can influence which treatment(s) a patient receives. Severe or chronic problems, such as schizophrenia, may be best addressed by two or more treatments, and some combined treatments may be more effective for that disorder than a particular single treatment (TADS Team, 2007). Each treatment may directly target a different factor.

Leon has two disorders: depression and social anxiety, and he might benefit from multiple treatments—one (or more) to target his depression, and one (or more) to target his social anxiety. One option would be to participate in group therapy for his social anxiety (the treatment modality of choice for that disorder) and wait to see the extent to which his depression lifts as his social anxiety diminishes. Alternatively, Leon might choose to initiate two types of treatment, one directed at his social anxiety and one at his depression. In this case, he might be in group therapy for his social anxiety and either take medication or begin CBT or another type of therapy for his depression.

Even people with one disorder may receive more than one type of treatment. For example, people with depression may benefit from a treatment that targets psychological factors while also being involved in couples therapy. Similarly, children with attention-deficit/hyperactivity disorder may take medication and also be in family therapy with their parents.

Some patients receive more than one treatment that targets the same type of factor. For instance, a depressed person may take more than one medication (targeting neurological factors), or an anxious woman might be in both couples therapy and interpersonal therapy (both targeting social factors). A given patient may initiate multiple treatments at the same time or start with one and add additional treatments as needed.

Treatments can directly target neurological, psychological, or social factors, but any successful treatment ultimately affects all three types of factors. Thus, a variety of paths can lead to the same general destination: reducing or eliminating symptoms and improving quality of life. However, as we shall see in subsequent chapters, some treatments are more effective for certain disorders than others.

Key Concepts and Facts About Creating a Treatment Plan ■

- The treatment or treatments given to a particular patient depend on the patient's willingness to receive particular treatments, on research results regarding specific treatments for the patient's problem, and on the expertise of the mental health clinician.

- Some patients may receive more than one type of treatment, depending on their specific problem(s), the effectiveness of a given treatment, the patient's interest in pursuing additional treatments, and the patient's insurance benefits and finances.

- Although any given treatment targets only one factor, changes brought about by an effective treatment in turn affect other factors.

SUMMING UP

Summary of Treatments That Target Neurological Factors

The goal of treatment is to reduce or eliminate problems or symptoms and/or to improve quality of life. Various procedures and substances are used to treat psychological disorders. Treatments that target neurological factors, sometimes referred to as biomedical treatments, include medications, brain stimulation, biofeedback, and, in rare cases, neurosurgery. Medications can alter synaptic activity in various ways.

Electroconvulsive therapy (ECT) induces a controlled brain seizure by passing current through electrodes on the scalp. ECT is most effective for treating severe depression. Transcranial magnetic stimulation (TMS) delivers very brief magnetic pulses into the cerebral cortex. Unlike ECT, TMS does not require anesthesia and it has fewer side effects.

Biofeedback is a technique by which patients can bring involuntary bodily activity, such as heart rate or muscle tension, under voluntary control. Neurosurgery, usually considered a treatment of last resort, is sometimes used to modify brain structures that contribute to severe disorders in cases where other treatments have not been sufficiently effective. Biomedical treatments used with adults may need to be modified for use with children or elderly patients.

Thinking like a clinician

Nita has been depressed for several weeks; although she's often teary and feels hopeless, she's able to function well enough at her job. She doesn't want to talk to a therapist about it ("I don't want any counseling or therapy"), but she's willing to see a psychiatrist for one visit ("Just to see whether there's anything that can help"). If the psychiatrist recommends a treatment that targets neurological factors, what is it likely to be and why? What would be the goal—in terms of neurological factors—of that particular type of treatment? Why would other treatments targeting neurological factors not be appropriate? What, in particular, should the psychiatrist want to know about Nita before making a recommendation?

Summary of Treatments That Target Psychological Factors

Psychodynamic therapy and psychoanalysis are intended to help each patient more adaptively manage unconscious conflicts that arise in large part from id-driven impulses and urges. They are supposed to do so by helping the patient develop insight into events in his or her past and how these events and unconscious forces influence current difficulties.

Client-centered therapy is designed to integrate the sense of self by decreasing the incongruence between a patient's real and ideal selves. According to the theory of client-centered therapy, with an integrated sense of self comes reduced emotional pain.

Behavioral treatments use both classical and operant conditioning techniques (including habituation and extinction) to change behavior. Behavioral methods often focus attention on the antecedents and consequences of a maladaptive behavior, as well as the behavior itself.

Cognitive methods based on Ellis's rational emotive behavior therapy (REBT) are designed to dispute beliefs that lead to maladaptive consequences. Methods based on Beck's cognitive restructuring challenge patients' maladaptive automatic negative thoughts, and encourage patients to test the accuracy of their beliefs through real-life experiments.

The behavioral aspects of cognitive-behavior therapy (CBT) are intended to transform maladaptive behaviors that stem from previous learning, whereas the cognitive aspects of CBT are intended to modify irrational thoughts and incorrect beliefs that influence feelings and behavior in a maladaptive way. Changing behaviors and thoughts in turn alters feelings as well.

Technology is being incorporated into treatment through the use of electronic methods for self-monitoring, cognitive restructuring, virtual exposure, and cybertherapy. However, cybertherapy has drawbacks: The therapist could be an imposter, confidential information may not remain private, and the lack of nonverbal cues for the therapist may skew the treatment in a less helpful direction.

Thinking like a clinician

After seeing the psychiatrist, Nita decides that she definitely doesn't want anyone "messing with my brain" and will try psychotherapy instead of a neurological intervention. List the types of questions a therapist with each theoretical orientation that targets psychological factors—psychodynamic, humanist, behavioral, and cognitive—might ask of Nita. What specific types of information would each therapist want, based on his or her orientation? What techniques might each type of therapist use in treating Nita's depression?

Summary of Treatments That Target Social Factors

Treatments that target social factors are designed to reduce symptoms and/or improve quality of life by changing a person's relationships for the better and by creating, expanding, or improving a person's sense of community. Interpersonal therapy (IPT) is intended to address a patient's problematic relationships and improve his or her interpersonal skills so that relationships become more satisfying; the theory is that as relationships improve, the symptoms of psychological disorders will lessen.

Family therapy can be conducted using most theoretical approaches; depending on the specific approach, the focus of family therapy may be an individual patient in the context of his or her family, or the family itself. In contrast, systems therapy views the entire family as the unit of change and is designed to improve communication or behavior patterns among family members and in doing so change the system.

Group therapy, in which patients with similar needs meet together with one or two therapists, can be based on various theoretical approaches, such as psychodynamic therapy or CBT.

Treatment can occur in different settings and with differing levels of intensity, ranging from once-a-week outpatient treatment to partial hospitalization, residential treatment, and inpatient treatment. People can also receive help for psychological disorders in self-help groups and through bibliotherapy. Prevention programs target those at risk for a variety of psychological disorders. Treatments for children and elderly patients that target social factors may need to be modified for those specific populations.

Therapists should try to be aware of—and discuss with patients—any cultural, demographic, or other significant difference between themselves and their patients that could affect the goals and expectations of treatment or create miscommunication and misunderstanding. Mental health services that are tailored to the needs of a specific cultural or ethnic group are more likely to be used by members of that group.

Thinking like a clinician

Community Psychiatric Hospital has had its budget slashed dramatically and thus is trying to help its highest functioning inpatients move into supervised housing in the community. What are the different types of living situations that might be available? Why might the hospital want to offer group therapy to those living outside the hospital? Some patients will live with their families; why might family therapy be offered to those families?

Summary of Creating a Treatment Plan

The treatment or treatments given to a particular patient depend on the patient's willingness to receive particular treatments, on research results regarding specific treatments for the patient's problem, and on the expertise of the mental health clinician. Some patients may receive more than one type of treatment, depending on their specific problem(s), the effectiveness of a given treatment, and the patient's interest in pursuing additional treatments. Although any given treatment targets only one factor, changes brought about by an effective treatment in turn affect other factors.

Thinking like a clinician

Now suppose that Nita, the woman with depression, is receiving CBT and taking medication. Why might she be receiving two types of treatment? What does—and doesn't—the fact that she's receiving more than one type of treatment indicate about the nature of her problem?

Key Terms

Treatment (for psychological disorders) (p. 110)

Biomedical treatments (p. 110)

Psychopharmacology (p. 110)

Agonists (p. 110)

Antagonists (p. 112)

Reuptake inhibitors (p. 113)

Antipsychotic medications (p. 113)

Benzodiazepines (p. 114)

Electroconvulsive therapy (ECT) (p. 114)

Transcranial magnetic stimulation (TMS) (p. 114)

Biofeedback (p. 115)

Psychoanalysis (p. 118)

Psychodynamic therapy (p. 118)

Therapeutic alliance (p. 119)

Free association (p. 119)

Interpretation (p. 119)

Dream analysis (p. 119)

Transference (p. 120)

Client-centered therapy (p. 121)

Behavior therapy (p. 122)

Cognitive therapy (p. 122)

Cognitive-behavior therapy (p. 122)

Habituation (p. 123)

Exposure (p. 123)

Systematic desensitization (p. 124)

Exposure with response prevention (p. 125)

Stimulus control (p. 125)

Behavior modification (p. 125)

Shaping (p. 126)

Extinction (p. 126)

Secondary reinforcers (p. 126)

Token economy (p. 126)

Rational-emotive behavior therapy (REBT) (p. 128)

Cognitive restructuring (p. 130)

Psychoeducation (p. 130)

Dialectical behavior therapy (DBT) (p. 131)

Cybertherapy (p. 133)

Interpersonal therapy (IPT) (p. 136)

Family therapy (p. 137)

Systems therapy (p. 137)

Validate (p. 138)

Reframe (p. 138)

Paradoxical intention (p. 138)

Group therapy (p. 139)

Outpatient treatment (p. 139)

Inpatient treatment (p. 140)

Partial hospitalization (p. 140)

Residential treatment (p. 140)

Bibliotherapy (p. 141)

Prevention programs (p. 141)

Managed care (p. 147)

More Study Aids

For additional study aids related to this chapter, go to:

www.worthpublishers.com/rosenberg

Researching Abnormality

Suppose you are a psychologist at a college counseling center. A student, Carlos, comes to the center because he's been depressed since his girlfriend, Liana, ended their relationship 5 weeks ago. Liana's rejection was a bolt out of the blue, as far as Carlos is concerned. He feels abandoned and alone. He has been spiraling downward since the breakup, feeling irritable and sad, sleeping a lot, and without appetite. He was just fired from his on-campus job because of his poor attitude. He doesn't care much about his classes or schoolwork. During your sessions with Carlos, he seems preoccupied with his relationship with Liana and worries that no other woman will ever love him.

Carlos is not the only student on campus to have this type of problem. You've noticed that a surprising number of students seeking help at the counseling center are depressed and have recently broken up with a boyfriend or a girlfriend. Like Carlos, these students frequently report feeling hurt, rejected, and unlovable. Some even think about suicide.

You wonder, though, whether the depression that many of these students are experiencing is a result specifically of their breakups. Perhaps they were depressed before the breakup—and that contributed to the failure of the relationship. In Carlos's case, perhaps his depression started earlier (although he hadn't realized it), and Liana got sick of his being down in the dumps. On the other hand, maybe a lot of the students would not have become depressed if their relationships had not ended.

How could you determine whether the students are depressed because their relationships ended, or whether their relationships ended because they were depressed (and this soured their relationships)? In this chapter, we explore specific methods that psychologists use to study psychopathology and its treatment, the challenges associated with the use of the different research methods, and the ways in which researchers address those challenges.

Using the Scientific Method to Understand Abnormality

Perhaps your observations about depression and relationship breakups are based simply on a coincidence: People—particularly young people—are frequently beginning and ending relationships, and

The scientific method is used to determine whether a hypothesis—such as whether a relationship's breaking up can lead to depression—has merit. The process of research on psychopathology often begins with observations that lead to a hypothesis about either the factors that may contribute to psychological disorders or the aspects of treatment that may be particularly helpful.

Scientists often collect quantitative data (numerical measurements, such as how many symptoms someone has, the number of weeks symptoms have been present, or how many people in the family have similar symptoms).

Scientific method

The process of gathering and interpreting facts that can lead to the formulation of a new theory or the validation or refutation of an existing theory.

Data

Methodical observations, which include numerical measurements of phenomena.

depression and breakups occur completely independently of each other. Many of the depressed students coming to the counseling center have had prior bouts of depression. In such cases, a breakup would not necessarily be the culprit, because those individuals might have had another bout of depression regardless. Alternatively, there may be a causal connection between breaking up and depression—but it could go either way, with either one leading to the other.

To determine whether your idea that the breaking up of a relationship can lead to depression is correct, you would use the **scientific method**, which is the process of gathering and interpreting facts that can lead to the formulation of a new theory or the validation or refutation of an existing theory. The steps of the scientific method normally are: observing relevent phenomena; identifying a question to be answered; developing a hypothesis that might answer the question; collecting new observations to test the hypothesis; drawing on the evidence to formulate a theory; and testing the theory.

The Scientific Method

Suppose that your casual observation is correct: Students who seek help for depression *are* more likely to have had a relationship breakup before the depression began. Knowing this, you are interested in understanding why some people get clinically depressed after a breakup (like Carlos), whereas other people bounce back. You may even have a hunch about why. But the scientific method of investigation relies on more than one individual's impressions and hunches. How can the scientific method help researchers learn more about the association between breakups in relationships and depression or, more generally, about how a psychological disorder such as depression arises?

Collect Initial Observations

The first step in the scientific method is observation. Sometimes the initial observations lead immediately to the next steps, but other times they lead the researcher to describe the phenomenon more carefully and systematically by collecting data. **Data** are methodical observations, which include numerical measurements of phenomena. Scientific facts are based on such data. Data about depression and breakups, for instance, might include responses to a questionnaire on which people who have recently gone through a breakup rate their moods and functioning.

In most scientific fields, properly collected data can be **replicated** under identical or nearly identical conditions: Any other researcher, using the same collection method, should obtain a second set of data with the same characteristics as the first. For example, if a researcher at another college's counseling center gave the same questionnaire about mood and functioning to a different group of students who'd recently suffered a breakup, that researcher would be trying to replicate the data.

Researchers collect data about *variables*: measurable characteristics of the object or event of interest. In the field of abnormal psychology, variables include activity in particular brain areas, hormone levels, the number of symptoms reported, the variety of abnormal behaviors exhibited, and types of observed interactions among family members. The list of variables of interest to researchers in psychopathology is long, as you will discover in this book. Variables can be *categorical* (for instance, someone either has or doesn't have an older sibling) or on a *continuum* (for instance, someone can have a phobia that can be characterized from mild to severe).

Identify a Question

The process of explaining a set of observations begins by asking a specific question. Let's say that your observations have led you to ask this question: "Why do some people get depressed after a relationship ends, rather than bounce back?" The question identifies an area where properly conducted research can point toward an answer.

Develop a Hypothesis

After identifying a question, a researcher then forms a *hypothesis*, which may or may not be the same as the original impression or hunch. A **hypothesis** is a preliminary idea that is proposed to answer the question about a set of observations. Hypotheses are important in part because they direct the researcher to make specific additional observations (which may include making precise measurements). The most common kinds of hypotheses propose a way to understand differences in measurements of a variable in different circumstances or to establish a relationship between variables. To develop a hypothesis, you need to propose some specific relationship for the variables in the question you've asked. For instance, a hypothesis might address *which people* are likely to get depressed or *why* some people are likely to get depressed. Let's say you develop this hypothesis: Individuals who suffered a major loss during childhood (such as the death of a parent) are more likely to get depressed after a relationship ends during adulthood. Your hypothesis involves two variables: one categorical (people either experienced a loss in childhood, or they didn't) and one continuous (depression can have different degrees of severity).

Collect Data to Test the Hypothesis

The next step involves systematically collecting data to test the hypothesis. For example, to test your hypothesis, you might recruit people who have just broken up with their spouse or partner. You might ask them to complete two questionnaires: one about any major losses they experienced in childhood, and the other about their current mood and functioning. Sometimes researchers compare two or more hypotheses, trying to determine which one best fits the data.

Develop a Theory

After enough data are collected and examined, the researcher proposes a **theory**, which is a principle or set of principles that explains a set of data. A theory provides an answer to the question identified by the researcher. For example, you might theorize that depression is particularly likely to arise in adults after a relationship breaks up if they, as children, suffered a loss and there was nothing they could do to control or manage the situation. In fact, as we saw in Chapter 2, when animals cannot control an aversive stimulus (a shock), they learn to become helpless; rather than try to escape from such a stimulus, they appear to give up. Such a process could underlie some forms of depression (Miller & Seligman, 1973, 1975). That is, according to this theory, the child forms an enduring association between loss and a sense of helplessness, and it is the feelings of helplessness that produce depression. Later in life, when the adult experiences a loss, this triggers the associations to helplessness, which in turn leads the adult to become depressed. This theory may apply to Carlos's case: His mother died of breast cancer when he was 6 years old, and he remembers feeling helpless during her illness and at her death.

Test the Theory

The next step of the scientific method is to test the theory by collecting and examining additional data. Your theory focuses on people who not only had a significant loss during childhood, but also felt helpless to control or manage the situation. The theory leads to **predictions**, hypotheses that should be confirmed if a theory is correct. So, for instance, the theory predicts that children who felt particularly helpless after a loss would be more likely as adults to become depressed after a relationship breaks up. Data can then be collected to address this specific prediction: In addition to questionnaires about early loss and mood and functioning, an additional questionnaire might ask about memories of feeling helpless. You could then test people who did or did not have an uncontrollable loss during childhood by giving them increasingly difficult puzzles; as a measure of helplessness, you would assess how easily participants give up trying to solve the puzzles. Figure 5.1 provides a summary of the steps of the scientific method.

Many methods can be used to test the predictions made by a theory, and we'll see what these are in the following section.

Replication
The process of repeating a study using the same data collection methods under identical or nearly identical conditions to obtain data that should have the same characteristics as those from the original study.

Hypothesis
A preliminary idea that is proposed to answer a question about a set of observations.

Theory
A principle or set of principles that explains a set of data.

Predictions
Hypotheses that should be confirmed if a theory is correct.

Figure 5.1

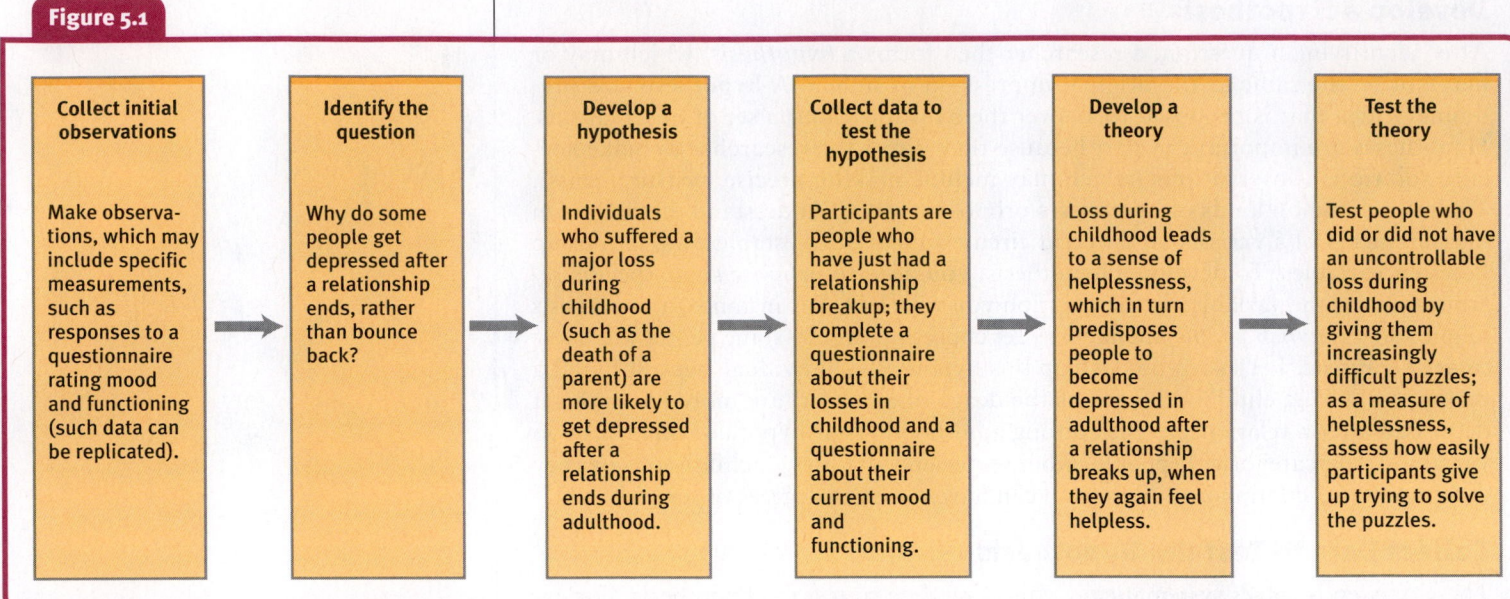

Collect initial observations	Identify the question	Develop a hypothesis	Collect data to test the hypothesis	Develop a theory	Test the theory
Make observations, which may include specific measurements, such as responses to a questionnaire rating mood and functioning (such data can be replicated).	Why do some people get depressed after a relationship ends, rather than bounce back?	Individuals who suffered a major loss during childhood (such as the death of a parent) are more likely to get depressed after a relationship ends during adulthood.	Participants are people who have just had a relationship breakup; they complete a questionnaire about their losses in childhood and a questionnaire about their current mood and functioning.	Loss during childhood leads to a sense of helplessness, which in turn predisposes people to become depressed in adulthood after a relationship breaks up, when they again feel helpless.	Test people who did or did not have an uncontrollable loss during childhood by giving them increasingly difficult puzzles; as a measure of helplessness, assess how easily participants give up trying to solve the puzzles.

5.1 ▶ Steps of the Scientific Method

Types of Scientific Research

Any individual researcher does not need to go through the entire sequence to be doing science. For instance, you went from having an observation to identifying a question—about relationship breakups and depression—to stating a full-fledged theory: Children who felt helpless in response to a loss grow up to be especially susceptible to becoming depressed after a relationship fails. However, your observation could have led you down many other research paths, depending on the specific question you developed. For instance, your question might have focused not on loss during childhood, but on the degree to which the adult was not totally surprised by the breakup of the relationship.

Psychologists employ different research methods when they pose and attempt to answer various questions; such methods include experiments, quasi-experiments, correlational research, case studies, and meta-analysis. As we review the various research methods, we will point out not only their strengths, but also their weaknesses. You might be tempted to conclude that the weaknesses are so severe that you can never understand anything with certainty from psychological research. Resist that temptation! Although each method has limitations, different methods have different limitations. Thus, if different methods produce the same answer to a question, we can be confident that the limitations of any one method are not responsible for the results. This method of *converging evidence*, where the same answer is produced using different techniques, has produced a wealth of knowledge about psychopathology.

Conducting Research with Experiments

Ideally, researchers prefer to employ **experiments**, which are research studies in which investigators intentionally manipulate one variable at a time, and measure the consequences of such manipulation on one or more other variables.

Independent Variables and Dependent Variables

You probably noticed that the definition of an experiment mentioned two kinds of variables: those that are manipulated and those that then are measured. In an experiment, researchers manipulate one variable at a time in order to observe possible changes in another variable. The variable that a researcher manipulates is called the **independent variable** (so named because it is free to change—it is independent). The variable that may change as a result is called the **dependent variable** (because its value *depends* on the independent variable). When the independent variable is changed, the accompanying changes in the dependent variable are the *effect*.

Experiments
Research studies in which investigators intentionally manipulate one variable at a time, and measure the consequences of such manipulation on one or more other variables.

Independent variable
A variable that a researcher manipulates.

Dependent variable
A variable that is measured and that may change its values as a result of manipulating the independent variable.

A researcher might separately manipulate several independent variables (always keeping all else constant while a single variable is changed), hoping to discover which ones cause the greatest effect on the dependent variable.

Of course, researchers could not use an experimental design to investigate the specific question about helplessness during early loss and subsequent depression after a breakup. A researcher ethically cannot cause a person to have a major loss during childhood (or to feel helpless at the time). Participants in an experimental study come as they are—with particular neurological, psychological, and social histories that can't be changed.

This is why most of the research on causes of psychological disorders does not use an experimental design. For ethical reasons as well as practical ones, researchers cannot alter participants' genes, subject participants to high levels of stress, cause traumatic experiences to occur in their lives, or create disruptive family events—all of which would involve intentionally manipulating independent variables. However, some aspects of psychopathology can be studied with an experimental design. For instance, an experimental design has been used to study learned helplessness in dogs (see Chapter 2; Overmier & Seligman, 1967); the independent variable was whether the dogs could escape an electrical shock, and the dependent variable was the number of attempts to escape.

Similarly, Watson and Rayner's experiment with Little Albert (1920; see Chapter 2), used an experimental design to test a theory about the etiology of a phobia. In that study, the independent variable was whether or not the conditioned (that is, the initially neutral) stimulus had been paired with an aversive unconditioned stimulus. The dependent variable was the presence of fear–related behaviors—as measured by Albert's crying and trying to get away from the white rat. When the conditioned stimulus (CS) and the unconditioned stimulus (UCS) had not yet been paired, Albert was not afraid of the rodent. His fear–related behaviors (the dependent variable) depended on his exposure to the pairing of CS and UCS.

Other examples of experimental designs in research on psychopathology include studies of people who have *panic attacks*—specific periods of intense dread or fear, accompanied by physical symptoms of fear; the independent variable is the situation or condition that may induce a panic attack, and the dependent variable is the number of such attacks. Further examples include studies of people who have substance abuse problems, where the independent variable is the type of *cues,* or stimuli, that trigger cravings to take the drug or to drink alcohol, and the dependent variable may be intensity of cravings for the drug or alcohol or physiological measures of arousal.

You could use an experimental design to conduct research that relates to the relationship between childhood loss and mood. You might, for instance, select three groups of participants: those who had a childhood loss but were able to cope with it, those who had a loss and experienced helplessness (like Carlos), and those who did not have a loss (note that you are not manipulating this variable, and thus composing the three groups is not part of the experiment itself). You could then have the independent variable be the type of movie viewed by participants; the film could involve either the theme of loss or some other theme that does not involve loss. The dependent variable might be participants' ratings of mood after viewing the movie. Your hypothesis for this study might be that participants who had suffered a loss and experienced helplessness during childhood would have the most negative mood after watching a movie with the theme of loss.

If changes in the independent variable do in fact change the measurements of the dependent variable (that is, they produce an effect), there is a *relation* between the variables. But if the experiment has not been carefully designed this relation could be more apparent than real. Factors that might inadvertently affect the variables of interest in the experiment are called **confounding variables,** or **confounds.** For example, suppose that you conducted an experiment in which the independent variable was the type of movie viewed by participants, with one movie involving the death of a loved one and the other not touching on the theme of loss. Then suppose that the movie involving loss was always shown immediately after a serious drama for the "loss-helplessness" group, whereas the movie that did not involve loss was always shown immediately after

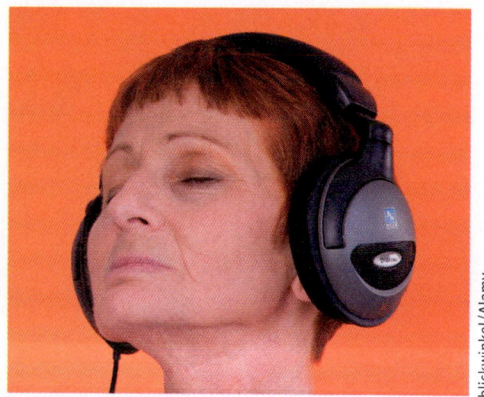

blickwinkel/Alamy

Some studies investigating psychopathology use an experimental design. Here the independent variable is different types of music and the dependent variable is depressed participants' self-reported mood after listening to the music.

Confounding variables (confounds)
Factors that might inadvertently affect the variables of interest in an experiment.

a comedy for the "loss-no helplessness" group. It could be the type of movie shown first—drama or comedy—and not differences between the groups that produces the effects on the dependent variable. Confounds lead to ambiguous or uncertain results. To minimize the possibility of confounds, the researcher should try to ensure that the experimental manipulation alters only the independent variables (and does not inadvertently affect other variables, such as the order in which the movies are presented) and that only those changes in the independent variables affect the dependent variable. It is not always possible to ensure that this is the case, however, and thus the experimenter must examine every reasonable hypothesis that might explain the effect.

Control Groups and Conditions

A common method for examining the possible effects of confounds in an experiment is to create a control group. The experimental group (or groups) and the control group are treated identically throughout the experiment, except that the independent variable is not manipulated for the **control group**. For example, say that your hypothesis was confirmed; the group of participants who had suffered an early loss and experienced helplessness did in fact have a more negative mood after watching a movie with the theme of loss. But here's a potential confound: Maybe these people are just very sensitive to depressing movies in general, not to themes of loss specifically. To rule out this possibility, you would control for this factor by testing another group of these people, showing them a depressing movie that has nothing to do with loss. (This movie should be as similar as possible to the first one in every way, except that it does not have the theme of loss.) If your hypothesis is correct, then you should find a much larger drop in mood following the movie about loss than following the movie that was merely depressing—which would provide evidence that it's the theme of loss itself that is important.

To use a control group appropriately, it must be as similar as possible to the experimental group. If the members of a control group differ significantly from members of the experimental group in terms of age, education, cultural background, temperament, or any other characteristic, one or more confounding variables has been introduced. Such a confound would cloud the interpretation of the results, because a difference in the dependent variable could be attributed to the confound instead of to the relation you intended to test. Perhaps the control group responded less strongly to the depressing movie simply because most of the participants in that group happened to be temperamentally placid.

You can imagine how hard it can be to match a control group perfectly to an experimental group. This difficulty often leads researchers to match the experimental group to the most similar possible control group: the experimental group itself! Sometimes, rather than having two separate groups that are treated differently, researchers have all participants take part in different *conditions*, or circumstances, which correspond to the different ways that experimental and control groups would be treated in a study that had both types of groups. For example, the same people could watch a movie about loss and at a different time watch a movie that was depressing but not about loss. However, when the same group of people take part in more than one condition, you need to avoid a confounding that might be introduced by the order of presentation of the conditions. For instance, if the "loss" film was always presented first, it could be that the participants were more alert during that part of the study, and that's why they responded differently. To avoid this, you would *counterbalance* the order of exposure to each condition: Half of the participants would watch the "loss" film first, and the other half would watch the "non-loss/depressing" film first. This procedure would ensure that each condition occurred equally often in each place in the order of presentation.

Bias

The way a study is set up can affect the assignment of participants into groups or influence the outcome of the experiment. For instance, suppose that you have two groups: members of one group see a "loss" film and members of the other see a "non-loss/depressing" film. When you assign participants to the groups, you

Control group
A group of participants in an experiment for which the independent variable is not manipulated, but which is otherwise treated identically to the experimental group.

Bias
A tendency that distorts data.

Corbis/Punchstock

inadvertently assign the people who smile at you to the "non-loss" group. Whether or not it is conscious (intentional) or unconscious (unintentional), a tendency or influence that distorts data—which ends up producing a confound—is called **bias**. This is why researchers place participants in groups using **random assignment**, assigning participants to each group by a procedure that relies on chance.

Even if you randomly assign participants to groups or have them take part in both conditions, other biases can interfere. Perhaps all your participants come from the same city, which recently experienced a devastating hurricane (and so the theme of loss is particularly salient for all participants). **Sampling bias** occurs when the participants are not drawn randomly from the relevant population. Sampling bias needs to be avoided if you want to be able to *generalize* (i.e., extrapolate) from the people in your study to the population at large. This brings us to an important distinction: The **population** is the complete set of possible participants (e.g., all rats or all people, or in certain cases all people of a particular age, gender, or race). The **sample** is the small portion of the population that is examined in a study.

Many of the same points also apply to the items that are selected to be used as stimuli in the study. For example, you might select a very powerful "loss" film and a limp "depressing" film—or vice versa. In this case, an irrelevant characteristic of the items—how powerful they are—might determine the results. Just as you need to be careful in sampling and assigning participants to groups, you need to be careful in selecting the items (such as the specific items in a questionnaire), ensuring that they are in fact representative of the types of items to which you want to generalize.

Internal and External Validity

A study has **internal validity** if it controls for possible confounding variables. Internal validity means that variations in the independent variable are in fact responsible for variations in the dependent variable (or variables, in studies in which more than one type of measurement is taken) and that the results are not a by-product of other, extraneous variables.

A study is said to have **external validity** when the results generalize from the sample (the particular participants who were tested) to the population from which it was drawn and from the conditions used in the study (such the particular movies shown, in the example study) to similar conditions outside the study. If a study does not have internal validity, it cannot have external validity. In contrast, even if a study has internal validity (its results have not been confounded), this does not guarantee that it will have external validity (that its results apply to relevant situations or other people).

Quasi-Experimental Design

Ideally, the participants in a study are randomly assigned to groups. But, in many cases, random assignment is not ethical, desirable, or possible. For instance, when trying to test hypotheses about why a disorder develops, researchers cannot "assign" one group to have a particular set of genes or brain functioning, a particular way of thinking, a particular type of traumatic experience, or particular friends or families. Therefore, in trying to understand possible causes of psychopathology, researchers often use *quasi-experimental designs*, which rely on groups that already exist. In fact, the "experiment" that we have been discussing is—like much research on psychopathology—a blend of experiment (manipulation of independent variable and measurement of dependent variable) and quasi-experiment (the selection of participants from pre-existing groups).

Suppose you want to know what the prevalence is in the United States of the type of depression that results from seasonal changes in the amount of daylight (sometimes referred to as *seasonal affective disorder*). You are a researcher in Portland, Oregon, and are collaborating on the study with researchers in Boston, New York, Chicago, and Detroit. Participants in the study are drawn from those five cities. Do you see the sampling bias problem? All these cities are in the northern half of the United States and therefore have a different number of daylight hours than does the southern half. Whatever prevalence rate was calculated would not reflect the entire United States.

Random assignment
Assigning participants to each group in a study using a procedure that relies on chance.

Sampling bias
The distortion that occurs when the participants in an experiment have not been drawn randomly from the relevant population under investigation.

Population
The complete set of possible relevant participants.

Sample
The small portion of a population that is examined in a study.

Internal validity
A characteristic of a study, indicating that it measures what it purports to measure because it has controlled for confounds.

External validity
A characteristic of a study, indicating that the results generalize from the sample to the population from which it was drawn and from the conditions used in the study to relevant conditions outside the study.

Correlation
The relationship between the measurements made of two variables in which a change in the value of one variable is associated with a change in the value of the other variable.

Correlation coefficient
A number that quantifies the strength of the correlation between two variables; the correlation coefficient is most typically symbolized by *r*.

Statistically significant
The condition in which the probability of obtaining the value of a statistical test is greater than what would be expected by chance alone.

A correlational study found that suicide is more likely to be the cause of death in high-altitude states, such as Colorado, than in lower altitude states (Cheng, 2002). This relationship may arise for any number of reasons, such as decreased levels of oxygen from the higher altitude (McCook, 2002), the challenges of mountain living, differences in the age and education levels of the populations, or perhaps the fact that depressed people seek a type of solitude more often found in high-altitude states. One possible confound the study did not control for was the amount of time those who committed suicide had lived at the higher altitude: Those who were born in high-altitude states would have adapted to the lower oxygen level. Researchers could have investigated one possible explanation by examining this variable (McCook, 2002).

Paul Chesley/Getty Images

To be a true experiment, you would need to have assigned participants randomly to the three groups (loss with helplessness, loss without helplessness, and no loss) *during childhood*. Obviously, this is undesirable and impossible. But in a quasi-experimental design, you can sort participants into groups—those who had a childhood loss and experienced helplessness, those who had a childhood loss but didn't experience helplessness, and those without a childhood loss. Then you would show people in all three groups a film that involves relationships breaking up. After viewing the film, participants in all three groups would rate their mood. Your hypothesis is that participants who experienced early loss and helplessness (like Carlos) will report greater sadness after seeing the film than will those in the other two groups. With a quasi-experimental design, you still try to control as many variables—such as age, health, education, and economic level—as you can in order to make the groups as similar as possible.

Correlational Research

Experiments and quasi-experiments allow researchers to zero in on which variables cause which effects. In some cases, however, manipulating the variables, even in a quasi-experiment, can be unethical or difficult. This is an issue for any study that involves participants' histories—such as medical histories, family histories, or experiences they had when younger. When independent variables can't or shouldn't be manipulated, researchers can study the relations among variables by looking for a **correlation**, a relationship between the measurements made of two variables in which a change in the value of one variable is associated with a change in the value of the other variable. A correlation compares two measurements and records the amount of similarity in their variations; the stronger the correlation, the more closely related the variables are. There are no independent and dependent variables in *correlational research*: Nothing is manipulated; instead, naturally occurring variations among measurements of different variables are compared. These comparisons can involve measures from different individuals or groups or measures from the same participants at different times. For example, if your study were correlational, your two variables of interest might be the extent to which a child experienced helplessness during a loss (perhaps rated by relatives who were present at the time or by the person's memory of how severe the sense of feeling helpless was) and the number of symptoms of depression experienced as an adult, after a breakup. Twin studies (discussed in Chapter 2) often involve correlational research.

Correlation Does Not Imply Causation

A major disadvantage of correlational methods is that they only indicate that two variables are related. A correlation does not demonstrate that either variable *causes* the other to change. In an experiment or in a quasi-experiment, the point is to show that changes in the independent variable *cause* changes in the dependent variable. In contrast, a correlational research study can only show that the values of two variables are related. For example, although the degree of helplessness felt during childhood loss and the amount of depression after an adult relationship breaks up may be correlated, the loss experienced after the breakup may not be the cause of the depression. As discussed earlier, it could be that depression comes first, and it causes the breakup! Simple correlations do not control for possible confounding variables. Perhaps experiencing helplessness as a result of an early loss leads people to be passive, and that in turn leads them to have fewer friends or family members who are supportive. It may be the relatively low amount of support received after a relationship breaks up that makes people vulnerable to depression. Such a factor could have contributed to Carlos's depression after his relationship with Liana ended.

Professors who teach statistics are fond of having their students memorize a simple statement: *Correlation does not imply causation*. To determine causation, a researcher must manipulate an independent variable while holding everything else constant. Only then can the results demonstrate that changes in the independent variable actually caused changes in the dependent variable.

Measuring a Correlation

The strength of the correlation between any two variables is quantified by a number called a **correlation coefficient** (most typically symbolized by r). When this number is positive, it signifies that the variables change in the same direction; both variables either increase or decrease in the same general pattern. A *positive relationship* is indicated by any correlation coefficient between 0 and +1. When the correlation coefficient is negative, it signifies that the variables change in opposite directions in the same general pattern; one goes up while the other goes down. A *negative relationship* is indicated by a correlation coefficient between 0 and −1. In either case, positive or negative, the stronger the relationship, the closer the coefficient is to +1 or −1. If the variables do not have any relationship at all, the correlation coefficient is 0.

If you plot two variables on a graph, putting one variable on each axis, you can see whether or not the variables change together. The closer the data points are to a straight line, the stronger the correlation. Figure 5.2 illustrates five possible correlations. When you draw a line through the data points as in the figure, you can measure the distance (parallel to the vertical axis) between each point and the line. The shorter these distances, on average, the stronger the correlation (leaning toward +1 or −1). Computer programs that perform statistical tests use a mathematical formula to calculate the correlation coefficient.

Statistical Significance

Even when variables are completely independent, they might vary in the same pattern simply by chance. In fact, the correlation coefficient between any two randomly selected sets of data is very seldom exactly 0. A correlation coefficient is **statistically significant** when it is greater than what would be expected by chance alone. Statistical significance is not the same thing as "importance." It simply means that the observed result is unlikely to be a quirk of random variation in the data. Suppose, for your participants, you calculated the correlation between age when experiencing a loss during childhood and symptoms of depression after an adult breakup, and the result was $r = -0.11$. This means the younger

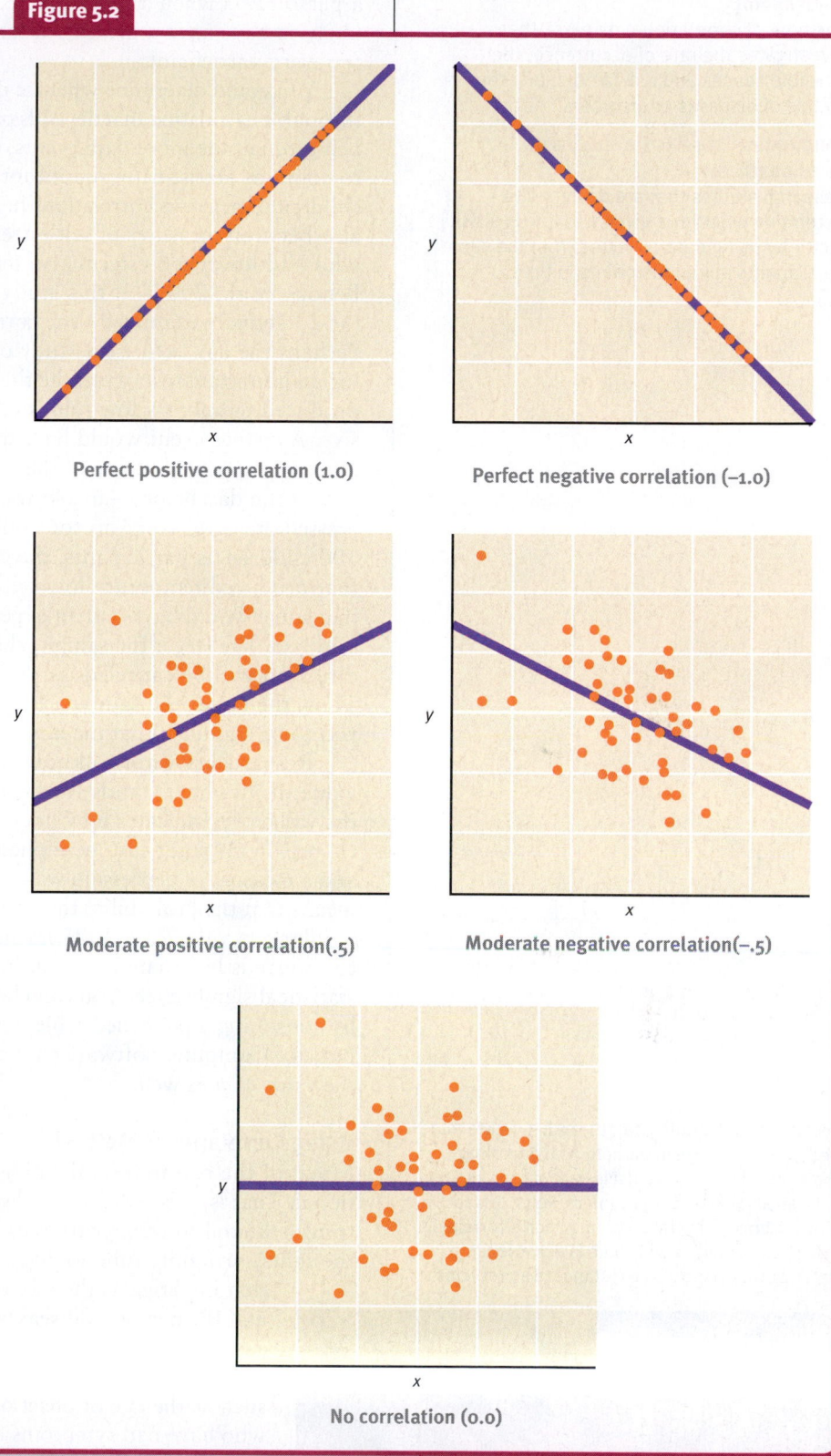

Figure 5.2

Perfect positive correlation (1.0)

Perfect negative correlation (−1.0)

Moderate positive correlation (.5)

Moderate negative correlation (−.5)

No correlation (0.0)

5.2 ▶ **Five Values of Correlation**

Epidemiology
The type of correlational research that investigates the rate of occurrence, the possible causes and risk factors, and the course of diseases or disorders.

Longitudinal studies (in studies of psychopathology)
Research studies that are designed to determine whether a given variable is a risk factor by using data collected from the same participants at various points in time.

a person was when a loss occurred, the more symptoms of depression he or she is likely to have after a breakup as an adult. However, this relationship may not hold for every participant.

You could determine whether the correlation coefficient is statistically significant through a calculation that depends partly on the number of data points you have. All else being equal, the more data points, the smaller the correlation coefficient needs to be to count as statistically significant. Why is this so? Consider the finding for gifted children of negative correlations between measures of self-esteem and depression and also between measures of self-esteem and aggression (in other words, gifted children who had lower self-esteem also tended to be depressed and to be more aggressive; Benony et al., 2007). If this study had involved only 4 gifted children (instead of the 23 actually examined), the correlations could easily reflect the luck of the draw: Perhaps the day before the study one of the 4 children had misread the instructions for an important test, which he then failed dramatically. That experience might have produced temporary low self-esteem and also made him feel depressed and aggressive. A chance event would have made the sample for this study nonrandom. Alternatively, suppose that one of the 4 children had absolutely aced an important test at school the day before—and so was feeling especially good about herself and not depressed or aggressive. This too could distort the results. In contrast, if the study had 100 children as participants, the chances that some would have had an experience that produced temporary low self-esteem would likely be balanced by the chances that some would have had an experience that produced the opposite effect. The bottom line: The larger the sample, the more likely that random variations going in one direction will be canceled out by random variations going in the other direction. Thus, the larger the sample, the smaller the correlation coefficient needs to be for you to be confident that the observed relationship is not a result of chance.

Researchers want to know not only the correlation coefficient, but also the value of p (which stands for *probability*) that is associated with that coefficient; the value of p indicates how likely it is that the correlation could have arisen due to chance. In the study just mentioned, the correlation between a measure of self-esteem and a measure of depression was $r = -.59$, and this coefficient was tied to $p < .01$. This means that the probability that the correlation is due to chance is less than 1 in 100. Similarly, a value of $p < .05$ means that the probability that the correlation is due to chance is less than 5 in 100. In fact, $p < .05$ is usually considered the cutoff for statistical significance. You can check the significance of the value of p for a data set by consulting a published table (which appears in appendixes of most statistics textbooks). Computer software that calculates the correlation coefficient usually gives the value of p as well.

Using Correlational Methods

Much of the research on defining and understanding psychopathology is correlational. That is, it is designed to discover whether one variable (a disorder or a symptom) is linked to other variables (such as alterations in neural activity, irrational thoughts, or family functioning). **Epidemiology** is a type of correlational research that investigates the rate of occurrence, the possible causes and risk factors, and the course of diseases or disorders. Thus, in epidemiological studies of psychopathology, researchers identify people with one (or more) disorder and correlate the presence or severity of the disorder with other variables, such as the age of onset of the disorder, the number of people in the family who have had symptoms of the disorder, or socioeconomic status.

Note that certain factors (such as having a relative with a disorder) can be *risk factors*, which increase the likelihood of developing a disorder. However, by definition, risk factors are simply that—risks, not destiny. How are such risks identified? Studies often use correlational data to determine whether people who have a psychological disorder are different in some way from people who don't have the disorder. Some of these studies are **longitudinal studies**, which are designed to determine whether a given variable is a risk factor by

Results of epidemiological research indicate that people who engage in pathological gambling—their gambling is compulsive—are at high risk to have an alcohol or drug problem (Petry, Stinson, & Grant, 2005). However, finding such a correlation does not tell us *why* there is a relationship between gambling and substance use problems.

Getty Images

using data collected from the same participants at multiple points in time. Specifically, such studies track a group of children or adults over time and observe whether a disorder develops. The presence or absence of the disorder is then correlated with a neurological factor (perhaps information about brain structure or function or hormone levels), a psychological factor (cognitive or emotional functioning, beliefs, or personality traits), or a social factor (family and other intimate relations, school performance, or socioeconomic status) that typically was assessed at an earlier point in time. Factors that are significantly correlated with the subsequent emergence of the disorder are taken to signal risk for developing that disorder. However, because such longitudinal studies are usually correlational, researchers cannot infer causality on the basis of the findings. As with virtually all correlational studies, many factors can explain differences observed in longitudinal studies.

AP Photo/Peter Dejong, Pool

Case Studies

Research on psychopathology may also rely on **case studies,** which focus in detail on one individual and the factors that underlie that person's psychological disorder or disorders. For instance, someone noticed that a patient had a very bad sore throat prior to developing symptoms of *obsessive-compulsive disorder* (OCD)—a disorder that is characterized by frequent and intrusive unwanted thoughts and behaviors that the individual feels compelled to engage in (we will say more about this in Chapter 7). Studies that were inspired by this observation found that OCD may sometimes develop from a particular type of streptococcal infection (Swedo et al., 1998), and eventually researchers identified *pediatric autoimmune neuropsychiatric disorder associated with streptococcal infection* (PANDAS; Giulino et al., 2002). PANDAS appears to arise, at least in part, when antibodies that attack the strep bacteria also attack the brain's basal ganglia. Antibiotics that treat the strep infection (leading to lower levels of antibodies) end up decreasing the OCD symptoms. The discovery of PANDAS began from a case study. However, additional crucial information could only be revealed by group studies. For example, parents and siblings of those who develop PANDAS-related OCD have a higher rate of OCD than does the general population (Lougee et al., 2000), which suggests that a person's neurological vulnerability affects whether he or she will develop the disorder when infected by this type of strep.

Case studies can alert clinicians to possible factors that may exacerbate symptoms of a particular disorder. Case 5.1 is about such a problem affecting a young woman with *autism*—a disorder that is diagnosed in childhood and involves significant problems with communication and social interactions (we'll discuss this disorder in more detail in Chapter 14).

Risk factors are usually variables that are associated—correlated—with the later emergence of psychological disorders. For instance, soldiers who fought in the Gulf War in 1991 were more likely to develop psychological disorders in the next year than were soldiers deployed elsewhere during that time period (Fiedler et al., 2006). However, the presence of risk factors doesn't guarantee that a disorder will develop.

CASE 5.1 ▸ FROM THE OUTSIDE: Menstruation-Related Exacerbation of Autism Symptoms

A 19-year-old nonverbal girl fulfilling *DSM-IV* criteria for autism and severe mental retardation was referred for aggression and SIB [self-injurious behavior]. At onset of menarche at age 12, agitation dramatically increased. Her mother recorded cyclical behavioral changes along with her menses. Before each menses, she became withdrawn, apathetic, quiet, irritable, and easily agitated with increased tantrums and appeared anxious. She also had a cyclical amplification of baseline autistic behaviors: stereotypies (rocking), sensitivity to changes, and sensitivity to noise. New-onset cyclical hand-biting was so intense that scarring resulted, and cyclical aggression directed at objects and others occurred several times daily. Teacher reports recorded and corroborated aggression and SIB that corresponded to the days before the onset of her menstrual period. Within 1 day of menstrual onset, mood symptoms and SIB abated. Neither behavioral therapy with positive or negative reinforcement nor treatment with acetaminophen or ibuprofen yielded improvement. Treatment with paroxetine [Paxil, an SSRI medication] 20 mg every morning resulted in improvement of premenstrual mood symptoms and premenstrual exacerbated SIB. On discontinuation of paroxetine on two distinct occasions, cyclical mood symptoms, aggression, and SIB returned.

(Lee, 2004, p. 1193)

Case studies (in studies of psychopathology)
A research method that focuses in detail on one individual and the factors that underlie that person's psychological disorder or disorders.

Uses and Limits of Case Studies

A case study focuses on a particular individual in detail, often describing neurological, psychological, and social factors: Such a study often provides information about a person's medical and family history, as well as his or her culture and the context of the problem. Mental health professionals use case studies for a variety of reasons:

• to demonstrate some aspect of diagnosis, etiology, or treatment;

• to provide support for (or evidence against) a particular hypothesis or theory; and

• to train other mental health professionals, who are given case studies and must then propose diagnoses and appropriate treatments.

This book includes numerous case studies so that you can gain a sense of how psychological disorders affect people's lives. Case studies with *From the Outside* in the title describe an individual with a disorder from a mental health professional's point of view. Case studies with *From the Inside* in the title are first-person accounts, allowing you to get a patient's point of view on what it is like to have a disorder or particular symptoms of a disorder.

Mental health clinicians and researchers must resist the temptation to generalize from a single case: Don't assume that the findings from a case study necessarily can be extended to other similar cases, let alone to the population at large. Sometimes the findings can be generalized, but sometimes they cannot be; every individual is unique, and a person's particular history presents many possible confounding factors. In addition, if a case study relies on correlations among variables, this method—as usual—prevents us from drawing conclusions about causality.

Single-Participant Experiments

Case studies are not necessarily limited to describing the values of variables and relations among them. In some situations, clinicians and researchers can actually perform experiments with only a single case. For instance, a researcher could treat someone suspected of having PANDAS-related OCD with antibiotics and determine whether the OCD symptoms improved. Experiments with only a single case are called **single-participant experiments**. Watson and Rayner conducted a single-participant experiment with Little Albert.

Single-participant experiments may rely on an *ABAB design*, which is often used to measure change in target behaviors as the result of some treatment. In many cases, the baseline condition is the first A, and administration of a treatment (e.g., behavior modification, or any other type of treatment) is B. A single participant receives both conditions: a baseline condition with no treatment (the first phase A of the ABAB design), and the treatment (phase B of the ABAB design) (Drotar, 2006). The data for the target behavior in the baseline phase (A) are compared to the data for that behavior in the next phase (B).

In the second A phase, the treatment in phase B is withdrawn, and researchers can determine whether, or how quickly, the person's targeted behavior returns to baseline (for example, withdrawing behavior modification treatment and observing what happens with extinction). This second A phase addresses the question "Will any behavior change from the previous phase persist once treatment is withdrawn?" The treatment is then presented again in the second B phase.

For instance, people with autism (such as the young woman in Case 5.1) have difficulty taking another person's perspective. One method to help them with this social skill is to tell them stories in which who, what, when, where, and why are clear—and ample information is given about the different characters' perspectives (Gray, 1996). Such stories are read aloud to the patient from a picture book. Results of previous research with social stories indicate that they can be helpful, but in most of those studies the stories were part of a comprehensive intervention that included other treatments such as social skills training (Swaggart et al., 1995).

A single-participant experiment was performed to determine whether social stories alone could help decrease tantrums in a 5-year-old boy, Gregg, diagnosed

Single-participant experiments
Experiments with only a single participant.

with autism (Lorimer et al., 2002). Gregg's tantrums involved screaming, kicking, and throwing things and were thought to be efforts to obtain attention. Before a tantrum, Gregg would "rev up" by shouting commands for attention, such as "Listen to me!"; these commands were referred to in the study as "interrupting verbalizations." When his parents or therapist ignored these commands (trying to extinguish the behavior), Gregg went into a tantrum; the episodes of interrupting verbalizations and tantrums would last at least 45 minutes. These episodes occurred about five times each day, usually when his parents or other adults weren't paying attention to him or when he had to wait to play with a particular object.

Social stories about adults talking to other adults and about having to wait were read to Gregg:

- each morning,
- at the beginning of each therapy session,
- right before the adult with him was to withdraw attention from him to talk to someone else, and
- when he was about to be asked to wait.

Then, when his interrupting behaviors began, Gregg was asked to look at his social storybook and figure out what appropriate behaviors would be.

Researchers collected data on the frequency of Gregg's target behaviors. In Gregg's case, the treatment was the use of social stories, and there were two dependent variables: the frequency of interrupting verbalizations and the frequency of temper tantrums. In the A phase of the ABAB design, no stories were told; in the B phase, the stories were told. Figure 5.3 illustrates the results: The social stories were an effective means of reducing Gregg's interrupting verbalizations and tantrums. Note that once the stories were withdrawn (the second A phase), the target behaviors increased the subsequent day. Moreover, by the end of the second B phase, Gregg's interrupting verbalizations decreased even more than they did in the first B phase.

Single-participant experiments can help clinicians who want to know the extent to which an intervention

Figure 5.3

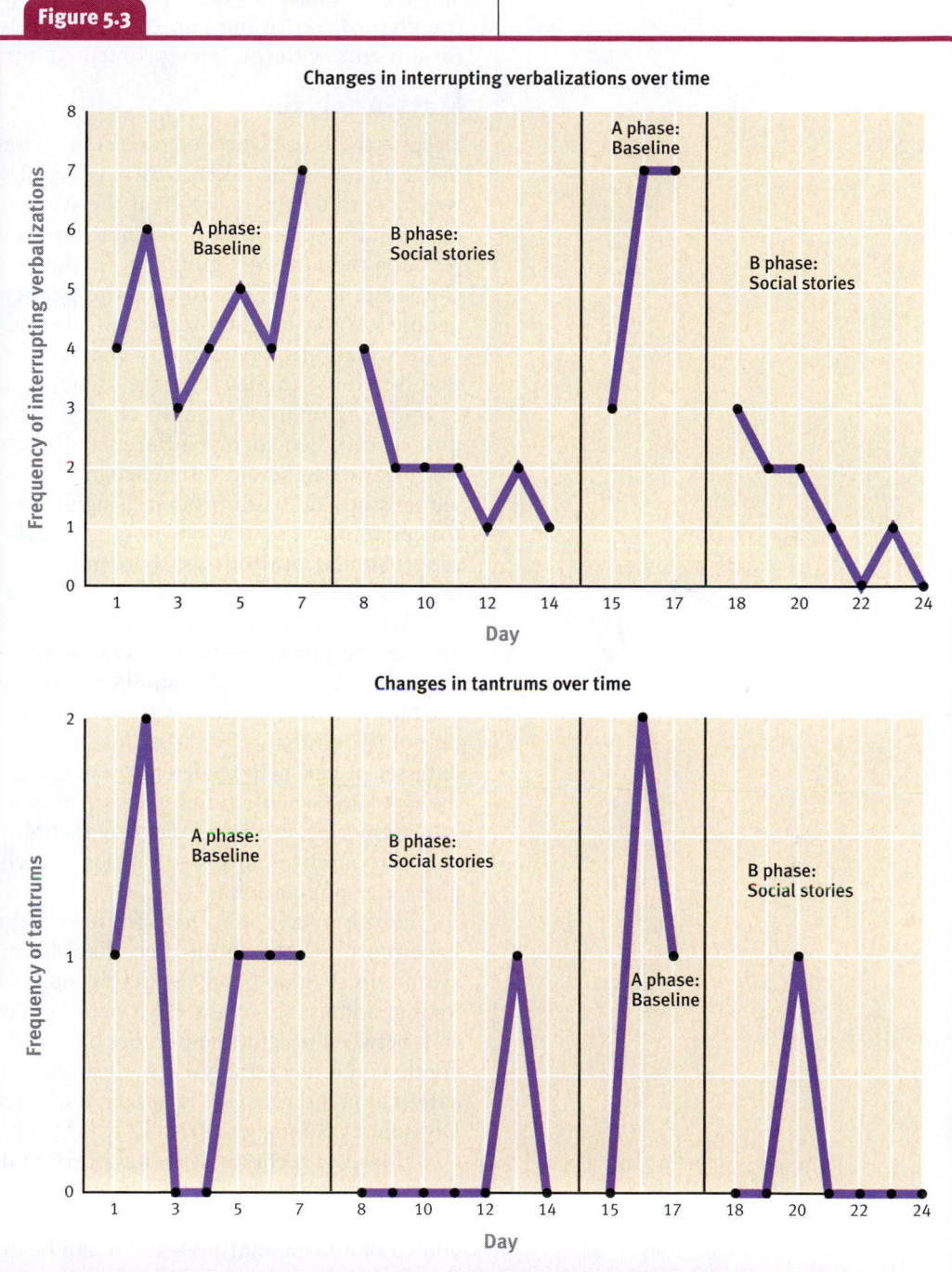

5.3 ▶ Results From a Single-Participant Experiment This single-participant experiment, using an ABAB design, shows the frequency of Gregg's interrupting verbalizations and tantrum behaviors over the course of the experiment.

Source: Lorimer, P.A., et al., 2002. Copyright 2002 by Sage Publications, Inc. For more information see the Permissions section.

can modify a patient's behavior. However, like case studies, single-participant experiments consider only one individual, so the results can be specific to that individual and based on neurological, psychological, or social factors that may not apply to others, or at least not in the same combination. Moreover, other confounding variables—such as the therapist's enthusiasm for the treatment, rather than the treatment itself—limit the generalizations that can be made. When the results of single-participant experiments are published, it is often with the goal of informing clinicians about possible interventions that might work for patients with the same problem and in similar circumstances.

Meta-Analysis

Despite the best efforts of researchers to minimize confounds, the results of any one study must be taken with a grain of salt—it's not clear whether researchers would obtain similar results if the study were undertaken in somewhat different circumstances. Perhaps the significant results found in one study were a fluke—or perhaps the lack of significant results in another study was a fluke. Such flukes can arise, in part, because of the particular people who were studied. Just as people vary in height and weight, they also vary in their behavioral tendencies, cognitive abilities, personality characteristics, and symptoms. This variety means that different samples from the same population can vary substantially, and when a sample is relatively small, chance variation can produce an appearance of a difference when such a difference doesn't really exist, or can obscure the measurement of an actual difference in the population. Moreover, sometimes an individual study does not produce a significant finding, but instead reports a near miss (for example, $p < .07$, which is above the critical .05 cutoff). If enough studies report similar near misses, there may be an effect, but it just isn't being measured well enough.

But how can researchers statistically evaluate more than one study that examines the same question? **Meta-analysis** is a research method that statistically combines the results of a number of studies that address the same question. This strategy can be especially valuable when some studies show an effect but others do not (Rosenthal, 1991). Because a meta-analysis increases the size of the overall data set, it can help to determine whether or not certain variables are related. In many cases, when studies are considered together in a single meta-analysis, the effect emerges loud and clear. A meta-analysis can uncover a relationship that is not apparent in any single study, which considers only a single sample from a particular population.

For instance, some clinicians have claimed that people with schizophrenia who have more insight about their disorder and its consequences also display fewer symptoms than do people with schizophrenia who have less insight. However, studies that address this claim have yielded inconsistent results: Some suggest a relationship between insight and number of symptoms, whereas others do not. Researchers conducted a meta-analysis of 40 studies on this relationship, and the results indicate that greater insight is in fact associated with fewer symptoms overall (Mintz, Dobson, & Romney, 2003).

However, meta-analyses have certain drawbacks. For one, there's the so-called *file drawer problem*. The results of studies that failed to find effects may linger in a researcher's file drawer, never making it to publication and thus never being included in a meta-analysis—and it can be difficult to estimate how many such negative findings there are. For another, not all studies are conducted equally well (e.g., some have more confounds than others). Some researchers have therefore asserted "garbage in, garbage out": If the individual studies are no good, why should we believe that aggregating them is a good idea? Thus, although meta-analyses can reveal underlying regularities in results from different studies, they must be followed up with new studies that directly test their conclusions.

Table 5.1 provides a summary of the different research methods we've discussed.

Meta-analysis
A research method that statistically combines the results of a number of studies that address the same question to determine the overall effect.

Table 5.1 ▶ Research Methods in Psychopathology

Research Method	Important Feature(s)	Drawback(s)
Experimental Design	Use of independent and dependent variables and random assignment allows researchers to infer cause and effect.	Most research on etiological factors that contribute to psychopathology cannot be studied with experiments (but experiments are often used to study the effects of treatment).
Quasi-experiments	Used when it is possible to identify independent and dependent variables, but random assignment of participants to groups is not possible; researchers can still infer cause and effect.	Because random assignment isn't possible, possible confounds are difficult to eliminate.
Correlational Research	Used when it is not possible to manipulate independent variables such as etiological factors; researchers can examine relationships between variables.	Results indicate only *related* factors, not *causal* factors.
Case Studies	Often descriptive, but can use any of the research methods applied to a single participant.	Caution must be exercised in generalizing from the sole participant to others; there are many possible confounding factors.
Single-Participant Experiments	An experiment with one participant (and so random assignment isn't possible); cause and effect can be inferred.	Caution must be exercised in generalizing from the sole participant to others; there are many possible confounding factors.
Meta-analysis	A statistical analysis that combines the results of a number of studies that examine the same general question to determine the overall effect.	It is difficult to estimate the number of studies that failed to find an effect and thus were not published and not included in the analysis; the studies analyzed are often not of equal quality but their results are nevertheless weighted equally in the analysis.

Ethical Guidelines for Research

In theory, you could use an experimental design to test your hypothesis about childhood loss and adult depression after a breakup. This would involve long-term planning. First, you would have to find children who volunteer (and understand what they are volunteering for) to participate in the research project. Then, you would have to randomly assign each of them to one of three different groups: (1) a group that would suffer an early loss in the family—such as their parents' divorcing and a parent's moving far away—and also experience helplessness; (2) a group that would suffer an early loss in their family without feeling helplessness (for instance, the experimenter might allow the child to convince a parent not to move away); or (3) a group that would not suffer an early loss in their family. During their college years, you could, in theory, randomly assign some participants in each group to be dumped by a boyfriend or girlfriend.

Obviously, were there such a study, people would not be clamoring to participate. But what if people did volunteer for the study—should it be conducted? What if parents volunteered their young children? In such cases, it's easy to say, "of course not!" It would be morally and ethically wrong to inflict such loss and emotional turmoil for the sake of a research study. More generally, certain methods are obviously unethical. Everyone would agree that it would be wrong to traumatize people in order to learn why some develop chronic psychological problems afterward and some don't. Similarly, it would be unethical to cause people to become addicted to drugs in order to do research on how easily they can overcome the addiction.

But most ethical issues are not so clear-cut. How, then, do researchers decide which research studies are ethical and which are not? To address this question,

Table 5.2 ▸ Information Provided for Obtaining Informed Consent

When obtaining informed consent from participants, a researcher must give participants the following information:

(1) the purpose of the research, expected duration, and procedures;

(2) their right to decline to participate and to withdraw from the research once participation has begun;

(3) the foreseeable consequences of declining or withdrawing;

(4) reasonably foreseeable factors that may be expected to influence their willingness to participate such as potential risks, discomfort, or adverse effects;

(5) any prospective research benefits;

(6) limits of confidentiality;

(7) incentives for participation; and

(8) whom to contact for questions about the research and research participants' rights.

Source: Copyright © American Psychological Association. For more information see the Permissions section.

psychologists have developed ethical guidelines for research, which are part of the overall ethical code for psychologists. For instance, before someone participates in a study, the investigator must provide information describing the study, as outlined in Table 5.2. If a person decides to participate after reading the information, he or she signs an *informed consent* form. By signing, the person acknowledges that he or she understands what is involved in the study and agrees to participate, knowing that he or she can withdraw from the study at any point (American Psychological Association, 2002).

Another ethical guideline for research is that investigators must *debrief* participants after a study is over. They must ask each participant about his or her experience, particularly about any negative aspects of the experience (in part so that the study can be adjusted to minimize possible negative experiences for future participants). Investigators must also clear up any misconceptions that the participant may have about the study (American Psychological Association, 2002).

In addition, agencies that fund research on psychopathology and treatment require that the study be reviewed and approved by an institutional review board (IRB) in the setting that hosts the study (e.g., hospital, university, or clinic). The IRB is composed of scientists, clinicians, and members of the community at large. The board evaluates each study's possible risks and benefits, and then decides whether the study should be approved. This serves as another check on any ethical issues that might arise while a study is being conducted or afterward.

Key Concepts and Facts About Using the Scientific Method to Understand Abnormality

- Researchers use the scientific method to understand and study psychopathology. In doing so, they observe relevant phenomena, identify a question to be answered, develop a hypothesis that might answer the question, collect new observations to test the hypothesis, draw on the evidence to formulate a reasonable theory, and test the theory.

- When conducting experiments, researchers systematically manipulate one or more independent variables (changing one at a time) and observe possible changes in one or more dependent variables. Researchers examine the possible contribution of confounds by using control groups or control conditions. To minimize unintentional bias, they randomly assign participants to groups. In addition, stimulus items are chosen to assess the relevant variables, and confounding characteristics are eliminated. Experiments should have both internal and external validity.

- Researchers may use a quasi-experimental design when random assignment is not ethical, desirable, or possible.

- Correlational research is used when independent variables cannot or should not be manipulated. Such studies allow researchers to investigate the relationship between two variables, specifically, whether a change in one variable is associated with a change in the other. However, a correlation does not imply causation; it only indicates that the two variables are related. The strength of the relationship is quantified by the correlation coefficient, r, which can range from −1 to +1, with a higher absolute value indicating a stronger relationship. Statistical significance indicates that the obtained measurement is greater than would be expected by chance alone. Longitudinal studies of psychopathology often use correlational data.

- Case studies allow a clinician or researcher to examine one individual in detail. Single-participant experiments (often using an ABAB design) provide information about how one variable affects another. However, information from a particular case may not generalize to others.

- Meta-analysis allows researchers to aggregate the results of a number of related studies in order to determine the relations among certain variables.

- Psychologists have developed an ethical code of conduct that lays out guidelines for research, including the requirements that informed consent must be obtained from participants and that participants must be debriefed after a study is over.

Research Challenges in Understanding Abnormality

Let's examine your hypothesis about the relationship between experiencing a childhood loss and feeling depressed after a breakup in adulthood. How can we use the neuropsychosocial approach to understand why breaking up can lead some people to become depressed? We could investigate neurological mechanisms by which early loss, associated with helplessness, might make people more vulnerable to later depression, perhaps through enduring changes to brain structure or function. We could investigate psychological effects resulting from early loss, such as learned helplessness, cognitive distortions, or problems with emotional regulation. We could investigate social mechanisms, such as the way the loss altered subsequent attachments to and relationships with others or how economic hardships arising from the early loss created a higher baseline of daily stress. And, crucially, we could propose ways in which these possible factors might interact with one another. For example, perhaps daily financial stress not only increases the degree of worrying about money, but also such worrying in turn changes neurological functioning as well as social functioning (as preoccupying financial worries alter social interactions).

Whatever type of factors researchers investigate, each type comes with its own challenges, which affect the way a study is undertaken and which limit the conclusions that can be drawn from a study's results. Let's examine the major types of challenges to research on the nature and causes of abnormality from the neuropsychosocial perspective.

Challenges in Researching Neurological Factors

DSM-IV-TR does not consider neurological factors when assigning diagnoses, but many researchers are exploring the possible role of neurological factors in causing psychological disorders. This research is yielding new insights into why some of us, in some circumstances, develop psychological problems. In fact, current findings about neurological factors are coming to play an increasingly large role in treatment.

With the exception of genetics, almost all techniques that assess neurological factors identify abnormalities in the structure or function of the brain. This assessment is done directly (e.g., with neuroimaging) or indirectly (e.g., with neuropsychological testing or measurements of the level of stress hormones in the bloodstream). Such abnormalities are associated (correlated) with specific disorders or symptoms. For instance, people with schizophrenia have larger than normal ventricles (the fluid-containing cavities in the brain) and other areas of the brain are correspondingly smaller (Vita et al., 2006). Like all correlational studies, the studies that revealed the enlarged ventricles cannot establish causation. That is, these results cannot establish whether:

• schizophrenia arises because of the effects of this brain abnormality;

• episodes of psychosis somehow create larger ventricles (in essence, schizophrenia, over time, creates the brain abnormality);

• the brain abnormality existed before symptoms of schizophrenia developed; or

• the brain abnormality arises from some other factor, such as the effects of medications for schizophrenia. (We will revisit these possible causes in Chapter 12, when we discuss schizophrenia in more detail.)

Another limitation of research using neuroimaging is that we do not yet have a complete understanding of what different parts of the brain do. Thus, researchers cannot be sure about the implications of structural abnormalities (e.g., enlarged ventricles) or functional abnormalities (e.g., why specific areas that are normally activated during a task are not activated when a person with a particular disorder performs the task). For example, the parietal lobes are involved in attention, in representing spatial information, in performing arithmetic, and in many other activities; simply knowing that these lobes are not activated to normal levels during a task does not tell us which particular processes they are failing to accomplish normally. Similarly, researchers don't know what it means when an area is activated when a person with a disorder performs a task but not when participants who don't have the disorder perform it.

Nevertheless, the outlook is far from hopeless. Researchers do know a considerable amount about what specific parts of the brain do (and are learning more every day). Also, they can use other techniques in combination with neuroimaging to learn which brain areas may play a role in causing or contributing to certain disorders. For example, if abnormal activation in the parietal lobe indicates that a person with schizophrenia is having to work harder to pay attention, then relatively low doses of transcranial magnetic stimulation (TMS) to the parietal lobe should disrupt the person's ability to pay attention more than would be the case for normal control participants. We will have more to say about neuroimaging research in subsequent chapters.

Challenges in Researching Psychological Factors

Scientists who study neurological factors examine the difficulties with the biological *mechanisms* that process information or that give rise to emotion. In contrast, scientists who study psychological factors examine specific mental contents, mental processes, behaviors, or emotions. As we noted in Chapter 3, information about psychological factors typically is obtained from patients' self-reports, from reports by others close to patients, or from direct observations.

Biases in Mental Processes That Affect Assessment

Assessing mental contents, emotions, and behaviors via self-report or report by others can yield inaccurate information because of biases in what people pay attention to remember, and report. Sometimes beliefs, expectations, or habits bias how participants respond, consciously or unconsciously. For instance, people who have anxiety disorders are more likely to be extremely attentive to stimuli that might be perceived as a threat (Cloitre et al., 1994; Mathews et al., 1989; Mogg, Millar, & Bradley, 2000). In contrast, people with depression do not have this particular bias but tend to be biased in what they recall—they are more likely than people who are not depressed to recall unpleasant events (Blaney, 1986; Murray, Whitehouse, & Alloy, 1999; Watkins, 2002; Williams et al., 1997). In fact, researchers have found that people in general are more likely to recall information consistent with their current mood than information that is inconsistent with their current mood (referred to as *mood-congruent memory bias*; Teasdale, 1983).

Biases not only influence attention and recall, but also can affect reporting. In one study, college students completed tests of cognitive abilities (including memory) and then were asked to complete a self-report scale to indicate how depressed they were. Participants who were more depressed *reported* that their cognitive functioning was impaired, but their cognitive test results did not support their reports (Wong, Wetterneck, & Klein, 2000): Their subjective experience was at odds with objective data. Thus, biases in attention, memory, and reporting can distort the results of research.

Research Challenges with Clinical Interviews

Patients' responses can be affected by whether they are asked questions by an interviewer or receive them in a written questionnaire (see Figure 5.4). Consider a study in which participants were asked questions about their symptoms of either OCD or social phobia. When the questions were first asked by a clinician as part of an interview, participants tended not to report certain avoidance-related symptoms that they later did report on a questionnaire. In contrast, when participants completed the questionnaire first, they reported these symptoms both on the questionnaire and in the subsequent interview (Dell'Osso et al., 2002).

Moreover, when interviewing family members or friends about a patient's behavior, clinicians should keep in mind that these people may have their own biases. They may pay more attention to, and so be more likely to remember, particular

Myrleen Ferguson Cate/Photo Edit

People with different disorders tend to have different biases in what they pay attention to, remember, and report. A man with depression, for instance, might report that he's not doing a very good job at work, but this may not be accurate. Because of his depression, he is more likely to remember aspects of his performance at work that did not meet his expectations and to forget about aspects of his performance that met or surpassed his expectations.

aspects of a patient's behavior, and they may have their own views as to the causes of the patient's behavior (Achenbach, 2008; Kirk & Hsieh, 2004). For example, when assessing children, clinicians usually rely heavily on reports from others, such as parents and teachers; however, these individuals often do not agree on the nature or cause of a child's problems (De Los Reyes & Kazdin, 2004).

In addition, some people, because of their level of intelligence, attention span, or life experiences, misunderstand the intent of questions on a questionnaire or in an interview. For instance, the question "What have you done today?" could refer to what important activities were accomplished (e.g., writing a paper or giving a presentation), or it could have a more literal meaning—"Tell me everything you've done today," including taking a shower and dressing (Schwarz, 1999). Responses to different meanings of a question will affect the data. One advantage of an interview is that the clinician can rephrase a question if the patient responds in a way that reveals that he or she misunderstood the intended meaning.

Figure 5.4

5.4 ▶ How the Question Is Asked Affects the Answer
Patients may respond differently to a question, depending on whether it is part of a questionnaire or asked by an interviewer (Dell'Osso et al., 2002).

Research Challenges with Questionnaires

In psychopathology research, questionnaires are a relatively inexpensive way to collect a lot of data quickly. However, questionnaires must be designed carefully in order to avoid various biases. For example, one sort of bias arises when a range of alternative responses are presented. Some questionnaires provide only two choices in response to an item ("yes" or "no"), whereas other questionnaires give participants more than two choices, such as "all the time," "frequently," "sometimes," "infrequently," or "never." With more choices comes more opportunities for bias: Twice a week might be interpreted as frequent by one person and infrequent by another. Moreover, the way the scale is defined is important. An example of this type of problem arose when people were asked to rate how successful they have been in life; simply changing the numeric values of the end points on the scale changed people's responses. When asked to respond on a rating scale with numbers from −5 to +5, like this:

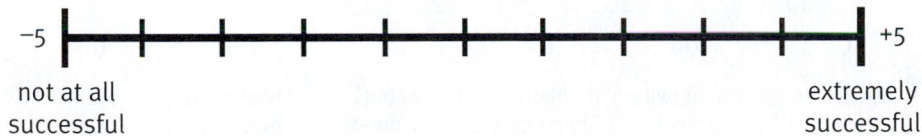

34% reported having been highly successful in life. When asked to respond on a scale with numbers from 0 to 10, like this:

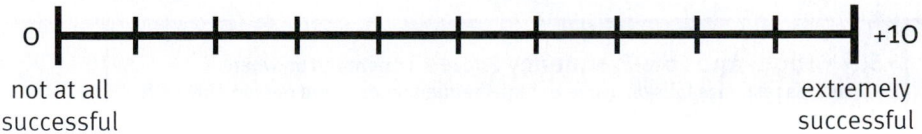

only 13% reported having been highly successful in life (Schwarz, Knäuper, Hippler, Noelle-Neumann, & Clark, 1991). To reduce the subjective aspect of rating scales, some questionnaires, such as the Posttraumatic Diagnostic Scale (Foa et al., 1997), define the frequency choices in terms of specific numerical values (such as having "frequently" defined as three times a week).

In addition, *response bias* is a major problem to avoid when designing questionnaires. **Response bias** refers to a tendency to respond in a particular way, regardless of what is being asked by the questions. For instance, some people, and members of some cultures in general, are more likely to check off "agree" than "disagree,"

Response bias
The tendency to respond in a particular way, regardless of what is being asked by the question.

regardless of the content of the statement (Javeline, 1999; Welkenhuysen-Gybels, Billiet, & Cambré, 2003). This type of response bias, called *acquiescence*, can be reduced by wording half the items negatively. Thus, if you were interested in assessing self-reported shyness in a questionnaire, you might include both the item "I often feel shy when meeting new people" and the item "I don't usually feel shy when meeting new people," which is simply a negative rewording of the first item.

Another type of response bias is **social desirability**: answering questions in a way that that the respondent thinks makes him or her "look good" (that is, in a way that he or she thinks is socially desirable), even if the answer is not true. For instance, some people might not agree with the statement "It is better to be honest, even if others don't like you for it." However, they may think that they *should* agree and respond accordingly. In contrast to a social desirability bias, some people answer questions in a way that they think makes them "look bad" or look worse than they actually are. People with malingering and factitious disorder (see Chapter 3) are likely to respond so that they appear more ill than they are. To compensate for these biases, many personality inventories have a scale that assesses the participant's tendency to answer in a socially desirable or falsely symptomatic manner. This scale is then used to adjust (or, in the language of testing, to "correct") the scores on the part of the inventory that measure traits.

Another type of response bias can occur because people generally assume that the center of the response scale is average. If a response scale is set up so that individuals believe that their responses are above (or below) average, they may shift their responses so that they are closer to average; see Figure 5.5 (Schwarz, 1999).

Figure 5.5

Low–Frequency Scale

( )	( )	( )	(X)	( )	( )
Less than once a month	About once a month	About once in two weeks	About once a week	About twice a week	More often

High–Frequency Scale

( )	(X)	( )	( )	( )	( )
Less than twice a week	About twice a week	About four times a week	About six times a week	About once every 24 hours	More often

5.5 ▶ **High- and Low-Frequency Scales** Depending on where someone's response falls on a low- or high-frequency scale, the person may shift the response closer to the assumed average—the center.

Source: Schwartz, 1999. Copyright © 1999 American Psychological Association. For more information see the Permissions section.

Challenges in Researching Social Factors

Challenges in researching social factors not only affect what can be learned about such factors themselves, but also affect what can be learned about other sorts of factors. Information obtained from and about people always has a context. For research on psychopathology, a crucial part of the context is defined by other people. Social factors arise from the setting (such as a home, hospital, outpatient clinic, or university),

Social desirability
A bias toward answering questions in a way that respondents think makes them "look good" (i.e., that he or she thinks is socially desirable), even if the responses are not true.

the people administering the study, and the cultural context writ large. Challenges to conducting research on social factors that affect psychopathology include the ways that the presence or behavior of the investigator and the beliefs and assumptions of a particular culture can influence the responses of participants.

Investigator-Influenced Biases

Like psychological factors, social factors are often assessed by self-report (such as patient's reports of financial problems), reports by others (such as family members' descriptions of family interactions or of a patient's behavior), and direct observation. Along with the biases we've already mentioned, the social interaction between investigator and participant can affect these kinds of data.

Experimenter Expectancy Effects

Experimenter expectancy effect refers to the investigator's intentionally or unintentionally treating participants in ways that encourage particular types of responses. The experimenter expectancy effect is slightly misnamed: it applies not only to experiments, but also to all psychological investigations in which an investigator interacts with participants. For instance, suppose that you are investigating whether a particular symptom of social phobia—a fear of being in social situations with strangers—is associated with a particular symptom of OCD—recurring intrusive thoughts or images. You are investigating whether these two symptoms—each of a different disorder—are correlated. You interview participants with social phobia and ask them about the nature of their fears. When they mention symptoms that are not of interest to you (such as their preference to be alone), you ask about how they feel in social situations with strangers. It's possible that you might ask with a particular tone of voice or facial expression, unintentionally suggesting the type of answer you hope to hear. Participants might, consciously or unconsciously, try to respond as they think you would like, perhaps exaggerating certain symptoms a bit. Such a social interaction can undermine the validity of the study.

Reducing Experimenter Expectancy Effects with a Double-Blind Design

To minimize the likelihood of experimenter expectancy effects, researchers often use a **double-blind design:** Neither the participant nor the investigator's assistant (who has contact with the participant) knows the group to which the participant has been assigned or the predicted results of the study. That is, both are blind to the participant's group assignment and the predicted results. Implementing double-blind designs has the following features:

- First and foremost, the assistant, who does not know the predictions, collects the information from participants.

- The investigator eliminates cues in the environment that might allow the assistant to infer the predictions.

- Instructions given to participants or questions asked of them are standardized, so that all participants are treated in the same way.

- A computer or other automated device delivers instructions and stimuli and scores the responses.

Although double-blind studies are a way to minimize experimenter expectancy effects, participants try to make sense of what is being asked of them in a study despite an investigator's best efforts. Participants often develop their own hypothesis about the nature of the study and may behave accordingly (Kihlstrom, 2002a).

Reactivity

Have you ever had the experience of being watched while you were doing something? Did you find that you behaved somewhat differently simply because you knew that you were being observed? If so, then you have experienced **reactivity**—a behavior change that occurs when one becomes aware of being observed. When participants in a study know that they are observed, they may subtly (or not so subtly) change their behavior, leading the study to have results that may not be valid. One way to counter such an effect is to use hidden cameras, but this may raise ethical issues—many people (rightfully) object to being "spied on."

Experimenter expectancy effect
The investigator's intentionally or unintentionally treating participants in ways that encourage particular types of responses.

Double-blind design
A research design in which neither the participant nor the investigator's assistant knows the group to which specific participants have been assigned or the predicted results of the study.

Reactivity
A behavior change that occurs when one becomes aware of being observed.

Although reactivity may be decreased by observing participants via video camera, they can still be aware that they are being observed by others and modify their behavior accordingly.

Reactivity can also occur when investigators observe family functioning. Suppose you were studying interaction patterns in families in which a parent is depressed. If the family members know that they are being observed (or at least the parents do), it is possible that this will change their behavior. Simply by giving you permission to observe their behavior, they may subtly change what they do and say. Thus, the behavior you observe may end up being different than it otherwise would have been.

Effects of Community Standards on Individual Behavior

Different communities can have different views of what thoughts, feelings, and behaviors are "normal" and "abnormal." These community views, or *standards*, in turn affect individuals' thoughts, feelings, and behaviors. However, as we have discussed earlier in this book, behavior that is "normal" in one context may not be so in another. Researchers and clinicians recognize the influence that community and cultural context can create and try to address these effects. For example, some widely administered tests, such as the MMPI-2, provide different norms on the basis of age, gender, ethnicity, education level, and occupation, against which individual participants can be compared. Such norms then allow researchers to compare study participants to the population from which they were drawn.

Cultural Differences in Evaluating Symptoms

Some researchers compare and contrast a given disorder in different cultures. Such studies can help distinguish universal symptoms from symptoms that are found only in certain cultures. Consider that some people in every culture may develop phobias, and so they fear specific stimuli or circumstances, but which particular specific stimuli or circumstances they fear tends to vary across cultures. For instance, people in India are twice as likely as people in England to have phobias of animals, darkness, and bad weather (types of *specific phobias*, discussed in Chapter 7), but are only half as likely to have phobias related to social matters (Chambers, Yeragani, & Keshavan, 1986).

Assessing psychological or social factors in other cultures can be challenging for researchers. Many words and concepts do not have exact equivalents across languages, making full translation impossible. Even when two cultures share a language, the meaning of a word may be different in each culture. For example, when a comprehensive set of interview questions was translated into Spanish and administered to residents of Puerto Rico and Mexico, 67% of the questions had to be changed because the meanings of some of the Spanish words were understood differently by the two populations (Kihlstrom, 2002b).

Key Concepts and Facts About Research Challenges to Understanding Abnormality

- Many studies that focus on neurological factors are correlational and so do not reveal how neurological factors may give rise to psychological disorders. They reveal only that certain neurological factors are associated with some disorders.

- Neuroimaging studies are becoming more common, and these studies may indicate differences in brain structure or function between those with a psychological disorder and those without a disorder. However, it is not always clear how such differences contribute to a disorder.

- Self-reports of patients or reports by others may be biased in what is paid attention to, remembered, or reported. In addition, participants may respond differently to questions that are asked during an interview and those that are presented on a questionnaire. Moreover, participants may misunderstand the intent of a question and hence answer in way that distorts the results. Researchers must take care in phrasing questions in order to minimize misinterpretation and various types of biases.

- Challenges in studying social factors can also create challenges in studying other types of factors. Such challenges include experimenter-influenced biases, such as experimenter expectancy effects (which can be reduced with a double-blind design) and reactivity. A major challenge for cross-cultural research on psychopathology is the difficulty of translating words or concepts across cultures.

Researching Treatment

Let's say that your interest in depression following breakups, plus your experiences at the counseling center helping students like Carlos, have led you to develop a new short-term treatment. In this treatment, which you have named "grief box therapy," you encourage patients to create "grief boxes"—boxes into which they place reminders of their recently ended relationships, and objects that symbolize their feelings of loss and hopelessness. Moreover, as part of the treatment, you strongly encourage patients to be with other people—friends, family members, or coworkers—as much as possible to counteract their feelings of loss. You—and other clinicians—will want to know whether your treatment is effective; that is, is it better for treating depression (specifically the sort following a breakup) than other treatments? What specific questions might you want to ask that research can help to answer? Research on treatment helps mental health professionals decide what treatments to use with a given patient who has a particular disorder.

As you will see in the following sections, research on treatment has challenges above and beyond those we've already discussed for research on psychopathology. And such research faces different challenges, depending on whether the target of treatment is neurological, psychological, or social factors.

Researching Treatments That Target Neurological Factors

Researchers and clinicians want to answer several questions when a new medication is developed, when an existing medication is used in a new way (to treat different symptoms), or when a new biomedical procedure is developed:

• Is the new treatment more effective than no treatment?

• If a treatment is effective, is it because of its actual properties (such as a medication's particular ingredients) or because of patients' expectations about what the treatment will do?

• Is the treatment more effective than other treatments currently used for those symptoms or problems?

• What are the treatment's side effects, and are they troubling enough that patients tend to stop the treatment? How does this dropout rate compare to that for the other treatments?

To assess a treatment, researchers first need to determine what specific variables should be measured and to define what it means to be "effective." Research on treatment frequently relies on an experimental or quasi-experimental design; in such studies, the independent variables might be the type of treatment, a specific technique, or type or dose of medication. And the dependent variables (the things measured) might be any of the variables listed in any column of Table 4.1 (on page 114), such as neural activity, specific mental contents, or family functioning. These variables are often related to the symptoms listed in the DSM-IV-TR criteria for the disorder under investigation.

Drug Effect or Placebo Effect?

One way to determine whether a treatment is effective is to compare it to no treatment. If people receiving the treatment are better off than those who don't receive any treatment, the treatment may have made the difference. But with biomedical treatments, such a comparison has a built-in problem: Patients know whether or not they have received the treatment. Perhaps people improve after taking a medication (or after ECT, TMS, or some other procedure) not because of the properties of the treatment itself, but because they expect to improve after receiving treatment. In fact, many studies have confirmed that expecting a treatment to be helpful leads to improvement, even if the individuals don't receive any actual treatment (Kirsch & Lynn, 1999). For example, having a TMS coil pressed on the scalp

Placebo effect
A positive effect of a medically inert substance or procedure.

Attrition
The reduction in the number of participants during a research study.

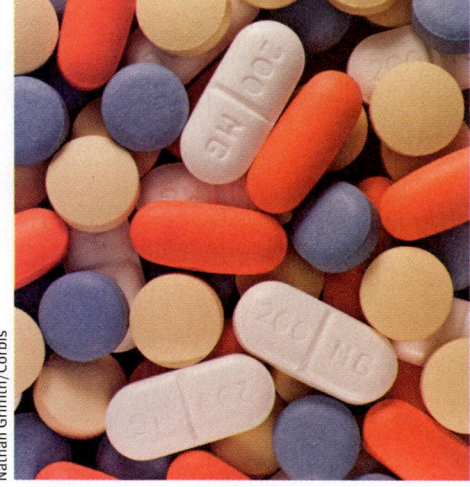

Nathan Griffith/Corbis

The color of a placebo pill can influence how effective it is. Red, pink, and yellow placebo pills work best when people believe them to be "stimulants," whereas blue placebo pills work best when people believe them to be "tranquilizers" (Buckalew & Ross, 1981).

and hearing loud clicking noises (like those produced during TMS when a magnetic field is discharged) can affect symptoms, whether or not magnetic pulses are actually sent to the brain (Loo, 2004; Nahas et al., 2003).

To discover whether a biomedical treatment is effective, researchers give a group of participants a *placebo*, an inert substance or a procedure that itself has no direct medical value. Often, a placebo is simply a sugar pill. A positive effect of such a medically inert substance or procedure is called a **placebo effect**. If patients who are given a sugar pill show the same improvement as patients who are given the pill with active ingredients, then a researcher can infer that the medication itself is not effective and that its apparent benefit is a result of the placebo effect.

The placebo effect can be strengthened or weakened by the outward qualities of the placebo and how it is administered: Taking more placebo pills generally has a greater effect; capsules do a better job than pills; and injections do better than capsules. The placebo can have an even greater effect when the person dispensing it shows interest in the patient's problems and is sympathetic and friendly (Shapiro & Morris, 1978). And placebos that patients are told cost more are more effective than are "less expensive" ones (Waber et al., 2008). If a study is not double-blind, an investigator's high expectations of a treatment's success also can cause a positive placebo effect (Shapiro, 1964). (In double-blind studies on treatment, the mental health clinician administering the treatment—as well as the patient—is blind to the patient's group assignment.

Thus, when investigators test the effects of any new medicine or other biomedical treatment, they invariably use some type of placebo treatment as a comparison. They may also include additional comparison groups, in which patient receive more established treatments, and researchers will likely use a double-blind design. Not all researchers are convinced, however, that patients and clinicians are truly "blind" in double-blind studies. In double-blind studies of medications for depression and anxiety, for instance, both patients and ("blind") clinicians may correctly guess whether patients are receiving a placebo or active medication based on the presence of side effects and changing symptoms (Margraf et al., 1991; White et al., 1992).

Some researchers have suggested that in order to evaluate the results of double-blind studies of medication, investigators should determine whether patients and their clinicians were actually blind to the treatment that the patients received (Piasecki et al., 2002); if not, the investigators should not consider the study to have been truly double-blind. Furthermore, some researchers also advocate using an *active placebo*—a placebo that mimics the side effects of an active medication but does not directly affect the psychological symptoms of the disorder being treated (Kirsch, Scoboria, & Moore, 2002; Moncrieff, 2001). For instance, when studying the effects of a tricyclic antidepressant, an investigator might use as an active placebo an antihistamine—an over-the-counter cold medicine that has some side effects that are similar to those of tricyclics.

The fact that people who suffer from certain disorders, including depression, sometimes improve following a placebo treatment (Kirsch, Scoboria, & Moore, 2002) does not mean that their problem was imaginary, or that they should throw away their medication. Rather, it seems that—for some people and for some disorders—the hope and positive expectations that go along with taking a medication (or undergoing a procedure) allow the body to mobilize its own resources to function better (Kirsch & Lynn, 1999; Scott et al., 2008).

Dropouts

On average, more than half of those who begin a treatment that is part of a research study do not complete the treatment—they drop out of the study (Kazdin, 1994). The reduction in the number of research participants during a study is called **attrition**. When attrition is different for different groups in a research study, researchers can't easily draw definitive conclusions about the treatment given to one group (Kendall, Holmbeck, & Verduin, 2004; Lambert & Ogles, 2004). Suppose, for example, that a group receiving medication (and experiencing its side effects) has more attrition than a group receiving a placebo (and not experiencing any side effects). To determine the medication's effects, should the researcher compare the placebo group to all those who *started* in the medication group (and thus include those who dropped out of the study), or should the researcher compare the placebo group only to those who *completed* the medication treatment? If you compare those who took the placebo to those who completed the medication treatment, the medication might look very promising. But if you compare the placebo group to all those who started the medication, the medication might not appear more effective than the placebo. This question of whether to include the results of those who drop out applies to research on all types of treatment—it isn't limited to research on biomedical treatments.

Researching Treatments That Target Psychological Factors

Many of the research issues that arise with biomedical treatments also arise in research on treatments that target psychological factors. In addition, as shown in Table 5.3, research on treatments that target psychological factors may be designed to investigate which aspects of therapy in general, or of particular types of therapy—such as your grief box therapy—are most helpful. Let's consider the sorts of factors that underlie the effects of treatments that targets psychological factors, how researchers control for confounding factors when they study such treatments, whether therapy is better than no treatment, whether one type of therapy is generally best, and which types of therapy are better for treating specific disorders.

Table 5.3 ▸ Treatment-Related Variables

Therapy Variables	Patient Variables	Therapist Variables	Patient-Therapist Interaction Variables
• Theoretical orientation • Specific techniques used	• Level of motivation and ability to change • Belief in the ability of treatment to help • Community resources available (social and financial support) • Preferred style of coping and relating to others • Preferred treatment focus: on symptoms (as in CBT) or on their meaning (as in psychodynamic therapy) • Personality traits	• Enthusiasm for and belief in the treatment • Usual style of interacting (such as supportive or challenging) • Treatment focus: on symptoms or on their meaning • Empathic ability • Personality traits • Experience with the particular type of treatment	• Structure of the relationship (therapist as expert vs. therapist as coach) • Fit between patient's and therapist's personalities • Fit between patient's and therapist's treatment focus (symptoms vs. their meaning) • Sense of alliance between patient and therapist

Common Factors

Just as placebos can provide relief even though they lack medically beneficial ingredients, the very act of seeing a therapist or counselor—or even setting up a meeting with one—may provide relief for some disorders (regardless of the specific techniques or theoretical approach of the therapist or counselor). Such relief may be due, at least in part, to **common factors,** which are helpful aspects of therapy that are shared by virtually all types of psychotherapy. According to results from numerous studies (Garfield & Bergin, 1994; Lambert & Ogles, 2004; Weinberger, 1995), common factors can include:

• opportunities to express problems;

• some explanation and understanding of the problems;

Common factors
Helpful aspects of therapy that are shared by virtually all types of psychotherapy.

- an opportunity to obtain support, feedback, and advice;

- encouragement to take (appropriate) risks and achieve a sense of mastery;

- hope; and

- a positive relationship.

Common factors, and certain patient characteristics—such as being motivated to change (Clarkin & Levy, 2004)—can contribute more to having a positive outcome from therapy than the specific techniques used. This means that Carl Rogers was on to something when he stressed the importance of a therapy relationship that is supportive and warm. Such qualities can amplify the therapeutic power of the common factors; however, the magnitude of the effect of common factors depends on the patient's specific problem (Roth & Fonagy, 2005). If your grief box therapy were effective, it might be because of such common factors and not something unique to your particular method.

Specific Factors

The existence of common factors creates a challenge for researchers who are interested in determining the benefits of a particular type of treatment or technique. These researchers must design studies in which the effects of common factors are accounted for and the unique benefits of the particular treatment or technique under investigation can be examined. The characteristics that give rise to these unique benefits are known as **specific factors**. For instance, when researching your grief box therapy, you might want to investigate whether the process of creating the grief box is a specific factor, providing benefit above and beyond the common factors that any therapy provides.

Such research has shown that common factors alone may not be *sufficient* to produce benefits in therapy for some disorders (Elliott, Greenberg, & Lietaer, 2004; Kirschenbaum & Jourdan, 2005; Lambert, 2004); at least for some disorders, specific factors play a key role in treatment. For example, research results suggest that for people with OCD, exposure with response prevention (a specific factor) is more important for successful treatment than common factors (Abramowitz, 1997; Chambless, 2002). However, for many disorders, including depression, the research results suggest that specific factors may be only as important as (or even *less* important than) common factors in the treatment of mild or moderate cases (Lambert, 2004). In fact, for some disorders, researchers have found that different types of therapy are about equally beneficial. The leftmost column in Table 5.3 notes specific factors—the therapy variables—that are the subject of research targeting psychological treatments. (In subsequent chapters, we will discuss research on treatments for specific disorders; such studies typically examine specific factors.)

Controlling Possible Confounding Variables with Analogue Studies

Many variables, such as those listed in Table 5.3, can influence the outcome of psychotherapy and may be confounding variables in specific studies. For instance, suppose you decide to undertake a study that compares your grief box therapy for depression after breakups to an older treatment for depression, such as cognitive-behavior therapy (CBT); you train some therapists at the counseling center to administer your new treatment, and they are very excited and enthusiastic about it. Other therapists at the counseling center administer CBT for depression, which they've been providing for years. These therapists may be less enthusiastic in their manner during therapy. If your new therapy does in fact benefit patients more than does CBT, a possible confounding variable would be the therapists' levels of enthusiasm for the two treatments. That is, it could be the manner in which the new therapy was provided that was particularly helpful to patients rather than the technique itself.

Specific factors
The characteristics of a particular treatment or technique that lead it to have unique benefits, above and beyond those conferred by common factors.

One way to study specific factors and also control for possible confounding factors that might influence treatment results is to carry out an analogue study. An **analogue study** is a type of research on treatment that is conducted under controlled conditions in a laboratory setting, thereby minimizing confounds. It is called an analogue study because the therapy is provided in a way that is *analogous* to the way therapy is usually provided. For example, one analogue study on family therapy sought to determine which method of questioning family members best facilitated each member's sense of alliance with the family therapist (Ryan & Carr, 2001). In this study, participating family members watched four 5-minute video clips of simulated family therapy sessions. In each clip, the therapist and family members remained the same; the clips differed only in the way the therapist questioned the family. Participants were asked to rate their perceptions of the alliances between the family members and the therapist in each of the four clips. Because the participants responded to video clips of simulated therapy sessions rather than directly experiencing different styles of asking questions (as would patients in actual family therapy sessions), the researchers could control for factors other than the therapist's style of questioning.

Is Therapy Better Than No Treatment?

Many kinds of treatments have been proposed for various disorders, but researchers have questioned whether people actually improve more by receiving therapy than they would have improved if they didn't receive any treatment. To address this question, researchers randomly assign participants to one of two groups: "treatment" and "no treatment." However, participants in the "no treatment" group are often assigned to a waiting list for treatment (which is ethically preferable to not providing any treatment at all), and thus this group is often called a *wait-list control group* (Kendall, Holmbeck, & Verduin, 2004, Lambert & Bergin, 1994). Researchers usually assess the dependent variable, such as level of symptoms, in both groups at the beginning of the study, before treatment begins—this is their *baseline assessment*. Then, researchers assess the same variables again after the treatment period (for the wait-list control group, this means assessing symptom level after the same duration of time as that over which the treatment group received treatment); this is called the *outcome assessment*. Researchers then compare the results of the two groups, and may also assess the variables at a later follow-up point, called a *follow-up assessment* (see Figure 5.6).

> **Analogue study**
> Research in which treatment is provided in a way that is analogous to the way it is usually provided, but that is conducted under controlled conditions in a laboratory setting, thereby minimizing confounds.

Figure 5.6

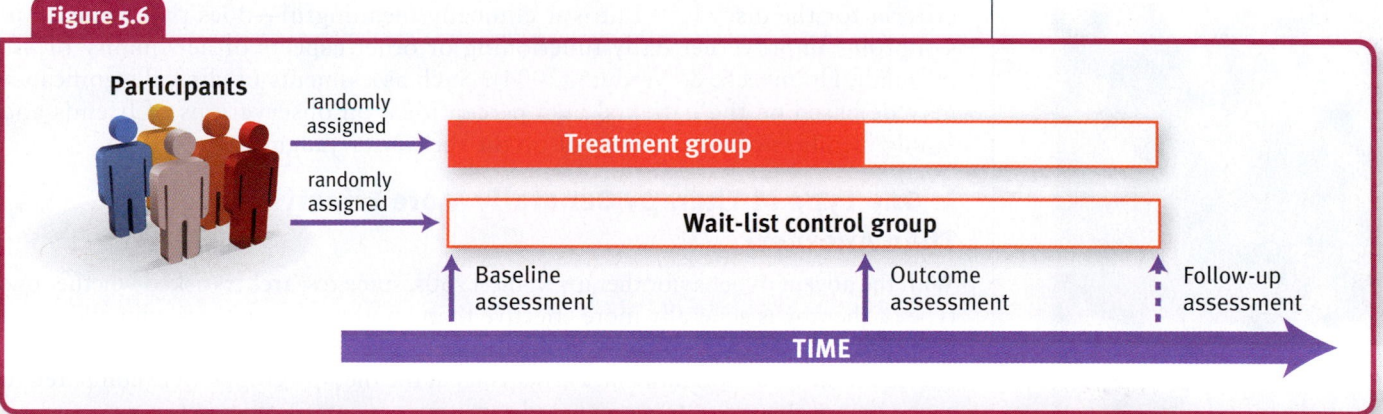

5.6 ▶ Comparing a Treatment Group to a Wait-List Control Group Participants are randomly assigned to one of two groups, a treatment group and a wait-list control group (although a study could have more than two groups). Generally, the dependent variables, such as intensity of symptoms, are assessed before the treatment period begins, to obtain a baseline. After treatment ends (or after the equivalent number of weeks for the wait-list control group), the dependent variables are again assessed (and may also be assessed later for follow-up) and the data from the two groups are compared.

Alternatively, instead of a "no treatment" or wait-list control group, researchers may use a placebo control group, the members of which meet with a "therapist" with the same frequency as the members of the treatment group. The "placebo therapist" refrains from using any of the active treatment techniques employed in the treatment group, but patients still receive attention and some level of support. For a study of your grief box therapy, a placebo control group might consist of patients who meet with therapists who listen to their concerns or complaints—without grief boxes, social support, or any other specific interventions.

With either type of control group—wait-list or placebo—researchers compare the level of symptoms in the treatment group with that in the control group before and after the treatment (or at equivalent times, if there was no treatment). It is possible that symptoms of members of the control group might diminish simply with the passage of time, and thus the crucial comparison is not whether people in the treatment group got better—but rather how much more they improved than did the people in the control group.

Researchers have conducted such studies for over half a century. How did they answer the question of whether therapy works? With a resounding "yes." Therapy really does make a difference (Lambert & Ogles, 2004). And, not surprisingly, treatment shows a larger effect when a treatment group is compared to a wait-list control group than when a treatment group is compared to a placebo group, which highlights the beneficial effects of common factors (Lambert & Ogles, 2004; Roth & Fonagy, 2005). However, studies with a wait-list control only reveal that all the myriad factors that go into treatment are more effective than no treatment at all. This sort of research doesn't identify which common factors or specific factors lead patients to improve (Borkovec & Miranda, 1999).

But what does it really mean to say that therapy works—that people who receive therapy are better off than those who don't receive therapy? How much better off are they? This is a complex question, and researchers currently frame it in terms of *clinical significance*, which may be either statistically meaningful or clinically meaningful. Consider a woman with the eating disorder bulimia nervosa, which typically involves compulsively eating large amounts of food (more than just "pigging out"—such *bingeing* consists of eating well past the point of normal fullness) and then vomiting to try to prevent weight gain. Suppose that, prior to treatment, the woman was bingeing and vomiting daily, but after treatment she was doing so only three times a week. This reduction may be statistically meaningful (although her symptoms are still over the threshold of the DSM-IV-TR criteria for the disorder). But is it clinically meaningful—does this decrease in symptoms improve her daily functioning or other aspects of her quality of life (Kendall, Holmbeck, & Verduin, 2004)? Such assessments of clinical significance may be based on the patients' own perceptions, on observations of friends and family members of the patients, or on the therapists' judgment.

Is One Type of Therapy Generally More Effective Than Another?

With the advent of behavior therapy in the 1960s, some researchers asked whether one type of therapy is generally more effective than another. Researchers who addressed this question randomly assigned participants to one of two groups, which received two different types of treatment. Participants in the therapy groups were compared to each other at the end of treatment, and sometimes at some later point in time.

The initial results of such research were surprising: No type of therapy appeared more effective than another, a finding that has been called the *Dodo bird verdict* of psychotherapy (Luborsky, Singer, & Luborsky, 1975). In the book *Alice's Adventures in Wonderland*, the Dodo Bird says: "Everybody has won, and all must have prizes." In this first generation of psychotherapy research, researchers did not investigate what actually transpired in the therapy sessions or whether some types of treatment were more effective for particular disorders.

Initially, studies designed to test the overall superiority of one form of psychotherapy over another did not find one type of therapy to be more effective. This finding has been called the *Dodo bird verdict*, in reference to the Dodo bird's proclamation in *Alice's Adventures in Wonderland*: "Everybody has won and all must have prizes." However, the Dodo bird verdict was based on research of particular therapies available at that time, using less rigorous research methods than those generally used today (Beutler, 2000).

Mary Evans Picture Library/Alamy

Is One Type of Therapy Better for Treating a Specific Disorder?

The first generation of research on treatment found that, in general, treatment of psychological disorders led to better outcomes compared to no treatment and no single treatment was superior to others. However, by the 1980s, a second generation of such research had begun, which examined both specific factors and specific disorders. This research sought to address whether any particular type of therapy was more effective than others in treating a specific disorder. (For instance, you would be addressing this question if you performed a study comparing your grief box therapy to CBT for people who became depressed after a breakup.) In order to address this research question, investigators refined the methods and procedures they used to provide therapy and assess its outcome. Let's briefly consider key advances in how researchers study the effects of various psychotherapies.

Randomized Clinical Trials

The second generation of research began with the landmark study by the National Institute of Mental Health (NIMH). The study was called the Treatment of Depression Collaborative Research Program (TDCRP; Elkin et al., 1985), and it marked a turning point in psychotherapy research. It used a research design analogous to the design used to measure the effect of a medication on symptoms of a medical disorder; this research design is referred to as a **randomized clinical trial** (**RCT**; also referred to as *randomized controlled trial*). RCTs have at least two groups, a treatment group and a control group (usually a placebo control), and participants are randomly assigned to groups (Kendall, Holmbeck, & Verduin, 2004). RCTs may also involve patients and therapists at multiple sites in a number of cities.

Researchers who conduct RCTs seek to use the scientific method to identify the specific factors that underlie a beneficial treatment. The independent variable is often the type of treatment or technique, as it was in the TDCRP, or any other variable listed in Table 5.3. The dependent variable is usually some aspect of patients' symptoms—such as frequency or intensity—or quality of life.

The TDCRP was designed to compare the benefits of four kinds of treatment for depression given over 16 weeks: interpersonal therapy (IPT), CBT, the tricyclic antidepressant medication *imipramine* (which was widely used before SSRIs became available) together with supportive sessions with a psychiatrist, and a placebo medication together with supportive sessions with a psychiatrist. Various dependent variables were measured. The main results told an interesting story: At the 18-month follow-up assessment, the CBT group had a larger sustained effect and fewer relapses, especially compared with the imipramine group (Elkin, 1994; Shea et al., 1992). But when the most severely depressed patients in each group were compared, IPT and imipramine were found to have been more effective than CBT (Elkin et al., 1995). However, most important in this study, the quality of the "collaborative bond" between therapist and patient (which was assessed by independent raters who viewed videotapes of sessions) had a stronger influence on treatment outcome than did the type of treatment (Krupnick et al., 1996).

The Importance of Follow-up Assessment

The TDCRP study followed patients for over 18 months after treatment ended, but some studies—because of financial or logistical constraints—do not make any follow-up assessment. This is unfortunate because the follow-up assessment imparts information about the enduring effects of treatment. One type of treatment may be more beneficial at the end of therapy, but those patients may have a higher rate of relapse a year later, leaving the patients in the other treatment group better off in the long run (Kendall, Holmbeck, & Verduin, 2004). Moreover, it is through follow-up assessments that investigators are best able to identify those at risk for relapse and learn how best to adjust treatment in order to help patients maintain their gains over the long term (Lambert & Ogles, 2004).

Randomized clinical trial (RCT)
A research design that has at least two groups—a treatment group and a control group (usually a placebo control)—to which participants are randomly assigned.

Exclusion Criteria

In most RCTs, including the TDCRP, researchers investigate treatments for patients who have a "pure" form of the DSM-IV-TR disorder of interest (Goldfried & Wolfe, 1998)—and *only* that one disorder. The decision to exclude people with an additional disorder or disorders makes many patients ineligible to participate. In reality, however, most patients have more than one disorder, which raises external validity questions about research using this exclusion criteria. In fact, after treatment, people with multiple disorders do not usually make the gains made by people who have only a single disorder (Coryell et al., 1988).

Manual-Based Treatment

One problem for researchers studying a particular type of therapy is that a therapist who claims to provide a particular type of therapy may in fact provide treatment that is remarkably similar to that of a therapist using a different theoretical orientation (Lambert & Bergin, 1994). This makes comparisons among types of therapies difficult. Suppose that some self-defined CBT therapists focus on relationship issues, and some self-defined IPT therapists give concrete suggestions for improving relationships. If there were no differences in outcomes between the two types of treatment, it could be because therapists in the two groups were all doing much the same thing!

In an effort to address this problem, RCTs generally require therapists to base their treatments on detailed manuals that provide session-by-session guidance and specify techniques to be used with patients. RCTs provide brief therapy, typically from 6 to 16 sessions. Different therapeutic approaches use different manuals; the most common theoretical approach for manual-based therapy is CBT. *Manual-based treatment* ensures that all therapists who use one particular approach provide similar therapy that is distinct from other types of therapy (Kendall, Holmbeck, & Verduin, 2004; Nathan, Skinstad, & Dolan, 2000).

In order to ensure that the particular type of therapy under investigation is, in fact, the type of therapy that is provided in the session, researchers may have therapists use manuals that specify in detail the goals of each session and the methods to be used.

Such research has led to more than 108 different treatment manuals for adults with 51 different DSM-IV-TR disorders (Beutler & Harwood, 2002; Chambless & Ollendick, 2001). Research aimed at identifying the unique specific components of a successful therapy has progressed by adding, subtracting, or otherwise changing specific components of a particular treatment manual, and then comparing the results from the two variations. For example, one RCT treatment group might receive CBT for depression, whereas another group would receive the same CBT *plus* an interpersonal component of treatment (similar to IPT). If patients in both groups fare the same, then the interpersonal component cannot be considered an active ingredient in this sort of treatment. Conversely, if the dual-component group fares better after treatment, then it can be inferred that the added interpersonal component made the treatment more effective. Similarly, to study your grief box therapy, you might have one group in which the members both make the boxes *and* reach out to friends and family and another group in which the members would only make the boxes without an emphasis on reaching out to friends and family.

In studies using this approach, the same therapist may perform both variants of a treatment (in contrast to earlier RCTs, in which a different group of therapists performed each type of therapy). By having each therapist perform different variants of treatment, researchers attempt to control for possible therapist variables that might affect treatment.

Allegiance Effect

Allegiance effect
A pattern in which studies conducted by investigators who prefer a particular theoretical orientation tend to obtain data that supports that particular orientation.

Another issue in RCT research is the **allegiance effect**, in which studies conducted by investigators who prefer a particular theoretical orientation tend to obtain data that support that particular orientation (Luborsky et al., 1999). Specifically, RCT investigators who support one type of treatment tend to have patients who do better with that type of treatment, whereas patients in the same study (using the same manuals) whose investigators support a different type of treatment tend to do better with that treatment. This means that even the use of manuals is not enough to control all types of confounds completely.

Empirically Supported Treatments and Evidence-Based Practice

When well-designed and well-conducted research studies, particularly those that rely on RCTs, show that a particular treatment or technique for a given disorder has a beneficial effect, that treatment or technique is said to be *empirically supported* (also referred to as *empirically validated*; Kendall, Holmbeck, & Verduin, 2004; Task Force on Promotion and Dissemination of Psychological Procedures, 1995). That is, research results support its beneficial effect. However, note that treatments or techniques that aren't designated as empirically supported may be equally beneficial—researchers just may not yet have documented their effects.

Suppose Carlos comes back to the counseling center a year after you first saw him, this time because he's having test anxiety. He gets so anxious before a test that he ends up doing poorly on the test even though he knows the material cold. How can you know which type of treatment or set of techniques to use to help him? Ideally, you have an *evidence-based practice*; that is, for each patient, you pick a treatment or set of techniques that research has shown to be effective for that patient's problem. (Such a judgment should also take into account the therapist's preference for—and training in—a particular method.) In the case of treating anxiety, for instance, various CBT methods such as relaxation training, cognitive restructuring, and exposure have been found to be effective for treating anxiety (Ergene, 2003).

Criticisms of RCTs

Research using RCTs has a number of critics and cautious observers (Messer, 2004). Their criticisms, discussed below, also apply to empirically supported treatments and evidence-based practices that are largely based on RCTs (Westen, Novotny, & Thompson-Brenner, 2004, 2005):

- *Exclusion criteria.* Excluding patients with more than one disorder limits the generalizability of a study's results (Westen & Morrison, 2001). For example, more than half of those with an anxiety disorder have at least one additional disorder, and 30–40% of those with depression also have been diagnosed with a personality disorder (Sleek, 1997). Moreover, researchers have shown that comorbid disorders affect the efficacy of treatment. For instance, treatment gains are generally more modest for those who have a personality disorder in addition to an Axis I disorder (Clarkin & Levy, 2004).

- *Homogenous samples.* Most of the patients in RCTs are White and middle-class. It is not clear how well such treatments generalize to patients with other ethnic backgrounds and from other socioeconomic levels (Bernal & Scharró-del-Rio, 2001). For example, when manual-based CBT—which was effective in an earlier RCT—was employed with depressed patients from an economically disadvantaged population, the treatment was not very effective (Miranda et al., 2003).

- *Overly rigid manual-based treatment.* Studies investigating the rigid use of manuals in RCTs suggest that strict adherence to manuals leads to less favorable results (Castonguay et al., 1996). Moreover, most therapists who are not part of a research study use manuals flexibly, if they use them at all. Thus, some critics ask, what knowledge is gained from RCTs that is applicable to the majority of therapists?

- *Therapy quality.* The quality of treatment in a RCT may vary even when the therapists are equally well trained and use the same manual, simply because therapists, as individuals, bring different levels of skill to their work (Garfield, 1998; Luborsky et al., 1997; Westen, Novotny, & Thompson-Brenner, 2005).

- *Common factors versus specific techniques.* For the treatment of some disorders, such as depression, the specific therapeutic approach or technique appears to contribute less toward successful therapy than do other factors, such as the quality of the therapist-patient relationship, the patient's motivation and readiness for change, and the alliance between therapist and patient (Horvath & Symonds,

Should a therapist use *aromatherapy*—having patients smell certain plant-based essential oils—to treat psychological disorders? Aromatherapy is not an empirically validated treatment for psychological disorders (Louis & Kowalski, 2002). This technique is in the realm of *pseudopsychology*, where claims are supported primarily by case studies or poorly designed studies with few participants, often without an appropriate control group.

Russell Sadur/Getty Images

Dose-response relationship
The association between more treatment (a higher dose) and greater improvement (a better response).

1991; Martin, Garske, & Davis, 2000; Messer, 2004; Messer & Wampold, 2002; Wampold, 2001). Thus, focusing on isolated components of treatment in an effort to enhance therapy may not be as effective as proponents had hoped. Moreover, RCTs generally do not assess patient variables, therapist variables, and patient-therapist interaction variables (Table 5.3), which may be important specific factors related to successful treatment (Beutler & Karno, 1999). For instance, those with more severe symptoms generally respond less well to treatment than do those with less severe symptoms, and those who are motivated to change make more positive change than do those less motivated (Clarkin & Levy, 2004; Garfield, 1994).

- *Length of treatment.* RCTs use short-term therapy, which may not be comparable to the type of therapy provided by most therapists. Moreover, research indicates that patients who have problems in only one sphere of life (for example, at work) receive greater benefit from brief psychotherapy than do those with problems in multiple spheres of life (Barkham & Shapiro, 1990; Klosko et al., 1990; Strupp & Binder, 1984)—perhaps in part because when a patient has problems in multiple spheres, fewer sessions are devoted to problems in each sphere.

- *Problems with DSM diagnostic groups.* We discussed some of the criticisms of DSM-IV-TR diagnostic groups in Chapter 3. Many of these criticisms also arise in the context of RCTs. For instance, it is possible that two people with the same disorder (according to DSM-IV-TR criteria)—but with different sets of symptoms—may respond differently to different treatments (Duncan, 2002).

- *Dependent variables.* What are appropriate dependent variables? Different types of therapy might be more (or less) effective with each of the variables listed in Table 5.3. Some RCTs focus exclusively on symptoms that pertain to DSM-IV-TR criteria. Perhaps treatments (or components of treatments) that reduce symptoms are different from those that improve relationships or quality of life. To the extent that researchers assess only DSM-IV-TR symptoms, such additional information will not be discovered.

- *Applying the results to individual patients.* Data from groups may not apply to a given individual sitting in a clinician's office. Each person has a unique background and a unique set of abilities, skills, and interests. In choosing a type of treatment for a given patient, clinicians often rely on their own experiences with similar patients (Pilkonis & Krause, 1999).

Some of the criticisms of RCTs—and therefore of empirically supported treatments—can be summed up by noting the difference between a treatment's *efficacy* and a treatment's *effectiveness*. Efficacy is assessed within the carefully controlled confines of RCTs in a research clinic. Effectiveness is assessed in nonresearch settings, the place where most clinicians treat patients, without excluding them because of multiple diagnoses. Thus, a treatment's effectiveness refers to the question of its generalizability to real-world settings, with no exclusion criteria, no set number of sessions, and usually no treatment manual (Kendall, Holmbeck, & Verduin, 2004; Lambert & Ogles, 2004; Roth & Fonagy, 2005). RCTs and evidence-based practices may overemphasize differences in technique among treatments while underemphasizing other factors that affect outcomes, such as the patient-therapist alliance and other common factors (Wampold & Bhati, 2004).

Ethical Research on Experimental Treatments

Any research on treatment conducted by a psychologist is bound by the ethical guidelines for research and usually must be approved by an IRB, discussed earlier in the chapter. As shown in Table 5.4, research on a new type of treatment—an *experimental* treatment such as your grief box therapy—is subject to additional guidelines because the researchers may not be aware of some of the risks and benefits of the new treatment at the outset of the study.

Table 5.4 ▶ Ethical Guidelines for Research on Experimental Treatments

Psychologists conducting research on experimental treatments must clarify to participants at the outset of the research:

(1) the experimental nature of the treatment;

(2) the services that will or will not be available to the control group(s) if appropriate;

(3) the means by which assignment to treatment and control groups will be made;

(4) available treatment alternatives if an individual does not wish to participate in the research or wishes to withdraw once a study has begun; and

(5) compensation for or monetary costs of participating.

Source: Copyright © American Psychological Association. For more information see the Permissions section.

The Therapy Dose-Response Relationship

We have been discussing research on treatment that uses experimental designs, randomly assigning participants to two or more groups and then comparing the results. Another approach relies on correlational methods. By definition, correlational studies of treatment do not include random assignment, nor do they have independent or dependent variables. Rather, a correlational research study determines whether changes in one variable are associated with changes in another variable.

Correlational research can answer a question like this: Is more treatment related to greater improvement? In other words, is a higher "dose" of therapy (more sessions) associated with a better "response"? This association between dose and response is referred to as the **dose-response relationship**, and research suggests that the general answer to this question is yes. More sessions are associated with a better outcome (Hansen, Lambert, & Forman, 2002; Shadish et al., 2000). In general, patients improve the most during the early phase of treatment (see Figure 5.7), and they continue to improve, but at diminishing rates, over time (Lutz et al., 2002). There are individual exceptions to this general pattern, as when someone with a specific phobia has an extremely good response to a single session of exposure therapy (Hellström & Öst, 1995; Öst, Grandberg, & Alm, 1997, Öst et al., 2001). However, people with more severe or entrenched problems, such as schizophrenia or personality disorders, may not show as much benefit in the early stages of outpatient treatment but rather tend to improve over a longer period of time.

Because the dose-response relationship is correlational, it does not indicate whether the increased number of sessions *causes* the increased response. It is possible that people who are feeling better during the course of treatment are more eager or more willing to attend additional sessions than those who are not responding as well. If this were the case, the response would be "causing" the increased dose

Figure 5.7

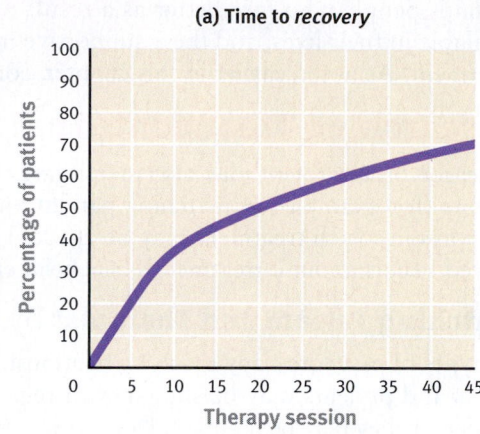
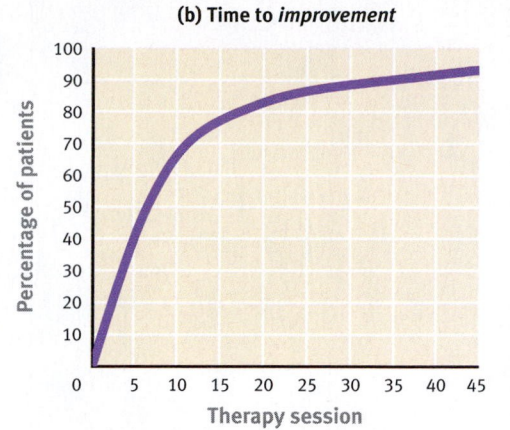

(a) Time to *recovery*

y-axis: Percentage of patients — 10, 20, 30, 40, 50, 60, 70, 80, 90, 100
x-axis: Therapy session — 0, 5, 10, 15, 20, 25, 30, 35, 40, 45

Among 10,000 patients with various psychological disorders, half attained clinically significant improvement (that is, *recovery*) by the 21st session. Another 25% attained clinically significant improvement by the 40th session. However, most people in RCTs, or in therapy in general, receive far fewer than 40 sessions.

(b) Time to *improvement*

y-axis: Percentage of patients — 10, 20, 30, 40, 50, 60, 70, 80, 90, 100
x-axis: Therapy session — 0, 5, 10, 15, 20, 25, 30, 35, 40, 45

Examining data using a lower standard of improvement—any positive change that was stable over time—and including patients who started out able to function reasonably well despite their disorder, yields different results: Half the patients attained this lower standard of improvement by the 7th session, with another 25% "improved" by the 14th session (Lambert, Hansen, & Finch, 2001).

5.7 ▸ The Dose-Response Relationship Comparing a more stringent definition of "improvement" (Figure 5.7a) to a more liberal one (Figure 5.7b) makes it clear that the exact criteria for improvemnt determine the particular height and shape of the curve for the dose-response relationship.

Source: Lambert et al., 2001. For more information see the Permissions section.

A curious finding invites speculation: People in the eastern part of the United States remain in treatment longer than those in the western part ("Fee, Practice, and Managed Care Survey," 2000). This is merely a correlation. One possible explanation is that people in the eastern part have a different definition of "improvement"; that is, they continue in treatment until their symptoms have improved more than those of their counterparts in the western part of the country. However, there are other possible explanations; perhaps you can think of some.

(increased number of sessions) (Otto, 2002; Tang & DeRubeis, 1999). Alternatively, both dose and response could be affected by some other factor. For example, perhaps people who fare better as a result of treatment have more social support available in their lives, and these supportive individuals encourage them to continue treatment. As noted earlier in this chapter, correlation does not imply causation.

Researching Treatments That Target Social Factors

Research on treatment may also investigate the possible benefits of targeting social factors (for example, by matching patient and therapist by gender or ethnicity) or the ways in which treatment may be affected by the larger social context (including shared beliefs about a treatment's beneficial effects).

Matching Patient and Therapist by Gender and Ethnicity

All types of psychotherapy involve a relationship between two (or more) people. Therapists and patients may be similar with regard to racial or ethnic background and gender, or they may be different. Does such a difference matter? Research suggests not: Differences between patient and therapist in ethnicity, gender, and age do not systematically alter therapy's beneficial effect (Beutler, Machado, & Neufeldt, 1994; Fiorentine & Hillhouse, 1999; Garfield, 1994; Lam & Sue, 2001; Maramba & Hall, 2002). However, with regard to gender, one study found that women and men are both less likely to drop out of treatment if they have a female therapist, although the study did not address the reason for this gender preference (Flaherty & Adams, 1998).

Nevertheless, some people prefer a therapist with a similar ethnic or racial background to their own. For those with a strong preference, such as some Asian Americans, matching the ethnicity of the patient and therapist may lead to better outcomes (Sue, Zane, & Young, 1994), and it can result in lower dropout rates among non-Whites (Flaherty & Adams, 1998; Flaskerud & Liu, 1991; Fiorentine & Hillhouse, 1999; Sue, Kuraski, & Srinivasan, 1999). However, not all studies have reported this result (Arcia, Sanchez-LaCay, & Fernandez, 2002).

Research on psychotherapy across different ethnic groups is complex, in part because of possible confounding factors. For instance, ethnicity is often associated with other demographic variables, such as socioeconomic status. Moreover, a patient's preference for a therapist from the same ethnic group may suggest that it's important for the patient and therapist to share *values*, not the same ethnic background per se (Ito & Maramba, 2002; Karlsson, 2005; Wong et al., 2003). In addition, research suggests that the more culturally assimilated a patient from a nonmajority ethnic group is, the less patient-therapist matching matters (Alvidrez, Azocar, & Miranda, 1996; Lamb & Jones, 1998). Finally, research on matching by ethnicity usually involves broad categories, such as patient and therapist who are both Asian American. However, when patients prefer a therapist from their own ethnic group, matching them with a therapist from a broadly similar group may not suffice. A Korean American patient, for instance, may prefer a Korean American therapist, but if such a therapist is not available, that patient may not prefer a Chinese American therapist over a therapist of any other background (Karlsson, 2005).

Culturally Sanctioned Placebo Effects

As we saw in Chapter 1, throughout time and across cultures, people in the role of healer have used different methods to treat abnormality. For some of the problems treated by healers—in the past and present—the placebo effect may be a key element of successful treatment. For instance, among the Shona people of Africa, those who have psychological problems often visit a *n'anga* (healer), who may recommend herbal remedies or steam baths or may throw bones to determine the source of a person's "bewitchment." Once the source is determined, the ill person's family is told how to mend community tensions that may have been caused by a family member's transgressing in some way (Linde, 2002). Westerners might consider the *n'anga*'s treatments, if effective, to work because of the placebo effect and the common factors that arise from any treatment (even a placebo): hope, support, and a framework for understanding the problem and its resolution.

Spencer Grant/Photo Edit

Some patients prefer a therapist who shares their ethnic background, and this common background may make a patient less likely to drop out of treatment. However, such matching does not appear to produce better treatment outcomes (Beutler, Machado, & Neufeldt, 1994; Garfield, 1994; Lam & Sue, 2001).

But members of nonindustrialized societies are not the only ones who are susceptible to such cultural forces. In Western cultures over the past two decades, people diagnosed with depression who are enrolled in studies to evaluate various medications have responded progressively more strongly to placebos (Walsh et al., 2002). Over that same two decades, pharmaceutical companies have increasingly advertised their medications directly to potential consumers, informing them about the possible benefits of the drugs. It is possible that the participants in these studies became more likely to believe that medication will be helpful than were participants 30 years ago, before direct advertising to consumers.

FEEDBACK LOOPS IN ACTION: **The Placebo Effect**

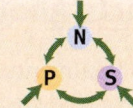

Successful treatments (including placebos) that target one type of factor in turn affect other types of factors; for example, medication (which targets neurological factors) affects symptoms related to psychological and social factors. Moreover, all types of treatment make use of a social factor—cultural norms about what kinds of interventions are appropriate, be they healer-induced possession trance or cognitive restructuring. In turn, these norms about appropriate treatment promote the patient's beliefs and expectations (psychological factor) regarding how effective the treatments are. Such beliefs and expectations then influence neurological and social factors, as well as other psychological factors. For example, a meta-analysis of studies on antidepressant treatments found that about 75–80% of the antidepressant's positive effects could be attributed to a placebo response, leaving at most only about 25% of the response due to the active ingredients of the medications. Thus, expectations that symptoms will improve may account for the lion's share of the positive response to an antidepressant (Kirsch & Lynn, 1999; Kirsch et al., 2002; Kirsch & Sapirstein, 1999; Walach & Maidhof, 1999). Indeed, more than half of studies of antidepressants that were funded by drug companies (which, if anything, may have biased the results towards supporting the effects of medication) found that a placebo was just as effective as the medication (Kirsch et al., 2002; Kirsch, Scoboria, & Moore, 2002; Moncrieff & Kirsch, 2005). In studies in which the placebo was designed to mimic the side effects of an antidepressant, the effects of the medication and the placebo were even more similar (Greenberg & Fisher, 1989).

These results do not necessarily show that placebos and actual antidepressant drugs have the same effects. Depressed people who responded well to SSRI medication, for instance, had a different pattern of brain activity than did patients who responded successfully to a placebo (Leuchter et al., 2002). Again, a patient's personal beliefs (psychological factor) about the effects of medication affect what happens in the brain, and these factors both affect, and are affected by, social factors.

Do the results regarding the placebo effect and antidepressants imply that depressed people should throw away their medication because they don't need it to attain the benefit? No! *Not taking any medication is not the same as taking a placebo medication.* There is something about the act of taking the medication that engages parts of the mind and brain to reduce depressive symptoms; without the placebo, these parts of the brain do not become active. There can't be a placebo effect without a placebo. So, if an antidepressant works for a patient, not taking it isn't at all the same as taking a placebo. (However, other nonmedical treatments may also be helpful for depression; we will discuss such treatments for that disorder in Chapter 6.)

What about Carlos and your hypotheses about loss and depression? As in the discovery of PANDAS, your observations about Carlos led you to identify questions about the etiology of his depression and about possible treatments. If you were interested in researching these matters, the particular design and procedure of your study would depend, in part, on the specific question you want to ask and hypothesis you want to test. You would use the scientific method to collect data (after obtaining approval from an IRB) and refine your hypothesis or formulate a theory.

If you wanted to test the efficacy of your grief box therapy, you would again use the scientific method, perhaps creating a treatment manual and organizing a RCT (in accordance with the guidelines for experimental treatments and with IRB approval). You might have four treatment groups: grief box only, encouraging social interactions only, grief box plus social interactions, and CBT (which serves as a nonexperimental comparison treatment). In this way, you could determine the relative effects of each component of your therapy, alone and in combination, and see how they fare against an established treatment. Depending on your results, you might refine your therapy.

Key Concepts and Facts About Researching Treatment

- When studying biomedical treatments, researchers should try to determine the extent to which a placebo effect—rather than a true drug effect—influences the results. Researchers should also take attrition rates into account when examining the effects of a treatment.

- Many of the challenges that arise in studying biomedical treatments, such as placebo effects and attrition, also arise when studying psychological treatments. A treatment may be effective because of common factors, as well as because of specific factors unique to that treatment. Control groups and analogue studies can allow researchers to examine specific factors and to rule out possible effects of some confounding factors. In general, research has demonstrated that therapy is more helpful than no treatment. Although the Dodo bird verdict found no one form of therapy superior *overall*, some specific therapies are better for some particular disorders.

- Randomized clinical trials (RCTs) are designed to investigate the efficacy of specific factors or treatments. RCTs typically in-volve manual-based treatment; some RCTs may have limited generalizability because of their exclusion criteria, homogenous samples, and other factors. Results of well-designed and well-conducted studies may indicate whether a particular treatment is empirically supported for a specific disorder. The results of research generally suggest a dose-response relationship. The code of ethics for psychologists includes specific guidelines for research on experimental treatments.

- Research on treatments that target social factors reveals that matching patients and therapists by ethnicity, gender, or age does not systematically alter the effectiveness of therapy. For patients with a strong preference, however, matching may lead to a better outcome. Cultural forces influence whether a treatment (including placebo) is effective.

- Any successful treatment, whatever type of neuropsychosocial factor it targets, also affects the other factors through feedback loops, inducing positive change. This is also true of changes that arise because of the placebo effect.

SUMMING UP

Summary of Using the Scientific Method to Understand Abnormality

Researchers use the scientific method to understand and study psychopathology. In doing so, they observe relevant phenomena, identify a question to be answered, develop a hypothesis that might answer the question, collect new observations to test the hypothesis, draw on the evidence to formulate a theory, and test the theory.

When conducting experiments, researchers systematically manipulate one or more independent variables and observe possible changes in one or more dependent variables. Researchers evaluate the possible contribution of confounds by using control groups or control conditions. To minimize unintentional bias, they randomly assign participants to groups. Experiments should have both inter-nal and external validity. Researchers may use a quasi-experimental design when random assignment is not ethical, desirable, or possible.

Correlational research is used when independent variables cannot or should not be manipulated. Such studies allow researchers to investigate the relationship between two variables, specifically, whether a change in one variable is associated with a change in the other. However, a correlation does not imply causation; it only indicates that the two variables are related. Statistical significance indicates that the obtained measurement is greater than would be expected to occur by chance alone. Longitudinal studies of psychopathology often use correlational data.

Case studies allow a clinician or researcher to examine one individual in detail. Single-participant experiments (often using an ABAB design) provide information about how one variable affects another. However, the results of case studies may not general-ize to other people. Meta-analysis allows researchers to aggregate the results of a number of studies that address the same question in order to determine the relations among certain variables.

Thinking like a researcher

Dr. Xavier studies compulsive gambling; she believes that people who begin gambling compulsively in their teens and early 20s have a different type of problem than those who begin gambling compulsively in their 40s or later. Based on what you have read about research methods, how would you state her question? What type of research design would you suggest she use (experimental, quasi-experimental, or correlational) and why? What might be some confounding variables for which she should try to control? How would Dr. Xavier go about ascertaining whether the study's results were statistically significant? What types of information would you want to know before generalizing from her results to other people with compulsive gambling?

Summary of Research Challenges to Understanding Abnormality

Many studies that focus on neurological factors are correlational and so do not reveal how neurological factors may give rise to psychological disorders. Neuroimaging studies may indicate differences in brain structure or function between those with a psychological disorder and those without a disorder. However, it is not always clear how such differences contribute to a disorder.

Self-reports of patients or reports by others may be biased in what is paid attention to, remembered, or reported. In addition, participants may respond differently to questions that are asked during an interview and those that are presented on a questionnaire. Researchers must take care in phrasing questions in order to minimize misinterpretation and various types of biases.

Challenges in studying social factors can also create challenges for studying other types of factors. Such challenges include experimenter-influenced biases, such as experimenter expectancy effects (which can be reduced with a double-blind design) and reactivity. A major challenge for cross-cultural research on psychopathology is the difficulty of translating words or concepts across cultures.

Thinking like a researcher

Suppose that you are investigating pyromania—the intense urge to start fires. Your participants come from two groups: those who've been arrested for arson, and those who have interacted in a chat room for people with urges to start fires. To collect your data, you could either have participants complete an anonymous survey online or arrange to interview them over the phone. Discuss biases that might uniquely affect each method and biases that might affect both. How could you try to minimize these biases? Suppose you had some participants who agreed to have images taken of their brains while they imagined lighting fires: How might you, as a researcher, use the neuroimaging information?

Summary of Researching Treatment

When studying biomedical treatments, researchers should try to determine the extent to which a placebo effect—rather than a true drug effect—influences the results. Many of the challenges that arise in studying biomedi-

cal treatments, such as placebo effects and attrition, also arise when studying psychological treatments. A treatment may be effective because of common factors, as well as because of specific factors that are unique to that treatment. In general, research has demonstrated that therapy is more helpful than no treatment. Although the Dodo bird verdict found no one form of therapy superior *overall*, some specific therapies are better for some particular disorders.

Randomized clinical trials (RCTs) are designed to investigate the efficacy of specific factors or treatments. RCTs typically involve manual-based treatment; some RCTs may have limited generalizability because of their exclusion criteria, homogenous samples, and other factors. Results of well-designed and well-conducted studies may indicate whether a particular treatment is empirically supported for a specific disorder. The results of research generally suggest a dose-response relationship.

Research on treatments that target social factors reveals that matching patients and therapists by ethnicity, gender, or age does not systematically alter the effectiveness of therapy. For patients with a strong preference, however, matching may lead to a better outcome. Any successful treatment, whatever type of neuropsychosocial factor it targets, also affects the other factors through feedback loops, inducing positive change. This is also true of change that arises because of the placebo effect.

Thinking like a researcher

Based on a survey, County Community College has found that 23% of their first-year students have anxiety or depression severe enough to meet the DSM-IV-TR criteria. The college would like to institute a treatment program for these students. In fact, the staff at the counseling center plans to conduct a research study and offer several different types of treatment: medication (if appropriate), CBT with an individual therapist, and CBT in group therapy. Students can sign up for whichever type of treatment they prefer and can even receive more than one type of treatment. The results will be recorded and used to guide how treatment is provided in the future. Is this study a randomized clinical trial—why or why not? What are some potential problems with the research design of this study? To learn whether each of the treatments is helpful to students, what questions should be asked of the students before and after the study?

Key Terms

Scientific method (p. 154)

Data (p. 154)

Replication (p. 155)

Hypothesis (p. 155)

Theory (p. 155)

Predictions (p. 155)

Experiments (p. 156)

Independent variable (p. 156)

Dependent variable (p. 156)

Confounding variables (confounds) (p. 157)

Control group (p. 158)

Bias (p. 158)

Random assignment (p. 159)

Sampling bias (p. 159)

Population (p. 159)

Sample (p. 159)

Internal validity (p. 159)

External validity (p. 159)

Correlation (p. 160)

Correlation coefficient (p. 160)

Statistically significant (p. 160)

Epidemiology (p. 162)

Longitudinal studies (in studies of psychopathology) (p. 162)

Case studies (in studies of psychopathology) (p. 163)

Single-participant experiments (p. 164)

Meta-analysis (p. 166)

Response bias (p. 171)

Social desirability (p. 172)

Experimenter expectancy effect (p. 173)

Double-blind design (p. 173)

Reactivity (p. 173)

Placebo effect (p. 176)

Attrition (p. 176)

Common factors (p. 177)

Specific factors (p. 178)

Analogue study (p. 179)

Randomized clinical trial (RCT) (p. 181)

Allegiance effect (p. 182)

Dose-response relationship (p. 184)

More Study Aids

For additional study aids related to this chapter, go to:

www.worthpublishers.com/rosenberg

Mood Disorders and Suicide

Kay Redfield Jamison, a psychologist who studies mood disorders, is uniquely qualified to report and reflect on such disorders. Not only has she made mood disorders her area of professional expertise, but she has also lived with such a disorder. In her memoir, *An Unquiet Mind* (1995), Jamison recounts her experiences. The youngest of three children in a military family, she and her siblings attended four different elementary schools—some in foreign countries—by the time she was in 5th grade. She describes her father, a meteorologist and Air Force officer, as expansive, with infectious good moods, and impulsive, often giving the children gifts. It was "like having Mary Poppins for a father" (Jamison, 1995, p. 17). However, he also suffered periods when he was immobilized by depression, and he generally had trouble regulating his emotions.

As we'll see in this chapter, Jamison herself developed difficulties regulating her emotions. She recounts that when she was a senior in high school, her mood became so dark that her thinking

> . . . was torturous. I would read the same passage over and over again only to realize that I had no memory at all for what I had just read. Each book or poem I picked up was the same way. Incomprehensible . . . I could not begin to follow the material presented in my classes. . . . It was very frightening . . . [my mind] no longer found anything interesting or enjoyable or worthwhile. It was incapable of concentrated thought and turned time and time again to the subject of death: I was going to die, what difference did anything make? Life's run was only a short and meaningless one, why live? I was totally exhausted and could scarcely pull myself out of bed in the mornings. . . . I wore the same clothes over and over again, as it was otherwise too much of an effort to make a decision about what to put on. I dreaded having to talk with people, avoided my friends whenever possible, and sat in the school library in the early mornings and late afternoons, virtually inert, with a dead heart and a brain as cold as clay.
>
> (Jamison, 1995, pp. 37–38)

In this passage, Jamison describes problems arising from her *mood*, a persistent emotion lurking in the background, regardless of what is occurring. The category of psychological disorders called **mood disorders** encompasses prolonged and marked disturbances in mood that affect how people feel, what they believe and expect, how they think and talk, and how they interact with others. In any particular year, about 8% of Americans experience a mood disorder (Substance Abuse and Mental Health Services Administration [SAMHSA], 2008). Mood disorders are among the leading causes of disability worldwide (World Health Organization [WHO], 2008).

Mood disorders
Psychological disorders characterized by prolonged and marked disturbances in mood that affect how people feel, what they believe and expect, how they think and talk, and how they interact with others.

Alan Witschonke

Psychologist Kay Redfield Jamison described being depressed: "My mind would . . . be drenched in awful sounds and images of decay and dying: dead bodies on the beach, charred remains of animals, toe-tagged corpses in morgues. During these agitated periods I became exceedingly restless, angry, and irritable, and the only way I could dilute the agitation was to run along the beach or pace back and forth across my room like a polar bear at the zoo" (1995, p. 45).

> **Table 6.1 ▸ Four Types of Mood Disorder Episodes**
>
> - A *major depressive episode* involves symptoms of depression.
> - A *manic episode* involves elated, irritable, or *euphoric* mood (mood that is extremely positive and may not necessarily be appropriate to the situation).
> - A *hypomanic episode* involves elated, irritable, or euphoric mood that is less distressing or severe than mania and is different than the individual's non-depressed state. That is, how a person behaves during a hypomanic episode is different from his or her usual state.
> - A *mixed episode* involves symptoms of both a major depressive episode and a manic episode.

Major depressive episode (MDE)
A mood episode characterized by severe depression that lasts for at least 2 weeks.

Anhedonia
A difficulty or inability to experience pleasure.

DSM-IV-TR distinguishes between two categories of mood disorders: depressive disorders and bipolar disorders. *Depressive disorders* are mood disorders in which someone's mood is consistently low; in contrast, *bipolar disorders* are mood disorders in which a person's mood is sometimes decidedly upbeat, perhaps to the point of being manic, and sometimes may be low. Note that the mood disturbances that are part of depressive disorders and bipolar disorders are not the normal ups and downs that we all experience; they are more intense and longer lasting than just feeling "blue" or "happy."

If such mood patterns are caused by substance abuse or a medical condition, a mental health clinician would not diagnose a mood disorder as the primary problem. Similarly, as with all clinical disorders, in order to be classified as a disorder, the symptoms of the mood disorder must cause significant distress, impair daily life, or put a person at risk of harm. The significant distress and suffering, along with a pervasive hopelessness that can arise with depression, sometimes lead people to contemplate or attempt suicide.

Using the DSM system to categorize mood disorders, a clinician must "build" a diagnosis based on a person's current and past history of disturbed moods. In DSM-IV-TR, each type of *episode* of a mood disorder is a "building block," with a diagnosis based on the presence or absence of different types of blocks. DSM-IV-TR defines four types of episodes: *major depressive episode, manic episode, hypomanic episode*, and *mixed episode* (see Table 6.1). Should a patient experience additional types of mood episodes over time, his or her diagnosis may change.

Let's first examine depressive disorders—what they are and their causes and treatments—and then consider bipolar disorders. Once we know more about mood disorders, we'll examine what is known about suicide and its prevention.

Depressive Disorders

Most people who read Jamison's description of her senior year in high school would think that she was depressed during that time. But what, exactly, does it mean to say someone is *depressed*? The diagnoses of depressive disorders are based on the building block referred to as a *major depressive episode*; people whose symptoms have met the criteria for a major depressive episode (see Table 6.2) are diagnosed with *major depressive disorder*.

The Building Block of Depressive Disorders: Major Depressive Episode

A clinician who uses the DSM-IV-TR system to categorize mood disorders builds a diagnosis based on a person's current and past history of episodes of disturbed moods. For depressive disorders, there is only one building block: **major depressive episode (MDE)**, which is characterized by severe depression that lasts for at least 2 weeks. MDE is not itself a diagnosis, but a building block toward a diagnosis (as we shall see later in this chapter, the diagnosis for other disorders typically requires several building blocks). Mood (which is a type of *affect*) is not the only symptom of a major depressive episode. Behavior and cognition are also affected by depression. These three spheres of functioning are sometimes referred to as the *ABCs*—affect, behavior, and cognition (but should not be confused with the ABCs of behavior therapy—antecedent, behavior, consequence).

Affect, the Mood Symptoms of Depression

During a major depressive episode, a person can feel unremitting sadness, hopelessness, or numbness. Some people also suffer from a loss of pleasure, referred to as **anhedonia**, a state in which activities and intellectual pursuits that were once enjoyable no longer are, or at least are not nearly as enjoyable as they had been. Someone who liked to go

Table 6.2 ▶ DSM-IV-TR Diagnostic Criteria for Major Depressive Episode

A. Five (or more) of the following symptoms have been present during the same 2-week period and represent a change from previous functioning; at least one of the symptoms is either (1) depressed mood (symptom 1, below) or (2) loss of interest or pleasure (symptom 2, below).

Note: Do not include symptoms that are clearly due to a general medical condition or mood-incongruent [i.e., not consistent with the mood] delusions or hallucinations.

(1) Depressed mood most of the day, nearly every day, as indicated by either subjective report (e.g., feels sad or empty) or observation made by others (e.g., appears tearful). Note: In children and adolescents, can be irritable mood.

(2) Markedly diminished interest or pleasure in all, or almost all, activities most of the day, nearly every day (as indicated by either subjective account or observation made by others).

(3) Significant weight loss when not dieting or weight gain (e.g., a change of more than 5% of body weight in a month) or decrease or increase in appetite nearly every day. Note: In children, consider failure to make expected weight gains.

(4) Insomnia or hypersomnia nearly every day.

(5) Psychomotor agitation or retardation nearly every day (observable by others, not merely subjective feelings of restlessness or being slowed down).

(6) Fatigue or loss of energy nearly every day.

(7) Feelings of worthlessness or excessive or inappropriate guilt (which may be delusional) nearly every day (not merely self-reproach or guilt about being sick).

(8) Diminished ability to think or concentrate, or indecisiveness, nearly every day (either by subjective account or as observed by others).

(9) Recurrent thoughts of death (not just fear of dying), recurrent suicidal ideation [i.e., thoughts about suicide] without a specific plan, or a suicide attempt or a specific plan for committing suicide.

B. The symptoms do not meet criteria for a mixed episode [discussed later in this chapter].

C. The symptoms cause clinically significant distress or impairment in social, occupational, or other important areas of functioning.

D. The symptoms are not due to the direct physiological effects of a substance (e.g., a drug of abuse, a medication) or a general medical condition (e.g., hypothyroidism).

E. The symptoms are not better accounted for by bereavement, i.e., after the loss of a loved one. The symptoms persist for longer than 2 months or are characterized by marked functional impairment, morbid preoccupation with worthlessness, suicidal ideation, psychotic symptoms, or psychomotor retardation.

Source: Reprinted with permission from the DSM-IV-TR Casebook: A Learning Companion to the Diagnostic and Statistical Manual of Mental Disorders, Fourth Edition, Text Revision, (Copyright 2002) American Psychiatric Association.

Major depressive episode includes affective/mood (green), behavioral/vegetative (orange), and cognitive (blue) symptoms.

to the movies, for instance, may no longer find it so interesting or fun and may feel that it is not worth the effort. Anhedonia can thus lead to social withdrawal. Other mood-related symptoms of depression include weepiness—crying at the drop of a hat or for no apparent reason—and decreased sexual interest or desire.

Behavioral and Physical Symptoms of Depression

People who are depressed make more negative comments, make less eye contact, are less responsive, speak more softly, and speak in shorter sentences than people who are not depressed (Gotlib & Robinson, 1982; Segrin & Abramson, 1994). Depression is also evident behaviorally in one of two ways: *psychomotor agitation* or *psychomotor retardation*. **Psychomotor agitation** is an inability to sit still, evidenced by pacing, hand wringing, or rubbing or pulling the skin, clothes, or other objects. In contrast, **psychomotor retardation** is a slowing of motor functions indicated by slowed bodily movements and speech (in particular, longer pauses in answering) and lower volume, variety, or amount of speech.

These two psychomotor symptoms, along with changes in appetite, weight, and sleep, are classified as **vegetative signs** of depression. Sleep changes can involve

Psychomotor agitation
An inability to sit still, evidenced by pacing, hand wringing, or rubbing or pulling the skin, clothes or other objects.

Psychomotor retardation
A slowing of motor functions indicated by slowed bodily movements and speech and lower volume, variety, or amount of speech.

Vegetative signs (of depression)
Psychomotor symptoms as well as changes in appetite, weight, and sleep.

insomnia or, less commonly, **hypersomnia**, which is sleeping more hours each day than normal. In addition, people who are depressed may feel less energetic than usual or feel tired or fatigued even when they don't physically exert themselves. In fact, many people who are depressed had sleep disturbances up to a month before the depression began, which suggests that sleep irregularities may be a harbinger of a depressive episode (Perlis et al., 1997; Perlis, Smith, et al., 2006). Sleep irregularities in depressed people are particularly notable during the phase when dreams primarily take place, known as *rapid eye movement* sleep (REM sleep) (Rao et al., 2002); REM sleep is involved in processing emotional memories (Marano, 2003).

In order to meet the diagnostic criteria, the vegetative signs should be observable by others, not just reported as subjective experiences. For instance, if a new patient reported difficulty getting to sleep, poor appetite, and feeling agitated, the clinician would ask the patient for more details before determining that these were vegetative signs of depression: How long does it actually take the patient to get to sleep? Has the patient's weight changed? The clinician would also observe the patient for signs of psychomotor agitation, such as a leg constantly bobbing up and down or fingers tapping on the armrest.

Cognitive Symptoms of Depression

When in the grip of depression, people often feel worthless or guilt-ridden, may evaluate themselves negatively for no objective reason, and tend to ruminate over their past failings (which they may exaggerate). They may misinterpret ambiguous statements made by other people as evidence of their worthlessness. For instance, a depressed man, Tyrone, might hear a colleague's question "How are you?" as an indication that he is incompetent and infer that the colleague is asking the question because Tyrone's incompetence is so obvious. Depressed patients can also feel unwarranted responsibility for negative events, to the point of having delusions that revolve around a strong sense of guilt, deserved punishment, worthlessness, or personal responsibility for problems in the world. They blame themselves for their depression and for the fact that they cannot function well. During a depressive episode, people may also report difficulty thinking, remembering, concentrating, and making decisions, as author William Styron describes, in Case 6.1. To others, the depressed person may appear distracted. Note, however, that depression is *heterogeneous*, which means that people with depression experience these symptoms in different combinations. No single set of symptoms is shared by all people with depression (Hasler et al., 2004).

CASE 6.1 ▸ FROM THE INSIDE: Major Depressive Episode

Another experience of depression was captured by the writer William Styron in his memoir, *Darkness Visible*.

In depression this faith in deliverance, in ultimate restoration, is absent. The pain is unrelenting, and what makes the condition intolerable is the foreknowledge that no remedy will come—not in a day, an hour, a month, or a minute. If there is mild relief, one knows that it is only temporary; more pain will follow. It is hopelessness even more than pain that crushes the soul. So the decision-making of daily life involves not, as in normal affairs, shifting from one annoying situation to another less annoying—or from discomfort to relative comfort, or from boredom to activity—but moving from pain to pain. One does not abandon, even briefly, one's bed of nails, but is attached to it wherever one goes.

(Styron, 1990, p. 62)

The symptoms of MDE develop over days and weeks. The **prodrome** is the early symptoms of the disorder, and the prodrome of an MDE may include anxiety or mild depressive symptoms that last for weeks to months before fully

Hypersomnia
Sleeping more hours each day than normal.

Prodrome
Early symptoms of a disorder.

Premorbid
Referring to the period of time prior to a patient's illness.

Major depressive disorder (MDD)
The mood disorder marked by five or more symptoms of an MDE lasting more than 2 weeks.

Age cohort
A group of people born in a particular range of years.

emerging as a major depressive episode. An untreated MDE typically lasts approximately 4 months or longer (American Psychiatric Association, 2000). The more severe the depression, the longer the episode is likely to last (Melartin et al., 2004). About two thirds of people who have an MDE eventually recover from the episode completely and return to their previous level of functioning—referred to as the **premorbid** level of functioning. About 20–30% of people who have an MDE find that their symptoms lessen over time to the point where they no longer meet the criteria for an MDE but don't completely resolve and may persist for years. One suggestion for DSM-V addresses the fact that some symptoms—but not enough for a diagnosis—persist for months or years: Evaluate depressive symptoms on two continua—how severe and how chronic the symptoms are—rather than with the current categorical system of whether or not symptoms meet the criteria (Klein, 2008).

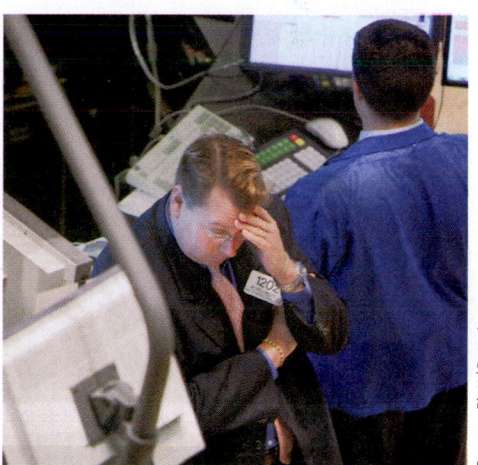

Tim Sloan/AFP/Getty Images

Normal bereavement has characteristics that are similar to symptoms of a major depressive episode: sad thoughts and feelings, problems in concentrating, and changes in appetite and sleep. However, bereaved people are not generally overcome with feelings of hopelessness or anhedonia.

What distinguishes depression from simply "having the blues"? One distinguishing feature is the number of symptoms. People who are sad or blue generally have fewer than five of the symptoms listed in the DSM-IV-TR diagnostic criteria for a major depressive episode (see Table 6.2). In addition, someone who is truly depressed has severe symptoms for a relatively long period of time and is unable to function effectively at home, school, or work. Moreover, pervasive hopelessness and loss of pleasure are usually absent in normal sadness.

Major Depressive Disorder

According to DSM-IV-TR, once someone's symptoms meet the criteria for a major depressive episode, he or she is diagnosed as having **major depressive disorder (MDD)**—five or more symptoms of an MDE lasting more than 2 weeks. Thus, once Kay Jamison had her first major depressive episode, she had the diagnosis of MDD, *single episode*. Unfortunately, more than half of those who have had a single depressive episode go on to have at least one additional episode, noted in DSM-IV-TR as MDD, *recurrent depression*. Some people have increasingly frequent episodes over time, others have clusters of episodes, and still others have isolated depressive episodes followed by several years without symptoms (American Psychiatric Association, 2000; McGrath et al., 2006). Research suggests that periods of remission last longer earlier in life. That is, as people with recurrent MDD grow older, they are free of depression for increasingly shorter periods (American Psychiatric Association, 2000).

MDD is very common in the United States: Up to 20% of Americans will experience it sometime in their lives (American Psychiatric Association, 2000; Kessler et al., 2003). Unfortunately, the documented rate of depression in the United States in increasing (Lewinsohn et al., 1993), perhaps because of increased stressors in modern life or decreased social support; in addition, at least part of this increase may simply reflect higher reporting rates. By 2020, depression will probably be ranked second among disabling diseases in the United States (right after heart disease; Schrof & Schultz, 1999); it is currently associated with more than $30 billion dollars of lost productivity among U.S. workers annually (Stewart et al., 2003).

Evidence also suggests that the risk of developing depression is increasing for each **age cohort**, a group of people born in a particular range of years. The risk of developing depression is higher among people born more recently than those born previously. In addition, if someone born more recently does develop depression, that individual probably will first experience it earlier in life than someone in an older cohort (American Psychiatric Association, 2000). Table 6.3 provides more facts about MDD.

Spencer Platt/Getty Images

Major depressive disorder leads to lowered productivity at work—both from missing days at work and from *presenteeism*, being present at work but less productive than normal (Adler et al., 2006; Druss, Schlesinger, & Allen, 2001; Stewart et al., 2003). For people whose jobs require high levels of cognitive effort, even mild memory or attentional difficulties may disrupt their ability to function adequately at work.

Table 6.3 ▸ Major Depressive Disorder Facts at a Glance

Prevalence

- Around 10–25% of women and 5–12% of men will develop MDD over their lifetimes. Before puberty, however, boys and girls develop MDD in equal numbers (Kessler et al., 2003).
- People with different ethnic backgrounds, education levels, incomes, and marital statuses are generally afflicted equally over their lives (American Psychiatric Association, 2000; Kessler et al., 2003; Weissman et al., 1991).

Comorbidity

- Most people with MDD also have an additional psychological disorder (Rush et al., 2005), such as an anxiety disorder (Barbee, 1998; Kessler et al., 2003) or substance abuse (Rush et al., 2005).

Onset

- MDD can begin at any age, with the average age of onset in the mid-20s, although people are developing MDD at increasingly younger ages.

Course

- Among individuals who have had a single MDE, approximately 50–65% will go on to have a second episode (Angst et al., 1999; American Psychiatric Association, 2000; Solomon et al., 2000).
- Those who have had two episodes have a 70% chance of having a third, and those who have had three episodes have a 90% chance of having a fourth.

Gender Differences

- As noted above, women are almost twice as likely as men to develop MDD (American Psychiatric Association, 2000; Kessler, 2003).
- Some women report that depressive symptoms become more severe premenstrually.

Source: Unless otherwise noted above, the source for information is American Psychiatric Association, 2000.

Because of the high comorbidity between depression and anxiety disorders (about 50%), researchers propose that the two types of disorders have a common cause, presently unknown. We will further discuss reasons for the high comorbidity between these two types of disorders when we consider anxiety disorders in Chapter 7.

Specifiers

The DSM-IV-TR criteria list includes *specifiers*—specific sets of symptoms that occur together or in particular patterns. Specifiers help clinicians and researchers identify or note variants of a disorder, which is important because each variant may respond best to a particular treatment or have a particular prognosis. For instance, depression with *melancholic features* includes complete anhedonia—the patient doesn't feel any better after positive events. When a patient experiences depression with melancholic features, the symptoms usually fluctuate during the day—he or she typically wakes early in the morning, feels worse in the morning, and loses his or her appetite. In contrast, *atypical depression* is characterized by depressed mood that brightens when good things happen, along with at least two of the following: hypersomnia, increased weight gain, heavy feelings in arms or legs, and persistent sensitivity to perceived rejection by others (American Psychiatric Association, 2000). Atypical depression is likely to respond to different medications than is depression with melancholic features (Rosenbaum et al., 2005).

Symptoms of depression may also include *catatonic features*, which are specific motor symptoms—rigid muscles that hold odd postures for long periods of time, or a physical restlessness. Although not common, depression can occur with *psychotic features*—hallucinations (e.g., in which a patient can feel that his or her body is decaying) or delusions (e.g., in which the patient believes that he or she is evil and living in hell).

Symptoms may also form a pattern over time. In contrast to recurrent depression, in which symptoms of an MDE disappear and then reemerge at a later time, *chronic depression* is the pattern in which the symptoms meet the criteria for an MDE continuously for over 2 years. In some cases, such as that of Marie Osmond in Case 6.2, depression emerges within 4 weeks of giving birth, designated as *postpartum onset*. However, the DSM-IV-TR cutoff of 4 weeks for postpartum onset may be too restrictive; 6 months to 1 year after giving birth may be a more useful diagnostic cutoff (Wisner et al., 2004), although some women develop symptoms as soon as 5 days after delivery (Adewuya, 2006) or even before the birth (Evans et al., 2001). Those most at risk for postpartum depression are women who have had recurrent depression before giving birth (Forty et al., 2006).

Although postpartum depression can arise after giving birth, for many women, "postpartum" depression may actually begin during pregnancy, particularly the latter half, and persist after the birth (Evans et al., 2001).

CASE **6.2** ▸ FROM THE INSIDE: Postpartum Onset of Depression

After the birth of her seventh child, Marie Osmond developed postpartum depression:

I'm collapsed in a pile of shoes on my closet floor. . . . I sit with my knees pulled up to my chest. I barely move. It's not that I want to be still. I am numb. I can tell I'm crying, but it's not like tears I've shed before. My eyes feel as though they have moved deep into the back of my head. There is only hollow space in front of them. Dark, hollow space. I am as empty as the clothing hanging above me. Despite my outward appearance, I feel like a lifeless form.

I can hear the breathing of my sleeping newborn son in his bassinet next to the bed. My ten-year-old daughter, Rachael, opens the bedroom door and whispers, "Mom?" into the room, trying not to wake the baby. Not seeing me, she leaves. She doesn't even consider looking in the closet on the floor. Her mother would never be there. She's right. This person sitting on the closet floor is nothing like her mother. I can't believe I'm here myself. I'm convinced that I'm losing my mind. This is not me.

I feel like I'm playing hide-and-seek from my own life, except that I just want to hide and never be found. I want to escape my body. I don't recognize it anymore. I have lost any resemblance to my former self. I can't laugh, enjoy food, sleep, concentrate on work, or even carry on a conversation. I don't know how to go on feeling like this: the emptiness, the endless loneliness. Who am I? I can't go on.

(Osmond, Wilkie, & Moore, 2001)

Sometimes recurrent depression follows a seasonal pattern, occurring at a particular time of year. Referred to as **seasonal affective disorder (SAD)**, this disorder manifests itself in two patterns:

- *Winter depression* is characterized by recurrent depressive episodes, hypersomnia, increased appetite (particularly for carbohydrates), weight gain, and irritability. These symptoms begin in autumn and continue through the winter months. The symptoms either disappear or are much less severe in the summer. Surveys find that approximately 4–6% of the general population experiences a winter depression, and the average age of onset is 23 years. The disorder is four times more common in women than in men (American Psychiatric Association, 2000). Winter depression often can be treated effectively with **phototherapy** (also called *light-box therapy*), in which full-spectrum lights are used as a treatment (Golden et al., 2005).

- *Summer depression*, which is less common, tends to appear in late spring. Symptoms often include poor appetite and weight loss, less sleep, and psychomotor changes (American Psychiatric Association, 2000). Treatment for summer depression usually includes antidepressant medication.

Seasonal affective disorder (SAD)
Recurrent depression that follows a seasonal pattern.

Phototherapy
Treatment for depression that uses full-spectrum lights; also called *light-box therapy*.

Phototherapy can be helpful to people who have winter depression. Typically, a person using phototherapy sits near special lights for an average of 30 minutes per day.

Depression in Children and Adolescents

In a given 6-month period, 1–3% of elementary-school children and 5–8% of teenagers are depressed (Garber & Horowitz, 2002; Lewinsohn & Essau, 2002). Moreover, some clinicians and researchers are reporting depression among preschool children, evidenced by avoidance, decreased enthusiasm and increased anhedonia (Luby et al., 2006). Younger children who are depressed are not generally considered to be at high risk to develop depression in adulthood (Harrington et al., 1990; Weissman, Wolk, Wickramaratne, et al., 1999). However, those who first get depressed as teenagers are considered to be at high risk for developing depression in adulthood (Lewinsohn, Rohde, et al., 1999; Weissman et al., 2006; Weissman, Wolk, et al., 1999). Teenage depression has far-reaching effects: Depressed teens are more likely than their nondepressed peers to drop out of school or to have an unplanned pregnancy (Waslick, Kandel, & Kakouros, 2002).

Dysthymic Disorder

Dysthymic disorder differs from major depressive disorder in that it involves fewer of the symptoms of a major depressive episode, but they persist for a longer period of time. Specifically, dysthymic disorder is characterized by depressed mood and as few as two other depressive symptoms that last for at least 2 years and that do not recede for longer than 2 months at any time during that period (see Table 6.4).

Because symptoms are chronic, people with dysthymic disorder often incorporate the symptoms into their enduring self-assessment, seeing themselves as incompetent or uninteresting. Whereas people with MDD see their symptoms as happening *to* them, people with dysthymic disorder view their symptoms as an integral part of themselves ("This is just how I am"), like Mr. A, in Case 6.3, below. If an individual diagnosed with dysthymic disorder develops an MDE, he or she is considered to have **double depression**. In that case, both MDD and dysthymic disorder are diagnosed. Individuals who have had double depression are likely to have more than one MDE. Double depression may require longer treatment than dysthymic disorder or MDD (Dunner, 2001).

CASE 6.3 ▶ FROM THE OUTSIDE: Dysthymic Disorder

Mr. A, a 28-year-old, single accountant, sought consultation because "I feel I am going nowhere with my life." Problems at work included a recent critical job review because of low productivity, conflicts with his boss, and poor management skills. His fiancée recently postponed their wedding because she has doubts about their relationship, especially his remoteness, critical comments, and lack of interest in sex.

Describing himself as a pessimist who has difficulty experiencing pleasure or happiness, Mr. A has long felt a sense of hopelessness—of life not being worth living. His mother was hospitalized with postpartum depression after the birth of his younger sister; his father had a drinking problem. His high school classmates found him gloomy and "not fun."

Although not troubled by thoughts of suicide nor significant vegetative signs of depression, Mr. A. does have months when his concentration is impaired, his energy level is lowered, and his interest in sex wanes. At such times, he withdraws from other people (although he always goes to work), staying in bed on weekends.

(Adapted from Frances & Ross, 1996, pp. 123–124)

Dysthymic disorder
A depressive disorder that involves fewer of the symptoms of a major depressive episode, but the symptoms persist for a longer period of time.

Double depression
Having both major depressive disorder and dysthymic disorder.

How would a clinician determine whether Mr. A, or someone else, suffered from dysthymic disorder or MDD—what differentiates the two disorders? People with dysthymic disorder are less likely to experience the vegetative signs associated

Table 6.4 ▶ DSM-IV-TR Diagnostic Criteria for Dysthymic Disorder

A. Depressed mood for most of the day, for more days than not, as indicated either by subjective account or observation by others, for at least 2 years.

Note: In children and adolescents, mood can be irritable and duration must be at least 1 year.

B. Presence, while depressed, of two (or more) of the following:

(1) poor appetite or overeating

(2) insomnia or hypersomnia

(3) low energy or fatigue

(4) low self-esteem

(5) poor concentration or difficulty making decisions

(6) feelings of hopelessness

C. During the 2-year period (1 year for children or adolescents) of the disturbance, the person has never been without the symptoms in Criteria A and B for more than 2 months at a time.

D. No major depressive episode has been present during the first 2 years of the disturbance (1 year for children and adolescents); i.e., the disturbance is not better accounted for by chronic major depressive disorder, or major depressive disorder, in partial remission.

Note: There may have been a previous major depressive episode provided there was a full remission (no significant signs or symptoms for 2 months) before development of the dysthymic disorder. In addition, after the initial 2 years (1 year in children or adolescents) of dysthymic disorder, there may be superimposed episodes of major depressive disorder, in which case both diagnoses may be given when the criteria are met for a major depressive episode.

E. There has never been a manic episode, a mixed episode, or a hypomanic episode, and criteria have never been met for cyclothymic disorder [all discussed later in the chapter].

F. The disturbance does not occur exclusively during the course of a chronic psychotic disorder, such as schizophrenia or delusional disorder [all discussed in Chapter 12].

G. The symptoms are not due to the direct physiological effects of a substance (e.g., a drug of abuse, a medication) or a general medical condition (e.g., hypothyroidism).

H. The symptoms cause clinically significant distress or impairment in social, occupational, or other important areas of functioning.

Source: Reprinted with permission from the DSM-IV-TR Casebook: A Learning Companion to the Diagnostic and Statistical Manual of Mental Disorders, Fourth Edition, Text Revision, (Copyright 2002) American Psychiatric Association.

with an MDE (psychomotor symptoms and changes in sleep, appetite, and weight; American Psychiatric Association, 2000). Other factors that can help a clinician distinguish between major depressive disorder and dysthymic disorder are age of onset (generally younger with dysthymic disorder), symptom duration (longer with dysthymic disorder), and number of symptoms (fewer with dysthymic disorder). See Table 6.5 for more facts about dysthymic disorder.

Understanding Depressive Disorders

How do depressive disorders arise? Why do some people, but not others, suffer from them? Like all psychological disorders, depressive disorders are best understood as arising from neurological, psychological, and social factors, and the feedback loops among them.

Neurological Factors

Neurological factors that contribute to depressive disorders can be classified into three categories: brain systems, neural communication, and genetics. Stress-related hormones—which underlie a specific kind of neural communication—are particularly important in understanding depressive disorders, and thus we consider them in a separate section below.

Table 6.5 ▶ Dysthymic Disorder Facts at a Glance

Prevalence

- In a given year, 3% of Americans have dysthmic disorder; 6% will have it over the course of their lives.

Comorbidity

- Among individuals with dysthymic disorder without a prior history of MDD, the risk of subsequently developing MDD is approximately 75% within 5 years of the onset of dysthymia.
- People with dysthymic disorder may also develop a substance-related disorder.

Onset

- The onset of dysthymia tends to be earlier than that of MDD.

Course

- The spontaneous remission rate (that is, the rate at which the disorder gets better by itself, without any treatment) for people with dysthymic disorder is only 10% per year.
- In one 10-year study, almost 75% of people with dysthymic disorder recovered within 5 years, but over 70% of the patients who recovered had a recurrence by the end of the study (Klein, Shankman, & Rose, 2006).
- Each year, approximately 10% of individuals with dysthymic disorder will have their first MDE.
- People whose dysthymic disorder precedes the onset of MDD, as occurs for 10–25% of people with MDD, are less likely to have a full recovery between episodes without treatment.

Gender Differences

- Boys and girls are equally likely to develop dysthymic disorder.
- In adulthood, women are two to three times more likely than men to develop dysthymic disorder.

Source: Unless otherwise noted, the source for information is American Psychiatric Association, 2000.

Brain Systems

Studies of depressed people have shown that they have unusually low activity in a part of the frontal lobe that has direct connections to the amygdala (which is involved in fear and other strong emotions) and to other brain areas involved in emotion (Kennedy et al., 1997). This finding hints that the depressed brain is not as able as the normal brain to regulate emotion. Moreover, this part of the frontal lobe has connections to the brain areas that produce the neurotransmitter substances dopamine, serotonin, and norepinephrine. Thus, this part of the frontal lobe may well be involved in regulating the amounts of such substances. This is important because these substances are involved in reward and emotion, which again hints that the brains of these people are not regulating emotion normally.

Researchers have refined this general observation and reported that one aspect of depression—lack of motivated behavior—is specifically related to reduced activity in the frontal (and parietal) lobes (Milak et al., 2005). In addition, these researchers report that depression does not simply reflect that the brain as a whole has become sluggish. Rather, they found that more severe depression is associated with *greater* activity in the emotion-related limbic system, which fits with the idea that emotions are not being effectively regulated. Moreover, these researchers found that some of the brain areas involved in attention (in particular, the thalamus) and in controlling movements (basal ganglia) are overactive in depressed people, which again suggests that the functions carried out by these brain areas are not being regulated normally.

Neural Communication

Researchers have long known that the symptoms of depression can be alleviated by medications that alter the activity of serotonin or norepinephrine (Arana & Rosenbaum, 2000). Indeed, when this fact was first discovered, some researchers thought that the puzzle of depression was nearly solved. However, we now know that the story is not that simple—depression is not caused by too much or too little of a specific neurotransmitter. Instead, the disorder arises in part from complex interactions among numerous neurotransmitter substances, which depend on how much of each is released into the synapses, how long each substance lingers in the synapse, and how the substances interact with receptors in other areas of the brain that are involved in the symptoms of depression (Nemeroff, 1998).

One of the early attempts to explain depression in terms of a single neurotransmitter is called the *catecholamine hypothesis*, which posits that symptoms of depression arise when levels of norepinephrine fall too low (Schildkraut, 1965). Support for this hypothesis came from studies showing that people who are depressed have fewer by-products of norepinephrine in their urine and cerebrospinal fluid (Nemeroff, 1998). Perhaps surprisingly, however, autopsies of the brains of people who were depressed found that many of them had a *higher* than normal density of norepinephrine receptors (Meana, Barturen, & Garcia-Sevilla, 1992). At first glance, this last finding may seem at odds with the first finding—why would people who have *less* norepinephrine have *more* receptors that respond to that neurotransmitter? This apparent paradox is resolved by knowing that when the brain doesn't produce enough of a neurotransmitter, it often attempts to compensate by increasing the number of receptors that respond to it. An increase in the number of receptors allows a given amount of neurotransmitter to have a larger effect.

Further support for the catecholamine hypothesis came from the finding that depression can be treated by drugs that block norepinephrine reuptake (Brunello & Racagni, 1998; Schatzberg, 2000). These drugs keep more norepinephrine in the synapse for a longer period of time, which means that less additional norepinephrine needs to be produced to affect the receptors.

But the neurotransmitter norepinephrine and the catecholamine hypothesis cannot be the whole story. Additional studies have implicated the neurotransmitter serotonin in depression (Booij & Van der Does, 2007; Munafò et al., 2006). Some researchers hypothesize that serotonin affects depression through its influence on norepinephrine activity (Schildkraut, 1965). However, other researchers have shown that serotonin directly affects the amygdala (which plays an important role in emotional expression; LeDoux, 2000), the hypothalamus (which is involved in vegetative signs of depression; Swaab, 2003), and cortical brain areas involved in thinking and judgment (Smith & Kosslyn, 2006). Moreover, measurements of cerebrospinal fluid and autopsy studies have shown that depressed people have lower levels of serotonin than normal (Sullivan et al., 2006). And, just as was documented for norepinephrine, lower levels of serotonin are associated with greater numbers of certain serotonin receptors, and drugs that block the reuptake of serotonin relieve symptoms of depression (Arroll et al., 2005).

Dopamine also appears to play several roles in depression (Nutt, 2008); too little of it not only can undermine the effects of reward (and hence can lead to lack of pleasure), but also can produce psychomotor retardation (Clausius, Born & Grunz, 2009; Martin-Soelch, 2009; Stein, 2008). In short, depression involves not only norepinephrine, but also serotonin and dopamine—and perhaps other neurotransmitters as well.

Stress-Related Hormones

The chemical story doesn't end with neurotransmitters. Nemeroff (1998, 2008) formulated the *stress–diathesis model* of depression (which is to be distinguished from the general *diathesis–stress model*, discussed in Chapter 1). The stress–diathesis model of depression focuses specifically on the hypothalamic-pituitary-adrenal axis (HPA axis; discussed in Chapter 2) and the role of cortisol, a hormone that is secreted in larger amounts when an individual experiences stress (see Figure 6.1). According to the stress–diathesis model, people with depression have an excess of cortisol circulating in their blood, which makes their brains prone to overreacting when they experience stress. Moreover, this stress reaction, in turn, alters the serotonin and norepinephrine systems, which underlie at least some of the symptoms of depression. Antidepressants

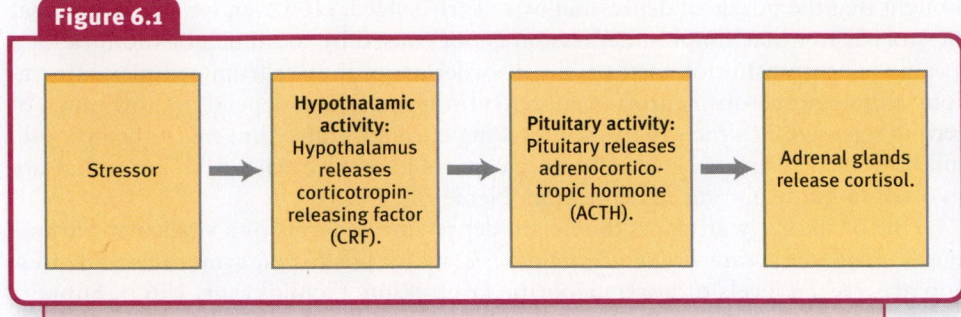

Figure 6.1

| Stressor | → | **Hypothalamic activity:** Hypothalamus releases corticotropin-releasing factor (CRF). | → | **Pituitary activity:** Pituitary releases adrenocortico-tropic hormone (ACTH). | → | Adrenal glands release cortisol. |

6.1 ▸ The HPA Axis Stress activates the hypothalamus, which releases corticotropin-releasing factor (CRF), which in turn stimulates the pituitary gland to release adrenocorticotropic hormone (ACTH), which then instructs the adrenal glands to release cortisol. According to the stress–diathesis model of depression, people who become depressed have high levels of cortisol, which lead to heightened reactivity to stress and increased serotonin levels.

and electroconvulsive therapy (ECT) can lower people's cortisol levels in addition to decreasing their depressive symptoms (Deuschle et al., 2003; Werstiuk et al., 1996).

The stress–diathesis model of depression receives support from several sources (Nemeroff, 2008). For one, higher levels of cortisol are associated with decreases in the size of the hippocampus, which thereby impairs the ability to form new memories (of the sort that later can be voluntarily recalled)—which in turn may contribute to the decreased cognitive abilities that characterize depression. And, in fact, researchers have reported that parts of this brain structure are smaller in depressed people than in those who are not depressed (Neumeister, Charney, & Drevets, 2005; Neumeister et al., 2005), which suggests that stress affects the symptoms of depression in part by altering levels of cortisol, which in turn impairs the functioning of the hippocampus.

In addition, the role of stress in setting the stage for depression receives support from studies of newborn rats that were separated from their mothers for brief periods of time each day (Plotsky et al., 2005). In adulthood, these stressed rats not only had more HPA axis activity and higher levels of corticotropin-releasing factor (CRF) than their nonstressed counterparts, but they also had a greater density of CRF receptors in certain brain areas. Consistent with these findings, Paxil, an antidepressant medication that targets serotonin, seems to decrease activation of the HPA axis in rats that have been deprived of their mother's presence (Plotsky, cited in Nemeroff, 1998). Moreover, when these rats are taken off Paxil, the increased activation resumes.

However, the stress–diathesis model describes only part of the neurological piece of depression. As noted earlier, dopamine also probably plays a role, and may do so independently of effects of stress. In addition, there's an intriguing twist to the finding that HPA axis activity is related to depression: Whereas HPA axis activity increases in typical depression, it decreases in atypical depression (Kasckow, Baker, & Geracioti, 2001). This finding suggests that the two forms of depression may arise in part from different neurological mechanisms.

Genetics

Twin studies show that when one twin of a monozygotic (identical) pair has MDD, the other twin has a risk of also developing the disorder that is four times higher than when the twins are dizygotic (fraternal; Bowman & Nurnberger, 1993; Kendler, Karkowski, & Prescott, 1999). Because monozygotic twins basically share all of their genes but dizygotic twins share only half of their genes, these results point to a role for genetics in the etiology of this disorder. One possibility is that genes influence how a person responds to stressful events (Costello et al., 2002; Kendler et al., 2005). If a person is sensitive to stressful events, the sensitivity could lead to increased HPA axis activation (Hasler et al., 2004), which in turn could contribute to depression.

However, genes are not destiny. The environment clearly plays an important role in whether a person will develop depression (Eley et al., 1998; Hasler et al., 2004; Rice, Harold, & Thaper, 2002; Wender et al., 1986). Even with identical twins, if one twin is depressed, this does not guarantee that the co-twin will also be depressed—in spite of their having basically the same genes. Whether a person gets depressed depends partly on his or her life experiences, including the presence of hardships and the extent of social support.

The environment plays a key role not only in whether the genes contribute to depression, but also in *how* the genes have their effects. In some cases, genetic factors may affect depression indirectly—by disrupting specific aspects of normal functioning that in turn trigger the disorder. For example, researchers have found that genetics may influence whether a person has disrupted sleep (Hasler et al., 2004; Modell et al., 2003), and adolescents who went on to develop the disorder (investigated in longitudinal studies) did have disrupted sleep.

Psychological Factors

Particular ways that people think about themselves and events, in concert with stressful or negative life experiences, can increase the risk of depression. In the following sections we consider psychological factors that can influence whether a person develops depression; these factors range from biases in attention to the effects of different ways of thinking to the results of learning.

Attentional Biases

Some people see a glass that is half full of water as being half empty. Similarly, some people focus their attention—consciously or unconsciously—on stimuli that are sad. People who are depressed are more likely to pay attention to sad and angry faces than to faces that display positive emotions (Gotlib, Kasch, et al., 2004; Gotlib, Krasnoperova, et al., 2004; Leyman et al., 2007); people who do not have a psychological disorder spend equal time looking at faces that express different emotions. This attentional bias has also been found for negative words and scenes, as well as for remembering depression-related—versus neutral—stimuli (Caseras et al., 2007; Gotlib, Kasch, et al., 2004; Matt, Vasquez, & Campbell, 1992; Mogg, Bradley, & Williams, 1995). Such an attentional bias may leave depressed people more sensitive to other people's sad moods and to negative feedback from others (or even a lack of positive feedback, as occurs when a person fails to smile when greeting you), compounding their depressive thoughts and feelings.

Dysfunctional Thoughts

As discussed in Chapter 2, Aaron Beck proposed that *cognitive distortions* are the root cause of many disorders. Beck (1967) has suggested that people with depression tend to have overly negative views about (1) the world, (2) the self, and (3) the future, referred to as the *negative triad of depression*. These distorted views can cause and maintain chronically depressed feelings and depression-related behaviors. For instance, a man who doesn't get the big raise he hoped for might respond with cognitive distortions that give rise to dysfunctional thoughts. He might think that he isn't "successful" because he didn't get the raise, and therefore that he must be worthless (notice the circular reasoning). This man is more likely to become depressed than he would be if he didn't have such dysfunctional thoughts.

Rumination

While experiencing negative emotions, some people reflect on these emotions; during such *ruminations*, they might say to themselves: "Why do bad things always happen to me?" or "Why did they say those hurtful things about me—is it something I did?" or "Should I have spoken more during the discussion?" (Nolen-Hoeksema & Morrow, 1991). Such ruminative thinking has been linked to depression (Just & Alloy, 1997; Nolen-Hoeksema, 2000; Nolen-Hoeksema & Morrow, 1991, 1993).

Studies have examined the relationship between depression and specific forms of rumination, such as *stress-reactive rumination*, which is ruminating about negative implications of stressful life events. Researchers assess this type of rumination by asking participants to agree or disagree with statements about what they "generally do when feeling down, sad, or depressed." Examples of such statements include:

- "Think about how the stressful event was all your fault"
- "Think about what the occurrence of the stressor means about you"
- "Think about how things like this always happen to you" (Robinson & Alloy, 2003).

To investigate the relationship between stress-reactive rumination and other cognitive vulnerabilities to depression (such as dysfunctional thoughts about oneself), researchers followed first-year college students who were not depressed at the time the study began (Robinson & Alloy, 2003). The investigators found that participants who *both* had a cognitive vulnerability for depression and engaged in stress-reactive rumination were, by senior year, more likely than participants who had only one or neither of these risk factors to (1) have experienced a depressive episode, (2) have had more depressive episodes, and (3) have had episodes of longer duration.

Attributional Style

When something bad happens, to what do you attribute the cause of the unfortunate turn of events? In general, people who consistently attribute negative events to their own qualities—called an *internal attributional style*—are more likely to become depressed. In one study, mothers-to-be who had an internal attributional style were more likely to be depressed 3 months after childbirth than were mothers-to-be who had an *external attributional style*—blaming negative events on qualities of others or on the environment (Peterson & Seligman, 1984). Similarly, college students who tended to blame themselves, rather than external factors for negative events, were more likely than those who did not to become depressed after receiving a bad grade (Metalsky et al., 1993).

Prison inmates who tended to attribute events to internal causes when they began to serve their sentences were more likely than other prisoners to become depressed after months of incarceration (Peterson & Seligman, 1984).

Three particular aspects of attributions are related to depression: whether the attributions are *internal* or *external, stable* (enduring causes) or *unstable* (local, transient causes), and *global* (general, overall causes) or *specific* (particular, precise causes) (see Table 6.6). Individuals who tend to attribute negative events to internal, global, and stable factors were most likely to become depressed when negative events occurred. This *depressive attributional style*, along with dysfunctional thoughts, is associated with being vulnerable to depression (Abramson, Seligman, & Teasdale, 1978). People who think this way make negative predictions about the future, for example: "Even if I find another boyfriend, he'll dump me too" (Abramson et al., 1999).

Internal (versus external), global (versus specific), and stable (versus unstable) attributions for negative events are associated with a cognitive vulnerability for depression (Abramson, Seligman, & Teasdale, 1978).

Table 6.6 ▶ Types of Attributions

Example attribution: "He broke up with me because . . . "

	Internal (personal)		External (environmental)	
	Stable	**Unstable**	**Stable**	**Unstable**
Global	I am inherently unlovable.	I was going through a rough period then.	He is a jerk.	He acted impulsively.
Specific	I am not flexible enough about letting people take a couple of days to respond to e-mails that I send.	I wasn't very flexible about his being late every time we arranged to get together last month.	He is incapable of being on time.	He didn't like that I was so annoyed when he was consistently late last week.

In fact, people who consistently make global and stable attributions for negative events—whether to internal or external causes—are more likely to feel hopeless in the face of negative events and come to experience *hopelessness depression*, a form of depression in which hopelessness is a central element (Abramson, Metalsky, & Alloy, 1989). Such people expect (1) that undesirable outcomes will occur (and that desirable ones won't) and (2) that they are helpless to change the situation. However, it is the depressive attributional style *in conjunction with* negative events that elicits hopelessness (Hankin et al., 2004). That is, the attributional style alone won't necessarily lead to depression; it is only when an individual with this style experiences negative events that depression is likely to follow. For instance, hopelessness depression is more common among those who experienced emotional abuse during childhood (Gibb et al., 2001).

Learned Helplessness

Hopelessness depression is not always based on incorrect attributions. It can arise from situations in which, in fact, undesirable outcomes *do* occur and the individual *is* helpless to change the situation, such as the situation of children who experience physical abuse or neglect (Widom, Dumont, & Czaja, 2007). Such circumstances lead to *learned helplessness*, in which a person gives up trying to change or escape from a negative situation (Overmier & Seligman, 1967; see Chapter 2 for a more detailed discussion and technical definition). For example, people in abusive relationships might become depressed if they feel that they cannot escape the relationship and that no matter what they do, the situation will not improve.

Social Factors

Depression is also associated with a variety of social factors, including stressful life events (such as in personal relationships), social exclusion, and social interactions (which are affected by culture). These social factors can affect whether depression develops or persists.

Stressful Life Events

In approximately 70% of cases, an MDE occurs after a significant life stressor, such as getting fired from a job or losing an important relationship. Such events are particularly likely to contribute to a first or second depressive episode (American Psychiatric Association, 2000; Lewinsohn et al., 1999; Tennant, 2002).

It might seem obvious that negative life events can lead to depression, but separating possible confounding factors and trying to establish causality have challenged researchers. For instance, people who are depressed (or have symptoms of depression) may have difficulty doing their job effectively; they may experience stressors such as problems with their coworkers and supervisors, job insecurity, or financial worries. In such cases, the depressive symptoms may *cause* the stressful life events. Alternatively, some people, by virtue of their temperament, may seek out situations or experiences that are stressful; for example, some soldiers volunteer to go to the front line (Foley, Neale, & Kendler, 1996; Lyons et al., 1993). The point is that the relationship between stressful life events and depression may not be as straightforward as it might seem.

In a longitudinal study examining the relationship between stressful life events and depression among teenagers, researchers found that participants who had three or more stressful life events in the previous year were more likely to

Researchers are trying to interpret the correlation between stressful life events and depression. Although stressful events may lead to depression, the symptoms of depression—such as a lack of energy, social isolation, and reduced productivity at work—can create stressful events. For instance, a man who is self-employed may be unable to maintain his usual level of work, so his income drops and financial worries increase.

develop depression than were those with fewer than three such events (Lewinsohn et al., 1999). Another study that examined the relationship between different types of stressful life events and subsequent depression among teenagers found that the recent breakup of a love relationship was the life event most closely associated with a first episode of depression (Monroe et al., 1999).

Several theories have been offered to explain how stressful life events can trigger depression in vulnerable people. Some researchers propose that such events can lead an individual to focus on discrepancies between the "real" and "ideal" selves; for example, the person's "ideal" self of being lovable or worthwhile may be challenged when a love relationship ends (Pyszczynski & Greenberg, 1987). Focusing on this kind of discrepancy can also happen after an injury or illness challenges the invulnerability of the "ideal" self. A person then tries to resolve the discrepancy between the "real" and "ideal" selves (perhaps by changing his or her concept of ideal self to one that isn't so lovable). When attempts to resolve the discrepancy are unsuccessful, a person may continue to focus on the discrepancy and become depressed. Later, we will discuss how the "stress" and "diathesis" parts of the stress-diathesis model relate to each other, and how they trigger a cascade of neurological events associated with depression.

Social Exclusion

Feeling the chronic sting of social exclusion—being pushed toward the margins of society—is also associated with depression. For instance, those who are the targets of prejudice, such as homosexuals who experience community alienation or violence (Mills et al., 2004), and those from lower socioeconomic groups (Field, Hernandez-Reif, & Diego, 2006; Henderson et al., 2005; Inaba et al., 2005), including the elderly (Hybels et al., 2006; Sachs-Ericsson, Plant, & Blazer, 2005), are more likely than others to become depressed.

Some studies find that Latinos and African Americans experience more depression than other ethnic groups in the United States; a closer look at the data, however, suggests that socioeconomic status, rather than ethnic or racial background, is the variable associated with depression (Bromberger et al., 2004; Gilmer et al., 2005). (Note that these individuals can be members of more than one group simultaneously.) People who become disabled in adulthood, through stroke or head trauma, are also more likely than others to become depressed (McDermott et al., 2005).

Social Interactions

To a certain extent, emotions can be contagious: People can develop depression, sadness, anxiety, or anger by spending time with someone who is already in such a state (Coyne, 1976; Hsee et al., 1990; Joiner, 1994; Segrin & Dillard, 1992; Sullins, 1991). For instance, one study found that roommates developed symptoms of depression after 3 weeks of living with someone who was depressed (Joiner, 1994).

Another factor associated with depression is the way some people typically interact in their personal relationships (Ainsworth et al., 1978; Bowlby, 1973, 1979). Patterns of *attachment* have been identified; such patterns begin in infancy and are partly based on the consistency and quality of the caregiver's interactions with the child. When infants are distressed, they tend to display one of the following three patterns that typically endure through adulthood:

1. *Secure attachment*, or seeking out and using a caregiver for comfort and support. (Adults with this style generally display a positive relationship style.)

2. *Avoidant attachment*, or actively avoiding the caregiver. (Adults with this style are emotionally distant from others.)

The quality of the bond between elderly partners can buffer against the negative effects of stressful life events (Kraaij & Garnefski, 2002).

3. *Anxious-ambivalent attachment*, or alternating between seeking support from the caregiver and withdrawing, often displaying anger. (Adults with this style chronically worry about their relationships.)

Adults who are characterized by the two insecure forms of attachment are more vulnerable to depression: Those with anxious-ambivalent attachment are the most likely to experience episodes of depression, followed by those with avoidant attachment. Adults with secure attachment are least likely to do so (Bifulco et al., 2002; Cooper, Shaver, & Collins, 1998; Fonagy et al., 1996).

Culture

A person's culture and context can influence how the person experiences and expresses depressive symptoms (Lam, Marra, & Salzinger, 2005). For instance, in Asian or Latin cultures, people with depression may not mention mood, but talk about "nerves" or describe headaches. Similarly, depressed people in Zimbabwe tend to complain about fatigue and headaches (Patel et al., 2001). In contrast, some depressed people from Middle Eastern cultures may describe problems with their heart, and depressed Native Americans of the Hopi people may report feeling heartbroken (American Psychiatric Association, 2000).

David Young-Wolff/Photo Edit

Culture influences which symptoms of depression people experience, express, and worry about most.

The influence of culture doesn't end with the way symptoms are described. Each culture—and subculture—also leads its members to take particular symptoms more or less seriously. For instance, in cultures that have strong prohibitions against suicide, having suicidal thoughts is a key symptom; in cultures that emphasize being productive at work, having difficulty functioning well at work is considered to be a key symptom (Young, 2001).

A particular culture can also be influenced by another culture and change accordingly. Consider that depressed people in China have typically reported mostly physical symptoms of depression, but these reports are changing as China becomes increasingly exposed to Western views of depression (Parker, Gladstone, & Chee, 2001).

Gender Difference

In North America, women are about twice as likely as men to be diagnosed with depression (American Psychiatric Association, 2000; Marcus et al., 2005), and studies in Europe find a similar gender difference (Angst et al., 2002; Dalgard et al., 2006). Research results indicate that the gender difference arises at puberty and continues into adulthood (Alloy & Abramson, 2007; Jose & Brown, 2008).

What might cause the gender difference? One explanation focuses on a ruminative response to stress: women are more likely than men to mull over a stressful situation, whereas men more often respond by distracting themselves and taking action (Nolen-Hoeksema, 1987; Nolen-Hoeksema & Morrow, 1993; Vajk et al., 1997). A ruminative pattern can be unlearned: College students who learned to use distraction more and rumination less improved their depressed mood (Nolen-Hoeksema & Morrow, 1993).

Another explanation for the gender difference in rates of depression is that girls' socialization into female roles can lead them to experience more body dissatisfaction, which in turn can make them more vulnerable to automatic negative thoughts that lead to depression (Cyranowski et al., 2000; Nolen-Hoeksema & Girgus, 1994). Another consideration is that women may be more likely than men to *report* symptoms of depression, although not necessarily to *experience* more of these symptoms (Sigmon et al., 2005). Such a bias in reporting symptoms isn't limited to self-reports: Family members are more likely to report female relatives as seeming depressed, even when the females themselves did not report feeling depressed (Brommelhoff et al., 2004).

Note also that biological differences—such as specific female hormonal changes involved in puberty—may contribute to this gender difference (Halbreich & Kahn, 2001; Steiner, Dunn, & Born, 2003). A role for this biological factor is consistent with the finding that, before puberty, boys and girls have similar rates of depression (Cohen et al., 1993). Additional evidence that hormones influence depression is the fact that women and men have similar rates of the disorder after women have reached menopause (and hence their levels of female hormone are greatly reduced; Hyde, Mezulis, & Abramson, 2008).

The different explanations for the gender difference are not mutually exclusive, and these factors may interact with one another (Hyde, Mezulis, & Abramson, 2008). For instance, girls who enter puberty early are more likely to become depressed (Kaltiala-Heino, Kosunen, & Rimpela, 2003), perhaps in part because their early physical development makes them more likely to be noticed and teased about their changing bodies, which in turn can lead to dissatisfaction with and rumination about their bodies. Let's examine more broadly how feedback loops contribute to depression.

FEEDBACK LOOPS IN ACTION: Depressive Disorders

How do neurological, psychological, and social factors interact through feedback loops to produce depression? As we noted earlier in the section on genetics, some people are more vulnerable to stress. For these people, the HPA axis is highly responsive to stress (and often the stress is related to social factors). For example, abuse or neglect at an early age, with accompanying frequent or chronic increase in the activity of the HPA axis, can lead cortisol-releasing cells to overrespond to any stressor—even mild ones (Nemeroff, 1998). In fact, college students with a history of MDD reported feeling more tension and responded less well after a stressful cognitive task (one that, unknown to these participants, was impossible to solve) than college students with no history of MDD (Ilgen & Hutchison, 2005). These results support the notion that stressors affect people vulnerable to MDD differently than they affect those without such a vulnerability (Hasler et al., 2004).

A cognitive factor that makes a person vulnerable to depression, such as a negative attributional style, a ruminative coping style, or dysfunctional thoughts (all psychological factors), can amplify the negative effects of a stressor. In fact, such cognitive factors can lead people to be hypervigilant for stressors or to interpret neutral events as stressors, which in turn activates the HPA axis. This neurological response then can lead such individuals to interact differently with others (social factor)—making less eye contact, being less responsive, and becoming more withdrawn.

Researchers have identified other ways that neurological, psychological, and social factors create feedback loops in depression. According to James Coyne's interactional theory of depression (Coyne, 1976; Coyne & Downey, 1991; Joiner, Coyne, & Blalock, 1999), someone who is neurologically vulnerable to depression (perhaps because of genes or neurotransmitter abnormalities) may, through verbal and nonverbal behaviors (psychological factor), alienate people who would otherwise be supportive (social factor; Nolan & Mineka, 1997). Such behaviors could arise from negative attributions and views about self and the environment (psychological factors), which in turn could arise from group interactions (social factors), such as being teased or ridiculed, or modeling the behavior of someone else. When someone who is depressed expresses consistently negative attitudes, exhibits a pattern of ignoring or failing to benefit from the help of others, or seems to become too

Girls are typically encouraged to cope with stressors by ruminating. In contrast, boys are typically encouraged to use activity and distraction. This gender difference may contribute to the higher rate of depression among women than among men (Nolen-Hoeksema, 1987, 2001).

Image Source/Jupiterimages

dependent on others, other people may eventually criticize and even reject the person, which could have the effect of confirming the person's negative view of self and his or her prospects for the future. Consider that researchers have found that depressed undergraduates are more likely than nondepressed undergraduates to solicit negative information from happy people; such a tendency can lead happier people to reject the depressed questioner, confirming negative beliefs about himself or herself (Wenzlaff & Beevers, 1998).

In short, people's psychological characteristics affect how they interpret events and how they behave, which in turn influences how they are treated in social interactions, which then influences their beliefs about themselves and others (Casbon et al., 2005). And all of this is modulated by whether or not the person is neurologically vulnerable to depression. Figure 6.2 illustrates the feedback loops.

Treating Depressive Disorders

As discussed in Chapter 4, different treatments target different factors. However, successful treatment of any one factor will affect the others. For example, improving disrupted brain functioning will alter a person's thoughts, mood, and behavior, and interactions with others.

Targeting Neurological Factors

In treating depressive disorders, clinicians rely on two major types of treatment that directly target neurological factors: medication and brain stimulation.

Medication

Several types of medications are commonly prescribed for depression; it can take weeks for one of these medications to bring about any change in depressed mood. Antidepressant medications include the following:

- **Selective serotonin reuptake inhibitors (SSRIs)**, such as *fluoxetine* (Prozac), *paroxetine* (Paxil), and *sertraline* (Zoloft). SSRIs slow the reuptake of serotonin from synapses. Because these antidepressants affect only certain receptors, they have fewer side effects than other types, which can make people less likely to stop taking them (Anderson, 2000; Beasley et al., 2000). However, SSRIs are the only type of antidepressant to have the side effect of decreased sexual interest, which can lead some patients to stop taking them (Brambilla et al., 2005; Gregorian et al., 2002). Many patients also find that the same dose of an SSRI brings less benefit over time (Arana & Rosenbaum, 2000)—an effect nicknamed *Prozac poop-out*. SSRIs are also used to treat anxiety disorders, (discussed in Chapter 7), as well as other disorders.

- **Tricyclic antidepressants (TCAs)**, such as *amitriptyline* (Elavil). TCAs are so named because their molecular structure contains three (*tri-*) rings of atoms; they have been used since the 1950s to treat depression and, until SSRIs became available, were the type of medication most commonly used for this purpose. TCAs are generally as effective as Prozac for depression (Agency for Health Care Policy and Research, 1999). The side effects of TCAs differ from those of SSRIs: The most common side effects include low blood pressure, blurred vision, dry mouth, and constipation, but diminished libido (sex drive) is not a significant side effect (Arana & Rosenbaum, 2000).

- **Monoamine oxidase inhibitors (MAOIs)**, such as *phenelzine* (Nardil). Some neurotransmitters, such as serotonin, dopamine, and norepinephrine, are classified as *monoamines*; monoamine oxidase is a naturally produced enzyme that breaks down monoamines in the synapse. *MAOIs* inhibit this chemical breakdown, so the net effect is to increase the amount of neurotransmitter in the synapse. MAOIs are more effective for treating atypical depression (Cipriani et al., 2007; Prien & Kocsis, 1995) than typical depression. These medications can be dangerous when patients

Selective serotonin reuptake inhibitors (SSRIs)
Medications that slow the reuptake of serotonin from the synapse.

Tricyclic antidepressants (TCAs)
Older antidepressants named after the three rings of atoms in their molecular structure.

Monoamine oxidase inhibitors (MAOIs)
Antidepressant medications that increase the amount of monoamine neurotransmitter in the synapse.

Figure 6.2

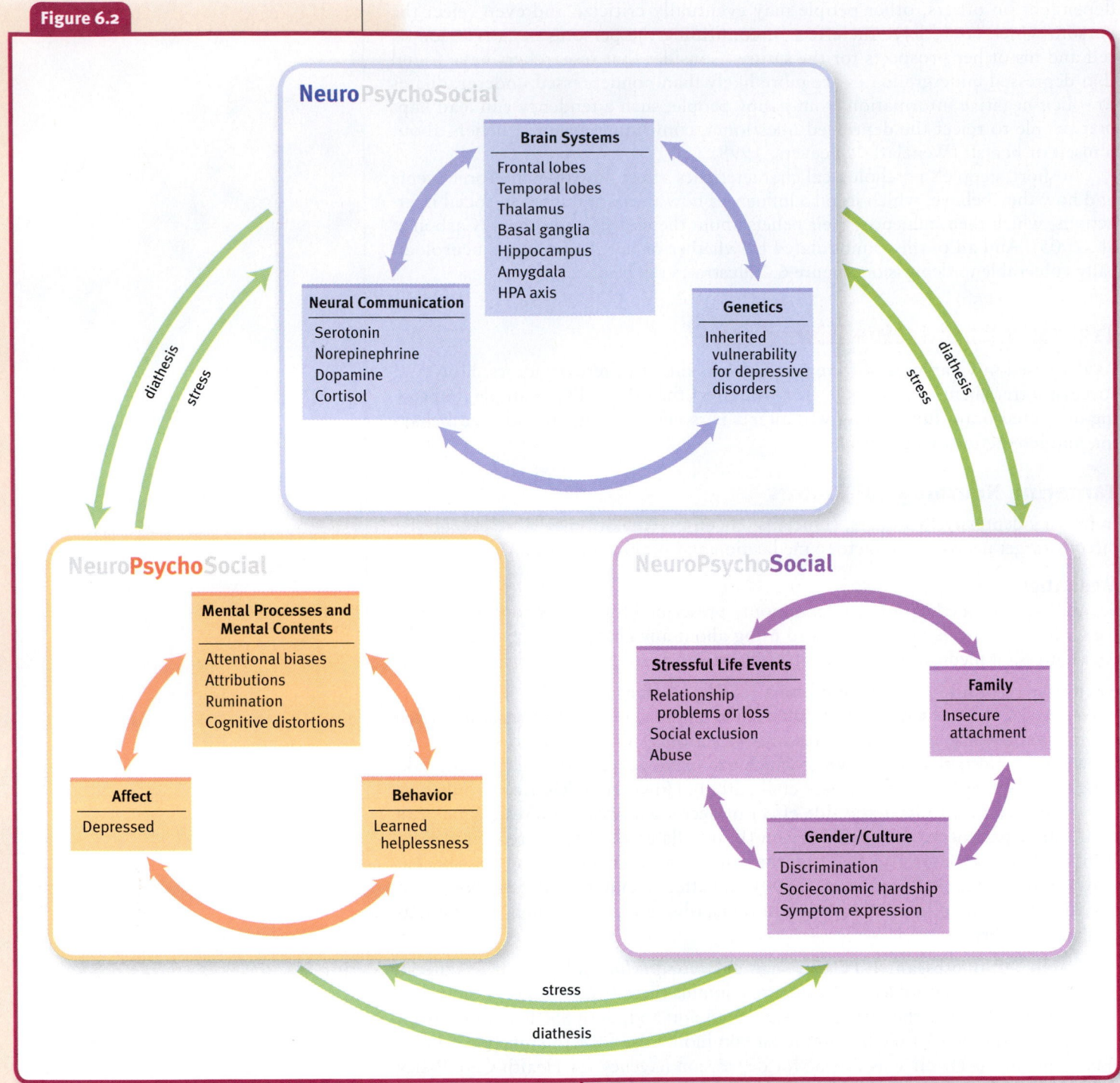

6.2 ▸ **Feedback Loops in Action: Depressive Disorders**

eat foods (such as wine and cheese) containing a substance called tyramine, which can cause fatal blood pressure changes. An MAOI is now available as a skin patch; the skin patch method of administering the medication avoids absorption via the gastrointestinal tract and thus reduces the risk associated with eating tyramine-rich foods (Patkar, Pae, & Masand, 2006).

Among the antidepressants, SSRIs have been the most popular, in part because they have the fewest side effects. By 2004, however, mental health professionals and laypeople raised concerns about whether SSRI use was associated with increased suicide rates. Studies comparing SSRIs to other antidepressants did, in fact, find a greater risk for suicidal thoughts and suicide attempts in children and adolescents taking such medications (Martinez et al., 2005); these findings led to a "black box" warning label, indicating that the medications may increase the risk of suicide in children who take them and that the children should be closely monitored for suicidal thoughts or behavior or for an increase in depressive symptoms. Since the warning label was mandated, additional research suggests that the benefits of SSRI antidepressants for youngsters outweigh any risk of suicide, although people taking them should continue to be carefully monitored (Bridge et al., 2007). Although studies of adults did not find an increased suicide risk with SSRIs generally (Fergusson et al., 2005; Gunnell, Saperia, & Ashby, 2005), they did find an increased suicide risk with the SSRI *paroxetine* (Paxil) (Aursnes et al., 2005). Moreover, studies of SSRI use by adults revealed an increased risk of nonlethal self-harming behavior (Martinez et al., 2005; Tihonen et al., 2006).

Medications for depression are continually being developed. Researchers seek to minimize the side effects of existing medications and to create new drugs for people who do not get sufficient relief from existing ones. For instance, some newer antidepressants, such as *venlafaxine* (Effexor) and *duloxetine* (Cymbalta), affect neurons that respond both to serotonin and norepinephrine; such medications are sometimes referred to as *serotonin/norepinephrine reuptake inhibitors* (SNRIs). Some other new antidepressants that affect noradrenaline (the alternative term for norepinephrine) and serotonin are referred to as *noradrenergic and specific serotonergic antidepressants* (NaSSAs, where *Na* stands for "noradrenergic"). The antidepressant *mirtazapine* (Remeron) is a NaSSa.

Clinicians may also prescribe any of the antidepressants discussed above for dysthymia. The decision regarding which antidepressant to prescribe for any depressive disorder is not yet based entirely on science—it is not presently possible to predict which antidepressant will be the most effective with the least side effects for a given individual (assuming that medication is the preferred treatment). Being able to predict side effects is important because they often lead patients to stop the medication. In fact, a majority of patients who receive medication for depression stop taking the medication before it has had a chance to be maximally effective either within the first few weeks, before it can take full effect, or during an extended period of better mood (Aikens, Nease, & Klinkman, 2008; National Committee for Quality Assurance, 2007).

Some people with depression who do not want to take prescription medication have successfully used an extract from a flowering plant called St. John's wort (*Hypericum perforatum*). Results of meta-analytic studies comparing St. John's wort to prescription antidepressants and placebos indicate that the herbal medication can help those with mild to moderate depression, and sometimes—but less commonly—even those with severe depression (Linde, Berner, & Krison, 2008; Linde et al., 2005). Patients taking St. John's wort report fewer side effects than do patients taking prescription medications (Linde, Berner, & Kriston, 2008); the most common side effect is dry mouth or dizziness.

Another medication for which a prescription is not necessary is *ademetionine*, or *S-adenosyl-L-methionine* (SAMe), which was found to be as effective as the TCA imiprimine and superior to a placebo (Agency for Health Care Policy and Research, 2002; Pancheri, Scapicchio, & Dell Chiaie, 2002). SAMe has been reported to reduce depression more quickly than other antidepressants—in about a week.

Valerie Giles/Photo Researchers

Don Farrall/Getty Images

St. John's wort, shown here as the plant and in capsule form, may lessen mild to moderate depression but may not be as effective as antidepressant medication for those with severe MDD (Linde et al., 2005).

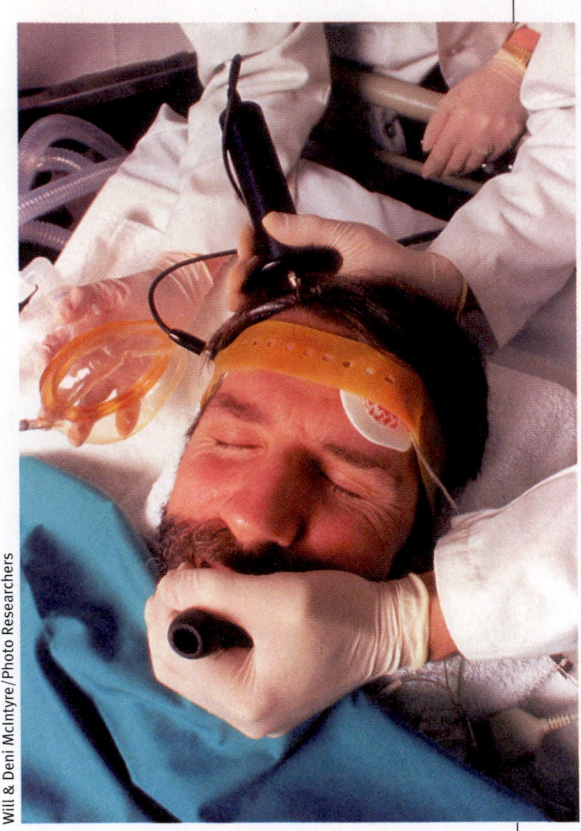

Will & Deni McIntyre/Photo Researchers

Eighty percent of all ECT treatment is given for depression (Sackheim et al., 1995).

Brain Stimulation

Not all patients with depression are helped by medication or by other commonly employed treatments, such as cognitive-behavior therapy (CBT). Electroconvulsive therapy (ECT; see Chapter 4) may be used when a patient's symptoms are severe and he or she (1) cannot take medication because of side effects or other medical reasons, (2) has a psychotic depression (depression with psychotic features) that does not respond to medication (Fink, 2001), or (3) has severe depression that has not improved significantly with either medication or psychotherapy (Lam et al., 1999). Unfortunately, some people receiving ECT suffer memory loss for events that occurred during a brief period of time before the procedure (Kho, VanVreeswijk, & Murre, 2006).

ECT for depression is usually administered 2 to 3 times a week over several weeks, for a total of 6 to 12 sessions (Shapira et al., 1998; Vieweg & Shawcross, 1998). Depressive symptoms lessen a few weeks after the treatment begins, although scientists don't yet understand exactly how ECT provides relief (Pagnin et al., 2004).

Unfortunately, depressed patients who hadn't responded to antidepressants commonly relapse after receiving ECT: At least half of these patients experience another episode of depression over the following 2 years (Gagne et al., 2000; Sackheim et al., 2001). To minimize the risk of a relapse, patients usually begin taking antidepressant medication after ECT ends. Some research suggests that relapse may be best prevented by beginning antidepressant medication *during* the course of ECT—rather than afterward—and by continuing ECT at a maintenance level (weekly sessions tapering to monthly sessions) for several months after the standard course of treatment is completed (Gagne et al., 2000).

Some patients with depression might benefit from transcranial magnetic stimulation (TMS; see Chapter 4), which involves sending high-intensity magnetic pulses through the brain. In some encouraging studies, about half of the depressed patients who did not improve with medication were treated successfully enough with TMS that they did not have to receive ECT (Epstein et al., 1998; Figiel et al., 1998; Klein et al., 1999). TMS is easier to administer and causes fewer side effects than ECT. However, unlike ECT, researchers have yet to establish definitive guidelines for TMS that govern critical features of the treatment, such as the positioning of the coils that deliver magnetic pulses and how often the treatment should be administered (Holtzheimer & Avery, 2005). In 2008, the Federal Drug Administration approved TMS as a treatment for depression to be used after medication treatments have failed.

Targeting Psychological Factors

Biomedical treatments are not the only ones available for depression. A variety of treatments are designed to alter psychological factors—changing the patient's behaviors, thoughts, and feelings.

Behavioral Methods

Behavioral methods focus on identifying depressive behaviors and then changing them. For instance, being socially isolated and avoiding daily activities can lead to depressive thoughts and feelings or can help maintain them (Emmelkamp, 1994). Changing these depressive behaviors can, in turn, increase the opportunities to receive positive reinforcement (Lewinsohn, 1974). Specific techniques to change depressive behaviors, collectively referred to as *behavioral activation* (Gortner et al., 1998), include self-monitoring, scheduling daily activities that lead to pleasure or a sense of mastery, and identifying and decreasing avoidant behaviors. Behavioral activation may also include problem solving—identifying obstacles that interfere with achieving a goal and then developing solutions to circumvent or eliminate those obstacles. For instance, a depressed college student may feel overwhelmed at the thought of asking for an extension for an already overdue paper. The student and therapist work together to solve the problem of how to go about asking for the extension—they come up with a realistic timetable to complete the paper and discuss how to talk with the professor. Behavioral activation techniques may initially feel aversive to a person with depression because they require more energy than he or she feels able to summon; however, mood improves in the long term. In fact, behavioral activation is superior to cognitive techniques in treating both moderate and severe depression (Dimidjian et al., 2006).

Cognitive Methods

Based on the premise that depressing thoughts lead to similar feelings and behaviors, cognitive methods aim to diminish or change such thoughts, which are often distortions of reality (see Chapter 4). Patients are encouraged to conduct their own experiments by collecting data to assess the accuracy of their beliefs, which are often irrational and untrue (Hollon & Beck, 1994). This process can relieve some patients' depression, and can prevent or minimize further episodes of depression (Teasdale & Barnard, 1993; Teasdale et al., 2002).

Consider Kay Jamison: She felt that she was a burden to her friends and family, and that they would all be better off if she were dead. Cognitive therapy would explore the accuracy of these beliefs: Why did she think she was a burden? What evidence did she have to support this conclusion? How might friends or family react if she told them that they'd be better off if she were dead? A cognitive therapist might even suggest that she talk to them about her beliefs and listen to their responses—was she accurate in her beliefs? Most likely, her friends and family would *not* agree that they'd be better off if she were dead.

However, successful short-term cognitive therapy is not necessarily a permanent cure. A meta-analysis of studies of manual-based, short-term therapy (usually 12–20 sessions) found that although CBT decreased symptoms, many patients still had significant symptoms at the conclusion of the treatment and were at risk for relapse. Of the patients who had improved, only about 35% retained that degree of improvement 18 months later; the others had at least some relapse of their depressive symptoms (Westen & Morrison, 2001).

Cognitive-Behavior Therapy Compared to Medication

CBT, particularly when it includes behavioral activation, is often about as successful as medication (Dimidjian et al., 2006; DeRubeis et al., 2005; Sava et al., 2009; TADS Team, 2007). In some ways CBT may be better than medication: The side effects of medication may lead patients to stop taking it; various studies have found that about 75% of patients either stop taking their antidepressant medication within the first 3 months, or they take less than an optimal dose (Mitchell, 2007). And when patients stop taking medication, a high proportion of them relapse. Furthermore, even when medication is successful, some research suggests that people at risk for further episodes should continue to take the medication for the rest of their lives to prevent relapses (Hirschfield et al., 1997).

In contrast, the beneficial effects of CBT can persist after treatment ends (Hollon et al., 2005); CBT is an alternative that need not be administered for life. Moreover, medication and CBT can be used together. In fact, studies have shown that a combination of medication and CBT is more effective than medication alone—even for severely depressed adolescents and adults (Macaskill & Macaskill, 1996; TADS Team, 2007; Thase et al., 1997). In addition, after treatment with antidepressants has ended, a patient's residual symptoms of depression can be reduced through CBT; this supplemental CBT can reduce the relapse rate (Fava et al., 1998a, 1998b).

Targeting Social Factors

Treatment for depression can also directly target a social factor—personal relationships. Such treatment is designed to increase the patient's positive interactions with others and minimize the negative interactions.

Interpersonal therapy seeks to improve patients' relationships, and thereby alleviate depression.

Interpersonal Therapy

Interpersonal therapy for depression (IPT, explained in Chapter 4) emphasizes the links between mood and events in a patient's recent and current relationships (Klerman et al., 1984). Relationships that function poorly can contribute to poor mood and depression, and improved relationships can reduce depression. IPT addresses four general aspects of relationships, generally in about 16 sessions:

• a deficiency in social skills or communication skills, which results in unsatisfying social relationships;

• persistent, significant conflicts in a relationship;

• grief about a loss; and

• changes in interpersonal roles (for example, a partner with a new job may have become less emotionally available).

IPT is effective in a wide range of circumstances and settings. For example, in an innovative study of depressed people in 30 Ugandan rural villages, researchers randomly assigned depressed residents from 15 villages to group IPT, consisting of 16 weeks of 90-minute sessions. The depressed residents from the other 15 villages received no treatment (the control group). Those who received group IPT had a significant decrease in their depressive symptoms (and were better able to provide for their families and participate in community activities) than those in the control group (Bolton et al., 2003). IPT has also successfully reduced the occurrence of postpartum depression in pregnant women at high risk for the disorder (Zlotnick et al., 2006). In addition to alleviating depressive symptoms, maintenance IPT—either alone or in combination with CBT—may also prevent relapse (Frank et al., 2007; Klein et al., 2004).

Family Systems Therapy

A family's functioning may be a target of treatment; this usually occurs when a family member's depression is related to either a maladaptive pattern of interaction within the family or a conflict that arose within the family. Conflicts—particularly over values—may arise within families that have immigrated to the United States; immigrant parents and their children who grow up in the United States may experience tension because what the parents want for their children conflicts with what the children (as they become adults) want for themselves. Immigrant parents from Mexico, for instance, may want to be very involved in their children's lives, just as they would be in their native hometown. But their children, growing up in the United States, may come to resent what the children perceive of as their parents' intrusive and controlling behavior (compared to the parents of their peers; Santisteban et al., 2002). The parents, in turn, may think that their children are rejecting both their Mexican heritage and the parents themselves. Caught between two cultures—the old and the new—and wanting to maintain aspects of their heritage but also feel "American," the resulting conflict can contribute to depression (Hovey, 1998, 2000; Hovey & King, 1996). Family systems therapy might help family members to talk about and understand the cultural and personal meaning of each others' behavior.

A similar cultural conflict can develop when members of a couple bump up against each other's different backgrounds (Baltas & Steptoe, 2000). As Ruben and Angie in Case 4.2 discovered, systems therapy can help clarify such a conflict and find adaptive ways to resolve it.

Spencer Grant/Photo Edit

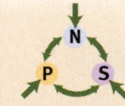

FEEDBACK LOOPS IN TREATMENT: **Depressive Disorders**

The goals of any treatment for depressive disorders are ultimately the same:

- to reduce symptoms of distress and depressed mood and negative or unrealistic thoughts about the self (psychological factors),

- to reduce problems related to social interactions—such as social withdrawal—and to make social interactions more satisfying and less stressful (social factors), and

- to correct imbalances in the brain associated with some of the symptoms, such as by normalizing neurotransmitter functioning or hormone levels (neurological factors).

Treatments that target one type of factor also affect other factors. CBT, for instance, not only can lessen psychological symptoms, but can also change brain activity (Goldapple et al., 2004), improve physical symptoms (including disrupted sleep, appetite, and psychomotor symptoms), and improve social relations. Moreover, as we saw in Chapter 5, medication for depression works not just through its effects on neurological functioning, but also through the placebo effect. Thus, a depressed patient's beliefs (psychological factor) can account for much of the effect of antidepressant medication. Figure 6.3 illustrates the various treatments discussed; the targets of treatments for depressive disorders, and the feedback loops that arise with successful treatment.

Note that Figure 6.3 lists the various types of treatment for depressive disorders, sorted into the three types of factors; in two cases—medication and CBT—we go one step further and list specific types of drugs and specific CBT methods. Why are we

Figure 6.3

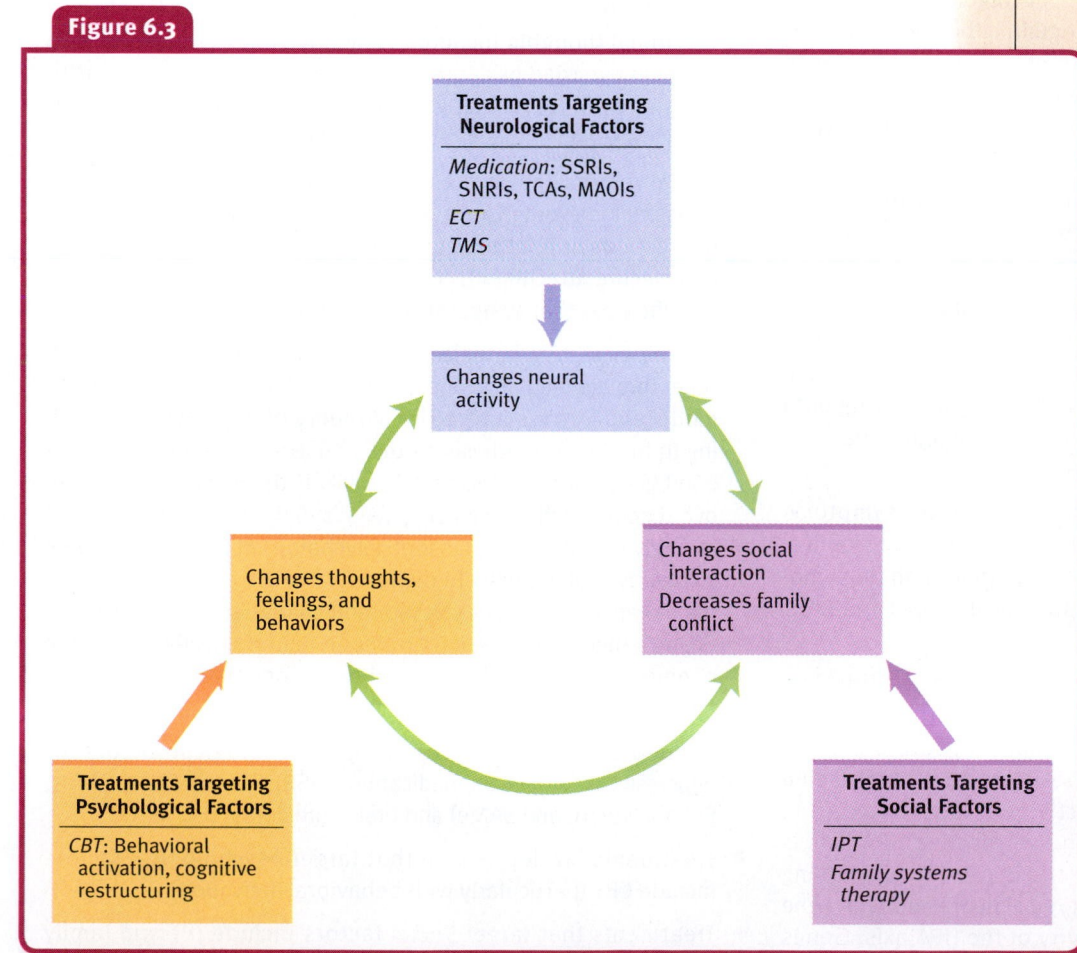

6.3 ▸ Feedback Loops in Treating Depressive Disorders

specific with only these two forms of treatment? Because the forms of treatment have been studied the most extensively, and hence more is known about which specific medications and CBT methods are most likely to reduce symptoms and improve quality of life. Rigorous studies of other types of treatments are less common, and hence less is known about the specific methods that are most likely to be effective. You will find this same disparity in knowledge reflected in subsequent figures that illustrate feedback loops of treatments for other disorders.

Now that we've discussed depressive disorders, let's look back at what we know about Kay Jamison thus far, and see whether MDD is the diagnosis that best fits her symptoms: She experienced depressed moods, anhedonia, fatigue, and feelings of worthlessness. She also had recurrent thoughts of death, as well as difficulty concentrating. Taken together, these symptoms seem to meet the criteria for MDD. However, she also has symptoms that may be building blocks for the diagnosis of another mood disorder. If her symptoms meet the criteria for any of those building blocks, her diagnosis would change. We examine those building blocks in the next section.

Key Concepts and Facts About Depressive Disorders

- A major depressive episode (MDE) is the building block for a diagnosis of major depressive disorder (MDD): When a person has an MDE, he or she is diagnosed with MDD. Symptoms of an MDE can arise in three areas: affect (anhedonia, weepiness, and decreased sexual interest), behavior (vegetative signs), and cognition (sense of worthlessness or guilt, difficulty concentrating, and recurrent thoughts of death or suicide). Most people who have an MDE return to their premorbid level of functioning after the episode, but some people will have symptoms that do not completely resolve even after several years.

- Depression is becoming increasingly prevalent in younger cohorts. Depression and anxiety disorders have a high comorbidity—around 50%.

- MDD may arise with melancholic features, catatonic features, or psychotic features. Symptoms may also fall into less common patterns, as in atypical depression and chronic depression. In some cases, depression is related to pregnancy and giving birth (postpartum onset) or to seasonal changes in light (seasonal affective disorder).

- A diagnosis of dysthymic disorder requires fewer symptoms than does a diagnosis of MDD; however, the symptoms of dysthymic disorder must persist for a longer time than do symptoms of MDD. People with both dysthymic disorder and MDD are said to have double depression.

- Neurological factors related to depression include low activity in the frontal lobes, and implicate abnormal functioning of various neurotransmitters (dopamine, serotonin, and norepinephrine). The stress–diathesis model of depression highlights the role of increased activity of the HPA axis and of excess cortisol in the blood; an overreactive HPA axis is thought to affect serotonin activity and impair the functioning of the hippocampus. People with atypical depression have the opposite pattern—decreased activity of the HPA axis. Genes can play a role in depression, perhaps by causing a person to have disrupted sleep patterns or by influencing how an individual responds to stressful events, which in turn affects activity of the HPA axis.

- Psychological factors that are associated with depression include a bias toward paying attention to negative stimuli, dysfunctional thoughts (including cognitive distortions related to the negative triad of depression), rumination, a negative attributional style (particularly attributing negative events to internal, global, and stable factors), and learned helplessness.

- Social factors that are associated with depression include stressful life events, social exclusion, and problems with social interactions or relationships (particularly for people who have an insecure attachment). Culture and gender can influence the specific ways that symptoms of depression are expressed.

- Neurological, psychological, and social factors can affect each other through feedback loops, as outlined by the stress–diathesis model and Coyne's interactional theory of depression. According to the stress–diathesis model, abuse or neglect during childhood (a stressor) and increased activity in the HPA axis can lead to overreactive cortisol-releasing cells (a diathesis), which respond strongly to even mild stressors. Psychological factors can create a cognitive vulnerability to depression, which in turn can amplify the negative effects of a stressor and change social interactions. Coyne's theory proposes that among neurologically vulnerable people, their depression-related behaviors may alienate other people, producing social stressors.

- Biomedical treatments that target neurological factors for depressive disorders are medications (SSRIs, TCAs, MAOIs, SNRIs, St. John's wort, and SAMe) and brain stimulation (ECT or TMS).

- Treatments for depression that target psychological factors include CBT (particularly with behavioral activation).

- Treatments that target social factors include IPT and family systems therapy.

continued on next page

Making a Diagnosis
- Reread Case 6.1 about William Styron, and determine whether or not his symptoms meet the criteria for an MDE. Specifically, list which criteria apply and which do not. If you would like more information to determine his diagnosis, what information—specifically—would you want, and in what ways would the information influence your decision?

- Reread Case 6.2 about Marie Osmond, and determine whether or not her symptoms meet the criteria for MDD, post-partum onset. Specifically, list which criteria apply and which do not. If you would like more information to determine her diagnosis, what information—specifically—would you want, and in what ways would the information influence your decision?

- Reread Case 6.3 about Mr. A, and determine whether or not his symptoms meet the criteria for dysthymic disorder. Specifically, list which criteria apply and which do not. If you would like more information to determine his diagnosis, what information—specifically—would you want, and in what ways would the information influence your decision?

Bipolar Disorders

After receiving her Ph.D. in psychology and joining the faculty of the Department of Psychiatry at UCLA, Kay Jamison went to a garden party for faculty. The man who would later become her psychiatrist was there, and years later they discussed the party:

> My memories of the garden party were that I had a fabulous, bubbly, seductive, assured time. My psychiatrist, however, in talking with me about it much later, recollected it very differently. I was, he said, dressed in a remarkably provocative way, totally unlike the conservative manner in which he had seen me dressed over the preceding year. I had on much more makeup than usual and seemed, to him, to be frenetic and far too talkative. He says he remembers having thought to himself, Kay looks manic. I, on the other hand, had thought I was splendid.
>
> (Jamison, 1995, p. 71)

The other set of mood disorders is **bipolar disorders**—in which a person's mood is often persistently and abnormally upbeat or shifts inappropriately from upbeat to markedly down. (Bipolar disorders were previously referred to as *manic-depressive illness* or simply *manic-depression*.) Jamison's behavior at the garden party indicates the opposite of depression—mania.

Building Blocks for Bipolar Disorders

Diagnoses of bipolar disorders are based on four building blocks, which are types of mood episodes. These four building blocks are major depressive episode (the building block of MDD), *manic episode, mixed episode*, and *hypomanic episode*. The configuration of an individual's particular mood episodes determines not only the diagnosis, but also the treatment and prognosis.

Manic Episode

The hallmark of a **manic episode**, such as the one Jamison apparently had when at the garden party, is a discrete period of at least 1 week of abnormally euphoric feelings, intense irritability, or an *expansive mood*. During an **expansive mood**, the person exhibits unceasing, indiscriminate enthusiasm for interpersonal or sexual interactions or for projects. The expansive mood and related behaviors contrast with the individual's usual state. For instance, a normally shy individual may, during a manic episode, have extensive, intimate conversations with strangers in public places. For some, though, the predominant mood during a manic episode may be irritability. Alternatively, during a manic episode, a person's mood can shift between abnormal and persistent euphoria and irritability, as it did for Jamison:

> There is a particular kind of pain, elation, loneliness, and terror involved in this kind of madness. When you're high, it's tremendous. The ideas and feelings are fast and frequent like shooting stars, and you follow them until you find better and brighter ones. Shyness goes, the right words and gestures are suddenly there, the power to

Bipolar disorders
Mood disorders in which a person's mood is often persistently and abnormally upbeat or shifts inappropriately from upbeat to markedly down.

Manic episode
A period of at least 1 week characterized by abnormal and persistent euphoria or expansive mood or irritability.

Expansive mood
A mood that involves unceasing, indiscriminate enthusiasm for interpersonal or sexual interactions or for projects.

captivate others a felt certainty. There are interests found in uninteresting people. Sensuality is pervasive and the desire to seduce and be seduced irresistible. Feelings of ease, intensity, power, well-being, financial omnipotence, and euphoria pervade one's marrow. But, somewhere, this changes. The fast ideas are far too fast, and there are far too many; overwhelming confusion replaces clarity. Memory goes. Humor and absorption on friends' faces are replaced by fear and concerns. Everything previously moving with the grain is now against—you are irritable, angry, frightened, uncontrollable, and enmeshed totally in the blackest caves of the mind. You never knew those caves were there. It will never end, for madness carves its own reality.

(1995, p. 67)

Table 6.7 lists the criteria for a manic episode.

Table 6.7 ▸ DSM-IV-TR Diagnostic Criteria for a Manic Episode

A. A distinct period of abnormally and persistently elevated, expansive, or irritable mood, lasting at least 1 week (or any duration if hospitalization is necessary).

B. During the period of mood disturbance, three (or more) of the following symptoms have persisted (four if the mood is only irritable) and have been present to a significant degree:

(1) inflated self-esteem or grandiosity

(2) decreased need for sleep (e.g., feels rested after only 3 hours of sleep)

(3) more talkative than usual or pressure to keep talking

(4) flight of ideas or subjective experience that thoughts are racing

(5) distractibility (i.e., attention too easily drawn to unimportant or irrelevant external stimuli)

(6) increase in goal-directed activity (either socially, at work or school, or sexually) or psychomotor agitation

(7) excessive involvement in pleasurable activities that have a high potential for painful consequences (e.g., engaging in unrestrained buying sprees, sexual indiscretions, or foolish business investments)

C. The symptoms do not meet criteria for a mixed episode [discussed later in the chapter].

D. The mood disturbance is sufficiently severe to cause marked impairment in occupational functioning or in usual social activities or relationships with others, or to necessitate hospitalization to prevent harm to self or others, or there are psychotic features.

E. The symptoms are not due to the direct physiological effects of a substance (e.g., a drug of abuse, a medication, or other treatment) or a general medical condition (e.g., hyperthyroidism).

Note: Manic-like episodes that are clearly caused by somatic antidepressant treatment (e.g., medication, electroconvulsive therapy, light therapy) should not count toward a diagnosis of bipolar I disorder [discussed later in the chapter].

Source: Reprinted with permission from the DSM-IV-TR Casebook: A Learning Companion to the Diagnostic and Statistical Manual of Mental Disorders, Fourth Edition, Text Revision, (Copyright 2002) American Psychiatric Association.

As noted in Table 6.7, in a manic episode, a person may begin projects (one type of goal-directed activity, see criterion B6 in Table 6.7), even though he or she doesn't possess the special knowledge or training required to complete the project; for instance, the person might try to install a dishwasher, despite knowing nothing about plumbing. Moreover, when manic, some people are uncritically grandiose—often believing themselves to have superior abilities or a special relationship to political or entertainment figures; these beliefs may reach delusional proportions, to the point where an individual may stalk a celebrity, believing that he or she is destined to marry that famous person.

During a manic episode, a person needs much less sleep—so much less that he or she may be able to go for days without it, yet not feel tired. Similarly, when manic, the affected person may speak rapidly or loudly and may be difficult to interrupt; he or she may talk nonstop for hours on end, not letting anyone else get a word in edgewise. Moreover, when manic, the individual rarely sits still (Cassano et al., 2009). Another symptom of mania is a **flight of ideas**, thoughts that race faster than they can be said. When speaking while in this state of mind, the person may flit from topic to topic, as illustrated in Case 6.4; flight of ideas has commonly been described as something like watching two or three television programs simultaneously.

CASE 6.4 ▶ FROM THE INSIDE: Flight of Ideas

Here is an example of a flight of ideas, which a man wrote in his diary during a manic episode:

I have to choose my words very carefully. For what I am doing is, I believe, something which has not very often been attempted (BEELZEBUB ON BED in form of blue fly). It is to think at precisely the same point in the space-time continuum by both methods of thought (Coughing, running at the nose, bottom of feet wet) (blue check handkerchief)—inductive and deductive (so hot, have to remove coat and purple pullover query CAESER'S) artistic and rational (itching), negative and positive—in the terminology expounded [previously] . . .

(Custace, 1952, pp. 138–139)

During a manic episode, the person may also be highly distractible and unable to screen out irrelevant details in the environment or in conversations, as evidenced by the parenthetical comment about the blue check handkerchief in Case 6.4. Another symptom of a manic episode is excessive planning of, and participation in, multiple activities. A college student with this symptom might participate in eight time-intensive extracurricular activities, including a theatrical production, a musical performance, a community service group, and a leadership position in a campus political group.

The expansiveness, unwarranted optimism, grandiosity, and poor judgment of a manic episode can lead to the reckless pursuit of pleasurable activities, such as spending sprees or unusual sexual behavior (infidelity or indiscriminate sexual encounters with strangers). These activities often lead to adverse consequences: credit card debt from the spending sprees or sexually transmitted diseases, including HIV, from unprotected sexual encounters.

People who have had a manic episode report afterward that they felt as if their senses were sharper during the episode—that their ability to smell or hear was better. Unfortunately, during a manic episode, individuals often don't recognize that they're ill; this was the case with Jamison, who, for many years, resisted getting treatment.

Typically, a manic episode begins suddenly, with symptoms escalating rapidly over a few days; symptoms can last from a few weeks to several months. Compared to an MDE, a manic episode is briefer and ends more abruptly.

Jack Sullivan/Alamy

During a manic episode, individuals may gamble excessively or act antisocially, behaviors they would never otherwise do. Similarly, people who are otherwise very ethical may behave unethically during a manic episode.

Mixed Episode

Another building block for diagnosing bipolar disorders is a *mixed episode*—an episode of mood disturbance characterized by symptoms of both manic *and* major depressive episodes. Prominent symptoms usually include:

• agitation,

• insomnia,

• appetite dysregulation,

• psychotic features, and

• suicidal thinking.

Flight of ideas
Thoughts that race faster than they can be said.

A mixed episode may last weeks to months, at which point all or some of the symptoms may disappear. Alternatively, a mixed episode may evolve into an MDE or, less often, into a manic episode. Mixed episodes are more common in young people and those over 60 years old, and they are more common among males than females (American Psychiatric Association, 2000).

Hypomanic Episode

The last building block for diagnosing bipolar disorders is a *hypomanic episode*, which is a distinct period of persistent and pervasive elated, irritable, or euphoric mood that is less distressing than mania and doesn't impair functioning, but it is clearly different from the individual's nondepressed state. Hypomania does not have psychotic features, nor does it require hospitalization; hypomania rarely includes the flight of ideas that bedevils someone in the grips of mania (American Psychiatric Association, 2000). In contrast to the grandiose thoughts people have about themselves during manic episodes, during hypomanic episodes people are uncritically self-confident but not grandiose. When hypomanic, some people may be more efficient and creative than they typically are (American Psychiatric Association, 2000). During a hypomanic episode, people may tend to talk loudly and rapidly, but, unlike what happens when people are manic, it is possible to interrupt them.

Two key features distinguish manic and hypomanic episodes:

1. Hypomania does not impair functioning; mania does.

2. Symptoms of a hypomanic episode must last for a minimum of 4 days, compared to 1 week for a manic episode.

Some research suggests that the 4-day minimum duration for a hypomanic episode specified in DSM-IV-TR may be too restrictive and that 2 days may be a more appropriate criterion for duration (Akiskal, 2003; Angst et al., 2003). Like a manic episode, a hypomanic episode begins suddenly; symptoms rapidly escalate during the first day or two but can last several weeks to months.

Kay Jamison remembered her episodes of hypomania fondly, which made it all the harder for her to continue to take the medication that evened out her moods:

> I tend to compare my current [medicated] self with the best I have been, which is when I have been mildly manic . . . most productive, most intense, most outgoing and effervescent. In short, for myself, I am a hard act to follow.
>
> (1995, p. 92)

The Two Types of Bipolar Disorder

The presence of different types of mood episodes—different building blocks—leads to different diagnoses. According to DSM-IV-TR, there are two types of bipolar disorder: bipolar I disorder and bipolar II disorder. Another disorder—cyclothymia (to be discussed later)—is characterized by symptoms of hypomania and depression that do not meet the criteria for the two types of bipolar disorder we are about to discuss.

Bipolar I Versus Bipolar II Disorder

The presence of manic *symptoms*—but not a manic episode—is the common element of the two types of bipolar disorder. The types differ in the severity of the manic symptoms. To receive the diagnosis of the more severe *bipolar I disorder*, a person must have a manic or mixed episode; an MDE may also occur with bipolar I. Thus, just as an MDE automatically leads to a diagnosis of MDD, having a mixed or manic episode automatically leads to a diagnosis of bipolar I. In contrast, to be diagnosed with *bipolar II disorder*, a person must alternate

During a hypomanic episode, which is less intense than a manic episode, an individual may go on spending sprees or make foolish investments.

David Woolley/Getty Images

Table 6.8 ▶ DSM-IV-TR Diagnostic Criteria for Bipolar II Disorder

A. Presence (or history) of one or more major depressive episodes.

B. Presence (or history) of at least one hypomanic episode.

C. There has never been a manic episode or a mixed episode.

D. The mood symptoms in Criteria A and B are not better accounted for by schizoaffective disorder and are not superimposed on schizophrenia, schizophreniform disorder, delusional disorder, or psychotic disorder not otherwise specified [all discussed in Chapter 12].

E. The symptoms cause clinically significant distress or impairment in social, occupational, or other important areas of functioning.

Source: Reprinted with permission from the Diagnostic and Statistical Manual of Mental Disorders, Fourth Edition, Text Revision, (Copyright 2002) American Psychiatric Association.

between hypomanic episodes and MDEs (see Table 6.8); bipolar II can be thought of as less severe because of the absence of manic episodes. Table 6.9 provides additional facts about bipolar disorders.

Both types of bipolar disorder can include **rapid cycling** of moods, defined as having four or more episodes that meet the criteria for any type of mood episode within 1 year (American Psychiatric Association, 2000). Rapid cycling is more common with bipolar II disorder and in women (Papadimitriou et al., 2005). Unfortunately, rapid cycling of either type of bipolar disorder is associated with more difficulty in finding an effective treatment (Ozcan, Shivakumar, & Suppes, 2006). The specifiers for MDD—features of psychosis, catatonia, melancholia, atypical, and postpartum onset—also apply to the MDEs experienced by people diagnosed with bipolar disorders.

Even for those who do not have rapid cycling, changes in the sleep-wake cycle (such as sleep deprivation and moving across time zones) can trigger or intensify a manic, mixed, or hypomanic episode (Johnson & Roberts, 1995; Leibenluft, 2008; Leibenluft et al., 1996). Moreover, those who are most likely to relapse have mood symptoms that do not completely clear up after a mood episode ends (although the symptoms do diminish enough that the criteria for a mood episode are no longer met; Judd et al., 2008).

As with depression, people of different races and ethnicities are equally likely to be afflicted with bipolar disorders (American Psychiatric Association, 2000). Some mental health clinicians, however, tend to diagnose schizophrenia instead of a bipolar disorder when evaluating black individuals (Neighbors et al., 2003).

From Jamison's descriptions, some of her experiences, such as those at the faculty garden party, appear to have been manic episodes. Because she had at least one manic episode, Jamison would be diagnosed with bipolar I disorder. The tentative diagnosis of MDD proposed earlier in the chapter would be changed to bipolar disorder in light of Jamison's history of at least one manic episode.

Bipolar Disorder and Creativity?

Are people with bipolar disorder more creative? Jamison and her colleagues (Goodwin & Jamison, 1990; Jamison, 1989; Jamison et al., 1980; see also Hershman & Lieb, 1988, 1998) have argued that a "loosening" of thought that occurs during a manic episode enhances creativity. However, studies supporting this argument often have had methodological problems. For instance, some studies have focused on historical figures (such as famous composers and writers), but these "participants" with bipolar disorder were selected *because*

Rapid cycling (of moods)
Having four or more episodes that meet the criteria for any type of mood episode within 1 year.

Table 6.9 ▸ Bipolar Disorders Facts at a Glance

Prevalence

- Between 0.4% and 1.6% of American suffer from bipolar I disorder.
- Approximately 0.5–1% of Americans will develop bipolar II disorder in their lifetimes (Merikangas et al., 2007).
- Approximately 10–15% of adolescents who are diagnosed as having recurrent MDEs will go on to develop bipolar I disorder.

Onset

- Both men and women begin to have symptoms of bipolar I disorder by the age of 20, on average, although the symptoms do not necessarily include full-blown manic attacks.

Comorbidity

- Up to 65% of those with any bipolar disorder are also diagnosed with another Axis I disorder (McElroy et al., 2001), such as anorexia nervosa, bulimia nervosa, attention deficit hyperactivity disorder, panic disorder, or social phobia (American Psychiatric Association, 2000; Merikangas et al., 2007).
- Around 60% of people with a bipolar disorder also have substance-related problems (Regier et al., 1990).

Course

- Individuals who have had one manic episode have a 90% chance of having at least one further manic episode.
- People who have bipolar II disorder are less likely to develop psychotic symptoms during an MDE than are people with bipolar I disorder.
- Bipolar II disorder typically has a more chronic, though less severe, course than bipolar I disorder (Judd et al., 2003).
- Approximately 60–70% of those with either type of bipolar disorder will have an MDE after a manic or hypomanic episode.
- People with either type of bipolar disorder have MDEs that are more severe and lead to more lost work days than do people with depressive disorders (Kessler et al., 2006).

Gender Differences

- Almost half of men with bipolar I disorder have their first full-blown manic episode by age 25; in contrast, only one third of women have their first manic episode by that age (Kennedy et al., 2005).
- Bipolar I disorder is equally common among males and females, but bipolar II disorder is more common among females than among males.
- In males, the number of manic episodes (or hypomanic in the case of bipolar II disorder) often equals or exceeds the number of MDEs, whereas in women, MDEs predominate.
- For women, having a bipolar disorder boosts the risk of developing mood episodes (of any kind) immediately after giving birth.
- As with depressive episodes, symptoms of any other type of mood episode (manic, hypomanic, or mixed) may get worse premenstrually.

Source: Unless otherwise noted, the source for information is American Psychiatric Association, 2000.

they had obvious creative genius; they were not randomly selected from a general population of people with bipolar disorder. Also, some of the studies have relied on biographical accounts of the family and friends of such creative people; such sources and the biographers typically are not mental health clinicians and so they may be less able to judge whether the creative person's behavior meets the criteria for a disorder. In an effort to circumvent such problems, some studies have examined the relationship between bipolar disorder and creativity by asking supposedly "blind" raters to assess various creative works, which included those of famous creative geniuses. However, the raters may have known whose works they were assessing, which would have biased their ratings (Richards et al., 1988; Rothenberg, 2001).

In contrast to the view of Jamison and her colleagues that mania enhances creativity, others have claimed that mental illness may be independent of creativity (Richards et al., 1988; Rothenberg, 2001). One study compared the creativity of people with bipolar disorder to the creativity of: (1) people who had a psychological disorder that was *not* a mood disorder; and, (2) people who did not have any psychological disorder. Bipolar disorder did not confer a creative advantage (Richards et al., 1988).

Cyclothymic Disorder

Just as dysthymia is a more chronic but less intense version of MDD, *cyclothymia* is a more chronic but less intense version of bipolar II disorder. The main feature of **cyclothymic disorder** is a chronic, fluctuating mood disturbance with numerous periods of hypomanic symptoms and numerous periods of depressive symptoms that do not meet the criteria for an MDE (see Table 6.10). Cyclothymia has a lifetime prevalence of 0.4–1.0% and affects men and women equally often (American Psychiatric Association, 2000). Some people may function particularly well during the hypomanic periods of cyclothymic disorder, but be impaired during depressive periods; this diagnosis is given only if the individual's depressed mood leads him or her to be distressed or impaired. Thus, someone with cyclothymic disorder may feel really upbeat and energetic when hypomanic and begin several projects at work or volunteer to complete projects ahead of schedule. However, when having symptoms of depression, he or she may have some difficulty concentrating or mustering the energy to work on the projects, and so fall behind on the deadlines.

Getty Images

Are people with bipolar disorders more creative? Although actress, author, and screenwriter Carrie Fisher has a bipolar disorder, many people with such a disorder are not exceptionally creative, and many creative people do not have such a disorder. Research suggests that the two variables—the presence of bipolar disorder and creativity—may be unrelated (Rothenberg, 2001).

Table 6.10 ▸ DSM-IV-TR Diagnostic Criteria for Cyclothymic Disorder
A. For at least 2 years, the presence of numerous periods with hypomanic symptoms and numerous periods with depressive symptoms that do not meet criteria for a major depressive episode.   Note: In children and adolescents, the duration must be at least 1 year.
B. During the above 2-year period (1 year in children and adolescents), the person has not been without the symptoms in Criterion A for more than 2 months at a time.
C. No major depressive episode, manic episode, or mixed episode has been present during the first 2 years of the disturbance.   Note: After the initial 2 years (1 year in children and adolescents) of cyclothymic disorder, there may be superimposed manic or mixed episodes (in which case both bipolar I disorder and cyclothymic disorder may be diagnosed) or major depressive episodes (in which case both bipolar II disorder and cyclothymic disorder may be diagnosed).
D. The symptoms in Criterion A are not better accounted for by schizoaffective disorder and are not superimposed on schizophrenia, schizophreniform disorder, delusional disorder, or psychotic disorder not otherwise specified [all these disorders are discussed in Chapter 12].
E. The symptoms are not due to the direct physiological effects of a substance (e.g., a drug of abuse, a medication) or a general medical condition (e.g., hyperthyroidism).
F. The symptoms cause clinically significant distress or impairment in social, occupational, or other important areas of functioning.

Source: Reprinted with permission from the Diagnostic and Statistical Manual of Mental Disorders, Fourth Edition, Text Revision, (Copyright 2002) American Psychiatric Association.

Cyclothymic disorder
A mood disorder characterized by chronic, fluctuating mood disturbance with numerous periods of hypomanic symptoms and numerous periods of depressive symptoms that do not meet the criteria for an MDE.

Cyclothymia usually unfolds slowly during early adolescence or young adulthood, and it has a chronic course, as Mr. F's history reveals (see Case 6.5). Approximately 15–50% of people with cyclothymia go on to develop some type of bipolar disorder (American Psychiatric Association, 2000).

CASE 6.5 ▶ FROM THE OUTSIDE: Cyclothymic Disorder

At his girlfriend's insistence, Mr. F., a 27-year-old single man, goes for a psychiatric evaluation. Mr. F. reports that he is excessively energetic, unable to sleep, irritable, and isn't satisfied with the humdrum nature of his work and personal life. He was often dissatisfied and irritable for periods of time ranging from a few days to a few weeks. These periods alternate with longer periods of feeling dejected, hopeless, worn out, and wanting to die; his moods can shift up to 20–30 times each year, and he describes himself as on an "emotional roller-coaster," and has been for as long as he can remember. He twice impulsively tried to commit suicide with alcohol and sleeping pills, although he has never had prominent vegetative symptoms, nor has he had psychotic symptoms.

(Adapted from Frances & Ross, 1996, p. 140)

Because Jamison had both MDEs and manic episodes, her symptoms do not meet the criteria for cyclothymic disorder. Figure 6.4 identifies the key mood episodes that are the diagnostic building blocks of the various mood disorders.

Understanding Bipolar Disorders

> Manic-depression . . . is an illness that is biological in its origins, yet one that feels psychological in the experience of it; an illness that is unique in conferring advantage and pleasure, yet one that brings in its wake almost unendurable suffering and, not infrequently, suicide.
>
> I am fortunate that I have not died from my illness, fortunate in having received the best medical care available, and fortunate in having the friends, colleagues, and family that I do.
>
> (Jamison, 1995, p. 6)

Kay Jamison made her professional life into a quest to understand mood disorders and why some people develop them. Let's examine what is known about bipolar disorders using the neuropsychosocial approach.

Neurological Factors

As with depressive disorders, both distinctive brain functioning and genetics are associated with bipolar disorders.

Brain Systems

One hint about a neurological factor that may contribute to bipolar disorders is the finding that the amygdala is enlarged in people who have been diagnosed with a bipolar disorder (Altshuler et al., 1998). This finding is pertinent because the amygdala is involved in expressing emotion, as well as regulating mood and accessing emotional memories (LeDoux, 1996). A larger amygdala may be a more emotionally reactive amygdala. Consistent with this idea, researchers have also found that the amygdala is more active in people who

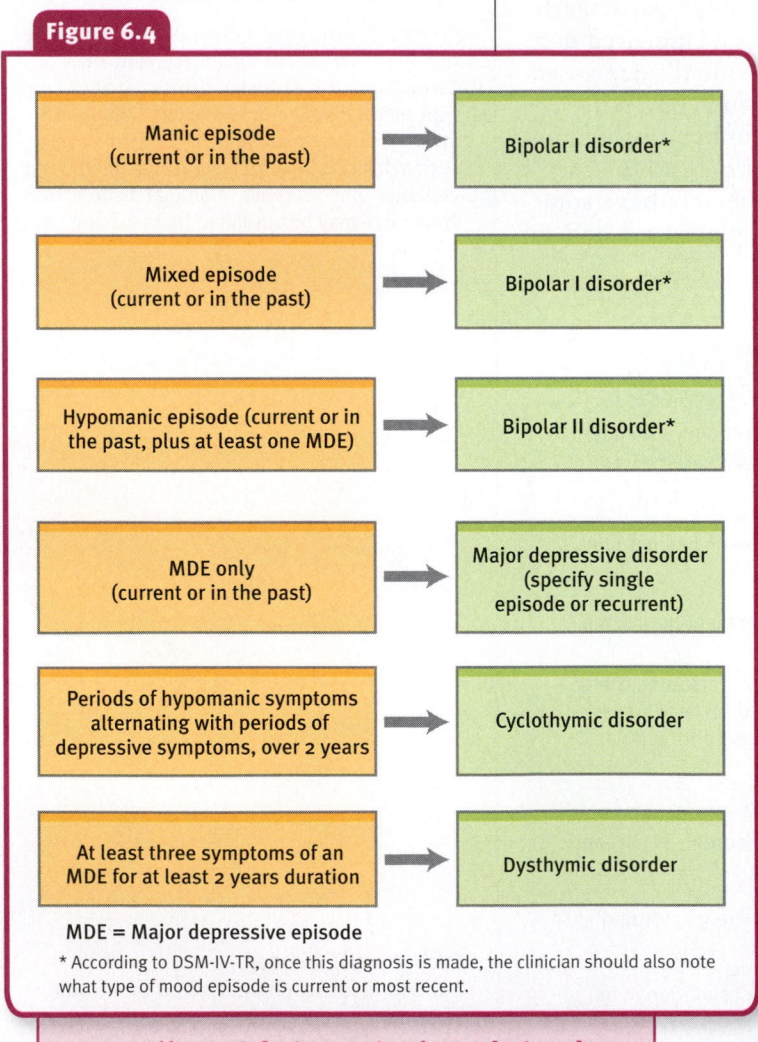

Figure 6.4

Manic episode (current or in the past)	→	Bipolar I disorder*
Mixed episode (current or in the past)	→	Bipolar I disorder*
Hypomanic episode (current or in the past, plus at least one MDE)	→	Bipolar II disorder*
MDE only (current or in the past)	→	Major depressive disorder (specify single episode or recurrent)
Periods of hypomanic symptoms alternating with periods of depressive symptoms, over 2 years	→	Cyclothymic disorder
At least three symptoms of an MDE for at least 2 years duration	→	Dysthymic disorder

MDE = Major depressive episode

* According to DSM-IV-TR, once this diagnosis is made, the clinician should also note what type of mood episode is current or most recent.

6.4 ▶ Differential Diagnosis of Mood Disorders

are experiencing a manic episode than it is in a control group of people who are not manic (Altshuler et al., 2005). The more reactive the amygdala, the more readily it triggers strong emotional reactions—and hence the fact that it is especially active during a manic episode makes sense.

Neural Communication

As we've discussed earlier in this chapter and in Chapter 2, imbalances in the levels of certain chemicals in the brain can contribute to psychological disorders. There's reason to believe that serotonin (Goodwin & Jamison, 1990) and norepinephrine play a role in bipolar disorders. For example, treatment with lithium (discussed shortly) not only lowers norepinephrine levels, but also reduces the symptoms of a bipolar disorder (Rosenbaum et al., 2005). As noted in Chapter 2, serotonin is an inhibitory neurotransmitter, and low levels of it are associated with depression (Mundo et al., 2000). However, we've also emphasized that glitches in neural communication contribute to psychological disorders in complex ways; the problem rarely (if ever) is limited to an imbalance of a single substance, but rather typically involves complex interactions among substances. In fact, researchers have also reported that the left frontal lobes of patients with mania produce too much of the excitatory neurotransmitter glutamate (Michael et al., 2003), so at least three neurotransmitters—serotonin, norepinephrine, and glutamate—are involved in bipolar disorders. Thus, changing the level of any one of these substances above is not likely to be sufficient.

Genetics

One day, Jamison and another scientist who does research on mood disorders sat down together, and Jamison drew her family tree: circles represented women, squares represented men, and darkened shapes noted family members who had a mood disorder. Here is what Jamison remembers about this:

> I was amazed at how many of my squares and circles were darkened, or darkened with a question mark placed underneath (I knew, for instance, that my great-uncle had spent virtually all of his adult life in an asylum, but I didn't know what his diagnosis had been). Manic-depressive illness occurred repeatedly, throughout the three generations I had knowledge of, on my father's side of the family; asterisks, representing suicide attempts, showed up like a starfield. My mother's side of the family, in comparison, was squeaky clean.

(p. 189)

Jamison's discovery of her paternal relatives' mood disorders mirrors the results of research on the frequency of mood disorders in families: Twin and adoption studies suggest that genes influence who will develop bipolar disorders. If one monozygotic twin has a bipolar disorder, the co-twin has a 40–70% chance of developing the disorder; if one dizygotic twin has the disorder, the co-twin has only about a 5% chance of developing the disorder, which is still over twice the prevalence in the population in general (Fridman et al., 2003; Kieseppä et al., 2004; McGuffin et al., 2003). In general, if you have a first-degree relative who has bipolar disorder, you have a 4–24% risk of developing the disorder (American Psychiatric Association, 2000).

Depressive disorders and bipolar disorders—even though they now are considered distinct disorders—may be different manifestations of the same genetic vulnerability (Akiskal, 1996; Angst, 1998). When a dizygotic twin has a bipolar disorder, the other twin has an 80% chance of developing any mood disorder (MDD, dysthymia, a bipolar disorder, or cyclothymia; Karkowski & Kendler, 1997; McGuffin et al., 2003; Vehmanen, Kaprio, & Loennqvist, 1995). Even so, researchers do not know how specific genes contribute to an inherited vulnerability for mood disorders. But they do know that genes alone cannot account for the development of such disorders—and thus, we next will examine the role that psychological factors play in bipolar disorders.

Psychological Factors: Thoughts and Attributions

Most research on the contribution of psychological factors to bipolar disorders focuses on cognitive distortions and automatic negative thoughts, which not only are common among people with depression but also plague people with a bipolar disorder during MDEs. In fact, research suggests that when depressed, people with either MDD or a bipolar disorder have a similar internal attributional style for negative events (Lyon, Startup, & Bentall, 1999; Scott et al., 2000). Mirroring these results, people with cyclothymia or dysthymia have a similar negative attributional style (Alloy et al., 1999).

In addition, even after a manic episode is completely resolved, up to a third of people may have residual cognitive deficits, ranging from difficulties with attention, learning, and memory to problems with executive functioning (planning and decision making) and problem solving (Martínez-Arán et al., 2000, 2005; Kolur et al., 2006; Rubinztein et al., 2000; Scott et al., 2000; Thompson et al., 2005; Zubieta et al., 2001). Moreover, the more mood episodes a person has, the more severe these deficits tend to be. Researchers propose that the persistent cognitive deficits associated with mania should become part of the diagnostic criteria for bipolar disorders, in addition to criteria on mood-related behaviors (Phillips & Frank, 2006).

Research results have not yet established a cause-and-effect relationship between the cognitive deficits and the mood symptoms of bipolar disorders. For instance, it is possible that having more episodes of mania or depression somehow causes the enduring cognitive deficits. But it is also possible that aspects of their cognitive deficits lead some people to be more likely to have additional mood episodes. Alternatively, it is possible that some other, as yet unidentified, variable leads to both the enduring cognitive deficits and the frequency of mood episodes.

Social Factors: Social and Environmental Stressors

Social factors such as starting a new job or moving to a different city can also affect the course of bipolar disorders (Goodwin & Jamison, 1990; Malkoff-Schwartz et al., 1998). Stress appears to be part of the process that leads to a first episode (Kessing, Agerbo, & Mortensen, 2004); people who develop a bipolar disorder experience significant stressors in their lives before their first episode (Goodwin & Ghaemi, 1998; Tsuchiya, Agerbo, & Mortensen, 2005). Stress can also worsen the course of the disorder (Johnson & Miller, 1997). In addition, stress—in particular, family-related stress—may contribute to relapse; people who live with family members who are critical of them are more likely to relapse than those whose family members are not critical (Honig et al., 1997; Miklowitz et al., 1988).

Social factors can also have indirect effects, as occurs when a new job disrupts a person's sleep pattern, which in turn triggers neurological factors that can lead to a mood episode (American Psychological Association, 2000).

FEEDBACK LOOPS IN ACTION: Bipolar Disorders

Bipolar disorders have a clear genetic and neurological basis, but feedback loops still operate among the neurological, psychological, and social factors associated with these disorders (see Figure 6.5). Consider the effects of sleep deprivation. It may directly or indirectly affect neurological functioning, making the individual more vulnerable to a manic or depressive episode. Moreover, like people with depression, people with a bipolar disorder tend to have an attributional style (psychological factor) that may make them more vulnerable to becoming depressed. In turn, their attributional style may affect how these people interact with others (social factor), such as their responses to problems in relationships. Even after a mood episode is over, residual problems with cognitive functioning—which affects problem solving, planning, or decision making—can adversely influence the work and social life of a person with a bipolar disorder.

Figure 6.5

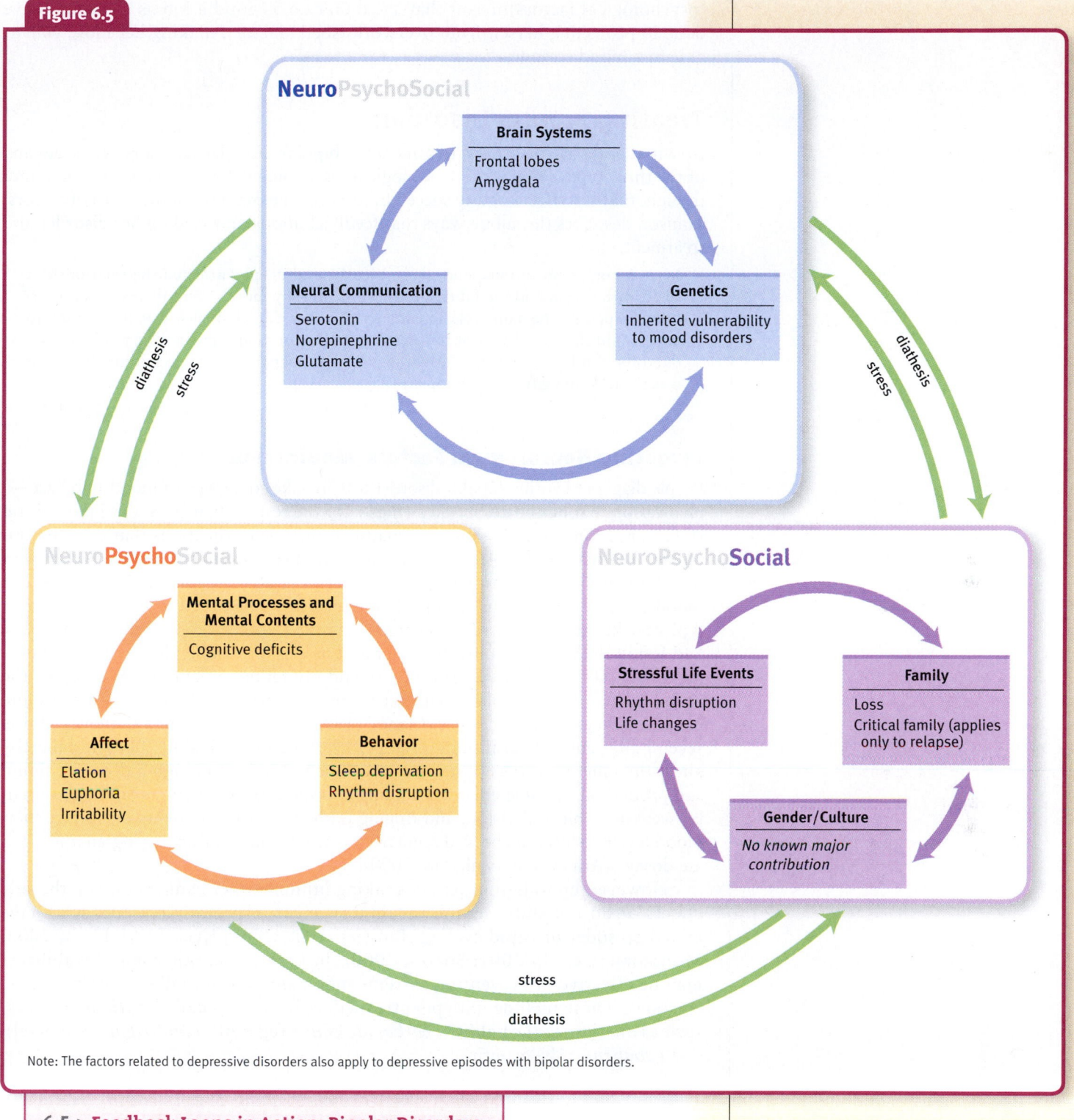

NeuroPsychoSocial

Brain Systems

Frontal lobes
Amygdala

Neural Communication

Serotonin
Norepinephrine
Glutamate

Genetics

Inherited vulnerability
to mood disorders

diathesis
stress

diathesis
stress

NeuroPsychoSocial

**Mental Processes and
Mental Contents**

Cognitive deficits

Affect

Elation
Euphoria
Irritability

Behavior

Sleep deprivation
Rhythm disruption

NeuroPsychoSocial

Stressful Life Events

Rhythm disruption
Life changes

Family

Loss
Critical family (applies
only to relapse)

Gender/Culture

*No known major
contribution*

stress

diathesis

Note: The factors related to depressive disorders also apply to depressive episodes with bipolar disorders.

6.5 ▶ Feedback Loops in Action: Bipolar Disorders

We can now understand Jamison's bipolar disorder as arising from a confluence of neuropsychosocial factors and feedback loops. Her family history provided a strong genetic component to her illness, which has a clear neurological basis (neurological factors). Her struggle against recognizing that she had an illness (psychological factors) meant that she didn't do as good a job as she could have done in protecting herself from overwork (social factor), making her more vulnerable to a mood episode.

Treating Bipolar Disorders

As with depressive disorders, treatment for bipolar disorders can directly target any of the three types of factors—neurological, psychological, and social. Keep in mind, though, that the effects of any successful treatment extend to all the types of factors. Jamison describes the subtle ways that feedback loops operated on her disorder and treatment:

> My temperament, moods, and illness clearly, and deeply, affected the relationships I had with others and the fabric of my work. But my moods were themselves powerfully shaped by the same relationships and work. The challenge was in learning to understand the complexity of this mutual beholdenness and in learning to distinguish the roles of lithium, will, and insight in getting well and in leading a meaningful life. It was the task and gift of psychotherapy.
>
> (1995, p. 88)

Targeting Neurological Factors: Medication

People diagnosed with a bipolar disorder usually take some type of **mood stabilizer**—a medication that minimizes mood swings—for the rest of their lives. (The term *mood stabilizer* is sometimes used more broadly to include medications that decrease impulsive behavior and violent aggression.) Mood stabilizers can reduce recurrences of both manic and depressive episodes (Arana & Rosenbaum, 2000). The oldest mood stabilizer is **lithium;** technically the medication is called *lithium carbonate*, a type of salt. Jamison describes her response to the drug: "I took [lithium] faithfully and found that life was a much stabler and more predictable place than I had ever reckoned. My moods were still intense and my temperament rather quick to the boil, but I could make plans with far more certainty and the periods of absolute blackness were fewer and less extreme" (1995, p. 153). Lithium apparently affects several different neurotransmitters (Jope, 1999; Lenox & Hahn, 2000) and thereby alters the inner workings of neurons (Friedrich, 2005). Too high a dose of lithium can produce severe side effects, including coordination problems, vomiting, muscular weakness, blurred vision, and ringing in the ears; thus, patients must have their blood levels of lithium checked regularly to ensure that they are taking an appropriate dosage (Arana & Rosenbaum, 2000).

However, up to half of patients taking lithium either cannot tolerate the side effects or do not show significant improvement, especially patients who have mixed episodes or rapid cycling (Burgess et al., 2001; Keck & McElroy, 2003; Montgomery et al., 2001; Soares, 2000). In such cases, other mood stabilizers may be effective in preventing extreme mood shifts, especially recurring manic episodes. These include antiepileptic medications (also called *anticonvulsants*) such as *divalproex* (Depakote), *carbamazepine* (Tegretol), *lamotrigine* (Lamictal), and *gabapentin* (Neurontin).

Some people with bipolar disorders stop taking mood stabilizers, not necessarily because of the common side effects (such as thirst, frequent urination, and diarrhea), but because the medication does what it's supposed to do—evens out their moods (Arana & Rosenbaum, 2000; Rosa et al., 2007). Some of these people report that they miss aspects of their manic episodes and feel that the medication blunts their emotions.

Mood stabilizers aren't the only medications given for bipolar disorders. Patients with a bipolar disorder may be given antidepressant medication for depression, but such medications can induce mania and so should be taken along with a mood stabilizer; in addition, patients with a bipolar disorder who take antidepressant

Mood stabilizer
A category of medication that minimizes mood swings.

Lithium
The oldest mood stabilizer; it is administered as a salt.

medication should take it for as brief a period as possible (Rosenbaum et al., 2005). Antidepressants may not be prescribed for people with rapid cycling, however, because these drugs can exacerbate the cycling (Schneck et al., 2008). For a manic episode, an antipsychotic medication such as *olanzapine* (Zyprexa) or *aripiprazole* (Ablify), or a high dose of a benzodiazepine may be given (Arana & Rosenbaum, 2000; Keck et al., 2009).

Despite the number of medications available to treat bipolar disorders, mood episodes still recur; in one study, half of the participants developed a subsequent mood episode within 2 years of recovery from an earlier episode (Perlis, Ostacher, et al., 2006).

Targeting Psychological Factors: Thoughts, Moods, and Relapse Prevention

Medication can be an effective component of treatment for bipolar disorders, but often it isn't the only component. Treatment that targets psychological factors focuses on helping patients develop patterns of thought and behavior that minimize the risk of relapse (Fava et al., 2001; Jones, 2004; Scott & Gutierrez, 2004), including consistently taking medication. CBT can help patients to stick with their medication schedules, develop better sleeping strategies, and recognize early signs of mood episodes, such as needing less sleep (Ball et al.,

Figure 6.6

Daily Log of Social Rhythms

Directions:
- Write the ideal target time you would like to do these daily activities.
- Record the time you actually did the activity each day.
- Record the people involved in the activity: 0=Alone; 1=Others present; 2=Others actively involved; 3=Others very stimulating

Date (week of):

Activity	Target Time	Sunday		Monday		Tuesday		Wednesday		Thursday		Friday		Saturday	
		Time	People	Time	People	Time	People	Time	People	Time	People	Time	People	Time	People
Out of bed															
First contact with other person															
Start work/school/ volunteer/family care															
Dinner															
To bed															
Rate MOOD each day from −5 to +5 −5=very depressed +5=very elated															

6.6 ▸ Assessing Social Rhythms One component of interpersonal and social rhythm therapy helps patients determine what types of social rhythm disruptions are likely to trigger a mood episode. A daily social rhythm log, like this one, can help patients identify the disruptions that increase their mood symptoms. Once they identify these disruptions, they can develop strategies to minimize them.

Source: Frank, Gonzalez, & Fagiolini, 2006, p. 984, Figure 2. For more information see the Permissions section.

2006; Brondolo & Mas, 2001; Frank et al., 2005; Miklowitz, 2008; Miklowitz et al., 2007).

Targeting Social Factors: Interacting with Others

Treatments that target social factors are designed to help patients minimize disruptions in their social patterns and develop strategies for better social interactions (Lam et al., 2000). One such treatment *interpersonal and social rhythm therapy* (IPSRT), was adapted from interpersonal therapy specifically for people with bipolar disorders (Frank et al., 1999) to address social factors that contribute toward relapse of mania. As in IPT, IPSRT sessions focus on identifying themes of social stressors, such as a relationship conflict (a *role dispute* in IPT; see Chapter 4) that arises because the partners have different expectations of the relationship. Treatment can then focus on developing effective ways for the patient to minimize such social stressors. In addition, IPSRT focuses on the timing of events (such as arranging weekend activities so that the patient wakes up at the same time each morning and goes to sleep at the same time each night—weekend and weekday), on increasing overall regularity in daily life (such as having meals at relatively fixed times during the day; see Figure 6.6), and helping the patient *want* to maintain regularity. IPSRT plus medication is more effective than medication alone (Frank et al., 1999; Miklowitz, 2008; Miklowitz et al., 2007).

Other treatments that target social factors focus on the family, educating family members about bipolar disorder and providing emergency counseling during crises (Miklowitz et al., 2000, 2003, 2007). Also, family therapy that reduces the critical behavior of family members can reduce relapses (Honig et al., 1997). Another treatment with a social focus is group therapy or a self-help group, either of which can decrease the sense of isolation or shame that people with bipolar disorders may experience; group members support each other as they try to make positive changes.

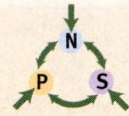

FEEDBACK LOOPS IN TREATMENT: Bipolar Disorder

Both Jamison and her psychiatrist understood that treatment could affect multiple factors:

> No pill can help me deal with the problem of not wanting to take pills; likewise, no amount of psychotherapy alone can prevent my manias and depressions. I need both. It is an odd thing, owing life to pills, one's own quirks and tenacities, and this unique, strange, and ultimately profound relationship called psychotherapy.
>
> (1995, p. 89)

We have seen that successful treatments for bipolar disorders can address multiple factors—for example, CBT can result in more consistent medication use and IPSRT can reduce triggers of relapse. Successful treatment can also affect interpersonal relationships. As patients begin to recover from a bipolar disorder, they interact differently with others, develop a more regular schedule, and come to view themselves differently. They change the attributions they make about events and even change how reliably they take medication for the disorder. Figure 6.7 summarizes the feedback loops involved in the treatment of bipolar disorders.

Jamison's treatment involved interactions among the factors: Her therapy helped her to recognize and accept her illness and encouraged her to take care of herself more appropriately (psychological and social factors), including sticking with a daily regimen of lithium (neurological factor). Furthermore, the successful lithium treatment allowed her to have better relationships with others (social factor), which led to a positive change in how she saw herself (psychological factor).

Figure 6.7

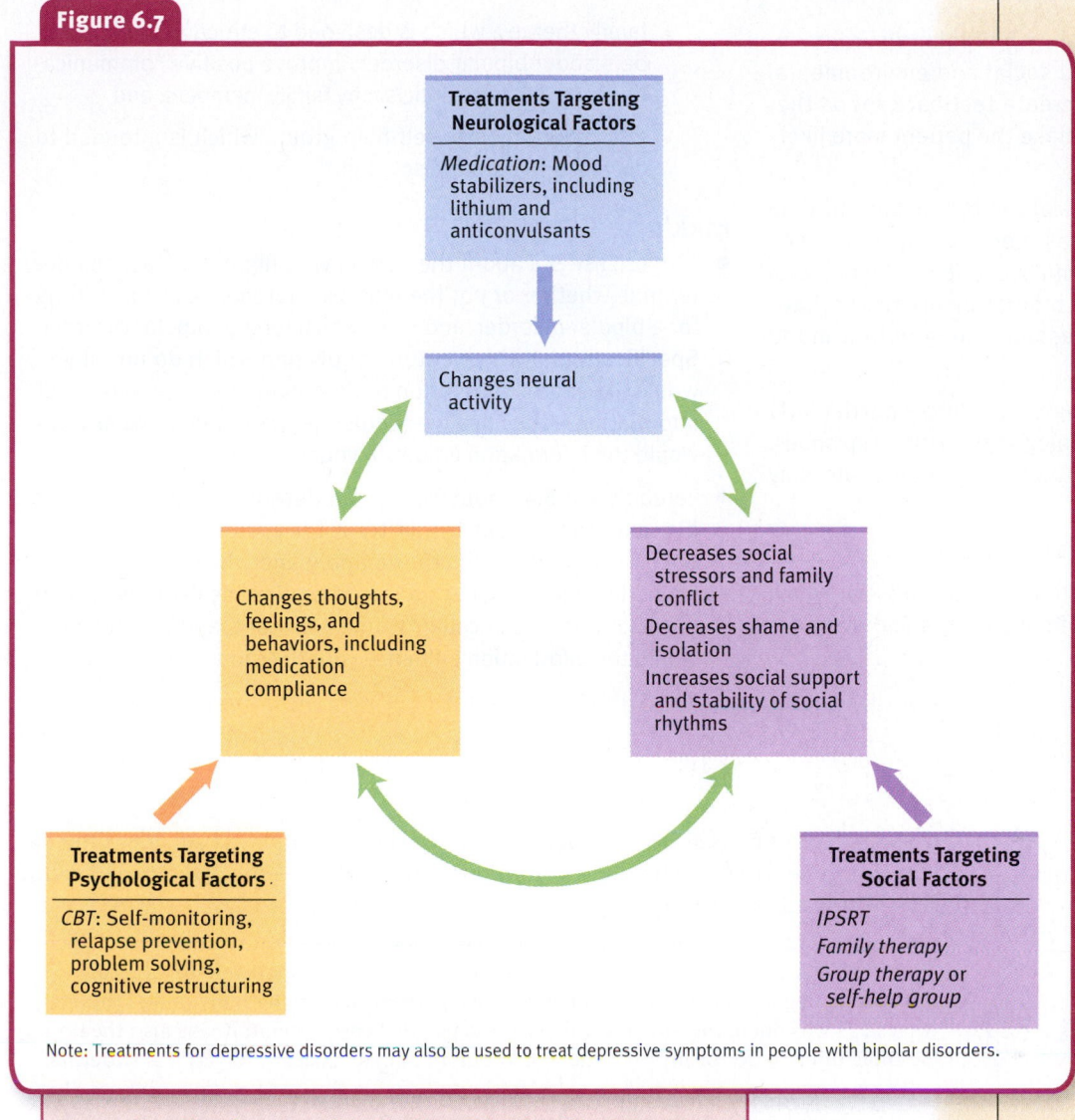

Treatments Targeting Neurological Factors

Medication: Mood stabilizers, including lithium and anticonvulsants

Changes neural activity

Changes thoughts, feelings, and behaviors, including medication compliance

Decreases social stressors and family conflict
Decreases shame and isolation
Increases social support and stability of social rhythms

Treatments Targeting Psychological Factors

CBT: Self-monitoring, relapse prevention, problem solving, cognitive restructuring

Treatments Targeting Social Factors

IPSRT
Family therapy
Group therapy or *self-help group*

Note: Treatments for depressive disorders may also be used to treat depressive symptoms in people with bipolar disorders.

6.7 ▶ Feedback Loops in Treating Bipolar Disorders

Key Concepts and Facts About Bipolar Disorders

- The four building blocks for diagnosing bipolar disorders are major depressive episode (MDE), manic episode, mixed episode, and hypomanic episode. Symptoms of a manic episode include grandiosity, pressured speech, flight of ideas, distractibility, poor judgment, decreased need for sleep, and psychomotor agitation. A mixed episode is characterized by symptoms of both an MDE and a manic episode and may include psychotic features and suicidal thinking. A hypomanic episode involves mood that is persistently elated, irritable, or euphoric; unlike other mood episodes, hypomanic episodes do not impair functioning.

- There are two types of bipolar disorder. Bipolar I disorder—usually more severe—requires only a manic or mixed episode; an MDE may occur but is not necessary for this diagnosis. Bipolar II

disorder requires alternating hypomanic episodes and MDEs and no history of manic or mixed episodes. Both disorders may involve rapid cycling. Cyclothmic disorder is a more chronic but less intense version of bipolar II disorder.

- Neurological factors that are associated with bipolar disorders include an enlarged and more active amygdala. Norepinephrine, serotonin, and glutamate are also involved. Bipolar disorders are influenced by genetic factors, which may influence mood disorders in general.

- Psychological factors that are associated with bipolar disorders include the cognitive distortions and negative thinking associated with depression. Moreover, some people with bipolar I disorder may have residual cognitive deficits after a manic episode is over.

continued on next page

- Social factors that are associated with bipolar disorders include disruptive life changes and social and environmental stressors. The different factors create feedback loops that can lead to a bipolar disorder or make the patient more likely to relapse.

- Treatments that target neurological factors include lithium and anticonvulsants, which act as mood stabilizers. When manic, patients may receive an antipsychotic medication or a benzodiazepine. Patients with a bipolar disorder who have MDEs may receive an antidepressant along with a mood stabilizer.

- Treatment that targets psychological factors—particularly CBT—helps patients recognize warning signs of mood episodes, develop better sleeping strategies, and, when appropriate, stay on medication.

- Treatments that target social factors include:
  - interpersonal and social rhythm therapy (IPSRT), which can increase the regularity of daily events and decrease social stressors;

- family therapy, which is designed to educate family members about bipolar disorder, improve positive communication, and decrease criticism by family members; and

- group therapy or a self-help group, which is intended to decrease shame and isolation.

Making a Diagnosis

- Reread Case 6.4 about the person with flight of ideas, and determine whether or not the man's symptoms meet the criteria for a bipolar disorder, and if so, which type of bipolar disorder. Specifically, list which criteria apply and which do not. If you would like more information to determine his diagnosis, what information—specifically—would you want, and in what ways would the information influence your decision?

- Reread Case 6.5 about Mr. F., and determine whether or not his symptoms meet the criteria for cyclothymic disorder. Specifically, list which criteria apply and which do not. If you would like more information to determine his diagnosis, what information—specifically—would you want, and in what ways would the information influence your decision?

Suicide

On more than one occasion, Kay Jamison seriously contemplated suicide. One day, when deeply depressed, she did more than think about it—she attempted suicide. Here she describes her motivation:

> I could not stand the pain any longer, could not abide the bone-weary and tiresome person I had become, and felt that I could not continue to be responsible for the turmoil I was inflicting upon my friends and family. In a perverse linking with my mind I thought that . . . I was doing the only fair thing for the people I cared about; it was also the only sensible thing to do for myself. One would put an animal to death for far less suffering.
>
> (Jamison, 1995, p. 115)

When Jamison attempted suicide, she was already receiving treatment for her disorder; in contrast, a majority of people who die by suicide have an untreated mental disorder, most commonly depression. Fortunately, Jamison's attempt was foiled. She later describes being grateful that she continued living. The hopelessness that she had felt went away, and she was able to enjoy life again.

Suicidal Thoughts and Suicide Risks

In the United States and Canada, suicide is ranked 11th among causes of death (McIntosh, 2003; Statistics Canada, 2005). Approximately 32,000 people die by suicide each year in the United States (Centers for Disease Control and Prevention [CDC], 2005), which constitutes about 1% of all deaths per year (McIntosh, 2003). Worldwide, suicide is the second most frequent cause of death among women under 45 years old (tuberculosis ranks first), and it is the fourth most frequent cause among men under 45 (after road accidents, tuberculosis, and violence; WHO, 1999). Table 6.11 lists more facts about suicide.

Thinking About, Planning, and Attempting Suicide

When suffering from a mood disorder, people may have thoughts of death or thoughts about committing suicide, known as **suicidal ideation** (Rihmer, 2007). But suicidal ideation does not necessarily indicate the presence of a psychological disorder or an actual suicide risk. Approximately 10–18% of the general population—including

Past research suggested that suicide rates peak in the spring for both men and women, with another peak in the autumn for women (Barraclough & White, 1978a, 1978b; Meares et al., 1981). However, more recent research suggests that such a relationship may be weakening over time (Hakko, Räsänen, & Tiihonen, 1998; Jessen, Steffensen, & Jensen, 1998; Parker et al., 2001; Rihmer et al., 1998; Yip, Callahan, & Yuen, 2000; Yip, Chao, & Ho, 1998; Yip, Yang, & Qin, 2006), perhaps because the effects of seasonal differences are minimized by modern artificial environments (Simkins et al., 2003).

Craig Tuttle/Corbis

Suicidal ideation
Thoughts of suicide.

Table 6.11 ▶ Suicide Facts at a Glance

Prevalence

- Approximately 1.3% of all deaths in the United States are considered to be suicides—over 32,000 people annually (CDC, 2005).
- Worldwide, the elderly (65 and older) are three times as likely to commit suicide as are those under 25 years old (WHO, 1999).
- In the United States, suicide is most likely to occur among the elderly, particularly white men; young people (under 26) are the next most likely to commit suicide (CDC, 2005; Miniño et al., 2002; CDC, 2000).
- From 1950 to 1995, worldwide suicide rates increased by 60%, particularly among young men (WHO, 1999), making it the third leading cause of death for teenagers, particularly males (Waters, 2000).

Gender Differences

- Worldwide, women are more likely to attempt suicide than are men (Nock et al., 2008).
- In the United States, although women are more likely to attempt suicide, men are four times more likely to die from an attempt (CDC, 2005).

Cultural Differences

- Hanging is the most common method of suicide worldwide, but guns are the most common method in the United States (particularly among men), undoubtedly because access to them is easier than in other countries (De Leo, 2002a; Moscicki, 1995; Romero & Wintemute, 2002).
- Internationally, Eastern European countries, as a region, have the highest rates of suicide; examples are Belarus (41.5 per 100,000) and Lithuania (51.6 per 100,000). Latin American countries tend to have the lowest rates; examples are Paraguay (4.2 per 100,000) and Colombia (4.5 per 100,000) (WHO, 2002).

both those with and without disorders—has at some point had suicidal thoughts (Weissman, Bland, et al., 1999). One study found that 6% of people who were healthy and had never been depressed occasionally thought about suicide (Farmer et al., 2001). Suicidal thoughts may range from believing that others would be better off if the person were dead (which Jamison had) to vague ideas of dying by suicide to specific plans to commit suicide.

Approximately 30% of those who have thoughts of suicide have also conceived of a plan (Kessler, Borges, & Walters, 1999). Even having a plan, though, does not by itself indicate that an individual is at risk for suicide. One person with a specific plan to commit suicide may not actually attempt it, whereas another person who had not previously had a serious intention or plan to die by suicide may do so (Kessler, Borges, & Walters, 1999). There are, however, certain behaviors that can suggest serious suicidal intent and can serve as warning signs (Packman et al., 2004):

- giving away possessions,

- saying goodbye to friends or family,

- talking about death or suicide generally or about specific plans to commit suicide,

- making threats of suicide, and

- rehearsing a plan for suicide.

Unfortunately, not everyone who plans or is about to commit suicide displays warning signs.

For some people, suicidal thoughts or plans turn into actions. Certain methods of suicide are more lethal than others, and the more lethal the method, the more likely it is that the suicide attempt will result in death or serious medical problems. For instance, shooting, hanging or jumping from a high place are more lethal than _family_

I'm so sorry for what I've put you through I never meant to hurt all of you so much and I don't blame any one of you for disowning me I just cant be a burden to you and my friends any longer you are all better off without me. I'm so sorry for this.

I've just snapped I cant take this meaningless existence anymore I've been in constant disappointment and that trend would have only continued. just remember the good times we had together

I love you mommy

I love you dad

I love you Kira

I love you Valancia

I love you Cynthia

I love you Zach

I love you Cayla

I love you Mark (ps. I'm really sorry)

A body of research examines suicide notes to evaluate what leads some people to try to kill themselves. Any conclusions drawn from such data, however, are limited. Fewer than 40% of the people who commit suicide leave notes, and there may be important differences between those who leave notes and those who don't (Leenaars, 1988; O'Connor, Sheeby & O'Connor, 1999). Moreover, suicide notes are subject to various self-report biases, including the desire to leave a particular impression and to elicit a particular reaction from the readers (Leenaars, 2003).

taking pills or cutting a vein. In the latter situations, the individual often has at least a few minutes to seek help after having acted. Some people may be very ambivalent about suicide and so may attempt suicide with a less lethal method or try to ensure that they are found by others before any lasting damage is done. Unfortunately, these suicide attempts may still end in death because the help the individuals had anticipated did not materialize. Other people who attempt suicide do not appear to be ambivalent; they may or may not display warning signs, but will follow through unless someone or something intervenes (Maris, 2002). One suggestion for DSM-V is that a sixth axis be added for the evaluation of a patient's suicidal risk, just as clinicians and researchers evaluate a patient's level of functioning on Axis V (see Chapter 3) (Oquendo et al., 2008).

Not all acts associated with suicide—such as certain types of skin cutting —are, in fact, suicide attempts. Such deliberate self-harming is usually potentially less lethal and is sometimes referred to as _parasuicidal behavior_. People may harm themselves without any suicidal impulse because they feel numb, or because such self-harming behaviors allow them to "feel something" (Linehan, 1981). Alternatively, some people deliberately harm themselves to elicit particular reactions from others. Parasuicidal behavior is discussed in more detail in Chapter 13.

Risk and Protective Factors for Suicide

The risk of suicide is higher for people who have a psychological disorder—whether officially diagnosed or not—than for those who do not have a disorder. The three most common types of disorders among those who commit suicide are (Brown et al., 2000; Duberstein & Conwell, 1997; Isometsä, 2000; Moscicki, 2001):

- major depressive disorder (50%),
- personality disorders (40%), and
- substance-related disorders (up to 50% of those who commit suicide are intoxicated by alcohol at the time of their death).

People who commit suicide may have more than one of these disorders.

Substance use or abuse plays a pivotal role in many suicide attempts because drugs and alcohol can cloud an individual's judgment and ability to reason. Also, as we'll see in Chapter 9, some substances, such as alcohol, are depressants: They depress the central nervous system and can lead to depressed mood (Rosenbaum et al., 2005). If someone is already depressed and drinks to "take away the pain," he or she may momentarily feel somewhat better when the blood alcohol level reaches a certain point, but soon thereafter his or her mood will be even worse than before drinking.

A history of being impulsive is another significant risk factor for suicide (Sanchez, 2001). Impulsive people may not exhibit warning signs of serious suicidal intent.

Beyond the presence of specific psychological disorders or impulsivity, another strong predictor of completed suicide is a history of past suicide attempts (Elliott et al., 1996; Moscicki, 1997; Oquendo et al., 2007). Specifically, people who have made serious attempts are more likely subsequently to die by suicide than are those who have made less serious attempts (Ivarsson et al., 1998; Krupinski et al., 1998; Stephens, Richard, & McHugh, 1999). Additional risk factors are listed in Table 6.12. Those at risk may benefit from early evaluation and treatment.

One group at higher risk for suicide is gays and lesbians, particularly during adolescence (Ramafedi, 1999). The increased risk, however, stems primarily from the social exclusion and discrimination experienced by these individuals (Igartua, Gill, & Montoro, 2003). Among homosexuals, suicide is most likely during the

Table 6.12 ▸ Risk and Protective Factors for Suicide

Risk Factors

- Mental disorder associated with suicidal behavior (depression, schizophrenia, substance abuse, or personality disorder)
- Feeling hopeless
- Being male (in the United States)
- Prior suicidal behavior (suicide threats, suicide attempts)
- Specific behaviors that suggest suicide planning (giving away possessions, saying goodbye to friends, talking about death or suicide, talking about specific plans to commit suicide, rehearsing a suicidal act, and/or accumulating medications)
- Family history of suicidal behavior
- Chronic impulsivity or aggression and low stress tolerance
- Poor coping and problem-solving skills
- Poor judgment and rigid, distorted thinking
- Major life stressors (physical or sexual assault, threats against life, diagnosis of serious medical problem, dissolution of a significant relationship, or sexual identity issues)
- Breakdown of support systems or social isolation
- Changes in mental status (acute deterioration in mental functioning, onset of major mental illness, extreme anxiety, paranoia, or severe depression)
- Unsatisfying relationship history (never married, separated, divorced, or lack of significant relationships)
- Poor work history (spotty work history or chronic unemployment)
- Childhood abuse
- History of violent behavior

Protective Factors

- Being married (or having a significant relationship)
- Employed or involved in a structured program (educational or vocational training program)
- Presence of a support system (family, friends, church, and/or social clubs)
- Having children who are under 18 years of age
- Constructive use of leisure time (enjoyable activities)
- General purpose for living
- Involved in mental health treatment
- Effective problem-solving skills

Source: Adapted from Sánchez, 2001, Appendix A.

period when disclosing their homosexuality to immediate family members (Igartua, Gill, & Montoro, 2003).

Despite such risks, most people who are depressed or have thoughts of suicide do not actually try to kill themselves. Even when in the blackest suicidal despair, specific factors can lessen the risk of a suicide attempt: receiving support from family and friends, holding religious or cultural beliefs that discourage suicide, and getting prompt and appropriate treatment for any depression or substance abuse. Additional protective factors are listed in Table 6.12.

Understanding Suicide

Adding risk factors and subtracting protective factors does not sum up to a definitive probability that a given individual will attempt or complete suicide. Rather, the presence or absence of such factors may create feedback loops over years, the effects of which may or may not culminate in suicide. To understand why some people commit suicide, we now turn to examine relevant neurological, psychological, and social factors and their feedback loops.

Neurological Factors

Because the main risk factors for suicide are associated with depression and impulsivity (as well as past suicide attempts), it's difficult to identify neurological factors that uniquely contribute to suicide (as distinct from factors that contribute to depression and impulsivity). Nevertheless, progress is being made in understanding the neurological factors that contribute to suicide.

Brain Systems and Neural Communication

The frontal lobes may play a key role in suicide, which makes sense because they normally inhibit behavior (and hence disrupted frontal lobe function may be related to impulsivity). In particular, postmortem studies have documented that the frontal lobes of suicide victims have structural abnormalities, such as greater-than-normal neural density (Rajkowska, 1997) and abnormal serotonin receptors (Brunner & Bronisch, 1999).

Many researchers believe that mood disorders in general reflect, at least in part, levels of the neurotransmitter serotonin. Guided by this idea, Bielau and colleagues (2005) reported a suggestive trend: They found that people who committed suicide tended to have fewer neurons in the part of the brain that produces serotonin than did people who died of other causes. In addition, researchers have found that people who commit suicide may have had fewer serotonin receptors in their brains (Boldrini et al., 2005). Notably, impulsivity is also associated with low serotonin levels. Given the role of serotonin in impulsivity and aggression (van Heeringen, 2003), its relation to suicide is not surprising: The low levels of serotonin associated with impulsivity may lead a person to act on a thought or emotion that normally would be ignored—and might even facilitate a horrible act of aggression against the self (after all, suicide is murder—the most aggressive of all acts—but directed toward oneself).

Genetics

Suicide seems to "run in families" (Correa et al., 2004), but it is difficult to discern a *specific* role of genes in influencing people to commit suicide. Depression has a genetic component, which may account for the higher rates of suicide among both twins in monozygotic pairs (13%) compared to dizygotic pairs (<1%; Zalsman et al., 2002). Given the apparent role of serotonin in suicide, studying genes related to serotonin is an obvious way to begin to look for genetic contributions to this behavior. However, such investigations have so far been fruitless. Researchers cannot yet identify genes that specifically influence whether a person will commit suicide (Sibille et al., 2004; Stefulj et al., 2004; Tsai et al., 2004).

Psychological Factors: Hopelessness and Impulsivity

Why might individuals think seriously about suicide? The obstacles in their lives may seem to be insurmountable, or suicide may appear to be the only way to end their excruciating emotional pain. However, suicide is a "permanent solution to a temporary problem" (National Depressive and Manic Depressive Association, 2002). When people are in the midst of despair, possible solutions to life's problems may seem elusive, but these feelings typically will lessen or disappear.

A number of the risk factors in Table 6.12 are psychological factors, such as poor coping skills (e.g., behaving impulsively) and poor problem-solving skills (e.g., difficulty identifying obstacles that interfere with meeting goals or failing to develop ways to work around obstacles), distorted and rigid thinking (thought patterns associated with depression), and hopelessness. Hopelessness, with its bleak thoughts of the future, is especially associated with suicide (Beck et al., 1985; Beck et al., 1990). Moreover, to some extent having depressed thoughts is self-perpetuating: When depressed, people are more likely to remember other bad times (Eich, Macaulay, & Lam, 1997). Their thoughts become populated with a string of bad times, from past to present, and onward to the future. They cannot see past their current hopelessness to envision better times or alternative solutions to their problems. And if they

Table 6.13 ▸ Suicide Rates in Selected Countries

Country or area	Year	Total number of suicides	Suicide rate per 100 000 population			
			Total	Male	Female	Male: female ratio
Argentina	1996	2 245	8.7	14.2	3.9	3.6
Australia	1998	2 633	17.9	28.9	7.0	4.1
Brazil	1995	6 584	6.3	10.3	2.5	4.1
Canada	1997	3 681	15.0	24.1	6.1	3.9
China	1999	16 836	18.3	18.0	18.8	1.0
Cuba	1997	2 029	23.0	32.1	14.2	2.3
Czech Republic	1999	1 610	17.5	30.1	6.3	4.8
Finland	1998	1 228	28.4	45.8	11.7	3.9
France	1998	10 534	20.0	31.3	9.9	3.2
Germany	1999	11 160	14.3	22.5	6.9	3.3
Ireland	1997	466	16.8	27.4	6.3	4.3
Israel	1997	379	8.7	14.6	3.3	4.4
Italy	1997	4 694	8.4	13.4	3.8	3.5
Japan	1997	23 502	19.5	28.0	11.5	2.4
Kazakhstan	1999	4 004	37.4	67.3	11.6	5.8
Puerto Rico	1998	321	10.8	20.9	2.0	10.4
Republic of Korea	1997	6 024	17.1	25.3	10.1	2.5
Russian Federation	1998	51 770	43.1	77.8	12.6	6.2
Singapore	1998	371	15.7	18.8	12.7	1.5
Thailand	1994	2 333	5.6	8.0	3.3	2.4
Ukraine	1999	14 452	33.8	61.8	10.1	6.1
United Kingdom	1999	4 448	9.2	14.6	3.9	3.8
United States	1998	30 575	13.9	23.2	3.3	4.4
Venezuela	1994	1 089	8.l	13.7	2.7	5.0

Source: World Health Organization (2002), *World Report on Violence and Health*, p. 187; http://www.who.int/violence_injury_prevention/violence/global_campaign/en/chap7.pdf.

are prone to impulsive behavior, such hopelessness sets them up to be like "an accident just waiting to happen."

Social Factors: Alienation and Cultural Stress

Suicide rates vary across countries (see Table 6.13; De Leo, 2002a; Vijayakumar et al., 2005; WHO, 1999), which suggests that social and cultural factors affect these rates. In some developing countries, the presence or history of a psychological disorder poses less of a risk for suicide than it does in developed countries (Vijayakumar et al., 2005). Note, however, that social and cultural differences may partly reflect different genetic vulnerabilities to certain risk factors (such as certain psychological disorders). For instance, the residents of one country could have a higher suicide rate, in part, because more people in the country tend to have genes

Natalie Forbes/Corbis

Cultural norms and customs can influence suicide rates. Among the Yuit Eskimos of St. Lawrence, when someone requests suicide three times, relatives are supposed to help the person kill himself or herself (Leighton & Hughes, 1955). In contrast, among the Tiv of Nigeria, suicide reportedly never occurs (Evans & Farberow, 1988). Such cultural norms about suicide can affect individuals' beliefs and expectations about suicide.

associated with depression. Alternatively, the suicide rates across countries could depend, in part, on the socioeconomic circumstances of citizens; suicide risk increases with economic adversity (Agerbo et al., 2007; Preti, 2003).

How might cultural factors affect suicide rates? The French sociologist Émile Durkheim (1897/1951) formulated a theory after comparing suicide rates in different countries across several periods of time. Durkheim proposed that suicide is more likely when a society is too "individualistic," and its citizens do not feel enough of a sense of being part of a community or group; that is, they feel alienated from others. Durkheim's theory may, in part, account for the increasing worldwide suicide rate among young men. That is, young men may feel an increasing sense of alienation and thus become more likely to commit suicide as their society modernizes, and as the social rituals and traditional societal organization that binds young people more closely to their family and community disintegrate. Conversely, Durkheim proposed that during times of stress, a community may pull together to grapple with the common challenge; when this happens an individual's sense of belonging to a cohesive group can protect against suicide. Other possible factors that may account for the increased suicide rate among youth are listed in Table 6.14.

Table 6.14 ▸ Possible Causes of the Increased Suicide Rate Among Youth
• Earlier and easier access to alcohol, drugs, and firearms
• Neurological damage to fetuses, from nutritional deficiencies, alcohol, nicotine, or cocaine use in pregnant mothers
• Longer survival of premature babies, with increased vulnerability of their nervous system (as a result of their low birth weight)
• The decrease in the average age of puberty
• The younger age at which depression first occurs
• Actual rates of depression may have increased over time
• More accurate reporting of suicides—thus the actual increase may be smaller than it appears
Source: De Leo, 2002a.

Support for Durkheim's theory comes from the decrease in suicide rates during good economic times or times of optimism within a culture (Weyerer & Wiedenmann, 1995). For example, in the final years of the Soviet Union (from 1984 to 1988), the suicide rate there decreased by over a third, as its citizens became hopeful about the future (Wasserman & Varnik, 1998).

Another important social factor that influences suicidal behavior is religion. Countries where the citizens are more religious tend to have lower suicide rates than do countries where citizens are less religious. Countries with a large Muslim population are among those with the lowest suicide rates in the world, followed by countries with a large Roman Catholic population; the tenets of both of these religions forbid suicide (De Leo, 2002a; Simpson & Conklin, 1989). Moreover, individuals who are more committed to their religion and more involved with it are less likely to commit suicide, which is consistent with Durkheim's theory that being an active member of a community decreases alienation, and therefore suicide (Stack 1983; Stack & Wasserman, 1992).

The difference in suicide rates between the sexes provides another example of the ways that culture can contribute to suicide. The ratio of men to women among those who commit suicide is five to one in some Eastern European countries and up to ten to one in Puerto Rico (WHO, 1999). This pattern of more men than women committing suicide is the rule, but there are exceptions. In India, the suicide rate for men and women is about the same (Mayer & Ziaian, 2002). And in China, particularly in rural areas, women are more likely to commit suicide than men (Ji, Kleinman, & Becker, 2001; Jianlin, 2000; Phillips, Li, & Zhang, 2002). Several explanations have been proposed for China's unique pattern. One is that Chinese women use more lethal methods (such as ingesting insecticides) than non-Chinese women do. In addition, medical facilities are widely scattered in rural China, so even if a woman were found by a friend or family member after she took the poison, there might not be enough time to get her to medical help (Phillips, 2001). Another explanation is that in rural China women are viewed as far inferior to men, leading to a sense of greater frustration and hopelessness among some women (Qin & Mortensen, 2001).

What might explain the gender differences in suicide rates in general? One possibility is that socially related protective factors may be more common or effective among women; that is, women may have better support systems, greater emotional awareness, and may be more willing to seek help (Canetto, 1992; De Leo, 2002a).

FEEDBACK LOOPS IN ACTION: **Suicide**

Suicide can best be understood as arising from the confluence of neurological, psychological, and social factors. A neurological vulnerability, such as abnormal neurotransmitter functioning, serves as the backdrop. Add to that the psychological factors: depression or feelings of hopelessness, beliefs about suicide, poor coping skills, and perhaps impulsive or violent personality traits. In turn, these factors affect, and are affected by, social and cultural forces—such as economic realities, wars, cultural beliefs and norms about suicide, religion, stressful life events, and social support. The dynamic balance among all these factors will influence the likelihood of an individual's suicidal ideation, plans, and behavior (Sánchez, 2001; Wenzel et al., 2009). Figure 6.8 summarizes the factors that may contribute to suicide, as well as the feedback loops between them.

Preventing Suicide

Suicide prevention efforts can focus on immediate safety or longer-term prevention. Immediate crisis intervention provides resources to help people when they are on the verge of committing suicide; for example, suicide hotlines are available for people who are seriously contemplating killing themselves. Longer-term interventions can help those at increased risk—people who have attempted suicide in the past. Prevention can also encompass treating related disorders, such as substance abuse, which in turn is associated with increased impulsivity and poor judgment. Such prevention efforts can target all three types of factors: neurological, psychological, and social. As we saw with the treatment of mood disorders, successfully changing one type of factor leads to changes in the others.

However, it is difficult to gauge the success of suicide prevention efforts. In the usual studies that evaluate treatments of DSM-IV-TR clinical disorders, potential participants can be identified through a clinical interview or questionnaire and assigned to a treatment group or a control group. However, there are many stumbling blocks in using similar research designs to evaluate suicide prevention methods. It's not clear, for instance, which participants should be included in a

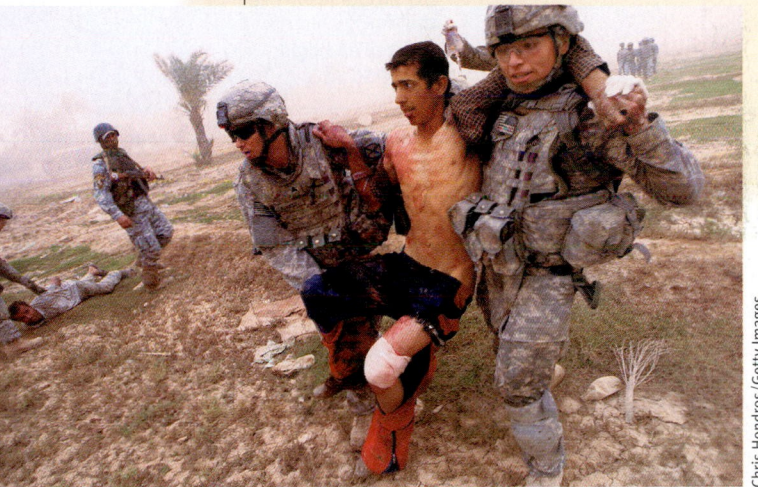

Chris Hondros/Getty Images

In 2007, U.S. soldiers on active duty in Iraq and Afghanistan attempted or committed suicide at the highest level since records for military personnel began to be kept in 1980 (Priest, 2008). On average, five soldiers attempted suicide every day. Reasons for the high suicide rate include the strain on family relationships caused by long and repeated tours of duty, combat-related stress, and legal and financial problems. The Army's suicide prevention efforts include hiring additional mental health providers and instituting a program to teach junior Army leaders how to recognize signs of suicide intention in their troops and how to then intervene (Tyson, 2008).

Figure 6.8

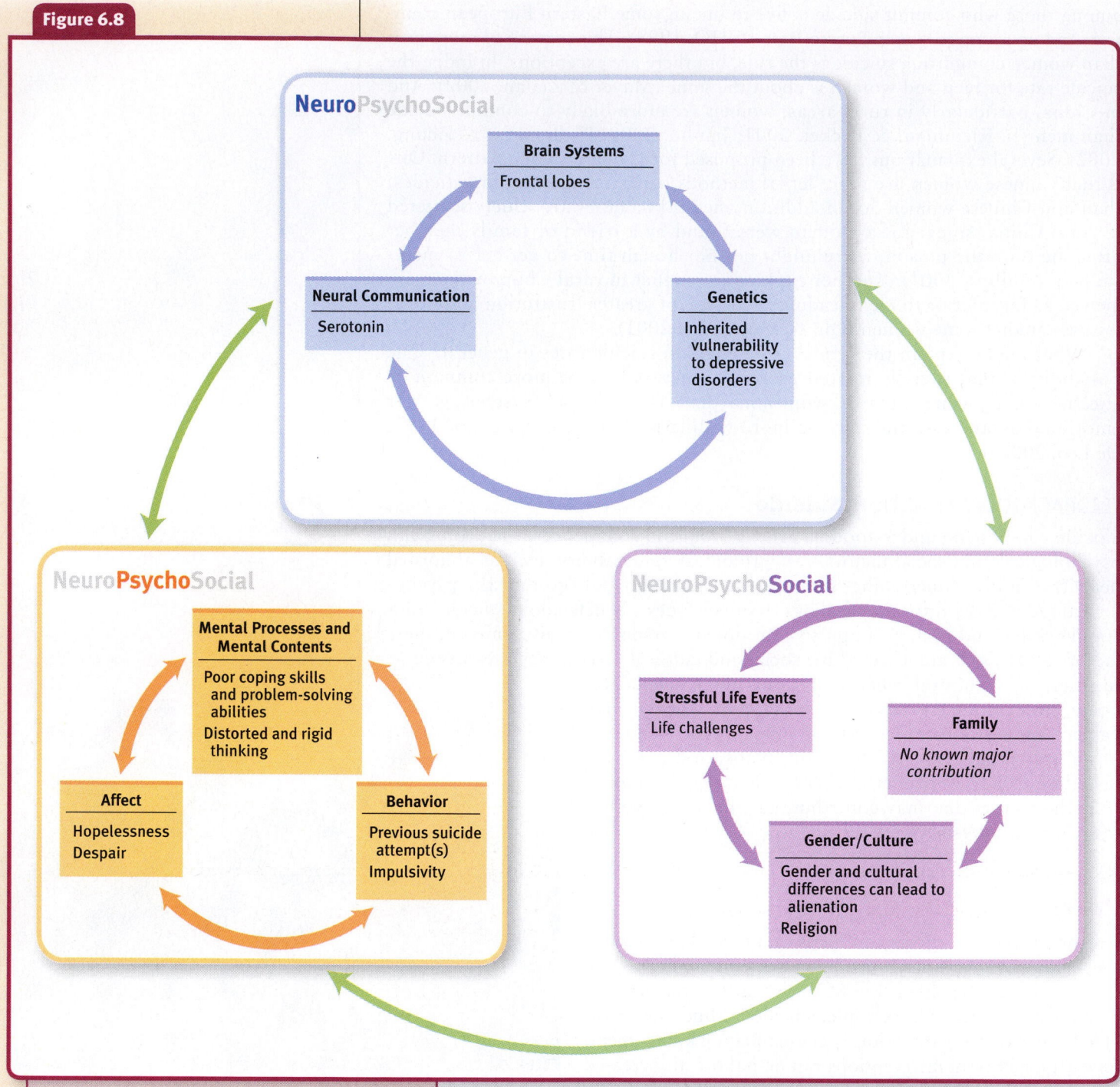

NeuroPsychoSocial

Brain Systems
Frontal lobes

Neural Communication
Serotonin

Genetics
Inherited vulnerability to depressive disorders

NeuroPsychoSocial

Mental Processes and Mental Contents
Poor coping skills and problem-solving abilities
Distorted and rigid thinking

Affect
Hopelessness
Despair

Behavior
Previous suicide attempt(s)
Impulsivity

NeuroPsychoSocial

Stressful Life Events
Life challenges

Family
No known major contribution

Gender/Culture
Gender and cultural differences can lead to alienation
Religion

6.8 ▸ Feedback Loops in Action: Suicide

study on suicide prevention: Those with any suicidal ideation, only those with a concrete plan, or those who have already tried once? Moreover, people who have already made at least one attempt may differ from those whose first attempt results in death. Another problem is determining what constitutes an appropriate control group. It would be unethical not to offer suicidal individuals in a control group the same level of services as those in the treatment group (De Leo, 2002b).

Despite such challenges in carrying out research, progress has been made in studying suicide prevention; let's review this progress.

Targeting Neurological Factors: Medication

Interventions that most commonly target neurological factors are medications (usually antidepressants) and, to a lesser extent, ECT for severe suicidal thoughts that do not respond to other treatments. However, it is unclear to what extent medications do prevent suicide. Khan and colleagues (2000) examined the U.S. Food and Drug Administration database that compared RCTs (randomized clinical trials) of newer antidepressants with placebos. The rates of both attempted and completed suicides were essentially the same for both groups. Nonetheless, before deciding that antidepressants have no effect on suicide, remember that people with serious suicidal intent are often excluded from RCTs that use placebo medications (see Chapter 4 for a discussion about exclusion criteria in RCTs). Thus, participants in the government database who attempted or completed suicide were probably not actively suicidal at the time they enrolled in the study.

Targeting Psychological Factors: Reducing Feelings of Hopelessness

For a person who is actively suicidal and who has contacted a mental health or medical professional, the first aim of suicide prevention is to make sure that the individual is safe. After this, crisis intervention helps the person to see past the hopelessness and rigidity that pervades his or her thinking, identifies whatever stressors have brought the individual to this point, helps him or her develop new solutions to the problems, and enhances the ability to cope.

In addition, a clinician tries to discover whether the person is depressed or abusing substances; if so, these problems, which may lead to suicidal thoughts or behaviors, should be treated (Reifman & Windle, 1995). Because most people who die by suicide had untreated depression, treatment for depression that targets psychological factors—typically CBT—can play a key role in suicide prevention.

Targeting Social Factors: Social Programs, Social Awareness

Ideally, prevention programs that decrease socially related risk factors and increase socially related protective factors should decrease the suicide rate. Thus, programs to prevent child abuse, to provide affordable access to mental health care (and so make it easier to obtain treatment for psychological disorders), to decrease substance abuse, and to increase employment may all help prevent suicides in the long term.

Part of the national suicide prevention plan in the United States is to increase awareness about suicide (Satcher, 1999), both among individuals who may feel suicidal and among the friends and family of someone feeling suicidal. The hope is that suicidal individuals will receive appropriate help before they commit suicide (see Table 6.15).

Table 6.15 ► Suicide Prevention: What to Do

What can you do if someone you know seems to be suicidal? According to the National Institute of Mental Health (Goldsmith et al., 2002), don't leave the person alone; get help by calling 911 or other trained emergency professionals. Also, try to make sure that potential means for committing suicide such as firearms or poisons are not easily accessible. Let the person know that you're concerned, and try not to be judgmental.

If you, or someone you know, are at risk for suicide, the following organizations can help:

- The National Hope Line Network
  Phone: 800-SUICIDE. This will connect you with a crisis center in your area.
  Website: **http://www.hopeline.com/**

- American Foundation for Suicide Prevention
  Phone: 212-363-3500
  Web site: **http://www.afsp.org**

- Suicide Prevention Advocacy Network
  Phone: 770-998-8819
  Web site: **http://www.spanusa.org**

FEEDBACK LOOPS IN PREVENTION: Suicide

To see how the three types of factors interact via feedback loops, let's examine a comprehensive suicide prevention program. From 1990 to 1995, the suicide rate among U.S. Air Force personnel aged 24–35 increased significantly. Recognizing

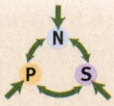

that those most likely to need help were often the least likely to seek it, the Air Force instituted a comprehensive program to prevent suicide. The program was designed to provide mental health services at the initial signs of distress or dysfunction and to change the norms about seeking help within the Air Force. The hope was that personnel could take advantage of such help without feeling stigmatized; the Air Force publicized that seeking help, either for oneself or for another, was a sign of responsibility and strength (Knox et al., 2003).

Taking advantage of this "experiment," researchers compared the number of suicides among Air Force personnel in the 7 years before the program was fully instituted (1990–1996) with the number during the first 6 years after it was in full swing (1997–2002). As seen in Figure 6.9, the suicide rate fell by 33% after the program was fully instituted (McIntosh, 2003). (The emphasis on early intervention and decreased stigma had an added bonus: There was also a decrease in the homicide rate and in severe family violence among Air Force personnel from the first time period to the second. Thus, the prevention program yielded additional changes in social factors.) The Air Force has continued this suicide prevention program, and in the decade since the program was launched, the average annual suicide rate decreased by almost 30% compared to the decade before the program was launched (Pflanz, 2008). In the wake of increased suicide rates among soldiers who served in Iraq and Afghanistan, other branches of the military have stepped up their suicide prevention programs (Lorge, 2008). The Air Force program is being adapted by some college campuses in hopes of lowering the suicide rate among students (Koplewicz et al., 2007). Figure 6.10 illustrates the feedback loops involved in the prevention of suicide.

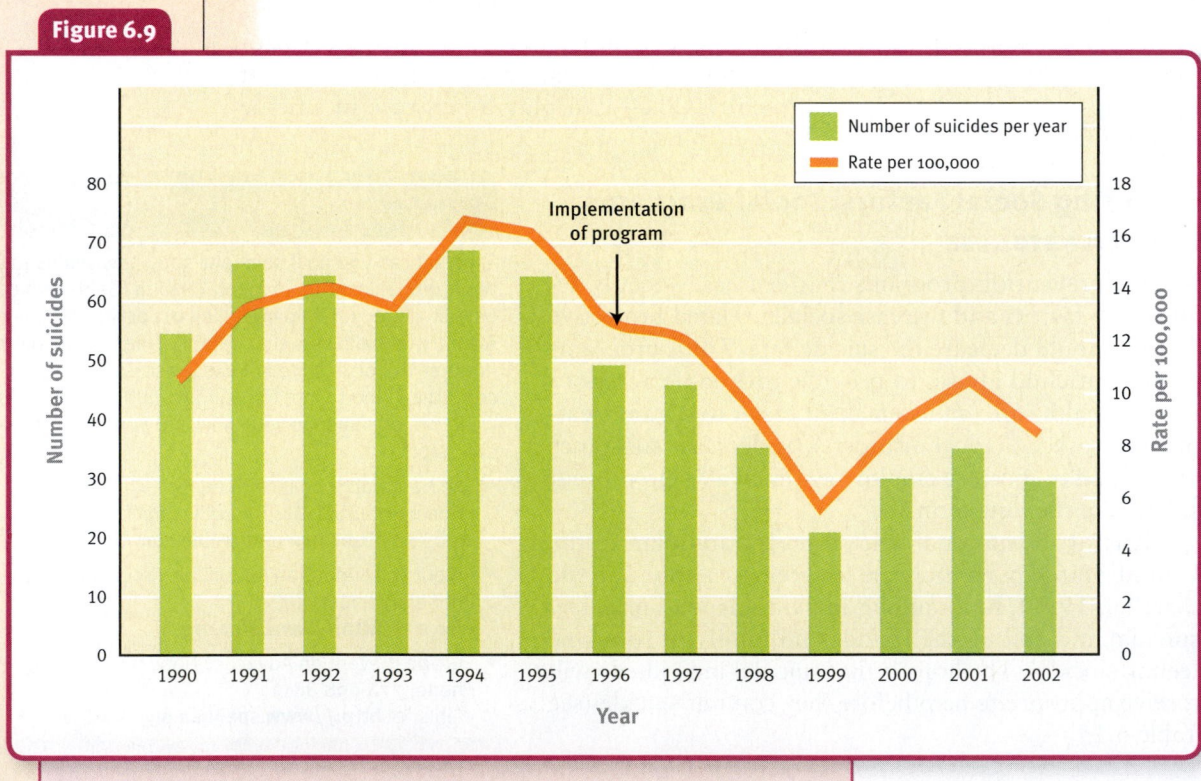

Figure 6.9

6.9 ▶ Successful Suicide Prevention? The number of suicides in the U.S. Air Force decreased after a suicide prevention program was implemented in 1996.

Source: Knox et al., 2003.

Figure 6.10

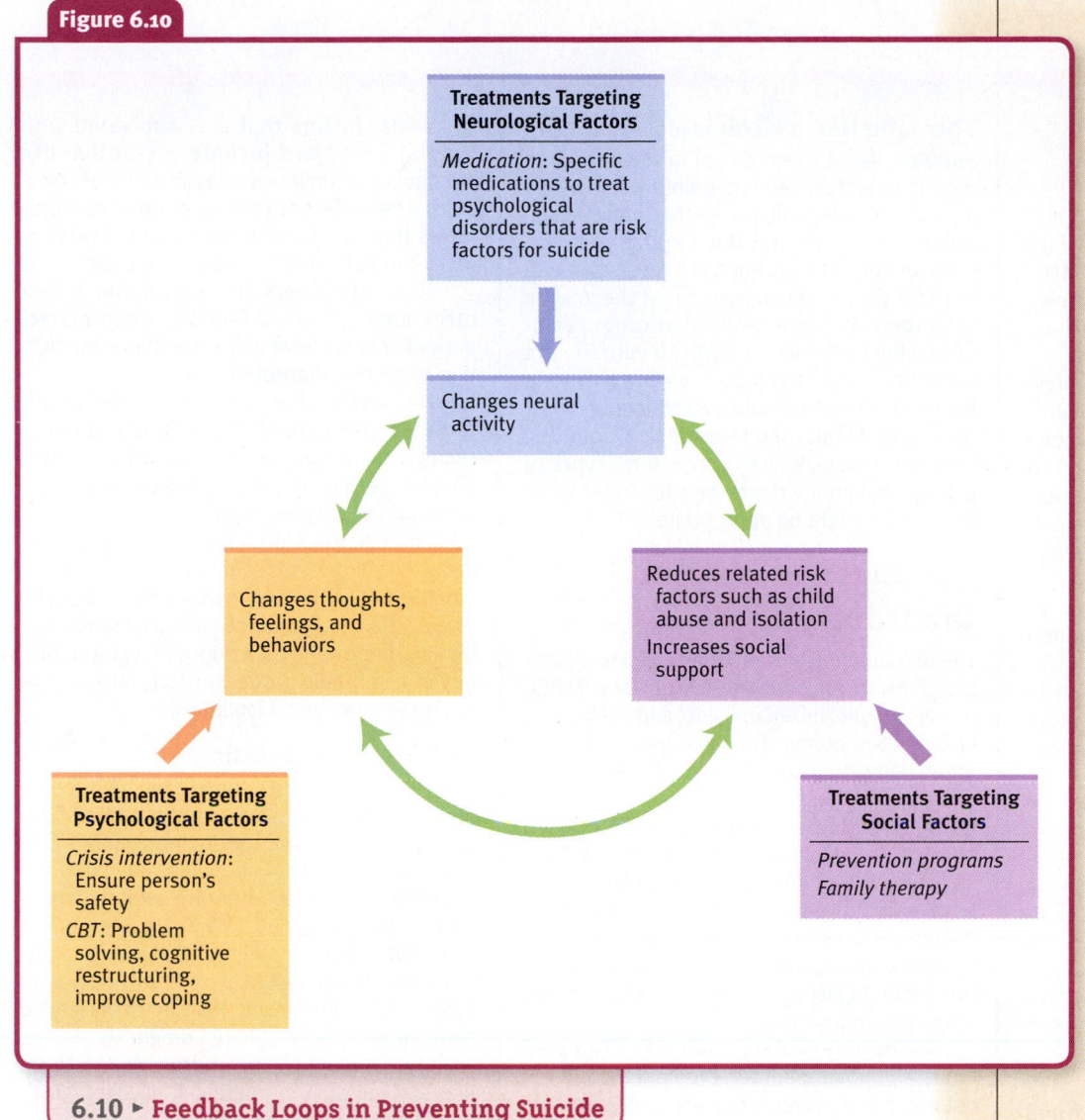

6.10 ▶ Feedback Loops in Preventing Suicide

Key Concepts and Facts About Suicide

- Suicide is ranked 11th among causes of death in North America. Having thoughts of suicide or making a plan to carry it out may indicate a risk for suicide; behavioral changes (such as giving away possessions) may indicate a more serious risk. However, not everyone who attempts or commits suicide displays warning signs. In addition, certain self-harming behaviors may be parasuicidal behaviors rather than suicide attempts. The presence of certain psychological disorders, such as MDD, and a history of previous serious suicide attempts increase an individual's risk for suicide.

- Neurological factors that are associated with suicide include structural abnormalities in the frontal lobes and altered serotonin activity. In addition, suicide may be associated with a genetic risk for mood disorders. Psychological risk factors for suicide include poor coping and problem-solving skills, distorted and rigid thinking, and a sense of hopelessness. Variations in suicide rates across countries point to the role of social factors in influencing people to commit suicide.

- Suicide prevention efforts target neurological, psychological, and social factors. Neurological factors are targeted by medications. Treatments that target psychological factors are designed to ensure that the suicidal individual is safe and then to help the person see past the hopelessness and rigidity that pervade his or her thinking. Suicide prevention may also help the patient identify the stressors that led him or her to feel suicidal and develop new solutions to the problems. To address social factors, prevention programs may target risk factors that are associated with suicide, such as child abuse.

SUMMING UP

Summary of Depressive Disorders

A major depressive episode (MDE) is the building block for a diagnosis of major depressive disorder (MDD); when a person has an MDE, he or she is diagnosed with MDD. Symptoms of an MDE can arise in three areas: affect, behavior, and cognition.

Depression is becoming increasingly prevalent in younger cohorts. Depression and anxiety disorders have a high comorbidity—around 50%. MDD may arise with melancholic features, catatonic features, or psychotic features. Symptoms may also fall into less common patterns, as in atypical depression and chronic depression.

A diagnosis of dysthymic disorder requires fewer symptoms than does a diagnosis of MDD; however, the symptoms of dysthymic disorder must persist for a longer time than do symptoms of MDD. People who have both dysthymic disorder and MDD are said to have double depression.

Neurological factors related to depression include low activity in the frontal lobes, and abnormal functioning of dopamine, serotonin, and norepinephrine. The stress–diathesis model of depression highlights the role of increased activity of the HPA axis and of excess cortisol in the blood, but people with atypical depression have the opposite pattern—decreased activity in the HPA axis. Genes can play a role in depression.

Psychological factors that are associated with depression include a bias toward paying attention to negative stimuli, dysfunctional thoughts, rumination, a negative attributional style and learned helplessness.

Social factors that are associated with depression include stressful life events, social exclusion, and problems with social interactions or relationships. Culture and gender can influence the specific ways that symptoms of depression are expressed.

Neurological, psychological and social factors can affect each other through feedback loops, as outlined by the stress–diathesis model and Coyne's interactional theory of depression.

Biomedical treatments that target neurological factors for depressive disorders are medications and brain stimulation. Treatments for depression that target psychological factors include CBT. Treatments that target social factors include IPT and family systems therapy.

Thinking like a clinician

Suppose that a friend began to sleep through morning classes, seemed uninterested in going out and doing things together, and became quiet and withdrawn. What could you conclude or not conclude based on these observations? If you were concerned that these were symptoms of depression, what other symptoms would you look for? What if your friend's symptoms did not appear to meet the criteria for an MDE—what could you conclude or not conclude? If your friend was, in fact, suffering from depression, how might the three types of factors explain the depressive episode? What treatments might be appropriate?

Summary of Bipolar Disorders

The four building blocks for diagnosing bipolar disorders are major depressive episode (MDE), manic episode, mixed episode, and hypomanic episode. Symptoms of a manic episode include grandiosity, pressured speech, flight of ideas, distractibility, poor judgment, decreased need for sleep, and psychomotor agitation. A mixed episode is characterized by symptoms of both an MDE and a manic episode and may include psychotic features and suicidal thinking. A hypomanic episode involves mood that is persistently elated, irritable, or euphoric; unlike other mood episodes, hypomanic episodes do not impair functioning.

Researchers have characterized two types of bipolar disorder. Bipolar I disorder—usually more severe—requires only a manic or mixed episode; an MDE may occur but is not necessary for this diagnosis. Bipolar II disorder requires alternating hypomanic episodes and MDEs and no history of manic or mixed episodes. Both disorders may involve rapid cycling. Cyclothmic disorder is a more chronic but less intense version of bipolar II disorder.

Neurological factors that are associated with bipolar disorders include an enlarged and more active amygdala. Norepinephrine, serotonin, and glutamate are also involved. Bipolar disorders are influenced by genetic factors, which may influence mood disorders in general.

Psychological factors that are associated with bipolar disorders include the cognitive distortions and negative thinking associated with depression. Moreover, some people with bipolar I disorder may have residual cognitive deficits after a manic episode is over.

Social factors that are associated with bipolar disorders include disruptive life changes and social and environmental stressors. The different factors create feedback loops that can lead to a bipolar disorder or make the patient more likely to relapse.

Mood stabilizers are one treatment that targets neurological factors; when manic, patients may receive an antipsychotic medication or a benzodiazepine.

Treatment that targets psychological factors—particularly CBT—helps patients recognize warning signs of mood episodes, develop better sleeping strategies, and, when appropriate, stay on medication.

Treatments that target social factors include interpersonal and social rhythm therapy (IPSRT), which can increase the regularity of daily events and decrease social stressors; family therapy and education; and group therapy or a self-help group, which is intended to decrease shame and isolation.

Thinking like a clinician

You get in touch with a friend from high school who tells you that she recently had a hypomanic episode. What are two possible DSM-IV-TR diagnoses that she might have had (be specific)? What will determine which diagnosis is most appropriate? What are a few of the symptoms that are hallmarks of a hypomanic episode? What would be the difference in symptoms if your friend instead experienced a manic episode? Would her diagnosis change or stay the same? Explain. How do the three types of factors (neurological, psychological, and social) explain why bipolar disorders develop? What would be the most appropriate ways to treat bipolar disorders?

Summary of Suicide

Having thoughts of suicide or making a plan to carry it out may indicate a risk for suicide; behavioral changes (such as giving away possessions) may indicate a more serious risk. However, not everyone who attempts or commits suicide displays warning signs. In addition, certain self-harming behaviors may be parasuicidal behaviors rather than suicide attempts. The presence of certain psychological disorders, such as MDD, and a history of previous serious suicide attempts increase an individual's risk for suicide.

Neurological factors that are associated with suicide include structural abnormalities in the frontal lobes and altered serotonin activity. In addition, suicide may be associated with a genetic risk for mood disorders. Psychological risk factors for suicide include poor coping and problem-solving skills, distorted and rigid thinking, and a sense of hopelessness. Variations in suicide rates across countries point to the role of social factors in influencing people who commit suicide.

Suicide prevention efforts target neurological, psychological, and social factors. Neurological factors are targeted by medications. Treatments that target psychological factors are designed to ensure that the suicidal individual is safe and then to help the person see past the hopelessness and rigidity that pervade his or her thinking and develop new solutions to problems. To address social factors, prevention programs may target risk factors that are associated with suicide, such as child abuse and substance abuse.

Thinking like a clinician

Based on what you have learned about suicide, explain Kay Jamison's suicide attempt in terms of the three types of factors. Identify how the neurological, psychological and social factors might have influenced each other via feedback loops. From what you know of her, what were Jamison's risk and protective factors?

Key Terms

Mood disorders (p. 191)

Major depressive episode (MDE) (p. 192)

Anhedonia (p. 192)

Psychomotor agitation (p. 193)

Psychomotor retardation (p. 193)

Vegetative signs (of depression) (p. 193)

Hypersomnia (p. 194)

Prodrome (p. 194)

Premorbid (p. 194)

Major depressive disorder (MDD) (p. 194)

Age cohort (p. 194)

Seasonal affective disorder (SAD) (p. 197)

Phototherapy (p. 197)

Dysthymic disorder (p. 198)

Double depression (p. 198)

Selective serotonin reuptake inhibitors (SSRIs) (p. 209)

Tricyclic antidepressants (TCAs) (p. 209)

Monoamine oxidase inhibitors (MAOIs) (p. 209)

Bipolar disorders (p. 217)

Manic episode (p. 217)

Expansive mood (p. 217)

Flight of ideas (p. 219)

Rapid cycling (of moods) (p. 221)

Cyclothymic disorder (p. 223)

Mood stabilizer (p. 228)

Lithium (p. 228)

Suicidal ideation (p. 232)

More Study Aids

For additional study aids related to this chapter, go to:

www.worthpublishers.com/rosenberg

Anxiety Disorders

Howard Hughes is famous for many things: He was an industrialist, creating Hughes Aircraft Company and designing the planes his company built; he was an aviator who broke flying records; he was the owner of hotels and casinos; he was a reclusive billionaire who directed an Academy Award–winning film. Born in 1905 to wealthy parents in Houston, Texas, Hughes set his sights on accomplishing feats that people said couldn't be done, and he achieved them nonetheless. During his lifetime, people around the world recognized his name and his accomplishments.

Earl Campbell, born in 1955, gained considerable fame as a National Football League (NFL) running back from 1978 to 1985. Campbell was such an outstanding athlete that he was voted most valuable player for each of his first 3 years with the NFL. He was later inducted into the Football Hall of Fame and went on to achieve in other areas of life: He became a food manufacturer, restaurateur, and businessman.

Unlike Hughes, Campbell was not born to wealth and privilege. He grew up in a small Texas town with 10 brothers and sisters, all living in a three-bedroom house that had its bathroom outdoors. Between May and August, the whole family worked in the nearby rose fields, cutting the flowers; in the autumn, they hauled hay for local farmers. When Campbell was 11 years old, his father died of a heart attack; his mother held the family together with her strong sense of morality and work ethic, which she instilled in her children.

Both of these men—Hughes and Campbell—possessed remarkable talents and abilities and an unusually strong drive to achieve. But they also shared another characteristic—they both suffered from symptoms of anxiety disorders. *Anxiety disorders* involve significant fear, agitation, and nervousness and can impair functioning in any or all spheres of life, including school, work, and interpersonal relationships. Both Hughes and Campbell developed such severe anxiety symptoms that they were unable to work effectively. However, the specific forms taken by their anxiety symptoms differed, as we'll see.

In this chapter, we discuss six types of anxiety disorders that are described in DSM-IV-TR: generalized anxiety disorder, panic disorder, social phobia, specific phobias, obsessive compulsive disorder, and posttraumatic stress disorder. We'll start with a general discussion of what anxiety is and identify some of the common features of the

Don Kilpatrick/Morgan Gaynin

different anxiety disorders. In the process we'll first examine Earl Campbell—his life, the nature of his anxiety symptoms, the disorders most relevant to his symptoms, and how he responded to and handled his anxieties. Once we have examined the disorders most applicable to Campbell's symptoms, we then turn to Howard Hughes—the nature of his constellation of anxiety symptoms, the disorders most relevant to these symptoms, and how he responded to and handled his anxieties.

Common Features of Anxiety Disorders

Earl Campbell played high school football and, after graduating, became a star running back on the University of Texas–Austin football team. From there, he went on to play for the Houston Oilers in the NFL. At age 24, he married Reuna, a woman from his hometown whom he had been dating for 10 years. Five years later, they had their first child, and 2 years after that, at the age of 31, Campbell retired from football.

Campbell went on to work for the University of Texas–Austin as a goodwill ambassador, representing the school at various functions, and helping student-athletes commit to their studies. One day, when Campbell was driving from Austin to Dallas, he stopped at a traffic light and had an unusual experience:

> Out of the blue, my heart started racing. I felt my chest. Then I broke into a cold sweat, began hyperventilating, and became convinced I was having a heart attack. The people in the car next to mine seemed totally unaware that anything was wrong. My heart just kept racing. I couldn't stop it. I was going to die. How could I stop it? It was getting worse. I was dying! The driver behind me started blowing his horn. The light had turned green. I needed help. I couldn't get out of the car. "God help me!" I prayed. Then it stopped—just like that, my heart stopped racing. I put my hand to my heart again. It felt normal. My hands and arms were covered with a cold clammy sweat. I wiped the perspiration from my face and look[ed] at myself in the rearview mirror. For the first time in my life, I caught sight of a frightened Earl Campbell and I didn't like it . . .
>
> (Campbell & Ruane, 1999, pp. 83–84)

Not only did Campbell have frightening bodily sensations, he also developed worries about "the little details that most people don't even think about. They weigh on me and tie up my mind. I am continually inundated with intrusive thoughts related to everything I say or do. Do I look okay? Am I walking right? Did I do this right? That right? Why is everyone looking at me? Is it because I'm Earl Campbell, or is it because there's something wrong with me?" (Campbell & Ruane, 1999, p. 199).

Campbell's experiences involve anxiety. In this section, we consider in detail what anxiety is and its relation to the fight-or-flight response. We then examine the common cooccurrence of anxiety disorders and depression.

What Is Anxiety?

Like the term *depression*, the words *anxiety* and *anxious* are used in everyday speech. But what do mental health professionals and researchers mean when using these terms? **Anxiety** refers to a sense of agitation or nervousness, which is often focused on an upcoming potential danger.

We all feel afraid and anxious from time to time. These feelings can be adaptive, signaling the presence of a dangerous stimulus and leading us to be more alert, which heightens our senses. For instance, if you are walking alone down a dark, quiet street late at night, you might be able to hear particularly well or be more sensitive to another person's presence behind you. Such heightened senses can be adaptive on a dark street. Should you hear or sense someone, you may choose to head quickly for a well-lit and busier street. Similarly, a moderate level of anxiety before a test or presentation can enhance your performance (Deshpande & Kawane, 1982)—and, in fact, the absence of anxiety can lead to a lackluster

AP Photo

In his 30s, former NFL player Earl Campbell suddenly developed symptoms of anxiety—racing heart and trouble breathing—which frightened him, as they would most people.

Anxiety
A sense of agitation or nervousness, which is often focused on an upcoming possible danger.

performance, even if you know the material well. Thus, feeling afraid or anxious can be normal and adaptive. Extreme anxiety, however, is a persistent, vague sense of dread or foreboding when not in the presence of a feared stimulus (such as a snake or a plane trip). Such extreme anxiety can arise in response to a high level of fear of a particular stimulus and is sometimes called **anxious apprehension** (Barlow, 2002a). An **anxiety disorder** involves extreme anxiety, intense arousal, and extreme attempts to avoid stimuli that lead to fear and anxiety. These emotions, or the efforts to avoid experiencing them, can create a high level of distress, which can interfere with normal functioning.

The Fight-or-Flight Response Gone Awry

Campbell describes some of the frightening physical sensations he experienced in this way: "Visualize yourself just sitting back in a chair, relaxing. Suddenly, your heart starts racing as if you had just run a hundred-yard dash. You break into a cold sweat. You have trouble breathing. You feel there is nothing you can do to stop all of these things from happening" (Campbell & Ruane, 1999, p. i). Campbell was describing the effects of the **fight-or-flight response** (also called the *stress response*; see Chapter 2), which occurs when an individual perceives a threat. Suppose you think you see a mugger lurking on a dark doorstep as you are hurrying home, alone, late at night. Your brain and body respond as if you must either fight or take flight. The stress response prepares your body to exert physical energy for an action, either fighting the threat or running away from it. It does not matter whether there is an actual threat. Your body automatically responds because you *perceive* a threat. Your body responds in a number of ways (for a more complete list, see Figure 7.1), most notably by:

- increasing your heart rate and breathing rate (in order to provide more oxygen to your muscles and brain),

- increasing the sweat on your palms (a small amount, which helps you grip better — yet not so much as to make your palms become slippery), and

- dilating your pupils (in order to let in more light and help you to see better).

Your body responds this way even to threats that do not require a lot of physical energy, such as—for many people—speaking in front of a group of people (or even *thinking* about speaking in front of them) or taking a pop quiz. In such cases, your body gets prepared, but most of the physical preparations aren't really necessary.

This fight-or-flight response underlies the fear and anxiety involved in almost all anxiety disorders. Some people have an overactive stress response—they have higher levels of arousal during the stress response. Other people may not have an overactive stress response, but they may misinterpret their arousal during the fight-or-flight response and attribute the bodily sensations to a physical ailment. They might, for instance, interpret an increased heart rate as a heart attack. In either case, people come to feel afraid or anxious about the physical sensations of the stress response or the conditions that seem to have caused the response. When their arousal feels as if it is getting out of control, they may start to feel **panic**, which is an extreme sense (or fear) of imminent doom, together with an extreme stress response (Bouton, Mineka, & Barlow, 2001)—what Campbell experienced sitting in his car at a stoplight. Some people who become panicked develop a **phobia** (a term derived from the Greek word for fear, *phobos*), which is an exaggerated fear of an object or a situation, together with an extreme avoidance of the object or situation. Such avoidance can interfere with everyday life. For instance, at one point, Campbell avoided crowded rooms because he thought they might bring on the uncomfortable physical sensations he'd experienced.

Unfortunately, significant anxiety and phobias are not unusual or rare. In the United States, anxiety disorders are the most common kind of mental disorder (Barlow, 2002a); around 15% of people will have some type of anxiety disorder in their

Anxious apprehension
Anxiety that arises in response to a high level of fear of a particular stimulus.

Anxiety disorder
A category of psychological disorders in which the primary symptoms involve extreme anxiety, intense arousal, and/or extreme attempts to avoid stimuli that lead to fear and anxiety.

Fight-or-flight response
The automatic neurological and bodily response to a perceived threat; also called the *stress response*.

Panic
An extreme sense (or fear) of imminent doom, together with an extreme stress response.

Phobia
An exaggerated fear of an object or a situation, together with an extreme avoidance of the object or situation.

Figure 7.1

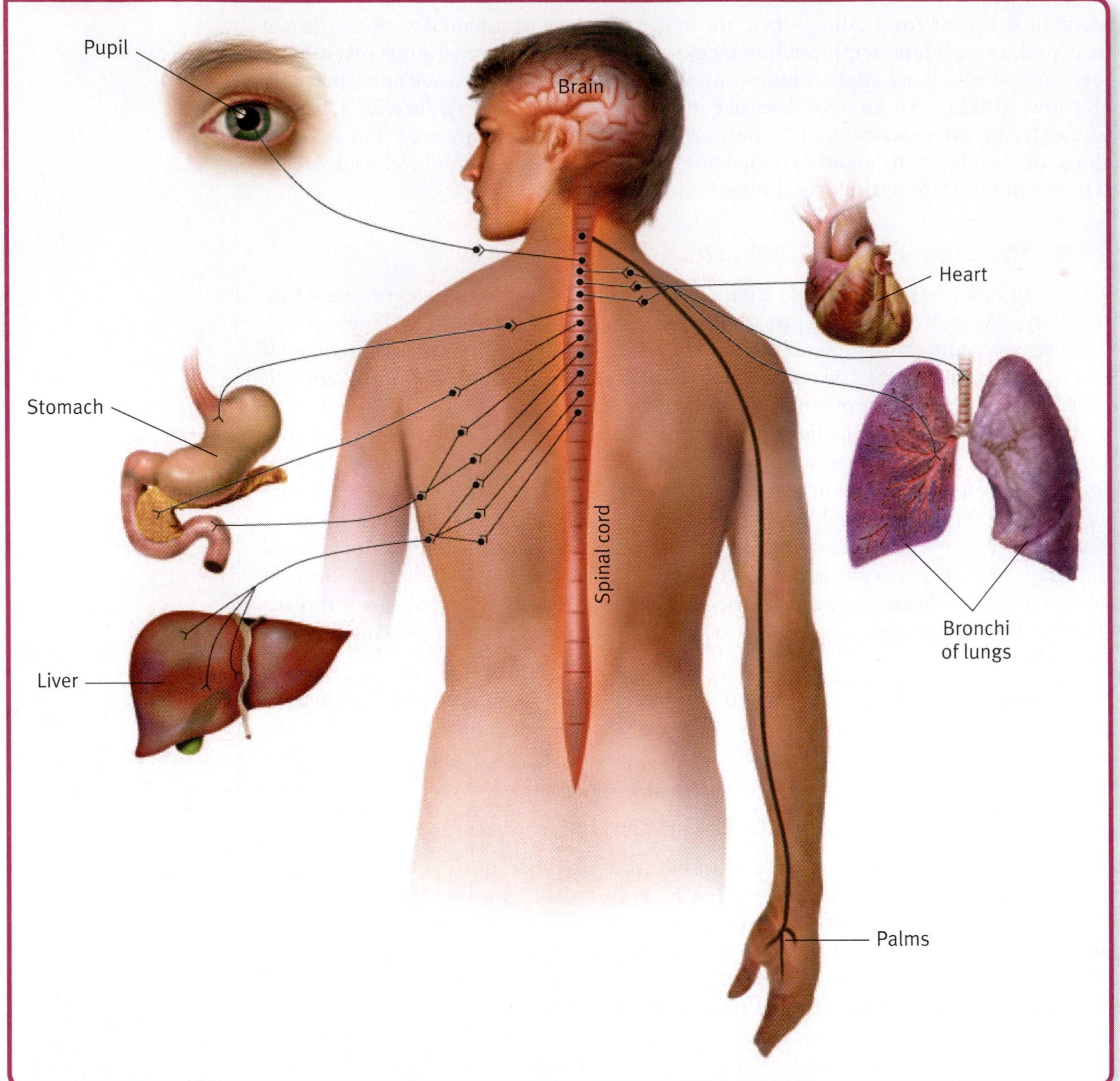

Pupil

Brain

Heart

Stomach

Spinal cord

Liver

Bronchi of lungs

Palms

7.1 ▸ The Fight-or-Flight Response The fight-or-flight response activates the sympathetic nervous system and prepares the body for a significant expenditure of physical energy. Specifically, the sympathetic nervous system gives rise to deeper and quicker breathing to deliver more oxygen to the blood, increased blood flow to muscles and brain (to give them more oxygen), decreased blood flow to skin (which is why people blanch when afraid), more glucose released from the liver into the blood (to provide energy for muscles, organs, and brain), increased sweat on the palms (a small amount, which improves the grip), pupil dilation for better visual acuity, slowed digestion in the stomach and intestines (and an urge to empty the system through urination, defecation, or vomiting). The parasympathetic nervous system typically brings these effects back to the normal state.

lifetimes (Somers et al., 2006). The prevalence rates of anxiety disorders diagnosed by family doctors almost doubled from 1990 to 2003, but it is not clear whether this trend represents a true increase in the number of cases, better recognition of anxiety disorders by the physicians, or both (Skaer, Sclar, & Robison, 2008). Women are twice as likely as men to be diagnosed with one of the anxiety disorders (Somers et al., 2006), although the reasons for this difference are not well understood. Some explanations point to biological differences, such as the hormonal shifts that occur during a woman's childbearing years (Ginsberg 2004); the gender difference in anxiety disorders coincides with the onset of puberty (as is the case with depression; see Chapter 6). Other explanations for the gender difference point to cultural factors (Pigott, 1999): Men tend to be reluctant to acknowledge symptoms of anxiety because they fear that admitting such feelings might undercut the masculine image they project to others.

Comorbidity of Anxiety Disorders

As you'll see throughout this text, symptoms of anxiety or avoidance may occur in many psychological disorders, including *mood disorders* (Chapter 6), *somatization disorder* (Chapter 8), *body dysmorphic disorder* (Chapter 8), and *anorexia nervosa* (Chapter 11). Clinicians must determine whether the anxiety and avoidance symptoms are the *primary* cause of the disturbance or a by-product of another type of problem. In the case of anorexia nervosa, for example, when someone gets anxious about eating high-calorie foods, the anxiety is *secondary* to larger concerns about food, weight, and appearance.

Anxiety and depression often occur together; about 50% of people with an anxiety disorder are also depressed (Brown et al., 2001). For Earl Campbell, depression followed anxiety. A couple of weeks after his first anxiety episode, on the first morning in his new house in Austin, Campbell experienced debilitating depression settling on him:

> The moment I woke up in the morning, a heaviness enveloped me. I couldn't avoid it. I would open my eyes and start crying. I would sit in the bedroom all day long, wearing pajamas and sunglasses, the curtains closed against the daylight. Life had slipped into slow motion. Sometimes I'd sit in a daze on the couch, watching Reuna unpacking boxes and organizing the house. I would just sit there in pain. I began to have terrible headaches. The depression would not let up. I told Reuna I was sure I was going to die. She knew I was quite serious.
>
> (Campbell & Ruane, 1999, p. 92)

Researchers and clinicians are trying to discover why there is such high comorbidity between anxiety disorders and depression. Some researchers have proposed a three-part model of anxiety and depression that specifies the ways in which the two kinds of disorders overlap and the ways in which they are distinct (Clark & Watson, 1991; Mineka, Watson, & Clark, 1998). This model has been supported by subsequent research (Joiner, 1996; Olino et al., 2008). The three parts of the model are as follows (see Figure 7.2):

1. *High level of negative emotions*, which include general distress. Both anxiety and depressive disorders can involve poor concentration, sleep disturbances, and irritability, as well as anxious apprehension. This part of the model represents the common factor shared by anxiety disorders and depression (and other disorders as well).

2. *Low level of positive emotions.* Symptoms of depression include a lack of enjoyment and slowed motor functioning. Low positive affect is a symptom of depression, but generally not a symptom of anxiety disorders.

3. *Physiological hyperarousal* (overarousal), which is found in anxiety disorders, but not in depression.

Approximately 10–25% of those with anxiety disorders also abuse or are dependent on alcohol (Bibb & Chambless, 1986; Otto et al., 1992). Among people with phobias, the alcohol use usually occurs *after* the anxiety symptoms develop. Among those with other kinds of anxiety disorders, alcohol use may either precede or follow the onset of the anxiety disorder (Swendsen et al., 1998).

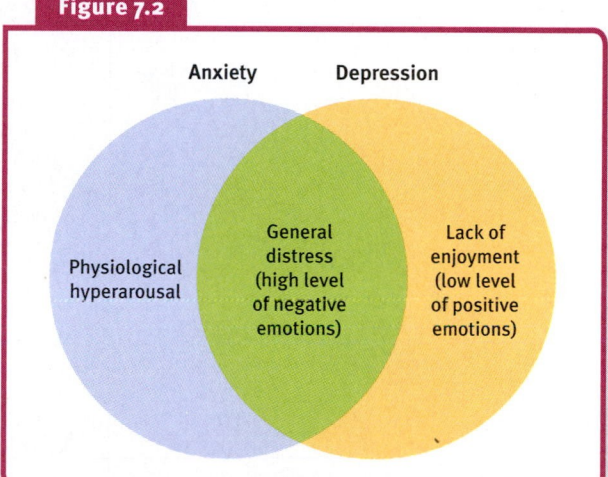

Figure 7.2

7.2 ► Tripartite Model of Anxiety and Depression Anxiety and depression have in common a high level of negative emotions, but each has unique elements: Anxiety generally involves a very high level of physiological arousal, whereas depression involves a low level of positive emotions.

People with phobias, such as musicians with performance anxiety (stage fright), may use alcohol to relieve their anxiety symptoms. However, using alcohol in this way can lead to abuse or dependence.

Dynamic Graphics/Jupiterimages

Key Concepts and Facts About Common Features of Anxiety Disorders

- The key symptoms of anxiety disorders are extreme anxiety, intense arousal, and attempts to avoid stimuli that lead to fear and anxiety.

- The fight-or-flight response arises when people perceive a threat; when the arousal feels out of control—either because the individual has an overactive stress response or because he or she misinterprets the arousal—the person may experience panic. In response to the panic, some people develop a phobia of stimuli related to their panic and anxiety symptoms.

- Anxiety disorders frequently co-occur with other psychological disorders, such as depression or substance-related disorders. Mental health clinicians must determine whether the anxiety symptoms are the primary cause of the problem or are the by-product of another type of disorder.

- The high comorbidity of depression and anxiety disorders suggests that the two disorders share some of the same features, specifically high levels of negative emotions and distress—which can lead to concentration and sleep problems and irritability.

Generalized Anxiety Disorder

Earl Campbell became a worrier—even during the best of times:

> On a day when life seems absolutely wonderful—say, a beautiful fall Saturday or Sunday when I'm watching one of my boys play football—I'll often be overcome by the fear that it will all come to an end somehow. It's just too good. Something bad is going to ruin it for me. This past year was the most difficult one I've had . . . Tyler [his son] was in the fifth grade, and I worried the entire year. I was in the fifth grade when my father died, and I thought my fate was sealed. I was scared I would die and my boys would have to go through life without a father, the way I did.
>
> (Campbell & Ruane, 1999, p. 204)

Worrying is a normal part of life, but some people worry more than others. How much is "too much" worrying?

What Is Generalized Anxiety Disorder?

Generalized anxiety disorder (GAD) is characterized by uncontrollable worry and anxiety about a number of events or activities (which are not solely the focus of another Axis I disorder, such as about having a panic attack) (see Table 7.1; American Psychiatric Association, 2000). The worry and anxiety among individuals suffering from GAD primarily focus on family, finances, work, and illness (Sanderson & Barlow, 1990); Earl Campbell worried mostly about family and illness; other people may worry about minor matters (Craske, Rapee, Jackel, & Barlow, 1989). In contrast to most people, people with GAD worry even when things are going well. Moreover, their worries intrude into their awareness when they are trying to focus on other thoughts—and they cannot stop worrying (American Psychiatric Association, 2000). Symptoms are present for at least half the days during a 6-month period. Like A. H., discussed in Case 7.1, people with GAD feel a chronic, low level of anxiety or worry about many things. Moreover, the fact that they constantly worry in itself causes them distress.

CASE 7.1 ▶ FROM THE OUTSIDE: Generalized Anxiety Disorder

A. H. was a 39-year-old divorced mother of two (son aged 12, daughter aged 7) who worked as a bank manager. However, she had become concerned about her ability to concentrate on and remember information while at work. A. H. had made some "financially disastrous" mistakes, and was now—at the suggestion of her supervisor—taking some vacation time to "get her head together." Because of her concentration and memory problems, it had been taking her longer to complete her work, so she had been arriving at work 30 minutes early each day, and often took work home. She reported being unable to relax, even outside of work, and at work it was hard to make decisions because she ruminated endlessly ("Is this the right decision, or should I do that?"), and hence tried to avoid making decisions altogether. Her concentration and memory problems were worst when she was worried about some aspect of life, which was most of the time. She reported that 75% of her waking life each day was spent in a state of anxiety and worry. In addition to worrying about

Generalized anxiety disorder (GAD)
The anxiety disorder characterized by uncontrollable worry and anxiety about a number of events or activities that are not solely the focus of another Axis I disorder.

her performance at work, she worried about her children's well being (whether they had been hurt or killed while out playing in the neighborhood). She also worried about her relationships with men, and minor things such as getting to work on time, keeping her house clean, and maintaining regular contact with friends and family. A. H. recognized that her fears were both excessive and uncontrollable, but she couldn't dismiss any worry that came to mind. She was irritable, had insomnia, frequent muscle tension and headaches, and felt generally on edge.

(Adapted from Brown & Barlow, 1997, pp. 1–3)

Table 7.1 ▶ DSM-IV-TR Diagnostic Criteria for Generalized Anxiety Disorder (GAD)

A. Excessive anxiety and worry (apprehensive expectation), occurring more days than not for at least 6 months, about a number of events or activities (such as work or school performance).

B. The person finds it difficult to control the worry.

C. The anxiety and worry are associated with three (or more) of the following six symptoms (with at least some symptoms present for more days than not for the past 6 months).

Note: Only one item is required in children.

(1) restlessness or feeling keyed up or on edge

(2) being easily fatigued

(3) difficulty concentrating or mind going blank

(4) irritability

(5) muscle tension

(6) sleep disturbance (difficulty falling or staying asleep, or restless unsatisfying sleep)

D. The focus of the anxiety and worry is not confined to features of an Axis I disorder, e.g., the anxiety or worry is not about having a Panic Attack (as in Panic Disorder [discussed later in this chapter]), being embarrassed in public (as in Social Phobia [discussed later in this chapter]), being contaminated (as in Obsessive-Compulsive Disorder [discussed later in this chapter]), being away from home or close relatives (as in Separation Anxiety Disorder [Chapter 14]), gaining weight (as in Anorexia Nervosa [Chapter 10]), having multiple physical complaints (as in Somatization Disorder [Chapter 8]), or having a serious illness (as in Hypochondriasis [Chapter 8]), and the anxiety and worry do not occur exclusively during Posttraumatic Stress Disorder [discussed later in this chapter].

E. The anxiety, worry, or physical symptoms cause clinically significant distress or impairment in social, occupational, or other important areas of functioning.

F. The disturbance is not due to the direct physiological effects of a substance (e.g., a drug of abuse, a medication) or a general medical condition (e.g., hyperthyroidism) and does not occur exclusively during a Mood Disorder [Chapter 6], a Psychotic Disorder [Chapter 12], or a Pervasive Developmental Disorder [Chapter 14].

Source: Reprinted with permission from the Diagnostic and Statistical Manual of Mental Disorders, Text Revision, Fourth Edition, (Copyright 2000) American Psychiatric Association.

The content of the worries of people with GAD is influenced by their culture and the types of catastrophic events most likely to occur in their locale. Those who live along the Gulf coast of the United States may worry about hurricanes; those who reside in California may worry about earthquakes.

Because the symptoms are chronic (lasting at least 6 months) and because many people with GAD can usually function adequately in some areas of their daily lives, they come to see their worrying and anxiety as a part of themselves, not as a disorder. However, as happened to A. H., not having control over anxious thoughts and worrying can lead to problems in work and social life. The worrying may be so intrusive that people feel restless, have difficulty concentrating or sleeping, and become irritable. See Table 7.2 for more facts about GAD.

As noted in Table 7.2, GAD and depression have an extremely high comorbidity. Among people who have both disorders at the same time, only 27% eventually experience remission, compared to 48% of those who have only GAD and 41% of those who have only depression (Schoevers et al., 2005). People with both disorders are also likely to have

AP Photo/Dave Martin

Table 7.2 ▸ Generalized Anxiety Disorder Facts at a Glance

Prevalence

- Approximately 5% of people will develop GAD in their lifetime, with women over age 40 at highest risk (approximately 10% of this group will develop the disorder) (American Psychiatric Association, 2000; Kessler et al., 2005; Somers et al., 2006).
- Primary care physicians report that their patients suffer from GAD more frequently than other anxiety disorders (Lieb, Becker, & Altamura, 2005; Wittchen & Hoyer, 2001).

Comorbidity

- GAD occurs very frequently with depression, with up to 80% of those having GAD during their lives also experiencing depression at some point (Judd et al., 1998).
- Approximately half of the people who have both GAD and depression during their lifetimes have both disorders at the same time (Ansseau et al., 2005).

Onset

- Approximately half the people with GAD develop the disorder between the ages of 10 and 19, whereas most others, particularly women, develop it sometime after turning 40 (Hoehn-Saric, Hazlett, & McLeod, 1993; Wittchen & Hoyer, 2001).

Course

- Once someone has GAD, its course is likely to be chronic, with symptoms fluctuating in response to stress.

Gender Differences

- Twice as many women as men are diagnosed with GAD.

Cultural Differences

- The content of the worries of people with GAD is shaped by their culture, their personal experiences, and the environment in which they live. Some people worry about catastrophic events, such as natural disasters; others worry about human-caused calamities, such as nuclear war or terrorist acts.

Source: Unless otherwise noted, the source for information is American Psychiatric Association, 2000.

had their symptoms arise at a younger age (Moffitt et al., 2007), to have more severe symptoms of each disorder, and to function less well than those who have only one of the two disorders (Zimmerman & Chelminski, 2003). Among people over 50 years old—the age group in which GAD is most common—depression often arises after GAD (Lenze et al., 2005; Schoevers et al., 2005). The high comorbidity also suggests that GAD and depression may reflect different facets of the same underlying problem, which is rooted in distress, worry, and rumination (Schoevers et al., 2003).

Understanding Generalized Anxiety Disorder

GAD can be best understood by using the neuropsychosocial approach to examine its etiology—by considering neurological, psychological, and social factors and the feedback loops among them. Each type of factor, by itself, seems to be necessary but not sufficient to give rise to this disorder. Neurological and psychological factors set the stage, and social factors can trigger the symptoms.

Neurological Factors

Let's examine the role of neurological factors in GAD. We'll see that the right hemisphere of the brain appears to play a special role in GAD, that a complex mix of neurotransmitters is involved in the disorder (largely by affecting the autonomic nervous system and brain areas involved in registering reward), and that genetics sets the stage by predisposing someone to develop GAD.

Brain Systems

The brain ultimately controls the body's responses, and thus GAD must involve the brain in some way. However, researchers are only beginning to identify the precise ways in which large-scale brain mechanisms are altered to produce GAD (Nutt, 2001). For example, they have found that patients with GAD have more gray and white matter in the superior temporal gyrus, an area used in hearing and language comprehension, than do individuals who do not have this disorder. Moreover, this brain area is strikingly larger in the right hemisphere than the left in patients with GAD, and the size difference is more extreme for people who have more severe anxiety (De Bellis et al., 2002). It is possible that this additional cortex leads people with GAD to form certain associations (such as of being in danger when in common situations or suffering dangerous consequences after performing common actions) more easily than do other people, but at present this is only a hypothesis.

The role of the right hemisphere was also evident in an fMRI study in which adolescent patients with GAD and adolescents in a control group viewed angry and neutral faces (Monk et al., 2006). The researchers found that a key part of the right frontal lobe was more strongly activated for the patients than for the controls when the participants saw angry faces. However, patients who showed greater activation in this area had less severe anxiety. These results are only suggestive, but might indicate that this area is involved in a coping activity, such as attempting to regulate bodily responses; in fact, the frontal lobes have many connections to the limbic system, including connections to the amygdala, which plays a key role in fear (e.g., LeDoux, 1996, 2000), and to the autonomic nervous system (Gabbott et al., 2005; Ghashghaei & Barbas, 2002; Teves et al., 2004).

The connections from the frontal lobes to the autonomic nervous system may play a particular role in GAD—but, unlike most types of anxiety disorders, GAD isn't associated with cranked up sympathetic nervous system activity (Marten et al., 1993). Instead, GAD is associated with decreased arousal that arises from an unusually responsive parasympathetic nervous system. The parasympathetic nervous system tends to cause effects opposite to those caused by the sympathetic nervous system. So, for instance, heightened parasympathetic activity slows heart rate, stimulates digestion and the bladder, and causes pupils to contract (Barlow, 2002a). When an individual with GAD perceives a threatening stimulus, his or her subsequent worry temporarily *reduces* any arousal (Borkovec & Hu, 1990), suppresses negative emotions (see Figure 7.2), and produces muscle tension (Barlow, 2002a; Pluess, Conrad, & Wilhelm, 2009). These facts are in stark contrast to Earl Campbell's symptoms, which suggest that he did not have GAD.

Neural Communication

Although the frontal lobes of patients with GAD are normal in size, the dopamine in the frontal lobes of these patients does not function normally (Stein, Westenberg, & Liebowitz, 2002). In fact, numerous studies suggest that a wide range of neurotransmitters, including gamma-aminobutyric acid (GABA), serotonin, and norepinephrine, may not function properly in people with GAD (Nutt, 2001). These neurotransmitters affect, among other things, people's response to reward, their motivation, and how effectively they can pay attention to stimuli and events.

Genetics

Studies of the genetics of GAD have produced solid evidence that GAD has a genetic component. The heritability estimate for GAD is at least 15–20% (Hettema, Prescott, & Kendler, 2001) and possibly almost 40% (Scherrer et al., 2000) and the disorder is equally heritable for men and women (Hettema, Prescott, & Kendler, 2001). However, much of this disorder may rest on a tendency to become anxious, which can be manifested in a number of different ways. For example, much of the genetic basis of GAD is shared with panic disorder (Chantarujikapong et al., 2001; Scherrer et al., 2000) and with posttraumatic stress disorder (Chantarujikapong et al., 2001). Moreover, if one family member has GAD, other family members are likely to have GAD or depression, which suggests a common underlying genetic vulnerability (Gorwood, 2004; Kendler et al., 2007).

Psychological Factors: Hypervigilance and the Illusion of Control

Psychological factors that contribute to GAD generally involve three characteristic modes of thinking and behaving: being particularly alert for possible threats, feeling that the worrying is out of control, and sensing that the worrying prevents panic.

1. People with GAD pay a lot of attention to stimuli in their environment, searching for possible threats. This heightened search for threats is called **hypervigilance.**

2. People with GAD typically feel that their worries are out of control and that they can't stop or alter the pattern of their thoughts, no matter what they do.

3. The mere act of worrying prevents anxiety from becoming panic (Craske, 1999), and thus the act of worrying is negatively reinforcing (Borkovec, 1994a; Borkovec et al., 1999). The worrying does not help the individual cope with the problem at hand, but it does give him or her the *illusion* of coping, which temporarily decreases anxiety about the perceived threat. Some people think that if they worry, they are actively addressing a problem. But they are not—worrying is not the same thing as effective problem solving; the original concern isn't reduced by the worrying and it remains a problem, along with the additional problem of chronic worrying.

Social Factors: Stressors

Stressful life events, such as a death in the family, friction in a close relationship, or trouble on the job, can trigger symptoms of GAD in someone who is neurologically and psychologically vulnerable to developing it. For people who develop GAD after age 40, the disorder often arises after a significant stressor occurs.

GAD also appears to be related more directly to relationships. In one interesting study, researchers found that college students with GAD rated themselves as having more severe global relationship problems (often being too compliant and deferential to others) than did college students in a control group. However, when friends of the students with GAD and friends of the control participants were asked to rate the severity of relationship problems of the participants in the study, the ratings did not differ for the GAD and control participants (Eng & Heimberg, 2006). This means that the GAD students felt that they had problems with relationships, but people close to them didn't see it that way. People with GAD may experience increased stress if they view themselves as having serious problems in relationships. Increased stress, in turn, can lead to distress and negative emotions that can be difficult to manage and regulate (Mennin, Turk et al., 2004).

FEEDBACK LOOPS IN ACTION:
Understanding Generalized Anxiety Disorder

Stressful life experiences (typically social factors) can trigger the onset of GAD, but most people who experience stressful periods in their lives—even extreme stress—never develop this disorder. Moreover, people who do develop GAD often report that they were afraid and avoidant as children (American Psychiatric Association, 2000), which may be explained by abnormal neurological or physiological (perhaps hormonal) functioning. However, such abnormal functioning in childhood could arise from genes, might develop in childhood because of early life experiences, or could be caused by some combination of the two. To develop GAD, a person probably must experience three factors (see Figure 7.3): abnormal neurological functioning (which may reflect abnormal levels of GABA or another neurotransmitter), learning certain kinds of worry-related behaviors such as hypervigilance for threats, and undergoing a highly stressful event or set of events such as a death in the family. Any one of these alone—and probably any two of these—will not cause GAD.

A construction forewoman talks with a member of her crew. People who have GAD may be hypervigilant for possible threats in their environment, for example, constantly scanning the boss's face for possible signs of displeasure.

Hypervigilance
A heightened search for threats.

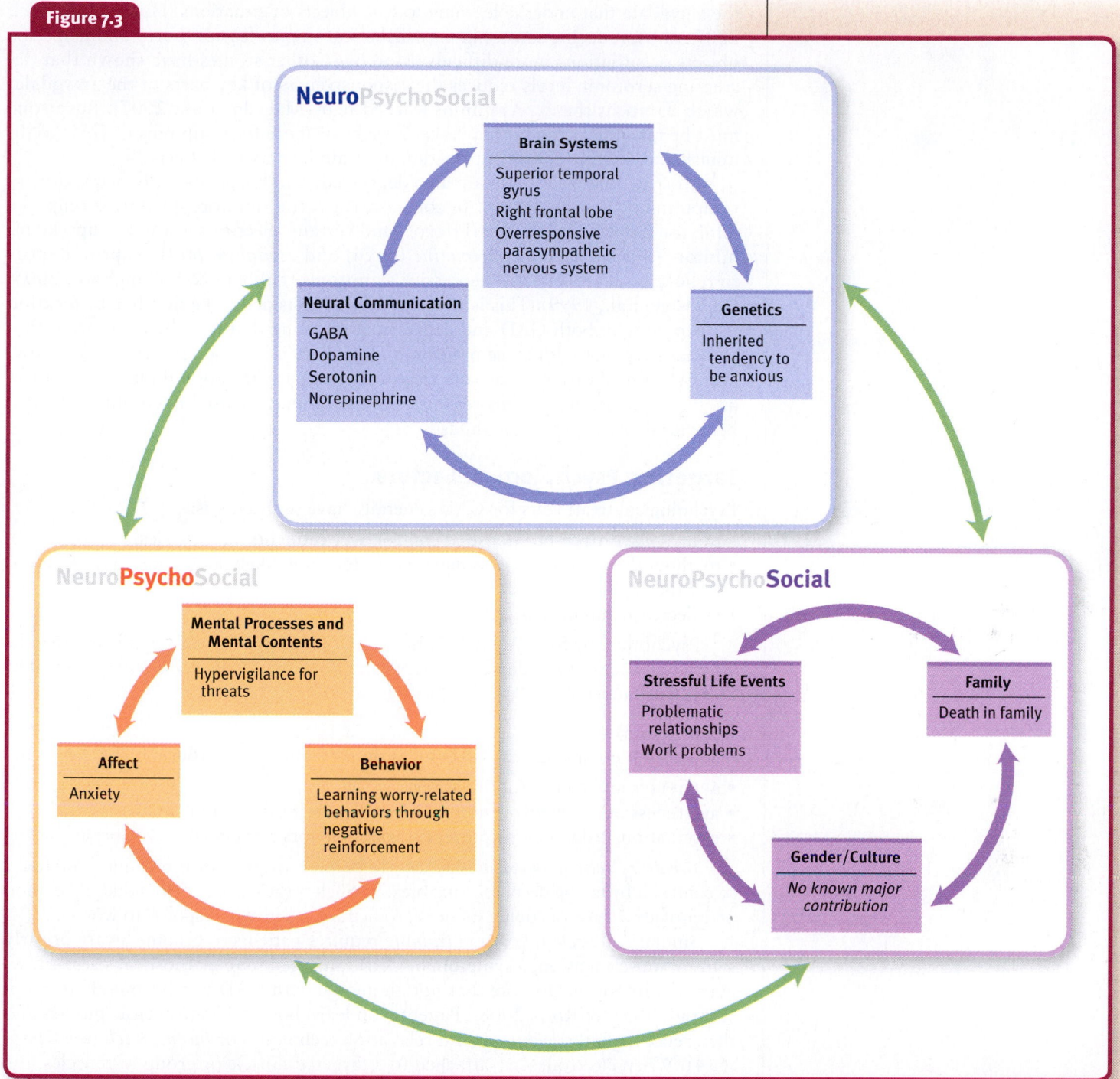

Figure 7.3

7.3 ▶ **Feedback Loops in Action: Generalized Anxiety Disorder**

Treating Generalized Anxiety Disorder

Treatment for GAD can target neurological, psychological, or social factors, although neurological or psychological factors are the predominant focus of treatments. As usual, interventions targeting any type of factor have ripple effects to the other factors.

Targeting Neurological Factors: Medication

The antianxiety medication *buspirone* (Buspar) effectively reduces the symptoms of GAD, probably by decreasing serotonin release. Serotonin facilitates changes in the amygdala that underlie learning to fear objects or situations (Huang & Kandel, 2007); thus, reducing serotonin may make learning to fear or worry about specific objects or situations more difficult. Moreover, other studies have shown that decreasing serotonin levels reduces the responsiveness of key parts of the amygdala, which dampens the expression of learned fear (Macedo et al., 2007). Buspirone must be taken daily, and it may take 2 weeks or more for symptoms of GAD to diminish and 6 weeks for the medication to attain its maximal effects.

Most people with GAD are also depressed, and buspirone only helps anxiety symptoms (Davidson, 2001). In contrast, the serotonin/norepinephrine reuptake inhibitor (SNRI) *venlafaxine* (Effexor) and certain selective serotonin reuptake inhibitors (SSRIs), such as *paroxetine* (Paxil) and *escitalopram* (Lexapro), appear to relieve both anxiety and depressive symptoms (Baldwin & Polkinghorn, 2005; Davidson et al., 1999). This is why an SNRI is considered the first-line medication for people with both GAD and depression, meaning that it is the medication that clinicians try first with these patients (unless there is a reason not to use it). However, when medication is the sole treatment and patients stop taking it, symptoms are likely to return. For this reason, medication may be used in conjunction with behavioral and cognitive methods.

Targeting Psychological Factors

Psychological treatments for GAD generally have several aims:

- to increase the person's sense of control over thoughts and worries,
- to allow the person to assess more accurately how likely and dangerous perceived threats actually are, and
- to decrease muscle tension.

Psychotherapy for GAD generally consists of behavioral and cognitive methods, which can successfully decrease symptoms (Borkovec & Ruscio, 2001; Cottraux, 2004; Durham et al., 2003).

Behavioral Methods

Behavioral methods to treat GAD focus on three main areas (Barlow, 2002a):

- awareness and control of breathing,
- awareness and control of muscle tension and relaxation, and
- elimination, reduction, or prevention of behaviors associated with worry.

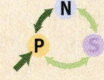

Breathing retraining requires patients to become aware of their breathing and to try to control it by taking deep, relaxing breaths. Such breathing can help induce relaxation and provide a sense of coping (of doing something positive in response to worry).

Similarly, *muscle relaxation training* requires patients to become aware of early signs of muscle tension, a symptom of GAD, and then to relax those muscles. (However, it is important to note that not all people with GAD exhibit muscle tension; Conrad, Isaac, & Roth, 2008.) Patients can learn how to identify tense muscles and then relax them through standard relaxation techniques or *biofeedback* (see Chapter 4). When electrodes are attached to a targeted muscle or group of muscles, the patient can see on a monitor or hear from a speaker signals that indicate whether the monitored muscles are tense or relaxed. This feedback helps the patient learn how to detect and reduce the tension, eventually without relying on the feedback.

People with GAD often develop behaviors that are associated with their worries. For instance, a patient who worries that "something bad" may happen to her family may call home several times each day. By calling home and finding out that everyone is fine, she temporarily lessens her anxiety, thus (negatively) reinforcing the calling behavior. People with GAD do not naturally habituate to such anxiety; as they worry about one set of concerns, they get increasingly anxious until they shift the focus of their worry to another set of concerns, never becoming habituated to any specific set of concerns.

Exposure is one method used to eliminate or reduce symptoms associated with GAD. Exposure relies on the principle of habituation (see Chapter 4) and when used to treat GAD, patients undergo prolonged exposure to their worries. They are asked to think about only one specific worry (this is the exposure) and to imagine their worst possible fears about the subject of that worry, such as the possible deaths of family members. Patients are asked to think about their worry continuously for about 30 minutes. After this half-hour of exposure, patients then list their rational responses to the worst outcomes they imagined. Patients' anxiety and level of worry should decrease both over the course of the session and across sessions. When patients can think about one set of concerns without much worry or anxiety, they move on to use the same procedure with another set of concerns (see Figure 7.4).

Figure 7.4

Worry exposure first involves evoking a particular worry as vividly as possible and trying to imagine the worst-case scenario related to that worry.

The patient then tries to stay focused on the single worry for about a half-hour; the patient should habituate to the anxiety caused by the worry.

Once the patient has habituated somewhat to the worry, the patient and therapist generate possible rational alternatives to the worst-case scenario.

After the patient has habituated to and developed a rational response to a particular worry, he or she is ready go through the same process with a new, specific worry.

7.4 ▶ Worry Exposure

Source: Adapted from Brown, O'Leary, & Barlow, 1993.

Cognitive Methods

Cognitive methods for treating GAD focus on first helping patients to identify the thought patterns that are associated with their worries and anxieties and then helping them to use cognitive restructuring and other methods to prevent these thought patterns from spiraling out of control. The methods can also decrease the *intensity* of patients' responses to their thought patterns, so that they are less likely to develop symptoms. Specific cognitive methods include the following:

- *Psychoeducation* about the nature of worrying and GAD symptoms and available treatment options and their possible advantages and disadvantages.

- *Meditation*, which helps patients learn to "let go" of thoughts and reduce the time spent thinking about worries (Evans et al., 2008; Lehrer & Woolfolk, 1994; Miller, Fletcher, & Kabat-Zinn, 1995).

- *Self-monitoring*, which helps patients become aware of cues that lead to anxiety and worry. For instance, patients may be asked to complete a daily log about their worries, identifying events or stimuli that lead them to worry more or worry less.

- *Problem solving*, which involves teaching the patient to think about worries in very specific terms—rather than global ones—so that they can be addressed through cognitive restructuring. Here's an exchange between a therapist and a patient with GAD. The patient starts out talking about a night when sleep had been particularly elusive; the phone had rung at 11:30 P.M., but it was a wrong number. Near the end of the exchange, the therapist tries to engage the patient in problem solving.

> Therapist: What did you think the call might be about?
>
> Patient: Well, you know, bad news of some sort, someone dying or something like that. After my visit home this summer, I have often worried that my father is getting up there in years, he turned 55 in July, and, well, since I moved to Albany I haven't seen my folks nearly as much as I would have liked to.
>
> Therapist: So, when the phone rang, you were worried that something may have happened with your father?
>
> Patient: I don't think just then because I picked up the phone real fast, but the phone ringing kind of startled me. But after I hung up, I wondered why I was so anxious and I realized that I must have thought that something happened to him. Once I realized that, I was worried about him the rest of the night.
>
> Therapist: If I recall from what you said before, he's in pretty good health, isn't he?
>
> Patient: Yeah, he had a mole removed a while ago. Since he's worked outside all of his life, I worry that all that sun will have caused him to get skin cancer some day.
>
> Therapist: What do you picture happening if your dad did pass away? [Note: Therapist attempts to help the patient frame the problem as a worst-case scenario; patient and therapist can then engage in problem solving.]
>
> Patient: What do you mean? Do you mean what would I do?
>
> (Brown, O'Leary & Barlow, 1993, p. 159)

- *Cognitive restructuring*, which involves helping the patient learn to identify and shift automatic, irrational thoughts related to worries (see the third panel in Figure 7.4). With the patient concerned about his father's health, the therapist could point out that the patient is using catastrophic thinking as well as overestimating the probability that something dire will occur (Brown, O'Leary & Barlow, 1993).

Targeting Social Factors

The neuropsychosocial approach leads us to notice whether certain kinds of treatments are available for particular disorders. For instance, at present, there are very few treatments for GAD that specifically target social factors.

Although CBT for GAD may be provided in a group format (Dugas et al., 2003), such groups seek to change thoughts, behaviors, and feelings; they do not directly focus on changing relationships, family dynamics, or other social factors. Similarly, family or couples therapy may be employed, but such treatment is usually a supplement to the primary treatment of medication or CBT.

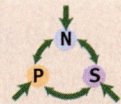

FEEDBACK LOOPS IN TREATMENT: **Generalized Anxiety Disorder**

Muscle relaxation training involves increasing the patient's awareness of muscle tension (psychological factor) and then using techniques to decrease that tension; this process leads to neurological changes (neurological factor), particularly when it reduces stress and thereby decreases the levels of stress hormones. In turn, as other behavioral methods and cognitive methods (psychological factors) reduce worry and anxiety, the patient can devote his or her attention to other matters, including relationships and work (social factors). For instance, with A. H. (the woman in Case 7.1), treatment consisted of psychoeducation, self-monitoring, exposure, and cognitive restructuring. Successful treatment also affected social factors: Her children found her "less moody" and "more fun to be with" (Brown & Barlow, 1997, p. 15). Thus, when behavioral methods and cognitive methods are successful, the individual develops a sense of mastery of and control over worries and anxiety (which decreases anxiety even further), and social interactions reinforce new behaviors. Similarly, medication directly targets neurological factors, which in turn reduces the individual's worries and anxiety; he or she becomes less preoccupied with these concerns, which increases the ability to focus at work and in relationships. These feedback loops are illustrated in Figure 7.5.

Did Earl Campbell develop GAD? Although his worries may seem excessive and uncontrollable at times, they do not appear to have had the effects necessary for the diagnosis, such as muscle tension, irritability, or difficulty sleeping (Criterion C, Table 7.1). Any irritability or sleep problems he had are better explained as symptoms of another anxiety disorder—panic disorder, which we discuss in the following section.

Figure 7.5

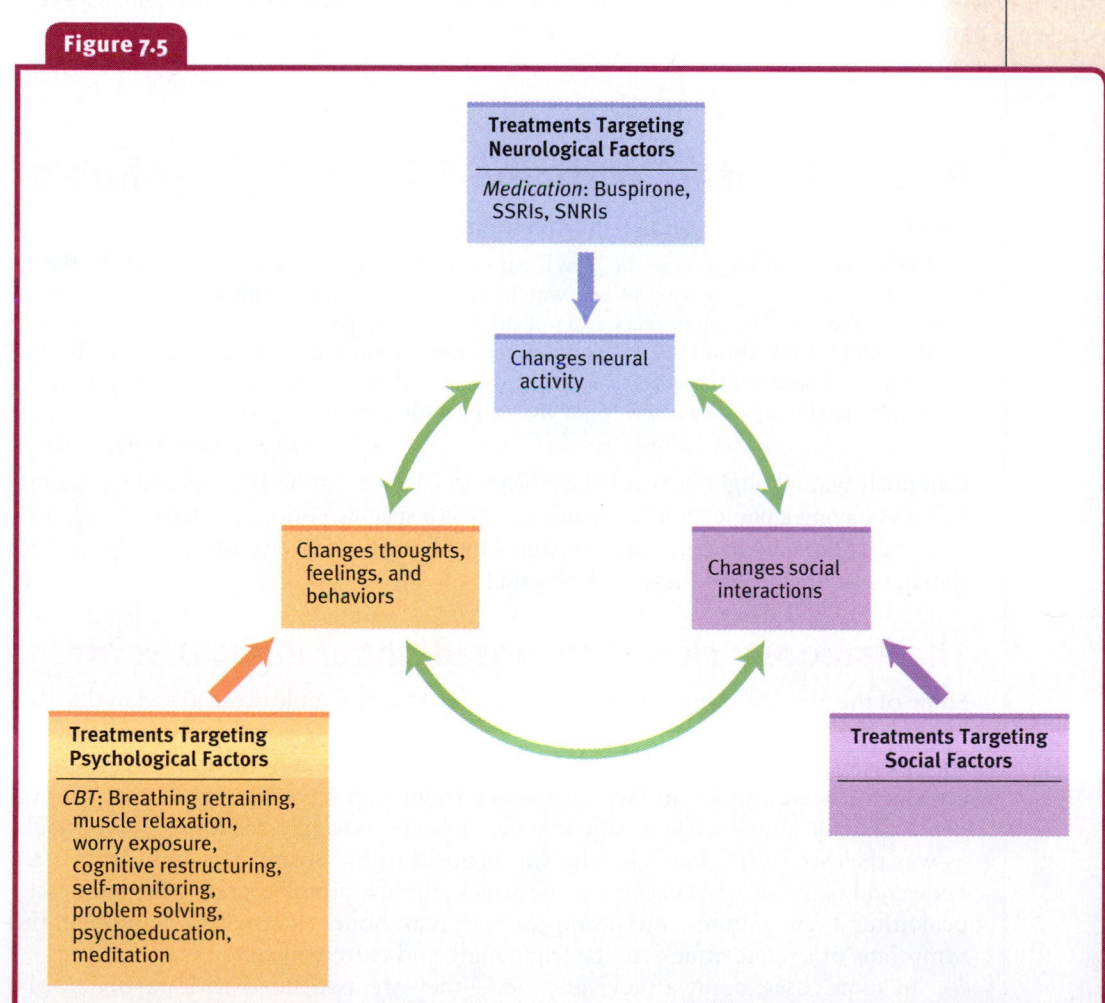

7.5 ▶ Feedback Loops in Treating Generalized Anxiety Disorder

Key Concepts and Facts About Generalized Anxiety Disorder

- Generalized anxiety disorder is marked by persistent uncontrollable worry about a number of events or activities that are not solely the focus of another Axis I disorder. Most people with GAD also have comorbid depression.

- Neurological factors associated with GAD include:
  - more gray and white matter in the areas of the brain related to hearing and language comprehension—the superior temporal gyrus—particularly in the right hemisphere. Moreover, unlike most other anxiety disorders, GAD is associated with *decreased* arousal because the parasympathetic nervous system is extremely responsive.
  - unusually strong activation in the right front lobe when viewing angry faces, which may be related to the operation of coping mechanisms;
  - abnormal activity of serotonin, dopamine, and other neurotransmitters, which in turn influences motivation, response to reward, and attention;
  - a genetic predisposition to become anxious and/or depressed. This predisposition, however, is not specific to GAD.

- Psychological factors that contribute to GAD include being hypervigilant for possible threats, a sense that the worrying is out of control, and the reinforcing experience that worrying prevents panic.

- Social factors that contribute to GAD include stressful life events, which can trigger the disorder.

- Treatments for GAD include:
  - medication (which targets neurological factors), such as buspirone or an SNRI or SSRI when depression is present as a comorbid disorder; and
  - CBT (which targets psychological factors), which may include breathing retraining, muscle relaxation training, worry exposure, cognitive restructuring, self-monitoring, problem solving, psychoeducation, and/or meditation. CBT may be employed in a group format.

Making a Diagnosis

- Reread Case 7.1 about A. H., and determine whether or not her symptoms meet the criteria for generalized anxiety disorder. Specifically, list which criteria apply and which do not. If you would like more information to determine her diagnosis, what information—specifically—would you want, and in what ways would the information influence your decision?

Panic Disorder (With and Without Agoraphobia)

Earl Campbell's uncomfortable episodes of anxiety didn't stop:

> The second night we were in the [new] house, I had my third episode. It felt just like the second one had. I was lying in bed watching television, and Reuna was sound asleep next to me. I was trying to relax and not think about my problem, but my problem was all I could think about. All of a sudden, my heart went crazy—pounding, pounding harder and harder. I thought it was going to leap right out of my chest. I sat up, struggling to regain my composure. It got worse. I couldn't breathe again.
>
> (Campbell & Ruane, 1999, p. 92)

Campbell again thought he was having heart attack and that his life was ending. Campbell was having a panic attack. A **panic attack** is a specific period of intense dread, fear, or a sense of imminent doom, accompanied by physical symptoms of a pounding heart, shortness of breath, shakiness, and sweating.

The Panic Attack—A Key Ingredient of Panic Disorder

Some of the physical symptoms of a panic attack may resemble those associated with a heart attack—heart palpitations, shortness of breath, chest pain, and a feeling of choking or being smothered (see Table 7.3), which is why Earl Campbell mistook his panic attacks for heart attacks. In fact, emergency room staff have learned to look for evidence of panic attack when a patient arrives who purportedly has had a heart attack, as was the case with Campbell, who was brought to the hospital by ambulance after his second panic attack. During a panic attack, the symptoms generally begin quickly, peak after a few minutes, and disappear within an hour. As noted by Campbell, the symptoms of a panic attack can be frightening and extremely aversive.

In some cases, panic attacks are *cued*—they are associated with particular objects, situations, or sensations. Although panic attacks are occasionally cued by

Panic attack
A specific period of intense dread, fear, or a sense of imminent doom, accompanied by physical symptoms of a pounding heart, shortness of breath, shakiness, and sweating.

Table 7.3 ▸ DSM-IV-TR Criteria for a Panic Attack

A discrete period of intense fear or discomfort, in which at least four of the following symptoms develop abruptly and reach a peak within 10 minutes:

• palpitations, pounding heart, or accelerated heart rate	• feeling dizzy, unsteady, lightheaded, or faint
• sweating	• derealization (feelings of unreality) or depersonalization (being detached from oneself)
• trembling or shaking	
• sensations of shortness of breath or smothering	• fear of losing control or going crazy
• feeling of choking	• fear of dying
• chest pain or discomfort	• paresthesias (numbness or tingling sensations)
• nausea or abdominal distress	• chills or hot flushes

Source: Reprinted with permission from the Diagnostic and Statistical Manual of Mental Disorders, Text Revision, Fourth Edition, (Copyright 2000) American Psychiatric Association.

a particular external stimulus (such as seeing a snake), they are more frequently cued by situations that are associated with internal sensations similar to panic. For example, grocery shopping in the winter—with the heat and stuffiness that comes from being under layers of clothing while inside of a store—may remind a person of sensations associated with a previous panic attack, which can lead to anxiety about having another panic attack. In other cases, panic attacks are *uncued*—they are spontaneous—they feel as though they come out of the blue, and are not associated with a particular object or situation. Panic attacks can occur at any time, even while sleeping (referred to as *nocturnal panic attacks*, which Campbell experienced). Infrequent panic attacks are not unusual; they affect 30% of adults at some point in their lives.

Recurrent panic attacks may interfere with daily life (for example, if they occur on a bus or at work) and cause the individual to leave the situation to return home or seek medical help. The symptoms of a panic attack are so unpleasant that people who suffer from this disorder may try to prevent another attack by avoiding environments and activities that increase their heart rates (hot places, crowded rooms, elevators, exercise, sex, mass transportation, or sporting events). They might even avoid leaving home (Bouton, Mineka, & Barlow, 2001).

What Is Panic Disorder?

Campbell describes *panic disorder*: ". . . the fear of having another panic attack, because the last thing in the world you want to face is one more of those horrible, frightening experiences. And the last thing you want to accept is the idea of living the rest of your life with panic. This condition caused me to shut myself up in the my house, where I would sit in the dark, frustrated, crying, afraid to go out. At one point, I even considered suicide" (Campbell & Ruane, 1999, p. ii).

To mental health clinicians, **panic disorder** is marked by frequent, unexpected panic attacks, along with fear of further attacks and possible restrictions of behavior in order to prevent such attacks (see Table 7.4). Note, however, that having panic attacks doesn't necessarily indicate a panic disorder. Panic attacks are distinguished from panic disorder by the frequency and unpredictability of the attacks and the individual's reaction to the attacks. Campbell's life changed as a result of his efforts to prevent additional attacks: "I remember all the places I've had an attack, and I make a concerted effort to avoid those places" (Campbell & Ruane, 1999, p. 201). Table 7.5 lists additional facts about panic disorder, and Case 7.2 provides a glimpse of a woman who suffers from panic attacks.

Panic disorder
The anxiety disorder characterized by frequent, unexpected panic attacks, along with fear of further attacks and possible restrictions of behavior in order to prevent such attacks.

CASE 7.2 ▶ FROM THE OUTSIDE: Panic Disorder

S was a 28-year-old married woman with two children, aged 3 and 5 years. S had experienced her first panic attack approximately 1 year prior to the time of the initial assessment. Her father had died 3 months before her first panic attack; his death was unexpected, the result of a stroke. In addition to grieving for her father, S became extremely concerned about the possibility of herself having a stroke. S reported [that before her father's death, she'd never had a panic attack nor been concerned about her health.] Apparently, the loss of her father produced an abrupt change in the focus of her attention, and a cycle of anxiety began [which led to a heightened] awareness of the imminence of her own death, given that "nothing in life was predictable." . . . S became increasingly aware of different bodily sensations. Following her first panic attack, S was highly vigilant for tingling sensation in her scalp, pain around her eyes, and numbness in her arms and legs. She interpreted all of these symptoms as indicative of impending stroke. Moreover, because her concerns became more generalized, she began to fear any signs of impending panic, such as shortness of breath and palpitations.

Her concerns led to significant changes in her lifestyle [and she avoided] unstructured time in the event she might dwell on "how she felt" and, by so doing, panic. . . . S felt that her life revolved around preventing the experience of panic and stroke.

(Craske, Barlow, & Meadows, 2000, pp. 45–46)

Symptoms of panic disorder are similar across cultures, but in some cultures, the symptoms focus on fear of magic or witchcraft (American Psychiatric Association, 2000); in other cultures, the physical symptoms may be expressed differently. For example, among Cambodian refugees, symptoms of panic disorder include a fear that "wind-and-blood pressure" (referred to as *wind overload*) may increase to the point of bursting the neck area, and patients may complain of a sore neck, along with headache, blurry vision, and dizziness (Hinton, Um, & Ba, 2001).

In some cultures, people experience symptoms that are similar—but not identical—to the classic symptoms of a panic attack. In the Caribbean, Puerto Rico, and some areas of Latin America, an anxiety-related problem called *ataque de nervios* can occur (usually in women). The most common symptoms are uncontrollable screaming and crying attacks, together with palpitations, shaking, and numbness. An *ataque*

Table 7.4 ▶ DSM-IV-TR Diagnostic Criteria for Panic Disorder (Without Agoraphobia)

A. Both (1) and (2):

(1) recurrent unexpected Panic Attacks

(2) at least one of the attacks has been followed by 1 month (or more) of one (or more) of the following:

    (a) persistent concern about having additional attacks

    (b) worry about the implications of the attack or its consequences (e.g., losing control, having a heart attack, "going crazy")

    (c) a significant change in behavior related to the attacks

B. Absence of Agoraphobia [discussed later in this section].

C. The Panic Attacks are not due to the direct physiological effects of a substance (e.g., a drug of abuse, a medication) or a general medical condition (e.g., hyperthyroidism).

D. The Panic Attacks are not better accounted for by another mental disorder, such as Social Phobia (e.g., occurring on exposure to feared social situations [discussed later in this chapter]), Specific Phobia (e.g., on exposure to a specific phobic situation [discussed later in this chapter]), Obsessive-Compulsive Disorder (e.g., on exposure to dirt in someone with an obsession about contamination [discussed later in this chapter]), Posttraumatic Stress Disorder (e.g., in response to stimuli associated with a severe stressor [discussed later in this chapter]), or Separation Anxiety Disorder (e.g., in response to being away from home or close relatives [Chapter 14]).

Source: Reprinted with permission from the Diagnostic and Statistical Manual of Mental Disorders, Text Revision, Fourth Edition, (Copyright 2000) American Psychiatric Association.

Table 7.5 ▶ Panic Disorder Facts at a Glance

Prevalence

- Up to 3% of people worldwide will experience panic disorder at some point in their lives (Rouillon, 1997; Somers et al., 2006). However, 30% of people will experience at least one panic attack in their lives. Up to 60% of people seen by cardiologists have panic disorder.

Comorbidity

- About 80% of people with panic disorder will have an additional Axis I disorder (Ozkan & Altindag, 2005). The two Axis I disorders mostly commonly associated with panic disorder are depression (up to 65% of cases) and substance abuse (up to 30% of cases) (Biederman et al., 2005; Keller & Hanks, 1994; Magee et al., 1996).
- Approximately 15–30% of those with panic disorder also have social phobia or GAD, and 2–20% have some other type of anxiety disorder (Goisman et al., 1995).
- Over a third of those with panic disorder also have a personality disorder—an Axis II disorder (Ozkan & Altindag, 2005).

Onset

- Panic disorder is most likely to arise during two phases of life: the teenage years or the mid-30s.

Course

- The frequency of panic attacks varies from person to person:
  - Some people get panic attacks once a week for months,
  - Others have attacks every day for a week.
- The frequency of panic attacks can vary over time:
  - After having regular panic attacks, a person can experience weeks or even years with less frequent attacks or no attacks at all,
  - Other patients come to have limited-symptom attacks—experiencing fewer than the minimum of four symptoms necessary for a diagnosis of panic attack (see Table 7.3),
  - Some people have no change over time in the frequency of their attacks.

Gender Differences

- Women are two to three times more likely than men to be diagnosed with panic disorder.

Cultural Differences

- Symptoms of panic disorder are generally similar across cultures, although people in some cultures may experience or explain the symptoms differently, such as "wind overload" among the Khmer (Hinton et al., 2002, 2003).

Source: Unless otherwise noted, information in the table is from American Psychiatric Association, 2000.

de nervios differs from a panic attack not only in the specific symptoms experienced, but also because it usually is triggered by a specific upsetting event, such as a funeral or a family conflict. Panic attacks that are part of panic disorder tend not to have such an obvious situational trigger. Furthermore, people who have had an *ataque de nervios* are usually not worried about recurrences (Guarnaccia, 1997b; Salmán et al., 1997).

Panic disorder, as well as *ataque de nervios* and other anxiety disorders, is diagnosed in at least twice as often in women as in men (American Psychiatric Association, 2000). A cultural explanation for this gender difference is that men may be less likely to report symptoms of anxiety or panic because they perceive them as inconsistent with how men are "supposed" to behave in their culture (Ginsburg & Silverman, 2000).

In short, panic disorder has a core of common symptoms across the world, centering on frequent, unexpected panic attacks and fear of further attacks, but culture does affect the specifics.

What Is Agoraphobia?

After Campbell's first panic attack, he refused to go out:

> . . . I knew I could not set foot outside my house. Until I learned what was wrong with me, the only place I would go was to a doctor's office or a hospital. . . . Reuna thought that was part of my problem. I was shutting myself off from the world. I was going to sleep very late, waking up at noon, spending the whole day in bed. She said I needed to pull my life back together or I would never get well. . . . The thing she failed to understand was the predicament I would be placing myself in if I did go out. What if I had another attack? What if it happened while I was in church? Or while I was walking down the aisle of a crowded grocery store? What would I do? How could I deal with the humiliation that such a loss of control would bring?
>
> (Campbell & Ruane, 1999, pp. 93–94)

Campbell had developed *agoraphobia*.

Agoraphobia (which literally means "fear of the marketplace") refers to the persistent avoidance of situations that might trigger panic symptoms or from which escape would be difficult. Moreover, many patients with agoraphobia may avoid places in which it would be embarrassing or hard to obtain help in case of a panic attack. For these reasons, tunnels, bridges, crowded theaters, and highways are typically avoided or entered with difficulty by people with agoraphobia.

Some people have agoraphobia without having panic attacks, but it is not common. These people avoid situations where they fear they might lose control of themselves for some other reason (such as incontinence) or where they fear they may experience symptoms that are less severe or numerous than the criteria for a panic attack (listed in Table 7.3). For instance, they might avoid types of situations that have, in the past, triggered palpatations and nausea (but experience less than the minimum of four symptoms necessary for a panic attack). However, people who only avoid particular kinds of stimuli (*only* bridges or *only* parties) are not diagnosed with agoraphobia, which is a more general pattern of avoiding many kinds of environments or situations. Table 7.6 lists the criteria for agoraphobia, but note that it is not a separate DSM-IV-TR diagnosis. A patient with agoraphobia will be

---

Table 7.6 ▸ DSM-IV-TR Criteria for Agoraphobia

A. Anxiety about being in places or situations from which escape might be difficult (or embarrassing) or in which help may not be available in the event of having an unexpected or situationally predisposed panic attack or panic-like symptoms. Agoraphobic fears typically involve characteristic clusters of situations that include being outside the home alone; being in a crowd or standing in a line; being on a bridge; and traveling in a bus, train, or automobile.

Note: Consider the diagnosis of Specific Phobia [discussed later in this chapter] if the avoidance is limited to one or only a few specific situations, or Social Phobia [discussed later in this chapter] if the avoidance is limited to social situations.

B. The situations are avoided (e.g., travel is restricted) or else are endured with marked distress or with anxiety about having a panic attack or panic-like symptoms, or require the presence of a companion.

C. The anxiety or phobic avoidance is not better accounted for by another mental disorder, such as Social Phobia (e.g., avoidance limited to social situations because of fear of embarrassment), Specific Phobia (e.g., avoidance limited to a single situation like elevators), Obsessive-Compulsive Disorder (e.g., avoidance of dirt in someone with an obsession about contamination), Posttraumatic Stress Disorder (e.g., avoidance of stimuli associated with a severe stressor [all disorders discussed later in this chapter], or separation anxiety disorder (e.g., avoidance of leaving home or relatives [discussed in Chapter 14]).

Source: Reprinted with permission from the Diagnostic and Statistical Manual of Mental Disorders, Text Revision, Fourth Edition, (Copyright 2000) American Psychiatric Association.

Agoraphobia
The persistent avoidance of situations that might trigger panic symptoms or from which escape would be difficult.

Agoraphobia is not a separate DSM-IV-TR disorder. Patients who meet the criteria for agoraphobia are diagnosed with either panic disorder with agoraphobia or agoraphobia without history of panic disorder, depending on the presence or absence of panic disorder.

diagnosed with either *panic disorder with agoraphobia* (if he or she also has panic disorder) or *agoraphobia without history of panic disorder* (if he or she had never had panic disorder). Between one third and one half of those with panic disorder also have agoraphobia. Some researchers suggest that agoraphobia—with no reference to panic disorder—should be a disorder in future diagnostic manuals (Bienvenu et al., 2006). Shirley B., in Case 7.3, suffered from symptoms of agoraphobia.

CASE 7.3 ▶ FROM THE INSIDE: Agoraphobia

"The Story of an Agoraphobic" by Shirley B.

As I am writing this I am a 46-year-old recovering agoraphobic. Whew! I never thought I could say that, let alone write it. But three weeks after I first admitted it in therapy, I crossed the street eight times on my own. Some people would say "That is no big deal." No, it's not a big deal—it's a MIRACLE! I wanted to shout, "Hello again world, I'm back. It's me, Shirley B.!!!" Living is what I do now. Not as fully as I plan to, but it is so much more than just being. . . .

There isn't much I can say about how I became agoraphobic. I just slipped a little day by day. . . . My daughter Nadeen was always by my side on those rare occasions when I ventured outside, forced to leave my home when I needed medical attention. In the past my fear kept me at home with all sorts of physical pains and ailments, as horrific as the pain was, the pain of facing the outside world was greater. When I had two abscessed teeth and my jaw was swollen to twice its normal size I was in such excruciating pain that I had to go to the dentist. So with my legs wobbling, my heart pounding, my hands sweating, and my throat choking, to the dentist I went. After examining my x-rays, the dentist said he wouldn't be able to do anything with my teeth because they were so infected, he prescribed medication for the pain and infection and said that I must return in ten days, not in two years. I felt as though those ten days were a countdown to my own execution. Each day passed at lightning speed—like a clock ticking away. The fear grew stronger and stronger. I had to walk around with my hand on my heart to keep it from jumping so hard, as if I were pledging allegiance, which I was—to my fears and phobia. I asked God to please give me strength to go back to the dentist. When the day came, I knew that my preparations would take me a little over four hours. I had to leave time, not just to bathe and dress, but to debate with myself about going.

Source: Anxiety Disorders Association of America.

People with extreme agoraphobia cannot function normally in daily life. They are totally housebound, too crippled by panic and fear to go to work, the supermarket, or the doctor. Others with agoraphobia are able to function better than Shirley B. and can enter many situations without triggering a panic attack. Relying on a friend or family member (often referred to as a "safe" person), such as Shirley's daughter Nadeen, can help the sufferer enter feared situations that otherwise might be avoided.

When agoraphobia develops, it usually does so within the first year of recurrent panic attacks (American Psychiatric Association, 2000). For some individuals, as panic attacks decrease, agoraphobia decreases; for others, there is no such relationship. Because people with agoraphobia avoid situations that are associated with past panic attacks, they do not learn that they can be in such situations and not have a panic attack.

Understanding Panic Disorder and Agoraphobia

"I still don't know what triggers a panic attack, but I can tell anyone reading this who has never experienced one that it is a devastating experience. I don't have many attacks these days, but when they come, they come hard and bring me to my knees. An attack may hit me on a day when I'm feeling relaxed and happy. That's when I think, 'Why me?' 'Why today?'" (Campbell & Ruane, 1999, p. 151). Let's use the neuropsychosocial approach to address Campbell's question about why panic disorder and agoraphobia arise and are maintained. Each type of factor makes an important and unique contribution.

Neurological Factors

Brain systems, neural communication, and genetics contribute to panic disorder and agoraphobia. Specifically, these three types of neurological factors appear to give rise to a heightened sensitivity to breathing changes.

Brain Systems

One key to explaining panic attacks came after researchers discovered that they could induce attacks in the laboratory. Patients who had had panic attacks volunteered to hyperventilate (that is, to breathe in rapid, short pants, decreasing carbon dioxide levels in the blood), which can trigger panic attacks. Moreover, researchers found that injections of some medically safe substances, such as sodium lactate (a salt produced in sweat) and caffeine, produced attacks—but only in people who have panic disorder (Nutt & Lawson, 1992; Pitts & McClure, 1967). Why do these substances induce panic attacks? One possibility is that they trigger a brain mechanism that warns us when we are suffocating (Klein, 1993). According to this theory, the brains of people who experience panic attacks have a low threshold for detecting decreased oxygen in the blood (Beck, Ohtake, & Shipherd, 1999; Papp, Klein, & Gorman, 1993; Papp et al., 1997).

As predicted by this theory, patients with panic disorder cannot hold their breath as long as control participants can (Asmundson & Stein, 1994). When triggered, the neural mechanism not only produces panic, but also leads to hyperventilation and a strong sense of needing to escape. The need to escape is consistent with the finding that the right frontal lobe is activated more than the left when people with panic disorder see stimuli that are likely to induce panic symptoms, such as a photograph of an emergency situation (Wiedemann et al., 1999). Why? Researchers have documented that a key part of the right frontal lobe is more strongly activated when people experience withdrawal emotions (such as fear) than when feeling approach emotions (such as joy) (Davidson, 1992). In addition, as noted earlier, the frontal lobes have direct connections to the amygdala (a subcortical structure that is involved in feeling strong emotions) and to the hypothalamus (a subcortical structure that is involved in the fight-or-flight response) (Gabbott et al., 2005; Ghashghaei & Barbas, 2002; Teves et al., 2004). Indeed, the frontal lobe helps to regulate the limbic system and hence plays a central role in both the triggering and modulating emotions (LeDoux, 1996, 2000).

Thus, the data suggest that withdrawal emotions—which prompt escape from a situation—are relatively easily induced in people with panic attacks. These emotions may be triggered by the sense of impending suffocation, which in turn may activate the limbic system and autonomic nervous system, as in the fight-or-flight response. However, research findings do not show that all panic attacks are a result of a suffocation reaction or that all such attacks are accompanied by activation of withdrawal mechanisms in the brain. In fact, researchers have documented two types of panic disorder, one based on a lower threshold for detecting suffocation (Abrams, Rassovsky & Kushner, 2006) and one based on learning (Acheson et al., 2007).

Neural Communication

Researchers have been investigating the role of neurotransmitters and neuromodulators in giving rise to panic disorder. One key neurotransmitter is norepinephrine, too much of which is apparently produced in people who have anxiety disorders (Nutt & Lawson, 1992). To explain this finding, some researchers have focused on a small subcortical structure called the *locus coeruleus*, which is located in the brainstem. The locus coeruleus produces norepinephrine, and some have theorized that it is too sensitive in people with panic disorder (Gorman et al., 1989) and thus may produce too much norepinephrine. The locus coeruleus and norepinepherine are important because they are central to the body's "alarm system," which causes the fight-or-flight response (including faster breathing, increased heart rate, and sweating), which can occur at times of panic. However, the picture is complicated by the fact that panic attacks do not increase levels of stress-related hormones (e.g., cortisol), which usually accompany the fight-or-flight response (Otte et al., 2002). Thus, panic is not the same thing as the ordinary stress response, although it may arise in part through some mechanisms that are also involved in helping us respond to emergencies.

Finally, serotonin may also play a role in panic disorder; this idea is supported by the fact that SSRIs can reduce the frequency and intensity of panic attacks (DeVane, 1997). Serotonin affects the locus coeruleus in complex ways, and it may exert its effects on panic attacks indirectly, by altering the operation of this brain structure (Bell & Nutt, 1998).

Genetics

Genetic factors appear to play a role in the emergence of panic disorder. In fact, first-degree biological relatives of people with panic disorder are up to eight times more likely to develop the disorder than are control participants, and up to 20 times more likely to do so if the relative developed it before 20 years of age (Crowe et al., 1983; Torgersen, 1983; van den Heuvel et al., 2000). Twin studies have yielded similar results by examining concordance rates; a **concordance rate** is the probability that both twins will have a characteristic or disorder, given that one of them has it. The concordance rate in pairs of female identical (monzygotic) twins is approximately 24%, in contrast to 11% for pairs of fraternal (dizygotic) twins (Kendler et al., 1993). However, the genetic predisposition is not specific for panic disorder. One twin study revealed that 20% of the heritability of panic disorder arises from factors that also lead to GAD and PTSD and another 20% is specific to panic disorder; the remaining 60% of the heritability was accounted for by nonshared environmental factors, such as particular traumatic experiences (Chantarujikapong et al., 2001). Earl Campbell wasn't the only one in his family to experience anxiety: His paternal aunt, maternal uncle and two of his sisters had significant anxiety symptoms.

Psychological Factors

We saw earlier that not all cases of panic disorder are related to a person's threshold for detecting suffocation—some cases of panic disorder arise from learning. Thus, behavioral and cognitive theories can also help us understand how panic disorder and agoraphobia arise and are perpetuated: People come to associate certain stimuli with the sensations of panic, and then develop maladaptive beliefs about those stimuli and the sensations that are related to anxiety and panic.

Learning: An Alarm Going Off

Learning theory offers one possible explanation for panic disorder. Initially, a person may have had a first panic attack in response to a stressful or dangerous life event (a *true alarm*). This experience produces conditioning, whereby the initial bodily sensations of panic (such as increased heart rate or sweaty palms) become *false alarms* associated with panic attacks. Thus, the individual comes to fear those *interoceptive cues* (that is, cues received from the interior of the body) or the external environment in which they had the panic attack. As these normal sensations that are part of the fight-or-flight response come to be associated with subsequent panic attacks, the bodily sensations of arousal themselves come to *elicit* panic attacks (*learned alarms*). The person then develops a *fear of fear*—a fear that the arousal symptoms of fear will lead to a panic attack (Goldstein & Chambless, 1978), much as S did in Case 7.2. Earl Campbell described his fear of fear: "Living with the thought that at any moment you may have to go through another attack is horrible. It creates an entirely new kind of anxiety" (Campbell & Ruane, 1999, p. 115). After developing this fear of fear, the person tries to avoid behaviors or situations where such sensations might occur (Mowrer, 1947; White & Barlow, 2002).

Concordance rate
The probability that both twins will have a characteristic or disorder, given that one of them has it.

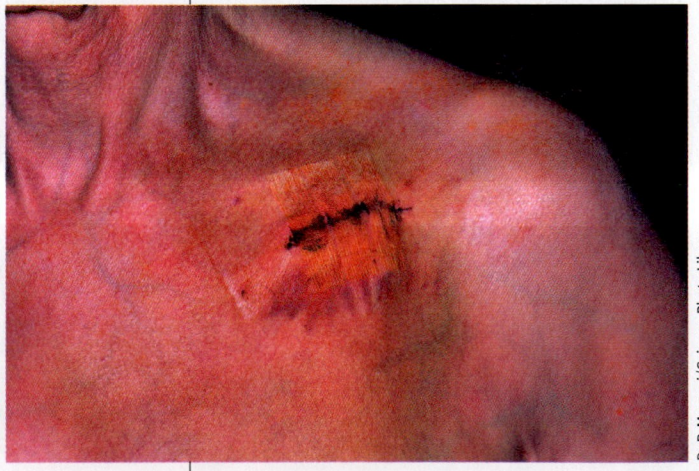

People whose hearts sometimes beat too quickly can be treated with a device implanted under the skin that shocks the heart, which causes it to beat at a normal speed again. However, the shocks can be uncomfortable and alarming. Research suggests that people who receive more frequent and intense shocks are more likely to develop panic disorder, which arises as a conditioned fear in response to the automatic shocks (Godemann et al., 2001).

Dr. P. Marazzi/Science Photo Library

Cognitive Explanations: Catastrophic Thinking and Anxiety Sensitivity

Cognitive theories, which focus on how a person *interprets* and then responds to alarm signals from the body, offer another possible explanation for panic disorder. People with panic disorder may misinterpret normal bodily sensations as indicating catastrophic effects (Salkovskis, 1988), which is referred to as *catastrophic thinking*. In essence, these interpretations can turn a panic attack into panic disorder. For instance, an increased heart rate may be (mis)interpreted as a signal of an impending heart attack. Such thoughts ("I'm going to have a heart attack") are frightening, and the fright increases autonomic arousal (faster and shallower breathing, sweating, increased heart rate), which then leads to more anxiety about a catastrophic bodily problem, more vigilance for changes in the body, and—as a result of all this anxiety and vigilance—more changes in the body. This process becomes a vicious cycle.

Evidence for this cognitive explanation comes from laboratory studies: Reading pairs of words that relate both to the body and catastrophic states or events (such as the words *breathless* and *suffocate*) increases the probability that a person who has had panic attacks in the past will have a panic attack again (Clark et al., 1988). Moreover, cognitive therapy that reduces the sort of automatic thoughts that lead to the vicious cycle can reduce symptoms of panic disorder (Beck & Emery, 1985; Clark et al., 1994). However, at least some people have panic attacks that are not a result of catastrophic thoughts, at least not conscious ones (Kenardy et al., 1992; Kenardy & Taylor, 1999).

A tendency toward catastrophic thinking is related to *anxiety sensitivity*, which is a tendency to fear bodily sensations that are related to anxiety, along with the belief that such sensations indicate that harmful consequences will follow (McNally, 1994; Reiss, 1991; Reiss & McNally, 1985; Schmidt, Lerew, & Jackson, 1997). For example, a person with high anxiety sensitivity is likely to believe—or fear—that an irregular heartbeat indicates a heart problem or that shortness of breath signals being suffocated. People with high anxiety sensitivity tend to know what has caused their bodily symptoms—for instance, that exercise caused a faster heart rate—but they become afraid anyway, believing that danger is indicated, even if it is not an immediate danger (Bouton, Mineka, & Barlow, 2001; Brown et al., 2003).

Many researchers view anxiety sensitivity and being prone to anxiety as enduring traits that leave individuals more vulnerable to develop panic disorder. One bit of evidence came from a study that followed first-year Air Force Academy cadets who were enrolled in a 5-week basic training course—training that is both physically and psychologically stressful. Those cadets who had more anxiety sensitivity at the beginning of training were the ones who were likely to develop spontaneous panic attacks later. This finding suggests that the mental stressors of basic training,

Researchers have shown that the mental stressors of basic military training are more challenging to people with preexisting anxiety sensitivity.

U.S. Air Force Academy

over and above the physical ones, were more challenging to people with preexisting anxiety sensitivity (Schmidt, Lerew, & Jackson, 1997). (Note, however, that this study examined spontaneous panic attacks, not panic disorder.)

Cognitive explanations can also explain nocturnal panic attacks. Nocturnal panic attacks occur in the first few hours of sleep during the transition into the stage of slow-wave (deep) sleep (Bouton, Mineka, & Barlow, 2001); they do not occur during REM sleep—the stage of sleep when rapid eye movements occur and during which most dreaming occurs. Thus, nocturnal panic attacks are not associated with dreams (or nightmares). What might cause these nighttime panic attacks? A cognitive explanation focuses on the individual's hypervigilance for bodily changes—such as alterations in breathing patterns—during sleep, as might occur during the transition to slow-wave sleep (Barlow, 2002b; Craske & Rowe, 1997). Support for this explanation comes from the finding that patients who experience nocturnal panic attacks report more breathing-related symptoms than do patients whose panic attacks occur solely while they are awake (Sarísoy et al., 2008).

Social Factors: Stressors, "Safe" People, and a Sign of the Times

Evidence suggests that social stressors contribute to panic disorder: People with panic disorder tend to have had a higher than average number of such stressful events during childhood and adolescence (Horesh et al., 1997). Moreover, 80% of people with panic disorder reported that the disorder developed after a stressful life event.

Social factors are often related to the ways patients cope with agoraphobia. The presence of a close relative or friend—a "safe person"—can help decrease catastrophic thinking and panicking when a person with agoraphobia feels anxious. The safe person can also decrease the sufferer's arousal (Carter et al., 1995). Although a safe person can make it possible for the patient with agoraphobia to go into situations that he or she wouldn't enter alone, reliance on a safe person can end up perpetuating the disorder: By venturing into anxiety-inducing situations only when a safe person is around, the patient never habituates to his or her anxiety symptoms. Campbell describes his feelings about being alone versus having another person with him: "I'm still afraid to be alone for long stretches of time: my fear is that I'll have an attack, no one will be there to help me, and I'll die. But because I used to enjoy spending time alone, I push that envelope hard" (Campbell & Ruane, 1999, p. 197).

Cultural factors can influence whether people develop panic disorder, perhaps through culture's influence on personality traits. Consider that over the last five decades, increasing numbers of Americans have developed the personality trait of anxiety-proneness (Spielberger & Rickman, 1990). The average child today scores higher on measures of this trait than did children who received psychiatric diagnoses in the 1950s (Twenge, 2000)! Specifically, the average anxiety score for children with psychological problems in 1957 was somewhat lower than the average anxiety score for children *without* psychological problem in the 1980s. The higher baseline level of anxiety in the United States may be a result of greater dangers in the environment—such as higher crime rates, new threats of terrorism, and new concerns about food safety.

FEEDBACK LOOPS IN ACTION: Understanding Panic Disorder

Cognitive explanations of panic disorder can help show how a few panic attacks can progress to panic disorder, but not everyone who has panic attacks develops panic disorder. It is only when neurological and psychological factors interact with bodily states that panic disorder develops (Bouton, Mineka, & Barlow, 2001). Cognitive processes such as catastrophic thinking and anxiety sensitivity (psychological factors) are triggered, in part, by environmental and social stressors (social factors). Indeed, such stressors may lead an individual to be aroused (neurological factor), but he or she then misinterprets the cause of this arousal (psychological factor). This misinterpretation may increase the arousal (Wilkinson et al., 1998), making it more likely that symptoms of panic—rapid heartbeat or shallow breathing—will follow.

For example, a man's argument with his wife might arouse his anger and increase his breathing rate. Breathing faster results in a lower carbon dioxide level in the blood, which then leads the blood vessels to constrict—which means less oxygen throughout the brain and body; the ensuing physical sensations (such as light-headedness) may be misinterpreted as the early stages of suffocation, leading the man to panic (Coplan et al., 1998). This is how such physical changes can serve as a false alarm (Beck, 1976). After many false alarms, the associated sensations may become learned alarms and trigger panic in the absence of a social stressor (Barlow, 1988). Also, this man may become hypervigilant for alarm signals of panic attacks,

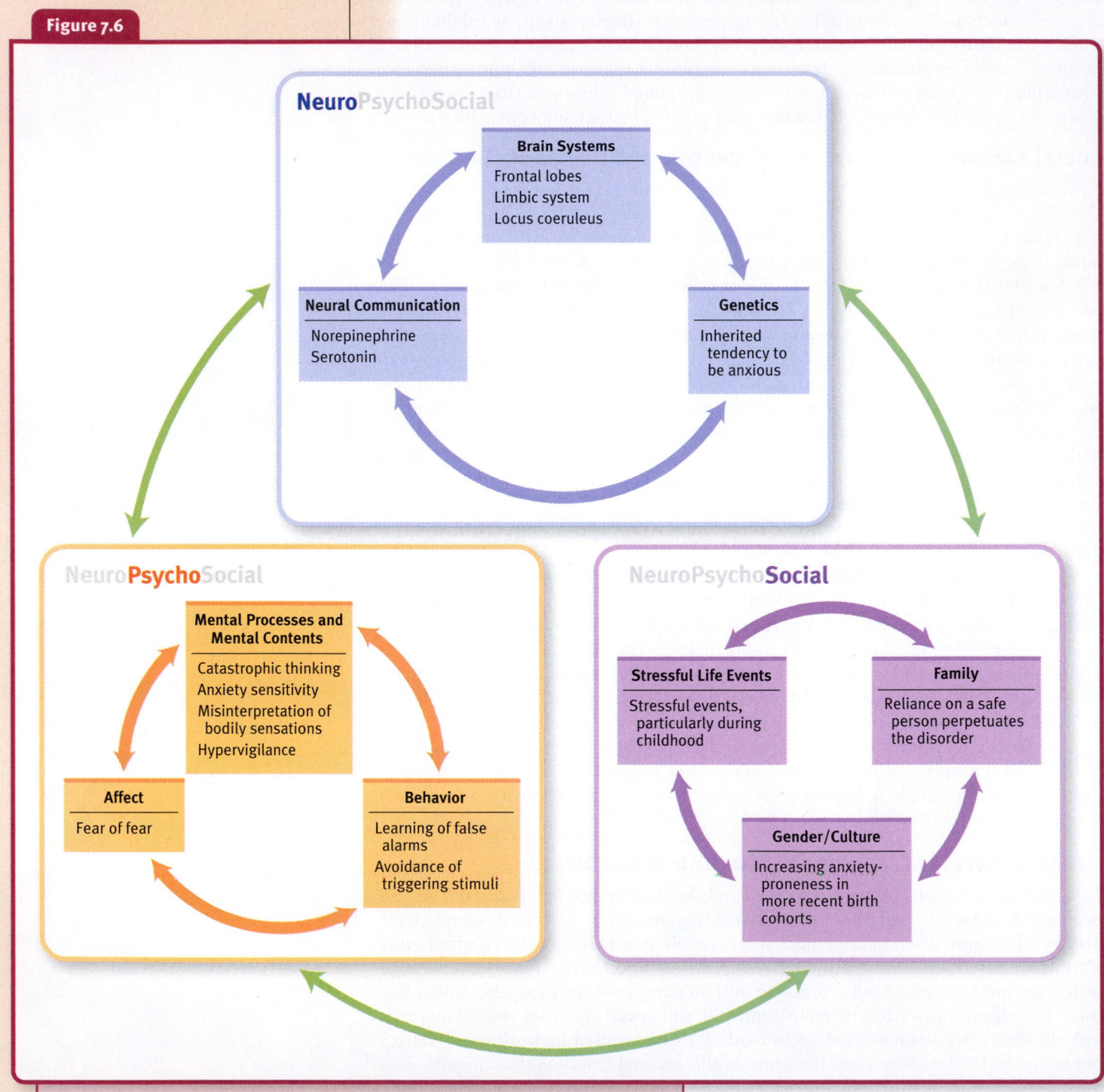

Figure 7.6

NeuroPsychoSocial

Brain Systems
Frontal lobes
Limbic system
Locus coeruleus

Neural Communication
Norepinephrine
Serotonin

Genetics
Inherited tendency to be anxious

NeuroPsychoSocial

Mental Processes and Mental Contents
Catastrophic thinking
Anxiety sensitivity
Misinterpretation of bodily sensations
Hypervigilance

Affect
Fear of fear

Behavior
Learning of false alarms
Avoidance of triggering stimuli

NeuroPsychoSocial

Stressful Life Events
Stressful events, particularly during childhood

Family
Reliance on a safe person perpetuates the disorder

Gender/Culture
Increasing anxiety-proneness in more recent birth cohorts

7.6 ▶ Feedback Loops in Action: Panic Disorder (With Agoraphobia)

leading to anticipatory anxiety. In turn, this anxiety increases activity in his sympathetic nervous system, which is what causes the breathing and heart rate changes that he feared. In this way, the man may trigger his own panic attack. Figure 7.6 illustrates these three factors and their feedback loops.

Treating Panic Disorder and Agoraphobia

Earl Campbell received treatment for his panic disorder—medication, cognitive-behavior therapy (CBT), and social support—which targeted all three types of neuropsychosocial factors. Let's examine the various types of treatments commonly used for panic disorder.

Targeting Neurological Factors: Medication

To treat panic disorder, a psychiatrist or another type of health care provider licensed to prescribe medication may recommend an antidepressant or a benzodiazepine. Benzodiazepines are prescribed as a short-term remedy; the benzodiazepines *alprazolam* (Xanax) and *clonazepam* (Klonapin) affect the targeted symptoms within 36 hours, and they need not be taken regularly. One of these drugs might be prescribed during a short but especially stressful period. Side effects of benzodiazepines mainly include drowsiness and slowed reaction times, and patients can suffer withdrawal or develop tolerance to the medications when they are taken for an extended period of time (see Chapter 4). For these reasons, an antidepressant such as an SNRI, an SSRI, or a TCA (tricyclic antidepressant) such as *clomipramine* may be a better long-term medication. These medications can take up to 10 days to have an effect and may be prescribed at a lower dose than is usual for depression (Gorman & Kent, 1999; Kasper & Resinger, 2001). After Campbell's panic attacks were diagnosed, he initially relied on medication as his sole treatment; like most people, though, when he stopped taking the medication or forgot to take a pill, his symptoms returned. Such recurrences motivated him to make use of other types of treatments.

Targeting Psychological Factors

CBT is the first-line treatment for panic disorder because it has the most enduring beneficial effects of any treatment (Cloos, 2005). In fact, patients with either type of panic disorder (that arising primarily because of learning or that arising primarily through a lower threshold for detecting suffocation) profit to equal degrees from CBT (Taylor, Woody, et al., 1996). Moreover, CBT methods can even be effective in a self-help format, with minimal therapist contact (Carlbring & Andersson, 2006; Carlbring et al., 2005).

Effective CBT methods can emphasize either the behavioral or the cognitive aspects of change. Specifically, as discussed in the following sections, behavioral methods focus on the bodily signals of arousal and panic and on the avoidance behaviors, whereas cognitive methods focus on the misappraisal of bodily sensations and on the mistaken inferences about them. A meta-analysis of the effects of treatment for panic disorder that combined behavioral and cognitive methods found that over half of patients who completed treatment improved and remained improved 2 years later (Westen & Morrison, 2001).

Behavioral Methods: Relaxation Training, Breathing Retraining, and Exposure

For people with panic disorder, any bodily arousal can lead to a fight-or-flight response. To help counter this excessive response to arousal, therapists may teach patients breathing retraining and relaxation techniques to stop the progression from bodily arousal to panic attack and to increase a sense of control over bodily sensations. Campbell reported how he learned to take "long deep breaths and relax my body completely when panic struck. This is very difficult; at first I didn't believe I could do it. I somehow had to convince myself that the attack was not really happening. I had to fight it off by relaxing myself" (Campbell & Ruane, 1999, p. 119).

Other behavioral methods, such as exposure, focus on the patient's tendency to avoid activities that produce certain bodily sensations (such as not exercising in order to prevent an increased heart rate) or to avoid situations associated with panic attacks (such as crowded theaters). Campbell, prior to his panic attacks, would jog 4–5 miles a day, but he stopped after his first panic attack: "I was afraid to go outside, afraid of having an attack right there on the street" (Campbell & Ruane, 1999, p. 108). Once he learned about panic disorder and how to combat it, he challenged himself to resume jogging. He began by walking alone down the block. Each day he went for a longer walk, and then he gradually started running.

Exposure for patients with agoraphobia addresses the particular situations they try to avoid. At the beginning of exposure treatment, patients may use *imaginal exposure*, exposure to mental images of the fear-inducing stimuli, progressing from least to most anxiety-inducing situations. They may then switch to **in vivo exposure**—direct exposure to the feared or avoided situation or stimulus (Barlow, Esler, & Vitali, 1998). The therapist or another person may accompany the patient on the first few in vivo exposures, or the patient may decide to have the experience alone. Not all patients, however, are willing or able to go through such exposure therapy; dropout rates have ranged from 3% to 25% (Chambless & Gillis, 1994; van Balkom et al., 1997). Of those patients who do undergo exposure treatment, 60–75% improve, and are still improved at follow-up 6–15 months later (Barlow, Esler, & Vitali, 1998). However, some patients continue to have residual symptoms of panic or avoidance, even though the treatment is largely successful.

To decrease a patient's reaction to bodily sensations associated with panic, behavioral therapists may use **interoceptive exposure**: They have the patient intentionally elicit the bodily sensations associated with panic so that he or she can habituate to those sensations and not respond with fear. During exposure to interoceptive cues, patients are asked to behave in ways that induce the long-feared sensation, such as spinning around to the point of dizziness or intentionally hyperventilating (see Table 7.7 for a more extensive list). Within approximately 30 minutes, the bodily arousal subsides. This procedure allows patients to learn that the bodily sensations pass and no harm befalls them. Because patients had previously avoided activities that were associated with the sensations, they never got to see (and believe) that such sensations did not lead to a heart attack or suffocation.

Cognitive Methods: Psychoeducation and Cognitive Restructuring

Cognitive methods for panic disorder help the patient to recognize misappraisals of bodily symptoms and to learn to correct mistaken inferences about such symptoms. First, psychoeducation for people with panic disorder involves helping them to understand how their physical sensations are symptoms of panic and not of a heart attack or some other harmful medical situation. The therapist describes the biology of panic and explains how catastrophic thinking and anxiety sensitivity can lead panic attacks to develop into panic disorder. Campbell read a pamphlet about panic disorder that described his symptoms perfectly. Having learned about the disorder in this way, he was better able to handle future panic attacks: "One of the most important things I have learned about my panic disorder over the years is that although my heart may be racing and I may feel like I'm having a heart attack, I know that I'm not. And I know it's going to stop" (Campbell & Ruane, 1999, p. 204).

Second, cognitive restructuring is then used to transform the patient's initial frightened thoughts of a medical crisis into more realistic thoughts, identifying the symptoms of panic, which may be uncomfortable but do not indicate danger (Beck et al., 1979). For instance, a therapist helps a patient identify the automatic negative thought about bodily arousal ("I won't be able to breathe . . . I'll pass out") and then challenges the patient about the belief: Was the patient truly unable to breath, or was breathing only difficult? Has the patient fainted before? In this way, each of the patient's automatic negative thoughts related to panic sensations are challenged and thereby reduced. Learning to interpret correctly both internal and external events can play a key role in preventing panic attacks that occur when a person experiences symptoms of suffocation (Clark, 1986; Taylor & Rachman, 1994).

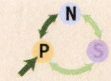

In vivo exposure
The behavioral therapy method that consists of direct exposure to a feared or avoided situation or stimulus.

Interoceptive exposure
The behavioral therapy method in which patients intentionally elicit the bodily sensations associated with panic so that they can habituate to those sensations and not respond with fear.

Table 7.7 ▸ Interoceptive Exposure Exercises for Treatment of Panic Disorder

Exercise	Duration (seconds)	Sensation intensity (0–8)	Anxiety (0–8)	Similarity (0–8)
Shake head from side to side	30			
Place head between legs and then lift	30			
Run on spot	60			
Hold breath	30, or as long as possible			
Completely tense body muscles	60, or as long as possible			
Spin in swivel chair	60			
Hyperventilate	60			
Breathe through narrow straw	120			
Stare at spot on wall or own mirror image	90			

Source: Craske & Barlow, 1993, Table 1.4, p. 36. Copyright 1993 by Guilford Publications, Inc. For more information see the Permissions section.

People receiving interoceptive exposure perform each of the exercises listed in this table for the indicated duration; such exercises are likely to elicit sensations typically associated with panic. After each exercise, they rate how intense the sensations were, their level of anxiety while doing the exercise, and how similar the sensations were to panic symptoms.

Targeting Social Factors: Group and Couples Therapy

Therapy groups (either self-help or conducted by a therapist) that focus specifically on panic disorder and agoraphobia can be a helpful addition to a treatment program (Galassi et al., 2007). Meeting with others who have similar difficulties and sharing experiences can help to decrease a patient's sense of isolation and shame. Moreover, couples or family therapy may be appropriate when a partner or other family member has been the safe person; as the patient gets better, he or she may rely less on that person, which can affect their relationship. In some cases, the patient's increasing independence is satisfying for everyone; but if the safe person has found satisfaction in tending to the patient, the patient's increased independence can be a stressful transition for that person. For Shirley B. (see Case 7.3), her relationship with her daughter Nadeen would undoubtedly change as her agoraphobia diminishes, because she will no longer need Nadeen to accompany her on excursions out of the house. The particular ways their relationship changes will depend on how each of them views Shirley's new independence.

Family members and friends can also be great sources of support, as Campbell noted: "When I'm traveling, my schedule frequently becomes so hectic that I get a bit run-down. Then, I can usually feel the panic sneaking up on me, and I'll pick up the phone right away to call Reuna. Just as it does at home, on the road it tends to attack me in the middle of the night" (Campbell & Ruane, 1999, p. 120). Reuna reminds him to take deep breaths and helps him get through it. He also remembered that, "I'd made one of my biggest steps towards recovery the day I called Janice [his assistant] into my office and exposed my illness to her. I strongly encourage anyone suffering from panic or anxiety to do the same. Start with a close friend you can trust completely, tell that person about your condition, and ask for support. Then do the same with a coworker. Next, approach a friend within your social network. Start small and work your way up" (Campbell & Ruane, 1999, p. 132).

FEEDBACK LOOPS IN TREATMENT: **Panic Disorder**

Invariably, medication—which changes neurological functioning—stops exerting its beneficial effect when the patient stops taking it. The positive changes in neural communication and brain activity, and the associated changes in thoughts, feelings, and behaviors do not endure. Eventually, the symptoms of panic disorder return. For some patients, though, medication is a valuable first step, providing enough relief from symptoms that they are motivated to obtain CBT, which can change their reactions (psychological factor) to perceived bodily sensations (neurological factor). When a patient receives both medication and CBT, however, the medication should be at a low enough dose that the patient can still feel the sensations that led to panic in the past (Taylor, 2000). In fact, the dose should be gradually decreased so that the patient can experience enough anxiety to be increasingly able to make use of cognitive-behavioral methods. It is the CBT that leads to enduring changes: Researchers have found that adding medication to CBT doesn't provide an advantage over CBT alone (de Beurs et al., 1999). This finding has led to CBT's being recommended even for those who prefer medication (Ellison & McCarter, 2002). Whether it involves medication or CBT or both, successful treatment will probably lead the patient, especially if he or she also has agoraphobia, to become more independent—which in turn can change the person's relationships, particularly with their safe people (social factor). These factors and their feedback loops are summarized in Figure 7.7.

Figure 7.7

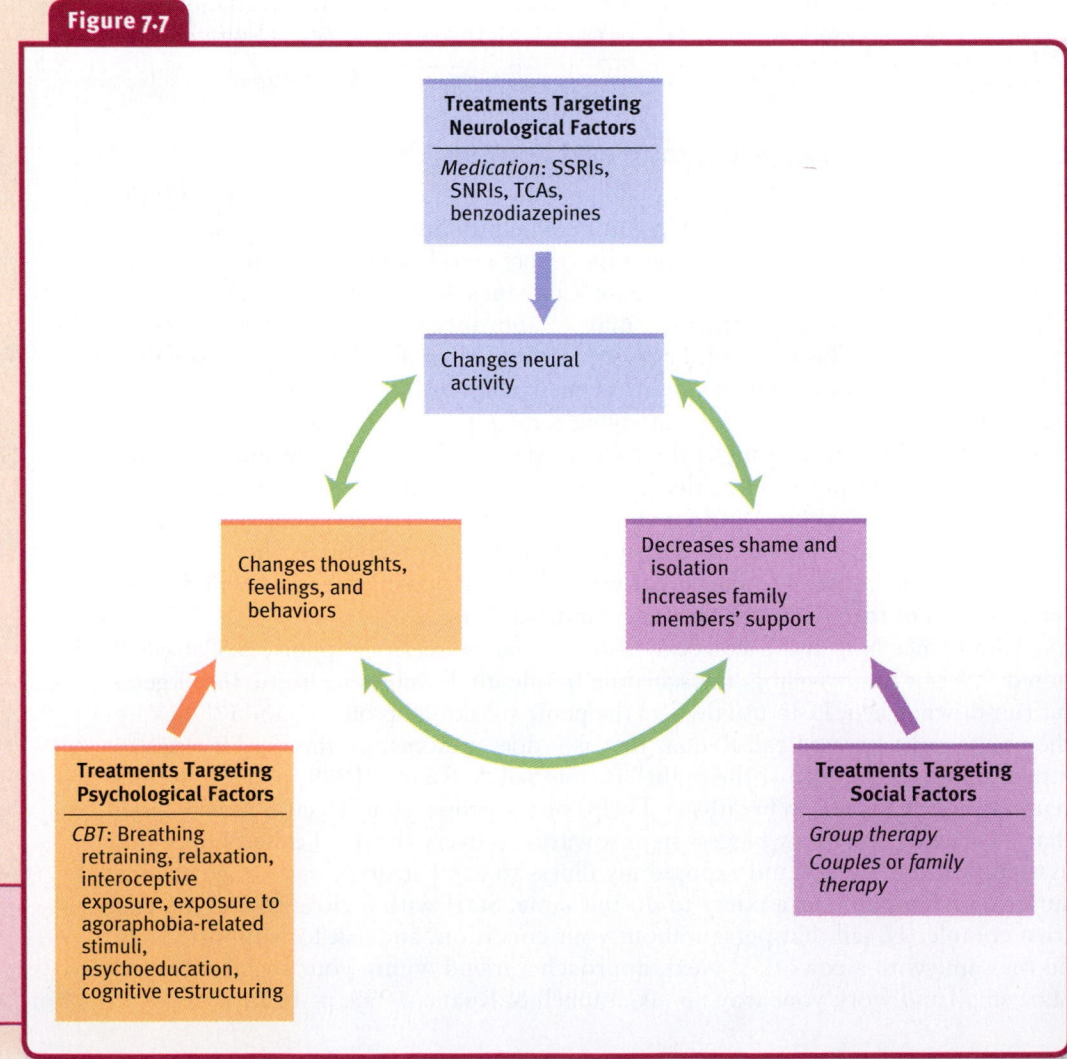

7.7 ▶ Feedback Loops in Treating Panic Disorder and Agoraphobia

Earl Campbell's Anxiety

The most appropriate diagnosis for Campbell appears to be panic disorder with agoraphobia. Despite using medication, Campbell continues to have some panic symptoms, but he makes good use of various cognitive and behavioral methods and of social support. He acknowledged his continuing efforts: "Even though crowds and noise bother me, I'll push myself to tolerate them for as long as I can. I know I must keep trying to get past the fear. It takes far more discipline for me to get through an average day with panic than it took for me to perform as a top running back in the NFL. The challenges of panic are greater" (Campbell & Ruane, 1999, p. 199).

In the rest of the chapter we examine other anxiety disorders, disorders not applicable to Campbell. As we discuss these other anxiety disorders, we consider Howard Hughes and his symptoms of anxiety, and the role these symptoms played in his life.

Key Concepts and Facts About Panic Disorder (With and Without Agoraphobia) ■

- The hallmark of panic disorder is recurrent panic attacks—periods of intense dread, fear, and feelings of imminent doom along with increased heart rate, shortness of breath, and other signs of hyperarousal. Panic attacks may be cued by particular stimuli (usually internal sensations), or they may arise without any clear cue. Panic disorder also involves fear of further attacks and, in some cases, restricted behavior in an effort to prevent further attacks.

- People in different cultures may have similar—but not identical—constellations of panic symptoms, such as *ataque de nervios* and wind-and-blood pressure.

- Some people with panic disorder also develop agoraphobia—avoiding situations that might trigger a panic attack or from which escape would be difficult, such as crowded locations or tunnels. Less commonly, people develop agoraphobia without panic disorder.

- Neurological factors that contribute to panic disorder and agoraphobia include:
  - A heightened sensitivity to detect breathing changes, which in turn leads to hyperventilation, panic, and a sense of needing to escape. This mechanism involves withdrawal emotions and the right frontal lobe, the amygdala, and the hypothalamus.
  - Too much norepinephrine (produced by an over-reactive locus coeruleus), which increases heart and respiration rates and other aspects of the fight-or-flight response.
  - A genetic predisposition to anxiety disorders, which makes some people vulnerable to panic disorder and agoraphobia.

- Psychological factors that contribute to panic disorder and agoraphobia include:
  - Conditioning of the initial bodily sensations of panic (interoceptive cues) or of external cues related to panic attacks, which leads them to become learned alarms and elicit panic symptoms. Some individuals then develop a fear of fear and avoid panic-related cues.
  - Heightened anxiety sensitivity and misinterpretation of bodily symptoms of arousal as symptoms of a more serious problem, such as a heart attack, which can, in turn, lead to hypervigilance for—and fear of—further sensations and cause increased arousal, creating a vicious cycle.

- Social factors related to panic disorder and agoraphobia include:
  - greater than average number of social stressors during childhood and adolescence;
  - the presence of a safe person, which can decrease catastrophic thinking and panic.
  - cultural factors, which can influence whether people develop panic disorder.

- The treatment that targets neurological factors is medication, specifically benzodiazepines for short-term relief and antidepressants for long-term use.

- CBT is the first-line treatment for panic disorder and targets psychological factors. Behavioral methods focus on the bodily signals of arousal, panic, and agoraphobic avoidance. Cognitive methods (psychoeducation and cognitive restructuring) focus on the misappraisal of bodily sensations and on mistaken inferences about them.

- Treatments that target social factors include group therapy focused on panic disorder, and couples or family therapy, particularly when a family member is a safe person.

Making a Diagnosis

- Reread Case 7.2 about S, and determine whether or not her symptoms meet the criteria for panic disorder. Specifically, list which criteria apply and which do not. If you would like more information to determine her diagnosis, what information—specifically—would you want, and in what ways would the information influence your decision?

- Reread Case 7.3 about Shirley B., and determine whether or not her symptoms meet the criteria for agoraphobia with or without panic disorder. Specifically, list which criteria apply and which do not. If you would like more information to determine her diagnosis, what information—specifically—would you want, and in what ways would the information influence your decision?

Social Phobia (Social Anxiety Disorder)

Earl Campbell and Howard Hughes were alike in that their anxiety symptoms did not significantly affect their lives until adulthood, after both men had already attained professional success. Although Howard Hughes did not appear to have experienced panic attacks, he had other anxiety-related problems. Let's examine his life and travails with anxiety.

Hughes grew up in Texas as an only child in a wealthy family; his father founded a tool company and was often traveling on business. As a child and teenager, Hughes was shy and had only one friend; he was "supersensitive"—he didn't seem to take teasing in stride as other children did—and he preferred to be alone or spend time with his mother. When he was almost 17, his mother, a homemaker, died unexpectedly of complications from a minor surgical procedure. Two years later, Hughes became an orphan: His father died unexpectedly of a heart attack. Hughes was independent and rich at the age of 19. Within the next 6 years, he'd have triumphs and disasters: He'd win an Academy Award and survive a horrific airplane crash that crushed his cheekbone. Four years later, he'd found Hughes Aircraft Company, and 3 years after that, set a world record for flight. During his lifetime, Howard Hughes was famous for these accomplishments. But after his death in 1976, he became famous for his bizarre behavior in the last decades of his life, portrayed in the films *The Aviator*, *Melvin and Howard*, and *The Amazing Howard Hughes*, among others.

As Hughes became more successful, he also became reclusive, seeing fewer and fewer people. But it wasn't simply that he became a hermit. He went through periods of time when he would do nothing but watch films, 24 hours a day, naked, moving only from bed to chair and back, with occasional forays to the bathroom. And "raised to believe in his own delicate nature and in the grave danger of being exposed to germs, he became obsessed about his health, and feared that he too was destined for an early death. The slightest change in his physical condition or the mildest illness now threw him into a panic. He began to take pills and resort to all sorts of precautions to insulate himself from disease and illness. It was an obsession that would grow with time" (Barlett & Steele, 1979, p. 52). When asked about this behavior, he defended it by saying, "Everybody carries germs around with them. I want to live longer than my parents, so I avoid germs" (Fowler, 1986).

Clearly, Hughes's behavior wasn't normal. But what was the matter with him? Where is the line drawn between normal shyness and an extreme reaction to social situations or any other feared object or situation? At what point did Hughes's concerns about health and germs become unreasonable? To answer these questions, let's explore social phobia (also called *social anxiety disorder*) and then examine other types of anxiety disorders from which Hughes may have suffered.

What Is Social Phobia?

Howard Hughes had always been quiet and shy, and he had problems relating normally to people. Even after he became famous as a film producer and aviator, he was still shy—to the point that, when dating the actress Katherine Hepburn and visiting her at her family's home, he refused to join the family for dinner and insisted on waiting to eat until everyone had left the table so that he could eat alone. His problems got worse: In his 50s and 60s, he refused to see anyone but his immediate aides, except for a few times when legal matters required him to interact face to face with a handful of other people. These behaviors are evidence of something more extensive than shyness; they are symptoms of social phobia.

Social phobia, also called *social anxiety disorder*, is an intense fear of public humiliation or embarrassment, together with the avoidance of social situations likely to cause this fear (American Psychiatric Association, 2000; see Table 7.8). Such social situations often include those where a person could be judged—for instance, public speaking. Social phobia may also arise in social situations in which

Social phobia
The anxiety disorder characterized by intense fear of public humiliation or embarrassment, together with the avoidance of social situations likely to cause this fear; also called *social anxiety disorder*.

Table 7.8 ▶ DSM-IV-TR Diagnostic Criteria for Social Phobia

A. A marked and persistent fear of one or more social or performance situations in which the person is exposed to unfamiliar people or to possible scrutiny by others. The individual fears that he or she will act in a way (or show anxiety symptoms) that will be humiliating or embarrassing.

Note: In children, there must be evidence of the capacity for age-appropriate social relationships with familiar people and the anxiety must occur in peer settings, not just in interactions with adults.

B. Exposure to the feared social situation almost invariably provokes anxiety, which may take the form of a situationally bound or situationally predisposed Panic Attack.

Note: In children, the anxiety may be expressed by crying, tantrums, freezing, or shrinking from social situations with unfamiliar people.

C. The person recognizes that the fear is excessive or unreasonable.

Note: In children, this feature may be absent.

D. The feared social or performance situations are avoided or else are endured with intense anxiety or distress.

E. The avoidance, anxious anticipation, or distress in the feared social or performance situation(s) interferes significantly with the person's normal routine, occupational (academic) functioning, or social activities or relationships, or there is marked distress about having the phobia.

F. In individuals under age 18 years, the duration is at least 6 months.

G. The fear or avoidance is not due to the direct physiological effects of a substance (e.g., a drug of abuse, a medication) or a general medical condition and is not better accounted for by another mental disorder (e.g., Panic Disorder With or Without Agoraphobia, Separation Anxiety Disorder [discussed in Chapter 14], Body Dysmorphic Disorder [Chapter 8], a Pervasive Developmental Disorder [Chapter 14], or Schizoid Personality Disorder [Chapter 13]).

H. If a general medical condition or another mental disorder is present, the fear in Criterion A is unrelated to it, e.g., the fear is not of Stuttering, trembling in Parkinson's disease, or exhibiting abnormal eating behavior in Anorexia Nervosa or Bulimia Nervosa [Chapter 10].

Source: Reprinted with permission from the Diagnostic and Statistical Manual of Mental Disorders, Text Revision, Fourth Edition, (Copyright 2000) American Psychiatric Association.

most people wouldn't think twice about being judged, such as eating in the presence of others or using public restrooms or dressing rooms. People with social phobia avoid such situations whenever possible—and may even avoid making eye contact with other people. When a social situation cannot be avoided and must be endured, the person with social phobia experiences panic or anxiety, sometimes including symptoms of upset stomach, diarrhea, sweating, muscle tension, and heart palpitations. DSM-IV-TR distinguishes between a social phobia that is limited to specific social performances where the individual is the center of attention—such as making a presentation—and *generalized social phobia*, which leads a person to fear and avoid all social situations, as does Rachel in Case 7.4. Table 7.9 lists additional facts about social phobia.

CASE 7.4 ▶ FROM THE OUTSIDE: Social Phobia

Rachel was a twenty-six-year-old woman who worked as an assistant manager of a small bookstore. [She sought treatment] for her intense anxiety about her upcoming wedding. Rachel wasn't afraid of being married (i.e., the commitment, living with her spouse, etc.); she was terrified of the wedding itself. The idea of being on display in front of such a large audience was almost unthinkable. In fact, she had postponed her wedding on two previous occasions because of her performance fears. . . .

She reported being shy from the time she was very young. When she was in high school, her anxiety around people had become increasingly intense and had affected her school life. She was convinced that her classmates would find her dull or boring or that they would notice her anxiety and assume that she was incompetent. Typically, she avoided doing oral reports

continued on next page

at school and didn't take any classes where she felt her performance might be observed or judged by her classmates (e.g., gym). On a few occasions, she even went out of her way to obtain special permission to hand in a written essay instead of doing an oral report. Despite being an excellent student, she generally tended to be very quiet in class and rarely asked questions or participated in class discussions.

Throughout college, Rachel had difficulty making new friends. Although people liked her company and often invited her to parties and other social events, she rarely accepted. She had a long list of excuses to get out of socializing with other people. She was comfortable only with her family and several longtime friends but aside from those, she tended to avoid significant contact with other people.

(Antony & Swinson, 2000a, pp. 5–6)

People who have social phobia also tend to be very sensitive to criticism and rejection and to worry about not living up to the perceived expectations of others. Thus, they often dread being evaluated or taking tests, and they may not perform up to their potential at school or work. Unfortunately, their diminished performance

Table 7.9 ▸ Social Phobia Facts at a Glance

Prevalence

- Social phobia is one of the most common anxiety disorders, with prevalence estimates ranging from 3% to 13%.
- Among all psychological disorders, it is the third most common, after major depression and alcohol abuse.
- A fear of public speaking or public performance is the most common symptom, followed by a fear of talking to strangers or meeting new people.

Comorbidity

- Among those with social phobia, over half will also have one other psychological disorder at some point in their lives, and 27% will have three or more disorders during their lives (Chartier, Walker, & Stein, 2003). Approximately 20–44% will have a mood disorder (Chartier, Walker, & Stein, 2003; Roth & Fonagy, 2005), and 23% will have alcohol or substance abuse or dependence (Chartier et al., 2003).

Onset

- Most people with social phobia were shy as children, and the more intense symptoms generally appear during adolescence.

Course

- Social phobia may develop gradually, or it may begin suddenly after a humiliating or stressful social experience.
- Symptoms typically are chronic, although they may lessen for some adolescents as they enter adulthood.

Gender Differences

- Three women develop social phobia for every two men with the disorder (Kessler et al., 1994).

Cultural Differences

- Culture can influence the specific form of social phobia symptoms; for instance, in Japan, some people with social phobia may fear that their body odor will offend others (Dinnel, Kleinknecht, & Tanaka-Matsumi, 2002), whereas people with social phobia in Hong Kong are more likely to be afraid of talking to individuals who are of a higher social status (Lee et al., in press).
- The prevalence of social phobia is increasing; people born more recently are more likely to develop social phobia in their lifetimes (Heimberg et al., 2000).

Source: Unless otherwise noted, information in the table is from American Psychiatric Association, 2000.

challenges their self-esteem, increasing their anxiety during subsequent performances or tests. Similarly, achievement at work may suffer because they avoid social situations that are important for advancement on the job, such as making presentations. People with social phobia are less likely to marry or have a partner than people who do not have this disorder. People with severe social phobia may quit school and be unable to get a job because the social interactions required at school or work are more than they feel they can endure.

Sometimes, a clinician or researcher cannot easily distinguish whether an individual's symptoms indicate that he or she has a social phobia or panic disorder with agoraphobia. However, there are two key features that distinguish these disorders:

1. People with social phobia fear other people's scrutiny.

2. People with social phobia rarely have panic attacks when alone.

In contrast, people who have panic disorder with agoraphobia do not exhibit these features.

Did Howard Hughes have social phobia? Biographical material suggests that he may well have: Although we don't know the degree of his fear of certain types of social situations (Criterion A), he is reported to have avoided parties and other occasions that involved meeting large numbers of people, whenever possible. However, in the first few decades of building his empire, he met with strangers or large groups of people when it served his business ends and he did not appear to have had panic attacks in the process. As a child, Hughes tried to avoid many social situations that seemed to make him anxious, and this preference continued throughout his adulthood (Barlett & Steele, 1979) (Criterion B).

Did Hughes recognize that his fear was excessive or unreasonable (Criterion C)? For a man as wealthy and powerful as Hughes, we can't know what he considered unreasonable or excessive. This was a man who accomplished achievements that others thought impossible or ridiculous. When he could, he avoided social situations that caused him anxiety, although when business required it, he endured uncomfortable situations (Criterion D). His social fears and avoidance significantly interfered with his life in the sense that they contributed to his becoming a recluse—he was last seen in public in 1958, when he was 53 years old ("The Hughes legacy," 1976).

These considerations lead us to infer that Hughes may have had social phobia as an adult, but this would not have been a lifelong diagnosis: For most of his adult life, the severity of his symptoms waxed and waned, and there were many periods when his symptoms do not appear to have met the criteria for this disorder.

Understanding Social Phobia

Social phobia is best understood as arising from interacting neuropsychosocial factors. Because of the very nature of this disorder, social factors are prominent contributors to it, along with neurological and psychological factors. As we'll see, Howard Hughes's history indicates that all three types of factors contributed to his problems: neurological and psychological vulnerabilities and social events that exacerbated his shyness.

Neurological Factors

Why does social phobia exist at all? Evolutionary psychologists speculate that social phobia may have its origins in behaviors of animals that are lower on a dominance hierarchy: Less powerful animals fear aggressive action from those more dominant and therefore behave submissively toward them. It is possible that social phobias arise when this innate mechanism becomes too sensitive or otherwise responds improperly (Hofmann, Moscovitch, & Heinrichs, 2002).

Various facts about the brains of people with social phobia are consistent with this conjecture. As we shall see, a variety of brain areas are overly active in these patients (including those involved in fear), neurotransmitter systems do not operate normally (particularly dopamine), and these people may even have a genetic predisposition for developing one of several disorders, including social phobia.

Brain Systems and Neural Communication

Social phobia involves fear, and researchers have shown repeatedly that the amygdala is strongly activated when animals—including humans—are afraid (Rosen & Donley, 2006). Thus, it's no surprise that the amygdala is more strongly activated when people with social phobia see faces with negative expressions (such as anger) than when they see happy faces, and that this difference is greater than observed in control participants who do not have the disorder (Phan et al., 2006). In addition, the more symptoms of social phobia a person has, the more strongly the amygdala is activated when the person views faces with negative expressions. Although it's not possible to identify cause and effect here, this correlation has the potential to provide an objective way to diagnose the severity of the disorder.

The amygdala is not the only brain area that responds differently in people with social phobia. Researchers have shown that a number of brain areas, including the hippocampus and cortical areas near it, do not function normally in people who have the disorder (Furmark et al., 2002). Moreover, the right hemisphere appears to play a part in this disorder, which is not surprising, given its role in withdrawal emotions (Davidson, 1992; see Chapter 2).

Virtually all of the major neurotransmitters may function abnormally in individuals who have social phobia, but impaired dopamine activity may be particularly important (Li, Chokka, & Tibbo, 2001). Researchers have examined regions of the brain that rely on dopamine and found that patients with social phobia show less activation in these regions than do control participants. Specifically, parts of the basal ganglia that control automatic behaviors, such as those learned when one becomes adept at playing the piano, rely on dopamine—and these areas are less activated in patients with social phobia than in control groups when participants are learning automatic behaviors (Sareen et al., 2007). But dopamine dysfunction cannot be the whole story; for example, evidence that people with social phobia have too little serotonin may suggest why SSRIs have sometimes been found to help these patients (Gorman & Kent, 1999; Lykouras, 1999).

Genetics

As is the norm for anxiety disorders, social phobia appears to arise from both genetic factors and environmental factors (Mathew, Caplan, & Groman, 2001; Stein, Jang, & Livesley, 2002). The heritability of social phobia is about 37% on average (with a range of 12–60% in various studies) (Beatty et al., 2002; Fyer, 2000; Kendler et al., 1992; Li, Chokka, & Tibbo, 2001; Neale et al., 1994). However, the genetic basis for this disorder appears not to lie in specific genes that affect only social behavior; rather, the genetic characteristics that predispose a person to develop this disorder may also predispose a person to develop autism or have fragile X syndrome (Coupland, 2001).

Given a general genetic predisposition, why would one person develop social phobia and another develop, say, autism? The answer may lie in the feedback loops among factors. Specifically, if a child is confronted with negative social events (such as those that occur in an abusive or overcontrolling family) and the social setting does not help him or her develop good ways to cope with such situations (as may occur when other family members exhibit poor ways to cope with anxiety), the child may respond by developing certain behavioral tendencies that (perhaps via reinforcement mechanisms, as discussed shortly) develop into social phobia.

Furthermore, we noted earlier that some people with social phobia were extremely shy as children; they had what is called a shy temperament, or *behavioral inhibition* (Biederman et al., 2001; Kagan, 1989), which has a genetic component. These patients cannot really be said to have *developed* a phobia, since they always had a basic level of discomfort in particular social situations (Coupland, 2001). This was certainly true of Howard Hughes, who was shy as a child and continued to be shy in his adult years; he preferred small dinner parties in people's homes to large social events.

Psychological Factors

Three types of psychological factors influence the emergence and maintenance of social phobia: cognitive biases and distortions, classical conditioning, and operant conditioning.

Cognitive Biases and Distortions

People who have social phobia have particular biases in attention and memory (Ledley & Heimberg, 2006; Lundh & Öst, 1996; Wenzel & Cochran, 2006). At the outset of one study, participants were shown photos of faces and asked to judge each facial expression as critical or accepting (Lundh & Öst, 1996). Following this, they were shown a larger set of faces and asked to pick out the ones that they had been shown initially. Those with social phobia were more likely to recognize the faces that they had earlier judged as critical, whereas those without social phobia were more likely to recognize faces that they had judged as accepting. Thus, people with social phobia seem to pay more attention to—and hence better remember—faces that they perceive as critical, which in turn feeds into their fears about being evaluated.

Similarly, cognitive distortions about the world can lead people with social phobia to see it as a very dangerous place; they then become chronically hypervigilant for potential social threats and negative evaluations by others (Beck & Emery, 1985; Joorman & Gotlib, 2006; Rapee & Heimberg, 1997). Of course, such anxious apprehension about social situations usually is not rational. People with social phobia also use distorted *emotional reasoning* as proof that they will be judged negatively: They evaluate the impression they made on others based on how anxious they became during the interaction, regardless of what actually transpired. So, for instance, a woman who is very nervous when giving a talk will base her evaluation of her performance not on how well she conveyed her message or by the response of the audience, but by how anxious she felt. People with social phobia interpret ambiguous cues as negative, which becomes proof that they were correct in their concerns. For example, people with social phobia are more likely than control participants to perceive neutral—and even happy—facial expressions as being negative (Stevens, Gerlach, & Rist, 2008). The anxious woman giving a talk may interpret the fact that some audience members in the front row are leaning forward in their seats during her talk as proof that they are "waiting for me to falter or make a jerk out of myself" rather than that they might be leaning in to hear her better or might be stretching their backs. People with social phobia also tend to have less positive beliefs about their own personality traits and social abilities compared to people who do not have this anxiety disorder (Rapee & Abbott, 2006; Wilson & Rapee, 2006). Such distorted thinking about self and social situations maintains the social phobia.

Unfortunately, such cognitive biases and distortions don't occur only during anxiety-provoking social encounters. People with social phobia persist in evaluating their social interactions long after others stop: Compared to nonanxious control participants, when asked to give an impromptu speech, those with social phobia were more like to assess their performance negatively and to ruminate on their performance a week later (Abbott & Rapee, 2004).

Classical Conditioning

In some cases, classical conditioning can contribute to the development of social phobia: A social situation (the conditioned stimulus) becomes paired with a negative social experience (such as public humiliation) to produce a conditioned emotional response (Mineka & Zinbarg, 1995). The conditioned response (fear or anxiety) may generalize to other, or even all, types of social situations. Based on letters from Hughes's mother to the director of the sleep-away camp he attended as a child, it seems that Hughes was teased by his campmates and took the teasing to heart. According to classical conditioning principles, it's possible that the sight of these campmates or the sound of their voices became a conditioned stimulus and induced in Hughes a powerful emotional response of humiliation or shame. He would then be likely to avoid similar stimuli.

Operant Conditioning

Operant conditioning principles apply to social phobia as well: Like a person with agoraphobia, a person with social phobia might avoid social situations in order to decrease the probability of an uncomfortable experience. The avoidant behavior does decrease anxiety and is thus reinforced (Mowrer, 1939). With each type of uncomfortable social situation that Hughes avoided, he learned that he could feel less anxious by staying away from those situations. And so, he avoided as many anxiety-provoking social situations as his money and power allowed.

Social Factors

Social factors that contribute to social phobia include the message some children receive from their interactions with family members—that social interactions can be a threat—and the influence of culture on people's concerns and fears about social interactions.

Parent-Child Interactions

Extreme overprotection by parents (as Hughes reportedly received from his mother) is associated with childhood anxiety (Hudson & Rapee, 2001; Wiborg & Dahl, 1997); such overprotection may lead children to cope with their anxiety through avoidance (Barrett et al., 1996). In Hughes's case, his mother was preoccupied and concerned about her son's shyness and his response to teasing, and she appears to have—perhaps inadvertently—reinforced his natural tendencies by letting him avoid social situations that made him uncomfortable (Fowler, 1986).

Culture

Different cultures emphasize different concerns about social interactions, and these concerns influence the specific nature of social phobia. For example, in certain Asian cultures, such as those of Korea and Japan, a person with social phobia may be especially afraid of offending others; in particular, he or she may fear that his or her body odor or blushing will be offensive. In Japan, this fear is known as *taijin kyofusho* (Dinnel, Kleinknecht, & Tanaka-Matsumi, 2002; Guarnaccia, 1997a). This contrasts with a fear among North Americans and Europeans of being humiliated by something they say or do (Lee & Oh, 1999).

Culture can influence the nature of the symptoms of social phobia. In Korea, for example, social fears called *taijin kyofusho* involve the possibility of offending others, perhaps through body odor or blushing.

The results from one study suggest that social phobias are becoming more common over time, and a higher proportion of people in more recent birth cohorts will develop the disorder (Heimberg et al., 2000).

FEEDBACK LOOPS IN ACTION: Understanding Social Phobia

A genetic or other neurological vulnerability, such as a shy temperament, can predispose people to developing social phobia (Bienvenu et al., 2007). The neurological vulnerability both contributes to and is affected by distorted thinking and conditioning to social situations (psychological factors). In addition, the anxiety and cognitive distortions may be triggered by a negative social event (social factor) and are then perpetuated by negative self-evaluations and avoidance of the feared social interactions (Antony & Barlow, 2002). Based on these psychological factors, people with social phobia may interact with others in ways that lead other people to rebuff them (Taylor & Alden, 2006), confirming their own negative view of themselves and of social interactions.

Furthermore, within the classical conditioning framework, both the unconditioned stimulus and the conditioned stimulus pertain to social interactions. Thus, the classical conditioning of social phobia is an event that involves social and psychological factors, as well as neurological ones—given that brain functioning is altered through the conditioning. Figure 7.8 illustrates these factors and their feedback loops.

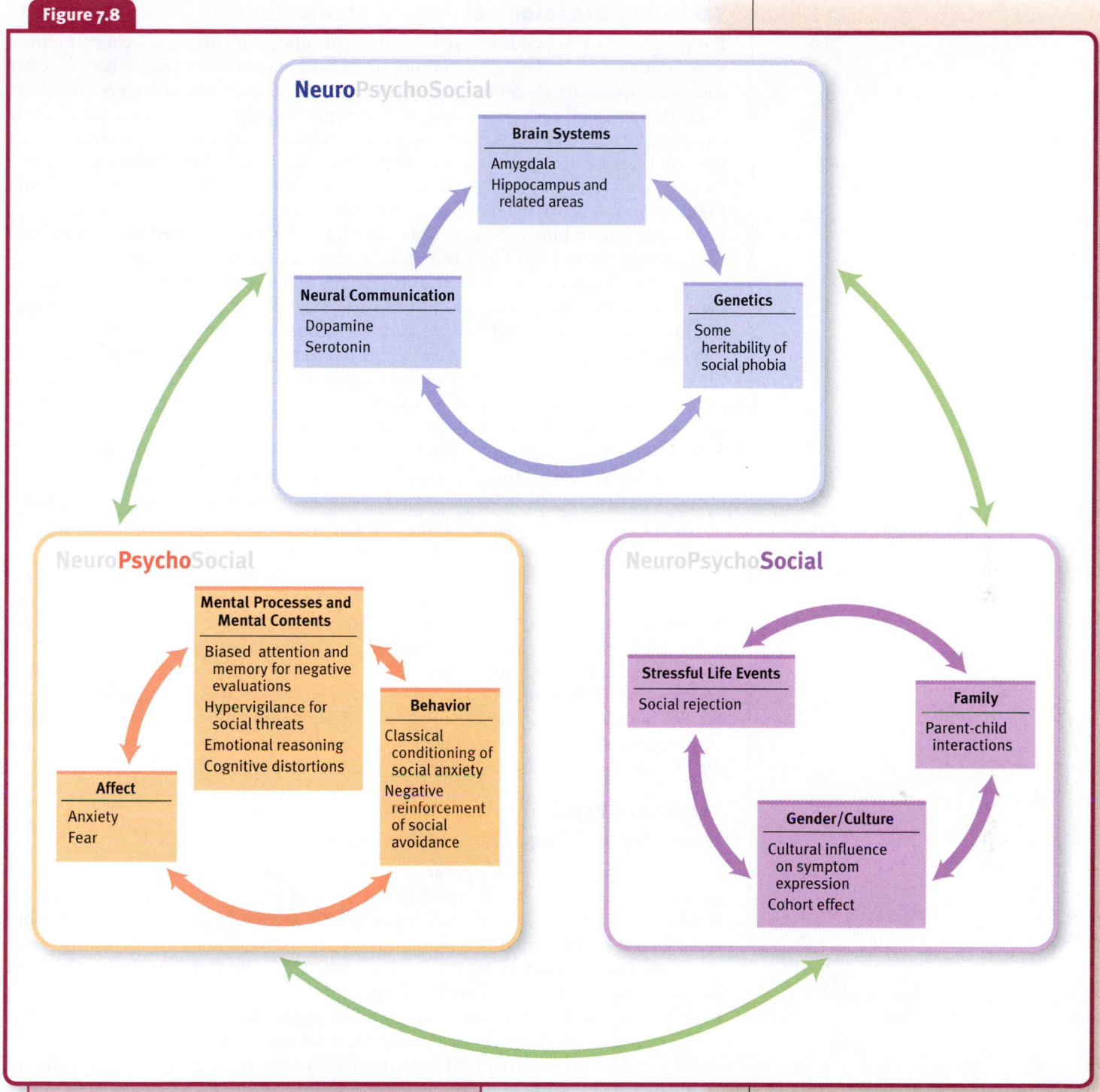

Figure 7.8

NeuroPsychoSocial

Brain Systems

Amygdala
Hippocampus and
related areas

Neural Communication

Dopamine
Serotonin

Genetics

Some
heritability of
social phobia

NeuroPsychoSocial

**Mental Processes and
Mental Contents**

Biased attention and
memory for negative
evaluations
Hypervigilance for
social threats
Emotional reasoning
Cognitive distortions

Behavior

Classical
conditioning of
social anxiety
Negative
reinforcement
of social
avoidance

Affect

Anxiety
Fear

NeuroPsychoSocial

Stressful Life Events

Social rejection

Family

Parent-child
interactions

Gender/Culture

Cultural influence
on symptom
expression
Cohort effect

7.8 ▶ Feedback Loops in Action: Social Phobia

Treating Social Phobia

Various forms of treatment are effective for social phobia; each one targets neuro-logical, psychological, or social factors, but will affect the other types of factors. Ultimately, the success of any form of treatment is reflected in diminished social fears and avoidance. Unfortunately, none of the treatments described here had been sufficiently developed when Hughes's symptoms were at their apex.

Targeting Neurological Factors: Medication

For people whose social fears are limited to periodic performances—whether a business presentation, a class presentation, or an onstage performance—a beta-blocker, such as *propranolol* (Inderal), is the medication of choice (Rosenbaum et al., 2005). Beta-blockers bind to some of the brain's receptors for epinephrine and norepinephrine, and hence make these receptors less sensitive. Both of these neurotransmitters are released during the fight-or-flight response. Thus, if the person perceives a "threat" and more epinephrine or norepinephrine is released as part of the fight-or-flight response, he or she will not experience its physical effects, such as increased heart rate, after taking a beta-blocker (see Figure 7.1 for a detailed list of the physical effects of the fight-or-flight response). Beta-blockers are not sedating.

For those whose social anxiety arises in a wider and more frequent set of circumstances, the medication of choice is the SSRI *paroxetine* (Paxil) or *sertraline* (Zoloft). Other SSRIs and SNRIs, such as *venlafaxine* (Effexor) and *nefazodone* (Serzone), and NaSSAs, such as *mirtazapine* (Remeron), can also help treat social phobia (Rivas-Vazques, 2001; Van der Linden, Stein, & van Balkom, 2000). However, higher doses of these medications are necessary to treat social phobia than to treat depression, and the medications may need to be taken for at least 6 months before the patient's fears and avoidance decrease (Rosenbaum et al., 2005). These medications affect the amygdala and the locus coeruleus, decreasing their activation. As with panic disorder, medication may be effective in treating social phobia in the short run (Federoff & Taylor, 2001), but symptoms generally return when medication is discontinued; thus, CBT is often also appropriate.

Hughes did take medication, but not specifically for his social phobia. Following a plane crash when he was about 40, he was so badly injured he wasn't expected to live through the night. He was given morphine for the pain. He did recover, although he remained in the hospital for 2 months, during which time he received increasing doses of morphine. His doctors later switched his pain medication to codeine, a drug he continued to take in ever-increasing quantities over the rest of this life. In his 50s, he also began taking the benzodiazepine Valium. Although the codeine and Valium may have taken the edge off his social phobia, they are very addictive and certainly interfered with his cognitive functioning.

Targeting Psychological Factors: Exposure and Cognitive Restructuring

CBT is used to treat social phobia, and there is evidence that such therapy has effects on the brain that are comparable to those of some medications; both sorts of treatments actually reduce the activity in certain key brain areas. For example, one study investigated two kinds of treatments with participants who had untreated social phobia (Furmark et al., 2002). The study began by scanning the participants' brains as they performed a public speaking task—which made them all anxious. Each participant was then randomly assigned to one of three groups: After the first scan, members of one group received the SSRI *citalopram*, members of another received CBT, and members of the third group were placed on a waiting list.

Nine weeks after the first scan, patients in the two treatment groups had improved by the same amount; however, patients in the waiting list group did not improve. At this point, all participants received a second brain scan, again while they performed the public speaking task. Comparison of the before and after brain scans revealed that a host of brain areas had less activity after treatment, particularly those involved in fear (and related emotions) and memory. Specifically, as shown in Figure 7.9, the amygdala, the hippocampus, and related areas were activated less strongly during the second scan, and the activation decreased comparably for the participants in the two treatment groups. The patients who responded best to treatment showed the greatest decrease in activation, which fits nicely

Some people with social phobia dread speaking in any group situation—such as a class or a meeting—to the extent that they are willing to be evaluated negatively for remaining quiet. Exposure and cognitive methods can help diminish the anxiety and avoidance.

image100/Alamy

Figure 7.9

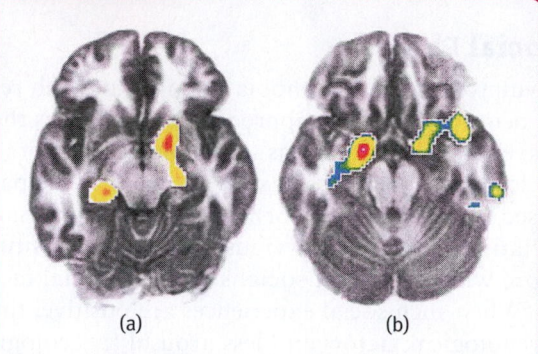

(a)   (b)

7.9 ▸ Effects of CBT and an SSRI on Brain Activity Results from a study by Furmark and colleagues (2002) show that activity in the amygdala, the hippocampus, and related areas was reduced by both CBT (a) and the SSRI citalopram (b). Brighter colors indicate greater reduction in activity. The scans are shown as viewed from the bottom.

Source: Furmark et al., 2002, Fig. 2-a. For more information see the Permissions section.

with other research results (Van der Linden et al., 2000). And perhaps most striking, 1 year later, the people who had the greatest reduction in activation from the first scan to the second scan were the most improved clinically. This means that the brain scans indicated how well the treatment worked for people with social phobia.

As shown by the study by Furmark and colleagues (2002), described above, cognitive methods can alleviate symptoms of social phobia. Such treatment helps individuals to identify irrational thoughts about social situations, develop more realistic thoughts and expectations, and test predictions about the consequences of engaging in specific behaviors (Antony & Barlow, 2002; Clark et al., 2006). For instance, let's say that a marketing manager is concerned that his voice might crack while making a presentation. Cognitive restructuring would address this concern: What would happen if his voice *did* crack? How could he resume his presentation? As the marketing manager identifies his automatic negative thoughts, he can develop more rational thoughts about giving presentations and develop possible solutions should his fears become reality.

In addition, the behavioral method of exposure can be very effective in treating people with social phobia: When people put themselves in social situations in order to habituate to their anxiety symptoms, their anxiety diminishes (Taylor, 1996). However, for those who do not want to participate in group therapy, or for those whose social anxiety is extremely high, exposure in individual sessions may allow them to habituate to less overwhelming stimuli that lead them to feel anxious. Following this, they are habituated to increasingly challenging stimuli. Table 4.3 (p. 127) provides an example of the kind of hierarchy of fear and avoidance of social situations that is used for exposure.

Targeting Social Factors: Group Interactions

Changing someone's thoughts and feelings about social interactions is an important part of treating social phobia (McEvoy et al., in press). However if the patient does not actually interact more with others after the treatment, then it cannot be considered a success. A patient might feel less anxious about social interactions but still avoid them out of habit. Because the very nature of the anxiety symptoms relate to social interactions, group therapy is the preferred mode of exposure treatment. Such therapy immerses people in the very type of experience that is associated with anxiety. *Cognitive-behavioral group therapy* uses exposure and cognitive restructuring in a group setting. This setting allows patients to try out their new skills immediately (Heimberg et al., 1990; Heimberg et al., 1998). Moreover, the exposure involved in group therapy helps to extinguish the conditioned bodily arousal (learned alarm) that arises in social situations. Cognitive-behavioral group therapy is as effective as medication (Davidson et al., 2004) and has the added benefit that the positive effects continue after treatment ends (Mörtberg et al., 2006).

In addition to therapy groups, there are self-help organizations for people who are afraid of speaking in public, such as Toastmasters, which give individuals an

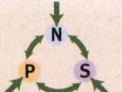

opportunity to practice making both spontaneous speeches and planned ones. (For more information, go to www.toastmasters.org.)

FEEDBACK LOOPS IN TREATMENT: **Social Phobia**

When medication is discontinued, symptoms of social phobia often recur. Such relapse is less likely after CBT. From a neuropsychosocial approach, CBT changes the way a patient thinks about and behaves in social situations (psychological factors). Viewing these situations more realistically and with less anxiety means that the patient does not get as physically aroused (neurological factor). This lowered arousal, along with positive or neutral expectations about the previously feared social situations, leads the patient to enter more willingly into a social situation (social factor), with less negative expectations. When such social experiences are positive, the patient feels increasing mastery (psychological factor) and less arousal (neurological factor), and perhaps receives reinforcement from others (social factor) for these changes. Figure 7.10 illustrates these factors and their feedback loops.

Figure 7.10

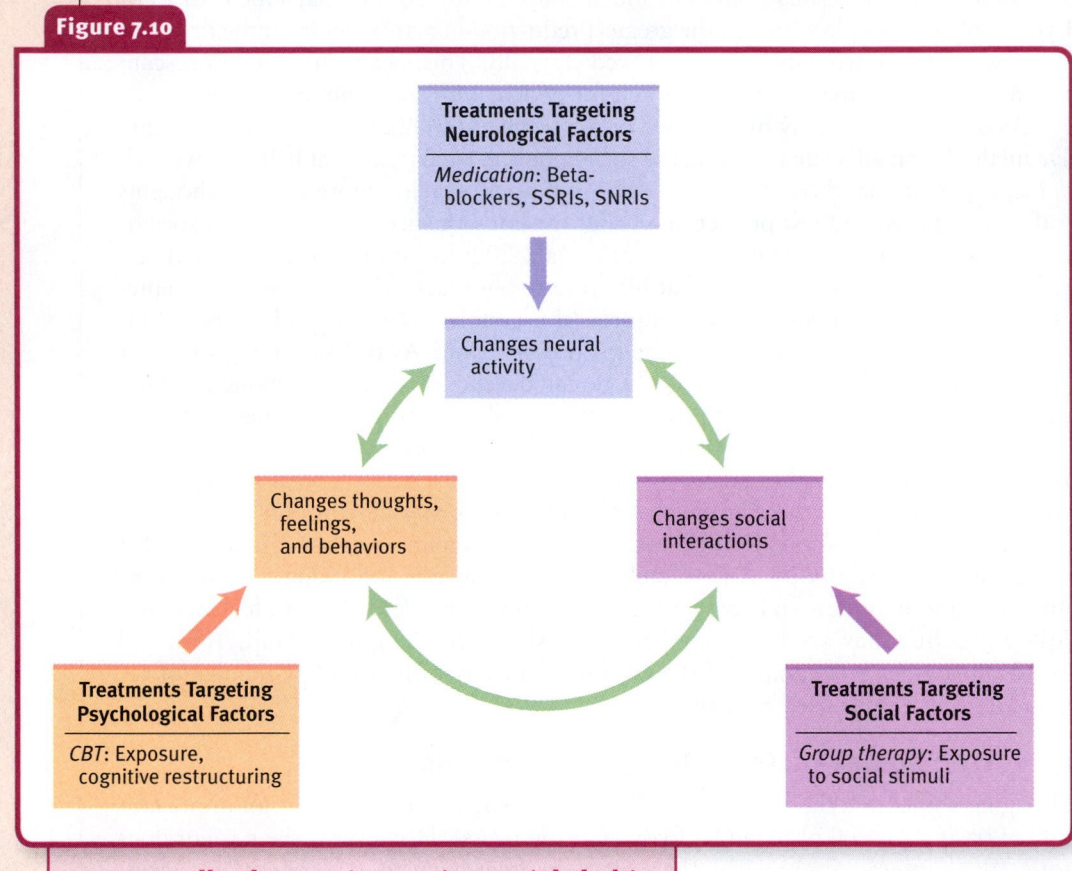

7.10 ▸ Feedback Loops in Treating Social Phobia

Key Concepts and Facts About Social Phobia (Social Anxiety Disorder)

- Social phobia is an intense fear of public humiliation or embarrassment, together with an avoidance of social situations likely to cause this fear. When such social situations cannot be avoided, they trigger panic or anxiety. Social phobia may be limited to specific types of performance-related situations or may be generalized to most social situations.

- The anxiety about performing poorly and being evaluated by others can, in turn, impair an individual's performance, creating a vicious cycle. The symptoms of social phobia may lead individuals with this disorder to be less successful than they could otherwise be, because they avoid job-related social interactions that are required for advancement.

- Neurological factors that give rise to social phobia include an amygdala that is more easily activated in response to social stimuli, too little dopamine in the basal ganglia, too little serotonin, and a genetic predisposition toward a shy temperament (behavioral inhibition).

- Psychological factors that give rise to social phobia include cognitive distortions and hypervigilance for social threats—particularly about being (negatively) evaluated. Classical conditioning of a fear response in social situations may contribute to social phobia; avoiding feared social situations is then negatively reinforced (operant conditioning).

- Social factors that give rise to social phobia include parents' modeling or encouraging a child to avoid anxiety-inducing social interactions. Moreover, people in different cultures may express their social fears somewhat differently (e.g., *taijin kyofusho*). The rate of social phobia appears to be increasing in more recent birth cohorts.

- Medication is the treatment that targets neurological factors, specifically, beta-blockers for periodic performance anxiety, and SSRIs or SNRIs for more generalized social phobia. The treatment that targets psychological factors is CBT, specifically, exposure and cognitive restructuring. Treatments that target social factors include group CBT and exposure to feared social stimuli.

Making a Diagnosis

- Reread Case 7.4 about Rachel, and determine whether or not her symptoms meet the criteria for social phobia. Specifically, list which criteria apply and which do not. If you would like more information to determine her diagnosis, what information—specifically—would you want, and in what ways would the information influence your decision?

Specific Phobias

During Hughes's convalescence after a near fatal plane crash at the age of 40, he grew concerned that he'd become afraid of flying. Before the crash, Hughes had loved to fly. But he knew that a number of his relatives had developed some extreme fears. For instance, his mother "had an intense fear of animals and was known to faint when one came near" (Barlett & Steeele, 1979, p. 30). Hughes's paternal grandmother "had developed a phobia about bugs, refusing to allow closets to be built in her new home for fear insects would nest in them" (Barlett & Steele, 1979, p. 45).

His mother also was extremely anxious about Hughes's health—she "watched for the slightest change in his physical condition. If she detected any abnormality in his feet, teeth, digestion, or bowels, she whisked him off to a doctor for an examination. During outbreaks of infectious diseases, the two of them often left Houston for some distant, uncontaminated place" (Barlett & Steele, 1979, p. 38). Hughes himself was afraid that he'd develop an illness: "Raised to believe in his own delicate nature and in the grave danger of being exposed to germs, he became obsessed about his health. . . . He began to take pills and resort to all sorts of precautions to insulate himself from disease and illness" (Barlett & Steele, 1979, p. 52). Mental health clinicians would probably consider Hughes's mother and grandmother—and likely Hughes himself—each to have had a *specific phobia*.

What Is Specific Phobia?

What distinguishes normal fear and avoidance of an object or situation from its "abnormal" counterpart? DSM-IV-TR describes the central element of a **specific phobia** as an excessive or unreasonable anxiety or fear related to a specific situation or object (American Psychiatric Association, 2000). People with a specific phobia know that their fear is excessive or unreasonable (see Table 7.10). (In contrast, a rational fear of being mugged in a large city park late at night and avoiding parks after dark would not be considered to be a specific phobia.) A person with a specific phobia works hard to avoid the feared stimulus, often significantly restricting his or her activity in the process (see Case 7.5). A person with an elevator phobia, for example, will choose to walk up many flights of stairs rather than take the elevator. Specific phobias you might recognize include claustrophobia (fear of small spaces), arachnophobia (spiders), and acrophobia (heights). DSM-IV-TR lists five types or categories of specific phobias: *animal*, *natural environment*, *blood-injection-injury*, *situational*, and "*other*" (American Psychiatric Association, 2000).

Specific phobia
The anxiety disorder characterized by excessive or unreasonable anxiety or fear related to a specific situation or object.

Table 7.10 ▸ DSM-IV-TR Diagnostic Criteria for Specific Phobia

A. Marked and persistent fear that is excessive or unreasonable, cued by the presence or anticipation of a specific object or situation (e.g., flying, heights, animals, receiving an injection, seeing blood).

B. Exposure to the phobic stimulus almost invariably provokes an immediate anxiety response, which may take the form of a situationally bound or situationally predisposed Panic Attack.

Note: In children, the anxiety may be expressed by crying, tantrums, freezing, or clinging.

C. The person recognizes that the fear is excessive or unreasonable.

Note: In children, this feature may be absent.

D. The phobic situation(s) is avoided or else is endured with intense anxiety or distress.

E. The avoidance, anxious anticipation, or distress in the feared situation(s) interferes significantly with the person's normal routine, occupational (or academic) functioning, or social activities or relationships, or there is marked distress about having the phobia.

F. In individuals under age 18 years, the duration is at least 6 months.

G. The anxiety, Panic Attacks, or phobic avoidance associated with the specific object or situation are not better accounted for by another mental disorder, such as Obsessive-Compulsive Disorder (e.g., fear of dirt in someone with an obsession about contamination [discussed later in this chapter]), Posttraumatic Stress Disorder (e.g., avoidance of stimuli associated with a severe stressor [discussed later in this chapter]), Separation Anxiety Disorder (e.g., avoidance of school [Chapter 14]), Social Phobia (e.g., avoidance of social situations because of fear of embarrassment), Panic Disorder with Agoraphobia, or Agoraphobia Without History of Panic Disorder.

Source: Reprinted with permission from the Diagnostic and Statistical Manual of Mental Disorders, Text Revision, Fourth Edition, (Copyright 2000) American Psychiatric Association.

CASE 7.5 ▸ FROM THE OUTSIDE: A Specific Phobia (Hydrophobia)

Kevin described an experience in which he almost drowned when he was 11. He and his parents were swimming in the Gulf of Mexico, in a place where there were underwater canyons with currents that would often pull a swimmer out to sea. He remembered the experience very distinctly. He was standing in water up to his neck, trying to see where his parents were. Suddenly, a large wave hit him and dragged him into one of the underwater canyons. Fortunately, someone on shore saw what had happened and rescued him. After the experience, he became very much afraid of the ocean, and the fear generalized to lakes, rivers, and large swimming pools. He avoided them all.

(McMullin, 1986, p. 165)

Animal Type

The *animal type* of specific phobia pertains to an extreme fear or avoidance of any variety of animal; commonly feared animals include snakes and spiders. Symptoms of the animal type of specific phobia usually emerge in childhood. People with a phobia for one kind of animal often also have a phobia for another kind of animal. Hughes's grandmother and mother had this type of phobia, although his mother's fainting in response to seeing an animal is unusual.

Natural Environment Type

The *natural environment* type of specific phobia typically focuses on heights, water, or storms. Kevin, in Case 7.5, had a fear of water. Phobias about the natural environment typically emerge during childhood.

Blood-Injection-Injury Type

The *blood-injection-injury type* of specific phobia produces a strong response to seeing blood, having injections, sustaining bodily injuries, or watching surgery. This type of phobia runs in families and emerges in early childhood. A unique response of this specific phobia involves first an increased arousal, then a rapid decrease in heart rate and blood pressure, which often causes fainting. Among people with this type of phobia, over half report having fainted in response to a feared stimulus (Öst, 1992).

Situational Type

A *situational type* of specific phobia involves a fear of a particular situation, such as being in an airplane, elevator, or enclosed space, or of driving a car. Some people develop this type of phobia in childhood, but in general it has a later onset, often in the mid-20s. People with this type tend to experience more panic attacks than do people with other types of specific phobia (Lipsitz et al., 2002). Situational phobia has a gender ratio, age of onset, and family history similar to those of panic disorder with agoraphobia.

Some researchers have argued that situational and natural environment fears overlap; for instance, fear of the dark is both a situational and a natural environment phobia. These researchers propose that these two types should be combined or that there should be no types, and mental health professionals should simply name the feared stimuli specifically (Antony & Swinson, 2000b).

Other Type

This category includes any *other type* of specific phobia that does not fall into the four categories already discussed. Examples of specific phobias that would be classified as "other" are a fear of falling down when not near a wall or some other type of support, a fear of costumed characters (such as clowns at a circus), and a phobic avoidance of situations that may lead to choking, vomiting, or contracting an illness—the last of which Hughes may have had.

Specifics About Specific Phobias

As noted in Table 7.11, the majority of people who have one sort of specific phobia are likely to have at least one more (Stinson et al., 2007). This high comorbidity among specific phobias has led some researchers to suggest that, like social phobia, specific phobia may take two forms: a focused type that is limited to a specific stimulus, and a more generalized type that involves fear of various stimuli (Stinson et al., 2007).

The unrealistic fears and extreme anxiety of a specific phobia occur in the presence of the feared stimulus but may even occur when simply thinking about it. Often, people with a specific phobia fear that something bad will happen as a result of contact with the stimulus: "What if I get stuck in the tunnel and it cracks open and floods?" "What if the spider bites me and I get a deadly disease?" People may also be afraid of the consequences of their reaction to the phobic stimulus, such as losing control of themselves or not being able to get help: "What if I mess my pants after the spider bites me?" or "What if I faint or have a heart attack while I'm in the tunnel?" In this sense, the fear of somehow losing control is similar to that in panic disorder (Horwath et al., 1993). The situation or object that causes fear and anxiety is related to the content of the worry about losing control: Someone who is afraid of heights may worry about getting dizzy when high up (and, as a result, plummeting to the ground).

There is a very long list of stimuli to which people have developed phobias (see www.phobialist.com), but people do not seem to develop specific phobias toward all kinds of stimuli. Humans, like other animals, have a natural readiness for certain stimuli to produce certain conditioned responses. This *preparedness* means that less learning from experience is needed to produce the conditioning (Öhman et al., 1976). Young children, for example, typically go through a period when they are easily afraid of the dark or of storms, which may suggest that such fears can more readily become specific phobias. In contrast, a fear of flowers is extremely unusual. Some psychologists (Menzies & Parker, 2001; Öhman, 1986; Stein & Matsunaga, 2006) propose that such preparedness has an evolutionary advantage—people are more readily afraid of objects or situations that could lead to death, such as being too close to the edge of a cliff (and falling off) or being bitten by a poisonous snake or spider. According to this view, those among our early ancestors who were afraid of these stimuli and avoided them were more likely to survive and reproduce—and thus pass on genes that led them to be prepared to fear these stimuli.

Table 7.11 ▶ Specific Phobia Facts at a Glance

Prevalence

- Approximately 10% of Americans will experience in their lifetime a fear severe enough to meet the criteria for specific phobia (Stinson et al., 2007).

Comorbidity

- Only a quarter of those with a diagnosis of specific phobia have a single specific phobia; 50% have three or more phobias. In addition, the more phobias a person has, the more likely he or she is to have another type of anxiety disorder (Curtis et al., 1998; Stinson et al., 2007).

Onset

- There are different ages of onset for the various types of specific phobias, although the average age is about 10 years (Stinson et al., 2007).
- Specific phobias that arise after trauma can occur at any age.

Course

- Specific phobias that arise during adolescence are likely to persist through adulthood; only 20% of persistent phobias that begin in adolescence will improve without treatment.

Gender Differences

- Twice as many women are diagnosed with specific phobias as men, although this ratio varies across type of specific phobias (Stinson et al., 2007). The gender difference in prevalence rates is more pronounced with animal, natural environment, and situational phobias. Men and women are equally likely to report blood-injection-injury phobia (Fredrikson et al., 1996).
- Gender differences may reflect a reporting bias: Women may be more likely to *report* symptoms, but not necessarily more likely to have them (Hartung & Widiger, 1998).

Cultural Differences

- The prevalence rates of the various types of specific phobias vary across countries, suggesting that cultural factors, such as the likelihood of coming into contact with various stimuli, affect the form that specific phobias take (Chambers, Yeragani, & Keshavan, 1986).

Source: Unless otherwise noted, information in the table is from American Psychiatric Association, 2000.

New Line Cinema/courtesy Everett Collection

Although many people fear some kind of animal, such as spiders or snakes, the fear and avoidance of that type of animal do not constitute a specific phobia unless they significantly interfere with normal functioning.

People also can have a natural disinclination to allow some particular conditioned stimuli to elicit certain conditioned responses, which is called *contrapreparedness*. For example, Marks (1969) describes a 43-year-old patient who, at the age of 10, saw a snake in a ditch just as a car door was accidentally slammed on her hand. Thirty years later, she still felt extremely afraid of snakes (preparedness), but she had no fear of car doors (contrapreparedness), despite a car door's having been the actual source of her pain.

Although Howard Hughes was worried about developing a fear of flying (specific phobia, situational type), the phobia didn't materialize. Because of his concern about becoming afraid of flying and the passion he had had for the activity, he pushed himself to get back in the cockpit as soon as he was physically able (Barlett & Steele, 1979), and then he flew repeatedly, successfully undergoing a self-imposed exposure treatment. However, Hughes may well have had a phobia of contracting an illness—his concerns were excessive and unreasonable, and his avoidance behaviors extreme.

Understanding Specific Phobias

Let's consider neurological, psychological, and social factors that contribute to specific phobias, as well as their feedback loops. For this disorder, neurological and psychological factors appear to weigh more heavily than social factors.

Neurological Factors

Researchers are making good headway in understanding the brain systems that underlie specific phobias, and there is evidence that an unusually reactive amygdala may predispose some people to develop these disorders. In addition, abnormal functioning of several neurotransmitters has been shown to contribute to specific phobias. Finally, researchers have provided solid evidence that genes play a role in specific phobias, and have also documented the role of environmental factors in triggering these genetic predispositions.

Brain Systems

Perhaps not surprisingly, our old friend the amygdala is again implicated in an anxiety disorder. In fact, the amygdala appears to have a hair-trigger in patients with specific phobia. For example, in one fMRI study, patients who were phobic of spiders and control participants were asked to match geometric figures. In this study, the trick was that in the background behind each figure—which was completely irrelevant to the task of matching the figures—was a picture of either a spider or a mushroom (because no one in the study was afraid of mushrooms). Even in this task, where the participants were not paying attention to the background pictures, the amygdala of the patients with the phobia was more strongly activated in response to the spiders than the mushrooms; this was not true for the control participants (Straube, Mentzel, & Miltner, 2006).

But the amygdala is not the only brain structure associated with the disorder. For example, in one PET study, people who had phobias of animals were shown pictures of those animals (e.g., snakes) while their brains were scanned (Rauch et al., 1995). The photos of animals not only activated various parts of the limbic system (including the amygdala), but also activated the part of the cortex (known as *somatosensory cortex*) that registers sensations on the body. One interpretation of this finding is that the pictures triggered mental imagery of bodily sensations (such as the feeling of a bug crawling on the skin); in fact, when interviewed afterward, all participants reported having both tactile sensations and visual imagery during the study.

Neural Communication

The sort of anxiety evoked by specific phobias is associated with too little of the inhibitory neurotransmitter substance GABA (File, Gonzalez, & Gallant, 1999). When a benzodiazepine (such as *diazepam*, or Valium) binds to the appropriate receptors, it facilitates the functioning of GABA. The drug thereby ultimately produces a calming effect.

In addition, lower levels of the neurotransmitter acetylcholine are associated with higher levels of anxiety (Degroot & Treit, 2002). Moreover, the systems that produce acetylcholine and serotonin appear to be linked, so that increases in the output of one are accompanied by decreases in the output of the other (File, Kenny, & Cheeta, 2000); thus, reducing the serotonin level raises the level of acetylcholine, which in turn decreases anxiety. This may be one reason why SSRIs, which lower the levels of serotonin, effectively treat anxiety disorders. Moreover, to make the situation even more complicated, norepinephrine is also implicated in anxiety. Clearly, anxiety does not result from a simple biochemical imbalance, and effective medications will need to target several different neurotransmitter substances.

Genetics

Researchers have discovered that some genes predispose individuals to develop a specific phobia (but not a particular one), whereas other genes underlie each specific type of phobia (Kendler et al., 2001; Lichtenstein & Annas, 2000). According to one theory, genetic differences may cause parts of the brain related to fear (in particular, the amygdala) to be too reactive to specific stimuli; that is, the amygdala is "prepared" to overreact to a specific stimulus, which leads to a specific phobia of that stimulus. Some people's brains may be more prepared than others', and so they are more likely to develop a specific phobia (LeDoux, 1996).

However, such a neural predisposition cannot be all there is to it: If it were, then when one identical twin has a specific phobia, so would the other twin, which is not always the case. As we've noted before, the genes predispose, but rarely determine. Rather, certain environmental events are necessary to trigger the disorder. Some theorists have hypothesized that brain damage, such as can occur in an auto accident if someone isn't wearing a seatbelt and suffers a head injury, may be one such triggering event. And, in fact, both specific phobia and panic disorder are more likely to develop if a person has had traumatic brain injury. In one study, researchers found that 30 years after a brain injury, over 8% of the people injured had a specific phobia (Koponen et al., 2002).

However, genes do not have equal effects for all specific phobias: The different specific phobias appear to be influenced to different degrees by genetics and the environment (see Figure 7.11 for the heritabilities of types of specific phobias). Family environment also has proven to be an important risk factor for specific phobias (Kendler et al., 2001).

Can genes shed light on the sex differences for specific phobias? Perhaps to a limited degree. Men and women have comparable genetic risk for animal phobia but may have different risks for agoraphobia, situational phobias, and blood-injection-injury phobia because different genes may underlie these disorders in the two sexes (Kendler et al., 2002). However, over the long run, genetics may only moderately influence whether a person will develop a specific phobia. Unique experiences (such as falling out of a tree and then becoming afraid of heights) appear to be very important (Kendler, Karkowski, & Prescott, 1999). In fact, animal and situational phobias are most likely to arise as a consequence of specific unique experiences with that particular animal or situation.

The sum of the research findings about neurological factors suggests that particular life experiences can lead to a particular specific phobia for people who—through genes or other life experiences—are neurologically vulnerable (Antony & Barlow, 2002; see *Feedback Loops in Action* section, below).

Psychological Factors

Life experiences always have their impact via how a person perceives and interprets them. Thus, psychological factors play a key role in whether a person will develop a specific phobia. Three primary psychological factors contribute to a specific phobia: a tendency to overestimate the probability of a negative event's occurring based on contact with the feared stimuli, classical conditioning, and operant conditioning.

Faulty Estimations

As we saw with social phobia, people who have a specific phobia have a particular cognitive bias—they believe strongly that something bad will happen when they

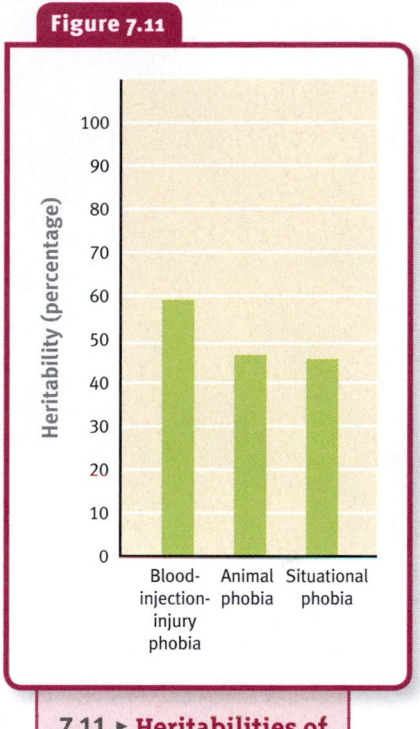

Figure 7.11

7.11 ▸ Heritabilities of Specific Phobias

Source: American Psychiatric Association, 2000.

encounter the feared stimulus (Tomarken, Mineka, & Cook, 1989). They also overestimate the probability that an unpleasant event, such as falling from a high place or an airplane's crashing into a tall building, will occur (Pauli, Wiedemann, & Montoya, 1998). People who have a specific phobia may also have perceptual distortions related to their feared stimulus. For example, a person with a spider phobia may perceive that a spider is moving straight toward him or her when it isn't (Riskind, Moore, & Bowley, 1995).

Conditioning: Classical and Operant

From a learning perspective, classical conditioning and operant conditioning could account for the development and maintenance of a specific phobia. Watson and Rayner's conditioning of Little Albert's fear of rats was the first experimental induction of a classically conditioned phobia (see Chapter 2). For Kevin, in Case 7.5, the ocean was the conditioned stimulus, the unconditioned stimulus was almost drowning, and the conditioned response was fear. Avoidance of the feared stimulus is negatively reinforced (Mowrer, 1939): The feared stimulus causes anxiety, which is then relieved by avoiding the stimulus. In Kevin's case, anxiety about water is reduced when he avoids water.

Some recent research, however, has questioned the importance of classical conditioning in the development of specific phobias. In studies of people with phobias of water, heights, and spiders, researchers usually have not found evidence that classical conditioning played the role that had been predicted (Jones & Menzies, 1995; Menzies & Clarke, 1993a, 1993b, 1995a, 1995b; Poulton et al., 1999). Further evidence for a limited role of classical conditioning comes from everyday observations: Many people experience the pairing of conditioned and unconditioned stimuli but do not become phobic.

Regardless of the extent of the role of classical conditioning, operant conditioning clearly plays a key role in maintaining a specific phobia: By avoiding the feared stimulus, a person can decrease the fear and anxiety that he or she would experience in the presence of it, which reinforces the avoidance. Hughes knew from experience with his social anxiety how easily such avoidance could narrow his life; his passion for flying motivated him to return to the skies after a disastrous plane crash.

Social Factors: Modeling and Culture

Sometimes, simply seeing other people exhibit fear of a particular stimulus is enough to make the observer become afraid of that stimulus (Mineka, Cook, & Miller, 1984). For example, if as a young child, you saw your older cousin become agitated and anxious when a dog approached, you might well learn to do the same. Similarly, repeated warnings about the dangers of a stimulus can increase the risk of developing a specific phobia of that stimulus (Antony & Barlow, 2002). After hearing about a plane crash on the news, it is no surprise that some people became afraid to fly—even though they had not been in a plane accident themselves.

Modeling is not the only way that culture can exert an effect on the content of specific phobias. Consider the fact that people in India are twice as likely as people in England to have phobias of animals, darkness, and bad weather, but are only half as likely to have social phobia or agoraphobia (Chambers, Yeragani, & Keshavan, 1986). One explanation for this finding is that women in India are apt to spend more time at home than their English counterparts, so they have less opportunity to encounter feared social situations. Similarly, dangerous and predatory animals are more likely to roam free in India than in England.

FEEDBACK LOOPS IN ACTION: Understanding Specific Phobias

A person may be neurologically vulnerable to developing a specific phobia (neurological factor), in part because of his or her genes. Through observing others' fear of a specific stimulus (social factor), the individual can become afraid and develop faulty cognitions, which can lead to anxious apprehension, distorted thinking, and the conditioning of false alarms to the feared stimulus (all psychological factors).

Given the neurological vulnerability, this set of events sets the stage for subsequent false alarms and anxious apprehension when the person is confronted with the stimulus (Antony & Barlow, 2002). And, of course, once the person begins to avoid the stimulus, the avoidance behavior is negatively reinforced. This behavior in turn affects not only the individual's beliefs but also his or her social interactions (social factors). These factors and feedback loops are illustrated in Figure 7.12.

Figure 7.12

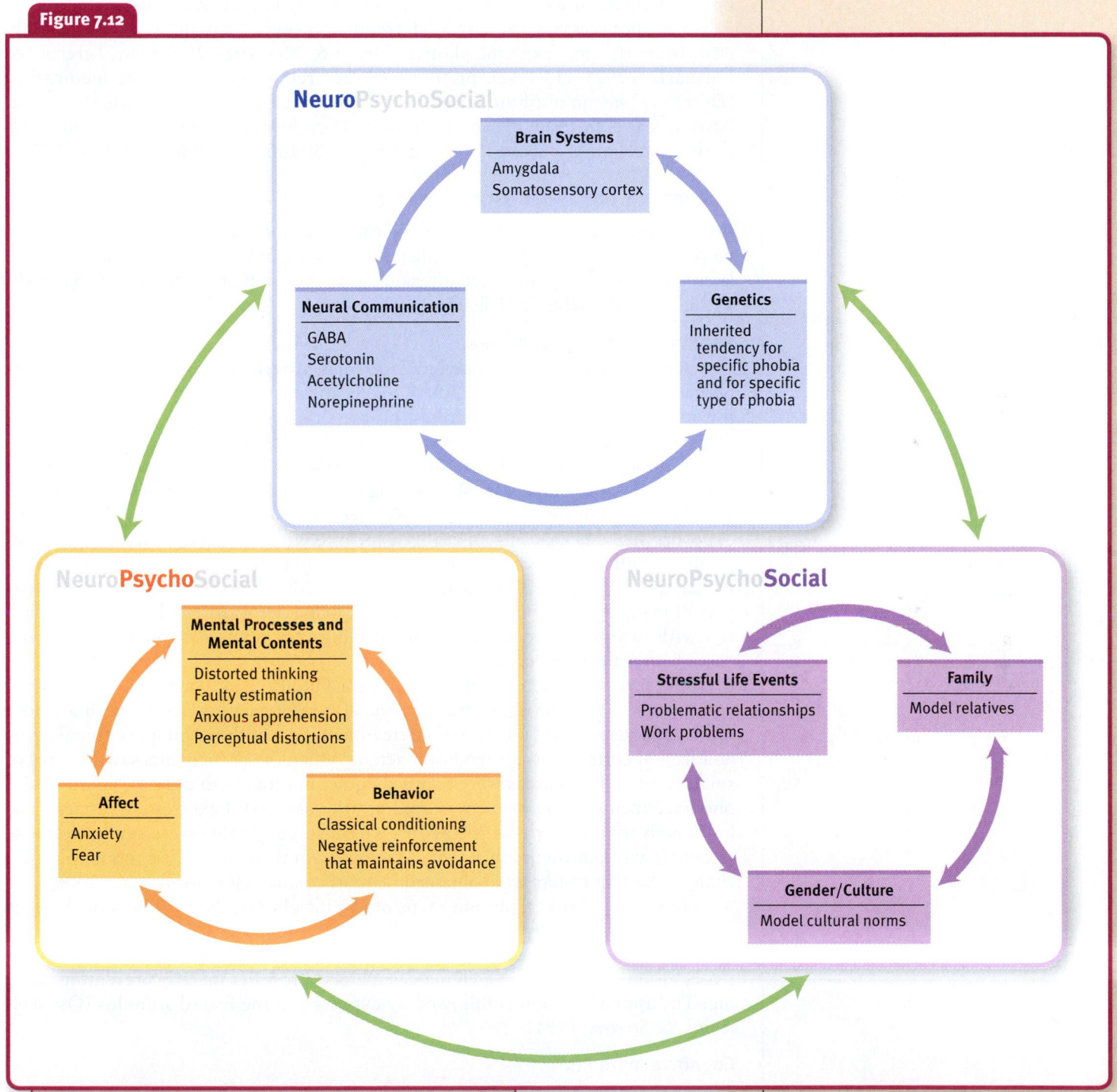

7.12 ▶ Feedback Loops in Action: Specific Phobia

Treating Specific Phobias

Treatment for specific phobias generally targets one type of factor, although the beneficial changes affect all the factors. Neurological or psychological factors are usually the primary target of treatments.

Targeting Neurological Factors: Medication

Medication, such as a benzodiazepine, may be prescribed for a specific phobia (alone or in combination with CBT), but this is generally not recommended. Medication is usually unnecessary because CBT treatment—even a single session—is highly effective in treating a specific phobia (Ellison & McCarter, 2002; Öst, Ferebee, & Furmark, 1997). However, preliminary research suggests that one medication (*D-cycloserine*, an antibiotic used to treat tuberculosis) may facilitate the neural basis of fear extinction; the combination of D-cycloserine and exposure is more effective than exposure alone (Norberg, Krystal, & Tolin, 2008; Ressler et al., 2004).

Targeting Psychological Factors

If you had to choose an anxiety disorder to have, specific phobia probably should be your choice. This is the anxiety disorder most treatable by CBT, with up to 90% lasting improvement rates even after only one session (Gitin, Herbert, & Schmidt, 1996; Öst, Salkovskis & Hellström, 1991).

Behavioral Method: Exposure

The behavioral method of *graded exposure* has proven effective in treating specific phobias (Vansteenwegen et al., 2007), and is considered a first-line treatment. With this method, the patient and therapist progress through an individualized hierarchy of anxiety-producing stimuli or events as fast as the patient can tolerate, as in exposure treatment for social anxiety (discussed earlier in the chapter and in Chapter 4; see Table 4.3), but in this case substituting the specific feared stimulus for the feared social situation or interaction. Moreover, recent research on treating phobias with exposure suggests that virtual reality exposure works as well, at least for certain phobias (Pull, 2005), such as of flying and heights (Coelho et al., in press; Emmelkamp et al., 2001, 2002; Rothbaum et al., 2001, 2002), and this technique is part of many treatment programs for fear of flying. Howard Hughes provided himself with in vivo exposure treatment by flying very often as soon as he was well enough after the plane crash.

Exposure clearly alters not only behavior but also neural activity. Consider the results from a neuroimaging study of the effects of treating people with a spider phobia (Paquette et al., 2003): Before treatment, part of the parahippocampal gyrus and frontal cortex showed significant activity when the participants saw pictures of spiders. These brain areas were relatively quiet in those who did not have a spider phobia. When viewing pictures of spiders after successful exposure treatment, the brain activation patterns of the people with a spider phobia were similar to those of people without the phobia. Thus, the behavioral treatment led to neurological changes. Similar results were obtained in another study (Johanson et al., 2006).

For the blood-injection-injury type of specific phobia, the treatment of choice is *applied tension* (Antony & Swinson, 2000b): To prevent changes in blood pressure and fainting before exposure to the feared (and faint-inducing) stimulus, the patient tenses all bodily muscles, which increases blood pressure, thereby preventing fainting. The applied tension is followed by exposure to the feared stimulus (Öst, Fellenius, & Sterner, 1991).

Cognitive Methods

Cognitive methods for treating a specific phobia are similar to those used to treat other anxiety disorders, such as panic disorder and social phobia. The therapist and patient identify illogical thoughts pertaining to the feared stimulus, and the therapist helps highlight discrepant information and challenges the patient to see the irrationality of his or her thoughts and expectations. Table 7.12 provides an example of thoughts that someone with claustrophobia—a fear of enclosed spaces—might have.

Group CBT may be appropriate for some kinds of phobias, such as fear of flying or of spiders (Götestam, 2002; Rothbaum et al., 2006; Van Gerwen, Spinhoven, & Van Dyck, 2006). However, unlike group CBT for social phobia, group treatment for specific phobia does not directly *target* social factors; rather, group CBT is a cost-effective way to teach patients behavioral and cognitive methods to overcome their fears.

Targeting Social Factors: A Limited Role for Observational Learning

Observational learning may play a role in the development of a specific phobia, but to many researchers' surprise, seeing others model how to interact normally with the feared stimulus generally is not an effective treatment for specific phobias. Perhaps observational learning is not effective because patients' cognitive distortions are powerful enough to negate any positive effects modeling might provide. For instance, someone with a spider phobia who observes someone else handling a spider might think, "Well, that person isn't harmed by the spider, but there's no guarantee that I'll be so lucky!" Nevertheless, such observational learning can be a helpful addition to CBT (Antony & Swinson, 2000b).

FEEDBACK LOOPS IN TREATMENT: **Specific Phobias**

When treatment is effective in creating lasting change in one type of factor, it causes changes in the other factors. Consider dental phobia and its treatment. Over 16% of people between the ages of 18 and 26 have significant dental anxiety, according to one survey (Locker, Thomson, & Poulton, 2001). One study examined the effect of a single session of CBT on dental phobia (Thom, Sartory, & Joehren, 2000). The treatment, which consisted of stress management training and imaginal exposure to dental surgery, occurred 1 week prior to the surgery, and patients were asked to practice daily during the intervening week. Another group of people with dental phobia was only given a benzodiazepine 30 minutes before surgery. A third group was given nothing; this was the control group. Both types of treatment led to less anxiety during the dental surgery than was reported by the control group. However, those in the CBT group continued to maintain and show further improvement at a 2-month follow-up: 70% of them went on to have subsequent dental work, whereas only 20% of those in the benzodiazepine group and 10% of the control group did so.

The neuropsychosocial approach leads us to consider how the factors and their feedback loops interact to produce such a specific phobia: The medication, although temporarily decreasing anxiety (neurological factor), did not lead to sustained change either in brain functioning or in thoughts about dental procedures. The CBT, in contrast, targeted psychological factors and also led to changes in a neurological factor—brain functioning associated with decreased anxiety and arousal related to dental surgery. In turn, these changes led to social changes—additional dental work. And the added dental visits presumably led to better health, which in turn affected the participants' view of themselves and their interactions with others. Indeed, if the visits had cosmetic effects (such as a nicer smile), their social benefits would be even more evident. Such feedback loops (see Figure 7.13) underlie the treatment of all specific phobias.

Table 7.12 ▸ Fearful Thoughts Related to Claustrophobia
• Many closed-in places, e.g., elevators, small rooms, do not have enough air.
• I will faint.
• If I go into a closed-in space, e.g., elevator or cave, I will not be able to get out.
• I will not be able to cope if I get stuck in a closed-in place.
• If I get too nervous, I may hurt myself.
• I will embarrass myself.
• I will lose control.
• I cannot think straight in enclosed places.
• I will go crazy.
• I will die.

Source: Antony, Craske, & Barlow, 1995, p. 105. For more information see the Permissions section.

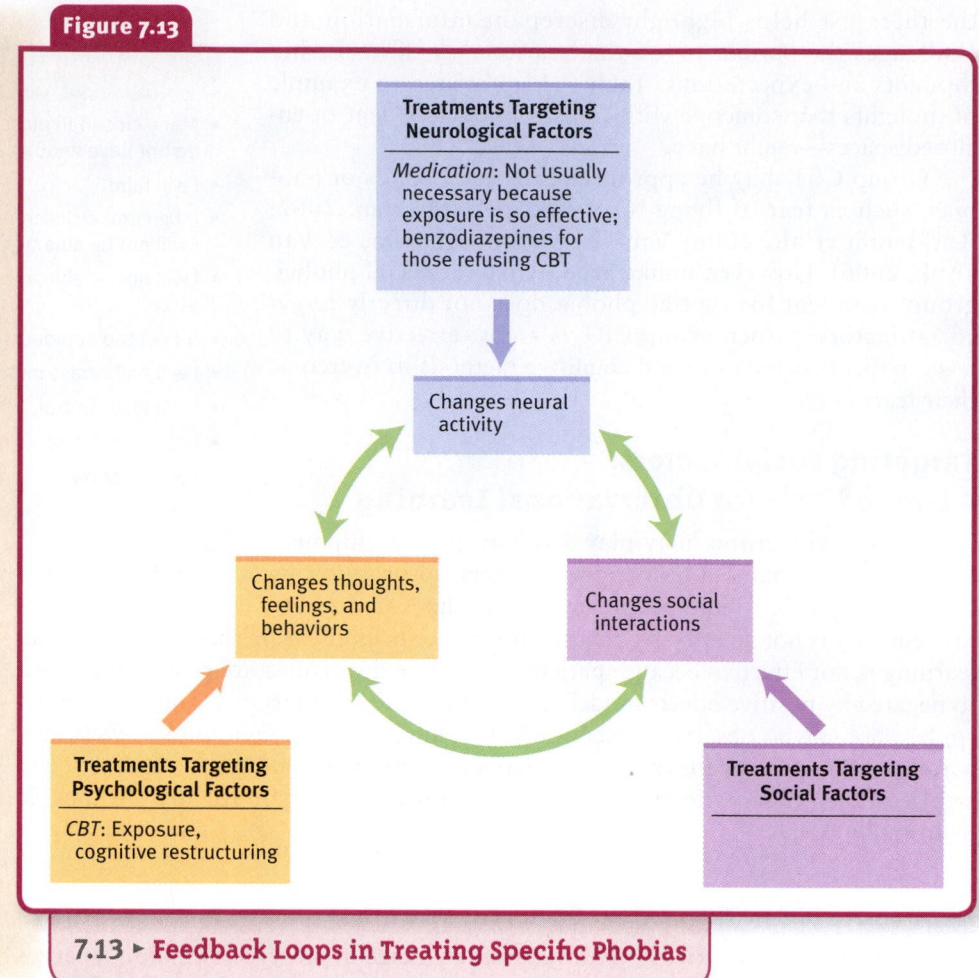

Figure 7.13

7.13 ▸ Feedback Loops in Treating Specific Phobias

Key Concepts and Facts About Specific Phobias

- Specific phobia involves excessive and irrational anxiety or fear related to a specific stimulus and avoidance of the feared stimulus. DSM-IV-TR specifies five types of specific phobias: animal, natural environment, blood-injection-injury, situational, and other.

- People are biologically prepared to develop specific phobias to certain stimuli as well as to resist developing phobias to certain other stimuli.

- Neurological factors, such as an overly reactive amygdala, appear to contribute to specific phobias. Neurotransmitters involved in specific phobias include GABA, serotonin, acetylcholine, and norepinephrine. Research suggests a role for genetics as well: Some genes are associated with specific phobias generally, whereas other genes are associated with particular types of specific phobias.

- Psychological factors that give rise to specific phobias include possibly classical conditioning (but rarely), operant conditioning (negative reinforcement of avoiding the feared stimulus), and cognitive biases related to the stimulus (such as overestimating the probability that a negative event will occur following contact with the feared stimulus).

- Observational learning—a social factor—can influence what particular stimulus a person comes to fear.

- Treatment for specific phobias can include medication (targeting neurological factors), specifically a benzodiazepine. However, medication is usually not necessary because CBT—the treatment of choice for specific phobia—is extremely effective (targeting psychological factors). CBT—particularly when exposure is part of the treatment—can work in just one session.

Making a Diagnosis

- Reread Case 7.5 about Kevin, and determine whether or not his symptoms met the criteria for specific phobia. Specifically, list which criteria apply and which do not. If you would like more information to determine his diagnosis, what information—specifically—would you want, and in what ways would the information influence your decision?

Obsessive-Compulsive Disorder

As we saw earlier, both Howard Hughes and his mother appeared to have a fear of Hughes contracting an illness. After his parents' deaths, Hughes's health concerns increased, and his profound fear of germs—and the rituals and behaviors that he used to limit what he believed were possible routes of contamination—became famous. But the protective rituals and behaviors extended beyond himself (and beyond rational thinking)—he made his aides and associates undertake similar precautions even though they were extreme and didn't, in fact, decrease his risk.

> He viewed anyone who came near as a potential germ carrier. Those whose movements he could control—his aides, drivers, and message clerks—were required to wash their hands and slip on thin white cotton gloves . . . before handing him documents or other objects. Aides who bought newspapers or magazines were instructed to buy three copies—Hughes took the one in the middle. To escape dust, he ordered unused windows and doors of houses and cars sealed with masking tape.
>
> (Bartlett & Steele, 1979, p. 175)

And it wasn't only germ prevention that Hughes tried to control. Throughout his life he'd been overly preoccupied with details; at one time or another, he concerned himself with every aspect of his companies—even demanding that employees conduct a detailed study of the vending machines at the Hughes Aircraft Company.

For most of his adulthood, Hughes wrote detailed memos about many things. In his 40s, he started doing so about trivial things. Here's an excerpt from a memo about an upcoming residential move:

> Any metal items of value should be protected against deterioration by putting them in a cabinet or a room that is dehydrated and kept dry. This is the new method of preserving metal articles. . . . Any keys found among his things which could not be identified were to be melted down.
>
> (Bartlett & Steele, 1979, p. 176)

Clearly, Hughes's preoccupations and ritualistic behaviors were not "normal." In fact, his preoccupations and behaviors are symptoms of obsessive-compulsive disorder.

What Is Obsessive-Compulsive Disorder?

Howard Hughes had obsessions and compulsions. **Obsessions** are thoughts, impulses, or images that persist or recur, are intrusive—and therefore difficult to ignore—and are inappropriate to the situation (American Psychiatric Association, 2000). For instance, Hughes had obsessions about germs—his preoccupations about them were intrusive and persistent. Worries about actual problems (such as "How can I pay my bills this month?" or "I don't think I can finish this project by the deadline") are not considered obsessions.

Whereas obsessions involve thoughts, impulses, and images, compulsions involve behaviors. A **compulsion** is a repetitive behavior (such as avoiding stepping on sidewalk cracks) or mental act (such as silently counting to 10) that a person feels driven to carry out; a compulsion usually corresponds thematically to an obsession. For instance, Howard Hughes was obsessed by the possibility that he might be exposed to germs and was compelled to behave in ways that he believed would protect him from such germs.

The key element of **obsessive-compulsive disorder (OCD)** is one or more obsessions, which may occur together with compulsions (American Psychiatric Association, 2000; see Table 7.13). The obsession can cause great distress and anxiety, despite a person's attempts to ignore or drive out the intrusive thoughts. People with OCD recognize that their obsessive thoughts do not originate from an external

Obsessions
Thoughts, impulses, or images that persist or recur, are intrusive—and therefore difficult to ignore—and are inappropriate to the situation.

Compulsions
Repetitive behaviors or mental acts that a person feels driven to carry out and that usually correspond thematically to an obsession.

Obsessive-compulsive disorder (OCD)
The anxiety disorder characterized by one or more obsessions, which may occur together with compulsions.

OCD can literally be life-threatening. Some people who compulsively hoard have died in fires in their homes. The hoarded objects took up so much space that it was difficult to leave once a fire started, or firefighters had to spend too much time trying to get in to the house (Kaplan, 2007).

Michael Maloney/San Fransisco Chronicle/Corb

Table 7.13 ▶ DSM-IV-TR Diagnostic Criteria for Obsessive-Compulsive Disorder

A. Either obsessions or compulsions:

Obsessions as defined by (1), (2), (3), and (4):

(1) recurrent and persistent thoughts, impulses, or images that are experienced, at some time during the disturbance, as intrusive and inappropriate and that cause marked anxiety or distress

(2) the thoughts, impulses, or images are not simply excessive worries about real-life problems

(3) the person attempts to ignore or suppress such thoughts, impulses, or images, or to neutralize them with some other thought or action

(4) the person recognizes that the obsessional thoughts, impulses, or images are a product of his or her own mind (not imposed from without, as in thought insertion)

Compulsions as defined by (1) and (2):

(1) repetitive behaviors (e.g., hand washing, ordering, checking) or mental acts (e.g., praying, counting, repeating words silently) that the person feels driven to perform in response to an obsession, or according to rules that must be applied rigidly

(2) the behaviors or mental acts are aimed at preventing or reducing distress or preventing some dreaded event or situation; however, these behaviors or mental acts either are not connected in a realistic way with what they are designed to neutralize or prevent or are clearly excessive.

B. At some point during the course of the disorder, the person has recognized that the obsessions or compulsions are excessive or unreasonable.

Note: This does not apply to children.

C. The obsessions or compulsions cause marked distress, are time consuming (take more than 1 hour a day), or significantly interfere with the person's normal routine, occupational (or academic) functioning, or usual social activities or relationships.

D. If another Axis I disorder is present, the content of the obsessions or compulsions is not restricted to it (e.g., preoccupation with food in the presence of an Eating Disorders [discussed in Chapter 10]; concern with appearance in the presence of Body Dysmorphic Disorder [Chapter 8]; preoccupation with drugs in the presence of a Substance Use Disorder [Chapter 9]; preoccupation with having a serious illness in the presence of Hypochondriasis [Chapter 8]; preoccupation with sexual urges or fantasies in the presence of a Paraphilia [Chapter 11]; or guilty ruminations in the presence of Major Depressive Disorder [Chapter 6]).

E. The disturbance is not due to the direct physiological effects of a substance (e.g., a drug of abuse, a medication) or a general medical condition.

Source: Reprinted with permission from the Diagnostic and Statistical Manual of Mental Disorders, Text Revision, Fourth Edition, (Copyright 2000) American Psychiatric Association.

source—for example, the thoughts aren't implanted by aliens from outer space, as some people with psychotic symptoms believe. Instead, they realize that the thoughts arise in their own minds, even though they can't control or suppress the thoughts.

Table 7.14 identifies common types of obsessions and compulsions. Obsessions (listed in the left side of Table 7.14) include preoccupations with *contamination, order, fear of losing control, doubts about whether the patient performed an action,* and *possible needs.* Compulsive behaviors are usually related to an obsession or anxiety associated with a particular situation or stimulus (also listed in Table 7.14) and include *washing, ordering, counting, checking, and hoarding* (Mataix-Cols, do Rosario-Campos, & Leckman, 2005). Performing the behavior temporarily prevents or relieves the anxiety. However, compulsions that relieve anxiety can take significant amounts of time to complete—sometimes more than an hour—and often create distress or impair functioning. DSM-IV-TR does not include subtypes of OCD.

Hughes clearly had compulsive symptoms of the contamination-washing type and had the ordering types of obsessions. At one point, he drafted a memo called "Notes on Notes," providing his assistant and secretaries with exact instructions for their typed notes:

Table 7.14 ▶ Common Types of Obsessions and Compulsions

Type of Obsession	Examples of obsessions: People with OCD may be preoccupied with anxiety-inducing thoughts about . . .	Type of Compulsion	Examples of compulsions: In order to decrease anxiety associated with an obsession, people may repeatedly be driven to . . .
Contamination	germs, dirt	Washing	wash themselves or objects in order to minimize any imagined contamination
Order	objects being disorganized, or a consuming desire to have objects or situations conform to a particular order or alignment	Ordering	order objects, such as canned goods in the cupboard, so that everything in the environment is "just so" (and often making family members and friends maintain this order)
Losing control	the possibility of behaving impulsively or aggressively, such as yelling during a funeral	Counting	count in response to an unwanted thought, which leads to a sense that the unwanted thought is neutralized (for instance, after each thought of blurting out an obscenity, methodically counting to 50)
Doubt	whether an action, such as turning off the stove, was performed	Checking	check that they did, in fact, perform a behavior about which they had doubts (such as repeatedly checking that the stove is turned off)
Possible need	the extremely remote likelihood that they will need a particular object at some undetermined point in the future as part of some unknown need (for instance, that they might need to look up something in today's newspaper in a few years)	Hoarding	hoard or collect objects that have no purpose (such as years' worth of newspapers) to the point where the behavior is clearly maladaptive (when piles of newspapers interfere with walking freely from room to room)

The word "shall" shall be used throughout instead of "will" in the third person singular and plural, making all sentences in the imperative rather than the indicative.

The infinitive verb shall not be used to express a major thought, except as an auxiliary to a main verb.

No changes or marks shall be made on the original pencil version.

The numbering system set forth in the notes shall not be a criterion for any future numbering system.

(Bartlett & Steele, 1979, p. 133)

Like the other anxiety disorders we've discussed, OCD often involves an unrealistic or disproportionate fear—in this case, of adverse consequences if the compulsive behavior is not completed. For instance, someone who hoards newspapers may be afraid that if she did not keep the papers, she would be unable to find an article that might later be crucial in some unforseen medical or legal matter. Or someone with an obsession about contamination, like Hughes, fears that if all germs aren't washed off, he will die of some disease. Additional facts about OCD are provided in Table 7.15, and Case 7.6 describes one woman's experience with OCD.

CASE 7.6 ▶ FROM THE INSIDE: Obsessive-Compulsive Disorder

For someone with OCD, just getting up in the morning and getting dressed can be filled with trials and tribulations:

Should I get up? It's 6:15. No, I better wait till 6:16, it's an even number. OK, 6:16, now I better get up, before it turns to 6:17, then I'd have to wait till 6:22.

OK, I'll get up, OK, I'm up, WAIT! I better do that again. One foot back in bed, one foot on the floor, now the other foot in bed and the opposite on the floor. OK. Let's take a shower, WAIT! That shoe on the floor is pointing in the wrong direction, better fix it. Oops, there's a piece of lint there, I better not set the shoe on top of it. . . . OH, JUST TOUCH THE SHOE TWICE AND GET OUTTA HERE!

continued on next page

All right, I got to the bedroom door without touching anything else, but I better step through and out again, just to be sure nothing bad will happen. THERE, THAT WAS EASY! Now to the bathroom. I better turn that light on, NO, off, NO, on, NO, off, NO, on, KNOCK IT OFF! All right, I'm done using the toilet, better flush it. OK, now spin around, wait for the toilet to finish a flush, now touch the handle, now touch the seat, remember you have to look at every screw on the toilet seat before you turn around again. OK, now turn around and touch the seat again, look at all the screws again. OK, now close the cover.

OK, let's pick out some clothes in the bedroom. First, I have to get out of the bathroom. Step in, step out, step in, step out, now look at all the hinges on the bathroom door. Do this on each step, both in and out of the bathroom.

OK, let's get some underwear. I want to wear the green ones because they fit the best, but they're lying on top of the T-shirt my grandmother gave me, and her husband (my grandfather) died last year, so I better wash those again before I wear them. If I wear them, something bad might happen.

(Steketee & White, 1990, pp. 4–5)

Understanding Obsessive-Compulsive Disorder

OCD can be understood by considering neuropsychosocial factors and their interactions. As with social phobia, neurological, psychological, and social factors influence one another. With OCD, however, social factors have less influence than neurological and psychological factors do. Howard Hughes had neurological and psychological vulnerabilities for the disorder that may have been exacerbated by psychological and social factors. Let's examine these factors in more detail.

Neurological Factors

Researchers have made much progress in understanding the neurological underpinnings of OCD. In the following sections we'll review how brain circuits have gone awry in this disorder, resulting in a loop of neural activity that may produce intrusive thoughts (obsessions) and lead one to repeat the same behavior over and over (compulsions); we'll also see that abnormalities in how neurotransmitters function (serotonin) play a role in this disorder. However, although genes also play a role, the genetic story is complex: Genes predispose people toward developing this disorder, but apparently by having an effect on anxiety disorders in general—not OCD in particular.

Brain Systems

When the frontal lobes trigger an action, there is feedback from the basal ganglia—and sometimes this feedback sets up a loop of repetitive activity, as shown in Figure 7.14 (Breiter et al., 1996; Jenike, 1984; Rauch et al., 1994, 2001). Many researchers now believe that this neural loop plays a key role in obsessive thoughts, which intrude and cannot be stopped easily. Performing a compulsion might temporarily stop the obsessive thoughts by reducing the repetitive neural activity (Insel, 1992; Jenike, 1984; Modell et al., 1989). (But soon after the compulsive behavior stops, the obsessions typically resume.)

Consistent with these ideas, Rapoport (1991) proposed that OCD symptoms can be caused by dysfunctional connections among the frontal lobes, the thalamus, and the basal ganglia (see Figure 7.14). Much research has focused on possible abnormalities in the basal ganglia and frontal lobes

Table 7.15 ▶ Obsessive-Compulsive Disorder Facts at a Glance

Prevalence

- Approximately 2–3% of Americans will develop OCD at some point in their lives (Burke & Regier, 1994), with generally similar prevalence rates worldwide (Horwath & Weissman, 2000).

Comorbidity

- Over 90% of those with OCD have another Axis I disorder, with the most frequent categories of comorbid disorders being mood disorders (81%) and other anxiety disorders (53%) (LaSalle et al., 2004). Eating disorders and some personality disorders are also relatively commonly diagnosed as comorbid with OCD.

Onset

- Among males with OCD, symptoms typically begin to emerge between the ages of 6 and 15.
- Among females, symptoms typically emerge between the ages of 20 and 29.

Course

- Symptoms typically build gradually until they reach a level that meets the diagnostic criteria. Over the course of a lifetime, symptoms wax and wane, becoming particularly evident in response to stress.

Gender Differences

- Men and women have an equal risk of developing OCD.

Cultural Differences

- Although the prevalence rates of OCD and the types of symptoms are about the same across cultures, the particular content of symptoms may differ as a function of cultural or religious prohibitions (Matsunaga et al., 2007; Millet et al., 2000).

Source: Unless otherwise noted, information in the table is from American Psychiatric Association, 2000.

Figure 7.14

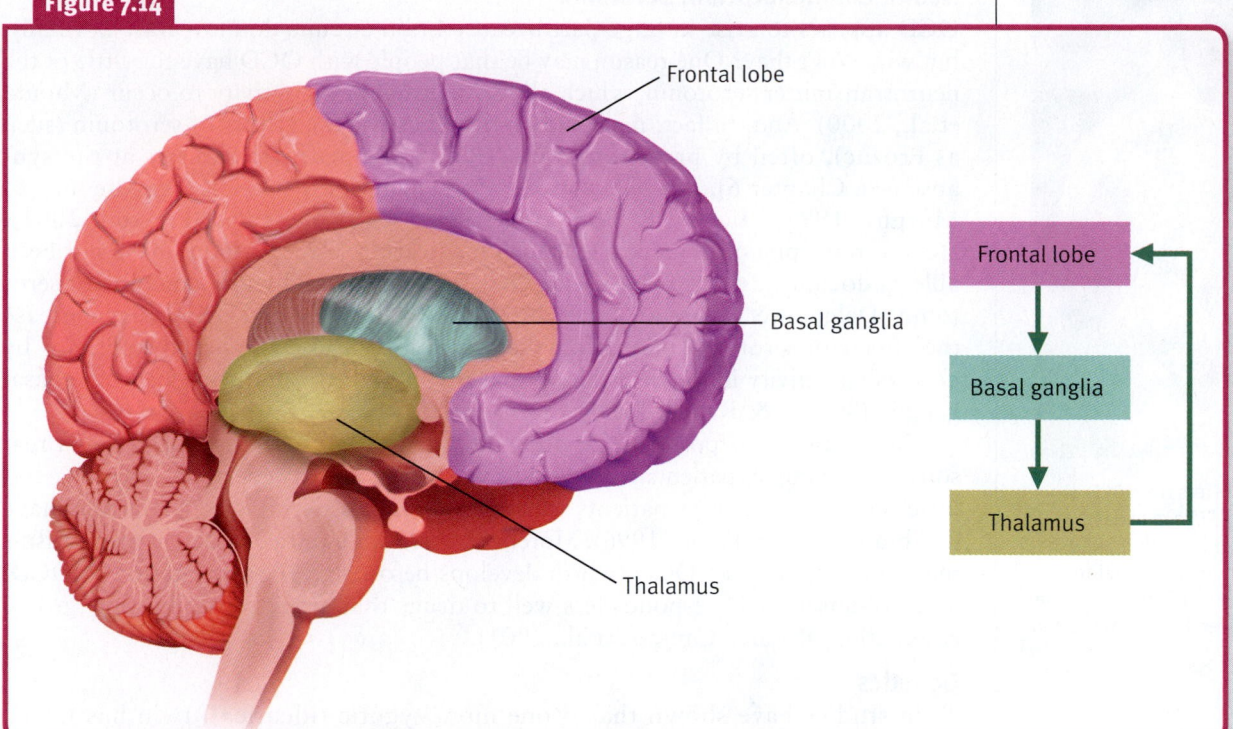

Frontal lobe

Basal ganglia

Thalamus

Frontal lobe

Basal ganglia

Thalamus

7.14 ▶ The Neural Loop That May Underlie Obsessive Thoughts The basal ganglia, the thalamus, and the frontal lobes are part of a neural loop of repeating brain activity associated with OCD.

in particular (Insel, 1992; Pigott, Myers, & Williams, 1996; Saxena & Rauch, 2000). In fact, as predicted by the theory, both the frontal cortex (especially the orbital frontal cortex—the lower parts of the cortex, behind the eyes) and the basal ganglia function abnormally in OCD patients (Baxter, 1992; Berthier et al., 2001; Saxena et al., 1998). This abnormal functioning could well prevent the frontal lobe from cutting off the loop of repetitive neural activity, as it appears to do in normal people.

Researchers have also suggested that OCD is associated with larger amounts of gray matter in the frontal lobes and smaller amounts in the posterior portions of the brain (Kim et al., 2001). Such structural abnormalities are consistent with the unusually large amount of activity in patients' frontal regions when they see a stimulus that provokes the OCD-related thoughts and behaviors (Adler et al., 2000). Furthermore, these patients have impaired visual-spatial abilities, which rely on similar areas of the brain (Micallef & Blin, 2001).

However, not all studies have found such brain abnormalities (Baxter, Schwarz, & Guze, 1991), which may suggest that there is more than one way OCD can arise (Hollander, Liebowitz, & Rosen, 1991). In fact, researchers have found that many (but not all) patients with OCD had an abnormal birth, epilepsy, head trauma, or infection of the brain or the membranes that cover it. For example, as we saw in Chapter 5, when children rapidly develop symptoms of OCD, the cause may be a particular type of streptococcal infection that leads to a disorder in the immune system, which is called *pediatric autoimmune neuropsychiatric disorder associated with streptococcal infection*. This disorder affects the basal ganglia (Swedo et al., 1998). Symptoms of OCD disappear when the children take the appropriate antibiotics.

Soccer star David Beckham suffers from OCD. His symptoms focus on ordering: "I have to have everything in a straight line or everything has to be in pairs.... I'll go into a hotel room. Before I can relax I have to move all the leaflets and all the books and put them in a drawer. Everything has to be perfect." (Dolan, 2006).

Neural Communication: Serotonin

OCD appears to arise in large part because brain circuits don't operate normally, but why don't they? One reason may be that people with OCD have too little of the neurotransmitter serotonin, which allows unusual brain activity to occur (Mundo et al., 2000). And, in fact, medications that increase the effects of serotonin (such as Prozac), often by preventing reuptake of this neurotransmitter at the synapse (see Chapter 6), can help to treat OCD symptoms (Greenberg, Altemus, & Murphy, 1997; Micallef & Blin, 2001; Thomsen, Ebbesen, & Persson, 2001). However, in spite of the efficacy of such medication, several studies have not been able to document that patients with OCD have abnormally low amounts of serotonin (Delgado & Moreno, 1998; Insel & Winslow, 1990). Drugs that increase the effects of serotonin may affect the symptoms of OCD indirectly, perhaps by decreasing activity in the neural loop that involves the frontal cortex and the basal ganglia (Saxena & Rauch, 2000).

In addition, it is possible that different varieties of OCD arise for different reasons. For example, patients who need to wash their hands repeatedly may have too little serotonin, whereas patients who have intense ordering obsessions may have had brain damage (Pigott, 1996). Moreover, there is a hint that different mechanisms may cause early-onset OCD (which develops before age 10) and later-onset OCD, as early-onset OCD responds less well to drugs that affect serotonin (Erzegovesi et al., 2001; Rosario-Campos et al., 2001).

Genetics

Twin studies have shown that if one monozygotic (identical) twin has OCD, the other is very likely (65%) to have it. As should be expected if this high rate reflects common genes, the rate is lower (only 15%) for dizygotic twins (Pauls, Raymond, & Robertson, 1991). Moreover, as you would expect from the results of the twin studies, OCD is more common among relatives of OCD patients (10.3% of whom also have OCD) than among relatives of control participants (of whom only 2% also have OCD) (Pauls et al., 1995).

However, although family studies have documented a genetic contribution to OCD, the link is neither simple nor straightforward: Members of the family of a person with OCD are more likely than other people to have an anxiety disorder, but that disorder need not be OCD specifically (Black et al., 1992; Smoller, Finn, & White, 2000; Torgersen, 1983).

Author Emily Colas, who has OCD, recounts her mother's struggle with symptoms of the disorder:

> I used to get frustrated at bedtime. My mother would sit on the edge of my bed, tuck me in, and kiss me good-night. Then she'd walk to the door and with her middle finger flick the light switch off. The hall light was on so I could see mom standing there a few minutes later still stroking the switch that was clearly by that time down. I'd yell "It's off!" to get her out of my room. She'd look back at me and then turn her head away, silently shut my door, and leave. Fifteen years later she explained to me that she knew the light was in fact off, but felt compelled to keep flicking the switch, in multiples of four, until it felt "right."
>
> (Colas, 1998, p. 31)

When many people first learn about OCD, they recognize tendencies they've noticed in themselves. If you've had this reaction while reading this section, you shouldn't worry: OCD may reflect extreme functioning of brain systems that function the same way in each of us to produce milder forms of such thinking. According to this view, OCD is not a qualitatively distinct disorder, with brain systems producing abnormal types of outputs (the way hallucinations may arise in some psychotic disorders), but rather is just one end of a continuum—with "normal" anchoring the other end. In fact, researchers found that the relatives of OCD patients were more likely than controls to have both OCD and OCD-like symptoms that were *subclinical* (not severe enough to qualify as the disorder) (Pauls et al., 1995). With subclinical symptoms, the brain produces the same kinds of thoughts, impulses, and images as found in OCD, but not frequently or strongly enough to disrupt daily life.

Psychological Factors

Psychological factors that help to explain OCD focus primarily on the way that operant conditioning affects compulsions and on the process by which normal obsessional thoughts become pathological.

Behavioral Explanations: Operant Conditioning and Compulsions

Compulsive behavior can provide short-term relief from anxiety that is produced by an obsession. Operant conditioning occurs when the behavior is negatively reinforced: Because it (temporarily) relieves the anxiety, it is more likely to recur when the thoughts arise again. All of Howard Hughes's various eccentric behaviors—his washing, his precautions against germs, his exerting control over the minute specifics of his memos (in "Notes on Notes"), his hoarding of newspapers and magazines—temporarily relieved his anxiety.

Cognitive Explanations: Obsessional Thinking

If you've ever had a crush on someone or been in love, you may have spent a lot of time thinking about the person—it may have even felt like an obsession. Such obsessions arise surprisingly frequently (Weissman et al., 1994), but they don't usually develop into a disorder. One theory about how a normal obsession becomes part of OCD is that the person decides that his or her thoughts refer to something unacceptable, such as killing someone or, as was the case with Howard Hughes, catching someone else's illness (Salkovskis, 1985). These obsessive thoughts, which the individual believes imply some kind of danger, lead to very uncomfortable feelings. Mental or behavioral rituals arise in order to reduce these feelings. A related theory is that for some people who develop OCD, a disturbing thought is the moral equivalent of actually performing the act, which leads to greater distress in response to the initial obsession (Rachman, 1997; Shafran, Thordarson, & Rachman, 1996). Both theories contrast a normal response to "unacceptable" thoughts (an awareness that such thoughts don't need to be controlled and an ability to let them fade from consciousness) with the belief of OCD patients that such thoughts must be controlled—and trying to do so amplifies the thoughts (Tolin, Worhunsky, & Maltby, 2006).

Consistent with this theoretical approach, researchers have found that some mental processes function differently in people with OCD than in people without the disorder. In particular, such patients are more likely to pay attention to and remember threat-relevant stimuli, and their processing of complex visual stimuli (as, for example, is necessary to decide whether an object has been touched by a dirty or clean tissue among people with contamination fears) is impaired (Constans et al., 1995; Muller & Roberts, 2005; Radomsky, Rachman, & Hammond, 2001). Such processing may make threatening stimuli easier to remember and harder to ignore, which keeps them in the patients' awareness longer (Muller & Roberts, 2005). Studies of memory also find that those with the checking type of OCD and those in a control group had equally accurate memories, but the OCD patients had less *confidence* in the accuracy of their recognition memories (MacDonald et al., 1997; McNally & Kohlbeck 1993; Muller & Roberts, 2005). Thus, because they are more likely to doubt their memories, they are more likely to want to go back and check.

Social Factors

Two types of social factors can contribute to OCD. One is stress, which can influence the onset and course of the disorder; the other is culture, which can influence the particular content of symptoms.

Stress

The onset of OCD often follows a stressor, and the severity of the symptoms is often proportional to the severity of the stressor (Turner & Beidel, 1988), which might range from taking a vacation at one end to the death of a family member at the other. However, such findings are not always easy to interpret. For example, one study found that people with more severe OCD tend to have more kinds of family stress and are more likely to be rejected by their families (Calvocoressi et al., 1995). Note, however, that the direction of causation is not clear: Although stress in the family may cause the greater severity of symptoms, it is also possible that the more severe symptoms led the families to reject the patients. In fact, a more recent study found that the more severe the patient's OCD symptoms, the less hopeful and more depressed were family members (Geffken et al., 2006). People with OCD often impose various restrictions on the behavior of friends and family members to ensure that it conforms to the patient's "rules," as Hughes did. For instance, someone who compulsively checks that doors and windows are locked may demand that family members similarly—and repeatedly—check the locks throughout the day.

Stress greatly affected the course of Hughes's symptoms. For much of his 20s, 30s, and early 40s, he was able to function relatively well, given the freedom his wealth and position provided. Although he was often preoccupied with work—staying up for 40 hours at a time to work on a film or on a design for a plane—he was able to keep his obsessions and compulsions at bay well enough to do his work. However, there were occasional periods of time when the external demands of his life became intense—deadlines, fights with associates, or legal problems—and his symptoms worsened. During one particularly stressful period in his late 30s, "Hughes began repeating himself at work and in casual conversations. In a series of memoranda on the importance of letter writing, he dictated, over and over again, 'a good letter should be immediately understandable . . . a good letter should be immediately understandable . . . a good letter should be immediately understandable . . .'" (Bartlett & Steele, 1979, p. 132).

By the time Hughes was in his 50s, however, the stressors increased and his functioning diminished. There were periods when he was so preoccupied with his germ phobia that he couldn't pay attention to anything else. At other times, his symptoms ebbed enough that he was able to focus somewhat on running his empire. But he couldn't reliably attend to the day-to-day demands of his businesses.

Culture

Different countries have about the same prevalence rates of OCD, although culture (Weissman et al., 1994) and religion can help determine the particular content of some obsessions or compulsions. For instance, religious obsessions and praying compulsions are more common among Turkish men than French men (Millet et al., 2000) and more common among Brazilians than Americans or Europeans (Fontenelle et al., 2004). And a devoutly religious patient's symptoms can relate to the specific tenets and practices of his or her religion (Shooka et al., 1998): Someone who is Catholic may have obsessional worries about having impure thoughts or feel a compulsion to go to confession multiple times each day. In contrast, devout Jews or Muslims may have symptoms that focus on extreme adherence to religious dietary laws.

FEEDBACK LOOPS IN ACTION:
Understanding Obsessive-Compulsive Disorder

One neurological underpinning of OCD appears to be a tendency toward increased activity in the neural loop that connects the frontal lobes and the basal ganglia (neurological factor). A person with such a neurological vulnerability might learn early in life to regard certain thoughts as dangerous because they can lead to obsessions. When these thoughts appear later in life at a time of stress, someone who is vulnerable may become distressed and anxious about the thoughts and try to suppress them. But a conscious attempt to suppress unwanted thoughts often has the opposite effect: The unwanted thoughts become more likely to persist (Salkovkis & Campbell, 1994; Wegner et al., 1987). Thus, the intrusive thoughts cause additional distress, and so the person tries harder to suppress them, creating a reinforcing cycle (psychological factor).

The content of a person's unwanted thoughts determine the extent to which those thoughts are unacceptable. When a person wants to suppress the unwanted thoughts, he or she develops rituals and avoidance behaviors to increase a sense of control and decrease anxiety; these behaviors temporarily lessen anxiety and are thus reinforced. Yet the thoughts cannot be fully controlled and become obsessive; the obsessions and compulsions impair functioning and can affect relationships as well. The person with OCD may expect family members and friends to conform to compulsive guidelines; these people and others can become frustrated and dismayed at the patient's rituals and obsessions (social factors). Figure 7.15 illustrates these factors and feedback loops.

Figure 7.15

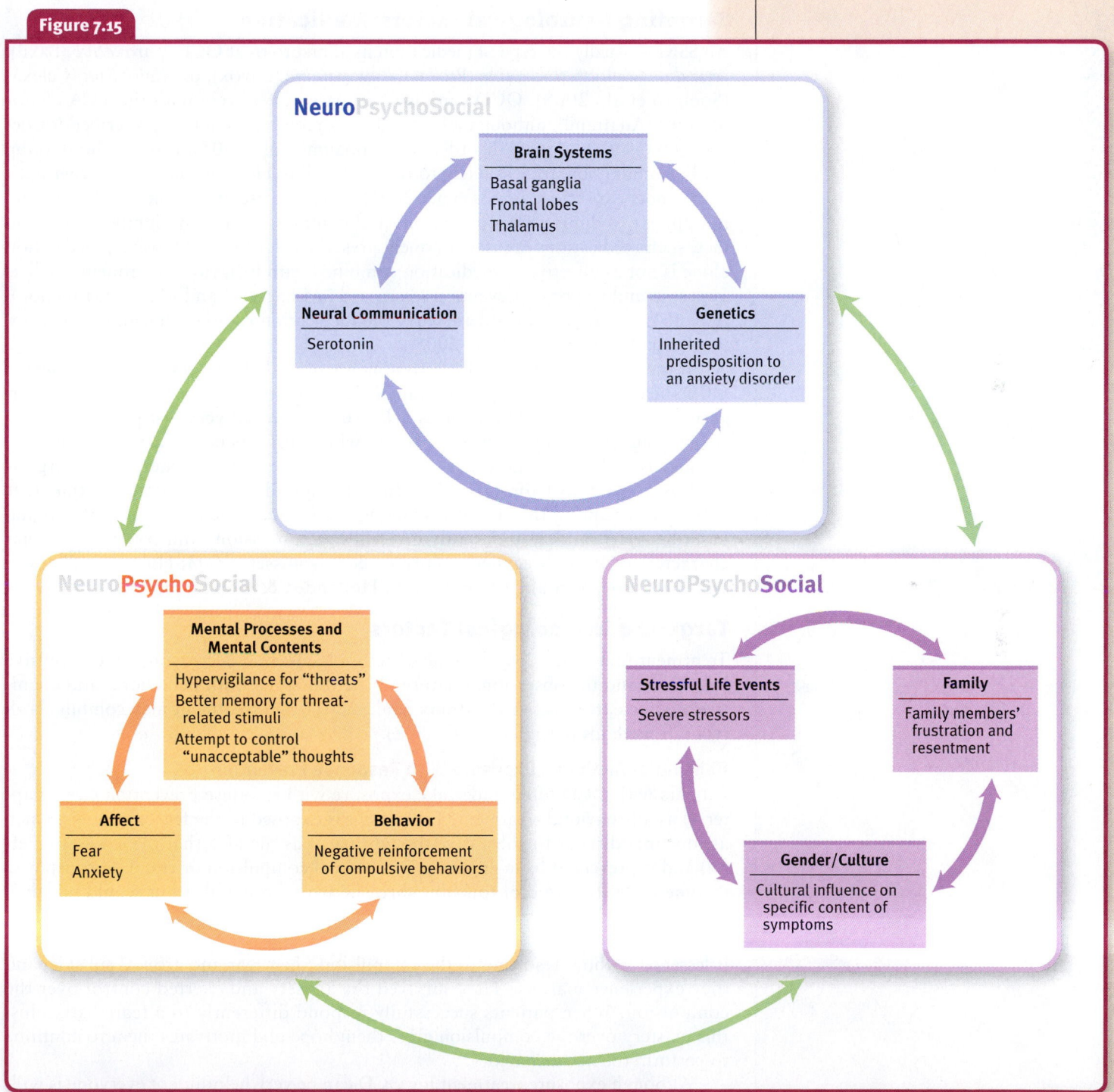

7.15 ▸ Feedback Loops in Action: Obsessive-Compulsive Disorder

Treating Obsessive Compulsive Disorder

The primary targets of treatment for OCD are usually either neurological or psychological factors. In Hughes's case, there was no one in his life with the clout and concern who could tell the powerful man that he needed help. As biographers Barlett and Steele (1979) note, his living situation was like a mental institution, but it was run by the patient, and no one was telling him that he had problems. His aides carried out whatever compulsive demands Hughes made, never challenging him about the irrationality of his orders.

Targeting Neurological Factors: Medication

An SSRI is usually the type of medication used first to treat OCD: *paroxetine* (Paxil), *sertraline* (Zoloft), *fluoxetine* (Prozac), *fluvoxamine* (Luvox), or *citalopram* (Celexa) (Soomro et al., 2008). OCD can also be treated effectively with the TCA *clomipramine* (Anafranil), although a higher dose is required than that prescribed for depression or other anxiety disorders (Rosenbaum et al., 2005). People who develop OCD in childhood are less likely to respond well to clomiprimine or to other antidepressants (Rosario-Campos et al., 2001). Hughes's use of codeine and Valium did not appear to diminish his obsessions and compulsions in any significant way; in fact, such medications are not routinely prescribed for OCD. However, medication alone is not as effective as medication combined with behavioral treatment, such as exposure and response prevention (discussed in Chapter 4 and in the next section). As with other anxiety disorders, when the medication is discontinued, OCD symptoms usually return (Foa et al., 2005).

If medication and behavioral treatments don't help a person who has *severe* OCD, he or she may receive transcranial magnetic stimulation (TMS) or neurosurgery (see Chapter 4). TMS involves delivering a series of very fast pulses of a very strong magnetic field to part of the brain, which disrupts neural activity. However, the jury is still out on the value of this treatment for this disorder. Neurosurgery, used as a last resort for cases that do not respond to less drastic treatment, is aimed at disrupting the circuit (involving the frontal lobe and the basal ganglia, described earlier) that apparently underlies the obsessions and compulsions that characterize OCD (Greenberg, Murphy, & Rasmussen, 2003; Husted & Shapira, 2004; Mantovani et al., 2006; Pallanti, Hollander, & Goodman, 2004).

Targeting Psychological Factors

Treatment that targets psychological factors focuses on decreasing the compulsive behaviors and the obsessional nature of the thoughts. Both behavioral and cognitive methods are effective (Cottraux et al., 2001), and treatment may combine both types of methods (Franklin et al., 2002).

Behavioral Methods: Exposure With Response Prevention

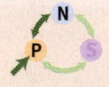

Patients with OCD often undertake exposure with response prevention (see Chapter 4) as a behavioral treatment. The patient is exposed to the feared stimulus (such as touching dirt) or the obsessive thought (such as the idea that the stove was left on) and is prevented from engaging in the usual compulsion or ritual. For instance, if someone were afraid of touching dirt, she would touch dirt but would not then wash her hands. Through exposure with response prevention, patients learn that nothing bad happens if they don't perform their compulsive behavior; the anxiety is lessened without resorting to the compulsion, their fear and arousal subside, and they experience mastery. They survived the anxiety and exerted control over the compulsion. When patients successfully respond differently to a feared stimulus, this mastery over the compulsion gives them hope and motivates them to continue to perform the new behaviors.

Although exposure treatment for OCD can be very helpful, not everyone is willing to use this form of treatment. Confronting a feared stimulus is, well, frightening! Medication may help such people when beginning exposure treatment—it can help them tolerate the anxiety that arises. Then, as the exposure treatment progresses, the medication is tapered off and the behavioral method is continued. This form of combined treatment may help minimize relapse when medication is stopped, compared to medication alone (Ellison & McCarter, 2002; Foa et al., 2005).

Cognitive Methods: Cognitive Restructuring

The goal of cognitive methods is to reduce the irrationality and frequency of the patient's intrusive thoughts and obsessions (Clark, 2005). Cognitive restructuring focuses on assessing the accuracy of these thoughts, making predictions based on them ("If I don't go back to check the locks, I will be robbed"), and testing whether these predictions come to pass.

Although CBT for OCD hadn't been sufficiently developed during Hughes's lifetime, consider how it might have been used: There were periods when Hughes daily and "painstakingly used Kleenex to wipe 'dust and germs' from his chair, ottoman, side table, and telephone. Sometimes he spent hours methodically cleaning the telephone, going over the earpiece, mouthpiece, base, and cord with Kleenex, repeating the cleaning procedure again and again, tossing the used tissues into a pile behind his chair" (Bartlett Steele, 1979, p. 233). At the same time, though, he didn't have his sheets changed for months at a time; to make the sheets last longer, he laid paper towels over them and slept on those. Moreover, he bathed only a few times a year. Clearly, such behavior was at odds with rational attempts to protect against germs. CBT would have focused on his overestimation of the probability of contracting an illness and the irrationality of his precautions.

Targeting Social Factors: Family Therapy

Although psychological or neurological factors are the primary targets of treatment for OCD, in some cases, social factors may also be addressed, for example, through family therapy or consultation with family members. This aspect of treatment educates family members about the patient's treatment and its goals and helps the family function in a more normal way. Family members and friends may have spent years conforming their behavior to the patient's illness (e.g., using clean tissues when handing an object to the patient), and they may be afraid to change their own behavior as the patient gets better, for fear of causing a relapse.

FEEDBACK LOOPS IN TREATMENT: **Obsessive-Compulsive Disorder**

As we've seen, medication can be effective in treating the symptoms of OCD (at least as long as the patient continues to take it). Medication works by changing neurochemistry, which in turn affects thoughts, feelings, and behaviors. We've also seen that CBT is effective. How does CBT have its effects? Could it be that therapy changes brain functioning in the same way that medication does? Until recently, such questions could not be answered. But neuroimaging has made it possible to begin to understand the positive effects of both medication and CBT on people with OCD. The neuropsychosocial approach leads us to examine the types of factors and their feedback loops (see Figure 7.16).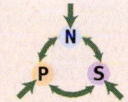

For example, in one study, researchers used PET scans to assess brain functioning in two groups of OCD patients. One group was given behavior therapy and the other group was given the SSRI fluoxetine (Prozac), which can reduce OCD symptoms. Both behavior therapy and Prozac decreased activity in a part of the basal ganglia that is involved in automatic behaviors (the right caudate). Prozac also affected activity in two parts of the brain involved in attention: the thalamus and the anterior cingulate (Baxter et al., 1992). Later research replicated the effects of behavior therapy on the brain (Schwartz et al., 1996).

In short, behavioral therapy or CBT changes the brain (neurological factor). As the patient improves, personal relationships change (social factor): The time and energy that had gone into the compulsions can be diverted to relationships. Moreover, the patient experiences mastery over the symptoms and develops hope and a new view of himself or herself (psychological factors). In turn, this makes the patient more willing to continue therapy, which further changes the brain, and so on, in a happy cycle of mutual feedback loops among neurological, psychological, and social factors.

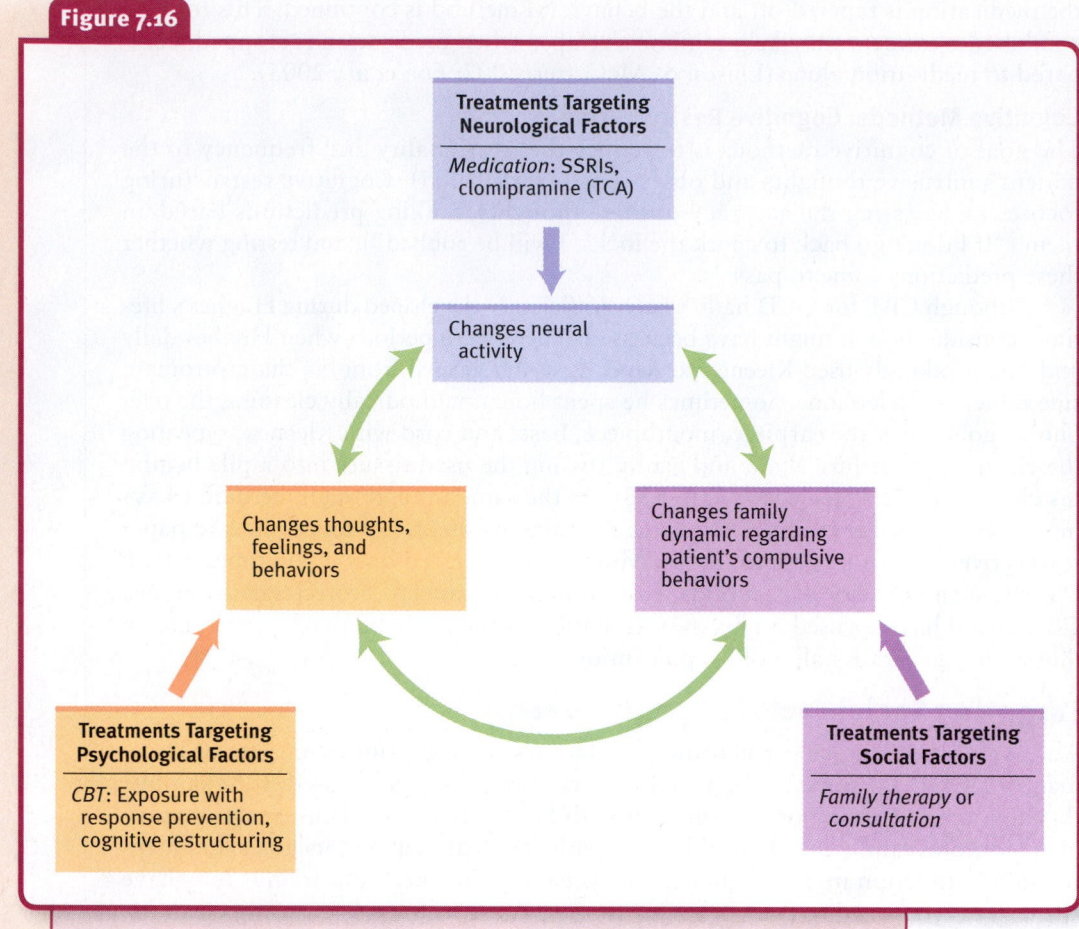

Figure 7.16

Treatments Targeting Neurological Factors

Medication: SSRIs, clomipramine (TCA)

Changes neural activity

Changes thoughts, feelings, and behaviors

Changes family dynamic regarding patient's compulsive behaviors

Treatments Targeting Psychological Factors

CBT: Exposure with response prevention, cognitive restructuring

Treatments Targeting Social Factors

Family therapy or *consultation*

7.16 ▸ Feedback Loops in Treating Obsessive-Compulsive Disorder

Key Concepts and Facts About Obsessive-Compulsive Disorder

- OCD is marked by persistent and intrusive preoccupations and—in most cases—repetitive, compelled behaviors that usually correspond to the obsessions. Although people with OCD recognize that their obsessions are irrational, they cannot turn off the preoccupying thoughts; they feel driven to engage in the compulsive behaviors, which provide only brief respite from the obsessions.

- Common obsessions include anxiety about contamination, order, losing control, doubts, and possible future need. Common compulsions include washing, ordering, counting, checking, and hoarding or collecting.

- Neurological factors associated with OCD include disruptions in the normal activity of the frontal lobes, the thalamus, and the basal ganglia; the frontal lobes do not turn off activity of the neural loop among these three brain areas, which may lead to the persistent obsessions. Lower than normal levels of serotonin also appear to play a role, although this may be more directly related to some types of OCD than others. Genes appear to make some people more vulnerable to anxiety disorders in general—not necessarily to OCD specifically.

- Psychological factors that may underlie OCD include negative reinforcement of the compulsive behavior, which temporarily relieves the anxiety that arises from the obsession. In addition, normal preoccupying thoughts may become obsessions when the thoughts are deemed "unacceptable" and hence require controlling. In turn, the thoughts lead to anxiety, which is then relieved by a mental or behavioral ritual. Like people with other anxiety disorders, people with OCD have cognitive biases related to their feared stimuli, in this case, regarding the theme of their obsessions.

- Social factors related to OCD include socially induced stress, which can influence the onset and course of the disorder, and culture, which can influence the particular content of obsessions and compulsions.

- Medication (such as an SSRI or clomipramine) is the treatment for OCD that directly targets neurological factors. The primary treatment for OCD—exposure with response prevention—directly targets psychological factors. Cognitive restructuring to reduce the irrationality and frequency of the patient's intrusive thoughts and obsessions may also be employed. Family education or therapy, targeting social factors, may be used as an additional treatment to help the patient's family function in a more normal way.

Making a Diagnosis

- Reread Case 7.6 about the woman who took a long time to get out of bed and get dressed in the morning, and determine whether or not her symptoms meet the criteria for obsessive-compulsive disorder. Specifically, list which criteria apply and which do not. If you would like more information to determine her diagnosis, what information—specifically—would you want, and in what ways would the information influence your decision?

Posttraumatic Stress Disorder

Within a 15-year span, Howard Hughes suffered more than his share of brushes with death—of his own and that of other people. He ran over and killed a pedestrian. He was the pilot in three plane accidents: In the first one, his cheekbone was crushed; in the second, two of his copilots died; in the third, he sustained such extensive injuries to his chest that his heart was pushed to the other side of his chest cavity and he wasn't expected to live through the night. Hughes did survive, but he clearly had endured a highly traumatic event.

Some people who experience a traumatic event go on to develop a *stress disorder*, which according to DSM-IV-TR (American Psychiatric Association, 2000) is marked by three types of persistent symptoms:

- *Reexperiencing the traumatic event*. Reexperiencing may involve flashbacks that can include illusions, hallucinations, or a sense of reliving the experience, as well as intrusive and distressing memories, dreams, or nightmares of the event.

- *Avoidance*. The individual avoids anything related to the trauma. The person may also experience a general emotional *numbness*.

- *Increased arousal and anxiety*. Arousal and anxiety symptoms include difficulty sleeping, hypervigilance, and a tendency to be easily startled (referred to as a heightened startle response).

DSM-IV-TR includes two types of stress disorders: *acute stress disorder*, which is the diagnosis when the above symptoms emerge within 4 weeks of a traumatic event and last less than 1 month and the person also experiences dissociation (to be discussed later); in contrast, *posttraumatic stress disorder (PTSD)* is the diagnosis if the symptoms last more than 1 month.

In this section we first explore the difference between everyday stress and the traumatic stress associated with stress disorders and then discuss posttraumatic stress disorder in detail. After that, we turn to the factors that give rise to stress disorders. At the end of the section, we explore treatments for posttraumatic stress disorder.

Howard Hughes survived several plane crashes, including the one shown above, and he ran over and killed a pedestrian (Fowler, 1986); any of these events would have been traumatic for most people. Some people who experience a traumatic event develop a stress disorder: acute stress disorder or posttraumatic stress disorder.

Stress Versus Traumatic Stress

Most people would agree that Hughes experienced a traumatic event when his airplane crashed and he was severely injured. But where is the line that separates a stressful event from a traumatic one? According to DSM-IV-TR, stress turns into traumatic stress when "the person has been exposed to a traumatic event in which both of the following were present:

1. the person experienced, witnessed, or was confronted with an event or events that involved actual or threatened death or serious injury, or a threat to the physical integrity of self or others [and]

This is the wreckage of one of the trains blasted by a bomb in the Attocha railway station in Madrid in March 2004; more than 130 people were killed. During times of political unrest, violence, or terrorism, rates of stress disorders are likely to increase.

2. the person's response involved intense fear, helplessness, or horror. Note: In children, this may be expressed instead by disorganized or agitated behavior." (American Psychiatric Association, 2000)

This definition has two components—the traumatic event itself, and the person's response to it. Let's examine both components.

Traumatic events are beyond the normal stressful events we all regularly encounter. Examples of traumatic events range from large-scale catastrophes with multiple victims (such as disasters and wars) to unintended acts or situations involving fewer people (such as motor vehicle accidents and life-threatening illnesses) to events that involve intentional and personal violence, such as rape and assault (Briere, 2004). Table 7.16 lists examples of various types of traumatic events. Traumatic events are relatively common: up to 30% of people will experience some type of disaster in their lifetime, and 25% have experienced a serious car accident (Briere & Elliott, 2000). Note that according to the DSM-IV-TR definition, emotional abuse is not a traumatic event, because it does not involve actual or threatened physical injury or death.

Several factors can affect whether a stress disorder will develop following a traumatic event:

- *The kind of trauma.* Trauma involving violence—particularly intended personal violence—is more likely to lead to a stress disorder than are natural disasters (Breslau et al., 1998; Briere & Elliott, 2000; Copeland et al., 2007; Dikel, Engdahl, & Eberly, 2005; Resnick et al., 1993).

- *The severity of the traumatic event, its duration, and its proximity* (American Psychiatric Association, 2000). Depending on the specifics of the traumatic event, those physically closer to it—nearer to the primary area struck by a tornado, for example—are more likely to develop a stress disorder (Blanchard et al., 2004; Middleton, Willmer, & Simmons, 2002), as are those who have experienced multiple traumatic events (Copeland et al., 2007). For instance, Vietnam veterans were more likely to develop PTSD if they had been wounded or if they spent more time in combat (Gallers et al., 1988; King et al., 1999). The same is true of veterans returning from Iraq and Afghanistan: Soldiers who were involved in combat were up to three times more likely to develop PTSD than soldiers who were not exposed to combat (Levin, 2007; Smith et al., 2008).

The types of traumatic events identified in Table 7.16 can lead to stress disorders, in part, because they challenge the basic assumptions that most people have about the world. These assumptions can be categorized into four types (Everly & Lating, 2004):

1. *The belief in a fair and just world*, where people get what they deserve and deserve what they get. When an individual who believes himself or herself to be a good person experiences a traumatic event, the person's basic beliefs about justice and fairness are called into question.

2. *The belief that it is possible to trust others and be safe.* Particularly when traumatic events are perpetrated by a known and previously liked or loved person, the victim often feels doubly betrayed or abandoned, thinking, "If I loved this person and he was able to hurt me this much, how can I trust my judgment about people?" (Janoff-Bulman, 1995).

3. *The belief that it is possible to be effective in the world.* When a traumatic event occurs, people often feel that they should have done something to prevent the event or at least somehow lessen its intensity ("If only I had . . ."). Thus, traumatic events challenge people's beliefs in their ability to protect themselves and others. People may develop a sense of learned helplessness (see Chapter 6)

Table 7.16 ▸ Types of Traumatic Events

Large-scale traumatic events, with multiple victims

- Disasters
  - ○ Natural disasters, such as earthquakes or hurricanes
  - ○ Human-caused disasters, such as chemical spills or nuclear accidents
- War and large-scale conflict, including police action against crowds
- Direct experience of injuring or killing others, or witnessing such events
- Mass violence against noncombatants, such as guerrilla-perpetrated atrocities and terrorist acts
- Large-scale transportation accidents, such as train derailments or airplane crashes

Unintended acts involving fewer people

- Motor vehicle accidents
- Exposure of emergency workers, such as firefighters and rescue workers, to a traumatic event
- Life-threatening illnesses, such as severe heart attack and cancer

Intended personal violence

- Rape and sexual assault (the perpetrator may or may not be known to victim)
- Physical assault (the perpetrator may or may not be known to victim)
- Violence, including sexual assault, perpetrated by a spouse or intimate partner
- Torture
- Physical stalking or cyber-stalking that causes the victim to feel threatened, intimidated, afraid, or terrorized
- Child abuse

Source: American Psychiatric Association, 2000; Briere, 2004.

and become depressed (Abramson, Metalsky, & Alloy, 1989; Bandura, 1997). In addition, when a person experiences the same traumatic event as others but suffers less physical harm or loss of property, the victim may develop *survivor guilt*, feeling guilty about faring better than others did.

4. *The sense that life has purpose and meaning.* Many people believe that life— their own lives or human existence in general—has a purpose. This belief may be spiritual or religious. Traumatic events can challenge these beliefs, leading victims to feel that their existence is pointless and meaningless (Everly & Lating, 2004).

Although certain types of traumatic events are more likely than others to lead to stress disorders, individuals differ in how they perceive the same traumatic event and how they respond to it. These differences will be based, in part, on previous experience with related events, appraisal of the stressors, and coping style. Thus, we need to consider the second component of the DSM-IV-TR definition of a traumatic event: a response of intense fear, helplessness, or horror. Unfortunately, DSM-IV-TR does not offer guidance on the degree of fear, helplessness or horror that qualifies, and given the horrific nature of a traumatic event, most people would respond with at least one of these emotions (Briere, 2004).

The stress disorders are two of only a small number of disorders in DSM-IV-TR for which the criteria *explicitly include a causal factor*—in this case, a traumatic event. However, experiencing a traumatic event is a necessary but not sufficient factor leading to a stress disorder (Everly & Lating, 2004). Let's examine posttraumatic stress disorder, and contrast it with acute stress disorder; in doing so we'll address other factors that can contribute to stress disorders.

What Is Posttraumatic Stress Disorder?

Posttraumatic stress disorder (PTSD) is diagnosed when people who have experienced a trauma persistently reexperience the traumatic event, avoid stimuli related to the event, and have symptoms of anxiety and hyperarousal; these symptoms must persist for at least a month (American Psychiatric Association, 2000). These three symptoms form the *posttrauma* criteria for PTSD, as shown in Table 7.17 (Criteria B, C, and D), and they may not emerge until months or years after the traumatic event. Table 7.18 presents other information about PTSD. Case 7.7 describes the experiences of a man with PTSD.

CASE **7.7** ▸ FROM THE OUTSIDE: Posttraumatic Stress Disorder

A. C. was a 42 year old single man, a recent immigrant who, one year before his appearance at the clinic, had walked into his place of work while an armed robbery was taking place. Two men armed with guns hit him over the head, threatened to kill him, tied him up and locked him in a closet with four other employees. He was released from the closet 4 hours later when another employee came in to work. The police were notified and A. C. was taken to the hospital where his head wound was sutured and he was released. For two weeks after the robbery A. C. continued to function as he had before the robbery with no increase in anxiety.

One day while waiting to meet someone on the street he was struck by the thought that he might meet his assailants again. He began to shiver, felt his heart race, felt dizzy, started to sweat and felt that he might pass out. He was brought to an emergency room, examined and released with a referral to victims' services. His anxiety increased so much that he was unable to return to work because it reminded him of the robbery. He started to have sleep difficulties, waking in the middle of the night to check the front door lock at home. He quit his job and dropped out of school due to his anxiety. He would have flashbacks of the guns that were used in the robbery and started to avoid people on the street who reminded him of the robbers. He began to feel guilty that he had entered the office while the robbery was in progress feeling that he somehow should have known what was occurring. His avoidance extended to the subway, exercising and socializing with friends.

(New York Psychiatric Institute, 2006)

A. C.'s symptoms didn't arise until 2 weeks after the robbery. If his symptoms had lasted for less than 4 weeks or if he had sought help from a mental health clinician within a month of the event, A. C. might have been diagnosed with acute stress disorder. Like PTSD, **acute stress disorder** also involves reexperiencing the traumatic event, avoiding stimuli related to the event, and exhibiting symptoms of anxiety and hyperarousal. However, unlike PTSD, the DSM-IV-TR criteria for acute stress disorder also involves symptoms of dissociation (American Psychiatric Association, 2000), namely:

- feeling emotionally detached or numb;
- feeling less aware of the environment, which some people describe as "being in a daze";
- *derealization*, in which the perception or experience of the external world seems strange or unreal, as though seen through a pane of glass;
- *depersonalization*, in which the perception or experience of oneself (either one's body or one's mental processes) is altered to the point of feeling like an observer, seeing oneself from the outside; and
- *dissociative amnesia*, or loss of memory of important elements of the traumatic event.

Moreover, the symptoms must occur within 4 weeks of the trauma (as A. C.'s did), last no more than 4 weeks, and must cause distress or impair functioning. Approximately 80% of those with acute stress disorder have symptoms that persist for more than a month, at which point the diagnosis then changes to PTSD (Harvey & Bryant, 2002). Unlike A. C., though, most people who experience trauma do not develop PTSD (Breslau et al., 1998; Resnick et al., 1993; Shalev et al., 1998).

Posttraumatic stress disorder (PTSD)
The anxiety disorder that arises a month or more after a traumatic event and that involves a persistent reexperiencing of the event, avoiding stimuli related to the event, and symptoms of anxiety and hyperarousal that persist for at least a month.

Acute stress disorder
The anxiety disorder that arises within a month after a traumatic event and that involves reexperiencing of the event, avoiding stimuli related to the event, and symptoms of anxiety, hyperarousal, and dissociation that last for less than a month.

Table 7.17 ▶ DSM-IV-TR Diagnostic Criteria for Posttraumatic Stress Disorder

A. The person has been exposed to a traumatic event in which both of the following were present:

(1) the person experienced, witnessed, or was confronted with an event or events that involved actual or threatened death or serious injury, or a threat to the physical integrity of self or others

(2) the person's response involved intense fear, helplessness, or horror.

Note: In children, this may be expressed instead by disorganized or agitated behavior

B. The traumatic event is persistently reexperienced in one (or more) of the following ways:

(1) recurrent and intrusive distressing recollections of the event, including images, thoughts, or perceptions.

Note: In young children, repetitive play may occur in which themes or aspects of the trauma are expressed.

(2) recurrent distressing dreams of the event.

Note: In children, there may be frightening dreams without recognizable content.

(3) acting or feeling as if the traumatic event were recurring (includes a sense of reliving the experience, illusions, hallucinations, and dissociative flashback episodes, including those that occur on awakening or when intoxicated).

Note: In young children, trauma-specific reenactment may occur.

(4) intense psychological distress at exposure to internal or external cues that symbolize or resemble an aspect of the traumatic event

(5) physiological reactivity on exposure to internal or external cues that symbolize or resemble an aspect of the traumatic event

C. Persistent avoidance of stimuli associated with the trauma and numbing of general responsiveness (not present before the trauma), as indicated by three (or more) of the following:

(1) efforts to avoid thoughts, feelings, or conversations associated with the trauma

(2) efforts to avoid activities, places, or people that arouse recollections of the trauma

(3) inability to recall an important aspect of the trauma

(4) markedly diminished interest or participation in significant activities

(5) feeling of detachment or estrangement from others

(6) restricted range of affect (e.g., unable to have loving feelings)

(7) sense of a foreshortened future (e.g., does not expect to have a career, marriage, children, or a normal life span)

D. Persistent symptoms of increased arousal (not present before the trauma), as indicated by two (or more) of the following:

(1) difficulty falling or staying asleep

(2) irritability or outbursts of anger

(3) difficulty concentrating

(4) hypervigilance

(5) exaggerated startle response

E. Duration of the disturbance (symptoms in Criteria B, C, and D) is more than 1 month.

F. The disturbance causes clinically significant distress or impairment in social, occupational, or other important areas of functioning.

Source: Reprinted with permission from the Diagnostic and Statistical Manual of Mental Disorders, Text Revision, Fourth Edition, (Copyright 2000) American Psychiatric Association.

Could Howard Hughes's problems have been related to an undiagnosed posttraumatic stress disorder? We don't know whether Hughes reexperienced any of his traumatic events (Criterion B), nor did he appear to have obvious avoidance symptoms related to the traumatic experiences (Criterion C): He continued flying after his last plane accident. He did have symptoms of increased arousal (Criterion D): irritability, hypervigilance, difficulty concentrating, and sleep problems, but these symptoms are better explained by his OCD and substance dependence. Thus, there is no evidence that Hughes suffered from PTSD.

Table 7.18 ▶ PTSD Facts at a Glance

Prevalence

- Among adults in the United States, approximately 8% develop PTSD, although this number varies depending on political events.

Comorbidity

- About 80% of those with PTSD also have another psychological disorder, most commonly a mood disorder, substance use disorder, or other anxiety disorder (Kessler et al., 1995).

Onset

- Symptoms usually begin within 3 months of the traumatic event, although people may go months or years before symptoms appear.
- However, people who develop PTSD usually show symptoms in the immediate aftermath of the trauma; approximately 80% of people with acute stress disorder go on to develop PTSD (Harvey & Bryant, 2002).

Course

- Duration of the symptoms varies. About half of those with PTSD recover within 3 months, whereas others continue to have persistent symptoms for more than a year after the traumatic event. Still others have symptoms that wax and wane.

Gender Differences

- Women who have been exposed to trauma develop PTSD more often than do men (American Psychiatric Association, 2000; Tolin & Foa, 2006), although males are more likely be victims of trauma (Tolin & Foa, 2006).

Cultural Differences

- Across cultures, people with PTSD may differ in the particular symptoms they express (e.g., more intrusive symptoms versus more arousal symptoms) depending on the coping styles that are encouraged in a given culture (Marsella, Friedman, & Spain, 1996).
- Black Americans, who are more likely to live in high-crime neighborhoods, develop PTSD at a higher rate than do white Americans (Himle et al., in press).

Source: Unless otherwise noted, information in the table is from American Psychiatric Association, 2000.

Criticisms of the DSM-IV-TR Criteria for Posttraumatic Stress Disorder

The diagnosis of PTSD was introduced into the DSM in the third edition (American Psychiatric Association, 1980), thereby officially recognizing the persistent mental suffering of some trauma victims. However, the diagnosis of PTSD is controversial for several reasons:

1. The distress and suffering experienced by people months after a traumatic event are not necessarily pathological, but including of them as criteria in the DSM defines the experiences as pathological (McHugh & Triesman, 2007; McNally, 2007; Spitzer, First, & Wakefield, 2007; Summerfield, 2001).

2. Many of the symptoms of PTSD (e.g., problems concentrating and sleeping, irritability) overlap with those of depression and anxiety, and therefore the apparent symptoms of PTSD may in fact be symptoms of those other disorders (Bodkin et al., 2007; Spitzer, First, & Wakefield, 2007).

3. The original criteria for PTSD involved traumatic events far outside those normally experienced during the ordinary course of life, such as war, rape,

kidnapping, or torture. The criteria were later altered to include more common traumatic events, such as car accidents and crime victimization (Summerfield, 2001), as experienced by A. C. in Case 7.7.

4. The criteria were altered for DSM-IV so that "second-hand victimization" is possible—that is, hearing about a traumatic event qualifies as having experienced it (McNally, 2003; Spitzer, First, & Wakefield, 2007).

5. What originally started as a way to understand war-related stress symptoms among soldiers has become something else—a way to seek the status of "victim" (Summerfield, 2001) for legal, financial, or psychological reasons (Spitzer, First, & Wakefield, 2007).

6. PTSD is the only diagnosis for which people can sue for compensation (Mezey & Robbins, 2001). Critics have claimed that the existence of a financial incentive means that PTSD is overdiagnosed, and people are intentionally or inadvertently encouraged to report being more traumatized than they really are (Mezey & Robbins, 2001; Spitzer, First, & Wakefield, 2007). Support for this claim comes from surveys that have found substantially lower rates of PTSD in people outside North America (Creamer, Burgess, & McFarlane, 2001; Perkonigg et al., 2000).

Taken together, these criticisms indicate that not all researchers agree with the DSM-IV-TR definition of a traumatic event or the specific diagnostic criteria for PTSD.

Understanding Posttraumatic Stress Disorder

Given that most people who experience a trauma do not go on to develop PTSD, the neuropsychosocial approach can help explain how neurological, psychological, and social factors can influence each other in particular ways and lead to PTSD. The various factors that contribute to PTSD may arise before the trauma, during the trauma, or after the trauma. Some form of combat-related stress disorder has been recognized for many decades, even centuries, giving researchers clues about possible factors to investigate more systematically.

Neurological Factors

The neurological factors that contribute to PTSD appear to arise, in large part, from interactions between the frontal lobe and the amygdala. In addition, the neurotransmitters norepinephrine and serotonin have been implicated in the disorder, and there is evidence that genes contribute to (but by no means determine) the likelihood that experiencing trauma will result in PTSD.

Brain Systems

Research has often shown that PTSD sufferers react more strongly to cues that they associate with their traumatic experience than do others. The cues can cause sweating or a racing heart (Orr, Metzger, & Pitman, 2002; Orr et al., 1993; Prins, Kaloupek, & Keane, 1995). Furthermore, the changes in heart rate are distinct from the changes found in control participants who have been asked to pretend having PTSD (Orr & Pitman, 1993). Thus, PTSD patients are not simply pretending, but do in fact react more strongly to the relevant cues than would be expected if they did not have a disorder.

In an effort to chart the mechanisms that give rise to these reactions, researchers have studied the brains of PTSD patients. First, MRI studies have shown that PTSD patients have smaller hippocampi than control participants (Bremner et al., 1995, 1997, 2003). Combat veterans with PTSD also had smaller hippocampi than other combat veterans who did not have PTSD (Gurvits et al., 1996). Second, the hippocampus apparently must work harder than normal in PTSD patients when they try to remember information, as shown by the fact that it is more strongly activated in these patients during memory tasks than in control participants (Shin et al.,

2004). The abnormal structure and function of the hippocampus in PTSD patients is important because that brain structure plays a crucial role in storing information in memory (Squire & Kandel, 2000), and thus an impaired hippocampus should impair memory. And, in fact, as expected, PTSD patients have trouble recalling autobiographical memories (McNally et al., 1995).

Note that correlation does not imply causation; perhaps the brain abnormality predisposes people to PTSD, or perhaps PTSD leads to the brain abnormality (McEwen, 2001; Pitman, Shin, & Rauch, 2001). A twin study provides an important hint about what causes what: In this study, researchers compared the sizes of the hippocampi in veterans who had served in combat and had PTSD with the sizes of hippocampi in their identical twins who had not served in combat and did not have PTSD. The results were clear: In both twins, the hippocampi were smaller than normal (Gilbertson et al., 2002). This finding implies that the trauma does not cause the hippocampus to become smaller, but rather the smaller size is a risk factor (or is correlated with some other factor that produces the risk) that makes a person vulnerable to the disorder.

Neuroimaging studies have focused not only on the hippocampus but also on the entire brain, in an effort to discover more generally which brain functions have been disrupted by PTSD (Rauch et al., 1996; Rauch, Shin & Phelps, 2006; Shin et al., 1999). For example, in some studies, researchers either show patients pictures of trauma-related stimuli (such as jungle scenes in Vietnam for Vietnam-war vets) or ask them to visualize such scenes. When PTSD patients visualize their own traumatic events, parts of the limbic system and related areas are activated, which is not surprising given the role these areas play in emotion. In addition, areas of the brain involved in visual perception are highly activated, which may indicate that these patients have particularly vivid visual mental images (Kosslyn, Thompson, & Ganis, 2006).

In addition, some studies have found that when PTSD patients see faces with fearful expressions (which can be presented so quickly that the participants aren't consciously aware of seeing them), their amygdalas become abnormally highly activated (Pitman, Shin, & Rauch 2001; Rauch, Shin, & Phelps, 2006; Rauch et al., 2000). Moreover, curiously, in three of these studies, patients with PTSD had less activation in Broca's area (in the left frontal lobe) when visualizing traumatic stimuli (Broca's area plays a key role in language production). Shin and colleagues (1997) suggest that these patients may be "scared speechless," which dampens down activity in this area. In fact, the more activated the amygdala, the less activated this area of the frontal lobe tends to be in these patients (Shin et al., 2005). It is possible that people who don't develop PTSD can use language to reinterpret trauma, and thereby lessen its impact—but PTSD patients may be overwhelmed by the sensory images, which interfere with using language in this way.

Neural Communication

Initially, researchers thought of PTSD as an extreme response to stressful situations. If so, then the brain would produce abnormal amounts of stress-related hormones, such as cortisol (Yehuda et al., 1991). But this turned out not to be the case—in fact, patients with PTSD actually have lower-than-normal levels of this hormone (Yehuda et al., 1995, 1996), even immediately after the traumatic event (McFarlane, Atchison, & Yehuda, 1997).

Even though the initial theory turned out not to be correct, it contained a grain of truth: PTSD patients do experience stress when they recall the traumatic event, and the brain does respond to stress in specific ways. In particular, when animals are forced to confront stressors, the locus coeruleus (a small structure in the brainstem) produces norepinephrine, a neurotransmitter that may be involved in PTSD (Charney et al., 1993; Southwick et al., 1994). Southwick and colleagues (1993) provided support for this theory. They gave a drug that allows norepinephrine levels to surge to volunteers with and without PTSD. When norepinephrine levels became very high, 70% of the PTSD patients had a panic attack, and 40% of them had a flashback to the traumatic event that precipitated their disorder. Moreover, this drug resulted in more extreme biochemical and cardiovascular effects for the PTSD patients than for the controls. However, neuroimaging studies have not documented abnormal activity in the locus coeruleus when these patients are confronted with the relevant stimulus cues. One possibility is that the locus coeruleus only creates abnormal levels of norepinephrine when the person is under larger amounts of stress than are induced by the usual stimuli. Another possibility is that stress itself is another sort of trigger for panic attacks in people with PTSD, operating along with images of the relevant stimuli.

Various types of evidence indicate that serotonin also plays a role in PTSD. For one, SSRIs can help treat the disorder, and apparently do so in part by allowing serotonin to moderate the effects of stress (Corchs, Nutt, Hodd, & Bernik, 2009). In addition, people who have certain alleles of genes that produce serotonin are susceptible to developing the disorder following trauma (Adamec, Holmes, & Blundell, 2008; Grabe et al., in press). However, research has shown that the effects of such genes may depend on a combination of factors, such as stressful environmental events in combination with low social support—and the same factors that affect whether people develop PTSD also affect whether they develop major depressive disorder (Kilpatrick et al., 2007). Thus, the effects of serotonin on PTSD are likely to be complex, and perhaps arise because of how it affects more general aspects of brain function.

Genetics

Some people may have a genetic predisposition to develop PTSD (Shalev et al., 1998; True et al., 1993). However, genes appear either to play a smaller role than the environment in predicting PTSD (McLeod et al., 2001) or to be relevant only in the context of complex interactions between genes and environment (Broekman, Olff, & Boer, 2007). Consider a study of twin pairs where all twins served in the military during the Vietnam War. Results of the study found that a twin was nine times more likely to develop PTSD if he had been in heavy combat in Vietnam than if he had not been in combat. Controlling for the amount of time in combat, researchers found that genes account for about one third of the variance in PTSD symptoms (True et al., 1993). Unique environmental experiences (such as being in a fierce battle) could account for the remaining variance.

Psychological Factors: History of Trauma, Comorbidity, and Conditioning

Psychological factors that exist before the traumatic event occurs affect whether a person will develop PTSD. Such factors include a history of depression or other psychological disorders (Brewin, Andrews, & Valentine, 2000), and the beliefs the person has about himself or herself and the world. Two specific beliefs that can create a vulnerability for PTSD are considering yourself unable to control stressors (Heinrichs et al., 2005; Joseph, Williams, & Yule, 1995) and the conviction that the world is a dangerous place (Keane et al., 1985; Kushner et al., 1992).

In addition, PTSD patients who have lower IQs tend to have more severe symptoms (Kremen et al., 2007; Macklin et al., 1998; McNally & Shin, 1995). However, this finding does not imply a causal relation in either direction. IQ might lead to some other factor, which in turn is responsible for the severity of symptoms. For example, one study found that children with IQs over 115 (more than 1 standard deviation above average; see Chapter 3) were less likely to experience a traumatic event by age 17 (Breslau, Lucia, & Alvarado, 2006). It may be that people with lower IQs are less adept at avoiding traumatic events. Alternatively, perhaps they believe that they cannot control traumatic events, and that's why there is a correlation between IQ and the severity of PTSD symptoms. In fact, perceiving that you have no control over the traumatic event as it is taking place or that your life is at risk during the event (whether or not the threat is that serious) can promote PTSD (Foa, Steketee, & Rothbaum, 1989).

Among individuals who experienced a common type of traumatic event—a car accident—those who coped during the accident by dissociating were more likely to go on to develop PTSD than those who did not (Shalev et al., 1996). Other factors that increase the likelihood of PTSD's developing after a car accident are ruminating about the accident afterward, consciously trying to suppress thoughts about it, and having intrusive, unwanted thoughts and memories about it (Ehlers, Mayou, & Bryant, 1998).

Corbis/Punchstock

People can be vulnerable to developing PTSD for a variety of reasons. For example, people with severe mental disorders such as bipolar disorder (see Chapter 6) and schizophrenia (Chapter 12) are also more likely to have PTSD, perhaps as a result of childhood abuse or assaults that occurred during episodes of mental illness. However, PTSD may go undiagnosed in this population (Mueser et al., 1998; Shevlin, Dorahy, & Adamson, 2007). PTSD is also more likely to develop in those who have some other type of anxiety disorder (Copeland et al., 2007), perhaps because most anxiety disorders involve hyperarousal and hypervigilance, which may lead people to respond to traumatic events in ways that promote a stress disorder. In addition, people who experience a traumatic event after having survived a prior traumatic event (for example, having been assaulted and then, years later, living through a hurricane) may be at risk.

During the traumatic event, people who cope by dissociating (disrupting the normal processes of perception, awareness, and memory) are more likely to develop PTSD (Shalev et al., 1996).

After the traumatic event, classical conditioning and operant conditioning may help to explain the avoidance symptoms of PTSD, in the same way that it can explain such behavior in other anxiety disorders (Mowrer, 1939). In terms of classical conditioning, the traumatic stress is the unconditioned stimulus, and both internal sensations and external objects or situations can become conditioned stimuli, which in turn can come to induce powerful and aversive conditioned emotional responses (Keane, Zimering, & Caddell, 1985).

As with other anxiety disorders, the avoidant symptoms of PTSD are negatively reinforced. In addition, drugs and alcohol can temporarily alleviate symptoms; such substance use is also negatively reinforced, and explains why people with PTSD have a higher incidence of substance abuse or dependence than do people who experienced a trauma but did not go on to develop PTSD (Chilcoat & Breslau, 1998; Jacobsen, Southwick, & Kosten, 2001). In one study of National Guard members who had been to Iraq, over half of those men and women who developed PTSD also reported problem drinking (Alvarez, 2008).

Social Factors

Social factors—both before the traumatic event and afterward—also help determine whether PTSD develops. Such factors include the additional stress of lower socioeconomic status and the level of social support provided to the trauma victim.

Socioeconomic Stress

As with other stressors in life, socioeconomic factors can influence an individual's ability to cope. People who need to worry about feeding, clothing, and housing themselves or their families have fewer emotional resources available to cope with a traumatic event and so are less likely than more fortunate individuals to weather it without developing PTSD (Mezey & Robbins, 2001).

In addition, those who are at a socioeconomic disadvantage may be more likely to experience trauma (Breslau et al., 1998; Himle et al., in press). For instance, poorer people are more likely to live in high-crime areas and so are more likely to witness crimes or become crime victims (Norris et al., 2003).

Social Support

People who receive support from others immediately after a trauma have a lower risk of developing PTSD (Kaniasty & Norris, 1992; Kaniasty, Norris & Murrell, 1990). For example, people who have experienced trauma during military service have a lower risk of developing PTSD if they have strong social support upon returning home (Jakupcak et al., 2006; King et al., 1999).

Cultural Expression of Symptoms

A person's culture can help determine which PTSD symptoms are more prominent. Cultural patterns might "teach" one coping style rather than another (Marsella et al., 1996). For example, Hurricane Paulina in Mexico and Hurricane Andrew in the United States were about equal in force, but the people who developed PTSD afterward did so in different ways (after controlling for the severity of an individual's trauma): Mexicans were more likely to have intrusive symptoms (Criterion B in Table 7.17), such as flashbacks about the hurricane and its devastation, whereas Americans were more likely to have arousal symptoms (Criterion D in Table 7.17), such as an exaggerated startle response or hypervigilance (Norris, Perilla, & Murphy, 2001). A similar finding was obtained from a study comparing Hispanic Americans to European Americans after Hurricane Andrew (Perilla, Norris, & Lavizzo, 2002).

FEEDBACK LOOPS IN ACTION:
Understanding Posttraumatic Stress Disorder

Neurological, psychological, and social differences among individuals lead to their different responses to traumatic events (Bowman, 1999). Neurological factors can make some people more vulnerable to developing PTSD after a trauma. For example, in a study of those training to be firefighters, trainees who had a larger startle response to loud bursts of noise at the beginning of training were more likely to develop PTSD after a subsequent fire-related trauma (Guthrie & Bryant, 2005). In another study of male Vietnam veterans who were fraternal or identical twins, researchers found that willingness to volunteer for combat and to accept riskier assignments is partly heritable (neurological factor; Lyons et al., 1993). This heritability may involve the dimension of temperament called *novelty seeking* (see Chapter 2). Someone high in novelty seeking pursues activities that are exciting and very stimulating, and a person with this characteristic may be more likely to volunteer for risky assignments (psychological factor), increasing the chance of encountering certain kinds of trauma. This means that neurological factors can influence both psychological and social factors, which in turn can increase the risk of trauma. At the same time, when a traumatic event is more severe (social factor), other types of factors are less important in influencing the onset of PTSD (Keane & Barlow, 2002).

Furthermore, ways of viewing the world and other personality traits (psychological factors) can influence the level of social support that is available to a person after suffering trauma (social factor). Because shy people are less likely have a wide social network, they tend to have less social support than do people who seek out social activities. Even when a traumatized person has sufficient social support, if others encourage him or her to suppress thoughts of the event ("just don't think about it any more"), he or she might inadvertently increase the amount of attention paid to the traumatic experience—which increases the risk of PTSD. Figure 7.17 illustrates these factors and their feedback loops.

Figure 7.17

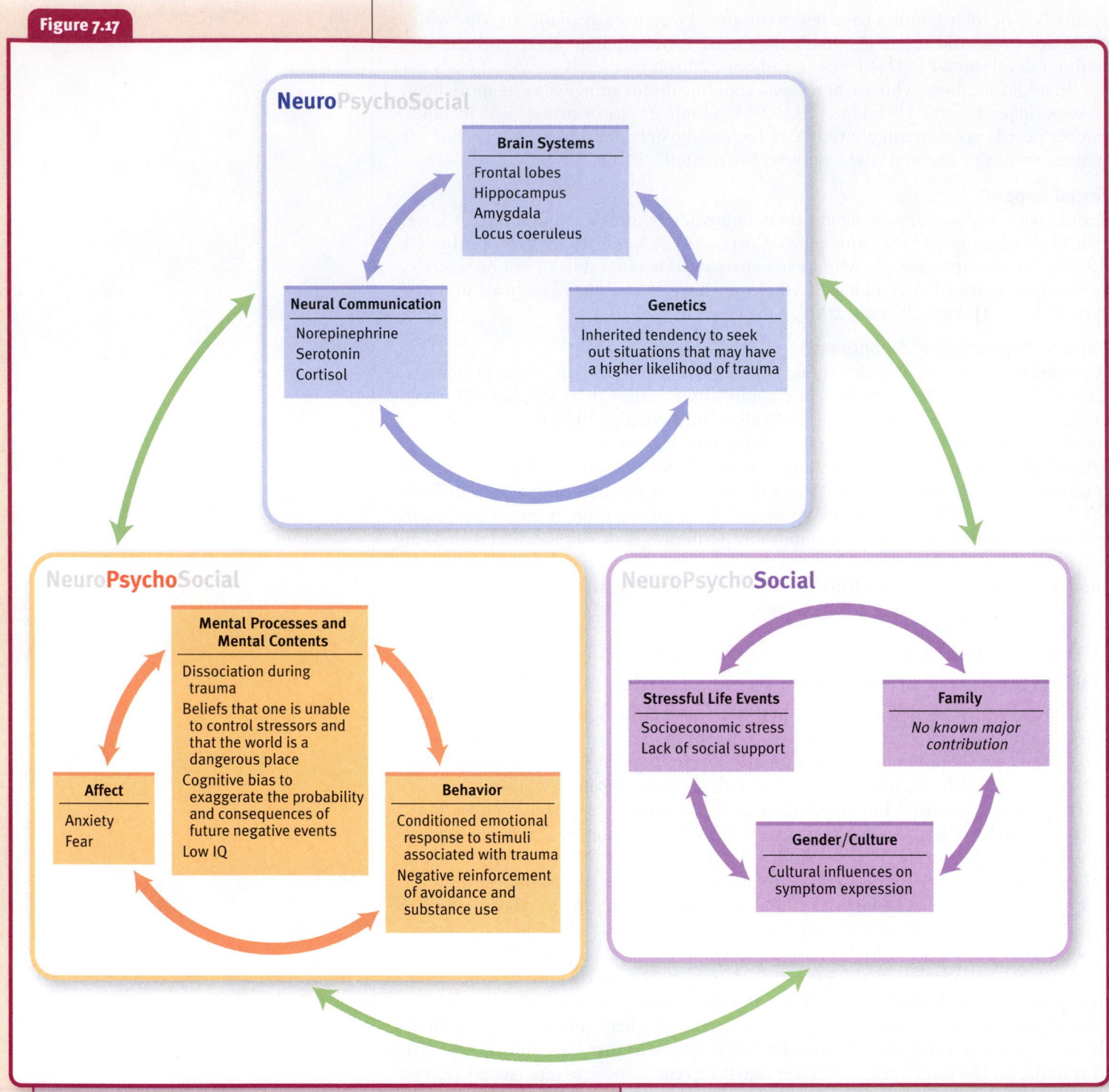

NeuroPsychoSocial

Brain Systems

Frontal lobes
Hippocampus
Amygdala
Locus coeruleus

Neural Communication

Norepinephrine
Serotonin
Cortisol

Genetics

Inherited tendency to seek
out situations that may have
a higher likelihood of trauma

NeuroPsychoSocial

**Mental Processes and
Mental Contents**

Dissociation during
trauma
Beliefs that one is unable
to control stressors and
that the world is a
dangerous place
Cognitive bias to
exaggerate the probability
and consequences of
future negative events
Low IQ

Affect

Anxiety
Fear

Behavior

Conditioned emotional
response to stimuli
associated with trauma
Negative reinforcement
of avoidance and
substance use

NeuroPsychoSocial

Stressful Life Events

Socioeconomic stress
Lack of social support

Family

*No known major
contribution*

Gender/Culture

Cultural influences on
symptom expression

7.17 ▶ Feedback Loops in Action: Posttraumatic Stress Disorder

Treating Posttraumatic Stress Disorder

Treatments for PTSD target neurological, psychological, and social factors; as usual, when a treatment is successful, changes in one factor affect the other factors. Patients may obtain treatment that specifically targets only one type of factor or more comprehensive treatment that targets two or even all three types of factors.

Targeting Neurological Factors: Medication

The SSRIs *sertraline* (Zoloft) and *paroxetine* (Paxil) are the first-line medications for treating the symptoms of PTSD (Brady et al., 2000; Davidson et al., 1997; Stein et al., 2000). In general, an SSRI should be taken continuously for at least 9 months for fullest symptom relief (Rosenbaum et al., 2005). An added advantage of SSRIs is that these medications can also help reduce comorbid symptoms of depression (Hidalgo & Davidson, 2000)—which is important because many people with PTSD also have depression. As with other anxiety disorders, when people discontinue the medication, the symptoms may return. This is why medication is not usually the sole treatment for PTSD, but rather is combined with treatment that directly addresses psychological and social factors (Rosenbaum et al., 2005).

Two experimental treatments that directly target neurological factors hold promise for helping people with PTSD. One is the use of *propranolol* (Inderal), a beta-blocker (also used to treat performance anxiety, as noted earlier in this chapter); preliminary studies suggest that when taken soon after a traumatic event, it may decrease the risk of subsequent PTSD by diminishing neural aspects of fear conditioning (Pitman & Delahanty, 2005; Vaiva et al., 2003), although not all studies find such preventative medication treatment to be more effective than placebo (Stein et al., 2007). The other experimental treatment for PTSD is transcranial magnetic stimulation (TMS; see Chapter 4). Preliminary results suggest that TMS can reduce PTSD symptoms, but these findings need to be replicated and further understood before TMS becomes part of the repertoire of standard treatments (Cohen et al., 2004; Osuch et al., 2008).

Targeting Psychological Factors

Treatments that target psychological factors generally employ a combination of behavioral methods and cognitive methods, which, separately or in combination, are about equally effective (Keane & Barlow, 2002; Marks et al., 1998; Schnurr et al., 2007; Tarrier et al., 1999). However, most studies of CBT for acute stress disorder or PTSD do not include lengthy follow-up (Bradley et al., 2005).

U.S. Navy/Getty Images

CBT conducted online helped people who developed PTSD as a result of the September 11, 2001, terrorist attack on the Pentagon (Litz et al., 2007).

Behavioral Methods: Exposure, Relaxation, and Breathing Retraining

A traumatic experience can leave someone who has PTSD with a diminished sense of control over the environment, and perhaps over himself or herself; this person may then go to unreasonable lengths to avoid stimuli associated with the trauma. This is why treatment aims to increase a sense of control over PTSD symptoms and to decrease avoidance. Just as exposure is used to decrease avoidance associated with other anxiety disorders, it is used for PTSD: Imaginal exposure or in vivo exposure (see Chapter 4) aims to induce habituation and to reduce the avoidance of internal and external cues associated with the trauma (Bryant & Harvey, 2000; Keane & Barlow, 2002). In this case, the specific stimuli in an exposure hierarchy are those associated with the trauma. As the individual becomes less aroused and fearful of these stimuli and avoids them less, mastery and control increase. To help with anxiety and reduce arousal symptoms, relaxation and breathing retraining are often included in treatment.

Cognitive Methods: Psychoeducation and Cognitive Restructuring

To diminish the difficult emotions that occur with PTSD, educating patients about the nature of their symptoms (psychoeducation) can be a first step. As patients learn about PTSD, they realize that their symptoms don't arise totally out of the blue; their experiences become more understandable and less frightening.

Cognitive methods can help patients understand the meaning of their traumatic experiences and the (mis)attributions they make about these experiences and the aftermath (Duffy, Gillespie, & Clark, 2007, Foa et al., 1991, 1999), such as "I deserved this happening to me because I should have walked down a different street."

Studies have examined whether CBT can help prevent acute stress disorder from evolving into PTSD. In fact, numerous studies have shown that CBT can significantly reduce the number of people who would have had their diagnosis change from acute stress disorder to PTSD (Bryant et al., 2005, 2006, 2008).

Targeting Social Factors: Safety, Support, and Family Education

Because the traumatic event is invariably a social stressor, the early focus of treatment is to ensure that the traumatized person is as safe as possible (Baranowsky, Gentry, & Schultz, 2005; Herman, 1992). For instance, in a case that involves domestic abuse and an ensuing stress disorder, the therapist and patient will spend time reviewing whether the woman is safe from further abuse, and if not, how to make her as safe as possible. For some types of traumatic events, such as combat-related trauma, group therapy—of any theoretical orientation—can provide support and diminish the sense of isolation, guilt, or shame about the trauma or the symptoms of PTSD (Schnurr et al., 2003). Moreover, family or couples therapy can help to educate family members and friends about PTSD and about ways in which they can support their loved one (Goff & Smith, 2005; Sherman, Zanatti, & Jones, 2005). Preliminary research suggests that interpersonal therapy (IPT; see Chapter 4), which focuses on relationship problems, may be a helpful alternative treatment for those who are not interested in CBT (Bleiberg & Markowitz, 2005).

Culture can help determine what kind of treatment for PTSD is appropriate. These Peruvian villagers were threatened by soldiers during a national state of emergency declared in 2003. Earlier, a study of Peruvians and Colombians exposed to traumatic experiences found that those from villages with a more individualist orientation felt that individual treatment was more appropriate, compared to those from more collectivist-oriented villages (Elsass, 2001).

Renzo Giraldo/El Comercio/AFP/Getty Images

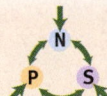

FEEDBACK LOOPS IN TREATMENT: Posttraumatic Stress Disorder

To appreciate the interactive nature of the neuropsychosocial approach, consider a study that treated people who developed PTSD after being in traffic accidents (as driver, passenger, or pedestrian) (Taylor et al., 2001). Most participants in the study had sustained injuries in the accident and had PTSD symptoms for over 2 years prior to treatment, so spontaneous remission of symptoms was unlikely. Prior to beginning the treatment, 15 of the 50 participants were taking an SSRI, a TCA, or a benzodiazepine for symptoms. Treatment consisted of 12 weeks of group CBT that involved: psychoeducation about traffic accidents, their aftereffects, and PTSD; cognitive restructuring focused on faulty thoughts (such as overrating the dangerousness of road travel); relaxation training; and imaginal and in vivo exposure.

After treatment, participants reported that they had less hyperarousal; that is, they experienced less autonomic reactivity, such as the startle response. In addition, they avoided the trauma-inducing stimuli less often and had fewer intrusive reexperiences of the trauma. These gains were maintained at the 3-month follow-up. So, an intervention that targets both social factors (group therapy with exposure to external trauma-related stimuli) and psychological factors (cognitive and behavioral interventions to change thinking and behavior) also apparently changed neurological functioning, as indicated by the reports of decreased hyperarousal. Successful treatments for PTSD that target one or two factors ultimately affect all three. Figure 7.18 illustrates these feedback loops in treatment.

Figure 7.18

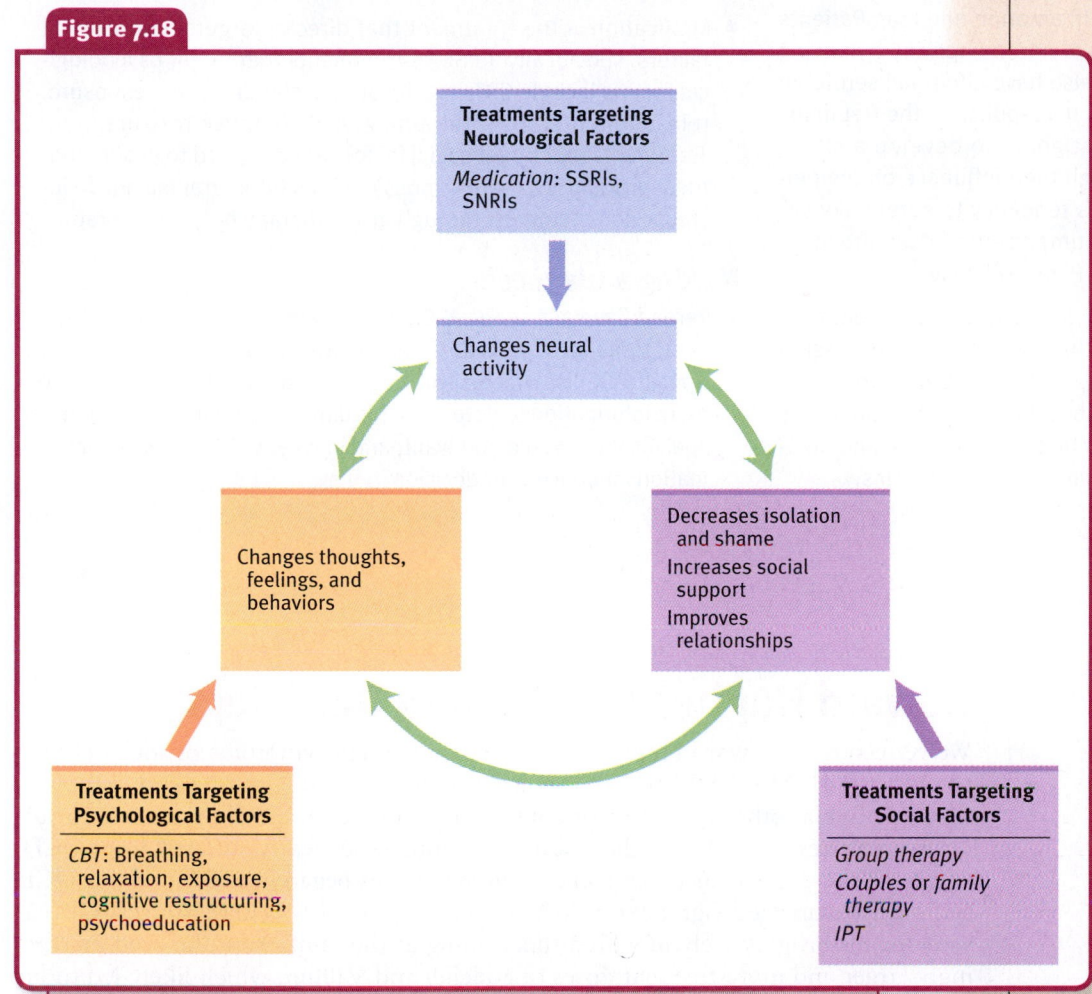

7.18 ▸ Feedback Loops in Treating Posttraumatic Stress Disorder

Key Concepts and Facts About Posttraumatic Stress Disorder

- Stress disorders are characterized by three types of persistent symptoms: reexperiencing the traumatic event avoidance of stimuli related to the event, and increased arousal and anxiety.

- DSM-IV-TR includes two types of stress disorder: acute stress disorder and posttraumatic stress disorder (PTSD). These two disorders are distinguished in part by the timing and duration of symptoms: Acute stress disorder is diagnosed when symptoms arise within 4 weeks of the stressor and have lasted for less than 4 weeks; when symptoms last more than 4 weeks the diagnosis is PTSD. The diagnostic criteria for acute stress disorder also include symptoms of dissociation.

- An event is considered traumatic if the individual experienced or witnessed an actual or threatened death or serious injury and responded with intense fear, helplessness, or horror. Types of traumatic events are large-scale events with multiple victims, unintended acts involving smaller numbers of people, and interpersonal violence. Interpersonal violence is more likely to lead to a stress disorder, as are other events in which the trauma is severe, of long duration, and of close proximity.

- The DSM-IV-TR diagnosis of PTSD has been criticized because the definition of traumatic stress is too broad, encompassing

continued on next page

normal responses to trauma, and because the symptoms specified in the criteria overlap with those for other disorders.

- Brain areas involved in PTSD include parts of the frontal lobe, the hippocampus, the locus coeruleus, and the amygdala—most of these areas are involved in emotion and fear. Patients with PTSD respond to high levels of norepinephrine by having panic attacks or flashbacks; they also have abnormal serotonin function and produce less cortisol in response to the traumatic event than do people who do not go on to develop a stress disorder. Although genes—through their influence on temperament—may affect an individual's tendency to enter risky situations, characteristics of the traumatic event itself are more important in determining whether PTSD will arise.

- Psychological factors that exist before a traumatic event contribute to PTSD; these factors include a history of depression or other psychological disorders, a belief in being unable to control stressors, the conviction that the world is a dangerous place, and lower IQ. After a traumatic event, classical and operant conditioning contribute to the avoidance symptoms.

- Social factors that contribute to PTSD include the stress of low socioeconomic status and a relative lack of social support for the trauma victim. Culture can influence the ways that individuals cope with traumatic stress.

- Medication is the treatment that directly targets neurological factors, specifically an SSRI. Treatments that target psychological factors include CBT, specifically psychoeducation, exposure, relaxation, breathing retraining, and cognitive restructuring. Treatments that target social factors are designed to ensure that the individual is as safe as possible from future trauma and to increase social support through group therapy or family therapy.

Making a Diagnosis

- Reread Case 7.7 about A. C., and determine whether or not his symptoms met the criteria for posttraumatic stress disorder. Specifically, list which apply and which do not. If you would like more information to determine his diagnosis, what information—specifically—would you want, and in what ways would the information influence your decision?

Howard Hughes and Anxiety Disorders

We've seen that Howard Hughes may have had enough symptoms of social phobia to meet the DSM-IV-TR criteria at some points in his life, and he may have had specific phobia, other type (fear of contracting an illness). He did not seem to suffer from a stress disorder. Without a doubt, though, he clearly suffered from OCD. Although there is evidence that some of his symptoms began in childhood, his OCD symptoms worsened significantly when he was in his 40s. There are several reasons for his progressively impaired functioning at this time. First, he used increasingly larger and more frequent doses of codeine and Valium, which likely led to his diminished cognitive functioning and control over his behavior—his compulsions. Second, he had by then suffered brain damage, which came about from two sources: (1) the 14 occurrences of head trauma Hughes withstood from various plane and car accidents (Fowler, 1986), and (2) the effects of advanced syphilis (Brown & Broeske, 1996).

Hughes contracted syphilis when in his 30s, before antibiotics were available (Brown & Broeske, 1996). To treat the disease, he underwent painful and risky mercury treatment; unfortunately, the treatment was not a complete success, and by the time he was in his 40s, the disease appears to have progressed. After Hughes's death, his autopsy indicated that significant brain cell death had occurred, which is a sign of advanced syphilis (a condition previously called *general paresis*; see Chapter 1). Symptoms can include gradual personality changes and poor judgment, which may take up to 15 years to emerge. For the first few decades of his adult life, then, Hughes was able to keep his OCD symptoms sufficiently in check that his functioning was far less impaired than it became in his 50s and afterward. It is possible that the effects of syphilis and the brain trauma from his accidents exacerbated his OCD. Thus, two physical factors contributed to the worsening of Hughes's OCD symptoms: brain damage, discussed in Chapter 15, and substance abuse, which is the focus of Chapter 9.

SUMMING UP

Summary of Common Features of Anxiety Disorders

The key symptoms of anxiety disorders are extreme anxiety, intense arousal, and attempts to avoid stimuli that lead to fear and anxiety. The fight-or-flight response arises when people perceive a threat; when the arousal feels out of control—either because the individual has an overactive stress response or because he or she misinterprets the arousal—the person may experience panic. In response to the panic, some people develop a phobia of the stimuli related to their panic and anxiety symptoms.

Anxiety disorders frequently co-occur with other psychological disorders, such as depression or substance-related disorders. Mental health clinicians must determine whether the anxiety symptoms are the primary cause of the problem or are the by-product of another type of disorder. The high comorbidity of depression and anxiety disorders suggests that the two disorders share some of the same features, specifically high levels of negative emotions and distress—which can lead to concentration and sleep problems and irritability.

Thinking like a clinician

What is the difference between fear and anxiety? Why (or when) might the fight-or-flight response become a problem? If people can have symptoms of anxiety when they have other types of disorders, what determines whether an anxiety disorder is the diagnosis?

Summary of Generalized Anxiety Disorder

Generalized anxiety disorder (GAD) is marked by persistent uncontrollable worry about a number of events or activities. A majority of people with GAD also have comorbid depression. Neurological factors associated with GAD include abnormal activity of dopamine and other neurotransmitters, which influences motivation, response to reward, and attention, and a genetic predisposition to become anxious and/or depressed.

Psychological factors that contribute to GAD include being hypervigilant for possible threats, a sense that the worrying is out of control, and the reinforcing experience that worrying prevents panic. Social factors that contribute to GAD include stressful life events, which can trigger the disorder.

Treatments for GAD include (1) medication such as buspirone or an SNRI or SSRI when depression is present as a comorbid disorder; and (2) CBT, which may be employed in a group format.

Thinking like a clinician

Based on what you have read, what differentiates a "worrywart"—someone who worries a lot—from someone with GAD? If having GAD is distressing, why don't patients simply stop worrying—what factors maintain the disorder? If someone you know with GAD asked you for advice about what kind of treatment to get, what would you recommend (based on what you have read) and why?

Summary of Panic Disorder (With and Without Agoraphobia)

The hallmark of panic disorder is recurrent panic attacks. Panic attacks may be cued by particular stimuli (usually internal sensations), or they may arise without any clear cue. Panic disorder also involves fear of further attacks and, in some cases, restricted behavior in an effort to prevent further attacks.

People in different cultures may have similar—but not identical—constellations of symptoms, such as *ataque de nervios* and wind-and-blood pressure. Some people with panic disorder also develop agoraphobia. Less commonly, people develop agoraphobia without panic disorder, but they fear triggering symptoms of panic.

Neurological factors contribute to panic disorder and agoraphobia, including: (1) A heightened sensitivity to detect breathing changes, which in turn leads to hyperventilation, panic, and a sense of needing to escape. (2) Too much norepinephrine, which increases heart and respiration rates and other aspects of the fight-or-flight response. (3) A genetic predisposition to anxiety disorders.

Psychological factors that contribute to panic disorder and agoraphobia include: (1) Conditioning of learned alarms that elicit panic symptoms. (2) Heightened anxiety sensitivity and misinterpretation of bodily symptoms of arousal in turn lead to a hypervigilance for—and fear of—further sensations, increasing arousal and creating a vicious cycle.

Social factors related to panic disorder and agoraphobia include: (1) a greater than average number of social stressors during childhood and adolescence; (2) the presence of a safe person, which can decrease catastrophic thinking and panic; and (3) cultural factors.

The treatment that targets neurological factors is medication, specifically benzodiazepines for short-term relief and antidepressants for long-term use. CBT is the first-line treatment for panic disorder and targets psychological factors. Treatments that target social factors include group therapy focused on panic disorder and couples or family therapy, particularly when a family member is a safe person.

Thinking like a clinician

All you know about Fiona is that she has had about ten panic attacks. Is this enough information to determine whether she has panic disorder? If it is, does she have the disorder? If this isn't enough information, what else would you want to know and why? Now suppose that Fiona starts missing Monday classes because of panic attacks on those days. She also stops going to parties on the weekend because she had a couple of panic attacks at parties. Would you change or maintain your answer about whether she has panic disorder—why or why not? Suppose Fiona does have panic disorder. Explain how she might have developed the disorder. By the end of the semester, Fiona no longer goes out of her apartment for fear of getting a panic attack. What might be appropriate treatments for Fiona?

Summary of Social Phobia (Social Anxiety Disorder)

Social phobia is an intense fear of public humiliation or embarrassment, together with an avoidance of social situations likely to cause this fear. When such social situations cannot be avoided, they trigger panic or anxiety. Social phobia may be limited to specific types of performance-related situations or may be generalized to most social situations. The anxiety about performing poorly and being evaluated by others can, in turn, impair an individual's performance, creating a vicious cycle.

Neurological factors that give rise to social phobia include an amygdala that is more easily activated in response to social stimuli, too little dopamine in the basal ganglia, too little serotonin, and a genetic predisposition toward a shy temperament, or behavioral inhibition. Psychological factors that give rise to social phobia include cognitive distortions and hypervigilance for social threats—particularly about being (negatively) evaluated. Classical conditioning of a fear response in social situations may contribute to social phobia; avoiding feared social situations is then negatively reinforced.

Social factors that give rise to social phobia include parents' modeling or encouraging a child to avoid anxiety-inducing social interactions. Moreover, people in different cultures may express their social fears somewhat differently.

Neurological factors are targeted by beta-blockers for periodic performance anxiety, and SSRIs or SNRIs for more generalized social phobia. The treatment that targets psychological factors is CBT, specifically, exposure and cognitive restructuring. Treatments that target social factors include group CBT and exposure to feared social stimuli.

Thinking like a clinician

Nick loved his job—he was a programmer and he worked from home. The thing he loved most about his job was that he didn't have to deal with people all day. However, his company was recently bought by a larger firm that wants Nick to start working in the central office a few days a week. His new boss tells him he'll have to attend several weekly meetings. Nick gets anxious about these changes. What determines whether Nick has a social phobia, or is just shy and nervous about the work changes? Explain your answer. If Nick gets so anxious that he can't attend the meetings, what would be an appropriate treatment for him?

Summary of Specific Phobias

Specific phobia involves excessive and irrational anxiety or fear related to a specific stimulus, and avoidance of the feared stimulus. DSM-IV-TR specifies five types of specific phobias: animal, natural environment, blood-injection-injury, situational, and other.

Neurological factors, such as an overreactive amygdala and genetics, appear to contribute to specific phobias. Neurotransmitters involved in specific phobias include GABA, serotonin, acetylcholine, and norepinephrine. Psychological factors that give rise to specific phobias include operant conditioning, possibly classical conditioning, and cognitive biases related to the stimulus. Observational learning—a social factor—can influence what particular stimulus a person comes to fear.

The medication for specific phobia is benzodiazepines. However, medication is usually not necessary because CBT—the treatment of choice for specific phobia—is extremely effective. CBT—particularly when exposure is

part of the treatment—can work in just one session.

Thinking like a clinician

Iqbal is horribly afraid of tarantulas, refusing to enter insect houses at zoos. Do you need any more information before determining whether Iqbal has a specific phobia of tarantulas? If so—what would you need to know? If not, do you think he has a specific phobia? Explain. How might Iqbal have developed his fear of tarantulas—what factors are likely to have been involved in its emergence and maintenance? Suppose Iqbal decided that he wants to "get rid of" his fear of tarantulas. What treatments are likely to be effective and what are the advantages and disadvantages of each?

Summary of Obsessive-Compulsive Disorder

Obsessive-compulsive disorder (OCD) is marked by persistent and intrusive preoccupations and—in most cases—repetitive behaviors that usually correspond to the obsessions. Although people with OCD recognize that their obsessions are irrational, they cannot turn off the preoccupying thoughts; they feel driven to engage in the compulsive behaviors, which provide only brief respite from the obsessions. Common obsessions include anxiety about contamination, ordering, losing control, doubts, and getting rid of objects. Common compulsions include washing, order, counting, checking, and hoarding or collecting.

Neurological factors associated with OCD include disruptions in the normal activity of a neural loop among frontal lobes, the thalamus, and the basal ganglia such that the frontal lobes do not turn off the neural loop, which may then lead to the persistent obsessions. Genes appear to make some people more vulnerable to anxiety disorders in general—not necessarily to OCD specifically.

Psychological factors that may underlie OCD include negative reinforcement of the compulsive behavior. In addition, normal preoccupying thoughts may become obsessions when the thoughts are deemed "unacceptable" and hence require controlling. In turn, the thoughts lead to anxiety, which is then relieved by a mental or behavioral ritual. Like people with other anxiety disorders, people with OCD have cognitive biases related to their feared stimuli, in this case, regarding the theme of their obsessions.

Social factors related to OCD include socially induced stress, which can influence the onset and course of the disorder, and culture,

which can influence the particular content of obsessions and compulsions.

Medication (such as an SSRI or clomipramine) is the treatment for OCD that directly targets neurological factors. The primary treatment for OCD—exposure with response prevention—directly targets psychological factors. Cognitive restructuring to reduce the irrationality and frequency of the patient's intrusive thoughts and obsessions may also be employed. Family education or therapy, targeting social factors, may be used as an additional treatment to help the patient's family function in a more normal way.

Thinking like a clinician

You visit a new friend. When you use her bathroom, you notice that all her toiletries seem very organized. Her kitchen is also neatly ordered. The next day, you notice that her classwork is well-organized—arranged neatly in color-coded folders and notebooks. You don't think twice about it until she drops her open backpack and all her stuff falls out, spilling all over the floor. She starts to cry. Based on what you have learned, do you think she has OCD? Why or why not? If she has OCD, is it because she has inherited the disorder? Explain your answer. If she does have OCD, what sorts of treatments should she consider?

Summary of Posttraumatic Stress Disorder

Stress disorders are characterized by three types of persistent symptoms: reexperiencing of the traumatic event avoidance of stimuli related to the event, and increased arousal and anxiety. DSM-IV-TR includes two types of stress disorder: acute stress disorder and posttraumatic stress disorder (PTSD). These two disorders are distinguished in part by the timing and duration of symptoms. The diagnostic criteria for acute stress disorder also include symptoms of dissociation.

An event is considered traumatic if the individual experienced or witnessed an actual or threatened death or serious injury and responded with intense fear, helplessness, or horror. Interpersonal violence is more likely to lead to a stress disorder, as are traumatic events that are severe, of long duration, and of close proximity. The DSM-IV-TR diagnosis of PTSD has been criticized because the definition of traumatic stress is too broad, encompassing normal responses to trauma, and because the symptoms specified in the criteria overlap with those of other disorders.

Brain areas involved in PTSD include parts of the frontal lobe, the hippocampus, the locus coeruleus, and the amygdala—most of these areas are involved in emotion and fear. Patients with PTSD respond unusually to high levels of norepinephrine, have disrupted serotonin function, and produce less cortisol in response to the traumatic event than do people who do not go on to develop a stress disorder.

Psychological factors that exist before a traumatic event contribute to PTSD; these factors include a history of depression or other psychological disorders, a belief in being unable to control stressors, the conviction that the world is a dangerous place, and lower IQ. After a traumatic event, classical and operant conditioning contribute to the avoidance symptoms. Social factors that contribute to PTSD include the stress of low socioeconomic status and a relative lack of social support for the trauma victim.

Medication is the treatment that directly targets neurological factors, specifically an SSRI. Treatments that target psychological factors include CBT. Treatments that target social factors are designed to ensure that the individual is as safe as possible from future trauma, and to increase social support through group therapy or family therapy.

Thinking like a clinician

Two friends, Farah and Michelle, came back from winter break. Each had been devastated by personal experiences that occurred during the break. Farah's house burned down after the boiler exploded; fortunately, everyone was safe. Michelle's house had also been destroyed in a fire, but the police believed it was set by an "enemy" of her father's. Six months pass, and by the time they go home for summer vacation, one of the friends has developed PTSD. Which friend do you think developed PTSD and why (based on what you have read)? What symptoms might she have and why? Based on what you have read, what do you think would be appropriate treatment for her?

Key Terms

Anxiety (p. 248)

Anxious apprehension (p. 249)

Anxiety disorder (p. 249)

Fight-or-flight response (p. 249)

Panic (p. 249)

Phobia (p. 249)

Generalized anxiety disorder (GAD) (p. 252)

Hypervigilance (p. 256)

Panic attack (p. 262)

Panic disorder (p. 263)

Agoraphobia (p. 266)

Concordance rate (p. 269)

In vivo exposure (p. 274)

Interoceptive exposure (p. 274)

Social phobia (p. 278)

Specific phobia (p. 289)

Obsessions (p. 299)

Compulsions (p. 299)

Obsessive-compulsive disorder (OCD) (p. 299)

Posttraumatic stress disorder (PTSD) (p. 314)

Acute stress disorder (p. 314)

More Study Aids

For additional study aids related to this chapter, go to:

www.worthpublishers.com/rosenberg

Dissociative and Somatoform Disorders

Anna O., a well-to-do 21-year-old woman living in Austria in the late 19th century, had been caring for her ill father for weeks. Anna and her mother alternated shifts, Anna taking the night shift, staying awake by his bedside. Her father was dying of tuberculosis, and Anna also began to feel sick. Her symptoms included severe vision problems, headaches, a persistent cough, paralysis (in her neck, right arm, and both legs), lack of sensation in her elbows, and daily periods of a state of consciousness similar to sleep-walking. After her cough developed, Anna was forbidden to take care of her father. Anna was diagnosed with **hysteria**, an emotional condition marked by extreme excitability and bodily symptoms for which there is no medical explanation.

For 2 years, Anna was treated by Dr. Joseph Breuer, a Viennese neurologist. Breuer became a colleague of Sigmund Freud and told Freud about Anna and her treatment, later described in *Studies in Hysteria* (Breuer & Freud, 1895/1955). Prior to Breuer's treatment of Anna, hypnosis was often used to treat hysteria. The physician hypnotized the patient (usually a woman) and then gave her a suggestion that the symptoms would go away. However, for some unknown reason, Breuer did not give Anna any suggestions, although he did hypnotize her. Instead, he asked her about her symptoms, and over time she told him about them. Anna and Breuer often met daily for treatment, sometimes twice a day. Anna's treatment usually involved Breuer's hypnotizing her and then asking her to tell him what she remembered about the origins of her symptoms. At other times, after being hypnotized, she simply told him what was on her mind. Anna referred to this process as the "talking cure." Freud was fascinated by Breuer's account of Anna's illness and her treatment; Breuer's "talking cure" was a precursor to psychoanalysis, and Freud's thoughts about Breuer and Anna led to the beginnings of his psychoanalytic theory (Freeman, 1980; see also Chapters 1 and 4).

Anna was diagnosed with hysteria—a common diagnosis at the time—but this term is a vague label for a condition that includes a wide range of symptoms. Hysteria is not a diagnosis in DSM-IV-TR; instead, DSM-IV-TR classifies symptoms that were once considered manifestations of hysteria as part of the diagnostic criteria for two categories of disorders: dissociative disorders and somatoform disorders. The central feature of *dissociative disorders* is **dissociation**, the separation of mental processes—such as perception, memory and self-awareness—that are normally integrated. Generally, each

Hysteria
An emotional condition marked by extreme excitability and bodily symptoms for which there is no medical explanation; hysteria is not a DSM-IV-TR disorder.

Dissociation
The separation of mental processes—such as perception, memory, and self-awareness—that are normally integrated.

Noma Bliss

Anna O. was diagnosed with hysteria, which is a vague condition that is not in the DSM-IV-TR classification system. Symptoms that were seen as part of hysteria are now generally considered to be symptoms of either dissociative disorders or somatoform disorders.

Amnesia
Memory loss, which is usually temporary but, in rare cases, may be permanent.

Identity problem
A dissociative symptom in which an individual is not sure who he or she is or may assume a new identity.

Derealization
A dissociative symptom in which the external world is perceived or experienced as strange or unreal.

Depersonalization
A dissociative symptom in which the perception or experience of self—either one's body or one's mental processes—is altered to the point of feeling like an observer, as though seeing oneself from the "outside."

individual mental process is not disturbed, but their normal integrated functioning is disturbed. (With schizophrenia, in contrast, it is the mental processes themselves, such as the form or pattern of thoughts, that are disturbed; see Chapter 12.) *Somatoform disorders* are marked by persistent bodily symptoms for which there is no medically identifiable cause. In this chapter we explore dissociative and somatoform disorders—their diagnostic criteria, criticisms of those criteria, the causes of the disorders, and treatments for them.

Dissociative Disorders

Breuer reported that Anna O. was an extremely bright young woman prone to "systematic day-dreaming, which she described as her 'private theatre.'" Anna lived "through fairy tales in her imagination; but she was always on the spot when spoken to, so that no one was aware of it. She pursued this activity almost continuously while she was engaged in her household duties" (Breuer & Freud, 1895/1955, p. 22). These dissociative states, or "absences," began in earnest when Anna became too weak to care for her father, and they became more prominent after his death in April 1881. Let's examine dissociative disorders in more detail, and then consider whether Anna's symptoms would meet the criteria for any of these disorders.

Dissociative Disorders: An Overview

Dissociation may arise suddenly or gradually, and it can be brief or chronic (Steinberg, 1994, 2001). Four types of dissociative symptoms are noted in DSM-IV-TR (American Psychiatric Association, 2000; Steinberg, 1994, 2001):

- **amnesia,** or memory loss, which is usually temporary but, in rare cases, may be permanent;
- **identity problems,** in which an individual isn't sure who he or she is or may assume a new identity;
- **derealization,** in which the external world is perceived or experienced as strange or unreal, and the individual feels "detached from the environment" or as if viewing the world through "invisible filters" or "a big pane of glass" (Simeon et al., 2000); and
- **depersonalization,** in which the perception or experience of self—either one's body or one's mental processes—is altered to the point of feeling like an observer, as though seeing oneself from the "outside," Individuals experiencing depersonalization may describe it as feeling is if "under water" or "floating," "like a dead person," "as if I'm here but not here," "detached from my body," "going through the motions," "like a robot," "emotionless," in a "brain fog," or "like my mind is a blank" (Simeon et al., 2000).

Anna O. appeared to experience derealization. After her father died, she recounted "that the walls of the room seemed to be falling over" (Breuer & Freud, 1895/1955, p. 23). She also reported having trouble recognizing faces and needing to make a deliberate effort to do so: "'this person's nose is such-and-such, his hair is such-and-such, so he must be so-and-so.' All the people she saw seemed like wax figures without any connection with her" (Breuer & Freud, 1895/1955, p. 26).

Normal Versus Abnormal Dissociation

Before you start worrying about whether you might have a dissociative disorder, you may be relieved to learn that experiencing symptoms of dissociation is not necessarily abnormal; occasional dissociating is a part of everyday life (Seedat, Stein, & Forde, 2003). For instance, you may find yourself in a class, but not remember walking to the classroom. Or, on hearing bad news, you may feel detached from yourself, as if you're watching yourself from the outside.

In some cases, periods of dissociation are part of religious or cultural rituals (Boddy, 1992). Consider the phenomenon of *possession trance* observed in some societies: During a hypnotic trance, a kind of spirit is believed to assume control of the person's body. Later, the person has amnesia for the experience. At first glance, possession trance may seem to be a psychotic experience (delusions of spirits taking over a body), but closer examination reveals that the "possessed" person doesn't exhibit any evidence of psychosis after the trance is over.

In some instances, dissociative experiences do indicate a disorder, but not necessarily a *dissociative* disorder; other psychiatric disorders can involve dissociative symptoms, such as when depersonalization or derealization occurs during a panic attack. DSM-IV-TR reserves the category of **dissociative disorders** for cases in which perception, consciousness, memory, or identity are dissociated to the point where the symptoms are pervasive, cause significant distress, and interfere with daily functioning. Research findings suggest that pathological dissociation is qualitatively different, not simply quantitatively different, from everyday types of dissociation, such as "spacing out" (Seedat, Stein, & Forde, 2003).

Only about 2% of the U.S. population reports having experienced dissociation to the extent that would be considered abnormal (Seedat, Stein, & Forde, 2003). Surveys indicate that 4–29% of individuals who have some other type of DSM-IV-TR diagnosis may also have a dissociative disorder (Coons, 1998; Foote et al., 2006; Johnson et al., 2006; Maaranen et al., 2005).

Anna's dissociative symptoms appear to have been abnormal; she had dissociations in perception, consciousness, memory, and identity:

> Two entirely distinct states of consciousness were present which alternated very frequently and without warning and which became more and more differentiated in the course of the illness. In one of these states she recognized her surroundings; she was melancholy and anxious, but relatively normal. In the other state she hallucinated and was "naughty"—that is to say, she was abusive, used to throw the cushions at people, . . . tore buttons off her bedclothes and linen with those of her fingers which she could move, and so on. At this stage of her illness if something had been moved in the room or someone had entered or left it [during her other state of consciousness] she would complain of having "lost" some time and would remark upon the gap in her train of conscious thoughts.
>
>   These "absences" had already been observed before she took to her bed; she [would] stop in the middle of a sentence, repeat her last words and after a short pause go on talking. These interruptions gradually increased till they reached the dimensions that have just been described. . . . At the moments when her mind was quite clear she would complain of the profound darkness in her head, of not being able to think, . . . of having two selves, a real one and an evil one which forced her to behave badly, and so on.
>
> (Breuer & Freud, 1895/1955, p. 24)

Anna's dissociative experiences were clearly beyond normal ones—they were pervasive and interfered with her daily functioning.

Cultural Variations in Pathological Dissociation

People in different cultures may express dissociative symptoms differently. For example, *latah*, experienced by people—mostly women—in Indonesia and Malaysia (Bartholomew, 1994), involves fleeting episodes in which the individual uses profanity and experiences amnesia and trancelike states.

Dissociative experiences have also varied across eras. Symptoms of hysteria were common among middle- and upper-class women of the Victorian era, the period in which Anna O. lived. Women of that time and social class led severely limited lives: They were expected to marry, have children, and run the home; they were allowed to pursue only a restricted range of other activities. Some researchers hypothesize that the hysterical symptoms of Victorian women like Anna who wanted a different life were one of the few means of social protest they could employ (Kimball, 2000). As we consider each type of dissociative disorder listed in DSM-IV-TR, we'll consider whether Anna's dissociative symptoms fit the contemporary diagnoses.

Types of Dissociative Disorders

DSM-IV-TR defines four types of dissociative disorders, described in the following sections: *dissociative amnesia, dissociative fugue, depersonalization disorder,*

Dissociative disorders
A category of psychological disorders in which perception, consciousness, memory, or identity are dissociated to the point where the symptoms are pervasive, cause significant distress, and interfere with daily functioning.

Dissociative amnesia
A dissociative disorder in which the sufferer has significantly impaired memory for important experiences or personal information that cannot be explained by ordinary forgetfulness.

JEWEL SAMAD/AFP/Getty Images

Soldiers with dissociative amnesia may forget combat experiences that were particularly troubling or traumatic. This soldier is attending a memorial service in Iraq for three of his comrades who were killed in a convoy attack.

and *dissociative identity disorder*. People whose symptoms do not fit neatly into the criteria of one of these disorders may be diagnosed with *dissociative disorder not otherwise specified* (DDNOS). Someone who has some, but not all, of the symptoms required for a diagnosis of one of the dissociative disorders, but whose functioning is nonetheless impaired because of those symptoms, will be diagnosed with DDNOS. The prevalence rate for DDNOS approaches those for the other dissociative disorders (Lipsanen et al., 2004), which means that as many people are diagnosed with DDNOS as are diagnosed with any of the other dissociative disorders.

The relatively high prevalence of DDNOS compared to the other four dissociative disorders suggests that the criteria for these four disorders may not adequately represent the underlying phenomena. That is, the diagnostic criteria for each of the dissociative disorders may be too narrow or strict, and thus the symptoms of some patients with significant dissociation don't "fit" the criteria neatly.

Dissociative Amnesia

Anna's native language was German, but as her condition began to worsen while she was nursing her father, she started to speak only English (a language in which she was also fluent). She developed complete amnesia for speaking the German language. Let's examine why her amnesia for speaking in her native language might be considered dissociative.

What Is Dissociative Amnesia?

Dissociative amnesia is a dissociative disorder in which the sufferer has significantly impaired memory for important experiences or personal information that cannot be explained by ordinary forgetfulness (see Table 8.1). The experiences or information typically involve traumatic or stressful events, such as occasions when the patient has been violent or tried to hurt herself or himself; the amnesia can come on suddenly. For example, soon after a bloody and dangerous battlefield situation, a soldier may not be able to remember what happened. To qualify as dissociative amnesia, the memory problem cannot be explained better by another psychological disorder, a medical disorder, or substance use; as with all dissociative disorders, it must also significantly impair functioning or cause distress (American Psychiatric Association, 2000). In Anna's case, her amnesia for speaking German could not really be considered as the loss of personal information, but conceivably could be construed as the loss of an important experience and couldn't be better explained by another disorder—and her father's illness and declining health had been extremely stressful for her. In this case—the forgotten material (how to speak German) is not directly related to the stressful event— her father's declining health. Nonetheless, her memory problems appear to be best explained as dissociative amnesia.

The memory problems in dissociative amnesia can take any of several forms:

- *Generalized amnesia*, in which the individual can't remember his or her entire life. Although common in television shows, this type of amnesia is, in fact, extremely rare.

- *Selective amnesia*, in which the individual can remember some of what happened in an otherwise forgotten period of time. For instance, a soldier may forget about a particularly traumatic battlefield skirmish, but remember what he and another person spoke about between phases of this skirmish.

- *Localized amnesia*, in which the individual has a memory gap for a specific period of time, often a period of time just prior to the stressful event, as occurred with Mrs. Y in Case 8.1.

Additional facts about dissociative amnesia are listed in Table 8.2.

Table 8.1 ▶ DSM-IV-TR Diagnostic Criteria for Dissociative Amnesia

A. The predominant disturbance is one or more episodes of inability to recall important personal information, usually of a traumatic or stressful nature, that is too extensive to be explained by ordinary forgetfulness.

B. The disturbance does not occur exclusively during the course of Dissociative Identity Disorder, Dissociative Fugue [both discussed later in this chapter], Posttraumatic Stress Disorder, Acute Stress Disorder [both in Chapter 7], or Somatization Disorder [discussed later in this chapter] and is not due to the direct physiological effects of a substance (e.g., a drug of abuse, a medication) or a neurological or other general medical condition (e.g., Amnestic Disorder Due to Head Trauma [discussed in Chapter 15]).

C. The symptoms cause clinically significant distress or impairment in social, occupational, or other important areas of functioning.

Source: R. Mayou and A. Farmer (2002) Functional somatic symptoms and syndromes. *British Medical Journal* 325, 265–268, Copyright 2002. For more information see the Permissions section.

CASE 8.1 ▸ FROM THE OUTSIDE: Dissociative Amnesia

Mrs. Y, a 51-year-old married woman . . . had a two-year history of severe depressive episodes with suicidal ideation, and reported total loss of memory for 12 years of her life . . . from the age of 37 to 49. [The amnesia began at age 49 when] she had had a car accident from which she sustained a very minor injury, but no loss of consciousness [nor any] posttraumatic stress symptoms. . . . She remembered what happened in the accident, and immediately preceding it, but suddenly had total loss of memory for the previous 12 years.

Mrs. Y had no problems recalling events which had occurred since the accident. She also had good autobiographical memory for her life events up to the age of 37.

Her parents and her grown-up children had told her that the . . . 12 years were painful for her. They would not tell her why, as they thought it would distress her even more. She was not only amnesic for these reputedly painful events, [but was unable] to recognize any of the friends she had made during that time. This included her present man friend, who was the passenger in her car at the time of the accident. Her family had told Mrs. Y that this gentleman (Mr. C) had been courting her for six years prior to the accident.

(Adapted from Degun-Mather, 2002, pp. 34–35)

Some people may spontaneously remember the forgotten experiences or information, particularly if their amnesia developed in response to a traumatic event and they leave the traumatic situation behind, as when a soldier with localized amnesia in response to combat leaves the battlefield. Anna O. recovered her ability to speak German at the end of her treatment with Dr. Breuer, after she reenacted a traumatic nightmare that she'd had when at her father's sickbed (and that marked the start of her problems).

Understanding Dissociative Amnesia

The following sections apply the neuropsychosocial approach as a framework for understanding the nature of dissociative amnesia. Unfortunately, because the disorder is so rare, not much is known about either the specific factors that give rise to it or how those factors might influence each other. In examining what is known or hypothesized about the origins of this disorder, we'll begin with neurological factors and focus on the possible role of the hippocampus (a brain structure that is crucial for storing new information in memory) and then consider the possible role of hormones. Next, we'll consider psychological factors, specifically the effects of traumatic events and the nature of dissociation itself. Finally, we'll turn to social factors and explore the possible role of abuse.

Neurological Factors: Brain Trauma?

Neurological factors are clearly involved in cases of amnesia that arise following brain injury, such as that suffered in a car accident (Piper & Merskey, 2004a). However, when amnesia follows brain injury, it is not considered to be *dissociative* amnesia. Neurological factors that may contribute to dissociative amnesia are less clear-cut, as we'll see.

Brain Systems Some researchers have suggested that dissociative amnesia may result in part from damage to the hippocampus, which is critically involved in storing new information about events in memory. These researchers assume that periods of prolonged stress affect the hippocampus so that it does not operate well when the person is highly aroused (Joseph, 1999). The arousal—which typically accompanies a traumatic event—will impair the ability to store new information about that event. Later, this process would lead to the symptoms of dissociative amnesia for that event.

However, the idea that damage to the hippocampus underlies dissociative amnesia cannot explain all cases of the disorder. Because such damage would prevent information from being stored in the first place, the subsequent amnesia would not be reversible: There would be no way to retrieve the memories later because the memories would not exist (Allen, Console, & Lewis, 1999). That is, the

Table 8.2 ▸ Dissociative Amnesia Facts at a Glance

Prevalence

- Dissociative amnesia is rare, and its prevalence is unknown.

Comorbidity

- Depression, anxiety, and substance-related disorders may be present along with dissociative amnesia. (Note: If the amnesia is a result of substance use, dissociative amnesia will not be the diagnosis.)

Onset

- Children or adults can develop this disorder.

Course

- Patients may have one or multiple episodes of amnesia.

Gender Differences

- No gender differences in the prevalence of dissociative amnesia have been reported.

Cultural Differences

- Dissociative amnesia may be a culture-related diagnosis; there are no reported cases of this disorder (due to a traumatic event by itself, in the absence of brain damage resulting from the trauma) prior to 1800 (Pope et al., 2007).

Source: Unless otherwise noted, the source is American Psychiatric Association, 2000. For more information see the Permissions section.

hippocampus is a critical gate-keeper of memory; without it, new information about facts cannot be stored. If damage to the hippocampus prevents new information from being stored, then such information is not available for later retrieval (even if the hippocampus itself recovers). Given that many cases of dissociative amnesia are characterized by "recovered" memories, it is not clear what brain systems would be involved.

Neural Communication How might the hippocampus get damaged, which then could lead to some cases of dissociative amnesia? Hormones could be the culprit. As discussed in Chapter 2, our adrenal glands respond to stress by producing the hormone cortisol. This hormone plays an important role in the fight-or-flight response, by allowing the body to use stored energy more efficiently; however, there are unfortunate consequences if too much cortisol is released for too long a period. Specifically, many researchers have shown in both monkeys and humans that excessive cortisol can reduce the size of the hippocampus (Bremner et al., 1995; Sapolsky, 1996, 1997).

However, as intriguing as this idea is, there is as yet no good evidence that such hippocampal damage has occurred in all patients with dissociative amnesia; further, as noted above, such damage would prevent memories from being stored, and thus reversible amnesia should not occur (but, at least in some cases, it does). Thus, it is unlikely that too much cortisol is in fact responsible for all cases of dissociative amnesia.

Psychological Factors: Disconnected Mental Processes

Researchers have focused on two theories of how cognitive disturbances—especially amnesia—arise with dissociative disorders: *dissociation theory* and *neodissociation theory*. Both theories focus on how dissociation can arise in response to traumatic experiences—specifically, how the normal processes of memory and its relation to other cognitive processes might be disrupted. Although neither theory can completely explain the phenomenon of dissociative amnesia, both offer some insight—and hence are worth considering. Let's examine these two theories.

Dissociation Theory The earliest theory of the origins of dissociative amnesia was dubbed the *dissociation theory* (Janet, 1907). From our perspective today, the dissociation theory appears poorly named, because it is the dissociation itself that must be explained by any theory; a more descriptive name like "arousal disruption theory" would seem more appropriate. Dissociation theory posits that very strong emotions (as occur in response to a traumatic stressor) narrow the focus of attention and also disorganize cognitive processes, which prevent them from being integrated normally. According to this theory, the poorly integrated cognitive processes allow memory to be dissociated from other aspects of cognitive functioning, leading to dissociative amnesia.

However, this theory does not specify whether the dissociation somehow blocks or alters information processing or only interferes with later retrieval of the information from memory (Guralnick, Schmeidler, & Simeon, 2000). At best the theory provides only a broad explanation for dissociative amnesia; it does not outline specific mechanisms to account for the dissociation and possible later reintegration of memory.

Neodissociation Theory In contrast, *neodissociation theory* (Hilgard, 1994; Woody & Bowers, 1994) proposes that an "executive monitoring system" normally coordinates various cognitive systems, much like a chief executive officer coordinates the various departments of a large company. However, in some circumstances (such as while a person is experiencing a traumatic event) the various cognitive systems can operate independently of the executive monitoring system. When this occurs, the executive system no longer has access to the information stored or processed by the separate cognitive systems. Memory thus operates as an independent cognitive system, and an "amnestic barrier" arises between memory and the executive system. This barrier causes the information in memory to be cut off from conscious awareness—that is, dissociated.

Although aspects of both dissociation and neodissociation theories have received some support from research (Green & Lynn, 1995; Hilgard, 1994; Kirsch & Lynn, 1998), neither theory explains the specific mechanisms involved in the dissociation or reintegration of memories.

Social Factors: Indirect Effects

Many traumatic events are social in nature, such as combat and abuse. These kinds of social traumas are likely to contribute to dissociative disorders, particularly dissociative amnesia. In fact, people with a dissociative disorder report childhood physical or sexual abuse almost three times more often than do people without a dissociative disorder (Foote et al., 2006). However, some researchers point out that traumatic events can also induce anxiety, which can lead people to have dissociative symptoms. Thus, traumatic events may not *directly* cause dissociative symptoms such as amnesia; rather such events may indirectly lead to such symptoms by triggering anxiety (Cardeña & Spiegel, 1993; Kihlstrom, 2001).

As noted in Table 8.2, some researchers propose that dissociative amnesia is a disorder of modern times, because there are no written accounts of its occurring before 1800 in any culture (Pope et al., 2007).

In sum, dissociative amnesia in the absence of physical trauma to the brain is extremely rare, which makes research on etiology and treatment similarly rare. Although researchers have proposed theories about why and how dissociative amnesia arises, these theories address dissociation generally; dissociative amnesia as a disorder is not well understood. These same deficiencies—a paucity of research and broad theories that do not adequately characterize the specific mechanisms—also limit our understanding of the other dissociative disorders.

Dissociative Fugue

The key features of **dissociative fugue** are sudden, unplanned travel and difficulty remembering the past. This combination can lead sufferers to be confused about who they are and sometimes to take on a new identity.

What Is Dissociative Fugue?

A person with dissociative fugue can have an episode that lasts anywhere from a few hours to weeks or even months. During a fugue state, an individual generally seems to function normally. Once the fugue state has subsided, however, the individual may not be able to remember what occurred during it (American Psychiatric Association, 2000). Table 8.3 lists the DSM-IV-TR diagnostic criteria for dissociative fugue. Table 8.4 provides more facts about this disorder, and Case 8.2 describes Joe, who had symptoms of dissociative fugue.

Table 8.3 ▶ DSM-IV-TR Diagnostic Criteria for Dissociative Fugue
A. The predominant disturbance is sudden, unexpected travel away from home or one's customary place of work, with inability to recall one's past.
B. Confusion about personal identity or assumption of a new identity (partial or complete).
C. The disturbance does not occur exclusively during the course of Dissociative Identity Disorder [discussed later in the chapter] and is not due to the direct physiological effects of a substance (e.g., a drug of abuse, a medication) or a general medical condition (e.g., temporal lobe epilepsy).
D. The symptoms cause clinically significant distress or impairment in social, occupational, or other important areas of functioning.

Source: Reprinted with permission from the Diagnostic and Statistical Manual of Mental Disorders, Text Revision, Fourth Edition, (Copyright 2000) American Psychiatric Association.

Dissociative fugue
A dissociative disorder that involves sudden, unplanned travel and difficulty remembering the past, which can lead patients to be confused about who they are and sometimes to take on a new identity.

Table 8.4 ▸ Dissociative Fugue Facts at a Glance

Prevalence

- This disorder is rare, occurring in approximately 0.2% of Americans. However, the prevalence may increase after widespread traumatic events such as natural disasters or wars.

Comorbidity

- People with dissociative fugue may also have a mood disorder, posttraumatic stress disorder (PTSD), or a substance-related disorder.

Onset

- The fugue state begins after a traumatic or overwhelming event, although it is not known how much time typically passes between the event and the onset of the fugue state.

Course

- Patients usually experience only a single episode, in response to high levels of stress, and recover quickly; however, some people may continue to have amnesia for events that transpired during the fugue state.
- Very little is known about the process by which people recover from dissociative fugue (Kihlstrom, 2001).

Gender Differences

- There does not appear to be any consistent gender difference in the prevalence of dissociative fugue.

Cultural Differences

- Dissociative fugue is not observed worldwide. Syndromes that are similar occur in some cultures, but these syndromes involve running or fleeing and different kinds of memory problems.

Source: Unless otherwise noted, the source is American Psychiatric Association, 2000.

CASE 8.2 ▸ FROM THE OUTSIDE: Dissociative Fugue

"Joe" went to work at his usual time [Monday morning, and on Tuesday night he] wandered into a K-Mart 150 miles from home and said, "Could you please help me? I don't know who I am or how I got here. Would you call the police for me?"

The police took his truck keys and located his truck. They discovered his identity, took him to the emergency room, and called his hometown where his wife had reported him missing. When he returned, he did not recognize his home, his wife, or his children. . . .

He described returning to his home and his wife as a déjà vu experience. He felt he had seen this woman before, but he couldn't quite place her. At work he did not recognize any of his coworkers. When he read papers that he had written, he indicated that he could understand about 10% of the material. He had some "vague recollection that it was familiar."

(Jasper, 2003, pp. 311, 313)

Joe's medical tests were negative, which ruled out a physical cause for his memory problems. He received treatment using hypnosis, and over time he remembered his life and the events that led up to his fugue state: He had become extremely angry at his boss and threatened to harm him physically, then ran out of the office. Apparently, the level of his anger and capacity for violence frightened Joe so much that he went into a fugue state.

An important fact about dissociative fugue, as noted in Table 8.4, is that it does not arise in all cultures. This simple observation implies a larger role for social factors than occurs for many other psychological disorders. For example, in some cultures, instead of the DSM-IV-TR diagnosis of dissociative fugue, people can develop a *running syndrome*. Although this condition has some symptoms that are similar to those of dissociative fugue, it typically involves a sudden onset of a trancelike state and dangerous behavior such as running or fleeing, which leads to exhaustion, sleep, and subsequent amnesia for the experience. Running syndromes include (American Psychiatric Association, 2000):

- *pibloktoq* among native Arctic people,
- *grisi siknis* among the Miskito of Nicaragua and Honduras, and
- *amok* in Western Pacific cultures.

These syndromes have in common with dissociative fugue part of Criterion A (Table 8.3)—unexpected travel—but the amnesia occurs after the running episode is over, so the individual doesn't remember that it happened. In contrast, with dissociative fugue, the memory problem arises during the fugue state, and the individual can't remember his or her past. In addition, Criteria B, C, and D for dissociative fugue do not necessarily apply to running syndromes.

Some cultures have syndromes that are similar to dissociative fugue, such as *grisi siknis*, which shares with dissociative fugue a sudden flight from home and problems with memory. This photo shows local healers of an indigenous Miskito community in Nicaragua treating people with grisi siknis.

EFE/Oscar Navarrete

Understanding Dissociative Fugue

In the following sections we describe the research findings related to dissociative fugue, focusing on the possible role of the frontal lobes, the relationship between the disorder and hypnotizability, and the role of traumatic events.

Neurological Factors

The findings from several studies suggest that frontal lobe problems may underlie dissociative fugue. In one study, Markowitsch and colleagues (1997) asked a patient with dissociative fugue and normal controls to recall aspects of their lives while their brains were being scanned. The patient's brain was not as strongly activated in the frontal and temporal regions as the control participants' brains were. Moreover, the right hemisphere was strongly activated in the control participants, but not in the patient. The right hemisphere is known to play a special role in the retrieval of autobiographical memories (Costello et al., 1998).

In another study (Glisky et al., 2004), researchers described a patient who lost not only his memory about his past but also his memory of German, which was his native language. This patient performed poorly on neuropsychological tests that assess frontal lobe function (such as the ability to organize behavior and inhibit responses). Moreover, as fMRI scans revealed, the frontal and parietal lobes of this patient were not as strongly activated as those of normal control participants when he judged whether letters formed words. The low activation in this patient's frontal lobes was particularly striking when he was asked to evaluate German words, which he claimed he could not do. In sharp contrast, when normal bilingual participants (who spoke German) were asked to pretend that they did not speak German when evaluating these words, they exhibited large amounts of activation in the frontal lobes—which shows that they worked hard to suppress their knowledge. Apparently, the patient wasn't simply pretending to have forgotten German, but actually had lost his memory.

The reduced activation in the frontal lobes of patients with dissociative fugue might be a result of high levels of stress-related hormones (Markowitsch, 1999), which could selectively affect processes that are involved in coordinating voluntary actions and mental events—including memory retrieval (Kopelman, 2002).

Psychological Factors: Related to Hypnotizability?

People who have had dissociative fugue are often more hypnotizable than the general population and may have a greater ability to dissociate (American Psychiatric Association, 2000). There are three possible implications of this relationship:

1. being more hypnotizable makes people more vulnerable to dissociative fugue after experiencing stress;

2. having experienced a fugue state, people became more hypnotizable and possibly more able to dissociate; or

3. dissociative fugue and hypnotizability are not directly related to each other; they are correlated, but their relationship is due to a third, unknown variable (for example, and purely hypothetically, a neurological condition that affects the frontal lobe).

Researchers have yet to begin to sort out the nature of this relationship, which is especially challenging because so few cases of the disorder are available to study.

Social Factors: Combat Stress

Dissociative fugue generally occurs in response to significant stressors that involve social factors, such as combat (American Psychiatric Association, 2000). That is, someone experiencing a dissociative fugue probably experienced a traumatic event beforehand. As with dissociative amnesia, the specific mechanism by which the traumatic event induces the fugue state is not clear.

To determine whether dissociative fugue is a phenomenon limited to Western cultures, one team of researchers attempted to discover whether the DSM-IV-TR definition of dissociative fugue applied to people in Uganda; in fact, it did not (van Dujil, Cardena, & de Jong, 2005). However, some symptoms of dissociative fugue overlapped with symptoms of possession trance and of other phenomena in the local culture, such as memory problems or temporarily assuming a new identity.

In sum, like dissociative amnesia, dissociative fugue is rare and poorly understood. Although there are clues as to possible factors that contribute to the disorder, the specific roles these factors may play and how they might influence each other are not known.

Depersonalization Disorder

Like many people, you may have experienced depersonalization. This does not mean that you have depersonalization disorder. A *persistent* feeling of being detached from one's mental processes or body is the key symptom of **depersonalization disorder**. Although the primary symptom is depersonalization, people who have this disorder may also experience derealization.

What Is Depersonalization Disorder?

People afflicted with depersonalization disorder may *feel* "detached from my body" or "like a robot," but they do not *believe* that they are truly detached or actually a robot. They still recognize reality. (In contrast, people who have a psychotic disorder may feel and believe such things; see Chapter 12.) In addition, people with depersonalization disorder may not react emotionally to events; they may feel that they don't control their behavior and are just being swept along by what is happening around them. Table 8.5 presents the DSM-IV-TR diagnostic criteria; symptoms meet the criteria for the disorder only when they occur independently of anxiety symptoms and they impair functioning or cause significant distress.

Some researchers point out that symptoms of depersonalization have much in common with symptoms of certain anxiety disorders (see Chapter 7)—a sense of being numb or detached, dizziness or faintness, and a tendency to avoid stimuli associated with increased anxiety (Hunter et al., 2003). Moreover, panic attacks can include depersonalization and derealization, and people with depersonalization disorder often have a comorbid anxiety disorder, which can make accurate diagnosis difficult. Typically, it is the comorbid anxiety symptoms, rather than the dissociative symptoms themselves, that lead individuals with depersonalization disorder to seek help. Table 8.6 provides more facts about depersonalization disorder.

Understanding Depersonalization Disorder

Researchers are beginning to chart the neurological factors that contribute to depersonalization disorder. Unfortunately, less is known about possible psychological or social factors, perhaps because the disorder is relatively rare. Let's examine what is known and how the different types of factors might influence one another.

Depersonalization disorder
A dissociative disorder whose primary symptom is a persistent feeling of being detached from one's mental processes or body, although people who have this disorder may also experience derealization.

Table 8.5 ▸ DSM-IV-TR Diagnostic Criteria for Depersonalization Disorder

A. Persistent or recurrent experiences of feeling detached from, and as if one is an outside observer of, one's mental processes or body (e.g., feeling like one is in a dream).

B. During the depersonalization experience, reality testing remains intact.

C. The depersonalization causes clinically significant distress or impairment in social, occupational, or other important areas of functioning.

D. The depersonalization experience does not occur exclusively during the course of another mental disorder, such as Schizophrenia [discussed in Chapter 12], Panic Disorder [Chapter 7], Acute Stress Disorder [Chapter 7], or another Dissociative Disorder [discussed later in this chapter], and is not due to the direct physiological effects of a substance (e.g., a drug of abuse, a medication) or a general medical condition (e.g., temporal lobe epilepsy).

Source: Reprinted with permission from the Diagnostic and Statistical Manual of Mental Disorders, Text Revision, Fourth Edition, (Copyright 2000) American Psychiatric Association.

Neurological Factors

As we'll see in the following sections, studies have addressed changes in brain systems and neural communication in people who have this disorder.

Brain Systems One PET study of patients with depersonalization disorder found unusual levels of activation (either too high or too low) in parts of the brain specifically involved in various phases of perception (Simeon et al., 2000). More specifically, the study found lower than normal activity in parts of the temporal lobe that are involved in visual and auditory recognition and higher than normal activity in parts of the parietal lobe, which is involved in orienting a person in space and representing the body. The researchers noted that these findings are consistent with the idea that depersonalization disorder involves dissociations in perception.

Researchers have investigated whether depersonalization disorder also involves abnormal emotional responses (Phillips & Sierra, 2003). Specifically, in one study, researchers scanned the brains of patients with this disorder and the brains of matched controls while participants viewed pictures of neutral or aversive scenes. The researchers found that the aversive stimuli produced less activation in brain regions involved in emotional reactions (specifically, disgust) in the patients than in the controls. However, the aversive pictures had the opposite effect on part of the right frontal lobe in the patients, causing it to be unusually activated; this area is involved in regulating emotion. The findings may suggest that patients with depersonalization disorder regulate their emotions more strongly than normal—which may be why they have weaker than normal emotional reactions (Phillips et al., 2001).

Other studies converge in providing evidence that depersonalization disorder arises, at least in part, from disruptions of emotional processing (Sierra et al., 2002). For example, when patients with this disorder viewed faces with highly emotional expressions, activity in the limbic system decreased—and this occurred in response to both very happy and very sad expressions (Lemche et al., 2007). This study also showed that the patients had unusually high levels of activity in the frontal lobes when viewing such facial expressions. This is important, because if the frontal lobes can suppress emotional responses, the result might be the sense of emotional detachment that such patients report. Such an effect might also explain why brain areas involved in emotion are not activated when patients with depersonalization disorder try to remember words that name emotions, whereas these brain areas are activated when normal control participants perform this task (Medford et al., 2006).

Neural Communication Patients with depersonalization disorder do not produce normal amounts of norepinephrine. In fact, the more strongly they exhibit symptoms of the disorder, the less norepinephrine they apparently produce (as measured in their urine; Simeon, Guralnick, et al., 2003). Norepinepherine is associated with activity of the autonomic nervous system, and thus this finding is consistent with the idea that these patients have blunted responses to emotion.

Table 8.6 ▶ Depersonalization Disorder Facts at a Glance

Prevalence

- The prevalence of depersonalization disorder is unknown, but thought to be extremely low.

Comorbidity

- People with depersonalization disorder may also have symptoms of anxiety (Bremner et al., 1998; Marshall et al., 2000; Segui et al., 2000). In one sample of 204 people with depersonalization disorder, almost three quarters had had an anxiety disorder (Baker et al., 2003).
- Other comorbid symptoms include depression, bodily concerns, and obsessive rumination.

Onset

- The average age of onset of depersonalization disorder is 16 years old.
- Episodes of depersonalization can be triggered by a wide range of events, including trauma, extreme stress, depression, panic, and the ingestion of a psychoactive drug such as marijuana or alcohol (Raimo et al., 1999; Simeon, Knutelska, et al., 2003).

Course

- Episodes of depersonalization can last from seconds to years.

Gender Differences

- Twice as many women as men are diagnosed with this disorder.

Source: Unless otherwise noted, the source is American Psychiatric Association, 2000.

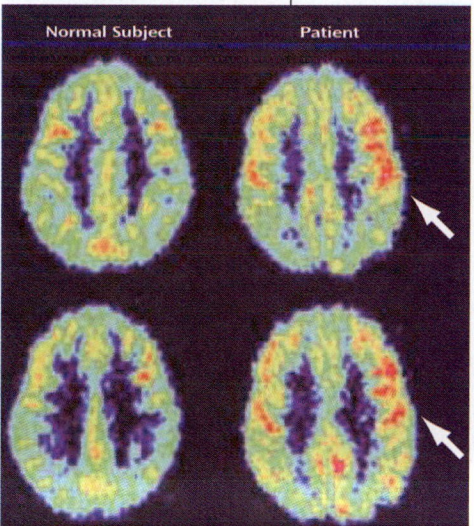

Daphne Simeon, M.D., et al., American Journal of Psychiatry 157:11782–1788, November 2000. © 2000 American Psychiatric Association

PET scans of the brain of a healthy person (left) and of the brain of a patient with depersonalization disorder (right). Note the increased activity in the parietal lobes of the patient; this part of the brain is involved in orienting a person in space and in representing the body.

Psychological Factors: Cognitive Deficits

Patients with depersonalization disorder have cognitive deficits that range from problems with short-term memory to impaired spatial reasoning, but the root cause of these difficulties appears to lie with attention: These patients cannot easily focus and sustain their attention (Guralnik et al., 2000, 2007). This is consistent with neuroimaging studies that reveal decreased activity in parts of the brain that register input from the senses. However, it is not clear whether the attentional problems are a cause or an effect of the disorder: On one hand, if a person is feeling disconnected from the world, he or she would not pay normal attention to objects and events; on the other hand, if a person had such attentional problems, this could contribute to feeling disconnected from the world. Moreover, given that many patients with depersonalization disorder also have depression or an anxiety disorder (Baker et al., 2003), it is not clear whether the problems with attention are specifically related to depersonalization disorder or arise from the comorbid disorder.

Social Factors: Childhood Emotional Abuse

We noted earlier that stressful events (often social in nature) can trigger depersonalization disorder. Moreover, a particular type of social stressor—severe and chronic emotional abuse experienced during childhood—seems to play a particularly important role in triggering depersonalization disorder (Simeon et al., 2001), although it is not clear why such abuse might lead to depersonalization disorder only in some cases. Once the disorder develops, factors such as negative mood, stress, the perception of threatening social interactions, and new environments can exacerbate its symptoms (Simeon, Knuteska, et al., 2003). For instance, if Mr. E in Case 8.3 had a fight with a friend, his depersonalization symptoms would probably become worse during the fight.

CASE **8.3** ▶ FROM THE OUTSIDE: Depersonalization Disorder

[Mr. E] was a 29-year-old, single man, employed as a journalist, who reported a 12-year history of depersonalization disorder. He described feeling detached from the world as though he was living "inside a bubble" and found it difficult to concentrate since he felt as though his brain had been "switched off." His body no longer felt solid and he could not feel himself walking on the ground. The world appeared two-dimensional and he reported his sense of direction and spatial awareness to be impaired. He described himself as having lost his "sense of himself" and felt that he was acting on "auto-pilot." He also reported symptoms of depression and some symptoms of OCD, which took the form of counting and stepping on cracks in the pavement, although he did not report the latter as a problem.

Prior to the onset of his [depersonalization disorder], he experienced transient [depersonalization] symptoms when intoxicated with cannabis. At the age of 17, he started at a new school and felt very anxious and experienced [depersonalization] symptoms when not under the influence of cannabis. He described the first time this happened as "terrifying" since he felt he had "gone into another world." He reported difficulty with breathing and believed he may have a brain tumor or that his "brain was traumatized into a state of panic." From the age of 17 to 19, the episodes of [depersonalization] became more frequent until they became constantly present. He reports the symptoms as "enormously restricting" his life in that he felt frustrated since he has been "unable to express or enjoy myself."

(Hunter et al., 2003, Appendix A, pp. 1462–1463)

FEEDBACK LOOPS IN ACTION: Depersonalization Disorder

One hypothesis for explaining depersonalization disorder is as follows: First, a significant stressor (often a social factor) elicits neurological events (largely in the frontal lobes) that suppress the normal emotional responses (Hunter et al., 2003; Sierra & Berrios, 1998; Simeon, Knutelska, et al., 2003). Following this, the disconnection between the intensity of the perceived stress and the lack of arousal may lead these patients to feel "unreal," which they may then attribute (a psychological factor) to being mentally ill (Baker et al., 2007; Hunter et al., 2003). And, in turn, the incorrect and catastrophic attributions that the patients make about their symptoms can lead to further anxiety (as occurs with panic disorder). The attributions can also lead to further depersonalization or derealization symptoms. Patients then become extremely sensitive to and hypervigilant for possible symptoms of "unreality" and come to fear that the symptoms indicate that they are going "round the bend." They may also avoid situations likely to elicit the symptoms.

Why might some people be more likely to interpret depersonalization symptoms as indicating that they are veering toward insanity? Perhaps because they had a family member with a major mental illness (social factor) (Hunter et al., 2003): When these people experience symptoms of depersonalization or derealization, rather than attributing such symptoms to external events, as normal responses to a stressor, they view the symptoms as confirming their mental illness. Figure 8.1 illustrates the three types of factors that arise in depersonalization disorder and their feedback loops.

Figure 8.1

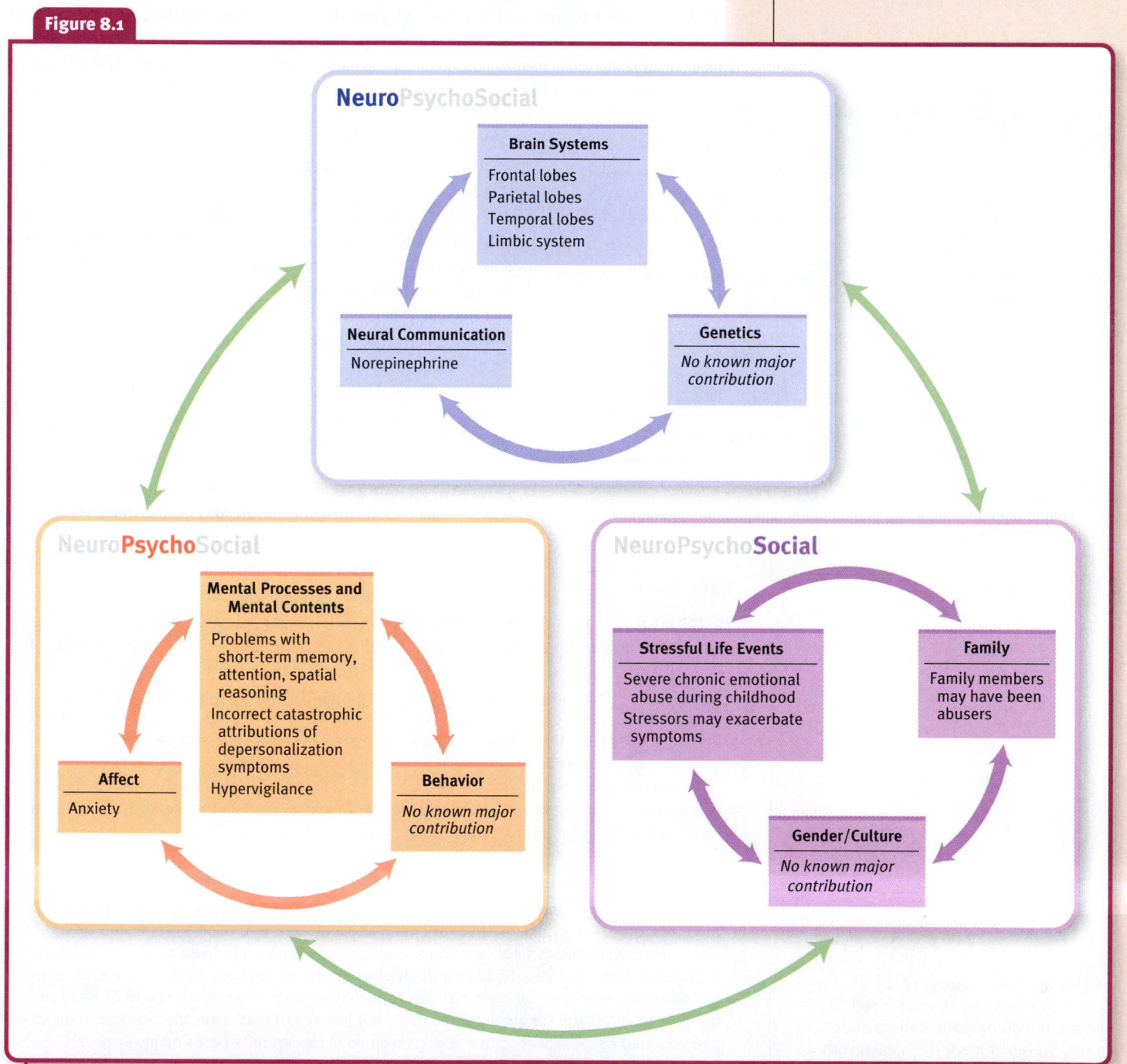

8.1 ▸ Feedback Loops in Action: Depersonalization Disorder

Dissociative Identity Disorder

Dissociative identity disorder, once known as *multiple personality disorder*, may be the most controversial of all DSM-IV-TR disorders. First we examine what dissociative identity disorder is, then some criticisms of the DSM-IV-TR diagnostic criteria, and then factors that may contribute to the disorder. In the process of examining these factors, we delve into the controversy about the disorder.

What Is Dissociative Identity Disorder?

The central feature of **dissociative identity disorder** (DID) is the presence of two or more distinct *alters* (personality states or identities), each with its own characteristics and history, that take turns controlling the person's behavior. For example, a person with this disorder might have an "adult" alter that is very responsible, thoughtful and considerate and a "child" alter that is irresponsible, impulsive and obnoxious. Each alter can have its own name, mannerisms, speaking style, and vocal pitch that distinguish it from other alters. Some alters report being unaware of the existence of other alters, and thus they experience amnesia (because the memory gaps are longer than ordinary forgetting). Perhaps the most compelling characteristic of alters is that, for a given patient, each alter can have unique medical problems and histories: One alter might have allergies, medical conditions, or even EEG patterns that the other alters do not have (American Psychiatric Association, 2000). Stressful events can precipitate a switch of alters, whereby the alter that was the dominant personality at one moment recedes and another alter becomes the dominant personality. Although the number of alters that have been reported ranges from 2 to 100, most people diagnosed with DID have 10 or fewer alters (American Psychiatric Association, 2000). Table 8.7 lists the DSM-IV-TR diagnostic criteria for DID, and Table 8.8 provides further information about the disorder. Case 8.4 presents the alters of someone with DID, which had previously been called *multiple personality disorder* (MPD).

Table 8.7 ▶ DSM-IV-TR Diagnostic Criteria for Dissociative Identity Disorder

A. The presence of two or more distinct identities or personality states (each with its own relatively enduring pattern of perceiving, relating to, and thinking about the environment and self).

B. At least two of these identities or personality states recurrently take control of the person's behavior.

C. Inability to recall important personal information that is too extensive to be explained by ordinary forgetfulness.

D. The disturbance is not due to the direct physiological effects of a substance (e.g., blackouts or chaotic behavior during alcohol intoxication) or a general medical condition. Note: In children, the symptoms are not attributable to imaginary playmates or other fantasy play.

Source: Reprinted with permission from the Diagnostic and Statistical Manual of Mental Disorders, Text Revision, Fourth Edition, (Copyright 2000) American Psychiatric Association.

CASE 8.4 ▶ FROM THE INSIDE: Dissociative Identity Disorder

In Robert B. Oxnam's memoir, *A Fractured Mind*, his various alters (11 in all) tell their stories. The following excerpts present recollections from two of the alters, beginning with Robert:

> This is Robert speaking. Today, I'm the only personality who is strongly visible inside and outside. . . . Fifteen years ago, I rarely appeared on the outside, though I had considerable influence on the inside; back then, I was what one might call a "recessive personality."
>
> Although [Bob, another alter] was the dominant MPD personality for thirty years, [he] did not have a clue that he was afflicted by multiple personality disorder until 1990, the very last year of his dominance. That was the fateful moment when Bob first heard that he had an "angry boy named Tommy" inside of him.

(Oxnam, 2005, p. 11)

Another alter, Bob, recounts:

> There were blank spots in my memory where I could not recall anything that happened for blocks of time. Sometimes when a luncheon appointment was canceled, I would go out at noon and come back at 3 P.M. with no knowledge of where I had been or what I had done. I returned tired, a bit sweaty, but I quickly showered and got back to work. Once, on a trip to Taiwan, a whole series of meetings was canceled because of a national holiday; I had zero memory of what I did for almost three days, but I do recall that, after the blank spot disappeared, I had a severe headache and what seemed to be cigarette burns on my arm.

(Oxnam, 2005, p. 31).

Dissociative identity disorder (DID)
The dissociative disorder characterized by the presence of two or more distinct *alters* (personality states or identities), each with their own characteristics and history, that take turns controlling the person's behavior.

Criticisms of the DSM-IV-TR Criteria

Significant problems plague the DSM-IV-TR diagnostic criteria for DID, including the following (Piper & Merskey, 2004b):

- DSM-IV-TR does not define "personality states" or "identities"; accordingly, a normal emotional state that emerges episodically—such as periodic angry outbursts—could be considered an "identity." By leaving "personality states" and "identities" undefined, the criteria allow the possibility that normal emotional fluctuations could be considered pathological.

- DSM-IV-TR does not indicate how clinicians can know when an alter has "taken control" (Criterion B) (Fahy, 1988). With no guidelines for how to make that judgment, there is apt to be little reliability in the diagnosis (see Chapter 3 for a discussion of reliability and diagnosis).

- DID—which is easy to role-play—can be difficult to distinguish from malingering (Labott & Wallach, 2002; Stafford & Lynn, 2002). When people can easily fake symptoms of a disorder, the validity of the disorder as a diagnostic entity can be questioned (see Chapter 3 for a discussion of validity and diagnosis).

- DID can be difficult to distinguish from rapid cycling bipolar disorder because both involve sudden changes in mood and demeanor. However, appropriate treatments for bipolar disorder differ from those for DID, which is why accurate diagnosis is important (Piper & Merskey, 2004b).

Some of Anna O.'s dissociative experiences seem similar to those of patients with DID, such as her "naughty" states (for which she had amnesia) and her feeling that she had two selves, a real one and an evil one, which would "take control."

Understanding Dissociative Identity Disorder

Research findings on various factors associated with DID can be at odds with each other, which only fuels the controversy over the validity of the diagnosis itself. As we shall see, much of the research on, and theorizing about, factors that may contribute to DID hinge on the fact that many people with this disorder report having been severely and chronically abused as children (Lewis et al., 1997; Ross et al., 1991). As usual, we'll begin by examining neurological factors and then consider psychological and social factors.

Neurological Factors: Alters in the Brain?

Research that investigates possible neurological differences between alters paints a mixed picture. On the one hand, the brain behaves differently when an alter who is aware of relevant information listens to a story than when an alter who is not aware of that information listens. As we note below, such differences in brain functioning could have something to do with early hormonal reactions to stress, and such reactions might contribute to the disorder in part because specific genes make certain people especially sensitive to stress. On the other hand, although one alter may profess to be ignorant of events experienced by other alters, rigorous testing often reveals that each alter does in fact have access to information acquired by other alters.

Brain Systems One hallmark of DID is that memories acquired by one alter are not directly accessible to other alters. However, in one study, the alters *reported* no memory for material that had been learned by other alters, but researchers nevertheless found no difference in either recall or recognition between the amnesic alters and normal control participants (Huntjens et al., 2003). Moreover, other studies suggest that although alters may report the subjective experience of amnesia, they do, in fact, have access to memories of other alters (Huntjens et al., 2005, 2006, 2007; Kong, Allen, & Glisky, 2008). Consistent with these findings, researchers have used changes in

Table 8.8 ► Dissociative Identity Disorder Facts at a Glance

Prevalence

- The prevalence rate for DID is difficult to specify, although several surveys estimate it to be about 1% (Johnson et al., 2006; Loewenstein, 1994). However, some researchers view this figure as a significant overestimate (Rifkin et al., 1998).

Comorbidity

- People with DID may also be diagnosed with a mood disorder, a substance-related disorder, PTSD, or a personality disorder (to be discussed in Chapter 13). DID may be difficult to distinguish from schizophrenia or bipolar disorder.

Onset

- It can take years to make the diagnosis of DID from the time that symptoms first emerge. Because of this long lag time and the rarity of the disorder, there is no accurate information about the usual age of onset.

Course

- DID is usually chronic.

Gender Differences

- Although women are more likely than men to develop DID, different studies have found varying gender ratios, with women three to nine times as likely as men to receive this diagnosis.

Cultural Differences

- DID is observed only in some Western cultures and was extremely uncommon before the 1976 television movie *Sybil*, which was about a "true case" of what was then called multiple personality disorder (Kihlstrom, 2001; Lilienfeld et al., 1999).

Source: Unless otherwise noted, the source is American Psychiatric Association, 2000.

electrical activity on the scalp to show that the brain responds as if the patient with DID recognizes previously learned words, even when the learning took place when one alter was dominant and the testing occurred when another alter was dominant (Allen & Movius, 2000). For example, if an adult alter were taught the words, a child alter might claim to have no memory of them—but the brain responses to the familiar words are the same, regardless of which alter is dominant when the test is done.

However, additional research has provided evidence that patients with DID are inhibited from recalling stored information when a different alter is dominant, even if they are capable of doing so (Elzinga et al., 2003). Why might some memories be made unavailable for easy recall by particular alters? Putnam (1995) has offered a theory, which other researchers have extended to specify brain mechanisms. Specifically, the orbital frontal cortex (the lower part of the frontal lobe, behind the eyes)—which regulates many other brain regions used in various cognitive and emotional processes—may play a key role in the development of DID (Forrest, 2001). According to this theory, early abuse may prevent this area of the brain from maturing normally, and hence it is not able to integrate representations of the self normally. If memories are associated with particular representations of the self (that is, with individual alters), each representation will cue only some specific memories—which will be easier to recall than ones that are not cued by that representation.

Perhaps the key characteristic of DID is that each alter has a different "sense of self." To the individual with DID, it feels as if different personalities "take over" in turn. To explore the neural bases of this phenomenon, Reinders and colleagues (2003) asked 11 DID patients to listen to stories about their personal traumatic history while their brains were scanned using PET. Each patient was scanned once when an alter who was aware of the past trauma was dominant and once when an alter who was not aware of the past trauma was dominant. Two results are of particular interest: First, and most basic, the brain responded differently for the two alters. This alone is evidence that something was neurologically different when the person was in the two states. Second, the traumatic history activated brain areas known to be activated by autobiographical information—but only when the alter that was aware of that information was dominant during the PET scanning. Moreover, a brain area known to process emotional information (the parietal operculum) was much more strongly activated when the participant was an alter that was aware of the trauma, compared to when the participant was an alter unaware of the trauma. Thus, from the brain's point of view, different information was in fact accessible to the two alters.

However, it is difficult to interpret the results of many studies that investigate neurological differences among alters because the studies do not include an appropriate control group (Merckelbach, Devilly, & Rassin, 2002). Researchers have found that hypnosis can alter brain activity (Kosslyn et al., 2000), so it is possible that at least some of the neurological differences between alters reflect a form of self-hypnosis. That is, the person with DID—perhaps unconsciously—hypnotizes himself or herself, which produces different neurological states when different alters come to the fore.

Neural Communication DID is thought to be associated with early childhood abuse, and it is well known that such abuse affects a wide range of stress-related hormones, cortisol being just one. These stress-related hormones clearly disrupt brain development and subsequent brain functioning, including that of the hippocampus and the frontal lobes—both of which play major roles in memory (Teicher et al., 2002). However, researchers do not yet understand what might cause stress-related hormones to affect specifically those brain systems that in turn would produce the symptoms of the disorder.

Genetics Using a questionnaire, a team of researchers assessed the capacity for dissociative experiences in monozygotic and dizygotic twins in the general population (Jang et al., 1998). This questionnaire did not address DID directly, but it did assess the capacity for both "normal" dissociations (such as becoming very absorbed in a television show or a movie) and "abnormal" dissociations (such as not recognizing your face in a mirror). These researchers found evidence that genetic influences account for 48% of the variance in measures of pathological dissociative experiences and 55% of the variance in measures of nonpathological experiences. In other words, almost half the variation in abnormal dissociations could be attributed to genes. Perhaps most interesting, the findings suggested that the same genetic influences underlie both sorts of dissociative experiences—which may suggest (counter to current thinking) that pathological experiences are simply an extreme on a continuum that also contains normal dissociative experiences.

Psychological Factors

The primary psychological factor associated with DID is hypnotizability—patients with this diagnosis are highly hypnotizable and can easily dissociate (Bliss, 1984; Frischholz et al., 1990, 1992). That is, they can spontaneously enter a trance state and frequently experience symptoms of dissociation, such as depersonalization or derealization. These abilities play a critical role in a psychologically based theory of DID, described in the upcoming section on feedback loops.

Social Factors: A Cultural Disorder?

Social factors have apparently affected the frequency of diagnosis of DID. From the beginning of the 20th century through the 1920s, DID was rarely diagnosed, and it continued to be rarely diagnosed until 1976 (Kihlstrom, 2001; Lilienfeld et al., 1999; Spanos, 1994). What happened in 1976? The television movie *Sybil* was aired and received widespread attention. This movie portrayed the "true story" of a woman with DID. The movie apparently affected either patients or therapists (who became more willing to make the diagnosis), or both. (Years later, it was revealed that the patient who was known as Sybil did not have alters, but rather had been encouraged by her therapist to "name" her different feelings as if they were alters; thus, what Sybil's therapist wrote about her alters was not based on Sybil's actual experiences [Borch-Jacobsen, 1997; Rieber, 1999].)

Consistent with the view that DID is a disorder induced by social factors present in some cultures, many countries, such as India and China, have an extremely low or zero prevalence rate of DID (Adityanjee, Raju, & Khandelwal, 1989; Draijer & Friedl, 1999; Xiao et al., 2006). In other countries, such as Uganda, people with DID symptoms are considered to be experiencing the culturally sanctioned possession trance, not suffering from DID (van Dujil, Cardeña, & de Jong, 2005).

FEEDBACK LOOPS IN ACTION: Two Models for the Emergence of Alters

Two models of dissociative identity disorder—the posttraumatic model and the sociocognitive model—are based on the existence of feedback loops among neurological, psychological, and social factors. However, the two models emphasize the roles of different factors and have different accounts of how the factors influence each other.

The Posttraumatic Model In addition to dissociating or entering hypnotic trances easily, most DID patients have at least one alter that reports having suffered severe, often recurring, physical abuse (which would imply a stress response; neurological factor) when young (Lewis et al., 1997; Ross et al., 1991). This trauma, induced by others (social factor), may increase the ease of dissociating (psychological factor), which in turn produces DID. In fact, children who experienced severe physical abuse later report that during the traumatic events their minds temporarily left their bodies as a way of coping; that is, they dissociated. Putting these observations together, the *posttraumatic model* (Gleaves, 1996) proposes that after frequent episodes of abuse with accompanying dissociation, the child's dissociated state can develop its own memories, identity, and way of interacting with the world, thus becoming an "alter" (Putnam, 1989).

Several studies support some aspects of the posttraumatic model. As would be expected from this model, some people with DID do have documented histories of severe physical abuse in childhood (Lewis et al., 1997; Putnam, 1989; Swica,

Courtesy Everett Collection

Some researchers attribute the increased prevalence of dissociative identify disorder since 1976 to the movie *Sybil*, based on the book of the same name, which claimed to portray the "true story" of a woman with DID. In a scene near the end of the movie, Sybil (played by Sally Field, lying down) and her psychiatrist (Joanne Woodward) work to "integrate" the different alters. In fact, it was later revealed that the real life "Sybil" had been explicitly encouraged to give names to different aspects of her personality, but did not actually dissociate, as her psychiatrist had declared she did.

Lewis, & Lewis, 1996) and also report having displayed signs of dissociation in childhood (Lewis et al., 1997). Moreover these patients report that they either don't remember being abused or remember very little of it (Lewis et al., 1997; Swica, Lewis, & Lewis, 1996). In addition, girls who were easy to hypnotize *and* able to dissociate readily were found to be the ones most likely to have been abused physically or sexually (Putnam et al., 1995).

However, if the posttraumatic model is correct, there should be a significant number of cases of childhood DID. In fact, very few such cases have been documented, and most studies of abused children have found only a great ability to dissociate, *not the presence of alters* (Piper & Merskey, 2004a). Moreover, most studies of adults with DID who experienced childhood abuse have not obtained independent corroborating evidence of abuse or trauma but rather rely solely on the patient's—or an alter's—report of abuse during childhood (Piper & Merskey, 2004a, 2000b). As we saw in Chapter 5, self-reports are subject to various cognitive biases. In short, mental health professionals are divided over whether childhood trauma is the root cause of DID (Dell, 1988; Pope et al., 1999).

The Sociocognitive Model In contrast to the posttraumatic model of DID, the *sociocognitive model* proposes that social interactions between therapist and patient (social factor) foster DID by influencing the beliefs and expectations of the patient (psychological factor). According to the sociocognitive model, the therapist unintentionally causes the patient to act in ways that are consistent with the symptoms of DID (Lilienfeld et al., 1999; Sarbin, 1995; Spanos, 1994). This explanation is plausible in part because hypnosis was commonly used to bring forth alters, and researchers have pointed out that suggestible patients can unconsciously develop alters (and ensuing neurological changes) in response to the therapist's promptings (Spanos, 1994). For instance, a therapist may encourage a patient to develop alters by asking specific questions ("Have people come up to you who seem to know you, but they are strangers to you?" or "Do you find clothes in your closet that you don't remember purchasing?") and then showing special interest when the patient answers "yes" to any such question. One finding that supports the sociocognitive model is that many people who have been diagnosed with DID had no notion of the existence of any alters before they entered therapy (Lilienfeld et al., 1999). In addition, cultural cues regarding DID (such as in portrayals in movies and memoirs or interviews of people with the disorder) may influence a patient's behavior.

The Debate About Dissociative Identity Disorder

After years of debate, the central issue regarding DID is not whether it exists, but rather how it arises and continues (McHugh, 1993). Is DID a natural response to severe and chronic childhood abuse, or is it mainly a product of influences from the

Dissociative identity disorder is described or portrayed in various films and memoirs; the photo shown here is a publicity shot for one of the earliest and best-known films, *The Three Faces of Eve*. According to the sociocognitive model of this disorder, such media portrayals can help create expectations in both patients and therapists about how people with the disorder behave. Therapists, in turn, unintentionally reinforce patients for behaving in ways consistent with such portrayals.

20thCentFox/Courtesy Everett Collection

media, the therapist, and general social expectations (Lilienfeld et al., 1999)? Proponents of the sociocognitive model recognize that childhood trauma can—at least in some cases—indirectly be associated with DID: it is possible that childhood trauma can lead people to become more suggestible or more able to fantasize, which can magnify the effects on their behavior of social interactions with a therapist (Lilienfeld et al., 1999). In other words, dissociation and DID symptoms may be *indirect* results of childhood trauma rather than direct posttraumatic results.

Proponents of the sociocognitive model point out that cultural influences, such as the airing of the movie *Sybil*, may have led therapists to ask leading questions regarding DID—and may have led highly suggestible patients to follow these leads unconsciously; such influences would account for the great variability in the number of cases over time. Proponents of the posttraumatic model counter that the increased prevalence of DID after 1976 simply reflects improved procedures for assessment and diagnosis. In support of their position, they point to the results of a study that is consistent with their model and contradicts the sociocognitive model: Women who reported having *recovered memories* (i.e., knowledge of prior events about which they previously had no memory) of childhood sexual abuse were *less* suggestible than women in a control group, not more suggestible, as would be predicted by the sociocognitive model (Leavitt, 1997). However, this study's support for the posttraumatic model isn't as strong as it might seem at first blush. Participants in the study were not DID patients, and so there may be some important difference between those who recover memories of childhood abuse and *don't* develop DID versus those who do go on to develop DID.

In sum, we do know that severe trauma can lead to dissociative disorders and can have other adverse effects (Putnam, 1989; Putnam et al., 1995). However, we do not know whether all of those who are diagnosed with DID have actually experienced traumatic events, nor even how severe an event must be in order to be considered "traumatic." Similarly, experiencing a traumatic event does not *specifically* cause DID (Kihlstrom, 2005); some people respond by developing depression or an anxiety disorder. Further, as noted in Chapter 7, many people who experience a traumatic event do not develop any psychological disorder.

Simply being sensitive to context or responding differently when in different emotional states does not mean that you have alters. For example, one study found that people who are bilingual responded differently to a personality test, depending on which language was used for the test (Ramírez-Esparza et al., 2006). Can you think of reasons for this result that do not involve alters?

Treating Dissociative Disorders

In general, dissociative disorders improve spontaneously, without treatment. This is especially true of dissociative amnesia and dissociative fugue. However, clinicians who encounter people with these disorders have used some of the treatments discussed below. Because dissociative disorders are so rare, few systematic studies of treatments have been conducted—and none have attempted to determine which treatments are most effective for a particular dissociative disorder. Thus, we consider treatments for dissociative disorders in general.

Targeting Neurological Factors: Medication

In general, medication is not used to treat the symptoms of dissociative disorders because research suggests that it is not helpful for dissociative symptoms (Sierra et al., 2003; Simeon, Stein, & Hollander, 1998). However, people with DID may receive medication for a comorbid disorders or for anxiety or mood symptoms that arise in response to the dissociative symptoms.

Targeting Psychological and Social Factors: Coping and Integration

Treatments that target the psychological factors underlying dissociative disorders focus on three elements: (1) reinterpreting the symptoms so that they don't create stress or lead the patient to avoid certain situations; (2) learning additional coping strategies to manage stress (Hunter et al., 2005); and (3) for DID patients, addressing the presence of alters and dissociated aspects of their memories or identities. The first two foci are similar to those for treating PTSD (Kluft, 1999; see Chapter 7).

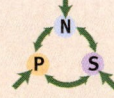

When addressing the presence of alters in those with DID, the type of treatment a clinician employs depends on which theory he or she accepts and thus guides treatment. Proponents of the posttraumatic model advise clinicians to identify in detail (or to "map") each alter's personality, recover memories of possible abuse, and then help the patient to integrate the different alters (Chu et al., 2005). In contrast, proponents of the sociocognitive model advise *against* mapping alters or trying to recover possible memories of abuse (Gee, Allen, & Powell, 2003). Instead, they recommend that the therapist use learning principles to extinguish patients' mention of alters: Alters are to be ignored, and the therapist doesn't discuss multiple identities. Alters are interpreted as creations inspired by the patient's desire for attention, and treatment focuses on current problems rather than on past traumas (Fahy, Abas, & Brown, 1989; McHugh, 1993).

In addition, hypnosis has sometimes been used as part of treatment, particularly by therapists who treat DID according to the posttraumatic model; in this case, hypnosis might be used to help the patient learn about his or her different alters and integrate them into a single, functional whole (Boyd, 1997; Kluft, 1999).

When using hypnosis to treat dissociative symptoms, the therapist may make suggestions such as "You will feel yourself becoming relaxed . . . you will notice yourself going into a state of trance . . . you will find yourself about to remember whatever was dissociated." One goal is to help reintegrate whatever has been dissociated, such as specific memories.

Will & Deni McIntyre/Photo Researchers, Inc.

Using hypnosis is, by its very nature, a social event: The therapist helps the patient achieve a hypnotic state through suggestions and bears witness to whatever the patient shares about the dissociated experience. However, using hypnosis to treat DID is controversial because the patient will probably be more suggestible when in a hypnotic trance, and the therapist may inadvertently make statements that the patient interprets as suggestions to produce more DID symptoms. Further, it is not clear that hypnosis can always help such patients, although there is some evidence that it sometimes might be useful (Powell & Gee, 1999).

Treatment may also focus on reducing the traumatic stress that can induce dissociative disorders. For instance, soldiers who experience dissociation during combat may be removed from the battlefield, which can then reduce the dissociation.

FEEDBACK LOOPS IN TREATMENT: **Dissociative Disorders**

When Breuer was treating Anna O., he relied on the "talking cure"—having her talk about relevant material, at first while in a hypnotic trance and later while not in a trance. This use of hypnosis continues today, and is often part of a treatment program for people with dissociative disorders (Butler et al., 1996), including dissociative amnesia (such as Mrs. Y in Case 8.1), dissociative fugue (such as Joe in Case 8.2), and DID (Putnam & Loewenstein, 1993). Hypnotic treatment for a dissociative disorder usually involves helping the individual to become aware of and integrate dissociated perceptions and memories, as well as to understand what may have led to the dissociation. Let's examine hypnotic treatment and how it leads to feedback loops among neurological, psychological, and social factors.

In the 1980s, researchers began to investigate the neurological changes that occur as a result of hypnosis and subsequently established that hypnosis alters brain events (Crawford et al., 1993; Kosslyn et al., 2000; Sabourin et al., 1990–1991; Spiegel, Bierre, & Rootenberg, 1989; Spiegel et al., 1985). The specific brain changes vary, however, depending on the task being performed during the hypnotic trance. When hypnotized, patients may be able to retrieve information that was previously dissociated; in turn, this may make them feel more like themselves and experience perceptions or memories in a more normal way (psychological factor).

In addition, hypnosis can be induced only when patients are willing to be hypnotized, and its beneficial effects occur when they go along with the therapist's hypnotic suggestions (social factor). In turn, the hypnotic state brings about changes in brain activity (neurological factor), which ultimately might play a role in integrating the stored information that was previously dissociated.

Figure 8.2 is a graphic representation of the three types of factors and their feedback loops in treating dissociative disorders.

Figure 8.2

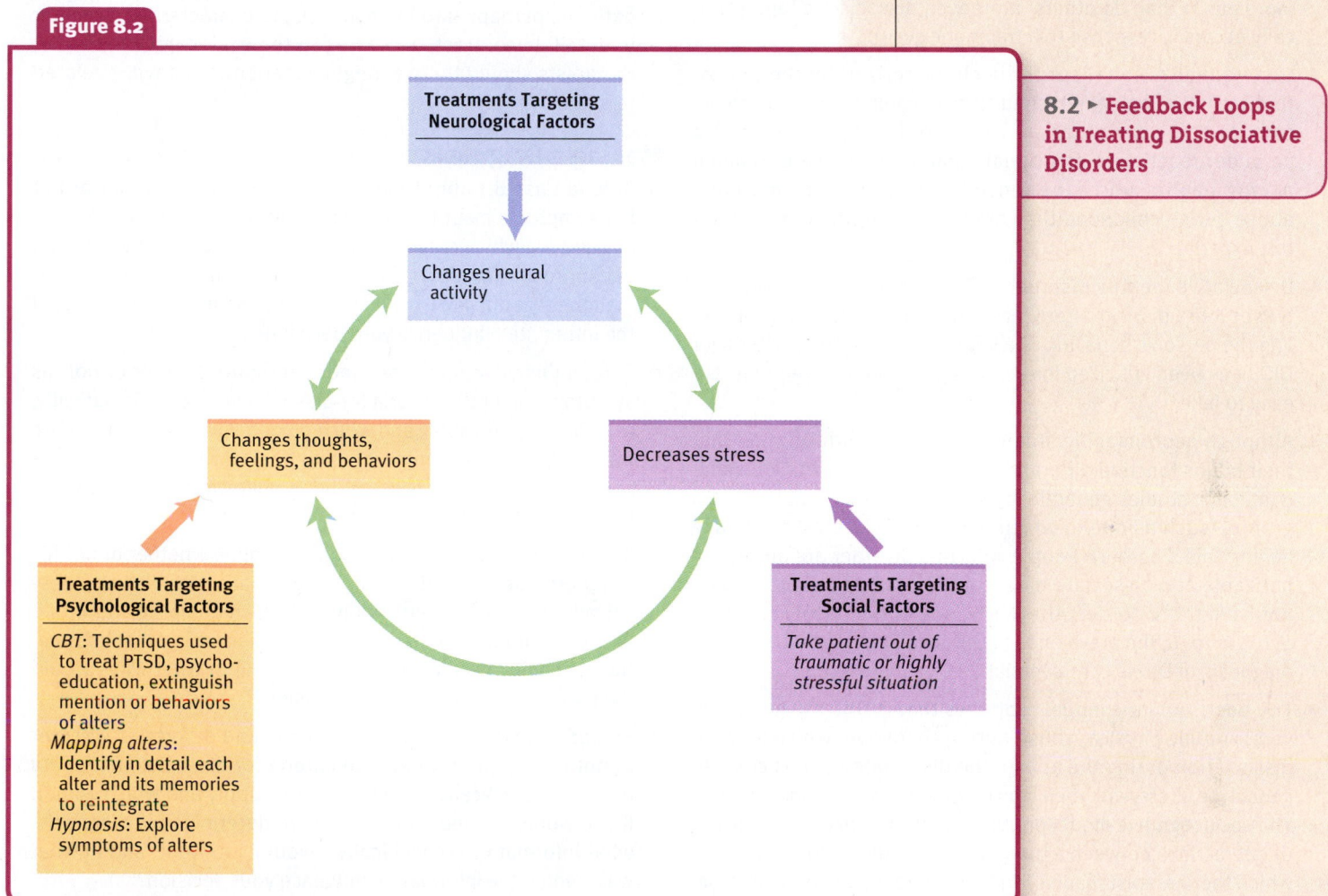

Treatments Targeting Neurological Factors

Changes neural activity

Changes thoughts, feelings, and behaviors

Decreases stress

Treatments Targeting Psychological Factors

CBT: Techniques used to treat PTSD, psycho-education, extinguish mention or behaviors of alters
Mapping alters: Identify in detail each alter and its memories to reintegrate
Hypnosis: Explore symptoms of alters

Treatments Targeting Social Factors

Take patient out of traumatic or highly stressful situation

8.2 ▶ Feedback Loops in Treating Dissociative Disorders

Key Concepts and Facts About Dissociative Disorders

- Dissociation involves a separation of mental processes that are normally integrated—a dissociation of perception, consciousness, memory, or identity. To qualify as a dissociative disorder, this separation must cause significant distress or impair functioning. Specific symptoms of dissociative disorders include amnesia, identity problems, derealization, and depersonalization. Dissociative disorders are rare and are often thought to arise in response to traumatic events.

- Dissociative amnesia is characterized by significantly impaired memory for important experiences or personal information that cannot be explained as ordinary forgetfulness or accounted for by another psychological disorder, substance use, or a medical condition. Dissociative amnesia most often occurs after some traumatic event. The amnesia may be generalized, selective, or localized. The amnesia may spontaneously disappear, particularly after the person leaves the traumatic situation.

continued on next page

- Dissociative fugue is characterized by sudden, unplanned travel and difficulty remembering the past, which in turn leads to identity confusion. Apparently, the frontal lobes of patients with this disorder are not as effective at accessing stored memories, particularly about the self; the reduced activation in the frontal lobes might be caused by stress-related hormones. People who have had this disorder are more hypnotizable and dissociate more easily than do others. Moreover, dissociative fugue typically occurs in response to a traumatic event.

- Depersonalization disorder is characterized by the persistent feeling of being detached from oneself, which may be accompanied by derealization. This disorder appears to involve an under-reaction to emotional stimuli, and is more common among people who experienced severe chronic emotional abuse during childhood than among people who did not have this experience.

- Dissociative identity disorder (DID) hinges on the presence of two or more distinct alters, each of which takes turns controlling the person's behavior. The DSM-IV-TR diagnostic criteria for DID have been criticized for being vague, and the symptoms are easy to fake.

- Although neuroimaging studies of patients with DID find that their brains function differently when different alters are dominant, such studies generally have not used appropriate control groups (such as one in which participants are asked to fake having this disorder). People with this disorder are more hypnotizable and dissociate more readily than do people who do not have this disorder. After the airing of the television movie *Sybil*, in 1976, the prevalence of DID increased dramatically. The diagnosis of DID is controversial.

- The posttraumatic model proposes that DID is caused by severe, chronic physical abuse during childhood, which leads to dissociation during the abuse; the dissociated states come to constitute alters, with their own memories and personality traits. The sociocognitive model proposes that DID arises as the result of interactions between a therapist and a suggestible patient, in which the therapist inadvertently encourages the patient to behave in ways consistent with the diagnosis. Both interpretations are consistent with the finding that severe childhood trauma is associated with the disorder.

- The goal of treatment for dissociative disorders ultimately is to reduce the symptoms themselves and lower the stress they induce. For patients with DID, the specific methods employed depend on what the clinician views as the cause of the disorder: According to the posttraumatic model, therapists should help patients, perhaps through hypnosis, to characterize each alter in detail. In contrast, according to the sociocognitive model, therapists should try to extinguish patients' behaviors related to alters.

Making a Diagnosis

- Reread Case 8.1 about Mrs. Y, and determine whether or not her symptoms meet the criteria for dissociative amnesia. Specifically, list which criteria apply and which do not. If you would like more information to determine her diagnosis, what information—specifically—would you want, and in what ways would the information influence your decision?

- Reread Case 8.2 about Joe, and determine whether or not his symptoms meet the criteria for dissociative fugue. Specifically, list which criteria apply and which do not. If you would like more information to determine his diagnosis, what information—specifically—would you want, and in what ways would the information influence your decision?

- Reread Case 8.3 about Mr. E, and determine whether or not his symptoms meet the criteria for depersonalization disorder. Specifically, list which criteria apply and which do not. If you would like more information to determine his diagnosis, what information—specifically—would you want, and in what ways would the information influence your decision?

- Reread Case 8.4 about Robert Oxnam, and determine whether or not his symptoms meet the criteria for dissociative identity disorder. Specifically, list which criteria apply and which do not. If you would like more information to determine his diagnosis, what information—specifically—would you want, and in what ways would the information influence your decision?

Somatoform Disorders

During the course of her illness, Anna O. developed medical symptoms that her doctors could not explain. For instance, she saw an eye doctor for problems with her vision, but he was unable to identify the cause (Breuer & Freud, 1895/1955). Similarly, doctors were unable to find a medical explanation for her cough. How might persistent medically unexplained physical symptoms such as these arise? How should they best be treated? Such bodily symptoms may fall under the category of *somatoform disorders* in DSM-IV-TR.

Somatoform Disorders: An Overview

The hallmark of **somatoform disorders** is complaints about physical well-being that cannot be entirely explained by a medical condition, substance use, or another psychological disorder. For example, one somatoform disorder is *hypochondriasis*, which is characterized by an individual's preoccupying belief that he or she has a serious illness, despite negative medical tests. By their very nature, however, somatoform disorders are "rule out" diagnoses, meaning that the clinician must make sure that there aren't medical conditions or other psychological disorders that can better explain the patients' physical symptoms. For instance, if a person repeatedly has panic attacks and complains of a racing heart, chest pain, and shortness of breath, he or she will not be considered to have a somatoform disorder, because the symptoms are explained by another psychological disorder—panic disorder.

In the absence of a medical condition or another psychological disorder, clinicians must judge the extent to which patients' physical symptoms (see Table 8.9) impair functioning, lead to significant distress, and are not under voluntary control, and decide whether the symptoms qualify as a somatoform disorder according to DSM-IV-TR criteria. Somatoform disorders are relatively rare in the general population but are the most common type of psychological disorder in medical settings (Bass, Peveler, & House, 2001): A third of patients visiting their primary care physician have symptoms that are not adequately explained by a medical condition (Kroenke, 2003). The medical costs of caring for patients with somatoform disorders are substantial; according to one estimate, patients with these disorders account for over $250 billion in medical costs each year (Barsky, Orav, & Bates, 2005).

Somatoform disorders are not a new phenomenon; they have a long history, although different labels have been given to them over time. They were described by the ancient Greek philosopher Hippocrates, who thought that somatoform symptoms—generally reported by women—were caused by a wandering uterus, from which the term *hysteria* is derived (*hystera* is Greek for "uterus"; Phillips, 2001). *Hysteria* was often used to refer to bodily symptoms that lack a medical explanation, as was true of Anna O.; in addition, patients with hysteria typically describe their symptoms dramatically.

Somatoform disorders must be distinguished from *factitious disorder*, mentioned in Chapter 3, in which people *intentionally* induce symptoms or falsely report symptoms that they do not in fact have to receive attention from others. Those with a somatoform disorder neither pretend to have symptoms nor intentionally induce physical symptoms for any type of gain.

Somatoform disorders share two common features (Looper & Kirmayer, 2002):

1. *bodily preoccupation*, which is similar to the heightened awareness of panic-related bodily sensations experienced by people with panic disorder (see Chapter 7), except that with somatoform disorders the patient can be preoccupied with any aspect of bodily functioning; and

2. *symptom amplification*, or directing attention to bodily symptoms such as those in Table 8.9, which in turn intensifies the symptoms (Kirmayer & Looper, 2006; Looper & Kirmayer, 2002). A common example of symptom amplification occurs when someone with a headache pays attention to the headache–and, invariably, the pain worsens.

Body dysmorphic disorder—a preoccupation with a *perceived* bodily defect—is the only somatoform disorder that does not include an actual somatic symptom.

The somatoform disorders involve dissociation; in these disorders, the processes of sensation and perception of bodily functioning are not integrated, but rather have become separated or altered. Somatoform disorders and dissociative disorders are classified separately only because of the bodily aspect of somatoform symptoms, but some researchers suggest that they should be combined into one category (Kihlstrom, 2001).

Somatoform disorders
A category of psychological disorders characterized by complaints about physical well-being that cannot be entirely explained by a medical condition, substance use, or another psychological disorder.

Table 8.9 ▶ Common Bodily Complaints of Patients with Somatoform Disorders

• Muscle and joint pain	• Palpitations
• Lower back pain	• Irritable bowel
• Tension headache	• Dizziness
• Atypical facial pain	• Insomnia
• Chronic fatigue	• Non-ulcer dyspepsia (indigestion)
• Non-cardiac chest pain	

Source: Mayou & Farmer, 2002. For more information see the Permissions section.

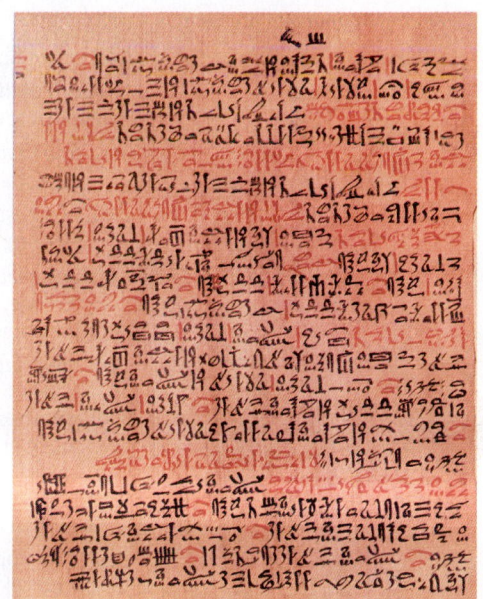

Symptoms of somatoform disorders have existed for millennia and were written about in the *Papyrus Ebers*, an ancient Egyptian medical document dating to 1600 B.C.E. However, the Egyptians believed that these symptoms had an underlying medical cause.

University Library, Leipzig, Germany/Archives Charmet/The Bridgeman Art Library

Somatization disorder (SD)
A somatoform disorder characterized by multiple physical symptoms that are medically unexplained and impair an individual's ability to function.

Pain disorder
A somatoform disorder that occurs when psychological factors significantly affect the onset, severity, or maintenance of significant pain.

Somatization Disorder

The hallmark of **somatization disorder** (**SD**) is multiple physical symptoms that are medically unexplained and impair an individual's ability to function (American Psychiatric Association, 2000). For example, Anna O.'s eye problems and her cough were both physical symptoms that impaired her daily life and that doctors could not explain. In this section we examine what somatization disorder is, and the various factors that are known to contribute to the disorder.

What Is Somatization Disorder?

To be diagnosed with SD according to DSM-IV-TR criteria, the individual must have had each of four different types of medically unexplained symptoms: pain symptoms, gastrointestinal symptoms, sexual symptoms, and pseudoneurological symptoms (the prefix *pseudo*—is used to indicate that the symptoms are similar to those of neurological disorders, but they do not have a neurological or other medical cause). Table 8.10 lists the DSM-IV-TR diagnostic criteria for SD.

As noted in Criterion C(2), sometimes people with SD *do* have a medical problem. In those cases, the clinician diagnoses SD only if the symptoms are more extreme than what would be expected based on the medical assessment. SD must be distinguished from neurological disorders, such as multiple sclerosis, other medical problems, and various other psychiatric disorders, including anxiety disorders and *pain disorder*.

According to DSM-IV-TR, **pain disorder** occurs when psychological factors significantly affect the onset, severity, or maintenance of significant pain (American Psychiatric Association, 2000). For a clinician to arrive at a diagnosis of pain disorder, the pain must cause significant distress or impair functioning, and malingering or factitious disorder must be ruled out. In some cases of pain disorder, examiners

---

Table **8.10** ▸ DSM-IV-TR Diagnostic Criteria for Somatization Disorder

A. A history of many physical complaints beginning before age 30 years that occur over a period of several years and result in treatment being sought or significant impairment in social, occupational, or other important areas of functioning.

B. Each of the following criteria must have been met, with individual symptoms occurring at any time during the course of the disturbance:

(1) *four pain symptoms:* a history of pain related to at least four different sites or functions (e.g., head, abdomen, back, joints, extremities, chest, rectum, during menstruation, during sexual intercourse, or during urination)

(2) *two gastrointestinal symptoms:* a history of at least two gastrointestinal symptoms other than pain (e.g., nausea, bloating, vomiting other than during pregnancy, diarrhea, or intolerance of several different foods)

(3) *one sexual symptom:* a history of at least one sexual or reproductive symptom other than pain (e.g., sexual indifference, erectile or ejaculatory dysfunction, irregular menses, excessive menstrual bleeding, vomiting throughout pregnancy)

(4) *one pseudoneurological symptom:* a history of at least one symptom or deficit suggesting a neurological condition not limited to pain (conversion symptoms such as impaired coordination or balance, paralysis or localized weakness, difficulty swallowing or lump in throat, aphonia [loss of voice], urinary retention, hallucinations, loss of touch or pain sensation, double vision, blindness, deafness, seizures; dissociative symptoms such as amnesia; or loss of consciousness other than fainting)

C. Either (1) or (2):

(1) after appropriate investigation, each of the symptoms in Criterion B cannot be fully explained by a known general medical condition or [as] the direct effects of a substance (e.g., a drug of abuse, a medication)

(2) when there is a related general medical condition, the physical complaints or resulting social or occupational impairment are in excess of what would be expected from the history, physical examination, or laboratory findings.

D. The symptoms are not intentionally feigned or produced (as in Factitious Disorder or Malingering).

Source: Reprinted with permission from the Diagnostic and Statistical Manual of Mental Disorders, Text Revision, Fourth Edition, (Copyright 2000) American Psychiatric Association.

cannot identify a medical cause for the pain; in other cases, a medical cause may underlie the pain, but psychological factors contribute significantly to the patient's experience of it. When the pain can be diagnosed as arising *predominantly* from a medical condition, pain disorder will not be diagnosed on Axis I, but the medical condition will be noted on Axis III, along with the specific location of the pain, such as the lower back (American Psychiatric Association, 2000).

Both pain disorder and somatization disorder involve genuine—as opposed to feigned—pain to which psychological factors are thought to contribute. However, SD requires that the individual have a history of four different locations of significant pain (as well as other types of bodily symptoms), whereas pain disorder requires only one location of significant pain (American Psychiatric Association, 2000).

Many laboratory tests and visits to doctors may be required to rule out other medical and psychological diagnoses, which is necessary before a diagnosis of SD can be made. When patients have more than one physical problem, arriving at such a diagnosis can be even more complicated and take even longer (Hilty et al., 2001). Table 8.11 lists additional facts about SD.

Table 8.11 ▸ Somatization Disorder Facts at a Glance

Prevalence

- An individual's symptoms rarely meet the stringent diagnostic criteria for SD; survey studies have found that at most approximately 1% of people will receive this diagnosis in their lifetimes.
- Although infrequent, SD is nonetheless a serious problem in medical settings; patients with this disorder use three times as many outpatient medical services and cost nine times more to treat than people who do not have this disorder (Hollifield et al., 1999).

Comorbidity

- People with SD often have other psychological disorders, most frequently an anxiety disorder (particularly panic disorder), depression, or borderline personality disorder (to be discussed in Chapter 13).
- Patients with SD who take benzodiazepines or narcotics for relief of bodily symptoms are at increased risk for developing a substance-related disorder (Holder-Perkins & Wise, 2001).

Onset

- Initial symptoms of SD usually emerge between adolescence and age 30; menstrual difficulties may be the earliest symptom in women.

Course

- The symptoms are chronic; they may fluctuate in location or in intensity (so that the criteria for SD are no longer met), but symptoms usually never completely disappear.
- Patients with SD often take many medications and receive numerous medical tests and diagnoses (Holder-Perkins & Wise, 2001).
- One study found that people in the United States who had this disorder spent, on average, 7 days in bed each month (Smith, Monson, & Ray, 1986).
- Over the course of a year, 50% of patients improve at least enough so that their symptoms no longer meet the full diagnostic criteria (Creed & Barsky, 2004).

Gender Differences

- Survey results differ: This disorder may occur equally often in women and men or may be as much as ten times more common among women as among men, depending on the survey (American Psychiatric Association, 2000; Toft et al., 2005).

Cultural Differences

- The specific symptoms of patients with SD vary across cultures, and some ethnic groups have a higher prevalence of this disorder than others.

Source: Unless otherwise noted, the source is American Psychiatric Association, 2000.

theboone/iStockphoto.com

In an effort to minimize their bodily symptoms, people with somatization disorder may restrict their activities. However, inactivity can create additional symptoms (such as back pain) or make existing symptoms worse (such as increased heart rate or difficulty breathing).

People with SD may avoid certain activities that they believe are associated with their bodily symptoms, such as any type of exercise. In so doing, patients attempt to minimize the physical sensations associated with the disorder. Unfortunately, they then become so out of shape that even normal daily activities, such as walking to the store from the parking lot, may lead them to experience bodily symptoms, creating a vicious cycle of avoidance and increased bodily symptoms. For people with SD, these symptoms impair daily life, which is what happened to Edward in Case 8.5.

CASE 8.5 ▶ FROM THE OUTSIDE: Somatization Disorder

As an infant, Edward had scarlet fever and a mild form of epilepsy, from which he recovered. By school age, he was complaining of stomachaches and joint pain and often missed school. There were many doctors, but no dire diagnosis: Edward was healthy, but many commented, a somewhat lonely and serious little boy.

Through high school and college Edward capitalized on those traits, achieving high grades and going into the insurance business. At forty-five, he is plagued by mysterious symptoms—heart palpitations, dizziness, indigestion, pain in his shoulders, back, and neck, and fatigue—and lives with his parents. His physical disabilities have made it impossible for Edward to hold a job, and his engagement was broken off. He remains on disability and spends much of his time in and out of hospitals undergoing various tests and procedures.

(Cantor, 1996, p. 54)

Criticism of the DSM-IV-TR Criteria

The DSM-IV-TR criteria for SD have been criticized on several grounds. First, the diagnosis is based on a simple counting of symptoms, so that each symptom is treated as equally important, regardless of how long it has persisted or how severe it is (Criterion B). However, some symptoms are more disabling than others, and chronic symptoms are likely to be more disabling than transient ones. Moreover, the minimum number of each type of symptom needed for the diagnosis was not based on research, but rather was set arbitrarily by the DSM-IV committee. That said, there is a simple defense of the method of counting symptoms used in DSM-IV-TR: studies find that the greater the number of medical symptoms an individual has, the more impaired he or she is likely to be (Barsky, Orav, & Bates, 2005; Jackson et al., 2006).

Second, the criteria do not address patients' behaviors nor their beliefs or attributions about their bodily symptoms (Holder-Perkins & Wise, 2001). Such factors are incorporated into the diagnostic criteria for panic disorder (see Chapter 7), and in some ways, SD is similar to panic disorder: Both involve a preoccupation with the body, and as we shall see, both involve catastrophic thinking about aspects of bodily functioning.

Third, for most patients with SD, their bodily symptoms—or at least some of them—may be better explained by a different psychological disorder, such as depression, an anxiety disorder, or a personality disorder, which makes the additional diagnosis of SD unnecessary. For instance, gastrointestinal symptoms may arise from significant anxiety. DSM-IV-TR does not distinguish between an individual who has enough physical symptoms to meet Criterion B but no comorbid psychological disorder and an individual for whom some symptoms are directly related to a comorbid disorder.

Understanding Somatization Disorder

Like other psychological disorders, somatization disorder can be fully understood only by considering multiple types of factors. These factors include genetics, bodily preoccupation, symptom amplification and catastrophic thinking, and other people's responses to illness. Let's examine the various factors and how they influence one another.

Neurological Factors: Genetics

Most of the progress in understanding the neurological factors that underlie SD has been in the area of genetics. For example, in a large-scale twin study, researchers found that genetic effects may account for as much as half of the variability in SD (Kendler et al., 1995). Note, however, that this finding does not imply that the disorder itself is necessarily inherited; it could be that temperament or other characteristics that are influenced by genetics predispose a person to develop the disorder in certain environments. (This same point can be made about most findings that link genes to disorders.) Kendler and colleagues (1995) also reported that characteristics of families have no consistent effect on whether members of the family develop this disorder. This finding suggests that—in addition to genes—specific experiences of an individual, not shared experiences among members of a family, affect whether a person develops the disorder.

An interesting hint about how genes might affect SD came from a study of relatives of people with another somatoform disorder, *hypochondriasis* (a preoccupying belief that the individual has serious illness, despite negative medical tests; this disorder was mentioned earlier, and will be discussed in more detail shortly). Researchers found that SD was more frequent in the relatives of people with hypochondriasis, compared to relatives of control participants (Fallon et al., 2000; Noyes et al., 1997). This finding might suggest an underlying genetic link between SD and hypochondriasis, which is consistent with the fact that both disorders involve abnormal attention to bodily symptoms.

Psychological Factors: Misinterpretation of Bodily Signals

Like all somatoform disorders, SD involves bodily preoccupation and symptom amplification, as well as catastrophic thinking—in this case, about physical sensations or fears of illness. These patients may believe, for example, that headaches indicate a brain tumor. Their mental processes—particularly attention—focus on bodily sensations, including the beating of their hearts (Barsky, Cleary, et al., 1993, 1994), leading to symptom amplification and catastrophic thinking. These effects also arise in part from faulty beliefs about their bodies and bodily sensations. For example, people with SD may erroneously believe that health is the absence of *any* uncomfortable physical sensations (Rief & Nanke, 1999). However, most people without SD experience some somatic symptoms, at least some of the time. The difference is that people who do not have a somatoform disorder do not habitually develop catastrophic misinterpretations of such sensations. Among a group of healthy college students, for example, 81% experienced at least one somatic symptom in a 3-day period (Gick & Thompson, 1997). For people with SD, their erroneous beliefs about health and illness can increase their level of arousal, which—because of their increased attention to bodily symptoms—can lead to further bodily sensations that are then misinterpreted (Mayou & Farmer, 2002).

Social Factors

Social factors that can contribute to SD include significant social stressors, the modeling and reinforcement of illness behavior, and cultural influences on symptoms. Let's examine these social factors.

Social Stress In many cases, somatoform disorders, including SD, develop after the death of a loved one or after another significant social stressor (Hiller, Rief, & Fichter, 2002). This is what happened to Anna O. after her father died. Somatic symptoms serve as a coping strategy, leading the person to focus attention away from the stressor and onto a bodily sensation.

Social Learning Observational learning can explain the finding that people with SD are more likely than those without the disorder to have had an ill parent (Bass & Murphy, 1995; Craig et al., 1993). In these cases, an ill parent may have inadvertently modeled illness behavior.

Moreover, operant conditioning can also be at work, when people provide reinforcement for an individual's illness behavior: During the patient's childhood, family members may have unintentionally reinforced illness behavior by paying extra attention to the child or buying special treats for the child when he or she was ill (Craig, 1978; Craig et al., 2004; Holder-Perkins & Wise, 2001). Similarly, adults with SD may be reinforced for their symptoms by the attention of medical personnel, family, friends, or coworkers (Maldonado & Spiegel, 2001).

Cultural Influences on Symptoms In many cultures, including that of the United States, somatic symptoms may be regarded as an acceptable way to express helplessness, such as by those who experienced abuse during childhood (Walling et al., 1994). The use of somatic symptoms to express helplessness may explain the bodily symptoms of Anna O. and other upper-middle class women of the Victorian era, whose lives were severely restricted by societal conventions. However, although symptoms of SD occur around the globe, the nature of the symptoms differs across cultures. For instance, symptoms of burning hands or feet are more common in Africa and South Asia than in Europe or North America (American Psychiatric Association, 2000).

In addition, culture influences the prevalence of SD: Although Hispanics in general are not more likely than others to develop the disorder, Puerto Ricans are ten times more likely to do so than the general U.S. population (Canino et al., 1992; Escobar, 1987; Shrout et al., 1992). Moreover, economic status influences prevalence. In contrast to Vienna during Anna O.'s lifetime, people from lower SES groups today are more likely to develop the disorder than those from higher SES groups (Wool & Barsky, 1994). One possible explanation is that those in lower SES groups may feel more helpless.

FEEDBACK LOOPS IN ACTION: **Somatization Disorder**

It is common for people with SD to have had a disease, illness, accident, or other form of trauma prior to developing the disorder. In fact, people with this disorder are more likely to report a history of childhood abuse than are other medical patients (Brown, Schrag, & Trimble, 2005). In individuals who are genetically predisposed to SD (neurological factor), the bodily sensations caused by an illness or accident are interpreted as signaling a catastrophic illness (psychological factor). In turn, this misinterpretation may cause the person to change his or her behavior in a way that ultimately becomes dysfunctional, restricting activities and straining relationships.

Such misinterpretations may initially grow out of modeling. For example, consider that children whose parents have chronic pain are more likely to report abdominal pain themselves and to use more pain relievers than a comparison group of children (Jamison & Walker, 1992). These children's experiences with their ill parent (social factor) may influence their body via their brains (perhaps they have more stomach acid because they are more anxious and stressed; neurological factor), their attention to and attributions for bodily sensations (psychological factors), and their reporting of pain (social factor).

Moreover, a patient's symptoms may have been unintentionally reinforced by friends and family (social factor). A similar shift in interpretation of sensations (psychological factor) can occur after stressful life events (social factor). In addition, frustrating interactions with health care providers, family members, or friends can increase stress (social factor). As with panic disorder (see Chapter 7), the physiological arousal that occurs in response to stress can increase troubling bodily sensations that then become the focus of preoccupations (see Figure 8.3).

Figure 8.3

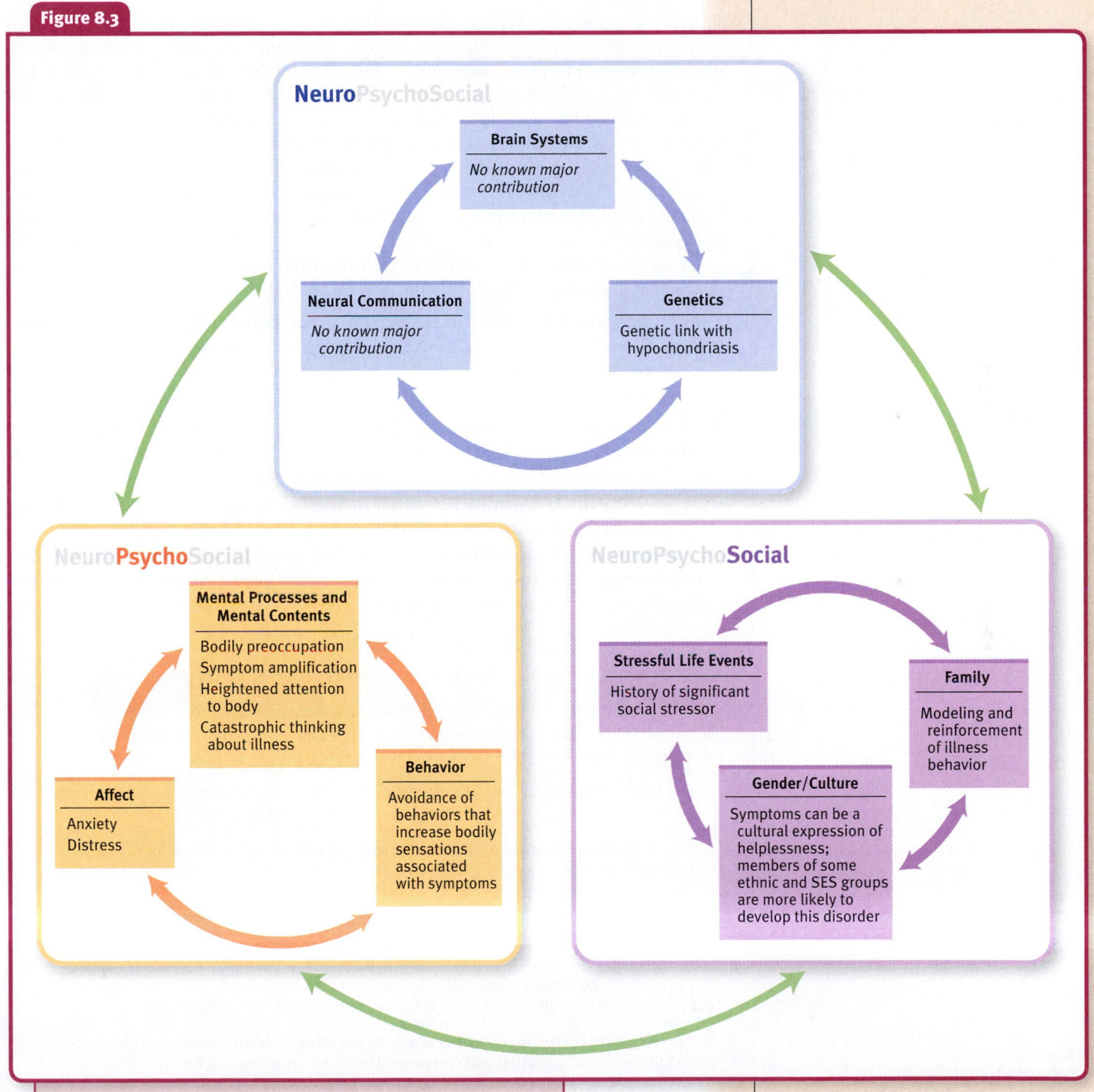

NeuroPsychoSocial

Brain Systems

No known major contribution

Neural Communication

No known major contribution

Genetics

Genetic link with hypochondriasis

NeuroPsychoSocial

Mental Processes and Mental Contents

Bodily preoccupation
Symptom amplification
Heightened attention to body
Catastrophic thinking about illness

Behavior

Avoidance of behaviors that increase bodily sensations associated with symptoms

Affect

Anxiety
Distress

NeuroPsychoSocial

Stressful Life Events

History of significant social stressor

Family

Modeling and reinforcement of illness behavior

Gender/Culture

Symptoms can be a cultural expression of helplessness; members of some ethnic and SES groups are more likely to develop this disorder

8.3 ▶ Feedback Loops in Action: Somatization Disorder

Conversion Disorder

Conversion disorder involves sensory or motor symptoms that do not correspond to those that arise from known medical conditions. We'll first explore what conversion disorder is, then review criticisms of the criteria for this disorder and discuss whether it is more similar to somatoform disorders or dissociative disorders. Following this, we review the neurological, psychological, and social factors that can lead to this disorder.

What Is Conversion Disorder?

Patients who have conversion disorder do not consciously produce the symptoms they experience (as in factitious disorder or malingering) and these patients are significantly distressed or their functioning is impaired by the symptoms (see Table 8.12). Conversion disorder is similar to SD in that both involve physical symptoms that are not explained by a medical condition; however, conversion disorder is limited to sensory and motor symptoms that appear to be neurological (that is, related to the nervous system) but, on closer examination, do not correspond to effects of known neurological pathways (see Figure 8.4). A diagnosis of conversion disorder can only be made after physicians rule out all possible medical causes, and this process can take years.

Conversion disorder is characterized by three types of symptoms (American Psychiatric Association, 2000; Maldonado & Speigel, 2001):

- *Motor symptoms*. Examples include tremors that worsen when attention is paid to them, tics or jerks, muscle spasms, swallowing problems, staggering, and paralysis (sometimes referred to as *pseudoparalysis*, which may also involve significant muscle weakness).

- *Sensory symptoms*. Examples include blindness, double vision, deafness, auditory hallucinations, and lack of feeling on the skin that doesn't correspond to what is produced by malfunctioning of an actual nerve path.

- *Seizures*. Examples include twitching or jerking of some part of the body and loss of consciousness with uncontrollable spasms of the large muscles in the body, causing the person to writhe on the floor. These seizures are often referred to as *pseudoseizures* because they do not have a neurological origin and are not usually affected by seizure medication. Pseudoseizures are likely to occur when other

Table 8.12 ▶ DSM-IV-TR Diagnostic Criteria for Conversion Disorder

A. One or more symptoms or deficits affecting voluntary motor or sensory function that suggest a neurological or other general medical condition.

B. Psychological factors are judged to be associated with the symptom or deficit because the initiation or exacerbation of the symptom or deficit is preceded by conflicts or other stressors.

C. The symptom or deficit is not intentionally produced or feigned (as in Factitious Disorder or Malingering).

D. The symptom or deficit cannot, after appropriate investigation, be fully explained by a general medical condition, or by the direct effects of a substance, or as a culturally sanctioned behavior or experience.

E. The symptom or deficit causes clinically significant distress or impairment in social, occupational, or other important areas of functioning or warrants medical evaluation.

F. The symptom or deficit is not limited to pain or sexual dysfunction, does not occur exclusively during the course of Somatization Disorder, and is not better accounted for by another mental disorder.

Source: Reprinted with permission from the Diagnostic and Statistical Manual of Mental Disorders, Text Revision, Fourth Edition, (Copyright 2000) American Psychiatric Association.

Conversion disorder
A somatoform disorder that involves sensory or motor symptoms that do not correspond to symptoms that arise from known medical conditions.

Figure 8.4

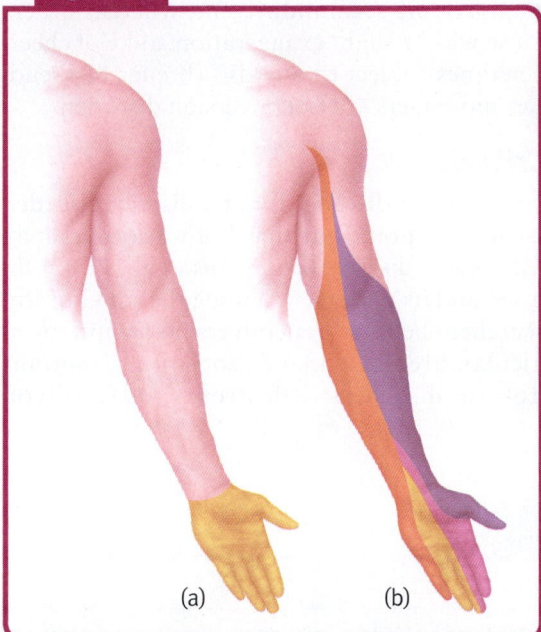

(a)   (b)

8.4 ▶ Conversion Disorder: Glove Anesthesia Patients suffering from conversion disorder have sensory or motor symptoms that at first may appear to be neurological but on further investigation do not correspond to true neurological damage. One example is *glove anesthesia,* in which the person reports that his or her hand—and only the hand—has no sensation, as shown in (a). However, the neural pathways that would create such an anesthesia in the hand would also create a lack of sensation in the arm (b); the color-coded regions show the areas served by different nerves. Thus, conversion disorder may be the appropriate diagnosis when a patient reports glove anesthesia in the absence of anesthesia of the arm.

people are present; patients don't hurt their heads, bite their tongues, or urinate, as during true seizures.

Anna O. had both motor conversion symptoms (paralysis of her neck, arm, and legs) and sensory conversion symptoms (problems with vision, a lack of sensation in her elbows). Breuer did not report any seizure-like symptoms.

In conversion disorder, muscle symptoms do not correspond to what would be produced by the relevant nerve pathways, but rather they arise from the patients' *perception* of what would happen if certain nerve pathways were disrupted. Thus, a patient may not be able to write but can scratch an itch, which would be impossible with true paralysis of the hand muscles. Similarly, when the sensory symptom of blindness occurs in conversion disorder, medical tests reveal that all parts of the visual system function normally. This was true for Mary, described in Case 8.6.

CASE 8.6 ▶ FROM THE INSIDE: Conversion Disorder

On graduating from high school, Mary decided to enter a convent and by the age of twenty-one had taken her vows of poverty, chastity, and obedience. This came as a shock to her family who, although they were practicing Catholics, had been far from religious. "I had a great need to help people and do something spiritual and good," Mary recalls. . . .

For the first decade she enjoyed the sense of community and the studious aspect of convent life. . . . But as time went on she became disenchanted with the church, which she felt was "out of touch with real people. . . . The church required blind obedience and no disagreement."

Mary began feeling nervous and anxious. She was rarely sick, but one day [when she was 36 years old] developed soreness in the back of her eye. Every time she moved it, she'd feel pins and needles. . . . By the fourth day she couldn't see out of one eye. A neurologist said it was optic neuritis, a diagnosis of nerve inflammation of unknown origin. She was hospitalized and given cortisone, but her sight didn't improve.

. . . Mary took a leave of absence and spent the good part of a year at a less stressful convent in the countryside. She began meeting regularly with a psychologist. . . . "I discovered I was a perfectionist, overworking to avoid my growing doubts.". . . Her eyesight gradually came back, and shortly after that she left the church.

. . . "During that period in my life I was undergoing deep psychological trauma. I was so unhappy, and I literally didn't want to see," she says. "I believed then, as I do today, that the body was telling me something, and I had to listen to it."

(Cantor, 1996, pp. 57–58)

People with conversion disorder may react in radically different ways to their symptoms and to what they might imply: Some seem indifferent, whereas others respond dramatically. Anna O.'s response was "a slight exaggeration, alike of cheerfulness and gloom; hence she was sometimes subject to moods" (Breuer & Freud, 1895/1955, p. 21). Table 8.13 provides more facts about conversion disorder.

Criticisms of the DSM-IV-TR Criteria

Some researchers have suggested that conversion disorder is not a distinct disorder, but rather a variant of SD; these researchers point out that both disorders may involve the bodily expression of psychological distress (Bourgeois et al., 2002). In fact, the diagnosis of conversion disorder, and its placement among the somatoform disorders, is controversial. Many researchers believe that conversion symptoms in general, and pseudoseizures in particular, are more like dissociative symptoms than like symptoms of other somatoform disorders (Kihlstrom, 2001; Mayou

---

Table 8.13 ► Conversion Disorder Facts at a Glance

Prevalence

- Conversion disorder is very rare, with prevalence estimates from 0.01% to 0.05% in the general population and up to 3% of those who are referred to outpatient mental health services.

Comorbidity

- Studies have found that up to 85% of people with conversion disorder also have major depressive disorder (Roy, 1980; Ziegler, Imboden, & Meyer, 1960).
- Patients with conversion disorder may also have a neurological disorder, such as multiple sclerosis or a condition that produces true seizures (Maldonado & Spiegel, 2001).
- A history of sexual or physical abuse is common among patients with conversion disorder (Bowman, 1993).

Onset

- This disorder frequently begins during late childhood or early adolescence, and rarely appears after age 35.
- Symptoms typically emerge suddenly after a significant stressor, such as the loss of a loved one, or a physical injury (American Psychiatric Association, 2000; Stone et al., 2009).
- For men, the disorder is most likely to develop in the context of the military or industrial accidents (American Psychiatric Association, 2000; Maldonado & Spiegel, 2001).

Course

- Symptoms typically last only a brief period of time.
- Between 25% and 67% of those with the disorder have a recurrence up to 4 years later (American Psychiatric Association, 2000; Maldonado & Spiegel, 2001).

Gender Differences

- Conversion disorder is two to ten times more common among women than men (Bowman, 1993; Raskin, Talbott, & Meyerson, 1966).
- Women with the disorder may later develop SD.
- Men with the disorder may also have antisocial personality disorder (to be discussed in Chapter 13).

Cultural Differences

- Conversion disorder is more common in rural populations, among those from lower SES backgrounds, and among those less knowledgeable about psychological and medical concepts.
- It is also more common in developing countries than in industrialized countries, and as a country becomes industrialized, the prevalence of conversion disorder decreases.
- Small "epidemics" of conversion disorder have been reported in countries undergoing cultural change or significant stress (Piñeros, Roselli, & Calderon, 1998; Cassady et al., 2005).

Source: Unless otherwise noted, the source is American Psychiatric Association, 2000.

et al., 2005). As they note, dissociation can affect not only memory and the sense of self, but can also disrupt the integration of sensory or motor functioning.

Other researchers argue that conversion disorder doesn't really exist, but is a type of factitious disorder: The patient is creating a socially sanctioned way to enact a sick role, thereby manipulating others and avoiding responsibilities (Celani, 1976). However, according to the DSM-IV-TR criteria, the symptoms would meet the criteria for factitious disorder only if they are voluntarily—that is, consciously—created. In many cases of conversion disorder, the symptoms do not appear to be consciously created, and so factitious disorder would not be an appropriate diagnosis.

Understanding Conversion Disorder

Research on neurological factors in conversion disorders focuses on how brain systems operate differently in people with the disorder. Psychological factors associated with the disorder include the role of self-hypnosis and dissociation. And a key social factor is the role of intense stressors. Unfortunately, not enough is known to understand how the various factors might influence each other.

Neurological Factors

By far, the bulk of neurologically oriented studies of conversion disorder have examined brain systems.

Brain Systems When contemplating the diagnosis of conversion disorder, clinicians must rule out simple malingering or faking of symptoms. (Patients are sometimes motivated to fake such illnesses in order to collect insurance, disability payments, and so on.) Could all cases of conversion disorder just be faking? Neuroimaging findings suggest that muscle weakness arising from conversion disorder is not the same as consciously simulated muscle weakness. For example, Stone and colleagues (2007) scanned the brains of patients with conversion disorder and of healthy controls while their ankles were flexed. The patients with conversion disorder all reported weakness in the manipulated ankle prior to the study; during the study, participants in the control group were asked to pretend that their ankles were weak. The results were clear: Some brain areas were more activated in the patients than in the controls (such as the insula, which is involved in registering input from the body) and some brain areas (including areas in the frontal lobes) were less activated in the patients than in the controls. These findings are good evidence that the patients were not simply faking their disorder.

In addition, some patients with chronic pain develop sensory deficits, a kind of "psychological" anesthesia. These patients often also have weakness (and sometimes paralysis) of a limb, and they are typically classified as having both conversion disorder and a pain disorder. In one study aimed at discovering whether such symptoms reflect changes in how brain systems operate, researchers scanned the brains of four such patients using fMRI, while sharp plastic fibers were pressed into the skin (Mailis-Gagnon et al., 2003). These patients had apparent sensory deficits in only one limb, and thus the researchers could directly compare stimulation of the normal and affected limbs. When the researchers stimulated the normal limb, the sharp plastic fibers activated a brain network that registers pain (which includes the thalamus, the anterior cingulate cortex, the insula, and part of the frontal lobe), as is normal. In contrast, this network was not activated when the researchers stimulated the affected limb, as is shown in Figure 8.5. Moreover, some brain areas—the somatosensory cortex (both the primary and secondary areas) and parts of the parietal and frontal lobes—were activated less than normally when the researchers stimulated the affected limb. These findings indicate that the "psychological" anesthesia actually affected the brain and inhibited activation in the brain areas that register sensation and pain.

Another neuroimaging study examined patients with conversion disorder who had a loss of sensation and motor control in one hand. These researchers used a vibration device to stimulate both hands while recording blood flow in the brain. They found decreased blood flow in the thalamus and the basal ganglia on the side

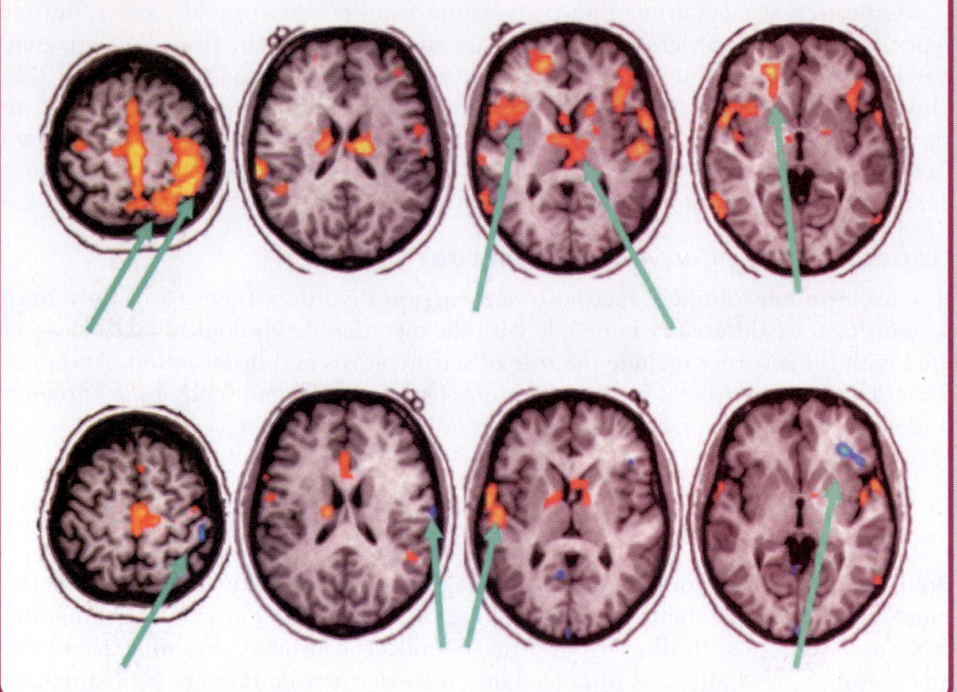

Figure 8.5

8.5 ▸ Brain Activation in Conversion Disorder: Healthy Limb Versus Affected Limb Brain areas activated when the skin of the healthy, nonaffected limb was stimulated (top row) compared to those activated when the skin of the affected limb was stimulated (bottom row); arrows show the key areas of activation (Mailis-Gagnon et al., 2003). It's clear that the scans in the bottom row show much less activation.

Source: A. Mailis-Gagnon, MD, et al., Neurology 2003;60:1501–1507. © 2003 American Academy of Neurology.

opposite the affected hand (each hemisphere of the brain controls and registers sensations from the opposite side of the body); these brain areas are involved in attention and motor control, respectively. When retested 2–4 months later, after the symptoms had disappeared, the patients' brains functioned normally (Vuilleumier et al., 2001). These findings suggest that the decreased sensitivity to stimuli that can occur in conversion disorder arises from decreased activity of sensory brain structures. Thus, at least for these patients, the disorder directly reflects brain events; it is not some form of malingering or faking of symptoms.

However, other researchers report that the brain *does* respond even though conscious perception is absent (for example, see Hoechstetter et al., 2002; Lorenz, Kunze, & Bromm, 1998). Taken together, the findings suggest that conversion disorder is not a direct consequence of impaired brain areas that *register* peripheral sensations, but rather reflects abnormal operation of brain areas that *interpret* sensations and *manage* other brain areas (that is, areas that are involved in "executive functions"). At least in some cases, abnormal processing in brain areas responsible for executive functions might inhibit brain areas that process sensation and pain or that produce movements, which in turn causes them to fail to function properly.

Finally, it is important to note that conversion disorder is sometimes incorrectly diagnosed. One study, for example, found that many patients who suffered seizures and were diagnosed with conversion disorder in fact had neurological abnormalities in one cerebral hemisphere, typically the right (Devinsky, Mesad, & Alper, 2001). Thus, in some cases, the symptoms of conversion disorder may reflect, at least in part, underlying medical problems. In fact, the results of one study of patients diagnosed with conversion motor paralysis suggest that as many as half of those patients may have a genuine medical problem (Heruti et al., 2002).

Genetics At least in some cases, conversion disorder may run in families, but it is difficult to disentangle the role of genes from that of modeling the behavior of family members (Schulte-Korne & Remschmidt, 1996). For example, if a parent never uses one hand, it is possible that a child may come to imitate that behavior, and thus not use that hand.

Psychological Factors: Self-Hypnosis?

There is no generally accepted explanation for how psychological factors might produce the selective bodily symptoms in conversion disorder (Halligan, Bass, & Wade, 2000). But self-hypnosis offers one possible explanation—that the disorder is the result of unintended self-hypnotic suggestion. According to this theory, patients have, consciously or unconsciously, "suggested" to themselves that they have symptoms. Thus, those who have a sensory conversion disorder may unknowingly hypnotize themselves so that they are not consciously aware of the sensations in some part of their body (Kozlowska, 2005); that is, such sensations have become dissociated. This theory receives support from the fact that people with conversion disorder are unusually hypnotizable (Roelofs, Hoogduin, et al., 2002).

The theory that conversion disorder results from self-hypnosis is supported by the finding that areas of the brain activated by hypnotically induced paralysis are similar to those activated by paralysis in patients with conversion disorder (Halligan et al., 2000; Oakley, 1999). The self-hypnosis explanation also is consistent with neodissociation theory, discussed in the section on dissociative amnesia: The sensory system is somehow disconnected from the executive monitoring system, creating the conscious experience of a lack of sensory input (Hilgard, 1994). Thus, conversion symptoms can be considered to be errors in the cognitive processing of sensation and movement (Kozlowska, 2005; Oakley, 1999).

Social Factors: Stress Response

Life stressors, such as combat, can trigger conversion disorder. Moreover, the greater the severity or number of stressors, the more severe the conversion symptoms (Roelofs et al., 2005). As we saw with SD, somatic symptoms can be a culturally accepted way to express feelings of helplessness (Celani, 1976), which may explain why some soldiers develop conversion disorder in combat. Conversion disorder can also be a way to obtain the attention associated with being sick. This was certainly true for Anna O., and for many other women of the Victorian era.

Hypochondriasis

People who are diagnosed with **hypochondriasis** are preoccupied with a fear or belief that they have a serious disease, but this preoccupation arises because they have misinterpreted their bodily sensations or symptoms (American Psychiatric Association, 2000). Despite the fact that physicians cannot identify a medical problem, patients with hypochondriasis persist in clinging strongly to their conviction that they have a serious disease. Although people with SD and those with hypochondriasis share a focus on bodily symptoms, only those with hypochondriasis believe that they have a serious illness despite reassurance from doctors. Moreover, people with hypochondriasis do not see that there are other possible explanations for their sensations (Smeets, de Jong, & Mayer, 2000).

What Is Hypochondriasis?

Patients with hypochondriasis may or may not realize that their worries are excessive for the situation; when they do not, they are said to have *poor insight* into their condition. Consider a man who sees floating "spots" and does not believe his eye doctor when told that such *floaters* are normal and nothing to worry about. The man probably doesn't think that the doctor is lying about the spots, but he may believe that the doctor didn't do a thorough enough eye examination; he may think that the floaters indicate that he is going blind or that he has a tumor. His worries about this problem are distressing and preoccupying to the point that he's functioning less well at work—not because of the floaters, but because of his frequent thoughts about the floaters. To be diagnosed with this disorder in DSM-IV-TR, this

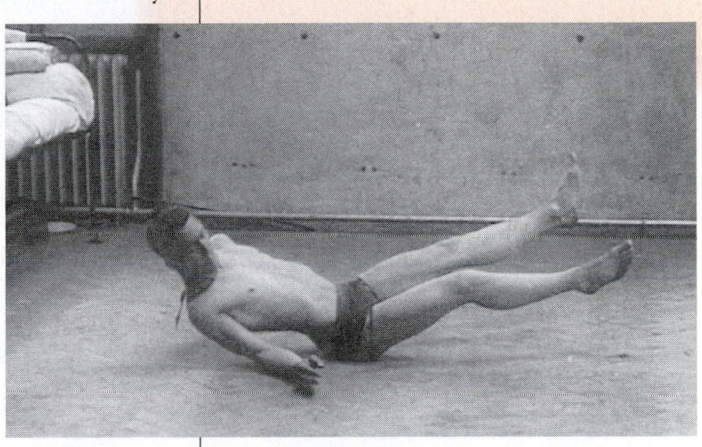

Symptoms of conversion disorder may be more common after significant psychological stressors, such as military combat. This soldier is displaying muscular spasms as part of his conversion disorder. Such symptoms among soldiers are thought to resolve a conflict between their loyalty to comrades and their fear of battle: Soldiers with such symptoms are unable to fight (Spiegel, 1974).

Hypochondriasis
A somatoform disorder marked by a preoccupation with a fear or belief of having a serious disease, but this preoccupation arises because the individual has misinterpreted his or her bodily sensations or symptoms.

Table 8.14 ▶ DSM-IV-TR Diagnostic Criteria for Hypochondriasis

A. Preoccupation with fears of having, or the idea that one has, a serious disease based on the person's misinterpretation of bodily symptoms.

B. The preoccupation persists despite appropriate medical evaluation and reassurance.

C. The belief in Criterion A is not of delusional intensity (as in Delusional Disorder, Somatic Type [discussed in Chapter 12]) and is not restricted to a circumscribed concern about appearance (as in Body Dysmorphic Disorder [discussed later in this chapter]).

D. The preoccupation causes clinically significant distress or impairment in social, occupational, or other important areas of functioning.

E. The duration of the disturbance is at least 6 months.

F. The preoccupation is not better accounted for by Generalized Anxiety Disorder, Obsessive-Compulsive Disorder, Panic Disorder [all discussed in Chapter 7], a Major Depressive Episode [Chapter 6], Separation Anxiety [Chapter 14], or another Somatoform Disorder.

Source: Reprinted with permission from the Diagnostic and Statistical Manual of Mental Disorders, Text Revision, Fourth Edition, (Copyright 2000) American Psychiatric Association.

kind of preoccupation with a perceived health problem must cause significant distress or impair the person's functioning in some way and must have continued for at least 6 months (see Table 8.14). Additional facts about hypochondriasis are presented in Table 8.15.

Like people with SD, those with hypochondriasis don't appreciate that even healthy people sometimes have aches and pains and other bodily discomforts. Instead, they unrealistically believe that having "good health" implies not having any unpleasant bodily symptoms (Barsky, Coeytaux, et al., 1993), as does the woman in Case 8.7.

CASE 8.7 ▶ FROM THE INSIDE: Hypochondriasis

I attended graduate school, held jobs, was married, had children. But my existence was peppered with episodes of illness. When the going got tough, I'd get sick. Or just the opposite: when things seemed to be going well, I'd come down with a symptom, or at least what I interpreted as one. It might be stomach pain, dizziness, black and blue marks, swollen glands, an achy heel. Anything. Whatever the symptoms, I always interpreted it as a precursor of some crippling illness: leukemia, Lou Gehrig's disease, scleroderma. I knew just enough about most diseases to cause trouble. Eventually I'd get past each episode, but it always took time—the cure a mysterious concoction of enough negative tests, a lessening of symptoms, some positive change in my life. And when the event was over, the realization that I was healthy and wasn't going to die, at least not immediately, was like a high, a reprieve, a new lease on life. That is, until the next time.

(Cantor, 1996, pp. 9–10)

Hypochondriasis and Anxiety Disorders: Shared Features

Hypochondriasis has many features in common with anxiety disorders. In fact, hypochondriasis and anxiety disorders are so similar that some researchers have advocated moving hypochondriasis from the category of somatoform disorders to the category of anxiety disorders, and renaming it *health anxiety disorder* (Mayou et al., 2005). Let's compare hypochondriasis with some anxiety disorders.

Hypochondriasis, phobias, and panic disorder are all characterized by high levels of fear and anxiety, as well as a faulty belief of harm or danger. However, with hypochrondriasis and panic disorder, the perceived danger is from an internal event that is thought to be producing a bodily sensation, whereas with phobias, it is from an external object (such as a snake) or a situation (such as giving a speech;

Table 8.15 ▸ **Hypochondriasis Facts at a Glance**

Prevalence

- In the general population, hypochondriasis is rare and its prevalence is unknown. Among medical patients, 1–5% are diagnosed with this disorder (Magarinos et al., 2002).

Comorbidity

- People with hypochondriasis also commonly suffer from an anxiety or depressive disorder or another somatoform disorder.

Onset

- Typically, hypochondriasis begins during early adulthood (Fallon et al., 1993).
- A stressful life event, such as the death of a loved one, can precipitate symptoms of hypochondriasis (Fallon & Feinstein, 2001).

Course

- Over the course of a year, 50% of people with hypochondriasis improve at least to some degree (Creed & Barsky, 2004; Olde Hartman et al., 2009).
- People most likely to recover fully from hypochondriasis do not have another psychological disorder; their symptoms developed quickly and are mild.

Gender Differences

- Nothing definitive can be said about whether one gender is more likely to suffer from this disorder than the other; the handful of relevant studies found contradictory results (Creed & Barsky, 2004; Toft et al., 2005).

Source: Unless otherwise noted, the source is American Psychiatric Association, 2000.

Fava, Mangelli, & Ruini, 2001). People with panic disorder, phobias, and hypochondriasis all may try to avoid certain stimuli or situations; with panic disorder and hypochondriasis, what is avoided may be an elevated heart rate (Hiller, Rief, & Fichter, 2002).

In addition, both patients with hypochondriasis and those with obsessive-compulsive disorder (OCD) have obsessions and compulsions (Abramowitz & Braddock, 2006). In particular, patients with hypochondriasis obsess about possible illnesses or diseases they believe they might have. They may compulsively ask doctors, friends, or family members for reassurance or compulsively "check" their body for particular sensations. If someone excessively probes, prods, or touches certain body parts, he or she can create lumps or bruises, which are then interpreted as a new "symptom" of disease. As Internet use has increased over the last decade, people with some forms of hypochondriasis spend hours compulsively consulting medical Web sites. (It's important to keep in mind that some medically related Internet chat rooms or Web sites can spread false or misleading information.)

Understanding Hypochondriasis

Let's again consider the neuropsychosocial factors. Most research on understanding hypochondriasis has examined psychological factors. Neurological and social factors are only beginning to be the focus of research and so not enough is known to understand the feedback loops among the types of factors.

Neurological Factors

Neurological factors that are associated with hypochondriasis involve brain systems, neural communication, and genetics.

Brain Systems Perhaps the most informative study of the brain systems that underlie hypochondriasis compared patients with this disorder to normal controls and also to patients who either had panic disorder or OCD (van den Heuvel et al.,

2005). The three types of patients had their brains scanned while they indicated the color of various printed words. The trick was that some words were related to OCD (e.g., "dirty," "messy"), and other words were related to symptoms of panic disorder (e.g., "crowd," "faint"). The meanings of the words thus could be distracting, perhaps to different degrees, for the patients. One relevant result of this study was that the amygdala was activated in the OCD patients when they viewed OCD-related words, but it was not activated in the patients with hypochondriasis—which shows that the two disorders are not the same. Moreover, in general the brain activation pattern of patients with hypochondriasis more closely resembled that of patients with panic disorder than patients with OCD. But even here, the patterns of activation were not identical, which indicates that the disorders are probably not precisely the same.

Neural Communication Some researchers have suggested that the neurotransmitter serotonin does not function properly in at least some cases of hypochondriasis (King, 1990). As we'll see in the section on treatment, there is some indirect support for this hypothesis, based on the observation that SSRIs (which selectively affect serotonin reuptake, as discussed in Chapter 4) appear to improve the disorder. That is, the mere fact that SSRIs can improve the symptoms is evidence that the symptoms arise, at least in part, from disruption of the activity of serotonin.

Genetics Results from one twin study suggest that genetic differences do contribute to hypochondriasis (Gillespie et al., 2000). These researchers found that genetics account for about a third of the variation in bodily symptoms that are not clearly related to a medical disorder. In addition, researchers have used genetic studies to examine the possible link between hypochondriasis and OCD; some studies find evidence for such a link (Bienvenu et al., 2000; Noyes, Happel & Yagla, 1999) and others don't (Fallon et al., 2000). One possible reason for these conflicting results is that there may be different types of hypochondriasis, only one of which is related to OCD (Barsky, 1992).

Psychological Factors: Catastrophic Thinking About the Body

People with hypochondriasis have specific biases in their reasoning: Not surprisingly, given their disorder, they not only tend to seek evidence of health threats but also may fail to consider evidence that such threats are minimal or nonexistent (Salkovskis, 1996; Smeets, de Jong, & Mayer, 2000). For instance, a man with hypochondriasis who notices a bruise on his leg might interpret it as an indicator of leukemia rather than trying to remember whether he had recently bumped into something that could cause a black-and-blue mark.

In addition, people afflicted with hypochondriasis focus attention closely on unpleasant sensations, even if those sensations are relatively weak or infrequent. They commonly focus on the functioning of body parts (such as the stomach or the heart), minor physical problems (such as a sore throat), and ambiguous physical sensations (such as "aching veins"). Moreover, they interpret bodily sensations as abnormal, pathological, and symptomatic of disease (Barsky, 1992; Barsky et al., 2000). In fact, like patients with SD, patients with hypochondriasis may engage in *catastrophic thinking* about their physical sensations or fears of illness, just as the woman in Case 8.7 did when she interpreted physical sensations as signs of "crippling illness." Furthermore, perhaps as a result of these attentional biases, people with hypochondriasis have better memory for health-related words than for non–health-related words (Brown et al., 1999).

As is the case with many anxiety disorders, people with hypochondriasis may engage in behaviors that temporarily reduce their anxiety. For example, they may repeatedly take their blood pressure, perform urine dipstick tests, feel body parts for cancerous lumps, or call their doctor about new symptoms. Such behaviors maintain their faulty beliefs and can, through negative reinforcement, sustain the anxiety in the long term.

Because of their particular cognitive biases regarding health and illness, for people with hypochondriasis, simply reading about an illness or hearing about someone who is sick can lead to becoming preoccupied with similar symptoms or diseases in their own bodies.

David Young-Wolff/PhotoEdit Inc.

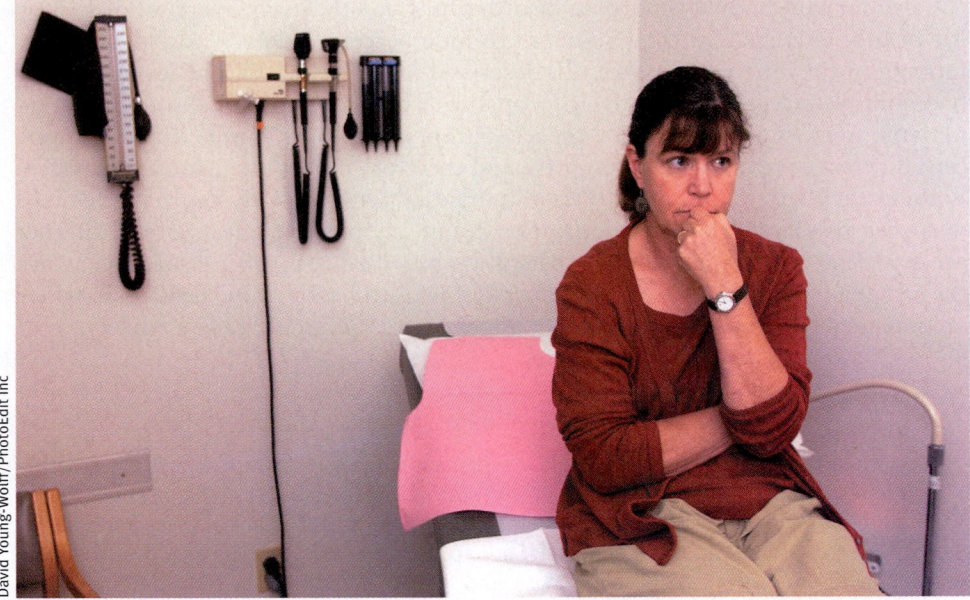

David Young-Wolff/PhotoEdit Inc

People with hypochondriasis fear that they have a serious illness and do not believe their doctors when told that they are healthy. Such patients may then "doctor-shop"—consulting many doctors in search of one who will confirm the presence of an illness.

Social Factors: Stress Response

As with other somatoform disorders, stressful events can precipitate hypochondriasis (Fallon & Feinstein, 2001). In addition, people with hypochondriasis are more likely than people without the disorder to report having experienced traumatic sexual contact, physical violence, or major familial upheaval (such as their parents' divorce) (Barsky, Wool, et al., 1994). In addition, through attention and concern, relatives and friends may unintentionally reinforce patients' symptoms.

Body Dysmorphic Disorder

Body dysmorphic disorder (sometimes called *dysmorphophobia*) is diagnosed when someone is excessively preoccupied with a *perceived* defect or defects in appearance. The preoccupation is excessive because a defect is either imagined or slight. In this section we examine body dysmorphic disorder in detail—the DSM-IV-TR criteria and the factors that contribute to the disorder.

What Is Body Dysmorphic Disorder?

It's a common experience to believe that a pimple on your forehead appears like a red beacon for others to see; many people will try to cover up or hide a pimple. It's also common for individuals with a receding hairline to change their hairstyle to make the hair loss less noticeable. What isn't common—and, in fact, signals a psychological disorder—is when an imperfection in appearance, even an imagined one, causes significant distress or takes up so much time and energy that daily functioning is impaired. These are the signs of body dysmorphic disorder. Table 8.16 lists the specific DSM-IV-TR diagnostic criteria for this disorder.

Common preoccupations for people with body dysmorphic disorder are thinning or excessive hair, acne, wrinkles, scars, complexion (too pale, too dark, too red, and so on), facial asymmetry, or the shape or size of some part of the face or body. The "defect" (or "defects") may change over the course of the illness (Phillips, 2001). People with body dysmorphic disorder may think that others are staring at them or talking about a "defect." Up to half of those with body dysmorphic disorder are delusional—that is, they believe their perception of a "defect" is accurate and not exaggerated (Phillips et al., 1994).

Table 8.16 ▸ DSM-IV-TR Diagnostic Criteria for Body Dysmorphic Disorder

A. Preoccupation with an imagined defect in appearance. If a slight physical anomaly is present, the person's concern is markedly excessive.

B. The preoccupation causes clinically significant distress or impairment in social, occupational, or other important areas of functioning.

C. The preoccupation is not better accounted for by another mental disorder (e.g., dissatisfaction with body shape and size in Anorexia Nervosa [discussed in Chapter 10]).

Source: Reprinted with permission from the Diagnostic and Statistical Manual of Mental Disorders, Text Revision, Fourth Edition, (Copyright 2000) American Psychiatric Association.

Body dysmorphic disorder
A somatoform disorder characterized by excessive preoccupation with a perceived defect or defects in appearance.

People with body dysmorphic disorder may compulsively exercise, diet, shop for beauty aids, pick at their skin, try to hide perceived defects, or spend hours looking in the mirror (like Mrs. A., described in Case 8.8, who believed that she had multiple defects). Alternatively, people with body dysmorphic disorder may try to avoid mirrors altogether. The preoccupation with—or attempts to hide—a perceived defect can be difficult to control and therefore devastating, consuming up to 8 hours each day (Phillips, 2001). An individual with body dysmorphic disorder may seek reassurance ("How do I look?"), but any positive effects of reassurance are transient; a half-hour later, the person with body dysmorphic disorder may ask the same question—even of the same person! Unfortunately, these behaviors, which are intended to decrease anxiety about appearance, end up increasing anxiety.

CASE 8.8 ▶ FROM THE OUTSIDE: Body Dysmorphic Disorder

Ms. A was an attractive 27-year-old single white female who presented with a chief complaint of "I look deformed." She had been convinced since she was a child that she was ugly, and her mother reported that she had "constantly been in the mirror" since she was a toddler. Ms. A was obsessed with many aspects of her appearance, including her "crooked" ears, "ugly" eyes, "broken out" skin, "huge" nose, and "bushy" facial hair. She estimated that she thought about her appearance for 16 hours a day and checked mirrors for 5 hours a day. She compulsively compared herself with other people, repeatedly sought reassurance about her appearance from her boyfriend and young son, applied and reapplied makeup for hours a day, excessively washed her face, covered her face with her hand, and tweezed and cut her facial hair. As a result of her appearance concerns, she had dropped out of high school and then college. She avoided friends and most social interactions. Ms. A felt chronically suicidal and had attempted suicide twice because, as she stated, "I'm too ugly to go on living."

(Phillips, 2001, pp. 75–76)

Individuals who have body dysmorphic disorder may feel so self-conscious about a perceived defect that they avoid social situations (American Psychiatric Association, 2000), which results in their having few (or no) friends nor a romantic partner. Some try to get medical or surgical treatment for a "defect," such as plastic surgery, dental work, or dermatological treatment. But surgery often does not help; in fact, the symptoms of the disorder can actually be worse after surgery (Veale, De Haro, & Lambrou, 2003). In extreme cases, when some people with body dysmorphic disorder can't find a doctor to perform the treatment they think they need, they may try to do it themselves (so-called D.I.Y., or do-it-yourself, surgery). Table 8.17 presents additional facts about body dysmorphic disorder.

Across cultures, features of body dysmorphic disorder are generally similar. However, *koro*, a condition that is observed in some people in Southeast Asia and that is somewhat similar to body dysmorphic disorder, has unique features: Those

Pop star Michael Jackson's face changed repeatedly over time, particularly his nose, chin, and cheeks, although he said that he only had surgery on his nose to help his singing. Might Michael Jackson have suffered from body dysmorphic disorder?

Michael Ochs Archives/Getty Images   Michael Ochs Archives/Getty Images   Chris Walter/Wireimage/Getty Images   Frazer Harrison/Getty Images   Michael A. Mariant-Pool/Getty Images

Table 8.17 ▶ Body Dysmorphic Disorder Facts at a Glance

Prevalence

- Approximately 0.7–2.3% of the general population has body dysmorphic disorder at any given time (Otto et al., 2001; Phillips, 2001).
- Among people having plastic surgery or dermatological treatment, prevalence rates range from 6% to 15% (Phillips, 2001).

Comorbidity

- Up to 60% of people with body dysmorphic disorder are also depressed; body dysmorphic disorder usually emerges first (Otto et al., 2001; Phillips, 2001).
- Thirty-eight percent of people with body dysmorphic disorder may also have social phobia (Coles et al., 2006).
- Up to 30% of people with body dysmorphic disorder also have OCD (Phillips, 2001).
- In one survey, almost half of those with body dysmorphic disorder had (at the time or previously) a substance-use disorder (Grant et al., 2005).
- Almost a third of those with body dysmorphic disorder will also develop an eating disorder (Ruffolo et al., 2006).

Onset

- Body dysmorphic disorder usually begins in adolescence (Phillips & Diaz, 1997; Phillips, Menard, et al., 2005), but it can go undiagnosed for several years if the person does not discuss the symptoms with anyone.

Course

- Body dysmorphic disorder is generally chronic, with fewer remissions than depression or most anxiety disorders (Phillips, Pagano et al., 2005, 2006; Phillips, Quinn, & Stout, 2008).
- The intensity of symptoms may ebb and flow (Phillips & Diaz, 1997).
- Over 25% of adults with body dysmorphic disorder have been housebound for at least 1 week; 8% were unable to work and received disability payments (Albertini & Phillips, 1999; Phillips et al., 1994).
- Two surveys found that about 30% of people with body dysmorphic disorder had attempted suicide (Phillips et al., 1994; Phillips, Coles, et al., 2005).

Gender Differences

- Body dysmorphic disorder affects both genders with approximately equal frequency, but men and women tend to differ with regard to the specific body parts they view as defective (Phillips, Menard, & Fay, 2006): Women are preoccupied with body weight, hips, breasts, and legs, and are more likely to pick their skin compulsively. In contrast, men are preoccupied with body build, genitals, height, excessive body hair, and thinning scalp hair, and are more likely to abuse or be dependent on alcohol.
- A variant of body dysmorphic disorder has been documented in some men who use anabolic steroids to build up their perceived weak muscles (Phillips, 2001).

Cultural Differences

- Generally, symptoms of body dysmorphic disorder are similar across cultures, although certain body attributes may be more likely to be the focus of concern, depending on what physical attributes are valued in a given culture (Pope et al., 1997, 2000).

with koro are preoccupied with their penis (in men) or labia, nipples, or breasts (in women), and fear that those body parts are shrinking or retracting and will disappear into their bodies, possibly resulting in death. In contrast to body dysmorphic disorder, koro is usually brief and symptoms disappear after reassurance.

Diagnosing Body Dysmorphic Disorder Versus Other Disorders

If some of the descriptions of the symptoms of body dysmorphic disorder seem to you to resemble those of anxiety disorders, you're right. Body dysmorphic disorder shares some features with anxiety disorders (see Chapter 7): (1) Like phobia disorders (agoraphobia, social phobia, and specific phobias), body dysmorphic disorder can involve an avoidance of anxiety-causing stimuli. (2) Like social phobia, it involves an excessive fear of being evaluated negatively. (3) Like OCD, body dysmorphic disorder involves obsessions (thoughts about a "defect"), as well as highly time-consuming compulsive behaviors. (As noted earlier, hypochondriasis also shares some of these features, although the compulsive behaviors are not usually as time-consuming.)

Because of these similarities and because patients with body dysmorphic disorder are highly anxious about the perceived deficit, some researchers advocate classifying body dysmorphic disorder as an anxiety disorder (Castle & Rossell, 2006; Mayou et al., 2005).

Understanding Body Dysmorphic Disorder

Research on the factors that contribute to body dysmorphic disorder has been limited thus far and has tended to focus on psychological factors. We now examine what is known about those factors as well as neurological and social ones.

Neurological Factors

One hint about the brain systems that underlie body dysmorphic disorder was provided by the tragic case of a young man whose brain became inflamed. This inflammation caused the frontal-temporal portions to atrophy, which in turn led to body dysmorphic disorder (Gabbay et al., 2003). These brain areas are involved in storing new information in memory—and thus abnormalities in them might explain why patients with body dysmorphic disorder have difficulty "updating" their impressions of themselves.

In addition, there is evidence that these patients have impaired functioning of serotonin (Marazziti et al., 1999). People who have anxiety disorders—including OCD—often have low levels of serotonin, and thus this finding is consistent with the idea that body dysmorphic disorder is related to anxiety disorders.

Finally, body dysmorphic disorder may arise, at least in part, from some of the same underlying genetic characteristics that give rise to OCD: When first-degree relatives of OCD patients were studied, many more of them had body dysmorphic disorder than in a comparable control group (Bienvenu et al., 2000). This finding is also consistent with the idea that body dysmorphic disorder is related to anxiety disorders (particularly OCD).

Psychological Factors: Focus on Imperfections

Patients with body dysmorphic disorder exhibit a variety of cognitive biases. Such patients:

- are easily distracted by emotional information, even when the information is unrelated to appearance (Buhlmann et al., 2002).

- tend to focus their attention on isolated body parts and are hypervigilant for any possible bodily imperfections.

- engage in *catastrophic thinking*, believing that such imperfections will lead to dire consequences, such as when a pimple acts as a neon light, calling attention to itself for all to see, which leads observers to think ill of the individual with the pimple (Buhlmann, Etcoff, & Wilhelm, 2008).

Like people with other somatoform disorders, people with body dysmorphic disorder often engage in behaviors that temporarily reduce their anxiety. For example, they might try to avoid mirrors (and possibly people) or develop new ways to hide a "defect"—with painstakingly applied makeup or contrived use of clothing or hats. However, just as avoidance of anxiety-inducing stimuli maintains faulty beliefs in people with phobias, so too with avoidance in body dysmorphic

Mauro Fermariello/Photo Researchers, Inc.

Compared to people with major depressive disorder, those with body dysmorphic disorder are more likely to have an education or job in art or design. However, don't infer causality from this correlation: Although it is possible that being immersed in art or design *causes* body dysmorphic disorder, it is also possible that people preoccupied with their body tend to pursue learning about or working in the arts (Veale, Ennis, & Lambrou, 2002).

disorder: Patients never have an opportunity to test their (irrational) beliefs. Through negative reinforcement, the behavior persists (see Chapters 2 and 7).

Social Factors: Cultural Emphasis on Certain Body Features

Although the features of body dysmorphic disorder are similar across cultures, the specific body parts that are the focus of patients' attention can vary, depending on the bodily attributes that are valued or emphasized in a given culture or subculture. For instance, many men with body dysmorphic disorder in the United States focus on the perception that they have small or inadequate muscles (Pope et al., 1997, 2000), whereas women tend to focus on their hips and weight (Phillips & Diaz, 1997).

Is Somatoform Disorder a Useful Concept?

Some researchers criticize the concept of somatoform disorders as a category (Mayou et al., 2005; Noyes et al., 2008). They point out that other disorders, such as mood and anxiety disorders, can also be accompanied by bodily symptoms, and so the distinction between bodily symptoms in those disorders and those in somatoform disorders is not clear. In fact, medically unexplained symptoms most frequently occur with depression and anxiety disorders (Smith, et al., 2005). More-over, many cultures reject the concept of somatoform disorders because body and mind are viewed as interrelated; the fact that there is no medical explanation for a bodily symptom is irrelevant (Lee, 1997).

Other researchers point out that different clinicians often decide on different diagnoses for the same patient with somatoform symptoms, making diagnos-tic reliability a problem (Simon & Gureje, 1999). Moreover, all four somatoform disorders are rare, particularly SD and hypochondriasis, which decreases their diag-nostic usefulness for clinicians using the DSM-IV-TR classification system (Creed, 2006; Creed & Barsky, 2004; Gureje, Ustun, & Simon, 1997; Lynch et al., 1999).

Another criticism notes that the relevant neurological, psychological, and social factors are all apt to contribute to many medical disorders (Bradfield, 2006), and that somatoform disorders are not necessarily best conceived of as psychological disorders. The primary symptoms of somatoform disorders are medical, and the fact that some of the other symptoms are psychological does not imply that the disorders themselves are psychological (Sykes, 2006). For instance, psychological factors may contribute to a heart attack, but heart attack is not included among the DSM-IV-TR list of psychological disorders.

Others point out that relying on the existence of medically *unexplained* symptoms—which underlies the diagnostic category of somatoform disorders—may only reflect the present state of knowledge about a particular set of symptoms (Merskey, 2004). That is, "medically unexplained" means "with present techniques, medically unexplained"—not "in principle, forever impossible to explain medi-cally." With the passage of time, two sorts of developments may lead the category of somatoform disorders to disappear. First, as more becomes known about the factors that contribute to each somatoform disorder, some of them may be moved to other categories, such as anxiety disorders or dissociative disorders. Second, as medical technology and diagnostic techniques improve, some patients who are cur-rently diagnosed with a somatoform disorder may be shown to have an underlying medical problem that explains their symptoms, and thus this category of psycho-logical diagnosis would no longer be appropriate.

Treating Somatoform Disorders

When treating any of the four somatoform disorders (SD, conversion disorder, hypochondriasis, or body dysmorphic disorder), clinicians target neurological, psychological, and social factors—individually or in combination. As we explain below, cognitive-behavioral therapy is generally the treatment of choice for soma-toform disorders. Let's examine similarities and differences in treatment for the four disorders.

Targeting Neurological Factors

Medications such as SSRI or St. John's wort may be used to treat some anxiety-related symptoms of somatoform disorders (see Table 8.18). As with anxiety disorders, however, when the medication is stopped, the symptoms usually return. There has not been much rigorous research on this form of treatment for somatoform disorders; the studies that have been reported have rarely included appropriate control groups, such as a placebo group or a wait-list control group to determine whether the disorder spontaneously improves with time. Other type of treatments, such as biofeedback, also target neurological factors (as shown in Table 8.18).

Were Anna O. to be treated by a mental health clinician today, she might receive medication. Anxiety or depression may have contributed to her symptoms, and if medication for these disorders did not alleviate her hallucinations, the clinician might recommend an antipsychotic medication (Martorano, 1984). Note that Anna O. *was* given medications frequently used at that time: morphine (typically given for pain relief) and chloral hydrate (a narcotic used to induce sleep). She became dependent on both of these substances, and after her "talking cure" with Breuer ended, she needed inpatient treatment to end her dependence.

Table 8.18 ▶ Targeting Neurological Factors for Somatoform Disorders

Disorder	Medication	Other Treatment	Comment
Somatization Disorder	SSRI[a] or St. John's Wort[b]	Biofeedback to decrease bodily tension or ECT	Medication studies often do not include appropriate placebo or wait-list control groups.
Conversion Disorder	For pseudoseizures, antianxiety medication (diazepam)[c]	ECT[d]; biofeedback[e] or TMS[f] for conversion paralysis	There have been very few rigorous medication studies.
Hypochondriasis	For obsessive and compulsive symptoms, an SSRI, particularly fluoxetine[g]		A wide range of medications can lead to improvement, including antipsychotics,[h] antidepressants, and antianxiety drugs,[i] suggesting that the specific medication is less important than the placebo effect of taking a medication.[j] Without CBT, relapse is likely when medication is stopped.
Body Dysmorphic Disorder	For obsessive and compulsive symptoms, an SSRI[k]		Without CBT, relapse is likely when medication is stopped.[l]

[a]Escobar et al., 1996; [b]Müller et al., 2004; [c]Ataoglu et al., 2003; [d]Giovanoli, 1988; [e]Fishbain et al., 1988; [f]Schonfeldt-Lecuona et al., 2003; [g]Fallon, 2004; Fallon et al., 1993, 2003; Magarinos et al., 2002; Mayou & Farmer, 2002; Phillips, 2001, Phillips, Albertini, & Rasmussen, 2002; [h]Fawcett, 2002; Weintraum & Robinson, 2000; [i]Kjernisted, Enns, & Lander, 2002; Oosterbaan et al., 2001; Stone, 1993; Wesner & Noyes, 1991; [j]Fallon et al., 1996; [k]Fallon, 2004; Jefferys & Castle, 2003; Magarinos et al., 2002; Mayou & Farmer, 2002; Phillips, Albertini, & Rasmussen, 2002; Phillips & Hollander, 2008; Phillips & Najjar, 2003; [l]Phillips, 2000.

Targeting Psychological Factors: Cognitive-Behavior Therapy

Research suggests that the treatment of choice for most somatoform disorders is cognitive-behavior therapy (CBT). As shown in Table 8.19, the foci of the cognitive and behavioral methods used in treating each of the disorders vary because each disorder has different symptoms. Cognitive methods focus on identifying and then modifying irrational thoughts and shifting attention away from the body and bodily symptoms. Behavioral methods focus on decreasing compulsive behaviors and avoidance.

Targeting Social Factors: Support and Family Education

Patients with a somatoform disorder can be helped, in part, merely by feeling that someone understands the pain and distress they feel (Looper & Kirmayer, 2002). For SD and conversion disorder, the therapist strives to understand the context of the symptoms and of their emergence and the way the symptoms affect the patient's interactions with others (Holder-Perkins & Wise, 2001); with these two disorders, treatment may focus on helping the patient communicate more assertively—which can help to relieve the social stressors that contribute to the disorders.

Table 8.19 ▶ Cognitive-Behavior Therapy for Somatoform Disorders

Disorder	Cognitive Focus	Behavioral Focus	Comment
Somatization Disorder	Psychoeducation; cognitive restructuring to modify faulty or irrational beliefs about bodily sensations; teach patients not to amplify the sensations	Identify and then decrease avoidant behaviors, sensations, and activities that lead to physical or psychological discomfort or restriction of activities[a]; relaxation to decrease physical tension	CBT is generally the most effective treatment for somatization disorder.[b]
Conversion Disorder	Psychoeducation; identify stressors or conflicts associated with the emergence of symptoms; develop alternative ways to resolve the conflict or cope with stressors (problem solving)[c]	Assertiveness training as appropriate; use paradoxical intention (suggesting that the patient continue to have the symptom) to decrease symptoms, as appropriate[d]	Insight-oriented treatment is sometimes used to help patients with conversion disorder understand the meaning of the symptoms. Once the meaning is understood, the symptoms may improve spontaneously.[e]
Hypochondriasis	Identify and modify faulty or irrational beliefs about health worries and bodily sensations (cognitive restructuring); teach patients not to amplify these sensations; decrease catastrophic attributions about sensations and illness worries	Identify sensations and activities that lead to discomfort; identify avoidant behaviors and decrease avoidance; use exposure with response prevention for compulsive behaviors such as bodily checking, seeking reassurance, or visiting doctors frequently	CBT is the most effective treatment for hypochondriasis.[f] Pilot studies have adapted IPT to treat hypochondriasis, and initial results are promising.[g]
Body Dysmorphic Disorder	Psychoeducation; identify and modify irrational body-related thoughts (cognitive restructuring); teach patients to shift attention away from body	Exposure with response prevention for compulsive bodily checking; exposure or systematic desensitization for body areas that are viewed as defective	Behavioral techniques are similar to those used to treat OCD. CBT is the treatment of choice for body dysmorphic disorder.[h]

[a]Mayou & Farmer, 2002; O'Malley et al., 1999; [b]Allen et al., 2006; Bass, Peveler, & House, 2001; [c]Maldonado & Spiegel, 2001; [d]Ataoglu et al., 2003; [e]Maldonado & Spiegel, 2001; [f]Barsky & Ahern, 2004; Taylor, Asmundson, & Coons, 2005; Wattar et al., 2005; [g]Stuart & Noyes, 2005; Stuart et al., 2008; [h]Williams, Hadjistavropoulos, & Sharpe, 2006.

Treatment may also focus on the family—educating family members about the disorder and the ways they may have inadvertently contributed to or reinforced the patient's symptoms. The therapist may teach family members how to reinforce positive change and to extinguish behavior related to the symptoms (Looper &

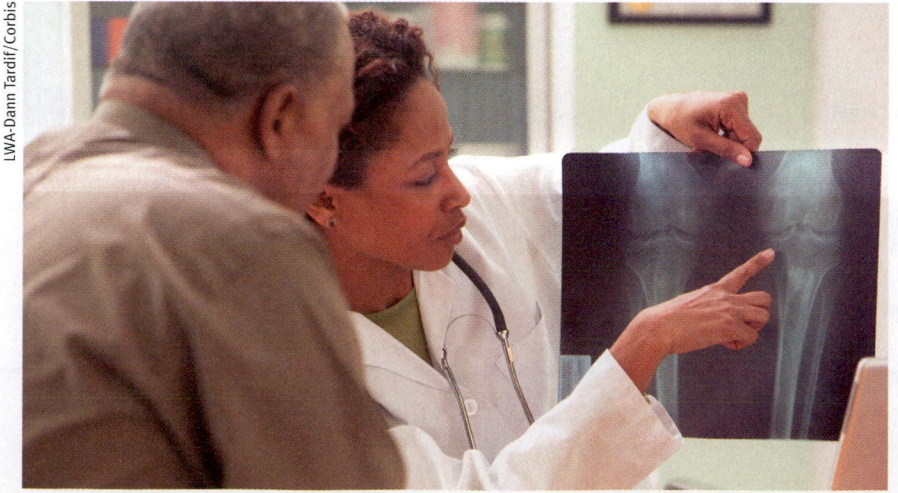

LWA-Dann Tardif/Corbis

Perhaps the most effective treatment for leg paralysis due to conversion disorder may be the simplest: Educate the patient about the nature of the symptoms. At least for three patients in one study, simply showing them their normal test results and contradictions from their physical exam did the trick. These patients walked out of the hospital unaided immediately after these results were given to them (Letonoff, Williams & Didhu, 2002).

Kirmayer, 2002; Maldonado & Spiegel, 2001). For instance, with SD, family members may be asked *not* to inquire about the patient's bodily symptoms. In addition, support groups may help patients feel less alone and isolated (Looper & Kirmayer, 2002).

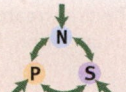

FEEDBACK LOOPS IN TREATMENT: **Somatoform Disorders**

Although biofeedback and medication primarily target neurological factors, such techniques can in turn affect the type and quality of attention paid to bodily sensations, and can change the meaning made of bodily sensations (psychological factors). CBT can provide new skills and ways of interpreting the sensations and modifying the preoccupying thoughts, which in turn can decrease the bodily symptoms (neurological factor) and the attention paid to them (psychological factor). Similarly, the relationship with a therapist (social factor) can provide reassurance and support, and as family members change how they respond to the patient's symptoms (social factor), positive change can be enhanced. Figure 8.6 shows how successful treatment of somatoform disorders affects the different types of factors directly and through their feedback loops.

Figure 8.6

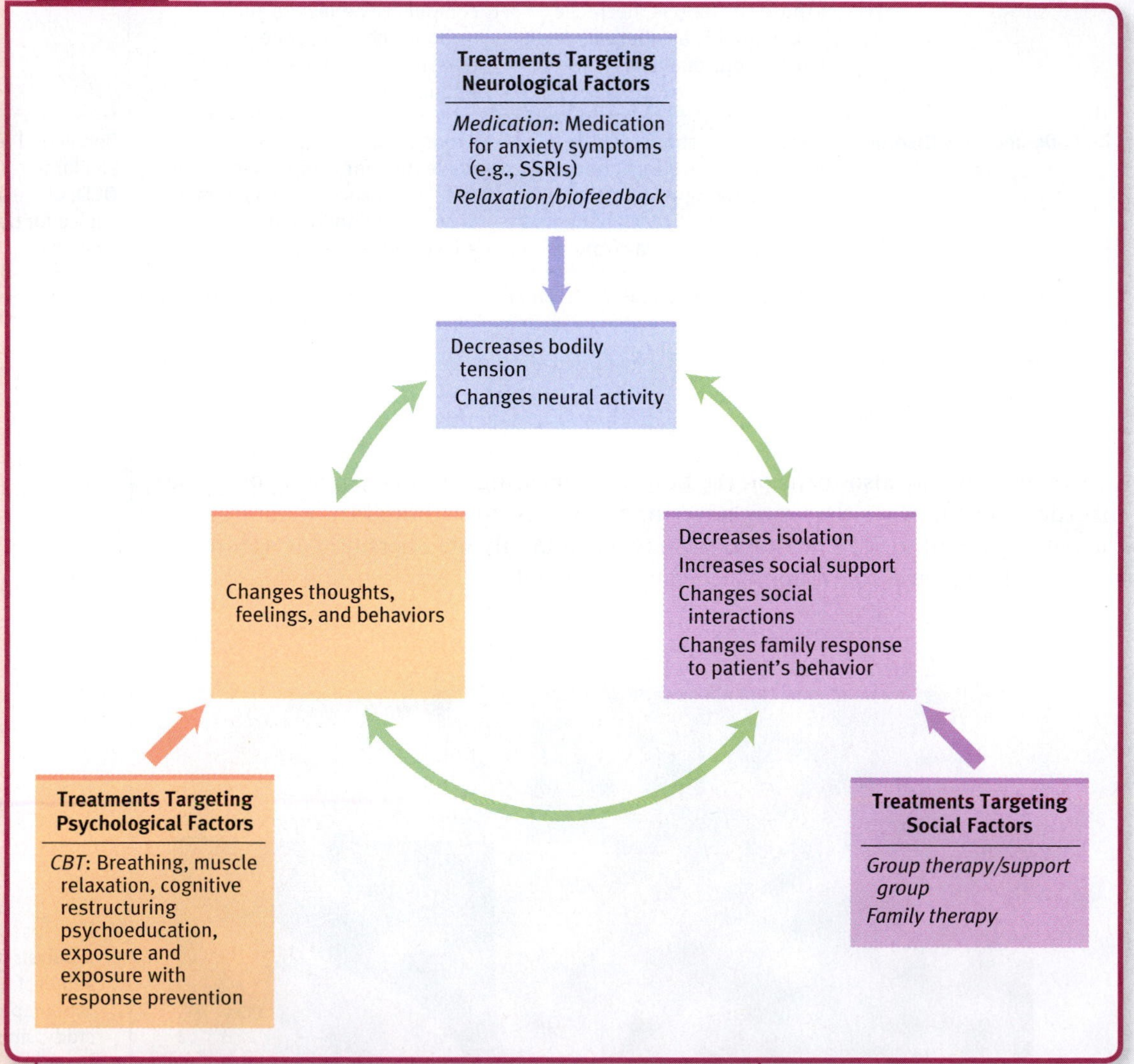

Treatments Targeting Neurological Factors

Medication: Medication for anxiety symptoms (e.g., SSRIs)
Relaxation/biofeedback

Decreases bodily tension
Changes neural activity

Changes thoughts, feelings, and behaviors

Decreases isolation
Increases social support
Changes social interactions
Changes family response to patient's behavior

Treatments Targeting Psychological Factors

CBT: Breathing, muscle relaxation, cognitive restructuring psychoeducation, exposure and exposure with response prevention

Treatments Targeting Social Factors

Group therapy/support group
Family therapy

8.6 ▸ Feedback Loops in Treating Somatization Disorder

Key Concepts and Facts About Somatoform Disorders

- Somatoform disorders involve complaints about physical well-being that cannot be entirely explained by a medical condition, substance use, or another psychological disorder and that cause significant distress or impair functioning. Diagnosing one of these disorders may require many medical tests or visits to physicians to ensure that the physical symptoms are not a result of a medical condition. Somatoform disorders are rare and are most likely to be observed in medical settings. All somatoform disorders involve bodily preoccupation, symptom amplification, and dissociation.

- Somatization disorder (SD) is characterized by multiple specific physical symptoms that are medically unexplained and impair an individual's ability to function. People with SD may avoid activities associated with their symptoms, which can create a vicious cycle as they become out of shape physically.

- The DSM-IV-TR criteria for diagnosing SD have been criticized on several grounds: (1) all symptoms are counted equally; (2) the minimum number of symptoms required is not based on research results; (3) patients' beliefs about their symptoms are not part of the criteria; and (4) the bodily symptoms may be better explained by other psychological disorders.

- Factors that contribute to SD include genes, catastrophic thinking about illness (along with symptom amplification and bodily preoccupation), other people's responses to illness, and the way symptoms function as a means of expressing helplessness.

- Conversion disorder involves sensory and motor symptoms that may initially appear to have neurological causes but in fact are not explained by a medical condition and are not consciously produced. There are three types of symptoms: motor symptoms, sensory symptoms, and seizures.

- Criticisms of DSM-IV-TR diagnostic criteria for conversion disorder include: (1) the prominent role of dissociation suggests that the disorder may be better grouped with dissociative disorders; and (2) many cases of conversion disorder may be a type of factitious disorder.

- Factors thought to contribute to conversion disorder include abnormal functioning of brain areas that interpret and manage other brain areas that process sensation and pain, self-hypnosis and dissociation, and intense social stressors.

- Hypochondriasis is characterized by misinterpretation of bodily sensations and symptoms, which leads to a belief that the individual has a serious illness—this despite no evidence of a medical problem and reassurance from health care personnel. Hypochondriasis has numerous features that are similar to those of anxiety disorders, including compulsions, obsessions, anxiety, and avoidance.

- The neural basis of hypochondriasis shares much with the neural basis of OCD and panic disorder (particularly the latter), but hypochondriasis has at least some distinct neural events. Parts of the brain involved in attention are more activated than normal, at least in certain circumstances.

- Psychological factors that contribute to hypochondriasis include attentional biases and catastrophic thinking (along with symptom amplification and bodily preoccupation).

- Body dysmorphic disorder is characterized by an excessive preoccupation with a perceived defect in appearance, which is either imagined or slight. Body dysmorphic disorder shares features with various anxiety disorders: a fear of being evaluated, obsessions (about a perceived defect), time-consuming compulsive behaviors (to hide or compensate for a perceived defect in some way), and avoidance of anxiety-inducing stimuli or situations. Some researchers advocate reclassifying body dysmorphic disorder as an anxiety disorder.

- Research on body dysmorphic disorder has focused on psychological factors, particularly cognitive biases and catastrophic thinking (along with symptom amplification and bodily preoccupation). A patient's perceived defect tends to be related to bodily attributes that are highly valued in his or her culture or subculture.

- CBT is generally the treatment of choice for somatoform disorders; medications, when used, target anxiety-related symptoms. Group and family therapy are generally used as supplementary treatments.

Making a Diagnosis

- Reread Case 8.5 about Edward, and determine whether or not his symptoms meet the criteria for somatization disorder. Specifically, list which criteria apply and which do not. If you would like more information to determine his diagnosis, what information—specifically—would you want, and in what ways would the information influence your decision?

- Reread Case 8.6 about Mary, and determine whether or not her symptoms meet the criteria for conversion disorder. Specifically, list which criteria apply and which do not. If you would like more information to determine her diagnosis, what information—specifically—would you want, and in what ways would the information influence your decision?

- Reread Case 8.7 about the unnamed woman, and determine whether or not her symptoms meet the criteria for hypochondriasis. Specifically, list which criteria apply and which do not. If you would like more information to determine her diagnosis, what information—specifically—would you want, and in what ways would the information influence your decision?

- Reread Case 8.8 about Ms. A, and determine whether or not her symptoms meet the criteria for body dysmorphic disorder. Specifically, list which criteria apply and which do not. If you would like more information to determine her diagnosis, what information—specifically—would you want, and in what ways would the information influence your decision?

Jewish Museum, Frankfurt am Main, Germany

Despite Breuer's poor prognosis for Anna's future, she went on to live a full life, becoming an accomplished advocate for and benefactor of poor women and children. In Anna's time, having a psychological disorder was neither a personal disaster nor a signal that life had to become constrained and unrewarding. This is still the case.

Follow-up on Anna O.

Anna O.'s symptoms do not fit neatly into any of the disorders discussed in this chapter. She had hallucinations and dissociative and bodily symptoms, but they probably wouldn't meet the diagnostic criteria for somatization disorder. Today, she would probably be diagnosed with more than one disorder.

Anna's symptoms cleared up near the end of her treatment with Breuer. However, after their final session, she had a major relapse, and Breuer refused to continue to treat her. He found the therapy sessions with Anna too time- and energy-consuming, and, given her relapse, he was not optimistic about her prognosis.

Anna's history for the 6 years after her treatment with Breuer remains largely unknown, although we do know that she was hospitalized several times, some of which were for her dependence on morphine and chloral hydrate, which Breuer had prescribed for her. Despite Breuer's negative prognosis, Anna O. went on to accomplish great things. Her real name was Bertha Pappenheim, and she became a social worker, the director of an orphanage, and the founder of a home for unwed mothers that was dedicated to teaching the women skills to support themselves and their children. For the rest of her life, she strove to improve the lives of poor women and children (Freeman, 1990).

SUMMING UP

Summary of Dissociative Disorders

Dissociation involves a separation of mental processes that are normally integrated—a dissociation of perception, consciousness, memory or identity. To qualify as a dissociative disorder, this separation must cause significant distress or impair functioning. Specific symptoms of dissociative disorders include amnesia, identity problems, derealization, and depersonalization. Dissociative disorders are rare and often may arise in response to traumatic events.

Dissociative amnesia is characterized by significantly impaired memory for important experiences or personal information that cannot be explained as ordinary forgetfulness or accounted for by another psychological disorder, substance use, or a medical condition. Dissociative amnesia most often occurs after some traumatic event. The amnesia may spontaneously disappear, particularly after the person leaves the traumatic situation.

Dissociative fugue is characterized by sudden, unplanned travel and difficulty remembering the past, which in turn leads to identity confusion. Apparently, the frontal lobes of patients with this disorder are not as effective at accessing stored memories, particularly about the self. Not much is known about the factors that contribute to dissociative fugue; what is known is that people who have had this disorder are more hypnotizable and dissociate more easily than do others.

Depersonalization disorder is characterized by the persistent feeling of being detached from oneself, which may be accompanied by derealization. This disorder appears to involve an under-reaction to emotional stimuli, and is more common among people who experienced severe chronic emotional abuse during childhood than among people who did not have this experience.

Dissociative identity disorder (DID) hinges on the presence of two or more distinct alters, each of which takes turns controlling the person's behavior; some alters seem to be unaware of the existence of other alters. The DSM-IV-TR diagnostic for DID criteria have been criticized for being vague and the symptoms are easy to fake. Although neuroimaging studies of patients with DID find that their brains function differently when different alters are dominant, such studies have not generally used appropriate control groups. People with this disorder are more hypnotizable and dissociate more readily than do people who do not have this disorder. The diagnosis of DID is controversial.

The posttraumatic model proposes that DID is caused by severe, chronic physical abuse during childhood, which leads to dissociation during the abuse; the dissociated states come to constitute alters, with their own memories and personality traits. The sociocognitive model proposes that DID arises as the result of interactions between a therapist and a suggestible patient, in which the therapist inadvertently encourages the patient to behave in ways consistent with the diagnosis. Both interpretations are consistent with the finding that severe childhood trauma is associated with the disorder.

The goal of treatment for DID, and for dissociative disorders in general, ultimately is to reduce the symptoms themselves and to lower the stress they induce; hypnosis may be used to help integrate dissociated perceptions and memories. According to the posttraumatic model, therapists should help patients, perhaps through hypnosis, to characterize each alter in detail. In contrast, according to the sociocognitive model, therapists should try to extinguish patients' behaviors related to alters.

Thinking like a clinician

How do mental health clinicians decide whether an individual's dissociative symptoms are normal or abnormal? Which of the two theories of DID do you think is most accurate and why?

The news reports that a 17-year-old boy murdered his stepfather. The boy says that his stepfather brutally abused him as a child, and local medical and emergency room records indicate numerous "accidents" that were consistent with such abuse. The boy also says that he has no memory of killing his stepfather; his defense attorney and several psychiatrists claim that the boy has DID and that an alter killed the stepfather. Based on what you have read in this chapter, how might this boy have developed this disorder? (Mention neurological, psychological, and social factors and possible feedback loops.) What would be appropriate treatments for him and why? Do think it is fair to punish a patient with DID for what an alter did? Why or why not?

Summary of Somatoform Disorders

Somatoform disorders involve complaints about physical well-being that cannot be entirely explained by a medical condition, substance use, or another psychological disorder and that cause significant distress or impair functioning. All somatoform disorders involve bodily preoccupation, symptom amplification, and dissociation.

Somatization disorder (SD) is characterized by multiple specific physical symptoms that are medically unexplained and impair an individual's ability to function. People with SD may avoid activities associated with their symptoms, which can create a vicious cycle as they become out of shape physically. Factors that contribute to SD include genes, catastrophic thinking about illness (along with symptom amplification and bodily preoccupation), other people's responses to illness, and the way symptoms function as a means to express helplessness.

Conversion disorder is characterized by sensory and motor symptoms, and seizures, which may initially appear to have neurological causes but in fact are not explained by a medical condition and are not consciously produced. Factors thought to contribute to conversion disorder include abnormal functioning of brain areas that process sensation and pain, self-hypnosis and dissociation, and intense social stressors.

Hypochondriasis is characterized by misinterpretation of bodily sensations and symptoms, which leads to a belief that the individual has a serious illness—this despite no evidence of a medical problem and reassurance from health care personnel. Hypochondriasis has numerous features that are similar to those of anxiety disorders, including compulsions, obsessions, anxiety, and avoidance; with hypochondriasis, the anxiety is focused on health-related matters.

The neural basis of hypochondriasis shares much with the neural basis of OCD and panic disorder, but the three disorders arise from at least some distinct neural events. Psychological factors that contribute to hypochondriasis include attentional biases and catastrophic thinking, along with symptom amplification and bodily preoccupation.

Body dysmorphic disorder is characterized by an excessive preoccupation with a perceived defect in appearance, which is either imagined or slight. Body dysmorphic disorder shares features with various anxiety disorders: a fear of being evaluated, obsessions (about a perceived defect), time-consuming compulsive behaviors to hide or compensate for a perceived defect in some way, and avoidance of anxiety-inducing stimuli or situations. Some researchers advocate reclassifying body dysmorphic disorder as an anxiety disorder.

CBT is generally the treatment of choice for somatoform disorders; medications, when used, target anxiety-related symptoms. Group and family therapy are generally used as supplementary treatments.

Thinking like a clinician

What do the four somatoform disorders have in common? What do body dysmorphic disorder and hypochondriasis—and not the other two somatoform disorders—have in common? Why might conversion disorder more appropriately be classified as a dissociative disorder? Do you think it should be—why or why not?

Now 57 years old, Mr. Andre left his native Haiti 5 years ago and moved to the United States. Unemployment rates in the U.S. were high at the time of his arrival and Mr. Andre had a hard time getting a job; he felt that he was being discriminated against. His wife supported the family for 2 years by cleaning homes. After 2 years of looking, Mr. Andre did get a job, delivering sandwiches to offices at lunchtime. Within 4 months of starting this job, though, he fell down a flight of stairs after making a delivery, and he has had persistent lower back pain since, leaving him bedridden and unable to work. Doctors have not found a medical explanation for this pain. What factors should (and shouldn't) clinicians take into account when evaluating Mr. Andre for a somatoform disorder? If they do think he has such a disorder, which one do you think it might be and why, and what treatment(s) should be recommended to Mr. Andre if you are correct? On what basis could some of the somatoform disorders be ruled out?

Key Terms

Hysteria (p. 331)

Dissociation (p. 331)

Amnesia (p. 332)

Identity problem (p. 332)

Derealization (p. 332)

Depersonalization (p. 332)

Dissociative disorders (p. 333)

Dissociative amnesia (p. 334)

Dissociative fugue (p. 337)

Depersonalization disorder (p. 340)

Dissociative identity disorder (DID) (p. 344)

Somatoform disorders (p. 353)

Somatization disorder (SD) (p. 354)

Pain disorder (p. 354)

Conversion disorder (p. 360)

Hypochondriasis (p. 365)

Body dysmorphic disorder (p. 369)

More Study Aids

For additional study aids related to this chapter, go to:

www.worthpublishers.com/rosenberg

Substance Use Disorders

The musical group the Beatles formed in 1957 and soared to international acclaim in 1963. The band's celebrity was so great that the four members—John Lennon, Paul McCartney, George Harrison, and Ringo Starr—found that they were essentially prisoners in their hotel rooms when on tour. Frenzied fans would try to steal into the rooms, going so far as to lower themselves down from the hotel roof! At Beatles' concerts, fans screamed so loudly that the band members could not hear themselves sing and play over the din. Sick of it all, the Beatles stopped touring in 1966 and just recorded music in the studio. Many of their songs broke all of the conventions of rock-and-roll music, and the Beatles developed the first themed rock album with *Sgt. Pepper's Lonely Hearts Club Band*. The album practically reeked of drug use and the band members then became famous both for their music and for their lifestyles—setting a model for a generation that experimented with mind-altering drugs. By 1968, however, tensions among the four band members had become severe, and they reached the breaking point in 1970, when the group officially dissolved. Beneath the musical history of the Beatles is a story of substance use, abuse, and dependence that illustrates the focus of this chapter.

Substance Use, Abuse, and Dependence

The Beatles used some drugs because that was what their peers did. For instance, almost all boys—and some girls—their age growing up in Liverpool, England smoked cigarettes. It was simply what was done. Similarly, the young band members drank alcohol; again, doing so was the norm. Sometimes they used a drug specifically for the effect it brought, such as when they took "uppers" (stimulants) to stay awake when performing late at night. When they toured in the early 1960s, they took drugs to relieve the monotony of life on the road; they would swallow a pill, "just to see what would happen" (Norman, 1997, p. 244). A few years later, they took "acid" (LSD) to help them understand the meaning of life and attain enlightenment and peace.

Richard Tuschman/Stock Illustration Source

Psychoactive substance
A chemical that alters mental ability, mood, or behavior.

Substance use disorders
Psychological disorders characterized by abuse of or dependence on psychoactive substances.

Substance intoxication
The reversible dysfunctional effects on thoughts, feelings, and behavior that arise from the use of a psychoactive substance.

All four members of the Beatles tried various psychoactive substances. A **psychoactive substance** is a chemical that alters mental ability, mood, or behavior. Psychoactive substances, commonly referred to as *drugs*, can be used for therapeutic purposes (for example, taking an antidepressant to diminish symptoms of depression), for nontherapeutic purposes (for example, drinking an alcoholic beverage to "unwind"), and for intoxication (for example, using a drug to get "wasted"). Frequent use of a psychoactive substance can proceed to abuse or dependence.

According to DSM-IV-TR, **substance use disorders** are characterized by abuse of or dependence on psychoactive substances. With substance use disorders, the psychoactive substance is taken either because of its effect on mood, behavior, or cognition or because it prevents uncomfortable withdrawal symptoms (American Psychiatric Association, 2000).

Why does a book on abnormal psychology include a discussion of substance use? For three reasons: First, when such use leads to abuse, it disrupts the individual's normal functioning. Substance abuse can lead to decidedly abnormal cognition or affect; not only can certain drugs produce delusions and hallucinations, but they can also induce paranoia and fear. Second, when a person becomes drug dependent, he or she may desire the substance to the point that the usual balance of motivations becomes skewed. He or she may forgo eating, sex, productive work, and all the other things that make life worth living in order to obtain the drug. Third, drug abuse may help to trigger various psychological disorders or exacerbate symptoms of a comorbid disorder. For instance, as we'll see, drug abuse is often comorbid with depression and other psychological disorders. In short, chronic substance abuse can have a ripple effect on a user's life, leading to impaired functioning in work, school, and relationships.

Is simply the act of trying a drug enough to meet the criteria for having a substance use disorder? What's the difference between use and abuse or between abuse and dependence? Moreover, does the context matter—does where and why someone uses a drug affect whether he or she would be diagnosed as abusing it? The answers to these questions help to determine whether drug use meets the criteria for a disorder and help to make decisions about treatment. Let's examine the differences among intoxication, use, abuse, and dependence.

Substance Use Versus Intoxication

The Beatles, individually and collectively, experimented with numerous drugs. Paul McCartney is generally described as having been the most cautious about drugs, whereas John Lennon used them regularly, sometimes continually. Lennon confessed to being "a drunk" in art school, and he began taking "pills" (stimulants) at age 17, when he became a musician. Why pills? "The only way to survive in Hamburg [Germany, where the band played at various periods in 1961, 1962, and 1963], to play eight hours a night, was to take pills. The waiters gave you them—the pills and drink" (Wenner, 1971). Lennon recounted how, during the filming of the Beatles' second movie, *Help!*, he and his bandmates

> turned on to pot, and we dropped drink, simple as that. I've always needed a drug to survive. The others, too, but I always had more, more pills, more of everything because I'm more crazy probably.
>
> (Wenner, 1971)

At one time or another, each Beatle could have been diagnosed with **substance intoxication**: reversible dysfunctional effects on thoughts, feelings, and behavior that arise from the ingestion of a psychoactive substance (see Table 9.1). The specific effects of substance intoxication depend on the substance and whether a person uses it only occasionally (getting drunk on Saturday night) or chronically (drinking to excess every night).

In contrast to substance intoxication, *substance use* is a general term that indicates simply that a person has used a substance—via smoking, swallowing, snorting, injecting it, or otherwise absorbing it. This term does not indicate the extent or effect of the exposure to the substance.

Table 9.1 ▶ DSM-IV-TR Criteria for Substance Intoxication

- The development of a reversible substance-specific syndrome that arises from the recent ingestion of (or exposure to) a substance.

Note: Different substances may produce similar or identical syndromes.

- The clinically significant maladaptive behavioral or psychological changes associated with intoxication (such as belligerence, rapidly changing mood, cognitive impairment, impaired judgment, impaired social or occupational functioning) are due to the direct physiological effects of the substance on the central nervous system and develop during or shortly after use of the substance.

Source: Reprinted with permission from the Diagnostic and Statistical Manual of Mental Disorders, Text Revision, Fourth Edition, (Copyright 2000) American Psychiatric Association.

Substance Abuse and Dependence

The Beatles used stimulants nightly when performing in Germany, but does that mean they were abusing the drugs? Were they dependent on the pills? Were they addicted? Some mental health clinicians and researchers avoid using the term *addiction*, partly because of its negative moral connotations and partly because the term is less exact than *abuse* or *dependence*. Moreover, *addiction* has been applied to other objects or behaviors such as chocolate, work, sex, love, and Internet use—which obscures its meaning. However, other clinicians and researchers believe that the upcoming revision of the DSM (DSM-V) should incorporate the term addiction in its classification system (O'Brien, Volkow, & Li, 2006). Those clinicians and researchers define *addiction* as the compulsion to seek and then use a psychoactive substance either for its pleasurable effects or, with continued use, for relief from negative emotions such as anxiety or sadness. These compulsive behaviors persist, despite negative consequences (National Institute on Drug Abuse [NIDA], 2007g).

Like this definition of addiction, the DSM-IV-TR definition of substance abuse focuses on the behaviors related to obtaining and using a drug, as well as the consequences of that use. According to DSM-IV-TR, **substance abuse** is a pattern of harmful use of a psychoactive substance that leads to harm or other adverse effects; see Table 9.2 (American Psychiatric Association, 1994, 2000). Whereas *intoxication* refers to the direct results of using a substance, *substance abuse* focuses more on the indirect effects of repeated use, such as legal problems, unmet obligations, or reckless behavior while using the substance (for instance, driving while under the influence). Although occasional illegal use of a substance may be associated with medical, legal, and psychological risks, it does not necessarily constitute *substance abuse* according to DSM-IV-TR. Consider someone who takes a stimulant such as Ritalin to stay awake only when cramming for exams during finals. Although such use could create medical, social, legal, or occupational problems, unless problems do arise and meet the criteria in Table 9.2, the use would not be considered abuse.

Use or abuse of a psychoactive substance can lead to **substance dependence**, the pattern of persistent and compulsive use of a psychoactive substance, despite its negative effects on work, relationships, health, or its legal consequences; Table 9.3 lists the specific DSM-IV-TR diagnostic criteria. Note that the criteria for substance abuse refer to the indirect effects of repeatedly using the substance—such as legal or social problems—whereas many of the criteria for substance dependence refer to the direct effects of compulsive and repeated substance use. According to DSM-IV-TR, patients cannot be diagnosed with both substance abuse and substance dependence; patients who meet the criteria for both disorders are only diagnosed with substance dependence.

That's Life

"I abuse chocolate."

DSM-IV-TR uses the terms *abuse* and *dependence* rather than *addiction*, in part because the word addiction has been overused. However, *abuse* and *dependence* may come to be similarly overused.

Table 9.2 ▸ DSM-IV-TR Diagnostic Criteria for Substance Abuse

A. A maladaptive pattern of substance use leading to clinically significant impairment or distress, as manifested by one (or more) of the following, occurring within a 12-month period:

(1) recurrent substance use resulting in a failure to fulfill major role obligations at work, school, or home (e.g., repeated absences or poor work performance related to substance use; substance-related absences, suspensions, or expulsions from school; neglect of children or household)

(2) recurrent substance use in situations in which it is physically hazardous to use the substance (e.g., driving an automobile or operating a machine when impaired by substance use)

(3) recurrent substance-related legal problems (e.g., arrests for substance-related disorderly conduct)

(4) continued substance use despite having persistent or recurrent social or interpersonal problems caused or exacerbated by the effects of the substance (e.g., arguments with spouse about consequences of intoxication, physical fights).

Source: Reprinted with permission from the Diagnostic and Statistical Manual of Mental Disorders, Text Revision, Fourth Edition, (Copyright 2000) American Psychiatric Association.

Substance abuse
A pattern of use of a psychoactive substance that leads to harm or other adverse effects.

Substance dependence
The persistent and compulsive use of a psychoactive substance, despite its negative effects on work, relationships, health, or its legal consequences.

Table 9.3 ▸ DSM-IV-TR Diagnostic Criteria for Substance Dependence

A maladaptive pattern of substance use, leading to clinically significant impairment or distress, as manifested by three (or more) of the following, occurring at any time in the same 12-month period:

(1) Tolerance, as defined by either of the following:
    (a) a need for markedly increased amounts of the substance to achieve intoxication or desired effect
    (b) markedly diminished effect with continued use of the same amount of the substance

(2) Withdrawal, as manifested by either of the following:
    (a) the characteristic withdrawal syndrome for the substance
    (b) the same (or a closely related) substance is taken to relieve or avoid withdrawal symptoms

(3) The substance is often taken in larger amounts or over a longer period than was intended

(4) There is a persistent desire or unsuccessful efforts to cut down or control substance use

(5) A great deal of time is spent in activities necessary to obtain the substance (e.g., visiting multiple doctors or driving long distances), use the substance (e.g., chain-smoking), or recover from its effects

(6) Important social, occupational, or recreational activities are given up or reduced because of substance use

(7) The substance use is continued despite knowledge of having a persistent or recurrent physical or psychological problem that is likely to have been caused or exacerbated by the substance (e.g., current cocaine use despite recognition of cocaine-induced depression, or continued drinking despite recognition that an ulcer was made worse by alcohol consumption).

Source: Reprinted with permission from the Diagnostic and Statistical Manual of Mental Disorders, Text Revision, Fourth Edition, (Copyright 2000) American Psychiatric Association.

Figure 9.1

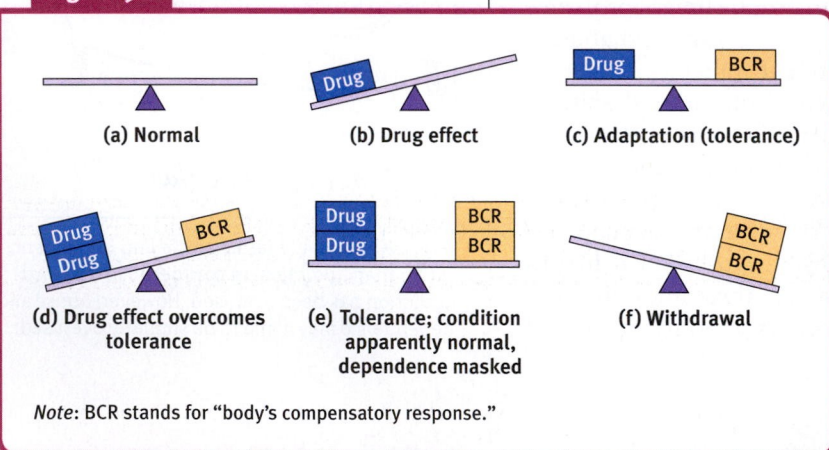

(a) Normal   (b) Drug effect   (c) Adaptation (tolerance)

(d) Drug effect overcomes tolerance   (e) Tolerance; condition apparently normal, dependence masked   (f) Withdrawal

Note: BCR stands for "body's compensatory response."

9.1 ▸ Tolerance and Withdrawal
Using a see-saw as a metaphor for the body's response to repeated drug use, this figure illustrates the progression to tolerance and withdrawal: (a) no drug use; (b) an imbalance arises from drug use; (c) the brain and body adapt to the drug, and tolerance begins; (d) more of the drug is taken to overcome tolerance; (e) the brain and body adapt to this higher level of drug use; (f) because of the adaptation, when drug use is discontinued (or reduced) that adaptation creates withdrawal symptoms.
Source: Adapted from Goldstein, 1994.

Two neurologically based symptoms of substance dependence can contribute to the diagnosis: *tolerance* and *withdrawal* (American Psychiatric Association, 2000). **Tolerance** occurs when, with repeated use, more of the substance is required to obtain the same effect (e.g., intoxication). For instance, someone who drinks alcohol regularly is likely to develop tolerance to alcohol and find that it takes more drinks to obtain a "buzz" and even more drinks to get drunk. As shown in Figure 9.1, with regular use of alcohol and some drugs, the body adapts and tries to compensate for the repeated influx of the substance.

Withdrawal refers to the set of symptoms that arises when a regular user decreases intake of the substance. As shown in Figure 9.1f, withdrawal arises because the body has compensated for the repeated influx of a drug and, when the person stops taking the drug, the neurological compensatory mechanisms are still in place, but the drug is no longer there to counterbalance them. Unfortunately, withdrawal symptoms can make it difficult for habitual users of some substances to cut back or stop their use: As they cut back, they may experience uncomfortable or even life-threatening symptoms that are temporarily alleviated by resuming use of the substance.

In most cases, substances that can lead to tolerance with regular use are also likely to produce withdrawal symptoms if stopped or taken at lower doses. There are some exceptions—substances for which tolerance may develop but withdrawal symptoms do not arise. For example, this is the case with LSD (lysergic acid diethylamide, a hallucinogen). In contrast, chronic marijuana use can lead to withdrawal symptoms, but the individual may not necessarily experience tolerance. Regular use of other substances, such as PCP (phencyclidine), causes neither tolerance nor withdrawal, and a diagnosis of dependence on this drug relies on other symptoms.

Use Becomes Abuse

People can develop substance abuse in three general ways. First, substance abuse can arise unintentionally, as can occur through environmental exposure. Consider a gas station attendant who daily inhales gasoline fumes.

Second, substance abuse (or dependence) can develop when the psychoactive element is a side effect, and the substance is taken for medicinal reasons unrelated to the psychoactive effect. For instance, former Chief Justice of the Supreme Court, William Rehnquist began taking the sedative-hypnotic drug *ethchlorvynol* (Placidyl) for insomnia and pain after back surgery in 1971 (Cooperman, 2007). Ten years later, it was clear to many that something was wrong: Rehnquist had become dependent on the drug, taking it in very large doses because he had developed a tolerance for it. In fact, the dose was so large that it impaired his speech. When he was abruptly taken off the medication, his withdrawal symptoms included paranoia and hallucinations; he was then put back on the medication and his use was gradually reduced (Mauro, 2007).

Third, substance abuse can develop as a result of the intentional use of a substance for its psychoactive effect, as the Beatles did when they took the stimulant Preludin during their nightly 8-hour gigs in Hamburg. The drug's stimulant properties gave them energy to perform these grueling sets (Spitz, 2005). In this third path toward substance abuse and dependence, someone may know the risks in using the substance but nonetheless underestimate his or her own level of risk (Weinstein, 1984, 1993). It is this third path toward developing substance abuse that has been the target of most research, and a number of different theories have tried to explain this type of slide from use to abuse.

Common Liabilities Model

The **common liabilities model** (also called the *problem behavior theory*; Donovan & Jessor, 1985) was developed in response to the results from a study that followed students from grades 7–9 into adulthood; the researchers found that adolescents who later developed substance abuse were likely to exhibit "problem behaviors" such as drug and alcohol use, early sexual intercourse, and delinquent behaviors (e.g., stealing and gambling). The researchers proposed that these various problem behaviors may stem from the same underlying factors—that is, the adolescents had *common liabilities*, related to neurological, psychological, or social factors or to feedback loops among these factors—hence the name given to this approach to understanding how use becomes abuse or dependence. Subsequent studies have supported this explanation (Agrawal et al., 2004; Ellickson et al., 2004).

Tolerance
The physiological response that arises from repeated use of a substance such that more of it is required to obtain the same effect.

Withdrawal
The set of symptoms that arises when a regular user decreases or stops intake of an abused substance.

Common liabilities model
The model that explains how neurological, psychological, and social factors make a person vulnerable to a variety of problematic behaviors, including substance abuse and dependence; also called *problem behavior theory*.

Substance use can become abuse in different ways, illustrated here left to right: through environmental exposure; when the psychoactive component is a side effect of a medication taken for medicinal purposes; or when people set out to use a substance for its psychoactive effects.

moodboard/Corbis   Punchstock/BananaStock   Chuck Savage/Corbis

One particularly important common liability is a problem with impulsivity—especially with difficulty restraining urges to engage in potentially harmful behaviors. Substance use disorders are not the only type of disorders that arise, in part, from problems with impulsivity. A variety of DSM-IV-TR disorders are characterized by impulsivity, including obsessive-compulsive disorder and the eating disorder, bulimia nervosa. In fact, DSM-IV-TR includes a separate category of impulse-control disorders that are not included in other categories. Such disorders involve compulsive or impulsive behaviors such as stealing (kleptomania), lighting fires (pyromania), and gambling, among others. Common liabilities may account for the high comorbidity between substance use disorders and these impulse-control disorders.

Gateway Hypothesis

Another theory that researchers have used to explain the progression from use to abuse or dependence is the gateway hypothesis, and the related *stage theory* (Kandel, 2002; Kandel & Logan, 1984). According to the **gateway hypothesis,** "entry" drugs such as cigarettes and alcohol serve as a gateway to (or the first stage in a progression to) use of "harder" drugs, such as cocaine, or illegal use of prescription medication. Researchers have found that some, though not all, adolescent users of entry drugs did go on to use marijuana (White et al., 2007), and some of these marijuana users moved on to harder drugs. Researchers have found that such adolescents usually first use tobacco, beer, or wine, and then progress to use marijuana and hard liquor (Kandel, 2002; Kandel & Logan, 1984). Teens are unlikely to experiment with marijuana unless they first experimented with legal—but restricted—substances such as alcohol. Similarly, adolescents and young adults don't generally try other illegal substances without having used marijuana (see Figure 9.2). The gateway hypothesis illuminates cases like that of Butch Jamieson (Case 9.1): He began with alcohol, moved on to marijuana, and then to heroin.

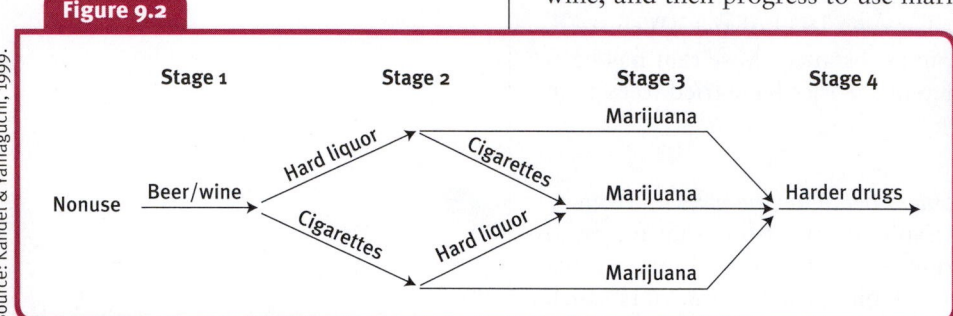

Figure 9.2

Source: Kandel & Yamaguchi, 1999.

9.2 ▸ Stages of Drug Use

CASE 9.1 ▸ FROM THE INSIDE: Progression from Alcohol to Heroin Dependence

My name is Butch Jamieson. This is my story. At this point in my life I have been clean 29 and a half years; before this I drank and used drugs for 23 years of my life. My first experience with any type of drug was alcohol at the tender age of 5. I stole some wine my mother was saving for some friends. I got extremely sick after drinking the whole bottle. From this point on I would look for the chance to steal drinks that were left behind after my parents would have people over for drinks. Everyone in my family drank, so I thought that this was normal behavior. My father had problems with drinking and he died when I was 15 years old as a result of his drinking; nine years later my mother died from the same thing. This did not tell me anything at all.

At age ten or 11, we moved to SE Washington DC where my drinking took off. At that time we did not get into the other drugs, because the older guys would not give it to us. A short time passed and this would soon change; the year was 1970, and pot was the big thing in town. We soon started to smoke pot and drink, and then at 21 years of age I allowed a sixteen year old boy to stick a needle in my arm and then my heroin addiction started. . . . Jails, Psych wards, OD-ing a few times did not stop me.

Source: Faces and Voices of Recovery, 2007a.

This general pattern of progression has been found in various countries and among different ethnic groups (Kandel & Yamaguchi, 1985). With any type of drug, there is also a typical progression of stages of use: initiation, experimentation, casual use, regular use, abuse, and dependence (Clayton, 1992; Werch & Anzalone, 1995). However, experimenting with drugs does not necessarily mean that an individual will march through this sequence to the end. Many people stop at one of the earlier stages, and most people who use entry drugs do not go on to develop substance

Gateway hypothesis
The proposal that use can become abuse when "entry" drugs serve as a gateway to (or the first stage in a progression to) use of "harder" drugs.

abuse or dependence. The gateway hypothesis is not a blueprint for all users; rather, it is a way to understand how people who abuse substances come to end up in that situation. In addition, even when people do come to abuse drugs or be dependent on them, they do not necessarily go through the specified sequence. In fact, some people with substance abuse problems had a reverse pathway: They started using harder drugs before softer ones (George & Moselhy, 2005), for example, using marijuana before using tobacco (Humfleet & Haas, 2004).

Factors Associated With Progressing from Entry Drugs to Hard Drugs

Two factors are associated with progressing from using entry drugs to using hard drugs:

1. *Age.* The younger a person is when he or she starts to use drugs or alcohol, the more likely he or she will be to abuse drugs later in life—and the less likely to decrease drug use or stop abusing drugs (D'Amico et al., 2001; Ginzler et al., 2003; Kandel & Yamaguchi, 1985; McGue & Iacono, 2005; Odgers et al., 2008; Sung et al., 2004);

2. *Quantity.* In general, the more drugs a person uses at the outset, the more likely he or she is to continue along the road to substance dependence (Bailey, 1992; D'Amico et al., 2001).

Note that the common liabilities model and the gateway hypothesis may both be correct, at least in some cases. And, in fact, they may be conceptually related: An underlying liability may lead some individuals to start experimenting with drugs earlier, or more intensely, than others. This earlier or more intense use of drugs may then lead some people with the underlying common liability to shift from entry drugs to harder drugs.

Substance Abuse as a Category or on a Continuum?

According to DSM-IV-TR, substance abuse and substance dependence are separate categories, and a habitual drug user is diagnosed with either substance abuse or substance dependence (or, in theory, does not meet the criteria for either diagnosis). However, some research suggests that the abuse/dependence distinction is artificial and that a more meaningful way to conceptualize harmful substance use, at least of alcohol, is on a continuum of severity (Heath et al., 2003; Langenbucher et al., 2004; Sher, Grekin, & Williams, 2005). According to this view, substance use, abuse, and dependence vary not qualitatively but rather quantitatively, with dependence on the extreme end of a continuum. This continuum is defined by the frequency, quantity, and duration of use (see Figure 9.3). The more frequent the use, the larger the quantity, and the longer the use has been going on, the more likely the use is to become abuse. And increasing frequency, quantity, or duration of use can push the diagnosis beyond abuse to dependence.

According to the continuum approach, we would determine whether any of the Beatles abused or was dependent on Preludin, for instance, based on how much, how often, and for how long each of them took the stimulant. This approach quantifies severity in a way that the DSM-IV-TR criteria do not (O'Malley, Johnston, & Bachman, 1999; H. A. Skinner, 1995).

Comorbidity

As we've noted in earlier chapters, many people with psychological disorders abuse substances, particularly alcohol, marijuana, cocaine, and opiates (Lingford-Hughes & Nutt, 2000). In a study specifically examining the prevalence of comorbid disorders among people with substance use disorders, almost half of those with alcohol abuse or dependence also had another DSM-IV-TR disorder—and almost three-quarters of those with drug abuse or dependence had another DSM-IV-TR disorder (Regier et al., 1993). Common comorbid disorders include mood disorders

Figure 9.3

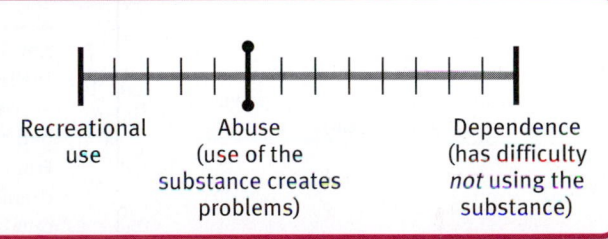

Recreational use   Abuse (use of the substance creates problems)   Dependence (has difficulty *not* using the substance)

9.3 ▸ A Continuum of Substance Use, Abuse, and Dependence Substance use, abuse, and dependence may be better conceptualized as occurring on a continuum rather than as discrete categories. Where an individual's use falls on the continuum would be determined by frequency, quantity, and duration.

Using or abusing more than one substance can increase the risk of accidental overdose; actor Heath Ledger died in 2008 from taking a combination of drugs, reportedly for his chronic insomnia. The autopsy results indicated that he'd taken pain killers, several benzodiazepines (used to decrease anxiety), and an over-the-counter antihistamine that can induce drowsiness. He may have developed tolerance to standard doses of these medications; in combination, they caused his heart or breathing to slow down so much that he died (Falco, 2008).

(most frequently depression), posttraumatic stress disorder (PTSD), schizophrenia, and *attention-deficit/hyperactivity disorder* (ADHD, discussed in Chapter 14), a disorder marked by problems sustaining attention or by physical hyperactivity (Brady & Sinha, 2005).

When substance abuse develops after another psychological disorder has developed, clinicians may infer that the person is using substances in an attempt to alleviate symptoms of the other disorder—to self-medicate. John Lennon struggled with depression at different points in his life; even at the height of Beatlemania, he had a bout of depression (revealed in his lyrics for the song "Help!"). It is possible that his drinking and later heroin use were attempts to alleviate his depression.

Polysubstance Abuse

As was true of the Beatles, some people abuse more than one substance, a behavior pattern that is called **polysubstance abuse**. One study found that among alcoholics, 64% also suffered from drug abuse or dependence (Staines et al., 2001). Polysubstance abuse is dangerous because of the ways that drugs can interact: One lethal combination occurs when someone takes a drug that slows down breathing, such as barbiturates (which are often used as sleeping pills), along with alcohol. A form of polysubstance abuse that is seldom recognized is the combination of alcohol and cigarettes (nicotine): Cigarettes are the biggest killer of all drugs, and this is particularly true among alcoholics. Most alcoholics are more likely to die from nicotine-related medical consequences, such as cardiovascular disease, than from alcohol-related ones (Hurt et al., 1996). Elaine W., the subject of Case 9.2, abused a variety of substances.

CASE 9.2 ▶ FROM THE INSIDE: Elaine W.'s Polysubstance Abuse

I remember my first experience with alcohol like it was yesterday. It was prom night, May 1969, and I was 16 years old. [My date had some wine he took from his house.] Although we had not discussed this prior to the prom, and without even giving it a second thought I turned the bottle up and drank when it was passed to me. I remember that warm, mellow glow that accompanied that first drink and the feeling of security in believing that I had found what I had been searching for all my life; feeling like I belonged and that all was well with my world. From then on, drinking on the weekends was a regular occurrence. I was always the one who drank just to get sloppy drunk and pass out. I recognized even then that once I drank the first one I couldn't stop. I didn't see that as a problem though; just thought it was the way it was supposed to be. One of my friends found out quite by accident that if she took a pain pill before drinking it made the high much better. Naturally when she shared that information with me I had to try it. They were her mother's pills and she was right—I loved it.

After graduation from high school, the love of my life went away to college. On one of his weekends home he brought some pot with him and I smoked for the first time. I thought it was pretty cool because I could get really high and not have a hangover the next day. I still continued to drink though. Because of the pot smoking, the good friends I had in high school wouldn't have much to do with me anymore, so I had found new friends that liked the same things I liked; acid, pot, cocaine, and lots of alcohol.

Source: Faces and Voices of Recovery, 2007b.

Elaine took a variety of different drugs on different occasions, and she also took alcohol and pain medication at the same time. Fortunately, Elaine's sisters were able to get her to seek treatment and her polysubstance abuse stopped.

Prevalence and Costs

Substance abuse and dependence are among the more common psychological disorders. In 2007, 9% of Americans aged 12 and older, or 22.3 million individuals, were estimated to have substance abuse or dependence (Substance Abuse and Mental Health Services Administration [SAMHSA], 2008). Generally, men are more likely than women to be diagnosed with a substance abuse or dependence disorder,

Polysubstance abuse
A behavior pattern of abusing more than one substance.

although women are more likely to be diagnosed with abuse of, or dependence on, legally obtained prescription medications (Simoni-Wastila, Ritter, & Strickler, 2004).

The prevalence of drug use, abuse, and dependence varies across ethnic and racial groups in the United States. For instance, Asian Americans have the lowest rates of alcohol abuse or dependence (4%), whereas Native Americans have the highest rate (13%). Although African Americans are more likely to abuse or be dependent on illegal substances, they are the least likely, after Asian Americans, to be diagnosed with alcohol abuse or dependence (SAMHSA, 2008). Note that these prevalence rates group people who have somewhat different ethnic backgrounds into the same broad category, but this is a simplification: Within each broad ethnic or racial category, there can be significant variation. For example, among Americans of Hispanic descent, the 1-month prevalence rate of heavy drinking (five or more drinks in a sitting) for Cuban Americans is 1.7%, whereas it is 7.4% for Mexican Americans (NIDA, 2003). Therefore, prevalence rates of racial and ethnic groups provide only a general overview, and do so only at a particular moment in time.

Substance abuse and dependence affects not only the user but also family members and friends, coworkers and colleagues. Substance abuse and dependence are associated with violence toward family members and neglect of children (Easton, Swan, & Sinha, 2000; Gruber & Taylor, 2006; Stuart et al., 2003). When the substance abuser is a parent, the abuse can create chaos and stress in the family. Parents who abuse substances may feel guilty and ashamed about their abuse, which ironically may lead them to increase their substance use to cope with these feelings (Gruber & Taylor, 2006). Children may find themselves shouldering adult tasks and responsibilities (Haber, 2000). Children of parents who abuse substances are at increased risk of developing emotional and behavioral problems (Grant, 2000; Kelley & Fals-Stewart, 2002).

A parent's substance abuse can affect children in other ways. The parent's behavior ends up inadvertently providing a model of coping that the child may come to imitate, as was the case for Barbara:

> With over 15 years of continuous sobriety I am still amazed at how my life has changed. As a young girl the message I received was: drinking, it was FUN, made people laugh and joke, not a care in the world. Later I would see it destroy our family due to an alcoholic mother. I swore I would never be like her. But I followed in her path, step by step. From my first drink to my last I was a blackout drinker. Somehow I managed to keep a job (sometimes) but I lost friends, respect and self esteem along the way. I never wanted to admit I had a problem, though I knew it all along.
>
> (Faces and Voices of Recovery, 2007c)

Substance abuse and dependence also have costs for society as a whole, both financially and in human capital. One estimate placed the total economic cost of alcohol and drug abuse in the United States at around $250 *billion a year*. These costs reflect the money spent by users in procuring the drugs, the government's costs in apprehending, bringing to trial, and incarcerating illegal drug users or dealing with the effects of illegal drug use (e.g., stealing in order to be able to buy drugs or driving under the influence of alcohol or drugs), and the costs of treating people for substance abuse and dependence (NIDA, 2006a). There is also a high correlation of substance abuse and dependence with unemployment, as is evident in Figure 9.4.

Culture and Context

The line between use and abuse, as well as that between abuse and dependence, shifts over time and across cultures and ethnic groups. For example, cocaine was used legally as a remedy for many ills in the second half of the 19th century, but it has now been illegal for decades. And, during the Prohibition era (1920–1933) in the United States, alcohol use was illegal.

Figure 9.4

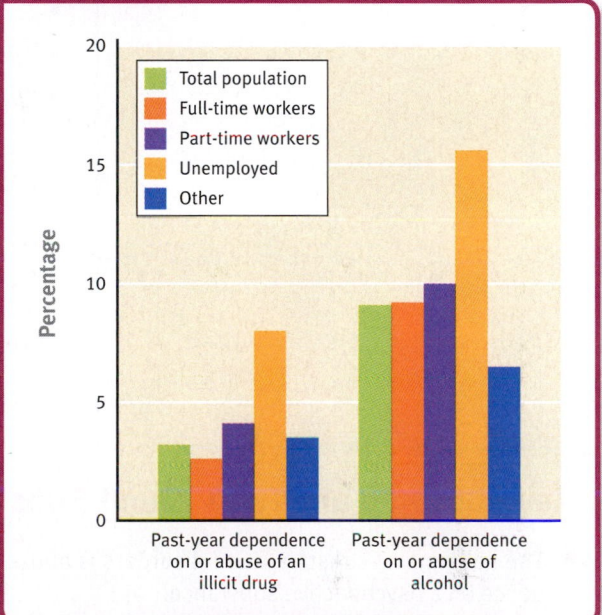

9.4 ▶ Abuse, Dependence, and Unemployment According to one national survey, 3% of Americans were dependent on or abused an illegal substance. Nine percent of those surveyed had alcohol abuse or dependence. As shown in the graph, a disproportionate number of people with abuse and dependence problems were unemployed at the time of the survey. The survey did not determine, however, whether their unemployment was a cause or a result of the substance abuse or dependence (SAMHSA, 2008).

Cultures may promote substance use in some contexts and not others. These Brazilian women are followers of Santo Daime, a spiritual practice that involves drinking *hoasca*, a tea made of plant-based hallucinogens. *Hoasca* is legal in Brazil and the United States when it is used as part of a religious practice.

BrazilPhotos.com / Alamy

Various cultures use psychoactive substances for different purposes. Some Native American tribes, for example, use peyote or psilocybin mushrooms (which, when eaten, produce vivid hallucinations) as part of sacred rituals. Similarly, tribal people in the South Pacific use *kava* (a beverage produced from the roots of a plant) and other substances as part of their rituals, which do not lead to substance abuse and dependence. Within these cultures, the use of psychoactive substances is strongly regulated, and there are penalties for abuse, including death (Trimble, 1994).

In addition, different cultures use alcohol differently. Patterns of use (or prohibition) can be divided into four categories (Room & Makela, 2000):

- *abstinence* (for example, in Muslim societies),
- *constrained* ritual use of alcohol (for example, among religious Jews),
- drinking as a *common* activity (as in some Mediterranean cultures), and
- *"fiesta" drunkenness* during community celebrations (such as Mardi Gras).

However, not all cultures fit neatly into one of these four categories, and within a given culture, subcultures may exhibit different patterns.

In the remaining sections of this chapter we discuss specific substances that are abused. We first describe what they are and consider the ways in which they have their effects. Because treatments for various types of substance abuse are similar, we consider treatment for all types of substance abuse in the final section of the chapter.

Key Concepts and Facts About Substance Use, Abuse, and Dependence

- The hallmark of substance use disorders is abuse of or dependence on a psychoactive substance.

- The term *addiction* focuses on the compulsive behaviors related to regular drug taking, but is not used in DSM-IV-TR.

- *Substance abuse* refers to the pattern of use of a psychoactive substance that leads to harmful effects; *substance dependence* refers to the persistent and compulsive use of a psychoactive substance, despite the ensuing negative consequences.

- Tolerance and withdrawal are common symptoms of substance dependence.

- Researchers have developed two compatible explanations of why substance use may lead to abuse. The common liabilities model focuses on underlying factors that may contribute to a variety of problem behaviors, including substance abuse. The gateway hypothesis focuses on factors that lead individuals to progress from using entry drugs to using harder drugs.

- In DSM-IV-TR, substance abuse and dependence are characterized as discrete categories; some researchers suggest

that they may be better conceptualized as being on a continuum.

- Substance use disorders frequently co-occur with mood disorders (particularly depression), PTSD, schizophrenia, and ADHD. Many people with substance use disorders engage in polysubstance abuse.

- Cultures can promote or regulate substance use through the use of rituals and penalties.

Making a Diagnosis

- Reread Case 9.1 about Butch Jamieson, and determine whether or not his symptoms meet the criteria for substance abuse or substance dependence. Specifically, list which criteria apply and which do not. If you would like more information to determine his diagnosis, what information—specifically—would you want, and in what ways would the information influence your decision?

Stimulants

In 1960, when the Beatles first started playing in Germany (before they became famous in England), they worked at a club in Hamburg called Indra, where they had to play for 8 hours nightly. As noted earlier, they got through their performances by taking a legal stimulant (Preludin). Band members later reported that they did not fully realize that they were ingesting a stimulant. A bouncer at the club simply handed pills to the boys and suggested that they take them. The pills had their effect: The musicians played for hours and then stayed up for hours afterward, going to other clubs (Spitz, 2005). And Preludin wasn't the only stimulant that they took. They drank coffee and tea, and all of them smoked cigarettes, as seen in the movie *A Hard Day's Night*. These stimulants are legal, but there are others that are illegal. We'll consider both types.

Stimulants are named for their effect on the central nervous system—they *stimulate* it, causing increased activity and arousal. Stimulants include nicotine and amphetamines (including Ritalin), which are restricted, as well as cocaine, crack, and MDMA (Ecstasy, or "e"), which are illegal. At low doses, a stimulant can make the user feel alert, less hungry, and more energetic, mentally and physically.

People may use stimulants repeatedly in an effort to feel more energetic. However, there is a significant cost to such repeated use: a high likelihood of dependence. Stimulants also can cause a rapid or irregular pulse and heart failure.

What Are Stimulants?

In this section we first consider the illegal drugs cocaine and crack, then consider drugs that have both legal and illegal uses—amphetamines, methamphetamines, Ritalin, and MDMA ("Ecstasy")—and end with a common substance that many people may not even realize *is* a stimulant—nicotine.

Cocaine and Crack

Derived from the coca leaf, cocaine was a popular medicine for various ailments in 18th-century Europe and North America. Its use was declared illegal at the beginning of the 20th century, after it became clear that the drug—and the quest for it—were impairing people's ability to function; it was being abused and leading to dependence (Rebec, 2000). Cocaine that is obtained in the form of a powder is typically inhaled, or "snorted"; as *crack*, a crystalline form, it is smoked.

Cocaine acts as a local anesthetic. Thus, when snorted, it leaves the user's nose feeling numb; repeated snorting can lead to diminished sense of smell and difficulty swallowing (NIDA, 2007b). Although the first few experiences of cocaine use may provide a heightened sense of well-being that can last for up to an hour, this positive state becomes increasingly harder to attain as tolerance develops (NIDA, 2007b).

Higher doses of cocaine bring many negative effects: paranoia, to the point of delusions; hallucinations, such as feeling insects crawling on the body when there are none; compulsive, repetitive behaviors such as teeth grinding; and increased heart rate and blood pressure with the accompanying risk of heart attack and sudden death. The hallucinations occur because cocaine causes sensory neurons to fire spontaneously. Users also lose their appetite, so those who are abusers or dependent on the drug may develop malnutrition. Table 9.4 lists these and additional effects of cocaine abuse. It is common for people with cocaine dependence to have alcohol dependence as well (Brady et al., 1995; Carroll, Rounsaville, & Bryant, 1993; Regier et al., 1990); when these two substances are used at the same time, the risk of sudden death increases (NIDA, 2007b).

Table 9.4 ▶ **Effects of Cocaine Abuse**

Long-term effects of cocaine	Medical consequences of cocaine abuse
Addiction Irritability and mood disturbances Restlessness Paranoia Hallucinations	Cardiovascular effects • disturbances in heart rhythm • heart attacks Respiratory effects • chest pain • respiratory failure Neurological effects • strokes • seizures and headaches Gastrointestinal complications • abdominal pain • nausea

Source: NIDA, 2004, p. 5.

Smoked crack acts more quickly than snorted cocaine and has more intense effects. Like snorting cocaine, smoking crack leads to a sense of well-being, energy, and mental clarity. However, this "high" usually lasts only minutes (NIDA, 2007b). As with other stimulants, when the high from crack evaporates, it leaves in its wake a sense of depression and craving for more of the drug, as related by Mr. R. in Case 9.3. These aftereffects may lead the user to take more of the drug, and may lead to dependence. Moreover, whereas dependence on cocaine may take months or even years to develop, dependence on crack can develop extremely rapidly—within weeks (NIDA, 2004; Rebec, 2000).

CASE 9.3 ▶ FROM THE INSIDE: Crack Dependence

Mr. R, a 28-year-old man, describes his dependence on crack.

I first started using cocaine about 4 years ago. I don't remember the first time I smoked the crack cocaine. It puts you in another world. I can't explain this euphoric feeling that it gives you, but it's a feeling I had never experienced before. I just want to sit there and enjoy the feeling and not think about anything or do anything. I have to keep doing it constantly to keep up the high.

I actually started staying out all night. I was smoking about 5 times a week and lost my apartment, lost everything. Everything was falling apart with my relationship, and I was starting to miss work a lot. But I just couldn't control it. You know, it overtook me. That's all I thought about and all I wanted to do was to keep smoking. Everything else was secondary.

An intense craving for me is when my heart starts beating fast—actually, I get a little sweaty—and all I think about doing is just going to smoke. That's it. Nothing else—everything that's on my mind just kind of disappears. First you start thinking about it, then your body almost reproduces the feeling that you get from a high.

The treatment center was an inpatient, intensive treatment program. It was a 6-month program and I stuck it out for 5 months. Then I moved into a halfway house and got myself a job. And one night, I wanted to smoke. I just said, "I want to smoke again. I want that feeling again." And I went out and picked up again.

From pretty much then on, I have been using regularly about once a week, once every 2 weeks. Today I have 9 days clean. During the past month, I've used only 2 or 3 times, so I'm curbing it down. I'm getting really sick and tired of it, honestly, of the consequences and of the using. And I don't think the high is what it used to be. It's kind of getting monotonous to me. It's getting old. I don't know what it's going to take [for me to stop]. I know I'm the only one who can do it. You know, everyone can tell me to do this and do that, but not until I make that decision that I'm going to get clean 100%.

(Hyman, 2001, p. 25–87)

As often happens when people become dependent on a drug, Mr. R.'s life became focused on obtaining and using crack, and his intense cravings made it difficult for him to stop using the drug.

Amphetamines

Amphetamines typically produce the same effects as does cocaine, although these effects last longer. Common amphetamines include *benzedrine* (racemic amphetamine sulfate), *dexedrine* (dextroamphetamine), and *adderall* (a combination of amphetamine salts). Amphetamines are usually available as pills, which typically are swallowed, although the contents of the pills may be snorted or diluted and injected. Amphetamines are legally used to treat some disorders, particularly ADHD and the sleep disorder *narcolepsy*, in which the sufferer spontaneously falls asleep for brief periods of time.

With repeated use of amphetamines, people may become hostile toward others or develop a sense of grandiosity, as well as exhibit disorganized thinking or behavior (Krystal et al., 2005). Because tolerance develops, repeat users may take high doses, which can cause *amphetamine psychosis*, a condition characterized by paranoid delusions and hallucinations (symptoms similar to those of paranoid schizophrenia; see Chapter 12). Abuse of, or dependence on, amphetamines can bring irreversible effects—including problems with memory and physical coordination—that arise from enduring changes in neurons (Volkow et al., 2001a), as well as reversible effects of irritability and violent behavior (Leccese, 1991; Wright & Klee, 2001). Withdrawal symptoms may include depression, fatigue, anxiety, and irritability. Mary Beth, discussed in Case 9.4, began using amphetamines not to experience a sense of euphoria, but to help her stay awake so that she could study more.

CASE 9.4 ▶ FROM THE OUTSIDE: Amphetamine Dependence

Mary Beth was a 20-year-old college student when she began using amphetamines to stay awake during the final exam period in the spring of her sophomore year. Although her exams didn't turn out very well (in part, because the drugs interfered with her ability to concentrate and remember), she continued to use them on and off over the next few months. Because tolerance gradually reduced the effects of the drug, she began taking more and more of it. Increasingly, the feelings of euphoria that at first had been induced by the drug were replaced by restlessness, irritability, and anger. People learned to stay away from her when she was studying late at night, because they knew she could lash out at them for the slightest provocation. Worse, though, were the profound feelings of depression that Mary Beth had begun to experience when the drug wore off. At those times, the best she could do (if she had no more drug to take) was to go to bed and try to fall asleep. The depression she experienced when she "crashed" was worse than anything she'd ever experienced before.

(Wilson et al., 1996, p. 286)

Methamphetamine

Another stimulant that is abused and leads to dependence is *methamphetamine* ("meth" or "speed"), which is chemically similar to amphetamines but has a greater and longer-lasting effect on the central nervous system. It can be inhaled, swallowed, smoked, or injected. Methamphetamine use can lead to an intense "rush" of pleasure, and use rapidly becomes abuse and then dependence as the person's life becomes focused on obtaining and using the drug. Both use of methamphetamine and the behaviors that are required to obtain it can impair functioning (NIDA, 2008a); as with all injected drugs, sharing needles increases the user's risk of contracting or spreading disease (such as HIV/AIDS). One man, Bill H., describes his dependence on methamphetamines after his first injection of the drug:

It was amazing. It also ruined my life. For the next 10 years my life went to hell. It was torture. I lost my job, family, respect, dignity, even my soul. I began doing things I still can't believe I've done. Lied, cheated, and screwed friend after friend until I had no friends at all. . . . I began to get paranoid, carried a 20-gauge sawed off shotgun around with me. . . . I saw people in trees, behind sofas, where there couldn't possibly be anybody there. It was a nightmare. That was 25 years ago; today I am a proud member of AA [Alcoholics Anonymous].

(Adapted from KCI, 2007)

Methamphetamine, like cocaine and amphetamines, can cause irritability, heart problems, hallucinations and paranoia at high doses (Ksir, 2000; NIDA, 2007e). Methamphetamine abuse can adversely affect the functioning of the neurotransmitters dopamine and serotonin, which leads to motor problems and impaired memory and emotional regulation; the increased blood pressure that results from taking the drug can cause strokes (NIDA, 2007e; Thompson et al., 2004). Table 9.5 summarizes the effects of long-term methamphetamine abuse. Some—but not all—of the brain damage inflicted by methamphetamine abuse is reversible with long-term abstinence (Volkow, Chang, et al., 2001a; Wang et al., 2004).

Table 9.5 ▶ Long-Term Effects of Methamphetamine Abuse

- Dependence
- Psychosis, including:
  - paranoia
  - hallucinations
- Repetitive motor activity
- Changes in brain structure and function
- Memory loss
- Aggressive or violent behavior
- Mood disturbances
- Severe dental problems
- Weight loss

Source: NIDA, 2008c.

Ritalin

Another legally restricted stimulant that is abused is *Ritalin* (methylphenidate hydrochloride), which—like amphetamines—is frequently prescribed for ADHD. Its neurological effect is similar to, but slower than, that of cocaine. Those who abuse Ritalin take the stimulant in any of three ways:

- swallowing pills, which does not usually lead to dependence;

- inhaling or snorting crushed pills, which leads to a quicker "high" and causes increased heart rate, stroke, or lung problems; and

- injecting the drug in liquid form, which is reported to produce an effect similar to that of cocaine.

Both inhaling and injecting Ritalin can lead to dependence. People who do not have ADHD may occasionally swallow Ritalin pills for the stimulant effects—heightened alertness, increased attention, and decreased appetite. Although such casual use does not meet the criteria for abuse or dependence, it still carries the risk of adverse medical side effects related to heart problems and stroke.

MDMA (Ecstasy)

Another stimulant drug that can be abused is *methylenedioxymethamphetamine* (MDMA), commonly called Ecstasy or simply "e." MDMA is usually taken in tablet form. It is chemically similar to both methamphetamine and the hallucinogen mescaline and has the effects of both types of drugs: the stimulant effect of increased energy and the hallucinogenic effect of distorted perceptions. With the first use, people report heightened feelings of empathy toward others and a greater sensitivity to touch. This experience is less pervasive with subsequent use. Other effects are a sense of well-being and warmth toward others, reduced anxiety, and distortions of time perception (NIDA, 2007e). Abuse can result in poor mood and difficulty regulating emotions, as well as anxiety and aggression, sleeping problems, and decreased appetite (NIDA, 2008b).

In addition, MDMA users can also develop impaired cognitive functioning, especially problems with memory, after the drug wears off. These cognitive deficits become more severe when the drug is abused (Verkes et al., 2001). One survey of MDMA users found that almost 60% reported withdrawal symptoms that included poor concentration, depression, decreased appetite, and fatigue; moreover, almost half of these users were dependent on the drug (NIDA, 2007e; Stone, Storr, & Anthony, 2006). Frequent users of MDMA may experience tolerance and withdrawal symptoms (Leung & Cottler, 2008). Lynn Smith recounts her experience of MDMA dependence:

> Sometimes I stopped eating and sleeping. I worked only two days a week to support my habit. The rest of the time was spent getting high, almost always on Ecstasy. The utter bliss of my first Ecstasy experience was a distant memory. Of course, I never could recapture that first high, no matter how much Ecstasy I took.
>
> In five months, I went from living somewhat responsibly while pursuing my dream to a person who didn't care about a thing—and the higher I got, the deeper I sank into a dark, lonely place. When I did sleep, I had nightmares and the shakes. I had pasty skin, a throbbing head and the beginnings of feeling paranoid.
>
> (Partnership for a Drug-Free America, 2007)

MDMA's side effects are similar to those of other stimulants, including increased blood pressure and heart rate. Excessive sweating, another side effect, can cause acute dehydration and hyperthermia (abnormally high body temperature). The effects of MDMA may be difficult to predict in part because the tablets often contain other drugs, such as ketamine, cocaine, or other stimulants; thus, many users' experiences with MDMA are a result of unintentional polysubstance use (Green, 2004). In addition, many people who take MDMA also use other substances—intentional polysubstance use.

Nicotine

Nicotine—the active ingredient in tobacco—is a stimulant that leads to abuse and dependence and tobacco use is associated with cancer. When inhaled via cigarettes, nicotine is absorbed into the lungs. Nicotine can also be absorbed through the mucus membranes in the mouth and throat when chewed (chewing tobacco) or when smoked but not inhaled (pipe or cigar tobacco). Nicotine causes increased alertness, but also dizziness, increased blood pressure, and irritability. Cigarette smoking delivers not only nicotine into the smoker's bloodstream, but also carbon monoxide and tar to the lungs; chronic smokers have a higher risk of developing lung cancer and other breathing-related problems than do people who do not smoke (NIDA, 2007a). According to the National Institute of Drug Abuse (NIDA, 2006c), tobacco abuse and dependence is the number-one preventable cause of death in the United States: Almost half a million Americans die each year as a result of cigarette smoking. The health effects of cigarette smoking are also costly: $75 billion is spent annually in the United States on related health care costs (NIDA, 2006c).

Nicotine withdrawal symptoms often include insomnia, anxiety, irritability, and concentration problems (Baker, Brandon, & Chassin, 2004). People who have nicotine dependence may report that the drug makes them feel relaxed. However, this may not be a direct effect of nicotine: Rather, when enough hours have elapsed since the last "hit" of nicotine, the dependent person may begin to have withdrawal symptoms, which include becoming irritable—and having another cigarette or wad of chewing tobacco produces the experience of "relaxation" as the irritability and jitteriness of withdrawal fade (NIDA, 2006c).

Many smokers try to quit several times before they are successful. George Harrison quit for a while but then resumed smoking until he was diagnosed with a smoking-related cancer, at which point he quit for good. Nicotine dependence can be so powerful that some people who develop smoking-related cancer continue the habit even after the cancer is diagnosed.

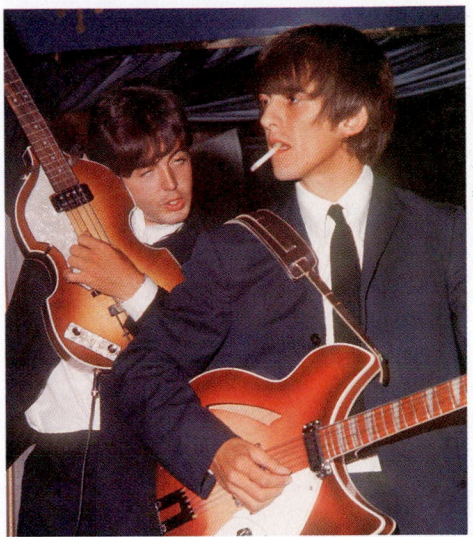

Although all the Beatles smoked cigarettes during their teenage years, some of them continued to smoke. George Harrison (at right) smoked heavily for almost all of his adult life, up to the point where he was diagnosed with throat cancer, in 1998. He also developed lung cancer, which led to his death in 2001.

DAVID MAGNUS/Rex Features courtesy Everett Collection

Understanding Stimulants

Each type of psychoactive substance can change the way the neurons function in specific brain areas. Depending on the substance, as well as the dose and the frequency of use, these brain changes can lead use to evolve into abuse and dependence. In turn, abuse and dependence can alter the way neurons communicate with each other and the ways various brain areas function and interact. With some substances, these changes may be permanent. In the following sections we examine how neurological factors contribute to stimulant abuse and stimulant dependence (and substance abuse more generally), again considering brain systems and neural communication. Because very little is known about how genes might influence stimulant abuse, that factor will not be considered. We'll begin by discussing the role of dopamine, which plays an important role with virtually all stimulants but especially with cocaine and methamphetamine. But dopamine isn't the whole story, as we shall see; we'll also consider additional general mechanisms and examine the bases of abuse of two particular substances: MDMA and nicotine. However, keep in mind that the major brain systems involved in substance abuse are not independent—they constantly influence each other through feedback loops, and these loops are probably at least as important as each system's individual contributions.

Brain Systems and Neural Communication I: Dopamine and Abuse

Particular brain structures have a role in stimulant abuse largely because of the effects of specific neurotransmitters, and so we consider brain systems and neural communication together.

The Dopamine Reward System

Dopamine plays a key role in both the pleasurable experience of taking stimulants and the abuse of stimulants (Kalivas & Volkow, 2005), as well as in the abuse of many other psychoactive substances. To see how, we need to consider the neural circuits that

Dopamine reward system
The system of neurons, primarily in the nucleus accumbens and ventral tegmental area, that relies on dopamine and gives rise to pleasant feelings.

rely on dopamine. To begin, let's consider one classic study. Researchers placed tiny electrodes in parts of rats' brains; when the rats pressed a lever, they got a small jolt of electricity, which activated neurons near the electrodes (Olds & Milner, 1954). The researchers discovered that the animals worked hard to receive electrical stimulation to certain parts of the brain. In fact, they sometimes seemed to prefer such stimulation to food or drink! (Which cannot help but remind us of some forms of drug abuse, in which users sacrifice food and drink for the drug.) This sort of finding eventually led researchers to define a "reward system" in the brain. This reward system includes the ventral tegmental area, which in turn activates the nucleus accumbens (see Figure 9.5). The neurons in this system rely on the neurotransmitter dopamine. In fact, if animals are given a drug that blocks the effects of dopamine, they will not work as hard to receive electrical stimulation in these areas (Fibiger & Phillips, 1988). For this reason, the reward system is usually referred to as the **dopamine reward system**.

A wide range of pleasurable activities, such as eating and having sex, activate the dopamine reward system. All stimulant drugs affect the dopamine reward system *directly* (Tomkins & Sellers, 2001). As we shall see when talking about other types of substances, some other types of substances (such as alcohol) also activate the dopamine reward system directly, and still other types of substances activate it indirectly

Figure 9.5

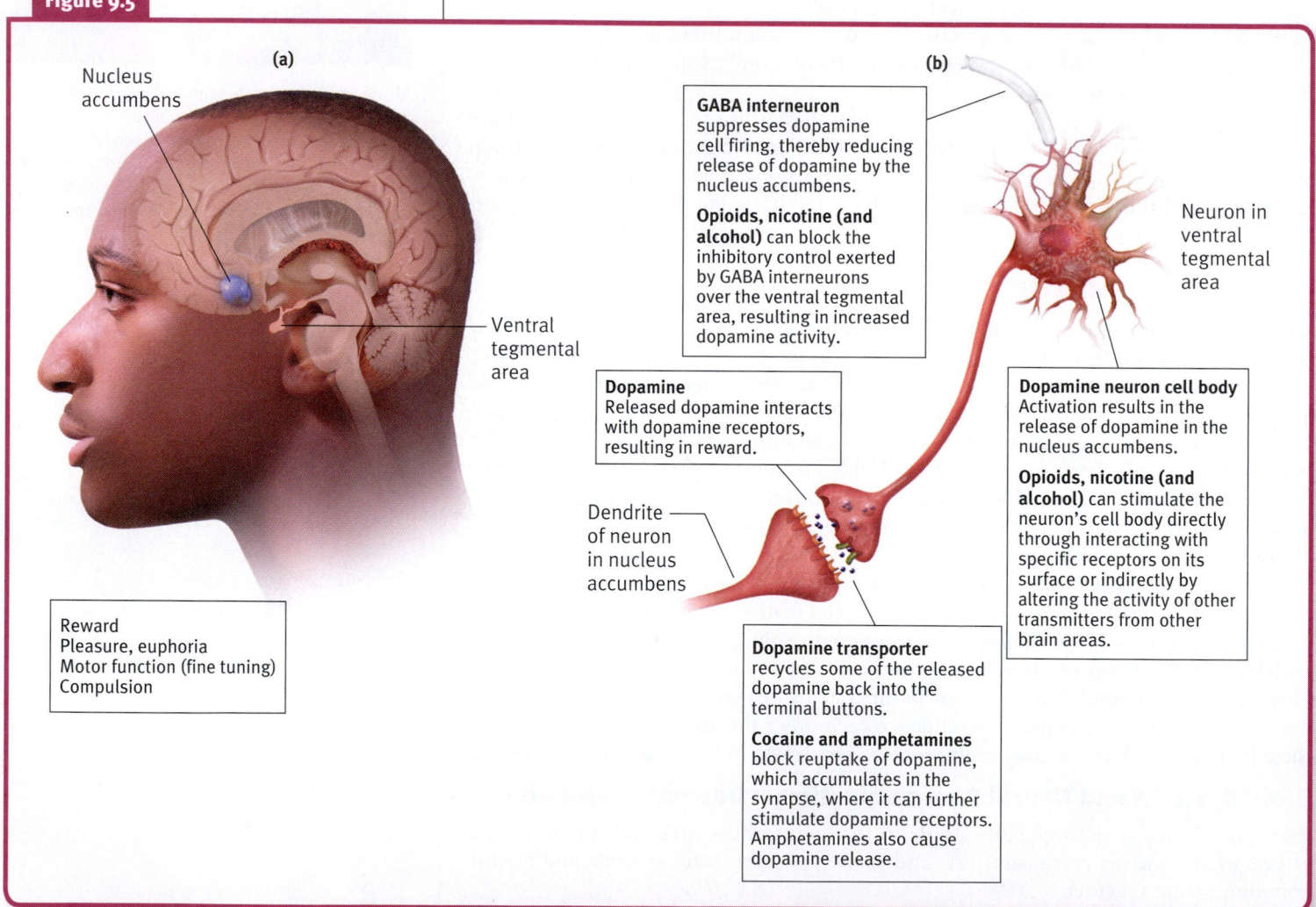

Nucleus accumbens

Ventral tegmental area

Reward
Pleasure, euphoria
Motor function (fine tuning)
Compulsion

GABA interneuron suppresses dopamine cell firing, thereby reducing release of dopamine by the nucleus accumbens.

Opioids, nicotine (and alcohol) can block the inhibitory control exerted by GABA interneurons over the ventral tegmental area, resulting in increased dopamine activity.

Neuron in ventral tegmental area

Dopamine Released dopamine interacts with dopamine receptors, resulting in reward.

Dendrite of neuron in nucleus accumbens

Dopamine neuron cell body Activation results in the release of dopamine in the nucleus accumbens.

Opioids, nicotine (and alcohol) can stimulate the neuron's cell body directly through interacting with specific receptors on its surface or indirectly by altering the activity of other transmitters from other brain areas.

Dopamine transporter recycles some of the released dopamine back into the terminal buttons.

Cocaine and amphetamines block reuptake of dopamine, which accumulates in the synapse, where it can further stimulate dopamine receptors. Amphetamines also cause dopamine release.

9.5 ▸ The Dopamine Reward System (a) Key brain areas and neural systems of the dopamine reward system. (b) Ways that the dopamine reward system is activated and altered by substance use, abuse, and dependence.

Note: Only the axon and synapse of the interneuron are shown, and for illustration purposes, there is only one terminal button of the dopamine neurons shown. In fact, the axon from the dopamine neuron has many terminal buttons.

by altering other brain areas or neurotransmitters that, in turn, affect dopamine (Leone, Pocock, & Wise, 1991).

Regular stimulant use (or other substance use) usually affects the dopamine reward system. Researchers have thus proposed the *dopaminergic hypothesis* of substance abuse: The rewarding effects of a drug arise directly or indirectly from the dopamine reward system (Koob & Le Moal, 2008; Robbins & Everitt, 1999a, 1999b; Tomkins & Sellers, 2001; Torrens & Martín-Santos, 2000). Because of the neural changes that occur with continued abuse, after a while, the person needs the substance to feel "normal" and experiences cravings when not using the drug.

As researchers have come to understand the dopamine reward system in more detail, they have begun to gain insight into an age-old puzzle: Why are some people more susceptible to becoming abusers than others? Do they have less "character" or a weak "moral compass"? No. In fact, at least part of the answer is that the dopamine reward system is more sensitive and responsive in some people. For example, in one study, participants were given an injection of the stimulant Ritalin. The researchers found that participants who rated the experience as pleasant had fewer dopamine receptors than those who found it unpleasant (Volkow et al., 1999). Such findings support the hypothesis that people with fewer dopamine receptors may be more vulnerable to drug use (and abuse); the smaller quantity of receptors means they have reduced activation in the reward system, which is boosted by substance use (Swanson & Volkow, 2002). In fact, rats bred so that they consume relatively high amounts of alcohol appear to have a less responsive dopamine reward system, which could explain why they drink more (McBride et al., 1990).

In addition, as we'll discuss shortly, stimuli related to taking a drug—such as the music, lighting, and crowds at a dance club where cocaine use occurs—can become associated with drug use. Connections among different brain areas, such as the amygdala and hippocampus, store associations between drug use and the stimuli related to drug use. Once such associations are established, these drug-related stimuli themselves can trigger the dopamine reward system (Tomkins & Sellers, 2001). Moreover, simply perceiving such aspects of the environment can activate structures in the limbic system (Dackis & O'Brien, 2001), which is tightly tied to the dopamine reward system. For example, one such structure is the anterior cingulate, and an fMRI study found that this structure was activated when cocaine addicts simply watched videotapes of cocaine-related objects and events (Wexler et al., 2001).

Effects of Cocaine and Methamphetamine on the Brain

To see how the dopamine reward system is involved in drug abuse, let's look at two abused drugs, cocaine and then methamphetamine. The effects of cocaine on the brain result from the way it affects dopamine levels. Specifically, cocaine binds to dopamine transporters—the molecules that take excess dopamine from the synapse and bring it back to dopamine containing sacs within the terminal buttons of the transmitting neuron (see Figure 9.6). When cocaine binds to these transporter molecules, they don't operate as effectively to remove dopamine from the synapses—and thus more dopamine

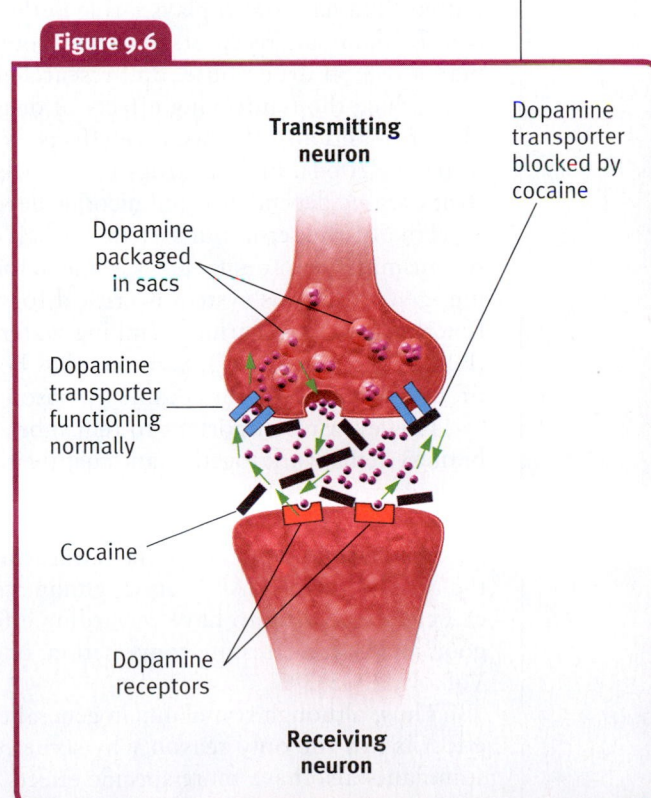

Figure 9.6

Transmitting neuron

Dopamine transporter blocked by cocaine

Dopamine packaged in sacs

Dopamine transporter functioning normally

Cocaine

Dopamine receptors

Receiving neuron

9.6 ▶ Cocaine Abuse and Dependence and Dopamine This schematic illustrates how cocaine binds to dopamine transporters, which prevents normal reuptake of dopamine back into the transmitting neuron and increases the amount of dopamine in the synapse, which thereby activates the dopamine reward system.

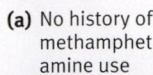

Figure 9.7

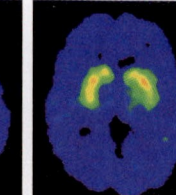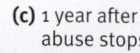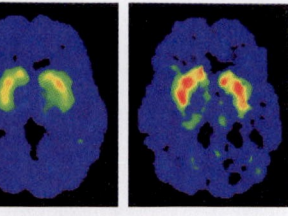

(a) No history of methamphetamine use   **(b)** 1 month after abuse stops   **(c)** 1 year after abuse stops

9.7 ▶ Methamphetamine Abuse: Reversible and Irreversible Brain Damage (a) This scan shows the distribution of dopamine transporters in a normal brain. (b) This scan shows the brain of a person who had used methamphetamine over a period of years; as is evident, even 1 month after this person stopped using the drug, the dopamine transporters are still in short supply. (c) This scan shows the brain of the same abuser more than a year after stopping the use of methamphetamine; although there is some recovery of function, the effects of chronic abuse are not completely reversed.

Source: Nora D. Volkow et al., The Journal of Neuroscience, December 1, 2001, 21 (23):9414–9418.

lingers there, which causes the receiving neuron to fire even when relatively little dopamine has been released by the sending neuron (Koob & Bloom, 1988; Koob, Sanna, & Bloom, 1998). Thus, relatively little stimulation can produce pleasurable sensations.

A similar mechanism is at work when someone takes methamphetamine. Again, the drug binds to the molecules that transport excess dopamine back to the terminal buttons and prevents them from operating effectively—thereby leaving more dopamine in the synapse, which in turn activates the dopamine reward system. Long-term use of methamphetamine disrupts the functioning of these transporter molecules. Moreover, as shown in Figure 9.7, not all of the damage inflicted on the brain by long-term methamphetamine abuse is reversible. The images in the figure show the distribution of dopamine transporters in the brain of a person who abused methamphetamine. As is evident, even 2 years after the person stopped using methamphetamine, the neurological effects of chronic abuse are not totally reversed.

Brain Systems and Neural Communication II: Beyond Dopamine

In this book we have emphasized that brain areas work together in systems, and often more than one system is involved in producing a particular behavior. This is true of stimulant abuse in particular, and substance abuse in general. Although the dopamine reward system plays a crucial role in leading people to abuse drugs, it is not the whole story. Many other neurotransmitters and their related brain systems have been implicated in drug abuse, but three are particularly important: gamma-aminobutyric acid (GABA), glutamate, and serotonin.

The GABAnergic system—the term used for the system of neurons that rely on the neurotransmitter GABA—appears to play a particular role in the shift from recreational use to abuse and dependence (Brady, 2005; Kalivas & Volkow, 2005). The GABAnergic system includes part of the frontal lobe—in particular, the prefrontal cortex—that is involved in motivated behavior (that is, behavior oriented toward a goal) and thus in drug-seeking behavior (Kalivas & Volkow, 2005).

The glutamate system—which consists of neurons that rely on the neurotransmitter glutamate—also plays a role in the shift from drug use to abuse and dependence. Glutamate receptors abound throughout the cortical and limbic regions that play a role in drug abuse, and researchers have shown that such receptors help to produce the reinforcing effects of drugs—which lead some people to become abusers—and also the negative effects experienced during withdrawal (Kenny & Markou, 2004). In fact, drugs that block glutamate receptors have been used to treat cocaine dependence and nicotine dependence (Ait-Daoud et al., 2006).

Finally, the serotonin system—which consists of neurons that rely on the neurotransmitter serotonin—plays a role in the abuse of stimulants. This is not surprising, given that this system is critical for the regulation of many basic biological functions, such as eating, drinking water, sexual behavior, and response to pain (Pihl & Peterson, 1995). Serotonin has been shown, for example, to play a role in producing the desire for cocaine (Aronson et al., 1995).

However, it's important to remember that the different neurotransmitters and brain systems work together and that their effects emerge from their interactions. As we have described, stimulants lead to increased dopamine production in the nucleus accumbens (and other dopamine-producing areas), and the higher level of dopamine not only has direct effects on the reward value of drugs but also indirectly modulates the activity of the GABAnergic, glutamate, and serotonin systems. These systems can cause the drug to have rewarding effects and make other rewards (such as a good meal, an interesting conversation, or a paycheck) feel less valuable (Kalivas & Volkow, 2005).

Thus, although stimulants in general engage the dopamine reward system, this effect is not the only reason why some people come to abuse such drugs. Some stimulants also have more specific effects on the brain. For example, MDMA not only causes dopamine to be released, but also binds to serotonin transporters and thereby creates excess serotonin in the synapse (analogous to the effect of cocaine on dopamine in a synapse; see Figure 9.6). This excess serotonin can have a calming, relaxing effect. However, high levels of serotonin in the synapse not only affect the receiving neuron, but also cause the sending neuron to produce less serotonin in the future. This effect persists even after the person has stopped using the drug. Moreover, in animals, even short-term use of MDMA can produce enduring damage to the terminal buttons of serotonin-releasing neurons, which in turn contributes to disrupted learning, memory, sleep, and appetite (NIDA, 2007e; Parrott, 2002). As a stimulant, then, MDMA not only affects the dopamine reward system, but also the serotonin system.

Finally, some stimulants operate on very specific receptors. For example, nicotine acts on a specific type of acetylcholine receptor called the *nicotinic receptor*. Such receptors are located on the cell bodies of dopamine-releasing neurons. Activation of these receptors leads to increased release of dopamine in the nucleus accumbens, as well as removing the inhibiting effect of other neurotransmitters (Picciotto, 1998; Tomkins & Sellers, 2001). The dopamine reward system is activated within 10 seconds of inhaling tobacco, which activates nicotinic receptors. Nicotine may activate brain areas in a pattern that parallels the brain areas affected by cocaine (Pich et al., 1997). Table 9.6 lists the neurological factors that contribute to the abuse of and dependence on stimulants.

Table 9.6 ▶ Neurological Factors That Contribute to the Abuse of and Dependence on Stimulants
• Stimulants bind to dopamine transporters, leading to increased dopamine in the synapse.
• Substance activates the dopamine reward system, specifically the nucleus accumbens and ventral tegmental area.*
• Associations between drug-related stimuli and drug use can activate the limbic system (and the dopamine reward system).*
• GABA, glutamate, and serotonin are involved in the shift from recreational drug use to abuse and dependence.*
*This factor is not unique to *stimulant* abuse and dependence.

Psychological Factors: From Learning to Coping

Various psychological factors contribute to stimulant abuse and dependence, and to substance abuse and dependence in general. One type of psychological factor is observational learning: Through observing others, people develop expectations about when to use drugs and what the experience of using a given substance should be like. These expectations in turn act as feedback that affects how the brain actually responds to a drug (Nitschke et al., 2006; Wager et al., 2004). Another psychological factor is operant conditioning: When the consequences (effects) of drug use are rewarding, the person is likely to use drugs again and again. Repeated drug use, in turn, can produce classical conditioning, whereby stimuli associated with drug use, such as the vial containing crack, elicit a *craving* (a strong urge or desire) for the drug (Epstein et al., 2009). Such factors affect each other and can become feedback loops that create a spiral of substance abuse and dependence.

Let's examine these psychological factors in more detail, first considering observational learning and then moving on to operant and classical conditioning—which are involved in the progression from use to abuse and dependence and in the maintenance of abuse and dependence once they develop.

Observational Learning

People may develop substance abuse or dependence, in part, through observing use or abuse of drugs by models—family members, peers, celebrities, or mentors. Not everyone who observes substance use or abuse will follow suit, but simply observing how other people use substances as a coping strategy can provide a model for that particular way to cope (Winfree & Bernat, 1998). For example, suppose a girl witnesses her respected older brother having an argument with their father. The brother and sister leave the house after the fight, and the brother proceeds to smoke crack while complaining about the father. Through observation, the younger sister learns that one way to cope with stress is through substance use. Similarly, studies have found that if a person's peers use or abuse substances, that person is likely to do the same (Dishion & Medici Skaggs, 2000; Fergusson, Swain-Campbell, & Horwood, 2002).

However, the relation between observing another person and then subsequently imitating his or her behavior is only a correlation—and, as we saw in Chapter 2, correlation does not imply causation. It is possible that those who are at risk for developing substance abuse (perhaps because of a family history) may be more likely to seek out peers who are substance users. For instance, consider that people who have a high need for social approval are more likely to model their peers' behavior. So, it is possible that if peers abuse drugs, those desperate for social approval are more likely to use or abuse drugs than are people who resist peer pressure and do not respond strongly to peer approval (Caudill & Kong, 2001).

In any event, observational learning is an established fact. And it is possible that by watching others—such as parents or peers, for instance—children and young adults learn to expect drugs to produce certain kinds of experiences, even if they do not use substances as a coping strategy (Brown et al., 1999; Colder et al., 1997; Zamboanga et al., 2005). For instance, when the Beatles began smoking cigarettes during their early teens, they did so in part because such behavior was modeled by their parents and their community; in addition, they probably developed the expectation that smoking would be fun and might make them appear more attractive to girls. These positive expectancies, developed through observational learning, may have led them to continue to smoke, even if smoking was initially unpleasant.

Operant Conditioning

Operant conditioning exerts its influence on stimulant use and abuse (and substance use, abuse, and dependence more generally) in several ways. First, if stimulant use is followed by pleasant consequences, those consequences act as positive reinforcement (which leads to recurrent use). Research on the dopamine reward system shows that aspects of this type of learning have neurological underpinnings. In fact, the dopamine reward system begins to be activated with the *expectation* of a drug's positive effects (that is, the expectation of reinforcement), which leads to **reward craving**—the desire for the gratifying effects of using a substance (Verheul, van den Brink, & Geerlings, 1999). Reward craving occurs even if recent experiences of drug use have not been positive.

Second, stimulant use and abuse can independently lead to negative reinforcement—alleviating a negative state, thereby producing a desirable experience (remember that negative reinforcement is not the same as punishment). In fact, such negatively reinforcing effects contribute to substance abuse among people trying to manage the psychological aftereffects of physical or emotional abuse (Bean, 1992; Catanzaro & Laurent, 2004; Ireland & Widom, 1994; Stewart, 1996); in particular, using drugs may (temporarily) distract them from painful memories or their present circumstances, and hence be reinforcing.

Drug use may provide transient relief from negative states, but persistently using substances as the means of gaining such relief (as the coping strategy)—which may have been learned, in part, through observing how other people cope—doesn't generally work, despite the fact that while the drug is in the system it may seem to the person that it helps. Substance use may temporarily make a person less aware of or make him or her care less about life's difficulties, but it doesn't make those difficulties go away. When the substance wears off, the person is in the same situation, if not worse off because of the consequences of the substance use (e.g., "crashing" after the high wears off or missing a deadline because of being high). These continuing life challenges in turn require more coping, and the person can enter a downward spiral. If substance use becomes the dominant coping strategy, it inevitably becomes substance abuse and possibly dependence.

The temporary emotional relief provided by substance use can create cravings for the drug when an individual experiences negative emotions; this type of craving is sometimes referred to as **relief craving** (Verheul, van den Brink, & Geerings, 1999). Both reward craving and relief craving can cause substance-dependent people to use drugs compulsively, even when they would like to quit. Thus, cravings are thought to play a primary role in maintaining substance dependence (Torrens & Martín-Santos, 2000).

A third way that operant conditioning contributes to substance abuse and dependence also involves negative reinforcement, but in this case because using the

Reward craving
The desire for the gratifying effects of using a substance.

Relief craving
The desire for the temporary emotional relief that can arise from using a substance.

substance can eliminate withdrawal symptoms. That is, once a substance develops dependence, he or she probably will experience withdrawal as the substance wears off—with symptoms that can range from mildly unpleasant to extremely unpleasant and potentially lethal. Substance use eliminates the unpleasant withdrawal state, which increases the likelihood of subsequent use. (Note that this type of desire to use a substance differs from relief craving, in which an individual has an urge to use a substance to reduce an uncomfortable state brought on by factors not related to withdrawal.)

Fourth, people who go on to abuse substances may respond more than others to a particular pattern of operant conditioning. Research has revealed that compared to people who don't abuse substances, people who do abuse substances are more likely to prefer smaller amounts of reinforcement that occur immediately after a behavior to larger amounts of delayed reinforcement (Bickel & Marsch, 2001). They also prefer larger but delayed losses (punishment) over smaller but more immediate losses (Higgins, Heil, & Lussier, 2004). Thus, when a substance abuser can choose between taking a drug (with immediate reinforcement, along with possible delayed losses or punishment) and not taking it (with a loss of immediate reinforcement), he or she may choose the immediate reward of drug use.

Classical Conditioning

Stimuli associated with drug use (such as drug paraphernalia) are referred to as **drug cues**, and they come to elicit conditioned responses through their repeated pairings with drug use. The drug cues are then associated with the reinforcing (positive or negative) effects of the drug and, in fact, drug cues can themselves elicit the activation of the dopamine reward system (Tomkins & Sellers, 2001). Being exposed to such cues—or even thinking about them—can lead to drug cravings (Hyman, 2005; Stewart, de Wit, & Eikelbloom, 1984). For example, people often handle money when buying cocaine and then use the cocaine shortly afterward; handling money can then become a conditioned stimulus. Thus, a person addicted to cocaine can come to crave it after handling money (Hamilton et al., 1998). Similarly, for cigarette smokers, certain conditioned stimuli—such as a full sensation in the belly after dinner—can lead to a craving for a cigarette among after-dinner smokers (Lazev, Herzog, & Brandon, 1999). Even after successful treatment for substance abuse, being exposed to drug cues can lead a former abuser to experience powerful cravings and can increase the risk of relapse (Hyman, 2005; Torrens & Martín-Santos, 2000).

Cravings do not last indefinitely, however. When a person craves a substance but does not use it, the craving normally disappears within an hour (Wertz & Sayette, 2001). Researchers have found that a person is more likely to feel the craving when he or she expects to be able to take the drug. Because expectations moderate cravings and cravings can lead to relapse, expectations play a role in causing relapses.

Table 9.7 summarizes the psychological factors that contribute to abuse of and dependence on stimulants.

A stimulus associated with substance use can lead a person to crave the substance. For some, simply handling money can cause a strong craving for cocaine.

Jonathan Torgovnik/Getty Images

Table 9.7 ▸ Psychological Factors That Contribute to Abuse of and Dependence on Stimulants

- Observational learning: People observe models using substances as a coping strategy and develop expectations about drug use.*
- Operant conditioning:
  - Positive reinforcement leads to subsequent expectations of reward, which in turn lead to reward craving.*
  - Substance use alleviates a negative state, which provides negative reinforcement and leads to relief craving; substance use can become a chronic coping strategy.*
- Classical conditioning: Drug cues elicit a craving*

*This factor is not unique to *stimulant* abuse and dependence.

Drug cues
The stimuli associated with drug use that come to elicit conditioned responses through their repeated pairings with use of the drug.

Social Factors

In addition to the neurological and psychological factors that contribute to stimulant abuse and dependence, various social factors can promote substance use, abuse and dependence. Specific negative patterns of family interactions and peer relations are associated with a higher risk of a subsequent substance use disorder. In addition, perceived social norms play a role, and less directly, sociocultural factors create a backdrop that makes some people more vulnerable to stimulant abuse and dependence, as well as to substance use disorders in general. Let's examine these social factors in more detail.

Family Relations

Research grounded in the stage theory (introduced earlier in this chapter), found that teenagers whose drug use progressed from marijuana to other illegal substances did not have close relationships with their parents (Andrews et al., 1991). However, this finding is only a correlation; it could be that the factors that led to drug abuse also soured relationships between teenager and parents or that bad relationships contributed to drug abuse—or that some third factor, such as a particular temperament, contributed to both factors. In addition, many studies have found that adolescents who have dysfunctional family interactions (for example, have experienced child abuse, violence in the household, or parental substance abuse) are more likely to use and abuse substances (Hawkins, Catalano, & Miller, 1992; Hesselbrock, 1986; Kilpatrick et al., 2000).

Peers

Friends do things together; they often have common views or activities they enjoy. It's not surprising, then, that peers' substance use can influence an individual's substance use and abuse (Brewer et al., 1998). The influence of peers can also help explain findings that support the gateway hypothesis about increasing drug use. Once a (susceptible) individual repeatedly uses an illicit entry drug, such as marijuana, he or she is then more likely to spend time with peers who also use this drug and become socialized into a subculture favorable to drug use. The person who sells the marijuana is also likely to sell harder drugs, such as cocaine, providing an opportunity to experiment with harder drugs (Hall & Lynskey, 2005).

Norms and Perceived Norms

Societies specify norms of behavior, which include the degree to which psychoactive substances can be taken without being considered abuse. The Beatles changed social norms, at least for a while, among some portions of the population, through their public association with drugs: their arrests for possession of illegal drugs, Paul McCartney's admission that he used LSD, and song lyrics referring to drug use, such as "I get high with a little help from my friends" from *Sgt. Pepper*. Many fans perceived that drug use was "in," that they would not be "hip" unless they used drugs too.

This observation highlights an important fact about social norms: It's a person's *perception* of the norms that is the key, not the actual social norms. Perceptions of social norms about drug use clearly affect drug use; that is, when people think that "everyone" in their school, neighborhood, social class, or clique uses drugs, they are more likely to use drugs themselves. In contrast, people who think that only a minority of their classmates, neighbors, or friends use drugs will be less likely to use drugs. The extent of the group's actual drug use is less important than what the individual *perceives* it to be.

Moreover, perceived norms can be distorted. Specifically, people tend to notice the behavior of others who are using substances (e.g., "They were high as kites") more than they do the behavior of those who do not use substances or use them only moderately (Perkins, 1997). This distortion may lead to an incorrect perception about the social norm of substance use—that it is more common than it actually is. This mistaken perception in turn can lead individuals to calibrate their substance use to the inaccurate norm and use drugs more heavily than the true norm.

Sociocultural Factors

In addition to family and friends, other social forces can nudge individuals closer to or further away from stimulant abuse and dependence as well as substance abuse generally. People who are experiencing economic hardship and are unemployed are more likely to develop substance use disorders (Reid et al., 2001; SAMHSA, 2000). Consider that children who grow up in economically disadvantaged neighborhoods are more likely to be exposed to ads for legal psychoactive substances (alcohol and cigarettes) and to have easier access to these legal psychoactive substances as well as to illegal ones. Children who live in such neighborhoods may also observe more substance abuse among family members, peers, or adults; as noted earlier, such modeling can have an adverse effect. Moreover, these children are also more likely to experience or witness traumatic events and develop PTSD (see Chapter 7), which is associated with substance abuse (Johnson, 2008; Stewart, 1996).

Society at large also influences substance use by establishing legal consequences (Torrens & Martín-Santos, 2000). Society's influence is also seen in how access to drug treatment centers is regulated and in the national policies that direct resources toward effective prevention and treatment programs. Table 9.8 summarizes the social factors associated with abuse of and dependence on stimulants.

As noted by the asterisks in Tables 9.6, 9.7, and 9.8, most of the factors that contribute to stimulant abuse and dependence also contribute to abuse of and dependence on other substances; the one exception is the specific neurological effects of stimulant drugs. Because most of the factors contribute to substance abuse and dependence generally, we do not examine the feedback loops among the factors until after we review all types of substance abuse and dependence.

Table 9.8 ▸ Social Factors That Contribute to Abuse of and Dependence on Stimulants

- Dysfunctional family interactions are correlated with the presence of substance use disorders.*
- An individual's substance use is related to that of his or her peers.*
- Norms and perceived norms influence substance use.*
- Substance use disorders are correlated with economic hardship and unemployment, perhaps in part because of easier access to drugs or more exposure to drugs in the environment.*

*This factor is not unique to *stimulant* abuse and dependence.

Key Concepts and Facts About Stimulants

- Stimulants, which increase arousal and brain activity, are the category of psychoactive substances most likely to lead to dependence. Unlike many other types of drugs, they act directly—rather then indirectly—on the dopamine reward system by binding to dopamine transporters in the synapse.

- Stimulants include cocaine and crack, amphetamines, methamphetamine, Ritalin, MDMA, and nicotine. Crack use is associated with the most rapid progression to dependence. In high doses, most of these stimulants can cause paranoia and hallucinations. With continued use, stimulants lead to tolerance and withdrawal.

- Neurological factors that contribute to abuse of and dependence on stimulants include activation of the dopamine reward system, which involves the nucleus accumbens and the ventral tegmental area.

- Psychological factors related to substance use disorders include learning: operant reinforcement of the effects of the drug,

classical conditioning of stimuli related to drug use (which leads to cravings), and observational learning of expectancies about both the effects of drugs and use of them to cope with problems.

- Social factors related to substance use disorders include the specific nature of an individual's relationships with family members, socioeconomic factors, and cultural and perceived norms about appropriate and inappropriate use of substances.

Making a Diagnosis

- Reread Case 9.4 about Mary Beth, and determine whether or not her symptoms meet the criteria for substance dependence on amphetamines. Specifically, list which criteria apply and which do not. If you would like more information to determine whether she has such a dependence, what information—specifically—would you want, and in what ways would the information influence your decision?

Depressants

Ringo Starr and John Lennon both had long periods of alcohol dependence. Starr reported that he "wasted" some years on alcohol, initially feeling that drinking gave him confidence but realizing later that it really didn't (Graff, 1989). And Lennon was frequently drunk during his 18-month separation from his wife, Yoko Ono.

What Are Depressants?

Alcohol is a depressant. Other depressants are opiates, barbiturates, and benzodiazepines such as *diazepam* (Valium). In contrast to stimulants, *depressants* tend to slow a person down, decreasing behavioral activity and level of awareness. Regular use of depressants tends to lead to tolerance, and discontinuing their use or cutting back on the dosage or frequency can produce withdrawal symptoms. In this section, we will discuss the effects of use, abuse of, and dependence on three types of depressants: alcohol, barbiturates, and benzodiazepines.

Alcohol

Approximately 50% of people in the United States aged 12 and older report that they have had at least one alcoholic beverage within the previous month (SAMHSA, 2008). But using a substance isn't the same as abusing it. Approximately 6% of Americans aged 12 or older (15 million people) are considered either to abuse or to be dependent on alcohol. Those who start to drink alcohol earlier in life are more likely to develop a disorder related to drinking (SAMHSA, 2008). But alcohol abuse and dependence aren't equally prevalent among all racial and ethnic groups: Native Americans have the highest prevalence of alcohol abuse and dependence (NIDA, 2003), and Blacks are 40% less likely than Whites to develop alcohol abuse (Grant et al., 2008).

Despite practice pouring the same quantity of liquid regardless of the shape of the glass, participants in one study poured more into shorter glasses than into taller ones (Wansink & Ittersum, 2005). Even professional bartenders are prone to estimate the quantities in differently shaped glasses incorrectly.

Daniel Templeton/Alamy

Blood Alcohol Concentration

The quantity of alcohol isn't the only variable that determines intoxication. In fact, the crucial variable is blood alcohol concentration, which is affected by the number of drinks consumed, the period of time over which they were consumed, the time since the individual has last eaten, the individual's body weight, and the individual's gender. Different concentrations of alcohol in the blood are associated with different neurological and psychological states (see Figure 9.8). In the United States, Canada, and Mexico, 0.08% is the legal limit of blood alcohol concentration for driving.

It can be harder than you might think to regulate just how much alcohol you drink. For example, pouring drinks into short, wide glasses may lead people to imbibe a larger dose of alcohol than intended. A study found that college students, as well as professional bartenders, were likely to pour 20% more alcohol into a shorter, wider glass than into a taller, narrower one. Even with practice, participants poured more into the wider glasses than the narrower ones (Wansink & Ittersum, 2005).

The same amount of alcohol will have a slightly greater effect on a woman than a man of the same size and weight, because men and women metabolize the drug differently (Frezza et al., 1990). This sex difference arises in part because women have, on average, less total water content in their bodies than do men, which means that ingested alcohol is less diluted (Greenfield, 2002; Van Thiel et al., 1988).

Not only do the effects of a given amount of alcohol differ by gender, but there are also individual differences. Some people have a more intense response to alcohol than do others. This variability appears to be mediated in part by genes (Schuckit, 1999), but it is also related to the level of tolerance an individual has acquired.

Binge Drinking

Binge drinking, or *heavy episodic drinking*, occurs when a person drinks until his or her blood alcohol concentration reaches at least 0.08% in a 2-hour period (which

Figure 9.8

Blood alcohol concentration (percentage)	Changes in thoughts, feelings, and behavior	Impaired functions and activities (continuum)
0.01 – 0.05	Relaxation Sense of well being Loss of inhibition	Alertness Judgment Coordination (especially fine motor skills)
0.06 – 0.10	Pleasure Numbing of feelings Nausea Sleepiness Emotional arousal	Visual tracking Reasoning and depth perception
0.11 – 0.20	Mood swings Anger Sadness Mania	Social behavior (e.g., obnoxiousness)
0.21 – 0.30	Aggression Reduced sensations Depression Stupor	Speech (slurred) Balance Temperature regulation
0.31 – 0.40	Unconsciousness Death possible Coma	Bladder control Breathing
0.41 and greater	Death	Heart rate (slowed)

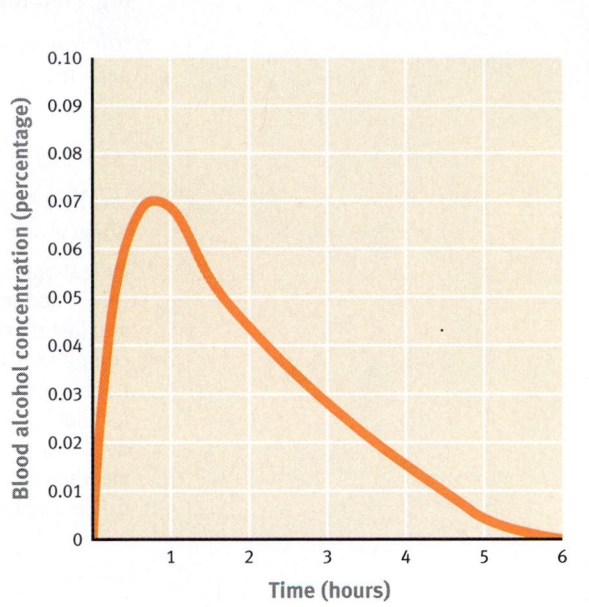

9.8 ▶ Blood Alcohol Concentration and Its Effects Different blood alcohol concentrations are on average associated with different effects. People may be motivated to drink alcohol because of the way it can affect thoughts, feelings, and behavior, but the same effects can impair functioning and, with repeated use, lead to alcohol abuse. As shown in the graph on the right, alcohol's effects—both desirable and undesirable—may be experienced within a few minutes and last a number of hours. The more someone has had to drink, the more impaired he or she will be for a longer period of time.

Source: Copyright © 2003 by BSCS. All rights reserved. Used with permission. For more information see the Permissions section.

generally translates into four or more drinks for women, five or more for men; one drink is equivalent to 12 ounces of beer, 5 ounces of wine, or 1.5 ounces of 80-proof liquor) (National Institute on Alcohol Abuse and Alcoholism National Advisory Council, 2004). Binge drinking is likely to occur when a person sets out to get drunk (Schulenberg et al., 1996). Repetitive binge drinking can lead to alcohol abuse or dependence.

The prevalence of binge drinking differs across the United States, often because of the type of colleges predominant in a state. For instance, students at colleges in California are less likely to binge drink than are college students in other states. California students tend to be older and are more often married (Wechsler et al., 1997), which may lead them to drink more responsibly. Men binge drink at higher rates than do women, and women at coeducational schools binge drink at higher rates than women at women's colleges (Dowdall, Crawford, & Wechsler, 1998). Binge drinkers are at increased risk for dangerous alcohol-related behaviors, such as driving while impaired (Wechsler et al., 1998), having unprotected sex, and engaging in more sexual activity than they would have when sober (Wechsler et al., 2002).

Alcohol Dependence
Chronic drinking leads to tolerance and withdrawal, and hence alcohol dependence. According to the National Institute on Alcohol Abuse and Alcoholism (2005), alcohol dependence is marked by four symptoms:

- *craving*, which is a strong need, or urge, to drink;

- *loss of control*, which consists of not being able to stop drinking once drinking has begun;

- *physical dependence*, which brings withdrawal symptoms, such as nausea, sweating, shakiness, and anxiety after stopping drinking; and

- *tolerance*, which causes a person to need to drink greater amounts of alcohol to get "high."

CASE 9.5 ▶ FROM THE INSIDE: Alcohol Dependence

Caroline Knapp describes her alcohol dependence in her memoir *Drinking: A Love Story* (1997):

By that point I don't even think the alcohol worked anymore. Certainly drinking was no longer fun. It had long ago ceased to be fun. A few glasses of wine with a friend after work could still feel reassuring and familiar, but drinking was so need driven by the end, so visceral and compulsive, that the pleasure was almost accidental. Pleasure just wasn't the point. At the end I didn't even feel like myself until I had a drink or two, and I remember that scared me a little: alcohol had become something I felt I needed in order to return to a sense of normalcy, in order to think straight. After one or two drinks I'd feel like I'd come back into my own skin—more clearheaded, more relaxed—but the feeling would last for only half an hour or so. Another few drinks and I'd be gone again, headed toward oblivion.

(p. 231)

In Case 9.5, above, Knapp describes the four elements of alcohol dependence: craving ("need driven"), loss of control (she would continue to drink until she was "headed toward oblivion"), physical dependence ("something I felt I needed in order to return to normalcy"), and tolerance (the alcohol didn't have as strong an effect as it had initially).

Alcohol abuse and dependence are also associated with memory problems, in particular, *blackouts*, periods of time during which the drinker cannot later remember what transpired while he or she was intoxicated. Knapp (1997) described her blackouts: "Sometimes I'd be so drunk at the end of the night I'd have to drive home with one eye shut, to avoid double vision. Sometimes I'd wake up at Sam's [a friend's] house, in his bed, wearing one of his T-shirts. I don't think we ever had sex but I can't say for sure" (p. 154).

Sedative-Hypnotic Drugs

Sedative-hypnotic drugs reduce pain and anxiety, relax muscles, lower blood pressure, slow breathing and heart rate, and induce sedation and sleep. In general, drugs in this class cause disinhibiting and depressant effects similar to those of alcohol (impaired physical coordination and mental judgment and increased aggressive or sexual behavior). Although these psychoactive substances can lower inhibitions and bring a sense of well-being, they also can cause memory problems, confusion, poor concentration, fatigue, and even respiratory arrest (NIDA, 2008e). When sedative-hypnotic drugs are mixed with another depressant, such as alcohol, the combined effect can be lethal: The person's breathing and heart rate can slow to dangerously low levels. Chronic use of these drugs can lead to tolerance. Two general types of drugs are in this class: *barbiturates* and *benzodiazepines*.

Barbiturates

Barbiturates, which include *amobarbital* (Amytal), *pentobarbital* (Nembutal), and *secobarbital* (Seconal), are usually prescribed to treat sleep problems. Although use of a barbiturate is legal with a prescription, this type of medication is commonly abused by both those with a prescription and those who obtain the drug illegally. As with other depressants, repeated barbiturate use leads to tolerance, so the person takes ever larger doses to get to sleep or reduce anxiety. Barbiturate abuse can also lead to withdrawal symptoms, including agitation and restlessness, hallucinations, confusion, and, in some cases, seizures (NIDA, 2005c). People who have become dependent on a barbiturate and want to discontinue or decrease their intake of the drug should do so only after medical consultation to determine an appropriate schedule for tapering off without inducing dangerous withdrawal symptoms; otherwise, abrupt discontinuation of the drug can lead to convulsions and death.

Benzodiapines

Benzodiazepines are usually prescribed to alleviate muscle pain, to aid sleep, or as a short-term treatment for anxiety (see Chapter 7); however, long-term use leads to tolerance and withdrawal. Examples of benzodiazepines include *lorazepam* (Ativan), *triazolam* (Halcion), *chlordiazepoxide* (Librium), *diazapam* (Valium), and *alprazolam* (Xanax). As with barbiturate dependence, a person with benzodiazepine dependence should gradually taper off of the drug, in consultation with a physician. For people who are dependent on these drugs, abruptly stopping use can lead to seizures and psychosis.

Understanding Depressants

In what follows, we will first discuss how brain systems and neural communication are affected by depressants in general and then turn to the effects of alcohol in particular. A considerable amount is known about the genetics of alcoholism, and we'll look closely at these findings before considering psychological and social factors.

Neurological Factors

In this section, we consider a set of closely related topics: the effects of depressants on the GABAnergic system, the neural bases of alcohol abuse and dependence, and the genetics of alcoholism.

Brain Systems and Neural Communication

Benzodiazepines (such as Valium), barbiturates, and alcohol directly affect the GABAnergic system, which is widespread in the brain and primarily activates inhibitory neurons. The resulting inhibition affects neurons in brain structures that are involved in anxiety, such as the amygdala. As we've noted before, the amygdala plays a key role in fear, and hence inhibiting it dulls the sense of fear and the related feeling of anxiety. Thus, it is not surprising that people who experience anxiety, for whatever reasons, find the use of depressants particularly reinforcing. In fact, those who suffer from phobias or panic disorders are at high risk to abuse alcohol and other depressants (Pihl, 1999). Depressants also indirectly affect the dopamine reward system.

Like other depressants, alcohol inhibits neurons, which has the net effect of dampening—or depressing—the nervous system so that it is less responsive. However, some of the brain systems that are most affected by alcohol normally inhibit other brain systems, which thereby become disinhibited—which is why people may seem "looser" after a couple of drinks, perhaps by talking more than usual or acting impulsively. Alcohol has a number of distinctive effects, which we consider in the remainder of this section: the nature of withdrawal, hangovers, and indirect effects on nutrition.

Chronic Alcohol Drinking and Withdrawal Although alcohol consumption induces the production of dopamine, which is rewarding, chronic use of alcohol stimulates the production of a type of neurotransmitter called *endogenous opioids*, sometimes referred to as "pleasure chemicals." (There is a class of drugs referred to as *opioids* or *opiates*, which we'll discuss later in the chapter. The word *endogenous*—means *originates within the body*—is used to distinguish the neurotransmitter opioids from the drugs of the same name.) Endogenous opioids are responsible for "runner's high," the feeling that occurs when someone has pushed herself or himself to a physical limit and experiences a sense of deep pleasure. In chronic drinkers, the activity of endogenous opioids occurs only in response to alcohol; when they stop drinking, their bodies no longer produce endogenous opioids. Thus, when a chronic drinker isn't consuming alcohol, he or she may experience symptoms related to opioid withdrawal, which are unpleasant. This experience in turn may induce the person to consume more alcohol to produce more opioids (Gianoulakis, 2001). In other words, with chronic use, drinking more alcohol may become negatively reinforcing—it removes an unpleasant state.

Biological By-products of Alcoholism People who frequently drink a lot of alcohol may become malnourished when the calories in alcohol substitute for calories from food (Mehta et al., 2006). Such malnourishment can include a deficiency in vitamin B1, which eventually causes several key parts of the brain to atrophy—including the mamillary bodies and the thalamus. Because these brain structures are important for storing new information in memory, drinking a lot of alcohol can indirectly lead to chronic memory problems (which produces a condition called *Korsakoff's syndrome*). Figure 9.9 shows a result of such brain atrophy: the increased size of the fluid-filled hollow areas, the ventricles, in the center of the brain.

Frequent high levels of alcohol use can also adversely affect the liver, which filters impurities from the blood; when a person drinks too much alcohol for too long a period of time, the liver develops scar tissue, which affects its ability to function. This condition is known as *cirrhosis* of the liver; it is potentially lethal and more likely to occur when malnutrition is present along with alcohol abuse or dependence (Lieber, 2003).

Why We Get Hangovers A hangover occurs the day after a person has been intoxicated by alcohol, and consists of a bad headache, nausea, and perhaps feeling dizzy and disoriented. These symptoms arise in part because alcohol is dehydrating: Alcohol is, essentially, a toxin, and the kidneys use water to remove toxins in the blood. Thus, the more alcohol a person drinks, the more water the kidneys use in the process of clearing out this toxin. But becoming dehydrated is only part of the reason we get hangovers. While the kidneys are working to remove the toxin, so is the liver. The liver relies on a two-step process to break down alcohol. First, the liver converts alcohol into a substance called acetaldehyde (a chemical that is related to formaldehyde), which is another toxin; second, it converts acetaldehyde to acetate, which is harmless. However, some people's livers cannot effectively carry out the second step, leaving their bodies subject to a toxin produced by their own livers!

If a person has become alcohol dependent, he or she may discover that one way to reduce the symptoms of a hangover is to drink more alcohol. For people with alcohol dependence, a hangover is more than simply being dehydrated or even having excess levels of acetaldehyde. It is also an indication that their bodies are going through alcohol withdrawal as the alcohol leaves the system (Cicero, 1978); drinking more alcohol can temporarily diminish the discomfort of the withdrawal symptoms. For a heavy drinker, withdrawal symptoms include headaches, weakness, tremors, anxiety, higher blood pressure, seizures, and increased heart and breathing rates. An extremely heavy drinker can also experience fever, agitation and irritability, as well as more severe symptoms such as confusion, convulsions, and visual hallucinations. All these alcohol withdrawal symptoms are collectively referred to as **delirium tremens**, or "the DTs." Such withdrawal symptoms normally begin within 4 days after the person last drank alcohol (Romach & Sellers, 1991). Delirium tremens can be potentially lethal; thus, when people with alcohol dependence are ready to stop drinking, they should have a physician supervise the process.

Genetics of Alcoholism
The tendency to abuse drugs is affected by genes. One sign of this is the fact that substance abuse disorders tend to run in families. However, only the genetics of alcoholism has been studied in depth. So, we will restrict our discussion of the genetics of depressant abuse and dependence to this single (very important) substance.

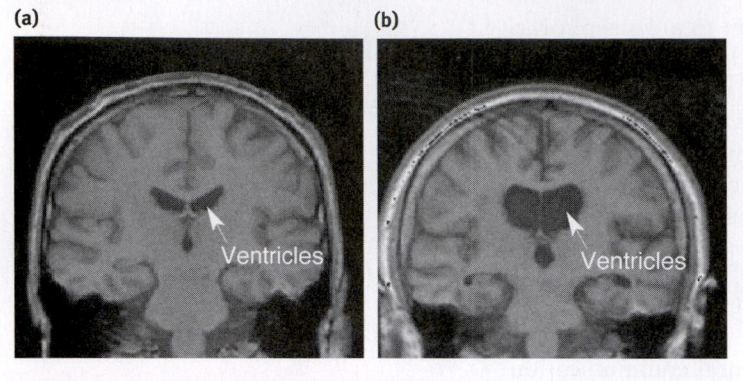

Figure 9.9

(a) (b)

Ventricles   Ventricles

9.9 ▸ Alcohol Abuse and Dependence: Effects on the Brain One of the effects of long-term alcohol dependence—alcoholism—is enlarged ventricles (the cavities in the brain filled with cerebrospinal fluid) (Rosenbloom, Sullivan, & Pfefferbaum, 2003). (a) The ventricles in this MRI scan are normal size; (b) the enlarged ventricles in this MRI scan are those of a man with alcohol dependence. The enlargement of the ventricles reflects the reduced size of a number of brain areas. These neurological changes may explain some of the memory problems associated with alcohol dependence.

Source: Rosenbloom, M., Sullivan, E.V., and Pfefferbaum, A. Using magnetic resonance imaging and diffusion tensor imaging to assess brain damage in alcoholics. Alcohol Research & Health 27(2):146–152, 2003.

Delirium tremens (DTs)
The symptoms of alcohol withdrawal marked by confusion, convulsions, visual hallucinations, and fever.

Family and Twin Studies For centuries, observers ranging from novelists to law enforcement officials have noted that members of some families are more likely to abuse alcohol than are members of other families. In fact, biological offspring of alcoholics are about twice as likely to become alcoholics as people without such a family history (Cloninger, Bohman, & Sigvardsson, 1981; Goodwin et al., 1974; Nurnberger et al., 2004; Russell, 1990).

Twin studies have also provided evidence for a genetic contribution to alcoholism (Cadoret, 1990; Carmelli, Heath, & Robinette, 1993). For example, one study investigated male twins who had registered with a Swedish Temperance Board because of problems with alcohol abuse. The results indicated that 54% of the variation in such abuse could be attributed to genetics and 14% to family environment (Kendler et al., 1997). Other studies suggest that the genetic influence may not be as high with females (McGue, Pickens, & Svikis, 1992).

Alcoholism and Adoption Studies Sometimes the offspring of alcoholics are adopted by parents who are not alcoholics, and researchers have studied some of these children after they've become adults. One striking finding is that even when they were raised by nonalcoholic parents, children whose biological parents were alcoholics are much more likely to abuse alcohol as adults than are those whose biological parents were not alcoholics. Another interesting finding from such adoption studies is evidence that there may be two distinct forms of alcoholism, which arise in part from different genes (Sigvardsson, Bohman, & Cloninger, 1996). Type 1 alcoholism is less severe and becomes evident later in life, and the effects of the genes associated with it can be moderated by environmental factors (such as whether the adoptive father had a skilled versus an unskilled job). Type 1 alcoholism occurs in both men and women. In contrast, Type 2 alcoholism apparently emerges early in life and occurs only in men, and the effects of the genes associated with it outweigh environmental factors. Some researchers have reported that Type 2 alcoholism arises in males who are (as were their fathers) impulsive and antisocial (Cloninger, 1987). If further data confirm that there are two distinct types of alcoholism, which are affected in different ways by genes, this would have implications for both diagnosis and treatment. For example, psychological treatment might be more effective for those with Type 1 alcoholism, whereas medications might be more important to prevent or treat Type 2 alcoholism.

Alcoholism and Chromosomal Markers Other evidence for the genetic bases of alcoholism comes from studies that link a genetic marker (i.e., a previously identified sequence of DNA at a particular location on a chromosome), particularly a portion of chromosome 11, to the disorder (Blum et al., 1990). But the genetic story is not all negative. Genes can make an individual more vulnerable to a disorder, but they can also have the opposite effect: They can protect against alcoholism by making drinking an aversive experience. For example, Asians often have a gene that give them forms of two liver enzymes that amplify the effects of alcohol (Higuchi et al., 1995), causing the person to have the negative consequences of drinking (including heart palpitations and nausea) after drinking even a little alcohol— bypassing the pleasant (and reinforcing) sensations that other people experience with a lower dose of alcohol. Researchers have shown that (probably because this gene leads alcohol to have larger effects) people with the gene drink less alcohol (Luczak et al., 2002) and are less likely to be binge drinkers (Luczak et al., 2001).

However, it is clear that more than one or two genes play a role in alcohol abuse and dependence; a number of genes, operating together, influence whether a person will develop problems with alcohol (Gordis, 1996; Sher, Grekin, & Wilkins, 2005).

Finally, just as we saw for stimulants, neurological factors that contribute to abuse of and dependence on depressants include activation of the dopamine reward system, neural-based associations between drug-related stimuli and drug use, and the role of GABA and glutamate in shifting recreational drug use to abuse and dependence. Table 9.9

Table 9.9 ▶ Neurological Factors That Contribute to the Abuse of and Dependence on Depressants

- Increased activity of the GABAnergic system leads to increased inhibition of anxiety-related brain structures.
- Depressants indirectly activate the dopamine reward system.
- Depressants generally cause the nervous system to be less responsive.
- Some substances directly activate the dopamine reward system, including the nucleus accumbens and the ventral tegmental area. *
- Associations between drug-related stimuli and drug use can activate the limbic system (and the dopamine reward system).*
- GABA and glutamate are involved in the shift from recreational drug use to abuse and dependence.*

*This factor is not unique to *depressant* abuse and dependence.

summarizes the neurological factors that contribute to the abuse of and dependence on depressants.

Psychological Factors

Many of the psychological factors that contribute to stimulant abuse and dependence also contribute to depressant abuse and dependence (see the starred items in Table 9.7); in particular:

- observational learning of depressant use, which promotes expectations about experiences from such use and promotes such use as a coping strategy;

- operant conditioning, in which

  - positive reinforcement leads to positive expectations of depressant use and to reward craving;

  - negative reinforcement can lead to relief craving and to depressant use becoming a chronic coping strategy; and

- classical conditioning, whereby drug cues elicit cravings.

Let's examine in a bit more detail the role of coping strategies and expectations in alcohol use.

Some people use alcohol as a way to cope with their problems. Consider Charles's experience:

> Charles, a high-school teacher with a long-standing problem of alcohol dependence, identified boredom and anger as key high-risk relapse factors. His problem with anger involved a pattern of avoiding interpersonal conflicts and letting his anger build up. Over time, Charles would reach a point of total frustration and use his angry thoughts and feelings to justify drinking binges. [He had perceived his anger to be a] "bad feeling that could only be expressed through drinking" . . . he often became upset and angry because of certain beliefs he held about how others "should" treat him.
>
> (Daley & Salloum, 1999, p. 258)

Like Charles, some people use alcohol to try to cope with particular emotions. In Charles's case, it was anger; for other people, the emotions might be sadness, anxiety, fear, shame, or any of a range of other emotions (Gaher et al., 2006).

Not all people use alcohol (or other drugs) to cope with life's ups and downs; particular factors lead some people to have a higher risk of using alcohol to cope. One such factor relates to the trait of anxiety sensitivity (see Chapter 7): People who are high in this trait find alcohol to be very calming, which explains why an anxiety disorder frequently precedes an alcohol use disorder in people who have both kinds of disorders (Sher et al., 1999; Stewart, Zvolensky, & Eifert, 2001).

Finally, even when they are not related to a coping strategy, expectations of what will happen as a result of drinking can also affect behavior after drinking (Kirsch & Lynn, 1999): People who drink to get "wasted" are in fact more likely to have that experience than are people who drink while having dinner with friends in a restaurant, even when people in both situations end up with the same blood alcohol concentration.

Social Factors

A variety of social factors can contribute to substance abuse and dependence (see the starred items in Table 9.8). For depressants, including alcohol, such factors include:

- dysfunctional family interactions (such as child abuse or neglect);

- peers' use of depressants;

- norms or perceived norms about depressant use (as in a subculture where drinking is the norm or is perceived to be so); and

- economic hardship and unemployment.

The relationship between alcohol use norms and perceived norms has been studied in depth. In the next sections we examine how alcohol abuse is affected by changing cultural norms about alcohol and differing community norms.

Cultural forces can influence substance use. In the reality television show *The Osbournes*, tobacco and alcohol use were verbally discouraged, but such substances were often apparent to viewers: packs of cigarettes or wine bottles on the table, a martini shaker in the background. These different types of communication sent mixed messages to viewers (Blair et al., 2005).

MTV/Courtesy: Everett Collection

Changing Cultural Norms and Alcohol Abuse

Culture affects both the degree of alcohol abuse and the ways in which alcohol is used. For example, the rate of alcohol dependence among American women has increased over time. Historically, women in the United States had much lower rates of alcoholism than did men, but as social mores and roles for women changed, the incidence of alcoholism among women has come to approach that of men (Greenfield, 2002).

Moreover, cultures create social norms for appropriate and inappropriate use of alcohol, such as allowing "fiesta" drunkenness on certain occasions (Finch, 2001; Room & Makela, 2000). The media provide another source of influence. One correlational study found that adolescents and young adults who saw more ads for alcohol drank more alcohol (Snyder et al., 2006), possibly because seeing more ads for alcohol led them to perceive the norm for alcohol use to be greater than it was.

Community Norms, Diversity, and Drinking

Some of the social factors that affect alcohol abuse may seem surprising at first glance. For example, in one study, researchers examined rates of alcohol use in the highest-risk college-aged group (white men) and found that white men who attended colleges that have more diverse students—minority, women, and older students— were less likely to binge drink, even if they had been binge drinkers in high school (Wechsler & Kuo, 2003). Moreover, white men who did not binge drink in high school and went to colleges with more diverse students bodies were less likely to start binge drinking than were their counterparts who attended colleges with less diverse student bodies. One possible explanation for this finding is that a more diverse student body–with a wider range of views about binge drinking—prevented a social norm of high levels of binge drinking from developing. The only ethnic group more likely to binge drink and have an alcohol disorder than white Americans is Native Americans. In contrast, Asian Americans and black Americans aged 20 and under are the least likely to binge drink (SAMHSA, 2008).

Most of the factors that contribute to depressant and stimulant abuse and dependence—and the mechanisms related to those factors—also contribute to abuse of, and dependence on, other types of substances. For this reason, we explain the feedback loops among the factors only after we discuss all types of substance abuse and dependence.

Key Concepts and Facts About Depressants

- Depressants decrease arousal, awareness, and nervous system activity level. Depressants include alcohol, barbiturates, and benzodiazepines.

- Continued use of depressants leads to tolerance and withdrawal. Some withdrawal symptoms are potentially lethal; people with a dependence on depressants should be medically supervised as they taper off their use of the drug. Using more than one depressant at the same time is also potentially lethal.

- The effects of alcohol depend on its concentration in the blood. Repeated binge drinking can lead to alcohol abuse or dependence. Long-term alcohol dependence is associated with a variety of cognitive problems, as well as atrophy of certain brain areas and enlarged ventricles. Withdrawal symptoms include delirium tremens.

- Depressants directly affect the GABAnergic system, which in turn dampens activity in key brain areas that give rise to anxiety; for this reason, people with anxiety symptoms are more likely than others to abuse depressants. Depressants also indirectly activate the dopamine reward system.

- Psychological factors related to depressant abuse and dependence include observational learning to expect specific effects from depressant use and to use depressants as a coping strategy, positive and negative reinforcement of the effects of the drug, and classical conditioning of drug cues that leads to cravings.

- Social factors related to abuse of and dependence on depressants include the nature of an individual's relationships with family members, peers' use of depressants, norms and perceived norms about appropriate and inappropriate use of depressants, and socioeconomic factors.

Making a Diagnosis

- Reread Case 9.5 about Caroline Knapp, and determine whether or not her symptoms meet the criteria for alcohol dependence. Specifically, list which criteria apply and which do not. If you would like more information to determine whether she has alcohol dependence, what information—specifically—would you want, and in what ways would the information influence your decision?

Other Abused Substances

This chapter has focused so far on stimulants and depressants because they are the most commonly abused substances. However, they are not the only substances that people abuse. In this section we briefly review three classes of other substances that are often abused: narcotic analgesics (such as codeine and heroin), hallucinogens (such as marijuana), and dissociative anesthetics (such as ketamine).

What Are Other Abused Substances?

By 1969, the Beatles had not performed for 3 years. In that year, they agreed to perform and have their rehearsals filmed. They spent a month in a recording studio composing and arranging songs, learning their parts, and rehearsing the songs. Rather than a true concert, however, the project culminated in a live, rooftop performance that was filmed. Some of this arduous process and the final concert were captured in the film *Let It Be*, which shows glimpses of the effects of John Lennon's heroin use. Lennon had difficulty remembering his lines from hour to hour and day to day, had trouble getting up each morning and arriving at the sessions on time, and had difficulty concentrating on writing and finishing songs (Spitz, 2005; Sulpy & Schweighardt, 1984). Such problems are typical of heroin use in particular and of the use of narcotic analgesics more generally.

Narcotic Analgesics

Narcotic analgesics are derived from the opium poppy plant or chemically related substances; narcotic analgesics are sometimes referred to as *opiates*, or *opioids*. To distinguish them from endogenous opioids, narcotic analgesics are sometimes referred to as *exogenous opioids* (*exogenous* means *arising from an outside source*). Exogenous opioids include methadone and heroin (to be discussed in more detail shortly), as well as codeine, morphine, and synthetic derivatives found in prescription pain relief medications such as *oxycodone* (OxyContin), *hydrocodone* (Vicodin), *meperidine hydrochloride* (Demerol), *propoxyphene* (Darvon), and *hydromorphone* (Dilaudid). These drugs can be injected, snorted, or taken by mouth. Legal but restricted narcotic analgesics are generally prescribed for persistent coughing, severe diarrhea, and severe pain. However, some people abuse these medications, taking them not for their medical effects but instead for the "high" they produce (NIDA, 2008a).

All analgesics relieve pain, and people who take analgesics for recreational purposes may temporarily experience pleasant, relaxing effects. However, this category of drugs is highly addictive—their use rapidly leads to tolerance and withdrawal and compulsive behavior related to procuring and taking the drug. Narcotics depress the central nervous system, and can cause drowsiness and slower breathing, which can lead to death if a narcotic analgesic is taken with a depressant. Although users may experience euphoria after taking a narcotic analgesic, that fades to apathy, unhappiness, impaired judgment, and psychomotor agitation (the "fidgets") or psychomotor retardation (sluggishness). Users may also experience confusion—as happened to John Lennon—as well as slurred speech, sedation, or unconsciousness.

Withdrawal from a narcotic analgesic begins within 8 hours after the drug was last used. Withdrawal symptoms peak within several days, but can last for a week or more. Physical symptoms of withdrawal include nausea and vomiting, muscle aches, tearing from the eyes, dilated pupils, sweating, fever, diarrhea, and insomnia; many of the symptoms are similar to those of a bad case of the flu. Depressed mood, irritability, and a sense of restlessness are also common during withdrawal.

Heroin

Heroin is one of the stronger opioids and is very addictive. Unfortunately, the contrast between the euphoria that the drug induces and the letdown that comes when its effects wear off can drive some individuals to crave the euphoria, and so they

Although some narcotic analgesics are derived from the opium poppy plant, others are synthetic derivatives. Repeated use of any type of narcotic analgesic rapidly leads to tolerance and withdrawal—signs of dependence.

Photodisc/Alamy

take the drug, again and again—which in turn leads to tolerance. Tolerance makes the same dose of heroin fall short: Instead of causing euphoria, it often causes irritability. Extraordinarily unpleasant withdrawal symptoms can arise within a few hours of the last dose, peak within 72 hours, and take up to a week to subside; symptoms include bouts of chills and hot flashes, diarrhea, and extreme restlessness (NIDA, 2007c). Debbie describes her first experience with heroin:

> [It's] as if you're drifting off into a deep, deep, deep, deep sleep. . . . You've got no feeling in a way. It feels like you're dead, you're [sic] body's dead in some ways but it's still warm. . . .You feel like you're in this little bubble and nobody can burst it but at the same time, you don't realise [sic] how much danger you're in.
>
> (Substancemisuse.net, 2007)

Debbie goes to describe heroin withdrawal, after 2 years of daily use:

> You're like a wild animal. You feel like you're climbing the ceiling. You're pulling your hair out. . . . You hit yourself, you know, to try and bring yourself out of it, to get that pain away. . . . you have stomach cramps, you feel sick. You don't know whether to put your arse on the toilet or your face down it. You can never get comfortable . . .
> . . . my skin was getting turned inside out and there were things crawling underneath it. . . . It felt like my head was going to blow up. . . . I didn't know what to do. I was having hot and cold [flashes]. I didn't know whether to get dressed and go out looking but there was nothing anywhere. . . . You get very nasty and violent coz I did and I'm not a very violent person . . . that day I really did go for it and, you know, "Without that [heroin] I can't live," that's what got into my head "Without that [heroin] I can't live."
>
> (Substancemisuse.net, 2007)

Debbie's experience with heroin withdrawal apparently involved many of the classic symptoms including chills and hot flashes, and restlessness.

Progression to Injection

Most people with substance abuse and dependence didn't begin by using a "hard" drug but progressed to such a drug over time; similarly, people who inject heroin ("shoot up") didn't necessarily start their heroin use that way. People rarely, if ever, *plan* to become addicted—rather, they just slip into this pathological state. Surveys of people who have used heroin find that the typical user starts out snorting heroin (as Lennon did), progresses to injecting heroin under the skin but not into blood vessels (termed *skin popping*), and then ends up injecting into blood vessels (termed *mainlining*). Injecting heroin causes a more intense experience: a "rush," a feeling of immediate intensity. Some users who inhale heroin do so because they mistakenly believe that this method of use is less likely to lead to tolerance and withdrawal (NIDA, 2005a). Most users proceed from occasional use to daily use, and their primary motivation in life becomes obtaining enough money to procure the next dose, or "fix." Because users become tolerant to the drug, they must increase the amount they use in order to get an effect. But their habit becomes a tightrope walk: Too great an amount is fatal.

Heroin abuse and dependence is associated with a variety of medical problems, such as pneumonia and liver disease. In addition, heroin often has various other substances added to it; these substances can clog blood vessels leading to vital organs. Moreover, abusers who inject the drug are at risk to develop AIDS and hepatitis as well as collapsed veins (NIDA 2007c).

Hallucinogens

In 1964, the Beatles began their search for the meaning of life through transcendental meditation, Hinduism, and "mind-altering" drugs such as lysergic acid diethylamide (LSD, also known as *acid*). George Harrison recounted that he had heard that hippies in the Haight-Ashbury district of San Francisco, California, were "dropping acid" in a similar search for meaning. Harrison flew there but was disgusted to find that the hippies generally weren't using LSD to seek enlightenment, but simply as another way to get high. Harrison was so disillusioned that he stopped using LSD in his search for meaning. Unlike other types of drugs we've discussed so far, hallucinogens are less predictable in their effects, and are more sensitive to the user's expectations as well as the context in which the drug is taken.

Hallucinogens are substances that induce sensory or perceptual distortions—hallucinations in any of the senses. That is, they lead users to think they see, hear, taste, or feel something that is not actually present or not present in the way it is perceived. Some hallucinogens also can induce mood swings. Hallucinogens frequently taken for recreational purposes include the following:

- *LSD* (a synthetic hallucinogen),
- *mescaline* (a psychoactive substance produced by some kinds of cacti),
- *psilocybin* (a psychoactive substance present in psilocybin mushrooms, commonly referred to as "magic mushrooms"), and
- *marijuana* (the dried leaves and flowers of the hemp plant).

The first three of these drugs are chemically similar to the neurotransmitter serotonin. A single moderate dose of any of these drugs (or a very high dose of marijuana) is enough to induce visual hallucinations. Let's examine the abuse of and dependence on LSD and marijuana.

LSD

All of the Beatles used LSD at one point or another, but John Lennon reported that he took LSD thousands of times—which surely would constitute abusing the drug. LSD is a hallucinogen because it alters the user's visual or auditory sensations and perceptions; it also induces shifting emotions. Users may also experience *synesthesia*, a blending of senses that might lead them to "see" musical notes or "hear" colors. At higher doses, LSD can lead to delusions and distortions of time (NIDA, 2007d). LSD normally has an effect within 30 to 90 minutes of being ingested, and the effects last up to 12 hours (NIDA, 2001).

However, the effects of LSD can be unpredictable. A "bad trip" (i.e., an adverse reaction to LSD) can include intense anxiety, fear, and dread; a user may feel as if he or she is totally losing control, going crazy, or dying. People who are alone when experiencing a bad trip may get hurt or kill themselves as they respond to the hallucinations. If other people are present, they can talk the user through the effects, constantly reminding him or her that the trip is actually a temporary, drug-induced state; alternatively, they may take the person to the emergency room of a hospital.

Two aftereffects can occur from LSD use, even after the pharmacological effects of the drug have worn off: psychosis (hallucinations and visual disturbances) and "flashbacks" (termed *hallucinogen persisting perception disorder* in DSM-IV-TR, which are involuntary and vivid memories of sensory distortions that occurred while under the influence of the drug). However, such aftereffects are rare.

Recurrent LSD use can rapidly lead to tolerance, meaning that the user needs larger doses. Tolerance disappears if the user stops taking the drug, and LSD does not cause withdrawal symptoms. Unfortunately, LSD abuse can induce enduring psychotic symptoms in a small number of people (NIDA, 2007d).

Marijuana

The Beatles also smoked *marijuana*, which is the dried leaves and flowers of the hemp plant (*cannabis sativa*). The resin from the hemp plant's flowering tops is made into another, more potent drug, *hashish*. The active ingredient of marijuana and hashish is *tetrahydrocannabinol* (THC). Both marijuana and hashish can be either smoked or ingested. George Harrison used hashish and was arrested for possessing it. Paul McCartney and John Lennon were arrested at different times for possessing marijuana.

Marijuana's effects are subtler than those of other hallucinogens, creating minor perceptual distortions that lead a person to experience more vivid sensations and to feel that time has slowed down (NIDA, 2005b). The user's cognitive and motor abilities are also slowed or temporarily impaired, which produces poor driving skills (Ramaekers et al., 2006). THC ultimately activates the dopamine reward system (NIDA, 2000).

Like the effects of LSD, marijuana's effects depend on the user's mood, expectations, and environment. For example, one study found that participants who were given THC and knew that they were receiving THC liked the effects and wanted more than did participants who were told they were receiving an antinausea drug but actually received THC (Kirk, Doty, & de Wit, 1998).

A user of marijuana who develops abuse or dependence will experience withdrawal symptoms after he or she stops using marijuana; such symptoms include irritability, anxiety, depression, decreased appetite, and disturbed sleep (Budney et al., 2004; Kouri & Pope, 2000). Studies have found that chronic marijuana use adversely affects learning, memory, and motivation—even when the user has not taken the drug recently and is not under its direct influence (Lane et al., 2005; Pope et al., 2001; Pope & Yurgelin-Todd, 1996). Smoking marijuana is also associated with an increased risk of heart attack (Mittleman et al., 2001). One survey found that of the approximately 7 million Americans who abuse or are dependent on an illegal substance, over half of them abuse or are dependent on marijuana (SAMHSA, 2004).

Dissociative Anesthetics

A *dissociative anesthetic* produces a sense of detachment from the user's surroundings—a *dissociation*. The word *anesthetic* in the name reflects the fact that many of these drugs were originally developed as anesthetics to be used during surgery. Dissociative anesthetics act like depressants and also affect gluamate activity (Kapur & Seeman, 2002). These drugs can distort visual and auditory perception. Drugs of this type have been referred to as "club drugs" because they tend to be taken before or during an evening of dancing at a nightclub. The most commonly abused members of this class of drugs are phencyclidine and ketamine, which we discuss in the following sections.

Phencyclidine (PCP)

Phencyclidine (PCP, also known as "angel dust" and "rocket fuel") became a street drug in the 1960s. It can be snorted, ingested, or smoked, and users can quickly begin to take it compulsively. PCP abusers may report feeling powerful and invulnerable while the drug is in their system, and they may become violent or suicidal, at which point they may end up in an emergency room (NIDA, 2007f). Possible medical effects of high doses include a decrease in breathing and heart rates, dizziness, nausea and vomiting, seizures, coma, and death; coma and death are more likely if PCP is used along with one or more other drugs. With abuse can come memory, speech, and cognitive problems, even up to a year after the last use (NIDA, 2007f).

PCP has deleterious effects even when taken at low to moderate doses. Medical effects include increased blood pressure, heart rate, and sweating, coordination problems, and numbness in the hands and feet. At higher doses, PCP users may experience symptoms of hallucinations, delusions, paranoia, disordered thinking, and other symptoms of schizophrenia (see Chapter 12), which may bring them to the attention of mental health professionals, as occurred for the man in Case 9.6. Repeated PCP use can lead to craving for, and compulsive use of, the drug (NIDA, 2008d).

CASE 9.6 ▶ FROM THE OUTSIDE: PCP Abuse

The patient is a 20-year-old man who was brought to the hospital, trussed in ropes, by his four brothers. This is his seventh hospitalization in the last 2 years, each for similar behavior. One of his brothers reports that he "came home crazy," threw a chair through a window, tore a gas heater off the wall, and ran into the street. The family called the police, who apprehended him shortly thereafter as he stood, naked, directing traffic at a busy intersection. He assaulted the arresting officers, escaped from them, and ran home screaming threats at his family. There his brothers were able to subdue him.

continued on next page

On admission, the patient was observed to be agitated, with his mood fluctuating between anger and fear. He had slurred speech and staggered when he walked. He remained extremely violent and disorganized for the first several days of his hospitalization, then began having longer and longer lucid intervals, still interspersed with sudden, unpredictable periods in which he displayed great suspiciousness, a fierce expression, slurred speech, and clenched fists.

After calming down, the patient denied ever having been violent or acting in an unusual way ("I'm a peaceable man") and said he could not remember how he got to the hospital. He admitted using alcohol and marijuana socially, but denied phencyclidine (PCP) use except for once, experimentally, 3 years previously. Nevertheless, blood and urine tests were positive for phencyclidine, and his brother believes "he gets dusted every day."

(American Psychiatric Association, 2002, pp. 121–122)

Ketamine

Ketamine ("Special K" or "vitamin K") induces anesthesia and hallucinations and can be injected or snorted. Ketamine is chemically similar to PCP but is shorter acting and has less intense effects. With high doses, some users experience a sense of dissociation so severe that they feel as if they are dying (NIDA, 2001). Ketamine use and abuse are associated with temporary memory loss, impaired thinking, a loss of contact with reality, violent behavior, and breathing and heart problems that are potentially lethal (Krystal et al., 2005; White & Ryan, 1996). Regular users of ketamine may develop tolerance and cravings (Jansen & Darracot-Cankovic, 2001).

Understanding Other Abused Substances

We first consider brain systems and neural communication for each separate class of abused substances and then look at genetics. We'll then examine psychological and social factors.

Neurological Factors

Depending on the abused substance, different brain systems and neural communication processes are critical, as we'll see in the following sections.

Brain Systems and Neural Communication

Narcotic analgesics (heroin, in particular), hallucinogens, and dissociative anesthetics have different effects on brain systems and neural communication.

Narcotic Analgesics Among the narcotic analgesics, researchers have focused most of their attention on heroin—in large part, because it poses the greatest problem.

Like other opioids, heroin slows down activity in the central nervous system. It directly affects the part of the brain involved in breathing and coughing—the brainstem—and thus historically was used to suppress persistent coughs. In addition, heroin binds to opioid receptors in the brain, which has the effect of decreasing pain, and indirectly activates the dopamine reward system (NIDA, 2000). Continued heroin use also decreases the production of endorphins, a class of neurotransmitters that act as natural painkillers. Opioids such as heroin bind to the same receptors as endorphins do. Thus, heroin abuse reduces the body's natural pain-relieving ability. Furthermore, someone with heroin dependence has his or her endorphin production reduced to the point that, when withdrawal symptoms arise, endorphins that would have kicked in to reduce pain are not able to do so, making the symptoms feel even worse than they otherwise would be. When the pain of withdrawal becomes particularly bad, the person may desperately crave more heroin in order to relieve the pain. These symptoms also motivate those with heroin dependence to make sure that they can get their next dose; they may steal or turn to prostitution (with its increased risk of HIV/AIDS) to finance their habit.

Hallucinogens THC, the active ingredient in marijuana, is chemically similar to the type of neurotransmitters known as *cannabinoids* (*anandamide* is one such cannabinoid), and it activates the dopamine reward system. For instance, in rats, cannabinoids trigger dopamine release in the nucleus accumbens (Tanda, Pontieri, & Di Chiara, 1997). People who began abusing marijuana at an early age have atrophy of brain areas that contain many receptors for cannabinoids (DeBellis et al., 2000; Ernst & Chefer, 2001; Wilson et al., 2000), especially the hippocampus and the cerebellum. Atrophy of the hippocampus can explain why chronic marijuana users develop memory problems, and atrophy of the cerebellum can explain why they develop balance and coordination problems. These brain areas are illustrated in Figure 9.10. Cannabinoids also modulate other neurotransmitters and affect pain and appetite (Wilson & Nicoll, 2001).

Dissociative Anesthetics PCP and ketamine alter the distribution in the brain of glutamate, a fast-acting excitatory neurotransmitter. Excitatory neurotransmitters induce brain activity and may underlie the violent, impulsive effects of these drugs. In addition, glutamate is involved in memory, pain perception, and responding to the environment (NIDA, 2007f). Glutamate can be toxic; it actually kills neurons if too much is present. Thus, by increasing levels of glutamate, dissociative anesthetics may, eventually, lead to cell death in brain areas that have receptors for this neurotransmitter—which would explain the memory and other cognitive deficits observed in people who abuse these drugs.

Genetics of Other Types of Substance Abuse

The genetic bases of abuse of other types of substances have not been studied in as much depth as those of alcohol abuse. However, one twin study of cannabis dependence (Lynskey et al., 2002) estimated that genes account for 45% of the variance in vulnerability to cannabis dependence, shared environmental factors account for 20%, and non-shared environmental factors account for the remaining 35%. Consistent with these findings, Tsuang and colleagues (2001) concluded from a study of over 3,330 male twins that genes, shared environment, and unique environmental factors all affect substance abuse (of illicit drugs).

Psychological Factors

Abuse of these other types of substances is affected by most of the same psychological factors that influence abuse of stimulants and depressants (see the starred items in Table 9.7): observational learning, operant conditioning, and classical conditioning all contribute to substance abuse as a maladaptive coping strategy. We examine here the unique aspects of classical conditioning associated with heroin abuse and dependence

Classical conditioning can help explain how some accidental heroin "overdoses" occur (Siegel, 1988; Siegel et al., 2000). The quotation marks around the word *overdoses* are meant to convey that, in fact, the user often has not taken more than usual but has taken a usual dose in the presence of novel stimuli (Siegel & Ramos, 2002). If a user normally takes heroin in a particular place, such as the basement of the house, he or she develops a conditioned response to being in that place: The brain triggers physiological changes to get ready for the influx of heroin, activating compensatory mechanisms to dampen the effect of the about-to-be-taken drug. This response creates a tolerance for the drug, but—and here's the most important point—only in that situation. The stimuli in a "neutral" setting (not associated with use of the drug), such as a bedroom, have not yet become paired with taking heroin—and hence the brain does not trigger these compensatory mechanisms before the person takes the drug. In this case, the conditioned stimulus (e.g., the basement) is not present to elicit the compensatory response. And, without this response, the same dose of heroin can have a greater effect if taken in the bedroom than it would have if taken in the basement, causing an "overdose."

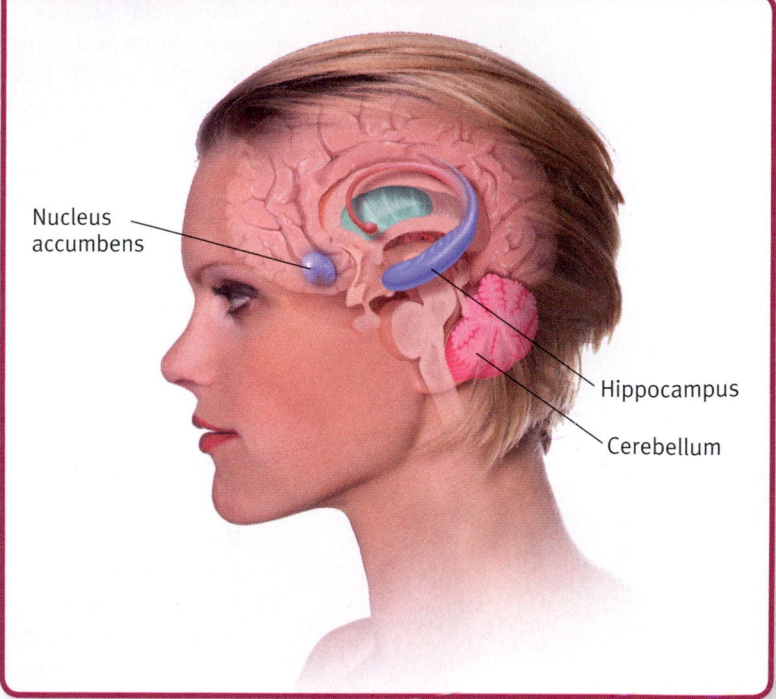

Figure 9.10

Nucleus accumbens

Hippocampus

Cerebellum

9.10 ▶ Marijuana's Effects on the Brain When marijuana is smoked, its active ingredient, THC, attaches to cannabinoid receptors in numerous brain areas, including in the nucleus accumbens, which is part of the dopamine reward system. People who began abusing marijuana at an early age eventually have atrophy of brain areas that have many cannabinoid receptors, especially the hippocampus and cerebellum.

Social Factors

The social factors that are commonly associated with abuse of or dependence on stimulants and depressants also apply to narcotic analgesics, hallucinogens, and dissociative anesthetics (see the starred items in Table 9.8). These include dysfunctional family interactions and a higher proportion of substance-abusing peers, which in turn affects the perceived norms of substance use and abuse (Kuntsche et al., 2009). Moreover, economic hardship and unemployment are associated with substance abuse and dependence, perhaps because of chronic stress that arises from economic adversity as well as increased exposure to substance abuse.

FEEDBACK LOOPS IN ACTION: Understanding Substance Use Disorders

The neurological, psychological, and social factors that contribute to substance abuse and dependence in general do not act in isolation but affect each other through various feedback loops (see Figure 9.11). For example, in one study, researchers examined children who did not have a substance use disorder, but whose parents had a history of either alcohol or drug dependence (Elkins et al., 2004). Children from the two types of families had different characteristics. Children whose parents had a history of *alcohol* dependence were more likely to have negative emotions such as sadness and anger and to be aggressive. They were also more likely to feel alienated and to react more strongly to stressful events (psychological factors). In contrast, children whose parents had a history of *drug* dependence reported lower self-control and showed lower levels of the temperamental trait *harm avoidance*; people who are low in harm avoidance are less responsive to signals of possible punishment.

One possible explanation for these results is that these personality differences in the children arose because of neurological differences (genetic or temperamental) between the two groups of parents. However, the researchers found that differences in the two groups resulted from all three types of factors and from interactions among them via feedback loops. For instance, some neurological factors tend to have a direct relationship with substance abuse and dependence: The effects that a given substance produces in the brain can be directly influenced by specific genes and an individual's prior exposure to the drug—either in the mother's womb or after birth. These factors affect everyone, although in different ways. As a specific example noted earlier in this chapter, participants who rated an injection of Ritalin as pleasant had fewer dopamine receptors, which suggests a neurological—and possibly genetic—vulnerability to stimulant abuse. But neurological factors, such as genes and their influence on temperament, can also have indirect effects: Someone who is high in the trait of novelty seeking, for instance, may be more willing to try a drug than someone low in that trait (DeJong, 2001). However, being high in novelty seeking doesn't necessarily *lead* to substance use and abuse; after all, most people who score high in this temperament do not abuse substances. As another example, some people have a temperament that leads them to be more responsive to reward (and to a drug's rewarding effects) than others are. In turn, this temperament leads them to be more easily affected by operant conditioning when using a drug (psychological factor): Someone who is more responsive to reward is likely to find a given blood alcohol concentration more enjoyable than might someone who is less responsive to reward.

And psychological factors and social factors also play a role in the development of substance use disorders. For instance, as noted previously, experiencing child abuse, neglect, or another significant social stressor increases the risk for substance abuse (Compton et al., 2005), although it does not inevitably lead to it. Moreover, as we saw for alcohol use, peer and family interactions and culture (social factors) help determine perceived social norms, which in turn alter a person's

Figure 9.11

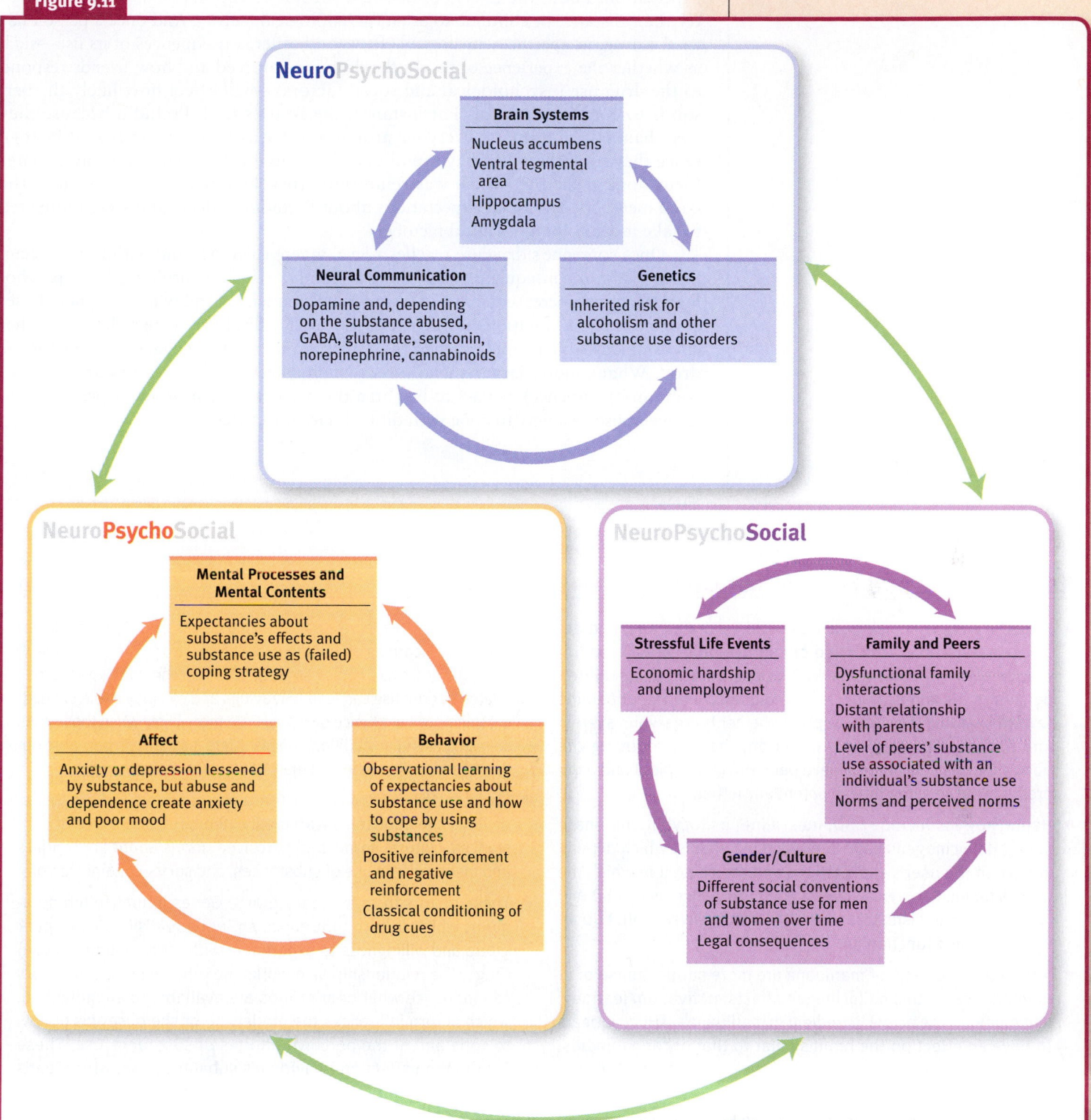

NeuroPsychoSocial

Brain Systems

Nucleus accumbens
Ventral tegmental area
Hippocampus
Amygdala

Neural Communication

Dopamine and, depending on the substance abused, GABA, glutamate, serotonin, norepinephrine, cannabinoids

Genetics

Inherited risk for alcoholism and other substance use disorders

NeuroPsychoSocial

Mental Processes and Mental Contents

Expectancies about substance's effects and substance use as (failed) coping strategy

Affect

Anxiety or depression lessened by substance, but abuse and dependence create anxiety and poor mood

Behavior

Observational learning of expectancies about substance use and how to cope by using substances
Positive reinforcement and negative reinforcement
Classical conditioning of drug cues

NeuroPsychoSocial

Stressful Life Events

Economic hardship and unemployment

Family and Peers

Dysfunctional family interactions
Distant relationship with parents
Level of peers' substance use associated with an individual's substance use
Norms and perceived norms

Gender/Culture

Different social conventions of substance use for men and women over time
Legal consequences

9.11 ▶ Feedback Loops In Action: Substance Use Disorders

expectations about the effects of taking a substance and his or her willingness to try the substance or continue to use it (psychological factor). And once a person has tried a drug, its specific neurological effects and other consequences of its use—such as whether the experience of taking the drug is reinforced and how friends respond to the drug use (psychological and social factors)—will affect how likely the person is to continue using it. For instance, the Beatles took Preludin because they were handed the pills and everyone around them was taking them (social factor). Once they took the pills, they found that they could play longer and stay up later (neurological factor), which was reinforcing (psychological factor). In turn, the band members developed expectations about Preludin's effects and were motivated to take it again (psychological factor).

Once someone's drug use reaches a level where tolerance and withdrawal occur, the unpleasant consequences of withdrawal and cravings (neurological and psychological factors) increase the risk of continued dependence. And when a former abuser goes into a social situation in which he or she previously abused drugs, the cues of that environment—the people, the bar, the drug paraphernalia—trigger cravings for the drug. What's more, larger social forces (such as economic stressors or family or community violence) can act to heighten the negatively reinforcing aspects of substance abuse as a way to cope with difficult circumstances.

Key Concepts and Facts About Other Abused Substances

- Narcotic analgesics, also called opioids, can dull pain and decrease awareness. Continued opioid use quickly leads to tolerance and withdrawal, as well as compulsive drug-related behaviors. Heroin is an opioid. Opioids activate the dopamine reward system. They also depress the central nervous system and decrease endorphin production, thereby reducing the body's inherent ability to relieve pain. Using an opioid and a depressant at the same time is potentially lethal.

- Hallucinogens include LSD, mescaline, psilocybin, and marijuana. Hallucinogens have unpredictable effects, which depend in part on the user's expectations and the context in which the drug is taken. People can have a "bad trip" when using LSD and can experience flashbacks long after the drug wears off. LSD affects serotonin functioning.

- Although the effects of marijuana are more subtle, abuse of or dependence on this hallucinogen affects motivation, learning, and memory. The active ingredient in marijuana—THC—appears to have an effect on the brain similar to that of cannabinoids, and activates the dopamine reward system. Chronic marijuana users may develop withdrawal.

- Dissociative anesthetics (sometimes referred to as "club drugs") are so named because they induce a sense of dissociation and cause anesthesia. They depress the central nervous system and affect glutamate activity. Dissociative anesthetics include PCP and ketamine. Use and abuse of this type of drug impairs cognitive functioning and can lead to violent behavior.

- Genes may predispose some people to develop abuse of or dependence on these substances.

- Psychological factors related to substance use disorders include observational learning of what to expect from taking the drugs and of using the drugs as a coping strategy. Classical conditioning of stimuli related to drug use can lead to cravings and can play a role in building tolerance (and hence overdoses are more likely when those cues are not present). In addition, the disorders may arise in part from operant conditioning (reinforcement of the effects of the drug).

- Social factors related to substance use disorders include the individual's relationships with family members, peers' use of substances, cultural norms and perceived norms about appropriate and inappropriate use of substances, and socioeconomic factors.

- These factors form feedback loops: Genes influence temperament, which in turn influences an individual's choice of peer group and willingness to experiment with (and continue to use) drugs. The relationship also works the other way: Social factors can influence what peer groups are available to an individual, which in turn influences the models he or she observes of how to cope and of the perceived norms of substance use. These factors then affect an individual's substance use, which leads to specific neurological effects (including tolerance and withdrawal), which further influence substance use behavior.

Making a Diagnosis

- Reread Case 9.6, and determine whether or not the young man's symptoms meet the criteria for abuse of or dependence on PCP. Specifically, list which criteria apply and which ones do not. If you would like more information to determine whether he is dependent on PCP, what information—specifically—would you want, and in what ways would the information influence your decision?

Treating Substance Use Disorders

Three of the four Beatles were known to have at least one type of substance dependence: George Harrison on nicotine (cigarettes), Ringo Starr on alcohol (for which he received treatment), and John Lennon on alcohol and heroin. It is not known whether any of the Beatles (other than Starr) received professional treatment for their abuse or dependence. Lennon reportedly quit using heroin all at once—*cold turkey*—without medical supervision.

We begin by considering the goals of treatment—what the best outcomes can be. Then we examine the treatments that target neurological, psychological, and social factors, and, when appropriate, note the use of specific treatments for particular types of substance abuse or dependence. However, as we shall see, many treatments that target psychological and social factors can effectively treat abuse of and dependence on more than one type of substance. Unfortunately, though, relapse rates after any type of treatment are high enough that people with substance abuse and dependence may need repeated episodes of treatment (NIDA, 2008f).

Goals of Treatment

Treatments for substance abuse and dependence can have two different ultimate goals. One goal is abstinence—leading the person to stop taking the substance entirely. When the goal of treatment is abstinence, relapse rates tend to be high (up to 60% by some estimates), particularly among patients with comorbid disorders (Brown & D'Amico, 2001; Curran et al., 2000; NIDA, 1999, 2008f). To help patients achieve abstinence, pharmaceutical companies have focused their efforts on developing two types of medications: (1) those that minimize withdrawal symptoms, and (2) those that block the "high" if the substance is used, thereby leading to extinction of the conditioned responses arising from substance abuse and dependence.

Given that abstinence-focused treatments have not been as successful as hoped, an alternative goal of treatment has emerged, which focuses on *harm reduction*—trying to reduce the harm to the individual and society that may come from substance abuse and dependence. For example, needle exchange programs give users a clean needle for each heroin injection, which decreases the transmission of HIV/AIDS because users don't need to share needles that may be contaminated with HIV. In some cases, harm reduction programs may also seek to find a middle ground between abuse and abstinence: controlled drinking or drug use. For those with symptoms of tolerance and withdrawal, which indicate dependence on alcohol or a drug, such a middle ground may be more difficult to achieve, however (Rosenberg & Melville, 2005). In the United States, most treatment programs have the goal of abstinence.

Targeting Neurological Factors

Treatments that are directed toward neurological factors approach substance use disorders as diseases, and thus select medications as the treatment. In this section we consider detoxification and then turn to medications used to treat abuse of and dependence on stimulants, depressants, narcotic analgesics, and hallucinogens.

Detoxification

Detoxification (also referred to as *detox*) is medically supervised withdrawal for those with substance dependence. Detoxification may involve a gradual decrease in dosage over a period of time to prevent potentially lethal withdrawal symptoms, such as seizures. People with alcohol, benzodiazepine, barbiturate, or opioid dependence should be medically supervised when they stop taking the substance particularly if they were using high doses. Use of other drugs, such as nicotine, cocaine, marijuana, and other hallucinogens, can be stopped abruptly without fear of medical

Two alternative goals guide treatments for substance abuse and dependence. One goal is abstinence—completely stopping the use of the substance. The other goal is harm reduction—lessening the harmful *effects* related to the substance abuse or dependence (for example, lowering the incidence of HIV/AIDS among heroin users by discouraging needle sharing).

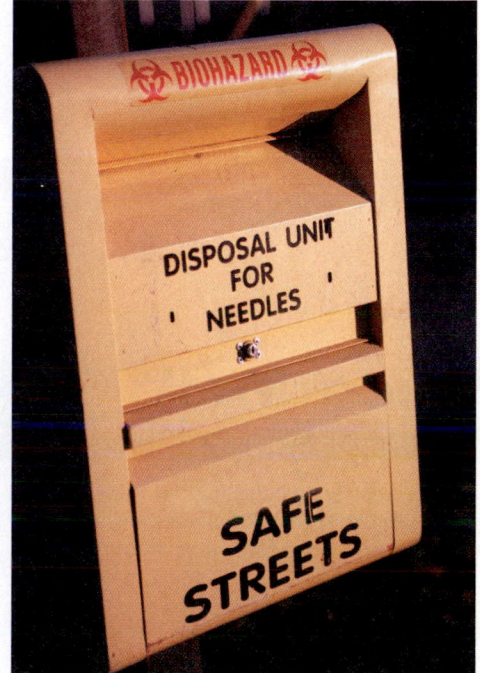

Jack Merritt/Alamy

Detoxification
Medically supervised withdrawal for those with substance dependence; also referred to as *detox*.

problems, although the withdrawal symptoms may be unpleasant. John Lennon was not medically supervised when he stopped using heroin, and he described his disturbing withdrawal experience in his song "Cold Turkey": "Thirty-six hours/ Rolling in pain/Praying to someone/Free me again." Because substance abuse and dependence cause permanent brain changes (which are evident even years after withdrawal symptoms have ceased; Hyman, 2005), O'Brien (2005) proposed that treatment for substance use and dependence should not end with detox, but rather should be a long-term venture, similar to long-term treatment for chronic diseases such as diabetes and hypertension.

Medications

Medications that treat substance abuse or dependence operate in any of several ways: (1) They interfere with the pleasant effects of drug use; (2) they reduce the unpleasant effects of withdrawal; or (3) they help maintain abstinence. Because of the high relapse rate among those who are dependent on a substance, however, medications should be supplemented with other relapse prevention strategies (O'Brien, 2005), described in the sections on treatments targeting psychological and social factors. We now turn to consider medications for specific types of drug abuse and dependence.

Stimulants

Of all drugs, stimulants have the most direct effects on the dopamine reward system. Unfortunately, medications that modify the action of the dopamine receptors per se (in the dopamine reward system) have not yet been developed. However, some medications do affect the functioning of dopamine. For example,

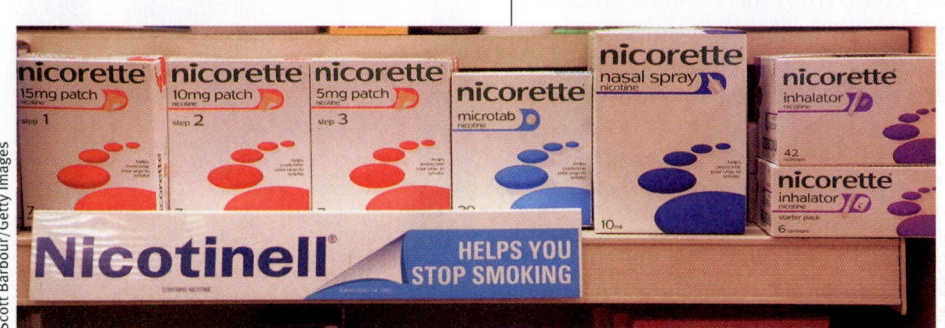

Scott Barbour/Getty Images

a medication that helps people stop smoking is *bupropion* (marketed as Zyban), which acts by affecting the functioning of several neurotransmitters—including dopamine. Bupropion can help to decrease cravings, both for nicotine and for methamphetamines (Killen et al., 2006; Newton et al., 2006). Alternatively, smoking can be treated by delivering nicotine through a form other than cigarettes, such as via skin patches, chewing gum, nasal inhalers, or sprays. These types of treatments are commonly referred to as *nicotine replacement therapy* because they replace a more harmful method of nicotine intake (smoking) with a less harmful method. After a period of time, the user tapers off nicotine by using less of the replacement form.

Nicotine replacement therapy—via skin patches, gum, nasal sprays, and inhalers—provides the user with nicotine in a less harmful manner than smoking cigarettes.

Depressants

Medication for dependence on depressants (such as alcohol) minimizes withdrawal symptoms by substituting a less harmful drug in the same category for the more harmful one. For example, longer-acting benzodiazepines, such as Valium, may be substituted for alcohol or other depressants.

Disulfiram (**Antabuse**), a medication for treating alcohol abuse and dependence, relies on a different approach. Antabuse causes violent nausea and vomiting when it is mixed with alcohol. When an alcoholic takes Antabuse and then drinks alcohol, the resulting nausea and vomiting should condition the person to have negative associations with drinking alcohol. When Antabuse is taken consistently, it leads people with alcohol dependence to drink less frequently, even though it does not make them more likely to become totally abstinent (Fuller et al., 1986; Sereny et al., 1986). Antabuse may also be effective in treating cocaine dependence (Baker, Jallow, & McCance-Katz, 2007; Carroll et al., 2004). However, many patients choose to stop taking Antabuse instead of giving up drinking alcohol (Suh et al., 2006).

Antabuse
A medication for treating alcohol abuse and dependence that induces violent nausea and vomiting when it is mixed with alcohol.

Naltrexone (reVia) is another medication used to treat alcohol abuse; after detox, it can help maintain abstinence. Naltrexone indirectly reduces activity in the dopamine reward system, making drinking alcohol less rewarding (O'Malley et al., 1992); it is the most widely used medication to treat alcoholism in the United States, and it has minimal side effects. Another medication, *acamprosate*, is more popular in Europe; acamprosate reduces cravings and acts by affecting a different type of receptors (NMDA receptors; Johnson & Ait-Daoud, 2000; Tomkins & Sellers, 2001). Researchers found that a combination of naltrexone and acamprosate is more effective in preventing relapse among those in recovery from alcohol abuse than is either drug alone (Brady, 2005; Kiefer et al., 2003).

Finally, people with alcohol dependence who are undergoing detox may develop seizures; to prevent seizures and decrease symptoms of DTs, patients may be given benzodiazepines, along with the beta-blocker *atenolol*. However, a patient with DTs should be hospitalized (Arana & Rosenbaum, 2000).

Narcotic Analgesics

Medications that are used to treat abuse of or dependence on narcotic analgesics are generally chemically similar to the drugs but that reduce or eliminate the "high"; treatments with these medications seek harm reduction because the medications are a safer substitute. For instance, patients with heroin dependence may be given *methadone*, a synthetic opiate that binds to the same receptors as heroin. For about 24 hours after a current or former heroin user has taken methadone, taking heroin will not lead to a high because methadone prevents the heroin molecules from binding to the receptors. Methadone also prevents heroin withdrawal symptoms and cravings (NIDA 2007c). Although patients on methadone are likely to abstain from using heroin, they are still using a substance, and so methadone doesn't promote complete abstinence, but rather heroin abstinence.

Because methadone can produce a mild high and is effective for only 24 hours, patients on methadone maintenance treatment generally must go to a clinic to receive a daily oral dose, a procedure that minimizes the sale of methadone on the black market. Methadone blocks only the effects of heroin, so those taking it might still use cocaine or alcohol to experience a high (El-Bassel et al., 1993). Another medication, *LAAM* (levo-alpha-acetyl-methadol), blocks the effects of narcotic analgesics for up to 72 hours (and so requires trips to a clinic only a few times a week) and does not produce a high. However, LAAM can cause heart problems and so is only prescribed for patients with a dependence on a narcotic analgesic for whom other treatments have proven inadequate.

Methodone and LAAM are generally available only in drug treatment clinics. In contrast, those seeking medication to treat abuse of or dependence on narcotic analgesics can receive a prescription for *buprenorphine* (Subutex) in a doctor's office. Buprenorphine is also available in combination with *naloxone* (Suboxone). In either preparation, buprenorphine has less potential for being abused than methadone because it does not produce a high. Treatment of opiate dependence with substitution medications, such as methadone, is generally more successful than promoting abstinence (D'Ippoliti et al., 1998; Strain et al., 1999; United Nations International Drug Control Programme, 1997).

Naltrexone is also used to treat alcohol dependence and often in combination with buprenorphine, to treat opiate dependence (Amass et al., 2004). Naltrexone is generally most effective for those who are highly motivated and willing to take medication that blocks the reinforcing effects of alcohol or opioids (Tomkins & Sellers, 2001).

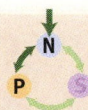

Finally, the beta-blocker *clonidine* (Catapres) may help with withdrawal symptoms (Arana & Rosenbaum, 2000). A summary of medications used to treat substance abuse and dependence is found in Table 9.10.

Table 9.10 ▸ Medications Used to Treat Withdrawal and Promote Maintenance in People with Substance Use Disorders

Class of Drugs	To Treat Withdrawal	To Promote Maintenance
Stimulants: Nicotine	*Nicotine products* (chewing gum, patch), *buproprion* (Zyban)	
Depressants	Longer-acting *depressants* (such as Valium) that block withdrawal symptoms	*Antabuse, acamprosate, naltrexone*
Narcotic Analgesics	*Methadone, buprenorphine, clonadine*	*Methadone* (technically, promotes maintenance by binding to receptors that would otherwise bind with heroin), *buprenorphine, LAAM, naltrexone*

Hallucinogens

Those who abuse LSD and want to quit can generally do so without withdrawal symptoms or significant cravings. Thus, marijuana is the only substance in this category that has been the focus of research on treatment, which generally targets psychological factors and social factors, not neurological ones (McRae, Budney, & Brady, 2003).

Targeting Psychological Factors

Treatments that target psychological factors focus on several elements: (1) increasing a user's motivation to cease or decrease substance use, (2) changing the user's expectations of the drug experience, (3) increasing the user's involvement in treatment, and (4) decreasing the (classically and operantly) conditioned behaviors associated with use of the drug.

Motivation

For those with substance abuse or dependence, stopping or decreasing use is, at best, unpleasant and, at worst, very painful and extremely aversive. Therefore, the user's motivation to stop or decrease strongly affects the ultimate success of any treatment.

Stages of Change

Extensive research has led to a theory of treatment that posits different stages of readiness for changing problematic behaviors of the sort associated with substance abuse and dependence. Research on this theory of **stages of change** has also led to methods that promote readiness for the next stage (Prochaska & DiClemente, 1994). Whereas most other treatments rely on a dichotomous view of substance use—users are either abstinent or not—this approach rests on the idea of intermediate states between theses two extremes; the five stages of readiness to change are as follows:

1. **Precontemplation.** The user does not admit that there is a problem and doesn't intend to change. A temporary decrease in use in response to pressure from others will be followed by a relapse when the pressure is lifted.

2. **Contemplation.** The user admits that there is a problem and may contemplate taking action. However, no actual behavioral change is undertaken at this stage; behavior change is something considered for the future. People with substance abuse and dependence may never get past this stage.

3. **Preparation.** The user is prepared to change. He or she has a specific commitment to change, a plan for change, and the ability to adjust the plan of action

Stages of change
A series of five stages that characterizes how ready a person is to change problematic behaviors: precontemplation, contemplation, preparation, action, and maintenance.

and intends to start changing the substance using behavior within a month. The user is very aware of the abuse, how it reached its current level, and available solutions. Although users in this stage are prepared to change, some are more ambivalent than others and may not implement the intended changes, essentially reverting to the contemplation stage.

4. **Action.** The user actually changes his or her substance use behavior and environment. At this stage, others most clearly perceive the user's intentions to stop or decrease substance use; it is during this stage that family members and friends generally offer the most help and support.

5. **Maintenance.** The user builds on gains already made in stopping or decreasing substance use and tries to prevent relapses. Former substance users who do not devote significant amounts of energy and attention to relapse prevention are likely to relapse all the way to the contemplation—or even the precontemplation—stage. Help and support from others, although important for maintenance, are usually less forthcoming at this stage; friends and family members usually mistakenly think that because the substance abuse has stopped or diminished, the former user is finished taking action. In fact, the former user must *actively* prevent relapses, and help and support from friends and family members is very important in this stage.

This description of the five steps suggests a lock-step model: Each stage has discrete tasks that allow entry to the next in a linear progression. Research, however, suggests that the stages are not mutually exclusive (Litrell & Girvin, 2002). For example, most people in the stage of action have occasional relapses and engage in the unwanted behavior, but they do not totally relapse into the old patterns. Also, uninterrupted forward progress is not the most typical path. People often regress before moving forward again. For example, only 5% of smokers who think about quitting go through all the stages of change within 2 years without a relapse (Prochaska, Velicer, et al., 1994).

Motivational Enhancement Therapy

Motivational enhancement therapy (also referred to as *motivational interviewing*) is specifically designed to boost patients' motivation to decrease or stop substance use (Hettema, Steeler, & Miller, 2005; Miller & Rollnick 1992). In this therapy, the patient (referred to as client in the original transcript) sets his or her own goals regarding substance use, and the therapist points out discrepancies between the user's stated personal goals and his or her current behavior. The therapist then elicits the user's desire to meet the goals, overriding the rewarding effects of drug use. Therapists using motivational enhancement therapy do not dispense advice or seek to increase any specific skills; rather, they focus on increasing the motivation to change drug use, discussing both positive and negative aspects of drug use, reasons to quit, and how change might begin (Miller, 2001). Below is a transcript from a motivational interviewing session that illustrates how such treatment is used.

Client:	So I see I need to cut down using cocaine, but it's not as big a deal as everyone seems to think. My husband nags me about it all the time, but it's not like he says.
Interviewer:	Well, let me ask you this: What are the good things about using cocaine?
Client:	What?
Interviewer:	I'm curious what's good about it.
Client:	You mean like . . .?
Interviewer:	What are the benefits in using it?
Client:	(pause) There is nothing like the high I get from a snort.
Interviewer:	(making a list) One good thing is the feeling that comes when you're high. Tell me more about that.
Client:	Total euphoria. I feel like I can accomplish anything I put my mind to. I'm Superwoman. Nothing bothers me, not even my whiny kids.

Motivational enhancement therapy
A form of treatment specifically designed to boost a patient's motivation to decrease or stop substance use by highlighting discrepancies between stated personal goals related to substance use and current behavior; also referred to as *motivational interviewing*.

Interviewer:	A feeling of total power and exhilaration, then.
Client:	Yeah, but when I come down I pay for it. It's a real downer, and it lasts forever. Then I just want to get high again, and the whole thing is a vicious cycle. And my kids are still whining.
Interviewer:	So in the short run, it's a big payoff, but in the long term the cost is too much.
Client:	Yeah, I've been thinking that I should cut it way back.
Interviewer:	You might want to change, but you're not sure.
Client:	No, I know I need to do something.
Interviewer:	You've already thought about changes you might make.

(Moyers, 2003, pp. 141–142)

Studies have shown that this treatment is more successful when patients have a positive relationship with their therapist and are at the outset strongly motivated to obtain treatment (Etheridge et al., 1999; Joe, Simpson, & Broome, 1999). As with most treatments, the beneficial effects of motivational interviewing tend to fade over the course of a year (Hettema, Steele, & Miller, 2005).

Cognitive-Behavior Therapy

Cognitive-behavior therapy (CBT) for substance abuse focuses on three general themes:

1. understanding and changing thoughts, feelings, and behaviors that lead to substance use (*antecedents*);

2. understanding and changing the *consequences* of the substance use; and

3. developing *alternative behaviors* to substitute for substance use (Carroll, 1998; Marlatt & Gordon, 1985).

Behavioral treatment may focus in particular on decreasing the positive consequences of drug use and on increasing the positive consequences of abstaining from drug use (referred to as *abstinence reinforcement*). As patients are able to change these consequences, they should be less motivated to abuse the substance. These principles may be used more generally for *contingency management*, in which reinforcement is contingent on the desired behavior occurring or the undesired behavior not occurring (Stitzer & Petry, 2006).

These principles have been applied to treatments for abuse of a variety of types of substances, including heroin and cocaine (Higgins et al., 1993; Higgins & Silverman, 1999). The desired behavior (such as attendance at treatment sessions or abstinence from using cocaine, as assessed by urine tests) is reinforced with one or more of these consequences:

- monetary vouchers, the value of which increases with continued abstinence (Jones et al., 2004; Silverman et al., 1999, 2001, 2004);

- decreasing the frequency of mandatory counseling sessions if treatment has been court ordered;

- more convenient appointment times; or

- being allowed to take home a small supply of methadone (requiring fewer trips to the clinic) for those being treated for heroin abuse.

Positive incentives (obtaining reinforcement for a desired behavior) are more effective than negative consequences (such as taking away privileges) in helping patients to stay in treatment and in decreasing substance use (Carroll & Onken, 2005). The cost of providing such rewards can be high, and relapse often increases once rewards are discontinued, which limits the practicality and effectiveness of abstinence reinforcement as a long-term treatment (Carroll & Onken, 2005). Figure 9.12 illustrates the effectiveness of monetary vouchers in promoting abstinence among cocaine users.

Once the patient has stopped abusing the substance, behavioral treatment may focus on preventing relapse by extinguishing the conditioned response

Figure 9.12

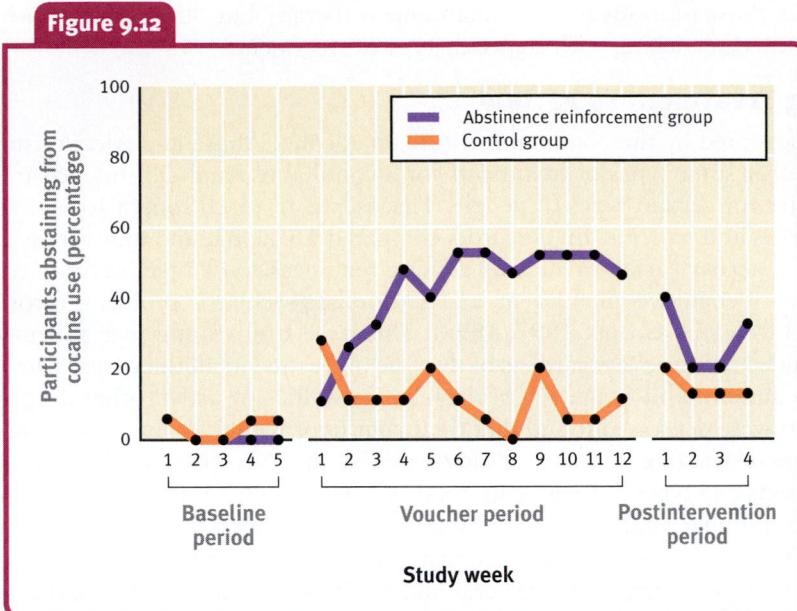

9.12 ▸ Abstinence Reinforcement Among Cocaine Users This graph illustrates the results of a 21-week study with cocaine users on the effects of reinforcing abstinence with vouchers. When patients' abstinence was reinforced with vouchers—compared to patients in a control group whose abstinence was not reinforced—they were more likely to stop using the drug. The abstinence reinforcement group and the control group were significantly different in their cocaine use in weeks 3–12 of the voucher period and weeks 1 and 4 of the postintervention period.

Source: Silverman et al., 2001. Copyright 2001 by the American Medical Association. For more information see the Permissions section.

(including cravings) to drug-related cues (see Chapter 4 for a detailed discussion of extinction). Treatment may also focus on decreasing the frequency or intensity of emotional distress, which can contribute to relapse (Vuchinich & Tucker, 1996). One way treatment can help patients regulate emotional distress is by helping them develop healthier coping skills, which will then increase self-control. Thus, many of the CBT methods used to treat depression and anxiety can be effective here; methods include self-monitoring, cognitive restructuring, problem solving, and various relaxation techniques.

Once (former) users come to understand the antecedents and consequences of their substance use and have developed alternative behaviors, they might be asked to complete a form that contains items like those in Table 9.11—which will help consolidate their ability to make healthier choices and prevent relapse.

Initially, CBT may focus narrowly on the substance use itself—that is, on how the patient copes when he or she has thoughts about using the substance. Later, the treatment expands to focus on related problem areas, such as employment or relationship difficulties.

Twelve-Step Facilitation (TSF)

Twelve-step facilitation (TSF) is based on the twelve steps or principles that form the basis of Alcoholics Anonymous (AA) (see Table 9.12). AA views alcohol abuse as a disease that can never be cured, although alcohol-related behaviors can be modified by the alcoholic's recognizing that he or she has lost control and is powerless over alcohol, turning to a higher power for help, and seeking abstinence. Research suggests that the AA approach can help those who are trying to stop their substance abuse (Laffaye et al., 2008).

AA's groups are leaderless, whereas TSF's groups are led by mental health professionals, whose goal is to help group members become ready to follow the twelve steps of AA. The twelve-step model has been used by those with narcotic abuse and dependence (Narcotics Anonymous, NA) and in numerous inpatient and outpatient treatment programs run by mental health professionals (Ries et al., 2008). Twelve-step facilitation targets *motivation* to adhere to the steps. In essence, its

Table 9.11 ▸ Decision Monitoring

When making any decision, whether large or small, do the following:

- Consider all the options you have.
- Think about all the consequences, both positive and negative, for each of the options.
- Select one of the options. Pick a safe decision that minimizes your risk of relapse.
- Watch for "red flag" thinking—thoughts like "I have to . . ." or "I can handle . . ." or "It really doesn't matter if . . . ."

Practice monitoring decisions that you face in the course of a day, both large and small, and consider safe and risky alternatives for each.

Sources: http://www.drugabuse.gov/TXManuals/CBT/CBTX8.html; adapted from Monti et al., 1989.

Table 9.12 ▸ Twelve Steps of Alcoholics Anonymous

(1) We admitted we were powerless over alcohol—that our lives had become unmanageable.

(2) Came to believe that a Power greater than ourselves could restore us to sanity.

(3) Made a decision to turn our will and our lives over to the care of God as we understood Him.

(4) Made a searching and fearless moral inventory of ourselves.

(5) Admitted to God, to ourselves and to another human being the exact nature of our wrongs.

(6) Were entirely ready to have God remove all these defects of character.

(7) Humbly asked Him to remove our shortcomings.

(8) Made a list of all persons we had harmed, and became willing to make amends to them all.

(9) Made direct amends to such people wherever possible, except when to do so would injure them or others.

(10) Continued to take personal inventory and when we were wrong promptly admitted it.

(11) Sought through prayer and meditation to improve our conscious contact with God as we understood Him, praying only for knowledge of His will for us and the power to carry that out.

(12) Having had a spiritual awakening as the result of these steps, we tried to carry this message to alcoholics, and to practice these principles in all our affairs.

Source: http://www.aa.org/en_pdfs/smf-121_en.pdf.

goals are like those of motivational enhancement therapy but the enhanced motivation focuses on sticking with a specific type of treatment.

Matching Treatment to Patient

Research sponsored by the National Institute on Alcohol Abuse and Alcoholism studied whether some types of treatments for alcohol abuse and dependence are more effective for certain types of people. That is, the research sought to *match* treatment types and patients. Investigators compared TSF, CBT, and motivational enhancement across variables such as gender, readiness to change, severity of abuse, degree of cognitive impairment, and additional psychiatric problems (Project MATCH Research Group, 1997, 1998). This large study found that patients generally tended to improve regardless of the type of treatment; all three treatments reduced the amount and frequency of drinking as well as of use of other drugs. Patients who were depressed found that treatment improved their mood, and the improved mood lasted for up to a year afterward. No matches were found between types of patients and types of treatments. Studies of treatments for abuse of cocaine have produced similar findings regarding matching (Beck, 1999).

Although studies have not shown a neat match between specific types of patients and specific treatments, two general findings have emerged: (1) For patients who abuse more than one substance, a single treatment program that focuses on polysubstance abuse tends to be more effective than a series of programs that focus on one substance at a time. (2) Patients who have substance abuse or dependence and another psychiatric disorder (which is true of many abusers) fared better when the other disorder was also treated.

Targeting Social Factors

Treatments that target social factors aim to change interpersonal and community antecedents and consequences of substance abstinence and use. Antecedents might be addressed by decreasing family tensions, increasing summer employment among teens, and decreasing community violence. Consequences might be addressed by increasing community support for abstinence and providing improved housing or employment opportunities for reduced use or for abstinence.

Residential Treatment

Some people who seek treatment for substance abuse may need more intensive help, such as the assistance that can be found in residential treatment, which provides a round-the-clock therapeutic environment (such as the Betty Ford Center in California). Because it is so intensive, residential treatment can help an individual more rapidly change how he or she thinks, feels, and behaves; some residential treatment programs have a spiritual component. Depending on the philosophy of the program, various combinations of methods—targeting neurological, psychological, and social factors—may be available.

Community-Based Treatment

Treatments that target social factors are usually provided in groups. One approach focuses on providing group therapy, which typically take place in residential programs, day-treatment programs (to which patients come during the day to attend groups and receive individual therapy but do not stay overnight), methadone clinics, and drug counseling centers. In addition, there are a number of self-help groups for people with substance abuse.

Group Therapy

CBT may be used in a group format to help those with substance abuse. The group provides peer pressure and support for abstinence (Crits-Christoph et al., 1999). Moreover, members may use role-playing to try out new skills, such as saying "no" to friends who offer drugs. Other types of groups include social-skills training groups, where members learn ways to communicate their feelings and desires more

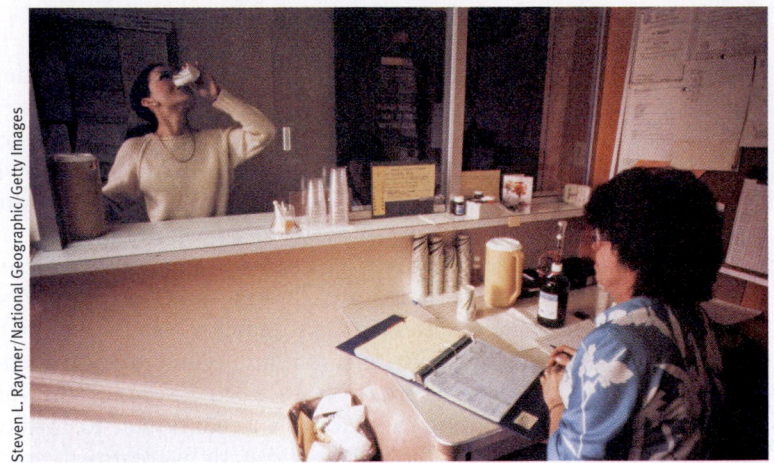

Steven L. Raymer/National Geographic/Getty Images

Various types of treatment for substance use disorders can be offered in the community, including day-treatment programs, methadone clinics (such as the one shown here), group therapy, and self-help groups.

effectively, and general support groups to decrease shame and isolation as members change their substance abuse patterns.

Self-Help Groups

Self-help groups (sometimes called support groups), such as the twelve-step programs of Alcoholics Anonymous and Narcotics Anonymous, hold regular meetings. Attending such a group might supplement other treatment or might be the only treatment a person pursues. As noted earlier, such groups often view belief in God or some other "higher power" as crucial to recovery, and even people who are not religious can improve through AA meetings (Humphreys & Moos, 2007; Moos & Timko, 2008; Timko, DeBenedetti, & Billow, 2006; Winzelberg & Humphreys, 1999). AA also provides social support, both from other group members and a *sponsor*—an individual with years of sobriety who serves as a mentor and can be called up when the newer member experiences cravings or temptations to drink again.

Other self-help organizations, such as Secular Organizations for Sobriety and Women for Sobriety, do not include spirituality or a religious component. Still other organizations offer groups that are led by trained professionals and so are technically not self-help groups; Rational Recovery and Smart Recovery are examples. These are based on cognitive-behavioral principles and do not use a twelve-step approach (Nowinski, 2003).

A meta-analysis showed that attending a self-help group at least once a week is associated with drug or alcohol abstinence (Fiorentine, 1999). Other research confirms that longer participation in AA is associated with better outcomes (Moos & Moos, 2004). Just like group therapy, a self-help group can be invaluable in decreasing feelings of isolation and shame. In general, self-help groups can be valuable sources of information and support, not only for the substance abuser but also for his or her relatives.

Family Therapy

To the extent that family interactions lead to or help sustain substance abuse, changing family patterns of interaction can modify these factors (Saatcioglu, Erim, & Cakmak, 2006; Stanton & Shadish, 1997). Among adolescents treated for substance abuse, outpatient family therapy appears to help them to abstain (Smith et al., 2006; Szapocznik, Hervis, & Schwartz, 2003; Williams & Chang, 2000), which suggests that changes in how parents and adolescents interact can promote and maintain abstinence. In fact, family therapy is usually a standard component of treatment for adolescents with substance use disorders (Austin, Macgowan, & Wagner, 2005). The goals of this type of therapy are tailored to the specific problems and needs of each family, but such therapy typically addresses issues related to communication, power, and control (see the discussion of family therapy in Chapter 4; Hogue et al., 2006).

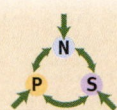

FEEDBACK LOOPS IN TREATMENT: **Substance Use Disorders**

At first glance, using medication to treat substance abuse or dependence might seem like the perfect solution. Substance abuse disrupts neurological factors, and how better to address that disruption than to use another substance? However, for medications to work effectively, they must be taken regularly, which means that users must remain motivated and willing to take them (psychological factor); in addition, the risk of relapse is reduced when a user minimizes contact with people and situations that trigger a desire to use the substance (social factors). Medications may target neural communication and the relevant brain systems, but they don't address the whole person or the person's context: friends, family, work and home environments, and the subculture and community in which the person lives.

The neuropsychosocial approach leads us to categorize the various treatments for substance abuse according to each one's direct target. Regardless of which type of factor is directly targeted, though, how exactly is treatment success determined? The following considerations help to determine whether an intervention was successful. Did the individual:

- complete the treatment, or is he or she still using or abusing the substance? (Is he or she abstinent—yes or no?)

- experience fewer harmful effects from the substance? (Is he or she using clean needles or no longer drinking to the point of passing out?)

- decrease use of the substance? (How much is the person using after treatment?)

- come to behave more responsibly? (Does he or she attend regular AA meetings or get to work on time?)

- feel better? (Is the person less depressed, anxious, "strung out," or are drug cravings less intense?)

- come to conform to societal norms? (Has he or she stayed out of jail?)

The treatments we've discussed can lead to improvement according to these considerations, but different types of treatments provide different paths toward improvement. Moreover, like most cigarette smokers, many substance abusers may quit multiple times. In addition, like studies of treatments for other types of disorders, studies of treatments for substance abuse have found a dose-response relationship: Longer treatment produces better outcomes than shorter treatment (Hubbard et al., 1989; Simpson, 1984, Simpson, Joe, & Broome, 2002). And for those people who abuse more than one type of substance, treatment is most effective when it addresses the entire set of substances.

The most robust finding about all of the treatments we've discussed is that they work, at least in the short term. Project MATCH showed that CBT, motivational enhancement therapy, and TSF were equally helpful. It also showed that medication and social interventions are effective. Ultimately, all successful treatments address all three types of factors that are identified in the neuropsychosocial approach. When people with substance abuse or dependence first stop abusing the substance, they will experience neurological changes that are, at minimum, uncomfortable (neurological and psychological factors). Moreover, how they think and feel about themselves will change (psychological factor)— from "abuser" or "addict" to "ex-abuser" or "in recovery". Their interactions with others will change (social factors): Perhaps they will make new friends who don't use drugs, avoid friends who abuse drugs, behave differently with family members (who in turn may behave differently toward them), perform better at work, or have fewer run-ins with the law. Other people's responses to them will also affect their motivation to continue to avoid using the substance and endure the uncomfortable withdrawal effects and ignore their cravings. Thus, as usual, treatment ultimately relies on feedback loops among the three types of factors (see Figure 9.13).

Figure 9.13

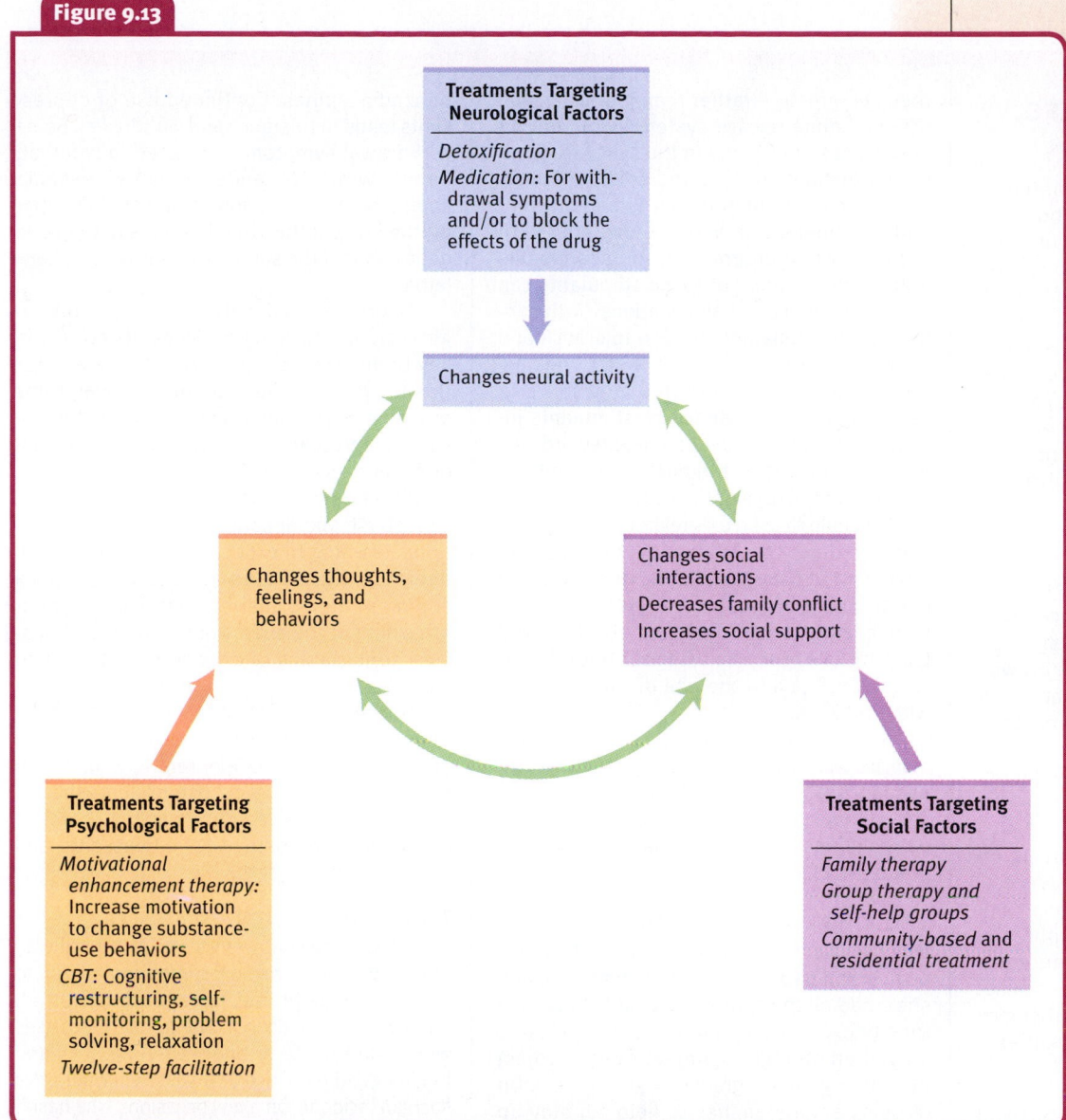

Treatments Targeting Neurological Factors

Detoxification Medication: For with-drawal symptoms and/or to block the effects of the drug

Changes neural activity

Changes thoughts, feelings, and behaviors

Changes social interactions
Decreases family conflict
Increases social support

Treatments Targeting Psychological Factors

Motivational enhancement therapy: Increase motivation to change substance-use behaviors

CBT: Cognitive restructuring, self-monitoring, problem solving, relaxation

Twelve-step facilitation

Treatments Targeting Social Factors

Family therapy
Group therapy and self-help groups
Community-based and residential treatment

9.13 ▶ Feedback Loops in Treating Substance Use Disorders

Key Concepts and Facts About Treating Substance Use Disorders

- Treatments that focus on neurological factors include detox to help reduce symptoms of withdrawal that come from dependence. Medications may reduce unpleasant withdrawal symptoms or block the pleasant effects of using the substance, which can help maintain abstinence.

- Treatments that target psychological factors, such as motivational enhancement therapy, are designed to motivate people to decrease substance use. CBT addresses antecedents, consequences, and specific behaviors related to substance use. Twelve-step facilitation provides structure and support to help patients to abstain.

- Social factors are targeted by residential treatment and other types of community-based treatment (group therapy and self-help groups), as well as family therapy to address issues of communication, power, and control.

SUMMING UP

Summary of Use, Abuse, and Dependence

The hallmark of substance use disorders is abuse of or dependence on a psychoactive substance. The term *addiction* focuses on the compulsive behaviors related to regular drug taking, but is not used in DSM-IV-TR. *Substance abuse* refers to the pattern of use of a psychoactive substance that leads to harmful effects; *substance dependence* refers to the persistent and compulsive use of a psychoactive substance, despite the ensuing negative consequences. Tolerance and withdrawal are common symptoms of substance dependence.

Researchers have developed two compatible explanations of why substance use may lead to abuse. The common liabilities model focuses on underlying factors that may contribute to a variety of problematic behaviors, including substance abuse. The gateway hypothesis focuses on factors that lead individuals to progress from using entry drugs to using harder drugs.

In DSM-IV-TR, substance abuse and dependence are characterized as discrete categories; some researchers suggest that they may be better conceptualized as being on a continuum. Substance use disorders frequently co-occur with mood disorders (particularly depression), PTSD, schizophrenia, and ADHD. Many people with substance use disorders engage in polysubstance abuse. Cultures can promote or regulate substance use through the use of rituals and penalties.

Thinking like a clinician

Jorge and his friend Rick worked hard and played hard in high school. On weekend evenings, usually their only free time, they'd binge drink, along with others in their group. They went to different colleges. Jorge kept up his "study hard, party hard" lifestyle; Rick didn't do much binge drinking in college, but he started smoking marijuana in the evenings when he was done studying and he'd go dancing on Saturday nights and sometimes take Ecstasy or stimulants. What information would you want to know in order to determine whether Jorge or Rick had a substance use disorder? How would you know whether either was dependent on a substance?

Summary of Stimulants

Stimulants, which increase arousal and brain activity, are the category of psychoactive substances most likely to lead to dependence. Unlike many other types of drugs, they act directly—rather than indirectly—on the dopamine reward system by binding to dopamine transporters in the synapse. Stimulants include cocaine and crack, amphetamines, methamphetamine, Ritalin, MDMA, and nicotine. Crack use is associated with the most rapid progression to dependence. In high doses, most of these stimulants can cause paranoia and hallucinations. With continued use, stimulants lead to tolerance and withdrawal.

Neurological factors that contribute to abuse of and dependence on stimulants include activation of the dopamine reward system, which involves the nucleus accumbens and the ventral tegmental area.

Psychological factors related to substance use disorders include learning: operant reinforcement of the effects of the drug, classical conditioning of stimuli related to drug use (which leads to cravings), and observational learning of expectancies about both the effects of drugs and the use of them to cope with problems.

Social factors related to substance use disorders include the specific nature of an individual's relationships with family members, socioeconomic factors, and cultural and perceived norms about appropriate and inappropriate use of substances.

Thinking like a clinician

One night before a major class project was due, Sierra had hours of work left to do, and she'd had all the coffee she could stand. She took one of her roommate's Ritalin pills and stayed up all night, completing the project by morning. Sierra gradually got in the habit of using amphetamines to help her stay up late and do course work. After college, Sierra took a job with lots of deadlines and lots of late hours. She continued to use stimulants to help her work, sometimes taking cocaine when she could get it.

At what point does Sierra's use of stimulants become abuse? Does she have a dependence—why or why not? What would be some specific symptoms that would indicate that she was abusing cocaine? What symptoms would you expect to see if Sierra were taking a high dose of stimulants? According to the neuropsychosocial approach, what factors might have led Sierra to abuse stimulants, if she were abusing them?

Summary of Depressants

Depressants decrease arousal, awareness, and nervous system activity level. Depressants include alcohol, barbiturates, and benzodiazepines. Continued use of depressants leads to tolerance and withdrawal. Some withdrawal symptoms are potentially lethal; people with a dependence on depressants should be medically supervised as they taper off their use of the drug. Using more than one depressant at the same time is also potentially lethal.

Depressants directly affect the GABAnergic system, which in turn dampens activity in key brain areas that give rise to anxiety; for this reason, people with anxiety symptoms are more likely than others to abuse depressants. Depressants also indirectly activate the dopamine reward system.

Psychological factors related to depressant abuse and dependence include observational learning to expect specific effects from depressant use and to use depressants as a coping strategy, positive and negative reinforcement of the effects of the drug, and classical conditioning of drug cues that leads to cravings.

Social factors related to abuse of and dependence on depressants include the specific nature of an individual's relationships with family members, peers' use of depressants, norms and perceived norms about appropriate and inappropriate use of depressants, and socioeconomic factors.

Thinking like a clinician

When you see your neighbor in the hallway in the evenings, she sometimes can't seem to walk in a straight line, her speech is slurred, and she reeks of alcohol. She frequently misses when she tries to put her key in the lock and begins giggling. Once you saw her vomit after such an incident. On a few occasions, she hasn't been so obviously "wasted" and has turned to you and roughly said, "What are you staring at?" One time, when you smirked as she tried to put her key in the lock, she came over to you and threatened to "kick your butt." Even during the daytime, though, she's not very nice or friendly.

Do you think your neighbor has a problem with alcohol, and if so, is it abuse or dependence? Why or why not—what supports or refutes the conclusion that she has an alcohol problem? What information would you want to know before making a confident decision? According to the neuropsychosocial approach, what factors might underlie your neighbor's use of alcohol?

Summary of Other Abused Substances

Narcotic analgesics, also called opioids, can dull pain and decrease awareness. Continued opioid use quickly leads to tolerance and withdrawal, as well as compulsive drug-related behaviors. Heroin is an opioid. Opioids activate the dopamine reward system. They also depress the central nervous system and decrease endorphin production, thereby reducing the body's inherent ability to relieve pain. Using an opioid and a depressant at the same time is potentially lethal.

Hallucinogens include LSD, mescaline, psilocybin, and marijuana. Hallucinogens have unpredictable effects, which depend in part on the user's expectations and the context in which the drug is taken. People can have a "bad trip" when using LSD and can experience flashbacks long after the drug wears off. Although the effects of marijuana are more subtle, abuse of or dependence on this hallucinogen affects motivation, learning, and memory. The active ingredient in marijuana, THC, appears to have an effect on the brain similar to that of cannabinoids, activating the dopamine reward system.

Dissociative anesthetics are so named because they induce a sense of dissociation and cause anesthesia. They depress the central nervous system and affect glutamate activity. Dissociative anesthetics include PCP and ketamine. Use and abuse of this type of drug impairs cognitive functioning, and can lead to violent behavior. Genes may predispose some people to develop abuse of or dependence on these substances.

Psychological factors related to substance use disorders include observational learning, and operant conditioning (reinforcement of the effects of the drug) and classical conditioning of stimuli related to drug use. Social factors related to substance use disorders include the individual's relationship with family members, peers' use of substances, cultural norms and perceived norms, and socioeconomic factors.

Thinking like a clinician

Nat didn't care much for drinking; his drugs of choice were ketamine and LSD. His friends worried about him, though, because every weekend he'd either be clubbing (and taking ketamine) or tripping on LSD.

What might be some of the sensations and perceptions that each drug induced in Nat, and why might his friends be concerned about him? Suppose he stopped using LSD, but started smoking marijuana daily. What symptoms might he experience, and why might his friends become concerned? If he switched from taking ketamine to snorting heroin before clubbing, what difference might it make in the long term?

How would you determine whether Nat was abusing or was dependent on these substances? What other information might you want to know before making such a judgment? Do you think he might develop withdrawal symptoms—why or why not? If so, which ones? According to the neuropsychosocial approach, what factors might underlie Nat's use of drugs?

Summary of Treating Substance Abuse

Treatments that focus on neurological factors include detox to help reduce symptoms of withdrawal that come from dependence. Medications may reduce unpleasant withdrawal symptoms or block the pleasant effects of using the substance, which can help maintain abstinence.

Treatments that target psychological factors, such as motivational enhancement therapy, are designed to motivate users to decrease substance abuse. CBT addresses antecedents, consequences, and specific behaviors related to substance use. Twelve-step facilitation provides structure and support to help patients abstain. Social factors are targeted by residential treatment and other types of community-based treatment, as well as family therapy to address issues of communication, power, and control.

Thinking like a clinician

Karl has been binge drinking and smoking marijuana every weekend for the past couple of years. He's been able to maintain his job, but Monday mornings he's in rough shape and sometimes he's had blackouts when he drinks. He's decided that he wants to quit drinking and smoking marijuana, but feels that he needs some help to do so. Based on what you've read in this chapter, what would you advise for Karl and why? What wouldn't you suggest to him as an appropriate treatment and why not?

Key Terms

Psychoactive substance (p. 382)

Substance use disorders (p. 382)

Substance intoxication (p. 382)

Substance abuse (p. 383)

Substance dependence (p. 383)

Tolerance (p. 385)

Withdrawal (p. 385)

Common liabilities model (p. 385)

Gateway hypothesis (p. 386)

Polysubstance abuse (p. 388)

Dopamine reward system (p. 396)

Reward craving (p. 400)

Relief craving (p. 400)

Drug cues (p. 401)

Delirium tremens (DTs) (p. 408)

Detoxification (p. 421)

Antabuse (p. 422)

Stages of change (p. 424)

Motivational enhancement therapy (p. 425)

More Study Aids

For additional study aids related to this chapter, go to:

www.worthpublishers.com/rosenberg

Eating Disorders

By the time she was 9 years old, Marya Hornbacher developed **bulimia nervosa,** which is an eating disorder characterized by binge eating along with vomiting or other behaviors to compensate for the large number of calories ingested. By the time she reached 15, she had **anorexia nervosa,** an eating disorder characterized by being at least 15% below expected body weight along with using various methods to prevent weight gain. For the next 5 years, she careened from one eating disorder to another. By Hornbacher's own account she had "been hospitalized six times, institutionalized once, had endless hours of therapy, been tested and observed and diagnosed . . . and fed and weighed for so long that I have begun to feel like a laboratory rat" (Hornbacher, 1998, p. 3). At the age of 23, Hornbacher wrote *Wasted: A Memoir of Anorexia and Bulimia* about her experiences with eating disorders, in which she wonders:

> Just what was I trying to prove, and to whom? This is one of the terrible, banal truths of eating disorders: when a woman is thin in this culture, she proves her worth, in a way that no great accomplishment, no stellar career, nothing at all can match. We believe she has done what centuries of a collective unconscious insist that no woman can do—control herself. A woman who can control herself is almost as good as a man. A thin woman can Have It All."
>
> (1998, pp. 81–82)

But as Hornbacher points out, eating disorders don't really help anyone have it all. An eating disorder

> . . . is an attempt to find an identity, but ultimately it strips you of any sense of yourself, save the sorry identity of "sick." It is a grotesque mockery of cultural standards of beauty that winds up mocking no one more than you. It is a protest against cultural stereotypes of women that in the end makes you seem the weakest, the most needy and neurotic of all women. It is the thing you believe is keeping you safe, alive, contained—and in the end, of course, you find it's doing quite the opposite. These contradictions begin to split a person in two. Body and mind fall apart from each other, and it is in this fissure that an eating disorder may flourish, in the silence that surrounds this confusion that an eating disorder may fester and thrive.
>
> (1998, p. 6)

Bulimia nervosa
An eating disorder characterized by binge eating along with vomiting or other behaviors to compensate for the large number of calories ingested.

Anorexia nervosa
An eating disorder characterized by being at least 15% below expected body weight along with using various methods to prevent weight gain.

Katherine Streeter/Frank Sturges Reps

Eating disorders
A category of psychological disorders characterized by abnormal eating and a preoccupation with body image.

Many people in Western culture try to attain or maintain a particular weight by dieting, exercising, or monitoring their food intake. Some of those people have—or will have—an eating disorder. An **eating disorder** is characterized by abnormal eating and a preoccupation with body image. Females make up 90% of those diagnosed with an eating disorder, and so in this chapter, we will refer to an individual with an eating disorder as "she" or "her;" however, the number of males with eating disorders has been slowly increasing (Hudson et al., 2007).

DSM-IV-TR lists two specific eating disorders: *anorexia nervosa* and *bulimia nervosa*. In this chapter, we examine the criteria for and the medical effects of these two disorders, and consider the criticisms of the criteria used to diagnose them. We also discuss research findings that can illuminate why eating disorders arise and the various methods used to treat them.

Anorexia Nervosa

After years of struggling with bulimia, Marya Hornbacher began "inching" toward anorexia; she gradually became significantly underweight by severely restricting her food intake, refusing to eat enough to obtain a healthy weight:

> Anorexia started slowly. It took time to work myself into the frenzy that the disease demands. There were an incredible number of painfully thin girls at [school], dancers mostly. The obsession with weight seemed nearly universal. Whispers and longing stares followed the ones who were visibly anorexic. We sat at our cafeteria tables, passionately discussing the calories of lettuce, celery, a dinner roll, rice. We moved between two worlds. When we pushed back our chairs and scattered to our departments, we transformed. I would watch girls who'd just been near tears in the dorm-room mirrors suddenly become rapt with life, fingers flying over a harp, a violin, bodies elastic with motion, voices strolling through Shakespeare's forest of words.
>
> (Hornbacher, 1998, p. 102).

Hornbacher wanted to be thin, to be in control of her eating, and to feel more in control of herself generally. She began to eat less and less, to the point where she began to pass out at school.

Let's investigate anorexia nervosa in more detail. In this section we discuss the specific DSM-IV-TR criteria for anorexia nervosa and its subtypes, the various medical consequences of the disorder, and criticisms of the DSM-IV-TR definition of anorexia nervosa.

What Is Anorexia Nervosa?

A key feature of *anorexia nervosa* (often referred to simply as *anorexia*) is that the person will not maintain at least a low normal weight and employs various methods to prevent weight gain (American Psychiatric Association, 2000). Despite medical and psychological consequences of a low weight, those with anorexia nervosa continue to pursue extreme thinness. Unfortunately, anorexia has a high risk of death, though not all by suicide: About 10–15% of people hospitalized with anorexia eventually die as a direct or indirect consequence of the disorder (American Psychiatric Association, 2000; Zipfel et al., 2000).

Anorexia Nervosa According to DSM-IV-TR

To be diagnosed with anorexia nervosa according to DSM-IV-TR, symptoms must meet four criteria:

1. *A refusal to obtain or maintain a healthy weight* (at least 85% of expected body weight, based on age and height).

2. *An intense fear of becoming fat or gaining weight*, despite being significantly underweight. This fear is often the primary reason that the person refuses to attain a healthy weight. Those who have anorexia are obsessed with their body

Individuals with anorexia nervosa have a very low weight and, despite medical consequences, refuse to maintain a healthy weight. This young woman had been on her college swim team when she suffered a heart attack; her anorexia persisted and she was considered to be a danger to herself and banned from campus.

and food, and their thoughts and beliefs about these topics are usually illogical or irrational, such as imagining that wearing a certain clothing size is "worse than death." Moreover, their feelings about themselves rise and fall with their caloric intake, their weight, or how their clothes seem to fit. If someone with anorexia eats 50 more calories (for comparison, a single pat of butter provides about 35 calories) than she had allotted for her daily intake, she may experience intense feelings of worthlessness. People who suffer from anorexia often deny that they have a problem and do not see their low weight as a source of concern.

3. *Distortions of body image* (the individual's view of her body). People with anorexia often feel that their bodies are bigger and "fatter" than they actually are (see Figure 10.1).

Figure 10.1

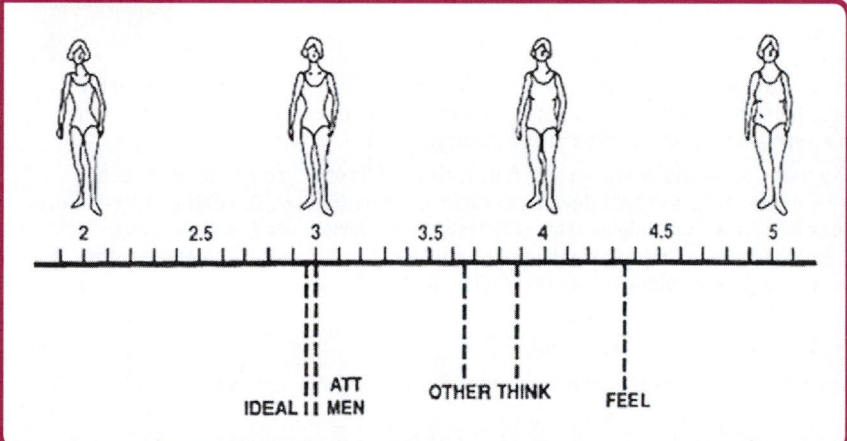

Amenorrhea
The suppression of menstruation; this condition is diagnosed after three consecutive missed menstrual cycles.

10.1 ▶ Body Image Distortion With respect to body image, women with anorexia may simply represent an extreme end of "normal" distortions; many other women do not assess their bodies accurately (Thompson, 1990). Here IDEAL is the average figure that women rated as ideal. ATT MEN ("attractive to men") shows the average figure that women rated as most attractive to men, whereas OTHER illustrates the average figure that men selected as most attractive. THINK depicts the average figure that women thought of as best matching their own, and FEEL depicts the average figure that women felt best matches their own.

Source: Thompson, 1990.

4. *The suppression of menstruation*, called **amenorrhea,** which is diagnosed after three consecutive missed menstrual cycles in females who have already begun menstruating. If a woman must take hormones to menstruate, she is considered to have amenorrhea. For children and adolescents who have not yet begun menstruating, this criterion does not apply. Table 10.1 lists the DSM-IV-TR diagnostic criteria for anorexia; additional facts about anorexia are provided in Table 10.2, and Case 10.1 provides a glimpse of life with anorexia.

Table 10.1 ▶ DSM-IV-TR Diagnostic Criteria for Anorexia Nervosa

A. Refusal to maintain body weight at or above a minimally normal weight for age and height (e.g., weight loss leading to maintenance of body weight less than 85% of that expected; or failure to make expected weight gain during period of growth, leading to body weight less than 85% of that expected).

B. Intense fear of gaining weight or becoming fat, even though underweight.

C. Disturbance in the way in which one's body weight or shape is experienced, undue influence of body weight or shape on self-evaluation, or denial of the seriousness of the current low body weight.

D. In postmenarcheal females [those who have already begun menstruating], amenorrhea, i.e., the absence of at least three consecutive menstrual cycles. (A woman is considered to have amenorrhea if her periods occur only following hormone, e.g., estrogen, administration.)

Source: Reprinted with permission from the Diagnostic and Statistical Manual of Mental Disorders, Text Revision, Fourth Edition, (Copyright 2000) American Psychiatric Association.

Table 10.2 ▸ Anorexia Nervosa Facts at a Glance

Prevalence

- In the course of a lifetime, about 1% of females and up to 0.3% of males will develop anorexia (Hoek & van Hoeken, 2003; Hudson et al., 2007).

Comorbidity

- Most studies find that at least half—but as high as 90%—of patients with anorexia have at least one comorbid psychological disorder. The most common types of comorbid disorders are depression, anxiety disorders, and personality disorders (Agras, 2001; Blinder, Cumella, & Sanathara, 2006; Cassin & van Ranson, 2005; Godart et al., 2003; Lucka, 2006).

Onset

- Anorexia typically emerges between the ages of 14 and 18 (American Psychiatric Association, 2000), although the disorder can make its first appearance at an earlier or a later age (Beck, Casper, & Anderson, 1996; Keith & Midlarsky, 2004).

Course

- Anorexia has the highest mortality rate of any psychological disorder—up to 15% (Zipfel et al., 2000). Half of the deaths are from suicide, and the others are from medical complications of the disorder. People with anorexia who also abuse substances have an even higher risk of death (Keel et al., 2003).
- According to some studies, fewer than 50% of those who survive fully recover (Keel et al., 2005; Von Holle et al., 2008), about 33% improve but do not recover, and 20% develop chronic anorexia (Fichter, Quadflieg, & Hedlund, 2006; Steinhausen, 2002); other studies have found higher rates of full recovery (Johnson, Lund, & Yates, 2003; Keski-Rahkonen et al., 2007). Some people with anorexia gain enough weight that they no longer meet the criteria for the disorder, but meet the criteria for bulimia nervosa (Keel et al., 2005).

Gender Differences

- Approximately 75–90% of those with anorexia nervosa are female (Hoek & van Hoeken, 2003; Hudson et al., 2007).

Cultural Differences

- The specific diagnostic criteria stated in DSM-IV-TR do not necessarily apply to all cultures. Many Chinese girls and women with anorexia have not reported the fear of becoming fat that is typical among people with anorexia in Western cultures. Rather, the reasons they give for their minimal food intake are discomfort when eating or the poor taste of the food (Lee & Lee, 1996).
- In the United States, females of black, Hispanic, or Asian background are less likely to be diagnosed with anorexia nervosa than are white females (Alegria et al., 2007; Nicdao, Hong, & Takeuchi, 2007; Striegel-Moore et al., 2003; Taylor et al., 2007).

CASE 10.1 ▸ FROM THE INSIDE: Anorexia Nervosa

Caroline Knapp suffered from both anorexia and alcohol dependence (see the excerpt from her book, *Drinking: A Love Story,* in Chapter 9, Case 9.5). In describing her relationship with food, she noted that people with anorexia nervosa develop bizarre eating habits and a kind of tunnel vision—focusing on food, on eating, and on not eating:

When you're starving . . . it's hard to think about anything else [except eating or not eating. It's] very hard to see the larger picture of options that is your life, very hard to consider what else you might need or want or fear were you not so intently focused on one crushing passion. I sat in my room every night, with rare exceptions, for three-and-a-half years. In secret, and with painstaking deliberation, I carved an apple and one-inch square of cheddar cheese into tiny bits, sixteen individual slivers, each one so translucently thin you could see the light shine through it if you held it up to a lamp. Then I lined up the apple slices on a tiny china saucer and placed a square of cheese on each. And then I ate them one by one, nibbled at them like a rabbit, edge by tiny edge, so slowly and with such concentrated precision the meal took two hours to consume. I planned for this ritual all day, yearned for it, carried it out with the utmost focus and care.

(Knapp, 2003, pp. 48–49)

If, as you read Knapp's description of her eating ritual, you were reminded of symptoms of obsessive-compulsive disorder (OCD, see Chapter 7), you're on to something. Some symptoms of anorexia overlap with certain symptoms of OCD: obsessions about symmetry, compulsions to order objects precisely, and hoarding. However, other symptoms of OCD, such as obsessions about contamination and checking and cleaning compulsions, do not overlap with those of anorexia (Halmi et al., 2003).

Two Types of Anorexia Nervosa: Restricting and Binge-Eating/Purging

People with anorexia become extremely thin and maintain their very low weight in either of two ways: through restricting what they eat or through binge eating and then purging. DSM-IV-TR categorizes two types of anorexia based on which pattern is present:

- *Restricting type.* Low weight is achieved and maintained through severe undereating; there is no binge eating or purging. This is the classic type of anorexia, and Knapp's description in Case 10.1 illustrates the pattern of eating that is common among people with the restricting type.

- *Binge-eating/purging type.* Some people with anorexia may engage in **binge eating**—eating much more food at one time than most people would eat in the same context, for example, a "snack" might consist of a pint or two of ice cream with a whole jar of hot fudge sauce. Among people with anorexia, binge eating is followed by **purging,** which is an attempt to reduce the ingested calories by vomiting or by using diuretics, laxatives, or enemas.

Medical, Psychological, and Social Effects of Anorexia Nervosa

Anorexia has serious negative effects on many aspects of bodily functioning. Because of the daily deficit between calories needed for normal functioning and calories taken in, the body tries to make do with less. However, this process comes at a high cost.

Anorexia's Medical Effects

One possible effect of anorexia is that the heart muscle becomes thinner as the body, searching for an energy source to meet the its caloric demands, cannibalizes muscle generally, and the heart muscle in particular. *Muscle wasting* is the term used when the body breaks down muscle in order to obtain needed calories. When people with anorexia exercise, they are not building muscle but *losing* it, especially heart muscle—which can be fatal. Excessive exercise is actively discouraged in people with anorexia, and even modest exercise may be discouraged, depending on the person's weight and medical status.

A physical examination and lab tests are likely to reveal other medical effects of anorexia, which arise through the body's adjustments to conserve energy. These include low heart rate and blood pressure, abdominal bloating or discomfort, constipation, loss of bone density (leading to osteoporosis and easily fractured bones), and a slower metabolism (which leads to lower body temperature, difficulty tolerating cold temperatures, and downy hairs forming on the body to provide insulation). More visible effects include dry and yellow-orange skin, brittle nails, and loss of hair on the scalp. Symptoms that

Binge eating
Eating much more food at one time than most people would eat in the same context.

Purging
Attempting to reduce calories that have already been consumed by vomiting or using diuretics, laxatives, or enemas.

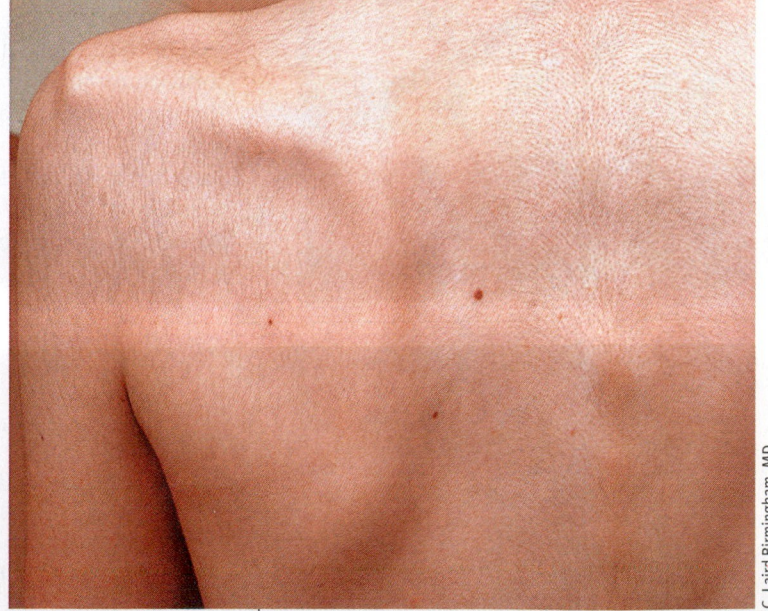
Underweight people may develop lanugo hair—fine downy hair similar to that of newborns—on the abdomen, back, and face. Lanugo disappears when normal weight is attained.

C. Laird Birmingham, MD

may not be as obvious to others include irritability, fatigue, and headaches (Mehler, 2003; Pomeroy, 2004). People, particularly females, with anorexia may also appear hyperactive or restless, which is probably a by-product of starvation, given that such behavior also occurs in starved animals (Klein & Walsh, 2005).

People with anorexia who purge may believe that they are getting rid of all the calories they've eaten, but they're wrong. In a starved state, the body so desperately needs calories that once food is in the mouth, the digestive process begins more rapidly than normal and calories may begin to be absorbed before the food reaches the stomach; even if vomiting occurs, some calories are still absorbed, although water the body needs is lost. Diuretics only decrease water in the body, not body fat or muscle, and laxatives and enemas simply get rid of water and the body's waste before it would otherwise be eliminated.

All four methods of purging—vomiting, diuretics, laxatives, and enemas—can result in dehydration, because they all deprive the body of needed fluids. And dehydration can create an imbalance in the body's *electrolytes*—salts that are critical for neural transmission and muscle contractions, including that of the heart muscle. When dehydration remains untreated, it can lead to death.

Psychological and Social Effects of Starvation

Researchers in the 1940s documented a number of unexpected psychological and social effects of extreme caloric restriction in what is sometimes called the *starvation study* (Keys et al., 1950). When healthy young men were given half their usual caloric intake for 6 months, they lost 25% of their original weight and suffered other changes: They became more sensitive to the sensations of light, cold, and noise; they slept less; they lost their sex drive; and their mood worsened. The men lost their sense of humor, argued with one another, and showed symptoms of depression and anxiety. They also became obsessed with food—talking and dreaming about food, collecting and sharing recipes. They began to hoard food and random items such as old books and knick-knacks. These striking effects persisted for months after the men returned to their normal diets. Such findings have since been substantiated by other researchers (Crisp et al., 1980). It is sobering that, even on this diet, the participants in the starvation study still ate more each day than do many people with anorexia.

The participants in the starvation study were psychologically healthy adult men, and they developed the noticeable symptoms after less than 6 months of caloric intake that would now be considered a relatively strict diet. Most people (females) with anorexia develop the disorder when they are younger than were the men in the study—and the consequences of restricting eating at a young age may be more severe than those noted in the starvation study. In fact, recent studies of the long-term consequences of starvation during puberty indicate an increased risk of heart disease (Sparén et al., 2004). Moreover, patients with anorexia generally maintain unhealthy eating patterns for much longer than the 6-month study period. The long-term effects of starvation can also lead people with anorexia to forget what it was like to live *without* the medical and psychological effects of the disorder. Marya Hornbacher described this kind of mental state:

> I was beginning to harbor [the] delusion . . . that I was superhuman. When you coast without eating for a significant amount of time, and you are still alive, you begin to scoff at those fools who believe they must eat to live. It seems blatantly obvious to you that this is not true. You get up in the morning, you do your work, you run, you do not eat, you live.
>
> You begin to forget what it means to live. You forget things. You forget that you used to feel all right. You forget what it means to feel all right because you feel like shit all of the time, and you can't remember what it was like before. People take the feeling of *full* for granted. They take for granted the feeling of steadiness, of hands that do not shake, heads that do not ache, throats not raw with bile and small rips from fingernails forced in haste to the gag spot.
>
> (1998, pp. 110–111)

In the starvation study Keys et al., (1950), men ate half their usual daily calories for 6 months. In this short amount of time, participants became preoccupied with food, as frequently occurs among people with anorexia. They also developed symptoms of depression and anxiety, which are often comorbid with anorexia. This photo shows a researcher obtaining information about a participant's physiology before the participant begins to restrict his caloric intake.

U. of MN School of Public Health CVD History Archive

Some people with anorexia may have such distorted thinking about their weight and body that they may come to believe that there's really nothing wrong with their weight or restricted food intake (Csipke & Horne, 2007; Gavin, Rodham, & Poyer, 2008). A minority may come to view anorexia as a lifestyle choice rather than a disorder. Unfortunately, anorexia has serious physical and mental health consequences, which are swept under the rug by such attempts to reframe the condition.

Problems With the DSM-IV-TR Definition of Anorexia Nervosa

Criticisms of the DSM-IV-TR definition of anorexia focus on the specific criteria and the classification of the two types: restricting and binge-eating/purging. In this section we first consider problems with the diagnostic criteria and then examine problems with the classification into the two types of anorexia.

Problems With the Diagnostic Criteria

Researchers and clinicians point to significant problems with three of the four DSM-IV-TR criteria for anorexia nervosa:

- *Refusal to maintain a healthy body weight* (Criterion A). Research suggests that this criterion may be of little value in predicting an individual's medical status, prognosis, or outcome (Garfinkel, Kennedy, & Kaplan, 1995). The extent to which someone is underweight does not accurately predict the degree or type of medical problems she will develop or how she will fare over time. Moreover, the body weight cutoff point of "85% of that expected" doesn't take into account the range of healthy weights in the population, changes in growth due to puberty, or cultural factors that can lead a person's weight to vary (Franko et al., 2004; Herzog & Delinsky, 2001).

- *Fear of becoming fat or of gaining weight* (Criterion B). Such fear may not characterize people with anorexia in non-Western cultures such as that of Hong Kong. Rather, a fear of gaining weight appears to be a by-product of a Western cultural value of thinness (Keel & Klump, 2003; Lee, Ho, & Hsu, 1993; Walsh & Kahn, 1997). Some researchers and clinicians propose that this criterion should instead highlight the overemphasis on the importance of controlling eating rather than focus on weight (Palmer, 2003). Further research can clarify whether people who are preoccupied with controlling eating (rather than being afraid of gaining weight) and meet the other three DSM-IV-TR criteria for anorexia are different in any other way from people who meet all four of the DSM-IV-TR criteria.

- *Amenorrhea* (Criterion D). Many researchers suggest that this diagnostic criterion should be deleted because it is not reliably associated with the degree of weight loss or the outcome of the eating disorder. Some women continue to menstruate at low weights; other women develop amenorrhea before losing a significant amount of weight (Cachelin & Maher, 1998; Garfinkel et al., 1996). Moreover, among females diagnosed with anorexia, those who have amenorrhea are similar to menstruating females with anorexia in terms of body image problems, depression, personality disorders, and the severity of the eating disorder (Garfinkel et al., 1996).

Problems With the Types

The goal of delineating types or subtypes of a disorder is to identify and organize useful information, such as distinguishing the prognosis or course of one type from another. The two types of anorexia in DSM-IV-TR do not achieve this goal. Patients diagnosed with one type often shift to the other type over time (Eddy et al., 2008). For example, at an 8-year follow-up, one study found that 62% of those with the restricting type had changed to the binge-eating/purging type; in fact, only 12% of those who had been restrictors never developed any binge/purge symptoms. These findings suggests that the restricting type may be an earlier phase of the disorder for some patients (Eddy et al., 2002).

Key Concepts and Facts About Anorexia Nervosa

- The hallmark of anorexia nervosa is a refusal to maintain a healthy weight; DSM-IV-TR defines the weight cutoff as less than 85% of expected body weight. Other criteria include an intense fear of becoming fat or gaining weight, distortions in body image, and amenorrhea. DSM-IV-TR includes two types of anorexia: restricting and binge-eating/purging.

- Anorexia can lead to significant medical problems, most importantly muscle wasting (particularly of heart muscle), as well as low heart rate, low blood pressure, loss of bone density, and decreased metabolism. Other symptoms include irritability, headaches, fatigue, and restlessness. All methods of purging—vomiting, diuretics, laxatives, and enemas—can cause dehydration because they primarily eliminate water, not calories, from the body.

- Starvation also leads to various psychological and social problems, including a heightened sensitivity to light, cold, and noise, poor sleep and mood, irritability, anxiety, and preoccupation with food.

- Critics of the DSM-IV-TR diagnostic criteria for anorexia point out that the criteria of low weight and amenorrhea aren't highly associated with general medical status, prognosis, or outcome. Also, the two types of anorexia—restricting and binge-eating/purging—may better represent stages of the disorder rather than distinct paths it can take.

Making a Diagnosis

- Reread Case 10.1 about Caroline Knapp, and determine whether or not her eating-related symptoms meet all of the criteria for anorexia nervosa. Specifically, list which criteria apply and which do not. If you would like more information to determine her diagnosis, what information—specifically—would you want, and in what ways would the information influence your decision? If you decide that her symptoms do meet the criteria, which DSM-IV-TR type of anorexia is the most appropriate and why?

Bulimia Nervosa

Marya Hornbacher describes her descent into bulimia nervosa:

> I woke up one morning with a body that seemed to fill the room. Long since having decided I was fat, it was a complete crisis when my body, like all girls' bodies, acquired a significantly greater number of actual fat cells than it had ever possessed. At puberty, what had been a nagging, underlying discomfort with my body became a full-blown, constant obsession. . . . When I returned [from the bathroom after throwing up], everything was different. Everything was calm, and I felt very clean. Everything was in order. Everything was as it should be. . . .
>
> I remember devouring piece after piece [of a loaf of bread, toasted with butter], my raging, insatiable hunger, the absolute absence of fullness. I remember cheerfully heading off for my bath. Night, I said. Locking the bathroom door, turning the water on, leaning over the toilet, throwing up in a heave of delight. . . . But the delight did not last long. The daily bingeing was making me heavier. . . . Though the purging was initially rare—maybe once or twice a week—it was right about this time that I began to get in trouble at school. With frequency. I got into fights. My grades fluctuated, notes were sent home about my disruptive behavior.
>
> (1998, pp. 40–44).

For Hornbacher, as for many people with bulimia, the maladaptive eating behaviors started off as an attempt to cope with negative feelings about weight, appearance, or eating "too much." As in her case, such behaviors can become entrenched and lead to additional negative feelings; the maladaptive eating behaviors and ensuing feelings can create their own problems. In this section we examine the criteria for bulimia nervosa, and the medical effects of the disorder; we then discuss criticisms of the diagnostic criteria and consider the disproportionately high prevalence of the related disorder, *eating disorder not otherwise specified*.

What Is Bulimia Nervosa?

A key feature of *bulimia nervosa* (often simply referred to as *bulimia*) is repeated episodes of binge eating followed by inappropriate efforts to prevent weight gain. Such inappropriate efforts to prevent weight gain are categorized by DSM-IV-TR as either purging or nonpurging:

- The *purging type* includes vomiting or using diuretics, laxatives, or enemas.
- The *nonpurging type* involves other behaviors to prevent weight gain, such as fasting or excessive exercise. Exercise is considered excessive by mental health clinicians if the individual feels high levels of guilt when she postpones or misses a workout (Mond et al., 2006).

As noted in the section on anorexia, a person with anorexia may purge or fast. In those cases, according to DSM-IV-TR, the symptoms that distinguish anorexia from bulimia are the low weight and related amenorrhea. Because women with bulimia nervosa are in the normal weight range—or possibly overweight—they generally continue to menstruate. Bulimia is twice as prevalent as anorexia (American Psychiatric Association, 2000) and, like anorexia, is much more prevalent among females (Keel et al., 2006). The DSM-IV-TR criteria for bulimia nervosa are presented in Table 10.3, and additional facts about the disorder are listed in Table 10.4.

Table 10.3 ▸ DSM-IV-TR Diagnostic Criteria for Bulimia Nervosa

A. Recurrent episodes of binge eating. An episode of binge eating is characterized by both of the following:

(1) eating, in a discrete period of time (e.g., within any 2-hour period), an amount of food that is definitely larger than most people would eat during a similar period of time and under similar circumstances

(2) a sense of lack of control over eating during the episode (e.g., a feeling that one cannot stop eating or control what or how much one is eating)

B. Recurrent inappropriate compensatory behavior in order to prevent weight gain, such as self-induced vomiting; misuse of laxatives, diuretics, enemas, or other medications; fasting; or excessive exercise.

C. The binge eating and inappropriate compensatory behaviors both occur, on average, at least twice a week for 3 months.

D. Self-evaluation is unduly influenced by body shape and weight.

E. The disturbance does not occur exclusively during episodes of Anorexia Nervosa.

Source: Reprinted with permission from the Diagnostic and Statistical Manual of Mental Disorders, Text Revision, Fourth Edition, (Copyright 2000) American Psychiatric Association.

Table 10.4 ▸ Bulimia Nervosa Facts at a Glance

Prevalence

- Over the course of a lifetime, 1–2% of women and 0.1–0.5% of men are likely to develop the disorder (Hoek & van Hoeken, 2003; Hudson et al., 2007).

Comorbidity

- Up to 75% of people with bulimia have at least one other disorder, often an anxiety disorder (Godart et al., 2003; Hinrichsen et al., 2003; Kaye et al., 2004; Keck et al., 1990; Milos et al., 2002; Schwalberg et al., 1992) or depression (American Psychiatric Association, 2000).
- About 30% of those with bulimia will also develop substance abuse or dependence at some point during their lifetime, which may evolve from initial use of stimulants for weight loss (American Psychiatric Association, 2000).

Onset

- Bulimia usually begins in late adolescence or early adulthood (American Psychiatric Association, 2000). It may develop in older adults, however (Beck et al., 1996).
- Those in more recent birth cohorts (that is, those born more recently) have a higher risk for developing bulimia (Hudson et al., 2007).

Course

- At a 15-month follow-up, almost a third of those diagnosed with bulimia still met the criteria for the diagnosis; at a 5-year follow-up, that proportion dropped to 15% (Fairburn et al., 2000). However, people who no longer meet the DSM-IV-TR criteria for the disorder may nevertheless continue to have persistent symptoms of bulimia, although not the number, frequency, or intensity specified by the criteria (Ben-Tovim, 2003; Keel & Mitchell, 1997; Keel et al., 1999; Wade et al., 2006).
- People who have less intense negative attitudes about their bodies and who function better in daily life are more likely to have a healthier outcome (Ben-Tovim, 2003; Collings & King, 1994; Keel et al., 1999).
- People with bulimia who also have or have had a substance use disorder generally do not fare as well as those without this comorbid disorder (Keel et al., 1999).

Gender Differences

- Approximately 75–90% of those with bulimia nervosa are female (Hoek & van Hoeken, 2003; Hudson et al., 2007).

Cultural Differences

- Some studies find significant differences in prevalence, frequency, and symptoms of eating disorders across ethnic groups within the United States. Specifically, black and Hispanic American women are less likely to be diagnosed with bulimia than are Asian American or white American women (Alegria et al., 2007; Nicdao et al., 2007; Striegel-Moore et al., 2003; Taylor et al., 2007). Other studies find fewer meaningful differences in symptoms and prevalence rates across ethnic groups (see Arriaza & Mann, 2001; Franko et al., 2007; Walcott, Pratt, & Patel, 2003).

Often, people with bulimia don't simply eat normally at meals and then binge between meals (Walsh, 1993). Rather, they try to control what they eat, restricting their caloric intake at meals (trying to be "good" and eat less), but later become ravenous and their hunger feels out of control. They then binge eat, which in turn makes them feel physically and emotionally "bad" because they "lost control" of themselves. As a result of such feelings, they may purge and subsequently strive to eat less, restricting their caloric intake at meals and creating a vicious cycle of restricting, bingeing, and usually purging. As one woman notes: "I don't eat all day and then I come home from work and binge. I always tell myself I'm going to eat a normal dinner, but it usually turns into a binge" (Fitzgibbon & Stolley, 2000). In Case 10.2, Gabriella tells a similar story.

CASE 10.2 ▸ FROM THE OUTSIDE: Bulimia Nervosa

[Gabriella is] a young Mexican woman whose parents moved to the U.S. when she was just a child. While her mother and father continue to speak Spanish at home and place a high value on maintaining their Mexican traditions, Gabriella wants nothing more than to fit in with her friends at school. She chooses to speak only English, looks to mainstream fashion magazines to guide her clothing and make-up choices, and wants desperately to have a fashion-model figure. In an attempt to lose weight, Gabriella has made a vow to herself to eat only one meal a day—dinner—but on her return home from school, she is rarely able to endure her hunger until dinnertime. She often loses control and ends up "eating whatever I can get my hands on." Frantic to keep her problem hidden from her family, she races to the store to replace all the food she has eaten.

(Fitzgibbon & Stolley, 2000)

Medical Effects of Bulimia Nervosa

Like anorexia, bulimia can lead to significant physical changes and medical problems. For instance, chronic vomiting, a purging method used by Marya Hornbacher, can cause the parotid and salivary glands (in the jaw area) to swell (creating a kind of "chipmunk" look) and can erode dental enamel, making teeth more vulnerable to cavities and other problems. Those who use syrup of ipecac (which is toxic) to induce vomiting may develop heart and muscle problems (Pomeroy, 2004; Silber, 2004).

Furthermore, many people with bulimia use laxatives regularly, which can lead to a permanent loss of intestinal functioning as the body comes to depend on the chemical laxatives to digest food and eliminate waste. In such cases, the malfunctioning intestinal section must be surgically removed (Pomeroy, 2004). Bulimia can also produce constipation, abdominal bloating and discomfort, fatigue, and irregular menstruation (Pomeroy, 2004). As noted earlier in the section on anorexia, all forms of purging can cause dehydration and an imbalance of the body's electrolytes, which disrupt normal neural transmission and heart conductance. Case 10.3 illustrates how the medical effects of bulimia can create significant—and enduring—problems.

Dr. Craig Mabrito

Frequent vomiting can permanently erode dental enamel, shown here, and lead to cavities and related problems.

CASE 10.3 ▸ FROM THE INSIDE: Bulimia Nervosa

A 32-year-old woman describes how bulimia nervosa has affected her:

My life revolves around food and exercise. Because of my abuse of diet pills and purging, I had a stroke when I was 23. I now have headaches. I am at risk of having another stroke, and this time I have a high chance of not coming out of it. Emotionally, it's a daily battle. I'm depressed because I want to eat, and I'm depressed because I know if I do eat, I'll get fat and gain all the weight back that I have lost.

> Everyone around me is terrified that I may die from this, and it has put a lot of stress on my marriage. I have no bedroom life anymore because I refuse to let my husband touch me or even look at my body. My kids are affected greatly by it because I usually have no energy to do anything with them, and when I do have energy, I am staying busy to burn the calories I have put in my body.
>
> (Anonymous, 2003, p. 382)

Problems With the DSM-IV-TR Diagnostic Criteria

Like that of anorexia, the DSM-IV-TR diagnosis of bulimia has received criticism. Specific criticisms focus on the definition of the term *binge eating*, the two types of bulimia that DSM-IV-TR specifies, and the issue of whether bulimia is sufficiently distinct from anorexia. Let's examine these criticisms.

Problems Defining Binge Eating

DSM-IV-TR's definition of binge eating (see Criterion A in Table 10.3) is subjective: Who determines whether the amount of food is larger than most people would eat, the patient or the therapist? In fact, research has found that calories consumed during "binge episodes" vary widely from episode to episode and person to person (Rossiter & Agras, 1990); thus, what some consider to be a binge, others might view as an unexceptional meal.

In addition, the elements of the DSM-IV-TR criteria that focus on the timing of binge eating (episodes occur within a 2-hour period and twice weekly for at least 3 months) are not based on research results and don't predict the course of the disorder or its prognosis (Franko et al., 2004; Garfinkel et al., 1995; Kendler et al., 1991). To see the implications of this criticism, let's compare two women, Tess, whose symptoms meet the timing criteria, and Jen, whose symptoms do not. Tess binges three times a week for 4 months and has enough of the other symptoms to be diagnosed with bulimia. Jen binges and purges once a week, usually in a 3-hour stint; however, twice every semester, during midterms and finals weeks, she binges and purges almost every day. She's been doing it since she was a freshman in high school, 7 years ago. Her bingeing and purging do not meet the timing criteria, and thus she would not be diagnosed with bulimia; however, her bingeing and purging cannot be considered "normal."

Problems With the Types of Bulimia

The classification of purging versus nonpurging types of bulimia doesn't appear to be useful: Comparisons of people who have the two types have not been able to document meaningful differences between the two groups, other than the specific compensatory behaviors used to prevent weight gain (Gleaves, Lowe, Green, et al., 2000; Gleaves, Lowe, Snow, et al., 2000; Williamson et al., 2002). That is, the two groups are similar in terms of the disorder's onset, course, outcome, and other variables. In fact, research has found that whether or not someone with bulimia is impulsive is the characteristic that best predicts course and prognosis, not whether her diagnosis is the purging or nonpurging type (Favaro et al., 2005). Examples of behaviors that indicate impulsivity include stealing, running away, and seeking out dangerous situations, as well as abusing substances (Fischer, Smith, & Anderson, 2003; Wonderlich & Mitchell, 2001).

Is Bulimia Distinct From Anorexia?

About half of people with anorexia go on to develop bulimia (Bulik et al., 1997; Tozzi et al., 2005), which may indicate that anorexia and bulimia are not distinct but rather represent phases of the same eating disorder, with the symptoms shifting over time. A person's diagnosis may better reflect where she is in the course of the eating disorder at the time she is diagnosed. Similarly, the types of each eating disorder—restricting and binge-eating/purging types for anorexia and purging and nonpurging types for bulimia—may represent different paths of the same underlying eating disorder. Consistent with this view, the two eating disorders and their types, as outlined in DSM-IV-TR, do not provide unique information about the course or prognosis of the disorder (Eddy et al., 2007; Franko et al., 2004).

In fact, the characteristics of the binge-eating/purging type of anorexia have more in common with those of bulimia than with those of the restricting type of anorexia (Gleaves, Lowe, Green, et al., 2000; Herzog et al., 1999). All that distinguishes the binge-eating/purging type of anorexia from bulimia is the low weight and consequent amenorrhea. In contrast, the restricting type of anorexia involves both a very different approach to eating (or not eating) and different coping styles, such as extreme self-regulation.

Eating Disorder Not Otherwise Specified

Many people with significantly disturbed eating don't meet all the criteria for anorexia or bulimia; those individuals are diagnosed with **eating disorder not otherwise specified** (**EDNOS**). Studies have found that as many patients are diagnosed with EDNOS, 4–6% of the general population of Americans (Herzog & Delinsky, 2001), as with anorexia and bulimia combined (Andersen, Bowers, & Watson, 2001; Fairburn & Bohn, 2005; Fairburn & Walsh, 2002; Ricca et al., 2001).

DSM-IV-TR defines EDNOS as follows: "The mental disorder appears to fall within the larger category [of eating disorders] but does not meet the criteria of any specific disorder within that category" (American Psychiatric Association, 2000). The definition of EDNOS does not specify particular criteria, and so people who are given this diagnosis have a wide range in the number and duration of symptoms. Nevertheless, people diagnosed with EDNOS often fall into one of three groups. One group consists of people with **partial cases**, meaning that their symptoms meet some of the diagnostic criteria for a specific disorder but not enough to justify the diagnosis of that disorder. An example of a partial case of anorexia would be a woman whose symptoms meet all the other criteria for the disorder but who is not amenorrheic; she would thus be diagnosed with EDNOS.

Another group consists of people with **subthreshold cases**; they have symptoms that fit all the diagnostic criteria for a specific disorder, but at levels lower than required for the diagnosis of that disorder. Jen, described earlier, has a subthreshold case of bulimia because she usually binges only once a week, which is less frequently than twice weekly as specified by the DSM-IV-TR criterion (Fairburn & Walsh, 2002); Jen would therefore be diagnosed with EDNOS if her symptoms impaired her functioning or caused her significant distress.

A third group consists of people who have a variant of an eating disorder that has received significant attention: **binge-eating disorder**, which is characterized by frequent episodes of rapid uncontrolled eating of large quantities of food, even when not hungry, without subsequent purging (American Psychiatric Association, 2000). Typically, those with binge-eating disorder feel distressed by their binge eating; people with this eating pattern are usually overweight (Grucza, Przybeck, & Cloninger, 2007; Hudson et al., 2007). Binge-eating disorder is *not* listed as an "official" eating disorder in DSM-IV-TR. Rather, it is a provisional diagnosis; ongoing research will help determine whether it should be included as a distinct disorder in DSM-V and, if so, what the specific diagnostic criteria should be. Research to date suggest that the prevalence of binge-eating disorder is more similar for males and females than is found for other eating disorders, and that this disorder is more common than anorexia nervosa and bulimia nervosa combined (Grucza, Przybeck, & Cloninger, 2007; Hudson et al., 2007).

Most people with EDNOS have attitudes and behaviors regarding weight, food, and body image that are similar to those of people with anorexia and bulimia. The only significant difference is that people with EDNOS don't meet the specific

Eating disorder not otherwise specified (EDNOS)
The diagnosis given when an individual's symptoms of disordered eating cause significant distress or impair functioning but do not meet the full criteria for a diagnosis of anorexia nervosa or bulimia nervosa.

Partial cases
The designation given to cases in which patients have symptoms that meet only some of the necessary criteria, but not enough symptoms to meet all the criteria for the diagnosis of a disorder.

Subthreshold cases
The designation given to cases in which patients have symptoms that fit all the necessary criteria, but at levels lower than required for the diagnosis of a disorder.

Binge-eating disorder
A provisional diagnosis of the variant of an eating disorder characterized by frequent episodes of rapid uncontrolled eating of large quantities of food, even when not hungry, without subsequent purging; according to DSM-IV-TR, patients with binge-eating receive a diagnosis of EDNOS.

DSM-IV-TR criteria for either of those other eating disorders (Fairburn, Palmer et al., in preparation; Turner & Bryant-Waugh, 2004). Some people diagnosed with EDNOS may have had anorexia or bulimia but then improved to the point where their symptoms no longer meet the criteria for either disorder. These people still have clinically significant symptoms of an eating disorder, however. This was true of Marya Hornbacher: As her eating disorder symptoms abated, she no longer met the criteria for either anorexia or bulimia, and her diagnosis was changed to EDNOS.

Based on research findings, an alternative system for categorizing anorexia and bulimia would require three fundamental changes (Gleaves, Lowe, Green, et al., 2000):

1. Eliminate the purging and nonpurging types of bulimia because they do not meaningfully distinguish course or outcome.

2. Create a separate diagnosis for bingeing and purging (both bulimia and binge-eating/purging type of anorexia) as distinct from a restricting type of anorexia. Moreover, this new diagnosis of bulimia (bingeing and purging, regardless of weight) may be better conceptualized on a continuum (Lowe et al., 1996), without a rigid cutoff of duration and frequency of symptoms; such a reformulation would reduce the number of EDNOS diagnoses.

3. Within the binge-eating/purging type, put those with anorexia and normal-weight bulimia on the same continuum, but at different points with regard to weight.

Key Concepts and Facts About Bulimia Nervosa

- Bulimia nervosa is characterized by recurrent episodes of binge eating followed by inappropriate efforts to prevent weight gain.

- DSM-IV-TR specifies two types of bulimia: the purging type (which is characterized by vomiting or the use of diuretics, laxatives, or enemas) and the nonpurging type (which involves fasting or excessive exercise).

- Bulimia is twice as prevalent as anorexia, and much more common among women than men.

- All purging methods can cause dehydration, which leads to electrolyte imbalances and possibly death. Chronic vomiting can lead to enlarged parotid and salivary glands and can erode dental enamel. Chronic laxative use can lead to permanent loss of intestinal functioning.

- Aspects of the DSM-IV-TR criteria for a diagnosis of bulimia have been criticized: The definition of "binge eating" is subjective, the purging/nonpurging distinction does not correlate meaningfully with course or prognosis, and bulimia and anorexia do not appear to be distinct disorders but rather may be different phases of the same disorder.

- Problems with the criteria for anorexia and bulimia are apparent in the prevalence of eating disorder not otherwise specified (EDNOS), which is greater than anorexia and bulimia combined. One subset of patients with EDNOS have binge-eating disorder.

Making a Diagnosis
- Reread Case 10.2 about Gabriella, and determine whether or not her symptoms meet the criteria for bulimia nervosa. Specifically, list which criteria apply and which do not. If you would like more information to determine her diagnosis, what information—specifically—would you want, and in what ways would the information influence your decision?

Understanding Eating Disorders

Why do eating disorders arise? Marya Hornbacher asked this question and ventured the following response:

> While depression may play a role in eating disorders, either as cause or effect, it cannot always be pinpointed directly, and therefore you never know quite what you're dealing with. Are you trying to treat depression as a cause, as the thing that has screwed up your life and altered your behaviors, or as an effect? Or simply *depressing*? Will drug therapy help, or is that a Band-Aid cure? How big a role do your upbringing and family play? Does the culture have anything to do with it? Is your personality just

problematic by nature, or is there, in fact, a faulty chemical pathway in your brain? If so, was it there before you started starving yourself, or did the starving put it there? . . . All of the above?

(1998, pp. 195–196)

In this passage, Hornbacher is trying to understand how, or why, some people—but not others—develop an eating disorder. Note that she mentions explanations that involve all three of the types of factors in the neuropsychosocial approach, although she does not consider ways in which such factors might interact. Given that up to half of the people with one of the eating disorders (anorexia, bulimia, or EDNOS) have had or will have another of these disorders, it makes sense to examine the etiology of these disorders collectively, rather than individually.

People with an eating disorder generally do not come to the attention of researchers until after they've developed the disorder. Yet once the eating disorder has developed, it is difficult to disentangle causal factors from factors that reflect the altered eating habits and poor nutrition that predated the full-blown disorder. In other words, it is challenging for researchers to distinguish the *causes* of eating disorders from the widespread *effects* of eating disorders on neurological (and, more generally, biological), psychological, and social functioning.

This difficulty in untangling cause and effect means that researchers do not know which of the neuropsychosocial factors that are associated with eating disorders actually give rise to the disorders. All that can be said at this time is that a number of factors are associated with the emergence and maintenance of eating disorders (Dolan-Sewall & Insel, 2005; Jacobi et al., 2004; Streigel-Moore & Cachelin, 2001).

An additional challenge to researchers is the high rate of comorbidity of other psychological and medical disorders with eating disorders, which makes it difficult to determine the degree to which risk factors uniquely lead to eating disorders, rather than being associated more generally with the comorbid disorders (Jacobi et al., 2004; Johnson, Cohen, Kasen et al., 2002).

Neurological Factors: Setting the Stage

We've already noted that the excessive caloric restriction in anorexia leads to specific medical effects, notably changes in hormones, metabolism, and body functioning. The eating changes and purging involved in bulimia (and anorexia, if purging occurs) bring their own medical effects and biological changes. Researchers try to determine whether neurological (or other biological) abnormalities they find among people with an eating disorder might have caused the disorder, might be caused by the disorder, or are simply correlated with the disorder (Franko et al., 2004; Jacobi et al., 2004).

Brain Systems

Neuroimaging studies have revealed many differences between the brains of people with eating disorders and those of control participants (Frank et al., 2004; Kaye, Frank, et al., 2005; Takano et al., 2001). Most notably, people who have anorexia have unusually low activity in several key areas of the brain: (1) the frontal lobes, which are involved in inhibiting responses and in regulating behavior more generally (a deficit in such processing may contribute to eating too much or eating too little); (2) the portions of the temporal lobes that include the amygdala, which is involved in fear and other strong emotions (fear helps prevent people from putting themselves in danger, and dampening this emotion may contribute to eating disorders); (3) the parietal lobes, which may play a key role in representing body size; and (4) the anterior (i.e., front) part of the cingulate cortex, which lies in the frontal lobes at the midline of the brain and is involved in monitoring for conflicts among competing responses or among competing information retrieved from memory (Kuhl et al., 2008); a deficit here may contribute to problems in learning to inhibit dysfunctional behavior.

Examining groups of patients can be useful, insofar as general patterns of brain differences can help to identify key characteristics associated with a disorder. However, if data from different groups (such as people with the restricting type of anorexia and people with the binge-eating/purging type) are averaged together, characteristics that are unique to one of the groups will not be detected. Thus, some research has focused specifically on particular groups, such as patients with the restricting type of anorexia. In one study, for example (Kojima et al., 2005), researchers examined the effects of weight gain in this one group. They found that some parts of the brain, in particular, the parietal lobes, became more active after these patients gained weight. The parietal lobes represent spatial properties, including size, and may be involved in representing the body image, which includes information about how large a person feels herself to be. However, other parts of the brain, such as the basal ganglia and the cerebellum, became less active after the patients gained weight—and the decreases in activation in both brain areas were larger for the patients who gained more weight. Both the basal ganglia and the cerebellum may be critical in controlling repetitive behaviors, such as those that underlie recurrent bingeing. The lower activation in these areas may indicate that the patients were less actively controlling their eating after gaining weight. However, even after gaining weight, the patients in this study still had less activity in the anterior cingulate cortex than did the control participants. As noted earlier, this brain area is involved in monitoring for conflicts either in actual responses or stored information. These patients may not be able to monitor accurately conflicts between different responses (such as eating versus not eating) or among stored information (such as about apearance versus health)—and this problem persists even after they have gained weight.

Neuroimaging studies not only have documented many abnormalities in the functioning of different parts of the brain in people who have eating disorders, but also have shown that the structure of the brain itself changes with these disorders. In fact, anorexia is associated with loss of both gray matter (cell bodies of neurons) and white matter (myelinated axons of the neurons) in the brain (see Chapter 2; Addolorato et al., 1997; Frank et al., 2004; Herholz, 1996). The gray matter carries out various sorts of cognitive and emotion-related processes (such as those involved in learning and in fear responses). Deficits in white matter may imply that different parts of the brain are not communicating appropriately, which could contribute to the problems patients with anorexia have when they try to convert an intellectual understanding of their disorder into changes in their behavior. Many of these structural deficits improve when the patient recovers, although they do not necessary disappear completely (Frank et al., 2004; Herholz, 1996). Thus, an eating disorder may have long-term consequences for a person's cognitive abilities and emotional responses.

Neural Communication: Serotonin

Losing large amounts of weight (as occurs in anorexia) and the associated malnutrition clearly change the amounts of serotonin and other neurotransmitters. We will focus here on serotonin because it is involved in regulating a wide variety of behaviors and characteristics that are associated with eating disorders, including binge eating and irritability (Hollander & Rosen, 2000; McElroy et al., 2000).

Neuroimaging research has shown that serotonin receptors function abnormally in patients with anorexia and bulimia (Kaye, Bailer et al., 2005; Kaye, Frank, et al., 2005). However, such research does not show that either eating disorder causes these abnormalities; the abnormalities in the serotonin receptors could be produced by the eating disorder itself or, instead, could be related to specific symptoms or characteristics (such as the impulsivity that is associated with bulimia). Thus, it is important that evidence seems to imply that the serotonin receptors are abnormal before patients develop anorexia. As discussed in Chapters 6 and 7, serotonin is related to mood and anxiety. Prior to developing anorexia, patients tend to be anxious and obsessional, and these traits persist even after recovery, which suggests a biologically based anxious temperament; this temperament may be related to serotonin levels or functioning (Kaye et al., 2003). Consistent with this view, researchers have found that people with anorexia are less responsive to serotonin than normal (Kaye, Bailer, et al., 2005).

In addition, some researchers suggest that eating less actually reduces anxiety, in part, by reducing serotonin levels. This reduction may be a result of lower levels of tryptophan in the diet, which occurs when food intake is reduced; tryptophan is a building block of serotonin. When young rats are fed severely restricted diets, their serotonin activity is reduced (Huether et al., 1997). Thus, the effects of reduced eating can affect the functioning of the serotonin system.

Researchers have also found that people with bulimia are not as responsive to serotonin as is typical (Kaye et al., 2000; Smith, Fairburn, & Cowen, 1999). In fact, the worse the symptoms of bulimia, the less responsive to serotonin the patient generally is (Jimerson et al., 1992). As with anorexia, tryptophan levels are related to symptoms of bulimia (Smith, Fairburn, & Cowen, 1999), and, as noted above, reduced tryptophan levels have the effect of reducing serotonin activity, which in turn can reduce anxiety.

The precise mechanism that underlies the dysregulation of serotonin and the abnormal behaviors found in eating disorders remains unknown, as do the reasons for its differing manifestations in anorexia and bulimia.

Genetics

When Marya Hornbacher told her parents that she had been making herself throw up, her mother said, "I used to do that." Did Hornbacher's genes predispose her to developing bulimia? If so, to what degree would genes play a role? As is true for those with mood disorders and anxiety disorders, people with an eating disorder are more likely than average to have family members with an eating disorder, but not necessarily the same one (Lilenfeld & Kaye, 1998; Strober et al., 2000).

Like genetic studies of other types of disorders, such studies of eating disorders compare identical twins to fraternal twins (see Chapter 2). The research findings indicate that anorexia has a substantial heritability, but estimates range from as little as 33% to as much as 88% (Bulik, 2005; Jacobi et al., 2004), depending on how the study was carried out. Twin studies of bulimia also indicate that the disorder in influenced by genes, and also yield a wide range of estimates of heritability, from 28% to 83% (Bulik 2005; Jacobi et al., 2004). Given that many people with bulimia previously had anorexia, it isn't surprising that both disorders have the same wide range of heritabilities—there is significant overlap in the two populations.

The large variation in heritabilities may simply indicate, once again, that genes aren't destiny; the way the environment interacts with the genes is also important. However, studies have shown that the shared family environment (such as how many books are in the house or how many meals a family eats all together) may not be as influential as the nonshared, unique environment (such as different relationships between each child and her father, the extent to which an individual is teased about weight, or unique peer group experiences) (Agliata, Tantleff-Dunn, & renk, 2007; Bulik, 2004; Klump et al., 2002). We'll examine such nonshared environmental factors in more detail in the next two sections.

Psychological Factors: Thoughts of and Feelings About Food

Eating and breathing are both essential to life, but eating provides more than sustenance. It can evoke powerful feelings, memories, and thoughts. Hornbacher recalls her associations to eating:

> My memories of childhood are almost all related to food. . . . I was my father's darling, and the way he showed love was through food. I would give away my lunch at school, then hop in my father's car, and we'd drive to a fast-food place and, essentially, binge.
>
> My mother was another story altogether. She ate, some. She would pick at cottage cheese, nibble at cucumbers, scarf down See's Candies. But she, like my father, and like me, associated food with love, and love with need.
>
> (1998, p. 27)

And once an eating disorder develops, the thoughts and behaviors associated with it can take on a life of their own, as Hornbacher reveals:

> I stood in the kitchen after school, scarfing down food without tasting it, staring at the television without seeing it. I would go through the perfunctory motions: washing my dishes, going into the bathroom, puking. In the bedroom, I'd stare at the mirror. When I entered junior high, at twelve, I'd been throwing up almost daily for three years. In the seventh grade, it increased to two or three times a day. I began to do it whenever I got the chance.

(1998, p. 59)

Many risk factors are not uniquely associated with eating disorders. Factors such as gender (female), ethnicity (White), negative self-evaluation, sexual abuse and other adverse experiences, the presence of comorbid disorders (e.g., depression and anxiety disorders; Jacobi et al., 2004), and using avoidant strategies to cope with problems (Pallister & Waller, 2008; Spoor et al., 2007) are also associated with psychological disorders more generally. Thus, many researchers have focused on factors that are specifically related to symptoms of eating disorders: factors associated with food, weight, appearance, and eating. In the following sections we examine research findings about these factors.

Thinking About Weight, Appearance, and Food

Based on what you've already read about eating disorders, it shouldn't come as a surprise to learn that people with eating disorders have irrational and illogical thoughts about weight, appearance, and food. Specifically, these automatic and irrational thoughts tend to be about their own weight and appearance and their moral evaluation of eating (Garfinkel et al., 1992; Striegel-Moore, 1993). We consider these two kinds of thoughts in the following sections.

Excessive Concern With Weight and Appearance

Some people with eating disorders have excessive concern with and tend to overvalue their weight, body shape, and eating (Fairburn, 1997; Fairburn, Cooper, & Cooper, 1986). For instance, they may weigh themselves multiple times a day and get depressed when the scale indicates that they've gained half a pound. The two characteristics that are among the most consistent predictors of the onset of an eating disorder are dieting and being dissatisfied with one's body (Thompson & Smolak, 2001). Some people are so concerned with weight and appearance that their food intake, weight, and body shape come to define their self-worth. Such concerns help maintain bulimia in that people believe that their compensatory behaviors reduce their overall caloric intake (Fairburn et al., 2003).

Abstinence Violation Effect

Many people who have an eating disorder engage in automatic, illogical, black-or-white thinking about food: Vegetables are "good," whereas desserts are "bad." They may come to view themselves in the same way: They are "good" when acting to lose weight, "bad" when eating a "bad" food or when they feel that their eating is out of control. Once they are "bad" in a given situation, they might allow themselves to continue to be "bad." Because they have violated their rules for abstaining from "bad" eating behavior, they then proceed to ignore the rules and binge. This pattern illustrates the **abstinence violation effect** (Polivy & Herman, 1993), in which the violation of a self-imposed rule about food restriction leads to feeling out of control with food, which then leads to overeating. For instance, having taken a taste of a friend's ice cream, an individual thinks, "I shouldn't have had any ice cream; I've blown it for the day, so I might was well have my own ice cream—in fact, I'll get a pint and eat the whole thing." Then, after she eats the ice cream, she tries to negate the calories ingested during the binge by purging or using some other compensatory behavior. Thus, the abstinence violation effect explains bingeing that occurs after the individual has "transgressed."

Abstinence violation effect
The condition that arises when the violation of a self-imposed rule about food restriction leads to feeling out of control with food, which then leads to overeating.

Operant Conditioning: Reinforcing Disordered Eating

As with many disorders, operant conditioning plays a role in the development and maintenance of symptoms—in this case, symptoms of disordered eating. Let's examine how.

First, the symptoms of eating disorders—anorexia, bulimia, or EDNOS—may inadvertently be reinforced through operant conditioning. As Hornbacher recounts:

> Eating disorders provide a little private drama. . . . And they are distracting. You don't have to think about any of the nasty minutiae of the real world, you don't get caught up in that awful boring thing called regular life, with its bills and its break-ups and its dishes and laundry and groceries and arguments over whose turn it is to change the litter box and bedtimes and bad sex and all that, because you are having a *real* drama, not a sitcom but a GRAND EPIC, all by yourself, and why would you bother with those foolish mortals when you could spend hours and hours with the mirror, when you are having the *most interesting* sado-masochistic affair with your own image?
>
> (1998, p. 281)

Hornbacher points out that the symptoms of eating disorders, such as preoccupations with food and weight or bingeing and purging, can provide distractions from work pressures, family conflicts, or social problems. The never-ending preoccupations with food, weight, and body are negatively reinforced (remember that negative reinforcement is still *reinforcement*, but it occurs when something aversive is removed, which is not the same as punishment) because they can provide relief from what the person might otherwise be thinking about—ongoing concerns about relationships, finances, or feeling social isolated.

Second, operant conditioning occurs when restricting behaviors are positively reinforced by the person's sense of power and mastery over her appetite, although such feelings of mastery are often short-lived as the disease takes over (Garner, 1997). Hornbacher noted: "The anorexic body seems to say: I do not need. It says: Power over the self" (1998, p. 85). A third way in which operant conditioning affects eating disorders occurs when people are positively reinforced for "losing control" of their appetite and bingeing. How can losing control be positively reinforcing? Easy: They've set up the rules so that they get to eat certain foods they enjoy (positive reinforcement) only when they let themselves lose control of their food intake. That is, during a binge, people eat foods that they normally don't eat at all or eat only in small quantities—typically fats, sweets, or carbohydrates. This means that the only way some people can eat foods they may enjoy—such as ice cream, cake, candy, or fried foods—is by being "out of control."

Fourth, like preoccupations with food, weight, and body, the act of bingeing itself turns off unpleasant thoughts or feelings—and so bingeing is negatively reinforced because the binge provides a respite from these thoughts or feelings. Fifth, bingeing can also induce an endorphin rush, which creates a pleasant feeling much like a "runner's high," which is positively reinforcing. Sixth, operant conditioning may occur because purging can be negatively reinforcing by relieving the anxiety and fullness that are created by overeating.

Finally, operant conditioning can contribute to symptoms of eating disorders because of the social isolation that can arise from the symptoms: Bingeing and purging are more often done alone, and people with restricting anorexia often prefer to eat alone. To the extent that social interactions are stressful to people with eating disorders, the isolation can be a relief, and thereby reinforcing.

Personality Traits as Risk Factors

Particular personality traits are associated with—and are considered risk factors for—eating disorders: perfectionism, harm avoidance, neuroticism, and low self-esteem. *Perfectionism* is a persistent striving to attain perfection and excessive self-criticism about mistakes (Antony & Swinson, 1998; Franco-Paredes et al., 2005). Numerous studies find perfectionism to be higher in people with eating disorders than in people who do not have these disorders (Forbush, Heatherton, & Keel, 2007). High scores on measures of perfectionism persist after people recover, which suggests that this personality trait may exist before an eating disorder arises and may increase the risk for developing such a disorder (Franco-Paredes et al., 2005); high perfectionism may lead to an intense drive to attain a desired weight or body shape, and thus contribute to the thoughts and behaviors that underlie an eating disorder. As illustrated in Figure 10.2, perfectionists are painfully aware of their imperfections, which is aversive for them. This heightened awareness of personal flaws—real or imagined—is called *aversive self-awareness* and leads to significant emotional distress, which may temporarily be dulled by focusing on immediate aspects of the environment, such as occurs with bingeing. Thus, bingeing may provide an escape from the emotional distress associated with perfectionism (Blackburn et al., 2006; Heatherton & Baumeister, 1991).

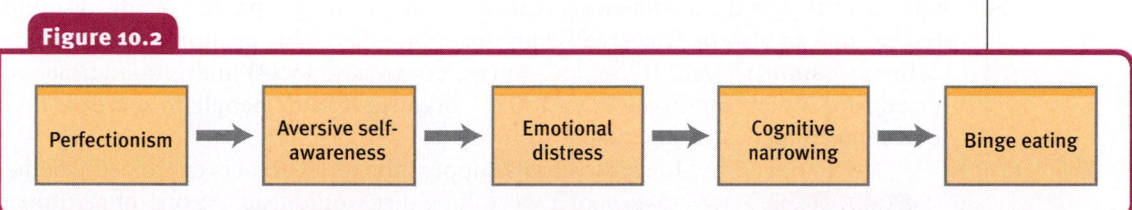

Figure 10.2

Perfectionism → Aversive self-awareness → Emotional distress → Cognitive narrowing → Binge eating

10.2 ▶ Bingeing as Escape For perfectionists, bingeing can be an escape from aversive feelings. Being aware of imperfections (referred to as *aversive self-awareness*) causes emotional distress. People high in perfectionism try to decrease the ensuing emotional distress by focusing on immediate aspects of the environment (referred to as *cognitive narrowing*), which they attain through bingeing (Blackburn et al., 2006; Heatherton & Baumeister, 1991).

People with eating disorders, more than other people, also tend to exhibit *harm avoidance*—the characteristic of trying to avoid potentially harmful situations or stimuli (Cassin & von Ranson, 2005). For instance, they are likely to be organized planners rather than carefree and spontaneous, which minimizes their exposure to potential danger. When people high in harm avoidance are preoccupied with stimuli related to food, weight, or appearance (perhaps because of a social factor such as a familial focus on such matters), they may be too concerned with their caloric intake and be more likely to perceive threats or dangers—such as eating "too much"—that other people don't see.

Another aspect of personality associated wtih eating disorders is *neuroticism* (see Chapter 2), which is characterized by a propensity toward anxiety and emotional reactivity (Eggert, Levendosky, & Klump, 2007; Miller et al., 2006). One Spanish study tracked females aged 12–21 who did not have an eating disorder. Those who had high levels of neuroticism were more likely to develop an eating disorder 18 months later (Cervera et al., 2003). People high in neuroticism may be more sensitive to criticism in general, and when this trait is combined with other risk factors (such as an overvaluation of weight and appearance), they may take to heart criticisms or comments related to their weight and appearance more than other people do (Davis, Claridge, & Fox, 2000).

Finally, people who have low self-esteem may try to raise their self-esteem by controlling their food intake, weight, and shape, believing that such changes will increase their self-worth (Geller et al., 2000; Striegel-Moore, Silberstein, & Rodin, 1986). For instance, they may think, "If I restrict my calories, that'll prove that I'm in control of myself and worthy of respect." However, efforts to increase self-worth in this way end up having a paradoxical effect: To the extent that attempts to control food intake, weight, and shape fail, self-esteem falls even lower; these people feel they've failed, yet again, to achieve something they wanted.

Dieting, Restrained Eating, and Disinhibited Eating

Frequently restricting the intake of specific foods—such as "fattening" foods—or overall caloric intake (as when dieting or trying to maintain one's current weight) is referred to as **restrained eating.** If you've ever been on some type of diet, you know that continuing to adhere to such restrictions can be challenging. And at times the diet may feel so constraining that you get discouraged and frustrated, and simply give up—which can lead to a bout of *disinhibited eating*, bingeing on a restricted type of food or simply eating more of a nonrestricted type of food (Polivy & Herman, 1985). In fact, it is common for dieters, and people with eating disorders, to alternate restrictive eating with disinhibited eating (Fairburn et al., 2005; Polivy & Herman, 1993, 2002).

In addition to dieting, researchers have identified other stimuli that may trigger disinhibited eating. One stimulus is eating more calories than intended or desired, which can trigger the abstinence violation effect. Seemingly paradoxically, disinhibited eating can also be triggered by an upcoming diet. This phenomenon is known as the *last supper effect* (Eldredge, Agras, & Arnow, 1994) and is sometimes referred to as "diet tomorrow, feast today" because it leads people to increase their food intake before starting a diet.

To study the last supper effect, researchers examined whether anticipation of a week-long diet would lead a group of restrained eaters (those with a significant history of failed attempts at dieting) to consume more than a group of restrained eaters not anticipating a diet (Urbszat, Herman, & Polivy, 2002). Volunteers (some of whom were restrained eaters, and some of whom were not) were assigned either to a group that would be on a low-fat diet for a week or to a group that would have no change in food intake. The participants were then asked to eat cookies from a plate and rate their taste; after they'd made their ratings, participants were allowed to finish the cookies on the plate if they wanted. As shown in Figure 10.3, results were consistent with the last supper effect: Restrained eaters who were anticipating the low-fat diet ate more cookies than did either their restrained counterparts not anticipating the diet or unrestrained eaters in either condition.

Restrained eaters can also become insensitive to internal cues of hunger and fullness. In order to maintain restricted eating, they may stop eating before they get a normal feeling of fullness and so end up trying to tune out sensations of hunger. If they binge, they may eat past the point of normal fullness. They therefore need to rely on external guides, such as portion size or elapsed time since their last meal, to control their food intake (Polivy & Herman, 1993). However, using external guides to direct food intake requires cognitive effort—to monitor the clock or to calculate how much food was last eaten and how much food should be eaten next—and when a person is thinking about other tasks (such as a job or homework assignment), he or she may temporarily stop using external guides and simply eat, which in turn may lead to disinhibited or binge eating (Baumeister et al., 1998; Kahan, Polivy, & Herman, 2003). In fact, the results of one study showed that restrained eaters ate more when they were asked to inhibit their emotional responses to a video clip (which required them to increase their cognitive effort) than when they did not inhibit their emotional responses (Vohs & Heatherton, 2000).

Figure 10.3

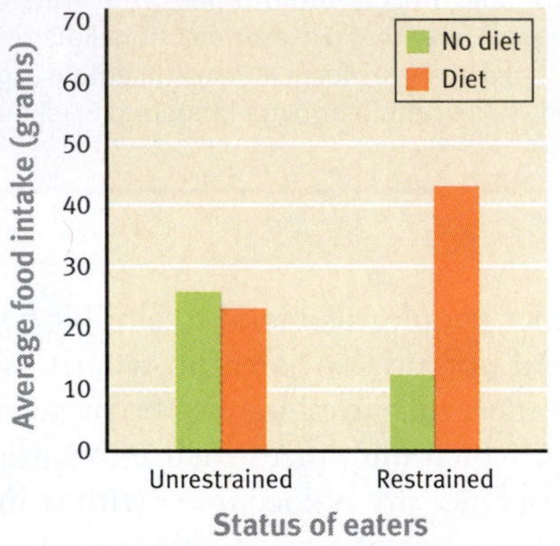

10.3 ▶ The Last Supper Effect
Restrained eaters who were about to diet ate more than did restrained eaters who were not about to diet. Unrestrained eaters ate comparable amounts, regardless of whether those participants were about to diet.

Source: Adapted from Urbszat, Herman, & Polivy, 2000.

Restrained eating
Restricting intake of specific foods or overall number of calories.

Other Psychological Disorders as Risk Factors

Another factor associated with the subsequent development of an eating disorder is the presence of a psychological disorder in early adolescence (see Figure 10.4), particularly depression. A longitudinal study of 726 adolescents found that having a depressive disorder during early adolescence was associated with a higher risk for later dietary restriction, purging, recurrent weight fluctuations, and the emergence of an eating disorder. This was the case even when researchers statistically controlled for other disorders or eating problems before adulthood (Johnson, Cohen, Kotler, et al., 2002).

Social Factors: The Body in Context

Various social factors contribute to eating disorders. One social factor is the role played by family and friends, who have the potential to minimize or amplify an individual's attention to food, weight, and body, and who can help shape individual's thoughts, feelings, and behaviors related to food, weight, and body. Another social factor is culture, which can contribute to eating disorders by promoting an ideal body shape; the media, in turn, propagate the cultural ideal. In this section we discuss these social factors as well as explanations of why so many more females than males develop eating disorders.

The Role of Family and Peers

As mentioned earlier, eating disorders tend to run in families. However, researchers have not found it easy to disentangle the influences of genes from those of the family itself for two main reasons:

1. Family members provide a model for eating, body image, and appearance concerns through their own behaviors (Stein, Woolley, Cooper, et al., 2006). For example, parents who spend a lot of time on their appearance before leaving the house model that behavior for their children.

2. Family members affect a child's concerns through their responses toward the child's body shape, weight, and food intake (Stein, Woolley, Senior, et al., 2006; Tantleff-Dunn, Gokee-LaRose, & Peterson, 2004; Thompson et al., 1999). For example, if a parent inquires daily about how much food his or her child ate at lunch or weighs the child daily, the child learns to pay close attention to caloric intake and daily fluctuations in weight.

Children whose parents are overly concerned about these matters are more likely to develop an eating disorder (Strober, 1995). Marya Hornbacher described her parents' eating styles:

> While my relationship to my parents has always been very complex, there is also the simple fact that both of them used food—one to excess, one to absence—as a means of communication, or comfort, or quest. Food was a problem in my family. A big problem. . . . My father was a periodic heavy drinker, ate constantly, and was forever obsessing about his weight—he would diet, berate himself for falling off his diet, call himself a pig. My mother was a former—or was it closet?—bulimic with strange eating habits. She'd eat normally for a while, then go on a diet, pick at her food, push it away, stare at her butt in the mirror.
>
> (1998, pp. 22–23)

Hornbacher was a keen observer of her parents' behaviors, especially those related to food, weight, and appearance. And she realized that she modeled her own behavior on theirs.

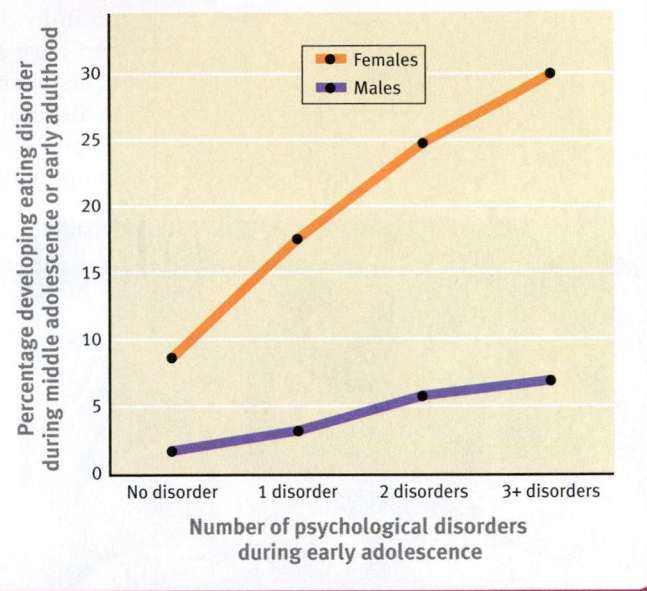

Figure 10.4

10.4 ▶ Psychiatric Disorders and the Risk of Developing an Eating Disorder The more psychological disorders an adolescent—particularly a female adolescent—has, the more likely he or she is to develop an eating disorder (Johnson, Cohen, Kasen, & Brook, 2002).

Children often pay attention to and imitate how their family members behave; when parents are concerned about food, weight, and appearance, they may intentionally or inadvertently pass on these concerns to their children.

David Young-Wolff/Photo Edit

Parents and siblings aren't the only ones who can shape a person's relationship to eating, food, and body. Friends also play a role, especially if they tease or criticize an individual concerning her weight, appearance, or food intake; such comments can have a lasting influence on her (dis)satisfaction with her body, her willingness to diet, and her self-esteem. Such influences can make a person more vulnerable to developing an eating disorder (Cash, 1995; Crowther et al., 2002; Fabian & Thompson, 1989; Keery et al., 2005; Muir, Wertheim, & Paxton, 1999; Tantleff-Dunn, Gokee-LaRose, & Peterson, 2004).

Unfortunately, many girls and women feel that symptoms of eating disorders—particularly preoccupations with food and weight—are "normal" and that talking about these topics is a way to bond with others. Hornbacher was aware of this social facet of eating disorders and its underlying drawback:

> Women use their obsession with weight and food as a point of connection with one another, a commonality even between strangers. Instead of talking about *why* we use food and weight control as a means of handling emotional stress, we talk ad nauseum about the fact that we don't like our bodies.
>
> (1998, p. 283)

For a teenage girl, her friends' comments can have a lasting influence on how she feels about her body, her willingness to diet, and her self-esteem.

M Nader/Getty Images

The Role of Culture

Many people believe that eating disorders have become more common and pervasive in recent decades. Hornbacher associated the increased prevalence with a cultural fad:

> Starving is the feminine thing to do these days, the way swooning was in Victorian times. In the 1920s, women smoked with long cigarette holders and flashed their toothpick legs. In the 1950s, women blushed and said tee-hee. In the 1960s, women swayed, eyes closed, with a silly smile on their faces. My generation and the last one feign disinterest in food. We are "too busy" to eat, "too stressed" to eat.
>
> (1998, p. 118)

Is Hornbacher right—are eating disorders a cultural phenomenon of modern times, as swooning was in the Victorian era? Yes and no. A meta-analysis of the incidence of eating disorders across cultures over the 20th century found only a small increase in the number of cases of anorexia. This finding indicates that Hornbacher was wrong to think that self-induced starvation—anorexia—is a type of "fad" in mental illness (Keel & Klump, 2003). Historically however, people who engaged in self-starvation were not obsessed about their weight; this weight concern has only been observed recently, suggesting that its inclusion in the DSM-IV-TR definition of anorexia may be related to a transient cultural fad.

However, Hornbacher seems to have been on the right track about the "fad" aspect of bulimia. In contrast to the stable incidence of anorexia over time, the incidence of bulimia significantly increased from 1970 to 1990 (Keel & Klump, 2003)—suggesting a cultural influence (Striegel-Moore & Cachelin, 2001)—and bulimia only arises in the context of concerns about weight.

Three elements come together to create the engine driving the culturally induced increase in eating disorders (Becker et al., 2002):

1. a cultural ideal of thinness,

2. repeated media exposure to this thinness ideal, and

3. an individual's assimilation of the thinness ideal.

In order to examine the cultural ideal of thinness, David Garner and colleagues (1980) undertook an innovative study: They tracked the measurements of Miss America contestants and *Playboy* centerfold playmates over time and found that their waists and hips gradually became smaller. Other studies have found similar results (Andersen & DiDomenico, 1992; Field et al., 1999; Nemeroff et al., 1994). In fact, while the size of playmates' bodies has decreased over time (as assessed by the body mass index, or BMI, an adjusted ratio of weight to height), the average BMI of women age 20–29 has increased (see Figure 10.5). During the same period studied by Garner and colleagues, the prevalence of eating disorders increased in the United States. It is not clear whether the contestants and playmates were creating or following a cultural trend in ideal body shape. What is clear is that society's pressure to be thin increases women's—and girls'—dissatisfaction with their bodies, which is a risk factor for eating disorders (Grabe & Hyde, 2006; Lynch et al., 2008; Stice et al., 2003).

The cultural influence on weight and appearance isn't limited to women: Men who regularly engage in activities such as modeling and wrestling, which draw attention to their appearance and weight, are increasingly likely to develop eating disorders (Brownell & Rodin, 1992; Garner, Rosen, & Barry, 1998; Sundgot-Borgen, 1999). Similarly, men who have a heightened awareness of appearance (Ousley, Cordero, & White, 2008), such as some in the gay community, are also more likely to develop an eating disorder (Carlat, Camargo, & Herzog, 1997; Russell & Keel, 2002).

Eating Disorders Across Cultures

Eating disorders occur throughout the world, but are found mainly in industrialized Western or Westernized countries (Kuboki et al., 1996; Lee, Chiu, & Chen, 1989; Lee, Hsu, & Wing, 1992; Pike & Walsh, 1996). Immigration to a Western country and internalization of Western norms increase the risk of developing symptoms of an eating disorder, as occurs among those immigrating from China and Egypt to Western countries (Bilukha & Utermohlen, 2002; Lee & Lee, 1996; Perez et al., 2002; Stark-Wroblewski, Yanico, & Lupe, 2005). Westernization (or modernization) of a culture similarly increases dieting (Gunewardene, Huon, & Zheng, 2001; Lee & Lee, 2000), which is a risk factor for eating disorders. In addition, as girls and women move into a higher socioeconomic bracket, they are more likely to develop an eating disorder (Lee & Lee, 2000; Polivy & Herman, 2002; Soomro et al., 1995).

Within the United States, prevalence rates of eating disorders vary across ethnic groups, based on different ideals of beauty and femininity: Native Americans have a higher risk for eating disorders than do other ethnic groups (Crago, Shisslak, & Estes, 1996) and black Americans have had the lowest risk (Andersen & Hay, 1985; Crago, Shisslak, & Estes, 1996; Mulholland & Mintz, 2001; Striegel-Moore et al., 2003). However, prevalence rates are increasing among black and Latina women (Franko et al., 2007; Gentile et al., 2007; Perez & Joiner, 2003; Shaw et al., 2004; Taylor et al., 2007), perhaps because of the growing number of ethnic models in mainstream ads who are as thin as their white counterparts (Brodey, 2005).

Finally, prevalence rates of eating disorders across ethnic groups may vary for people at different ages; studies with participants from younger cohorts find fewer differences across ethnic groups (Wade, 2007).

The Power of the Media

The power of the media to influence cultural ideals of beauty and femininity is illustrated by the results of an innovative study in Fiji by Anne Becker and colleagues (2002). Prior to 1995, there was no television in Fiji, a group of islands in the South Pacific. Traditional Fijian culture promoted robust body shapes and appetites, and there were no cultural pressures for thinness or dieting. Researchers collected data from adolescent girls shortly after the introduction of television in 1995 and again 3 years later. At the beginning of the study, when a large body size was the cultural

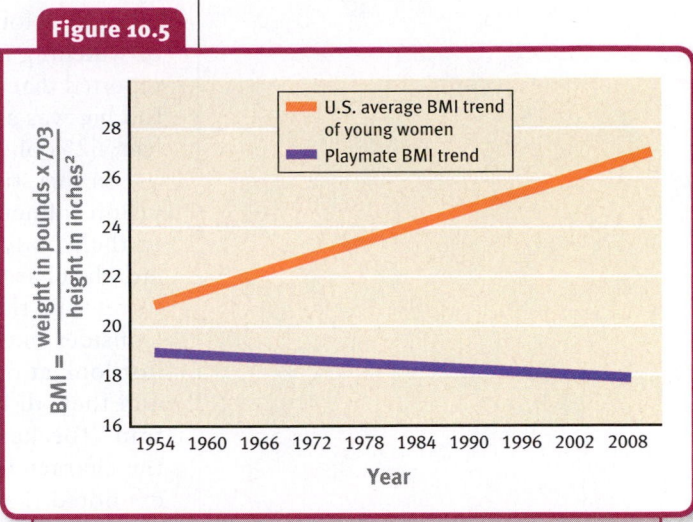

Figure 10.5

10.5 ▶ Women's Body Size Over Time: Playmates and Average Young Women Over the last four decades, the size (specifically, the body mass index, BMI) of the average young woman's body has become heavier (orange line); over the same period of time, the body size of *Playboy* playmates has become thinner (purple line), presenting an increasingly unattainable ideal.

When females move from a non-Western country to a Western country, their risk of developing an eating disorder increases.

Jeff Greenberg/Photo Edit

ideal, they found almost no one who felt they were "too big or fat." After 3 years of watching television (primarily shows from Western countries), however, 75% reported that they felt "too big or fat" at least some of the time. In addition, feeling too big was associated with dieting to lose weight, which had become very prevalent: 62% of the girls had dieted within the prior 4 weeks.

In this study in Fiji, over three quarters of the participants reported that television influenced their body image and that they wanted to change the shape of their body to resemble those of the Western television characters. To emulate the characters, they changed their hairstyles, clothes, and behavior and tried to reshape their bodies through dieting and, for some (11%), through purging. Consider one girl's comments: "When I look at the characters on TV . . . and I just look at the body, the figure of that body, so I say, 'look at them, they are thin and they all have this figure', so I myself want to become like that, to become thin" (Becker et al., 2002, p. 513). Moreover, 30% of the participants viewed the characters on TV as role models for work and career issues. The researchers noted that this profound change occurred over the course of only 3 years, which is particularly dramatic given the long history of a fuller figure as the Fijian cultural ideal.

A similar process might be occurring in industrialized societies, where ideals of thinness saturate the environment through television, movies, magazines, advertisements, books, and even cartoons. A number of studies have documented associations between media exposure and disordered eating (Bissell & Zhou, 2004; Kim & Lennon, 2007; Stice et al., 1994); for instance, the more time adolescent girls spent watching television, the more likely they were to report disordered eating a year later (Harrison & Hefner, 2006). However, not all females who view these media images end up with an eating disorder. Some people are more affected than others, perhaps because of their combination of neurological, psychological, and social risk factors. For them, chronic exposure to these types of images may tip the scales and set them on a course toward an eating disorder (Levine & Harrison, 2004).

Objectification Theory: Explaining the Gender Difference

How, exactly, the cultural ideal of thinness makes women vulnerable to eating disorders is explained by **objectification theory**, which posits that girls learn to consider their bodies as objects and commodities (Fredrickson & Roberts, 1997). Western culture promotes the view of male bodies as agents—instruments that perform tasks—and of female bodies as objects mainly to be looked at and evaluated in terms of appearance (see Figure 10.6). Marya Hornbacher recounted her sense of being objectified:

> I remember the body from the outside in. . . . There will be copious research on the habit of women with eating disorders perceiving themselves through other eyes, as if there were some Great Observer looking over their shoulder. Looking, in particular, at their bodies and finding, more and more often as they get older, countless flaws.
>
> (1998, p. 14)

Implicit in Hornbacher's musings about her perceptions of her body is the sense of her body as an object—to be looked at and evaluated and, all too frequently, found defective.

According to the theory, objectification encourages eating disorders because female bodies are evaluated according to the cultural ideal, and women strive to have their bodies conform so that they will be positively evaluated. As they internalize the ideal of thinness, they increase their risk for eating disorders (Calogero, Davis, & Thompson, 2005; Thompson & Stice, 2001)—especially in combination with learning to see their bodies as objects from the outside: As Hornbacher noted, if they hold an ideal of thinness and see their bodies as objects, they become more

Objectification theory
The theory that girls learn to consider their bodies as objects and commodities.

Figure 10.6

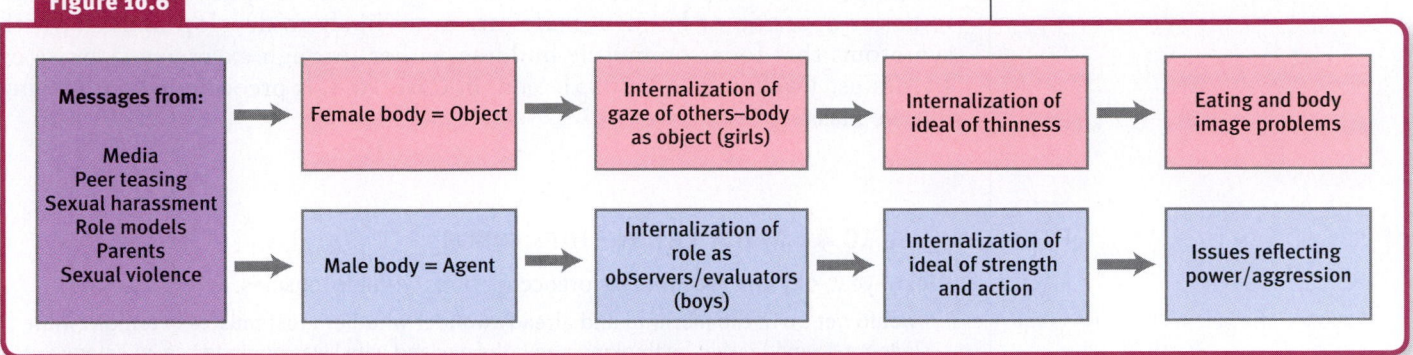

| Messages from:

Media
Peer teasing
Sexual harassment
Role models
Parents
Sexual violence | → | Female body = Object | → | Internalization of gaze of others–body as object (girls) | → | Internalization of ideal of thinness | → | Eating and body image problems |
| → | Male body = Agent | → | Internalization of role as observers/evaluators (boys) | → | Internalization of ideal of strength and action | → | Issues reflecting power/aggression |

10.6 ▸ Objectification and Eating Problems Objectification theory helps to explain the large gender difference in the prevalence of eating disorders. This theory proposes that whereas boys are encouraged to view their bodies as instruments that can perform tasks (agents), girls are encouraged to consider their bodies as objects and commodities to be evaluated (objects)—which makes girls more vulnerable to developing an eating disorder.

Source: Adapted from Smolak & Murmen, 2004.

likely to pay attention to their flaws and to feel ashamed of their bodies, and these feelings motivate restrained eating (Fredrickson & Roberts, 1997; Moradi, Dirks, & Matteson, 2005; Smolak & Murnen, 2004).

Consider this study: Female participants alone in a dressing room with a full-length mirror were asked to try on either a one-piece swimsuit or a sweater. While wearing the new clothing, the women completed a checklist assessing body shame (questions included: "I wish I were invisible," "I wish I could cover my body."). They then took part in a "food taste test" (cookies). Women who tried on bathing suits reported more shame about their bodies and subsequently ate less than their sweater-clad counterparts. Male participants who wore bathing suits did not exhibit this response (Fredrickson et al., 1998).

The objectification process typically begins before adulthood. As girls enter puberty, when female bodies are increasingly viewed in sexual terms, comments on their bodies—such as catcalls or whistles when they walk down the street—may increase their sense of bodies as objects or commodities (Bryant-Waugh, 1993; Larkin, Rice, & Russell, 1999). Children learn these cultural messages early. Today, even preschool children attribute more negative qualities to fat women than to fat men (Turnbull, Heaslip, & McLeod, 2000).

Another explanation for the gender difference in prevalence rates of eating disorders focuses on the politics of a cultural ideal of thinness for women. Some researchers note that as women's economic and political power has increased, female models have become thinner and less curvaceous, creating a physical ideal of womanhood that is harder—if not impossible—to meet. Women then spend significant time, energy, and money trying to emulate this thinner ideal through exercise, diet, medications, and even surgery, which in turn dissipates their economic and political power (Barber, 1998; Bordo, 1993).

Although today males are much less likely to develop any type of eating disorder than are women, this large gender discrepancy may not last. Data suggest that male physical ideals are increasingly unrealistic: Male film stars and Mr. Universe winners are increasingly muscular (Pope, Phillips, & Olivardia, 2000), paralleling the changes in women's bodies in the media. Just as females covet bodies similar to those promoted in the media, so do males (Ricciardelli et al., 2006): Two-thirds of men want their bodies to be more similar to cultural ideals of the male body (McCabe & Ricciardelli, 2001a, 2001b; Ricciardelli &

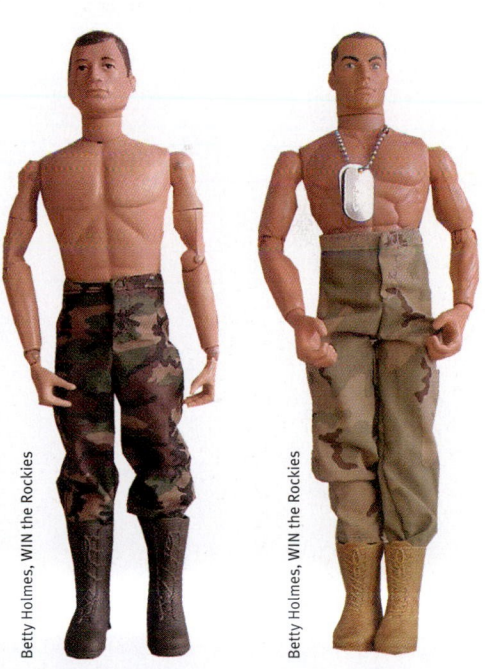

Betty Holmes, WIN the Rockies

Betty Holmes, WIN the Rockies

Many female dolls have unattainable physical proportions; this is increasingly also becoming true of male dolls. As seen in this comparison of a 1960 G. I. Joe action figure (left) with one from 2000 (right), male action figures have become more muscular over the last 25 years (Baghurst et al., 2006).

McCabe, 2001). However, rather than suffer from the specific sets of symptoms for anorexia or bulimia, males are more likely to develop EDNOS, with symptoms that focus on muscle building, either through excessive exercise or steroid use (Weltzin et al., 2005). Sam, in Case 10.4, is preoccupied with losing muscle mass.

CASE 10.4 ▶ FROM THE INSIDE: EDNOS

Forty-year-old Sam recounts his preoccupations with his muscles:

I would get up in the morning and already wonder whether I lost muscle overnight while sleeping. I would rather be thinking about the day and who I was going to see, et cetera. But instead, the thoughts always centered on my body. Throughout the day, I would think about everything I ate, every physical movement I did, and whether it contributed to muscle loss in any way. I would go to bed and pray that I would wake up and think about something else the next day. It's a treadmill I can't get off of.

(Olivardia, 2007, pp. 125–126)

FEEDBACK LOOPS IN ACTION: Eating Disorders

As we have seen, many neurological, psychological, and social factors are associated with the development and maintenance of eating disorders. Let's look at some theories about how these factors interact through feedback loops.

Most females in Western societies are exposed to images of thin women as ideals in the media, yet only some women develop an eating disorder. Why? Neurological factors (such as a genetic vulnerability) may make some individuals more susceptible to the psychological and social factors related to eating disorders (Bulik, 2005). For instance, researchers hypothesize that young women who are prone to anxiety (neuroticism)—which is both a psychological factor and a neurological factor—are more susceptible to the effects of a familial focus on appearance, a social factor (Davis et al., 2004). In turn, these two factors are associated with weight preoccupation, creating feedback loops: After statistically controlling for body size, researchers found that young women who were preoccupied with weight were more prone to anxiety and were more likely to have families that focused on appearance. That is, two factors—anxiety proneness and familial focus on appearance—were most associated with the young women's preoccupation with weight. This preoccupation in turn leads to anxiety focused on weight and appearance.

A preoccupation with weight can also lead to dieting, which can create its own neurochemical changes (neurological factor) that may lead to eating disorders (Walsh et al., 1995). In addition, the stringent rules that people may set for a diet can lead them to feel out of control with eating if they "violate" those rules (psychological factor). Further, people with higher levels of perfectionism and body dissatisfaction (psychological factors) may seek out comments about their appearance (social factor) or pay more attention to appearance-related comments (psychological factor) (Halmi et al., 2000). Figure 10.7 illustrates the feedback loops for eating disorders.

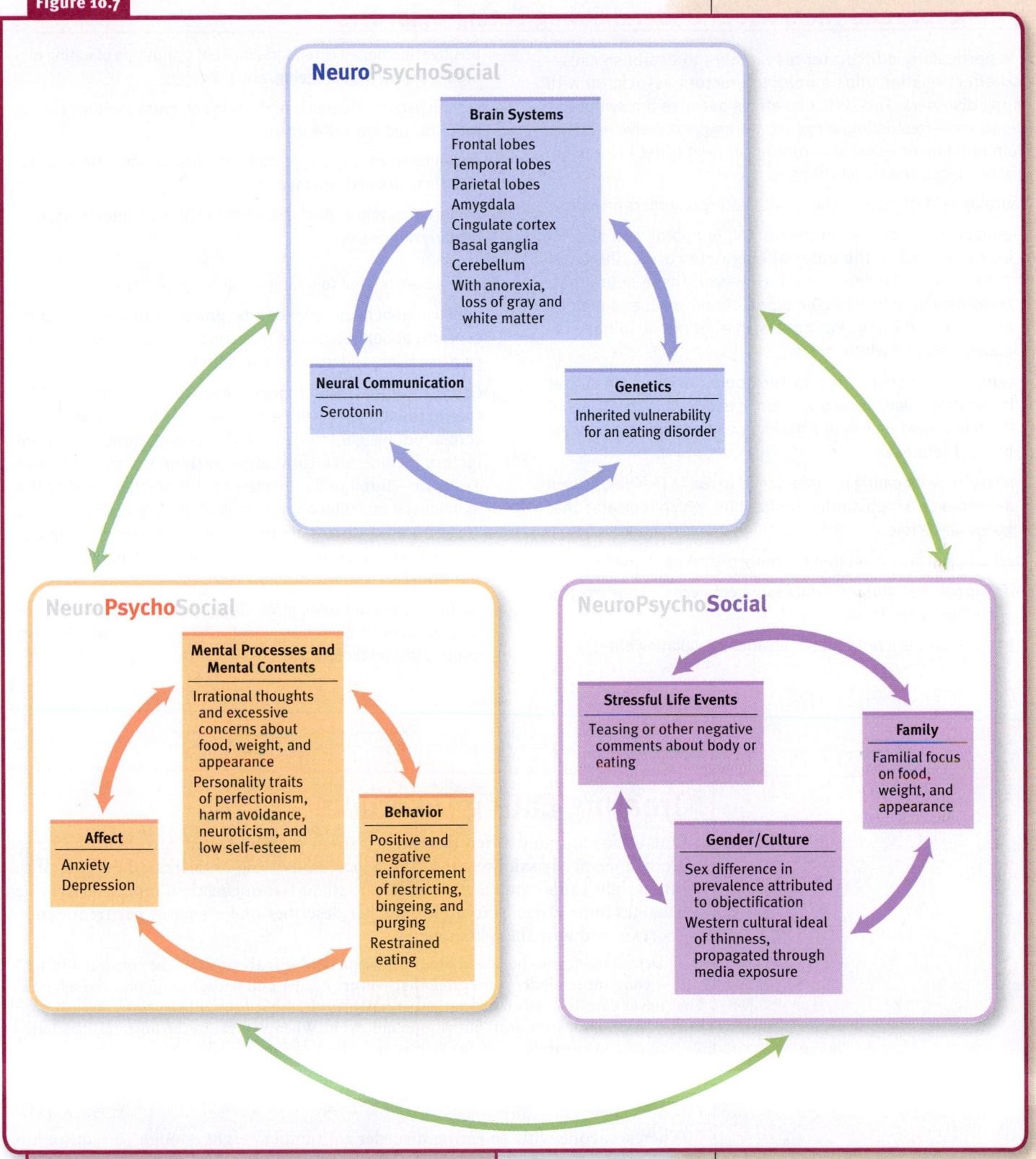

Figure 10.7

NeuroPsychoSocial

Brain Systems

Frontal lobes
Temporal lobes
Parietal lobes
Amygdala
Cingulate cortex
Basal ganglia
Cerebellum
With anorexia, loss of gray and white matter

Neural Communication

Serotonin

Genetics

Inherited vulnerability for an eating disorder

NeuroPsychoSocial

Mental Processes and Mental Contents

Irrational thoughts and excessive concerns about food, weight, and appearance

Personality traits of perfectionism, harm avoidance, neuroticism, and low self-esteem

Affect

Anxiety
Depression

Behavior

Positive and negative reinforcement of restricting, bingeing, and purging

Restrained eating

NeuroPsychoSocial

Stressful Life Events

Teasing or other negative comments about body or eating

Family

Familial focus on food, weight, and appearance

Gender/Culture

Sex difference in prevalence attributed to objectification

Western cultural ideal of thinness, propagated through media exposure

10.7 ▶ Feedback Loops in Action: Eating Disorders

Key Concepts and Facts About Understanding Eating Disorders

- It is particularly difficult for researchers to establish cause-and-effect relationships among the factors associated with eating disorders. This difficulty arises because the symptoms themselves—restricting, bingeing, purging, excessive exercise, malnourishment—create neurological (and other biological), psychological, and social changes.

- Neurological factors associated with eating disorders include:

  - unusually low activity in the frontal, temporal, and parietal lobes, as well as the anterior cingulate cortex, the basal ganglia, and the cerebellum. However, these neural patterns may vary for specific types of anorexia, and may be affected by dieting. Patients with anorexia also have reduced gray and white matter;

  - reduced responsiveness to serotonin, a neurotransmitter involved in mood, anxiety, and binge eating. One theory about the role of serotonin in bulimia involves tryptophan, a building block of serotonin;

  - a tendency for eating disorders tend to run in families, as well as evidence of substantial heritability, which indicates that genes play a role.

- Psychological factors related to eating disorders include:

  - irrational thoughts and excessive concerns about weight, appearance, and food;

  - binge eating as a result of the abstinence violation effect;

  - positive and negative reinforcement of symptoms of eating disorders (restricting, bingeing, and purging);

  - certain personality traits: perfectionism, harm avoidance, neuroticism, and low self-esteem;

  - disinhibited eating, triggered by the last supper effect, especially in restrained eaters; and

  - comorbid psychological disorders in female adolescents, particularly depression.

- Social factors related to eating disorders include:

  - family members and friends who provide a model for eating, concerns about weight, and focus on appearance through their own behaviors and responses to others;

  - cultural factors, which play a key role, as evidenced by the increased prevalence over time of bulimia and concern about weight that is part of anorexia. Specific cultural factors include a cultural ideal of thinness and repeated exposure—through the media—to this ideal, as well as the individual's assimilation of this ideal. People in Western and Westernized countries are more likely to develop eating disorders than are people from non-Western and developing countries;

  - conflicting gender roles in Western societies and a tendency to view women's bodies as objects and search for bodily flaws (objectification theory).

Treating Eating Disorders

One important goal when treating a patient with anorexia is to help the patient attain a medically safe weight through increased eating or decreased purging; if that safe weight cannot be reached with outpatient treatment, then inpatient treatment becomes imperative. Marya Hornbacher describes one aspect of her treatment for anorexia and how she felt about it:

> Denied food, your body and brain will begin to obsess about it. It's the survival instinct, a constant reminder to eat, one that you try harder and harder to ignore, though you never can. Instead of eating, you simply *think* about food all the time. You dream about it, you stare at it, but you do not eat it. When you get to the hospital, you have to eat, and as truly terrifying as it is, it is also welcome. Food is the sun and the moon and the stars, the center of gravity, the love of your life. Being forced to eat is the most welcome punishment there is.
>
> (1998, p. 151)

When someone with an eating disorder *isn't* underweight enough to require inpatient treatment, many different factors can be the initial targets of treatment. In this section we examine specific treatments that target neurological (and biological, more broadly), psychological, and social factors and the role of hospitalization.

Like treatment for other disorders, the intensity of treatment for eating disorders can range from hospitalization, day or evening programs, residential treatment, to outpatient treatment. In all these forms of treatment, cognitive-behavior therapy

(CBT) is generally considered the method of choice. Regardless of the severity of the eating disorder, frequent visits with an internist or family doctor are an important additional component of treatment. The physician determines whether a patient should be medically hospitalized and, if not, whether she is medically stable enough to partake in daily activities. Let's examine treatment options using the neuropsychosocial approach.

Targeting Neurological and Biological Factors: Nourishing the Body

Neurologically and biologically focused treatments are designed to create a pattern of normal healthy eating and to stabilize medical problems that arise from the eating disorder. Treatments that focus specifically on these goals include nutritional counseling to improve eating, medical hospitalization to address significant medical problems, and medication to diminish some symptoms of the eating disorder as well as symptoms of comorbid anxiety and depression.

A Focus on Nutrition

For people with any type of eating disorder, increasing the nutrition and variety of foods eaten—and not purged—is critical. A nutritionist will help develop meal plans for increasing caloric intake at a reasonable pace. In the process of nutritional counseling, the nutritionist may identify a patient's mistaken beliefs about food and weight; the nutritionist then seeks to educate the patient and thus help her correct such beliefs.

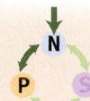

When very low weight patients with anorexia increase their food intake too aggressively, they can develop *refeeding syndrome*, in which rapidly shifting blood electrolyte levels can cause congestive heart failure, mental confusion, seizures, breathing difficulty, and possibly death (Mehler, 2001; Pomeroy, 2004; Swenne, 2000). For such low weight patients, caloric intake should increase at a moderate pace. Despite improved nutrition, menstruation may not restart (or begin) months after a woman's weight and body fat are in the normal range.

As people with anorexia begin to eat more, they may experience gastrointestinal discomfort. This may occur for two reasons: First, because of a lack of body fat, eating more may compress a section of the duodenum (a part of the intestine) that is on top of an important artery (Adson, Mitchell, & Trenkner, 1997). Second, when people eat no fat (or very small amounts of it), their ability to produce bile, which is necessary for the digestion of fats, diminishes. With reduced bile production, people may feel uncomfortable after eating fats. To minimize this discomfort, nutritionists suggest reintroducing fats slowly; bile production increases with increased fat consumption over the course of a couple of weeks.

Medical Hospitalization

The bodily effects of eating disorders—particularly anorexia—can be directly life-threatening. When medical problems related to eating disorders become severe, a *medical* hospitalization rather than a psychiatric hospitalization may be necessary. Medical hospitalization generally occurs in response to a medical crisis, such as a heart problem, gastrointestinal bleeding, or significant dehydration. The goal of medical hospitalization is to treat the specific medical problem and stabilize the patient's health.

Medication

Generally, various medications have not been found to help with the weight gain phase of treatment for anorexia (Crow et al., 2009; de Zwaan, Roerig, & Mitchell, 2004; Rivas-Vasquez, Rice, & Kalman, 2003; Walsh et al., 2006). However, once the patient's normal weight is restored, selective serotonin reuptake inhibitors (SSRIs) may help prevent the person from relapsing (developing anorexia again; Barbarich et al., 2004).

For bulimia, antidepressants—particularly SSRIs—may reduce some symptoms of the eating disorder. Compared to placebos, SSRIs can help decrease bingeing, vomiting, and weight and shape concerns, although other symptoms may still persist—including a fear of normal eating (Bacaltchuk, Hay, & Mari, 2000; Mitchell et al., 2001). Symptoms of comorbid depression may also be reduced by SSRIs. The SSRI prozac (*fluoxetine*) is the most widely studied medication for bulimia, and the FDA has approved it to treat this disorder. Studies of Prozac's effects on bulimia typically last no longer than 16 weeks, however, so it isn't clear how long the medication should be taken (de Zwaan, Roerig, & Mitchell, 2004). Moreover, as with other disorders, the beneficial effects of medication used to treat eating disorders typically stop soon after the medication is discontinued.

Targeting Psychological Factors: Cognitive-Behavior Therapy

Among the treatments that directly target psychological factors, CBT is the most extensively studied and is considered the treatment of choice (Pike, Devlin, & Loeb, 2004). CBT for eating disorders focuses primarily on changes in thoughts, feelings, and behaviors that are related to eating, food, and the body, at least in the initial stages. At the outset of treatment, the patient and therapist discuss who monitors the patient's weight and at what point inpatient treatment would be recommended and pursued (Pike, Devlin, & Loeb, 2004).

CBT for Anorexia

CBT for anorexia focuses on identifying and changing thoughts and behaviors that impede normal eating and that maintain the symptoms of the disorder. Cognitive restructuring can decrease the patient's irrational thoughts (such as the belief that starving means having self-control) and help the patient develop more realistic thoughts (for example, that appropriate eating indicates the ability to care for herself). The therapist also helps the patient to develop more adaptive coping strategies (Bowers & Ansher, 2008; Garner, Vitousek, & Pike, 1997; Wilson & Fairburn, 2007), such as expressing anger or disappointment directly to other people rather than hiding or denying such "negative" feelings. Treatment may also involve psychoeducation (about the disorder and its effects), training in self-monitoring (to notice hunger cues and become aware of problematic behaviors), and relaxation training (to decrease anxiety that arises with increased eating). Because low weight can affect cognitive functioning, irrational thoughts may not change substantially until the patient's weight increases (McIntosh et al., 2005). CBT can be effective in reducing symptoms of anorexia and has been shown to prevent relapses (Pike et al., 2003).

Because people with anorexia may not seek help voluntarily, motivation (or resistance) to change is often more of an issue than it is in the treatment of other disorders. Motivational enhancement therapy (see Chapter 9) may be employed to increase patients' willingness to change; with anorexia, this treatment might address the patient's goals that are unrelated to eating, food, and weight, and help her see how her behaviors—and the eating disorder symptoms—interfere with attaining those goals.

CBT for Bulimia

When used as a treatment for bulimia, CBT focuses on the thoughts, feelings, and behaviors that (1) prevent normal eating and (2) promote bingeing, purging, and other behaviors that are intended to offset the calories ingested during a binge. CBT also addresses thoughts, feelings, and behaviors that are related to body image and appearance and that maintain the symptoms of bulimia. In addition to focusing on symptoms of the disorder, CBT may address perfectionism, low self-esteem, and mood issues (Wilson & Fairburn, 2007). CBT for bulimia uses many of the same methods as for anorexia: psychoeducation, cognitive restructuring, self-monitoring, and relaxation. In addition, treatment may employ a method used to treat obsessive-compulsive disorder (OCD): *exposure with response prevention* (discussed in Chapters 4 and 7). For bulimia, this method generally involves exposing the patient to anxiety-provoking stimuli, such as foods she would typically eat only during a binge. Patients are asked to consume a moderate amount of the binge food during a therapy session (the exposure), and the response prevention involves *not purging* or responding in another usual way to compensate for the calories ingested. The benefits of CBT for bulimia are well documented (Agras, Crow, et al., 2000; Fairburn et al., 1995; Ghaderi, 2006; Walsh et al., 1997).

Researchers have proposed three possible mechanisms to explain the beneficial effects of CBT as a treatment for bulimia (Wilson et al., 2002):

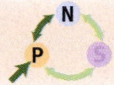

1. CBT leads to more normal eating.

2. CBT decreases patients' dietary restrictions, which reduces the risk of bingeing (and subsequent purging) because of hunger or inadequate nutrition.

3. CBT increases patients' ability to cope with potential *triggers* of bingeing and purging, which increases a sense of self-efficacy, which in turn further decreases bingeing and purging (Wilson & Fairburn, 2007).

Using CBT Manuals to Treat Eating Disorders

CBT manuals have been adapted for both anorexia and bulimia, although clinicians often need to deviate from the manuals (see Chapter 5 for a more general discussion about manual-based treatment). Such manuals provide a session-by-session guide with specific goals and techniques. As shown in Table 10.5, manual-based treatment may last 20 sessions or less, and generally consists of three phases, each of which has a different focus and uses different techniques. The first phase focuses on the behaviors themselves; the second focuses on the thoughts that underlie such behaviors; and the third focuses on how to prevent relapse. Research has shown that relapse is more likely to occur after treatment that uses behavioral techniques only and does not address the inappropriate thoughts about weight and appearance that underlie the problematic behaviors (Fairburn et al., 1993). Here's a therapeutic interchange from the second phase of treatment, addressing the underlying cognitive distortions that contribute to disordered eating behavior:

Therapist (T): Did you notice any situations leading to binge episodes or urges to binge in the past week that involve problem thoughts?

Patient (P) Well, I binged after skiing one day. I was upset, because I went skiing and the people were nicer to my friend than they were to me and I was sure that it was because she is thinner and prettier than I am.

T: I'm hearing some faulty reasoning here. Let's work to uncover the underlying problem thought.

Table 10.5 ▶ Three Phases of CBT for Bulimia

Phase of Treatment	Focus of Phase	Techniques Employed
Phase 1	Behavioral symptoms related to food and appearance	Psychoeducation; self-monitoring; assignments to normalize eating and decrease bingeing and purging, including exposure with response prevention
Phase 2	Cognitive symptoms related to the eating disorder	Cognitive restructuring of illogical thoughts pertaining to food, weight, appearance, purging, and self; problem solving
Phase 3	Relapse prevention	Problem solving about possible eating and appearance concerns or other factors likely to lead to relapse

Sources: Fairburn, Marcus, & Wilson, 1993; Pike, Devlin, & Loeb, 2004.

P: My friend is prettier than I am, so that means that people like her more and like me less, and she's thinner. So I guess the underlying problem thought is that people don't like me because I'm fat and ugly. [...]

T: What is the evidence to support the view that people don't like you because you are fat and ugly?

P: Well, I am fat and ugly.

T: I think you know that is subjective, not objective. [...]

P: More people talked to her than me.

      (Agras & Apple, 1997, pp. 95–96; Agras & Apple, 2008, pp. 107–108)

Notice the underlying circularity in the patient's reasoning: Because the patient believes that more people talked to her friend than talked to her, that is "proof" that it was because her friend is thinner and prettier.

Efficacy of CBT for Treating Eating Disorders

Most people with eating disorders who improve significantly with CBT do so within the first month of treatment (Agras, Crow, et al., 2000). Others may improve somewhat but may stop treatment because they feel that it isn't helping them. Although CBT helps decrease their bingeing, purging, and dieting behaviors, up to 50% of patients retain some symptoms after the treatment ends (Lundgren, Danoff-Burg, & Anderson, 2004). One study of 48 patients who completely abstained from bingeing and purging after CBT found that 44% had relapsed 4 months later (Halmi et al., 2002). Those who relapsed had more eating rituals, were more preoccupied with food-related thoughts, and were less motivated to change their behavior.

    Why does CBT not help everyone with an eating disorder? There's no simple answer. Some studies that examined the presence of comorbid disorders—particularly personality disorders—found that people with comorbid disorders tend to respond less well than those with only the eating disorder (Bandini et al., 2006; Bruce & Steiger, 2005). Although CBT may be the treatment of choice and helps many people with eating disorders, it clearly isn't a panacea.

Targeting Social Factors

Given the important role that social factors play in contributing to eating disorders, it is not surprising that various effective treatments directly target these factors. Treatments that target social factors include interpersonal therapy, family therapy, group-based inpatient treatment programs, and prevention programs.

Interpersonal Therapy

Interpersonal therapy (IPT) has been applied to eating disorders, in the form of manual-based treatment consisting of 4 to 6 months of weekly therapy (Fairburn, 1998). In any form of IPT, the focus is on problems in relationships that contribute to the onset, maintenance, and relapse of the disorder (Frank & Spanier, 1995; Klerman & Weissman, 1993). IPT thus is designed to improve current relationships and social functioning in general. Although IPT was originally developed to treat depression, the idea behind IPT for eating disorders is that as problems with relationships resolve, symptoms decrease, even though the symptoms are not addressed directly by the treatment (Swartz, 1999; Tantleff-Dunn, Gokee-LaRose, & Peterson, 2004).

    How does IPT work? The hypothesized mechanism is as follows: (1) IPT reduces longstanding interpersonal problems; and (2) the resulting improvement of relationships makes people feel hopeful and empowered, and increases their self-esteem. These changes have four effects: First, they lead people to change other aspects of their lives, such as disordered eating; second, they lead to less concern about appearance and weight, and therefore less dieting and bingeing (Fairburn, 1997); third, as relationships improve, people have more social contact and hence less time to engage in disordered eating behaviors; and finally, with less interpersonal stress, people don't need to expend as much effort on coping and have less need for bingeing and purging to manage their (less frequent) negative feelings.

Although IPT for anorexia has not yet been well researched, IPT for bulimia has been, and many studies have shown that it is an effective alternative to CBT for bulimia (Apple, 1999; Birchall, 1999; Fairburn, 1997, 2005). IPT may require more time than CBT to reduce symptoms, but at 1-year follow-up, its results are comparable to those with CBT (Fairburn et al., 1986, 1993; Wilfley et al., 1993). For example, Fairburn (1997) randomly assigned people with bulimia to one of three treatments: CBT, IPT, or behavior therapy (BT). All three treatments decreased participants' symptoms, but CBT was slightly more effective. Over time, however, the benefits of BT declined, while people in the CBT and IPT groups continued to improve. Other studies have reported similar findings (Agras, Walsh et al., 2000; Wilson et al., 2002).

Family Therapy

Prior to the 1970s, anorexia was treated psychodynamically, which was the type of psychological treatment most widely available at that time. But in the 1970s, psychiatrists Salvador Minuchin in the United States (Minuchin, Rosman, & Baker, 1978) and Mara Selvini Palazzoli in Italy (1974, 1988) began to treat girls and young women with anorexia using family therapy, treating the family as a system. As we saw in Chapter 4, systems therapy identifies the problem as maladaptive family interactional patterns and structures, and treatment is designed to change these patterns and roles. As with IPT, treatment does not specifically address the patient's eating and food issues. Family therapy for anorexia nervosa has been found to be most effective for young women and girls who live with their parents.

The most widely used family-oriented treatment for anorexia is called the *Maudsley approach* (Dare & Eisler, 1997; le Grange & Eisler, 2009; Lock et al., 2001), named after the hospital in which the treatment originated. This approach does not view the family as responsible for causing problems and in fact makes no assumptions about the causes of the disorder. Instead, the **Maudsley approach** focuses on the future by: (1) helping parents view the patient as distinct from her illness, and (2) supporting the parents as *they* figure out how to lead their daughter to eat so that she can proceed with her development to adulthood. The therapist asks the parents to unite to feed their daughter, despite her anxiety and protests. Once her weight is normal and she eats without a struggle, they gradually return control to her, and other family issues—including general ones of adolescent development—become the focus (Lock, 2004). The initial phase of treatment requires an enormous commitment on the part of the family: A parent must be home continuously to monitor the daughter's eating. Clearly, the Maudsley approach is not feasible for all families. But research results indicate that it is perhaps the most effective treatment for adolescents and young adults with anorexia (Keel & Haedt, 2008).

Psychiatric Hospitalization

In contrast to medical hospitalizations, psychiatric hospitalizations for eating disorders are often planned in advance, and they usually take place in units that specialize in treating people with eating disorders. Psychiatric hospitalization is recommended when less intensive treatments have failed to change disordered eating behaviors sufficiently. The hospital environment is a 24-hour community in which patients attend many different types of group therapy, including groups focused on body image, coping strategies, and relationships with food. These groups can decrease the isolation and shame patients may feel and give patients an opportunity to try out new ways of relating. Hospitalized patients also receive individual therapy and usually some type of family therapy; medication may also be administered, if deemed appropriate.

The short-term goals of psychiatric hospitalization for anorexia and bulimia include increasing the individual's weight to the normal range, establishing a normal eating pattern (three full meals and two snacks per day), curbing excessive exercise, and beginning to change irrational, maladaptive thoughts about food, weight, and body shape. For those who purge or otherwise try to compensate for their caloric intake, an additional goal is to stop or at least reduce such compensatory behaviors.

One type of family therapy for people with anorexia is the Maudsley approach. The first step of this family treatment is to empower the parents to figure out how best to lead their daughter to resume normal eating.

Maudsley approach
A family treatment for anorexia nervosa that focuses on supporting parents as they determine how to lead their daughter to eat appropriately.

Psychiatric hospitalization can improve eating symptoms and help to change distorted thoughts about food, weight, and body. But, in many cases, these positive changes are not enduring. Twelve months after discharge from a psychiatric hospitalization, 30–50% of patients relapse (Pike, 1998). Consider that in 1 year, Marya Hornbacher was hospitalized three times. Why is there such a high relapse rate? There are various explanations. One is that some patients are reluctant to change their behaviors, and they accept the intensive treatment for health reasons or because of pressure from family members—but once out of the hospital, they are not willing to continue the changes they began. For example, each time Hornbacher was released from the hospital, she reverted to her old eating behaviors. Some researchers have examined the amount of weight gained during hospitalization for anorexia. Patients who gain more weight during their hospitalizations are likely to fare better 1 year later. This finding could mean that patients who are more motivated to improve will gain more weight while in the hospital; alternatively, it could mean that a higher level of weight gain in and of itself starts an upward spiral of recovery (Lund et al., 2009).

A second reason for the high relapse rate after psychiatric hospitalization is that some patients do not receive appropriate outpatient care after they leave the hospital. This lack of care makes it more difficult for them to learn how to sustain their changed eating, weight, and views about their bodies when they are not in a supervised therapeutic environment.

A third reason for the high relapse rate focuses on economic pressures from insurance companies, which have cut the approved length of hospital stays for people with eating disorders (and for those with psychological disorders in general). Psychiatric hospitalizations have become increasingly short, which reduces the amount of change that can realistically be accomplished during a stay. For instance, one study found that the average stay of a patient who is hospitalized for an eating disorder fell dramatically from 149.5 days in 1984 to 23.7 days in 1998 (Wiseman et al., 2001), and this decreased average length of stay may continue (Calderon et al., 2007). Psychiatric hospitalization no longer provides long-term treatment that yields enduring changes in eating habits and in thoughts and feelings about food and weight; instead, hospitalization now responds to symptom-related problems by stabilizing people when their medical or eating disorder symptoms approach a danger point (Wiseman et al., 2001). The "dose" of inpatient treatment is shorter, and so it is not surprising that the "response" is shorter-lasting and relapse is likely to occur. Marya Hornbacher described her experience:

> In the last week of February, my vital [medical] signs stabilized and my [health] insurance pulled out. I was discharged on grounds of noncompliance and insufficient [insurance] coverage. Eating disorders are regarded, by the insurance companies, as temporary and cured once the heart speeds up a bit. I was returned to my parents' house, batty and sicker than when I'd gone in. The tiny bit of weight I'd gained in the hospital scared me, and once discharged, I just stopped eating altogether.
>
> (1998, p. 182)

Prevention Programs

Many mental health clinicians and researchers seek to *prevent* eating disorders, particularly for those individuals most at risk (Coughlin & Kalodner, 2006; Shaw et al., 2009; Stice & Hoffman, 2004): namely, those people who have some symptoms of an eating disorder but do not meet all the diagnostic criteria. Prevention programs often seek to challenge maladaptive beliefs about appearance and food and to decrease overeating, fasting, and avoidance of some types of foods. Prevention programs may take place as a single session or multiple sessions, may take the form of presentations or workshops, or may even be provided via the Internet (Zabinski et al., 2001, 2004).

At least under some circumstances, such programs can be helpful. Meta-analyses have found that certain aspects of prevention programs (such as multiple sessions rather than a single session) were associated with less disordered eating in participants, compared to those in a control group (Stice & Shaw, 2004; Stice, Shaw, & Marti, 2006). Unfortunately, not all studies and reviews find prevention programs to be effective (Pratt & Woolfenden, 2002).

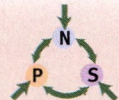

FEEDBACK LOOPS IN TREATMENT: **Eating Disorders**

With all eating disorders, successful treatment should resolve medical crises and normalize eating and nutrition, whether directly or indirectly. For a person with anorexia, this means increasing her eating. Better nutrition means improved brain functioning (neurological factor) and cognitive functioning (psychological factor). For a person with bulimia, it means normalizing her meals—making sure that she is not only eating adequately throughout the day but also getting enough of the various food groups. Eating in this way will decrease the likelihood of extreme hunger, binges, or eating that feels out of control (psychological factor) (Shah et al., 2005).

In most cases, enduring changes in eating arise from changes in the way the individual thinks about food, her beliefs about weight, appearance, femininity, efficacy, and control. These enduring changes may come about, in part, through CBT (psychological factor). In addition, the individual is not isolated from her social context. The support of family and friends and the improved quality of these relationships, which may arise from IPT or family therapy (social factor), can help her reject an overvaluation of appearance, weight, and body shape. Improved family interaction patterns can increase mood and satisfaction with relationships, which can decrease the level of attention that the person pays to cultural pressures toward an ideal body shape (psychological factor). The feedback loops involved in treating eating disorders are shown in Figure 10.8.

Figure 10.8

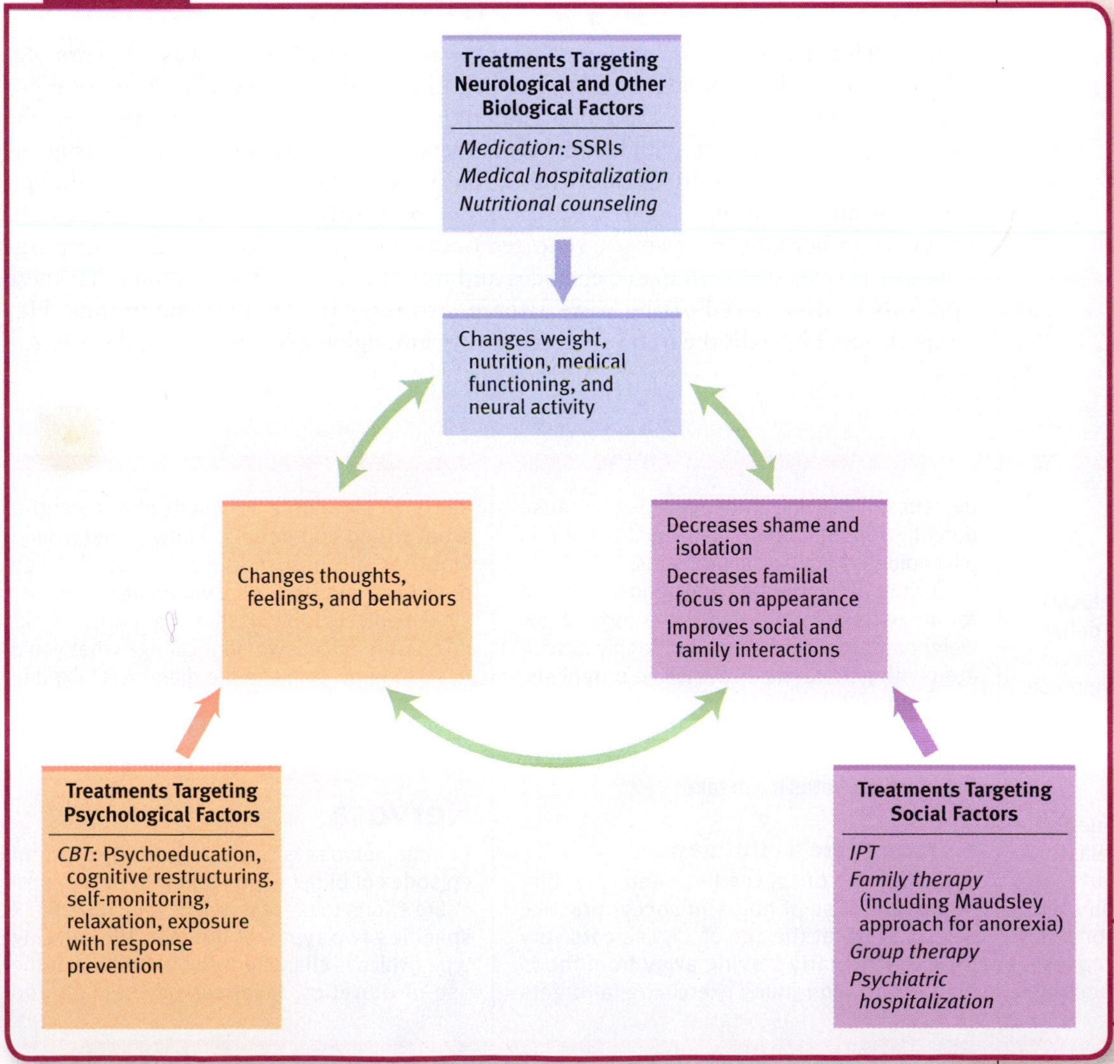

Treatments Targeting Neurological and Other Biological Factors

Medication: SSRIs
Medical hospitalization
Nutritional counseling

Changes weight, nutrition, medical functioning, and neural activity

Changes thoughts, feelings, and behaviors

Decreases shame and isolation
Decreases familial focus on appearance
Improves social and family interactions

Treatments Targeting Psychological Factors

CBT: Psychoeducation, cognitive restructuring, self-monitoring, relaxation, exposure with response prevention

Treatments Targeting Social Factors

IPT
Family therapy (including Maudsley approach for anorexia)
Group therapy
Psychiatric hospitalization

10.8 ▶ Feedback Loops in Treatment: Eating Disorders

Key Concepts and Facts About Treating Eating Disorders

- The treatments that target neurological and other biological factors include:
  - nutritional counseling to improve eating (and can also correct erroneous information about food and weight);
  - medical hospitalization for significant medical problems related to the disorder; and
  - medication to address some symptoms of the eating disorder and of anxiety and depression. Specifically, SSRIs may help prevent relapse in those with anorexia and can decrease symptoms of bingeing and purging in those with bulimia.
- The primary treatment that targets psychological factors is CBT, which is the treatment of choice for eating disorders. CBT addresses maladaptive thoughts, feelings, and behaviors that impede normal eating, promote bingeing and purging, and lead to body image dissatisfaction. CBT may include exposure with response prevention and help patients develop new coping strategies.

- Treatments that target social factors include:
  - interpersonal therapy, which is designed to improve the patient's relationships; as relationships become more satisfying, the eating disorder symptoms diminish;
  - family therapy, particularly the Maudsley approach, which can be helpful for adolescents with anorexia who live at home. Parents figure out how to feed their child, despite her protests, until she eats normally and without a struggle;
  - psychiatric hospitalization, which provides supervised mealtimes to increase normal eating, and a range of therapeutic groups to address various psychological and social factors (such as irrational beliefs about food and weight and social problems), plus individual therapy and possibly medication;
  - prevention programs, which have the goal of preventing eating disorders from developing, particularly in high-risk individuals.

Follow-up on Marya Hornbacher

Marya Hornbacher's first memoir, *Wasted*, was written when she was 23 years old. Within a year of its publication, she was diagnosed with a rapid cycling form of bipolar disorder (see Chapter 6 for a discussion of bipolar disorder). Hornbacher spent the next 10 years struggling with alcohol dependence and bipolar disorder; her struggles are recounted in her subsequent memoir, *Madness: A Bipolar Life* (2008). Although the flagrant symptoms of eating disorders were mostly behind her at the close of *Wasted*, in her later memoir she reported occasional periods of restricting or purging as she struggled with manic episodes and mixed episodes. She recounts that these periods of disordered eating were attempts to regulate her extreme moods. Her experiences highlight the frequent comorbidity among people with eating disorders.

SUMMING UP

Summary of Anorexia Nervosa

The hallmark of anorexia nervosa is a refusal to maintain a healthy weight; DSM-IV-TR defines the weight cutoff as less than 85% of expected body weight. Other criteria include an intense fear of becoming fat or gaining weight, distortions in body image, and amenorrhea. DSM-IV-TR includes two types of anorexia: restricting and binge-eating/purging.

Anorexia can lead to significant medical problems, most importantly muscle wasting (particularly of heart muscle), low heart rate, low blood pressure, loss of bone density, and decreased metabolism. Other symptoms include irritability, headaches, fatigue, and restlessness. All methods of purging—vomiting,

diuretics, laxatives, and enemas—can cause dehydration. Starvation also leads to various psychological and social problems.

Critics of the DSM-IV-TR diagnostic criteria for anorexia point out that the criteria of low weight and amenorrhea are not highly associated with general medical status, prognosis, or outcome. Also, the two types of anorexia—restricting and binge-eating/purging—may better represent stages of the disorder rather than distinct paths it can take.

Thinking like a clinician
Since the age of 12, Lee has been very thin, in part because of hours of soccer practice weekly. Now, at the age of 17, Lee eats very little (particularly staying away from foods high in fat), continues exercising, and gets

angry when people comment about weight. What would you need to know to determine whether Lee has anorexia nervosa? If Lee does have anorexia, what would be some possible medical problems that might arise? What if Lee were male—would it change what you'd need to know to make the diagnosis? Explain your answer.

Summary of Bulimia Nervosa

Bulimia nervosa is characterized by recurrent episodes of binge eating followed by inappropriate efforts to prevent weight gain. DSM-IV-TR specifies two types of bulimia: the purging type (which is characterized by vomiting or the use of diuretics, laxatives or enemas) and the nonpurging type (which involves fasting or excessive exercise). Bulimia is twice as prevalent as anorexia, and much more common among women than men.

All purging methods can cause dehydration, which lead to electrolyte imbalances and possibly death. Chronic vomiting can lead to enlarged parotid and salivary glands, and can erode dental enamel. Chronic laxative use can lead to permanent loss of intestinal functioning.

Aspects of the DSM-IV-TR criteria for a diagnosis of bulimia have been criticized: The definition of "binge eating" is subjective, the purging/nonpurging distinction does not correlate meaningfully with course or prognosis, and bulimia and anorexia do not appear to be distinct disorders but rather may be different phases of the same disorder. Problems with the criteria for anorexia and bulimia are apparent in the prevalence of eating disorder not otherwise specified (EDNOS), which has a higher prevalence than anorexia and bulimia combined. One subset of patients with EDNOS have binge-eating disorder.

Thinking like a clinician

Tanya had been dieting, but after a month or so, she began to pig out toward bedtime. After the first few of these gorging sessions, she felt both physically uncomfortable and ashamed of herself, and she would make herself vomit. After about a week, though, she stopped throwing up; instead she began exercising for about an hour each day. This pattern of daily exercising and pigging out in the evening has persisted for about 6 months. Does Tanya have bulimia nervosa, EDNOS, or just disordered eating but no DSM-IV-TR diagnosis? What were the key factors that determined your answer?

Summary of Understanding Eating Disorders

It is particularly difficult for researchers to establish cause-and-effect relationships among the factors associated with eating disorders because the symptoms themselves—restricting, bingeing, purging, excessive exercise, malnourishment—create neurological (and other biological), psychological, and social changes.

Neurological factors associated with eating disorders include unusually low activity in the frontal, temporal, and parietal lobes, as well as the anterior cingulate cortex, the basal ganglia, and the cerebellum. However, these neural patterns may vary for specific types of anorexia, and may be affected by dieting. Patients with anorexia also have reduced gray

and white matter. People with anorexia and bulimia are not as responsive to serotonin, a neurotransmitter involved in mood, anxiety, and binge eating. Eating disorders tend to run in families and have substantial heritability, which indicates a role for genes.

Psychological factors related to eating disorders include: irrational thoughts and excessive concerns about weight, appearance, and food; binge eating as a result of the abstinence violation effect; positive and negative reinforcement of symptoms of eating disorders (restricting, bingeing, and purging); certain personality traits (perfectionism, harm avoidance, neuroticism, and low self-esteem); disinhibited eating triggered by the last supper effect, especially in restrained eaters; and comorbid disorders in female adolescents, particularly depression.

Social factors related to eating disorders include: Family members and friends who provide a model for eating, concern about weight, and focus on appearance through their own behaviors and responses to others. Cultural factors play a key role, as evidenced by the increased prevalence over time of bulimia and concern about weight that is part of anorexia. Specific cultural factors include a cultural ideal of thinness and repeated exposure—through the media—to this ideal, as well as the individual's assimilation of this ideal.

Thinking like a clinician

Suppose scientists discover genes that are associated with eating disorders. What could—and couldn't—you infer about the role of genetics in eating disorders? How could genes contribute to eating disorders if bulimia is a relatively recent phenomenon? In what ways does the environment influence the development of eating disorders? Why do only some people who are exposed to familial and cultural emphases on weight, food, and appearance develop an eating disorder?

Summary of Treating Eating Disorders

The treatments that target neurological and other biological factors include: nutritional counseling; medical hospitalization for significant medical problems related to the disorder; and medication to address symptoms of the disorder and of anxiety and depression. Specifically, SSRIs may help prevent relapse in those with anorexia and can decrease symptoms of bingeing and purging in those with bulimia.

The primary treatment that targets psychological factors is CBT, which is the

treatment of choice for eating disorders. CBT addresses maladaptive thoughts, feelings, and behaviors that impede normal eating, promote bingeing and purging, and lead to body image dissatisfaction. CBT may include exposure with response prevention and help patients develop new coping strategies.

Treatments that target social factors include IPT, which is designed to improve the patient's relationships; as relationships become more satisfying, the eating disorder symptoms diminish. Family therapy, particularly with the Maudsley approach, can be helpful for adolescents with anorexia who live at home. Psychiatric hospitalization provides supervised mealtimes to increase normal eating and a range of therapeutic groups to address various psychological and social factors. Prevention programs have the goal of preventing eating disorders from developing, particularly in high-risk individuals.

Thinking like a clinician

Suppose your local hospital establishes an eating disorders treatment program. Based on what you have learned in this chapter, what services should they offer, and why? If your friend, who has bulimia nervosa, asked your advice about what type of treatment she should get, how would you respond, and why?

Key Terms

Bulimia nervosa (p. 435)

Anorexia nervosa (p. 435)

Eating disorders (p. 436)

Amenorrhea (p. 437)

Binge eating (p. 439)

Purging (p. 439)

Eating disorder not otherwise specified (EDNOS) (p. 446)

Partial cases (p. 446)

Subthreshold cases (p. 446)

Binge-eating disorder (p. 446)

Abstinence violation effect (p. 451)

Restrained eating (p. 454)

Objectification theory (p. 458)

Maudsley approach (p. 467)

More Study Aids

For additional study aids related to this chapter, go to:
www.worthpublishers.com/rosenberg

Gender and Sexual Disorders

Laura and Mike have been married for a couple of years. They generally get along well, but lately their relationship has been strained. They both work long hours and are tired when they get home. They spend weekends doing household chores or zoning out in front of the television or their computers. Laura and Mike aren't spending much quality time together, and their sex life has become nonexistent. They don't even snuggle with each other in bed anymore and rarely touch each other outside the bed. Their relationship has changed so much since they first started dating, when they were attracted to each other and enjoyed sexual relations. What went wrong, and what can they do to improve their relationship?

By its very nature, human sexuality emerges from a confluence of neuropsychosocial factors. Neurologically, sexuality relies on the actions of hormones and brain activity. Psychologically, sexuality arises from the desire to be sexual with a particular person, in a certain situation, at a specific moment. Fantasies and thoughts, body image, the subjective sense of being male or female—all of these factors and others influence sexuality. Similarly, concerns about reproduction, infertility, or sexually transmitted diseases and past experiences related to sex, such as sexual abuse or rape, also affect an individual's sexuality.

Woody Allen once commented that his favorite part of masturbation was the cuddling afterward. This joke only serves to emphasize that sexuality is ultimately social: It involves relationships. In fact, even during solitary masturbation, someone's thoughts and fantasies usually involve other people. Sexuality is influenced by general emotional satisfaction with a partner, how satisfied the partner has been, the context of a particular sexual encounter, moral and religious teachings about sexuality, and cultural views of appropriate sexual behavior (Malatesta & Adams, 2001). All of these conditions and circumstances are ultimately rooted in social factors.

Abnormalities in sexuality and sexual behavior are also influenced by neuropsychosocial factors. For instance, an individual's brain (and, as a result, his or her body) may not respond to sexual stimuli in the usual way or may respond sexually to stimuli that are not generally considered to be sexual in nature (such as shoes). Similarly, some individuals may have sexual fantasies that disturb them, or they may have difficulties with sexual functioning that lead

Stephen Tunney

Richard B. Levine/Newscom

What is viewed as normal and abnormal sexuality is partly based on the cultural views of appropriate sexual behavior.

Alaska Stock Images

Gender identity
The subjective sense of being male or female, as these categories are defined by the person's culture.

Gender identity disorder
A psychological disorder characterized by a cross-gender identification that leads the individual to be chronically uncomfortable with his or her biological sex.

Gender role
The outward behaviors, attitudes, and traits that a culture deems masculine or feminine.

to distress or problems in their relationships. In addition, families, communities, or cultures determine which sexual fantasies, urges, and behaviors are considered "deviant" or "abnormal." These socially defined sexual "abnormalities" differ across cultures and shift over time. For example, masturbation and oral sex were once considered to be deviant. More recently, homosexuality was considered a psychological disorder until 1973, when it was removed from the DSM. Moreover, like most other psychological problems and disorders, normal and abnormal sexuality and sexual behavior fall on a continuum. However, DSM-IV-TR uses the categorical approach to define sexual disorders; that is, according to DSM-IV-TR, sexual fantasies, urges, and behaviors are either normal or not normal.

As we'll see in this chapter, the diagnosis of most—though not all—sexual disorders in DSM-IV-TR hinges on the patient's experience of distress or impaired functioning as a result of the sexual symptoms (First & Frances, 2008). Simply having unusual or "deviant" sexual fantasies or engaging in unusual sexual behaviors is not generally sufficient for a diagnosis.

The diagnostic criteria for various disorders in the DSM-IV-TR category of sexual and gender disorders address neuropsychosocial factors. That said, some disorders have predominantly neurological and other biological criteria (the *sexual dysfunctions*) whereas others have primarily psychological and social criteria (the *paraphilias* and *gender identity disorder*). Let's examine these disorders.

Gender Identity Disorder

Last year, Mike became confused when his good friend, Sam, began to dress like and live as a woman. In fact, Sam was changing his name to Sandy and would, within the next couple of years, have surgery to acquire female genitals. Sam had dated girls occasionally in high school and seemed "normal," so Mike didn't know how to make sense of Sam's change. Seeing Sam as a woman made Mike uncomfortable, and now they only saw each other occasionally. Mike told Laura about Sam's change to Sandy, but he hasn't told her about his feelings about the change. Mike found himself wondering what life—and sex—had been like for Sam, and what it was like now for Sandy. Mike surfed the Internet for reputable information about Sam's condition, and discovered that it is called *gender identity disorder*.

What Is Gender Identity Disorder?

Like Sam, a small percentage of people who are born one sex (either a biological female or a biological male) do not feel comfortable with their corresponding gender identity. **Gender identity** is the subjective sense of being male or female, as these categories are defined by the person's culture. For instance, there are people like Sam, who have normal male sexual anatomy but *feel* as if they are female. Conversely, there are people with normal female anatomy who feel as if they are male. For people with these feelings, their sense of their gender identity does not correspond to their biological sex, a condition known as *cross-gender identification*. Such individuals are said to have a **gender identity disorder**, a cross-gender identification that leads them to be chronically uncomfortable with their biological sex. People with gender identity disorder are sometimes referred to as *transsexuals*.

People with gender identity disorder usually identify with the opposite biological sex in childhood, preferring to dress or play with toys in ways that are typical of children of the other gender. That is, they wish to behave in accordance with the gender role of the other sex; **gender role** refers to the outward behaviors, attitudes, and traits that a culture deems masculine or feminine. For instance, gender roles for females often allow a wider variety of emotions (anger, tears, and fear) to be displayed in public than do gender roles for males; in contrast, gender roles for males often allow more overtly aggressive or assertive behaviors than do gender roles for females. An individual with gender identity disorder desires to adopt the gender role of the opposite sex not because of perceived cultural advantages of becoming the other sex, but because the opposite gender role is consistent with the person's sense of self.

In children, gender identity disorder is not simply "tomboyishness" in girls or "sissy" behavior in boys. Rather, gender identity disorder reflects a profound sense of identifying with the other sex, to the point of denying one's own sexual organs; moreover, girls with gender identity disorder report that they don't want to develop breasts or menstruate. Most children diagnosed with gender identity disorder, however, do not continue to have the disorder into adulthood, although a sizable number may identify themselves as homosexual when adults (American Psychiatric Association, 2000; Drummond et al., 2008; Green, 1987; Zucker, 2005; Zucker & Bradley, 1995). For instance, studies of boys with gender identity disorder have found that only 2–12% had gender identity disorder as adults. However, 40–80% of boys with gender identity disorder reported being bisexual or homosexual in adulthood (the wide range noted here is due, in part, to the fact that different studies define adult sexuality in different ways); the number of girls with gender identity disorder in childhood who have been followed into adulthood is too small to obtain reliable statistics (Zucker, 2005). Thus, having a diagnosis of gender identity disorder in childhood is generally a poor predictor of the disorder persisting into adulthood. Some have criticized the childhood diagnosis as a way to pathologize early homosexual behavior or interest or a way to label with a mental illness those who don't conform to cultural norms of sex-appropriate behaviors (Hill et al., 2005; Langer & Martin, 2004).

Table 11.1 lists the criteria for gender identity disorder. Among adolescents and adults, symptoms may include discomfort from living publicly as their biological sex. In fact, these individuals may be preoccupied by the wish to *be* the other sex. They may take that wish further and live, at least some of the time, as someone of the other sex—dressing and behaving accordingly, whether at home or in public. Some adults with gender identity disorder have medical and surgical treatments to assume the appearance of the other sex.

Table 11.1 ▶ DSM-IV-TR Diagnostic Criteria for Gender Identity Disorder

A. A strong and persistent cross-gender identification (not merely a desire for any perceived cultural advantages of being the other sex). In adolescents and adults, the disturbance is manifested by symptoms such as a stated desire to be the other sex, frequent passing as the other sex, desire to live or be treated as the other sex, or the conviction that he or she has the typical feelings and reactions of the other sex.

In children, the disturbance is manifested by four (or more) of the following:

(1) repeatedly stated desire to be, or insistence that the person is, the other sex

(2) in boys, preference for cross-dressing or simulating female attire; in girls, insistence on wearing only stereotypical masculine clothing

(3) strong and persistent preferences for cross-sex roles in make-believe play or persistent fantasies of being the other sex

(4) intense desire to participate in the stereotypical games and pastimes of the other sex

(5) strong preference for playmates of the other sex.

B. Persistent discomfort with his or her sex or sense of inappropriateness in the gender role of that sex. In *children*, the disturbance is manifested by any of the following:

- In *boys*, assertion that his penis or testes are disgusting or will disappear or assertion that it would be better not to have a penis, or aversion toward rough-and-tumble play and rejection of male stereotypical toys, games, and activities;

- In *girls*, rejection of urinating in a sitting position, assertion that she has or will grow a penis, or assertion that she does not want to grow breasts or menstruate, or marked aversion toward normative feminine clothing.

In *adolescents* and *adults*, the disturbance is manifested by symptoms such as preoccupation with getting rid of primary and secondary sex characteristics (such as request for hormones, surgery, or other procedures to physically alter sexual characteristics to simulate the other sex) or belief that he or she was born the wrong sex.

C. The disturbance is not concurrent with a physical intersex condition [that is, a condition in which the individual has both male and female physical sexual characteristics].

D. The disturbance causes clinically significant distress or impairment.

Source: Reprinted with permission from the Diagnostic and Statistical Manual of Mental Disorders, Text Revision, Fourth Edition, (Copyright 2000) American Psychiatric Association.

Bless Bless Productions 1998

Teena Brandon was born female, yet felt like a male on the inside and came to live as a man, though without having sex reassignment surgery. As an adult, Brandon was raped and later killed by young men after they discovered that Brandon was biologically female. Brandon's life was the subject of the documentary film *The Brandon Teena Story* and the feature film *Boys Don't Cry*.

Females have a wider range of acceptable "masculine" behavior and dress than males have of acceptable "feminine" behavior and dress. Women can wear men's clothes without risk of being labeled as deviant, whereas men who wear women's clothes (when not as part of a performance) are often considered to have something wrong with them.

The final two DSM-IV-TR criteria require that the symptoms do not arise because the person is an *intersex* individual (someone who was born with both male and female sexual characteristics) and that the symptoms cause significant distress or impair functioning. However, the distress experienced by someone with gender identity disorder often arises because of *other people's responses* to the cross-gender behaviors. For instance, a biological male child with gender identity disorder may be ostracized or made fun of by children or even teachers for consistently "playing girl games"—and thus the child feels distress because of the reactions of others. In contrast, for most disorders in DSM-IV-TR, the distress the individual feels arises directly from the symptoms themselves (e.g., distress that is caused by feeling hopeless, or being afraid in social situations).

Most adolescents and adults with gender identity disorder report having had symptoms of the disorder in childhood (even though most people who had gender identity disorder in childhood do not have it later in life), like the person in Case 11.1. And like Mike's friend Sam, some people with gender identity disorder seek to change their sexual anatomy to match their gender identity; such surgery is called *sex reassignment surgery* (discussed later in the chapter, in the section on treatment).

CASE 11.1 ▶ FROM THE INSIDE: Gender Identity Disorder

In her memoir, *She's Not There: A Life in Two Genders* (2003), novelist and English professor Jenny Finney Boylan (who was born male) describes her experiences feeling, since the age of 3, as if she were a female in a male body:

> Since then, the awareness that I was in the wrong body, living the wrong life, was never out of my conscious mind—*never*, although my understanding of what it meant to be a boy, or a girl, was something that changed over time. Still, this conviction was present during my piano lesson with Mr. Hockenberry, and it was there when my father and I shot off model rockets, and it was there years later when I took the SAT, and it was there in the middle of the night when I woke in my dormitory at Wesleyan. And at every moment I lived my life, I countered this awareness with an exasperated companion thought, namely, Don't be an *idiot*. You're *not* a girl. Get over it.
>
> But I never got over it.
>
> [. . .] By intuition I was certain that the thing I knew to be true was something others would find both impossible and hilarious. My conviction, by the way, had nothing to do with a desire to be *feminine*, but it had everything to do with being *female*. Which is an odd belief for a person born male.

(pp. 19–21)

United Artists/Photofest

Bob Barkany/Getty Images

Most commonly, individuals with gender identity disorder are heterosexual relative to their gender identification. For instance, biological men who see themselves as women tend to be attracted to men, and thus feel as if they are heterosexual (Blanchard, 1989, 1990; Zucker & Bradley, 1995). Others are homosexual relative to their gender identification; a biological woman who sees herself as a man may be sexually attracted to men. However, some people with gender identity disorder are asexual—they have little or no interest in any type of sex.

As noted in Table 11.2 (along with other facts about gender identity disorder), gender identity disorder is about three times more common among biological males as biological females. One explanation for this difference is that in Western cultures, females have a wider range of acceptable "masculine" behavior and dress than males do of acceptable "feminine" behavior and dress. A woman dressed in "men's" clothes might not even get a second look, but a man dressed in "women's" clothes will likely be subjected to ridicule.

Table 11.2 ► Gender Identity Disorder Facts at a Glance

Prevalence

- The prevalence of gender identity disorder is unknown, but believed to be low.

Comorbidity

- In one survey of 31 patients who were diagnosed with gender identity disorder and had not yet begun the process of sex reassignment surgery, almost 75% had another psychiatric disorder at some point in their lives, most often either a mood disorder or a substance-related disorder (Hepp et al., 2005). However, only 39% had comorbid Axis I disorders after they began the sex reassignment process; this finding suggests that the previous high comorbidity was at least partly related to living as a gender that did not correspond to a person's gender identity.

Onset

- Symptoms of cross-gender identity almost always begin in childhood.
- During adolescence, relationships with parents and peers often become particularly strained, and teenagers with gender identity disorder may become depressed (Di Ceglie et al., 2002).

Course

- If symptoms persist into adulthood, they are likely to remain stable, leading many individuals to seek sex reassignment surgery.

Gender Differences

- The incidence of those seeking sex reassignment surgery in some European countries is 1 of every 30,000 males and 1 of every 100,000 females, which suggests that gender identity disorder may be three times more common among males.
- Biological males with this disorder may be rejected by family and peers, may experience physical abuse, substance abuse, prostitution, AIDS, or poverty, and may drop out of school (Seil, 1996).

Cultural Differences

- Cross-gender identification is not considered pathological in all cultures; in some Native American and traditional African cultures, such people have high status and are seen as especially spiritual (Jacobs, Thomas, & Lang, 1997; Langer & Martin, 2004; Roscoe, 1993).

Source: Unless otherwise noted, information is from American Psychiatric Association, 2000.

Criticisms of the DSM-IV-TR Definition

Some critics of the DSM-IV-TR diagnosis of gender identity disorder point out that the criteria don't specify the nature of the "distress" that the disorder causes. As mentioned earlier, with gender identity disorder, distress usually arises because of other people's reactions to the cross-gender behaviors associated with the symptoms (Langer & Martin, 2004). For instance, suppose family members respond negatively—perhaps with anger—to an individual's cross-gender behaviors, even disowning him or her. Understandably, the person might then experience distress or impaired functioning. In this case, the distress or impaired functioning doesn't arise from the symptoms of gender identity disorder; it arises as a (often reasonable) response to the negative reactions of others.

In addition, some critics claim that the concept of gender in DSM-IV-TR is too narrow. Critics also argue that the concept of "appropriate" behavior (especially for males) is too constrained.

Understanding Gender Identity Disorder

We now know that the brains of adults with gender identity disorder are different in some respects from the brains of people who do not have the disorder. Moreover, various psychological and social factors are associated with gender identity disorder. But research so far has not determined whether these factors *contribute* to the disorder or are early manifestations of the disorder. In the following sections we examine these neurological, psychological, and social factors.

Neurological Factors

Researchers know little about neurological factors that contribute to gender identity disorder. However, they have begun to document differences in specific brain structures in people who have the disorder versus those who do not, and have evidence that hormones during fetal development play a role in producing this disorder. In addition, genes can play a large role in contributing to this disorder.

Brain Systems and Neural Communication

The brains of transsexuals differ from typical brains in ways consistent with their gender identity. In particular, Kruijver and colleagues (2000) examined a specific type of neuron in a brain structure called the *bed nucleus of the stria terminalis* (which is often regarded as an extension of the amygdala). Typically, males have almost twice as many of these neurons as females do. In this study, the number of these neurons in the brains of male-to-female transsexuals was in the range typically found in female brains, and the number in the brains of female-to-male transsexuals was in the range typically found in male brains.

How might such brain alterations arise? Research suggests that prenatal exposure to hormones may affect later gender identity (Bradley & Zucker, 1997; Wallien et al., 2008; Zucker & Bradley, 1995). In particular, maternal stress during pregnancy could produce hormones that predispose a person to gender identity disorder (Zucker & Bradley, 1995). In rats, maternal stress raises the level of cortisol in both the pregnant rat and any male pups she is carrying. Such an increase in cortisol can disrupt the timing of prenatal developmental events in a way that leads to low levels of androgen in the fetus and changes certain brain areas (Ward, 1992; Zucker & Bradley, 1995, p. 155). The mother's male pups later exhibit less "male" behavior (less initiation of copulation, less rough play) and more "female" behavior (a sexual posturing typical of female but not male rats). One study found similar results in humans but with a different hormone, testosterone (which underlies many male sexual characteristics): Fetal levels of testosterone—measured from amniotic fluid—were positively associated with later stereotypical "male" play behavior in girls and, to a lesser extent, in boys; the higher the level of testosterone in the fluid, the more "male" play the children exhibited when they were between 6 and 10 years old (Auyeung et al., 2009).

Genetics

A hint that genetic factors contribute to gender identity disorder was reported by Sadeghi and Fakhrai (2000). These researchers described two 18-year-old female identical twins, both of whom had requested sex reassignment surgery. These young women had cross-dressed since childhood and had the hallmarks of gender identity disorder. That same year, Green (2000) reported ten pairs of close relatives (siblings or parent-child pairs) who had in common gender identity disorder. These case reports are intriguing, but they do not carry the force of full-scale studies such as the one conducted by Coolidge and colleagues (2002). These researchers studied 314 children who were either identical or fraternal twins and concluded that as much as 62% of the variance in gender identity disorder can be chalked up to genes! If this result is replicated, it will provide strong support for these researchers' view that the disorder "may be much less a matter of choice and much more a matter of biology" (p. 251). However, even in this study, almost 40% of the variance was ascribed to the effects of nonshared environment, and thus genes—once again—are not destiny.

In short, neurological factors—brain differences, prenatal hormones, and genetic predispositions—may contribute to gender identity disorder, but the presence of any one of these factors does not appear to be sufficient to lead to this disorder (Di Ceglie, 2000).

Psychological Factors: A Correlation With Play Activities?

In general, correlational studies have found that boys are more likely than girls to engage in rough-and-tumble play and to have a higher activity level. Biological boys with gender identity disorder, however, do not have as high an activity level as their counterparts without the disorder. Similarly, biological girls with gender identity disorder are more likely to engage in rough-and-tumble play than are other girls (Bates, Bentler, & Thompson, 1973, 1979; Zucker & Bradley, 1995). Both boys and girls with gender identity disorder are less likely to play with same-sex peers; instead, they seek out, feel more comfortable with, and feel themselves to be more similar to children of the other sex (Green, 1974, 1987). Of course, such findings should be interpreted with caution, for two reasons: (1) These very characteristics are part of the diagnostic criteria for gender identity disorder in children, so it is not at all surprising that these behaviors are correlated with having the disorder; (2) a diagnosis of gender identity disorder in childhood does not usually persist into adulthood. Thus, beyond symptoms that are part of the criteria for gender identity disorder, no psychological factors are clearly associated with the disorder.

Social Factors: Responses From Others

Social factors may be associated with gender identity disorder, but such factors are unlikely to be sufficient to *cause* the disorder (Bradley & Zucker, 1997; Di Ceglie, 2000). Nevertheless, one study found that mothers of boys with gender identity disorder remarked on their sons' physical beauty, which may have led the mothers to interact differently with these sons, treating them more as girls (Zucker et al., 1993). As shown in Figure 11.1(a), college students rated photographs of boys with gender identity disorder as cuter and prettier than photos of boys without the disorder; in contrast, Figure 11.1(b) shows that girls with gender identity disorder were rated as less attractive than girls who did not have the disorder (Zucker et al., 1993). These contrasting ratings of physical appearance may reflect the prenatal influence of hormones: Biological boys may have been exposed to more female hormones in the womb, leading to the feminization of their facial features; conversely, biological girls may have been exposed to more male hormones in the womb, leading to the masculinization of their facial features. In turn, the feminized or masculinized facial features may lead others to interact differently with people who then develop this disorder.

Figure 11.1

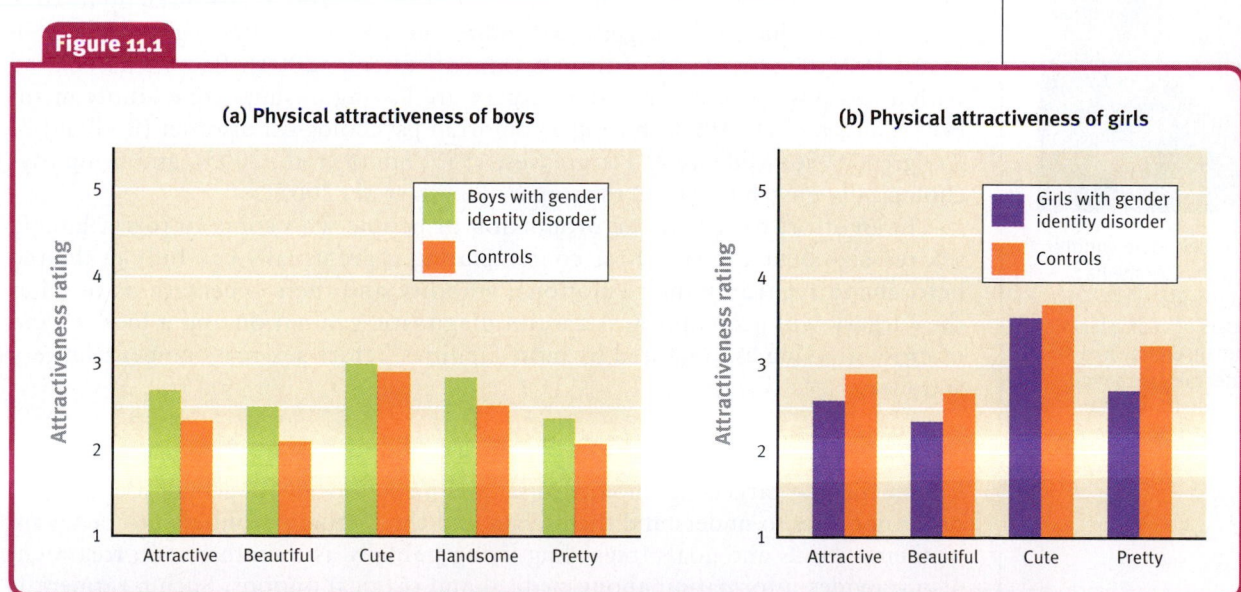

11.1 ▶ Physical Attractiveness Ratings of Children With Gender Identity Disorder
(a) Viewing photographs, college students rated boys with gender identity disorder as more attractive than boys without this disorder. (b) Girls with gender identity disorder were considered to be less attractive than girls who did not have the disorder (Zucker et al., 1993).

Source: Adapted from Zucker & Bradley, 1995.

Given how little is known about the neurological, psychological, and social factors that contribute to gender identity disorder, we cannot comment on the nature of any feedback loops among them.

Treating Gender Identity Disorder

Treatments for gender identity disorder can target neurological (and other biological), psychological, or social factors.

Targeting Neurological and Other Biological Factors: Altered Appearance

One way for people with gender identity disorder to achieve greater congruence between the gender they feel themselves to be and the sex of their bodies is to alter some or all of their biological sexual characteristics. This sort of treatment may involve taking hormones: In biological women, taking androgens (i.e., male sex hormones) will lower the voice, stop menstruation, and begin facial hair growth. In biological men, taking estrogen or progesterone (i.e., female sex hormones) will enlarge breasts, and redistribute fat to the hips and buttocks.

Some people with gender identity disorder go a step further and have **sex reassignment surgery**, a procedure in which the genitals (and breasts, for biological women) are surgically altered to appear like those of the other sex. Sex reassignment surgery for biological males involves creating breasts and removing most of the penis and testes and then creating a clitoris and vagina. For biological females, surgery involves the removal of breasts, ovaries, and uterus and then creating a penis. Patients may also have subsequent surgeries to make their facial features more similar to those of the other sex. These surgical treatments can be prohibitively expensive, however.

Sex reassignment surgery is technically more effective for biological men than for biological women, in part because it is difficult to create an artificial penis that provides satisfactory sexual stimulation (Steiner, 1985). Regardless of biological sex, however, most people who have gender identity disorder are satisfied with the outcome of their sex reassignment surgery, despite possible difficulty in attaining orgasm (Cohen-Kettenis & Gooren, 1999; Smith et al., 2005). However, up to 10% of people who have this surgery (depending on the study) later regret it (Landen et al., 1998; Smith, Van Goozen, & Cohen-Kettenis, 2001). Factors associated with a less positive outcome after surgery are having unsupportive family members (Landen et al., 1998), having a comorbid psychological disorder (Bodlund & Kullgren, 1996; Midence & Hargreaves, 1997; Smith et al., 2005), and being psychologically unstable prior to the surgery (Smith et al., 2005).

In an effort to reduce the proportion of people who come to regret having sex reassignment surgery, those contemplating it are usually carefully evaluated beforehand regarding their emotional stability and their expectations of what the surgery will accomplish. A careful diagnostic evaluation and a long period of cross-dressing are required by most facilities before sex reassignment surgery is done.

Targeting Psychological Factors: Understanding the Choices

Treatment that targets psychological factors helps those with gender identity disorder not only to understand themselves and their situation but also to be aware of their options and goals (regarding living publicly as the other sex); treatment also provides information about medical and surgical options. Such treatment is typically provided by mental health clinicians specially trained in diagnosing and helping people with gender identity disorder. These clinicians also help patients identify and obtain treatment for any other mental health concerns, such as depression or anxiety (Carroll, 2000). For those who choose to live part-time or

Ian Spratt

Caroline Cossey, born Barry Cossey, increasingly felt during adolescence that although she had a male body, she was a female inside. When 20 years old, after a couple of years of taking female hormones and living as a woman, Cossey had sex reassignment surgery and later became a model and actress.

Sex reassignment surgery
The procedure in which an individual's genitals (and breasts, for biological women) are surgically altered to appear like those of the other sex.

full-time as the other sex, the clinician helps them discover whether doing so feels more consistent with how they feel and how they see themselves. Moreover, the clinician helps the patient with problem solving related to living as the other sex—identifying and developing possible solutions to issues that might arise regarding other people's responses.

Targeting Social Factors: Family Support

Family members of those with gender identity disorder may not understand the disorder or know how to be supportive. Educating the family about gender identity disorder and standard family therapy techniques that focus on communication (see Chapter 4) can help family members develop more effective ways to discuss problems.

In addition, groups for people with gender identity disorder can provide support and information. Group therapy may also focus on relationship difficulties or problems that may arise as a result of living as the other sex, such as experiencing sexual harassment for those newly living as a woman, or being taunted by other men for those newly living as a man (Di Ceglie, 2000).

In sum, treatment for gender identity disorder first targets psychological factors—helping individuals determine whether they want to live as the other sex. If they decide to do so, then treatment targeting social factors comes into play, to address problems with family members and interactions with other people in general. Finally, treatment targeting neurological and other biological factors is provided when individuals wish to have medical or surgical procedures.

Key Concepts and Facts About Gender Identity Disorder

- Gender identity disorder is characterized by a persistent cross-gender identification that leads to chronic discomfort with one's biological sex. Symptoms of gender identity disorder often emerge in childhood, but most children diagnosed with the disorder no longer have the disorder by the time they become adults. However, most adults with gender identity disorder report that their symptoms began in childhood.

- In children, symptoms of gender identity disorder include cross-dressing and otherwise behaving in ways typical of the other sex, such as engaging in other-sex types of play, choosing other-sex playmates, and even claiming to be the other sex. In adults, symptoms include persistent and extreme discomfort from living publicly as their biological sex, which leads many to live (at least some of the time) as someone of the other sex.

- Criticisms of the diagnostic criteria in DSM-IV-TR for this disorder point to the overly narrow concept of gender and appropriate behavior (particularly for males) and the ambiguous requirement about distress. With gender identity disorder, the person's distress often arises because of other people's reactions to the cross-gender behaviors.

- Some brain areas in adults with gender identity disorder are more similar to the corresponding brain areas of members of their desired sex than they are to those of their biological sex. Results from animal studies suggest that one explanation for

this disorder is that prenatal exposure to hormones causes the brain to develop in ways more similar to the other sex, although the sexual characteristics of the body are unchanged. Beyond symptoms that are part of the diagnostic criteria for the disorder, no psychological or social factors are clearly associated with the disorder.

- Treatments may target neurological (and other biological), psychological, or social factors:

  - Treatments that target neurological (and other biological) factors include hormone treatments and sex reassignment surgery.

  - Treatments that target psychological factors include psychoeducation, helping the patient choose among gender-related lifestyle options, and problem solving about potential difficulties.

  - Treatments that target social factors include family education, support groups, and group therapy.

Making a Diagnosis

- Reread Case 11.1 about Jenny Boylan, and determine whether or not her symptoms meet the criteria for gender identity disorder. Specifically, list which criteria apply and which do not. If you would like more information to determine whether the diagnosis fits, what information—specifically—would you want, and in what ways would the information influence your decision?

Paraphilias

One of the reasons that Mike was so disturbed about Sam's transformation into Sandy was that it reminded Mike of his secret pastime during his teenage years: He'd secretly "borrow" some of his older sister's clothes from her room, dress up as a girl, and admire himself in front of the mirror. He'd found this extremely erotic, but also terrifying. He worried that he'd get caught and felt that it somehow wasn't "right." Throughout his adulthood, Mike struggled to overcome his urge to dress in women's clothes, usually successfully. During most of his marriage to Laura, he'd managed to keep this urge at bay, and he never told his wife about it. However, once he heard about Sam, his urge became stronger—which affected his relationship with Laura because he thought it best to avoid sexual relations with her until he felt more in control of himself. He'd felt alone in his worries and concerns until he frequented online chat rooms. Now he's spending a lot of time "chatting" with other men who like to cross-dress; he bought some women's clothes (which he kept hidden) and puts them on and masturbates when Laura is out. What's going on with Mike? To find out, we need to consider another category of sexual disorders, called *paraphilias*.

What Are Paraphilias?

Gender identity disorder focuses on the mismatch between an individual's gender identity and biological sex. In contrast, the DSM-IV-TR set of **paraphilias** (from the Greek *para-*, meaning "beside" or "beyond," and *philos*, meaning "fondness" or "love") focuses on "deviant" fantasies, objects, or behaviors that play a role in sexual arousal. Specifically, a paraphilia is characterized by intense recurrent sexual fantasies or urges related to:

- nonconsenting partners or children,
- nonhuman objects (such as women's shoes), or
- suffering or humiliating oneself or one's partner; the diagnosis of a paraphilia would apply only when such experiences are not part of sexual role-playing.

These fantasies, urges, or behaviors together form a predictable pattern of arousal that is consistent for an individual (referred to as an *arousal pattern*). To be considered more than a normal variation in sexual fantasies, urges, or behaviors, this arousal pattern must:

- interfere with the ability for mutual sexual activity involving affection,
- impair functioning in some other way,
- cause significant distress, or
- involve a person who did not consent (as when exhibitionists "flash" unsuspecting strangers).

In addition, the diagnostic criteria for all paraphilias require that the arousal pattern has been present for at least 6 months (American Psychiatric Association, 2000). However, the arousal pattern doesn't necessarily affect all areas of functioning—people with a paraphilia may not be impaired at work or even necessarily in their family life.

Sexuality—both normal and abnormal—is best thought of as being represented by a continuum, but DSM-IV-TR uses a categorical approach, which means drawing a line to separate "normal" from "abnormal." For some paraphilias, DSM-IV-TR draws the line at the point where the sexual arousal pattern causes significant distress or impairs functioning. Someone who becomes aroused in response to pornography or in response to particular items of clothing, for instance, would not be diagnosed as having a paraphilia unless this arousal pattern caused significant distress or impaired functioning.

The specific arousal patterns of the types of paraphilias are listed in Table 11.3, along with their DSM-IV-TR diagnostic criteria. Paraphilic disorders are often classified into two groups: those that involve nonconsenting individuals, and those

Paraphilia
A sexual disorder characterized by deviant fantasies, objects, or behaviors that play a role in sexual arousal.

that involve objects or consenting adults. Paraphilic disorders are almost exclusively diagnosed in men; the only paraphilia observed in a significant percentage of women is *sexual masochism*. Because of the extremely high prevalence of the other paraphilias

Table 11.3 ▸ Paraphilias: An Overview and the DSM-IV-TR Diagnostic Criteria

Disorder	Specific Sexual Fantasies, Urges, or Activities to Enhance Sexual Arousal	DSM-IV-TR Diagnostic Criteria
Exhibitionism	Exposing genitals to an unsuspecting stranger	A. Over a period of at least 6 months, recurrent, intense sexually arousing fantasies, sexual urges, or behaviors involving exposing one's genitals to an unsuspecting stranger. B. The person has acted on these urges, or the sexual urges or fantasies cause marked distress or interpersonal difficulty.
Voyeurism	Observing an unsuspecting person who is disrobing or having sex	A. Over a period of at least 6 months, recurrent, intense sexually arousing fantasies, sexual urges, or behaviors involving the act of observing an unsuspecting person who is naked, in the process of disrobing, or engaging in sexual activity. B. The person has acted on these urges, or the sexual urges or fantasies cause marked distress or interpersonal difficulty.
Frotteurism	Touching or rubbing against a nonconsenting person	A. Over a period of at least 6 months, recurrent, intense sexually arousing fantasies, sexual urges, or behaviors involving touching and rubbing against a nonconsenting person. B. The person has acted on these urges, or the sexual urges or fantasies cause marked distress or interpersonal difficulty.
Pedophilia	Sexual activity with a prepubescent child	A. Over a period of at least 6 months, recurrent, intense sexually arousing fantasies, sexual urges, or behaviors involving sexual activity with a prepubescent child or children (generally age 13 years or younger). B. The person has acted on these urges, or the sexual urges or fantasies cause marked distress or interpersonal difficulty. C. The person is at least age 16 years and at least 5 years older than the child or children in Criterion A.
Sexual Sadism	Inflicting psychological or physical pain on another person	A. Over a period of at least 6 months, recurrent, intense sexually arousing fantasies, sexual urges, or behaviors involving acts (real, not simulated) in which the psychological or physical suffering (including humiliation) of the victim is sexually exciting to the person. B. The person has acted on these urges with a nonconsenting person, or the sexual urges or fantasies cause marked distress or interpersonal difficulty.
Sexual Masochism	Being humiliated, bound, or made to suffer in other ways	A. Over a period of at least 6 months, recurrent, intense sexually arousing fantasies, sexual urges, or behaviors involving the act (real, not simulated) of being humiliated, beaten, bound, or otherwise made to suffer. B. The fantasies, sexual urges, or behaviors cause clinically significant distress or impairment in functioning.
Fetishism	Using a nonliving object to become aroused	A. Over a period of at least 6 months, recurrent, intense sexually arousing fantasies, sexual urges, or behaviors involving the use of nonliving objects (such as female undergarments). B. The fantasies, sexual urges, or behaviors cause clinically significant distress or impairment in functioning. C. The fetish objects are not limited to articles of female clothing used in cross-dressing (as in Transvestic Fetishism, below) or devices designed for the purpose of tactile genital stimulation (such as a vibrator).
Transvestic Fetishism	Cross-dressing (dressing in clothes of the other gender for sexual arousal)	A. Over a period of at least 6 months, in a heterosexual male, recurrent, intense sexually arousing fantasies, sexual urges, or behaviors that involve cross-dressing. B. The fantasies, sexual urges, or behaviors cause clinically significant distress or impair functioning.

Paraphilias include deviant sexual fantasies, urges, and activities that can be classified into three types: Those that involve nonconsenting partners or children (in **purple**); those that involve suffering or humiliating oneself or a partner (in **gray**); and those that involve nonhuman animals or objects (in **yellow**). Note that sexual sadism involves nonconsenting people. Nonetheless, DSM-IV-TR groups sexual sadism with sexual masochism, rather than with the other paraphilias that involve nonconsenting people. Note also that the specifics of Criterion B—distress, impaired functioning, interpersonal problems, or acting on the sexual fantasies and urges—vary across the paraphilic disorders, depending in part on the whether the disorder involves nonconsenting individuals.

Source: Adapted from American Psychiatric Association, 2000; McAnulty, Adams, & Dillon, 2001, p. 751. For more information see the Permissions section.

among men, in this section we use the masculine pronouns (e.g., *him*) when discussing patients with these disorders. (In the section on understanding paraphilias, we will examine possible reasons for this extreme gender difference.)

Mental health researchers believe that, based on the number of Web sites and online chat rooms, the prevalence of paraphilic disorders is higher than had been previously thought, but the actual prevalence is unknown. Most research on paraphilias has been conducted with men whose disorders involve nonconsenting individuals (such as child molesters, rapists, and exhibitionists) and who have come to the attention of mental health clinicians and researchers through the criminal justice system or at the urging of family members. We examine that type of paraphilias first.

Paraphilias Involving Nonconsenting Individuals

The common feature of the paraphilic disorders discussed in this section is that the person with the disorder has sexual fantasies, urges, or behaviors that involve nonconsenting individuals—children in the case of pedophilia. Specifically, if the patient has recurrent fantasies or urges involving a nonconsenting person *but does not act on them*, a diagnosis of the paraphilic disorder is given only if the fantasies and urges cause significant distress or interpersonal difficulties. In contrast, if the man did act on those recurrent fantasies and urges with a nonconsenting individual, the diagnosis would be made, even if the patient did not experience distress or other interpersonal difficulties. For instance, someone who "flashes" others, who molests children, or who sadistically sexually assaults victims would be diagnosed with a paraphilic disorder if the duration criterion (at least 6 months) for the behavior were met.

Thus, men who engage in some criminal sexual behaviors could qualify for the diagnosis of a paraphilia, which creates confusion about what constitutes criminal behavior versus mental illness. However, psychiatrists who helped to create the diagnostic criteria for paraphilias in DSM-IV-TR point out that they never intended to allow paraphilias to be diagnosed solely on the basis of sexual *behaviors*, because doing so "blurs the distinction between mental disorder and ordinary criminality" (First & Frances, 2008, p. 1240). This problem is likely to be addressed in the next edition of the DSM, DSM-V.

Exhibitionism: Physically Exposing Oneself

The paraphilia **exhibitionism** is characterized by sexual fantasies, urges, or behaviors that hinge on a person's exposing his genitals to a stranger, usually as a surprise (see Table 11.3). Moreover, to be considered a disorder, the man must either experience distress or relationship problems as a result of the fantasies and urges or have actually exposed himself. People who expose themselves for money (such as nude dancers or artists' models) are not considered exhibitionists because they do so for compensation, not for sexual arousal (McAnulty, Adams, & Dillon, 2001).

A man with exhibitionism typically gets an erection and may masturbate while exposing himself. Men with this disorder commonly report that they don't intend to frighten or shock strangers, but hope that strangers will enjoy or be aroused by seeing their genitals (Lang et al., 1987; Langevin et al., 1979). Men with exhibitionism may rehearse beforehand; they may achieve orgasm during the exhibitionistic episode or later, when they think about it. One study found that, over the course of his life, the typical man with this disorder had "flashed" an average of 514 people (Abel et al., 1987). (However, some very active men skew the average; the median number of people flashed is 34.) Case 11.2 examines one man's experience.

CASE 11.2 ▸ FROM THE OUTSIDE: Exhibitionism

Tom was a 39-year-old married businessman who was referred for . . . assessment because of persistent dependence on phone sex, video pornography, and compulsive masturbation despite relapse prevention sex offender group therapy and individual psychodynamic psychotherapy. Tom had been arrested for exhibitionism 2 years before as well and was on probation. In an attempt to control his urges to expose himself, he had made a behavioral contract with

Exhibitionism
A paraphilic disorder in which sexual fantasies, urges, or behaviors hinge on exposing one's genitals to a stranger, usually as a surprise.

his wife that he would immediately tell her if he had urges to expose himself or if he had done so. He had agreed to take a lie detector test any time she requested it. He had a signed agreement with his wife that he would live separately from her if his exhibitionism relapsed. He reported that this behavioral contracting intervention was helpful in assisting him to refrain from exposing himself, but had not stopped his [other compulsive sexual behaviors]. He also still had recurrent urges to expose himself as well. He reported that his hypersexual fantasies, urges, and activities distracted him for 1 to 2 hours a day although he currently denied a high frequency of genital/sexual behavior.

(Kafka, 2000, pp. 493–494)

Voyeurism: Watching Others

Voyeurism is the paraphilia characterized by sexual fantasies, urges, or behaviors that involves *observing* someone who is in the process of undressing, is nude, or is engaged in sexual activity. The person being watched has neither consented to nor is aware of being observed (see Table 11.3). As with exhibitionism, for voyeurism to be a disorder, the person's urges and fantasies must cause distress or relationship problems, or the person must have acted on those fantasies and urges.

The voyeur rarely has physical contact with the observed person. Moreover, voyeurism is distinguished from looking at pornography or watching nude dancing; voyeurism involves observing someone *who does not know that he or she is being observed*. A man with this disorder might use binoculars to "spy" on a woman, masturbating while observing her through her window as she undresses, or might plant hidden cameras and watch the video later or via an Internet feed.

David Young-Wolff/Photo Edit

People with voyeurism tend not to have physical contact with the people they observe.

Frotteurism: Touching a Stranger

Frotteurism (from the French, *frotter*, "to rub") is characterized by recurrent, intense, sexually arousing fantasies, sexual urges, or behaviors that involve touching or rubbing against a nonconsenting person (see Table 11.3). As with exhibitionism and voyeurism, the urges and fantasies must cause distress or relationship problems, or the man must have acted on those fantasies and urges. This diagnosis has two types: men who like to rub, and men who like to touch ("touchers"). On crowded public transportation, men with frotteurism try to stand or sit next to attractive females and rub their genitals against the victims' buttocks, thighs, or crotch, often while fantasizing that they are having consensual sex, as Charles, in Case 11.3, did. When discovered, men with frotteurism flee from the train or bus.

CASE 11.3 ▶ FROM THE OUTSIDE: Frotteurism

Charles was 45 when he was referred for psychiatric consultation by his parole officer following his second arrest for rubbing up against a woman in the subway. According to Charles, he had a "good" sexual relationship with his wife of 15 years when he began, 10 years ago, to touch women in the subway. A typical episode would begin with his decision to go into the subway to rub against a woman, usually in her 20s. He would select the woman as he walked into the subway station, move in behind her, and wait for the train to arrive at the station. He would be wearing plastic wrap around his penis so as not to stain his pants after ejaculating while rubbing up against his victim. As riders moved on to the train, he would follow the woman he had selected. When the door closed, he would begin to push his penis up against her buttocks, fantasizing that they were having intercourse in a normal, noncoercive manner. In about half the episodes, he would ejaculate and then go on to work. If he failed to ejaculate, he would either give up for that day or change trains and select another victim. According to Charles, he felt guilty immediately after each episode, but would soon find himself ruminating about and anticipating the next encounter. He estimated that he had done this about twice a week for the last 10 years and thus had probably rubbed up against approximately a thousand women.

(Spitzer et al., 2002, pp. 164–165)

Voyeurism
A paraphilia characterized by sexual fantasies, urges, or behaviors that involve observing someone who is in the process of undressing, is nude, or is engaged in sexual activity, when the person being observed has neither consented to nor is aware of being observed.

Frotteurism
A paraphilia characterized by recurrent, intense, sexually arousing fantasies, sexual urges, or behaviors that involve touching or rubbing against a nonconsenting person.

Pedophilia: Sexually Abusing Children

Child sexual abuse is a crime, but the DSM-IV-TR diagnosis for those who fantasize about, have urges, or actually engage in sexual activity with a child (typically one who has not yet gone through puberty) is **pedophilia** (see Table 11.3). For this diagnosis, the person with pedophilia must be at least 16 years old, and at least 5 years older than the child. Thus, someone is diagnosed with pedophilia if he has had sexual activity with a child (and so would also be considered a *child molester*) *or* if he has sexual fantasies about or urges to do so and these impulses significantly impair his relationships or cause distress. Someone with pedophilia may or may not sexually molest children; a child molester may or may not be diagnosed with pedophilia, depending on the duration of the related fantasies, urges, or behaviors (Camilleri & Quinsey, 2008).

The sexual behaviors range from fondling to oral-genital contact to penetration. Approximately 25% of victims (who are more likely to be girls than boys; McAnulty et al., 2001) are under 6 years of age, 25% are between 6 and 10 years old, and 50% are between 11 and 13 (Erickson, Walbeck, & Seely, 1988). People with pedophilia often say that they believe that adult sexual contact with children has positive effects for the child. Compared to rapists, people with pedophilia who have molested children view themselves as less responsible for the abuse and view the child as more responsible (Stermac & Segal, 1989)—claiming that the child "seduced" them. In fact, some child molesters with pedophilia report that they didn't think they were harming the children they molested, but were "sharing pleasure" (Spitzer et al., 2002). Studies suggest that men with pedophilia who are sex offenders are likely to have at least one other paraphilia (Heil & Simons, 2008; Raymond et al., 1999).

Pedophilia often begins in adolescence, and it tends to be a chronic condition. The relapse rate for pedophiles drawn to boys is twice that of those drawn to girls (American Psychiatric Association, 2000). Although pedophilia typically involves sexual behavior with a minor, the disorder may be limited to fantasies, viewing pornography, or voyeurism directed toward minors.

Note that not all sexual abuse of children occurs because of a consistent sexual arousal pattern: Children may be sexually abused because the abuser has another sort of psychological disorder, such as a substance abuse problem (often alcohol, which as we saw in Chapter 9 can disinhibit behavior), or the sexual abuse is an act of aggression (Dorr, 1998; Fagan et al., 2002; Marshall, 1997). (The effects of child sexual abuse and other forms of child maltreatment are discussed in Chapter 2.)

Sexual Sadism and Sexual Masochism: Pain and Humiliation

Sexual sadism and sexual masochism are two complementary sides of a mode of sexual interaction in which pain, suffering, or humiliation creates or enhances sexual excitement. People who do not experience significant distress or interpersonal problems because of their sadistic or masochistic sexual fantasies, urges, and behavior and whose sexual partners are consenting adults would not be diagnosed with either of these disorders. Let's examine the DSM-IV-TR criteria for these two disorders.

Sexual Sadism: Inflicting the Pain

A person who feels sexually aroused by fantasies, urges, and behaviors that inflict physical or psychological suffering on another person is said to have **sexual sadism** (see Table 11.3). Note that sexual sadism involves *real* acts that cause someone else to suffer (versus simulated acts, where no real suffering occurs). There are two sets of circumstances in which someone would be diagnosed with sexual sadism: (1) The recurrent sadistic fantasies or urges cause the individual significant distress, such as occurs when a man is horrified to discover that he is consistently aroused when fantasizing about hurting his partner; or (2) the individual has repeatedly subjected a nonconsenting partner to sexually sadistic acts (as occurs with sadistic rape)—such behavior is also a criminal act.

Pedophilia
A paraphilia characterized by recurrent sexually arousing fantasies, sexual urges, or behaviors involving a child who has not yet gone through puberty (typically aged 13 or younger).

Sexual sadism
A paraphilia characterized by recurrent sexually arousing fantasies, urges, and behaviors that inflict physical or psychological suffering on another person.

Any type of rape is a criminal act; sadistic rape—while criminal—is also a type of sexual sadism, as defined in DSM-IV-TR. What distinguishes sadistic rape from other forms of rape is that in the former the offender becomes sexually aroused by gratuitous violence or the victim's suffering or humiliation (Heil & Simons, 2008). In contrast, nonsadistic rape occurs when the rapist uses force in order to get his victim to "comply," but not because such force is a critical element of his sexual arousal pattern (Yates, Hucker, & Kingston, 2008).

For those diagnosed with sexual sadism, the sadistic sexual fantasies were often present in childhood, and the sadistic behavior commonly began in early adulthood—as occurred with the man in Case 11.4. Sexual sadism is usually chronic, and the severity of the sadistic behaviors increases over time (American Psychiatric Association, 2000).

CASE 11.4 ▶ FROM THE OUTSIDE: Sexual Sadism

A physician, raised alone by his widowed mother since age 2, has been preoccupied with spanking's erotic charge for him since age 6. Socially awkward during adolescence and his 20s, he married the first woman he dated and gradually introduced her to his secret arousal pattern of imagining himself spanking women. Although horrified, she episodically agreed to indulge him on an infrequent schedule to supplement their frequent ordinary sexual behavior. He ejaculated only when imagining spanking. Following her sixth episode of anxious, sullen depression in 20 years of marriage, her psychologist instructed her to tell him "No more." He fell into despair, was diagnosed with a major depressive disorder, and wrote a long letter to her about why he was entitled to spank her. He claimed to have had little idea that her participation in this humiliation was negatively affecting her mental health ("She even had orgasms sometimes after I spanked her!"). He became suicidal as a solution to the dilemma of choosing between his or her happiness and becoming conscious that what he was asking was abusive. He was shocked to discover that she had long considered suicide as a solution to her marital trap of loving an otherwise good husband and father who had an unexplained sick sexual need.

(Sadock & Sadock, 2007, pp. 709–710)

Sexual Masochism: Receiving the Pain

Whereas sexual sadism involves hurting others, **sexual masochism** is characterized by recurrent sexual arousal in response to fantasies, urges, or behaviors related to being hurt—specifically, being humiliated or made to suffer in other ways (see Table 11.3; American Psychiatric Association, 2000). Moreover, for a diagnosis of sexual masochism, the sexual fantasies, urges, and behavior must cause significant distress or impair functioning.

Sexual masochism is diagnosed in both men and women and is, in fact, the only paraphilia that occurs at measurable rates among women (Levitt, Moser, & Jamison, 1994). One study found that about a quarter of women who engage in sexually masochistic behavior reported a history of sexual abuse during childhood, which suggests that the abuse made them more likely to be aroused by masochistic acts (Nordling, Sandnabba, & Santtila, 2000). However, these women did not necessarily have sexual masochism, because they did not report distress or impaired functioning because of their sexual preferences.

Some people with sexual masochism inflict the pain or humiliation on themselves, whereas others rely on someone else to do this to them. Some people with sexual masochism may also have sexual sadism, alternating the role they assume. They may also have fetishism or transvestic fetishism, which we discuss next.

Paraphilias Involving Nonhuman Objects

Two paraphilic disorders—fetishism and transvestic fetishism—are characterized by persistent sexual fantasies, urges, and behaviors that focus on nonhuman animals or objects, such as clothing, which lead to significant distress or impair functioning.

Sexual masochism
A paraphilia in which the individual repeatedly becomes sexually aroused by fantasies, urges, or behaviors related to being hurt—specifically, being humiliated or made to suffer in other ways—and this arousal pattern causes significant distress or impairs functioning.

Newscom

The hallmark of the paraphilia fetishism is being sexually aroused by inanimate objects, such as footwear or mannequins.

Fetishism
A paraphilia in which the individual repeatedly uses nonliving objects to achieve or maintain sexual arousal and such an arousal pattern causes significant distress or impairs functioning.

Transvestic fetishism
A paraphilia in which a heterosexual man cross-dresses in women's clothes for sexual arousal and experiences distress or impaired functioning because of the cross-dressing; formerly called *transvestism*.

Fetishism: Sexually Arousing Objects

Fetishism is the paraphilia characterized by the repeated use of nonliving objects, such as women's shoes or undergarments, in sexual fantasies, urges, or behaviors, which in turn leads to distress or impaired functioning (see Table 11.3). The object—termed a *fetish*—may be used to achieve sexual arousal or to maintain an erection with a partner or alone. For instance, a man with a shoe fetish will become aroused by seeing or smelling women's footwear. He may steal women's shoes and use them to masturbate (Shiah et al., 2006). When fetishism is severe, he may be unable to have sexual relations with a partner unless the fetish is part of the sexual experience. When the fetish is a nonsexual body part, such as a foot, the paraphilia may be referred to as *partialism*. The DSM-IV-TR definition of fetishism, however, does not include partialism (and so a foot fetish is technically classified as a paraphilia not otherwise specified).

A survey of hospital discharge summaries of men with fetishism (Chalkley & Powell, 1983) found that:

- 60% preferred items of clothing (as did the man in Case 11.5);
- 25% were aroused by items of rubber;
- 15% were aroused by footwear;
- 15% had partialism; and
- 37% regularly stole items of their preferred fetish.

People with fetishism generally come to the attention of mental health professionals only after being apprehended for the theft of their fetish.

CASE 11.5 ▶ FROM THE OUTSIDE: Fetishism

A single, 32-year-old male free-lance photographer presented with the chief complaint of "abnormal sex drive." The patient related that although he was somewhat sexually attracted by women, he was far more attracted by "their panties" . . . His first ejaculation occurred at 12 via masturbation to fantasies of women wearing panties. He masturbated into his older sister's panties, which he had stolen without her knowledge. Subsequently he stole panties from her friends and other women he met socially. He found pretexts to "wander" into bedrooms of women during social occasions, and would quickly rummage through their possessions until he found a pair of panties to his satisfaction. He later used these to masturbate into and then "saved them" in a "private cache." The pattern of masturbating into women's underwear had been his preferred method of achieving sexual excitement and orgasm from adolescence until the present consultation . . . he felt anxious and depressed because his social life was limited by his sexual preference.

(Spitzer et al., 2002, p. 247)

Transvestic Fetishism: Cross-Dressing for Sexual Arousal

Formerly called *transvestism*, **transvestic fetishism** is the diagnosis given to heterosexual men who cross-dress in women's clothes for sexual arousal and experience distress or impaired functioning because of it (Table 11.3), as Mike did. (Note that this is in contrast to men with gender identity disorder, who dress as women *not* for sexual arousal but to make their outward appearance more congruent with their internal experience; see Table 11.4.) Moreover, men with transvestic fetishism use female clothing differently than those with a nontransvestic fetish that involves female apparel, such as an underwear fetish. Men with a nontransvestic fetish may wear female clothes to achieve sexual arousal, but only if the clothes were previously worn by a woman; they do not try to appear female, as Jenny Boylan, in Case 11.1, did. In contrast, men with transvestic fetishism wear *new* female clothes and try to appear as female, as Mike did.

Transvestic fetishism usually begins in childhood; most men with this disorder began cross-dressing before age 10. As adults, the cross-dressing usually is not limited to the privacy of the home: Almost three quarters of men with this disorder who

Table 11.4 ▶ Transvestic Fetishism Versus Gender Identity Disorder

Transvestic Fetishism	Gender Identity Disorder
Gender identity same as biological sex	Gender identity opposite of biological sex
Comfortable with own biological sex	Want to be the other sex
Cross-dress for sexual arousal or to feel "calmer"	Cross-dress for congruence between appearance and gender identity

were surveyed reported that they had appeared in public while dressed as women. Almost two thirds are married, often with children; you may assume that they hide their fetish from their wives, but as with Mr. A., in Case 11.6, the wives often know about the cross-dressing. Most wives are ambivalent about it, and less than a third accept it (Docter & Prince, 1997).

CASE 11.6 ▶ FROM THE OUTSIDE: Transvestic Fetishism

Mr. A., [is] a 65-year-old security guard [married and with grown children], formerly a fishing-boat captain. . . . His first recollection of an interest in female clothing was putting on his sister's [underwear] at age 12, an act accompanied by sexual excitement. He continued periodically to put on women's underpants—an activity that invariably resulted in an erection, sometimes a spontaneous emission, and sometimes masturbation, but was never accompanied by fantasy. Although he occasionally wished to be a girl, he never fantasized himself as one. He was competitive and aggressive with other boys and always acted "masculine." During his single years he was always attracted to girls, but was shy about sex. Following his marriage at age 22, he had his first heterosexual intercourse.

His involvement with female clothes was of the same intensity even after his marriage. Beginning at age 45, after a chance exposure to a magazine called *Transvestia*, he began to increase his cross-dressing activity. He learned there were other men like himself, and he became more and more preoccupied with female clothing in fantasy and progressed to periodically dressing completely as a woman. . . . Over time [his cross-dressing] has become less eroticized and more an end in itself, but it still is a source of some sexual excitement. He always has an increased urge to dress as a woman when under stress; it has a tranquilizing effect. If particular circumstances prevent him from cross-dressing, he feels extremely frustrated.

(Spitzer et al., 2002, pp. 257–258)

Assessing Paraphilic Disorders

The paraphilias are usually assessed by examining neurological (sometimes reflected by bodily responses), psychological, or social factors. Sexual arousal in men can be measured by a *penile plethysmograph*, which is an indirect measure of neurological events. The device is placed on a man's penis and measures penile rigidity. The man is then shown "normal" and "deviant" stimuli (such as photos of footwear or whips), and the rigidity of the penis is measured after each stimulus is presented. If the plethysmograph registers unusual amounts of arousal when the man views deviant stimuli, compared to stimuli that induce arousal in men without a paraphilia, this response suggests that he has a paraphilia.

In addition, researchers have recorded brain electrical activity while "normal" heterosexual men and men with paraphilias viewed "normal" erotic, "deviant" erotic (such as typical fetish objects), or neutral stimuli (such as a street scene). Men with paraphilias showed greater activation in the left frontal lobe (which typically reflects the presence of an "approach emotion," Davidson, 2002) when viewing deviant erotic stimuli than men without paraphilias, but men without paraphilias showed greater activation in the right parietal lobe when viewing normal erotic stimuli (which may reflect increased attention or other visual processing; Waismann et al., 2003).

Self-reports of arousal (psychological factor) are also used to assess paraphilic disorders: Men describe what they find sexually arousing, either to a mental health clinician or in response to a questionnaire. Finally, assessment of paraphilias may rely on reports from partners or the criminal justice system (social factor), when men are apprehended for engaging in illegal sexual activity such as exhibitionism or pedophilia (McAnulty, Adams, & Dillon, 2001).

Criticisms of the DSM-IV-TR Paraphilias

Critics of the set of paraphilic disorders identified in DSM-IV-TR point out that such disorders are, in essence, behaviors and fantasies that Western culture currently labels as "deviant"; such deviance is relative to the current cultural concept of "normal" sexual behavior or fantasies (Moser & Kleinplatz, 2005). Normal sexual behavior typically has been defined by the church, the government, or the medical community. Moreover, labeling certain sexual behaviors or urges as deviant has been done throughout history, although the specific behaviors or urges have varied across cultures and over time. For instance, homosexuality, masturbation, and oral sex have at various points in time in various cultures been considered unacceptable deviations from normal sexuality. Sexual deviations have been considered sinful, criminal, or sick, and the responses to such deviations have included penitence, punishment, or "cure" (McAnulty, Adams, & Dillon, 2001; Moser, 2001).

However, we must stress that, according to DSM-IV-TR, the issue isn't simply having unusual sexual interests, but rather that these interests or their related behaviors cause significant distress or significantly impair functioning (Moser, 2009).

Another criticism is that some sex crimes are included as just another type of paraphilia. Such crimes that may meet the criteria for a paraphilia include exhibitionism, voyeurism, frotteurism, pedophilia, and sexual sadism. As one researcher in the field points out:

> Some sex crimes are not diagnoses (e.g., rape) and some Paraphilia diagnoses are not crimes (e.g., Fetishism, Sexual Masochism, consensual Sexual Sadism, and Transvestic Fetishism). Some sexual interests were both crimes and diagnoses, but are no longer (e.g., homosexuality). . . . Some sexual behaviors were psychiatric disorders and were believed to cause a variety of physical disorders, but are now considered healthy (e.g., masturbation). . . . What is defined as "normal" sexual behavior, what is a mental disorder, what is a crime, and what constitutes a sex crime do change over time.
>
> (Moser, 2009, p. 324)

Including such a large range of diverse disorders limits the kinds of generalizations that can be made about the paraphilias. Specifically, the diagnosis of some of the paraphilias depends on the fact that the object of desire does not consent to the sexual interaction, whereas others paraphilias do not involve coercion—and may not involve another person at all.

And even among patients with paraphilias that are directed toward nonconsenting victims, we can further distinguish distinct groups of patients. For instance, some patients prefer normal sexual activity but have deviant fantasies of coercing others, which cause them distress; in contrast, other patients meet the criteria solely because of their behavior (that is, they may molest children or sadistically rape someone), but they may not feel any distress about this behavior. Both types of individuals would be diagnosed with a paraphilic disorder directed toward nonconsenting partners (McAnulty, Adams, & Dillon, 2001).

Similarly, DSM-IV-TR does not take into consideration how well an individual can overcome his urges and *not* engage in a paraphilic behavior. The capacity to restrain the behavior should be particularly important with paraphilias that involve nonconsenting partners. A man may have fantasies of exposing himself or fondling a child, but if he is always able to restrain himself from acting out those fantasies, he is not a danger to anyone; nevertheless, if his fantasies and urges cause him distress or impair his ability to function, he would be diagnosed with pedophilia.

Finally, as we discuss in the following section, some researchers have suggested that paraphilias should be considered a type of obsessive-compulsive disorder (OCD).

Understanding Paraphilias

Researchers are only just beginning to learn why paraphilias emerge and persist, and not enough is known to understand how feedback loops might arise among neurological, psychological, and social factors. However, some facts related to these factors—and their interactions—have been reported, including neurological similarities to OCD and the role of classical conditioning in sexual arousal.

Neurological Factors

Many theorists who have considered the neurological underpinnings of paraphilias have noted the apparent similarities between these disorders and OCD, both of which involve obsessions and compulsions. As discussed in Chapter 7, OCD appears to arise from abnormal functioning in a neural system that includes the basal ganglia (which play a central role in producing automatic, repetitive behaviors) and the frontal lobes (which normally inhibit such behaviors). In fact, researchers found that people with pedophilia have very specific cognitive deficits when performing tasks that rely on this neural system (Tost et al., 2004). For example, these patients were strikingly impaired in inhibiting responses and in working memory—both of which rely heavily on the frontal lobes (Smith & Kosslyn, 2006).

In addition, evidence suggests that the neurotransmitters that are used in this neural system, such as dopamine and serotonin, do not function properly in people who have paraphilias (Kafka, 2003). Indeed, SSRIs decrease the sexual fantasies and behaviors related to paraphilias, which is consistent with the view that neural interactions involved in OCD are also involved in the paraphilias (Abouesh & Clayton, 1999; Bradford, 2001; Kafka & Hennen, 2000; Roesler & Witztum, 2000).

Finally, there is a hint that genes contribute to the paraphilic disorders. For example, researchers have identified monozygotic twins who have both paraphilias and OCD (Cryan, Butcher & Webb, 1992). In addition, researchers have found that paraphilias have a slight tendency to run in families; moreover, pedophilia occurs more frequently in families in which a member has pedophilia than in families in which members have another sort of paraphilia (Gaffney, Lurie, & Berlin, 1984). If such findings are replicated, they would suggest that distinct sets of genes contribute to pedophilia.

Psychological Factors: Conditioned Arousal

Both psychodynamic and cognitive-behavioral theories have been invoked to explain paraphilias, but research to date does not generally support either type of explanation (Osborne & Wise, 2005). Behavioral theory, though, can answer one intriguing question about paraphilias: Why are almost all people with paraphilias male? One contributing factor may simply stem from male physiology: The position of the penis and testicles on the body can easily lead to their being inadvertently stimulated (Munroe & Gauvain, 2001); this is important because such stimulation can result in classical conditioning.

Classical conditioning principles can explain how certain objects or situations come to produce sexual arousal in general, and paraphilias in males in particular (Domjan, Cusato, & Krause, 2004; Köksal et al., 2004). Consider this example: A fetish for objects such as women's shoes can develop when an unconditioned stimulus that led to sexual arousal became paired with a conditioned stimulus (women's shoes). Thus, a boy who coincidentally saw his mother's shoes before—intentionally or accidentally—touching his penis may come to have a conditioned response of sexual arousal to women's shoes in the future. Moreover, the pleasurable consequence of arousal and possible orgasm provides positive reinforcement (Laws & Marshall, 1991). And, as discussed in Chapter 2, classical conditioning alters neural communication so that neurons that store particular associations come to fire together more easily. In fact, humans—or at least human males—may be biologically prepared to develop classically conditioned sexual arousal to some situations or objects (Osborne & Wise, 2005), which would explain why a pillow fetish is not a common fetish.

Punchstock/Photodisc

Some men who fought in World War II developed what would be considered a paraphilia: These men, who were in their formative years during the war, spent time with women who wore gas masks and bathrobes, and such attire became a sexual turn-on for the men (Kaplan, 1991).

Classical conditioning may be amplified by the *Zeigarnik effect* (Deutsch, 1968), which makes people more likely both to recall interrupted activities than ones that they finished and to try to complete interrupted activities when later allowed to do so. Applied to paraphilias, sexual arousal that has been associated with an object or situation may be such an interrupted activity: Sexual arousal at a young age that isn't allowed expression at that time becomes "interrupted"; the person is later driven to "complete" the interrupted activity. A sexual Zeigarnik effect is more likely to occur in males because of the nature of male anatomy, thus accounting for the predominance of men among those with paraphilias (Munroe & Gauvain, 2001).

Social Factors: More Erotica?

The Zeigarnik effect can also help explain why traditional, nonindustrialized societies have lower prevalence of paraphilias than do Western societies: Western societies provide many erotic stimuli—in magazines, in movies, and on billboards and television—to which males can become aroused. In turn, males, particularly boys, are thus more likely to be "interrupted," leading to a desire to complete the task (Munroe & Gauvain, 2001).

To summarize, three main factors appear to contribute to paraphilias: a neurological similarity to OCD, classical conditioning of sexual arousal, and the Zeigarnik effect. One hypothesis for the almost exclusive prevalence of these disorders among males pertains to how the male anatomy promotes more frequent and easier accidental sexual arousal, along with the consequences of being interrupted while aroused (the Zeigarnik effect).

Treating Paraphilias

Only some people who have paraphilias receive treatment—typically those who engaged in predatory paraphilic behavior with nonconsenting individuals and so were brought into the criminal justice system (where they are classified as *sex offenders*). The goal of treatment, which may be ordered by a judge, is to decrease paraphilic impulses and behaviors by targeting neurological, psychological, and social factors; research on treatments for paraphilic disorders is not yet advanced enough to indicate how feedback loops arise as a result of treatment.

Targeting Neurological and Other Biological Factors: Medication

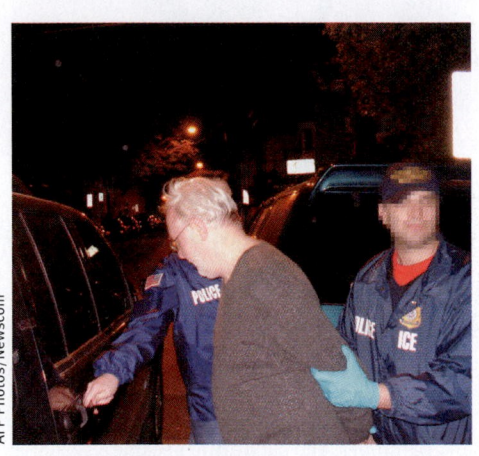

Most men who receive treatment for a paraphilia do so after coming to the attention of the criminal justice system, as did this man.

One goal of treatment for men who have engaged in predatory paraphilic behaviors with nonconsenting individuals is to decrease or eliminate their sex drive. *Chemical castration* refers to the use of medications to achieve this goal. Medications include antiandrogen drugs such as *medroxyprogesterone acetate* (Depo-Provera) and *cyprotereone acetate* (Androcur), which decrease testosterone levels. In turn, decreased testosterone levels lead to decreased sexual urges, fantasies, and behaviors in sexual offenders (Bradford, 2000; Gijs & Gooren, 1996; Robinson & Valcour, 1995). However, these medications don't necessarily diminish men's paraphilic *interests* along with sex drive. Moreover, within a few weeks of stopping the medication, the men again experience the urges and may engage in the predatory behaviors (Bradford, 2000; Gijs & Gooren, 1996).

In addition, as noted earlier, SSRIs may help decrease the sexual fantasies, urges, and behaviors in men whose paraphilic disorder has obsessive-compulsive elements (Abouesh & Clayton, 1999; Bradford, 2001; Kafka & Hennen, 2000; Roesler & Witztum, 2000). Thus, a treatment that targets neurological factors can affect thoughts (fantasies), which are psychological factors.

Targeting Psychological Factors: Cognitive-Behavior Therapy

CBT may be used to decrease cognitive distortions that promote paraphilic fantasies, urges, and behaviors. For example, such distortions might include the belief that sexual actions directed toward nonconsenting individuals are not harmful. Behavioral

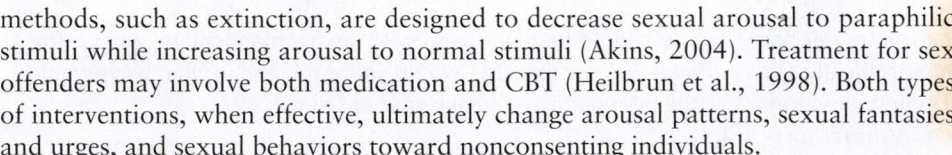

methods, such as extinction, are designed to decrease sexual arousal to paraphilic stimuli while increasing arousal to normal stimuli (Akins, 2004). Treatment for sex offenders may involve both medication and CBT (Heilbrun et al., 1998). Both types of interventions, when effective, ultimately change arousal patterns, sexual fantasies and urges, and sexual behaviors toward nonconsenting individuals.

In addition, treatment may sometimes include *relapse prevention training*, which teaches men to identify and recognize high-risk situations and learn strategies to avoid them. Such training also involves learning new coping skills, such as anger management or assertiveness (Pithers, 1990). However, such treatments tend not to reduce subsequent offenses among those sex offenders who are also *psychopaths*—people who lack empathy, show little remorse or guilt about hurting others, and shirk responsibility for their actions (Barbaree, 2005; Langton et al., 2006).

Targeting Social Factors

Some treatments for sex offenders target social factors, for example, by training these men to empathize with victims in the hopes that they will be less likely to reoffend in the future (Marshall, O'Sullivan, & Fernandez, 1996). However, many offenders do not complete psychosocial treatments (Hanson, Bloom, & Stevenson, 2004; Langevin, 2006). Furthermore, such treatments have not been found to be very successful (Hanson, Bloom, & Stephenson, 2004).

In sum, most men who receive treatment—of any type—for a paraphilic disorder do so because their paraphilic behavior involves nonconsenting people; treatment typically is instigated by the criminal justice system. In this context, the goal of treatment is to reduce the likelihood of reoffending—of *acting* on the paraphilic urges. Treatments that target neurological factors primarily influence the behaviors, but not the underlying fantasies or urges; CBT addresses both the behaviors and the fantasies.

Key Concepts and Facts About Paraphilias

- Paraphilias are characterized by a predictable sexual arousal pattern regarding "deviant" fantasies, objects, or behaviors. Paraphilias can involve (1) nonconsenting partners or children (exhibitionism, voyeurism, frotteurism, and pedophilia), (2) suffering or humiliating oneself or one's partner (sexual masochism and sexual sadism), or (3) arousal by nonhuman objects (fetishism and transvestic fetishism). To be diagnosed with a paraphilia, either the person must have acted on these sexual urges and fantasies, or these arousal patterns must cause the patient significant distress.

- Assessments of paraphilias may involve the use of a penile plethysmograph to determine the sorts of stimuli that arouse a man, as well as self-reports of arousing stimuli and reports from partners and from the criminal justice system for those apprehended for sexual crimes.

- Criticisms of the DSM-IV-TR paraphilia classification include the following: What is determined to be sexually "deviant" varies across cultures and over time; the diagnostic criteria are overly broad (e.g., fantasies or behavior, distress or no distress) and thereby lead clinicians to group together very different disorders (that is, to create a heterogeneous group); and the criteria do not address the ability to control the paraphilic urges.

- Research shows that paraphilias share similarities with OCD. Additional possible contributing factors include classically conditioned arousal and the Zeigarnik effect.

- Most frequently, men who receive treatment for paraphilias were ordered to do so by the criminal justice system. Treatments that target neurological factors decrease paraphilic behaviors through medication; however, although the behaviors may decrease, the interests often do not. Treatments that target psychological factors are designed to change cognitive distortions about the predatory sexual behaviors, especially the false belief that the behavior is not harmful to the nonconsenting victims. A goal of such treatments is to change sexual arousal patterns using behavioral methods, as well as to prevent relapse. Although social factors may be the target of treatment for sex offenders, they have not generally been successful.

Making a Diagnosis

- Reread Case 11.2 about Tom, and determine whether or not his symptoms meet the diagnostic criteria for exhibitionism. Specifically, list which criteria apply and which do not. If you would like more information to determine his diagnosis, what information—specifically—would you want, and in what ways would the information influence your decision?

continued on next page

- Reread Case 11.3 about Charles, and determine whether or not his symptoms meet the criteria for frotteurism. Specifically, list which criteria apply and which do not. If you would like more information to determine his diagnosis, what information—specifically—would you want, and in what ways would the information influence your decision?

- Reread Case 11.4 about the physician who spanked his wife, and determine whether or not his symptoms meet the criteria for sexual sadism. Specifically, list which criteria apply and which do not. If you would like more information to determine his diagnosis, what information—specifically—would you want, and in what ways would the information influence your decision?

- Do you think the physician's wife should be diagnosed with sexual masochism? List the criteria that apply to her, and which do not. If you would like more information to determine whether she should be diagnosed with sexual masochism, what information—specifically—would you want, and in what ways would the information influence your decision?

- Reread Case 11.5 about the 32-year-old man, and determine whether or not his symptoms meet the criteria for fetishism. Specifically, list which criteria apply and which do not. If you would like more information to determine his diagnosis, what information—specifically—would you want, and in what ways would the information influence your decision?

- Reread Case 11.6 about Mr. A, and determine whether or not his symptoms meet the criteria for transvestic festishism. Specifically, list which criteria apply and which do not. If you would like more information to determine his diagnosis, what information—specifically—would you want, and in what ways would the information influence your decision?

Sexual Dysfunctions

Let's return to Laura and Mike, the married couple whose relationship—and sex life—had become strained. Laura found that she didn't particularly miss having sexual relations with Mike. She did wonder how they had gotten to this point. In fact, Laura didn't have any sex drive, and the few times she and Mike had made love, nothing "happened" for her—she didn't have an orgasm or even find herself aroused. She couldn't pinpoint where things had gone astray; she'd like to feel desire, to *want* to have sexual relations with her husband, but she just didn't know where to start or how to get herself worked up about it. Was there something wrong with their relationship, or with her? Or is such lack of interest entirely "normal"?

An Overview of Sexual Functioning and Sexual Dysfunctions

People engage in sexual relations for two general reasons: to create babies (reproductive sex) and for pleasure (recreational sex). The vast majority of sexual acts are for pleasure, as opposed to procreation. Researchers have defined the "normal" progression of sexual pleasure as the *human sexual response cycle*, discussed below. **Sexual dysfunctions** are characterized by problems in the sexual response cycle. Let's first examine this cycle and then consider various ways in which it can go awry for men and women.

The Normal Sexual Response Cycle

What is a normal sexual response? In the 1950s and 1960s, researchers William Masters and Virginia Johnson sought to answer this question by measuring in their laboratory the sexual responses of thousands of volunteers. Based on their research, Masters and Johnson outlined the **sexual response cycle** for both women and men as consisting of four stages (see Figure 11.2): excitement, plateau, orgasm, and resolution (Masters & Johnson, 1966). Although it is convenient to organize these events into stages, the boundaries between these stages are not clear-cut (Levin, 1994):

1. *Excitement.* Excitement occurs in response to sensory-motor, cognitive, and emotional stimulation that leads to erotic sensations or feelings. Such arousal includes muscle tension throughout the body and engorged blood vessels, especially in the genital area. In men, this means that the penis swells; in women, this means that the clitoris and external genital area swell and vaginal lubrication occurs.

2. *Plateau.* Bodily changes that began in the excitement phase become more intense and then level off when the person reaches the highest level of arousal.

Sexual dysfunctions
Sexual disorders that are characterized by problems in the sexual response cycle.

Sexual response cycle
The four stages of sexual response—excitement, plateau, orgasm, and resolution—outlined by Masters and Johnson.

3. *Orgasm.* The arousal triggers involuntary contractions of internal genital organs, followed by ejaculation in men. In women, responses range from extended or multiple orgasms (without falling below the plateau level) to resolution.

4. *Resolution.* Following orgasm is a period of relaxation, of release from tension. For men, this period is often referred to as a *refractory period*, during which it is impossible to have an additional orgasm. Women rarely have such limitations and can often return to the excitement phase with effective sexual stimulation.

Other researchers have developed Masters and Johnson's ideas further. In particular, researchers now recognize that before the excitement phase, the person must first experience sexual attraction, which should lead to sexual desire, which in turn leads to the first stage of the sexual response cycle: excitement (Kaplan, 1981). According to DSM-IV-TR, *desire* consists of fantasies and thoughts about sexual activity along with an inclination or interest in being sexual (American Psychiatric Association, 2000). Sexual problems can occur when individuals experience a diminished—or even a lack of—sexual desire, or when they have difficulties related to sexual arousal or performance (the last three stages of sexual response). Laura appears to lack any sexual desire.

Figure 11.2

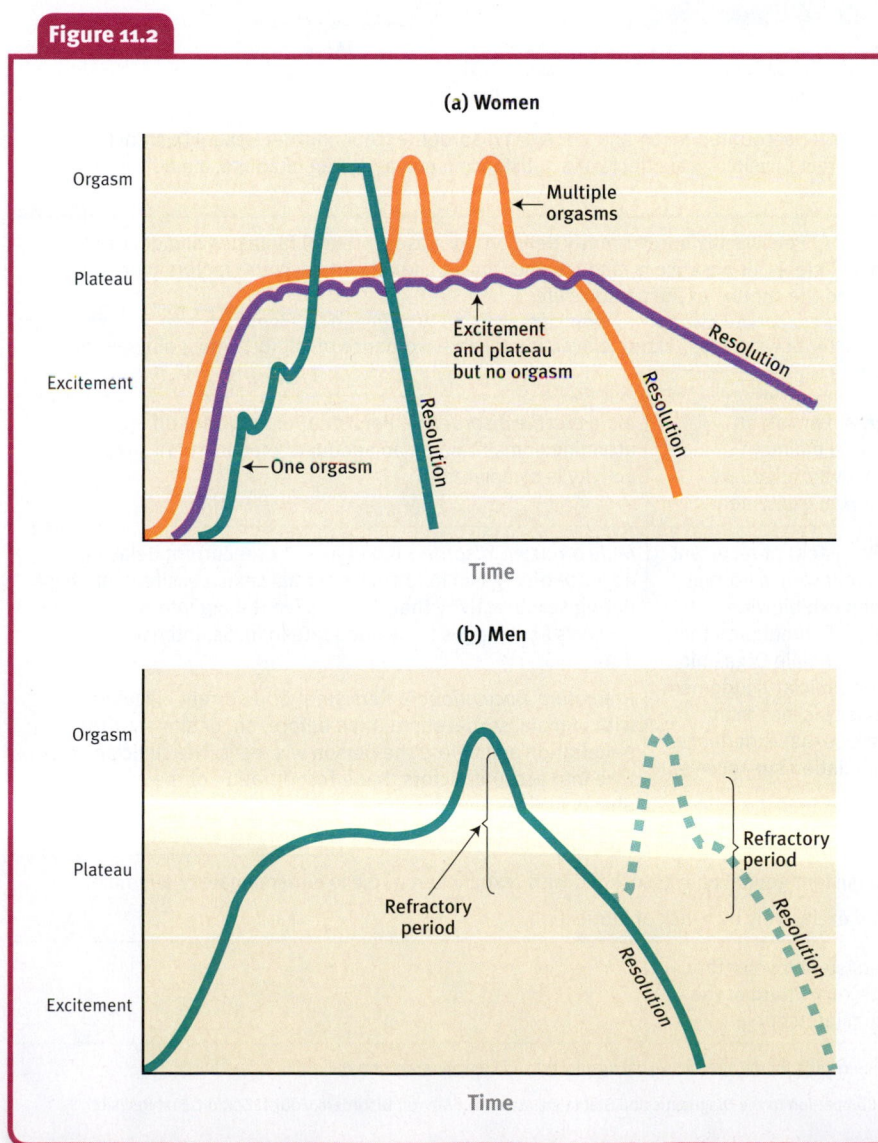

(a) Women

Orgasm
Plateau
Excitement

Multiple orgasms
Excitement and plateau but no orgasm
Resolution
Resolution
Resolution
One orgasm

Time

(b) Men

Orgasm
Plateau
Excitement

Refractory period
Refractory period
Resolution
Resolution

Time

11.2 ▸ The Human Sexual Response Cycle According to Masters and Johnson (1966), during the normal sexual response cycle, women and men go through four stages: excitement, plateau, orgasm, and resolution. However, women can experience multiple orgasms without a refractory period **(a)**, whereas men must experience a refractory period before a subsequent orgasm **(b)**.

Source: Masters & Johnson, 1966. For more information see the Permissions section.

Sexual Dysfunctions According to DSM-IV-TR

The DSM-IV-TR categories of disorders of sexual dysfunction were partly inspired by Masters and Johnson's sexual response cycle. Disorders of sexual dysfunction are divided into four categories: *sexual desire disorders*, *sexual arousal disorders*, *orgasmic disorders*, and *sexual pain disorders*. These disorders can arise in individuals of various sexual orientations: heterosexuals, lesbians, gay men, or bisexuals.

Someone can have more than one kind of sexual dysfunction, as when a man with premature ejaculation becomes nervous about having sexual relations and so develops a dysfunction of desire or arousal. Moreover, sexual dysfunction may have existed for an individual's entire adult life or been acquired after a period of normal sexual functioning, as happened to Laura. In addition, the dysfunction may occur in all circumstances (*generalized*) or only in certain situations, with specific partners or types of stimulation (*situational*). DSM-IV-TR also allows clinicians and researchers to note whether the sexual dysfunction is thought to be due to psychological rather than medical factors or due to a combination of psychological and medical factors. Table 11.5 lists the sexual dysfunctions and their diagnostic criteria.

As noted in Table 11.5, for a sexual dysfunction to be considered a disorder, the specific sexual symptoms must cause significant distress or relationship problems

Table 11.5 ▶ DSM-IV-TR Diagnostic Criteria for Sexual Dysfunctions

Type of Sexual Dysfunction	Female	Male
General Criteria	A. The sexual dysfunction causes significant distress or interpersonal difficulties.	
	B. The sexual dysfunction is not better accounted for by another Axis I disorder (except another Sexual Dysfunction) and is not due exclusively to the direct physiological effects of a substance (such as a drug of abuse, a medication) or a general medical condition.	
Desire	*Hypoactive sexual desire disorder:* A. Persistently or recurrently deficient (or absent) sexual fantasies and desire for sexual activity. The judgment of deficiency or absence is made by the clinician, taking into account factors that affect sexual functioning, such as age and the context of the person's life.	
	Sexual aversion disorder: A. Persistent or recurrent extreme aversion to, and avoidance of, all (or almost all) genital sexual contact with a sexual partner.	
Arousal	*Female sexual arousal disorder:* A. Persistent or recurrent inability to attain, or to maintain until completion of the sexual activity, adequate lubrication or swelling during sexual excitement.	*Male erectile disorder:* A. Persistent or recurrent difficulty attaining or maintaining an adequate erection until sexual activity is completed.
Orgasm	*Female orgasmic disorder:* A. Persistent or recurrent delay in, or absence of, orgasm following a normal sexual excitement phase. Women exhibit wide variability in the type or intensity of stimulation that triggers orgasm. The diagnosis of Female Orgasmic Disorder should be based on the clinician's judgment that the woman's orgasmic capacity is less than would be reasonable for her age, sexual experience, and the adequacy of sexual stimulation she receives.	*Male orgasmic disorder:* A. Persistent or recurrent delay in, or absence of, orgasm following a normal sexual excitement phase during sexual activity that the clinician (taking into account the person's age) judges to be adequate in focus, intensity, and duration.
		Premature ejaculation: A. Persistent or recurrent ejaculation with minimal sexual stimulation before, on, or shortly after penetration and before the person wishes it. The clinician must take into account factors that affect duration of the excitement phase, such as age, novelty of the sexual partner or situation, and recent frequency of sexual activity.
Pain	*Dyspareunia:* A. Recurrent or persistent genital pain associated with sexual intercourse in either a male or a female.	
	B. The disturbance is not caused exclusively by a lack of lubrication.	
	Vaginismus: A. Recurrent or persistent involuntary spasm of the musculature of the outer third of the vagina that interferes with sexual intercourse.	

Note: To be diagnosed with a sexual dysfunction, the person must meet both the criteria for the specific sexual dysfunction and the general criteria.

Source: Reprinted with permission from the DSM-IV-TR Casebook: A Learning Companion to the Diagnostic and Statistical Manual of Mental Disorders, Fourth Edition, Text Revision, (Copyright 2002) American Psychiatric Association.

(American Psychiatric Association, 2000). This means that someone may have a problem with any aspect of sexual response but would not be diagnosed as having a sexual dysfunction disorder unless the problem caused the individual marked distress or led to problems in his or her relationships.

Many, if not most, problems in the sexual response cycle have psychological causes rather than physical causes relating to the sex organs. This is true of both Mike and Laura, and somewhat true for Sarah and Benjamin, in Case 11.7. Table 11.6 provides more information about sexual dysfunctions.

CASE 11.7 ▸ FROM THE OUTSIDE: Sexual Dysfunctions

More than a decade [earlier], Sarah had experienced a very traumatic childbirth, with lacerations and ripping in the vaginal canal, which created extensive scarring and a lack of sensation. Since then she had found it difficult to become aroused and reach orgasm with intercourse. Before the delivery she had been fine.

Sarah had lost all interest in sex, but she was willing to be sexual for the sake of intimacy, which she still enjoyed. Her husband, Benjamin, however, had a hard time not taking it personally that she couldn't have an orgasm, and began to fixate on the problem, bringing it up in and out of the bedroom. But all the time and effort he was spending on her arousal only made her more anxious and less likely to become aroused at all. He started to feel inadequate as a result and began to find it difficult to maintain his erection. They had gone on in this way for years, and now were close to a separation.

(Berman et al., 2001, p. 168)

To understand better the problems Sarah and Benjamin were having, let's examine sexual dysfunctions in more detail.

Sexual Desire Disorders

Sexual desire is a multifaceted experience. It can be thought of as having at least three components: (1) a neurological and other biological component (related to hormones and brain activity, which lead to a genital response); (2) a cognitive component (related to an inclination or desire to be sexual); and (3) an emotional and relational component (related to being willing to engage in sex with a particular person at a specific place and time) (Levine, 1988). Any of these components can lead to either of two disorders, hypoactive sexual desire disorder or sexual aversion disorder.

Hypoactive Sexual Desire Disorder

As specified in DSM-IV-TR, one type of desire problem is **hypoactive sexual desire disorder**, whose hallmark is a persistent or recurrent lack of sexual fantasies or an absence of desire for sexual activity (see Table 11.5). This lack of desire may be lifelong or more recently acquired, and it may occur in all situations (generalized) or only in particular situations (such as with a specific person), but it must cause distress or impair functioning. Laura seems to have such a lack of sexual desire—a lack of any interest in sexual relations with Mike—but she wishes to feel desire.

Hypoactive sexual desire focuses primarily on a person's cognitive (fantasies) and emotional/relational (desire) state (Malatesta & Adams, 2001). People with hypoactive sexual desire disorder may lack sexual desire and be unwilling to engage in sexual behavior with a partner, or they may lack desire but still be willing to engage in sexual behavior with a partner, as was Sarah in Case 11.7. However, someone who is depressed and, as part of the depression, has little or no sexual desire (a symptom of depression) is not considered to have hypoactive sexual desire disorder because the low desire is caused by another disorder.

Women are more likely than men to have hypoactive sexual desire disorder. This sex difference may arise in part because, for women, desire may be more closely tied to the emotional nuances of a relationship than for men—as illustrated

Hypoactive sexual desire disorder
A sexual dysfunction characterized by a persistent or recurrent lack of sexual fantasies or an absence of desire for sexual activity.

Table 11.6 ▶ Sexual Dysfunctions Facts at a Glance

Prevalence

- According to one survey of 1065 female and 447 male patients in a general medical practice, 22% of the men and 40% of the women had a "sexual dysfunction" in the preceding 4 weeks (Nazareth, Boynton, & King, 2003). However, the true prevalence of sexual dysfunctions is difficult to determine: Many surveys either equate sexual dissatisfaction—for any reason—with sexual dysfunction or use criteria that are different from those in DSM-IV-TR.

- In another survey, 35% of men and 54% of women who had at least one heterosexual partner in the previous year reported at least one sexual problem lasting 1 month (Mercer et al., 2003). Note, however, that this is not long enough for a diagnosis of sexual dysfunction.

- Only a small minority of respondents (6% of men, 16% of women) had persistent sexual problems that lasted more than 6 months (Mercer et al., 2003).

- According to one survey, although 40% of women reported sexual problems, only 12% reported *distress* about their problems (Shifren et al., 2008). Without distress (or impaired functioning), the diagnosis of a sexual dysfunction would not be made.

Comorbidity

- People with sexual dysfunctions may also have a co-occurring mood or anxiety disorder.

Onset

- A sexual dysfunction may arise from specific circumstances, or it may be lifelong.

Course

- As women age, sexual problems other than desire problems tend to decrease, except for hormonally induced lubrication problems.

- The opposite is true for men: As they age, their sexual problems tend to increase, usually because of erectile difficulties that are associated with prostate problems, cardiovascular problems, or other medical causes (Hackett, 2008; Heiman, 2002b).

Gender Differences

- In one study, the most common problems among men were lack of interest, premature orgasm, and performance anxiety.

- Among women the most common problems were failure to achieve orgasm and painful intercourse.

Cultural Differences

- Cultural norms about sexuality affect the extent to which a sexual problem leads to enough distress or relationship difficulties for it to be considered a disorder (Hartley, 2006). For example, Japanese women have a low prevalence of problems with sexual desire, perhaps because Japanese women do not consider no or little sexual desire to be a problem (Kameya, 2001).

Source: Unless otherwise noted, the source for the table material is American Psychiatric Association, 2000.

in Case 11.8. In addition, as women age, decreased desire is probably related to women's hormonal shift with menopause: Women who have gone through menopause tend to report diminished desire more so than other women (Eplov et al., 2007). In fact, women who enter menopause abruptly and at an earlier age because of the surgical removal of their uterus and ovaries are more likely to report low sexual desire than are their same-age counterparts who have not yet entered menopause (Dennerstein et al., 2006).

In addition, psychological and social factors account for a given woman's *distress* about decreased desire, and women in different European countries report different levels of distress in response to decreased desire (Graziottin, 2007).

CASE 11.8 ▸ FROM THE OUTSIDE: Hypoactive Sexual Desire Disorder

Crystal is a 35-year-old married software engineer who is a team leader in a highly competitive company. She works 12-hour days and says she has no time for exercise or relaxation. Her husband is also an engineer. She has been trying to get pregnant for the past 8 months. They have been having scheduled intercourse on the 13th and 15th days of her regular cycle without success. She states that sex seems like work and she just wants to get it over with. When she married 5 years ago, her sex life was satisfying and she had no difficulty with interest or orgasm.

(Candib, cited in Hicks, 2005)

Sexual Aversion Disorder

Another type of desire disorder is **sexual aversion disorder,** whose hallmark is a persistent or recurrent extreme aversion to and avoidance of most genital sexual contact with a partner (see Table 11.5). People with this disorder may have normal desire, interest, and sexual fantasies and may masturbate. However, even the idea of contact with a partner's genitals or of being touched by a partner makes them anxious, like the man in Case 11.9; if such sexual physical contact occurs, they may panic (Kaplan, 1987).

CASE 11.9 ▸ FROM THE OUTSIDE: Sexual Aversion Disorder

A 33-year-old stockbroker sought treatment because of "impotence." Five months previously, a close male friend had died of a coronary occlusion, and within the following week the patient developed anxiety about his own cardiac status. Whenever his heart beat fast because of exertion, he became anxious that he was about to have a heart attack. He had disturbing dreams from which he would awaken anxious and unable to get back to sleep. He stopped playing tennis and running.

The patient began to avoid sexual intercourse, presumably because of his anxiety about physical exertion. This caused difficulties with his wife, who felt that he was deliberately depriving her of sexual outlets and was also preventing her from becoming pregnant, which she very much desired. In the past month, although no longer worried about his heart, the patient had avoided sexual intercourse entirely. He claimed to have some desire for sex, but when the situation arose, he could not bring himself to do it. He became so upset about his sexual difficulties that he began to have trouble concentrating at work. He felt himself to be a failure both as a husband and as a man. . . .

Four years previously, at 29 and after 3 years of marriage, he had presented himself for treatment with the complaint that he had never attempted to have sexual intercourse with his wife. Sexual activity consisted of his obtaining an erection without either his wife or himself touching his penis, and ejaculation occurred by rubbing his penis on his wife's abdomen. He was unable to touch his wife's genitalia. [He and his wife had treatment at that time, using behavioral techniques discussed below in the treatment section; treatment was a dramatic success.]

(Spitzer et al., 2002, p. 288)

Sexual Arousal Disorders

Sexual arousal disorders occur when a person cannot become aroused or cannot maintain arousal during a sexual encounter. These disorders can arise when the normal progression through the excitement phase is disrupted. This disruption can happen in three ways: (1) when *the pleasurable stimulation gets interrupted* (e.g., when a couple stops their sexual behavior because their young child enters their bedroom), (2) when *other external stimuli interfere* (e.g., when a car alarm goes off outside), or (3) when *internal stimuli interfere* (e.g, when the person becomes anxious, afraid, sad, or angry or has thoughts that intrude) (Malatesta & Adams, 2001).

Like sexual desire, sexual arousal involves neurological and other biological components (responses to stimuli and stimulation), cognitive components (thoughts), and emotional components, including a subjective sense that a response to a particular stimulus is "sexual" (Rosen & Beck, 1988). And any, or any combination, of these components can contribute to the problem. For example, a man

Sexual aversion disorder
A sexual dysfunction characterized by a persistent or recurrent extreme aversion to and avoidance of most genital sexual contact with a partner.

can have an adequate erection but think that he is inadequate because he believes that his penis is not hard enough. Similarly, a woman may respond to the biological sensations of sexual arousal by being afraid of losing control (Malatesta & Adams, 2001). Despite the influence of cognitive and emotional components, the DSM-IV-TR criteria for arousal disorders are exclusively biological (Malatesta & Adams, 2001). They focus on blood flow problems that interfere with sexual arousal.

Female Sexual Arousal Disorder

Two arousal disorders are included in DSM-IV-TR, one for men and one for women. The hallmark of **female sexual arousal disorder** (formerly known as *frigidity*) is persistent or recurrent difficulty attaining or maintaining engorged genital blood vessels in response to adequate stimulation (see Table 11.5). Normally with arousal, some of the fluid in these blood vessels (not the blood itself; Giraldi & Levin, 2006) is exuded into the genital area, serving as a lubricant. With female arousal disorder, however, the less than normal engorgement leads to decreased lubrication.

Menopause can lead to vaginal dryness and inadequate lubrication during sexual activity. In some sense, this makes female sexual arousal disorder a natural part of aging for women. In fact, female arousal disorder is most likely to occur in those who have been through menopause, particularly among women who have adequate sexual desire and can attain orgasm (Heiman, 2002b; Laumann, Paik, & Rosen, 1999). When the arousal problem is not a result of menopause-related hormonal changes, it frequently occurs along with desire and/or orgasm problems; this comorbidity means that it is rare for a woman to have *only* arousal problems that do not arise from hormone-related dryness. Note that DSM-IV-TR focuses exclusively on the neurological and other biological aspect of sexual arousal, not the subjective experience—which may be more significant for many women (Basson et al., 2001; Rosen & Leiblum, 1995).

As with all sexual dysfunctions, the diagnosis of sexual arousal disorder requires that the arousal problem cause distress or relationship difficulties and not be due exclusively to some other psychological disorder or to a medical disorder (see Table 11.5).

Male Erectile Disorder

The hallmark symptom of **male erectile disorder** (*impotence*, in nontechnical language) is a persistent or recurrent inability to attain or maintain an adequate erection until the end of sexual activity (American Psychiatric Association, 2000; see Table 11.5). Some men with male erectile disorder are able to have erections during foreplay but not during actual penetration. Others are not able to obtain a full erection with a new partner or in some situations; still others, such as Harry, in Case 11.10, have the problem during any type of sexual activity. If the man is able to have a full erection during masturbation, biological causes are unlikely. More than half of men over 40 years old have at least some erection problem (Feldman et al., 1994); thus, male erectile disorder, like its counterpart, female arousal disorder, can be seen as a normal by-product of aging. It is estimated that 300 million men worldwide will develop male erectile disorder by the year 2025, in part because of the increased aging of the population (cited in Shabsigh et al., 2003).

Female sexual arousal disorder
A sexual dysfunction marked by a woman's persistent or recurrent difficulty attaining or maintaining engorged genital blood vessels in response to adequate stimulation; formerly referred to as *frigidity*.

Male erectile disorder
A sexual dysfunction characterized by a man's persistent or recurrent inability to attain or maintain an adequate erection until the end of sexual activity; sometimes referred to as *impotence*.

CASE 11.10 ▶ FROM THE OUTSIDE: Male Erectile Disorder

Harry [had been married for 2 years when] he found out his wife had been involved in numerous extramarital affairs and divorced her. He said his friends all knew but were reluctant to tell him. Following the divorce he encountered erectile problems with all partners—even those to whom he felt close.

(Althof, 2000, p. 261)

Clearly, psychological factors can contribute to male erectile disorder; it is not always a neurological or other biological problem or a consequence of normal aging.

Orgasmic Disorders

An *orgasmic disorder* is diagnosed when a clinician determines that the individual has experienced normal excitement and adequate stimulation for orgasm in normal circumstances (based on the person's age and other factors)—but fails to have an orgasm. If a man or woman cannot achieve orgasm with intercourse but can do so through other types of sexual stimulation, the individual is not necessarily considered to have an orgasmic disorder. Like sexual arousal disorders, DSM-IV-TR includes separate diagnoses for males and for females who have difficulty reaching orgasm: female orgasmic disorder and male orgasmic disorder. A third disorder in this category, called *premature ejaculation*, is characterized by the opposite problem in males—coming to orgasm too quickly, with little stimulation. Disorders in this category may involve neurological (and other biological), cognitive, and emotional components.

Female Orgasmic Disorder

Female orgasmic disorder is diagnosed when a woman's normal sexual excitement does not lead to orgasm or when orgasm is delayed following a normal amount of stimulation (see Table 11.5). Women who experience occasional difficulty achieving orgasm do not have this disorder. The problem with achieving orgasm must be persistent and must exceed what would be expected based on the woman's age and sexual experience. Moreover, the clinician should make sure that the problem with orgasm is not caused by inadequate sexual stimulation. As with all sexual dysfunctions, female orgasmic disorder is only diagnosed if the problem concerning orgasm causes relationship problems or distress. Approximately 5–24% of women may have adequate sexual desire and excitement but nonetheless have female orgasmic disorder (Laumann et al., 1994; Spector & Carey, 1990).

Clinicians distinguish between two types of female orgasmic disorder: absolute and situational. If female orgasmic disorder is *absolute*, the woman does not have an orgasm in any circumstance. If female orgasmic disorder is *situational*, the woman may have an orgasm only in certain circumstances, for example, when masturbating. Lola, described in Case 11.11, has the absolute type of female orgasmic disorder.

CASE 11.11 ▶ FROM THE OUTSIDE: Female Orgasmic Disorder

Lola, a 25-year-old laboratory technician, has been married to a 32-year-old cabdriver for 5 years. The couple has a 2-year-old son, and the marriage appears harmonious.

The presenting complaint is Lola's lifelong inability to experience orgasm. She has never achieved orgasm, although during sexual activity she has received what should have been sufficient stimulation. She has tried to masturbate, and on many occasions her husband has manually stimulated her patiently for lengthy periods of time. Although she does not reach climax, she is strongly attached to her husband, feels erotic pleasure during lovemaking, and lubricates copiously. According to both of them, the husband has no sexual difficulty.

Exploration of her thoughts as she nears orgasm reveals a vague sense of dread of some undefined disaster. More generally, she is anxious about losing control over her emotions, which she normally keeps closely in check. She is particularly uncomfortable about expressing any anger or hostility.

(Spitzer et al., 2002, pp. 238–239)

Male Orgasmic Disorder

Male orgasmic disorder is a delay or absence of orgasm in men; Table 11.5 lists the specific criteria. Male orgasmic disorder is different from female orgasmic disorder in several respects: (1) Male orgasmic disorder typically involves problems reaching orgasm with a partner, even though the man can easily reach orgasm during masturbation (Apfelbaum, 1989, 2000); (2) male orgasmic disorder typically involves problems with orgasm only during vaginal intercourse (some men, however, cannot

Female orgasmic disorder
A sexual dysfunction characterized by a woman's persistent problem in progressing from normal sexual excitement to orgasm, such that orgasm is delayed or does not occur, despite a normal amount of appropriate stimulation.

Male orgasmic disorder
A sexual dysfunction characterized by a man's delay or absence of orgasm.

ever reach orgasm); and (3) its prevalence (less than 10% of the general male population) is lower than that of female orgasmic disorder (Spector & Carey, 1990).

Men with orgasmic disorder—particularly those who only have difficulty achieving orgasm with vaginal intercourse—do not necessarily seek treatment because couples may not view it as a significant problem; both partners may come to orgasm, although the man may do so through sexual activities other than vaginal intercourse, as the man in Case 11.12 does. Usually what brings men with this sexual dysfunction to seek treatment is the desire to have a baby, at which point male orgasm during vaginal intercourse becomes necessary.

CASE 11.12 ▸ FROM THE OUTSIDE: Male Orgasmic Disorder

[A man, 43 and never married, had sexual relationships with many women and was proud that he could sustain erections for a long time.] He nevertheless found masturbation more satisfying and had never come close to [having an orgasm during vaginal intercourse.] He had only reached orgasm four times with a partner, all with the same partner, by masturbating and then switching to fellatio only at the point of ejaculatory inevitability. . . . He was afraid that if he reached orgasm [during vaginal intercourse], he would be "under a woman's dominion."

(Apfelbaum, 2000, pp. 236–237)

Premature Ejaculation

A second type of orgasm-related problem for men is **premature ejaculation**, which is characterized by orgasm and ejaculation that occur earlier than the man expects— usually before, immediately during, or shortly after penetration (American Psychiatric Association, 2000; see Table 11.5 for the diagnostic criteria). Criterion A in Table 11.5 uses the phrase "minimal sexual stimulation" to indicate that the man ejaculates after less intense or briefer stimulation than would normally result in orgasm. Premature ejaculation is the most common male sexual dysfunction (Hellstrom et al., 2006; Laumann, Paik, & Rosen, 1999; Spector & Carey, 1990). According to Masters and Johnson (1970), premature ejaculation occurs when the man is unable to control his ejaculation sufficiently to satisfy his partner at least 50% of the time. Another definition is that premature ejaculation occurs when the man cannot voluntarily delay the ejaculation reflex (Kaplan, 1981).

Premature ejaculation is considered by some to be a *couple's* problem, as with Mr. and Mrs. Albert in Case 11.13. That is, it is a problem only insofar as the couple prefers the man to ejaculate in a particular phase of his partner's sexual response cycle: Some couples try to have both partners achieve orgasm at around the same time, but this is difficult with premature ejaculation. Other couples do not find early ejaculation a problem: The partner is sexually stimulated to orgasm in other ways after the man ejaculates (Malatesta & Adams, 2001).

CASE 11.13 ▸ FROM THE OUTSIDE: Premature Ejaculation

Mr. and Ms. Albert are an attractive, gregarious couple, married for 15 years, who [are in] the midst of a crisis over their sexual problems. Mr. Albert, a successful restaurateur, is 38. Ms. Albert, who since marriage has devoted herself to child rearing and managing the home, is 35. She reports that throughout their marriage she has been extremely frustrated because sex has "always been hopeless for us." She is now seriously considering leaving her husband.

The difficulty is the husband's rapid ejaculation. Whenever any lovemaking is attempted, Mr. Albert becomes anxious, moves quickly toward intercourse, and reaches orgasm either immediately upon entering his wife's vagina or within one or two strokes. He then feels humiliated and recognizes his wife's dissatisfaction, and they both lapse into silent suffering. He has severe feelings of inadequacy and guilt, and she experiences a mixture of frustration and resentment toward his "ineptness and lack of concern." Recently, they have developed a pattern of avoiding sex, which leaves them both frustrated, but which keeps overt hostility to a minimum. . . . [Mr. Albert's] inability to control his ejaculation is a source of intense shame, and he finds himself unable to talk to his wife about his sexual "failures." Ms. Albert is highly

Premature ejaculation
A sexual dysfunction characterized by orgasm and ejaculation that occur earlier than the man expects, usually before, immediately during, or shortly after penetration.

sexual and easily aroused in foreplay but has always felt that intercourse is the only "acceptable" way to reach orgasm.

In other areas of their marriage, including rearing of their two children, managing the family restaurant, and socializing with friends, the Alberts are highly compatible. Despite these strong points, however, they are near separation because of the tension produced by their mutual sexual disappointment.

(Spitzer et al., 2002, pp. 266–267)

Sexual Pain Disorders

Some people experience significant pain with sexual activity, particularly with sexual intercourse. DSM-IV-TR specifies two sexual dysfunctions that are related to consistent pain associated with sexual intercourse, dyspareunia and vaginismus, which are discussed in the following sections.

Dyspareunia

Dyspareunia is characterized by recurrent or persistent genital pain that is associated with sexual intercourse (see Table 11.5). In men, dyspareunia is rare (Bancroft, 1989; Sadock, 1995). When it does occur in men, the pain occurs after ejaculation and is often related to a medical condition. Up to 10–20% of women have dyspareunia (Laumann, Paik, & Rosen, 1999; Rosen et al., 1993). In women, dyspareunia may be related to a physical condition, such as surgical scar tissue or infection, or to insufficient lubrication, as can occur with menopause. When the pain persists, it can lead to problems with desire or excitement.

Vaginismus

Vaginismus consists of recurrent or persistent involuntary spasms of the musculature of the outer third of the vagina, which interfere with sexual intercourse (American Psychiatric Association, 2000; see Table 11.5). These spasms may be so strong that it is impossible to insert the penis into the vagina, or at least not without significant discomfort. Such spasms may also occur when trying to insert a tampon, finger, or *speculum* (the device inserted vaginally during a pelvic medical examination). This difficulty can lead some women to become afraid of any type of vaginal penetration. A fear of penetration related to vaginismus is distinguished from sexual aversion: With vaginismus, the woman only avoids sexual activities that involve vaginal insertion, not all sexual activities.

Most women with vaginismus also have dyspareunia (Heiman, 2002b). Dyspareunia can make vaginismus worse as a woman tenses certain vaginal muscles when she anticipates intercourse (Carey & Gordon, 1995; Tollison & Adams, 1979). Although vaginismus can lead to problems in the desire phase or excitement phase of the sexual response cycle, it typically does not (Kolodny, Masters, & Johnson, 1979). Further, other forms of sexual stimulation are usually satisfying. As with premature ejaculation, the desire to become pregnant is the most common reason why women with vaginismus seek treatment (Leiblum, Pervin, & Campbell, 1989). Like most women with vaginismus, Lynn in Case 11.14 also has dyspareunia.

CASE 11.14 ▶ FROM THE INSIDE: LYNN Vaginismus and Dyspareunia

We've been married for nine years and have two great kids. Unfortunately, family responsibilities and high stress jobs really cut into our together time. Exhaustion makes sex seem like an extra chore—just one more thing to do that we don't have time to enjoy and now can't. I don't know if it's from the busy, stressful lifestyle or not, or from being "out of practice," but about a year ago intercourse began to really hurt. It started with a burning sensation some of the time during sex. I found myself getting more anxious that it would hurt again and it usually did. Trips to the doctor revealed little besides the standard "do more foreplay or use more lubricant" advice. Now it seems like my body just "tightens up" and we can hardly have sex at all. Entry is painful and besides burning I feel tightness, spasms, discomfort and anxiety. The

continued on next page

Dyspareunia
A sexual dysfunction characterized by recurrent or persistent genital pain that is associated with sexual intercourse.

Vaginismus
A sexual dysfunction in females in which recurrent or persistent involuntary spasms of the musculature of the outer third of the vagina interfere with sexual intercourse.

pleasure is gone, and there is only the expectation of discomfort and frustration. Our marriage is suffering and it feels like a deep chasm is growing between us as sex has become impossible. My husband and I fight a lot more and I know he is growing impatient. I don't want my children to be another statistic of divorce because of this. I just don't know what to do.

(Vaginismus.com, 2007)

Criticisms of the Sexual Dysfunctions in DSM-IV-TR

Criticisms of the DSM-IV-TR classification of and criteria for sexual dysfunctions focus on several issues:

1. The sexual dysfunctions are based on the lock-step, sequential progression in Masters and Johnson's model of the sexual response cycle. However, this may not be the best model for understanding sexual dysfunctions in women. As shown in Figure 11.3, for women, arousal and desire often occur at the same time, or arousal can lead to desire rather than desire always preceding arousal. In this alternative model for females, emotional and physical satisfaction may include orgasm, although not all women need to have an orgasm to feel satisfied.

Figure 11.3

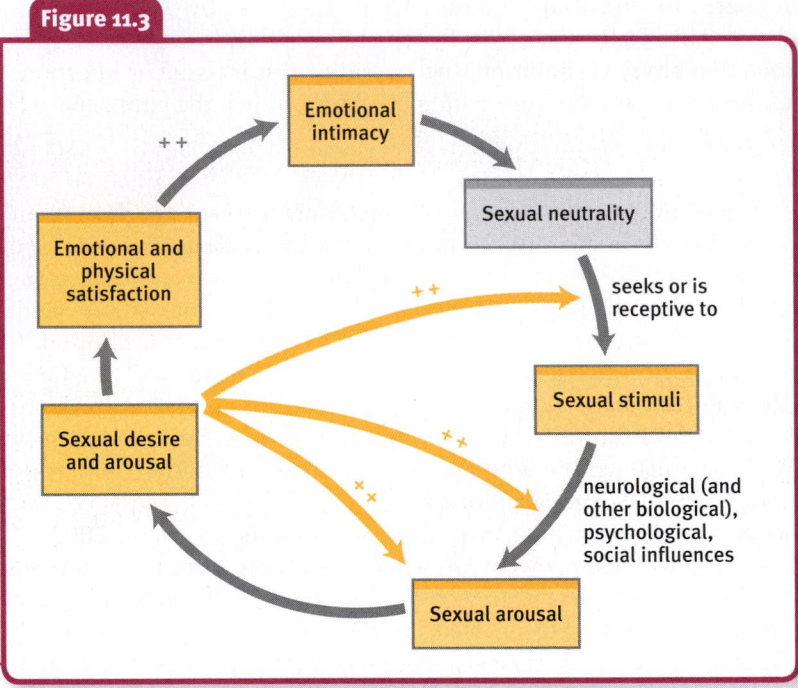

11.3 ▶ An Alternative Female Sexual Response Cycle An alternative model of the female sexual response cycle (Basson, 2001)—in the context of relationships—is analogous to a circle. The cycle starts with sexual neutrality: not feeling very sexual, but with an openness to seek or be receptive to sexual stimuli. In turn, such sexual stimuli may, depending on neurological (and other biological), psychological, and social factors operating at that moment, lead to sexual arousal, which in turn leads to a sense of desire and further arousal. The desire creates positive feedback loops (+ +) that lead to heightened arousal, which then leads to emotional and physical satisfaction. This satisfaction in turn produces a sense of emotional intimacy with her partner, making her more likely to be receptive to or seek out sexual stimuli in the future. She may also feel spontaneous sexual desire, which leads to positive feedback loops among the first three phases.

Source: Adapted from Basson, 2001. For more information see the Permissions section.

2. DSM-IV-TR focuses on body parts (heart rate, genital engorgement) rather than the whole person (Apfelbaum, 2000; Kleinplatz, 2001). Psychological and social factors—such as the subjective experience, thoughts and feelings, the quality of the relationship with the partner and the interaction of the couple, and the context of sexual activity—are generally overlooked (Tiefer, 1991). These factors play a larger role for women than is recognized by the DSM-IV-TR criteria (Basson, 2005; Basson et al., 2004, 2005).

3. The emphasis is on orgasm as the conclusion of sexual activity (Tiefer, 1991). Sexual activity that does not end in orgasm is implicitly considered not satisfying (Kleinplatz, 2001). Nevertheless, as noted above, some women feel satisfied even without having an orgasm.

4. The DSM-IV-TR criteria rest on a cultural definition of "normal" to define abnormal sexual functioning (Moynihan, 2003). Critics note that the norm promoted by American culture is that of an adolescent male, ever ready for

sexual encounters, and able to have erections on demand (Kleinplatz, 2001). As women and men age, they are more likely to meet the criteria for a sexual dysfunction even when there is no real "dysfunction"—only the body's growing older (Tiefer, 1987, 1991).

5. The criteria do not include any specific duration; people with symptoms that are transient, perhaps as a result of the aftereffects of surgery or a difficult time in a relationship, are grouped together with people whose symptoms are chronic (Balo, Segraves, & Clayton, 2007).

6. The DSM-IV-TR definitions of various sexual dysfunctions for women are not necessarily the ones used by those who specialize in the field of human sexuality (Basson, 2001).

7. Hypoactive sexual desire disorder in particular has been criticized on several grounds (Basson, 2001). First, it is left to the clinician to determine whether desire is sufficiently lacking (accounting for the individual's age and the context of the problem), and clinicians from diverse cultural and religious or spiritual backgrounds differ in their assessments. Second, the DSM-IV-TR criteria can lead to the diagnosis of a sexual dysfunction when there may be no actual dysfunction, but rather the couple may have a *discrepancy* in desire, where one partner desires sexual relations more or less often than the other (Rosen & Leiblum, 1989). In fact, diminished sexual desire may be an appropriate response to a relationship that isn't functioning well (Basson et al., 2001). Finally, different types of problems with desire (such as lifelong versus acquired or situational versus generalized) may require different treatments. Nevertheless, DSM-IV-TR clumps all variations of hypoactive sexual desire disorder together (Heiman, 2002a).

8. Many researchers in the field believe that dyspareunia should not be considered a *sexual* disorder, but rather a type of *pain* disorder (Binik, 2005; Binik et al., 2002).

When a relationship has significant problems, a lack of sexual desire may be appropriate and not a sign of a disorder.

Rob Wilkinson/Alamy

Understanding Sexual Dysfunctions

In a sense, we can view Laura's lack of sexual desire as being related, at least in part, to Mike's sexual difficulties: As Mike pulled back from Laura, Laura's desire for sexual intimacy with Mike waned. Their experiences highlight the fact that sexuality does not exist in a vacuum. Sexuality and any problems related to it develop through feedback loops among neurological (and other biological), psychological, and social factors.

Neurological and Other Biological Factors

In this section, we first consider how disease, illness, surgery, and medication can, directly and indirectly, disrupt normal sexuality. We then turn to the effects of normal aging, which can produce sexual difficulties.

Sexual Side Effects: Disease, Illness, Surgery, and Medication

Disease or illness can produce sexual dysfunction directly, as occurs with prostate cancer or cervical cancer. In addition, surgery can lead to sexual problems: Half of women who survive major surgeries for gynecological-related cancer develop sexual difficulties that do not become better over time (Andersen, Andersen, & DeProsse, 1989).

Disease or illness can also cause side effects of sexual dysfunction *indirectly*, as occurs with diabetes or circulation problems that limit blood flow to genital areas. Some physical problems can lead to sexual problems even more indirectly: People who have had a heart attack may be afraid to engage in sexual activity for fear that it will bring on another attack.

Prolonged bike riding can sometimes crush the nerves and arteries to the penis or clitoris, leading to arousal problems.

Richard Price/Getty Images

Some medications can interfere with normal sexual response, including:

• SSRIs and other dopamine-blocking medications such as traditional antipsychotics,

• beta-blockers and other medications that treat high blood pressure,

• antiseizure medication,

• estrogen and progesterone medications,

• HIV medications, and

• narcotics and sedative-hypnotics.

Alcohol can also disrupt the normal sexual response cycle.

Aging

Researchers have found that normal aging can affect sexual functioning among older people (George & Weiler, 1981). For instance, as we've seen, older women often have a vaginal lubrication problem that arise with menopause; when the lubrication problem is not addressed (for instance, with an over-the-counter lubricant such as Astroglide or K-Y Jelly), the dryness can cause intercourse to be painful and lead to dyspareunia.

In addition, as men age, their testosterone levels decrease significantly, often making prolonged tactile stimulation necessary to attain erections. Older men are likely to experience reduced penile hardness, decreased urgency to reach climax, and a longer refractory period (Butler & Lewis, 2002; Masters & Johnson, 1966).

In addition to the normal biological changes that arise with age, older people of both sexes may develop illnesses or diseases that make sexual activity physically more challenging. They also may take medications that have side effects that interfere with their sexual response. However, most older people say that they continue to enjoy sex.

Nick Daly/Jupiter Images

Men and women often experience changes in aspects of sexual performance as they get older, which may disrupt sexual activity. However, most will still experience pleasure from sexual activities (Leiblum & Seagraves, 2000).

Psychological Factors: Predisposing, Precipitating, and Maintaining Sexual Dysfunctions

Certain beliefs and experiences can *predispose* individuals to develop sexual dysfunctions (see Table 11.7). For example, a woman may believe that women in general lose their sexual desire as they age and a man may believe that "real men" have intercourse twice a day and that only rock-hard erections will satisfy women (Nobre & Pinto-Gouveia, 2006). Such a belief can lead to a self-fulfilling prophecy, if the belief produces the perception of a dysfunction and that perception in turn leads to a real dysfunction. For example, a man who believes that women are only

Table 11.7 ▶ Predisposing Events for Sexual Dysfunctions

Event	Effect
The view that sex is dirty and sinful	Early learning of such negative attitudes toward sex and misinformation leads to fears and inhibitions, which can lead to problems of desire, arousal, orgasm, and vaginismus.
Early negative conditioning experiences	In men, premature ejaculation can develop after hurrying to have an orgasm quickly for fear of being "caught." In women, a fear of pregnancy or being "caught" can lead to anxiety that contributes to sexual dysfunction.
Sexual trauma	Sexual trauma can produce negative conditioning and can lead to a fear of sex, as well as arousal and desire problems.

Sources: Bartoi & Kinder, 1998; Becker & Kaplan, 1991; Kaplan, 1981; Laumann, Paik, & Rosen, 1999; LoPiccolo & Friedman, 1988; Masters & Johnson, 1970; Silverstein, 1989.

satisfied by very hard erections may develop a problem as he ages: He may notice that his erections are not as hard as they were when he was younger and then become self-conscious and preoccupied during sex, which does in fact lead him to fail to satisfy his partner.

In addition, having been sexually abused as a child also predisposes a person later to develop sexual dysfunctions. Consider the fact that male victims of childhood sexual abuse are three times more likely to have erection problems and twice as likely to have desire problems and premature ejaculation than their peers who did not experience childhood sexual abuse (Laumann, Paik, & Rosen, 1999). Similarly, women who were victims of childhood sexual abuse are more likely than women who were not abused to report sexual problems (although not necessarily problems that meet the DSM-IV-TR criteria for sexual dysfunctions; Westerlund, 1992).

Factors that are thought to *precipitate*, or trigger, sexual dysfunctions generally involve sexual situations in which an individual feels anxious—for example, situations in which a man becomes nervous about not "performing" adequately. Such preoccupations can lead to disorders of sexual desire and arousal. Here are some examples of different types of problematic preoccupations:

- focusing attention on sex-related fears and worries, which distract and detract during a sexual encounter;

- feeling uncomfortable with how one's body may look or feel to a partner (Berman & Berman, 2001); and

- worrying about nonsexual matters, such as work or family problems.

Once someone has a problem with desire, arousal, or orgasm, he or she may become anxious that it will happen again, which sets up a self-fulfilling prophecy and becomes a *maintaining factor*. For instance, when a single sexual experience was perceived as a "failure," an individual may become anxious during subsequent sexual experiences, monitoring his or her responsiveness (and so *thinking* about the sexual response rather than *experiencing* it)—which in turn can interfere with a normal sexual response and create a sexual dysfunction (Bach, Brown, & Barlow, 1999).

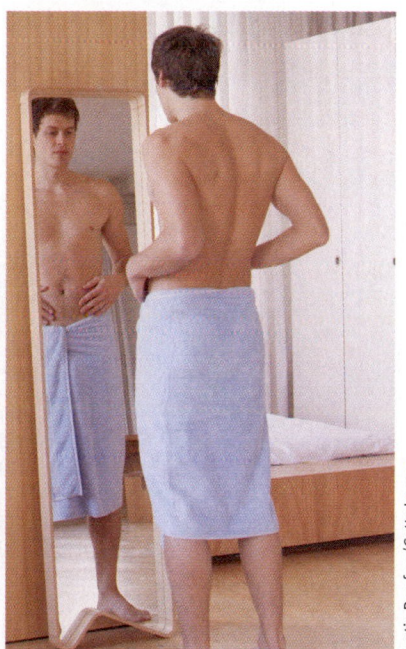

Social Factors

Although sexuality involves how we see ourselves, it usually also involves other people. The sexual relations of a couple are influenced by how the partners relate to each other, specifically: (1) how conflict is expressed and resolved, (2) how they communicate their needs and desires, their likes and dislikes, (3) how they handle stress, and (4) how strongly attracted they each are to each other (Tiefer, 2001). For example, Mike's sexual secret from Laura led him to pull away from her sexually. She thought he wasn't interested in sex. That is, from her vantage point, he appeared to have a sexual desire problem, and she herself then lost interest.

Being chronically preoccupied and anxious about something—including how your body might look or feel to a partner—while engaged in sexual activity can interfere with the normal sexual response cycle, and lead to a sexual dysfunction.

FEEDBACK LOOPS IN ACTION: **Sexual Dysfunctions**

Just as neurological, psychological, and social factors influence each other and contribute to a normal sexual response, feedback loops among these factors can contribute to sexual dysfunctions (see Figure 11.4). Such feedback loops best explain why some people, and not others, develop sexual dysfunctions. For instance, people's sexual beliefs ("My body looks ugly" or "I won't be able to have an orgasm"; psychological factors) can influence their sexual functioning: The beliefs create fears

Jeff Greenberg/Photo Edit

Justin Pumfrey/Getty Images

and anxieties that can lead to high levels of sympathetic nervous system activity (neurological factor), which physically interferes with sexual arousal and orgasm (Apfelbaum, 2001; Kaplan, 1981; Masters & Johnson, 1970). Current problems in a relationship (social factors) similarly affect sexual functioning, as can having been sexually abused (Bartoi & Kinder, 1998; Becker, 1989; DiLillo, 2001; Laumann, Paik, & Rosen, 1999).

Familial and cultural views of sexuality (social factors) can also influence sexual functioning (psychological and neurological factors): We are all taught various lessons about sexuality both directly (what our parents, teachers, religious leaders, and

Figure 11.4

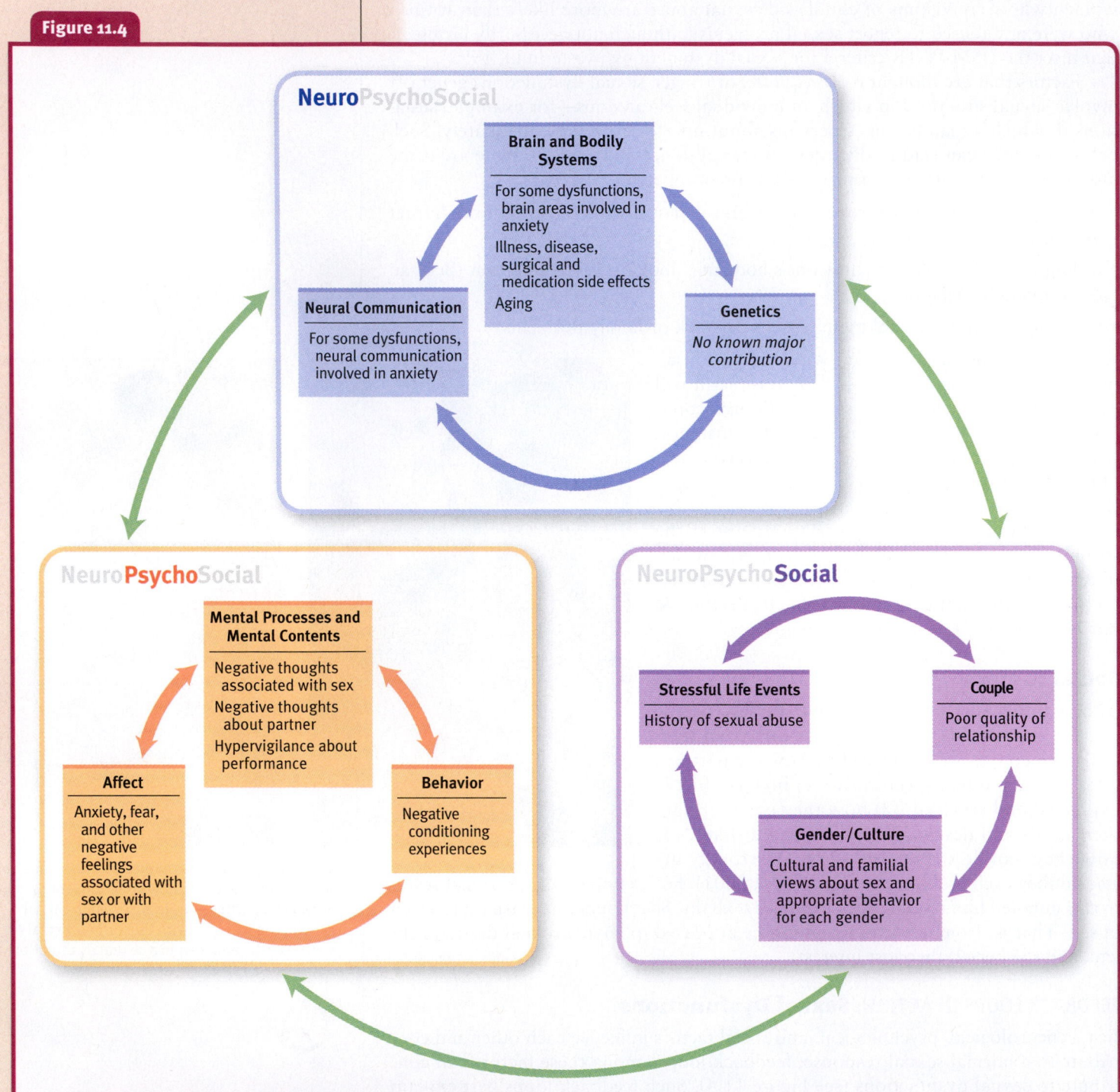

11.4 ► Feedback Loops in Action: Sexual Dysfunctions

peers told us) and indirectly (through observations of family members or friends and from television, movies, books, and the Internet). Some people are taught that sexual relations outside of marriage are wrong, whereas other people are taught that sexual experimentation before marriage is a good thing. Such direct and indirect lessons help shape each person's notion of appropriate or normal sexuality. Depending on what an individual learned about sex, he or she may be primed to have sexual difficulties in some situations.

The interplay of factors is seen in the contrasting examples of two men, each of whom has an experience of erectile dysfunction. One man has a history of poor self-esteem and worry (psychological factors), as well as anxiety about his sexual performance (neurological and psychological factors). Although he is very attracted to his partner and generally has a positive view of sex (psychological and social factors), he worries that his partner may get annoyed at his "performance failure" and perhaps leave him. This leads him to be even more anxious the next time they have a sexual encounter (neurological and social factors), and he again has difficulty attaining or maintaining an erection, and thus develops persistent erectile dysfunction. In contrast, the other man, who also has a positive attitude toward sex and is attracted to his partner, drinks too much—which leads to an episode of erectile dysfunction. However, this man does not have the general "performance" worries of the first man, nor is he anxious about how his partner may respond. He expects (psychological factor) later to have his usual erections and to be able to satisfy his partner, which is in fact what happens.

Thus, neurological, psychological, and social factors influence each other in complex ways that predispose an individual to develop a sexual dysfunction, and that precipitate and maintain it once it develops.

Assessing Sexual Dysfunctions

Many people first seek help for sexual problems from a physician, who may investigate the extent to which medical factors—rather than psychological or social factors—contribute to the problems. A physician, in turn, may refer the patient to a specialist. Patients may see a *sex therapist*—usually a mental health clinician—trained to assess and treat problems related to sexuality and sexual activity. Before sex therapists begin to treat people for sexual dysfunctions, they usually make sure that the patients have a thorough assessment to identify specific factors that contribute to the dysfunction. The results of the assessment guide which factor(s) are targeted for treatment and which specific treatments the therapist suggests. Sexual dysfunctions can be assessed by examining neurological and other biological factors, as well as psychological and social factors.

Assessing Neurological and Other Biological Factors

Mental health professionals who assess and treat sexual problems want to know about an individual's health status and sexual response cycle. Such information may be obtained through lab tests that measure endocrine and hormone levels, ultrasound imaging to assess internal organs, and tests to assess the functioning of sensory nerves. Testing for men may include a plethysmograph to assess penile response, and testing for women may include vaginal probes to measure lubrication and the vagina's ability to relax and dilate. Genital swelling and lubrication—or their lack—in a woman do not necessarily reflect her subjective sense of sexual arousal or pleasure (Basson, 2005).

Assessing Psychological Factors

An assessment by a sex therapist may include personality tests and inventories such as the MMPI-2 (see Chapter 3), as well as questions about symptoms of depression (which can lead to problems of sexual desire). In addition, the sex therapist will assess the patient's thoughts, feelings, and expectations regarding his or her partner and about sexual activity, as well as past masturbatory and other sexual experiences that might bear on the current difficulties. This information helps the sex therapist determine what specific psychological factors contribute to the patient's sexual dysfunction. For example, Lola in Case 11.11 was concerned about losing control during orgasm, and the man in Case 11.12 was afraid that he'd be "under a woman's dominion" if he had orgasm during vaginal intercourse.

Assessing Social Factors

A sex therapist investigates how relationship issues affect a patient's sexuality and whether the sexual difficulties occur only with the patient's partner or more generally. For instance, the therapist might ask what function sex serves in the relationship and how unresolved conflict and power issues affect the sexual aspect of the relationship (Stock & Moser, 2001). Other questions might address how the couple decides on the timing, duration, or specific activities of sexual relations. Depending on the answers, the sex therapist may target specific social factors as part of the treatment.

Treating Sexual Dysfunctions

Once the specific nature of the sexual problem has been determined, treatment can target the relevant factors. Depending on the nature of the problem and the types of treatments the patient—and his or her partner—are interested in, treatment may include medication, cognitive-behavioral therapy, sex therapy (which may provide specific guidance and techniques to treat sexual problems), couples therapy, or some other type of therapy.

Targeting Neurological and Other Biological Factors: Medications

There has been an increasing trend toward the *medicalization* of sex therapy, that is, a tendency to target neurological and other biological factors (see Table 11.8) and pay less attention to other factors. In the 1990s, medical treatments for erectile dysfunction began in earnest with the advent of the drug Viagra and the marketing campaign for it, which brought the topic of erectile dysfunction from a rarely discussed but relatively common problem among older men to a topic of everyday conversation. Viagra (*sildenafil citrate*) is one of the class of drugs called *phosphodiesterase type 5 inhibitors*, or *PDE-5 inhibitors*. Viagra doesn't cause an erection directly; instead, the drug operates by increasing the flow of blood to the penis only when a man is sexually excited. Viagra (and its competitors, such as Cialis) is not a cure but a treatment for impotence, and it is effective only if the man takes a pill before sexual activity.

Table 11.8 ▸ Medications for Sexual Dysfunctions

Sexual phase	Female	Male
Desire	*Hypoactive sexual desire disorder:* Testosterone pills or cream; Wellbutrin (*bupropion*) may counteract diminished desire that is a side effect of SSRIs taken for another disorder *Sexual aversion disorder:* Antianxiety medication for the phobia or panic component	
Arousal	*Female sexual arousal disorder:* PDE-5 inhibitors when arousal problems have a medical cause	*Erectile disorder:* PDE-5 inhibitors
Orgasm		*Premature ejaculation:* SSRIs
Pain	*Vaginismus:* Antianxiety medication *Dyspareunia:* Estrogen cream	

Some women with arousal disorders use PDE-5 inhibitors because these medications have an analogous effect on the clitoris. However, PDE-5 inhibitors are most effective with women who—for medical reasons—have reduced blood flow to the clitoral area, which leads to decreased physical arousal (Berman et al., 2001). Critics point out that prescribing this type of medication for a woman will not improve sexual functioning when the problem is with her relationship, not her body (Bancroft, 2002).

At least in some cases, PDE-5 inhibitors (and the medicalization of treatment more generally) may actually produce sexual problems. For example, consider a middle-aged man with erectile dysfunction who is given Viagra and resumes sexual intercourse with his postmenopausal wife. However, his wife cannot maintain adequate lubrication or interest during intercourse given her husband's (now) extended erections. In this situation, according to DSM-IV-TR, she may be viewed as having sexual arousal disorder, but this "disorder" may only exist because her partner is taking medication to counter effects of aging. Many researchers and clinicians maintain that in such cases the woman does not have a disorder, although she may have a relationship problem (Basson et al., 2001).

Targeting Psychological Factors: Shifting Thoughts, Learning New Sexual Behaviors

Two types of treatment directly target psychological factors: *Sex therapy*, which provides specific guidance and techniques to treat sexual problems, and psychological therapies—such as CBT or psychodynamic therapy—which address feelings and thoughts about oneself and others and how they may relate to sexual problems.

One of the main goals of treatments that directly target psychological factors related to sexual dysfunctions is to educate patients about sexuality and the human sexual response. Another goal is to help patients develop strategies to counter negative thoughts, beliefs, or attitudes that may interfere with sexual desire, arousal, or orgasm (Carey & Gordon, 1995). For instance, during sexual activity, some people are preoccupied with nonsexual thoughts that prevent them from reaching full arousal or orgasm. These nonsexual thoughts might be work-related worries, thoughts about household tasks that need to be done, or worries that someone will interrupt the sexual encounter. Cognitive treatment may involve teaching a patient how to filter out such thoughts and (re)focus on the sexual interaction. The therapist might encourage the patient to apply standard cognitive methods (see Chapter 4) to sexual encounters, such as problem solving ("You could turn the phone off") or cognitive restructuring ("Are you likely to think of a solution to your work problem while making love? If not, you can let your mind focus on the physical sensations you are experiencing").

In addition to addressing very specific sex-related thoughts and feelings, the treatment may also address the patient's view of himself or herself. Sometimes the sense of being dysfunctional or inadequate generalizes from the sexual realm to the whole self, and the individual with a sexual dysfunction comes to have low self-esteem and self-doubts generally. In such cases, the therapy may use cognitive and behavioral methods (see Chapter 4), to address the thoughts and feelings of being inadequate in multiple spheres of life.

Behavioral treatment typically involves "homework." Depending on the nature of the problem, the homework may be completed by the patient or by the patient and his or her partner together. Homework for women with female orgasmic disorder (as well as other sexual dysfunctions) may include masturbation in order to learn more about what sensations and fantasies facilitate arousal and orgasm (Meston et al., 2004). For many patients, a first step is to begin to (re)discover pleasurable sensations through specific homework exercises. In the beginning of behavioral treatment, homework may include **sensate focus exercises**, which are designed to increase awareness of pleasurable sensations, but preclude orgasm. Such exercises may prohibit genital touching, intercourse, or orgasm; rather partners take turns touching other parts of each others' bodies so that each can discover what kinds of stimulation feel most enjoyable (Baucom et al., 1998; LoPiccolo & Stock, 1986).

Sensate focus exercises
A behavioral technique that is assigned as homework in sex therapy, in which an individual or couple seeks to increase awareness of pleasurable sensations that do not involve genital touching, intercourse, or orgasm.

Sex therapists may recommend sensate focus exercises—a graduated series of tasks that focus on body awareness and sexual sensations. One such task might be a sensual bath, either alone or with a partner; the goal is not to come to orgasm but rather to become aware of pleasurable sensations.

Comstock/Punchstock

Typically, the therapist explains a homework assignment during a session, and the patient or couple reports the results during the following session. The goals of behavioral techniques are to help patients develop a more relaxed awareness of their bodies and increase their orgasmic responding and control. Treatment may also involve a realistic look at an individual's or couple's daily work schedule, which is followed by a discussion of how to create the time and energy to begin a sexual encounter so that the partners are not tired or busy. In addition, therapists typically use specific behavioral techniques for different sexual dysfunctions. For instance, people with sexual aversion disorder may undergo desensitization as part of their treatment, gradually exposing themselves to frightening or aversive elements of the sexual situation (Kaplan, 1995).

Researchers have examined how well specific psychosocial treatments (that is, treatments that directly target psychological and social factors) help people with particular sexual disorders. For erectile dysfunction, treatments such as psychoeducation and behavioral homework assignments (such as increasing communication skills) can help to increase satisfaction with erectile functioning, sexual frequency, and satisfaction with the relationship (Heiman & Meston, 1997). Premature ejaculation is significantly helped by behavioral techniques (de Carufel & Trudel, 2006), such as the *squeeze technique* (Kaplan, 1989): Right before ejaculation, the man squeezes the base of the tip (just below the head) of his erect penis for about 4 seconds. When he feels his ejaculation to be under control, he begins stimulation again. Once he has mastered this technique during masturbation, he tries sexual relations with his partner; if necessary for control, he can employ the squeeze technique during sexual relations with his partner (Heiman & Meston, 1997).

Women with vaginismus may be helped by systematic desensitization, which involves gradual dilation of the vaginal opening until vaginal spasms no longer occur. Biofeedback may be helpful for some women with dyspareunia.

For orgasmic disorders, treatments that target psychological factors are more effective for people who have never experienced orgasm; people who have infrequent orgasms, or situational problems achieving orgasm, may be better treated by methods that target the couple's interactions or biological problems (depending on the specific reason for the inconsistency of orgasms; Heiman, 2000). Unfortunately, there are, as yet, few well-designed studies that have assessed specific psychosocial treatments for women's sexual dysfunctions (Heiman, 2002a) in part because research on these treatments is not sponsored by an industry (as is research on the effectiveness of medications).

Targeting Social Factors: Couples Therapy

The sex therapy techniques discussed in the previous section may be implemented alone (by the individual with a sexual dysfunction) or with a partner. Sex therapy may involve teaching couples specific cognitive and behavioral techniques. However, implementing such techniques with a partner requires motivation and willingness to be open with the partner about sexual matters and to experiment sexually. Moreover, how a couple interacts sexually occurs against the backdrop of their overall relationship. Treatment may focus on the couple's relationship issues (couples therapy, rather than sex therapy per se) and include teaching communication, intimacy, and relationship skills (Baucom et al., 1998; Beck, 1995; Heiman, 2002b; Masters & Johnson, 1970), such as assertiveness, problem solving, negotiation, and conflict management (Malatesta & Adams, 2001). Couples therapy may also address issues of power, control, and lifestyle as they relate to the sexual dysfunction; for example, the therapist may employ techniques from systems therapy (see Chapter 4) to focus on assertiveness within the sexual aspects of the relationship. Treatment for a sexual dysfunction in a partner of a lesbian or gay couple may also address special issues that affect their sexual relationship, such as living "in the closet" or sexual intimacy when one partner is HIV positive (Nichols, 2000).

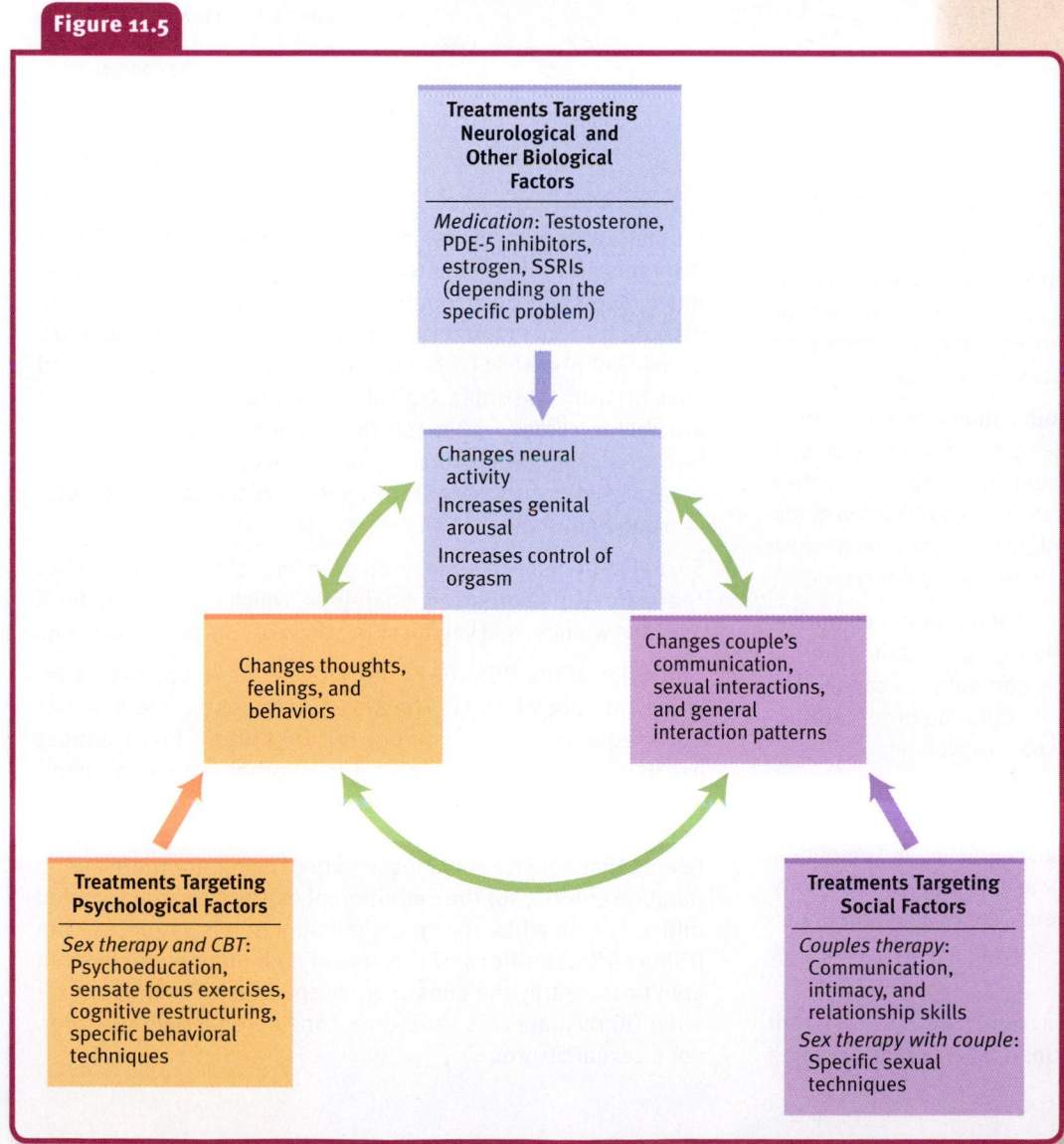

FEEDBACK LOOPS IN TREATMENT: **Sexual Dysfunctions**

Like successful treatment for any psychological disorder, successful treatment of sexual dysfunctions ultimately affects all the neuropsychosocial factors (see Figure 11.5). For instance, CBT for female orgasmic disorder targets psychological factors (the thoughts, beliefs, and feelings related to sex or orgasm and behaviors such as masturbation) (Heiman, 2002a). In turn, changes in these factors lead, through feedback loops, to changes in neurological and other biological factors (which underlie orgasm) as well as social factors (the meaning for both partners of an orgasm and the changes in their interactions). A similar set of feedback loops occurs with CBT for vaginismus (ter Kuile et al., 2007): CBT changes thoughts and feelings about penetration, and the responses of the vaginal muscles, making vaginal intercourse with a partner possible.

Although all the techniques mentioned may alleviate sexual dysfunctions, the definition of "success" is less clear-cut than for treatments of most psychological disorders. As we noted at the beginning of this chapter, sexuality and sexual dysfunctions typically involve other people besides the patient, and a treatment that the patient views as successful may not be perceived that way by the partner. Let's go back to the older gentleman whose erectile dysfunction was treated with Viagra. He may have been pleased by his response to the drug treatment (Althof et al., 2006), only to discover that his wife was now unhappy about his sustained erections and more frequent desire for intercourse. She, then, might be diagnosed with a sexual

Figure 11.5

Treatments Targeting Neurological and Other Biological Factors

Medication: Testosterone, PDE-5 inhibitors, estrogen, SSRIs (depending on the specific problem)

Changes neural activity
Increases genital arousal
Increases control of orgasm

Changes thoughts, feelings, and behaviors

Changes couple's communication, sexual interactions, and general interaction patterns

Treatments Targeting Psychological Factors

Sex therapy and CBT: Psychoeducation, sensate focus exercises, cognitive restructuring, specific behavioral techniques

Treatments Targeting Social Factors

Couples therapy: Communication, intimacy, and relationship skills
Sex therapy with couple: Specific sexual techniques

11.5 ▶ Feedback Loops in Treatment: Sexual Dysfunctions

desire problem. Yet she might explain that when her husband had difficulty with his erections, he was much more affectionate, sexually attentive to her, and creative in their sexual interactions. Now he is goal-directed, focusing almost exclusively on intercourse. Solving his erectile dysfunction led to changes in the couple's sexual relations that were not viewed as positive by his wife. Treatments that directly target only one type of factor, such as medication, may seem to resolve the problem for the patient, but instead can—via feedback loops among the three types of factors—have unexpected negative consequences for the couple.

Steve Kelley/Cartoonist Group

Targeting only a neurological (or other biological) factor in one partner may not improve the overall sexual functioning and satisfaction of the couple.

Key Concepts and Facts About Sexual Dysfunctions

- Sexual dysfunctions are psychological disorders marked by problems in the human sexual response cycle. The response cycle traditionally has been regarded as having four parts: excitement, plateau, orgasm, and resolution—but it is now commonly regarded as beginning with sexual attraction and desire.

- Sexual dysfunctions fall into one of four categories: disorders of desire, arousal, orgasm, and pain. The dysfunctions may be situational or generalized and may arise from neurological (and other biological) factors, psychological factors, or a combination of factors. However, to be classified as dysfunctions they must cause significant distress or problems in the person's relationships.

- Sexual desire disorders involve three components: cognitive, emotional, and, to a lesser extent, neurological (and other biological). Problems with any of these components can lead to hypoactive sexual desire or sexual aversion disorder. Both of these disorders may be diagnosed in men or women.

- Sexual arousal disorders arise when the normal progression through the excitement phase is disrupted. Arousal disorders involve neurological (or other biological), cognitive, and emotional components, although DSM-IV-TR focuses solely on the neurological (or other biological) component. The two disorders pertaining to arousal are female sexual arousal disorder and male erectile disorder.

- Sexual orgasmic disorders are characterized by persistent problems with the orgasmic response after experiencing a normal excitement phase and adequate stimulation. These disorders may involve neurological (and other biological), cognitive, and emotional components. DSM-IV-TR includes three disorders in this category. Two of these involve an absence or delay of orgasmic response: female orgasmic disorder and male orgasmic disorder. Typically, men with orgasmic disorder are able to climax with masturbation but not with vaginal intercourse. The third disorder, premature ejaculation, involves orgasm that occurs persistently with minimal sexual stimulation and before the man wishes it.

- Sexual pain disorders hinge on pain with sexual intercourse. There are two disorders: dyspareunia, which can occur in both men and women, and vaginismus, which occurs only in women.

- Criticisms of the DSM-IV-TR sexual dysfunction disorders include the following: (1) The sexual response cycle may not apply equally well to women; (2) the criteria focus almost exclusively on the neurological (and other biological) components; (3) the end goal is orgasm, not satisfaction; (4) the criteria rest on a particular definition of normal sexual functioning that doesn't encompass normal aging; (5) there are no duration criteria; (6) the definition of distress or interpersonal difficulty caused by the sexual dysfunction is vague; (7) the DSM-IV-TR definitions of the sexual dysfunctions for women aren't necessarily the ones used by specialists in human sexuality; (8) dyspareunia should be considered a pain disorder, not a sexual disorder.

- Various factors contribute to sexual dysfunctions. Neurological (and other biological) factors include disease, illness, surgery or medications, and the normal aging process.

- Psychological factors can be divided into three types: predisposing factors, such as negative attitudes toward sex, negative conditioning experiences, and a history of sexual abuse; precipitating factors, such as anxiety about sex and distraction because of sexual or nonsexual matters; and maintaining factors, such as worrying about future sexual problems.

- Social factors include: the quality of the partners' relationship (how stress, conflict, and communication are handled, and how attracted the partners are to one another); the partner's sexual functioning; a history of abuse; and sexual mores in the individual's subculture (e.g., religious teachings).

- Neurological (and other biological) factors that may contribute to sexual dysfunctions are assessed through tests of endocrine and hormone levels and of the functioning of sensory nerves, internal organs, and the genitals. Psychological factors are sometimes assessed through personality tests and inventories; a clinician will also consider possible comorbid disorders and assess a patient's thoughts and feelings about sexual activities. Social factors include the ways that sexual problems interact with any relationship problems a couple may have.

- Treatments that target neurological (and other biological) are medications for erectile dysfunction and for analogous arousal problems in women.

- Treatments that target psychological factors include psychoeducation, sensate focus exercises, and CBT to counter negative thoughts, beliefs, and behaviors associated with sexual dysfunction. For certain sexual dysfunctions, specific techniques may be particularly helpful.

- Treatments that target social factors address problematic issues in a couple's relationship as well as teach the couple specific sex-related cognitive or behavioral strategies.

- Treatments that focus on one type of factor for a given patient can create complex feedback loops, which sometimes have unexpected—and perhaps negative—consequences for the couple. Successful treatment for a patient might create problems for the partner.

Making a Diagnosis

- Reread Case 11.7 about Sarah and Benjamin, and determine whether either of them meet the criteria for any sexual dysfunction(s). Specifically, examine the criteria for each disorder and determine whether Sarah or Benjamin's symptoms meet each of the criteria for each disorder appropriate to their sex. If you would like more information to determine their diagnoses, what information—specifically—would you want, and in what ways would the information influence your decision?

- Reread Case 11.8 about Crystal, and determine whether her symptoms meet the criteria for hypoactive sexual desire disorder. Specifically, list which criteria apply and which do not. If you would like more information to determine her diagnosis, what information—specifically—would you want, and in what ways would the information influence your decision?

- Reread Case 11.9 about the stockbroker, and determine whether his symptoms meet the criteria for sexual aversion disorder. Specifically, list which criteria apply and which do not. If you would like more information to determine his diagnosis, what information—specifically—would you want, and in what ways would the information influence your decision?

- Reread Case 11.10 about Harry, and determine whether his symptoms meet the criteria for hypoactive sexual desire disorder. Specifically, list which criteria apply and which do not. If you would like more information to determine his diagnosis, what information—specifically—would you want, and in what ways would the information influence your decision?

- Reread Case 11.11 about Lola, and determine whether her symptoms meet the criteria for female orgasmic disorder. Specifically, list which criteria apply and which do not. If you would like more information to determine her diagnosis, what information—specifically—would you want, and in what ways would the information influence your decision?

- Reread Case 11.12 about the man who didn't generally reach orgasm during vaginal intercourse, and determine whether his symptoms meet the criteria for male orgasmic disorder. Specifically, list which criteria apply and which do not. If you would like more information to determine his diagnosis, what information—specifically—would you want, and in what ways would the information influence your decision?

- Reread Case 11.13 about Mr. Albert, and determine whether his symptoms meet the criteria for premature ejaculation. Specifically, list which criteria apply and which do not. If you would like more information to determine his diagnosis, what information—specifically—would you want, and in what ways would the information influence your decision?

- Reread Case 11.14 about Lynn, and determine whether her symptoms meet the criteria for vaginismus and/or dyspareunia. Specifically, list which criteria of each disorder apply and which do not. If you would like more information to determine her diagnosis, what information—specifically—would you want, and in what ways would the information influence your decision?

SUMMING UP

Summary of Gender Identity Disorder

Gender identity disorder is characterized by a persistent cross-gender identification that leads to chronic discomfort with one's biological sex. Symptoms of gender identity disorder often emerge in childhood, but most children diagnosed with the disorder no longer have the disorder by the time they are adults. However, most adults with gender identity disorder report that their symptoms began in childhood.

In children, symptoms of gender identity disorder include cross-dressing, engaging in other-sex types of play, choosing other-sex playmates, and even claiming to be the other sex. In adults, symptoms include persistent and extreme discomfort from living publicly as their biological sex, which leads many to live (at least some of the time) as someone of the other sex.

Criticisms of the diagnostic criteria in DSM-IV-TR for this disorder point to the overly narrow concept of gender and appropriate behavior (particularly for males) and the ambiguous requirement about distress. With gender identity disorder, the person's distress often arises because of other people's reactions to the cross-gender behavior.

Some brain areas in adults with gender identity disorder are more similar to the corresponding brain areas of members of their desired sex than to those of their biological sex. Results from animal studies suggest that one explanation for this disorder is that prenatal exposure to hormones causes the brain to develop in ways more similar to the other sex, although the sexual characteristics of the body are unchanged. Beyond symptoms that are part of the diagnostic criteria for the disorder, no psychological or social factors are clearly associated with the disorder.

Treatments may target neurological (and other biological), psychological, or social factors. Treatments that target neurological and other biological factors include hormone treatments and sex reassignment surgery. Treatments targeting psychological factors include psychoeducation and helping the patient choose among gender-related lifestyle options and problem solve about potential difficulties. Treatments that target social factors include family education, support groups, and group therapy.

Thinking like a clinician

When Nico was a boy, he hated playing with the other boys; he detested sports and loved playing with the girls—playing "house" and "dress up"—except when the girls made him dress up as "the man" of the group. Sometimes he got to be the princess, and that thrilled him. As a teenager, Nico's closest friends continued to be females. Although Nico shied away from playing with boys, he felt himself sexually attracted to them. To determine whether Nico had gender identity disorder, transvestic fetishism, or no gender or sexual disorder, what information would a clinician want? What specific information would count heavily? Should that fact that Nico is attracted to males affect the assessment? Why or why not?

Summary of The Paraphilias

Paraphilias are characterized by a predictable sexual arousal pattern regarding "deviant" fantasies, objects, or behaviors. Paraphilias can involve (1) nonconsenting partners or children (exhibitionism, voyeurism, frotteurism, and pedophilia), (2) suffering or humiliating oneself or one's partner (sexual masochism and sexual sadism), or (3) arousal by nonhuman objects (fetishism and transvestic fetishism). To be diagnosed with a paraphilia, either the person must have acted on these sexual urges and fantasies, or these arousal patterns must cause the patient significant distress.

Assessments of paraphilias may involve the use of a penile plethysmograph to determine the sorts of stimuli that arouse a man, as well as self-reports of arousing stimuli and reports from partners and from the criminal justice system for those apprehended for sexual crimes.

Criticisms of the DSM-IV-TR paraphilia classification include the following: What is determined to be sexually "deviant" varies across cultures and over time; the diagnostic criteria are overly broad and thereby lead clinicians to group together very different disorders; and the criteria do not address the ability to control the paraphilic urges.

Research shows that paraphilias share similarities with OCD. Additional possible contributing factors include classically conditioned arousal and the Zeigarnik effect.

Most frequently, men who receive treatment for paraphilias because they were ordered to do so by the criminal justice system. Treatments that target neurological factors decrease paraphilic behaviors through medication; however, although the behaviors may decrease, the interests often do not. Treatments that target psychological factors are designed to change cognitive distortions about the predatory sexual behaviors, especially the false belief that the behavior is not harmful to the nonconsenting victims. A goal of such treatments is to change sexual arousal patterns using behavioral methods, as well as to prevent relapse. Although social factors may be the target of treatment for sex offenders, they have not generally been successful.

Thinking like a clinician

Ben was getting distracted at work because he kept fantasizing about having sexual relations with young boys. He'd think about a neighbor's son or a boy in an advertisement. He hadn't *done* anything about his fantasies, but they were getting increasingly harder to turn off. According to DSM-IV-TR, what paraphilic disorder, if any, does Ben have? On what is your decision based? If Ben wasn't getting distracted by his fantasies, would your diagnosis change or stay the same, and why? Do you think that illegal acts (such as child sex abuse or sexual acts with nonconsenting individuals) should be part of the DSM criteria, as they presently are? Explain your answer. What treatment options are available to Ben?

Summary of Sexual Dysfunctions

Sexual dysfunctions are psychological disorders marked by problems in the human sexual response cycle. The response cycle traditionally has been regarded as having four parts: excitement, plateau, orgasm, and resolution—but it is now commonly regarded as beginning with sexual attraction and desire. Sexual dysfunctions fall into one of four categories: disorders of desire, arousal, orgasm, and pain. The dysfunctions may be situational or generalized and may arise from neurological (and other biological) factors, psychological factors, or a combination of factors. However, to be classified as dysfunctions they must cause significant distress or problems in the person's relationships.

Each sexual dysfunction involves cognitive, emotional, and neurological (and other biological) components to varying degrees; the DSM-IV-TR diagnostic criteria, however, generally focus on neurological and other biological components.

Various factors contribute to sexual dysfunctions. Neurological (and other biological) factors include disease, illness, surgery or medications, and the normal aging process. Psychological factors are divided into predisposing, precipitating, and maintaining factors. Social factors include the quality of the partners' relationship, the partner's sexual functioning, a history of abuse, and sexual mores in the individual's subculture. All the factors interact via feedback loops. An assessment of sexual dysfunctions may evaluate neurological (and other biological), psychological, and social factors.

Treatments that target neurological (and other biological) factors are medications for erectile dysfunction and for analogous arousal problems in women. Treatments that target psychological factors include psychoeducation and sensate focus exercises, and CBT to counter negative thoughts, beliefs, and behaviors associated with sexual dysfunction. Treatments that target social factors address problematic issues in a couple's relationship as well as teach the couple specific sex-related cognitive or behavioral strategies. Treatments that focus on one type of factor for a given patient can create complex feedback loops, which sometimes have unexpected—and perhaps negative—consequences for the couple.

Thinking like a clinician

Chi-Ling and Yinong were in their 30s and had been trying to have a baby for a year. Their sexual relations were strained: They had sex when the ovulation predictor test kit indicated that they should, and each month's attempt and subsequent failure made them anxious. There was no joy or love in their sexual relations, and most of the time Chi-Ling was barely aroused and lubricated; she rarely had orgasms anymore. She just wanted Yinong to hurry up and ejaculate, and he was finding it increasingly difficult to do so. Based on what you have read, do you think that Chi-Ling or Yinong has any sexual dysfunctions, and if so, which one(s)? Support your position. If you could obtain additional information before you decide, what would you want to know and why?

Key Terms

Gender identity (p. 474)

Gender identity disorder (p. 474)

Gender role (p. 474)

Sex reassignment surgery (p. 480)

Paraphilia (p. 482)

Exhibitionism (p. 484)

Voyeurism (p. 485)

Frotteurism (p. 485)

Pedophilia (p. 486)

Sexual sadism (p. 486)

Sexual masochism (p. 487)

Fetishism (p. 488)

Transvestic fetishism (p. 488)

Sexual dysfunctions (p. 494)

Sexual response cycle (p. 494)

Hypoactive sexual desire disorder (p. 497)

Sexual aversion disorder (p. 499)

Female sexual arousal disorder (p. 500)

Male erectile disorder (p. 500)

Female orgasmic disorder (p. 501)

Male orgasmic disorder (p. 501)

Premature ejaculation (p. 502)

Dyspareunia (p. 503)

Vaginismus (p. 503)

Sensate focus exercises (p. 511)

More Study Aids

For additional study aids related to this chapter, go to:

www.worthpublishers.com/rosenberg

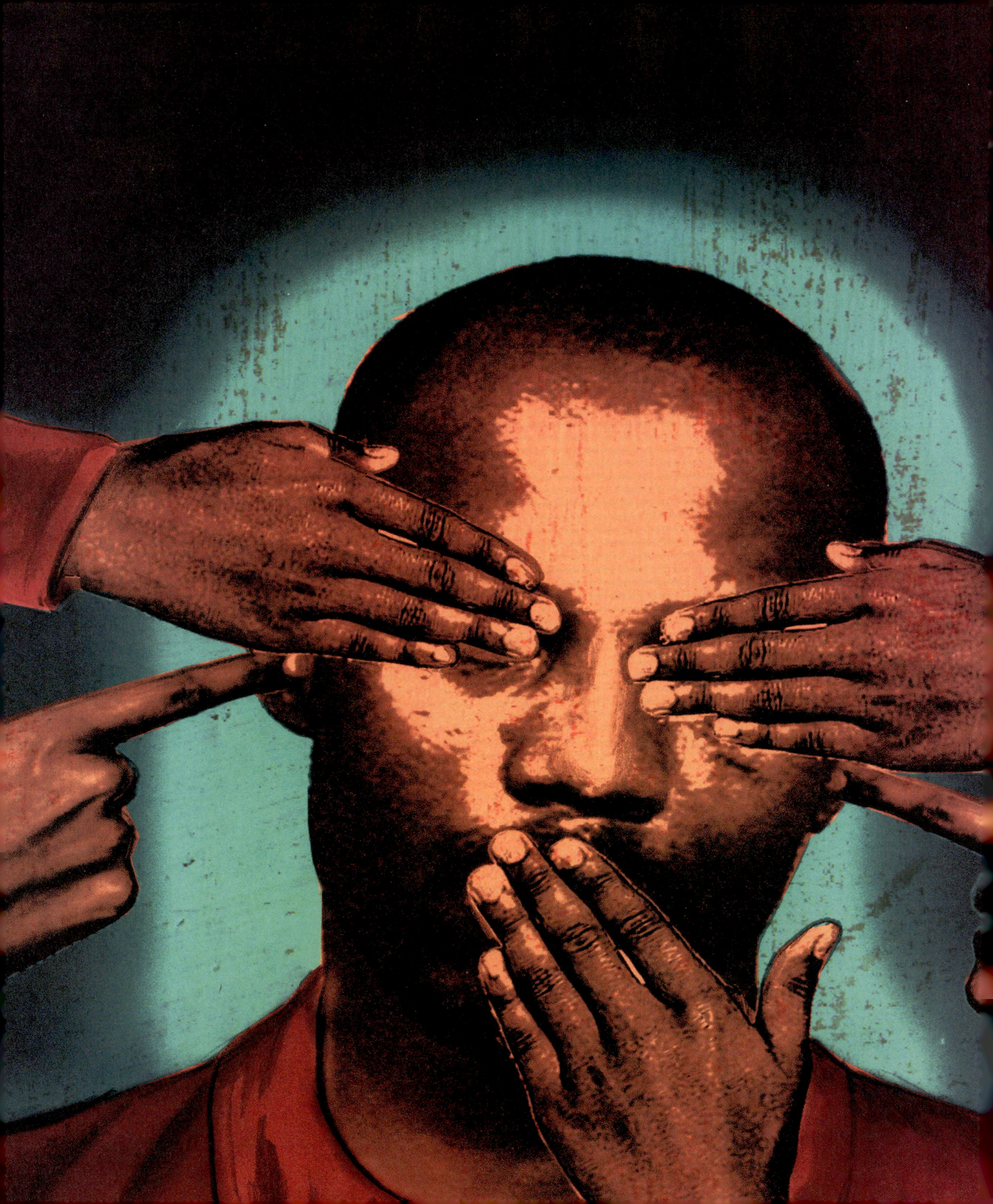

Schizophrenia and Other Psychotic Disorders

In 1930, female quadruplets were born in a small Midwestern city. All four survived, which at that time was remarkable. This set of quadruplets (or quads) was also remarkable in two other ways: All four developed from a single fertilized egg and so basically were genetically identical. In addition, all four went on to develop symptoms of schizophrenia as young adults. In the psychological literature, the quadruplets came to be known by pseudonyms they were given to protect their privacy: Nora, Iris, Myra, and Hester Genain.

The quads were born to parents of limited financial means. Their father, Henry, was abusive, violent, and alcoholic. He also exhibited some symptoms of schizophrenia. Their mother, Maud, had been a nurse. Maud was very strict with the girls, but she was a better parent than Henry.

By the time the quads were in their early 20s, three had been hospitalized for schizophrenia at least once, and the fourth was exhibiting symptoms of schizophrenia. Also around that time, Mrs. Genain was recovering from bladder surgery, and it was becoming increasingly difficult for her to care for the young women. The family's problems were brought to the attention of researchers at the National Institute of Mental Health (NIMH), and the family was invited to move to a research and treatment facility in Washington, DC. At the facility, the sisters were treated, studied, and written about extensively. In fact, the pseudonyms the quads were given related to the initials of NIMH: Nora, Iris, Myra, and Hester. Their false last name, Genain, means "dire birth" in Greek.

The fact that all four of the Genain sisters developed symptoms of schizophrenia was by no means an inevitable result. For identical twins, the chance of both twins's developing schizophrenia is about 48%. For identical quads, the odds of all four developing schizophrenia are about one in six, or 16% (Rosenthal, 1963). The quads' story offers possible clues about why all four of them developed schizophrenia and provides some understanding of what causes the disorder. In this chapter, we discuss the symptoms of schizophrenia, what is known about its causes, and current treatments for this disorder.

Nora, Iris, Myra, and Hester Genain were identical quadruplets. All four suffered from schizophrenia, although this outcome is statistically unlikely. The symptoms and course of the disorder were different for each sister, illustrating the range of ways it can affect people.

What Are Schizophrenia and Other Psychotic Disorders?

Schizophrenia is a psychological disorder characterized by psychotic symptoms— hallucinations and delusions—that significantly affect emotions, behavior, and most notably, mental processes and mental contents. The symptoms of schizophrenia can interfere with a person's abilities to comprehend and respond to the world in a normal way. DSM-IV-TR lists schizophrenia as a single disorder (see Chapter 3, and Table 12.1), but research suggests that schizophrenia is not a unitary disorder (Blanchard, Horan, & Collins, 2005; Turetsky et al., 2002). Instead, like depression (see Chapter 6), schizophrenia is a set of related disorders. Research findings suggest that each variant of schizophrenia has different symptoms, causes, course of development, and, possibly, response to treatments. Let's examine in more detail the symptoms and types of schizophrenia and other related psychotic disorders.

The Symptoms of Schizophrenia

The criteria for schizophrenia in DSM-IV-TR fall into two clusters:

- *positive symptoms*, consisting of delusions and hallucinations and disorganized speech and behavior;

- *negative symptoms*, consisting of the absence or reduction of normal mental processes, mental contents, feelings, or behaviors, including speech, emotional expressiveness, and/or movement.

Let's examine in detail the DSM-IV-TR criteria (Table 12.1), criticisms of these criteria, and an alternative way to diagnose schizophrenia.

Positive Symptoms

Positive symptoms are so named because they are marked by the *presence* of abnormal or distorted mental processes, mental contents, or behaviors. Positive symptoms of schizophrenia are

- hallucinations (distortions of perception),

- delusions (distortions of thought),

- disorganized speech, and

- disorganized behavior.

Schizophrenia
A psychological disorder characterized by psychotic symptoms that significantly affect emotions, behavior, and mental processes and mental contents.

Positive symptoms
Symptoms of schizophrenia that are marked by the *presence* of abnormal or distorted mental processes, mental contents, or behaviors.

Table 12.1 ► DSM-IV-TR Diagnostic Criteria for Schizophrenia

A. *Characteristic symptoms*: Two (or more) of the following, each present for a significant portion of time during a 1-month period (or less if successfully treated):

(1) delusions

(2) hallucinations

(3) disorganized speech

(4) grossly disorganized or catatonic behavior

(5) negative symptoms, i.e., affective flattening, alogia, or avolition

Note: Only one Criterion A symptom is required if delusions are bizarre or hallucinations consist of a voice keeping up a running commentary on the person's behavior or thoughts or two or more voices conversing with each other.

B. *Social/occupational dysfunction*: For a significant portion of the time since the onset of the disturbance, one or more major areas of functioning, such as work, interpersonal relations, or self-care, are markedly below the level achieved prior to the onset (or when the onset is in childhood or adolescence, failure to achieve expected level of interpersonal, academic, or occupational achievement).

C. *Duration*: Continuous signs of the disturbance persist for at least 6 months. This 6-month period must include at least 1 month of symptoms (or less if successfully treated) that meet Criterion A (i.e., active-phase symptoms) and may include periods of prodromal or residual symptoms. During these prodromal or residual periods, the signs of the disturbance may be manifested by only negative symptoms or two or more symptoms listed in Criterion A present in an attenuated form (e.g., odd beliefs, unusual perceptual experiences).

Source: Reprinted with permission from the Diagnostic and Statistical Manual of Mental Disorders, Text Revision, Fourth Edition, (Copyright 2000) American Psychiatric Association.

Although DSM-IV-TR divides symptoms of schizophrenia into two categories (positive and negative), current research suggests that the symptoms fall into three clusters, or dimensions: positive, in green (A1 and A2), disorganized, in orange (A3 and A4), and negative, in blue (A5).

These symptoms are distinguished by their extreme quality. From time to time, we all have hallucinations, such as thinking we hear the doorbell ring when it didn't. But the hallucinations experienced by people with schizophrenia are intrusive—they may be voices that talk constantly or scream at the patient. Similarly, a delusion of someone with schizophrenia isn't an isolated, one-time false belief (e.g., "My roommate took my sweater and that's why it's missing"). With schizophrenia and other psychotic disorders, the delusions are extensive, although they often focus on one topic (e.g., "My roommate is out to get me, and the fact that she has taken my sweater is just one more example").

The positive symptoms of disorganized speech and disorganized behavior are apparent from watching or talking to an individual who has them—it's difficult, if not impossible, to understand what's being said, and the individual's behavior is clearly odd (wearing a coat during a heat wave, for example). Let's examine the four positive symptoms in more detail.

Hallucinations

As discussed in Chapter 1, **hallucinations** are sensations so vivid that the perceived objects or events seem real even though they are not. Any of the five senses can be involved in a hallucination, although auditory hallucinations—specifically, hearing voices—are the most common type experienced by people with schizophrenia. Pamela Spiro Wagner describes one of her experiences with auditory hallucinations:

> [The voices] have returned with a vengeance, bringing hell to my nights and days. With scathing criticism and a constant scornful commentary on everything I do, they sometimes order me to do things I shouldn't. So far, I've stopped myself, but I might not always be able to. . . .

(Wagner & Spiro, 2005, p. 2)

Research that investigates possible underlying causes of auditory hallucinations finds that people with schizophrenia, and to a lesser extent their unaffected siblings, have difficulty distinguishing between verbal information that is internally generated

Hallucinations
Sensations that are so vivid that the perceived objects or events seem real, even though they are not.

(as when imagining a conversation or talking to oneself) and verbal information that is externally generated (as when another person is actually talking) (Brunelin et al., 2007). People with schizophrenia are also more likely to (mis)attribute their own internal conversations to another person (Brunelin, Combris, et al., 2006; Keefe et al., 1999); this misattribution apparently contributes to the experience of auditory hallucinations.

Delusions

People with schizophrenia may also experience **delusions**—incorrect beliefs that persist, despite evidence to the contrary. Delusions often focus on a particular theme, and several types of themes are common among these patients. For one, *paranoid delusions* involve the theme of being persecuted by others. Pamela Spiro Wagner's paranoid delusions involved extraterrestrials:

> I barricade the door each night for fear of beings from the higher dimensions coming to spirit me away, useless as any physical barrier would be against them. I don't mention the NSA, DIA, or Interpol surveillance I've detected in my walls or how intercepted conversations among these agencies have intruded into TV shows.
>
> (Wagner & Spiro, 2005, p. 2)

In contrast, *delusions of control* revolve around the belief that the person is being controlled by other people (or aliens), who literally put thoughts into his or her head, called *thought insertion*:

> I came to believe that a local pharmacist was tormenting me by inserting his thoughts into my head, stealing mine, and inducing me to buy things I had no use for. The only way I could escape the influence of his deadly radiation was to walk a circuit a mile in diameter around his drugstore, and then I felt terrified and in terrible danger.
>
> (Wagner, 1996, p. 400)

In this example, note that Wagner believed that it is possible for the pharmacist to insert his thoughts into her head and thus control her.

Another delusional theme is believing oneself to be significantly more powerful, knowledgeable, or capable than is actually the case, referred to as *delusions of grandeur*. Someone with this type of delusion may believe that he or she has invented a new type of computer when such an achievement by that person is clearly impossible. Delusions of grandeur may also include the mistaken belief that the individual is a different—often famous and powerful—person, such as the president or a prominent religious figure.

Yet another delusional theme is present in *delusions of reference*: the belief that external events have special meaning for the individual. Someone who believes that a song playing in a movie is in some kind of code that has special meaning *just for* him or her, for instance, is having a delusion of reference.

Whatever the theme of the delusion, according to DSM-IV-TR, if it is bizarre or clearly implausible, then additional symptoms are not needed for a diagnosis of schizophrenia. An example would be a patient's belief that his or her organs have been replaced, despite the absence of a surgical scar.

Disorganized Speech

People with schizophrenia can sometimes speak incoherently, although they may not necessarily be aware that other people cannot understand what they are saying. Speech can be disorganized in a variety of different ways. One type of disorganized speech is **word salad**, which is a random stream of seemingly unconnected

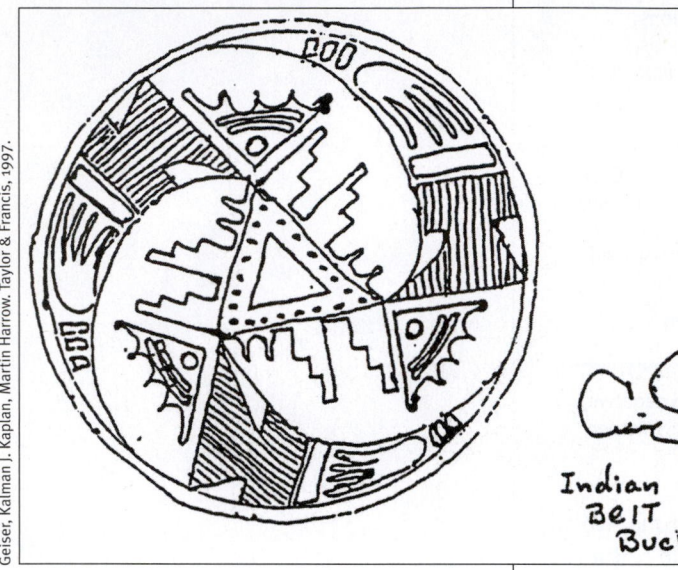

Drawing by Craig Geiser from Living with Schizophrenia by Stuart Emmons, Craig Geiser, Kalman J. Kaplan, Martin Harrow. Taylor & Francis, 1997.

The man who made this drawing said, "This belt buckle symbolized safety for me in my stay in the hospital. I felt no harm would come to me while I wore it. I also left it visible to me on my nightstand next to my bed at night. I thought several times the belt buckle saved me from whatever was going on. My belt buckle seemed as though it was wearing thinner, using up its strength a little at a time in helping me" (Emmons et al., 1997, p. 183). Although many people have a good luck charm, the fact that this man believed that his belt buckle was getting thinner because it was "using up its strength" suggests that he had a delusional belief about it.

Delusions
Persistent false beliefs that are held despite evidence that the beliefs are incorrect or exaggerate reality.

Word salad
Disorganized speech consisting of a random stream of seemingly unconnected words.

words. For example, a patient might say something like "Pots dog small is tabled." Another type of disorganized speech involves many *neologisms*, or words that the patient makes up:

> That's *wish-bell*. Double vision. It's like walking across a person's eye and reflecting personality. It works on you, like dying and going to the spiritual world, but landing in the *Vella* world.

(Marengo et al., 1985, p. 423)

In this case, "wish-bell" is the neologism; it doesn't exist, nor does it have an obvious meaning or function as a metaphor.

Disorganized Behavior

Another positive symptom (and recall that *positive* in this context means "present," not "good") of schizophrenia is *disorganized behavior*, behavior that is so unfocused and disconnected from a goal that the person cannot successfully accomplish a basic task, or the behavior is inappropriate in the situation. Disorganized behavior can range from laughing inappropriately in response to a serious matter or masturbating in front of others, to being unable to perform normal daily tasks such as washing oneself, putting together a simple meal, or even selecting appropriate clothes to wear.

Hester Genain had symptoms of schizophrenia that began in childhood, including disorganized behavior: "Hester did a lot of strange things. Once Mrs. Genain bought each girl four pairs of new panties, and Hester put on all four pairs over the dirty one she was wearing" (Rosenthal, 1963, p. 52).

The category of disorganized behavior also includes **catatonia** (also referred to as *catatonic behavior*), which occurs when an individual remains in an odd posture or position, with rigid muscles, for hours. For example, during her early 20s, Iris Genain's symptoms included standing in the same position for hours each evening.

These positive symptoms—hallucinations, delusions, disorganized speech, and disorganized behavior—constitute four of the five DSM-IV-TR symptom criteria for schizophrenia; the fifth criterion is any negative symptom (discussed in the following section). DSM-IV-TR requires that a person have a total of two—out of the five—of these symptoms (see Table 12.1) to be diagnosed with schizophrenia. In order to receive such a diagnosis, then, an individual must have a least one positive symptom.

Negative Symptoms

In contrast to positive symptoms, **negative symptoms** are marked by the *absence* or reduction of normal mental processes, mental contents, or behaviors. DSM-IV-TR specifies three types of negative symptoms: *flat affect*, *alogia*, and *avolition*. Each of these reflects the lack of a normal mental process, expression of feeling, or behavior, but they differ in what—specifically—is lacking. Let's look more closely at these negative symptoms.

Flat Affect: Muted Expression

Some people with schizophrenia exhibit **flat affect**, which occurs when a person does not display a great range of emotion and hence often seems emotionally neutral. Such people may not express or convey much information through their facial expressions or body language, and they tend to refrain from making eye contact (although they may smile somewhat and do not necessarily come off as "cold").

Although people with schizophrenia may not display much emotion, that doesn't necessarily mean that they don't *experience* much emotion. Studies suggest that their experience of emotion is much like that of other people (Aghevli, Blanchard, & Horan, 2003; Chattopadhyay, 2005; Myin-Germeys, Delespaul, & deVries, 2000). However, this is not apparent from casual observation.

Catatonia
A condition in which an individual remains in an odd posture or position, with rigid muscles, for hours.

Negative symptoms
Symptoms of schizophrenia that are marked by the *absence* or reduction of normal mental processes, mental contents, or behaviors.

Flat affect
A lack of, or considerably diminished, emotional expression, such as occurs when someone speaks robotically and shows little facial expression.

People with schizophrenia may exhibit flat affect—an extremely limited range of emotional expression—which can make them appear emotionally unresponsive. However, these people report experiencing emotions to the same degree as others do.

Alogia: Poverty of Speech

People with schizophrenia who have **alogia**, or poverty of speech, may respond slowly or minimally to questions and generally speak less than do most other people. A person with alogia will take a while to muster the mental effort necessary to respond to a question. Even choosing among words can be challenging. For example, if asked how he or she liked a television show that just ended, a person with alogia might nod once very briefly. If pushed to explain why the show was enjoyable, he or she might take 5–10 seconds to think and then just say "Funny."

Avolition: Difficulty Initiating or Following Through

In movies portraying people with schizophrenia, hospitalized patients are often shown sitting in chairs apparently doing nothing all day, not even talking to others. This portrayal suggests **avolition**, the term for difficulty in initiating or following through with activities. For example, Hester Genain would often sit for hours, seemingly staring into space, and had difficulty beginning her chores.

The sets of positive and negative symptoms in DSM-IV-TR grew out of decades of clinical observations of patients with schizophrenia; these symptoms can generally be observed or can be inferred by a trained individual. However, research has revealed that cognitive deficits—which are not part of the DSM-IV-TR criteria—also play a crucial role in schizophrenia. Let's examine these deficits.

Cognitive Deficits: The Specifics

Research has revealed the important role that cognitive deficits (also called *neurocognitive deficits*) play in the course and prognosis of schizophrenia (Barch, 2005; Green, 2001). In this section, we examine specific deficits in attention, memory, and executive functioning that arise in most people with schizophrenia (Keefe, Eesley, & Poe, 2005; Wilk et al., 2005).

Deficits in Attention

Cognitive deficits include difficulties in sustaining and focusing attention, which can involve distinguishing relevant from irrelevant stimuli (Gur et al., 2007). One individual with schizophrenia recounted: "If I am talking to someone they only need to cross their legs or scratch their heads and I am distracted and forget what I was saying" (Torrey, 2001, p. 29).

Deficits in Working Memory

Another area of cognitive functioning adversely affected in people with schizophrenia is *working memory*, which consists of short-term memory and a set of executive processes that operate on information in short-term memory (for example, by ordering it in new ways). Working memory organizes and transforms incoming information so that it will be available to be remembered later and also is involved in reasoning and related mental activities (Baddeley, 1986). For example, if you are trying to remember items you need to buy at the store, you will probably use working memory to organize the items into easy-to-recall categories. People with schizophrenia do not organize information effectively, which indicates that their working memories are impaired; they may not remember something they were told or shown once or even a few times.

However, when presented with information on multiple occasions, people with schizophrenia are able to store the information in long-term memory. Once the information is successfully stored, they will remember it as well as people who do not have schizophrenia (Chan et al., 2000; Green, 2001). Deficits in working memory may also lead to disruptions in reasoning—and hence to disorganized speech (Melinder & Barch, 2003).

Deficits in Executive Functioning

The problems with working memory apparently arise because people with schizophrenia often have difficulty with **executive functions**, which are mental processes involved in planning, organizing, problem solving, abstract thinking, and exercising good judgment (Cornblatt et al., 1997; Erlenmeyer-Kimling et al., 2000; Kim et al.,

Alogia
A negative symptom of schizophrenia marked by speaking less than most other people and responding slowly or minimally to questions.

Avolition
A negative symptom of schizophrenia marked by difficulty in initiating or following through with activities.

Executive functions
Mental processes involved in planning, organizing, problem solving, abstract thinking, and exercising good judgment.

2004). Executive functions are required to organize, interpret, and transform information in working memory—and hence a problem with such functioning will disrupt working memory. But more than this, the problems with executive functioning have far-reaching consequences for cognition in general. For instance, Hester had the most severe symptoms of the Genain quads, and her deficits in executive functioning were prominent much of the time. She had difficulty performing household chores that required multiple steps—such as making mashed potatoes by herself, which required peeling the potatoes, then boiling them, knowing when to take them out of the water, and mashing them with other (measured) ingredients. When Hester was not actively psychotic, she would be able to perform the first step of a multistep task, but only after she had finished that step could she begin to plan and implement a second step. After she completed each step, she needed to receive instructions for the next one. Obviously, deficits in executive functioning can impair a person's overall ability to function.

Cognitive Deficits Endure Over Time

Neurocognitive deficits do not necessarily make their first appearance at the same time that the DSM-IV-TR symptoms of schizophrenia first emerge. For many people who develop schizophrenia, cognitive deficits exist in childhood, well before a first episode of schizophrenia (Cannon et al., 1999; Erlenmeyer-Kimling et al., 2000; Fish et al., 1992; Fuller et al., 2002; Ott et al., 2002; Torrey, 2002). In addition to predating symptoms of schizophrenia, cognitive deficits often persist after the DSM-IV-TR symptoms improve (Hoff & Kremen, 2003; Hughes et al., 2003; Rund et al., 2004; Tsuang, Stone, & Faraone, 2000).

The lives of Genain sisters illustrate both the importance of cognitive deficits and their variety. Hester had the most difficulty academically and was held back in 5th grade because of her inadequate school performance. Moreover, she had difficulty carrying out simple household tasks and seemed to suffer from deficits in attention, memory, and executive functioning. The cognitive functioning of the other quads did not appear to be as impaired. In fact, Myra did not exhibit any significant cognitive deficits, and she graduated from high school, held a job, married, and had two children. Nora and Iris had moderate levels of cognitive deficits; they could perform full-time work for periods of time but could not function independently for long stretches (Mirsky & Quinn, 1988; Mirsky et al., 1987, 2000).

Limitations of DSM-IV-TR Criteria

Although the DSM-IV-TR criteria provide a relatively reliable way to diagnose schizophrenia, a number of researchers point to drawbacks of those criteria—both of the specific criteria and of the grouping of positive and negative symptoms (Fauman, 2006; Green, 2001). A more diagnostically and prognostically relevant set of symptoms, these researchers suggest, would focus on the extent of cognitive deficits and the breadth and severity of the DSM-IV-TR symptoms.

Absence of Focus on Cognitive and Social Functioning

Cognitive deficits are not specifically addressed by the DSM-IV-TR criteria, despite their importance. Specifically, although the DSM-IV-TR set of positive symptoms includes disorganized speech and disorganized behavior (see Table 12.1), research suggests that these two symptoms together form an important cluster, independent of hallucinations and delusions. Moreover, these symptoms arise from underlying cognitive deficits that contribute to disorganized thinking. For instance, cognitive deficits can cause thoughts to skip from one topic to another, topics that are related to each other only tangentially if at all (this problem is referred to as a *loosening of associations*). Thus, disorganized speech arises from disorganized thinking, but such thinking is not part of the DSM-IV-TR criteria. Similarly, disorganized behavior, such as laughing at a funeral or putting on four pairs of underwear, can arise because the individual's cognitive deficits prevent him or her from organizing social experiences into categories covered by general rules of behavior or conventions.

Cognitive deficits can also lead to unusual, although not necessarily disorganized, social behavior. As we'll discuss in more detail later, people with schizophrenia may be socially isolated and avoid contact with others because such interactions can be overwhelming or confusing. People with schizophrenia can have difficulty understanding the usual, unspoken rules of social convention. Also, even after an episode of schizophrenia has abated, they may not understand when someone is irritated because they do not notice or correctly interpret the other person's facial expression or tone of voice. When irritation erupts into anger, it can seem to come out of the blue, frightening and overwhelming people with schizophrenia. So, they may try to tread a safer path and avoid others as much as possible.

The poor social skills and social isolation that are frequently a part of schizophrenia are not included in the DSM-IV-TR criteria, although they are related to an impaired ability to work (Dickinson, Bellack, & Gold, 2007). The disorganized behavior, social isolation and poor social skills, and perhaps avolition, all are indicators of underlying cognitive deficits (Farrow et al., 2005).

Categorical, Not Continual

The DSM-IV-TR definition of schizophrenia (and other disorders; see Chapter 3) is categorical—that is, someone's symptoms either meet the criteria (in this case, indicate that he or she has schizophrenia) or do not. Some researchers in the field question whether schizophrenia is best described as a category and suggest that instead it should be regarded as located on a continuum (Tsuang, Stone, & Faraone, 2000; Westen et al., 2002). Recognizing this limitation, DSM-IV-TR does provide an alternative way to diagnose schizophrenia, allowing the clinician to rate the symptoms as absent, mild, moderate, or severe (American Psychiatric Association, 2000).

Moreover, the list of symptoms is divided into three dimensions: positive (hallucinations and delusions), disorganized (speech and behavior, and inappropriate affect), and negative (alogia, avolition, or flat affect), and each dimension is rated separately. These dimensions better reflect how the symptoms cluster together: Symptoms within each of these dimensions tend to vary with each other more than they do with symptoms on other dimensions. Thus, someone with severe hallucinations is more likely to have severe delusions as well, but not necessarily to have severe negative symptoms. As shown in Figure 12.1, the alternative system in DSM-IV-TR enables clinicians and researchers to note that someone with schizophrenia has differing levels of symptom severity across each of the three dimensions. In keeping with current research, this chapter discusses disorganized symptoms as a separate symptom cluster.

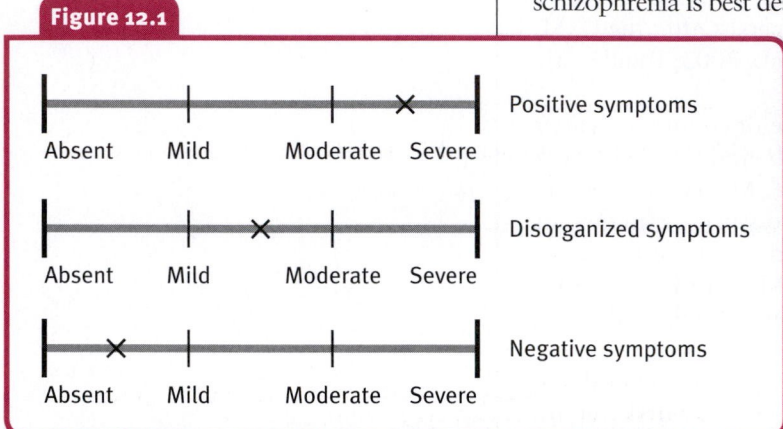

Figure 12.1

12.1 ▶ Symptoms of Schizophrenia as Positions on Continuous Dimensions In DSM-IV-TR's alternative way of diagnosing schizophrenia, symptoms within the three symptom clusters are rated on a continuum from absent to severe. Symptoms within each cluster tend to vary together, but independently of the other clusters. In the example shown, the individual has severe positive symptoms, moderate disorganized symptoms, and only mild negative symptoms.

Subtypes of Schizophrenia

DSM-IV-TR specifies a set of subtypes of schizophrenia, which are based on the presence or absence of particular positive symptoms. Over time, the diagnosis of subtype may change, as the prominence of different symptoms shifts (Reichenberg, Reickmann, & Harvery, 2005). Information on the importance of cognitive deficits in schizophrenia has led many researchers to use an alternative set of subtypes. Let's examine both sets.

DSM-IV-TR Subtypes

DSM-IV-TR identifies five subtypes of schizophrenia: paranoid, disorganized, catatonic, undifferentiated, and residual.

Paranoid Schizophrenia

Paranoid schizophrenia is characterized by the presence of delusions and auditory hallucinations that are limited to specific topics that have a coherent paranoid or

Paranoid schizophrenia
The subtype of schizophrenia characterized by the presence of delusions and auditory hallucinations that are limited to specific topics that have a coherent paranoid or grandiose theme.

grandiose theme. An example of a paranoid theme is that the person believes that he or she is being hunted by the CIA; an example of a grandiose theme is that the person believes that he or she is God. Pamela Spiro Wagner describes one of her paranoid delusions, which involves being hunted by "the Five People":

> The computers at the drugstore across the street, programmed by the Five People, have tapped into my TV set and monitor my activities with special radar. If I go out, special agents keep every one of my movements under surveillance. A man lighting a cigarette near the drugstore uses his lighter to signal to another just down the street, warning him of my approach. Another alerts conspirators inside. Nothing I do, indoors or out, goes unremarked.

> (Wagner & Spiro, 2005, p. 205)

People with paranoid schizophrenia can have relatively intact cognitive and emotional functioning when the content of their thoughts and experiences does not relate to their delusion.

Diagnosing people with paranoid schizophrenia can be difficult because they may seem normal if they don't talk about the topic of their delusions. Although the paranoid subtype has the best recovery rate (Fenton & McGlashan, 1991), it is also the subtype most associated with aggressive behavior. People with this subtype of schizophrenia can act aggressively toward either themselves or others, and they have the highest suicide rate, 13%, among all patients with schizophrenia (Fenton & McGlashan, 1991).

Disorganized Schizophrenia

Disorganized speech and behavior and inappropriate emotional expression are typical of the subtype called **disorganized schizophrenia**. People with disorganized schizophrenia may giggle, dress strangely, speak obscenely or incoherently (like Emilio in Case 12.1), or urinate or defecate in public. People with disorganized schizophrenia generally have a poor prognosis and, because of their inability to care for themselves, may require constant care.

CASE 12.1 ▶ FROM THE OUTSIDE: Disorganized Schizophrenia

Emilio is a 40-year-old man who looks 10 years younger. He is brought to the hospital, his twelfth hospitalization, by his mother because she is afraid of him. He is dressed in a ragged overcoat, bedroom slippers, and a baseball cap and wears several medals around his neck. His affect ranges from anger at his mother ("She feeds me shit . . . what comes out of other people's rectums") to a giggling, obsequious seductiveness toward the interviewer. His speech and manner have a childlike quality, and he walks with a mincing step and exaggerated hip movements. His mother reports that he stopped taking his medication about a month ago and has since begun to hear voices and to look and act more bizarrely. When asked what he has been doing, he says, "eating wires and lighting fires." His spontaneous speech is often incoherent and marked by frequent rhyming and clang associations (speech in which sounds, rather than meaningful relationships, govern word choice).

Emilio's first hospitalization occurred after he dropped out of school at age 16, and since that time he has never been able to attend school or hold a job. He has been treated with neuroleptics [antipsychotic medications] during his hospitalizations but doesn't continue to take medication when he leaves, so he quickly becomes disorganized again. He lives with his elderly mother, but sometimes disappears for several months at a time and is eventually picked up by the police as he wanders in the streets. There is no known history of drug or alcohol abuse.

(Spitzer et al., 2002, pp. 189–190)

Catatonic Schizophrenia

Catatonic schizophrenia is characterized by catatonic (stiff or seemingly "frozen") postures or poses, bizarre jerky movements, or frozen facial expressions. A person with catatonic schizophrenia also may not speak, may involuntarily and senselessly repeat words or phrases said by others, or may mimic other people's bodily movements. Because they are unable to take care of themselves, such as by eating and washing, people with catatonic schizophrenia require constant care.

Disorganized schizophrenia
The subtype of schizophrenia characterized by disorganized speech and behavior and inappropriate emotional expression.

Catatonic schizophrenia
The subtype of schizophrenia characterized by stiff or "frozen" postures or poses, bizarre jerky movements, or frozen facial expression.

Grunnitus Studio/Photo Researchers

This woman suffers from catatonic schizophrenia. People diagnosed with this subtype of schizophrenia assume odd postures or poses for hours at a time, and may senselessly repeat words or remain mute. People with catatonic schizophrenia typically cannot care for themselves and require constant attention.

Undifferentiated Schizophrenia

When someone's symptoms lead to the diagnosis of schizophrenia but do not completely match those specified for paranoid, disorganized, or catatonic schizophrenia, the individual will be diagnosed with the subtype **undifferentiated schizophrenia**.

Residual Schizophrenia

Regardless of the subtype of schizophrenia that someone has, when the positive (and disorganized) symptoms have subsided but the negative symptoms persist, the full criteria for schizophrenia are no longer met; the person's subtype classification changes to *residual schizophrenia*, which indicates that there is a residue of (negative) symptoms but the pronounced positive symptoms have faded away. Residual schizophrenia may also be diagnosed when prominent negative symptoms are absent but two or more mild positive symptoms, such as odd beliefs that are not delusional, are present (American Psychiatric Association, 2000). The diagnosis of residual schizophrenia may apply only during a brief period, for example, during an individual's transition from a psychotic state to remission. Sometimes, though, an individual's symptoms may be such that the diagnosis of residual schizophrenia is assigned indefinitely.

Deficit/Nondeficit Subtypes

In contrast to the DSM-IV-TR subtypes of schizophrenia, an alternative set of subtypes is based on the presence or absence of neurocognitive deficits (Horan & Blanchard, 2003; Kirkpatrick et al., 1989). The *deficit subtype* requires the presence of severe neurocognitive deficits in attention, memory, and executive functioning, as well as the positive and negative symptoms that are manifestations of these deficits, such as disorganized speech and behavior and alogia. Such patients are generally more impaired than are other patients with schizophrenia, their symptoms are less likely to improve with currently available treatments, and they have a poorer prognosis.

The *nondeficit subtype* requires the presence of primarily positive symptoms, such as hallucinations and delusions, in conjunction with relatively intact cognitive functioning. People with this subtype are generally less impaired, and they have a better prognosis (McGlashan & Fenton, 1993). Someone with the paranoid subtype in DSM-IV-TR is considered to have the nondeficit subtype.

Distinguishing Between Schizophrenia and Other Disorders

Positive or negative symptoms may arise in schizophrenia or in the context of other disorders. Clinicians and researchers must determine whether the positive or negative symptoms reflect schizophrenia, another disorder, or, in some cases, schizophrenia *and* another disorder. Let's examine the other disorders that have symptoms similar to those of schizophrenia and consider how these disorders are distinguished from schizophrenia. We will contrast schizophrenia with mood disorders, substance-related disorders, and a set of various psychotic disorders—including schizophreniform and brief psychotic disorders, schizoaffective disorder, delusional disorder, shared psychotic disorder, and schizotypal personality disorder.

Psychotic Symptoms in Schizophrenia, Mood Disorders, and Substance-Related Disorders

Other psychological disorders, most notably mood disorders and substance-related disorders, may involve symptoms such as hallucinations and delusions. (Mood disorders with psychotic features are discussed in Chapter 6, and substance-induced hallucinations and delusions are discussed in Chapter 9.) The nature of these psychotic symptoms is usually consistent with the characteristics of the mood disorder

Undifferentiated schizophrenia
The subtype of schizophrenia characterized by symptoms that do not completely match those specified for the paranoid, disorganized, or catatonic subtype.

or substance-related disorder, and the psychotic symptoms only arise during a mood episode or with substance use or withdrawal. For instance, people with mania may become psychotic, developing grandiose delusions about their abilities. Psychotic mania is distinguished from schizophrenia by the presence of other symptoms of mania—such as pressured speech or little need for sleep. Psychotically depressed people may have delusions or hallucinations; the delusions usually involve themes of the depressed person's worthlessness or the "badness" of certain body parts (e.g., "My intestines are rotting").

Substance-related disorders can lead to delusions (see Chapter 9), such as the paranoid delusions that arise from chronic use of stimulants. Substances (and withdrawal from them) can also induce hallucinations, such as the tactile hallucinations that can arise with cocaine use (e.g., the feeling that bugs are crawling over a person's arms).

Some negative symptoms of schizophrenia can be difficult to distinguish from symptoms of other disorders, notably depression: People with schizophrenia or depression may show little interest in activities, hardly speak at all, give minimal replies to questions, and avoid social situations (American Psychiatric Association, 2000). As noted in Table 12.2, although both of these disorders may involve similar outward behaviors, the behaviors arise from different causes. With schizophrenia, these behavioral symptoms stem from the cognitive deficits associated with the disorder. In general, people with schizophrenia but not depression do not have other symptoms of depression, such as changes in weight or sleep or feelings of worthlessness and guilt (American Psychiatric Association, 2000). Of course, people with schizophrenia may develop comorbid disorders, such as depression or substance abuse. The presence of any comorbid disorder can make it more difficult to determine the correct diagnoses.

Table 12.2 ▶ Behavioral Symptoms Common to Depression and Schizophrenia

Behavioral Symptoms	Causes in Depression	Causes in Schizophrenia
Little or no interest in activities, staring into space for long periods of time	Lack of pleasure in activities (anhedonia), difficulty making decisions	Difficulty initiating behavior (avolition)
Short or "empty" replies to questions	Lack of energy	Difficulty organizing thoughts to speak
Social isolation	Lack of energy, anhedonia, feeling undeserving of companionship	Feeling overwhelmed by social situations, lack of social skills

Psychotic Disorders

Although mood disorders and substance-related disorders may involve psychotic symptoms, the diagnostic criteria for these two categories of disorders do not specifically require the presence of psychotic symptoms. In contrast, the criteria for the disorders collectively referred to as *psychotic disorders* specifically require the presence of psychotic symptoms. Psychotic disorders are considered to lie on a spectrum, related to each other in their symptoms and risk factors but differing in their specific constellations of symptoms, duration, and severity. In addition to schizophrenia, these disorders include schizophreniform disorder, brief psychotic disorder, schizoaffective disorder, delusional disorder, and shared psychotic disorder. Although it is not classified as a psychotic disorder, the personality disorder *schizotypal personality disorder* (discussed in Chapter 13) is thought to be part of the spectrum of schizophrenia-related disorders (Kendler, Neale, & Walsh, 1995). Let's examine each of these disorders in turn.

Schizophreniform and Brief Psychotic Disorders

In some cases, an individual's symptoms may meet most, but not all, of the criteria for a diagnosis of schizophrenia. The individual clearly suffers from some psychotic symptoms and has significant difficulty in functioning as a result of his or her psychological problems. However, the impaired functioning hasn't been present for the minimum 6-month duration required for a diagnosis of schizophrenia. Two disorders fall into this class, depending on the specifics of the symptoms and their duration.

Schizophreniform disorder is the diagnosis given when a person's symptoms meet all the criteria for schizophrenia *except* that the symptoms have been present for only 1–6 months (American Psychiatric Association, 2000). In addition, daily functioning may or may not have declined over that period of time. If the symptoms persist for more than 6 months (and daily functioning significantly declines, if it hasn't already), the diagnosis shifts to schizophrenia.

In contrast, **brief psychotic disorder** refers to the sudden onset of psychotic symptoms (hallucinations and delusions), symptoms of disorganized speech or behavior, or catatonic behavior, that last between a day and a month and are followed by a full recovery (American Psychiatric Association, 2000). With this disorder, no negative symptoms should be present during the episode. Rather, brief psychotic disorder is marked by intense emotional episodes and confusion, during which the person may be so disorganized that he or she can't function safely and independently; he or she also has a higher risk of suicide during the time of the episode. Once recovered, people who had this disorder have a good prognosis for full recovery (Pillman et al., 2002).

Schizoaffective Disorder

Schizoaffective disorder is characterized by the presence of both schizophrenia *and* a depressive, manic, or mixed mood episode (see Chapter 6). Because schizoaffective disorder involves mood episodes, negative symptoms such as flat affect are not common, and the diagnosis is likely to be made solely on the basis of positive symptoms. Because of their mood episodes, people with schizoaffective disorder are at greater risk for committing suicide than are people with schizophrenia (Bhatia et al., 2006; De Hert, McKenzie, & Peuskens, 2001). The prognosis for recovery from schizoaffective disorder is better than that for recovery from schizophrenia, particularly when stressors or events clearly contribute to the disorder (American Psychiatric Association, 2000).

Delusional Disorder

When a person's sole symptom is that he or she adheres to nonbizarre but demonstrably incorrect beliefs—those that are theoretically plausible, such as believing that someone is following you—and those beliefs have persisted for more than 1 month, that person is diagnosed with **delusional disorder**. Note that the assessment of the bizarreness of the beliefs distinguishes schizophrenia (bizarre) from delusional disorder (nonbizarre). What is interpreted as being bizarre will vary across clinicians, depending on their experience with people from different subcultures, ethnic groups, or countries; what may seem bizarre to a clinician, though, may be understandable given a particular patient's background and experience (Mullen, 2003). Clinicians and researchers have identified the following types of nonbizarre delusions (American Psychiatric Association, 2000):

- *Erotomanic.* The belief that another person is in love with the patient. This delusion usually focuses on romantic or spiritual union rather than sexual attraction. It is common for people with erotomania to try to contact the person who is the object of their delusion.

- *Grandiose.* The belief that the patient has a great (but unrecognized) ability, talent, or achievement.

- *Persecutory.* The belief that the patient is being spied on, drugged, harassed, or otherwise conspired against. Small snubs or slights are magnified in the patient's eyes, and he or she may seek legal action to redress these perceived insults. People with this delusion sometimes become violent against those whom they perceive as harming them.

Schizophreniform disorder
The psychotic disorder characterized by symptoms that meet all the criteria for schizophrenia *except* that the symptoms have been present for only 1–6 months and daily functioning may or may not have declined over that period of time.

Brief psychotic disorder
The psychotic disorder characterized by the sudden onset of positive or disorganized symptoms that last between a day and a month and are followed by a full recovery.

Schizoaffective disorder
The psychotic disorder characterized by the presence of both schizophrenia *and* a depressive, manic, or mixed mood episode.

Delusional disorder
The psychotic disorder characterized by the presence of nonbizarre but demonstrably incorrect beliefs that have persisted for more than 1 month.

Diana Napolis suffered from persecutory delusions about filmmaker Stephen Spielberg and singer and actress Jennifer Love Hewitt; she believed that both were controlling her brain (Soto, 2003).

- *Somatic.* The false belief that the patient is experiencing bodily sensations (such as insects on the skin) or bodily malfunctions (such as a foul odor coming from a body cavity).

- *Jealous.* The belief that the patient's partner is unfaithful. This belief is based on tiny amounts of "evidence," such as the partner's arriving home a few minutes late. The patient is likely to confront his or her partner with the "evidence" and may try to "prevent" further unfaithful acts by following or attacking the partner.

People with delusional disorder—like those with the paranoid subtype of schizophrenia—may appear normal when they are not talking about their delusions: Their behavior may not be particularly odd nor their functioning otherwise impaired. The prognosis for people with this disorder is mixed. For some, the delusions may ebb and flow, sometimes interfering with daily life and sometimes fading into the background and not having any effect; for others, the delusions may dwindle away and not reappear.

Henry Genain, the quads' father, exhibited some signs of delusional disorder of the jealous type: Soon after he met Maud, the Genains' mother, he asked her to marry him, but she refused. He pestered her for months, threatening that if she didn't marry him, neither of them would live to marry anyone else. On multiple occasions, he threatened to kill himself or her. After she consented to marry him (because his family begged her to), he didn't want her to socialize with anyone else, including her family: "I want you with me. I'm not going to let you go among other people. . . . I wouldn't trust no woman. All women are weak. I'm not going to trust you either" (Rosenthal, 1963, p. 33). His jealousy was so extreme that he didn't want her to go out of the house because people walking down the street might smile at her. When the quads were 7 years old, Mrs. Genain thought of leaving Henry, but he told her, "If you leave me, I will find you where you go and I'll kill you" (Rosenthal, 1963, p. 69). She believed him and stayed with him.

Shared Psychotic Disorder

Have you ever worried about "catching" a psychological disorder? Probably not. However, in rare cases, something very much like this seems to occur. Perhaps the most exotic psychotic disorder is **shared psychotic disorder** (or *folie à deux*, which is French for "paired madness"), which occurs when an individual develops delusions as a result of his or her close relationship with another person who has delusions as

Shared psychotic disorder
The psychotic disorder in which an individual develops delusions as a result of his or her close relationship with another person who has delusions as part of a psychotic disorder; also known as *folie à deux*.

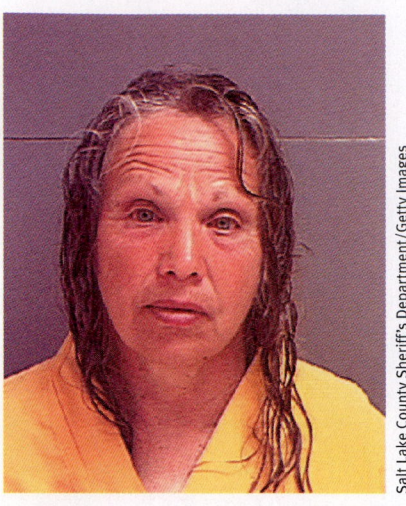

Salt Lake County Sheriff's Department/Getty Images

Salt Lake County Sheriff's Department/Getty Images

Wanda Barzee and her husband, Brian David Mitchell, kidnapped 14-year-old Elizabeth Smart in 2002. Mitchell believed he was God, and Barzee apparently came to share his belief. Although diagnosing Barzee was difficult, some doctors who examined her believed that she had shared psychotic disorder.

part of a psychotic disorder. The person who had the disorder at the outset is referred to as the primary person and is usually diagnosed with schizophrenia or delusional disorder. The individual diagnosed with shared psychotic disorder comes to adopt the delusions of his or her close friend or family member. The delusions of the primary person may be shared by more than one other person, as can occur in families when the primary person is a parent. When the primary person's delusions subside, the other person's shared delusions may or may not subside as well.

For example, in one case of shared psychotic disorder, the primary person was a young woman with hallucinations and delusions; she was later diagnosed with schizophrenia. She believed that God was sending messages to her. She lived with her two older sisters and convinced them that God was talking to her and that they should join her in taking over a nearby house because God wished it. Her sisters came to share the delusions; they attempted to burglarize the house but were arrested. When the older sisters were separated from their ill sister, their delusions abated (Joshi, Frierson, & Gunter, 2006).

Schizotypal Personality Disorder

Eccentric behaviors and difficulty with relationships are the hallmarks of *schizotypal personality disorder*, to be discussed in more detail with the other personality disorders in Chapter 13. Although schizotypal personality disorder is not technically a psychotic disorder, we mention it here because some research suggests that it may in fact be a milder form of schizophrenia (Dickey, McCarley, & Shenton, 2002). With this personality disorder, problems in relationships may become evident in early adulthood, marked by discomfort when relating to others as well as by being stiff or inappropriate in relationships. However, before you start to become concerned for yourself or someone you know, keep in mind that relationship difficulties are not enough for a diagnosis of schizotypal personality disorder; eccentric behavior, such as having unusual mannerisms or difficulty following social conventions, must also be present. For example, people with schizotypal personality disorder may not make eye contact and may look to one side of a person's face when they speak to him or her (and, to complicate things a bit, to be considered a symptom of schizotypal personality disorder, such behavior should not be due to social anxiety disorder). A person with schizotypal personality disorder may have very few if any close friends, may feel that he or she doesn't fit in, and may experience social anxiety. Schizotypal personality disorder, unlike schizophrenia, does not involve psychotic symptoms. Table 12.3 summarizes the features of the psychotic disorders.

Figure 12.2 shows a decision tree for diagnosing psychotic disorders.

Schizophrenia Facts in Detail

In this section we will discuss additional facts about schizophrenia—how common it is, the disorders that are most frequently comorbid with it, gender and cultural factors related to the disorder, and the prognosis for patients with the disorder.

Prevalence

The world over—from China or Finland to the United States or New Guinea—approximately 1% of the population will develop schizophrenia at some point in their lives (Gottesman, 1991; Perälä et al., 2007).

Schizophrenia is one of the top five causes of disability among adults in developed nations, ranking with heart disease, arthritis, drug use, and HIV (Murray & Lopez, 1996). In the United States, about 5% of people with schizophrenia (about

Figure 12.2

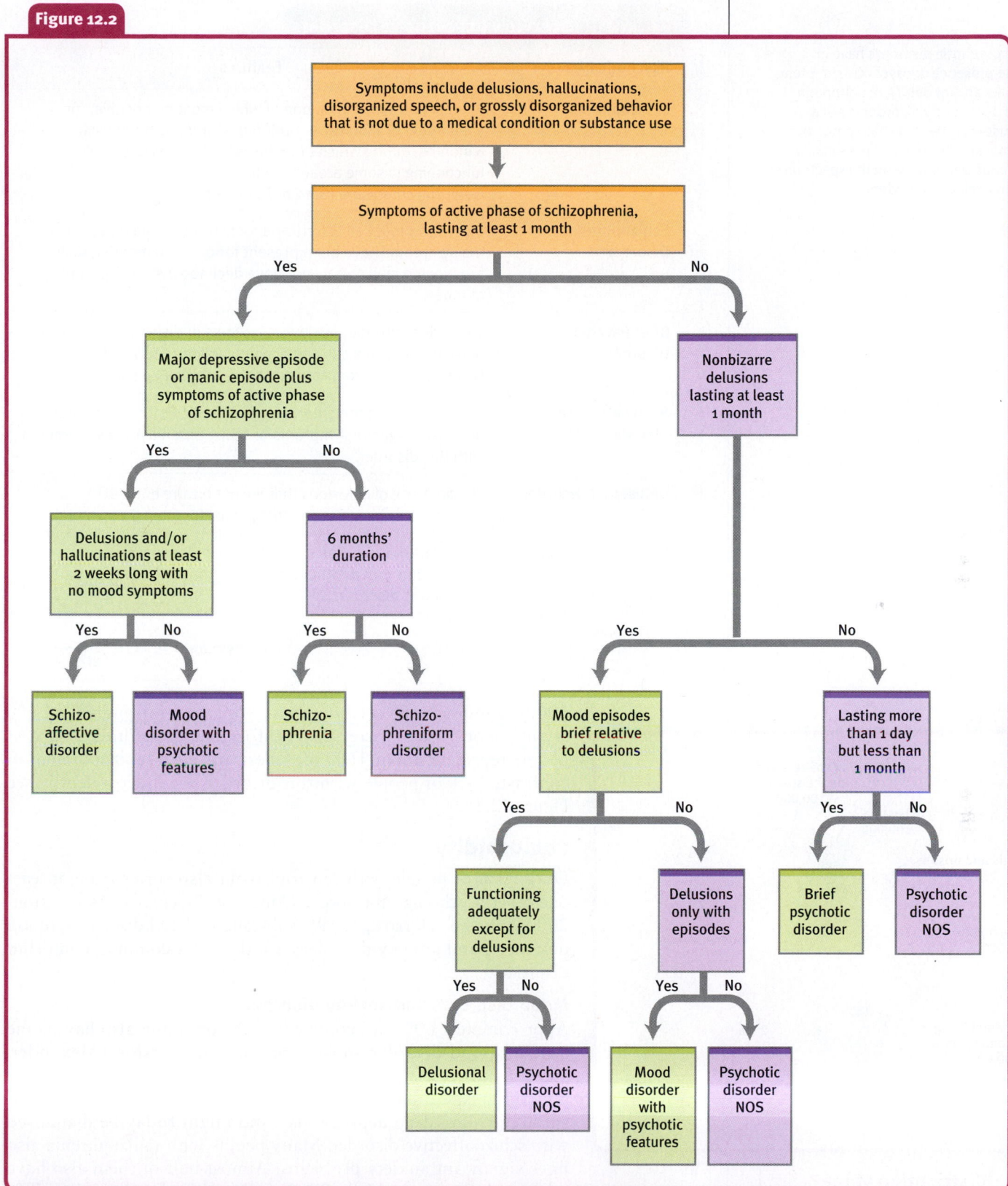

12.2 ▶ Differential Diagnosis Decision Tree for Psychotic Disorders

Note: NOS stands for "not otherwise specified." A psychotic disorder NOS is one in which psychotic symptoms significantly cause distress or impair functioning but do not match the full criteria for any other disorder in this category.

Source: Adapted from American Psychiatric Association, 2000, Appendix A, pp. 750–751.

The various psychotic disorders have in common the presence of psychotic symptoms: hallucinations and/or delusions. Although schizotypal personality disorder is not a psychotic disorder (because hallucinations and delusions are absent), this personality disorder is considered to be on the spectrum of schizophrenia-related disorders.

Table 12.3 ▸ Overview of Psychotic Disorders

Psychotic Disorder	Features
Schizophrenia	At least two symptoms, one of which must be positive, for a minimum of 1 month; continuous symptoms for at least 6 months, during which time the individual has impaired functioning in some area(s) of life. *Note: Full criteria are listed in Table 12.1.*
Schizophreniform Disorder	Symptoms meet all the criteria for schizophrenia *except* that the symptoms have been present for only 1–6 months; daily functioning may or may not have declined over that period of time.
Brief Psychotic Disorder	The sudden onset of positive symptoms or disorganization, which persists between a day and a month, followed by a full recovery. No negative symptoms are present during the episode.
Schizoaffective Disorder	Symptoms meet the criteria for both schizophrenia and mood disorder. Negative symptoms of schizophrenia are less common with this disorder.
Delusional Disorder	The presence of delusions that are not bizarre but are demonstrably incorrect and that persist for more than 1 month.
Shared Psychotic Disorder (folie à deux)	Delusions that arise as a result of the individual's close relationship with another person who has delusions as part of a psychotic disorder.

Source: Torrey, 2001.

Figure 12.3

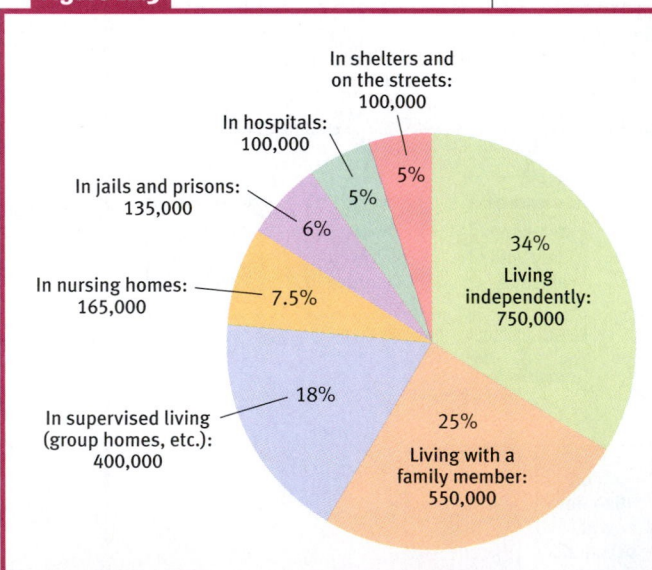

12.3 ▸ Distribution of the 2.2 Million Americans with Schizophrenia

100,000 individuals) are homeless, 5% are in hospitals, and 6% are in jail or prison (Torrey, 2001). Together, these three groups of people represent about 16% of Americans with schizophrenia; in contrast, 34% of people with this disorder live independently (see Figure 12.3).

Comorbidity

Over 90% of people with schizophrenia also suffer from at least one other psychological disorder (American Psychiatric Association, 2000; Sands & Harrow, 1999). Substance-related disorders, mood disorders, and anxiety disorders are the most common comorbid disorders.

Mood Disorders and Anxiety Disorders

Approximately 80% of people with schizophrenia also have some type of mood disorder, most commonly depression (Alexander, 1996; Sands & Harrow, 1999). As noted earlier, such individuals are said to have a *schizoaffective disorder*. Iris Genain, for instance, suffered from "deep depressions" and might today be diagnosed with schizoaffective disorder. Many people with schizophrenia also have significant anxiety problems: Almost half of them also have panic attacks (Goodwin, Lyons, & McNally, 2002) and anxiety disorders (Cosoff & Hafner, 1998).

Substance-Related Disorders

Up to 60% of people with schizophrenia have a substance abuse problem that is not related to tobacco (Swartz et al., 2006). Moreover, 90% of those with schizophrenia smoke cigarettes (Regier et al., 1990), and they tend to inhale more deeply than do other smokers (Tidey et al., 2005). One hypothesis for the high comorbidity with nicotine dependence is that the cigarette use is a form of self-medication, because the nicotine affects certain receptors in the brain related to symptoms of schizophrenia (Kumari & Postma, 2005).

In addition, some people with schizophrenia may use alcohol and other drugs to alleviate their symptoms:

> The voices are like people having a conversation inside my head of which I am not a part. They can be like scratching, whispers, or real loud, like shouting. They clutter my mind and I cannot think straight until I am unable to do anything. . . . When I first heard the voices, I would drink until I passed out. When I woke up with a vicious hangover, the voices would be there like thunder, and I would start drinking again.
>
> **(Hummingbird, 1999, pp. 863–864)**

As is clear from this patient's description, drinking brought temporary relief from intrusive and persistent auditory hallucinations.

Researchers have also noted that even before their positive symptoms emerged, some people with schizophrenia abused drugs, particularly nicotine (cigarettes), marijuana, amphetamines, phencyclidine (PCP), mescaline, and lysergic acid diethylamide (LSD) (Bowers et al., 2001; Weiser et al., 2004). For example, a study of Swedish males found that those who used marijuana in adolescence were more likely later to develop schizophrenia. The more a person used marijuana, the more likely he or she was to develop schizophrenia, particularly if the drug was used more than 50 times (Moore et al., 2007; Zammit et al., 2002). Similarly, a longitudinal study found that girls who used marijuana by age 18 and then later developed schizophrenia had more symptoms of schizophrenia at age 26 than did controls; other studies have found similar results (Arseneault et al., 2002; Verdoux et al., 2003).

Without question, frequent use of marijuana is associated with subsequent schizophrenia; moreover, people with schizophrenia who also use marijuana are more likely to have aggravated symptoms and more relapses (Johns, 2001). However, keep in mind the correlation between using marijuana and subsequent schizophrenia does not show that the drug *causes* schizophrenia. Perhaps marijuana use leads to schizophrenic symptoms only in those who were likely to develop the disorder anyway, or some aspect of a predisposition to develop schizophrenia also might make drug use attractive. It is also possible that marijuana "tips the scales" in those who are vulnerable but who would not develop schizophrenia if they did not use the drug. Or, perhaps some other factor affects both substance abuse and subsequent schizophrenia (Bowers et al., 2001). Researchers do not yet know enough to be able to choose among these possibilities, and true experiments designed to investigate them would obviously be unethical.

One study may be able to shed some light on the relationship between using marijuana and later developing schizophrenia: The study compared marijuana use by those who have a "predisposition" toward psychosis (e.g., a pattern of odd or paranoid thoughts) versus those who do not have such a predisposition (Henquet et al., 2005). The researchers began the study before any of the participants had developed the disorder, and thus they were able to examine marijuana use prior to emergence of the symptoms. The study not only found that marijuana use was associated with later development of psychosis, but also that it had a greater effect on those who were predisposed to develop schizophrenia. Moreover, the more extensively marijuana was used, the more likely psychosis was to develop. Finally, this study did not support the notion that those who are predisposed to develop schizophrenia use marijuana in an attempt to medicate themselves: Those who were predisposed were not more likely to use marijuana 4 years later.

Why might people with, or at risk for, schizophrenia be drawn to use marijuana at all? Glimmers of an answer come from a neuropsychological study of people with schizophrenia who used marijuana with varying frequencies. Those who used

Guitarist Peter Green (lying down), cofounder of the rock group Fleetwood Mac, developed schizophrenia after using LSD frequently. Although Green attributes his illness to his drug abuse, researchers cannot yet definitively state that such abuse *causes* schizophrenia in people who might not otherwise develop the disorder.

Araldo Di Crollalanza/Rex Features, Courtesy Everett Collection marijuana more frequently and more recently actually performed better on various neuropsychological tests, which suggests that marijuana use may enhance the cognitive functioning of people with schizophrenia (Coulston et al., 2007). Results from an fMRI study suggest that marijuana affects people with schizophrenia by increasing the activity of the frontal lobe, which counteracts some of the cognitive deficits and impaired brain functioning that can accompany the disorder (Callicott et al., 2003; Freedman, 2008).

Course

Typically, schizophrenia develops in phases. In the premorbid phase, before symptoms develop, some people may display personality characteristics that later evolve into negative symptoms. During the **prodromal phase**, which occurs before the onset of a psychological disorder, symptoms may develop gradually but do not meet all the criteria for the disorder. In the **active phase**, a person has full-blown positive and negative symptoms that meet all of the criteria for the disorder. Over time, the individual may fully recover, may have intermittent episodes, or may develop chronic symptoms that interfere with normal functioning.

Premorbid Phase

In the premorbid phase, a person who later goes on to develop schizophrenia may appear odd or eccentric and may have difficulty interacting with other people appropriately. This was the case for the Genain quads; during the premorbid phase, the sisters, with the possible exception of Myra, were seen as odd, and lacked the skills to make and sustain relationships with nonfamily members. However, it is important to note that most people who are odd or have eccentric tendencies do not develop schizophrenia. In addition, many people who develop schizophrenia, and particularly those who develop schizoaffective disorder, did not have odd or eccentric characteristics before the illness emerged.

Prodromal Phase

The prodromal phase, which may last from months to years, is marked by signs of suspiciousness, some disorganized thinking or behavior, poor hygiene, angry outbursts, and social withdrawal. These behaviors can be seen as precursors of the symptoms of schizophrenia, but they have not reached the level of positive and negative symptoms necessary for a diagnosis of schizophrenia (Heinssen et al., 2001; Maurer & Häfner, 1995).

The prodromal phase was a bit different for each Genain sister. Hester may have begun her prodromal phase as early as age 11, when her cognitive functioning was sufficiently impaired that she could no longer keep up in school and was held back. Moreover, even in elementary school, she was described as socially inept (Rosenthal, 1963; Mirsky et al., 2000). By 11th grade, her symptoms progressed to the point that she could no longer function well enough to attend school. In spring of that year, she was on her way to the active phase: "She complained of feeling insecure, was temperamental, began making sighing noises, clicking her tongue, and 'hatefully' combed her hair" (Rosenthal, 1963, p. 104). The tongue clicking and sighing continued for months, and she became destructive, breaking things. Instead of attending 12th grade, she stayed home, helping her mother around the house. Hester dressed and fed herself, but she was very slow at these tasks and would sometimes simply sit and stare into space.

In contrast, Nora's prodromal symptoms emerged later. After high school, she was employed as a stenography clerk in the same building as her father's office. However, after 1 year of working there, she began to have crying spells and increasing agitation. Her father criticized her for working too hard and told her to quit her job. During the time she held the job, Nora successfully fought off an attempted rape by a client of the company she worked for; her parents' (and boss's) response was that she should keep quiet about it and go on as if nothing happened. After that, she became increasingly agitated and disorganized until she quit her job several months later. Her illness progressed to the active phase; she developed

Prodromal phase
The phase that precedes the onset of a psychological disorder (such as schizophrenia) when symptoms do not yet meet all the criteria for the disorder.

Active phase
The phase of a psychological disorder (such as schizophrenia) in which the individual exhibits symptoms that meet all the criteria for the disorder.

psychotic symptoms, one of which was her complaint that the bones in her neck were slipping out of place.

Active Phase

During the active phase (which is also sometimes referred to as an *episode of schizophrenia* or *psychotic episode*), symptoms become full-blown, thereby meeting the diagnostic criteria for schizophrenia. It is usually positive symptoms that lead to the diagnosis. For up to 80% of people having a first episode of schizophrenia, the symptoms subside after treatment—they go into *remission* (Robinson et al., 1999).

However, for some people, the symptoms persist, even with medication; these patients are chronically ill. Approximately 60–70% of people who have had an episode of schizophrenia go on to have additional episodes (Torrey, 2001), but keep in mind that this also means that 30–40% of people who experience one episode never have another.

Middle-to-Late Phase

For people who continue to have active episodes of schizophrenia, cognitive functioning may decline significantly during the first 5 years of the illness; also, as they remain or become more disorganized, their ability to care for themselves declines. For example, they may reach a point where they cannot keep themselves properly groomed, or even dress themselves. However, by 10 years after the first episode, these people usually stabilize and seldom become worse. By 30 years after schizophrenia first developed, their functioning may have improved somewhat (see Table 12.4), particularly when some type of treatment has been effective. In fact, most of the Genain sisters improved (Mirsky et al., 2000). Iris and Nora were able to work part-time as volunteers; in their 40s and beyond, these two sisters were able to live outside of a hospital setting (Rosenthal, 1963; Mirsky et al., 2000).

Table 12.4 ▶ 10-Year and 30-Year Course of Schizophrenia

	10 Years Later	30 Years Later
Completely recovered	25%	25%
Much improved, relatively independent	25%	35%
Improved, but requiring extensive support network	25%	15%
Hospitalized, unimproved	15%	10%
Dead, mostly by suicide	10%	15%

Source: Torrey, 2001, p. 130.

Gender Differences

Men are somewhat more likely to develop schizophrenia than are women (McGrath, 2006) and do so at an earlier age. Specifically, men are more likely to develop the disorder between the ages of 18 and 25, whereas women are more likely to develop the disorder later in life, between the ages of 26 and 45. Compared to men, women usually have fewer negative symptoms of schizophrenia (Maric et al., in press; McGorry, 2001) and more mood symptoms (Maurer, 2001), and they are less likely to have substance abuse problems or to exhibit suicidal or violent behavior (Seeman, 2000). Moreover, women generally functioned at higher levels before their illness developed.

Culture

Two findings bear on the role of culture and schizophrenia. First, across various countries, schizophrenia is more common among people in urban areas and lower socioeconomic classes than among people in rural areas and higher socioeconomic classes (Freeman, 1994; Mortensen et al., 1999), as we'll discuss in more detail later in this chapter. Moreover, there are ethnic differences in prevalence rates in the United States: Blacks are twice as likely as Whites or Latinos to develop schizophrenia (Dassori et al., 1995; Keith et al., 1991). These prevalence differences may reflect the influence of a variety of moderating variables, such as social class and different rates of help seeking among the ethnic groups.

Second, people with schizophrenia in non-Western countries are generally better able to function in their societies than are their Western counterparts; that is, they have a better prognosis (American Psychiatric Association, 2000). We'll discuss possible reasons for this finding in the *Understanding Schizophrenia* section on social factors.

Table 12.5 provides a summary of facts about schizophrenia.

Table 12.5 ▸ Schizophrenia Facts at a Glance
Prevalence
• Approximately 1% of people worldwide have schizophrenia (Gottesman, 1991; Tandon, Keshavan, & Nasrallah, 2008).
Comorbidity
• Over 90% of people with schizophrenia also have another disorder. The most frequent comorbid disorders are mood, anxiety, and substance-related disorders.
Onset
• Men are more likely to develop the disorder between 18 and 25, whereas women are more likely to develop it between 26 and 45 years old.
Course
• About two thirds of people who have had one episode will go on to have subsequent episodes.
• About a third of people with schizophrenia become chronically ill, without much reduction of symptoms; for most others, the symptoms subside.
Gender Differences
• Schizophrenia affects men more frequently than women (1.4:1 male-to-female ratio; McGrath, 2006), and—as noted above—women tend to develop the disorder at older ages than do men.
• Women have fewer negative symptoms than do men.
Cultural Differences
• Schizophrenia is more common among those living in urban areas and those from lower socioeconomic groups (Freeman, 1994; Mortensen et al., 1999; Saha et al., 2005).
• In non-Western countries, people with schizophrenia generally function better in society than do those in Western countries (Hopper et al., 2007).
• In a given country, immigrants are almost twice as likely to develop schizophrenia as are native-born residents (Saha et al., 2005).
• Within the United States, Latinos and Whites are less likely to develop schizophrenia than are Blacks (Zhang & Snowden, 1999).

Source: Unless otherwise noted, citations for above table are: American Psychiatric Association, 2000.

Prognosis

In general, the long-term prognosis for schizophrenia follows the rule of thirds:

• one third of patients improve significantly;

• one third basically stay the same, having episodic relapses and some permanent deficits in functioning, but able to hold a "sheltered" job—a job designed for people with mild to moderate disabilities; and

• one third become chronically and severely disabled by their illness.

Table 12.6 summarizes factors associated with a better prognosis in Western countries. However, this table does not indicate a crucial fact about the prognosis for people with schizophrenia: Over the course of their lives, people with schizophrenia are more likely than others to die by suicide or to be victims of violence. Let's examine these risks in greater detail.

Table 12.6 ▸ Factors Associated With a Better Prognosis for Individuals With Schizophrenia

People with schizophrenia who significantly improve often have one or more of the following characteristics:

- They functioned at a relatively high level before their first episode.
- The symptoms had a sudden onset.
- They developed symptoms later in life.
- They have a family history of mood disorders, not schizophrenia.
- They have the paranoid subtype (in the DSM-IV-TR categorization) or the nondeficit subtype, with relatively good cognitive functioning.
- They have fewer negative symptoms.
- They are aware of their symptoms and recognize that the symptoms are caused by an illness.
- They are women (whose symptoms also respond better to medication).

Sources: Amador et al., 1991; Fenton & McGlashan, 1994; Green, 2001.

Suicide

People with schizophrenia have a higher risk of dying by suicide than do other people: As Table 12.4 shows, 10–15% of people with schizophrenia commit suicide (Caldwell & Gottesman, 1990; Siris, 2001). Those with the paranoid subtype are at the highest risk for suicide. Perhaps paradoxically, patients at risk for committing suicide are those who are most likely to be aware of their symptoms: They have relatively few negative symptoms but pronounced positive symptoms; they are highly intelligent with career goals, are aware of their deterioration, and have a pattern of relapsing and then getting better, with many episodes; and—like other people who die by suicide—they are more likely to be male (Fenton, 2000; Funahashi et al., 2000; Moussaoui et al., 1999; Siris, 2001). Ironically, some of these factors—a high level of premorbid functioning, few negative symptoms, and an awareness of the symptoms and their effects—are associated with a better prognosis (see Table 12.6). As researchers have identified these risk factors, they have used them to focus suicide prevention efforts.

Violence

Suicide is often the result of some form of self-inflicted violence, but this does not imply that patients with schizophrenia are generally violent. Although the afflicted individual may threaten to become violent during an episode of schizophrenia, contrary to sensational headlines, these patients rarely actually engage in violent behavior. Risk factors associated with violent behavior include being male, having comorbid substance abuse, not taking medication, and having engaged in criminal behavior or having had psychopathic tendencies before schizophrenia developed (Hunt et al., 2006; Monahan et al., 2001; Skeem & Mulvey, 2001; Tengström, Hodgins, & Kullren, 2001). Only one of these factors pertains to schizophrenia directly; rather, it is the comorbid disorders that increase the risk of violent behavior (Angermeyer, 2000; Erkiran et al., 2006; Swanson et al., 2006). Note that less than 10% of violent acts reported to the police are caused by people with schizophrenia, and most of these offenders are people with schizophrenia who also abuse alcohol or drugs (Walsh, Buchanan, & Fahy, 2002).

Rather than being perpetrators of violence, people with schizophrenia have a much greater likelihood of being victims of violence. One survey found that almost 20% of people with a psychotic disorder had been victims of violence in the previous 12 months. Those who were more disorganized and functioned less well were more likely to have been victimized (Chapple et al., 2004), perhaps because their impaired functioning made them easier "marks" for perpetrators.

Key Concepts and Facts About What are Schizophrenia and Other Psychotic Disorders? ▪

- According to DSM-IV-TR, schizophrenia is characterized by two or more symptoms, at least one of which must be positive; these symptoms must be present for a minimum of 6 months and must significantly impair functioning.

- Positive symptoms are delusions, hallucinations, disorganized speech, and disorganized behavior. However, research findings suggest that the disorganized symptoms form their own distinct cluster and should be grouped separately from delusions and hallucinations.

- Negative symptoms are flat affect, alogia, and avolition.

- Research studies have indicated that cognitive deficits underlie negative and disorganized symptoms of schizophrenia. Such deficits include problems with attention, working memory, and executive functioning. The DSM-IV-TR criteria have been criticized for omitting important cognitive and social deficits that lead to positive and negative symptoms and that are closely associated with prognosis.

- DSM-IV-TR distinguishes five subtypes of schizophrenia: paranoid, disorganized, catatonic, undifferentiated, and residual schizophrenia. However, because the symptoms of schizophrenia often shift over time, an individual's subtype can change. Many researchers argue that a more meaningful way to distinguish subtypes of schizophrenia would be based on whether the individual has a deficit or nondeficit subtype.

- Symptoms of schizophrenia can appear to overlap with those of other disorders, notably mood disorders and substance-related disorders. The category of psychotic disorders specifically requires symptoms of hallucinations or delusions; disorders in this category are schizophrenia, schizophreniform disorder, brief psychotic disorder, schizoaffective disorder, delusional disorder, and shared psychotic disorder. These disorders, along with schizotypal personality disorder, are part of a spectrum of schizophrenia-related disorders.

- Schizophrenia occurs in approximately 1% of the population worldwide, and most people with schizophrenia have at least one comorbid disorder. Men have an earlier onset of the disorder than do women. Symptoms of the disorder typically evolve in phases: premorbid, prodromal, active, and then middle-to-late phases.

- Up to 15% of people with schizophrenia commit suicide. People with this disorder who behave violently are most likely to have a comorbid disorder that is associated with violent behavior, such as a substance-related disorder. People with schizophrenia are more likely than other people to be victims of violence.

Making a Diagnosis

- Reread Case 12.1 about Emilio, and then determine whether or not his symptoms met the minimum criteria for a diagnosis of schizophrenia. Specifically, list which criteria apply and which ones do not. If you would like more information to determine his diagnosis, what information—specifically—would you want, and in what ways would the information influence your decision? If you decide that a diagnosis of schizophrenia is appropriate for Emilio, do you think he has the deficit or nondeficit subtype, and why?

Understanding Schizophrenia

Despite the low odds that all four of the Genain quads would develop schizophrenia, it did happen. Why? The neuropsychosocial approach helps us to understand the factors that lead to schizophrenia and how these factors influence each other. As we shall see, although neurological factors (including genes) can make a person vulnerable to the disorder, psychological and social factors also contribute to its development—which may help explain not only why all four Genain quads ended up with schizophrenia, but also why the disorder affected them differently.

The quads shared the same genes, looked alike, and at least in their early years, were often treated similarly, especially by Mrs. Genain. However, Hester was smaller and frailer than the others; she weighed only 3 pounds at birth and could not always keep up with her sisters. Because of Hester's difficulties, it wasn't always possible to treat the four girls the same, and so Mr. and Mrs. Genain sometimes treated them as two pairs of twins: Nora and Myra were paired together (they were seen as most competent), and Iris—who in fact was almost as competent as Nora and Myra—was paired with Hester.

Let's look at the specific neurological, psychological, and social factors that give rise to schizophrenia and then examine how these factors affect one another.

Neurological Factors in Schizophrenia

Perhaps more than for any other psychological disorder, neurological factors play a crucial role in the development of schizophrenia. These factors involve brain systems, neural communication, and genetics.

Brain Systems

People who have schizophrenia have abnormalities in the structure and function of their brains. Early research on this topic came from autopsy studies in which researchers compared the brains of people who had schizophrenia with those of people who did not (Rosanoff, 1914; Southard, 1910). These researchers found that the brains of people who had schizophrenia were atrophied (shrunken) relative to the brains of people without the disorder. Neuroimaging studies have since documented more specific differences in brain structure and function between those with schizophrenia and those who do not have the disorder.

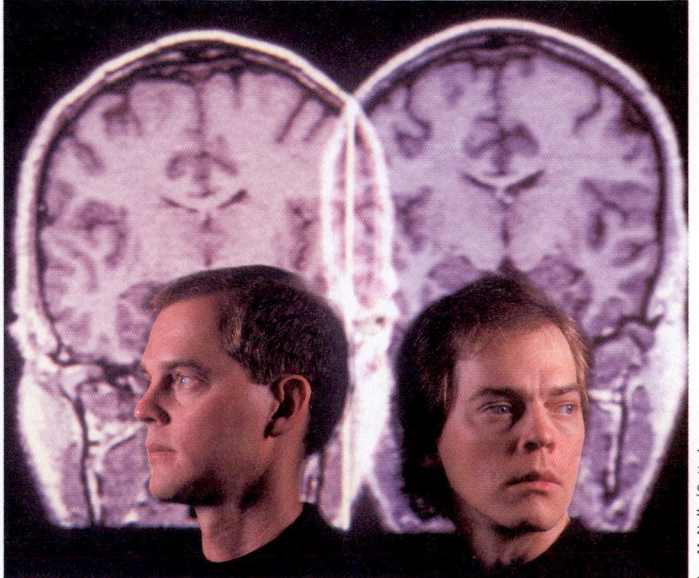

These brain scans of identical twins show, for one of them, the enlarged ventricles that typically are associated with schizophrenia. The twin on the right has schizophrenia, the twin on the left does not.

The most striking example of a structural abnormality in the brains of people with schizophrenia is enlarged ventricles, which are cavities in the center of the brain that are filled with cerebrospinal fluid (Vita et al., 2006). Larger ventricles means that the size of the brain itself is reduced. This reduction in size is especially significant for people with schizophrenia because, in general, even before developing the disorder, they have brains that are smaller than normal. This is true, in part, because their brains never grew to "full" size. In addition, research suggests that schizophrenia causes parts of the brain to shrink (DeLisi et al., 1997; Gur, Ragland, & Gur, 1997; Rapoport et al., 1999).

One possible reason for the differences in brain structure (and brain functioning) between those who have schizophrenia and those who do not could be effects of the medications used to treat schizophrenia—and not the disorder itself. With the development of neuroimaging techniques, scientists began to address this possibility. Researchers used longitudinal studies to follow people from the time of their first schizophrenic episode. Such studies have shown that even at the time of their first episode, people who have schizophrenia have smaller overall brain volume and less cerebral cortex than people who have no known risk of developing schizophrenia (Velakoulis et al., 1999). In fact, the less cortical matter patients had, the more poorly they fared 2 years after their first episode (Cahn et al., 2002). Thus, these abnormalities in brain structure are not primarily a result of taking medication.

In 1981, the Genain sisters, then 51 years old, returned to NIMH for a 3-month evaluation; during that time they were taken off their medications. CT scans of the quads showed similar brain abnormalities in all four sisters (Mirsky & Quinn, 1988). However, even though they were basically genetically identical, their performance on neuropsychological tests varied: Nora and Hester showed more evidence of neurological difficulties, and they were more impaired in their daily functioning when not taking medication. Thus, once again, we see that genes are not destiny and that brain function cannot be considered in isolation. The brain is a mechanism, but how it performs depends in part on how it is "programmed" by learning and experience—which are psychological factors.

In the following sections, we consider the likely role of the following brain abnormalities: a frontal lobe defect, an impaired temporal lobe and thalamus, an abnormal hippocampus, and abnormal interactions among brain areas. We then turn to possible causes of such abnormalities in the brain, considering the effects of the mother's diet or illness, as well as early oxygen deprivation. Finally, we examine possible "biological markers"; telltale neurological, bodily, or behavioral signs that may indirectly reveal that a person is vulnerable to developing schizophrenia.

A Frontal Lobe Defect?

Many studies have set out to discover whether people with schizophrenia have impaired frontal lobe functioning. The root of such impairment may lie in the fact that the brain has too many connections among neurons at birth, and part of normal maturation is the elimination, or *pruning*, of unneeded connections (Huttenlocher, 2002). Results suggest that an excess of such pruning takes place during adolescence for people who develop schizophrenia: Too many of the neural connections in the frontal lobes are eliminated, which may account for some of the neurocognitive deficits that typically accompany this disorder (Keshavan, Anderson, & Pettegrew, 1994; Pantelis et al., 2003; Walker et al., 2004).

In addition, some symptoms of schizophrenia are associated with abnormal activity in specific brain areas; for example, people with schizophrenia often have too little activity in part of the left frontal lobe, a lack that is associated with avolition. Moreover, studies have shown that disorganized symptoms are associated with abnormal activity in the right frontal lobe (Liddle et al., 1992; Perlstein et al., 2001).

Impaired Temporal Lobe and Thalamus?

Enlarged ventricles are associated with decreased size of the temporal lobes. This is significant for people with schizophrenia because the temporal lobes process auditory information, some aspects of language, and visual recognition (Levitan, Ward, & Catt, 1999; Sanfilipo et al., 2002). Abnormal functioning of the temporal lobes may underlie some positive symptoms, notably auditory hallucinations, in people with schizophrenia.

The thalamus, which transmits sensory information to other parts of the brain, also appears to be smaller and to function abnormally in people with schizophrenia (Andreasen et al., 1994; Andrews et al., 2006; Konick & Friedman, 2001). Abnormal functioning of the thalamus is associated with difficulties in focusing attention, in distinguishing relevant from irrelevant stimuli, and in particular types of memory difficulties, all of which are cognitive deficits that can arise with schizophrenia.

Abnormal Hippocampus?

The hippocampus—a subcortical brain structure crucially involved in storing new information in memory—has also been a focus of schizophrenia research. Studies have found that the hippocampi of people with schizophrenia and their first-degree relatives (parents and siblings) are smaller than those of control participants (Nelson et al., 1998; Seidman et al., 2002; Vita et al., 2006), which may contribute to the deficits in memory often experienced by some people with schizophrenia (Holthausen et al., 2003; Olson et al., 2006; Yoon et al., 2008).

Interactions Among Brain Areas

Some researchers propose that schizophrenia arises from disrupted interactions among the frontal lobes, the thalamus, and the cerebellum—which may act as a timekeeper, synchronizing and coordinating signals from many brain areas (Andreasen, 2001; Andreasen et al., 1999). According to this theory, the thalamus fails to screen out sensory information, which overwhelms subsequent processing, and the form and content of the person's thoughts become confused. In addition, many patients with schizophrenia have abnormal interconnections between the anterior cingulate cortex in the frontal lobe (which is involved in attention) and the hippocampus (Benes, 2000), which may contribute to some of the disrupted cognitive functions.

Possible Causes of Brain Abnormalities

How might these brain abnormalities arise? Researchers have identified several possible causes. Some researchers have focused on factors that could affect the developing brain of a fetus or a newborn. The growing fetus can be affected if the mother is malnourished. Similarly, development of the brain can be disrupted if the mother is significantly ill during her pregnancy. In addition, the brain can become impaired if oxygen is cut off from the infant before or during birth. Let's consider each of these possible causes.

Maternal Malnourishment One possible cause of brain abnormalities is *maternal malnourishment* during pregnancy, particularly during the first trimester (Brown et al., 1999; Wahlbeck et al., 2001). It is possible, for example, that Mrs. Genain's poor diet contributed to the quads' schizophrenia: During the first trimester of her pregnancy, Maud Genain had such bad nausea that her weight dropped from 150 pounds before her pregnancy to 117 pounds a few months into her pregnancy (Rosenthal, 1963). However, we must note that the research results are based on data from many people, and thus we must always be careful when applying data from a group (the members of which varied) to specific individuals (the Genains).

Maternal Illness and Stress A second possible cause of brain abnormalities is *maternal illness* (Brown et al., 2004; Buka et al., 1999; Ellman, 2008; Mednick et al., 1998). Maternal illness during the 6th month of pregnancy is of particular concern. During fetal development, neurons travel to their final destination in the brain and establish connections with other neurons (this process is called *cell migration*). If the mother catches the flu or another viral infection in the second trimester, this may disrupt cell migration in the developing fetus's brain, which causes some neurons to fall short of their intended destinations. Because the neurons are not properly positioned, they form different connections than they would have formed if they had been in the correct locations—leading to abnormal neural communication (Arnold et al., 1991; David, 1994; Green, 2001; McGlashan & Hoffman, 2000). The cognitive deficits associated with schizophrenia could be related to such abnormalities in cell migration: Various brain areas may not be set up properly to allow smooth communication within and among them. However, among those who have no family history of schizophrenia or related disorders, maternal malnutrition or illness accounts for only a small percentage of cases of schizophrenia (Green, 2001).

Significant maternal stress in the first trimester (such as the death of the mother's parent) has also been associated with higher rates of schizophrenia in the children (Ellman, 2008; Khashan et al., 2008).

Oxygen Deprivation Another possible source of the abnormal brain structure and function found in schizophrenia is prenatal or birth-related medical complications that lead to oxygen deprivation (Cannon, 1997, 1998; Geddes & Lawrie, 1995; McNeil, Cantor-Graae, & Weinberger, 2000; Zornberg, Buka, & Tsuang, 2000). Studies have shown that people with schizophrenia who did not receive enough oxygen at specific periods before birth have smaller hippocampi than do people with schizophrenia who were not deprived of oxygen during or before birth (van Erp et al., 2002). As noted earlier, the hippocampus plays a role in memory, and thus a reduced size of this brain structure may help explain some of the problems with working memory that can arise in people with schizophrenia.

Although inadequate oxygen before or during birth may contribute to making a person vulnerable to schizophrenia, it does not cause the disorder. A relatively large number of infants experience this problem during birth and do not go on to develop schizophrenia (Clarke, Harley, & Cannon, 2006).

Biological Markers

People with schizophrenia, and even some of their unaffected family members, may exhibit distinctive behaviors in specific situations or when performing specific tasks—behaviors that are not displayed by other people. When a neurological, bodily, or behavioral characteristic distinguishes people with a psychological disorder (or people with a first-degree relative with the disorder) from people who do not have the disorder, it is said to be a **biological marker** for the disorder. One biological marker for schizophrenia, but not other psychological disorders, is difficulty in maintaining smooth, continuous eye movements when tracking a light as it moves across the visual field—such tracking is called *smooth pursuit eye movements* (Clementz & Sweeney, 1990; Holzman et al., 1984; Iacono et al., 1992). This difficulty reflects underlying neurological factors, and is associated with irregularities in brain activation during motion processing (Hong et al., 2005). Although it is not clear exactly why people with schizophrenia and their family members have this specific difficulty (Holzman et al., 1988), researchers believe that it can help to identify people who are vulnerable for developing schizophrenia. Figure 12.4 shows the results of smooth pursuit eye movement recordings for the Genain sisters.

Biological marker
A neurological, bodily, or behavioral characteristic that distinguishes people with a psychological disorder (or a first-degree relative with the disorder) from those without the disorder.

Figure 12.4

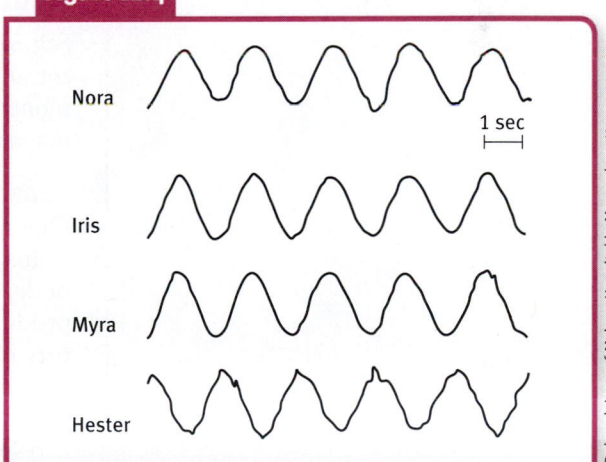

Nora

Iris

Myra

Hester

1 sec

Dr. Deborah Levy of McLean Hospital in Massachusetts obtained this data.

12.4 ▶ Genain Sisters' Smooth Pursuit Eye Movements The Genain sisters completed this test in 1981. The results show that Nora and Hester had more irregularities in their eye movements and they also performed more poorly on some of the neuropsychological tests, indicating that they were more neurologically impaired.

Another biological marker for schizophrenia is *sensory gating* (Freedman et al., 1996), which is assessed as follows: Participants hear two clicks, one immediately after the other. Normally, the brain responds less strongly to the second click than to the first. However, people with schizophrenia and their first-degree relatives don't show the normal large drop in the brain's response to the second click. This has been interpreted as a manifestation of the difficulties that people with schizophrenia can have in filtering out unimportant stimuli.

A third type of biological marker for schizophrenia has been reported by researchers who performed careful analyses of home movies of children who were later diagnosed with schizophrenia (Grimes & Walker, 1994; Walker et al., 1993). They found that the children who went on to develop schizophrenia were different from their siblings: They made more involuntary movements, such as writhing or excessive movements of the tongue, lips, or arms. This tendency for involuntary movement was particularly evident from birth to age 2, but could be seen even through adolescence in individuals who later developed the disorder (Walker, Savoie, & Davis, 1994). Moreover, those who displayed more severe movements of this type later developed more severe symptoms of schizophrenia (Neumann & Walker, 1996).

These researchers also found that the children who displayed more involuntary movements also cried more when coming into contact with adults. Similar results were reported by researchers who studied Finnish people with schizophrenia. Looking back at the patients' school performance, these researchers found that the children who went on to develop schizophrenia did not do significantly worse academically than other children—but they were significantly worse at sports and handicrafts, both of which require motor coordination (Cannon et al., 1999). Further support for the relationship between movement abnormalities and schizophrenia comes from a study in which researchers compared the extent of abnormal movements in two groups of people: One group consisted of people with schizotypal personality disorder—a disorder on the schizophrenia spectrum—and the other group was composed of healthy control participants or people who had another type of personality disorder. Only people with schizotypal personality disorder had abnormal movements (Mittal et al., 2008).

This said, we note that not everyone who is clumsy or uncoordinated goes on to develop schizophrenia. Biological markers are correlated with underlying problems—but sometimes can also arise for other reasons.

Neural Communication

Schizophrenia is likely to involve a complex interplay of many brain systems and neurotransmitters, including dopamine, serotonin, and glutamate, as well as the stress hormone, cortisol. Let's look more closely at these neurotransmitter substances and their interactions, as well as the possibility that sex hormones may play a role in this disorder.

Dopamine

One neurotransmitter that is clearly involved in schizophrenia is dopamine: Neuroimaging studies of people with schizophrenia have found abnormally low numbers of dopamine receptors in their frontal lobes (Okubo et al., 1997), as well as increased production of dopamine (possibly to compensate for the reduced numbers of receptors in the frontal lobes) in the striatum (parts of the basal ganglia that produce dopamine; Heinz, 2000). The **dopamine hypothesis** proposes that an overproduction of dopamine or an increase in the number or sensitivity of dopamine receptors is responsible for schizophrenia. According to this hypothesis, the excess dopamine or extra sensitivity to this neurotransmitter triggers a flood of unrelated thoughts, feelings, and perceptions. Delusions are then attempts to organize these disconnected events into a coherent, understandable experience (Gottesman, 1991; Kapur, 2003). This hypothesis was supported by the discovery that medications that decrease dopamine levels also reduce the positive symptoms of schizophrenia (but not the negative symptoms; Rosenbaum et al., 2005). Further support for the dopamine hypothesis comes from studies of people who do not have schizophrenia: When they are given LSD, an hallucinogenic that increases dopamine activity (as well as blocking the

Walker © 1994. Used by permission of Oxford University Press.

The child in this photo went on to develop schizophrenia. Notice the unusual hand postures (indicating involuntary movement) of the child; studies of home movies of the child who later developed schizophrenia revealed many such involuntary movements, particularly of the tongue, lips, or arms.

Dopamine hypothesis
The view that schizophrenia arises from an overproduction of dopamine or an increase in the number or sensitivity of dopamine receptors.

neurotransmitter serotonin), they report schizophrenia-like experiences (Syvalathi, 1994). (As noted in Chapter 9, LSD affects both serotonin and dopamine activity.)

Clearly, dopamine is involved in schizophrenia, but research has definitively documented that the dopamine hypothesis was an oversimplification (McDermott & de Silva, 2005). Rather than being a primary cause of the disorder, dopamine affects, and is affected by, other neurotransmitters whose activity, along with the structural and functional abnormalities of various brain areas, gives rise to some of the symptoms of schizophrenia (Laruelle et al., 1993; Nestler, 1997; Syvalathi, 1994; Vogel et al., 2006; Walker & Diforio, 1997; Weinberger & Lipska, 1995).

Serotonin and Glutamate

Medications that affect serotonin levels can decrease both positive and negative symptoms in people with schizophrenia. Research studies suggest complex interactions among serotonin, dopamine, and glutamate (Andreasen, 2001). For example, serotonin has been shown to enhance the effect of glutamate, which is the most common fast-acting excitatory transmitter in the brain (Aghajanian & Marek, 2000). This is relevant to understanding schizophrenia because the N-methyl-D-aspartate (NMDA) glutamate receptor has been shown to play a crucial role in learning and memory, and hence abnormalities in its functioning may explain some of the deficits associated with schizophrenia, such as deficits in working memory. In particular, studies have found unusually high levels of glutamate in people with schizophrenia, particularly in the frontal lobe (Abbott & Bustillo, 2006; van Elst et al., 2005); such an excess of glutamate may disrupt the timing of neural activation in the frontal lobe, which in turn may impair cognitive activities that depend on the smooth coordination of different operations, such as working memory, where information a must be actively retained in short-term memory as it is operated upon (Lewis & Moghaddam, 2006).

Stress and Cortisol

Research findings suggest that stress can contribute to schizophrenia, because stress affects cortisol production, which in turn affects the brain; the effects of stress probably start well before the first episode of schizophrenia emerges. The relationship with cortisol appears even in childhood. Children who are at risk for schizophrenia react more strongly to stress, and their baseline levels of cortisol are higher than those of other children (Walker, Logan, & Walker, 1999). The relationship between stress, cortisol, and symptoms of schizophrenia has also been noted during adolescence, the time when prodromal symptoms often emerge: A 2-year longitudinal study of adolescents with schizotypal personality disorder found that cortisol levels—and symptoms of schizophrenia—increased over the 2 years (Walker, Walder, & Reynolds, 2001).

Thus, people who develop schizophrenia appear to be more biologically reactive to stressful events. A hypothesized mechanism for this relationship is that the biological changes and stressors of adolescence promote higher levels of cortisol, which is thought to affect dopamine activity. Even after adolescence, people with schizophrenia have higher levels of stress-related hormones, including cortisol (Zhang et al., 2005). In one study, the siblings of people with schizophrenia exhibited a larger stress response than did healthy control participants but a smaller stress response than did participants with schizophrenia; these findings not only provide evidence that genes play a role in how strongly a person will respond to stress, but also suggest that the genetic contribution to the stress response may play a role in the development of schizophrenia (Brunelin et al., 2008).

Effects of Estrogen

We noted earlier that when women develop schizophrenia, they often have different symptoms than men do and tend to function better. Such findings have led to the *estrogen protection hypothesis* (Seeman & Lang, 1990). According to this hypothesis, the hormone estrogen, which occurs at higher levels in women, protects against symptoms of schizophrenia through its effects on serotonin and dopamine activity. This protection may explain why women are likely to have a later onset of the disorder than do men. Evidence for the estrogen protection hypothesis comes from two sources. One is the finding that women with schizophrenia who had higher levels of estrogen also had better cognitive functioning (Hoff et al., 2001). The other is the finding that providing constant doses of estrogen through a skin patch (in addition to antipsychotic medication) reduced the positive symptoms of women with severe schizophrenia more than did antipsychotic medication without supplementary estrogen (Kulkarni et al., 2008).

Genetics

Various twin, family, and adoption studies indicate that genes play a role in schizophrenia (Gottesman, 1991; Kendler & Diehl, 1993; Tienari, Wahlberg, & Wynne, 2006; Wynne et al., 2006). The more genes that a person shares with a relative who has schizophrenia, the higher the risk that that person will also develop schizophrenia (see Table 12.7). However, even for those who have a close relative with schizophrenia, the chance of developing the disorder is still relatively low: More than 85% of people who have one parent or one sibling (who is not a twin) with the disorder do not go on to develop it themselves (Gottesman & Moldin, 1998), and this percentage is even lower for people with a grandparent, aunt, or uncle (second-degree relatives) with the disorder (Gottesman & Erlenmeyer-Kimling, 2001). Nonetheless, a family history of schizophrenia is still the strongest known risk factor for developing the disorder (Hallmayer, 2000).

Table 12.7 ▶ Degree of Relatedness and Risk of Developing Schizophrenia	
Family Member(s) with Schizophrenia	**Risk of Developing Schizophrenia**
First cousin	2%
Half-sibling	6%
Full sibling	9%
One parent	13%
Two parents	46%
Fraternal twin	14–17%
Identical twin	46–53%

Sources: Gottesman, 1991; Kendler, 1983.

If the cause of schizophrenia were entirely genetic, then when one identical twin developed the disorder, the co-twin would also develop the disorder; that is, the co-twin's risk of developing schizophrenia would be 100%—if schizophrenia were entirely caused by genes. But this is not what happens; the actual risk of a co-twin developing schizophrenia ranges from 46 to 53% (in different studies), as shown in Table 12.7. However, identical twins have the same *predisposition* for developing schizophrenia, although only one of them may develop it. This means that even if only one twin in a pair develops the disorder, the children of both twins (the one with the disorder and the one without) have the same risk of developing it. That is, both the affected and the unaffected twin transmit the same genetic vulnerability to their offspring (Gottesman & Bertelsen, 1989).

Another risk factor that may be related to genes does not involve the usual patterns of inheritance, but may hinge on genetic defects in the sperm of older fathers (Tsuchiya et al., 2005; Wohl & Gorwood, 2007; Zammit et al., 2003): Children whose fathers were over 45 years old when they were born were almost three times as likely to develop schizophrenia as children whose fathers were between the ages of 20 and 24 when they were born. One possibility is that mutations in the sperm of older fathers may be responsible for this increased rate, but there is no solid evidence yet that such mutations are in fact responsible for this effect.

Researchers have begun to make inroads in identifying specific genes that create various vulnerabilities for schizophrenia (Craddock, O'Donovan, & Owen, 2005; Stefansson et al., 2008; Xu et al., 2008). However, the results of studies that examine specific genes thought to be related to schizophrenia have generally been disappointing—any given gene accounts for only a small minority of cases of schizophrenia (Hamilton, 2008; Sanders et al., 2008). Nevertheless, some aspects of the disorder have been linked to specific genes; for example, some patients with schizophrenia exhibit symptoms of agitation, and a specific mutation of one gene has been linked to this symptom (Sachs, 2006).

Clearly, genes alone do not determine whether someone will develop schizophrenia. In order to examine the influences of both genes and environment, a Finnish adoption study tracked two groups of adopted children: those whose biological mothers had schizophrenia, and those whose mothers did not (the control group). None of the adoptive parents of these children had schizophrenia, but some adoptive families were dysfunctional (Tienari et al., 1994, 2006). In the control group, the incidence of schizophrenia was no higher than in the general population, regardless of the characteristics of the adoptive families. In contrast, the children whose biological mothers had schizophrenia and whose adoptive families were dysfunctional were much more likely to develop schizophrenia than were the children whose biological mothers had schizophrenia but whose adoptive families were not dysfunctional. Thus, better parenting appeared to protect children who were genetically at risk for developing schizophrenia.

Psychological Factors in Schizophrenia

We have seen that schizophrenia is not entirely a consequence of brain structure, brain function, or genetics. As the neuropsychosocial approach implies, schizophrenia arises from a combination of different sorts of factors. For example, the neurocognitive deficits that plague individuals with schizophrenia also affect how they perceive the social world, and their perceptions affect their ability to function in that world (Sergi et al., 2006). If we understand their experiences, their behaviors do not appear so bizarre. Let's examine in detail the psychological underpinnings of schizophrenia so that we can better understand how all four Genain quadruplets developed the disorder, despite the odds against this outcome. Note that not every person with schizophrenia experiences each type of difficulty we discuss (Walker et al., 2004).

Mental Processes and Cognitive Difficulties: Attention, Memory, and Executive Functions

We've already noted problems with attention, working memory, and executive function in schizophrenia. Let's now consider how such problems may contribute to the disorder.

The cognitive difficulties of people with schizophrenia arise before the DSM-IV-TR symptoms emerge, and the difficulties persist even after the DSM-IV-TR symptoms have diminished (Hughes et al., 2003; Rund et al., 2004). The difficulties with attention—in distinguishing relevant from irrelevant stimuli, for example (Nuechterlein, 1991)—occur even when the person is taking medication and isn't psychotic (Cornblatt et al., 1997; Dawson et al., 1993). This attentional problem can make it hard for individuals with schizophrenia to discern which stimuli are important and which aren't; such individuals may feel overwhelmed by a barrage of stimuli. This leads to problems in organizing what they are perceiving and experiencing, which would contribute to their difficulties with perception and memory (Sergi et al., 2006).

Furthermore, as noted earlier, problems with working memory lead people with schizophrenia often to exhibit deficits in problem solving, planning, judgment, and other executive functions. It may be hard for them to plan and complete the various steps of a multistep task, such as making mashed potatoes.

Another cognitive problem common to people with schizophrenia is that they often don't realize that they are having problems; this inability is referred to as a *lack of insight*. They do not recognize that they are behaving abnormally or having unusual experiences. Thus, they are unaware of their disorder or the specific problems it creates for themselves and others (Amador & Gorman, 1998) and see no need for treatment (Buckley, Wirshing et al., 2007). In Case 12.2, psychologist Fred Frese discusses his lack of insight into his own schizophrenia and its effects.

Performance in a virtual maze classified people with symptoms of schizophrenia versus healthy controls. Participants had to remember which combination of three features—color, shape, and sound—would open each door in the maze. Participants who did poorly also reported more symptoms of schizophrenia—both positive and negative (Sorkin et al., 2006).

Sorkin, A., Weinshall, D., Modai, I., & Peled, A. (2006). Improving the accuracy of the diagnosis of schizophrenia by means of virtual reality. American Journal of Psychiatry, 163, 512–520. Reprinted with permission from the American Journal of Psychiatry.

CASE 12.2 ▶ FROM THE INSIDE: Schizophrenia

Psychologist Fred Frese describes his history with schizophrenia:

I was 25 years old, and I was in the Marine Corps at the time, and served two back to back tours in the Far East, mostly in Japan. And when I came back I was a security officer in charge of a Marine Corps barracks with 144 men. And we had responsibilities for security for atomic weapons . . . and a few other duties. About six months into that assignment, I made

continued on next page

Courtesy of Fred Frese

Psychologist Fred Frese was diagnosed with paranoid schizophrenia in 1965 when he was a Marine Corps security officer. He was hospitalized many times over the next 10 years but was able to earn a Ph.D. in psychology in 1978. Over the past 30 years, he has written about mental illness from both sides of the experience, been an advocate for the mentally ill, and served as Director of Psychology at Western Reserve Psychiatric Hospital.

a discovery—to me it was a discovery—that somehow the enemy had developed a new weapon by which they could psychologically hypnotize certain high-ranking officials. And I became very confident that I had stumbled onto this discovery. And because it was a psychological sort of thing I would share this with a person who would be likely to know most about this kind of stuff and that was the base psychiatrist. So I called him up and he agreed to see me right away, and I went down and told him about my discovery, and he listened very politely and when I got finished to get up and leave there were these two gentlemen in white coats on either side of me—either shoulder. And I often say I think one of them looked like he might be elected governor of Minnesota somewhere along the way. But they escorted me down into a seclusion padded room [sic]. And within a day or two I discovered that they had me labeled as paranoid schizophrenic. Of course I immediately recognized that the psychiatrist was under the control of the enemies with their new weapons. I spent about five months mostly in Bethesda, which is the Navy's major hospital, and was discharged with a psychiatric condition. However, that was my discovery that I was diagnosed with . . . schizophrenia. The way the disorder works is, I didn't have a disorder, I had "made this discovery". So it was a number of years before I came to this conclusion that there was something wrong here and I was hospitalized about ten times, almost always involuntarily . . . over about a ten year period of time.

(WCPN, 2003).

To develop a sense of the consequences of having such cognitive difficulties, imagine the experience of a man with these deficits who tries to go shopping for ingredients for dinner. He may find himself in the supermarket, surrounded by hundreds of food items; because of his attentional problems, each item on a shelf may capture the same degree of his attention. Because of deficits in executive functioning, he loses track of why he is there—what was he supposed to buy? And if he remembers why he is there ("I need to get chicken, rice, and vegetables"), he may not be able to exercise good judgment about how much chicken to buy or which vegetables. Or, because of the combination of his cognitive deficits, he may find the whole task too taxing and leave without the dinner ingredients.

Beliefs and Attributions

As mentioned earlier, cognitive difficulties often develop before symptoms of schizophrenia emerge. The early influence of the cognitive deficits affects what the person comes to believe. For example, because children with these cognitive deficits may do poorly in school and often are socially odd, they may be ostracized or teased by their classmates; they may then come to believe that they are inferior and proceed to act in accordance with those beliefs, perhaps by withdrawing from others (Beck & Rector, 2005).

In addition, if people with schizophrenia have delusional beliefs, the delusions almost always relate to themselves and their extreme cognitive distortions (e.g., "The FBI is out to get me"). These distortions influence what they pay attention to and what beliefs go unchallenged. People with schizophrenia may be inflexible in their beliefs or may jump to conclusions, and their actions based on their beliefs can be extreme (Garety et al., 2005). Moreover, they may be very confident that their (false) beliefs are true (Moritz & Woodward, 2006). For example, a man with paranoid schizophrenia might attribute a bad connection on a cell phone call to interference by FBI agents or aliens; he searches for and finds "confirming evidence" of such interference ("There's a bad connection when I call my friend and they want to listen in, but there's no static when I call directory assistance and there's no need for them to listen in"). Disconfirming evidence—that cell phone service is weak in the spot where he was standing when he made the call to his friend—is ignored (Beck & Rector, 2005).

People with paranoid schizophrenia tend to blame negative events on others, specifically the subjects of their delusions (Garety & Freeman, 1999). So, for instance, if a man with paranoid schizophrenia is waiting for a commuter train and hears an announcement that the train is delayed, he might think, "The FBI is trying

to prevent me from reaching my destination, and they've instructed the transit system to delay my train." People with paranoid schizophrenia are often unwilling to test the veracity of their beliefs, perhaps believing that such tests would be "rigged" and the results therefore meaningless.

Similarly, people with schizophrenia who have auditory hallucinations do not generally try to discover where the sounds of the hallucinations are coming from. For example, they don't check whether the radio is on or whether people are talking in the hallway. They are less likely to question the reality of an unusual experience (that is, whether it arises from something outside themselves) and so do not correct their distorted beliefs (Johns, Hemsley, & Kuipers, 2002).

Negative symptoms can also give rise to unfounded beliefs; specifically, people who have negative symptoms are particularly likely to have low expectations of themselves. Although such low expectations could indicate an accurate assessment of their abilities, research suggests that this is generally not the case: When cognitive therapy successfully addresses the negative self-appraisals of people with schizophrenia, their functioning subsequently improves (Rector, Seeman, & Segal, 2003). This finding suggests that the negative self-appraisals are distorted beliefs that became self-fulfilling prophecies (Beck & Rector, 2005).

Emotional Expression

Another psychological factor is the facial expressions of people with schizophrenia, which are less intense than those of people who do not have the disorder (Brozgold et al., 1998; Kring & Neale, 1996). Moreover, people with schizophrenia are less accurate than control participants in labeling the emotions expressed by faces they are shown (Penn & Combs, 2000; Schneider et al., 2006). Part of the explanation for problems related to emotional expression may be the cognitive deficits: In general, people with schizophrenia often have difficulty recognizing emotions that are conveyed by tone of voice (such as the quaver in a voice filled with fear), facial expression (such as an annoyed frown), or body language (such as a defensive, withdrawn crossing of the arms; Green, 2001). Because they cannot "read" nonverbal communication well, they are confused when someone's words and subsequent behavior are at odds. People with schizophrenia are likely to miss the nonverbal communication that helps most people make sense of the apparent inconsistency between what others say and what they do (Greig, Bryson, & Bell, 2004). In fact, even biological relatives of people with schizophrenia have problems in understanding other people's nonverbal communication (Janssen et al., 2003), which suggests that neurological factors are involved.

Social Factors in Schizophrenia

We've seen that schizophrenia often entails difficulty in understanding and navigating the social world. We'll now examine this difficulty in more detail and also consider the ways that economic circumstances and cultural factors can influence schizophrenia.

Understanding the Social World

Each of us develops a **theory of mind**—a theory about other people's mental states (their beliefs, desires, feelings) that allows us to predict how they will react in a given situation. People with schizophrenia have difficulty with tasks that require an accurate theory of mind (Russell et al., 2006) and may thus find relating to others confusing. Because people with schizophrenia have difficulty interpreting emotional expression in others, they don't fully understand the messages people convey. The symptoms of paranoia and social withdrawal in people with schizophrenia may be a direct result of this social confusion (Frith, 1992). To a person with schizophrenia, other people can seem to behave in random and unpredictable ways. Thus, it makes sense that he or she tries to come up with an explanation for other people's

Theory of mind
A theory about other people's mental states (their beliefs, desires, and feelings) that allows a person to predict how other people will react in a given situation.

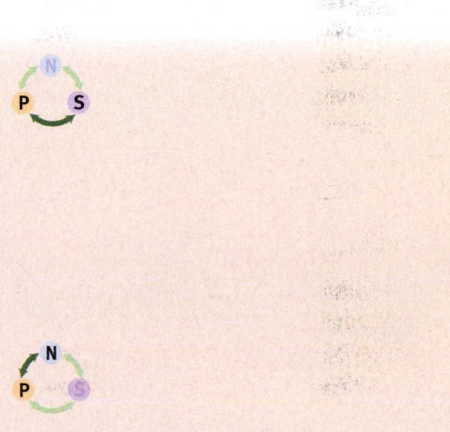

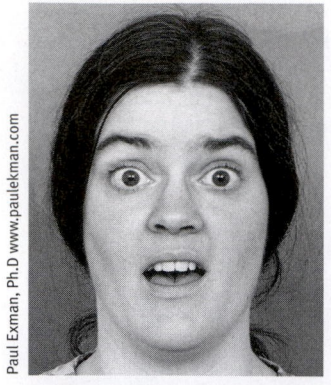
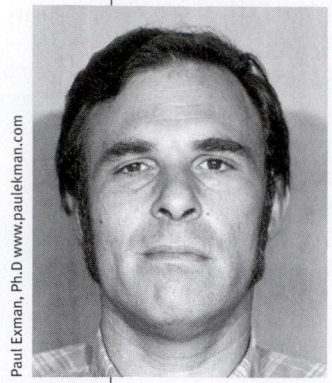

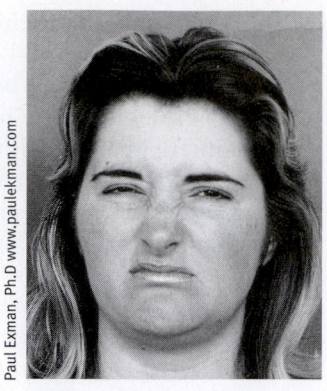

Paul Exman, Ph.D www.paulekman.com

People with schizophrenia may have difficulty accurately "reading" other people's emotional expressions, which can make social interactions confusing and lead them to respond inappropriately.

behavior (a paranoid delusion) or else tries to minimize contact with others because their behavior seems inexplicable.

In spite of the fact that they basically were genetically identical, the Genain quads did not have the same level of social skills or ability to navigate the social world. For instance, Myra was able to work as a secretary for most of her life—a job that requires social awareness and social skills (Mirsky et al., 2000). She had markedly better social skills and stronger social desires than Hester—qualities that enabled her to have a boyfriend at school (Rosenthal, 1963).

Stressful Groups

Orphanages are notoriously stressful environments, which may be a major reason why being raised in an orphanage increases the likelihood of later developing schizophrenia in those who are genetically vulnerable. In fact, children born to a parent with schizophrenia are more likely to develop schizophrenia as adults if they were raised in an institution than if they were raised by the parent with schizophrenia. In addition, genetically vulnerable children raised by foster parents who do not have schizophrenia are even less likely to develop the disorder than are vulnerable children raised in an orphanage or raised by a parent with schizophrenia (Mednick et al., 1998). These findings suggest that, of the three types of environments in which an individual with a vulnerability to schizophrenia can grow up, a foster family is the least stressful.

Stress also contributes to whether someone who recovered from schizophrenia will relapse (Gottesman, 1991; Ventura et al., 1989). Almost two thirds of people hospitalized with schizophrenia live with their families after leaving the hospital. These families can create a stressful environment for a person with schizophrenia, especially if the family is high in expressed emotion. The concept of **high expressed emotion (high EE)** is not aptly named: It's not just that the family with this characteristic expresses emotion in general, but rather that family members express critical and hostile emotions and are over-involved (for example, by frequently criticizing or nagging the patient to change his or her behavior; Wuerker et al., 2002). In fact, hospitalized patients who return to live with a family high in EE are more likely to have a relapse than patients who do not return to live with such a family (Butzlaff & Hooley, 1998; Kavanagh, 1992; Vaughn & Leff, 1976). However, note that high EE does not cause schizophrenia in the first place.

The Genain quads certainly experienced significant stress, and—as you can guess from what you've read so far—their family would be considered high in EE. Psychologist David Rosenthal (1963) reported that the quads' father was particularly critical, almost constantly angry, and extremely controlling—in fact, so extreme was his need to control his children that he forbade his daughters to close any doors, even the one to the bathroom.

The relationship between high EE and relapse of schizophrenia is a correlation. Although it's possible that the critical and controlling behaviors of family members, in part, cause a relapse, it is also equally possible that the causality goes the other way—that people whose symptoms of schizophrenia are more severe between episodes elicit

High expressed emotion (high EE)
A family interaction style characterized by hostility, unnecessary criticism, or emotional overinvolvement.

more attempts by their family members to try to minimize the psychotic, disorganized, or negative symptoms. And then these behaviors lead the family to be classified as high in EE. This explanation may apply, in part, to the Genain family: Among the four sisters, Hester's symptoms were the most chronic and debilitating. She received the most physical punishment, including being whipped and having her head dunked in water, often in response to behaviors that her father wanted her to stop.

Researchers have also discovered ethnic differences in how patients perceive critical and intrusive family behaviors. Among black American families, for instance, behaviors by family members that focus on problem solving are associated with a better outcome for the schizophrenic individual, perhaps because the behavior is interpreted as reflecting caring and concern (Rosenfarb, Bellack, & Aziz, 2006). Thus, what is important is not the family behavior *in and of itself*, but how such behavior is perceived and interpreted by family members.

Immigration

A well-replicated finding is that schizophrenia is more common among immigrants, compared both to people who stayed in the immigrants' original country and to people who are natives in the immigrants' adopted country (Cantor-Graae & Selten, 2005; Lundberg et al., 2007). This higher rate of schizophrenia among immigrants occurs among people who have left a wide range of countries and among people who find new homes in a range of European countries. In fact, one meta-analysis found that being an immigrant was the second largest risk factor for schizophrenia, after a family history of this disorder (Cantor-Graae & Selten, 2005). Both first-generation immigrants—that is, those who left their native country and moved to another country—and their children have relatively high rates of schizophrenia; this is especially true for immigrants and their children who have darker skin color than the natives of the adopted country, which is consistent with the role of social stressors (discrimination in particular) in schizophrenia (Selten, Cantor-Graae, & Kahn, 2007). For instance, the increased rate of schizophrenia among African-Caribbean immigrants to Britain (compared to British and Caribbean residents who are not immigrants) may arise from the stresses of immigration, socioeconomic disadvantage, and racism (Jarvis, 1998). Researchers have sought to rule out potential confounds such as illness or nutrition, but have yet to find such an explanation for the higher risk of schizophrenia among immigrants. Case 12.3 describes the symptoms of schizophrenia in an immigrant from Haiti to the United States.

CASE 12.3 ▶ FROM THE OUTSIDE: Schizophrenia

Within a year after immigrating to the United States, a 21-year-old Haitian woman was referred to a psychiatrist by her schoolteacher because of hallucinations and withdrawn behavior. The patient was fluent in English, although her first language was Creole. Her history revealed that she had seen an ear, nose, and throat specialist in Haiti after her family doctor could not find any medical pathology other than a mild sinus infection. No hearing problems were noted and no treatment was offered. Examination revealed extensive auditory hallucinations, flat affect, and peculiar delusional references to voodoo. The psychiatrist wondered if symptoms of hearing voices and references to voodoo could be explained by her Haitian background, although the negative symptoms seem unrelated. As a result, he consulted with a Creole-speaking, Haitian psychiatrist.

The Haitian psychiatrist interviewed the patient in English, French, and Creole. Communication was not a problem in any language. He discovered that in Haiti, the patient was considered "odd" by both peers and family, as she frequently talked to herself and did not work or participate in school activities. He felt that culture may have influenced the content of her hallucinations and delusions (i.e., references to voodoo) but that the bizarre content of the delusions, extensive hallucinations, and associated negative symptoms were consistent with the diagnosis of schizophrenia.

(Takeshita, 1997, pp. 124–125)

Schizophrenia occurs more frequently among immigrants (and their children) than among people who live in their native country. The various stresses of the immigration process, including financial problems and discrimination, are thought to account, at least in part, for this increased risk. The people in this photo are beginning the process of becoming legal immigrants.

Spencer Platt/Getty Images

In Case 12.3, notice that, although the women had odd and prodromal behaviors in Haiti, her full-blown symptoms did not emerge until she immigrated to the United States. Also notice that these symptoms could have emerged when she got older, even if she had stayed in Haiti. As compelling as single cases can be, full–scale studies—with adequate controls—must play a central role in helping us understand psychological disorders.

Economic Factors

Another social factor associated with schizophrenia is socioeconomic status: A disproportionately large number of people with schizophrenia live in urban areas and among lower economic classes (Hudson, 2005; Mortensen et al., 1999). As discussed in Chapter 2, researchers have offered two possible explanations for this association between the disorder and economic status: social selection and social causation (Dauncey et al., 1993). The **social selection** hypothesis proposes that those who are mentally ill "drift" to a lower socioeconomic level because of their impairments (and hence social selection is sometimes called *social drift*). Most vulnerable to social selection would be those whose illness prevents them from working or those who do not have—or do not make use of—family members who can care for them (Dohrenwend et al., 1992). Consider a young woman who grows up in a middle-class family and moves to a distant city after college, and where, after she graduates, she supports herself reasonably well working full time. She subsequently develops schizophrenia, but refuses to return home to her family, who cannot afford to send her much money. Her income now consists primarily of meager checks from governmental programs—barely enough to cover food and housing in a poor section of town where rent is cheapest. She has drifted from the middle class to a lower class.

Another explanation is **social causation**: The daily stressors of urban life, especially for the poor, trigger mental illness in those who are vulnerable (Freeman, 1994; Hudson, 2005). Social causation would explain cases of schizophrenia in people who grew up in a lower social class. The stressors these people experience include poverty or financial insecurity, as well as and living in neighborhoods with higher crime rates.

In a study designed to investigate the influence of social selection versus social causation, researchers in Ireland examined the relationship between social class at birth and later schizophrenia. These researchers found no differences in the rates of schizophrenia among the children of those in different social classes in Ireland (Mulvany et al., 2001). If social causation were at work, there should be more cases of schizophrenia among children born into lower social classes.

However, the data on this issue are not clear-cut. A similar study that included a more ethnically diverse sample in Israel found a higher rate of schizophrenia among those born into a lower social class, as would be predicted by social causation (Werner, Malaspina, & Rabinowitz, 2007). Note, however, that the social causation hypothesis focuses solely on social class. It does not address ethnicity or race, and so does not take into account the stressful effects of discrimination that arise for non-White immigrants.

Cultural Factors: Recovery in Different Countries

Although the prevalence of schizophrenia is remarkably similar across countries and cultures, the same cannot be said about recovery rates. Some studies report that people in developing countries have higher recovery rates than do people in industrialized countries (American Psychiatric Association, 2000; Kulhara & Chakrabarti, 2001), although this was not found in all earlier studies (Edgerton & Cohen, 1994; von Zerssen et al., 1990).

What accounts for this cultural difference? The important distinction may not be the level of industrial and technological development of a country, but how individualist its culture is. *Individualist cultures* stress values of individual autonomy and independence. In contrast, *collectivist cultures* emphasize the needs of the group, group cohesion, and interdependence. People with schizophrenia in collectivist cultures, such as those of Japan, Hong Kong, and Singapore, have a more favorable course and prognosis than people with schizophrenia in individualist cultures such as that of the United States (Lee et al., 1991; Ogawa et al., 1987; Tsoi & Wong, 1991).

Social selection
The hypothesis that those who are mentally ill "drift" to a lower socioeconomic level because of their impairments.

Social causation
The hypothesis that the daily stressors of urban life, especially as experienced by people in a lower socioeconomic level, trigger mental illness in those who are vulnerable.

The collectivist characteristics of a culture may help a patient to recover for several reasons. Consider that people in collectivist countries may:

1. be more tolerant of those with schizophrenia and therefore less likely to be critical, hostile, and controlling toward those individuals. That is, the families of patients with schizophrenia may be more likely to have lower levels of expressed emotion, decreasing the risk of relapse and leading to better recoveries (El-Islam, 1991).

2. elevate the importance of community and, in so doing, provide a social norm that creates more support for people with schizophrenia and their families.

3. have higher expectations of people with schizophrenia—believing that such individuals can play a functional role in society—and these expectations become a self-fulfilling prophecy (Mathews, Basily, & Mathews, 2006).

Thus, collectivism and strong family values may best explain the better recovery rates in less developed countries, which are generally more collectivist (Weisman, 1997). In such countries, to preserve family harmony, family members may be more tolerant of odd behaviors in a relative with schizophrenia, and they may be more willing to live with that person. In fact, for Latino patients, increasing their perception of the cohesiveness of the family (increased collectivism) is associated with fewer psychiatric symptoms and less distress (Weisman et al., 2005).

FEEDBACK LOOPS IN ACTION: Schizophrenia

No individual risk factor by itself accounts for a high percentage of the cases of schizophrenia. It is true that genetics, prenatal environmental events (such as maternal malnutrition and maternal illness), and birth complications affect fetal development (neurological factors) and can increase the likelihood that a person will develop schizophrenia. But many people who have these risk factors do not develop the disorder. Similarly, a dysfunctional family or another type of stressful environment (social factors) can contribute to, but do not cause, schizophrenia. And cognitive deficits (psychological factors) can contribute to the disorder because they create cognitive distortions but, again, such factors do not actually cause schizophrenia.

As usual, in determining the origins of psychopathology, no one factor reigns supreme in producing schizophrenia; instead, the feedback loops among the three types of factors provide the best explanation (Mednick et al., 1998; Tienari, Wahlberg, & Wynne, 2006). To get a more concrete sense of the effects of the feedback loops, consider the fact that economic factors (which are social) can influence whether a pregnant woman is likely to be malnourished, which in turn affects the developing fetus (and his or her brain). And various social factors create consistently high levels of stress among immigrants or among children raised in an orphanage. Thus, social events influence the degree of stress the individual experiences (a psychological factor), which can trigger factors that affect brain function, including increased cortisol levels. Coming full circle, these psychological and neurological factors are affected by culture (a social factor), which influences the prognosis, how people with schizophrenia are viewed, and how they come to view themselves (psychological factors).

Numerous studies have documented specific ways in which the three types of factors affect one another. For example, in one study (Tienari, Wahlberg, & Wynne, 2006), the researchers tracked adopted children over 21 years; some of them had biological mothers who had schizophrenia (genetic/neurological factor), others had biological mothers without schizophrenia. Some adoptive families exhibited a particular type of dysfunctional communication (social factor), in which the adoptive parent's way of communicating leaves the child puzzled and unsure what the parent means. This style of communication tends to be confusing and stressful to the children (neurological and psychological factors).

Among these adopted children, those with a low genetic risk of schizophrenia were unlikely to develop any schizophrenia spectrum disorder regardless of whether the adoptive parents' style of communication was healthy or dysfunctional. In contrast, the parents' style of communication made a big difference for those children with a higher genetic risk—those whose mothers did have schizophrenia: Those raised in a stressful environment, with confusing and unpredictable communication from adoptive parents, were almost nine times more likely to develop the disorder than those who were raised by adoptive parents with a better communication style; the rates were 13% compared to 1.5% (Tienari, Wahlberg, & Wynne, 2006).

These interactions through feedback loops (see Figure 12.5) illustrate the diathesis–stress model. Researchers explain how stress can affect those who have

Figure 12.5

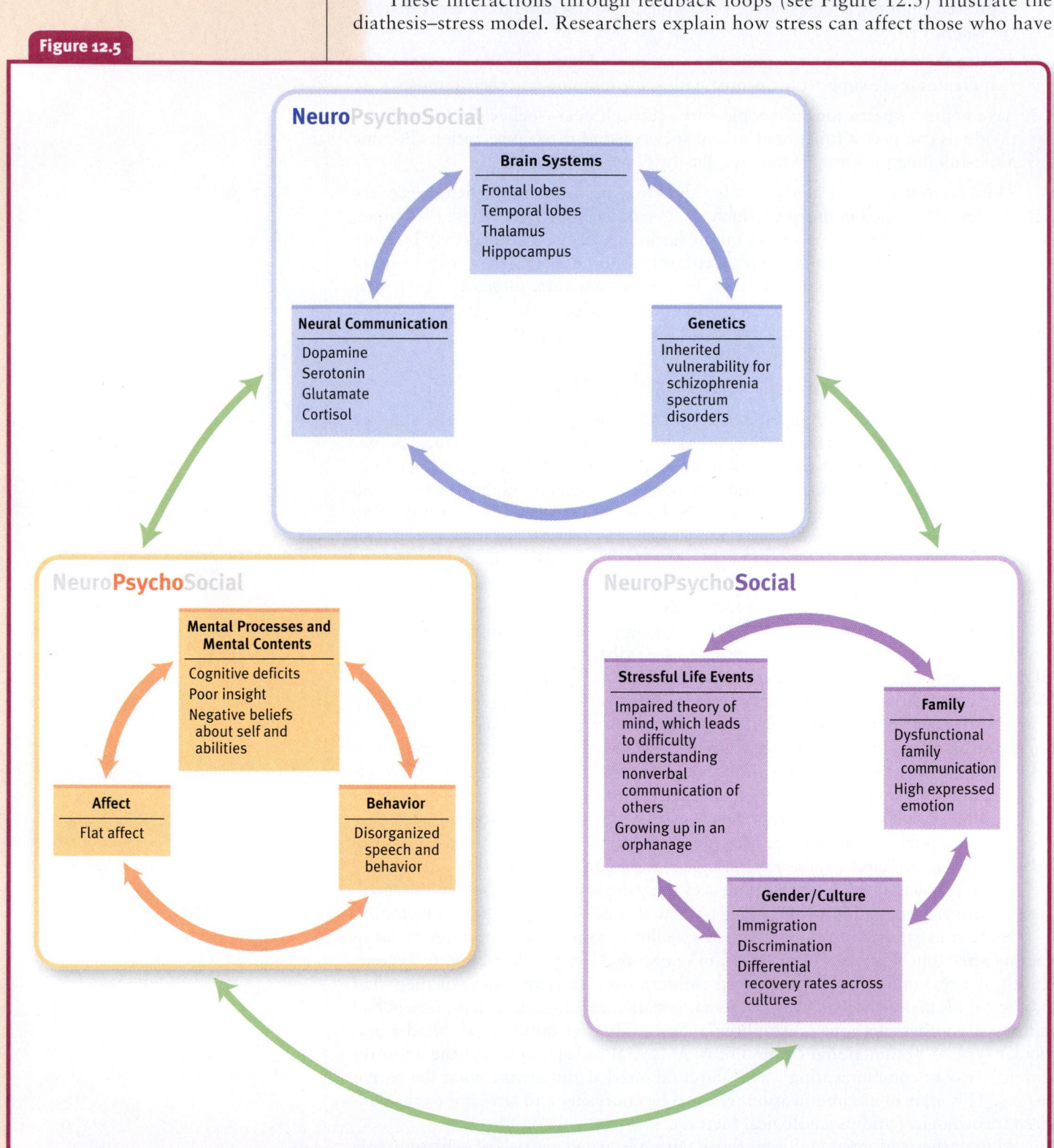

12.5 ► Feedback Loops in Action: Schizophrenia

an underlying vulnerability to schizophrenia (Walker & Diforio, 1997). The key idea is that vulnerable people are biologically predisposed either to produce too much stress hormones or to be too sensitive to the effects of such hormones when they encounter a stressful event (van Os & Delespaul, 2003). The excess hormones or the excessive sensitivity to them can activate certain dopamine pathways too strongly, which then exacerbates schizophrenia symptoms. The social withdrawal common among people with schizophrenia may thus be an attempt to decrease stress (Walker & Diforio, 1997). Consistent with this view, people with schizophrenia who took part in a stress management program had fewer hospital admissions 1 year later (Norman et al., 2002). Moreover, as this model predicts, people with schizophrenia have higher baseline levels of cortisol, as do people at risk for schizophrenia. And antipsychotic medications lower the high cortisol levels in people with schizophrenia.

In addition, the neurocognitive deficits that accompany schizophrenia leave these patients with fewer cognitive resources to cope with stressful events. For example, their lack of insight and impaired theory of mind make it difficult for them to plan adequately. Cognitive deficits give rise to cognitive distortions, which can give rise to delusions that ultimately lead to social withdrawal (Beck & Rector, 2005). And the distorted ways of thinking about self and the world create stress, which produces higher levels of cortisol as a result of the hyperactivation of the hypothalamic-pituitary-adrenal (HPA) axis, which leads to a cascade of neurological events that further decreases cognitive functioning.

The Genain quads illustrate the effects of these feedback loops. A family history of schizophrenia as well as prenatal complications made the quads neurologically vulnerable to developing schizophrenia. They were socially isolated, were teased by other children, and experienced physical and emotional abuse. Had the Genain quads grown up in a different home environment, with parents who treated them differently, it is possible that some of them might not have developed schizophrenia and those who did might have suffered fewer relapses.

Key Concepts and Facts About Understanding Schizophrenia

- A variety of neurological factors are associated with schizophrenia:

  - Abnormalities in brain structure and function have been found in the frontal and temporal lobes, the thalamus, and the hippocampus. Moreover, certain brain areas do not appear to interact with each other properly. People with schizophrenia are more likely to have enlarged ventricles than are other people. The brain abnormalities give rise to biological markers in some individuals.

  - These brain abnormalities appear to be a result of, at least in some cases, maternal malnourishment or illness during pregnancy or to fetal oxygen deprivation.

  - Schizophrenia is associated with abnormalities in dopamine, serotonin, and glutamate activity, as well as a heightened stress response and increased cortisol production.

  - Less than 15% of people with schizophrenia have a first-degree relative (who is not a twin) who also has the disorder, but genetics is still the strongest predictor that a given individual will develop schizophrenia. Genetics alone, though, cannot explain why a given individual develops the disorder.

- Psychological factors that are associated with schizophrenia and shape the symptoms of the disorder include:

  - cognitive deficits in attention, memory, and executive functioning;

  - dysfunctional beliefs and attributions; and

  - difficulty recognizing and conveying emotions.

- Various social factors are also associated with schizophrenia:

  - an impaired theory of mind, which makes it difficult to understand other people's behavior, which in turn means that that other people's behavior routinely appears to be unpredictable;

  - a stressful home environment, such as being raised in an orphanage or by a parent with schizophrenia;

  - the stresses of immigration—particularly for people likely to encounter discrimination—and economic hardship; and

  - the individualist nature of the culture, which is associated with lower recovery rates for people with schizophrenia.

Treating Schizophrenia

The Genain sisters were treated at NIMH and then subsequently in hospitals, residential settings, and community mental health centers. During the early years of the quads' illness, antipsychotic medications were only just beginning to be used, and treatments that target psychological and social factors have changed substantially since then. Today, treatment for schizophrenia occurs in steps, with different symptoms and problems targeted in each step (Green, 2001).

STEP 1: When the patient is actively psychotic, first reduce the positive symptoms.

STEP 2: Reduce the negative symptoms.

STEP 3: Improve neurocognitive functioning.

STEP 4: Reduce the person's disability and increase his or her ability to function in the world.

As we'll see, the last step is the most challenging.

Targeting Neurological Factors in Treating Schizophrenia

At present, interventions targeting neurological factors generally focus on the first two steps of treatment: reducing positive symptoms and reducing negative symptoms. Some such treatments focus on the third step: improving cognitive function.

Medication

The first progress in using medication to treat symptoms of schizophrenia began in the 1950s, with the development of the first antipsychotic (also called *neuroleptic*) medication, thorazine. Since then, various antipsychotic medications have been developed, and two general types of these medications are now used widely, each with its own set of side effects. In this section we examine these medications and their side effects. We begin with the traditional antipsychotic medications, and discuss their potential drawbacks; we then consider the new generations of medications, and their benefits and drawbacks; following this, we examine what happens when people with schizophrenia stop taking their medication; finally, we consider whether it would be helpful to give medication to people with early signs of schizophrenia.

Traditional Antipsychotics

Thorazine (chlorpromazine) and other similar antipsychotics are dopamine antagonists, which effectively block the action of dopamine. Positive symptoms—hallucinations and delusions—diminish in approximately 75–80% of people with schizophrenia who take such antipsychotic medications (Green, 2001). Since their development, traditional antipsychotics have been the first step in treating schizophrenia. When taken regularly, they can reduce the risk of relapse: Only 25% of those who took antipsychotic medication for 1 year had a relapse, compared to 65–80% of those not on medication for a year (Rosenbaum et al., 2005). Traditional antipsychotics have sedating properties, which affect patients quickly; above and beyond such sedation, improvement in psychotic symptoms can take anywhere from 5 days to 6 weeks (Rosenbaum et al., 2005).

Some of the side effects of traditional antipsychotics create problems when a person takes them regularly for an extended period of time. Patients can develop **tardive dyskinesia**, an enduring side effect that produces involuntary lip smacking and odd facial contortions as well as other movement-related symptoms. Although tardive dyskinesia typically does not go away even when traditional antipsychotics are discontinued, its symptoms can be reduced with another type of medication. It is interesting to note, however, that decades before antipsychotic medications existed, clinicians described motor symptoms very similar to those of tardive dyskinesia in some patients who had what would now be labeled schizophrenia (Turner, 1989). This observation implies that it is possible that at least in some cases of tardive

Tardive dyskinesia
An enduring side effect of traditional antipsychotic medications that produces involuntary lip smacking and odd facial contortions as well as other movement-related symptoms.

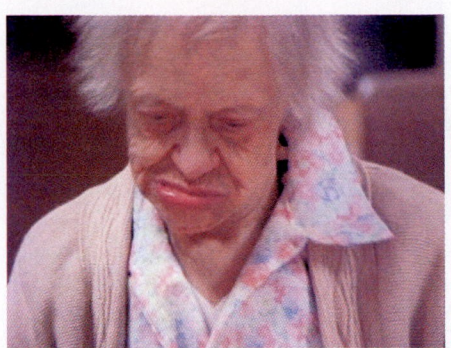

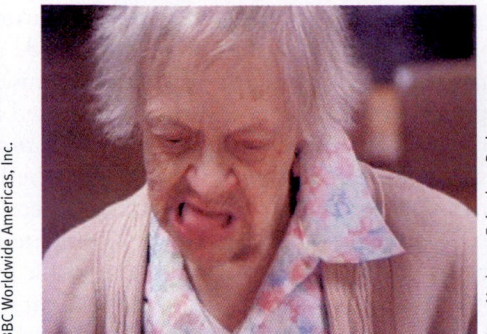

From Madness, Episode 3, Brainwaves. BBC Worldwide Americas, Inc.

dyskinesia are a by-product of schizophrenia itself, not a side effect of the medications. Other side effects of traditional antipsychotics include tremors, weight gain, and a sense of physical restlessness.

Atypical Antipsychotics: A New Generation

More recently, a different class of medications has become available for the treatment of schizophrenia: **atypical antipsychotics** (also referred to as *second-generation antipsychotics*), which affect dopamine and serotonin and do not affect the motor areas of the brain as much as traditional antipsychotics. Because of how they work, they do not pose a risk of tardive dyskinesia. Examples of atypical antipsychotics include *Risperdal* (risperidone), *Zyprexa* (olanzapine), and *Seroquel* (quetiapine). In contrast to typical antipsychotics, with long-term use these newer drugs appear to reduce both positive and negative symptoms (Corrigan et al., in press) and may reduce cognitive deficits (Geddes et al., 2000; Keefe, Bollini, & Silva, 1999; Keefe et al., 2006). However, the beneficial effects of atypical antipsychotics on cognitive functioning are less robust than was initially thought (Green, 2007; Keefe, Sweeney, et al., 2007), and some studies have found that traditional antipsychotics work as well as atypical antipsychotics for those patients who can tolerate the side effects (Kahn et al., 2008).

Nonetheless, atypical antipsychotics have several advantages over traditional antipsychotics: (1) As yet, they have not been found to lead to tardive dyskinesia; (2) they can reduce comorbid symptoms of anxiety and depression (Marder, Davis, & Chouinard, 1997); and, (3) they improve daily functioning (Keefe, Bilder, et al., 2007). Like traditional antipsychotics, they decrease the likelihood of relapse, at least for 1 year (which is the longest period studied; Csernansky, Mahmoud, & Brenner, 2002; Lauriello & Bustillo, 2001). However, the benefits of newer antipsychotics must be weighed against medical costs: Side effects include changes in metabolism that cause significant weight gain and increased risk of heart problems, and these side effects can become so severe or problematic that some people won't or shouldn't continue to use these medications (McEvoy et al., 2007).

In order to compare the effects and side effects of traditional and second-generation antipsychotic medications, NIMH funded the Clinical Antipsychotic Trials of Intervention Effectiveness (CATIE) research program. This large-scale study examined 1,460 patients in 57 U.S. cites. This landmark study did not apply many of the exclusion criteria common to previous studies typically conducted by drug companies, and thus it included a more representative sample of participants. Moreover, the medication phase of CATIE was extended to 18 months. Analyzing the results of the study will take years, but the most striking result thus far is the high rate of patients who stopped taking the medication they were taking at the beginning of the study. More than two thirds of the participants stopped, either because the medication they were taking didn't sufficiently help reduce symptoms or because of the side effects. Disappointingly, continued use of second-generation antipsychotics was not significantly better overall, primarily because of their side effects (Lieberman et al., 2005). Among these newer antipsychotics, no particular medication stood out as superior (McEvoy et al., 2006; Tamminga, 2006).

This woman is exhibiting signs of tardive dyskinesia—involuntary lip smacking and odd facial grimaces that can be an enduring side effect of long-term use of traditional antipsychotic medication. Such side effects can persist even after the antipsychotic medication is discontinued. Symptoms of tardive dyskinesia can be reduced with other medications.

Atypical antipsychotics
A relatively new class of antipsychotic medications that affect dopamine and serotonin activity but create fewer movement-related side effects than do traditional antipsychotics; also referred to as *second-generation antipsychotics*.

Either type of antipsychotic medication is considered "successful" when it significantly reduces symptoms and the side effects can be tolerated. However, sometimes medication is not successful because it wasn't really given a fighting chance: patients often stop taking their prescribed medication without consulting their doctor, which is referred to as *noncompliance*. As in the CATIE study, many people who stop taking their medication—whether in consultation with their doctor or not—cite significant unpleasant side effects as the main reason.

A unique study set out to investigate the side effects of antipsychotic medications in *healthy* participants, who took a single dose of each of the following, in random order: a traditional antipsychotic (haloperidol), an atypical antipsychotic (risperidone), and a placebo. Both types of antipsychotic medication caused some side effects that were similar to the negative symptoms of schizophrenia, particularly, but not limited to, alogia, which in this case was due to drowsiness (Artaloytia et al., 2006). Clearly, there is a need for medications that can reduce symptoms while not creating side effects that lead people to stop taking the drug.

Discontinuing Medication

Given how often patients stop taking their medication, we need to understand the effects of discontinuing medication. When people with schizophrenia discontinue their medication, they are more likely to relapse. One study found that among those who were stable for over 1 year and then stopped taking their medication, 78% had symptoms return within a year after that and 96% had symptoms return after 2 years (Gitlin et al., 2001). Various studies have found similar results (Cunningham et al., 2001; Perkins, 1999; Weiden & Zygmunt, 1997). And even up to 5 years after discharge, patients who had been hospitalized for schizophrenia and then discontinued their medication were five times as likely to relapse as those who didn't (Robinson et al., 1999). With enough relapses, though, some people begin to understand the need for treatment:

> I thought I could live my life without taking medication, but I ended up in the hospital again. Then it got worse. I started losing my concentration and my memory got bad. That's when I finally realized I had to take medication.
>
> (Miller & Mason, 2002, p. 25)

Preventive Medication?

Acute episodes of psychosis appear to create long-lasting disturbances in brain activation, cognitive functioning, and social relations. In addition, research suggests that pharmacological treatment administered soon after the first psychotic episode is associated with a better long-term prognosis, compared to treatment begun later (Harris et al., 2005; Marshall et al., 2005). Some clinicians and researchers are investigating whether early and aggressive use of antipsychotic medication can prevent or minimize the long-term damage that psychotic episodes appear to inflict (Lieberman, 1999). Moreover, as noted in Chapter 3, some researchers are exploring whether people who have prodromal symptoms of schizophrenia (but not enough symptoms to meet the diagnostic criteria for the disorder) can reduce the likelihood of a later psychotic episodes by taking antipsychotic medication preemptively (McGorry & Edwards, 2002; McGorry et al., 2002). That is, researchers have asked whether preventive medication can help children and adolescents who have some symptoms but for whom the number and intensity of those symptoms do not meet the criteria for a psychotic disorder (Gosden, 2000; Gottesman & Erlenmeyer-Kimling, 2001; Warner, 2002).

Small pilot studies of early intervention with risperidone with at-risk groups have found some benefits, such as decreased positive symptoms (Cannon et al., 2002; Cornblatt, Lencz, & Obuchowski, 2002; McGorry et al., 2002; Wade et al., 2006). However, some researchers are concerned about whether adolescents or children, whose brains are still undergoing rapid development, should be given antipsychotic medications in the absence of a psychotic episode. All four of the Genain sisters were treated with medication; only Myra had long stretches of time when she did not need medication (Mirsky & Quinn, 1988). By 1995, Nora, Iris, and Hester were continuing to take traditional antipsychotics; Myra was on a low dose of an atypical antipsychotic. These medications helped reduce their symptoms (Mirsky et al., 2000).

Brain Stimulation: ECT and TMS

Medication is not the only treatment that targets neurological factors. As mentioned in Chapter 1, electroconvulsive therapy (ECT) was originally used to treat schizophrenia, but generally was not successful. Although currently used only infrequently to treat this disorder, a course of ECT may be administered to people with active schizophrenia who are not helped by medications. ECT may reduce symptoms, but its effects are short-lived; furthermore, "maintenance" ECT—that is, regular although less frequent treatments—may be necessary for long-term improvement (Keuneman, Weerasundera, & Castle, 2002). Three of the Genain sisters—Nora, Iris, and Hester—received numerous sessions of ECT before antipsychotic medication was available. After ECT, their symptoms improved at least somewhat but, usually within months if not weeks, worsened again until the symptoms were so bad that a course of ECT was again administered (Mirsky et al., 1987; Rosenthal, 1963).

In experimental studies with small numbers of patients, transcranial magnetic stimulation (TMS) appears to decrease hallucinations, at least in the short term (Brunelin, Poulet, et al., 2006; d'Alfonso et al., 2002; Hoffman et al., 2000; Poulet et al., 2005). However, not all studies have found TMS to have this positive effect (McNamara et al., 2001; Saba et al., 2006). The specifics of ECT and TMS administration are discussed in Chapter 4.

Targeting Psychological Factors in Treating Schizophrenia

Treatments for schizophrenia that target psychological factors address the four general treatment steps; they (1) reduce psychotic symptoms through cognitive-behavior therapy (CBT); (2) reduce negative symptoms through CBT; (3) improve neurocognitive functioning through cognitive rehabilitation; and (4) improve overall functioning and quality of life through psychoeducation and motivational enhancement (Tarrier & Bobes, 2000).

Cognitive-Behavior Therapy

CBT addresses the patient's symptoms and the distress that they cause. Treatment may initially focus on understanding and managing symptoms, by helping patients to:

- learn to distinguish hallucinatory voices from people actually speaking,
- highlight the importance of taking effective medications,
- discuss issues that interfere with compliance, and
- develop more effective coping strategies.

When a therapist uses CBT to address problems arising from delusions, he or she would not try to challenge the delusions themselves, but instead would try to help the patient move forward in life despite these beliefs. For instance, if someone believes that the CIA is after him, the CBT therapist might focus on the effects of that belief: What if the CIA were following him? How can he live his life more fully in spite this belief? Patient and therapist work together to implement new coping strategies and monitor medication compliance. In fact, such uses of CBT not only improve overall functioning (Step 4), but also can decrease positive symptoms (Step 1) (Bustillo et al., 2001; Pfammatter, Junghan, & Brenner, 2006; Rector & Beck, 2002a, 2002b) as well as negative symptoms (Step 2) (Dickerson, 2004; Tarrier et al., 2001; Turkington et al., 2006).

Cognitive Rehabilitation

Once psychotic symptoms have subsided, people with schizophrenia often continue to struggle with neurocognitive deficits that limit their ability to function. **Cognitive rehabilitation** (also called *neurocognitive remediation* or *cognitive mediation*)

Cognitive rehabilitation
A form of psychological treatment that is designed to strengthen cognitive abilities through extensive and focused practice; also called *neurocognitive remediation* or *cognitive mediation*.

is designed to strengthen cognitive abilities through extensive and focused practice (Wexler et al., 1997). Researchers have reported that such practice enhances the abilities to shift attention voluntarily, to sustain attention, and to reason, and increases mental flexibility (Krabbendam & Aleman, 2003; McGurk et al., 2007; Penadés et al., 2006; Wexler & Bell, 2005; Wykes et al., 2003). However, this treatment is expensive, and some studies find that its effects do not generalize beyond the specific tasks that are practiced (Silverstein et al., 2005). If in fact such practice does not generalize, then this treatment will have only minimal effects on the patient's functioning in the real world. Research efforts are under way to determine which specific rehabilitation techniques work to improve the general life skills of people with schizophrenia.

Treating Comorbid Substance Abuse: Motivational Enhancement

Because many people with schizophrenia also abuse drugs or alcohol, recent research has focused on developing treatments for people with both schizophrenia and substance-related disorders; motivational enhancement is one facet of such treatment. As we discussed in Chapter 9, patients who receive motivational enhancement therapy develop their own goals, and then clinicians help them meet those goals. For people who have both schizophrenia and substance-related disorders, one goal might be to take medication regularly (Lehman et al., 1998). For people who have two disorders, treatment that targets both of them appears to be more effective than treatment that targets one or the other alone (Barrowclough et al., 2001).

Targeting Social Factors in Treating Schizophrenia

Treatments that target social factors address three of the four general treatment steps: They identify early warning signs of positive and negative symptoms through family education and therapy; when necessary, such treatments involve hospitalizing people whose symptoms make them unable to care for themselves or whose symptoms put themselves or others at high risk of harm. These treatments also reduce certain negative symptoms through social skills training and improve overall functioning and quality of life through community-based interventions. Community-based interventions include work-related and residential programs (Tarrier & Bobes, 2000).

Family Education and Therapy

By the time a person is diagnosed with schizophrenia, family members typically have struggled for months—or even years—to understand and help their loved one. Psychoeducation for family members can provide practical information about the illness and its consequences, how to recognize early signs of relapse, how to recognize side effects of medications, and how to manage crises that may arise. Such education can decrease relapse rates (Pfammatter, Junghan, & Brenner, 2006; Pilling et al., 2002; Pitschel-Walz et al., 2001). In addition, family-based treatments may provide emotional support for family members (Dixon, Adams, & Luckstead, 2000). Moreover, family therapy, as noted in Chapter 4, can create more adaptive family interaction patterns:

> In 1989, my older sister and I joined Mom in her attempts to learn more about managing symptoms of her illness. Mom's caseworkers met with us every 6 to 8 weeks for over 8 years. Mom, who had never been able to admit she had an illness, now told us that she did not want to die a psychotic. This was one of the many positive steps that we observed in her recovery. Over the years, other family members have joined our group. . . . With the help of the treatment team, we can now respond *effectively* to Mom's symptoms and identify stress-producing situations that, if left unaddressed, can lead to episodes of hospitalization. With Mom's help we have identified the different stages of her illness. In the first stage, we listed withdrawal, confusions, depression, and sleeping disorder. Fifteen years ago when mom reported her symptoms to me, I just told her everything would be okay. Today we respond immediately. For 8 years she has maintained a low dosage of medications, with increases during times of stress.
>
> (Sundquist, 1999, p. 620)

Family therapy can also help high EE families change their pattern of interaction, so that family members are less critical of the patient, which can lower the relapse rate from 75% to 40% (Leff et al., 1990). However, as noted earlier in this chapter, not all families with high EE have such high relapse rates, especially in certain cultures (Cheng, 2002). Thus, treatment that changes a family's high EE pattern of interaction can help patients in some situations but is not always appropriate.

Group Therapy: Social Skills Training

Given the prominence of social deficits in many people with schizophrenia, clinicians often try to improve a patient's social skills. Social skills training usually occurs in a group setting, and its goals include learning to "read" other people's behaviors, learning what behaviors are expected in particular situations, and responding to others in a more adaptive way. Social skills training teaches these skills by breaking down complex social behaviors into their components: maintaining eye contact when speaking to others, taking turns speaking, learning to adjust how loudly or softly to speak in different situations, and learning how to behave when meeting someone new. The leader and members of a group take turns role playing these different elements of social interaction.

In contrast to techniques that focus specifically on behaviors, cognitive techniques focus on group members' irrational beliefs about themselves, their knowledge of social conventions, the beliefs that underlie their interactions with other people, and their ideas about what others may think; such beliefs often prevent people with schizophrenia from attempting to interact with others. These social skills may be applied to interactions with mental health professionals, such as discussing with a psychiatrist the side effects a medication is causing. Each element of the training is repeated several times, to help overcome patients' neurocognitive problems when learning new material. Research has shown that although social skills training does improve social skills and daily functioning that depends on social skills, it is less effective in preventing relapse or directly increasing employment (Bustillo et al., 2001; Kurtz & Mueser, 2008). Apparently such training is not sufficient to remove enough stress or reduce other contributing factors that may trigger a relapse.

Inpatient Treatment

Short-term or long-term hospitalization is sometimes necessary for people with schizophrenia. A short-term hospital stay may be required when someone is having an acute schizophrenic episode (is actively psychotic, extremely disorganized, or otherwise unable to care for himself or herself) or is suicidal or violent. The goal is to reduce symptoms and stabilize the patient. Inpatient treatment includes various therapy groups, such as a group to discuss medication side effects. Once the symptoms are reduced to the point where appropriate self-care is possible and the risk of harm is minimized, the patient will probably be discharged. Long-term hospitalization may occur only when other treatments have not significantly reduced symptoms and the patient needs full-time intensive care.

Legal measures have made it difficult to hospitalize people against their will (Torrey, 2001). Although these tougher standards protect people from being hospitalized simply because they do not conform to common social conventions (see Chapter 1), they also mean that people who have a disorder that *by its very nature* limits their ability to comprehend that they have an illness may not receive appropriate help until their symptoms have become so severe that normal functioning is impossible. Early intervention for ill adults who do not want help but do not realize that they are ill is legally almost impossible today. This issue will be discussed in more detail in Chapter 16.

Minimizing Hospitalizations: Community-Based Interventions

In Chapter 1 we noted that asylums and other forms of 24-hour care, treatment, and containment for those with severe mental illness have met with mixed success over the past several hundred years. Traditionally, people with chronic schizophrenia were likely to end up in such institutions. However, beginning in the 1960s with the widespread use of antipsychotic medications and building into the 1970s, the U.S. government

Joseph Schwartz/Corbis

Deinstitutionalization was mandated without adequate funding for communities to take care of people with schizophrenia and other serious mental illnesses. One result has been increased poverty and homelessness among those with such disorders.

established the social policy of *deinstitutionalization*—trying to help those with severe mental illness live in their communities rather than remain in the hospital. Not everyone thinks that deinstitutionalization was a good idea, at least not in the way it has been implemented. The main problem is that the patients were sent out into communities without adequate social, medical, or financial support. It is now common in many U.S. cities to see such individuals on street corners, begging for money or loitering, with no obvious social safety net.

The good news is that some communities have adequately funded programs to help people with chronic schizophrenia and other chronic and debilitating psychological disorders live outside of institutions. **Community care** (also known as *assertive community treatment*) programs allow mental health staff to visit patients in their homes at any time of the day or night (Mueser et al., 1998; Stein & Test, 1980). Patients who receive such community care report greater satisfaction with their care; however, such treatment may not necessarily lead to better outcomes (Killaspy et al., 2006).

Residential Settings

Some people with schizophrenia may be well enough not to need hospitalization but are still sufficiently impaired that they cannot live independently or with family members. Alternative housing includes a range of supervised residential settings. At one extreme is highly supervised housing, in which a small number of people live with a staff member. Residents take turns shopping for and making meals. They also have household chores and attend house meetings to work out the normal annoyances of group living. Those able to handle somewhat more responsibility may live in an apartment building filled with people of similar abilities, with a staff member available to supervise any difficulties that arise. In independent living, in contrast, a staff member provides periodic home visits to patients living on their own. As patients improve, they transition to less supervised settings.

Vocational Rehabilitation

A variety of programs assist people with schizophrenia to acquire job skills; such programs are specifically aimed at helping patients who are relatively high-functioning but have residual symptoms that interfere with functioning at, or near, a normal level. Those who are more impaired may participate in *sheltered employment*, working in settings that are specifically designed for people with emotional or intellectual problems who cannot hold a regular job. Individuals in such programs may work in a hospital coffee shop or create craft items that are sold in shops. Those who are less impaired may be part of *supported employment* programs, which place individuals in regular work settings and provide an on-site job coach to help them adjust to the demands of the job itself and the social interactions involved in having a job (Bustillo et al., 2001). Examples of supported employment jobs might include work in a warehouse packaging items for shipment, or restocking items in an office or a store ("Project search," 2006). What predicts how well a patient with schizophrenia can live and work in the world? Researchers have found that an individual's ability to live and perhaps work outside of a hospital is associated with a specific cognitive function: his or her ability to use working memory (Dickinson & Coursey, 2002).

Details of the treatment that the Genain sisters received are only available for their time at NIMH, in the 1950s, when less was known about the disorder and how to treat it effectively. During the sisters' stay at NIMH, therapists tried to reduce the parents' level of emotional expressiveness and criticism; however, such attempts do not appear to have been effective. After their departure from NIMH, the sisters lived in a variety of settings: Nora lived first with Mrs. Genain, and subsequently in a supervised apartment with Hester. Iris was less able to live independently and lived in the hospital, in supervised residential settings, or at home with Mrs. Genain; she died in 2002. Myra, long divorced, generally lived independently; after Mrs. Genain died in 1983, Myra moved into her mother's house with her older son. Like Iris, Hester spent many years in the hospital, then with Mrs. Genain. She lived with Nora in a supervised apartment until she died in 2003 (Mirsky & Quinn, 1988; Mirsky et al., 1987, 2000).

Community care
Programs that allow mental health care providers to visit patients in their homes at any time of the day or night; also known as *assertive community treatment*.

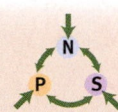

FEEDBACK LOOPS IN TREATMENT: Schizophrenia

To be effective, treatment for people with schizophrenia must employ interventions that induce interactions among neurological, psychological, and social factors (see Figure 12.6). When successful, medication (treatment targeting neurological factors) can reduce the positive and negative symptoms, and even help improve cognitive functioning. These changes in neurological and psychological factors, in turn, make it possible for social treatments, such as social skills training and vocational rehabilitation, to be more effective. If patients are not psychotic and have improved cognitive abilities, they can better learn social and vocational skills that allow them to function more effectively and independently.

Figure 12.6

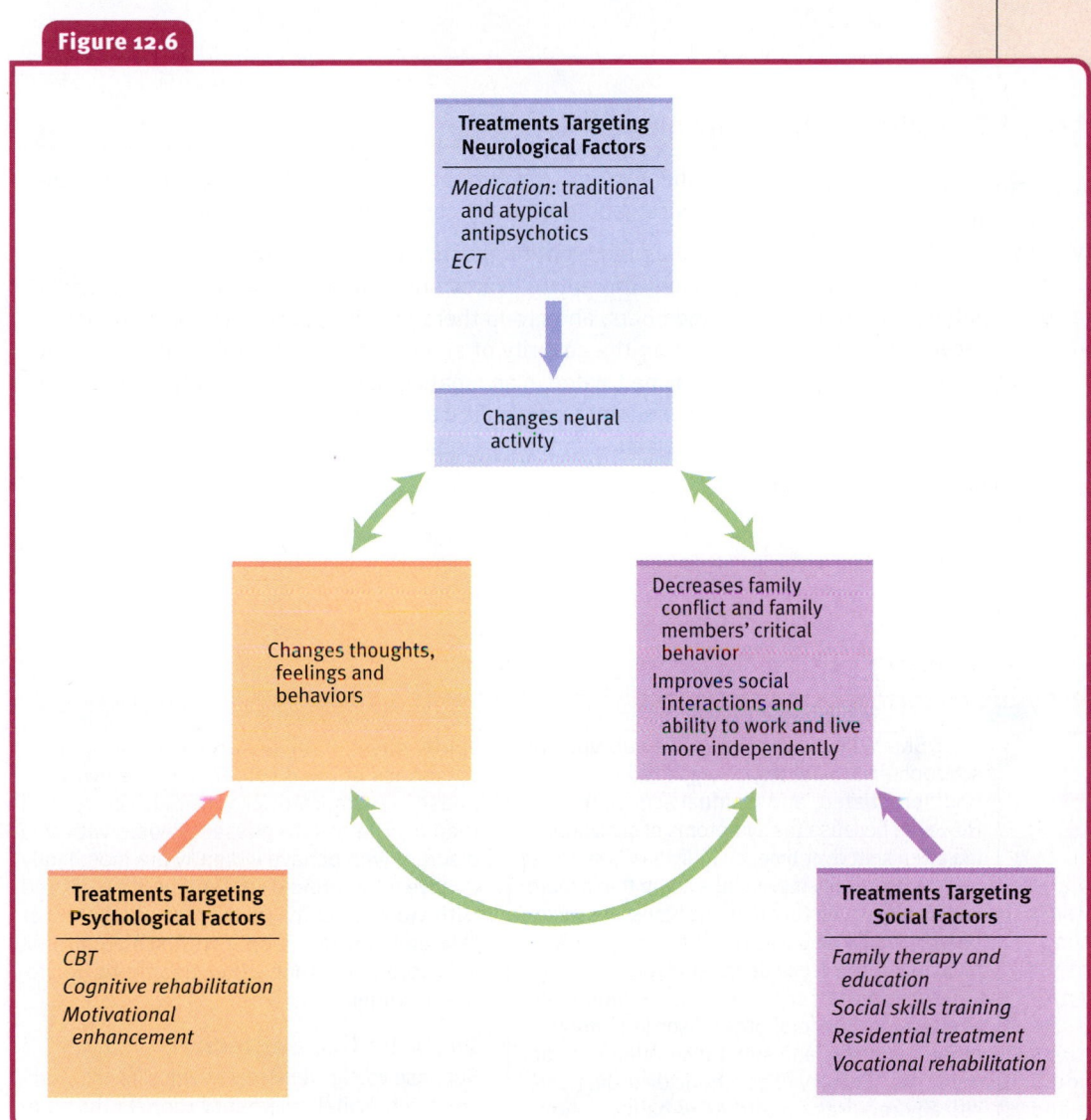

12.6 ▸ Feedback Loops in Treating Schizophrenia

Treatments that target psychological factors (CBT and cognitive rehabilitation) address steps 1, 3 and 4 of treatment: decreasing positive symptoms and cognitive deficits (psychological) and improving overall functioning and quality of life (social factor). Moreover, even when CBT may not *decrease* psychotic symptoms per se (step 1), it teaches patients how to function (step 4) despite these symptoms. In turn, as psychotic symptoms become more manageable, stress levels—and cortisol production—should decrease and thereby have fewer effects on brain functioning.

Similarly, treatments that target social factors, such as family therapy and psychoeducation, social skills groups, and vocational rehabilitation, also address step 4: improving the patient's overall functioning and quality of life. As family and social interactions become less stressful, cortisol levels should decrease.

However, although medication can improve symptoms, it is not a panacea—in part because many patients stop taking it—which leaves an important role for psychosocial treatments. For instance, CBT (which addresses medication compliance and psychotic symptoms) focuses on motivation and beliefs, which are often not affected by medication. And treatments that target social factors (such as family therapy to change a high EE interaction pattern) can lower relapse rates (presumably via psychological and neurological factors associated with decreased stress). Therefore, each type of treatment for schizophrenia is a part of a larger whole.

Key Concepts and Facts About Treating Schizophrenia

- Treatments that target neurological factors include traditional and atypical antipsychotics; when these medications do not significantly decrease positive symptoms, ECT may be used. Although antipsychotic medications can decrease positive and, in some cases, negative symptoms, many patients discontinue such treatment because of side effects or because the medication did not help them enough. People who stop taking medication are much more likely to relapse.

- Treatments that target psychological factors include CBT to help patients better manage their psychotic symptoms, cognitive

rehabilitation to reduce cognitive deficits, and motivational enhancement to decrease comorbid substance abuse.

- Treatments that target social factors include family education, family therapy to improve the interaction pattern among family members, and group therapy to improve social skills. Depending on the severity of an episode of schizophrenia, a patient may be treated in an inpatient facility or as an outpatient in the community. Community-based interventions include residential care and vocational rehabilitation.

SUMMING UP

Summary of What Are Schizophrenia and Other Psychotic Disorders?

According to DSM-IV-TR, schizophrenia is marked by two or more symptoms, at least one of which must be a positive symptom. These symptoms must be present for a minimum of 6 months and must significantly impair functioning. Research findings suggest that the disorganized symptoms form their own distinct cluster and should be grouped separately from delusions and hallucinations.

Research studies have indicated that cognitive deficits underlie negative and disorganized symptoms of schizophrenia. The DSM-IV-TR criteria have been criticized for omitting important cognitive and social deficits that lead to positive and negative symptoms and that are closely associated with prognosis.

DSM-IV-TR distinguishes five subtypes of schizophrenia: paranoid, disorganized, catatonic, undifferentiated, and residual schizophrenia. However, because the symptoms of schizophrenia often shift over time, an individual's subtype can change. Many researchers argue that a more useful way to distinguish subtypes of schizophrenia would be based on whether the individual has a deficit or nondeficit subtype.

Symptoms of schizophrenia can appear to overlap with those of other disorders, notably mood disorders and substance-related disorders. The category of psychotic disorders specifically requires symptoms of hallucinations or delusions; disorders in this category are schizophrenia, schizophreniform disorder, brief psychotic disorder, schizoaffective disorder, delusional disorder, and shared psychotic disorder. These disorders, along with schizotypal personality disorder, are part of a spectrum of schizophrenia-related disorders.

Most people with schizophrenia have at least one comorbid disorder. Men have an

earlier onset of the disorder than do women. Symptoms of the disorder typically evolve in phases: premorbid, prodromal, active, and then middle-to-late phases. People with this disorder who behave violently are most likely to have a comorbid disorder that is associated with violent behavior, such as a substance-related disorder. People with schizophrenia are more likely than other people to be victims of violence.

Thinking like a clinician

Suppose you are a mental health clinician working in a hospital emergency room in the summer; a woman is brought in for you to evaluate. She's wearing a winter coat, and in the waiting room, she talks—or shouts—to herself or an imaginary person. You think that she may be suffering from schizophrenia. What information would you need in order to make that diagnosis? What other psychological disorders could, with only brief observation, appear similar to schizophrenia?

Summary of Understanding Schizophrenia

A variety of neurological factors are associated with schizophrenia: (1) Abnormalities in brain structure and function have been found in the frontal and temporal lobes, the thalamus, and the hippocampus. Moreover, certain brain areas do not appear to interact with each other properly. People with schizophrenia are more likely to have enlarged ventricles than are other people. The brain abnormalities give rise to biological markers in some individuals. (2) These brain abnormalities appear to be a result of, at least in some cases, maternal malnourishment, illness during pregnancy, or fetal oxygen deprivation. (3) Schizophrenia is associated with abnormalities in dopamine, serotonin, and glutamate activity, as well as a heightened stress response and increased production of cortisol. (4) Genetics is the strongest predictor that a given individual will develop schizophrenia. Genetics alone, though, cannot explain why a given individual develops the disorder.

Psychological factors that are associated with schizophrenia and shape the symptoms of the disorder include: (1) cognitive deficits in attention, memory, and executive functioning; (2) dysfunctional beliefs and attributions; and (3) difficulty recognizing and conveying emotions.

Various social factors are also associated with schizophrenia: (1) an impaired theory of mind, which means that that other people's behavior routinely appears to be unpredictable; (2) a stressful home environment, such as being raised in an orphanage or by a parent with schizophrenia; (3) the stresses of immigration—particularly for people likely to encounter discrimination—and economic hardship; and (4) the individualist nature of the culture, which is associated with lower recovery rates for people with schizophrenia.

Thinking like a clinician

Using the neuropsychosocial approach, explain in detail how the three types of factors and their feedback loops may have led all four Genain sisters to develop schizophrenia.

Summary of Treating Schizophrenia

Treatments that target neurological factors include traditional and atypical antipsychotics; when these medications do not significantly decrease positive symptoms, ECT may be used. Although antipsychotic medications can decrease positive and, in some cases, negative symptoms, many patients discontinue such treatment because of side effects or because the medication did not help them enough. People who stop taking medication are much more likely to relapse.

Treatments that target psychological factors include CBT to help patients better manage their psychotic symptoms, cognitive rehabilitation to reduce cognitive deficits, and motivational enhancement to decrease comorbid substance abuse.

Treatments that target social factors include family education, family therapy to improve the interaction pattern among family members, and group therapy to improve social skills. Depending on the severity of an episode of schizophrenia, a patient may be treated in an inpatient facility or as an outpatient in the community. Community-based interventions include residential care and vocational rehabilitation.

Thinking like a clinician

Suppose you are designing a comprehensive treatment program for people with schizophrenia. Although you'd like to provide each program participant with many types of services, budgetary constraints mean that you have to limit the types of treatments your program offers. Based on what you have read about the treatment of schizophrenia, what would you definitely include in your treatment program, and why? Also list the types of treatment you'd like to include if you had a bigger budget.

Key Terms

Schizophrenia (p. 520)

Positive symptoms (p. 520)

Hallucinations (p. 521)

Delusions (p. 522)

Word salad (p. 522)

Catatonia (p. 523)

Negative symptoms (p. 523)

Flat affect (p. 523)

Alogia (p. 524)

Avolition (p. 524)

Executive functions (p. 524)

Paranoid schizophrenia (p. 526)

Disorganized schizophrenia (p. 527)

Catatonic schizophrenia (p. 527)

Undifferentiated schizophrenia (p. 528)

Schizophreniform disorder (p. 530)

Brief psychotic disorder (p. 530)

Schizoaffective disorder (p. 530)

Delusional disorder (p. 530)

Shared psychotic disorder (p. 531)

Prodromal phase (p. 536)

Active phase (p. 536)

Biological marker (p. 543)

Dopamine hypothesis (p. 544)

Theory of mind (p. 549)

High expressed emotion (high EE) (p. 550)

Social selection (p. 552)

Social causation (p. 552)

Tardive dyskinesia (p. 556)

Atypical antipsychotics (p. 557)

Cognitive rehabilitation (p. 559)

Community care (p. 562)

More Study Aids

For additional study aids related to this chapter, go to:

www.worthpublishers.com/rosenberg

Personality Disorders

Rachel Reiland wrote a memoir called *Get Me Out of Here*, about living with a personality disorder. In the opening of the book, Reiland remembers Cindy, the golden-haired grade-school classmate who was their teacher's favorite. At the end of a painting class, Cindy's painting was beautiful, with distinctive trees. Unfortunately, Rachel's painting looked like a "putrid blob." Rachel then recounts:

> I seethed with jealousy as Mrs. Schwarzheuser showered Cindy with compliments. Suddenly, rage overwhelmed me. I seized a cup of brown paint and dumped half of it over my picture. Glaring at Cindy, I leaned across the table and dumped the other half over her drawing. I felt a surge of relief. Now Cindy's picture looked as awful as mine.
>
> "Rachel!" Mrs. Schwarzheuser yelled. "You've completely destroyed Cindy's beautiful trees. Shame on you. You are a *horrible* little girl. The paint is everywhere—look at your jeans."
>
> My blue jeans were soaked with brown paint. They looked ugly. I looked ugly. Mrs. Schwarzheuser frantically wiped up paint to keep it from dripping onto the floor. Everyone was watching.
>
> I felt my body go numb. My legs, arms, and head were weightless. Floating. It was the same way I felt when Daddy pulled off his belt and snapped it. Anticipation of worse things to come—things I had brought on myself because I was different.
>
> "In all my years, I've never seen a child like you. You are the *worst* little girl I've ever taught. Go sit in the corner, immediately."
>
> Shame on Rachel. That language I understood. And deserved. . . .
> Mrs. Schwarzheuser was right. I was horrible.
>
> (2004, pp. 1–2)

Reiland's actions toward Cindy that day were troublesome and troubling, but many children have episodes of feeling intensely jealous and angry toward others and then act out those feelings. Such episodes don't necessarily indicate that a child, or the adult he or she grows up to be, has a disorder.

But some children and teenagers exhibit problems with relationships that persist into adulthood—problems that interfere with an aspect of daily life, such as work or family life. These problems have existed for so long that they seem to be a part of who the person is, a part of his or her personality. Such persistent problems indicate **personality disorders**, a category of psychological disorders characterized by a pattern of inflexible and maladaptive thoughts, feelings, and behaviors that arise across a range of situations and lead to distress or dysfunction.

Personality disorders
A category of psychological disorders characterized by a pattern of inflexible and maladaptive thoughts, feelings, and behaviors that arise across a range of situations and lead to distress or dysfunction.

Illustration by Sean Rodwell/Photography by Paul Hampartsoumian/Advocate Art

Diagnosing Personality Disorders

Unfortunately, Rachel Reiland's troublesome behavior continued as she grew older, at least when she was outside the house. Her teachers were frustrated with her, and angry at her; for instance, she vividly remembers when she was 12 years old, in her Catholic school, and sent, yet again, to the principal's office for breaking the rules:

> "Miss Marsten [Reiland's maiden name]," Sister Luisa said disapprovingly. "I see you have managed to get yourself thrown out of the classroom again. What was it this time? A smart remark? Or just your usual disrespect?"
>
> (Reiland, 2004, pp. 3–4)

It's not unusual for children to act out in school, as Reiland did. But as children get older, they mature. In Reiland's case, she went on to do well academically in high school and college, but in the nonacademic areas of her life things didn't go as well. While in high school, she developed anorexia nervosa. In high school and college, she frequently got drunk and was sexually promiscuous. She hadn't yet grown out of the maladaptive childhood patterns of behavior that got her into so much trouble with Sister Luisa.

In her mid-20s, Reiland unintentionally became pregnant when dating a man named Tim. They decided to marry and did so, even though she had a miscarriage before the wedding. They then had two children, first Jeffrey and 2 years later, Melissa. It seemed that Reiland had straightened out her life and that her childhood problems were behind her.

She temporarily stopped working while the children were young. When they were 2- and 4-years old, she found herself overwhelmed—alternately angry and needy. One day during this period of her life, her husband called to say he'd be late at work and wouldn't be home until 6 or 7 p.m. She responded by asking whether his coming home late was her fault. Reiland recounts their ensuing exchange:

> "I didn't say it's your fault, honey. It's just that . . . well, I've got to get some stuff done." I began to twist the phone cord around my finger, tempted to wrap it around my neck.
>
> "I'm a real pain in the ass, aren't I? You're pissed, aren't you?"
> Tim tried to keep his patience, but I could still hear him sigh.
> "Please, Rachel. I've got to make a living."
> "Like I don't do anything around here? Is that it? Like I'm some kind of stupid housewife who doesn't do a god-damned thing? Is that what you're getting at?"
> Another sigh.
> "Okay. Look, sweetheart, I've got to do this presentation this afternoon because it's too late to cancel. But I'll see if I can reschedule the annuity guy for tomorrow. I'll be home by four o'clock, and I'll help you clean up the house."
> "No, no, no!"
> I was beginning to cry.
> "What now?"
> "God, Tim. I'm such an idiot. Such a baby. I don't do a thing around this house, and here I am, wanting you to help me clean. I must make you sick."
> "You don't make me sick, sweetheart. Okay? You don't. Look, I'm really sorry, but I've got to go."
> The tears reached full strength. The cry became a moan that turned to piercing screams. *Why in the hell can't I control myself? The man has to make a living. He's such a good guy; he doesn't deserve me—no one should have to put up with me!*
> "Rachel? Rachel? Please calm down. Please! Come on. You're gonna wake up the kids; the neighbors are gonna wonder what in the hell is going on. Rachel?"
> "[Screw you!] Is that all you care about, what the *neighbors* think? [Screw] you, then. I don't need you home. I don't want you home. Let this [damn] house rot; let the [damn] kids starve. I don't give a shit. And I don't need your shit!"
>
> (2004, pp. 11–12)

When Tim responds by saying he's going to cancel all his appointments and can be home in a few minutes, she sobs, "You must really hate me . . . you really hate me, don't you?" (Reiland, 2004, p. 12).

Personality
Enduring traits and characteristics that lead a person to behave in relatively predictable ways across a range of situations.

Reiland's behavior seems extreme, but is it so extreme that it indicates a personality disorder, or is it just an emotional outburst from a mother of young children who is feeling overwhelmed? In order to understand the nature of Reiland's problems and see how a clinician determines whether an individual's problems merit a diagnosis of personality disorder, we must focus on *personality*, and contrast normal versus abnormal variations of personality.

When you describe your roommate or new friends to your parents, you usually describe his or her **personality**—enduring traits and characteristics that lead a person to behave in relatively predictable ways across a range of situations. Similarly, when you imagine how family members will react to bad news you're going to tell them, you are probably basing your predictions of their reactions on your sense of their personality characteristics. Such characteristics—or *personality traits*—are generally thought of as being on a continuum, with a trait's name, such as "interpersonal warmth," at one end of the continuum and its opposite, such as "standoffishness," at other end of the continuum. Each person is unique in terms of the combination of his or her particular personality traits—and how those traits affect his or her behavior in various situations.

In this section we examine in more detail the DSM-IV-TR category of personality disorders and then the specific personality disorders that it contains.

What Are Personality Disorders?

Some people consistently and persistently exhibit extreme versions of personality traits, for example, being overly conscientious and rule-bound or, like Reiland, being overly emotional and quick to anger. Such extreme and inflexible traits that arise across a variety of situations can become maladaptive and cause distress or dysfunction—characteristics of a personality disorder. Let's examine the definition of personality disorders more closely.

As Table 13.1 notes, personality disorders reflect persistent thoughts, feelings, and behaviors that are significantly different from the norms in the individual's culture (Criterion A). Specifically, these differences involve the ABCs of psychological functioning:

- *affect*, which refers to the range, intensity, and changeability of emotions and emotional responsiveness and the ability to regulate emotions;

- *behavior*, which refers to the ability to control impulses and interactions with others; and

- *cognition (mental processes and mental contents)*, which refers to the perceptions and interpretations of events, other people, and oneself.

In addition, the differences in the ABCs of psychological functioning are relatively inflexible and persist across a range of situations (Criterion B in Table 13.1). Criterion B highlights how central these maladaptive personality traits are to the way the individual functions—the traits exert an influence in a wide variety of situations and the individual has extreme difficulty thinking, feeling, and behaving any differently. This rigidity across situations in turn leads to distress or impaired functioning, as it did for Sarah, in Case 13.1. To be diagnosed with a personality disorder, the maladaptive traits

Personality disorders are characterized by a pattern of inflexible and maladaptive thoughts, feelings, and behaviors that arise across a range of situations. This woman might be diagnosed with a personality disorder if she consistently got angry with little provocation and had difficulty controlling her anger in a variety of settings.

Billy E. Barnes/Photo Edit

Table 13.1 ▶ DSM-IV-TR General Diagnostic Criteria for a Personality Disorder

A. An enduring pattern of inner experience and behavior that deviates markedly from the expectations of the individual's culture. This pattern is manifested in two (or more) of the following areas:

(1) cognition (i.e., ways of perceiving and interpreting self, other people, and events)

(2) affectivity (i.e., the range, intensity, lability, and appropriateness of emotional response)

(3) interpersonal functioning

(4) impulse control

B. The enduring pattern is inflexible and pervasive across a broad range of personal and social situations.

C. The enduring pattern leads to clinically significant distress or impairment in social, occupational, or other important areas of functioning.

D. The pattern is stable and of long duration and its onset can be traced back at least to adolescence or early adulthood.

E. The enduring pattern is not better accounted for as a manifestation or consequence of another mental disorder.

F. The enduring pattern is not due to the direct physiological effects of a substance (e.g., a drug of abuse, a medication) or a general medical condition (e.g., head trauma).

Source: Reprinted with permission from the Diagnostic and Statistical Manual of Mental Disorders, Text Revision, Fourth Edition, (Copyright 2000) American Psychiatric Association.

typically should date back at least to early adulthood and should not primarily arise from a substance-related or medical disorder or another psychological disorder (American Psychiatric Association, 2000). We can now answer the question of whether Reiland's difficulties were more than those of an overwhelmed mother of young children. Specifically, her problems—in all four areas of functioning listed in Criterion A (cognition, affectivity, interpersonal functioning, and impulse control) as well as those listed in Criteria B through F—indicate that she has a personality disorder.

CASE 13.1 ▶ FROM THE OUTSIDE: Personality Disorder

Sarah, a 39-year-old single female, originally requested therapy at . . . an outpatient clinic, to help her deal with chronic depression and inability to maintain employment. She had been unemployed for over a year and had been surviving on her rapidly dwindling savings. She was becoming increasingly despondent and apprehensive about her future. She acknowledged during the intake interview that her attitude toward work was negative and that she had easily become bored and resentful in all of her previous jobs. She believed that she might somehow be conveying her negative work attitudes to prospective employers and that this was preventing them from hiring her. She also volunteered that she detested dealing with people in general. . . .

Sarah had a checkered employment history. She had been a journalist, a computer technician, a night watch person, and a receptionist. In all of these jobs she had experienced her supervisors as being overly critical and demanding, which she felt caused her to become resentful and inefficient. The end result was always her dismissal or her departure in anger. Sarah generally perceived her co-workers as being hostile, unfair, and rejecting. However, she would herself actively avoid them, complaining that they were being unreasonable and coercive when they tried to persuade her to join them for activities outside of work. For example, she would believe that she was being asked to go for drinks purely because her co-workers wanted her to get drunk and act foolishly. Sarah would eventually begin to take "mental health" days off from work simply to avoid her supervisors and colleagues.

(Thomas, 1994, p. 211)

Although personality disorders are generally considered to be stable, at least from adolescence into adulthood, research suggests that (as shown in Figure 13.1) these disorders are not as enduring as previously thought (Clark, 2009; Durbin & Klein, 2006; Lenzenweger, Johnson, & Willett, 2004; Zanarini et al., 2005); rather symptoms can improve over time for some people (Grilo et al., 2004; Johnson et al., 2000; Lenzenweger, 1999). Nevertheless, these disorders are typically among the most resistant to treatment.

As a group, people with personality disorders obtain less education (Torgersen, Kringlen, & Cramer, 2001) and are more likely never to have married or to be separated or divorced (Torgersen, 2005) than people who don't have such disorders. Personality disorders are associated with suicide: Among people who die by suicide, about 30% are thought to have had a personality disorder; among people who attempt suicide, about 40% are thought to have a personality disorder (American Psychiatric Association Work Group on Suicidal Behaviors, 2003).

Why Are Personality Disorders on Axis II Instead of Axis I?

When the five-axis diagnostic system of DSM was instituted, mental retardation and personality disorders were placed on Axis II because both involved persistent conditions that began in childhood and were believed to be stable—in contrast to the fluctuations observed with most Axis I disorders (Oldham, 2005). However, subsequent research indicates that personality disorders and Axis I disorders don't differ significantly on these two variables (Livesley, 2001). As discussed in previous chapters, many Axis I disorders involve symptoms that emerge in adolescence or young adulthood, or even in childhood (such as depression and eating disorders).

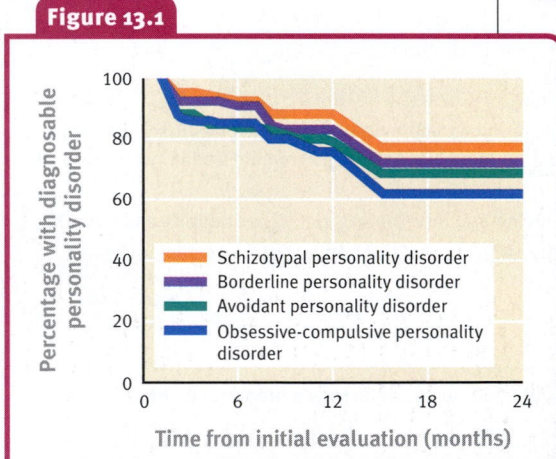

Figure 13.1

13.1 ▶ Stability of Personality Disorders Within 2 years of being diagnosed with a personality disorder, around one quarter to one third of the people in one study no longer met the diagnostic criteria for 12 consecutive months (Grilo et al., 2004). This finding indicates that personality disorders are not as stable as once thought.

Source: Grilo et al., 2004. For more information see the Permissions section.

Moreover, as just noted, personality disorders can fluctuate over time. Thus, the reasons for putting personality disorders on a separate axis have not been borne out by research.

However, symptoms of personality disorders do contrast with those of Axis I disorders, in that they can be difficult to diagnose in a first interview, largely because patients may not be aware of the symptoms. In many cases, people who have a personality disorder are so familiar with their lifelong pattern of emotional responses, behavioral tendencies, and mental processes and contents that the ways in which this pattern is maladaptive may not be apparent to them. In fact, most people with a personality disorder identify *other* people or situations as being the problem, not something about themselves.

Assessing Personality Disorders

Given that many people with personality disorders are not aware of the nature of their problems, clinicians may diagnose a patient with a personality disorder based both on what the patient says and on patterns in the way he or she says it (Skodol, 2005). For instance, Sarah, in Case 13.1, probably had specific complaints about her co-workers, but the key information lies in the *pattern of her complaints*—in her claim that most of her co-workers, in various companies, were hostile and rejecting. More patient visits may be required to identify such a pattern and to diagnose a personality disorder than to diagnose an Axis I disorder. And more so than with other diagnoses, clinicians must make inferences about the patient in order to diagnose a personality disorder. However, clinicians must be careful not to assume that their inferences are correct without further corroboration; for example, a clinician should not assume that Sarah's problems with her co-workers were Sarah's fault without obtaining further information (Skodol, 2005).

To help assess personality disorders, clinicians and researchers may have patients complete personality inventories or questionnaires. To diagnose a personality disorder, the clinician may also talk with someone in the patient's life, such as a family member—who often describes the patient very differently than does the patient (Clark, 2007; Clifton, Turkehimer, & Oltmanns, 2004). The picture that emerges of someone with a personality disorder is a pattern of chronic *interpersonal* difficulties or chronic problems with *self*, such as a feeling of emptiness (Livesley, 2001).

According to DSM-IV-TR, when clinicians assess personality disorders, they should take into account the individual's culture, ethnicity, and social background. For instance, a woman who appears unable to make any decisions independently (even about what to make for dinner) and constantly defers to family members might have a personality disorder. However, for some immigrants, this pattern of behavior may be within a normal range for their ethnic or religious group. When immigrants have problems that are related to the challenges of adapting to a new culture or that involve behaviors or a worldview that is typical of people with their background, a personality disorder shouldn't be diagnosed. A clinician who isn't familiar with a patient's background should get more information from other sources. Sometimes it may not be obvious that a person is an immigrant, and sometimes the children of immigrants have incorporated a different set of social norms than those of the mainstream culture. If at all possible, clinicians should assess a patient's level of acculturation to determine whether he or she values and follows mainstream cultural norms—and if not, which norms he or she values and follows.

Although an individual may exhibit a pattern of problems that indicates a personality disorder, clinicians should take into consideration the individual's ethnicity, social background, and culture. If the individual's pattern of thoughts, feelings, and behaviors are characteristic of people from his or her background, a diagnosis of a personality disorder is not warranted.

Andrew Fox/Corbis

DSM-IV-TR Personality Clusters

DSM-IV-TR lists ten personality disorders, divided into three clusters. Each cluster of personality disorders shares a common

Table 13.2 ▸ DSM-IV-TR Personality Disorders, by Cluster

Cluster A involves odd or eccentric behaviors:	*Paranoid personality disorder* is characterized by mistrust and suspicion of others.
	Schizoid personality disorder is characterized by few close relationships and a limited range of emotional expression.
	Schizotypal personality disorder is characterized by few close relationships and eccentric perceptions, thoughts, and behaviors.
Cluster B involves emotional, dramatic, or erratic behaviors:	*Antisocial personality disorder* is characterized by repeated violation of or disregard for the rights of others.
	Borderline personality disorder is characterized by rapidly changing emotions, unstable relationships, and impulsivity.
	Histrionic personality disorder is characterized by exaggerated emotions and excessive attention-seeking behaviors.
	Narcissistic personality disorder is characterized by an excessive sense of self-importance and difficulty appreciating other people's perspectives.
Cluster C involves anxious and fearful behaviors:	*Avoidant personality disorder* is characterized by a heightened sensitivity to rejection and social inhibition.
	Dependent personality disorder is characterized by submissive, clingy behavior intended to elicit care from others, along with dependence on others for decision making and reassurance.
	Obsessive-compulsive personality disorder is characterized by orderliness, perfectionism, and control at the expense of spontaneity and flexibility.

Source: Reprinted with permission from the Diagnostic and Statistical Manual of Mental Disorders, Text Revision, Fourth Edition, (Copyright 2000) American Psychiatric Association.

feature (see Table 13.2). **Cluster A personality disorders** are characterized by odd or eccentric behaviors that have elements related to those of schizophrenia. **Cluster B personality disorders** are characterized by emotional, dramatic, or erratic behaviors that involve problems with emotional regulation. **Cluster C personality disorders** are characterized by anxious or fearful behaviors.

Table 13.3 provides an overview of facts about personality disorders in general. In the subsequent discussions of the individual personality disorders, you may notice that adding the prevalence rates for the various disorders gives a higher total than the overall prevalence rate of 14% listed in Table 13.3. This mathematical discrepancy is explained by the high comorbidity, also noted in the table: Half of people who have a personality disorder will be diagnosed with at least one other personality disorder (and in some cases, with more than one other personality disorder).

Criticisms of the DSM-IV-TR Category of Personality Disorders

The category of personality disorders, as defined in DSM-IV-TR, has been criticized on numerous grounds. One criticism is that DSM-IV-TR treats personality disorders as categorically distinct from normal personality (Livesley, 2001; Saulsman & Page, 2004; Widiger & Costa, 2002; Widiger & Lowe, 2008; Widiger & Trull, 2007). In contrast, most psychological researchers currently view normal personality and personality disorders as being on continua. In DSM-IV-TR terms, two people might differ only slightly in the degree to which they exhibit a personality trait, but one person would be considered to have a personality disorder and the other person would not. A related criticism is that the DSM-IV-TR criteria for personality disorders create an arbitrary cutoff on the continuum between normal and abnormal (Livesley, 2001; Widiger & Trull, 2007).

Another criticism pertains to the clusters, which were organized by superficial commonalities. Research does not necessarily support the organization of personality disorders into these clusters (Blais et al., 1997; Sheets & Craighead, 2007). Moreover, the specific personality disorders are not clearly distinct from each other

Cluster A personality disorders
Personality disorders characterized by odd or eccentric behaviors that have elements related to those of schizophrenia.

Cluster B personality disorders
Personality disorders characterized by emotional, dramatic, or erratic behaviors that involve problems with emotional regulation.

Cluster C personality disorders
Personality disorders characterized by anxious or fearful behaviors.

Table 13.3 ▸ An Overview: Personality Disorder Facts at a Glance

Prevalence

- Researchers estimate that up to 14% of Americans will have at least one personality disorder over the course of their lives (Grant, Hasin, et al., 2004; Lenzenweger, 2006; Samuels et al., 2002; Torgersen et al., 2001).

Comorbidity

- Up to 75% of those with a personality disorder will also be diagnosed with an Axis I disorder (Dolan-Sewell, Krueger, & Shea, 2001; Lenzenweger, 2006).
- Common comorbid disorders from Axis I are mood disorders, anxiety disorders, and substance-related disorders (Grant, Stinson, et al., 2004; Johnson, Cohen, Kasen, & Brook, 2006a; Lenzenweger, 2006).
- Around 50% of people with a personality disorder will be diagnosed with at least one other personality disorder (Skodol, 2005).

Onset

- The DSM-IV-TR diagnostic criteria require that symptoms arise by young adulthood.
- For one personality disorder—antisocial personality disorder—a diagnostic criterion requires that symptoms arise before age 15.

Course

- Symptoms of personality disorders are often relatively stable, but they may fluctuate or improve as people go through adulthood.

Gender Differences

- Specific personality disorders have gender differences in prevalence, but there is no such difference across all personality disorders.

Source: Unless otherwise noted, the source is American Psychiatric Association, 2000.

(Blais & Norman, 1997; Kupfer, First, & Regier, 2002). For instance, schizoid and schizotypal personality disorders share a number of features, including a pattern of poor social skills and abilities and a small number of social contacts. Similarly, histrionic and narcissistic personality disorders share a pattern of grandiosity and the desire to be the center of attention.

In addition, some personality disorders are not clearly distinct from related Axis I disorders (Widiger & Trull, 2007). The diagnostic criteria for avoidant personality disorder, for example, overlap considerably with those for social phobia, as we'll discuss in detail in the section on avoidant personality disorder. Similarly, critics point out that the general criteria for personality disorders (Table 13.1, Criteria A through D) could apply to some Axis I disorders such as dysthymia and schizophrenia (Oldham, 2005).

The process by which the DSM-IV-TR criteria were determined is another target of criticism. The minimum number of symptoms needed to make a diagnosis, as well as the specific criteria, aren't necessarily supported by research results (Widiger & Trull, 2007). Moreover, different personality disorders require different numbers of symptoms and different levels of impairment (Livesley, 2001; Skodol, 2005; Tyrer & Johnson, 1996; Westen & Shedler, 2000).

The high comorbidity among personality disorders invites another criticism: that the specific personality disorders do not capture the appropriate underlying problems, and so clinicians must use more than one diagnosis to describe the types of problems exhibited by patients (Widiger & Mullins-Sweatt, 2005). In fact, the most frequently diagnosed personality disorder is *personality disorder not otherwise specified*, which is often diagnosed along with an additional personality disorder (Verheul, Bartak, & Widiger, 2007; Verheul & Widiger, 2004). As with other categories of disorders, the *not otherwise specified* diagnosis is used when a patient's symptoms cause distress or impair functioning but do not fit the criteria for any of the disorders within the relevant category—in this case, one of the ten specific personality disorders.

Understanding Personality Disorders in General

At one point, Reiland became impatient with her 4-year-old son Jeffrey and "lost it." She slapped, then cursed him. As he cried, she commanded him to stop crying. He didn't, and she proceeded to spank him so hard that it hurt her hand.

> He had stopped crying, his fright overcoming his need to express his emotions. But his eyes were wide open, as big as I'd ever seen them. And absolutely, unequivocally horrified. That look stopped me.
>
> The familiar feeling of weightlessness overtook me again. I knew Jeffrey's look. I knew that feeling.
>
> It had been a common part of my childhood—enduring rages that began and ended just as unpredictably. The reality slowly sunk in. I had beaten my child. Just as my father had beaten his. Just as I swore I never ever would. A wave of nausea rose within me. *I was just like my father.* Even my children would be better off without me. There was no longer any reason to stay alive.
>
> (Reiland, 2004, p. 19)

Reiland's realization was relatively unusual for someone with a personality disorder: She recognized in this instance that it was *she* who created a problem—*she* who had done something wrong, although her father never recognized his responsibility. He too was quick to anger and hit her and her siblings. Do personality disorders run in families? If so, to what extent do genes and environment lead to personality disorders? How might personality disorders arise?

Neurological Factors in Personality Disorders: Genes and Temperament

Perhaps the most influential neurological factor associated with personality disorders is genes (Cloninger, 2005; Paris, 2005). Researchers have not produced evidence that genes underlie specific personality disorders, but they have shown that genes clearly influence *temperament*, which is the aspect of personality that reflects a person's typical affective state and emotional reactivity (see Chapter 2). Temperament, in turn, plays a major role in personality disorders. Genes influence temperament via their effects on brain structure and function, including neurotransmitter activity.

It is possible that the genes that affect personality traits can predispose some people to develop a personality disorder. For instance, some people are genetically predisposed to seek out novel and exciting stimuli, such as those associated with stock trading, race car driving, or bungee jumping, whereas other people are predisposed to become easily overstimulated and habitually prefer low-key, quiet activities, such as reading, writing, or walking in the woods. Such differences in temperament are the foundation on which different personality traits are built—and, at their extremes, temperaments can give rise to inflexible personality traits that are associated with personality disorders. Examples include a novelty seeker (temperament) who compulsively seeks out ever more exciting activities (inflexible behavior pattern), regardless of the consequences, and a person who avoids overstimulation (temperament) and turns down promotions because the new position would require too many activities that would be overstimulating (inflexible behavior pattern).

Reiland may well have inherited a tendency to develop certain aspects of temperament, which increased the likelihood of her behaving like her father in certain types of situations. However, her genes and her temperament don't paint the whole picture; psychological and social factors also influenced how she thought, felt, and behaved.

Psychological Factors in Personality Disorders: Temperament and the Consequences of Behavior

Two psychological factors significantly contribute to personality disorders: temperament and operant conditioning. Although influenced by genes, temperament is also shaped by the environment—and ultimately is best conceptualized as a psychological factor. As just noted, temperament influences the types of situations to which individuals are likely to gravitate and to avoid—and how they are likely to behave in those situations. The consequences of their behaviors (operant conditioning) will influence the likelihood that they will repeat the behaviors. Furthermore, the consequences can lead to pervasive dysfunctional beliefs—which can form the foundation for some types of personality disorders.

The Role of Temperament

Temperaments—and their contribution to personality disorders—can be classified in two different ways. As discussed in Chapter 2, Cloninger (1987) proposed four basic dimensions on which temperaments vary (see Figure 13.2; left side). The strength of each dimension varies across individuals, and each cluster of personality disorders is characterized by an extreme on a particular dimension.

In particular, people with Cluster A (odd/eccentric) personality disorders are not strongly motivated by relationships with other people—they avoid social risk taking and are generally indifferent to normal social rewards, such as attention from others. They tend to score low on reward dependence. Indeed, it's not just that being with other people isn't rewarding and doesn't motivate their behavior; rather, such people have the opposite motivation, preferring to be alone. People with Cluster B (dramatic/erratic) personality disorders tend to score high on novelty seeking and tend to engage in new, highly stimulating, or intensely demanding activities, perhaps leading them to get into arguments more frequently. People with Cluster C (fearful/anxious) personality disorders tend to be high on harm avoidance; they have in common a fear of uncertainty that leads them to withdraw from relationships, situations, or activities that most other people view as relatively safe. For instance, Sarah, in Case 13.1, generally perceived her co-workers as threatening and tried to avoid them.

Cloninger also proposed three character dimensions (see Figure 13.2; right side), which can help illuminate the nature of personality disorders; most personality disorders are marked by low levels of *cooperativeness, self-directedness*, and *self-transcendence*, which translate behaviorally into personality characteristics of being uncooperative, having difficulty regulating and adapting behavior, and being

Figure 13.2

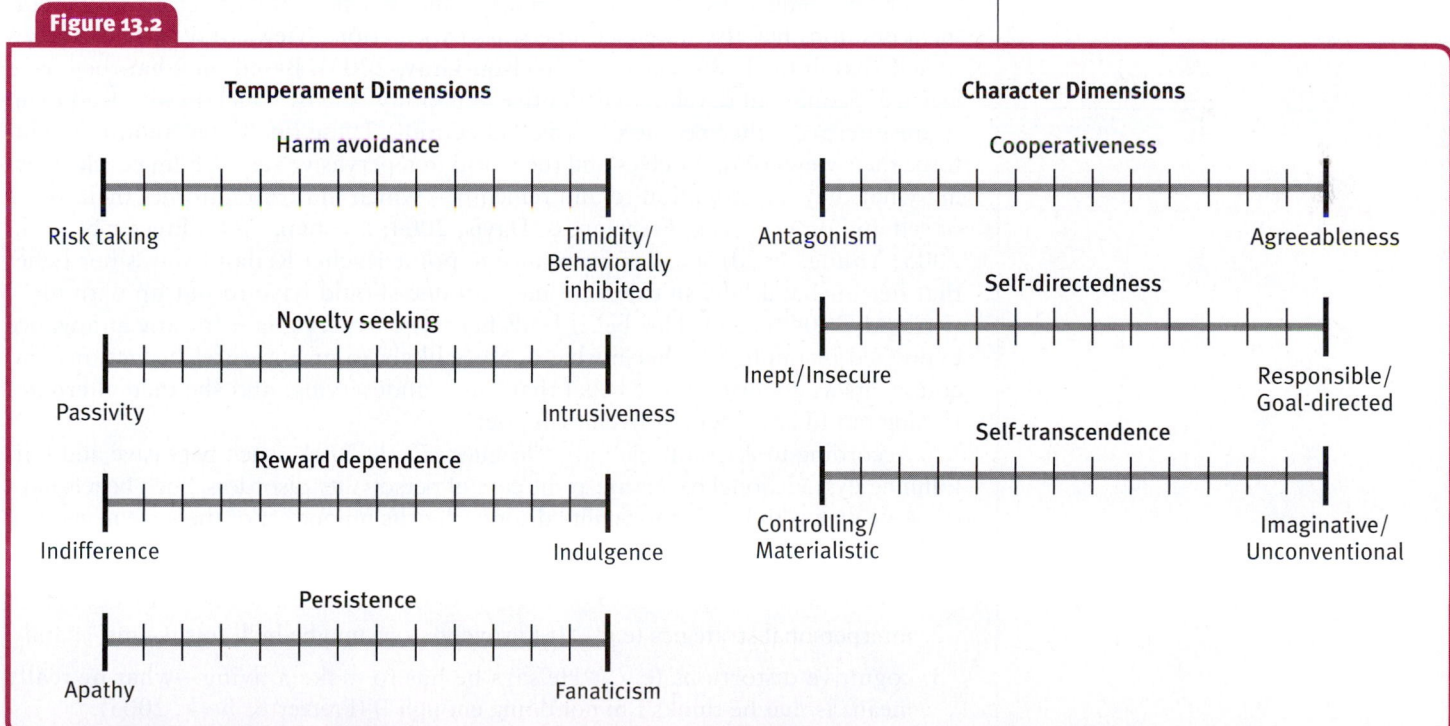

13.2 ▶ Cloninger's Four Basic Temperaments and Three Character Dimensions Personality disorders are characterized by extremes on dimensions of temperament and character.

controlling. Each particular personality disorder within a cluster is associated with a combination of the temperament and character dimensions. For example, borderline personality disorder—characterized by emotional dysregulation and impulsivity—involves high levels of novelty seeking and reward dependence as well as low scores on the three character dimensions (Cloninger, 2005).

A second way to classify how temperaments relate to personality disorders is to group them according to the most basic characteristics that underlie the disorders. Mathematical techniques allow researchers to discover dimensions that cut across a set of measurements, which can reveal such underlying characteristics. Research that uses these techniques consistently yields four basic dimensions that are related to personality disorders (Mulder & Joyce, 1997; Trull & Durrett, 2005):

- *emotional dysregulation*, rapidly changing moods and irritability;

- *dissocial behavior (or psychopathy)*, a lack of moral conscience and an ability to manipulate others;

- *inhibitedness (or social withdrawal)*, a desire to avoid social interactions; and

- *compulsivity*, an overly developed sense of conscientiousness.

These four dimensions are heritable (Livesley, Jang, & Vernon, 1998).

The Consequences of Behavior

Although an infant may be born with a bias to develop certain temperamental characteristics, these characteristics—and personality traits—evolve through experience in interacting with the world. Personality traits involve sets of learned behaviors and emotional reactions to specific stimuli; what is learned is in part shaped by the consequences of behavior, including how other people respond to the behavior. The mechanisms of operant conditioning are at work whenever an individual experiences consequences of behaving in a certain way: If the consequences are positive, the behavior is reinforced (and hence likely to recur); if the consequences are negative, the behavior is punished (and hence likely to be dampened down).

The consequences of behaving in a specific way not only affect how temperament develops but also influence a person's expectations, views of others, and views of self (Bandura, 1986; Farmer & Nelson-Gray, 2005). Based on what they have learned, people can develop maladaptive and faulty beliefs, which in turn lead them to misinterpret other people's words and actions. These (mis)interpretations reinforce their views of themselves and the world in a pervasive self-fulfilling cycle, biasing what they pay attention to and remember, which in turn reinforces their views of self and others (Beck, Freeman, & Davis, 2004; Linehan, 1993; Pretzer & Beck, 2005; Young, 1990). For instance, at one point Rachel Reiland states her belief that her husband "doesn't deserve me—no one should have to put up with me!" (Reiland, 2004, p. 11). This belief leads her to be hypervigilant for any annoyance expressed or implied by her husband. She's likely to misinterpret his actions and comments as confirming her belief that she is undeserving, and she then alternates lashing out in anger with groveling in grief.

According to Aaron Beck and colleagues (2001, 2004), such pervasive and self-fulfilling dysfunctional beliefs are at the core of personality disorders. Such beliefs have three elements, and each personality disorder has its unique set of these elements:

1. automatic thoughts (e.g., "No one should have to put up with me because I'm so bad");

2. interpersonal strategies (e.g., "If I grovel or cry, maybe he'll forgive me"); and

3. cognitive distortions (e.g., "He says he has to make a living—what he really means is that he thinks I'm not doing enough") (Pretzer & Beck, 2005).

Social Factors in Personality Disorders: Insecurely Attached

Another factor that influences whether a person will develop a personality disorder is *attachment style*—the child's emotional bond and way of interacting with (and thinking about) his or her primary caretaker (Bowlby, 1969; see Chapter 1).

The attachment style established during childhood often continues into adulthood, affecting how the individual relates to others (Waller & Shaver, 1994). Most children develop a *secure attachment* (Schmitt et al., 2004), which is marked by a positive view of their own worth and of the availability of others. However, a significant minority of children develop an *insecure attachment*, which can involve a negative view of their own worth, the expectation that others will be unavailable, or both (Bretherton, 1991). People with personality disorders are more likely to have insecure attachment (Crawford et al., 2006).

People can develop insecure attachments for a variety of reasons, such as childhood abuse (sexual, physical, or verbal), neglect, or inconsistent discipline (Johnson, Bromley, & McGeoch, 2005; Johnson, Cohen, Chen, et al., 2006; Paris, 2001). Consider Reiland's experience with her father:

Insecure attachment to a parent can make a child vulnerable to developing a personality disorder. Insecure attachment can arise from abuse, neglect, or inconsistent discipline.

plainpicture

> My father hadn't spared me because I was Daddy's little girl. It was because he worked such long hours and because I had witnessed so much I had become adept at avoiding him. Often his explosive violence had been irrational and triggered by the slightest provocation; a facial expression he found disrespectful, tears he didn't want to see, any expression of emotion he didn't have patience for. And the rules changed all the time. Something that could bring him to smile or laugh one day could provoke him to angrily pull off his belt a few days or hours later. . . . Dad had been far harsher on his daughters than his sons, particularly verbally. To a man who coveted control and saw any emotion, particularly tears, as weakness, his daughters could provoke the worst in him. In his mind, women were weak, manipulative, overemotional, and inferior.
>
> (2004, p. 84)

Reiland's father abused her physically and verbally, alternating the abuse with bouts of neglect. However, such social risk factors may lead to psychopathology in general, not personality disorders in particular (Kendler et al., 2000). A single traumatic event does not generally lead to a personality disorder (Rutter, 1999).

FEEDBACK LOOPS IN ACTION: **Understanding Personality Disorders**

Neurological, psychological, and social factors create feedback loops with each other (see Figure 13.3). As with other kinds of psychological disorders, no one factor reigns supreme as the underlying basis of personality disorders. People must have several adverse factors—whether neurological, psychological, or social—to develop a personality disorder, and social adversity will have the biggest effect on those who are neurologically vulnerable (Paris, 2005). Careful examination of social risk factors, for instance, shows the importance of their influence on other factors: People with personality disorders tend to have parents with Axis I or II disorders (Bandelow et al., 2005; Siever & Davis, 1991). In Reiland's case, her father's unpredictable rages suggest some type of disorder, and neither parent functioned very well at home. Parents' dysfunctional behavior clearly creates a stressful social environment for children, and the children may also inherit a predisposition toward a specific temperament (neurological factor). Similarly, chronic stress and abuse, such as Reiland experienced, affects brain structure and function (neurological factor; Teicher et al., 2003), which in turn affects mental processes (psychological factor).

The specific personality disorder an individual develops depends on his or her temperament and family members' reactions to that temperament (Linehan, 1993; Rutter & Maughan, 1997). For instance, children with difficult temperaments—particularly behaviorally inhibited or passive temperaments—tend to have more conflict with their parents and peers (Millon, 1981; Rutter & Quinton, 1984), which leads them to experience a higher incidence of physical abuse and social rejection. These children may then come to expect (psychological factor) to be treated poorly by others (social factor). Thus, social factors can amplify underlying temperaments

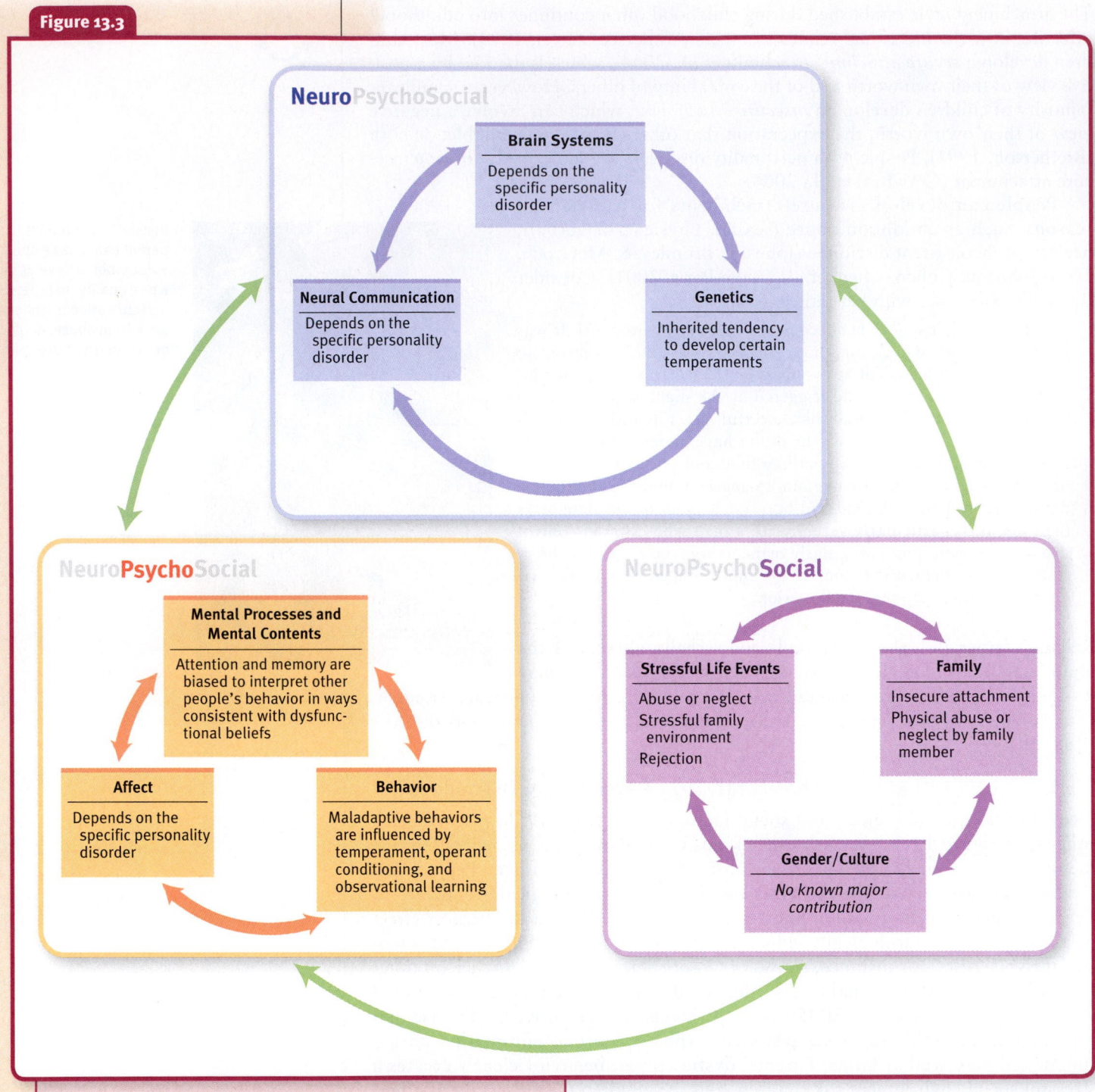

Figure 13.3

NeuroPsychoSocial

Brain Systems

Depends on the specific personality disorder

Neural Communication

Depends on the specific personality disorder

Genetics

Inherited tendency to develop certain temperaments

NeuroPsychoSocial

Mental Processes and Mental Contents

Attention and memory are biased to interpret other people's behavior in ways consistent with dysfunctional beliefs

Affect

Depends on the specific personality disorder

Behavior

Maladaptive behaviors are influenced by temperament, operant conditioning, and observational learning

NeuroPsychoSocial

Stressful Life Events

Abuse or neglect
Stressful family environment
Rejection

Family

Insecure attachment
Physical abuse or neglect by family member

Gender/Culture

No known major contribution

13.3 ▶ Feedback Loops in Action: Personality Disorders

and traits so that they subsequently form the foundation for a personality disorder (Caspi et al., 2002; Paris, 1996, 2005).

We earlier noted that temperament is partly inherited, but even so, not all children will be like their parents. When the child's temperament differs dramatically from the parents', they may not abuse or neglect the child, but the parents may not know how to relate or bond with the child (Chess & Thomas, 1996; Graybar &

Boutilier, 2002). A shy and retiring boy may retreat from taking risks; his parents may force him into anxiety-provoking social situations, where he may get rejected by peers, increasing his trepidation about venturing into such situations again. His parents may then get angry at him for being afraid. In contrast, parents who understand their son's temperament might gently encourage him to take social risks in a gradual way, so that he might come to see that the feared humiliation or rejection doesn't materialize. Thus, two shy boys, growing up with different types of parenting, can readily develop different views of themselves and the world (Pretzer & Beck, 2005). And some of the resulting beliefs and attitudes may contribute to the child's developing a personality disorder.

Treating Personality Disorders: General Issues

Rachel Reiland wanted to kill herself. She called a church-sponsored hotline, and the hotline counselor convinced her not to be alone and to talk to her pastor. If she didn't show up at the pastor's by a certain time, the counselor said that he'd call an ambulance to get her. She arranged for a babysitter to watch the kids. Her pastor persuaded her to go with him to the emergency room, where she was seen by mental health clinicians and began treatment.

People with Axis I disorders often say that their problems "happened" to them—the problems are overlaid on their "usual" self. They want the problems to get better so that they can go back to being that usual self, and thus they seek treatment. In contrast, people with personality disorders don't see the problem as overlaid on their usual self; by its very nature, a personality disorder is integral to the way a person functions in the world. And so people with these disorders are less likely to seek treatment unless they also have an Axis I disorder (in which case, they typically seek help for the Axis I disorder; however, people with both a personality disorder and an Axis I disorder generally respond less well to treatments that target the Axis I disorder; Piper & Joyce, 2001).

Addressing and reducing the symptoms of a personality disorder can be challenging because patients' entrenched maladaptive beliefs and behaviors can lead them to be less motivated during treatment and less likely to collaborate with the therapist. Treatment that targets personality disorders generally lasts longer than does treatment for Axis I disorders. Unfortunately, there is little research on treatment for most personality disorders. The next section summarizes what is known about treating personality disorders in general; later in the chapter we discuss treatments for the specific personality disorders for which there are substantial research results.

Targeting Neurological Factors in Personality Disorders

Treatments for personality disorders that target neurological factors include antipsychotics, antidepressants, mood stabilizers, or other medications. Generally, however, such medications are only effective for comorbid Axis I symptoms and not very helpful for symptoms of personality disorders *per se* (Paris, 2005; 2008). Nevertheless, some of these medications may provide temporary relief of some symptoms (Paris, 2003; Soloff, 2000).

Targeting Psychological Factors in Personality Disorders

Both cognitive-behavior therapy (CBT) and psychodynamic therapy have been used to treat personality disorders. Both therapies focus on core issues that are theorized to give rise to the disorders; they differ in terms of the specific nature of the inferred core issues. Psychodynamic therapy addresses unconscious drives and motivations, whereas CBT addresses maladaptive views of self and others and negative beliefs that give rise to the problematic feelings, thoughts, and behaviors of the personality disorder (Beck, Freeman, & Davis, 2004). In treating all personality disorders, CBT is intended to increase the patient's sense of self-efficacy and mastery and to modify the negative, unrealistic beliefs that lead to maladaptive behaviors.

In addition, because people with personality disorders may not be motivated to address the problems associated with the disorder, treatment may employ motivational enhancement strategies to help patients identify goals and become willing to work with the therapist. In general, guidelines for treating personality disorders should be comprehensive, consistent, and flexible enough to address the myriad types of problems that these disorders create for the person and for others (Critchfield & Benjamin, 2006; Livesley, 2007).

Treatment that targets psychological factors has been studied in depth only for borderline personality disorder; we examine such treatment in the section discussing that personality disorder.

Targeting Social Factors in Personality Disorders

Guidelines for treating personality disorders also stress the importance of the relationship between therapist and patient, who must collaborate on the goals and methods of therapy (Critchfield & Benjamin, 2006). In fact, the relationship between patient and therapist may often become a focus of treatment as the patient's typical style of interacting with others plays out in the therapy relationship. This relationship often provides an opportunity for the patient to become aware of his or her interaction style and to develop new ways to interact with others (Beck, Freeman, & Davis, 2004).

Family education, family therapy, or couples therapy can provide a forum for family members to learn about the patient's personality disorder and to receive practical advice about how to help the patient—for example, how to respond when the patient gets agitated or upset. Family therapy can provide support for families as they strive to change their responses to the patient's behavior, thereby changing the reinforcement contingencies (Ruiz-Sancho, Smith, & Gunderson, 2001). For instance, if family members are trying to respond differently to a patient's overly dramatic and emotional requests for money ("I just have to buy that dress, or I won't be able to go out in public"), family therapy can help them use more effective and less punitive ways of communicating and learn to set limits (for instance, not give more money to the patient).

In addition, interpersonal or group therapy can highlight and address the maladaptive ways in which patients relate to others. Therapy groups also provide a forum for patients to try out new ways of interacting (Piper & Ogrodniczuk, 2005). For example, if a man thinks and acts as if he is better than others, the comments and responses of other group members can help him understand how his haughty and condescending way of interacting creates problems for him.

Key Concepts and Facts About Diagnosing Personality Disorders

- A personality disorder is characterized by maladaptive personality traits that begin by young adulthood and continue through adulthood; these traits are relatively inflexible, are expressed across a wide range of situations, and lead to distress or impaired functioning. A personality disorder affects three areas of functioning: affect, behavior (including social behavior), and cognition.

- The diagnostic criteria for personality disorders were based on the assumptions that maladaptive personality traits begin in childhood and are stable throughout life. These assumptions

led to the disorders' being placed on a separate axis (Axis II) of DSM-IV-TR. Subsequent research indicates that some Axis I disorders begin in childhood and that symptoms of personality disorders may improve over time.

- Personality disorders may be assessed through diagnostic interviews, personality inventories, or questionnaires. The clinician may make the diagnosis based on the pattern of the patient's behavior and, given the preponderance of interpersonal problems that arise with personality disorders, may also rely on supplemental reports from family or friends.

- In DSM-IV-TR, personality disorders are grouped into three clusters: Cluster A, characterized by odd or eccentric behaviors related to features of schizophrenia; Cluster B, characterized by dramatic and erratic behaviors and problems with emotional regulation; and Cluster C, characterized by anxious or fearful behaviors.

- The category of personality disorders in DSM-IV-TR has been criticized on numerous grounds: The disorders are categorical and not continuous; the clusters are based on common superficialities not necessarily supported by research; the criteria for the disorders within a cluster overlap substantially; some of the disorders are not distinguished sufficiently from Axis I disorders; the criteria for specific disorders aren't supported by research; and the disorders and the criteria do not correspond to the types of personality problems observed by mental health clinicians, as is evident in the high prevalence of personality disorder not otherwise specified.

- The neuropsychosocial approach explains how personality disorders develop by highlighting the interactions among three sorts of factors:

- Neurological factors involve the effects of genes on temperament.

- Psychological factors include temperament, operant conditioning, and dysfunctional beliefs.

- Social factors include insecure attachment that can result from childhood abuse or neglect.

- Treatments for personality disorders include medications for comorbid symptoms, CBT or psychodynamic therapy, and family education and therapy, as well as couples, interpersonal, and group therapy.

Making a Diagnosis

- Reread Case 13.1 about Sarah, and determine whether or not her symptoms meet the general diagnostic criteria for a personality disorder, as noted in Table 13.1. Specifically, list which criteria apply and which do not. If you would like more information to determine whether she had a personality disorder, what information—specifically—would you want, and in what ways would the information influence your decision?

Odd/Eccentric Personality Disorders

Cluster A personality disorders involve odd or eccentric behaviors and ways of thinking. Patients who have a Cluster A personality disorder are likely to develop an Axis I disorder that involves psychosis, such as schizophrenia or delusional disorder (Oldham et al., 1995; see Chapter 12). The three personality disorders in this cluster—paranoid, schizoid, and schizotypal personality disorders—are considered to be on the less severe end of the spectrum of schizophrenia-related disorders. We'll examine each of the three Cluster A personality disorders in turn and then consider what is known about the factors that give rise to them and about how to treat them. Rachel Reiland did not exhibit symptoms characteristic of this group of personality disorders, and so we will not discuss her again until we discuss Cluster B personality disorders.

Paranoid Personality Disorder

The essential feature of **paranoid personality disorder** is persistent and pervasive mistrust and suspiciousness, accompanied by a bias to interpret other people's motives as hostile (see Table 13.4, Criterion A). Someone with this personality disorder may distrust co-workers and family members, and even (falsely) believe that his or her partner is having an affair, despite the partner's denials. The patient's accusations create a difficult situation for the partner who is not having an affair but can't "prove" it to the patient's satisfaction.

Paranoid personality disorder
A personality disorder characterized by persistent and pervasive mistrust and suspiciousness, accompanied by a bias to interpret other people's motives as hostile.

Table 13.4 ▸ DSM-IV-TR Diagnostic Criteria for Paranoid Personality Disorder

A. A pervasive distrust and suspiciousness of others such that their motives are interpreted as malevolent, beginning by early adulthood and present in a variety of contexts, as indicated by four (or more) of the following:

(1) suspects, without sufficient basis, that others are exploiting, harming, or deceiving him or her

(2) is preoccupied with unjustified doubts about the loyalty or trustworthiness of friends or associates

(3) is reluctant to confide in others because of unwarranted fear that the information will be used maliciously against him or her

(4) reads hidden demeaning or threatening meanings into benign remarks or events

(5) persistently bears grudges (i.e., is unforgiving of insults, injuries, or slights)

(6) perceives attacks on his or her character or reputation that are not apparent to others and is quick to react angrily or to counterattack

(7) has recurrent suspicions, without justification, regarding fidelity of spouse or sexual partner

B. Does not occur exclusively during the course of schizophrenia [Chapter 12], a mood disorder with psychotic features [Chapter 6], or another psychotic disorder [Chapter 12] and is not due to the direct physiological effects of a general medical condition.

Source: Reprinted with permission from the Diagnostic and Statistical Manual of Mental Disorders, Text Revision, Fourth Edition, (Copyright 2000) American Psychiatric Association.

People with paranoid personality disorder are better able to evaluate whether their suspicions are based on reality than are people with paranoid schizophrenia. Moreover, the sources of their perceived threats are not likely to be strangers or bizarre types of signals (such as radio waves), as is the case with paranoid schizophrenia, but rather known individuals (Skodol, 2005). If the symptoms arise while a person is using substances or during a psychotic episode of schizophrenia or a mood disorder, then paranoid personality disorder is not diagnosed. As you'll see in Case 13.2, about Ms. X., it may not be immediately apparent from a patient's report what is "true" and what is a paranoid belief.

CASE 13.2 ▸ FROM THE OUTSIDE: Paranoid Personality Disorder

The Case of Ms. X. by Daphne C. Brazile, MD

Ms. X. is a middle-aged African-American woman who has lived in the area all of her life. She began seeking treatment . . . after her family members had noted that, to them, she was acting strangely. Ms. X. stated that she believed that her family members were out to make her crazy and convince her neighbors of the same. She stated the reason for this was because she was the "darkest one" in her family. Ms. X. was a fair-skinned black woman. She was born to a dark-skinned black mother and a white father. She was the darkest sibling of her family. Because of this, she felt that her family had treated her and her mother unjustly. She stated that as a child, she was instructed to look after her lighter-skinned older sisters, whom the family held in high regard. She stated that she did not complete high school because she had to care for her older sister's children. She described that she would be instructed to "cook and clean" for them, as though she were their slave, and be available to them whenever they needed her. . . . Because of this, [she claimed] she was not able to have a social life. After Ms. X. married, she continued to receive the same treatment from her sisters. She stated that her children were treated unfairly, because of their darker skin as well. . . . As she got older, Ms. X. stated that her sisters, who were part of the elite society, would "embarrass" her while around their socialite friends. She believed this to be due to her darker skin color. She stated that her sisters convinced her neighbors that she was a "bad" person, and because of this, her neighbors would do "evil" things to spite her.

Ms. X. met with her sisters to discuss this issue. When confronted, the sisters denied that they were treating her negatively. They acknowledged that their skin was fairer than hers but denied that they were treating her in such a way. They believed that their sister was "delusional." Ms. X. refused to believe her sisters, and when confronted with the idea that her family was not in any way harming her, she would shift the conversation to another topic.

(Paniagua, 2001, pp. 135–136)

People with paranoid personality disorder distrust others and tend to interpret other people's remarks or behaviors as having malevolent intent. They are likely to maintain these interpretations despite evidence to the contrary.

David Young-Wolff/Photo Edit

As was the case with Ms. X.'s refusal to believe her sisters, people with paranoid personality disorder cannot readily be persuaded that their paranoid beliefs do not reflect reality, although they can recognize that there are multiple ways to interpret other people's reactions and behaviors. Although less obvious in the case of Ms. X., other common characteristics of people with this personality disorder include a strong desire to be self-sufficient and in control, which stems from a distrust of others, and a tendency to be critical of others and blame them for problems that arise. People with this disorder may also be unable to accept criticism *from* others. In response to stress, they may become briefly psychotic, with their paranoid beliefs reaching delusional proportions.

In addition, people with paranoid personality disorder tend to be difficult to get along with because their suspiciousness frequently leads them to be secretive or "cold," argumentative, or complaining or to bear a grudge. These behaviors often elicit hostility or anger in others, which then confirms the individual's suspicious beliefs. Table 13.5 provides additional information about paranoid personality disorder.

Table 13.5 ▶ Paranoid Personality Disorder Facts at a Glance

Prevalence

- Between 0.5% and 4.5% of the general population is estimated to have paranoid personality disorder (American Psychiatric Association, 2000; Grant, Hasin, et al., 2004).
- Among patients receiving treatment in outpatient mental health clinics, prevalence estimates are higher (2–10%), and among hospitalized patients, prevalence estimates are in the range of 10–30%.

Comorbidity

- People with paranoid personality disorder may also have another Axis II personality disorder, usually another Cluster A (odd/eccentric) personality disorder (schizoid or schizotypal) or narcissistic, avoidant, or borderline personality disorder.

Onset

- Symptoms can first appear in childhood or adolescence, when the individual appears hypersensitive, has difficulties with peers, and has odd thoughts or fantasies or uses language unconventionally.

Course

- The symptoms of paranoid personality disorder are relatively stable over time (Seivewright, Tyrer, & Johnson, 2002).

Gender Differences

- Based on surveys in the general population, there is no clear gender difference in the prevalence of paranoid personality disorder. However, among people with this disorder, men are more likely than women to come to the attention to mental health professionals (Morey, Alexander, & Boggs, 2005).

Source: Unless otherwise noted, the source is American Psychiatric Association, 2000.

Part of the challenge for clinicians is that the symptoms of paranoid personality disorder may not always imply that a person has the disorder. When the suspicious beliefs of someone with paranoid personality disorder center on racial or ethnic conflicts, as they did for Ms. X., it may be difficult for a clinician to determine the extent to which such beliefs may reflect the actual state of affairs or, alternatively, are pervasive misperceptions and misinterpretations (Paniagua, 2001). Similarly, the clinician must try to understand how an individual's life events might give rise to beliefs and behaviors that, in error, could be considered paranoid. For example, an immigrant who experienced harassment might exhibit appropriately guarded behavior patterns in unfamiliar circumstances, such as not speaking much or responding to others with minimal bodily or facial expressions of emotion; such behaviors may in turn inadvertently elicit negative emotions and behaviors from others who don't understand the person's cultural context.

To summarize, paranoid personality disorder involves a chronic pattern of suspiciousness and mistrust that often creates interpersonal problems because of the guarded ways in which the patient interacts with others.

Schizoid Personality Disorder

Schizoid personality disorder is characterized by a restricted range of emotions in social interactions and few—if any—close relationships (American Psychiatric Association). Table 13.6 lists the DSM-IV-TR diagnostic criteria. People with schizoid personality disorder often lack social skills and may not pick up on or understand the normal social cues required for smooth social interactions—for instance, they may return someone's smile with a stare. Such difficulties with social cues can lead to problems in jobs that require interacting with others.

In addition, people with schizoid personality disorder may react passively to adverse events: They may seem to lack initiative and drift through life. People with

Schizoid personality disorder
A personality disorder characterized by a restricted range of emotions in social interactions and few—if any—close relationships.

Table 13.6 ▶ DSM-IV-TR Diagnostic Criteria for Schizoid Personality Disorder

A. A pervasive pattern of detachment from social relationships and a restricted range of expression of emotions in interpersonal settings, beginning by early adulthood and present in a variety of contexts, as indicated by four (or more) of the following:

(1) neither desires nor enjoys close relationships, including being part of a family

(2) almost always chooses solitary activities

(3) has little, if any, interest in having sexual experiences with another person

(4) takes pleasure in few, if any, activities

(5) lacks close friends or confidants other than first-degree relatives

(6) appears indifferent to the praise or criticism of others

(7) shows emotional coldness, detachment, or flattened affectivity

B. Does not occur exclusively during the course of schizophrenia [Chapter 12], a mood disorder with psychotic features [Chapter 6], another psychotic disorder [Chapter 12], or a pervasive developmental disorder [Chapter 14] and is not due to the direct physiological effects of a general medical condition.

Source: Reprinted with permission from the Diagnostic and Statistical Manual of Mental Disorders, Text Revision, Fourth Edition, (Copyright 2000) American Psychiatric Association.

this disorder appear to be emotionless and often don't express anger, even when provoked. And in fact, they often report that they rarely experience strong emotions such as joy and anger (Livesley, 2001). In contrast to those with paranoid personality disorder, people with schizoid personality disorder generally aren't suspicious and are indifferent to other people (Skodol, 2005).

Not surprisingly, patients with this personality disorder function best when isolated from others, which is true for the woman in Case 13.3; in fact, people with this personality disorder generally don't marry or express a desire for sexual intimacy. In response to stress, they may have a very brief psychotic episode (from minutes to hours). Table 13.7 presents some additional facts about schizoid personality disorder.

CASE 13.3 ▶ FROM THE OUTSIDE: Schizoid Personality Disorder

A 33-year-old woman with three children became a cause of concern to social services because of her limited caring abilities. Investigations led to two of her children being taken into [foster] care and, after a further period of 2 years, her third child was also taken away. At this time she was referred to psychiatric services because she was felt to be isolated from society and had such poor social function. It proved very difficult to engage her as she would go to great length to avoid contact and it was uncertain to what extent she required compulsory treatment. Eventually, she was admitted under a compulsory order after threatening a community worker. . . . After discharge from [the] hospital she was transferred to supportive housing but resented the frequent monitoring of her progress, which she perceived as intrusion and tried to avoid contact. . . . She also developed a marked tremor on antipsychotic drugs and these were steadily withdrawn and stopped altogether after 1 year and she remained completely free of psychotic symptoms. However, the improvement revealed marked schizoid personality features and she found it difficult to adjust to interacting with others in her [community residence] and tried wherever possible to avoid them. . . . She functioned better with no contact and so a transfer was agreed to a supported [apartment] where she would be left undisturbed apart from one visit each week from a support worker and a full review every 6 months. After 2 years she remains well on no treatment and is very happy with her life, which despite little interaction with other people now includes regular contact with her family.

(Tyrer, 2002, p. 470)

Table 13.7 ▶ Schizoid Personality Disorder Facts at a Glance

Prevalence

- Approximately 3% of the general population is estimated to have schizoid personality disorder (Grant, Hasin, et al., 2004).

Comorbidity

- A common comorbid Axis I disorder is major depressive disorder.
- Common comorbid Axis II disorders are the other Cluster A (odd/eccentric) personality disorders (paranoid and schizotypal personality disorders) and avoidant personality disorder. Half of the people diagnosed with schizoid personality disorder will also be diagnosed with schizotypal personality disorder (McGlashan et al., 2000).

Onset

- Those who develop schizoid personality disorder were often socially isolated underachievers who were teased by their classmates as children and adolescents.

Course

- Schizoid personality disorder is relatively stable over time (Seivewright, Tyrer, & Johnson, 2002).

Gender Differences

- This personality disorder is diagnosed more often in men than in women.
- Women with this personality disorder are often more impaired than their male counterparts.

Source: Unless otherwise noted, the source is American Psychiatric Association, 2000.

As with paranoid personality disorder, mental health clinicians need to make sure that the diagnosis of schizoid personality disorder isn't applied to people from different cultural backgrounds because of behaviors that are appropriate in their culture of origin. For instance, among the Hindu of India, it is considered saintly to be detached from and unmoved by events, and such traits would thus not be considered symptoms of a personality disorder in that culture (Castillo, 1997). Similarly, symptoms of schizoid personality disorder must be distinguished from superficially similar behaviors exhibited by immigrants or people who move from rural to urban environments and find the experience so overstimulating that they "shut down" emotionally for the first few months: Such individuals may engage in solitary activities and appear emotionally flat as they attempt to cope with the novel and demanding environment (American Psychiatric Association, 2000).

In sum, schizoid personality disorder involves a chronic pattern of limited emotional expression and diminished social understanding, few relationships, and little desire for relationships.

Schizotypal Personality Disorder

People with **schizotypal personality disorder** have eccentric thoughts, perceptions, and behaviors, in addition to having very few close relationships, like those with schizoid personality disorder (American Psychiatric Association, 2000).

What Is Schizotypal Personality Disorder?

According to the DSM-IV-TR diagnostic criteria, schizotypal personality disorder has nine symptoms (see Table 13.8, Criterion A), which can be organized into three distinct groups (Calkins et al., 2004; Raine, 2006; Reynolds et al., 2000):

- *Cognitive-perceptual*
  - magical thinking, in which the person believes that he or she has control over external events, as occurs with superstitious beliefs
  - unusual perceptual experiences, such as sensing the presence of another person when no one is there or hearing a voice on the radio murmuring one's name

Schizotypal personality disorder
A personality disorder characterized by eccentric thoughts, perceptions, and behaviors, in addition to having very few close relationships.

- *ideas of reference*, in which the individual interprets ordinary events to have particular meaning for him or her (a milder form of delusions of reference, described in Chapter 12)
    - suspiciousness or paranoid ideation, which consists of paranoid beliefs that are less entrenched than paranoid delusions
- *Interpersonal*
    - no close friends because of a preference for being alone
    - constricted affect, showing only a narrow range of emotions
    - social anxiety that arises because of a general suspiciousness about other people
    - suspiciousness or paranoid ideation about other people
- *Disorganized*
    - odd/eccentric behaviors, such as wearing mismatched or unkempt clothing, avoiding eye contact, or being unable to make conversation
    - odd speech, such as being overly vague or elaborate or using words idiosyncratically (as in "My co-worker isn't talkable")

IK, in Case 13.4, had symptoms that represent all three groups highlighted in Table 13.8. Additional facts about schizotypal personality disorder are listed in Table 13.9.

Table 13.8 ▸ DSM-IV-TR Diagnostic Criteria for Schizotypal Personality Disorder

A. A pervasive pattern of social and interpersonal deficits marked by acute discomfort with, and reduced capacity for, close relationships as well as by cognitive or perceptual distortions and eccentricities of behavior, beginning by early adulthood and present in a variety of contexts, as indicated by five (or more) of the following:

(1) ideas of reference (excluding delusions of reference)

(2) odd beliefs or magical thinking that influences behavior and is inconsistent with subcultural norms (e.g., superstitiousness, belief in clairvoyance, telepathy, or "sixth sense"; in children and adolescents, bizarre fantasies or preoccupations)

(3) unusual perceptual experiences, including bodily illusions

(4) odd thinking and speech (e.g., vague, circumstantial, metaphorical, overly elaborate, or stereotyped)

(5) suspiciousness or paranoid ideation

(6) inappropriate or constricted affect

(7) behavior or appearance that is odd, eccentric, or peculiar

(8) lack of close friends or confidants other than first-degree relatives

(9) excessive social anxiety that does not diminish with familiarity and tends to be associated with paranoid fears rather than negative judgments about self.

B. Does not occur exclusively during the course of schizophrenia [Chapter 12], a mood disorder with psychotic features [Chapter 6], another psychotic disorder [Chapter 12], or a pervasive developmental disorder [Chapter 14].

Note: Cognitive-perceptual symptoms are in green, interpersonal symptoms are in purple, and disorganized symptoms are in orange. Note also that Criterion A5 is considered to be both a cognitive-perceptual symptom and an interpersonal symptom.

Source: Reprinted with permission from the Diagnostic and Statistical Manual of Mental Disorders, Text Revision, Fourth Edition, (Copyright 2000) American Psychiatric Association.

CASE 13.4 ▸ FROM THE OUTSIDE: Schizotypal Personality Disorder

IK is a 33-year-old man who had both schizotypal personality disorder and obsessive-compulsive disorder (OCD) for at least 17 years.

His schizotypal symptoms included poor interpersonal relatedness, ideas of reference (not delusional), social anxiety, unusual perceptual experiences (such as seeing things in the periphery, but not there when viewed directly), constricted affect, and some paranoid ideation (in particular with regard to police officers, but his father reported that this was unrealistic).

IK's social skills deficits were primarily conversation skills, inappropriate affect, poor assertion skills, and lack of eye contact with the therapist and family members. He was also prone to aggressive outbursts in the home, often breaking objects due to frustration.

(McKay & Neziroglu, 1996, pp. 190–191)

Table 13.9 ▸ Schizotypal Personality Disorder Facts at a Glance

Prevalence

• Approximately 2–3% of the general population has schizotypal personality disorder.

Comorbidity

• Common comorbid Axis I disorders are major depressive disorder, social phobia, and panic disorder (American Psychiatric Association, 2000; Raine, 2006).

• Common comorbid Axis II disorders include other Cluster A (odd/eccentric) personality disorders (schizoid and paranoid; McGlashan et al., 2000), as well as borderline, avoidant, and obsessive-compulsive personality disorders (American Psychiatric Association, 2000; Raine, 2006).

Onset

• Symptoms arise by early adulthood.

• In childhood and adolescence, symptoms may include social isolation and social anxiety, academic underachievement, hypersensitivity, odd fantasies and thoughts, and idiosyncratic use of language.

Course

• Although schizotypal personality disorder most commonly has a stable course, symptoms may improve over time for some people (Fossati, Madeddu, & Maffei, 2003). In fact, for almost a quarter of patients, symptoms improve to the point where they no longer meet all the diagnostic criteria (Grilo et al., 2004).

• Among other patients with this disorder the opposite is true: A small percentage go on to develop schizophrenia or another psychotic disorder (Grilo et al., 2004).

Gender Differences

• Schizotypal personality disorder is slightly more common among men than women.

Source: Unless otherwise noted, the source is American Psychiatric Association, 2000.

Distinguishing Between Schizotypal Personality Disorder and Other Disorders

Schizotypal personality disorder differs from schizoid personality disorder in that the former includes cognitive-perceptual symptoms—such as IK's ideas of reference and seeing things with peripheral vision that could not be seen with a direct gaze—and odd behavior. Nevertheless, research suggests that these two disorders may not be distinct from each other; half of those with schizoid personality disorder are also diagnosed with schizotypal personality disorder (McGlashan et al., 2000). Some researchers propose that schizoid personality disorder may simply be a subtype of schizotypal personality disorder (Raine, 2006).

Schizotypal personality disorder is generally thought of as a milder form of schizophrenia, and some researchers propose moving this disorder to Axis I, with schizophrenia (First et al., 2002). Sometimes, it can be difficult to determine whether a person's symptoms are severe enough to merit a diagnosis of schizophrenia. To help with diagnosis, clinicians may assess the degree to which patients are convinced of the reality of their perceptions or beliefs by probing their ability to recognize other interpretations (Skodol, 2005). When under stress, people with schizotypal personality disorder may become psychotic for minutes to hours.

The DSM-IV-TR explicitly notes that cognitive and perceptual distortions may occur as part of culturally sanctioned or religious rituals or practices, and these should be distinguished from symptoms of schizotypal personality disorder. Examples include voodoo experiences, mind reading, and receiving "the evil eye" (Campinha-Bacote, 1992; Paniagua, 2001).

Understanding Odd/Eccentric Personality Disorders

The odd or eccentric elements of Cluster A personality disorders are less intense manifestations of features of schizophrenia (Chapter 12): Paranoid personality disorder involves paranoid beliefs; schizoid personality disorder involves flat affect and a detachment from others; and schizotypal personality disorder involves cognitive alterations similar to those that arise in schizophrenia—delusions and unusual perceptions. Schizotypal personality disorder is the most thoroughly researched among the odd/eccentric personality disorders; thus, in this section we focus predominantly on the neuropsychosocial factors that give rise to this particular disorder but also include information about the other odd/eccentric personality disorders where appropriate.

Neurological Factors in Odd/Eccentric Personality Disorders

Most of the neurological factors that contribute to schizophrenia have also been found to contribute to schizotypal personality disorder: genes and prenatal environment, such as maternal illness and malnourishment, and birth complications (Raine, 2006; Torgersen et al., 2000). In both disorders, researchers have documented abnormalities in brain structure (in the frontal and temporal lobes, the thalamus, and the hippocampus) and abnormalities in neural function (activity of dopamine, serotonin, and glutamate). These abnormalities are generally not as severe in people with schizotypal personality disorder as in people with schizophrenia (Buchsbaum et al., 2002; Siever & Davis, 2004).

Genes play a role in all Cluster A personality disorders (paranoid, schizoid, and schizotypal): First-degree relatives of patients with Cluster A personality disorders are more likely to develop a schizophrenia-related disorder than are people who are not related to such patients (Chang et al., 2002; Siever & Davis, 1991). This makes sense given that schizophrenia shares some symptoms with each of the odd/eccentric personality disorders. Additional evidence that genes play a role is the fact that the rates of schizotypal personality disorder are higher among family members of people with schizophrenia than among the general population (Siever & Davis, 2004; Tienari et al., 2003).

Psychological Factors in Odd/Eccentric Personality Disorders

Like people with schizophrenia, those with schizotypal personality disorder tend to have specific cognitive deficits. These include problems with attention (distinguishing relevant from irrelevant stimuli), memory, and executive function (used in problem solving, planning, and judgment) (Voglmaier et al., 2000). According to Beck and colleagues (2004), schizotypal personality disorder is unusual among the personality disorders in that the primary distortions are in mental processes (e.g., perceptions) rather than in mental contents. However, problems with social interactions can arise from the cognitive deficits: People with this personality disorder tend to have an impaired *theory of mind*—as reflected by difficulty recognizing emotions in others (Waldeck & Miller, 2000) and taking another's point of view or recognizing another's mental state (Langdon & Coltheart, 2001). Although people with schizotypal personality disorder have cognitive deficits, they generally have better cognitive skills than do people with schizophrenia (Trestman et al., 1995).

In addition, core maladaptive beliefs and strategies of people with each of the odd/eccentric personality disorders may differ (see Table 13.10), but all these patients

Table 13.10 ▸ Maladaptive Views, Beliefs, and Strategies of Individuals with Odd/Eccentric Personality Disorders

Personality Disorder	View of Self	View of Others	Main (Negative) Beliefs	Main Strategies (Overt Behavior)
Paranoid	Righteous, innocent, vulnerable	Interfering, malicious, discriminatory, malevolent	"People are dangerous." "Others' motives are suspect." "I must always be on guard." "I cannot trust people."	Remain wary. Look for hidden motives, accuse, counterattack.
Schizoid	Self-sufficient, loner	Intrusive	"I need plenty of space." "Others are unrewarding." "Relationships are messy and undesirable."	Maintain isolation.
Schizotypal	Unreal, detached, loner; vulnerable, socially conspicuous; supernaturally sensitive and gifted	Untrustworthy, malevolent	The patient holds odd or superstitious beliefs such as a belief in telepathy or "sixth sense." "It's better to be isolated from others."	Watch for and neutralize malevolent attention from others. Keep to oneself. Be vigilant for supernatural forces or events.

Source: Beck, Freeman, & Davis, 2004, pp. 21, 36, 48–49. Copyright 2004 by Guilford Publications, Inc. For more information see the Permissions section.

tend to avoid others and isolate themselves (Beck, Freeman, & Davis, 2004; Farmer & Nelson-Gray, 2005). People with any of these three disorders also often behave in unusual ways (hence the label "odd/eccentric"), and these behaviors then make them noticeable to others. And their obvious unusual behavior can make other people more likely to mistreat them (intentionally or not), confirming their beliefs about themselves and other people. People with these disorders also pay attention to, remember, and interpret stimuli in ways that are consistent with their beliefs and that thus reinforce their isolation and avoidance of other people.

Social Factors in Odd/Eccentric Personality Disorders

In contrast to their lesser role in schizophrenia, certain social factors appear to play a relatively large role in the onset of schizotypal personality disorder. These social factors include physical abuse or neglect, insecure attachment to parents, and discrimination (Berenbaum et al., 2008; Raine, 2006; Wilson & Constanzo, 1996)—all stressful events. In fact, some of these social factors may be related to each other: Insecure attachment may, at least in part, arise from abuse or neglect. Children who develop schizotypal personality disorder are more likely to have experienced trauma, abuse, and neglect than are those who went on to develop most other personality disorders (Yen et al., 2002). These negative childhood experiences influence patients' views of other people as untrustworthy and having malevolent motives.

FEEDBACK LOOPS IN ACTION: Understanding Schizotypal Personality Disorder

With schizotypal personality disorder, as with schizophrenia (Chapter 12), neuropsychosocial factors create feedback loops (see Figure 13.4). For instance, early social stressors such as neglect and trauma can contribute to brain abnormalities, particularly if a genetic or other neurological vulnerability exists before birth. The neurological changes, in turn, contribute to disturbances in cognitive and emotional functioning (Raine, 2006). These cognitive and emotional disturbances then can lead to problems in social interactions and increased stress (Skodol, Gunderson et al., 2002), which then affect neurological functioning. Moreover, trauma, neglect, and insecure attachment may give rise to a paranoid attributional style and a discomfort with others (Raine, 2006).

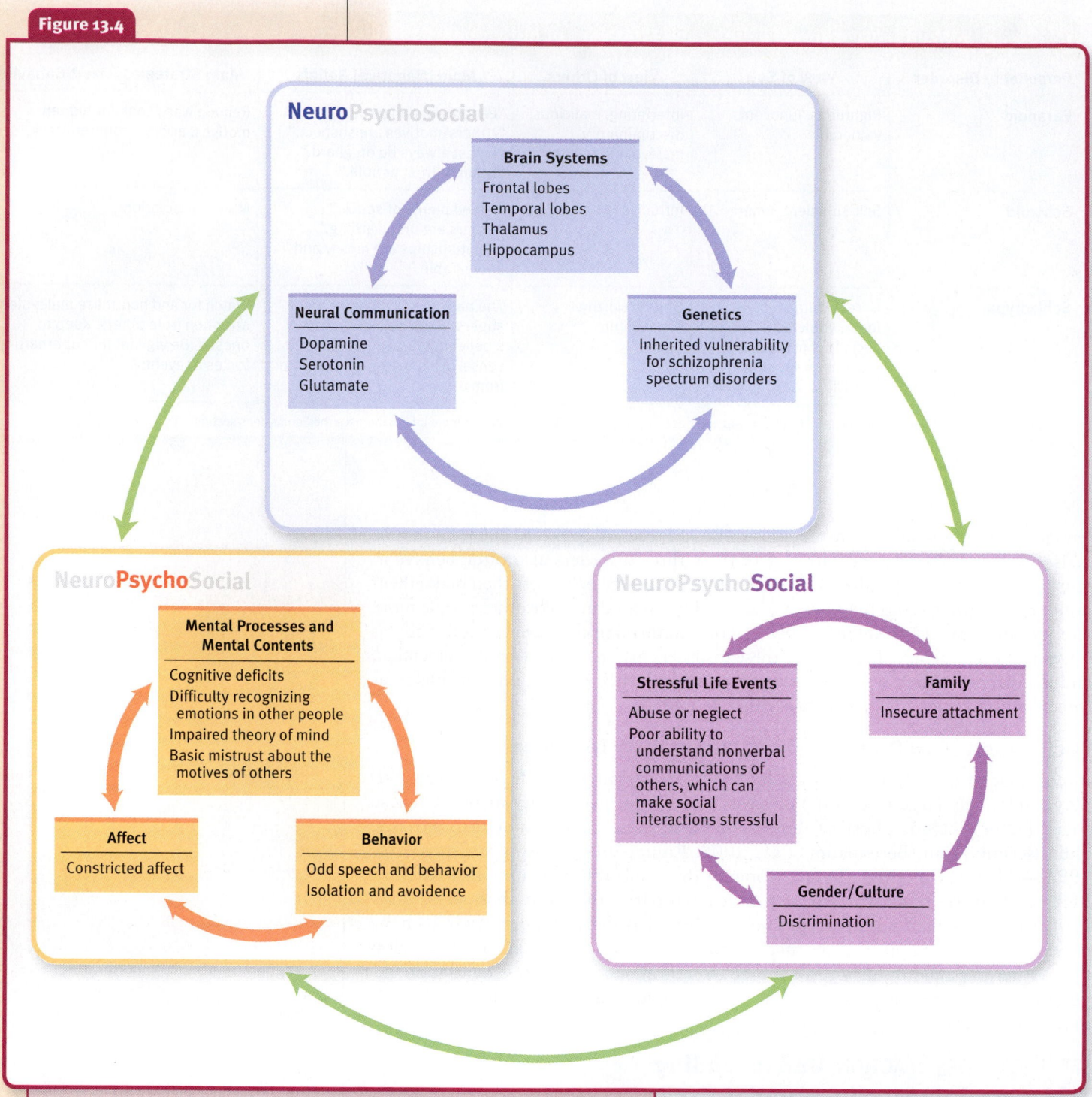

Figure 13.4

NeuroPsychoSocial

Brain Systems

Frontal lobes
Temporal lobes
Thalamus
Hippocampus

Neural Communication

Dopamine
Serotonin
Glutamate

Genetics

Inherited vulnerability
for schizophrenia
spectrum disorders

NeuroPsychoSocial

**Mental Processes and
Mental Contents**

Cognitive deficits
Difficulty recognizing
emotions in other people
Impaired theory of mind
Basic mistrust about the
motives of others

Affect

Constricted affect

Behavior

Odd speech and behavior
Isolation and avoidance

NeuroPsychoSocial

Stressful Life Events

Abuse or neglect
Poor ability to
understand nonverbal
communications of
others, which can
make social
interactions stressful

Family

Insecure attachment

Gender/Culture

Discrimination

13.4 ▸ Feedback Loops in Action: Schizotypal Personality Disorder

Treating Odd/Eccentric Personality Disorders

Unfortunately, very little research has been conducted to evaluate treatments for these personality disorders. People with an odd/eccentric personality disorder tend not to be interested in treatment and, if urged or coerced into it, are often reluctant participants at best. Treatment may create significant anxiety for the patient. Thus, the particular challenge of treating people with odd/eccentric personality disorders is their tendency not to collaborate with the therapist to develop goals for treatment (Beck, Freeman, & Davis, 2004; Farmer & Nelson-Gray, 2005).

Nevertheless, when such patients do participate in CBT, they can develop more adaptive strategies, such as improved social skills (which makes them less likely to be conspicuous, and in turn leads them to feel safer when with others). CBT may also employ relaxation techniques, exposure to avoided social situations, and cognitive restructuring of distorted views of self and others and of dysfunctional beliefs (Beck, Freeman, & Davis, 2004; Farmer & Nelson-Gray, 2005).

Most of the medications that effectively treat symptoms of schizophrenia can also treat symptoms of schizotypal personality disorder, although the medications are often taken at a lower doses (Koenigsberg et al., 2003; Raine, 2006; see Chapter 12). The psychosocial treatments employed with people who have schizophrenia—CBT, social skills training, and family therapy—may be employed with people who have schizotypal personality disorder, but very few studies have evaluated the use of such treatments for people diagnosed with schizotypal personality disorder. One preliminary study investigated such treatments for people who had some symptoms of schizotypal personality—but not enough symptoms to receive the diagnosis of the personality disorder; the results suggest that social skills training can be effective (Liberman & Robertson, 2005).

Key Concepts and Facts About Odd/Eccentric Personality Disorders

- The essential feature of paranoid personality disorder is a persistent and pervasive mistrust and suspiciousness, which is accompanied by a bias to interpret other people's motives as hostile. Although paranoid personality disorder and paranoid schizophrenia both involve suspicious beliefs, people with the personality disorder have some capacity to evaluate whether their suspicions are based on reality; they also tend to be suspicious about people they know. In contrast, the beliefs of people with paranoid schizophrenia are delusional, and they perceive threats as coming from strangers or objects.

- Schizoid personality disorder is characterized by a restricted range of emotions in social interactions and few—if any—close relationships; people with this disorder have poor social skills. They report rarely experiencing strong emotions, and they prefer to be—and function best when—isolated from others.

- Schizotypal personality disorder is marked by eccentric thoughts, perceptions, and behaviors, as well as by having very few close relationships. This personality disorder is characterized by three groups of symptoms: cognitive-perceptual, interpersonal, and disorganized.

- Schizotypal personality disorder is viewed as a milder form of schizophrenia. Many of the factors that give rise to schizophrenia also appear to give rise to schizotypal personality disorder: genes and the prenatal environment; problems with attention, memory, and executive function as well as an impaired theory of mind; and physical abuse or neglect in childhood, insecure attachment, and discrimination.

- Paranoid, schizoid, and schizotypal personality disorders are on the spectrum of schizophrenia-related disorders, and close relatives of people with any of these odd/eccentric personality disorders are more likely to have schizophrenia. Schizotypal personality disorder involves neurological abnormalities that are less severe than those associated with schizophrenia.

- People with odd/eccentric personality disorders are reluctant participants in treatment. Treatment may address fundamental issues, such as isolation and suspiciousness. Treatment for schizotypal personality disorder may include antipsychotic medication (although at lower doses than used for psychotic disorders), CBT, social skills training, and family therapy.

Making a Diagnosis

- Reread Case 13.2 about Ms. X., and determine whether or not her symptoms meet the criteria for paranoid personality disorder. Specifically, list which criteria apply and which do not. If you would like more information to determine her diagnosis, what information—specifically—would you want, and in what ways would the information influence your decision?

- Reread Case 13.3 about the 33-year-old woman, and determine whether or not her symptoms meet the criteria for schizoid personality disorder. Specifically, list which criteria apply and which do not. If you would like more information to determine her diagnosis, what information—specifically—would you want, and in what ways would the information influence your decision?

- Reread Case 13.4 about IK, and determine whether or not his symptoms meet the criteria for schizotypal personality disorder. Specifically, list which criteria apply and which do not. If you would like more information to determine his diagnosis, what information—specifically—would you want, and in what ways would the information influence your decision?

Dramatic/Erratic Personality Disorders

In her memoir, Rachel Reiland recalls an occasion when a minor matter set off an escalating fight between her and her husband. She raged at him until she realized that she might drive him away. Then, she decided to leave him before he had a chance to leave her. She ran out of the house barefoot, then ran for miles through the city on glass-strewn sidewalks. After several hours, her husband and children—who had been searching for her—pulled up their car beside her and brought her home (Reiland, 2004).

Reiland's response to this fight with her husband exemplifies the typical reactions of people with Cluster B personality disorders—impulsive, dramatic, and erratic behaviors, which arise because of difficulty regulating their emotions. In fact, emotional dysregulation and impulsive and dramatic behaviors are common to all Cluster B (dramatic/erratic) personality disorders. This commonality can sometimes make it difficult to determine which specific Cluster B personality disorder a given patient has; many of the symptoms specified in the diagnostic criteria are not unique to a single personality disorder in the cluster (Blais, Hilsenroth, & Fowler, 1999; Fosatti, Madeddu, & Maffei, 1999; Zanarini & Gunderson, 1997; Zittell & Westen, 1998). People with a dramatic/erratic personality disorder also tend to have certain types of Axis I disorders, namely substance-related disorders, mood disorders, anxiety disorders, or eating disorders (Dolan-Sewell, Krueger, & Shea, 2001; McGlashan et al., 2000; Oldham et al., 1995; Skodol, Oldham, & Gallaher, 1999; Skodol et al., 1993; Tyrer et al., 1997; Zanarini, Gunderson, & Frankenburg, 1989; Zanarini et al., 1998).

Let's examine the four Cluster B (dramatic/erratic) personality disorders: antisocial, borderline, histrionic, and narcissistic.

Antisocial Personality Disorder

One day, Reiland was in a particularly angry mood and she put the following note on the front door: *"You need to pick up the kids. I'm upstairs in the attic. Don't even think of going up there if you know what's good for you!"* At the bottom of the stairs to the attic, she taped another note: *"Stay away! Don't mess with me! You don't know what I might have up here!"* The last note was on the attic door, which was locked: *"I might die anyway, but if you dare come in here, you might all be dead! You don't know what I have up here!"* (Reiland, 2004, p. 148).

Some might say that Reiland's behavior—and her apparent lack of concern for how her husband and children might respond to the notes—had elements of **antisocial personality disorder**, which involves a persistent disregard for the rights of others. As noted in Criterion A in Table 13.11, people with antisocial personality disorder may violate rules or laws (for example, by stealing) and may lie or act aggressively, hurting others (American Psychiatric Association, 2000). They may also act impulsively, putting themselves or others at risk of harm. In addition to these behaviors, people with antisocial personality disorder shirk their responsibilities—they don't pay their bills or show up for work on time, for instance. They may also exhibit a fundamental lack of regret for or guilt about their antisocial behaviors, seeming to lack a conscience, a moral sense, or a sense of empathy. In Reiland's case, holing up

Table 13.11 ▸ DSM-IV-TR Diagnostic Criteria for Antisocial Personality Disorder

A. There is a pervasive pattern of disregard for and violation of the rights of others occurring since age 15 years, as indicated by three (or more) of the following:

(1) failure to conform to social norms with respect to lawful behaviors as indicated by repeatedly performing acts that are grounds for arrest

(2) deceitfulness, as indicated by repeated lying, use of aliases, or conning others for personal profit or pleasure

(3) impulsivity or failure to plan ahead

(4) irritability and aggressiveness, as indicated by repeated physical fights or assaults

(5) reckless disregard for safety of self or others

(6) consistent irresponsibility, as indicated by repeated failure to sustain consistent work behavior or honor financial obligations

(7) lack of remorse, as indicated by being indifferent to or rationalizing having hurt, mistreated, or stolen from another

B. The individual is at least age 18 years

C. There is evidence of conduct disorder [Chapter 14] with onset before age 15 years

D. The occurrence of antisocial behavior is not exclusively during the course of schizophrenia [Chapter 12] or a manic episode [Chapter 6].

Source: Reprinted with permission from the Diagnostic and Statistical Manual of Mental Disorders, Text Revision, Fourth Edition, (Copyright 2000) American Psychiatric Association.

in the attic and writing the threatening notes probably resulted from uncontrollable emotions that ended up hurting other people (and Reiland) rather than from a disregard for others.

The diagnostic criteria for antisocial personality disorder are the most behaviorally specific of the criteria for personality disorders and even include overt criminal behaviors (Skodol, 2005). Because of this specificity, antisocial personality disorder is the most reliably diagnosed personality disorder (Skodol, 2005). Clinicians may, however, be biased in how they diagnosis this disorder: One study found that clinicians in the United Kingdom were more likely to rate a man described in a case report as having antisocial personality disorder when the man was identified as White than when he was identified as Black (Mikton & Grounds, 2007). And although the criteria are behaviorally specific, it is not clear whether people with this personality disorder who perpetrate a criminal act have a unique constellation of personality traits not shared by people with this disorder who do not perpetrate a criminal act (Silverstein, 2007).

Like other personality disorders, antisocial personality disorder manifests itself in childhood or adolescence, but DSM-IV-TR is again very specific about antisocial personality disorder: The symptoms must have arisen by age 15 (although the diagnosis cannot be made until the individual is at least 18 years old). The diagnosis for people who exhibit a similar pattern of symptoms but are younger than 18 is **conduct disorder**, which is characterized by consistently violating the rights of others (through lying, threatening, destructive and aggressive behaviors) or violating societal norms. (In Chapter 14 we discuss conduct disorder in detail.) Table 13.12 provides additional facts about antisocial personality disorder.

Table 13.12 ▶ Antisocial Personality Disorder Facts at a Glance

Prevalence
- Between 1% and 4% of Americans are diagnosed with antisocial disorder (American Psychiatric Association, 2000; Grant, Hasin, et al., 2004).
- Around 60% of male prisoners in a number of countries have antisocial personality disorder (Moran, 1999).

Comorbidity
- The most common comorbid Axis I disorders are anxiety disorders, mood disorders, substance-related disorders, and somatization disorders (American Psychiatric Association, 2000; Compton et al., 2005; Sareen et al., 2004).
- In a clinical setting, most patients who meet the criteria for antisocial personality disorder also are diagnosed with at least one other personality disorder, typically another dramatic/erratic personality disorder (Widiger & Corbitt, 1997).

Onset
- As required by the DSM-IV-TR criteria, symptoms of conduct disorder emerge before age 15, and specific symptoms of antisocial behavior occur since age 15. The specific antisocial behaviors then continue into adulthood.

Course
- Antisocial personality disorder has a chronic course, but symptoms may improve as patients age, particularly in their 40s (Seivewright, Tyrer, & Johnson, 2002)

Gender Differences
- Antisocial personality disorder is diagnosed three times more often in men than in women.

Source: Unless otherwise noted, citations are to American Psychiatric Association, 2000.

CASE 13.5 ▶ FROM THE OUTSIDE: Antisocial Personality Disorder

John and his sister were adopted by the same family when they were respectively 1.5 and 3 years of age. From the very beginning, John was severely physically abused by his adoptive father as a result of just minor misbehaviors. Furthermore, John felt that he and his sister were neglected (lack of warmth and attention) by his adoptive parents and that he and his sister were thought of much less highly by them than their only biological son. From age 10 John and his sister were sexually abused on a regular basis by his adoptive father, and John was forced to watch when his father raped his sister. He demonstrated more and more oppositional and angry behavior, and he became a notorious thief. John left junior secondary technical school prematurely and had many short-term jobs, but he was dismissed every time because of lack of motivation, disobedience, and/or theft. As a consequence of his deviant behavior, John was placed in a juvenile correctional and observation institute when he was 16 years of age. A psychiatric report from this episode described him as a socially, emotionally, morally, and sexually underdeveloped person who was very suspicious and angry. He projected his discomfort on the outside world. After his release from the juvenile correctional institute (when he was 18 years of age), John was arrested because of violent pedophilic rape, theft, and fraud. John was sentenced to forensic psychiatric treatment. But soon after his release, when he was 24, John was sentenced to life imprisonment because he committed an excessively violent sexual homicide on a 9-year-old boy.

(Martens, 2005, pp. 117–118)

Antisocial personality disorder
A personality disorder characterized by a persistent disregard for the rights of others.

Conduct disorder
A psychological disorder that typically arises in childhood and is characterized by the violation of the basic rights of others or of societal norms that are appropriate to the individual's age.

The Role of Conduct Disorder

One of the diagnostic criteria for antisocial personality disorder is evidence of conduct disorder in childhood. Although a person need not have been *diagnosed* with that disorder during childhood, the person should have exhibited symptoms of it, as John in Case 13.5 did. Given this diagnostic requirement, it is not surprising that having conduct disorder in childhood is strongly associated with antisocial personality disorder in adulthood.

However, although most men with antisocial personality disorder had serious conduct-related problems as children (that is, they are reported to have exhibited symptoms of conduct disorder as children or teenagers), most boys with conduct problems do not go on to develop antisocial personality disorder (Hill, 2003; Maugham & Rutter, 2001). As shown in Figure 13.5, though, the more symptoms of conduct disorder a boy has, the more likely it is that he will develop antisocial personality disorder in young adulthood.

Most women with antisocial personality disorder did not have serious conduct problems when they were younger (Burnette & Newman, 2005). Even without meeting the diagnostic criteria for conduct disorder, however, girls who show a pattern of interpersonal and physical aggression are more likely to develop antisocial personality disorder as women. Although Reiland had conduct problems as a girl and as an adult she displayed some elements of antisocial personality disorder—impulsivity and irritability—she did not exhibit enough symptoms to meet the diagnostic criteria for this disorder.

Another risk factor that may lead conduct disorder to progress to antisocial personality disorder is socioeconomic status (SES): People with conduct disorder from lower SES groups have an increased risk of developing antisocial personality disorder (Lahey, Loeber et al., 2005).

Psychopathy: Is It Different Than Antisocial Personality Disorder?

The term *psychopath* (or *sociopath*, which was used in the first DSM) has often been used to refer to someone with symptoms of antisocial personality disorder. These two terms are not exactly the same, however. As illustrated in Figure 13.6, the

Figure 13.5

13.5 ▶ Conduct Disorder and Its Relation to Antisocial Personality Disorder Boys 7–12 years old who have more symptoms of conduct disorder are more likely to develop antisocial personality disorder by age 19.

Source: Lahey et al., 2005, Figure 2, p. 394. For more information see the Permissions section.

Figure 13.6

13.6 ▶ Symptoms of Psychopathy The criteria for psychopathy are organized into two general groups, each of which has two clusters of criteria. The criteria for antisocial personality disorder (italicized) are much broader than those for psychopathy. For instance, most of the affective characteristics of psychopathy are not included in the criteria for antisocial personality disorder. The diagnosis of antisocial personality disorder is therefore likely to result in a more heterogeneous grouping than is psychopathy.

Source: Adapted from Hare, 2003. For more information see the Permissions section.

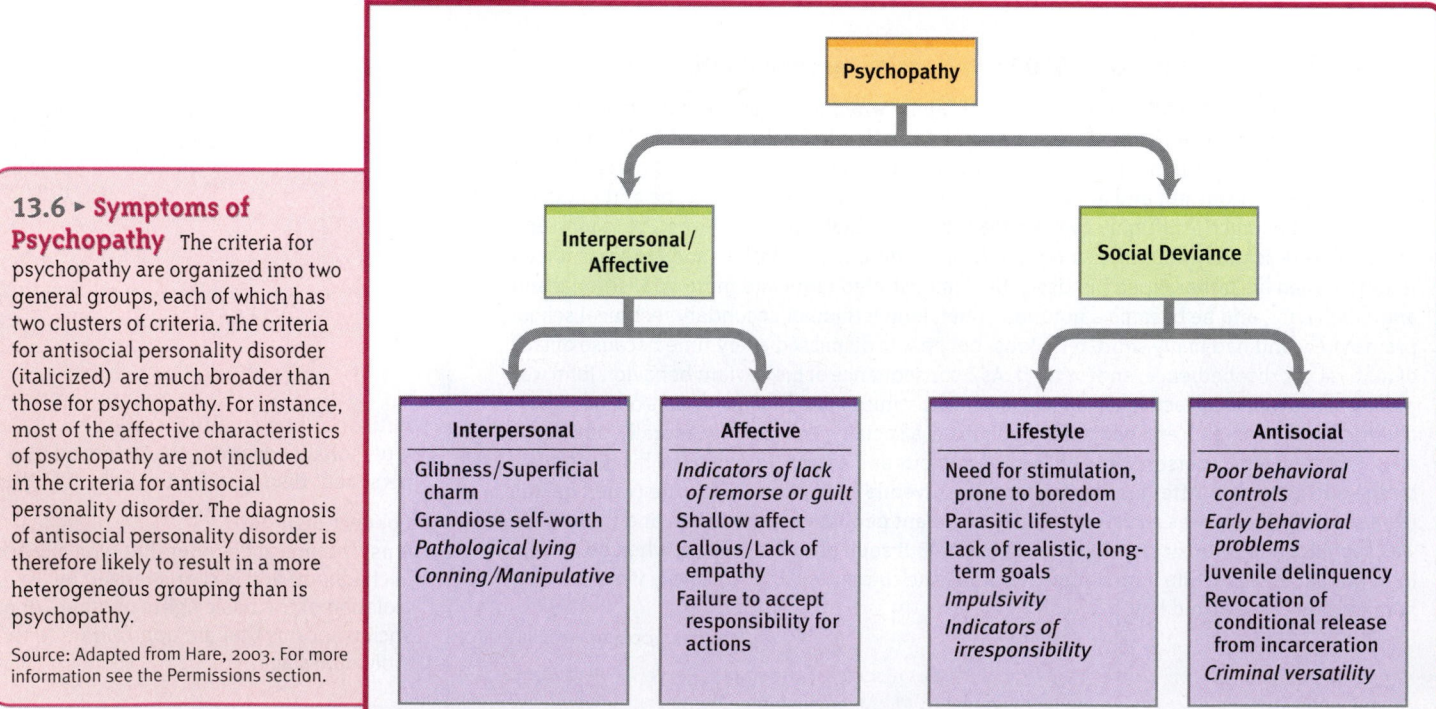

diagnosis of antisocial personality disorder is broader (i.e., less restrictive, because there are fewer criteria) than the diagnosis of psychopathy. Moreover, the diagnosis of antisocial personality disorder tends to focus more on *behaviors*—mostly criminal ones, such as stealing or breaking other laws—than on the personality traits that may underlie the behaviors. In contrast, **psychopathy** emphasizes specific emotional and interpersonal characteristics, such as a lack of empathy, an unmerited feeling of high self-worth, and a refusal to accept responsibility for one's actions—as well as antisocial behaviors. Psychopathy is generally considered to be a more universal concept than antisocial personality disorder; most cultures recognize a similar cluster of psychopathic characteristics (Cooke, 1998; Gacono et al., 2001).

Research findings reflect the relative breadth of the criteria for antisocial personality disorder compared to those for psychopathy: Although only a minority of prisoners (15% of male prisoners, 7.5% of female prisoners) meet the specific criteria for psychopathy, a majority of prisoners (50–80%) meet the broad behavioral criteria for antisocial personality disorder (Hare, 2003). And approximately 81% of people diagnosed with psychopathy also meet criteria for antisocial personality disorder, but only 38% of people diagnosed with antisocial personality disorder meet the criteria for psychopathy (Hart & Hare, 1989; Hildebrand & de Ruiter, 2004; Stålenheim & von Knorring, 1996; Sutker & Allain, 2001). In other words, although psychopathy and antisocial personality disorder have elements in common, psychopathy is defined more narrowly than antisocial personality disorder and with a different emphasis.

Understanding Antisocial Personality Disorder

The concept of psychopathy has been employed longer than the diagnosis of antisocial personality disorder. Hence, more research has addressed psychopathy and criminality than antisocial personality disorder—and the relative lack of research on antisocial personality disorder makes it difficult to identify the factors that contribute to the disorder (Ogloff, 2006). Moreover, most research that does examine factors that contribute to antisocial personality disorder has studied participants who are or have been in prisons or jails or who have comorbid substance abuse problems, which makes it difficult to sort out the factors that contribute solely to antisocial personality disorder. Therefore, the following sections examine neurological, psychological, and social factors—and the feedback loops among them—that contribute to antisocial personality disorder and/or psychopathy, keeping in mind the limitations of existing research.

Neurological Factors in Antisocial Personality Disorder and Psychopathy

People with antisocial personality disorder or psychopathy (and the groups have not been rigorously separated in most of this research) may have abnormal brain *structures* as well as abnormal brain *function* (Pridmore, Chambers, & McArthur, 2005). There is also evidence that these people are genetically biased to develop certain temperaments, which may contribute to their disorder.

Brain Systems First, regarding brain structure, people with antisocial personality disorder or psychopathy tend to have unusually small frontal lobes (Raine et al, 2000) and unusually small hippocampi (Laakso et al., 2001), but they have greater than normal amounts of white matter (the fatty insulation on axons, see Chapter 2) in the corpus callosum (the fibers that form the primary connection between the two cerebral hemispheres; Raine et al., 2003). The smaller frontal lobes might suggest problems in inhibiting and planning behavior. It is tempting to suggest that the smaller hippocampus reflects the effects of stress (see the discussion of posttraumatic stress disorder in Chapter 7), but people with this personality disorder do not generally perceive their situations as stressful, as other people would. Thus, it is not clear how to interpret this brain abnormality.

Second, regarding brain function, the frontal and temporal lobes of these patients tend to show less activation than normal—especially when the patients participate in tasks that involve classical conditioning (Schneider et al., 2000), tasks that require inhibiting responses (Smith, 2000; Völlm et al., 2004), and tasks that

Although the concepts of psychopathy and antisocial personality disorder overlap, they are not the same. Most prisoners meet the criteria for the diagnosis of antisocial personality disorder, but only 15% at most meet the criteria for psychopathy, which is defined more narrowly.

Psychopathy
A set of emotional and interpersonal characteristics marked by a lack of empathy, an unmerited feeling of high self-worth, and a refusal to accept responsibility for one's actions.

require processing emotional pictures and words (Intrator et al., 1997; Kiehl et al., 2001). Moreover, these patients exhibit deficits on tasks that rely on the frontal lobes, such as those requiring planning or discovering that a rule has been changed (Dolan & Park, 2002). Such deficits probably contribute to their problems in inhibiting and planning behavior, and may also suggest that these people would have difficulty learning emotion-related information.

Neural Communication Antisocial personality disorder has been linked to genes that regulate dopamine production (Prichard et al., 2007) and also to genes that regulate serotonin (Lyons-Ruth et al., 2007). In fact, the dopamine and serotonin systems may not interact in normal ways in these patients. In one study, a novel drug that affects the balance of these systems (in complex ways) improved a range of psychological symptoms in patients with borderline personality disorder (Nickel et al., 2006)—such a study has yet to be conducted to examine antisocial personality disorder, but researchers speculate that the results would tell the same story.

Abnormal brain functioning may reflect or contribute to underlying differences in temperament. For instance, men diagnosed with antisocial personality disorder in adulthood were, at 3 years old, identified as distractible, impulsive, and restless (Caspi et al., 1996); these same qualities are observed in children with conduct disorder, which is to be expected, given the diagnostic criteria for antisocial personality disorder. However, these qualities are also evident in attention-deficit/hyperactivity disorder, which is not a precursor to the personality disorder (Satterfield, 1987).

Genetics As just noted, genes that affect dopamine and serotonin have been linked to this disorder, and these genes may influence temperament; thus, it is interesting that people with antisocial personality disorder consistently exhibit a number of specific temperament dimensions. One such dimension is high *reward dependence*—being highly motivated by the possibility of reward (Gray, 1987). Another is low *harm avoidance*, which can be thought of as low anxiety or as not being strongly motivated by the threat of punishment (Cloninger, 1987; Cloninger, Svrakic, & Przybeck, 1993; Gray, 1987; Lykken, 1995). A third temperament dimension shared by these people is low *persistence*—low frustration tolerance—which often leads to impulsive behavior and a tendency to take shortcuts.

And, in fact, researchers have reported evidence that genes contribute to these distinctive temperament dimensions (Zuckerman, 1991). Although few genetic studies focus on antisocial personality disorder specifically, what studies there are generally reveal that genetic factors bias a person to develop conduct disorder and criminality (Cadoret et al., 1995; Nigg & Goldsmith, 1994; Slutske et al., 1997). Adoption studies have found that the environment in which a child is raised influences the risk of criminal behavior or antisocial personality disorder only if the child is biologically vulnerable, as shown in Table 13.13. When a child's biological parents were not criminals, the child's later criminal behavior was unaffected by environmental influences, such as the number of foster placements before adoption or the adoptive parents' criminality (Caspi et al., 2002; Mednick, Gabrielli, & Hutchings, 1984).

Table 13.13 ▶ Percentage of Children Who Later Committed Crimes: The Role of Biology and Family Environment in Criminality

Exposure to Environmental Forces Associated with Criminality	Biological Parents' Criminality	
	High	Low
High	40.0%	6.7%
Low	12.1%	2.9%

Note: Environmental forces associated with criminality include variables such as the number of foster placements before adoption and the adoptive father's socioeconomic status.

Source: Brock et al., 1996. For more information see the Permissions section.

Psychological Factors in Antisocial Personality Disorder and Psychopathy

Antisocial personality disorder and psychopathy appear to arise, in part, because of problems with classical and operant conditioning processes. These processes normally help to socialize children into law-abiding citizens who learn from their mistakes and who develop the ability to empathize with others. Instead, people with antisocial personality disorder view others as "marks" and look for opportunities to exploit them (Beck, Freeman, & Davis, 2004).

Whereas classical conditioning and operant conditioning lead most people to learn to avoid encounters with a painful stimulus (such as a shock), criminals with psychopathic traits do not learn to avoid painful stimuli—but when such criminals are given medication to increase the activity of their sympathetic nervous system, they *do* learn to avoid shocks at the same rate as control participants (Schachter & Latane, 1964). Thus, when not medicated, they cannot easily learn from punishing experiences (Eysenck, 1957) and are likely to repeat behavior associated with a negative consequence, despite receiving punishment (such as a prison sentence; Zuckerman, 1999). Moreover, their temperament of low harm avoidance means that they are less likely to be afraid of the threat of punishment. And because they are highly motivated by rewarding activities, they are less inclined to inhibit themselves to avoid punishment; they thus behave in ways that are impulsive, have difficulty delaying gratification, and have poor judgment (Silverstein, 2007).

Social Factors in Antisocial Personality Disorder and Psychopathy

One risk factor for conduct disorder and subsequent antisocial personality disorder is a child's relationship with his or her parents or primary caretakers. Each parent or other primary caretaker has a style of interacting with the child from infancy. Some parents abuse or neglect their children or are inconsistent in disciplining them, which can lead to an insecure attachment (Bowlby, 1969). These children have a relatively high risk of developing conduct disorder and later antisocial personality disorder (Levy & Orlans, 1999, 2000; Ogloff, 2006). Note, however, that this finding is simply a correlation and does not necessarily mean that attachment difficulties *cause* later antisocial behavior; it is possible that some other variable makes it difficult for the children to develop normal attachment *and* more likely to develop antisocial behaviors.

Other childhood factors associated with the later development of antisocial personality disorder include poverty, family instability, and—in those who are genetically vulnerable—adoptive parents' criminality (Raine et al, 1996).

FEEDBACK LOOPS IN ACTION: Antisocial Personality Disorder and Psychopathy

The various factors create feedback loops that ultimately produce psychopathy or antisocial personality disorder (see Figure 13.7). Twin and adoption studies reveal that some people have a predisposition toward criminality or associated temperaments (neurological factor), but the environment in which children grow up (social factor) influences whether that predisposition is likely to lead to criminal behavior. One study found that children with conduct disorder who were punished for their offenses were less likely to develop antisocial personality disorder later in life, confirming the contribution of operant conditioning to the disorder (Black, 2001).

Moreover, the types of temperaments that are associated with antisocial personality disorder and psychopathy can impede the normal classical and operant conditioning processes that promote empathy and discourage antisocial behaviors (psychological factor; Kagan & Reid, 1986; Martens, 2005; Pollock et al., 1990). Finally, the experience of abuse or neglect by parents (social factor) may contribute to a tendency toward underarousal (Schore, 2003), which in turn leads people to seek out more arousing (and reckless) activities that may increase their risk of seeing or experiencing violence (Jang, Vernon, & Livesley, 2001)—which they may find stimulating, and hence which may reinforce such behavior (making it more likely to occur in the future).

Treating Antisocial Personality Disorder and Psychopathy

Medication is usually prescribed to people with antisocial personality disorder or psychopathy only for comorbid disorders such as depression or a substance-use disorder (Gacono et al., 2001). The psychosocial treatments offered to these people

Figure 13.7

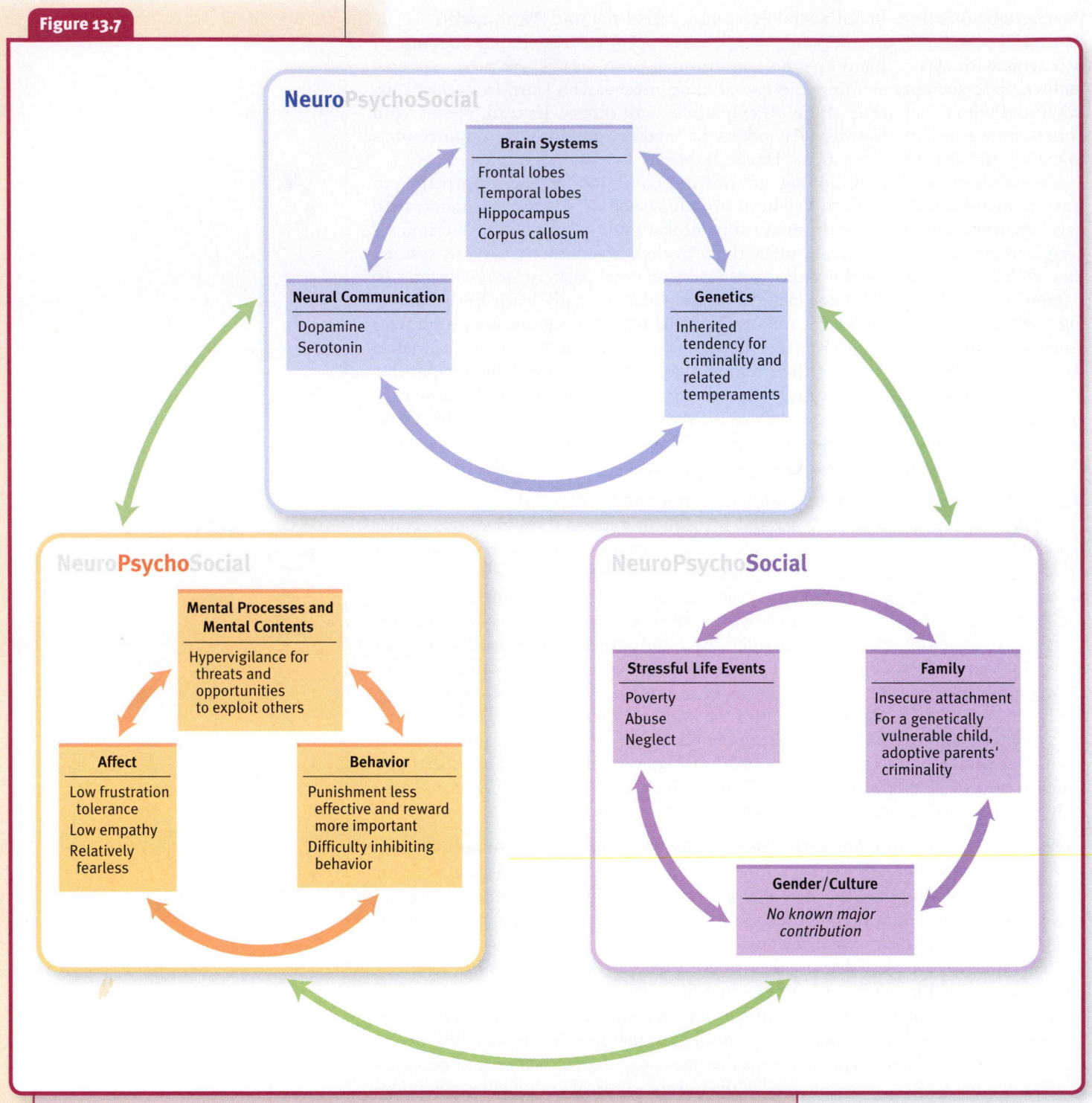

NeuroPsychoSocial

Brain Systems

Frontal lobes
Temporal lobes
Hippocampus
Corpus callosum

Neural Communication

Dopamine
Serotonin

Genetics

Inherited
tendency for
criminality and
related
temperaments

NeuroPsychoSocial

Mental Processes and Mental Contents

Hypervigilance for
threats and
opportunities
to exploit others

Affect

Low frustration
tolerance
Low empathy
Relatively
fearless

Behavior

Punishment less
effective and reward
more important
Difficulty inhibiting
behavior

NeuroPsychoSocial

Stressful Life Events

Poverty
Abuse
Neglect

Family

Insecure attachment
For a genetically
vulnerable child,
adoptive parents'
criminality

Gender/Culture

*No known major
contribution*

13.7 ▸ Feedback Loops in Action: Antisocial Personality Disorder and Psychopathy

depend on the setting: Those who are less violent are more likely to be seen in out-patient settings; those who are more violent are seen in prisons and jails.

Most research on treatment involves people diagnosed with psychopathy, not antisocial personality disorder specifically. Some of the personality traits associated with psychopathy interfere with a therapeutic collaboration: problems in delaying gratification, lack of empathy, and low frustration tolerance. Psychopathy has a poor prognosis, and treatments developed thus far are not likely to alter behavior or reduce symptoms (Gacono et al., 2001; Rice, Harris, & Cormier, 1992; Serin, 1991). People with psychopathy who are in prison are likely to commit additional crimes after their release (Ogloff, Wong, & Greenwood, 1990; Seto & Barbaree, 1999). When an individual with psychopathy is violent, *managing* the patient, rather than *treating* the patient's personality problems, may be the more realistic and appropriate goal (Ogloff, 2006).

People with antisocial personality disorder who are most likely to respond to treatment have a comorbid anxiety disorder, and this capacity for anxiety may suggest that such people are not psychopaths (Meloy, 1988). A challenge in treating people with antisocial personality disorder is their utter lack of motivation. Because they aren't disturbed by their behavior, they are rarely genuinely motivated to change, which makes any real collaboration between therapist and patient unlikely; patients often will attend therapy only when required to do so. Treatment generally focuses on changing overt behaviors (Farmer & Nelson-Gray, 2005).

Treatments for people with antisocial personality disorder who are not psychopathic have some success—at least in the short term. These treatments focus on comorbid substance abuse and aggressive behavior (Henning & Frueh, 1996). The most effective treatments provide clear rules about behavior (including clear and consistent consequences for rule violations) and target behavior change and behavioral control, as is addressed with CBT. Such treatment programs teach patients to recognize triggers for problematic behaviors, devise more adaptive solutions, and foster impulse control (Fabiano, Robinson, & Porporino, 1990; MacKenzie, 2001). In contrast, treatments that target emotional and social factors, such as empathy training or social skills training, are less effective (Gacono et al., 2001).

Treatments that target social factors include family therapy aimed at decreasing inadvertent support from family members for antisocial behavior. These social treatments teach the patient and family members new ways of interacting (Gacono et al., 2001). In jail (or as a court-mandated alternative to jail time), some people may participate in *therapeutic communities*, 24-hour programs that tightly control the patient's behavior; some therapeutic communities are situated in prisons or jails. Research indicates that therapeutic communities can be effective for people who have both antisocial personality disorder and substance abuse (McKendrick et al., 2007; Woodall et al., 2007).

In sum, there is little research on treatments for antisocial personality disorder in people who do not also have comorbid substance use disorders. Treatment is usually court-ordered, and its effectiveness depends on whether the individual also has psychopathy or other psychological problems, and hinges in large part on his or her motivation to change.

Borderline Personality Disorder

The term "**borderline personality**" originally was used by psychodynamic therapists to describe patients whose personality was on the border between neurosis and psychosis (Kernberg, 1967). Now, however, it is generally used to describe the DSM-IV-TR personality disorder that includes some features of that type of personality: **borderline personality disorder**, which is characterized by volatile emotions, an unstable self-image, and impulsive behavior in relationships (American Psychiatric Association, 2000). The diagnostic criteria for borderline personality disorder are noted in Table 13.14. A key criterion is emotional dysregulation (also known as affective instability, Criterion 6), which leads the individual frequently to respond more emotionally than a situation warrants and to display quickly changing emotions (Glenn & Klonsky, 2009). Another prominent criterion refers to a relationship pattern of idealizing the other person at the beginning of the relationship, spending a lot of time with the person and revealing much, thus creating an intense intimacy. But then positive feelings quickly switch to negative ones, which leads the individual with this disorder to devalue the other person (Criterion 2). Rachel Reiland's pattern of thoughts, feelings, and behaviors meet the criteria for borderline personality disorder. Reiland describes the switch in how she viewed other people:

> I saw people as either good or evil. When they were "good," I vaulted them to the top of a pedestal. They could do no wrong, and I loved them with all of my being. When they were "bad," they became objects of scorn and revenge.

Borderline personality disorder
A personality disorder characterized by volatile emotions, an unstable self-image, and impulsive behavior in relationships.

People with borderline personality disorder may engage in parasuicidal behaviors, such as cutting their arms, to help regulate their emotions. These scars on a 50-year-old woman are a result of such parasuicidal behavior. Self-harming behavior may also occur in an attempt to commit suicide.

Lauren Shear/Photo Researchers

Table 13.14 ▶ DSM-IV-TR Diagnostic Criteria for Borderline Personality Disorder

A pervasive pattern of instability of interpersonal relationships, self-image, and affects, and marked impulsivity beginning by early adulthood and present in a variety of contexts, as indicated by five (or more) of the following:

(1) frantic efforts to avoid real or imagined abandonment. Note: Do not include suicidal or self-mutilating behavior covered in Criterion 5.

(2) a pattern of unstable and intense interpersonal relationships characterized by alternating between extremes of idealization and devaluation.

(3) identity disturbance: markedly and persistently unstable self-image or sense of self.

(4) impulsivity in at least two areas that are potentially self-damaging (e.g., spending, sex, substance abuse, reckless driving, binge eating). Note: This impulsivity does not include suicidal or self-mutilating behavior covered in Criterion 5.

(5) recurrent suicidal behavior, gestures, or threats, or self-mutilating behavior.

(6) affective instability due to a marked reactivity of mood (e.g., intense episodic dysphoria [poor mood], irritability, or anxiety usually lasting a few hours and only rarely more than a few days).

(7) chronic feelings of emptiness.

(8) inappropriate, intense anger or difficulty controlling anger (e.g., frequent displays of temper, constant anger, recurrent physical fights).

(9) transient, stress-related paranoid ideation or severe dissociative symptoms.

Note: The criteria for borderline personality disorder involves four domains: Interpersonal (in green); cognitive (in orange); behavior (in purple); and emotional (in blue).

Source: Reprinted with permission from the Diagnostic and Statistical Manual of Mental Disorders, Text Revision, Fourth Edition, (Copyright 2000) American Psychiatric Association.

In relationships with those closest to me, the "good" and "bad" assessments could alternate wildly, sometimes from one hour to the next. The unrealistic expectations of perfection that came with the good-guy pedestal were destined to be unfulfilled, which led to disappointment and sense of betrayal.

(2004, p. 88)

The highly fluid and impulsive behaviors that are part of borderline personality disorder arise, in part, because of the patient's strong responses to emotional stimuli. For example, if a patient with borderline personality disorder has to wait for someone who is late for an appointment, the patient often cannot regulate the ensuing powerful feelings of anger, anxiety, or despair, which can last for days. Moreover, the person with this personality disorder is extremely sensitive to any hint of being abandoned, which also can cause strong emotions that are then difficult to bring under control.

When not in the throes of intense emotions, people with borderline personality disorder may feel chronically empty, lonely, and isolated (Klonsky, 2008). When feeling empty, they may harm themselves in some nonlethal way—such as superficial cutting of skin—in order to feel "something"; such behavior has been called *parasuicidal* rather than suicidal because the intention is *not* to commit suicide, but rather to gain relief from feeling emotionally numb. The parasuicidal behavior usually occurs when the person is in a dissociated state, often after he or she has felt rejected or abandoned (Livesley, 2001). More worrying to clinicians, family members, and friends is when the self-harming behavior is a suicide attempt. In fact, almost 10% of people with borderline personality disorder die by suicide (Linehan & Heard, 1999; Paris, 1993).

Table 13.15 provides additional facts about borderline personality disorder. The table notes that this disorder is more commonly diagnosed in women than in men, but this difference may be due to diagnostic bias on the part of clinicians: Given identical cases and symptoms, clinicians are more likely to diagnose women with borderline personality disorder than men; clinicians may see women with symptoms of borderline personality disorder as more ill than their male counterparts (Becker & Lamb, 1994; Strain, 2003).

Table 13.15 ▸ Borderline Personality Disorder Facts at a Glance

Prevalence

- Borderline personality disorder occurs in 2% of the general population, 10% of outpatients, and 20% of inpatients.
- Among the personality disorders, borderline personality disorder is the most common: 30–60% of those diagnosed with a personality disorder have borderline personality disorder (Adams, Bernat, & Luscher, 2001; Widiger & Frances, 1989; Widiger & Trull, 1993).
- Borderline personality disorder is five times more common among first-degree relatives of someone with the disorder than in the general population.

Comorbidity

- Common comorbid disorders include mood disorders, substance-related disorders, eating disorders (especially bulimia), and anxiety disorders (Grilo et al., 2004; Gunderson, Weinberg, et al., 2006; Zanarini et al., 2004).

Onset

- As with all personality disorders, symptoms for borderline personality disorder emerge in childhood or adolescence.

Course

- There is a high suicide rate among people with borderline personality disorder, with almost 10% dying by suicide (Linehan & Heard, 1999; Paris, 1993).
- The early adulthood years of people with this disorder are marked by mood episodes and serious impulse control problems, including suicide attempts; the risk of suicide peaks during early adulthood.
- Those who survive into their 20s and 30s are likely to improve within 10 years (Paris & Zweig-Frank, 2001; Zanarini, Frankenburg, Hennen, et al., 2006; Zanarini et al., 2007). Not all people improve, however (Skodol, Gunderson, et al., 2005).
- Those patients who meet fewer of the diagnostic criteria and who don't have a history of childhood trauma have a better prognosis 2 years after diagnosis (Gunderson, Daversa, et al., 2006).

Gender Differences

- Around 75% of those diagnosed with borderline personality disorder are female.

Cultural Differences

- The diagnostic criteria for borderline personality disorder—and its conceptual underpinnings— may not apply equally well in all cultures, especially Asian cultures (Lee, 2008).

Source: Unless otherwise noted, citations should be for American Psychiatric Association, 2000.

People with borderline personality disorder may have comorbid depression, as this individual does:

> Thoughts of the past are prominent in my head. Bad person, naughty baby, no wonder my birth mother didn't want me. I'm not deserving of anything good in my life. I need to be punished just because I'm alive. Mind swirling, too many thoughts at once, can't cope. Worthless, burden, angry. The anger is initially directed at the right people. However, it doesn't stay there for long. I soon turn it around and, consequently, the anger returns to me, as it should do, because that's my lot in life. I should be used to it by now. Once more a failure.

(Castillo, 2003, p. 120)

Comorbid depression frequently contributes to increased suicidal thoughts, plans, or attempts. As borderline personality disorder symptoms diminish—including a decrease in emotional sensitivity—depression is likely to improve (Gunderson et al., 2004). Donna, in Case 13.6, exhibits extreme emotional sensitivity.

CASE 13.6 ▸ FROM THE OUTSIDE: Borderline Personality Disorder

[A woman, Donna, exhibited] episodes of explosive anger and bitter tirades, along with weekly (sometimes daily) expressions of bitterness and resentment. Frustrations and disappointments, which are inevitable within any relationship and would only be annoying inconveniences to most people, were perceived by Donna as outrageous mistreatments or exploitations. Even when she recognized that they did not warrant a strong reaction, she still had tremendous difficulty stifling her feelings of anger and resentment. Her tendency to misperceive innocent remarks as being intentionally inconsiderate (at times even malevolent) further exacerbated her propensity to anger. She acknowledged that she would often push, question, and test her friends and lovers so hard for signs of disaffection, reassurances of affection, or admissions of guilt, that they would become frustrated and exasperated and might eventually lash out against her. She would often find herself embroiled in fruitless arguments that she subsequently regretted. She had no long-standing relationships, but there were numerous people who remained embittered toward her. Three marriages had, in fact, all ended in acrimonious divorce.

(Widiger, Costa, & McCrae, 2002, p. 443)

Distinguishing Between Borderline Personality Disorder and Other Disorders

Symptoms of borderline personality disorder overlap with symptoms of other psychological disorders. Borderline personality disorder and posttraumatic stress disorder, for instance, share the symptoms of dissociation, a feeling of numbness, and quickly shifting emotions. However, for people with borderline personality disorder, the most common emotion is anger; for people with posttraumatic stress disorder, it is fear or anxiety.

People with borderline personality disorder may occasionally have psychotic symptoms, such as hearing voices, but in contrast to people who have schizophrenia, they recognize that the voices are produced by their own minds and so they don't respond to them (Paris, 1999). Bipolar disorder and borderline personality disorder share the symptom of mood alteration. However, with borderline personality disorder, a mood change typically occurs over a period of hours, not weeks or months. Moreover, for people with borderline personality disorder, the mood changes come about in response to a clear trigger, such as feeling rejected or abandoned or disappointed by someone's behavior, as Reiland was when her husband didn't return home the moment she asked him to do so. Once triggered, the predominant unregulated emotion is anger (Paris, 1999).

Borderline personality disorder and antisocial personality disorder share the symptoms of impulsivity, instability in relationships, and manipulation of others. In general, people with borderline personality disorder manipulate others in order to meet emotional needs, whereas people with antisocial personality disorder manipulate others for personal gain. However, people can engage in both sorts of manipulation. In fact, up to 15% of people diagnosed with borderline personality disorder are also diagnosed with antisocial personality disorder (Grilo & McGlashan, 2005).

Understanding Borderline Personality Disorder

The neuropsychosocial approach allows us to appreciate the complexity of borderline personality disorder. In fact, this approach underlies the most comprehensive analysis that has been made of the disorder and its treatment (Linehan, 1993). Let's examine the elements of what Linehan (1993) calls the *biosocial theory* of borderline personality disorder and also consider research related to it.

Neurological Factors: Born to Be Wild?

Considerable research has been reported on the neurological bases of borderline personality disorder.

Brain Systems First, the frontal lobes, hippocampus, and amgydala are unusually small in people with borderline personality disorder (Driessen et al., 2000; Lyoo, Han, & Cho, 1998; Schmahl, Vermetten, et al., 2003; Tebartz van Elst et al., 2003). Second, these structures are part of a network of brain areas that functions abnormally in people with this disorder; this network includes the orbitofrontal and dorsolateral regions of the frontal lobe, the anterior cingulate, the amygdala, and the hippocampus (De la Fuente et al., 1997; Juengling et al., 2003; Lieb et al., 2004; Soloff, Meltzer, et al., 2003).

Dysfunction of the anterior cingulate is particularly interesting because this structure plays a role in controlling affect: When normal control participants experience emotional and stressful situations, this area is activated; it is not activated in patients with borderline personality disorder (Schmahl, Elzinga, et al., 2003; Schmahl et al., 2004). This abnormality might contribute to the problems that people with this disorder have in regulating their emotions.

In contrast to the frontal lobes and the anterior cingulate, the amygdala (which is involved in the perception and production of strong emotions, notably fear) is *more* strongly activated than normal in these patients when they see faces with negative expressions (Donegan et al., 2003). This finding makes sense because the frontal lobes normally inhibit the amygdala (LeDoux, 1996); thus, if the frontal lobes are not working properly, they may fail to keep activation of the amygdala within a normal range.

In addition, consistent with findings from neuroimaging studies, numerous studies have shown that people who have borderline personality disorder have difficulty performing tasks that rely on the frontal lobes (LeGris & van Reekum, 2006). For example, they typically have difficulty inhibiting responses, such as is required in the Stroop task, where participants name the color of the ink (e.g., the word "red" is printed in blue ink) used to print the name of a color and the name conflicts with the color of the ink—and thus responses based on the name of the color must be inhibited (Kunert et al., 2003; Sprock et al., 2000). People with this disorder also have difficulty focusing attention, organizing visual material, and making decisions, and their visual and verbal memory is impaired (LeGris & van Reekum, 2006).

Neural Communication Relatively low levels of serotonin are related to impulsivity, which is characteristic of borderline personality disorder. Thus, it is not surprising that these patients have been shown to have abnormal serotonin functioning (Soloff et al., 2000); in particular, their serotonin receptors apparently are not as sensitive as normal, and thus the effects of serotonin are diminished (Hansenne et al., 2002). In addition, this dysfunction involving serotonin is apparently greater in women than in men with the disorder (Leyton et al., 2001; New et al., 2003; Soloff, Kelly et al., 2003)—and many more women than men receive this diagnosis.

But problems with serotonin alone cannot explain the abnormal brain functioning (Lieb et al., 2004). For instance, Rinne and colleagues (2002) showed that the hypothalamic-pituitary-adrenal (HPA) axis in at least some of these patients is unusually responsive, which results in excess amounts of cortisol.

The overall effect of these various brain abnormalities is consistent with Linehan's theory. According to this theory, people with borderline personality disorder are likely to be neurologically vulnerable to emotional dysregulation. This vulnerability is usually expressed as a low threshold for emotional responding, with responses that are often extreme and intense. In addition, the brains of these people are relatively slow to return to a normal baseline of arousal.

Genetics Genetic studies do not find a specific transmission of borderline personality disorder itself (Torgersen et al., 2000). However, they do reveal a genetic vulnerability to components of this disorder, such as impulsivity, emotional volatility, and anxiety (Adams et al., 2001; Heim & Westen, 2005; Skodol, Siever, et al., 2002).

Psychological Factors: Emotions on a Yo-Yo

The core feature of borderline personality disorder is dysregulation—of emotion, of sense of self, of cognition, and of behavior (Robins, Ivanoff, & Linehan, 2001). For instance, people with this disorder feel unsure of themselves, of their goals and values; the one thing they are often sure of, however, is that they are in some way "bad" or "defective." They may have been told repeatedly that they're "too sensitive." Their behaviors can be extreme: In one instant, they will fly into a rage over some inconsequential thing, but in the next instant, they will break down in tears and beg for reassurance, as Reiland did. These behaviors may inadvertently be reinforced by family members' attention.

Other behaviors exhibited by people with this disorder—including substance use or abuse, binge eating, and parasuicidal behaviors—are more directly self-destructive and are often instigated with the goal of feeling better after interpersonal stress (Paris, 1999). Unfortunately, such maladaptive behaviors can be reinforcing because they *do* temporarily relieve emotional pain. Because of such temporary relief, these behaviors are negatively reinforced.

When highly emotionally aroused—by fear or anger, for instance—all of us are likely to have cognitive dysfunctions: difficulties in focusing attention and keeping long-term goals in mind, which makes impulsive urges more difficult to put in a larger context. Moreover, when in such an aroused state, people are more likely to distort or misinterpret what others say and do and to engage in black-and-white thinking, overlooking ambiguities or subtleties (Fonagy & Bateman, 2008). Both of these problems are more severe for people with borderline personality disorder. For example, when aroused, Reiland apparently did not pay attention to the actual cues her husband provided and would get so wrapped up in the emotions of the moment that she could not think about what was best for their relationship. And when aroused, Reiland interpreted her husband as not loving her, when all he was doing was asking questions in order to understand the situation.

Although online message boards may provide support for adolescent girls and young women, they may also encourage or normalize the self-harming behavior that is associated with borderline personality disorder (Whitlock, Powers, & Eckenrode, 2006).

Social Factors: Invalidation

Borderline personality disorder also involves interpersonal dysregulation—relationships are typically intense, chaotic, and difficult (Robins, Ivanoff, & Linehan, 2001). One explanation for the interpersonal problems suggests that they arose in childhood—that family members and friends were likely to *invalidate* the patient's experience (Linehan, 1993). For instance, a parent might tell a child "You're too sensitive" or "You're overreacting." During childhood, such dismissals may have led to fear of rejection and abandonment, if not actual rejection. Such experiences may have sensitized the child, leading him or her subsequently to overreact to the slightest hint of being invalidated.

In addition, this interpersonal dysregulation may arise in part because of patients' emotional and cognitive dysregulation (Fonagy & Bateman, 2008). When people with borderline personality disorder meet someone who is positive or helpful, they often begin by depending on that person to help calm their emotions, as Reiland did with her husband. But, paradoxically, once they feel dependent, they fear being abandoned—which leads them to behave in ways likely to lead to rejection! Friends and family members may come to respond with caring and concern only when the patient exhibits self-destructive behaviors (which, in turn, inadvertently reinforces those behaviors).

FEEDBACK LOOPS IN ACTION: Understanding Borderline Personality Disorder

Linehan's (1993) theory of borderline personality disorder rests on a series of feedback loops (like those illustrated in Figure 13.8): Some children have brain systems (neurological factor) that lead them to have extreme emotional reactions (psychological factor), and their parents may have difficulty soothing them (social factor) when they are emotionally aroused (Graybar & Boutelier, 2002; Linehan, 1993). Either because the parents create an invalidating environment ("It's not as bad as you're making it out to be"; social factor) or because they engage in outright abuse or neglect (as occurred with Reiland), the children may become insecurely attached to their parents. In turn, the children don't learn to regulate their emotions or behaviors (and cognitions) and elicit untoward reactions from others, which then confirms their view of themselves and others.

This invalidating process, according to Linehan, leaves the person feeling punished for his or her thoughts, feelings, and behaviors—they are trivialized, dismissed, disrespected (Linehan & Kehrer, 1993). Such people therefore have a hard time identifying and labeling their emotions accurately and coming to trust their own experiences and perceptions as valid (psychological factor). They don't learn effective problem solving or distress tolerance.

Figure 13.8

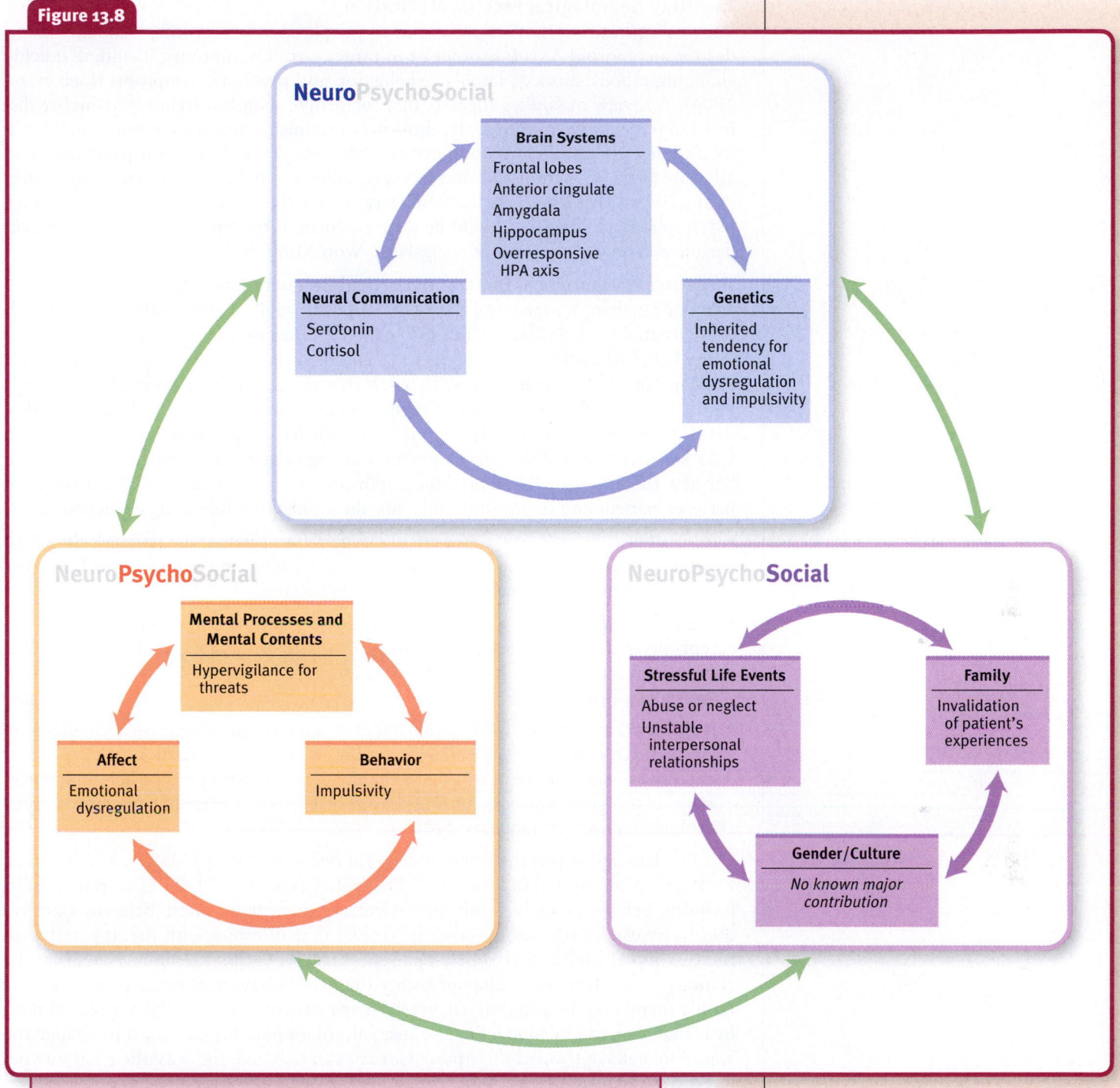

13.8 ▶ Feedback Loops in Action: Borderline Personality Disorder

Treating Borderline Personality Disorder: New Treatments

Borderline personality disorder is among the most challenging personality disorders to treat (Robins, Ivanoff, & Linehan, 2001). In part, treatment is challenging because of the patient's parasuicidal or suicidal thoughts and behaviors. It can also be challenging because of the intense anger that a patient may direct at the mental health clinician. Let's examine the various targets of treatment—neurological factors, psychological factors, and social factors—paying particular attention to a comprehensive psychological treatment that is the treatment of choice: *dialectical behavior therapy.*

Targeting Neurological Factors: Medication

Various medications may be prescribed to people with borderline personality disorder for a comorbid Axis I disorder or to target certain symptoms, including quickly changing moods, anxiety, impulsive behavior, and psychotic symptoms (Lieb et al., 2004). A review of studies suggests that for people with borderline personality disorder, SSRIs—compared to a placebo—may diminish symptoms of emotional lability and anxiety and help with anger management. In addition, antipsychotics can alleviate psychotic symptoms, and mood stabilizers may help some symptoms (Binks et al., 2006a). Although medications may reduce the intensity of some symptoms, psychopharmacology should not be the only form of treatment for people with borderline personality disorder (Koenigsberg, Woo-Ming, & Siever, 2007).

Targeting Psychological Factors: Dialectical Behavior Therapy

Marsha Linehan, a pioneer in the treatment of borderline personality disorder, initially treated such patients with CBT, which focuses on identifying and correcting faulty beliefs (Linehan, 1993; Beck et al., 2003). Unfortunately, this led some people to drop out of treatment because they felt that the focus on changing faulty beliefs implicitly criticized and invalidated them (Dimeff & Linehan, 2001). Linehan (1993) developed a new treatment for people with borderline personality disorder. From CBT she incorporated skill development and cognitive restructuring. In addition, in her new therapy she underscored the importance of a warm and collaborative bond between patient and therapist; to this mix she addded the following elements:

- *An emphasis on validating the patient's experience.* That is, the patient's thoughts, feelings, and behaviors in a given situation make sense in the context of his or her life, past experiences, and strengths and weaknesses.

- *A Zen Buddhist approach.* Patients should see, and then without judgment, accept any painful realities of their lives. Patients are encouraged to "let go" of emotional attachments that cause them suffering. Mindfulness, or nonjudgmental awareness, is the goal.

- *A dialectics component. Dialectics* refers to a synthesis of opposing elements; in this context, it refers to the patient's coming to accept the situation and aspects of it that he or she does not feel able to change (e.g., validating his or her experience) while at the same time recognizing that in order to feel better, change must occur (Robins, Ivanoff, & Linehan, 2001).

Linehan called this treatment *dialectical behavior therapy* (DBT), and it entails both group and individual therapy. The initial priority of DBT is to reduce self-harming behaviors such as burning or cutting oneself. As these behaviors are reduced, treatment focuses on other behaviors that interfere with therapy and with the quality of life, and also helps patients develop skills to change what can be changed (e.g., their own behavior rather than the behavior of other people such as family members). In addition, treatment helps patients to recognize aspects of their lives that they can't change: For instance, although patients can learn to change the way they behave toward their parents, they can't change the way their parents behave toward them. Treatment lasts about 1 year.

Researchers have conducted many studies to evaluate DBT over the years and have noted impressive results for patients with borderline personality disorder: DBT does decrease suicidal thoughts and behaviors (Binks et al., 2006b; Bohus et al., 2000, 2004; Linehan et al., 2006; Shearin & Linehan, 1994) and has lower dropout and hospitalization rates than other specialized treatments for this disorder (Linehan et al., 2006). DBT benefits people with borderline personality disorder and comorbid substance abuse (Linehan et al., 1999; van den Bosch et al., 2005), and it has been adapted to treat people with Axis I disorders that involve impulsive symptoms, such as bulimia (Palmer et al., 2003; Telch, Agras, & Linehan, 2001).

Intensive (and manual-based) forms of psychodynamically oriented psychotherapy have also been shown to be effective for patients with borderline personality disorder (Bateman & Fonagy, 2004; Clarkin et al., 2007; Gregory & Remen, 2008).

Similarly, research indicates that cognitive therapy can be effective (Brown et al., 2004; Davidson et al., 2006; Wenzel et al., 2006).

Targeting Social Factors: Interpersonal Therapy

Interpersonal therapy (IPT) has been adapted to treat borderline personality disorder. The goal of IPT for this personality disorder is to help the patient develop more adaptive interpersonal skills so that he or she feels and functions better. This therapy tries to help patients integrate their extreme but opposed feelings about an individual: When they talk about feeling one way about someone ("He's perfect"), the therapist tries to discuss opposite feelings as well, underscoring that no individual is all good or all bad (Markowitz, 2005; Markowitz, Skodol, & Bleiberg, 2006). A course of IPT for borderline personality disorder typically lasts about 8 months. Social interactions are also a focus of the group therapy component of DBT.

FEEDBACK LOOPS IN TREATMENT: **Borderline Personality Disorder**

Successful treatment of borderline personality disorder may target more than one factor; positive changes in any factor, though, affect other factors via feedback loops (see Figure 13.9). For example, one goal of DBT is to help patients regulate their emotions (psychological factor). When the therapy is successful, better emotional regulation allows patients to calm themselves more effectively when they are anxious

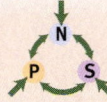

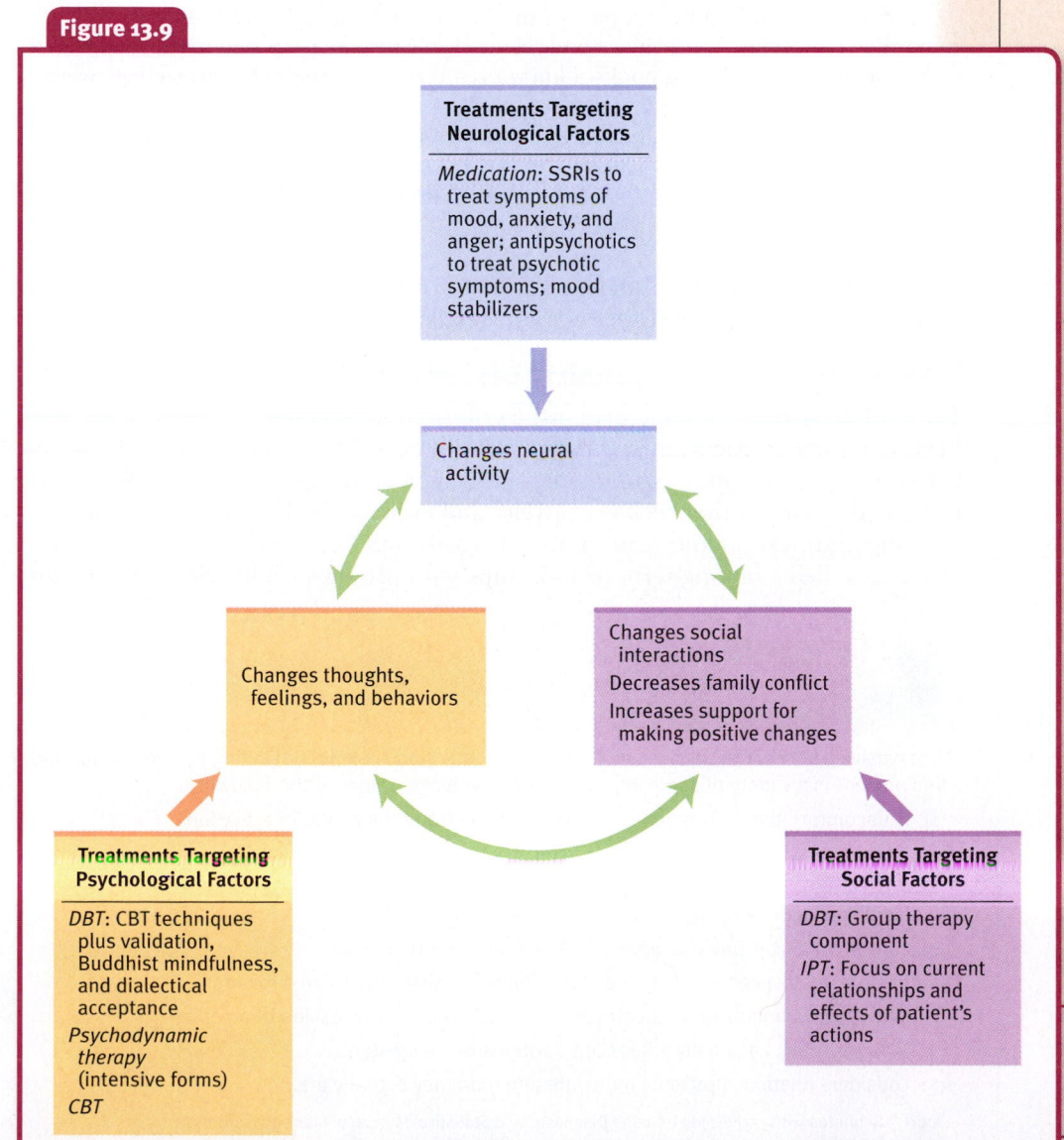

Figure 13.9

Treatments Targeting Neurological Factors

Medication: SSRIs to treat symptoms of mood, anxiety, and anger; antipsychotics to treat psychotic symptoms; mood stabilizers

Changes neural activity

Changes thoughts, feelings, and behaviors

Changes social interactions
Decreases family conflict
Increases support for making positive changes

Treatments Targeting Psychological Factors

DBT: CBT techniques plus validation, Buddhist mindfulness, and dialectical acceptance
Psychodynamic therapy (intensive forms)
CBT

Treatments Targeting Social Factors

DBT: Group therapy component
IPT: Focus on current relationships and effects of patient's actions

13.9 ▸ Feedback Loops in Treatment: Borderline Personality Disorder

or angry, which directly affects brain mechanisms (neurological factor) and in turn makes their relationships less volatile (social factors). Similarly, the honest and caring feedback from others within the therapeutic environment (part of DBT, IPT, and intensive psychodynamic therapy) challenges patients to alter their behaviors and ways of thinking about themselves and their relationships (psychological and social factors), which in turn decreases their emotional reactivity (neurological and psychological factors).

Histrionic Personality Disorder

You may know someone who initially seemed charming, open, enthusiastic—maybe even flirtatious. After a while, did he or she seem to go to great lengths to be the center of attention, behaving too dramatically? Did the person have temper tantrums, sobbing episodes, or other dramatic displays of emotion that appeared to turn on and off like a light switch? These are the qualities of people with **histrionic personality disorder**, who seek attention and exaggerate their emotions (American Psychiatric Association, 2000).

Rachel Reiland relates her desire to be the center of attention and the dramatic behaviors she engaged in to obtain that attention:

> I wanted to be the entire focus of any person I was obsessed with. My incessant hunger for attention had been a part of my life for as long as I could remember. The burning heartache of emptiness obsessed me even when my peers had been taken with Barbie dolls and coloring books. I knew even then that these constant feelings were not normal. . . .
>
> When the object of my longing—the teacher, the coach, the boss—was present in the room, I geared everything to that person. I contrived every word, action, inflection, and facial expression for him. *Does he see me laughing? Does he see how funny everybody thinks I am?*

(2004, pp. 335–336)

Reiland's behavior involved some features of histrionic personality disorder; in what follows we examine the disorder in more detail.

What Is Histrionic Personality Disorder?

Table 13.16 lists the specific diagnostic criteria for histrionic personality disorder. Beyond the overt attention seeking and dramatic behavior, people with histrionic personality disorder may exhibit more subtle indications of the disorder: When they feel bored or empty, they seek out novelty and excitement. They may have difficulty delaying gratification and tend to become easily and excessively frustrated by life's challenges. Being in long-term relationships with people with histrionic personality

Histrionic personality disorder
A personality disorder characterized by attention-seeking behaviors and exaggerated and dramatic displays of emotion.

Table 13.16 ▶ DSM-IV-TR Diagnostic Criteria for Histrionic Personality Disorder

A pervasive pattern of excessive emotionality and attention seeking, beginning by early adulthood and present in a variety of contexts, as indicated by five (or more) of the following:

(1) is uncomfortable in situations in which he or she is not the center of attention

(2) interaction with others is often characterized by inappropriate sexually seductive or provocative behavior

(3) displays rapidly shifting and shallow expression of emotions

(4) consistently uses physical appearance to draw attention to self

(5) has a style of speech that is excessively impressionistic and lacking in detail

(6) shows self-dramatization, theatricality, and exaggerated expression of emotion

(7) is suggestible, i.e., easily influenced by others or circumstances

(8) considers relationships to be more intimate than they actually are.

Source: Reprinted with permission from the Diagnostic and Statistical Manual of Mental Disorders, Text Revision, Fourth Edition, (Copyright 2000) American Psychiatric Association.

disorder can be challenging because they usually don't recognize their symptoms; they don't feel as though they are overreacting or being overly dramatic or seductive, although—like the woman in Case 13.7—they clearly are. Table 13.17 provides additional facts about the personality disorder.

CASE 13.7 ▸ FROM THE OUTSIDE: Histrionic Personality Disorder

A 23-year-old single woman was referred for a psychological assessment by her gynecologist. The patient had been described as "outgoing, effusive, and 'dressed to kill'."

She had been experiencing debilitating pain for over half a year, but the pain seemed to be medically unexplainable. Throughout the interview, she used facial and other nonverbal expressiveness to dramatize the meaning of her words. In describing her pain, for example, she said she felt as though "I will absolutely expire" as she closed her eyes and dropped her head forward to feign death. However, when asked about her pain, she became coquettish and was either unable or unwilling to provide details. She talked freely about topics tangential to the interview, skipping quickly from topic to topic and periodically inserting sexual double entendres. She described her family as happy and well-adjusted but acknowledged conflict with her mother and complained that her older brothers treated her like a baby. She described herself as close to her parents and said that she calls home every day. She was not currently in a serious relationship, but stated with a giggle that most boys "find me very attractive," adding that they "just want me for my body." She also reported that she found it easy to get to know others. At the time of the interview, she was working as a dancer at an adult club; she particularly liked the attention and the money that the job provided. She felt that, in contrast to the other girls, she was an artist. Her family believed that she was teaching ballet.

(Millon & Davis, 2000, p. 237; quoted in Horowitz, 2004, pp. 190–191)

Distinguishing Between Histrionic Personality Disorder and Other Disorders

Although people with antisocial personality disorder, borderline personality disorder, and histrionic personality disorder are all manipulative and impulsive, their motivations differ: People with histrionic personality disorder desire attention; people with antisocial personality disorder seek power or material gain; and people with borderline personality disorder want nurturance (Skodol, 2005). Moreover, although both histrionic and borderline personality disorders involve rapidly shifting emotions, only with the latter are the emotions usually related to anger.

Reiland's behavior fit some of the criteria for histrionic personality disorder, in that some of her dramatic displays seemed to be motivated by a desire for attention. She might be diagnosed with histrionic personality disorder as a comorbid disorder; however, the elements of her behavior that indicate borderline personality disorder overshadow the features of histrionic personality disorder. A clinician trying to make a definitive diagnosis (or diagnoses) would want to find out more about any thoughts, feelings, or behaviors that might indicate or rule out histrionic personality disorder.

Understanding Histrionic Personality Disorder

Unfortunately, little formal research has been conducted on histrionic personality disorder, but clinical observations have led to theories about how this disorder arises. Various psychological and social factors are theorized to contribute to the disorder. First, patients with this disorder are thought to believe themselves to be special, view other people as potential admirers, and apparently are sensitive to negative evaluation (Farmer & Nelson-Gray, 2005),

Table 13.17 ▸ Histrionic Personality Disorder Facts at a Glance

Prevalence
- Approximately 2–3% of the general population will have histrionic personality disorder at some point during their lives (American Psychiatric Association, 2000; Grant, Hasin et al., 2004).
- Among people seeking treatment in inpatient and outpatient mental health settings, the prevalence of this disorder is 10–15%.

Comorbidity
- Common comorbid Axis I disorders are somatoform disorders and major depressive disorder.
- Common comorbid Axis II disorders are borderline, narcissistic, antisocial, and dependent personality disorders (Skodol, 2005).

Onset
- As with other personality disorders, symptoms must emerge by young adulthood.

Course
- Symptoms of histrionic personality disorder typically improve over time (Seivewright, Tyrer, & Johnson, 2002).

Gender Differences
- Some studies find histrionic personality disorder to occur as frequently in men as in women, but others find that it is diagnosed more frequently in women.
- Men with histrionic personality disorder may appear "macho" and seek attention for their athletic skills, not their appearance.

Source: Unless otherwise noted, the source is American Psychiatric Association, 2000.

perhaps because of a temperament that is high in reward dependence. This personality disorder—in fact all four of the dramatic/erratic personality disorders—involve a sense of entitlement that drives the manipulative behavior ("I deserve this so I can do whatever it takes to get it") and a poor tolerance of negative emotions (Beck, Freeman, & Davis, 2004). When frustrated or angry, people with histrionic personality disorder tend to have dramatic outbursts; others may, in turn, respond with attention, inadvertently reinforcing these outbursts (Farmer & Nelson-Gray, 2005).

Social factors that are thought to contribute to this disorder include the childrearing practices of the parents. Specifically, one possibility is that people who develop histrionic personality disorder received significantly less attention than they desired during childhood; their subsequent inappropriate attempts (dramatic demands) to obtain attention were inadvertently reinforced, leading to a (maladaptive) belief that they must make an extraordinary effort to obtain attention (Kraus & Reynolds, 2001; Turner, 1994).

Treating Histrionic Personality Disorder

A goal of treatment for histrionic personality disorder is to help patients recognize and then modify their maladaptive beliefs and strategies (which are outlined in Table 13.20). Specifically, using techniques from CBT or psychodynamic therapy, the therapist tries to help patients increase their capacity to tolerate distress, develop more adaptive ways of responding to frustration, recognize the negative impact that their actions have on their relationships, and shift their view of themselves and other people (Beck, Freeman, & Davis, 2004; Farmer & Nelson-Gray, 2005). Like other patients with dramatic/erratic personality disorders, those with histrionic personality disorder often do not remain in treatment for long; they become bored or frustrated and continue to see other people as the primary problem.

Narcissistic Personality Disorder

People with **narcissistic personality disorder** have an inflated sense of their own importance, they expect—and demand—praise and admiration, and they lack empathy (American Psychiatric Association, 2000). This sense of self-importance, however, masks mixed feelings. On the one hand, they are preoccupied with their own concerns and expect others to be as well, and they get angry when other people don't defer to them. They overvalue themselves and undervalue other people, which is true of Patricia in Case 13.8. On the other hand, their self-esteem can be fragile, leading them to fish for compliments. They are relatively insensitive to others' feelings and points of view. Table 13.18 lists the diagnostic criteria for narcissistic personality disorder, and Table 13.19 presents additional information about this disorder.

Narcissistic personality disorder
A personality disorder is characterized by an inflated sense of importance, an excessive desire to be admired, and a lack of empathy.

CASE 13.8 ▶ FROM THE OUTSIDE: Narcissistic Personality Disorder

Patricia was a 41-year-old married woman who presented at an outpatient mental health clinic complaining of interpersonal difficulties at work and recurring bouts of depression. She described a series of jobs in which she had experienced considerable friction with coworkers, stating that people generally did not treat her with the respect she deserved. She attributed her depression to the recent suspicion that perhaps people did not like her because of her behavior. . . . Patricia reported a long history of banking jobs in which she had experienced interpersonal discord. Shortly before her entrance into treatment, Patricia was demoted from a supervisory capacity at her current job because of her inability to effectively interact with those she was supposed to supervise. She described herself as always feeling out of place with her coworkers and indicated that most of them failed to adequately appreciate her skill or the amount of time she put in at work. She reported that she was beginning to think that perhaps she had something to do with their apparent dislike of her. Patricia stated several times . . . that the tellers at the bank were jealous of her status and abilities as a loan officer and that this made them dislike her.

(Corbitt, 2002, pp. 294–295)

Table 13.18 ▶ DSM-IV-TR Diagnostic Criteria for Narcisstic Personality Disorder

A pervasive pattern of grandiosity (in fantasy or behavior), need for admiration, and lack of empathy, beginning by early adulthood and present in a variety of contexts, as indicated by five (or more) of the following:

(1) has a grandiose sense of self-importance (e.g., exaggerates achievements and talents, expects to be recognized as superior without commensurate achievements)

(2) is preoccupied with fantasies of unlimited success, power, brilliance, beauty, or ideal love

(3) believes that he or she is "special" and unique and can only be understood by, or should associate with, other special or high-status people (or institutions)

(4) requires excessive admiration

(5) has a sense of entitlement, i.e., unreasonable expectations of especially favorable treatment or automatic compliance with his or her expectations

(6) is interpersonally exploitative, i.e., takes advantage of others to achieve his or her own ends

(7) lacks empathy: is unwilling to recognize or identify with the feelings and needs of others

(8) is often envious of others or believes that others are envious of him or her

(9) shows arrogant, haughty behaviors or attitudes

Source: Reprinted with permission from the Diagnostic and Statistical Manual of Mental Disorders, Text Revision, Fourth Edition, (Copyright 2000) American Psychiatric Association.

Note that Patricia, in Case 13.8, said that people didn't treat her with the respect that she felt she deserved and that she didn't feel adequately appreciated; people with narcissistic personality disorder often report such feelings. Although all of the dramatic/erratic personality disorders in Cluster B have criteria that involve callous and demanding behaviors, narcissistic personality disorder stands out for its features of grandiosity and a general *lack* of impulsivity or clear-cut self-destructive behaviors. In addition, people with narcissistic personality disorder fear abandonment less than do people with borderline personality disorder (Skodol, 2005).

Although Reiland had symptoms of each of the dramatic/erratic personality disorders, her symptoms do not meet the criteria for a diagnosis of narcissistic personality disorder; her problematic behaviors were often impulsive and self-destructive. Although her symptoms clearly met the criteria for borderline personality disorder, a clinician would need additional information to determine whether she had a comorbid dramatic/erratic personality disorder.

Understanding Narcissistic Personality Disorder

As is true for histrionic personality disorder, very little research has been conducted on narcissistic personality disorder, and so, again, we examine clinically based theories about how the disorder arises. The same psychological and social factors that are theorized to contribute to histrionic personality disorder are also theorized to contribute to narcissistic personality disorder. In fact, patients with these disorders share the belief that they are special and impressive, view other people as potential admirers, and are especially sensitive to negative evaluation (Farmer & Nelson-Gray, 2005). However, the two disorders are not the same: People with these disorders have distinct biases in their views of themselves versus others, tend to hold different maladaptive beliefs, and rely on different maladaptive strategies (see Table 13.20).

Table 13.19 ▶ Narcissistic Personality Disorder Facts at a Glance

Prevalence
- Approximately 1% of the general population will have narcissistic personality disorder at some point in their lifetimes.

Comorbidity
- Common Axis I comorbid disorders are substance-related disorders and anorexia nervosa.
- Common comorbid personality disorders include paranoid personality disorder and the other Cluster B (dramatic/erratic) personality disorders: histrionic, borderline, and antisocial personality disorders.

Onset
- As with other personality disorders, symptoms must emerge by early adulthood.

Course
- People with narcissistic personality disorder may have a hard time adjusting to physical or occupational limitations that arise with advancing age.
- People with this disorder may function at a lower level than they seem capable of, because they are unwilling to risk possible defeat.

Gender Differences
- Between 50% and 75% of those diagnosed with narcissistic personality disorder are male.

Source: Unless otherwise noted, the source is American Psychiatric Association, 2000.

Table 13.20 ▸ Maladaptive Views, Beliefs, and Strategies of Individuals with Narcissistic and Histrionic Personality Disorders

Personality Disorder	View of Self	View of Others	Main Beliefs	Main Strategies (Overt Behavior)
Histrionic	Glamorous, impressive	Seducible, receptive, admiring	"I need to impress others." "People are there to serve and admire me." "People have no right to deny me my just desserts."	Dramatics, charm, temper tantrums, crying; suicidal gestures
Narcissistic	Special, unique; above the rules	Inferior, admiring	"I am special." "Since I'm special, I *deserve* special rules." "I'm better than others."	Self-aggrandize, use others; transcend rules; manipulate; compete

Source: Beck, Freeman, & Davis, 2004, pp. 21, 36, 48–49.

As for histrionic personality disorder, parents' child-rearing practices are thought to contribute to an adult's subsequent narcissistic personality disorder. However, one theory about how narcissistic personality disorder arises proposes that parents were too attentive and permissive, leading the child to have an overinflated sense of self-worth and to expect others to give him or her the same unqualified positive responses as did the parents (Millon, 1998).

Treating Narcissistic Personality Disorder

Treatment for narcissistic personality disorder is basically the same as treatment for histrionic disorder. Again, the therapist seeks to help patients recognize and then modify their maladaptive beliefs and strategies (as outlined in Table 13.20), using techniques of CBT or psychodynamic therapy. However, as for all patients with dramatic/erratic personality disorders, those with narcissistic personality disorder usually do not remain in treatment for long—and typically continue to see other people as the primary problem rather than their own beliefs or behaviors.

Key Concepts and Facts About Dramatic/Erratic Personality Disorders

- The hallmark of antisocial personality disorder is a persistent disregard for the rights of others, which may lead these people to violate rules or laws or to act aggressively. To be diagnosed with this personality disorder, an individual must have exhibited symptoms of conduct disorder before the age of 15.

- The diagnostic criteria for antisocial personality disorder overlap with aspects of psychopathy. However, psychopathy is defined by a more restrictive set of criteria, which focus on emotional and interpersonal characteristics, such as a lack of empathy, as well as antisocial behaviors. In contrast, the criteria for antisocial personality disorder tends to focus on behaviors, particularly criminal behaviors. More criminals are diagnosed with antisocial personality disorder than with psychopathy.

- Psychopathy and antisocial personality disorder are thought to arise from feedback loops among various factors, including genes and temperament, lack of empathy, classical and operant conditioning, abuse or neglect or inconsistent discipline in childhood, parents' criminal behavior, and attachment style. Treatment for psychopathy has generally not been successful; treatment for antisocial personality disorder focuses on

modifying specific behaviors and has some degree of success, at least temporarily, in motivated individuals.

- Borderline personality disorder is characterized by volatile emotions, an unstable self-image, and impulsive behavior in relationships. People with this disorder have problems with emotional regulation—which is probably related to their temperament—and may engage in self-harming behaviors or try to commit suicide.

- Factors that contribute to borderline personality disorder include the genetic and neurological underpinnings of emotional dysregulation, a relatively low threshold for emotional responsiveness, an easily changeable sense of self, cognitive distortions, and a history of abuse, neglect, or feeling invalidated by others.

- Treatment for borderline personality may include medication, CBT, DBT, intensive psychodynamic therapy, and IPT.

- The hallmark of histrionic personality disorder is attention seeking, usually through exaggerated emotional displays. Symptoms may also include a sense of boredom or emptiness and a low tolerance for frustration.

- Narcissistic personality disorder is characterized by a grandiose sense of self-importance and a constant desire for praise and admiration. People with this disorder may also feel a sense of entitlement, behave arrogantly, and have difficulty understanding other people's points of view.

- Histrionic and narcissistic personality disorders are theorized to arise from a combination of temperament, maladaptive beliefs and behaviors, and social interactions. Patients with these personality disorders often drop out of treatment early, in part because they are reluctant to shift from viewing others as the cause of their problems to viewing or acknowledging their own role in creating their problems.

Making a Diagnosis

- Reread Case 13.5 about John, and determine whether or not his symptoms meet the criteria for antisocial personality disorder. Specifically, list which criteria apply and which do not. If you would like more information to determine his diagnosis, what information—specifically—would you want, and in what ways would the information influence your decision?

- Reread Case 13.6 about Donna, and determine whether or not her symptoms meet the criteria for borderline personality disorder. Specifically, list which criteria apply and which do not. If you would like more information to determine her diagnosis, what information—specifically—would you want, and in what ways would the information influence your decision?

- Reread Case 13.7 about the 23-year-old woman, and determine whether or not her symptoms meet the criteria for histrionic personality disorder. Specifically, list which criteria apply and which do not. If you would like more information to determine her diagnosis, what information—specifically—would you want, and in what ways would the information influence your decision?

- Reread Case 13.8 about Patricia, and determine whether or not her symptoms meet the criteria for narcissistic personality disorder. Specifically, list which criteria apply and which do not. If you would like more information to determine her diagnosis, what information—specifically—would you want, and in what ways would the information influence your decision?

Fearful/Anxious Personality Disorders

The personality disorders in Cluster C—avoidant, dependent, and obsessive-compulsive personality disorders—share the feature of anxiety or fear. Although they have this superficial commonality, there is little overlap among the diagnostic criteria for these three disorders; this is in sharp contrast to the disorders within Cluster A (odd/eccentric) and those within Cluster B (dramatic/erratic), which have overlapping criteria.

Avoidant Personality Disorder

The predominant characteristic of people with **avoidant personality disorder** is *social inhibition*—extreme shyness—that usually stems from feeling inadequate and being overly sensitive to negative evaluation (American Psychiatric Association, 2000). People with avoidant personality disorder are often characterized as shy, isolated, timid, or lonely.

What Is Avoidant Personality Disorder?

The diagnostic criteria for avoidant personality disorder (see Table 13.21) all relate to the individual's predominant concern about embarrassing himself or herself during social interactions—perhaps by blushing or crying—and being socially rejected or humiliated. These fears, in turn, lead the individual to try to limit social interactions.

People with avoidant personality disorder are so reluctant to engage in social interactions that they may turn down a promotion if the position requires increased social contact. And they are often hypervigilant for any indication of criticism or rejection. Unfortunately, their social fears and anxieties cause them to behave in tense and fearful ways—for example, not talking about themselves for fear of what others might think—when they

Avoidant personality disorder
A personality disorder characterized by extreme social inhibition (i.e., extreme shyness) that usually stems from feeling inadequate and being overly sensitive to negative evaluation.

Table 13.21 ▶ DSM-IV-TR Diagnostic Criteria for Avoidant Personality Disorder

A pervasive pattern of social inhibition, feelings of inadequacy, and hypersensitivity to negative evaluation, beginning by early adulthood and present in a variety of contexts, as indicated by four (or more) of the following:

(1) avoids occupational activities that involve significant interpersonal contact, because of fears of criticism, disapproval, or rejection.

(2) is unwilling to get involved with people unless certain of being liked.

(3) shows restraint within intimate relationships because of the fear of being shamed or ridiculed.

(4) is preoccupied with being criticized or rejected in social situations.

(5) is inhibited in new interpersonal situations because of feelings of inadequacy.

(6) views self as socially inept, personally unappealing, or inferior to others.

(7) is unusually reluctant to take personal risks or to engage in any new activities because they may prove embarrassing

Source: Reprinted with permission from the Diagnostic and Statistical Manual of Mental Disorders, Text Revision, Fourth Edition, (Copyright 2000) American Psychiatric Association.

Table 13.22 ▸ Avoidant Personality Disorder Facts at a Glance

Prevalence

- Approximately 0.5–2.5% of the general American population has avoidant personality disorder (American Psychiatric Association, 2000; Grant, Hasin, et al., 2004).
- Up to 10% of those seen in outpatient clinics have this disorder.

Comorbidity

- Common comorbid Axis I disorders are mood disorders or anxiety disorders.
- Because the diagnostic criteria overlap with those of social phobia, comorbidity between the two disorders is very high (Shea et al., 2004; Skodol, 2005; Skodol et al., 1995); in one study, 43% of people diagnosed with social phobia were also diagnosed with avoidant personality disorder (Faravelli et al., 2000).
- Common comorbid Axis II personality disorders are dependent personality disorder (because patients are dependent on the few friends they have), borderline personality disorder, and the Cluster A (odd/eccentric) personality disorders.

Onset

- Based on the diagnostic criteria, symptoms such as shyness or a fear of strangers or new situations must emerge by early adulthood.

Course

- Two years after diagnosis, approximately 50% of people with avoidant personality disorder improve enough with treatment that their symptoms no longer meet the criteria (Grilo et al., 2004).

Gender Differences

- Men and women do not consistently differ in their prevalence rates for avoidant personality disorder (Torgersen, 2005).

Source: Unless specifically noted, citations are to American Psychiatric Association, 2000.

do interact with other people. This anxious way of relating to others may inadvertently elicit a mild version of the very reaction they fear—that others will evaluate them in a negative light. Among all people with personality disorders, those with avoidant personality disorder report the lowest quality of life (Cramer, Torgersen, & Kringlen, 2003; Wilberg et al., 2009). Table 13.22 provides additional facts about this disorder, and Case 13.9 describes one individual's experience.

CASE 13.9 ▸ FROM THE OUTSIDE: Avoidant Personality Disorder

Marcus is a 33-year-old man who recently divorced.

His marriage deteriorated over several years and primarily as the result of his wife's increasing frustration with his unwillingness to do anything to improve his situation. He is employed as a warehouse manager and has held the same position for 9 years. He sees others doing more with their lives and wishes that he could as well. Although he hates that his wife chose to leave the marriage, he cannot blame her for doing so. Each evening after work he is filled with feelings of self-contempt and anguish. He would like to go out and be with other people, but he is certain that no one wants his company. He finds that drinking alcohol and watching television usually takes his mind off this unfulfilling life. Marcus thinks of committing suicide frequently.

(Rasmussen, 2005, p. 201)

Distinguishing Between Avoidant Personality Disorder and Other Disorders

If you're thinking that you've read about a disorder that seems similar to avoidant personality disorder earlier in this textbook, you're correct. Avoidant personality disorder has much in common with social phobia (Chapter 7), and the symptoms

Dependent personality disorder
A personality disorder characterized by submissive and clingy behaviors, based on fear of separation.

of the two disorders overlap (Chambless, Fydrich, & Rodebaugh, 2008; Tillfors et al., 2004). However, the criteria for avoidant personality disorder are broader than those for social phobia, and the symptoms include a more pervasive sense of inadequacy or inferiority and a reluctance to take risks (Skodol, 2005), as was true of Marcus in Case 13.9.

When making the diagnosis of avoidant personality disorder, clinicians must take cultural factors into account (American Psychiatric Association, 2000). For example, recent immigrants may exhibit symptoms of this disorder, perhaps because of language barriers or concerns about safety, and so clinicians must be sure to ask whether the behavior predates immigration. Similarly, ethnic and religious groups have different norms about appropriate levels of social contact and avoidance, and so clinicians should ascertain whether social norms, and not a true fear of social contact, drive the behaviors. For example, among deeply observant Muslims, the norm is for women to shun social contact with men who are not family members, and such behavior by a woman in this group should not be taken to indicate avoidant personality disorder. Because the three fearful/anxious personality disorders have not been studied in depth, we will discuss the underlying bases for and treatment of all three disorders after we consider specific features of each of them separately.

Patrick Ryan/Getty Images

Symptoms of avoidant personality disorder and social phobia overlap, and people with either disorder are excessively concerned about being rejected by others or behaving in a way that leads them to feel humiliated. However, the social difficulties and feelings of inadequacy of people with avoidant personality disorder are generally more pervasive than those of people with the Axis I disorder, and can make meetings like this extremely uncomfortable or even impossible.

Dependent Personality Disorder

Dependent personality disorder is characterized by submissive and clingy behaviors, based on fear of separation. The DSM-IV-TR definition notes that the clingy behaviors are intended to elicit attention, reassurance, and decisive behaviors from other people (American Psychiatric Association, 2000). These behaviors are not a temporary bid for attention or reassurance (like the behaviors of those with borderline or histrionic personality disorder), but are part of a chronic pattern of helpless behavior.

What Is Dependent Personality Disorder?

People with dependent personality disorder are chronically plagued by self-doubt and consistently underestimate their abilities (see Table 13.23 for the list of diagnostic criteria). Thus, they have a hard time making all kinds of decisions, from life-altering ones about what career to pursue to mundane decisions about what clothes to wear. They prefer to have other people make such choices for them. And because they are so quick to believe they are wrong, they are likely to see any criticism or disapproval as proof of their basic negative beliefs about themselves.

People with dependent personality disorder often don't learn the skills needed to function independently and so are, in fact, dependent on others; they have reason to be concerned about living on their own. When a relationship ends, they typically leap into another one in order to ensure that they are not alone. Even while in an intimate relationship, they are often preoccupied with the possibility that the relationship will end and they will have to fend for themselves. Individuals with dependent personality disorder are

Table 13.23 ▶ DSM-IV-TR Diagnostic Criteria for Dependent Personality Disorder

A pervasive and excessive need to be taken care of that leads to submissive and clinging behavior and fears of separation, beginning by early adulthood and present in a variety of contexts, as indicated by five (or more) of the following:

(1) has difficulty making everyday decisions without an excessive amount of advice and reassurance from others.

(2) needs others to assume responsibility for most major areas of his or her life.

(3) has difficulty expressing disagreement with others because of fear of loss of support or approval. Note: Do not include realistic fears of retribution.

(4) has difficulty initiating projects or doing things on his or her own (because of a lack of self-confidence in judgment or abilities rather than a lack of motivation or energy).

(5) goes to excessive lengths to obtain nurturance and support from others, to the point of volunteering to do things that are unpleasant.

(6) feels uncomfortable or helpless when alone because of exaggerated fears of being unable to care for himself or herself.

(7) urgently seeks another relationship as a source of care and support when a close relationship ends.

(8) is unrealistically preoccupied with fears of being left to take care of himself or herself

Source: Reprinted with permission from the Diagnostic and Statistical Manual of Mental Disorders, Text Revision, Fourth Edition, (Copyright 2000) American Psychiatric Association.

Table 13.24 ▶ Dependent Personality Disorder Facts at a Glance

Prevalence

- The prevalence of dependent personality disorder in the general population is less than 1% (Grant, Hasin, et al., 2004).

Comorbidity

- Common Axis I disorders are mood disorders and anxiety disorders.
- Common comorbid personality disorders are avoidant, borderline, and histrionic personality disorders.

Onset

- As required by the diagnostic criteria, symptoms must emerge by young adulthood.

Course

- Symptoms may improve over time, to the point where the individual no longer meets the criteria for the disorder (Markowitz et al., 2005).

Gender Differences

- In the general population, women tend to be diagnosed with dependent personality disorder more often than men (Torgersen, 2005); in a clinical setting, however, men and women may have similar prevalence rates (American Psychiatric Association, 2000).

Source: Unless otherwise noted, citations are to American Psychiatric Association, 2000.

most comfortable in relationships with people who take the initiative—and take responsibility. Not surprisingly, then, they often choose overprotective and dominating people to be their friends and partners, becoming passive in those relationships. Generally, people who have dependent personality disorder have a limited social circle, consisting of only a few people on whom they depend, as is true of Matthew in Case 13.10. Once they have established a relationship, people with dependent personality disorder are hesitant to disagree with the other person for fear that he or she will withdraw emotional support. In fact, an individual with this personality disorder may go to great lengths to maintain the extensive support that the other person provides, even tolerating mental or physical abuse (American Psychiatric Association, 2000).

It is important to note that even if an individual possesses enough of the characteristics to meet the diagnostic criteria in Table 13.23, he or she will not be diagnosed with dependent personality disorder unless these characteristics significantly impair functioning in major areas of life. Table 13.24 provides additional information about this disorder.

CASE 13.10 ▶ FROM THE OUTSIDE: Dependent Personality Disorder

Matthew is a 34-year-old single man who lives with his mother and works as an accountant. He is seeking treatment because he is very unhappy after having just broken up with his girlfriend. His mother had disapproved of his marriage plans, ostensibly because the woman was of a different religion. Matthew felt trapped and forced to choose between his mother and his girlfriend, and because "blood is thicker than water," he had decided not to go against his mother's wishes. . . . Matthew is afraid of disagreeing with his mother for fear that she will not be supportive of him and he will then have to fend for himself. He criticizes himself for being weak, but also admires his mother and respects her judgment. . . . He feels that his own judgment is poor.

Matthew works at a job several grades below what his education and talent would permit. On several occasions he has turned down promotions because he didn't want the responsibility of having to supervise other people or make independent decisions. . . . He has two very close friends whom he has had since early childhood. He has lunch with one of them every single workday and feels lost if his friend is sick and misses a day.

Matthew is the youngest of four children and the only boy. . . . He had considerable separation anxiety as a child—he had difficulty falling asleep unless his mother stayed in the room, mild school refusal, and unbearable homesickness when he occasionally tried "sleepovers." . . . He has lived at home his whole life except for 1 year of college, from which he returned because of homesickness.

(Spitzer, Gibbon, et al., 2002, pp. 179–180)

Distinguishing Between Dependent Personality Disorder and Other Disorders

Avoidant and dependent personality disorders share the characteristics of desire for reassurance, feelings of inadequacy, and submissive behaviors (Leising, Sporberg, & Rehbein, 2006). However, with avoidant personality disorder, these characteristics focus on feeling socially inept, whereas with dependent personality disorder, they focus on feeling incapable of taking care of oneself (Skodol, 2005), as Matthew in Case 13.10 felt.

When considering the diagnosis of dependent personality disorder, clinicians need to keep in mind that cultures have different norms about appropriate dependent behaviors; moreover, these norms may vary for men and women and for people of different ages. For instance, some Asian cultures may promote more deference or passivity than is the norm in North America, and some Latino cultures promote *marianismo* (the opposite of machismo), where women are expected to be submissive to and dependent on men. These behaviors, normal within those cultures, should be distinguished from symptoms of dependent personality disorder (Paniagua, 2001).

Obsessive-Compulsive Personality Disorder

Obsessive-compulsive personality disorder is characterized by preoccupations with perfectionism, orderliness, and self-control as well as low levels of flexibility and efficiency (American Psychiatric Association, 2000). It is the personality disorder associated with the least disability (Skodol, Gunderson, et al., 2002) and the highest obtained educational level (Torgersen, Kringlen, & Cramer, 2001). Rachel Reiland describes her father as having some elements of obsessive-compulsive personality disorder: He was strict, "coveted control," and became enraged when events weren't to his liking. Reiland herself had some elements of this disorder: "Once upon a time perfectionism was my noble aspiration. My perfectionism extended beyond academics or career. I also aspired to be the perfect mother, lover, and friend, always appropriate in all my emotional expressions" (2004, p. 361).

What Is Obsessive-Compulsive Personality Disorder?

People with obsessive-compulsive personality disorder can get so bogged down in details that they leave the most important elements to the last minute (see Table 13.25 for the complete diagnostic criteria). For instance, when preparing a presentation, people with this disorder might spend hours creating a single PowerPoint slide, trying to get it perfect, and end up running out of time for organizing their talk. They can't see the forest for the trees. For people with obsessive-compulsive personality disorder, decision making is a painful, long process; thus, once they've made a decision, they're not likely to change their minds—which can end up making them appear rigid and inflexible. And, like Reiland's father, when they are unable to control a situation, they may become angry, irritable, or upset.

Some (but not all) people who are workaholics may have obsessive-compulsive personality disorder—they may feel uncomfortable on vacations unless they take work along with them. Alternatively, others with obsessive-compulsive personality disorder may spend inordinate amounts of time on hobbies or household chores, striving for perfection and adhering to rules inflexibly. They may hold others to these same unrealistically stringent standards.

The relationships of people with obsessive-compulsive personality disorder are normally formal and serious; they are preoccupied with logic and intellect, are overly conscientious, and are intolerant of emotional or "illogical" behavior in others. Typically, people with obsessive-compulsive personality disorder feel uncomfortable with others who express emotions easily and openly. People with this disorder are not likely to express tender feelings or pay compliments. Other people often feel frustrated by their rigidity. In turn, people with

Obsessive-compulsive personality disorder
A personality disorder characterized by preoccupations with perfectionism, orderliness, and self-control as well as low levels of flexibility and efficiency.

Table 13.25 ▶ DSM-IV-TR Diagnostic Criteria for Obsessive-Compulsive Personality Disorder

A pervasive pattern of preoccupation with orderliness, perfectionism, and mental and interpersonal control, at the expense of flexibility, openness, and efficiency, beginning by early adulthood and present in a variety of contexts, as indicated by four (or more) of the following:

(1) is preoccupied with details, rules, lists, order, organization, or schedules to the extent that the major point of the activity is lost

(2) shows perfectionism that interferes with task completion (e.g., is unable to complete a project because his or her own overly strict standards are not met)

(3) is excessively devoted to work and productivity to the exclusion of leisure activities and friendships (not accounted for by obvious economic necessity)

(4) is overconscientious, scrupulous, and inflexible about matters of morality, ethics, or values (not accounted for by cultural or religious identification)

(5) is unable to discard worn-out or worthless objects even when they have no sentimental value

(6) is reluctant to delegate tasks or to work with others unless they submit to exactly his or her way of doing things

(7) adopts a miserly spending style toward both self and others; money is viewed as something to be hoarded for future catastrophes

(8) shows rigidity and stubbornness

Source: Reprinted with permission from the Diagnostic and Statistical Manual of Mental Disorders, Text Revision, Fourth Edition, (Copyright 2000) American Psychiatric Association.

Table 13.26 ▶ Obsessive-Compulsive Personality Disorder Facts at a Glance

Prevalence

- Approximately 1–8% of the general population has obsessive-compulsive personality disorder (American Psychiatric Association, 2000; Grant, Hasin, et al., 2004).
- Around 3–10% of people receiving treatment in mental health clinics have obsessive-compulsive personality disorder.

Comorbidity

- People with an anxiety disorder are more likely to develop obsessive-compulsive personality disorder than are members of the general population.
- Most people with obsessive-compulsive disorder (OCD) do not also have obsessive-compulsive personality disorder.

Onset

- The diagnostic criteria specify that symptoms must emerge by early adulthood.

Course

- Symptoms of up to a third of patients may improve over time to the point that they no longer meet the diagnostic criteria (Grilo et al., 2004).

Gender Differences

- Twice as many men as women are diagnosed with obsessive-compulsive personality disorder.

Source: Unless otherwise noted, citations should be American Psychiatric Association, 2000.

Some workaholics have obsessive-compulsive personality disorder: They are perfectionistic and extremely orderly and organized. However, they can become so preoccupied with doing a job perfectly that they are inefficient or can't complete the task. Moreover, when problems arise, they can be rigid and inflexible.

obsessive-compulsive personality disorder have difficulty acknowledging the perspectives of others, as is true of Mr. V in Case 13.11. Table 13.26 provides additional information about this disorder.

CASE 13.11 ▶ FROM THE OUTSIDE:
Obsessive-Compulsive Personality Disorder

Mr. V, a 25-year-old philosophy graduate student, began twice-weekly psychotherapy. His presenting complaint was difficulty with completing work effectively, particularly writing tasks, due to excessive anxiety and obsessionality. . . . When he came for treatment, he was struggling to make progress on his master's thesis. Although Mr. V socialized quite a bit, he reported that intimate relationships often felt "wooden." He was usually overcommitted, with an endless list of "shoulds" that he would constantly mentally review and remind himself how much he was failing to satisfy his obligations. A central theme throughout treatment was his tendency to be self-denigrating, loathing himself as a person deserving of punishment in some way yet being extremely provocative. . . . He also held very strong political beliefs, sure that his way of viewing things was superior to others.

(Bender, 2005, p. 413)

Distinguishing Between Obsessive-Compulsive Personality Disorder and Other Disorders

Obsessive-compulsive personality disorder is distinguished from OCD by the absence of true obsessions and compulsions. Rather, those with obsessive-compulsive personality disorder are preoccupied with details—as was Mr. V when writing his master's thesis—and are inflexible. Researchers are still trying to determine whether obsessive-compulsive personality disorder and OCD differ quantitatively or qualitatively. Research studies addressing this question have reported mixed findings (Albert et al., 2004; Eisen et al., 2006; Wu, Clark, & Watson, 2006). Most people with one of the two disorders do not have the other (Mancebo et al., 2005).

Understanding Fearful/Anxious Personality Disorders

Virtually nothing is known about the neurological bases of fearful/anxious personality disorders, but the apparent similarity between these disorders and anxiety disorders might indicate that the amygdala is involved. At present, however, this is merely inference and speculation. In contrast, psychological factors associated with these disorders have been identified. In particular, fear and anxiety underlie the three fearful/anxious disorders. Temperament—specifically being high in the dimension of harm avoidance—can contribute to the development of one of these disorders, especially avoidant personality disorder (Joyce et al., 2003; Taylor, Laposa, & Alden, 2004). In fact, many of the factors related to social phobia are also involved in avoidant personality disorder, which makes sense, given the overlap in the symptoms of the two disorders. For instance, people with social phobia are also high in the dimension of harm avoidance (Marteinsdottir et al., 2003). Moreover, people with both disorders have similar negative beliefs about themselves in relation to other people and avoid social situations for fear of embarrassing themselves (Meyer, 2002; Morey et al., 2003).

Cognitive and behavioral factors are thought to contribute to all three fearful/anxious personality disorders, as outlined in Table 13.27. For all three, patients avoid situations that lead to discomfort and anxiety: With avoidant personality disorder, patients avoid social situations; with dependent personality disorder, they avoid making decisions and having responsibility; and with obsessive-compulsive personality disorder, they avoid making mistakes and experiencing strong emotions. The avoidance perpetuates the cognitive distortions because the patients' fears go unchallenged (Beck, Freeman, & Davis, 2004; Farmer & Nelson-Gray, 2005).

Finally, social factors also contribute to these personality disorders. These factors include anxious or avoidant attachment style, which may have arisen in childhood as a result of particular interaction patterns with parents (Gude et al., 2004; Pincus & Wilson, 2001).

Treating Fearful/Anxious Personality Disorders

As for most other personality disorders, there is little research on the treatment of fearful/anxious personality disorders, and what research there is has focused primarily on avoidant personality disorder. The findings suggest that the treatment that is effective with social phobia—CBT that uses exposure to avoided stimuli as well as

Table 13.27 ▶ Maladaptive Views, Beliefs, and Strategies of Individuals with Fearful/Anxious Personality Disorders

Personality Disorder	View of Self	View of Others	Main Beliefs	Main Strategies
Avoidant	Socially inept, incompetent, vulnerable to rejection	Critical, demeaning, superior	"I may get hurt." "If people know the 'real' me, they will reject me." "It's terrible to be rejected, put down." "I can't tolerate unpleasant feelings."	Avoid evaluative situations and unpleasant thoughts or feelings
Dependent	Needy, weak, helpless, incompetent	Idealized as nurturant, supportive, competent	"I am helpless." "I need people to survive, to be happy."	Cultivate relationships in which dependence is accepted
Obsessive-Compulsive	Responsible, accountable, fastidious, competent	Irresponsible, casual, incompetent, self-indulgent	"I must not err." "I know what's best." "Details are crucial." "People *should* do better, try harder."	Perfectionism, control, criticism, punishment, thinks in terms of "shoulds"

Source: Beck, Freeman, & Davis, 2004, pp. 21, 36, 48–49.

cognitive restructuring of maladaptive beliefs and strategies—can also help people with avoidant personality disorder (Beck, Freeman, & Davis, 2004; Emmelkamp et al., 2006; Farmer & Nelson-Gray, 2005; Reich, 2000; Van Velzen, Emmelkamp, & Scholing, 1997). Treatment may also include family or couples therapy to help family members change their responses to—and thus the consequences of—the patient's maladaptive behaviors.

Table 13.28 summarizes the contrasting characteristics of the ten personality disorders.

Table 13.28 ▸ The Personality Disorders: A Summary

Personality Disorders	Affect	Behavior	Cognition	Social Functioning
Odd/Eccentric: Cluster A				
Paranoid	Easily feels betrayed and angry	Hypervigilant for betrayal	Distrustful/suspicious of others; reads malevolent meaning into neutral remarks	Generally avoids relationships
Schizoid	Emotionally constricted, detached	Avoids people when possible	Views relationships as messy and undesirable	Indifferent to praise or criticism; generally avoids relationships
Schizotypal	Generally emotionally constricted, but displays inappropriate affect and anxiety	Avoids people whenever possible	Perceptual distortions, ideas of reference, magical thinking	Generally avoids relationships
Dramatic/Erratic: Cluster B				
Antisocial	Aggressive feelings toward others, lack of empathy	Generally poor impulse control	Believes that he or she is entitled to break rules	Dominant in relationships
Borderline	Emotionally expressive, with inappropriately strong and rapid reactions	Poor impulse control	Dramatic shifts between overvaluing and undervaluing others; may develop paranoid thinking under stress	Alternately dominant and submissive in relationships
Histrionic	Rapidly shifting but shallow emotions	Relatively poor impulse control; strives to be center of attention	Some grandiosity, believes that he or she should be admired	Dominant in relationships
Narcissistic	No empathy; haughty towards others	Manipulates others	Grandiosity	Dominant in relationships
Fearful/Anxious: Cluster C				
Avoidant	Anxiety in social situations	Overcontrol of behavior	Excessively negative self-opinion; worries about being rejected or criticized	Submissive in relationships
Dependent	Anxiety about possible separations from others and having to function independently	Overcontrol of behavior	Believes that he or she is helpless and incompetent and so must rely on others	Submissive in relationships
Obsessive-Compulsive	Constricted in expression of emotion to others	Overcontrol of behavior	Perfectionism; rigid thinking; preoccupation with details, rules, and lists	Dominant and somewhat detached in relationships

Source: Pretzer & Beck, 2005; Skodol, 2005.

Key Concepts and Facts About Fearful/Anxious Personality Disorders

- The hallmark of avoidant personality disorder is social inhibition, which usually stems from feeling inadequate and being overly sensitive to negative evaluation. Although similar to social phobia, avoidant personality disorder has criteria that are more pervasive and involve a more general reluctance to take risks. CBT methods that are used to treat social phobia can also be effective with avoidant personality disorder.

- Dependent personality disorder is characterized by submissive and clingy behaviors, based on fear of separation; these behaviors are intended to elicit attention, reassurance, and decision making from other people. People with dependent personality disorder are chronically plagued by self-doubt and consistently underestimate their abilities; in fact, they may not know how to function independently.

- Obsessive-compulsive personality disorder is characterized by preoccupations with perfectionism, orderliness, and self-control and by low levels of flexibility and efficiency. These rigid personality traits may lead these people to have difficulty prioritizing and making decisions, and they are often intolerant of emotional or "illogical" behavior in others.

- Psychological and social factors that contribute to social phobia also contribute to avoidant personality disorders.

Making a Diagnosis

- Reread Case 13.9 about Marcus, and determine whether or not his symptoms meet the criteria for avoidant personality disorder. Specifically, list which criteria apply and which do not. If you would like more information to determine his diagnosis, what information—specifically—would you want, and in what ways would the information influence your decision?

- Reread Case 13.10 about Matthew, and determine whether or not his symptoms meet the criteria for dependent personality disorder. Specifically, list which criteria apply and which do not. If you would like more information to determine his diagnosis, what information—specifically—would you want, and in what ways would the information influence your decision?

- Reread Case 13.11 about Mr. V, and determine whether or not his symptoms meet the criteria for obsessive-compulsive personality disorder. Specifically, list which criteria apply and which do not. If you would like more information to determine his diagnosis, what information—specifically—would you want, and in what ways would the information influence your decision?

Follow-up on Rachel Reiland

We can say with certainty that Rachel Reiland suffered from borderline personality disorder. In addition, she displayed significant elements of two other personality disorders: histrionic personality disorder (her dramatic behaviors may have been motivated by excessive emotional reactivity and a desire for attention) and obsessive-compulsive personality disorder (her rigid thoughts and behaviors may have been motivated by perfectionism). However, it is difficult to determine whether these aspects of her personality met the criteria for the diagnosis of a comorbid personality disorder. Her symptoms of borderline personality disorder were so pronounced that they might have masked additional personality disorders.

If a clinician interviewing Reiland had sought to assess the presence of possible comorbid personality disorders, he or she might have spoken with Reiland's husband for his perspective, asked Reiland specific questions related to the other personality disorders under consideration, or asked her to complete a personality inventory or questionnaire (described in Chapter 3).

What happened to Reiland? In her memoir, she notes that she was hospitalized three times; the first time because of significant suicidal impulses. After discharge from that first hospitalization, she spent 4 years in intensive outpatient therapy with a psychiatrist—three times a week during the first 2 years of treatment. She was hospitalized twice more over the course of her therapy and again developed anorexia for a period of time. Her symptoms were sufficiently severe that her therapist imposed strict limits on their interactions; for instance, he banned physical contact of any kind. Although her therapist used psychodynamic therapy, he also incorporated elements of CBT and DBT into the treatment. For instance, the therapist addressed Reiland's black-and-white thinking and validated her experiences while trying to help her accept her feelings without judging herself. In addition to the hospitalizations and outpatient therapy, Reiland tried various medications, settling on antidepressants that she gradually stopped before her therapy ended.

Her treatment was successful. She wrote her memoir 8 years after her therapy ended; she developed and sustained the ability to regulate her moods, to control her impulses, and to have productive and enjoyable relationships.

SUMMING UP

Summary of Diagnosing Personality Disorders

A personality disorder is characterized by maladaptive personality traits that begin by young adulthood and continue through adulthood; these traits are relatively inflexible, are expressed across a wide range of situations, and lead to distress or impaired functioning. A personality disorder affects three areas of functioning: affect, behavior (including social behavior), and cognition. The diagnostic criteria for personality disorders were based on the assumptions that the maladaptive personality traits begin in childhood and are stable throughout life. These assumptions led to the disorders being placed on a separate axis (Axis II) of DSM-IV-TR. Subsequent research indicates that some Axis I disorders begin in childhood and that symptoms of personality disorders may improve over time.

Personality disorders may be assessed through diagnostic interviews, personality inventories, or questionnaires. The clinician may make the diagnosis based on the pattern of the patient's behavior and, given the preponderance of interpersonal problems that arise with personality disorders, may also rely on supplemental reports from family or friends.

In DSM-IV-TR, personality disorders are grouped into three clusters: Cluster A, characterized by odd or eccentric behaviors related to features of schizophrenia; Cluster B, characterized by dramatic and erratic behaviors and problems with emotional regulation; and Cluster C, characterized by anxious or fearful behaviors. The category of personality disorders in DSM-IV-TR has been criticized on numerous grounds.

The neuropsychosocial approach explains how personality disorders develop by highlighting the interactions among three sorts of factors: the effects of genes on temperament and the interaction of temperament, operant conditioning, dysfunctional beliefs, and insecure attachment that can result from childhood abuse or neglect. Treatments for personality disorders include medications for comorbid symptoms, CBT or psychodynamic therapy, and family education and therapy, as well as couples, interpersonal, and group therapy.

Thinking like a clinician

V.J. was 50 years old, never married, and had never been very successful professionally. He

was a salesman, and changed companies every few years, either because he was passed over for a promotion and quit, or because he didn't like the new rules—or the way that the rules were enforced—at the job. He'd been in love a few times, but it never worked out. He chalked it up to difficulty finding the right woman. He had some friends, but they were really people he'd known over the years and saw occasionally. Most of his positive social interactions happened in chat rooms or via e-mail, not face to face.

Is there anything about the information presented that would lead you to wonder whether he might have a personality disorder—if so, what was the information? (And if not, why not?) Based on what you have read, how should mental health clinicians go about determining whether V.J. might have a personality disorder or whether his personality traits are in the normal range? Do you agree with the way that DSM-IV-TR goes about classifying personality disorders—why or why not?

Summary of Odd/Eccentric Personality Disorders

The essential feature of paranoid personality disorder is a persistent and pervasive mistrust and suspiciousness, which is accompanied by a bias to interpret other people's motives as hostile. Although paranoid personality disorder and paranoid schizophrenia both involve suspicious beliefs, people with the personality disorder have some capacity to evaluate whether their suspicions are based on reality; they also tend to be suspicious about people they know. In contrast, the beliefs of people with paranoid schizophrenia are delusional, and they perceive threats as coming from strangers or objects.

Schizoid personality disorder is characterized by a restricted range of emotions in social interactions and few—if any—close relationships; people with this disorder have poor social skills. They report rarely experiencing strong emotions, and they prefer to be—and function best when—isolated from others.

Schizotypal personality disorder is marked by eccentric thoughts, perceptions, and behaviors, as well as by having very few close relationships. This personality disorder is characterized by three groups of symptoms:

cognitive-perceptual, interpersonal, and disorganized. Schizotypal personality disorder is viewed as a milder form of schizophrenia. Many of the factors that give rise to schizophrenia also appear to give rise to schizotypal personality disorder: genes and the prenatal environment; problems with attention, memory, and executive function as well as an impaired theory of mind; and physical abuse or neglect in childhood, insecure attachment, and discrimination.

Paranoid, schizoid, and schizotypal personality disorders are on the spectrum of schizophrenia-related disorders, and close relatives of people with any of these odd/eccentric personality disorders are more likely to have schizophrenia. Schizotypal personality disorder involves neurological abnormalities that are less severe than those associated with schizophrenia.

People with odd/eccentric personality disorders are reluctant participants in treatment. Treatment may address fundamental issues, such as isolation and suspiciousness. Treatment for schizotypal personality disorder may include antipsychotic medication (although at lower doses than used for psychotic disorders), CBT, social skills training, and family therapy.

Thinking like a clinician

Shawna has few friends; most of the time she's quiet and shy, avoiding eye contact. Occasionally, she mentions that her troubles—work, social, and financial—are because of the radiation coming out of the computer. She says it with a straight face, but it's hard to tell whether she's joking. When asked whether she's being serious, she reluctantly says that she's not, but it's not clear whether she's being honest. If you were asked to determine whether she has a personality disorder, what kinds of questions would you ask? Based on what you have read, what types of answers would distinguish somewhat quirky behavior from the truly odd behavior that characterizes a Cluster A personality disorder? If you determined that her behavior was odd enough to merit a diagnosis of a Cluster A (odd/eccentric) personality disorder, what would you look for in order to decide which of those disorders might be the best diagnosis? Could Shawna have more than one personality disorder? If not, why not? And if so, what might her other symptoms be?

Summary of Dramatic/Erratic Personality Disorders

The hallmark of antisocial personality disorder is a persistent disregard for the rights of others, which may lead these people to violate rules or laws or to act aggressively. To be diagnosed with this personality disorder, an individual must have exhibited symptoms of conduct disorder before the age of 15. The diagnostic criteria for antisocial personality disorder overlap with aspects of psychopathy. However, psychopathy is defined by a more restrictive set of criteria, which focus on emotional and interpersonal characteristics, such as a lack of empathy, as well as antisocial behaviors. In contrast, for antisocial personality disorder, the focus is on behaviors, particularly criminal behaviors. More criminals are diagnosed with antisocial personality disorder than with psychopathy.

Psychopathy and antisocial personality disorder are thought to arise from feedback loops among various factors, including genes and temperament, lack of empathy, classical and operant conditioning, abuse or neglect or inconsistent discipline in childhood, parents' criminal behavior, and attachment style. Treatment for psychopathy has generally not been successful; treatment for antisocial personality disorder focuses on modifying specific behaviors and has some degree of success, at least temporarily, in motivated individuals.

Borderline personality disorder is characterized by volatile emotions, an unstable self-image, and impulsive behavior in relationships. People with this disorder have problems with emotional regulation—which is probably related to their temperament—and may engage in self-harming behaviors or try to commit suicide. Factors that contribute to borderline personality disorder include the genetic and neurological underpinnings of emotional dysregulation, a relatively low threshold for emotional responsiveness, an easily changeable sense of self, cognitive distortions, and a history of abuse, neglect, or feeling invalidated by others. Treatment for borderline personality may include medication, CBT, DBT, intensive psychodynamic therapy, and IPT.

The hallmark of histrionic personality disorder is attention seeking, usually through exaggerated emotional displays. Symptoms may also include a sense of boredom or emptiness and a low tolerance for frustration.

Narcissistic personality disorder is characterized by a grandiose sense of self-importance and a constant desire for praise and admiration. People with this disorder may also feel a sense of entitlement, behave arrogantly, and have difficulty understanding other people's points of view.

Thinking like a clinician

In high school and college, Will acted in school plays. Now in his 30s, he travels a lot, making presentations for his job, and so has a lot of independence. He likes the freedom of not having a boss looking over his shoulder all the time, and he enjoys making presentations. Because no one really knows how many hours he works, he sometimes starts late in the morning or quits early; then, he heads for a bar to down a few beers. Occasionally, he takes whole days off—after he's had too much to drink the night before. He's been through a series of girlfriends, never staying with one for more than 6 months. Lately, though, his single status has been bothering him, and he's been wondering why there don't seem to be any decent women out there.

In what ways does Will seem typical of someone with a Cluster B (dramatic/erratic) personality disorder? In what ways is he unusual? What would you need to know before you could decide whether he had a dramatic/erratic personality disorder? Which specific personality disorder seems most likely from the description of him, and why? Why is—or isn't—this information enough to make a diagnosis?

Summary of Fearful/Anxious Personality Disorders

The hallmark of avoidant personality disorder is social inhibition, which usually stems from feeling inadequate or being overly sensitive to negative evaluation. Although similar to social phobia, avoidant personality disorder has criteria that are more pervasive and involves a more general reluctance to take risks. CBT methods that are used to treat social phobia can also be effective with avoidant personality disorder.

Dependent personality disorder is characterized by submissive and clingy behaviors, based on fear of separation; these behaviors are intended to elicit attention, reassurance, and decision making from other people. People with dependent personality disorder are chronically plagued by self-doubt and consistently underestimate their abilities; in fact, they may not know how to function independently.

Obsessive-compulsive personality disorder is characterized by preoccupations with perfectionism, orderliness, and self-control and by low levels of flexibility and efficiency. These rigid personality traits may lead these people to have difficulty prioritizing and making decisions, and they are often intolerant of emotional or "illogical" behavior in others.

Thinking like a clinician

Juan and his wife, Beatriz, are from Argentina. They have been referred to mental health services by their family doctor. Beatriz always brings her husband with her to her doctor's appointments, and she wants her husband in the room during the examination, although her English is more than sufficient to express herself and understand the doctor.

Beatriz and Juan happened to mention at her last medical visit that she never leaves the house if Juan isn't with her. She didn't see why she should, because Juan is happy to go with her wherever she needs to go. She said that she likes it this way—that she doesn't feel "stuck" at home and that Juan pretty much takes care of whatever she doesn't feel able to do.

Before thinking about a possible diagnosis, what specific areas of Beatriz's functioning would you want to know more about, and why? What other types of information would you want to have (for example, about cultural issues), and why? Might Beatriz be suffering from an Axis I disorder? If so, which one, and what would you need to know to be relatively certain of that? If not, why not? What personality disorder or disorders might she have (or does she have none)? On what information do you base your judgment?

Key Terms

Personality disorders (p. 567)

Personality (p. 568)

Cluster A personality disorders (p. 572)

Cluster B personality disorders (p. 572)

Cluster C personality disorders (p. 572)

Paranoid personality disorder (p. 581)

Schizoid personality disorder (p. 583)

Schizotypal personality disorder (p. 585)

Antisocial personality disorder (p. 593)

Conduct disorder (p. 593)

Psychopathy (p. 595)

Borderline personality disorder (p. 599)

Histrionic personality disorder (p. 608)

Narcissistic personality disorder (p. 610)

Avoidant personality disorder (p. 613)

Dependent personality disorder (p. 614)

Obsessive-compulsive personality disorder (p. 617)

More Study Aids

For additional study aids related to this chapter, go to:

www.worthpublishers.com/rosenberg

Childhood Disorders

Lela and Carlos Enriquez have three children: Javier, Pia, and Richie. It's been a very challenging year for the family, full of heartache. All three children have been having various difficulties at home or at school. Lela and Carlos are trying to figure out what, exactly, the problems are and what can be done about them.

The most troubling problem concerns their youngest son, Richie. He's almost 2 years old, but he has yet to smile at his parents—or anyone. He's not talking either, and although he seems to understand what people say to him, he is a bit slow to respond. Whereas most toddlers are talking in (at least) 2- or 3-word sentences, Richie doesn't even say single words. His doctor wasn't that worried when she saw him at his last physical exam a few months ago: "Well, kids sometimes take a while to talk. Let's give him a few more months and if he hasn't started talking by then, give me a call." Richie also seems shy in the extreme—he doesn't even look people in the eye.

Richie's older siblings have also been having problems. Javier is 10 years old, and he's had both academic and social problems at school; his teacher suggested he receive a thorough evaluation. His 8-year-old sister, Pia, has been a bit of a puzzle. On her last report card, her teacher noted that she's very bright but doesn't seem to be working as hard as she could.

Like Richie, Pia, and Javier, many children have problems socially or academically or achieve developmental milestones, such as walking and talking, later than the average child. When are such difficulties part of the range of normal development, and when do they signal a larger problem? This chapter addresses this question by exploring various disorders listed in DSM-IV-TR that typically are first diagnosed during infancy, childhood, or adolescence. For these disorders, the timing of the diagnosis contrasts with that of most of the disorders discussed in previous chapters (e.g., anxiety, depression, substance-related disorders), which typically are first diagnosed during adulthood. Nonetheless, children can be diagnosed with many of the Axis I disorders discussed in previous chapters.

We begin this chapter by examining mental retardation—a disorder that can profoundly affect the lives of children and their families and that may require special schools or residential placements as well as other special services. We then examine a set of disorders referred to as *pervasive developmental disorders*, which are often comorbid with mental retardation and may require special school placements and special services. We next turn to disorders that may

Alan Baker/Heart Agency

Mental retardation
Intelligence that is significantly below normal—an IQ approximately equal to or less than 70 (where the mean IQ is set at 100)—and that impairs daily functioning; also referred to as *intellectual disability*.

not affect children and their families as much, although they still cause significant distress and/or impair functioning: learning disorders and disorders of disruptive behavior and attention. In the final section, we examine briefly other disorders of childhood, which have symptoms that can overlap with those of other psychological disorders or problems.

Some of the disorders discussed in this chapter are lifetime diagnoses. Individuals and their family members can become adept at managing, compensating for, and working around the symptoms of these disorders. Neurological factors are often the most direct cause of many of the disorders discussed in this chapter, such as mental retardation and learning disorders; psychological and social factors may play a role, but often only an indirect one. For instance, poor pregnant mothers and children raised in poverty (social factor) may be more likely to be exposed to substances that cause certain types of mental retardation in children. Psychological and social factors also play a role in how well an individual adapts to and compensates for his or her disorder.

For many of the disorders in this chapter, the specific mechanisms of feedback loops among the three factors are not as well documented as they are for disorders discussed in most other chapters. For this reason, some of the sections that describe the contributions of neurological, psychological, and social factors do not include information on feedback loops among these factors.

Mental Retardation

When either Lela or Carlos calls Richie's name, he often seems to ignore it. They can tell that he's not deaf—he clearly notices street noises and other sounds and he startles in response to loud noises. He seems to understand *some* of what people say to him, but his cognitive abilities are less developed than Javier's and Pia's were when they were his age; Richie's intellectual functioning definitely doesn't seem normal. Could he be mentally retarded?

In this section we examine mental retardation in more detail—its criteria and causes and the treatments provided to people with this disorder.

What Is Mental Retardation?

Mental retardation refers to intelligence that is significantly below normal—an IQ approximately equal to or less than 70 (where the mean IQ is set at 100)—and that impairs daily functioning. The deficits in intellectual ability and daily functioning (see Table 14.1) must have begun before 18 years of age, and thus cannot be the result of brain trauma in adulthood. The IQ cutoff of 70 or less is two standard deviations or more below average ability. Mental retardation, along with personality disorders, is an Axis II diagnosis because the authors of DSM-IV wanted to ensure that symptoms of Axis I disorders do not overshadow the possibility that a given individual has comorbid mental retardation (or a personality disorder) (American Psychiatric Association, 2000). The term *intellectual disability* is sometimes used as a synonym for mental retardation.

DSM-IV-TR specifies the following four levels of mental retardation, which are set by ranges of IQ scores (Criterion A). In general, the lower the IQ score, the more impaired the individual is likely to be. However, an individual's IQ scores can vary by about 5 points because of testing error, so the ranges generally allow a 5-point leeway for assigning the level of retardation and level of adaptive functioning:

- *Mild mental retardation.* The IQ score can range from 50–55 to 70; 85% of people with mental retardation fall into this group. People in this mild

Table 14.1 ▶ DSM-IV-TR Diagnostic Criteria for Mental Retardation

A. Significantly subaverage intellectual functioning: an IQ of approximately 70 or below on an individually administered IQ test (for infants, a clinical judgment of significantly subaverage intellectual functioning).

B. Concurrent deficits or impairments in present adaptive functioning (i.e., the person's effectiveness in meeting the standards expected for his or her age by his or her cultural group) in at least two of the following areas:

communication,
self-care,
home living,
social/interpersonal skills,
use of community resources,
self-direction,
functional academic skills,
work,
leisure,
health, and
safety.

C. The onset is before age 18 years.

Source: Reprinted with permission from the Diagnostic and Statistical Manual of Mental Disorders, Text Revision, Fourth Edition, (Copyright 2000) American Psychiatric Association.

range may be able to function relatively independently with training but usually need additional help and support during stressful periods.

- *Moderate mental retardation.* The IQ score can range from 35–40 to 50–55; 10% of people with mental retardation fall into this group. Although they are not able to function independently, with training and supervision, people in this group may be able to perform unskilled work and take basic care of themselves.

- *Severe mental retardation.* The IQ score can range from 20–25 to 35–40; approximately 3–4% of people with mental retardation fall into this group. Adults in this group are likely to live with their family or in a supervised setting and are able to perform simple tasks only with close supervision. They may be able to learn to read a few basic words and do simple counting. During childhood, they may begin speaking later than other children.

- *Profound mental retardation.* The IQ score falls below 20 or 25; 1–2% of those with mental retardation fall into this group. People in this group need constant supervision or help to perform simple tasks; they are likely to have significant neurological problems.

Like Sean Penn's character in the movie *I Am Sam*, people with mild mental retardation can, with training, learn to function independently. In this scene Penn is shown with Michelle Pfeiffer, who plays his lawyer in his fight to retain custody of his young daughter.

Figure 14.1 illustrates the IQ scores associated with the four levels of mental retardation.

Although an individual's IQ score serves as a guide, the most important criterion for determining the level of mental retardation is the level of adaptive functioning (Criterion B), which indicates how well the person can cope with life's daily demands compared to others of the same age and cultural background. Information from parents and teachers may help the clinician to determine the individual's ability to function. Depending on IQ and level of adaptive functioning, someone with mental retardation may require anywhere from minimal supervision to constant care. Many, like Larry in Case 14.1, have needs and abilities that fall somewhere in the middle.

CASE **14.1** ▶ FROM THE OUTSIDE: Mental Retardation

Larry, a 34-year-old man with moderate mental retardation . . . had been referred for complaints of seeing "monsters," "scary faces," and "the bogeyman." He initially appeared paranoid and delusional, describing the feared bogeyman in detail. An assessment of possible neurochemical or physical factors that might help explain the recent onset of these symptoms yielded no significant diagnostic information. . . .

Larry's perception of monsters was specific to certain situations, such as being alone in a dark room. . . .

Specifically, when asked to go alone to any dark place [including the dark stairwell in his group home, where Larry must go to carry out his assigned chore of taking down the trash], he became agitated, resisted, and made loud statements about monsters and scary faces. . . .

Larry's monsters could be attributed to his limited means of communicating his fear of being alone in the dark. [It appears, then, that Larry has a phobic response to the dark.] . . .

Even if the residence staff excused him from this task, Larry would remain agitated because he believed he was shirking an important responsibility.

(Nezu, Nezu, & Gill-Weiss, 1992, pp. 78, 164)

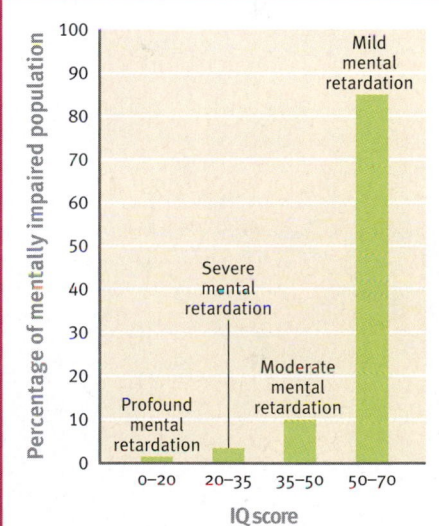

Figure 14.1

Note: The high-end cutoff for profound, severe, and moderate mental retardation can be 5 IQ points higher than noted in this graph if the individual has a low level of functioning for that IQ score.

14.1 ▶ The Four Levels of Mental Retardation There are four levels of mental retardation, each of which corresponds to a range of IQ scores. As the graph indicates, most people with mental retardation fall in the *mild* range, with increasingly smaller numbers of people having more severe retardation.

Larry had two disorders: mental retardation and a specific phobia. Because of his mental retardation, he had difficulty explaining his fears. He received CBT treatment for his phobia, which was successful, and he became able to go down to the basement without fear.

Like people of normal intelligence, people with mental retardation exhibit a wide variety of personality characteristics: Some are passive or easygoing, and others are impulsive or aggressive; those who have severe or profound mental retardation—or even moderate mental retardation, like Larry—may have difficulty communicating

Table 14.2 ▸ Mental Retardation Facts at a Glance

Prevalence

- Approximately 1% of the general population has mental retardation; however, prevalence estimates vary depending on the survey method used and the particular population studied.

Onset

- Severe and profound retardation are generally identified at birth, although in some cases, mental retardation is caused by a medical condition later in childhood, such as head trauma.
- Mild retardation is sometimes not diagnosed until relatively late in childhood, although the onset may have been earlier.

Comorbidity

- Compared to the general population, people with mental retardation are three to four times more likely to have an additional psychological disorder.
- Among the most common comorbid disorders are major depressive disorder and attention-deficit/hyperactivity disorder.
- Symptoms of mental retardation may affect the presentation of symptoms of a comorbid disorder; people with severe or profound mental retardation, for instance, may not be able to report feelings of hopelessness or depressed mood.

Course

- The diagnosis is typically lifelong for moderate to profound mental retardation, but beneficial environmental factors can improve adaptive functioning for those with mild mental retardation to the point where they no longer meet all the criteria for the disorder.
- Educational opportunities, support, and stimulation can improve the level of functioning.

Gender Differences

- Mental retardation occurs more frequently in males, with a male-to-female ratio of 1.5 to 1.

Cultural Differences

- Although the criteria for mental retardation used in other countries are similar to those used in the United States, they are not always the same; such differences may account for the higher prevalence rates in some other countries, such as 4.5% in France (Oakland et al., 2003).

Source: Unless otherwise noted, the source for information is American Psychiatric Association, 2000.

verbally, which can heighten aggressive or impulsive tendencies. Unfortunately, people with mental retardation are more likely than average to be exploited or abused by others. Table 14.2 lists additional facts about mental retardation.

Understanding Mental Retardation

There are many neurological paths to mental retardation, some of which arise because the fetus is exposed to certain types of substances (such as drugs or a virus) or to other stimuli (such as radiation); such harmful substances and stimuli are referred to as **teratogens**. Mental retardation may also arise from particular complications during labor (such as occurs when a newborn receives insufficient oxygen during birth) or from exposure to high levels of lead prenatally or during childhood (which can occur when young children eat lead-based paint chips or inhale lead-based dust from sanded paint; prior to 1978, lead was an ingredient used in paints).

Neurological Factors: Teratogens and Genes

One type of teratogen is environmental toxins, to which a fetus typically is exposed through the placenta after the toxin has entered the mother's bloodstream. Examples of environmental toxins include synthetic chemicals such as methyl mercury,

Teratogens
Substances or other stimuli that are harmful to a fetus.

Table 14.3 ▸ Genetic Causes of Mental Retardation

Cause of Mental Retardation	Genetic Abnormality
• *Down syndrome*	• Abnormality in chromosome 21
• *Rett's disorder* (females only)	• Abnormality in X chromosome (which is lethal for male fetuses)
• *Fragile X* (the most common cause of inherited mental retardation)	• Repetition of a piece of genetic code on the X chromosome that becomes progressively more severe in each generation
• *Prader-Willi* and *Angelman Syndromes*	• Deletion on chromosome 15 that has different consequences depending on which parent's genes contribute the deletion
• *Phenylketonuria* (PKU)	• A genetically based defect in an enzyme, *phenylalanine hydroxylase*, that leads to a failure to convert phenylalanine to tyrosine. Unconverted phenylalanine is toxic to brain cells, leading to mental retardation. Mental retardation can be prevented if PKU is identified (through a blood test at birth) and the individual adheres to a diet that restricts phenylalanine.
• *Congenital hypothyroidism*	• Inadequate production of thyroid hormone caused by a genetic mutation. The fetus gets thyroid hormone from the mother, but after birth the deficiency leads to defects in the developing brain. If hypothyroidism is not detected within the first 3 months of life, the damage is not reversible even with thyroid hormone replacement.

polychlorinated biphenyls (PCBs), and mixtures of chemicals such as those found in pesticides. Exposure to these toxins in the first trimester of pregnancy can affect important early developmental processes of the central nervous system (Lanphear, Vorhees, & Bellinger, 2005). Mental retardation may also arise because of a variety of genetic abnormalities, listed in Table 14.3.

The cognitive and behavioral deficits observed in people with mental retardation arise because the brain does not process information appropriately, often because of abnormal brain structure. In fact, using evidence from autopsies and neuroimaging, researchers report that people with some forms of mental retardation have larger heads, which may suggest larger brains (Herbert, 2005), which in turn could result from any number of factors, including larger fluid-filled ventricles in the center of the brain, bulkier white matter (myelin around the axons), or greater numbers of glial cells.

In contrast, with other forms of mental retardation, people have smaller than normal heads. For example, this occurs in people who suffer from *fetal alcohol syndrome*. This syndrome is a set of birth defects caused by the mother's alcohol use during pregnancy (alcohol is a teratogen). Moreover, smaller head size may arise because the sizes of some specific brain areas are reduced. In fetal alcohol syndrome, the cerebellum, the basal ganglia, and the corpus callosum are affected (Riley & McGee, 2005), all of which are involved in coordination and smooth motor movement. The frontal lobes are also affected, specifically the portions involved in planning, carrying out tasks, and controlling impulsive behavior. All of these activities are difficult for many children with fetal alcohol syndrome.

Although severe or profound mental retardation often involves global abnormalities, each case of mild or moderate mental retardation may present a unique profile of specific impaired abilities, related to the particular cause of the retardation.

Psychological Factors: Problem Behaviors

Individuals with mental retardation often show two types of problematic behaviors that are not specifically mentioned in the DSM-IV-TR criteria: (1) **stereotyped behaviors** (also referred to as *stereotypies*), which are repetitive behaviors that don't serve a function, such as hand flapping, slight but fast finger and hand motions,

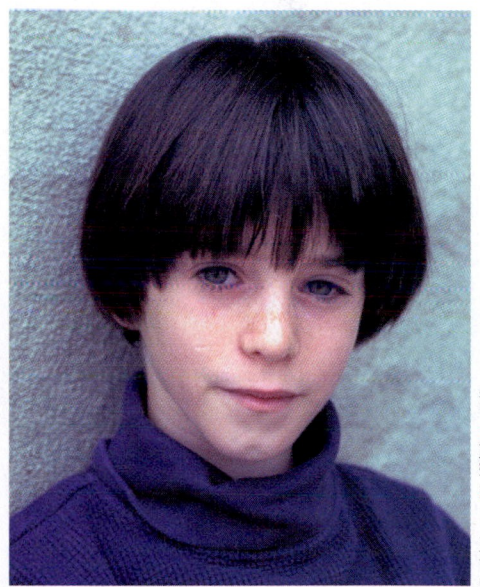

David Young-Wolff/Photo Edit

The characteristic facial features associated with fetal alcohol syndrome include small eyes, a proportionately large smooth space between the upper lip and the nose, and a thin upper lip.

Stereotyped behaviors
Repetitive behaviors—such as body rocking—that do not serve a function; also referred to as *stereotypies*.

When this child gets excited, she engages in the stereotyped behavior of hand-flapping. Other stereotyped behaviors exhibited by people with mental retardation include rocking back and forth and repeatedly moving a finger.

Maria Platt-Evans/Photo Researchers

and body rocking (American Psychiatric Association, 2000); and (2) *self-injurious behaviors*, such as hitting the head against something and hitting or biting oneself. People with mental retardation who exhibit both stereotypic behaviors and self-injurious behaviors have greater deficits in nonverbal social skills than those with only one type of problematic behavior (Matson et al., 2006). Other problematic behaviors that often go along with mental retardation include consistently choosing to interact with objects rather than people, inappropriately touching others, and resisting physical contact or affection. How or why all these behaviors arise is not yet known.

Social Factors: Understimulation

Another way in which mental retardation can arise is when an infant's environment is severely understimulating or the infant is undernourished (Dennis, 1973; Dong & Greenough, 2004; Skeels & Dye, 1939). However, in 30–40% of cases, there is no clear cause for the mental retardation; when there are clear etiological factors, the diagnosis is generally in the severe or profound range.

In sum, most cases of mental retardation arise primarily from neurological factors—genes or teratogens, which in turn lead to abnormal brain structure and function, leading to cognitive deficits. Moreover, children with mental retardation may exhibit stereotyped or self-injurious behaviors.

Treating Mental Retardation

Mental retardation cannot be "cured," but interventions can help people to function more independently in daily life. Such interventions are designed to improve the person's ability to communicate and other skills. But more than that, clinicians try to prevent mental retardation from arising in the first place. Prevention efforts seek to avert or reduce the factors that cause mental retardation.

Targeting Neurological Factors: Prevention

Because the key causes of mental retardation are neurological, this type of factor is the target of prevention efforts. Two successful prevention efforts focus on *phenylketonuria* (PKU) and exposure to lead. Since the 1950s, virtually all newborns in the United States receive a test to detect whether they have PKU, which consists of a problem metabolizing the enzyme phenylalanine hydroxylase. For newborns testing positive, lifelong dietary modifications can prevent any brain damage, thus preventing mental retardation. Another successful prevention effort involves childhood exposure to lead, which can lead to brain abnormalities. As noted earlier, lead was banned as an ingredient in paint in 1978; laws were passed that required landlords and homeowners to inform any prospective renters or buyers of any known lead paint on the property. Beginning in the 1970s, lead was also phased out as an additive to gasoline. As a result of these measures, lead exposure—and lead-induced mental retardation—has decreased.

There are no neurological treatments for mental retardation, although symptoms of comorbid disorders may respond to medication.

Targeting Psychological and Social Factors: Communication

Given the deficits and heterogeneous symptoms that accompany mental retardation, no single symptom is the focus of all psychological and social treatments. Rather, psychological and social treatments depend on the individual's specific constellation of symptoms of mental retardation and possible comorbid disorders. In some cases, treatment is designed to target significant communication deficits. Such treatment may teach nonvocal communication, for example, using a technique called the Picture Exchange Communication System (PECS) (Bondy & Frost, 1994). With this system, children learn to give a picture of the desired item to someone in exchange for that item. Important elements of the program include learning to recognize which picture corresponds to what is wanted (cognitive skill), going over to someone to give the picture (social skill), and responding appropriately to the question "What do you want?" (social and communication skills).

Targeting Social Factors: Accommodation in the Classroom—It's the Law

With the passage of the Americans with Disabilities Act in 1990 and the subsequent Individuals with Disabilities Education Act (IDEA) in 1997, eligible children with disabilities between the ages of 3 and 21 are guaranteed special education and related services that are individually tailored to the child's needs, at no cost to the parents. Each child with disabilities receives a comprehensive evaluation, and the child is placed in the least restrictive environment that responds to his or her needs. An *individualized education program* (IEP) specifies educational goals as well as supplementary services or products that should be used to help the student utilize the regular curriculum.

For many children, one goal of the IEP is to facilitate **inclusion**—placing students with disabilities in a regular classroom, with guidelines for any accommodations that the regular classroom teacher or special education teacher should make. Note that *mainstreaming* is not the same as inclusion; mainstreaming simply refers to placing a child with disabilities into a regular classroom, with no curriculum adjustments to accommodate the disability. With inclusion, a child with mild mental retardation placed in a regular classroom may take much longer than his or her classmates to learn to read, and his or her reading fluency will not be as high as that of classmates. At school, such children may meet regularly with a speech and language therapist and a reading and math specialist during periods when the rest of the class is doing work that is beyond their ability.

Legal mandates have also brought people with mental retardation (and other disabilities) out from the shadows of institutional living into society: Depending on the severity of their retardation, they live in communities, hold jobs, and have families.

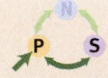

Photo Courtesy of Pyramid Educational Consultants, Inc. reserves all rights to this photo

With the Picture Exchange Communication System, a child who has mental retardation with poor verbal communication skills can make his or her desires known: The child presents a card with the picture of the desired object to another person, who then may give the actual object to the child.

Paul Conklin/Photo Edit

Like this girl with Down syndrome, youngsters with mild to moderate mental retardation may be placed in regular classrooms, either as part of inclusion (in which the teacher makes specific accommodations based on the child's special needs) or mainstreaming (in which the teacher doesn't make specific accommodations).

Inclusion
The placement of students with disabilities in a regular classroom, with guidelines for any accommodations that the regular classroom teacher or special education teacher should make.

In some cases, children with mental retardation (or other disabilities) may frequently behave in ways that disrupt the class—yelling, having temper tantrums, and acting aggressively toward others. In such cases, the children may be transferred to schools for students with special needs who cannot be accommodated in a regular classroom.

Is mental retardation an appropriate diagnosis for Richie Enriquez? It may well be—his language abilities are significantly delayed. However, he also has additional symptoms that are not explained by mental retardation—he avoids eye contact and hardly smiles. In the next section, we'll examine a set of disorders that might better account for these problems.

Key Concepts and Facts About Mental Retardation

- The diagnosis of mental retardation requires both an IQ score at or below 70 *and* impaired daily functioning. The four levels of mental retardation are mild, moderate, severe, and profound. Some people with mental retardation—particularly at the severe or profound level—may have difficulty communicating verbally.

- Neurological factors are the primary direct cause of most cases of mental retardation—usually a genetic abnormality or prenatal exposure to a teratogen such as alcohol. In turn, the genetic abnormality or teratogen alters brain structure and function.

- Although mental retardation cannot be cured, many types can be prevented, including PKU-related retardation (through early detection and dietary modification) and retardation caused by lead poisoning (by removing lead from the environment). Interventions are designed to improve the person's functioning by increasing his or her communication and daily living skills.

- Children whose symptoms make verbal communication difficult may be taught alternative methods of communication, such as the Picture Exchange Communication System (PECS).

- Legally, children with mental retardation are entitled to special education and related services, tailored to their individual needs through an individualized education program (IEP).

Making a Diagnosis

- Reread Case 14.1 about Larry, and determine whether or not his symptoms meet the criteria for mental retardation. Specifically, list which criteria apply and which do not. If you would like more information to determine his diagnosis, what information—specifically—would you want, and in what ways would the information influence your decision? If you think he did have mental retardation, what level of retardation do you think he has and why—on what do you base your decision?

Pervasive Developmental Disorders

Richie Enriquez exhibits some behaviors that are not typical of individuals diagnosed with mental retardation: He avoids making eye contact with people and can spend hours—literally hours—playing with a glittery plastic ball. When his mother, Lela, takes the toy away from him, perhaps because it's time for lunch, he has a nuclear-sized temper tantrum: "He screams, he cries, he hits his head against the wall. . . . I don't know what to do. When I try to hold him, to comfort him, it seems to make things even worse. I've never seen a child like him." Carlos notes that "if the evening routine—dinner, bath, three books, bed—varies, if I forget to read the third book, Richie freaks out, rocking himself and screaming. And he has no interest in playing with Javier and Pia—even though they try so hard to get him to play or to laugh." From these descriptions, Richie's behaviors sound like symptoms of autism, a pervasive developmental disorder.

Pervasive developmental disorders are a set of disorders that have in common severe deficits in communication and in social interaction skills, and may also involve stereotyped behaviors and narrow interests. The word *pervasive* indicates that the symptoms affect all areas of the individual's life. Pervasive developmental disorders primarily arise from neurological abnormalities and dysfunctions (Kundert & Trimarchi, 2006; Ozonoff, Rogers, & Hendren, 2003). Most pervasive developmental disorders become evident during infancy or early childhood, and many children also have comorbid mental retardation, which may be true of Richie. Children for whom mental retardation is the only psychological

Pervasive developmental disorders
A set of developmental disorders that have in common severe deficits in communication and in social interaction skills and may also involve stereotyped behaviors and narrow interests.

disorder usually look people in the eye, and they tend to respond when hearing their names and to smile at other people. In contrast, children with a pervasive developmental disorder—with or without mental retardation—generally avoid eye contact and shy away from social interactions.

Four specific disorders are included in the DSM-IV-TR category of pervasive developmental disorders: *autistic disorder, Asperger's disorder, childhood disintegrative disorder*, and *Rett's disorder*. Children who have symptoms of a pervasive developmental disorder that impairs their functioning but do not meet the criteria for any of these four disorders will be diagnosed with *pervasive developmental disorder not otherwise specified*.

We first examine *autism spectrum disorders*—what they are, their causes and treatments—and then briefly consider the two less common pervasive developmental disorders that include profound neurological abnormalities: *childhood disintegrative disorder* and *Rett's disorder*.

Autism Spectrum Disorders

The term *autism spectrum disorders* is sometimes used as a synonym for *pervasive developmental disorders*; however, many researchers and clinicians consider autistic spectrum disorders to include only the two disorders that have related symptoms and etiology: autistic disorder and Asperger's disorder (Towbin, Mauk, & Batshaw, 2002). This is how we will use the term in this chapter. By "spectrum" we imply that there is a continuum, from mild to severe, and a given individual can fall somewhere along that continuum.

Autism: What Is Autistic Disorder?

Autism, or as is it named in DSM-IV-TR, **autistic disorder**, is characterized by delayed or impaired communication and social skills, along with restricted and repetitive behaviors and interests. The dysfunction is pervasive: It is severe and spans a number of areas of childhood development. Table 14.4 lists the DSM-IV-TR criteria. Among the pervasive developmental disorders, autistic disorder has the most specific diagnostic criteria.

People with autism tend to be oblivious to—and so appear to ignore—others. Younger children with autism appear to be uninterested in making friends. Some older children may want to make friends, but they don't understand the basic rules of social interaction; thus, their attempts are unlikely to be successful. To understand how symptoms of autism translate into daily life, consider the following list of "peculiarities" that a mother compiled about her 4-year-old son, George, before he was diagnosed with autism (quoted verbatim from Moore, 2006, pp. 94–95):

- He talks [by reciting] quotations and by imitating adult speech.
- Has poor social interaction. Doesn't know how to play with others.
- Avoids eye contact with strangers.
- He is very excitable (easily aroused, not easy to calm).

Autistic disorder
A pervasive developmental disorder that arises in childhood and is characterized by delayed or impaired communication and social skills, along with restricted and repetitive behaviors and interests; also referred to as *autism*.

Table 14.4 ▸ DSM-IV-TR Diagnostic Criteria for Autistic Disorder

A. A total of six (or more) items from (1), (2), and (3), with at least two from (1), and one each from (2) and (3):

(1) qualitative impairment in social interaction, as manifested by at least two of the following:

    (a) marked impairment in the use of multiple nonverbal behaviors such as eye-to-eye gaze, facial expression, body postures, and gestures to regulate social interaction;

    (b) failure to develop peer relationships appropriate to developmental level;

    (c) a lack of spontaneous seeking to share enjoyment, interests, or achievements with other people (e.g., by a lack of showing, bringing, or pointing out objects of interest);

    (d) lack of social or emotional reciprocity.

(2) qualitative impairments in communication as manifested by at least one of the following:

    (a) delay in, or total lack of, the development of spoken language (not accompanied by an attempt to compensate through alternative modes of communication such as gesture or mime);

    (b) in individuals with adequate speech, marked impairment in the ability to initiate or sustain a conversation with others;

    (c) stereotyped and repetitive use of language or idiosyncratic language;

    (d) lack of varied, spontaneous make-believe play or social imitative play appropriate to developmental level.

(3) restricted repetitive and stereotyped patterns of behavior, interests, and activities, as manifested by at least one of the following:

    (a) encompassing preoccupation with one or more stereotyped and restricted patterns of interest that is abnormal either in intensity or focus;

    (b) apparently inflexible adherence to specific, nonfunctional routines or rituals;

    (c) stereotyped and repetitive motor mannerisms (e.g., hand or finger flapping or twisting, or complex whole-body movements);

    (d) persistent preoccupation with parts of objects.

B. Delays or abnormal functioning in at least one of the following areas, with onset prior to age 3 years:

(1) social interaction;

(2) language as used in social communication;

(3) symbolic or imaginative play.

C. The disturbance is not better accounted for by Rett's Disorder or Childhood Disintegrative Disorder [both discussed later in this chapter].

Source: Reprinted with permission from the Diagnostic and Statistical Manual of Mental Disorders, Text Revision, Fourth Edition, (Copyright 2000) American Psychiatric Association.

- He complains about strong stimuli, such as the sun, loud noises.
- Abnormalities of attention, including the ability to shut people out and be absorbed in something trivial for a long time.
- Loves nature, will stand and look at the moon for as long as he is allowed, despite freezing weather.
- Has a strong aversion to strangers, groups, and crowds.
- Obsessive.
- Ritualistic.
- Lines up [Lego bricks or matches them by color, but] doesn't build. Always destroys.
- Occasionally plays with feces.
- Doesn't dress or undress—just beginning to put on trousers and coat.
- Could recognize simple words at twenty months.
- Has a strong reaction to colors.
- Never asks questions except where is Mummy, Daddy, Sam.
- Only just starting to correlate facial expressions of others to emotion.

These behaviors might not be that unusual for a toddler, but they are definitely not typical for a 4-year-old. The items on George's mother's list span the problem areas that are the hallmarks of autism: impaired social interactions, impaired communication, and restricted and repetitive behaviors. Some of George's symptoms—symptoms of autism—overlap with symptoms of childhood schizophrenia; playing with feces, not dressing oneself, and becoming very upset in response to unwanted change could be signs of disorganized symptoms of schizophrenia. However, symptoms of autism are present before age 3, and symptoms of childhood schizophrenia arise *after* age 3.

When assessed with an intelligence tests that includes both verbal and visual elements, many individuals with autism are also diagnosed as having mental retardation. When researchers use an intelligence test that does not rely on verbal instructions or responses, however, intelligence scores of individuals with autism are often significantly higher—in or above the average intelligence range (Dawson et al., 2005). Moreover, unlike those with mental retardation, people with autism may not be impaired in all domains (though, as a rule, the impairments are general enough to be considered "pervasive"). In fact, about 20% of people with autism have pockets of unique skills relating to art, music, numbers, or calendars, such as the ability to identify the day of the week on which a given date fell, even when the date is many years in the past (Hermelin, 2001); such people are sometimes referred to as *autistic savants*. James, the person described in Case 14.2, has a remarkable ability to remember information he has heard.

CASE 14.2 ▶ FROM THE OUTSIDE: Autistic Disorder

James was the third of four children, born following an uncomplicated pregnancy and labor. His health during the first 3 months of life was good, but shortly thereafter his mother expressed concern because of his sensitivities to light and sound, his failure to make an anticipatory response to being picked up, his fluctuating moods between inconsolable crying and extreme passiveness, and his failure to look at her when she fed him. She reported that he preferred lying in his crib, staring at the mobile, to being held or played with. Because his motor milestones appeared at the appropriate times, James's pediatrician reassured his mother that his development was fine. By age 16 months, James had not begun to babble or say single words, and spent most of his time in a corner, repetitively moving toy cars back and forth. At 20 months, other symptoms emerged: he developed unusual hand movements and body postures; his obliviousness to people increased; he reacted to even the most subtle interruption in his routine or other changes in the world with extreme disorganization and panic; he developed a fascination with light switches and with studying tiny bits of paper and twigs.

At 4 years, James had not yet begun to speak socially to others, but could identify by name many numbers and all of the letters of the alphabet. . . . He persisted in lining up objects in the most complex patterns, but could never use objects appropriately. . . . At about the age of

4½ years, he began to echo long and complicated sentences, some of which his mother reported he may have heard days or even weeks before. He was able to complete puzzles designed for 8- and 9-year olds quickly, but was unable to reproduce a line or circle.

At about age 5, James made his first spontaneous statement. His mother reported that he had been looking at the sky and said, "It looks like a flower." He did not speak again for 8 months, but then began talking in full sentences. . . . When he met strangers, he mechanically introduced himself without ever establishing eye contact, and then rushed on to ask what the person's birthday, anniversary, and social security number were, often appearing to pause long enough to get the answers. Years later, upon re-meeting the person, he was able to recite back these facts.

(Caparulo & Cohen, 1977, pp. 623–624; case printed in Sattler, 1982, p. 474)

Asperger's disorder
A psychological disorder on the autism spectrum characterized by problems with social interaction and narrowed behaviors—similar to but less severe than autism—but in which language and cognitive development are in the normal range; also referred to as *Asperger's syndrome*.

Like children with mental retardation (but unlike other children), children who have autism (1) tend to engage in very repetitive play and (2) often display stereotyped behaviors. They insist on repeating the same behaviors or activities for much longer periods than other children do. People with autism also become distressed when certain routines are not carried out or completed, as was Richie when his father varied the evening activities in any way; to calm themselves down, they may rock themselves, as did Richie.

For the most part, people with autism do not go through childhood milestones (language, social, or motor) in a normal fashion. They may speak with a monotone voice, and the rhythm of their speech may be odd. Moreover, they often have a variety of problems with attention and may be impulsive or aggressive; they may be more sensitive to sensory stimuli, leading them to shun physical contact with others. Typically, children with autism have only one narrow interest, such as the names of subway stations. Richie probably has mental retardation *and* autism: Mental retardation best explains his general cognitive slowing and his language problems, which are not limited to social interactions. His other odd behaviors—such as avoidance of eye contact, lack of social interest in his siblings, and extreme preoccupation with his ball—are best accounted for by autism. Table 14.5 provides additional facts about autism.

What Is Asperger's Disorder?

A disorder related to autism, but less severe, is **Asperger's disorder** (also referred to as *Asperger's syndrome*, or simply, *Asperger's*), which involves similar types of problems with social interaction and narrowed behaviors. However, unlike individuals with autism, the diagnostic criteria specify that those with Asperger's have language and cognitive abilities that are within the normal range—and so mental retardation cannot be present.

Children with Asperger's disorder often have problems with the relatively subtle social cues related to language—the indirect or implied meanings behind words. For instance, someone with Asperger's might interpret "I'd

Table 14.5 ▶ Autistic Disorder Facts at a Glance

Prevalence

- Significantly less than 1% of the population has this disorder; prevalence estimates range from 0.02% to 0.2%.
- The reported prevalence of autism is increasing (Atladóttir, 2007; Hertz-Picciotto & Delwiche, 2009), at least in part because of earlier diagnosis of the disorder (Parner, Schendel, & Thorsen, 2008).

Onset

- Symptoms usually arise during infancy and include an indifference or aversion to physical contact, no eye contact or smiles, a lack of response to parents' voices, a lack of emotional attachment to parents, and the unusual use of toys (Ozonoff et al., 2008).
- According to the DSM-IV-TR criteria, symptoms must arise by age 3.
- Autism may be diagnosed as early as 14 months of age (Landa, Holman, & Garrett-Mayer, 2007).

Comorbidity

- Mental retardation is a common comorbid disorder—between 50% and 70% of those with autism also have mental retardation (Sigman, Spence, & Wang, 2006). However, some researchers believe the high comorbidity is an overestimate (Edelson, 2006), particularly because individuals with autism tend to have higher IQs when tested using nonverbal IQ tests.
- Some researchers make a distinction between autism that co-occurs with mental retardation, which leads to a relatively low level of functioning, and autism without mental retardation, which is not generally associated with as low a level of functioning (Koyama et al., 2007).

Course

- Children with autism often improve in some areas of functioning during the elementary school years (Shattuck et al., 2007).
- During adolescence, some children's symptoms worsen, whereas other children's symptoms improve (American Psychiatric Association, 2000; Shattuck et al., 2007).

Gender Differences

- Males are four to five times more likely than females to develop autism.

Source: Unless otherwise noted, the source for information is American Psychiatric Association, 2000.

Table 14.6 ▶ DSM-IV-TR Diagnostic Criteria for Asperger's Disorder

A. Qualitative impairment in social interaction, as manifested by at least two of the following:

(1) marked impairment in the use of multiple nonverbal behaviors such as eye-to-eye gaze, facial expression, body postures, and gestures to regulate social interaction;

(2) failure to develop peer relationships appropriate to developmental level;

(3) a lack of spontaneous seeking to share enjoyment, interests, or achievements with other people (e.g., by a lack of showing, bringing, or pointing out objects of interest to other people);

(4) lack of social or emotional reciprocity.

B. Restricted repetitive and stereotyped patterns of behavior, interests, and activities, as manifested by at least one of the following:

(1) encompassing preoccupation with one or more stereotyped and restricted patterns of interest that is abnormal either in intensity or focus;

(2) apparently inflexible adherence to specific, nonfunctional routines or rituals;

(3) stereotyped and repetitive motor mannerisms (e.g., hand or finger flapping or twisting, or complex whole-body movements);

(4) persistent preoccupation with parts of objects.

C. The disturbance causes clinically significant impairment in social, occupational, or other important areas of functioning.

D. There is no clinically significant general delay in language (e.g., single words used by age 2 years, communicative phrases used by age 3 years).

E. There is no clinically significant delay in cognitive development or in the development of age-appropriate self-help skills, adaptive behavior (other than in social interaction), and curiosity about the environment in childhood.

F. Criteria are not met for another specific Pervasive Developmental Disorder or Schizophrenia [discussed in Chapter 12].

Source: Reprinted with permission from the Diagnostic and Statistical Manual of Mental Disorders, Text Revision, Fourth Edition, (Copyright 2000) American Psychiatric Association.

like to borrow that" not as a request to borrow the object but simply as an expressed wish. Table 14.6 lists the complete diagnostic criteria.

People with Asperger's often avoid sustained eye contact, and don't use other nonverbal behaviors, such as facial expressions or body language, in normal ways (Criterion A1). And because they don't understand social conventions, their behavior can (inadvertently) communicate disinterest in others. Whereas autism is characterized by an indifference to others, Asperger's tends to involve a lack of awareness of other people's *responses*. For example, someone with Asperger's may continue talking about a topic long past the point at which the listener's interest has waned. The person with Asperger's doesn't notice— doesn't pick up on the social cues that indicate that the other person is no longer listening.

To be diagnosed with Asperger's, the individual must have symptoms that impair the ability to function at school and care for himself or herself. Unlike those with autism, however, children with Asperger's develop in all areas (including language) except social functioning. In fact, the disorder often isn't diagnosed in early childhood because all other areas of functioning are relatively normal. DSM-IV-TR includes Asperger's disorder in the category of pervasive developmental disorders in order to group it with autism. However, Asperger's does *not* involve pervasive deficits. Table 14.7 provides additional facts about this disorder.

Like people with autism, people with Asperger's often develop an all-consuming but narrow interest, spending large amounts of time on it, to the point of neglecting other activities. Josh, described in Case 14.3, has a consuming passion about directions.

CASE 14.3 ▶ FROM THE OUTSIDE: Asperger's Disorder

Josh is described by his older brother Ryan, a college student.

Josh, a lot of the times is to himself [sic]. He's off to the side, he likes to be in his own little world. And he's got kind of . . . I want to say, a downward pull, he wants to think that everyone wants to threaten him. For the longest time I'd yell at him because I'd say, "Stop crying, why are you crying? There's no need to cry. I didn't say anything!" But to him, it's a threat if you say something and . . . he can't control the way he feels. . . .

. . . when he needs his time, you give him his time. And when he's ready to come out and be social again, then he'll come out.

And I try my best to introduce him to all the people that I know so he doesn't feel uncomfortable and alone.

. . . when he's doing something that he wants to learn about or that he's interested in or that I've done, he's extraordinarily lively. He's very happy. And that's when he gets to his loud stages where he'll laugh and he's way up there. I love to see him laugh, but when something is funny he is, horrendously loud, he's over the top . . . sometimes I'll take his hand and I'll give him a little squeeze on the hand and that's kind of his cue to kind of like ease it down a little bit.

Josh is amazing at directions . . . he can give directions to anybody to anything, if you are anywhere in the US, he'll tell you where you are. . . . I get lost all the time, directions are not my thing and . . . I'll call Josh, now . . . when like, I'm out on the road. . . . I'm like "Josh, I don't know where I'm at" and he'll say like, "What's around you?" and I'll tell him and he'll know exactly where I am. It's really cool.

(Coulter, 2007)

Josh is not aware when he is too loud, because he isn't able to read other people's nonverbal signals appropriately. Such social communication problems can lead to depression and anxiety in people with Asperger's: They are unable to understand and respond to others appropriately and thus may be rejected or ridiculed (Meyer et al., 2006). Their problems in understanding social cues can also lead to difficulty in feeling empathy (Lawson, Baron-Cohen, & Wheelwright, 2004).

People with Asperger's often fall into one of two social patterns: (1) They become socially isolated, minimizing contact with others (they are similar to people with autism in this regard); or (2) they become socially annoying, seeking out interactions with others but, because of their limited social skills, imposing their desires on others. Children with Asperger's often do best socially when interacting either with adults (who are more tolerant of their social foibles) or with younger children, who are willing to be bossed around by an older child (Kundert & Trimarchi, 2006).

Distinguishing Between Asperger's Disorder and Other Disorders

Asperger's disorder can sometimes be difficult to distinguish from other disorders, particularly autism without comorbid mental retardation. However, two factors typically arise in autism but not in Asperger's disorder:

1. language problems in addition to social difficulties, and
2. extreme distress when change is foisted upon them.

Even in the area of social functioning there can be differences: An individual with autism is often uninterested in social interactions, whereas an individual with Asperger's may be interested but does not possess the social skills necessary for smooth interactions.

Some symptoms of Asperger's disorder overlap with those of schizoid personality disorder (Chapter 13): Both disorders involve a lack of close friendships and a preference for solitary activities. However, older children and adolescents with Asperger's are more interested in social interactions and relationships than are people with schizoid personality disorder.

People with Asperger's are distinguished from those with normal social awkwardness by their difficulty in understanding social cues. Furthermore, the all-consuming

Table 14.7 ▶ Asperger's Disorder Facts at a Glance

Prevalence

- The estimated prevalence for Asperger's disorder is around 0.25–0.8% (Fombonne, 2005; Ozonoff, Rogers, & Hendren, 2003), depending on the exact criteria used, the research methods used, and the population studied.

Onset

- Although symptoms may emerge during early childhood, Asperger's is often not diagnosed until the child is in elementary or middle school because academic performance is normal. In some cases, the child's difficulty in social situations is not understood as a deficit but viewed as willful behavior.

Comorbidity

- Depression and anxiety disorders are the most common comorbid disorders. Attention-deficit/hyperactivity disorder may also co-occur.
- Asperger's is the only pervasive developmental disorder that cannot be comorbid with mental retardation—the DSM-IV-TR criteria stipulate normal cognitive development.

Course

- As children with Asperger's disorder enter adolescence and adulthood they may become aware of their social difficulties and isolation; this awareness may contribute to comorbid depression. However, many children with Asperger's are able to improve their social skills.
- Asperger's disorder has a good prognosis, and the higher the individual's IQ, the better the prognosis. Most people with Asperger's are able to work and be self-sufficient.

Gender Differences

- At least five times more males than females are diagnosed with Asperger's disorder.

Source: Unless otherwise noted, the source for information is American Psychiatric Association, 2000.

focus on a narrow interest is different from a normal "passion" for a hobby or activity in that people with Asperger's have significant difficulty putting aside their interest to attend to necessary tasks, such as eating and going to school.

Understanding Autism Spectrum Disorders

Let's examine the factors that give rise to the autism spectrum disorders (autism and Asperger's). Autism is the pervasive developmental disorder that has been the most widely investigated (and, as noted in Table 14.5, the prevalence rate is increasing), whereas the factors that give rise to Asperger's disorder have only recently been the focus of study. Therefore, most of the discussion that follows pertains to autism, unless otherwise noted.

Autism appears to be rooted primarily in neurological factors, which interact with psychological and social factors. The symptoms themselves involve a range of psychological and social factors.

Neurological Factors

Like schizophrenia, autism is marked by significant abnormalities in brain structure and function. Genetics also appears to play a role in this disorder.

Brain Systems Children who have autism have an unusually large head circumference, which is probably due to an above-average increase in white and gray matter during infancy (Hardan et al., 2006). However, adults with autism do not have larger than average heads, so the early accelerated growth is followed by slower growth during childhood (Herbert, 2005).

The connections and communication among brain areas also appear abnormal in autism (Minshew & Williams, 2007). Brain areas in the same region appear to communicate excessively, while there is too little communication among distant areas (Courchesne & Pierce 2005), in particular, between the frontal lobes and other brain areas (Murias et al., 2006). In addition, parts of the frontal lobe are less active among those with autism than among control group participants, which is consistent with the deficits in executive function that have been documented in autism (Silk et al., 2006). Asperger's is associated with a variety of problems with motor coordination, which suggests abnormalities in the central nervous system; these coordination problems continue into adulthood (Tani et al., 2006) and are also seen in people with high-functioning autism (Jansiewicz et al., 2006).

Genetics How might these abnormalities arise? Genes appear to play a role. Researchers have long observed that autism tends to run in families; 8% of siblings of affected children will also have the disorder (compared to at most 0.2% of the general population; Muhle, Trentacoste, & Rapin, 2004). Even stronger evidence comes from twin studies: Monozygotic twin-pairs are up to nine times more likely to have the disorder than are dizygotic twin pairs (Bailey et al., 1995; Folstein & Rutter, 1977; Le Couteur et al., 1996; Steffenburg et al., 1989).

However, researchers have not located a single gene that always gives rise to autism (Weiss et al., 2008). Instead, most forms of autism probably arise from interactions among genes—perhaps 15 or more of them (Santangelo & Tsatsanis, 2005). Research suggests that one possible cause of the genetic mutations associated with some cases of autism is the father's age at conception (Croen et al., 2007): Fathers who were 40 or older were almost six times more likely to have children with autism than fathers younger than 30 (Reichenberg et al., 2006). Older mothers were also more likely to have children with an autism spectrum disorder (Croen et al., 2007).

Certain stimuli may trigger autism in genetically vulnerable children (Waldman et al., 2008). Although researchers had earlier suggested that the cause of autism might be *thimerisol*, an ingredient in a widely used vaccine for measles-mumps-rubella, no studies have so far been able to document a causal link between this vaccine and the disorder (Muhle, Trentacoste, & Rapin, 2004; Thompson et al., 2007). In fact, autism rates continue to increase even among children who received vaccines without thimerisol (Schechter & Grether, 2008), which indicates that factors other than thimerisol are at work. Another possibility was suggested by the discovery that in 2005 more children had autism in counties of the Northwest states (California, Oregon, and Washington) that had more days of rain from 1987 to 2001. The researchers conjectured that bad weather may lead children to spend more time indoors, possibly increasing their television viewing, their risk for a vitamin D deficiency, or their exposure to household cleaning products.

Like autism, Asperger's disorder appears to have a genetic basis: Compared to the general population, relatives of someone with Asperger's are more likely to have an autism spectrum disorder (Cederlund & Gillberg, 2004).

Psychological Factors: Cognitive Deficits

Neurological factors give rise to psychological symptoms, particularly cognitive deficits in shifting attention and in mental flexiblilty (Ozonoff & Jensen, 1999). These deficits underlie the extreme difficulty in transitioning from one activity to another that individuals with autism spectrum disorders experience; people with autism also tend to focus on details at the expense of the broader picture (Frith, 2003). However, these deficits are not part of the DSM-IV-TR diagnostic criteria.

Another problem—also not noted in the DSM-IV-TR criteria—is difficulty in recognizing facial expressions of emotions (Serra et al., 2003). For example, in one study 3- and 4-year-olds' brain activity was assessed with EEG while they were shown photographs of faces that either expressed fear or had neutral expressions. Normal children exhibited greater brain activity in response to the fear expressions than to the neutral expressions. But children with autism responded to both types of facial expressions with the same pattern of brain activity (Dawson et al., 2004).

People with autism also have difficulty viewing the world from another person's perspective—with using a **theory of mind**, which is a theory about other people's mental states (their beliefs, desires, and feelings) that allows each of us to predict how others will react in a given situation (Tager-Flusberg, 1999). Because a theory of mind requires thinking about somebody else, by definition, this ability involves both psychological and social factors. An impaired theory of mind is demonstrated with the *false belief test* (Baron-Cohen, Leslie, & Frith, 1985), which requires that the participant keep in mind the point of view of someone else: Two dolls, Sally and Anne, are used to act out a scene. Sally puts a marble in a basket and then leaves the room without taking the basket. Anne then quietly moves the marble from the basket into a box. The child is then asked to say where Sally will look for the marble when she comes back in the room. The correct answer, that Sally will look in the basket, requires the participant to appreciate the point of view of Sally, who does not know that the marble was moved. In this study, 80% of the children with autism answered incorrectly that Sally would look in the box. These children were not able to override what they knew and take Sally's perspective. Although some individuals with milder symptoms of autism may be able to answer correctly on the false belief test, they are not able to do so when the task involves more complex processing of social cues, such as understanding white lies or irony (Happé, 1994).

People with Asperger's disorder also have an impaired theory of mind. However, these problems are less severe than in people with autism (Ziatas, Durkin, & Pratt, 2003). In addition, even the normal siblings of individuals with Asperger's have an impaired theory of mind (Dorris et al., 2004), which provides further support for the inference that genes play a role in this disorder.

Social Factors: Communication Problems

The earliest indications of autism arise in interactions with other people: Children with autism pay attention to other people's mouths, not their eyes (Dawson, Webb, & McPartland, 2005) and don't respond to their own name or to parents' voices (Baranek, 1999). Moreover, they don't develop normal communication skills—verbal or nonverbal. As they get older, they don't develop the typical ability to recognize faces, and they also have problems recognizing emotion, both in voices (Rutherford, Baron-Cohen, & Wheelwright, 2002) and in facial expressions (Bölte & Poustka, 2003). These cognitive deficits make social interactions confusing and unpredictable.

Theory of mind
A theory about other people's mental states (their beliefs, desires, and feelings) that allows a person to predict how other people will react in a given situation.

Even older children with autism who have developed some communication skills may still have deficits that prevent normal conversation. And, despite adequate verbal skills, adults with autism often don't understand elements of conversation involving a back-and-forth exchange of information and interest in the other person, and so cannot interact normally.

Asperger's disorder involves similar—although less severe—problems with social communication. However, there is very little research on how various factors might contribute to autism as compared to Asperger's disorder.

In sum, autism and Asperger's disorder are primarily caused by neurological factors (including those that are consequences of genetics); the neurological factors give rise to symptoms of the disorder, which are psychological and social in nature. As noted earlier, psychological and social factors also influence the course of these disorders—indeed, every social interaction has the potential to change the brain, if only by inducing learning (which occurs because of neural changes). However, at present, it appears that psychological and social factors contribute to autism and Asperger's disorder only indirectly (e.g., by influencing where a person lives, which in turn may be a risk factor for exposure to certain stimuli). For this reason, in this section we do not discuss feedback loops for autism spectrum disorders.

Treating Autism Spectrum Disorders

Treatment of autism generally focuses on increasing communication skills and appropriate social behaviors. Unfortunately, there is no cure for autism, and no one type of intervention is helpful for all those with the disorder. The treatments that are most effective are time-intensive (at least 25 hours per week), have strong family involvement, are individualized to the child, and begin as early in the child's life as possible (Rogers, 1998). Early treatment depends on early diagnosis of the disorder; to ensure early diagnosis, the American Academy of Pediatrics recommends that all children receive screening tests for autism before the age of 2 (Johnson, Meyers, & Council on Children with Disabilities, 2007).

Targeting Neurological Factors

No treatments successfully target the neurological factors that appear to underlie autism spectrum disorders. Medication may help treat symptoms of comorbid disorders or of agitation or aggression. The medications most likely to be prescribed are antipsychotics and selective serotonin-reuptake inhibitors (SSRIs; des Portes, Hagerman, & Hendern, 2003). Some research suggests that people with autism may be more likely than other people to experience side effects from medications (Harden & Lubetsky, 2005). Medication is not usually prescribed for people with Asperger's disorder (Campbell & Morgan, 1998), unless it is for a comorbid disorder.

Targeting Psychological Factors: Applied Behavior Analysis

The technique most widely used to modify the maladaptive behaviors associated with autism is called **applied behavior analysis**. This method uses shaping (described in Chapter 4) to help individuals learn complex behaviors. The key idea is that a complex behavior is divided into short, simple actions that are reinforced and then ultimately strung together. For example, many children with autism eat with their hands and resist eating with utensils, which can create problems when eating with classmates or when the family goes out to eat. Thus, learning to use a spoon is one behavior that is often shaped via applied behavior analysis. Initially, the therapist looks for any spoon-related behavior—such as a glance at the spoon or the child's moving a hand near the spoon—and responds with verbal reinforcement ("That's right, there is the spoon, good job") and perhaps some concrete reward, such as a few small candies. After a few successful attempts at approaching the spoon, the child is reinforced for picking up the spoon, then for putting the spoon

AP Photo/The Daily Messenger, Eric Sucar

Jason McElwain, at 17, was manager of his high school's basketball team; he was thought to be too small to be on the team. At the final home game, which his team was losing, with 4 minutes to go, he was allowed to play. Here he is being cheered by his teammates and the crowd after he went on to score 20 points and win the game. Jason was diagnosed with autism when he was 2 years old; he didn't begin speaking until he was 5 years old (Associated Press, 2006). As he grew older his social skills improved (McElwain & Paisner, 2008).

Applied behavior analysis
A technique used to modify maladaptive behaviors by reinforcing new behaviors through shaping.

in the mouth, and finally for using it with food. Parents of children with autism are encouraged to use this method at home.

Targeting Social Factors: Communication

Treatment for autism and Asperger's disorder that addresses social factors often focuses, in one way or another, on facilitating communication and interpersonal interactions. For example, when an individual with autism has severe communication difficulties, treatment may include the use of PECS, the picture system for facilitating communication mentioned in the section on mental retardation. For people with high-functioning autism or Asperger's, treatment may focus on training appropriate social behaviors through social skills groups or through individual instruction and modeling—observing others engaging in appropriate social behavior and then role-playing such behaviors (Bock, 2007). For instance, when Richie enters elementary school, he might attend a social skills group for selected kindergarteners and first-graders; the psychologist who leads such groups explicitly teaches the children appropriate social behavior—such as making eye contact and asking and answering questions—and has the children practice with each other. Parents are asked to continue social skills training at home by modeling desired social behaviors and reinforcing their children for improved behavior (Kransny et al., 2003).

In addition, various training programs have been developed to help people with Asperger's or autism who do not also have mental retardation; such programs help them perceive and interpret social cues—facial expressions and body language—more accurately. In fact, there is a pilot project that uses a computer game to provide such training (Golan & Baron-Cohen, 2006). Another tool to develop the ability to read social cues is social stories, which are stories in which the important social cues and responses are made explicit (Konstantareas, 2006). Although intriguing, research on the outcomes of various training programs and their tools is in its infancy. The extent to which a change in one factor affects another factor is unknown for the autism spectrum disorders. Thus, we do not include a discussion of treatment-related feedback loops among the three types of factors.

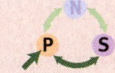

Other Pervasive Developmental Disorders

DSM-IV-TR includes two other disorders in the subcategory of pervasive developmental disorders: *childhood disintegrative disorder* and *Rett's disorder*. Both disorders are extremely rare, and are caused by neurological factors.

Childhood Disintegrative Disorder

In contrast to autism, which involves deficits in communication and interest in others since birth, **childhood disintegrative disorder** is characterized by normal development until at least 2 years old, followed by a profound loss of communication skills, normal types of play, and bowel control. The loss of normal functioning may occur as early as 2 years old or as late as 10 years old. DSM-IV-TR requires a loss of skills in at least two of five areas: language, social skills, bowel or bladder control, play, and motor skills. Normal functioning is often lost in all five areas (American Psychiatric Association, 2000). Thus, a clinician can distinguish childhood disintegrative disorder from autism by the age of the child when the symptoms began and by the course of the symptoms: Symptoms of childhood disintegrative disorder usually do not improve over time (Ozonoff, Rogers, & Hendren, 2003), whereas symptoms of autism can improve with interventions. Childhood disintegrative disorder is a rare neurological disorder that is caused by factors that appear to be unrelated to those of autism.

Rett's Disorder

Similar to childhood disintegrative disorder, Rett's disorder—which afflicts only females—involves a loss of skills already mastered. Specifically, **Rett's disorder** is characterized by normal prenatal development and normal functioning after birth through at least 5 months of age (up to about 2 years), after which the growth of

Childhood disintegrative disorder
A pervasive developmental disorder characterized by normal development until at least 2 years old, followed by a profound loss of communication skills, normal types of play, and bowel control.

Rett's disorder
A pervasive developmental disorder that affects only females and is characterized by normal prenatal development and functioning after birth through at least 5 months of age, after which the growth of the child's head slows and she loses the ability to control normal muscle movements, interest in other people, and previously developed skills.

the girl's head slows and she loses the ability to control normal muscle movements, interest in other people, and previously developed skills. The skills that are lost include the voluntary movement of hands (which is replaced by recurrent hand gestures that resemble hand-washing or hand-wringing) and coordination of the trunk. In addition to the loss of skills, a girl with Rett's disorder has language problems and psychomotor retardation. Mental retardation is an inevitable consequence of this disorder.

Although Rett's disorder includes some of the problems in communicating that mark autism and childhood disintegrative disorder, it has three unique features: a slowed rate of growth of the child's head circumference, coordination problems, and the loss of hand skills. Moreover, symptoms of Rett's disorder emerge by 2 years of age, at the latest; childhood disintegrative disorder symptoms emerge between 2 and 10. Rett's disorder occurs only in females because it is an X-linked genetic disorder that impedes normal brain development related to movement and cognition (Amir et al., 1999; Matijevic et al., 2009). Male fetuses with this mutation typically do not survive until birth.

Key Concepts and Facts About Pervasive Developmental Disorders

- Pervasive developmental disorders involve two types of problems: (1) significant deficits in communication and social interaction skills, and (2) stereotyped behaviors or narrow interests. Disorders in this category are autistic disorder, Asperger's disorder, childhood disintegrative disorder, and Rett's disorder.

- Autistic disorder (or simply, autism) is characterized by significant problems with communication, social interactions, and language use. Individuals with autism are oblivious to other people and do not pay attention to or understand basic social rules and cues. They may have extremely narrow interests involving repetitive play. Many people with autism also have comorbid mental retardation when tested with conventional intelligence tests; on tests that do not rely on verbal abilities, however, people with autism tend to score in the average range or higher. In addition, some people with autism have unique skills.

- Asperger's disorder is characterized by problems that are similar to—though less severe than—those associated with autism. With Asperger's, however, language and cognitive development are in the normal range. People with Asperger's avoid eye contact and are often unaware of other people's responses. They may be interested in social relationships but because they do not generally understand conventional social rules, forming and maintaining relationships is difficult.

- Neurological factors that underlie autism include abnormal connections and communication among different brain areas, in particular, between the frontal lobe and the rest of the brain. Genes play a role in the development of autism and Asperger's.

- Psychological symptoms of autism include deficits in shifting attention and in mental flexibility, and an impaired theory of mind. People with Asperger's have less severe problems in using a theory of mind than do people with autism. Social symptoms of autism include problems in recognizing emotion in the voices or faces of others and in understanding the give and take of social communication.

- Interventions for autism include medication for comorbid disorders or symptoms of anxiety, agitation, and aggression. Medication is not usually prescribed for symptoms of Asperger's disorder. Treatment for autism that targets psychological factors includes applied behavior analysis to modify maladaptive behaviors. Treatments that target psychological and social factors focus on teaching the individual to communicate, to recognize conventional social cues, and to read the emotional expressions of others, as well as how to initiate and respond in social situations.

- In contrast to autism and Asperger's disorder, childhood disintegrative disorder is characterized by normal development up to at least 2 years of age, followed by a profound loss of communication skills, normal types of play, and bowel control.

- Rett's disorder also involves the loss of skills already mastered, but the onset of the disorder occurs between 5 months and 2 years of age. The child loses interest in other people and the ability to control normal muscle movements. Mental retardation always accompanies Rett's disorder, which affects only females.

Making a Diagnosis

- Reread Case 14.2 about James, and determine whether or not his symptoms meet the criteria for autism. Specifically, list which criteria apply and which do not. If you would like more information to determine his diagnosis, what information—specifically—would you want, and in what ways would the information influence your decision?

- Reread Case 14.3 about Josh, and determine whether or not his symptoms meet the criteria for Asperger's disorder. Specifically, list which criteria apply and which do not. If you would like more information to determine his diagnosis, what information—specifically—would you want, and in what ways would the information influence your decision?

Learning Disorders: Problems with the Three Rs

Richie Enriquez's older brother, Javier, is in the 4th grade. Javier's teacher has noted that his reading ability doesn't seem up to what it should be. Javier is a bright boy, but when the students take turns reading aloud, Javier isn't able to read as well as his classmates. Javier generally has things he wants to say in class—sometimes raising his hand so high and waving it so energetically that he practically hits the heads of nearby children; his comments often show a keen understanding of what the teacher has said. His apparent reading problem seems to be at odds with his general intelligence. Could Javier have a learning disorder?

What Are Learning Disorders?

A **learning disorder** is characterized by a significant disparity between an individual's academic performance and the expected level of performance based on the individual's age, intelligence (assessed through an IQ test), and education level. Achievement that is at least two standard deviations below the level of a person's IQ score is the general guideline for diagnosing learning disorders. However, a gap less than that may be applicable when a comorbid anxiety disorder interferes with performance on an IQ test or when an individual's ethnic or cultural background decreases his or her familiarity with the items on the IQ test. DSM-IV-TR specifies three types of learning disorders: *reading, mathematics,* and *written expression*. The reading disorder is also referred to as **dyslexia**. Table 14.8 lists the DSM-IV-TR criteria for learning disorders generally.

Table 14.8 ▸ DSM-IV-TR Diagnostic Criteria for Learning Disorders

A. The specific ability, as measured by individually administered standardized tests, is substantially below that expected given the person's chronological age, measured intelligence, and age-appropriate education.

B. The disturbance in Criterion A significantly interferes with academic achievement or activities of daily living that require reading skills.

C. If a sensory deficit is present, the learning difficulties are in excess of those usually associated with the sensory deficit.

Source: Adapted from American Psychiatric Association, 2000.

DSM-IV-TR lists specific deficits for each type of learning disorder (American Psychiatric Association, 2000):

- *Reading disorder* is characterized by difficulty with reading accuracy, speed, or comprehension, to the point that the difficulty interferes with academic achievement or activities of daily functioning that involve reading.

- *Mathematics disorder* is characterized by difficulty with recognizing numbers or symbols, paying attention to and remembering all the different steps in a math problem, particular arithmetic skills such as multiplication, or translating written problems into arithmetic symbols.

- *Disorder of written expression* is diagnosed when poor spelling or handwriting occurs *along with* significant grammatical or punctuation mistakes or problems in paragraph organization. (This is the least studied of the learning disorders.)

Nancy, in Case 14.4, has a reading disorder. Additional facts about learning disorders are presented in Table 14.9.

Learning disorder
A psychological disorder characterized by a significant disparity between an individual's academic performance and the expected level of performance based on his or her age, intelligence, and education level.

Dyslexia
A learning disorder characterized by difficulty with reading accuracy, speed, or comprehension that interferes with academic achievement or activities of daily functioning that involve reading.

Table 14.9 ▶ Learning Disorders Facts at a Glance

Prevalence

- Between 2% and 10% of Americans are estimated to have a learning disorder.
- Five percent of public school students in the United States are diagnosed with a learning disorder.

Onset

- Symptoms of learning disorders do not usually emerge until early in elementary school (typically kindergarten through 3rd grade), when the relevant academic skills are needed.
- Children with a high IQ and a reading or mathematics disorder may not be diagnosed until the 4th grade or later.
- Symptoms appear rapidly when they arise from a serious medical problem.

Comorbidity

- Common comorbid disorders include depressive disorders and attention-deficit/hyperactivity disorder.
- Mathematics disorder and written expression disorder commonly co-occur with reading disorder.

Course

- With early identification and intervention, a significant number of children with reading disorder can overcome their difficulties.

Gender Differences

- Between 60% and 80% of people with reading disorder are male; however, males may be more likely to be diagnosed because of their disruptive behavior, which calls attention to their difficulties.

Cultural Differences

- In the United States, Hispanic children are least likely to be diagnosed with a learning disorder, perhaps because language barriers make it more difficult to diagnose (National Center for Health Statistics, 2008).

Source: Unless otherwise noted, the source for information is American Psychiatric Association, 2000.

CASE 14.4 ▶ FROM THE INSIDE: Learning Disorder (Reading)

Nancy Lelewer, author of *Something's Not Right: One Family's Struggle With Learning Disabilities* (1994), describes what having a learning disorder was like for her:

I began public elementary school in the early 1940s. . . . Reading was taught exclusively by a whole-word method dubbed "Look, Say" because of its reliance on recognizing individual words as whole visual patterns, rather than focusing on letters or letter patterns. In first grade, I listened to my classmates, and when it was my turn, I read the pictures, not the words, "Oh Sally! See Spot. Run. Run. Run." When we were shown flash cards and responded in unison to them, I mouthed something.

Then came our first reading test. The teacher handed each student a sheet of paper, the top half of which was covered with writing. I looked at it and couldn't read a word. . . . The room grew quiet as the class began to read.

As I stared at the page, total panic gripped me. My insides churned, and I began to perspire as I wondered what I was going to do. As it happened, the boy who sat right in front of me was the most able reader in my class. Within a few minutes, he had completed the test and had pushed his paper to the front of his desk, which put it in my full view. . . . [I copied his answers and] passed the test and was off on a track of living by my wits rather than being able to read.

The "wits track" is a nerve-wracking one. I worried that the boy would be out sick on the day we had a reading test. I worried that the teacher might change the location of my desk. I worried that I would get caught copying another student's answers. I knew that something was wrong with me, but I didn't know what. Why couldn't I recognize words that my classmates read so easily? Because everyone praised me when I did well on tests, I did my best to hide my inadequate reading skills. (pp. 15–17)

Unfortunately, learning disorders may cast a long shadow over many areas of life for many years. People with learning disorders are 50% more likely to drop out of school than are other people in the general population, and work and social relationships are also more likely to suffer (American Psychiatric Association, 2000). They are also more likely to suffer from poor self-esteem.

Social factors can lead a child to be incorrectly diagnosed with a learning disorder. For example, immigrant children may not have English language skills advanced enough to allow their reading, writing, or math skills to approach the expected level of performance. Children who have frequently been absent from school may also be incorrectly diagnosed with a learning disorder—the problem may simply be that they missed so much school that they didn't receive adequate instruction in those skills. At Javier's school, when a teacher thinks that a child may have a learning disorder, the relevant staff members meet: The teacher, the school learning specialist, the speech and language therapist, and the school psychologist discuss the teacher's concerns and decide what steps should be taken. These next steps may include observing the child in the classroom, recommending a formal evaluation, and/or talking with the parents.

Understanding Learning Disorders

Like mental retardation and pervasive developmental disorders, learning disorders arise in large part because of neurological factors. But psychological and social factors also play a role.

Neurological Factors

Among the three types of learning disorders, dyslexia has been studied the most extensively. Evidence is growing that impaired brain systems underlie this disorder and that genes contribute to these impaired systems.

Brain Systems

In most forms of dyslexia, the brain systems involved in auditory processing do not function as they should (Marshall et al., 2008; Ramus et al., 2003). For example, one study used electrodes placed on the scalp to examine the brain waves of infants while they listened to syllables coming out of a speaker. Eight years later, the children's reading abilities were assessed, and the children classified as dyslexic, poor readers, or normal readers. The children who were classified as dyslexic at 8 years old had brain-wave patterns in infancy (while they listened to spoken syllables) that were different from those of the children whose reading ability was classified as normal, which suggests that the children with dyslexia were born with processing problems in the auditory system (Molfese, 2000). Further research has suggested that these brain-wave differences continue at least through the first 4 years of life (Espy et al. 2004).

The results of many neuroimaging studies have converged to identify a set of brain areas that is disrupted in people who have dyslexia (Shaywitz, Lyon, & Shaywitz, 2006). First, two rear areas in the left hemisphere are not as strongly activated during reading tasks in people with dyslexia as they are in people who read normally. One of these areas, at the junction of the parietal and temporal lobes, appears to be involved in converting visual input to sounds (Friedman, Ween, & Albert, 1993). The other area, at the junction of the parietal and occipital lobes, appears to be used to recognize whole words, based on their visual forms (Cao et al., 2006; McCandliss, Cohen, & Dehaene, 2003). Moreover, these areas are not activated normally even in young children with dyslexia, and thus the malfunction observed in adults cannot be a result of not reading properly over the course of many years but probably contributes to reading disorder (Shaywitz et al., 2002). Second, two other brain areas (the bottom part of the frontal lobe and the right occipital-temporal region) are more activated in people with a reading disorder than in people who read normally. These areas appear to be used in carrying out compensatory strategies, which rely on stored information instead of the usual vision-sound conversion process.

Consistent with the neuroimaging results, researchers have also reported structural differences between the brains of people with dyslexia and normal readers. Compared to people who read normally, people with dyslexia have reduced gray matter (which includes the cell bodies of neurons) in the temporal lobes, particularly the left temporal lobe (Vinckenbosch, Robichon, & Eliez, 2005), and portions of their frontal lobes are relatively large (Vinckenbosch, Robichon, & Eliez, 2005; Zadina et al., 2006). Moreover, people who have relatively large occipital lobes (which are specialized for vision) tend to read better than those with smaller occipital lobes (Zadina et al., 2006); this difference may suggest that at least some people with dyslexia have impaired visual abilities. (Fine et al., 2007).

However, the precise brain areas involved in dyslexia are influenced by culture, as manifested by the language spoken in a society. Specifically, part of the left frontal lobe is impaired in dyslexic children who speak Chinese, instead of the areas just discussed (which were assessed in English-speaking children). Chinese writing does not depend on an alphabet, but instead requires memorizing specific characters that correspond to words (Siok et al., 2004). The frontal lobes are involved in using stored information to help register current stimuli, and such processing may play a large role in reading Chinese characters.

At least some forms of dyslexia also appear to reflect a specific problem in processing visual stimuli—independent of problems in connecting those stimuli to sounds—which may be why some people with dyslexia reverse letters when they write (Vidyasagar, 2005). Thus, findings regarding brain systems suggest that there are probably different forms of dyslexia, with different underlying causes.

Genetics

Reading disorder, and possibly the other learning disorders, are moderately to highly heritable (Hawke, Wadsworth, & DeFries, 2006; Schulte-Körne, 2001), and at least four specific genes are thought to affect the development of these disorders

(Fisher & Francks, 2006; Marino et al., 2007). Some of these genes affect how neurons are connected during brain development (Rosen et al., 2007), and some may affect the functioning of neurons or influence the activity of neurotransmitters (Grigorenko, 2001).

However, there is evidence that environmental factors—such as attending a low-quality school or coming from a disadvantaged family—can contribute to at least some forms of dyslexia (Olson et al., 1999; Shaywitz, Lyon, & Shaywitz, 2006; Wadsworth et al., 2000).

Psychological Factors

Although learning disorders arise from neurological abnormalities, this is not the end of the story. Some children with learning disorders succeed in situations where others fail. Why? In order to address this question, researchers interviewed college students with learning disorders and specifically asked about their experiences as young children (Miller, 2002). These people reported a number of psychological factors that played important roles in shaping their *motivation* to overcome their disorder; these factors included success experiences, self-determination, recognizing particular areas of strength, identifying the learning disability, and developing ways to cope with it. One person recounted, "I like to do things on my own, and if I [I'm] going to learn it, I'm going to keep drilling myself and doing it on my own . . . until it sinks in" (Miller, 2002, p. 295).

Social Factors

Social factors play a role in shaping motivation to persist in the face of difficulties (Miller, 2002). Other people, such as parents and teachers, were important in supporting and encouraging children who later succeeded in overcoming their learning disabilities. Social factors such as support and encouragement can thus affect a psychological factor—motivation to persist despite problems with learning. However, it is not clear whether the various factors—neurological, psychological, and social—have other interactions via feedback loops.

In sum, research findings suggest that impaired brain systems underlie learning disorders. Dyslexia—the most extensively studied learning disorder—appears to involve problems in the brain systems that process language and in brain systems that process visual stimuli. However, other factors also affect the nature and course of the disorder: Motivation and social support influence an individual's ability to overcome and compensate for a learning disorder.

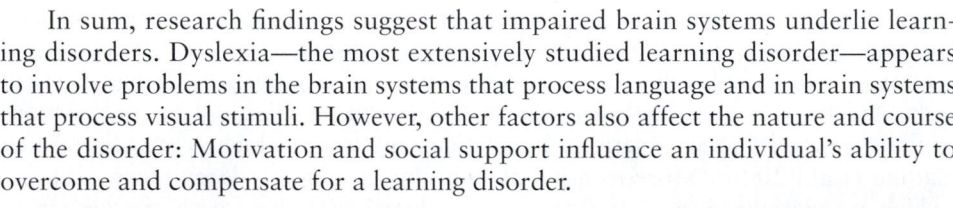

Treating Learning Disorders

Children with learning disorders are eligible for the accommodations and services mandated by the Individuals with Disabilities Education Act (IDEA), as described earlier. As with the other childhood disorders discussed thus far in this chapter, neurological factors are generally not directly targeted for treatment (unless the treatment is for a comorbid disorder). Dyslexia has been the subject of the most research on treatment, and researchers have reported successful interventions for this disorder.

Treating Dyslexia

Some techniques for helping people with dyslexia include phonological practice, which consists of learning to divide words into individual sounds and to identify rhyming words. Another technique focuses on teaching children the *alphabetic principle*, which governs the way in which letters signal elementary speech sounds (Shaywitz et al., 2004). In fact, various forms of training using these techniques have been shown not only to improve performance but also to improve the functioning of brain areas that were impaired prior to the training (Gaab et al., 2007; Simos et al., 2007; Temple et al., 2003).

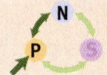

Treating Other Learning Disorders

Various techniques have been developed to help people cope with the other learning disorders. However, finding the most helpful technique for a given individual may be a trial-and-error process because numerous distinct problems can often underlie a deficit. In some cases, simply allowing an individual to have more time to complete a task can make a dramatic difference. In other cases, structuring the activity can help. For example, techniques to help people with mathematics disorder include the use of cue cards, breaking down the concepts into smaller steps, and giving immediate feedback for each step in a problem (Brosvic et al., 2006).

Unlike children with mental retardation and pervasive developmental disorders, children with a learning disorder and no comorbid disorder may not behave in a way that would cause them to be labeled as "different." Although not being able to read well or do mathematical computations as well as peers can affect a child's self-esteem and ability to succeed in several areas of life, it is also possible that a learning disorder may not influence other parts of life as strongly as mental retardation or autism generally do.

What do (left to right) singer Jewel, TV star Patrick Dempsey, martial artist Billy Blanks, business mogul Richard Branson, and actress Keira Knightley have in common? They all have dyslexia, which has not stopped them from attaining success in their fields.

Key Concepts and Facts About Learning Disorders

- A learning disorder is characterized by a substantial disparity between an individual's performance on a standardized test and the expected level of performance based on the individual's age, intelligence (assessed by an IQ test) and education level. DSM-IV-TR includes three types of learning disorders: reading disorder (dyslexia), mathematics disorder, and disorder of written expression.

- Genes contribute to learning disorders. Dyslexia appears to result from disruptions in brain systems that process language and in brain systems that process visual stimuli. Motivation and social support influence an individual's ability to overcome and compensate for a learning disorder.

- Treatment for learning disorders may involve accommodations and services mandated by the Individuals with Disabilities Education Act (IDEA). Various cognitive techniques can help a person learn to compensate for a learning disorder. Depending on the specific learning disorder and the individual, some techniques may be more effective than others.

Making a Diagnosis

- Reread Case 14.4 about Nancy, and determine whether or not her symptoms meet the criteria for a learning disorder. Specifically, list which criteria apply and which do not. If you would like more information to determine her diagnosis, what information—specifically—would you want, and in what ways would the information influence your decision?

Disorders of Disruptive Behavior and Attention

In addition to Javier Enriquez's apparent difficulties reading, his teacher has commented—not very positively—on Javier's high energy level. He doesn't always stay in his chair during class, and when he's working on a group project, other kids seem to get annoyed at him: "He can get 'in their face' a bit." Javier's mother, Lela, and his father, Carlos, acknowledge that Javier is a very active, energetic boy. But Carlos says, "I was that way when I was a kid, but I grew out of it as I got older." Javier's teacher recently mentioned the possibility of his having attention-deficit/hyperactivity disorder.

In contrast, Javier's sister, 8-year-old Pia, is definitely not energetic. Like her brother, Pia is clearly bright, but her teacher says she seems to "space out" in class. The teacher thinks that Pia is simply not applying herself, but her parents wonder whether she's underachieving because she's bored and understimulated in school. At home, Pia has defied her parents increasingly often—not doing her chores or performing simple tasks they ask her to do. Lela and Carlos then get frustrated and angry. At other times, Pia is off in her own world, "kind of like an absent-minded professor."

Hounding Pia to do her chores (and getting angry when she doesn't) is not a new pattern. For a number of years, her parents frequently had to remind Pia to clean up her room, make her bed, and help set the table. They thought she was intentionally defying them. Is Pia's behavior in the normal range, or does it signal a problem? If so, what might the problem be?

And what about Javier's behavior—is it in the normal range? Most children are disruptive some of the time. But in some cases, the disruptive behavior is much more frequent and obtrusive and becomes a cause for concern. The most common reason that children are referred to a clinician is because of disruptive behavior at home, at school, or both (Frick & Silverthorn, 2001). The clinician's task is to distinguish between normal behavior and pathologically disruptive behavior and, if the behavior falls outside the normal range, determine which disorder(s) might be the cause (Christophersen & Mortweet, 2001). The disruptive behaviors may not necessarily distress the individual who performs them. But the behaviors often distress other people or violate social norms (Christophersen & Mortweet, 2001).

Three disorders are associated with disruptive behavior: *conduct disorder*, *oppositional defiant disorder*, and *attention-deficit/hyperactivity disorder* (which is characterized mainly by problems with attention but sometimes by disruptive behavior as well). As we'll see, symptoms of these three disorders commonly—though not always—occur together.

What Is Conduct Disorder?

The hallmark of **conduct disorder** is a violation of the basic rights of others or of societal norms that are appropriate to the individual's age (American Psychiatric Association, 2000). As outlined in Table 14.10, 15 types of behaviors are listed in the diagnostic criteria for conduct disorder; these behaviors are sorted into four categories:

- aggression to people and animals;
- destruction of property;
- deceitfulness or theft; and
- serious violation of rules.

Just as the criteria for antisocial personality disorder (Chapter 13) focus almost exclusively on behavior that violates the rights of others, so do the criteria for conduct disorder. To be diagnosed with antisocial personality disorder, the individual must be at least 18 years old. Although adults may be diagnosed with conduct disorder, it is most commonly diagnosed in children.

DSM-IV-TR requires the presence of a minimum of 3 out of the 15 types of behavior listed in Criterion A within the last 12 months; at least one type of behavior must have occurred during the last 6 months. Although the diagnosis requires impaired functioning in some area of life, it does *not* require distress.

Most individuals diagnosed with conduct disorder are under 18 years old; if the behaviors persist into adulthood, the individual usually meets the criteria for antisocial personality disorder; in some cases, however, an individual may not meet all the criteria for that disorder and so retains the diagnosis of conduct disorder.

Like people with antisocial personality disorder, people with conduct disorder appear to lack empathy and concern for others, and they don't exhibit genuine remorse for their misdeeds. In fact, when the intent of another person's behavior is ambiguous, an individual with conduct disorder is likely to (mis)attribute the other's motives as threatening or hostile and then feel justified in his or her own aggressive behavior. People with conduct disorder typically blame others for their inappropriate behaviors ("He made me do it"). And though appearing self-confident, some people with conduct disorder may, in fact, have low self-esteem; however, other people with this disorder have overinflated self-esteem. Outbursts of anger, recklessness, and poor frustration tolerance also frequently occur, although these characteristics are not part of the DSM-IV-TR criteria.

DSM-IV-TR specifies three levels of intensity for the symptoms of conduct disorder; the symptoms may progress from mildly disruptive to severely disruptive behaviors:

- *Mild.* The individual has only the minimum number of symptoms to meet the criteria, and the disruptive behaviors cause minimal harm to others (for example, lying or staying out after curfew).

Table 14.10 ▶ DSM-IV-TR Diagnostic Criteria for Conduct Disorder

A. A repetitive and persistent pattern of behavior in which the basic rights of others or major age-appropriate societal norms or rules are violated, as manifested by the presence of three (or more) of the following criteria in the past 12 months, with at least one criterion present in the past 6 months:

Aggression to people and animals
(1) often bullies, threatens, or intimidates others;
(2) often initiates physical fights;
(3) has used a weapon that can cause serious physical harm to others (e.g., a bat, brick, broken bottle, knife, gun);
(4) has been physically cruel to people;
(5) has been physically cruel to animals;
(6) has stolen while confronting a victim (e.g., mugging, purse snatching, extortion, armed robbery);
(7) has forced someone into sexual activity.

Destruction of property
(8) has deliberately engaged in fire setting with the intention of causing serious damage;
(9) has deliberately destroyed others' property (other than by fire setting).

Deceitfulness or theft
(10) has broken into someone else's house, building, or car;
(11) often lies to obtain goods or favors or to avoid obligations (i.e., "cons" others);
(12) has stolen items of nontrivial value without confronting a victim (e.g., shoplifting, but without breaking and entering; forgery).

Serious violations of rules
(13) often stays out at night despite parental prohibitions, beginning before age 13 years;
(14) has run away from home overnight at least twice while living in parental or parental surrogate home (or once without returning for a lengthy period);
(15) is often truant from school, beginning before age 13 years.

B. The disturbance in behavior causes clinically significant impairment in social, academic, or occupational functioning.

C. If the individual is age 18 years or older, criteria are not met for Antisocial Personality Disorder [discussed in Chapter 13].

Source: Reprinted with permission from the Diagnostic and Statistical Manual of Mental Disorders, Text Revision, Fourth Edition, (Copyright 2000) American Psychiatric Association.

Conduct disorder
A psychological disorder that typically arises in childhood and is characterized by the violation of the basic rights of others or of societal norms that are appropriate to the individual's age.

- *Moderate.* The individual has a number of conduct problems, and their effect on other people is between mild and severe (for example, vandalism or stealing objects that were left unattended).

- *Severe.* The individual has many conduct problems, or the conduct problems create considerable harm to others (for example, forced sex, using a weapon, or stealing while confronting a victim).

People with conduct disorder are also likely to use—and abuse—substances at an earlier age than are people without this disorder. Similarly, they are more likely to have problems in school (such as suspension or expulsion), legal problems, unplanned pregnancies and sexually transmitted diseases, and physical injuries that result from fights. Because of their behavioral problems, children with conduct disorder may live in foster homes or attend special schools. They may also have poor academic achievement and score lower than normal on verbal intelligence tests. Problems with relationships, financial woes, and psychological disorders may persist into adulthood (Colman et al., 2009).

When clinicians assess whether conduct disorder might be an appropriate diagnosis for an individual, they will of course talk with the person; however, the nature of conduct disorder is such that a child may not provide complete information about his or her behavior. Thus, clinicians try to obtain additional information from other sources, usually school officials or parents, although even these people may not know the full extent of a child's conduct problems. Usually, the behaviors that characterize conduct disorder are not limited to one setting but occur in a variety of settings: in school, at home, in the neighborhood. This was true for Brad, as described in Case 14.5.

CASE 14.5 ▶ FROM THE OUTSIDE: Conduct Disorder

Brad was [a teenager and] small for his age but big on fighting. For him, this had gone beyond schoolyard bullying. He had four assault charges during the previous six months, including threatening rape and beating up a much younger boy who was mentally challenged. The family was being asked to leave their apartment complex because of Brad's aggressive behavior and several stealing incidents. Other official arrests included burglaries and trespassing. Brad had participated in a number of outpatient services, including anger management classes in which he had done well, but obviously he was not applying what he had learned to everyday life. He was referred to the [a treatment] program by the juvenile court judge.

Prior to placement, Brad had lived with his mother and older brother. Their family life had been characterized by many disruptions, including contact with several abusive father figures and frequent moves. Mrs. B had epilepsy that was not controlled with medication. She experienced several seizures per week. Brad's older brother also had a record with the juvenile authorities, but his offenses were confined to property crimes and the use of alcohol. He had graduated from an inpatient substance abuse program. Brad and his brother had a history of physical fighting. Prior to the boys' births, Mrs. B had had two children removed from her custody by state protective services. Mrs. B was very protective of Brad. She felt that the police and schools had it "in for him" and regularly defended him as having been provoked or blamed falsely. Although she was devastated at having Brad removed from her home, Mrs. B reported that she could no longer deal with Brad's aggression.

(Chamberlain, 1996, pp. 485–486)

In addition to specifying the intensity of the symptoms, DSM-IV-TR also uses the timing of onset to define two types of conduct disorder, each of which typically has a different course and prognosis:

- *adolescent-onset type*, in which no symptoms were present before age 10; and

- *childhood-onset type*, which is more severe and in which the first symptoms appeared when the child was younger than 10 years old.

Let's examine these two types of the disorder in more detail.

Adolescent-Onset Type

For people with adolescent-onset type, the symptoms of conduct disorder emerge with or after—but not before—puberty. The disruptive behaviors are not likely to be violent and typically include minor theft, public drunkenness, and property offenses, rather than violence against people and robbery, which are more likely with childhood-onset type (Moffit et al., 2002). The behaviors associated with adolescent-onset type of conduct disorder can be thought of as exaggerations of normal adolescent behaviors (Moffitt & Caspi, 2001). With this type, the disruptive behaviors are usually transient, and adolescents with this disorder are able to maintain relationships with peers (who may behave disruptively along with them). This type of conduct disorder has been found to have a small sex difference; the male to female ratio is 1.5 to 1 (Moffitt & Caspi, 2001).

Childhood-Onset Type

DSM-IV-TR distinguishes only two types of conduct disorder based on the time of onset—adolescence or childhood. But researchers have further identified two variants of childhood-onset conduct disorder, each with different features and pathways to the disorder (Frick & Muñoz, 2006): Some people with childhood-onset type exhibit *callous* and *unemotional* traits (Caputo, Frick, & Brodsky, 1999; Frick, Bodin, & Barry, 2000), which are features of psychopathy (discussed in Chapter 13), and others with childhood-onset type do not possess these traits.

Childhood-Onset Type With Callous and Unemotional Traits

Children and teenagers with callous and unemotional traits are likely to be more aggressive, both when responding to real or perceived provocations and when exhibiting disruptive behavior for some type of gain, such as premeditated theft (Kruh, Frick, & Clements, 2005). This variant of conduct disorder has the highest heritability (Viding et al., 2005). Like adults with psychopathy, these young people seek out exciting and dangerous activities, are relatively insensitive to threat of punishment (Frick et al., 2003), and are strongly oriented toward the possibility of reward (Pardini, Lochman, & Frick, 2003). Moreover, they are less reactive to threatening or distressing stimuli (Frick et al., 2003; Loney et al., 2003).

Researchers propose that the decreased sensitivity to punishment—associated with low levels of fear—underlies the unique constellation of callousness and increased aggression (Frick, 2006; Pardini, Obradovic, & Loeber, 2006). Individuals with this variant of conduct disorder are not concerned about the negative consequences of their violent behaviors. And lacking fear and the bodily arousal that goes along with it, they don't learn to refrain from certain behaviors and thereby fail to internalize social norms or develop a conscience or empathy for others (Frick & Morris, 2004; Pardini, 2006; Pardini, Lochman, & Frick, 2003). In fact, those with conduct disorder with callous and unemotional traits are less likely to recognize emotional expressions of sadness (Blair et al., 2001).

Childhood-Onset Type Without Callous and Unemotional Traits

Some individuals with conduct disorder that arises before puberty do not possess callous or unemotional traits. These people are less likely to be aggressive in general. When they are aggressive, it is usually as a *reaction* to a perceived or real threat; it is not premeditated (Frick et al., 2003). People with this variant of childhood-onset conduct disorder have difficulty regulating their negative emotions: They have high levels of emotional distress (Frick & Morris, 2004; Frick et al., 2003), and they react more strongly to other people's distress (Pardini, Lochman, & Frick, 2003) and to negative emotional stimuli generally (Loney et al., 2003). In addition, they process social cues less accurately, and so are more likely to misperceive such cues and respond aggressively when (mis)perceiving threats (Dodge & Pettit, 2003). Because of their problems in regulating negative emotions, they are more likely to act aggressively and antisocially in *impulsive* ways when distressed. They often feel bad afterward, but still can't control their behavior (Pardini, Lochman, & Frick, 2003). These people may fall into a negative interaction pattern with parents: When a parent brings up the child's past or present misconduct, the child becomes agitated and then doesn't appropriately process what the parent says, becomes more distressed, and then impulsively behaves in an aggressive manner. The parent may respond with aggression (verbal or physical), creating a vicious cycle (Gauvain & Fagot, 1995).

This variant of conduct disorder is influenced less by genes and more by maladaptive parenting (Oxford, Cavell, & Hughes, 2003); moreover, it is more likely to arise in children with poor verbal reasoning abilities (Loney et al., 1998).

As noted in Table 14.11, the two DSM-IV-TR types of conduct disorder—adolescent- and childhood-onset—differ not only in the timing of onset, but also in other respects.

Table 14.11 ▸ Conduct Disorder Facts at a Glance

Prevalence

- Studies find a wide range of prevalence rates in the general population (1–10%), depending on how the study was conducted and the exact composition of the population studied. About 10% of Americans will be diagnosed with conduct disorder during their lives (Nock et al., 2006).
- Conduct disorder is more likely to occur in urban than in rural areas.
- Conduct disorder is one of the more frequently diagnosed psychological disorders in children.

Onset

- DSM-IV-TR specifies that symptoms of the disorder begin in childhood or adolescence. When symptoms arise before age 10, the diagnosis is childhood-onset type; when there are no symptoms before age 10, it is adolescent-onset type.

Comorbidity

- With the childhood-onset type, common comorbid disorders include oppositional defiant disorder and attention-deficit/hyperactivity disorder (Costello et al., 2003); some studies estimate that up to 90% of children with conduct disorder exhibit symptoms of attention-deficit/hyperactivity disorder (Frick & Muñoz, 2006).
- Among teenagers with conduct disorder, comorbid mood disorders are common (Christophersen & Mortweet, 2001).

Course

- The earlier the onset and the more severe the disruptive behaviors, the worse the prognosis (Barkley et al., 2002; Frick & Loney, 1999).
- Individuals with childhood-onset conduct disorder are likely to develop additional symptoms of the disorder by puberty and continue to have the disorder through adolescence.
- Those with the childhood-onset type are more likely than those with the adolescent-onset type to be diagnosed with antisocial personality disorder in adulthood.

Gender Differences

- During their lives, about 12% of American males and 7% of American females will have had conduct disorder (Nock et al., 2006).
- Although more males than females are diagnosed with this disorder (both types), the sex difference is more marked for the childhood-onset type, with ten males diagnosed for each female (Moffitt & Caspi, 2001).
- Males with conduct disorder tend to be confrontationally aggressive (engaging in fighting, stealing, vandalism, and school-related problems); females tend to be nonconfrontational (lying, truancy, running away, substance use, and prostitution).

Source: Unless otherwise noted, the source for information is American Psychiatric Association, 2000.

What Is Oppositional Defiant Disorder?

The defining features of **oppositional defiant disorder** are overt disobedience, hostility, defiance, and negativity toward people in authority. As noted in Table 14.12, for a diagnosis of oppositional defiant disorder, DSM-IV-TR requires that the individual exhibit four out of eight forms of defiant behavior (Criterion A), many of which are confrontational behaviors, such as arguing with adults, intentionally annoying others, and directly refusing to comply with an adult's request. Pia did not comply with her parents' requests to complete her chores or help with other tasks. Her teacher has commented on a similar behavior pattern at school.

Other examples of defiant behaviors include refusing to negotiate, compromise, or adhere to reasonable directions and testing the limits of rules; young children with oppositional defiant disorder may have intense and frequent temper tantrums. (Violent confrontations are not usually part of oppositional defiant disorder.) These behaviors must have been exhibited for at least 6 months, must occur more frequently than would be expected for the individual's age and developmental level, and must impair functioning.

The disruptive behaviors of oppositional defiant disorder are different in several important ways from those characterizing conduct disorder. Oppositional defiant disorder involves only a subset of the symptoms of conduct disorder—the overtly defiant behaviors—and these are often verbal. The disruptive behaviors of oppositional defiant disorder are

- generally directed toward authority figures;
- not usually violent and do not usually cause severe harm; and
- often exhibited only in specific situations with parents or other adults the individual knows well (Christophersen & Mortweet, 2001).

According to DSM-IV-TR, if an individual meets the diagnostic criteria for both oppositional defiant disorder and conduct disorder, only conduct disorder is diagnosed.

During a clinical interview, the young person may not behave disruptively. In fact, children and adolescents with oppositional defiant disorder often do not feel they are being oppositional, but rather believe that they are responding to unreasonable demands being made of them. It is important for the clinician, then, to obtain information from others when assessing disruptive behaviors. It is also important that the clinician keep in mind any cultural factors that might influence which sorts of behaviors are deemed acceptable or unacceptable. Figure 14.2 illustrates the possible paths for disruptive behavior disorder diagnoses. Table 14.13 lists additional facts about oppositional defiant disorder, and Case 14.6 describes Danny, a 6-year-old with oppositional defiant disorder, whose symptoms are atypical in that he hits his peers.

Table 14.12 ▸ DSM-IV-TR Diagnostic Criteria for Oppositional Defiant Disorder

A. A pattern of negativistic, hostile, and defiant behavior lasting at least 6 months, during which four (or more) of the following are often present:
(1) loses temper
(2) argues with adults
(3) actively defies or refuses to comply with adults' requests or rules
(4) deliberately annoys people
(5) blames others for his or her mistakes or misbehavior
(6) is touchy or easily annoyed by others
(7) is angry and resentful
(8) is spiteful or vindictive

Note: Consider a criterion met only if the behavior occurs more frequently than is typically observed in individuals of comparable age and developmental level.

B. The disturbance in behavior causes clinically significant impairment in social, academic, or occupational functioning.

C. The behaviors do not occur exclusively during the course of a psychotic disorder [Chapter 12] or mood disorder [Chapter 6].

D. Criteria are not met for conduct disorder, and, if the individual is age 18 years or older, criteria are not met for antisocial personality disorder [Chapter 13].

Source: Reprinted with permission from the Diagnostic and Statistical Manual of Mental Disorders, Text Revision, Fourth Edition, (Copyright 2000) American Psychiatric Association.

CASE 14.6 ▸ FROM THE OUTSIDE: Oppositional Defiant Disorder

Danny is 6 years old and is exhibiting behavior problems in his kindergarten classroom and the child-care after-school program. He is disruptive, hits and touches peers, argues with teachers, becomes easily frustrated, and has temper tantrums when things do not go his way. Danny is considered explosive and unpredictable. He is socially immature and disliked by his peers. Danny's parents had divorced several years earlier and are both remarried. He lives with his mother but sees his father regularly. The communication between Danny's parents is strained, and they differ in their opinions on how to handle Danny's behavior. The parents have different parenting styles and do not always provide Danny with clear and consistent boundaries across the two households.

(August et al., 2007, p. 137)

Oppositional defiant disorder
A psychological disorder that typically arises in childhood or adolescence and is characterized by overt disobedience, hostility, defiance, and negativity toward people in authority.

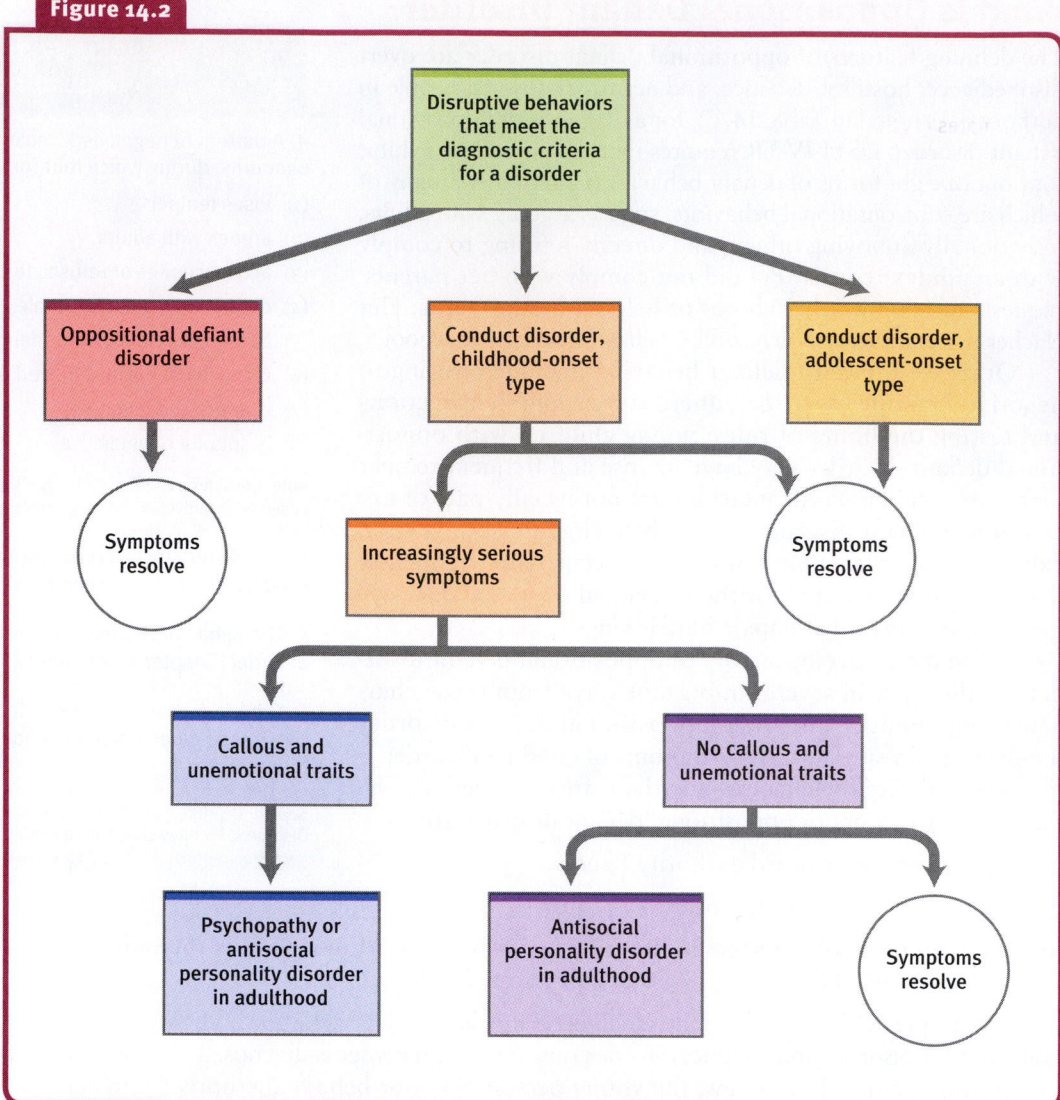

Figure 14.2

14.2 ▸ Typical Paths Related to Disruptive Behavior Disorders Several diagnostic paths are possible for individuals who exhibit significantly disruptive behaviors. Oppositional defiant disorder and conduct disorder can arise either in childhood or in adolescence. Once symptoms reach a level that meets the diagnostic criteria for either disorder, symptoms may (1) remain relatively stable (and hence do not progress to a different part of the diagram), (2) resolve so that the diagnosis no longer applies, or (3) shift, so that a different diagnosis is more appropriate. Although a patient's symptoms can shift from oppositional defiant disorder to conduct disorder, this is not typical. Nevertheless, most research on oppositional defiant disorder has studied the small subset of people who go on to develop conduct disorder.

Oppositional behavior is common among toddlers and adolescents; a clinician must be careful not to make the diagnosis of oppositional defiant disorder unless the disruptive behaviors occur significantly more often or with more intensity than is expected for the individual's age group. Critically, normal oppositional behavior does not impair functioning.

Moreover, symptoms of other disorders may be mistaken for symptoms of oppositional defiant disorder. For instance, a young patient who is psychotic may become angry and defiant, or a depressed individual may become irritable. When disruptive behaviors arise only in the context of a psychotic or mood disorder, oppositional defiant disorder is not the appropriate diagnosis. As another

Table 14.13 ▶ **Oppositional Defiant Disorder Facts at a Glance**

Prevalence

- Estimates of prevalence rates for this disorder vary widely, from 2% to 16%, depending on the specific population investigated and the specific research methods used.

Onset

- Symptoms usually emerge before 8 years of age, although they may become evident as late as 13.
- Symptoms are typically observed at home before occurring in other contexts.
- The onset progresses gradually, over months or even years, until the symptoms reach the point where the diagnostic criteria are met.

Comorbidity

- Attention-deficit/hyperactivity disorder is the most common comorbid disorder (Costello et al., 2003; Lahey, McBurnett, & Loeber, 2000); up to 90% of children with oppositional defiant disorder also exhibit symptoms of attention-deficit/hyperactivity disorder (Frick & Muñoz, 2006).
- Learning disorders may also co-occur with oppositional defiant disorder.

Course

- Most people with the childhood-onset type of conduct disorder were previously diagnosed with oppositional defiant disorder (Whittinger et al., 2007); however, most people with oppositional defiant disorder do not go on to develop conduct disorder.

Gender Differences

- Before puberty, more males than females are diagnosed with oppositional defiant disorder. After puberty there is no sex difference in prevalence.
- Males exhibit more persistent and more confrontational symptoms than females do.

Cultural Differences

- Different cultures may have different norms concerning what defiant behaviors are considered inappropriate or unacceptable.

Source: Unless otherwise noted, the source for information is American Psychiatric Association, 2000.

example, people with attention-deficit/hyperactivity disorder may, as a result of their impulsivity or hyperactivity, annoy other people or ignore a request to "calm down" or "sit down." However, in this context, the behaviors are not expressing defiance but are a result of attention-deficit/hyperactivity disorder.

Sometimes, disruptive behaviors arise as a response to still other disorders or problems, and this possibility should be kept in mind by a clinician. For instance, a child who is having difficulties with schoolwork, perhaps because of dyslexia or another learning disorder, may act up, or be defiant in an effort to hide the problem by distracting the teacher and classmates.

What Is Attention-Deficit/Hyperactivity Disorder?

Individuals who have oppositional defiant disorder or conduct disorder behave disruptively because they want to defy rules, authority figures, or social norms. Those who have a third type of disorder, *attention-deficit/hyperactivity disorder*, often behave disruptively but do so unintentionally. People with attention-deficit/hyperactivity disorder are unusually impulsive and/or are hyperactive, which is why they have difficulty conforming to rules and social norms that call for restraint or calm behavior.

Attention-deficit/hyperactivity disorder (ADHD) is characterized by inattention, hyperactivity, and/or impulsivity. People diagnosed with this disorder vary in which set of symptoms is most dominant; some primarily have difficulty maintaining

Attention-deficit/hyperactivity disorder (ADHD)
A psychological disorder that typically arises in childhood and is characterized by inattention, hyperactivity, and/or impulsivity.

Table 14.14 ▸ DSM-IV-TR Diagnostic Criteria for Attention-Deficit/Hyperactivity Disorder

A. Either (1) or (2):

(1) *inattention*: six (or more) of the following symptoms of inattention have persisted for at least 6 months to a degree that is maladaptive and inconsistent with developmental level:
  (a) often fails to give close attention to details or makes careless mistakes in schoolwork, work, or other activities;
  (b) often has difficulty sustaining attention in tasks or play activities;
  (c) often does not seem to listen when spoken to directly;
  (d) often does not follow through on instructions and fails to finish schoolwork, chores, or duties in the workplace (not due to oppositional behavior or failure to understand instructions);
  (e) often has difficulty organizing tasks and activities;
  (f) often avoids, dislikes, or is reluctant to engage in tasks that require sustained mental effort (such as schoolwork or homework);
  (g) often loses things necessary for tasks or activities (e.g., toys, school assignments, pencils, books, or tools);
  (h) is often easily distracted by extraneous stimuli;
  (i) is often forgetful in daily activities.

(2) *hyperactivity-impulsivity*: six (or more) of the following symptoms of hyperactivity-impulsivity have persisted for at least 6 months to a degree that is maladaptive and inconsistent with developmental level:

Hyperactivity
  (a) often fidgets with hands or feet or squirms in seat;
  (b) often leaves seat in classroom or in other situations in which remaining seated is expected;
  (c) often runs about or climbs excessively in situations in which it is inappropriate (in adolescents or adults, may be limited to subjective feelings of restlessness);
  (d) often has difficulty playing or engaging in leisure activities quietly;
  (e) is often "on the go" or often acts as if "driven by a motor";
  (f) often talks excessively.

Impulsivity
  (g) often blurts out answers before questions have been completed;
  (h) often has difficulty awaiting turn;
  (i) often interrupts or intrudes on others (e.g., butts into conversations or games).

B. Some hyperactive-impulsive or inattentive symptoms that caused impairment were present before age 7 years.

C. Some impairment from the symptoms is present in two or more settings (e.g., at school [or work] and at home).

D. There must be clear evidence of clinically significant impairment in social, academic, or occupational functioning.

E. The symptoms do not occur exclusively during the course of a Pervasive Developmental Disorder, Schizophrenia [Chapter 12], or other Psychotic Disorder [Chapter 12] and are not better accounted for by another mental disorder (e.g., Mood Disorder [Chapter 6], Anxiety Disorder [Chapter 7], Dissociative Disorders [Chapter 8], or a Personality Disorder [Chapter 13]).

Source: Reprinted with permission from the Diagnostic and Statistical Manual of Mental Disorders, Text Revision, Fourth Edition, (Copyright 2000) American Psychiatric Association.

attention, and others primarily have difficulty with hyperactivity and impulsivity. Still others have all three types of symptoms. To meet the criteria for the diagnosis (see Table 14.14), the symptoms must impair functioning in at least two settings, such as at school and at home. The impulsive and hyperactive symptoms are most noticeable and disruptive in a classroom setting. Javier's difficulty staying in his chair at school, which disrupted the class, may have reflected this disorder. In Case 14.7, an adult recounts how he recognized his own ADHD.

CASE **14.7** ▸ FROM THE INSIDE: **Attention Deficit/Hyperactivity Disorder**

Attention-deficit disorder (ADD) was the term used in the third edition of the DSM. In his book *Driven to Distraction: Recognizing and Coping with Attention Deficit Disorder from Childhood Through Adulthood*, psychiatrist Edward Hallowell recounts what happened when he learned about the disorder:

> I discovered I had ADD when I was thirty-one years old, near the end of my training in child psychiatry at the Massachusetts Mental Health Center in Boston. As my teacher in neuropsychiatry began to describe ADD in a series of morning lectures during a steamy Boston summer, I had one of the great "Aha!" experiences of my life.
>
> "There are some children," she said, "who chronically daydream. They are often very bright, but they have trouble attending to any one topic for very long. They are full of energy and have trouble staying put. They can be quite impulsive in saying or doing whatever comes to mind, and they find distractions impossible to resist."
>
> So there's a name for what I am! I thought to myself with relief and mounting excitement. There's a term for it, a diagnosis, an actual condition, when all along I'd thought I was just slightly daft. . . . I wasn't all the names I'd been called in grade school—"a daydreamer," "lazy," "an underachiever," "a spaceshot"—and I didn't have some repressed unconscious conflict that made me impatient and action-oriented.
>
> What I had was an inherited neurological syndrome characterized by easy distractibility, low tolerance for frustration or boredom, a greater-than-average tendency to say or do whatever came to mind . . . and a predilection for situations of high intensity. Most of all, I had a name for the overflow of energy I so often felt—the highly charged, psyched-up feeling that infused many of my waking hours in both formative and frustrating ways.
>
> (Hallowell & Ratey, 1994, pp. ix–x)

Because the sets of symptoms vary, clinicians find it useful to classify ADHD into different types. The hyperactive/impulsive type is associated with disruptive behaviors, accidents, and rejection by peers, whereas the inattentive type of ADHD is associated with academic problems that are typical of deficits in executive functions: difficulty remembering a sequence of behaviors, monitoring and shifting the direction of attention, organizing material to be memorized, and inhibiting interference during recall. A third group of patients, with the combined type, has symptoms of each of the other two types.

However, symptoms may change over time; as some children get older, the particular set of symptoms they exhibit can shift, most frequently from hyperactive/impulsive to the combined type (Lahey et al., 2005). Children with ADHD often have little tolerance for frustration, as was true of Edward Hallowell in Case 14.7; such children tend to have temper outbursts, changeable moods, and symptoms of depression. Once properly diagnosed and treated, such symptoms often decrease.

Problems with attention are likely to become more severe when sustained attention is necessary or when a task is thought to be boring, which is what happened to Javier. Various factors (psychological and social) can reduce symptoms, including:

• frequent rewards for appropriate behavior;
• close supervision;
• being in a new situation or setting;
• doing something interesting; and
• having someone else's undivided attention.

In contrast, symptoms are likely to become more severe in group settings, where the individual receives less attention or rewards.

Socially, people with ADHD may initiate frequent shifts in the topic of a conversation, either because they are not paying consistent attention to the conversation or they are not following implicit social rules: Those with symptoms of hyperactivity may talk so much that others can't get a word in edgewise, or they may inappropriately start conversations. These symptoms can make peer relationships difficult.

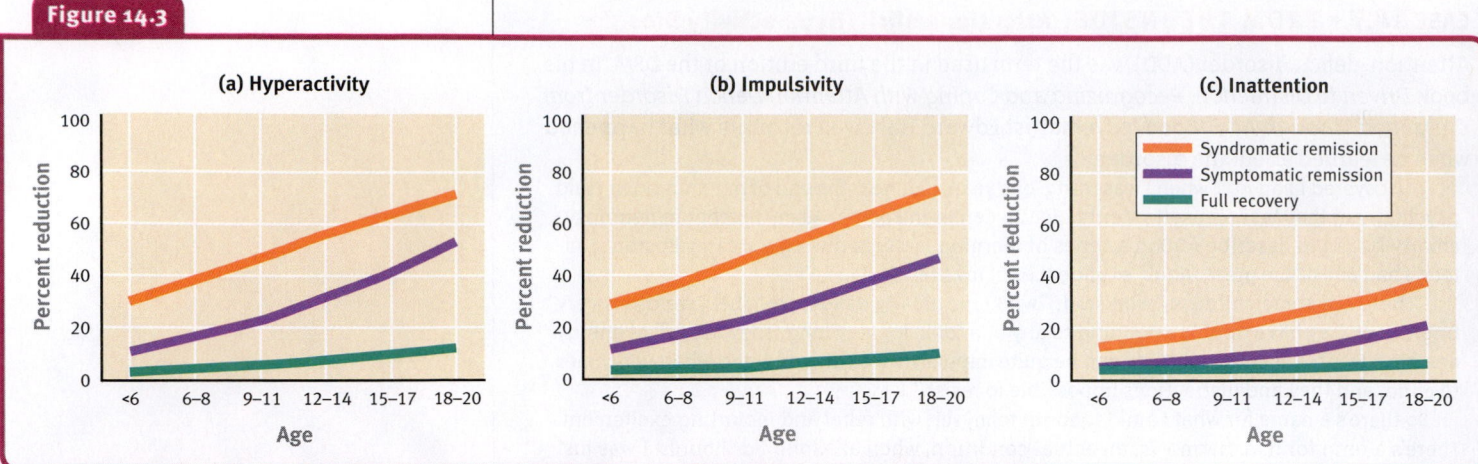

Figure 14.3

14.3 ▸ Reduction in ADHD Symptoms From Childhood to Adulthood By adulthood, the symptoms of (a) hyperactivity and (b) impulsivity diminish more in people with ADHD than do the symptoms of (c) inattention (Biederman, Mick, & Faraone, 2000). In *syndromatic remission,* symptoms improve and no longer meet diagnostic criteria; in *symptomatic remission,* symptoms improve but diagnostic criteria are still met (Biederman et al., 2000).

In addition, symptoms of impulsivity can lead to increased risk of harm. As shown in Figure 14.3, as the child heads into adulthood, hyperactive and impulsive symptoms tend to decrease but not disappear. Symptoms of inattention, however, do not tend to decrease as much (Biederman, Mick, & Faraone, 2000). Additional facts about ADHD are presented in Table 14.15.

Distinguishing Between Attention-Deficit/Hyperactivity Disorder and Other Disorders

Some symptoms of ADHD overlap with those of other disorders. For instance, the hyperactive and impulsive symptoms of ADHD may appear similar to those of hypomania or mania (bipolar disorder, Chapter 6) or to anxiety symptoms (such as those that may arise with anxiety disorders, Chapter 7). In addition, symptoms of inattention may overlap with some of the symptoms of dissociative disorders (Chapter 8). Moreover, symptoms of substance-related disorders (Chapter 9) and personality disorders (Chapter 13) may overlap with both inattention and hyperactive/impulsive symptoms.

However, two factors distinguish ADHD from the other disorders: (1) childhood onset, and (2) the relatively large number of symptoms of inattention and/or hyperactivity/impulsivity necessary for the diagnosis. But even these two factors may not allow a clinician to distinguish disruptive behaviors that arise from hyperactivity or impulsivity from disruptive behaviors that arise from defiance associated with oppositional defiant disorder or conduct disorder. The extremely high comorbidity between ADHD and oppositional defiant disorder or conduct disorder requires clinicians to assess carefully the reason for a child's persistent disruptive behavior. A general rule of thumb is that individuals with ADHD and *not* oppositional defiant disorder or conduct disorder do not intentionally violate the rights of others. For instance, Javier didn't hurt others physically, nor had his parents or teachers noticed any significant lying or stealing. Moreover, his disruptive behaviors in the classroom did not seem willful; rather, it seemed as though he couldn't help himself when he jumped out of his seat. And when he stood 5 inches from his classmates' faces while talking to them, he seemed happy and excited, not threatening. However, many children are diagnosed with both conduct disorder and ADHD, indicating that they intentionally violate rules *and* are also impulsive and hyperactive or have problems with attention.

Table 14.15 ▸ Attention-Deficit/Hyperactivity Disorder Facts at a Glance

Prevalence

- The estimated prevalence of ADHD in school-aged children increased from 6% in 1997 to 9% in 2006 (National Center for Health Statistics, 2008).
- Prevalence among American adults is about 4% (Kessler et al., 2006).

Comorbidity

- Common comorbid disorders include mood and anxiety disorders and learning disorders.
- Children with hyperactive and impulsive symptoms are more likely to be diagnosed with oppositional defiant disorder or conduct disorder than are those with inattentive symptoms (Christophersen & Mortweet, 2001): In surveys of the general population, 50–75% of children with ADHD also meet the criteria for conduct disorder (Kazdin, 1995). Another study found that over half of children with ADHD had comorbid oppositional defiant disorder (Biederman et al., 1996).

Onset

- Children are not usually diagnosed before age 4 or 5 because the range of normal behavior for preschoolers is very wide.
- In younger children, the diagnosis is generally based more on hyperactive and impulsive symptoms than on inattention symptoms.
- DSM-IV-TR requires that the disorder have its onset by age 7; however, research suggests that onset may occur up to age 12. Note, however, that diagnosis may occur much later.

Course

- Symptoms of ADHD become obvious during the elementary school years, when attentional problems interfere with schoolwork.
- By early adolescence, the more noticeable signs of hyperactivity—difficulty sitting still, for example—typically diminish to a sense of restlessness or a tendency to fidget.
- Children who had ADHD but not oppositional defiant disorder or conduct disorder in childhood have a higher risk of developing adolescent-onset conduct disorder than do peers who had none of those disorders in childhood (Mannuzza et al., 2004).
- As adults, people with ADHD may avoid sedentary jobs because of their restlessness.

Gender Differences

- Males are more likely—in one survey, more than twice as likely—to be diagnosed with ADHD, particularly the hyperactive/impulsive type, although this gender difference may reflect a bias in referrals to mental health clinicians rather than any actual difference in prevalence (Biederman et al., 2005; National Center for Health Statistics, 2008).

Cultural Differences

- In the United States, non-Hispanic white children are more likely to be diagnosed with ADHD than are Hispanic or black children (Havey et al., 2005; Stevens, Harman, & Kelleher, 2005).
- Worldwide, the prevalence of the disorder among children averages about 5% (Polanczyk & Rohde, 2007), although some studies find higher prevalence rates (Bird, 2002; Ofovwe, Ofovwe, & Meyer, 2006); the variability across countries can be explained by the different thresholds at which behaviors are judged as reaching a symptomatic level, as well as somewhat different diagnostic criteria (Bird, 2002).

Source: Unless otherwise noted, the source for information is American Psychiatric Association, 2000.

Criticisms of the DSM-IV-TR Diagnostic Criteria

Clinicians and researchers have pointed out numerous problems with the DSM-IV-TR criteria for ADHD. First, the diagnostic criteria for children do not necessarily apply very well to adults; adults with less than five symptoms can be clearly impaired, even though they don't exhibit the minimum number (six) of symptoms required for a diagnosis (McGough & McCracken, 2006). Second, according to the DSM criteria, if symptoms don't arise until after age 7, the diagnosis of ADHD is not, strictly speaking, applicable (American Psychiatric Association, 2000). However, research studies that examined people whose symptoms arose after age 7 (but generally by age 12) found that the symptoms were virtually identical to those of people with an earlier onset of the disorder, which suggests that the age cutoff is not meaningful (Faraone et al., 2006; McGough & Barkley, 2004).

Third, symptoms of hyperactivity may be different in females than in males: Girls who have hyperactive symptoms may talk more than other girls or may be more emotionally reactive, rather than hyperactive with their bodies (Quinn, 2005). Some researchers propose that ADHD is underdiagnosed in girls, who are less likely to have behavioral problems at school and so are less likely to be referred for evaluation (Quinn, 2005). In fact, female teenagers with ADHD are likely to be diagnosed with and treated for depression before the ADHD is diagnosed (Harris International, 2002, cited in Quinn, 2005).

Teachers are often the ones who first raise the possibility that a particular child has ADHD, and they are more likely to refer for evaluation children who disrupt the class (hyperactive/impulsive type). One study found that teachers were more likely to identify students as having ADHD when their class size was larger, and non-Hispanic white children were more likely to be identified than were Hispanic children (Havey et al., 2005). Other studies find that white children are more often diagnosed—and treated—than black children (Stevens, Harman, & Kelleher, 2005).

Before diagnosing ADHD, however, a mental health clinician should be sure that any difficulties in finishing tasks are a result of attentional problems, and not an oppositional attitude or difficulty in understanding the instructions. For instance, it turns out that Pia Enriquez simply hadn't been paying attention when her parents reminded her of her chores or asked her to set the table. Pia's "absent-minded professor" demeanor masked that fact that she has difficulty paying attention and becomes bored easily (particularly in the classroom, where she quickly grasps the underlying concepts in the material the teacher presents). When diagnosing adults with ADHD, clinicians should seek corroboration from school records or family members.

Understanding Disorders of Disruptive Behavior and Attention

Given the high comorbidity and symptom overlap among the three disorders—conduct disorder, oppositional defiant disorder, and ADHD—we'll focus on the disorder that is best understood, ADHD. Studies of factors related to oppositional defiant disorder and conduct disorder probably include participants who also have ADHD, which makes it difficult to determine which factors are uniquely associated with oppositional defiant disorder and conduct disorder and *not* ADHD.

Neurological Factors

Research on ADHD has revealed that people who have this disorder have abnormal brain structure and function, and also has begun to characterize the role that neurotransmitters and genes have in these brain abnormalities. Unfortunately, researchers are only beginning to consider the different possible types of the disorder separately—and thus at present only a very coarse picture is beginning to emerge.

ADHD and Brain Systems

As noted earlier, people with ADHD may have impaired executive function (Kiliç et al., 2007; Stuss et al., 1994). In addition, children and adults with ADHD cannot estimate time accurately, which affects their ability to plan and follow through on commitments (Barkley et al., 2001; Kerns, McInerney, & Wilde, 2001; McInerney & Kerns, 2003; Riccio et al., 2005). Such functions rely in part on the frontal lobes.

In fact, researchers have proposed that the behavioral problems that characterize people with ADHD may arise, at least in part, from impaired frontal lobe functioning. Two sorts of findings that support this view focus on brain structure and on brain function. Regarding brain structure, children and adolescents with this disorder have smaller brains than do children and adolescents without the disorder, and the deficit in size is particularly marked in the frontal lobes (Schneider, Retz et al., 2006; Sowell et al., 2003; Valera et al., 2007). Indeed, particular parts of the frontal lobes have been shown to be smaller in adults with ADHD (Durston et al., 2004; Hesslinger et al., 2002). However, the anatomical abnormalities are not restricted to the frontal lobes. Parts of the temporal lobes are smaller than normal in children and adolescents who have the disorder (Sowell et al., 2003), as are portions of the corpus callosum, the basal ganglia, and the cerebellum (Castellanos et al., 2002; Schrimsher et al., 2002; Valera et al., 2007). The cerebellar deficit is particularly interesting because this brain structure is crucial to attention and timing; in fact, the smaller this structure, the worse the symptoms of ADHD are (Castellanos et al., 2002; Mackie et al., 2007).

Some of the brain differences between people who have ADHD and those who do not may actually arise because the brain has attempted to compensate for the impaired regions. Perhaps critically, at least some of the differences found in the brains of children—notably those in the basal ganglia—do not persist into adulthood (Castellanos et al., 2002; Schneider et al., 2006). This finding is consistent with the fact that over half of the children who are diagnosed with ADHD do not meet the diagnostic criteria when they become adults (Schneider et al., 2006).

Regarding brain function, the research results indicate that ADHD is not a result of impaired functioning in any single brain area, but rather emerges from how different areas interact. As the anatomical abnormalities would suggest, neuroimaging studies have revealed many patterns of abnormal brain functioning in people who have ADHD (Rubia et al., 2007; Stevens, Pearlson, & Kiehl, 2007; Vance et al., 2007). In general, neural structures involved in attention, including portions of the frontal and parietal lobes, tend not to be activated as strongly (during relevant tasks) in people with this disorder as in people without it (e.g., Stevens, Pearlson, & Kiehl, 2007; Schneider et al., 2006; Vance et al., 2007). However, virtually every lobe in the brains of individuals with ADHD has been shown not to function normally during tasks that draw on their functions (e.g., Mulas et al., 2006; Schneider et al., 2006; Vance et al., 2007).

In addition, abnormal brain functioning can influence the autonomic nervous system (see Chapter 2): ADHD (and some types of conduct disorder) has been associated with unusually low arousal in response to normal levels of stimulation (Crowell et al., 2006), a response that could explain some of the stimulation-seeking behavior seen in individuals with this disorder. That is, these people could engage in stimulation-seeking behavior in order to obtain an optimal level of arousal.

ADHD and Neural Communication

The overall pattern of difficulties that characterizes ADHD suggests problems with multiple neurotransmitters that are involved in coordinating and organizing cognition and behavior. For one, dopamine apparently does not function effectively in the brains of people with this disorder (Volkow et al., 2007). This malfunction may arise for any of various reasons, including too few of the relevant receptors or problems in removing dopamine from the synapse (Swanson et al., 2007). But dopamine functioning is not the only issue: Imbalances in serotonin and norepinephrine may also contribute to the disorder (Arnsten, 2006; Gainetdinov et al., 1999; Waldman & Gizer, 2006), and the activity of other neurotransmitters may also be disrupted (Pattij & Vanderschuren, 2008). Given the number of brain areas that are involved, it is not surprising that problems with multiple neurotransmitters are likely to be associated with the disorder.

ADHD and Genetics

Genes may be one reason why people with ADHD have abnormal brain systems and disrupted neural communication. Indeed, not only does this disorder runs in families, but also parent and teacher reports indicate that it is highly correlated among monozygotic twins (with correlations ranging from 0.60 to 0.90). In addition, a large set of data reveals that this disorder is among the most heritable of psychological disorders (Martin et al., 2006; Stevenson et al., 2005; Waldman & Gizer, 2006).

However, as with most psychological disorders that are influenced by genes, a combination of genes—not a single gene—probably contributes to it (Faraone et al., 2005). In fact, over a dozen different genes have so far been identified as possibly contributing to this disorder (Guan et al., in press; Swanson et al., 2007; Waldman & Gizer, 2006). Many of these genes have been shown to affect the activity of the neurotransmitters that likely are involved in the disorder. In addition, some of these genes may also contribute to conduct disorder and oppositional defiant disorder, which would, at least in part, account for the high comorbidity among these disorders (Dick et al., 2005; Jain et al., 2007).

Genetic factors do not occur in a vacuum. In fact, such factors often interact with environmental events, which lead a given individual to be more or less sensitive to teratogens prenatally or to environmental exposure during early childhood (Jacobson et al., 2006; Kahn et al. 2003; Pineda et al., 2007; Swanson et al., 2007). Researchers have identified several environmental risk factors. For example, children whose mothers smoked while pregnant are much more likely to develop ADHD than are children whose mothers did not smoke (Braun et al., 2006), and this relationship appears to be particularly strong for children who have a specific gene (Neuman et al., 2007).

Neurological Factors in Conduct and Oppositional Defiant Disorders

Finally, although ADHD is by far the best-understood of the disruptive disorders, researchers have begun to investigate the other two. Much of what is known about neurological factors related to oppositional defiant disorder and conduct disorder overlaps with what is known about antisocial personality disorder (see Figure 13.6). This is not surprising, given the fact that most people with antisocial personality disorder or psychopathy had oppositional defiant disorder and/or conduct disorder during childhood or adolescence. Moreover, many, if not most, of the participants in those studies probably also had comorbid ADHD (although most people with ADHD don't develop oppositional defiant disorder, conduct disorder, or antisocial personality disorder). It is clear that genes play a role (Gelhorn et al., 2006; Hudziak et al., 2005; Maes et al., 2007): Both oppositional defiant disorder and conduct disorder are more common among children whose biological parents were criminals or had been diagnosed with oppositional defiant disorder, conduct disorder, ADHD, antisocial personality disorder, a substance use disorder, or a mood disorder (Frick & Muñoz, 2006; Haber, Jacobs, & Heath, 2005). All of these disorders except depression are considered to reflect externalizing problems, related to undercontrol (see Chapter 3).

Conduct disorder with callous and unemotional traits is accompanied by decreased sensitivity to—and arousal by—punishment, which is associated with a temperament referred to as low harm avoidance (Frick et al., 2003). This temperament in turn impedes the ability to internalize appropriate social norms and develop a conscience (Pardini, 2006). Moreover, individuals with this type of conduct disorder are likely to be high in another aspect of temperament, reward dependence; they are strongly motivated by the possibility of reward. But at the same time they are also low in persistence; they have a low tolerance for frustration (Gray, 1987; Zuckerman, 1991).

Psychological Factors: Recognizing Facial Expressions, Keeping Track of Time

We'll first examine the psychological factors of the best understood of the disorders that involve disruptive behavior—ADHD. In addition to problems with attention and executive function, people with ADHD may have other, perhaps less obvious, difficulties. As with autism, one problem is recognizing emotions in facial expressions—not all emotions, but anger and sadness in particular. Why? The answer isn't known, but one suggestion is that these people might have had very negative experiences with others who are sad or angry, and these unpleasant experiences motivate them to tune out such expressions (Pelc et al., 2006).

In addition, children with ADHD appear to have an attributional style that leaves them vulnerable to low self-esteem. In one study (Milich, 1994), children with ADHD initially overestimated their ability to succeed in a challenging task, and—when confronted with failure—boys with ADHD became more frustrated and were less likely to persist with the challenging task than were boys in a control group. Moreover, in another study (Collett & Gimpel, 2004), children with ADHD attributed the cause of negative events to global and stable characteristics about themselves ("I am a failure") rather than external, situational factors ("That was a very challenging task"). Conversely, children with ADHD were more likely than children without a psychological disorder to attribute positive events to external, situational causes. These attribution patterns were observed regardless of whether children were taking medication for ADHD. And such patterns are often seen in people who experience low self-esteem (Sweeney, Anderson, & Bailey, 1986; Tennen & Herzberger, 1987).

Low self-esteem among those with ADHD isn't restricted to children. One study compared college students with and without ADHD and matched them to control participants who had comparable demographic variables and grade-point averages; students with ADHD reported lower self-esteem and social skills than did students without ADHD (Shaw-Zirt et al., 2005). Other studies report lower self-esteem among adolescents with ADHD (Slomkowski, Klein, & Mannuzza, 1995).

Furthermore, problems with self-esteem are not limited to people with ADHD but are also present in those who have other disorders of disruptive behavior. However, people with oppositional defiant disorder and conduct disorder often fall at the ends of a self-esteem continuum: They either have low self-esteem or they have overly inflated self-esteem—believing themselves to be superior in ways that are not corroborated by their characteristics or behavior.

People with ADHD can have difficulty picking up on certain social cues—specifically, they may not recognize the facial expressions that correspond to anger and sadness.

Social Factors: Blame and Credit

The self-esteem of children with ADHD may also be related to their parents' attributions: Although parents don't necessarily blame their children for ADHD-related behaviors, they don't give their children as much credit for positive behaviors as do parents of children without ADHD (Johnston & Freeman, 1997). The parents of children with ADHD tend to attribute children's positive behaviors to random situational factors.

Parents of children with ADHD may also feel frustrated and pessimistic about their children's abilities and behavior. In a study aimed at exploring these emotions, researchers compared the feelings of parents of children (aged 7 to 12) with and without ADHD while each child-parent pair was engaged in either "getting ready" activities (such as getting ready to leave the house to go to school) or "other" activities (Whalen et. al. 2006). Each parent carried around a personal digital assistant (PDA) that beeped at unpredictable times. At the sound of the beep, parents filled in an electronic diary that asked about the current activity and parents' feelings. Parents of children with ADHD reported spending more time on "getting ready" activities. They also reported more feelings of anger and stress, were less likely to be in a good mood, and had more arguments with their children during such activities than did parents of children without ADHD. Although the researchers did not observe the actual behaviors of the parents, it is reasonable to surmise that any parent who reported negative feelings may have acted toward his or her child in ways that reflected these feelings—either overtly and explictly, or by being irritable or impatient.

For people diagnosed with oppositional defiant disorder or conduct disorder, all of the social factors associated with ADHD play a role, as do many of the factors that give rise to antisocial personality disorder: harsh or inconsistent punishment and a family history of substance abuse or antisocial personality disorder. In fact, studies have demonstrated that psychological and social factors play a larger role in oppositional defiant disorder and conduct disorder than in ADHD (Frick & Muñoz, 2006). However, genetic factors can also account for part of the effect of these social

factors: Parents who develop substance use disorders or antisocial personality disorder may have temperaments (influenced by genes) that increase the likelihood that these disorders will emerge; however, such parents may also pass the genes to their children, making it difficult to distinguish among the different influences.

Other social factors related to oppositional defiant disorder and conduct disorder—with or without comorbid ADHD—are intertwined with psychological factors (Levy & Orlans, 1999, 2000; Ogloff, 2006). Children exposed to neglect or violence—in the neighborhood, among peers, or at home—observe others showing a disregard for social norms; through observational learning, they may come to imitate those behaviors (psychological factor). Parental neglect or inconsistent parenting is also associated with a child's disruptive behavior: Children may receive positive attention or praise rarely and negative attention more frequently—when breaking rules or being disruptive. They then learn to obtain attention by acting up. Moreover, parents may be inconsistent in setting limits on inappropriate behavior, and so children learn that nothing bad usually happens if they break rules (and if parents do intervene, the children receive attention!) (Dodge & Pettit, 2003; Loeber & Farrington, 2000; Moffitt, 2003; Raine, 2002). Thus, as we saw with antisocial personality disorder and psychopathy, genes may predispose someone toward certain types of behavior, but the environment in which a child is raised and how the child is treated influence whether such behavior is exhibited (Caspi et al., 2002; Mednick, Gabriella, & Hutchings, 1984).

Finally, social factors can indirectly influence the development of these disorders. For example, children typically are raised in homes selected by their parents—based on various social factors such as parents' financial status, proximity to extended family, and community resources. If children are raised in a house where lead paint has been applied, they may be more vulnerable to ADHD. In fact, children whose hair contains higher levels of lead (which is a measure of exposure to lead, perhaps from lead paint in one's home environment) are more likely to have ADHD than are children who have lower levels of lead in their hair (Tuthill, 1996). Even children who were exposed to very low levels of lead in their environment are more likely to develop ADHD than are children who were not exposed (Nigg, 2006).

FEEDBACK LOOPS IN ACTION:
Attention-Deficit/Hyperactivity Disorder

In this section, we examine how the different factors related to attention-deficit/hyperactivity disorder create feedback loops (see Figure 14.4). Current research suggests that psychological and social factors contribute to the development of ADHD in those who are neurologically vulnerable to the disorder because of genetics, prenatal factors (such as the mother's smoking), or environmental factors (such as exposure to lead in early childhood; Laucht et al., 2007).

Consider the finding that children with ADHD are less accurate at recognizing sad and angry facial expressions (Pelc et al., 2006). Such deficits, particularly difficulty in recognizing anger, are associated with more interpersonal problems. These results suggest that when peers or adults (typically parents or teachers) show—rather than tell—their displeasure about the behavior of a child who has ADHD, that child is less likely to perceive (psychological factor) the social cue (social factor) than is a child who does not have the disorder. The inability to perceive others' displeasure in turn creates additional tension for both the child and those who interact with him or her. In fact, children with ADHD are more likely than those without the disorder to be rejected by their peers (Mrug et al., 2009). Moreover, other people's responses to the child's behavior (social factor) in turn influence how the child comes to feel about himself or herself (psychological factor; Brook & Boaz, 2005).

Other research results suggest that the family environment is associated with ADHD. In particular, family conflict is higher in families that include a child

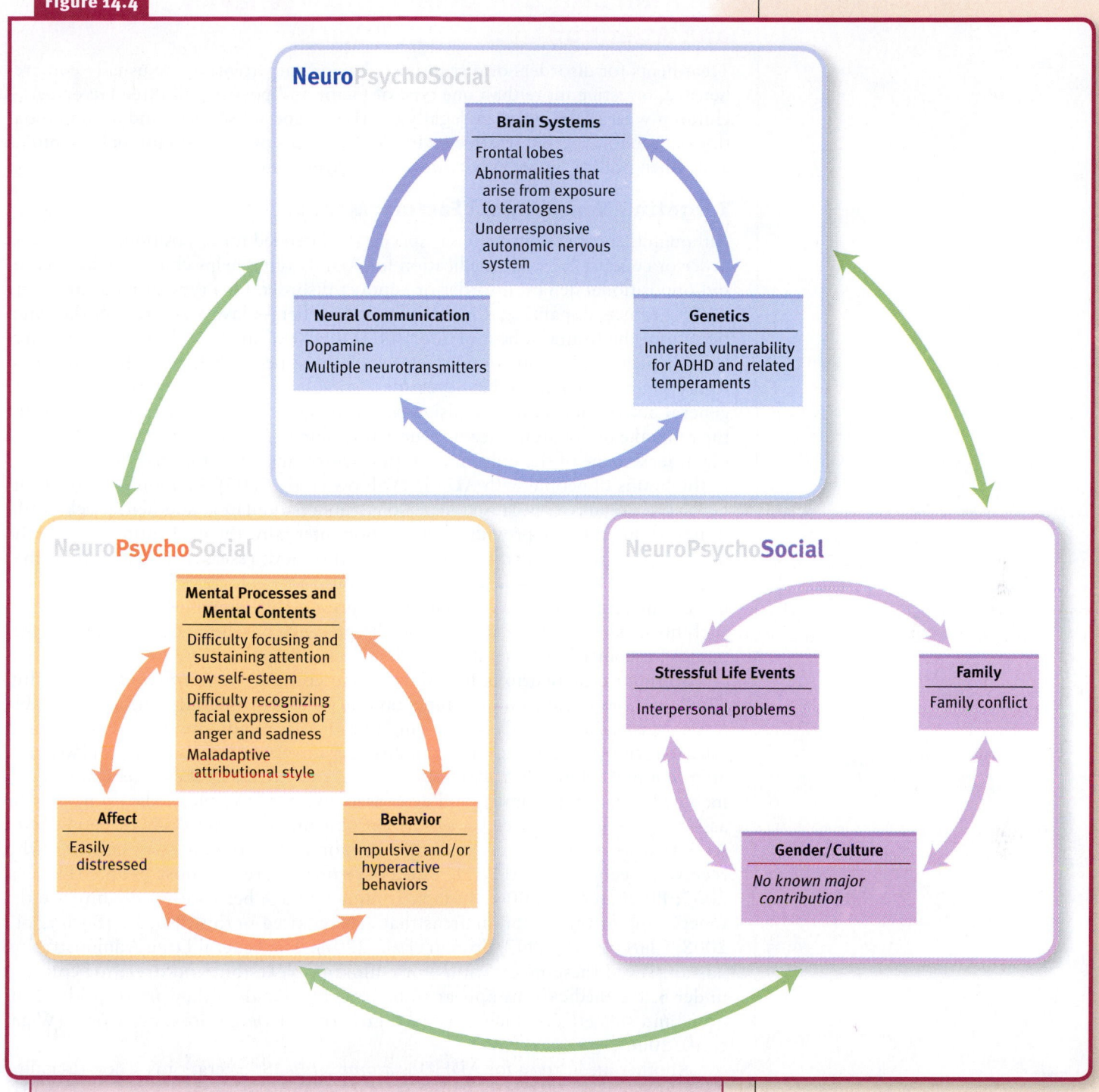

Figure 14.4

14.4 ▶ Feedback Loops in Action: Attention-Deficit/Hyperactivity Disorder

with ADHD than in control families (Pressman et al., 2006). However, do family environments that are higher in conflict *contribute* to ADHD in those who are vulnerable? Or do the symptoms of the disorder—inattention, hyperactivity, or impulsivity—create more tension in the family? Or do difficulties associated with the disorder, such as difficulty in recognizing angry or sad facial expressions, increase family tension? It may be that all these possible influences occur.

Treating Disorders of Disruptive Behavior and Attention

Treatments for disorders of disruptive behavior and attention are usually comprehensive, targeting more than one type of factor and possibly all three factors. And children with ADHD may be legally entitled to special services and accommodations in school. Specific treatments for ADHD focus on both attentional symptoms and, when present, hyperactivity/impulsivity symptoms.

Targeting Neurological Factors: Medication

Although there are no medications specifically intended for oppositional defiant disorder or conduct disorder, medication for ADHD often helps children with comorbid oppositional defiant disorder or conduct disorder. One type of medication for ADHD targets dopamine, which—as noted earlier—plays a key role in the functioning of the frontal lobe (Solanto, 2002). Many of these medications are stimulants, which may sound counterintuitive because people with ADHD don't seem to need more stimulation. However, these stimulants increase attention and reduce general activity level and impulsive behavior. The medications appear to disrupt the reuptake of dopamine, leaving more dopamine in the synapse and thus correcting at least some of the imbalance in this neurotransmitter that has been observed in the brains of people with ADHD (Volkow et al., 2005). In addition, this disorder may arise in part because the person is understimulated, and hence seeks additional stimulation; by providing stimulation internally, the medications reduce the need to seek it externally. Consistent with this view, researchers have found that people with ADHD perform memory and verbal tasks better when auditory white noise is present in the background (which presumably stimulates them) than when such noise is not present; in contrast, the presence of white noise impairs performance for control participants (Söderlund, Sikström, & Smart, 2007).

Stimulant medications for ADHD may contain *methylphenidate* (Ritalin, Concerta, and Focalin) or an amphetamine (such as Adderall), and are available in shorter-lasting formulas (requiring two or three daily doses) and in a timed-release formula (requiring only one dose per day). Methyphenidate is also available as a daily skin patch. For some people, side effects of these medications can include headache, insomnia, and decreased appetite, and the medications may be associated with increased risk of heart problems. About 65–75% of people with ADHD who receive stimulants improve (compared to 4–30% of controls who receive placebos), and the side effects are not severe for most people (Pliszka, 2007; Pliszka et al., 2006). In fact, stimulants have been shown to improve the functioning of various brain areas that are impaired in this disorder (Bush et al., 2008; Clarke et al., 2007; Epstein et al., 2007). The Federal Drug Administration has approved these medications for children 6 years old and over; for children under 6, the medications appear to be less effective than they are for older children, and side effects, such as slowed growth and weight loss, are worse (Wigal et al., 2006).

Another medication for ADHD is *atomoxetine* (Strattera); it is a noradrenaline reuptake inhibitor, not a stimulant. Atomoxetine has effects and side effects similar to those of the stimulant medications (Kratochvil et al., 2002) and currently is the medication of choice for people with both ADHD and substance abuse.

Medications for ADHD reduce impulsive behaviors, which seems to decrease related aggressive behaviors (Frick & Morris, 2004). This effect can have wide-ranging consequences. In particular, as noted earlier, for some children, the symptoms of ADHD give rise to feedback loops involving interactions with their families or with peers that cause the disruptive behaviors to escalate. Successful treatment with medication disrupts these feedback loops, reducing the frequency and intensity of disruptive behaviors, which in turn leads family members or peers not to become as irritated and angry, which thereby reduces their undercutting the child's self-esteem (Frick & Muñoz, 2006; Hinshaw et al., 1993; Jensen et al., 2001).

Targeting Psychological Factors: Treating Disruptive Behavior

Treatments that target psychological factors have been developed for oppositional defiant disorder, conduct disorder, and ADHD. These treatments usually employ behavioral and cognitive methods to address disruptive behaviors. One reason for such behaviors is that children with any of these disorders tend to have low frustration tolerance and difficulty in working for delayed—rather than immediate—reward. Thus, behavioral methods may focus on helping such children restrain their behavior and accept a delayed reward. Specific techniques include a reinforcement program that uses concrete rewards, such as a toy, and social rewards, such as praise or special time with a parent. These methods slowly increase the delay until the child receives either a concrete reward ("Now you can have that toy") or a social reward ("You did a great job, I'm proud of you"), which should motivate the child to control behavior for a delayed reward in the future (Sonuga-Barke, 2006).

Behavioral methods for treating all three disorders may also be used to modify social behaviors, such as not responding to others aggressively or not interrupting others. For example, when children enter preschool or kindergarten, it may be the first time they have to sit quietly for a length of time and wait for a turn to participate. Often the teacher will ask children to raise a hand and wait until called on to answer a question. A child with ADHD will be more likely than other children to speak out of turn or to keep vigorously waving a raised hand, trying to get the teacher's attention. 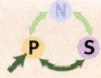 A program of rewarding the child for increasingly longer times of not speaking out or waving frantically can teach the child to behave with more restraint, which can ease relations with classmates.

Cognitive methods seek to enhance children's social problem-solving abilities. Specifically, the therapist helps the child interpret social cues in a more realistic way—for instance, acknowledging that the other person may not have hostile motives when he asked you to move your backpack—and develop more appropriate social goals and responses (Dodge & Pettit, 2003). Through skills-building, modeling, and role-playing, the treatment also shows the child how to inhibit angry or impulsive reactions and to learn more effective ways to respond to others. The therapist praises the child's successes in these areas. To enhance the generalizability of the new skills to life outside the therapy session, parents and teachers may be asked to help with role-playing and modeling and to use praise in their contacts with the child.

When a child's symptoms interfere with functioning in school, an IEP may specify classroom accommodations, such as increased time to complete tests and more frequent but shorter breaks throughout the day.

Targeting Social Factors: Reinforcement in Relationships

Most of the treatments that target social factors are designed to help parents—and teachers when necessary—to make more systematic and consistent use of operant conditioning principles: reinforcement, punishment, and extinction. Through operant conditioning, such treatment is designed to shape a child's prosocial behavior and decrease defiant or impulsive behavior. In addition, group therapy and various other techniques may be used to improve social skills.

Contingency Management: Changing Parents' Behavior

Contingency management is a procedure for modifying behavior by changing the conditions that lead to, or are produced by, it. Treatment may target parents of children with ADHD, to help them set up a contingency management program with their child—particularly in cases in which the parents have been inconsistent in their use of praise and other reinforcers as well as punishment (Frick & Muñoz, 2006).

Contingency management
A procedure for modifying behavior by changing the conditions that led to, or are produced by, it.

The first step of contingency management training with parents is psychoeducation—teaching the parents that the symptoms are not the result of intentional misbehavior but part of a disorder (Barkley, 1997, 2000). The training then is intended to:

1. change parents' beliefs about the reasons for their child's behavior so that parents approach their child differently and develop realistic goals for their child's behavior;

2. help parents to institute behavior modification, which includes paying attention to desired behaviors, being consistent and clear about directions, and developing reward programs; and

3. teach parents to respond consistently to misbehavior.

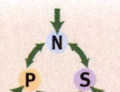

Parent training, then, targets social factors—interactions between parents and child. Changes in the way parents think about and interact with their child, in turn, change the child's ability to control behavior (psychological factor). Parent training may be the best treatment for families who have children with mild ADHD or preschoolers with ADHD (Kratochvil et al., 2004).

Parent Management Training

Parent management training is designed to combine contingency management techniques with additional techniques that focus on improving parent-child interactions generally—improving communication and facilitating real warmth and positive interest in the parent for his or her child (Kazdin, 1995).

Multisystemic Therapy

Multisystemic therapy (Henggeler et al., 1998) is based on family systems therapy and focuses on the context in which the child's behavior occurs: with peers, in school, in the neighborhood, and in the family. This comprehensive treatment may involve family and couples therapy, interventions with peers, CBT with the child, and an intervention in the school (such as meeting with the child's teacher or directly assisting in the classroom to help the child manage his or her behavior). The specific techniques employed are tailored to the systems in the child's life that need to be changed.

A substantial minority of children with conduct disorder and oppositional defiant disorder don't respond to a given treatment or, if they do, their disruptive behaviors may decrease only to the point where the diagnostic criteria for a disruptive behavior disorder are no longer met; usually, though, the disruptive behaviors do not decrease to normal levels (Kazdin, 1995). Moreover, success in changing a child's behavior in one setting—at home, for example—does not necessarily generalize to other settings, such as the classroom. Younger children who have relatively minor symptoms are most likely to benefit from the treatments that target social factors.

FEEDBACK LOOPS IN TREATMENT: Treating Attention-Deficit/Hyperactivity Disorder

Let's take a closer look at treatment for ADHD, examining the feedback loops among the various factors (see Figure 14.5).

At first glance, medication might seem to have its effects solely through neurological mechanisms, but this isn't so. Taking medication (neurological factor) not only leads to increased control of attention and hyperactive or impulsive behaviors, but it is also associated with higher levels of self-esteem (psychological factor; Frankel et al., 1999) and improved social functioning (social factor; Chacko et al., 2005). And better social functioning feeds back to improve self-esteem, which can lead a child not to seek attention as vigorously.

Other feedback loops originate from programs for parents or the family (which target social factors); such interventions in turn create feedback loops with psychological factors—improving the child's thoughts, feelings, and behaviors.

Figure 14.5

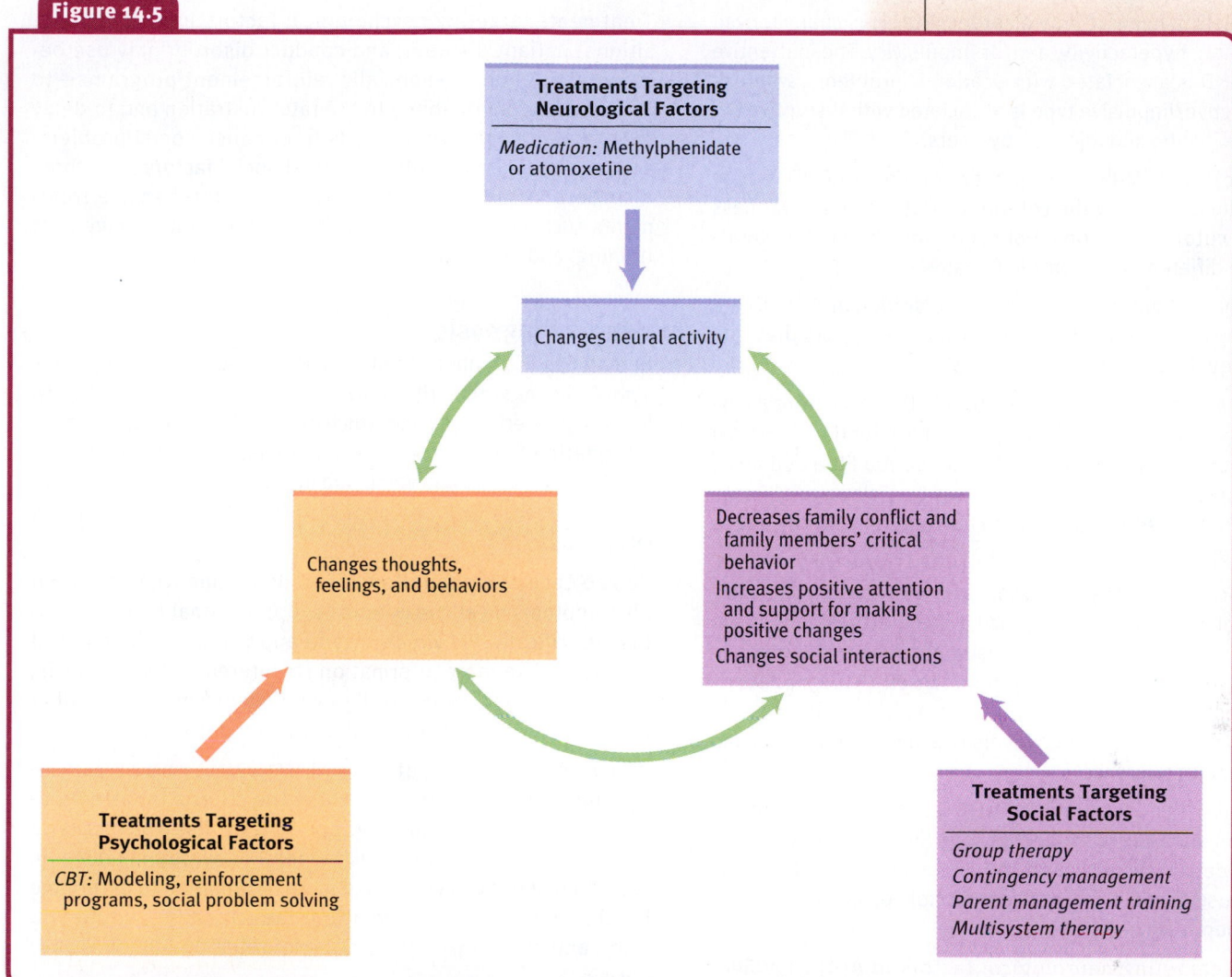

Treatments Targeting
Neurological Factors

Medication: Methylphenidate
or atomoxetine

Changes neural activity

Changes thoughts,
feelings, and behaviors

Decreases family conflict and
family members' critical
behavior
Increases positive attention
and support for making
positive changes
Changes social interactions

Treatments Targeting
Psychological Factors

CBT: Modeling, reinforcement
programs, social problem solving

Treatments Targeting
Social Factors

Group therapy
Contingency management
Parent management training
Multisystem therapy

14.5 ▸ Feedback Loops in Treatment: Attention-Deficit/Hyperactivity Disorder

Key Concepts and Facts About Disorders of Disruptive Behavior and Attention ▪

- Conduct disorder is characterized by a violation of the basic rights of others or of societal norms that are appropriate to the individual's age. Conduct disorder involves four types of behavior: aggression to people and animals, destruction of property, deceitfulness or theft, and serious violation of rules. Symptoms may be mild, moderate, or severe, and the disorder may begin in childhood or adolescence. Conduct disorder is commonly comorbid with attention-deficit/hyperactivity disorder and substance use or abuse.

- Childhood-onset conduct disorder with callous and unemotional traits has the highest heritability among the various types of conduct disorder; this variant is also associated with more severe symptoms. Individuals with childhood-onset

conduct disorder *without* callous and unemotional traits are less aggressive, although they are likely to be aggressive impulsively, in response to (mis)perceived threats. Adolescent-onset conduct disorder tends to involve mild symptoms that are usually transient.

- Oppositional defiant disorder is characterized by a behavioral pattern of disobedience, hostility, defiance, and negativity toward people in authority. The behaviors are usually not violent nor do they cause severe harm, and they often occur only in certain contexts. Some people with oppositional defiant disorder go on to develop conduct disorder; if an individual's behaviors meet the criteria for both oppositional defiant disorder and conduct disorder, only conduct disorder is diagnosed.

continued on next page

- Attention-deficit/hyperactivity disorder (ADHD) is characterized by inattention, hyperactivity, and/or impulsivity. The inattentive type of ADHD is associated with academic problems, whereas the hyperactive/impulsive type is associated with disruptive behaviors, accidents, and rejection by peers.

- Criticisms of the DSM-IV-TR diagnostic criteria for ADHD include the difficulty in applying the criteria to adults, the arbitrariness of the age cutoff for the onset of symptoms, and failure to acknowledge different symptoms in females.

- Oppositional defiant disorder, conduct disorder, and ADHD are highly comorbid, making it difficult to sort out factors that contribute uniquely to one of the disorders.

- Neurological factors that contribute to ADHD include frontal lobe problems (which lead to the symptoms of inattention, impaired executive function and memory difficulties). Too little dopamine and imbalances in other transmitters may also play a role. Genes also contribute to ADHD and conduct disorder, in part by affecting temperament.

- Psychological factors that are associated with ADHD include low self-esteem and difficulty recognizing facial expressions of anger and sadness. People with oppositional defiant disorder and conduct disorder tend to have either low self-esteem or overly high self-esteem, are relatively unresponsive to the threat of punishment, and exhibit high levels of emotional distress and poor frustration tolerance.

- Social factors that contribute to ADHD include parents' not giving children enough credit for their positive behaviors. For oppositional defiant disorder and conduct disorder, social factors include abuse, neglect, inconsistent discipline, and lack of positive attention.

- Treatment targeting neurological factors in ADHD involves medication—typically methylphenidate or atomoxetine.

Treatments targeting psychological factors in ADHD, oppositional defiant disorder, and conduct disorder may use behavioral methods—especially reinforcement programs—to increase a person's ability to tolerate frustration and to delay reward, and cognitive methods to enhance social problem-solving ability. Treatments that target social factors in all three disorders include group therapy and comprehensive treatments such as contingency management, parent management training, and multisystemic therapy.

Making a Diagnosis

- Reread Case 14.5 about Brad, and determine whether or not his symptoms meet the criteria for conduct disorder. Specifically, list which criteria apply and which do not. If you would like more information to determine his diagnosis, what information—specifically—would you want, and in what ways would the information influence your decision? How severe do you consider his symptoms to be?

- Reread Case 14.6 about Danny, and determine whether or not his symptoms meet the criteria for oppositional defiant disorder. Specifically, list which criteria apply and which do not. If you would like more information to determine his diagnosis, what information—specifically—would you want, and in what ways would the information influence your decision?

- Reread Case 14.7 about Edward Hallowell, and determine whether or not his symptoms meet the criteria for attention-deficit/hyperactivity disorder. Specifically, list which criteria apply and which do not. Which type(s) of symptoms does he seem to have? If you would like more information to determine his diagnosis, what information—specifically—would you want, and in what ways would the information influence your decision?

Other Disorders of Childhood

Children can exhibit a wide variety of odd or unusual behaviors that in and of themselves do not necessarily indicate psychopathology:

- Many children become anxious (temporarily) about separating from loved ones such as parents, particularly during early childhood and adolescence. Younger children may put up a fuss about being dropped off at school; older children may "freak out" about going away from home for the summer.

- Some children learn to speak and understand language quickly; others learn verbal communication skills more slowly.

- Children may go through phases that involve odd eating habits such as being picky eaters or occasionally chomping on a crayon.

- Children who have been toilet-trained can have accidents and "go" in places other than the toilet.

- Some children may, from time to time, exhibit repetitive movements, such as abnormally frequent eye blinking or repetitive vocal sounds such as throat clearing or odd noises.

These behaviors or constellations of behaviors are common enough to be considered normal patterns of infancy, childhood, and adolescence, but sometimes they may indicate any of a number of disorders. In the following sections we discuss the circumstances in which such behaviors would lead a clinician to diagnose a disorder. First, we'll explore an anxiety disorder that most typically arises in children—*separation anxiety disorder*. Then, we'll briefly review other types of disorders that can arise in children. Most of these disorders come to the attention of a pediatrician, who may treat the problem or, if needed, recommend a specialist; depending on the nature of the problem, the pediatrician might refer the child to a speech therapist, urologist, nutritionist, gastroenterologist, mental health clinician, or some other type of specialist.

Separation Anxiety Disorder

Although anxiety disorders form a distinct category in DSM-IV-TR (see Chapter 7), one anxiety disorder is placed among disorders pertaining to infancy, childhood, and adolescence because DSM-IV-TR specifies that it must begin in childhood. That disorder is **separation anxiety disorder,** which is characterized by excessive anxiety about separation from home or from someone to whom the child has become attached. In this section the word *parent* refers to the individual from whom the child fears separation; that individual may be the mother, father, some other family member, caretaker, or other person involved in the child's life. We'll examine separation anxiety disorder in detail, then turn to its causes and treatment.

What Is Separation Anxiety Disorder?

During different phases of development, an infant or toddler will normally become distressed on separating (or even thinking about separating) from a parent. To qualify for a diagnosis of separation anxiety disorder, the anxiety, distress, or impaired functioning must be excessive and must be exhibited over a period of at least 4 weeks (see Table 14.16).

Separation anxiety is more than a child's getting upset about temporarily saying goodbye to a parent. Children with separation anxiety disorder may become so homesick when away from home that activities—such as a sleepover at a friend's or a stay at overnight camp—are interrupted in order to return home. Or these children may want to know the parent's whereabouts at all times, using a cell phone to make frequent contact during any physical separation. And when away from the parent, they may also manifest physical symptoms of anxiety (see Chapter 7): dizziness, stomachaches, nausea and vomiting, and feeling faint (American Psychiatric Association, 2000). When the disorder emerges in children younger than 6 years old, the clinician can specify "early onset."

Some children with separation anxiety disorder fear that they will get permanently "lost" from their parents, and their dreams have similar themes. And like people with agoraphobia (see Chapter 7), they may be unable to leave the house alone (at an age when it would be appropriate to do so) or even to be in their room alone. Such children often try to stay within a few feet of the parent, moving from room to room as the parent moves from room to room. At bedtime, they may be unable to fall asleep unless someone else is in the room with them, and during the night, they may crawl into bed with parents or a sibling. If parents lock their bedroom door at night, the child may sleep on the floor right outside the door. If children with this disorder are separated from their parent, they may have persistent

Separation anxiety disorder
A psychological disorder that typically arises in childhood and is characterized by excessive anxiety about separation from home or from someone to whom the individual has become attached.

Table 14.16 ▸ DSM-IV-TR Diagnostic Criteria for Separation Anxiety Disorder

A. Developmentally inappropriate and excessive anxiety concerning separation from home or from those to whom the individual is attached, as evidenced by three (or more) of the following:

(1) recurrent excessive distress when separation from home or major attachment figures occurs or is anticipated;

(2) persistent and excessive worry about losing, or about possible harm befalling, major attachment figures;

(3) persistent and excessive worry that an untoward event will lead to separation from a major attachment figure (e.g., getting lost or being kidnapped);

(4) persistent reluctance or refusal to go to school or elsewhere because of fear of separation;

(5) persistently and excessively fearful or reluctant to be alone or without major attachment figures at home or without significant adults in other settings;

(6) persistent reluctance or refusal to go to sleep without being near a major attachment figure or to sleep away from home;

(7) repeated nightmares involving the theme of separation;

(8) repeated complaints of physical symptoms (such as headaches, stomachaches, nausea, or vomiting) when separation from major attachment figures occurs or is anticipated.

B. The duration of the disturbance is at least 4 weeks.

C. The onset is before age 18 years.

D. The disturbance causes clinically significant distress or impairment in social, academic (occupational), or other important areas of functioning.

E. The disturbance does not occur exclusively during the course of a Pervasive Developmental Disorder, Schizophrenia or another Psychotic Disorder [Chapter 12] and, in adolescents and adults, is not better accounted for by Panic Disorder with Agoraphobia [Chapter 7].

Source: Reprinted with permission from the Diagnostic and Statistical Manual of Mental Disorders, Text Revision, Fourth Edition, (Copyright 2000) American Psychiatric Association.

fantasies about reuniting. Also, like individuals with generalized anxiety disorder (see Chapter 7), they may have recurrent fears about harm befalling their parent or themselves, as JC did, in Case 14.8. Table 14.17 lists additional facts about separation anxiety disorder.

CASE 14.8 ▸ FROM THE OUTSIDE: Separation Anxiety Disorder

JC is a 9-year-old boy who lives with his mother and attends the third grade, where he is an A student. During the last 2 weeks, he has refused to go to school and has missed 6 school days. He is awake almost all night worrying about going to school. As the start of the school day approaches, he cries and screams that he cannot go, chews holes in his shirt, pulls his hair, digs at his face, punches the wall, throws himself on the floor, and experiences headaches, stomachaches, and vomiting. If he attends school, he is less anxious until bedtime. As his separation anxiety has increased, he has become gloomy, has stopped reading for fun, and frequently worries about his mother's tachycardia [rapid heart rate].

JC was seen once by a psychiatrist at age 3 years for problems with separation anxiety. He did well in preschool and kindergarten. He was seen at a community mental health center during the first grade for school refusal, but did well again during the second grade. In addition to having recurrent symptoms of separation anxiety disorder, he is phobic of dogs, avoids speaking and writing in public, and has symptoms of generalized anxiety disorder and obsessive-compulsive disorder. His mother has a history of panic disorder.

(Hanna, Fischer, & Fluent, 2006, pp. 56–57)

Table 14.17 ▸ Separation Anxiety Disorder Facts at a Glance

Prevalence

- About 4% of adults experienced separation anxiety disorder in childhood (Shear et al., 2006).
- Separation anxiety disorder is the most prevalent anxiety disorder among children.

Onset

- As required by DSM-IV-TR, the disorder must emerge before an individual is 18 years old, although it can begin as early as the preschool years.
- Separation anxiety disorder may emerge after some type of stressful event, such as a move, the death of a pet, or the illness of a relative.

Comorbidity

- Children with separation anxiety disorder are more likely to experience other anxiety disorders than are children in the general population (Brückl et al., 2006; Verduin & Kendall, 2003).

Course

- Symptoms often wax and wane.
- As the child gets older, symptoms tend to lessen; at some point before adulthood, most individuals no longer meet the criteria for the disorder (Foley, Pickles et al., 2004; Shear et al., 2006).

Gender Differences

- In the general population, more females than males have this disorder; however, comparable numbers of males and females with this disorder are treated as outpatients.

Cultural Differences

- Different ethnic groups and cultures have different norms about what constitutes appropriate responses to separation in children, which can affect parents' inclination to perceive a separation problem and create different thresholds for diagnosis across cultures.

Source: Unless otherwise noted, the source for information is American Psychiatric Association, 2000.

Distinguishing Between Separation Anxiety Disorder and Other Disorders

As they did for JC, the symptoms of separation anxiety disorder can overlap with those of generalized anxiety disorder and social phobia. Both separation anxiety disorder and generalized anxiety disorder involve worries that are difficult to control, such as a fear that family members may be harmed. With separation anxiety disorder, however, the worries are restricted to separation from the parent; with generalized anxiety disorder, the worries involve a variety of topics, most of which are unrelated to separation issues. Similarly, although both social phobia and separation anxiety disorder may involve a reluctance to leave the house (and attend school), with social phobia, the fear is about performing or being evaluated by others.

When separated from the parent, children with separation anxiety disorder may exhibit symptoms of various other disorders. For instance, a child or adolescent with separation anxiety disorder may, on occasion, have panic attacks when forced to separate from the parent; however, the attacks do not indicate panic disorder unless the child or adolescent comes to fear having additional panic attacks. In addition, such children may appear depressed—seeming sad, apathetic and withdrawn—and have difficulty concentrating. In fact, some may become clinically depressed. Children with this disorder worry about death and may have persistent fears of monsters, kidnappers, or other harmful figures or acts, particularly when alone. They may even report that no one loves them—perhaps because their parents do not allow them to sleep in the parents' bed or because the parents force them to attend school. When forced to separate from the parent, children with separation anxiety disorder may get angry and hit other people. Parents, siblings, teachers, and others may report that a child with separation anxiety disorder is particularly needy or "high maintenance," which can lead to tension and frustration for all concerned. In some cases, the child's behavior may resemble that of those with oppositional defiant disorder; however, children with separation anxiety disorder, unlike those with oppositional defiant disorder, generally comply with requests that do not require them to be separated from the parent.

Finally, we note that refusal to attend school is not always caused by separation anxiety disorder, however. It may arise because of a mood disorder, social phobia, or oppositional defiant disorder. Clinicians must thoroughly evaluate the reasons for the school refusal before diagnosing separation anxiety disorder.

Understanding Separation Anxiety Disorder

Separation anxiety disorder most commonly arises in children who are part of tight-knit families (American Psychiatric Association, 2000). Separation anxiety disorder is more common among first-degree relatives (parents and siblings) than in the general population, and the disorder is considered to be moderately heritable (Cronk et al., 2004). However, the heritability probably reflects a heritability of anxiety in general: Separation anxiety is more common among children whose mothers have panic disorder than among children whose mothers don't have that disorder (Cronk et al., 2004).

But other factors create feedback loops: Tight-knit families may reinforce behaviors associated with anxiety about separation and may punish behaviors associated with actual separation. If so, then children in such families who have temperaments that are high in harm avoidance and reward dependence may be especially vulnerable, because they will be relatively responsive to reward and punishment. Moreover, separation anxiety disorder is more common in children whose fathers are absent (Cronk et al., 2004), perhaps because that absence leads the child to have a heightened fear of losing the remaining parent.

Treating Separation Anxiety Disorder

As with other anxiety disorders, treatment of separation anxiety disorder may involve CBT (with exposure and cognitive restructuring; see Chapter 7). Family therapy is often another component of treatment; the therapist identifies any family patterns that maintain the disorder and helps parents change their interaction patterns to encourage and reinforce their child for engaging in appropriate separation behaviors (Siqueland, Rynn, & Diamond, 2005).

Other Types of Disorders of Childhood, in Brief

Let's now consider four subcategories of DSM-IV-TR disorders that typically arise in childhood: *communication disorders, feeding and eating disorders, elimination disorders,* and *tic disorders.* Disorders in these subcategories involve behaviors that are on an extreme end of a continuum, and thus represent abnormal rather than normal behaviors.

Communication Disorders

Some children evidence **communication disorders,** which are disorders characterized by significant problems in understanding language or in expressing themselves with language. (Children with hearing problems are not considered to have problems in understanding language unless they have clear difficulty learning sign language or other forms of language that do not require hearing.) A mental health clinician may be asked to help determine whether a child's apparent difficulty comprehending language or expressing himself or herself is abnormal—outside the normal range—and, if so, whether a disorder other than a communication disorder might better account for the problems. For instance, a child might willfully refuse to speak or appear to misunderstand others (oppositional defiant disorder) or might be so anxious that he or she is "scared speechless." Alternatively, a child might exhibit problems with coherently expressing himself or herself because of childhood-onset schizophrenia,

Communication disorders
A set of psychological disorders characterized by significant problems in understanding language or using language to express oneself.

a pervasive developmental disorder, mental retardation, or another disorder (American Psychiatric Association, 2000).

Feeding and Eating Disorders

Feeding and eating disorders are characterized by problems with eating or with feeding in the case of infants or young children whose diet consists entirely or mainly of liquids, such as formula or milk (American Psychiatric Association, 2000). Disorders in this subcategory include those that arise when a child does not eat enough (and so either loses weight or fails to gain adequate weight), disorders that lead the child to exhibit bizarre eating habits (such as eating nonfood objects, including dirt), as well as the eating disorders anorexia nervosa and bulimia nervosa (discussed in Chapter 10).

When the eating problem results from a medical problem or another psychological disorder, the diagnosis of a feeding or eating disorder is not made. Mental health clinicians may be asked to help determine whether feeding or eating problems arise from another psychological disorder, such as depression, anxiety, or oppositional defiant disorder, or from other causes. Mental health clinicians may also treat the child with a feeding or eating disorder and his or her family.

Elimination Disorders

Humans are not born knowing how to use the toilet; we must learn to do so. Most children learn by the age of 5 years, although they may have occasional accidents. But some children who are 5 years old or older do not routinely use the toilet appropriately to urinate or defecate, indicating an **elimination disorder.**

DSM-IV-TR includes two types of elimination disorders. **Encopresis** is the elimination disorder characterized by a child's persistently defecating in improper locations—neither in a toilet nor in a diaper (American Psychiatric Association, 2000). Encopresis often arises, paradoxically, as the result of constipation (Loening-Baucke, 1996): The colon and large intestine become full of hard stool, which makes bowel movements painful; children may then put off defecating as long as possible, which makes the constipation worse. The intestines cannot function properly because they are so full of stool (Partin et al., 1992), and the passage of feces becomes uncontrolled as looser stool from the small intestine leaks out around the mass of stool in the large intestine, colon, and rectum. Parents may then think their child is willfully refusing to use the toilet or has diarrhea, even though the real problem is the opposite—a large, hard stool that is difficult to pass. Encopresis that results from hard stool is often resolved through changes in diet, such as increasing the child's intake of fluids and high-fiber foods.

Enuresis is another elimination disorder, which is characterized by a child's persistently urinating in bed or into his or her clothes; nighttime enuresis, or bedwetting, is common: Approximately a tenth of children between 5 and 16 years old wet their beds, although not necessarily nightly (Mellon & McGrath, 2000). As children age, this problem becomes less common. Nighttime enuresis usually involves abnormal sleep patterns that cause children to sleep so deeply that they are not aware of the sensations of a full bladder or cannot rouse themselves to get out of bed and get to the bathroom (Nield & Kamat, 2004).

The most successful treatment for enuresis is based on behavioral principles and uses a bed-wetting alarm, as shown in Figure 14.6 (Mellon & McGrath, 2000; Mikkelsen, 2001): This treatment helps the child learn to control his or her bladder at night (some models of the equipment, such as that in Figure 14.6, also work for daytime enuresis). The alarm goes off immediately after its sensor (attached to underwear) detects wetness. Initially, the child wakes up from the alarm *after* wetting the bed but is instructed to try to urinate in the toilet after being awakened by the alarm's going off. With motivation and repeated experience, the child learns to wake up increasingly earlier in the process of bed-wetting; within 6 months (but often in less time), the child usually learns to wake up and go to the bathroom

---

Feeding and eating disorders
A set of psychological disorders characterized by problems with feeding or eating.

Elimination disorders
A set of psychological disorders characterized by inappropriate urination or defecation.

Encopresis
An elimination disorder characterized by a child's persistent defecation in improper locations—neither in a toilet nor in a diaper.

Enuresis
An elimination disorder characterized by a child's persistent urination in bed or into his or her clothes.

Figure 14.6

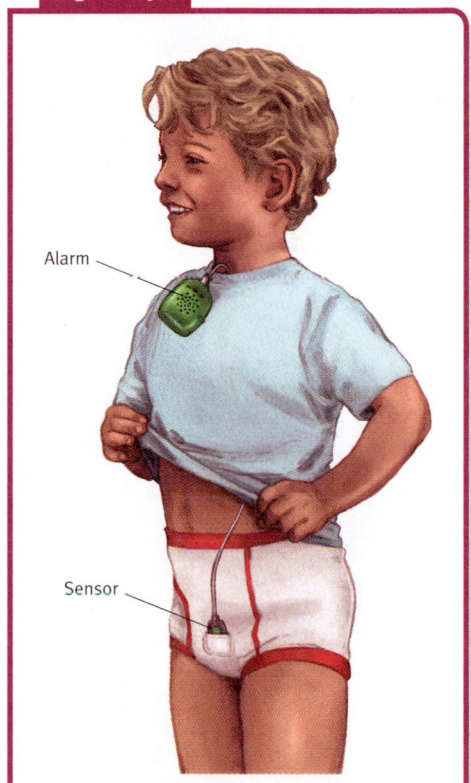

14.6 ▶ Behavioral Treatment of Enuresis A bed-wetting alarm is the treatment of choice for nighttime enuresis. In the model shown here, the sensor immediately detects any wetness, triggering the alarm, which is near enough to the child's ear that it will probably wake the child up when it goes off. Although initially the child wakes up after wetting the bed, with motivation and experience, he or she will learn to wake up increasingly closer in time to the release of urine. Soon thereafter, the child becomes able to wake up *before* urine is released and thus urinate in the toilet.

before urinating in the bed. That is, the child learns to detect the sensations of a full bladder even during sleep.

Although children may willfully refuse to use the toilet (which could be a symptom of oppositional defiant disorder; Christophersen, 1994) or have severe anxiety about using the toilet, both enuresis and encopresis usually arise from biological factors. Consultation with the child's pediatrician and implementation of the recommended strategies often resolve these disorders. Children with elimination problems may come to the attention of a mental health professional because the parents are worried not only about the problem itself but also that it may be a sign of another type of problem, such as oppositional defiant disorder, significant anxiety, or sexual abuse (perhaps by a child care provider).

Tic Disorders

A **tic** is rapid but repetitive involuntary movement or vocalization. Many people develop some kind of tic—they may have an episodic but persistent eye blink or shoulder shrug (motoric tics), or a recurrent "hmmm" of throat clearing or grunting sound (vocal tics). Tics are relatively common in children, but a **tic disorder** may be diagnosed when the tic (motor or vocal) is persistent and occurs many times a day on most days. In fact, up to 12% of children between 6 and 15 years old have a tic disorder at some point in their lives (Khalifa & von Knorring, 2003; Zhu et al., 2003).

One tic disorder is *Tourette's disorder* (also referred to as *Tourette syndrome*), named for the psychiatrist Gilles de la Tourette (1857–1904), who first described the constellation of symptoms. **Tourette's disorder** involves recurrent motoric *and* vocal tics. A rare type of vocal tic is the involuntary shouting of obscenities (referred to as *coprolalia*); only 10% of people with Tourette's disorder exhibit coprolalia (American Psychiatric Association, 2000).

Tic disorders are generally evaluated and treated by a neurologist. Children with these disorders can come to the attention of a mental health professional because parents may be concerned that the symptoms either represent willful oppositional behavior (as in oppositional defiant disorder) or are a manifestation of anxiety.

A tic may be difficult to distinguish from a stereotyped behavior that arises as part of a pervasive developmental disorder. However, stereotypies generally seem intentional and rhythmic, and they appear to soothe the individual exhibiting the behavior. In contrast, tic behaviors generally arise in clusters, and although they may sometimes feel voluntary, they are typically involuntary. Tics can also be difficult to distinguish from compulsions, especially if comorbid obsessive-compulsive disorder (OCD) is present. However, the compulsive behaviors of OCD are usually more elaborate and also more normal-seeming than a tic, and they are associated with corresponding obsessions. Vocal tics should be distinguished from the psychotically disorganized speech that is associated with schizophrenia: In the absence of other disorganized or psychotic behavior, a tic disorder is the more likely diagnosis.

Depending on the individual and the type and severity of tics, the effects can range from no distress or impaired functioning to severe distress and/or impaired functioning. Young children may not be aware of their tics and usually do not experience distress or impaired functioning, in part because their peers do not call attention to their problem. For older children and adults, the more noticeable the tics, the more social rejection they may experience and the more self-conscious and ashamed they are likely to become, perhaps leading them to avoid social interactions whenever possible. Frequent tics or those that involve complex behaviors (such as deep knee bends) may interfere with normal functioning. In such cases, medication for the tic disorder may decrease the frequency and intensity of the symptoms (Davies et al., 2006; Shavitt et al., 2006). Behavioral treatment for tics may help patients increase their ability to control the behaviors for short periods of time (Carr & Chong, 2005; Cook & Blacher, 2007; Phelps, Brown, & Power, 2002).

Tic disorders
A set of disorders characterized by persistent tics (motor or vocal) that occur many times a day on most days.

Tourette's disorder
A tic disorder characterized by recurrent motoric and vocal tics; also referred to as *Tourette syndrome*.

Key Concepts and Facts About Other Disorders of Childhood

- Separation anxiety disorder is characterized by excessive anxiety about separation from home or from someone to whom the child is strongly attached. Separation anxiety disorder is moderately heritable and is more likely to arise in tight-knit families, whose members may inadvertently reinforce behaviors associated with separation anxiety and punish behaviors associated with actual separation. Separation anxiety disorder is treated with methods used to treat other anxiety disorders: CBT that includes exposure and cognitive restructuring, along with family therapy.

- Communication disorders are characterized by problems in understanding or using language.

- Feeding and eating disorders are characterized by problems with attaining or maintaining adequate weight and nutrition or by bizarre eating habits.

- The elimination disorders are enuresis and encopresis, which are characterized, respectively, by accidental or intentional failure to urinate and failure to defecate appropriately in a toilet.

- Tic disorders are characterized by persistent motor or vocal tics. Tourette's disorder involves recurrent motoric and vocal tics.

Making a Diagnosis

- Reread Case 14.8 about JC, and determine whether or not his symptoms meet the criteria for separation anxiety disorder. Specifically, list which criteria apply and which do not. If you would like more information to determine his diagnosis, what information—specifically—would you want, and in what ways would the information influence your decision?

SUMMING UP

Summary of Mental Retardation

The diagnosis of mental retardation requires both an IQ score at or below 70 *and* impaired daily functioning. The four levels of mental retardation are mild, moderate, severe, and profound. Some people with mental retardation—particularly at the severe or profound level—may have difficulty communicating verbally.

Neurological factors are the primary direct cause of most cases of mental retardation—usually a genetic abnormality or prenatal exposure to a teratogen such as alcohol. In turn, the genetic abnormality or teratogen alters brain structure and function.

Although mental retardation cannot be cured, many types can be prevented, including those due to PKU and lead poisoning. Interventions are designed to improve the person's functioning by increasing his or her communication and daily living skills. Legally, children with mental retardation are entitled to special education and related services, tailored to their individual needs through an IEP.

Thinking like a clinician

Clare just graduated from college and started working in a center for adults with various intellectual disabilities. She is trying to get to know each client—his or her strengths and weaknesses. The clients with mental retardation are classified in the moderate to severe range. Based on what you've learned, what can—and can't—you assume about those clients? Why might people with mild or profound mental retardation not be at the center?

Summary of Pervasive Developmental Disorders

Pervasive developmental disorders involve two types of problems: (1) significant deficits in communication and social interaction skills, and (2) stereotyped behaviors or narrow interests. Disorders in this category are autistic disorder, Asperger's disorder, childhood disintegrative disorder, and Rett's disorder.

Autistic disorder (or simply, autism) is characterized by significant problems with communication, social interactions, and language use. Individuals with autism are oblivious to other people and do not pay attention to or understand basic social rules and cues. They may have extremely narrow interests involving repetitive play. Many people with autism also have comorbid mental retardation when tested with conventional intelligence tests; on tests that do not rely on verbal abilities, however, people with autism tend to score in the average range or higher. In addition, some people with autism have unique skills.

Asperger's disorder is characterized by problems that are similar to—though less severe than—those associated with autism. With Asperger's, however, language and cognitive development are in the normal range.

Neurological factors that underlie autism include abnormal connections and communication among different brain areas, in particular, between the frontal lobe and the rest of the brain. Genes play a role in the development of autism and Asperger's. Psychological symptoms of autism include deficits in shifting attention and in mental flexibility, and problems in using a theory of mind. People with Asperger's have less severe problems with their theory of mind than people with autism. Social symptoms include problems in recognizing emotion in the voices or faces of others and in understanding the give and take of social communication.

Interventions for autism include medication for comorbid disorders or symptoms of anxiety, agitation, and aggression. Treatment for autism that targets psychological factors includes applied behavior analysis to modify maladaptive behaviors. Treatments that target psychological and social factors focus on teaching the individual to communicate, to recognize conventional social cues, to read the emotional expressions of others, and how to initiate and respond in social situations.

In contrast to autism and Asperger's disorder, childhood disintegrative disorder is characterized by normal development up to at least 2 years of age, followed by a profound loss of communication skills, normal types of play, and bowel control.

Rett's disorder also involves the loss of skills already mastered, but the onset of the disorder occurs between 5 months and 2 years of age. Mental retardation always accompanies Rett's disorder, which affects only females.

Thinking like a clinician

The center where Clare works also has clients with pervasive developmental disorders. Based on what you have learned, what is the most important information that Clare should know about people with pervasive developmental disorders, and why? What particular pervasive developmental disorders would be most and least likely to be seen in people who need the type of care that Clare's workplace provides? How might Clare use her knowledge about pervasive developmental disorders— and autism in particular—when she is working with the center's clients?

Summary of Learning Disorders

A learning disorder is characterized by a substantial disparity between an individual's performance on a standardized test and the expected level of performance based on the individual's age, intelligence, and education level. DSM-IV-TR includes three types of learning disorders: reading disorder (dyslexia), mathematics disorder, and disorder of written expression.

Genes contribute to learning disorders. Dyslexia appears to result from disruptions in brain systems that process language and in brain systems that process visual stimuli. Motivation and social support influence an individual's ability to overcome and compensate for a learning disorder.

Treatment for learning disorders may involve accommodations and services mandated by IDEA. Various cognitive techniques can help a person learn to compensate for a learning disorder.

Thinking like a clinician

Nikhil recently graduated from college and is about to start working in the *Teach for America* program. He's been assigned to teach at an inner city school. Nikhil was a math major in college and doesn't know much about learning disorders. However, he was a peer tutor in college and saw that some people had a *really*

hard time understanding different elements of math. Based on what you've read, what information should Nikhil know (and hopefully will be taught as part of his training) about learning disorders before he walks into a classroom, and why should he learn this?

Summary of Disorders of Disruptive Behaviors and Attention

Conduct disorder is characterized by a violation of the basic rights of others or of societal norms that are appropriate to the individual's age. The disorder may begin in childhood or adolescence. Conduct disorder is commonly comorbid with ADHD and substance use or abuse.

Childhood-onset conduct disorder with callous and unemotional traits has the highest heritability among the various types of conduct disorder. Individuals with this type of conduct disorder often have more severe symptoms. People with childhood-onset conduct disorder *without* callous and unemotional traits are less aggressive, although they are likely to be aggressive impulsively, in response to (mis)perceived threats. Adolescent-onset conduct disorder tends to involve mild symptoms that are usually transient.

Oppositional defiant disorder is characterized by a behavioral pattern of disobedience, hostility, defiance, and negativity toward people in authority. The behaviors are usually not violent nor do they cause severe harm, and they often occur only in certain contexts.

Attention-deficit/hyperactivity disorder (ADHD) is characterized by inattention, hyperactivity, and/or impulsivity. The inattentive type of ADHD is associated with academic problems, whereas the hyperactive/impulsive type is associated with disruptive behaviors, accidents, and rejection by peers. Criticisms of the DSM-IV-TR diagnostic criteria for ADHD include the difficulty in applying the criteria to adults, the arbitrariness of the age cutoff for the onset of symptoms, and failure to acknowledge different symptoms in females. Oppositional defiant disorder, conduct disorder, and ADHD are highly comorbid, making it difficult to sort out factors that contribute uniquely to one of the disorders.

Neurological factors that contribute to ADHD include frontal lobe problems (which lead to the symptoms of inattention, impaired executive function, and memory difficulties). Too little dopamine, and imbalances in other transmitters may also play a role. Genes also contribute to ADHD and conduct disorder, in part by affecting temperament.

Psychological factors that are associated with ADHD include low self-esteem and

difficulty recognizing facial expressions of anger and sadness. People with oppositional defiant disorder and conduct disorder tend to have either low self-esteem or overly high self-esteem, are relatively unresponsive to the threat of punishment, and exhibit high levels of emotional distress and poor frustration tolerance.

Social factors that contribute to ADHD include parents' not giving children enough credit for their positive behaviors. For oppositional defiant disorder and conduct disorders, social factors include abuse, neglect, inconsistent discipline, and lack of positive attention.

Treatment targeting neurological factors in ADHD involves medication—typically methylphenidate, or atomoxetine. Treatments targeting psychological factors in ADHD, oppositional defiant disorder, and conduct disorder may use behavioral methods—especially reinforcement programs—to increase a person's ability to tolerate frustration and to delay reward, and cognitive methods to enhance social problem-solving ability. Treatments that target social factors in all three disorders include group therapy and comprehensive treatments such as contingency management program, parent management training, and multi-systemic therapy.

Thinking like a clinician

Nikhil has some first-hand familiarity with oppositional defiant disorder and conduct disorder—he went to a large middle school and large high school, where some kids always acted up and got into trouble. And during high school and college, some of his friends and then one of his roommates had ADHD. Even though Nikhil may think he knows something about disruptive behavior disorders and ADHD, based on what you have read, what information about these disorders should he be given before he begins to teach, and why?

Summary of Other Disorders of Childhood

Separation anxiety disorder is characterized by excessive anxiety about separation from home or from someone to whom the child is strongly attached. Separation anxiety disorder is moderately heritable and is more likely to arise in tight-knit families. Separation anxiety disorder is treated with methods used to treat other anxiety disorders: CBT that includes exposure and cognitive restructuring, along with family therapy.

Communication disorders are characterized by problems in understanding or using language. Feeding and eating disorders are characterized by problems with attaining or maintaining adequate weight and nutrition or by bizarre eating habits. The elimination disorders are enuresis and encopresis, which are characterized, respectively, by accidental or intentional failure to urinate and failure to defecate appropriately in a toilet. Tic disorders are characterized by persistent motor or vocal tics. Tourette's disorder involves recurrent motoric and vocal tics.

Thinking like a clinician

Nia is 12 years old and going through puberty. Lately she's been coming home right after school and staying home during the weekend, no longer hanging out with her friends. In fact, she's unhappy when her mother (her parents are divorced) leaves her alone to go shopping or to go out in the evening; sometimes she tearfully begs her mother not to leave, but won't—or can't—explain why she feels so upset. Based on what you have learned, how do you think Nia—and her mother—should proceed? Should they wait and hope the symptoms pass or try to find out more? Explain your answer in detail.

Key Terms

Mental retardation (p. 626)

Teratogens (p. 628)

Stereotyped behaviors (p. 629)

Inclusion (p. 631)

Pervasive developmental disorders (p. 632)

Autistic disorder (p. 633)

Asperger's disorder (p. 635)

Theory of mind (p. 639)

Applied behavior analysis (p. 640)

Childhood disintegrative disorder (p. 641)

Rett's disorder (p. 641)

Learning disorder (p. 643)

Dyslexia (p. 643)

Conduct disorder (p. 649)

Oppositional defiant disorder (p. 653)

Attention-deficit/hyperactivity disorder (ADHD) (p. 655)

Contingency management (p. 667)

Separation anxiety disorder (p. 671)

Communication disorders (p. 674)

Feeding and eating disorders (p. 675)

Elimination disorders (p. 675)

Encopresis (p. 675)

Enuresis (p. 675)

Tic disorders (p. 676)

Tourette's disorder (p. 676)

More Study Aids

For additional study aids related to this chapter, go to:

www.worthpublishers.com/rosenberg

Cognitive Disorders

Mrs. B. was an 87-year-old woman at the time that she was referred for neuropsychological testing. Mrs. B. wasn't always able to get to the toilet in time to urinate, her hearing and vision weren't as good as they had been, and, because of an inner-ear problem, she sometimes felt off-balance and fell. A neuropsychologist was asked to determine the nature of Mrs. B.'s problems—specifically the extent to which a cognitive disorder might account for at least some of her difficulties. The neuropsychologist noted that Mrs. B. required

". . . assistance in several self-care activities (meal preparation, shopping, transportation, ambulation [moving around], dressing, and bathing), principally because of gait, balance, and sensory changes. . . . [She] had moved from another state several months earlier at the urging of her daughter, who had been receiving reports from neighbors and relatives that she was unable to care for herself or her home and was increasingly suspicious and argumentative. Her first residence in her new community was . . . a nursing home, but it soon became apparent that she was functioning at a higher level than other residents and she moved to a small board-and-care home [a small residential facility for elders who need round-the-clock help with daily functioning and personal care]. With only a few persons in the home and a low resident-to-staff ratio, this seemed a good arrangement for an older person who needed an intermediate level of assistance. Mrs. B. apparently thought otherwise.

"She often refused to admit staff to her room or to accept assistance with activities such as bathing, despite an unsteady gait and several recent falls. She had arguments with other residents that sometimes escalated into shouting matches. A private-duty companion was hired to assist her for several hours a day and to take her on excursions outside of the home. This was helping somewhat, but accusations and arguments continued at an unsettling rate. Mrs. B. sometimes seemed to forget plans that she had agreed to and was occasionally tearful and sad."

(LaRue & Watson, 1998, pp. 6, 10)

What might account for Mrs. B.'s disruptive behavior and memory problems? One possibility is some type of cognitive disorder. According to DSM-IV-TR, **cognitive disorders** are a category of psychological disorders in which the primary symptom is significantly reduced mental abilities, relative to a prior level of functioning.

Impaired cognitive abilities are not unique to cognitive disorders. Many of the disorders discussed in previous chapters involve a change in cognitive functioning: People who are depressed or anxious

Cognitive disorders
A category of psychological disorders in which the primary symptom is significantly reduced mental abilities, relative to a prior level of functioning.

can have impaired attention, concentration, and memory; those with a psychotic disorder have impaired perception and judgment; and substance abuse and dependence can lead to a wide variety of cognitive impairments. The cognitive changes associated with these disorders, however, are secondary to the other symptoms that characterize the disorders: depressed mood, anxiety and fear, psychotic symptoms, or behaviors related to substance abuse and dependence.

In contrast, with cognitive disorders, the changes in cognitive functioning—in mental processes—constitute the primary set of symptoms. Patients may (or may not) also exhibit disturbances in behavior, mood, or mental contents. Usually, the undesired cognitive changes arise from a medical disease such as Parkinson's disease, a medical condition such as a *stroke*, or the use of or withdrawal from a psychoactive substance (which may include exposure to a toxic substance). When substance use or withdrawal causes the cognitive symptoms, according to DSM-IV-TR, the symptoms must be in excess of those typically experienced with intoxication or withdrawal from a substance in order to be considered a cognitive disorder (American Psychiatric Association, 2000).

The three types of cognitive disorders discussed in this chapter are *delirium, amnestic disorder*, and *dementia*. Delirium involves impaired cognition and a marked change in awareness (as occurs when someone who is drinking alcohol doesn't recognize friends or drinks to the point of being in a stupor). Amnestic disorder involves impaired cognition that is confined to memory. Dementia involves impaired memory plus at least one other impaired cognitive function—such as perception, attention, or language use. Cognitive disorders are almost exclusively due to neurological factors.

In most cases, these disorders afflict older adults rather than younger adults. So, part of the job of diagnosing these disorders is to distinguish the symptoms of these disorders from changes that occur with normal aging. Let's first examine the changes in cognitive functioning that arise during the normal aging process, which will allow us to contrast these effects with those described in subsequent sections.

Normal Versus Abnormal Aging and Cognitive Functioning

The neuropsychologist assessing Mrs. B. needed to determine whether her disturbances in memory, mood, and behavior were normal for an 87-year-old, particularly one with a variety of medical problems. And, if her memory, mood, and behavior weren't in the normal range, given her circumstances, what, specifically, could account for her difficulties? The neuropsychologist initially assessed Mrs. B. using a clinical interview (discussed in Chapter 3), observing her as well as noting her responses to questions:

> "Mrs. B. arrived promptly for her appointment, accompanied by her private-duty nurse. She was well-groomed and alert but ambulated slowly, leaning against the railing on the wall to maintain her balance; she was also unsteady on rising and standing from a chair. She was fluent and willing to talk at great length about her situation, although her speech was often repetitive and tangential. Mood was . . . positive during the interview. She denied hallucinations, delusions, or suicidal ideation but admitted to some depression, which she felt had improved somewhat on antidepressant medication. She was able to describe some aspects of her experience at the [nursing home] and gave several examples of the types of things that annoyed her at the current board-and-care home."
>
> (LaRue & Watson, 1998, p. 6)

Mrs. B. was able to remember aspects of her nursing home experience that she didn't like, but she forgot other types of information, such as upcoming plans to which she had agreed. In the normal course of events, however, various cognitive functions tend to decline with advancing age. Mental health clinicians must compare the individual's current cognitive functioning both to the person's prior abilities and to the normal changes in functioning that occur with age. Even healthy older adults have some cognitive deficits, compared to their younger counterparts, and these must be taken into account when attempting to determine whether an older individual has a disorder. Thus, the neuropsychologist must assess whether Mrs. B.'s functioning has declined and, if so, whether this decline is beyond what occurs with the normal aging process. In this section, we examine what happens to cognitive functioning during normal aging and then examine the neurological factors that can disrupt cognitive functioning.

Cognitive Functioning in Normal Aging

Most—though not all—aspects of cognitive functioning remain relatively stable during older adulthood. Let's first examine intelligence, which can be divided into two sets of abilities, or types of intelligence (Cattell, 1971): **Crystallized intelligence** relies on using knowledge to reason; such knowledge has "crystallized" from previous experience. Normally, crystallized intelligence, such as the ability to understand what various words mean, remains stable or increases with age, even among older adults; crystallized intelligence is often assessed through tests that measure verbal ability, and these tests often allow ample time for people to respond to questions. In contrast, **fluid intelligence** relies on the ability to create new strategies to solve new problems, without relying solely on information previously learned. Fluid intelligence relies on *executive functions*, which include the abilities to think abstractly, to plan, and to exert good judgment. Fluid intelligence is typically assessed with tests of visual-motor skills, problem solving, and perceptual speed (Salthouse, 2005); these tests usually are timed, and points are lost for taking "too long" to respond with the right answer. If Mrs. B. took such tests, even if she gave the correct answer, her scores would be lower if she took more than a "normal" amount of time. As adults age, they respond more slowly, and so their scores on most measures of fluid intelligence decline. Specifically, these kinds of test scores begin to decline noticeably at around age 55, with a more significant decline at around age 65 (Harvey, 2005a). When tests are not timed, however, the decline in fluid intelligence is less pronounced, particularly on tests that involve executive functioning (Jennings et al., 2007).

Of course, normal cognitive decline is always judged in relation to the individual's baseline. An older adult who starts out with a high IQ and has functioned well will probably be able to continue to function well even with the normal decline of aging. In contrast, the functioning of someone who has a lower IQ initially (such as in the low normal range, or an IQ of 85 or lower) will be affected more dramatically—perhaps to the point where his or her ability to function independently is curtailed (Harvey, 2005a).

Let's examine in more detail some of the specific mental processes that are affected by normal aging: memory, processing speed, attention, and executive functions.

Memory

Memory is not a single ability, and various aspects of it are affected in different ways by aging. We can distinguish between implicit and explicit memories. *Implicit memories* consist of unconscious stored information that guides a person to behave in certain ways. Classical and operant conditioning produce implicit memories; habits, such as those used by someone who is adept at cooking or trout fishing, are implicit memories. Implicit memories are not affected very much by aging (Fleischman et al., 2004). Older people often remember how to perform well-learned tasks such as driving or typing.

In contrast, *explicit memories* can be voluntarily brought to mind, as words or mental images. For example, remembering where you left your house keys, the name of your best friend, or the facts you learned earlier in this book relies on explicit memories. The elderly (generally considered to be people aged 65 and older; World Health Organization [WHO], 2009) tend to have problems with some aspects of explicit memories. In particular, they have problems in recalling stored explicit information. To *recall* information is to activate that information after voluntarily

Aging normally only minimally affects crystallized intelligence, which relies on knowledge based on previous experience.

Rick Gomez/Corbis

Crystallized intelligence
A type of intelligence that relies on using knowledge to reason; such knowledge has "crystallized" from previous experience.

Fluid intelligence
A type of intelligence that relies on the ability to create new strategies to solve new problems, without relying solely on information previously learned.

An older person may sometimes be unable to recall the name of a common object but be able to recognize the name if someone else says it. This and other normal aging-related cognitive changes do not usually impair daily functioning.

attempting to "look it up" in memory, and so to become aware of it. For instance, essay tests assess a person's ability to recall information about a topic. In contrast, to *recognize* information requires first perceiving it and then comparing it to information stored in memory; if what you perceive matches something you've previously stored in memory, you've recognized the stimulus. For instance, multiple-choice tests assess a person's ability to recognize a correct answer to a question.

Healthy older people often have little difficulty with recognition but do have problems with some aspects of recall. In particular, older people sometimes have trouble recalling the names of common objects on demand. Thus, they might say, "I went to the store to buy a 'thingamajig' this morning." The person can describe the object or recognize the correct word when someone else says it, and he or she may even recall the correct word a few minutes later when talking about something else (Nicholas et al., 1985). In addition, the elderly often have trouble remembering the source of information—where or when they learned it (Schacter et al., 1991, 1997).

However, in spite of these difficulties, healthy older people can often recall temporarily forgotten names of common things when given cues or hints. Moreover, with normal aging, the ability to recall personal information is preserved; people can recall important episodes from their past.

Processing Speed, Attention, and Working Memory

Memory involves storing information and then later accessing it. Specific mental processes are used to store and access information, and these processes can take varying amounts of time. Older adults have a slower processing speed, so they generally learn new information at a slower rate, need more exposure to the to-be-learned material, and need more practice in retrieving the information after they have learned it. For these reasons, the elderly may be impaired when carrying out tasks that require rapid responses (Filit et al., 2002; Salthouse, 2001). One explanation for the slowed processing that comes with advanced age is that the myelin sheaths coating the axons degrade or disappear, which then causes the neurons' signals to dissipate, and hence communication among brain areas is impaired (Andrews-Hanna et al., 2007).

Attention involves selecting some information for more careful analysis: what a person pays attention to gets processed more fully than what he or she does not pay attention to. The ability to sustain attention or to divide attention sequentially among multiple tasks (known as *multitasking*) is also likely to decline as people age (Parasuraman, Nestor, & Greenwood, 1989). Thus, older adults may have a harder time performing tasks such as balancing a checkbook while talking on the phone.

Many tasks—as well as the tests used in neuropsychological assessments—require both sustained attention and the faster processing speed typical of younger people. For instance, one test that requires both abilities is the *Trail Making Test* (Reitan, 1958), a timed test that requires the individual to connect dots in a particular sequence; one version involves dots with alternating numbers and letters, and test-takers are asked to connect the dots in ascending and alphabetical order (see Figure 15.1 for a similar task). The average 25-year-old takes 26 seconds to complete the task, whereas the average 72-year-old takes 70 seconds to complete it (Spreen & Straus, 1998). Mrs. B. was not able to complete the test as instructed; she connected only the numbered dots and omitted the lettered dots entirely (LaRue & Watson, 1998).

Figure 15.1

15.1 ▶ Trail Making Test The Trail Making Test (Reitan, 1958), similar to this figure, involves connecting dots in a particular fashion—alternating numbers and letters in ascending and alphabetical order. The test-taker is to make a line from 1 to A, then from A to 2, from 2 to B, and so on.

If you tried our version of the Trail Making Test in Figure 15.1, you probably noticed that it's a bit of a mental juggling act. Such mental juggling is typical of tasks that rely on *working memory*. Working memory requires keeping information activated (so that you are aware of it) while operating on it in a specific way; for example, counting backwards by 3 from 100 requires working memory (holding in mind the number 100, subtracting 3, then holding in mind 97, subtracting 3, and so on). Working memory relies on the frontal lobes, and the key parts of frontal lobes don't operate as effectively in elderly people as they do in younger people—and hence the elderly typically have problems using working memory (De Beni & Palladino, 2004; Li, Lindenberger, & Silkström, 2001).

In sum, normal aging typically leads to problems in recall, slower mental processing, difficulty sustaining high levels of attention and in dividing attention, and problems with working memory. These abilities are necessary for fluid intelligence, which usually declines with age but generally not enough to impair daily functioning. In contrast, crystallized intelligence, which includes recognition memory for vocabulary and memory for personal events, typically does not decline dramatically with age.

Psychological Disorders and Cognition

Contrary to popular belief, most older adults don't have a psychological disorder; in fact, older adults have the lowest prevalence of psychological disorders of any age group (American Psychological Association, Working Group on Older Adults, 1998). But when an older person does have a psychological disorder, its symptoms can impair cognitive functioning. Thus, before assuming that an individual's deteriorated cognitive functioning is due to a *cognitive* disorder—delirium, amnestic disorder, or dementia—the clinician must first determine whether the deterioration could be due to another psychological disorder. For instance, Mrs. B. had a history of depression and described herself as having a "hot temper" even as a young adult. Mrs. B.'s daughter described her mother "as always somewhat self-centered and suspicious of the motives of others, but this had worsened noticeably in recent years, to the point where she had been isolated within her own home," which led to the move to the nursing home (LaRue & Watson, 1998, p. 6).

The neuropsychologist must determine whether Mrs. B.'s memory problems might reflect a psychological disorder such as depression. Let's briefly review the psychological disorders that most commonly diminish cognitive functioning in older adults: depression, anxiety disorders, and schizophrenia.

Depression

Older adults are less likely than their younger counterparts to be diagnosed with depression. When they are depressed, however, the symptoms often differ from those of younger adults: Older depressed adults have more anxiety, agitation, and memory problems (Segal, 2003). Thus, cognitive functioning is affected by depression both directly (memory problems) and indirectly (anxiety and agitation affect attention, concentration, and other mental processes; see Table 15.1). When depressed, a particular group of older adults is at high risk for suicide: Older White men who live alone have the highest suicide rate of any age group (WHO, 2002).

A mental health clinician must also determine whether symptoms of depression in an older person could be *caused* by a cognitive disorder: Some symptoms of depression, such as fatigue, may be caused by brain changes associated with a cognitive disorder (Puente, 2003). Mr. Rosen, in Case 15.1, was being treated for depression and experienced cognitive problems that may or may not have been related to his depression.

Table 15.1 ▶ Common Cognitive Deficits in Late-Life Depression

Information processing speed
- Slow to respond or initiate behavior; incomplete grasp of complex information (because of a lag in processing)

Attention and concentration
- Absentmindedness for daily activities, events, and appointments; tasks left incomplete; decreased attentiveness for reading or conversation, which can also disrupt memory

Executive function
- Difficulty with calculating, sequencing, multitasking, and other novel problem solving; inflexible behavior or thinking; perseverative or ruminative thinking; decline in organization and planning; indecisiveness, decreased initiation of behavior

Memory
- Forgetfulness and absentmindedness, but should improve with prompts, cues, or explicit memory aids

Source: Potter & Steffens, 2007. For more information see the permissions section.

CASE 15.1 ▶ FROM THE OUTSIDE: Normal Aging or Something More?

Maurice Rosen was 69 when he made an appointment for a neurological evaluation. He had recently noticed that his memory was slipping and he had problems with concentration that were beginning to interfere with his work as a self-employed tax accountant. He complained of slowness and losing his train of thought. Recent changes in the tax laws were hard for him to learn, and his wife said he was becoming more withdrawn and reluctant to initiate activities. However, he was still able to take care of his personal finances and accompany his wife on visits to friends. Although mildly depressed about his disabilities, he denied other symptoms of depression, such as disturbed sleep or appetite, feelings of guilt, or suicidal ideation.

Mr. Rosen has a long history of treatment for episodes of depression, beginning in his 20s. He has taken a number of different antidepressants and once had a course of electroconvulsive therapy. As recently as 6 months before this evaluation, he had been taking an antidepressant.

(Spitzer et al., 2002, p. 70)

Like Mr. Rosen, Mrs. B. had a history of depression and was taking antidepressant medication. However, the neuropsychologist who assessed Mrs. B.'s cognitive functioning determined that the difficulties she was having were not due to depression (LaRue & Watson, 1998).

Anxiety Disorders

Like depression, anxiety disorders are less common among older adults than among younger adults. The anxiety disorder most prevalent among older adults is generalized anxiety disorder (Segal, 2003). About 5% of older adults have generalized anxiety disorder, most often along with depression; in about half the cases, the anxiety disorder was not present when the individual was younger (Flint, 2005). The fears and worries that accompany generalized anxiety disorder can impair cognitive functioning, in part because they give rise to preoccupations and decreased attention and concentration.

Schizophrenia

Although not common, about 15% of people with schizophrenia have their first psychotic episode when older than 44 (Cohen et al., 2000). Schizophrenia can involve both positive symptoms (delusions and hallucinations) and negative symptoms, such as speaking minimally (alogia) and an absence of initiative (avolition; see Chapter 12); these symptoms can also arise with cognitive disorders.

Medical Factors That Can Affect Cognition

The typical older adult has one or more medical conditions that can diminish cognitive functioning. In this section we review medical problems that affect cognitive functioning and that can cause cognitive disorders—delirium, amnestic disorder, and dementia.

Diseases and Illnesses

Various physical diseases and illnesses can affect cognition—directly or indirectly. Some medical illnesses, such as encephalitis (a viral infection of the brain) and brain tumors, directly affect the brain and, in doing so, affect cognition. The specific cognitive deficits that arise depend on the particular features of the illness, such as the size and location of a brain tumor.

Some chronic diseases or illnesses indirectly affect cognition by creating pain, which can disrupt attention, concentration, and other mental processes. For example, arthritis can cause chronic pain, and the aftermath of surgery can cause acute pain. In addition, pain can interfere with sleep, which further impairs mental processes. The detrimental effects on cognition of some illnesses may be temporary, so that cognitive functioning improves as the symptoms resolve or the pain recedes. In other cases, though, the person may never return to his or her prior level of functioning.

In still other cases, an older adult may *appear* to have impaired cognitive functioning but actually has undiagnosed or uncorrected sensory problems, such as hearing loss or vision problems. If someone chronically mishears what is said, he or she will seem "not with it" or "senile" when, in fact, the problem is simply that the individual thinks the topic of conversation is something other than what it actually is.

Stroke

A **stroke** (so named because it was originally assumed to be a "stroke of God") is the interruption of normal blood flow to or within the brain (often because of an obstruction—such as a blood clot—in a blood vessel). The result is that part of the brain fails to receive oxygen and nutrients, and the neurons in that area die. The cognitive, emotional, and behavioral consequences of a stroke depend crucially on which specific group of neurons is affected; depending on their location, different deficits are produced. In the following sections, we briefly consider some of the more common deficits.

Aphasia

Aphasia is a problem in using language. (The word *aphasia* literally means "an absence of speech.") Traditionally, there are two main types of aphasia, each named after a neurologist who first characterized it in detail. **Broca's aphasia** is characterized by problems producing speech and often occurs after damage to part of the left frontal lobe. Patients with Broca's aphasia speak haltingly, and their speech can be very telegraphic—consisting of only the main words. In addition, they typically don't use grammar correctly; for example, these patients often omit words such as *and, or,* and *of.* In contrast, **Wernicke's aphasia** is characterized by problems with both comprehension of language and production of meaningful utterances. This disorder often occurs after damage to part of the rear portions of the left temporal lobe. Although these patients may appear to speak fluently, they often order words incorrectly and sometimes make up nonsense words. For instance, when asked to describe his occupation prior to suffering a stroke, one patient with Wernicke's aphasia said, "Never, now mista oyge I wanna tell you this happened when happened when he rent" (Kertesz, 1981, p. 73, as cited in Carlson, 1994, p. 517). Clinicians sometimes have difficulty distinguishing between schizophrenia and Wernicke's aphasia. However, people with schizophrenia (except perhaps when extremely psychotic) can understand speech and name objects better than can patients with Wernicke's aphasia (Mendez & Cummings, 2004).

Agnosia

Patients who have *agnosia* have difficulty understanding what they perceive, although neither their sensory abilities nor their knowledge about objects is impaired. Many forms of agnosia can arise, but two are most common. *Apperceptive agnosia* occurs when a person cannot organize visual input into objects and their spatial relations. As a consequence, a person with apperceptive agnosia cannot determine whether two shapes are the same or different and thus cannot copy a drawing. (This disorder may arise following carbon monoxide poisoning, which produces diffuse damage in the occipital lobe.) This disorder can lead to disorientation, which must be distinguished from disorientation that occurs with dementia (to be discussed shortly).

The other common form of agnosia, *associative agnosia*, occurs when a person can visually organize shapes appropriately, and hence can see objects, but cannot associate the shape with its meaning—and hence cannot understand what he or she is seeing. Thus, someone with associative agnosia is able to tell whether two objects are the same or different, and can copy a drawing of a stick figure, but doesn't understand that the lines and circle of the stick figure represent a human. Here's another example of the type of problems that arise with associative agnosia: One of

A stroke is an interruption of normal blood flow to the brain that causes neurons in that part of the brain to die. The effect of a stroke depends on its location in the brain and the size of the brain area that it affects. This image shows a colored MRI scan of the brain of a woman who had a stroke, with red indicating dead brain tissue and green indicating healthy tissue.

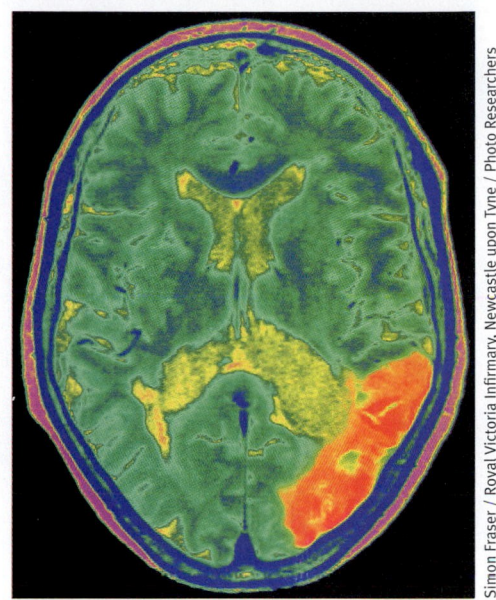

Simon Fraser / Royal Victoria Infirmary, Newcastle upon Tyne / Photo Researchers

Stroke
The interruption of normal blood flow to or within the brain, which results in neuronal death.

Aphasia
A neurological condition characterized by problems in producing or comprehending language.

Broca's aphasia
A neurological condition characterized by problems producing speech.

Wernicke's aphasia
A neurological condition characterized by problems comprehending language and producing meaningful utterances.

us (SMK) once saw a patient who could not name a comb when shown it but could say what color it was and could reach for it and hold it properly. Moreover, as soon as the patient felt the comb with his fingers, he could name it easily. The problem was not that he had forgotten the name or that he was unable to retrieve or say the name—rather, it was an inability to make the connection between (that is, to associate) the visual form and the appropriate information stored in memory (Farah, 2004; Kosslyn & Koenig, 1995). Clinicians must distinguish between this kind of problem with object recognition and the sort of disorientation that may accompany severe psychosis, as sometimes occurs with schizophrenia.

Apraxia

Another medical condition that can affect cognitive functioning is **apraxia** (Kosslyn & Koenig, 1995), which involves problems in organizing and carrying out voluntary movements even though the muscles themselves are not impaired. The problem is in the brain, not in the muscles. Apraxia can take a variety of forms; some patients have trouble with individual components of a series of movements (such as pinching thumb and forefinger to pick up a coin), whereas others have trouble sequencing movements (such as the movements necessary to light a candle, that is, taking out a match, striking it, and holding the flame to the wick). Clinicians must distinguish between such problems with voluntary movements and the avolition (difficulty initiating or following through with activities) that may accompany schizophrenia (noted in Chapter 12).

Head Injury

Cognitive disorders can arise from head injuries—which may result from a car accident, from a fall, or in a variety of other ways. The specific cognitive deficits that develop depend on the exact nature of the head injury. The same kinds of deficits that follow a stroke can also occur after a head injury.

Substance-Induced Changes in Cognition

We saw in Chapter 9 that some people take substances (including prescribed medications) to alter their level of awareness or their emotional or cognitive state. But medications or exposure to toxic substances can produce unintended changes in attention, memory, judgment, or other cognitive functions, particularly when a high dose is taken. In fact, older people are more sensitive to the effects of medications, and so a dose appropriate for a younger adult is more likely to have negative effects or side effects in an older adult (Mort & Aparasu, 2002). Even anesthesia for surgery can subsequently affect cognitive functioning (Thompson, 2003).

To determine whether psychological or medical disorders are causing an individual's decline in cognitive functioning, the clinician may take a number of steps (Harvey, 2005a; Rabin et al., 2006). Specifically, he or she may

- interview and observe the patient;
- speak with the patient's family or friends or someone else who knows the patient and his or her history;
- obtain a medical examination by an internist or neurologist;
- ask for laboratory testing to be performed, such as blood tests or neuroimaging tests;
- review the patient's recent and current medications;
- assess the patient's ability to function in daily life; and
- obtain neuropsychological testing to determine the specific cognitive abilities that are impaired.

All of these steps were taken when Mrs. B. was being diagnosed in order to determine the nature of her problems—her memory difficulties and her disruptive behaviors that made it difficult for her to live in supervised residential settings.

Apraxia
A neurological condition characterized by problems in organizing and carrying out voluntary movements even though the muscles themselves are not impaired.

Delirium
A cognitive disorder characterized by a disturbance in consciousness and changes in cognitive functioning, particularly in attention.

Key Concepts and Facts About Normal Versus Abnormal Aging and Cognitive Functioning

- Most aspects of cognitive functioning remain stable during the normal course of aging. However, fluid intelligence and the related abilities of processing speed, recalling verbal information on demand, maintaining attention, and multitasking do decline in older adults. But these declines do not generally impair daily functioning.

- Although older adults are less likely than younger adults to have a psychological disorder, the disorders that are most common among older adults are depression and generalized anxiety disorder. A small percentage of adults develop schizophrenia and have their first psychotic episode after the age of 44. These disorders can lead to impaired cognitive functioning that may superficially resemble symptoms of a cognitive disorder.

- Brain injury, most commonly from a stroke, can produce various cognitive deficits that may resemble those related to psychological disorders. Among the deficits that may follow a stroke or a head injury are aphasia (problems with producing and comprehending language), agnosia (problems in interpreting what is perceived), and apraxia (problems in organizing and producing voluntary movements).

- Legally prescribed medications or illegal substances can alter awareness, emotional states, and cognitive functioning. A dose that is standard for a younger person can adversely affect an older adult.

Making a Diagnosis

- Reread Case 15.1 about Maurice Rosen, and determine whether or not his symptoms are probably the result of normal aging or might indicate a psychological disorder. Specifically, list which symptoms seem to result from normal aging and which ones may indicate a disorder. If you would like more information to determine his diagnosis, what information—specifically—would you want, and in what ways would the information influence your decision?

Delirium

Mrs. B.'s cognitive difficulties emerged gradually over time. Although she forgot appointments, she never forgot—and was never confused about—who and where she was. Moreover, she did not experience unusual or rapid changes in consciousness or in the ability to focus her attention. If she had, these symptoms might have indicated that she was delirious, as are many residents of nursing homes who are 75 years old or older (American Psychiatric Association, 2000). In this section we look at delirium in detail.

What Is Delirium?

Delirium is characterized by two main symptoms: a disturbance in consciousness and changes in cognitive functioning, particularly in attention. These symptoms develop rapidly—over hours to days—and fluctuate within a 24-hour period. The disturbance in consciousness is evidenced by decreased awareness of the external environment; the person may appear "stoned" or seem to be focusing on internally generated stimuli, such as mental images. Attentional problems include difficulties in focusing on external stimuli as well as problems in sustaining and shifting attention. A delirious patient may have a hard time understanding a question, or may have trouble shifting attention to a new question and remain focused on the previous one. Alternatively, he or she may be distracted and unable to pay attention to any question.

These attentional problems can make it difficult for a clinician to interview the delirious patient; the clinician must infer the patient's mental state from his or her behavior and unusual responses and then seek information from family members or friends. The DSM-IV-TR diagnostic criteria are summarized in Table 15.2, and Case 15.2 describes one woman's experience with delirium.

Table 15.2 ▶ DSM-IV-TR General Diagnostic Criteria for Delirium

A. Disturbance of consciousness (i.e., reduced clarity of awareness of the environment) with reduced ability to focus, sustain, or shift attention.

B. A change in cognition (such as memory deficit, disorientation, language disturbance) or the development of a perceptual disturbance that is not better accounted for by a preexisting, established, or evolving dementia.

C. The disturbance develops over a short period of time (usually hours to days) and tends to fluctuate during the course of the day.

D. There is evidence from the history, physical examination, or laboratory findings that the symptoms in Criteria A and B are (one or more of the below):

1. Caused by medication;

2. Caused by a general medical condition;

3. Developed during substance intoxication;

4. Developed during, or shortly after, a withdrawal syndrome.

Source: Reprinted with permission from the Diagnostic and Statistical Manual of Mental Disorders, Text Revision, Fourth Edition, (Copyright 2000) American Psychiatric Association. For more information see the Permissions section.

CASE 15.2 ▸ FROM THE OUTSIDE: Delirium

A 74-year-old African American woman, Ms. Richardson, was brought to a city hospital emergency room by the police. She is unkempt, dirty, and foul-smelling. She does not look at the interviewer and is apparently confused and unresponsive to most of his questions. She knows her name and address, but not the day or the month. She is unable to describe the events that led to her admission.

The police reported that they were called by neighbors because Ms. Richardson had been wandering around the neighborhood and not taking care of herself. The medical center mobile crisis unit went to her house twice but could not get in . . . they broke into the apartment . . . and then found Ms. Richardson hiding in the corner, wearing nothing but a bra. The apartment was filthy. . . .

[Ms. Richardson was diabetic, and her diabetes was out-of-control when she was admitted to the hospital. They begin to stabilize her medically and decided to transfer her the next day to a medical unit. Before the transfer, she was interviewed by a psychiatrist, who noted:]

Her facial expression was still mostly unresponsive, and she still didn't know the month and couldn't say what hospital she was in. She reported that the neighbors had called the police because she was "sick," and indeed she had felt sick and weak, with pains in her shoulder; in addition, she had not eaten for 3 days. [Her mental state improved when the diabetes was treated.]

(Spitzer et al., 2002, pp. 13–14)

When delirious, individuals may also be disoriented, not knowing where they are or what the time, day, or year is; this was the case with Ms. Richardson in Case 15.2. Less frequently, when delirious, people may not know *who* they are. In addition, they may have difficulty speaking clearly, naming objects, or writing. The content of their speech may resemble that of someone in a manic episode: pressured and nonsensical, or flitting from topic to topic.

Delirious people may also experience perceptual alterations, including:

- *misinterpretations* (correctly perceiving a sensory stimuli but making the incorrect interpretation of what it is, such as correctly identifying the smell of smoke but incorrectly attributing the smell to a roaring fire rather than to an extinguished match);

- *illusions* (misperceiving an object, as in perceiving the form of a pair of pants crumpled on the floor as a dog); and

- *hallucinations* (seeing—or hearing—someone or something that isn't actually there).

The perceptual disturbances are most frequently visual. Delirious individuals may believe that their perceptual experiences are real and behave accordingly. Hallucinations that are threatening may make them afraid, and they may respond by attacking others. Sometimes people in a delirious state are injured while responding to their altered perceptions, and their behavior can appear bizarre. Because of the perceptual difficulties, such patients may not consent to appropriate treatment.

People experiencing delirium may also have problems with their sleep cycle, or they may become physically restless and agitated. Perceptual alterations are more likely when patients are in this state. Alternatively, delirious patients may exhibit the opposite pattern, becoming sluggish, with diminished physical activity; perceptual disturbances are less likely during this state. During a 24 hour period, a patient may shift between these two patterns. Emotions may run the gamut, rapidly shifting from elation and euphoria to depression, fear, anxiety, and apathy.

Delirium is most common among the elderly, the terminally ill, and patients who have just had surgery; it is not yet known why delirium is more likely among these groups, but it may arise from neurological changes related to aging that make

Table 15.3 ▶ Delirium Facts at a Glance

Prevalence

- Older adults are more likely than others to develop delirium.
- At any given time, 0.4% of adults over the age of 18 may be delirious; among those 55 years of age or older, the prevalence almost triples, to 1.1%.
- Among elderly patients in hospitals, 10–15% are delirious when admitted and 10–40% may be diagnosed with delirium during their stay.
- Among residents in nursing homes who are age 75 and older, up to 60% may be delirious at any point in time.
- Up to 80% of terminally ill patients will become delirious, particularly when they are close to death (Brown & Boyle, 2002).

Comorbidity

- Delirium may occur along with another cognitive disorder or a substance-related disorder.

Onset

- When delirium is caused by certain drugs, such as cocaine or hallucinogens (see Chapter 9), symptoms usually emerge within minutes to hours. When delirium arises from other substances, such as benzodiazepines, symptoms may take longer to emerge.
- Delirium can arise after head trauma, in which case symptoms often develop immediately.

Course

- Symptoms of delirium typically fluctuate over the course of the day.
- For most people, symptoms completely subside within a few hours or days; for others, especially the elderly, symptoms may persist for months or longer.
- A shorter course occurs when the cause of delirium is contained and brief, as with substance intoxication.
- People who had relatively good health and cognitive functioning before their delirium began are likely to make a better recovery.
- People with previous episodes of delirium are more vulnerable to subsequent episodes.

Gender Differences

- Among the elderly, men are more likely than women to become delirious.

Cultural Differences

- Countries have different guidelines for diagnosing delirium, which can prohibit making meaningful comparisons across countries (Leentjens & Diefenbacher, 2006).

Source: Unless otherwise noted, the source for information is American Psychiatric Association, 2000.

the elderly more vulnerable to develop delirium. Table 15.3 provides additional information about delirium.

Symptoms of delirium can also occur with other disorders, which may make it difficult to provide a definitive—or even a tentative—diagnosis. The following symptoms may seem similar to those of delirium:

- *Psychotic symptoms.* In schizophrenia or a mood disorder with psychotic features, the psychotic elements (i.e., delusions and hallucinations) are often integral to the symptoms of the disorder. In contrast, in delirium, the aspects of symptoms that appear psychotic are not as systematic.

- *Mood, anxiety, or dissociative symptoms.* With mood, anxiety, or dissociative disorders, the symptoms of fear, anxiety, or dissociation are relatively stable and tend not to vary with cognitive symptoms. In contrast, with delirium, symptoms of fear, anxiety, or dissociation tend to fluctuate along with the cognitive symptoms, and attentional problems are prominent.

If the clinician has reason to suspect that the symptoms arise because of a medical condition, as in the case of Ms. Richardson, or substance use, delirium is a tentative diagnosis, pending physical or laboratory tests. In addition, the clinician should take care when diagnosing delirium in people from another culture or a different background. Such individuals may respond to the clinician's questions in ways that suggest delirium, but the clinician should consider whether a patient's culture or background, along with anxiety or symptoms of other disorders, might better account for the apparent cognitive difficulties.

Understanding Delirium: A Side Effect?

Delirium can arise from ingestion of a substance, such as alcohol or a prescribed medication, or as a result of a medical condition, such as an infection.

Delirium That Arises From Substance Use

Delirium can arise from the effects of a psychoactive substance such as alcohol or a medication, or from withdrawal from such a substance. According to DSM-IV-TR, intoxication or withdrawal are considered to give rise to delirium only when the symptoms are significantly more severe than those that usually occur during intoxication or withdrawal. The symptoms must be severe enough that they require more than the usual attention and treatment provided to someone who used the substance in question. If the symptoms are not severe enough to reach the level needed for a diagnosis of delirium, the appropriate diagnosis is a substance-related disorder, either intoxication or withdrawal (see Chapter 9).

Delirium That Arises From Intoxication

When intoxication causes delirium, only a brief time elapses between taking the substance and the emergence of delirium symptoms—minutes to hours. Among older adults, delirium often arises after taking medication on doctor's orders: One study found that up to 20% of older adults are prescribed potentially inappropriate medications (Zhan et al., 2001), which can create unnecessary side effects and interact with other medications to affect cognition and mood.

Most frequently, when the intoxication has worn off, the delirium ends. There are exceptions, however: Some substances, such as PCP, can produce extended delirium. Moreover, some people may have persistent symptoms of delirium even when no longer intoxicated.

Delirium That Arises From Substance Withdrawal

Sometimes, a chronic user of a substance such as alcohol or a hypnotic-sedative can become delirious after stopping the substance use. In fact, delirium tremens (the DTs) arises from withdrawal after alcohol dependence. Depending on the individual and the substance involved, the symptoms of delirium can last from a few hours to 2–4 weeks. The diagnosis of delirium is made only when the cognitive problems associated with withdrawal are significantly more severe than is usual upon withdrawal from the substance, and the symptoms require the attention of medical or mental health professionals.

Delirium Due to a General Medical Condition

Like a fever, delirium can arise for a variety of medical reasons:

- infection,
- dehydration,
- electrolyte imbalance (which can arise from an eating disorder; see Chapter 10),
- stroke,
- brain tumor,
- pneumonia,
- heart attack,
- head trauma, or
- surgery (arising from anesthesia).

Some of these causes, such as dehydration, can be fatal if not treated (Brown & Boyle, 2002).

How do clinicians determine the underlying cause of an individual's delirium? From a physical examination, a consultation with someone who knows the patient and may know something about what led to the symptoms, results of laboratory tests, and a review of the patient's medical history. In some cases, the clinician may need to evaluate the patient a number of times over the course of a day or over several days to determine the specific cause of the delirium (or whether, in fact, the diagnosis of delirium is most appropriate; Kessler, 2006). Delirium can be caused by more than one factor; for example, if someone with alcohol dependence develops an infection and doesn't drink alcohol while the fever is raging, that person's delirium might well arise from both the DTs and the fever.

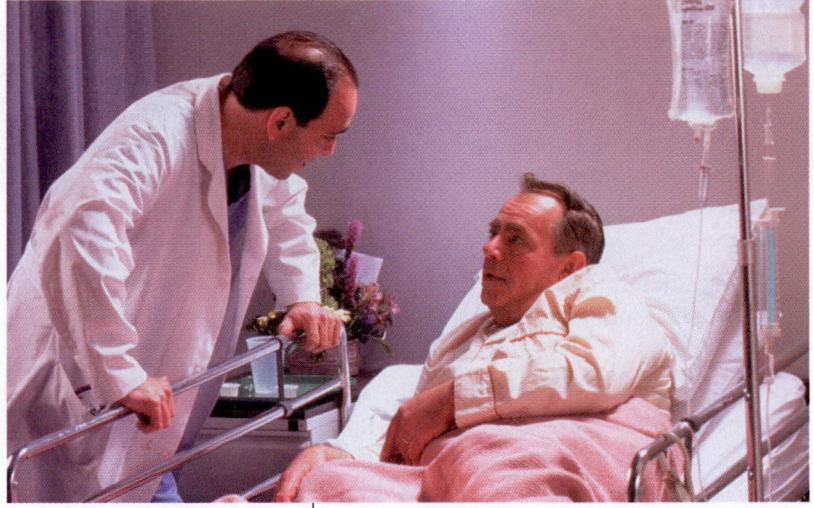

Delirium can arise from a variety of medical problems, including dehydration, or after receiving anesthesia. A percentage of surgery patients—particularly elderly ones—become temporarily delirious in response to anesthesia.

Treating Delirium: Rectify the Cause

Most often, treatment for delirium targets neurological factors—treating the underlying medical condition or substance use that affects the brain and gives rise to the delirium. In most cases, as the medical condition improves or the substance intoxication or withdrawal resolves, the delirium ends. In some cases, though, treatment for the underlying medical problem—for example, administering antibiotics to treat bacterial pneumonia—can take days to affect the delirium; in other cases, as arises when people are close to death, doctors may not be able to treat the underlying cause of the delirium. For temporary relief, the patient may be given antipsychotic medication for the delirious symptoms, usually haloperidol or risperidone (Leentjens & van der Mast, 2005). In fact, studies find that giving haloperidol preventatively to elderly patients about to undergo surgery can decrease the severity and duration of postoperative delirium (Kalisvaart et al., 2005).

Treatment may also target psychological and social factors. Such interventions for people with delirium include (Brown & Boyle, 2002):

- providing hearing aids or eyeglasses to eliminate sensory and perceptual impairments;

- teaching the patient to focus on the here and now, by providing very visible clocks and calendars or other devices and encouraging the patient to use them;

- creating an environment that optimizes stimulation, perhaps by providing adequate lighting and reducing unnecessary noise;

- ensuring that the patient is fed and warm;

- making the environment safe by removing objects with which the patient could harm himself or herself or others; and

- educating the people who interact with the patient (residential staff, friends, and family members) about delirium.

Key Concepts and Facts About Delirium

- According to DSM-IV-TR, delirium is characterized by a disturbance in consciousness and changes in cognitive functioning (particularly in attention). These symptoms develop rapidly and fluctuate over the course of a 24-hour period.

- When delirious, people may not know where they are, who they are, or what day (or year) it is. They may also misinterpret stimuli and experience illusions or have hallucinations. Because they believe that these perceptual alterations are real, patients

continued on next page

may behave accordingly and get hurt—or hurt other people—in the process.

- Delirious people may become either restless and agitated or sluggish and lethargic, or they may rapidly alternate between these two states. Delirium most commonly occurs among the elderly, the terminally ill, and patients who have just had surgery.

- Symptoms of depression, anxiety, dissociation, psychosis, and substance use can appear similar to some symptoms of delirium.

- Delirium can arise from substance intoxication or withdrawal; however, for a diagnosis of delirium related to substance use, the symptoms must be more severe than would normally arise from intoxication produced by, or withdrawal from, the particular substance. Delirium can also arise from a medical condition such as an infection or head trauma or following surgery.

- Treatment for delirium that targets neurological factors often addresses the underlying physical cause, typically through medication. Antipsychotic medication may be given when treatment for the underlying condition isn't possible or will take time to take effect.

- Treatments that target psychological and social factors include correcting sensory impairments, helping patients increase their awareness of the here and now, and educating people who interact with the delirious patient about the symptoms of the disorder.

Making a Diagnosis

- Reread Case 15.2 about Ms. Richardson, and determine whether or not her symptoms meet the criteria for delirium. Specifically, list which criteria apply and which do not. If you would like more information to determine her diagnosis, what information—specifically—would you want, and in what ways would the information influence your decision?

Amnestic Disorder

Mrs. B. was not delirious and had not been delirious in the nursing home; she knew who and where she was and her cognitive difficulties—her memory problems—were not transient. In addition to forgetting about planned activities, she'd been forgetting whether she'd taken her medications and forgetting doctor's appointments. The neuropsychologist needed to determine the extent of her memory problems and whether they were worse than those normally associated with aging.

> "When questioned about her memory and thinking, she reported that she had "been off track" some before her move and attributed this to [an] "imbalance" resulting from the many stresses that she had experienced in her life. She was vague in describing what she had found stressful, naming the death of her husband (many years before) and the loss or theft of some belongings (how and when unclear). . . .
>
> "Mrs. B. had some reservations at first about being asked more questions about her memory and mood, but as the interview continued, she became more comfortable and worked with good effort. Testing proceeded very slowly because of her tendency to digress, reminiscing about events from her early life or about current circumstances. In general, she was more willing to talk than to participate in structured assessment."
>
> (LaRue & Watson, 1998, p. 6)

For some older people, the only significant cognitive function that is impaired is memory—in particular, the ability to store new information or to recall or recognize information already stored. Mrs. B.'s memory problems seem to be limited to recent events—such as scheduling appointments—rather than events in her distant past. Either type of memory problem may indicate *amnestic disorder*. In this section we examine amnestic disorder and its neurological causes in more detail.

What Is Amnestic Disorder?

The key characteristic of **amnestic disorder** is impaired memory while other mental processes remain relatively intact. The memory problem may involve difficulty storing new information or recalling previously stored information. DSM-IV-TR allows the clinician to specify whether the memory impairment is *transient* (lasting from a few days to a maximum of 1 month—a type that may arise as a result of seizures), or is *chronic* (lasting for longer than 1 month). The memory problem is

Amnestic disorder
A cognitive disorder characterized by impaired memory while other mental processes remain relatively intact.

Confabulate
To create stories in order to fill in gaps in memory.

most obvious when the person must spontaneously recall information, such as remembering a friend's telephone number. The specific types of memory that are most impaired (such as visual versus verbal and recent versus distant past) depend on the brain areas that have been affected. People with extreme memory problems may need closely supervised care every day. According to DSM-IV-TR, amnestic disorder is characterized only by memory problems and not problems with other cognitive functions. Table 15.4 lists the specific criteria.

Memory problems that arise with amnestic disorder are less likely to affect implicit memory. For instance, a previously acquired ability to type or to drive is often preserved, but someone with amnestic disorder may be unable to explain how to drive or even to remember that he or she *can* drive. Nonetheless, once behind a wheel, the person knows what to do. In spite of being able to perform certain basic tasks that rely on implicit memory, the patient cannot remember factual information—particularly new information—which clearly impairs functioning. As one man with chronic amnestic disorder notes:

> I lead a basic lifestyle. I strenuously avoid what I would call "high-risk" situations. That is, situations in which my memory difficulties would leave me lost and disoriented. I don't even travel to unfamiliar places unless I am accompanied or have a detailed written guide. . . . If I visit the cinema or theater, I must make sure that I won't have to leave my seat during the screening as I would not be able to find my way back.
>
> I don't read novels. I will never be able to take a job. Familiarizing myself with the location of the workplace, the nature of the job, the names of my employers and colleagues, the plan of the building, the extent of my responsibilities, etc. would take many weeks. In fact it would not be possible.
>
> (Wilson, 1999, p. 42)

Imagine what it might be like to have serious gaps in your memory: Your wallet isn't where you thought you left it but is on the kitchen counter instead; at a party, someone who you think is a stranger seems to know a lot about you. To create a sense of coherence in their lives, people with memory problems may **confabulate**—create stories to fill in the blanks in memory. For example, an individual with impaired memory may come to believe that his or her wallet ended up on the kitchen counter because someone else in the family moved it. When a mental health clinician asks such a patient about his or her life or problems, the patient's report may be a confabulation and hence be inaccurate. One man, Jack, recounts his experience with memory problems, beginning with being asked by a professor to relay a message to a classmate:

> I left the room and promptly forgot the message, where to go, the name of the lecturer who'd sent me, and how to return to the room I originally been sent from. I was lost. And I can't recall what came of the incident . . . many of my recent memories are like this. I start off relatively clear and then fade off as I related the story to myself. And I often find that as faithful to the truth as many of my recollections may be, some are tinged with pure fiction, as if without even realizing it, I am filling in the gaps, the empty times with fabricated notions of the past. . . . But then I am in no position to say whether this is in fact the case. I cannot gauge how accurate any of my memories are.
>
> (Wilson, 1999, p. 41)

Friends or family members may thus be the best source of information about an amnestic patient's symptoms. Case 15.3 describes a woman with amnestic disorder who did not noticeably confabulate. Additional facts about amnestic disorder are listed in Table 15.5.

Table 15.4 ▶ DSM-IV-TR General Diagnostic Criteria for Amnestic Disorder

A. The development of memory impairment as manifested by impairment in the ability to learn new information or the inability to recall previously learned information.

B. The memory disturbance causes significant impairment in social or occupational functioning and represents a significant decline from a previous level of functioning.

C. The memory disturbance does not occur exclusively during the course of a Delirium or a Dementia [discussed later in this chapter] or persists beyond the usual duration of substance delirium or withdrawal.

D. There is evidence from the history, physical examination, or laboratory findings that the disturbance is:

- the direct physiological consequence of a general medical condition (including physical trauma); or,
- etiologically related to the persisting effects of substance use (e.g., a drug of abuse, a medication).

Source: Adapted from American Psychiatric Association, 2000.

Brand X Photography/Veer

People with amnestic disorder may try to fill the holes in their memories by confabulating—creating stories that make a coherent narrative of their circumstances. For instance, a woman with amnestic disorder might not remember how her underwear came to be in her pocketbook; she might then create a story to explain its presence.

Table 15.5 ▸ Amnestic Disorder Facts at a Glance

Prevalence

- The prevalence of amnestic disorder is unknown.

Comorbidity

- Substance-related disorders may contribute to amnestic disorder in some cases.

Onset

- The age of onset varies, depending on the cause of the memory problems.
- Symptoms may emerge rapidly or gradually, depending on the cause of the memory problems.
- Prior to the emergence of the memory problems, the person may be confused or disoriented and have attentional problems, which may lead to a diagnosis of delirium.

Course

- Depending on the cause of the memory problems, symptoms may last anywhere from a few hours to indefinitely.
- When the disorder is due to head trauma, symptoms improve the most within the first few months, and may continue to improve for up to 2 years after the trauma.
- When memory problems begin, the person may confabulate; as the problems persist, the person usually confabulates less or not at all.
- People may deny that they have memory problems, even when presented with "proof"; they may, in turn, accuse others of manufacturing the "proof."

Gender Differences

- Given the lack of research on the prevalence of this disorder, it is unknown whether a sex difference exists.

Source: American Psychiatric Association, 2000.

CASE 15.3 ▸ FROM THE OUTSIDE: Amnestic Disorder

A 55-year-old woman, whom we shall call Ms. A.,

. . . began to experience progressive difficulties remembering. Her past medical history was unremarkable. There was no family history of neurodegenerative disease. An example of her problem was that she saw the same movie twice within a few days without noticing that she had seen it the first time. Despite her severe memory impairment, she lived independently and continued managing her own shop. She was extremely aware of her predicament and concerned about her future.

Neurological consultation was sought 3 years after the onset of her memory problem. Elementary neurological examination [and tests] were normal . . . her only deficit was an amnestic syndrome with amnesia [for recent events. She had a] normal attention span, preserved memory for events that occurred before the onset of her disorder, and no confabulation or false recognition.

Her complaints increased over the following 2 years. Examination 5 years after the onset showed that learning of verbal and nonverbal material was severely impaired. Other cognitive functions were normal. . . . At this time she had to give up working because of her memory problem. She remained independent but had to use strategies, to compensate for her disorder. She continued traveling by herself. On one occasion she left her suitcase at one hotel and, not remembering where she had left it, slept at another hotel.

During the following years her memory problems remained unchanged and she was very conscious of her deficit. . . . Formal assessment of memory, 13 years after her initial complaint, revealed no additional change in her performance. . . . No behavioral change was observed and she remained alert and well groomed. She was fully aware of her predicament and continued caring for herself.

(Didic et al., 1998, pp. 526–527)

What distinguishes amnestic disorder from delirium, which may involve memory problems? With amnestic disorder, the memory problem is the *sole* cognitive impairment—there is no significant change in consciousness or attention or other mental processes—as was the case for Ms. A in Case 15.3. Impaired memory is also the key symptom of dissociative amnesia (see Chapter 8), but with that disorder, the impairment is generally limited to particular types of memories—traumatic or otherwise stressful ones. Moreover, amnestic disorder is diagnosed only when there is strong reason to believe that the memory problems are related to a medical condition or substance use; in contrast, the impaired memory of dissociative amnesia is thought to be caused by psychological trauma. And, although it is normal to have some memory problems with advanced age, a diagnosis of amnestic disorder indicates memory problems that are significantly more severe than those due simply to aging.

Is amnestic disorder an appropriate diagnosis for Mrs. B.'s problems? No; she has other cognitive problems—revealed by her poor performance on the Trail Making Test.

Understanding Amnestic Disorder

Amnestic disorder is caused exclusively by one of two types of neurological factors: substance use or a medical condition. However, the disorder typically has different courses of development in the two cases: When the disorder is caused by chronic substance abuse or exposure to a toxin, memory usually becomes impaired gradually. (One medical condition that gradually leads to amnestic disorder is chronic malnutrition.) In contrast, when amnestic disorder is caused by stroke or trauma to the head, memory becomes impaired rapidly. Let's consider the two types of causes in more detail.

Substance-Induced Persisting Amnestic Disorder

When substance use causes the memory impairment and the amnesia lasts significantly longer than the period of intoxication or withdrawal, the disorder falls under the DSM-IV-TR diagnosis of *substance-induced persisting amnestic disorder*. To make this diagnosis, there must be evidence from the individual's history, a physical examination, or laboratory tests that the impaired memory was caused by substance use, exposure to certain toxins, or the effect of a medication.

Typically, people with this disorder have, or have had, substance dependence. Alcohol is the most common substance that leads to amnestic disorder; in DSM-IV-TR it is referred to as *alcohol-induced persisting amnestic disorder*. Alcohol reduces the absorption of the vitamin *thiamine* from food; thiamine is found in nuts, bread, and some fruits, vegetables, and meats (Hochhalter et al., 2001). Severe thiamine deficiency can lead to significant memory problems, specifically the amnestic disorder called *Korsakoff's syndrome*. Memory symptoms often emerge after age 40, usually abruptly, although subtle memory problems are often evident earlier. Unfortunately, the symptoms are likely to remain stable or diminish only somewhat over time, even with sustained sobriety (Kapur & Graham, 2002; Victor, Adams, & Collins, 1989).

Amnestic disorder can also be caused by environmental toxins such as lead, mercury, and carbon monoxide. In addition, relatively high doses and prolonged intake of a barbiturate (such as Seconal) or a benzodiazepine (such as Valium; see Chapter 9) may cause amnestic disorder. Amnestic disorder caused by such substances has a better prognosis than does that caused by alcohol. Once the individual tapers off the use of the drug, the memory problems usually clear up.

Amnestic Disorder Due to a General Medical Condition

A variety of medical conditions can lead to amnestic disorder (O'Conner & Lafleche, 2006) by damaging brain areas involved in memory: the hippocampus,

Figure 15.2

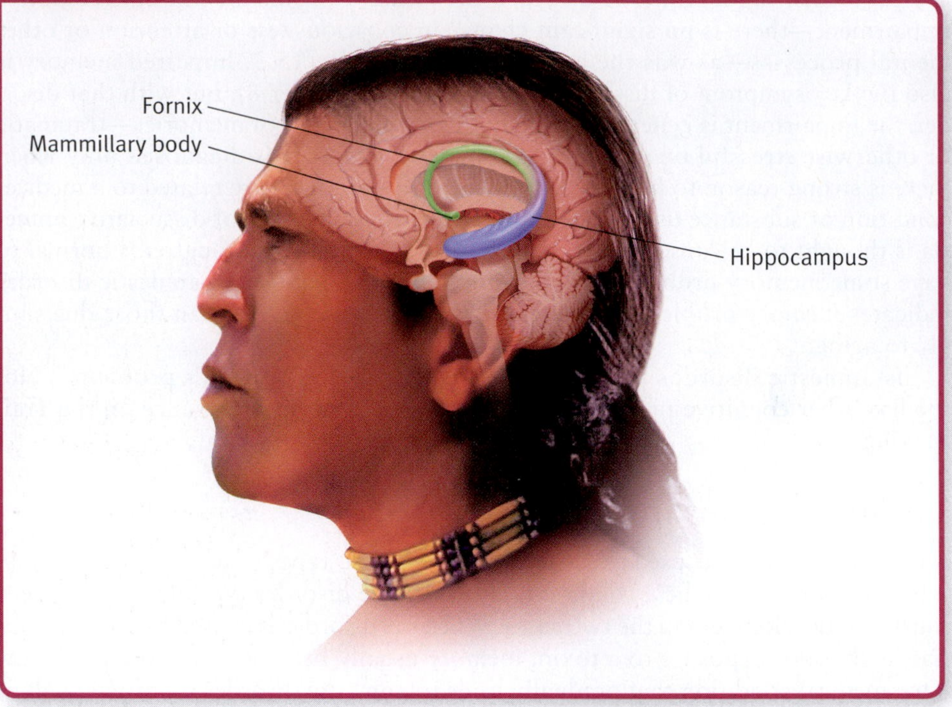

Fornix
Mammillary body
Hippocampus

15.2 ▶ Brain Areas Affected by Medical Conditions That Cause Amnestic Disorder Medical conditions such as a stroke or a head injury can damage the hippocampus, the mammillary bodies, and the fornix; this damage can lead to amnestic disorder.

the mammillary bodies, and the fornix (see Figure 15.2 for the locations of these brain areas). The clinician determines whether *amnestic disorder due to a medical condition* is the most appropriate diagnosis after reviewing the patient's history—including results of laboratory tests or a physical examination—and determining that the symptoms are not better accounted for by another disorder, such as dissociative disorder or depression.

Treating Amnestic Disorder

No treatment can cure amnestic disorder. However, depending on the specific brain damage and the areas affected, partial or full memory function can sometimes return over time; when memory returns, it usually does so within a couple of years of the onset of the disorder (Wilson, 2004). In most cases, the goal of treatment is *rehabilitation*—helping the patient learn to function as well as possible given the symptoms.

Currently, there are no medications that improve memory in patients with amnestic disorder, although patients may receive medication for comorbid disorders. Rehabilitation of the patient with amnestic disorder typically targets psychological and social factors: (1) helping the patient to develop strategies to compensate for impaired memory, and (2) changing the physical environment so that the patient does not need to rely as much on memory in order to function.

Targeting Psychological Factors: Developing and Implementing New Strategies

Rehabilitation teaches patients techniques and strategies to use to compensate for their memory problems (Wilson, 2004), particularly ways of organizing information so that it can later be retrieved from memory more readily. One such strategy is the use of *mnemonics*, which may help people to remember simple information, such as where the car is parked at the mall. For example, someone whose visual memory is not significantly impaired might imagine the location of the car in the parking lot, which will help him or her retain this information. Another strategy is to write down any information that must be retrieved later, such as by making a note about where in the parking lot the car is parked.

Depending on the patient's abilities and inclinations, he or she may use a variety of memory aids: diaries, notebooks, alarms, calendars, or hand-held electronic personal digital assistants (PDAs). A PDA-type device can be a very effective memory aid because an alarm can be set to go off at the appropriate time, and the device can display a text message telling the patient what he or she needs to do at that moment ("Take red pill now" or "Go to Dr. Gabi's office at 23 Main Street") (Kapur, Glisky & Wilson, 2004). In contrast to memory aids that require the patient to remember to use the tools (as in remembering to look at written notes), PDAs do not require the patient to remember as much information. Table 15.6 lists various memory aids.

If a patient has not previously used such memory aids, however, he or she must be taught how to use them, which can create a paradox: Even after learning how to use a memory aid, the patient must later remember how to use it and then remember to use it in the appropriate situation. Depending on the specific nature of the memory problems, though, many patients can learn new strategies and use them. To ensure that a patient has learned a technique or strategy, the clinician should do the following (Wilson, 2004):

- Explain the to-be-learned information as simply as possible.

- Ask the patient to remember only one piece of information or one procedure at a time. For instance, a patient who had never used a PDA before, such as Ms. A. in Case 15.3, should first learn how to use the device to access stored information (such as a grocery list) before learning how to enter new information into it.

- Make sure that the patient understands the information—if the information is verbal, he or she should paraphrase the information and repeat it back to the clinician. For instance, after the clinician explained to Ms. A. how to access information on the PDA, such as the grocery list, Ms. A. should paraphrase those instructions.

- Link the new information to something the patient already knows. For instance, the clinician could program the PDA so that pressing and holding the G key accesses the grocery list and pressing and holding the M key accesses a medication schedule.

- Have the patient rehearse and practice the learned information frequently. For example, Ms. A. should repeatedly access the grocery list while with the clinician. Once she has mastered this step, she can proceed to learn how to add information to the grocery list.

- Make sure that the patient is actively thinking about the information, not simply parroting it.

Patients are more likely to remember their own actions than the corrections of errors they make. Thus, mental health professionals may use **errorless learning techniques** to teach patients new information (Kessels & de Haan, 2003): Patients are explicitly guided in learning a new skill rather than being allowed to figure it out through trial and error. For instance, if using errorless learning to teach Ms. A. how to enter a grocery list into a PDA, the clinician would discourage guessing and give as much information as Ms. A. needed to enter the list correctly the first time. If she didn't know what to do at a given step, the clinician would show her or provide help ranging from very specific guidance ("Now press the green button") to hints or prompts ("What do you do first to add an item?"), depending on her ability to take the next step correctly.

Electronic devices can serve as memory aids for patients with amnestic disorder. They can be programmed so that an alarm goes off at a particular time, when the screen displays a message about some action the patient should take.

Mint Photography

Table 15.6 ▸ Memory Aids for People With Memory Problems

- Alarm clock for waking up
- Clock or watch to tell the date as well as the time
- Watch with a timer (for elapsed time)
- An appointment diary
- A journal (to write about and later read about events or experiences that otherwise would be forgotten)
- A notebook for writing notes to self
- Lists of things to do or buy, such as groceries
- Labels on cabinets and drawers
- Sticky notes with reminders about chores to be done
- A tape recorder for creating auditory notes to self
- Asking other people to provide reminders
- A PDA

Source: Adapted from Wilson, 1999, p. 35, Table 3.4.

Errorless learning techniques
Techniques by which patients are explicitly guided in learning a new skill rather than being allowed to figure it out through trial and error.

John Livzey/Getty Images

This man has significant memory problems. The notes on his dresser drawers label the type of items in each drawer. Such modifications to his environment can reduce the impact of his memory problems, and make his experience getting dressed each morning less confusing or frustrating.

The challenge with memory aids is to overcome the patient's difficulty in remembering to use the strategies and devices in real-life settings. To facilitate such generalization, the clinician may teach family members or others how to use the strategies and devices and how to help the patient use them in his or her home environment.

Targeting Social Factors: Organizing the Environment

One way to reduce the cognitive load of someone with amnestic disorder is to enlist others to structure the patient's environment so that memory is less important. For instance, family members can place labels on the outside of cupboard doors and room doors at home or at a residential facility; each label identifies what is on the other side of the door (for example, "dishes," "kitchen," "Sally Johnson's room"). In some rehabilitation centers, the doors to bathrooms are painted a distinctive color, and arrows on the walls or floors show the direction to a bathroom, so patients don't need to rely as much on memory to get around the facility (Wilson, 2004).

Key Concepts and Facts About Amnestic Disorder

- Amnestic disorder is characterized by significant deficits solely in memory—other cognitive functions remain relatively intact. People with amnestic disorder may confabulate to fill in memory gaps, and they may not be able to report their history accurately during a clinical interview. Amnestic disorder can be transient or chronic.

- When trying to determine whether amnestic disorder is the most appropriate diagnosis for a patient with memory problems, the clinician must rule out other disorders that can give rise to memory problems, including delirium and dissociative amnesia; the clinician must also determine that the memory impairment is more severe than would be expected from normal aging.

- Amnestic disorder is caused exclusively by two types of neurological factors: (1) substance use (leading to substance-induced persisting amnesia, which most frequently occurs with severe and chronic alcohol dependence), or (2) a medical condition, such as stroke, head trauma, or the effects of surgery.

- Rehabilitation focuses on helping amnestic patients learn to use organizational strategies (such as mnemonics or writing down information) and memory aids (such as diaries and PDAs). A patient's environment can be structured in order to minimize the amount of information that needs to be remembered to function in daily life—for example, by putting identifying labels on doors.

Making a Diagnosis

- Reread Case 15.3 about Ms. A., and determine whether or not her symptoms meet the criteria for amnestic disorder. Specifically, list which criteria apply and which do not. If you would like more information to determine her diagnosis, what information—specifically—would you want, and in what ways would the information influence your decision?

Dementia

Mrs. B. seemed to have some memory problems, but memory was not the only aspect of her cognitive functioning that had declined. During neuropsychological testing, "the principal areas of difficulty on [certain] tests were in mental control, as evidenced by tangential and repetitive speech; psychomotor slowing [in this case, slow movements based on mental processes, not reflexes]; and reduced flexibility in thought and action" (LaRue & Watson, p. 9). Some of these difficulties are characteristic of *dementia*. Could Mrs. B. have dementia?

In this section we focus on dementia: what it is, what neurological factors give rise to it, and what treatments are available for it.

What Is Dementia?

Dementia is the general term for a set of cognitive disorders that is characterized by deficits in learning new information or recalling information already learned *plus* at least one of the following types of impaired cognition (American Psychiatric Association, 2000):

- *Aphasia.* In dementia, aphasia often appears as overuse of the words *thing* and *it* because of difficulty remembering the correct specific words.

- *Apraxia.* Problems with executing motor tasks (even though there isn't anything wrong with the appropriate muscles, limbs, or nerves) can lead to problems dressing and eating, at which point self-care becomes impossible.

- *Agnosia.* People with dementia may not recognize friends, family members, or even the face in the mirror.

- *Executive function problems.* These problems lead to difficulties in planning, initiating, organizing, abstracting, and sequencing or even in recognizing that one has memory problems. (These problems arise primarily in dementia that affects the frontal lobes.) These deficits can make it impossible to meet the demands of daily life. Mrs. B. evidenced some difficulties in tasks that required executive functions.

We discussed aphasia, apraxia, and agnosia earlier, in the context of effects of brain damage on cognition. Unlike the effects of a stroke or a head injury, however, dementia is not caused by an isolated incident. Rather, it arises over a period of time, as brain functioning degrades; symptoms of dementia often change over time, typically becoming worse, but sometimes remaining static or even reversing course.

To be diagnosed as having dementia, a person must have cognitive deficits severe enough to impair daily functioning, and these deficits must contrast with a prior, more adaptive level of functioning. Table 15.7 summarizes the DSM-IV-TR diagnostic criteria for dementia.

Mild symptoms of dementia may go unnoticed in people whose cognitive functioning started out at a very high level. Such a patient may detect his or her compromised ability to function, but neuropsychological testing is likely to show that the patient's abilities are within the normal range for his or her age—and so the early signs of dementia would go undiagnosed (Harvey, 2005a). Most people with dementia are over 65 years of age when symptoms emerge, and in these cases, DSM-IV-TR specifies that the disorder has *late onset*. When symptoms begin before age 65, the disorder is said to have *early onset*. Early onset, particularly before age 50, is rare and is usually hereditary (Ikeuchi et al., 2008).

Depending on the specific mental processes that are impaired, a patient with dementia may

- behave inappropriately (for instance, tell unsuitable jokes or be overly familiar with strangers);

Dementia
A set of cognitive disorders characterized by deficits in learning new information or recalling information already learned *plus* at least one other type of cognitive impairment.

Table 15.7 ▸ DSM-IV-TR General Diagnostic Criteria for Dementia

A. Multiple cognitive deficits are present, including the following:

1. memory impairment (new learning or recall) *and*

2. one or more of aphasia, apraxia, agnosia, or executive dysfunction.

B. The cognitive deficits significantly impair social or occupational functioning and reflect a significant decline from a previous level of higher functioning.

C. The cognitive deficits are not exclusively present during delirium.

D. The cognitive deficits cannot be better attributed to another Axis I disorder, such as depression [Chapter 6] or schizophrenia [Chapter 12].

Source: Rabin et al., 2006, p. 211, Exhibit 10.1; based on American Psychiatric Association, 2000.

- misperceive reality (for instance, think that a caretaker is an intruder); or
- wander away while trying to get "home" (a place where he or she lived previously).

Impaired cognitive functioning can lead many patients to feel easily overwhelmed or confused and become agitated. The agitation or confusion may cause a patient to become violent, which can make it difficult or potentially dangerous for the patient to remain living at home with family members—and hence the patients may be moved to a residential care facility.

The most common cause of dementia is **Alzheimer's disease** (also called "dementia of the Alzheimer's type," or simply Alzheimer's), in which the afflicted individual initially has problems with both memory and executive function (such as difficulty with abstract thinking and impaired judgment). As the disease advances, memory problems worsen, and attention and language problems emerge, and spatial abilities may deteriorate; the patient may even develop psychotic symptoms, such as hallucinations and delusions (particularly delusions of persecution). In the final stage, the patient's memory loss is complete—he or she doesn't recognize family members and friends, can't communicate, and is completely dependent on others for care. In Case 15.4, Diana Friel McGowin describes her experience with Alzheimer's disease; additional facts about dementia are provided in Table 15.8.

Table 15.8 ▸ Dementia Facts at a Glance

Prevalence

- About 5 million older Americans are estimated to have dementia (Alzheimer's Association, 2007).
- Among those between 65 and 69 years of age, 1–2% are diagnosed with dementia; the prevalence doubles with every additional 4 years of age.
- Dementia occurs most frequently in those over 85 years old; 16–30% of people in this age group are diagnosed with dementia (Knopman, Boeve, & Petersen, 2003; Ritchie & Lovestone, 2002).

Comorbidity

- Depression (Kales et al., 2005; Snow et al., 2005) and psychotic symptoms such as hallucinations and delusions (Tractenberg et al., 2003) commonly co-occur with dementia.

Onset

- Onset usually occurs late in life.
- Cognitive deterioration can be rapid or gradual, depending on the cause of the dementia.
- Impaired learning and recall are early signs of some types of dementia.

Course

- People with dementia may be unable to perform complex tasks in new situations but still be able to perform simple ones in familiar surroundings.
- Some types of dementia, such as that caused by Alzheimer's disease, get progressively worse (these types are referred to as *progressive dementias*); other types of dementia, such as that caused by HIV infection, can get better with treatment of the underlying cause. Still other types remain relatively unchanging.

Gender Differences

- Dementia is slightly more common in males than in females.

Cultural Differences

- Some cultures and ethnic groups—such as African Americans, Asian Americans, and Hispanic Americans—may be more tolerant of impaired memory and other cognitive dysfunctions that affect the elderly, in some cases, viewing these changes as a normal part of aging. Family members thus may wait longer before seeking medical assistance for an older person with dementia (Cox, 2007).

Source: Unless otherwise noted, the source for information is American Psychiatric Association, 2000.

Alzheimer's disease
A medical condition in which the afflicted individual initially has problems with both memory and executive function and which leads to progressive dementia.

CASE 15.4 ▶ FROM THE INSIDE: Dementia

Diana Friel McGowin was 45 years old when she became aware of memory problems. She got lost on the way home because no landmarks looked familiar; she was unable to remember her address or to recognize her cousin. After neuropsychological and neuroimaging tests, she was diagnosed with early-onset Alzheimer's disease (because the disorder emerged before age 65). In her memoir about the progressive nature of this disease, *Living in the Labyrinth* (1993), McGowin describes sharing with her neurologist some of the symptoms she was having:

I showed him the burns on my wrists and arms sustained because I forgot to protect myself when inserting or removing food from the oven. I told him of becoming lost in the neighborhood grocery store where I had shopped for over twenty years. I showed him my scribbled notes and sketched maps of how to travel to the bank, the post office, the grocery, and work. (p. 41)

She describes other memory problems as the disease progressed:

I sometimes lost my thread of thought in mid-sentence. Memories of childhood and long ago events were quite clear, yet I could not remember if I ate that day. On more than one occasion when my grandchildren were visiting, I forgot they were present and left them to their own devices. Moreover, on occasions when I had picked them up to come play at my house, the small children had to direct me home. (pp. 64–65)

Further into her memoir, she notes:

As my grip upon the present slips, more and more comfort is found within my memories of the past. Childhood nostalgia is so keen I can actually smell the aroma of the small town library where I spent so many childhood hours. (p. 109)

Painfully lonely, I still contrarily, deliberately, sit alone in my home. The radio and TV are silent. I am suspended. Somewhere there is that ever-present reminder list of what I am supposed to do today. But I cannot find it. (p. 112)

In the early phases of a progressive dementia, when the person has relatively little decline in executive function, he or she may become so depressed about the diagnosis and its prognosis that he or she attempts suicide. Diana McGowin, in Case 15.4, became acutely aware of her symptoms during the early phase of the disease and worked hard to try to compensate by making maps and lists.

Distinguishing Between Dementia and Other Psychological Disorders

The symptoms of dementia—impaired memory and other cognitive dysfunctions—also occur with other disorders and can resemble symptoms of other disorders, which sometimes makes an accurate diagnosis challenging. The following disorders have symptoms that may seem similar to those of dementia:

- *Mental retardation.* However, mental retardation does not primarily involve memory problems; moreover, mental retardation is diagnosed in young people. Clinicians must keep in mind that people whose intellectual functioning in early and middle adulthood was in the low average range or below (an IQ of 85 or less) may have difficulty functioning as the normal changes with aging are superimposed on the lower baseline level of cognitive abilities. Such people may technically meet the criteria for dementia in older adulthood (Heaton, Grant, & Matthews, 1991).

- *Schizophrenia.* Although both dementia and schizophrenia often involve hallucinations and delusions, schizophrenia is usually diagnosed earlier in adulthood. Moreover, schizophrenia has a standard set of positive and negative symptoms

(Harvey, 2005b; see Chapter 12). Although some people develop schizophrenia later in life (which can make it difficult to distinguish it from dementia by the age of onset), such later-onset schizophrenia often progresses rapidly from the prodromal phase—when symptoms are just beginning to emerge—to a full psychotic episode, whereas psychotic symptoms are likely to emerge more gradually with dementia (Harvey, 2005c).

- *Depression.* A clinician may find it particularly difficult to distinguish between depression and dementia in elderly patients—both disorders can involve memory problems, poor concentration, and other cognitive dysfunctions. The timing of the onset of symptoms can help distinguish the two disorders: Patients with depression often have relatively normal cognitive functioning before becoming depressed and then rapidly decline. In contrast, those with dementia may have a slower cognitive decline.

- *Delirium.* With some patients, the particular symptoms can make it difficult for mental health clinicians to determine whether delirium, dementia, or both are present (see Table 15.9). Friends or family members may be called on to provide a more accurate history of a patient's symptoms than the patient can provide.

- *Amnestic disorder.* Both amnestic disorder and dementia involve memory problems. However, a diagnosis of dementia requires that additional cognitive deficits be present.

- *Normal aging.* It is normal for adults to experience some decline in cognitive functioning with increasing age; to be considered as dementia, an elderly person's cognitive problems must be significantly worse than would be normally expected and must be caused by a medical condition or related to substance use.

Table 15.9 ▸ Symptoms Unique and Common to Delirium and Dementia

Unique to Delirium	Unique to Dementia	Common to Both Delirium and Dementia
• Delirium has a rapid onset. • Symptoms (including changes in consciousness) fluctuate within a 24-hour period. • Hallucinations—frequently visual—are present. • Symptoms often gradually improve. • The person is not alert and focused.	• Dementia has a gradual onset. • Symptoms typically do not fluctuate within a 24-hour period. • Hallucinations are often absent. • Symptoms rarely improve. • The person is consistently alert.	• Memory problems • Problems with other types of cognitive functioning

Understanding Dementia

Dementia is caused by a variety of neurological factors, and according to DSM-IV-TR, each of these factors corresponds to a specific dementia diagnosis. Let's review the most common types of dementia: dementia of the Alzheimer's type, vascular dementia, and dementia due to other general medical conditions.

Dementia of the Alzheimer's Type

Almost three quarters of dementia cases are caused by Alzheimer's disease (Plassman et al., 2007). There is no routine lab test for diagnosing this disease at present, and so this type of dementia is diagnosed by excluding or ruling out other possible causes.

The Progression of Alzheimer's Disease

The onset of Alzheimer's disease is gradual, with symptoms becoming more severe over time. Often, the early signs of dementia of the Alzheimer's type involve difficulty remembering recent events or newly learned information. In fact, in the early stages of Alzheimer's, the memory problems may be diagnosed as amnestic disorder (Petersen & O'Brien, 2006); it is only as the disease progresses that other cognitive dysfunctions emerge.

Within a few years of onset, symptoms may include aphasia, apraxia, and agnosia. Spatial abilities may deteriorate markedly. Patients may also become irritable and their personality may change, and such changes may become more pronounced as cognitive functioning declines. In the final stage of the disease, motor problems arise, creating difficulties with walking, talking, and self-care. Generally, these patients die about 8–10 years after the first symptoms emerge. Table 15.10 describes normal functioning with aging and the five stages of the disorder's progression in more detail.

In some cases, people with dementia also exhibit behavioral disturbances, such as agitation or wandering about, which arise because of the cognitive deficits—they get lost or, like Ms. McGowin, they can't remember their destination. DSM-IV-TR

Table 15.10 ▶ Normal Functioning and the Five Stages of Dementia of the Alzheimer's Type

Level of Cognitive Impairment	Clinical Phase	Clinical Characteristics	Diagnosis
1 = No Cognitive Decline	Normal	No subjective complaints of memory deficit. No memory deficit evident on clinical interview.	Normal
2 = Very Mild Cognitive Decline	Forgetfulness	Subjective complaints of memory deficits. No objective deficits in employment or social situations. Appropriate concern with respect to symptomatology.	Normal aged
3 = Mild Cognitive Decline	Early confusional	Earliest clear-cut deficits. Decreased performance in demanding employment and social settings. Objective evidence of memory deficit obtained only with an intensive interview. Mild to moderate anxiety accompanies symptoms. When introduced to new people, has increased difficulty remembering their names. Word-finding problems noticeable to other people. Loses objects.	Compatible with incipient Alzheimer's disease
4 = Moderate Cognitive Decline	Late confusional	Clear-cut deficit on careful clinical interview. Inability to perform complex tasks. Although patient has significant memory problems, denies them or blames others for problems. Flattening of affect and withdrawal from challenging situations occur. Inability to perform complex tasks such as paying bills.	Mild Alzheimer's disease
5 = Moderately Severe Cognitive Decline	Early dementia	Patients can no longer survive without some assistance. Patients are unable during interview to recall a major relevant aspect of their current lives. Persons at this stage retain knowledge of many major facts regarding themselves and others. They invariably know their own names and generally know their spouses and children's names. They require no assistance with toileting or eating, but may have some difficulty choosing the proper clothing to wear.	Moderate Alzheimer's disease
6 = Severe Cognitive Decline	Middle dementia	May occasionally forget the name of the spouse upon whom they are entirely dependent for survival. Will be largely unaware of all recent events and experiences in their lives. Will require some assistance with activities of daily living. Personality and emotional changes occur, such as suspiciousness; may develop psychotic symptoms, wander, and become lost.	Moderately severe Alzheimer's disease
7 = Very Severe Cognitive Decline	Late dementia	All verbal abilities are lost. Frequently there is no speech at all— only grunting. Incontinent of urine; requires assistance toileting and feeding. Loses basic psychomotor skills (e.g., ability to walk).	Severe Alzheimer's disease

Source: Adapted from Reisberg et al., 1982, Table 12.1.

Table 15.11 ▸ Prevalence of Dementia of the Alzheimer's Type From Age 65 On

Age (in years)	Prevalence Among Males	Prevalence Among Females
65	0.6%	0.8%
85	11%	14%
90	21%	25%
95	36%	41%

As people age beyond 65 years old, they are increasingly likely to develop Alzheimer's disease. About half the cases in each age group have moderate to severe cognitive impairment (American Psychiatric Association, 2000).

allows clinicians to note whether the individual's dementia occurs *with behavioral disturbance* or *without behavioral disturbance.* One woman describes her husband's recent behavioral disturbances:

> My husband used to be such an easy-going, calm person. Now, he suddenly lashes out at me and uses awful language. Last week, he got angry when our daughter and her family came over and we sat down to eat. I never know when it's going to happen. He's changed so much—it scares me sometimes.
>
> (National Institute on Aging, 2003, p. 47)

People with Alzheimer's who exhibit behavioral disturbances are more likely to have greater declines in cognitive functioning and to need institutional care sooner than patients whose behavior causes less concern (Scarmeas et al., 2007). As noted in Table 15.11, slightly more females than males develop this form of dementia, and it accounts for progressively more cases of dementia in older age groups.

Brain Abnormalities Associated With Alzheimer's Disease: Neurofibrillary Tangles and Amyloid Plaques

Two brain abnormalities are associated with Alzheimer's disease: *neurofibrillary tangles* and *amyloid plaques.* In the following we consider each of these abnormalities.

The internal support structure of a neuron includes microtubules, which are tiny hollow tubes that create tracks from the cell body to the end of the axon; nutrients are distributed within the cell via these microtubules. A protein, called *tau,* helps stabilize the structure of these tracks (see Figure 15.3). With Alzheimer's disease, the tau proteins become twisted together in what are called **neurofibrillary tangles,** and these proteins no longer hold together the microtubules—which thereby disrupts the neuron's distribution system for nutrients. In addition, the collapse of this support structure prevents normal communication with other neurons. This process may also contribute to the death of neurons. In fact, people with Alzheimer's have smaller brains than normal (Henneman et al., 2009).

The brains of people with Alzheimer's disease are abnormal in another way— they have **amyloid plaques,** which are fragments of proteins (one type of which

Figure 15.3

15.3 ▸ Neurofibrillary Tangles in Alzheimer's Disease Tau proteins stabilize the structure of a neuron from the cell body through the end of the axon. With Alzheimer's disease, these proteins become entangled, destroying the structure of the neuron and disrupting its communication with other neurons.

Source: National Institute of Aging.

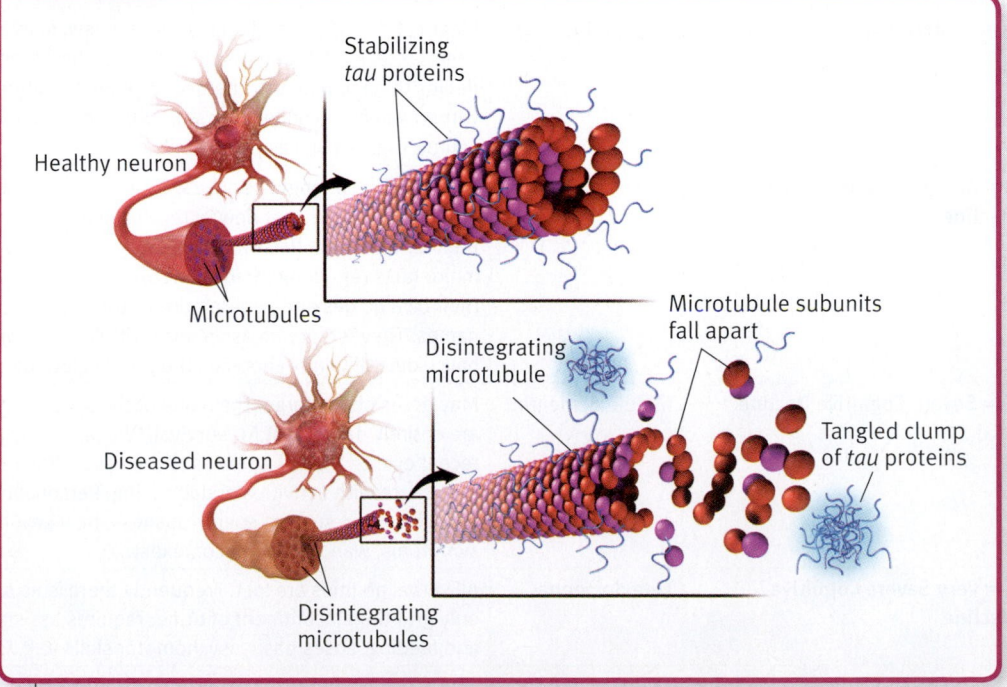

Neurofibrillary tangles
The mass created by tau proteins that become twisted together and destroy the microtubules, leaving the neuron without a distribution system for nutrients.

Galerie Beckel-Odille-Boicos

Galerie Beckel-Odille-Boicos

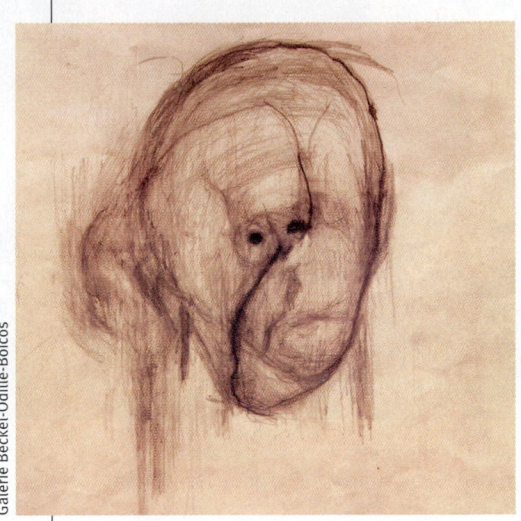

Galerie Beckel-Odille-Boicos

Artist William Utermohlen learned in 1995 that he had Alzheimer's disease—which causes a type of progressive dementia. He responded to the news by painting self-portraits. Alzheimer's can specifically affect brain areas involved in spatial abilities, which are crucial for painting. As his dementia progressed, Utermohlen's images became less distinct and more abstract; these three portraits were done in (left to right) 1998, 1999, and 2000. Although he recognized that his paintings weren't what he wanted, he said that he "could not figure out how to correct them" (Grady, 2006).

is called *amyloid*) that accumulate on the outer surfaces of neurons, particularly neurons in the hippocampus (the brain area predominately involved in storing new information in memory).

Researchers have not yet determined whether the neurofibrillary tangles and plaques *cause* Alzheimer's disease or are a by-product of some other process that causes the disease (National Institute of Aging, 2003). However, neurofibrillary tangles and amyloid plaques are generally discovered during autopsies, and PET scanning that used a particular chemical marker has been able to detect the amyloid plaques and neurofibrillary tangles that distinguish Alzheimer's disease from other causes of memory problems in living patients (Small et al., 2006). Additional studies have corroborated the potential of such PET scanning to detect Alzheimer's disease (Ikonomovic et al., 2008). And other experimental biomedical tests have been designed to identify biological markers that distinguish patients with Alzheimer's. For example, one test compares blood samples and cerebrospinal fluid from patients with Alzheimer's disease, patients with dementia due to Parkinson's disease (which we will discuss shortly), and healthy control participants (Neale, 2008). Preliminary studies using this test have been successful in distinguishing among the types of participants.

Genetics

People who have a specific version of one gene, *apo E*, are more susceptible to late-onset Alzheimer's disease than those who don't have this particular gene. However, someone can have this version of the apo E gene and not develop Alzheimer's; conversely, someone can develop Alzheimer's and not have this version of the gene.

In contrast, early-onset Alzheimer's is caused by mutation of one of three other genes, and two of these mutations lead to Alzheimer's disease in 100% of cases. However, the third type of mutation, a rare form called *presenilin 2*, does not always cause the disease (Bird et al., 1996; Williamson-Catania, 2007), which suggests that other neurological factors and/or psychosocial factors play a role.

Vascular Dementia

Vascular refers to blood vessels, and *vascular diseases* refer to problems with blood vessels, such as high blood pressure or high cholesterol. Vascular disease can reduce or block blood supply to the brain, which in turn can cause **vascular dementia**. Blood vessels are involved in dementia in two possible ways: (1) plaque

Amyloid plaques
Fragments of protein that accumulate on the outside surfaces of neurons, particularly neurons in the hippocampus.

Vascular dementia
A type of dementia caused by reduced or blocked blood supply to the brain, which arises from plaque buildup or blood clots.

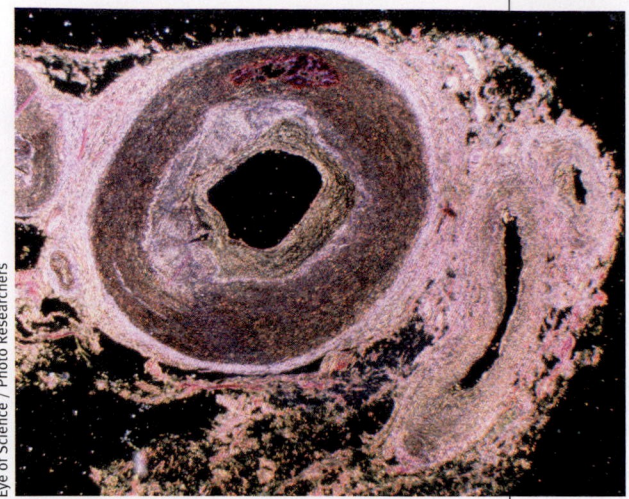

Eye of Science / Photo Researchers

A buildup of plaque in the arteries can lead to decreased blood supply to the brain, which can cause vascular dementia.

builds up on artery walls, making the arteries narrower, which then diminishes blood flow to the brain, or (2) bits of clotted blood block the inside of arteries, which then prevents blood from reaching the brain—which, as we noted earlier, produces a stroke. Such clots can cause a series of small strokes (sometimes referred to as *transient ischemic attacks* or *ministrokes*) in which blood supply to parts of the brain is temporarily blocked, leading to transient impaired cognition or consciousness. When multiple ministrokes occur over time, dementia can arise as brain areas involved in cognitive functioning become impaired. This form of dementia can have a gradual onset. In contrast, a single, large stroke inflicts more brain damage than a series of ministrokes; in such cases, vascular dementia has an abrupt onset.

A clinician makes the diagnosis of vascular dementia based on the patient's laboratory test results and on abnormal reflexes or responses during a neurological examination (for instance, weakness in a limb or problems in walking). Symptoms of vascular dementia can wax and wane over a given 24-hour period, but even the patient's highest level of functioning is lower than it was before dementia set in (Puente, 2003). In addition, neuroimaging may reveal lesions in particular brain areas. People with vascular dementia may also have Alzheimer's disease, particularly if they are very old (Kalaria & Ballard, 1999). Vascular dementia is more common in men than women.

The course of the disorder is variable, depending on the specific brain areas affected; when symptoms become more severe, they worsen in a stepwise fashion, with more deficits apparent after each instance of reduced blood supply to the brain. Aggressive treatment of the underlying vascular disease (typically via medication) may prevent additional strokes or reduced blood flow to brain areas.

Dementia Due to Other General Medical Conditions

Dementia can also be caused by a variety of other medical conditions, including Parkinson's disease, late-stage HIV infection, and Huntington's disease. With these and certain other medical conditions, the onset can be gradual or sudden, the course can range from acute to chronic, and the patient may also develop behavioral disturbances. Let's look at some of the general medical conditions that can cause dementia.

Dementia Due to Parkinson's Disease

Parkinson's disease is characterized by a slow, progressive loss of motor function; typical symptoms are trembling hands, a shuffling walk, and muscular rigidity. About 1 million Americans have Parkinson's disease, and around 50% of people with Parkinson's disease develop dementia due to this disease. Those who develop dementia are usually older (age of onset is about 65 years old) or are in a more advanced stage of the disease (Papapetropoulos et al., 2005). The dementia generally involves problems in memory and executive functions. Comorbid depression can cause even more cognitive dysfunctions.

Parkinson's disease causes damage to dopamine-releasing neurons in an area of the brain known as the *substantia nigra*. As a consequence, the brains of these patients do not have normal amounts of this neurotransmitter, which is critically involved in motor functions as well as executive functions. Parkinson's disease is thought to arise from a combination of genetic inheritance and other neurological factors, such as brain damage caused by exposure to toxins (for example, pesticides).

Dementia Due to Lewy Bodies

Another type of progressive dementia is **dementia due to Lewy bodies**. *Lewy bodies* consist of a type of protein that, in some people, builds up inside neurons that produce dopamine and acetylcholine and can eventually cause the neurons to die. The neurons most often affected are involved in memory and motor control (but neurons associated with other functions can also be affected).

Dementia due to Lewy bodies
A type of progressive dementia caused by a type of protein (referred to as Lewy bodies) that builds up inside some types of neurons and can eventually cause them to die.

The early stage of dementia due to Lewy bodies is marked by visual hallucinations, fluctuations in attention and consciousness throughout the day (with long periods of time spent staring into space or being drowsy), and a stiffness of movement that is similar to that of people with Parkinson's disease (rigid muscles, tremors, slowed movements, and a shuffling style of walking). Clinicians may have difficulty distinguishing this form of dementia from Alzheimer's, and about 20% of people who were diagnosed with Alzheimer's were found also to have abnormal Lewy bodies (which were discovered on autopsy; Rabin et al., 2006). The main features that are present in dementia due to Lewy bodies but tend not to be as marked in dementia due to Alzheimer's disease are:

(1) the presence of (visual) hallucinations early in the course of the disorder,

(2) a tendency to retain the ability to name objects,

(3) very poor visuospatial ability, and

(4) impaired executive functions (Kaufer, 2002; Knopman, Boeve, & Petersen, 2003; Walker & Stevens, 2002).

Like patients with Alzheimer's disease, patients with dementia due to Lewy bodies progressively deteriorate until death, which on average occurs about 8–10 years after diagnosis.

Dementia Due to HIV Disease

The human immunodeficiency virus (HIV) can cause widespread destruction of white matter and of subcortical brain areas; this damage gives rise to dementia. The symptoms of this form of dementia include impaired memory, concentration, and problem solving, as well as cognitive slowing. Moreover, patients may exhibit signs of apathy and social withdrawal or delirium, delusions, or hallucinations. They may develop tremors or repetitive movements or have balance problems (McArthur et al., 2003; Price, 2003; Shor-Posner et al., 2000). Antiretroviral medications that treat HIV infection slow and in some cases may actually reverse the brain damage, improving cognitive functioning (Sacktor et al., 2006).

Dementia Due to Huntington's Disease

Huntington's disease is a progressive disease that kills neurons and affects cognition, emotion, and motor functions; it leads to dementia and eventually results in death. Early symptoms of Huntington's include bipolar-like mood swings between mania and depression, irritability, and psychotic symptoms (e.g., hallucinations or delusions). Motor symptoms include slow or restless movements, and the symptoms of dementia include memory problems (which become severe as the disease progresses), executive dysfunction, and poor judgment.

Between 5 and 7 people per 100,000 develop Huntington's disease (Folstein, 1989). Men and women are equally affected; the disease is usually diagnosed when patients are in their late 30s or early 40s, but the age of onset can range from 4 years old to 85 years old.

Huntington's disease is inherited and is based on a single gene. If a parent has Huntington's disease, his or her children each have a 50% chance of developing it. Genetic testing can assess whether the gene is present. However, even if the gene is present, the disorder does not always develop.

Dementia Due to Head Trauma

Just as head trauma can cause amnestic disorder, it can also cause dementia. The precise deficits and their severity depend on which brain areas are affected and to what degree. The individual with this form of dementia may also exhibit behavioral disturbances, such as agitation or anxiety. Such a patient may have amnesia for events during and after the trauma, as well as other persistent memory problems. In addition, he or she may exhibit sensory or motor problems and even personality changes (becoming increasingly aggressive or apathetic or suffering severe mood swings) (American Psychiatric Association, 2000).

Huntington's disease
A progressive disease that kills neurons and affects cognition, emotion, and motor functions; it leads to dementia and eventually results in death.

This form of dementia is most common among young males, who are more likely to engage in risk-taking behaviors (including reckless drinking). In some cases, the dementia is caused by a single trauma to the head (such as a car accident) and is unlikely to get worse; when the dementia is caused by multiple traumas (as occurs with boxers) it may become worse over time (American Psychiatric Association, 2000).

Substance-Induced Persisting Dementia

When the cognitive deficits of dementia are caused by substance use but persist beyond the period of intoxication or withdrawal, the clinician makes the diagnosis of *substance-induced persisting dementia*. A patient who receives this diagnosis usually has a long history of substance dependence, and symptoms rarely occur in patients younger than 20 years old. The onset is slow, as is the progression of deficits—the first symptoms arise while the person has substance dependence. The deficits are often not reversible and may even get worse when the substance use is discontinued, although there are exceptions (American Psychiatric Association, 2000).

As we've noted, dementia may be caused by any number of medical illnesses or conditions, and these causes are not mutually exclusive; in a given individual, dementia may have more than one cause. For example, someone may have both vascular dementia *and* Alzheimer's disease. When this occurs, the clinician diagnoses each type (cause) separately. Table 15.12 summarizes key facts about the different types of dementia.

Table 15.12 ▶ Key Facts About Different Types of Dementia

Dementia due to . . .	Approximate percentage of dementia cases	Prognosis/Course	Onset	Gender difference
Alzheimer's Disease	70%	Poor	Gradual, often after age 65; early onset is rare.	Slightly more common among females than males
Vascular Disease	15% (often comorbid with Alzheimer's type)	Cognitive loss may remain stable or worsen in a stepwise fashion.	Abrupt; earlier age of onset than Alzheimer's	More common among men
Lewy Bodies	15% (can be comorbid with Alzheimer's type)	Poor	Gradual; age of onset is between 50 and 85.	Slightly more common among men than women
HIV Infection	Less than 10%	Poor unless treated with antiretroviral medication	Gradual; depends on age at which HIV infection is acquired	Estimates of sex ratios vary, depending in part on the sex difference in HIV prevalence and the availability of antiretroviral treatment at the time a study is undertaken.
Parkinson's Disease	Less than 10%; often comorbid with Alzheimer's type and/or vascular dementia; about 50% of patients with Parkinson's disease develop dementia.	Poor	Gradual; typical age of onset is in the 70s.	More men than women develop Parkinson's disease, and so men are more likely to develop this type of dementia.
Huntington's Disease	Less than 10%	Poor	Gradual; onset usually occurs in the 40s or 50s.	No sex difference
Head Trauma	Unknown	Depends upon the specific nature of the trauma	Usually abrupt, after the head injury	Unknown, but most common among young males
Substance-Induced	Unknown	Variable, depends on the specific substance and deficits	Gradual; in the 30s and beyond	Unknown

Note: Most cases of dementia are caused by Alzheimer's disease. However, dementia in a given individual can arise from more than one cause, and the percentages in the second column reflect these comorbidities; for this reason, the numbers add up to more than 100%.

Treating Dementia

With most types of dementia, such as the Alzheimer's type and vascular dementia, no treatments can return cognitive functioning to normal. There is one exception to this general situation: antiretroviral medications sometimes can significantly reduce symptoms of dementia caused by HIV infection. However, as with amnestic disorder, for most other types of dementia, treatment largely consists of rehabilitation. Given the high proportion of dementia that is caused by Alzheimer's disease (see Table 15.12), in the following sections we focus on treatment for that type of dementia, unless otherwise noted.

Targeting Neurological Factors

Medications have been developed to delay the progression of cognitive difficulties in people with Alzheimer's disease. One class of drugs, *cholinesterase inhibitors*, such as *galantamine* (Razadyne) or *donepezil* (Aricept), is used for mild to moderate cognitive symptoms; these medications increase levels of acetylcholine (American Association of Geriatric Psychiatry, 2006; Lanctôt et al., 2003; Lyle et al., 2008; Poewe, Wolters, & Emre, 2006; Ritchie et al., 2004). Another type of drug, *memantine* (Namenda), affects levels of glutamate (Tariot et al., 2004) and is used to treat moderate to severe Alzheimer's dementia (Kavirajan, 2009; Laks & Engelhardt, 2008). Although these drugs can help some patients (Atri et al., 2008; Cummings, Mackell, & Kaufer, 2008; Homma et al., 2008), they are new, and few carefully controlled studies of these medications have been completed. Moreover, it is unknown what the long-term effects of these drugs may be (Langa, Foster, & Larson, 2004; Ringman & Cummings, 2006). These medications may also be given to patients with dementia due to Parkinson's disease.

Antipsychotic medications are sometimes given for psychotic symptoms or behavioral disturbances, but the side effects of both traditional and atypical antipsychotics have led researchers to be cautious in advising their long-term use (Ballard & Howard, 2006; Schneider, Dagerman, & Insel, 2006). Patients with dementia due to Lewy bodies should not be given antipsychotic medication for behavioral disturbances because this type of medication makes their symptoms worse.

When patients have high blood pressure (which increases the risk of co-occurring vascular dementia), they may also receive medications to treat that problem.

Targeting Psychological Factors

The American Association for Geriatric Psychiatry (2006) recommends that the first line of intervention for dementia should help patients maintain as high a quality of life as is possible given the symptoms. Such interventions focus on psychological and social factors.

To target psychological factors, people in the early stages of dementia—and their friends and relatives—may be taught strategies and given devices to compensate for memory loss (such as those used for people with amnestic disorder, described earlier). In addition, structured and predictable daily activities can reduce patients' confusion (Spector et al., 2000). Moreover, patients may be given a GPS tracking device to wear so that they can be found relatively quickly and easily if they get lost (Rabin et al., 2006).

The early stages of progressive dementias are often associated with significant anxiety and depression (Porter et al., 2003; Ross, Arnsberger, & Fox, 1998). One type of treatment that may alleviate these comorbid conditions is *reality orientation therapy* (Woods, 2004). This therapy is designed to decrease a patient's confusion by focusing on the here and now. For example, the clinician may frequently repeat the patient's name ("Good morning, Mr. Rodrigues; how are you on this Monday morning,

People with dementia can wander off and become confused about who they are and where their home is. Some people with dementia wear small GPS tracking devices, like the one in this sneaker, so that if they wander off they can be found relatively quickly and easily.

Monitoring whereabouts

Antennas

GPS and battery device can be moved between different pairs

1 Wearer's movements picked up by satellite, relayed to monitoring center and made accessible to care takers by internet or phone

2 Electronic alert automatically issued if wearer enters or breaks a pre-defined area

© 2007 MCT
Source: Images: GTX Corporation   Graphic: Elsebeth Nielsen, Eeli Polli

Newscom

Mr. Rodrigues?") and remind the patient of the day and time; calendars and clocks are located where the patient can see them easily. Patients whose cognitive functioning is impaired to the point where they are in residential centers are encouraged to join in activities rather than isolate themselves.

Another method that may decrease the depression and anxiety that can accompany progressive cognitive decline is *reminiscence therapy*, which stimulates the patients' memories that are least affected by dementia—those of their early lives. When providing this treatment, the therapist focuses on patients' life histories and asks patients to explore and share their experiences with group members or with the therapist; patients may feel relief at being able to remember some information, and their anxiety decreases and their mood then improves (Woods et al., 1998).

To treat behavioral disturbances such as agitation and aggression that sometimes arise with dementia, caregivers—family members and paid caretakers—may first be asked to identify the antecedents and consequences of the problematic behavior (Ayalon et al., 2006; Livingston et al., 2005; Spira & Edelstein, 2006); then, they are advised on how to modify those aspects of the environment or the interactions, when feasible. For instance, if a patient becomes aggressive only at night after waking up to go to the bathroom, a night-light in his or her room may help reduce any anxiety that arises because the patient is confused upon awakening.

Targeting Social Factors

As cognitive and physical functioning declines, patients with dementia may receive services that target social factors—such as *elder day care*, which is a day treatment program for older adults with cognitive or physical impairments. Such day treatment provides a respite for family members who care for the patient and an opportunity for the patient to interact with other people. As the patient continues to decline, however, he or she may require live-in caretakers or full-time care in a nursing home or other residential facility. In addition, the methods used with amnestic patients to create a less cognitively taxing physical environment (for example, labeling doors) may also be used with patients who have dementia.

Taking care of a family member who has Alzheimer's disease is often extremely stressful, and this stress increases the caretaker's risk of developing a psychological or medical disorder. (For example, patients may not recognize a family member, and so believe that the family member is an intruder and try to attack him or her or cower in fear.) In recent years, those involved in treating patients with dementia have also reached out to family members who act as caretakers to provide education, support, and, when needed, treatment to help these people develop less stressful ways of interacting with the patients. Such interventions help family members (and indirectly, the patients themselves) function as well as possible under the circumstances.

Diagnosing Mrs. B.'s Problems

Let's reconsider the specific nature of Mrs. B.'s problems. The neuropsychologist recounted that Mrs B. knew who and where she was and understood the test instructions. Results of tests of her ability to remember information both immediately after learning it and after a 30-minute delay were normal for her age, which indicated that she probably did not have Alzheimer's disease or another disorder that involves significant memory impairment (such as amnestic disorder). Instead, the neuropsychologist suggested that Mrs. B.'s problems reflected a mild dementia combined with depression and chronic pain. The neuropsychologist wrote in her report:

> "Feedback to Mrs. B. reinforced her belief that her current memory problems do not suggest [Alzheimer's disease]. She was asked about activities that she enjoys, and we explored ways of increasing her opportunities for these activities with her attendant (e.g., she has recently visited a senior day-care program and hopes to attend one or two days a week). She was encouraged to give her current living situation a longer try, working

with her daughter and staff to improve the most bothersome aspects of the situation. Written reports were provided to the daughter (who is Mrs. B.'s legal guardian) and other medical professionals involved in her care. Feedback was also provided by telephone to the daughter and the referring psychiatrist to answer questions about results and to further discuss approaches to care. Recommendations included continuing psychotherapy and antidepressant medication, negotiating brief written contracts between Mrs. B. and staff members at the board-and-care home to clarify mutual expectations in problem areas, and considering low-dose antispychotic medication in the event that aggressive and accusatory behaviors escalated despite behavioral intervention. Neither returning home nor moving into the daughter's home was recommended. . . .

"For Mrs. B., things got worse before they got better. Her "fit" in the board-and-care home continued to deteriorate, and after much discussion, she moved back to a nursing home. For a time, she was taking multiple psychoactive medications and her cognitive function deteriorated at a rapid rate. [She was taken off her medications] and her [cognitive functioning] rebounded. A year later, after an intervening small stroke, her memory function is slightly worse, but her mood is brighter, she communicates well, and she has fewer complaints about staff and other residents than she did in the board-and-care home."

(LaRue & Watson, 1998, p. 11)

Key Concepts and Facts About Dementia

- Dementia is the umbrella term for a set of cognitive disorders that involve deficits in memory *and* aphasia, apraxia, agnosia, or problems with executive functions.

- Dementia can give rise to hallucinations and delusions. Conversely, deficits in memory and other cognitive functions may resemble symptoms of dementia but actually arise from mental retardation, schizophrenia, depression, delirium, or amnestic disorder.

- All types of dementia are caused by neurological factors. The most common type of dementia—that due to Alzheimer's disease—is a progressive disorder characterized by neurofibrillary tangles and amyloid plaques in the brain. Although symptoms may emerge before age 65 (early onset, which is highly heritable), the late-onset form (which also has a genetic basis but is less heritable) is much more common. Patients with Alzheimer's may or may not exhibit behavioral disturbances.

- Vascular dementia is caused by reduced or blocked blood flow to the brain, usually because of narrowed arteries or strokes. Vascular dementia can be caused by a series of ministrokes (gradual onset) or a single large stroke (rapid onset); contributory medical problems such as high blood pressure and high cholesterol are often treated aggressively to decrease the likelihood of further brain damage.

- Other types of dementia are caused by medical conditions:
  - Parkinson's disease is a progressive disorder that affects motor functions.
  - Lewy bodies build up inside certain types of neurons and cause the neurons to die, leading to progressive, irreversible dementia.

- HIV disease can eventually destroy white matter and subcortical brain areas; in some cases, this type of dementia can be arrested and even reversed with antiretroviral medication.

- Huntington's disease is a progressive disease that involves death of neurons in brain areas that are involved in cognition, emotion, and motor control.

- Head trauma is caused by accidents or incurred as part of an athletic sport.

- Substance use or dependence can lead to temporary or persistent dementia.

- Treatments for dementia that target neurological factors include medications that affect the levels of acetylcholine and glutamate. Behavioral disturbances that do not decrease with behavioral treatment may be targeted with antipsychotic medications.

- Psychological and social interventions for people with dementia are designed to improve the patients' quality of life. Methods include the use of memory aids, reality orientation therapy, reminiscence therapy, and restructuring the environment.

Making a Diagnosis

- Reread Case 15.4 about Diana Friel McGowin, and determine whether or not her symptoms meet the criteria for dementia. Specifically, list which criteria apply and which do not. If you would like more information to determine her diagnosis, what information—specifically—would you want, and in what ways would the information influence your decision?

SUMMING UP

Summary of Normal Versus Abnormal Aging and Cognitive Functioning

Most aspects of cognitive functioning remain stable during the normal course of aging. However, fluid intelligence and the related abilities of processing speed, recalling verbal information on demand, maintaining attention and multitasking do decline in older adults. But these declines do not generally impair daily functioning.

Although older adults are less likely than younger adults to have a psychological disorder, the disorders that are most common in older adults are depression and generalized anxiety disorder; symptoms of these disorders and of schizophrenia may superficially resemble symptoms of a cognitive disorder.

Brain injury, most commonly from a stroke, can produce various cognitive deficits that may resemble those related to psychological disorders. Among the deficits that may follow a stroke or a head injury are aphasia, agnosia, and apraxia.

In addition, legally prescribed medications or illegal substances can alter awareness, emotional states, and cognitive functioning. A dose that is standard for a younger person can adversely affect an older adult.

Thinking Like a Clinician

Evan is a first-year college student who lives with his grandmother because her home is near his school. Before he started living with her, he had spent only a few days at a time with her, usually on trips with his mother. Now that he's spending more time with his grandmother, he has noticed that she frequently tells him the same stories from her childhood. When she asks him to do an errand, she sometimes forgets the words of the objects she wants him to bring home or the shop she wants him to visit. And sometimes when he enters a room that she's in, she seems momentarily confused about who he is and why he's there. Evan is concerned that there is something "not right" with his grandmother, and is wondering whether he should suggest that she be evaluated by a doctor. Based on what you've learned about normal versus abnormal changes with aging, what specific advice would you give to Evan to help him determine whether his grandmother's cognitive problems are likely to be those of normal aging (and so Evan need not urgently suggest that she see her doctor)?

Summary of Delirium

According to DSM-IV-TR, delirium is characterized by a disturbance in consciousness and changes in cognitive functioning, particularly mental processes that rely on attention. These symptoms develop rapidly and fluctuate over the course of a 24-hour period. When delirious, people may not know where they are, who they are, or what day (or year) it is. They may also misinterpret stimuli and experience illusions or have hallucinations. Because they believe that these perceptual alterations are real, patients may behave accordingly and get hurt—or hurt other people—in the process. Delirious people may become either restless and agitated or sluggish and lethargic, or they may rapidly alternate between these two states.

Symptoms of depression, anxiety, dissociation, psychosis, and substance use can appear similar to some symptoms of delirium. Delirium can arise from substance intoxication or withdrawal, as well as from a medical condition such as an infection, head trauma, or following surgery.

Treatment for delirium that targets neurological factors often addresses the underlying physical cause, typically through medication. Antipsychotic medication may be given when treatment for the underlying condition isn't possible or will take time to take effect. Treatments that target psychological and social factors include correcting sensory impairments, helping patients increase their awareness of the here and now, and educating people who interact with the delirious patient about the symptoms of the disorder.

Thinking like a clinician

Drew is on his college's football team and had to have surgery on his knee. For the procedure, he had general anesthesia. His mom was with him right after the surgery, and Drew was delirious and remained so for hours. What can you assume, and what should you not assume, about Drew's consciousness, cognitive functions, and emotions? What might be a likely cause of his delirium?

Summary of Amnestic Disorder

Amnestic disorder is characterized by significant deficits solely in memory—other cognitive functions remain relatively intact. People with amnestic disorder may confabulate to fill in memory gaps, and they may not be able to report their history accurately during a clinical interview. Amnestic disorder can be transient or chronic. Amnestic disorder is caused exclusively by two types of neurological factors: (1) substance use, or (2) a medical condition, such as stroke, head trauma, or the effects of surgery.

Rehabilitation focuses on helping amnestic patients learn to use organizational strategies and memory aids. A patient's environment can be structured in order to minimize the amount of information that needs to be remembered to function in daily life.

Thinking like a clinician

Sixty-five-year-old Lucinda recently retired from her job as corporate vice-president of marketing. Lucinda lives alone but frequently visits her son, his wife, and their young daughter. She's noticed lately that she is losing things and often forgets things—such as where her keys are, lunch dates with friends, and other appointments. She's chalking up these problems to her retirement and the resulting changes in her daily patterns. At what point might losing and forgetting things indicate a cognitive disorder? For Lucinda to be diagnosed with amnestic disorder, what should her symptoms be, what should they not be, and why?

Summary of Dementia

Dementia is the umbrella term for a set of cognitive disorders that involve deficits in memory *and* aphasia, apraxia, agnosia, or problems with executive functions. Dementia can give rise to hallucinations and delusions. Conversely, deficits in memory and other cognitive functions may resemble symptoms of dementia but actually arise from mental retardation, schizophrenia, depression, delirium, or amnestic disorder.

All types of dementia are caused by neurological factors. The most common type of dementia—that due to Alzheimer's disease—is a progressive disorder characterized by neurofibrillary tangles and amyloid plaques in the brain. Although symptoms may emerge before age 65, the late-onset form is much more common. Patients with Alzheimer's may or may not exhibit behavioral disturbances. Vascular dementia is caused by reduced or blocked blood flow to the brain, usually because of narrowed arteries or strokes. Vascular dementia can be caused by a series of ministrokes (gradual onset) or a single large stroke (rapid onset); contributory medical problems such as high blood pressure and high cholesterol are often treated aggressively to decrease the likelihood of further brain damage. Other types of dementia are caused by medical conditions: Parkinson's disease, Lewy bodies, HIV disease (this type of dementia can be arrested or even reversed with antiretroviral medications), Huntington's disease, head trauma, or substance use or withdrawal.

Treatments for dementia that target neurological factors include medications that affect the levels of acetylcholine and glutamate. Behavioral disturbances that do not decrease with behavioral treatment may be targeted with antipsychotic medications.

Psychological and social interventions for people with dementia are designed to improve the patients' quality of life. Methods include the use of memory aids, reality orientation therapy, reminiscence therapy, and restructuring their environment.

Thinking like a clinician

What symptoms would Lucinda, described above, need to display in order to be diagnosed with dementia? If you knew only that Lucinda had been diagnosed with dementia, what should and shouldn't you assume about its cause(s) and her prognosis?

Key Terms

Cognitive disorders (p. 681)

Crystallized intelligence (p. 683)

Fluid intelligence (p. 683)

Stroke (p. 687)

Aphasia (p. 687)

Broca's aphasia (p. 687)

Wernicke's aphasia (p. 687)

Apraxia (p. 688)

Delirium (p. 688)

Amnestic disorder (p. 694)

Confabulate (p. 694)

Errorless learning techniques (p. 699)

Dementia (p. 701)

Alzheimer's disease (p. 702)

Neurofibrillary tangles (p. 706)

Amyloid plaques (p. 707)

Vascular dementia (p. 707)

Dementia due to Lewy bodies (p. 708)

Huntington's disease (p. 709)

More Study Aids

For additional study aids related to this chapter, go to:

www.worthpublishers.com/rosenberg

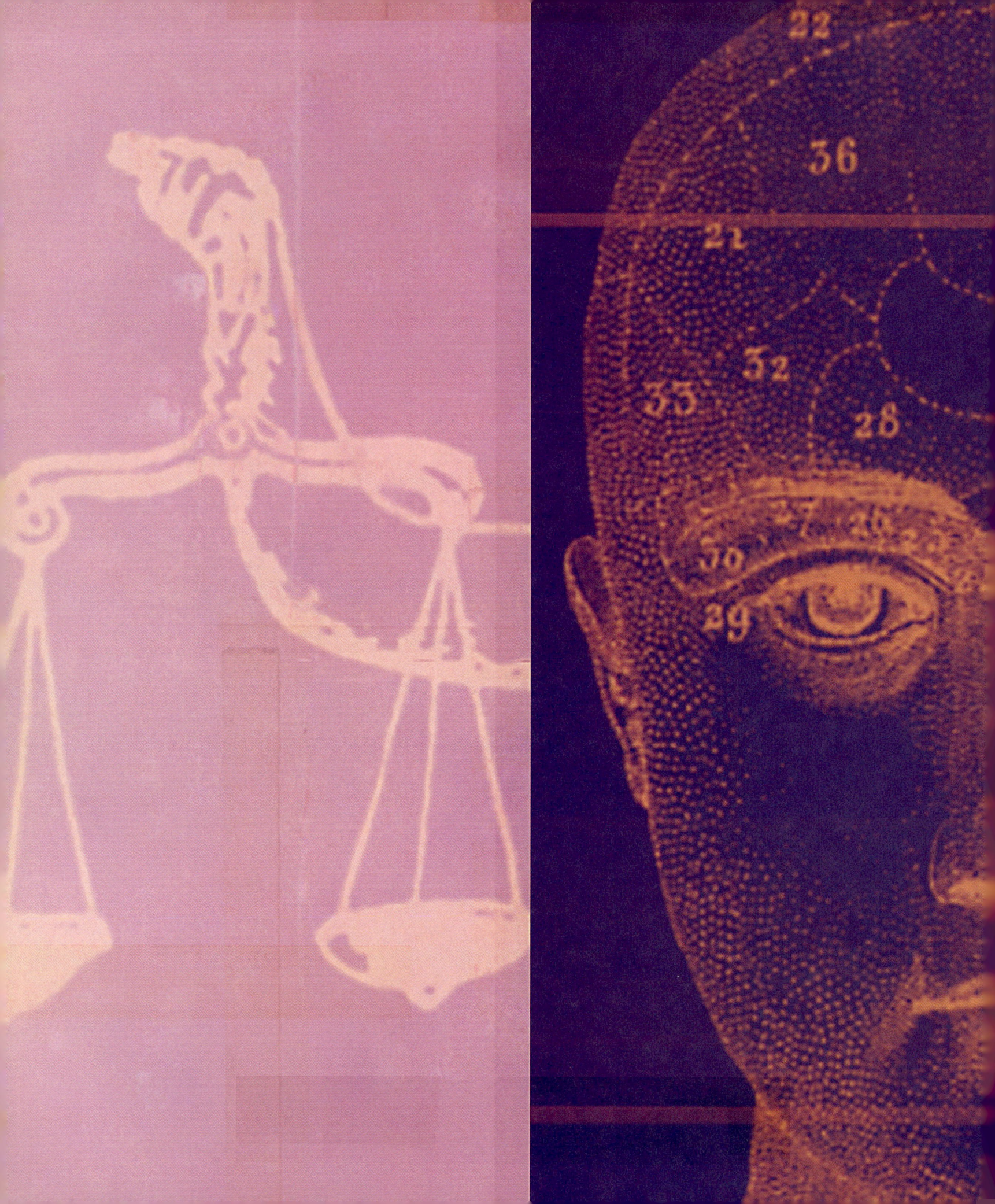

Ethical and Legal Issues

I t's the early evening rush hour in New York City in January 1998. People are waiting in a subway station for a train to take them home, to meet friends, or to go out to dinner. Kendra Webdale, a 32-year-old woman, is among the people waiting at the platform. Andrew Goldstein, a 29-year-old man, comes up from behind her and pushes her in front of an oncoming train as it enters the station. He murdered her, as many witnesses later testified. This might seem an open-and-shut criminal case, but it's not. Goldstein had a 10-year history of mental illness, had been in and out of psychiatric units and hospitals, and was diagnosed with paranoid schizophrenia.

If Goldstein wasn't in his "right mind" when he pushed Webdale, should he face a trial? And if found guilty, should he go to jail, or perhaps be executed? Or should he be judged and treated as someone who is mentally ill—and if so, why? Are those who commit criminal acts dealt with differently if they are mentally ill? Moreover, what if Goldstein had been seeing a psychotherapist and had mentioned that he might do something like this? Should the therapist have reported his statement to the police? Mental health clinicians are bound by a code of ethics and by state and federal laws. What are the relevant ethical guidelines and laws that affect how mental health clinicians treat their patients? These are the types of questions that address the relationships among the law, ethics, and the reality of mental illness and its treatment.

The laws and ethical codes pertaining to mental illness, treatment, and criminal behavior by the mentally ill evolve over time. As we shall see, even when the law is clear about the type of treatment an individual should receive, financial constraints may prevent the individual from receiving that treatment.

In this chapter, we examine the legal and ethical issues that can affect mental health professionals and their patients, paying particular attention to criminal actions by people who are mentally ill—the circumstances under which they are considered insane, what happens to them when they are dangerous to themselves or others, and whether and when they receive treatment.

Clifford Alejandro

Ethical Issues

Various mental health professionals had some contact with Andrew Goldstein during the years that led up to his pushing Kendra Webdale to her death. Any mental health professional may at times have to balance ethical and legal obligations to a patient against the safety of others. Suppose Goldstein had confided to a mental health professional that he sometimes had impulses to hurt people—impulses that he felt he might not be able to control. How should the clinician treat such information? If Goldstein gave specifics about when, where, or with whom he was likely to become violent, would that affect how the clinician should treat such information? What is the clinician ethically bound to do in such instances? We address these questions in the following sections.

An Ethical Principle: The Role of Confidentiality

Different types of mental health professionals assess, and provide treatment for, psychological problems. Each profession has its own code of ethics, although there are commonalities among all of the codes (Web sites containing the specific codes of ethics for the different types of mental health professionals are listed in Table 16.1). The most important commonality is the ethical requirement to maintain **confidentiality**—not to

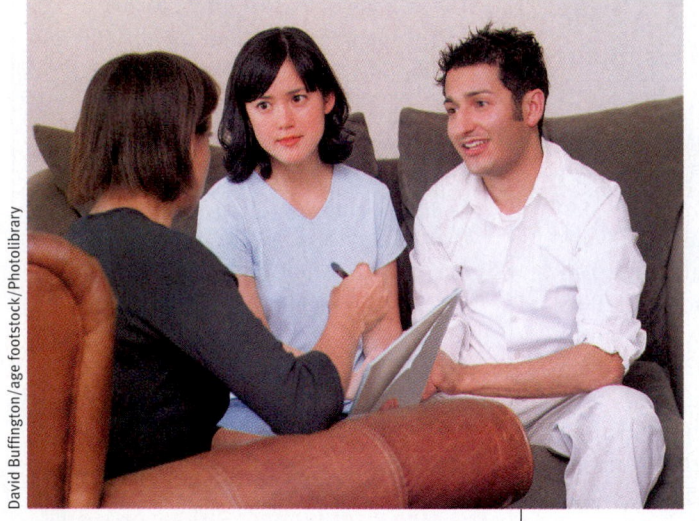

David Buffington/age footstock/Photolibrary

A mental health clinician is bound by confidentiality, but each member of a couple participating in couples therapy is not.

disclose information about a patient (even whether someone *is* a patient) to others unless legally mandated to do so. Let's look closely at the ethical principle of confidentiality.

The ethical principles and code of conduct of the American Psychological Association requires that mental health records remain confidential. In addition, the clinician must inform patients about the limits of confidentiality—that is, under what circumstances confidentiality may be broken. At first glance, this ethical rule might seem to imply that a clinician would have been required to keep anything Goldstein discussed confidential, even if it concerned violent impulses he felt unable to control. However, the situation is not quite so simple.

Ambiguities Regarding Confidentiality

The principle of confidentiality appears to be straightforward, but some clinical situations are thorny and difficult to resolve. When a therapist is treating a couple, for instance, the therapist is bound by confidentiality, but each person in the couple is not; this means that each partner may tell other people about what transpires in therapy sessions. Similarly, in group therapy, although the therapist is bound by confidentiality, each member is not (although group members are asked not to talk about anything they hear from other members). However, when a patient is a minor (under 18 years of age), the clinician may inform the parents about information that the child has told the clinician. The clinician usually discusses the limits of confidentiality with a child old enough to understand them—or at least discusses possible circumstances in which the clinician may need to share information with parents or others.

Table 16.1 ▸ Web Sites for the Ethical Codes of Various Mental Health Professions	
Mental Health Profession	**URL of Web Site Presenting Ethical Code**
Psychologist	www.apa.org/ethics
Psychiatrist	www.psych.org/psych_pract/ethics/ppaethics.cfm
Social worker	http://www.socialworkers.org/pubs/code/code.asp
Psychiatric nurse	http://nursingworld.org/mods/mod580/code.pdf
List of specific types of mental health clinicians	http://kspope.com/ethcodes/index.php

Limits of Confidentiality: HIPAA in Action

Congress passed the Health Insurance Portability and Accountability Act in 2002 (HIPAA; U.S. Department of Health and Human Services, 2002), and in doing so widened the set of circumstances under which confidential information could be shared with other individuals and organizations participating in the care or monitoring of a patient. No longer was the patient's permission to share information with other health providers legally required. HIPAA does recognize the special nature of psychotherapy provided by a mental health clinician, however; patients must provide written consent before clinicians can share notes from their psychotherapy sessions. Without a patient's consent, the clinician can share only limited information—such as the dates of treatment, the patient's diagnosis and prognosis, and the medications prescribed—with other people or organizations involved in the treatment or monitoring of the patient.

Through HIPAA, patients lost an element of control over the distribution of their health records (Appelbaum, 2002). The circumstances under which health care information can be shared without a patient's consent (or even without the patient's being told about it) now include the following (U.S. Department of Health and Human Services, 2002):

1. *During litigation.* The opposing lawyer in a lawsuit can request health information from a provider and must only state that he or she made reasonable attempts to notify the patient about the request for information. During litigation, lawyers can even request the medical records of witnesses!

2. *When the person is a police suspect.* Police officers can request health information about a suspect without having a warrant or being under any judicial oversight.

3. *Marketing efforts by health providers (and their business associates) to patients.* For instance, if a community mental health center were initiating a variety of therapy groups, for people with depression, social phobia, and ADHD, the center would be able to send a brochure about the groups to patients currently receiving treatment at the facility.

4. *Research.* When investigators have approval for a study that uses patients' medical records, the investigators may have access to those records without the patients' explicit permission.

However, unless the sharing of information is specifically to facilitate treatment, the law specifies that the provider should disclose only the minimum necessary information.

Legal Restrictions on Confidentiality

States usually have laws to protect confidentiality. However, most states have exceptions to those rules. Typically, confidentiality can be violated in certain situations:

• when a patient gives the clinician permission to violate confidentiality, for example by explicitly giving permission to a therapist to speak to the patient's spouse;

• when a clinician has reasonable cause to suspect abuse of children, the elderly, or the disabled (in such cases, the clinician usually must report the suspected abuse to the appropriate authorities so that steps can be taken to protect those who cannot otherwise protect themselves);

• when a clinician has reasonable cause to believe that a patient is likely to harm himself or herself significantly or attempt suicide (in this situation, the clinician must take steps to protect the patient); and

• when a clinician has good reason to believe that a patient is likely to inflict significant harm on a specified other person (in this case, the clinician must take steps to protect that other person).

Thus, a clinician should not have violated Goldstein's confidentiality if he spoke in generalities about his violent urges. Even if Goldstein had said that he had

Confidentiality
The ethical requirement not to disclose information about a patient (even whether someone *is* a patient) to others unless legally compelled to do so.

violent impulses that he couldn't control when in subway stations or when around blond-haired women, such a statement would probably not be viewed as posing a specific enough danger to violate confidentiality. The clinician would have been legally compelled to violate Goldstein's confidentiality, however, if he had specifically named Kendra Webdale as someone he planned to harm.

Privileged Communication

Confidentiality is an ethical term. A related *legal* term is **privileged communication**, which refers to confidential information that is protected from being disclosed during legal proceedings. Just as a priest cannot legally be compelled to reveal what was said by a parishioner in the confessional, the Supreme Court has ruled that communication between a patient and a therapist is privileged (*Jaffee v. Redmond*, 1996; Mosher & Swire, 2002). However, not all confidential information is privileged, and vice versa.

The person who shared information with the clinician is usually the one who decides whether it can be revealed, but others can make this decision in certain circumstances. For example, if a judge orders that a defendant must undergo a mental health evaluation, as happened to Goldstein after he was taken into custody, the communication between the mental health clinician(s) doing the evaluation and the defendant may not be considered privileged in some courts, depending on the jurisdiction (Meyer & Weaver, 2006; Myers, 1998). In such a circumstance, in order to comply with the law and behave ethically, the mental health clinician should explain to the defendant at the very beginning of the evaluation that anything said to the clinician may be disclosed to the judge. That is, the defendant should be made aware at the outset about the limits of confidentiality. Whenever the law regarding privileged communication conflicts with the ethics of confidentiality, patients should be told of the limits of confidentiality as soon as possible (Meyer & Weaver, 2006).

Another type of exception to the laws governing privileged communication occurs when a patient (or former patient) initiates a civil lawsuit against another party and raises the issue of personal injury (with mental health consequences) in the suit. An example of this type of case would be one in which a woman sues her employer for anguish that resulted from harassment at work. In these sorts of lawsuits for personal injury, the mental health clinician is legally bound to testify if his or her testimony is relevant to the case (Bartol & Bartol, 2004).

It is not always clear who owns a privileged communication that arises in the context of group therapy. In this situation, the therapist may not be compelled to testify about what transpired, but group members may be. At present, judges decide on a case-by-case basis whether a therapist must testify, depending on the specific circumstances (Meyer & Weaver, 2006).

Informed Consent to Participate in Research on Mental Illness: Can Patients Truly Be Informed?

In Chapter 5, we touched on ethical issues related to research, including the issue of informed consent. But can someone who is mentally ill give truly informed consent to participate in psychological research pertaining to his or her disorder? People who have anxiety disorders may be able to understand fully the research procedure and possible adverse effects, but what about people with schizophrenia? Are such patients' mental processes impaired to the extent that their consent isn't really informed? What about people who are having a first episode of psychosis and agree to participate in a study before the psychotic episode has abated?

The general rule of thumb for researchers is that potential participants must be capable of understanding and reasoning about what they are consenting to (Meyer & Weaver, 2006). Thus, the ability to understand and reason about the research procedure may be more important to informed consent than whether the person is psychotic at the time of consent (Kovnick et al., 2003; Misra & Ganzini, 2004).

Privileged communication
Confidential information that is protected from being disclosed during legal proceedings.

Researchers are developing ways to ensure that patients who may be cognitively impaired by a psychological disorder adequately understand the benefits and risks of their participation in research. For instance, Wirshing and colleagues (2005) developed an educational video to increase awareness about informed consent among patients with schizophrenia. Among other points, the video explained that participants can withdraw from the study at any time. Researchers continue to develop and assess methods to ensure that participants give truly informed consent to participate in research (Eyler, Mirzakhanian, & Jeste, 2005).

Key Concepts and Facts About Ethical Issues

- Each type of mental health professional works under his or her own discipline's ethical code; all disciplines include in their ethical code the principle of confidentiality, which applies to information that patients share with mental health professionals.

- Although the clinician is bound by confidentiality, patients in couples therapy, family therapy, and group therapy are not. When a patient is a minor, the clinician may inform the parents about what the child has said; however, most clinicians discuss the limits of confidentiality with a child old enough to understand.

- Because of HIPAA, the limits of confidentiality have been redefined. Now limited information about a patient may be shared with the patient's other health providers in order to facilitate treatment.

- Although laws protect confidentiality, confidentiality may be violated against a patient's wishes when a clinician has reasonable cause to (1) suspect abuse of children, the elderly, or the disabled or (2) believe that a patient is likely to do significant harm to himself or herself (including attempting suicide) or a specified other person.

- The legal counterpart of the ethical principle of confidentiality is privileged communication—the protection of confidential information from disclosure during legal proceedings; however, in some circumstances, other people can decide whether the information about a patient should be disclosed.

- Patients who have impaired cognitive processes because of a psychological disorder (such as schizophrenia) may be able to provide informed consent to participate in research if they can understand what they are consenting to and can reason about it.

Criminal Actions and Insanity

After Andrew Goldstein pushed Kendra Webdale in front of the oncoming subway train, other passengers detained him until the police arrived. When taken to the police station, he explained in a signed statement why he pushed her: "I felt a sensation like something was entering me like a ghost or a spirit or something like that. . . . When I have the sensation that something is entering me, I get the urge to push, shove, or sidekick" (Rohde, 1999b).

Goldstein then said he "watched in 'horror'" as the train ran over Webdale, after which he is reported to have turned to the man next to him, "raised his arms in the air and said, 'I don't know'" (Rohde, 1999b). When police came, he told them he was a "'psychotic patient' who had suffered a 'psychotic attack'" (Rohde, 1999b) and asked to be taken to the hospital.

Goldstein was arraigned on the charge of second-degree murder and then, perhaps because he seemed to be mentally ill or because of his long psychiatric history, he was taken to a hospital rather than taken to jail. As we shall see, if someone who allegedly committed a crime was mentally ill during or after the criminal act, jail may not be the appropriate place for that person to be. Moreover, treatment—rather than detention—may be an appropriate goal for such a defendant's immediate future. In this section we review the legal and clinical issues that arise after a crime has been committed by someone who is mentally ill.

As discussed in Chapter 1, the term *insanity* is a legal term and is not used in DSM-IV-TR. The legal concept of insanity addresses the question of whether a person was, at the time he or she committed a crime, *criminally responsible*—which involves both action and intention: To be **criminally responsible** means that a defendant's crime was the product of both an *action* or attempted action (the alleged criminal behavior) and his or her *intention* to perform that action (Greene et al., 2007; Meyer & Weaver, 2006).

After a crime has been committed and a person has been arrested, the legal system provides two discrete opportunities to determine whether the defendant is suffering from a mental illness: (1) What was the defendant's mental state at the time he or she (allegedly) committed the act? Might the insanity defense be appropriate? (2) What is the defendant's mental state during the time of assessment, leading up to the trial? Can the person adequately assist in his or her own defense? Is the person competent to stand trial? We next discuss each of these circumstances in turn.

While Committing the Crime: Sane or Insane?

In the United States, the legal definition of insanity corresponds to a "test" that is used to determine whether a person is insane. The particular test has changed over time. In the following sections we review the five tests of insanity that have been used, beginning with the first—the M'Naghten test.

The M'Naghten Test

In England in 1841, a Scottish man named Daniel M'Naghten believed that the British Prime Minister, Sir Robert Peel, was personally responsible for M'Naghten's woes. M'Naghten attempted to shoot Peel, but missed him and killed Peel's secretary. During M'Naghten's trial, witnesses testified that he was insane, and the jury found him *not guilty by reason of insanity* (NGBI). This verdict did not sit well with Queen Victoria, reigning monarch at the time, who had been the intended victim of a number of assassination attempts; she asked that it be reviewed. In response, the judges narrowed the insanity defense by limiting the relevance of the defendant's mental state to the time the alleged crime was committed. In what came to be known as the **M'Naghten test (or rule)**, the question asked at a trial became whether, *at the time of committing the act,* the defendant knew what he or she was doing and, if so, knew that the act was wrong—and if he or she did not know this, it was because of "a defect of reason, from disease of the mind." With this narrower test, the judges reversed the verdict and found M'Naghten guilty.

The Irresistible Impulse Test

The M'Naghten test of insanity was adopted in the United States and continued to be used until 1886, when the definition of insanity was widened. The new definition, specified by the **irresistible impulse test**, focused on whether the defendant knew that the criminal behavior was wrong but nonetheless performed it because of an irresistible impulse.

Since the irresistible impulse test was introduced, changes in the legal definition of insanity have centered around the extent to which the criminal behavior was "uncontrollable"; that is, someone might know that the behavior was wrong but nevertheless be unable to stop it (*Parsons v. Alabama,* 1886).

The Durham Test

In 1954, the Supreme Court ruled on a case, *Durham v. U.S.*, and again broadened the test for the insanity defense. The **Durham test** was designed to determine whether the irresistible impulse was *due to mental defect or disorder* present at the time of the alleged crime. The Durham ruling shifted the insanity defense so that it hinged on evidence that the behavior did not arise entirely from free will. The Durham ruling moved away from consideration about morality (knowing "right from wrong") and into the realm of science (having a mental impairment).

There was major drawback to the Durham ruling, however: It left unclear what constituted a mental defect or disorder. For instance, it is possible that someone who was drunk at the time that a crime was committed might be considered to

The Granger Collection, New York

PORTRAIT OF DANIEL M'NAUGHTEN.

The earliest insanity defense case was that of Daniel M'Naghten, a Scottish man whose delusions about the British Prime Minister led him, in 1841, to commit murder. After M'Naghten was found not guilty by reason of insanity, the House of Lords narrowed the criteria for determining insanity; these criteria came to be known as the M'Naghten test.

Criminally responsible
The determination that a defendant's crime was the product of both an *action* or attempted action (the alleged criminal behavior) and his or her *intention* to perform that action.

M'Naghten test (or rule)
The legal test in which a person is considered insane if, because of a "defect of reason, from disease of the mind," he or she did not know what he or she was doing (at the time of committing the act) and did not know that it was wrong.

have a mental defect. And what about someone with antisocial personality disorder (or psychopathy)—might the disorder make that individual able to use the insanity defense? Moreover, how could the court decide whether the criminal behavior was *caused by* the disorder or defect (Greene et al., 2007; Meyer & Weaver, 2006)? This drawback is so significant that most states use other definitions of insanity; only New Hampshire still uses the Durham test (Wrightsman & Fulero, 2005).

The American Legal Institute Test

To address some of the thorny issues that arose from the Durham test, the American Legal Institute (ALI) proposed two alternative criteria for insanity:

1. The person lacks a *substantial capacity* to appreciate that the behavior was wrong (versus has *no* capacity); or
2. the person has a diminished ability to make his or her behavior conform to the law, that is, an irresistible impulse.

These elements comprise the **American Legal Institute (ALI) test**, and are sometimes referred to as *knowledge (cognition)* and *impulse (volition)* criteria. The ALI test broadened the test for insanity because it provided these two possible criteria (Greene et al., 2007; Meyer & Weaver, 2006). The ALI test also specified that if an individual's only defect or disorder is criminal behavior, the insanity defense cannot be used. This prevented people with antisocial personality disorder (or psychopathy) and people whose only crime is using illegal substances from using these problems as the basis for an insanity defense. The ALI test, or definition, continues to be used by many states.

Insanity Defense Reform Acts

In federal courts, the insanity test changed again in 1984 as a result of John Hinckley's 1981 assassination attempt of then-President Ronald Reagan and Hinckley's subsequent acquittal as not guilty by reason of insanity. Hinckley was a young man with a history of mental illness; he reported that he shot the president in order to impress actress Jodie Foster, about whom he had obsessive delusions (*erotomanic delusions*, described in Chapter 12). In addition to wounding Reagan, Hinckley also shot the president's press secretary (who suffered brain damage and paralysis), as well as a Secret Service agent and a police officer.

The jury found Hinckley insane on the basis of the impulse (volition) element of the ALI test. This means that the jury decided that Hinckley knew it was wrong to shoot the president, but that he was not able to restrain himself. He was sent to a psychiatric hospital, not prison. The fact that Hinckley would serve no prison time greatly disturbed some lawmakers, who, through the Insanity Defense Reform Acts of 1984 and 1988, proceeded to restrict the test for insanity. The new test for insanity, used only in federal court, is most similar to the M'Naghten test—it asks whether the individual, because of a *severe* mental defect or disorder, has a diminished capacity to understand right from wrong (cognition). In an effort to make it more difficult to enter a plea of NGBI, Congress also put an end to the irresistible impulse element (volition) in federal courts. Defendants with mental retardation, psychotic disorders, or mood disorders may qualify for the insanity defense under these new rules, depending on the circumstances of the crime and the defendant's state of mind at the time, but having a disorder *in and of itself* does not constitute an insanity defense. Table 16.2 provides an overview of the various tests of insanity, and Case 16.1 describes a woman who entered a plea of insanity in a murder case.

Irresistible impulse test
The legal test in which a person is considered insane if he or she knew that his or her criminal behavior was wrong but nonetheless performed it because of an irresistible impulse.

Durham test
The legal test in which a person is considered insane if an irresistible impulse to perform criminal behavior was due to a mental defect or disorder present at the time of the crime.

American Legal Institute test (ALI test)
The legal test in which a person is considered insane if a defendant either lacks a substantial capacity to appreciate that his or her behavior was wrong or has a diminished ability to make his or her behavior conform to the law.

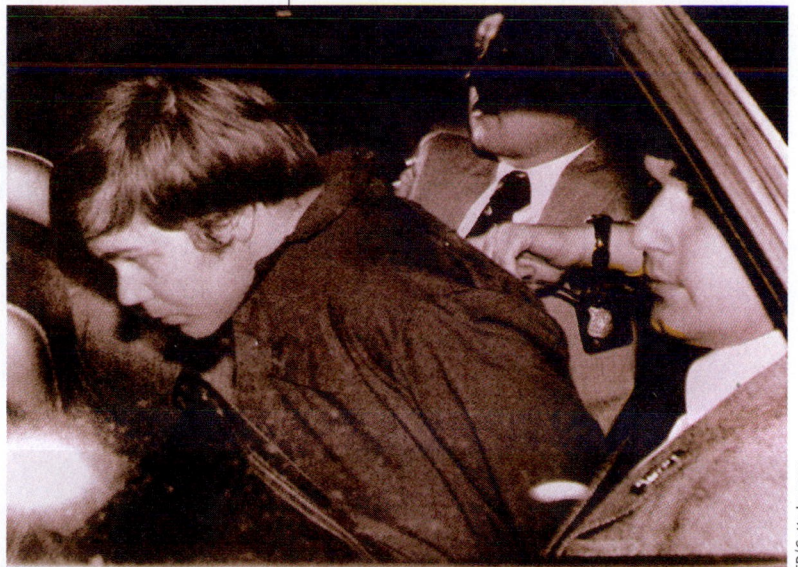

John Hinckley developed an obsessive preoccupation with actress Jodie Foster and repeatedly tried to communicate with her by phone and letter. After his attempts were rebuffed, he developed the delusional belief that assassinating President Ronald Reagan would impress Foster and induce her to pay attention to him. In 1981, he acted on that belief and shot the President and three other people.

AFP/Getty Images

Andrea Yates, who was tried for murdering her five children, said she drowned them in order to save them from hell. Her lawyers used the insanity defense.

CASE 16.1 ▶ FROM THE OUTSIDE: The Insanity Defense

In 2001, Andrea Yates confessed to police that she drowned her five children, ages 6 months to 7 years old, in her bathtub. She reported that she believed Satan was inside her, and she drowned them to try to save them from hell. Yates's lawyers said that she had been psychotic at the time of the murders and that she did not know that her actions were wrong. (According to Texas state law, the key element of the insanity defense is knowing that the actions were wrong at the time of the crime.) Her lawyers pointed to her history of mental illness: two previous suicide attempts and four psychiatric hospitalizations for schizophrenia and postpartum depression.

During her trial, an expert witness for the prosecution, psychiatrist Dr. Park Dietz, agreed with previous witnesses that Yates had been psychotic at the time of the drownings, but testified that she was still able to know right from wrong and therefore not insane under Texas law. To support his position, Dr. Dietz brought up the television series *Law and Order*, which he had been told Yates had watched. Dietz, who also served as a consultant to the producers of that television series, testified that shortly before she drowned her children, an episode of *Law and Order* aired that involved a woman with postpartum depression who drowned her children in a bathtub and was declared insane. Prosecutors used Dietz's testimony about the television show to indicate that Yates knew her actions were wrong (Greene et al., 2007).

It turns out, however, that no such episode had been aired; this error was discovered after the jury convicted Yates of murder but before they began deliberating about her punishment. Rather than declare a mistrial, the judge simply told the jurors about the error. Yates was given a life sentence in prison. The appeals court ruled that a mistrial had occurred, and Yates was retried. She was ultimately found not guilty by reason of insanity and placed in a state mental hospital, where she will remain until she is no longer considered a danger to others or herself (Ewing & McCann, 2006).

Table 16.2 ▶ Tests for the Insanity Defense Used Over Time

Test	Legal Standard
M'Naghten (1843)	"Didn't know what he or she was doing or didn't know it was wrong"
Irresistible impulse (1886)	"Could not control conduct"
Durham (1954)	"Criminal act was caused by mental illness"
American Legal Institute (ALI; 1962)	"Lacks substantial capacity to appreciate the wrongfulness of the conduct *or* to control it" [emphasis added]
Present federal law (1984 and 1988)	"Lacks capacity to appreciate the wrongfulness of his or her conduct"

Source: Meyer & Weaver, 2006, p. 123, which was adapted in part from Morris, 1986.

The Insanity Defense: Current Issues

The federal requirements for the insanity defense have been narrowed, but ambiguities about its definition have not yet been addressed by the courts. In particular, the courts have yet to resolve two issues about how this defense can be applied:

• whether the person knew the act was *wrong* (a moral question) versus *illegal* (a legal question); and

- whether the person knew *in the abstract* that the act was wrong versus knew *that the specific behavior* was wrong in a particular circumstance (for instance, someone can know that killing people is wrong but, because of a mental illness, believe that killing a particular person for a specific reason is justified: "He was the devil, tempting me, so I had to kill him").

Let's examine how these issues about the insanity defense apply to Andrew Goldstein, who pleaded not guilty by reason of insanity. At the trial, an eyewitness to the murder, Ms. Lorenzino, who was standing nearby on the platform, testified that she:

> entered the subway station . . . just behind Mr. Goldstein and immediately noticed that he was acting strangely. "I saw a man walking in front of me walking oddly," Ms. Lorenzino said. She said Mr. Goldstein would take a few "baby steps" on his "tip toes" and then stumble. Mr. Goldstein then started walking normally, then paced furiously back and forth on the southern end of the platform. He mumbled to himself and eyed Ms. Lorenzino and Ms. Webdale, who was reading a magazine about six feet away from Ms. Lorenzino, each time he passed them. Mr. Goldstein's pacing was so intense that it prompted one man to cry out: "Yo buddy, can you stop pacing? You're making us nervous," Ms. Lorenzino said.
>
> As the wait for a train dragged on, Mr. Goldstein walked up to Ms. Lorenzino and stood beside her, she said. "I felt very uncomfortable that he was standing next to me. . . . I said, 'What are you looking at?' Then he backed off as if he was frustrated." Mr. Goldstein paced for a few more minutes, Ms. Lorenzino said, looked down the track as if checking for a train and then walked down the platform to Ms. Webdale. "Do you have the time?" he asked her. Ms. Webdale glanced at her watch and answered, "a little after five," Ms. Lorenzino said. Mr. Goldstein then positioned himself against the wall behind Ms. Webdale, who returned to her magazine, Ms. Lorenzino said.
>
> When the train sped into the station, she said, Mr. Goldstein "darted" off the wall and violently pushed Ms. Webdale. Ms. Lorenzino said she was struck by how well-planned the push seemed. It gave Ms. Webdale no time to escape. "It was perfect," she said, referring to the timing. Ms. Webdale's body never hit the rails, she said, "she just flew right under the train."
>
> Police Officer Raymond McLoughlin, who also testified yesterday, said he arrived at the station to find people shouting "He's right here! He's right here!" He found Mr. Goldstein, who made no effort to escape, sitting on the platform with his legs crossed, surrounded by 20 enraged people who were berating him, he said.
>
> (Rohde, 1999c)

After the murder, during Goldstein's confession, the prosecutor tried to understand whether Goldstein understood what he was doing, that is, whether his

> mental illness caused him to lack a "substantial capacity" to know or appreciate "the nature and consequence" of the attack or know that it was wrong. On the videotape, [the prosecutor] pointedly asks Mr. Goldstein if he thinks it was wrong to push Ms. Webdale. Mr. Goldstein nods and then appears confused. The prosecutor asks him if he understands. Mr. Goldstein says no, and then [the prosecutor] asks him again if he thinks the attack was wrong. "I wasn't thinking about anything when I pushed her," Mr. Goldstein said. "It's like an attack. You don't really think. . . . It's like whoosh, whoosh" he added, referring to what he repeatedly described during the confession as the sensation of a "spirit" or "ghost" entering his body that gave him an overwhelming desire to push, kick or shove. Mr. Goldstein says that he pushed Ms. Webdale only "slightly," but then seems confused again. He blurts out that "I didn't push her thinking she would end up on tracks" and that he did not know in what direction he was pushing Ms. Webdale.
>
> Mr. Goldstein then says, "I wouldn't push anyone onto the tracks."
>
> "Because you know its wrong?" [the prosecutor] asks.
>
> "Yes," Mr. Goldstein replies.
>
> (Rohde, 1999a)

The prosecutor continues to try to clarify whether Goldstein understood that what he had done to Webdale was wrong:

> "But you knew," says the interrogator, "that if you pushed her off the platform, she might get . . ."
>
> "Killed, yeah," Mr. Goldstein says.

"And you also knew that if you did that, it would be the wrong thing to do?"

"Yeah, definitely," Mr. Goldstein says. "I would never do something like that."

"Well, you did."

"I know, but the thing is I would never do it on purpose."

(Winerip, 1999b)

The questioning continues:

"You certainly agree," [the prosecutor] says, "that you knew what you were doing and you knew it was wrong."

"Uh-huh," Mr. Goldstein says.

"When you pushed her onto the tracks to cause her death," [the prosecutor] says.

"I see," Mr. Goldstein says.

"No, tell me, did you?"

"Oh, no. I'm sorry?"

"Were you really listening to what I was saying?" [the prosecutor] asks.

"Oh no."

"Do you agree or disagree that you knew at the time that you pushed her, that it could cause her death?"

"I wasn't thinking about anything about pushing," Mr. Goldstein says. "When it happens, I don't think, it just goes whoosh, whoosh, push, you know," he says, adding, "It's like a random variable."

(Winerip, 1999b)

Assessing Insanity for the Insanity Defense

Interactions such as the one between Goldstein and the prosecutor may illustrate that the defendant's mental illness affects his or her testimony while on trial. But how does a jury go about determining whether a defendant was insane at the time a crime was perpetrated? The members of a jury rely on testimony about the defendant's mental state during the time leading up to the crime. Such testimony may come from friends and family members or from witnesses. In Goldstein's case, witnesses testified that he was acting strangely before pushing Ms. Webdale in front of the train. Jurors may hear about a defendant's history of mental illness prior to the crime (as occurred for both Goldstein and Hinckley). Expert witnesses who are mental health clinicians may give testimony or submit reports.

How do mental health clinicians determine whether a defendant was insane at the time of the criminal act? What information do they obtain? They may interview the defendant in jail and administer and interpret psychological tests (see Chapter 3). However, such after-the-fact assessments of the defendant's mental state should take into account events that occurred after the crime and before the clinician's evaluation. Specifically, the defendant's mental state may be affected by his or her experiences in jail, medications he or she may be taking, decision to plead NGBI, reactions to the crime, coaching from the defendant's lawyer or other inmates, and even responses to various assessment methods (Meyer & Weaver, 2006). For example, imagine that a man killed someone when he ran a red light. After the crime, he becomes guilt-ridden and depressed, even suicidal, requiring medication. Assessing his mental status in jail may not shed much light on his mental status at the time of the crime.

Past psychiatric history doesn't necessarily indicate a person's mental state at the time he or she committed a crime, but a history of mental illness can provide a context for evaluating the person at the time when the crime was committed. In Goldstein's case, symptoms of schizophrenia arose when he was 16 years old, and he was committed to a state psychiatric facility when he was in college. Following this stay, he had a lengthy history of mostly brief hospital stays, each stay lasting only until he was "stabilized" (not actively psychotic), and he was then released to outpatient treatment. However, because of a lack of state funds for mental health care, Goldstein's outpatient treatment usually consisted of almost no treatment. For most of the time he was ill and while an outpatient, he did not have close supervision or monitoring and did not reliably take his medication (Kleinfeld & Roane, 1999). He would eventually deteriorate to the point where he needed to be hospitalized, was stabilized and released again, and then the cycle would be repeated—a process often referred to as a "revolving door."

States' Rights: Doing Away With the Insanity Defense

Some states have abolished the insanity defense, replacing it with some other type of defense that recognizes that a defendant did not have "free will" while committing a crime (Meyer & Weaver, 2006). Two alternative options are:

- *Diminished capacity*, whereby a person, due to mental illness or defect, was less able to understand that the criminal behavior was wrong or to formulate a specific intention. With this defense, the person is still considered guilty but receives a lesser sentence, is convicted of a lesser crime, or receives a modified form of punishment. This defense contains variations on the two elements of the ALI test of insanity.

- *Guilty but mentally ill*, whereby a convicted defendant is often sent to a psychiatric facility and, if his or her mental state improves over time, may also serve time in prison; alternatively, the defendant may be sent to a prison immediately, where he or she may or may not receive psychiatric care. Note that with guilty but mentally ill, the person isn't acquitted (that is, found not guilty of a crime), and there is no guarantee that mental health services will be provided (Meyer & Weaver, 2006). In fact, in many states, prisoners who have been found guilty but mentally ill receive no more psychological treatment than do other prisoners (Wrightsman & Fulero, 2005).

With the Insanity Defense, Do People Really "Get Away With Murder"?

After the Hinckley trial, some people perceived the insanity defense as a way to "get away with murder." But this perception isn't very accurate. Consider a landmark study of 9,000 felony cases across eight states from 1976 to 1987 (Steadman et al., 1993). Among those cases, only 1% used the insanity defense. Further, only one quarter of that 1% of defendants were acquitted (that is, found not guilty of the crime). And of this 0.25%, only 7%—2 cases—were acquitted by a jury rather than a judge. This indicates that the defense of not guilty by reason of insanity was rare and, even where it was employed, was not very successful. Researchers have also compared the average time spent in jail by defendants who were found guilty (5 years) versus the average time spent in a mental hospital by those who were found NGBI (4.7 years) and concluded that when the insanity defense is used successfully, people do not "get away with murder" (Meyer & Weaver, 2006).

After Committing the Crime: Competent to Stand Trial?

Whereas the insanity defense refers to a defendant's mental state at the time the crime was committed, his or her **competency to stand trial** is based on an evaluation of mental state during the time leading up to the trial. That is, does a mental defect or disorder prevent the defendant from participating in his or her own defense?

Competency to stand trial usually entails being able to

- understand the proceedings that will take place,

- understand the facts in the case and the legal options available,

- consult with his or her "lawyer with a reasonable degree of rational understanding" (*Dusky v. United States*, 1960), and

- assist the lawyer in building the defense.

These aspects of competency can be independent of each other; someone can have one ability impaired, but have the others intact (McArthur Research Network, 2006). Until recently, the courts and lawyers have viewed competency to stand trial as an all-or-nothing condition—a defendant either can or can't. With the all-or-nothing standard, Goldstein was found competent to stand trial.

Competency to stand trial
The mental state during the time leading up to the trial that enables a defendant to participate in his or her own defense.

The same all-or-nothing standard is used to determine whether a defendant is *competent to plead guilty* as well as *competent to waive the right to an attorney* (*Godinez v. Moran*, 1993; Perlin, 2000a). If a person is found not competent to stand trial, he or she would also be considered to be not competent to plead guilty or to waive the right to an attorney. Someone who is found not competent is referred for mental health treatment (*Dusky v. United States*, 1960). Some scholars have proposed an alternative term to address the mental competency of all defendants who are nearing legal proceedings: *adjudicative competence* (MacArthur Research Network on Mental Health and the Law, 2001b). Case 16.2 examines the issue of competency to stand trial and waive counsel.

CASE 16.2 ▶ FROM THE OUTSIDE: Competent to Stand Trial and Waive Counsel

On December 7, 1993, Colin Ferguson intentionally killed 6 people and injured 19 others on a New York commuter train. After his arrest, Ferguson was diagnosed with paranoid personality disorder. Because he was assessed as rational and not delusional, he was deemed competent to stand trial; he fired his attorney when the attorney stated that he would propose an insanity defense. Ferguson then chose to represent himself but did not use the insanity defense. The legal system allowed a mentally ill man to be his own legal counsel, although he did not defend himself adequately. Those following the trial witnessed an intelligent but clearly mentally ill man state that he would call as a witness an exorcist who would testify that a microchip—supposedly planted by the governor of New York—had been lasered out of Ferguson's head by a remote control device (McQuiston, 1995; Perlin, 2000a). That witness was never called to the stand.

Ferguson was convicted on 6 counts of murder and 19 counts of attempted murder.

The MacArthur Foundation has funded a number of research projects investigating legal issues relevant to the mentally ill. For example, *The MacArthur Adjudicative Competence Study* (Hoge et al., 1992, 1997; MacArthur Research Network on Mental Health and the Law, 2001a) found that criminal defense attorneys viewed 15% of their clients as possibly having impaired competence (among 122 randomly selected felony cases). Those defendants most likely to have diminished competence were much less helpful to their attorneys than were those who were clearly competent: They were less actively involved in making decisions and in establishing the facts of the case. Nevertheless, the attorneys didn't always request that possibly impaired clients be referred for an official mental health evaluation, although the more serious the crime—and more severe the penalty—the more likely the attorneys were to seek an evaluation.

When defendants are found not competent to stand trial, they sometimes are medicated to reduce the symptoms of their mental illness and make them able to stand trial. Occasionally, defendants do not want to take the medication but are given it against their will, perhaps by injection. However, the Supreme Court ruled that mentally ill patients accused of nonviolent crimes could not be forced to take medication in order to become competent to stand trial (*Sell v. United States*, 2003). If it appears unlikely that a person will become competent to stand trial, he or she may be released—but may be civilly committed to a psychiatric facility if deemed a danger to self or others.

In 2002, while suffering from delusions, Brian David Mitchell kidnapped young Elizabeth Smart (see the discussion of the Smart case in Chapter 12). He was apprehended 9 months later (Smart was found alive and returned to her parents) and continues to have delusions. In 2009, he had yet to be found competent to stand trial. A judge had ruled against forcing Mitchell to take medication in order to be competent to stand trial because the judge did not believe that the treatment would succeed (Carlisle, 2009).

AP Photo/George Frey, pool

Key Concepts and Facts About Criminal Actions and Insanity ■

- Various tests have been used to determine whether a defendant is insane. The first was the M'Naghten test in 1843, followed by the irresistible impulse test. After almost 70 years came the Durham test. Many states presently use the American Legal Institute (ALI) test, which requires either impaired knowledge that the behavior was wrong (cognition) or impaired capacity to resist the impulse to act illegally (volition). The Insanity Defense Reform Acts of the 1980s did away with the volition element to determine insanity in federal courts.

- Two issues are still to be clarified by the courts: (1) whether someone who is legally insane must have known that the act was "wrong" versus "illegal" and (2) whether insanity depends on knowing in the abstract that an act is wrong versus knowing that the specific behavior is wrong in the particular circumstance.

- To assess insanity, a jury may rely on testimony about the defendant's mental state during the time leading up to the crime, the defendant's history of mental illness prior to the crime, and testimony or reports from expert witnesses about the defendant's mental state or mental illness.

- Mental health clinicians may assess a defendant's sanity through interviews with the person, psychological tests and questionnaires, and interviews with family members and friends. However, such measures may be affected by the defendant's experiences in jail, medications he or she may be taking, the decision to plead not guilty by reason of insanity (NGBI), reactions to the crime, coaching from the defendant's lawyer or other inmates, and the way the defendant responds to various assessment methods. But none of this information necessarily indicates the defendant's mental state at the time of the crime.

- Some states offer alternatives to the insanity defense, including those of diminished capacity and guilty but mentally ill.

- Research indicates that acquittal on the basis of the insanity defense is extremely rare, particularly when the decision is made by a jury rather than a judge.

- Competency to stand trial addresses the defendant's mental state before the trial and whether the defendant is competent to participate in his or her own defense; someone who is not competent to stand trial would also be deemed not competent to plead guilty and not competent to waive the right to an attorney.

Making a Determination

- Do you think that Andrew Goldstein was insane, according to the legal definition (cognition or volition), at the time of the crime? Specifically, how did you arrive at your decision? If you would like more information to determine whether he was legally insane, what information—specifically—would you want, and in what ways would the information influence your decision?

- Reread Case 16.2 about Colin Ferguson, and determine whether or not he should have been deemed competent (to stand trial and to waive counsel). Specifically, how did you arrive at your decision? If you would like more information to determine whether he was legally competent, what information—specifically— would you want, and in what ways would the information influence your decision?

Dangerousness: Legal Consequences

Andrew Goldstein's attack on Kendra Webdale wasn't the first time he had engaged in dangerous behavior, and his dangerous behavior wasn't a secret.

> In the two years before Kendra Webdale was instantly killed on the tracks, Andrew Goldstein attacked at least 13 other people. The hospital staff members who kept treating and discharging Goldstein knew that he repeatedly attacked strangers in public places.
>
> He was hospitalized after assaulting a psychiatrist at a Queens clinic. [The clinic note from November 14, 1997, reads]: "Suddenly, without any warning, patient springs up and attacks one of [the] doctors, pushing her into a door and then onto the floor. He was hospitalized after threatening a woman, [again] after attacking two strangers at a Burger King [and yet again] after fighting with an apartment mate." [A note from March 2, 1998, says]: "Broke down roommate's door because he could not control the impulse." And particularly chilling, six months before Kendra Webdale's death, he was hospitalized for striking another woman he did not know on a New York subway.
>
> (Winerip, 1999a)

Goldstein's history indicates that he had become dangerous. **Dangerousness**, a legal term, refers to someone's potential to harm self or others. Determining whether someone is dangerous, in this sense, rests on assessing threats of violence to self

Dangerousness
The legal term that refers to someone's potential to harm self or others.

or to others, or establishing an inability to care for oneself. Dangerousness can be broken down into four components regarding the potential harm (Brooks, 1974; Perlin, 2000c):

1. severity (how much harm might the person inflict?),

2. imminence (how soon might the potential harm occur?),

3. frequency (how often is the person likely to be dangerous?), and

4. probability (how likely is the person to be dangerous?)

Evaluating Dangerousness

Clinicians are sometimes asked to evaluate how dangerous a patient may be—specifically, the severity, imminence, and likelihood of potential harm (Meyer & Weaver, 2006). Such evaluations are either/or in nature—the individual is either deemed not to be dangerous (or at least not dangerous enough to violate confidentiality) or deemed to be dangerous, in which case, confidentiality is broken in order to protect the individual from self-harm or to protect others (Otto, 2000; Quattrocchi & Schopp, 2005). Prior to each discharge from a hospital or psychiatric unit, Goldstein had to be evaluated for dangerousness; he was then discharged because he was deemed not dangerous, or not dangerous enough.

Researchers set out to determine the risk factors that could best identify which patients discharged from psychiatric facilities would subsequently act violently. A summary of the findings appears in Table 16.3. Here are the most notable findings:

- Almost 20% of the patients studied committed at least one violent act within 5 months of their discharge from the psychiatric hospital.

- Men were only somewhat more likely than women to be violent; when female patients were violent, it was generally family members who were victims.

- A history of violent behavior—assessed through hospital records, arrest records, and self-reports—was a strong risk factor for later violence. Part of the problem in evaluating whether Andrew Goldstein was dangerous was that he received care in different facilities, and each facility only had access to information about his violent behavior that led to his admittance to that facility, or his violent behavior while in that facility.

- Persistent thoughts about harming others and higher scores on an anger scale predicted later violence.

- Childhood experiences of serious and frequent abuse, as well as having a father who was a criminal or who engaged in substance abuse, predicted future violent behavior.

- Certain diagnoses, such as substance abuse and antisocial personality disorder, were relatively good predictors of future violence; schizophrenia predicted a *lower* rate of violence. In general, the presence of delusions or hallucinations was not associated with later violence; however, delusions involving suspicions of others and hallucinations that "commanded" a violent act did predict later violence (Steadman et al., 1998).

Confining individuals deemed to be dangerous involves taking away their liberty—their freedom—and is not done lightly. Loitering or yelling at "voices" should not be considered legally dangerous. Rather, the legal system allows an individual to be incarcerated or hospitalized, or to continue to be incarcerated or hospitalized, in only two types of situations:

1. when the individual has not yet committed a violent crime but is perceived to be at imminent risk to do so, or

2. when the individual has already served a prison term or received mandated treatment in a psychiatric hospital and is about to be released but is perceived to be at imminent risk of behaving violently.

Table 16.3 ▶ Major Risk Factors For a Patient to Act Violently

Patient's Prior Arrests
- More serious crimes
- Greater frequency of crimes

Patient Experienced Child Abuse
- Experienced more serious abuse
- Experienced greater frequency of abuse

Patient's Father . . .
- Used drugs
- Was absent during patient's childhood

Patient's Demographics
- Younger
- Male
- Unemployed

Patient's Diagnosis
- Antisocial personality disorder

Other Clinical Information About Patient
- Has substance abuse problems
- Has problems controlling anger
- Has violent fantasies
- Has had loss of consciousness
- Has been brought to the attention of mental health professionals involuntarily, through the legal system

Source: Monahan et al., 2001. For more information see the Permissions section.

To prevent such people from harming themselves or others, the law provides that they can be confined as long as they (continue to) pose a significant danger.

When clinicians evaluate present and future dangerousness, they base their judgment (in part) on an individual's history of such behavior, but such information provides only limited guidance (Perlin, 2000c; Schopp & Quattrocchi, 1984). In fact, whether someone is an imminent danger to self or others is often not clear. For example, although the possible dangerous acts the person may commit should be "imminent," exactly how this word is defined remains unclear (Meyer & Weaver, 2006).

Actual Dangerousness

Mentally ill individuals who engage in criminal acts receive a lot of media attention, which may lead people to believe that criminal behavior by those with mental illnesses is more common than it really is (Pescosolido et al., 1999). In fact, criminal behavior among the mentally ill population is no more common than it is in the general population (Fazel & Grann, 2006). However, two sets of circumstances related to mental illness do increase dangerousness: (1) when the mental illness involves psychosis, and the person may be a danger to self as well as others (Fazel & Grann, 2006; Steadman et al., 1998; Wallace, Mullen, & Burgess, 2004), and especially (2) when serious mental illness is combined with substance abuse (Maden et al., 2004). The relationship between various major mental illnesses, substance use disorders, and violence is shown in Figure 16.1.

It is worth stressing a cautionary note: Although in this section we have focused on the relation between some forms of mental illness and violence, as occurred with Goldstein, most mentally ill people are *not* violent. Indeed, if they are in jail or prison, it is usually for minor nonviolent offenses related to either trying to survive (e.g., stealing food) or to substance abuse—the mental illness is not a direct cause of the incarceration (Hiday & Wales, 2003).

Adam Sylvester/Photo Researchers, Inc.

Although some people with mental illness may create a public nuisance, like this man yelling at voices that only he can hear, such public displays are not dangerous and should not, in and of themselves, lead to hospitalization (Perlin, 2000c).

Figure 16.1

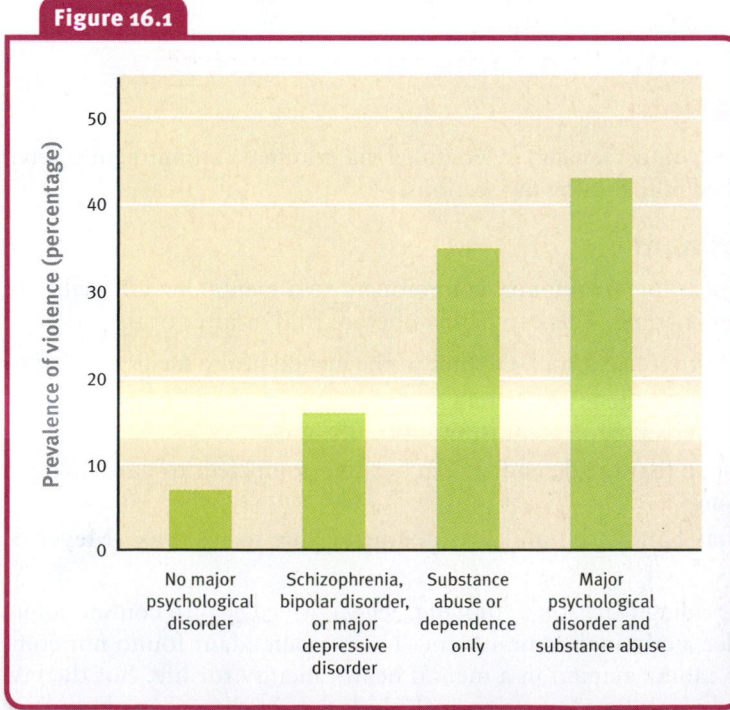

16.1 ▶ Lifetime Prevalence of Violent Behavior
Substance use disorders (with or without a comorbid major psychological disorder) are associated with a much higher rate of violent behaviors (such as the use of a weapon in a fight or coming to blows with another person) than is observed in the general population (Swanson, 1994).

Source: Monahan et al., 1994. For more information see the Permissions section.

Confidentiality and the Dangerous Patient: Duty to Warn and Duty to Protect

In the 1960s, University of California college student Prosenjit Poddar liked fellow student Tatiana Tarasoff. However, his interest in her was greater than was hers in him. He became depressed by her rejection and began treatment with a psychologist. During the course of his treatment, his therapist became concerned that Mr. Poddar might hurt or kill Ms. Tarasoff (Poddar had purchased a gun for that purpose). The therapist informed campus police that Poddar might harm Tarasoff. The police briefly restrained him, but they determined that he was rational and not a threat to Tarasoff. Ms. Tarasoff was out of the country at the time, but neither she nor her parents were alerted to the potential danger. Two months later, Poddar killed Tarasoff.

Her parents sued the psychologist, saying that Tarasoff should have been protected either by warning her or by having Poddar committed to a psychiatric facility. In what has become known as the **Tarasoff rule**, the Supreme Court of California (and later courts in other states) ruled that psychologists have a duty to protect potential victims who are in imminent danger (*Tarasoff v. Regents of the University of California*, 1974, 1976). This rule has been extended to other mental health clinicians. There are a few options for mental health professionals who decide that a patient is about to harm a specific person (Quattrocchi & Schopp, 2005):

- warn the intended victim or someone else who can warn the victim,

- notify law enforcement agencies, and

- take other reasonable steps, depending on the situation, such as having the patient voluntarily or involuntarily committed to a psychiatric facility for an extended evaluation (that is, have the patient confined).

The Tarasoff rule effectively extended a clinician's *duty to warn* of imminent harm to a *duty to protect*. The clinician must violate confidentiality in order to take reasonable care to protect an identifiable—or reasonably foreseeable—victim (*Brady v. Hopper*, 1983; *Cairl v. State*, 1982; Egley, 1991; *Emerich v. Philadelphia Center for Human Development*, 1998; Schopp, 1991; *Thompson v. County of Alameda*, 1980). Note, however, that potential danger to property is not sufficient to compel clinicians to violate confidentiality (Meyer & Weaver, 2006).

Maintaining Safety: Confining the Dangerously Mentally Ill Patient

A dangerously mentally ill person can be confined via criminal commitment or civil commitment, described in the following sections.

Criminal Commitment

Criminal commitment is the involuntary commitment to a mental health facility of a person charged with a crime. This can happen before trial or after trial:

- If the defendant hasn't yet had a trial, the time at the mental health facility is used to
  - evaluate whether he or she is competent to proceed with the legal process (for instance, is the defendant competent to stand trial?) and
  - provide treatment so that the defendant can become competent to participate in the legal proceedings.
- If the defendant has had a trial and was acquitted due to insanity (Meyer & Weaver, 2006).

Based on a 1972 ruling (*Jackson v. Indiana*, 1972), it is illegal to confine someone indefinitely under a criminal commitment. Thus, a defendant found not competent to stand trial cannot remain in a mental health facility for life. But the law is unclear as to exactly how long is long enough. Judges have discretion about how

Tarasoff rule
A ruling by the Supreme Court of California (and later other courts) that psychologists have a duty to protect potential victims who are in imminent danger.

Criminal commitment
The involuntary commitment to a mental health facility of a person charged with a crime.

long they can commit a defendant to a mental health facility to determine whether treatment may lead to competence to stand trial. Such treatment may last several years. If the defendant does not become competent, he or she may not remain committed for the original reason—to receive treatment in order to become competent. In this case, the process of deciding whether he or she should be released from the mental health facility proceeds just as it does for anyone who hasn't been criminally charged. If the individual is deemed to be dangerous, however, he or she may be civilly committed.

Civil Commitment

When an individual hasn't committed a crime but is deemed to be at significant risk of harming himself or herself, or of harming a specific other person, the judicial system can confine that individual in a mental health facility, which is referred to as a **civil commitment**. This is the more common type of commitment.

There are two types of civil commitment: (1) inpatient commitment to a 24-hour inpatient facility, and (2) outpatient commitment to some type of monitoring and/or treatment program (Meyer & Weaver, 2006). Civil commitment grows out of the idea that the government can act as a caregiver, functioning as a "parent" to people who are not able to care for themselves; this legal concept is called *parens patriae*.

The interplay between dangerousness, duty to warn, and civil commitment is illustrated by what happened to Mr. Smith, described in Case 16.3.

CASE 16.3 ▶ FROM THE OUTSIDE: Civil Commitment and Duty to Warn

Smith has experienced a life-long pattern of difficulty in interacting with others and in functioning effectively in social and occupational situations. He tends to be emotionally uncomfortable and interpersonally awkward. He is inclined to interpret the words and actions of others idiosyncratically, and he characteristically avoids situations that require interpersonal exchanges. He manages to provide for his basic tangible needs, but he remains emotionally withdrawn and interpersonally isolated. He works as a janitor who cleans office buildings at night after closing. He lives in a rooming house populated primarily by residents who have had mental health difficulties. He has no friends among the residents, but he ordinarily gets along in the house without serious difficulty by limiting interaction with the other residents.

Smith has been convicted of assault on three occasions. In each of the first two incidents, he struck another individual, causing minor injuries involving bruises and abrasions. Following the first assault, he was convicted and placed on probation. Following the second conviction, he served 60 days in the county jail and was released on parole. In the third incident, he struck a coworker with a wrench, causing serious but not permanent or life-threatening injuries. He served 6 months in the county jail for that offense. During legal proceedings following each assault, various participants in the legal system realized that he suffered some psychological disorder, but none believed that his impairment was sufficient to support an insanity defense or civil commitment. These individuals recommended that Smith seek treatment after release.

He refused to seek treatment after the first conviction, but he began attending weekly psychotherapy sessions as a condition of his release on parole following the second conviction, and he returned to therapy following release from jail following the third offense. The treating psychologist has diagnosed Smith as suffering from a personality disorder with schizoid and paranoid features. Although he is no longer on parole, Smith has continued attending the weekly sessions. During these sessions, he expressed his belief that the convictions were unfair because in each case he had struck out to protect himself from others who had begun watching him, picking on him, and looking for an opportunity to harm him.

During the last few sessions, Smith told the psychologist that "now, they're starting again." He reported having missed work twice during the previous couple of weeks because a coworker named Brown had made comments that Smith interpreted as either warnings or threats. As they were leaving work early in the morning, Brown stated, "be careful" and "watch your step out there." Smith reported that he was uncertain whether Brown was threatening him or warning him about others who might harm him.

The psychologist encouraged Smith to consider alternative interpretations of Brown's comments. When Smith seemed unable to consider any alternative interpretation, the psychologist became increasingly concerned that Smith's reality testing was deteriorating and that

continued on next page

Civil commitment
The involuntary commitment to a mental health facility of a person deemed to be at significant risk of harming himself or herself or a specific other person.

his persecutory ideation was increasing. The psychologist considered the possibility that a joint session with Smith and Brown might help reduce the risk of another assault. Specifically, Smith might consider alternate interpretations and become reassured that these remarks were innocent, or Brown might realize that it would be advisable to discontinue making such remarks to Smith. Smith responded to the psychologist's suggestion for a joint meeting by becoming increasingly agitated, and he yelled that he had thought their conversations were secret and that he would never again see the psychologist if their conversations were shared with anyone.

The psychologist considered the following [types of] interventions, some of which are mutually compatible: (a) increase the frequency of therapy sessions; (b) emphasize a cognitive reframing of Smith's interpretations of Brown's comments; (c) encourage Smith to explore alternate means of protecting himself from the perceived danger, such as always leaving work at the same time other people leave or always walking home from work on well-lit streets; (d) refer Smith to the clinic psychiatrist for medication review; (e) encourage Smith to consider voluntary inpatient care, particularly if the apparent deterioration worsens.

The psychologist realized that if such approaches failed to ameliorate Smith's deterioration, or if she believed that the risk of another assault was severe or imminent, delegated preventive action [such as civil commitment] might be warranted. Because Smith's functioning seemed unlikely to meet the jurisdiction's criteria for civil commitment, a warning of some kind would be the available delegated intervention. She would be hesitant to warn, however, because she knew of no empirical evidence that warnings reduce violence, and she believed that Smith would view such action as a betrayal and discontinue therapy. Further isolation might also occur if the warning resulted in his dismissal from his job or in counterproductive responses from Brown. The psychologist's prior clinical interventions, primarily cognitive reframing and support, had been effective in ameliorating her client's inclination toward persecutory interpretations of events and in managing the risk associated with exacerbation of these tendencies. She realized that she had no [step-by-step procedure] that allowed her to measure the absolute severity of the risk or the effectiveness of warnings or of these clinical interventions. She weighed the potential costs and benefits of various interventions as she monitored the risk represented by Smith's current functioning.

(Quattrocchi & Schopp, 2005)

Do you think that Smith was dangerous? Did he make a threat regarding an identifiable—or foreseeable—victim? Could Smith's statements be taken in a way to indicate to the psychologist that Brown was the target? If so, the psychologist might be obligated to take steps to warn the victim or to restrain Smith through a civil commitment (although the extent of this obligation differs among various states). But as you can see from this example, some components related to dangerousness—severity, imminence, probability of potential harm, and past frequency of dangerous behavior—are not always known or knowable. (In fact, the article that presented the case of Mr. Smith did not provide information about what the psychologist decided or about what happened to Smith.) Mental health clinicians must base their judgments as best they can, in part on known risk factors.

Civil commitments can conflict with individual rights, so guidelines have been created to protect patients' rights by establishing the circumstances necessary for an involuntary commitment, the duration of such a commitment—and who decides when it ends—as well as the right to refuse a specific type of treatment or treatment in general (Meyer & Weaver, 2006). It may seem that civil commitments are always forced or coerced, but that is not necessarily so. Some civil commitments are voluntary (that is, the patient agrees to the hospitalization); however, some "voluntary" hospitalizations may occur only after substantial coercion (Meyer & Weaver, 2006).

Most people who are civilly committed belong to a subset of the mentally ill population—those who are overrepresented in the revolving door that leads to jails or hospitals. This revolving door evolved because lawmakers and clinicians wanted a more humane approach to dealing with the dangerous mentally ill, by treating them in the least restrictive setting before their condition deteriorates to the point where they harm themselves or others (Hiday, 2003).

Inpatient Commitment

The MacArthur Coercion Study (MacArthur Research Network on Mental Health and the Law, 2001b) found that half of inpatients who initially reported that they didn't need hospitalization and treatment later shifted their views. Looking back, they realized that they did, in fact, need to be hospitalized. The other half of the study's participants continued to believe that they didn't need hospitalization. Participants also noted that family, friends, and mental health professionals' attempts to persuade them by using inducements (for example, saying that voluntarily going along with a hospitalization would give them more control over the process) did not feel like coercion, whereas attempts to persuade them by the use of force or threats (such as the threat of involuntary commitment) did feel like coercion. Moreover, patients were more likely to feel coerced when they believed that they weren't allowed to tell their side of the story or when they believed that others weren't acting out of concern and with respect for them.

Mandated Outpatient Commitment

Mandated outpatient commitment developed in the 1960s and 1970s, along with increasing deinstitutionalization of patients from mental hospitals; the goal was to develop less restrictive alternatives to inpatient care (Hiday, 2003). Such outpatient commitment may consist of legally mandated treatment that includes some type of psychotherapy, medication, or periodic monitoring of the patient by a mental health clinician. The hope is that mandated outpatient commitment will preempt a cycle observed in many patients who have been committed: (1) getting discharged from inpatient care, (2) stopping their medication, (3) becoming dangerous, and (4) ending up back in the hospital through a criminal or civil commitment or landing in jail.

Researchers have investigated whether mandated outpatient commitment is effective: Are the patient and the public safer than if the patient was allowed to obtain voluntary treatment after discharge from inpatient care? Does mandated treatment result in less frequent hospitalizations or incarcerations for the patient? To address these questions, one study compared involuntarily hospitalized patients who either were offered psychosocial treatment and services upon discharge or who were court-ordered to obtain outpatient treatment for 6 months—and made frequent use of services (between 3 and 10 visits/month) (Hiday, 2003; Swartz et al., 2001). The results indicated that those who received mandated outpatient treatment:

- went back into the hospital less frequently and for shorter periods of time,

- were less violent,

- were less likely to be victims of crime themselves, and

- were more likely to take their medication or obtain other treatment, even when the mandated treatment period ended.

(Note, however, that patients in this study were not randomly assigned, so there may have been confounds.) Other studies have found similar benefits of mandated outpatient commitment (Hough & O'Brien, 2005). When people know that they will end up back in the hospital if they don't participate in treatment, they are more likely to comply with that treatment. That said, it is also clear that mandated outpatient commitment is not effective without adequate funding for increased therapeutic services (Perlin, 2003; Rand Corporation, 2001). Let's examine what happens without adequate funding.

The Reality of Treatment for the Chronically Mentally Ill

Coercion to be hospitalized was not an issue for Andrew Goldstein. In fact, he had the opposite problem: He generally *wanted* to be hospitalized and tried repeatedly to make that happen.

> He signed himself in voluntarily for all 13 of his hospitalizations. His problem was what happened after discharge. The social workers assigned to plan his release knew he shouldn't have been living on his own, and so did Goldstein, but everywhere they looked they were turned down. They found waiting lists for long-term care at state

hospitals, waiting lists for supervised housing at state-financed group homes, waiting lists for a state-financed intensive-case manager, who would have visited Goldstein daily at his apartment to make sure he was coping and taking his meds.

More than once he requested long-term hospitalization at Creedmoor, the state hospital nearby. In 1997, he walked into the Creedmoor lobby, asking to be admitted. "I want to be hospitalized," he said. "I need a placement." But in a cost-cutting drive, New York [had] been pushing hard to reduce its patient census and to shut state hospitals. Goldstein was instead referred to an emergency room, where he stayed overnight and was released.

Again, in July 1998, Goldstein cooperated with psychiatrists, this time during a month-long stay at Brookdale Hospital, in hopes of getting long-term care at Creedmoor. Brookdale psychiatrists had a well-documented case. In a month's time, Goldstein committed three violent acts: punching the young woman on the subway; attacking a Brookdale therapist, a psychiatrist, a social worker and a ward aide; striking a Brookdale nurse in the face. This time, Creedmoor officials agreed in principle to take him, but explained that there was a waiting list, that they were under orders to give priority to mental patients from prison and that they did not know when they would have an opening. Days later, Goldstein was discharged from Brookdale.

(Winerip, 1999a)

Those who work with the mentally ill said that Mr. Goldstein seemed poorly served by the system. "We're really concerned that there are huge gaps in the mental health system," said Jody Silver, director of advocacy for Community Access, a Manhattan program that provides supported housing for people with psychiatric disabilities. "He had a place to live, but he didn't have support. It sounds like he needed a program with an intensive support service, where he would be visited daily by a caseworker who would monitor his medication and help him with his life. He was totally alone in the community. This person was grossly underserved."

(Kleinfield & Roane, 1999)

Not only was Goldstein underserved, but so was the public at large. When appropriate services were available to him, Goldstein made good use of them. He spent a year in a residential setting on the grounds of the state hospital—he did well, was cooperative and friendly, and regularly took his medications. But personnel at state hospitals are under pressure to move patients to less expensive programs, even if the patients aren't ready. Goldstein was considered too low-functioning to qualify for a program that provided less supervision, but he was discharged from the residential program nonetheless—to a home where he received almost no support. A year before the murder he tried, without success, to return to a supervised group but no spaces were available (Winerip, 1999a).

Unfortunately, Goldstein's history with the mental health system in New York is not unique (see Case 16.4). People with severe mental illness generally don't receive the care they need (which is also in society's interest for them to receive) unless their families are wealthy and willing to pay for needed services—long-term hospitalization, supervised housing, or intensive daytime supervision. Even when a defendant is deemed to be mentally ill and ordered to be transferred to a psychiatric facility, space may not be available in such a facility; the options then are to hold the defendant in jail or to release him or her and provide a less intensive form of mental health treatment (Goodnough, 2006).

As discussed in Chapter 12, deinstitutionalization is a reasonable option for those who can benefit from newer, more effective treatments, and providing treatment in the least restrictive alternative setting is also a good idea. Unfortunately, however, such community-based forms of care are not adequately funded, which forces facilities to prioritize and provide treatment only to the sickest, leaving everyone else to make their own way in the system. Thus, most people with severe mental illness lack adequate supervision, care, or housing. They may be living on their own in tiny rented rooms, on the street, in homeless shelters that are not equipped to handle mentally ill people, or they may be in jail. The law may mandate treatment for severely mentally ill individuals, but that doesn't mean they receive it.

After the murder of Kendra Webdale, New York State passed *Kendra's law*, allowing family members, roommates, and mental health clinicians to request court-mandated outpatient treatment for a mentally ill person who refuses treatment; a judge makes the final decision about mandating treatment. The unfortunate irony is that Goldstein sought further treatment, but the lack of social support and available treatment allowed his illness to interfere with his taking medication. In his case, the real culprit may have been the lack of resources to provide the type of support and services that he and others like him—such as the man described Case 16.4—need.

CASE 16.4 ▶ FROM THE OUTSIDE: A Failed Mandated Outpatient Treatment

On February 12, 2008, David Tarloff murdered psychologist Kathryn Faughey and injured psychiatrist Kent Shinbach in a delusional plan to steal money to fly to Hawaii with his elderly mother. Tarloff, who had been a patient of Shinbach, was hospitalized over a dozen times since 1991, when he was diagnosed with paranoid schizophrenia. In the year leading up to the murders, Tarloff received psychiatric care three times after violent or threatening behavior; he was stabilized on medication and released, despite his family's request for continued inpatient treatment. After release each time, he stopped taking his medication. His family even made use of Kendra's law, so that Tarloff was supposed to receive mandated outpatient treatment, but he avoided the periodic outpatient visits. He was released from a psychiatric unit 10 days before he murdered Faughey.

(Konigsberg & Farmer, 2008).

Eight months after David Tarloff committed murder, the judge hearing the case declared Tarloff unfit to stand trial. Tarloff was sent to a psychiatric facility (Eligon, 2008).

The problems in obtaining appropriate treatment for people with chronic and severe mental illnesses are described by parents of an individual with schizophrenia:

> We are the parents of the throwaway schizophrenics, the disposables, the ones who are the most difficult to treat; who are often, as a result of their disability, unable to ask for or accept help. They refuse it.
>
> Left without treatment they continue to suffer. Relatives must stand by and watch, unable to alleviate the suffering which in the main is ignored by the mental health care system until it is too late. It seems to be the same story the world over. We are the people who are told you can't help those who won't help themselves, and we reply under our breath that is seems to us that you won't help those who can't help themselves.
>
> We are the people who mop up the blood of our sons and daughters when they have killed themselves, released from hospital all too soon, or not considered sick enough to be hospitalised. . . . When we ask psychiatrists why they do not declare our obviously ill relatives incompetent, they reply that [mental health law] ties their hands. When we ask the bureaucrats and the politicians how such a law can be passed, they tell us that the psychiatrists are interpreting the law too narrowly. When we turn to the lawyers they tell us that the rights of the individual are paramount. . . . We are left helpless and hopeless, alone in our struggle to save the lives of our children.

(Deveson, 1991, p. 244)

Sexual Predator Laws

People who are repeat sexual offenders—often referred to as *sexual predators*—are clearly dangerous. How do they fit into the legal concept of dangerousness? Are they to be treated as mentally ill? How do the criminal justice and mental health systems view such individuals?

The answers to these questions have evolved over time. Before the 1930s, a sexual offense was viewed as a criminal offense: The perpetrator was seen as able to control the behavior although he or she didn't do so. In the 1930s, sexual offenses were viewed as related to mental illness (sexual psychopaths), and treatment programs for those who committed such offenses proliferated. Unfortunately, the treatments were not effective. By the 1980s, sexual offenses were again seen as crimes for which prison sentences were appropriate consequences. In the 1990s, after highly publicized cases of sexual mutilation and murder of children, some states passed laws to deal with sexually violent predators, who were seen as having no or poor ability to control their impulses. Rather than emphasizing treatment (which had not been effective), the new laws called for incarcerating these individuals as a preventative measure.

Patrick Andrade/The New York Times/Redux

In 1997, the Supreme Court upheld the constitutionality of state laws regarding sexual predators (*Kansas v. Hendricks*, 1997); these laws are based on the concept of *parens patriae,* under which the government, as "parent," has the power to protect the public from threats, as well as the duty to care for those who cannot take care of themselves (Perlin, 2000c). These laws were intended to prevent sex offenders from committing similar offences, in some cases by ensuring that offenders do not reenter society while there is a significant risk that they will reoffend. At the end of a prison term, if a sexual predator was deemed likely to reoffend *and* was suffering from a mental abnormality or personality disorder, that person could be committed to a psychiatric hospital indefinitely (Winick, 2003).

However, some people viewed such laws as too restrictive, and in 2002, the Supreme Court ruled that in order to commit a sexual offender indefinitely after a jail or prison sentence has been served, it must be demonstrated that the person has difficulty controlling the behavior (*Kansas v. Crane*, 2002; the Supreme Court did not say how to demonstrate this, other than pointing to the individual's past history). In prison, treatment is voluntary, whereas with commitment it is mandatory.

Key Concepts and Facts About Dangerousness ■

- Dangerousness has four components related to the potential harm the person may inflict: severity, imminence, frequency, and probability.

- Risk factors for dangerousness include a patient's prior arrests and violent acts, experience of child abuse, diagnosis of antisocial personality disorder or substance abuse, and the criminal and substance abuse history of the patient's father. A combination of serious mental illness and substance abuse leads to the highest risk of violence.

- Mental health clinicians have a legal duty to warn and to protect specified potential victims who are judged to be in imminent danger of being harmed by a patient. The clinician may warn the intended victim, notify law enforcement agencies, and/or take other reasonable steps, such as have the patient confined to a psychiatric facility. Clinicians may violate confidentiality to fulfill these duties.

- Criminal commitment may occur before a defendant's trial to evaluate his or her competence for upcoming legal proceedings or to obtain treatment for the defendant so that he or she can become competent to take part in legal proceedings. When criminal commitment occurs after a trial, it is because the defendant was acquitted for the reason of insanity.

- Civil commitments occur before a crime has been committed, in order to prevent harm to the patient or others deemed to be at significant risk of harm. Patients may be committed to inpatient or outpatient facilities. Unfortunately, civil commitments do not guarantee appropriate treatment.

- State sexual predator laws are designed to keep indefinitely committed to a psychiatric hospital those sex offenders who are considered to be likely to re-offend. The Supreme Court has upheld such state laws, provided that the state can show that the person has difficulty controlling the behavior.

Making a Determination

- Reread Case 16.3 about Mr. Smith, and determine whether or not his behavior seems to call for civil commitment and create a duty to warn. Specifically, how did you arrive at your decision? If you would like more information to determine whether he should be civilly committed or whether the therapist has a duty to warn, what information—specifically—would you want, and in what ways would the information influence your decision?

Legal Issues Related to Treatment

In the 1960s and 1970s, the courts decided several landmark cases regarding the rights of the mentally ill. These cases addressed the right to treatment and the right to refuse treatment.

Right to Treatment

In 1966 (*Lake v. Cameron*), the Supreme Court ruled that people who are forced to receive treatment through civil commitment should be given the least restrictive alternative treatment available. That is, they should have the type of treatment that infringes the least on their individual liberties. If an individual doesn't need the 24-hour monitoring and care of an inpatient unit, that person should be treated in a less restrictive environment (such as in a residential setting and with outpatient treatment).

One year after this ruling, the Supreme Court ruled that civil commitment must entail more than warehousing or confining people; the Court ruled that appropriate treatment must also be provided, while recognizing that treatment might not necessarily be successful (*Rouse v. Cameron*, 1967). In subsequent cases during the 1970s, courts in various jurisdictions outlined specific minimal criteria for such treatment—including the minimum staffing ratio (number of patients per care provider) and number of hours per week of treatment, as well as the need for each patient to have an individualized treatment plan (*Wyatt v. Stickney*, 1971). The specifics of these requirements differ from jurisdiction to jurisdiction.

The Supreme Court also ruled that civil commitment may not be used simply to confine people against their will indefinitely (except as previously noted with some sexual predators). When patients no longer meet the criteria for commitment (that is, they are no longer dangerous) and can survive independently or with help from willing family members, then they must be discharged (*O'Connor v. Donaldson*, 1975). The reasoning behind this ruling is that the purpose of the confinement is treatment, and so when inpatient treatment is no longer required, the person should be released.

Right to Refuse Treatment

A federal district court in New Jersey set another standard when it ruled that a civilly committed patient has the right to refuse treatment (*Rennie v. Klein*, 1978). Generally, this ruling has been applied to a patient's right to refuse to take medications, most frequently traditional antipsychotics that carry the risk of a serious side effect called *tardive dyskinesia* (see Chapter 12) (Perlin, 2000b). However, the court did not establish the right to refuse treatment in all situations. As long as there has been a fair and adequate hearing of the issues involved for a given patient, his or her refusal can be overridden after weighing certain factors (Meyer & Weaver, 2006):

- the patient is physically threatening to others (which may include patients and staff members),
- the proposed treatment carries only a small risk of irreversible side effects,
- there are no less restrictive treatment alternatives available, and
- the patient's capacity to decide rationally about particular treatments is significantly diminished.

Competence to Refuse Treatment

One of the acceptable circumstances for overriding a committed patient's refusal of a treatment is that he or she does not have the capacity to decide rationally about treatment. How can mental health clinicians and the courts determine whether someone is competent to refuse treatment? (Being competent to refuse treatment is different from being competent to stand trial, although both competencies involve some of the same mental processes and abilities.) One study that investigated the general question of competence to refuse treatment (Appelbaum & Grisso, 1995; Grisso & Appelbaum, 1995) found that about half of patients with schizophrenia performed reasonably well on several tasks assessing decision-making ability. Not surprisingly, those with more severe symptoms of schizophrenia did less well. After 2 weeks of treatment, those whose symptoms had improved also improved in their decision-making abilities related to competence. An even greater proportion of patients hospitalized for depression—about 75%—performed adequately on the tasks that assess decision making. Unlike the patients with more severe symptoms of schizophrenia, those with more severe depression were not necessarily less competent to make decisions. Thus, having a severe mental illness did not routinely make these patients "not competent to refuse treatment."

Some legal scholars and mental health advocates argue that the right to refuse treatment is at odds with outpatient commitment laws, whereby individuals can be forced to take medication, be committed to an inpatient facility, or put in jail if they don't adhere to their outpatient treatment (Perlin, 2003). In fact, although some individuals who receive outpatient commitment may be competent to refuse treatment, the law may not allow them to refuse.

Mental Health and Drug Courts

Federal, state, and local court dockets are filled with cases awaiting a hearing or trial. In order to hasten the speed with which cases are resolved, municipalities have instituted specialized courts, such as divorce courts, to address particular types of problems. Two such special courts are particularly relevant to the mentally ill: drug courts and mental health courts.

Drug courts were developed in Miami in 1989 for first-time drug abusers—those whose substance abuse was viewed as the underlying motivation for their crime (Miethe, Lu, & Reese, 2000). Soon after arrest, these people were offered an alternative to jail: They could attend a drug treatment program, submit to random and frequent drug testing by urinalysis, and meet with the drug court judge regularly. If they did not show up for a court hearing, a bench warrant would be issued within hours and they could be sent to jail. The overall goal of drug courts is to help defendants reintegrate into society.

Drug court programs do not simply aim to decrease substance abuse; they recognize the complex nature of the factors that contribute to such abuse. Thus, drug courts not only promote intensive treatment for drug abuse and relapse prevention—they also encourage education and employment. In fact, participants typically are asked to earn a GED (high school graduate equivalency diploma) and to hold a steady job. Moreover, participants are required to develop a relationship with a mentor in the community and to meet all their financial obligations, such as child support. Some drug court programs also require community service. Abstinence is assessed through frequent random drug testing, and during their time in such a program, less than 10% of participants use drugs.

Relapse rates are between 4% and 20% for those entering a program and even lower (less than 4%) for those who complete one. Many communities have extended drug court programs to include individuals who were previously jailed for substance abuse–related crimes, with equivalent success (Drug Court Clearinghouse and Technical Assistance Project, 1998).

The success of drug courts led to the development of mental health courts, which began in Florida and now exist in most states, but not necessarily in most

Drug courts recognize that maintaining abstinence can depend on a complex interplay of factors, such as educational opportunities and employment.

John Sundlof/Alamy

districts (Council of State Governments, 2005). Mental health courts seek to treat, rather than incarcerate, mentally ill people who are charged with a misdemeanor. Here are some common types of cases heard in mental health courts and the features of such courts (Goldkamp & Irons-Guynn, 2000):

- The defendant's mental illness seems to contribute to the alleged criminal behavior.

- The defendant's behavior has raised concern for public safety.

- The specialized court is voluntary—the defendant must consent to be part of that court rather than the usual court.

- The mental health court tries *not* to send those who are mentally ill to prison.

Some mental health courts do not accept a defendant who has been violent. Other mental health courts will accept violent defendants but will put the defendants in jail if they do not adhere to the plan for treatment (Redlich et al., 2005). Studies report the same basic finding: When mentally ill people receive treatment, they are subsequently less likely to become violent or to reoffend (McNiel & Binder, 2007; Steadman et al., 1998).

Key Concepts and Facts About Treatment and the Legal System

- The Supreme Court has ruled that people who are civilly committed should be given the least restrictive alternative *treatment* available—not simply confinement—while recognizing that treatment might not necessarily be successful. In addition, civil commitments may not be used solely to confine people against their will indefinitely.

- Patients usually have a right to refuse treatment, such as medication. However, patients who have physically threatened other people may be forced to take medication or receive other treatment, as long as there has been a fair and adequate hearing of the issues involved. In addition, the right to refuse treatment may be overridden in certain circumstances, such as when a patient does not have sufficient capacity to decide rationally about particular treatments.

- Defendants may be sent to drug courts if their drug use was the underlying motivation for the crime; in drug court programs, defendants are offered treatment for their substance abuse or dependence, along with random drug testing and educational and job training opportunities. Drug courts have been successful in decreasing rates of relapse and reoffending.

- Mental health courts can mandate treatment for mentally ill defendants; such programs have been found to decrease violence and repeat offending.

The Wheels of Justice: Follow-up on Andrew Goldstein

The jury that heard Andrew Goldstein's case was deadlocked—some jurors voted to convict and some voted him not guilty by reason of insanity. The deadlocked jury meant that another trial was necessary. This time, with Goldstein's permission, his lawyers took him off his medication several weeks before he was to testify so that jurors could see the extent of his mental illness. However, his mental state at the time of trial could not be used to determine his mental status at the time he committed the crime. This strategy was very controversial, and the judge allowed it, provided that Goldstein be asked daily whether he wanted to receive medication and that he be given medication forcibly if he appeared to become not competent to stand trial (Rohde, 2000). Goldstein hit his social worker within several weeks of stopping his medication, which meant that he resumed taking it and did not take the stand. The jury found Goldstein guilty, although they acknowledged that he was mentally ill. They decided that he knew what he was doing when he threw Kendra Webdale onto the tracks, and that he knew it was wrong.

[The witness] Ms. Lorenzino testified that Mr. Goldstein did not simply push Ms. Webdale, but that he picked her up bodily and threw her in front of the train. In interviews, jurors said that his apparent deliberateness and preparation, as well as the fact that he caught himself before falling in front of the train, helped convince them that he was not psychotic, that he knew what he was doing was wrong.

(Barnes, 2000a)

After his trial, Goldstein was sent to prison, where he was evaluated to determine whether he needed to be admitted to a psychiatric hospital to become stable. If so, once stable, he would be returned to prison. In such cases, hospitalizations are brief, only long enough to get the defendant well enough to return to prison. In 2006, 8 years after the murder, Goldstein's conviction was overturned because of a technical misstep during the second trial. In a third trial, Goldstein's lawyers entered a plea of guilty, with the understanding that he would serve 23 years in prison, followed by 5 years of psychiatric oversight and supervision after his release.

SUMMING UP

Summary of Ethical Issues

Each type of mental health professional works under his or her own discipline's ethical code; all disciplines include in their ethical code the principle of confidentiality, which applies to information that patients share with mental health professionals. Although the clinician is bound by confidentiality, patients in couples therapy, family therapy, and group therapy are not. When a patient is a minor, the clinician may inform the parents about what the child has said; however, most clinicians discuss the limits of confidentiality with a child who is old enough to understand.

Because of HIPAA, the limits on confidentiality have been redefined. Now limited information about a patient may be shared with the patient's other health providers in order to facilitate treatment. Although laws protect confidentiality, confidentiality may be violated against the patient's wishes when a clinician has reasonable cause to (1) suspect abuse of children, the elderly, or the disabled or (2) believe that a patient is likely to do significant harm to himself or herself (including suicide attempts) or a specified other person.

The legal counterpart to the ethical principle of confidentiality is privileged communication—the protection of confidential information from disclosure during legal proceedings; however, in some circumstances, other people can decide whether the information about a patient should be disclosed.

Patients who have impaired cognitive processes because of a psychological disorder (such as schizophrenia) may be able to provide informed consent to participate in research if they can understand what they are consenting to and can reason about it.

Thinking like a clinician

Rina is taking medication and seeing a therapist for depression. During one therapy session, she remarks, "Sometimes I think my family would be better off if I were dead." Based on what you have read, should Rina's therapist violate confidentiality and take steps to prevent Rina from hurting herself? Why or why not?

What if, instead, Rina had said about her multiply handicapped brother, "Sometimes I think my family would be better off if he were dead"? Would your view of whether Rina's therapist should violate confidentiality change—why or why not? What would Rina need to do or say to provide a *clear* indication that the therapist should violate confidentiality?

Summary of Criminal Actions and Insanity

Various tests have been used to determine whether a defendant is insane. The first was the M'Naghten test in 1843, followed by the irresistible impulse test. After almost 70 years came the Durham test. Many states presently use the American Legal Institute (ALI) test, which requires either impaired knowledge that the behavior was wrong (cognition) or impaired capacity to resist the impulse to act illegally (volition). The Insanity Defense Reform Acts of the 1980s did away with the volition element to determine insanity in federal courts.

Two issues are still to be clarified by the courts: (1) whether someone who is legally insane must have known that the act was "wrong" versus "illegal," and (2) whether insanity depends on knowing in the abstract that an act is wrong versus knowing that the specific behavior is wrong in the particular circumstance. To assess insanity, a jury may rely on testimony about the defendant's mental state during the time leading up to the crime, the defendant's history of mental illness prior to the crime, testimony or reports from expert witnesses about the defendant's mental state or mental illness.

Mental health clinicians may assess a defendant's sanity through interviews with the person, psychological tests and questionnaires, and interviews with family members and friends. However, such measures may be affected by the defendant's experiences in jail, medications he or she may be taking, the decision to plead not guilty by reason of insanity (NGBI), reactions to the crime, coaching from the defendant's lawyer or other inmates, and the way the defendant responds to various assessment methods. But none of this information necessarily indicates the defendant's mental state at the time of the crime. Some states offer alternatives to the insanity defense, including those of diminished capacity and guilty but mentally ill. Research indicates that acquittal on the basis of the insanity defense is extremely rare, particularly when the decision is made by a jury rather than a judge.

Competency to stand trial addresses the defendant's mental state before the trial and whether the defendant is competent to participate in his or her own defense; someone who is not competent to stand trial would also be deemed not competent to plead guilty and not competent to waive the right to an attorney.

Thinking like a clinician

Jon has been arrested for disturbing the peace and destroying private property; at 2 a.m. last night, he was yelling and kicking over trash cans on Main Street, and broke several store windows. His rant went on for 25 minutes, until the police arrived. Jon initially resisted arrest and then cooperated. It seemed to the police that Jon was behaving as if he were having a manic episode, and, in fact, he had a history of bipolar disorder. How might mental health clinicians and the legal system go about determining whether Jon was "insane" at the time of the crime? What information would you want to know in order to determine whether he was insane? What if, rather than a history of bipolar disorder, Jon had a history of alcohol abuse and dependence and was drunk the night of the crime. Would that change your opinions? Why or why not?

Summary of Dangerousness

Dangerousness has four components related to the potential harm the person may inflict: severity, imminence, frequency, and probability. Risk factors for dangerousness include a patient's prior arrests and violent acts, experience of child abuse, diagnosis of antisocial personality disorder or substance abuse, and the criminal and substance abuse history of the patient's father. A combination of serious mental illness and substance abuse leads to the highest risk of violence.

Mental health clinicians have a legal duty to warn and to protect specified potential victims who are judged to be in imminent danger of being harmed by a patient. The clinician may warn the intended victim, notify law enforcement agencies, and/or take other reasonable steps, such as have the patient confined to a psychiatric facility. Clinicians may violate confidentiality to fulfill these duties.

Criminal commitment may occur before a defendant's trial to evaluate his or her competence for upcoming legal proceedings or to obtain treatment for the defendant so that he or she can become competent to take part in legal proceedings. When criminal commitment occurs after a trial, it is because the defendant was acquitted for the reason of insanity.

Civil commitments occur before a crime has been committed, in order to prevent harm to the patient or others deemed to be at significant risk of harm. Patients may be committed to inpatient or outpatient facilities.

Unfortunately, civil commitments do not guarantee appropriate treatment.

State sexual predator laws are designed to keep indefinitely committed to a psychiatric hospital those sex offenders who are likely to re-offend. The Supreme Court has upheld such state laws, provided that the state can show that the person has difficulty controlling the behavior.

Thinking like a clinician

Tyrone was diagnosed with schizoaffective disorder when he was 25; his mother, ill with diabetes herself, couldn't supervise and take care of him to the extent that he needed. Cutbacks in mental health services in his community meant that he couldn't receive adequate services outside of a hospital ("We don't have any available beds in residential care," and "We don't have any available places in the day treatment center—we're full"). By age 30, he was living on the streets, in jail for petty crimes such as stealing food from a grocery store, and had been treated for brief periods in a psychiatric facility. Based on what you have read, do you think Tyrone is dangerous—why or why not? Suppose, during psychotic episodes, he darts across busy streets—causing car accidents as drivers quickly brake to avoid hitting him. Would he be dangerous then—why or why not? What would be the advantages and disadvantages to him, and to society, of committing him to inpatient treatment? To outpatient treatment?

Summary of Legal Issues Related to Treatment

The Supreme Court has ruled that people who are civilly committed should be given the least restrictive alternative *treatment* available—not simply confinement—while recognizing that treatment might not necessarily be successful. In addition, civil commitments may not be used solely to confine people against their will indefinitely.

Patients usually have a right to refuse treatment, such as medication. However, patients who have physically threatened other people may be forced to take medication or receive other treatment, as long as there has been a fair and adequate hearing of the issues involved. In addition, the right to refuse treatment may be overridden in certain circumstances, such as when a patient does not

have sufficient capacity to decide rationally about particular treatments.

Defendants may be sent to drug courts if their drug use was the underlying motivation for the crime; in drug court programs, defendants are offered treatment for their substance abuse or dependence, along with random drug testing and educational and job training opportunities. Drug courts have been successful in decreasing rates of relapse and reoffending. Mental health courts can mandate treatment for mentally ill defendants; such programs have been found to decrease violence and repeat offending.

Thinking like a clinician

Ella is in the throes of a psychotic episode and is in the hospital. At times, she feels bugs crawling under her skin, and so she viciously scratches herself until she bleeds. At other times, she thinks she has superpowers and can fly—if there were an open window, she'd jump out of it. Her psychiatrist has prescribed an antipsychotic medication, but she won't take it: "I don't like the way it makes me feel." Based on what you have read, do you think Ella has the right to refuse treatment? Why or why not?

Key Terms

Confidentiality (p. 719)

Privileged communication (p. 720)

Criminally responsible (p. 722)

M'Naghten test (or rule) (p. 722)

Irresistible impulse test (p. 723)

Durham test (p. 723)

American Legal Institute test (ALI test) (p. 723)

Competency to stand trial (p. 727)

Dangerousness (p. 729)

Tarasoff rule (p. 732)

Criminal commitment (p. 732)

Civil commitment (p. 733)

More Study Aids

For additional study aids related to this chapter, go to:

www.worthpublishers.com/rosenberg

°A°

Abnormal psychology The subfield of psychology that studies the causes and progression of psychological disorders; also referred to as *psychopathology*.

Abstinence violation effect The condition that arises when the violation of a self-imposed rule about food restriction leads to feeling out of control with food, which then leads to overeating.

Action potential The wave of chemical activity that moves from the cell body down the axon when a neuron fires.

Active phase The phase of a psychological disorder (such as schizophrenia) in which the individual exhibits symptoms that meet all the criteria for the disorder.

Acute stress disorder The anxiety disorder that arises within a month after a traumatic event and that involves reexperiencing of the event, avoiding stimuli related to the event, and symptoms of anxiety, hyperarousal, and dissociation that last for less than a month.

Affect An emotion that is associated with a particular idea or behavior, similar to an attitude.

Age cohort A group of people born in a particular range of years.

Agonists Medications that mimic the effects of a neurotransmitter or neuromodulator and activate a particular type of receptor.

Agoraphobia The persistent avoidance of situations that might trigger panic symptoms or from which escape would be difficult.

Allegiance effect A pattern in which studies conducted by investigators who prefer a particular theoretical orientation tend to obtain data that supports that particular orientation.

Alogia A negative symptom of schizophrenia marked by speaking less than most other people and responding slowly or minimally to questions.

Alzheimer's disease A medical condition in which the afflicted individual initially has problems with both memory and executive function and which leads to progressive dementia.

Amenorrhea The suppression of menstruation; this condition is diagnosed after three consecutive missed menstrual cycles.

American Legal Institute test (ALI test) The legal test in which a person is considered insane if a defendant either lacks a substantial capacity to appreciate that his or her behavior was wrong or has a diminished ability to make his or her behavior conform to the law.

Amnesia Memory loss, which is usually temporary but, in rare cases, may be permanent.

Amnestic disorder A cognitive disorder characterized by impaired memory while other mental processes remain relatively intact.

Amyloid plaques Fragments of protein that accumulate on the outside surfaces of neurons, particularly neurons in the hippocampus.

Analogue study Research in which treatment is provided in a way that is analogous to the way it is usually provided, but that is conducted under controlled conditions in a laboratory setting, thereby minimizing confounds.

Anhedonia A difficulty or inability to experience pleasure.

Anorexia nervosa An eating disorder characterized by being at least 15% below expected body weight along with using various methods to prevent weight gain.

Antabuse A medication for treating alcohol abuse and dependence that induces violent nausea and vomiting when it is mixed with alcohol.

Antagonists Medications that bind to a receptor site on a dendrite (or cell body) and prevent the neurotransmitter in the synapse from binding to that receptor or cause less of it to bind.

Antipsychotic medications Medications that reduce certain psychotic symptoms; also called *neuroleptic medications*.

Antisocial personality disorder A personality disorder characterized by a persistent disregard for the rights of others.

Anxiety A sense of agitation or nervousness, which is often focused on an upcoming possible danger.

Anxiety disorder A category of psychological disorders in which the primary symptoms involve extreme anxiety, intense arousal, and/or extreme attempts to avoid stimuli that lead to fear and anxiety.

Anxious apprehension Anxiety that arises in response to a high level of fear of a particular stimulus.

Aphasia A neurological condition characterized by problems in producing or comprehending language.

Applied behavior analysis A technique used to modify maladaptive behaviors by reinforcing new behaviors through shaping.

Apraxia A neurological condition characterized by problems in organizing and carrying out voluntary movements even though the muscles themselves are not impaired.

Asperger's disorder A psychological disorder on the autism spectrum characterized by problems with social interaction and narrowed behaviors—similar to but less severe than autism—but in which language and cognitive development are in the normal range; also referred to as *Asperger's syndrome*.

Asylums Institutions to house and care for people who are afflicted with mental illness.

Attention-deficit/hyperactivity disorder (ADHD) A psychological disorder that typically arises in childhood and is characterized by inattention, hyperactivity, and/or impulsivity.

Attrition The reduction in the number of participants during a research study.

Atypical antipsychotics A relatively new class of antipsychotic medications that affect dopamine and serotonin activity but create fewer movement-related side effects than do traditional antipsychotics; also referred to as *second-generation antipsychotics*.

Autistic disorder A pervasive developmental disorder that arises in childhood and is characterized by delayed or impaired communication and social skills, along with restricted and repetitive behaviors and interests; also referred to as *autism*.

Avoidant personality disorder A personality disorder characterized by extreme social inhibition (i.e., extreme shyness) that usually stems from feeling inadequate and being overly sensitive to negative evaluation.

Avolition A negative symptom of schizophrenia marked by difficulty in initiating or following through with activities.

°B°

Behavior modification The use of operant conditioning principles to change maladaptive behavior.

Behavior therapy The form of treatment that rests on the ideas that (1) maladaptive behaviors, cognitions, and emotions stem from previous learning and (2) new learning can allow patients to develop more adaptive behaviors, cognitions, and emotions.

Behavioral genetics The field that investigates the degree to which the variability of characteristics in a population arises from genetic versus environmental factors.

Behaviorism The approach to psychology that focuses on understanding directly observable behaviors in order to understand mental illness and other psychological phenomena.

Benzodiazepines A class of medications commonly known as tranquilizers.

Bias A tendency that distorts data.

Bibliotherapy The use of self-help materials as part of therapy.

Binge eating Eating much more food at one time than most people would eat in the same context.

Binge-eating disorder A provisional diagnosis of the variant of an eating disorder characterized by frequent episodes of rapid uncontrolled eating of large quantities of food, even when not hungry, without subsequent purging; according to DSM-IV-TR, patients with binge-eating disorder receive a diagnosis of EDNOS.

Biofeedback A technique by which a person is trained to bring normally involuntary or unconscious bodily activity, such as heart rate or muscle tension, under voluntary control.

Biological marker A neurological, bodily, or behavioral characteristic that distinguishes people with a psychological disorder (or a first-degree relative with the disorder) from those without the disorder.

Biomedical treatments Treatments that are designed to reduce target symptoms and/or improve quality of life by changing brain functioning, hormonal activity, or another aspect of bodily functioning.

Biopsychosocial approach The view that a psychological disorder arises from the combined influences of three types of factors—biological, psychological, and social.

Bipolar disorders Mood disorders in which a person's mood is often persistently and abnormally upbeat or shifts inappropriately from upbeat to markedly down.

Body dysmorphic disorder A somatoform disorder characterized by excessive preoccupation with a perceived defect or defects in appearance.

Borderline personality disorder A personality disorder characterized by volatile emotions, an unstable self-image, and impulsive behavior in relationships.

Brain circuits Sets of connected neurons that work together to accomplish a basic process.

Brain systems Sets of brain circuits that work together to accomplish a complex function.

Brief psychotic disorder The psychotic disorder characterized by the sudden onset of positive or disorganized symptoms that last between a day and a month and are followed by a full recovery.

Broca's aphasia A neurological condition characterized by problems producing speech.

Bulimia nervosa An eating disorder characterized by binge eating along with vomiting or other behaviors to compensate for the large number of calories ingested.

○ **C** ○

Case studies (in studies of psychopathology) A research method that focuses in detail on one individual and the factors that underlie that person's psychological disorder or disorders.

Catatonia A condition in which an individual remains in an odd posture or position, with rigid muscles, for hours.

Catatonic schizophrenia The subtype of schizophrenia characterized by stiff or "frozen" postures or poses, bizarre jerky movements, or frozen facial expression.

Cerebral cortex The outer layer of cells on the surface of the brain.

Childhood disintegrative disorder A pervasive developmental disorder characterized by normal development until at least 2 years old, followed by a profound loss of communication skills, normal types of play, and bowel control.

Civil commitment The involuntary commitment to a mental health facility of a person deemed to be at significant risk of harming himself or herself or a specific other person.

Classical conditioning A type of learning that occurs when two stimuli are paired so that a neutral stimulus becomes associated with another stimulus that elicits a reflexive behavior; also referred to as *Pavlovian conditioning*.

Client-centered therapy A humanistic therapy developed by Carl Rogers that is intended to promote personal growth so that a client can reach his or her full potential.

Clinical assessment The process of obtaining relevant information and making a judgment about mental illness based on the information.

Clinical interview A meeting between clinician and patient during which the clinician asks questions related to the patient's symptoms and functioning.

Clinical psychologist A mental health professional who has a doctoral degree that requires several years of related coursework and several years of treating patients while receiving supervision from experienced clinicians.

Cluster A personality disorders Personality disorders characterized by odd or eccentric behaviors that have elements related to those of schizophrenia.

Cluster B personality disorders Personality disorders characterized by emotional, dramatic, or erratic behaviors that involve problems with emotional regulation.

Cluster C personality disorders Personality disorders characterized by anxious or fearful behaviors.

Cognitive disorders A category of psychological disorders in which the primary symptom is significantly reduced mental abilities, relative to a prior level of functioning.

Cognitive distortions Dysfunctional, maladaptive thoughts that are not accurate reflections of reality and contribute to psychological disorders.

Cognitive rehabilitation A form of psychological treatment that is designed to strengthen cognitive abilities through extensive and focused practice; also called *neurocognitive remediation* or *cognitive mediation*.

Cognitive restructuring The process of reorganizing how a person interprets situations and events, which relies on replacing dysfunctional or irrational automatic thoughts with more rational ones.

Cognitive therapy The form of treatment that rests on the ideas that (1) mental contents influence feelings and behavior; (2) irrational thoughts and incorrect beliefs lead to psychological problems; and, (3) correcting such thoughts and beliefs will therefore lead to better mood and more adaptive behavior.

Cognitive-behavior therapy The form of treatment that combines methods from cognitive and behavior therapies.

Common factors Helpful aspects of therapy that are shared by virtually all types of psychotherapy.

Common liabilities model The model that explains how neurological, psychological, and social factors make a person vulnerable to a variety of problematic behaviors, including substance abuse and dependence; also called *problem behavior theory*.

Communication disorders A set of psychological disorders characterized by significant problems in understanding language or using language to express oneself.

Community care Programs that allow mental health care providers to visit patients in their homes at any time of the day or night; also known as *assertive community treatment*.

Comorbidity The presence of more than one disorder at the same time in a given patient.

Competency to stand trial The mental state during the time leading up to the trial that enables a defendant to participate in his or her own defense.

Complex inheritance The transmission of traits that are expressed along a continuum by the interaction of sets of genes.

Compulsions Repetitive behaviors or mental acts that a person feels driven to carry out and that usually correspond thematically to an obsession.

Computerized axial tomography (CT) A neuroimaging technique that uses X-rays to build a three-dimensional image (CT or CAT scan) of the brain.

Concordance rate The probability that both twins will have a characteristic or disorder, given that one of them has it.

Conditioned emotional responses Emotions and emotion-related behaviors that are classically conditioned.

Conditioned response (CR) A response that comes to be elicited by the previously neutral stimulus that has become a conditioned stimulus.

Conditioned stimulus (CS) A neutral stimulus that, when paired with an unconditioned stimulus, comes to elicit the reflexive behavior.

Conduct disorder A psychological disorder that typically arises in childhood and is characterized by the violation of the basic rights of others or of societal norms that are appropriate to the individual's age.

Confabulate To create stories in order to fill in gaps in memory.

Confidentiality The ethical requirement not to disclose information about a patient (even whether someone *is* a patient) to others unless legally compelled to do so.

Confounding variables (confounds) Factors that might inadvertently affect the variables of interest in an experiment.

Contingency management A procedure for modifying behavior by changing the conditions that led to, or are produced by, it.

Control group A group of participants in an experiment for which the independent variable is not manipulated, but which is otherwise treated identically to the experimental group.

Conversion disorder A somatoform disorder that involves sensory or motor symptoms that do not correspond to symptoms that arise from known medical conditions.

Correlation The relationship between the measurements made of two variables in which a change in the value of one variable is associated with a change in the value of the other variable.

Correlation coefficient A number that quantifies the strength of the correlation between two variables; the correlation coefficient is most typically symbolized by *r*.

Counseling psychologist A mental health professional who has either a Ph.D. degree from a psychology program that focuses on counseling or an Ed.D. degree from a school of education.

Criminal commitment The involuntary commitment to a mental health facility of a person charged with a crime.

Criminally responsible The determination that a defendant's crime was the product of both an *action* or attempted action (the alleged criminal behavior) and his or her *intention* to perform that action.

Crystallized intelligence A type of intelligence that relies on using knowledge to reason; such knowledge has "crystallized" from previous experience.

Culture The shared norms and values of a society that are explicitly and implicitly conveyed to its members by example and through the use of reward and punishment.

Cybertherapy Internet-based therapy.

Cyclothymic disorder A mood disorder characterized by chronic, fluctuating mood disturbance with numerous periods of hypomanic symptoms and numerous periods of depressive symptoms that do not meet the criteria for an MDE.

° **D** °

Dangerousness The legal term that refers to someone's potential to harm self or others.

Data Methodical observations, which include numerical measurements of phenomena.

Defense mechanisms Unconscious processes that work to transform psychological conflict so as to prevent unacceptable thoughts and drives from reaching consciousness.

Delirium A cognitive disorder characterized by a disturbance in consciousness and changes in cognitive functioning, particularly in attention.

Delirium tremens (DTs) The symptoms of alcohol withdrawal marked by confusion, convulsions, visual hallucinations, and fever.

Delusional disorder The psychotic disorder characterized by the presence of nonbizarre but demonstrably incorrect beliefs that have persisted for more than 1 month.

Delusions Persistent false beliefs that are held despite evidence that the beliefs are incorrect or exaggerate reality.

Dementia A set of cognitive disorders characterized by deficits in learning new information or recalling information already learned *plus* at least one other type of cognitive impairment.

Dementia due to Lewy bodies A type of progressive dementia caused by a type of protein (referred to as Lewy bodies) that builds up inside some types of neurons and can eventually cause them to die.

Dependent personality disorder A personality disorder characterized by submissive and clingy behaviors, based on fear of separation.

Dependent variable A variable that is measured and that may change its values as a result of manipulating the independent variable.

Depersonalization A dissociative symptom in which the perception or experience of self—either one's body or one's mental processes—is altered to the point of feeling like an observer, as though seeing oneself from the "outside."

Depersonalization disorder A dissociative disorder whose primary symptom is a persistent feeling of being detached from one's mental processes or body, although people who have this disorder may also experience derealization.

Derealization A dissociative symptom in which the external world is perceived or experienced as strange or unreal.

Detoxification Medically supervised withdrawal for those with substance dependence; also referred to as *detox*.

Diagnosis The identification of the nature of a disorder.

Diagnostic bias A systematic error in diagnosis.

Dialectical behavior therapy (DBT) The form of treatment that includes elements of CBT as well as an emphasis on validating the patient's experience, a Zen Buddhist approach, and a dialectics component.

Diathesis–stress model The model that proposes that a psychological disorder is triggered when a person with a predisposition—a diathesis—for the particular disorder experiences an environmental event that causes significant stress.

Disorganized schizophrenia The subtype of schizophrenia characterized by disorganized speech and behavior and inappropriate emotional expression.

Dissociation The separation of mental processes—such as perception, memory, and self-awareness—that are normally integrated.

Dissociative amnesia A dissociative disorder in which the sufferer has significantly impaired memory for important experiences or personal information that cannot be explained by ordinary forgetfulness.

Dissociative disorders A category of psychological disorders in which perception, consciousness, memory, or identity are dissociated to the point where the symptoms are pervasive, cause significant distress, and interfere with daily functioning.

Dissociative fugue A dissociative disorder that involves sudden, unplanned travel and difficulty remembering the past, which can lead patients to be confused about who they are and sometimes to take on a new identity.

Dissociative identity disorder (DID) The dissociative disorder characterized by the presence of two or more distinct *alters* (personality states or identities), each with their own characteristics and history, that take turns controlling the person's behavior.

Dizygotic twins Twins who developed from two fertilized eggs and so have the same overlap in genes (50%) as do siblings not conceived at the same time; also referred to as *fraternal twins*.

Dopamine hypothesis The view that schizophrenia arises from an overproduction of dopamine or an increase in the number or sensitivity of dopamine receptors.

Dopamine reward system The system of neurons, primarily in the nucleus accumbens and ventral tegmental area, that relies on dopamine and gives rise to pleasant feelings.

Dose-response relationship The association between more treatment (a higher dose) and greater improvement (a better response).

Double depression Having both major depressive disorder and dysthymic disorder.

Double-blind design A research design in which neither the participant nor the investigator's assistant knows the group to which specific participants have been assigned or the predicted results of the study.

Dream analysis The psychodynamic technique in which the therapist interprets the content of a patient's dreams.

Drug cues The stimuli associated with drug use that come to elicit conditioned responses through their repeated pairings with use of the drug.

Durham test The legal test in which a person is considered insane if an irresistible impulse to perform criminal behavior was due to a mental defect or disorder present at the time of the alleged crime.

Dyslexia A learning disorder characterized by difficulty with reading accuracy, speed, or comprehension that interferes with academic achievement or activities of daily functioning that involve reading.

Dyspareunia A sexual dysfunction characterized by recurrent or persistent genital pain that is associated with sexual intercourse.

Dysthymic disorder A depressive disorder that involves fewer of the symptoms of a major depressive episode, but the symptoms persist for a longer period of time.

º E º

Eating disorder not otherwise specified (EDNOS) The diagnosis given when an individual's symptoms of disordered eating cause significant distress or impair functioning but do not meet the full criteria for a diagnosis of anorexia nervosa or bulimia nervosa.

Eating disorders A category of psychological disorders characterized by abnormal eating and a preoccupation with body image.

Ego According to Freud, the psychic structure that is charged with mediating between the id's demands for immediate gratification and the superego's high standards of morality, as well as the constraints of external reality.

Electroconvulsive therapy (ECT) A procedure that causes a controlled brain seizure in an effort to reduce or eliminate the symptoms of certain psychological disorders.

Elimination disorders A set of psychological disorders characterized by inappropriate urination or defecation.

Emotion A short-lived experience evoked by a stimulus that produces a mental response, a typical behavior, and a positive or negative subjective feeling.

Encopresis An elimination disorder characterized by a child's persistent defecation in improper locations—neither in a toilet nor in a diaper.

Enuresis An elimination disorder characterized by a child's persistent urination in bed or into his or her clothes.

Epidemiology The type of correlational research that investigates the rate of occurrence, the possible causes and risk factors, and the course of diseases or disorders.

Errorless learning techniques Techniques by which patients are explicitly guided in learning a new skill rather than being allowed to figure it out through trial and error.

Etiology The factors that lead a person to develop a psychological disorder.

Executive functions Mental processes involved in planning, organizing, problem solving, abstract thinking, and exercising good judgment.

Exhibitionism A paraphilic disorder in which sexual fantasies, urges, or behaviors hinge on exposing one's genitals to a stranger, usually as a surprise.

Expansive mood A mood that involves unceasing, indiscriminate enthusiasm for interpersonal or sexual interactions or for projects.

Experimenter expectancy effect The investigator's intentionally or unintentionally treating participants in ways that encourage particular types of responses.

Experiments Research studies in which investigators intentionally manipulate one variable at a time, and measure the consequences of such manipulation on one or more other variables.

Exposure The behavioral technique that involves repeated contact with a feared or arousing stimulus in a controlled setting.

Exposure with response prevention The behavioral technique in which a patient is carefully prevented from engaging in his or her usual maladaptive response after being exposed to a stimulus that usually elicits the response.

External validity A characteristic of a study, indicating that the results generalize from the sample to the population from which it was drawn and from the conditions used in the study to relevant conditions outside the study.

Extinction The process of eliminating a behavior by not reinforcing it.

∘ F ∘

Factitious disorder A psychological disorder marked by the false reporting or inducing of medical or psychological symptoms in order to assume a "sick" role and receive attention.

Family therapy The form of treatment that involves either the family as a whole or some portion of it.

Feeding and eating disorders A set of psychological disorders characterized by problems with feeding or eating.

Female orgasmic disorder A sexual dysfunction characterized by a woman's persistent problem in progressing from normal sexual excitement to orgasm, such that orgasm is delayed or does not occur, despite a normal amount of appropriate stimulation.

Female sexual arousal disorder A sexual dysfunction marked by a woman's persistent or recurrent difficulty attaining or maintaining engorged genital blood vessels in response to adequate stimulation; formerly referred to as *frigidity*.

Fetishism A paraphilia in which the individual repeatedly uses nonliving objects to achieve or maintain sexual arousal and such an arousal pattern causes significant distress or impairs functioning.

Fight-or-flight response The automatic neurological and bodily response to a perceived threat; also called the *stress response*.

Flat affect A lack of, or considerably diminished, emotional expression, such as occurs when someone speaks robotically and shows little facial expression.

Flight of ideas Thoughts that race faster than they can be said.

Fluid intelligence A type of intelligence that relies on the ability to create new strategies to solve new problems, without relying solely on information previously learned.

Free association The psychodynamic technique in which patients report aloud their train of thought, uncensored.

Frotteurism A paraphilia characterized by recurrent, intense, sexually arousing fantasies, sexual urges, or behaviors that involve touching or rubbing against a nonconsenting person.

Functional magnetic resonance imaging (fMRI) A neuroimaging technique that uses MRI to obtain images of brain functioning, which reveal the extent to which different brain areas are activated during particular tasks.

∘ G ∘

Gateway hypothesis The proposal that use can become abuse when "entry" drugs serve as a gateway to (or the first stage in a progression to) use of "harder" drugs.

Gender identity The subjective sense of being male or female, as these categories are defined by the person's culture.

Gender identity disorder A psychological disorder characterized by a cross-gender identification that leads the individual to be chronically uncomfortable with his or her biological sex.

Gender role The outward behaviors, attitudes, and traits that a culture deems masculine or feminine.

Generalized anxiety disorder (GAD) The anxiety disorder characterized by uncontrollable worry and anxiety about a number of events or activities that are not solely the focus of another Axis I disorder.

Genes Segments of DNA that control the production of particular proteins and other substances.

Genotype The sum of an organism's genes.

Group therapy The form of treatment in which several patients with similar needs meet together with one or two therapists.

∘ H ∘

Habituation The process by which the emotional response to a stimulus that elicits fear, or anxiety is reduced by exposing the patient to the stimulus repeatedly.

Hallucinations Sensations that are so vivid that the perceived objects or events seem real, although they are not.

Heritability An estimate of how much of the variation in a characteristic within a population (in a specific environment) can be attributed to genetics.

High expressed emotion A family interaction style characterized by hostility, unnecessary criticism, or emotional overinvolvement.

Histrionic personality disorder A personality disorder characterized by attention-seeking behaviors and exaggerated and dramatic displays of emotion.

Hormones Neurotransmitter substances that are released directly into the bloodstream and often function primarily as neuromodulators.

Huntington's disease A progressive disease that kills neurons and affects cognition, emotion, and motor functions; it leads to dementia and eventually results in death.

Hypersomnia Sleeping more hours each day than normal.

Hypervigilance A heightened search for threats.

Hypoactive sexual desire disorder A sexual dysfunction characterized by a persistent or recurrent lack of sexual fantasies or an absence of desire for sexual activity.

Hypochondriasis A somatoform disorder marked by preoccupation with a fear or belief of having a serious disease, but this preoccupation arises because the individual has misinterpreted his or her bodily sensations or symptoms.

Hypothesis A preliminary idea that is proposed to answer a question about a set of observations.

Hysteria An emotional condition marked by extreme excitability and bodily symptoms for which there is no medical explanation; hysteria is not a DSM-IV-TR disorder.

∘ I ∘

Id According to Freud, the seat of sexual and aggressive drives, as well as the desire for immediate gratification of physical and psychological needs.

Identity problem A dissociative symptom in which an individual is not sure who he or she is or may assume a new identity.

Inappropriate affect An expression of emotion that is not appropriate to what a person is saying or not appropriate to the situation.

Inclusion The placement of students with disabilities in a regular classroom, with guidelines for any accommodations that the regular classroom teacher or special education teacher should make.

Independent variable A variable that a researcher manipulates.

Inpatient treatment Treatment that occurs while a patient is in a psychiatric hospital or in a psychiatric unit of a general hospital.

Internal validity A characteristic of a study, indicating that it measures what it purports to measure because it has controlled for confounds.

Interoceptive exposure The behavioral therapy method in which patients intentionally elicit the bodily sensations associated with panic so that they can habituate to those sensations and not respond with fear.

Interpersonal therapy (IPT) The form of treatment that is intended to improve the patient's skills in relationships so that they become more satisfying.

Interpretation The psychodynamic technique in which the therapist infers the unconscious meaning or motivation behind a patient's words and behaviors and shares these inferences with the patient.

In vivo exposure The behavioral therapy method that consists of direct exposure to a feared or avoided situation or stimulus.

Irresistible impulse test The legal test in which a person is considered insane if he or she knew that his or her criminal behavior was wrong but nonetheless performed it because of an irresistible impulse.

◦ L ◦

Learned helplessness The state of "giving up" that arises when an animal is in an aversive situation where it seems that no action can be effective.

Learning disorder A psychological disorder characterized by a significant disparity between an individual's academic performance and the expected level of performance based on his or her age, intelligence, and education level.

Lithium The oldest mood stabilizer; it is administered as a salt.

Longitudinal studies (in studies of psychopathology) Research studies that are designed to determine whether a given variable is a risk factor by using data collected from the same participants at various points in time.

◦ M ◦

Magnetic resonance imaging (MRI) A neuroimaging technique that creates especially sharp images of the brain by measuring the magnetic properties of atoms in the brain; MRI allows more precise diagnoses when brain abnormalities are subtle.

Magnetic resonance spectroscopy (MRS) A neuroimaging technique that uses magnetic resonance to assess levels of neurotransmitter substances in the brain.

Major depressive disorder (MDD) The mood disorder marked by five or more symptoms of an MDE lasting more than 2 weeks.

Major depressive episode (MDE) A mood episode characterized by severe depression that lasts for at least 2 weeks.

Male erectile disorder A sexual dysfunction characterized by a man's persistent or recurrent inability to attain or maintain an adequate erection until the end of sexual activity; sometimes referred to as *impotence*.

Male orgasmic disorder A sexual dysfunction characterized by a man's delay or absence of orgasm.

Malingering Intentional false reporting of symptoms or exaggeration of existing symptoms, either for material gain or to avoid unwanted events.

Managed care A type of health insurance plan that restricts access to specialized medical care by limiting benefits or reimbursement.

Manic episode A period of at least 1 week characterized by abnormal and persistent euphoria or expansive mood or irritability.

Maudsley approach A family treatment for anorexia nervosa that focuses on supporting parents as they determine how to lead their daughter to eat appropriately.

Mendelian inheritance The transmission of traits by separate elements (genes).

Mental contents The specific material that is stored in the mind and operated on by mental processes.

Mental processes The internal operations that underlie cognitive and emotional functions (such as perception, memory, and guilt feelings) and most human behavior.

Mental retardation Intelligence that is significantly below normal—an IQ approximately equal to or less than 70 (where the mean IQ is set at 100)—and that impairs daily functioning; also referred to as *intellectual disability*.

Meta-analysis A research method that statistically combines the results of a number of studies that address the same question to determine the overall effect.

M'Naghten test (or rule) The legal test in which a person is considered insane if, because of a "defect of reason, from disease of the mind," he or she did not know what he or she was doing (at the time of committing the act) and that it was wrong.

Monoamine oxidase inhibitors (MAOIs) Antidepressant medications that increase the amount of monoamine neurotransmitter in the synapse.

Monozygotic twins Twins who have basically the same genetic makeup (although it may differ in how often specific genes are repeated) because they began life as a single fertilized egg (zygote), which then divided into two embryos; also referred to as *identical twins*.

Mood A persistent emotion that is not attached to a stimulus; it exists in the background and influences mental processes, mental contents, and behavior.

Mood disorders Psychological disorders characterized by prolonged and marked disturbances in mood that affect how people feel, what they believe and expect, how they think and talk, and how they interact with others.

Mood stabilizer A category of medication that minimizes mood swings.

Moral treatment The treatment of the mentally ill that provided an environment in which people with mental illness were treated with kindness and respect and functioned as part of a community.

Motivational enhancement therapy A form of treatment specifically designed to boost a patient's motivation to decrease or stop substance use by highlighting discrepancies between stated personal goals related to substance use and current behavior; also referred to as *motivational interviewing*.

◦ N ◦

Narcissistic personality disorder A personality disorder is characterized by an inflated sense of importance, an excessive desire to be admired, and a lack of empathy.

Negative punishment The type of punishment that takes place when a behavior is followed by the removal of a pleasant or desired event or circumstance, which decreases the probability of that behavior's recurrence.

Negative reinforcement The type of reinforcement that occurs when an aversive or uncomfortable stimulus is *removed* after a behavior, which makes that behavior more likely to be produced again in the future.

Negative symptoms Symptoms of schizophrenia that are marked by the *absence* or reduction of normal mental processes, mental contents, or behaviors.

Neurofibrillary tangles The mass created by tau proteins that become twisted together and destroy the microtubules, leaving the neuron without a distribution system for nutrients.

Neuromodulators Chemicals that modulate (alter) the way neurotransmitters affect the receiving neuron. Some chemicals that act as neurotransmitters can also act as neuromodulators in certain circumstances, and vice versa.

Neurons Brain cells that process information related to physical, mental, and emotional functioning.

Neuropsychological testing The employment of assessment techniques that use behavioral responses to test items in order to draw inferences about brain functioning.

Neuropsychosocial approach The view that a psychological disorder arises from the combined influences of neurological, psychological, and social factors—which affect and are affected by one another through feedback loops.

Neurosis According to psychoanalytic theory, a pattern of thoughts, feelings, or behavior that expresses an unresolved conflict between the ego and the id or between the ego and the superego.

Neurotransmitters Chemicals that are released at the terminal buttons and cross the synaptic cleft.

○ O ○

Objectification theory The theory that girls learn to consider their bodies as objects and commodities.

Observational learning The process of learning through watching what happens to others; also referred to as *modeling*.

Obsessions Thoughts, impulses, or images that persist or recur, are intrusive—and therefore difficult to ignore—and are inappropriate to the situation.

Obsessive-compulsive disorder (OCD) The anxiety disorder characterized by one or more obsessions, which may occur together with compulsions.

Obsessive-compulsive personality disorder A personality disorder characterized by preoccupations with perfectionism, orderliness, and self-control as well as low levels of flexibility and efficiency.

Operant conditioning A type of learning in which the likelihood that a behavior will be repeated depends on the consequences associated with the behavior.

Oppositional defiant disorder A psychological disorder that typically arises in childhood or adolescence and is characterized by overt disobedience, hostility, defiance, and negativity toward people in authority.

Outpatient treatment Treatment that does not involve an overnight stay in a hospital.

○ P ○

Pain disorder A somatoform disorder that occurs when psychological factors significantly affect the onset, severity, or maintenance of significant pain.

Panic An extreme sense (or fear) of imminent doom, together with an extreme stress response.

Panic attack A specific period of intense dread, fear, or a sense of imminent doom, accompanied by physical symptoms of a pounding heart, shortness of breath, shakiness, and sweating.

Panic disorder The anxiety disorder characterized by frequent, unexpected panic attacks, along with fear of further attacks and possible restrictions of behavior in order to prevent such attacks.

Paradoxical intention A systems therapy technique in which the therapist suggests that the problem behavior be allowed to continue or even increase in intensity or frequency.

Paranoid personality disorder A personality disorder characterized by persistent and pervasive mistrust and suspiciousness, accompanied by a bias to interpret other people's motives as hostile.

Paranoid schizophrenia The subtype of schizophrenia characterized by the presence of delusions and auditory hallucinations that are limited to specific topics that have a coherent paranoid or grandiose theme.

Paraphilia A sexual disorder characterized by deviant fantasies, objects, or behaviors that play a role in sexual arousal.

Partial cases The designation given to cases in which patients have symptoms that meet only some of the necessary criteria, but not enough symptoms to meet all the criteria for the diagnosis of a disorder.

Partial hospitalization Treatment is provided at a hospital or other facility, but the patient does not sleep there.

Pedophilia A paraphilia characterized by recurrent sexually arousing fantasies, sexual urges, or behaviors involving a child who has not yet gone through puberty (typically aged 13 or younger).

Personality Enduring traits and characteristics that lead a person to behave in relatively predictable ways across a range of situations.

Personality disorders A category of psychological disorders characterized by a pattern of inflexible and maladaptive thoughts, feelings, and behaviors that arise across a range of situations and lead to distress or dysfunction.

Pervasive developmental disorders A set of developmental disorders that have in common severe deficits in communication and in social interaction skills and may also involve stereotyped behaviors and narrow interests.

Phenotype The sum of an organism's observable traits.

Phobia An exaggerated fear of an object or a situation, together with an extreme avoidance of the object or situation.

Phototherapy Treatment for depression that uses full-spectrum lights; also called *light-box therapy*.

Placebo effect A positive effect of a medically inert substance or procedure.

Polysubstance abuse A behavior pattern of abusing more than one substance.

Population The complete set of possible relevant participants.

Positive punishment The type of punishment that takes place when a behavior is followed by an undesirable consequence, which makes the behavior less likely to recur.

Positive reinforcement The type of reinforcement that occurs when a desired reinforcer is received after a behavior, which makes the behavior more likely to occur again in the future.

Positive symptoms Symptoms of schizophrenia that are marked by the *presence* of abnormal or distorted mental processes, mental contents, or behaviors.

Positron emission tomography (PET) A neuroimaging technique that measures blood flow (or energy consumption) in the brain and requires introducing a very small amount of a radioactive substance into the bloodstream.

Posttraumatic stress disorder (PTSD) The anxiety disorder that arises a month or more after a traumatic event and that involves a persistent reexperiencing of the event, avoiding stimuli related to the event, and symptoms of anxiety and hyperarousal that persist for at least a month.

Predictions Hypotheses that should be confirmed if a theory is correct.

Premature ejaculation A sexual dysfunction characterized by orgasm and ejaculation that occur earlier than the man expects, usually before, immediately during, or shortly after penetration.

Premorbid Referring to the period of time prior to a patient's illness.

Prevalence The number of people who have a disorder in a given period of time.

Prevention programs Programs that are designed to prevent or inhibit the development or progression of psychological problems or disorders.

Privileged communication Confidential information that is protected from being disclosed during legal proceedings.

Prodromal phase The phase that precedes the onset of a psychological disorder (such as schizophrenia) when symptoms do not yet meet all the criteria for the disorder.

Prodrome Early symptoms of a disorder.

Prognosis The likely course and outcome of a disorder.

Projective test A tool for personality assessment in which the patient is presented with ambiguous stimuli (such as inkblots or stick figures) and is asked to make sense of and explain them.

Psychiatric nurse A mental health professional who has an M.S.N. degree, plus a C.S. certificate in psychiatric nursing.

Psychiatrist A mental health professional who has an M.D. degree and has completed a residency that focuses on mental disorders.

Psychoactive substance A chemical that alters mental ability, mood, or behavior.

Psychoanalysis The intensive psychotherapy based on Freud's view that psychopathology arises from unconscious conflict.

Psychoanalytic theory The theory that thoughts, feelings, and behaviors are a result of conscious and unconscious forces continually interacting in the mind.

Psychodynamic therapy A form of psychotherapy based on psychoanalysis but that involves less frequent sessions, less emphasis on aggressive and sexual drives, and more attention to present experiences.

Psychoeducation The process of educating patients about research findings and therapy procedures relevant to their situation.

Psychological disorder A pattern of thoughts, feelings, or behaviors that causes significant personal *distress*, significant *impairment* in daily life, and/or significant *risk of harm*, any of which is unusual for the context and culture in which it arises.

Psychomotor agitation An inability to sit still, evidenced by pacing, hand wringing, or rubbing or pulling the skin, clothes or other objects.

Psychomotor retardation A slowing of motor functions indicated by slowed bodily movements and speech and lower volume, variety, or amount of speech.

Psychopathy A set of emotional and interpersonal characteristics marked by a lack of empathy, an unmerited feeling of high self-worth, and a refusal to accept responsibility for one's actions.

Psychopharmacology The use of medication to reduce or eradicate symptoms of psychological disorders; also the study of such treatment.

Psychosexual stages According to Freud, the sequence of five distinct stages of development (oral, anal, phallic, latency, and genital) through which children proceed from infancy to adulthood; each stage has a key task that must be completed successfully for healthy psychological development.

Psychosis An impaired ability to perceive reality to the extent that normal functioning is not possible. The two types of psychotic symptoms are hallucinations and delusions.

Punishment The process by which an event or object that is the consequence of a behavior *decreases* the likelihood that the behavior will occur again.

Purging Attempting to reduce calories that have already been consumed by vomiting or using diuretics, laxatives, or enemas.

◦ R ◦

Random assignment Assigning participants to each group in a study using a procedure that relies on chance.

Randomized clinical trial (RCT) A research design that has at least two groups—a treatment group and a control group (usually a placebo control)—to which participants are randomly assigned.

Rapid cycling (of moods) Having four or more episodes that meet the criteria for any type of mood episode within 1 year.

Rational-emotive behavior therapy (REBT) The form of treatment in which a patient's irrational thoughts are transformed into rational ones, which in turn leads to more positive emotions and adaptive behaviors.

Reactivity A behavior change that occurs when one becomes aware of being observed.

Receptors Specialized sites on dendrites and cell bodies that respond only to specific molecules.

Reframe A systems therapy technique in which the therapist offers new ways to conceive of, or frame, the family's or identified patient's problem.

Reinforcement The process by which the consequence of a behavior *increases* the likelihood of the behavior's recurrence.

Reliable Classification systems (or measures) that consistently produce the same results.

Relief craving The desire for the temporary emotional relief that can arise from using a substance.

Replication The process of repeating a study using the same data collection methods under identical or nearly identical conditions to obtain data that should have the same characteristics as those from the original study.

Residential treatment Treatment in which patients stay in a staffed facility where they sleep, eat breakfast and dinner, and perhaps take part in evening groups.

Response bias The tendency to respond in a particular way, regardless of what is being asked by the question.

Restrained eating Restricting intake of specific foods or overall number of calories.

Rett's disorder A pervasive developmental disorder that affects only females and is characterized by normal prenatal development and functioning after birth through at least 5 months of age, after which the growth of the child's head slows and she loses the ability to control normal muscle movements, interest in other people, and previously developed skills.

Reuptake The process of moving leftover neurotransmitter molecules in the synapse back into the sending neuron.

Reuptake inhibitors Medications that partially block the process by which a neurotransmitter is reabsorbed into the terminal button, thus increasing the amount of the neurotransmitter in the synaptic cleft.

Reward craving The desire for the gratifying effects of using a substance.

∘ **S** ∘

Sample The small portion of a population that is examined in a study.

Sampling bias The distortion that occurs when the participants in an experiment have not been drawn randomly from the relevant population under investigation.

Schizoaffective disorder The psychotic disorder characterized by the presence of both schizophrenia *and* a depressive, manic, or mixed mood episode.

Schizoid personality disorder A personality disorder characterized by a restricted range of emotions in social interactions and few—if any—close relationships.

Schizophrenia A psychological disorder characterized by psychotic symptoms that significantly affect emotions, behavior, and mental processes and mental contents.

Schizophreniform disorder The psychotic disorder characterized by symptoms that meet all the criteria for schizophrenia *except* that the symptoms have been present for only 1–6 months and daily functioning may or may not have declined over that period of time.

Schizotypal personality disorder A personality disorder characterized by eccentric thoughts, perceptions, and behaviors, in addition to having very few close relationships.

Scientific method The process of gathering and interpreting facts that can lead to the formulation of a new theory or the validation or refutation of an existing theory.

Seasonal affective disorder (SAD) Recurrent depression that follows a seasonal pattern.

Secondary reinforcers Objects and events that do not directly satisfy a biological need but are desirable nonetheless.

Selective serotonin reuptake inhibitors (SSRIs) Medications that slow the reuptake of serotonin from the synapse.

Sensate focus exercises A behavioral technique that is assigned as homework in sex therapy, in which an individual or couple seeks to increase awareness of pleasurable sensations that do not involve genital touching, intercourse, or orgasm.

Separation anxiety disorder A psychological disorder that typically arises in childhood and is characterized by excessive anxiety about separation from home or from someone to whom the individual has become attached.

Sex reassignment surgery The procedure in which an individual's genitals (and breasts, for biological women) are surgically altered to appear like those of the other sex.

Sexual aversion disorder A sexual dysfunction characterized by a persistent or recurrent extreme aversion to and avoidance of most genital sexual contact with a partner.

Sexual dysfunctions Sexual disorders that are characterized by problems in the sexual response cycle.

Sexual masochism A paraphilia in which the individual repeatedly becomes sexually aroused by fantasies, urges, or behaviors related to being hurt—specifically, being humiliated or made to suffer in other ways—and this arousal pattern causes significant distress or impairs functioning.

Sexual response cycle The four stages of sexual response—excitement, plateau, orgasm, and resolution—outlined by Masters and Johnson.

Sexual sadism A paraphilia characterized by recurrent sexually arousing fantasies, urges, and behaviors that inflict physical or psychological suffering on another person.

Shaping The process of reinforcing a small component of behavior at a time and then progressively adding components until the desired complex behavior occurs.

Shared psychotic disorder The psychotic disorder in which an individual develops delusions as a result of his or her close relationship with another person who has delusions as part of a psychotic disorder; also known as *folie à deux*.

Single-participant experiments Experiments with only a single participant.

Social causation The hypothesis that the daily stressors of urban life, especially as experienced by people in a lower socioeconomic level, trigger mental illness in those who are vulnerable.

Social desirability A bias toward answering questions in a way that respondents think makes them "look good" (i.e., that he or she thinks is socially desirable), even if the responses are not true.

Social phobia The anxiety disorder characterized by intense fear of public humiliation or embarrassment, together with the avoidance of social situations likely to cause this fear; also called *social anxiety disorder*.

Social selection The hypothesis that those who are mentally ill "drift" to a lower socioeconomic level because of their impairments; also referred to as *social drift*.

Social support The comfort and assistance that an individual receives through interactions with others.

Social worker A mental health professional who has an M.S.W. degree and may have had training to provide psychotherapy to help individuals and families.

Somatization disorder (SD) A somatoform disorder characterized by multiple physical symptoms that are medically unexplained and impair an individual's ability to function.

Somatoform disorders A category of psychological disorders characterized by complaints about physical well-being that cannot be entirely explained by a medical condition, substance use, or another psychological disorder.

Specific factors The characteristics of a particular treatment or technique that lead it to have unique benefits, above and beyond those conferred by common factors.

Specific phobia The anxiety disorder characterized by excessive or unreasonable anxiety or fear related to a specific situation or object.

Stages of change A series of five stages that characterizes how ready a person is to change problematic behaviors: precontemplation, contemplation, preparation, action, and maintenance.

Statistically significant The condition in which the probability of obtaining the value of a statistical test is greater than what would be expected by chance alone.

Stereotyped behaviors Repetitive behaviors—such as body rocking—that do not serve a function; also referred to as *stereotypies*.

Stimulus control The behavioral technique for changing the frequency of a maladaptive conditioned response by controlling the frequency or intensity of exposure to the stimulus that elicits the response.

Stimulus generalization The process whereby responses come to be elicited by stimuli that are similar to the conditioned stimulus.

Stroke The interruption of normal blood flow to or within the brain, which results in neuronal death.

Substance abuse A pattern of use of a psychoactive substance that leads to harm or other adverse effects.

Substance dependence The persistent and compulsive use of a psychoactive substance, despite its negative effects on work, relationships, health, or its legal consequences.

Substance intoxication The reversible dysfunctional effects on thoughts, feelings, and behavior that arise from the use of a psychoactive substance.

Substance use disorders Psychological disorders characterized by abuse of or dependence on psychoactive substances.

Subthreshold cases The designation given to cases in which patients have symptoms that fit all the necessary criteria, but at levels lower than required for the diagnosis of a disorder.

Suicidal ideation Thoughts of suicide.

Superego According to Freud, the seat of the conscience, which works to impose morality.

Synapse The place where the tip of the axon of one neuron sends signals to another neuron.

Systematic desensitization The behavioral technique of learning to relax in the presence of a feared stimulus.

Systems therapy The form of treatment that is designed to change the communication or behavior patterns of one or more family members in the context of the family as a whole; also known as *family systems therapy*.

∘ T ∘

Tarasoff rule A ruling by the Supreme Court of California (and later other courts) that psychologists have a duty to protect potential victims who are in imminent danger.

Tardive dyskinesia An enduring side effect of traditional antipsychotic medications that produces involuntary lip smacking and odd facial contortions as well as other movement-related symptoms.

Temperament The various aspects of personality that reflect a person's typical emotional state and emotional reactivity (including the speed and strength of reactions to stimuli).

Teratogens Substances or other stimuli that are harmful to a fetus.

Theory A principle or set of principles that explains a set of data.

Theory of mind A theory about other people's mental states (their beliefs, desires, and feelings) that allows a person to predict how other people will react in a given situation.

Therapeutic alliance The positive relationship between the therapist and the patient.

Tic disorders A set of disorders characterized by persistent tics (motor or vocal) that occur many times a day on most days.

Token economy A treatment program that uses "tokens" or chits as secondary reinforcers to change behavior.

Tolerance The physiological response that arises from repeated use of a substance such that more of it is required to obtain the same effect.

Tourette's disorder A tic disorder characterized by recurrent motoric and vocal tics; also referred to as *Tourette syndrome*.

Transcranial magnetic stimulation (TMS) A procedure that sends sequences of short, strong magnetic pulses into the cerebral cortex via a coil placed on the scalp.

Transference The psychodynamic process by which patients interact with the therapist in the same manner that they did with their parents or other important figures in their lives.

Transvestic fetishism A paraphilia in which a heterosexual man cross-dresses in women's clothes for sexual arousal and experiences distress or impaired functioning because of the cross-dressing; formerly called *transvestism*.

Treatment (for psychological disorders) The use of a procedure or substance to reduce or eliminate psychological problems or symptoms of psychological disorders and/or improve quality of life.

Tricyclic antidepressants (TCAs) Older antidepressants named after the three rings of atoms in their molecular structure.

∘ U ∘

Unconditioned response (UCR) A behavior that is reflexively elicited by a stimulus.

Unconditioned stimulus (UCS) A stimulus that reflexively elicits a behavior.

Undifferentiated schizophrenia The subtype of schizophrenia characterized by symptoms that do not completely match those specified for the paranoid, disorganized, or catatonic subtype.

∘ V ∘

Vaginismus A sexual dysfunction in females in which recurrent or persistent involuntary spasms of the musculature of the outer third of the vagina interfere with sexual intercourse.

Valid Classification systems (or measures) that actually characterize what they are supposed to characterize.

Validate A systems therapy technique by which the therapist demonstrates an understanding of each family member's feelings and desires.

Vascular dementia A type of dementia caused by reduced or blocked blood supply to the brain, which arises from plaque buildup or blood clots.

Vegetative signs (of depression) Psychomotor symptoms as well as changes in appetite, weight, and sleep.

Voyeurism A paraphilia characterized by sexual fantasies, urges, or behaviors that involve observing someone who is in the process of undressing, is nude, or is engaged in sexual activity, when the person being observed has neither consented to nor is aware of being observed.

∘ W ∘

Wernicke's aphasia A neurological condition characterized by problems comprehending language and producing meaningful utterances.

Withdrawal The set of symptoms that arises when a regular user decreases or stops intake of an abused substance.

Word salad Disorganized speech consisting of a random stream of seemingly unconnected words.

Abbott, C., Bustillo, J. (2006). What have we learned from proton magnetic resonance spectroscopy about schizophrenia? A critical update. *Current Opinion in Psychiatry, 19,* 135–139.

Abbott, M. J., & Rapee, R. M. (2004). Post-event rumination and negative self-appraisal in social phobia before and after treatment. *Journal of Abnormal Psychology, 113,* 136–144.

Abel, G. G., Becker, J. V., Mittelman, M., Cunningham-Rathner, J., Rouleau, J. L., & Murphy, W. D. (1987). Self-reported sex crimes of nonincarcerated paraphiliacs. *Journal of Interpersonal Violence, 2,* 3–25.

Abouesh, A., & Clayton, A. (1999). Compulsive voyeurism and exhibitionism: A clinical response to paroxetine. *Archives of Sexual Behavior, 28,* 23–30.

Abraham, S. F., Brown, T., Boyd, C., Luscombe, G., & Russell, J. (2006). Quality of life: Eating disorders. *Australian and New Zealand Journal of Psychiatry, 40,* 150–155.

Abramowitz, J. S. (1997). Effectiveness of psychological and pharmacological treatments for obsessive-compulsive disorder: A quantitative review. *Journal of Consulting and Clinical Psychology, 65,* 44–52.

Abramowitz, J. S., & Braddock, A. E. (2006). Hypochondriasis: Conceptualization, treatment, and relationship to obsessive-compulsive disorder. *Psychiatric Clinics of North America, 29,* 503–519.

Abrams, K., Rassovsky, Y., & Kushner, M. G. (2006). Evidence for respiratory and nonrespiratory subtypes in panic disorder. *Depression and Anxiety, 23,* 474–481.

Abramson, L. Y., Alloy, L. B., Hogan, M. E., Whitehouse, W. G., Donovan, P., Rose, D. T., et al. (1999). Cognitive vulnerability to depression: Theory and evidence. *Journal of Cognitive Psychotherapy, 13,* 5–20.

Abramson, L. Y., Metalsky, G. I., & Alloy, L. B. (1989). Hopelessness depression: A theory-based subtype of depression. *Psychological Review, 96,* 358–372.

Abramson, L. Y., Seligman, M. E., & Teasdale, J. D. (1978). Learned helplessness in humans: Critique and reformulation. *Journal of Abnormal Psychology, 87,* 49–74.

Abreu, J. M. (1999). Conscious and nonconscious African American stereotypes: Impact on first impression and diagnostic ratings by therapists. *Journal of Consulting and Clinical Psychology, 67,* 387–393.

Achenbach, T. M. (2008). Multicultural perspectives on developmental psychopathology. In J. J. Hudziak (Ed.), *Developmental psychopathology and wellness: Genetic and environmental influences* (pp. 23–47). Arlington, VA: American Psychiatric Publishing.

Achenbach, T. M., Krukowski, R. A., Dumenci, L., & Ivanova, M. Y. (2005). Assessment of adult psychopathology: Meta-analyses and implications of cross-informant correlations. *Psychological Bulletin, 131,* 361–382.

Achenbach, T. M., McConaughy, S. H., & Howell, C. T. (1987). Child/adolescent behavioral and emotional problems: Implications of cross-informant correlations for situational specificity. *Psychological Bulletin, 101,* 213–232.

Acheson, D. T., Forsyth, J. P., Prenoveau, J. M., & Bouton, M. E. (2007). Interoceptive fear conditioning as a learning model of panic disorder: An experimental evaluation using 20% CO_2-enriched air in a non-clinical sample. *Behaviour Research and Therapy, 45,* 2280–2294.

Ackerman, N.J. (1980). The family with adolescents. In E.A. Carter & M. McGoldrick (Eds.), *The family life cycle* (p. 181). New York: Gardner Press.

Adams, H. E., Bernat, J. A., & Luscher, K. A. (2001). Borderline personality disorder: An overview. In P. B. Sutker & H. E. Adams (Eds.), *Comprehensive handbook of psychopathology* (3rd ed., pp. 491–507). New York: Kluwer Academic/Plenum.

Adamec, R., Holmes, A., & Blundell, J. (2008). Vulnerability to lasting anxiogenic effects of brief exposure to predator stimuli: sex, serotonin and other factors—relevance to PTSD. *Neuroscience and Biobehavioural Reviews, 32,* 1287–1292.

Addolorato, G., Taranto, C., De Rossi, G., & Gasbarrini, G. (1997). Neuroimaging of cerebral and cerebellar atrophy in anorexia nervosa. *Psychiatry Research: Neuroimaging, 76,* 139–141.

Adewuya, A. O. (2006). Early postpartum mood as a risk factor for postnatal depression in Nigerian women. *American Journal of Psychiatry, 163,* 1435–1437.

Adityanjee, Raju, G. S., & Khandelwal, S. K. (1989). Current status of multiple personality disorder in India. *American Journal of Psychiatry, 146,* 1607–1610.

Adler, C. M., McDonough-Ryan, P., Sax, K. W., Holland, S. K., Arndt, S., & Strakowski, S. M. (2000). fMRI of neuronal activation with symptom provocation in unmedicated patients with obsessive compulsive disorder. *Journal of Psychiatric Research, 34,* 317–324.

Adler, D. A., McLaughlin, T. J., Rogers, W. H., Chang, H., Lapitsky, L., & Lerner, D. (2006). Job performance deficits due to depression. *American Journal of Psychiatry, 163,* 1569–1576.

Adler, N. E., Epel, E. S., Castellazzo, G., & Ickovics, J. R. (2000). Relationship of subjective and objective social status with psychological and physiological functioning: Preliminary data in healthy white women. *Health Psychology, 19,* 586–592.

Adson, D. E., Mitchell, J. E., & Trenkner, S. W. (1997). The superior mesenteric artery syndrome and acute gastric dilatation in eating disorders: A report of two cases and a review of the literature. *International Journal of Eating Disorders, 21,* 103–114.

Afifi, T. O., Brownridge, D. A., Cox, B. J., & Sareen, J. (2006). Physical punishment, childhood abuse and psychiatric disorders. *Child Abuse & Neglect, 30,* 1093–1103.

Agency for Health Care Policy and Research. (1999). *Newer antidepressant drugs are equally as effective as older-generation drug treatments, research shows.* AHCPR Pub. No. 99-E013. Rockville, MD: Author.

Agency for Health Care Policy and Research. (2002). *S-adenosyl-L-methionine for treatment of depression, osteoarthritis, and liver disease.* AHRQ Publication No. 02-E033, August 2002. Rockville, MD: Author. Retrieved October 24, 2008, from http://www.ahrq.gov/clinic/epcsums/samesum.htm

Agerbo, E., Gunnell, D., Bonde, J. P., Mortensen, P. B., & Nordentoft, M. (2007). Suicide and occupation: The impact of socio-economic, demographic and psychiatric differences. *Psychological Medicine, 37,* 1131–1140.

Aghajanian, G. K., & Marek, G. J. (2000). Serotonin model of schizophrenia: Emerging role of glutamate mechanisms. *Brain Research Reviews, 31,* 302–312.

Aghevli, M. A., Blanchard, J. J., & Horan, W. P. (2003). The expression and experience of emotion in schizophrenia: A study of social interactions. *Psychiatry Research, 119,* 261–270.

Agliata, A. K., Tantleff-Dunn, S., & Renk, K. (2007). Interpretation of teasing during early adolescence. *Journal of Clinical Psychology, 63,* 23–30.

Agosti, V., & Levin, F. R. (2006). The effects of alcohol and drug dependence on the course of depression. *The American Journal on Addictions, 15,* 71–75.

Agras, W. S. (2001). The consequences and costs of the eating disorders. *Psychiatric Clinics of North America, 24,* 371–379.

Agras, W. S., & Apple, R. F. (1997). *Overcoming eating disorders—therapist guide.* Graywind/The Psychological Corporation.

Agras, W. S., & Apple, R. F. (2008). *Overcoming Eating Disorders- Therapist Guide.* 2nd edition. New York: Oxford University Press.

Agras, W. S., Crow, S. J., Halmi, K. A., Mitchell, J. E., Wilson, G. T., & Kraemer, H. C. (2000). Outcome predictors for the cognitive behavior treatment of bulimia nervosa: Data from a multisite study. *American Journal of Psychiatry, 157,* 1302–1308.

Agras, W. S., Walsh, B. T., Fairburn, C. G., Wilson, G. T., & Kraemer, H. C. (2000). A multicenter comparison of cognitive-behavioral therapy and interpersonal psychotherapy. *Archives of General Psychiatry, 54,* 459–465.

Agrawal, A., Neale, M. C., Prescott, C. A., & Kendler, K. S. (2004). A twin study of early cannabis use and subsequent use and abuse/dependence of other illicit drugs. *Psychological Medicine, 34,* 1227–1237.

Aikens, J. E., Nease Jr., D. E., & Klinkman, M. S. (2008). Explaining patients' beliefs about the necessity and harmfulness of antidepressants. *Annals of Family Medicine, 6,* 23–29.

Ainsworth, M. (1989), Attachments beyond infancy. *American Psychologist, 44,* 709–716.

Ainsworth, M. D. S., & Bell, S. M. (1970). Attachment, exploration, and separation: Illustrated by the behavior of one-year-olds in a strange situation. *Child Development, 41,* 49–67.

Ainsworth, M. D. S., Blehar, M. C., Waters, E., & Wall, S. (1978). *Patterns of attachment: A psychological study of the strange situation.* Hillsdale, NJ: Lawrence Erlbaum.

Ait-Daoud, N., Dameron, Z. C., III, Marzani-Nissen, G. R., Wells, L. T., & Johnson, B. A. (2006). Glutaminergic agents for the treatment of alcohol and substance abuse disorders. *Primary Psychiatry, 13,* 56–64.

Akins, C. K. (2004). The role of Pavlovian conditioning in sexual behavior: A comparative analysis of human and nonhuman animals. *International Journal of Comparative Psychology, 17,* 241–262.

Akiskal, H. S. (1996). The prevalent clinical spectrum of bipolar disorders: Beyond DSM-IV. *Journal of Clinical Psychopharmacology, 16*(Suppl. 1), 4S–14S.

Akiskal, H. S. (2003). Validating "hard" and "soft" phenotypes within the bipolar spectrum: Continuity or discontinuity? *Journal of Affective Disorder, 73,* 1–5.

Albert, U., Maina, G., Forner, F., & Bogetto, F. (2004). DSM-IV-TR obsessive-compulsive personality disorder: Prevalence in patients with anxiety disorders and in healthy comparison subjects. *Comprehensive Psychiatry, 45,* 325–332.

Albertini, R. S., & Phillips, K. A. (1999). Thirty-three cases of body dysmorphic disorder in children and adolescents. *Journal of the American Academy of Child & Adolescent Psychiatry, 38,* 453–459.

Alegría, M., Canino, G., Shrout, P. E., Woo, M., Duan, N., Vila, D., et al. (2008). Prevalence of mental illness in immigrant and non-immigrant U.S. Latino groups. *American Journal of Psychiatry, 165,* 359–369.

Alegría, M., Woo, M., Cao, Z., Torres, M., Meng, X., & Striegel-Moore, R. (2007). Prevalence and correlates of eating disorders in Latinos in the United States. *International Journal of Eating Disorders, 40,* S15–S21.

Alexander, F., & French, T. M. (1946). *Psychoanalytic therapy: Principles and application.* Oxford, England: Ronald Press.

Alexander, W. (1996). Strong relationship found between schizophrenia, mood disorders. *Psychiatric Times, 13,* n.p.

Alford, G. S., & Karns, L. (2000). Psychosis. In A. E. Kazdin (Ed.), *Encyclopedia of psychology* (Vol. 6, pp. 452–456). Washington, DC: American Psychological Association.

Allen, J. G., Console, D. A., & Lewis, L. (1999). Dissociative detachment and memory impairment: Reversible amnesia or encoding failure? *Comparative Psychiatry, 40,* 160–171.

Allen, J. J., & Movius, H. L., II (2000). The objective assessment of amnesia in dissociative identity disorder using event-related potentials. *International Journal of Psychophysiology, 38,* 21–41.

Allen, L. A., Woolfolk, R. L., Escobar, J. I., Gara, M. A., & Hamer, R. M. (2006). Cognitive-behavioral therapy for somatization disorder: A randomized controlled trial. *Archives of Internal Medicine, 166,* 1512–1518.

Allison, P. D., & Furstenberg, F. F., Jr. (1989). How marital dissolution affects children: Variations by age and sex. *Developmental Psychology, 25,* 540–549.

Alloy, L. B., & Abramson, L. Y. (2007). The adolescent surge in depression and emergence of gender differences: A biocognitive vulnerability-stress model in developmental context. In D. Romer & E. Walker (Eds.), *Adolescent psychopathology and the developing brain: Integrating brain and prevention science* (pp. 284–312). New York: Oxford University Press.

Alloy, L. B., Reilly-Harrington, N., Fresco, D. M., Whitehouse, W. G., & Zechmeister, J. S. (1999). Cognitive styles and life events in subsyndromal unipolar and bipolar disorders: Stability and prospective prediction of depressive and hypomanic mood swings. *Journal of Cognitive Psychotherapy, 13,* 21–40.

Allyne, R. (2007, October 31). Man who had sex with bike in court. Telegraph. Retrieved on April 17, 2009 from http://www.telegraph.co.uk/news/uknews/1567410/Man-who-had-sex-with-bike-in-court.html

Alonso, P., Pujol, J., Cardoner, N., Benlloch, L., Deus, J., Menchon, et al. (2001). Right prefrontal repetitive transcranial magnetic stimulation in obsessive-compulsive disorder: A double-blind, placebo-controlled study. *American Journal of Psychiatry, 158,* 1143–1145.

Althof, S. E. (2000). Erectile dysfunction: Psychotherapy with men and couples. In S. R. Leiblum & R. C. Rosen (Eds.), *Principles and practice of sex therapy* (3rd ed., pp. 242–275). New York: Guilford Press.

Althof, S. E., O'Leary, M. P., Cappelleri, J. C., Glina, S., King, R., Tseng, L., et al. (U.S. and International SEAR study group). (2006). Self-esteem, confidence, and relationships in men treated with sildenafil citrate for erectile dysfunction. *Journal of General Internal Medicine, 21,* 1069–1074.

Altshuler, L., Bookheimer, S., Proenza, M. A., Townsend, J., Sabb, F., Firestine, A., et al. (2005). Increased amygdala activation during mania: A functional magnetic resonance imaging study. *American Journal of Psychiatry, 162,* 1211–1213.

Altshuler, L. L., Bartzokis, G., Grieder, T., Curran, J., & Mintz, J. (1998). Amygdala enlargement in bipolar disorder and hippocampal reduction in schizophrenia: An MRI study demonstrating neuroanatomic specificity. *Archives of General Psychiatry, 55,* 663–664.

Altshuler, L. L., Bauer, M., Frye, M. A., Gitlin, M. J., Mintz, J., Szuba, M. P., et al. (2001). Does thyroid supplementation accelerate tricyclic antidepressant response? A review and meta-analysis of the literature. *American Journal of Psychiatry, 158,* 1617–1622.

Alvarez, L. (2008, July 8). After the battle, fighting the bottle at home. *New York Times.* Retrieved November 12, 2008, from http://www.nytimes.com/2008/07/08/us/08vets.html?sq=ptsd%20AND%20Afghanistan%20AND%20iraq&st=nyt&scp=1&pagewanted=all

Alvidrez, J., Azocar, F., & Miranda, J. (1996). Demystifying the concept of ethnicity for psychotherapy research. *Journal of Consulting and Clinical Psychology, 64,* 903–908.

Alzheimer's Association. (2007). *Alzheimer's disease facts and figures 2007.* Retrieved December 2, 2007, from http://www.alz.org/national/documents/report_alzfactsfigures2007.pdf

Amador, X. F., & Gorman, J. M. (1998). Psychopathologic domains and insight in schizophrenia. *Psychiatric Clinics of North America, 21,* 27–42.

Amador, X. F., Strauss, D. H., Yale, S. A., & Gorman, J. M. (1991). Awareness of illness in schizophrenia. *Schizophrenia Bulletin, 17,* 113–132.

Amass, L., Ling, W., Freese, T. E., Reiber, C., Annon, J. J., Cohen, A. J., et al. (2004). Bringing buprenorphine-naloxone detoxification to community treatment providers: The NIDA Clinical Trials Network Field Experience. *American Journal on Addictions, 13*, S42–S66.

Amat, J., Matus-Amat, P., Watkins, L. R., & Maier, S. F. (1998). Escapable and inescapable stress differentially and selectively alter extracellular levels of 5-HT in the ventral hippocampus and dorsal periaqueductal gray of the rat. *Brain Research, 797*, 12–22.

Amat, J., Sparks, P. D., Matus-Amat, P., Griggs, J., Watkins, L. R., & Maier, S. F. (2001). The role of habenular complex in the elevation of dorsal raphe nucleus serotonin and the changes in the behavioral responses produced by uncontrollable stress. *Brain Research, 917*, 118–126.

American Association of Geriatric Psychiatry. (2006). *American Journal of Geriatric Psychiatry, 14*, 561–572. Retrieved December 4, 2007, from http://www.aagponline.org/prof/position_caredmnalz..asp

American Psychiatric Association Work Group on Suicidal Behaviors (Jacobs, D. G., Baldessarini, R. J., Conwell, Y., Fawcett, J. A., Horton, L., Meltzer, H., Pfeffer, C. R., & Simon, R. I.). (2003). Practice guideline for the assessment and treatment of patients with suicidal behaviors. *American Journal of Psychiatry, 160*(Suppl.), 1–60.

American Psychiatric Association. (1952). *Diagnostic and Statistical Manual of Mental Disorders.* Washington, DC: Author.

American Psychiatric Association. (2000). *Diagnostic and statistical manual of mental disorders* (4th ed., text revision). Washington, DC: Author.

American Psychological Association, Working Group on the Older Adult. (1998). What practitioners should know about working with older adults. *Professional Psychology: Research and Practice, 29*, 413–427.

American Psychological Association. (2002). *Ethical principles of psychologists and code of conduct.* Retrieved September 9, 2008, from http://www.apa.org/ethics/code2002.pdf

Amir, R. E., Van den Veyver, I. B., Wan, M., Tran, C. Q., Francke, U., & Zoghbi, H. (1999). Rett syndrome is caused by mutations in X-linked MECP2, encoding methyl CpG binding protein 2. *Nature Genetics, 23*, 185–188.

Anastasi, A. (1988). *Psychological testing* (6th ed.). New York: Macmillan.

Andersen, A. E., & DiDomenico, L. (1992). Diet vs. shape content of popular male and female magazines: A dose-response relationship to the incidence of eating

disorders? *International Journal of Eating Disorders, 11*, 283–287.

Andersen, A. E., & Hay, A. (1985). Racial and socioeconomic influences in anorexia nervosa and bulimia. *International Journal of Eating Disorders, 4*, 479–487.

Andersen, A. E., Bowers, W. A., & Watson, T. (2001). A slimming program for eating disorders not otherwise specified: Reconceptualizing a confusing, residual diagnostic category. *Psychiatric Clinics of North America, 24*, 271–280.

Andersen, B. L., Anderson, B., & DeProsse, C. (1989). Controlled prospective longitudinal study of women with cancer: I. Sexual functioning outcomes. *Journal of Consulting and Clinical Psychology, 57*, 683–691.

Anderson, I. M. (2000). Selective serotonin reuptake inhibitors versus tricyclic antidepressants: A meta-analysis of efficacy and tolerability. *Journal of Affective Disorders, 58*, 19–36.

Anderson, P. L., Zimand, E., Hodges, L. F., & Rothbaum, B. O. (2005). Cognitive behavioral therapy for public-speaking anxiety using virtual reality for exposure. *Depression and Anxiety, 22*, 156–158.

Andersson, G., Carlbring, P., Holmström, A., Sparthan, E., Furmark, T., Nilsson-Ihrfelt, E., et al. (2006). Internet-based self-help with therapist feedback and in vivo group exposure for social phobia: A randomized controlled trial. *Journal of Consulting and Clinical Psychology, 74*, 677–686.

Andreasen, N. C. (1979). Thought, language, and communication disorders: Clinical assessment, definition of terms, and assessment of their reliability. *Archives of General Psychiatry 36*, 1315–1321.

Andreasen, N. C. (2001). *Brave new brain: Conquering mental illness in the era of the genome.* New York: Oxford University Press.

Andreasen, N. C., Arndt, S., Swayze, V., Cizadlo, T., Flaum, M., O'Leary, D., et al. (1994). Thalamic abnormalities in schizophrenia visualized through magnetic resonance image averaging. *Science, 266*, 294–298.

Andreasen, N. C., Nopoulos, P., O'Leary, D. S., Miller, D. D., Wassink, T., & Flaum, M. (1999). Defining the phenotype of schizophrenia: Cognitive dysmetria and its neural mechanisms. *Biological Psychiatry, 46*, 908–920.

Andrews, J. A., Hops, H., Ary, D., Lichtenstein, E., & Tildesley, E. (1991). The construction, validation and use of the Guttman scale of adolescent substance use: An investigation of family relationships. *Journal of Drug Issues, 21*, 557–572.

Andrews, J., Wang, L., Csernansky, J. G., Gado, M. H., & Barch, D. M. (2006).

Abnormalities of thalamic activation and cognition in schizophrenia. *American Journal of Psychiatry, 163*, 463–469.

Andrews-Hanna, J. R., Snyder, A. Z., Vincent, J. L., Lustig, C., Head, D., Raichle, M. E., et al. (2007). Disruption of large-scale brain systems in advanced aging. *Neuron, 56*, 924–935.

Angermeyer, M. C. (2000). Schizophrenia and violence. *Acta Psychiatrica Scandinavica, 102*, 63–67.

Angst, J. (1998). The emerging epidemiology of hypomania and bipolar II disorder. *Journal of Affective Disorders, 50*, 143–151.

Angst, J. (1999). Major depression in 1998: Are we providing optimal therapy? *Journal of Clinical Psychiatry, 60*, 5–9.

Angst, J., Angst, F., & Stassen H. H. (1999). Suicide risk in patients with major depressive disorder. *Journal of Clinical Psychiatry, 60*(Suppl 2), 57–62.

Angst, J., Gamma, A., Benazzi, B., Ajdacica, V., Eich, D., & Rössler, W. (2003). Toward a re-definition of subthreshold bipolarity: Epidemiology and proposed criteria for bipolar-II, minor bipolar disorders and hypomania. *Journal of Affective Disorders, 73*, 133–146.

Angst, J., Gamma, A., Gastpar, M., Lépine, J.-P., Mendlewicz, J., & Tylee, A. (2002). Gender differences in depression: Epidemiological findings from the European DEPRES I and II studies. *European Archives of Psychiatry and Clinical Neuroscience, 252*, 201–209.

Anonymous (2003, August 16). Commentary. *British Medical Journal, 327*, 382–383.

Ansbacher, H. L., & Ansbacher, R. R. (Eds.). (1956). *The individual psychology of Alfred Adler: A systematic presentation of selections from his writings.* New York: Basic Books.

Ansseau, M., Fischler, B., Dierick, M., Mignon, A., & Leyman, S. (2005). Prevalence and impact of generalized anxiety disorder and major depression in primary care in Belgium and Luxemburg: The GADIS study. *European Psychiatry, 20*, 229–235.

Antonuccio, D. O., Burns, D., Danton, W. G., & O'Donohue, W. (2000). The rumble in Reno: The psychosocial perspective on depression. *Psychiatric Times, 17*, 24–28. http://www.mhsource.com/pt/p000824.html.

Antonuccio, D. O., Burns, D. D., & Danton, W. G. (2002). Antidepressants: A triumph of marketing over science? *Prevention & Treatment, 5*, Article 25. http://www.journals.apa.org/prevention/volume5/pre0050025c.html

Antonuccio, D. O., Danton, W. G., & DeNelsky, G. Y. (1995). Psychotherapy versus medication for depression: Challenging the conventional wisdom with data. *Professional Psychology: Research & Practice, 26,* 574–585.

Antony, M. M., & Barlow, D. H. (Eds.). (2002). *Handbook of assessment and treatment planning for psychological disorders.* New York: Guilford Press.

Antony, M. M., & Swinson, R. P. (1998). *When perfect isn't good enough: Strategies for coping with perfectionism.* Oakland, CA: New Harbinger.

Antony, M. M., & Swinson, R. P. (2000). *The shyness & social anxiety workbook: Proven techniques for overcoming your fears.* Oakland, CA: New Harbinger.

Antony, M. M., & Swinson, R. P. (2000). *The shyness and social anxiety workbook.* Oakland, CA: New Harbinger Publications.

Antony, M. M., & Swinson, R. P. (2000a). Specific phobia. In M. M. Antony & R. P. Swinson (Eds.), *Phobic disorders and panic in adults: A guide to assessment and treatment* (pp. 79–104). Washington, DC: American Psychological Association.

Antony, M. M., Craske, M. G., & Barlow, D. H. (1995). *Mastery of your specific phobia.* New York: Graywind Publications.

Anxiety Disorders Association of America. Retrieved September 23, 2002, from http://www.adaa.org/GettingHelp/Articles/ShirlyB.asp

Apfelbaum, B. (1989). Retarded ejaculation: A much-misunderstood syndrome. In S. R., Leiblum & R. C. Rosen (Eds.), *Principles and practice of sex therapy: Update for the 1990s* (2nd ed., pp. 168–206). New York: Guilford Press.

Apfelbaum, B. (2000). Retarded ejaculation: A much misunderstood syndrome. In S. R. Leiblum & R. C. Rosen (Eds.), *Principles and practice of sex therapy* (3rd ed., pp. 205–241). New York: Guilford Press.

Apfelbaum, B. (2001). What the sex therapies tell us about sex. In P. J. Kleinplatz (Ed.), *New directions in sex therapy: Innovations and alternatives.* (pp. 5–28). Philadelphia: Taylor and Rutledge.

Appelbaum, P. S. (2002). Privacy in psychiatric treatment: Threats and responses. *American Journal of Psychiatry, 159,* 1809–1818.

Appelbaum, P. S., & Grisso, T. (1995). The MacArthur Treatment Competence Study: I. Mental illness and competence to consent to treatment. *Law and Human Behavior, 19,* 105–126.

Apple, R. F. (1999). Interpersonal therapy for bulimia nervosa. *Journal of Clinical Psychology, 55,* 715–725.

Arana, G. W., & Rosenbaum, J. F. (2000). *Handbook of psychiatric drug therapy.* Philadelphia: Lippincott Williams & Wilkins.

Arcia, E., Sánchez-LaCay, A., & Fernández, M. C. (2002). When worlds collide: Dominican mothers and their Latina clinicians. *Transcultural Psychiatry, 39,* 74–96.

Arnold, S. E., Hyman, B. T., Van Hoesen, G. W., & Damasio, A. R. (1991). Some cytoarchitectural abnormalities of the entorhinal cortex in schizophrenia. *Archives of General Psychiatry, 48,* 625–632.

Arnsten, A. F. (2006). Fundamentals of attention-deficit/hyperactivity disorder: Circuits and pathways. *Journal of Clinical Psychiatry, 67*(Suppl. 8), 7–12.

Aronson, S. C., Black, J. E., McDougle, C. J., Scanley B. E., Heninger, G. R., Price, L. H., et al. (1995). Serotonergic mechanisms of cocaine effects in humans. *Psychopharmacology, 119,* 179–185.

Arriaza, C. A., & Mann, T. (2001). Ethnic differences in eating disorder symptoms among college students: The confounding role of body mass index. *Journal of American College Health, 49,* 309–315.

Arroll, B., Macgillivray, S., Ogston, S., Reid, I., Sullivan, F., Williams, B., et al. (2005). Efficacy and tolerability of tricyclic antidepressants and SSRIs compared with placebo for treatment of depression in primary care: A meta-analysis. *Annals of Family Medicine, 3,* 449–456.

Arseneault, L., Cannon, M., Poulton, R., Murray, R., Caspi, A., & Moffitt, T. E. (2002). Cannabis use in adolescence and risk for adult psychosis: Longitudinal prospective study. *British Medical Journal, 325,* 1195–1199.

Arseneault, L., Milne, B. J., Taylor, A., Adams, F., Delgado, K., Caspi, A., et al. (2008). Being bullied as an environmentally mediated contributing factor to children's internalizing problems: A study of twins discordant for victimization. *Archives of Pediatric Adolescent Medicine, 162,* 145–150.

Artaloytia, J. F., Arango, C., Lahti, A., Sanz, J., Pascual, A., Cubero, P., et al. (2006). Negative signs and symptoms secondary to antipsychotics: A double-blind, randomized trial of a single dose of placebo, haloperidol, and risperidone in healthy volunteers. *American Journal of Psychiatry, 163,* 488–493.

Asmundson, G. J. G., & Stein, M. B. (1994). Triggering the false suffocation alarm in panic disorder patients by using a voluntary breath-holding procedure. *American Journal of Psychiatry, 151,* 264–266.

Associated Press. (2006). Autistic hoops star going Hollywood. *MSNBC,* March 2. Retrieved December 30, 2006, from http://www.msnbc.msn.com/id/11526448/

Ataoglu, A., Ozcetin, A., Icmeli, C., & Ozbulut, O. (2003). Paradoxical therapy in conversion reaction. *Journal of Korean Medical Science, 18,* 581–584.

Atladóttir, H. O. (2007). Time trends in reported diagnoses of childhood neuropsychiatric disorders: A Danish cohort study. *Archives of Pediatric and Adolescent Medicine, 161,* 193–198.

Atri, A., Shaughnessy, L. W., Locascio, J. J., & Growdon, J. H. (2008). Long-term course and effectiveness of combination therapy in Alzheimer disease. *Alzheimer Disease & Associated Disorders, 22,* 209–221

August, G. J., Bloomquist, M. L., Realmuto, G. M., & Hektner, J. M. (2007). The Early Risers "Skills for Success" Program: A targeted intervention for preventing conduct problems and substance abuse in aggressive elementary school children. In P. Tolan, J. Szapocznik, & S. Sambrano (Eds.), *Preventing youth substance abuse: Science-based programs for children and adolescents* (pp. 137–158). Washington, DC: American Psychological Association.

Aursnes, I., Tvete, I. F., Gaasemyr, J., & Natvig, B. (2005). Suicide attempts in clinical trials with paroxetine randomized against placebo. *BMC Medicine, 3,* 3–14.

Austin, A. M., Macgowan, M. J., & Wagner, E. F. (2005). Effective family-based interventions for adolescents with substance use problems: A systematic review. *Research on Social Work Practice, 15,* 67–83.

Auyeung, B., Baron-Cohen, S., Ashwin, E., Knickmeyer, R., Taylor, K., Hackett, G., et al. (2009). Fetal testosterone predicts sexually differentiated childhood behavior in girls and in boys. *Psychological Science, 20,* 144–148.

Avery, D. H., Holtzheimer, P. E. III, Fawaz, W., Russo, J., Neumaier, J., Dunner, D. L., et al. (2006). A controlled study of repetitive transcranial magnetic stimulation in medication-resistant major depression. *Biological Psychiatry, 59,* 187–194.

Ayalon, L., Gum, A., Feliciano, L., & Areán, P. A. (2006). Effectiveness of nonpharmacological interventions for the management of neuropsychiatric symptoms in patients with dementia: A systematic review. *Archives of Internal Medicine, 166,* 2182–2188.

Aziz, A. (2004). Sources of perceived stress among American medical doctors: A cross-cultural perspective. *Cross Cultural Management, 11,* 28–39.

Bacaltchuk, J., Hay, P., & Mari, J. J. (2000). Antidepressants versus placebo for the treatment of bulimia nervosa: A systematic review. *Australian and New Zealand Journal of Psychiatry, 34,* 310–317.

Bach, A. K., Brown, T. A., & Barlow, D. H. (1999). The effects of false negative feedback on efficacy expectancies and sexual arousal in sexually functional males. *Behavior Therapy, 30,* 79–95.

Baddeley, A. (1986). *Working memory.* New York: Clarendon Press/Oxford University Press.

Baden, A. L., & Wong, G. (2008). Assessment issues for working with diverse populations of elderly: Multiculturally sensitive perspectives. In L. A. Suzuki & J. G. Ponterotto (Eds.), *Handbook of multicultural assessment: Clinical, psychological, and educational applications* (pp. 594–623). San Francisco: Jossey-Bass.

Baer, J. C., & Martinez, C. D. (2006). Child maltreatment and insecure attachment: A meta-analysis. *Journal of Reproductive and Infant Psychology, 24,* 187–197.

Baghurst, T., Hollander, D. B., Nardella, B., & Haff, G. G. (2006). Change in sociocultural ideal male physique: An examination of past and present action figures. *Body Image, 3,* 87–91.

Bailey, A., Le Couteur, A., Gottesman, I., & Bolton, P. (1995). Autism as a strongly genetic disorder: Evidence from a British twin study. *Psychological Medicine, 25,* 63–77.

Bailey, S. L. (1992). Adolescents' multisubstance use patterns: The role of heavy alcohol and cigarette use. *American Journal of Public Health, 82,* 1220–1224.

Baker, D., Earle, M., Medford, N., Sierra, M., Towell, A., & David, A. (2007). Illness perceptions in depersonalization disorder: Testing an illness attribution model. *Clinical Psychology & Psychotherapy, 14,* 105–116.

Baker, D., Hunter, E. C. M., Lawrence, E., Medford, N., Sierra, M., Lambert, et al. (2003). Depersonalisation disorder: Clinical features of 204 cases. *British Journal of Psychiatry, 182,* 428–433.

Baker, J. R., Jatlow, P., & McCance-Katz, E. F. (2007). Disulfiram effects on responses to intravenous cocaine administration. *Drug and Alcohol Dependence, 87,* 202–209.

Baker, T. B., Brandon, T. H., & Chassin, L. (2004). Motivational influences on cigarette smoking. *Annual Review of Psychology, 55,* 463–491.

Baldwin, D. S., & Polkinghorn, C. (2005). Evidence-based pharmacotherapy of generalized anxiety disorder. *International Journal of Neuropsychopharmacology, 8,* 293–302.

Ball, J. R., Mitchell, P. B., Corry, J. C., Skillecorn, A., Smith, M., & Malhi, G. S. (2006). A randomized controlled trial of cognitive therapy for bipolar disorder: Focus on long-term change. *Journal of Clinical Psychiatry, 67,* 277–286.

Ball, S., Smolin, J., & Shekhar, A. (2002). A psychobiological approach to personality: Examination within anxious outpatients. *Journal of Psychiatric Research, 36,* 97–103.

Ballard, C., & Howard, R. (2006). Neuroleptic drugs in dementia benefits and harm. *Nature Reviews Neuroscience, 7,* 492–500.

Balon, R., Segraves, R. T., Clayton, A. (2007). Issues for DSM-V: Sexual dysfunction, disorder, or variation along normal distribution: Toward rethinking DSM criteria of sexual dysfunctions. *American Journal of Psychiatry, 164,* 198–200.

Baltas, Z., & Steptoe, A. (2000). Migration, culture conflict and psychological well-being among Turkish-British married couples. *Ethnicity and Health, 5,* 173–180.

Bancroft, J. (1989). Man and his penis—a relationship under threat? *Journal of Psychology & Human Sexuality, 2,* 7–32.

Bancroft, J. (2002). The medicalization of female sexual dysfunction: The need for caution. *Archives of Sexual Behavior, 31,* 451–455.

Bandelow, B., Krause, J., Wedekind, D., Broocks, A., Hajak, G., & Rüther, E. (2005). Early traumatic life events, parental attitudes, family history, and birth risk factors in patients with borderline personality disorder and healthy controls. *Psychiatry Research, 134,* 169–179.

Bandini, S., Antonelli, G., Moretti, P., Pampanelli, S., Quartesan, R., & Perriello, G. (2006). Factors affecting dropout in outpatient eating disorder treatment. *Eating and Weight Disorders, 11,* 179–184.

Bandura, A. (1986). The explanatory and predictive scope of self-efficacy theory. *Journal of Social & Clinical Psychology, 4,* 359–373.

Bandura, A. (1997). *Self-efficacy: The exercise of control.* New York: W. H. Freeman/Times Books/Henry Holt & Co.

Bandura, A., Ross, D., & Ross, S. A. (1961). Transmission of aggression through imitation of aggressive models. *Journal of Abnormal and Social Psychology, 63,* 575–582.

Baranek, G. T. (1999). Autism during infancy: A retrospective video analysis of sensory-motor and social behaviors at 9–12 months of age. *Journal of Autism and Developmental Disorders, 29,* 213–224.

Baranowsky, A. B., Gentry, J. E., & Schultz, D. F. (2005). *Trauma practice: Tools for stabilization and recovery.* Ashland, OH: Hogrefe & Huber.

Barbaree, H. E. (2005). Psychopathy, treatment behavior, and recidivism: An extended follow-up of Seto and Barbaree. *Journal of Interpersonal Violence, 20,* 1115–1131.

Barbarich, N. C., McConaha, C. W., Halmi, K. A., Gendall, K., Sunday, S. R., Gaskill, J., et al. (2004). Use of nutritional supplements to increase the efficacy of fluoxetine in the treatment of anorexia nervosa. *International Journal of Eating Disorders, 35,* 10–15.

Barbee, J. G. (1998). Mixed symptoms and syndromes of anxiety and depression: Diagnostic, prognostic, and etiologic issues. *Annals of Clinical Psychiatry, 10,* 15–29.

Barber, C. (2008, February). The medicated Americans: Antidepressant prescriptions on the rise. *Scientific American.* Retrieved October 11, 2008, from http://www.sciam.com/article.cfm?id=the-medicated-americans

Barber, N. (1998). The slender ideal and eating disorders: An interdisciplinary "telescope" model. *International Journal of Eating Disorders, 23,* 295–307.

Barch, D. M. (2005). The cognitive neuroscience of schizophrenia. *Annual Review of Clinical Psychology, 1,* 321–353.

Barkham, M., & Shapiro, D. A. (1990). Brief psychotherapeutic interventions for job-related distress: A pilot study of prescriptive and explanatory therapy. *Counselling Psychology Quarterly, 3,* 133–147.

Barkley, R. A. (1997). *Defiant children: A clinician's manual for assessment and parent training* (2nd ed.). New York: Guilford Press.

Barkley, R. A. (2000). *Taking charge of ADHD: The complete authoritative guide for parents* (rev. ed.). New York: Guilford Press.

Barkley, R. A., Edwards, G., Laneri, M., Fletcher, K., & Metevia, L. (2001). Executive functioning, temporal discounting, and sense of time in adolescents with attention-deficit hyperactivity disorder (ADHD) and oppositional defiant disorder (ODD). *Journal of Abnormal Child Psychology, 29,* 541–556.

Barkley, R. A., Shelton, T. L., Crosswait, C., Moorehouse, M., Fletcher, K., Barrett, S., et al. (2002). Preschool children with disruptive behavior: Three-year outcome as a function of adaptive disability. *Development and Psychopathology, 14,* 45–67.

Barlett, D. L., & Steele, J. B. (1979). *Howard Hughes: His life and madness.* New York: Norton.

Barlow, D. H. (2002). *Anxiety and its disorders* (2nd ed.). New York: Guilford Press.

Barlow, D. H. (2002a). The experience of anxiety: Shadow of intelligence or specter of death? In D. H. Barlow (Ed.), *Anxiety and its disorders: The nature and treatment of anxiety and panic* (pp. 1–36). New York: Guilford Press.

Barlow, D. H. (2002b). True alarms, false alarms, and learned (conditioned) anxiety: The origins of panic and phobia. In D. H. Barlow (Ed.), *Anxiety and its disorders: The nature and treatment of anxiety and panic* (pp. 219–251). New York: Guilford Press.

Barlow, D. H. (1988). *Anxiety and its disorders: The nature and treatment of anxiety and panic.* New York: Guilford Press.

Barlow, D. H. & Chorpita, B. F. (1998). The development of anxiety. *Psychological Bulletin, 124,* 3–21.

Barlow, D. H., Esler, J. L., & Vitali, A. E. (1998). Psychosocial treatments for panic disorders, phobias, and generalized anxiety disorder. In P. E. Nathan & J. M. Gorman (Eds.), *A guide to treatments that work* (pp. 288–318). New York: Oxford University Press.

Barnes, J. (2000a, March 25). Insanity defense fails for man who threw woman onto track. *The New York Times*, p. A1.

Barnes, J. (2000b, March 24). Subway killer to be treated in cell or in hospital, or both. *The New York Times*, p. B3.

Barnett, J. E., & Scheetz, K. (2003). Technological advances and telehealth: Ethics, law, and the practice of psychotherapy. *Psychotherapy: Theory, Research, Practice, Training, 40*, 86–93.

Baron-Cohen S., Leslie, A. M., & Frith, U. (1985). Does the autistic child have a "theory of mind"? *Cognition, 21,* 37–46.

Barraclough, B. M., & White, S. J. (1978a). Monthly variation of suicide and undetermined death compared. *British Journal of Psychiatry, 132*, 275–278.

Barraclough, B. M., & White, S. J. (1978b). Monthly variation of suicidal, accidental and undetermined poisoning deaths. *British Journal of Psychiatry, 132*, 279–282.

Barrett, P. M., Rapee, R. M., Dadds, M. R., & Ryan, S. M. (1996). Family enhancement of cognitive style in anxious and aggressive children. *Journal of Abnormal Child Psychology, 24,* 187–203.

Barrowclough, C., Haddock, G., Tarrier, N., Lewis, S. W., Moring, J., O'Brien, R., et al. (2001). Clinical outcome following neuroleptic discontinuation in patients with remitted recent-onset schizophrenia. *American Journal of Psychiatry, 158*, 1835–1842.

Barsky, A. J. (1992). Hypochondriasis and obsessive compulsive disorder. *Psychiatric Clinics of North America, 15*, 791–801.

Barsky, A. J., & Ahern, D. K. (2004). Cognitive behavior therapy for hypochondriasis: A randomized controlled trial. *JAMA: Journal of the American Medical Association, 291*, 1464–1470.

Barsky, A. J., Bailey, E. D., Fama, J. M., & Ahern, D. K. (2000). Predictors of remission in DSM hypochondriasis. *Comprehensive Psychiatry, 41*, 179–183.

Barsky, A. J., Cleary, P. D., Sarnie, M. K., & Klerman, G. L. (1993). The course of transient hypochondriasis. *American Journal of Psychiatry, 150*, 484–488.

Barsky, A. J., Cleary, P. D., Sarnie, M. K., & Ruskin, J. N. (1994). Panic disorder, palpitations, and the awareness of cardiac activity. *Journal of Nervous & Mental Disease, 182*, 63–71.

Barsky, A. J., Coeytaux, R. R., Sarnie, M. K., & Cleary, P. D. (1993). Hypochondriacal patients' beliefs about good health. *American Journal of Psychiatry 150*, 1085–1089.

Barsky, A. J., Orav, E. J., & Bates, D. W. (2005). Somatization increases medical utilization and costs independent of psychiatric and medical comorbidity. *Archives of General Psychiatry, 62*, 903–910.

Barsky, A. J., Wool, C., Barnett, M. C., & Cleary, P. D. (1994). Histories of childhood trauma in adult hypochondriacal patients. *American Journal of Psychiatry, 151*, 397–401.

Bartholomew, R. E. (1994). Disease, disorder, or deception? *Latah* as habit in a Malay extended family. *Journal of Nervous and Mental Disease, 182*, 331–338.

Bartholomew, R. E. (1998). The medicalization of exotic deviance: A sociological perspective on epidemic koro. *Transcultural Psychiatry, 35*, 5–38.

Bartoi, M. G., & Kinder, B. N. (1998). Effects of child and adult sexual abuse on adult sexuality. *Journal of Sex & Marital Therapy, 24*, 75–90.

Bartol, C. R., & Bartol, A. M. (2004). *Psychology and law: Theory, research, and application.* Belmont, CA: Thomson/Wadsworth.

Basic Behavioral Science Task Force of the National Advisory Mental Health Council (1996). Basic behavioral science research for mental health, *American Psychologist, 51*, 722–731.

Bass, C., & Murphy, M. (1995). Somatoform and personality disorders: Syndromal comorbidity and overlapping developmental pathways. *Journal of Psychosomatic Research*, *39*, 403–427.

Bass, C., Peveler, R., & House, A. (2001). Somatoform disorders: Severe psychiatric illnesses neglected by psychiatrists. *British Journal of Psychiatry, 179*, 11–14.

Basson, R. (2001). Using a different model for female sexual response to address women's problematic low sexual desire. *Journal of Sex & Marital Therapy, 27,* 395–403.

Basson, R. (2005). Women's sexual dysfunction: Revised and expanded definitions. *Canadian Medical Association Journal, 172*, 1327–1333.

Basson, R., Berman, J., Burnett, A., Derogatis, L., Ferguson, D., Fourcroy, J., et al. (2001). Report of the International Consensus Development Conference on Female Sexual Dysfunction: Definitions and classifications. *Journal of Sex & Marital Therapy, 27*, 83–94.

Basson, R., Brotto, L. A., Laan, E., Redmond, G., & Utian, W. H. (2005). Assessment and management of women's sexual dysfunctions: Problematic desire and arousal. *Journal of Sexual Medicine, 2*, 291–300.

Basson, R., Leiblum, S., Brotto, L., Derogatis, L., Fourcroy, J., Fugl-Meyer, K., et al. (2004). Revised definitions of women's sexual dysfunction. *Journal of Sexual Medicine, 1*, 40–48.

Bateman, A. W., & Fonagy, P. (2004). *Psychotherapy for borderline personality disorder: Mentalization based treatment.* Oxford, England: Oxford University Press.

Bates, J. E., Bentler, P. M., & Thompson, S. K. (1973). Measurement of deviant gender development in boys. *Child Development, 44*, 591–598.

Bates, J. E., Bentler, P. M., & Thompson, S. K. (1979). Gender-deviant boys compared with normal and clinical control boys. *Journal of Abnormal Child Psychology, 7*, 243–259.

Battle, C. L., Shea, M. T., Johnson, D. M., Yen, S., Zlotnick, C., Zanarini, M. C., et al. (2004). Childhood maltreatment associated with adult personality disorders: Findings from the collaborative longitudinal personality disorders study. *Journal of Personality Disorders, 18*, 193–211.

Baucom, D. H., Shohan, V., Mueser, D. T., Daiuto, A. D., & Stickle, T. R. (1998). Empirically supported couple and family interventions for marital distress and adult mental health problems. *Journal of Consulting and Clinical Psychology, 66*, 53–88.

Baumeister, R. F., Bratslavsky, E., Muraven, M., & Tice, D. M. (1998). Ego depletion: Is the active self a limited resource? *Journal of Personality and Social Psychology, 74*, 1252–1265.

Baxter, L. R. (1992). Neuroimaging studies of obsessive compulsive disorder. *Psychiatric Clinics of North America, 15*, 871–884.

Baxter, L. R., Schwartz, J. M., Bergman, K. S., Szuba, M. P., Guze, B. H., Mazziotta, J. C., et al. (1992). Caudate glucose metabolic rate changes with both drug and behavior therapy for obsessive-compulsive disorder. *Archives of General Psychiatry, 49*, 681–689.

Baxter, L. R., Schwartz, J. M., & Guze, B. H. (1991). Brain imaging: Toward a neuroanatomy of OCD. In J. Zohar, T. Insel, & S. Rasmussen (Eds.), *The psychobiology of obsessive-compulsive disorder.* New York: Springer.

Bean, N. M. (1992). Elucidating the path toward alcohol and substance abuse by adolescent victims of sexual abuse. *Journal of Applied Social Sciences, 17*, 57–94.

Beasley, C. M., Jr., Koke, S. C., Nilsson, M. E., & Gonzales, J. S. (2000). Adverse events and treatment discontinuations in clinical trials of fluoxetine in major depressive disorder: An updated meta-analysis. *Clinical Therapeutics: The International Journal of Drug Therapy, 22*, 1319–1330.

Beasley, C. M. Jr., Sutton, V. K., Taylor, C. C., Sethuraman, G., Dossenbach, M., & Naber, D. (2006). Is quality of life among minimally symptomatic patients with schizophrenia better following withdrawal or continuation of antipsychotic treatment? *Journal of Clinical Psychopharmacology, 26*, 40–44.

Beatty, M. J., Heisel, A. D., Hall, A. E., Levine, T. R., & La France, B. H. (2002). What can we learn from the study of twins about genetic and environmental influences on interpersonal affiliation, aggressiveness, and social anxiety? A meta-analytic study. *Communication Monographs, 69,* 1–18.

Beck, A. (1967). *Depression.* New York: Harper & Row.

Beck, A., & Emery, G. (1985). *Anxiety disorders and phobias.* New York: Basic Books.

Beck, A. T. (1967). *Depression: Causes and treatment.* Philadelphia: University of Pennsylvania Press.

Beck, A. T. (1976). *Cognitive therapy and the emotional disorders.* Oxford, England: International Universities Press.

Beck, A. T. (1999, February). *From the president's corner: New research in cognitive therapy.* Bala Cynwyd, PA: Beck Institute for Cognitive Therapy and Research.

Beck, A. T. (2005). The current state of cognitive therapy: A 40-year retrospective. *Archives of General Psychiatry, 62,* 953–959.

Beck, A. T., Brown, G., Berchick, R. J., Stewart, B. L., & Steer, R. A. (1990). Relationship between hopelessness and ultimate suicide: A replication with psychiatric outpatients. *American Journal of Psychiatry, 147,* 190–195.

Beck, A. T., Butler, A. C., Brown, G. K., Dahlsgaard, K. K., Newman, C. F., & Beck, J. S. (2001). Dysfunctional beliefs discriminate personality disorders. *Behaviour Research and Therapy, 39,* 1213–1225.

Beck, A. T., Emery, G., & Greenberg, R. L. (2005). *Anxiety disorders and phobias: A cognitive perspective.* New York: Basic Books.

Beck, A. T., Freeman, A., & Davis, D. D. (2004). *Cognitive therapy of personality disorders* (2nd ed.). New York: Guilford Press.

Beck, A. T., & Rector, N. A. (2005). Cognitive approaches to schizophrenia: Theory and therapy. *Annual Review of Clinical Psychology, 1,* 577–606.

Beck, A. T., Rush, A. J., Shaw, B. F., & Emery, G. (1979). *Cognitive therapy of depression: A treatment manual.* New York: Guilford Press.

Beck, A. T., Steer, R. A., & Brown, G. K. (1996). *BDI–II: Beck Depression Inventory Manual,* (2nd ed.). San Antonio, TX: The Psychological Corporation.

Beck, A. T., Steer, R. A., Kovacs, M., & Garrison, B. (1985). Hopelessness and eventual suicide: A 10-year prospective study of patients hospitalized with suicidal ideation. *American Journal of Psychiatry, 142,* 559–563.

Beck, A. T. (2003). From the President: Synopsis of the Cognitive Model of Borderline Personality Disorder. The Beck Institute. Retrieved October 6th, 2009, from http://www.beckinstitute.org/InfoID/56/RedirectPath/Add1/FolderID/165/SessionID/{018DB423-1F38-4EBC-9156-03D1A34B14E8}/InfoGroup/Main/InfoType/Article/PageVars/Library/InfoManage/Zoom.htm

Beck, D., Casper, R., & Anderson, A. (1996). Truly late onset of eating disorders: A study of 11 cases averaging 60 years of age at presentation. *International Journal of Eating Disorders, 20,* 389–395.

Beck, J. G. (1995). Hypoactive sexual desire disorder: An overview. *Journal of Consulting and Clinical Psychology, 63,* 919–927.

Beck, J. G., Ohtake, P. J., & Shipherd, J. C. (1999). Exaggerated anxiety is not unique to CO_2 in panic disorder: A comparison of hypercapnic and hypoxic challenges. *Journal of Abnormal Psychology, 108,* 473–482.

Becker, A., & Hamburg, P. (1996). Culture, the media, and eating disorders. *Cross-Cultural Psychiatry, 4,* 163–167.

Becker, A. E. (1994). Nurturing and negligence: Working on others' bodies in Fiji. In T. J. Csordas (Ed.), *Embodiment and experience: The existential ground of culture and self* (pp. 100–115). New York: Cambridge University Press.

Becker, A. E., Burwell, R. A., Herzog, D. B., Hamburg, P., & Gilman, S. E. (2002). Eating behaviours and attitudes following prolonged exposure to television among ethnic Fijian adolescent girls. *British Journal of Psychiatry, 180,* 509–514.

Becker, D., & Lamb, S. (1994). Sex bias in the diagnosis of borderline personality disorder and posttraumatic stress disorder. *Professional Psychology: Research and Practice, 25,* 55–61.

Becker, J. V. (1989). Impact of sexual abuse on sexual functioning. In S. R. Leiblum & R. C. Rosen (Eds.), *Principles and practice of sex therapy: Update for the 1990s* (2nd ed., pp. 298–318). New York: Guilford Press.

Becker, J. V., & Kaplan, M. S. (1991). Rape victims: Issues, theories, and treatment. *Annual Review of Sex Research, 2,* 267–292.

Beech, A., & Ford, H. (2006). The relationship between risk, deviance, treatment outcome and sexual reconviction in a sample of child sexual abusers completing residential treatment for their offending. *Psychology, Crime & Law, 12,* 685–701.

Bell, C. J., & Nutt, D. J. (1998). Serotonin and panic. *British Journal of Psychiatry, 172,* 465–471.

Bellgrove, M. A., Chambers, C. D., Vance, A., Hall, N., Karamitsios, M., & Bradshaw, J. L. (2006). Lateralized deficit of response inhibition in early-onset schizophrenia. *Psychological Medicine, 36,* 495–505.

Bellgrove, M. A., Hawi, Z., Lowe, N., Kirley, A., Robertson, I. H., & Gill, H. (2005). DRD4 gene variants and sustained attention in attention deficit hyperactivity disorder (ADHD): Effects of associated alleles at the VNTR and -521 SNP. *American Journal of Medical Genetics: Part B Neuropsychiatry Genetics, 136,* 81–86.

Bender, D. S. (2005). Therapeutic alliance. In J. M. Oldham, A. E. Skodol, & D. S. Bender (Eds.), *The American Psychiatric Publishing textbook of personality disorders* (pp. 405–420). Washington, DC: American Psychiatric Publishing.

Bender, L. (1963). *Bender visual motor Gestalt test.* New York: American Orthopsychiatric Corporation.

Benes, F. M. (2000). Emerging principles of altered neural circuitry in schizophrenia. *Brain Research Reviews, 31,* 251–269.

Benony, H., Van Der Elst, D., Chahraoui, K., Benony, C., & Marnier, J. P. (2007). Link between depression and academic self-esteem in gifted children. *Encephale, 33,* 11–20.

Benton, A. L., Hamsher, N. R., Varney, N. R., & Spreen, O. (1983). *Contributions to neuropsychological assessment.* Oxford, UK: Oxford University Press.

Ben-Tovim, D. I. (2003). Eating disorders: Outcome, prevention and treatment of eating disorders. *Current Opinion in Psychiatry, 16,* 65–69.

Berenbaum, H., Thompson, R. J., Milanek, M. E., Boden, M. T., & Bredemeier, K. (2008). Psychological trauma and schizotypal personality disorder. *Journal of Abnormal Psychology, 117,* 502–519.

Berman, J., & Berman, L. (with Bumiller, E.). (2001). *For women only: A revolutionary guide to reclaiming your sex life.* New York: Holt.

Berman, L. A., Berman, J. R., Bruck, D., Pawar, R. V., & Goldstein, I. (2001). Pharmacotherapy or psychotherapy? Effective treatment for FSD related to unresolved childhood sexual abuse. *Journal of Sex & Marital Therapy, 27,* 421–425.

Bernal, G., & Scharró-del-Río, M. R. (2001). Are empirically supported treatments valid for ethnic minorities? Toward an alternative approach for treatment research. *Cultural Diversity and Ethnic Minority Psychology, 7,* 328–342.

Berthier, M. L., Kulisevsky, J., Gironell, A., & López, O. L. (2001). Obsessive-compulsive disorder and traumatic brain injury: Behavioral, cognitive, and neuroimaging findings. *Neuropsychiatry, Neuropsychology, & Behavioral Neurology, 14,* 23–31.

Beutler, L. E. & Karno, M. (1999). Psychotherapy research: Basic or applied? *Journal of Clinical Psychology, 55,* 171–180.

Beutler, L. E. (2000). David and Goliath: When empirical and clinical standards of practice meet. *American Psychologist, 55,* 997–1007.

Beutler, L. E. (2002). The dodo bird is extinct. *Clinical Psychology: Science and Practice, 9,* 30–34.

Beutler, L. E., & Harwood, T. M. (2002). What is and can be attributed to the therapeutic relationship?. *Journal of Contemporary Psychotherapy, 32,* 25–33.

Beutler, L. E., Harwood, T. M., Alimohamed, S. & Malik, M. (2002). Functional impairment and coping style: Patient moderators of therapeutic relationships. In J. N. Norcross (Ed.), *Empirically supported therapeutic relationships* (pp. 145–170). New York: Oxford University Press.

Beutler, L. E., Machado, P. P. P., & Neufeldt, S. A. (1994). Therapist variables. In A. E. Bergin & S. L. Garfield (Eds.), *Handbook of psychotherapy and behavior change* (4th ed., pp. 229–269). Oxford, England: John Wiley & Sons.

Beutler, L. E., & Malik, M. L. (2002). *Rethinking the DSM: A psychological perspective.* Washington, DC: American Psychological Association.

Bhatia, T., Thomas, P., Semwal, P., Thelma, B. K., Nimgaonkar, V. L., & Deshpande, S. N. (2006). Differing correlates for suicide attempts among patients with schizophrenia or schizoaffective disorder in India and USA. *Schizophrenia Research, 86,* 208–214.

Bhugra, D., & Ayondrinde, O. (2001). Racism, racial life events and mental ill health. *Advances in Psychiatric Treatment, 7,* 343–349.

Bhui, K., Stansfeld, S., McKenzie, K., Karlsen, S., Nazroo, J., & Weich, S. (2005). Racial/ethnic discrimination and common mental disorders among workers: Findings from the EMPIRIC Study of Ethnic Minority Groups in the United Kingdom. *American Journal of Public Health, 95,* 496–501.

Bibb, J. L., & Chambless, D. L. (1986). Alcohol use and abuse among diagnosed agoraphobics. *Behaviour Research and Therapy, 24,* 49–58.

Bickel, W. K., & Marsch, L. A. (2001). Toward a behavioral economic understanding of drug dependence: Delay discounting processes. *Addiction, 96,* 73–86.

Bieberich, A. A., & Morgan, S. B. (1998). Affective expression in children with autism or Down syndrome. *Journal of Autism and Developmental Disorders, 28,* 333–338.

Bieberich, A. A., & Morgan, S. B. (2004). Self-regulation and affective expression during play in children with autism or Down syndrome: A short-term longitudinal study. *Journal of Autism and Developmental Disorders, 34,* 439–448.

Biederman, J., Faraone, S. V., Milberger, S., Jetton, J. G., Chen, L., Mick, E., et al. (1996). Is childhood oppositional defiant disorder a precursor to adolescent conduct disorder? Findings from a four-year follow-up study of children with ADHD. *Journal of the American Academy of Child & Adolescent Psychiatry, 35,* 1193–1204.

Biederman, J., Hirshfeld-Becker, D. R., Rosenbaum, J. F., Hérot, C., Friedman, D., Snidman, N., et al. (2001). Further evidence of association between behavioral inhibition and social anxiety in children. *American Journal of Psychiatry, 158,* 1673–1679.

Biederman, J., Kwon, A., Aleardi, M., Chouinard, V., Marino, T., Cole, H., et al. (2005). Absence of gender effects on attention-deficit hyperactivity disorder: Findings in nonreferred subjects. *American Journal of Psychiatry, 162,* 1083–1089.

Biederman, J., Mick, E., & Faraone, S. V. (2000). Age-dependent decline of symptoms of attention-deficit hyperactivity disorder: Impact of remission definition and symptom type. *American Journal of Psychiatry, 157,* 816–818.

Biederman, J., Petty, C., Faraone, S. V., Hirshfeld-Becker, D. R., Henin, A., Pollack, M. H., et al. (2005). Patterns of comorbidity in panic disorder and major depression: Findings from a nonreferred sample. *Depression and Anxiety, 21,* 55–60.

Bielau, H., Mawrin, C., Krell, D., Agelink, M. W., Trübner, K., Davis, R., et al. (2005). Differences in activation of the dorsal raphé nucleus depending on performance of suicide. *Brain Research, 1039,* 43–52.

Bienvenu, O. J., Hettema, J. M., Neale, M. C., Prescott, C. A., & Kendler, K. S. (2007). Low extraversion and high neuroticism as indices of genetic and environmental risk for social phobia, agoraphobia, and animal phobia. *American Journal of Psychiatry, 164,* 1714–1721.

Bienvenu, O. J., Nestadt, G., Samuels, J. F., Costa, P. T., Howard, W. T., & Eaton, W. W. (2001). Phobic, panic, and major depressive disorders and the five-factor model of personality. *Journal of Nervous and Mental Disease, 189,* 154–161.

Bienvenu, O. J., Onyike, C. U., Stein, M. B., Chen, L. S., Samuels, J., Nestadt, G., et al. (2006). Agoraphobia in adults: Incidence and longitudinal relationship with panic. *British Journal of Psychiatry, 188,* 432–438.

Bienvenu, O. J., Samuels, J. F., Riddle, M. A., Hoehn-Saric, R., Liang, K. Y., Cullen, B. A., et al. (2000). The relationship of obsessive-compulsive disorder to possible spectrum disorders: Results from a family study. *Biological Psychiatry, 48,* 287–293.

Bierer, L. M., Yehuda, R., Schmeidler, J., Mitropoulou, V., New, A. S., Silverman, J. M., et al. (2003). Abuse and neglect in childhood: Relationship to personality disorder diagnoses. *CNS Spectrums, 8,* 737–740, 749–754.

Bifulco, A., Moran, P. M., Ball, C., & Bernazzani, O. (2002). Adult attachment style.1: Its relation to clinical depression. *Social Psychiatry & Psychiatric Epidemiology, 37,* 50–59.

Bilich, L. L., Deane, F. P., Phipps, A. B., Barisic, M., & Gould, G. (2008). Effectiveness of bibliotherapy self-help for depression with varying levels of telephone helpline support. *Clinical Psychology & Psychotherapy, 15,* 61–74.

Bilukha, O. O., & Utermohlen, V. (2002). Internalization of Western standards of appearance, body dissatisfaction and dieting in urban educated Ukrainian females. *European Eating Disorders Review, 10,* 120–137.

Binik, Y. M. (2005). Should dyspareunia be retained as a sexual dysfunction in DSM-V? A painful classification decision. *Archives of Sexual Behavior, 34,* 11–21.

Binik, Y. M., Reissing, E., Pukall, C., Flory, N., Payne, K. A., & Khalifé, S. (2002). The female sexual pain disorders: Genital pain or sexual dysfunction? *Archives of Sexual Behavior, 31,* 425–429.

Binks, C. A., Fenton, M., McCarthy, L., Lee, T., Adams, C. E., & Duggan, C. (2006a). Pharmacological interventions for people with borderline personality disorder. *Cochrane Database of Systematic Reviews, 25*(1): CD005653.

Binks, C. A., Fenton, M., McCarthy, L., Lee, T., Adams, C. E., & Duggan, C. (2006b). Psychological therapies for people with borderline personality disorder. *Cochrane Database of Systematic Reviews, 25*(1): CD005652.

Birchall, H. (1999). Interpersonal psychotherapy in the treatment of eating disorders. *European Eating Disorders Review, 7,* 315–320.

Bird, H. R. (2002). The diagnostic classification, epidemiology, and cross-cultural validity of ADHD. In P. S. Jensen & J. R. Cooper (Eds.), *Attention deficit hyperactivity disorder: State of the science-best practices* (pp. 2-1–2-16). Kingston, NJ: Civic Research Institute.

Bird, T. D., Levy-Lahad, E., Poorkaj, P., Sharma, V., Nemens, E., Lahad, A., et al. (1996). Wide range in age of onset for chromosome 1-related familial Alzheimer's disease. *Annals of Neurology, 40,* 932–936.

Bissell, K., & Zhou, P. (2004). Must-see TV or ESPN: Entertainment and sports media exposure and body-image distortion in college women. *Journal of Communication, 54,* 5–21.

Black, D. W. (2001). Antisocial personality disorder: The forgotten patients of psychiatry. *Primary Psychiatry, 8,* 30–81.

Black, D. W., Noyes, R., Goldstein, R. B., & Blum, N. (1992). A family study of obsessive-compulsive disorder. *Archives of General Psychiatry, 49,* 362–368.

Blackburn, S., Johnston, L., Blampied, N., Popp, D., & Kallen, R. (2006). An application of escape theory to binge eating. *European Eating Disorders Review, 14,* 23–31.

Blair, N. A., Yue, S. K., Singh, R., & Bernhardt, J. M. (2005). Depiction of substance use in reality television: A content analysis of *The Osbournes. British Medical Journal, 331,* 1517–1519.

Blair, R. J. R., Colledge, E., Murray, L. K., & Mitchell, D. G. V. (2001). Selective impairment in the processing of sad and fearful expressions by children with psychopathic tendencies. *Journal of Abnormal Child Psychology, 29,* 491–498.

Blais, M. A., Hilsenroth, M. J., & Fowler, J. C. (1999). Diagnostic efficiency and hierarchical functioning of the DSM-IV borderline personality disorder criteria. *Journal of Nervous and Mental Disease, 187,* 167–173.

Blais, M. A., McCann, J. T., Benedict, K. B., & Norman, D. K. (1997). Toward an empirical/theoretical grouping of the DSM-III-R personality disorders. *Journal of Personality Disorders, 11,* 191–198.

Blais, M. A., & Norman, D. K. (1997). A psychometric evaluation of the DSM-IV personality disorder criteria. *Journal of Personality Disorders, 11,* 168–176.

Blanchard, E. B. (2000). Biofeedback. In A. E. Kazdin (Ed.), *Encyclopedia of psychology* (Vol. 1, pp. 417–420). Washington, DC: American Psychological Association.

Blanchard, E. B., Kuhn, E., Rowell, D. L., Hickling, E. J., Wittrock, D., Rogers, R. L., et al. (2004). Studies of the vicarious traumatization of college students by the September 11th attacks: Effects of proximity, exposure and connectedness. *Behaviour Research and Therapy, 42,* 191–205.

Blanchard, E. B., Lackner, J. M., Gusmano, R., Gudleski, G. D., Sanders, K., Keefer, L., et al. (2006). Prediction of treatment outcome among patients with irritable bowel syndrome treated with group cognitive therapy. *Behaviour Research and Therapy, 44,* 317–337.

Blanchard, J. J., Horan, W. P., & Collins, L. M. (2005). Examining the latent structure of negative symptoms: Is there a distinct subtype of negative symptom schizophrenia? *Schizophrenia Research, 77,* 151–165.

Blanchard, R. (1989). The classification and labeling of nonhomosexual gender dysphorias. *Archives of Sexual Behavior, 18,* 315–334.

Blanchard, R. (1990). Gender identity disorders in adult men. In R. Blanchard & B. W. Steiner (Eds.), *Clinical management of gender identity disorders in children and adults* (pp. 47–76). Washington, DC: American Psychiatric Press.

Blaney, P. H. (1986). Affect and memory: A review. *Psychological Bulletin, 99,* 229–246.

Blatt, S. J., Sanislow, C. A., Zuroff, D. C., & Pilkonis, P. A. (1996). Characteristics of effective therapists: Further analyses of data from the National Institute of Mental Health Treatment of Depression Collaborative Research Program. *Journal of Consulting and Clinical Psychology, 64,* 1276–1284.

Blazer, D. G., Hybels, C. F., Simonsick, E. M., & Hanlon, J. T. (2000). Marked differences in antidepressant use by race in an elderly community sample: 1986–1996. *American Journal of Psychiatry, 157,* 1089–1094.

Blazer, D. G., Landerman, L. R., Hays, J. C., Simonsick, E. M., & Saunders, W. B. (1998). Symptoms of depression among community-dwelling elderly African-American adults. *Psychological Medicine, 28,* 1311–1320.

Bleiberg, K. L., & Markowitz, J. C. (2005). A pilot study of interpersonal psychotherapy for posttraumatic stress disorder. *American Journal of Psychiatry, 162,* 181–183.

Blinder, B. J., Cumella, E. J., & Sanathara, V. A. (2006). Psychiatric comorbidities of female inpatients with eating disorders. *Psychosomatic Medicine, 68,* 454–462.

Bliss, E. L. (1984). Spontaneous self-hypnosis in multiple personality disorder. *Psychiatric Clinics of North America, 7,* 135–148.

Block, J. J. (2008). Issues for DSM-V: Internet addiction. *American Journal of Psychiatry, 165,* 306–307.

Bloom, B. L. (1997). *Planned short-term psychotherapy: A clinical handbook* (2nd ed.). Boston: Allyn & Bacon.

Bloom, J. W. (1998). The ethical practice of Web counseling. *British Journal of Guidance & Counselling, 26,* 53–59.

Blum, K., Noble, E. P., Sheridan, P. J., Montgomery, A., Ritchie, T., Jagadeeswaran, P., et al. (1990). Allelic association of human dopamine D2 receptor gene in alcoholism. *Journal of the American Medical Association, 263,* 2055–2060.

Bock, M. A. (2007). The impact of social-behavioral learning strategy training on the social interaction skills of four students with Asperger syndrome. *Focus on Autism and Other Developmental Disabilities, 22,* 88–95.

Boddy, J. (1992). Comment on the proposed DSM-IV criteria for trance and possession disorder. *Transcultural Psychiatric Research Review, 29,* 323–330.

Bodkin, J. A., Pope, H. G., Detke, M. J., & Hudson, J. I. (2007). Is PTSD caused by traumatic stress? *Journal of Anxiety Disorders, 21,* 176–182.

Bodlund, O., & Kullgren, G. (1996). Transsexualism—general outcome and prognostic factors: A five-year follow-up study of nineteen transsexuals in the process of changing sex. *Archives of Sexual Behavior, 25,* 303–316.

Bohus, M., Haaf, B., Simms, T., Limberger, M. F., Schmahl, C., Unckel, C., et al. (2004). Effectiveness of inpatient dialectical behavioral therapy for borderline personality disorder: A controlled trial. *Behaviour Research and Therapy, 42,* 487–499.

Bohus, M., Haaf, B., Stiglmayr, C., Pohl, U., Böhme, R., & Linehan, M. (2000). Evaluation of inpatient dialectical-behavioral therapy for borderline personality disorder—a prospective study. *Behaviour Research and Therapy, 38,* 875–887.

Boldrini, M., Underwood, M. D., Mann, J. J., & Arango, V. (2005). More tryptophan hydroxylase in the brainstem dorsal raphé nucleus in depressed suicides. *Brain Research, 1041,* 19–28.

Bölte, S., & Poustka, F. (2003). The recognition of facial affect in autistic and schizophrenic subjects and their first-degree relatives. *Psychological Medicine, 33,* 907–915.

Bolton, P., Bass, J., Neugebauer, R., Verdeli, H., Clougherty, K. F., Wickramaratne, P., et al. (2003). Group interpersonal psychotherapy for depression in rural Uganda: A randomized controlled trial. *JAMA: Journal of the American Medical Association, 289,* 3117–3124.

Bondy, A. S., & Frost, L. A. (1994). The Picture Exchange Communication System. *Focus on Autism and Other Developmental Disabilities, 9*(3), 1–19.

Booij, L., & Van der Does, A. J. W. (2007). Cognitive and serotonergic vulnerability to depression: Convergent findings. *Journal of Abnormal Psychology, 116,* 86–94.

Borch-Jacobsen, M. (1997), "Sybil: The making of a disease: An interview with Dr. Herbert Spiegel," *The New York Review,* April 27, 1997, p. 60.

Bordo, S. (1993). *Unbearable weight: Feminism, Western culture, and the body.* Berkeley: University of California Press.

Borkovec, T. D. (1994). The nature, functions, and origins of worry. In G. C. L. Davey & F. Tallis (Eds.), *Worrying: Perspectives on theory, assessment and treatment.* (pp. 5–33). Oxford, England: John Wiley & Sons.

Borkovec, T. D., & Castonguay, L. G. (1998). What is the scientific meaning of empirically supported therapy? *Journal of Consulting and Clinical Psychology, 66,* 136–142.

Borkovec, T. D., Hazlett-Stevens, J., & Diaz, M. L. (1999). The role of positive beliefs about worry in generalized anxiety disorder and its treatment. *Clinical Psychology and Psychotherapy, 6,* 126–138.

Borkovec, T. D., & Hu, S. (1990). The effect of worry on cardiovascular response to phobic imagery. *Behaviour Research and Therapy, 28,* 69–73.

Borkovec, T. D., & Miranda, J. (1999). Between-group psychotherapy outcome research and basic science. *Journal of Clinical Psychology, 55,* 147–158.

Borkovec, T. D., & Ruscio, A. M. (2001). Psychotherapy for generalized anxiety disorder. *Journal of Clinical Psychiatry, 62* (Suppl. 11), 37–42.

Bourgeois, J. A., Chang, C. H., Hilty, D. M., & Servis, M. E. (2002). Clinical manifestations and management of conversion disorders. *Current Treatment Options in Neurology, 4,* 487–497.

Bourguignon, E. (2004). Suffering and healing, subordination and power: Women and possession trance. *Ethos, 32,* 557–574.

Bouton, M. E., Mineka, S., & Barlow, D. H. (2001). A modern learning theory perspective on the etiology of panic disorder. *Psychological Review, 108,* 4–32.

Bowen, M. (1978). *Family therapy in clinical practice* (2nd ed.). Northvale, NJ: Jason Aronson.

Bower, G. H., & Forgas, J. P. (2000). Affect, memory, and social cognition. In E. Eich, J. F. Kihlstrom, G. H. Bower, J. P. Forgas, & P. M. Niedenthal (Eds.), *Cognition and emotion* (pp. 87–168). New York: Oxford University Press.

Bowers, M., Jr., Boutros, N., D'Souza, D. C., & Madonick, S. (2001). Substance abuse as a risk factor for schizophrenia and related disorders. *International Journal of Mental Health, 30,* 33–57.

Bowers, W. A., & Ansher, L. S. (2008). The effectiveness of cognitive behavioral therapy on changing eating disorder symptoms and psychopathy of 32 anorexia nervosa patients at hospital discharge and one year follow-up. *Annals of Clinical Psychiatry, 20,* 79–86.

Bowlby, J. (1969). *Attachment and loss: Vol. 1. Attachment.* New York: Basic Books.

Bowlby, J. (1973). *Attachment and loss: Vol. 2, Separation.* New York: Basic Books.

Bowlby, J. (1979). *The making and breaking of affectional bonds.* London: Tavistock.

Bowman, E. S. (1993). Etiology and clinical course of pseudoseizures: Relationship to trauma, depression, and dissociation. *Psychosomatics: Journal of Consultation and Liaison Psychiatry, 34,* 333–342.

Bowman, E. S., & Nurnberger, J. I. (1993). Genetics of psychiatry diagnosis and

treatment. In D. L. Dunner (Ed.), *Current psychiatric therapy* (pp. 46–56). Philadelphia: Saunders.

Bowman, M. L. (1999). Individual differences in posttraumatic distress: Problems with the DSM-IV model. *The Canadian Journal of Psychiatry/La Revue canadienne de psychiatrie, 44,* 21–33.

Boyd, J. D. (1997). Clinical hypnosis for rapid recovery from dissociative identity disorder. *American Journal of Clinical Hypnosis, 40,* 97–110.

Boylan, J. F. (2003). *She's not there: A life in two genders.* New York: Broadway Books.

Boyle, M. (2000). Kraepelin, Emil. In A. E. Kazdin (Ed.), *Encyclopedia of psychology* (Vol. 4, pp. 458–460). Washington, DC: American Psychological Association.

Bradfield, J. W. B. (2006). A pathologist's perspective of the somatoform disorders. *Journal of Psychosomatic Research, 60,* 327–330.

Bradford, J. M. (2001). The neurobiology, neuropharmacology, and pharmacological treatment of the paraphilias and compulsive sexual behaviour. *Canadian Journal of Psychiatry, 46,* 24–25.

Bradford, J. M. W. (2000). The treatment of sexual deviation using a pharmacological approach. *Journal of Sex Research, 37,* 248–257.

Bradley, R., Greene, J., Russ, E., Dutra, L., & Westen, D. (2005). A multidimensional meta-analysis of psychotherapy for PTSD. *American Journal of Psychiatry, 162,* 214–227.

Bradley, S. J., & Zucker, K. J. (1997). Gender identity disorder: A review of the past 10 years. *Journal of the American Academy of Child & Adolescent Psychiatry, 36,* 872–880.

Brady v. Hopper, 570 F. Supp. 1333 (D. Colo. 1983).

Brady, K. (2005). *New pharmacological approaches to addiction.* Medscape. Retrieved February 15, 2006, from http://www.medscape.com/viewarticle/507191

Brady, K., Pearlstein, T., Asnis, G. M., Baker, D., Rothbaum, B., Sikes, C. R., et al. (2000). Efficacy and safety of sertraline treatment of posttraumatic stress disorder: A randomized controlled trial. *JAMA: Journal of the American Medical Association, 283,* 1837–1844.

Brady, K., & Sinha, R. (2005). Co-occurring mental and substance use disorders: The neurobiological effects of chronic stress. *American Journal of Psychiatry, 162,* 1483–1493.

Brady, K. T., Sonne, E., Randall, C.L., Adinoff, B., & Malcolm, R. (1995). Features of cocaine dependence with concurrent alcohol abuse. *Drug and Alcohol Dependence, 39,* 69–71.

Brambilla, P., Cipriani, A., Hotopf, M., & Barbui, C. (2005). Side-effect profile

of fluoxetine in comparison with other SSRIs, tricyclic and newer antidepressants: A meta-analysis of clinical trial data. *Pharmacopsychiatry, 38,* 69–77.

Brannigan, G. G., & Decker, S. L. (2003). *Bender visual-motor Gestalt test* (2nd ed.). Itasca, IL: Riverside Publishing.

Brannigan, G. G., & Decker, S. L. (2006). The Bender-Gestalt II. *American Journal of Orthopsychiatry, 76,* 10–12.

Braun, J., Kahn, R. S., Froehlich, T., Auinger, P., & Lanphear, B. P. (2006). Exposures to environmental toxicants and attention deficit hyperactivity disorder in US children. *Environmental Health Perspectives, 114,* 1904–1909.

Breiter, H. C., Rauch, S. L., Kwong, K. K., Baker, J. R., Weisskoff, R. M., Kennedy, D. N., et al. (1996). Functional magnetic resonance imaging of symptom provocation in obsessive-compulsive disorder. *Archives of General Psychiatry, 53,* 595–606.

Breiter, H. C., & Rosen, B. R. (1999). Functional magnetic resonance imaging of brain reward circuitry in the human. In J. F. McGinty (Ed.), *Advancing from the ventral striatum to the extended amygdala: Implications for neuropsychiatry and drug use: In honor of Lennart Heimer* (pp. 523–547). New York: New York Academy of Sciences.

Bremner, J. D., Krystal, J. H., Putnam, F. W., Southwick, S. M., Marmar, C., Charney, D. S., et al. (1998). Measurement of dissociative states with the Clinician-Administered Dissociative States Scale (CADSS). *Journal of Traumatic Stress, 11,* 125–136.

Bremner, J. D., Krystal, J. H., Southwick, S. M., & Charney, D. S. (1995). Functional neuroanatomical correlates of the effects of stress on memory. *Journal of Trauma and Stress, 8,* 527–553.

Bremner, J. D., Randall, P., Scott, T. M., Bronen, R. A., Seibyl, J. P., Southwick, S. M., et al. (1995). MRI-based measurement of hippocampal volume in patients with combat-related posttraumatic stress disorder. *American Journal of Psychiatry, 152,* 973–981.

Bremner, J. D., Randall, P., Vermetten, E., Staib, L., Bronen, R. A., Mazure, C., et al. (1997). Magnetic resonance imaging-based measurement of hippocampal volume in posttraumatic stress disorder related to childhood physical and sexual abuse: A preliminary report. *Biological Psychiatry, 41,* 23–32.

Bremner, J. D., Vermetten, E., Afzal, N., & Vythilingam, M. (2004). Deficits in verbal declarative memory function in women with childhood sexual abuse-related posttraumatic stress disorder. *Journal of Nervous and Mental Disease, 192,* 643–649.

Bremner, J. D., Vythilingam, M., Vermetten, E., Southwick, S. M., McGlashan, T., Nazeer, A., et al. (2003). MRI and PET study of deficits in hippocampal structure and function in women with childhood sexual abuse and posttraumatic stress disorder. *American Journal of Psychiatry, 160,* 924–932.

Breslau, J., Aguilar-Gaxiola, S., Kendler, K. S., Su, M., Williams, D., & Kessler, R. C. (2006). Specifying race-ethnic differences in risk for psychiatric disorder in a USA national sample. *Psychological Medicine, 36,* 57–68.

Breslau, J., Kendler, K. S., Su, M., Aguilar-Gaxiola, S., & Kessler, R. C. (2005). Lifetime risk and persistence of psychiatric disorders across ethnic groups in the United States. *Psychological Medicine, 35,* 317–327.

Breslau, N., Kessler, R. C., Chilcoat, H. D. Schultz, L. R., Davis, G. C., & Andreski, P. (1998). Trauma and posttraumatic stress disorder in the community: The 1996 Detroit Area Survey of Trauma. *Archives of General Psychiatry, 55,* 626–632.

Breslau, N., Lucia, V. C., & Alvarado, G. F. (2006). Intelligence and other predisposing factors in exposure to trauma and posttraumatic stress disorder. *Archives of General Psychiatry, 63,* 1238–1245.

Breslau, N., Peterson, E., & Schultz, L. R. (2008). A second look at prior trauma and the posttraumatic stress disorder effects of subsequent trauma: A prospective epidemiological study. *Archives of General Psychiatry, 65,* 431–437.

Bressan, R. A., & Crippa, J. A. (2005). The role of dopamine in reward and pleasure behaviour—review of data from preclinical research. *Acta Psychiatrica Scandinavica, 111,* 14–21.

Bretherton, I. (1991). The roots and growing points of attachment theory. In C. M. Parkes, J. Stevenson-Hinde, & P. Marris (Eds.), *Attachment across the life cycle* (pp. 9–32). New York: Tavistock/Routledge.

Bretlau, L. G., Lunde, M., Lindberg, L., Undén, M., Dissing, S., & Bech, P. (2008). Repetitive transcranial magnetic stimulation (rTMS) in combination with escitalopram in patients with treatment-resistant major depression. A double-blind, randomised, sham-controlled trial. *Pharmacopsychiatry, 41,* 41–47.

Breuer, J., & Freud, S. (1955). *Studies on hysteria* (Vol. 2). (J. Strachey, Trans.). London: Hogarth Press. (Original work published 1895.)

Brewer, D. D., Catalano, R. F., Haggerty, K., Gainey, R. R., & Fleming, C. B. (1998). A meta-analysis of predictors of continued drug use during and after treatment for opiate addiction. *Addiction, 93,* 73–92.

Brewer, K. R., & Wann, D. L. (1998). Observational learning effectiveness as a function of model characteristics: Investigating the importance of social power. *Social Behavior & Personality, 26,* 1–10.

Brewin, C. R., Andrews, B., & Valentine, J. D. (2000). Meta-analysis of risk factors for posttraumatic stress disorder in trauma-exposed adults. *Journal of Consulting and Clinical Psychology, 68,* 748–766.

Bridge, J. A., Iyengar S., Salary, C. B., Barbe, R. P., Birmaher, B., Pincus, H. A., et al. (2007). Clinical response and risk for reported suicidal ideation and suicide attempts in pediatric antidepressant treatment: A meta-analysis of randomized controlled trials. *Journal of the American Medical Association, 297,* 1683–1696.

Briere, J. (2004). Trauma types and characteristics. In J. Briere (ed.), *Psychological assessment of adult posttraumatic states: Phenomenology, diagnosis, and measurement* (2nd ed., pp. 5–37). Washington, DC: American Psychological Association.

Briere, J., & Elliott, D. (2000). Prevalence, characteristics and long-term sequelae of natural disaster exposure in the general population. *Journal of Traumatic Stress, 13,* 661–679.

Briere, J., Scott, C., & Weathers, F. (2005). Peritraumatic and persistent dissociation in the presumed etiology of PTSD. *American Journal of Psychiatry, 162,* 2295–2301.

Brodey, D. (2005, September 20). Blacks join the eating-disorder mainstream. *New York Times.* Retrieved August 31, 2007, from http://www.nytimes.com/2005/09/20/health/psychology/20eat.html?ex=1188792000&en=07d24d3f858c7fc5&ei=5070

Brody, A. L., Saxena, S., Stoessel, P., Gillies, L. A., Fairbanks, L. A., Alborzian, S., et al. (2001). Regional brain metabolic changes in patients with major depression treated with either paroxetine or interpersonal therapy: Preliminary findings. *Archives of General Psychiatry, 58,* 631–640.

Broekman, B. F. P., Olff, M., & Boer, F. (2007). The genetic background to PTSD. *Neuroscience & Biobehavioral Reviews, 31,* 348–362.

Bromberg, W. (1937). *The mind of man: The story of man's conquest of mental illness.* New York: Harper.

Bromberger, J. T., Harlow, S., Avis, N., Kravitz, H. M., & Cordal, A. (2004). Racial/ethnic differences in the prevalence of depressive symptoms among middle-aged women: The Study of Women's Health Across the Nation (SWAN). *American Journal of Public Health, 94,* 1378–1385.

Brommelhoff, J. A., Conway, K., Merikangas, K., & Levy, B. R. (2004). Higher rates of depression in women: Role of gender bias within the family. *Journal of Women's Health, 13,* 69–76.

Brondolo, E., & Mas, F. (2001). Cognitive-behavioral strategies for improving medication adherence in patients with bipolar disorder. *Cognitive and Behavioral Practice, 8,* 137–147.

Brook, U., & Boaz, M. (2005). Attention-deficit and hyperactivity disorder (ADHD) and learning disabilities (LD): Adolescents' perspective. *Patient Education and Counseling, 58,* 187–191.

Brooks, A. (1974). *Law, psychiatry, and the mental health system.* Boston: Little, Brown.

Brosvic, G. M., Dihoff, R. E., Epstein, M. L., & Cook, M. L. (2006). Feedback facilitates the acquisition and retention of numerical fact series by elementary school students with mathematics learning disabilities. *Psychological Record, 56,* 35–54.

Brown, A. S., Begg, M. D., Gravenstein, S., Schaefer, C. A., Wyatt, R. J., Bresnahan, M., et al. (2004). Serologic evidence of prenatal influenza in the etiology of schizophrenia. *Archives of General Psychiatry, 61,* 774–780.

Brown, A. S., van Os, J., Driessens, C., Hoek, H. W., & Susser, E. S. (1999). Prenatal famine and the spectrum of psychosis. *Psychiatric Annals, 29,* 145–150.

Brown, G. K., Beck, A. T., Steer, R. A., & Grisham, J. R. (2000). Risk factors for suicide in psychiatric outpatients: A 20-year prospective study. *Journal of Consulting and Clinical Psychology, 68,* 371–377.

Brown, G. K., Newman, C. F., Charlesworth, S. E., Crits-Christoph, P., & Beck, A. T. (2004). An open clinical trial of cognitive therapy for borderline personality disorder. *Journal of Personality Disorders, 18,* 257–271.

Brown, H. D., Kosslyn, S. M., Delamater, B., Fama, J., & Barsky, A. J. (1999). Perceptual and memory biases for health-related information in hypochondriacal individuals. *Journal of Psychosomatic Research, 47,* 67–78.

Brown, M., Smits, J., Powers, M. B., & Telch, M. J. (2003). Differential factors in predicting panic disorder patients' subjective and behavioral hyperventilation challenge. *Journal of the Anxiety Disorders, 17,* 583–591.

Brown, P. H., & Broeske, P. H. (1996). *Howard Hughes: The untold story.* Cambridge, MA: Da Capo Press.

Brown, R. J., Schrag, A., & Trimble, M. R. (2005). Dissociation, childhood interpersonal trauma, and family functioning in patients with somatization disorder. *American Journal of Psychiatry, 162,* 899–905.

Brown, S. A., & D'Amico, E. J. (2001). Outcomes of alcohol treatment for adolescents. *Recent Developments in Alcoholism Research, 15,* 307–327.

Brown, S. A., Tate, S. R., Vik, P. W., Haas, A. L., & Aarons, G. A. (1999). Modeling of alcohol use mediates the effect of family history of alcoholism on adolescent alcohol expectancies. *Experimental and Clinical Psychopharmacology, 7,* 20–27.

Brown, T. A., & Barlow, D. H. (1997). *Casebook in abnormal psychology*. New York: Brooks/Cole.

Brown, T. A., & Barlow, D. H. (2002). Classification of anxiety and mood disorders. In D. H. Barlow (Ed.), *Anxiety and its disorders* (2nd ed., pp. 292–327). New York: Guilford Press.

Brown, T. A., Campbell, L. A., Lehman, C. L., Grisham, J. R., & Mancill, R. B. (2001). Current and lifetime comorbidity of the DSM-IV-TR anxiety and mood disorders in a large clinical sample. *Journal of Abnormal Psychology, 100,* 585–599.

Brown, T. A., O'Leary, T. A., & Barlow, D. H. (1993). Generalized anxiety disorder. In D. H. Barlow (Ed.), *Clinical handbook of psychological disorders: A step-by-step treatment manual* (2nd ed., pp. 137–188). New York: Guilford Press.

Brown, T. M., & Boyle, M. F. (2002). The ABC of psychological medicine: Delirium. *BMJ: British Medical Journal, 325,* 644–647.

Brown, W. A. (2002). Are antidepressants as ineffective as they look? *Prevention & Treatment, 5,* Article 26. http://www.journals.apa.org/prevention/volume5/pre0050026c.html

Brownell, K. D., & Rodin, J. (1992). Prevalence of eating disorders in athletes. In K. D. Brownell, J. Rodin, & J. H. Wilmore (Eds.), *Eating, body weight, and performance in athletes: Disorders of modern society* (pp. 128–145). Philadelphia: Lea & Febiger.

Brozgold, A. Z., Borod, J. C., Martin, C. C., Pick, L. H., Alpert, M., & Welkowitz, J. (1998). Social functioning and facial emotional expression in neurological and psychiatric disorders. *Applied Neuropsychology, 5,* 15–23.

Bruce, K. R., & Steiger, H. (2005). Treatment implications of Axis-II comorbidity in eating disorders. *Eating Disorders: Journal of Treatment & Prevention, 13,* 93–108.

Bruch, H. (1966). Anorexia nervosa and its differential diagnosis. *Journal of Nervous and Mental Disease, 141,* 555–566.

Brückl, T. M., Wittchen, H., Höfler, M., Pfister, H., Schneider, S., & Lieb, R. (2006). Childhood separation anxiety and the risk of subsequent psychopathology: Results from a community study. *Psychotherapy and Psychosomatics, 76,* 47–56.

Bruder, C. E., Piotrowski, A., Gijsbers, A. A., Andersson, R., Erickson, S., de Ståhl, T. D., et al. (2008). Phenotypically concordant and discordant monozygotic twins display different DNA copy-number-variation profiles. *American Journal of Human Genetics, 82,* 763–771.

Brunelin, J., Combris, M., Poulet, E., Kallel, L., d'Amato, T., Dalery, J., et al. (2006). Source monitoring deficits in hallucinating compared to non-hallucinating patients with schizophrenia. *European Psychiatry, 21,* 259–261.

Brunelin, J., d'Amato, T., Brun, P., Bediou, B., Kallel, L., Senn, M., et al. (2007). Impaired verbal source monitoring in schizophrenia: An intermediate trait vulnerability marker? *Schizophrenia Research, 89,* 287–292.

Brunelin, J., d'Amato, T., van Os, J., Cochet, A., Suaud-Chagny, M., & Saoud, M. (2008). Effects of acute metabolic stress on the dopaminergic and pituitary-adrenal axis activity in patients with schizophrenia, their unaffected siblings and controls. *Schizophrenia Research, 100,* 206–211.

Brunelin, J., Poulet, E., Bediou, B., Kallel, L., Dalery, J., d'Amato, T., et al. (2006). Low frequency repetitive transcranial magnetic stimulation improves source monitoring deficit in hallucinating patients with schizophrenia. *Schizophrenia Research, 81,* 41–45.

Brunello, N., & Racagni, G. (1998). Rationale for the development of noradrenaline reuptake inhibitors. *Human Psychopharmacology Clinical & Experimental, 13,* S13–S19.

Brunner, J., & Bronisch, T. (1999). Neurobiological correlates of suicidal behavior. Facharzt für Psychiatrie und Psychotherapie, 67, 391–412.

Bryant, R. A., & Harvey, A. G., (2000). *Acute stress disorder: A handbook of theory, assessment and treatment.* Washington, DC: American Psychological Association.

Bryant, R. A., Mastrodemenico, J., Felmingham, K. L., Hopwood, S., Kenny, L., Dandris, E., et al. (2008). Treatment of acute stress disorder: A randomized controlled trial. *Archives of General Psychiatry, 65,* 659–667.

Bryant, R. A., Moulds, M. L., Guthrie, R. M., & Nixon, R. D. V. (2005). The additive benefit of hypnosis and cognitive-behavioral therapy in treating acute stress disorder. *Journal of Consulting and Clinical Psychology, 73,* 334–340.

Bryant, R. A., Moulds, M. L., Nixon, R. D. V., Mastrodomenico, J., Felmingham, K., & Hopwood, S. (2006). Hypnotherapy and cognitive behaviour therapy of acute stress disorder: A 3-year follow-up. *Behaviour Research and Therapy, 44,* 1331–1335.

Bryant-Waugh, R. (1993). Epidemiology. In B. Lask & R. Bryant-Waugh, (Eds.), *Childhood onset anorexia nervosa and related eating disorders* (pp. 55–68). Hillsdale, NJ: Lawrence Erlbaum.

Buchsbaum, M. S., Christian, B. T., Lehrer, D. S., Narayanan, T. K., Shi, B., Mantil, J., et al. (2006). D2/D3 dopamine receptor binding with [F-18]fallypride in thalamus and cortex of patients with schizophrenia. *Schizophrenia Research, 85,* 232–244.

Buchsbaum, M. S., Nenadic, I., Hazlett, E. A., Spiegal-Cohen, J., Fleischman, M. B., Akhavan, A., et al. (2002). Differential metabolic rates in prefrontal and temporal Brodmann areas in schizophrenia and schizotypal personality disorder. *Schizophrenia Research, 54,* 141–150.

Buckalew, L. W., & Ross, S. (1981). Relationship of perceptual characteristics to efficacy of placebos. *Psychological Reports, 49,* 955–961.

Buckley, P. F., Wirshing, D. A., Bhushan, P., Pierre, J. M., Resnick, S. A., & Wirshing, W. C. (2007). Lack of insight in schizophrenia: Impact on treatment adherence. *CNS Drugs, 21,* 129–141.

Budney, A. J., Hughes, J. R., Moore, B. A., & Vandrey, R. (2004). Review of the validity and significance of cannabis withdrawal syndrome. *American Journal of Psychiatry, 161,* 1967–1977.

Buhlmann, U., Etcoff, N. L., & Wilhelm, S. (2006). Emotion recognition bias for contempt and anger in body dysmorphic disorder. *Journal of Psychiatric Research, 40,* 105–111.

Buhlmann, U., Etcoff, N. L., & Wilhelm, S. (2008). Facial attractiveness ratings and perfectionism in body dysmorphic disorder and obsessive-compulsive disorder. *Journal of Anxiety Disorders, 22,* 540–547.

Buhlmann, U., McNally, R. J., Wilhelm, S., & Florin, I. (2002). Selective processing of emotional information in body dysmorphic disorder. *Journal of Anxiety Disorders, 16,* 289–298.

Buka, S. L., Goldstein, J. M., Seidman, L. J., Zornberg, G. L., Donatelli, J. A., Denny, L. R., et al. (1999). Prenatal complications, genetic vulnerability and schizophrenia: The New England longitudinal studies of schizophrenia. *Psychiatric Annals, 29,* 151–156.

Bulik, C. M. (2004). Genetic and biological risk factors. In J. K. Thompson (Ed.), *Handbook of eating disorders and obesity* (pp. 3–16). Hoboken, NJ: John Wiley & Sons.

Bulik, C. M. (2005). Exploring the gene-environment nexus in eating disorders. *Journal of Psychiatry & Neuroscience, 30,* 335–339.

Bulik, C. M., Sullivan, P. F., Fear, J., & Pickering, A. (1997). Predictors of the development of bulimia nervosa in women with anorexia nervosa. *Journal of Nervous and Mental Disease, 185,* 704–707.

Burgess, S., Geddes, J., Hawton, K., Townsend, E., Jamison, K., & Goodwin, G. (2001). Lithium for maintenance treatment of mood disorders. *Cochrane Database System Review,* CD003013.

Burke, A. W. (1984). Racism and psychological disturbance among West

Indians in Britain. *International Journal of Social Psychiatry, 30*, 50–68.

Burke, J. D., Jr., & Regier, D. A. (1994). Epidemiology of mental disorders. In R. E. Hales, S. C. Yudofsky, & J. A. Talbott (Eds.), *The American Psychiatric Press textbook of psychiatry* (2nd ed., pp. 81–104). Washington, DC: American Psychiatric Association.

Burnette, M. L., & Newman, D. L. (2005). The natural history of conduct disorder symptoms in female inmates: On the predictive utility of the syndrome in severely antisocial women. *American Journal of Orthopsychiatry, 75*, 421–430.

Burns, D. (1980). *Feeling good: The new mood therapy.* New York: Signet.

Bush, G., Spencer, T. J., Holmes, J., Shin, L. M., Valera, E. M., Seidman, L. J., et al. (2008). Functional magnetic resonance imaging of methylphenidate and placebo in attention-deficit/hyperactivity disorder during the multi-source interference task. *Archives of General Psychiatry, 65*, 102–114.

Buss, A. H. (1995). *Personality: Temperament, social behavior, and the self.* Needham Heights, MA: Allyn & Bacon.

Bustillo, J. R., Lauriello, J., Horan, W. P., & Keith, S. J. (2001). The psychosocial treatment of schizophrenia: An update. *American Journal of Psychiatry, 158*, 163–175.

Butcher, J. N., & Rouse, S. V. (1996). Personality: Individual difference and clinical assessment. *Annual Review of Psychology, 47*, 87–111.

Butler, L. D., Duran, R. E. F., Jasiukaitis, P., Koopman, C., & Spiegel, D. (1996). Hypnotizability and traumatic experience: A diathesis-stress model of dissociative symptomatology. *American Journal of Psychiatry, 153*, 42–46.

Butler, R. N., & Lewis, M. I. (2002). *The new love and sex after 60.* New York: Ballantine Books.

Butzlaff, R. L., & Hooley, J. M. (1998). Expressed emotion and psychiatric relapse. *Archives of General Psychiatry, 55*, 547–552.

Cachelin, F. M., & Maher, B. A. (1998). Is amenorrhea a critical criterion for anorexia nervosa? *Journal of Psychosomatic Research, 44*, 435–440.

Cadoret, R. J. (1990). Genetics of alcoholism. In R. L. Collins, K. E. Leonard, & J. S. Searles (Eds.), *Alcohol and the family: Research and clinical perspectives* (pp. 39–78). New York: Guilford Press.

Cadoret, R. J., Yates, W. R., Troughton, E., Woodworth, G., & Stewart, M. A. (1995). Adoption study demonstrating two genetic pathways to drug abuse. *Archives of General Psychiatry, 52,* 42–52.

Cahn, W., Hulshoff Pol, H. E., Lems, E. B. T. E., van Haren, N. E. M., Schnack, H. G., van

der Linden, J. A., et al. (2002). Brain volume changes in first-episode schizophrenia: A 1-year follow-up study. *Archives of General Psychiatry, 59*, 1002–1012.

Cairl v. State, 323 N.W.2d 20 (Minn. 1982).

Calderon, R., Vander Stoep, A., Collett, B., Garrison, M. M., & Toth, K. (2007). Inpatients with eating disorders: Demographic, diagnostic, and service characteristics from a nationwide pediatric sample. *International Journal of Eating Disorders, 40*, 622–628.

Caldwell, C., & Gottesman, I. (1990). Schizophrenics kill themselves too: A review of risk factors for suicide. *Schizophrenia Bulletin, 16*, 571–589.

Calkins, M. E., Curtis, C. E., Grove, W. M., & Iacono, W. G. (2004). Multiple dimensions of schizotypy in first degree biological relatives of schizophrenia patients. *Schizophrenia Bulletin, 30*, 317–325.

Callicott, J. H., Mattay, V. S., Verchinski, B. A., Marenco, S., Egan, M. F., & Weinberger, D. R. (2003). Complexity of prefrontal cortical dysfunction in schizophrenia: More than up or down. *American Journal of Psychiatry, 160*, 2209–2215.

Calogero, R. M., Davis, W. N., & Thompson, J. K. (2005). The role of self-objectification in the experience of women with eating disorders. *Sex Roles, 52*, 43–50.

Calvocoressi, L., Lewis, B., Harris, M., Trufan, S. J., Goodman, W. K., McDougle, C. J., et al. (1995). Family accommodation in obsessive-compulsive disorder. *American Journal of Psychiatry, 152,* 441–443.

Camilleri, J. A., & Quinsey, V. L. (2008). Pedophilia: Assessment and treatment. In D. R. Laws & W. T. O'Donohue (Eds.), *Sexual deviance: Theory, assessment, and treatment* (2nd ed., pp. 183–212). New York: Guilford Press.

Campbell, E., & Ruane, J. (1999). *The Earl Campbell story.* Toronto: ECW Press.

Campbell, J. M., & Morgan, S. B. (1998). Asperger's disorder. In L. Phelps (Ed.), *Health-related disorders in children and adolescents: A guidebook for understanding and educating* (pp. 68–73). Washington, DC: American Psychological Association.

Campbell, L. F., & Smith, T. P. (2003). Integrating self-help books into psychotherapy. *Journal of Clinical Psychology/In Session, 59*(2), 177–186.

Campinha-Bacote, J. (1992). Voodoo illness. *Perspectives in Psychiatric Care, 28*, 11–17.

Canetto, S. S. (1992). Gender and suicide in the elderly. *Suicide and Life-Threatening Behavior, 22*, 80–97.

Canino, I. A., Rubio-Stipec, M., Canino, G. J., & Escobar, J. I. (1992). Functional somatic symptoms: A cross-

ethnic comparison. *American Journal of Orthopsychiatry, 62*, 605–68.

Cannon, M., Jones, P., Huttunen, M. O., Tanskanen, A., Huttunen, T., Rabe-Hesketh, S., et al. (1999). School performance in Finnish children and later development of schizophrenia: A population-based longitudinal study. *Archives of General Psychiatry, 56*, 457–463.

Cannon, T. D. (1997). On the nature and mechanisms of obstetric influences in schizophrenia: A review and synthesis of epidemiologic studies. *International Review of Psychiatry, 9*, 387–397.

Cannon, T. D. (1998). Neurodevelopmental influences in the genesis and epigenesis of schizophrenia: An overview. *Applied & Preventive Psychology, 7*, 47–62.

Cannon, T. D., Huttunen, M. O., Dahlstroem, M., Larmo, I., Raesaenen, P., & Juriloo, A. (2002). Antipsychotic drug treatment in the prodromal phase of schizophrenia. *American Journal of Psychiatry, 159*, 1230–1232.

Cantor, C. (1996). *Phantom illness: Shattering the myth of hypochondria.* Boston: Houghton Mifflin.

Cantor-Graae, E., & Selten, J. (2005). Schizophrenia and migration: A meta-analysis and review. *American Journal of Psychiatry, 162*, 12–24.

Cao, F., Bitan, T., Chou, T., Burman, D. D., & Booth, J. R. (2006). Deficient orthographic and phonological representations in children with dyslexia revealed by brain activation patterns. *Journal of Child Psychology and Psychiatry, 47*, 1041–1050.

Caparulo, B. K., & Cohen, D. J. (1977). Cognitive structures, language, and emerging social competence in autistic and aphasic children. *Journal of the American Academy of Child Psychiatry, 16*, 620–645.

Caplan, P. J. (1995). *They say you're crazy: How the world's most powerful psychiatrists decide who's normal.* Reading, MA: Addison Wesley Longman.

Caputo, A. A., Frick, P. J., & Brodsky, S. L. (1999). Family violence and juvenile sex offending: The potential mediating role of psychopathic traits and negative attitudes toward women. *Criminal Justice and Behavior, 26*, 338–356.

Cardeña, E., & Spiegel, D. (1993). Dissociative reactions to the San Francisco Bay Area earthquake of 1989. *American Journal of Psychiatry, 150*, 474–478.

Carey, M. P., & Gordon, C. M. (1995). Sexual dysfunction among heterosexual adults: Description, epidemiology, assessment, and treatment. In L. Diamant & R. D. McAnulty (Eds.), *The psychology of sexual orientation, behavior, and identity: A handbook* (pp. 165–196). New York: Greenwood.

Carlat, D. J., Camargo, C. A., Jr., & Herzog, D. B. (1997). Eating disorders in males: A report on 135 patients. *American Journal of Psychiatry, 154,* 1127–1132.

Carlbring, P., & Andersson, G. (2006). Internet and psychological treatment. How well can they be combined? *Computers in Human Behavior, 22,* 545–553.

Carlbring, P., Furmark, T., Steczkó, J., Ekselius, L., & Andersson, G. (2006). An open study of internet-based bibliotherapy with minimal therapist contact via email for social phobia. *Clinical Psychologist, 10,* 30–38.

Carlbring, P., Nilsson-Ihrfelt, E., Waara, J., Kollenstam, C., Buhrman, M., Kaldo, V., et al. (2005). Treatment of panic disorder: Live therapy vs. self-help via the Internet. *Behaviour Research and Therapy, 43,* 1321–1333.

Carlisle, N. (2009, February 13). Elizabeth Smart kidnap case: Mitchell booked into Salt Lake Country jail. *The Salt Lake Tribune.* Retrieved on February 28, 2009, from http://www.sltrib.com/faith/ci_11697926

Carlson, N. R. (1994). *Physiology of behavior.* Needham Heights, MA: Allyn & Bacon.

Carmelli, D., Heath, R., & Robinette, D. (1993). Genetic analysis of drinking behavior in World War II veteran twins. *Genetic Epidemiology, 10,* 201–213.

Carr, J. E., & Chong, I. M. (2005). Habit reversal treatment of tic disorders: A methodological critique of the literature. *Behavior Modification, 29,* 858–875.

Carroll, K. M. (1998). *A cognitive-behavioral approach: Treating cocaine addiction.* National Institute on Drug Abuse. NIH Publication Number 98–4308. Retrieved Month October 6th, 2009, from http://www.drugabuse.gov/TXManuals/CBT/CBT1.html

Carroll, K. M., & Onken, L. S. (2005). Behavioral therapies for drug abuse. *American Journal of Psychiatry, 162,* 1454–1460.

Carroll, K. M., Ball, S. A., Martino, S., Nich, C., Babuscio, T. A., Nuro, K. F., et al. (2008). Computer-assisted delivery of cognitive-behavioral therapy for addiction: A randomized trial of CBT4CBT. *American Journal of Psychiatry, 165,* 881–888.

Carroll, K. M., Fenton, L. R., Ball, S. A., Nich, C., Frankforter, T. L., Shi, J., et al. (2004). Efficacy of disulfiram and cognitive behavior therapy in cocaine-dependent outpatients. *Archives of General Psychiatry, 61,* 264–272.

Carroll, K. M., Rounsaville, B. J., & Bryant, K. J. (1993). Alcoholism in treatment-seeking cocaine abusers: Clinical and prognostic significance. *Journal of Studies on Alcohol, 54,* 199–208.

Carroll, R. A. (2000). Gender dysphoria. In S. R. Leiblum & R. C. Rosen (Eds.), *Principles and practice of sex therapy* (3rd ed., pp. 368–397). New York: Guilford Press.

Carter, B., & McGoldrick, M. (1999). Overview: The expanded family life cycle: Individual, family, and social perspectives. In B. Carter & M. McGoldrick (Eds.), *The expanded family life cycle: Individual, family, and social perspectives* (3rd ed., pp. 1–26). Boston: Allyn & Bacon.

Carter, M. M., Hollon, S. D., Carson, R., & Shelton, R. C. (1995). Effects of a safe person on induced distress following a biological challenge in panic disorder with agoraphobia. *Journal of Abnormal Psychology, 104,* 156–163.

Casbon, T. S., Burns, A. B., Bradbury, T. N., & Joiner, T. E., Jr. (2005). Receipt of negative feedback is related to increased negative feedback seeking among individuals with depressive symptoms. *Behaviour Research and Therapy, 43,* 485–504.

Caseras, X., Garner, M., Bradley, B. P., & Mogg, K. (2007). Biases in visual orienting to negative and positive scenes in dysphoria: An eye movement study. *Journal of Abnormal Psychology, 116,* 491–497.

Cash, T. F. (1995). Developmental teasing about physical appearance: Retrospective descriptions and relationships with body image. *Social Behavior and Personality, 23,* 123–129.

Caspi, A., McClay, J., Moffitt, T. E., Mill, J., Martin, J., Craig, I. W., et al. (2002). Role of genotype in the cycle of violence in maltreated children. *Science, 297,* 851–854.

Caspi, A., Moffitt, T. E., Newman, D. L., & Silva, P. A. (1996). Behavioral observations at age 3 predict adult psychiatric disorders: Longitudinal evidence from a birth cohort. *Archives of General Psychiatry, 53,* 1033–1039.

Cassady, J. D., Kirschke, D. L., Jones, T. F., Craig, A. S., Bermudez, O. B., & Schaffner, W. (2005). Case series: Outbreak of conversion disorder among Amish adolescent girls. *Journal of the American Academy of Child & Adolescent Psychiatry, 44,* 291–297.

Cassano, G. B., Mula, M., Rucci, P., Miniati, M., Frank, E., Kupfer, D. J., et al. (2009). The structure of lifetime manic-hypomanic spectrum. *Journal of Affective Disorders, 112,* 59–70.

Cassin, S. E., & von Ranson, K. M. (2005). Personality and eating disorders: A decade in review. *Clinical Psychology Review, 25,* 895–916.

Castellanos, F. X., Lee, P. P., Sharp, W., Jeffries, N. O., Greenstein, D. K., Clasen, L. S., et al. (2002). Developmental trajectories of brain volume abnormalities in children and adolescents with attention deficit/hyperactivity disorder. *Journal of*

the *American Medical Association, 288,* 1740–1748.

Castillo, H. (2003). *Personality disorder: Temperament or trauma?* London: Jessica Kingsley.

Castillo, R. J. (1997). *Culture & mental illness: A client-centered approach.* Belmont, CA: Thomson/Brooks/Cole.

Castle, D. J., & Rossell, S. L. (2006). An update on body dysmorphic disorder. *Current Opinion in Psychiatry, 19,* 74–78.

Castonguay, L. G., Goldfried, M. R., Wiser, S., Raue, P. J., & Hayes, A. M. (1996). Predicting the effect of cognitive therapy for depression: A study of unique and common factors. *Journal of Consulting and Clinical Psychology, 64,* 497–504.

Catanzaro, S. J., & Laurent, J. (2004). Perceived family support, negative mood regulation expectancies, coping, and adolescent alcohol use: Evidence of mediation and moderation effects. *Addictive Behaviors, 29,* 1779–1797.

Cattell, R. B. (1971). *Abilities: Their structure, growth, and action.* New York: Houghton Mifflin.

Caudill, B. D., & Kong, F. H. (2001). Social approval and facilitation in predicting modeling effects in alcohol consumption. *Journal of Substance Abuse, 13,* 425–441.

Cederlund, M., & Gillberg, C. (2004). One hundred males with Asperger syndrome: A clinical study of background and associated factors. *Developmental Medicine & Child Neurology, 46,* 652–660.

Celani, D. (1976). An interpersonal approach to hysteria. *American Journal of Psychiatry, 133,* 1414–1418.

Centers for Disease Control and Prevention, National Center for Health Statistics. (2000, July 24). Death and death rates for the 10 leading causes of death specified in age groups, by race and sex: United States, 1998. *Monthly Vital Statistics Reports, 48*(11), 26. Retrieved October, 6, 2002, from http://www.cdc.gov/nchs/fastats/suicide.htm

Centers for Disease Control and Prevention, National Center for Injury Prevention and Control. (2005). Web-based injury statistics query and reporting system (WISQARS) [Online]. Retrieved October 20, 2008, from www.cdc.gov/ncipc/wisqars/default.htm

Cervera, S., Lahortiga, F., Martinez-Gonzalez, M. A., Gual, P., Irala-Estevez, J. D., & Alonso, Y. (2003). Neuroticism and low self-esteem as risk factors for incident eating disorders in a prospective cohort study. *International Journal of Eating Disorders, 33,* 271–280.

Chacko, A., Pelham, W. E., Jr., Gnagy, E. M., Greiner, A., Vallano, G., Bukstein, O., et al. (2005). Stimulant medication effects in a summer treatment program among young children with attention-deficit/hyperactivity disorder. *Journal of the American Academy of Child & Adolescent Psychiatry, 44,* 249–257.

Chakraborty, A., & McKenzie, K. (2002). Does racial discrimination cause mental illness? *British Journal of Psychiatry, 180,* 475–477.

Chalkley, A. J., & Powell, G. E. (1983). The clinical description of forty-eight cases of sexual fetishism. *British Journal of Psychiatry, 142,* 292–295.

Chamberlain, P. (1996). Intensified foster care: Multi-level treatment for adolescents with conduct disorders in out-of-home care. In E. D. Hibbs & P. S. Jensen (Eds.), *Psychosocial treatments for child and adolescent disorders: Empirically based strategies for clinical practice* (pp. 475–495). Washington, DC: American Psychological Association.

Chambers, J., Yeragani, V. K., & Keshavan, M. S. (1986). Phobias in India and the United Kingdom: A trans-cultural study. *Acta Psychiatrica Scandinavica, 74,* 388–391.

Chambless, D. L. (2002). Beware the dodo bird: The dangers of overgeneralization. *Clinical Psychology: Science & Practice, 9,* 13–16.

Chambless, D. L. (2002). Identification of empirically supported counseling psychology interventions: Commentary. *Counseling Psychologist, 30,* 302–308.

Chambless, D. L., Fydrich, T., & Rodebaugh, T. L. (2008). Generalized social phobia and avoidant personality disorder: Meaningful distinction or useless duplication? *Depression and Anxiety, 25,* 8–19.

Chambless, D. L., & Gillis, M. M. (1994). A review of psychosocial treatments for panic disorder. In B. E. Wolfe & J. D. Maser (Eds.), *Treatment of panic disorder: A consensus development conference* (pp. 149–173). Washington, DC: American Psychiatric Association.

Chambless, D. L., & Hollon, S. D. (1998). Defining empirically supported therapies. *Journal of Consulting and Clinical Psychology, 66,* 7–18.

Chambless, D. L., & Ollendick, T. H. (2001). Empirically supported psychological interventions: Controversies and evidence. *Annual Review of Psychology, 52,* 685–716.

Chan, A. S., Kwok, I. C., Chiu, H., Lam, L., Pang, A., & Chow, L. (2000). Memory and organizational strategies in chronic and acute schizophrenic patients. *Schizophrenia Research, 41,* 431–445.

Chang, C., Chen, W. J., Liu, S. K., Cheng, J. J., Yang, W. O., Chang, H., et al. (2002). Morbidity risk of psychiatric disorders among the first degree relatives of schizophrenia patients in Taiwan. *Schizophrenia Bulletin, 28,* 379–392.

Chantarujikapong, S. I., Scherrer, J. F., Xian, H., Eisen, S. A., Lyons, M. J., Goldberg, J., et al. (2001). A twin study of generalized anxiety disorder symptoms, panic disorder symptoms and post-traumatic stress disorder in men. *Psychiatry Research, 103,* 133–146.

Chapple, B., Chant, D., Nolan, P., Cardy, S., Whiteford, H., & McGrath, J. (2004). Correlates of victimisation amongst people with psychosis. *Social Psychiatry and Psychiatric Epidemiology, 39,* 836–840.

Charney, D. S., Deutch, A. Y., Krystal, J. H., Southwick, S. M., & Davis M. (1993). Psychobiologic mechanisms of posttraumatic stress disorder. *Archives of General Psychiatry, 50,* 294–305.

Chartier, M. J., Walker, J. R., & Stein, M. B. (2003). Considering comorbidity in social phobia. *Social Psychiatry and Psychiatric Epidemiology, 38,* 728–734.

Chattopadhyay, S. (2005). Do schizophrenics experience emotion but differ in expression? *Internet Journal of Mental Health, 2,* 1–6.

Chaves, J. F. (2000). Hypnosis. In A. E. Kazdin (Ed.), *Encyclopedia of psychology* (Vol. 4, pp. 211–216). Washington, DC: American Psychological Association.

Cheng, A. T. A. (2002). Expressed emotion: A cross-culturally valid concept? *British Journal of Psychiatry, 181,* 466–467.

Cheng, D. (2002, October 7). Moderate altitude increases suicide deaths. Poster presented at the Research Forum Educational Program, American College of Emergency Physicians, Seattle, Washington.

Chess, S., & Thomas, A. (1996). *Temperament: Theory and practice.* Philadelphia: Brunner/Mazel.

Cheung, V. Y., Bocking, A. D., & Dasilva, O. P. (1995). Preterm discordant twins: What birth weight difference is significant? *American Journal of Obstetrics & Gynecology, 172,* 955–959.

Chilcoat, H. D., & Breslau, N. (1998). Posttraumatic stress disorder and drug disorders: Testing causal pathways. *Archives of General Psychiatry, 55,* 913–917.

Christophersen, E. R. (1994). *Pediatric compliance: A guide for the primary care physician.* New York: Plenum Medical Book Co/Plenum Publishing Corp.

Christophersen, E. R., & Mortweet, S. L. (2001). Diagnosis and management of disruptive behavior disorders. In *Treatments that work with children: Empirically supported strategies for managing childhood problems* (pp. 11–48). Washington, DC: American Psychological Association.

Chu, J. A., & International Society for the Study of Dissociation. (2005). Guidelines for treating dissociative identity disorder in adults. *Journal of Trauma & Dissociation, 6,* 69–149.

Chung, H. (2002). The challenges of providing behavioral treatment for Asian Americans. *Western Journal of Medicine, 176*(4), 222–223.

Cicchetti, D., & Toth, S. L. (1991). *Internalizing and externalizing expressions of dysfunction.* Hillsdale, NJ: Lawrence Erlbaum.

Cicchetti, D., & Toth, S. L. (2005). Child maltreatment. *Annual Review of Clinical Psychology, 1,* 409–438.

Cicero, T. J. (1978). Tolerance to and physiological dependence on alcohol: Behavioral and neurobiological mechanisms. In M. A. Lipton, A. DiMascio, & K. F. Killman (Eds.), *Psychopharmacology.* New York: Raven.

Cipriani, A., Geddes, J. R., Furukawa, T. A., & Barbui, C. (2007). Meta-review on short-term effectiveness and safety of antidepressants for depression: An evidence-based approach to inform clinical practice. *The Canadian Journal of Psychiatry/La Revue canadienne de psychiatrie, 52,* 553–562.

Citron, M., Solomon, P., & Draine, J. (1999). Self-help groups for families of persons with mental illness: Perceived benefits of helpfulness. *Community Mental Health Journal, 35,* 15–30.

Claes, S. J. (2004). Corticotropin-releasing hormone (CRH) in psychiatry: From stress to psychopathology. *Annals of Medicine, 36,* 50–61.

Clark, D. A. (2005). Focus on "cognition" in cognitive behavior therapy for OCD: Is it really necessary? *Cognitive Behaviour Therapy, 34,* 131–139.

Clark, D. M. (1986). A cognitive approach to panic. *Behaviour Research and Therapy, 24,* 461–470.

Clark, D. M., Ehlers, A., Hackmann, A., McManus, F., Fennell, M., Grey, N., et al. (2006). Cognitive therapy versus exposure and applied relaxation in social phobia: A randomized controlled trial. *Journal of Consulting and Clinical Psychology, 74,* 568–578.

Clark, D. M., Salkovskis, P. M., Gelder, M. G., Koehler, C., Martin, M., Anastasiades, P., et al. (1988). Tests of a cognitive theory of panic. In I. Hand & H. U. Wittchen (Eds.), *Panic and phobias II.* New York: Springer-Verlag.

Clark, D. M., Salkovskis, P. M., Hackmann, A., Middleton, H., Anastasiades, P., & Gelder, M. (1994). A comparison of cognitive therapy, applied relaxation and imipramine in the treatment of panic disorder. *British Journal of Psychiatry, 164,* 759–769.

Clark, L. A. (2007). Assessment and diagnosis of personality disorder: Perennial issues and an emerging reconceptualization. *Annual Review of Psychology, 58,* 227–257.

Clark, L. A. (2009). Stability and change in personality disorder. *Current Directions in Psychological Science, 18,* 27–31.

Clark, L. A., & Watson, D. (1991). Tripartite model of anxiety and depression: Evidence and taxonomic implications. *Journal of Abnormal Psychology, 100,* 316–336.

Clarke, A. R., Barry, R. J., McCarthy, R., Selikowitz, M., & Johnstone, S. J. (2007). Effects of stimulant medications on the EEG of girls with attention-deficit/hyperactivity disorder. *Clinical Neurophysiology, 118,* 2700–2708.

Clarke, M. C., Harley, M., & Cannon, M. (2006). The role of obstetric events in schizophrenia. *Schizophrenia Bulletin, 32,* 3–8.

Clarkin, J. F., & Levy, K. N. (2004). The influence of client variables on psychotherapy. In M. J. Lambert (Ed.), *Bergin & Garfield's handbook of psychotherapy and behavior change* (5th ed., pp. 194–226). New York: John Wiley & Sons.

Clarkin, J. F., Levy, K. N., Lenzenweger, M. F., & Kernberg, O. F. (2007). Evaluating three treatments for borderline personality disorder: A multiwave study. *American Journal of Psychiatry, 164,* 922–928.

Clausius, N., Born, C., & Grunze H. (2009). The relevance of dopamine agonists in the treatment of depression. Neuropsychiatrie: Klinik, Diagnostik, Therapie und Rehabilitation: Organ der Gesellschaft Osterreichischer Nervenarzte und Psychiater, 23, 15–25.

Clayton, R. R. (1992). Transitions in drug use: Risk and protective factors. In M. Glantz & R. Pickens (Eds.), *Vulnerability to drug abuse* (pp. 15–51). Washington, DC: American Psychological Association.

Clementz, B. A., & Sweeney, J. A. (1990). Is eye movement dysfunction a biological marker for schizophrenia? A methodological review. *Psychological Bulletin, 108,* 77–92.

Clifton, A., Turkheimer, E., & Oltmanns, T. F. (2004). Contrasting perspectives on personality problems: Descriptions from the self and others. *Personality and Individual Differences, 36,* 1499–1514.

Cloitre, M., Shear, M. K., Cancienne, J., & Zeitlin, S. B. (1994). Implicit and explicit memory for catastrophic associations to bodily sensation words in panic disorder. *Cognitive Therapy & Research, 18,* 225–240.

Cloninger, C. R. (1987). A systematic method for clinical description and classification of personality variants: A proposal. *Archives of General Psychiatry, 44,* 573–588.

Cloninger, C. R. (1987). Neurogenetic adaptive mechanisms in alcoholism. *Science, 236,* 410–416.

Cloninger, C. R. (2005). Genetics. In J. M. Oldham, A. E. Skodol, & D. S. Bender (Eds.). *The American Psychiatric Publishing textbook of personality disorders* (pp. 143–154). Washington, DC: American Psychiatric Publishing.

Cloninger, C. R., Bohman, M., & Sigvardsson, S. (1981). Inheritance of alcohol abuse: Cross-fostering analysis of adopted men. *Archives of General Psychiatry, 38,* 861–868.

Cloninger, C. R., Svrakic, D. M., & Przybeck, T. R. (1993). A psychobiological model of temperament and character. *Archives of General Psychiatry, 50,* 975–990.

Cloos, J. (2005). The treatment of panic disorder. *Current Opinion in Psychiatry, 18,* 45–50.

Cobb, H. C., Reeve, R. E., Shealy, C. N., Norcross, J. C., Schare, M. L., Rodolfa, E. R., et al. (2004). Overlap among clinical, counseling, and school psychology: Implications for the profession and combined-integrated training. *Journal of Clinical Psychology, 60,* 939–955.

Coelho, C. M., Waters, A. M., Hine, T. J., & Wallis, G. (in press). The use of virtual reality in acrophobia research and treatment. *Journal of Anxiety Disorders, np.*

Cohen, C. I., Cohen, G. D., Blank, K., Gaitz, C., Katz, I. R., Leuchter, A., et al. (2000). Schizophrenia and older adults: An overview: Directions for research and policy. *American Journal of Geriatric Psychiatry, 8,* 19–28.

Cohen, H., Kaplan, Z., Kotler, M., Kouperman, I., Moisa, R., & Grisaru, N. (2004). Repetitive transcranial magnetic stimulation of the right dorsolateral prefrontal cortex in posttraumatic stress disorder: A double-blind, placebo-controlled study. *American Journal of Psychiatry, 161,* 515–524.

Cohen, P., Cohen, J., Kasen, S., Velez, C., Hartmark, C., Johnson, J., et al. (1993). An epidemiological study of disorders in late childhood and adolescence: I. Age- and gender-specific prevalence. *Journal of Child Psychology and Psychiatry, 34,* 851–867.

Cohen-Kettenis, P. T., & Gooren, L. J. G. (1999). Transsexualism: A review of etiology, diagnosis and treatment. *Journal of Psychosomatic Research, 46,* 315–333.

Colas, E. (1998). *Just checking: Scenes from the life of an obsessive-compulsive.* New York: Pocket Books.

Colder, C. R., Chassin, L., Stice, E. M., & Curran, P. J. (1997). Alcohol expectancies as potential mediators of parent alcoholism effects on the development of adolescent heavy drinking. *Journal of Research on Adolescence, 7,* 349–374.

Coles, J. (2007, March 9). Mechanic: I have sex with cars. *The Sun.* Retrieved on April 17, 2009 from http://www.thesun.co.uk/sol/homepage/news/article21242.ece

Coles, M. E., Phillips, K. A., Menard, W., Pagano, M. E., Fay, C., Weisberg, R. B., et al. (2006). Body dysmorphic disorder and social phobia: Cross-sectional and prospective data. *Depression and Anxiety, 23,* 26–33.

Collett, B. R., & Gimpel, G. A. (2004). Maternal and child attributions in ADHD versus non-ADHD populations. *Journal of Attention Disorders, 7,* 187–196.

Collings, S., & King, M. (1994). Ten year follow-up of 50 patients with bulimia nervosa. *British Journal of Psychiatry, 164,* 80–87.

Colman, I., Murray, J., Abbott, R., Maughan, B, Kuh, D., Croudace, T. J., et al. (2009). Outcomes of conduct problems in adolescence: 40 year follow-up of national cohort. *British Medical Journal, 338,* a2981.

Combs, D. R., Basso, M. R., Wanner, J. L., & Ledet, S. N. (2008). Schizophrenia. In M. Hersen & J. Rosqvist (Eds.), *Handbook of psychological assessment, case conceptualization, and treatment, Vol 1: Adults* (pp. 352–402). Hoboken, NJ: John Wiley & Sons.

Compton, W. M., Conway, K. P., Stinson, F. S., Colliver, J. D., & Grant, B. F. (2005). Prevalence, correlates, and comorbidity of DSM-IV-TR antisocial personality syndromes and alcohol and specific drug use disorders in the United States: Results from the National Epidemiologic Survey on Alcohol and Related Conditions. *Journal of Clinical Psychiatry, 66,* 677–685.

Compton, W. M., Thomas, Y. F., Conway, K. P., & Colliver, J. D. (2005). Developments in the epidemiology of drug use and drug use disorders. *American Journal of Psychiatry, 162,* 1494–1502.

Conger, R. D., & Donnellan, M. B. (2007). An interactionist perspective on the socioeconomic context of human development. *Annual Review of Psychology, 58,* 175–199.

Conrad, A., Isaac, L., & Roth, W. T. (2008). The psychophysiology of generalized anxiety disorder: 1. Pretreatment characteristics. *Psychophysiology, 45,* 366–376.

Constans, J. I., Foa, E. B., Franklin, M. E., & Mathews, A. (1995). Memory for actual and imagined events in OC checkers. *Behavior Research and Therapy, 33,* 665–671.

Cook, C. R., & Blacher, J. (2007). Evidence-based psychosocial treatments for tic disorders. *Clinical Psychology: Science and Practice, 14,* 252–267.

Cook-Darzens, S., Doyen, C., Falissard, B., & Mouren, M. (2005). Self-perceived family functioning in 40 French families of anorexic adolescents: Implications for therapy. *European Eating Disorders Review, 13,* 223–236.

Cooke, D. (1998). Psychopathy across cultures. In D. Cooke, A. Forth, & R. Hare (Eds.), *Psychopathy: Theory, research and implications for society* (pp. 13–45). NATO AS1 Series. Netherlands: Kluwer Academic.

Cooke, D. J., Hart, S. D., & Michie, C. (2004). Cross-national differences in the assessment of psychopathy: Do they reflect variations in raters' perceptions of symptoms? *Psychological Assessment, 16,* 335–339.

Coolidge, F. L., Thede, L. L., & Young, S. E. (2002). The heritability of gender identity disorder in a child and adolescent twin sample. *Behavior Genetics, 32,* 251–257.

Coons, P. M. (1998). The dissociative disorders. Rarely considered and underdiagnosed. *Psychiatric Clinics of North America, 21,* 637–648.

Cooper, M. L., Shaver, P. R., & Collins, N. L. (1998). Attachment styles, emotion regulation, and adjustment in adolescence. *Journal of Personality and Social Psychology, 74,* 1380–1397.

Cooperman, A. (2007, January 5). Sedative withdrawal made Rehnquist delusional in '81. *Washington Post,* p. A1.

Cooper-Patrick, L., Powe, N. R., Jenckes, M. W., Gonzales, J. J., Levine, D. M., & Ford, D. E. (1997). Identification of patient attitudes and preferences regarding treatment of depression. *Journal of General Internal Medicine, 12,* 431–438.

Copeland, W. E., Keeler, G., Angold, A., & Costello, E. J. (2007). Traumatic events and posttraumatic stress in childhood. *Archives of General Psychiatry, 64,* 577–584.

Coplan, J. D., Goetz, R., Klein, D. F., Papp, L. A., Fyer, A. J., Liebowitz, M. R., et al. (1998). Plasma cortisol concentrations preceding lactate-induced panic: Psychological, biochemical, and physiological correlates. *Archives of General Psychiatry, 55,* 130–136.

Corbitt, E. M. (2002). Narcissism from the perspective of the five-factor model. In P. T. Costa, Jr., & T. A. Widiger (Eds.), *Personality disorders and the five-factor model of personality* (2nd ed., pp. 293–298). Washington, DC: American Psychological Association.

Corchs, F., Nutt, D.J., Hood, S., & Bernik, M. (2009). Serotonin and sensitivity to trauma-related exposure in selective serotonin reuptake inhibitors-recovered posttraumatic stress disorder. *Biological Psychiatry, 66,* 17–24.

Cornblatt, B., & Obuchowski, M. (1997). Update of high-risk research: 1987–1997. *International Review of Psychiatry, 9,* 437–447.

Cornblatt, B., Lencz, T., & Obuchowski, M. (2002). The schizophrenia prodrome: Treatment and high-risk perspectives. *Schizophrenia Research, 54,* 177–186.

Cornblatt, B., Obuchowski, M., Schnur, D. B., & O'Brien, J. (1997). Attention and clinical symptoms in schizophrenia. *Psychiatric Quarterly, 68,* 343–359.

Cornblatt, B. A., Lenzenweger, M. F., Dworkin, R. H., & Erlenmeyer-Kimling, L. (1992). Childhood attentional dysfunctions predict social deficits in unaffected adults at risk for schizophrenia. *British Journal of Psychiatry, 161,* Suppl. 18, 59–64.

Correa, H., Campi-Azevedo, A. C., De Marco, L., Boson, W., Viana, M. M., Guimarães, M. M., et al. (2004). Familial suicide behaviour: Association with probands suicide attempt characteristics and 5-HTTLPR polymorphism. *Acta Psychiatrica Scandinavica, 110,* 459–464.

Corrigan, P. W., Reinke, R. R., Landsberger, S. A., Charate. A., & Toombs, G. A. (in press). The effects of atypical antipsychotic medications on psychosocial outcomes. *Schizophrenia Research,* n.p.

Corrigan, P. W., & Watson, A. C. (2001). Paradox of self-stigma and mental illness. *Clinical Psychological Science Practice, 9,* 35–53.

Coryell, W., Endicott, J., Andreasen, N. C., Keller, M. B., Clayton, P. J., Hirschfeld, R. M., et al. (1988). Depression and panic attacks: The significance of overlap as reflected in follow-up and family study data. *American Journal of Psychiatry, 145,* 293–300.

Cosoff, S. J., & Hafner, R. J. (1998). The prevalence of comorbid anxiety in schizophrenia, schizoaffective disorder and bipolar disorder. *Australian & New Zealand Journal of Psychiatry, 32,* 67–72.

Costello, A., Fletcher, P. C., Dolan, R. J., Frith, C. D., & Shallice, T. (1998). The origins of forgetting in a case of isolated retrograde amnesia following a haemorrhage: Evidence from functional imaging. *Neurocase, 4,* 437–446.

Costello, E. J., Angold, A., Burns, B. J., Stangl, D. K., Tweed, D. L., Erkanli, A., et al. (1996). The Great Smoky Mountains Study of youth: Goals, design, methods, and the prevalence of DSM-III-R disorders. *Archives of General Psychiatry, 53,* 1129–1136.

Costello, E. J., Compton, S. N., Keeler, G., & Angold, A. (2003). Relationships between poverty and psychopathology: A natural experiment. *JAMA: Journal of the American Medical Association, 290,* 2023–2029.

Costello, E. J., Mustillo, S., Erkanli, A., Keeler, G., & Angold, A. (2003). Prevalence and development of psychiatric disorders in childhood and adolescence. *Archives of General Psychiatry, 60,* 837–844.

Costello, E. J., Pine, D. S., Hammen, C., March, J. S., Plotsky, P. M., Weissman, M. M., et al. (2002). Development and natural history of mood disorders. *Biological Psychiatry, 52,* 529–542.

Cottraux, J. (2004). Recent developments in the research on generalized anxiety disorder. *Current Opinion in Psychiatry, 17,* 49–52.

Cottraux, J., Note, I., Yao, S. N., Lafont, S., Note, B., Mollard, E., et al. (2001). A randomized controlled trial of cognitive therapy versus intensive behavior therapy in obsessive compulsive disorder. *Psychotherapy & Psychosomatics, 70,* 288–297.

Coughlin, J. W., & Kalodner, C. (2006). Media literacy as a prevention intervention for college women at low- or high-risk for eating disorders. *Body Image, 3,* 35–43.

Coulston, C. M., Perdices, M., & Tennant, C. C. (2007). The neuropsychological correlates of cannabis use in schizophrenia: Lifetime abuse/dependence, frequency of use, and recency of use. *Schizophrenia Research, 96,* 169–184.

Coulter, D. (2007). Brothers and sisters and Asperger's syndrome. Retrieved October 23, 2007, from http://home.att.net/~coultervideo/assibessay.htm

Council of State Governments. (2005). Mental health courts: A national snapshot. Retrieved October 15, 2007, from http://www.ojp.usdoj.gov/BJA/pdf/MHC_National_Snapshot.pdf

Coupland, N. J. (2001). Social phobia: Etiology, neurobiology, and treatment. *Journal of Clinical Psychiatry, 62,* 25–35.

Courchesne, E., & Pierce, K. (2005). Why the frontal cortex in autism might be talking only to itself: Local over-connectivity but long-distance disconnection. *Current Opinion in Neurobiology, 15,* 225–230.

Cox, C. B. (2007). Culture and dementia. In C. B. Cox (Ed.), *Dementia and social work practice: Research and interventions* (pp. 173–187). New York: Springer.

Cox, T., Jack, N., Lofthouse, S., Watling, J., Haines, J., & Warren, M. (2005). King George III and porphyria: An elemental hypothesis and investigation. *The Lancet, 366,* 332–335.

Coyne, J. C. (1976). Toward an inter-actional description of depression. *Psychiatry: Journal for the Study of Interpersonal Processes, 39,* 28–40.

Coyne, J. C., & Downey, G. (1991). Social factors and psychopathology: Stress, social support, and coping processes. *Annual Review of Psychology, 42,* 401–425.

Crabtree, A. (2000). Mesmer, Franz Anton. In A. E. Kazdin (Ed.), *Encyclopedia of psychology* (Vol. 5, pp. 200–201). Washington, DC: American Psychological Association.

Craddock, N., & Owen, M. J. (2005). The beginning of the end for the Kraepelinian dichotomy. *British Journal of Psychiatry, 186,* 364–366.

Crago, M., Shisslak, C. M., & Estes, L. S. (1996). Eating disturbances among American minority groups: A review. *International Journal of Eating Disorders, 19,* 239–248.

Craig, K. (1978). Social modeling influences on pain. In R. Sternback (Ed.), *The psychology of pain* (pp. 67–95). New York: Raven Press.

Craig, T. K., Boardman, A. P., Mills, K., Daly-Jones, O., & Drake. H. (1993). The South London Somatisation Study. I: Longitudinal course and the influence of early life experiences. *British Journal of Psychiatry, 163,* 579–588.

Craig, T. K. J., Bialas, I., Hodson, S., & Cox, A. D. (2004). Intergenerational transmission of somatization behaviour: 2. Observations of joint attention and bids for attention. *Psychological Medicine, 34,* 199–209.

Cramer, V., Torgersen, S., & Kringlen, E. (2003). Personality disorders, prevalence, socio-demographic correlations, quality of life, dysfunction, and the question of continuity. *PTT: Persönlichkeitsstörungen Theorie und Therapie, 7,* 189–198.

Craske, M. G. (1999). *Anxiety disorders: Psychological approaches to theory and treatment.* Boulder, CO: Westview Press.

Craske, M. G., & Barlow, D. H. (1993). Panic disorder and agoraphobia. In D. H. Barlow (Ed.), *Clinical handbook of psychological disorders: A step-by-step treatment manual* (2nd ed., pp. 1–47). New York: Guilford Press.

Craske, M. G., Barlow, D. H., & Meadows, E. A. (2000). *Mastery of your anxiety and panic: Therapist guide for anxiety, panic, and agoraphobia* (3rd ed.). New York: Graywind Publications.

Craske, M. G., Rapee, R. M., Jackel, L., & Barlow, D. H. (1989). Qualitative dimensions of worry in DSM-III-R generalized anxiety disorder subjects and nonanxious controls. *Behaviour Research and Therapy, 27,* 397–402.

Craske, M. G., & Rowe, M. K. (1997). Nocturnal panic. *Clinical Psychology: Science and Practice, 4,* 153–174.

Crawford, H. J., Gur, R. C., Skolnick, B., Gur, R. E., & Benson, D. M. (1993). Effects of hypnosis on regional cerebral blood flow during ischemic pain with and without suggested hypnotic analgesia. *International Journal of Psychophysiology, 15,* 181–195.

Crawford, T. N., Shaver, P. R., Cohen, P., Pilkonis, P. A., Gillath, O., & Kasen, S. (2006). Self-reported attachment, interpersonal aggression, and personality disorder in a prospective community sample of adolescents and adults. *Journal of Personality Disorders, 20,* 331–351.

Creamer, M., Burgess, P., & McFarlane, A. C. (2001). Post-traumatic stress disorder: Findings from the Australian National Survey of Mental Health and Well-Being. *Psychological Medicine, 31,* 1237–1247.

Creed, F. (2006). Can DSM-V facilitate productive research into the somatoform disorders? *Journal of Psychosomatic Research, 60,* 331–334.

Creed, F., & Barsky, A. (2004). A systematic review of the epidemiology of somatisation disorder and hypochondriasis. *Journal of Psychosomatic Research, 56,* 391–408.

Crisp, A. H., Hsu, L. K., Harding, B., & Hartshorn, J. (1980). Clinical features of anorexia nervosa: A study of a consecutive series of 102 female patients. *Journal of Psychosomatic Research, 24,* 179–191.

Critchfield, K. L., & Benjamin, L. S. (2006). Principles for psychosocial treatment of personality disorder: Summary of the APA Division 12 Task Force/NASPR Review. *Journal of Clinical Psychology, 62,* 661–674.

Crits-Christoph, P., Siqueland, L., Blaine, J., Frank, A., Luborsky, L., Onken, L. S., et al. (1999). Psychosocial treatments for cocaine dependence: National Institute on Drug Abuse Collaborative Cocaine Treatment Study. *Archives of General Psychiatry, 56,* 493–502.

Croen, L. A., Najjar, D. V., Fireman, B., & Grether, J. K. (2007). Maternal and paternal age and risk of autism spectrum disorders. *Archives of Pediatric and Adolescent Medicine, 161,* 334–340.

Cronk, N. J., Slutske, W. S., Madden, P. A. F., Bucholz, K. K., & Heath, A. C. (2004). Risk for separation anxiety disorder among girls: Paternal absence, socioeconomic disadvantage, and genetic vulnerability. *Journal of Abnormal Psychology, 113,* 237–247.

Crow, S. J., Mitchell, J. E., Roerig, J. D., & Steffen, K. (2009). What potential role is there for medication treatment in anorexia nervosa? *International Journal of Eating Disorders, 42,* 1–8.

Crowe, R., Noyes, R., Pauls, D., & Slyman, D. (1983). A family study of panic disorder. *Archives of General Psychiatry, 40,* 1065–1069.

Crowell, S. E., Beauchaine, T. P., Gatzke-Kopp, L., Sylvers, P., Mead, H., & Chipman-Chacon, J. (2006). Autonomic correlates of attention-deficit/hyperactivity disorder and oppositional defiant disorder in preschool children. *Journal of Abnormal Psychology, 115,* 174–178.

Crowther, J. H., Kichler, J. C., Shewood, N. E., & Kuhnert, M. E. (2002). The role of familial factors in bulimia nervosa. *Eating Disorders: The Journal of Treatment & Prevention, 10,* 141–151.

Cryan, E. M., Butcher, G. J., and Webb, M. G. (1992). Obsessive-compulsive disorder and paraphilia in a monozygotic twin pair. *British Journal of Psychiatry, 161,* 694–698.

Csernansky, J. G., Mahmoud, R., & Brenner, R. (2002). A comparison of risperidone and haloperidol for the prevention of relapse in patients with schizophrenia. *New England Journal of Medicine, 346,* 16–22.

Csipke, E., & Horne, O. (2007). Pro-eating disorder websites: Users' opinions. *European Eating Disorders Review, 15,* 196–206.

Cuijpers, P. (1997). Bibliotherapy in unipolar depression: A meta-analysis. *Journal of Behavior Therapy and Experimental Psychiatry, 28,* 139–147.

Cuijpers, P. (1998). A psychoeducational approach to the treatment of depression: A meta-analysis of Lewinsohn's "Coping with depression" course. *Behavior Therapy, 29,* 521–533.

Cukrowicz, K. C., White, B. A., Reitzel, L. R., Burns, A. B., Driscoll, K. A., Kemper, T. S., et al. (2005). Improved treatment outcome associated with the shift to empirically supported treatments in a graduate training clinic. *Professional Psychology: Research and Practice, 36,* 330–337.

Cummings, J. L., Mackell, J., & Kaufer, D. (2008). Behavioral effects of current Alzheimer's disease treatments: A descriptive review. *Alzheimer's & Dementia, 4,* 49–60.

Cunningham Owens, D. G., Carroll, S., Fattah, Z., Clyde, Z., Coffey, I., & Johnstone, E. C. (2001). A randomized, controlled trial of a brief interventional package for schizophrenic outpatients. *Acta Psychiatrica Scandinavica, 103,* 362–371.

Curran, G. M., Flynn, H. A., Kirchner, J., & Booth, B. M. (2000). Depression after alcohol treatment as a risk factor for relapse among male veterans. *Journal of Substance Abuse Treatment, 19,* 259–265.

Curtis, G. C., Magee, W. J., Eaton, W. W., Wittchen, H. U., & Kessler, R. C. (1998). Specific fears and phobias: Epidemiology and classification. *British Journal of Psychiatry, 173,* 212–217.

Custace, J. (1952). *Wisdom, madness and folly.* New York: Pellegrini & Cudahy.

Cyranowski, J., Frank, E., Young, E., & Shear, K. (2000). Adolescent onset of the gender difference in lifetime rates of major depression: A theoretical model. *Archives of General Psychiatry, 57,* 21–27.

Czermak, C., Lehofer, M., Renger, H., Wagner, E. M., Lemonis, L, Rohrhofer, A., et al. (2004). Dopamine receptor D3 mRNA expression in human lymphocytes is negatively correlated with the personality trait of persistence. *Journal of Neuroimmunology, 150,* 145–149.

Dackis, C. A., & O'Brien, C. P. (2001). Cocaine dependence: A disease of the brain's reward centers. *Journal of Substance Abuse Treatment, 21,* 111–117.

Daley, D. C., & Salloum, I. (1999). Relapse prevention. In P. J. Ott, R. E. Tarter, & R. T. Ammerman (Eds.), *Sourcebook on substance abuse: Etiology, epidemiology, assessment, and treatment* (pp. 255–263). Needham Heights, MA: Allyn & Bacon.

d'Alfonso, A. A., Aleman, A., Kessels, R. P., Schouten, E. A., Postma, A., van Der Linden, J. A., et al. (2002). Transcranial magnetic stimulation of left auditory cortex in patients with schizophrenia: Effects on hallucinations and neurocognition. *Journal of Neuropsychiatry and Clinical Neuroscience, 14,* 77–79.

Dalgard, O. S., Dowrick, C., Lehtinen, V., Vazquez-Barquero, J. L., Casey, P., Wilkinson, G., et al. (The ODIN Group). (2006). Negative life events, social support and gender difference in depression: A multinational community survey with data from the ODIN study. *Social Psychiatry and Psychiatric Epidemiology, 41,* 444–451.

D'Amico, E. J., Metrik, J., McCarthy, D. M., Frissell, K. C., Applebaum, M., & Brown, S. A. (2001). Progression into and out of binge drinking among high school students. *Psychology of Addictive Behaviors, 15,* 341–349.

Dannon, P. N., Dolberg, O. T., Schreiber, S., & Grunhaus, L. (2002). Three- and six-month outcome following courses of either ECT or rTMS in a population of severely depressed individuals—preliminary report. *Biological Psychiatry, 51,* 687–690.

Dao, T. K., & Prevatt, F. (2006). A psychometric evaluation of the Rorschach Comprehensive System's Perceptual Thinking Index. *Journal of Personality Assessment, 86,* 180–189.

Dare, C., & Eisler, I. (1997). Family therapy for anorexia nervosa. In D. M. Garner & P. E. Garfinkel (Eds.), *Handbook of treatment for eating disorders* (2nd ed., pp. 307–324). New York: Guilford Press.

Dare, C., Eisler, I., Russell, G., Treasure, J., & Dodge, L. (2001). Psychological therapies for adults with anorexia nervosa: Randomised controlled trial of out-patient treatments. *British Journal of Psychiatry, 178,* 216–221.

Dassori, A. M., Miller, A. L., & Saldana, D. (1995). Schizophrenia among Hispanics: Epidemiology, phenomenology, course, and outcome. *Schizophrenia Bulletin, 21,* 303–312.

Dauncey, K., Giggs, J., Baker, K., & Harrison, K. (1993). Schizophrenia in Nottingham: Lifelong residential mobility of a cohort. *British Journal of Psychiatry, 163,* 613–619.

Davey, G. (Ed.). (1987). *Cognitive processes and Pavlovian conditioning in humans.* Oxford, England: John Wiley & Sons.

David, A. S. (1994). Schizophrenia and the corpus callosum: Developmental, structural and functional relationships. *Behavioural Brain Research, 64,* 203–211.

Davidovsky, A. S., Fleta, J. L. H., & Moreno, T. S. (2007). Neurosurgery and refractory obsessive-compulsive disease: A case report. *Actas Españolas de Psiquiatría, 35,* 336–337.

Davidson, J. R. T. (2001). Pharmacotherapy of generalized anxiety disorder. *Journal of Clinical Psychiatry, 62,* 46–50.

Davidson, J. R. T., DuPont, R. L., Hedges, D., & Haskins, J. T. (1999). Efficacy, safety, and tolerability of venlafaxine extended release and buspirone in outpatients with generalized anxiety disorder. *Journal of Clinical Psychiatry, 60,* 528–535.

Davidson, J. R. T., Foa, E. B., Huppert, J. D., Keefe, F. J., Franklin, M. E., Compton, J. S., et al. (2004). Fluoxetine, comprehensive cognitive behavioral therapy, and placebo in generalized social phobia. *Archives of General Psychiatry, 61,* 1005–1013.

Davidson, J. R. T., Landburg, P. D., Pearlstein, T., Weisler, R., Sikes, C., & Farfel, G. M. (1997). Double-blind comparison of sertraline and placebo in patients with posttraumatic stress disorder (PTSD). *Abstracts of the American College of Neuropsychopharmacology.* Paper presented at the 36th annual meeting, San Juan, Puerto Rico.

Davidson, K., Norrie, J., Tyrer, P., Gumley, A., Tata, P., Murray, H., et al. (2006). The effectiveness of cognitive behavior therapy for borderline personality disorder: Results from the borderline personality disorder study of cognitive therapy (BOSCOT) trial. *Journal of Personality Disorders, 20,* 450–465.

Davidson, R. J. (1992a). Emotion and affective style: Hemispheric substrates. *Psychological Science, 3,* 39–43.

Davidson, R. J. (1992b). A prolegomenon to the structure of emotion: Gleanings from neuropsychology. *Cognition and Emotion, 6,* 245–268.

Davidson, R. J. (1993). Parsing affective space: Perspectives from neuropsychology and psychophysiology. *Neuropsychology, 7,* 464–475.

Davidson, R. J. (1994a). Honoring biology in the study of affective style. In P. Ekman & R. J. Davidson (Eds.), *The nature of emotion: Fundamental questions* (pp. 321–328). New York: Oxford University Press.

Davidson, R. J. (1998). Affective style and affective disorders: Perspectives from affective neuroscience. *Cognition and Emotion, 12,* 307–330.

Davidson, R. J. (2002). Anxiety and affective style: Role of prefrontal cortex and amygdala. *Biological Psychiatry, 51,* 68–80.

Davidson, R. J., Abercrombie, H., Nitschke, J. B., & Putnam, K. (1999). Regional brain function, emotion and disorders of emotion. *Current Opinion in Neurobiology, 9,* 228–234.

Davidson, R. J., Jackson, D. C., & Kalin, N. H. (2000). Emotion, plasticity, context, and regulation: Perspectives from affective neuroscience. *Psychological Bulletin, 126,* 890–909.

Davies, L., Stern, J. S., Agrawal, N., & Robertson, M. M. (2006). A case series of patients with Tourette's Syndrome in the United Kingdom treated with aripiprazole. *Human Psychopharmacology: Clinical and Experimental, 21,* 447–453.

Davis, C., Claridge, G., & Fox, J. (2000). Not just a pretty face: Physical attractiveness and perfectionism in the risk for eating disorders. *International Journal of Eating Disorders, 27,* 67–73.

Davis, C., Shuster, B., Blackmore, E., & Fox, J. (2004). Looking good—family focus on appearance and the risk for eating disorders. *International Journal of Eating Disorders, 35,* 136–144.

Davis, J. H. (1969). *The Bouviers: Portrait of an American family.* New York: Doubleday.

Davis, J. H. (1996). *Jacqueline Bouvier: An intimate memoir.* New York: Wiley.

Davison, G. C. (2005). Issues and nonissues in the gay-affirmative treatment of patients who are gay, lesbian, or bisexual. *Clinical Psychology: Science and Practice, 12,* 25–28.

Dawson, G., Webb, S. J., Carver, L., Panagiotides, H., & McPartland J. (2004). Young children with autism show atypical brain responses to fearful versus neutral facial expressions of emotion. *Developmental Science, 7,* 340–359.

Dawson, G., Webb, S. J., & McPartland, J. (2005). Understanding the nature of face processing impairment in autism: Insights from behavioral and electrophysiological studies. *Developmental Neuropsychology, 27,* 403–424.

Dawson, M., Mottron, L., Jelenic, P., & Soulières, I. (2005, May). Superior performance of autistics on RPM and PPVT relative to Wechsler scales provides evidence for the nature of autistic intelligence. Poster presented at the International Meeting for Autism Research, Boston, MA.

Dawson, M. E., Hazlett, E. A., Filion, D. L., Nuechterlein, K. H., & Schell, A. M. (1993). Attention and schizophrenia: Impaired modulation of the startle reflex. *Journal of Abnormal Psychology, 102,* 633–641.

De Bellis, M. D., Clark, D. B., Beers, S. R., Soloff, P. H., Boring, A. M., Hall, J., et al. (2000). Hippocampal volume in adolescent-onset alcohol use disorders. *American Journal of Psychiatry, 157,* 737–744.

De Bellis, M. D., Keshavan, M. S., Shifflett, H., Iyengar, S., Dahl, R. E., Axelson, D. A., et al. (2002). Superior temporal gyrus volumes in pediatric generalized anxiety disorder. *Biological Psychiatry, 51,* 553–562.

De Beni, R., & Palladino, P. (2004). Decline in working memory updating through ageing: Intrusion error analyses. *Memory, 12,* 75–89.

de Beurs, E., van Balkom, A. J. L. M., Van Dyck, R., & Lange, A. (1999). Long-term outcome of pharmacological and psychological treatment for panic disorder with agoraphobia: A 1-year naturalistic follow-up. *Acta Psychiatrica Scandinavica, 99,* 59–67.

de Carufel, F., & Trudel, G. (2006). Effects of a new functional-sexological treatment for premature ejaculation. *Journal of Sex & Marital Therapy, 32,* 97–114.

De Hert, M., McKenzie, K., & Peuskens, J. (2001). Risk factors for suicide in young people suffering from schizophrenia: A long-term follow-up study. *Schizophrenia Research, 47,* 127–134.

De la Fuente, J. M., Goldman, S., Stanus, E., Vizuete, C., Morlan, I., Bobes, J., et al. (1997). Brain glucose metabolism in borderline personality disorder. *Journal of Psychiatry Research, 31,* 531–541.

De Leo, D. (2002a). Struggling against suicide: The need for an integrative approach. *Crisis: The Journal of Crisis Intervention and Suicide Prevention, 23,* 23–31.

De Leo, D. (2002b). Why are we not getting any closer to preventing suicide? *British Journal of Psychiatry, 181,* 372–374.

De Los Reyes, A., & Kazdin, A. E. (2004). Measuring informant discrepancies in clinical child research. *Psychological Assessment, 16,* 330–334.

de Zwaan, M., Roerig, J. L., & Mitchell, J. E. (2004). Pharmacological treatment of anorexia nervosa, bulimia nervosa, and binge eating disorder. In J. K. Thompson (Ed.), *Handbook of eating disorders and obesity* (pp. 186–217). Hoboken, NJ: John Wiley & Sons.

Deckersbach, T., Rauch, S., Buhlmann, U., & Wilhelm, S. (2006). Habit reversal versus supportive psychotherapy in Tourette's disorder: A randomized controlled trial and predictors of treatment response. *Behaviour Research and Therapy, 44,* 1079–1090.

Degroot, A., & Treit, D. (2002). Dorsal and ventral hippocampal cholinergic systems modulate anxiety in the plus-maze and shock-probe tests. *Brain Research, 949,* 60–70.

Degun-Mather, M. (2002). Hypnosis in the treatment of a case of dissociative amnesia for a 12-year period. *Contemporary Hypnosis, 19,* 33–41.

DeJong, W. (2001). Finding common ground for effective campus-based prevention. *Psychology of Addictive Behaviors, 15,* 292–296.

Delgado, P. L., & Moreno, F. A. (1998). Different roles for serotonin in anti-obsessional drug action and the pathophysiology of obsessive-compulsive disorder. *British Journal of Psychiatry, 173,* 21–25.

DeLisi, L. E., Sakuma, M., Tew, W., Kushner, M., Hoff, A. L., & Grimson, R. (1997). Schizophrenia as a chronic active brain process: A study of progressive brain structural change subsequent to the onset of schizophrenia. *Psychiatry Research: Neuroimaging, 74,* 129–140.

Dell, P. F. (1988). Professional skepticism about multiple personality. *Journal of Nervous and Mental Disorders, 176,* 537–555.

Dell'Osso, L., Rucci, P., Cassano, G. B., Maser, J. D., Endicott, J., Shear, M. K., et al. (2002). Measuring social anxiety and obsessive-compulsive spectra: Comparison of interviews and self-report instruments. *Comprehensive Psychiatry, 43,* 81–87.

Dennerstein, L., Koochaki, P., Barton, I., & Graziottin, A. (2006). Hypoactive sexual desire disorder in menopausal women: A survey of Western European women. *Journal of Sexual Medicine, 3,* 212–222.

Dennis, W. (1973). *Children of the creche.* New York: Appleton-Century-Crofts.

DeRubeis, R. J., Hollon, S. D., Amsterdam, J. D., Shelton, R. C., Young, P. R., Salomon, R. M., et al. (2005). Cognitive therapy vs medications in the treatment of moderate to severe depression. *Archives of General Psychiatry, 62,* 409–416.

des Portes, V., Hagerman, R. J., & Hendren, R. L. (2003). Pharmacotherapy. In S. Ozonoff, S. J. Rogers, & R. L. Hendren (Eds.), *Autism spectrum disorders: A research review for practitioners.* (pp. 161–186). Washington, DC: American Psychiatric Publishing.

Deshpande, S. W., & Kawane, S. D. (1982). Anxiety and serial verbal learning: A test of the Yerkes-Dodson Law. *Asian Journal of Psychology & Education, 9,* 18–23.

Deuschle, M., Hamann, B., Meichel, C., Krumm, B., Lederbogen, F., Kniest, A., et al. (2003). Antidepressive treatment with amitriptyline and paroxetine: Effects on saliva cortisol concentrations. *Journal of Clinical Psychopharmacology, 23,* 201–205.

Deutsch, M. (1968). Field theory in social psychology. In G. Lindzey & E. Aronson (Eds.), *Handbook of social psychology* (Vol. 1, pp. 412–487). Cambridge, MA: Addison-Wesley.

DeVane, C. L. (1997). The place of selective serotonin reuptake inhibitors in the treatment of panic disorder. *Pharmacotherapy, 17,* 282–292.

Deveson, A. (1991). *Tell me I'm here: One family's experience of schizophrenia.* New York: Penguin Books.

Devinsky, O., Mesad, S., & Alper, K. (2001). Nondominant hemisphere lesions and conversion nonepileptic seizures. *Journal of Neuropsychiatry and Clinical Neuroscience, 13,* 367–373.

Di Ceglie, D. (2000). Gender identity disorder in young people. *Advances in Psychiatric Treatment, 6,* 458–466.

Di Ceglie, D., Freedman, D., McPherson, S., & Richardson, P. (2002). Children and adolescents referred to a specialist gender identity development service: Clinical features and demographic characteristics. *International Journal of Transgenderism, 6,* n.p.

Dick, D. M., Viken, R. J., Kaprio, J., Pulkkinen, L., & Rose, R. J. (2005). Understanding the covariation among childhood externalizing symptoms: Genetic and environmental influences on conduct disorder, attention deficit hyperactivity disorder, and oppositional defiant disorder symptoms. *Journal of Abnormal Child Psychology, 33,* 219–229.

Dickerson, F. B. (2004). Update on cognitive behavioral psychotherapy for schizophrenia: Review of recent studies. *Journal of Cognitive Psychotherapy, 18,* 189–205.

Dickey, C. C., McCarley, R. W., & Shenton, M. E. (2002). The brain in schizotypal personality disorder: A review of structural MRI and CT findings. *Harvard Review of Psychiatry, 10,* 1–15.

Dickinson, D., & Coursey, R. D. (2002). Independence and overlap among neurocognitive correlates of community functioning in schizophrenia. *Schizophrenia Research, 56,* 161–170.

Dickinson, D., Bellack, A. S., & Gold, J. M. (2007). Social/communication skills, cognition, and vocational functioning in schizophrenia. *Schizophrenia Bulletin, 33,* 1213–1220.

Didic, M., Ali Chérif, A., Gambarelli, D., Poncet, M., & Boudouresques, J. (1998). A permanent pure amnestic syndrome of insidious onset related to Alzheimer's disease. *Annals of Neurology, 43,* 526–530.

Dikel, T. N., Engdahl, B., & Eberly, R. (2005). PTSD in former prisoners of war: Prewar, wartime, and postwar factors. *Journal of Traumatic Stress, 18,* 69–77.

DiLillo, D. (2001). Interpersonal functioning among women reporting a history of childhood sexual abuse: Empirical findings and methodological issues. *Clinical Psychology Review, 21,* 553–576.

Dimeff, L., & Linehan, M. M. (2001). Dialectical behavior therapy in a nutshell. *The California Psychologist, 34,* 10–13.

Dimidjian, S., Hollon, S. D., Dobson, K. S., Schmaling, K. B., Kohlenberg, R. J., Addis, M. E. et al. (2006). Randomized trial of behavioral activation, cognitive therapy, and antidepressant medication in the acute treatment of adults with major depression. *Journal of Consulting and Clinical Psychology, 74,* 658–670.

Dinnel, D. L., Kleinknecht, R. A., & Tanaka-Matsumi, J. (2002). A cross-cultural comparison of social phobia symptoms. *Journal of Psychopathology & Behavioral Assessment, 24,* 75–84.

D'Ippoliti, D., Davoli, M., Perucci, C. A., Pasqualini, F., & Bargagli, A. M. (1998).

Retention in treatment of heroin users in Italy: The role of treatment type and of methadone maintenance dosage. *Drug and Alcohol Dependence, 52,* 167–171.

Dishion, T. J., & Medici Skaggs, N. (2000). An ecological analysis of monthly "bursts" in early adolescent substance use. *Applied Developmental Science, 4,* 89–97.

Dishion, T. J., & Stormshak, E. A. (2007). *Intervening in children's lives: An ecological, family-centered approach to mental health care.* Washington, DC: American Psychological Association.

Dixon, L., Adams, C., & Lucksted, A. (2000). Update on family psychoeducation for schizophrenia. *Schizophrenia Bulletin, 26,* 5–20.

Docter, R. F., & Prince, V. (1997). Transvestism: A survey of 1032 cross-dressers. *Archives of Sexual Behavior, 26,* 589–605.

Dodge, K. A., & Pettit, G. S. (2003). A biopsychosocial model of the development of chronic conduct problems in adolescence. *Developmental Psychology, 39,* 349–371.

Dodge, R., Sindelar, J., & Sinha, R. (2005). The role of depression symptoms in predicting drug abstinence in outpatient substance abuse treatment. *Journal of Substance Abuse Treatment, 28,* 189–196.

Doerfel-Baasen, D., & Rauh, H. (2001). Parents and teachers of young children under conditions of sociopolitical change. *American Behavioral Scientist, 44,* 1818–1842.

Dohrenwend, B. P., Levav, I., Shrout, P. E., Schwartz, S., Naveh, G., Link. B. G., et al. (1992). Socioeconomic status and psychiatric disorders: The causation-selection issue. *Science, 255,* 946–952.

Dolan, A. (2006, April 3). The obsessive disorder that haunts my life. *Daily Mail.* Retrieved on February 25 2009 from http://www.dailymail.co.uk/pages/live/articles/showbiz/showbiznews.html?in_article_id=381802&in_page_id=1773

Dolan, M., & Park, I. (2002). The neuropsychology of antisocial personality disorder. *Psychological Medicine, 32,* 417–427.

Dolan-Sewell, R., & Insel, T. R. (2005). Special issue on anorexia nervosa. *International Journal of Eating Disorders, 37,* S1–S9.

Dolan-Sewell, R. T., Krueger, R. F., & Shea, M. T. (2001). Co-occurrence with syndrome disorders. In J. W. Livesley (Ed.), *Handbook of personality disorders: Theory, research, and treatment* (pp. 84–104). New York: Guilford Press.

Domjan, M., Cusato, B., & Krause, M. (2004). Learning with arbitrary versus ecological conditioned stimuli: Evidence from sexual conditioning. *Psychonomic Bulletin & Review, 11,* 232–246.

Domjan, M., Cusato, B., & Krause, M. (2004). Learning with arbitrary versus ecological conditioned stimuli: Evidence from sexual conditioning. *Psychonomic Bulletin & Review, 11,* 232–246.

Donegan, N. H., Sanislow, C. A., Blumberg, H. P., Fulbright, R. K., Lacadie, C., Skudlarski, P., et al. (2003). Amygdala hyperreactivity in borderline personality disorder: Implications for emotional dysregulation. *Biological Psychiatry, 54,* 1284–1293.

Dong, W. K., & Greenough, W. T. (2004). Plasticity of nonneuronal brain tissue: Roles in developmental disorders. *Mental Retardation and Developmental Disabilities Research Reviews, 10,* 85–90.

Donovan, J., & Jessor, R. (1985). Structure of problem behavior in adolescence and young adulthood. *Journal of Consulting and Clinical Psychology, 53,* 890–904.

Dorcus, R. M., & Shaffer, G. W. (1945). Functional psychoses. In R. M. Dorcus & G. W. Shaffer, *Textbook of abnormal psychology* (3rd ed., pp. 304–330). Baltimore: Williams & Wilkins.

Dorr, D. (1998). Psychopathy in the pedophile. In T. Millon, E. Simonsen, M. Birket-Smith, & R. D. Davis (Eds.), *Psychopathy: Antisocial, criminal, and violent behavior* (pp. 304–320). New York: Guilford Press.

Dorris, L., Espie, C. A. E., Knott, F., & Salt, J. (2004). Mind-reading difficulties in the siblings of people with Asperger's syndrome: Evidence for a genetic influence in the abnormal development of a specific cognitive domain. *Journal of Child Psychology and Psychiatry, 45,* 412–418.

Double, D. (2002). The limits of psychiatry. *BMJ: British Medical Journal, 324,* 900–904.

Dowdall, G. W., Crawford, M., & Wechsler, H. (1998). Binge drinking among American college women: A comparison of single-sex and coeducational institutions. *Psychology of Women Quarterly, 22,* 705–715.

Dowling, J. E. (1992). *Neurons and networks: An introduction to neuroscience.* Cambridge, MA: Harvard University Press.

Draijer, N., & Friedl, M. (1999). The prevalence of dissociative disorders and DID among psychiatric inpatients: A meta-analysis of prevalence studies. In A. Aukamp, R. Blizard, J. Chu, G. Fair, & S. Gold (Eds.), *Proceedings of the 16th International Fall Conference of the International Society for the Study of Dissociation.*

Driessen, M., Herrmann J., Stahl, K., Zwaan, M., Meier, S., Hill, A., et al. (2000). Magnetic resonance imaging volumes of the hippocampus and the amygdala in women with borderline personality disorder and early traumatization. *Archives of General Psychiatry, 57,* 1115–1122.

Drotar, D. (2006). Research design considerations for psychological interventions. In D. Drotar, *Psychological interventions in childhood chronic illness* (pp. 59–83). Washington, DC: American Psychological Association.

Drug Court Clearinghouse and Technical Assistance Project. (1998, June). *Looking at a decade of drug courts* (Publication No. NCJ 171140).

Drummond, K. D., Bradley, S. J., Peterson-Badali, M., & Zucker, K. J. (2008). A follow-up study of girls with gender identity disorder. *Developmental Psychology, 44,* 34–45.

Druss, B. G., Schlesinger, M., & Allen, H. M., Jr. (2001). Depressive symptoms, satisfaction with health care, and 2-year work outcomes in an employed population, *American Journal of Psychiatry, 158,* 731–734.

Duberstein, P. R., & Conwell, Y. (1997). Personality disorders and completed suicide: A methodological and conceptual review. *Clinical Psychology: Science and Practice, 4,* 359–376.

Duffy, M., Gillespie, K., & Clark, D. M. (2007). Post-traumatic stress disorder in the context of terrorism and other civil conflict in Northern Ireland: Randomised controlled trial. *British Medical Journal, 334,* 1147.

Dugas, M. J., Ladouceur, R., Léger, E., Freeston, M. H., Langolis, F., Provencher, M. D., et al. (2003). Group cognitive-behavioral therapy for generalized anxiety disorder: Treatment outcome and long-term follow-up. *Journal of Consulting and Clinical Psychology, 71,* 821–825.

Dukakis, K. (2002). *Kitty Dukakis Speaks Out About Shock Therapy.* CNN, airdate May 21, 2:21pm EST.

Dukakis, K., & Scovell, J. (1991). *Now you know.* New York: Simon and Shuster.

Dukakis, K., & Tye, L. (2006). *Shock.* New York: Avery.

Duncan, B. L. (2002). The Legacy of Saul Rosenzweig: The Profundity of the Dodo Bird. *Journal of Psychotherapy Integration, 12,* 32–57.

Dunner, D. L. (2001). Acute and maintenance treatment of chronic depression. *Journal of Clinical Psychiatry, 62,* 10–16.

Durbin, C. E., & Klein, D. N. (2006). Ten-year stability of personality disorders among outpatients with mood disorders. *Journal of Abnormal Psychology, 115,* 75–84.

Durham, R. C., Chambers, J. A., MacDonald R. R., Power, K. G., & Major, K. (2003). Does cognitive-behavioural therapy influence the long-term outcome of generalized anxiety disorder? An 8–14 year follow-up of two clinical trials. *Psychological Medicine, 33,* 499–509.

Durkheim, E. (1951). *Suicide: A study in sociology*. New York: Free Press. (Original work published 1897)

Durston, S., Hulshoff Pol, H. E., Schnack, H. G., Buitelaar, J. K., Steenhuis, M. P., Minderaa, R. B., et al. (2004) Magnetic resonance imaging of boys with attention-deficit/hyperactivity disorder and their unaffected siblings. *Journal of the American Academy of Child and Adolescent Psychiatry, 43*, 332–340.

Dusky v. United States, 362 U.S. 402 (1960), quoted in *Godinez, 509 U.S. 398.*

Dwight-Johnson, M., Sherbourne, C. D., Liao, D., & Wells, K. B. (2000). Treatment preferences among primary care patients. *Journal of General Internal Medicine, 15*, 527–534.

Dzokoto, V. A., & Adams, G. (2005). Understanding genital-shrinking epidemics in West Africa: Koro, juju, or mass psychogenic illness? *Culture, Medicine and Psychiatry, 29*, 53–78.

Eakin, E. (2000, January 15). Bigotry as mental illness or just another norm. *New York Times*, pp. 1, 31.

Easton, C. J., Swan, S., & Sinha, R. (2000). Prevalence of family violence in clients entering substance abuse treatment. *Journal of Substance Abuse Treatment, 18*, 23–28.

Eaton, W., & Kessler, L. (1985). The NIMH Epidemiologic Catchment Area Study. *Epidemiological Field Methods in Psychiatry.* New York: Academic Press.

Eddy, K. T., Dorer, D. J., Franko, D. L., Tahilani, K., Thompson-Brenner, H., & Herzog, D. B. (2007). Should bulimia nervosa be subtyped by history of anorexia nervosa? A longitudinal validation. *International Journal of Eating Disorders, 40*, S67–S71.

Eddy, K. T., Dorer, D. J., Franko, D. L., Tahilani, K., Thompson-Brenner, H., & Herzog, D. B. (2008). Diagnostic crossover in anorexia nervosa and bulimia nervosa: Implications for DSM-V. *American Journal of Psychiatry, 165*, 245–250.

Eddy, K. T., Keel, P. K., Dorer, D. J., Delinsky, S. S., Franko, D. L., & Herzog, D. B. (2002). Longitudinal comparison of anorexia nervosa subtypes. *International Journal of Eating Disorders, 31*, 191–201.

Edelson, M. G. (2006). Are the majority of children with autism mentally retarded? A systematic evaluation of the data. *Focus on Autism and Other Developmental Disabilities, 21*, 66–83.

Edgerton, R. B., & Cohen, A. (1994). Culture and schizophrenia: The DOSMD challenge. *British Journal of Psychiatry, 164*, 222–231.

Edwards, E., Kornrich, W., Houtten, P. V., & Henn, F. A. (1992). Presynaptic serotonin mechanisms in rats subjected to inescapable shock. *Neuropharmacology, 31*, 323–330.

Eger, E. I., II, Gong, D., Xing, Y., Raines, D. E., & Flood, P. (2002). Acetylcholine receptors and thresholds for convulsions from flurothyl and 1,2-dichlorohexafluorocyclobutane. *Anesthesia & Analgesia, 95*, 1611–1615.

Eggert, J., Levendosky, A., & Klump, K. (2007). Relationships among attachment styles, personality characteristics, and disordered eating. *International Journal of Eating Disorders, 40*, 149–155.

Egley, L. C. (1991). Defining the Tarasoff duty. *The Journal of Psychiatry and Law, 19*, 99–133.

Ehlers, A., Mayou, R. A., & Bryant, B. (1998). Psychological predictors of chronic posttraumatic stress disorder after motor vehicle accidents. *Journal of Abnormal Psychology, 107*, 508–519.

Eich, E., Macaulay, D., & Lam, R. W. (1997). Mania, depression, and mood dependent memory. *Cognition and Emotion, 11*, 607–618.

Eich, E., Macaulay, D., & Ryan, L. (1994). Mood dependent memory for events of the personal past. *Journal of Experimental Psychology: General, 123*, 201–215.

Eisen, J. L., Coles, M. E., Shea, M. T., Pagano, M. E., Stout, R. L., Yen, S., et al. (2006). Clarifying the convergence between obsessive compulsive personality disorder criteria and obsessive compulsive disorder. *Journal of Personality Disorders, 20*, 294–305.

Eisen, K. P., Allen, G. J., Bollash, M., & Pescatello, L. S. (2008). Stress management in the workplace: A comparison of a computer-based and an in-person stress-management intervention. *Computers in Human Behavior, 24*, 486–496.

Eisman, E. J., Dies, R. R., Finn, S. E., Eyde, L. D., Kay, G. G., Kubiszyn, T. W., et al. (2000). Problems and limitations in using psychological assessment in the contemporary health care delivery system. *Professional Psychology: Research and Practice, 31*, 131–140.

Ekman, P. (1984). Expression and the nature of emotion. In K. R. Scherer & P. Ekman (Eds.), *Approaches to emotion* (pp. 319–343). Hillsdale, NJ: Erlbaum.

El-Bassel, N., Schilling, R., Turnbull, J., & Su, K. (1993). Correlates of alcohol use among methadone patients. *Alcoholism, Clinical and Experimental Research, 17*, 681–686.

Eldredge, K. L., Agras, W. S., & Arnow, B. (1994). The last supper: Emotional determinants of pretreatment weight fluctuations in obese binge eaters. *International Journal of Eating Disorders, 16*, 83–88.

Eley, T. C., Deater-Deckard, K., Fombone, E., Fulker, D. W., & Plomin, R. (1998). An adoption study of depressive symptoms in middle childhood. *Journal of Child Psychology & Psychiatry & Allied Disciplines, 39*, 337–345.

Eligon, J. (2008, October 15). Suspect in therapist death is to be institutionalized. *The New York Times.* Retrieved on March 2, 2009, from http://www.nytimes.com/2008/10/15/nyregion/15tarloff.html?pagewanted=print

El-Islam, M. F. (1991). Transcultural aspects of schizophrenia and ICD-10. *Psychiatria Danubina, 3*, 485–494.

Elkin, I. (1994). The NIMH Treatment of Depression Collaborative Research Program: Where we began and where we are. In A. E. Bergin & S. L. Garfield (Eds.), *Handbook of psychotherapy and behavior change* (4th ed., pp. 114–139). Oxford, England: John Wiley & Sons.

Elkin, I., Gibbons, R. D., Shea, M. T., Sotsky, S. M., Watkins, J. T., Pilkonis, P. A., et al. (1995). Initial severity and differential treatment outcome in the National Institute of Mental Health Treatment of Depression Collaborative Research Program. *Journal of Consulting and Clinical Psychology, 63*, 841–847.

Elkin, I., Parloff, M. B., Hadley, S. W., & Autry, J. H. (1985). NIMH Treatment of Depression Collaborative Research Program: Background and research plan. *Archives of General Psychiatry, 42*, 305–316.

Elkins, I. J., McGue, M., Malone, S., & Iacono, W. G. (2004). The effect of parental alcohol and drug disorders on adolescent personality. *American Journal of Psychiatry, 161*, 670–676.

Ellickson, P. L., Tucker, J. S., Klein, D. J., & Saner, H. (2004). Antecedents and outcomes of marijuana use initiation during adolescence. *Preventive Medicine: An International Journal Devoted to Practice and Theory, 39*, 976–984.

Elliott, A. J., Pages, K. P., Russo, J., & Wilson, L. G. (1996). A profile of medically serious suicide attempts. *Journal of Clinical Psychiatry, 57*, 567–571.

Elliott, G. C., Cunningham, S. M., Linder, M., Colangelo, M., & Gross, M. (2005). Child physical abuse and self-perceived social isolation among adolescents. *Journal of Interpersonal Violence, 20*, 1663–1684.

Elliott, R., Greenberg, L. S., & Lietaer, G. (2004). Research on experiential psychotherapies. In M. J. Lambert (Ed.), *Bergin & Garfield's handbook of psychotherapy and behavior change* (5th ed., pp. 493–540). New York: John Wiley & Sons.

Ellis, A., & MacLaren, C. (1998). *Rational emotive behavior therapy: A therapist's guide.* Atascadero, CA: Impact Publishers.

Ellison, J. M., & McCarter, R. H. G. (2002). Combined treatment for anxiety disorders. In D. J. Stein & E. Holland (Eds.), *Textbook of anxiety disorders* (pp. 93–106). Washington DC: American Psychiatric Publishing.

Ellman, L. M. (2008). Pre and perinatal factors in the neurodevelopmental course of schizophrenia: Neurocognitive and clinical outcomes. *Dissertation Abstracts International: Section B: The Sciences and Engineering, 69(1),* 673B.

Elsass, P. (2001). Individual and collective traumatic memories: A qualitative study of post-traumatic stress disorder symptoms in two Latin American localities. *Transcultural Psychiatry, 38,* 306–316.

Elzinga, B. M., Phaf, R. H., Ardon, A. M., & van Dyck, R. (2003). Directed forgetting between, but not within, dissociative personality states. *Journal of Abnormal Psychology, 112,* 237–243.

Emerich v. Philadelphia Center for Human Development, 720 A.2d 1032 (Pa. 1998).

Emmelkamp, P. M. G. (1994). Behavior therapy with adults. In A. E. Bergin & S. L. Garfield (Eds.), *Handbook of psychotherapy and behavior change* (4th ed., pp. 379–427). Oxford, England: John Wiley & Sons.

Emmelkamp, P. M. G. (2004). Behavior therapy with adults. In M. J. Lambert (Ed.), *Bergin and Garfield's handbook of psychotherapy and behavior change* (5th ed., pp. 393–446). New York: John Wiley & Sons.

Emmelkamp, P. M. G., Benner, A., Kuipers, A., Feiertag, G. A., Koster, H. C., & van Apeldoorn, F. J. (2006). Comparison of brief dynamic and cognitive-behavioural therapies in avoidant personality disorder. *British Journal of Psychiatry, 189,* 60–64.

Emmelkamp, P. M. G., Bruynzeel, M., Drost, L., & Van Der Mast, C. A. P. G. (2001). Virtual reality treatment in acrophobia: A comparison with exposure in vivo. *CyberPsychology & Behavior, 4,* 335–339.

Emmelkamp, P. M. G., Krijn, M., Hulsbosch, A. M., de Vries, S., Schuemie, M. J., & van der Mast, C. A. P. G. (2002). Virtual reality treatment versus exposure in vivo: A comparative evaluation in acrophobia. *Behaviour Research & Therapy, 40,* 509–516.

Emmons, S., Geiser, C., Kaplan, K., & Harrow, M. (1997). *Living with schizophrenia.* Washington, DC: Taylor & Francis.

Eng, W., & Heimberg, R. G. (2006). Interpersonal correlates of generalized anxiety disorder: Self versus other perception. *Journal of Anxiety Disorders, 19,* 143–156.

Engel, G. L. (1977). The need for a new medical model: A challenge to biomedicine. *Science, 196,* 129–136.

Engel, G. L. (1980). The clinical application of the biopsychosocial model. *American Journal of Psychiatry, 137,* 535–544.

Entwisle, D. R. (1972). To dispel fantasies about fantasy-based measures of achievement motivation. *Psychological Bulletin, 77,* 377–391.

Eplov, L., Giraldi, A., Davidsen, M., Garde, K., & Kamper-Jorgensen, F. (2007). Sexual desire in a nationally representative Danish population. *Journal of Sexual Medicine, 4,* 47–56.

Epstein, C. M., Figiel, G. S., McDonald, W. M., Amazon-Leece, J., & Figiel, L. (1998). Rapid rate transcranial magnetic stimulation in young and middle-aged refractory depressed patients. *Psychiatric Annals, 28,* 36–39.

Epstein, D. H., Willner-Reid, J., Vahbzadeh, M., Mezghanni, M., Lin, J.-L., & Preston, K. L. (2009). Real-time electronic diary reports of cue exposure and mood in the hours before cocaine and heroin craving and use. *Archives of General Psychiatry, 66,* 88–94.

Epstein, J. N., Casey, B. J., Tonev, S. T., Davidson, M. C., Reiss, A. L., Garrett, A., et al. (2007). ADHD- and medication-related brain activation effects in concordantly affected parent-child dyads with ADHD. *Journal of Child Psychology and Psychiatry, 48,* 899–913.

Ergene, T. (2003). Effective interventions on test anxiety reduction: A meta-analysis. *School Psychology International, 24,* 313–328.

Erickson, W. D., Walbeck, N. H., & Seely, R. K. (1988). Behavior patterns of child molesters. *Archives of Sexual Behavior, 17,* 77–87.

Eriksen, K., & Kress, V. E. (2005). *Beyond the DSM story: Ethical quandaries, challenges, and best practices.* Thousand Oaks, CA: Sage Publications.

Erkiran, M., Özünalan, H., Evren, C., Aytaçlar, S., Kirisci, L., & Tarter, R. (2006). Substance abuse amplifies the risk for violence in schizophrenia spectrum disorder. *Addictive Behaviors, 31,* 1797–1805.

Erlenmeyer-Kimling, L., Rock, D., Roberts, S. A., Janal, M., Kestenbaum, C., Cornblatt, B., et al. (2000). Attention, memory, and motor skills as childhood predictors of schizophrenia-related psychoses: The New York High-Risk Project. *American Journal of Psychiatry, 157,* 1416–1422.

Ernst, A. M., & Chefer, S. (2001). Neuroimaging and substance abuse disorders in the year 2000. *Current Opinion in Psychiatry, 14,* 179–185.

Erzegovesi, S., Cavallini, M. C., Cavedini, P., Diaferia, G., Locatelli, M., & Bellodi, L. (2001). Clinical predictors of drug response in obsessive-compulsive disorder. *Journal of Clinical Psychopharmacology, 21,* 488–492.

Escobar, J. I. (1987). Cross-cultural aspects of the somatization trait. *Hospital and Community Psychiatry, 38,* 174–180.

Escobar, J. I. (1996). Pharmacological treatment of somatization/hypochondriasis. *Psychopharmacology Bulletin, 32,* 589–596.

Escobar, J. I., Nervi, C. H., & Gara, M. A. (2000). Immigration and mental health: Mexican Americans in the United States. *Harvard Review of Psychiatry, 8,* 64–72.

Espy, K. A., Molfese, D. L., Molfese, V. J., & Modglin, A. (2004). Development of auditory event-related potentials in young children and relations to word-level reading abilities at age 8 years. *Annals of Dyslexia, 54,* 9–38.

Etheridge, R. M., Craddock, S. G., Hubbard, R. L., & Rounds-Bryant, J. L. (1999). The relationship of counselling and self-help participation to patient outcomes in DATOS. *Drug and Alcohol Dependence, 57,* 99–112.

Eubanks-Carter, C., Burckell, L. A., & Goldfried, M. R. (2005). Enhancing therapeutic effectiveness with lesbian, gay, and bisexual clients. *Clinical Psychology: Science and Practice, 12,* 1–18.

Evans, G., & Farberow, N. L. (1988). *The encyclopedia of suicide.* New York: Facts on File.

Evans, G. W., & Stecker, R. (2004). Motivational consequences of environmental stress. *Journal of Environmental Psychology, 24,* 143–165.

Evans, J., Heron, J., Francomb, H., Oke, S., & Golding, J. (2001). Cohort study of depressed mood during pregnancy and after childbirth. *British Medical Journal, 323,* 257–260.

Evans, S., Ferrando, S., Findler, M., Stowell, C., Smart, C., & Haglin, D. (2008). Mindfulness-based cognitive therapy for generalized anxiety disorder. *Journal of Anxiety Disorders, 22,* 716–721.

Everly Jr., G. S., & Lating, J. M. (2004). The defining moment of psychological trauma: What makes a traumatic event traumatic? In G. S. Everly, Jr., & J. M. Lating (Eds.), *Personality-guided therapy for posttraumatic stress disorder* (pp. 33–51). Washington, DC: American Psychological Association.

Ewing, C. P., & McCann, J. T. (2006). *Minds on trial: Great cases in law and psychology.* New York: Oxford University Press.

Exner, J. E. (1974). *The Rorschach: A comprehensive system.* Oxford, UK: John Wiley.

Eyler, L. T., Mirzakhanian, H., & Jeste, D. V. (2005). A preliminary study of interactive questioning methods to assess and improve understanding of informed consent among patients with schizophrenia. *Schizophrenia Research, 75,* 193–198.

Eysenck, H. J. (1957). *The dynamics of anxiety and hysteria: An experimental application of modern learning theory topsychiatry*. Oxford, England: Praeger.

Eysenck, H. J. (1990). Genetic and environmental contributions to individual differences: The three major dimensions of personality. *Journal of Personality, 58,* 245–261.

Fabian, L. J., & Thompson, J. K. (1989). Body image and eating disturbance in young females. *International Journal of Eating Disorders, 8,* 63–74.

Fabiano, E., Robinson, D., & Porporino, F. (1990). *A preliminary assessment of the cognitive skills training program: A component of living skills programming: Program description, research findings and implementation strategy*. Ottawa: Correctional Service of Canada.

Faces and Voices of Recovery (2007a). Retrieved on July 30, 2007 from http://www.facesandvoicesofrecovery.org/resources/story_jamieson.php.

Faces and Voices of Recovery (2007b). Retrieved on July 30, 2007 from http://www.facesandvoicesofrecovery.org/resources/story_elaine.php.

Faces and Voices of Recovery (2007c). Retrieved on July 30, 2007 from http://www.facesandvoicesofrecovery.org/resources/story_brown.php.

Fagan, P. J., Wise, T. N., Schmidt, C. W., Jr., & Berlin, F. S. (2002). Pedophilia. *JAMA: Journal of the American Medical Association, 288,* 2458–2465.

Fahy, T. A. (1988). The diagnosis of multiple personality disorder: A critical review. *British Journal of Psychiatry, 153,* 597–606.

Fahy, T. A., Abas, M., & Brown, J. C. (1989). Multiple personality: A symptom of psychiatric disorder. *British Journal of Psychiatry, 154,* 99–101.

Fairburn, C., Cooper, Z., Doll, H., Norman, P., & O'Conner, M. (2000). The natural course of bulimia nervosa and binge eating disorder in young women. *Archives of General Psychiatry, 57,* 659–665.

Fairburn, C. G. (1997). Interpersonal psychotherapy for bulimia nervosa. In D. M. Garner & P. E. Garfinkel (Eds.), *Handbook of treatment for eating disorders* (2nd ed., pp. 278–294). New York: Guilford Press.

Fairburn, C. G. (1998). Interpersonal psychotherapy for bulimia nervosa. In J. C. Markowitz (Ed.), *Interpersonal psychotherapy* (pp. 99–128). Washington, DC: American Psychiatric Association.

Fairburn, C. G. (2005). Evidence-based treatment of anorexia nervosa. *International Journal of Eating Disorders, 37,* S26–S30.

Fairburn, C. G., & Bohn, K. (2005). Eating disorder NOS (EDNOS): An example of the troublesome "not otherwise specified" (NOS) category in DSM-IV-TR. *Behaviour Research and Therapy, 43,* 691–701.

Fairburn, C. G., Cooper, Z., & Cooper, P. (1986). The clinical features and maintenance of bulimia nervosa. In K. D. Brownell & J. Foreyt (Eds.), *Physiology, psychology, and treatment of eating disorders* (pp. 389–404). New York: Basic Books.

Fairburn, C. G., Cooper, Z., Doll, H. A., & Davies, B. A. (2005). Identifying dieters who will develop an eating disorder: A prospective, population-based study. *American Journal of Psychiatry, 162,* 249–2255.

Fairburn, C. G., Jones, R., Peveler, R. C., Hope, R. A., & O'Connor, M. (1993). Psychotherapy and bulimia nervosa: Longer-term effects of interpersonal psychotherapy, behavior therapy, and cognitive behavior therapy. *Archives of General Psychiatry, 50,* 419–428.

Fairburn, C. G., Kirk, J., O'Connor, M., & Cooper, P. J. (1986). A comparison of two psychological treatments for bulimia nervosa. *Behaviour Research and Therapy, 24,* 629–643.

Fairburn, C. G., Marcus, M. D., & Wilson, G. T. (1993). Cognitive-behavioral therapy for binge eating and bulimia nervosa: A comprehensive treatment manual. In C. G. Fairburn & G. T. Wilson (Eds.), *Binge eating: Nature, assessment, and treatment* (pp. 361–404). New York: Guilford Press.

Fairburn, C. G., Norman, P. A., Welch, S. L., O'Connor, M., Doll, H., & Peveler, R. (1995). A prospective study of outcome in bulimia nervosa and the long-term effects of three psychological treatments. *Archives of General Psychiatry, 52,* 304–312.

Fairburn, C. G., Palmer, R. L., Bohn, K., Doll, H. A., & O'Connor, M. E. (in preparation). The clinical features of patients with Eating Disorders NOS.

Fairburn, C. G., Peveler, R. C., Jones, R., Hope, R. A., & Doll, H. A. (1993). Predictors of 12-month outcome in bulimia nervosa and the influence of attitudes to shape and weight. *Journal of Consulting and Clinical Psychology, 61,* 696–698.

Fairburn, C. G., Stice, E., Cooper, Z., Doll, H. A., Norman, P. A., & O'Connor, M. E. (2003). Understanding persistence of bulimia nervosa: A 5-year naturalistic study. *Journal of Consulting and Clinical Psychology, 71,* 103–109.

Fairburn, C. G., & Walsh, B. T. (2002). Atypical eating disorders (eating disorder not otherwise specified). In C. G. Fairburn & K. D. Brownell (Eds.), *Eating disorders and obesity* (2nd ed., pp. 171–182). New York: Guilford Press.

Falco, M. (2008, February 7). Sad lessons from Heath Ledger's death. CNN. Retrieved December 23, 2008, from http://www.cnn.com/HEALTH/blogs/paging.dr.gupta/2008/02/sad-lessons-from-heath-ledgers-death.html

Falicov, C. J. (1998). *Latino families in therapy: A guide to multicultural practice*. New York: Guilford Press.

Fallon, B. A. (2004). Pharmacotherapy of somatoform disorders. *Journal of Psychosomatic Research, 56,* 455–460.

Fallon, B. A., & Feinstein, S. (2001). Hypochondriasis. In K. A. Phillips (Ed.), *Somatoform and factitious disorders* (pp. 27–65). Washington, DC: American Psychiatric Association.

Fallon, B. A., Liebowitz, M. R., Salman, E. M., Schneier, F. R., Jusino, C., Hollander, E., et al. (1993). Fluoxetine for hypochondriacal patients without major depression. *Journal of Clinical Psychopharmacology, 13,* 438–441.

Fallon, B. A., Qureshi, A. I., Laje, G., & Klein, B. (2000). Hypochondriasis and its relationship to obsessive-compulsive disorder. *Psychiatric Clinics of North America, 23,* 605–616.

Fallon, B. A., Qureshi, A. I., Schneier, F. R., Sanchez-Lacay, A., Vermes, D., Feinstein, R., et al. (2003). An open trial of fluvoxamine for hypochondriasis. *Psychosomatics: Journal of Consultation and Liaison Psychiatry, 44,* 298–303.

Fallon, B. A., Schneier, F. R., Marshall, R., Campeas, R., Vermes, D., Goetz, D., et al. (1996). The pharmacotherapy of hypochondriasis. *Psychopharmacology Bulletin, 32,* 607–611.

Fan, A. P., & Eaton, W. W. (2001). Longitudinal study assessing the joint effects of socio-economic status and birth risks on adult emotional and nervous conditions. *British Journal of Psychiatry, 178,* s78–s83.

Farah, M. J. (2004). *Visual agnosia* (2nd ed.). Cambridge, MA: MIT Press/Bradford Books.

Faraone, S. V., Biederman, J., Spencer, T., Mick, E., Murray, K., Petty, C., et al. (2006). Diagnosing adult attention deficit hyperactivity disorder: Are late onset and subthreshold diagnoses valid? *American Journal of Psychiatry, 163,* 1720–1729.

Faraone, S. V., Perlis, R. H., Doyle, A. E., Smoller, J. W., Goralnick, J. J., Holmgren, M. A., et al. (2005). Molecular genetics of attention-deficit/hyperactivity disorder. *Biological Psychiatry, 57,* 1313–1323.

Faraone, S. V., Tsuang, M. T., & Tsuang, D. W. (2001) *Genetics of mental disorders: What practitioners and students need to know*. New York: Guilford Press.

Faravelli, C., Zucchi, T., Viviani, B., Salmoria, R., Perone, A., Paionni, A., et al. (2000). Epidemiology of social phobia: A clinical approach. *European Psychiatry, 15,* 17–24.

Farmer, A., Redman, K., Harris, T., Webb, R., Mahmood, A., Sadler, S., et al. (2001). The Cardiff sib-pair study. *Crisis, 22,* 71–73.

Farmer, R. F., & Nelson-Gray, R. O. (2005). Behavioral treatment of personality disorders. In R. F. Farmer & R. O. Nelson-Gray, *Personality-guided behavior therapy* (pp. 203–243). Washington, DC: American Psychological Association.

Farrow, T. F. D., Hunter, M. D., Wilkinson, I. D., Green, R. D. J., & Spence, S. A. (2005). Structural brain correlates of unconstrained motor activity in people with schizophrenia. *British Journal of Psychiatry, 187,* 481–482.

Fauman, M. A. (2006). Defining a DSM infrastructure. *American Journal of Psychiatry, 163,* 1873–1874.

Fava, G. A., Bartolucci, G., Rafanelli, C., & Mangelli, L. (2001). Cognitive-behavioral management of patients with bipolar disorder who relapsed while on lithium prophylaxis. *Journal of Clinical Psychiatry, 62,* 556–559.

Fava, G. A., Mangelli, L., & Ruini, C. (2001). Assessment of psychological distress in the setting of medical disease. *Psychotherapy and Psychosomatics 70,* 171–175.

Fava, G. A., Rafanelli, C., Grandi, S., Conti, S., & Belluardo, P. (1998a). Prevention of recurrent depression with cognitive behavioral therapy: Preliminary findings. *Archives of General Psychiatry, 55,* 816–820.

Fava, G. A., Rafanelli, C., Grandi, S., Canestrari, R., & Morphy, M. A. (1998b). Six-year outcome for cognitive behavioral treatment of residual symptoms in major depression. *American Journal of Psychiatry, 155,* 1443–1445.

Favaro, A., Zanetti, T., Tenconi, E., Degortes, D., Ronzan, A., Veronese, A., et al. (2005). The relationship between temperament and impulsive behaviors in eating disordered subjects. *Eating Disorders: The Journal of Treatment & Prevention, 13,* 61–70.

Fawcett, R. G. (2002). Olanzapine for the treatment of monosymptomatic hypochondriacal psychosis. *Journal of Clinical Psychiatry, 63,* 169.

Fazel, S., & Grann, M. (2006). The population impact of severe mental illness on violent crime. *American Journal of Psychiatry, 163,* 1397–1403.

Federoff, I. C., & Taylor, S. (2001). Psychological and pharmacological treatments of social phobia: A meta-analysis. *Journal of Clinical Psychopharmacology, 21,* 311–324.

Fee, practice and managed care survey. (2000). *Psychotherapy Finances, 10*(318), 10.

Feldman, H. A., Goldstein, I., Hatzichristou, D. G., Krane, R. J., & McKinlay, J. B. (1994). Impotence and its medical and psychosocial correlates: Results of the Massachusetts Male Aging Study. *Journal of Urology, 151,* 54–61.

Fenton, W., & McGlashan, T. (1991). Natural history of schizophrenia subtypes: I. Longitudinal study of paranoid, hebephrenic, and undifferentiated schizophrenia. *Archives of General Psychiatry, 48,* 969–977.

Fenton, W. S. (2000). Depression, suicide, and suicide prevention in schizophrenia. *Suicide and Life-Threatening Behavior, 30,* 34–49.

Fenton, W. S., & McGlashan, T. H. (1994). Antecedent, symptoms progression, and long-term outcome of the deficit syndrome in schizophrenia. *American Journal of Psychiatry, 151,* 351–356.

Fergusson, D., Doucette, S., Glass, K. C., Shapiro, S., Healy, D., Hebert, P., et al. (2005). Association between suicide attempts and selective serotonin reuptake inhibitors: Systematic review of randomised controlled trials. *British Medical Journal, 330,* 396–369.

Fergusson, D. M., Swain-Campbell, N. R., & Horwood, L. J. (2002). Deviant peer affiliations, crime and substance use: A fixed effects regression analysis. *Journal of Abnormal Child Psychology, 30,* 419–430.

Fibiger, H. C., & Phillips, A. G. (1988). Mesocorticolimbic dopamine systems and reward. *Annals of the New York Academy of Sciences, 537,* 206–215.

Fichter, M. M., Quadflieg, N., & Hedlund, S. (2006). Twelve-year course and outcome predictors of anorexia nervosa. *International Journal of Eating Disorders, 39,* 87–100.

Fick, D. M., Cooper, J. W., Wade, W. E., Waller, J. L., Maclean, J. R., & Beers, M. H. (2003). Updating the Beers criteria for potentially inappropriate medication use in older adults: Results of a US consensus panel of experts. *Archives of Internal Medicine, 163,* 2716–2724.

Fiedler, N., Ozakinci, G., Hallman, W., Wartenberg, D., Brewer, N. T., Barrett, D. H., et al. (2006). Military deployment to the Gulf War as a risk factor for psychiatric illness among US troops. *British Journal of Psychiatry, 188,* 453–459.

Field, A. E., Camargo, C. A., Jr., Taylor, C. B., Berkey, C. S., Frazier, L., Gillman, M. W., et al. (1999). Overweight, weight concerns, and bulimic behaviors among girls and boys. *Journal of the American Academy of Child & Adolescent Psychiatry, 38,* 754–760.

Field, T., Hernandez-Reif, M., & Diego, M. (2006). Risk factors and stress variables that differentiate depressed from nondepressed pregnant women. *Infant Behavior & Development, 29,* 169–174.

Figiel, G. S., Epstein, C., McDonald, W. M., Amazon-Leece, J., Figiel, L., Saldivia, A., et al. (1998). The use of rapid-rate transcranial magnetic stimulation (rTMS) in refractory depressed patients. *Journal of Neuropsychiatry & Clinical Neurosciences, 10,* 20–25.

File, S. E., Gonzalez, L. E., & Gallant, R. (1999). Role of the dorsomedial hypothalamus in mediating the response to benzodiazepines on trial 2 in the elevated plus-maze test of anxiety. *Neuropsychopharmacology, 21,* 312–320.

File, S. E., Kenny, P. J., & Cheeta, S. (2000). The role of the dorsal hippocampal serotonergic and cholinergic systems in the modulation of anxiety. *Pharmacology, Biochemistry & Behavior, 66,* 65–72.

Fillit, H. M., Butler, R. N., O'Connel, A. W., Albert, M. S., Birren, J. E., Cotman, C. W., et al. (2002). Achieving and maintaining cognitive vitality with aging. *Proceedings of the Mayo Clinic, 77,* 681–696.

Finch, A. E., Lambert, M. J., & Brown, G. (2000). Attacking anxiety: A naturalistic study of a multimedia self-help program. *Journal of Clinical Psychology, 56,* 11–21.

Finch, E. (2001). Social and transcultural aspects of substance misuse. *Current Opinion in Psychiatry, 14,* 173–177.

Fine, J. G., Semrud-Clikeman, M., Keith, T. Z., Stapleton, L. M., & Hynd, G. W. (2007). Reading and the corpus callosum: An MRI family study of volume and area. *Neuropsychology, 21,* 235–241.

Fink, M. (2001). Convulsive therapy: A review of the first 55 years. *Journal of Affective Disorders, 63,* 1–15.

Finn, J., & Banach, M. (2000). Victimization online: The down side of seeking services for women on the Internet. *CyberPsychology & Behavior, 3,* 243–254.

Finzi-Dottan, R., & Karu, T. (2006). From emotional abuse in childhood to psychopathology in adulthood: A path mediated by immature defense mechanisms and self-esteem. *Journal of Nervous and Mental Disease, 194,* 616–621.

Fiorentine R., & Hillhouse M. P. (1999). Drug treatment effectiveness and client-counselor empathy. *Journal of Drug Issues, 29,* 59–74.

Fiorentine, R. (1999). After drug treatment: Are 12-step programs effective in maintaining abstinence? *American Journal of Drug and Alcohol Abuse, 25,* 93–116.

Fiorentine, R., & Hillhouse, M. P. (1999). Drug treatment effectiveness and client-counselor empathy. *Journal of Drug Issues, 29,* 59–74.

First, M. B. (2006, July 26–28). *Dimensional approaches in diagnostic classification: A critical appraisal.* Dimensional Conference. Retrieved January 17, 2007, from http://dsm5.org/conference13.cfm

First, M. B., Bell, C. C., Cuthbert, B., Krystal, J. H., Malison, R., Offord, D. R., et al. (2002). Personality disorders and relational disorders: A research agenda for addressing crucial gaps in DSM. In D. J. Kupfer, M. B. First, & D. A. Regier (Eds.), *A research agenda for DSM-V* (pp. 123–199). Washington, DC: American Psychiatric Association.

First, M. B., & Frances, A. (2008). Issues for DSM-V: Unintended consequences of small changes: The case of paraphilias. *American Journal of Psychiatry, 165*, 1240–1241.

First, M. B., Spitzer, R. L., Williams, J. B. W., & Gibbon, M. (1997). *Structured clinical interview for DSM-IV Axis II personality disorders (SCID-II), user's guide and interview.* Washington, DC: American Psychiatric Press.

First, M. B., Spitzer, R. L., Gibbon, M., & Williams, J. B. W. (2002). *Structured clinical interview for DSM-IV Axis I disorders, research version, non-patient edition (SCID-I/NP).* New York: Biometrics Research, New York State Psychiatric Institute.

Fischer, S., Smith, G. T., & Anderson, K. G. (2003). Clarifying the role of impulsivity in bulimia nervosa. *International Journal of Eating Disorders, 33*, 406–410.

Fish, B., Marcus, B., Hans, S. L., Auerbach, J. G., & Perdue, S. (1992). Infants at risk for schizophrenia: Sequelae of a genetic neurointegrative defect. A review and replication analysis of pandysmaturation in the Jerusalem Infant Development Study. *Archives of General Psychiatry, 49*, 221–235.

Fishbain, D. A., Goldberg, M., Khalil, T. M., Asfour, S. S., Abdel-Moty, E., Meagher, B. R., et al. (1988). The utility of electromyographic biofeedback in the treatment of conversion paralysis. *American Journal of Psychiatry, 145*, 1572–1575.

Fisher, S. E., & Francks, C. (2006). Genes, cognition and dyslexia: Learning to read the genome. *Trends in Cognitive Sciences, 10*, 250–257.

Fitzgibbon, M. L., & Stolley, M. R. (2000). Minority women: The untold story. *Nova: Dying to be thin.* Retrieved august 31, 2007, from http://www.pbs.org/wgbh/nova/thin/minorities.html

Flaherty, J., & Adams, S. (1998). Therapist-patient race and sex matching: Predictors of treatment duration. *Psychiatric Times, 15*, n.p. Retrieved March 12, 2008, from http://www.psychiatrictimes.com/display/article/10168/49886

Flaskerud, J. H. (1991). Effects of an Asian client-therapist language, ethnicity and gender match on utilization and outcome of therapy. *Community Mental Health Journal, 27*, 31–42.

Flaskerud, J. H., & Liu, P. Y. (1991). Effects of an Asian client-therapist language, ethnicity and gender match on utilization and outcome of therapy. *Community Mental Health Journal, 27*, 31–42.

Fleischman, D. A., Wilson, R. S., Gabrieli, J. D. E., Bienias, J. L., & Bennett, D. A. (2004). A longitudinal study of implicit and explicit memory in old persons. *Psychology and Aging, 19*, 617–625.

Flint, A. J. (2005). Generalised anxiety disorder in elderly patients: Epidemiology, diagnosis and treatment options. *Drugs and Aging, 22*, 101–114.

Foa, E. B., Cashman, L., Jaycox, L., & Perry, K. (1997). The validation of a self-report measure of posttraumatic stress disorder: The Posttraumatic Diagnostic Scale. *Psychological Assessment, 9*, 445–451.

Foa, E. B., Dancu, C. V., Hembree, E. A., Jaycox, L. H., Meadows, E. A., & Street, G. P. (1999). A comparison of exposure therapy, stress inoculation training, and their combination for reducing posttraumatic stress disorder in female assault victims. *Journal of Consulting and Clinical Psychology, 67*, 194–200.

Foa, E. B., Gilboa-Schechtman, E., Amir, N., & Freshman, M. (2000). Memory bias in generalized social phobia: Remembering negative emotional expressions. *Journal of Anxiety Disorders, 14*, 501–519.

Foa, E. B., & Goldstein, A. J. (1978). Continuous exposure and complete response prevention in the treatment of obsessive-compulsive neurosis. *Behavior Therapy, 9*, 821–829.

Foa, E. B., Liebowitz, M. R., Kozak, M. J., Davies, S., Campeas, R., Franklin, M. E., et al. (2005). Randomized, placebo-controlled trial of exposure and ritual prevention, clomipramine, and their combination in the treatment of obsessive-compulsive disorder. *American Journal of Psychiatry, 162*, 151–161.

Foa, E. B., Rothbaum, B. O., Riggs, D. S., & Murdock, T. B. (1991). Treatment of posttraumatic stress disorder in rape victims: A comparison between cognitive-behavioral procedures and counseling. *Journal of Consulting and Clinical Psychology, 59*, 715–723.

Foa, E. B., Steketee, G., & Rothbaum, B. O. (1989). Behavioral/cognitive conceptualizations of post-traumatic stress disorder. *Behavior Therapy, 20*, 155–176.

Foley, D. L., Neale, M. C., & Kendler, K. S. (1996). A longitudinal study of stressful life events assessed at personal interview with an epidemiologic sample of adult twins: The basis of individual variation in event exposure. *Psychological Medicine, 26*, 1239–1252.

Foley, D. L., Pickles, A., Maes, H. M., Silberg, J. L., & Eaves, L. J. (2004). Course and short-term outcomes of separation anxiety disorder in a community sample of twins. *Journal of the American Academy of Child & Adolescent Psychiatry, 43*, 1107–1114.

Foley, D., Rutter, M., Pickles, A., Angold, A., Maes, H., Silberg, J., et al. (2004). Informant disagreement for separation anxiety disorder. *Journal of the American Academy of Child & Adolescent Psychiatry, 43*, 452–460.

Folstein, S., & Rutter, M. (1977). Infantile autism: A genetic study of 21 twin pairs. *Journal of Child Psychology and Psychiatry, 18*, 297–321.

Folstein, S. E. (1989). *Huntington's disease: A disorder of families.* Baltimore: Johns Hopkins University Press.

Fombonne, E. (2005). The changing epidemiology of autism. *Journal of Applied Research in Intellectual Disabilities, 18*, 281–294.

Fonagy, P., & Bateman, A. (2008). The development of borderline personality disorder—a mentalizing model. *Journal of Personality Disorders, 22*, 4–21.

Fonagy, P., Leigh, T., Steele, M., Steele, H., Kennedy, R., Mattoon, G., et al. (1996). The relation of attachment status, psychiatric classification, and response to psychotherapy. *Journal of Consulting and Clinical Psychology, 64*, 22–31.

Fontenelle, L. F., Mendlowicz, M. V., Marques, C., & Versiani, M. (2004). Trans-cultural aspects of obsessive-compulsive disorder: A description of a Brazilian sample and a systematic review of international clinical studies. *Journal of Psychiatric Research, 38*, 403–411.

Foote, B., Smolin, Y., Kaplan, M., Legatt, M. E., & Lipschitz, D. (2006). Prevalence of dissociative disorders in psychiatric outpatients. *American Journal of Psychiatry, 163*, 623–629.

Forbush, K., Heatherton, T. F., & Keel, P. K. (2007). Relationships between perfectionism and specific disordered eating behaviors. *International Journal of Eating Disorders, 40*, 37–41.

Forgas, J. P. (1995). Strange couples: Mood effects on judgments and memory about prototypical and atypical relationships. *Personality and Social Psychology Bulletin, 21*, 747–765.

Forrest, K. A. (2001). Toward an etiology of dissociative identity disorder: A neurodevelopmental approach. *Consciousness and Cognition, 10*, 259–293.

Forty, L., Jones, L., Macgregor, S., Caesar, S., Cooper, C., Hough, A., et al. (2006). Familiality of postpartum depression in unipolar disorder: Results of a family study. *American Journal of Psychiatry, 163*, 1549–1553.

Fossati, A., Madeddu, F., & Maffei, C. (1999). Borderline personality disorder and childhood sexual abuse: A meta-analytic study. *Journal of Personality Disorders, 13,* 268–280.

Fosse, G. K., & Holen, A. (2004). Cohabitation, education, and occupation of psychiatric outpatients bullied as children. *Journal of Nervous and Mental Disease, 192,* 385–388.

Fowler, R. D. (1986). Howard Hughes: A psychological autopsy. *Psychology Today, 20,* 22–33.

Fox, N. A., Nichols, K. E., Henderson, H. A., Rubin, K., Schmidt, L., Hamer, D., et al. (2005). Evidence for a gene-environment interaction in predicting behavioral inhibition in middle childhood. *Psychological Science, 16,* 921–926.

Fraley, R. C., & Shaver, P. R. (1997). Adult attachment and the suppression of unwanted thoughts. *Journal of Personality and Social Psychology, 73,* 1080–1091.

Frances, A., First, M. B., & Pincus, H. A. (1995). *DSM-IV guidebook.* Washington, DC: American Psychiatric Association.

Frances, A., & Ross, R. (1996). *DSM-IV case studies: A clinical guide to differential diagnosis.* Washington, DC: American Psychiatric Press.

Franco-Paredes, K., Mancilla-Díaz, J. M., Vázquez-Arévalo, R., López-Aguilar, X., & Álvarez-Rayón, G. (2005). Perfectionism and eating disorders: A review of the literature. *European Eating Disorders Review, 13,* 61–70.

Frank, E., Gonzalez, J. M., & Fagiolini, A. (2006). The importance of routine for preventing recurrence in bipolar disorder. *American Journal of Psychiatry, 163,* 981–985.

Frank, E., Hlastala, S., Ritenour, A., Houck, P., Tu, X. M., Monk, T. H., et al. (1997). Inducing lifestyle regularity in recovering bipolar disorder patients: Results from the maintenance therapies in bipolar disorder protocol. *Biological Psychiatry, 41,* 1165–1173.

Frank, E., Kupfer, D. J., Buysse, D. J., Swartz, H. A., Pilkonis, P. A., Houck, P. R., et al. (2007). Randomized trial of weekly, twice-monthly, and monthly interpersonal psychotherapy as maintenance treatment for women with recurrent depression. *American Journal of Psychiatry, 164,* 761–767.

Frank, E., Kupfer, D. J., Thase, M. E., Mallinger, A. G., Swartz, H. A., Eagiolini, A. M., et al. (2005). Two-year outcomes for interpersonal and social rhythm therapy in individuals with bipolar I disorder. *Archives of General Psychiatry, 62,* 996–1004.

Frank, E., & Spanier, C. (1995). Interpersonal psychotherapy for depression: Overview, clinical efficacy, and future directions. *Clinical Psychology: Science and Practice, 2,* 349–369.

Frank, E., Swartz, H. A., Mallinger, A. G., Thase, M. E., Weaver, E. V., & Kupfer, D. J. (1999). Adjunctive psychotherapy for bipolar disorder: Effects of changing treatment modality. *Journal of Abnormal Psychology, 108,* 579–587.

Frank, G. K., Bailer, U. F., Henry, S., Wagner, A., & Kaye, W. H. (2004). Neuroimaging studies in eating disorders. *CNS Spectrums, 9,* 539–548.

Frank, G. K., Kaye, W. H., Weltzin, T. E., Perel, J., Moss, H., McConaha, C., et al. (2001). Altered response to meta-chlorophenylpiperazine in anorexia nervosa: Support for a persistent alteration of serotonin activity after short-term weight restoration. *International Journal of Eating Disorders, 30,* 57–68.

Frankel, F., Cantwell, D. P., Myatt, R., & Feinberg, D. T. (1999). Do stimulants improve self-esteem in children with ADHD and peer problems? *Journal of Child and Adolescent Psychopharmacology, 9,* 185–194.

Franklin, M. E., Abramowitz, J. S., Bux, D. A., Zoellner, L. A. & Feeny, N. C. (2002). Cognitive-behavioral therapy with and without medication in the treatment of obsessive-compulsive disorder. *Professional Psychology: Research and Practice, 33,* 162–168.

Franko, D. L., Becker, A. E., Thomas, J. J., & Herzog, D. B. (2007). Cross-ethnic differences in eating disorder symptoms and related distress. *International Journal of Eating Disorders, 40,* 156–164.

Franko, D. L., Wonderlich, S., Little, D., & Herzog, D. B. (2004). Diagnosis and classification of eating disorders: What's new? In J. K. Thompson (Ed.), *Handbook of eating disorders and obesity.* New York: Wiley.

Fraser, A. (2000). *The houses of Hanover and Saxe-Coburg.* Berkeley: University of California Press.

Fredrickson, B. L., & Roberts, T. (1997). Objectification theory: Toward understanding women's lived experiences and mental health risks. *Psychology of Women Quarterly, 21,* 173–206.

Fredrickson, B. L., Roberts, T.-A., Noll, S. M., Quinn, D. M., & Twenge, J. M. (1998). That swimsuit becomes you: Sex differences in self-objectification, restrained eating, and math performance. *Journal of Personality & Social Psychology, 75,* 269–284.

Fredrikson, M., Annas, P., Fischer, H., & Wik, G. (1996). Gender and age differences in the prevalence of specific fears and phobias. *Behaviour Research and Therapy, 34,* 33–39.

Freedman, R. (2008). Cannabis, inhibitory neurons, and the progressive course of schizophrenia. *American Journal of Psychiatry, 165*(4), 416–419.

Freedman, R. Adler, L. E., Myles-Worsley, M., Nagamoto, H. T., Miller, C., Kesley, M., et al. (1997). Inhibitory gating of an evoked response to repeated auditory stimuli in schizophrenic and normal subjects. Human recordings, computer simulation, and an animal model. *Archives of General Psychiatry, 53,* 1114–1121.

Freedman, R., Adler, L. E., Myles-Worsley, M., Nagamoto, H. T., Miller, C., Kisley, M., McRae, K., Cawthra, E., & Waldo, M. (1996). Inhibitory gating of an evoked response to repeated auditory stimuli in schizophrenic and normal subjects: Human recordings, computer simulation, and an animal model. *Archives of General Psychiatry, 53,* 1114–1121.

Freels, S. A., Richman, J. A., & Rospenda, K. M. (2005). Gender differences in the causal direction between workplace harassment and drinking. *Addictive Behaviors, 30,* 1454–1458.

Freeman, H. (1994). Schizophrenia and city residence. *British Journal of Psychiatry, 164,* 39–50.

Freeman, H. (1994). Schizophrenia and city residence. *British Journal of Psychiatry, 164,* 39–50.

Freeman, L. (1980). *Freud rediscovered.* New York: Arbor House.

Freeman, L. (1990). *The story of Anna O.* New York: Paragon House.

Freemantle, N., Anderson, I. M., & Young, P. (2000). Predictive value of pharmacological activity for the relative efficacy of antidepressant drugs: Meta-regression analysis. *British Journal of Psychiatry, 177,* 292–302.

Frerikson, M., Annas, P., Fischer, H., & Wik, G. (1996). Gender and age differences in the prevalence of specific fears and phobias. *Behaviour Research and Therapy 34,* 33–39.

Freud, S. (1900/1958). *The interpretation of dreams.* New York: Basic Books.

Freud, S. (1920). Fear and anxiety. In S. Freud, *A general introduction to psychoanalysis* (pp. 340–355). New York: Liveright.

Freud, S. (1938). *Moses and monotheism.* New York: W. W. Norton.

Freud, S. (1955). Three essays on the theory of sexuality. In J. Strachey (Ed. & Trans.), *The standard edition of the complete psychological works of Sigmund Freud* (Vol. 7, pp. 125–245). London: Hogarth Press. (Original work published 1905)

Freud, S. (1961). *The ego and the id.* New York: W. W. Norton. (Original work published 1923)

Frezza, M., Di Padova, C., Pozzato, G., Terpin, M., Baraona, E., & Lieber, C. S. (1990). High blood alcohol levels in women. *New England Journal of Medicine, 322,* 95–99.

Frick, P. J. (2006). Developmental pathways to conduct disorder. *Child and Adolescent Psychiatric Clinics of North America, 15,* 311–331.

Frick, P. J., & Loney, B. R. (1999). Outcomes of children and adolescents with oppositional defiant disorder and conduct disorder. In H. C. Quay & A. E. Hogan (Eds.), *Handbook of the disruptive behavior disorders* (pp. 507–524). New York: Kluwer Academic/Plenum.

Frick, P. J., & Morris, A. S. (2004). Temperament and developmental pathways to conduct problems. *Journal of Clinical Child and Adolescent Psychology, 33,* 54–68.

Frick, P. J., & Muñoz, L. (2006). Oppositional defiant disorder and conduct disorder. In C. A. Essau (Ed.), *Child and adolescent psychopathology: Theoretical and clinical implications* (pp. 26–51). New York: Routledge/Taylor & Francis.

Frick, P. J., & Silverthorn, P. (2001). Psychopathology in children. In P. B. Sutker & H. E. Adams (Eds.), *Comprehensive handbook of psychopathology* (3rd ed., pp. 881–920). New York: Kluwer Academic/Plenum.

Frick, P. J., Bodin, S. D., & Barry, C. T. (2000). Psychopathic traits and conduct problems in community and clinic-referred samples of children: Further development of the Psychopathy Screening Device. *Psychological Assessment, 12,* 382–393.

Frick, P. J., Cornell, A. H., Bodin, S. D., Dane, H. E., Barry, C. T., & Loney, B. R. (2003). Callous-unemotional traits and developmental pathways to severe conduct problems. *Developmental Psychology, 39,* 246–260.

Fridman, C., Ojopi, &. P. B., Gregório, S. P., Ikenaga, E. H., Moreno, D. H., Demetrio, F. N., Guimarães, P. E. M., Vallada, H. P., Gattaz, W. F., & Dias Neto, E. (2003). Association of a new polymorphism in ALOX12 gene with bipolar disorder. *European Archives of Psychiatry & Clinical Neuroscience, 253,* 40–43.

Friedman, R. F., Ween, J. E., & Albert, M. L. (1993). Alexia. In K. M. Heilman & E. Valenstein (Eds.), *Clinical neuropsychology* (3rd ed., pp. 37–62). New York: Oxford University Press.

Friedrich, M. J. (2005) Molecular studies probe bipolar disorder. *Journal of the American Medical Association, 293,* 545–546.

Frink, H. W. (1921). Psychology of the compulsion neurosis. In H. W. Frink (Ed.), *Morbid fears and compulsions: Their psychology and psychoanalytic treatment* (pp. 163–185). London: Kegan Paul.

Frischholz, E. J., Braun, B. G., Sachs, R. G., Hopkins, L., Shaeffer, D. M., Lewis, J., et al. (1990). The Dissociative Experiences Scale: Further replication and validation. *Dissociation: Progress in the Dissociative Disorders, 3,* 151–153.

Frischholz, E. J., Lipman, L. S., Braun, B. G., & Sachs, R. G. (1992). Psychopathology, hypnotizability, and dissociation. *American Journal of Psychiatry, 149,* 1521–1525.

Frith, C. D. (1992). *The cognitive neuropsychology of schizophrenia.* Hillsdale, NJ: Lawrence Erlbaum Associates.

Frith, U. (2003). *Autism: Explaining the enigma* (2nd ed.). Malden, MA: Blackwell Publishing.

Frosch, A. (2002). Transference: Psychic reality and material reality. *Psychoanalytic Psychology, 19,* 603–633.

Fuller, R. K., Branchey, L., Brightwell, D. R., Derman, R. M., Emrick, C. D., Iber, F. L., et al. (1986). Disulfiram treatment of alcoholism: A Veterans Administration cooperative study. *Journal of the American Medical Association 256,* 1449–1455.

Fuller, R., Nopoulos, P., Arndt, S., O'Leary, D., Ho, B.-C., & Andreasen, N. C. (2002). Longitudinal assessment of premorbid cognitive functioning in patients with schizophrenia through examination of standardized scholastic test performance. American Journal of Psychiatry, 159, 1183–1189.

Funahashi, T., Ibuki, Y., Domon, Y., Nishimura, T., Akehashi, D., & Sugiura, H. (2000). A clinical study on suicide among schizophrenics. Psychiatry and Clinical Neuroscience, 54, 173–179.

Furmark, T., Tillfors, M., Marteinsdottir, I., Fischer, H., Pissiota, A., Langstroem, B., & Fredrikson, M. (2002). Common changes in cerebral blood flow in patients with social phobia treated with citalopram or cognitive-behavioral therapy. *Archives of General Psychiatry, 59,* 425–433.

Fyer, A. J. (2000). Heritability of social anxiety: A brief review. *Journal of Clinical Psychiatry, 54,* 10–12.

Gaab, N., Gabrieli, J. D. E., Deutsch, G. K., Tallal, P., & Temple, E. (2007). Neural correlates of rapid auditory processing are disrupted in children with developmental dyslexia and ameliorated with training: An fMRI study. *Restorative Neurology and Neuroscience, 25,* 295–310.

Gabbay, V., Asnis, G. M., Bello, J. A., Alonso, C. M., Serras, S. J., & O'Dowd, M. A. (2003) New onset of body dysmorphic disorder following frontotemporal lesion. *Neurology, 61,* 123–125.

Gabbott, P. L., Warner, T. A., Jays, P. R., Salway, P., & Busby, S. J. (2005). Prefrontal cortex in the rat: Projections to subcortical autonomic, motor, and limbic centers. *Journal of Comparative Neurology, 492,* 145–177.

Gacono, C. B., Nieberding, R. J., Owen, A., Rubel, J., & Bodholdt, R. (2001). Treating conduct disorder, antisocial, and psychopathic personalities. In J. B. Ashford, B. D. Sales, & W. H. Reid (Eds.), *Treating adult and juvenile offenders with special needs* (pp. 99–129). Washington, DC: American Psychological Association.

Gaffney, G. R., Lurie, S. F., & Berlin, F. S. (1984). Is there familial transmission of pedophilia? *Journal of Nervous and Mental Disease, 172,* 546–548.

Gagne, G. G., Furman, M. J., Carpenter, L. L., & Price, L. H. (2000). Efficacy of continuation ECT and antidepressant drugs compared to long-term antidepressants alone in depressed patients. *American Journal of Psychiatry, 157,* 1960–1965.

Gaher, R. M., Simons, J. S., Jacobs, G. A., Meyer, D., & Johnson-Jimenez, E. (2006). Coping motives and trait negative affect: Testing mediation and moderation models of alcohol problems among American Red Cross disaster workers who responded to the September 11, 2001 terrorist attacks. *Addictive Behaviors, 31,* 1319–1330.

Gainetdinov, R. R., Wetsel, W. C., Jones, S. R., Levin, E. D., Jaber, M., & Caron, M. G. (1999). Role of serotonin in the paradoxical calming effect of psychostimulants on hyperactivity. *Science, 283,* 397–401.

Galassi, F., Quercioli, S., Charismas, D., Niccolai, V., & Barciulli, E. (2007). Cognitive-behavioral group treatment for panic disorder with agoraphobia. *Journal of Clinical Psychology, 63,* 409–416.

Gallers, J., Foy, D. W., Donahoe, C. P., & Goldfarb, J. (1988). Post-traumatic stress disorder in Vietnam combat veterans: Effects of traumatic violence exposure with military adjustment. *Journal of Traumatic Stress, 1,* 181–192.

Garb, H. N. (1997). Race bias, social class bias, and gender bias in clinical judgment. *Clinical Psychology: Science & Practice, 4,* 99–120.

Garb, H. N., Wood, J. M., Lilienfeld, S. O., & Nezworski, M. T. (2005). Roots of the Rorschach controversy. *Clinical Psychology Review, 25,* 97–118.

Garber, J., & Horowitz, J. L. (2002). Depression in children. In I. H. Gotlib & C. L. Hammen (Eds.), *Handbook of depression* (pp. 510–540). New York: Guilford Press.

Garcia-Palacios, A., Botella, C., Hoffman, H., & Fabregat, S. (2007). Comparing acceptance and refusal rates of virtual reality exposure vs. in vivo exposure by patients with specific phobias. *CyberPsychology & Behavior, 10,* 722–724.

Garety, P. A., & Freeman, D. (1999). Cognitive approaches to delusions: A critical review of theories and evidence. British Journal of Clinical Psychology, 38, 113–154.

Garety, P. A., Freeman, D., Jolley, S., Dunn, G., Bebbington, P. E., Fowler, D. G., Kuipers, E., & Dudley, R. (2005). Reasoning, emotions, and delusional conviction in psychosis. Journal of Abnormal Psychology, 114, 373–384.

Garfield, S. L. (1994). Research on client variables in psychotherapy. In A. E. Bergin & S. L. Garfield (Eds.). Handbook of psychotherapy and behavior change (4th ed.). (pp. 190–228). Oxford, England: John Wiley & Sons.

Garfield, S. L. (1994). Research on client variables in psychotherapy. In A. E. Bergin & S. L. Garfield (Eds.), Handbook of psychotherapy and behavior change (4th ed.). Oxford, England: John Wiley & Sons.

Garfield, S. L. (1998). Some Comments on Empirically Supported Treatments. Journal of Consulting and Clinical Psychology, 66, 121–125.

Garfield, S. L. (1998). Some comments on empirically supported treatments. Journal of Consulting & Clinical Psychology, 66, 121–125.

Garfield, S. L., & Bergin, A. E. (1994). Introduction and historical overview. In A. E. Bergin & S. L. Garfield (Eds.), Handbook of psychotherapy and behavior change (4th ed., pp. 3–18). Oxford, England: John Wiley & Sons.

Garfinkel, P. E., Goldbloom, D., Davis, R., Olmsted, M. P., Garner, D. M., & Halmi, K. A. (1992). Body dissatisfaction in bulimia nervosa: Relationship to weight and shape concerns and psychological functioning. International Journal of Eating Disorders, 11, 151–161.

Garfinkel, P. E., Kennedy, S. H., & Kaplan, A. S. (1995). Views on classification and diagnosis of eating disorders. Canadian Journal of Psychiatry, 40, 445–456.

Garfinkel, P. E., Lin, E., Goering, P., Spegg, C., Goldbloom, D., Kennedy, S., Kaplan, A. S., & Woodside, D. B. (1996). Should amenorrhoea be necessary for the diagnosis of anorexia nervosa? Evidence from a Canadian community sample. British Journal of Psychiatry, 168, 500–506.

Garner, D. M. (1997). Psychoeducational principles in treatment. In D. M. Garner & P. E. Garfinkel (Eds.), Handbook of treatment for eating disorders (2nd ed., pp. 147–177). New York: Guilford Press.

Garner, D. M., Garfinkel, P. E., Schwartz, D., & Thompson, M. (1980). Cultural expectations of thinness in women. Psychological Reports, 47, 483–491.

Garner, D. M., Rosen, L. W., & Barry, D. (1998). Eating disorders among athletes: Research and recommendations. Child and Adolescent Psychiatric Clinics of North America, 7, 839–857.

Garner, D. M., Vitousek, K. M., & Pike, K. M. (1997). Cognitive-behavioral therapy for anorexia nervosa. In Garner, David M.

(Ed.); Garfinkel, Paul E. (Ed.), Handbook of treatment for eating disorders (2nd ed.). (pp. 94–144). New York, NY: Guilford Press.

Gaser, C., Nenadic, I., Buchsbaum, B. R., Hazlett, E. A., & Buchsbaum, M. S. (2004). Ventricular enlargement in schizophrenia related to volume reduction of the thalamus, striatum, and superior temporal cortex. American Journal of Psychiatry, 161, 154–156.

Gauvain, M., & Fagot, B. (1995). Child temperament as a mediator of mother-toddler problem solving. Social Development, 4, 257–276

Gavin, J., Rodham, K., & Poyer, H. (2008). The presentation of "pro-anorexia" in online group interactions. Qualitative Health Research, 18, 325–333.

Geddes, J. R., & Lawrie, S. M. (1995). Obstetric complications: A meta-analysis. British Journal of Psychiatry, 67, 786–793.

Geddes, J., Freemantle, N., Harrison, P., & Bebbington, P. (2000). Atypical antipsychotics in the treatment of schizophrenia: Systematic overview and meta-regression analysis. British Medical Journal, 321, 1372–1376.

Gee, T., Allen, K., & Powell, R. A. (2003). Questioning premorbid dissociative symptomatology in dissociative identity disorder: Comment on Gleaves, Hernandez, and Warner (1999). Professional Psychology: Research and Practice, 34, 114–116.

Geffken, G. R., Storch, E. A., Duke, D. C., Monaco, L., Lewin, A. B., & Goodman, W. K. (2006). Hope and coping in family members of patients with obsessive-compulsive disorder. Journal of Anxiety Disorders, 20, 614–629.

Gega, L., Marks, I., & Mataix-Cols, D. (2004). Computer-aided CBT self-help for anxiety and depressive disorders: Experience of a London clinic and future directions. Journal of Clinical Psychology, 60, 147–157.

Gelhorn, H., Stallings, M., Young, S., Corley, R., Rhee, S. H., Hopfer, C., & Hewitt, J. (2006). Common and specific genetic influences on aggressive and nonaggressive conduct disorder domains. Journal of the American Academy of Child & Adolescent Psychiatry, 45, 570–577.

Geller, J., Srikameswaran, S., Cockell, S. J., & Zaitsoff, S. L. (2000). Assessment of shape- and weight-based self-esteem in adolescents. International Journal of Eating Disorders, 28, 339–345.

Gentile, K., Raghavan, C., Rajah, V., & Gates, K. (2007). It doesn't happen here: Eating disorders in an ethnically diverse sample of economically disadvantaged, urban college students. Eating Disorders: The Journal of Treatment & Prevention, 15, 405–425.

George, L. K., & Weiler, S. J. (1981). Sexuality in middle and late life: The effects of age, cohort, and gender. Archives of General Psychiatry, 38, 919–923.

George, M. S., Lisanby, S. H., & Sackheim, H. A. (1999). Transcranial magnetic stimulation: Applications in neuropsychiatry. Archives in General Psychiatry, 56, 300–311.

George, S., & Moselhy, H. (2005). "Gateway hypothesis"—A preliminary evaluation of variables predicting non-conformity. Addictive Disorders & Their Treatment, 4, 39–40.

Geracioti, T. D., Jr., Carpenter, L. L., Owens, M. J., Baker, D. G., Ekhator, N. N., Horn, P. S., Strawn, J. R., Sanacora, G., Kinkead, B., Price, L. H., & Nemeroff, C. B. (2006). Elevated cerebrospinal fluid substance p concentrations in posttraumatic stress disorder and major depression. American Journal of Psychiatry, 163, 637–643.

Ghaderi, A. (2006). Does individualization matter? A randomized trial of standardized (focused) versus individualized (broad) cognitive behavior therapy for bulimia nervosa. Behaviour Research and Therapy, 44, 273–288.

Ghashghaei, H. T., & Barbas, H. (2002). Pathways for emotion: Interactions of prefrontal and anterior temporal pathways in the amygdala of the rhesus monkey. Neuroscience, 115, 1261–1279.

Gianoulakis, C. (2001). Influence of the endogenous opioid system on high alcohol consumption and genetic predisposition to alcoholism. Journal of Psychiatry & Neuroscience, 26, 304–318.

Gibb, B. E., Alloy, L. B., Abramson, L. Y., Rose, D. T., Whitehouse, W. G., Donovan, P., Hogan, M. E., Cronholm, J., & Tierney, S. (2001). History of childhood maltreatment, negative cognitive styles, and episodes of depression in adulthood. Cognitive Therapy & Research, 25, 425–446.

Gick, M. L., & Thompson, W. G. (1997). Negative affect and the seeking of medical care in university students with irritable bowel syndrome. Journal of Psychosomatic Research, 43, 535–540.

Gijs, L., & Gooren, L. (1996). Hormonal and psychopharmacological interventions in the treatment of paraphilias: An update. Journal of Sex Research, 33, 273–290.

Gilbertson, M. W., Shenton, M. E., Ciszewski, A., Kasai, K., Lasko, N. B., Orr, S. P., & Pitman, R. K. (2002). Smaller hippocampal volume predicts pathologic vulnerability to psychological trauma. Nature Neuroscience, 5, 1242–1247.

Gillespie, N. A., Cloninger, C. R., Heath, A. C., & Martin, N. G. (2003). The genetic and environmental relationship between Cloninger's dimensions of temperament and character. Personality and Individual Differences, 35, 1931–1946.

Gillespie, N. A., Zhu, G., Heath, A. C., Hickie, I. B., & Martin, N. G. (2000). The genetic aetiology of somatic distress. *Psychological Medicine, 30,* 1051–1061.

Gilmer, W. S., Trivedi, M. H., Rush, A. J., Wisniewski, S. R., Luther, J., Howland, R. H., Yohanna, D., Khan, A., & Alpert, J. (2005). Factors associated with chronic depressive episodes: A preliminary report from the STAR-D project. *Acta Psychiatrica Scandinavica, 112,* 425–433.

Gilmour, H., Gibson, F., & Campbell, J. (2003). Living alone with dementia: A case study approach to understanding risk. *Dementia: The International Journal of Social Research and Practice, 2,* 403–420.

Ginsberg, D. L. (Ed.). (2004). Women and anxiety disorders: Implications for diagnosis and treatment. *CNS Spectrums, 9,* 1–16.

Ginsburg, G. S., & Silverman, W. K. (2000). Gender role orientation and fearfulness in children with anxiety disorders. *Journal of Anxiety Disorders, 14,* 5–67.

Ginzler, J. A., Cochran, B. N., Domenech-Rodríguez, M., Cauce, A. M., & Whitbeck, L. B. (2003). Sequential progression of substance use among homeless youth: An empirical investigation of the gateway theory. *Substance Use & Misuse, 38,* 725–758.

Giovanoli, E. J. (1988). ECT in a patient with conversion disorder. *Convulsive Therapy, 4,* 236–242.

Giraldi, A., & Levin, R. J. (2006). Vascular physiology of female sexual function. In: I. Goldstein, C. M. Meston, S. R. Davis, & A. M. Traish. (Eds.), *Women's Sexual Function and Dysfunction—Study, Diagnosis and Treatment.* London: Taylor and Francis. pp. 174–180.

Gitin, N. M., Herbert, J. D., & Schmidt, C. (1996, November). One-session in vivo exposure for odontophobia. Paper presented at the 30th annual convention of the Association for the Advancement of Behavior Therapy, New York.

Gitlin, M., Nuechterlein, K., Subotnik, K. L., Ventura, J., Mintz, J., Fogelson, D. L., Bartzokis, G., & Aravagiri, M. (2001). Clinical outcome following neuroleptic discontinuation in patients with remitted recent-onset schizophrenia. American Journal of Psychiatry, 158, 1835–1842.

Giuffrida, A., Leweke, F. M., Gerth, C. W., Schreiber, D., Koethe, D., Faulhaber, J., Klosterkötter, J., & Piomelli, D. (2004). Cerebrospinal anandamide levels are elevated in acute schizophrenia and are inversely correlated with psychotic symptoms. *Neuropsychopharmacology, 29,* 2108–2114.

Giulino, L., Gammon, P., Sullivan, K., Franklin, M., Foa, E., Maid, R., & March, J. S. (2002). Is parental report of upper respiratory infection at the onset of obsessive-compulsive disorder suggestive of pediatric autoimmune neuropsychiatric disorder associated with streptococcal infection? *Journal of Child & Adolescent Psychopharmacology, 12,* 157–164.

Givens, J. L., Houston, T. K., Van Voorhees, B. W., Ford, D. E., & Cooper, L. A. (2007). Ethnicity and preferences for depression treatment. *General Hospital Psychiatry, 29,* 182–191.

Gladis, M. M., Gosch, E. A., Dishuk, N. M., & Crits-Christoph, P. (1999). Quality of life: Expanding the scope of clinical significance. *Journal of Consulting and Clinical Psychology, 67,* 320–331.

Glass, R. M. (2001). Electroconvulsive therapy: Time to bring it out of the shadows. *JAMA: Journal of the American Medical Association, 285,* 1346–1348.

Gleaves, D. H., Lowe, M. R., Green, B. A., Cororve, M. B., & Williams, T. L. (2000). Do anorexia and bulimia nervosa occur on a continuum? A taxometric analysis. *Behavior Therapy, 31,* 195–219.

Gleaves, D. H., Lowe, M. R., Snow, A. C., Green, B. A., & Murphy-Eberenz, K. P. (2000). Continuity and discontinuity models of bulimia nervosa: A taxometric investigation. *Journal of Abnormal Psychology, 109,* 56–68.

Gleaves, D. H. (1996). The sociocognitive model of dissociative identity disorder: A reexamination of the evidence. *Psychological Bulletin, 120,* 42–59.

Glenn, C. R., & Klonsky, E. D. (2009). Emotion dysregulation as a core feature of borderline personality disorder. *Journal of Personality Disorders, 23,* 20–28.

Glisky, E. L., Ryan, L., Reminger, S., Hardt, O., Hayes, S. M., & Hupbach, A. (2004). A case of psychogenic fugue: I understand, aber ich verstehe nichts. *Neuropsychologia, 42,* 1132–1147.

Godart, N. T., Flament, M. F., Curt, F., Perdereau, F., Lang, F., Venisse, J. L., Halfon, O., Bizouard, P., Loas, G., Corcos, M., Jeammet, P., & Fermanian, J. (2003). Anxiety disorders in subjects seeking treatment for eating disorders: A DSM-IV-TR controlled study. *Psychiatry Research, 117,* 245–258.

Goddard, A. W., Mason, G. F., Almai, A., Rothman, D. L., Behar, K. L., Petroff, O. A. C., Charney, D. S., & Krystal, J. H. (2001). Reductions in the occipital cortex GABA levels in panic disorder detected with 1H-magnetic resonance spectroscopy. *Archives of General Psychiatry 58,* 556–561.

Godemann, F., Ahrens, B., Behrens, S., Berthold, R., Gandor, C., Lampe, F., & Linden, M. (2001). Classic conditioning and dysfunctional cognitions in patients with panic disorder and agoraphobia treated with an implantable cardioverter/defibrillator. *Psychosomatic Medicine, 63,* 231–238.

Godinez v. Moran, 509 U.S. 389 (1993).

Goff, B. S. N., & Smith, D. B. (2005). Systemic traumatic stress: The couple adaptation to traumatic stress model. *Journal of Marital & Family Therapy, 31,* 145–157.

Goisman, R. M., Goldenberg, I., Vasile, R. G., & Keller, M. B. (1995). Comorbidity of anxiety disorders in a multicenter anxiety study. *Comprehensive Psychiatry, 36,* 303–311.

Golan, O., & Baron-Cohen, S. (2006). Systemizing empathy: Teaching adults with Asperger syndrome or high-functioning autism to recognize complex emotions using interactive multimedia. *Development and Psychopathology, 18,* 591–617.

Goldapple, K., Segal, Z., Garson, C., Lau, M., Bieling, P., Kennedy, S., & Mayberg, H. (2004). Modulation of cortical-limbic pathways in major depression: Treatment-specific effects of cognitive behavior therapy. *Archives of General Psychiatry, 61,* 34–41.

Golden, C. J., Hammeke, T. A., & Purisch, A. D. (1980). *The Luria-Nebraska Neuropsychological Battery: manual.* Los Angeles: Western Psychological Services.

Golden, R. N., Gaynes, B. N., Ekstrom, R. D., Hamer, R. M., Jacobsen, F. M., Suppes, T., Wisner, K. L., & Nemeroff, C. B. (2005). The efficacy of light therapy in the treatment of mood disorders: A review and meta-analysis of the evidence. *American Journal of Psychiatry, 162,* 656–662.

Goldfried, M. R., & Wolfe, B. E. (1998). Toward a more clinically valid approach to therapy research. *Journal of Consulting and Clinical Psychology, 66,* 143–150.

Goldfried, M. R., & Wolfe, B. E. (1998). Toward a more clinically valid approach to therapy research. *Journal of Consulting and Clinical Psychology, 66,* 143–150.

Goldkamp, J. S., & Irons-Guynn, C. (2000). Emerging judicial strategies for the mentally ill in the criminal caseload: Mental health courts in Fort Lauderdale, Seattle, San Bernardino, and Anchorage. U.S. Department of Justice, Office of Justice Programs; Bureau of Justice Assistance.

Goldsmith, S. K., Pellmar, T. C., Kleinman, A. M., & Bunney, W. E. (Eds.). (2002). *Reducing suicide: A national imperative.* Washington, DC: National Academies Press.

Goldstein, A. (1994) *Addiction: From Biology to Drug Policy.* New York: Freeman.

Goldstein, A. J., & Chambless, D. L. (1978). A reanalysis of agoraphobia. *Behavior Therapy, 9,* 47–59.

Goldstein, D. S. (2000). *The autonomic nervous system in health and disease.* New York: Marcel Dekker.

Goodnough, A. (2006, November 15). Officials clash over mentally ill in Florida jails. *The New York Times,* p. A1.

Goodwin, D. W., Schulsinger, F., Moller, N., Hermansen, L., Winokur, G., & Guze, S. B. (1974). Drinking problems in adopted and nonadopted sons of alcoholics. *Archives of General Psychiatry, 31,* 164–169.

Goodwin, F. K., & Ghaemi, S. N. (1998). Understanding manic-depressive illness. *Archives of General Psychiatry, 55,* 23–25.

Goodwin, F. K., & Jamison, K. R. (1990). *Manic-depressive illness.* New York: Oxford University Press.

Goodwin, J., Hill, S., & Attias, R. (1990). Historical and folk techniques of exorcism: Applications to the treatment of dissociative disorders. *Dissociation: Progress in the Dissociative Disorders, 3,* 94–101.

Goodwin, R., Lyons, J. S., & McNally, R. J. (2002). Panic attacks in schizophrenia. *Schizophrenia Research, 58,* 213–220.

Gordis, E. (1996). Alcohol research: At the cutting edge. *Archives of General Psychiatry, 53,* 199–201.

Gorman, J. M., & Kent, J. M. (1999). SSRIs and SNRIs: Broad spectrum of efficacy beyond major depression. *Journal of Clinical Psychiatry, 60,* 33–39.

Gorman, J. M., & Kent, J. M. (1999). SSRIs and SNRIs: Broad spectrum of efficacy beyond major depression. *Journal of Clinical Psychiatry, 60,* 33–39.

Gorman, J. M., Liebowitz, M. R., Fyer, A. J., & Stein, J. (1989). A neuroanatomical hypothesis for panic disorder. *American Journal of Psychiatry, 146,* 148–161.

Gortner, E. T., Gollan, J. K., Dobson, K. S., & Jacobson, N. S. (1998). Cognitive-behavioral treatment for depression: Relapse prevention. *Journal of Consulting and Clinical Psychology, 66,* 377–384.

Gorwood, P. (2004). Generalized anxiety disorder and major depressive disorder comorbidity: An example of genetic pleiotropy? *European Psychiatry, 19,* 27–33.

Gosden, R. (2000). Prepsychotic treatment for schizophrenia: A rejoinder. Reply. *Ethical Human Sciences & Services, 2,* 211–214.

Götestam, K. G. (2002). One session group treatment of spider phobia by direct or modelled exposure. *Cognitive Behaviour Therapy, 31,* 18–24.

Gotlib, I. H., & Robinson, L. A. (1982). Responses to depressed individuals: Discrepancies between self-report and observer rated behavior. *Journal of Abnormal Psychology, 91,* 231–240.

Gotlib, I. H., Kasch, K. L., Traill, S., Joormann, J., Arnow, B. A., & Johnson, S. L. (2004). Coherence and specificity of information-processing biases in depression and social phobia. *Journal of Abnormal Psychology, 113,* 386–398.

Gotlib, I. H., Krasnoperova, E., Yue, D. N., & Joormann, J. (2004). Attentional biases for negative interpersonal stimuli in clinical depression. *Journal of Abnormal Psychology, 113,* 127–135.

Gottesman, I. I. (1991) *Schizophrenia genesis: The origin of madness.* New York: Freeman.

Gottesman, I. I. (1991) *Schizophrenia genesis: The origin of madness.* New York: Freeman.

Gottesman, I. I., & Bertelsen, A. (1989). Confirming unexpressed genotypes for schizophrenia: Risks in the offspring of Fischer's Danish identical and fraternal discordant twins. *Archives of General Psychiatry, 46,* 867–872.

Gottesman, I. I., & Erlenmeyer-Kimling, L. (2001). Family and twin strategies as a head start in defining prodromes and endophenotypes for hypothetical early-interventions in schizophrenia. *Schizophrenia Research, 51,* 93–102.

Gottesman, I. I., & Moldin, S. O. (1998). Genotypes, genes, genesis, and pathogenesis in schizophrenia. In M. F. Lenzenweger & R. H. Dworkin (Eds.), *Origins and development of schizophrenia* (pp. 5–11). Washington, DC: American Psychological Association.

Gould, R. A., & Clum, G. A. (1993). A meta-analysis of self-help treatment approaches. *Clinical Psychology Review, 13,* 169–186.

Grabe, H. J., Spitzer, C., Schwahn, C., Marcinek, A., Frahnow, A., Barnow, S., et al. (in press). Serotonin transporter gene (SLC6A4) promoter polymorphisms and the susceptibility to Posttraumatic Stress Disorder in the general population. *American Journal of Psychiatry, np.*

Grabe, S., & Hyde, J. S. (2006). Ethnicity and body dissatisfaction among women in the United States: A meta-analysis. *Psychological Bulletin, 132,* 622–640.

Grady, D. (2006). Self-portraits chronicle a descent into Alzheimer's. *The New York Times,* Oct. 24. (Accessed 10/24/06).

Grady, D. (2006, October 24). Self-portraits chronicle a descent into Alzheimer's. *New York Times.* Retrieved February 21, 2007, from http://www.nytimes.com/2006/10/24/health/24alzh.html

Graff, G. (1989). A Starr is reborn. Retrieved July 16, 2002, from http://members.aol.com/applescruff33/ringoastarrisreborninterview.html

Graham, K. G. (1976, April). Interview with Little Edie. *Interview Magazine* In A. Mayles (Director/Producer) & D. Mayles (Director/Producer), *Grey Gardens* (disc 2).

Grant, B. F. (2000). Estimates of U.S. children exposed to alcohol abuse and dependence in the family. *American Journal of Public Health, 90,* 112–115.

Grant, B. F., Goldstein, R. B., Chou, S. P., Huang, B., Stinson, F. S., Dawson, D. A., et al. (2008). Sociodemographic and psychopathologic predictors of first incidence of DSM-IV substance use, mood, and anxiety Disorders: Results from the Wave 2 National Epidemiologic Survey on Alcohol and Related Conditions. *Molecular Psychiatry, 13,* 1–16.

Grant, B. F., Hasin, D. S., Stinson, F. S., Dawson, D. A., Chou, S. P., Ruan, W. J., & Pickering, R. P. (2004). Prevalence, correlates, and disability of personality disorders in the United States: Results from the National Epidemiologic Survey on Alcohol and Related Conditions. *Journal of Clinical Psychiatry, 65,* 948–958.

Grant, B. F., Stinson, F. S., Dawson, D. A., Chou, S. P., Ruan, W. J., & Pickering, R. P. (2004). Co-occurrence of 12-month alcohol and drug use disorders and personality disorders in the United States: Results from the National Epidemiologic Survey on Alcohol and Related Conditions. *Archives of General Psychiatry, 61,* 361–368.

Grant, J. E., Menard, W., Pagano, M. E., Fay, C., & Phillips, K. A. (2005). Substance use disorders in individuals with body dysmorphic disorder. *Journal of Clinical Psychiatry, 66,* 309–316.

Gratz, K. L., Rosenthal, M. Z., Tull, M. T., Lejuez, C. W., & Gunderson, J. G. (2006). An experimental investigation of emotion dysregulation in borderline personality disorder. *Journal of Abnormal Psychology, 115,* 850–855.

Gray, C. A. (1996) Social stories and comic strip conversations with students with Asperger syndrome and high functioning autism. In E. Schopler, G. B. Mesibov, & L. Kunce (Eds.), *Asperger syndrome and high functioning autism* (pp. 1–10). New York: Plenum.

Gray, J. A. (1987). Perspectives on anxiety and impulsiveness: A commentary. *Journal of Research in Personality, 21,* 493–509.

Gray, J. A. (1987). Perspectives on anxiety and impulsivity: A commentary. *Journal of Research in Personality, 21,* 493–510.

Gray, J. A. (1991). The neuropsychology of temperament. In J. Strelau & A. Angleitner (Eds.), *Explorations in temperament: International perspectives on theory and measurement* (pp. 105–128). New York: Plenum Press.

Graybar, S. R., & Boutilier, L. R. (2002). Nontraumatic pathways to borderline personality disorder. *Psychotherapy: Theory, Research, Practice, Training, 39,* 152–162.

Graziottin, A. (2007). Prevalence and evaluation of sexual health problems—HSDD in Europe. *Journal of Sexual Medicine, 4,* 211–219.

Green, A. R. (2004). MDMA: Fact and fallacy, and the need to increase knowledge in both the scientific and popular press. *Psychopharmacology, 173,* 231–233.

Green, J. P., & Lynn, S. J. (1995). Hypnosis, dissociation, and simultaneous-task performance. *Journal of Personality and Social Psychology, 69,* 728–735.

Green, M. F. (2001). *Schizophrenia revealed: From neurons to social interactions.* New York: W.W. Norton.

Green, M. F. (2007). Cognition, drug treatment, and functional outcome in schizophrenia: A tale of two transitions. *American Journal of Psychiatry, 164,* 992–994.

Green, M. F. (2007). Cognition, drug treatment, and functional outcome in schizophrenia: A tale of two transitions. *American Journal of Psychiatry, 164,* 992–994.

Green, R. (1974). The behaviorally feminine male child: Pretranssexual? Pretransvestic? Prehomosexual? Preheterosexual? In R. C. Friedman, R. M. Richart, R. L. Vande Wiele, & L. O. Stern (Eds.), *Sex differences in behavior.* (pp. 33–52). Oxford, England: John Wiley & Sons

Green, R. (1987). Gender identity in childhood and later sexual orientation: Follow-up of 78 males. In S. Chess & A. Thomas (Eds.), *Annual progress in child psychiatry and child development* (pp. 214–220). Philadelphia: Brunner/Mazel.

Green, R. (2000). Family cooccurrence of "gender dysphoria": Ten siblings or parent-child pairs. *Archives of Sexual Behavior, 29,* 499–507.

Greenberg, B. D., Altemus, M., & Murphy, D. L. (1997). The role of neurotransmitters and neurohormones in obsessive-compulsive disorder. *International Review of Psychiatry, 9,* 31–44.

Greenberg, B. D., Murphy, D. L., & Rasmussen, S. A. (2003) Neuroanatomically based approaches to obsessive-compulsive disorder. Neurosurgery and transcranial magnetic stimulation. *Psychiatric Clinics of North America, 23,* 671–686.

Greenberg, J. R., & Mitchell, S. A. (1983). *Object relations in psychoanalytic theory.* Cambridge, MA: Harvard University Press.

Greenberg, R. P. (2002). Reflections on the emperor's new drugs. *Prevention & Treatment, 5,* Article 27. Available on the World Wide Web: http://www.journals.apa.org/prevention/volume5/pre0050027c.html.

Greenberg, R. P., & Fisher, S. (1989). Examining antidepressant effectiveness: Findings, ambiguities, and some vexing puzzles. In S. Fisher & R. P. Greenberg (Eds.), *The limits of biological treatments for psychological distress: Comparisons with psychotherapy and placebo* (pp. 1–37). Hillsdale, NJ: Lawrence Erlbaum.

Greene, E., Heilbrun, K., Fortune, W. H., & Nietzel, M. T. (2007). *Wrightsman's psychology and the legal system* (6th ed.). Belmont, CA: Thomson/Wadsworth.

Greene, R. L. (2000). *The MMPI-2: An interpretive manual* (2nd ed.). Needham Heights, MA: Allyn & Bacon.

Greenfield, S. F. (2002). Women and alcohol use disorders. *Harvard Review of Psychiatry, 10,* 76–85.

Greenhouse, L. (2006, February 22). Sect allowed to import its hallucinogenic tea. *New York Times.* Retrieved February 22, 2006, from http://www.nytimes.com/2006/02/22/politics/22scotus.html?_r=1&oref=slogin

Greenwood, T. A., & Kelsoe, J. R. (2003). Promoter and intronic variants affect the transcriptional regulation of the human dopamine transporter gene. *Genomics, 82,* 511–520.

Gregorian, R. S., Golden, K. A., Bahce, A., Goodman, C., Kwong, W. J., & Khan, Z. M. (2002). Antidepressant-induced sexual dysfunction. *The Annals of Pharmacotherapy, 36,* 1577–1589.

Gregory, R. J., & Remen, A. L. (2008). A manual-based psychodynamic therapy for treatment-resistant borderline personality disorder. *Psychotherapy: Theory, Research, Practice, Training, 45,* 15–27.

Greig, T. C., Bryson, G. J., & Bell, M. D. (2004). Theory of mind performance in schizophrenia: Diagnostic, symptom, and neuropsychological correlates. *Journal of Nervous and Mental Disorders, 192,* 12–18.

Grigorenko, E. L. (2001). Developmental dyslexia: An update on genes, brains, and environments. *Journal of Child Psychology and Psychiatry, 42,* 91–125.

Grilo, C. M., & McGlashan, T. H. (2005). Course and outcome of personality disorders. In Oldham, John M. (Ed.); Skodol, Andrew E. (Ed.); Bender, Donna S. (Ed.). *The American Psychiatric Publishing Textbook of Personality Disorders.* (pp. 103–115). Washington, DC, US: American Psychiatric Publishing, Inc.

Grilo, C. M., Sanislow, C. A., Gunderson, J. G., Pagano, M. E., Yen, S., Zanarini, M. C., Shea, M. T., Skodol, A. E., Stout, R. L., Morey, L. C., & McGlashan, T. H. (2004). Two-year stability and change of schizotypal, borderline, avoidant, and obsessive-compulsive personality disorders. *Journal of Consulting and Clinical Psychology, 72,* 767–775.

Grimes, K., & Walker, E. F. (1994). Childhood emotional expressions, educational attainments, and age at onset of illness in schizophrenia. *Journal of Abnormal Psychology, 103,* 784–790.

Grisaru, N., Amir, M., Cohen, H., & Kaplan, Z. (1998). Effect of transcranial magnetic stimulation in posttraumatic stress disorder: A preliminary study. *Biological Psychiatry, 44,* 52–55.

Grisso, T., & Appelbaum, P. S. (1995). The MacArthur Treatment Competence Study: III. Abilities of patients to consent to psychiatric and medical treatment. *Law and Human Behavior, 19,* 149–174.

Grove, L. (2005, May 25). Tom to Brooke: Don't be a woman of substance. *New York Daily News.* Retrieved January 18, 2007, from http://www.nydailynews.com/news/gossip/story/312036p-266946c.html

Gruber, K. J., & Taylor, M. F. (2006). A family perspective for substance abuse: Implications from the literature. *Journal of Social Work Practice in the Addictions, 6,* 1–29.

Grucza, R. A., Przybeck, T. R., & Cloninger, C. R. (2007). Prevalence and correlates of binge eating disorder in a community sample. *Comprehensive Psychiatry, 48,* 124–131.

Guan, L., Wang, B., Chen, Y., Yang, L., Li, J., Qian, Q., Wang, Z., Faraone, S. V., & Wang, Y. (in press). A high-density single-nucleotide polymorphism screen of 23 candidate genes in attention deficit hyperactivity disorder: Suggesting multiple susceptibility genes among Chinese Han population. *Molecular Psychiatry.*

Guarnaccia, P. J. (1997a). A cross-cultural perspective on anxiety disorders. In S. Friedman (Ed.), *Cultural issues in the treatment of anxiety* (pp. 3–20). New York: Guilford Press.

Guarnaccia, P. J. (1997b). Social stress and psychological distress among Latinos in the United States. In I. Al-Issa & M. Tousignant (Eds.), *Ethnicity, immigration, and psychopathology* (pp. 71–94). New York: Plenum Press.

Gude, T., Hoffart, A., Hedley, L., & Ro, O. (2004). The dimensionality of dependent personality disorder. *Journal of Personality Disorders, 18,* 604–610.

Gujar, S. K., Maheshwari, S., Bjorkman-Burtscher, I., & Sundgren, P. C. (2005). Magnetic resonance spectroscopy. *Journal of Neuroophthalmology, 25,* 217–226.

Gunderson, J. G., Daversa, M. T., Grilo, C. M., McGlashan, T. H., Zanarini, M. C., Shea, M. T., Skodol, A. E., Yen, S., Sanislow, C. A., Bender, D. S., Dyck, I. R., Morey, L. C., & Stout, R. L. (2006). Predictors of 2-year outcome for patients with borderline personality disorder. *American Journal of Psychiatry, 163,* 822–826.

Gunderson, J. G., Morey, L. C., Stout, R. L., Skodol, A. E., Shea, M. T., McGlashan, T. H., Zanarini, M. C., Grilo, C. M., Sanislow, C. A., Yen, S., Daversa, M. T., & Bender, D. S. (2004). Major depressive disorder and borderline personality disorder revisited: Longitudinal interactions. *Journal of Clinical Psychiatry, 65,* 1049–1056.

Gunderson, J. G., Weinberg, I., Daversa, M. T., Kueppenbender, K. D., Zanarini, M. C., Shea, M. T., Skodol, A. E., Sanislow, C. A., Yen, S., Morey, L. C., Grilo, C. M.,

McGlashan, T. H., Stout, R. L., & Dyck, I. (2006). Descriptive and longitudinal observations on the relationship of borderline personality disorder and bipolar disorder. *American Journal of Psychiatry, 163,* 1173–1178.

Gunewardene, A., Huon, G. F., & Zheng, R. (2001). Exposure to Westernization and dieting: A cross-cultural study. *International Journal of Eating Disorders, 29,* 289–293.

Gunnell, D., Saperia, J., & Ashby, D. (2005). Selective serotonin reuptake inhibitors (SSRIs) and suicide in adults: Meta-analysis of drug company data from placebo controlled, randomised controlled trials submitted to the MHRA's safety review. *British Medical Journal, 330,* 385–388.

Gur, R. C., Ragland, J. D., & Gur, R. E. (1997). Cognitive changes in schizophrenia—a critical look. *International Review of Psychiatry, 9,* 449–457.

Gur, R. E., Turetsky, B. I., Loughead, J., Snyder, W., Kohler, C., Elliott, M., Pratiwadi, R., Ragland, J. D., Bilker, W. B., Siegel, S. J., Kanes, S. J., Arnold, S. E, & Gur, R. C. (2007). Visual attention circuitry in schizophrenia investigated with oddball event-related functional Magnetic Resonance Imaging. *American Journal of Psychiatry, 164,* 442–449.

Guralnik, O., Giesbrecht, T., Knutelska, M., Sirroff, B., & Simeon, D. (2007). Cognitive functioning in depersonalization disorder. *Journal of Nervous and Mental Disease, 195,* 983–988.

Guralnik, O., Schmeidler, J., & Simeon, D. (2000). Feeling unreal: Cognitive processes in depersonalization. *American Journal of Psychiatry, 157,* 103–109.

Gureje, O., Ustun, T. B., & Simon, G. E. (1997). The syndrome of hypochondriasis: A cross-national study in primary care. *Psychological Medicine, 27,* 1001–1010.

Gurman, A. S. (2000). Family therapy. In A. E. Kazdin (Ed.), *Encyclopedia of psychology* (Vol. 3, pp. 329–333). Washington, DC: American Psychological Association.

Gurvits, T. V., Shenton, M. E., Hokama, H., & Ohta, H. (1996). Magnetic resonance imaging study of hippocampal volume in chronic, combat-related posttraumatic stress disorder. *Biological Psychiatry, 40,* 1091–1099.

Guthrie, R. M., & Bryant, R. A. (2005). Auditory startle response in firefighters before and after trauma exposure. *American Journal of Psychiatry, 162,* 283–290.

Gyulai, L., Abass, A., Broich, K., & Reilley, J. (1997). I-123 lofetamine single-photon computer emission tomography in rapid cycling bipolar disorder: A clinical study. *Biological Psychiatry, 41,* 152–161.

Haber, J. (2000). Management of substance abuse and dependence problems in families.

In M. A. Naegle & C. E. D'Avanzo (Eds.), *Addictions & substance abuse: Strategies for advanced practice nursing* (pp. 305–331). Englewood Cliffs, NJ: Prentice Hall.

Haber, J. Hamera, E., Hillyer, D., Limandri, B., Panel, S., Staten, R., & Zimmerman, M. (2003). Advanced practice psychiatric nurses: 2003 legislative update. *Journal of the American Psychiatric Nurses Association, 9,* 205–216.

Haber, J. R., Jacob, T., & Heath, A. C. (2005). Paternal alcoholism and offspring conduct disorder: Evidence for the "common genes" hypothesis. *Twin Research and Human Genetics, 8,* 120–131.

Hackett, G. I. (2008). Erectile dysfunction predicts cardiovascular risk in men. *British Medical Journal, 337,* a2166.

Hakko, H., Räsänen, P., & Tiihonen, J. (1998). Secular trends in the rates and seasonality of violent and nonviolent suicide occurrences in Finland during 1980–95. *Journal of Affective Disorders, 50,* 49–54.

Halbreich, U., & Kahn, L. (2001). Role of estrogen in the aetiology and treatment of mood disorders. *CNS Drugs, 15,* 797–817.

Hall, W. D., & Lynskey, M. (2005). Is cannabis a gateway drug? Testing hypotheses about the relationship between cannabis use and the use of other illicit drugs. *Drug and Alcohol Review, 24,* 39–48.

Halligan, P. W., Athwal, B. S., Oakley, D. A., & Frackowiak, R. S. J. (2000). The functional anatomy of a hypnotic paralysis: Implications for conversion hysteria. *Lancet, 355,* 986–987.

Halligan, P. W., Bass, C., & Wade, D. T. (2000). New approaches to conversion hysteria: Functional imaging may improve understanding and reduce morbidity. *British Medical Journal, 320,* 1488–1489.

Hallmayer, J. (2000). The epidemiology of the genetic liability for schizophrenia. *Australian & New Zealand Journal of Psychiatry, 34*(Suppl.), S47–S55.

Hallowell, E. M., & Ratey, J. J. (1994). *Driven to distraction: Recognizing and coping with attention deficit disorder from childhood through adulthood.* New York: Touchstone.

Halmi, K. A. (1995). Current concepts and definitions. In G. I. Szmukler, C. Dare, & J. Treasure (Eds.), *Handbook of eating disorders: Theory, treatment and research* (pp. 29–42). Oxford, England: John Wiley & Sons.

Halmi, K. A., Agras, W. S., Mitchell, J., Wilson, G. T., Crow, S., Bryson, S. W., & Kraemer, H. (2002). Relapse predictors of patients with bulimia nervosa who achieved abstinence through cognitive behavioral therapy. *Archives of General Psychiatry, 59,* 1105–1109.

Halmi, K. A., Sunday, S. R., Klump, K. L., Strober, M., Leckman, J. F., Fichter, M., Kaplan, A., Woodside, B., Treasure, J., Berrettini, W. H., Al Shabboat, M., Bulik, C. M., & Kaye, W. H. (2003). Obsessions and compulsions in anorexia nervosa subtypes. *International Journal of Eating Disorders, 33,* 308–319.

Halmi, K. A., Sunday, S. R., Strober, M., Kaplan, A., Woodside, D. B., Fichter, M., Treasure, J., Berrettini, W. H., & Kaye, W. H. (2000). Perfectionism in anorexia nervosa: Variation by clinical subtype, obsessionality, and pathological eating behavior. *American Journal of Psychiatry, 157,* 1799–1805.

Hamilton, M. E., Voris, J. C., Sebastian, P. S., Singha, A. K., Krejci, L. P., Elder, I. R., Allen, J. E., Beitz, J. E., Covington, K. R., Newton, A. E., Price, L. T., Tillman, E., & Hernandez, L. L. (1998). Money as a tool to extinguish conditioned responses to cocaine in addicts. *Journal of Clinical Psychology, 54,* 211–218.

Hamilton, S. R. (2008). Schizophrenia candidate genes: Are we really coming up blank? *American Journal of Psychiatry, 165,* 420–423.

Hankin, B. L., Abramson, L. Y., Miller, N., & Haeffel, G. J. (2004). Cognitive vulnerability-stress theories of depression: Examining affective specificity in the prediction of depression versus anxiety in three prospective studies. *Cognitive Therapy and Research, 28,* 309–345.

Hanna, G. L., Fischer, D. J., & Fluent, T. E. (2006). Separation anxiety disorder and school refusal in children and adolescents. *Pediatrics in Review, 27,* 56–63.

Hansen, N. B., Lambert, M. J., & Forman, E. M. (2002). The psychotherapy dose-response effect and its implications for treatment delivery services. *Clinical Psychology: Science and Practice, 9,* 329–343.

Hansenne, M., Pitchot, W., Pinto, E., Reggers, J., Scantamburlo, G., Fuchs, S., Pirard, S., & Ansseau, M. (2002). 5-HT1A dysfunction in borderline personality disorder. *Psychological Medicine, 32,* 935–941.

Hanson, R. K., Bloom, I., & Stephenson, M. (2004). Evaluating community sex offender treatment programs: A 12-year follow-up of 724 offenders. *Canadian Journal of Behavioural Science, 36,* 87–96.

Happé, F. G. E. (1994). An advanced test of theory of mind: Understanding of story characters' thoughts and feelings by able autistic, mentally handicapped, and normal children and adults. *Journal of Autism and Developmental Disorders, 24,* 129–154.

Hardan, A. Y., Muddasani, S., Vernulapalli, M., Keshavan, M. S., & Minshew, N. J. (2006). An MRI study of increased cortical thickness in autism. *American Journal of Psychiatry, 163,* 1290–1292.

Harden, B. L., & Lubetsky, M. (2005). Pharmacotherapy in autism and related disorders. *School Psychology Quarterly, 20,* 155–171.

Hare, R. D. (2003). *Manual for the Hare Psychopathy Checklist* (2nd ed. rev.). Toronto, Canada: Multi-Health Systems.

Harrington, R., Fudge, H., Rutter, M., Pickles, A., & Hill, J. (1990). Adult outcomes of childhood and adolescent depression: I. Psychiatric status. *Archives of General Psychiatry, 47,* 465–473.

Harris, M. G., Henry, L. P., Harrigan, S. M., Purcell, R., Schwartz, O. S., Farrelly, S. E., et al. (2005). The relationship between duration of untreated psychosis and outcome: An eight-year prospective study. *Schizophrenia Research, 79,* 85–93.

Harrison, K., & Hefner, V. (2006). Media exposure, current and future body ideals, and disordered eating among preadolescent girls: A longitudinal panel study. *Journal of Youth and Adolescence, 35,* 153–163.

Hart, S. D., & Hare, R. D. (1989). Discriminant validity of the Psychopathy Checklist in a forensic psychiatric population. *Psychological Assessment, 1,* 211–218.

Hartley, H. (2006). The "pinking" of Viagra culture: Drug industry efforts to create and repackage sex drugs for women. *Sexualities, 9,* 363–378.

Hartmann, H. (1939). *Ego psychology and the problem of adaptation.* New York: International Universities Press.

Hartung, C. M., & Widiger, T. A. (1998). Gender differences in the diagnosis of mental disorders: Conclusions and controversies of the DSM-IV. *Psychological Bulletin, 123,* 260–278.

Harvey, A. G., & Bryant, R. A. (2002). Acute stress disorder: A synthesis and critique. *Psychological Bulletin, 128,* 886–902.

Harvey, P. D. (2005a). Aging in healthy individuals. In *Schizophrenia in late life: Aging effects on symptoms and course of illness* (pp. 17–34). Washington, DC: American Psychological Association.

Harvey, P. D. (2005b). Dementia and schizophrenia: Similarities and differences. In *Schizophrenia in late life: Aging effects on symptoms and course of illness* (pp. 101–116). Washington, DC: American Psychological Association.

Harvey, P. D. (2005c). Late-onset schizophrenia. In *Schizophrenia in late life: Aging effects on symptoms and course of illness* (pp. 89–99). Washington, DC: American Psychological Association.

Haskett, M. E., Nears, K., Ward, C. S., & McPherson, A. V. (2006). Diversity in adjustment of maltreated children: Factors associated with resilient functioning. *Clinical Psychology Review, 26,* 796–812.

Hasler, G., Drevets, W. C., Manji, H. K., & Charney, D. S. (2004). Discovering endophenotypes for major depression. *Neuropsychopharmacology, 29,* 1765–1781.

Hasler, G., Drevets, W. C., Manji, H. K., & Charney, D. S. (2004). Discovering endophenotypes for major depression. *Neuropsychopharmacology, 29,* 1765–1781.

Havey, J. M., Olson, J. M., McCormick, C., & Cates, G. L. (2005). Teachers' perceptions of the incidence and management of attention-deficit hyperactivity disorder. *Applied Neuropsychology, 12,* 120–127.

Hawke, J. L., Wadsworth, S. J., & DeFries, J. C. (2006). Genetic influences on reading difficulties in boys and girls: The Colorado twin study. *Dyslexia: An International Journal of Research and Practice, 12,* 21–29.

Hawkins, J., Catalano, R., & Miller, J. (1992). Risk and protective factors for alcohol and other drug problems in adolescence and early adulthood: Implications for substance abuse prevention. *Psychological Bulletin, 112,* 64–105.

Hayden, D. (2003). *Pox: Genius, madness, and the mysteries of syphilis.* New York: Basic Books.

Heath, A. C., Madden, P. A. F., Bucholz, K. K., Nelson, E. C., Todorov, A., Price, R. K., Whitfield, J. B., & Martin, N. G. (2003). Genetic and environmental risks of dependence on alcohol, tobacco, and other drugs . In R. Plomin, J. C. DeFries, I. W. Craig, & P. McGuffin (Eds.), *Behavioral genetics in the postgenomic era* (pp. 309–334). Washington, DC: American Psychological Association.

Heatherton, T. F., & Baumeister, R. F. (1991). Binge eating as escape from self-awareness. *Psychological Bulletin, 110,* 86–108.

Heaton, R. K., Grant, I., & Matthews, C. G. (1991). Comprehensive norms for an expanded Halstead-Reitan Battery: Demographic corrections, research findings, and clinical applications. Odessa, FL: Psychological Assessment Resources.

Heil, P., & Simons, D. (2008). Multiple paraphilias: Prevalence, etiology, assessment, and treatment. In D. R. Laws & W. T. O'Donohue (Eds.), *Sexual deviance: Theory, assessment, and treatment* (2nd ed., pp. 527–556). New York: Guilford Press.

Heilbrun, K., Nezu, C. M., Keeney, M., Chung, S., & Wasserman, A. L. (1998). Sexual offending: Linking assessment, intervention, and decision making. *Psychology, Public Policy, and Law, 4,* 138–174.

Heim, A., & Westen, D. (2005). Theories of personality and personality disorders. In J. M. Oldham, A. E. Skodol, & D. S. Bender (Eds.), *The American Psychiatric Publishing textbook of personality disorders* (pp. 17–33). Washington, DC: American Psychiatric Publishing.

Heiman, J. R. (2000). Orgasmic disorders in women. In S. R. Leiblum & R. C. Rosen (Eds.), *Principles and practice of sex therapy* (3rd ed., pp. 118–153). New York: Guilford Press.

Heiman, J. R. (2002a). Psychologic treatments for female sexual dysfunction: Are they effective and do we need them? *Archives of Sexual Behavior, 31,* 445–450.

Heiman, J. R. (2002b). Sexual dysfunction: Overview of prevalence, etiological factors, and treatments. *Journal of Sex Research, 39,* 73–78.

Heiman, J. R., & Meston, C. M. (1997). Evaluating sexual dysfunction in women. *Clinical Obstetrics and Gynecology, 40,* 616–629.

Heimberg, R. G., Dodge, C. S., Hope, D. A., Kennedy, C. R., Zollo, L. J., & Becker, R. E. (1990). Cognitive behavioral group treatment for social phobia: Comparison with a credible placebo control. *Cognitive Therapy and Research, 14,* 1–23.

Heimberg, R. G., Liebowitz, M. R., Hope, D. A., Schneier, F. R., Holt, C. S., Welkowitz, L. A., Juster, H. R., Campeas, R., Bruch, M. A., Cloitre, M., Fallon, B., & Klein, D. F. (1998). Cognitive behavioral group therapy vs phenelzine therapy for social phobia: 12-week outcome. *Archives of General Psychiatry, 55,* 1133–1141.

Heimberg, R. G., Stein, M. B., Hiripi, E., & Kessler, R. C. (2000). Trends in the prevalence of social phobia in the United States: A synthetic cohort analysis of changes over four decades. *European Psychiatry, 15,* 29–37.

Heinlen, K. T., Welfel, E. R., Richmond, E. N., & O'Donnell, M. S. (2003). The nature, scope, and ethics of psychologists' e-therapy Web sites: What consumers find when surfing the Web. *Psychotherapy: Theory, Research, Practice, Training, 40,* 112–124.

Heinrichs, M., Wagner, D., Schoch, W., Soravia, L. M., Hellhammer, D. H., & Ehlert, U. (2005). Predicting posttraumatic stress symptoms from pretraumatic risk factors: A 2-year prospective follow-up study in firefighters. *American Journal of Psychiatry, 162,* 2276–2286.

Heinssen, R. K., Perkins, D. O., Appelbaum, P. S., & Fenton, W. S. (2001). Informed consent in early psychosis research: NIMH workshop, November 15, 2000. *Schizophrenia Bulletin, 27,* 571–584.

Heinz, A. (2000). Dopaminhypothese der Schizophrenien: Neue Befunde fur eine alte Theorie. [The dopamine hypothesis of schizophrenia: New findings for an old theory]. *Nervenarzt, 71,* 54–57.

Hellström, K., & Öst, L. (1995). One-session therapist directed exposure vs two forms of manual directed self-exposure in the treatment of spider phobia. *Behaviour Research and Therapy, 33,* 959–965.

Hellstrom, W. J. G., Nehra, A., Shabsigh, R., & Sharlip, I. D. (2006). Premature ejaculation: The most common male sexual dysfunction. *Journal of Sexual Medicine, 3,* 1–3.

Helms, J. E., & Cook, D. A. (1999). *Using race and culture in counseling and psychotherapy: Theory and process.* Needham Heights, MA, US, Allyn & Bacon.

Henderson, C., Roux, A. V. D., Jacobs, D. R., Jr., Kiefe, C. I., West, D., & Williams, D. R. (2005). Neighbourhood characteristics, individual level socioeconomic factors, and depressive symptoms in young adults: The CARDIA study. *Journal of Epidemiology & Community Health, 59,* 322–328.

Hendin, H. (1995). Assisted suicide, euthanasia, and suicide prevention: The implications of the Dutch experience. *Suicide and Life-Threatening Behavior, 25,* 193–204.

Henggeler, S. W., Schoenwald, S. K., Borduin, C. M., Rowland, M. D., & Cunningham, P. B. (1998). *Multisystemic treatment of antisocial behavior in children and adolescents.* New York: Guilford Press.

Henneman, W. J. P., Sluimer, J. D., Barnes, J., van der Flier, W. M., Cluimer, I. C., Fox, N. C., Scheltens, P., Vreken, K. & Barkhof, F. (2009). Hippocampal atrophy rates in Alzheimer's disease. *Neurology, 72,* 999–1007.

Henning, K. R., & Frueh, B. C. (1996). Cognitive-behavioral treatment of incarcerated offenders. *Criminal Justice and Behavior, 23,* 523–541.

Henquet, C., Krabbendam, L., Spauwen, J., Kaplan, C., Lieb, R., Wittchen, H. U., & van Os, J. (2005). Prospective cohort study of cannabis use, predisposition for psychosis, and psychotic symptoms in young people. *British Medical Journal, 330,* 11–16.

Hepp, U., Kraemer, B., Schnyder, U., Miller, N., & Delsignore, A. (2005). Psychiatric comorbidity in gender identity disorder. *Journal of Psychosomatic Research, 58,* 259–261.

Herbert, M.R. (2005). Large brains in autism: The challenge of pervasive abnormality. *The Neuroscientist, 11,* 417–440.

Herek, G. M., & Garnets, L. D. (2007). Sexual orientation and mental health. *Annual Review of Clinical Psychology, 3,* 105–127.

Herholz, K. (1996). Neuroimaging in anorexia nervosa . *Psychiatry Research, 62,* 105–110.

Herman, J. (1992). *Trauma and recovery.* New York: Basic Books.

Hermelin, B. (2001). *Bright splinters of the mind: A personal story of research with autistic savants.* London: Jessica Kingsley.

Hershman, D. J., & Lieb, J. (1988). *The key to genius/manic-depression and the creative life.* New York: Prometheus.

Hershman, D. J., & Lieb, J. (1998). *Manic depression and creativity.* New York: Prometheus.

Hertz-Picciotto, I., & Delwiche, L. (2009). The rise in autism and the role of age at diagnosis. *Epidemiology, 20,* 84–90.

Heruti, R. J., Levy, A., Adunski, A., & Ohry, A. (2002). Conversion motor paralysis disorder: Overview and rehabilitation model. *Spinal Cord, 40,* 327–334.

Herzog, D. B., & Delinsky, S. S. (2001). Classification of eating disorders. In R. H. Striegel-Moore & L. Smolak (Eds.), *Eating disorders: Innovative directions in research and practice* (pp. 31–50). Washington, DC: American Psychological Association.

Herzog, D. B., Dorer, D. J., Keel, P. K., Selwyn, S. E., Ekeblad, E. R., Flores, A. T., et al. (1999). Recovery and relapse in anorexia and bulimia nervosa: A 7.5-year follow-up study. *Journal of the American Academy of Child & Adolescent Psychiatry, 38,* 829–837.

Hesselbrock, V. (1986). Family history of psychopathology in alcoholics: A review and issues. In R. Meyer (Ed.), *Psychopathology and Addictive Disorders* (pp. 41–56). New York: Guilford Press.

Hesslinger, B., Tebartz van Elst, L., Thiel, T., Haegele, K., Hennig, J., & Ebert, D. (2002) Frontoorbital volume reductions in adult patients with attention deficit hyperactivity disorder. *Neuroscience Letters, 328,* 319–321.

Hestad, K., Ellertsen, B., & Klove, H. (1998). Neuropsychological assessment in old age. In Nordhus, I. H. (Ed); VandenBos, G. R. (Ed); Berg, S. (Ed); Fromholt, P. (Ed), *Clinical Geropsychology.* (pp. 259–288). Washington, DC: American Psychological Association.

Hettema, J. M., Neale, M. C., & Kendler, K. S. (2001). A review and meta-analysis of the genetic epidemiology of anxiety disorders. *American Journal of Psychiatry, 158,* 1568–1578.Nemeroff, C. (1998). The neurobiology of depression. *Scientific American, 278,* 28–35.

Hettema, J. M., Prescott, C. A., & Kendler, K. S. (2001). A population-based twin study of generalized anxiety disorder in men and women. *Journal of Nervous & Mental Disease, 189,* 413–420.

Hettema, J., Steele, J., & Miller, W. R. (2005). Motivational interviewing. *Annual Review of Clinical Psychology, 1,* 91–111.

Heyman, I., Mataiz-Cols, D., & Fineberg, N. A. (2006). Obsessive-compulsive disorder. *British Medical Journal, 333,* 424–429.

Hicks, K. M. (2005). The "new view" approach to women's sexual problems. Medscape. Retrieved September 28, 2007, from http://www.medscape.com/viewprogram/4705_pnt

Hidalgo, R. B., & Davidson, R. T. (2000). Selective serotonin reuptake inhibitors in post-traumatic stress disorder. *Journal of Psychopharmacology, 14,* 70–76.

Hiday, V. A. (2003). Outpatient commitment: The state of empirical research on its outcomes. *Psychology, Public Policy, and Law, 9,* 8–32.

Hiday, V. A., & Wales, H. W. (2003). Civil commitment and arrests. *Current Opinion in Psychiatry, 16,* 575–580.

Higgenbotham, H. N., West, S., & Forsyth, D. (1988). *Psychotherapy and behavior change: Social, cultural and methodological perspectives.* New York: Pergamon.

Higgins, S. T., & Silverman, K. (1999). *Motivating behavior change among illicit-drug abusers: Research on contingency management interventions.* Washington, DC: American Psychological Association.

Higgins, S. T., Budney, A. J., Bickel, W. K., Hughes, J. R., Foerg, F., & Badger, G. (1993). Achieving cocaine abstinence with a behavioral approach. *American Journal of Psychiatry, 150,* 763–769.

Higgins, S. T., Heil, S. H., & Lussier, J. P. (2004). Clinical implications of reinforcement as a determinant of substance use disorders. *Annual Review of Psychology, 55,* 431–461.

Higuchi, S., Matsushita, S., Murayama, M., Takagi, S., & Hayashida, M. (1995). Alcohol and aldehyde dehydrogenase polymorphisms and the risk for alcoholism. *American Journal of Psychiatry, 152,* 1219–1221.

Hildebrand, M., & de Ruiter, C. (2004). PCL-R psychopathy and its relation to DSM-IV-TR Axis I and II disorders in a sample of male forensic psychiatric patients in the Netherlands. *International Journal of Law and Psychiatry, 27,* 233–248.

Hilgard, E. R. (1994). Neodissociation theory. In S. J. Lynn & J. W. Rhue (Eds.), *Dissociation: Clinical and theoretical perspectives* (pp. 32–51). New York, Guilford Press.

Hill, C. E., & Lambert, M. J. (2004). Methodological issues in studying psychotherapy processes and outcomes. In M. J. Lambert (Ed.) *Bergin and Garfield's Handbook of Psychotherpy and Behavior Change* (5th edition). (pp. 84–135). New York: Wiley and Sons.

Hill, D. B., Rozanski, C., Carfagnini, J., & Willoughby, B. (2005). Gender identity disorders in childhood and adolescence: A critical inquiry. *Journal of Psychology & Human Sexuality, 17,* 7–33.

Hill, J. (2003). Early identification of individuals at risk for antisocial personality disorder. *British Journal of Psychiatry, 182,* s11–s14.

Hiller, W., Rief, W., & Fichter, M. M. (2002). Dimensional and categorical approaches to hypochondriasis. *Psychological Medicine, 32,* 707–718.

Hilty, D. M., Bourgeois, J. A., Chang, C. H., & Servis, M. E. (2001). Somatization disorder. *Current Treatment Options in Neurology, 3,* 305–320.

Himle, J. A., Baser, R. E., Taylor, R. J., Campbell, R. D, & Jackson, J. S. (in press). Anxiety disorders among African Americans, blacks of Caribbean descent, and non-Hispanic whites in the United States. *Journal of Anxiety Disorders, np.*

Hinrichsen, H., Wright, F., Waller, G., & Meyer, C. (2003). Social anxiety and coping strategies in the eating disorders. *Eating Behaviors, 4,* 117–126.

Hinshaw, S. P., Erhardt, D., Murphy, D. A., Greenstein, J. J., & Pelham, W. E. (1993). Part 7: Attention-deficit hyperactivity disorder. In V. B. Van Hasselt & M. Hersen (Eds.), *Handbook of behavior therapy and pharmacotherapy for children: A comparative analysis* (pp. 233–271). Needham Heights, MA: Allyn & Bacon.

Hinton, D., Hinton, S., Pham, T., Chau, H., & Tran, M. (2003). 'Hit by the wind' and temperature-shift panic among Vietnamese refugees. *Transcultural Psychiatry, 40,* 342–376.

Hinton, D., Hinton, S., Um, K., Chea, A. S., & Sak, S. (2002). The Khmer "weak heart" syndrome: Fear of death from palpitations. *Transcultural Psychiatry, 39,* 323–344.

Hinton, D., Um, K., & Ba, P. (2001). A unique panic-disorder presentation among Khmer refugees: The sore-neck syndrome. *Culture, Medicine and Psychiatry, 25,* 297–316.

Hirai, M., & Clum, G. A. (2006). A meta-analytic study of self-help interventions for anxiety problems. *Behavior Therapy, 37,* 99–111.

Hirai, M., & Clum, G. A. (2008). Self-help therapies for anxiety disorders. In P. L. Watkins & G. A. Clum (Eds.), *Handbook of self-help therapies* (pp. 77–107). New York: Lawrence Erlbaum Associates.

Hirschfeld, R. M., Keller, M. B., Panico, S., Arons, B. S., Barlow, D., Davidoff, F., et al. (1997). The National Depressive and Manic-Depressive Association consensus statement on the undertreatment of depression. *JAMA: Journal of the American Medical Association, 277,* 333–340.

Hochhalter, A. K., Sweeney, W. A., Savage, L. M., Bakke, B. L., & Overmier, J. B. (2001). Using animal models to address the memory deficits of Wernicke-Korsakoff syndrome. In M. E. Carroll & J. B. Overmier (Eds.), *Animal research and human health: Advancing human welfare through behavioral science* (pp. 281–292). Washington, DC: American Psychological Association.

Hoechstetter, K., Meinck, H. M., Henningsen, P., Scherg, M., & Rupp, A. (2002). Psychogenic sensory loss: Magnetic source imaging reveals normal tactile evoked activity of the human primary and secondary somatosensory cortex. *Neuroscience Letters, 323,* 137–140.

Hoehn-Saric, R., Hazlett, R. L., & McLeod, D. R. (1993). Generalized anxiety disorder with early and late onset of anxiety symptoms. *Comprehensive Psychiatry, 34,* 291–298.

Hoek, H. W., & van Hoeken, D. (2003). Review of the prevalence and incidence of eating disorders. *International Journal of Eating Disorders, 34,* 383–396.

Hoff, A. L., & Kremen, W. S. (2003). Neuropsychology in schizophrenia: An update. *Current Opinion in Psychiatry, 16,* 149–155.

Hoff, A., Kremen, W. S., Wieneke, M. H., Lauriello, J., Blankfeld, H. M., Faustman, W. O., Csernansky, J. G., & Nordahl, T. E. (2001). Association of estrogen levels with neuropsychological performance in women with schizophrenia. *American Journal of Psychiatry, 158,* 1134–1139.

Hoffman, L. W. (1991). The influence of the family environment on personality: Accounting for sibling differences. *Psychological Bulletin, 110,* 187–203.

Hoffman, R. E., Boutros, N. N., Hu, S., Berman, R. M., Krystal, J. H., & Charney, D. S. (2000). Transcranial magnetic stimulation and auditory hallucinations in schizophrenia. *Lancet, 355,* 1073–1075.

Hoffman, R. E., Gueorguieva, R., Hawkins, K. A., Varanko, M., Boutros, N. N., Wu, Y., et al. (2005). Temporoparietal transcranial magnetic stimulation for auditory hallucinations: Safety, efficacy and moderators in a fifty patient sample. *Biological Psychiatry, 58,* 97–104.

Hofmann, S. G., Moscovitch, D. A., & Heinrichs, N. (2002). Evolutionary mechanisms of fear and anxiety. *Journal of Cognitive Psychotherapy, 16,* 317–330.

Hoge, S. K., Bonnie, R. J., Poythress, N., & Monahan, J. (1992). Attorney-client decision-making in criminal cases: Client competence and participation as perceived by their attorneys. *Behavioral Sciences & the Law, 10,* 385–394.

Hoge, S., Poythress, N., Bonnie, R., Monahan, J., Eisenberg, M., & Feucht-Haviar, T. (1997). *The MacArthur Adjudicative Competence Study*: Diagnosis, psychopathology, and adjudicative competence-related abilities. *Behavioral Sciences and the Law, 15,* 329–345.

Hogue, A., Dauber, S., Samuolis, J., & Liddle, H. A. (2006). Treatment techniques and outcomes in multidimensional family therapy for adolescent behavior problems. *Journal of Family Psychology, 20,* 535–543.

Holder-Perkins, V., & Wise, T. N. (2001). Somatization disorder. In K. A. Phillips (Ed.), *Somatoform and factitious disorders* (pp. 1–26). Washington, DC: American Psychiatric Association.

Hollander, E., & Rosen, J. (2000). Impulsivity. *Journal of Psychopharmacology, 14,* S39–S44.

Hollander, E., Liebowitz, M. R., & Rosen, W. G. (1991). Neuropsychiatric and neuropsychological studies in obsessive-compulsive disorder. In J. Zohar, T. Insel, & S. Rasmussen (Eds.), *The psychobiology of obsessive-compulsive disorder.* (pp. 126–145). New York: Springer.

Hollier, L. M., McIntire, D. D., & Leveno, K. J. (1999). Outcome of twin pregnancies according to intrapair birth weight differences. *Obstetrics & Gynecology, 94,* 1006–1010.

Hollifield, M., Paine, S., Tuttle, L., & Kellner, R. (1999). Hypochondriasis, somatization, and perceived health and utilization of health care services. *Psychosomatics: Journal of Consultation and Liaison Psychiatry, 40,* 380–386.

Hollon, S. D., & Beck, A. T. (1994). Cognitive and cognitive-behavioral therapies. In A. E. Bergin & S. L. Garfield (Eds.), *Handbook of psychotherapy and behavior change* (4th ed., pp. 428–466). New York: John Wiley & Sons.

Hollon, S. D., & Beck, A. T. (2004). Cognitive and cognitive behavior therapies. In M. J. Lambert (Ed.), *Bergin and Garfield's handbook of psychotherapy and behavior change* (5th ed., pp. 447–492). New York: John Wiley & Sons.

Hollon, S. D., DeRubeis, R. J., Shelton, R. C., & Weiss, B. (2002). The emperor's new drugs: Effect size and moderation effects. *Prevention & Treatment, 5,* Article 28. http://www.journals.apa.org/prevention/volume5/pre0050028c.html.

Hollon, S. D., DeRubeis, R. J., Shelton, R. C., Amsterdam, J. D., Salomon, R. M., O'Reardon, J. P., et al. (2005). Prevention of relapse following cognitive therapy vs medications in moderate to severe depression. *Archives of General Psychiatry, 62,* 417–422.

Holtzheimer, P. E., III, & Avery, D. H. (2005). Focal brain stimulation for treatment-resistant depression: Transcranial magnetic stimulation, vagus-nerve stimulation, and deep-brain stimulation. *Primary Psychiatry, 12,* 57–64.

Holthausen, E. A., Wiersma, D., Sitskoorn, M. M., Dingemans, P. M., Schene, A. H., & van den Bosch, R. J. (2003). Long-term memory deficits in schizophrenia: primary or secondary dysfunction? *Neuropsychology, 17,* 539–547.

Holzman, P. S., Kringlen, E., Matthysse, S., Flanagan, S. D., Lipton, R. B., Cramer, G., et al. (1988). A single dominant gene can account for eye tracking dysfunctions and schizophrenia in offspring of discordant twins. *Archives of General Psychiatry, 45,* 641–647.

Holzman, P. S., Solomon, C. M., Levin, S., & Waternaux, C. S. (1984). Pursuit eye movement dysfunctions in schizophrenia: Family evidence for specificity. *Archives of General Psychiatry 41*, 136–139.

Homma, A., Imai, Y., Tago, H., Asada, T., Shigeta, M., Iwamoto, et al. (2008). Donepezil treatment of patients with severe Alzheimer's disease in a Japanese population: Results from a 24-week, double-blind, placebo-controlled, randomized trial. *Dementia and Geriatric Cognitive Disorders, 25*, 399–407.

Hong, L. E., Tagamets, M., Avila, M., Wonodi, I., Holcomb, H., & Thaker, G. K. (2005). Specific motion processing pathway deficit during eye tracking in schizophrenia: A performance-matched functional magnetic resonance imaging study. *Biological Psychiatry, 57*, 726–732.

Honig, A., Hofman, A., Rozendaal, N., & Dingemans, P. (1997). Psycho-education in bipolar disorder: Effect on expressed emotion. *Psychiatry Research, 72*, 17–22.

Hopper, K., Harrison, G., Janca, A., & Sartorius, N. (2007). *Recovery from schizophrenia: An international perspective. A Report from the WHO Collaborative Project, The International Study of Schizophrenia.* New York: Oxford University Press.

Horan, W. P., & Blanchard, J. J. (2003). Neurocognitive, social, and emotional dysfunction in deficit syndrome schizophrenia. *Schizophrenia Research, 65*, 125–137.

Horesh, N., Amir, M., Kedem, P., Goldberger, Y., & Kotler, M. (1997). Life events in childhood, adolescence and adulthood and the relationship to panic disorder. *Acta Psychiatrica Scandinavica, 96*, 373–378.

Hornbacher, M. (1998). *Wasted: A memoir of anorexia and bulimia.* New York: HarperPerennial.

Hornbacher, M. (2008). *Madness: A bipolar life.* New York: Houghton Mifflin.

Horney, K. (1937). *The neurotic personality of our times.* Oxford, England: Norton.

Horowitz, L. M. (2004). Diffuse identity and lack of long-term direction: The histrionic personality disorder and other related disorders. In L. M. Horowitz (Ed.), *Interpersonal foundations of psychopathology* (pp. 189–203). Washington, DC: American Psychological Association.

Horvath, A. O., & Symonds, B. D. (1991). Relation between working alliance and outcome in psychotherapy: A meta-analysis. *Journal of Counseling Psychology, 38*, 139–149.

Horwath, E., & Weissman, M. M. (2000). The epidemiology and cross-national presentation of obsessive-compulsive disorder. *Psychiatric Clinics of North America, 23*, 493–507.

Horwath, E., Lish, J. D., Johnson, J., Hornig, C. D., & Weissman, M. M. (1993). Agoraphobia without panic: Clinical reappraisal of an epidemiologic finding. *American Journal of Psychiatry, 150*, 1496–1501.

Hough, W. G., & O'Brien, K. P. (2005). The effect of community treatment orders on offending rates. *Psychiatry, Psychology and Law, 12*, 411–423.

Houts, A. C. (2002). Discovery, invention, and the expansion of the modern Diagnostic and Statistical Manual of Mental Disorders. In L. E. Beutler & M. L. Malik (Eds.), *Rethinking the DSM: A psychological perspective* (pp. 17–65). Washington, DC: American Psychological Association.

Hovey, J. D. (1998). Acculturative stress, depression, and suicidal ideation among Mexican-American adolescents: Implications for the development of suicide prevention programs in schools. *Psychological Reports, 83*, 249–250.

Hovey, J. D. (2000). Acculturative stress, depression, and suicidal ideation in Mexican immigrants. *Cultural Diversity & Ethnic Minority Psychology, 6*, 134–151.

Hovey, J. D., & King, C. A. (1996). Acculturative stress, depression, and suicidal ideation among immigrant and second-generation Latino adolescents. *Journal of the American Academy of Child and Adolescent Psychiatry, 35*, 1183–1192.

Howard, K. I., Lueger, R. J., Maling, M. S., & Martinovich, Z. (1993). A phase model of psychotherapy outcome: Causal mediation of change. *Journal of Consulting & Clinical Psychology, 61*, 678–685.

Hsee, C. K., Hatfield, E., Carlson, J. G., & Chemtob, C. (1990). The effect of power on susceptibility to emotional contagion. *Cognition & Emotion, 4*, 327–340.

http://transcripts.cnn.com/TRANSCRIPTS/0205/21/lt.24.html, accessed April 3, 2007.

Huang, Y. Y., & Kandel, E. R. (2007) 5-Hydroxytryptamine induces a protein kinase A/mitogen-activated protein kinase-mediated and macromolecular synthesis-dependent late phase of long-term potentiation in the amygdala. *Journal of Neuroscience, 27*, 3111–3119.

Hubbard, R. L., Marsden, M. E., Rachal, J. V., Harwood, H. G., Cavanaugh, E. R., & Ginzburg, H. M. (1989). *Drug abuse treatment: A national study of effectiveness* (pp. 90–92). Chapel Hill: University of North Carolina Press, 1989.

Hudson, C. G. (2005). Socioeconomic status and mental illness: Tests of the social causation and selection hypotheses. *American Journal of Orthopsychiatry, 75*, 3–18.

Hudson, J. I., Hiripi, E., Pope, H. G., Jr., & Kessler, R. C. (2007). The prevalence and correlates of eating disorders in the National Comorbidity Survey Replication. *Biological Psychiatry, 61*, 348–358.

Hudson, J., & Rapee, R. M. (2001). Parent-child interactions and anxiety disorders: An observational study. *Behaviour Research and Therapy, 39*, 1411–1427.

Hudziak, J. J., Derks, E. M., Althoff, R. R., Copeland, W., & Boomsma, D. I. (2005). The genetic and environmental contributions to oppositional defiant behavior: A multi-informant twin study. *Journal of the American Academy of Child & Adolescent Psychiatry, 44*, 907–914.

Huether, G., Zhou, D., Schmidt, S., Wiltfang, J., & Eckart, R. (1997). Long-term food restriction down-regulates the density of serotonin transporters in the rat frontal cortex. *Biological Psychiatry, 41*, 1174–1180.

Hugdahl, K. (2001). *Psychophysiology: The mind-body perspective* (2nd ed.). Cambridge, MA: Harvard University Press.

Hughes, C., Kumari, V., Soni, W., Das, M., Binneman, B., Drozd, S., et al. (2003). Longitudinal study of symptoms and cognitive function in chronic schizophrenia. *Schizophrenia Research, 59*, 137–146.

Hui, C. H., & Triandis, H. C. (1986). Individualism-collectivism: A study of cross-cultural researchers. *Journal of Cross-Cultural Psychology, 17*, 225–248.

Humfleet, G. L., & Haas, A. L. (2004). Is marijuana use becoming a "gateway" to nicotine dependence? *Addiction, 99*, 5–6.

Hummingbird. (1999). First person account: Schizophrenia, substance abuse, and HIV. *Schizophrenia Bulletin, 25*, 863–866.

Humphreys, K., & Moos, R. H. (2007). Encouraging posttreatment self-help group involvement to reduce demand for continuing care services: Two-year clinical and utilization outcomes. *Alcoholism: Clinical and Experimental Research, 31*, 64–68.

Humphreys, K., Winzelberg, A., & Klaw, E. (2000). Psychologists' ethical responsibilities in Internet-based groups: Issues, strategies, and a call for dialogue. *Professional Psychology: Research and Practice, 31*, 493–496.

Hunt, I. M., Kapur, N., Windfuhr, K., Robinson, J., Bickley, H., Flynn, S., Parsons, R., Burns, J., Shaw, J., & Appleby, L. (National Confidential Inquiry into Suicide and Homicide by People with Mental Illness). (2006). Suicide in schizophrenia: Findings from a national clinical survey. *Journal of Psychiatric Practice, 12*, 139–147.

Hunter, E. C. M., Baker, D., Phillips, M. L., Sierra, M., & David, A. S. (2005). Cognitive-behaviour therapy for depersonalisation disorder: An open study. *Behaviour Research and Therapy, 43*, 1121–1130.

Hunter, E. C. M., Phillips, M. L., Chalder, T., Sierra, M., & David, A. S. (2003). Depersonalisation disorder: A cognitive-behavioural conceptualisation. *Behaviour Research and Therapy, 41,* 1451–1467.

Huntjens, R. J. C., Peters, M. L., Postma, A., Woertman, L., Effting, M., & van der Hart, O. (2005). Transfer of newly acquired stimulus valence between identities in dissociative identity disorder (DID). *Behaviour Research and Therapy, 43,* 243–255.

Huntjens, R. J. C., Peters, M. L., Woertman, L., Bovenschen, L. M., Martin, R. C., & Postma, A. (2006). Inter-identity amnesia in dissociative identity disorder: A simulated memory impairment? *Psychological Medicine, 36,* 857–863.

Huntjens, R.J.C., Peters, M., Woertman, L., van der Hart, O., & Postma, A. (2007). Memory transfer for trauma-related words between identities in dissociative identity disorder. *Behaviour Research and Therapy, 45,* 775–789.

Huntjens, R. J. C., Postma, A., Peters, M. L., Woertman, L., & van der Hart, O. (2003). Interidentity amnesia for neutral, episodic information in dissociative identity disorder. *Journal of Abnormal Psychology, 112,* 290–297.

Hurt, R. D., Offord, K. P., Croghan, I. T., Gomez-Dahl, L., Kottke, T. E., Morse, R. M., et al. (1996). Mortality following inpatient addictions treatment: Role of tobacco use in a community-based cohort. *Journal of the American Medical Association, 275,* 1097–1103.

Husted, D. S., & Shapira, N. A. (2004). A review of the treatment for refractory obsessive-compulsive disorder: From medicine to deep brain stimulation. *CNS Spectrums, 9,* 833–847.

Huttenlocher, P. R. (2002). *Neural plasticity: The effects of environment on the development of the cerebral cortex.* Cambridge, MA: Harvard University Press.

Hybels, C. F., Blazer, D. G., Pieper, C. F., Burchett, B. M., Hays, J. C., Fillenbaum, G. G., Kubzansky, L. D., & Berkman, L. F. (2006). Sociodemographic characteristics of the neighborhood and depressive symptoms in older adults: Using multilevel modeling in geriatric psychiatry. *American Journal of Geriatric Psychiatry, 14,* 498–506.

Hyde, J. S., Mezulis, A. H., & Abramson, L. Y. (2008). The ABCs of depression: Integrating affective, biological, and cognitive models to explain the emergence of the gender difference in depression. *Psychological Review, 115,* 291–313.

Hyman, S. E. (2001). A 28-year-old man addicted to cocaine. *Journal of the American Medical Association, 286,* 2586–2594.

Hyman, S. E., (2005). Addiction: A disease of learning and memory. *American Journal of Pyschiatry, 162,* 1414–1422.

Hyman, S. E., & Nestler, E. J. (1993). *The molecular foundations of psychiatry.* Washington, DC: American Psychiatric Press.

Hyman, S. M., Gold, S. N., & Cott, M. A. (2003). Forms of social support that moderate PTSD in childhood sexual abuse survivors. *Journal of Family Violence, 18,* 295–300.

Iacono, W. G., Moreau, M., Beiser, M., Fleming, J. A. E., & Lin, T. (1992). Smooth-pursuit eye tracking in first-episode psychotic patients and their relatives. *Journal of Abnormal Psychology, 101,* 104–116.

Igartua, K. J., Gill, K., & Montoro, R. (2003). Internalized homophobia: A factor in depression, anxiety, and suicide in the gay and lesbian population. *Canadian Journal of Community Mental Health, 22,* 15–30.

Ikeuchi, T., Kaneko, H., Miyashita, A., Nozaki, H., Kasuga, K., Tsukie, T., et al. (2008). Mutational analysis in early-onset familial dementia in the Japanese population: The role of PSEN1 and MAPT R406W mutations. *Dementia and Geriatric Cognitive Disorders, 26,* 43–49.

Ikonomovic, M. D., Klunk, W. E., Abrahamson, E. E., Mathis, C. A., Price, J. C., Tsopelas, N. D., et al. (2008). Post-mortem correlates of in vivo PiB-PET amyloid imaging in a typical case of Alzheimer's disease. *Brain: A Journal of Neurology, 131,* 1630–1645.

Ilgen, M. A., & Hutchison, K. E. (2005). A history of major depressive disorder and the response to stress. *Journal of Affective Disorders, 86,* 143–150.

Inaba, A., Thoits, P. A., Ueno, K., Gove, W. R., Evenson, R. J., & Sloan, M. (2005). Depression in the United States and Japan: Gender, marital status, and SES patterns. *Social Science & Medicine, 61,* 2280–2292.

Insel, T. R. (1992). Toward a neuroanatomy of obsessive-compulsive disorder. *Archives of General Psychiatry, 49,* 739–744.

Insel, T. R., & Winslow, J. T. (1990). Neurobiology of obsessive-compulsive disorder. In M. A. Jenike, L. Baer, & W. E. Minichiello (Eds.), *Obsessive-compulsive disorders: Theory and management.* (pp. 118–131). Chicago: Year Book Medical.

Intrator, J., Hare, R., Strizke, P., & Brichtswein, K. (1997). A brain imaging (single photon emission computerized tomography) study of semantic and affective processing in psychopaths. *Biological Psychiatry, 42,* 96–103.

Ireland, T., & Widom, C. S. (1994). Childhood victimization and risk for alcohol and drug arrests. *International Journal of the Addictions, 29,* 235–274.

Isometsä, E. T. (2000). Suicide. *Current Opinion in Psychiatry, 13,* 143–147.

Ito, K. L., & Maramba, G. G. (2002). Therapeutic beliefs of Asian American therapists: Views from an ethnic-specific clinic. *Transcultural Psychiatry, 39,* 33–73.

Ivarsson, T., Larsson, B., & Gillberg, C. (1998). A 2–4 year follow-up of depressive symptoms, suicidal ideation, and suicide attempts among adolescent psychiatric inpatients. *European Child and Adolescent Psychiatry, 7,* 96–104.

Ivry, R. B., Spencer, R. M., Zelaznik, H. N., & Diedrichsen, J. (2002). The cerebellum and event timing. In S. M. Highstein & W. T. Thach (Eds.). *The cerebellum: Recent developments in cerebellar research* (pp. 302–317). New York: New York Academy of Sciences.

Jackson v. Indiana, 406 U.S. 715 (1972).

Jackson, J., Fiddler, M., Kapur, N., Wells, A., Tomenson, B., & Creed, F. (2006). Number of bodily symptoms predicts outcome more accurately than health anxiety in patients attending neurology, cardiology, and gastroenterology clinics. *Journal of Psychosomatic Research, 60,* 357–363.

Jacobi, C., Hayward, C., de Zwaan, M., Kraemer, H. C., & Agras, W. S. (2004). Coming to terms with risk factors for eating disorders: Application of risk terminology and suggestions for a general taxonomy. *Psychological Bulletin, 130,* 19–65.

Jacobs, M. K., Christensen, A., Snibbe, J. R., Dolezal-Wood, S., Huber, A., & Polterok, A. (2001). A comparison of computer-based versus traditional individual psychotherapy. *Professional Psychology: Research & Practice, 32,* 92–96.

Jacobs, S.-E., Thomas, W., & Lang, S. (1997). *Two-spirit people: Native American gender identity, sexuality, and spirituality.* Champaign: University of Illinois Press.

Jacobsen, L. K., Southwick, S. M., & Kosten, T. R. (2001). Substance use disorders in patients with posttraumatic stress disorder: A review of the literature. *American Journal of Psychiatry, 158,* 1184–1190.

Jacobson, N. S., Martell, C. R., & Dimidjian, S. (2001). Behavioral activation treatment for depression: Returning to contextual roots. *Clinical Psychology: Science and Practice, 8,* 255–270.

Jacobson, S. W., Carr, L. G., Croxford, J., Sokol, R. J., Li, T.-K., & Jabobson, J. L. (2006). Protective effect of the alcohol dehydrogenase-ADH1B allele in children exposed to alcohol during pregnancy. *Journal of Pediatrics, 148,* 30–37.

Jaffee v. Redmond, 518 U.S. 1 (1996).

Jain, M., Palacio, L. G., Castellanos, F. X., Palacio, J. D., Pineda, D., Restrepo, M. I., et al. (2007). Attention-deficit/hyperactivity disorder and comorbid disruptive behavior disorders: Evidence of pleiotropy and new susceptibility loci. *Biological Psychiatry, 61,* 1329–1339.

Jakupcak, M., Osborne, T. L., Michael, S., Cook, J. W., & McFall, M. (2006). Implications of masculine gender role stress in male veterans with posttraumatic stress disorder. *Psychology of Men & Masculinity, 7*, 203–211.

Jamison, K. R. (1989). Mood disorders and patterns of creativity in British writers and artists. *Psychiatry, 52*, 125–134.

Jamison, K. R. (1993). *Touched with Fire: Manic-Depressive Illness and the Artistic Temperament*. New York: Free Press.

Jamison, K. R. (1993). *Touched with fire: Manic-depressive illness and the artistic temperament*. New York: Free Press.

Jamison, K. R. (1995). *An unquiet mind: A memoir of moods and madness*. New York: Vintage Books.

Jamison, K. R., Gerner, R. H., Hammen, C., & Padesky, C. (1980). Clouds and silver linings: Positive experiences associated with primary affective disorders. *American Journal of Psychiatry, 137*, 198–202.

Jamison, R. N., & Walker, L. S. (1992). Illness behavior in children of chronic pain patients. *International Journal of Psychiatry in Medicine, 22*, 329–342.

Janet, P. (1907). *The major symptoms of hysteria*. New York: Macmillan.

Jang, K. L., Paris, J., Zweig-Frank, H., & Livesley, W. J. (1998). Twin study of dissociative experience. *Journal of Nervous and Mental Disease, 186*, 345–351.

Jang, K. L., Vernon, P. A., & Livesley, W. J. (2001). Behavioural-genetic perspectives on personality function. *The Canadian Journal of Psychiatry, 46*, 234–244.

Janoff-Bulman, R. (1995). *Victims of violence*. In G. S. Everly, Jr., & J. M. Lating (Eds.), *Psychotraumatology: Key papers and core concepts in post-traumatic stress* (pp. 73–86). New York: Plenum Press.

Jansen, A., Nederkoorn, C., & Mulkens, S. (2005). Selective visual attention for ugly and beautiful body parts in eating disorders. *Behaviour Research and Therapy, 43*, 183–196.

Jansen, K. L., & Darracot-Cankovic, R. (2001). The nonmedical use of ketamine, part two: A review of problem use and dependence. *Journal of Psychoactive Drugs 33*, 151–158.

Jansiewicz, E. M., Goldberg, M. C., Newschaffer, C. J., Denckla, M. B., Landa, R., & Mostofsky, S. H. (2006). Motor signs distinguish children with high functioning autism and Asperger's syndrome from controls. *Journal of Autism and Developmental Disorders, 36*, 613–621.

Janssen, I., Krabbendam, L., Jolles, J., & van Os, J. (2003). Alterations in theory of mind in patients with schizophrenia and non-psychotic relatives. *Acta Psychiatrica Scandinavica, 108*, 110–117.

Janus, E. S. (2003). Treatment and the civil commitment of sex offenders. In B. J. Winick & J. Q. La Fond (Eds.), *Protecting society from sexually dangerous offenders: Law, justice, and therapy* (pp. 119–129). Washington, DC: American Psychological Association.

Jarret, R. B., Kraft, D., Doyle, J., Foster, B. M., Eaves, G. G., & Silver, P. C. (2001). Preventing recurrent depression using cognitive therapy with and without a continuation phase: A randomized clinical trial. *Archives of General Psychiatry, 58*, 381–388.

Jarvis, E. (1998). Schizophrenia in British immigrants: Recent findings, issues and implications. *Transcultural Psychiatry, 35*, 39–74.

Jasper, F. J. (2003). Working with dissociative fugue in a general psychotherapy practice: A cautionary tale. *American Journal of Clinical Hypnosis, 45*, 311–322.

Javeline, D. (1999). Response effects in polite cultures: A test of acquiescence in Kazakhstan. *Public Opinion Quarterly, 63*, 1–28.

Jefferys, D. E., & Castle, D. J. (2003). Body dysmorphic disorder—a fear of imagined ugliness. *Australian Family Physician, 32*, 722–755.

Jenike, M. A. (1984). Obsessive-compulsive disorder: A question of a neurologic lesion. *Comprehensive Psychiatry, 25*, 298–304.

Jenike, M., Baer, L., & Minichiello, W. (Eds.) (1998). *Obsessive-compulsive disorders: Practical management*. St. Louis: Mosby.

Jenkins-Hall, K., & Sacco, W. P. (1991). Effects of client race and depression on evaluations by white therapists. *Journal of Social Clinical Psychology, 10*, 322–333.

Jennings, J. M., Dagenbach, D., Engle, C. M., & Funke, L. J. (2007). Age-related changes and the attention network task: An examination of alerting, orienting, and executive function. *Aging, Neuropsychology, and Cognition, 14*, 353–369.

Jensen, P. S., Hinshaw, S. P., Kraemer, H. C., Lenora, N., Newcorn, J. H., Abikoff, H. B., et al. (2001). ADHD comorbidity findings from the MTA study: Comparing comorbid subgroups. *Journal of the American Academy of Child & Adolescent Psychiatry, 40*, 147–158.

Jerome, L. W., & Zaylor, C. (2000). Cyberspace: Creating a therapeutic environment for telehealth applications. *Professional Psychology: Research & Practice, 31*, 478–483.

Jessen, G., Steffensen, P., & Jensen, B. (1998). Seasons and meteorological factors in suicidal behaviour: Findings and methodological considerations from a Danish study. *Archives of Suicide Research, 4*, 263–280.

Ji, J., Kleinman, A., & Becker, A. E. (2001). Suicide in contemporary China: A review of China's distinctive suicide demographics in their sociocultural context. *Harvard Review of Psychiatry, 9*, 1–12.

Jianlin, J. (2000). Suicide rates and mental health services in modern China. *Crisis, 21*, 118–121.

Jimerson, D. C., Lesem, M. D., Kaye, W. H., & Brewerton, T. D. (1992). Low serotonin and dopamine metabolite concentrations in cerebrospinal fluid from bulimic patients with frequent binge episodes. *Archives of General Psychiatry, 49*, 132–138.

Joe, G. W., Simpson, D. D., & Broome, K. M. (1999). Retention and patient engagement models for different treatment modalities in DATOS. *Drug and Alcohol Dependence, 57*, 113–125.

Johanson, A., Risberg, J., Tucker, D. M., & Gustafson, L. (2006). Changes in frontal lobe activity with cognitive therapy for spider phobia. *Applied Neuropsychology, 13*, 34–41.

Johns, A. (2001). Psychiatric effects of cannabis. *British Journal of Psychiatry, 178*, 116–122.

Johns, L. C., Hemsley, D., & Kuipers, E. (2002). A comparison of auditory hallucinations in a psychiatric and non-psychiatric group. *British Journal of Clinical Psychology, 41*, 81–86.

Johnson, B. A., & Ait-Daoud, N. (2000). Neuropharmalogical treatments for alcoholism: Scientific basis and clinical findings. *Psychopharmacology, 149*, 327–344.

Johnson, C. L., Lund, B. C., & Yates, W. R. (2003). Recovery rates for anorexia nervosa. *American Journal of Pyschiatry, 160*, 798.

Johnson, C. P., Myers, S. M., & the Council on Children with Disabilities (2007). Identification and evaluation of children with autism spectrum disorders. *Pediatrics, 120*, 1183–1215.

Johnson, J. G., Bromley, E., & McGeoch, P. G. (2005). Role of childhood experiences in the development of maladaptive and adaptive personality traits. In J. M. Oldham, A. E. Skodol, & D. S. Bender, Donna S. (Eds.), *The American Psychiatric Publishing textbook of personality disorders* (pp. 209–221). Washington, DC: American Psychiatric Publishing.

Johnson, J. G., Cohen, P., Chen, H., Kasen, S., & Brook, J. S. (2006b). Parenting behaviors associated with risk for offspring personality disorder during adulthood. *Archives of General Psychiatry, 63*, 579–587.

Johnson, J. G., Cohen, P., Dohrenwend, B. P., Link, B. G., & Brook, J. S. (1999). A longitudinal investigation of social causation and social selection processes involved in the association between socioeconomic status and psychiatric disorders. *Journal of Abnormal Psychology, 108*, 490–499.

Johnson, J. G., Cohen, P., Kasen, S., & Brook, J. S. (2002). Childhood adversities associated with risk for eating disorders or weight problems during adolescence or early adulthood. *American Journal of Psychiatry, 159*, 394–400.

Johnson, J. G., Cohen, P., Kasen, S., & Brook, J. S. (2006). Dissociative disorders among adults in the community, impaired functioning, and axis I and II comorbidity. *Journal of Psychiatric Research, 40*, 131–140.

Johnson, J. G., Cohen, P., Kasen, S., & Brook, J. S. (2006a). Personality disorders evident by early adulthood and risk for anxiety disorders during middle adulthood. *Journal of Anxiety Disorders, 20*, 408–426.

Johnson, J. G., Cohen, P., Kasen, S., Skodol, A. E., Hamagami, F., & Brook, J. S. (2000). Age-related change in personality disorder trait levels between early adolescence and adulthood: A community-based longitudinal investigation. *Acta Psychiatrica Scandinavica, 102*, 265–275.

Johnson, J. G., Cohen, P., Kotler, L., Kasen, S., & Brook, J. S. (2002). Psychiatric disorders associated with risk for the development of eating disorders during adolescence and early adulthood. *Journal of Consulting and Clinical Psychology, 70*, 1119–1128.

Johnson, S. L., & Roberts, J. E. (1995). Life events and bipolar disorder: Implications from biological theories. *Psychological Bulletin, 117*, 434–449.

Johnson, S. D. (2008). Substance use, post-traumatic stress disorder and violence. *Current Opinion in Psychiatry, 21*, 242–246.

Johnson, S. L., & Miller, I. (1997). Negative life events and time to recovery from episodes of bipolar disorder. *Journal of Abnormal Psychology, 106*, 449–457.

Johnston, C., & Freeman, W. (1997). Attributions for child behavior in parents of children with behavior disorders and children with attention-deficit/hyperactivity disorder. *Journal of Consulting and Clinical Psychology, 65*, 636–645.

Joiner, T. E. (1994). Contagious depression: Existence, specificity to depressed symptoms, and the role of reassurance seeking. *Journal of Personality & Social Psychology, 67*, 287–296.

Joiner, T. E., Jr. (1996). A confirmatory factor-analytic investigation of the tripartite model of depression and anxiety in college students. *Cognitive Therapy and Research, 20*, 521–539.

Joiner, T., Coyne, J. C., & Blalock, J. (1999). On the interpersonal nature of depression: Overview and synthesis. In T. Joiner & J. C. Coyne (Eds.), *The interactional nature of depression: Advances in interpersonal approaches* (pp. 3–19). Washington, DC: American Psychological Association.

Jones H. E., Johnson, R. E., Bigelow, G. E., Silverman, K., Mudric, T., & Strain, E. C. (2004). Safety and efficacy of L-tryptophan and behavioral incentives for treatment of cocaine dependence: A randomized clinical. *American Journal on Addictions, 13*, 421–437.

Jones, M. K., & Menzies, R. G. (1995). The etiology of fear of spiders. *Anxiety, Stress & Coping: An International Journal, 8*, 227–234.

Jones, S. (2004). Psychotherapy of bipolar disorder: A review. *Journal of Affective Disorders, 80*, 101–114.

Joormann, J., & Gotlib, I. H. (2006). Is this happiness I see? Biases in the identification of emotional facial expressions in depression and social phobia. *Journal of Abnormal Psychology, 115*, 705–714.

Jope, R. S. (1999). Anti-bipolar therapy: Mechanism of action of lithium. *Molecular Psychiatry, 4*, 117–128.

Jose, P. E., & Brown, I. (2008). When does the gender difference in rumination begin? Gender and age differences in the use of rumination by adolescents. *Journal of Youth and Adolescence, 37*, 180–192.

Joseph, R. (1999). The neurology of traumatic "dissociative" amnesia: Commentary and literature review. *Child Abuse and Neglect, 23*, 715–727.

Joseph, S., Williams, R., & Yule, W. (1995). Psychosocial perspectives on post-traumatic stress. *Clinical Psychology Review, 15*, 515–544.

Joshi, K. G., Frierson, R. L., & Gunter, T. D. (2006). Shared psychotic disorder and criminal responsibility: A review and case report of folie à trois. *Journal of the American Academy of Psychiatry and the Law, 34*, 511–517.

Joyce, P. R., McKenzie, J. M., Luty, S. E., Mulder, R. T., Carter, J. D., Sullivan, P. F., & Cloninger, C. R. (2003). Temperament, childhood environment and psychopathology as risk factors for avoidant and borderline personality disorders. *Australian and New Zealand Journal of Psychiatry, 37*, 756–764.

Judd, L. L., Akiskal, H. S., Schettler, P. J., Coryell, W., Maser, J., Rice, J. A., et al. (2003). The comparative clinical phenotype and long term longitudinal episode course of bipolar I and II: A clinical spectrum or distinct disorders? *Journal of Affective Disorders, 73*, 19–32.

Judd, L. L., Kessler, R. C., Paulhus, M. P., Zeller, P. V., Wittchen, H. U., & Kinovac, J. L. (1998). Cormorbidity as a fundamental feature of generalized anxiety diorders: Results from the National Comorbidity Study (NCS). *Acta Psychiatrica Scandinavia, 393*(Suppl.), 6–11.

Judd, L. L., Schettler, P. J., Akiskal, H. S., Coryell, W., Leon, A. C., Maser, J., et al.

(2008). Residual symptom recovery from major affective episodes in bipolar disorders and rapid episode relapse/recurrence. *Archives of General Psychiatry, 65*, 386–394.

Juengling, F. D., Schmahl, C., Hesslinger, B., Ebert, D., Bremner, J. D., Gostomzyk, J., et al. (2003). Positron emission tomography in female patients with borderline personality disorder. *Journal of Psychiatry Research, 37*, 109–115.

Jung, C. G. (1983). *The essential Jung* (A. Storr, Ed.). Princeton, NJ: Princeton University Press.

Just, N., & Alloy, L. B. (1997). The response styles theory of depression: Tests and an extension of the theory. *Journal of Abnormal Psychology, 106*, 221–229.

Kafka, M. P. (2000). The paraphilia-related disorders: Nonparaphilic hypersexuality and sexual compulsivity/addiction. In S. R. Leiblum & R. C. Rosen (Eds.), *Principles and practice of sex therapy* (3rd ed., pp. 471–503). New York: Guilford Press.

Kafka, M. P. (2003). The monoamine hypothesis for the pathophysiology of paraphilic disorders: An update. *Annals of the New York Academy of Science, 989*, 86–94.

Kafka, M. P., & Hennen, J. (2000). Psychostimulant augmentation during treatment with selective serotonin reuptake inhibitors in men with paraphilia-related disorders: A case series. *Journal of Clinical Psychiatry, 61*, 664–670.

Kagan, J. (1989). Temperamental contributions to social behavior. *American Psychologist, 44*, 668–674.

Kagan, R. M., & Reid, W. J. (1986). Critical factors in the adoption of emotionally disturbed youths. *Child Welfare Journal, 65*, 63–73.

Kahan, D., Polivy, J., & Herman, C. P. (2003). Conformity and dietary disinhibition: A test of the ego-strength model of self-regulation. *International Journal of Eating Disorders, 33*, 165–171.

Kahn, R. S., Fleischhacker, W. W., Boter, H., Davidson, M., Vergouwe, Y., Keet, I. P. M., et al. (2008). Effectiveness of antipsychotic drugs in first-episode schizophrenia and schizophreniform disorder: An open randomised clinical trial. *Lancet, 371*, 1085–1097.

Kahn, R. S., Khoury, J., Nichols, W. C., & Lanphear, B. P. (2003). Role of dopamine transporter genotype and maternal prenatal smoking in childhood hyperactive-impulsive, inattentive, and oppositional behaviors. *Journal of Pediatrics, 143*, 104–110.

Kahn. E. (1998). A critique of nondirectivity in the person-centered approach. *Journal of Humanistic Psychology, 39*, 94–110.

Kalaria, R. N., & Ballard, C. (1999). Overlap between pathology of Alzheimer disease and vascular dementia. *Alzheimer Disease & Associated Disorders, 13*, S115–S123.

Kales, H. C., Chen, P., Blow, F. C., Welsh, D. E., & Mellow, A. M. (2005). Rates of clinical depression diagnosis, functional impairment, and nursing home placement in coexisting dementia and depression. *American Journal of Geriatric Psychiatry, 13*, 441–449.

Kalisvaart, K. J., de Jonghe, J. F. M., Bogaards, M. J., Vreeswijk, R., Egberts, T. C. G., Burger, B. J., et al. Haloperidol prophylaxis for elderly hip-surgery patients at risk for delirium: A randomized placebo-controlled study. *Journal of the American Geriatrics Society, 53*, **1658**–1666.

Kalivas, P. W., & Volkow, N. D. (2005). The neural basis of addiction: A pathology of motivation and choice. *American Journal of Psychiatry, 162*, 1403–1413.

Kaltiala-Heino, R., Kosunen, E., & Rimpela, M. (2003). Pubertal timing, sexual behaviour and self-reported depression in middle adolescence. *Journal of Adolescence, 26*, 531–545.

Kaltiala-Heino, R., Rimpelä, M., Rantanen, P., & Rimpelä, A. (2000). Bullying at school—an indicator of adolescents at risk for mental disorders. *Journal of Adolescence, 23*, 661–674.

Kameya, Y. (2001). How Japanese culture affects the sexual functions of normal females. *Journal of Sex & Marital Therapy, 27*, 151–152.

Kandel, D., & Logan, J. (1984). Patterns of drug use from adolescence to young adulthood: Periods of risk for initiation, continued use and discontinuation. *American Journal of Public Health, 74*, 660–666.

Kandel, D. B. (2002). *Stages and pathways of drug involvement: Examining the gateway hypothesis.* Cambridge, England: Cambridge University Press.

Kandel, D. B., & Yamaguchi, K. (1985). Developmental patterns of the use of legal, illegal and medically prescribed psychotropic drugs from adolescence to young adulthood. In C. L. Jones & R. Battjes (Eds.), *Etiology of drug abuse: Implications for prevention* (pp. 193–235). Washington DC: Superintendent of Documents, U.S. Government Printing Office. [NIDA Research Monograph 56, DHHS Pub. No. ADM 85–1335.]

Kandel, E. R., Schwartz, J. H., & Jessell, T. M. (Eds.). (2007). *Principles of neural science* (5th ed.). New York: Elsevier Science.

Kaniasty, K. Z., Norris, F. H., & Murrell, S. A. (1990). Received and perceived social support following natural disaster. *Journal of Applied Social Psychology, 20*, 85–114.

Kaniasty, K., & Norris, F. H. (1992). Social support and victims of crime: Matching event, support, and outcome. *American Journal of Community Psychology, 20*, 211–241.

Kansas v. Crane, 122 S. Ct. 867 (2002).

Kansas v. Hendricks, 521 U.S. 346 (1997).

Kaplan, A. (2007). Hoarding: Studies characterize phenotype, demonstrate treatment. *Psychiatric Times, 24*(6). Retrieved on February 25, 2009, from http://www.psychiatrictimes.com/showArticle.jhtml?articleId=199202770

Kaplan, A. (2007). Mental illness in US Latinos addressed in survey, outreach efforts. *Psychiatric Times, 24*, n.p. Retrieved April 3, 2007, from http://www.psychiatrictimes.com/showArticle.jhtml;jsessionid=0V0Y2JR5R5CX0QSNDLPCKH0CJUNN2JVN?articleID=198001928&pgno=2

Kaplan, H. S. (1981). *The new sex therapy.* New York: Brunner/Mazel.

Kaplan, H. S. (1987). *Sexual aversion, sexual phobias, and panic disorder.* New York: Brunner/Mazel.

Kaplan, H. S. (1989). *How to overcome premature ejaculation.* New York: Brunner-Routledge.

Kaplan, H. S. (1995). Sexual aversion disorder: The case of the phobic virgin, or an abused child grows up. In R. C. Rosen & S. R. Leiblum (Eds.), *Case studies in sex therapy* (pp. 65–80). New York: Guilford Press.

Kaplan, L. J. (1991). *Female perversions.* Northvale, NJ: Jason Aronson.

Kapur, N., & Graham, K. S. (2002). Recovery of memory function in neurological disease. In A. D. Baddeley, M. D. Kopelman, & B. A. Wilson (Eds.), *Handbook of memory disorders* (2nd ed., pp. 233–248). Chichester, England: Wiley.

Kapur, N., Glisky, E. L., & Wilson, B. A. (2004). External memory aids and computers in memory rehabilitation. In A. D. Baddeley, M. D. Kopelman, & B. A. Wilson (Eds.), *Essential handbook of memory disorders for clinicians* (pp. 301–328). New York: Wiley.

Kapur, S. & Seeman, P. (2002) NMDA receptor antagonists ketamine and PCP have direct effectson the deopamine D(2) and serotonin 5-HT(2) receptors: Implications for models of schizophrenia. *Molecular Psychiatry, 7*, 837–844.

Kapur, S. (2003). Psychosis as a state of aberrant salience: A framework linking biology, phenomenology, and pharmacology in schizophrenia. *American Journal of Psychiatry, 160*, 13–23.

Kar, N. (2005). Chronic koro-like symptoms—two case reports. *BioMed Central Psychiatry, 5*, 34. Retrieved February 19, 2007, from http://www.pubmedcentral.nih.gov/articlerender.fcgi?artid=1266381

Karkowski, L. M., & Kendler, K. S. (1997). An examination of the genetic relationship between bipolar and unipolar illness in an epidemiological sample. *Psychiatric Genetics, 7*, 159–163.

Karlsson, R. (2005). Ethnic matching between therapist and patient in psychotherapy: An overview of findings, together with methodological and conceptual issues. *Cultural Diversity and Ethnic Minority Psychology, 11*, 113–129.

Kasckow, J. W., Baker, D., & Geracioti, T. D., Jr. (2001). Corticotropin-releasing hormone in depression and post-traumatic stress disorder. *Peptides, 22*, 845–851.

Kasper, S., & Resinger, E. (2001). Panic disorder: The place of benzodiazepines and selective serotonin reuptake inhibitors. *European Neuropsychopharmacology, 11*, 307–321.

Katerndahl, D., Burge, S., & Kellogg, N. (2005). Predictors of development of adult psychopathology in female victims of childhood sexual abuse. *Journal of Nervous and Mental Disease, 193*, 258–264.

Kaufer, D. I. (2002). Pharmacologic therapy of dementia with Lewy bodies. *Journal of Geriatric Psychiatry and Neurology, 15*, 224–232.

Kaufman, A. S., Kaufman, J. C., & McLean, J. E. (1995). Factor structure of the Kaufman Adolescent and Adult Intelligence Test (KAIT) for Whites, African Americans, and Hispanics. *Educational and Psychological Measurement, 55*, 365–376.

Kavanagh, D. J. (1992). Recent developments in expressed emotion and schizophrenia. *British Journal of Psychiatry, 160*, 601–620.

Kavirajan, H. (2009). Memantine: A comprehensive review of safety and efficacy. *Expert Opinion in Drug Safety, 8*, 89–109.

Kaye, W. H., Bailer, U. F., Frank, G. K., Wagner, A., & Henry, S. E. (2005). Brain imaging of serotonin after recovery from anorexia and bulimia nervosa. *Physiology & Behavior, 86*, 15–17.

Kaye, W. H., Barbarich, N. C., Putnam, K., Gendall, K. A., Fernstrom, J., Fernstrom, M., et al. (2003). Anxiolytic effects of acute tryptophan depletion in anorexia nervosa. *International Journal of Eating Disorders, 33*, 257–267.

Kaye, W. H., Bulik, C. M., Thornton, L., Barbarich, N., Masters, K., & Price Foundation Collaborative Group. (2004). Comorbidity of anxiety disorders with anorexia and bulimia nervosa. *American Journal of Psychiatry, 161*, 2215–2221.

Kaye, W. H., Frank, G. K., Bailer, U. F., & Henry, S. E. (2005). Neurobiology of anorexia nervosa: Clinical implications of alterations of the function of serotonin and other neuronal systems. *International Journal of Eating Disorders, 37*, S15–S19.

Kaye, W. H., Gendall, K. A., Fernstrom, M. H., Fernstrom, J. D., McConaha, C. W., & Weltzin, T. E. (2000). Effects of acute tryptophan depletion on mood in bulimia nervosa. *Biological Psychiatry, 47*, 151–157.

Kazdin, A. E. (1994). Methodology, design, and evaluation in psychotherapy research. In A. E. Bergin & S. L. Garfield (Eds.), *Handbook of psychotherapy and behavior change* (4th ed., pp. 19–71). Oxford, England: John Wiley & Sons.

Kazdin, A. E. (1995). *Conduct disorders in childhood and adolescence* (2nd ed.). Thousand Oaks, CA: Sage Publications.

Kazdin, A. E., & Weisz, J. R. (1998). Identifying and developing empirically supported child and adolescent treatments. *Journal of Consulting and Clinical Psychology, 66,* 19–36.

KCI. (2007, June–July). *KCI: The Anti-Meth Site.* Methamphetamine: Stories and letters of the hidden costs. Retrieved October 10, 2007, from http://www.kci.org/meth_info/letters/2007/June-July_2007.htm

Keane, T. M., & Barlow, D. H. (2002). Posttraumatic stress disorder. In D. H. Barlow (Ed.), *Anxiety and its disorders: The nature and treatment of anxiety and panic* (2nd ed., pp. 418–452). New York: Guilford Press.

Keane, T. M., Scott, W. O., Chavoya, G. A., Lamparski, D. M., & Fairbank, J. A. (1985). Social support in Vietnam veterans with posttraumatic stress disorder: A comparative analysis. *Journal of Consulting and Clinical Psychology, 53,* 95–102.

Keane, T. M., Zimering, R. T., & Caddell, J. M. (1985). A behavioral formulation of posttraumatic stress disorder in Vietnam veterans. *The Behavior Therapist, 8,* 9–12.

Keck, P. E., Jr., & McElroy, S. L. (2003). Redefining mood stabilization. *Journal of Affective Disorders, 73,* 163–169.

Keck, P. E., Orsulak, P. J., Cutler, A. J., Sanchez, R., Torbeyns, A., Marcus, R. N., et al. CN138–135 Study Group (2009). Aripiprazole monotherapy in the treatment of acute bipolar I mania: A randomized, double-blind, placebo- and lithium-controlled study. *Journal of Affective Disorders, 112,* 36–49.

Keck, P. E., Pope, H. G., Hudson, J. I., McElroy, S. L., Yurgelun-Todd, D., & Hundert, E. M. (1990). A controlled study of phenomenology and family history in outpatients with bulimia nervosa. *Comprehensive Psychiatry, 31,* 275–283.

Keefe, R. S., Bilder, R. M., Davis, S. M., Harvey, P. D., Palmer, B. W., Gold, J. M., et al. (2007). Neurocognitive effects of antipsychotic medications in patients with chronic schizophrenia in the CATIE trial. *Archives of General Psychiatry, 64,* 633–647.

Keefe, R. S. E., Arnold, M. C., Bayen, U. J., & Harvey, P. D. (1999). Source monitoring deficits in patients with schizophrenia: A multinomial modelling analysis. *Psychological Medicine, 29,* 903–914.

Keefe, R. S. E., Bollini, A. M., & Silva, S. G. (1999). Do novel antipsychotics improve cognition? A report of a meta-analysis. *Psychiatric Annals, 29,* 623–629.

Keefe, R. S. E., Eesley, C. E., & Poe, M. P. (2005). Defining a cognitive function decrement in schizophrenia. *Biological Psychiatry, 57,* 688–691.

Keefe, R. S. E., Silva, S. G., Perkins, D. O., & Lieberman, J. A. (1999). The effects of atypical antipsychotic drugs on neurocognitive impairment in schizophrenia: A review and meta-analysis. *Schizophrenia Bulletin, 25,* 201–222.

Keefe, R. S. E., Sweeney, J. A., Gu, H., Hamer, R. M., Perkins, D. O., McEvoy, J. P., & Lieberman, J. A. (2007). Effects of olanzapine, quetiapine, and risperidone on neurocognitive function in early psychosis: A randomized, double-blind 52-week comparison. *American Journal of Psychiatry, 164,* 1061–1071.

Keefe, R. S. E., Young, C. A., Rock, S. L., Purdon, S. E., Gold, J. M., Breier, A., & HGGN Study Group. (2006). One-year double-blind study of the neurocognitive efficacy of olanzapine, risperidone, and haloperidol in schizophrenia. *Schizophrenia Research, 81,* 1–15.

Keel, P. K., Mitchell, J. E., Miller, K. B., Davis, T. L., & Crow, S. J. (1999). Long-term outcome of bulimia nervosa. *Archives of General Psychiatry, 56,* 63–69.

Keel, P. K., & Haedt, A. (2008). Evidence-based psychosocial treatments for eating problems and eating disorders. *Journal of Clinical Child and Adolescent Psychology, 37,* 39–61.

Keel, P. K., & Klump, K. L. (2003). Are eating disorders culture-bound syndromes? Implications for conceptualizing their etiology. *Psychological Bulletin, 129,* 747–769.

Keel, P. K., & Mitchell, J. E. (1997). Outcome in bulimia nervosa. *American Journal of Psychiatry, 154,* 313–321.

Keel, P. K., Dorer, D. J., Eddy, K. T., Franko, D., Charatan, D. L., & Herzog, D. B. (2003). Predictors of mortality in eating disorders. *Archives of General Psychiatry, 60,* 179–183.

Keel, P. K., Dorer, D. J., Franko, D. L., Jackson, S. C., & Herzog, D. B. (2005). Postremission predictors of relapse in women with eating disorders. *American Journal of Psychiatry, 162,* 2263–2268.

Keel, P. K., Heatherton, T. F., Dorer, D. J., Joiner, T. E., & Zalta, A. K. (2006). Point prevalence of bulimia nervosa in 1982, 1992, and 2002. *Psychological Medicine, 36,* 119–127.

Keery, H., Boutelle, K., van den Berg, P., & Thompson, J. K. (2005). The impact of appearance-related teasing by family members. *Journal of Adolescent Health, 37,* 120–127.

Keith, J. A., & Midlarsky, E. (2004). Anorexia nervosa in postmenopausal women: Clinical and empirical perspectives. *Journal of Mental Health and Aging, 10,* 287–299.

Keith, S., Regier, D., & Rae, D. (1991). Schizophrenic disorderes. In L. N. Robins & D. S. Rae (Eds.), *Psychiatric disorders in America: The Epidemiological Catchment Area Study.* New York: Free Press.

Keller, M. B., & Hanks, D. L. (1994). The natural history and heterogeneity of depressive disorders: Implications for rational antidepressant therapy. *Journal of Clinical Psychiatry, 55,* 25–31.

Kelley, M.L., & Fals-Stewart, W. (2002). Couple- versus individual-based therapy for alcohol and drug abuse: Effects on children's psychosocial functioning. *Journal of Consulting & Clinical Psychology, 70,* 417–427.

Kelsey, J. E., Newport, J., & Nemeroff, C. B. (2006). *Principles of psychopharmacology for mental health professionals.* Hoboken, NJ: John Wiley & Sons.

Keltikangas-Järvinen, L., Puttonen, S., Kivimäki, M., Rontu, R., & Lehtimäki, T. (2006). Cloninger's temperament dimensions and epidermal growth factor A61G polymorphism in Finnish adults. *Genes, Brain & Behavior, 5,* 11–18.

Kemp, S. (2000). Psychology: The Middle Ages. In A. E. Kazdin (Ed.), *Encyclopedia of psychology* (Vol. 6, pp. 382–385). Washington, DC: American Psychological Association.

Kenardy, J., & Taylor, C. B. (1999). Expected versus unexpected panic attacks: A naturalistic prospective study. *Journal of Anxiety Disorders, 13,* 435–445.

Kenardy, J., Fried, L., Kraemer, H. C., & Taylor, C. B. (1992). Psychological precursors of panic attacks. *British Journal of Psychiatry, 160,* 668–673.

Kendall, P. C., Holmbeck, G. N., & Verduin, T. (2004). Methodology, design, and evaluation in psychotherapy research. In M. J. Lambert (Ed.), *Bergin & Garfield's handbook of psychotherapy and behavior change* (5th ed., pp. 16–43). New York: John Wiley & Sons.

Kendell, R., & Jablensky, A. (2003). Distinguishing between the validity and utility of psychiatric diagnoses. *American Journal of Psychiatry, 160,* 4–12.

Kendler, K. S. (1983) Overview: A current perspective on twin studies of schizophrenia. *American Journal of Psychiatry 140,* 1413–1425.

Kendler, K. S., & Diehl, S. R. (1993). The genetics of schizophrenia: A current genetic-epidemiologic perspective. *Schizophrenia Bulletin, 19,* 87–112.

Kendler, K. S., Bulik, C. M., Silberg, J., Hettema, J. M., Myers, J., & Prescott, C. A.

(2000). Childhood sexual abuse and adult psychiatric and substance use disorders in women: An epidemiological and cotwin control analysis. *Archives of General Psychiatry, 57,* 953–959.

Kendler, K. S., Gardner, C. O., Gatz, M., & Pedersen, N. L. (2007). The sources of co-morbidity between major depression and generalized anxiety disorder in a Swedish national twin sample. *Psychological Medicine, 37,* 453–462.

Kendler, K. S., Jacobson, K. C., Myers, J., & Prescott, C. A. (2002). Sex differences in genetic and environmental risk factors for irrational fears and phobias. *Psychological Medicine, 32,* 209–217.

Kendler, K. S., Karkowski, L. M., & Prescott, C. A. (1999). Causal relationship between stressful life events and the onset of major depression. *American Journal of Psychiatry, 156,* 837–848.

Kendler, K. S., Karkowski, L. M., & Prescott, C. A. (1999). Fears and phobias: Reliability and heritability. *Psychological Medicine, 29,* 539–553.

Kendler, K. S., Kuhn, J. W., Vittum, J., Prescott, C. A., & Riley, B. (2005). The interaction of stressful life events and a serotonin transporter polymorphism in the prediction of episodes of major depression: A replication. *Archives of General Psychiatry, 62,* 529–535.

Kendler, K. S., MacLean, C., Neale, M., Kessler, R. C., Heath, A. C. & Eaves, L. (1991). The genetic epidemiology of bulimia nervosa. American Journal of Psychiatry, 148, 1627–1637.

Kendler, K. S., Myers, J., & Prescott, C. A. (2002). The etiology of phobias: An evaluation of the stress-diathesis model. *Archives of General Psychiatry, 59,* 242–248.

Kendler, K. S., Myers, J., Prescott, C. A., & Neale, M. C. (2001). The genetic epidemiology of irrational fears and phobias in men. *Archives of General Psychiatry, 58,* 257–265.

Kendler, K. S., Neale, M. C., & Walsh, D. (1995). Evaluating the spectrum concept of schizophrenia in the Roscommon Family Study. *American Journal of Psychiatry, 152,* 749–754.

Kendler, K. S., Neale, M. C., Kessler, R. C., Heath, A. C., & Eaves, L. J. (1992). The genetic epidemiology of phobias in women: The interrelationship of agoraphobia, social phobia, situational phobia, and simple phobia. *Archives of General Psychiatry, 49,* 273–281.

Kendler, K. S., Neale, M. C., Kessler, R. C., Heath, A. C., & Eaves, L. J. (1993). Panic disorder in women: A population-based twin study. *Psychological Medicine, 23,* 397–406.

Kendler, K. S., Prescott, C. A., Neale, M. C., & Pedersen, N. L. (1997). Temperance

board registration for alcohol abuse in a national sample of Swedish male twins, born 1902–1949. *Archives of General Psychiatry, 54,* 178–184.

Kendler, K. S., Walters, E. E., Truett, K. R., Heath, A. C., Neale, M. C., Martin, N. G., & Eaves, L. J. (1995). A twin-family study of self-report symptoms of panic-phobia and somatization. *Behavior Genetics 25,* 499–515.

Kennedy, N., Boydell, J., Kalidindi, S., Fearon, P., Jones, P. B., van Os, J., & Murray, R. M. (2005). Gender differences in incidence and age at onset of mania and bipolar disorder over a 35-year period in Camberwell, England. *American Journal of Psychiatry, 162,* 257–262.

Kennedy, S. H., Javanmard, M., & Vaccarino, F. J. (1997). A review of functional neuroimaging in mood disorders: Positron emission tomography and depression. *The Canadian Journal of Psychiatry, 42,* 467–475.

Kennedy, S. H., Javanmard, M., Franco, J., & Vaccarino, F. J. (1997). A review of functional neuroimaging in mood disorders: Positron emission tomography and depression. *Canadian Journal of Psychiatry, 42,* 467–475.

Kenny, P. J., & Markou, A. (2004). The ups and downs of addiction: Role of metabotropic glutamate receptors. *Trends in Pharmacological Science, 25,* 265–272.

Kernberg, O. (1967). Borderline Personality Organization. *Journal of the American Psychoanalytic Association, 15,* 641–685.

Kernberg, O. F. (1986). *Severe personality disorders: Psychotherapeutic strategies.* New Haven, CT: Yale University Press.

Kerns, K. A., McInerney, R. J., & Wilde, N. J. (2001). Time reproduction, working memory, and behavioral inhibition in children with ADHD. *Child Neuropsychology, 7,* 21–31.

Keshavan, M. S., Anderson, S. A., & Pettegrew, J. W. (1994). Is schizophrenia due to excessive synaptic pruning in the prefrontal cortex? The Feinberg hypothesis revisited. *Journal of Psychiatric Research, 28,* 239–265.

Keski-Rahkonen, A., Hoek, H. W., Susser, E. S., Linna, M. S., Sihvola, E., Raevuori, A., et al. (2007). Epidemiology and course in anorexia nervosa in the community. *American Journal of Psychiatry, 164,* 1259–1265.

Kessels, R. P. C., & de Haan, E. H. F. (2003). Implicit learning in memory rehabilitation: A meta-analysis on errorless learning and vanishing cues methods. *Journal of Clinical and Experimental Neuropsychology, 25,* 805–814.

Kessing, L. V., Agerbo, E., & Mortensen, P. B. (2004). Major stressful life events and other risk factors for first admission with mania. *Bipolar Disorders, 6,* 122–129.

Kessler, H. R. (2006). The bedside neuropsychological examination. In P. J. Snyder, P. D. Nussbaum, & D. L. Robins (Eds.), *Clinical neuropsychology: A pocket handbook for assessment* (2nd ed., pp. 75–101). Washington, DC: American Psychological Association.

Kessler, R. C. (2003). Epidemiology of women and depression. *Journal of Affective Disorders, 74,* 5–13.

Kessler, R. C., & Frank, R. G. (1997). The impact of psychiatric disorders on work loss days. *Psychological Medicine, 27,* 861–873.

Kessler, R. C., Adler, L., Barkley, R., Biederman, J., Conners, C. K., Demler, O., Faraone, S. V., Greenhill, L. L., Howes, M. J., Secnik, K., Spencer, T., Ustun, T. B., Walters, E. E., & Zaslavsky, A. M. (2006). The prevalence and correlates of adult ADHD in the United States: Results from the National Comorbidity Survey replication. *American Journal of Psychiatry, 163,* 716–723.

Kessler, R. C., Akiskal, H. S., Ames, M., Birnbaum, H., Greenberg, P., Hirschfeld, R. M. A., Jin, R., Merikangas, K. R., Simon, G. E., & Wang, P. S. (2006). Prevalence and effects of mood disorders on work performance in a nationally representative sample of U.S. workers. *American Journal of Psychiatry, 163,* 1561–1568.

Kessler, R. C., Berglund, P., Demler, O., Jin, R., & Walters, E. E. (2005). Lifetime prevalence and age-of-onset distributions of DSM-IV disorders in the National Comorbidity Survey Replication. *Archives of General Psychiatry, 62,* 593–602.

Kessler, R. C., Berglund, P., Demler, O., Jin, R., Koretz, D., Merikangas, K. R., et al. (2003). The epidemiology of major depressive disorder: Results from the National Comorbidity Survey Replication (NCS-R). *JAMA: Journal of the American Medical Association, 289,* 3095–3105.

Kessler, R. C., Berglund, P., Demler, O., Jin, R., Koretz, D., Merikangas, K. R., et al. (2003). The epidemiology of major depressive disorder: Results from the National Comorbidity Survey Replication (NCS-R). *JAMA: Journal of the American Medical Association, 289,* 3095–3105.

Kessler, R. C., Borges, G., & Walters, E. E. (1999). Prevalence of and risk factors for lifetime suicide attempts in the National Comorbidity Survey. *Archives of General Psychiatry, 56,* 617–626.

Kessler, R. C., Brandenburg, N., Lane, M., Roy-Byrne, P., Stang, P. D., Stein, D. J., et al.. (2005). Rethinking the duration requirement for generalized anxiety disorder: Evidence from the National Comorbidity Survey Replication. *Psychological Medicine, 35,* 1073–1082.

Kessler, R. C., Chiu, W. T., Demler, O., & Walters, E. E. (2005). Prevalence, severity, and comorbidity of 12-Month DSM-IV disorders in the National Comorbidity Survey Replication. *Archives of General Psychiatry, 62,* 617–627.

Kessler, R. C., Foster, C. L., Saunders, W. B., & Stang, P. E. (1995). Social consequences of psychiatric disorders I: Educational attainment. *American Journal of Psychiatry, 152,* 1026–1032.

Kessler, R. C., McGonagle, K. A., Zhao, S., Nelson, C. B., Hughes, M., Eshelman, S., et al. (1994). Lifetime and 12-month prevalence of DSM-III-R psychiatric disorders in the United States. *Archives of General Psychiatry, 51,* 8–19.

Kessler, R. C., Mickelson, K. D., & Williams, D. R. (1999). The prevalence, distribution, and mental health correlates of perceived discrimination in the United States. *Journal of Health and Social Behavior, 40,* 208–230.

Kessler, R. C., Sonnega, A., Bromet, E., Hughes, M., & Nelson, C. B. (1995). Posttraumatic stress disorder in the National Comorbidity Survey. *Archives of General Psychiatry, 52,* 1048–1060.

Kessler, R. C., McGonagle, K. A., Zhao, S., Nelson, C. B., Hughes, M., Eshleman, S., et al. (1994). Lifetime and 12-month prevalence of DSM-III-R psychiatric disorders in the USA. *Archives of General Psychiatry 51,* 8–19.

Keuneman, R., Weerasundera, R., & Castle, D. (2002). The role of ECT in schizophrenia. *Australasian Psychiatry, 10,* 385–388.

Keyes, C. L. M. (2007). Promoting and protecting mental health as flourishing: A complementary strategy for improving national mental health. *American Psychologist, 62,* 95–108.

Keys, A., Brozek, J., Henschel, A., Mickelsen, O., & Taylor, H. L. (1950). *The biology of human starvation* (Vols. 1–2). Oxford, England: University of Minnesota Press.

Khalifa, N., & von Knorring, A. (2003). Prevalence of tic disorders and Tourette syndrome in a Swedish school population. *Developmental Medicine & Child Neurology, 45,* 315–319.

Khan A., Leventhal, R. M., Khan, S. R., & Brown, W. A. (2002). Severity of depression and response to antidepressants and placebo: An analysis of the Food and Drug Administration database. *Journal of Clinical Psychopharmacology, 22,* 40–45.

Khan, A., Warner, H. A., & Brown, W. A. (2000). Symptom reduction and suicide risk in patients treated with placebo in antidepressant clinical trials: An analysis of the Food and Drug Administration database. *Archives of General Psychiatry, 57,* 311–317.

Khashan, A. S., Abel, K. M., McNamee, R., Pedersen, M. G., Webb, R. T., Baker, P. N., et al. (2008). Higher risk of offspring schizophrenia following antenatal maternal exposure to severe adverse life events. *Archives of General Psychiatry, 65,* 146–152.

Kho, K. H., VanVreeswijk, M. F., & Murre, J. M. J. (2006). A retrospective controlled study into memory complaints reported by depressed patients after treatment with electroconvulsive therapy and pharmacotherapy or pharmacotherapy only. *Journal of ECT, 22,* 199–205.

Kiefer, F., Jahn, H., Tarnaske, T., Helwig, H., Briken, P., Holzbach, R., et al. (2003). Comparing and combining naltrexone and acamprosate in relapse prevention of alcoholism: A double-blind, placebo-controlled study. *Archives of General Psychiatry, 60,* 92–99.

Kiehl, K. A., Smith, A. M., Hare, R. D., Mendrek, A., Forster, B. B., Brink, J., et al. (2001). Limbic abnormalities in affective processing by criminal psychopaths as revealed by functional magnetic resonance imaging. *Biological Psychiatry, 50,* 677–684.

Kieseppä, T., Partonen, T., Haukka, J., Kaprio, J., & Lönnqvis, J. (2004). High concordance of bipolar I disorder in a nationwide sample of twins. *American Journal of Psychiatry, 161,* 1814–1821.

Kihlstrom, J. F. (2001). Dissociative disorders. In P. B. Sutker & H. E. Adams (Eds.), *Comprehensive handbook of psychopathology* (3rd ed., pp. 259–276). New York: Kluwer Academic/Plenum.

Kihlstrom, J. F. (2002a). Demand characteristics in the laboratory and the clinic: Conversations and collaborations with subjects and patients. *Prevention and Treatment, 5,* Article 36c.

Kihlstrom, J. F. (2002b). Demand characteristics in the laboratory and the clinic: Conversations and collaborations with subjects and patient. *Prevention & Treatment, 5, np.*

Kihlstrom, J. F. (2002b). To honor Kraepelin: From symptoms to pathology in the diagnosis of mental illness. In L. E. Beutler & M. L. Malik (eds.), *Rethinking the DSM: A psychological perspective* (pp. 279–303). Washington, DC: American Psychological Association.

Kihlstrom, J. R. (2005). Dissociative disorders. *Annual Review of Clinical Psychology, 1,* 227–253.

Kiliç, B. G., Sener, S., Koçkar, A. I., & Karakas, S. (2007). Multicomponent attention deficits in attention deficit hyperactivity disorder. *Psychiatry and Clinical Neurosciences, 61,* 142–148.

Killaspy, H., Bebbington, P., Blizard, R., Johnson, S., Nolan, F., Pilling, S., et al. (2006). The REACT study: Randomised evaluation of assertive community treatment in north London. *BMJ: British Medical Journal, 332,* 815–820.

Killen, J. D., Fortmann, S. P., Murphy Jr., G. M., Hayward, C., Arredondo, C., Cromp, D., et al. (2006). Extended treatment with Bupropion SR for cigarette smoking cessation. *Journal of Consulting and Clinical Psychology, 74,* 286–294.

Kilpatrick, D. G., Acierno, R., Saunders, B., Resnick, H. S., Best, C. L., et al. (2000). Risk factors for adolescent substance abuse and dependence: Data from a national sample. *Journal of Consulting and Clinical Psychology, 68,* 19–30.

Kilpatrick, D. G., Koenen, K. C., Ruggiero, K. J., Acierno, R., Galea, S., Resnick, H. S., et al. (2007). The serotonin transporter genotype and social support and moderation of posttraumatic stress disorder and depression in hurricane-exposed adults. *American Journal of Psychiatry, 164,* 1693–1699.

Kim, J.-H., & Lennon, S. J. (2007). Mass media and self-esteem, body image, and eating disorder tendencies. *Clothing and Textiles Research Journal, 25,* 3–23.

Kim, J-J., Lee, M. C., Kim, J., Kim, I. Y., Kim, S. I., Han, M. H., et al. (2001). Grey matter abnormalities in obsessive-compulsive disorder: Statistical parametric mapping of segmented magnetic resonance images. *British Journal of Psychiatry, 179,* 330–334.

Kim, M., Kwon, J. S., Kang, S., Youn, T., & Kang, K. (2004). Impairment of recognition memory in schizophrenia: Event-related potential study using a continuous recognition task. *Psychiatry and Clinical Neurosciences, 58,* 465–472.

Kimball, M. M. (2000). From "Anna O." to Bertha Pappenheim: Transforming private pain into public action. *History of Psychology, 3,* 20–43.

Kimble, G. A. (1981). Biological and cognitive constraints of learning. In L. T. Benjamin, Jr. (Ed.), *The G. Stanley Hall lecture series* (Vol. 1). Washington, DC: American Psychological Association.

King, B. H. (1990). Hypothesis: Involvement of the serotonergic system in the clinical expression of monosymptomatic hypochondriasis. *Pharmacopsychiatry, 23,* 85–89.

King, D. W., King, L. A., Foy, D. W., Keane, T. M., & Fairbank, J. A. (1999). Posttraumatic stress disorder in a national sample of female and male Vietnam veterans: Risk factors, war-zone stressors, and resilience-recovery variables. *Journal of Abnormal Psychology, 108,* 164–170.

King, L. A., King, D. W., Fairbank, J. A., Keane, T. M., & Adams, G. A. (1998). Resilience-recovery factors in post-traumatic stress disorder among female and male Vietnam veterans: Hardiness, postwar social support, and additional stressful life events.

Journal of Personality and Social Psychology, 74, 420–434.

King, S. A., Engi, S., & Poulos, S. T. (1998). Using the Internet to assist therapy. *British Journal of Guidance and Counselling, 26*, 43–52.

Kirk, J. M., Doty, P., & de Wit, H. (1998). Effects of expectancies on subjective responses to oral d$_9$-tetrahydrocannabinol. *Pharmacology, Biochemistry and Behavior, 59*, 287–293.

Kirk, S. A., & Hsieh, D. K. (2004). Diagnostic consistency in assessing conduct disorder: An experiment on the effect of social context. *American Journal of Orthopsychiatry, 74*, 43–55.

Kirkpatrick, B., Buchanan, R. W., McKenney, P. D., Alphs, L. D., & Carpenter, W. T., Jr. (1989). The Schedule for the Deficit Syndrome: An instrument for research in schizophrenia. *Psychiatry Research, 30*, 119–123.

Kirmayer, L. J., & Looper, K. J. (2006). Abnormal illness behaviour: Physiological, psychological and social dimensions of coping with distress. *Current Opinion in Psychiatry, 19*, 54–60.

Kirsch, I., & Lynn, S. J. (1998). Dissociation theories of hypnosis. *Psychological Bulletin, 123*, 100–111.

Kirsch, I., & Lynn, S. J. (1999). Automaticity in clinical psychology. *American Psychologist, 54*, 504–515.

Kirsch, I., & Sapirstein, G. (1998). Listening to Prozac but hearing placebo: A meta-analysis of antidepressant medication. *Prevention & Treatment, 1*, Article 0002a.

Kirsch, I., & Sapirstein, G. (1999). Listening to Prozac but hearing placebo: A meta-analysis of antidepressant medications. In I. Kirsch (Ed.), *How expectancies shape experience* (pp. 303–320). Washington, DC: American Psychological Association.

Kirsch, I., Moore, T. J., Scoboria, A., & Nicholls, S. S. (2002). The emperor's new drugs: An analysis of antidepressant medication data submitted to the U.S. Food and Drug Administration. *Prevention & Treatment, 5*, Article 23. Available on the World Wide Web: http://www.journals.apa.org/prevention/volume5/pre0050023a.html.

Kirsch, I., Moore, T. J., Scoboria, A., & Nicholls, S. S. (2002). The emperor's new drugs: An analysis of antidepressant medication data submitted to the U.S. Food and Drug Administration. *Prevention & Treatment, 5*, n.p.

Kirsch, I., Scoboria, A., & Moore, T. J. (2002). Antidepressants and placebos: Secrets, revelations, and unanswered questions. *Prevention & Treatment, 5*, n.p.

Kirsch, L. G., & Becker, J. V. (2006). Sexual offending: Theory of problem, theory of change, and implications for treatment effectiveness. *Aggression and Violent Behavior, 11*, 208–224.

Kirschenbaum, H., & Jourdan, A. (2005). The current status of Carl Rogers and the person-centered approach. *Psychotherapy: Theory, Research, Practice, Training, 42*, 37–51.

Kitzmann, K. M. (2000). Effects of marital conflict on subsequent triadic family interactions and parenting. *Developmental Psychology, 36*, 3–13.

Kjernisted, K. D., Enns, M. W., & Lander, M. (2002). An open-label clinical trial of nefazodone in hypochondriasis. *Psychosomatics: Journal of Consultation and Liaison Psychiatry, 43*, 290–294.

Klassen, A. F., Miller, A., & Fine, S. (2006). Agreement between parent and child report of quality of life in children with attention-deficit/hyperactivity disorder. *Child: Care, Health and Development, 32*, 397–406.

Klein, D. A., & Walsh, B. T. (2005). Translational approafches to understanding anorexia nervosa. *International Journal of Eating Disorders, 37*, S10–S14.

Klein, D. F. (1993). False suffocation alarms, spontaneous panics, and related conditions: An integrative hypothesis. *Archives of General Psychiatry, 50*, 306–317.

Klein, D. N. (2008). Classification of depressive disorders in the DSM-V: Proposal for a two-dimension system. *Journal of Abnormal Psychology, 117*, 552–560.

Klein, D. N., Santiago, N. J., Vivian, D., Blalock, J. A., Kocsis, J. H., Markowitz, J. C., et al. (2004). Cognitive-behavioral analysis system of psychotherapy as a maintenance treatment for chronic depression. *Journal of Consulting & Clinical Psychology, 72*, 681–688.

Klein, D. N., Shankman, S. A., & Rose, S. (2006). Ten-year prospective follow-up study of the naturalistic course of dysthymic disorder and double depression. *American Journal of Psychiatry, 163*, 872–880.

Klein, E., Kreinin, I., Chistyakov, A., Koren, D., Mecz, L., Marmur, S., et al. (1999). Therapeutic efficacy of right prefrontal slow repetitive transcranial magnetic stimulation in major depression: A double-blind controlled study. *Archives of General Psychiatry, 56*, 315–320.

Klein, M. (1932). *The Psycho-analysis of children*. London: Hogarth.

Kleinfield, N. R., & Roane, K. R. (1999, January 11). Subway killing casts light on suspect's mental torment. *The New York Times*, p. A1.

Kleinknecht, R. A. (2002). Comments on: Non-associative fear acquisition: A review of the evidence from retrospective and longitudinal research. *Behaviour Research and Therapy, 40*, 159–163.

Kleinman, A. (1988). *Rethinking psychiatry: From cultural category to personal experience*. New York: Free Press.

Kleinplatz, P. J. (2001). A critical evaluation of sex therapy: Room for improvement. In P. J. Kleinplatz (Ed.), *New directions in sex therapy: Innovations and alternatives* (pp. xi–xxxiii). Philadelphia: Taylor and Rutledge.

Klerman, G. L., & Weissman, M. M. (Eds.). (1993). *New applications of interpersonal psychotherapy*. Washington, DC: American Psychiatric Association.

Klerman, G. L., Weismann, M. M., Rounsaville, B. J., & Chevron, E. S. (1984). *Interpersonal psychotherapy for depression*. New York: Basic Books.

Klerman, G., Weissman, M., Rounseville, B., & Chevron, E. (1984). *Interpersonal psychotherapy of depression*. New York: Basic Books.

Klin, A., Pauls, D., Schultz, R., & Volkmar, F. (2005). Three diagnostic approaches to Asperger syndrome: Implications for research. *Journal of Autism and Developmental Disorders, 35*, 221–234.

Klinger, L. G., Dawson, G., & Renner, P. (2003). Autistic disorder. In E. J. Mash & R. A. Barkley (Eds.), *Child psychopathology* (2nd ed., pp. 409–454). New York: Guilford Press.

Klonsky, E. D. (2008). What is emptiness? Clarifying the 7th criterion for borderline personality disorder. *Journal of Personality Disorders, 22*, 418–426.

Klosko, J. S., Barlow, D. H., Tassinari, R., & Cerny, J. A. (1990). A comparison of alprazolam and behavior therapy in treatment of panic disorder. *Journal of Consulting and Clinical Psychology, 58*, 77–84.

Kluft, R. P. (1999). An overview of the psychotherapy of dissociative identity disorder. *American Journal of Psychotherapy, 53*, 289–319.

Klump, K. L., Wonderlich, S., Lehoux, P., Lilenfeld, L. R. R., & Bulik, C. M. (2002). Does environment matter? A review of nonshared environment and eating disorders. *International Journal of Eating Disorders, 31*, 118–135.

Knapp, C. (1997). *Drinking: A love story*. New York: Dial Press.

Knapp, C. (2003). *Appetites: Why women want*. New York: Counterpoint.

Knopman, D. S., Boeve, B. F., & Petersen, R. C. (2003). Essentials of the proper diagnoses of mild cognitive impairment, dementia, and major subtypes of dementia. *Mayo Clinic Proceedings, 78*, 1290–1308.

Knox, K. L., Litts, D. A., Talcott, G. W., Feig, J. C., & Caine, E. D. (2003). Risk of suicide and related adverse outcomes after exposure to a suicide prevention programme in the US Air Force: Cohort study. *British Medical Journal, 327,* 1376–1380.

Koenigsberg, H. W., Reynolds, D., Goodman, M., New, A. S., Mitropoulou, V., Trestman, R. L., Silverman, J., & Siever, L. J. (2003). Risperidone in the treatment of schizotypal personality disorder. *Journal of Clinical Psychiatry, 64,* 628–634.

Koenigsberg, H. W., Woo-Ming, A. M., & Siever, L. J. (2007). Psychopharmacological treatment of personality disorders. In P. E. Nathan & J. M. Gorman (Eds.), *A guide to treatments that work* (3rd ed., pp. 659–680). New York: Oxford University Press.

Kohen, R., Neumaier, J. F., Hamblin, M. W., & Edwards, E. (2003). Congenitally learned helpless rats show abnormalities in intracellular signaling. *Biological Psychiatry, 53,* 520–529.

Kohn, R. (2002). Belonging to two worlds: The experience of migration. Commentary. *South African Psychiatry Review, 5,* 6–8.

Kohut, H. (1971). *Analysis of the self: Systematic approach to treatment of narcissistic personality disorders.* New York: International Universities Press,

Kohut, H. (1977). *The restoration of the self.* New York: International Universities Press.

Kojima, S., Nagai, N., Nakabeppu, Y., Muranaga, T., Deguchi, D., Nakajo, M., Masuda, A., Nozoe, S., & Naruo, T. (2005). Comparison of regional cerebral blood flow in patients with anorexia nervosa before and after weight gain. *Psychiatry Research: Neuroimaging, 140,* 251–258.

Köksal, F., Domjan, M., Kurt, A., Sertel, Ö., Örüng, S., Bowers, R., et al. (2004). An animal model of fetishism. *Behaviour Research and Therapy, 42,* 1421–1434.

Kolodny, R., Masters, W., & Johnson, V. (1979). *A textbook of sexual medicine.* Boston: Little Brown and Company.

Kolur, U. S., Reddy, Y. C. J., John, J. P., Kandavel, T., & Jain, S. (2006). Sustained attention and executive functions in euthymic young people with bipolar disorder. *British Journal of Psychiatry, 189,* 453–458.

Kong, L. L., Allen, J. J. B., & Glisky, E. L. (2008). Interidentity memory transfer in dissociative identity disorder. *Journal of Abnormal Psychology, 117,* 686–692.

Konick, L. C., & Friedman, L. (2001). Meta-analysis of thalamic size in schizophrenia. *Biological Psychiatry, 49,* 28–38.

Konigsberg, E., & Farmer, A. (2008, February 20). Father tells of slaying suspect's long ordeal. *The New York Times.* Retrieved July 21, 2008, from http://www.nytimes.com/2008/02/20/nyregion/20commit.html?8br

Konstantareas, M. M. (2006). Social skills training in high functioning autism and Asperger's disorder. *Hellenic Journal of Psychology, 3,* 39–56.

Koob, G. F., & Bloom, F. E. (1988). Cellular and molecular mechanisms of drug dependence. *Science, 242,* 715–723.

Koob, G. F., & Le Moal, M. (2008). Addiction and the brain antireward system. *Annual Review of Psychology, 59,* 29–53.

Koob, G. F., Sanna, P. P., & Bloom, F. E. (1998). Neuroscience of addiction. *Neuron, 21,* 467–476.

Kopelman, M. D. (1999). Clinical and neuropsychological studies of patients with amnesic disorders. In M. A. Ron & A. S. David (Eds.), *Disorders of mind and brain* (Vol. 1, pp. 147–176). Cambridge: Cambridge University Press.

Kopelman, M. D. (2002). Psychogenic fugue. In A. D. Baddeley, M. D. Kopelman, & B. A. Wilson (Eds.), *The handbook of memory disorders* (2nd ed., pp. 451–471). Chichester, England: Wiley.

Koplewicz, H. S., Shatkin, J. P., Kadison, R., Nielsen, J., Girard, K., & Sood, A. A. (2007). *College mental health.* Symposium 24 at the American Academy of Child & Adolescent Psychiatry 54th Annual Meeting, October 23–28, 2007.

Koponen, S., Taiminen, T., Portin, R., Himanen, L., Isoniemi, H., Heinonen, H., et al. (2002). Axis I and II psychiatric disorders after traumatic brain injury: A 30-year follow-up study. *American Journal of Psychiatry, 159,* 1315–1321.

Kosslyn, S. M., & Koenig, O. (1995). *Wet mind: The new cognitive neuroscience.* New York: Free Press.

Kosslyn, S. M., Thompson, W. L., & Ganis, G. (2006). *The case for mental imagery.* New York: Oxford University Press.

Kosslyn, S. M., Thompson, W. L., Costantini-Ferrando, M. F., Alpert, N. M., & Spiegel, D. (2000). Hypnotic visual illusion alters color processing in the brain. *American Journal of Psychiatry, 157,* 1279–1284.

Kouri, E. M., & Pope, H. G. (2000). Abstinence symptoms during withdrawal from chronic marijuana use. *Experimental & Clinical Psychopharmacology, 8,* 483–492.

Kovnick, J. A., Appelbaum, P. S., Hoge, S. K., & Leadbetter, R. A. (2003). Competence to consent to research among long-stay inpatients with chronic schizophrenia. *Psychiatric Services, 54,* 1247–1252.

Koyama, T., Tachimori, H., Osada, H., Takeda, T., & Kurita, H. (2007). Cognitive and symptom profiles in Asperger's syndrome and high-functioning autism. *Psychiatry and Clinical Neurosciences, 61,* 99–104.

Kozlowska, K. (2005). Healing the disembodied mind: Contemporary models of conversion disorder. *Harvard Review of Psychiatry, 13,* 1–13.

Kraaij, V., & Garnefski, N. (2002). Negative life events and depressive symptoms in late life: Buffering effects of parental and partner bonding? *Personal Relationships, 9,* 205–214.

Krabbendam, L., & Aleman, A. (2003). Cognitive rehabilitation in schizophrenia: A quantitative analysis of controlled studies. *Psychopharmacology, 169,* 376–382.

Kram, M. L., Kramer, G. L., Steciuk, M., Ronan, P. J., & Petty, F. (2000). Effects of learned helplessness on brain GABA receptors. *Neuroscience Research, 38,* 193–198.

Kransny, L., Williams, B. J., Provencal, S., & Ozonoff, S. (2003). Social skills interventions for the autism spectrum: Essential ingredients and a model curriculum. *Child and Adolescent Psychiatric Clinics of North America, 12,* 107–122.

Kratochvil, C. J., Greenhill, L. L., March, J. S., Burke, W. J., & Vaughan, B. S. (2004). Current opinion: The role of stimulants in the treatment of preschool children with attention-deficit hyperactivity disorder. *CNS Drugs, 18,* 957–966.

Kratochvil, C. J., Heiligenstein, J. H., Dittmann, R., Spencer, T. J., Biederman, J., Wernicke, J., et al. (2002). Atomoxetine and methylphenidate treatment in children with ADHD: A prospective, randomized, open-label trial. *Journal of the American Academy of Child & Adolescent Psychiatry, 41,* 776–784.

Kraus, G., & Reynolds, D. J. (2001). The "A-B-C's" of the Cluster B's: Identifying, understanding, and treating Cluster B personality disorders. *Clinical Psychology Review, 21,* 345–373.

Kravitz, H. M., Fawcett, J., McGuire, M., Kravitz, G. S., & Whitney, M. (1999). Treatment attrition among alcohol-dependent men: is it related to novelty seeking personality traits? *Journal of Clinical Psychopharmacology, 19,* 51–56.

Kremen, W. S., Koenen, K. C., Boake, C., Purcell, S., Eisen, S. A., Franz, C. E., Tsuang, M. T., & Lyons, M. J. (2007). Pretrauma cognitive ability and risk for posttraumatic stress disorder. *Archives of General Psychiatry, 64,* 361–368.

Krijn, M., Emmelkamp, P. M. G., Biemond, R., de Wilde de Ligny, C., Schuemie, M. J., & van der Mast, C. A. P. G. (2004). Treatment of acrophobia in virtual reality: The role of immersion and presence. *Behaviour Research and Therapy, 42,* 229–239.

Kring, A. M., & Neale, J. M. (1996). Do schizophrenic patients show a disjunctive relationship among expressive, experiential, and psychophysiological components of emotion? *Journal of Abnormal Psychology, 105,* 249–257.

Kringelbach, M. L., Araujo, I., & Rolls, E. T. (2001). Face expression as a reinforcer activates the orbitofrontal cortex in an emotion-related reversal task. *Neuroimage, 13(6),* S433.

Kroenke, K. (2003). Patients presenting with somatic complaints: Epidemiology, psychiatric co-morbidity and management. *International Journal of Methods in Psychiatric Research, 12,* 34–43.

Kruh, I. P., Frick, P. J., & Clements, C. B. (2005). Historical and personality correlates to the violence patterns of juveniles tried as adults. *Criminal Justice and Behavior, 32,* 69–96.

Kruijver, F. P., Zhou, J. N., Pool, C. W., Hofman, M. A., Gooren, L. J. G., & Swaab, D. F. (2000). Male-to-female transsexuals have female neuron numbers in a limbic nucleus. *Journal of Clinical Endocrinology and Metabolism, 85,* 2034–2041.

Kruijver, I. P. M., Kerkstra, A., Francke, A. L., Bensing, J. M., & van de Wiel, H. B. M. (2000). Evaluation of communication training programs in nursing care: A review of the literature. *Patient Education and Counseling, 39,* 129–145.

Krupinski, J., Tiller, J. W. G., Burrows, G. D., & Mackenzie, A. (1998). *Predicting suicide risk among young suicide attempters.* In R. J. Kosky, H. S. Eshkevari, R. D. Goldney, & R. Hassan (Eds.), *Suicide prevention: The global context* (pp. 93–97). New York: Plenum Press.

Krupnick, J. L., Sotsky, S. M., Simmens, S., Moyer, J., Elkin, I., Watkins, J., et al. (1996). The role of the therapeutic alliance in psychotherapy and pharmacotherapy outcome: Findings in the National Institute of Mental Health Treatment of Depression Collaborative Research Program. *Journal of Consulting and Clinical Psychology, 64,* 532–539.

Krystal, J. H., Perry, E. B., Jr., Gueorguieva, R., Belger, A., Madonick, S. H., Abi-Dargham, A., et al. (2005). Comparative and interactive human psychopharmacologic effects of ketamine and amphetamine: Implications for glutamatergic and dopaminergic model psychoses and cognitive function. *Archives of General Psychiatry, 62,* 985–995.

Ksir, C. (2000). Drugs. In A. E. Kazdin (Ed.), *Encyclopedia of psychology* (Vol. 3, pp. 98–101). Washington, DC: American Psychological Association.

Kuboki, T., Nomura, S., Ide, M., Suematsu, H., & Araki, S. (1996). Epidemiological data on anorexia nervosa in Japan. *Psychiatry Research, 62,* 11–16.

Kuhl, B. A., Kahn, I., Dudukovic, N. M., & Wagner, A. D. (2008). Overcoming suppression in order to remember: Contributions from anterior cingulated and ventrolateral prefrontal cortex. *Cognitive, Affective, & Behavioral Neuroscience, 8,* 211–221.

Kulhara, P., & Chakrabarti, S. (2001). Culture and schizophrenia and other psychotic disorders. *Psychiatric Clinics of North America, 24,* 449–464.

Kulkarni, J., de Castella, A., Fitzgerald, P. B., Gurvich, C. T., Bailey, M., Bartholomeusz, C., et al. (2008). Estrogen in severe mental illness: A potential new treatment approach. *Archives of General Psychiatry, 65,* 955–960.

Kumari, V., & Postma, P. (2005). Nicotine use in schizophrenia: The self medication hypotheses. *Neuroscience & Biobehavioral Reviews, 29,* 1021–1034.

Kumpulainen, K., Räsänen, E., Henttonen, I., Almqvist, F., Kresanov, K., Linna, S., et al. (1998). Bullying and psychiatric symptoms among elementary school-age children. *Child Abuse & Neglect, 22,* 705–717.

Kundert, D. K., & Trimarchi, C. L. (2006). Pervasive developmental disorders. In L. Phelps (Ed.), *Chronic health-related disorders in children: Collaborative medical and psychoeducational interventions* (pp. 213–235). Washington, DC: American Psychological Association.

Kunen, S., Niederhauser, R., Smith, P. O., Morris, J. A., & Marx, B. D. (2005). Race disparities in psychiatric rates in emergency departments. *Journal of Consulting & Clinical Psychology, 73,* 116–126.

Kunert, H. J., Druecke, H. W., Sass, H., & Herpertz, S. C. (2003). Frontal lobe dysfunctions in borderline personality disorder? Neuropsychological findings. *Journal of Personality Disorders, 17,* 497–509.

Kuntsche, E., Simons-Morotn, B., Fotiou, A., ter Bogt, T., & Kokkevi, A. (2009). Decrease in adolescent cannabis use from 2002 to 2006 and links to evenings out with friends in 31 European and North American Countries and Regions. *Archives of Pediatric Adolescent Medicine, 163,* 119–125.

Kupfer, D. J., First, M. B., & Regier, D. A. (Eds.). (2002). *A research agenda for DSM-V.* Washington, DC: American Psychiatric Association.

Kurihara, T., Kato, M., Reverger, R., & Yagi, G. (2000). Outcome of schizophrenia in a non-industrialized society: Comparative study between Bali and Tokyo. *Acta Psychiatrica Scandinavica, 101,* 148–152.

Kurtz, M. M., & Mueser, K. T. (2008). A meta-analysis of controlled research on social skills training for schizophrenia. *Journal of Consulting and Clinical Psychology, 76,* 491–504.

Kurtz, M. M., Seltzer, J. C., Shagan, D. S., Thime, W. R., & Wexler, B. E. (2007). Computer-assisted cognitive remediation in schizophrenia: What is the active ingredient? *Schizophrenia Research, 89,* 251–260.

Kushner, M. G., Riggs, D. S., Foa, E. B., & Miller, S. (1992). Perceived controllability and the development of PTSD in crime victims. *Behaviour Research and Therapy, 31,* 105–110.

Kutchins, H., & Kirk, S. A. (1997). *Making us crazy: DSM: The psychiatric bible and the creation of mental disorders.* New York: Free Press.

La Rue, A., & Watson, J. (1998). Psychological assessment of older adults. *Professional Psychology: Research and Practice, 29,* 5–14.

Laakso, M., Vaurio, O., Koivisto, E., Savolainen, L., Eronen, M., & Aronen, H. J. (2001). Psychopathy and the posterior hippocampus. *Brain Behavior and Research, 118,* 187–193.

Labott, S. M., & Wallach, H. R. (2002). Malingering dissociative identity disorder: Objective and projective assessment. *Psychological Reports, 90,* 525–538.

Laffaye, C., McKellar, J. D., Ilgen, M. A., & Moos, R. H. (2008). Predictors of 4-year outcome of community residential treatment for patients with substance use disorders. *Addiction, 103,* 671–680.

Lagges, A. M., & Dunn, D. W. (2003). Depression in children and adolescents. *Neurologic Clinics, 21,* 953–960.

Lahey, B. B., Loeber, R., Burke, J. D., & Applegate, B. (2005). Predicting future antisocial personality disorder in males from a clinical assessment in childhood. *Journal of Consulting and Clinical Psychology, 73,* 389–399.

Lahey, B. B., McBurnett, K., & Loeber, R. (2000). Are attention-deficit/hyperactivity disorder and oppositional defiant disorder developmental precursors to conduct disorder? In A. J. Sameroff, M. Lewis, & S. M. Miller (Eds.), *Handbook of developmental psychopathology* (2nd ed., pp. 431–446). Dordrecht, Netherlands: Kluwer Academic.

Lahey, B. B., Pelham, W. E., Loney, J., Lee, S. S., & Willcutt, E. (2005). Instability of the DSM-IV subtypes of ADHD from preschool through elementary school. *Archives of General Psychiatry, 62,* 896–902.

Lake v. Cameron, 124 U.S. App. D. C. 264; 364 F.2d 657; 1966 U.S. App. LEXIS 6103 (1966).

Laks, J., & Engelhardt, E. (2008). Reports in pharmacological treatments in geriatric psychiatry: Is there anything new or just adding to old evidence? *Current Opinion in Psychiatry, 21,* 562–567.

Lam, A. G., & Sue, S. (2001). Client diversity. *Psychotherapy: Theory, Research, Practice, Training, 38,* 479–486.

Lam, D. H., Bright, J., Jones, S., Hayward, P., Schuck, N., Chisholm, D., & Sham, P. (2000). Cognitive therapy for bipolar illness—a pilot study of relapse prevention. *Cognitive Therapy and Research, 24,* 503–520.

Lam, K., Marra, C., & Salzinger, K. (2005). Social reinforcement of somatic versus psychological description of depressive events. *Behaviour, Research and Therapy*, 1203–1218.

Lam, R. W., Bartley, S., Yatham, L. N., Tam, E. M., & Zis, A. P. (1999). Clinical predictors of short-term outcome in electroconvulsive therapy. *The Canadian Journal of Psychiatry/La Revue canadienne de psychiatrie*, 44, 158–163.

Lamb, W. K., & Jones, E. E. (1998). *A meta-analysis of racial matching in psychotherapy*. Unpublished manuscript, University of California–Berkeley.

Lambert, K., & Kinsley, C. H. (2005). *Clinical neuroscience*. New York: Worth.

Lambert, M. J. (Ed.). (2004). *Bergin & Garfield's handbook of psychotherapy and behavior change* (5th ed.). New York: John Wiley & Sons.

Lambert, M. J., & Bergin, A. E. (1994). The effectiveness of psychotherapy. In A. E. Bergin & S. L. Garfield (Eds.), *Handbook of psychotherapy and behavior change* (4th ed., pp. 143–189). Oxford, England: John Wiley & Sons.

Lambert, M. J., & Ogles, B. M. (2004). The efficacy and effectiveness of psychotherapy. In M. J. Lambert (Ed.), *Bergin and Garfield's handbook of psychotherapy and behavior change* (5th ed., pp. 139–193). New York: John Wiley &Sons.

Lambert, M. J., Hansen, N. B., & Finch, A. E. (2001). Patient-focused research: Using patient outcome data to enhance treatment effects. *Journal of Consulting & Clinical Psychology*, 69, 159–172.

Lampropoulos, G. K. (2001). Bridging technical eclecticism and theoretical integration: Assimilative integration. *Journal of Psychotherapy Integration*, 11, 5–19.

Lanctôt, K. L., Herrmann, N., Yau, K. K., Kahn, L. R., Liu, B. A., LouLou, M. M., et al. (2003). Efficacy and safety of cholinesterase inhibitors in Alzheimer's disease: A meta-analysis. *Canadian Medical Association Journal*, 169, 557–564.

Landa, R. J., Holman, K. C., & Garrett-Mayer, E. (2007). Social and communication development in toddlers with early and later diagnosis of autism spectrum disorders. *Archives of General Psychiatry*, 64, 853–864.

Landen, M., Walinder, J., Hambert, G., & Lundstrom B. (1998). Factors predictive of regret in sex reassignment. *Acta Psychiatrica Scandinavica*, 97, 284–289.

Lane, S. D., Cherek, D. R., Pietras, C. J., & Steinberg, J. L. (2005). Performance of heavy marijuana-smoking adolescents on a laboratory measure of motivation. *Addictive Behaviors*, 30, 815–828.

Lang, P. J. (1995). The emotion probe: Studies of motivation and attention. *American Psychologist*, 50, 372–385.

Lang, R. A., Langevin, R., Checkley, K. L., & Pugh, G. (1987). Genital exhibitionism: Courtship disorder or narcissism? *Canadian Journal of Behavioural Science/Revue canadienne des sciences du comportement*, 19, 216–232.

Langa, K. M., Foster, N. L., & Larson, E. B. (2004). Mixed dementia: Emerging concepts and therapeutic implications. *JAMA: Journal of the American Medical Association*, 292, 2901–2908.

Langdon, R., & Coltheart, M. (2001). Visual perspective-taking and schizotypy: Evidence for a simulation-based account of mentalizing in normal adults. *Cognition*, 82, 1–26.

Lange, A., van de Ven, J.-P., Schrieken, B., & Emmelkamp, P. M. G. (2001). Interapy. Treatment of posttraumatic stress through the Internet: A controlled trial. *Journal of Behavior Therapy & Experimental Psychiatry*, 32, 73–90.

Langenbucher, J. W., Labouvie, E., Martin, C. S., Sanjuan, P. M., Bavly, L., Kirisci, L., et al. (2004). An application of item response theory analysis to alcohol, cannabis, and cocaine criteria in DSM-IV. *Journal of Abnormal Psychology*, 113, 72–80.

Langer, S. J., & Martin, J. I. (2004). How dresses can make you mentally ill: Examining gender identity disorder in children. *Child & Adolescent Social Work Journal*, 21, 5–23.

Langevin, R. (2006). Acceptance and completion of treatment among sex offenders. *International Journal of Offender Therapy and Comparative Criminology*, 50, 402–417.

Langevin, R., Paitich, D., Ramsay, G., Anderson, C., Kamrad, J., Pope S., et al. (1979). Experimental studies of the etiology of genital exhibitionism. *Archives of Sexual Behavior*, 8, 307–331.

Langton, C. M., Barbaree, H. E., Harkins, L., & Peacock, E. J. (2006). Sex offenders' response to treatment and its association with recidivism as a function of psychopathy. *Sexual Abuse: Journal of Research and Treatment*, 18, 99–120.

Lanphear, B. P., Vorhees, C. V., & Bellinger, D. C. (2005) Protecting children from environmental toxins. Public Library of Science Medicine, e61. Retrieved January 17, 2007, from http://medicine.plosjournals.org/perlserv/?request=get-document&doi=10.1371%2Fjournal.pmed.0020061

Larkin, J., Rice, C., & Russell, V. (1999). Sexual harassment, education and the prevention of disordered eating. In N. Piran, M. Levine, & C. Steiner-Adair (Eds.), *Preventing eating disorders: Ahandbook of intervention and special challenges* (pp. 194–207). Philadelphia: Brunner/Mazel.

Larson, C. L., Schaefer, H. S., Siegle, G. J., Jackson, C. A. B., Anderle, M. J.,

& Davidson, R. J. (2006). Fear is fast in phobic individuals: Amygdala activation in response to fear-relevant stimuli. *Biological Psychiatry*, 60, 410–417.

Laruelle, M., Abi-Dargham, A., Casanova, M. F., Toti, R., Weinberger, D. R., & Kleinman, J. E. (1993). Selective abnormalities of prefrontal serotonergic receptors in schizophrenia: A postmortem study. *Archives of General Psychiatry*, 50, 810–818.

Larzelere, R. E., & Kuhn, B. R. (2005). Comparing child outcomes of physical punishment and alternative disciplinary tactics: A meta-analysis. *Clinical Child and Family Psychology Review*, 8, 1–37.

LaSalle, V. H., Cromer, K. R., Nelson, K. N., Kazuba, D., Justement, L., & Murphy, D. L. (2004). Diagnostic interview assessed neuropsychiatric disorder comorbidity in 334 individuals with obsessive-compulsive disorder. *Depression and Anxiety*, 19, 163–173.

Lau, A., & Zane, N. (2000). Examining the effects of ethnic-specific services: An analysis of cost-utilization and treatment outcome for Asian American clients. *Journal of Community Psychology*, 28, 63–77.

Laucht, M., Skowronek, M. H., Becker, K., Schmidt, M. H., Esser, G., Schulze, T. G., et al. (2007). Interacting effects of the dopamine transporter gene and psychosocial adversity on attention-deficit/hyperactivity disorder symptoms among year-olds from a high-risk community sample. *Archives of General Psychiatry*, 64, 585–590.

Laumann, E. O., Paik, A., & Rosen, R. C. (1999). Sexual dysfunction in the United States: Prevalence and predictors. *Journal of the American Medical Association*, 281, 537–544.

Laumann, E., Gagnon, J. H., Michael, R. T., & Michaels, S. (1994). *The social organization of sexuality: Sexual practices in the United States*. Chicago: University of Chicago Press.

Lauriello, J., & Bustillo, J. (2001). Medication treatments for schizophrenia: Translating research findings into better outcomes. *Journal of Psychiatric Practice*, 7, 260–265.

LaVeist, T. A., Nickerson, K. J., & Bowie, J. V. (2000). Attitudes about racism, medical mistrust and satisfaction with care among African American and White cardiac patients. *Medical Care Research and Review*, 57, 146–161.

Laws, D. R., & Marshall, W. L. (1991). Masturbatory reconditioning with sexual deviates: An evaluative review. *Advances in Behaviour Research & Therapy*, 13, 13–25.

Lawson, J., Baron-Cohen, S., & Wheelwright, S. (2004). Empathising and systemising in adults with and without

Asperger syndrome. *Journal of Autism and Developmental Disorders, 34,* 301–310.

Lazev, A. B., Herzog, T. A., & Brandon, T. H. (1999). Classical conditioning of environmental cues to cigarette smoking. *Experimental and Clinical Psychopharmacology, 7,* 56–63.

Le Couteur, A., Bailey, A., Goode, S., Pickles, A., Robertson, S., Gottesman, I., et al. (1996). A broader phenotype of autism: The clinical spectrum in twins. *Journal of Child Psychology and Psychiatry, 37,* 785–801.

le Grange, D., & Eisler, I. (2009). Family interventions in adolescent anorexia nervosa. *Child and Adolescent Psychiatric Clinics of North America, 18,* 159–173.

Leavitt, F. (1997). False attribution of suggestibility to explain recovered memory of childhood sexual abuse following extended amnesia. *Child Abuse and Neglect, 21,* 265–272.

Leccese, A. P. (1991). *Drugs and society: Behavioral medicines and abusable drugs.* Englewood Cliffs, NJ: Prentice Hall.

Ledley, D. R., & Heimberg, R. G. (2006). Cognitive vulnerability to social anxiety. *Journal of Social & Clinical Psychology, 25,* 755–778.

LeDoux, J. (1996). *The emotional brain.* New York: Simon & Schuster.

LeDoux, J. E. (1996). *The emotional brain: The mysterious underpinnings of emotional life.* New York: Simon & Schuster.

LeDoux, J. E. (2000). Emotion circuits in the brain. *Annual Review of Neuroscience, 23,* 155–184.

Lee S. A. (1997). Chinese perspective of somatoform disorders. *Journal of Psychosomatic Research, 43,* 115–119.

Lee, A. M., & Lee, S. (1996). Disordered eating and its psychosocial correlates among Chinese adolescent females in Hong Kong. *International Journal of Eating Disorders, 20,* 177–183.

Lee, B. Y., & Newberg, A. B. (2005). Religion and health: A review and critical analysis. *Zygon, 40,* 443–468.

Lee, D. O. (2004). Menstrually related self-injurious behavior in adolescents with autism. *Journal of the American Academy of Child & Adolescent Psychiatry, 43,* 1193.

Lee, P. W. H., Lieh Mak, F., Yu, K. K., & Spinks, J. A. (1991). Pattern of outcome in schizophrenia in Hong Kong. *Acta Psychiatrica Scandinavica. 84,* 346–352.

Lee, S. H., & Oh, D. S. (1999). Offensive type of social phobia: Cross-cultural perspectives. *International Medical Journal, 6,* 271–279.

Lee, S., & Lee, A. M. (2000). Disordered eating in three communities of China: A comparative study of female high school students in Hong Kong, Shenzhen, and rural Hunan. *International Journal of Eating Disorders, 27,* 317–327.

Lee, S., Chiu, H. F., & Chen, C. (1989). Anorexia nervosa in Hong Kong: Why not more in Chinese? *British Journal of Psychiatry, 154,* 683–688.

Lee, S., Ho, T. P., & Hsu, L. K. (1993). Fat phobic and non-fat phobic anorexia nervosa: A comparative study of 70 Chinese patients in Hong Kong. *Psychological Medicine, 23,* 999–1017.

Lee, S., Hsu, L. G., & Wing, Y. K. (1992). Bulimia nervosa in Hong Kong Chinese patients. *British Journal of Psychiatry, 161,* 545–551.

Lee, S., Ng, K. L. Kwok, K. P. S., & Tsang, A. (in press). Prevalence and correlates of social fears in Hong Kong. *Journal of Anxiety Disorders, np.*

Lee, Y. H. (2008). The diagnosis of borderline personality disorder in Asian cultures. *Dissertation Abstracts International B: Sciences and Engineering, 68*(12), 8402B.

Leenaars, A. A. (1988). Are women's suicides really different from men's? *Women & Health, 14,* 17–33.

Leenaars, A. A. (2003). Can a theory of suicide predict all "suicides" in the elderly? *Crisis: The Journal of Crisis Intervention and Suicide Prevention, 24,* 7–16.

Leentjens, A. F. G., & van der Mast, R. C. (2005). Delirium in elderly people: An update. *Current Opinion in Psychiatry, 18,* 325–330.

Leentjens, A. F., & Diefenbacher, A. (2006). A survey of delirium guidelines in Europe. *Journal of Psychosomatic Research, 61,* 123–128.

Leff, J., Berkowitz, R., Shavit, N., Strachan, A., Glass, I., & Vaughn, C. (1990). A trial of family therapy versus a relatives' group for schizophrenia. Two-year follow-up. *British Journal of Psychiatry, 157,* 571–577.

LeGris, J., & van Reekum, R. (2006). Neuropsychological correlates of borderline personality disorder and suicidal behavior. *Canadian Journal of Psychiatry, 51,* 131–142.

Lehman, A. F., Steinwachs, K. M., & Survey Co-Investigators of the PORT Project. (1998). Patterns of usual care for schizophrenia: Initial results from the Schizophrenia Patient Outcomes Research Team (PORT) Client Survey. *Schizophrenia Bulletin, 24,* 11–20.

Lehrer, P. M., & Woolfolk, R. L. (1994). Respiratory system involvement in Western relaxation and self-regulation. In B. H. Timmons & R. Ley (Eds.), *Behavioral and psychological approaches to breathing disorders* (pp. 191–203). New York: Plenum Press.

Leibenluft, E. (2008). Chronobiological evaluation of rapid-cycling bipolar disorder. NIMH Grant Number: 1Z01MH02614-07. Manuscript in preparation.

Leibenluft, E., Albert, P. S., Rosenthal, N. E., & Wehr, T. A. (1996). Relationship between sleep and mood in patients with rapid-cycling bipolar disorder. *Psychiatry Research, 63,* 161–168.

Leiblum, S. R., & Segraves, R. T. (2000). Sex therapy with aging adults. In S. R. Leiblum & R. C. Rosen (Eds), *Principles and practice of sex therapy* (3rd ed., pp. 423–448). New York: Guilford Press.

Leiblum, S. R., Pervin, L. A., & Campbell, E. H. (1989). The treatment of vaginismus: Success and failure. In S. R. Leiblum & R. C. Rosen (Eds.), *Principles and practice of sex therapy: Update for the 1990s* (2nd ed., pp. 113–138). New York: Guilford Press.

Leighton, A. H., & Hughes, C. C. (1955). Notes on Eskimos patterns of suicide. *Southwestern Journal of Anthropology, 11,* 327–338.

Leising, D., Sporberg, D., & Rehbein, D. (2006). Characteristic interpersonal behavior in dependent and avoidant personality disorder can be observed within very short interaction sequences. *Journal of Personality Disorders, 20,* 319–330.

Lelewer, N. (1994). *Something's not right: One family's struggle with learning disabilities.* Acton, MA: VanderWyk & Burnham.

Lemche, E., Surguladze, S. A., Giampietro, V. P., Anilkumar, A., Brammer, M. J., Sierra, M., et al. (2007). Limbic and prefrontal responses to facial emotion expressions in depersonalization. *Neuroreport, 18,* 473–477.

Lenox, R. H., & Hahn, C. G. (2000). Overview of the mechanism of action of lithium in the brain: 50-year update. *Journal of Clinical Psychiatry, 61,* 5–15.

Lenze, E. J., Mulsant, B. H., Mohlman, J., Shear, M. K., Dew, M. A., Schulz, R., et al. (2005). Generalized anxiety disorder in late life: Lifetime course and comorbidity with major depressive disorder. *American Journal of Geriatric Psychiatry, 13,* 77–80.

Lenzenweger, M. F. (1999). Stability and change in personality disorder features: The Longitudinal Study of Personality Disorders. *Archives of General Psychiatry, 56,* 1009–1015.

Lenzenweger, M. F. (2006). The longitudinal study of personality disorders: History, design considerations, and initial findings. *Journal of Personality Disorders, 20,* 645–670.

Lenzenweger, M. F., Johnson, M. D., & Willett, J. B. (2004). Individual growth curve analysis illuminates stability and change in personality disorder features: The longitudinal study of personality disorders. *Archives of General Psychiatry, 61,* 1015–1024.

Leone, P., Pocock, D., & Wise, R. A. (1991). Morphine-dopamine interaction: Ventral tegmental morphine increases nucleus accumbens dopamine release. *Pharmacology Biochemistry & Behavior, 39,* 469–472.

Letonoff, E. J., Williams, T. R., & Sidhu, K. S. (2002). Hysterical paralysis: A report of three cases and a review of the literature. *Spine, 27,* E441–E445.

Leuchter, A. F., Cook, I. A., Witte, E. A., Morgan, M., & Abrams, M. (2002). Change in brain function of depressed subjects during treatment with placebo. *American Journal of Psychiatry, 159,* 122–129.

Leung, K. S., & Cottler, L. B. (2008). Ecstasy and other club drugs: A review of recent epidemiologic studies. *Current Opinion in Psychiatry, 21,* 234–241.

Levenson, J. S. (2004). Sexual predator civil commitment: A comparison of selected and released offenders. *International Journal of Offender Therapy and Comparative Criminology, 48,* 638–648.

Levin, A. (2007). Multiple physical illnesses common in Iraq war veterans with PTSD. *Psychiatric News, 42*(2), 4.

Levin, R. J. (1994). Human male sexuality: Appetite and arousal, desire and drive. In C. R. Legg & D. A. Booth (Eds.), *Appetite: Neural and behavioural bases* (pp. 127–164). New York: Oxford University Press.

Levine, M. P., & Harrison, K. (2004). Media's role in the perpetuation and prevention of negative body image and disordered eating. In J. K. Thompson (Ed.), *Handbook of eating disorders and obesity* (pp. 695–717). Hoboken, NJ: John Wiley & Sons.

Levine, S. B. (1988). Intrapsychic and individual aspects of sexual desire. In S. R. Leiblum & R. C. Rosen (Eds.), *Sexual desire disorders* (pp. 21–44). New York: Guilford Press.

Levitan, C., Ward, P. B., & Catts, S. V. (1999). Superior temporal gyral volumes and laterality correlates of auditory hallucinations in schizophrenia. *Biological Psychiatry, 46,* 955–962.

Levitt, E. E., Moser, C., & Jamison, K. V. (1994). The prevalence and some attributes of females in the sadomasochistic subculture: A second report. *Archives of Sexual Behavior, 23,* 465–473.

Levy, T. M., & Orlans, M. (1999). Kids who kill: Attachment disorder, antisocial personality and violence. *The Forensic Examiner, 8,* 19–24.

Levy, T. M., & Orlans, M. (2000). Attachment disorder as an antecedent to violence and antisocial patterns in children. In T. M. Levy (Ed.), *Handbook of attachment interventions* (pp. 1–26). San Diego, CA: Academic Press.

Lewinsohn, P. M. (1974). A behavioral approach to depression. In R. J. Friedman & M. M. Katz (Eds.), *The psychology of depression: Contemporary theory and research* (pp. 157–186). Washington, DC: Winston.

Lewinsohn, P. M., & Essau, C. A. (2002). Depression in adolescents. In I. H. Gotlib & C. L. Hammen (Eds.), *Handbook of depression.* (pp. 541–559). New York: Guilford Press.

Lewinsohn, P. M., Allen, N. B., Seeley, J. R., & Gotlib, I. H. (1999). First onset versus recurrence of depression: Differential processes of psychosocial risk. *Journal of Abnormal Psychology, 108,* 483–489.

Lewinsohn, P. M., Rohde, P., Klein, D. N., & Seeley, J. R. (1999). Natural course of adolescent major depressive disorder: I. Continuity into young adulthood. *Journal of the American Academy of Child & Adolescent Psychiatry, 38,* 56–63.

Lewinsohn, P. M., Rohde, P., Seeley, J. R., & Fischer, S. A. (1993). Age-cohort changes in the lifetime occurrence of depression and other mental disorders. *Journal of Abnormal Psychology, 102,* 110–120.

Lewis, D. A., & Moghaddam, B. (2006). Cognitive dysfunction in schizophrenia: Convergence of gamma-aminobutyric acid and glutamate alterations. *Archives of Neurology, 63,* 1372–1376.

Lewis, D. O., Yeager, C. A., Swica, Y., Pincus, J. H., & Lewis, M. (1997). Objective documentation of child abuse and dissociation in 12 murderers with dissociative identity disorder. *American Journal of Psychiatry, 154,* 1703–1710.

Lewis, P. A., & Critchley, H. D. (2003). Mood-dependent memory. *Trends in Cognitive Sciences, 7,* 431–433.

Lewontin, R. C. (1976). Race and intelligence. In N. J. Block & G. G. Dworkin (Eds.), *The IQ controversy* (pp. 78–92). New York: Pantheon Books.

Leyman, L., De Raedt, R., Schacht, R., & Koster, E. H. W. (2007). Attentional biases for angry faces in unipolar depression. *Psychological Medicine, 37,* 393–402.

Leyton, M., Okazawa, H., Diksic, M., Paris, J., Rosa, P., Mzengeza, S., et al. (2001). Brain regional alpha-[C-11] methyl-(L)-tryptophan trapping in impulsive subjects with borderline personality disorder. *American Journal of Psychiatry, 158,* 775–782.

Li, D., Chokka, P., & Tibbo, P. (2001). Toward an integrative understanding of social phobia. *Journal of Psychiatry & Neuroscience, 26,* 190–202.

Li, D., Sham, P. C., Owen, M. J., & He, L. (2006). Meta-analysis shows significant association between dopamine system genes and attention deficit hyperactivity disorder (ADHD). *Human Molecular Genetics, 15,* 2276–2284.

Li, S-C., Lindenberger, U., & Sikström, S. (2001). Aging cognition: From neuro-modulation to representation. *Trends in Cognitive Sciences, 5,* 479–486.

Liberman, R. P., & Robertson, M. J. (2005). A pilot, controlled skills training study of schizotypal high school students. *Verhaltenstherapie, 15,* 176–180.

Lichtenstein, P., & Annas, P. (2000). Heritability and prevalence of specific fears and phobias in childhood. *Journal of Child Psychology & Psychiatry & Allied Disciplines, 41,* 927–937.

Liddle, P. F., Friston, K. J., Frith, C. D., Hirsch, S. R., Jones, T., & Frackowiak, R. S. (1992). Patterns of cerebral blood flow in schizophrenia. *British Journal of Psychiatry, 160,* 179–186.

Lieb, K., Zanarini, M. C., Schmahl, C., Linehan, M. M., & Bohus, M. (2004). Borderline personality disorder. *Lancet, 364,* 453–461.

Lieb, R., Becker, E., & Altamura, C. (2005). The epidemiology of generalized anxiety disorder in Europe. *European Neuropsychopharmacology, 15,* 445–452.

Lieber, C. S. (2003). Relationships between nutrition, alcohol use, and liver disease. *Alcohol Research & Health, 27,* 220–231.

Lieberman, J. A. (1999). Is schizophrenia a neurodegenerative disorder? A clinical and pathophysiological perspective. *Biological Psychiatry, 46,* 729–739.

Lieberman, J. A., Stroup, T. S., McEvoy, J. P., Swartz, M. S., Rosenheck, R. A., Perkins, D. O., et al. (for the Clinical Antipsychotic Trials of Intervention Effectiveness (CATIE) Investigators). (2005). Effectiveness of antipsychotic drugs in patients with chronic schizophrenia. *New England Journal of Medicine, 353,* 1209–1223.

Liebowitz, M. R. (1999). Update on the diagnosis and treatment of social anxiety disorder. *Journal of Clinical Psychiatry, 60*(Suppl. 18), 22–26.

Lilenfeld, L. R., & Kaye, W. H. (1998). Genetic studies of anorexia and bulimia nervosa. In H. Hoek, J. Treasure, & M. Katzman (Eds.), *Neurobiology in the treatment of eating disorders* (pp. 169–194). Chichester, England: John Wiley & Sons.

Lilienfeld, S. O., Wood, J. M., & Garb, H. N. (2000). The scientific status of projective techniques. *Psychological Science in the Public Interest, 1,* 27–66.

Lilienfeld, S. O., Kirsch, I., Sarbin, T. R., Lynn, S. J., Chaves, J. F., Ganaway, G. K., et al. (1999). Dissociative identity disorder and the sociocognitive model: Recalling the lessons of the past. *Psychological Bulletin, 125,* 507–523.

Lin, E. H. B., Katon, W. J., Simon, G. E., Von Korff, M., Bush, T. M., Walker, E. A., et al. (2000). Low-intensity treatment of depression in primary care: Is it problematic? *General Hospital Psychiatry, 22,* 78–83.

Lin, K. M., & Cheung, F. (1999). Mental health issues for Asian Americans. *Psychiatric Services 50,* 774–780.

Lin, K. M., Cheung, F., Smith, M., & Poland, R. E. (1997). The use of psychotropic medications in working with Asian patients. In E. Lee (Ed.), *Working with Asian Americans: A guide for clinicians* (pp. 388–399). New York: Guilford Press.

Lindblom, K. M., Linton, S. J., Fedeli, C., & Bryngelsson, I. (2006). Burnout in the working population: Relations to psychosocial work factors. *International Journal of Behavioral Medicine, 13,* 51–59.

Linde, K., Berner, M. M., & Kriston, L. (2008). St. John's wort for major depression. *Cochrane Database of Systematic Reviews,* Issue 4. Art. No.: CD000448.

Linde, K., Berner, M., Egger, M., & Mulrow, C. (2005). St John's wort for depression: Meta-analysis of randomised controlled trials. *British Journal of Psychiatry, 186,* 99–107.

Linde, P. (2002). *Of spirits and madness: An American psychiatrist in Africa.* New York: McGraw-Hill.

Linehan, M. M. (1981). A social-behavioral analysis of suicide and parasuicide: Implications for clinical assessment and treatment. In J. Clarkin & H. Glazer (Eds.), *Depression: Behavioral and directive intervention strategies* (pp. 229–294). New York: Garland Press.

Linehan, M. M. (1993). *Cognitive-behavioral treatment of borderline personality disorder.* New York: Guilford Press.

Linehan, M. M., & Heard, H. L. (1999). Borderline personality disorder: Costs, course, and treatment outcomes. In N. E. Miller & K. M. Magruder (Eds.), *Cost-effectiveness of psychotherapy: A guide for practitioners, researchers, and policymakers* (pp. 291–305). New York: Oxford University Press.

Linehan, M. M., & Kehrer, C. A. (1993). Borderline personality disorder. In D. H. Barlow (Ed.), *Clinical handbook of psychological disorders: A step-by-step treatment manual* (2nd ed., pp. 396–441). New York: Guilford Press.

Linehan, M. M., Comtois, K. A., Murray, A. M., Brown, M. Z., Gallop, R. J., Heard, H. L., Korslund, K. E., Tutek, D. A., Reynolds, S. K., & Lindenboim, N. (2006). Two-year randomized controlled trial and follow-up of dialectical behavior therapy vs therapy by experts for suicidal behaviors and borderline personality disorder. *Archives of General Psychiatry, 63,* 757–766.

Linehan, M. M., Schmidt, H., III, Dimeff, L. A., Craft, J. C., Kanter, J., & Comtois, K. A. (1999). Dialectical behavior therapy for patients with borderline personality disorder and drug-dependence. *The American Journal on Addictions, 8,* 279–292.

Lingford-Hughes, A., & Nutt, D. (2000). Alcohol and drug abuse. *Current Opinion in Psychiatry, 13,* 291–298.

Lipsanen, T., Korkeila, J., Peltola, P., Järvinen, J., Langen, K., & Lauerma, H. (2004). Dissociative disorders among psychiatric patients: Comparison with a nonclinical sample. *European Psychiatry, 19,* 53–55.

Lipsitz, J. D., Barlow, D. H., Mannuzza, S., Hofmann, S. G., & Fyer, A. J. (2002). Clinical features of four DSM-IV-specific phobia subtypes. *Journal of Nervous and Mental Disease, 190,* 471–478.

Littrell, J. H., & Girvin, H. (2002). Stages of change: A critique. *Behavior Modification, 26,* 223–273.

Litz, B. T., Engel, C. C., Bryant, R. A., & Papa, A. (2007). A randomized, controlled proof-of-concept trial of an Internet-based, therapist-assisted self-management treatment for posttraumatic stress disorder. *American Journal of Psychiatry, 164,* 1676–1683.

Litz, B. T., Engel, C. C., Bryant, R. A., & Papa, A. (2007). A randomized, controlled proof-of-concept trial of an Internet-based, therapist-assisted self-management treatment for posttraumatic stress disorder. *American Journal of Psychiatry, 164,* 1676–1684.

Livesley, W. J. (2001). Conceptual and taxonomic issues. In W. J. Livesley (Ed.), *Handbook of personality disorders: Theory, research, and treatment* (pp. 3–38). New York: Guilford Press.

Livesley, W. J. (2007). An integrated approach to the treatment of personality disorder. *Journal of Mental Health, 16,* 131–148.

Livesley, W. J., Jang, K. L., & Vernon, P. A. (1998). Phenotypic and genetic structure of traits delineating personality disorder. *Archives of General Psychiatry, 55,* 941–948.

Livingston, G., Johnston, K., Katona, C., Paton, J., & Lyketsos, C. G. (Old Age Task Force of the World Federation of Biological Psychiatry). (2005). Systematic review of psychological approaches to the management of neuropsychiatric symptoms of dementia. *American Journal of Psychiatry, 162,* 1996–2021.

Lock, J. (2004). Family approaches for anorexia nervosa and bulimia nervosa. In J. K. Thompson (Ed.), *Handbook of eating disorders and obesity* (pp. 218–231). Hoboken, NJ: John Wiley & Sons.

Lock, J., Le Grange, D., Agras, W. S., & Dare, C. (2001). Treatment manual for anorexia nervosa: A family-based approach. *Family Therapy, 29,* 190–191.

Locker, D., Thomson, W. M., & Poulton, R. (2001). Psychological disorder, conditioning experiences, and the onset of dental anxiety in early adulthood. *Journal of Dental Research, 80,* 1588–1592.

Loeber, R., & Farrington, D. P. (2000). Young children who commit crime: Epidemiology, developmental origins, risk factors, early interventions, and policy implications. *Development and Psychopathology, 12,* 737–762.

Loening-Baucke, V. (1996). Encopresis and soiling. *Pediatric Clinics of North America, 43,* 279–298.

Loewenstein, R. J. (1994). Diagnosis, epidemiology, clinical course, treatment, and cost effectiveness of treatment for dissociative disorders and MPD: Report submitted to the Clinton Administration Task Force on Health Care Financing Reform. *Dissociation: Progress in the Dissociative Disorders, 7,* 3–11.

Loney, B. R., Frick, P. J., Clements, C. B., Ellis, M. L., & Kerlin, K. (2003). Callous-unemotional traits, impulsivity, and emotional processing in adolescents with antisocial behavior problems. *Journal of Clinical Child and Adolescent Psychology, 32,* 66–80.

Loney, B. R., Frick, P. J., Ellis, M., & McCoy, M. G. (1998). Intelligence, callous-unemotional traits, and antisocial behavior. *Journal of Psychopathology and Behavioral Assessment, 20,* 231–247.

Loo, C. (2004). Transcranial magnetic stimulation: Promise for the future? *Australasian Psychiatry, 12,* 409–410.

Looper, K. J., & Kirmayer, L. J. (2002). Behavioral medicine approaches to somatoform disorders. *Journal of Consulting and Clinical Psychology, 70,* 810–827.

Lopez, S. R., Nelson, K. A., Polo, J. A., Jenkins, J., Karno, M., & Snyder, K. (1998, August). *Family warmth and the course of schizophrenia of Mexican Americans and Anglo Americans.* Paper presented at the International Congress of Applied Psychology, San Francisco.

LoPiccolo, J., & Friedman, J. M. (1988). Broad-spectrum treatment of low sexual desire: Integration of cognitive, behavioral, and systemic therapy. In S. R. Leiblum & R. C. Rosen (Eds.), *Sexual desire disorders* (pp. 107–144). New York: Guilford Press.

LoPiccolo, J., & Stock, W. E. (1986). Treatment of sexual dysfunction. *Journal of Consulting and Clinical Psychology, 54,* 158–167.

Lorenz, J., Kunze, K., & Bromm, B. (1998). Differentiation of conversive sensory loss and malingering by P300 in a modified oddball task. *Neuroreport, 9,* 187–191.

Lorge, E. (2008, January 31). Army responds to rising suicide rates. *Army Behavioral Health.* Retrieved December 2, 2008, fromhttp://www.behavioralhealth.army.mil/news/20080131armyrespondstosuicide.html

Lorimer, P. A., Simpson, R. L., Myles, B. S., & Ganz, J. B. (2002). The use of social stories as a preventative behavioral intervention in a home setting with a child with autism. *Journal of Positive Behavior Interventions, 4,* 53–60.

Lougee, L., Perlmutter, S. J., Nicolson, R., Garvey, M. A., & Swedo, S. E. (2000). Psychiatric disorders in first-degree relatives of children with pediatric autoimmune neuropsychiatric disorders associated with streptococcal infections (PANDAS). *Journal of the American Academy of Child & Adolescent Psychiatry, 39,* 1120–1126.

Louis, M., & Kowalski, S. D. (2002). Use of aromatherapy with hospice patients to decrease pain, anxiety, and depression and to promote an increased sense of well-being. *American Journal of Hospice & Palliative Care, 19,* 381–386.

Louis, M., & Kowalski, S. D. (2002). Use of aromatherapy with hospice patients to decrease pain, anxiety, and depression and to promote an increased sense of well-being. *American Journal of Hospice & Palliative Care, 19,* 381–386.

Lowe, M. R., Gleaves, D. H., DiSimone-Weiss, R. T., Furgueson, C., Gayda, C. A., Kolsky, P. A., et al. (1996). Restraint, dieting, and the continuum model of bulimia nervosa. *Journal of Abnormal Psychology, 105,* 508–517.

Luborsky, L., Barber, J., Siqueland, L., McLellan, A. T., Woody, G. (1997). Establishing a therapeutic alliance with substance abusers. In L. S. Onken, J. D. Blaine, & J. J. Boren (Eds.), *Beyond the therapeutic alliance: Keeping the drug-dependent individual in treatment* (pp. 223–240). National Institute on Drug Abuse Research Monograph 165. NIH publication no. 97–4142. Washington: DC: U.S. Government Printing Office.

Luborsky, L., Diguer, L., Seligman, D. A., Rosenthal, R., Krause, E. D., Johnson, S., et al. (1999). The researcher's own therapy allegiances: A "wild card" in comparisons of treatment efficacy. *Clinical Psychology: Science & Practice 6,* 95–106.

Luborsky, L., Rosenthal, R., Diguer, L., Andrusyna, T. P., Berman, J. S., Levitt, J. T., et al. (2002). The dodo bird verdict is alive and well—mostly. *Clinical Psychology: Science and Practice, 9,* 2–12.

Luborsky, L., Singer, B., & Luborsky, L. (1975). Comparative studies of psychotherapies: Is it true that "everyone has won and all must have prizes"? *Archives of General Psychiatry, 32,* 995–1008.

Luby, J. L., Sullivan, J., Belden, A., Stalets, M., Blankenship, S., & Spitznagel, E. (2006). An observational analysis of behavior in depressed preschoolers: Further validation of early-onset depression. *Journal of the American Academy of Child & Adolescent Psychiatry, 45,* 203–212.

Lucka, I. (2006). Depressive disorders in patients suffering from anorexia nervosa. *Archives of Psychiatry and Psychotherapy, 8,* 55–61.

Luczak, S. E., Elvine-Kreis, B., Shea, S. H., Carr, L. G., & Wall, T. L. (2002). Genetic risk for alcoholism relates to level of response to alcohol in Asian-American men and women. *Journal of Studies on Alcohol, 63,* 74–82.

Luczak, S. E., Wall, T. L., Shea, S. H., Byun, S. M., & Carr, L. G. (2001). Binge drinking in Chinese, Korean, and White college students: Genetic and ethnic group differences. *Psychology of Addictive Behaviors, 15,* 306–309.

Ludman, E. J., Simon, G. E., Tutty, S., & Von Korff, M. (2007). A randomized trial of telephone psychotherapy and pharmacotherapy for depression: Continuation and durability of effects. *Journal of Consulting and Clinical Psychology, 75,* 257–266.

Lund, B. C., Hernandez, E. R., Yates, W. R., Mitchell, J. R., McKee, P. A., & Johnson, C. L. (2009). Rate of inpatient weight restoration predicts outcome in anorexia nervosa. *International Journal of Eating Disorders, 42,* 301–305.

Lundberg, P., Cantor-Graae, E., Kahima, M., & Östergren, P. (2007). Delusional ideation and manic symptoms in potential future emigrants in Uganda. *Psychological Medicine, 37,* 505–512.

Lundgren, J. D., Danoff-Burg, S., & Anderson, D. A. (2004). Cognitive-behavioral therapy for bulimia nervosa: An empirical analysis of clinical significance. *International Journal of Eating Disorders, 35,* 262–274.

Lundh, L., & Öst, L. (1996). Recognition bias for critical faces in social phobics. *Behaviour Research & Therapy, 34,* 787–794.

Lutz, W., Martinovich, Z., Howard, K. I., & Leon, S. C. (2002). Outcome management, expected treatment response, and severity-adjusted provider filing in outpatient psychotherapy. *Journal of Clinical Psychology, 58,* 1291–1304.

Lutz, W., Martinovich, Z., Howard, K. I., & Leon, S. C. (2002). Outcomes management, expected treatment response, and severity-adjusted provider profiling in outpatient psychotherapy. *Journal of Clinical Psychology, 58,* 1291–1304.

Lykken, D. T. (1995). *The antisocial personalities.* Mahwah, NJ: Erlbaum.

Lykouras, L. (1999). Pharmacotherapy of social phobia: A critical assessment. *Psychiatriki, 10,* 35–41.

Lyle, S., Grizzell, M., Willmott, S., Benbow, S., Clark, M., & Jolley, D. (2008). Treatment of a whole population sample of Alzheimer's disease with donepezil over a 4-year period: Lessons learned. *Dementia and Geriatric Cognitive Disorders, 25,* 226–231.

Lynch, D. J., McGrady, A., Nagel, R., & Zsembik, C. (1999). Somatization in family practice: Comparing 5 methods of classification. *Primary Care Companion to the Journal of Clinical Psychiatry, 1,* 85–89.

Lynch, W. C., Heil, D. P., Wagner, E., & Havens, M. D. (2008). Body dissatisfaction mediates the association between body mass index and risky weight control behaviors among White and Native American adolescent girls. *Appetite, 51,* 210–213.

Lynskey, M. T., Heath, A. C., Nelson, E. C., Bucholz, K. K., Madden, P. A. F., Slutske, W. S., et al. (2002). Genetic and environmental contributions to cannabis dependence in a national young adult twin sample. *Psychological Medicine, 32,* 195–207.

Lyon, H. M., Startup, M., & Bentall, R. P. (1999). Social cognition and the manic defense: Attributions, selective attention, and self-schema in bipolar affective disorder. *Journal of Abnormal Psychology, 108,* 273–282.

Lyons, M. J., Eisen, S. A., Goldberg, J., True, W., Lin, N., Meyer, J. M., et al. (1998). A registry-based twin study of depression in men. *Archives of General Psychiatry, 55,* 468–472.

Lyons, M. J., Goldberg, J., Eisen, S. A., True, W., & Tsuang, M. T. (1993). Do genes influence exposure to trauma? A twin study of combat. *American Journal of Medical Genetics, 48,* 22–27.

Lyons, M. J., Goldberg, J., Eisen, S. A., True, W., Tsuang, M. T., Meyer, J. M., et al. (1993). Do genes influence exposure to trauma? A twin study of combat. *American Journal of Medical Genetics (Neuropsychiatric Genetics), 48,* 22–27.

Lyons-Ruth, K., Holmes, B. M., Sasvari-Szekely, M., Ronai, Z., Nemoda, Z., & Pauls, D. (2007). Serotonin transporter polymorphism and borderline or antisocial traits among low-income young adults. *Psychiatric Genetics, 17,* 339–343.

Lyoo, I. K., Han, M. H., & Cho, D. Y. (1998). A brain MRI study in subjects with borderline personality disorder. *Journal of Affective Disorders, 50,* 235–243.

Maaranen, P., Tanskanen, A., Honkalampi, K., Haatainen, K., Hintikka, J., & Viinamäki, H. (2005). Factors associated with pathological dissociation in the general population. *Australian and New Zealand Journal of Psychiatry, 39,* 387–394.

MacArthur Research Network on Mental Health and the Law. (2001a). *The*

MacArthur Adjudicative Competence Study. Retrieved January 21, 2006, from http://macarthur.virginia.edu/adjudicate.html

MacArthur Research Network on Mental Health and the Law. (2001b). *The MacArthur Coercion Study*. Retrieved October 27, 2006, from http://www.macarthur.virginia.edu/coercion.html

MacArthur Research Network on Mental Health and the Law. (2001c). *The MacArthur Violence Risk Assessment Study*. Retrieved January 24, 2006, fromhttp://www.macarthur.virginia.edu/risk.html

Macaskill, N. D., & Macaskill, A. (1996). Rational-emotive therapy plus pharmacotherapy versus pharmacotherapy alone in the treatment of high cognitive dysfunction depression. *Cognitive Therapy & Research, 20,* 575–592.

MacDonald, P. A., Antony, M. M., MacLeod, C. M., & Richter, M. M. (1997). Memory and confidence in memory judgments among individuals with obsessive compulsive disorder and nonclinical controls. *Behaviour Research and Therapy, 35,* 497–505.

Macedo, C. E., Martinez, R. C., Albrechet-Souza, L., Molina, V. A., & Brandao, M. L. (2007). 5-HT2- and D1-mechanisms of the basolateral nucleus of the amygdala enhance conditioned fear and impair unconditioned fear. *Behavioural Brain Research, 177,* 100–108.

MacKay, D. G., & Ahmetzanov, M. V. (2005). Emotion, memory, and attention in the taboo Stroop paradigm: An experimental analogue of flashbulb memories. *Psychological Science, 16,* 25–32.

MacKenzie, K. R. (2001). Group psychotherapy. In W. J. Livesley (Ed.), *Handbook of personality disorders: Theory, research, and treatment* (pp. 497–526). New York: Guilford Press.

Mackie, S., Shaw, P., Lenroot, R., Pierson, R., Greenstein, D. K., Nugent, T. F., III, Sharp, W. S., et al. (2007). Cerebellar development and clinical outcome in attention deficit hyperactivity disorder. *American Journal of Psychiatry, 164,* 647–655.

Macklin, M. L., Metzger, L. J., Litz, B. T., McNally, R. J., Lasko, N. B., Orr, S. P., et al. (1998). Lower precombat intelligence is a risk factor for posttraumatic stress disorder. *Journal of Consulting and Clinical Psychology, 66,* 323–326.

Maden, A., Scott, F., Burnett, R., Lewis, G. H., & Skapinakis, P. (2004). Offending in psychiatric patients after discharge from medium secure units: Prospective national cohort study. *BMJ: British Medical Journal, 328,* 1534.

Maes, H. H., Silberg, J. L., Neale, M. C., & Eaves, L. J. (2007). Genetic and cultural transmission of antisocial behavior: An extended twin parent model. *Twin Research and Human Genetics, 10,* 136–150.

Magarinos, M., Zafar, U., Nissenson, K., & Blanco, C. (2002). Epidemiology and treatment of hypochondriasis. *CNS Drugs, 16,* 9–22.

Magee, W. J., Eaton, W. W., Wittchen, H., McGonagle, K. A., & Kessler, R. C. (1996). Agoraphobia, simple phobia, and social phobia in the national comorbidity survey. *Archives of General Psychiatry, 53,* 159–168.

Maier, M. A., Bernier, A., Pekrun, R., Zimmermann, P., Strasser, K., & Grossmann, K. E. (2005). Attachment state of mind and perceptual processing of emotional stimuli. *Attachment & Human Development, 7,* 67–81.

Mailis-Gagnon, A., Giannoylis, I., Downar, J., Kwan, C. L., Mikulis, D. J., Crawley, A. P., et al. (2003). Altered central somatosensory processing in chronic pain patients with "hysterical" anesthesia. *Neurology, 13,* 1501–1507.

Main, M., & Solomon, J. (1986). Discovery of an insecure-disorganized/disoriented attachment pattern. In T. B. Brazelton & M. W. Yogman (Eds.), *Affective development in infancy* (pp. 95–124). Westport, CT: Ablex.

Malan, D. H. (1976). *The frontier of brief psychotherapy: An example of the convergence of research and clinical practice.* New York: Plenum Medical.

Malatesta, V. J., & Adams, H. E. (2001). Sexual dysfunctions. In P. B. Sutker & H. E. Adams (Eds.), *Comprehensive handbook of psychopathology* (3rd ed., pp. 713–748). New York: Academic/Plenum.

Maldonado, J. R., & Spiegel, D. (2001). Conversion disorder. In K. A. Phillips (Ed.), *Somatoform and factitious disorders* (pp. 95–128). Washington, DC: American Psychiatric Association.

Malik, M. L., & Beutler, L. E. (2002). The emergence of dissatisfaction with the DSM. In L. E. Beutler & M. L. Malik (Eds.), *Rethinking the DSM: A psychological perspective* (pp. 3–15). Washington, DC: American Psychological Association.

Malik, S., & Velazquez, J. (2002, July/August). Cultural competence and the "New Americans." *Children's Voice.* Retrieved September 1, 2005, from http://www.cwla.org/articles/default.htm

Malkoff-Schwartz, S., Frank, E., et al. (1998). Stressful life events and social rhythm disruption in the onset of manic depressive bipolar episodes: A preliminary investigation. *Archives of General Psychiatry, 55,* 702–707.

Mancebo, M. C., Eisen, J. L., Grant, J. E., & Rasmussen, S. A. (2005). Obsessive compulsive personality disorder and obsessive compulsive disorder: Clinical characteristics, diagnostic difficulties, and treatment. *Annals of Clinical Psychiatry, 17,* 197–204.

Manfro, G. G., Otto, M. W., McArdle, E. T., Worthington III, J. J., Rosenbaum, J. F., &

Pollak, M. H. (1996). Relationship of antecedent stressful life events to childhood and family history of anxiety and the course of panic disorder. *Journal of Affective Disorders, 41,* 135–139.

Mannuzza, S., Klein, R. G., Abikoff, H., & Moulton, J. L., III. (2004). Significance of childhood conduct problems to later development of conduct disorder among children with ADHD: A prospective follow-up study. *Journal of Abnormal Child Psychology, 32,* 565–573.

Mantovani, A., Lisanby, S. H., Pieraccini, F., Ulivelli, M., Castrogiovanni, P., & Rossi, S. (2006). Repetitive transcranial magnetic stimulation (rTMS) in the treatment of obsessive-compulsive disorder (OCD) and Tourette's syndrome (TS). *International Journal of Neuropsychopharmacology, 9,* 95–100.

Maramba, G. G., & Hall, G. C. N. (2002). Meta-analyses of ethnic match as a predictor of dropout, utilization, and level of functioning. *Cultural Diversity and Ethnic Minority Psychology, 8,* 290–297.

Maramba, G. G., & Nagayama Hall, G. C. (2002). Meta-analyses of ethnic match as a predictor of dropout, utilization, and level of functioning. *Cultural Diversity & Ethnic Minority Psychology, 8,* 290–297.

Marano, H. E. (2003). Bedfellows: Insomnia and depression. *Psychology Today,* July/August, n.p. Retrieved May 4, 2007, from http://psychologytoday.com/articles/pto-20030715-000001.html

Marazziti, D., Dell'Osso, L., Presta, S., Pfanner, C., Rossi, A., Masala, I., et al. (1999). Platelet [3H]paroxetine binding in patients with OCD-related disorders. *Psychiatry Research, 89,* 223–228.

Marcus, S. M., Young, E. A., Kerber, K. B., Kornstein, S., Farabaugh, A. H., Mitchell, J., et al. (2005). Gender differences in depression: Findings from the STAR*D study. *Journal of Affective Disorders, 87,* 141–150.

Marder, S. R., Davis, J. M., & Chouinard, G. (1997). The effects of risperidone on the five dimensions of schizophrenia derived by factor analysis: Combined results of the North American trials. *Journal of Clinical Psychiatry, 58,* 538–546.

Marengo, J. T., Harrow, M., Lannin-Kettering, I.B., & Wilson, A. (1985). The assessment of bizarre-idiosyncratic thinking: A manual for scoring responses to verbal tests. In M. Harrow & D. Quinlan (Eds.), *Disordered thinking and schizophrenic psychopathology* (pp. 394–449). New York: Gardner Press.

Margraf, J., Ehlers, A., Roth, W. T., Clark, D. B, Sheikh, J., Agras, W. S., et al. (1991). How "blind" are double-blind studies? *Journal of Consulting and Clinical Psychology, 59,* 184–187.

Maric, N., Krabbendam, L., Vollebergh, W., de Graaf, R., & van Os, J. (in press). Sex differences in symptoms of psychosis in a non-selected, general population sample. *Schizophrenia Research*, n.p.

Marino, C., Citterio, A., Giorda, R., Facoetti, A., Menozzi, G., Vanzin, L., et al. (2007). Association of short-term memory with a variant within DYX1C1 in developmental dyslexia. *Genes, Brain & Behavior, 6*, 640–646.

Maris, R. W. (2002). Suicide. *The Lancet, 360*, 319–326.

Markowitsch, H. J. (1999). Functional neuroimaging correlates of functional amnesia. *Memory, 7*, 561–583.

Markowitsch, H. J., Fink, G. R., Thöne, A., Kessler, J., & Heiss, W.-D. (1997). A PET study of persistent psychogenic amnesia covering the whole life span. *Cognitive Neuropsychiatry, 22*, 135–158.

Markowitz, J. C. (2005). Interpersonal therapy. In J. M. Oldham, A. E. Skodol, & D. S. Bender (Eds.). *The American Psychiatric Publishing textbook of personality disorders* (pp. 321–334). Washington, DC: American Psychiatric Publishing.

Markowitz, J. C., Skodol, A. E., & Bleiberg, K. (2006). Interpersonal psychotherapy for borderline personality disorder: Possible mechanisms of change. *Journal of Clinical Psychology, 62*, 431–444.

Markowitz, J. C., Skodol, A. E., Petkova, E., Xie, H., Cheng, J., Hellerstein, D. J., et al. (2005). Longitudinal comparison of depressive personality disorder and dysthymic disorder. *Comprehensive Psychiatry, 46*, 239–245.

Marks, I. M. (1969). *Fears and phobias*. New York: Academic Press.

Marks, I., Lovell, K., Noshirvani, H., Livanou, M., & Thrasher, S. (1998). Treatment of posttraumatic stress disorder by exposure and/or cognitive restructuring: A controlled study. *Archives of General Psychiatry, 55*, 317–325.

Marlatt, G. A., & Gordon, J. R. (Eds.). (1985). *Relapse prevention: Maintenance strategies in the treatment of addictive behaviors*. New York: Guilford Press.

Marsella, A., Friedman, M., & Spain, E. (1996). Ethnocultural aspects of posttraumatic stress disorder: An overview of issues and research directions. In A. Marsella, M. Friedman, E. Gerrity, & R. Scurfield (Eds.), *Ethnocultural aspects of posttraumatic stress disorder: Issues, research, and clinical applications* (pp. 105–130). Washington, DC: American Psychological Association.

Marshall, C. R., Harcourt-Brown, S., Ramus, F., & van der Lely, H. K. (2008). The link between prosody and language skills in children with specific language impairment (SLI) and/or dyslexia. *International Journal of Language Communication Disorders, 23*, 1–23.

Marshall, J. C., Halligan, P. W., Fink, G. R., Wade, D. T., & Frackowiak, R. S. (1997). The functional anatomy of a hysterical paralysis. *Cognition, 64*, B1–B8.

Marshall, M., Lewis, S., Lockwood, A., Drake, R., Jones, P., & Croudace, T. (2005). Association between duration of untreated psychosis and outcome in cohorts of first-episode patients. *Archives of General Psychiatry, 62*, 975–983.

Marshall, R. D., Schneier, F. R., Lin, S., Simpson, H. B., Vermes, D., & Leibowitz, M. (2000). Childhood trauma and dissociative symptoms in panic disorder. *American Journal of Psychiatry, 157*, 451–453.

Marshall, R. D., Spitzer, R., & Liebowitz, M. R. (1999). Review and critique of the new DSM-IV diagnosis of acute stress disorder. *American Journal of Psychiatry, 156*, 1677–1685.

Marshall, W. L. (1997). Pedophilia: Psychopathology and theory. In D. R. Laws, & W. T. O'Donohue (Eds.), *Sexual deviance: Theory, assessment, and treatment.* (pp. 152–174). New York: Guilford Press.

Marshall, W. L., O'sullivan, C., & Fernandez, Y. M. (1996). The enhancement of victim empathy among incarcerated child molesters. *Legal and Criminological Psychology, 1*, 95–102.

Marteinsdottir, I., Tillfors, M., Furmark, T., Anderberg, U. M., & Ekselius, L. (2003). Personality dimensions measured by the Temperament and Character Inventory (TCI) in subjects with social phobia. *Nordic Journal of Psychiatry, 57*, 29–35.

Marten, P. A., Brown, T. A., Barlow, D. H., Borkovec, T. D., Shear, M. K., & Lydiard, R. B. (1993). Evaluation of the ratings comprising the associated symptom criterion of DSM-III-R generalized anxiety disorder. *Journal of Nervous and Mental Disease, 181*, 676–682.

Martens, W. H. J. (2005). Multidimensional model of trauma and correlated antisocial personality disorder. *Journal of Loss & Trauma, 10*, 115–129.

Martin, D. (2002, January 25). Edith Bouvier Beale, 84, "Little Edie," Dies. *The New York Times*, p. A20.

Martin, D. J., Garske, J. P., & Davis, M. K. (2000). Relationship of alliance with outcome and other variables. *Journal of Consulting and Clinical Psychology, 68*, 438–450.

Martin, N. C., Levy, F., Pieka, J., & Hay, D. A. (2006). A genetic study of attention deficit hyperactivity disorder, conduct disorder, oppositional defiant disorder and reading disability: Aetiological overlaps and implications. *International Journal of Disability, Development and Education, 53*, 21–34.

Martin-Soelch, C. (2009). Is depression associated with dysfunction of the central reward system? Biochemical Society Transactions, 37(Pt 1), 313–317.

Martinez, C., Rietbrock, S., Wise, L., Ashby, D., Chick, J., Moseley, J., et al. (2005). Antidepressant treatment and the risk of fatal and non-fatal self harm in first episode depression: nested case-control study. *British Medical Journal, 330*, 389–393.

Martínez-Arán, A., Vieta, E., Colom, F., Reinares, M., Benabarre, A., Gasto, C., & Salamero, Met al. (2000). Cognitive dysfunctions in bipolar disorder: Evidence of neuropsychological disturbances. *Psychotherapy & Psychosomatics, 69*, 2–18.

Martínez-Arán, A., Vieta, E., Colom, F., Torrent, C., Reinares, M., Goikolea, J. M., Benabarre, A., et al. (2005). Do cognitive complaints in euthymic bipolar patients reflect objective cognitive impairment? *Psychotherapy and Psychosomatics, 74*, 295–302.

Martorano, J. T. (1984). The psychological treatment of Anna O. In M. Rosenbaum & M. Muroff (Eds.), *Anna O.: Fourteen contemporary reinterpretations* (pp. 85–100). New York: Free Press.

Maslach, C. (2003). Job burnout: New directions in research and intervention. *Current Directions in Psychological Science, 12*, 189–192.

Maslow, A. H. (1968). *Toward a psychology of being* (2nd ed.). Oxford, England: D. Van Nostrand.

Masters, W. H., & Johnson, V. E. (1966). *Human sexual response*. Oxford, England: Little, Brown.

Masters, W. H., & Johnson, V. E. (1970). *Human sexual inadequacy*. New York: Bantam Books.

Mataix-Cols, D., do Rosario-Campos, M. C., & Leckman, J. F. (2005). A multidimensional model of obsessive-compulsive disorder. *American Journal of Psychiatry, 162*, 228–238.

Mather, C. (2005). Accusations of genital theft: A case from northern Ghana. *Culture, Medicine and Psychiatry, 29*, 33–52.

Mathew, S. J., Coplan, J. D., & Gorman, J. M. (2001). Neurobiological mechanisms of social anxiety disorder. *American Journal of Psychiatry, 158*, 1558–1567.

Mathews, A., Mogg, K., May, J., & Eysenck, M. (1989). Implicit and explicit memory bias in anxiety. *Journal of Abnormal Psychology, 98*, 236–240.

Mathews, M., Basily, B., & Mathews, M. (2006). Better outcomes for schizophrenia in non-Western countries. *Psychiatric Services, 57*, 143–144.

Matijevic, T., Knezevic, J., Slavica, M., & Pavelic, J. (2009). Rett syndrome: From the gene to the disease. *European Neurology, 61,* 3–10.

Matson, J. L., Minshawi, N. F., Gonzalez, M. L., & Mayville, S. B. (2006). Relationship of comorbid problem behaviors to social skills in persons with profound mental retardation. *Behavior Modification, 30,* 496–506.

Matsunaga, H., Maebayashi, K., Hayashida, K., Okino, K., Matsui, T., Iketani, T., et al. (2007). Symptom structure in Japanese patients with obsessive-compulsive disorder. *American Journal of Psychiatry, 165,* 251–253.

Matt, G. E., Vazquez, C., & Campbell, W. K. (1992). Mood-congruent recall of affectively toned stimuli: A meta-analytic review. *Clinical Psychology Review, 12,* 227–255.

Maughan, B., & Rutter, M. (2001). Antisocial children grown up. In J. Hill & B. Maughan (Eds.), *Conduct disorders in childhood and adolescence* (pp. 507–552). New York: Cambridge University Press.

Maurer, K. (2001). Overview of the oestrogen protection hypothesis in schizophrenia 2001 [abstract S47]. *Archives of Women's Mental Health, 3(suppl 2),* 12.

Maurer, K., & Häfner, H. (1995). Methodological aspects of onset assessment in schizophrenia. *Schizophrenia Research, 15,* 265–276.

Mauro, T. (2007, January 4). Rehnquist FBI File sheds new light on drug dependence, confirmation battles. *Legal Times.* Retrieved August 1, 2007, from http://www.law.com/jsp/law/LawArticleFriendly.jsp?id=1167818524831

Mausner-Dorsch, H., & Eaton, W. W. (2000). Psychosocial work environment and depression: Epidemiologic assessment of the demand-control model. *American Journal of Public Health, 90,* 1765–1770.

Mayer, P., & Ziaian, T. (2002). Suicide, gender, and age variations in India: Are women in Indian society protected from suicide? *Crisis, 23,* 98–103.

Mayou, R., & Farmer, A. (2002). Functional somatic symptoms and syndromes. *British Medical Journal, 325,* 265–268.

Mayou, R., Kirmayer, L. J., Simon, G., Kroenke, K., & Sharpe, M. (2005). Somatoform disorders: Time for a new approach in DSM-V. *American Journal of Psychiatry, 162,* 847–855.

Mays, V. M., & Cochran, S. D. (2001). Mental health correlates of perceived discrimination among lesbian, gay, and bisexual adults in the United States. *American Journal of Public Health, 91,* 1869–1876.

Maysles, A. (Director). (2006). *The Beales of Grey Gardens.* Available from The Criterion Collection, New York, NY.

Maysles, D. (Director/Producer), & Maysles, A. (Director/Producer). (1976). *Grey Gardens* [Motion picture]. (Available from The Criterion Collection, Irvington, NY)

McAnulty, R. D., Adams, H. E., & Dillon, J. (2001). Sexual deviations: Paraphilias. In P. B. Sutker & H. E. Adams (Eds.), *Comprehensive handbook of psychopathology* (3rd ed., pp. 749–773). New York: Academic/Plenum.

McArthur, J. C., Haughey, N., Gartner, S., Conant, K., Pardo, C., Nath, A., et al. (2003). Human immunodeficiency virus-associated dementia: An evolving disease. *Journal of Neurovirology, 9,* 205–221.

McBride, W. J., Murphy, J. M., Lumeng, L., & Li, T.-K. (1990). Serotonin, dopamine and GABA involvement in alcohol drinking of selectively bred rats. *Alcohol, 7,* 199–205.

McCabe, M. P., & Ricciardelli, L. A. (2001a). Body image and body change techniques among young adolescent boys. *European Eating Disorders Review, 9,* 335–347.

McCabe, M. P., & Ricciardelli, L. A. (2001b). Parent, peer and media influences on body image and strategies to both increase and decrease body size among adolescent boys and girls. *Adolescence, 36,* 225–240.

McCabe, O. L. (2004). Crossing the quality chasm in behavioral health care: The role of evidence-based practice. *Professional Psychology: Research & Practice, 35,* 571–579.

McCandliss, B., Cohen, L., & Dehaene, S. (2003). The visual word form area: Expertise in reading in the fusiform gyrus. *Trends in Cognitive Sciences, 7,* 293–299.

McCook, A. (2002, October 8). More suicide deaths in high altitude U.S. states. *Reuters-Health.* Retrieved November 4, 2002, from http://www.nlm.nih.gov/medlineplus/news/fullstory_9779.html

McDermott, E., & de Silva, P. (2005). Impaired neuronal glucose uptake in pathogenesis of schizophrenia—can GLUT 1 and GLUT 3 deficits explain imaging, post-mortem and pharmacological findings? *Medical Hypotheses, 65,* 1076–1081.

McDermott, S., Moran, R., Platt, T., Issac, T., Wood, H., & Dasari, S. (2005). Depression in adults with disabilities, in primary care. *Disability and Rehabilitation: An International, Multidisciplinary Journal, 27,* 117–123. McElawin, J. & Paisner, D. (2008). *The Game of My Life.* New York: New American Library.

McElroy, S. L., Altshuler, L. L., Suppes, T., Keck, P. E., Jr., Frye, M. A., Denicoff, K. D., Nolen, W. A., Kupka, R. W., Leverich, G. S., Rochussen, J. R., Rush, A. J., & Post, R. M. (2001). Axis I psychiatric comorbidity and its relationship to historical illness variables in 288 patients with bipolar disorder. *American Journal of Psychiatry, 158,* 420–426.

McElroy, S. L., Casuto, L. S., Nelson, E. B., Lake, K. A., Soutullo, C. A., Keck, P. E., Jr., & Hudson, J. I. (2000). Placebo-controlled trial of sertraline in the treatment of binge eating disorder. *American Journal of Psychiatry, 157,* 1004–1006.

McEvoy, . M., Mahoney, A., Perini, S. J., & Kingsep, P. (in press). Changes in post-event processing and metacognitions during cognitive behavioral group therapy for social phobia. *Journal of Anxiety Disorders, np.*

McEvoy, J. P., Lieberman, J. A., Perkins, D. A., Hamer, R. M., Gu, H., Lazarus, A., Sweitzer, D., Olexy, C., Weiden, P., & Strakowski, S. D. (2007). Efficacy and tolerability of olanzapine, quetiapine, and risperidone in the treatment of early psychosis: A randomized, double-blind 52-week comparison. *American Journal of Psychiatry, 164,* 1050–1060.

McEvoy, J. P., Lieberman, J. A., Stroup, T. S., Rosenheck, R., Swartz, M. S., Perkins, D. O., et al. (for the CATIE Investigators). (2006). Effectiveness of clozapine versus olanzapine, quetiapine, and risperidone in patients with chronic schizophrenia who did not respond to prior atypical antipsychotic treatment. *American Journal of Psychiatry, 163,* 600–612.

McEwen, B. S. (2001). Commentary on PTSD discussion. *Hippocampus, 11,* 82–84.

McFarlane, A. C., Atchison, M., & Yehuda, R. (1997). The acute stress response following motor vehicle accidents and its relations to PTSD. *Annals of the New York Academy of Science, 821,* 437–441.

McGlashan, T. H., & Fenton, W. S. (1993). Subtype progression and pathophysiologic deterioration in early schizophrenia. *Schizophrenia Bulletin, 19,* 71–84.

McGlashan, T. H., & Hoffman, R. E. (2000). Schizophrenia as a disorder of developmentally reduced synaptic connectivity. *Archives of General Psychiatry, 57,* 637–648.

McGlashan, T. H., Grilo, C. M., Skodol, A. E., Gunderson, J. G., Shea, M. T., Morey, L. C., Zanarini, M. C., & Stout, R. L. (2000). The Collaborative Longitudinal Personality Disorders Study: Baseline Axis I/II and II/II diagnostic co-occurrence. *Acta Psychiatrica Scandinavica, 102,* 256–264.

McGoldrick, M., Giordano, J., & Pearce, J. K. (Eds.). (1996). *Ethnicity and family therapy* (2nd ed.). New York: Guilford Press.

McGorry, P. (2001). Early psychosis—gender aspects of treatment. Presentation at 1st World Congress on Women's Mental Health, March 27–31, Berlin, Germany.

McGorry, P. D., & Edwards, J. (2002). Response to "The prevention of schizophrenia: What interventions are safe and effective?" *Schizophrenia Bulletin, 28,* 177–180.

McGorry, P. D., Yung, A. R., Phillips, L. J., Yuen, H. P., Francey, S., Cosgrave, E. M., Dominic, D., Bravin, J., McDonald, T., Blair, A., Adlard, S., & Jackson, H. (2002). Randomized controlled trial of interventions designed to reduce the risk of progression to first-episode psychosis in a clinical sample with subthreshold symptoms. *Archives of General Psychiatry, 59,* 921–928.

McGough, J. J., & Barkley, R. A. (2004). Diagnostic controversies in adult attention deficit hyperactivity disorder. *American Journal of Psychiatry, 161,* 1948–1956.

McGough, J. J., & McCracken, J. T. (2006). Adult attention deficit hyperactivity disorder: Moving beyond DSM-IV. *American Journal of Psychiatry, 163,* 1673–1675.

McGowin, D. (1993). *Living in the labyrinth: A personal journal through the maze of Alzheimer's.* New York: Delacorte Press.

McGowin, D. F. (1993). *Living in the Labyrinth: A Personal Journey Through the Maze of Alzheimer's.* San Francisco: Elder Press.

McGrath, J. J. (2006). Variations in the incidence of schizophrenia: Data versus dogma. *Schizophrenia Bulletin, 32,* 195–197.

McGrath, P. J., Stewart, J. W., Quitkin, F. M., Chen, Y., Alpert, J. E., Nierenberg, A. A., et al. (2006). Predictors of relapse in a prospective study of fluoxetine treatment of major depression. *American Journal of Psychiatry, 163,* 1542–1548.

McGue, M., & Iacono, W. G. (2005). The association of early adolescent problem behavior with adult psychopathology. *American Journal of Psychiatry, 162,* 1118–1124.

McGue, M., Pickens, R. W., & Svikis, D. S. (1992). Sex and age effects on the inheritance of alcohol problems: A twin study. *Journal of Abnormal Psychology, 101,* 3–17.

McGuffin, P., Katz, R., Aldrich, J., & Bebbington, P. (1988). The Camberwell Collaborative Depression Study. II. Investigation of family members. *British Journal of Psychiatry, 152,* 766–774.

McGuffin, P., Rijsdijk, F., Andrew, M., Sham, P., Katz, R., & Cardno, A. (2003). The heritability of bipolar affective disorder and the genetic relationship to unipolar depression. *Archives of General Psychiatry, 60,* 497–502.

McGurk, S. R., Twamley, E. W., Sitzer, D. I., McHugo, G. J., & Mueser, K. T. (2007). A meta-analysis of cognitive remediation in schizophrenia. *American Journal of Psychiatry, 164,* 1791–1802.

McHugh, P. (1993). Multiple personality disorder. *Harvard Medical School Mental Health Letter, 10,* 4–6.

McHugh, P. R., & Treisman, G. (2007). PTSD: A problematic diagnostic category. *Journal of Anxiety Disorders, 21,* 211–222.

McInerney, R. J., & Kerns, K. A. (2003). Time reproduction in children with ADHD: Motivation matters. *Child Neuropsychology, 9,* 91–108.

McIntosh, J. L. (2003). *U.S.A. suicide: Official final data 2001.* Retrieved January 19, 2004, from http://www.suicidology.org/associations/1045/files/2001datapg.pdf

McIntosh, V. V. W., Jordan, J., Carter, F. A., Luty, S. E., McKenzie, J. M., Bulik, C. M., Frampton, C. M. A., & Joyce, P. R. (2005). Three psychotherapies for anorexia nervosa: A randomized, controlled trial. *American Journal of Psychiatry, 162,* 741–747.

McKay, D., & Neziroglu, F. (1996). Social skills training in a case of obsessive-compulsive disorder with schizotypal personality disorder. *Journal of Behavior Therapy and Experimental Psychiatry, 27,* 189–194.

McKendrick, K., Sullivan, C., Banks, S., & Sacks, S. (2007). Modified therapeutic community treatment for offenders with MICA disorders: Antisocial personality disorder and treatment outcomes. *Journal of Offender Rehabilitation, 44,* 133–159.

McKenna, K. (2004). *Talk to her: Interview.* Seattle, WA: Fantagraphics Books.

McLeod, D. S., Koenen, K. C., Meyer, J. M., Lyons, M. J., Eisen, S., True, W., et al. (2001). Genetic and environmental influences on the relationship among combat exposure, posttraumatic stress disorder symptoms, and alcohol use. *Journal of Traumatic Stress, 14,* 259–275.

McMullin, R. E. (1986). *Handbook of cognitive therapy techniques.* New York: Norton.

McNally, R. J. (1994). *Panic disorder: A critical analysis.* New York: Guilford Press.

McNally, R. J. (2002). On nonassociative fear emergence. *Behaviour Research and Therapy, 40,* 169–172.

McNally, R. J. (2003) Progress and controversy in the study of posttraumatic stress disorder. *Annual Review of Psychology, 54,* 229–252.

McNally, R. J. (2007). Can we solve the mysteries of the National Vietnam Veterans Readjustment Study? *Journal of Anxiety Disorders, 21,* 192–200.

McNally, R. J., & Kohlbeck, P. A. (1993). Reality monitoring in obsessive-compulsive disorder. *Behaviour Research and Therapy, 31,* 249–253.

McNally, R. J., & Shin, L. M. (1995). Association of intelligence with severity of posttraumatic stress disorder symptoms in Vietnam combat veterans. *American Journal of Psychiatry, 152,* 936–938.

McNally, R. J., Lasko, N. B., Macklin, M. L., & Pitman, R. K. (1995). Autobiographical memory disturbance in combat-related posttraumatic stress disorder. *Behaviour Research and Therapy, 33,* 619–630.

McNamara, B., Ray, J. L., Arthurs, O. J., & Boniface S. (2001). Transcranial magnetic stimulation for depression and other psychiatric disorders. *Psychological Medicine, 31,* 1141–1146.

McNeil, T. F., Cantor-Graae, E., & Weinberger, D. R. (2000). Relationship of obstetric complications and differences in size of brain structures in monozygotic twin pairs discordant for schizophrenia. *American Journal of Psychiatry, 157,* 203–212.

McNiel, D. E., & Binder, R. L. (2007). Effectiveness of a mental health court in reducing criminal recidivism and violence. *American Journal of Psychiatry, 164,* 1395–1403.

McQuiston, J. T. (1995, February 17). Commuter killing trial goes to jury: Ferguson gives incoherent summation. *Houston Chronicle,* p. A2.

McRae, A. L., Budney, A. J., & Brady, K. T. (2003). Treatment of marijuana dependence: A review of the literature. *Journal of Substance Abuse Treatment, 24,* 369–376.

Meana, J. J., Barturen, F., & Garcia-Sevilla, J. J. (1992). 1a$_2$-Adrenoceptors in the brain of suicide victims: Increased receptor density associated with major depression. *Biological Psychiatry, 31,* 471–490.

Meana, J. J., Barturen, F., & Garcia-Sevilla, J. J. (1992). 1a-sub-2-Adrenoceptors in the brain of suicide victims: Increased receptor density associated with major depression. *Biological Psychiatry, 31,* 471–490.

Meares, R., Mendelsohn, F. A., & Milgrom-Friedman, J. (1981). A sex difference in the seasonal variation of suicide rate: A single cycle for men, two cycles for women. *British Journal of Psychiatry, 138,* 321–325.

Medford, N., Brierley, B., Brammer, M., Bullmore, E. T., David, A. S., & Phillips, M. L. (2006). Emotional memory in depersonalization disorder: A functional MRI study. *Psychiatry Research, 148,* 93–102.

Mednick, S. A., Gabrielli, W. F., & Hutchings, B. (1984). Genetic influences in criminal convictions: Evidence from an adoption cohort. *Science, 224,* 891–894.

Mednick, S. A., Watson, J. B., Huttunen, M., Cannon, T. D., Katila, H., Machon, R., et al. (1998). A two-hit working model of the etiology of schizophrenia. In M. F. Lenzenweger & R. H. Dworkin (Eds.), *Origins and development of schizophrenia: Advances in experimental psychopathology* (pp. 27–66). Washington, DC: American Psychological Association.

Meehl, P. (1960). The cognitive activity of the clinician. *American Psychologist, 15,* 19–27.

Meehl, P. E. (1962). Schizotaxia, schizotypy, schizophrenia. *American Psychologist, 12,* 827–838.

Mehler, P. S. (2001). Diagnosis and care of patients with anorexia nervosa in primary care settings. *Annals of Internal Medicine, 134,* 1048–1059.

Mehler, P. S. (2003). Osteoporosis in anorexia nervosa: Prevention and treatment. *International Journal of Eating Disorders, 33,* 113–126.

Mehta, M. M., Moriarty, K. J., Proctor, D., Bird, M., & Darling, W. (2006). Alcohol misuse in older people: Heavy consumption and protean presentations. *Journal of Epidemiology & Community Health, 60,* 1048–1052.

Melartin, T. K., Rytsälä, H. J., Leskelä, U. S., Lestelä-Mielonen, P. S., Sokero, T. P., & Isometsä, E. T. (2004). Severity and comorbidity predict episode duration and recurrence of DSM-IV major depressive disorder. *Journal of Clinical Psychiatry, 65,* 810–819.

Melfi, C., Croghan, T., Hanna, M., & Robinson, R. (2000). Racial variation in antidepressant treatment in a Medicaid population. *Journal of Clinical Psychiatry, 61,* 16–21.

Melinder, M. R., & Barch, D. M. (2003). The influence of a working memory load manipulation on language production in schizophrenia. *Schizophrenia Bulletin, 29,* 473–485.

Mellon, M. W., & McGrath, M. L. (2000). Empirically supported treatments in pediatric psychology: Nocturnal enuresis. *Journal of Pediatric Psychology, 25,* 193–214.

Meloy, J. R. (1988). *The psychopathic mind: Origins, dynamics, and treatment.* Northvale, NJ: Aronson.

Mendez, M. F., & Cummings, J. L. (2004). Neuropsychiatric aspects of aphasia. In S. C. Yudofsky & R. E. Hales (Eds.), *Essentials of neuropsychiatry and clinical neurosciences* (pp. 189–200). Arlington, VA: American Psychiatric Publishing.

Mennin, D. S., Turk, C. L., Heimberg, R. G., & Carmin, C. (2004). Regulation of emotion in generalized anxiety disorder. In M. A. Reinecke & D. A. Clark (Eds.), *Cognitive therapy across the lifespan: Evidence and practice* (pp. 60–89). New York: Cambridge University Press.

Menzies, R. G., & Clarke, J. C. (1993a). The etiology of childhood water phobia. *Behaviour Research and Therapy, 31,* 499–501.

Menzies, R. G., & Clarke, J. C. (1993b). The etiology of fear of heights and its relationship to severity and individual response patterns. *Behaviour Research and Therapy, 31,* 355–365.

Menzies, R. G., & Clarke, J. C. (1995a). The etiology of phobias: A nonassociative account. *Clinical Psychology Review, 15,* 23–48.

Menzies, R. G., & Clarke, J. C. (1995b). The etiology of acrophobia and its relationship to severity and individual response patterns. *Behaviour Research and Therapy, 33,* 795–803.

Menzies, R. G., & Parker, L. (2001). The origins of height fear: An evaluation of neoconditioning explanations. *Behaviour Research and Therapy, 39,* 185–199.

Mercer, C. H., Fenton, K. A., Johnson, A. M., Wellings, K., Macdowall, W., McManus, S., et al. (2003). Sexual function problems and help seeking behaviour in Britain: National probability sample survey. *British Medical Journal, 327,* 426–427.

Merckelbach, H., Devilly, G. J., & Rassin, E. (2002). Alters in dissociative identity disorder: Metaphors or genuine entities? *Clinical Psychology Review, 22,* 481–497.

Merikangas, K. R., Akiskal, H. S., Angst, J., Greenberg, P. E., Hirschfeld, R. M. A., Petukhova, M., et al. (2007). Lifetime and 12-month prevalence of bipolar spectrum disorder in the National Comorbidity Survey Replication. *Archives of General Psychiatry, 64,* 543–552.

Merskey, H. (2004). Somatization, hysteria, or incompletely explained symptoms? *Canadian Journal of Psychiatry, 49,* 649–651.

Messer, S. B. (1992). A critical examination of belief structures in integrative and eclectic psychotherapy. In J. C. Norcross & M. R. Goldfried (Eds.), *Handbook of psychotherapy integration* (pp. 130–165). New York: Basic Books.

Messer, S. B. (2003). Introduction to the special issue on assimilative integration. *Journal of Psychotherapy Integration, 11,* 1–4.

Messer, S. B. (2004). Evidence-based practice: Beyond empirically supported treatments. *Professional Psychology: Research & Practice, 35,* 580–588.

Messer, S. B., & Wampold, B. E. (2002). Let's face facts: Common factors are more potent than specific therapy ingredients. *Clinical Psychology: Science and Practice, 9,* 21–25.

Messias, E., & Kirkpatrick, B. (2001). Summer birth and deficit schizophrenia in the Epidemiological Catchment Area study. *Journal of Nervous and Mental Disease, 189,* 608–612.

Meston, C. M., Hull, E., Levin, R. J., & Sipski, M. (2004). Disorders of orgasm in women. *Journal of Sexual Medicine, 1,* 66–68.

Metalsky, G. I., Joiner, T. E., Hardin, T. S., & Abramson, L. Y. (1993). Depressive reactions to failure in a naturalistic setting: A test of the hopelessness and self-esteem

theories of depression. *Journal of Abnormal Psychology, 102,* 101–109.

Meyer, B. (2002). Personality and mood correlates of avoidant personality disorder. *Journal of Personality Disorders, 16,* 174–188.

Meyer, G. J. (2002). Exploring possible ethnic differences and bias in the Rorschach Comprehensive System. *Journal of Personality Assessment, 78,* 104–129.

Meyer, G. J. (2002). Implications of information-gathering methods for a refined taxonomy of psychopathology. In L. E. Beutler & M. L. Malik (Eds.), *Rethinking the DSM: A psychological perspective* (pp. 69–105). Washington, DC: American Psychological Association.

Meyer, G. J., & Archer, R. P. (2001). The hard science of Rorschach research: What do we know and where do we go? *Psychological Assessment, 13,* 486–502.

Meyer, J. A., Mundy, P. C., van Hecke, A. V., & Durocher, J. S. (2006). Social attribution processes and comorbid psychiatric symptoms in children with Asperger syndrome. *Autism, 10,* 383–402.

Meyer, R. G., & Weaver, C. M. (2006). *Law and mental health: A case-based approach.* New York: Guilford Press.

Mezey, G. & Robbins, I. (2001). Usefulness and validity of post-traumatic stress disorder as a psychiatric category. *British Medical Journal, 323,* 561–563.

Mezulis, A. H., Abramson, L. Y., Hyde, J. S., & Hankin, B. L. (2004). Is there a universal positivity bias in attributions? A meta-analytic review of individual, developmental, and cultural differences in the self-serving attributional bias. *Psychological Bulletin, 130,* 711–747.

Micallef, J., & Blin, O. (2001). Neurobiology and clinical pharmacology of obsessive-compulsive disorder. *Clinical Neuropharmacology, 24,* 191–207.

Michael, N., Erfrth, A., Ohrmann, P., Gössling, M., Arold, V., Heindel, W., et al. (2003). Acute mania is accompanied by elevated glutamate/glutamine levels within the left dorsolateral prefrontal cortex. *Psychopharmacology, 168,* 344–346.

Middleton, K. L., Willner, J., & Simmons, K. M. (2002). Natural disasters and post-traumatic stress disorder symptom complex: Evidence from the Oklahoma tornado outbreak. *International Journal of Stress Management, 9,* 229–236.

Midence, K., & Hargreaves, I. (1997). Psychosocial adjustment in male-to-female transsexuals: An overview of the research evidence. *Journal of Psychology: Interdisciplinary and Applied, 131,* 602–614.

Miethe, T. D., Lu, H., & Reese, E. (2000). Reintegrative shaming and recidivism risk in drug court: Explanations for some unexpected findings. *Crime and Delinquency, 46,* 522–541.

Mikkelsen, E. J. (2001). Enuresis and encopresis: Ten years of progress. *Journal of the American Academy of Child & Adolescent Psychiatry, 40,* 1146–1158.

Miklowitz, D. J. (2004). The role of family systems in severe and recurrent psychiatric disorders: A developmental psychopathology view. *Development and Psychopathology, 16,* 667–688.

Miklowitz, D. J. (2008). Adjunctive psychotherapy for bipolar disorders: State of the evidence. *American Journal of Psychiatry, 165,* 1408–1419.

Miklowitz, D. J., George, E. L., Richards, J. A., Simoneau, T. L., & Suddath, R. L. (2003). A randomized study of family-focused psychoeducation and pharmacotherapy in the outpatient management of bipolar disorder. *Archives of General Psychiatry, 60,* 904–912.

Miklowitz, D. J., Goldstein, M. J., Nuechterlein, K. H., Snyder, K. S., & Mintz, J. (1988). Family factors and the course of bipolar affective disorder. *Archives of General Psychiatry, 45,* 225–231.

Miklowitz, D. J., Otto, M. W., Frank, E., Reilly-Harrington, N. A., Kogan, J. N., Sachs, G. S., et al. (2007). Intensive psychosocial intervention enhances functioning in patients with bipolar depression: Results from a 9-month randomized controlled trial. *American Journal of Psychiatry, 164,* 1340–1347.

Miklowitz, D. J., Simoneau, T. L., George, E. L., Richards, J. A., Kalbag, A., Sachs-Ericsson, N., et al. (2000). Family-focused treatment of bipolar disorder: 1-year effects of a psychoeducational programme in conjunction with pharmacotherapy. *Biological Psychiatry 48,* 582–592.

Mikton, C., & Grounds, A. (2007). Cross-cultural clinical judgment bias in personality disorder diagnosis by forensic psychiatrists in the UK: A case-vignette study. *Journal of Personality Disorders, 21,* 400–417.

Mikulincer, M. (1994). *Human learned helplessness: A coping perspective.* New York: Plenum Press.

Milak, M. S., Parsey, R. V., Keilp, J., Oquendo, M. A., Malone, K. M., & Mann, J. J. (2005). Neuroanatomic correlates of psychopathologic components of major depressive disorder. *Archives of General Psychiatry, 62,* 397–408.

Milich, R. (1994). The response of children with ADHD to failure: If at first you don't succeed, do you try, try, again? *School Psychology Review, 23,* 11–18.

Miller, J. J., Fletcher, K., & Kabat-Zinn, J. (1995). Three-year follow-up and clinical implications of a mindfulness meditation-based stress reduction intervention in the treatment of anxiety disorders. *General Hospital Psychiatry, 17,* 192–200.

Miller, J. L., Schmidt, L. A., Vaillancourt, T., McDougall, P., & Laliberte, M. (2006). Neuroticism and introversion: A risky combination for disordered eating among a non-clinical sample of undergraduate women. *Eating Behaviors, 7,* 69–78.

Miller, M. (2002). Resilience elements in students with learning disabilities. *Journal of Clinical Psychology, 58,* 291–298.

Miller, R., & Mason, S. E. (2002). *Diagnosis: Schizophrenia.* New York: Columbia University Press.

Miller, W. R. (2001). Motivational enhancement therapy: Description of counseling approach. In J. J. Boren, L. S. Onken, & K. M. Carroll (Eds.), *Approaches to drug abuse counseling* (pp. 89–93). Bethesda, MD: National Institute on Drug Abuse. Available at http://www.dualdiagnosis.org/library/nida_00-4151/8.html

Miller, W. R., & Rollnick, S. (1992). *Motivational interviewing* (2nd ed.). New York: Guilford Press.

Miller, W. R., & Seligman, M. E. (1973). Depression and the perception of reinforcement. *Journal of Abnormal Psychology, 82,* 62–73.

Miller, W. R., & Seligman, M. E. (1975). Depression and learned helplessness in man. *Journal of Abnormal Psychology, 84,* 228–238.

Miller, W. R., & Seligman, M. E. (1975). Depression and learned helplessness in man. *Journal of Abnormal Psychology, 84,* 228–238.

Millet, B., Leclaire, M., Bourdel, M. C., Loo, H., Tezcan, E., & Kuloglu, M. (2000). Comparison of sociodemographic, clinical and phenomenological characteristics of Turkish and French patients suffering from obsessive-compulsive disorder. *Canadian Journal of Psychiatry, 45,* 848.

Millon, T. (1981). *Disorders of personality, DSM-III: Axis II.* New York: Wiley.

Millon, T. (1998). DSM-IV narcissistic personality disorder: Historical reflections and future directions. In E. Ronningstam (Ed.), *Disorders of narcissism: Diagnostic, clinical, and empirical implications* (pp. 75–101). Washington, DC: American Psychiatric Press.

Millon, T., & Davis, R. D. (2000). *Personality disorders in modern life.* New York: Wiley.

Mills, T. C., Paul, J., Stall, R., Pollack, L., Canchola, J., Chang, Y. J., Moskowitz, J. T., & Catania, J. A. (2004). Distress and depression in men who have sex with men: The Urban Men's Health Study. *American Journal of Psychiatry, 161,* 278–285.

Mills, T. C., Paul, J., Stall, R., Pollack, L., Canchola, J., Chang, Y. J., et al. (2004). Distress and depression in men who have sex with men: The Urban Men's Health Study. *American Journal of Psychiatry, 161,* 278–285.

Milos, G., Spindler, A., Ruggiero, G., Klaghofer, R., & Schnyder, U. (2002). Comorbidity of obsessive-compulsive disorders and duration of eating disorders. *International Journal of Eating Disorders, 31,* 284–289.

Minde, K. (2003). Assessment and treatment of attachment disorders. *Current Opinion in Psychiatry, 16,* 377–381.

Mineka, S., & Zinbarg, R. (1995). Conditioning and ethological models of social phobia. In R. G. Heimberg, M. R. Liebowitz, D. A. Hope, & F. R. Schneier (Eds.), *Social phobia: Diagnosis, assessment, and treatment* (pp. 134–162). New York: Guilford Press.

Mineka, S., & Zinbarg, R. (1995). Conditioning and ethological models of social phobia. In R. G. Heimberg, M. R. Liebowitz, D. A. Hope, & F. R. Schneier (Eds.), *Social phobia: Diagnosis, assessment, and treatment* (pp. 134–162). New York: Guilford Press.

Mineka, S., Cook, M., & Miller, S. (1984). Fear conditioned with escapable and inescapable shock: Effects of a feedback stimulus. *Journal of Experimental Psychology: Animal Behavior Processes, 10,* 307–323.

Mineka, S., Watson, D., & Clark, L. A. (1998). Comorbidity of anxiety and unipolar mood disorders. *Annual Review of Psychology, 49,* 377–412.

Miniño, A. M., Arias, E., Kochanek, K. D., Murphy, S. L., & Smith, B. L. (2002). Deaths: Final data for 2000. *National Vital Statistics Reports, 50*(15). Hyattsville, MD: National Center for Health Statistics.

Minshew, N. J., & Williams, D. L. (2007). The new neurobiology of autism: Cortex, connectivity, and neuronal organization. *Archives of Neurology, 64,* 945–950.

Mintz, A. R., Dobson, K. S., & Romney, D. M. (2003). Insight in schizophrenia: A meta-analysis. *Schizophrenia Research, 61,* 75–88.

Minuchin, S. (1974). *Families and family therapy.* Cambridge, MA: Harvard University Press.

Minuchin, S., Rosman, B. L., & Baker, L. (1978). *Psychosomatic families: Anorexia nervosa in context.* Oxford, England: Harvard University Press.

Miranda, J., Azocar, F., Organista, K. C., Dwyer, E., & Areane, P. (2003). Treatment of depression among impoverished primary care patients from ethnic minority groups. *Psychiatric Services, 54,* 219–225.

Miranda, J., Azocar, F., Organista, K., Dwyer, E., & Arean, P. (2000). Treatment of depression in disadvantaged medical patients. Presented at the tenth NIMH international conference on Mental Health Problems in the General Health Care Sector. Bethesda, Maryland.

Miranda, J., Azocar, F., Organista, K., Dwyer, E., & Areane, P. (2003). Treatment of depression among impoverished primary care patients from ethnic minority groups. *Psychiatric Services, 54*, 219–225.

Mirsky, A. F., & Quinn, O. W. (1988). The Genain quadruplets. *Schizophrenia Bulletin, 14*, 595–612.

Mirsky, A. F., Bieliauskas, L. A., French, L. M., Van Kammen, D. P., Joensson, E., & Sedvall, G. (2000). A 39-year followup on the Genain quadruplets. *Schizophrenia Bulletin, 26*, 699–708.

Mirsky, A., F., Quinn, O. W., DeLisi, L. E., Schwerdt, P., & Buchsbaum, M. S. (1987). The Genain quadruplets: A 25-year follow-up of four monozygous women discordant for the severity of schizophrenic illness. In N. E. Miller & G. D. Cohen (Eds.), *Schizophrenia and aging: Schizophrenia, paranoia, and schizophreniform disorders in later life* (pp. 83–94). New York: Guilford Press.

Misra, S., & Ganzini, L. (2004). Capacity to consent to research among patients with bipolar disorder. *Journal of Affective Disorders, 80*, 115–123.

Mitchell, A. J. (2007). Understanding medication discontinuation in depression. *Psychiatric Times, 24*. Retrieved October 20, 2008, fromhttp://www.psychiatrictimes.com/display/article/10168/54731

Mitchell, J. E., Peterson, C. B., Myers, T., & Wonderlich, S. (2001). Combining pharmacotherapy and psychotherapy in the treatment of patients with eating disorders. *Psychiatric Clinics of North America, 24*, 315–323.

Mittal, V. A., Neumann, C., Saczawa, M., & Walker, E. F. (2008). Longitudinal progression of movement abnormalities in relation to psychotic symptoms in adolescents at high risk of schizophrenia. *Archives of General Psychiatry, 65*, 165–171.

Mittendorfer-Rutz, E., Rasmussen, F., & Wasserman, D. (2004). Restricted fetal growth and adverse maternal psychosocial and socioeconomic conditions as risk factors for suicidal behaviour of offspring: A cohort study. *Lancet, 364*, 1135–1140.

Mittleman, M. A., Lewis, R. A., Maclure, M., Sherwood, J. B., & Muller, J. E. (2001). Triggering myocardial infarction by marijuana. *Circulation, 103*, 2805–2809.

Miura, Y., Mizuno, M., Yamashita, C., Watanabe, K., Murakami, M., & Kashima, H. (2004). Expressed emotion and social functioning in chronic schizophrenia. *Comprehensive Psychiatry, 45*, 469–474.

Modell, J. G., Mountz, J. M., Curtis, G. C., & Greden, J. F. (1989). Neurophysiologic dysfunction in basal ganglia/limbic striatal and thalamocortical circuits as a pathogenetic mechanism of obsessive-compulsive disorder. *Journal of Neuropsychiatry & Clinical Neurosciences, 1*, 27–36.

Modell, S., Huber, J., Holsboer, F., & Lauer, C. J. (2003). The Munich Vulnerability Study on Affective Disorders: Risk factors for unipolarity versus bipolarity. *Journal of Affective Disorders, 74*, 173–184.

Moffitt, T. E. (2003). Life-course-persistent and adolescence-limited antisocial behavior: A 10-year research review and a research agenda. In B. B. Lahey, T. E. Moffitt, & A. Caspi (Eds.), *Causes of conduct disorder and juvenile delinquency* (pp. 49–75). New York: Guilford Press.

Moffitt, T. E., & Caspi, A. (2001). Childhood predictors differentiate life-course persistent and adolescence-limited antisocial pathways among males and females. *Development and Psychopathology, 13*, 355–375.

Moffitt, T. E., Caspi, A., Harrington, H., & Milne, B. J. (2002). Males on the life-course-persistent and adolescence-limited antisocial pathways: Follow-up at age 26 years. *Development and Psychopathology, 14*, 179–207.

Moffitt, T. E., Caspi, A., Harrington, H., Milne, B. J., Melchior, M., Goldberg, D., & et al. (2007). Generalized anxiety disorder and depression: Childhood risk factors in a birth cohort followed to age 32. *Psychological Medicine, 37*, 441–452.

Mogg, K., & Bradley, B. P. (2005). Attentional bias in generalized anxiety disorder versus depressive disorder. *Cognitive Therapy and Research, 29*, 29–45.

Mogg, K., Bradley, B. P., & Williams, R. (1995). Attentional bias in anxiety and depression: The role of awareness. *British Journal of Clinical Psychology, 34*, 17–36.

Mogg, K., Millar, N., & Bradley, B. P. (2000). Biases in eye movements to threatening facial expressions in generalized anxiety disorder and depressive disorder. *Journal of Abnormal Psychology, 109*, 695–704.

Mogg, K., Millar, N., & Bradley, B. (2000). Biases in eye movements to threatening facial expressions in generalized anxiety disorder and depressive disorder. *Journal of Abnormal Psychology, 109*, 695–704.

Mohr, D. C., Hart, S. L., Julian, L., Catledge, C., Honos-Webb, L., Vella, L., et al. (2005). Telephone-administered psychotherapy for depression. *Archives of General Psychiatry, 62*, 1007–1014.

Molfese, D. L. (2000). Predicting dyslexia at 8 years of age using neonatal brain responses. *Brain and Language, 72*, 238–245.

Monahan, J., Steadman, H., Silver, E., Appelbaum, P. S., Robbins, P. C., Mulvey, E. P., et al. (2001). *Rethinking risk assessment: The MacArthur study of mental disorder and violence.* New York: Oxford University Press.

Moncrieff, J. (2001). Are antidepressants overrated? A review of methodological problems in antidepressant trials. *Journal of Nervous and Mental Disease, 189*, 288–295.

Moncrieff, J. (2002). The antidepressant debate. *British Journal of Psychiatry, 180*, 193–194.

Moncrieff, J., & Kirsch, I. (2005). Efficacy of antidepressants in adults. *British Medical Journal, 331*, 155–157.

Moncrieff, J., Wessely, S., & Hardy, R. (2001). Antidepressants using active placebos. *Cochrane Database Systematic Review, 2*, CD003012.

Mond, J. M., Hay, P. J., Rodgers, B., & Owen, C. (2006). An update on the definition of "excessive exercise" in eating disorders research. *International Journal of Eating Disorders, 39*, 147–153.

Monk, C. S., Nelson, E. E., McClure, E. B., Mogg, K., Bradley, B. P., Leibenluft, E., et al. (2006). Ventrolateral prefrontal cortex activation and attentional bias in response to angry faces in adolescents with generalized anxiety disorder. *American Journal of Psychiatry, 163*, 1091–1097.

Monroe, S. M., & Simons, A. D. (1991). Diathesis-stress theories in the context of life-stress research: Implications for the depressive disorders. *Psychological Bulletin, 110*, 406–425.

Monroe, S. M., Rohde, P., Seeley, J. R., & Lewinsohn, P. M. (1999). Life events and depression in adolescence: Relationship loss as a prospective risk factor for first onset of major depressive disorder. *Journal of Abnormal Psychology, 108*, 606–661.

Montgomery, S. A., Schatzberg, A. F., Guelfi, J. D., Kasper, S., Nemeroff, C., Swann, A., et al. (2001). Pharmacotherapy of depression and mixed states in bipolar disorder. *Journal of Affective Disorders, 59*(Suppl. 1), S39–S56.

Monti, P. M., Abrams, D. B., Kadden, R. M., & Cooney, N. L. (1989). *Treating alcohol dependence: A coping skills training guide in the treatment of alcoholism.* New York: Guilford Press.

Moore, C. (2006). *George & Sam: Two boys, One family, and autism.* New York: St. Martin's Press.

Moore, T. H. M., Zammit, S., Lingford-Hughest, A., Barnes, T. R. E., Jones, P. B., Burke, M., et al. (2007). Cannabis use and risk of psychotic or affective mental health outcomes: A systematic review. *Lancet, 370,* 319–328.

Moos, R. H., & Moos, B. S. (2004). Long-term influence of duration and frequency of participation in Alcoholics Anonymous on individuals with alcohol use disorders. *Journal of Consulting and Clinical Psychology, 72,* 81–90.

Moos, R. H., & Timko, C. (2008). Outcome research on 12-step and other self-help programs. In M. Galanter & H. D. Kleber (Eds.), *The American Psychiatric Publishing textbook of substance abuse treatment* (4th ed., pp. 511–521). Arlington, VA: American Psychiatric Publishing.

Moos, R., & Moos, B. (1986). *Family Environment Scale Manual* (2nd ed.). Palo Alto, CA: Consulting Psychologists Press.

Moradi, B., Dirks, D., & Matteson, A. V. (2005). Roles of sexual objectification experiences and internalization of standards of beauty in eating disorder symptomatology: A test and extension of objectification theory. *Journal of Counseling Psychology, 52,* 420–428.

Moran, P. (1999). The epidemiology of antisocial personality disorder. *Social Psychiatry and Psychiatric Epidemiology, 34,* 231–242.

Morey, L. C., Alexander, G. M., & Boggs, C. (2005). Gender. In J. M. Oldham, A. E. Skodol, & D. S. Bender (Eds.), *The American Psychiatric Publishing textbook of personality disorders* (pp. 541–559). Washington, DC: American Psychiatric Publishing.

Morey, L. C., Warner, M. B., Shea, M. T., Gunderson, J. G., Sanislow, C. A., Grilo, C., et al. (2003). The representation of four personality disorders by the schedule for nonadaptive and adaptive personality dimensional model of personality. *Psychological Assessment, 15,* 326–332.

Morey, R. A., Inan, S., Mitchell, T. V., Perkins, D. O., Lieberman, J. A., & Belger, A. (2005). Imaging frontostriatal function in ultra-high-risk, early, and chronic schizophrenia during executive processing. *Archives of General Psychiatry, 62,* 254–262.

Morgan, C. D., & Murray, H. A. (1935). A method for investigating fantasies: The Thematic Apperception Test. *Archives of Neurological Psychiatry, 34,* 289–306.

Morgan, J. F., & Crisp, A. H. (2000). Use of leukotomy for intractable anorexia nervosa: A long-term follow-up study. *International Journal of Eating Disorders, 27,* 249–258.

Moritz, S., & Woodward, T. S. (2006). The contribution of metamemory deficits to schizophrenia. *Journal of Abnormal Psychology, 115,* 15–25.

Morris, N. (1986). *Insanity defense* (National Institute of Justice Crime File Study Guide).

Washington, DC: U.S. Department of Justice, National Institute of Justice/Criminal Justice Reference Service.

Mort, J. R., & Aparasu, R. R. (2002). Prescribing of psychotropics in the elderly: Why is it so often inappropriate? *CNS Drugs, 16,* 99–109.

Mörtberg, E., Karlsson, A., Fyring, C., & Sundin, Ö. (2006). Intensive cognitive-behavioral group treatment (CBGT) of social phobia: A randomized controlled study. *Journal of Anxiety Disorders, 20,* 646–660.

Mortensen, P. B., Pedersen, C. B., Westergaard, T., Wohlfahrt, J., Ewald, H., Mors, O., et al. (1999). Effects of family history and place and season of birth on the risk of schizophrenia. *New England Journal of Medicine, 340,* 603–608.

Moscicki, E. (2001). Epidemiology of suicide. In S. Goldsmith(Ed.), *Risk factors for suicide* (pp. 1–4). Washington, DC: National Academy Press.

Moscicki, E. K. (1995). Epidemiology of suicidal behavior. In M. M. Silverman & R. W. Maris (Eds.), *Suicide prevention: Toward the year 2000* (pp. 22–35). New York: Guilford Press.

Moscicki, E. K. (1997). Identification of suicide risk factors using epidemiologic studies. *Psychiatric Clinics of North America, 20,* 499–517.

Moser, C. (2001). Paraphilia: A critique of a confused concept. In P. J. Kleinplatz (Ed.), *New directions in sex therapy: Innovations and alternatives* (pp. 91–108). Philadelphia: Taylor and Rutledge.

Moser, C. (2009). When is an unusual sexual interest a mental disorder? *Archives of Sexual Behavior, 38,* 323–325.

Moser, C., & Kleinplatz, P. J. (2005). DSM-IV-TR and the paraphilias: An argument for removal. *Journal of Psychology & Human Sexuality, 17,* 91–109.

Mosher, P. W., & Swire, P. P. (2002). The ethical and legal implications of Jaffee v. Redmond and the HIPAA medical privacy rule for psychotherapy and general psychiatry. *Psychiatric Clinics of North America, 25,* 575–584.

Moussaoui, D., el Kadiri, M. Agoub, M., Tazi, I., & Kadri, N. (1999). Depression, suicidal ideation and schizophrenia. *Encephale, 25,* 9–11.

Mowrer, O. H. (1939). A stimulus-response analysis of anxiety and its role as a reinforcing agent. *Psychological Review, 46,* 553–565.

Mowrer, O. H. (1947). On the dual nature of learning: A re-interpretation of "conditioning" and "problem-solving." *Harvard Educational Review, 17,* 102–148.

Moyers, T. (2003). Motivational interviewing. In J. L. Sorensen, R. A. Rawson, J. Guydish, & J. E. Zweben (Eds.),

Drug abuse treatment through collaboration: Practice and research partnerships that work (pp. 139–150). Washington, DC: American Psychological Association.

Moynihan, R. (2003). The making of a disease: Female sexual dysfunction. *British Medical Journal, 326,* 45–47.

Mrazek, P., & Haggerty, R. (1994). *Reducing risks for mental disorders: Frontiers for preventive intervention research.* Washington, DC: National Academy Press.

Mrug, S., Hoza, B., Gerdes, A. C., Hinshaw, S., Arnold, L. E., Hechtman, L., et al. (2009). Discriminating between children with ADHD and classmates using peer variables. *Journal of Attention Disorders, 12,* 372–380.

Mueser, K. T., Bond, G. R., Drake, R. E., & Resnick, S. G. (1998). Models of community care for severe mental illness: A review of research on case management. *Schizophrenia Bulletin, 24,* 37–74.

Mueser, K. T., Goodman, L. B., Trumbetta, S. L., Rosenberg, S. D., Osher, F. C., Vidaver, R., et al. (1998). Trauma and posttraumatic stress disorder in severe mental illness. *Journal of Consulting and Clinical Psychology, 66,* 493–499.

Muhle, R., Trentacoste, S. V., & Rapin, I. (2004). The genetics of autism. *Pediatrics, 113,* e472–e486.

Muir, S. L., Wertheim, E. H., & Paxton, S. J. (1999). Adolescent girls' first diets: Triggers and the role of multiple dimensions of self-concept. *Eating Disorders: The Journal of Treatment & Prevention, 7,* 259–227.

Mulas, F., Capilla, A., Fernández, S., Etchepareborda, M. C., Campo, P., Maestú, F., et al. (2006). Shifting-related brain magnetic activity in attention-deficit/hyperactivity disorder. *Biological Psychiatry, 59,* 373–379.

Mulder, R. T., & Joyce, P. R. (1997). Temperament and the structure of personality disorder symptoms. *Psychological Medicine, 27,* 99–106.

Mulholland, A. M., & Mintz, L. B. (2001). Prevalence of eating disorders among African American women. *Journal of Counseling Psychology, 48,* 111–116.

Mullen, R. (2003). The problem of bizarre delusions. *Journal of Nervous and Mental Disease, 191,* 546–548.

Muller, J., & Roberts, J. E. (2005). Memory and attention in obsessive-compulsive disorder: A review. *Journal of Anxiety Disorders, 19,* 1–28.

Muller, N., & Schwarz, M. (2006). Schizophrenia as an inflammation-mediated dysbalance of glutamatergic neurotransmission. *Neurotox Research, 10,* 131–148.

Müller, T., Mannel, M., Murck, H., & Rahlfs, V. W. (2004). Treatment of somatoform disorders with St. John's wort: A randomized, double-blind and placebo-controlled trial. *Psychosomatic Medicine, 66,* 538–547.

Mulvany, F., O'Callaghan, E., Takei, N., Byrne, M., Fearon, P., & Larkin, C. (2001). Effect of social class at birth on risk and presentation of schizophrenia: Case-control study. *BMJ: British Medical Journal, 323,* 1398–1401.

Munafò, M. R., Clark, T. G., Roberts, K. H., & Johnstone, E. C. (2006). Neuroticism mediates the association of the serotonin transporter gene with lifetime major depression. *Neuropsychobiology, 53,* 1–8.

Mundo, E., Richter, M. A., Sam, F., Macciardi, F., & Kennedy, J. L. (2000). Is the 5-HT-sub(1Dß) receptor gene implicated in the pathogenesis of obsessive-compulsive disorder? *American Journal of Psychiatry, 157,* 1160–1161.

Mundo, E., Walker, M., Tims, H., Macciardi, F., & Kennedy, J. L. (2000). Lack of linkage disequilibrium between serotonin transporter protein gene (SLC6A4) and bipolar disorder. *American Journal of Medical Genetics, 96,* 379–383.

Munroe, R. L. & Gauvain, M. (2001). Why the paraphilias? Domesticating strange sex. *Cross-Cultural Research: The Journal of Comparative Social Science, 35,* 44–64.

Murias, M. A., Webb, S. J., Merkle, K., Greenson, J., & Dawson, G. (2006, October 14). Spontaneous EEG coherence in adults with autism. Poster presented at *Neuroscience 2006* Georgia World Congress Center..

Murphy, L. J., & Mitchell, D. L. (1998). When writing helps to heal: E-mail as therapy. *British Journal of Guidance and Counseling, 26,* 21–32

Murray, C. J. L., & Lopez, A. D. (Eds.). (1996). *The global burden of disease. A comprehensive assessment of mortality and disability from diseases, injuries, and risk factors in 1990 and projected to 2020.* Cambridge, MA: Harvard School of Public Health.

Murray, H. A. (1943). *Thematic Apperception Test manual.* Cambridge, MA: Harvard University Press.

Murray, L. A., Whitehouse, W. G., & Alloy, L. B. (1999). Mood congruence and depressive deficits in memory: A forced-recall analysis. *Memory, 7,* 175–196.

Myers, J. E. B. (1998). Legal issues in child abuse and neglect practice. Thousand Oaks, CA: Sage.

Myin-Germeys, I., Delespaul, P. A. E. G., & deVries, M. W. (2000). Schizophrenia patients are more emotionally active than is assumed based on their behavior. *Schizophrenia Bulletin, 26,* 847–853.

Nahas, Z., Kozel, F. A., Li, X., Anderson, B., & George, M. S. (2003). Left prefrontal transcranial magnetic stimulation (TMS) treatment of depression in bipolar affective disorder: A pilot study of acute safety and efficacy. *Bipolar Disorders, 5,* 40–47.

Nahas, Z., Kozel, F. A., Li, X., Anderson, B., George, M. S. (2003). Left prefrontal transcranial magnetic stimulation (TMS) treatment of depression in bipolar affective disorder: A pilot study of acute safety and efficacy. *Bipolar Disorders, 5,* 40–47.

Nathan, P. E., Skinstad, A. H., & Dolan, S. L. (2000). Clinical psychology II. Psychological treatments: Research and practice. In K. Pawlik & M.R. Rosenzweig (Eds.), *International handbook of psychology* (pp. 429–451). Thousand Oaks, CA: Sage Publications.

Nathan, P. E., Stuart, S. P., & Dolan, S. L. (2000). Research on psychotherapy efficacy and effectiveness: Between Scylla and Charybdis? *Psychological Bulletin, 126,* 964–981.

National Center for Health Statistics. (2008). *Diagnosed attention deficit hyperactivity disorder and learning disability: United States, 2004–2006.* DHHS Publication No. (PHS) 2008-1565, Series 10, No. 237. Retrieved on February 15, 2009, from http://www.cdc.gov/nchs/data/series/sr_10/sr10_237.pdf

National Committee for Quality Assurance. (2007). *The state of health care quality 2007.* Washington, DC: Author.

National Depressive and Manic Depressive Association. (2002). *Suicide prevention.* Retrieved Month 00, 200X, from http://www.ndmda.org/suicide.html

National Institute on Aging. (2003). *Alzheimer's disease: Unraveling the mystery.* NIH Pub. No: 02-3782. Retrieved December 4, 2007, from http://www.nia.nih.gov/NR/rdonlyres/A294D332-71A2-4866-BDD7-A0DF216DAAA4/0/Alzheimers_Disease_Unraveling_the_Mystery.pdf

National Institute on Alcohol Abuse and Alcoholism, National Advisory Council. (2004). NIAAA Council approves definition of binge drinking. *NIAAA Newsletter, 3.* Retrieved February 22, 2006, from http://pubs.niaaa.nih.gov/publications/Newsletter/winter2004/Newsletter_Number3.htm#council

National Institute on Alcohol Abuse and Alcoholism. (2005). What is alcoholism? Retrieved December 12, 2005, from http://www.niaaa.nih.gov/FAQs/General-English/FAQ1.htm

National Institute on Drug Abuse (2000). *The brain: Understanding neurobiology through the study of addiction.* [NIH Publication No. 00-4871]. Bethesda, MD: Author.

National Institute on Drug Abuse. (1999). *Principles of drug addiction treatment: A research-based guide* [NIH Publication No. 00-4180]. Bethesda, MD: Author.

National Institute on Drug Abuse. (2001). *NIDA research report series: Hallucinogens and dissociative drugs* [NIH Publication No. 01-4209]. Retrieved December 24, 2008, from http://www.drugabuse.gov/PDF/PODAT/PODAT.pdf

National Institute on Drug Abuse. (2003). *Drug use among racial/ethnic minorities* [NIH Publication No. 03-3888]. Bethesda, MD: Author.

National Institute on Drug Abuse. (2004). *NIDA research report series: Cocaine: Abuse and addiction* [NIH publication number 99-4342]. Bethesda, MD: Author.

National Institute on Drug Abuse. (2005a). *NIDA research report series: Heroin: Abuse and addiction* [NIH Publication No. 05-4165]. Bethesda, MD: Author.

National Institute on Drug Abuse. (2005b). *NIDA research report series: Marijuana abuse* [NIH publication number 05-3859]. Bethesda, MD: Author.

National Institute on Drug Abuse. (2005c). *NIDA research report series: Prescription drugs: Abuse and addiction* [NIH Publication No. 05-4881]. Bethesda, MD: Author.

National Institute on Drug Abuse. (2006a). NIDA InfoFacts: Costs to society. Retrieved March 12, 2009, from http://www.drugabuse.gov/Infofacts/costs.html

National Institute on Drug Abuse. (2006b). NIDA InfoFacts: Methylphenidate (Ritalin). Retrieved March 12, 2009, from www.drugabuse.gov/Infofacts/ADHD.html

National Institute on Drug Abuse. (2006c). NIDA research report series: Tobacco addiction [NIH Publication No. 06-4342]. Bethesda, MD: Author.

National Institute on Drug Abuse. (2007a). NIDA InfoFacts: Cigarettes and Other Tobacco Products. Retrieved on March 12, 2009, from http://www.drugabuse.gov/Infofacts/tobacco.html.

National Institute on Drug Abuse. (2007b). NIDA InfoFacts: Crack and cocaine. Retrieved March 12, 2009, from http://www.drugabuse.gov/Infofacts/cocaine.html.

National Institute on Drug Abuse. (2007c). NIDA InfoFacts: Heroin. Retrieved March 12, 2009, from http://www.drugabuse.gov/Infofacts/heroin.html.

National Institute on Drug Abuse. (2007d). NIDA InfoFacts: LSD. Retrieved March 12, 2009, from http://www.drugabuse.gov/pdf/infofacts/Hallucinogens08.pdf.

National Institute on Drug Abuse. (2007e). NIDA InfoFacts: MDMA (Ecstasy). Retrieved March 12, 2009, from http://www.drugabuse.gov/Infofacts/ecstasy.html

National Institute on Drug Abuse. (2007f). NIDA InfoFacts: PCP (Phencyclidine). Retrieved March 12, 2009, from http://www.drugabuse.gov/Infofacts/hallucinogens.html.

National Institute on Drug Abuse. (2007g). *The science of addiction: Drugs, brains, and behavior* [NIH Publication No. 07-5605]. Bethesda, MD: Author.

National Institute on Drug Abuse. (2008a). NIDA InfoFacts: Nationwide trends. Retrieved December 20, 2008, from http://www.drugabuse.gov/Infofacts/NationTrends08.pdf

National Institute on Drug Abuse. (2008b). NIDA InfoFacts: MDMA (Ecstasy). Retrieved December 20, 2008, from http://www.drugabuse.gov/PDF/Infofacts/MDMA08.pdf

National Institute on Drug Abuse. (2008c). NIDA InfoFacts: Methamphetamine. Retrieved December 20, 2008, from http://www.drugabuse.gov/Infofacts/methamphetamine.html

National Institute on Drug Abuse. (2008d). NIDA InfoFacts: Hallucinogens—LSD, peyote, psilocybin and PCP. Retrieved December 20, 2008, from http://www.drugabuse.gov/Infofacts/hallucinogens.html

National Institute on Drug Abuse. (2008e). InfoFacts: Prescription and over-the-counter medications. Retrieved December 23, 2008, from http://www.nida.nih.gov/PDF/Infofacts/PainMed08.pdf

National Institute on Drug Abuse. (2008f). NIDA InfoFacts: Treatment approaches for drug addiction. Retrieved December 24, 2008, from http://www.nida.nih.gov/PDF/InfoFacts/Treatment08.pdf

Nazareth, I., Boynton, P., & King, M. (2003). Problems with sexual function in people attending London general practitioners: Cross sectional study. *British Medical Journal, 327,* 423–426.

Neal-Barnett, A. M., & Smith Sr., J. (1997). African Americans. In S. Friedman (Ed.), *Cultural issues in the treatment of anxiety.* (pp. 154–174). New York: Guilford Press.

Neale, M. C., Walter, E. E., Eaves, L. J., Kessler, R. C., Heath, A. C., & Kendler, K. S. (1994). Genetics of blood-injury fears and phobias: A population-based twin study. *American Journal of Medical Genetics, 54,* 326–334.

Neale, T. (2008). ICAD: Biomarkers may help identify pre-clinical Alzheimer's. *Medscape.* Retrieved on July 31, 2008, from http://www.medpagetoday.com/MeetingCoverage/ICAD/tb/10323

Nebelkopf, E., & Phillips, M. (2004). *Healing and mentat health for Native Americans: Speaking in red.* Walnut Creek, CA: Altamira Press.

Neighbors, H. W., Trierweiler, S. J., Ford, B. C., & Muroff, J. R. (2003). Racial

differences in DSM diagnosis using a semi-structured instrument: The importance of clinical judgment in the diagnosis of African Americans. *Journal of Health & Social Behavior, 44,* 237–256.

Neighbors, H. W., Trierweiler, S. J., Ford, B. C., & Muroff, J. R. (2003). Racial differences in DSM-IV-TR diagnosis using a semi-structured instrument: The importance of clinical judgment in the diagnosis of African Americans. *Journal of Health & Social Behavior, 44,* 237–256.

Nelson, M. D., Saykin, A. J., Flashman, L. A., & Riordan, H. J. (1998). Hippocampal volume reduction in schizophrenia as assessed by magnetic resonance imaging: A meta-analytic study. *Archives of General Psychiatry, 55,* 433–440.

Nemeroff, C. (1998). The neurobiology of depression. *Scientific American, 278,* 28–35.

Nemeroff, C. B. (2008). Recent findings in the pathophysiology of depression. *Focus, 6,* 3–14.

Nemeroff, C. J., Stein, R. I., Diehl, N. S., & Smilack, K. M. (1994). From the Cleavers to the Clintons: Role choices and body orientation as reflected in magazine article content. *International Journal of Eating Disorders, 16,* 167–176.

Nestadt, G., Samuels, J., Riddle, M., Bienvenu, J., Liang, K-Y., LaBuda, M., et al. (2000). A family study of obsessive-compulsive disorder. *Archives of General Psychiatry, 57,* 358–363.

Nestler, E. J. (1997). Schizophrenia: An emerging pathophysiology. *Nature, 385,* 578–579.

Neuman, R. J., Lobos, E., Reich, W., Henderson, C. A., Sun, L. W., & Todd, R. D. (2007). Prenatal smoking exposure and dopaminergic genotypes interact to cause a severe ADHD subtype. *Biological Psychiatry, 61,* 1320–1328.

Neumann, C., & Walker, E. F. (1996). Childhood neuromotor soft signs, behavior problems, and adult psychopathology. In T. Ollendick & R. Prinz (Eds.), *Advances in clinical child psychology* (pp. 173–203). New York: Plenum Press.

Neumeister, A., Charney, D. S., & Drevets, W. C. (2005). Depression and the hippocampus. *American Journal of Psychiatry, 162,* 1057.

Neumeister, A., Wood, S., Bonne, O., Nugent, A. C., Luckenbaugh, D. A., Young, T., Bain, E. E., Charney, D. S., & Drevets, W. C. (2005). Reduced hippocampal volume in unmedicated, remitted patients with major depression versus control subjects. *Biological Psychiatry, 57,* 935–937.

New York Psychiatric Institute. (2006). Retrieved November 1, 2006, from http://nypisys.cpmc.columbia.edu/anxiety/PTSDCASE.HTM.

New, A. S., Hazlett, E. A., Buchsbaum, M. S., Goodman, M., Koenigsberg, H. W., & Iskander, L. (2003). M-CPP PET and impulsive aggression in borderline personality disorder. *Biological Psychiatry, 53,* 104S.

Newman, C. F., Leahy, R. L., Beck, A. T., Reilly-Harrington, N. A., & Gyulai, L. (2002). *Bipolar disorder: A cognitive therapy approach.* Washington, DC: American Psychological Association.

Newman, C.F., Leahy, R.L., Beck, A.T., Reilly-Harrington, N.A., & Gyulai, L., (2001). *Bipolar disorder: A cognitive therapy approach.* Washington, DC: American Psychological Association.

Newman, M. G., Kenardy, J., Herman, S., & Taylor, C. B. (1997). Comparison of palmtop-computer-assisted brief cognitive-behavioral treatment to cognitive behavioral treatment for panic disorder. *Journal of Consulting and Clinical Psychology, 65,* 178–183.

Newton, T. F., Roache, J. D., De La Garza II, R., Fong, T., Wallace, C. L., Li, S., Elkashef, A., Chiang, N., & Kahn, R. (2006). Bupropion reduces methamphetamine-induced subjective effects and cue-induced craving. *Neuropsychopharmacology, 31,* 1537–1544.

Nezu, C. M., Nezu, A. M., & Gill-Weiss, M. J. (1992). Psychopathology in persons with mental retardation: Clinical guidelines for assessment and treatment. Champaign, IL: Research Press.

Ng, C. H. (1997). The stigma of mental illness in Asian cultures. *Australian and New Zealand Journal of Psychiatry, 31,* 382–390.

Nguyen, H. H. (2006). Acculturation in the United States. In D. L. Sam & J. W. Berry (Eds.), *The Cambridge handbook of acculturation psychology* (pp. 311–330). New York: Cambridge University Press.

Nicdao, E. G., Hong, S., & Takeuchi, D. T. (2007). Prevalence and correlates of eating disorders among Asian Americans: Results from the National Latino and Asian American Study. *International Journal of Eating Disorders, 40,* S22–S26.

Nicholas, M., Obler, L., Albert, M., & Goodglass, H. (1985). Lexical retrieval in healthy aging. *Cortex, 21,* 595–606.

Nichols, M. (2000). Special populations. In S. R. Leiblum & R. C. Rosen (Eds.), *Principles and practice of sex therapy* (3rd ed., pp. 335–367). New York: Guilford Press.

Nickel, M. K., Muehlbacher, M., Nickel, C., Kettler, C., Gil, F. P., Bachler, E., Buschmann, W., Rother, N., Fartacek, R., Egger, C., Anvar, J., Rother, W. K., Loew, T. H., & Kaplan, P. (2006). Aripiprazole in the treatment of patients with borderline personality disorder: A double-blind, placebo-controlled study. *American Journal of Psychiatry, 163,* 833–838.

Nield, L. S., & Kamat, D. (2004). Enuresis: How to evaluate and treat. *Clinical Pediatrics, 43,* 409–415.

Nigg, J. T. (2006). Temperament and developmental psychopathology. *Journal of Child Psychology and Psychiatry, 47,* 395–422.

Nigg, J. T. (2006). *What causes ADHD? Toward a multi-path model for understanding what goes wrong and why.* New York: Guilford Press.

Nigg, J. T., & Goldsmith, H. H. (1994). Genetics of personality disorders: Perspectives from personality and psychopathology research. *Psychological Bulletin, 115,* 346–380.

Nigg, J. T., Hinshaw, S. P., & Huang-Pollock, C. (2006). Disorders of attention and impulse regulation. In D. Cicchetti & D. J. Cohen (Eds.), *Developmental psychopathology, Vol. 3: Risk, disorder, and adaptation* (2nd ed., pp. 358–403). Hoboken, NJ: John Wiley & Sons.

Nigg, J., Nikolas, M., Friderici, K., Park, L., & Zucker, R. A. (2007). Genotype and neuropsychological response inhibition as resilience promoters for attention-deficit/hyperactivity disorder, oppositional defiant disorder, and conduct disorder under conditions of psychosocial adversity. *Development and Psychopathology, 19,* 767–786.

Nitschke, J. B., Dixon, G. E., Sarinopoulos, I., Short, S. J., Cohen, J. D., Smith, E. E., et al. (2006). Altering expectancy dampens neural response to aversive taste in primary taste cortex. *Nature Neuroscience, 9,* 435–442.

Nobre, P. J., & Pinto-Gouveia, J. (2006). Dysfunctional sexual beliefs as vulnerability factors for sexual dysfunction. *Journal of Sex Research, 43,* 68–75.

Nock, M. K., Borges, G., Bromet, E. J., Alonso, J., Angermeyer, M., Beautrais, A., et al. (2008). Cross-national prevalence and risk factors for suicidal ideation, plans and attempts. *British Journal of Psychiatry, 192,* 98–105.

Nock, M. K., Kazdin, A. E., Hiripi, E., & Kessler, R. C. (2006). Prevalence, subtypes, and correlates of DSM-IV conduct disorder in the National Comorbidity Survey replication. *Psychological Medicine, 36,* 699–710.

Nolan, S. A., & Mineka, S. (1997, November). Verbal, nonverbal, and genderrelated factors in the interpersonal consequences of depression and anxiety. Presented at the annual meeting of the Association for the Advancement of Behavior Therapy, Miami Beach, FL.

Nolen-Hoeksema, S. (1987). Sex differences in unipolar depression: Evidence and theory. *Psychological Bulletin, 101,* 259–282.

Nolen-Hoeksema, S. (2000). The role of rumination in depressive disorders and mixed anxiety/depressive symptoms. *Journal of Abnormal Psychology, 109,* 504–511.

Nolen-Hoeksema, S. (2001). Gender differences in depression. *Current Directions in Psychological Science, 10,* 173–176.

Nolen-Hoeksema, S., & Girgus, J. (1994). The emergence of gender differences in depression during adolescence. *Psychological Bulletin, 115,* 424–443.

Nolen-Hoeksema, S., & Morrow, J. (1991). A prospective study of depression and posttraumatic stress symptoms after a natural disaster: The 1989 Loma Prieta earthquake. *Journal of Personality and Social Psychology, 61,* 115–121.

Nolen-Hoeksema, S., & Morrow, J. (1993). Effects of rumination and distraction on naturally occurring depressed mood. *Cognition & Emotion, 7,* 561–570.

Nomura, M., Kusumi, I., Kaneko, M., Masui, T., Daiguji, M., Ueno, T., Koyama, T., & Nomura, Y. (2006). Involvement of a polymorphism in the 5-HT2A receptor gene in impulsive behavior . *Psychopharmacology, 187,* 30–35.

Norberg, M. M., Krystal, J. H., & Tolin, D. F. (2008). A meta-analysis of D-cycloserine and the facilitation of fear extinction and exposure therapy. *Biological Psychiatry, 63,* 1118–1126.

Norcross, J. C., Hedges, M., & Castle, P. H. (2002). Psychologists conducting psychotherapy in 2001: A study of the Division 29 membership. *Psychotherapy: Theory, Research, Practice, Training, 39,* 97–102.

Norcross, J. C., Sayette, M. A., Mayne, T. J., Karg, R. S., & Turkson, M. A. (1998). Selecting a doctoral program in professional psychology: Some comparisons among PhD counseling, PhD clinical, and PsyD clinical psychology programs. *Professional Psychology: Research and Practice, 29,* 609–614.

Nordling, N., Sandnabba, N. K., & Santtila, P. (2000). The prevalence and effects of self-reported childhood sexual abuse among sadomasochistically oriented males and females. *Journal of Child Sexual Abuse, 9,* 53–63.

Norman, P. (1997). *Shout! The Beatles in their generation.* New York: Fireside.

Norman, R. M. G., Malla, A. K., McLean, T. S., McIntosh, E. M., Neufeld, R. W. J., Voruganitia, L. P., & Cortese, L. (2002). An evaluation of a stress management program for individuals with schizophrenia. *Schizophrenia Research, 58,* 293–303.

Norris, F. H., Murphy, A. D., Baker, C. K., Perilla, J. L., Rodriguez, F. G., & Rodriguez, J. D. J. G. (2003). Epidemiology of trauma and posttraumatic stress disorder in Mexico.

Journal of Abnormal Psychology, 112, 646–656.

Norris, F. H., Perilla, J. L., & Murphy, A. D. (2001). Postdisaster stress in the United States and Mexico: A cross-cultural test of the multicriterion conceptual model of posttraumatic stress disorder. *Journal of Abnormal Psychology, 110,* 553–563.

Nowinski, J. (2003). Self-help groups. In J. L. Sorensen, R. A. Rawson, J. Guydish & J. E. Zweben (Eds.). *Drug abuse treatment through collaboration: Practice and research partnerships that work* (pp. 55–70). Washington, DC: American Psychological Association.

Noyes, R., Jr., Happel, R. L., & Yagla, S. J. (1999). Correlates of hypochondriasis in a nonclinical population. *Psychosomatics, 40,* 461–469.

Noyes, R., Jr., Holt, C. S., Happel, R. L., Kathol, R. G., & Yagla, S. J. (1997). A family study of hypochondriasis. *Journal of Nervous and Mental Disorders, 185,* 223–232.

Noyes, R., Jr., Stuart, S. P., & Watson, D. B. (2008). A reconceptualization of the somatoform disorders. *Psychosomatics: Journal of Consultation Liaison Psychiatry, 49,* 14–22.

Nuechterlein, K. H. (1991). Vigilance in schizophrenia and related disorders. In S. R. Steinhauer, J. H. Gruzelier, & J. Zubin (Eds.), *Neuropsychology, psychophysiology, and information processing* (pp. 397–433). New York: Elsevier Science.

Nurnberger, J. I. Jr., Wiegand, R., Bucholz, K., O'Connor, S., Meyer, E. T., Reich, T., et al. (2004). A family study of alcohol dependence: Coaggregation of multiple disorders in relatives of alcohol-dependent probands. *Archives of General Psychiatry, 61,* 1246–1256.

Nutt, D. J. (2001). Neurobiological mechanisms in generalized anxiety disorder. *Journal of Clinical Psychiatry, 62,* 22–27.

Nutt, D. J. (2008). Relationship of neurotransmitters to the symptoms of major depressive disorder. Journal of Clinical Psychiatry, 69 (Suppl E1), 4–7.

Nutt, D., & Lawson, C. (1992). Panic attacks: A neurochemical overview of models and mechanisms. *British Journal of Psychiatry, 160,* 165–178.

Nutt, D., & Lawson, C. (1992). Panic attacks: A neurochemical overview of models and mechanisms. *British Journal of Psychiatry, 160,* 165–178.

O'Malley, P. G., Jackson, J. L., Santoro, J., Tomkins, G., Balden, E., & Kroenke, K. (1999). Antidepressant therapy for unexplained symptoms and symptom syndromes. *Journal of Family Practice, 48,* 980–990.

Oakland, T., Mpofu, E., Glasgow, K., & Jumel, B. (2003). Diagnosis and administrative interventions for students with mental retardation in Australia, France, United States, and Zimbabwe 98 years after Binet's first intelligence test. *International Journal of Testing, 3*, 59–75.

Oakley, D. A. (1999). Hypnosis and conversion hysteria: A unifying model. *Cognitive Neuropsychiatry, 4*, 243–265.

O'Brien, C. P. (2005). Anticraving medications for relapse prevention: A possible new class of psychoactive medications. *American Journal of Psychiatry, 162*, 1423–1431.

O'Brien, C. P., Volkow, N., & Li, T. (2006). What's in a word? Addiction versus dependence in DSM-V. *American Journal of Psychiatry, 163*, 764–765.

O'Connor v. Donaldson, 422 U.S. 563 (1975).

O'Connor, M. G., & Lafleche, G. (2006). Amnesic syndromes. In P. J. Snyder, P. D. Nussbaum, & D. L. Robins (Eds.), *Clinical neuropsychology: A pocket handbook for assessment* (2nd ed., pp. 463–488). Washington, DC: American Psychological Association.

O'Connor, R. C., Sheehy, N. P., & O'Connor, D. B.. (1999). A thematic analysis of suicide notes. *Crisis: The Journal of Crisis Intervention and Suicide Prevention, 20*, 106–114.

Odgers, C. L., Caspi, A., Nagin, D., Piquero, A. R., Slutske, W. S., Milne, B., Dickson, N., Poulton, R., & Moffitt, T. E. (2008). Is it important to prevent early exposure to drugs and alcohol among teens? *Psychological Science, 19*, 1037–1044.

Ofovwe, C. E., Ofovwe, G. E., & Meyer, A. (2006). The prevalence of attention-deficit/hyperactivity disorder among school-aged children in Benin City, Nigeria. *Journal of Child and Adolescent Mental Health, 18*, 1–5.

Ogawa, K., Miya, M., Watarai, A., Nakazawa, K. M., Yuasa, S., & Utena, H. (1987). A long-term follow up study of schizophrenia in Japan—with special reference to the course of social adjustment. *British Journal of Psychiatry, 151*, 758–765.

Ogden, C. A., Rich, M. E., Schork, N. J., Paulus, M. P., Geyer, M. A., Lohr, J. B., Kuczenski, R., & Niculescu, A. B. (2004). Candidate genes, pathways and mechanisms for bipolar (manic-depressive) and related disorders: An expanded convergent functional genomics approach. *Molecular Psychiatry, 9*, 1007–1029.

Ogloff, J. R. P. (2006). Psychopathy/antisocial personality disorder conundrum. *Australian and New Zealand Journal of Psychiatry, 40*, 519–528.

Ogloff, J. R. P. (2006). Psychopathy/antisocial personality disorder conundrum. *Australian and New Zealand Journal of Psychiatry, 40*, 519–528.

Ogloff, J. R., Wong, S., & Greenwood, A. (1990). Treating criminal psychopaths in a therapeutic community program. *Behavioral Sciences & the Law, 8*, 181–190.

Öhman, A. (1986). Face the beast and fear the face: Animal and social fears as prototypes for evolutionary analyses of emotion. *Psychophysiology, 23*, 123–145.

Öhman, A., Fredrikson, M., Hugdahl, K., & Rimmo, P.-A. (1976). The premise of equipotentiality in human classical conditioning: Conditioned electrodermal responses to potentially phobic stimuli. *Journal of Experimental Psychology: General, 105*, 313–337.

Okubo, Y., Suhara, T., Suzuki, K., Kobayashi, K., Inoue, O., Terasaki, O., Someya, Y., Sassa, T., Sudo, Y., Matsushima, E., Iyo, M., Tateno, Y., & Toru, M. (1997) Decreased prefrontal dopamine D1 receptors in schizophrenia revealed by PET. *Nature, 385*, 578–579.

Okubo, Y., Suhara, T., Suzuki, K., Kobayashi, K., Inoue, O., Terasaki, O., et al. (1997). Decreased prefrontal dopamine D1 receptors in schizophrenia revealed by PET. *Nature, 385*, 578–579.

olde Hartman, T. C., Borghuis, M. S., Lucassen, P. L. B. J., can de Laar, F. A., Speckens, A. E., & van Weel, C. (2009). Medically unexplained symptoms, somatization disorder, and hypochondriasis: Course and Progrnoisis. A systematic review. *Journal of Psychosomatic Research, 66*, 363–377.

Oldham, J. M. (2005). Personality disorders: Recent history and future directions. In J. M. Oldham, A. E. Skodol, & D. S. Bender (Eds.), *The American Psychiatric Publishing textbook of personality disorders* (pp. 3–16). Washington, DC: American Psychiatric Publishing.

Oldham, J. M., Skodol, A. E., Kellman, H. D., Hyler, S. E., Doidge, N., Rosnick, L., et al. (1995). Comorbidity of Axis I and Axis II disorders. *American Journal of Psychiatry, 152*, 571–578.

Olds, J., & Milner, P. (1954). Positive reinforcement produced by electrical stimulation of the septal area and other regions of rat brain. *Journal of Comparative and Physiological Psychology, 47*, 419–427.

Olino, T. M., Klein, D. N., Lewinsohn, P. M., Rohde, P., & Seeley, J. R. (2008). Longitudinal associations between depressive and anxiety disorders: A comparison of two trait models. *Psychological Medicine, 38*, 353–363.

Olivardia, R. (2007). Muscle dysmorphia: Characteristics, assessment, and treatment. In J. K. Thompson, J. Kevin, & G. Cafri (Eds.), *The muscular ideal: Psychological, social, and medical perspectives* (pp. 123–139). Washington, DC: American Psychological Association.

Olson, D. H., McCubbin, H. I., Barnes, H., Larsen, A., Muxen, M., & Wilson, M. (1985). *Family inventories*. St. Paul, MN: Family Social Science, University of Minnesota.

Olson, I.R., Page, K, Moore, K., Chatterjee, A., & Verfaellie, M. (2006). Working memory for conjunctions relies on the medial temporal lobe. *Journal of Neuroscience, 26*, 4596–4601.

Olson, R., Forsberg, H., Gayan, J., & DeFries, J. (1999). A behavioral-genetic analysis of reading disabilities and component processes. In R. Klein & P. McMullen (Eds.), *Converging methods for understanding reading and dyslexia* (pp. 133–153). Cambridge, MA: MIT Press.

O'Malley, P. M., Johnston, L. D., & Bachman, J. G. (1999). Epidemiology of substance abuse in adolescence. In P. J. Ott, R. E. Tarter, & R. T. Ammerman (Eds.), *Sourcebook on substance abuse: Etiology, epidemiology, assessment, and treatment* (pp. 14–31). Needham Heights, MA: Allyn & Bacon.

O'Malley, S. S., Jaffe, A. J., Chang, G., & Schottenfeld, R. S. (1992). Naltrexone and coping skills therapy for alcohol dependence: A controlled study. *Archives of General Psychiatry, 49*, 881–887.

Oniszcenko, W., Zawadzki, B., Strelau, J., Riemann, R., Angleitner, A., & Spinath, F. M. (2003). Genetic and environmental determinants of temperament: A comparative study based on Polish and German samples. *European Journal of Personality, 17*, 207–220.

Oniszczenko, W., & Dragan, W. L. (2005). Association between dopamine D4 receptor exon III polymorphism and emotional reactivity as a temperamental trait. *Twin Research and Human Genetics, 8*, 633–637.

Oosterbaan, D. B., van Balkom, A. J., van Boeijen, C. A., de Meij, T. G., & van Dyck, R. (2001). An open study of paroxetine in hypochondriasis. *Progress in Neuro-Psychopharmacology & Biological Psychiatry, 25*, 1023–1033.

Open Minds. (1999). Over 72% of insured Americans are enrolled in MBHOs: Magellan Behavioral Health continues to dominate the market. *Open Minds: The Behavioral Health and Social Service Industry Analyst, 11*, 9.

Oquendo, M. A., Baca-García, E., Mann, J., & Giner, J. (2008). Issues for DSM-V: Suicidal behavior as a separate diagnosis on a separate axis. *American Journal of Psychiatry, 165*, 1383–1384.

Oquendo, M. A., Bongiovi-Garcia, N. E., Galfalvy, H., Goldberg, P. H., Grunebaum, M. F., Burke, A. K., & Mann, J. J. (2007). Sex differences in clinical predictors of suicidal acts after major depression: A prospective study. *American Journal of Psychiatry, 164*, 134–141.

Orr, S. P., & Pitman, R. K. (1993). Psychophysiologic assessment of attempts to simulate posttraumatic stress disorder. *Biological Psychiatry, 33*, 127–129.

Orr, S. P., Metzger, L. J., & Pitman, R. K. (2002). Psychophysiology of post-traumatic stress disorder. *Psychiatric Clinics of North America, 25*, 271–293.

Orr, S. P., Pitman, R. K., Lasko, N. B., & Herz, L. R. (1993). Psychophysiological assessment of posttraumatic stress disorder imagery in World War II and Korean combat veterans. *Journal of Abnormal Psychology, 102*, 152–159.

Osborne, C. & Wise, T. (2005). Paraphilias. In R. Balon & T. Segraves (Eds.), *Handbook of sexual dysfunction*. Boca Raton, FL: Taylor & Francis.

Osmond, M., Wilkie, M., & Moore, J. (2001). *Behind the smile: My journey out of postpartum depression*. New York: Warner.

Öst, L. (1992). Blood and injection phobia: Background and cognitive, physiological, and behavioral variables. *Journal of Abnormal Psychology, 101*, 68–74.

Öst, L. G., Ferebee, I., & Furmark, T. (1997). One-session group therapy of spider phobia: Direct versus indirect treatments. *Behaviour Research & Therapy, 35*, 721–732.

Öst, L., Brandberg, M., & Alm, T. (1997). One versus five sessions of exposure in the treatment of flying phobia. *Behaviour Research and Therapy, 35*, 987–996.

Öst, L., Fellenius, J., & Sterner, U. (1991). Applied tension, exposure in vivo, and tension-only in the treatment of blood phobia. *Behaviour Research and Therapy, 29*, 561–574.

Öst, L., Salkovskis, P. M., & Hellström, K. (1991). One-session therapist-directed exposure vs. self-exposure in the treatment of spider phobia. *Behavior Therapy, 22*, 407–422.

Öst, L., Svensson, L., Hellström, K., & Lindwall, R. (2001). One-session treatment of specific phobias in youths: A randomized clinical trial. *Journal of Consulting and Clinical Psychology, 69*, 814–824.

Osuch, E. A., Benson, B. E., Luckenbaugh, D. A., Garaci, D. A., Post, R. M., & McCann, U. (2008). Repetitive TMS combined with exposure therapy for PTSD: a preliminary study. *Journal of Anxiety Disorders, 23*, 54–59.

Ott, S. L., Roberts, S., Rock, D., Allen, J., & Erlenmeyer-Kimling, L. (2002). Positive and negative thought disorder and psychopathology in childhood among subjects with adulthood schizophrenia. *Schizophrenia Research, 58*, 231–239.

Otte, C., Kellner, M., Arlt, J., Jahn, H., Holsboer, F., & Wiedemann, K. (2002). Prolactin but not ACTH increases during sodium lactate-induced panic attacks. *Psychiatry Research, 109*, 201–205.

Otto, M. W. (2002). The dose and delivery of psychotherapy: A commentary on Hansen et al. *Clinical Psychology: Science and Practice, 9*, 348–349.

Otto, M. W., Pollack, M. H., Sachs, G. S., O'Neil, C. A., & Rosenbaum, J. (1992). Alcohol dependence in panic disorder patients. *Journal of Psychiatric Research, 26*, 29–38.

Otto, M. W., Wilhelm, S., Cohen, L. S., & Harlow, B. L. (2001). Prevalence of body dysmorphic disorder in a community sample of women. *American Journal of Psychiatry, 158*, 2061–2063.

Otto, R. K. (2000). Assessing and managing violence risk in outpatient settings. *Journal of Clinical Psychology, 56*, 1239–1262.

Ousley, L., Cordero, E. D., & White, S. (2008). Eating disorders and body image of undergraduate men. *Journal of American College Health, 56*, 617–621.

Overmier, J. B., & Seligman, M. E. (1967). Effects of inescapable shock upon subsequent escape and avoidance responding. *Journal of Comparative and Physiological Psychology, 63*, 28–33.

Overmier, J. B., & Seligman, M. E. (1967). Effects of inescapable shock upon subsequent escape and avoidance responding. *Journal of Comparative and Physiological Psychology, 63*, 28–33.

Oxford, M., Cavell, T. A., & Hughes, J. N. (2003). Callous/unemotional traits moderate the relation between ineffective parenting and child externalizing problems: A partial replication and extension. *Journal of Clinical Child and Adolescent Psychology, 32*, 577–585.

Oxnam, R. B. (2005). *A fractured mind: My life with multiple personality disorder*. New York: Hyperion Books.

Ozcan, M. E., Shivakumar, G., & Suppes, T. (2006). Treating rapid cycling bipolar disorder with novel medications. *Current Psychiatry Reviews, 2*, 361–369.

Ozkan, M., & Altindag, A. (2005). Comorbid personality disorders in subjects with panic disorder: Do personality disorders increase clinical severity? *Comprehensive Psychiatry, 46*, 20–26.

Ozonoff, S., & Jensen, J. (1999). Specific executive function profiles in three neuro-developmental disorders. *Journal of Autism and Developmental Disorders, 29*, 171–177.

Ozonoff, S., Macari, S., Young, G. S., Goldring, S., Thompson, M., Rogers, S. J. (2008). Atypical object exploration at 12 months of age is associated with autism in a prospective sample. *Autism, 12*, 457–472.

Ozonoff, S., Rogers, S. J., & Hendren, R. L. (2003). *Autism spectrum disorders: A research review for practitioners*. Arlington, VA: American Psychiatric Publishing.

Packman, W. L., Marlitt, R. E., Bongar, B., & Pennuto, T. O. (2004). A comprehensive and concise assessment of suicide risk. *Behavioral Sciences & the Law, 22*, 667–680.

Pagnin, D., de Queiroz, V., Pini, S., & Cassano, G. B. (2004). Efficacy of ECT in depression: A meta-analytic review. *Journal of ECT, 20*, 13–20.

Palazzoli, M. S. (1974). Self-starvation: From the intrapsychic to the transpersonal approach to anorexia nervosa. (A. Pomerans, Trans.). Oxford, England: Chaucer.

Palazzoli, M. S. (1988). The family of the anorexic patient: A model system. In M. S. Palazzoli & M. Selvini (Eds.), *The work of Mara Selvini Palazzoli* (A. Pomerans, Trans., pp. 183–197). Lanham, MD: Jason Aronson.

Pallanti, S., Hollander, E., & Goodman, W. K. (2004). A qualitative analysis of nonresponse: Management of treatment-refractory obsessive-compulsive disorder. *Journal of Clinical Psychiatry, 65*, 6–10.

Pallister, E., & Waller, G. (2008). Anxiety in the eating disorders: Understanding the overlap. *Clinical Psychology Review, 28*, 366–386.

Palmer, R. L. (2003). Concepts of eating disorders. In J. Treasure, U. Schmidt, & E. van Furth (Eds.), *Handbook of eating disorders* (pp. 1–10). Chichester, England: Wiley.

Palmer, R. L., Birchall, H., Damani, S., Gatward, N., McGrain, L., & Parker, L. (2003). A dialectical behavior therapy program for people with an eating disorder and borderline personality disorder-description and outcome. *International Journal of Eating Disorders, 33*, 281–286.

Pancheri, P., Scapicchio, P., & Dell Chiaie, R. (2002). A double-blind, randomized parallel-group, efficacy and safety study of intramuscular S-adenosyl-L-methionine 1,4-butanedisulphonate (SAMe) versus imipramine in patients with major depressive disorder. *International Journal of Neuropsychopharmacology, 5*, 287–294.

Paniagua, F. A. (2001). *Diagnosis in a multicultural context*. Thousand Oaks, CA: Sage Publications.

Pantelis, C., Velakoulis, D., McGorry, P. D., Wood, S. J., Suckling, J., Phillips, L. J., Yung, A. R., Bullmore, E. T., Brewer, W., Soulsby, B., Desmond, P., & McGuire, P. K. (2003). Neuroanatomical abnormalities before and after onset of psychosis: a cross-sectional and longitudinal MRI comparison. *Lancet, 361*, 281–288.

Pantelis, C., Velakoulis, D., McGorry, P. D., Wood, S. J., Suckling, J., Phillips, L. J., Yung, A. R., Bullmore, E. T., Brewer, W., Soulsby, B., Desmond, P., & McGuire, P. K. (2003). Neuroanatomical abnormalities before and after onset of psychosis: A cross-sectional and longitudinal MRI comparison. *Lancet, 361,* 281–288.

Papadimitriou, G. N., Calabrese, J. R., Dikeos, D. G., & Christodoulou, G. N. (2005). Rapid cycling bipolar disorder: Biology and pathogenesis. *International Journal of Neuropsychopharmacology, 8,* 281–292.

Papapetropoulos, S., Gonzalez, J., Lieberman, A., Villar, J. M., & Mash, D. C. (2005). Dementia in Parkinson's disease: A post-mortem study in a population of brain donors. *International Journal of Geriatric Psychiatry, 20,* 418–422.

Papp, L. A., Klein, D. F., & Gorman, J. M. (1993). Carbon dioxide hypersensitivity, hyperventilation, and panic disorder. *American Journal of Psychiatry, 150,* 1149–1157.

Papp, L. A., Martinez, J. M., Klein, D. F., Coplan, J. D., Norman, R. G., Cole, R., de Jesus, M. J., Ross, D., Goetz, R., & Gorman, J. M. (1997). Respiratory psychophysiology of panic disorder: Three respiratory challenges in 98 subjects. *American Journal of Psychiatry, 154,* 1557–1565.

Paquette, V., Lévesque, J., Mensour, B., Leroux, J. M., Beaudoin, G., Bourgouin, P., & Beauregard, M. (2003). "Change the mind and you change the brain": Effects of cognitive-behavioral therapy on the neural correlates of spider phobia. *Neuroimage, 18,* 401–409.

Parasuraman, R., Nestor, P. G., & Greenwood, P. (1989). Sustained-attention capacity in young and older adults. *Psychology and Aging, 4,* 339–345.

Pardini, D. A. (2006). The callousness pathway to severe violent delinquency. *Aggressive Behavior, 32,* 590–598.

Pardini, D. A., Lochman, J. E., & Frick, P. J. (2003). Callous/unemotional traits and social-cognitive processes in adjudicated youths. *Journal of the American Academy of Child & Adolescent Psychiatry, 42,* 364–371.

Pardini, D., Obradovic, J., & Loeber, R. (2006). Interpersonal callousness, hyperactivity/impulsivity, inattention, and conduct problems as precursors to delinquency persistence in boys: A comparison of three grade-based cohorts. *Journal of Clinical Child and Adolescent Psychology, 35,* 46–59.

Paris, J. (1993). The treatment of borderline personality disorder in light of the research on its long term outcome. *The Canadian Journal of Psychiatry, 38,* 28–34.

Paris, J. (1996). Cultural factors in the emergence of borderline pathology. *Psychiatry: Interpersonal and Biological Processes, 59,* 185–192.

Paris, J. (1999). Borderline personality disorder. In T. Millon, P. H. Blaney, &

R. D. Davis (Eds), *Oxford textbook of psychopathology* (pp. 628–652). New York: Oxford University Press.

Paris, J. (2001). Psychosocial adversity. In W. J. Livesley (Ed.), *Handbook of personality disorders: Theory, research, and treatment* (pp. 231–241). New York: Guilford Press.

Paris, J. (2003). *Personality disorders over time: Precursors, course, and outcome.* Arlington, VA: American Psychiatric Publishing.

Paris, J. (2005). A current integrative perspective on personality disorders. In J. M. Oldham, A. E. Skodol, & D. S. Bender (Eds.), *The American Psychiatric Publishing textbook of personality disorders* (pp. 119–128). Washington, DC: American Psychiatric Publishing.

Paris, J. (2008). Clinical trials of treatment for personality disorders. *Psychiatric Clinics of North America, 31,* 517–526.

Paris, J., & Zweig-Frank, H. (2001). The 27-year follow-up of patients with borderline personality disorder. *Comprehensive Psychiatry, 42,* 482–487.

Parker, G., Gladstone, G., & Chee, K. T. (2001). Depression in the planet's largest ethnic group: The Chinese. *American Journal of Psychiatry, 158,* 857–864.

Parner, E. T., Schendel, D. E., & Thorsen, P. (2008). Autism prevalence trends over time in Denmark. *Archives of Pediatrics & Adolescent Medicine, 162,* 1150–1156.

Parpura, V., & Haydon, P. G. (2000). Physiological astrocytic calcium levels stimulate glutamate release to modulate adjacent neurons. *Proceedings of the National Academy of Sciences USA, 97,* 8629–8634.

Parrott, A. C. (2002). Recreational Ecstasy/MDMA, the serotonin syndrome, and serotonergic neurotoxicity. *Pharmacology, Biochemistry & Behavior, 71,* 837–844.

Parsons v. Alabama, 81 Ala. 577, So. 854 (1886).

Partin, J. C., Hamill, S. K., Fischel, J. E., & Partin, J. S. (1992). Painful defecation and fecal soiling in children. *Pediatrics, 89,* 1007–1009.

Partnership for a Drug-Free America. (2007). *Agony from Ecstasy.* Retrieved October 20, 2007, from http://www.drugfree.org/Portal/Stories/Agony

Patel, V., Abas, M., Broadhead, J., Todd, C., & Reeler, A. (2001). Depression in developing countries: Lessons from Zimbabwe. *British Medical Journal, 322,* 482–484.

Patkar, A. A., Pae, C., & Masand, P. S. (2006). Transdermal selegiline: The new generation of monoamine oxidase inhibitors. *CNS Spectrum, 11,* 363–375.

Pattij, T., & Vanderschuren, L. J. (2008). The neuropharmacology of impulsive behaviour. *Trends in Pharmacological Sciences, 29,* 192–199.

Pauli, P., Wiedemann, G., & Montoya, P. (1998). Covariation bias in flight phobics. *Journal of Anxiety Disorders, 12,* 555–565.

Pauls, D. L., Alsobrook, J. P., Goodman, W., Rasmussen, S., & Leckman, J. F. (1995). A family study of obsessive-compulsive disorder. *American Journal of Psychiatry, 152,* 76–84.

Pauls, D. L., Raymond, C. L., & Robertson, M. (1991). The genetics of obsessive-compulsive disorder: A review. In J. Zohar, T. Insel, & S. Rasmussen (Eds.), *The psychobiology of obsessive-compulsive disorder (*pp. 89–100). New York: Springer.

Pavlov, I. (1936). *Lectures on conditioned reflexes.* Oxford, England: Liveright.

Pavlov, I. P. (1927). *Conditioned reflexes: An investigation of the physiological activity of the cerebral cortex* (Trans. G. V. Anrep). London: Oxford University Press.

Paxton, S. J., Schutz, H. K., Wertheim, E. H., & Muir, S. L. (1999). Friendship clique and peer influences on body image concerns, dietary restraint, extreme weight-loss behaviors, and binge eating in adolescent girls. *Journal of Abnormal Psychology, 108,* 255–266.

Pelc, K., Kornreich, C., Foisy, M. L., & Dan, B. (2006). Recognition of emotional facial expressions in attention-deficit hyperactivity disorder. *Pediatric Neurology, 35,* 93–97.

Penadés, R., Catalán, R., Salamero, M., Boget, T., Puig, O., Guarch, J., & Gastó, C. (2006). Cognitive remediation therapy for outpatients with chronic schizophrenia: A controlled and randomized study. *Schizophrenia Research, 87,* 323–331.

Pengilly, J. W., & Dowd, E. T. (2000). *Hardiness and social support as moderator of stress in college students. Journal of Clinical Psychology, 56,* 813–820.

Penn, D. L., & Combs, D. (2000). Modification of affect perception deficits in schizophrenia. *Schizophrenia Research, 46,* 217–229.

Pennebaker, J. W. (1999). The effects of traumatic disclosure on physical and mental health: The values of writing and talking about upsetting events. *International Journal of Emergency Mental Health, 1,* 9–18.

Perälä, J., Suvisaari, J., Saarni, S. I., Kuoppasalmi, K., Isometsä, E., Pirkola, S., Partonen, T., Tuulio-Henriksson A., Hintikka, J., Kieseppä, T., Härkänen, T., Koskinen, S., & Lönnqvist, J. (2007). Lifetime prevalence of psychotic and bipolar I disorders in a general population. *Archives of General Psychiatry, 64,* 19–28.

Perez, M., & Joiner, T. E., Jr. (2003). Body image dissatisfaction and disordered eating in black and white women. *International Journal of Eating Disorders, 33,* 342–350.

Perez, M., Voelz, Z. R., Pettit, J. W., & Joiner Jr., T. E. (2002). The role of acculturative stress and body dissatisfaction in predicting bulimic symptomatology across ethnic groups. *International Journal of Eating Disorders, 31,* 442–454.

Perilla, J. L., Norris, F. H., & Lavizzo, E. A. (2002). Ethnicity, culture, and disaster response: Identifying and explaining ethnic differences in PTSD six months after Hurricane Andrew. *Journal of Social & Clinical Psychology, 21,* 20–45.

Perkins, D. O. (1999). Adherence to antipsychotic medications. *Journal of Clinical Psychiatry, 60,* 25–30.

Perkins, H. W. (1997). College student misperceptions of alcohol and other drug use norms among peers. In *Designing alcohol and other drug prevention programs in higher education: Bringing theory into practice* (pp. 177–206). Newton, MA: Higher Education Center for Alcohol and Other Drug Abuse and Violence Prevention.

Perkonigg, A., Kessler, R. C., Storz, S., & Wittchen, H. U. (2000). Traumatic events and post-traumatic stress disorder in the community: Prevalence, risk factors and comorbidity. *Acta Psychiatrica Scandinavica, 101,* 46–59.

Perlick, D., & Silverstein, B. (1994). Faces of female discontent: Depression, disordered eating, and changing gender roles. In P. Fallon M. Katzman, & S. C. Wooley (Eds.), *Feminist perspectives on eating disorders* (pp. 77–93). New York: Guilford Press.

Perlin, M. L. (2000a). The competence to plead guilty and the competence to waive counsel. In M. L. Perlin (Ed.), *The hidden prejudice: Mental disability on trial* (pp. 205–221). Washington, DC: American Psychological Association.

Perlin, M. L. (2000b). The right to refuse treatment. In M. L. Perlin (ed.) *The Hidden Prejudice: Mental Disability on Trial.* (pp. 125–156). Washington, DC: American Psychological Association.

Perlin, M. L. (2000c). Involuntary civil commitment law. In M L. Perlin, (Ed.), *The Hidden Prejudice: Mental Disability on Trial.*(pp. 79–112). Washington, DC, US: American Psychological Association.

Perlin, M. L. (2003). Therapeutic jurisprudence and outpatient commitment law: Kendra's Law as case study. *Psychology, Public Policy, and Law, 9,* 183–208.

Perlis, M. L., Giles, D. E., Buysse, D. J., Tu, X., & Kupfer, D. J. (1997). Self-reported sleep disturbance as a prodromal symptom in recurrent depression. *Journal of Affective Disorders, 42,* 209–212.

Perlis, M. L., Smith, L. J., Lyness, J. M., Matteson, S. R., Pigeon, W. R., Jungquist,

C. R., et al. (2006). Insomnia as a risk factor for onset of depression in the elderly. *Behavioral Sleep Medicine, 4,* 104–113.

Perlis, R. H., Ostacher, M. J., Patel, J. K., Marangell, L. B., Zhang, H., Wisniewski, S. R., et al. (2006). Predictors of recurrence in bipolar disorder: Primary outcomes from the Systematic Treatment Enhancement Program for Bipolar Disorder (STEP-BD). *American Journal of Psychiatry, 163,* 217–224.

Perlstein, W. M., Carter, C. S., Noll, D. C., & Cohen, J. D. (2001). Relation of prefrontal cortex dysfunction to working memory and symptoms in schizophrenia. *American Journal of Psychiatry, 158,* 1105–1113.

Pescosolido, B. A., Monahan, J., Link, B. G., Stueve, A., & Kikuzawa, S. (1999). The public's view of the competence, dangerousness, and need for legal coercion of persons with mental health problems. *American Journal of Public Health, 89,* 1339–1345.

Petersen, R. C., & O'Brien, J. (2006). Mild cognitive impairment should be considered for DSM-V. *Journal of Geriatric Psychiatry and Neurology, 19,* 147–154.

Peterson, C., & Seligman, M. E. (1984). Causal explanations as a risk factor for depression: Theory and evidence. *Psychological Review, 91,* 347–374.

Peterson, T. J., Feldman, G., Harley, R., Fresco, D. M., Graves, L., Holmes, A., Bogdan, R., Papakostas, G. I., Bohn, L., Lury, R. A., Fava, M., & Segal, Z. V. (2007). Extreme response style in recurrent and chronically depressed patients: Change with antidepressant administration and stability during continuation treatment. *Journal of Consulting and Clinical Psychology, 75,* 145–153.

Petkova, E., Quitkin, F. M., McGrath, P. J., Stewart, J. W., & Klein, D. F. (2000). A method to quantify rater bias in antidepressant trials. *Neuropsychopharmacology, 22,* 559–565.

Petry, N. M., Stinson, F. S., & Grant, B. F. (2005). Comorbidity of DSM-IV pathological gambling and other psychiatric disorders: Results from the National Epidemiologic Survey on Alcohol and Related Conditions. *Journal of Clinical Psychiatry, 66,* 564–574.

Petty, F., Kramer, G. L., & Wilson, L. (1992). Prevention of learned helplessness: In vivo correlation with cortical serotonin. *Pharmacology, Biochemistry and Behavior, 43,* 361–367.

Pfammatter, M., Junghan, U. M., & Brenner, H. D. (2006). Efficacy of psychological therapy in schizophrenia: Conclusions from meta-analyses. *Schizophrenia Bulletin, 32,* S64–S80.

Pfennig, A., Frye, M. A., Köberle, U., & Bauer, M. (2004). The mood spectrum and hypothalamic-pituitary-thyroid axis. *Primary Psychiatry, 11,* 42–47.

Pflanz, S. (2008). *Talking paper on Air Force Suicide Prevention Program.* Retrieved December 2, 2008, fromhttp://afspp.afms. mil/idc/groups/public/documents/afms/ ctb_101896.pdf

Phan, K. L., Fitzgerald, D. A., Nathan, P. J., & Tancer, M. E. (2006). Association between amygdala hyperactivity to harsh faces and severity of social anxiety in generalized social phobia. *Biological Psychiatry, 59,* 424–429.

Phelps E. A., O'Connor, K. J., Cunningham, W. A., Funayama, E. S., Gatenby, J. C., Gore, J. C., & Banaji, M. R. (2000). Performance on indirect measures of race evaluation predicts amygdala activation. *Journal of Cognitive Neuroscience, 12,* 729–738.

Phelps, L., Brown, R. T., & Power, T. J. (2002). Tics and Tourette's disorder. In L. Phelps, R. T. Brown, & T. J. Power (Eds.), *Pediatric psychopharmacology: Combining medical and psychosocial interventions* (pp. 203–229). Washington, DC: American Psychological Association.

Phillips, K. A. (2000). Body dysmorphic disorder: Diagnostic controversies and treatment challenges. *Bulletin of the Menninger Clinic, 64,* 18–35.

Phillips, K. A. (2001) Body dysmorphic disorder. In K. A. Phillips (Ed.), *Somatoform and factitious disorders* (pp. 67–94). Washington, DC: American Psychiatric Press.

Phillips, K. A., & Diaz, S. F. (1997). Gender differences in body dysmorphic disorder. *Journal of Nervous and Mental Disease, 185,* 570–577.

Phillips, K. A., & Hollander, E. (2008). Treating body dysmorphic disorder with medication: Evidence, misconceptions, and a suggested approach. *Body Image, 5,* 13–27.

Phillips, K. A., & Najjar, F. (2003). An open-label study of citalopram in body dysmorphic disorder. *Journal of Clinical Psychiatry, 64,* 715–720.

Phillips, K. A., Albertini, R. S., & Rasmussen S. A. (2002). A randomized placebo-controlled trial of fluoxetine in body dysmorphic disorder. *Archives of General Psychiatry, 59,* 381–388.

Phillips, K. A., Coles, M. E., Menard, W., Yen, S., Fay, C., & Weisberg, R. B. (2005). Suicidal ideation and suicide attempts in body dysmorphic disorder. *Journal of Clinical Psychiatry, 66,* 717–725.

Phillips, K. A., McElroy, S. L., Keck, P. E., Jr., Hudson, J. I., & Pope, H. G., Jr. (1994). A comparison of delusional and nondelusional body dysmorphic disorder in 100 cases. *Psychopharmacology Bulletin, 30,* 179–186.

Phillips, K. A., Menard, W., & Fay, C. (2006). Gender similarities and differences in 200 individuals with body dysmorphic disorder. *Comprehensive Psychiatry, 47,* 77–87.

Phillips, K. A., Menard, W., Fay, C., & Pagano, M. E. (2005). Psychosocial functioning and quality of life in body dysmorphic disorder. *Comprehensive Psychiatry, 46,* 254–260.

Phillips, K. A., Pagano, M. E., Menard, W., & Stout, R. L. (2006). A 12-month follow-up study of the course of body dysmorphic disorder. *American Journal of Psychiatry, 163,* 907–908.

Phillips, K. A., Pagano, M. E., Menard, W., Fay, C., & Stout, R. L. (2005). Predictors of remission from body dysmorphic disorder: A prospective study. *Journal of Nervous and Mental Disease, 193,* 564–567.

Phillips, K. A., Quinn, G., & Stout, R. L. (2008). Functional impairment in body dysmorphic disorder: A prospective, follow-up study. *Journal of Psychiatric Research, 42,* 701–707.

Phillips, M. (2001, September 22–26). *The participation of China to the WHO/SUPRE-MISS project.* Paper read at the XXIst Congress of the International Association for Suicide Prevention, Chennai, India.

Phillips, M. L., & Frank, E. (2006). Redefining bipolar disorder: Toward DSM-V. *American Journal of Psychiatry, 163,* 1135–1136.

Phillips, M. L., & Sierra, M. (2003). Depersonalization disorder: A functional neuroanatomical perspective. *Stress, 6,* 157–165.

Phillips, M. L., Medford, N., Senior, C., Bullmore, E. T., Suckling, J., Brammer, M. J., Andrew, C., Sierra, M., Williams, S. C., & David, A. S. (2001). Depersonalization disorder: Thinking without feeling. *Psychiatry Research, 108,* 145–160.

Phillips, M. R., Li, X., & Zhang, Y. (2002). Suicide rates in China, 1995–99. *The Lancet, 359,* 835–840.

Phillips, M. R., West, C. L., Shen, Q., & Zheng, Y. (1998). Comparison of schizophrenic patients' families and normal families in China, using Chinese versions of FACES-II and the Family Environment Scales. *Family Process, 37,* 95–106.

Piasecki, M. P., Antonuccio, D. O., Steinagel, G. M., Kohlenberg, B. S., & Kapadar, K. (2002). Penetrating the blind in a study of an SSRI. *Journal of Behavior Therapy and Experimental Psychiatry, 33,* 67–71.

Piasecki, M., Antonuccio, D. O., Steinagel, G., & Kohlenberg, B. S. (2002). Penetration of the blind in a controlled study of Paxil used to treat cocaine addiction. *Journal of Behavior Therapy and Experimental Psychiatry, 33,* 67–71.

Picciotto, M. R. (1998). Common aspects of the action of nicotine and other drugs of abuse. *Drug and Alcohol Dependence, 51,* 165–172.

Pich, E. M., Pagliusi, S. R., Tessari, M., Talabot-Ayer, D., van Huijsduijnen, R. H., & Chiamulera, C. (1997). Common neural substrates for the addictive properties of nicotine and cocaine. *Science, 275,* 83–86.

Pigott, T. A., Myers, K. R., & Williams, D. A. (1996). Obsessive-compulsive disorder: A neuropsychiatric perspective. In R. M. Rapee (Ed.), *Current controversies in the anxiety disorders.* (pp. 13–160). New York: Guilford Press.

Pigott, T. A. (1996). OCD: Where the serotonin selectivity story begins. *Journal of Clinical Psychiatry, 57,* 11–20.

Pigott, T. A. (1999). Gender differences in the epidemiology and treatment of anxiety disorders. *Journal of Clinical Psychiatry, 60*(Suppl. 18), 4–15.

Pihl, R. O. (1999). Substance abuse: Etiological considerations. In T. Millon, P. H. Blaney, & R. D. Davis (Eds.), *Oxford textbook of psychopathology* (pp. 249–276). New York: Oxford University Press.

Pihl, R. O., & Peterson, J. B. (1995). Alcoholism: The role of different motivational systems. *Journal of Psychiatry & Neuroscience, 20,* 372–396.

Pike, K. M. (1998). Long-term course of anorexia nervosa: Response, relapse, remission, and recovery. *Clinical Psychology Review, 18,* 447–475.

Pike, K. M., & Walsh, T. (1996). Ethnicity and eating disorders: Implications for incidence and treatment. *Psychopharmacology Bulletin, 32,* 265–274.

Pike, K. M., Devlin, M. J., & Loeb, K. L. (2004). Cognitive-behavioral therapy in the treatment of anorexia nervosa, bulimia nervosa, and binge eating disorder. In J. K. Thompson (Ed.), *Handbook of eating disorders and obesity* (pp. 130–162). Hoboken, NJ: John Wiley & Sons.

Pike, K. M., Walsh, B. T., Vitousek, K., Wilson, G. T., & Bauer, J. (2003). Cognitive behavior therapy in the posthospitalization treatment of anorexia nervosa. *American Journal of Psychiatry, 160,* 2046–2049.

Pilkonis, P. A., & Krause, M. S. (1999). Summary: Paradigms for psychotherapy outcome research. *Journal of Clinical Psychology, 55,* 201–205.

Pilling, S., Bebbington, P., Kuipers, E., Garety, P., Geddes, J., Orbach, G., & Morgan, C. (2002). Psychological treatments in schizophrenia: I. Meta-analysis of family intervention and cognitive behaviour therapy. *Psychological Medicine, 32,* 763–782.

Pillmann, F., Haring, A., Balzuweit, S., & Marneros, A. (2002). A comparison of DSM-IV brief psychotic disorder with "positive" schizophrenia and healthy controls. *Comprehensive Psychiatry, 43,* 385–392.

Pilowsky, D. J., Wickramaratne, P., Nomura, Y., & Weissman, M. M. (2006). Family discord, parental depression, and psychopathology in offspring: 20-year follow-up. *Journal of the American Academy of Child & Adolescent Psychiatry, 45,* 452–460.

Pincus, A. L., & Wilson, K. R. (2001). Interpersonal variability in dependent personality. *Journal of Personality, 69,* 223–251.

Pine, D. S., Wasserman, G. A., Miller, L., Coplan, J. D., Bagiella, E., Kovelenku, P., Myers, M. M., & Sloan, R. P. (1998). Heart period variability and psychopathology in urban boys at risk for delinquency. *Psychophysiology, 35,* 521–529.

Pineda, D. A., Palacio, L. G., Puerta, I. C., Merchán, V., Arango, C. P., Galvis, A. Y., Gómez, M., Aguirre, D. C., Lopera, F., & Arcos-Burgos, M. (2007). Environmental influences that affect attention-deficit/hyperactivity disorder: Study of a genetic isolate. *European Child & Adolescent Psychiatry, 16,* 337–346.

Piñeros, M., Rosselli, D., & Calderon, C. (1998). An epidemic of collective conversion and dissociation disorder in an indigenous group of Colombia: Its relation to cultural change. *Social Science & Medicine, 46,* 1425–1428.

Pinkerman, J. E., Haynes, J. P., & Keiser, T. (1993). Characteristics of psychological practice in juvenile court clinics. *American Journal of Forensic Psychology, 11,* 3–12.

Piper, A., & Merskey, H. (2004a). The persistence of folly: A critical examination of dissociative identity disorder. Part I. The excesses of an improbable concept. *Canadian Journal of Psychiatry, 49,* 592–600.

Piper, A., & Merskey, H. (2004b). The persistence of folly: A critical examination of dissociative identity disorder. Part II. The defense and decline of multiple personality or dissociative identity disorder. *Canadian Journal of Psychiatry, 49,* 678–683.

Piper, W. E., & Joyce, A. S. (2001). Psychosocial treatment outcome. In W. J. Livesley (Ed.), *Handbook of personality disorders: Theory, research, and treatment* (pp. 323–343). New York: Guilford Press.

Piper, W. E., & Ogrodniczuk, J. S. (2005). Group treatment. In J. M. Oldham, A. E. Skodol, & D. S. Bender (Eds.), *The American Psychiatric Publishing textbook of personality disorders* (pp. 347–357). Washington, DC: American Psychiatric Publishing.

Piran, N., Jasper, K., & Pinhas, L. (2004). Feminist therapy and eating disorders. In J. K. Thompson (Ed.), *Handbook of eating disorders and obesity* (pp. 263–278). Hoboken, NJ: John Wiley & Sons.

Pissiota, A., Frans, O., Michelgård, A., Appel, L., Långström, B. Flaten, M.A., & Fredrikson,

M. (2003). Amygdala and anterior cingulate cortex activation during affective startle modulation: a PET study of fear. *European Journal of Neuroscience, 18,* 1325–1331.

Pissiota, A., Frans, Ö., Michelgård, Å., Appel, L., Långström, B., Flaten, M. A., & Fredrikson, M. (2003). Amygdala and anterior cingulate cortex activation during affective startle modulation: A PET study of fear. *European Journal of Neuroscience, 18,* 1325–1331.

Pithers, W. D. (1990). Relapse prevention with sexual aggressors: A method for maintaining therapeutic gain and enhancing external supervision. In W. L. Marshall, D. R. Laws, & H. E. Barbaree (Eds.), *Handbook of sexual assault: Issues, theories, and treatment of the offender* (pp. 343–361). New York: Plenum Press.

Pitman, R. K., & Delahanty, D. L. (2005). Conceptually driven pharmacologic approaches to acute trauma. *CNS Spectrums, 10,* 99–106.

Pitman, R. K., Shin, L. M., & Rauch, S. L. (2001). Investigating the pathogenesis of posttraumatic stress disorder with neuroimaging. *Journal of Clinical Psychiatry, 62,* 47–54.

Pitschel-Walz, G., Leucht, S., Baeuml, J., Kissling, W., & Engel, R. R. (2001). The effect of family interventions on relapse and rehospitalization in schizophrenia—a meta-analysis. *Schizophrenia Bulletin, 27,* 73–92.

Pitts, F. M., & McClure, J. N. (1967) Lactate metabolism anxiety neurosis. *New England Journal of Medicine, 277,* 1329–1336

Plassman, B. L., Langa, K. M., Fisher, G. G., Heeringa, S. G., Weir, D. R., Ofsedal, M. B., Burke, J. R., Hurd, M. D., Potter, G. G., Rodgers, W. L., Steffens, D. C., Willis, R. J., & Wallace, R. B. (2007). Prevalence of dementia in the United States: The Aging, Demographics, and Memory Study. *Neuroepidemiology, 29,* 125–132.

Plaze, M., Bartrés-Faz, D., Martinot, J., Januel, D., Bellivier, F., De Beaurepaire, R., Chanraud, S., Andoh, J., Lefaucheur, J., Artiges, E., Pallier, C., & Paillère-Martinot, M. (2006). Left superior temporal gyrus activation during sentence perception negatively correlates with auditory hallucination severity in schizophrenia patients. *Schizophrenia Research, 87,* 109–115.

Pliszka, S. R. (2007). Pharmacologic treatment of attention-deficit/hyperactivity disorder: Efficacy, safety and mechanisms of action. *Neuropsychology Review, 17,* 61–72.

Pliszka, S. R., Matthews, T. L., Braslow, K. J., & Watson, M. A. (2006). Comparative Effects of Methylphenidate and Mixed Salts Amphetamine on Height and Weight in Children With Attention-Deficit/

Hyperactivity Disorder. *Journal of the American Academy of Child & Adolescent Psychiatry, 45,* 520–526.

Plomin, R., DeFries, J. C., Craig, I. W., & McGuffin, P. (Eds). (2003). *Behavioral genetics in the postgenomic era.* Washington, DC: APA Books.

Plomin, R., DeFries, J. C., McClearn, G. E., & Rutter, M. (1997). *Behavioral genetics* (3rd ed.). New York: Freeman.

Plotsky, P. M., Thrivikraman, K. V., Nemeroff, C. B., Caldji, C., Sharma, S., & Meaney, M. J. (2005). Long-term consequences of neonatal rearing on central corticotropin-releasing factor systems in adult male rat offspring. *Neuropsychopharmacology. 30,* 2192–2204.

Pluess, M., Conrad, A., & Wilhelm, F. H. (2009). Muscle tension in generalized anxiety disorder: A critical review of the literature. *Journal of Anxiety Disorders, 23,* 1–11.

Poewe, W., Wolters, E., & Emre, M. (2006). Long-term benefits of rivastigmine in dementia associated with Parkinson's disease: An active treatment extension study. *Movement Disorders, 21,* 456–461.

Polanczyk, G., & Rohde, L. A. (2007). Epidemiology of attention-deficit/hyperactivity disorder across the lifespan. *Current Opinion in Psychiatry, 20,* 386–392.

Polanczyk, G., de Lima, M. S., Horta, B. L., Biederman, J., Rohde, L. A. (2007). The worldwide prevalence of ADHD: A systematic review and metaregression analysis. *American Journal of Psychiatry, 164,* 942–948.

Polivy, J., & Herman, C. P. (1993). Etiology of binge eating: Psychological mechanisms. In C. G. Fairburn, & G. T. Wilson (Eds.), *Binge eating: Nature, assessment, and treatment* (pp. 173–205). New York: Guilford Press.

Polivy, J., & Herman, C. P. (2002). Causes of eating disorders. *Annual Review of Psychology, 53,* 187–213.

Polivy, J., & Herman, C. P. (1985). Dieting and binge eating: A causal analysis. *American Psychologist, 40,* 193–204.

Pollak, S. D., Cicchetti, D., Hornung, K., & Reed, A. (2000). Recognizing emotion in faces: Developmental effects of child abuse and neglect. *Developmental Psychology, 36,* 679–688.

Pollock, V. E., Briere, J., Schneider, L., Knop, J., Mednick, S. A., & Goodwin, D. W. (1990). Childhood antecedents of antisocial behavior: Parental alcoholism and physical abusiveness. *American Journal of Psychiatry, 147,* 1290–1293.

Pomeroy, C. (2004). Assessment of medical status and physical factors. In J. K. Thompson (Ed.), *Handbook of eating disorders and obesity* (pp. 81–111). Hoboken, NJ: John Wiley & Sons.

Poortinga, Y. H. (1995). Cultural bias in assessment: Historical and thematic issues. *European Journal of Psychological Assessment, 11,* 140–146.

Pope, H. G., & Yurgelin-Todd D. (1996). The residual cognitive effects of heavy marijuana use in college students. *JAMA: Journal of the American Medical Association, 275,* 521–527.

Pope, H. G., Gruber, A. J., Hudson, J. I., Huestis, M. A., & Yurgelun-Todd, D. (2001). Neuropsychological performance in long-term cannabis users. *Archives of General Psychiatry, 58,* 909–915.

Pope, H. G., Jr., Gruber, A. J., Choi, P., Olivardia, R., & Phillips, K. A. (1997). Muscle dysmorphia: An underrecognized form of body dysmorphic disorder. *Psychosomatics: Journal of Consultation and Liaison Psychiatry, 38,* 548–557.

Pope, H. G., Jr., Gruber, A. J., Mangweth, B., Bureau, B., deCol, C., Jouvent, R., & Hudson, J. I. (2000). Body image perception among men in three countries. *American Journal of Psychiatry, 157,* 1297–1301.

Pope, H. G., Jr., Oliva, P. S., Hudson, J. I., Bodkin, J. A., & Gruber, A. J. (1999). Attitudes toward DSM-IV-TR dissociative disorders diagnoses among board-certified American psychiatrists. *American Journal of Psychiatry, 156,* 321–323.

Pope, H. G., Jr., Poliakoff, M. B., Parker, M. P., Boynes, M., & Hudson, J. I. (2007). Is dissociative amnesia a culture-bound syndrome? Findings from a survey of historical literature. *Psychological Medicine, 37,* 225–233.

Pope, H. G., Phillips, K. A., & Olivardia, R. (2000). *The Adonis complex: The secret crisis of male body obsession.* Sydney: Free Press.

Porter, R. (2002). *Madness: A brief history.* New York: Oxford University Press.

Porter, V. R., Buxton, W. G., Fairbanks, L. A., Strickland, T., O'Connor, S. M., Rosenberg-Thompson, S., & Cummings, J. L. (2003). Frequency and characteristics of anxiety among patients with Alzheimer's disease and related dementias. *Journal of Neuropsychiatry & Clinical Neurosciences, 15,* 180–186.

Potter, G. G., & Steffens, D. C. (2007, November 1). Depression and cognitive impairment in older adults. *Psychiatric Times, 24.* Retrieved January 10, 2008, from http://www.psychiatrictimes.com/showArticle.jhtml;jsessionid=Z3DNXGDTEZBJAQSNDLOSKH0CJUNN2JVN?articleId=202602111

Poulet, E., Brunelin, J., Bediou, B., Bation, R., Forgeard, L., Dalery, J., D'Amato, T., & Saoud, M. (2005). Slow transcranial magnetic stimulation can rapidly reduce resistant auditory hallucinations in schizophrenia. *Biological Psychiatry, 57,* 188–191.

Poulton, R., & Menzies, R. G. (2002). Non-associative fear acquisition: A review of the evidence from retrospective and longitudinal research. *Behaviour Research and Therapy, 40,* 127–149.

Poulton, R., Menzies, R. G., Craske, M. G., Langley, J. D., & Silva, P. A. (1999). Water trauma and swimming experiences up to age 9 and fear of water at age 18: A longitudinal study. *Behaviour Research and Therapy, 37,* 39–48.

Powell, R. A., & Gee, T. L. (1999). The effects of hypnosis on dissociative identity disorder: A reexamination of the evidence. *Canadian Journal of Psychiatry, 44,* 914–916.

Powers, M. B., & Emmelkamp, P. M. G. (2008). Virtual reality exposure therapy for anxiety disorders: A meta-analysis. *Journal of Anxiety Disorders, 22,* 561–569.

Powers, P. S., Santana, C. A., & Bannon, Y. S. (2002). Olanzapine in the treatment of anorexia nervosa: An open label trial. *International Journal of Eating Disorders, 32,* 146–154.

Pratt, B., & Woolfenden, S. (2002). Interventions for preventing eating disorders in children and adolescents. *Cochrane Database of Systematic Reviews (2):* CD002891.

Pressman, L. J., Loo, S. K., Carpenter, E. M., Asarnow, J. R., Lynn, D., McCracken, J. T., McGough, J. J., Lubke, G. H., Yang, M. H., & Smalley, S. L. (2006). Relationship of family environment and parental psychiatric diagnosis to impairment in ADHD. *Journal of the American Academy of Child & Adolescent Psychiatry, 45,* 346–354.

Preti, A. (2003). Unemployment and suicide. *Journal of Epidemiology & Community Health, 57,* 557–558.

Pretzer, J. L., & Beck, A. T. (2005). A cognitive theory of personality disorders. In M. F. Lenzenweger & J. F. Clarkin (Eds.), *Major theories of personality disorder* (2nd ed., pp. 43–113). New York: Guilford Press.

Price, B. H., Baral, I., Cosgrove, G. R., Rauch, S. L., Nierenberg, A. A., Jenike, M. A., & Cassem, E. H. (2001). Improvement in severe self-mutilation following limbic leucotomy: A series of 5 consecutive cases. *Journal of Clinical Psychiatry, 62,* 925–932.

Price, D. D., Finniss, D. G., & Benedetti, F. (2008). A comprehensive review of the placebo effect: Recent advances and current thought. *Annual Review of Psychology, 59,* 565–590.

Price, R. W. (2003). Editorial comment: Diagnosis of focal brain lesions—old lessons retaught. *AIDS Reader, 13,* 553.

Prichard, Z. M., Jorm, A. F., Mackinnon, A., & Easteal, S. (2007). Association analysis of 15 polymorphisms within 10 candidate genes for antisocial behavioural traits. *Psychiatric Genetics, 17,* 299–303.

Pridmore, S., Chambers, A., & McArthur, M. (2005). Neuroimaging in psychopathy. *Australian and New Zealand Journal of Psychiatry, 39,* 856–865.

Prien, R. F. & Kocsis, J. H. (1995). Long-term treatment of mood disorders. In *Psychopharmacology: the Fourth Generation of Progress.* F. E. Bloom & D. J. Kupfer (Eds.), (pp. 1067–1079). New York: Raven Press.

Priest, D. (2008). Soldier suicides at record level. *Washington Post, 130*(422).

Prins, A., Kaloupek, D. G., & Keane, T. M. (1995). Psychophysiological evidence for autonomic arousal and startle in traumatized adult populations. In M. J. Friedman D. S. Charney, & A. Y. Deutch (Eds.), *Neurobiological and clinical consequences of stress: From normal adaptation to post-traumatic stress disorder* (pp. 291–314). Philadelphia: Lippincott Williams & Wilkins.

Prochaska, J. O., Norcross, J. C., & DiClemente, C. C. (1994). *Changing for good.* New York: Morrow.

Prochaska, J. O., Velicer, W. F., Rossi, J. S., Goldstein, M. G., Marcus, B. H., Rakowski, W., et al. (1994). Stages of change and decisional balance for 12 problem behaviors. *Health Psychology, 13,* 39–46.

Project MATCH Research Group. (1997). Matching alcoholism treatments to patient heterogeneity: Project MATCH posttreatment drinking outcomes. *Journal of Studies on Alcohol, 58,* 7–29.

Project MATCH Research Group. (1998). Matching alcoholism treatments to patient heterogeneity: Project MATCH three-year drinking outcomes. *Alcoholism: Clinical & Experimental Research, 22,* 1300–1311.

Project search. (2006). *The Advance* (APSE newsletter), *17.* Retrieved August 2, 2007, from http://www.apse.org/docs/falladvance2006.pdf

Propper, C., & Moore, G. A. (2006). The influence of parenting on infant emotionality: A multi-level psychobiological perspective. *Developmental Review, 26,* 427–460.

Pruett, M. K., Insabella, G. M., & Gustafson, K. (2005). The Collaborative Divorce Project: A court-based intervention for separating parents with young children. *Family Court Review, 43,* 38–51.

Przeworski, A., & Newman, M. G. (2004). Palmtop computer-assisted group therapy for social phobia. *Journal of Clinical Psychology, 60,* 179–188.

Puente, A. E. (2003). Neuropsychology: Introducing aging into the study of brain and behavior. In S. K. Whitbourne & J. C. Cavanaugh (Eds.), *Integrating aging topics into psychology: A practical guide for teaching* (pp. 29–42). Washington, DC: American Psychological Association.

Pull, C. B. (2005). Current status of virtual reality exposure therapy in anxiety disorders. *Current Opinion in Psychiatry, 18,* 7–14.

Putnam, F. W. (1989). Pierre Janet and modern views of dissociation. *Journal of Traumatic Stress, 2,* 413–429.

Putnam, F. W. (1995). Development of dissociative disorders. In: D. Cicchetti & D. J. Cohen (Eds.), *Developmental psychopathology* (Vol. 2, pp. 581–608). New York: Wiley.

Putnam, F. W., & Loewenstein, R. J. (1993). Treatment of multiple personality disorder: A survey of current practices. *American Journal of Psychiatry, 150,* 1048–1052.

Putnam, F. W., Helmers, K., Horowitz, L. A., & Trickett, P. K. (1995). Hypnotizability and dissociativity in sexually abused girls. *Child Abuse & Neglect, 19,* 645–655.

Pyszczynski, T., & Greenberg, J. (1987). Self-regulatory perseveration and the depressive self-focusing style: A self-awareness theory of reactive depression. *Psychological Bulletin, 102,* 1–17.

Qin, P., & Mortensen, P. B. (2001). Specific characteristics of *suicide* in China. *Acta Psychiatrica Scandinavica, 103,* 117–121.

Quattrocchi, M. R., & Schopp, R. F. (2005). *Tarasaurus rex:* A standard of care that could not adapt. *Psychology, Public Policy, and Law, 11,* 109–137.

Quinn, P. O. (2005). Treating adolescent girls and women with ADHD: Gender-specific issues. *Journal of Clinical Psychology, 61,* 579–587.

Rabheru, K. (2001). The use of electroconvulsive therapy in special patient populations. *The Canadian Journal of Psychiatry/La Revue canadienne de psychiatrie, 46,* 710–719.

Rabin, L. A., Wishart, H. A., Fields, R. B., & Saykin, A. J. (2006). The dementias. In P. J. Snyder, P. D. Nussbaum, & D. L. Robins (Eds.), *Clinical neuropsychology: A pocket handbook for assessment* (2nd ed., pp. 210–239). Washington, DC: American Psychological Association.

Rachman, S. (1997). A cognitive theory of obsessions. *Behaviour Research and Therapy, 35,* 793–802.

Radomsky, A. S., Rachman, S., & Hammond, D. (2001). Memory bias, confidence and responsibility in compulsive checking. *Behaviour Research and Therapy, 39,* 813–822.

Raimo, E. B., Roemer, R. A., Moster, M., & Shan, Y. (1999). Alcohol-induced depersonalization. *Biological Psychiatry, 45,* 1523–1526.

Raine, A. (2002). Biosocial studies of antisocial and violent behavior in children and adults: A review. *Journal of Abnormal Child Psychology, 30,* 311–326.

Raine, A. (2006). Schizotypal personality: Neurodevelopmental and psychosocial trajectories. *Annual Review of Clinical Psychology, 2,* 291–326.

Raine, A., Brennan, P., Mednick, B., & Mednick, S. A. (1996). High rates of violence, crime, academic problems, and behavioral problems in males with both early neuromotor deficits and unstable family environments. *Archives of General Psychiatry, 53,* 544–549.

Raine, A., Lencz, T., Bihrle, S., LaCasse, L, & Colletti, P. (2000). Reduced prefrontal gray matter volume and reduced autonomic activity in antisocial personality disorder. *Archives of General Psychiatry, 57,* 119–127.

Raine, A., Lencz, T., Taylor, K., Hellige, J. B., Bihrle, S., Lacasse, L., Lee, M., Ishikawa, S. S., & Colletti, P. (2003). Corpus callosum abnormalities in psychopathic antisocial individuals. *Archives of General Psychiatry, 60,* 1134–1142.

Rajkowska, G. (1997). Morphometric methods for studying the prefrontal cortex in suicide victims and psychiatric patients. *Annals of the New York Academy of Sciences, 836,* 253–268.

Rajska-Neumann, A., & Wieczorowska-Tobis, K. (2007). Polypharmacy and potential inappropriateness of pharmacological treatment among community-dwelling elderly patients. *Archives of Gerontology and Geriatrics, 44,* 303–309.

Rakoff, D. (2002, December 29). The lives they lived; The debutante's staying-in party. *The New York Times,* p. 00.

Raleigh, M. J., McGuire, M. T., Brammer, G. L., & Yuwiler, A. (1984). Social and environmental influences on blood serotonin concentrations in monkeys. *Archives of General Psychiatry, 41,* 405–410.

Ramaekers, J. G., Kauert, G., van Ruitenbeek, P., Theunissen, E. L., Schneider, E., & Moeller, M. R. (2006). High-potency marijuana impairs executive function and inhibitory motor control. *Neuropsychopharmacology, 31,* 2296–2303.

Ramafedi, G. (1999). Suicide and sexual orientation: Nearing the end of a controversy? *Archives of General Psychiatry, 56,* 885–886.

Ramirez, M., III. (1999). *Multicultural psychotherapy: An approach to individual and cultural differences* (2nd ed.). Needham Heights, MA: Allyn & Bacon.

Ramírez-Esparza, N., Gosling, S. D., Benet-Martínez, V., Potter, J. P., & Pennebaker, J. W. (2006). Do bilinguals have two personalities? A special case of cultural frame switching. *Journal of Research in Personality, 40,* 99–120.

Ramus, F. Rosen, S., Dakin, S., Day, B., Castellote, J., White, S., et al. (2003).

Theories of developmental dyslexia: Insights from a multiple case study of dyslexic adults. *Brain, 126,* 841–865.

Rand Corporation. (2001). Retrieved October 27, 2006, from http://www.rand.org/news/Press/ca.mental.htmlRedlich, A. D., Steadman, H. J., Monahan, J., Petrila, J., & Griffin, P. A. (2005). The second generation of mental health courts. *Psychology, Public Policy, and Law, 11,* 527–538.

Rao V., & Lyketsos, C. G. (1998). Delusions in Alzheimer's disease. *Journal of Neuropsychiatry & Clinical Neurosciences, 10,* 373–382.

Rao, U., Dahl, R. E., Ryan, N. D., Birmaher, B., Williamson, D. E., Rao, R., & Kaufman, J. (2002). Heterogeneity in EEG sleep findings in adolescent depression: Unipolar versus bipolar clinical course. *Journal of Affective Disorders, 70,* 273–280.

Rapee, R. M., & Abbott, M. J. (2006). Mental representation of observable attributes in people with social phobia. *Journal of Behavior Therapy and Experimental Psychiatry, 37,* 113–126.

Rapee, R. M., & Heimberg, R. G. (1997). A cognitive-behavioral model of anxiety in social phobia. *Behaviour Research and Therapy, 35,* 741–756.

Raphael, F. J., & Lacey, J. H. (1992). Sociocultural aspects of eating disorders. *Annals of Medicine, 24,* 293–296.

Rapoport, J. L. (1991). Recent advances in obsessive-compulsive disorder. *Neuropsychopharmacology, 5,* 1–10.

Rapoport, J. L., Giedd, J. N., Blumenthal, J., Hamburger, S., Jeffries, N., Fernandez, T., Nicolson, R., Bedwell, J., Lenane, M., Zijdenbos, A., Paus, T., & Evans, A. (1999). Progressive cortical change during adolescence in childhood-onset schizophrenia: A longitudinal magnetic resonance imaging study. *Archives of General Psychiatry, 56,* 649–654.

Rapoport, M. J., Mamdani, M., & Herrmann, N. (2006). Electroconvulsive therapy in older adults: 13-year trends. *The Canadian Journal of Psychiatry/La Revue canadienne de psychiatrie, 51,* 616–619.

Raskin, M., Talbott, J. A., & Meyerson, A. T. (1966). Diagnosis of conversion reactions: Predictive value of psychiatric criteria. *Journal of the American Medical Association, 197,* 530–534.

Rasmussen, H. B., Timm, S., Wang, A. G., Soeby, K., Lublin, H., Fenger, M., Hemmingsen, R., & Werge, T. (2006). Association between the CCR5 32-bp deletion allele and late onset of schizophrenia. *American Journal of Psychiatry, 163,* 507–511.

Rasmussen, P. R. (2005). The avoidant prototype. In P. R. Rasmussen (Ed.), *Personality-guided cognitive-behavioral*

therapy (pp. 191–213). Washington, DC: American Psychological Association.

Rauch, S. L., Dougherty, D. D., Cosgrove, G. R., Cassem, E. H., Alpert, N. M., Price, B. H., Nierenberg, A. A., Mayberg, H. S., Baer, L., Jenike, M. A., & Fischman, A. J. (2001). Cerebral metabolic correlates as potential predictors of response to anterior cingulotomy for obsessive compulsive disorder. *Biological Psychiatry, 50,* 659–667.

Rauch, S. L., Dougherty, D. D., Malone, D., Rezai, A., Friehs, G., Fischman, A. J., Alpert, N. M., Haber, S. N., Stypulkowski, P. H., Rise, M. T., Rasmussen, S. A., & Greenberg, B. D. (2006). A functional neuroimaging investigation of deep brain stimulation in patients with obsessive-compulsive disorder. *Journal of Neurosurgery, 104,* 558–565.

Rauch, S. L., Jenike, M. A., Alpert, N. M., Baer, L., Breiter, H. C., Savage, C. R., et al. (1994). Regional cerebral blood flow measured during symptom provocation in obsessive-compulsive disorder using oxygen 15-labeled carbon dioxide and positron emission tomography. *Archives of General Psychiatry, 51,* 62–70.

Rauch, S. L., Savage, C. R., Alpert, N. M., Miguel, E. C., Baer, L., Breiter, H. C., et al. (1995). A positron emission tomographic study of simple phobic symptom provocation. *Archives of General Psychiatry, 52,* 20–28.

Rauch, S. L., Savage, C. R., Brown, H. D., Curran, T., Alpert, N. M., Kendrick, A., et al. (1995). A PET investigation of implicit and explicit sequence learning. *Human Brain Mapping, 3,* 271–286.

Rauch, S. L., Shin, L. M., & Phelps, E. A. (2006). Neurocircuitry models of post-traumatic stress disorder and extinction: Human neuroimaging research—past, present, and future. *Biological Psychiatry, 60,* 376–382.

Rauch, S. L., van der Kolk, B. A., Fisler, R. E., & Alpert, N. M. (1996). A symptom provocation study of posttraumatic stress disorder using positron emission tomography and script-driven imagery. *Archives of General Psychiatry, 53,* 380–387.

Rauch, S. L., Whalen, P. J., Shin, L. M., McInerney, S. C., Macklin, M. L., Lasko, N. B., Orr, S. P., & Pitman, R. K. (2000). Exaggerated amygdala response to masked facial stimuli in posttraumatic stress disorder: A functional MRI study. *Biological Psychiatry, 47,* 769–776.

Raymond, N. C., Coleman, E., Ohlerking, F., Christenson, G. A., & Miner, M. (1999). Psychiatric comorbidity in pedophilic sex offenders. *American Journal of Psychiatry, 156,* 786–788.

Ready, D. J., Pollack, S., Rothbaum, B. O., & Alarcon, R. D. (2006). Virtual reality exposure for veterans with posttraumatic stress disorder. *Journal of Aggression, Maltreatment & Trauma, 12,* 199–220.

Rebec, G. V. (2000). Cocaine. In A. E. Kazdin (Ed.), *Encyclopedia of psychology* (Vol. 2, pp. 130–131). Washington, DC: American Psychological Association.

Rector, N. A., & Beck, A. T. (2002a). A clinical review of cognitive therapy for schizophrenia. *Current Psychiatry Report, 4,* 284–292.

Rector, N. A., & Beck, A. T. (2002b). Cognitive therapy for schizophrenia: From conceptualisation to intervention. *Canadian Journal of Psychiatry, 47,* 39–48.

Rector, N. A., Seeman, M. V., & Segal, Z. V. (2003.) Cognitive therapy of schizophrenia: A preliminary randomized controlled trial. *Schizophrenia Research, 63,* 1–11.

Reger, G. M., & Gahm, G. A. (2008). Virtual reality exposure therapy for active duty soldiers. *Journal of Clinical Psychology, 64,* 940–946.

Regier, D. A., Farmer, M. E., Rae, D. S., Locke, B. Z., Keith, S. J., Judd, L. L., & Goodwin, F. K. (1990). Comorbidity of mental disorders with alcohol and other drug abuse: Results from the Epidemiologic Catchment Area (ECA) study. *Journal of the American Medical Association, 264,* 2511–2518.

Regier, D. A., Farmer, M. E., Rae, D. S., Locke, B. Z., Keith, S. J., Judd, L. L., & Goodwin, F. K. (1990). Comorbidity of mental disorders with alcohol and other drug use: Results from the Epidemiological Catchment Area (ECA) Study. *Journal of the American Medical Association, 264,* 2511–2518.

Regier, D. A., Farmer, M. E., Rae, D. S., Locke, B. Z., Keith, S. J., Judd, L. L., & Goodwin, F. K. (1990). Comorbidity of mental disorders with alcohol and other drug abuse. Results from the Epidemiologic Catchment Area (ECA) Study. *Journal of the American Medical Association, 264,* 2511–2518.

Regier, D. A., Narrow, W. E., Rae, D. S., Manderscheid, R. W., Locke, B. Z., & Goodwin, F. K. (1993). The de facto US mental and addictive disorders service system: Epidemiologic Catchment Area prospective 1-year prevalence rates of disorders and services. *Archives of General Psychiatry, 50,* 85–94.

Rehm, L. P. (2002). How can we better disentangle placebo and drug effects? *Prevention & Treatment, 5,* Article 31. http://www.journals.apa.org/prevention/volume5/pre0050031c.html.

Reich, J. (2000). The relationship of social phobia to avoidant personality disorder: A proposal to reclassify avoidant personality disorder based on clinical empirical findings. *European Psychiatry, 15,* 151–159.

Reichenberg, A., Gross, R., Weiser, M., Bresnahan, M., Silverman, J., Harlap, S., Rabinowitz, J., Shulman, C., Malaspina, D., Lubin, G., Knobler, H. Y., Davidson, M., & Susser, E. (2006). Advancing paternal age and autism. *Archives of General Psychiatry, 63,* 1026–1032.

Reichenberg, A., Rieckmann, N., & Harvey, P. D. (2005). Stability in schizophrenia symptoms over time: Findings from the Mount Sinai Pilgrim Psychiatric Center longitudinal study. *Journal of Abnormal Psychology, 114,* 363–372.

Reid, G., Aitken, C., Beyer, L., & Crofts, N. (2001). Ethnic communities' vulnerability to involvement with illicit drugs. *Drugs: Education, Prevention & Policy, 8,* 359–374.

Reifman, A., & Windle, M. (1995). Adolescent suicidal behaviors as a function of depression, hopelessness, alcohol use, and social support: A longitudinal investigation. *American Journal of Community Psychology, 23,* 329–354.

Reiland, R. (2004). *Get me out of here: My recovery from borderline personality pisorder.* Center City, MN: Hazeldon.

Reinders, A. A., Nijenhuis, E. R., Paans, A. M., Korf, J., Willemsen, A. T., & den Boer, J. A. (2003). One brain, two selves. *Neuroimage, 20,* 2119–2125.

Reiner, R. (2008). Integrating a portable biofeedback device into clinical practice for patients with anxiety disorders: Results of a pilot study. *Applied Psychophysiology and Biofeedback, 33,* 55–61.

Reisberg, B., Ferris, S. H., de Leon, M. J., & Crook, T. (1982). The Global Deterioration Scale for the assessment of primary degenerative dementia. *American Journal of Psychiatry, 139,* 1136–1139.

Reiss, S. (1991). Expectancy model of fear, anxiety, and panic. *Clinical Psychology Review, 11,* 141–153.

Reiss, S., & McNally, R. J. (1985). Expectancy model of fear. In S. Reiss and R. R. Bootzin (Eds.), *Theoretical issues in behavior therapy* (pp. 107–121). New York: Academic Press.

Reitan, R. M. (1958). Validity of the Trail Making Test as an indicator of organic brain damage. *Perceptual and Motor Skills, 8,* 271–276.

Reitan, R. M., & Davison, L. A. (1974). *Clinical neuropsychology: Current status and applications. The series in clinical psychology* (Vol. 2). Washington, DC: V. H. Winston.

Remafedi, G. (1999). Sexual orientation and youth suicide. *JAMA: Journal of the American Medical Association, 282,* 1291–1292.

Rende, R., & Plomin, R. (1992). Diathesis-stress models of psychopathology: A quantitative genetic perspective. *Applied & Preventive Psychology, 1,* 177–182.

Rende, R., & Plomin, R. (1992). Diathesis-stress models of psychopathology: A quantitative genetic perspective. *Applied & Preventative Psychology, 1,* 177–182.

Renner, L. M., & Slack, K. S. (2006). Intimate partner violence and child maltreatment: Understanding intra- and intergenerational connections. *Child Abuse & Neglect, 30,* 599–617.

Rennie v. Klein, 462 F. Supp. 1131; 1978 U.S. Dist. LEXIS 14441 (1978).

Resnick, H. S., Kilpatrick, D. G., Dansky, B. S., Saunders, B. E., & Best, C. L. (1993). Prevalence of civilian trauma and posttraumatic stress disorder in a representative national sample of women. *Journal of Consulting and Clinical Psychology, 61,* 984–991.

Ressler, K. J., Rothbaum, B. O., Tannenbaum, L., Anderson, P., Graap, K., Zimand, E., Hodges, L., & Davis, M. (2004). Cognitive enhancers as adjuncts to psychotherapy: Use of D-cycloserine in phobic individuals to facilitate extinction of fear. *Archives of General Psychiatry, 61,* 1136–1144.

Rettew, D. C., & McKee, L. (2005). Temperament and its role in developmental psychopathology. *Harvard Review of Psychiatry, 13,* 14–27.

Rettew, D. C., Doyle, A. C., Kwan, M., Stanger, C., & Hudziak, J. J. (2006). Exploring the boundary between temperament and generalized anxiety disorder: A receiver operating characteristic analysis. *Journal of Anxiety Disorders, 20,* 931–945.

Reynolds, C. A., Raine, A., Mellingen, K., Venables, P. H., & Mednick, S. A. (2000.) Three-factor model of schizotypal personality: Invariance across culture, gender, religious affiliation, family adversity, and psychopathology. *Schizophrenia Bulletin, 26,* 603–618.

Reynolds, S., Stiles, W. B., Barkham, M., Shapiro, D. A., Hardy, G. E., & Rees, A. (1996). Acceleration of changes in session impact during contrasting time-limited psychotherapies. *Journal of Consulting and Clinical Psychology, 64,* 577–586.

Ricca, V., Mannucci, E., Mezzani, B., Di Bernardo, M., Zucchi, T., Paionni, A., Placidi, G. P. A., Rotella, C. M., & Faravelli, C. (2001). Psychopathological and clinical features of outpatients with an eating disorder not otherwise specified. *Eating & Weight Disorders, 6,* 157–165.

Ricciardelli, L. A., & McCabe, M. P. (2001). Self-esteem and negative affect as moderators of sociocultural influences on body dissatisfaction strategies to decrease weight and strategies to increase muscle tone among adolescent boys and girls. *Sex Roles, 44,* 189–207.

Ricciardelli, L. A., McCabe, M. P., Lillis, J., & Thomas, K. (2006). A Longitudinal

Investigation of the Development of Weight and Muscle Concerns Among Preadolescent Boys. Journal of Youth and Adolescence, 35, 177–187.

Riccio, C. A., Wolfe, M., Davis, B., Romine, C., George, C., & Lee, D. (2005). Attention–deficit hyperactivity disorder: Manifestation in adulthood. Archives of Clinical Neuro-psychology, 20, 249–269.

Rice, F., Harold, G., & Thaper, A. (2002). The genetic aetiology of childhood depression: A review. Journal of Child Psychology & Psychiatry, 43, 65–79.

Rice, M. E., Harris, G., & Cormier, C. (1992). An evaluation of a maximum security therapeutic community for psychopaths and other mentally disordered offenders. Law and Human Behavior; 16, 399–412.

Rice, M. J., & Moller, M. D. (2006). Wellness outcomes of trauma psychoeducation. Archives of Psychiatric Nursing, 20, 94–102.

Richards, J. C., Edgar, L. V., & Gibbon, P. (1996). Cardiac acuity in panic disorder. Cognitive Therapy and Research, 20, 361–376.

Richards, R., Kinney, D. K., Lunde, I., Benet, M., & Merzel, A. P. C. (1988). Creativity in manic-depressives, cyclothymes, their normal relatives, and control subjects. Journal of Abnormal Psychology 97, 281–288.

Rieber, R. W. (1999). Hypnosis, false memory and multiple personality: A trinity of affinity. History of Psychiatry, 10, 3–11.

Rief, W., & Nanke, A. (1999). Somatization disorder from a cognitive-psychobiological perspective. Current Opinion in Psychiatry, 12, 733–738.

Rief, W., Heuser, J., Mayrhuber, E., Stelzer, I., Hiller, W., & Fichter, M. M. (1996). The classification of multiple somatoform symptoms. Journal of Nervous and Mental Disease, 184, 680–687. Rosenbloom, M., Sullivan, E. V., & Pfefferbaum, A. (2003). Using magnetic resonance imaging and diffusion tensor imaging to assess brain damage in alcoholics. Alcohol Research & Health 27, 146–152.

Ries, R. K., Galanter, M., & Tonigan, J. S. (2008). Twelve-step facilitation. In M. Galanter, & H. D. Kleber, (Eds.), The American Psychiatric Publishing textbook of substance abuse treatment (4th ed.). (pp. 373–386). Arlington, VA: American Psychiatric Publishing, Inc.

Rifkin, A., Ghisalbert, D., Dimatou, S., Jin, C., & Sethi, M. (1998). Dissociative identity disorder in psychiatric inpatients. American Journal of Psychiatry, 155, 844–845.

Rihmer, Z. (2007). Suicide risk in mood disorders. Current Opinion in Psychiatry, 20, 17–22.

Rihmer, Z., Rutz, W., Pihlgren, H., & Pestality, P. (1998). Decreasing tendency of seasonality in suicide may indicate lowering rate of depressive suicides in the population. Psychiatry Research, 81, 233–240.

Riley, E. P., & McGee, C. L. (2005). Fetal alcohol spectrum disorders: An overview with emphasis on changes in brain and behavior. Experimental Biology and Medicine, 230, 357–365.

Ringman, J. M., & Cummings, J. L. (2006). Current and emerging pharmacological treatment options for dementia. Behavioral Neurology, 17, 5–16.

Rinne, T., de Kloet, E. R., Wouters, L., Goekoop, J. G., DeRijk, R. H., & van den Brink, W. (2002). Hyperresponsiveness of hypothalamic-pituitary adrenal axis to combined dexamethasone/corticotropin-releasing hormone challenge in female borderline personality disorder subjects with a history of sustained childhood abuse. Biological Psychiatry, 52, 1102–1112.

Riskind, J. H., & Alloy, L. B. (2006). Cognitive vulnerability to psychological disorders: Overview of theory, design, and methods. Journal of Social & Clinical Psychology, 25, 705–725.

Riskind, J. H., Moore, R., & Bowley, L. (1995). The looming of spiders: The fearful perceptual distortion of movement and menace. Behavior Research and Therapy, 33, 171–178.

Ritchie, C. W., Ames, D., Clayton, T., & Lai, R. (2004). Meta-analysis of randomized trials of the efficacy and safety of donepezil, galantamine, and rivastigmine for the treatment of Alzheimer disease. American Journal of Geriatric Psychiatry, 12, 358–369.

Ritchie, K., & Lovestone, S. (2002). The dementias. Lancet, 360, 1767–1769.

Ritterband, L. M., Gonder-Frederick, L. A., Cox, D. J., Clifton, A. D., West, R. W., & Borowitz, S. M. (2003). Internet interventions: In review, in use, and into the future. Professional Psychology: Research & Practice, 34, 527–534.

Rivas-Vazques, R. A. (2001). Antidepressants as first-line agents in the current pharma-cotherapy of anxiety disorders. Professional Psychology: Research and Practice, 32, 101–104.

Rivas-Vazquez, R. A. (2001). Antidepressants as first-line agents in the current pharmacotherapy of anxiety disorders. Professional Psychology: Research and Practice, 32, 101–104.

Rivas-Vazquez, R. A., Rice, J., & Kalman, D. (2003). Pharmacotherapy of obesity and eating disorders. Professional Psychology: Research & Practice, 34, 562–566.

Robbins, T. W. (2000). Chemical neuromodulation of frontal-executive functions in humans and other animals. Experimental Brain Research, 133, 130–138.

Robbins, T. W., & Everitt, B. J. (1999a). Drug addiction: Bad habits add up. Nature, 398, 567–570.

Robbins, T. W., & Everitt, B. J. (1999b). Interaction of the dopaminergic system with mechanisms of associative learning and cognition: Implications for drug abuse. Psychological Science, 10, 199–202.

Robins, C. J., Ivanoff, A. M., & Linehan, M. M. (2001). Dialectical behavior therapy. In W. J. Livesley (Ed.), Handbook of personality disorders: Theory, research, and treatment (pp. 437–459). New York: Guilford Press.

Robins, C. J., Ivanoff, A. M., & Linehan, M. M. (2001). Dialectical behavior therapy. In W. J. Livesley (Ed.), Handbook of personality disorders: Theory, research, and treatment (pp. 437–459). New York: Guilford Press.

Robins, L. N., & Regier, D. A. (1991). Psychiatric disorders in America: The Epidemiological Catchment Area Study. New York: Free Press.

Robins, L. N., & Regier, D. A. (1991). Psychiatric Disorders in America: The Epidemiologic Catchment Area Study. New York: Free Press.

Robinson, D., Woerner, M. G., Alvir, J. M., Bilder, R., Goldman, R., Geisler, S., Koreen, A., Sheitman, B., Chakos, M., Mayerhoff, D., & Lieberman, J. A. (1999). Predictors of relapse following response from a first episode of schizophrenia or schizoaffective disorder. Archives of General Psychiatry, 56, 241–247.

Robinson, M. S., & Alloy, L. B. (2003). Negative cognitive styles and stress-reactive rumination interact to predict depression: A prospective study. Cognitive Therapy and Research, 27, 275–292.

Robinson, T., & Valcour, F. (1995). The use of depo-provera in the treatment of child molesters and sexually compulsive males. Sexual Addiction & Compulsivity, 2, 277–294.

Roelofs, K., Hoogduin, K. A. L., Keijers, G. P. J., Näring, G. W. B., Moene, G. C., & Sandijck, P. (2002). Hypnotic susceptibility in patients With conversion disorder. Journal of Abnormal Psychology, 111, 390–395.

Roelofs, K., Spinhoven, P., Sandijck, P., Moene, F. C., & Hoogduin, K. A. L. (2005). The impact of early trauma and recent life-events on symptom severity in patients with conversion disorder. Journal of Nervous and Mental Disease, 193, 508–514.

Roelofs, K., van Galen, G. P., Keijsers, G. P., & Hoogduin, C. A. (2002). Motor initiation and execution in patients with conversion paralysis. Acta Psychologica, 110, 21–34.

Roesler, A. & Witztum, E. (2000). Pharmacotherapy of paraphilias in the next millennium. Behavioral Sciences & the Law, 18, 43–56.

Rogan, R. G., & Hammer, M. R. (1998). An exploratory study of message affect behavior:

A comparison between African Americans and Euro-Americans. *Journal of Language and Social Psychology, 17,* 449–464.

Rogers, C. R. (1942). *Counseling and psychotherapy: Newer concepts in practice.* Oxford, England: Houghton Mifflin.

Rogers, C. R. (1951). *Client-centered therapy: Its current practice, implications, and theory.* Boston: Houghton Mifflin.

Rogers, S. J. (1998). Neuropsychology of autism in young children and its implications for early intervention. *Mental Retardation and Developmental Disabilities Research Reviews, 4,* 104–112.

Rohde, D. (1999a, October 16). Jury hears a confession in killing. *The New York Times,* p. B2.

Rohde, D. (1999b, March 4). Man claims "ghost" drove him to push woman to her death. *The New York Times,* p. B2.

Rohde, D. (1999c, October 9). Witness tearfully describes fatal subway shoving. *The New York Times* p. B2,.

Rohde, D. (2000, February 23). For retrial, subway defendant goes off medication. *The New York Times,* p. B1.

Roisman, G. I., & Fraley, R. C. (2006). The limits of genetic influence: A behavior-genetic analysis of infant-caregiver relationship quality and temperament. *Child Development, 77,* 1656–1667.

Romach, M. K., & Sellers, E. M. (1991). Management of the alcohol withdrawal syndrome. *Annual Review of Medicine, 42,* 323–340.

Romero, M. P., & Wintemute, G. J. (2002). The epidemiology of firearm suicide in the United States. *Journal of Urban Health, 79,* 39–48.

Room, R., & Makela K. (2000). Typologies of the cultural position of drinking. *Journal of Studies on Alcohol, 61,* 475–483.

Rosa, A. R., Marco, M., Fachel, J. M. G., Kapczinski, F., Stein, A. T., & Barros, H. M. T. (2007). Correlation between drug treatment adherence and lithium treatment attitudes and knowledge by bipolar patients. *Progress in Neuro-Psychopharmacology & Biological Psychiatry, 31,* 217–224.

Rosa, M. A., Gattaz, W. F., Pascual-Leone, A., Fregni, F., Rosa, M. O., Rumi, D. O., Myczkowski, M., Silva, M. F., Mansur, C., Rigonatti, S. P., Teixeira, M. J., & Marcolin, M. A. (2006). Comparison of repetitive transcranial magnetic stimulation and electroconvulsive therapy in unipolar non-psychotic refractory depression: A randomized, single-blind study. *International Journal of Neuropsychopharmacology, 9,* 667–676.

Rosanoff, A. J. (1914). A study of brain atrophy in relation to insanity. *American Journal of Insanity, 71,* 101–132.

Rosario-Campos, M. C., Leckman, J. F., Mercadante, M. T., Shavitt, R. G., da Silva Prado, H., Sada, P., Zamignani, D., & Miguel, E. C. (2001). Adults with early-onset obsessive-compulsive disorder. *American Journal of Psychiatry 158,* 1899–1903.

Roscoe, W. (1993). How to become a berdache: Toward a unified analysis of gender diversity. In G. Herdt (Ed.), *Third sex, third gender: Beyond sexual dimorphism in culture and history* (pp. 329–372). New York: Zone Books.

Rosen, G. D., Bai, J., Wang, Y., Fiondella, C. G., Threlkeld, S. W., LoTurco, J. J., & Galaburda, A. M. (2007). Disruption of neuronal migration by RNAi of Dyx1c1 results in neocortical and hippocampal malformations. *Cerebral Cortex, 17,* 2562–2572.

Rosen, J. B., & Donley, M. P. (2006). Animal studies of amygdala function in fear and uncertainty: Relevance to human research. *Biological Psychology, 73,* 49–60.

Rosen, R. C., & Beck, J. G. (1988). *Patterns of sexual arousal: Psychophysiological processes and clinical applications.* New York: Guilford Press.

Rosen, R. C., & Leiblum, S. R. (1989). Assessment and treatment of desire disorders. In S. R. Leiblum & R. C. Rosen (Eds.), *Principles and practice of sex therapy: Update for the 1990s* (2nd ed., pp. 19–47). New York: Guilford Press.

Rosen, R. C., & Leiblum, S. R. (Eds.). (1995). *Case studies in sex therapy.* New York: Guilford Press.

Rosen, R. C., Taylor, J. F., Leiblum, S. R., & Bachmann, G. A. (1993). Prevalence of sexual dysfunction in women: Results of a survey study of 329 women in an outpatient gynecological clinic. *Journal of Sex & Marital Therapy, 19,* 171–188.

Rosenbaum, B., Valbak, K., Harder, S., Knudsen, P., Koster, A., Lajer, M., Lindhardt, A., Winther, G., Petersen, L., Jorgensen, P., Nordentoft, M., & Andreasen, A. H. (2005). The Danish National Schizophrenia Project: Prospective, comparative longitudinal treatment study of first-episode psychosis. *British Journal of Psychiatry, 186,* 394–399.

Rosenbaum, J. F., Arana, G. W., Human, S. E., Labbate, L. A., & Fava, M. (2005). *Handbook of psychiatric drug therapy.* New York: Lippincott Williams & Wilkins.

Rosenbaum, J. F., Arana, G. W., Hyman, S. E., Labbate, L. A., & Fava, M. (2005). *Handbook of psychiatric drug therapy* (5th ed.). New York: Lippincott, Williams, & Wilkins.

Rosenberg, H., & Melville, J. (2005). Controlled drinking and controlled drug use as outcome goals in British treatment services. *Addiction Research and Theory, 13,* 85–92.

Rosenbloom, M., Sullivan, E.V., & Pfefferbaum, A. (2003). Using magnetic resonance imaging and diffusion tensor imaging to assess brain damage in alcoholics. *Alcohol Research & Health 27,* 146–152.

Rosenfarb, I. S., Bellack, A. S., & Aziz, N. (2006). Family interactions and the course of schizophrenia in African American and White patients. *Journal of Abnormal Psychology, 115,* 112–120.

Rosenfarb, I. S., Bellack, A. S., & Aziz, N. (2006). Family interactions and the course of schizophrenia in African American and white patients. *Journal of Abnormal Psychology, 115,* 112–120.

Rosenthal, D. (Ed.). (1963). *The Genain quadruplets: A case study and theoretical analysis of heredity and environment in schizophrenia.* New York: Basic Books.

Rosenthal, R. (1991). *Meta-analytic procedures for social research.* Beverly Hills, CA: Sage Publications.

Rospenda, K. (2002). Workplace harassment, services utilization, and drinking outcomes. *Journal of Occupational Health Psychology, 7,* 141–155.

Ross, C. A., Miller, S. D., Bjornson, L., Reagor, P., Fraser, G. A., & Anderson, G. (1991). Abuse histories in 102 cases of multiple personality disorder. *The Canadian Journal of Psychiatry/La Revue canadienne de psychiatrie, 36,* 97–101.

Ross, L. K., Arnsberger, P., & Fox, P. J. (1998). The relationship between cognitive functioning and disease severity with depression in dementia of the Alzheimer's type. *Aging & Mental Health, 2,* 319–327.

Ross, L. T., & Hill, E. M. (2004). Comparing alcoholic and nonalcoholic parents on the family unpredictability scale. *Psychological Reports, 94,* 1385–1391.

Rossiter, E. M., & Agras, W. S. (1990). An empirical test of the DSM-III-R definition of binge. *International Journal of Eating Disorders, 9,* 513–518.

Roth, A., & Fonagy, P. (2005). *What works for whom: A critical review of psychotherapy research* (2nd ed.). New York,: Guilford Press.

Roth, A., & Fonagy, P. (2005). *What works for whom: A critical review of psychotherapy research* (2nd ed.). New York: Guilford Press.

Roth, A., & Fonagy, P. (2005). *What works for whom: A critical review of psychotherapy research* (2nd ed.). New York: Guilford.

Rothbaum, B. O., Anderson, P., Zimand, E., Hodges, L., Lang, D., & Wilson, J. (2006). Virtual reality exposure therapy and standard (in vivo) exposure therapy in the treatment of fear of flying. *Behavior Therapy, 37,* 80–90.

Rothbaum, B. O., Anderson, P., Zimand, E., Hodges, L., Lang, D., & Wilson, J. (2006). Virtual reality exposure therapy and standard (in vivo) exposure therapy in the treatment of fear of flying. *Behavior Therapy, 37,* 80–90.

Rothbaum, B. O., Hodges, L., Anderson, P. L., Price, L., & Smith, S. (2002). Twelve-month follow-up of virtual reality and standard exposure therapies for the fear of flying. *Journal of Consulting & Clinical Psychology, 70,* 428–432.

Rothbaum, B. O., Hodges, L., Smith, S., Lee, J. H., & Price, L. (2001). A controlled study of virtual reality exposure therapy for the fear of flying. *Journal of Consulting & Clinical Psychology, 68,* 1020–1026.

Rothbaum, F., Weisz, J., Pott, M., Miyake, K., & Morelli, G. (2000). Attachment and culture: Security in the United States and Japan. *American Psychologist, 55,* 1093–1104.

Rothenberg, A. (2001). Bipolar illness, creativity, and treatment. *Psychiatric Quarterly, 72,* 131–147.

Rothman, A. J., Haddock, G., & Schwarz, N. (2001). "How many partners is too many?" Shaping perceptions of personal vulnerability. *Journal of Applied Social Psychology, 31,* 2195–2214.

Rothman, E. (1995, December 15). What's in a name? *Focus Online: News from Harvard Medical, Dental, and Public Health Schools.* Retrieved April 25, 2007, from http://focus.hms.harvard.edu/1995/Dec15_1995/On_Becoming_A_Doctor.html

Rouillon, F. (1997). Epidemiology of panic disorder. *Human Psychopharmacology: Clinical and Experimental, 12,* S7–S12.

Rouse v. Cameron, 373 F.2d 451 (D. C. Cir. 1966); later proceeding, 387 F.2d 241 (1967).

Roy, A. (1980). Hysteria. *Journal of Psychosomatic Research, 24,* 53–56.

Rubia, K., Smith, A. B., Brammer, M. J., & Taylor, E. (2007). Temporal lobe dysfunction in medication-naïve boys with attention-deficit/hyperactivity disorder during attention allocation and its relation to response variability. *Biological Psychiatry, 62,* 999–1006.

Rubin, L., Fitts, M., & Becker, A. E. (2003) Whatever feels good in my soul: Body ethics and aesthetics among African American and Latina women. *Culture, Medicine, and Psychiatry, 27,* 49–75.

Rubinsztein, J. D., Michael, A., Paykel, E. S., & Sahakian, B. J. (2000). Cognitive impairment in remision of bipolar affective disorder. *Psychological Medicine, 30,* 1025–1036.

Ruffolo, J. S., Phillips, K. A., Menard, W., Fay, C., & Weisberg, R. B. (2006). Comorbidity of body dysmorphic disorder and eating disorders: Severity of psychopathology and body image disturbance. *International Journal of Eating Disorders, 39,* 11–19.

Ruiz-Sancho, A. M., Smith, G. W., & Gunderson, J. G. (2001). Psychoeducational approaches. In W. J. Livesley (Ed.), *Handbook of personality disorders: Theory, research, and treatment* (pp. 460–474). New York: Guilford Press.

Rund, B. R., Melle, I., Friis, S., Larsen, T. K., Midboe, L. J., Opjordsmoen, S., Simonsen, E., Vaglum, P., & McGlashan, T. (2004). Neurocognitive dysfunction in first-episode psychosis: Correlates with symptoms, premorbid adjustment, and duration of untreated psychosis. *American Journal of Psychiatry, 161,* 466–472.

Rush, A. J., Zimmerman, M., Wisniewski, S. R., Fava, M., Hollon, S. D., Warden, D., Biggs, M. M., Shores-Wilson, K., Shelton, R. C., Luther, J. F., Thomas, B., & Trivedi, M. H. (2005). Comorbid psychiatric disorders in depressed outpatients: Demographic and clinical features. *Journal of Affective Disorders, 87,* 43–55.

Russell, C. J., & Keel, P. K. (2002). Homosexuality as a specific risk factor for eating disorders in men. *International Journal of Eating Disorders, 31,* 300–306.

Russell, M. (1990). Prevalence of alcoholism among children of alcoholics. In M. Windle, & J. S. Searles (Eds.), *Children of alcoholics: Critical perspectives* (pp. 9–38). New York: Guilford Press.

Russell, T. A., Reynaud, E., Herba, C., Morris, R., & Corcoran, R. (2006). Do you see what I see? Interpretations of intentional movement in schizophrenia. *Schizophrenia Research, 81,* 101–111.

Rutherford, M. D., Baron-Cohen, S., & Wheelwright, S. (2002). Reading the mind in the voice: A study with normal adults and adults with Asperger syndrome and high functioning autism. *Journal of Autism and Developmental Disorders, 32,* 189–194.

Rutter, M. (2003). Poverty and Child Mental Health: Natural experiments and social causation. *JAMA: Journal of the American Medical Association, 290,* 2063–2064.

Rutter, M. L. (1999). Psychosocial adversity and child psychopathology. *British Journal of Psychiatry, 174,* 480–493.

Rutter, M., & Maughan, B. (1997). Psychosocial adversities in childhood and adult psychopathology. *Journal of Personality Disorders, 11,* 4–18.

Rutter, M., & Quinton, D. (1984). Parental psychiatric disorder: Effects on children. *Psychological Medicine, 14,* 853–880.

Ruwaard, J., Lange, A., Bouwman, M., Broeksteeg, J., & Schrieken, B. (2007). E-mailed standardized cognitive behavioural treatment of work-related stress: A randomized controlled trial. *Cognitive Behaviour Therapy, 36,* 179–192.

Ryan, D., & Carr, A. (2001). A study of the differential effects of Tomm's questioning styles on therapeutic alliance. *Family Process, 40,* 67–77.

Ryan, D., & Carr, A. (2001). A study of the differential effects of Tomm's questioning styles on therapeutic alliance. *Family Process, 40,* 67–77.

Rybakowski, F., Slopien, A., Dmitrzak-Weglarz, M., Czerski, P., Rajewski, A., & Hauser, J. (2006). The 5-HT2A -1438 A/G and 5-HTTLPR polymorphisms and personality dimensions in adolescent anorexia nervosa: Association study. *Neuropsychobiology, 53,* 33–39.

Saatcioglu, O., Erim, R., & Cakmak, D. (2006). Role of family in alcohol and substance abuse. *Psychiatry and Clinical Neurosciences, 60,* 125–132.

Saba, G., Verdon, C. M., Kalalou, K., Rocamora, J. F., Dumortier, G., Benadhira, R., Stamatiadis, L., Vicaut, E., Lipski, H., & Januel, D. (2006). Transcranial magnetic stimulation in the treatment of schizophrenic symptoms: A double blind sham controlled study. *Journal of Psychiatric Research, 40,* 147–152.

Sabourin, M. E., Cutcomb, S. D., Crawford, H. J., & Pribram, K. (1990–1991). EEG correlates of hypnotic susceptibility and hypnotic trance: Spectral analysis and coherence. *International Journal of Psychophysiology, 10,* 125–142.

Sachdev, P. S. (1985). Koro epidemic in north-east India. *Australia New Zealand Journal of Psychiatry, 19,* 433–438.

Sachs, G. S. (2006). A review of agitation in mental illness: Burden of illness and underlying pathology. *Journal of Clinical Psychiatry, 67*(Suppl. 10), 5–12.

Sachs-Ericsson, N., Plant, E. A., & Blazer, D. G. (2005). Racial differences in the frequency of depressive symptoms among community dwelling elders: The role of socioeconomic factors. *Aging & Mental Health, 9,* 201–209.

Sackeim, H. A., Devanand, D. P., & Nobler, M. S. (1995). Electroconvulsive therapy. In F. E. Bloom & D. J. Kupfer (Eds.), *Psychopharmacology: The fourth generation of progress* (pp. 1123–1141). New York: Raven Press.

Sackheim, H. A., Haskett, R. F., Mulsant, B. H., Thase, M. E., Mann, J. J., Pettinati, H. M., Greenberg, R. M., Crowe, R. R., Cooper, T. B., & Prudic, J. (2001). Continuation pharmacotherapy in the prevention of relapse following electroconvulsive therapy: A randomized controlled trial. *Journal of the American Medical Association, 285,* 1299–1307.

Sackheim, H. A., Devanand, D. P., & Nobler, M. S. (1995). Electroconvulsive therapy. In F. E. Bloom & D. J. Kupfer (Eds.), *Psychopharmacology: The Fourth Generation of Progress.* New York: Raven Press. pp. 1123–1141.

Sacktor, N., Nakasujja, N., Skolasky, R., Robertson, K., Wong, M., Musisi, S., Ronald, A., & Katabira, E. (2006). Antiretroviral therapy improves cognitive impairment in HIV+ individuals in sub-Saharan Africa. *Neurology, 67,* 311–314.

Sadeghi, M., & Fakhrai, A. (2000). Transsexualism in female monozygotic twins: A case report. *Australian and New Zealand Journal of Psychiatry, 34,* 862–864.

Sadock, B. J., & Sadock, V. A. (2007). *Kaplan and Sadock's synopsis of psychiatry: Behavioral sciences/clinical psychiatry* (10th ed.). Philadelphia: Lippincott, Williams, & Wilkins.

Sadock, B. J., and Sadock, V. A. (2007). *Kaplan and Sadock's Synopsis of Psychiatry: Behavioral Sciences/Clinical Psychiatry* 10th edition. Philadelphia: Wolters Kluwer Health.

Sadock, V. (1995). Psychotropic drugs and sexual dysfunction. *Primary Psychiatry, 4,* 16–17.

Safer, D. L., Telch, C. F., & Agras, W. S. (2001). Dialectical behavior therapy for bulimia nervosa. *American Journal of Psychiatry, 158,* 632–634.

Saha, S., Chant, D., Welham, J., & McGrath, J. (2005). A systematic review of the prevalence of schizophrenia. *PLoS Medicine, 2,* e141.

Salamone, J. D. (2002). Antidepressants and placebos: Conceptual problems and research strategies. *Prevention & Treatment, 5,* Article 24. http://www.journals.apa.org/prevention/volume5/pre0050024c.html.

Salkovskis, P. M. (1985). Obsessional-compulsive problems: A cognitive-behavioural analysis. *Behaviour Research and Therapy, 23,* 571–583.

Salkovskis, P. M. (1988). Phenomenology, assessment, and the cognitive model of panic. In S. Rachman & J. D. Maser (Eds.), *Panic: Psychological perspectives* (pp. 111–136). Hillsdale, NJ: Lawrence Erlbaum.

Salkovskis, P. M. (1996). The cognitive approach to anxiety: Threat beliefs, safety-seeking behavior, and the special case of health anxiety and obsessions. In P. M. Salkovskis (Ed.), *Frontiers of cognitive therapy* (pp. 48–74). New York: Guilford Press.

Salkovskis, P. M., & Campbell, P. (1994). Thought suppression induces intrusion in naturally occurring negative intrusive thoughts. *Behaviour Research and Therapy, 32,* 1–8.

Salmán, E., Diamond, K., Jusino, C., Sánchez-LaCay, A., & Liebowitz, M. R. (1997). Hispanic Americans. In S. Friedman (Ed.), *Cultural issues in the treatment of anxiety* (pp. 59–80). New York: Guilford Press.

Salthouse, T. A. (2001). General and specific age-related influences on neuropsychological variables. In F. Boiler & S. Cappa (Eds.), *Handbook of neuropsychology: Vol. 6. Aging and dementia.* (pp. 39–50) London: Elsevier.

Salthouse, T. A. (2005). Relations between cognitive abilities and measures of executive functioning. *Neuropsychology, 19,* 532–545.

Salthouse, T. A. (2005). Relations between cognitive abilities and measures of executive functioning. *Neuropsychology, 19,* 532–545.

Samuels, J., Eaton, W. W., Bienvenu, O. J., III, Brown, C., Costa, P. T., Jr., & Nestadt, G. (2002). Prevalence and correlates of personality disorders in a community sample. *British Journal of Psychiatry, 180,* 536–542.

Sánchez, H. G. (2001). Risk factor model for suicide assessment and intervention. *Professional Psychology: Research and Practice, 32,* 351–358.

Sandberg, S. (2002). *Hyperactivity and attention disorders of childhood.* New York: Cambridge University Press.

Sanders, A. R., Duan, J., Levinson, D. F., Shi, J., He, D., Hou, C., Burrell, G. J., Rice, J. P., Nertney, D. A., Olincy, A., Rozic, P., Vinogradov, S., Buccola, N. G., Mowry, B. J., Freedman, R., Amin, F., Black, D. W., Silverman, J. M., Byerley, W. F., Crowe, R. R., Cloninger, C. R., Martinez, M., & Gejman, P. V. (2008). No significant association of 14 candidate genes with schizophrenia in a large European ancestry sample: Implications for psychiatric genetics. *American Journal of Psychiatry, 165,* 497–506.

Sanderson, W. C., & Barlow, D. H. (1990). A description of patients diagnosed with DSM-III-R generalized anxiety disorder. *Journal of Nervous and Mental Disease, 178,* 588–591.

Sands, J. R., & Harrow, M. (1999). Depression during the longitudinal course of schizophrenia. *Schizophrenia Bulletin, 25,* 157–171.

Sanfilipo, M., Lafargue, T., Rusinek, H., Arena, L., Loneragan, C., Lautin, A., Rotrosen, J., & Wolkin, A. (2002). Cognitive performance in schizophrenia: Relationship to regional brain volumes and psychiatric symptoms. *Psychiatry Research: Neuroimaging, 116,* 1–23.

Santangelo, S. L., & Tsatsanis, K. (2005). What is known about autism: Genes, brain, and behavior. *American Journal of Pharmacogenomics, 5,* 71–92.

Santhiveeran, J., & Grant, B. (2005). Use of communication tools and fee-setting in e-therapy: A Web site survey. *Social Work in Mental Health, 4,* 31–45.

Santisteban, D. A., Muir-Malcolm, J. A., Mitrani, V. B., & Szapocznik, J. (2002). Integrating the study of ethnic culture and family psychology intervention science. In H. A. Liddle, D. A. Santisteban, R. F. Levant, & J. H. Bray (Eds), *Family psychology: Science-based interventions* (pp. 331–351).

Washington, DC: American Psychological Association.

Sapolsky, R. M. (1996). Why stress is bad for your brain. *Science, 273,* 749–750.

Sapolsky, R. M. (1997). *Why zebras don't get ulcers.* New York: Freeman.

Sarbin, T. R. (1995). On the belief that one body may be host to two or more personalities. *International Journal of Clinical and Experimental Hypnosis, 43,* 163–183.

Sareen, J., Campbell, D. W., Leslie, W. D., Malisza, K. L., Stein, M. B., Paulus, M. P., Kravetsky, L. B., Kjernisted, K. D., Walker, J. R., & Reiss, J. P. (2007). Striatal function in generalized social phobia: A functional magnetic resonance imaging study. *Biological Psychiatry, 61,* 396–404.

Sareen, J., Stein, M. B., Cox, B. J., & Hassard, S. T. (2004). Understanding comorbidity of anxiety disorders with antisocial behavior: Findings from two large community surveys. *Journal of Nervous and Mental Disease, 192,* 178–186.

Sarísoy, G., Böke, Ö., Arík, A. C., & Sahin, A. R. (2008). Panic disorder with nocturnal panic attacks: Symptoms and comorbidities. *European Psychiatry, 23,* 195–200.

Sarró, R. (1956). Spain as the cradle of psychiatry. In *Centennial papers: Saint Elizabeth's Hospital 1855–1955* (pp. 85–96). Washington, DC: Centennial Commission, Saint Elizabeth's Hospital.

Satcher, D. (1999). *The Surgeon General's call to action to prevent suicide, 1999.* Washington, DC: U.S. Public Health Service.

Satterfield, J. H. (1987). Childhood diagnostic and neurophysiological predictors of teenage arrest rates: An 8-year prospective study. In S. A. Mednick, T. E. Moffit, & S. A. Stack (Eds.), *The causes of crime: New biological approaches* (pp. 146–167). Cambridge, England: Cambridge University Press.

Sattler, J. M. (1982). *Assessment of children's intelligence and special abilities* (2nd ed.). Boston: Allyn & Bacon.

Saudino, K. J. (2005). Special article: Behavioral genetics and child temperament. *Journal of Developmental & Behavioral Pediatrics, 26,* 214–223.

Saulsman, L. M., & Page, A. C. (2004). The five-factor model and personality disorder empirical literature: A meta-analytic review. *Clinical Psychology Review, 23,* 1055–1085.

Sava, F. A., Yates, B. T., Lupu, V., Szentagotai, A., & David, D. (2009). Cost-effectiveness and cost-utility of cognitive therapy, rational emotive behavioral therapy, and fluoxetine (Prozac) in treating clinical depression: A randomized clinical trial. *Journal of Clinical Psychology, 65,* 36–52.

Saxena, S., & Rauch, S. L. (2000). Functional neuroimaging and the neuroanatomy of obsessive-compulsive disorder. *Psychiatric Clinics of North America, 23,* 563–586.

Saxena, S., Brody, A. L., Schwartz, J. M., & Baxter, L. R. (1998). Neuroimaging and frontal-subcortical circuitry in obsessive-compulsive disorder. *British Journal of Psychiatry, 173,* 26–37.

Scahill, L., & Schwab-Stone, M. (2000). Epidemiology of ADHD in school-age children. *Child and Adolescent Psychiatric Clinics of North America, 9,* 541–555.

Scarmeas, N., Brandt, J., Blacker, D., Albert, A., Hadjigerogious, G., Dubois, B., Devanand, D., Honig, L., & Stern, Y. (2007). Disruptive behavior as a predictor in Alzheimer's disease. *Archives of Neurology, 64,* 1755–1761.

Scarpa, A., Haden, S. C., & Hurley, J. (2006). Community violence victimization and symptoms of posttraumatic stress disorder: The moderating effects of coping and social support. *Journal of Interpersonal Violence, 21,* 446–469.

Scarr, S., & McCartney, K. (1983). How people make their own environments: A theory of genotype-environment effects. *Child Development, 54,* 424–435.

Schachter, S., & Latane, B. (1964). Crime, cognition, and the autonomic nervous system. *Nebraska Symposium on Motivation, 12,* 221–275.

Schacter, D. L., Kaszniak, A. K., Kihlstrom, J. F., & Valdiserri, M. (1991). The relation between source memory and aging. *Psychology and Aging, 6,* 559–568.

Schacter, D. L., Koutstaal, W., & Norman, K. A. (1997). False memories and aging. *Trends in Cognitive Sciences, 1,* 229–236.

Schaefer, K. (Interviewer). (2003, May 29). Ideastream Focus on Mental Health: Frese Family Album. [Radio broadcast]. Cleveland, OH: WPCN.

Schafe, G. E., & LeDoux, J. E. (2004). The neural basis of fear. In M. S. Gazzaniga (Ed.), *The cognitive neurosciences* (3rd ed.), (pp. 987–1003). Cambridge, MA: MIT Press.

Schatzberg, A. F. (2000). Clinical efficacy of reboxetine in major depression. *Journal of Clinical Psychiatry, 61,* 31–38.

Schechter, R., & Grether, J. K. (2008). Continuing increases in autism reported to California's developmental services system: Mercury in retrograde. *Archives of General Psychiatry, 65,* 19–24.

Schena, M., Shalon, D., Davis, R. W., & Brown, P. O. (1995). Quantitative monitoring of gene expression patterns with a complementary DNA microarray. *Science, 270,* 467–470.

Scherrer, J. F., True, W. R., Xian, H., Lyons, M. J., Eisen, S. A., Goldberg, J., Lin, N., & Tsuang, M. T. (2000). Evidence for genetic influences common and specific to symptoms

of generalized anxiety and panic. *Journal of Affective Disorders, 57,* 25–35.

Schildkraut, J. J. (1965). The catecholamine hypothesis of affective disorders: A review of supporting evidence. *American Journal of Psychiatry, 122,* 509–522.

Schmahl, C. G., Elzinga, B. M., Vermetten, E., Sanislow, C., McGlashan, T. H., & Bremner, J. D. (2003). Neural correlates of memories of abandonment in women with and without borderline personality disorder. *Biological Psychiatry, 54,* 142–151.

Schmahl, C. G., Vermetten, E., Elzinga, B. M., & Bremner, J. D. (2004). A positron emission tomography study of memories of childhood abuse in borderline personality disorder. *Biological Psychiatry, 55,* 759–765.

Schmahl, C. G., Vermetten, E., Elzinga, B. M., & Douglas, B. J. (2003). Magnetic resonance imaging of hippocampal and amygdala volume in women with childhood abuse and borderline personality disorder. *Psychiatry Research, 122,* 193–198.

Schmaling, K. B., & Hernandez, D. V. (2005). Detection of depression among low-income Mexican Americans in primary care. *Journal of Health Care for the Poor and Underserved, 16,* 780–790.

Schmidt, N. B., Lerew, D. R., & Jackson, R. J. (1997). The role of anxiety sensitivity in the pathogenesis of panic: Prospective evaluation of spontaneous panic attacks during acute stress. *Journal of Abnormal Psychology, 106,* 355–364.

Schmitt, D. P., Alcalay, L., Allensworth, M., Allik, J., Ault, L., Austers, I., et al. (2004). Patterns and universals of adult romantic attachment across 62 regions: Are models of self and other pancultural constructs? *Journal of Cross-cultural Psychology, 35*(4), 367–402.

Schneck, C. D., Miklowitz, D. J., Miyahara, S., Araga, M., Wisniewski, S., Gyulai, L., et al. (2008). The prospective course of rapid-cycling bipolar disorder: Findings from the STEP-B. *American Journal of Psychiatry, 165,* 370–377.

Schneider, F. R., Blanco, C., Antia, S. X., & Liebowitz, M. R. (2002). The social anxiety spectrum. *Psychiatric Clinics of North America, 25,* 757–774.

Schneider, F., Gur, R. C., Koch, K., Backes, V., Amunts, K., Shah, N. J., Bilker, W., Gur, R. E., & Habel, U. (2006). Impairment in the specificity of emotion processing in schizophrenia. *American Journal of Psychiatry, 163,* 442–447.

Schneider, F., Habel, U., Kessler, C., Posse, S., Grodd, W., & Muller-Gartner, H. (2000). Functional imaging of conditioned aversive emotional responses in antisocial personality disorder. *Neuropsychobiology, 42,* 192–201.

Schneider, L. S., Dagerman, K. S., & Insel, P. (2006). Risk of death with atypical

antipsychotic drug treatment for dementia: Meta-analysis of randomized placebo-controlled trials: Reply. *JAMA: Journal of the American Medical Association, 295,* 496–497.

Schneider, L. S., Dagerman, K., & Insel, P. S. (2006). Efficacy and adverse effects of atypical antipsychotics for dementia: Meta-analysis of randomized, placebo-controlled trials. *American Journal of Geriatric Psychiatry, 14,* 191–210.

Schneider, M., Retz, W., Coogan, A., Thome, J., & Rösler, M. (2006). Anatomical and functional brain imaging in adult attention-deficit/hyperactivity disorder (ADHD)—a neurological view. *European Archives of Psychiatry and Clinical Neuroscience, 256*(Suppl. 1): I/32–I/41.

Schneider-Axmann, T., Kamer, T., Moroni, M., Maric, N., Tepest, R., Dani, I., Honer, W. G., Scherk, H., Rietschel, M., Schulze, T. G., Müller, D. J., Cordes, J., Schönell, H., Steinmetz, H., Gaebel, W., Vogeley, K., Kühn, K., Wagner, M., Maier, W., Träber, F., Block, W., Schild, H. H., & Falkai, P. (2006). Relation between cerebrospinal fluid, gray matter and white matter changes in families with schizophrenia. *Journal of Psychiatric Research, 40,* 646–655.

Schnurr, P. P., Friedman, M. J., Engel, C. C., Foa, E. B., Shea, M. T., Chow, B. K., Resick, P. A., Thurston, V., Orsillo, S. M., Haug, R., & Turner, C. (2007). Cognitive behavioral therapy for posttraumatic stress disorder in women: A randomized controlled trial. *JAMA: Journal of the American Medical Association, 297,* 820–830.

Schnurr, P. P., Friedman, M. J., Foy, D. W., Shea, M. T., Hsieh, F. Y., Lavori, P. W., Glynn, S. M., Wattenberg, M., & Bernardy, N. C. (2003). Randomized trial of trauma-focused group therapy for posttraumatic stress disorder: Results from a Department of Veterans Affairs cooperative study. *Archives of General Psychiatry, 60,* 481–489.

Schoevers, R. A., Beekman, A. T. F., Deeg, D. J. H., Jonker, C., & van Tilburg, W. (2003). Comorbidity and risk-patterns of depression, generalised anxiety disorder and mixed anxiety-depression in later life: Results from the AMSTEL study. *International Journal of Geriatric Psychiatry, 18,* 994–1001.

Schoevers, R. A., van Tilburg, W., Beekman, A. T. F., & Deeg, D. J. H. (2005). Depression and generalized anxiety disorder: Co-occurrence and longitudinal patterns in elderly patients. *American Journal of Geriatric Psychiatry, 13,* 31–39.

Schonfeldt-Lecuona, C., Connemann, B. J., Spitzer, M., & Herwig, U. (2003). Transcranial magnetic stimulation in the reversal of motor conversion disorder. *Psychotherapy & Psychosomatics, 72,* 286–288.

Schopp, R. F. (1991). The psychotherapist's duty to protect the public: The appropriate standard and the foundation in legal theory and empirical premises. *Nebraska Law Review, 70,* 327–360.

Schopp, R. F., & Quattrocchi, M. R. (1984). Tarasoff, the doctrine of special relationships and the psychotherapist's duty to warn. *The Journal of Psychiatry and Law, 12,* 13–37.

Schore, A. N. (2003). *Affect dysregulation and disorders of the self.* New York: Norton.

Schrimsher, G. W., Billingsley, R. L., Jackson, E. F., & Moore, B. D., III. (2002). Caudate nucleus volume asymmetry predicts attention-deficit hyperactivity disorder (ADHD) symptomatology in children. *Journal of Child Neurolology, 17,* 877–884.

Schrof, J. M., & Schultz, S. (1999, March 8). Melancholy nation. *U.S. News and World Report,* pp. 56–63.

Schuckit, M. A. (1999). New findings on the genetics of alcoholism. *JAMA: Journal of the American Medical Association, 281,* 1875–1876.

Schulenberg, J., Wadsworth, K. N., O'Malley, P. M., Bachman, J. G., & Johnston, L. D. (1996). Adolescent risk factors for binge drinking during the transition to young adulthood: Variable- and pattern-centered approaches to change. *Developmental Psychology, 32,* 659–674.

Schulte-Körne, G. (2001). Genetics of reading and spelling disorder. *Journal of Child Psychology and Psychiatry, 42,* 985–997.

Schulte-Korne, G., & Remschmidt, H. (1996). Familial clustering of conversion disorder. *Nervenartz, 67,* 794–798.

Schwalberg, M. D., Barlow, D. H., Alger, S. A., & Howard, L. J. (1992). Comparison of bulimics, obese binge eaters, social phobics, and individuals with panic disorder on comorbidity across DSM-III-R anxiety disorders. *Journal of Abnormal Psychology, 101,* 675–681.

Schwartz, J. M., Stoessel, P. W., Baxter, L. R., Martin, K. M., & Phelps, M. E. (1996). Systematic changes in cerebral glucose metabolic rate after successful behavior modification treatment of obsessive-compulsive disorder. *Archives of General Psychiatry, 53,* 109–113.

Schwartz, R. C. (2001). Racial profiling in medical research. *New England Journal of Medicine, 344,* 1392–1393.

Schwarz, N. (1999). Self-reports: How the questions shape the answers. *American Psychologist, 54,* 93–105.

Schwarz, N. (1999). Self-Reports: How the questions shape the answers. *American Psychologist, 54,* 93–105.

Schwarz, N., Knäuper, B., Hippler, H. J., Noelle-Neumann, E., & Clark, F. (1991). Rating scales: Numeric values may change the meaning of scale labels. *Public Opinion Quarterly, 55,* 570–582.

Schwarz, N., Knäuper, B., Hippler, H., Noelle-Neumann, E., & Clark, L. (1991). Rating scales: Numeric values may change the meaning of scale labels. *Public Opinion Quarterly, 55,* 570–582.

Sclar, D. A., Robison, L. M., Skaer, T. L, & Galin, R. S. (1999). Ethnicity and the prescribing of antidepressant pharmacotherapy: 1992–1995. *Harvard Review of Psychiatry, 7,* 29–36.

Scogin, F., Bynum, J., Stephens, G., & Calhoon, S. (1990). Efficacy of self-administered treatment programs: Meta-analytic review. *Professional Psychology: Research and Practice, 21,* 42–47.

Scott, D. J., Stohler, C. S., Egnatu, C. M., Wang, H., Koeppe, R. A., & Zubieta, J. (2008). Placebo and nocebo effects are defined by opposite opioid and dopaminergic responses. *Archives of General Psychiatry, 65,* 220–231.

Scott, J., & Gutierrez, M. J. (2004). The current status of psychological treatments in bipolar disorders: A systematic review of relapse prevention. *Bipolar Disorders, 6,* 498–503.

Scott, J., Stanton, B., Garland, A., & Ferrier, I. N. (2000). Cognitive vulnerability in patients with bipolar disorder. *Psychological Medicine, 30,* 467–472.

Scott, W. D., Ingram, R. E., & Shadel, W. G. (2003). Hostile and sad moods in dysphoria: Evidence for cognitive specificity in attributions. *Journal of Social & Clinical Psychology, 22,* 233–252.

Seedat, S., Stein, M. B., & Forde, D. R. (2003). Prevalence of dissociative experiences in a community sample: Relationship to gender, ethnicity, and substance use. *Journal of Nervous and Mental Disease, 191,* 115–120.

Seeman, M. V. (2000). Women and psychosis. *Medscape Women's Health, 5,* n.p. Retrieved February 9, 2009, from http://www.medscape.com/viewarticle/408912

Seeman, M., & Lang, M. (1990) The role of estrogens in schizophrenia gender differences. *Schizophrenia Bulletin, 16,* 185–194.

Segal, D. L. (2003). Abnormal psychology. In S. K. Whitbourne & J. C. Cavanaugh (Eds.), *Integrating aging topics into psychology: A practical guide for teaching* (pp. 141–158). Washington, DC: American Psychological Association.

Segal, Z. V., Pearson, J. L., & Thase, M. E. (2003). Challenges in preventing relapse in major depression: Report of a National Institute of Mental Health Workshop on state of the science of relapse prevention in major depression. *Journal of Affective Disorders, 77,* 97–108.

Segrin, C., & Abramson, L. Y. (1994). Negative reactions to depressive behaviors: A communication theory analysis. *Journal of Abnormal Psychology, 103,* 655–668.

Segrin, C., & Dillard, J. P. (1992). The interactional theory of depression: A meta-analysis of the research literature. *Journal of Social & Clinical Psychology, 11,* 43–70.

Segui, J., Maruez, M., Garcia, L., Canet, J., Salvador-Carulla, L., & Ortiz, M. (2000). Depersonalization in panic disorder: A clinical study. *Comprehensive Psychiatry, 41,* 172–178.

Seidman, L. J., Faraone, S. V., Goldstein, J. M., Kremen, W. S., Horton, N. J., Makris, N., Toomey, R., Kennedy, D., Caviness, V. S., & Tsuang, M. T. (2002). Left hippocampal volume as a vulnerability indicator for schizophrenia: A magnetic resonance imaging morphometric study of nonpsychotic first-degree relatives. *Archives of General Psychiatry, 59,* 839–849.

Seil, D. (1996). Transsexuals: The boundaries of sexual identity and gender. In R. P. Cabaj & T.S. Stein (Eds.), *Textbook of Homosexuality and Mental Health.* (pp. 743–762). Washington, DC: American Psychiatric Press.

Seivewright, H., Tyrer, P., & Johnson, T. (2002). Change in personality status in neurotic disorders. *Lancet, 359,* 2253–2254.

Sell v. United States, 539 U.S. 166 (2003). (No. 02-5664).

Selten, J., Cantor-Graae, E., & Kahn, R. S. (2007). Migration and schizophrenia. *Current Opinion in Psychiatry, 20,* 111–115.

Sentell, J. W., Lacroix, M., Sentell, J. V., & Finstuen, K. (1997). Predictive patterns of suicidal behavior: The United States armed services versus the civilian population. *Military Medicine, 162,* 162–171.

Sereny, G., Sharma, V., Holt. J., & Gordis, E. (1986). Mandatory supervised Antabuse therapy in an outpatient alcoholism program: A pilot study. *Alcoholism, 10,* 290–292.

Sergi, M. J., Rassovsky, Y., Nuechterlein, K. H., & Green, M. F. (2006). Social perception as a mediator of the influence of early visual processing on functional status in schizophrenia. *American Journal of Psychiatry, 163,* 448–454.

Serin, R. C. (1991). Psychopathy and violence in criminals. *Journal of Interpersonal Violence, 6,* 423–431.

Serra, M., Althaus, M., de Sonneville, L. M. J., Stant, A. D., Jackson, A. E., & Minderaa, R. B. (2003). Face recognition in children with a pervasive developmental disorder not otherwise specified. *Journal of Autism and Developmental Disorders, 33,* 303–317.

Seto, M. C., & Barbaree, H. E. (1999). Psychopathy, treatment behavior, and sex offender recidivism. *Journal of Interpersonal Violence, 14,* 1235–1248.

Shabsigh, R., Seftel, A. D., Kloner, R. A., Rosen, R. C., & Montorsi, F. (2003). The emerging frontier for management of erectile sysfunction: Strategies for patient care on the horizon. Symposium held at the Hilton Chicago in Chicago on April 25, 2003.

Shadish, W. R, Navarro, A. M., Matt, G. E., & Phillips, G. (2000). The effects of psychological therapies under clinically representative conditions: A meta-analysis. *Psychological Bulletin, 126*, 512–529.

Shadish, W. R., Cook, T. D., & Campbell, D. T. (2002). *Experimental and quasi-experimental designs for causal inference.* Boston: Houghton Mifflin.

Shadish, W. R., Navarro, A. M., Matt, G. E., & Phillips, G. (2000). The effects of psychological therapies under clinically representative conditions: A meta-analysis. *Psychological Bulletin, 126*, 512–529.

Shaffer, G. W., & Lazarus, R. S. (1952). Historical development. In G. W. Shaffer & R. S. Lazarus (Eds.), *Fundamental concepts in clinical psychology* (pp. 1–31). New York: McGraw-Hill.

Shafran, R., Thordarson, D. S., & Rachman, S. (1996). Thought-action fusion in obsessive compulsive disorder. *Journal of Anxiety Disorders, 10*, 379–391.

Shah, N., Passi, V., Bryson, S., & Agras, W. S. (2005). Patterns of eating and abstinence in women treated for bulimia nervosa. *International Journal of Eating Disorders, 38*, 330–334.

Shalev, A. Y., Peri, T., Canetti, L., & Schreiber, S. (1996). Predictors of PTSD in injured trauma survivors: A prospective study. *American Journal of Psychiatry, 153*, 219–225.

Shalev, A. Y., Sahar, T., Freedman, S., Peri, T., Glick, N., Brandes, D., Orr, S. P., & Pitman, R. K. (1998). A prospective study of heart rate response following trauma and the subsequent development of posttraumatic stress disorder. *Archives of General Psychiatry, 55*, 553–559.

Shapira, B., Tubi, N., Drexler, H., Lidsky, D., Calev, A., & Lerer, B. (1998). Cost and benefit in the choice of ECT schedule: Twice versus three times weekly ECT. *British Journal of Psychiatry, 172*, 44–48.

Shapiro, A. K. (1964). Factors contributing to the placebo effect: Their significance for psychotherapy. *American Journal of Psychotherapy, 18*, 73–88.

Shapiro, A. K., & Morris, L. A. (1978). The placebo effect in medical and psychological therapies. In S. L. Garfield & A. E. Bergin (Eds.), *Handbook of psychotherapy and behavior change: An empirical analysis* (2nd ed.). New York: John Wiley & Sons.

Shattuck, P. T., Seltzer, M. M., Greenberg, J. S., Orsmond, G. I., Bolt, D., Kring, S., Lounds, J., & Lord, C. (2007). Change in autism symptoms and maladaptive behaviors in adolescents and adults with an autism spectrum disorder. *Journal of Autism and Developmental Disorders, 37*, 1735–1747.

Shavitt, R. G., Hounie, A. G., Campos, M. C. R., & Miguel, E. C. (2006). Tourette's syndrome. *Psychiatric Clinics of North America, 29*, 471–486.

Shaw, D. S., Winslow, E. B., Owens, E. B., & Hood, N. (1998). Young children's adjustment to chronic family adversity: A longitudinal study of low-income families. *Journal of the American Academy of Child & Adolescent Psychiatry, 37*, 545–553.

Shaw, H., Ramirez, L., Trost, A., Randall, P., & Stice, E. (2004). Body image and eating disturbances across ethnic groups: More similarities than differences. *Psychology of Addictive Behaviors, 18*, 12–18.

Shaw, H., Stice, E., & Becker, C. B. (2009). Preventing eating disorders. *Child and Adolescent Psychiatric Clinics of North America, 18*, 199–207.

Shaw-Zirt, B., Popali-Lehane, L., Chaplin, W., & Bergman, A. (2005). Adjustment, social skills, and self-esteem in college students with symptoms of ADHD. *Journal of Attention Disorders, 8*, 109–120.

Shaywitz, B. A., Shaywitz, S. E., Blachman, B. A., Pugh, K. R., Fulbright, R. K., Skudlarski, P., et al. (2004). Development of left occipito-temporal systems for skilled reading in children after a phonologically-based intervention. *Biological Psychiatry, 55*, 926–933.

Shaywitz, B. A., Shaywitz, S. E., Pugh, K. R., Mencl, W. E., Fulbright, R. K., Skudlarski, P., et al. (2002). Disruption of posterior brain systems for reading in children with developmental dyslexia. *Biological Psychiatry, 52*, 101–110.

Shaywitz, B.A., Lyon, G. R., & Shaywitz, S.E. (2006). The role of functional magnetic resonance imaging in understanding reading and dyslexia. *Developmental Neuropsychology, 30*, 613–632.

Shea, M. T., Elkin, I., Imber, S. D., Sotsky, S. M., Watkins, J. T., Collins, J. F., et al. (1992). Course of depressive symptoms over follow-up: Findings from the National Institute of Mental Health Treatment of Depression Collaborative Research Program. *Archives of General Psychiatry, 49*, 782–787.

Shea, M. T., Stout, R. L., Yen, S., Pagano, M. E., Skodol, A. E., Morey, L. C., et al. (2004). Associations in the course of personality disorders and Axis I disorders over time. *Journal of Abnormal Psychology, 113*, 499–508.

Shear, K., Jin, R., Ruscio, A. M., Walters, E. E., & Kessler, R. C. (2006). Prevalence and correlates of estimated DSM-IV child and adult separation anxiety disorder in the National Comorbidity Survey replication. *American Journal of Psychiatry, 163*, 1074–1083.

Shearin, E. N., & Linehan, M. M. (1994). Dialectical behavior therapy for borderline personality disorder: Theoretical and empirical foundations. *Acta Psychiatrica Scandinavica, 89*, 61–68.

Sheehy, G. (1972, January 10). The secret of Grey Gardens. *New York Magazine*, pp. 24–30.

Sheehy, G. (2006). A return to Grey Gardens. *New York Magazine*, November 6. Retrieved December 27, 2006, from http://nymag.com/arts/theater/features/23484/

Sheets, E., & Craighead, W. E. (2007). Toward an empirically based classification of personality pathology. *Clinical Psychology: Science and Practice, 14*, 77–93.

Shepherd, G. M. (1999). Information processing in dendrites. In M. J. Zigmond, F. E. Bloom, S. C. Landis, J. L. Roberts, & L. R. Squire (Eds.), *Fundamental neuroscience* (pp. 363–388). New York: Academic Press.

Shepherd, M. D., Schoenberg, M., Slavich, S., Wituk, S., Warren, M., & Meissen, G. (1999). Continuum of professional involvement in self-help groups. *Journal of Community Psychology, 27*, 39–53.

Sher, K. J., Grekin, E. R., & Williams, N. A. (2005). The development of alcohol use disorders. *Annual Review of Clinical Psychology, 1*, 493–523.

Sher, K. J., Trull, T. J., Bartholow, B. D., & Vieth, A. (1999). Personality & alcoholism: Issues, methods and etiological processes. In K. E. Leonard & H. T. Blane (Eds.), *Psychological theories of drinking and alcoholism.* (pp. 54–105). New York: Guilford Press.

Sherman, M. D., Zanotti, D. K., & Jones, D. E. (2005). Key elements in couples therapy with veterans with combat-related posttraumatic stress disorder. *Professional Psychology: Research and Practice, 36*, 626–633.

Shevlin, M., Dorahy, M. J., & Adamson, G. (2007). Trauma and psychosis: an analysis of the National Comorbidity Survey. *American Journal of Psychiatry, 164*, 166–169.

Shiah, L., Chao, C., Mao, W., & Chuang, Y. (2006). Treatment of paraphilic sexual disorder: The use of topiramate in fetishism. *International Clinical Psychopharmacology, 21*, 241–243.

Shifren, J. L., Russo, P. A., Segreti, A., & Johannes, C. B. (2008). Sexual problems and distress in United States women: Prevalence and correlates. *Obstetrical Gynecology, 112*, 970–978.

Shin, L. M., Kosslyn, S. M., McNally, R. J., Alpert, N. M., Thompson, W. L., Rauch, S. L., et al. (1997). Visual imagery and perception in posttraumatic stress disorder: A positron emission tomographic investigation. *Archives of General Psychiatry, 54*, 233–241.

Shin, L. M., McNally, R. J., Kosslyn, S. M., Thompson, W. L., Rauch, S. L., Alpert,

N. M., et al. (1999). Regional cerebral blood flow during script-driven imagery in childhood sexual abuse-related PTSD: A PET investigation. *American Journal of Psychiatry, 156,* 575–584.

Shin, L. M., Shin, P. S., Heckers, S., Krangel, T. S., Macklin, M. L., Orr, S. P., et al. (2004). Hippocampal function in posttraumatic stress disorder. *Hippocampus, 14,* 292–300.

Shin, L. M., Wright, C. I., Cannistraro, P. A., Wedig, M. M., McMullin, K., Martis, B., et al. (2005). A functional magnetic resonance imaging study of amygdala and medial prefrontal cortex responses to overtly presented fearful faces in posttraumatic stress disorder. *Archives of General Psychiatry, 62,* 273–281.

Shiraishi, H., Suzuki, A., Fukasawa, T., Aoshima, T., Ujiie, Y., Ishii, G., et al. (2006). Monoamine oxidase A gene promoter polymorphism affects novelty seeking and reward dependence in healthy study participants. *Psychiatric Genetics, 16,* 55–58.

Shooka, A., Al-Haddad, M. K., & Raees, A. (1998). OCD in Bahrain: A phenomenological profile. *International Journal of Social Psychiatry, 44,* 147–154.

Shor-Posner, G., Lecusay, R., Miguez-Burbano, M. J., Quesada, J., Rodriguez, A., Ruiz, P., et al. (2000). Quality of life measures in the Miami HIV-1 infected drug abusers cohort: Relationship to gender and disease status. *Journal of Substance Abuse, 11,* 395–404.

Shrout, P. E., Canino, G. J., Bird, H. R., Rubio-Stipec, M., Bravo, M., & Burnam, M. A. (1992). Mental health status among Puerto Ricans, Mexican Americans, and non-Hispanic whites. *American Journal of Community Psychology, 20,* 729–752.

Sibille, E., Arango, V., Galfalvy, H. C., Pavlidis, P., Erraji-Benchekroun, L., Ellis, S. P., et al. (2004). Gene expression profiling of depression and suicide in human prefrontal cortex. *Neuropsychopharmacology, 29,* 351–361.

Siegel, S. (1988). State dependent learning and morphine tolerance. *Behavioral Neuroscience, 102,* 228–232.

Siegel, S., & Ramos, B. M. C. (2002). Applying laboratory research: Drug anticipation and the treatment of drug addiction. *Experimental and Clinical Psychopharmacology, 10,* 162–183.

Siegel, S., Baptista, M. A. S., Kim, J. A., McDonald, R. V., & Weise-Kelly, L. (2000). Pavlovian psychopharmacology: The associative basis of tolerance. *Experimental and Clinical Psychopharmacology, 8,* 276–293.

Sierra, M., & Berrios, G. E. (1998). Depersonalization: Neurobiological perspectives. *Biological Psychiatry, 44,* 898–908.

Sierra, M., Phillips, M. L., Ivin, G., Krystal, J., & David, A. S. (2003). A placebo-controlled, cross-over trial of lamotrigine in depersonalization disorder. *Journal of Psychopharmacology, 17,* 103–105.

Sierra, M., Senior, C., Dalton, J., McDonough, M., Bond, A., Phillips, M. L., et al. (2002). Autonomic response in depersonalization disorder. *Archives of General Psychiatry, 59,* 833–838.

Siever, L. J., & Davis, K. L. (1991). A psychobiological perspective on the personality disorders. *American Journal of Psychiatry, 148,* 1647–1658.

Siever, L. J., & Davis, K. L. (2004). The pathophysiology of schizophrenia disorders: Perspectives from the spectrum. *American Journal of Psychiatry, 161,* 398–413.

Sifneos, P. E. (1992). *Short-term anxiety-provoking psychotherapy: A treatment manual.* New York: Basic Books.

Sigman, M., Spence, S. J., & Wang, A. T. (2006). Autism from developmental and neuropsychological perspectives. *Annual Review of Clinical Psychology, 2,* 327–355.

Sigmon, S. T., Pells, J. J., Boulard, N. E., Whitcomb-Smith, S., Edenfield, T. M., Hermann, B. A., et al. (2005). Gender differences in self-reports of depression: The response bias hypothesis revisited. *Sex Roles, 53,* 401–411.

Sigvardsson, S., Bohman, M., & Cloninger, C. R. (1996). Replication of the Stockholm Adoption Study of alcoholism: Confirmatory cross-fostering analysis. *Archives of General Psychiatry, 53,* 681–687.

Silber, T. J. (2004). Ipecac Abuse, morbidity and mortality: Is it time to repeal its over the counter status? paper presented at the conference on eating disorders, April 29–May 2, Caribe Royale All-Suites Resort and Convention Center, Orlando FL. [Abstract in the *International Journal of eating Disorders, 35,* 375.]

Silk, T. J., Rinehart, N., Bradshaw, J. L., Tonge, B., Egan, G., O'Boyle, M., et al. (2006). Visuospatial processing and the function of prefrontal-parietal networks in autism spectrum disorders: A functional MRI study. *American Journal of Psychiatry, 163,* 1440–1443.

Silver, E., & Teasdale, B. (2005). Mental disorder and violence: An examination of stressful life events and impaired social support. *Social Problems, 52,* 62–78.

Silverman, K., Chutuape, M. A., Bigelow, G. E., & Stitzer, M. L. (1999). Voucher-based reinforcement of cocaine abstinence in treatment-resistant methadone patients: Effects of reinforcement magnitude. *Psychopharmacology, 146,* 128–138.

Silverman, K., Robles, E., Mudric, T., Bigelow, G. E., & Stitzer, M. L. (2004). A randomized trial of long-term reinforcement of cocaine abstinence in methadone-maintained patients who inject drugs. *Journal of Consulting Clinical Psychology, 72,* 839–854.

Silverman, K., Svikis, D., Robles, E., Stitzer, M. L., & Bigelow, G. E. (2001). A reinforcement-based therapeutic workplace for the treatment of drug abuse: Six-month abstinence outcomes. *Experimental & Clinical Psychopharmacology, 9,* 14–23.

Silverstein, J. L. (1989). Origins of psychogenic vaginismus. *Psychotherapy and Psychosomatics, 52,* 197–204.

Silverstein, M. L. (2007). Descriptive psychopathology and theoretical viewpoints: Dependent, histrionic, and antisocial personality disorders. In M. L. Silverstein, *Disorders of the self: A personality-guided approach* (pp. 145–170). Washington, DC: American Psychological Association.

Silverstein, S. M., Hatashita-Wong, M., Solak, B. A., Uhlhaas, P., Landa, Y., Wilkniss, S. M., et al. (2005). Effectiveness of a two-phase cognitive rehabilitation intervention for severely impaired schizophrenia patients. *Psychological Medicine, 35,* 829–837.

Sim, L., & Zeman, J. (2005). Emotion regulation factors as mediators between body dissatisfaction and bulimic symptoms in early adolescent girls. *Journal of Early Adolescence, 25,* 478–496.

Simeon, D., Guralnik, O., Hazlett, E. A., Spiegel-Cohen, J., Hollander, E., & Buchsbaum M. S. (2000). Feeling unreal: A PET study of depersonalization disorder. *American Journal of Psychiatry, 157,* 1782–1788.

Simeon, D., Guralnik, O., Knutelska, M., Yehuda, R., & Schmeidler, J. (2003). Basal norepinephrine in depersonalization disorder. *Psychiatry Research, 121,* 93–97.

Simeon, D., Guralnik, O., Schmeidler, J., Sirof, B., & Knutelska, M. (2001). The role of childhood interpersonal trauma in depersonalization disorder. *American Journal of Psychiatry, 158,* 1027–1033.

Simeon, D., Knutelska, M., Nelson, D., & Guralnik, O. (2003). Feeling unreal: A depersonalization disorder update of 117 cases. *Journal of Clinical Psychiatry, 64,* 990–997.

Simeon, D., Stein, D. J., & Hollander E. (1998). Treatment of depersonalization disorder with clomipramine. *Biological Psychiatry, 15,* 302–303.

Simkins, S., Hawton, K., Yip, P. S. F., & Yam, C. H. K. (2003). Seasonality in suicide: A study of farming suicides in England and Wales. *Crisis: The Journal of Crisis Intervention and Suicide Prevention, 24,* 93–97.

Simon, G. E., & Gureje, O. (1999). Stability of somatization disorder and somatization symptoms among primary care patients. *Archives of General Psychiatry, 56,* 90–95.

Simoni-Wastila, L., Ritter, G., & Strickler, G. (2004). Gender and other factors associated with the nonmedical use of abusable prescription drugs. *Substance Use & Misuse, 39,* 1–23.

Simons, R. L., Murry, V., McLoyd, V., Lin, K., Cutrona, C., & Conger, R. D. (2002). Discrimination, crime, ethnic identity, and parenting as correlates of depressive symptoms among African American children: A multilevel analysis. *Development and Psychopathology, 14,* 371–393.

Simos, P. G., Fletcher, J. M., Sarkari, S., Billingsley, R. L., Denton, C., & Papanicolaou, A. C. (2007). Altering the brain circuits for reading through intervention: A magnetic source imaging study. *Neuropsychology, 21,* 485–496.

Simpson, D. D. (1984) National treatment system evaluation based on the drug abuse reporting program (DARP) follow-up research. *NIDA Research Monograph, 51,* 29–41.

Simpson, D. D., Joe, G. W., & Broome, K. M. (2002). A national 5-year follow-up of treatment outcomes for cocaine dependence. *Archives of General Psychiatry, 59,* 538–544.

Simpson, M. E., & Conklin, G. H. (1989). Socio-economic development, suicide and religion: A test of Durkheim's theory of religion and suicide *Social Forces, 67,* 945–964.

Siok, W. T., Perfetti, C. A., Jin, Z., & Tan, L. H. (2004). Biological abnormality of impaired reading is constrained by culture. *Nature, 431,* 71–76.

Siqueland, L., Rynn, M., & Diamond, G. S. (2005). Cognitive behavioral and attachment based family therapy for anxious adolescents: Phase I and II studies. *Journal of Anxiety Disorders, 19,* 361–381.

Siris, S. G. (2001). Suicide and schizophrenia. *Journal of Psychopharmacology, 15,* 127–135.

Skaer, T. L., Sclar, D. A., & Robison, L. M. (2008). Trend in anxiety disorders in the USA 1990–2003. *Primary Care & Community Psychiatry, 13,* 1–7.

Skeels, H., & Dye, H. (1939). A study of the effects of differential stimulation on mentally retarded children. *American Journal of Mental Deficiency, 44,* 114–136.

Skeem, J. L., & Mulvey, E. P. (2001). Psychopathy and community violence among civil psychiatric patients: Results from the MacArthur violence risk assessment study. *Journal of Consulting and Clinical Psychology, 69,* 358–374.

Skinner, B. F. (1965). *Science and human behavior.* New York: Free Press.

Skinner, B. F. (1986). What is wrong with daily life in the Western world? *American Psychologist, 41,* 568–574.

Skinner, B. F. (1987). Whatever happened to psychology as the science of behavior? *American Psychologist, 42,* 780–786.

Skinner, H. A. (1995). Critical issues in the diagnosis of substance use disorders. In J. D. Blaine, A. M. Horton, & L. H. Towle (Eds.), *Diagnosis and severity of drug abuse and dependence.* (NIH Publication No. 95–3884).

Skodol, A. E. (2005). Manifestations, clinical diagnosis, and comorbidity. In J. M. Oldham, A. E. Skodol, & D. S. Bender (Eds.), *The American Psychiatric Publishing textbook of personality disorders* (pp. 57–87). Washington, DC: American Psychiatric Publishing.

Skodol, A. E., Gunderson, J. G., McGlashan, T. H., Dyck, I. R., Stout, R. L., Bender, D. S., et al. (2002). Functional impairment in patients with schizotypal, borderline, avoidant, or obsessive-compulsive personality disorder. *American Journal of Psychiatry, 159,* 276–283.

Skodol, A. E., Gunderson, J. G., Shea, M. T., McGlashan, T. H., Morey, L. C., Sanislow, C. A., et al. (2005). The Collaborative Longitudinal Personality Disorders Study (CLPS): Overview and implications. *Journal of Personality Disorders, 19,* 487–504.

Skodol, A. E., Oldham, J. M., & Gallaher, P. E. (1999). Axis II comorbidity of substance use disorders among patients referred for treatment of personality disorders. *American Journal of Psychiatry, 156,* 733–738.

Skodol, A. E., Oldham, J. M., Hyler, S. E., Kellman, H. D., Doidge, N., & Davies, M. (1993). Comorbidity of DSM-III-R eating disorders and personality disorders. *International Journal of Eating Disorders, 14,* 403–416.

Skodol, A. E., Oldham, J. M., Hyler, S. E., Stein, D. J., Hollander, E., Galagher, P. E., et al. (1995). Patterns of anxiety and personality disorder comorbidity. *Journal of Psychiatric Research, 29,* 361–374.

Skodol, A. E., Pagano, M. E., Bender, D. S., Shea, M. T., Gunderson, J. G., Yen, S., et al. (2005). Stability of functional impairment in patients with schizotypal, borderline, avoidant, or obsessive-compulsive personality disorder over two years. *Psychological Medicine, 35,* 443–451.

Skodol, A. E., Siever, L. J., Livesley, W. J., Gunderson, J. G., Pfohl, B., & Widiger, T. A. (2002). The borderline diagnosis II: Biology, genetics, and clinical course. *Biological Psychiatry, 51,* 951–963.

Sleek, S. (1997). Treating people who live life on the borderline. *APA Monitor, 7,* 20–22.

Sloan, D. M., Mizes, J. S., & Epstein, E. M. (2005). Empirical classification of eating disorders. *Eating Behaviors, 6,* 53–62.

Slomkowski, C., Klein, R. G., & Mannuzza, S. (1995). Is self-esteem an important outcome in hyperactive children? *Journal of Abnormal Child Psychology, 23,* 303–315.

Slutske, W. S., Heath, A. C., Dinwiddie, S. H., Madden, P. A. F., Bucholz, K. K.,

Dunne, M. P., et al. (1997). Modeling genetic and environmental influences in the etiology of conduct disorder: A study of 2,682 adult twin pairs. *Journal of Abnormal Psychology, 106,* 266–279.

Small, G. W., Kepe, V., Ercoli, L. M., Siddarth, P., Bookheimer, S. Y., Miller, K. J., et al. (2006). PET of brain amyloid and tau in mild cognitive impairment. *New England Journal of Medicine, 355,* 2652–2653.

Smeets, G., de Jong, P. J., & Mayer, B. (2000). If you suffer from a headache, then you have a brain tumour: Domain-specific reasoning "bias" and hypochondriasis. *Behavioral Research and Therapy, 38,* 763–776.

Smith A. (2000). An fMRI investigation of frontal lobe functioning in psychopathy and schizophrenia during a go/no go task (Doctoral dissertation, The University of British Columbia, Canada). *Dissertation Abstracts International B, Physical Sciences and Engineering.* 61 (01), 128.

Smith G. R., Jr., Monson, R. A., & Ray, D. C. (1986). Patients with multiple unexplained symptoms: Their characteristics, functional health, and health care utilization. *Archives of Internal Medicine, 146,* 69–72.

Smith, D. C., Hall, J. A., Williams, J. K., An, H., & Gotman, N. (2006). Comparative efficacy of family and group treatment for adolescent substance abuse. *American Journal on Addictions, 15,* 131–136.

Smith, E. E., & Kosslyn, S. M. (2006). *Cognitive psychology: Mind and brain.* Upper Saddle River, NJ: Prentice Hall.

Smith, K. A., Fairburn, C. G., & Cowen, P. J. (1999). Symptomatic relapse in bulimia nervosa following acute tryptophan depletion. *Archives of General Psychiatry, 56,* 171–176.

Smith, L. M., Chang, L., Yonekura, M. L., Gilbride, K., Kuo, J., Poland, R. E., Walot, I., & Ernst, T. (2001). Brain proton magnetic resonance spectroscopy and imaging in children exposed to cocaine in utero. *Pediatrics, 107,* 227–231.

Smith, R. C., Gardiner, J. C., Lyles, J. S., Sirbu, C., Dwamena, F. C., Hodges, A., et al. (2005). Exploration of DSM-IV-TR criteria in primary care patients with medically unexplained symptoms. *Psychosomatic Medicine, 67,* 123–129.

Smith, T. C., Ryan, M. A. K., Wingard, D. L., Slymen, D. J., Sallis, J. F., & Kritz-Silverstein, D. (2008). New onset and persistent symptoms of posttraumatic stress disorder self reported after deployment and combat exposures: Prospective population based US military cohort study. *British Medical Journal, 336,* 366–371.

Smith, Y. L. S., van Goozen, S. H. M., & Cohen-Kettenis, P. T. (2001). Adolescents with gender identity disorder who were accepted or rejected for sex reassignment surgery: A prospective follow-up study. *Journal of the American Academy of Child & Adolescent Psychiatry, 40*, 472–481.

Smith, Y. L. S., Van Goozen, S. H. M., Kuiper, A. J., & Cohen-Kettenis, P. T. (2005). Sex reassignment: Outcomes and predictors of treatment for adolescent and adult transsexuals. *Psychological Medicine, 35*, 89–99.

Smolak, L., & Murnen, S. K. (2004). A feminist approach to eating disorders. In J. K. Thompson (Ed.), *Handbook of eating disorders and obesity* (pp. 590–605). Hoboken, NJ: John Wiley & Sons.

Smoller, J. W., Finn, C., & White, C. (2000). The genetics of anxiety disorders: An overview. *Psychiatric Annals, 30*, 745–753.

Snow, A. L., Dani, R., Souchek, J., Sullivan, G., Ashton, C. M., & Kunik, M. E. (2005). Comorbid psychosocial symptoms and quality of life in patients with dementia. *American Journal of Geriatric Psychiatry, 13*, 393–401.

Snowden, L. R. (2007). Explaining mental health treatment disparities: Ethnic and cultural differences in family involvement. *Culture, Medicine and Psychiatry, 31*, 389–402.

Snowden, L. R., & Cheung, F. K. (1990). Use of inpatient mental health services by members of ethnic minority groups. *American Psychologist, 45*, 347–355.

Snowden, L. R., & Pingitore, D. (2002). Frequency and scope of mental health service delivery to African Americans in primary care. *Mental Health Services Research, 4*, 123–130.

Snyder, L. B., Milici, F. F., Slater, M., Sun, H., & Strizhakova, Y. (2006). Effects of alcohol advertising exposure on drinking among youth. *Archives of Pediatric Adolescent Medicine, 160*, 18–24.

Soares, J. C. (2000). Recent advances in the treatment of bipolar mania, depression, mixed states, and rapid cycling. *International Clinical Psychopharmacology, 15*, 183–196.

Söderlund, G., Sikström, S., & Smart, A. (2007). Listen to the noise: Noise is beneficial for cognitive performance in ADHD. *Journal of Child Psychology and Psychiatry, 48*, 840–847.

Solanto, M. V. (2002). Dopamine dysfunction in AD/HD: Integrating clinical and basic neuroscience research. *Behavioural Brain Research 130*, 65–71.

Soloff, P. H. (2000). Psychopharmacology of borderline personality disorder. *Psychiatric Clinics of North America, 23*, 169–192.

Soloff, P. H., Kelly, T. M., Strotmeyer, S. J., Malone, K. M., & Mann, J. J. (2003). Impulsivity, gender, and response to fenfluramine challenge in borderline personality disorder. *Psychiatry Research, 119*, 11–24.

Soloff, P. H., Meltzer, C. C., Becker, C., Greer, P. J., Kelly, T. M., & Constantine, D. (2003). Impulsivity and prefrontal hypometabolism in borderline personality disorder. *Psychiatry Research, 123*, 153–163.

Soloff, P. H., Meltzer, C. C., Greer, P. J., Constantine, D., & Kelly, T. M. (2000). A fenfluramine-activated FDG-PET study of borderline personality disorder. *Biological Psychiatry, 47*, 540–547.

Solomon, D. A., Keller, M. B., Leon, A. C., Mueller, T. I., Lavori, P. W., Shea, M. T., et al. (2000). Multiple recurrences of major depressive disorder. *American Journal of Psychiatry, 157*, 229–233.

Somers, J. M., Goldner, E. M., Waraich, P., & Hsu, L. (2006). Prevalence and incidence studies of anxiety disorders: A systematic review of the literature. *Canadian Journal of Psychiatry, 51*, 100–113.

Sonuga-Barke, E. J. S., Thompson, M., Abikoff, H., Klein, R., & Brotman, L. M. (2006). Nonpharmacological interventions for preschoolers with ADHD: The case for specialized parent training. *Infants & Young Children 19*, 142–153.

Soomro, G. M., Altman, D., Rajagopal, S., & Oakley-Browne, M. (2008). Selective serotonin re-uptake inhibitors (SSRIs) versus placebo for obsessive compulsive disorder (OCD). *Cochrane Database of Systematic Reviews, 2008, 1*, Article Number CD001765.

Sorkin, A., Weinshall, D., Modai, I., & Peled, A. (2006). Improving the accuracy of the diagnosis of schizophrenia by means of virtual reality. *American Journal of Psychiatry, 163*, 512–520.

Soto, O. R. (2003, November 8). Stalker of actress to be freed from jail. *San Diego Union-Tribune*. Retrieved September 25, 2008, from http://www.signonsandiego.com/news/metro/20031106-9999_2m6stalk.html

Southard, E. E. (1910). A study of the dementia praecox group in the light of certain cases showing anomalies or scleroses in particular brain regions. *American Journal of Insanity, 67*, 119–176.

Southwick, S. M., Bremner, D., Krystal, J. H., & Charney, D. S. (1994). Psychobiologic research in post-traumatic stress disorder. *Psychiatric Clinics of North America, 17*, 251–264.

Southwick, S. M., Krystal, J. H., Morgan, C. A., Johnson, D., Nagy, L. M., Nicolaou, A., et al. (1993). Abnormal noradrenergic function in posttraumatic stress disorder. *Archives of General Psychiatry, 50*, 266–274.

Sowell, E. R., Thompson, P. M., Welcome, S. E., Henkenius, A. L., Toga, A. W., & Peterson, B. S. (2003). Cortical abnormalities in children and adolescents with attention-deficit hyperactivity disorder. *Lancet, 362*, 1699–1707.

Spanos, N. P. (1994). Multiple identity enactments and multiple personality disorder: A sociocognitive perspective. *Psychological Bulletin, 116*, 143–165.

Sparén, P., Vågerö, D., Shestov, D. B., Plavinskaja, S., Parfenova, N., Hoptlar, V., et al. (2004). Long term mortality after severe starvation during the siege of Leningrad: Prospective cohort study. *British Medical Journal, 328*, 11.

Spector, A., Davies, S., Woods, B., & Orrell, M. (2000). Reality orientation for dementia: A systematic review of the evidence of effectiveness from randomized controlled trials. *The Gerontologist, 40*, 206–212.

Spector, I. P., & Carey, M. P. (1990). Incidence and prevalence of the sexual dysfunctions: A critical review of the empirical literature. *Archives of Sexual Behavior, 19*, 389–408.

Spiegel, D., Bierre, P., & Rootenberg, J. (1989). Hypnotic alteration of somatosensory perception. *American Journal of Psychiatry, 146*, 749–754.

Spiegel, D., Cutcomb, S., Ren, C., & Pribram, K. (1985). Hypnotic hallucination alters evoked potentials. *Journal of Abnormal Psychology, 94*, 249–255.

Spiegel, H. (1974). The grade 5 syndrome: The highly hypnotizable person. *International Journal of Clinical and Experimental Hypnosis, 22*, 303–319.

Spielberger, C. D., & Rickman, R. L. (1990). Assessment of state and trait anxiety in cardiovascular disorders. In D. G. Byrne and R. H. Rosenman (Eds.), *Anxiety and the heart* (pp. 73–92). New York: Hemisphere Publishing.

Spira, A. P., & Edelstein, B. A. (2006). Behavioral interventions for agitation in older adults with dementia: An evaluative review. *International Psychogeriatrics, 18*, 195–225.

Spira, A. P., & Edelstein, B. A. (2006). Behavioral interventions for agitation in older adults with dementia: An evaluative review. *International Psychogeriatrics, 18*, 195–225.

Spitz, B. (2005). *The Beatles: The biography*. New York: Little, Brown.

Spitzer, R. L., First, M. B., & Wakefield, J. C. (2007). Saving PTSD from itself in DSM-V. *Journal of Anxiety Disorders, 21*, 233–241.

Spitzer, R. L., First, M. B., Williams, J. B. W., & Gibbon, M. (2002). *DSM-IV-TR Casebook*. Washington, DC: American Psychiatric Publishers.

Spitzer, R. L., Gibbon, M., Skodol, A. E., Williams, J. B. W., & First, M. B. (Eds). (2002). *DSM-IV-TR casebook: A learning companion to the Diagnostic and Statistical Manual of Mental Disorders, 4th edition, text revision*. Arlington, VA: American Psychiatric Publishing.

Spitzer, R. L., Gibbon, M., Skodol, A. E., Williams, J. B. W., & First, M. B. (2002). *DSM-IV-TR casebook: A learning companion to the Diagnostic and Statistical Manual of Mental Disorders, fourth edition, text revision*. Arlington, VA: American Psychiatric Publishing.

Spitzer, R. L., Gibbon, M., Skodol, A. E., Williams, J. B. W., & First, M. B. (2002). *DSM-IV-TR casebook: A learning companion to the diagnostic and statistical manual of mental disorders, fourth edition, text revision*. Arlington, VA: American Psychiatric Publishing, Inc.

Spitzer, R. L., Gibbon, M., Skodol, A. E., Williams, J. B. W., & First, M. B. (Eds.). (2002). *DSM-IV-TR casebook: A learning companion to the Diagnostic and Statistical Manual of Mental Disorders,* 4th edition, text revision. Arlington, VA: American Psychiatric Publishing.

Spoor, S. T. P., Bekker, M. H. J., Van Strien, T., & van Heck, G. L. (2007). Relations between negative affect, coping, and emotional eating. *Appetite, 48,* 368–376.

Sporn, A., & Lisanby, S. H. (2006). Non-pharmacological treatment modalities in children and adolescents: A review of electro-convulsive therapy, transcranial magnetic stimulation, vagus nerve stimulation, magnetic seizure therapy, and deep brain stimulation. *Clinical Neuropsychiatry: Journal of Treatment Evaluation, 3,* 230–244.

Spreen, O., & Strauss, E. (1998). *A compendium of neuropsychological tests: Administration norms and commentary* (2nd ed.). New York: Oxford University Press.

Sprock, J., Rader, T. J., Kendall, J. P., & Yoder, C. Y. (2000). Neuropsychological functioning in patients with borderline personality disorder. *Journal of Clinical Psycholology, 56,* 1587–1600.

Squire, L. R. (2004). Memory systems of the brain: A brief history and current perspective. *Neurobiology of Learning and Memory, 82,* 171–177.

Squire, L. R., & Kandel, E. (2000). *Memory: From mind to molecules.* New York: Scientific American Library.

Sramek, J. J., Frackiewicz, E. J., & Cutler, N. R. (1997). Efficacy and safety of two dosing regimens of buspirone in the treatment of outpatients with persistent anxiety. *Clinical Therapeutics, 19,* 498–506.

Stack, S. (1983). The effect of religious commitment of suicide: A cross-national analysis. *Journal of Health and Social Behavior, 24,* 362–274.

Stack, S., & Wasserman, I. (1992). The effect of religion on suicide ideology: An analysis of the networks perspective *Journal of Scientific Study of Religion, 31,* 457–466.

Stafford, J., & Lynn, S. J. (2002). Cultural scripts, memories of childhood abuse, and multiple identities: A study of role-played enactments. *International Journal of Clinical and Experimental Hypnosis, 50,* 67–85.

Staines, G. L., Magura, S., Foote, J., Deluca, A., & Kosanke, N. (2001). Polysubstance use among alcoholics. *Journal of Addictive Diseases, 20,* 53–69.

Stålenheim, E. G., & von Knorring, L. (1996). Psychopathy and Axis I and Axis II psychiatric disorders in a forensic psychiatric population in Sweden. *Acta Psychiatrica Scandinavica, 94,* 217–223.

Stanton, M. D. (1981). Strategic approaches to family therapy. In A. S. Gurman & D. P. Kniskern (Eds.), *Handbook of family therapy* (pp. 361–402). New York: Brunner/Mazel.

Stanton, M. D., & Shadish, W. R. (1997). Outcome, attrition, and family-couples treatment for drug abuse: A meta-analysis and review of the controlled, comparative studies. *Psychological Bulletin, 122,* 170–191.

Starker, S. (1988). Psychologists and self-help books: Attitudes and prescriptive practices of clinicians. *American Journal of Psychotherapy, 42,* 448–455.

Stark-Wroblewski, K., Yanico, B. J., & Lupe, S. (2005). Acculturation, internalization of western appearance norms, and eating pathology among Japanese and Chinese international student women. *Psychology of Women Quarterly, 29,* 38–46.

Statistics Canada. (2005). *Selected leading causes of death by sex, 1997.* Retrieved December 3, 2006, from http://www.statcan.ca/english/Pgdb/health36.htm

Steadman, H. J., McGreevy, M. A., Morrissey, J. P., Callahan, L. A., Robbins, P. C., & Cirincione, C. (1993). *Before and after Hinckley: Evaluating insanity defense reform.* New York: Guilford Press.

Steadman, H., Mulvey, E., Monahan, J., Robbins, P., Appelbaum, P., Grisso, T., Roth, L., & Silver, E. (1998). Violence by people discharged from acute psychiatric inpatient facilities and by others in the same neighborhoods. *Archives of General Psychiatry, 55,* 393–401.

Stefansson, H., Rujescu, D., Cichon, S., Pietiläinen, O. P., Ingason, A., Steinberg, S., et al. (2008). Large recurrent microdeletions associated with schizophrenia. *Nature, 455,* 232–236.

Steffenburg, S., Gillberg, C., Hellgren, L., Andersson, L., Gillberg, I. C., Jakobsson, G., & Bohman, M. (1989). A twin study of autism in Denmark, Finland, Iceland, Norway and Sweden. *Journal of Child Psychology and Psychiatry, 30,* 405–416.

Stefulj, J., Büttner, A., Kubat, M., Zill, P., Balija, M., Eisenmenger, W., Bondy, B., & Jernej, B. (2004). 5HT-2C receptor polymorphism in suicide victims: Association studies in German and Slavic populations. *European Archives of Psychiatry & Clinical Neuroscience, 254,* 224–227.

Stein, A., Woolley, H., Cooper, S., Winterbottom, J., Fairburn, C. G., & Cortina-Borja, M. (2006a). Eating habits and attitudes among 10-year-old children of mothers with eating disorders: Longitudinal study. *British Journal of Psychiatry, 189,* 324–329.

Stein, A., Woolley, H., Senior, R., Hertzmann, L., Lovel, M., Lee, J., et al. (2006). Treating disturbances in the relationship between mothers with bulimic eating disorders and their infants: A randomized, controlled trial of video feedback. *American Journal of Psychiatry, 163,* 899–906.

Stein, D.J. (2008). Depression, anhedonia, and psychomotor symptoms: the role of dopaminergic neurocircuitry. *CNS Spectrums, 3,* 561–565.

Stein, D. J., & Matsunaga, H. (2006). Specific phobia: A disorder of fear conditioning and extinction. *CNS Spectrums, 11,* 248–251.

Stein, D. J., Seedat, S., van der Linden, G. J. H., & Zungu-Dirwayi, N. (2000). Selective serotonin reuptake inhibitors in the treatment of post-traumatic stress disorder: A meta-analysis of randomized controlled trials. *International Clinical Psychopharmacology, 15*(Suppl. 2), S31–S39.

Stein, D. J., Westenberg, H. G. M., & Liebowitz, M. R. (2002). Social anxiety disorder and generalized anxiety disorder: Serotonergic and dopaminergic neurocircuitry. *Journal of Clinical Psychiatry, 63,* 12–19.

Stein, D., Weizman, A., & Bloch, Y. (2006). Electroconvulsive therapy and Transcranial Magnetic Stimulation: Can they be considered valid modalities in the treatment of pediatric mood disorders? *Child and Adolescent Psychiatric Clinics of North America, 15,* 1035–1056.

Stein, L. I., & Test, M. A. (1980). Alternative to mental hospital treatment: I. Conceptual model, treatment program, and clinical evaluation. *Archives of General Psychiatry, 37,* 392–397.

Stein, M. B., Jang, K. L., & Livesley, W. J. (2002). Heritability of social anxiety-related concerns and personality characteristics: A twin study. *Journal of Nervous and Mental Disease, 190,* 219–224.

Stein, M. B., Kerridge, C., Dimsdale, J. E., & Hoyt, D. B. (2007). Pharmacotherapy to prevent PTSD: Results from a randomized controlled proof-of-concept trial in physically injured patients. *Journal of Traumatic Stress, 20,* 923–932.

Stein, M. B., McQuaid, J. R., Pedrelli, P., Lenox, R., & McCahill, M. E. (2000). Posttraumatic stress disorder in the primary care medical setting. *General Hospital Psychiatry, 22,* 261–269.

Steinberg, M. (1994). *Handbook for the assessment of dissociation*. Washington, DC: American Psychiatric Publishers.

Steinberg, M. (2001). *The stranger in the mirror: Dissociation—the hidden epidemic*. Washington, DC: American Pyschiatric Publishing.

Steiner, B. W. (1985). *Gender dysphoria: Development, research, management*. New York: Plenum Press.

Steiner, M., Dunn, E., & Born, L. (2003). Hormones and mood: From menarche to menopause and beyond. *Journal of Affective Disorders, 74*, 67–83.

Steinhausen, H. (2002). The outcome of anorexia nervosa in the 20th century. *American Journal of Psychiatry, 159*, 1284–1293.

Steketee, G., & White, K. (1990). *When once is not enough*. Oakland, CA: New Harbinger Publications.

Stephens, J. H., Richard, P., & McHugh, P. R. (1999). Suicide in patients hospitalized for schizophrenia: 1913–1940. *Journal of Nervous and Mental Disease, 187*, 10–14.

Stermac, L. E., & Segal, Z. V. (1989). Adult sexual contact with children: An examination of cognitive factors. *Behavior Therapy, 20*, 573–584.

Stevens, J., Harman, J. S., & Kelleher, K. J. (2005). Race/ethnicity and insurance status as factors associated with ADHD treatment patterns. *Journal of Child and Adolescent Psychopharmacology, 15*, 88–96.

Stevens, M. C., Pearlson, G. D., & Kiehl, K. A. (2007). An fMRI auditory oddball study of combined-subtype attention deficit hyperactivity disorder. *American Journal of Psychiatry, 164*, 1737–1749.

Stevens, S., Gerlach, A. L., & Rist, F. (2008). Effects of alcohol on ratings of emotional facial expressions in social phobics. *Journal of Anxiety Disorders, 22*, 940–948.

Stevenson, J., Asherson, P., Hay, D., Levy, F., Swanson, J., Thapar, A., et al. (2005). Characterizing the ADHD phenotype for genetic studies. *Developmental Science, 8*, 115–121.

Stewart, J., deWit, H., & Eikelbloom, R. (1984). Role of unconditioned and conditioned drug effects in the self-administration of opiates and stimulants. *Psychological Review, 91*, 251–268.

Stewart, S. (1996). Alcohol abuse in individuals exposed to trauma: A critical review. *Psychological Bulletin, 120*, 83–112.

Stewart, S., Zvolensky, M. J., & Eifert, G. H. (2001). Negative-reinforcement drinking motives mediate the relation between anxiety sensitivity and increased drinking behavior. *Personality & Individual Differences, 31*, 157–171.

Stewart, W. F., Ricci, J. A., Chee, E., Hahn, S. R., & Morganstein, D. (2003). Cost of lost productive work time among US workers with depression. *JAMA: Journal of the American Medical Association, 289*, 3135–3144.

Stice, E., & Hoffman, E. (2004). Eating disorder prevention programs. In J. K. Thompson (Ed.), *Handbook of eating disorders and obesity* (pp. 33–57). Hoboken, NJ: John Wiley & Sons.

Stice, E., & Shaw, H. (2004). Eating disorder prevention programs: A meta-analytic review. *Psychological Bulletin, 130*, 206–227.

Stice, E., Maxfield, J., & Wells, T. (2003). Adverse effects of social pressure to be thin on young women: An experimental investigation of the effects of "fat talk." *International Journal of Eating Disorders, 34*, 108–117.

Stice, E., Schupak-Neuberg, E., Shaw, H. E., & Stein, R. I. (1994). Relation of media exposure to eating disorder symptomatology: An examination of mediating mechanisms. *Journal of Abnormal Psychology, 103*, 836–840.

Stice, E., Shaw, H., & Marti, C. N. (2006). A meta-analytic review of eating disorder prevention programs: Encouraging findings. *Annual Review of Clinical Psychology, 3*, 233–257.

Stinson, F. S., Dawson, D. A., Chou, S. P., Smith, S., Goldstein, R. B., Ruan, W. J., & et al. (2007). The epidmiology of DSM-IV specific phobia in the USA: Result from the National Epidemiologic Survey on Alcohol and Related Conditions. *Psychological Medicine, 37*, 1047–1059.

Stitzer, M., & Petry, N. (2006). Contingency management for treatment of substance abuse. *Annual Review of Clinical Psychology, 2*, 411–434.

Stock, W., & Moser, C. (2001). Feminist sex therapy in the age of Viagra. In P. J. Kleinplatz (Ed.), *New directions in sex therapy: Innovations and alternatives* (pp. 130–162) Philadelphia: Taylor and Rutledge.

Stone, A. B. (1993). Treatment of hypochondriasis with clomipramine. *Journal of Clinical Psychiatry, 54*, 200–201.

Stone, A. L., Storr, C. L., & Anthony, J. C. (2006). Evidence for a hallucinogen dependence syndrome developing soon after onset of hallucinogen use during adolescence. *International Journal of Methods in Psychiatric Research, 15*, 116–130.

Stone, J., Carson, A., Aditya, H., Prescott, R., Zaubi, M., Warlow, C., & Sharpe, M. (2009). The role of physical injury in motor and sensory conversion symptoms: A systematic and narrative review. *Journal of Psychosomatic Research, 66*, 383–390.

Stone, J., Zeman, A., Simonotto, E., Meyer, M., Azuma, R., Flett, S., et al. (2007). fMRI in patients with motor conversion symptoms and controls with simulated weakness. *Psychosomatic Medicine, 69*, 961–969.

Strain, B. A. (2003). Influence of gender bias on the diagnosis of borderline personality disorder. *Dissertation Abstracts International B: Sciences and Engineering, 64* (6), 2941B.

Strain, E. C., Bigelow, G. E., Liebson, I. A., & Stitzer, M. L. (1999). Moderate- vs high-dose methadone in the treatment of opioid dependence: A randomized trial. *JAMA: Journal of the American Medical Association, 281*, 1000–1005.

Strakowski, S. M., Adler, C. M., & DelBello, M. P. (2002). Volumetric MRI studies of mood disorders: Do they distinguish unipolar and bipolar disorder? *Bipolar Disorders, 4*, 80–88.

Strakowski, S. M., Shelton, R. C., & Kolbrener, M. L. (1993). The effects of race and comorbidity on clinical diagnosis in patients with psychosis. *Journal of Clinical Psychiatry, 54*, 96–102.

Straube, T., Mentzel, H., & Miltner, W. H. R. (2006). Neural mechanisms of automatic and direct processing of phobogenic stimuli in specific phobia. *Biological Psychiatry, 59*, 162–170.

Striegel-Moore, R. H. (1993). Etiology of binge eating: A developmental perspective. In C. G. Fairburn & G. T. Wilson (Eds.), *Binge eating: Nature, assessment, and treatment* (pp. 144–172). New York: Guilford Press.

Striegel-Moore, R. H., & Cachelin, F. M. (2001). Etiology of eating disorders in women. *Counseling Psychologist, 29*, 635–661.

Striegel-Moore, R. H., Dohm, F. A., Kraemer, H. C., Taylor, C. B., Daniels, S., Crawford, P. B., et al. (2003). Eating disorders in White and Black women. *American Journal of Psychiatry, 160*, 1326–1331.

Striegel-Moore, R. H., Silberstein, L. R., & Rodin, J. (1986). Toward an understanding of risk factors for bulimia. *American Psychologist, 41*, 246–263.

Strober, M. (1995). Family-genetic influences on anorexia nervosa and bulimia nervosa. In K. D. Brownell & C. G. Fairburn (Eds.), *Eating disorders and obesity: A comprehensive handbook*. New York: Guilford Press.

Strober, M., Freeman, R., Lampert, C., Diamond, J., & Kaye, W. (2000). Controlled family study of anorexia nervosa and bulimia nervosa: Evidence of shared liability and transmission of partial syndromes. *American Journal of Psychiatry, 157*, 393–401.

Strupp, H., & Binder, J. (1984). *Psycho-therapy in a new key: A guide to time-limited dynamic psychotherapy*. New York: Basic Books.

Stuart, G. L., Moore, T. M., Ramsey, S. E., & Kahler, C. W. (2003). Relationship aggression and substance use among women court-referred to domestic violence intervention programs. *Addictive Behaviors, 28*, 1603–1610.

Stuart, S., & Noyes, R., Jr. (2005). Treating hypochondriasis with interpersonal psychotherapy. *Journal of Contemporary Psychotherapy, 35*, 269–283.

Stuart, S., Noyes, R., Jr., Starcevic, V., & Barsky, A. (2008). Integrative approach to somatoform disorders combining interpersonal and cognitive-behavioral theory and techniques. *Journal of Contemporary Psychotherapy, 38*, 45–53.

Stunkard, A., Allison, K., & Lundgren, J. (2008). Issues for DSM-V: Night eating syndrome. *American Journal of Psychiatry, 165*, 424.

Stuss, D. T., Alexander, M. P., Palumbo, C. L., Buckle, L., Sayer, L., & Pogue, J. (1994). Organizational strategies with unilateral or bilateral frontal lobe injury in word learning tasks. *Neuropsychology, 8*, 355–373.

Styron, W. (1990). *Darkness visible: A memoir of madness*. New York: Random House.

Substance Abuse and Mental Health Services Administration, Office of Applied Studies. (2008). *National survey on drug use and health, 2003 and 2004*. Retrieved October 20, 2008, fromhttp://oas. samhsa.gov/NSDUH/2k4nsduh/2k4tabs/ Sect6peTabs1to81.htm#tab6.59a

Substance Abuse and Mental Health Services Administration. (2000). *National household survey on drug abuse main findings 1998: Office of applied studies*. Rockville, MD: National Clearinghouse for Alcohol and Drug Information.

Substance Abuse and Mental Health Services Administration. (2008). *Results from the 2007 national survey on drug use and health: National findings*. (Office of Applied Studies, NSDUH Series H-34, DHHS Publication No. SMA 08-4343). Rockville, MD: Department of Health and Human Services. Retrieved December 18, 2008, from http://oas.samhsa. gov/nsduh/2k7nsduh/2k7Results.pdf

Substance Abuse and Mental Health Services Administration. (2004). *Results from the 2003 national survey on drug use and health: National findings*. [NHSDA Series H-25. DHHS Pub. No. (SMA) 04-3964]. Rockville, MD: Department of Health and Human Services.

Substancemisuse.net. (2007). Debbie's story. Retrieved August 2, 2007, from http://www. substancemisuse.net/problem-users/pustories/ debbiesstory.htm

Sue, S., Fujino, D. C., Hu, L. T., Takeuchi, D. T., & Zane, N. W. S. (1991). Community mental health services for ethnic minority groups: A test of the cultural responsiveness hypothesis. *Journal of Consulting and Clinical Psychology, 59*, 533–540.

Sue, S., Kuraski, K. S., & Srinivasan, S. (1999). Ethnicity, gender, and cross-cultural issues in clinical research. In P. C. Kendall, J. N. Butcher, & G. N. Holmbeck (Eds.), *Handbook of research methods in clinical psychology* (2nd ed., pp. 54–71). Hoboken, NJ: John Wiley & Sons.

Sue, S., Zane, N., & Young, K. (1994). Research on psychotherapy with culturally diverse populations. In A. E. Bergin & S. L. Garfield (Eds.), *Handbook of psychotherapy and behavior change* (4th ed., pp. 783–817). Oxford, England: John Wiley & Sons.

Suh, J. J., Pettinati, H. M., Kampman, K. M., & O'Brien, C. P. (2006). The status of disulfiram: A half of a century later. *Journal of Clinical Psychopharmacology, 26*, 290–302.

Sullins, E. S. (1991). Emotional contagion revisited: Effects of social comparison and expressive style on mood convergence. *Personality and Social Psychology Bulletin, 17*, 166–174.

Sullivan, G. M., Mann, J. J., Oquendo, M. A., Lo, E. S., Cooper, T. B., & Gorman, J. M. (2006). Low cerebrospinal fluid transthyretin levels in depression: Correlations with suicidal ideation and low serotonin function. *Biological Psychiatry, 60*, 500–506.

Sullivan, H. S. (1953). *The interpersonal theory of psychiatry*. New York: W.W. Norton.

Sullivan, H. S. (1953). *The interpersonal theory of psychiatry*. Oxford, England: Norton.

Sullivan, P. F., Bulik, C. M., & Kendler, K. S. (1998). The epidemiology and classification of bulimia nervosa. *Psychological Medicine, 28*, 599–610.

Sulpy, D., & Schweighardt, R. (1994). *Drugs, divorces, and a slipping image: The unauthorized story of the Beatles' "Get Back" sessions*. Princeton Junction, NJ: The 910.

Sultan, S., Andronikof, A., Réveillère, C., & Lemmel, G. (2006). A Rorschach stability study in a nonpatient adult sample. *Journal of Personality Assessment, 87*, 330–348.

Summerfield, D. (2001). The invention of post-traumatic stress disorder and the social usefulness of a psychiatric category. *British Medical Journal, 322*, 95–98.

Sundgot-Borgen, J. (1999). Eating disorders among male and female elite athletes. *British Journal of Sports Medicine, 33*, 434.

Sundquist, A. (1999). First person account: Family psychoeducation can change lives. *Schizophrenia Bulletin, 25*, 619–621.

Sung, M., Erkanli, A., Angold, A., & Costello, E. J. (2004). Effects of age at first substance use and psychiatric comorbidity on the development of substance use disorders. *Drug and Alcohol Dependence, 75*, 287–299.

Surguladze, S. A., Young, A. W., Senior, C., Brébion, G., Travis, M. J., & Phillips, M. L. (2004). Recognition accuracy and response bias to happy and sad facial expressions in patients with major depression. *Neuropsychology, 18*, 212–218.

Sutker, P. D., & Allain, A. N., Jr. (2001). Antisocial personality disorder. In H. E. Adams & P. B. Sutker (Eds.), *Comprehensive handbook of psychopathology* (3rd ed., pp. 445–490). New York: Kluwer Academic/ Plenum.

Sutton, C. T., & Broken Nose, M. A. (1996). American Indian families: An overview. In M. McGoldrick, J. Giordano, & J. K. Pearce (Eds.), *Ethnicity and family therapy* (2nd ed., pp. 31–44). New York: Guilford Press.

Svartberg, M., & Stiles, T. C. (1991). Comparative effects of short-term psychodynamic psychotherapy: A meta-analysis. *Journal of Consulting & Clinical Psychology, 59*, 704–714.

Swaab, D. F. (2003). *The human hypothalamus: Basic and clinical aspects. Part 1: Nuclei of the human hypothalamus*. Amsterdam: Elsevier.

Swaab, D. F. (2003). *The human hypothalamus: Basic and clinical aspects. Part 1: Nuclei of the human hypothalamus*. Amsterdam: Elsevier.

Swaggart, B., Gagnon, E., Bock, S. J., Earles, T. L., Quinn, C., & Myles, B. S. (1995). Using social stories to teach social and behavioral skills to children with autism. *Focus on Autistic Behavior, 10*, 1–16.

Swanson, J. M., & Volkow, N. D. (2002). Pharmacokinetic and pharmacodynamic properties of stimulants: Implications for the design of new treatments for ADHD. *Behavioural Brain Research, 130*, 73–78.

Swanson, J. M., Casey, B. J., Nigg, J., Castellanos, F. X., Volkow, N. D., & Taylor, E. (2004). Clinical and cognitive definitions of attention deficits in children with attention-deficit/hyperactivity disorder. In M. I. Posner (Ed.), *Cognitive neuroscience of attention* (pp. 430–445). New York: Guilford.

Swanson, J. M., Kinsbourne, M., Nigg, J., Lanphear, B., Stefanatos, G. A., Volkow, N., et al. (2007). Etiologic subtypes of attention-deficit/hyperactivity disorder: Brain imaging, molecular genetic and environmental factors and the dopamine hypothesis. *Neuropsychology Review, 17*, 39–59.

Swanson, J. W. (1994). Mental disorder, substance abuse, and community violence: an epidemiological approach. In J. Monahan & H. J. Steadman (Eds.), *Violence and mental disorder: Developments in risk assessment* (pp. 101–136). Chicago: University of Chicago Press.

Swanson, J. W., Swartz, M. S., Van Dorn, R. A., Elbogen, E. B., Wagner, H. R., Rosenheck, R. A., et al. (2006). A national study of violent behavior in persons with schizophrenia. *Archives of General Psychiatry, 63,* 490–499.

Swanson, J., Flodman, P., Kennedy, J., Spence, M. A., Moyzis, R., Schuck, S., et al. (2000). Dopamine genes and ADHD. *Neuroscience and Biobehavioral Reviews, 24,* 21–25.

Swartz, H. A. (1999). Interpersonal psychotherapy. In M. Hersen, & A. S. Bellack (Eds.), *Handbook of comparative interventions for adult disorders* (2nd ed., pp. 139–155). Hoboken, NJ: John Wiley & Sons.

Swartz, M. S., Swanson, J. W., Hiday, V. A., Wagner, H. R., Burns, B. J., & Borum, R. (2001). A randomized controlled trial of out patient commitment in North Carolina. *Psychiatric Services, 52,* 325–329.

Swartz, M. S., Wagner, H. R., Swanson, J. W., Stroup, T. S., McEvoy, J. P., Canive, J. M., et al. (2006). Substance use in persons with schizophrenia: Baseline prevalence and correlates from the NIMH CATIE study. *Journal of Nervous and Mental Disease, 194,* 164–172.

Swedo, S. E., Leonard, H. L., Garvey, M., Mittleman, B., Allen, A. J., Perlmutter, S., et al. (1998). Pediatric autoimmune neuropsychiatric disorders associated with streptococcal infections: Clinical description of the first 50 cases. *American Journal of Psychiatry, 155,* 264–271.

Swedo, S. E., Leonard, H. L., Garvey, M., Mittleman, B., Allen, A. J., Perlmutter, S., et al. (1998). Pediatric autoimmune neuropsychiatric disorders associated with streptococcal infections: Clinical description of the first 50 cases. *American Journal of Psychiatry, 155,* 264–271.

Sweeney, P. D., Anderson, K., & Bailey, S. (1986). Attributional style in depression: A meta-analytic review. *Journal of Personality and Social Psychology, 50,* 974–991.

Swendsen, J. D., Merikangas, K. R., Canino, G. J., Kessler, R. C., Rubio-Stipec, M., & Anglst, J. (1998). The comorbidity of alcoholism with anxiety and depressive disorders in four geographic communities. *Comprehensive Psychiatry, 39,* 176–184.

Swenne, I. (2000). Heart risk associated with weight loss in anorexia nervosa and eating disorders: Electrocardiographic changes during the early phase of refeeding. *Acta Paediatrica, 89,* 447–452.

Swica, Y., Lewis, D. O., & Lewis, M. (1996). Child abuse and dissociative identity disorder/multiple personality disorder: The documentation of childhood maltreatment and the corroboration of symptoms. *Child and Adolescent Psychiatric Clinics of North America, 5,* 431–447.

Swift, A., & Wright, M. O. (2000). Does social support buffer stress for college

women: When and how? *Journal of College Student Psychotherapy, 14,* 23–42.

Sykes, R. (2006). Somatoform disorders in DSM-IV: Mental or physical disorders? *Journal of Psychosomatic Research, 60,* 341–344.

Syvalathi, E. K. G. (1994). Biological factors in schizophrenia: Structural and functional aspects. *British Journal of Psychiatry, 164*(Suppl. 23), 9–14.

Szapocznik, J., Hervis, O., & Schwartz, S. (2003). *Brief strategic family therapy for adolescent drug abuse.* (NIH Publication 03-4751). Bethesda, MD: National Institute on Drug Abuse.

Szasz, T. S. (1960). The myth of mental illness. *American Psychologist, 15,* 113–118.

TADS Team (2007). The Treatment for Adolescents with Depression Study (TADS): Long-term effectiveness and safety outcomes. *Archives of General Psychiatry, 64,* 1132–1144.

Tager-Flusberg, H. (1999). A psychological approach to understanding the social and language impairments in autism. *International Review of Psychiatry, 11,* 325–334.

Takano, A., Shiga, T., Kitagawa, N., Koyama, T., Katoh, C., Tsukamoto, E., et al. (2001). Abnormal neuronal network in anorexia nervosa studied with I-123-IMP SPECT. *Psychiatry Research, 107,* 45–50.

Takeshita, J. (1997). Psychosis. In W-S. Tseng & J. Streltzer (Eds.), Culture and psychopathology: A guide to clinician assessment (pp. 124–138). New York: Brunner/Mazel.

Tamminga, C. A. (2006). Practical treatment information for schizophrenia. *American Journal of Psychiatry, 163,* 563–565.

Tanda, G., Pontieri, F., & Di Chiara, G. (1997). Cannabinoid and heroin activation of mesolimbic dopamine transmission by a common opioid receptor mechanism. *Science, 276,* 2048–2050.

Tandon, R., Keshavan, M. S., & Nasrallah, H. A. (2008). Schizophrenia, "just the facts": What we know in 2008. 2. Epidemiology and etiology. *Schizophrenia Research, 102,* 1–18.

Tang, T. Z., & DeRubeis, R. J. (1999). Sudden gains and critical sessions in cognitive-behavioral therapy for depression. *Journal of Consulting and Clinical Psychology, 67,* 894–904.

Tani, P., Lindberg, N., Appelberg, B., Wendt, T. N., Wendt, L. V., & Porkka-Heiskanen, T. (2006). Clinical neurological abnormalities in young adults with Asperger syndrome. *Psychiatry and Clinical Neurosciences, 60,* 253–255.

Tanielian, T., & Jaycox, L. H. (2008). *Invisible wounds of war: Psychological and cognitive injuries, their consequences, and services to assist recovery.* Rand Center for

Military Health Policy Research. Retrieved September 4, 2008, from http://www.rand.org/pubs/monographs/2008/RAND_MG720.sum.pdf

Tantleff-Dunn, S., Gokee-LaRose, J., & Peterson, R. D. (2004). Interpersonal psychotherapy for the treatment of anorexia nervosa, bulimia nervosa, and binge eating disorder. In J. K. Thompson (Ed.), *Handbook of eating disorders and obesity* (pp. 163–185). Hoboken, NJ: John Wiley & Sons.

Tarasoff v. Regents of the University of California, 529 P.2d 553 (Cal. 1974).

Tarasoff v. Regents of the University of California, 551 P.2d 334 (Cal. 1976).

Tareen, A., Hodes, M., & Rangel, L. (2005). Non-fat-phobic anorexia nervosa in British South Asian adolescents. *International Journal of Eating Disorders, 37,* 161–165.

Tariot, P. N., Farlow, M. R., Grossberg, G. T., Graham, S. M., McDonald, S., Gergel, I. (2004). Memantine treatment in patients with moderate to severe Alzheimer disease already receiving donepezil: A randomized controlled trial. *Journal of the American Medical Association, 291,* 317–324.

Tarrier, N., & Bobes, J. (2000). The importance of psychosocial interventions and patient involvement in the treatment of schizophrenia. *International Journal of Psychiatry in Clinical Practice, 4,* S35–S51.

Tarrier, N., Kinney, C., McCarthy, E., Wittkowski, A., Yusupoff, L., Gledhill, A., et al. (2001). Are some types of psychotic symptoms more responsive to cognitive-behavior therapy? *Behavioural & Cognitive Psychotherapy, 29,* 45–55.

Tarrier, N., Pilgrim, H., Sommerfield, C., Faragher, B., Reynolds, M., Graham, E., & Barrowclough, C. (1999). A randomized trial of cognitive therapy and imaginal exposure in the treatment of chronic posttraumatic stress disorder. *Journal of Consulting & Clinical Psychology, 67,* 13–18.

Tarullo, A. R., & Gunnar, M. R. (2006). Child maltreatment and the developing HPA axis. *Hormones and Behavior, 50,* 632–639.

Task Force on Promotion and Dissemination of Psychological Procedures. (1995). Training in and dissemination of empirically-validated psychological treatments: Report and recommendations. *The Clinical Psychologist, 48,* 3–23.

Tate, D. F., & Zabinski, M. F. (2004). Computer and Internet applications for psychological treatment: Update for clinicians. *Journal of Clinical Psychology, 60,* 209–220.

Tauscher, J., Bagby, R.M., Javanmard, M., Christensen, B.K., Kasper, S., and Kapur, S. (2001). Inverse relationship between serotonin 5-HT(1A) receptor binding and anxiety: A [(11)C]WAY-100635 PET investigation in healthy volunteers. *American Journal of Psychiatry, 158,* 1326–1328.

Taylor, C. T., & Alden, L. E. (2006). Parental overprotection and interpersonal behavior in generalized social phobia. *Behavior Therapy, 37,* 14–24.

Taylor, C. T., Laposa, J. M., & Alden, L. E. (2004). Is avoidant personality disorder more than just social avoidance? *Journal of Personality Disorders, 18,* 571–594.

Taylor, J. Y., Caldwell, C. H., Baser, R. E., Faison, N., & Jackson, J. S. (2007). Prevalence of eating disorders among Blacks in the national survey of American life. *International Journal of Eating Disorders, 40,* S10–S14.

Taylor, S. (1996). Meta-analysis of cognitive-behavioral treatment for social phobia. *Journal of Behavior Therapy and Experimental Psychiatry, 27,* 1–9.

Taylor, S. (2000). *Understanding and treating panic disorder: Cognitive-behavioural approaches.* New York: Wiley.

Taylor, S., & Rachman, S. J. (1994). Klein's suffocation theory of panic. *Archives of General Psychiatry, 51,* 505–506.

Taylor, S., Asmundson, G. J. G., & Coons, M. J. (2005). Current directions in the treatment of hypochondriasis. *Journal of Cognitive Psychotherapy, 19,* 285–304.

Taylor, S., Fedoroff, I. C., Koch, W. J., Thordarson, D. S., Fecteau, G., & Nicki, R. M. (2001). Posttraumatic stress disorder arising after road traffic collisions: Patterns of response to cognitive-behavior therapy. *Journal of Consulting & Clinical Psychology, 69,* 541–551.

Taylor, S., Woody, S., Koch, W. J., McLean, P. D., & Anderson, K. W. (1996). Suffocation false alarms and efficacy of cognitive behavioral therapy for panic disorder. *Behavior Therapy, 27,* 115–126.

Tcheremissine, O. V., Lane, S. D., Cherek, D. R., & Pietras, C. J. (2003). Impulsiveness and other personality dimensions in substance use disorders and conduct disorders. *Addictive Disorders & Their Treatment, 2,* 1–7.

Teasdale, J. D. (1983). Negative thinking in depression: Cause, effect, or reciprocal relationship. *Advances in Behaviour Research & Therapy, 5,* 3–25.

Teasdale, J. D., & Barnard, P. J. (1993). *Affect, cognition, and change: Re-modelling depressive thought.* Hillsdale, NJ: Lawrence Erlbaum.

Teasdale, J. D., Moore, R. G., Hayhurst, H., Pope, M., Williams, S., & Segal, Z. V. (2002). Metacognitive awareness and prevention of relapse in depression: empirical evidence. *Journal of Consulting and Clinical Psychology, 70,* 275–287.

Tebartz van Elst, L., Hesslinger, B., Thiel, T., Geiger, E., Haegele, K., Lemieux, L., et al. (2003). Frontolimbic brain abnormalities in patients with borderline personality disorder: A volumetric magnetic resonance imaging study. *Biological Psychiatry, 54,* 163–171.

Teicher, M. H., Andersen, S. L., Polcari, A., Anderson, C. M., & Navalta, C. P. (2002). Developmental neurobiology of childhood stress and trauma. *Psychiatric Clinics of North America, 25,* 397–426.

Teicher, M. H., Andersen, S. L., Polcari, A., Anderson, C. M., Navalta, C. P., & Kim, D. M. (2003). The neurobiological consequences of early stress and childhood maltreatment. *Neuroscience & Biobehavioral Reviews, 27,* 33–44.

Tek, C., Kirkpatrick, B., Kelly, C., & McCreadie, R. G. (2001). Summer birth and deficit schizophrenia in Nithsdale, Scotland. *Journal of Nervous and Mental Disease, 189,* 613–617.

Telch, C. F., Agras, W. S., & Linehan, M. M. (2001). Dialectical behavior therapy for binge eating disorder. *Journal of Consulting and Clinical Psychology, 69,* 1061–1065.

Temple, E., Deutsch, G. K., Poldrack, R. A., Miller, S. L., Tallal, P., Merzenich, M. M., et al. (2003). Neural deficits in children with dyslexia ameliorated by behavioral remediation: Evidence from functional MRI. *Proceedings of the National Academy of Sciences, USA, 100,* 2860–2865.

Tengström, A., Hodgins, S., & Kullgren, G. (2001). Men with schizophrenia who behave violently: The usefulness of an early- versus late-start offender typology. *Schizophrenia Bulletin, 27,* 205–218.

Tennant, C. (2002). Life events, stress and depression: A review of the findings. *Australian & New Zealand Journal of Psychiatry, 36,* 173–182.

Tennen, H., & Herzberger, S. (1987). Depression, self-esteem, and the absence of self-protective attributional biases. *Journal of Personality and Social Psychology, 52,* 72–80.

ter Kuile, M., van Lankveld, J. J. D. M., de Groot, E., Melles, R., Neffs, J., & Zandbergen, M. (2007). Cognitive-behavioral therapy for women with lifelong vaginismus: Process and prognostic factors. *Behaviour Research and Therapy, 45,* 359–373.

Teves, D., Videen, T. O., Cryer, P. E., & Powers, W. J. (2004) Activation of human medial prefrontal cortex during autonomic responses to hypoglycemia. *Proceedings of the National Academy of Sciences USA, 101,* 6217–6221.

Thase, M. E. (2002). Antidepressant effects: The suit may be small, but the fabric is real. *Prevention & Treatment, 5,* Article 32. http://www.journals.apa.org/prevention/volume5/pre0050032c.html.

Thase, M. E., Greenhouse, J. B., Frank, E., Reynolds, C. F., III, Pilkonis, P. A., Hurley, K., et al. (1997). Treatment of major depression with psychotherapy or psychotherapy-pharmacotherapy combinations. *Archives of General Psychiatry, 54,* 1009–1015.

The Hughes legacy: Scramble for the billions. (1976, April 19). *Time Magazine.* Retrieved June 28, 2007, from http://www.time.com/time/magazine/article/0,9171,914059,00.html

Thom, A., Sartory, G., & Joehren, P. (2000). Comparison between one-session psychological treatment and benzodiazepine in dental phobia. *Journal of Consulting & Clinical Psychology, 68,* 378–387.

Thomas, G. V. (1994). Mixed personality disorder with passive-aggressive and avoidant features. In P. T. Costa, Jr., & T. A. Widiger (Eds.), *Personality disorders and the five-factor model of personality* (pp. 211–215). Washington, DC: American Psychological Association.

Thompson v. County of Alameda, 614 P.2d 728 (Cal. 1980).

Thompson, J. K. (1990). *Body image disturbance: Assessment and treatment.* New York: Pergamon Press.

Thompson, J. K., & Smolak, L. (2001). *Body image, eating disorders, and obesity in youth: Assessment, prevention, and treatment.* Washington, DC: American Psychological Association.

Thompson, J. K., & Stice, E. (2001). Thin-ideal internalization: Mounting evidence for a new risk factor for body-image disturbance and eating pathology. *Current Directions in Psychological Science, 10,* 181–183.

Thompson, J. K., Heinberg, L. J., Altabe, M., & Tantleff-Dunn, S. (1999). *Exacting beauty: Theory, assessment, and treatment of body image disturbance.* Washington, DC: American Psychological Association.

Thompson, J. M., Gallagher, P., Hughes, J. H., Watson, S., Gray, J. M., Ferrier, I. N., et al. (2005). Neurocognitive impairment in euthymic patients with bipolar affective disorder. *British Journal of Psychiatry, 186,* 32–40.

Thompson, P. M., Hayashi, K. M., Simon, S. L., Geaga, J. A., Hong, M. S., Sui, Y., et al. (2004). Structural abnormalities in the brains of human subjects who use methamphetamine. *Journal of Neuroscience, 24,* 6028–6036.

Thompson, R. F. (1993). *The brain, a neuroscience primer* (2nd ed.). New York: W. H. Freeman.

Thompson, S. B. N. (2003). General anaesthesia and cognitive functioning. *Chinese Journal of Clinical Psychology, 11,* 71–72.

Thompson, W. W., Price, C., Goodson, B., Shay, D. K., Benson, P., Hinrichsen, V. L., et al. (2007). Early thimerosal exposure and neuropsychological outcomes at 7 to 10 years. *New England Journal of Medicine, 357,* 1281–1292.

Thomsen, P. H., Ebbesen, C., & Persson, C. (2001). Long-term experience with citalopram in the treatment of adolescent OCD. *Journal of the American Academy of Child & Adolescent Psychiatry, 40,* 895–902.

Thorberg, F. A., & Lyvers, M. (2006). Negative Mood Regulation (NMR) expectancies, mood, and affect intensity among clients in substance disorder treatment facilities. *Addictive Behaviors, 31,* 811–820.

Thorn, B. L., & Gilbert, L. A. (1998). Antecedents of work and family role expectations of college men. *Journal of Family Psychology, 12,* 259–267.

Tomkins, D. M., & Sellers, E. M. (2001). Addiction and the brain: The role of neurotransmitters in the cause and treatment of drug dependence. *Canadian Medical Association Journal, 164,* 817–821.

Tidey, J. W., Rohsenow, D. J., Kaplan, G. B., & Swift, R. M. (2005). Cigarette smoking topography in smokers with schizophrenia and matched non-psychiatric controls. *Drug and Alcohol Dependence, 80,* 259–265.

Tiefer, L. (1987). Social constructionism and the study of human sexuality. In P. Shaver & C. Hendrick (Eds.), *Sex and gender* (pp. 70–94). Thousand Oaks, CA: Sage Publications.

Tiefer, L. (1991). Historical, scientific, clinical and feminist criticisms of "the human sexual response cycle" model. *Annual Review of Sex Research, 2,* 1–23.

Tiefer, L. (2001). Feminist critique of sex therapy: Foregrounding the politics of sex. In P. J. Kleinplatz (Ed.), *New directions in sex therapy: Innovations and alternatives.* Philadelphia: Taylor and Rutledge.

Tienari, P., Wahlberg, K., & Wynne, L. C. (2006). Finnish Adoption Study of Schizophrenia: Implications for family interventions. *Families, Systems, & Health, 24,* 442–451.

Tienari, P., Wynne, L. C., Läksy, K., Moring, J., Nieminen, P., Sorri, A., et al. (2003). Genetic boundaries of the schizophrenia spectrum: Evidence from the Finnish adoptive family study of schizophrenia. *American Journal of Psychiatry, 160,* 1587–1594.

Tienari, P., Wynne, L. C., Moring, J., Lahti, I., Naarala, M., Sorri, A., et al. (1994). The Finnish adoptive family study of schizophrenia. Implications for family research. *British Journal of Psychiatry, 164,* 20–26.

Tihonen, J., Lönnqvist, J. Wahlbeck, K., Klaukka, T., Tanskanen, A., & Kaukka, J. (2006). Antidepressants and the risk of suicide, attempted suicide, and overall mortality in a nationwide cohort. *Archives of General Psychiatry, 63,* 1358–1367.

Tillfors, M., Furmark, T., Ekselius, L., & Fredrikson, M. (2004). Social phobia and avoidant personality disorder: One spectrum disorder? *Nordic Journal of Psychiatry, 58,* 147–152.

Tillfors, M., Furmark, T., Marteinsdottir, I., Fischer, H., Pissiota, A., Langstrom, B., et al. (2001). Cerebral blood flow in subjects with social phobia during stressful speaking tasks: A PET study. *American Journal of Psychiatry 158,* 1220–1226.

Tillfors, M., Furmark, T., Marteinsdottir, I., Fischer, H., Pissiota, A., Langstroem, B., et al. (2001). Cerebral blood flow in subject with social phobia during stressful speaking tasks: A PET study. *American Journal of Psychiatry, 158,* 1220–1226.

Timko, C., DeBenedetti, A., & Billow, R. (2006). Intensive referral to 12-step self-help groups and 6-month substance use disorder outcomes. *Addiction, 101,* 678–688.

Tisher, M., & Dean, S. (2000). Family therapy with the elderly. *Australian and New Zealand Journal of Family Therapy, 21,* 94–101.

Toft, T., Fink, P., Oernboel, E., Christensen, K., Frostholm, L., & Olesen, F. (2005). Mental disorders in primary care: Prevalence and co-morbidity among disorders. Results from the Functional Illness in Primary Care (FIP) study. *Psychological Medicine, 35,* 1175–1184.

Tolin, D. F., & Foa, E. B. (2006). Sex differences in trauma and posttraumatic stress disorder: A quantitative review of 25 years of research. *Psychological Bulletin, 132,* 959–992.

Tolin, D. F., Worhunsky, P., & Maltby, N. (2006). Are "obsessive" beliefs specific to OCD? A comparison across anxiety disorders. *Behaviour Research and Therapy, 44,* 469–480.

Tollison, C. D., & Adams, H. E. (1979). *Sexual disorders: Treatment, theory, and research.* New York: Gardner.

Tomarken, A. J., Mineka, S., & Cook, M. (1989). Fear-relevant selective associations and covariation bias. *Journal of Abnormal Psychology, 98,* 381–394.

Tomkins, D. M., & Sellers, E. M. (2001). Addiction and the brain: The role of neurotransmitters in the cause and treatment of drug dependence. *Canadian Medical Association Journal, 164,* 817–821.

Torgersen, S. (2005). Epidemiology. In J. M. Oldham, A. E. Skodol, & D. S. Bender (Eds.), *The American Psychiatric Publishing textbook of personality disorders* (pp. 129–141). Washington, DC: American Psychiatric Publishing.

Torgersen, S. G. (1983). Genetic factors in anxiety disorders. *Archives of General Psychiatry, 40,* 1085–1089.

Torgersen, S., Kringlen, E., & Cramer, V. (2001). The prevalence of personality disorders in a community sample. *Archives of General Psychiatry, 58,* 590–596.

Torgersen, S., Lygren, S., Oien, P. A., Skre, I., Onstad, S., Edvardsen, J., Tambs, K., & Kringlen, E. (2000). A twin study of personality disorders. *Comprehensive Psychiatry, 41,* 416–425.

Torrens, M., & Martín-Santos, R. (2000). Why do people abuse alcohol and drugs? *Current Opinion in Psychiatry, 13,* 285–289.

Torrens, M., Fonseca, F., Mateu, G., & Farré, M. (2005). Efficacy of antidepressants in substance use disorders with and without comorbid depression: A systematic review and meta-analysis. *Drug and Alcohol Dependence, 78,* 1–22.

Torrey, E. F. (2001). *Surviving schizophrenia: A manual for families, consumers, and providers* (4th ed.). New York: Quill.

Torrey, E. F. (2002). Studies of individuals with schizophrenia never treated with antipsychotic medications: A review. *Schizophrenia Research, 58,* 101–115.

Tost, H., Vollmert, C., Brassen, S., Schmitt, A., Dressing, H., & Braus, D. F. (2004). Pedophilia: Neuropsychological evidence encouraging a brain network perspective. *Medical Hypotheses, 63,* 528–531.

Towbin, K. E., Mauk, J. E., & Batshaw, M. L. (2002). Pervasive developmental disorders. In M. L. Batshaw (Ed.), *Children with disabilities* (5th ed., pp. 365–387). Baltimore: Brookes Publishing.

Tozzi, F., Thornton, L. M., Klump, K. L., Fichter, M. M., Halmi, K. A., Kaplan, A. S., et al. (2005). Symptom fluctuation in eating disorders: Correlates of diagnostic crossover. *American Journal of Psychiatry, 162,* 732–740.

Tractenberg, R. E., Weiner, M. F., Patterson, M. B., Teri, L., & Thal, L. J. (2003). Comorbidity of psychopathological domains in community-dwelling persons with Alzheimer's disease. *Journal of Geriatric Psychiatry and Neurology, 16,* 94–99.

Trestman, R. L., Keefe, R. S. E., Mitropoulou, V., Harvey, P. D., deVegvar, M. L., Lees-Roitman, S., et al. (1995). Cognitive function and biological correlates of cognitive performance in schizotypal personality disorder. *Psychiatry Research, 59,* 127–136.

Trierweiler, S. J., Muroff, J. R., Jackson, J. S., Neighbors, H. W., & Munday, C. (2005). Clinician race, situational attributions, and diagnoses of mood versus schizophrenia disorders. *Cultural Diversity & Ethnic Minority Psychology, 11,* 351–364.

Trimble, J. E. (1994). Cultural variations in the use of alcohol and drugs. In W. J. Lonner & R. S. Malpass (Eds.), *Psychology and culture* (pp. 79–84). Boston: Allyn & Bacon.

True, W. R., Rice, J., Eisen, S. A., Heath, A. C., Goldberg, J., Lyons, M. J., et al. (1993). A twin study of genetic and environmental contributions to liability for posttraumatic stress symptoms. *Archives of General Psychiatry, 50,* 257–264.

Trull, T. J., & Durrett, C. A. (2005). Categorical and dimensional models of personality disorder. *Annual Review of Clinical Psychology, 1,* 355–380.

Tsai, S., Hong, C., Yu, Y. W.-Y., Chen, T., Wang, Y., & Lin, W. (2004). Association study of serotonin 1B receptor (A-161T) genetic polymorphism and suicidal behaviors and response to fluoxetine in major depressive disorder. *Neuropsychobiology, 50,* 235–238.

Tsoi, W. F., & Wong, K. E. (1991). A 15 year follow up study of Chinese schizophrenic patients. *Acta Psychiatrica Scandinavica. 84,* 217–220.

Tsuang, M. T., Bar, J. L., Harley, R. M., & Lyons, M. J. (2001). The Harvard Twin Study of Substance Abuse: What we have learned. *Harvard Review of Psychiatry, 9,* 267–279.

Tsuang, M. T., Stone, W. S., & Faraone, S. V. (2000). Toward reformulating the diagnosis of schizophrenia. *American Journal of Psychiatry, 157,* 1041–1050.

Tsuchiya, K. J., Agerbo, E., & Mortensen, P. B. (2005). Parental death and bipolar disorder: A robust association was found in early maternal suicide. *Journal of Affective Disorders, 86,* 151–159.

Tsuchiya, K. J., Takagai, S., Kawai, M., Matsumoto, H., Nakamura, K., Minabe, Y., et al. (2005). Advanced paternal age associated with an elevated risk for schizophrenia in offspring in a Japanese population. *Schizophrenia Research, 76,* 337–342.

Turetsky, B. I., Moberg, P. J., Mozley, L. H., Moelter, S. T., Agrin, R. N., Gur, R. C., et al. (2002). Memory-delineated subtypes of schizophrenia: Relationship to clinical, neuroanatomical, and neurophysiological measures. *Neuropsychology, 16,* 481–490.

Turkington, D., Kingdon, D., & Weiden, P. J. (2006). Cognitive behavior therapy for schizophrenia. *American Journal of Psychiatry, 163,* 365–373.

Turnbull, J. D., Heaslip, S., & McLeod, H. A. (2000). Pre-school children's attitudes to fat and normal male and female stimulus figures. *International Journal of Obesity, 24,* 1705–1706.

Turner, H., & Bryant-Waugh, R. (2004). Eating disorder not otherwise specified (eating disorder NOS): Profiles of clients presenting at a community eating disorder service. *European Eating Disorders Review, 12,* 18–26.

Turner, R. M. (1994). Borderline, narcissistic, and histrionic personality disorders. In M. Hersen & R. T. Ammerman (Eds.),

Handbook of prescriptive treatments for adults (pp. 393–420). New York: Plenum Press.

Turner, S. M., & Beidel, D. C. (1988). *Treating obsessive-compulsive disorder.* Elmsford, NY: Pergamon Press.

Turner, T. (1989). Rich and mad in Victorian England. *Psychological Medicine, 19,* 29–44.

Tuthill, R. W. (1996). Hair lead levels related to children's classroom attention-deficit behavior. *Archives of Environmental Health, 51,* 214–220.

Twenge, J. M. (2000). The age of anxiety? Birth cohort change in anxiety and neuroticism, 1952–1993. *Journal of Personality and Social Psychology, 79,* 1007–1021.

Tyrer, P. (2002). Nidotherapy: A new approach to the treatment of personality disorder. *Acta Psychiatrica Scandinavica, 105,* 469–472.

Tyrer, P., & Johnson, T. (1996). Establishing the severity of personality disorder. *American Journal of Psychiatry, 153,* 1593–1597.

Tyrer, P., Gunderson, J., Lyons, M., & Tohen, M. (1997). Extent of comorbidity between mental state and personality disorders. *Journal of Personality Disorders, 11,* 242–259.

Tyson, A. S. (2008, September 5). Soldiers' suicide rate on pace to set record. *The Washington Post,* p. A02.

U.S. Census Bureau. (2000). *Changing shape of the nation's income distribution, 1947–1998.* Retrieved April 4, 2001, from http:// www.census.gov/prod/2000pubs/p60-204.pdf

U.S. Census Bureau. (2001) *Census 2000 redistricting [Public Law 94–171] summary file.* Washington, DC: Author.

U.S. Department of Health and Human Services, Office of the Secretary. (2002). Standards for privacy of individually identifiable health information. *Federal Register, 67:* 53182–53273.

U.S. Department of Health and Human Services. (1999). *Mental health: A report of the Surgeon General.* Rockville: MD: Author. Retrieved January 15, 2007, from http:// mentalhealth.samhsa.gov/cre/ch2.asp

U.S. Department of Health and Human Services. (2001). *Mental health: Culture, race, and ethnicity. A supplement to mental health: A report of the Surgeon General.* Rockville, MD: U.S. Department of Health and Human Services, Substance Abuse and Mental Health Services Administration, Center for Mental Health Services. Retrieved October 12, 2008, from http://www. surgeongeneral.gov/library/mentalhealth/cre/ sma-01-3613.pdf

U.S. National Library of Medicine. (2005). The balance of passions. In *History of*

medicine and disease: Emotions and disease. Retrieved February 19, 2007, from http:// www.nlm.nih.gov/hmd/emotions/balance.html

United Nations International Drug Control Programme. (1997). *Worlddrug report.* Oxford: Oxford University Press.

United States Public Health Service. (2001). *Mental health: Culture, race, and ethnicity. A supplement to mental health: A report of the Surgeon General.* Retrieved January 12, 2007, from http://www.surgeongeneral.gov/ library/mentalhealth/cre/

Urbszat, D., Herman, C. P., & Polivy, J. (2002). Eat, drink, and be merry, for tomorrow we diet: Effects of anticipated deprivation on food intake in restrained and unrestrained eaters. *Journal of Abnormal Psychology, 111,* 396–401.

Vaginismus.com. (2007). Burning and tightness from no apparent cause: Lynn. Retrieved October 1, 2007, from http://www. vaginismus.com/vaginismus-stories

Vaiva, G., Ducrocq, F., Jezequel, K., Averland, B., Lestavel, P., Brunet, A., et al. (2003). Immediate treatment with propranolol decreases posttraumatic stress disorder two months after trauma. *Biological Psychiatry, 54,* 947–949.

Vajk, F. C., Craighead, W. E., Craighead, L. W., & Holley, C. (1997, November). Risk of major depression as a function of response styles to depressed mood. Poster presented at the annual meeting of the Association for the Advancement of Behavior Therapy, Miami Beach, FL.

Valera, E. M., Faraone, S. V., Murray, K. E., & Seidman, L. J. (2007). Meta-analysis of structural imaging findings in attention-deficit/hyperactivity disorder. *Biological Psychiatry, 61(12),* 1361–1369.

van Balkom, A. J. L. M., Bakker, A., Spinhoven, P., Blaauw, B. M. J. W., Smeenk, S., et al. (1997). A meta-analysis of the treatment of panic disorder with or without agoraphobia: A comparison of psychopharmacological, cognitive-behavioral, and combination treatments. *Journal of Nervous and Mental Disease, 185,* 510–516.

van den Bosch, L. M. C., Koeter, M. W. J., Stijnen, T., Verheul, R., & van den Brink, W. (2005). Sustained efficacy of dialectical behaviour therapy for borderline personality disorder. *Behaviour Research and Therapy, 43,* 1231–1241.

van den Bosch, L. M.C., Koeter, M. W. J., Stijnen, T., Verheul, R., & van den Brink, W. (2005). Sustained efficacy of dialectical behaviour therapy for borderline personality disorder. *Behaviour Research and Therapy, 43,* 1231–1241.

van den Heuvel, O. A., van de Wetering, B. J., Veltman, D. J., & Pauls, D. L. (2000). Genetic studies of panic disorder: A review. *Journal of Clinical Psychiatry, 61,* 756–766.

van den Heuvel, O. A., Veltman, D. J., Groenewegen, H. J., Witter, M. P., Merkelbach, J., Cath, D. C., van et al. (2005). Disorder-specific neuroanatomical correlates of attentional bias in obsessive-compulsive disorder, panic disorder, and hypochondriasis. *Archives of General Psychiatry*, 62, 922–933.

van den Heuvel, O.A., Veltman, D.J., Groenewegen, H.J., Witter, M.P., Merkelbach, J., Cath, D.C., et al. (2005). Disorder-specific neuroanatomical correlates of attentional bias in obsessive-compulsive disorder, panic disorder, and hypochondriasis. *Archives of General Psychiatry*, 62, 922–933.

Van der Linden, G. J. H., Stein, D. J., & van Balkom, A. J. L. M. (2000). The efficacy of the selective serotonin reuptake inhibitors for social anxiety disorder (social phobia): A meta-analysis of randomized controlled trials. *International Clinical Psychopharmacology*, 15(Suppl. 2), S15–S23.

Van der Linden, G., Van Heerden, B., Warwick, J., Wessels, C., Van Kradenburg, J., Zungu-Dirwayi, N., et al. (2000). Functional brain imaging and pharmacotherapy in social phobia: Single photon emission computer tomography before and after treatment with the selective serotonin reuptake inhibitor citalopram. *Progress in Neuro-Psychopharmacology & Biological Psychiatry*, 24, 419–438.

van Duijl, M., Cardeña, E., & de Jong, J. (2005). The validity of DSM-IV-TR dissociative disorders categories in south-west Uganda. *Transcultural Psychiatry*, 42, 219–241.

van Elst, L. T., Valerius, G., Büchert, M., Thiel, T., Rüsch, N., Bubl, E., et al. (2005). Increased prefrontal and hippocampal glutamate concentration in schizophrenia: Evidence from a magnetic resonance spectroscopy study. *Biological Psychiatry*, 58, 724–730.

van Erp, T. G. M., Saleh, P. A., Rosso, I. M., Huttunen, M., Lönnqvist, J., Pirkola, T., et al. (2002). Contributions of genetic risk and fetal hypoxia to hippocampal volume in patients with schizophrenia or schizoaffective disorder, their unaffected siblings, and healthy unrelated volunteers. *American Journal of Psychiatry*, 159, 1514–1520.

Van Gerwen, L. J., Spinhoven, P., & Van Dyck, R. (2006). Behavioral and cognitive group treatment for fear of flying: A randomized controlled trial. *Journal of Behavior Therapy and Experimental Psychiatry*, 37, 358–371.

van Heeringen, K. (2003). The neurobiology of suicide and suicidality. *Canadian Journal of Psychiatry*, 48, 292–300.

van Os, J., & Delespaul, P. (2003). Psychosis research at Maastricht University, The Netherlands. *British Journal of Psychiatry*, 183, 559–560.

Van Thiel, D. H., Tarter, R. E., Rosenblum, E., & Gavaler, J. S. (1988). Ethanol, its metabolism and gonadal effects: Does sex make a difference? *Advances in Alcohol and Substance Abuse* 7, 131–169.

Van Velzen, C. J. M., Emmelkamp, P. M. G., & Scholing, A. (1997). The impact of personality disorders on behavioral treatment outcome for social phobia. *Behaviour Research and Therapy*, 35, 889–900.

Vance, A., Silk, T. J., Casey, M., Rinehart, N. J., Bradshaw, J. L., Bellgrove, M. A., et al. (2007). Right parietal dysfunction in children with attention deficit hyperactivity disorder, combined type: A functional MRI study. *Molecular Psychiatry*, 12, 826–832.

Vansteenwegen, D., Vervliet, B., Hermans, D., Thewissen, R., & Eelen, P. (2007). Verbal, behavioural and physiological assessment of the generalization of exposure-based fear reduction in a spider-anxious population. *Behaviour Research and Therapy*, 45, 291–300.

Vaughn, C., & Leff, J. (1976). Measurement of expressed emotion in the families of psychiatric patients. *British Journal of Social and Clinical Psychology*, 15, 1069–1177.

Veale, D., De Haro, L., & Lambrou, C. (2003). Cosmetic rhinoplasty in body dysmorphic disorder. *British Journal of Plastic Surgery*, 56, 546–551.

Veale, D., Ennis, M., & Lambrou, C. (2002). Possible association of body dysmorphic disorder with an occupation or education in art and design. *American Journal of Psychiatry*, 159, 1788–90.

Vehmanen, L., Kaprio, J., & Loennqvist, J. (1995). Twin studies on concordance for bipolar disorder. *Psychiatria Fennica*, 26, 107–116.

Velakoulis, D., Pantelis, C., McGorry, P. D., Dudgeon, P., Brewer, W., Cook, M., et al. (1999). Hippocampal volume in first-episode psychoses and chronic schizophrenia: A high resolution magnetic resonance imaging study. *Archives of General Psychiatry*, 56, 133–141.

Ventura, J., Nuechterlein, K. H., Lukoff, D., & Hardesty, J. P. (1989). A prospective study of stressful life events and schizophrenic relapse. *Journal of Abnormal Psychology*, 98, 407–411.

Verdoux, H., Sorbara, F., Gindre, C., Swendsen, J. D., & van Os, J. (2003). Cannabis use and dimensions of psychosis in a nonclinical population of female subjects. *Schizophrenia Research*, 59, 77–84.

Verduin, T. L., & Kendall, P. C. (2003). Differential occurrence of comorbidity within childhood anxiety disorders. *Journal of Clinical Child and Adolescent Psychology*, 32, 290–295.

Verheul, R., & Widiger, T. A. (2004). A meta-analysis of the prevalence and usage

of the personality disorder not otherwise specified (PDNOS) diagnosis. *Journal of Personality Disorders*, 18, 309–319.

Verheul, R., Bartak, A., & Widiger, T. A. (2007). Prevalence and construct validity of personality disorder not otherwise specified (PDNOS). *Journal of Personality Disorders*, 21, 359–370.

Verheul, R., van den Brink, W., & Geerlings, P. (1999). A three-pathway psychobiological model of craving for alcohol. *Alcohol Alcoholism*, 34, 197–222.

Verkes, R. J., Gijsman, H. J., Pieters, M. S. M., Schoemaker, R. C., de Visser, S., Kuijpers, M., et al. (2001). Cognitive performance and serotonergic function in users of Ecstasy. *Psychopharmacology*, 153, 196–202.

Victor, M., Adams, R. D., & Collins, G. H. (1989). *The Wernicke-Korsakoff syndrome and related neurological disorders due to alcoholism and malnutrition* (2nd ed.). Philadelphia: F. A. Davis.

Vidal, C. N., Rapoport, J. L., Hayashi, K. M., Geaga, J. A., Sui, Y., McLemore, L. E., et al. (2006). Dynamically spreading frontal and cingulate deficits mapped in adolescents with schizophrenia. *Archives of General Psychiatry*, 63, 25–34.

Viding, E., Blair, R. J. R., Moffitt, T. E., & Plomin, R. (2005). Evidence for substantial genetic risk for psychopathy in 7-year-olds. *Journal of Child Psychology and Psychiatry*, 46, 592–597.

Vidyasagar, T. R. (2005). Attentional gating in primary visual cortex: A physiological basis for dyslexia. *Perception*, 34, 903–911.

Vieweg, R., & Shawcross, C. R. (1998). A trial to determine any difference between two and three times a week ECT in the rate of recovery from depression. *Journal of Mental Health (UK)*, 7, 403–409.

Vijayakumar, L., John, S., Pirkis, J., & Whiteford, H. (2005). Suicide in developing countries. 2. Risk factors. *Crisis*, 26, 112–119.

Villaseñor, Y., & Waitzkin, H. (1999). Limitations of a structured psychiatric diagnostic instrument in assessing somatization among Latino patients in primary care. *Medical Care*, 37, 637–646.

Vinckenbosch, E., Robichon, F., & Eliez, S. (2005). Gray matter alteration in dyslexia: Converging evidence from volumetric and voxel-by-voxel MRI analyses. *Neuropsychologia*, 43, 324–331.

Viney, W. (2000). Dix, Dorothea Lynde. In A. E. Kazdin (Ed.), *Encyclopedia of psychology* (Vol. 3, pp. 65–66). Washington, DC: American Psychological Association.

Vita, A., De Peri, L., Silenzi, C., & Dieci, M. (2006). Brain morphology in first-episode schizophrenia: A meta-analysis of quantitative magnetic resonance imaging studies. *Schizophrenia Research*, 82, 75–88.

Vita, A., De Peri, L., Silenzi, C., & Dieci, M. (2006). Brain morphology in first-episode schizophrenia: A meta-analysis of quantitative magnetic resonance imaging studies. *Schizophrenia Research, 82,* 75–88.

Vogel, M., Busse, S., Freyberger, H. J., & Grabe, H. J. (2006). Dopamine D3 receptor and schizophrenia: A widened scope for the immune hypothesis. *Medical Hypotheses, 67,* 354–358.

Voglmaier, M. M., Seidman, L. J., Niznikiewicz, M. A., Dickey, C. C., Shenton, M. E., & McCarley, R. W. (2000). Verbal and nonverbal neuropsychological test performance in subjects with schizotypal personality disorder. *American Journal of Psychiatry, 157,* 787–793.

Vohs, K. D., & Heatherton, T. F. (2000). Self-regulatory failure: A resource-depletion approach. *Psychological Science, 11,* 249–254.

Volkow, N. D., Chang, L., Wang, G. J., Fowler, J. S., Franceschi, D., Sedler, M., et al. (2001). Loss of dopamine transporters in methamphetamine abusers recovers with protracted abstinence. *Journal of Neuroscience, 21,* 9414–9418.

Volkow, N. D., Chang, L., Wang, G., Fowler, J. S., Franceschi, D., Sedler, M. J., et al. (2001a). Higher cortical and lower subcortical metabolism in detoxified methamphetamine abusers. *American Journal of Psychiatry, 158,* 383–389.

Volkow, N. D., Chang, L., Wang, G.-J., Fowler, J. S., Ding, Y.-S., Sedler, M., Loganet et al. (2001). Low level of brain dopamine D2 receptors in methamphetamine abusers: Association with metabolism in the orbitofrontal cortex. *American Journal of Psychiatry, 158,* 2015–2021.

Volkow, N. D., Wang, G., Fowler, J. S., & Ding, Y. (2005). Imaging the effects of methylphenidate on brain dopamine: New model on its therapeutic actions for attention-deficit/hyperactivity disorder. *Biological Psychiatry, 57,* 1410–1415.

Volkow, N. D., Wang, G., Newcorn, J., Telang, F., Solanto, M. V., Fowler, J. S., et al. (2007). Depressed dopamine activity in caudate and preliminary evidence of limbic involvement in adults with attention-deficit/hyperactivity disorder. *Archives of General Psychiatry, 64,* 932–940.

Volkow, N. D., Wang, G.-J., Fowler, J. S., Logan, J., Gatley, S. J., Gifford A., et al. (1999). Prediction of reinforcing responses to psychostimulants in humans by brain dopamine D2 receptor levels. *American Journal of Psychiatry, 156,* 1440–1443.

Völlum, B., Richardson, P., Stirling, J., Elliott, R., Dolan, M., Chaudhry, I., et al. (2004). Neurobiological substrates of antisocial and borderline personality disorder: Preliminary results of a functional fMRI study. *Criminal Behaviour and Mental Health, 14,* 39–54.

Von Holle, A., Pinheiro, A. P., Thornton, L. M., Klump, K. L., Berrettini, W. H., Brandt, H., et al. (2008). Temporal patterns of recovery across eating disorder subtypes. *Australian and New Zealand Journal of Psychiatry, 42,* 108–117.

von Zerssen, D., Leon, C. A., Moller, H., Wittchen, H., Pfister, H., & Sartorius, N. (1990). Care strategies for schizophrenic patients in a transcultural comparison. *Comprehensive Psychiatry, 31,* 398–408.

Voth, H. M., & Orth, M. H. (1973). *Psychotherapy and the role of the environment.* New York: Behavioral Press.

Vuchinich, R. E. & Tucker, J. A. (1996). Alcoholic relapse, life events, and behavioral theories of choice: A prospective analysis. *Experimental and Clinical Psychopharmacology, 4,* 19–28.

Vuilleumier, P., Chicherio, C., Assal, F., Schwartz, S., Slosman, D., & Landis, T. (2001). Functional neuroanatomical correlates of hysterical sensorimotor loss. *Brain, 124,* 1077–1090.

Waas, G. A., & Kleckler, D. M. (2000). Play therapy. In A. E. Kazdin (Ed.), *Encyclopedia of psychology* (Vol. 6, pp. 218–223). Washington, DC: American Psychological Association.

Waber, R. L., Shiv, B., Carmon, Z., & Ariely, D. (2008). Research letter: Commericial features of placebo and therapeutic efficacy. *Journal of the American Medical Association, 299*(9), 1016–1017.

Wada, T., Kawakatsu, S., Komatani, A., Okuyama, N., & Otani, K. (1999). Possible association between delusional disorder, somatic type and reduced regional cerebral blood flow. *Progress in Neuro-Psychopharmacology & Biological Psychiatry, 23,* 353–357.

Wade, D., Harrigan, S., Harris, M. G., Edwards, J., & McGorry, P. D. (2006). Treatment for the initial acute phase of first-episode psychosis in a real-world setting. *Psychiatric Bulletin, 30,* 127–131.

Wade, T. D. (2007). Epidemiology of eating disorders: Creating opportunities to move the current classification paradigm forward. *International Journal of Eating Disorders, 40,* S27–S30.

Wade, T. D., Bergin, J. L., Tiggemann, M., Bulik, C. M., & Fairburn, C. G. (2006). Prevalence and long-term course of lifetime eating disorders in an adult Australian twin cohort. *Australian and New Zealand Journal of Psychiatry, 40,* 121–128.

Wadsworth, S. J., Olson, R. K., Pennington, B. F., & DeFries, J. C. (2000). Differential genetic etiology of reading disability as a function of IQ. *Journal of Learning Disabilities, 33,* 192–199.

Wager, T. D., Rilling, J. K., Smith, E. E., Sokolik, A., Casey, K. L., Davidson, R. J., et al. (2004). Placebo-induced changes in fMRI in the anticipation and experience of pain, *Science, 303,* 1162–1167.

Wagner, P. S. (1996). First person account: A voice from another closet. *Schizophrenia Bulletin, 22,* 399–401.

Wagner, P. S., & Spiro, C. S. (2005). *Divided minds: Twin sisters and their journey through schizophrenia.* New York: St. Martin's Press.

Wahl, O. F. (1999). Mental health consumers' experience of stigma. *Schizophrenia Bulletin, 25,* 467–478.

Wahl, O. F. (1999). Mental health consumers' experience of stigma. *Schizophrenia Bulletin, 25,* 467–478.

Wahlbeck, K., Forsén, T., Osmond, C., Barker, D. J. P., & Eriksson, J. G. (2001). Association of schizophrenia with low maternal body mass index, small size at birth and thinness during childhood. *Archives of General Psychiatry, 58,* 48–52.

Waismann, R., Fenwick, P. B., Wilson, G. D., Hewett, T. D., & Lumsden, J. (2003). EEG responses to visual erotic stimuli in men with normal and paraphilic interests. *Archives of Sexual Behavior, 32,* 135–144.

Walach, H., & Maidhof, C. (1999). Is the placebo effect dependent on time? A meta-analysis. In I. Kirsch (Ed.), *How Expectancies Shape Experience* (pp. 321–332). Washington, DC: American Psychological Association.

Walcott, D. D., Pratt, H. D., & Patel, D. R. (2003). Adolescents and eating disorders: Gender, racial, ethnic, sociocultural and socioeconomic issues. *Journal of Adolescent Research, 18,* 223–243.

Waldeck, T. L., & Miller, L. S. (2000). Social skills deficits in schizotypal personality disorder. *Psychiatry Research, 93,* 237–246.

Waldman, I. D., & Gizer, I. R. (2006). The genetics of attention deficit hyperactivity disorder. *Clinical Psychology Review, 26,* 396–432.

Waldman, M., Nicholson, S., Adilov, N., & Williams, J. (2008). Autism prevalence and precipitation rates in California, Oregon, and Washington counties. *Archives of Pediatric Adolescent Medicine, 162,* 1026–1034.

Waldron, V. R., Lavitt, M., & Kelley, D. (2000). The nature and prevention of harm in technology-mediated self-help settings: Three exemplars. *Journal of Technology in Human Services, 17,* 267–293.

Walker, E. F., & Diforio, D. (1997). Schizophrenia: A neural diathesis-stress model. *Psychological Review, 104,* 667–685.

Walker, E. F., Grimes, K. E., Davis, D., & Smith, A. (1993). Childhood precursors of schizophrenia: Facial expressions of emotion. *American Journal of Psychiatry, 150,* 1654–1660.

Walker, E. F., Logan, C. B., & Walder, D. (1999). Indicators of neurdevelopmental abnormality in schizotypal personality disorder. *Psychiatric Annals, 29,* 132–136.

Walker, E. F., Savoie, T., & Davis, D. (1994). Neuromotor precursors of schizophrenia. *Schizophrenia Bulletin, 148,* 661–666.

Walker, E. F., Walder, D. J., & Reynolds, F. (2001). Developmental changes in cortisol secretion in normal and at-risk youth. *Development & Psychopathology, 13,* 721–732.

Walker, E., Kestler, L., Bollini, A., & Hochman, K. M. (2004). Schizophrenia: Etiology and course. *Annual Review of Psychology, 55,* 401–430.

Walker, Z., & Stevens, T. (2002). Dementia with Lewy bodies: Clinical characteristics and diagnostic criteria. *Journal of Geriatric Psychiatry and Neurology, 15,* 188–194.

Wallace, C., Mullen, P. E., & Burgess, P. (2004). Criminal offending in schizophrenia over a 25-year period marked by deinstitutionalization and increasing prevalence of comorbid substance use disorders. *American Journal of Psychiatry, 161,* 716–727.

Waller, N. G., & Shaver, P. R. (1994). The importance of nongenetic influences on romantic love styles: A twin-family study. *Psychological Science, 5,* 268–274.

Wallien, M. S. C., Zucker, K. J., Steensma, T. D., & Cohen-Kettenis, P. T. (2008). 2D:4D finger-length ratios in children and adults with gender identity order. *Hormones and Behavior, 54,* 450–454.

Walling, M.K., Reiter, R.C., O'Hara, M.W., Milburn, A.K., Lilly, G. & Vincent, S.D. (1994). Abuse history and chronic pain in women: I. Prevalences of sexual abuse and physical abuse. *Obstetrics and Gynecology, 84,* 193–199.

Walls, J. (2005). *The glass castle.* New York: Scribner's.

Walsh, A. E., Oldman, A. D., Franklin, M., Fairburn, C. G., & Cowen, P. J. (1995). Dieting decreases plasma tryptophan and increases the prolactin response to d-fenfluramine in women but not men. *Journal of Affective Disorders, 21,* 89–97.

Walsh, B. T. (1993). Binge eating in bulimia nervosa. In C. G. Fairburn & G. T. Wilson (Eds.), *Binge eating: Nature, assessment, and treatment* (pp. 37–49). New York: Guilford Press.

Walsh, B. T., & Kahn, C. B. (1997). Diagnostic criteria for eating disorders: Current concerns and future directions. *Psychopharmacology Bulletin, 33,* 369–372.

Walsh, B. T., Kaplan, A. S., Attia, E., Olmsted, M., Parides, M., Carter, J. C., et al. (2006). Fluoxetine after weight restoration in anorexia nervosa: A randomized controlled trial. *Journal of the American Medical Association, 295,* 2605–2612.

Walsh, B. T., Seidman, S. N., Sysko, R., & Gould, M. (2002). Placebo response in studies of major depression: Variable, substantial, and growing. *Journal of the American Medical Association, 287,* 1840–1847.

Walsh, B. T., Seidman, S. N., Sysko, R., & Gould, M. (2002). Placebo response in studies of major depression: Variable, substantial, and growing. *JAMA: Journal of the American Medical Association, 287,* 1840–1847.

Walsh, B. T., Wilson, G. T., Loeb, K. L., Devlin, M. J., Pike, K. M., Roose, S. P., et al. (1997). Medication and psychotherapy in the treatment of bulimia nervosa. *American Journal of Psychiatry, 154,* 523–531.

Walsh, E., Buchanan, A., & Fahy, T. (2002). Violence and schizophrenia: Examining the evidence. *British Journal of Psychiatry, 180,* 490–495.

Wampold, B. E. (2001). Practical interpretations of outcome research in psychotherapy through the examination of effect sizes. *Clinician's Research Digest, Supp. 24,* n.p.

Wampold, B. E. (2001). *The Great Psychotherapy Debate: Models, Methods, and Findings.* Mahwah, NJ, US: Lawrence Erlbaum Associates, Publishers.

Wampold, B. E., & Bhati, K. S. (2004). Attending to the omissions: A historical examination of evidence-based practice movements. *Professional Psychology: Research & Practice, 35,* 563–570.

Wang G-J, Volkow, N. D., Chang, L., Miller, E., Sedler, M., Hitzemann, R., Zhu, W., Logan, J., Ma, Y., & Fowler, J. S. (2004). Partial recovery of brain metabolism in methamphetamine abusers after protracted abstinence. *American Journal of Psychiatry, 161,* 242–248.

Wang, P. S., Lane, M., Olfson, M., Pincus, H. A., Wells, K. B., & Kessler, R. C. (2005). Twelve-month use of mental health services in the United States: Results from the National Comorbidity Survey Replication. *Archives of General Psychiatry, 62,* 629–640.

Wansink, B., & Ittersum, K. (2005). Shape of glass and amount of alcohol poured: Comparative study of effect of practice and concentration. *British Medical Journal, 331,* 1512–1514.

Ward, O. B. (1992). Fetal drug exposure and sexual differentiation of males. In A. A. Gerall, H. Moltz, & I. L. Ward (Eds.), *Sexual differentiation* (pp. 181–219). New York: Plenum Press.

Warner, R. (2002). Response to McGorry and Edwards. *Schizophrenia Bulletin, 28,* 181–185.

Waslick, B. D., Kandel, R., & Kakouros, A. (2002). Depression in children and adolescents: An overview. In D. Shaffer & B. Waslick (Eds.), *The many faces of depression in children and adolescents* (pp. 1–36). Arlington, VA: American Psychiatric Publishing.

Wasserman, D., & Varnick A. (1998). Reliability of statistics on violent death and suicide in the Former USSR, 1970–1990. *Acta Psychiatrica Scandinavica Supplement, 394,* 34–41.

Waters, M. (2000). Psychologists spotlight growing concern of higher suicide rates among adolescents. *Monitor on Psychology, 31,* n.p.

Watkins, P. C. (2002). Implicit memory bias in depression. *Cognition and Emotion, 16,* 381–402.

Watson, J. B. (1931). *Behaviorism* (2nd ed.). Oxford, England: Kegan Paul.

Watson, J. B., & Rayner, R. (1920). Conditioned emotional reactions. *Journal of Experimental Psychology, 3,* 1–14.

Watson, J. C., Goldman, R. N., & Greenberg, L. S. (2007). *Case studies in emotion-focused treatment of depression: A comparison of good and poor outcomes.* Washington, DC: American Psychological Association.

Wattar, U., Sorensen, P., Buemann, I., Birket-Smith, M., Salkovskis, P. M., Albertsen, M., & Strange, S. (2005). Outcome of cognitive-behavioural treatment for health anxiety (hypochondriasis) in a routine clinical setting. *Behavioural and Cognitive Psychotherapy, 33,* 165–175.

Watts-English, T., Fortson, B. L., Gibler, N., Hooper, S. R., & DeBellis, M. D. (2006). The psychobiology of maltreatment in childhood. *Journal of Social Issues, 62,* 717–736.

Wechsler, H., & Kuo, M. (2003). Watering down the drinks: The moderating effect of college demographics on alcohol use of high-risk groups. *American Journal of Public Health, 93,* 1929–1933.

Wechsler, H., Dowdall, G. W., Maenner, G., Gledhill-Hoyt, J., & Lee, H. (1998). Changes in binge drinking and related problems among American college students between 1993 and 1997. *Journal of American College Health, 47,* 57–68.

Wechsler, H., Fulop, M., Padilla, A., Lee, H., & Patrick, K. (1997). Binge drinking among college students: A comparison of California with other states. *Journal of American College Health, 45,* 273–277.

Wechsler, H., Lee, J. E., Nelson, T. F., & Kuo, M. (2002). Underage college students' drinking behavior, access to alcohol, and the influence of deterrence policies. *Journal of American College Health, 50,* 223–236.

Wegner, D. M., Schneider, D. J., Carter, S. R., & White, T. L. (1987). Paradoxical effects of thought suppression. *Journal of Personality & Social Psychology, 53,* 5–13.

Weiden, P. J., & Zygmunt, A. (1997). Medication noncompliance in schizophrenia: Part I, assessment. *Journal of Practical Psychiatry and Behavioral Health, 3,* 106–112.

Weinberger, D. R., & Lipska, B. K. (1995). Cortical maldevelopment, antipsychotic drugs, and schizophrenia: A search for common ground. *Schizophrenia Research, 16,* 87–110.

Weinberger, J. (1995). Common factors aren't so common: The common factors dilemma. *Clinical Psychology: Science and Practice, 2,* 45–69.

Weinstein, N. (1993). Testing four competing theories of health-protective behavior. *Health Psychology, 12,* 324–333.

Weinstein, N. D. (1984). Why it won't happen to me: Perceptions of risk factors and illness susceptibility. *Health Psychology, 3,* 431–457.

Weintraub, E., & Robinson, C. (2000). A case of monosymptomatic hypochondriacal psychosis treated with olanzapine. *Annals of Clinical Psychiatry, 12,* 247–249.

Weiser, M., Reichenberg, A., Grotto, I., Yasvitzky, R., Rabinowitz, J., Lubin, G., et al. (2004). Higher rates of cigarette smoking in male adolescents before the onset of schizophrenia: A historical-prospective cohort study. *American Journal of Psychiatry, 161,* 1219–1223.

Weisman, A. G. (1997). Understanding cross-cultural prognostic variability for schizophrenia. *Cultural Diversity and Mental Health, 3,* 23–35.

Weisman, A. G., Rosales, G., Kymalainen, J., & Armesto, J. (2005). Ethnicity, family cohesion, religiosity and general emotional distress in patients with schizophrenia and their relatives. *Journal of Nervous and Mental Disease, 193,* 359–368.

Weiss, L. A., Shen, Y., Korn, J. M., Arking, D. E., Miller, D. T., Fossdal, R., et al. (2008). Association between microdeletion and microduplication at 16p11.1 and autism. *New England Journal of Medicine, 358,* 667–675.

Weissman, M. M., Bland, R. C., Canino, G. J., Greenwald, S., Hwu, H. G., Lee, C. K., et al. (1994). The cross national epidemiology of obsessive compulsive disorder: The Cross National Collaborative Group. *Journal of Clinical Psychiatry, 55,* 5–10.

Weissman, M. M., Bland, R. C., Canino, G. J., Greenwald, S., Hwu, H. G., Joyce, P. R., et al. (1999). Prevalence of suicide ideation and suicide attempts in nine countries. *Psychological Medicine, 29,* 9–17.

Weissman, M. M., Bruce, M. L., Leaf, P. J., Florio, L., & Holzer, C. (1991). Affective disorders. In L. N. Robins & D. A. Regier (Eds.), *Psychiatric disorders in America* (pp. 53–80). New York: Free Press.

Weissman, M. M., Markowitz, J. C., & Klerman, G. L. (2000). *Comprehensive guide to interpersonal therapy.* New York: Basic Books.

Weissman, M. M., Pilowsky, D. J., Wickramaratne, P. J., Talati, A., Wisniewski, S. R., Fava, M., et al. (2006). Remissions in maternal depression and child psychopathology: A STAR*D-child report. *JAMA: Journal of the American Medical Association, 295,* 1389–1398.

Weissman, M. M., Wickramaratne, P., Nomura, Y., Warner, V., Pilowsky, D., & Verdeli, H. (2006). Offspring of depressed parents: 20 years later. *American Journal of Psychiatry, 163,* 1001–1008.

Weissman, M. M., Wolk, S., Goldstein, R. B., Moreau, D., Adams, P., Greenwald, S., et al. (1999). Depressed adolescents grown up. *JAMA: Journal of the American Medical Association, 281,* 1707–1713.

Weissman, M. M., Wolk, S., Wickramaratne, P., Goldstein, R. B., Adams, P., Greenwald, S., et al. (1999). Children with prepubertal-onset major depressive disorder and anxiety grown up. *Archives of General Psychiatry, 56,* 794–801.

Weisz, J. R., Jensen-Doss, A., & Hawley, K. M. (2006). Evidence-based youth psychotherapies versus usual clinical care. *American Psychologist, 61,* 671–689.

Weisz, J. R., McCarty, C. A., Eastman, K. L., Chaiyasit, W., & Suwanlert, S. (1997). Developmental psychopathology and culture: Ten lessons from Thailand. In S. S. Luthar, J. A. Burack, D. Cicchetti, & J. R. Weisz (Eds.), *Developmental psychopathology: Perspectives on adjustment, risk, and disorder* (pp. 568–592). New York: Cambridge University Press.

Weisz, J. R., Suwanlert, S., Chaiyasit, W., & Walter, B. R. (1987). Over- and undercontrolled referral problems among children and adolescents from Thailand and the United States: The *wat* and *wai* of cultural differences. *Journal of Consulting and Clinical Psychology, 55,* 719–726.

Welkenhuysen-Gybels, J., Billiet, J., & Cambré, B. (2003). Adjustment for acquiescence in the assessment of the construct equivalence of Likert-type score items. *Journal of Cross-Cultural Psychology, 34,* 702–722.

Weltzin, T. E., Weisensel, N., Franczyk, D., Burnett, K., Klitz, C., & Bean, P. (2005). Eating disorders in men: Update. *Journal of Men's Health & Gender, 2,* 186–193.

Wender, P. H., Kety, S. S., Rosenthal, D., Schulsinger, F., Ortmann, J., & Luhde, I. (1986). Psychiatric disorders in the biological and adoptive families of adopted individuals with affective disorders. *Archives of General Psychiatry, 43,* 923–929.

Wender, P. H., Rosenthal, D., Kety, S. S., Schulsinger, F., & Weiner, J. (1973). Social class and psychopathology in adoptees: A natural experimental method for separating the role of genetic and experimental factors. *Archives of General Psychiatry, 28,* 318–325.

Wenner, J. S. (1971). John Lennon interview with Rolling Stone magazine. Retrieved on March 12, 2009 from, http://members.tripod.com/~taz4158/johnint.html

Wenzel, A., & Cochran, C. K. (2006). Autobiographical memories prompted by automatic thoughts in panic disorder and social phobia. *Cognitive Behaviour Therapy, 35,* 129–137.

Wenzel, A., Brown, G. K., & Beck, A. T. (2009). *Cognitive therapy for suicidal patients: Scientific and clinical applications.* (pp. 53–77). Washington, DC: American Psychological Association.

Wenzel, A., Chapman, J. E., Newman, C. F., Beck, A. T., & Brown, G. K. (2006). Hypothesized mechanisms of change in cognitive therapy for borderline personality disorder. *Journal of Clinical Psychology, 62,* 503–516.

Wenzlaff, R. M., & Beevers, C. G. (1998). Depression and interpersonal responses to others' moods: The solicitation of negative information about happy people. *Personality & Social Psychology Bulletin, 24,* 386–398.

Werch, C. E., & Anzalone, D. A. (1995). Stage theory and research on tobacco, alcohol, and other drug use. *Journal of Drug Education, 25,* 81–98.

Werneke, U., Horn, O., & Taylor, D. M. (2004). How effective is St. John's wort? The evidence revisited. *Journal of Clinical Psychiatry, 65,* 611–617.

Werner, S., Malaspina, D., & Rabinowitz, J. (2007). Socioeconomic status at birth is associated with risk of schizophrenia: Population-based multilevel study. *Schizophrenia Bulletin, 33,* 1373–1378.

Werstiuk, E. S., Coote, M., Griffith, L., Shannon, H., & Steiner, M. (1996). Effects of electroconvulsive therapy on peripheral adrenoceptors, plasma, noradrenaline, MHPG, and cortisol in depressed patients. *British Journal of Psychiatry, 169,* 758–765.

Wertz, J. M., & Sayette, M. A. (2001). A review of the effects of perceived drug use opportunity on self-reported urge. *Experimental and Clinical Psychopharmacology, 1,* 3–13.

Wesner, R. B., & Noyes, R. (1991). Imipramine: An effective treatment for illness phobia. *Journal of Affective Disorders, 22,* 43–48.

Westen, D., & Morrison, K. (2001). A multidimensional meta-analysis of treatments for depression, panic, and generalized anxiety disorder: An empirical examination of the status of empirically supported treatments. *Journal of Consulting and Clinical Psychology, 69,* 875–899.

Westen, D., & Shedler, J. (2000). A prototype matching approach to diagnosing personality disorders: Toward DSM-V. *Journal of Personality Disorders, 14,* 109–126.

Westen, D., & Weinberger, J. (2004). When clinical description becomes statistical prediction. *American Psychologist, 59,* 595–613.

Westen, D., Heim, A. K., Morrison, K., Patterson, M., & Campbell, L. (2002). Simplifying diagnosis using a prototype-matching approach: Implications for the next edition of the DSM. In L. E. Beutler & M. L. Malik (Eds.), *Rethinking the DSM: A psychological perspective* (pp. 221–250). Washington, DC: American Psychological Association.

Westen, D., Novotny, C. M., & Thompson-Brenner, H. (2004). The empirical status of empirically supported psychotherapies: Assumptions, findings, and reporting in controlled clinical trials. *Psychological Bulletin, 130,* 631–663.

Westen, D., Novotny, C. M., & Thompson-Brenner, H. (2005). EBP ≠ EST: Reply to Crits-Christoph et al. (2005) and Weisz et al. (2005). *Psychological Bulletin, 131,* 427–433.

Westerlund, E. (1992). *Women's sexuality after childhood incest.* New York: W. W. Norton & Co.

Wexler, B. E., & Bell, M. D. (2005). Cognitive remediation and vocational rehabilitation for schizophrenia. Schizophrenia Bulletin, 31, 931–941.

Wexler, B. E., Gottschalk, C. H., Fulbright, R. K., Prohovnik, I., Lacadie, C. M., Rounsaville, B. J., & Gore, J. C. (2001). Functional magnetic resonance imaging of cocaine craving. *American Journal of Psychiatry, 158,* 86–95.

Wexler, B. E., Hawkins, K. A., Rounsaville, B., Anderson, M., Sernyak, M. J., & Green, M. F. (1997). Normal neurocognitive performance after extended practice in patients with schizophrenia. Schizophrenia Research, 26, 173–180.

Weyerer, S., & Wiedenmann, A. (1995). Economic factors and the rate of suicide in Germany between 1881 to 1989. *Psychological Report, 76,* 1331–1341.

Whalen, C. K, Henker, B., Ishikawa, S. S., Jamner, L. D., Floro, J. N., Johnston, J. A., & Swindle, R. (2006). An electronic diary study of contextual triggers and ADHD: Get ready, get set, get mad. *Journal of the American Academy of Child Adolescent Psychiatry, 45,* 166–174.

Whitaker, R. (2002). *Mad in America: Bad science, bad medicine, and the enduring mistreatment of the mentally ill.* Cambridge, MA: Perseus.

White, H. R., Jarrett, N., Valencia, E. Y., Loeber, R., & Wei, E. (2007). Stages and sequences of initiation and regular substance use in a longitudinal cohort of black and white male adolescents. *Journal of Studies on Alcohol and Drugs, 68,* 173–181.

White, J. M., & Ryan, C. F. (1996). Pharmacological properties of ketamine. *Drug and Alcohol Review, 15,* 145–155.

White, K. H., & Barlow, D. H. (2002). Panic disorder and agoraphobia. In D.H. Barlow (Ed.), *Clinical handbook of psychological disorders* (2nd ed., pp. 328–379). New York: Guilford Press.

White, K., Kando, J., Park, T., Waternaux, C., & Brown, W. A. (1992). Side effects and the "blindability" of clinical drug trials. *American Journal of Psychiatry, 149,* 1730–1731.

White, R. W. (1948). *The abnormal personality: A textbook.* New York: Ronald Press.

Whitehead, W. E. (2006). Hypnosis for irritable bowel syndrome: The empirical evidence of therapeutic effects. *International Journal of Clinical and Experimental Hypnosis, 54,* 7–20.

Whitlock, J. L., Powers, J. L., & Eckenrode, J. (2006). The virtual cutting edge: The Internet and adolescent self-injury. *Developmental Psychology, 42,* 407–417.

Whittinger, N. S., Langley, K., Fowler, T. A., Thomas, H. V., & Thapar, A. (2007). Clinical precursors of adolescent conduct disorder in children with attention-deficit/hyperactivity disorder. *Journal of the American Academy of Child & Adolescent Psychiatry, 46,* 179–187.

WHO World Mental Health Survey Consortium. (2004). Prevalence, severity, and unmet need for treatment of mental disorders in the World Health Organization World Mental Health Surveys. *JAMA: Journal of the American Medical Association, 291,* 2581–2590.

Wiborg, I. M., & Dahl, A. A. (1997). The recollection of parental rearing styles in patients with panic disorder. *Acta Psychiatrica Scandinavica, 96,* 58–63.

Wiborg, I. M., Falkum, E., Dahl, A. A., & Gullberg, C. (2005). Is harm avoidance an essential feature of patients with panic disorder? *Comprehensive Psychiatry, 46,* 311–314.

Widiger, T. A., & Corbitt, E. M. (1997). Comorbidity of antisocial personality disorder with other personality disorders. In D. M. Stoff, J. Breiling, &J. D. Maser (Eds.), *Handbook of antisocial behavior* (pp. 75–82). Hoboken: John Wiley.

Widiger, T. A., & Costa, P. T., Jr. (2002). Five-factor model personality disorder research. In P. T. Costa, Jr., & T. A. Widiger (Eds.), *Personality disorders and the five-factor model of personality* (2nd ed., pp. 59–87). Washington, DC: American Psychological Association.

Widiger, T. A., & Frances, A. J. (1989). Epidemiology, diagnosis, and comorbidity of borderline personality disorder. In A. Tasman, R. E. Hales, & A. J. Frances (Eds.), *Review of psychiatry* (Vol. 8). Washington, DC: American Psychiatric Press.

Widiger, T. A., & Lowe, J. R. (2008). A dimensional model of personality disorder: Proposal for DSM-V. *Psychiatric Clinics of North America, 31,* 363–378.

Widiger, T. A., & Mullins-Sweatt, S. N. (2005). Categorical and dimensional models of personality disorders. In J. M. Oldham, A. E. Skodol, & D. S. Bender (Eds.), *The American Psychiatric Publishing textbook of personality disorders* (pp. 35–53). Washington, DC: American Psychiatric Publishing.

Widiger, T. A., & Trull, T. J. (1993). Borderline and narcissistic personality disorders. In P. B. Sutker & H. E. Adams (Eds.), *Comprehensive handbook of psychopathology* (2nd ed., pp. 371–394). New York: Plenum Press.

Widiger, T. A., & Trull, T. J. (2007). Plate tectonics in the classification of personality disorder: Shifting to a dimensional model. *American Psychologist, 62,* 71–83.

Widiger, T. A., Costa, P. T., Jr., & McCrae, R. R. (2002). A proposal for Axis II: Diagnosing personality disorders using the five-factor model. In P. T. Costa, Jr., & T. A. Widiger (Eds.), *Personality disorders and the five-factor model of personality* (2nd ed., pp. 431–456). Washington, DC: American Psychological Association.

Widom, C. S., DuMont, K., & Czaja, S. J. (2007). A prospective investigation of major depressive disorder and comorbidity in abused and neglected children grown up. *Archives of General Psychiatry, 64,* 49–56.

Wiedemann, G., Pauli, P., Dengler, W., Lutzenberger, W., Birbaumer, N., & Buchkremer, G. (1999). Frontal brain asymmetry as a biological substrate of emotions in patients with panic disorders. *Archives of General Psychiatry, 56,* 78–84.

Wigal, T., Greenhill, L., Chuang, S., McGough, J., Vitiello, B., Skrobala, A., et al. (2006). Safety and tolerability of methylphenidate in preschool children with ADHD. *Journal of the American Academy of Child and Adolescent Psychiatry, 45,* 1294–1303.

Wilberg, T., Karterud, S., Pedersen, G., & Urnes, O. (2009). The impact of avoidant personality disorder on psychosocial functioning is substantial. *Nordic Journal of Psychiatry, 30,* 1–7.

Wilfley, D. E., Agras, W. S., Telch, C. F., Rossiter, E. M., Schneider, J. A., Cole, A. G., et al. (1993). Group cognitive-behavioral therapy and group interpersonal psychotherapy for the nonpurging bulimic individual: A controlled comparison. *Journal of Consulting and Clinical Psychology, 61,* 296–305.

Wilk, C. M., Gold, J. M., McMahon, R. P., Humber, K., Iannone, V. N., & Buchanan, R. W. (2005). No, it is not possible to be schizophrenic yet neuropsychologically normal. Neuropsychology, 19, 778–786.

Wilkinson, D. J. C., Thompson, J. M., Lambert, G. W., Jennings, G. L., Schwarz, R. G., Jefferys, D., et al. (1998). Sympathetic activity in patients with panic disorder at rest, under laboratory mental stress, and during panic attacks. *Archives of General Psychiatry, 55,* 511–520.

Williams, D. R., & Williams-Morris, R. (2000). Racism and mental health: The African American experience. *Ethnicity & Health, 5,* 243–268.

Williams, J. M. G., Watts, F. N., MacLeod, C. & Mathews, A. (1997). *Cognitive Psychology and Emotional Disorders* (2nd ed.). Chichester, England: Wiley.

Williams, J., Hadjistavropoulos, T., & Sharpe, D. (2006). A meta-analysis of psychological and pharmacological treatments for body dysmorphic disorder. *Behaviour Research and Therapy, 44,* 99–111.

Williams, R. J., & Chang, S. Y. (2000). A comprehensive and comparative review of adolescent substance abuse treatment outcome. *Clinical Psychology: Science & Practice, 7,* 138–166.

Williamson, D. A., Womble, L. G., Smeets, M. A. M., Netemeyer, R. G., Thaw, J. M., Kutlesic, V., & Gleaves, D. H. (2002). Latent structure of eating disorder symptoms: A factor analytic and taxometric investigation. *American Journal of Psychiatry, 159,* 412–418.

Williamson-Catania, J. (2007). Genetics of neurodegenerative disease: Alzheimer's diease, frontotemporal dementia. In K. L. Bell (Dir.), *Dementia: Update for the practitioner.* Columbia University College of Physicians and Surgeons, Continuing Medical Education. Retrieved December 20, 2007, from http://ci.columbia.edu/c1182/web/sect_8/c1182_s8_2.html

Wilson, B. A. (1999). *Case studies in neuropsychological rehabilitation.* New York: Oxford University Press.

Wilson, B. A. (2004). Management and remediation of memory probems in brain-injured adults. In A. D. Baddeley, M. D. Kopelman, & B. A. Wilson (eds.), *Essential handbook of memory disorders for clinicians* (pp. 199–226). New York: Wiley.

Wilson, G. T., & Fairburn, C. G. (2007). Treatments for eating disorders. In P. Nathan & J. M. Gorman (Eds.), *A guide to treatments that work* (3rd ed., pp. 579–609). New York: Oxford University Press.

Wilson, G. T., Fairburn, C. C., Agras, W. S., Walsh, B. T., & Kraemer, H. (2002). Cognitive-behavioral therapy for bulimia nervosa: Time course and mechanisms of change. *Journal of Consulting & Clinical Psychology, 70,* 267–274.

Wilson, G. T., Nathan, P. E., O'Leary, K. D., & Clark, L. A. (1996). *Abnormal psychology: Integrating perspectives.* Boston: Allyn & Bacon.

Wilson, I., Duszynski, K., & Mant, A. (2003). A 5-year follow-up of general practice patients experiencing depression. *Family Practice, 20,* 685–689.

Wilson, J. K., & Rapee, R. M. (2006). Self-concept certainty in social phobia. *Behaviour Research and Therapy, 44,* 113–136.

Wilson, J. S., & Costanzo, P. R. (1996). A preliminary study of attachment, attention, and schizotypy in early adulthood. *Journal of Social & Clinical Psychology, 15,* 231–260.

Wilson, R. I., & Nicoll, R. A. (2001). Endogenous cannabinoids mediate retrograde signaling at hippocampal synapses. *Nature, 410,* 588–592.

Wilson, W., Mathew, R., Turkington, T., Hawk, T., Coleman, R. E., & Provenzale, J. (2000). Brain morphological changes and early marijuana use: a magnetic resonance and positron emission tomography study. *Journal of Addictive Diseases, 19,* 1–22.

Winerip, M. (1999a, May 23). Bedlam on the street. *The New York Times.*

Winerip, M. (1999b, October 18). Oddity and normality vie in subway killer's confession. *The New York Times,* p. B1.

Winfree, L. T., & Bernat, F. P. (1998). Social learning, self-control, and substance abuse by eighth grade students: A tale of two cities. *Journal of Drug Issues, 28,* 539–338.

Winick, B. J. (2003). A therapeutic jurisprudence assessment of sexually violent predator laws. In B. J. Winick & J. Q. La Fond (Eds.), *Protecting society from sexually dangerous offenders: Law, justice, and therapy* (pp. 317–331). Washington, DC: American Psychological Association.

Winnicott, D.W. (1958). *Through paediatrics to psycho-analysis: Collected papers.* New York: Basic Books, 1958.

Winzelberg, A., & Humphreys, K. (1999). Should patients' religiosity influence clinicians' referral to 12-step self-help groups? Evidence from a study of 3,018 male substance abuse patients. *Journal of Consulting and Clinical Psychology, 67,* 790–794.

Wirshing, D. A., Sergi, M. J., & Mintz, J. (2005). A videotape intervention to enhance the informed consent process for medical and psychiatric treatment research. *American Journal of Psychiatry, 162,* 186–188.

Wise, T. N., & Birket-Smith, M. (2002). The somatoform disorders for DSM-V: The need for changes in process and content. *Psychosomatics: The Journal of Consultation and Liaison Psychiatry, 43,* 437–440.

Wiseman, C. V., Sunday, S. R., Klapper, F., Harris, W. A., & Halmi, K. A. (2001). Changing patterns of hospitalization in eating disorder patients. *International Journal of Eating Disorders, 30,* 69–74.

Wisner, K. L., Perel, J. M., Peindl, K. S., & Hanusa, B. H. (2004). Timing of depression recurrence in the first year after birth. *Journal of Affective Disorders, 78,* 249–252.

Wittchen, H. U., & Hoyer, J. (2001). Generalized anxiety disorder: Nature and course. *Journal of Clinical Psychiatry, 62,* 15–19.

Wohl, M., & Gorwood, P. (2007). Paternal ages below or above 35 years old are associated with a different risk of schizophrenia in the offspring. European Psychiatry, 22, 22–26.

Wolchik, S. A., Sandler, I. N., Millsap, R. E., Plummer, B. A., Greene, S. M., Anderson, E. R., et al. (2002). Six-year follow-up of preventive interventions for children of divorce: A randomized controlled trial. *JAMA: Journal of the American Medical Association, 288,* 1874–1881.

Wolpe, J. (1997). Thirty years of behavior therapy. *Behavior Therapy, 28,* 633–635.

Wonderlich, S., & Mitchell, J. E. (2001). The role of personality in the onset of eating disoders and treatment implications. *Psychiatric Clinics of North America, 24,* 249–258.

Wong, E. C., Kim, B. S. K., Zane, N. W. S., Kim, I. J., & Huang, J. S. (2003). Examining culturally based variables associated with ethnicity: Influences on credibility perceptions of empirically supported interventions. *Cultural Diversity & Ethnic Minority Psychology, 9,* 88–96.

Wong, E. C., Kim, B. S. K., Zane, N. W. S., Kim, I. J., & Huang, J. S. (2003). Examining culturally based variables associated with ethnicity: Influences on credibility perceptions of empirically supported interventions. *Cultural Diversity & Ethnic Minority Psychology, 9,* 88–96.

Wong, J. L., Wetterneck, C., & Klein, A. (2000). Effects of depressed mood on verbal memory performance versus self-reports of cognitive difficulties. *International Journal of Rehabilitation & Health, 5,* 85–97.

Wood, J. M., Lilienfeld, S. O., Nezworski, M. T., & Garb, H. N. (2001). Coming to grips with negative evidence for the comprehensive system for the Rorschach: A comment on Gacono, Loving, and Bodholdt; Ganellen; and Bornstein. *Journal of Personality Assessment, 77,* 48–70.

Wood, J. M., Nezworski, M. T., Garb, H. N., & Lilienfeld, S. O. (2001). Problems with the norms of the comprehensive system for the Rorschach: Methodological and conceptual considerations. *Clinical Psychology: Science & Practice, 8,* 397–402.

Woodall, W. G., Delaney, H. D., Kunitz, S. J., Westerberg, V. S., & Zhao, H. (2007). A randomized trial of a DWI intervention program for first offenders: Intervention outcomes and interactions with antisocial personality disorder among a primarily American-Indian sample. *Alcoholism: Clinical and Experimental Research, 31,* 974–987.

Woods, B. (2004). Reducing the impact of cognitive impairment in dementia. In A. D. Baddeley, M. D. Kopelman, & B. A. Wilson (Eds.), *Essential handbook of memory disorders for clinicians* (pp. 285–300) New York: Wiley.

Woods, B., Spector, A., Jones, C., Orrell, M., & Davies, S. (1998). Reminiscence therapy for dementia. *Cochrane Database of Systematic Reviews, 3:* CD001120. DOI: 10.1002/14651858.CD001120.pub2.

Woody, E. Z., & Bowers, K. S. (1994). A frontal assault on dissociated control. In S. L. Lynn & J. Rhue (Eds.), *Dissociation: Clinical and theoretical perspectives* (pp. 52–79). New York: Guilford.

Wool, C. A., & Barsky, A. J. (1994). Do women somatize more than men? Gender differences in somatization. *Psychosomatics: Journal of Consultation and Liaison Psychiatry, 35,* 445–452.

World Health Organization, (2002). *World report on violence and health.* Retrieved October 20, 2008, fromhttp://www.who.int/violence_injury_prevention/violence/global_campaign/en/chap7.pdf

World Health Organization. (1948) *Constitution of the World Health Organization.* Retrieved January 26, 2009, from Jawww.searo.who.int/LinkFiles/About_SEARO_const.pdf

World Health Organization. (1999). *Figures and facts about suicide.* Technical Report. Geneva: Author.

World Health Organization. (2002). *Distribution of suicides rates (per 100,000) by gender and age, 2000.* Retrieved February 22, 2009, from http://www.who.int/mental_health/prevention/suicide/suicide_rates_chart/en/index.html

World Health Organization. (2008). *Depression.* Retrieved October 20, 2008, fromhttp://www.who.int/mental_health/management/depression/definition/en/

World Health Organization. (2009). *Definition of an older or elderly person.* Retrieved February 21, 2009, from http://www.who.int/healthinfo/survey/ageingdefnolder/en/index.html

Wright, L. (2007). *My life at Grey Gardens: Thirteen months and beyond* Lois Wright, Publisher.

Wright, S., & Klee, H. (2001). Violent crime, aggression and amphetamine: What are the implications for drug treatment services? *Drugs: Education, Prevention & Policy, 8,* 73–90.

Wrightsman, L. S., & Fulero, S. M. (2005). *Forensic psychology* (2nd ed.). Belmont, CA: Wadsworth.

Wu, K. D., Clark, L. A., & Watson, D. (2006). Relations between obsessive-compulsive disorder and personality: Beyond Axis I-Axis II comorbidity. *Journal of Anxiety Disorders, 20,* 695–717.

Wuerker, A. K., Long, J. D., Haas, G. L., & Bellack, A. S. (2002). Interpersonal control, expressed emotion, and change in symptoms in families of persons with schizophrenia, Schizophrenia Research, 58, 281–292.

Wyatt v. Stickney, 334 F. Supp. 1341 (M. D. Ala. 1971).

Wykes, T., Reeder, C., Williams, C., Corner, J., Rice, C., & Everitt, B. (in press). Are the effects of cognitive remediation therapy (CRT) durable? Results from an exploratory trial in schizophrenia. *Schizophrenia Research, 61,* 163–174.

Wynne, L. C., Tienari, P., Nieminen, P., Sorri, A., Lahti, I., Moring, J., et al. (2006). I. Genotype-environment interaction in the schizophrenia spectrum: Genetic liability and global family ratings in the Finnish Adoption Study. *Family Process, 45,* 419–434.

Xiao, Z., Yan, H., Wang, Z., Zou, Z., Xu, Y., Chen, J., et al. (2006). Trauma and dissociation in China. *American Journal of Psychiatry, 163,* 1388–1391.

Xu, B., Roos, J. L., Levy, S., van Rensburg, E. J., Gogos, J. A., & Karalorgou, M. (2008). Strong association of de novo copy number mutations with sporadic schizophrenia. *Nature Genetics, 40,* 880–885.

Yang, L. H., Phillips, M. R., Licht, D. M., & Hooley, J. M. (2004). Causal attributions about schizophrenia in families in China: Expressed emotion and patient relapse. *Journal of Abnormal Psychology, 113,* 592–602.

Yates, P. M., Hucker, S. J., & Kingston, D. A. (2008). Sexual sadism: Psychopathy and theory. In D. R. Laws & W. T. O'Donohue (Eds.), *Sexual deviance: Theory, assessment, and treatment* (2nd ed., pp. 213–230). New York: Guilford Press.

Yehuda, R., Boisoneau, D., Lowy, M. T., & Giller, E. L. (1995). Dose-response changes in plasma cortisol and lymphocyte glucocorticoid receptors following dexamethasone administration in combat veterans with and without posttraumatic stress disorder. *Archives of General Psychiatry, 52,* 583–593.

Yehuda, R., Giller, E. L., Southwick, S. M., Lowy, M. T., & Mason, J. W. (1991). Hypothalamic-pituitary-adrenal dysfunction in posttraumatic stress disorder. *Biological Psychiatry, 30,* 1031–1048.

Yehuda, R., Kahana, B., Binder-Brynes, K., Southwick, S. M., Mason, J. W., & Giller, E. L. (1995). Low urinary cortisol excretion in Holocaust survivors with posttraumatic stress disorder. *American Journal of Psychiatry, 152,* 982–986.

Yehuda, R., Teicher, M. H., Trestman, R. L., Levengood, R. A., & Siever, L. J. (1996). Cortisol regulation in posttraumatic stress disorder and major depression: A chronobiological analysis. *Biological Psychiatry, 40,* 79–88.

Yen, S., Sr., Shea, M. T., Battle, C. L., Johnson, D. M., Zlotnick, C., Dolan-Sewell, R., et al. (2002). Traumatic exposure and posttraumatic stress disorder in borderline, schizotypal, avoidant and obsessive-compulsive personality disorders: Findings from the Collaborative Longitudinal Personality Disorders Study. *Journal of Nervous and Mental Disease, 190,* 510–518.

Yip, P. S. F., Callanan, C., & Yuen, H. P. (2000). Urban/rural and gender differentials in suicide rates: East and west. *Journal of Affective Disorders, 57,* 99–106.

Yip, P. S. F., Chao, A., & Ho, T. P. (1998). A re-examination of seasonal variation in suicides in Australia and New Zealand. *Journal of Affective Disorders, 47,* 141–150.

Yip, P. S. F., Yang, K. C. T., & Qin, P. (2006). Seasonality of suicides with and without psychiatric illness in Denmark. *Journal of Affective Disorders, 96,* 117–121.

Yoo, H. J., Kim, M., Ha, J. H., Chung, A., Sim, M. E., Kim, S. J., et al. (2006). Biogenetic temperament and character and attention deficit hyperactivity disorder in Korean children. *Psychopathology, 39,* 25–31.

Yoon, T., Okada, J., Jung, M. W., & Kim, J. J. (2008). Prefrontal cortex and hippocampus subserve different components of working memory in rats. *Learning & Memory, 15,* 97–105.

Young, D. M. (2001). Depression. In W. S. Tseng & J. Streltzer (Eds.), *Culture and psychopathology: A guide to clinical assessment* (pp. 28–45). New York: Brunner/Mazel.

Young, J. E. (1990). *Cognitive therapy for personality disorders: A schema-focused approach.* Sarasota, FL: Professional Resource Exchange.

Young, K. S. (2005). An empirical examination of client attitudes towards online counseling. *CyberPsychology & Behavior, 8*, 172–177.

Yovel, I., & Mineka, S. (2005). Emotion-congruent attentional biases: The perspective of hierarchical models of emotional disorders. *Personality and Individual Differences, 38*, 785–795.

Yudofsky, S. C. (2005). *Fatal Flaws: Navigating Destructive Relationships With People with Disorders of Personality and Character*. Washington, DC, US: American Psychiatric Publishing, Inc.

Zabinski, M. F., Pung, M. A., Wilfley, D. E., Eppstein, D. L., Winzelberg, A. J., Celio, A., et al. (2001). Reducing risk factors for eating disorders: Targeting at-risk women with a computerized psychoeducational program. *International Journal of Eating Disorders, 29*, 401–408.

Zabinski, M. F., Wilfley, D. E., Calfas, K. J, Winzelberg, A. J., & Taylor, C. B. (2004). An interactive psychoeducational intervention for women at risk of developing an eating disorder. *Journal of Consulting and Clinical Psychology, 72*, 914–919.

Zadina, J. N., Corey, D. M., Casbergue, R. M., Lemen, L. C., Rouse, J. C., Knaus, T. A., et al. (2006). Lobar asymmetries in subtypes of dyslexic and control subjects. *Journal of Child Neurology, 21*, 922–931.

Zalsman, G., Frisch, A., Apter, A., & Weizman, A. (2002). Genetics of suicidal behavior: Candidate association genetic approach. *Israel Journal of Psychiatry & Related Sciences, 39*, 252–261.

Zamboanga, B. L., Bean, J. L., Pietras, A. C., & Pabón, L. C. (2005). Subjective evaluations of alcohol expectancies and their relevance to drinking game involvement in female college students. *Journal of Adolescent Health, 37*, 77–80.

Zammit, S., Allebeck, P., Andreasson, S., Lundberg, I., & Lewis, G. (2002). Self reported cannabis use as a risk factor for schizophrenia in Swedish conscripts of 1969: Historical cohort study. *British Medical Journal, 325*, 1199–1212.

Zammit, S., Allebeck, P., Dalman, C., Lundberg, I., Hemmingson, T., Owen, M. J., et al. (2003). Paternal age and risk for schizophrenia. *British Journal of Psychiatry, 183*, 405–408.

Zanarini, M. C., & Gunderson, J. G. (1997). Differential diagnosis of antisocial and borderline personality disorders. In D. M. Stoff, J. Breiling, & J. D. Maser (Eds.), *Handbook of antisocial behavior* (pp. 83–91). Hoboken, NJ: John Wiley.

Zanarini, M. C., Frankenburg, F. R., DeLuca, C. J., Hennen, J., Khera, G. S., & Gunderson, J. G. (1998). The pain of being borderline: Dysphoric states specific to borderline personality disorder. *Harvard Review of Psychiatry, 6*, 201–207.

Zanarini, M. C., Frankenburg, F. R., Hennen, J., Reich, B., & Silk, K. R. (2005). The McLean Study of Adult Development (MSAD): Overview and implications of the first six years of prospective follow-up. *Journal of Personality Disorders, 19*, 505–523.

Zanarini, M. C., Frankenburg, F. R., Hennen, J., Reich, D. B., & Silk, K. R. (2004). Axis I comorbidity in patients with borderline personality disorder: 6-year follow-up and prediction of time to remission. *American Journal of Psychiatry, 161*, 2108–2114.

Zanarini, M. C., Frankenburg, F. R., Hennen, J., Reich, D. B., & Silk, K. R. (2006). Prediction of the 10-year course of borderline personality disorder. *American Journal of Psychiatry, 163*, 827–832.

Zanarini, M. C., Frankenburg, F. R., Reich, D. B., & Silk, K. R., Hudson, J. I., & McSweeney, L. B. (2006). The subsyndromal phenomenology of borderline personality disorder: A 10-year follow-up study. *American Journal of Psychiatry, 164*, 929–935.

Zanarini, M. C., Gunderson, J. G., & Frankenburg, F. R. (1989). Axis I phenomenology of borderline personality disorder. *Comprehensive Psychiatry, 30*, 149–156.

Zane, N., Hall, G. C. N., Sue, S., Young, K., & Nunez, J. (2004). Research on psychotherapy with culturally diverse populations. In M. J. Lambert (Ed.), *Bergin and Garfield's handbook of psychotherapy and behavior change* (5th ed., pp. 805–821). New York: John Wiley & Sons.

Zarrinpar, A., Deldin, P., and Kosslyn, S. M. (2006). Effects of depression on sensory/motor vs. central processing in visual mental imagery. *Cognition & Emotion, 20*, 737–758.

Zhan, C., Sangl, J., Bierman, A., Miller, M., Friedman, B., Wickizer, S., et al. (2001). Potentially inappropriate medication use in the community-dwelling elderly: Findings from the 1996 medical expenditure panel survey. *Journal of the American Medical Association, 286*, 2823–2829.

Zhang, A. Y., Snowden, L. R., & Sue, S. (1998). Differences between Asian and White Americans' help seeking and utilization patterns in the Los Angeles area. *Journal of Community Psychology, 26*, 317–326.

Zhang, A., & Snowden, L. R. (1999). Ethnic characteristics of mental disorders in five U.S. communities. *Cultural Diversity and Ethnic Minority Psychology, 5*, 134–146.

Zhang, X. Y., Zhou, D. F., Cao, L. Y., Wu, G. Y., & Shen, Y. C. (2005). Cortisol and cytokines in chronic and treatment-resistant patients with schizophrenia: Association with psychopathology and response to antipsychotics. *Neuropsychopharmacology, 30*, 1532–1538.

Zhu, Y., Wang, K., Zhang, J., Long, Y., Su, L., & Zhou, M. (2003). A survey on tic disorder of children aged 6–15 years. *Chinese Mental Health Journal, 17*, 363–366.

Zhukov, D. A., & Vinogradova, E. P. (1998). Agonistic behavior during stress prevents the development of learned helplessness in rats. *Neuroscience and Behavioral Physiology, 28*, 206–210.

Ziatas, K., Durkin, K., & Pratt, C. (2003). Differences in assertive speech acts produced by children with autism, Asperger syndrome, specific language impairment, and normal development. *Development and Psychopathology, 15*, 73–94.

Ziegler, F. J., Imboden, J. B., & Meyer, E. (1960). Contemporary conversion reactions: A clinical study. *American Journal of Psychiatry, 116*, 901–910.

Zimmerman, M., & Chelminski, I. (2003). Generalized anxiety disorder in patients with major depression: Is DSM-IV's hierarchy correct? *American Journal of Psychiatry, 160*, 504–521.

Zipfel, S., Loewe, B., Reas, D. L., Deter, H.-C., & Herzog, W. (2000). Long-term prognosis in anorexia nervosa: Lessons from a 21-year follow-up study. *Lancet, 355*, 721–722.

Zittel, C., & Westen, D. (1998). Conceptual issues and research findings on borderline personality disorder: What every clinician should know. *In Session, 4*, 5–20.

Zlotnick, C., Miller, I. W., Pearlstein, T., Howard, M., & Sweeney, P. (2006). A preventive intervention for pregnant women on public assistance at risk for postpartum depression. *American Journal of Psychiatry, 163*, 1443–1445.

Zornberg, G. L., Buka, S. L., & Tsuang, M. T. (2000). Hypoxic-ischemia-related fetal/neonatal complications and risk of schizophrenia and other nonaffective psychoses: A 19-year longitudinal study. *American Journal of Psychiatry 157*, 196–202.

Zorumski, C. F. (2005). Neurobiology, neurogenesis, and the pathology of psychopathology. In C. F. Zorumski & E. H. Rubin (Eds.), *Psychopathology in the genome and neuroscience era* (pp. 175–187). Washington, DC: American Psychiatric Publishing.

Zubieta, J.-K., Huguelet, P., O'Neil, R. L., & Giordani, B. J. (2001). Cognitive function in euthymic bipolar I disorder. *Psychiatry Research, 102*, 9–20.

Zucker, K. J. (2005). Gender identity disorder in children and adolescents. *Annual Review of Clinical Psychology, 1,* 467–492.

Zucker, K. J., & **Bradley, S. J.** (1995). *Gender identity disorder and psychosexual problems in children and adolescents.* New York: Guilford Press.

Zucker, K. J., Wild, J., Bradley, S. J., & **Lowry, C. B.** (1993). Physical attractiveness of boys with gender identity disorder. *Archives of Sexual Behavior, 22,* 23–36.

Zuckerman, M. (1991). Biotypes for basic personality dimensions? "The Twilight Zone" between genotype and social phenotype. In J. Strelau & A. Angleitner (Eds.), *Explorations in temperament: International perspectives on theory and measurement* (pp. 129–146). New York: Plenum Press.

Zuckerman, M. (1991). *Psychobiology of personality.* New York: Cambridge University Press.

Zuckerman, M. (1994). *Behavioural expressions and biosocial bases of sensation seeking.* New York: Cambridge University Press.

Zuckerman, M. (1999). Antisocial personality disorder. In M. Zuckerman, *Vulnerability to psychopathology: A biosocial model* (pp. 209–253). Washington, DC: American Psychological Association.

Chapter 1

Figure 1.3 (p. 26) After Monroe et al. (1991) Diathesis – stress theories in the context of life-stress research: Implications for the depressive disorders. *Psychological Bulletin, 110,* 406–425. Copyright © 1991 American Psychological Association.

Chapter 2

Table 2.2 (p. 54) Permission by FEELING GOOD: THE NEW MOOD THERAPY by DAVID D. BURNS, M.D. COPYRIGHT © 1980 BY DAVID D. BURNS, M.D. Reprinted by permission of HarperCollins Publishers, WILLIAM MORROW, pp. 40–41.

Case 2.1 (p. 63) From Watson et al. (2007) Case studies in emotion – focused treatment of depression: A comparison of good and poor outcome. Copyright © 2007 American Psychological Association.

Chapter 3

Case 3.1 (p. 76) From Ellen Rothman, excerpt from "What's in a Name?" *Focus Online: News From Harvard Medical, Dental, and Public Health Schools*, December 15, 1995. Copyright © 1995 Reprinted by permission of the author.

Table 3.1 (p. 80) Reprinted with permission from the Diagnostic and Statistical Manual of Mental Disorders, Text Revision, Fourth Edition, (Copyright 2000) American Psychiatric Association.

Table 3.2 (p. 80) Reprinted with permission from the Diagnostic and Statistical Manual of Mental Disorders, Text Revision, Fourth Edition, (Copyright 2000) American Psychiatric Association.

Table 3.3 (p. 81) Reprinted with permission from the DSM-IV-TR Casebook: A Learning Companion to the Diagnostic and Statistical Manual of Mental Disorders, Fourth Edition, Text Revision, (Copyright 2002) American Psychiatric Association.

Table 3.4 (p. 82) Reprinted with permission from the Diagnostic

and Statistical Manual of Mental Disorders, Text Revision, Fourth Edition, (Copyright 2000) American Psychiatric Association.

Table 3.6 (p. 100) Excerpted from the MMPI-2 Booklet of Abbreviated Items. Copyright © 2005 by the Regents of the University of Minnesota. All rights reserved. Used by permission of the University of Minnesota Press. "MMPI-2" and "Minnesota Multiphasic Personality Inventory 2" are trademarks owned by the Regents of the University of Minnesota.

Figure 3.4 (p. 104) Reprinted by permission of the American Medical Association from the *Journal of the American Medical Association 291*: 2581–2590. Copyright 2004.

Chapter 4

Excerpt: "Leon is a 45-year-old postal employee…" (p. 109) Reprinted with permission from the DSM-IV-TR Casebook: A Learning Companion to the Diagnostic and Statistical Manual of Mental Disorders, Fourth Edition, Text Revision, (Copyright 2002) American Psychiatric Association.

Case 4.1 (p. 120) Frosch et al. (2002) Transference: Psychic reality and material reality. *Psychoanalytic Psychology 19* Copyright © 2002 American Psychological Association.

Case 4.2 (p. 138) Excerpt from ETHNICITY AND FAMILY THERAPY by Sutton and Broken Nose. Copyright © 1996 by Guilford Publications, Inc. Reprinted by permission.

Chapter 5

Case 5.1 (p. 163) From Lee et al. (2004), Menstrually related self-injurious behavior in adolescents with autism. *Journal of the American Academy of Child & Adolescent Psychiatry* Copyright 2004. Reprinted by permission of Wolters Kluwer Health via Rightslink.

Figure 5.3 (p. 165) From JOURNAL OF POSITIVE INTERVENTIONS by Lorimer et al. Copyright 2002 by Sage Publications, Inc. Journals.

Reproduced with permission of Sage Publications in the format Textbook via Copyright Clearance Center.

Table 5.2 (p. 168) From Ethical principles of psychologists and code of conduct. *American Psychologist 57*, 1060–73. Copyright © American Psychological Association.

Figure 5.5 (p. 172) After Schwartz (1999) Self reports: How the questions shape the answers. *American Psychologist 54*, 93–105. Copyright © 1999 American Psychological Association.

Table 5.4 (p. 184) From Ethical principles of psychologists and code of conduct. *American Psychologist 57*, 1060–73 Copyright © American Psychological Association.

Figure 5.7 (p. 185) From Lambert et al. (2001) Patient focused research: Using patient outcome data to enhance treatment effects. *Journal of Consulting and Clinical Psychology 69* Copyright © 2001 American Psychological Association.

Chapter 6

Excerpts from *An Unquiet Mind* (pp. 191, 217, 218, 220, 224, 225, 228, 230, and 232) From AN UNQUIET MIND by Kay Redfield Jamison, copyright © 1995 by Kay Redfield Jamison. Used by permission of Alfred A. Knopf, a division of Random House, Inc.

Table 6.2 (p. 193) Reprinted with permission from the DSM-IV-TR Casebook: A Learning Companion to the Diagnostic and Statistical Manual of Mental Disorders, Fourth Edition, Text Revision, (Copyright 2002) American Psychiatric Association.

Case 6.1 (p. 194) From DARKNESS VISIBLE: A MEMOIR OF MADNESS by William Styron, copyright © 1990 by William Styron. Used by permission of Random House, Inc.

Table 6.3 (p. 196) Reprinted with permission from the DSM-IV-TR Casebook: A Learning Companion to the Diagnostic and Statistical Manual of Mental Disorders, Fourth Edition, Text Revision, (Copyright 2002) American Psychiatric Association.

Chapter 7

Chapter 8

and Statistical Manual of Mental Disorders, Text Revision, Fourth Edition, (Copyright 2000) American Psychiatric Association.

Table 8.16 (p. 369) Reprinted with permission from the Diagnostic and Statistical Manual of Mental Disorders, Text Revision, Fourth Edition, (Copyright 2000) American Psychiatric Association.

Table 8.17 (p. 371) Reprinted with permission from the Diagnostic and Statistical Manual of Mental Disorders, Text Revision, Fourth Edition, (Copyright 2000) American Psychiatric Association.

Chapter 9

Table 9.1 (p. 382) Reprinted with permission from the Diagnostic and Statistical Manual of Mental Disorders, Text Revision, Fourth Edition, (Copyright 2000) American Psychiatric Association.

Table 9.2 (p. 383) Reprinted with permission from the Diagnostic and Statistical Manual of Mental Disorders, Text Revision, Fourth Edition, (Copyright 2000) American Psychiatric Association.

Table 9.3 (p. 384) Reprinted with permission from the Diagnostic and Statistical Manual of Mental Disorders, Text Revision, Fourth Edition, (Copyright 2000) American Psychiatric Association.

Case 9.1 (p. 386) Reprinted by permission of Faces & Voices of Recovery.

Case 9.2 (p. 388) Reprinted by permission of Faces & Voices of Recovery.

Excerpt: "With over 15 years of continuous sobriety…" (p. 389) Reprinted by permission of Faces & Voices of Recovery.

Case 9.3 (p. 392) Permission by Hyman, S. E. (2001) A 28-year-old man addicted to cocaine. *Journal of the American Medical Association*, 286, 2586–94. Copyright © 2001. Reprinted by permission.

Figure 9.8 (p. 405) Permission by NIH module – "Understanding Alcohol: Investigations into Biology and Behavior". Copyright © 2003 by

BSCS. All rights reserved. Used with permission.

Case 9.6 (p. 415) Reprinted with permission from the DSM-IV-TR Casebook: A Learning Companion to the Diagnostic and Statistical Manual of Mental Disorders, Fourth Edition, Text Revision, (Copyright 2002) American Psychiatric Association.

Fig 9.12 (p. 427) Permission by Silverman et al., Sustained cocaine abstinence in methadone maintenance patients through voucher-based reinforcement therapy. *Archives of General Psychiatry*, 53, 409–15. Copyright 2001. Reprinted by permission.

Chapter 10

Excerpts from *Wasted: A Memoir of Anorexia and Bulimia* (pp. 436, 436, 440, 442, 447, 450, 451, 452, 455, 456, 458, 462, and 468) Excerpts from WASTED: A MEMOIR OF ANOREXIA AND BULIMIA by MARYA HORNBACHER. Copyright © 1998 by Marya Hornbacher-Beard. Reprinted by permission of HarperCollins Publishers.

Table 10.1 (p. 437) Reprinted with permission from the Diagnostic and Statistical Manual of Mental Disorders, Text Revision, Fourth Edition, (Copyright 2000) American Psychiatric Association.

Case 10.1 (p. 438) From Knapp, DRINKING: A LOVE STORY. Copyright © 2003, pages 48–49.

Table 10.3 (p. 443) Reprinted with permission from the Diagnostic and Statistical Manual of Mental Disorders, Text Revision, Fourth Edition, (Copyright 2000) American Psychiatric Association.

Figure 10.2 (p. 453) After Blackburn, S. et al. (2006), An application of escape theory to binge eating. *European Eating Disorders Review, 14*, 23–31, Figure 1, page 27 in Heatherton, T. F. and Baumeister, R. F. (1991), Binge eating as escape from self-awareness. *Psychological Bulletin*, 110, 86–108. Copyright © 1991 American Psychological Association.

Chapter 11

Table 11.1 (p. 475) Reprinted with permission from the Diagnostic and Statistical Manual of Mental Disorders, Text Revision, Fourth Edition, (Copyright 2000) American Psychiatric Association.

Case 11.3 (p. 485) Reprinted with permission from the DSM-IV-TR Casebook: A Learning Companion to the Diagnostic and Statistical Manual of Mental Disorders, Fourth Edition, Text Revision, (Copyright 2002) American Psychiatric Association.

Case 11.3 (p. 488) Reprinted with permission from the DSM-IV-TR Casebook: A Learning Companion to the Diagnostic and Statistical Manual of Mental Disorders, Fourth Edition, Text Revision, (Copyright 2002) American Psychiatric Association.

Case 11.6 (p. 489) Reprinted with permission from the DSM-IV-TR Casebook: A Learning Companion to the Diagnostic and Statistical Manual of Mental Disorders, Fourth Edition, Text Revision, (Copyright 2002) American Psychiatric Association.

Figures 11.2a & 11.2b (p. 495) From HUMAN SEXUAL RESPONSE by William H. Masters and Virginia E. Johnson. Copyright © 1966. Reprinted by permission of The Estate of Masters and Johnson.

Table 11.5 (p. 496) Reprinted with permission from the DSM-IV-TR Casebook: A Learning Companion to the Diagnostic and Statistical Manual of Mental Disorders, Fourth Edition, Text Revision, (Copyright 2002) American Psychiatric Association.

Case 11.9 (p. 499) Reprinted with permission from the DSM-IV-TR Casebook: A Learning Companion to the Diagnostic and Statistical Manual of Mental Disorders, Fourth Edition, Text Revision, (Copyright 2002) American Psychiatric Association.

Case 11.11 (p. 501) Reprinted with permission from the DSM-IV-TR Casebook: A Learning Companion to the Diagnostic and Statistical Manual of Mental Disorders, Fourth Edition, Text Revision, (Copyright 2002) American Psychiatric Association.

Case 11.13 (p. 502) Reprinted with permission from the DSM-IV-TR Casebook: A Learning Companion to the Diagnostic and Statistical Manual of Mental Disorders, Fourth Edition, Text Revision, (Copyright 2002) American Psychiatric Association.

Figure 11.3 (p. 504) Permission by JOURNAL OF SEX & MARITAL THERAPY by Basson et al. Copyright © 2001 by Taylor & Francis Informa UK Ltd – Journals. Reproduced with permission of Taylor & Francis Informa UK Journals in the format Textbook via Copyright Clearance Center.

Chapter 12

Case 12.1 (p. 527) Reprinted with permission from the DSM-IV-TR Casebook: A Learning Companion to the Diagnostic and Statistical Manual of Mental Disorders, Fourth Edition, Text Revision, (Copyright 2002) American Psychiatric Association.

Case 12.2 (p. 547) Reprinted by permission of Fred Frese, Ph.D. Associate Professor of Psychology in Psychiatry, Northeastern Ohio University College of Medicine, Coordinator, Recovery Project.

Case 12.3 (p. 551) From CULTURE AND PSYCHOPATHOLOGY: A GUIDE TO CLINICAL ASSESSMENT by Tseng et al. Copyright © 1997 by Taylor & Francis Group LLC Books. Reproduced with permission of Taylor & Francis Group LLC – Books in the format Textbook by Copyright Clearance Center.

Chapter 13

Excerpts from Get Me Out of Here: My Recovery From Borderline Personality Disorder (pp. 567, 568, 574, 577, 599, 608) Excerpt from Get Me Out of Here: My Recovery From Borderline Personality Disorder by Rachel Reiland. Copyright © 2005 by HAZELDEN FOUNDATION. Reprinted by permission of Hazelden Foundation, Center City, MN.

Table 13.1 (p. 569) Reprinted with permission from the Diagnostic and Statistical Manual of Mental

Disorders, Text Revision, Fourth Edition, (Copyright 2000) American Psychiatric Association.

Figure 13.1 (p. 570) After Grilo et al. (2004), Two to four year stability and change of schizotypal, borderline, avoidant and obsessive-compulsive personality disorders. Journal of Consulting and Clinical Psychology 72, 767–75. Copyright © 2004 American Psychological Association.

Table 13.2 (p. 572) Reprinted with permission from the Diagnostic and Statistical Manual of Mental Disorders, Text Revision, Fourth Edition, (Copyright 2000) American Psychiatric Association.

Table 13.4 (p. 581) Reprinted with permission from the Diagnostic and Statistical Manual of Mental Disorders, Text Revision, Fourth Edition, (Copyright 2000) American Psychiatric Association.

Table 13.8 (p. 586) Reprinted with permission from the Diagnostic and Statistical Manual of Mental Disorders, Text Revision, Fourth Edition, (Copyright 2000) American Psychiatric Association.

Table 13.10 (p. 589) From COGNITIVE THERAPY OF PERSONALITY DISORDERS by Beck et al. Copyright 2004 by Guilford Publications, Inc. Reprinted by permission.

Table 13.11 (p. 592) Reprinted with permission from the Diagnostic and Statistical Manual of Mental Disorders, Text Revision, Fourth Edition, (Copyright 2000) American Psychiatric Association.

Figure 13.5 (p. 594) After Lahey et al. (2005), Predicting anti-social behavior disorder in males from a clinical assessment in childhood. Journal of Consulting and Clinical Psychology, 73. Copyright © 2005 American Psychological Association.

Figure 13.6 (p. 594) After Figure 1: Scale structure of PCL-R in Hare (2003), THE PSYCHOPATHY CHECKLIST, REVISED MANUAL 2/E. Copyright © 2003. Reprinted by permission of MHS.

Table 13.13 (p. 596) From Brock et al., Genetics of Criminal and

Antisocial_Behaviour. Copyright 1996. Reprinted by permission of Elsevier Science via Rightslink.

Table 13.14 (p. 600) Reprinted with permission from the Diagnostic and Statistical Manual of Mental Disorders, Text Revision, Fourth Edition, (Copyright 2000) American Psychiatric Association.

Table 13.16 (p. 608) Reprinted with permission from the Diagnostic and Statistical Manual of Mental Disorders, Text Revision, Fourth Edition, (Copyright 2000) American Psychiatric Association.

Table 13.18 (p. 611) Reprinted with permission from the Diagnostic and Statistical Manual of Mental Disorders, Text Revision, Fourth Edition, (Copyright 2000) American Psychiatric Association.

Table 13.21 (p. 613) Reprinted with permission from the Diagnostic and Statistical Manual of Mental Disorders, Text Revision, Fourth Edition, (Copyright 2000) American Psychiatric Association.

Table 13.23 (p. 615) Reprinted with permission from the Diagnostic and Statistical Manual of Mental Disorders, Text Revision, Fourth Edition, (Copyright 2000) American Psychiatric Association.

Case 13.10 (p. 616) Reprinted with permission from the DSM-IV-TR Casebook: A Learning Companion to the Diagnostic and Statistical Manual of Mental Disorders, Fourth Edition, Text Revision, (Copyright 2002) American Psychiatric Association.

Table 13.25 (p. 617) Reprinted with permission from the Diagnostic and Statistical Manual of Mental Disorders, Text Revision, Fourth Edition, (Copyright 2000) American Psychiatric Association.

Chapter 14

Table 14.1 (p. 626) Reprinted with permission from the Diagnostic and Statistical Manual of Mental Disorders, Text Revision, Fourth Edition, (Copyright 2000) American Psychiatric Association.